AMERICAN NATIONAL BIOGRAPHY

AMERICAN NATIONAL BIOGRAPHY

Published under the auspices of the
AMERICAN COUNCIL OF LEARNED SOCIETIES

General Editors

John A. Garraty
Mark C. Carnes

VOLUME 1

OXFORD UNIVERSITY PRESS
New York 1999 Oxford

OXFORD UNIVERSITY PRESS

Oxford New York
Athens Auckland Bangkok Bogotá
Buenos Aires Calcutta Cape Town Chennai
Dar es Salaam Delhi Florence Hong Kong Istanbul
Karachi Kuala Lumpur Madrid Melbourne Mexico City
Mumbai Nairobi Paris São Paulo Singapore
Taipei Tokyo Toronto Warsaw
and associated companies in
Berlin Ibadan

Published by Oxford University Press, Inc.,
198 Madison Avenue, New York, New York 10016
http://www.oup-usa.org

Funding for this publication was provided in part by
the Andrew W. Mellon Foundation, the Rockefeller Foundation,
and the National Endowment for the Humanities,
a federal agency.

Library of Congress Cataloging-in-Publication Data

American national biography / general editors, John A. Garraty, Mark C. Carnes
p. cm.
"Published under the auspices of the American Council of Learned Societies."
Includes bibliographical references and index.
1. United States—Biography—Dictionaries. I. Garraty, John Arthur,
1920– . II. Carnes, Mark C. (Mark Christopher), 1950– .
III. American Council of Learned Societies.
CT213.A68 1998 98-20826 920.073—dc21 CIP
ISBN 0-19-520635-5 (set)
ISBN 0-19-512780-3 (vol. 1)

Printing (last digit): 9 8 7 6 5 4 3

Printed in the United States of America
on acid-free paper

CONSTITUENT SOCIETIES OF THE AMERICAN COUNCIL OF LEARNED SOCIETIES

African Studies Association

American Academy of Arts and Sciences

American Academy of Religion

American Anthropological Association

American Antiquarian Society

American Association for the Advancement of Slavic Studies

American Comparative Literature Association

American Dialect Society

American Economic Association

American Folklore Society

American Historical Association

American Musicological Society

American Numismatic Society

American Oriental Society

American Philological Association

American Philosophical Association

American Philosophical Society

American Political Science Association

American Psychological Association

American Schools of Oriental Research

American Society for Aesthetics

American Society for Eighteenth Century Studies

American Society for Legal History

American Society for Theatre Research

American Society of Comparative Law

American Society of International Law

American Sociological Association

American Studies Association

Archaeological Institute of America

Association for Asian Studies

Association for Jewish Studies

Association for the Advancement of Baltic Studies

Association of American Geographers

Association of American Law Schools

Bibliographical Society of America

College Art Association

College Forum of the National Council of Teachers of English

Dictionary Society of North America

Economic History Association

German Studies Association

Hispanic Society of America

History of Science Society

Latin American Studies Association

Law and Society Association

Linguistic Society of America

Medieval Academy of America

Metaphysical Society of America

Middle East Studies Association

Modern Language Association

National Communication Association

Organization of American Historians

Renaissance Society of America

Sixteenth Century Studies Conference

Society for Cinema Studies

Society for Ethnomusicology

Society for French Historical Studies

Society for the History of Technology

Society of Architectural Historians

Society of Biblical Literature

Society of Dance History Scholars

Sonneck Society for American Music

EDITORS AND ADVISERS

GENERAL EDITORS

EDITORIAL ADVISORY BOARD

SENIOR AND ASSOCIATE EDITORS

Lois Scharf, *Case Western Reserve University*
Harvard Sitkoff, *University of New Hampshire*
Ronald H. Spector, *George Washington University*
Ralph E. Weber, *Marquette University*

Politics, Diplomacy, and the Military, 1945–1995

SENIOR EDITOR
Lloyd C. Gardner, *Rutgers University*

ASSOCIATE EDITORS
Fraser Harbutt, *Emory University*
Richard H. Immerman, *Temple University*
Robert J. McMahon, *University of Florida*
David Oshinsky, *Rutgers University*
David S. Patterson
Athan G. Theoharis, *Marquette University*
Betty Miller Unterberger, *Texas A&M University*

Religion

SENIOR EDITOR
Albert J. Raboteau, *Princeton University*

ASSOCIATE EDITORS
Henry Warner Bowden, *Rutgers University*
Randall Burkett, *Emory University*
Jay P. Dolan, *University of Notre Dame*
Robert S. Ellwood, *University of Southern California*
E. Brooks Holifield, *Emory University*
Paula E. Hyman, *Yale University*
James H. Moorhead, *Princeton Theological Seminary*
Marc Lee Raphael, *College of William and Mary*
Jonathan D. Sarna, *Brandeis University*
Stephen J. Stein, *Indiana University*
Harry S. Stout, *Yale University*
James M. Washington, *Union Theological Seminary*
Peter W. Williams, *Miami University*

Education

SENIOR EDITOR
Patricia Albjerg Graham, *Harvard University*

ASSOCIATE EDITORS
Jeanne E. Amster, *San Francisco University High School*
Barbara Brenzel, *Wellesley College*
Robert P. Cohen, *University of Georgia*
Linda Eisenmann, *University of Massachusetts at Boston*
Barbara Finkelstein, *University of Maryland*
G. Michael Fultz, *University of Wisconsin–Madison*
Lynn D. Gordon, *University of Rochester*
Thomas James, *Brown University*
Bruce A. Kimball, *University of Rochester*
Ellen Condliffe Lagemann, *New York University*
Linda M. Perkins, *Hunter College, City University of New York*
William J. Reese, *University of Wisconsin–Madison*
John L. Rury, *DePaul University*
Kathleen Underwood, *University of Texas at Arlington*

Business

SENIOR EDITOR
Louis P. Galambos, *Johns Hopkins University*

ASSOCIATE EDITORS
Ronald W. Edsforth, *Dartmouth College*
John A. Heitmann, *University of Dayton*
John N. Ingham, *University of Toronto*
K. Austin Kerr, *Ohio State University*
Albro Martin, *Bradley University*
G. H. Mattersdorff, *Lewis and Clark College*
John J. McCusker, *Trinity University*
Russell R. Menard, *University of Minnesota*
Daniel Nelson, *University of Akron*
Edward C. Papenfuse, *Maryland State Archives*
Stephen M. Salsbury, *University of Sydney*

Law and the Judiciary

SENIOR EDITOR
Michal R. Belknap, *California Western School of Law*

ASSOCIATE EDITORS
Norma Basch, *Rutgers University–Newark*
Beverly Blair Cook, *University of Wisconsin–Milwaukee*
Paul Finkelman, *University of Akron*
Kermit L. Hall, *Ohio State University*
Jonathan Lurie, *Rutgers University*
R. Michael McReynolds, *National Archives*
John V. Orth, *University of North Carolina at Chapel Hill*
Michael E. Parrish, *University of California, San Diego*
Donald M. Roper, *State University of New York at New Paltz*
Philippa Strum, *Brooklyn College, City University of New York*
Mark Tushnet, *Georgetown University*

EDITORIAL AND PRODUCTION STAFF

MANAGING EDITOR
Paul Betz (1994–1999)

PROJECT MANAGER
Michael R. Kornegay (1989–1994)

PROJECT EDITORS
Margaret J. Dietrich, Sara Lawrence, Susan Baker Monroe,
Matthew E. Van Atta, Joel T. Van Pelt,
Anne H. Wimer

COPY CHIEFS
Jennifer N. Rozgonyi, Leslie Watkins

COPYEDITORS
Stacey Hamilton, Beth Snowberger,
Lee Baldwin, Katherine B. Becker, Sandra Eisdorfer, Geoffrey T. Garvey,
Geoffrey Gneuhs, Martha Graedel, Sharon Harless, Kathryn B. Haywood, Leslie T. Henry,
Jean Fortune Kaplan, Noel Kinnamon, Corrie Lisk, James L. Lux, Laura Mansberg,
Jay Mazzocchi, Jane McGary, Robert Mirandon, Barbara Norton, Rita Signorelli Pappas,
Donna Grear Parker, Joann Petilli, Martha A. Schutz, Curtis R. Scott, Merryl A. Sloane,
Chris Stamey, Martha Dimes Toher, Kathleen J. Travers, Benjamin T. Turney,
Janet Wagner, Paula J. Wald, Fay Washington, Patricia J. Watson,
Stephanie Wenzel, Caroline Winterer

EDITORIAL ASSISTANTS
L. Paige Battle, Thomas W. Collins, Joy Cox, Tina C. Gallatin, Julie Peery,
Laura C. Rudolph, Shane Speer, Julie A. Steiner,
Lisbeth G. Svendsgaard

COMPUTER SYSTEMS MANAGER
Catherine A. Guldner

GRAPHIC DESIGNER
Joan Greenfield

INDEXERS
Arden Alexander, Elisabeth B. Parker

PROOFREADERS
Marion Laird, Carol Wengler

FACTCHECKERS

David Anderson, Ladan Atai, Susan Baker, Mark Beck, Martha Jane Brazy, Anthony B. Cashman III, Sandy L. Chaney, Derek Chang, Thomas Devine, John Donahue, Ayse Erginer, Elif Erginer, Kathleen Feeney, Jeana K. Foley, Mark E. Gammon, Lars Golumbic, James Halpin, Tim J. Henderson, Matt Jacobs, Catherine Kempf, Marie-Claire Kirch, Andrew J. Kirkendall, Kelli M. Kobor, Edward L. Lach, Jr., Michael Lanham, Joshua L. McKaughan, Farrell O'Gorman, Michelle Osborn, Jennifer Parchesky, Douglas Carl Peifer, Scott Philyaw, Jessica Ryan, Katayoun Sadri, Dan Salemson, Michael Sistrom, Greg Smith, Brian Steele, Margaret Swezey, Martha Temkin, Anne Townsend, Michael Trotti

INTERNS

Akin T. Akinli, Scott Blanton, Cindy E. Burda, Christian S. Dick, Devin Fergus, Charles W. Gaddy, Joanna L. Grant, Yancey R. Hall, Lisa M. Harper, Sehoya E. Harris, William E. Hoke, David Jackson, Amy L. Kiger, Andrea P. Kinney, Paul Mandl, Sarah McCarty, Susan W. McMichaels, Locke A. Monroe, Elise J. Morgan, Kristin M. Morphy, Aaron W. Morrison, Jennifer R. Nacca, Jennifer N. Scherer, Yvette M. Stillwell, Erin D. Sullivan, Angela J. Switzer, David L. Webb, William B. Wetzell, Elizabeth Zoe Vicary, Amasa Wainwright, Sarah E. Wall, Sara Graves Wheeler

FOREWORD

In 1986 R. M. Lumiansky, my predecessor as president of the American Council of Learned Societies (ACLS), discussed with me the need to replace the *Dictionary of American Biography* (*DAB*), one of the first projects that the ACLS had undertaken after its creation in 1919. The *DAB* was fifty years old, its original twenty volumes having been published between 1926 and 1937. Lumiansky told me that Columbia University professor John A. Garraty, the editor of supplements 4–8 of the *DAB*, felt strongly that the ACLS should sponsor an entirely new biographical work. Garraty argued that because the supplements covered more recent periods of American history they could not serve to update the roughly fifteen thousand articles in the original, nor could they conveniently include the many important figures such as Sojourner Truth, Scott Joplin, Charles Guiteau, and Martha Washington who had been left out of the original.

Since my own field is American history, I needed no convincing. Furthermore, I did not have to think twice about finding a general editor for the new work, so great was my respect for Professor Garraty both as a historian and as the person responsible for the *DAB* supplements from the early 1970s onward. After becoming ACLS president in July 1986, I began to consult with him about the possibilities for a new biographical dictionary, and our plans fell into place quickly. All that remained was the search for a publisher and for the funding necessary to underwrite the costs of the project.

The search for a publisher was more complicated than we had anticipated. The original publisher of the *DAB*, Charles Scribner's Sons, had been taken over by a larger firm, which at the time was not interested in producing a new biographical dictionary. So we began to seek a publisher with the capacity to take on such a big project, to carry it off with the requisite professional standards, and to deal with the potential for an electronic edition. The quest ended, happily, in a contract with Oxford University Press, Inc. We anticipated that Oxford, with its long history of academic publishing and with its exceptionally strong list of authors in American history, would be an unusually congenial partner in publishing a reference work of so vast a scope as the *American National Biography* (*ANB*). And indeed that has been the case.

But the project would not have been realized without substantial investment. For its part, Oxford was to invest several million dollars and many years of labor by a sizable staff. And the ACLS had to raise more than three million dollars in order to pay the authors and editors of the *ANB*. We could not have done so without a grant from the Rockefeller Foundation and without a continuing series of sizable grants from the Andrew W. Mellon Foundation and the National Endowment for the Humanities. The *ANB* would not now be in your hands except for the generosity of these funders and the confident support of Oxford University Press. The entire project is a wonderful example of the potential of public-private collaboration in major humanities efforts.

It also goes without saying that the *ANB* would not have come into existence but for the expertise, dedication, and professionalism of John A. Garraty and his fellow general editor, Mark C. Carnes, professor of history at Barnard College. Garraty, the obvious choice to direct the project, did his work brilliantly. It will be hard for readers to imagine the challenges and frustrations of putting together twenty-four volumes comprising nearly 17,500 biographies. Carnes has worked on the *ANB* with Garraty from the first day and has been equally essential to the project.

The ACLS owes a similar debt of gratitude to our publishers. Edward Barry, president of Oxford University Press, Inc., took a personal interest in every aspect of the project and was unwavering in his determination that it be successfully completed. Claude Conyers, editorial director of Oxford's Scholarly and Professional Reference Division, brought to bear exceptional experience in the publication of reference works and marshaled the forces needed to sustain years of effort. Michael Kornegay, project manager of the *ANB*, supervised the administration of the project from the Oxford University Press offices in Cary, North Carolina, during the first five years of its development. Subsequently, Paul Betz, as managing editor, directed the day-to-day editing and production of the work, surmounting the stresses and details of a very complicated process with professionalism, dignity, and expertise.

Even with the contributions of those I have already mentioned, the *ANB* would not have come to pass if it were not for the skill and dedication of my ACLS colleagues Douglas Greenberg and Steven Wheatley. Greenberg was there from the start, helping to negotiate the publishing contract and arranging the operational details of ACLS participation. Wheatley took over when Greenberg moved on to the presidency of the Chicago Historical Society and has brought the project to completion. Greenberg and then Wheatley chaired our management committee meetings, which regularly addressed questions of format, organization, and other publishing issues.

Finally, let me note that the *ANB* represents a collective effort of enormous magnitude by the often invoked, but rarely manifest, scholarly community. This work is spectacular evidence of that community. The editorial advisory board helped develop the basic design of the project. The senior editors identified and shaped the substantive areas to be covered. Our associate editors were essential in the recruitment of authors and the review of their manuscripts. Most important were the thousands of historians and other scholars who contributed their research and analysis to what is, I am sure, this generation's major reference work in American biography.

Stanley N. Katz
President Emeritus, ACLS

The publication of the *American National Biography* powerfully demonstrates the close connection between historical and humanistic scholarship and our larger public life. Sponsoring the publication of major scholarly reference works, conspicuously useful to a wide readership, is one important way in which the ACLS fulfills its mission of advancing humanistic scholarship. It is a pleasure to recognize my predecessors, R. M. Lumiansky and Stanley N. Katz, for the vision and commitment that led to the development of the *ANB*; and to pay tribute to Stan Katz for his leadership in seeing this extraordinary collaborative project to completion. The ACLS looks forward to working with Oxford University Press in the future to keep the *ANB*, in both print and electronic editions, the most current and comprehensive work of American biography.

John H. D'Arms
President, ACLS

PREFACE

The *American National Biography* was conceived as the successor to the *Dictionary of American Biography*, first published between 1926 and 1937. The editors of the *DAB* saw no reason to defend its focus on great and significant persons or to justify the American nation as the context for the undertaking. In recent decades, however, historians intent on examining the past "from the bottom up" have emphasized the experiences of ordinary men and women, often members of ethnic groups or racial minorities that were neglected by previous scholars. As such people and their particular communities have come into clearer focus, the national frame of reference has often slipped from view. Some have argued that the "nation" is an artificial construct that inhibits understanding the past. To such scholars, the need for a biographical collection of the American *nation* is no longer self-evident.

Yet biography remains indispensable to historical understanding. The *ANB* is not a history, but the basic materials of historical inquiry tend to collect around prominent people, whose lives illuminate the human dimensions of the past and reveal its larger processes. For that reason a biographical dictionary can be a valuable source for almost any work of history. The American nation, moreover, constitutes an essential structure for understanding this vast and diverse material. Many people who did not think of themselves as "Americans" have nevertheless left their imprint on its history. The American nation is thus a product of its many pasts. The *ANB* brings together the diverse voices of the past without claiming that they blend harmoniously.

But while the value of a national biographical reference work has endured, the character of such an undertaking has changed considerably since the *DAB* was published. The number of professional historians has increased dramatically, and the discipline has expanded its horizons with the development of new research methods, the discovery of new primary sources, and the growth of new fields of study, such as the history of African Americans, women, immigrants, workers, and others. Virtually all aspects of the past are now seen from a different perspective. Today, historians do not regard the slave-plantation South with nostalgia or dismiss women's participation in politics as quaint or deride the doctrinal views of small religious sects or deny the cultural importance of dolls or pop music. Nor do most historians assume a proprietary omniscience in regard to their subjects or believe that history is merely a collection of facts. Nearly all acknowledge that history consists of many different stories and interpretations.

Compared to the *DAB*, the *ANB* has substantially broadened the criteria for the inclusion of subjects. An "American" is loosely defined as someone whose significant actions occurred during his or her residence within what is now the United States or whose life or career directly influenced the course of American history. "Significance" includes achievement (superior accomplishment as judged by contemporaries), fame (celebrity or notoriety), or influence (effect on one's own time despite lack of public notice). Even some "ordinary" persons have been included if they left autobiographies, diaries, or other artifacts that attracted posthumous attention. An example is Martha Ballard, an eighteenth-century midwife whose diary has proven invaluable to scholars. The only invariant rule is that all subjects must have died prior to 1996. To apply these criteria, we made utility our fundamental principle: would readers and researchers want to know something more about a particular figure? At the margins, priority was given to persons, especially women and minorities, about whom new information or new ways of interpreting old data had become available.

To create the database from which *ANB* subjects were selected, scores of reference works were examined. Also included were the subjects of books, dissertations, and essays of a biographical character that have appeared in recent decades. The directors of every state historical society were asked for suggestions, as were the presidents of all of the nation's scholarly societies. In addition, individual scholars nominated thousands of possible subjects of entries.

All potential subjects were placed in categories, mostly occupational (politics, the military, and diplomacy; art and architecture; the performing arts; business; journalism and literature; law; medicine; science and technology; religion; education; the social sciences; social reform; and sports). Native Americans, whose study requires archaeological, anthropological, and linguistic skills, were put into a single category and reviewed by specialists in the field. Otherwise, the *ANB* did not group potential subjects in ethnic or racial groups or by cultural or social affiliations. For example, the *ANB* did not establish a category for gays and lesbians. Harvey Milk was included in "politics" not for his local standing as a member of the San Francisco Board of Supervisors but because his advocacy of gay rights had national significance. In all, nearly thirty thousand people from all walks of life eventually were considered.

The task of selecting from among all these potential subjects was the work of nearly two hundred associate editors, each assigned to a topical category. For persons selected, the associate editors recommended a length ranging from 750 to 7,500 words and proposed several biographers. When completed, each essay was reviewed by the associate editor who made the assignment and then by the *ANB* staff at Columbia University. If substantial revision was required, the manuscript was returned to the author with suggestions and queries. After the staff at Columbia University had approved an essay, it was factchecked under the supervision of the *ANB* staff of Oxford University Press in Cary, North Carolina. (The Oxford factcheckers generated well over a hundred thousand queries, and their work has immeasurably strengthened the factual foundation of our understanding of the American past.) The Oxford staff also supervised the copyediting of manuscripts to ensure uniformity of style and format, and they sent manuscripts back to authors for a final check.

This complicated procedure was time-consuming and expensive, but necessary. Its chief purpose, aside from promoting factual accuracy, was to ensure that the *ANB* reflected a national breadth of judgment and opinion. The simplest measure of this is statistical. While the original *DAB* was written by 2,243 authors, the *ANB* is the work of almost 6,100, drawn from nearly every discipline and located throughout the nation. By virtue of its decentralized editorial structure and the diversity of its editors and authors, the *American National Biography* has earned its name.

In summing up the contribution of the *DAB* in his introduction to volume 20 of that work, Dumas Malone stressed the effort of the editors to consider American life and culture broadly, covering "all sects and sections, races, classes, and parties." The editors of the *ANB* have pursued this goal with, we trust, equal determination. But just as the authors and editors of the 1920s and 1930s wrote from the perspective of their times, we write and edit from ours. These volumes contain and reflect current knowledge and views about the significant figures of our national past. With time, what is known of these and other figures will expand and be modified, but here is the record as the twentieth century ends.

The American Council of Learned Societies and Oxford University Press are nevertheless committed to ensuring that the *ANB* will remain a vital reference well into the next century. They have established a Center for American Biography, whose charge is to update and enlarge the *ANB* so that generations ahead can continue to turn to a standard, reliable source of biographical information.

We would like to express our heartfelt gratitude to the staff that assisted us in our project office at Columbia University. Patrick G. Williams, Sandra Opdycke, Steven West, Charles Forcey, and Walter Friedman were stalwart reviewers of manuscripts on our behalf. The mainstay in the management of our office was Dorothy McCann. We also benefited from research conducted by Susanne Pichler and Jennifer Sharpe.

John A. Garraty
Mark C. Carnes
General Editors

EDITORIAL NOTE

The format of articles in the *American National Biography* is based on chronology. A given article traces a person's life through the sequence of significant events as they occurred from birth to death. Childhood and education are, as a rule, briefly discussed at the outset; then the course of the subject's career is mapped out, with the emphasis on the key achievements and the essential details of private life. Wherever possible, contextual or explanatory information has been given in order to orient the general reader, who may be unaware of the historical circumstances surrounding an event or unfamiliar with the particulars of a field of endeavor, such as physics or educational theory or agriculture. In articles on people who were engaged in a variety of careers or important activities that overlapped, allowance has been made for a more thematic approach to their biographies. The concluding paragraph of the text is usually meant to put the subject's life in historical perspective, as seen from the vantage point of the late twentieth century.

Appended to each article is a descriptive bibliography, which may include mention of primary sources, the most useful published biographies, articles or monographs about specific aspects of the person's career, and obituaries. The aim is not to be comprehensive but rather to offer the interested reader guidance on where to begin to look for more information.

The articles are arranged in alphabetical order according to headword, which usually consists of a surname and given names. Whether or not a surname is separated into parts, such as van der Kemp, or is prefixed with a particle like Mac or Mc, the sequence is always strictly letter by letter: Mabie, for example, precedes MacArthur, which comes before McAdoo. In the case of duplicate names, such as Benjamin Henry Latrobe, precedence is given to the person born first. For spellings of names and for the division between surname and given names, we have usually followed the authority of the Library of Congress catalog. In general, the headword, or entry term, of an article is the name by which the subject is best known: thus "RUTH, Babe" heads the article on the famous baseball player, rather than "RUTH, George Herman." If a subject is known by more than one name, a blind entry will direct the reader to the actual entry term: for example, "ZITKALA-SA. *See* Bonnin, Gertrude Simmons." Blind entries also serve to point readers to group entries, as in the instance of "ONIZUKA, Ellison S. *See* Challenger Shuttle Crew."

Every effort has been made to confirm the birth and death dates following the entry term of an article. The full extent of a person's life may, however, not always be known. We have therefore sometimes had to resort to giving approximate dates or to providing only the year or years that the person flourished. With regard to Old Style and New Style dates, we have adopted an expediency recommended by several of our associate editors. The dating of George Washington's birth can serve as an illustration. At the time that Washington was born, Great Britain and the American colonies still observed the Julian, or Old Style, calendar, which read 11 February 1731 on the day in question. Two decades later, the British and the colonists adopted the Gregorian, or New Style, calendar, which necessitated a forward shift in dates by eleven days. Thus Washington's birthday is now typically said to have occurred on 22 February 1732. It might appear that the Old Style and New Style dates of his birth are a year apart, but that is because under the Julian calendar January, February, and March were the last three months of the year and under the Gregorian calendar they became the first three months of the year. To alleviate possible confusion about the dating of events prior to the calendar shift of 1752, we usually cite the Old Style day and month and the New Style year. In the *ANB*, the date of Washington's birth is given as 11 February 1732; any event dated later in 1732, through the month of December, can then be understood as having taken place in the same year.

With regard to technical matters of style, such as capitalization of names of organizations, events, and eras, we have generally followed the thirteenth edition of *The Chicago Manual of Style*, which was in use at the time that the editorial principles of the *ANB* were formulated. Although our aim has been to establish consistency in format, style, and usage, we have not attempted to impose a uniform manner of expression on our more than six thousand contributors.

Special thanks are owed to Kathi Pittman and Bill Edstrom of Auto-Graphics, Inc., Pomona, California, for coordinating the typesetting of the *ANB*.

Paul Betz
Managing Editor

AMERICAN NATIONAL BIOGRAPHY

A

AARONS, Alexander A. (15 May 1890–14 Mar. 1943), theatrical producer, was born in Philadelphia, Pennsylvania, the son of Alfred E. Aarons, a theatrical composer and producer, and Josephine Hall. He was educated in New York schools. Aarons, whose producing career lasted only thirteen years, did not immediately take up his father's profession, but after hearing George Gershwin's songs in 1919 he determined to feature the young composer in a show of his own. Aarons's father had planned *La La Lucille* (1919) with Victor Herbert as composer, but he allowed his son to follow his instincts, hire Gershwin as composer, and produce the show himself. The show was a moderate success but closed quickly because of an actors' strike.

Even after *The Hole in the Wall* (1920), Aarons remained part owner of a Manhattan men's clothing store. Influenced by the Bolton-Wodehouse-Kern Princess Theatre musical comedies, Aarons produced *Oui Madame* in a small Philadelphia playhouse in 1920, with music by Herbert and with composer Vincent Youmans as rehearsal pianist. The show never left Philadelphia. Aarons's dream of a new Princess series did not progress until he persuaded Fred and Adele Astaire, then appearing in *The Love Letter*, to perform in *For Goodness' Sake* (1922) by William Daly and Paul Lannin. During the show's New York run Aarons convinced the Astaires to take the show to London. Renamed *Stop Flirting*, with Gershwin interpolations, the production ran for 455 performances, longer than any other Astaire show. Aarons then joined forces with producer Vinton Freedley. After producing *The New Poor* (1923) they signed George and Ira Gershwin and the Astaires for *Lady, Be Good!* (1924). (In the meantime, writing as "Arthur Francis," Ira Gershwin and Youmans had written songs for *Piccadilly to Broadway* [1920]. George Gershwin played their songs for Aarons, who signed them to write *Two Little Girls in Blue* [1922], but he sold the show to booking agent Abe Erlanger. Youmans also composed the score for Aarons's 1925 production of *A Night Out*, including "Sometimes I'm Happy," but the show closed on the road.)

The Princess-derived manifesto of the Aarons-Freedley musical comedies included everyday characters caught in comic situations, snappy contemporary dialogue, no intrusive "star turns," and songs arising from plot and character. Wishing to fill larger theaters, the producers used a larger chorus and youthful stars, relying on comics such as Victor Moore. The Gershwins became virtual "house composers." Gershwin biographer Edward Jablonski remarked, "The kind of 'smart show' that Aarons and Freedley aimed at provided [them] with the chance to compose songs for a knowing, literate, contemporary audience."

Lady, Be Good! was a major hit, marking for the noted financial backer, "angel" Otto Kahn, "a unique experience—the first time [Kahn] had ever received any return from a theatrical venture." It was followed by *Tip-Toes* (1925), *Oh, Kay!* (1926), which featured the American debut of English star Gertrude Lawrence, and *Funny Face* (1927), starring the Astaires. All scores were written by the Gershwins. In 1928 Aarons and Freedley produced *Here's Howe*, featuring the music of Gus Kahn, Joseph Meyer, and Irving Caesar; *Hold Everything!*, with a score by Buddy DeSylva and Ray Brown; and *Treasure Girl*, with music by the Gershwins. In 1929 followed *Spring Is Here* and *Heads Up!*, both with songs by Richard Rodgers and Lorenz Hart. The last Aarons-Freedley-Gershwin hit was *Girl Crazy* (1930). Following *Singin' the Blues* (1931), a well-received musical about African Americans composed by Jimmy McHugh and Dorothy Fields, and *Pardon My English* (1932), with score by the Gershwins, Aarons and Freedley ended their partnership.

According to Fred Astaire, Aarons was so anxious on opening nights that he hid in the men's room until the curtain fell. He once remarked, "You know, I just feel like throwing up all the time the show is on." With his wife Ella Mulligan—they had no children—Aarons enjoyed a transatlantic society that included Noël Coward, Tallulah Bankhead, Lord Ned Lathom, Jules Glaenzer of Cartiers, Paul Whiteman, Georges Carpentier, Florenz Ziegfeld, Fanny Brice, Charles Chaplin, and Marilyn Miller. Aarons always invited friends to his office for five o'clock cocktails, and Rodgers called him a "bald, bespectacled man with a great fund of jokes and an enormous love for music."

Called by Ira Gershwin "one of the keenest judges of a smart tune," Aarons insisted that George Gershwin expand a fragment he had written in London for *Lady, Be Good!* The song became the legendary "Fascinating Rhythm." Ira Gershwin said:

> Alex was fond . . . of at least 20 of George's songs which had not yet been written up lyrically, so he had no means of calling for any one of them by numeral or title. But he could request what he wanted to hear this way: whisking his hand across George's shoulder, he would say: "Play me the one that goes like *that*." Or: "Play the tune that smells like an onion." Or: "*You* know, the one that reminds me of the Staten Island Ferry." And so on.

Freedley once expressed dislike for an improvised Rodgers melody, but Aarons overruled him. The tune became "With a Song in My Heart," which went on to earn considerable fame.

The Aarons-Freedley partnership thrived on Aarons's musical instincts and Freedley's business sense. Both partners wrongly believed the Gershwin score for *Funny Face* to be substandard, but Aarons also understood that Robert Benchley's book, originally called *Smarty*, was the real problem. Consequently he extended the tryout and hired Paul Gerard Smith and Fred Thompson as new librettists. In 1927 the show opened the new Alvin Theater (derived from the first syllables of their given names; now the Neil Simon Theater) on Fifty-second Street west of Broadway, built specifically for the kinds of shows they produced. *Funny Face* succeeded in both New York and London.

Freedley gave actor Bert Lahr his first musical comedy starring role in *Hold Everything!*, but the show lost money in its tryout, and, according to theater critic and biographer (and Bert's son) John Lahr, Aarons viewed Freedley's "little flop" as "just one of those things I'd close up on the road." The show ended up running for two years, and Aarons and Freedley signed Lahr to a (never completed) five-year contract. Despite a charming score and the presence of Gertrude Lawrence, *Treasure Girl*, which centered on the unappealing side of fortune hunting, was the first Gershwin-Aarons-Freedley flop. Aarons subsequently recruited Rodgers and Hart, but before the opening of *Heads Up!* he reportedly charged down the aisles shouting, "Boys, you can forget about the show. You can forget about everything. The bottom's just dropped out of the market."

Girl Crazy was a great success, but the depression made the partners cautious, and Aarons's judgment failed. In 1932, short of funds and against Freedley's advice, he insisted on casting Jack Buchanan, the former Andre Charlot revue star, in a book musical called *Pardon My English*, which ignored Buchanan's intimate charm. Buchanan left the show during tryouts, Freedley took over, and in ten weeks the show lost $50,000. Discussions about another Gershwin show led nowhere, and the Gershwins became involved in *Of Thee I Sing* and *Porgy and Bess*. The Aarons-Freedley partnership formally ended in February 1933. Freedley went on to produce *Anything Goes*; Aarons never produced another Broadway show. He moved to Hollywood, where his only film credit was as assistant producer of *The Broadway Melody of 1936*. After working for various agencies, he was a producer at RKO Pictures, advising on the Gershwin film biography, when he died in Beverly Hills of a heart attack. Innovative, gregarious, and emotional, Aarons advanced the early careers of George Gershwin, Vincent Youmans, Richard Rodgers, and Lorenz Hart. In association with Vinton Freedley, he built the Alvin Theater, teamed Fred and Adele Astaire with the Gershwins, and produced the 1920s' most stylish and successful musical comedies.

• There is no known collection of Aarons papers. Aarons is fondly remembered in many biographies and books of memoirs. Among these are Fred Astaire, *Steps in Time* (1960); Gerald Bordman, *Days to Be Happy, Years to Be Sad: The Life and Music of Vincent Youmans* (1982); Ira Gershwin, *Lyrics on Several Occasions* (1959); Edward Jablonski, *Gershwin: A Biography* (1987); John Lahr, *Notes on a Cowardly Lion: The Biography of Bert Lahr* (1969); and Richard Rodgers, *Musical Stages: An Autobiography* (1975).

JAMES ROSS MOORE

AARONS, Alfred E. (16 Nov. 1865–16 Nov. 1936), theatrical manager and producer, was born in Philadelphia, Pennsylvania, the son of Aaron Aarons, a clothier, and Elizabeth (maiden name unknown). Educated in Philadelphia public schools, at age fifteen he began working in the box office of the Central Theater. After several other theatrical jobs, Aarons established a dramatic and vaudeville agency in Philadelphia; he opened an office in New York City after moving there in 1890. There in the same year he married Josephine Hall, an actress. They had three children.

Beginning in 1892 Aarons worked for Oscar Hammerstein, first as the manager of the Manhattan Roof Garden above Hammerstein's Manhattan Opera House and then at Koster and Bial's Music Hall on Thirty-fourth Street. Among many European acts making their debut at Koster and Bial's was Britain's saucy singer, Marie Lloyd. When Hammerstein bought America's largest variety theater, the Victoria, and turned it over to his son Willie, Aarons became its European representative. Between 1893 and 1895 Aarons sent back such star acts as the Moulin Rouge singer Yvette Guilbert and the classical dancer Cléo de Merode, noted for her flawless skin, heart-shaped face, and chignon hairstyle—"le style Cléo," which became an American fad.

Never a man to put all his eggs in one basket, upon his return in 1897 Aarons joined the organization of Mark Klaw and Abraham Erlanger, the core of the recently formed Theatrical Syndicate that came to dominate legitimate theater bookings. He also leased Harriman's Theater in New York City and briefly produced international vaudeville. He began to write songs. In 1898 Aarons leased Krause's Music Hall on Thirty-fourth Street and renamed it the Savoy Theater.

An early Aarons composition, "Rag Time Liz," was interpolated into his production of the musical comedy *Wine, Women and Song* (1898), one of Eva Tanguay's earliest American shows. In 1900 Aarons produced and wrote the score for *The Military Maid*, a show in which Josephine Hall sang a showstopping number called "Sister Mary Has the Measles." It closed in a week. In the same year his score and production of *Mam'selle Hawkins* were called sprightly; the show ran slightly more than a month. His luck at producing musical comedies did not improve with *The Ladies' Paradise* (1901) for Hall, despite a score by Ivan Caryll; equally unsuccessful were his scores for Hall's *The Knickerbocker Girl* (1903) and, collaborating with the prolific Harry B. Smith, *A China Doll* (1904). Perhaps Aarons's most successful musical enterprise in these years was *The Babes and the Baron* (1905), an English musical comedy with interpolations by Aarons and Jerome Kern. Turning to straight drama, Aarons successfully produced *His Honor, the Mayor* (1906).

For Klaw and Erlanger, Aarons organized the International Theater Managers Association, covering the United States and Canada. He was thus credited with the Syndicate's stranglehold on theatrical road shows. He served on the board of trustees of the Actors Fund of America and became an increasingly powerful presence inside the Broadway power structure. In 1915, following the death of his first wife, Aarons married actress Leila Hughes. They had no children.

In 1919 Aarons was planning another musical comedy, which eventually was called *La La Lucille: A New, Up to the Minute Musical Comedy of Class and Distinction*, its score to be composed by Victor Herbert. Aarons's son Alex, a clothing store proprietor who had become interested in producing musical comedy, introduced him to a young composer named George Gershwin. Gershwin took over the show—his first complete theatrical score—and the elder Aarons stepped partially aside; when the show took the road, Alex A. Aarons got his first production credit in collaboration with George Seitz.

Gershwin was invited to write Aarons's next show; instead he suggested Vincent Youmans and his own brother Ira, who was still writing as "Arthur Francis." This became *Two Little Girls in Blue* (1921), the first full theatrical score for both. Before the show opened, Erlanger bought Aarons out. Three nonmusical productions of the elder Aarons at this time were *Yama* and *The Drums of Jeopardy* (both 1922) and *Magnolia* (1923). Both elder and younger Aarons shared the misery of the pre-Broadway closing of the British hit *A Night Out* (1925). Later in 1925 the elder Aarons produced the Gershwins' *Tell Me More*. This followup to the younger Aarons's *Lady, Be Good!* (1924) for Fred and Adele Astaire ran 100 performances in New York City but 263 (under Alex Aarons's name) in London.

By this time Jake and Lee Shubert had broken the Syndicate's monopoly on legitimate theater and substituted their own. Aarons's most ambitious musical, *My Princess*, a Sigmund Romberg–Dorothy Donnelly operetta that seemed dated by contrast to the Gershwins' peppy shows, was further unlucky in its choice of opening night: 6 October 1927, the first night of the talking film *The Jazz Singer*. Aarons's subsequent ventures into straight drama were largely unsuccessful: *Headquarters* (1929), a "derivative police drama"; *The Girl Outside* (1932), a "stale and pedestrian minor theatrical romance"; and *$25 an Hour* (1933), a "grim comedy" of European tenors that nevertheless managed to show off Jean Arthur in blue pajamas.

Aarons went on to manage New York City's most important theaters: the New Amsterdam, the Broadhurst, the Vanderbilt, and the National. In the early days of the depression, Aarons, still a part of the theatrical establishment, chaired the special committee representing theater within the New York mayor's Committee on Unemployment Relief. Aarons died in New York City.

• Information on Aaron's career can be found in Gerald Bordman, *Days to Be Happy, Years to Be Sad* (1982), and Vincent Sheean, *The Amazing Oscar Hammerstein* (1956). An obituary is in the *New York Times*, 17 Nov. 1936.

JAMES ROSS MOORE

AARONS, Edward Sidney (1916–16 June 1975), mystery writer, was born in Philadelphia, Pennsylvania. Aarons (also known by the pen names Paul Ayres and Edward Ronns) worked variously as a newspaper reporter, millhand, salesman, and fisherman to support himself while attending Columbia University. In 1933 he won a collegiate short story contest. In 1936, with the publication of his first mystery novel, he decided to make writing his career.

Under the name Edward Ronns, he wrote hard-boiled detective novels such as *Death in a Lighthouse* (1938), *Murder Money* (1938), and *The Corpse Hangs High* (1939). During this period and until 1956, when he turned exclusively to the novel form and his popular "Assignment" series, he wrote many magazine stories and novellas that appeared in publications such as *Detective Story Magazine*, *The Shadow*, and *Scarab*. Throughout this period of his career his fiction is set in the large eastern cities where he had spent much of his life before settling in Washington, Connecticut, in the mid-1950s. As a newspaper reporter in Philadelphia, for example, he gained an intimate knowledge of a big city's inner workings that is reflected in his early novels and short stories. Also during this period, with such novels as *No Place to Live* (1947) and *Gift of Death* (1948), Aarons began to develop a series hero named Jerry Benedict. In 1956, with great success, Aarons returned to the notion of a series hero—Sam Durrell, who first appears in *Assignment to Disaster*.

Aarons's writing career was sidetracked in 1941 when, after the bombing of Pearl Harbor, he enlisted in the coast guard. After having attained the rank of chief petty officer, Aarons returned to civilian life in 1945. He went back to school at Columbia University, where he received a bachelor's degree in 1947, with a concentration on ancient history and literature. He also met his first wife, Ruth Ives. After her death, he subsequently married Grace Dyer. There were no children from either marriage.

Although he abandoned the local settings of his early work with his Assignment series, there was a similar eye for detail and a concern for topical issues. These were most often set in the faraway places that Aarons researched on annual trips in search of new and vivid material. Along with their topical appeal, these later books also reflected Aarons's appreciation for each region's historical background.

Moving his fiction from a domestic to an international setting certainly helped its popularity. The Assignment series sold more than 23 million copies and has been reprinted in seventeen languages. In the *New York Times Book Review*, Anthony Boucher referred to the series as "among the best modern adventure stories of espionage and international intrigue." The series follows the fictional adventures of Sam Durrell, a

Yale-educated Central Intelligence Agency agent—code named Cajun, for his Louisiana upbringing—who crisscrosses the globe fighting villains who threaten international or regional security. During his missions Durrell dishes out and receives large doses of graphically depicted violence. Despite Durrell's callous zeal in his pursuit of duty, he often reveals a soft spot for the women with whom he works. Readers of the series learned to depend on its formula. Each novel begins with a chapter of violent intrigue. Durrell is then introduced and situated in a foreign country, where, after confronting a series of obstacles, he beats the arch-villain, averts a catastrophe, and wins the lady.

The series format does allow for some variations within the broader formula, however. Early in the series, the villains are sometimes women. Later in the series, female characters who possess varying degrees of refinement become admiring accomplices in Durrell's heroic exploits. Although his depiction of women often displays the chauvinism typical of the spy novel of the 1950s and 1960s, some readers find that the women who aid Durrell's later efforts display a fair amount of independent strength and intelligence.

Of Aarons's eighty-odd novels, it was the Assignment series along with its protagonist, Sam Durrell, that caught the public's attention. In fact, the series was so popular that a member of Aarons's family briefly continued it after the author's death in New Milford, Connecticut.

Through his Assignment series Aarons helped to create the American variant of the spy hero popularized by Ian Fleming's James Bond. Scholar Roger Handberg has suggested that Aarons's Americanization of the spy novel—along with Donald Hamilton's Matt Helm series (1960–1974) and Philip Atlee's Joe Gall series (1964–1973)—is a significant part of a distinctly American response to the tensions and increasing complexity of the Cold War.

• There is an extended listing of Aarons's writings, together with an assessment, in John M. Reilly, ed., *Twentieth-Century Crime and Mystery Writers*, 2d ed. (1985). Aarons's Sam Durrell series is briefly considered in Roger Handberg, "Know Thy Enemy: Changing Images of the Enemy in Popular Literature," *North Dakota Quarterly* 53 (Winter 1985): 121–27. An obituary is in the *New York Times*, 20 June 1975.

SERGIO RIZZO

ABBE, Cleveland (3 Dec. 1838–28 Oct. 1916), meteorologist and astronomer, was born in New York City, the eldest of seven children of George Waldo Abbe, a merchant, and Charlotte Colgate. He was educated at the New York Free Academy, now City College of New York (part of CUNY), where he earned his bachelor's degree in 1857 and a master's degree in 1860.

Abbe taught at Trinity Grammar School in New York from 1857 to 1858 and at Michigan State Agricultural College and the University of Michigan from 1859 to 1860. While in Ann Arbor, he studied with the German astronomer Franz Brunnow.

He was rejected for military service because of myopia and spent the Civil War years computing telegraphic longitudes for the U.S. Coast Survey under Benjamin Gould (1824–1896) in Cambridge, Massachusetts. In 1865 and 1866 he studied astronomy with Otto Struve at Nicholas Central Observatory in Pulkova, Russia. Upon his return to the United States he served briefly as a computer, reducing data for the *Nautical Almanac*, and as an assistant observer at the U.S. Naval Observatory.

In 1868 Abbe became director of the Cincinnati Observatory where he developed a telegraphic meteorological service covering the greater part of the Ohio Valley and serving the commercial and agricultural interests of the region. His first weather bulletin was issued in 1869, several months before Congress passed a national weather service bill and a year before the U.S. Army Signal Office began issuing daily national weather reports. Abbe left the observatory in 1870 and became a civilian employee of the Signal Office, in Washington, D.C., where, as professor of meteorology, he was one of the nation's highest paid scientists.

From 1891 until his retirement in 1916 Abbe spent the rest of his career with the U.S. Weather Bureau in the Department of Agriculture. He was the founder and long-time editor of the *Monthly Weather Review*, author of numerous official reports, and translator of many European works. He was a pioneer in weather map analysis and forecasting, proponent of a national time standard, and meteorology editor for several encyclopedias, including *Britannica*. He wrote many articles on the history of meteorology. As an adjunct professor at Columbian (now George Washington) University and a lecturer at Johns Hopkins University, he tried, unsuccessfully, to establish meteorology's place in the academy. The first college departments of meteorology were not established until the 1930s, and meteorology was not fully professionalized until after World War II. Although he did not make original theoretical contributions to the science of meteorology, Abbe was a dedicated scientist in the federal service who kept the practical work of weather forecasting abreast of the latest physical theories, promoted the field of meteorology and its history, and served as a bridge between scientists in Europe and America.

Abbe was active in international scientific and learned societies and received several awards, including the Symons Medal of the Royal Meteorological Society, the Longstreth Medal of the Franklin Institute, and the Hartley Medal of the National Academy of Sciences.

Abbe was married to Frances Martha Neal in 1870; they had three sons. Frances died in 1908, and he married Margaret Augusta Percival in 1909. Abbe's hobbies included oriental archaeology and music. He died in Chevy Chase, Maryland.

• Most of Abbe's personal papers are in the Library of Congress. Smaller collections are located in Eisenhower Library at the Johns Hopkins University, at the Cincinnati Observatory, and in the library of the City University of New York.

Many of his official documents are in the Records of the Weather Bureau in the National Archives.

William J. Humphreys, "Biographical Memoir of Cleveland Abbe, 1838–1916," *Biographical Memoirs of the National Academy of Sciences* 8 (1919): 469–508, contains Abbe's curriculum vita and a bibliography with 290 items. There is a short article about Abbe in the *Dictionary of Scientific Biography*. Truman Abbe, *Professor Abbe and the Isobars: The Story of Cleveland Abbe, America's First Weatherman* (1955), was written by his son, who used his father's papers to prepare the book.

On Abbe's early career see Nathan Reingold, "Cleveland Abbe at Pulkowa: Theory and Practice in the Nineteenth Century Physical Sciences," *Archives Internationales d'Histoire des Sciences* 17 (1964): 133–47. On his work in Cincinnati see William J. Humphreys, "Origin and Growth of the Weather Service of the United States, and Cincinnati's Part Therein," *Scientific Monthly* 18 (1924): 372–82, and James Rodger Fleming, *Meteorology in America, 1800–1870* (1990). See also Cecil J. Alter, "National Weather Service Origins," *Bulletin of the Historical and Philosophical Society of Ohio* 7 (1949): 139–85.

JAMES RODGER FLEMING

ABBEY, Edward (29 Jan. 1927–14 Mar. 1989), essayist, novelist, and radical ecologist, was born in Home, Pennsylvania, the son of Paul Revere Abbey, a farmer, and Mildred Postlewaite, a public schoolteacher. He was raised, with four siblings, on a hardscrabble farm. A turning point in late adolescence came out of some months of hitchhiking around the western United States, with which he ever after fervently identified himself.

He was drafted into the U.S. Army (1945–1947), which he later wrote of as arbitrary and despised servitude—an insistently repeated theme. After discharge, he used the GI Bill to major in philosophy at the University of New Mexico (B.A., 1951). He worked at marginal living, varied jobs, and writing and intermittently did graduate work, studying Enlightenment thought on a Fulbright Fellowship at the University of Edinburgh (1951–1952) and philosophy at the University of New Mexico (M.A., 1956; thesis on ethics of violence in nineteenth-century anarchism).

For many years Abbey worked, somewhat intermittently, as a Forest Service fire-lookout and national park ranger in the mountain West (1956–1971). For brief periods he disconsolately tried being a social caseworker and technical writer in New York City. Primarily living in and writing about the mountain-desert West, he also made excursions, personal and literary, into wilderness areas in Appalachia, Alaska, Mexico, and Australia. Abbey's wives included Rita Deanin, whom he married in 1952 and divorced in 1965 (they had two children); Judy Pepper, whom he married in 1965 and who died in 1970 (they had one child); and Clarke (maiden name unknown), who survived him with her two children. In his later years, he taught writing at the University of Arizona, until his death in Oracle, Arizona.

Abbey held that his main vocation was as iconoclastic litterateur defending natural wilderness and freedom. So with his eight novels. *Jonathan Troy* (1954), in the manner of socially critical naturalism, is about an adolescent growing up in rural poverty and disillusionment in the East. The others are mostly western in scene and theme. *The Brave Cowboy* (1956) centered on a quixotic, anti-authority contemporary cowboy and his defiant flight from police and military, ending with techno-destruction, in intensely realized mountain wilderness scenes. (It was also the source for an unusual western movie with Kirk Douglas, *Lonely Are the Brave* [1962].) The slight *Fire on the Mountain* (1962; made into a movie of that title in 1981) told the story of an individualistic old rancher being dispossessed by military-technological development—a favorite theme.

More vivid description of the mountain scene and of physical sensation, around a middle-aged fire-lookout and his ill-fated love affair with an upper-class adolescent woman, shapes the pathos of the novella *Black Sun* (1971). Less autobiographical is *Good News* (1980), a rather cartoonishly done satiric dystopia of the near-future civil war in Phoenix of vestigial rebels against stereotypical American fascists "after the Great Collapse" of ecologically disintegrating America. The more personal *The Fool's Progress: An Honest Novel* (1988) episodically recounts the pilgrimage, through varied bohemian and yuppie scenes, of an Abbey-like, aging and ailing macho character, with old pickup truck and dog, from a Tucson suburb to a Pennsylvania farm in search of his roots in simple, marginal living and brotherly compassion.

"Cactus Ed's" best-known novel, and intended handbook of troublemaking, *The Monkey-Wrench Gang* (1975), along with its posthumously published continuation *Hayduke Lives!* (1990), is dedicated to the Luddite anarchism of sabotaging American technocracy in the remaining open West. Comic and hyperbolic picaresque, the two novels center on psychopathic-heroic George Washington Hayduke, war veteran and lower-class westerner, and his "eco-warrior" buddies battling the "development" machines and authorities. Abbey argues for a "healthy hatred" of "technotyranny" and for ingenious "creative destruction" (but no violence against persons) for a "counter-industrial revolution" against "the planetary Empire of Growth and Greed," a "megamachine" destroying all being.

Such dissidence ("Society is like a stew—if you don't keep it stirred up you get a lot of *scum* on top") was also a major aspect of his half-dozen collections of nonfictional prose. These wilderness accounts and "personal history" essays may be some of Abbey's best writing, not only in the intensely vivid (yet antimystical) nature experiences, but in presenting a richly responsive, whether wry or angry, iconoclast. *Desert Solitaire* (1968), the best known, centers with tough candor on his times as a fire-lookout and park ranger. Here, and increasingly in later essays (influenced to more overt sabotage by post-1960s protest), he revived anarchist Propaganda of the Deed (destroying surveyors' markers, burning billboards, disabling diesels, protectively tree-spiking in old-growth forests, satiric sloganeering, and other measures). This became an acknowledged impetus for his friends founding in 1980 a radical environmentalist protest movement called Earth First! Defiant "direct action" is personally as well as socially therapeutic and positively "transforms the human personality," Abbey typically insisted.

But in fact Abbey was more of a sardonic commentator than a political activist. His defense of wilderness expresses not just conservation but a larger libertarian ethic: "The domination of nature leads to the domination of human nature." Power is "the natural enemy of truth," and thus we need radical depowering, especially from the "mad cancer of growth for its own sake." To achieve a properly decentralized and egalitarian society, he argued, Americans must reduce their population by more than half and develop a simpler, steady-state, limited-tech society "keeping true to the earth."

Abbey's commitment was not to "fine" literature but to combining "art" with "sedition." "Occupation? Criminal anarchy." His defiance gave his writings, with their immediacy of nature experience, wry and hyperbolic humor, and libertarian demands for limiting population, techno-organization, and other domination, a distinctive role, as did his diatribes against the "diseases" he labeled tourism, consumerism, and "mediaism." (Abbey did not own a TV.) The anarchist mockeries were broad scale: "Recorded history is largely an account of the crimes and disasters committed by banal little men at the levers of imperial machines." Some effects seem evident in his esteem in current radical environmentalist literature and movements.

Abbey's self-conscious role was to combine, in both person and writings, the ecologically sensitive wilderness westerner with the Enlightenment rebel-skeptic in a post–World War II he-man manner (he had trouble with "new feminism" and other "chicken-shit liberalism"). In spite of his considerable macho western mode—including boots and vest over flannel shirt, six-pack of beer and cigar, pickup and .357 magnum, full beard and fully scornful tongue—he was also attempting a libertarian revision of western mythology. His late twentieth-century apocalyptic social concern as well as his personal responsiveness in a wry western style may convey a distinctive American rebelliousness.

• Manuscripts, letters, and other Abbey materials are in the Special Collections of the University of Arizona. In addition to the eight novels cited above, Abbey's writings include the self-edited *The Best of Edward Abbey* (1988)—not always his best. The travel and personal essay collections are *Desert Solitaire* (1968), *The Journey Home: Some Words in Defense of the American West* (1977), *Abbey's Road* (1979), *Down the River with Henry David Thoreau and Friends* (1982), *Beyond the Wall* (1984), and *One Life at a Time, Please* (1988). A late collection of aphorisms is *A Voice Crying in the Wilderness* (1989). His texts to collections of photographs include *Appalachian Wilderness: The Great Smokey Mountains*, with Eliot Porter (1970), *Slickrock: Endangered Canyons of the Southwest*, with Philip Hyde (1971), *Cactus Country* (1973), *The Hidden Canyon: A River Journey*, with John Blaustein (1977), and *Desert Images*, with David Muench (1979).

Some biographical material is in an introductory monograph by Garth McCann, *Edward Abbey* (1977). An interesting memoir is Edward Hoagland, "Abbey's Road," in *Balancing Acts* (1992). Brief recollections are in the miscellany by James Hepworth and Gregory McNamee, eds., *Resist Much, Obey Little: Some Notes on Edward Abbey* (1985). A survey of some of the writings is Ann Ronald, *The New West of Edward Abbey* (1982). The radical environmental context is presented in Dave Foreman, *Confessions of an Eco-Warrior* (1991). See also Dave Foreman and Bill Haywood, eds., *Ecodefense: A Field Guide to Monkeywrenching*, 2d ed., with foreword by Abbey (1987). For fuller background, see *Earth First! Journal* (1980–1990); also, Christopher Manes, *Green Rage: Radical Environmentalism and the Unmaking of Civilization* (1990); Rik Scarce, *Eco-Warriors: Understanding the Radical Environmental Movement* (1990); Susan Zakin, *Coyotes and Town Dogs: Earth First!* (1993); and Kingsley Widmer, "Edward Abbey," in *Contemporary American Activists*, ed. David De Leon (1993).

KINGSLEY WIDMER

ABBEY, Edwin Austin (1 Apr. 1852–1 Aug. 1911), artist, was born in Philadelphia, Pennsylvania, the son of William Maxwell Abbey, a commercial broker, and Margery Ann Kiple. Abbey's sole formal artistic training took place in 1868 at the Pennsylvania Academy of the Fine Arts, where he took night classes under Christian Schussele.

In 1871 Abbey began a lifelong association as an illustrator for the publishing firm Harper & Brothers in New York City. Abbey entered the publishing business at a fortunate time, as popular magazines were increasing their use of illustrations accompanying news stories, feature articles, and works of literature. When he started at Harper, the firm used wood engraving to translate drawings to publication. The most successful illustrators were skilled draftsmen who could convey a scene succinctly without losing details in the print. As Abbey honed his drawing abilities, his assignments advanced in complexity—from news and feature articles to historical and travel material to plays and poetry. Strong contour lines, tonal contrasts, and simple yet evocative costumes and settings were hallmarks of Abbey's early work. His first drawing to accompany a literary topic was for Robert Herrick's poem "Corinna's Going A-Maying," published in *Harper's New Monthly Magazine* (May 1874); the poem was the subject as well of Abbey's first oil painting (1890). Harper also published books illustrated by Abbey (usually after the drawings ran in the magazines), including editions of Charles Dickens's *Christmas Stories* (1875), *Selections from the Poetry of Robert Herrick* (1882), Oliver Goldsmith's *She Stoops to Conquer* (1887), and *Old Songs* (1889).

Abbey occasionally drew for other publishers, including Scribner, Armstrong & Co. Bryant and Gay's *Popular History of the United States* (1876–1881) featured work by some of the best illustrators of the time, including Winslow Homer, Alfred Kappes, and Charles Mente as well as Abbey.

British art and history fascinated Abbey. His well-executed drawings for the volume of Herrick's poetry and an assignment to illustrate an article on Stratford-on-Avon prompted, in 1878, a trip to England, where he would remain for the rest of his life and where he befriended fellow expatriates James McNeill Whistler, John Singer Sargent, and Henry James. Influenced by the mid-nineteenth-century British painters known as the Pre-Raphaelites, Abbey incorporated their representational painting style, attention to historical detail, and dramatic subjects into his own work.

Around the beginning of 1888 Abbey began his largest commission for Harper—illustrating all of Shakespeare's comedies, tragedies, and histories. His striving for historical accuracy was satisfied by several trips throughout Europe to view firsthand the plays' various settings, by the careful study and collection of period costumes and furniture, and by the re-creation of scenes in his studio in Gloucestershire, which he occasionally shared with Sargent. Abbey also regularly attended Shakespeare theater productions. Harper published the series in its monthly magazine between 1889 and 1908 using new photomechanical processes that benefited Abbey's fluid and detailed style. The comedies were published in book form in 1896. Several of Abbey's finest oil paintings were inspired by the Shakespeare series, including *The Play Scene in "Hamlet"* (1897) and *King Lear's Daughters* (1898).

The decision in 1890 to hire Abbey, a novice painter, to complete a large mural for the Boston Public Library was probably prompted by the artist's friendship with architect-in-chief Charles Follen McKim and with Sargent and sculptor Augustus Saint-Gaudens, both of whom also contributed to the library's decoration. Also in 1890, Abbey married Mary Gertrude Mead, with whom he had no children. Abbey's contiguous series of oil paintings that hang in the delivery room of the library illustrates the theme of the Holy Grail set in twelfth-century France. The completed series, unveiled in 1901, was met with mixed reviews. Some critics preferred the flat, decorative quality of Puvis de Chavannes's legend of St. Genevieve to Abbey's theatrical scenes and elusive symbolism.

In 1896 Abbey was elected an associate of the Royal Academy and, in 1898, a royal academician. He exhibited his Shakespeare paintings and American commissions at the Academy before shipping them abroad. His dedication to British subject matter and his academic painting style overrode any hesitation the other members might have had about Abbey because of his American origins.

Abbey's international success warranted his election to several other distinguished associations, including the Institute of American Architects (1895), the Société Nationale des Beaux-Arts (1896), the National Academy of Design (1901), and the American Academy of Arts and Letters (1905). In 1896 Abbey was awarded the Cross of the Légion d'honneur. He also received two honorary degrees, an M.A. from Yale University (1897) and an LL.D from the University of Pennsylvania (1902). In 1908 the Pennsylvania Academy of the Fine Arts gave Abbey a Gold Medal of Honor.

In 1902 Abbey began work on the decoration of the new state capitol in Harrisburg, Pennsylvania, his last major commission. The project's scope required Abbey to hire several assistants, make hundreds of figure studies, and use lantern slides to transfer his drawings to the large canvases. Combining allegorical and historical imagery, the largest painting is the 35-foot-tall *Apotheosis of Pennsylvania* in the state house of representatives; historical paintings *Penn's Treaty with the Indians* and *The Reading of the Declaration of Independence* accompany the *Apotheosis*. Lunettes in the rotunda represent the "treasures" of the state, from landscape to religious freedom to iron and steel workers. Because the paintings were unfinished when Abbey died in London, Sargent supervised their completion.

Abbey's most prestigious British commissions included a panel for the Royal Exchange in London and the official painting of King Edward VII's coronation (both completed in 1904). The Royal Exchange painting depicts the reconciliation of the Merchant Taylors Company and the Skinners Company in front of Richard III. The coronation painting, now in the Royal Collection, presents a friezelike formation of royal, government, and religious participants at the 1902 event.

Abbey's popularity waned in the twentieth century with the decline of magazine illustration and the advent of new painting styles and as historic and literary themes lost favor to the contemporary realism of the ashcan school and regionalism and to the art-for-art's sake fervor of abstraction. His position in history relegated him to being a follower of rather than a contributor to the Pre-Raphaelites. As a master of the graphic medium, however, Abbey is still revered for his imaginative and sensitive compositions.

• The Yale University Art Gallery owns the bulk of Abbey's work, and there are three main catalogs on portions of the collection: *Paintings, Drawings, and Pastels by Edwin Austin Abbey* (1939), *Edwin Austin Abbey* (1973), and Lucy Oakley, *Unfaded Pageant: Edwin Austin Abbey's Shakespearean Subjects* (1994). A plaster bas relief of Abbey by William Rudolph O'Donovan belongs to the Yale University Art Gallery, and a painting by John White Alexander is owned by the National Academy of Design. The major source on Abbey's life and work is E. V. Lucas, *Edwin Austin Abbey, Royal Academician: The Record of His Life and Work* (1921).

N. ELIZABETH SCHLATTER

ABBEY, Henry Eugene (27 June 1846–17 Oct. 1896), theatrical and operatic manager and impresario, was born in Akron, Ohio, the son of Henry Stephen Abbey, a clockmaker and partner in a jewelry business, and Elizabeth Smith. After graduating with honors from Akron High School, where he showed a keen interest in music, Abbey worked in his father's jewelry store until he launched his artistic management career in 1869 at the Sumner Opera House in Akron. In 1871 he became manager of the newly opened Akron Academy of Music, where he stayed for one season before moving to work first at John Ellsler's Euclid Avenue Opera House in Cleveland and then as treasurer of the Ellsler Opera House in Pittsburgh. While still in Akron, Abbey and Ellsler managed the tours of the singing and dancing Worrell Sisters, Edwin Adams, and Jane Coombs. Abbey's father died in 1873, leaving him the family jewelry store, which he apparently managed while still managing theatrical attractions on tour, including John T. Raymond and Lotta Crabtree. In 1876 Abbey sold the jewelry business (while retaining a real estate interest in Akron) and joined John B. Schoeffel in managing the Academy of Music in Buffalo, a business association that lasted until his death. In the same year he married Kate Kingsley of Massachusetts; they had two children.

With the backing of Crabtree, Abbey and Schoeffel took over management of New York's Park Theater in 1876, followed by the Park Theater in Boston in 1879. During this period Abbey managed Edward A. Sothern and brought together actors William H. Crane and Stuart Robson, who developed a successful stage partnership. In 1880 Abbey leased Booth's Theater in New York, where he presented Edwin Booth in Shakespeare plays. Abbey also scored a theatrical coup by starring Sarah Bernhardt in her American debut. Then at the height of her career, Bernhardt played 164 times under his management for a fee of $100,000.

In 1881 Abbey began his association with opera by managing Adelina Patti's concert tour for a profit in excess of $100,000 as well as producing comic operas and concerts at the Metropolitan Casino. In 1882 the Park Theater in New York burned, and the firm added the Grand Opera House and Star Theater (the second Wallack's theater) to its holdings. At this time Abbey brought Christine Nilsson from Europe for a farewell tour and furnished the season's sensation by introducing Lillie Langtry to the American stage.

Abbey's wife died unexpectedly in 1883, the same year Abbey became manager of the Metropolitan Opera House. It had been established that year by some of the nouveaux riches who were dissatisfied with the number of available boxes at the Academy of Music. Thus began the celebrated operatic war between the two opera houses and their supporters, with both houses ending the season with large deficits. Among the Met's established stars of the season were Christine Nilsson, Sofia Scalchi, Italo Campanini, Franco Novara, and Giuseppi Del Puente; in addition, Marcella Sembrich made her debut. Because he would not continue without restitution of his losses, Abbey's first term of managing the Metropolitan Opera lasted only one year. Because it was thought to be less expensive than Italian opera to produce, seven seasons of German opera followed, much to the delight of the thriving ethnic German populace in New York and to the consternation of many socialites. Also in 1883 Abbey presented Mary Anderson (1859–1940) at the London Lyceum, another theater he managed, and Henry Irving in New York. In 1884, in partnership with Langtry, Abbey became manager of the Princess Theatre in London. The next year a third partner, Maurice Grau, was added to the firm, which became Abbey, Schoeffel and Grau. For the next ten years it was one of the most important producing organizations in the theatrical world. Also in 1885 Abbey relinquished the Grand Opera House and suffered the untimely death of his young son.

Abbey was married a second time in 1886, to Florence Gerard, an actress. They had no children. After managing Wallack's (third) theater in 1887–1888, in 1889 he opened the Tremont Theater in Boston. Among the famous performers Abbey managed during the latter part of his career were Josef Hofmann, Benoit-Constant Coquelin, Lillian Russell, Lawrence Barrett, Jane Hading, Ellen Terry, Jean Mounet-Sully, Helena Modjeska, Fanny Janauschek, and the London Gaiety.

Abbey and Grau returned to the Metropolitan Opera in 1891 to restore Italian opera after the seven-year run of German opera, and in the following years stars such as Patti, Emma Albani, Lillian Nordica, the de Reszke brothers, Emma Eames, Lilli Lehmann, Jean Lasalle, Marie van Zandt, Emma Calvé, Nellie Melba, and Pol Plançon sang on its stage. In 1892 the Metropolitan Opera House burned, reopening in 1893. A theater bearing Abbey's name also opened in 1893 (known as the Knickerbocker after his death) and was used mainly for legitimate theater and comic opera, mostly foreign attractions.

But the 1890s also brought Abbey several reverses, including the failures of the visit of the great tragedian Mounet-Sulley and the spectacle "America," which was originally produced to great acclaim at the 1893 World's Columbian Exposition but later failed on the road. In 1896 a combination of the effects of the establishment of the so-called Theatrical Syndicate, the depression of mid-decade, and his own failing health left the firm with a total indebtedness of $365,000. A physically broken and financially bankrupt Abbey tried to reorganize the firm, retaining interests in only the Boston Tremont and the Metropolitan Opera. Suffering from Bright's disease, Abbey died in New York.

Personally modest and not well known even in his own time, Abbey experienced many vagaries in his career because of his willingness to take risks. However, he usually succeeded in presenting the musical and theatrical stars that a demanding public desired. This he did not only in New York but in many smaller cities in North America, Europe, and elsewhere. Between 1870 and 1900 the entertainment business felt the effects of many changes, including immigration, the rising social, cultural, and financial aspirations of the middle and upper classes, and the centralization of show business through theatrical circuits and booking agencies. Combining the qualities of showman, speculator, and businessman, Abbey studied public demand and served it.

• There is an Abbey clippings file at the New York Public Library. The most important study of Abbey's life and contributions is Richard J. Hossala, "Henry E. Abbey, Commercial-Manager: A Study of Producing Management in the Theatre of the Late Nineteenth Century (1870–1900)" (Ph.D. diss., Kent State Univ., 1972). A thesis by John Daniel Collins, "Henry Eugene Abbey: Akron Impresario" (Univ. of Akron, 1959), also is useful. Two studies of the operatic "war" in 1883–1884 are also available: Michael J. Pisoni, "Operatic War in New York City, 1883–84: Colonel James H. Mapleson at the Academy of Music vs. Henry E. Abbey at the Metropolitan Opera House" (Ph.D. diss., Indiana Univ., 1975), and John Frederick Cone, *First Rival of the Metropolitan Opera* (1983). Many accounts of the Metropolitan Opera have been written. Among the best of the general histories is Irving Kolodin, *The Metropolitan Opera, 1883–1966* (1966); Henry E. Krehbiel, *Chapters of Opera* (1908), gives a more contemporary account. Obituaries are in the 18 Oct. 1896 issues of the *New York Times* and the *New York Tribune*.

HARVEY R. BRENNEISE

ABBOT, Charles Greeley (31 May 1872–17 Dec. 1973), astronomer, was born in Wilton, New Hampshire, the son of Harris Abbot and Caroline Ann Greeley, farmers. Abbott began the study of chemistry and physics at Phillips Andover Academy and graduated from the Massachusetts Institute of Technology in 1894 with a thesis in chemical physics under the direction of A. A. Noyes. He then applied for teaching jobs but, failing to secure a position, decided to stay at MIT for postgraduate studies and in 1895 received an M.Sc. with a thesis on osmotic pressure. During this year, however, his name was suggested to Samuel Pierpont Langley, the secretary of the Smithsonian Institution as well as the director of its Astrophysical Observatory. Abbot thus secured a position as Langley's assistant, knowing nothing of astronomy when he arrived in Washington in June 1895 to work as an observatory aide. In 1897 he married Lillian E. Moore.

The primary aim of the Astrophysical Observatory, created by Langley in the early 1890s, was to study the amount and character of solar radiation. Langley had developed sensitive devices to measure the heat energy received from the sun and used these for bolometric studies of the so-called solar constant, as well as for spectroscopic studies, combining his detectors with spectrometers to map out the infrared spectrum of the sun. After Langley's death, Abbot became in 1906 the second director of the Astrophysical Observatory and in 1928 also became the fifth secretary of the Smithsonian Institution. He served in both positions until 1944. Abbot was a deft instrument designer and observer, whose lifelong goal soon became the refinement of Langley's determination of the solar constant. He was preoccupied, again following Langley, with proving a conviction that the solar constant varied and influenced terrestrial weather.

Abbot's primary strength was his ability to build devices such as bolometers and pyrheliometers to measure the heat received from the sun. He and his staff built instruments and made daily observations from Washington, D.C., as well as from a network of observing stations he built at various times around the world. Again following Langley's mode of operation, Abbot attempted observations from high mountains. But he added the use of unmanned balloonsondes, developing a special lightweight automated pyrheliometer for the task, which established the modern range for the solar constant.

When Abbot began working for Langley, and later with F. E. Fowle, values for the solar constant varied from Claude-Servais-Mathias Pouillet's 1.76, to Langley's 3.0, and to Knut Ångstrom's 4.0 calories per square centimeter per minute. This divergence was due to a lack of instrument standardization as well as poor knowledge of the amount of terrestrial atmospheric absorption influencing the observations. From about 1900 to 1915 Abbot designed a properly insulated thermometer chamber that also ensured greater heat conductivity to the thermometer bulb. These refinements, in conjunction with his balloon observations taken at altitudes of some twenty-five kilometers, allowed him to establish a value for the solar constant, 1.938, which established the range of the modern value and remained the standard for decades.

Abbot's search for an astronomical method of weather prediction was never successful in his lifetime. He had been convinced by the meteorologist H. H. Clayton, using Smithsonian data, that correlations between solar variations and terrestrial weather existed. Supported by Clayton's deductions, Abbot always insisted that he had detected the variation and ardently defended his observational and reduction techniques in the face of criticism throughout his life. Even when his scientific ally and patron C. F. Marvin, chief of the Weather Bureau, pointed to serious flaws in his technique in the 1920s, Abbot remained steadfast in his conviction.

Abbot possessed considerable charm, but he could also be an aggressive debater and convincing orator when he thought his conclusions were being threatened. Through his scientific friends, such as George Ellery Hale, who particularly admired his instrumental capabilities, Abbot obtained early recognition and prominence, including many endorsements for continuing solar-constant research at the Smithsonian. His constant proselytizing for support, which often included strong hints at his work's application to weather prediction, gained him patronage from Congress and from John A. Roebling of the Roebling Iron Works (grandson and son of the builders of the Brooklyn Bridge), who was particularly impressed with the possibility of finding clues to weather behavior. Abbot's single-minded scientific interests continued during his tenure as Smithsonian secretary, a period when both federal support and private patronage were on the decline. While he managed to maintain his astrophysical activities, the Smithsonian overall suffered considerably during the depression from lack of money and poor administration.

Because of his professional position and general predilections, Abbot campaigned to promote the image of science in service to humanity. Anxious to apply science to practical needs, Abbot harbored a fascination with the uses of solar energy. He built solar cookers and furnaces, which he used during his visits to

Mount Wilson Observatory in southern California. His World War I activities included studies of ballistics and searchlight design as well as brokering projects by Robert Goddard, which ranged from a recoilless gun to rocket ordnance. He was also known to dabble in lay preaching, and he loved to sing and was known to play the cello. His first wife died in 1944 and in 1954 he married a second time, to Virginia A. Johnston. He died in Washington, D.C., at the age of 101.

• An extensive collection of Charles Greeley Abbot Papers is housed in the Smithsonian Institution Archives. He also left an autobiographical account in Charles Greeley Abbot, *Adventures in the World of Science* (1958). A history of the Smithsonian Astrophysical Observatory, placing Abbot into institutional context, is Bessie Zaban Jones, *Lighthouse of the Skies* (1965), chapters 9–12. See also Deborah Jean Warner, "Charles Greeley Abbot," *Year Book of the American Philosophical Society* (1975), pp. 111–16; Peggy Aldrich Kidwell, "Prelude to Solar Energy: Pouillet, Herschel, Forbes and the Solar Constant," *Annals of Science* 38 (1981): 457–76; and David DeVorkin, "Defending a Dream: Charles Greeley Abbot's Years at the Smithsonian," *Journal for the History of Astronomy 21* (1990): 121–36.

DAVID DEVORKIN

ABBOT, Francis Ellingwood (6 Nov. 1836–23 Oct. 1903), Unitarian clergyman and philosopher, was born in Boston, the son of Joseph Hale Abbot and Fanny Ellingwood Larcom. The senior Abbot was a schoolmaster and amateur scientist who reflected the strict moralism of early nineteenth-century Unitarianism, while his wife displayed a strong poetical bent, and Abbot's life and career were influenced by both. After being educated at the Boston Latin School he entered Harvard College and graduated in 1859. While there he underwent a strong religious conversion, at least partly through the influence of his college friend William Reed Huntington and his professor Frederic Dan Huntington, and decided to study for the Unitarian ministry. During his college years he met Katharine Fearing Loring, whom he married in 1859; they had eight children, three of whom survived infancy.

He began his ministerial studies at Harvard Divinity School, but his need to support a family led him to transfer in 1860 to Meadville (Unitarian) Theological School, where he could also serve as principal of a local female seminary. While at Meadville he began to abandon his conservative Christian Unitarian faith and to undertake his subsequent lifelong goal of anchoring religious faith in science and philosophy rather than in revelation. He also strove to combine a strong loyalty to theism and moralism with an opposition to the doctrinal aspects of Christianity. Abbot graduated from Meadville in 1863 and was called in 1864 as minister of the first Unitarian Society of Dover, New Hampshire.

During his ministry at Dover, Abbot's criticism of traditional Christianity increased, and he became an important figure in the debate at the Unitarian National Conference meeting at Syracuse in 1866 over whether Unitarianism should understand itself as a Christian community. The defeat of the radicals at Syracuse led Abbot to help found in 1867 the Free Religious Association, in which he was an active participant until 1880.

Abbot's alienation from Christianity led to divisions within his congregation in Dover, and in 1868 he resigned from the Unitarian ministry. The First Independent Society of Dover, an independent free religious congregation, was founded by his supporters, and a protracted legal case developed over control of the church property. As a result of this case (*Hale v. Everett*), the radicals were excluded from control of the property. In 1869 he was chosen to be minister of the Unitarian Society of Toledo, Ohio, which, at his insistence, severed its connections with Unitarianism. His ministry in Toledo was not successful, and the society was largely moribund by 1873.

While in Toledo, Abbot became in 1870 editor of the *Index*, a weekly paper associated with the Free Religious Association and throughout the 1870s one of the leading journalistic voices for radical religion. In 1873 Abbot (and the *Index*) relocated to Boston. Under his editorship the *Index* sharply criticized both evangelical Protestantism and Roman Catholicism and advocated the secularist agenda of the National Liberal League, of which Abbot was president between 1876 and 1878. In 1878 Abbot broke with the NLL over the question of the Comstock laws against obscenity. As a strong opponent of "free love," he desired that these laws be reformed but still retained, but in the meeting of the NLL in Syracuse in 1878 a majority called for their outright repeal. In protest, Abbot and others in 1878 founded the National Liberal League of America (later called the American Liberal Union) as an alternative organization.

In the 1880s he began to concentrate his efforts more on the formal questions of philosophy. He received a Ph.D. in philosophy from Harvard in 1881 and was an active member of the Cambridge circle of philosophers. In consequence, however, of both his reputation for religious radicalism and his prickly personality, he was unable to procure a university teaching position and was instead forced to earn his livelihood running the Home School for Boys, a classical school for young men. But a legacy acquired in 1892 allowed him to dedicate his efforts full time to philosophy.

Abbot's philosophy can be characterized as a form of critical realism that attempted to bring together science and religion and refute the popular philosophical trends toward Kantianism and idealism. His Harvard dissertation was on the subject of "scientific realism," which was also the subject of his best-known philosophical work, *Scientific Theism* (1885). In contrast to both idealism and Kantianism, Abbot maintained that reality lay neither in the mind nor in experience, but in the objective relations of universals, or, as he called it, *universalia inter res*. This insight, he continued, was central to the achievements of science and should in turn be foundational for philosophy.

In the spring of 1888 he temporarily replaced Josiah Royce (who was away for health reasons) on the Harvard faculty, and his lectures were published in 1890 under the title *The Way Out of Agnosticism.* Royce published a devastating review of this volume in the *International Journal of Ethics*, which dismissed Abbot's theory of universals, claimed that he had borrowed his ideas from Hegel, and accused him of "philosophical pretensions." The review provoked great controversy within the Boston philosophical community. Upon the completion of his last philosophical treatise, *The Syllogistic Philosophy* (published posthumously in 1906), and on the tenth anniversary of his wife's death, Abbot committed suicide by taking poison and died on her grave. Recent scholars have noted the power of much of Abbot's religious and philosophical thought but have cited both the radical nature of his teachings, which stood so far out of the mainstream of religious and philosophical currents, and his difficult personality as preventing him from having any major impact on his generation.

• Abbot's papers are in the possession of Harvard University. A chronology of his life and a full list of his publications can be found in Sydney E. Ahlstrom and Robert B. Mullin, *The Scientific Theist: A Life of Francis Ellingwood Abbot* (1987). Obituaries are in the *Boston Transcript*, 24 Oct. 1903, and the *Christian Register*, 12 Nov. 1903.

ROBERT BRUCE MULLIN

ABBOT, Gorham Dummer (3 Sept. 1807–3 Aug. 1874), educator of women and clergyman, was born in Brunswick, Maine, the son of "Squire" Jacob Abbot, a land trustee and sometime merchant, and his wife and second cousin, Betsey Abbot. Gorham Abbot grew up in the nearby town of Hallowell and, like his four brothers, graduated from Bowdoin College (A.B., 1826; A.M., 1829) and studied at Andover Theological Seminary. All of the Abbot brothers became teachers and clergymen, the two eldest, Jacob Abbott and John Stevens Cabot Abbott, also distinguishing themselves as prolific authors. (The boys had added a second *t* to the family name; Gorham, however, employed the original spelling later in life.)

Gorham Abbot married Rebecca Leach in 1834. Their only child died at age ten after an accident. Ordained in 1837, Abbot served as pastor of a New Rochelle, New York, Presbyterian church from 1837 to 1841. He was also active in the American Tract Society and the American Society for the Diffusion of Useful Knowledge, which sought to distribute suitable literature to public schools. However, it was as a teacher and as a promoter of the higher education of women that he most distinguished himself. From 1831 to 1833, he and his brother Jacob ran the Mount Vernon School for girls in Boston. In 1843, Gorham, Jacob, and their brother Charles E. Abbott founded an institute in New York City for the instruction of "young ladies" in "all the branches of a finished education, including the elementary and higher English studies, the French and Latin languages, vocal music, and drawing" (Institution for the Education of Young Ladies, Announcement [1845], p. 5). In 1845 Gorham Abbot left the school and with a number of its senior pupils established a separate institute devoted to the advanced liberal education of young women, Abbott's Collegiate Institution for the Education of Young Ladies. The school became known as the Spingler Institute after it moved, in 1848, to a building on Union Square constructed for its use by the heirs of Henry Spingler.

Though the Spingler Institute also offered primary and secondary education, Abbot was most intent on meeting a rising demand for college-level training for women. He endeavored to provide both a comprehensive curriculum—with a pronounced religious orientation—and well-appointed facilities. Subjects taught at Spingler Institute included mental and moral philosophy, ancient and modern history, mathematics, chemistry, physiology, literature, modern languages, and music. Drawing pupils not only from New York City, but from over two dozen states and a number of nations, the institute thrived until the 1860s. The war years brought hard times as well as several changes in location. Conflict scattered the student body; attendant economic disarray and Abbot's own unhappy business dealings crippled the institute's finances. Abbot retired at the end of the decade and died in South Natick, Massachusetts.

Throughout his career Abbot argued for women's right to an education equal to that offered to men in private colleges. "We have between one and two hundred colleges in our country," he stated at the laying of the Spingler Institute's cornerstone, "but where is the Yale, Harvard, or Princeton for the education of females?" (*Abbot Memorial Book*, p. 41). "The great aim of the Institution," its annual announcement declared in 1861, "has always been to provide for *daughters*, privileges of education equal to those of *sons* in our Universities, Colleges, and Halls" (p. 12). Abbot wished to sway public opinion in favor of expanded opportunity, and, indeed, many who knew him, including his nephew Lyman Abbott, believed he had helped hasten American acceptance of the liberal education of women and credited him with influencing Vassar College's patron, Matthew Vassar.

However, Abbot seems not to have questioned prevailing conceptions of gender roles. He argued that any educated, cultivated woman could most benefit a household and best minister to her family as wife and mother. The Spingler Institute's principal attention, its announcements repeated year after year, would be devoted to studies "which are to qualify the pupil for daily duty as long as she lives, to fit woman for woman's sphere." Abbot apparently did not seek to reform the methods or goals of nineteenth-century education itself. Though renouncing compulsion or reward as the best means to motivate pupils, he sought to bring "wayward wills" to heel and to inculcate "habits of order, system, obedience, submission to Parents and to Teachers, and of moral self control" (Abbott's Collegiate Institution for the Education of Young Ladies, Announcement [1848], p. 4).

• A number of the annual announcements of Abbot's institutes can be found in the research collections of the New York Public Library. Abbot's publications include *Memoir of Nathan W. Dickerman* (1830) and *The Family at Home; or, Familiar Illustrations of the Various Domestic Duties* (1834). His *Mexico and the United States; Their Mutual Relations and Common Interests* (1869) reveals an interest in history and politics, a strong sympathy for Mexican nationalism, especially in the figure of Benito Juárez, and an apparent antipathy toward the Roman Catholic church. Biographical information can be gleaned from Edward Abbott, ed., *Of Gorham D. Abbot, Rebecca S., His Wife, and Elizabeth R., Their Daughter, A Brief Memorial* (1876); Abbot Memorial Committee, *The Abbot Memorial Book* (1902?); Emma Nason, *Old Hallowell on the Kennebec* (1909); Lyman Abbott, *Reminiscences* (1923); *General Catalogue of Bowdoin College and the Medical School of Maine; A Biographical Record of Alumni and Officers, 1794–1950* (1950); and *General Catalogue of the Theological Seminary, Andover, Massachusetts, 1808–1908* (1909). An obituary, with some inaccuracies, is in the *New York Evening Post*, 5 Aug. 1874. The *New York Times* obituary of the following day merely quotes the *Post* piece.

PATRICK G. WILLIAMS

ABBOT, Henry Larcom (13 Aug. 1831–1 Oct. 1927), Union soldier and engineer, was born in Beverly, Massachusetts, the son of Joseph Hale Abbot and Fanny Ellingwood. Abbot's father, a fellow of the American Academy of Arts and Sciences, was an educator and school principal. From 1850 to 1854 Abbot attended the U.S. Military Academy at West Point, graduating second in his class. As a second lieutenant in the U.S. Army Corps of Topographical Engineers, Abbot served first in the Office of Pacific Railroad Explorations and Surveys in Washington, D.C., and then in 1855 in California and Oregon surveying a railroad route.

From May 1857 to July 1861, First Lieutenant Abbot assisted Captain Andrew A. Humphreys on a survey of the Mississippi River delta designed to seek the best way to protect the land against inundation and to provide a reliable navigation passage through the river's mouth. His work was so valuable that Humphreys made him the report's coauthor. Their *Report upon the Physics and Hydraulics of the Mississippi River* (1861) significantly advanced the knowledge of river hydraulics, although their belief that levees alone could prevent disastrous flooding along the river proved faulty.

In April 1856 Abbot married Mary Susan Everett of Cambridge, Massachusetts. The couple had at least three children. Their son Frederic Vaughan Abbot also became a distinguished officer in the Corps of Engineers. In 1861 Abbot began his Civil War service as assistant topographical engineer on the staff of Brigadier General Irvin McDowell. Wounded in 1861 at the Battle of First Manassas, Abbot was rewarded for his "gallant and meritorious service" with a promotion to brevet captain. He thereupon assisted John G. Barnard, the chief engineer in charge of the Department of Washington, with the construction of fortifications south of the Potomac. He served as Barnard's aide-de-camp during the Peninsula Campaign, from March to July 1862, and afterward continued to assist Barnard in constructing fortifications to guard the southern approaches to Alexandria, Virginia. From November 1862 to February 1863, Abbot served as chief topographical engineer for Major General Nathaniel Banks's expedition to New Orleans and the lower Mississippi region. In early 1863 he was commissioned a colonel, 1st Connecticut Artillery Volunteers, and he commanded a regiment in charge of maintaining the defenses of Washington. From 1864 to 1865 he commanded the siege artillery of the Army of the James, which was then involved in operations against Petersburg and Richmond. His work earned him the brevet rank of major general, U.S. volunteers, by the war's conclusion. He was discharged from volunteer service in September 1865 and assumed his regular rank of major in the U.S. Army Corps of Engineers.

After the war Abbot became commander of the newly established Engineer School of Application and Engineer Battalion at Willet's Point, New York. During his twenty-year tenure (1866–1886), the engineer school became both an important training center for army engineers and a major center for research in military engineering. Charged by the Board of Engineers for Fortifications, on which he also served, to devise a submarine mine system, Abbot industriously set to work, training engineer troops while addressing a practical and important problem. Abbot tested all known high explosives to select the one best suited for underwater use, developed a new spherical mine, and devised an electrically controlled system of submarine mining. He analyzed and deduced the distance mines must be from each other to avoid accidental detonation yet prevent passage of enemy vessels. The system was satisfactorily tested during the Spanish-American War. Abbot published his detailed report on submarine mines in 1881 as Number 23 of the *Professional Papers of the U.S. Army Corps of Engineers*. Other duties assigned Abbot included observing a solar eclipse in Sicily in 1870; contracting for torpedo cable in Europe in 1873, during which time he also acquired knowledge of British, German, Austrian, and French torpedo systems; and visiting Europe again in 1883–1884 as a member of the joint Army-Navy Gun Foundry Board to report on the development of large steel cannon. In October 1886, Abbot was promoted to colonel and became the division engineer for the northeastern part of the United States. He remained in that position until August 1895, when he retired because of age.

In retirement Abbot became a consulting engineer to the Wisconsin Central Railroad, which was preparing plans for a harbor at Manitowoc, Wisconsin; he helped establish a car ferry connecting Manitowoc with the Pere Marquette railroad in Michigan. He served as president on a board of consulting engineers for a project to build a ship canal to link Lake Erie with the Ohio River (1895–1896) and was a member of the technical committee of the New French Panama Canal Company from 1897 to 1904, during which time he resided part-time in Paris and in Panama. When the

United States took over the isthmus in 1904 and began work on the Panama Canal, Abbot became a member of the American board of consulting engineers. He was influential in convincing the government to accept the board's minority report favoring a lock-canal over the sea-level canal recommended by the majority. He became a professor of hydraulic engineering at George Washington University in 1905 and taught until 1910. In 1915 he served on the special Panama Canal Slide Committee appointed by the National Academy of Sciences at President Woodrow Wilson's request.

A dedicated and skillful engineer, Abbot authored many significant professional papers. These include studies of coastal defense and submarine mines, floods on the Mississippi, Panama Canal construction, and siege artillery in the Civil War, as well as specific technical studies dealing with hydraulic engineering, astronomical observations, and the use of high explosives. During his long life he wrote the obituaries for many of his contemporaries, some of which provide important information about the U.S. Army Corps of Engineers. In his many positions, Abbot proved to be a master of tact and diplomacy, able to mediate disputes and resolve controversies, both in military and civilian life. Abbot died in Cambridge, Massachusetts.

• Most of Abbot's personal papers (and some official correspondence) are at the Houghton Library at Harvard University; the extensive collection includes letter books and diaries. Abbot's field notebooks dealing with his survey work in Oregon and California in the years 1855–1856 are in the possession of the Oregon Historical Society, Portland. Abbot's August–November 1855 diary was published by Robert W. Sawyer, "Henry Larcom Abbot—and Pacific Railroad Surveys in Oregon, 1855," *Oregon Historical Quarterly* 33 (March and June 1932): 1–24, 115–133. There is no biography of Abbot, but the Office of History, Headquarters of the U.S. Army Corps of Engineers, has some biographical material and also holds some of Abbot's correspondence, diplomas, and a large number of photographs once in his possession. See also *Who's Who in Engineering* and G. W. Cullum's *Biographical Register* (1891). A partial bibliography of Abbot's writings is in *The Centennial of the United States Military Academy at West Point, New York*, vol. 2 (1904). Abbot's work with Humphreys on the Mississippi River report is discussed in Martin Reuss, "Andrew A. Humphreys and the Development of Hydraulic Engineering: Politics and Technology in the Army Corps of Engineers," *Technology and Culture* 26, no. 1 (Jan. 1985): 1–33.

MARTIN REUSS

ABBOT, John (31 May 1751–c. 1840), artist-naturalist, was born in London, England, the son of John Abbot, an attorney in the court of King's Bench, Plea side, and Ann Clousinger. (Although baptismal records list his birth date as 31 May, Abbot, in his "Notes on My Life" [1834], claimed he was born on 1 June.) Little is known about Abbot's early education. The family rented a country home near London where young John read books and studied insects in the field. His father had a collection of good paintings and encouraged his son's interests with books and arranged for home art lessons under the engraver and drawing master Jacob Bonneau. Nevertheless, Abbot's career was assumed to be in law, and in February 1769 he began to clerk in his father's law office. In his free time he continued to study insects, purchase books that illustrated insects and birds, and paint pictures. In 1770 Abbot exhibited two lepidoptera watercolors at the Society of Artists of Great Britain in London. By early 1773 he had determined to go to North America to collect and paint insects. The Royal Society of London and two English naturalists, Thomas Martyn and Dru Drury, commissioned Abbot to collect natural history specimens.

Abbot left England in July 1773 and landed in Virginia in September. Shipboard friends, the Parke Goodalls, invited him to stay with them in Hanover County, and there he began his collections in America. In 1774–1775 he sent three different insect collections to his English sponsors, but only one lepidoptera collection for Martyn arrived safely. Disturbed by the unrest in Virginia prior to the American Revolution, Abbot departed for Georgia in early December 1775. After a journey of about two months by horse-drawn carriage, he reached Georgia and settled down along Brier Creek in present-day Burke County, where he recommenced his insect study and painting. The name of Abbot's wife is uncertain, but he did marry and they had one child. During the military campaigns in Georgia and South Carolina in 1779–1780, Abbot and his family were probably refugees. He saw no military service, either in the militia or the Continental line (some historians have confused him with an illiterate man with the same name).

Abbot secured a land grant on the north side of Brier Creek in 1785 and moved his family there. He engaged in subsistence farming and worked as a schoolmaster. With his cabin as a base, he collected insect, bird, and spider specimens in the valleys of the Savannah and Ogeechee rivers, Brier Creek in Burke and Screven counties, and Black Creek in Bulloch County. He noted ecological changes in his field notes and wrote essays on foods, behavior, and bird migration that were of great use to his British correspondents, who now included John Francillon and John Latham. He met Aloysius Enslen, the botanical collector for Prince Maurice-Joseph of Liechtenstein, and he knew Robert Squibb, who assisted Thomas Walter with his *Flora Caroliniana* (1788). His fellow Briton, John Lyon, visited him at his cabin in 1803 and subsequently praised Abbot's drawings as "elegant and masterly." Abbot first sketched his natural history subjects in graphite and then meticulously applied watercolor that enabled him to capture textures. His artistic style was influenced by other artist-naturalists, especially George Edwards, John Latham, and Eleazer Albin, and the preferences of his customers, but at his best, Abbot created original and elegant compositions.

In 1806 Abbot moved to Savannah, where he could more easily secure his supplies and ship paintings and specimens to customers. There he came into more frequent contact with others interested in natural history. Augustus Gottlieb Oemler, a pharmacist and naturalist, and Stephen Elliott, author of *A Sketch of the Botany of South Carolina and Georgia* (1821–1824) were among those he met. Abbot exchanged specimens with them, and both men bought a set of his paintings. In 1809 Abbot met Alexander Wilson, who was writing *American Ornithology*, and accompanied him on several collecting trips near Savannah. Wilson found Abbot "a very good observer" who "paints well." Thomas Nuttall, an English plant collector, had heard of Abbot while in Savannah in 1815 but had not seen him. William Baldwin, an ardent amateur botanist, studied the plants in some of Abbot's paintings but never met him. Abbot knew Titian Ramsey Peale, who later noted that Abbot often purchased caterpillars from boys in Savannah. While Abbot did many watercolors on commission for John Eatton LeConte of Liberty County, Georgia, most of their business apparently was done by mail. Increasingly, Abbot's specimens and paintings found their way to American and European enthusiasts and into various natural history publications.

One hundred and four of Abbot's insect watercolors were published in James Edward Smith, *The Natural History of the Rarer Lepidopterous Insects of Georgia* (1797). Additional paintings or figures from them appeared in Jean Alphonse Boisduval and John Eatton LeConte, *Histoire générale et iconographie des lépidoptères et des chenilles de l'Amerique Septentrionale* (1833); William Swainson, *Zoological Illustrations* (1820–1821); and Edward Doubleday, *The Entomologist* (1840). Charles Athanase, Baron Walckenaer, *Histoire naturelle des insectes: Aptères* (1847), used Abbot's spider watercolors to describe new species, and Thomas Martyn, *Psyche* (1797), illustrated insects collected by Abbot. Johann Christian Fabricius, *Entomologica systematica emendata et aucta* (1793), and Jacob Hübner, *Sammlung exotischer Schmetterlinge* (1806) and *Zutrage sur Sammlung exotischer Schmetterlinge bestehend in Bekindigung einzelner Fliegmuster neue oder rarer nicht europaischer Gattungen* (1818–1837, completed by Carl Geyer between 1825 and 1837), published descriptions of insect species from specimens prepared by Abbot.

Abbot's bird watercolors or his natural history observations were used in John Latham, *Supplement to the General Synopsis of Birds* (1787–1801), *Index Ornithologicus* (1790), and *A General History of Birds* (1821–1828); Alexander Wilson, *American Ornithology* (1808–1814); and John James Audubon, *Ornithological Biography* (1831–1839). Charles Darwin referred to Abbot in his *Journal during the Voyage of the HMS Beagle Round the World* (1845).

The War of 1812 interrupted Abbot's natural history shipments to England, and, discouraged and disgusted, he sought solace in the rural areas of Screven and Bulloch counties. To his dismay, war and illness continued to disrupt his work. After his wife died in 1817, he disposed of his property in Savannah and moved to Bulloch County near the tiny settlement of Arcola about four miles east of Brooklet, where he continued as an artist-naturalist. During his lifetime, Abbot completed in excess of 3,000 paintings. His correspondents now included the naturalists Heinrich Escher, William Swainson, George Ord, and Frederic de Lafresnaye. He was living on the William McElveen farm in a small house at the time of the 1840 census and died there shortly afterward.

Abbot was a shy and retiring person who preferred the solitude of field, forest, and swamp to the bustle of Savannah. His primary interest lay in collecting, observing, and painting insects, arachnids, and birds. He accepted monetary payment for his efforts but never actively pursued publication of his discoveries as Alexander Wilson and John James Audubon did. Abbot's observations, detailed in his notes and essays, his watercolors, and his collected specimens were of great value to his European and American correspondents but were never widely known during his lifetime. Abbot's research in natural history meant that the insect, arachnid, and bird species of Georgia were more thoroughly recorded at an earlier date than those in any other region of North America. His notes and watercolors now provide us with valuable records of species that are, in some instances, endangered or extinct or have not been seen in Georgia in many years. In his best watercolors, Abbot created fresh and elegant compositions that he drew with accuracy and colored with an eye for detail and beauty. Abbot's recognition as a pioneer artist-naturalist came belatedly, as his influence on the developing sciences of arachnology, ornithology, entomology, and botany became known.

• Abbot's brief autobiography, "Notes on My Life" (1834), is in the Museum of Comparative Zoology, Harvard University. Other Abbot manuscripts are in the Alexander Turnbull Library, Wellington, New Zealand; Atlanta (Ga.) Historical Society; Bibliothèque Centrale du Museum National d'Histoire Naturelle, Paris; British Library, London; British Museum (Natural History), London; Carnegie Museum of Natural History, Pittsburgh, Pa.; Cornell University Libraries, Ithaca, N.Y.; Emory University, Atlanta, Ga.; Johns Hopkins University, Baltimore, Md.; Knowsley Hall Library, Prescot, Merseyside, England; the Linnean Society of London; Smithsonian Institution Archives, Washington, D.C.; University of Georgia Libraries, Athens; and University of South Carolina Library, Columbia. A pioneering work on Abbot was Elsa G. Allen, *Georgia Historical Quarterly* 41 (June 1957): 143–57. Abbot is described in Arnold Mallis, *American Entomologists* (1971). Of special note are Vivian Rogers-Price's monograph *John Abbot's "Birds of Georgia"* (1997) and the illustrated catalog of a 1983 exhibition of Abbot at the Madison-Morgan Cultural Center, Madison, Ga., published as Rogers-Price, *John Abbot in Georgia: The Vision of a Naturalist Artist (1751–c. 1840)*. Articles on Abbot include Joseph Ewan in *Bartonia* 51 (1985): 37–45; M. J. Largen and Rogers-Price in *Archives of Natural History* 12, pt. 2 (Oct. 1985): 231–52; Phil Parkinson in *Turnbull Library Record* 11 (May 1978): 26–36; V. Rogers in *Atlanta Historical Journal* 22 (1978): 29–44: Rogers-Price in *Turnbull Library Record* 17 (Oct. 1984): 60–80; Rogers-Price and William W. Griffin in *Antiques* (Oct. 1983): 768–75; Marcus B. Simpson in *Archives of Natural History* 20, pt. 2 (1993): 197–212; and Ronald S. Wilkinson in *Entomologists Record* 96 (1984): 110–23, 165–76, 222–29, and 273–85.

VIVIAN ROGERS-PRICE

ABBOTT, Anderson Ruffin (7 Apr. 1837–29 Dec. 1913), surgeon, was born in Toronto, Upper Canada (now Ontario), the son of Wilson Ruffin Abbott, a businessman and properties investor, and Mary Ellen Toyer. The Abbotts had arrived in Toronto about 1835, coming from Mobile, Alabama, via New Orleans and New York; Wilson Abbott became one of the wealthiest African Canadians in Toronto. Anderson received his primary education in Canadian public and private schools. Wilson Abbott moved his family to the Elgin Settlement in 1850, providing his children with a classical education at the famed Buxton Mission School. Anderson Abbott, a member of the school's first graduating class, continued his studies at the Toronto Academy as one of three African Americans there. He then attended the Preparatory Department at Oberlin College from 1856 through 1858, afterward returning to Toronto to start his medical training.

At age twenty-three Abbott graduated from the Toronto School of Medicine, having spent four years under the tutelage of a black physician, Alexander T. Augusta. He became a licentiate of the Medical Board of Upper Canada in 1861. In 1863 he petitioned U.S. secretary of war Edwin Stanton and was commissioned as an assistant surgeon, assuming the rank of captain.

From 1863 to 1866 Abbott served in the Washington, D.C., area, first at Camp Barker, a "contraband camp" that accommodated runaway slaves, under the command of his former mentor, A. T. Augusta. The establishment of Freedmen's Hospital in Washington, D.C., in 1863, the first public hospital for African Americans in the United States, has been attributed to the work of these two doctors. When Augusta was transferred to another posting, Abbott for some time assumed the position of executive in charge of the contraband hospitals in Washington, which provided medical care to emancipated slaves and soldiers. In 1864 he moved to Abbott's Hospital, in the Freedmen's Village, the Union-controlled estate seized from Robert E. Lee in northern Virginia.

While in Washington Abbott had the opportunity to meet Abraham Lincoln. In a memoir he described the stir that he and Augusta made when attending a White House levee during the winter of 1863–1864. After Lincoln's assassination in April 1865, Mary Todd Lincoln gave Abbott the plaid shawl that Lincoln had often worn about town.

At the end of the Civil War, Abbott signed a contract with the Freedmen's Bureau to serve at the Freedmen's Hospital in Washington. He remained there until he resigned on 5 April 1866.

Returning to Canada, Abbott resumed his medical studies at the Toronto University, standing for the primary examination for the degree of medicine in 1867. In 1869 he was made a member of the province's College of Physicians and Surgeons. From 1869 to 1871 he continued to practice; for a time he was acting resident at the Toronto General Hospital.

In 1871 Abbott married Mary Ann Casey, with whom he would have three sons and four daughters, five of whom survived infancy. He also moved that year to Chatham, Ontario, to practice medicine, remaining in the area until 1881. He held numerous public positions in Chatham: he was president of the Wilberforce Educational Institute (1873–1880); coroner of the County of Kent (1874), possibly the first person of African descent to hold such a position in Canada; associate editor of the *Missionary Messenger*, the organ of the British Methodist Episcopal Church, (1874); president of the Chatham Literary and Debating Society; president of the Chatham Medical Society (1878); and worth chief templar of the Masonic lodge.

Abbott considered intellect the noblest part of human nature. This ideal would direct the course of the remainder of his life. While continuing to practice medicine, he also became known in North America and abroad for his pursuits as a champion of education and the rights of African Americans, as well as a civic leader and orator. In Chatham, Abbott was active in the fight against segregated schools; at Wilberforce, a predominantly African-Canadian school, he strove to ensure that the students received a good classical education.

In 1881 Abbott moved his family to Dundas, Ontario, where in his medical practice, he continued to be involved in the local educational system and civic arena, even though the population was primarily white. He served as an officer of the Dundas Mechanics' Institute, a high school trustee, a warden for St. James Anglican Church, and a registrar of the St. James Guild.

The Abbotts left Dundas in 1889, moving to Oakville, Ontario, where they remained for one year before returning to Toronto. In the spring of 1890 Abbott, although still residing in Toronto, was elected a member of the predominantly white James S. Knowlton Post No. 532 of the Grand Army of the Republic, New York State; he was made surgeon of the post in 1892 and appointed aide de camp to the commanding officer of the Department of New York. His appointment gave him the distinction of becoming the highest-ranking man of African descent in the organization (Robinson, 1980).

When the renowned cardiologist Daniel Hale Williams left Provident Hospital and Training School in Chicago in 1894, Abbott, who had been residing in Chicago with his family since 1891, was persuaded to come out of retirement and accept the position of medical superintendent for the facility. As a holder of medical licenses for both Illinois and Michigan, he was able to practice in the United States. He remained at Provident for approximately three years, apparently resigning in the spring of 1897 for business reasons. Following his father's example, Abbott was an astute businessman and had acquired several properties. The Abbotts remained in Chicago until they returned to Toronto around 1900.

An avid writer, lecturer, and poet, Abbott expounded on such topics as Darwinism, race, the medical profession, the integration of schools, and many other interests. Over the years, in addition to writing for the

Missionary Messenger, he contributed to such papers as the *Chatham Planet*, *Dundas Banner*, and *New York Age*. He died in Toronto, leaving a legacy in the field of medicine and in literary circles.

• Abbott's papers, including his scrapbooks, articles, family photos, and an autobiographical piece, "History of A. R. Abbott," which covers his life until 1899, are held in the Metropolitan Toronto Reference Library. His records related to his medical service are in the National Archives, Record Group 94, Adjutant General's Office, Personal Papers of Medical Officers and Physicians, prior to 1912; and in the Records of the Bureau of Refugees, Freedmen, and Abandoned Lands (Record Group 105). The best biographical article on Abbott is Henry S. Robinson, "Medical History: Anderson Ruffin Abbott, MD, 1837–1913", *Journal of the National Medical Association* 72 (1980): 713–16. See also Gwendolyn Robinson and John W. Robinson, *Seek the Truth: A Story of Chatham's Black Community* (1989); and Daniel G. Hill, *The Freedom-Seekers: Blacks in Early Canada* (1981).

M. DALYCE NEWBY

ABBOTT, Berenice (17 July 1898–10 Dec. 1991), photographer, was born in Springfield, Ohio, the daughter of Charles E. Abbott and Alice Bunn. Her parents were divorced soon after Abbott's birth, and she was raised by her mother in Columbus, Ohio. After attending public schools there and in Cleveland, she entered Ohio State University but withdrew after one semester (1917–1918). She traveled to New York City, where she supported herself by working as a waitress, as an artist's model, and as a bit player at the Provincetown Playhouse. She became interested in sculpture and in the course of her work met surrealist photographer Man Ray. By 1921 Abbott had scraped together enough money to go to Europe, where she continued her study of sculpture in Paris and Berlin until she suddenly abandoned art.

In 1923 Man Ray (now working in Paris) offered her a job as his darkroom assistant and taught her the basics of photography. Despite their later break, Abbott always acknowledged that she owed her career to him. He also introduced her to Eugène Atget, whose long-neglected photographs of Paris she later rescued from oblivion. In 1926 Abbott set up her own portrait studio and achieved acclaim for her revealing psychological studies of writers and artists of the 1920s. A number of these were shown in her first solo exhibition, Portraits photographiques, held at the Galerie Au Sacre du Printemps in 1926; Jean Cocteau (one of her sitters) wrote an introductory statement for the accompanying catalog, calling attention to the "chess game" of dark and light in Abbott's work. Often reproduced, these portraits (notably the one of James Joyce, seated, with hat and cane) have acquired the status of canonical likenesses. In 1928 Abbott and Man Ray were among those chosen to exhibit at the first formal group photography show ever held in Paris.

In 1929 Abbott returned to the United States, bringing with her the thousands of Atget's negatives and prints that she had purchased from his executor after the photographer's death in 1927. Until she sold the collection to the Museum of Modern Art in 1968, she devoted a large part of her time to printing and publishing this archive, thereby assuring Atget's recognition as a seminal figure in the history of photography. Her monograph on his work, *The World of Atget* (1964), is thought by many to be "the finest piece of writing by one photographer on another" (O'Neal, p. 30). Inspired by Atget's straight documentary work, Abbott determined to chronicle the rapidly changing appearance of her own city. Between 1929 and 1939 she produced a body of black-and-white photographs that capture both the beauty and the complex morphology of urban structures with a devotion to realism that characterizes all her work. Always opposed to the subjective "pictorialism" of art photography (as in the work of Alfred Stieglitz or Paul Strand), she contended that "photography cannot grow up if it imitates some other medium. It has to walk alone, it has to be itself" (unpublished catalog, N.Y. Public Library).

Setting up a studio in Greenwich Village, where she lived and worked for three decades, Abbott supported herself first by means of magazine assignments, allowing herself one day a week for her New York project. In 1934 the first exhibition of some of these photographs was held at the Museum of the City of New York, and she finally found (after many failed attempts) a sponsor for the work: the Federal Art Project of the Works Projects Administration. In the meantime, architectural historian Henry-Russell Hitchcock invited her to collaborate on another urban documentary project, recording remaining pre–Civil War buildings. An exhibition of these photographs, Urban Vernacular of the Forties, Fifties and Sixties, was shown at Yale University in 1934. The following year Abbott began to teach photography at the New School for Social Research. She remained on the faculty until 1958, credited with having established one of the first academic photography programs in the country.

Abbott's New York chronicle was completed with the publication of *Changing New York* (1939), now regarded as a classic text: a selection of ninety-seven of her hundreds of prints, accompanied by brief interpretative texts by her longtime companion, art critic Elizabeth McCausland. Notwithstanding the physical and mental exertion that had gone into the work, Abbott's belief was that "excitement about the subject is the voltage which pushes me over the mountain of drudgery to produce the final photograph" (unpublished catalog, N.Y. Public Library). Although fearful of heights, she had forced herself to look down from neighboring skyscrapers to shoot photographs such as "Nightview" (1935), a gridwork of midtown office buildings and one of her most famous works. To compensate for the sway of high buildings in the wind, and to assure clarity of focus in wide-angle shots, 'she had to make technological adaptations as she went along. Except for her collection published as *Greenwich Village Today and Yesterday* (1949), she made no further studies of New York, however. Instead, beginning in 1939, she turned to physics and biology as subjects for the camera, convinced that science was "the phenomenon of the age most in need of interpretation" (unpublished catalog, N.Y. Public Library).

Her new photographs of, for example, objects in motion, magnetic fields, soap bubbles, and penicillin growing in a petri dish not only reveal otherwise hidden, exquisite geometric patterns but provide exact illustrations of scientific principles and phenomena. As with her city photographs, Abbott frequently had to devise her own techniques and pieces of equipment (several of which she subsequently patented) to facilitate her work. As critic John Canaday pointed out, she was the artist "who most completely mastered the totality of the photographic discipline" (O'Neal, p. 32).

From 1944 to 1949 Abbott was picture editor of *Science Illustrated*, but not for another ten years did she find a sponsor for her own science photography. In 1954 she turned, for a time, to another project, driving down U.S. Route 1 from Maine to Florida, taking some 400 photographs to record new structures and vanishing small-town life along the way. With the exception of reproductions of some individual prints—a dramatic shot of the massive thrust of Norris Dam in Tennessee, for example—this work remains unpublished and largely unknown. Finally, in 1958, Abbott joined the Physical Science Study Committee of Educational Services, Inc., at the Massachusetts Institute of Technology, helping plan a new high school physics curriculum. A selection of her photographs was used to illustrate their textbook, *Physics* (1960). Between 1959 and 1961 the Smithsonian Institution sponsored a traveling exhibition of her Images of Physics, in recognition of which the Professional Photographers of America named Abbott as one of the top ten women photographers in the United States. Some critics now believe that these science photographs are her most significant.

With money earned from her MIT assignment, Abbott purchased an old house in Monson, Maine, and for reasons of health moved there permanently in 1966. Asked once what she thought was her best photograph, she replied, "The one I will take tomorrow" (O'Neal, p. 32). She remained active professionally up to her death, making prints from her negatives, overseeing the publication of limited-edition portfolios of her photographs, and teaching darkroom techniques to students who came to work with her. She died at her home in Monson. Abbott never married.

Despite her early difficulties in finding backing for her projects, Abbott was eventually recognized internationally as teacher, technical innovator, and—both in her own right and as sponsor of Atget's work—contributor to the development of documentary photography. A member of the American Association and Institute of Arts and Letters, she was also appointed by the French government, in 1988, to the Order of Arts and Letters.

• Commerce Graphics, Ltd., Inc., in East Rutherford, N.J., was founded by Abbott in 1984–1985 to house her photographic archives and to oversee loans and reproductions of this material. Other archives of her work are at the International Museum of Photography/George Eastman House, Rochester, N.Y.; the Museum of Modern Art and the New York Public Library; and the Smithsonian Institution. The Archives of American Art has some papers relating to Abbott. In addition to *Changing New York* (reprinted under the title *New York in the Thirties* [1973]) and other books cited above, she wrote *A Guide to Better Photography* (1941); *The View Camera Made Simple* (1948); *A Portrait of Maine*, with text by Chenoweth Hall (1968); and several periodical articles, including "It Has to Walk Alone," *American Society of Magazine Photographers News* 1 (Nov. 1951), and "The Image of Science," *Art in America* 47 (Winter 1959). Prints of her photographs are in public collections throughout the United States. A major retrospective show was held at the New York Public Library in 1989; the accompanying catalog, *Berenice Abbott, Photographer: A Modern Vision*, ed. Julia Van Haaften, with essays by Abbott, is an essential monograph. Another major study (with some biographical material) is Hank O'Neal, *Berenice Abbott, American Photographer* (1982), with introduction by John Canaday and extensive commentaries by Abbott. Elizabeth McCausland, "The Photography of Berenice Abbott," *Trend* 3 (Spring 1935), was the first critical review of her work. An obituary is in the *New York Times*, 11 Dec. 1991.

ELEANOR F. WEDGE

ABBOTT, Bud (2 Oct. 1895–24 Apr. 1974), and **Lou Costello** (6 Mar. 1906–3 Mar. 1959), a team of comedians on stage, radio, film, and television, were born, respectively, in Asbury Park and Paterson, New Jersey. Abbott (born William Alexander Abbott) was the son of Harry Abbott, a circus advance agent, and Rae Fisher, a circus bareback rider. Costello (born Louis Francis Cristillo) was the son of Sebastian Cristillo, an Italian-born silk weaver and insurance sales agent, and Helen Rege.

As a child, Abbott moved with his family to Coney Island, New York, where he was quickly attracted to the entertainment world of his parents. He dropped out of grade school to work various jobs at the local amusement park, including selling candy, painting signs, and luring customers inside a mirrored maze, then earning extra money by showing them the way out. At sixteen, Abbott, with his father's help, was hired as assistant treasurer for a Brooklyn burlesque hall. When not working in the box office, Abbott would study the routines and delivery of the comedians onstage. He held similar positions in other theaters during the next several years, eventually working his way up to treasurer at the National Theater in Washington, D.C. While there, he met Jennie Mae Pratt, a young dancer whose professional name was Betty Smith, whom he married in 1918. They had two children. His wife remained in show business until the early 1930s, performing as a dancer, singer, and comedian. The couple moved to Cleveland and then to Detroit, where Abbott worked as a theater producer, staging shows and hiring performers. Occasionally filling in for comedians who failed to appear, Abbott began to perfect his role as straight man, using his tall, thin frame, dapper appearance, and smooth talk to contrast with the slapstick routines of his burlesque partners. By the early 1930s, he had become a well-known straight man on the Minsky burlesque circuit, playing opposite a variety of comics including Harry Steppe, Harry Evanson, and sometimes even his wife.

Although Costello's father had hoped his children would become well educated, Costello never completed high school. Instead, he was more interested in athletics, excelling in basketball (despite his 5′4″ height) and amateur boxing, competing briefly as an amateur under the name of Lou King. From an early age, however, Costello had dreamed of appearing in movies, so in 1927 he hitchhiked with a friend from Paterson to Hollywood in search of work. When acting jobs could not be found, Costello first worked as a carpenter at Metro-Goldwyn-Mayer and then used his athletic skills and determination to land a job as a stunt double. But after eighteen months Costello's body had suffered too many injuries, so he and his friend decided to return east. Stopping off in St. Joseph, Missouri, Costello talked his way into getting hired as a Dutch comic in a burlesque theater, even though he was neither Dutch nor experienced onstage. He learned quickly, however, and by the mid-1930s Costello (having by then changed his birth name) was a promising baggy-pants comedian in burlesque halls around the country. While performing in New York, he met Anne Battler, a dancer in the chorus line, whom he married in 1934. They had four children.

Working in many of the same theaters around the country, Abbott and Costello crossed paths at least by 1933 in New York and even performed (in separate acts) in the same theater in 1935. The following year they joined together and immediately made an effective team, Costello's roly-poly effervescence serving as the perfect comic foil for Abbott's debonair smoothness. Known as Abbott and Costello (the straight man always received top billing), the pair performed in amusement parks, nightclubs, and vaudeville houses around the country. Their first national exposure was a ten-minute radio debut on *The Kate Smith Hour* in 1938, followed by frequent guest spots on other programs and eventually their own weekly series, *The Abbott and Costello Program* (1941–1949).

Capitalizing on their initial radio success, Abbott and Costello were headliners in a popular Broadway show, *The Streets of Paris*, in 1939–1940, then moved to Hollywood to display their talents on the screen. Their first film, *One Night in the Tropics* (1940) won them a long-term contract with Universal Pictures, but it was their follow-up, *Buck Privates* (1941), that not only grossed $10 million (a Universal record at the time) but also earned them critical accolades and extraordinary popularity. They averaged more than two films a year throughout the 1940s, most of them following the same formula: Abbott and Costello as "fish out of water," creating havoc in the army, the navy, college, and high society. The routines began to vary slightly in 1948, when Abbott and Costello started to "meet" Frankenstein, the Invisible Man, Dr. Jekyll and Mr. Hyde, Captain Kidd, and the Mummy. Altogether, they starred in twenty-eight films for Universal and eight more for other studios, all made over the course of only sixteen years. Many of their best ideas were recycled for the fifty-two half-hour CBS television episodes of *The Abbott and Costello Show* (1952–1954), which continue to air in syndication.

The team's best-known routine, "Who's on First," which they employed on stage, radio, film, and television, illustrates their technique: Abbott insisting without a smile that a baseball infield consists of players named Who, What, and I Don't Know, while Costello works himself into a frenzy of exasperation trying to make some sense of this improbable situation. Of course, the verbal sparring of debonair wise-guy with childlike buffoon did not originate with Abbott and Costello, but few other comedians did it so well in so many different media.

Except for a brief separation in 1945, Abbott and Costello remained together until early 1957, when they amicably dissolved the partnership so that Costello could pursue more serious dramatic roles. Audiences, however, seemed to prefer him as the childlike fat man who was always the butt of the joke. Two years after the team split, Costello died of a heart attack in Los Angeles. Abbott meanwhile continued to make a few appearances on television, but his plans for retirement were complicated by financial difficulties with the Internal Revenue Service. Two years after Costello's death, Abbott went on the road with Candy Candido, a veteran comic who closely impersonated Costello's voice and appearance. But after several stops, Abbott became too ill to continue the tour. His final role came in 1967 as the voice for cartoon episodes of *The Abbott and Costello Show*. Abbott died at his home in Woodland Hills, a suburb of Los Angeles.

• The only biography devoted to either Abbott or Costello singly was written by Costello's youngest daughter, Chris Costello, with Raymond Strait, *Lou's on First* (1981), but the lives of both have been surveyed in Bob Thomas, *Bud and Lou* (1977). On the team's output in all media, the best source is Jim Mulholland, *The Abbott and Costello Book* (1975), but for additional details on their films together, see Bob Furmanek and Ron Palumbo, *Abbott and Costello in Hollywood* (1991); Richard J. Anobile, *Who's on First?* (1972); and Leonard Maltin, *Movie Comedy Teams* (1970). Costello's obituary is in the *New York Times*, 4 March 1959, Abbott's on 25 April 1974.

JAMES I. DEUTSCH

ABBOTT, Charles Conrad (4 June 1843–27 July 1919), naturalist and archaeologist, was born in Trenton, New Jersey, the son of Timothy Abbott, a banker, and Susan Conrad. As a child he loved nature and began a lifelong fascination with the flora and fauna of the Delaware River Valley. Like many young men drawn to natural history, he saw no prospects for turning his passion into a livelihood and so chose to study medicine.

Entering the medical department of the University of Pennsylvania in 1860, he pursued the curriculum "in a half-hearted way." His Civil War service as a private in the New Jersey militia in 1863 consisted largely of guarding bridges on the Susquehanna River. While in medical school he also published his first articles on natural history, mostly in the fields of ornithology and ichthyology. Abbott graduated in 1865 but never practiced medicine. In 1867 he married Julia Boggs Olden, with whom he had three children. For a time he engaged in the manufacture of chemicals, but he soon abandoned this to devote most of his life to studying and writing on nature. Apparently his earnings as an author and his family's money supported him comfortably for life.

According to Abbott, his earliest publications were rejected by the scientific journals because of his youth, and they subsequently appeared in the local press. In 1868 his paper on the birds of New Jersey was included in a book on the state's geology. Although considered the best of his ornithological writings, it apparently made some notable mistakes in identification. Abbott refused to acknowledge that he was wrong, as he would continue to do throughout his career.

Abbott was a member of several scientific organizations, including the Academy of Natural Sciences of Philadelphia, the New York Academy of Sciences, and the Nuttall Ornithological Club. But his stubbornness and the caustic comments that he directed at his critics drove a wedge between him and leading American scientists. Moreover, his tendency to aim his many books and articles at a popular audience—works that contained little new information, much that was disputed by the scientific establishment, and some errors—also kept him from the inner circles of the nation's natural history establishment.

Abbott based most of his writings on observations and collections made on the family estate, "Three Beeches," located south of Trenton, which he inherited in 1874. Among his best known books were *A Naturalist's Rambles about Home* (1884), *Upland and Meadow* (1886), *Cyclopedia of Natural History* (1887), *The Model Book of Natural History* (1888), *Days Out of Doors* (1889), *Travels in a Tree-Top* (1894), *The Freedom of the Fields* (1898), *Clear Skies and Cloudy* (1899), *In Nature's Realm* (1900), and *The Rambles of an Idler* (1906). Although the public and popular press regarded these works well, the scientific press was less enthusiastic. Then and later the serious scientists objected to the overly theoretical and conjectural content of Abbott's books and articles and to his insistence that animal behavior depended on intelligence as well as instinct. Witmer Stone considered *Upland and Meadow* "probably his best effort."

Although Abbott published in such respectable natural history journals as the *Proceedings of the Academy of Natural Sciences of Philadelphia*, he more often wrote for a wider public in periodicals like *Popular Science Monthly*, *Forest and Stream*, *Lippincott's*, and the British periodical *Science Gossip*. He reached younger audiences in *St. Nicholas* and other juvenile magazines. His attempts at fiction included *A Colonial Wooing* (1895), but neither his novels nor his short stories were critical successes.

Abbott's work in archaeology, however, was well regarded in his own time and continues to be so. As with his natural history studies, his archaeological pursuits began early in his career and were confined largely to the vicinity of Trenton. There he unearthed a great many implements and other artifacts that shed light on the culture of prehistoric peoples of North America, both paleolithic and neolithic, in gravel deposited by glaciers. The first significant publication of his findings was in the 1875 *Annual Report* of the Smithsonian Institution. His major contribution to this branch of knowledge was *Primitive Industry; or, Illustrations of the Handiwork, in Stone, Bone and Clay, of the Native Races of the Northern Atlantic Seaboard* (1881). Abbott donated most of his artifacts to Harvard's Peabody Museum.

Abbott's continuing quarrels with the scientific community, along with the burning of his New Jersey home, made his last years particularly trying. He moved to Bristol, Pennsylvania, where he died.

Abbott's sentimental, romantic approach to natural history no doubt appealed to Americans witnessing the disappearance of the nation's rural character, but the popularity of his works did not extend far beyond his lifetime.

• The Abbott Family Papers at the Princeton University Library contain much of Abbott's correspondence; letters for the period from 1895 to 1900 are at the Academy of Natural Sciences of Philadelphia. An anonymous article, "Sketch of Charles C. Abbott," *Popular Science Monthly*, Feb. 1887, pp. 547–53, is a favorable assessment of Abbott's work at mid-career. Also sympathetic is Ernest Ingersoll, "Charles Conrad Abbott, M.D., at Trenton," *The Critic*, 28 Dec. 1897, pp. 373–75. More critical is the obituary notice by Witmer Stone in the *Auk*, Jan. 1920, pp. 183–84. A defense of Abbott's archaeological efforts is G. Frederick Wright, "Charles Conrad Abbott and Ernest Volk," *Science*, 14 Nov. 1919, pp. 451–53. Other information on Abbott is in Lucy Aiello, "Charles Conrad Abbott, M.D.: New Jersey's Pick and Shovel Scientist," *New Jersey History* 85:208–16.

MICHAEL J. BRODHEAD

ABBOTT, Edith (26 Sept. 1876–28 July 1957), social reformer, social work educator, and author, was born in Grand Island, Nebraska, the daughter of Othman Ali Abbott, a lawyer and first lieutenant governor of Nebraska, and Elizabeth Maletta Griffin, a woman suffrage advocate. Abbott grew up in a comfortable and politically progressive household on the American prairie. However, the severe economic depression that began in 1893 caused Abbott to postpone her college plans after graduation from an Omaha girls' boarding school. Instead, at the age of seventeen she became a teacher at the Grand Island High School.

Through summer sessions, correspondence courses, and finally full-time study, Abbott received her undergraduate degree from the University of Nebraska in 1901. While attending a summer session at the University of Chicago in 1902, she so impressed the faculty, including the renowned economist Thorstein Veblen, that she won a fellowship for full-time study. In

1903 Abbott began work on her Ph.D. in political economics, graduating with honors in 1905. Her dissertation focused on unskilled labor and wages in the nineteenth century.

After a brief stint as the secretary for the Boston Women's Trade Union League, Abbott spent six months as a researcher for the Carnegie Institution, working in both Washington, D.C., and New York City, concentrating on the problems women faced as industrial workers. In 1906 she published a series of articles based on her research in the *Journal of Political Economy*. That same year she received a Carnegie fellowship as well as a scholarship from the Association of Collegiate Alumnae for postdoctoral study at the London School of Economics. There Abbott met the English social reformers Beatrice and Sidney Webb and was swayed by the Webbs' insistence that reform, not charity, was the most efficient route to alleviating poverty. Returning to the United States in 1907, she taught for one year at Wellesley College before joining her sister Grace Abbott, also a social reformer and later (1921–1934) director of the U.S. Children's Bureau, in Chicago. Together, the two sisters lived for the next dozen years at Hull-House, the settlement founded by Jane Addams almost two decades earlier. As a part of this vibrant, predominantly female circle of Progressive reformers, Abbott pursued her interests in the professionalization of social work.

In 1908 Abbott became the assistant to Sophonisba Breckinridge, director of the Chicago School of Civics and Philanthropy. Together, the two led the effort to establish social work as a profession at the same time emphasizing the need for rational state planning rather than haphazard private charity in addressing the needs of the poor. Abbott and Breckinridge also co-authored two studies examining juvenile delinquency, child labor laws, and compulsory education laws. *The Delinquent Child and the Home* was published in 1912, followed by *Truancy and Non-Attendance in the Chicago Schools* in 1917.

A prolific author in her own right, Abbott published more than 100 articles and books during her lifetime, including the classic *Women in Industry* (1910). That work, based in part on her earlier research for the Carnegie Institution, was a comprehensive look at working women in the United States from the colonial era to the early years of the twentieth century. Predating the work of modern labor historians by several decades, Abbott used corporate records and census data to document how the industrialization of the American economy affected women by creating low wages and harsh working conditions.

Abbott applied the same painstaking research methods in the cause of woman suffrage before the Nineteenth Amendment gave women the unqualified right to vote. In Illinois, where women had limited suffrage rights, Abbott was able to track voting patterns because women were given different ballots and tabulations were broken down by gender. Analyzing the results of municipal elections in Chicago between 1915 and 1917, Abbott argued that women, unlike men, consistently voted not out of loyalty for a particular political party but for reform-minded candidates. In two articles published in the progressive journal *National Municipal Review*, she joined the chorus of those demanding full suffrage for women as part of the social reform effort.

But it was as an educator that Edith Abbott made her most remembered contribution. In 1920, when the Chicago School of Civics and Philanthropy began to experience financial difficulties, Abbott and Breckinridge persuaded the University of Chicago to take over its administration. Now known as the School of Social Service Administration, it became the first university-sponsored graduate program in the field. Abbott felt strongly that social workers should be trained in the most up-to-date scientific methods of social inquiry and service, combining fieldwork with course work. Appointed dean of the School of Social Service Administration in 1924, Abbott designed the curriculum that professionalized social work. Still true to her social reform roots, she sought to impress upon students the ever-increasing need for statistical evidence in formulating state policy. To gain the widest audience possible, Abbott collaborated with Breckinridge in the formation of the *Social Service Review* in 1927. In addition to this professional journal, the two also published case studies as part of the prestigious University of Chicago Social Service Series.

During the 1920s many Americans became increasingly hostile to the perceived negative effects of unrestricted immigration. In 1924 Congress passed the Immigration Restriction Act, which set quotas on immigration by country. At the same time, Abbott was calling for legislation to prohibit exploitation of recent immigrants. In 1924 she published *Immigration: Select Documents and Case Records* and, two years later, *Historical Aspects of the Immigration Problem: Select Documents*. In 1929 President Herbert Hoover appointed Abbott to the Wickersham Commission on Law Observance and Enforcement. She focused on the issue of criminal acts among immigrants and, through exhaustive research, concluded that contrary to popular belief immigrants actually committed far fewer crimes in proportion to their numbers in the general population. Published in 1931 as the *Report on Crime and Criminal Justice in Relation to the Foreign Born*, the publication announced that "charging our high crime rates against the foreign born . . . is the 'easy way'—the line of least resistance. . . . But an attempt to face squarely the more difficult problems of life is more in line with our American traditions."

Always an advocate of public assistance administered by government rather than by private agencies, Abbott applauded the initial efforts of the New Deal to respond to the national emergency known as the Great Depression. However, she criticized the fact that most administrative authority was left to the individual states. She feared that in their haste to distribute much-needed relief, New Deal agencies would establish poor guidelines for social services. She welcomed the proposal of Harry Hopkins, head of the Federal

Emergency Relief Administration (FERA), to establish a federal scholarship program to train state-level FERA administrators at accredited schools of social work. In 1934 Abbott saw the enrollment at her graduate school swell and its national reputation grow. Her own reputation as a leader in social work education was recognized when she was elected president of the National Conference of Social Work in 1936.

Although the 1930s brought professional success to Edith Abbott, her personal life became increasingly trying. After fighting a rare form of cancer for several years, Edith's sister Grace Abbott died in 1939. The two sisters had been remarkably close all their lives, and the death of her younger sister devastated Abbott. She found some solace in her remaining family and a few close friends, but she sought to ease her grief primarily through her work. In 1941 she published her last book, *Public Assistance*. A year later she stepped down as dean of the School of Social Service Administration though she continued teaching and editing the *Social Service Review*.

The death of Abbott's mentor and close friend, Sophonisba Breckinridge, in 1948 was another personal blow. A year later she was invited to live at Hull-House again, and though the community of which she had been such a vital part forty years earlier was long gone, she was relieved to no longer live alone. In 1951, at the age of seventy-five, she received the National Conference of Social Work's Survey Award in recognition of her "imaginative and constructive contributions to social work." True to form, she used her acceptance speech as another opportunity to demand continued reform of government services to the poor. Suffering from glaucoma during her final years, Abbott returned to her family's home in Grand Island, Nebraska, where she died.

• Edith Abbott's papers, along with those of her sister Grace, are held by the Regenstein Library, University of Chicago. Abbott's dozens of articles and books are annotated by Rachel Marks in "The Published Writings of Edith Abbott: A Bibliography," *Social Service Review* 32 (Mar. 1958): 51–56. Abbott's life and career are ably discussed in Lela B. Costin, *Two Sisters for Social Justice: A Biography of Grace and Edith Abbott* (1983). An obituary is in the *New York Times*, 30 July 1957.

KATHLEEN BANKS NUTTER

ABBOTT, Emma (9 Dec. 1850–5 Jan. 1891), soprano and opera impresario, was born in Chicago, Illinois, the daughter of Seth Abbott, an itinerant musician and music teacher, and Almira Palmer. Abbott's father encouraged her and her brother George to develop the musical ability that they demonstrated at an early age. Emma, who sang constantly as a child, chose the guitar as her instrument; her brother studied the violin. In 1854 the family moved from Chicago to Peoria, Illinois, and their fortunes declined. To supplement the family income Seth Abbott and the two musical children began to give concerts in Peoria and elsewhere starting in 1859; according to contemporary biographical lexicographer F. O. Jones, the trio performed hundreds of concerts during this period.

Abbott began teaching guitar at the age of thirteen. When she was sixteen she joined the Lombard Concert Company of Chicago and went on the road with them, performing in Iowa, Illinois, Michigan, and Wisconsin. When the troupe disbanded in Grand Haven, Michigan, Abbott was stranded. Undaunted, she worked her way to New York by giving parlor concerts in hotels in exchange for room and board. In New York, Abbott continued to perform in hotel parlors, but she was not particularly successful. She subsequently attempted various concert tours, again in the Midwest. In 1867 soprano Clara Louise Kellogg heard Abbott sing in Toledo, Ohio, and was sufficiently impressed with her ability that she provided Abbott with letters of introduction, personally interceded on her behalf with voice teacher Achille Errani, and gave her an appropriate performance wardrobe once Abbott reached New York. Abbott commenced study with Errani in 1870, and she secured employment singing in the choirs of Henry Ward Beecher's church in Brooklyn and Edwin H. Chapin's Church of the Divine Paternity in Manhattan. Abbott's New York debut took place at a benefit concert on 12 December 1871; for the event she was publicized as a protégée of Kellogg. Members of Chapin's congregation contributed some $10,000 to a fund to enable Abbott to study in Europe. She went first to Milan, where she studied under Antonio Sangiovanni, and later to Paris, where she was a pupil of Mathilde Marchesi. In Paris Abbott was befriended by Baroness Rothschild, who made possible further vocal study, with Pierre Francois Wartel and Enrico Delle Sedie.

Contact with soprano Adelina Patti led to Abbott's operatic debut in London at Covent Garden on 2 May 1876, with James Mapleson's company, in the role of Marie in Donizetti's *La Fille du régiment* (in Italian). Abbott's contract with the company was later broken, however, when she refused to sing the role of Violetta in Verdi's *La Traviata*, contending that the opera was immoral. In 1875 Abbott secretly married Eugene Wetherell, a New York druggist and member of Chapin's congregation who had followed her to Europe. The couple had no children. In the autumn of 1876 they returned to the United States. Abbott, who retained her given name throughout her life, gave concerts in various cities, including Baltimore, New York, Washington, and Philadelphia. Her American operatic debut was at the New York Academy of Music on 23 February 1877, again as Marie in *La Fille du régiment*.

In 1878 Abbott formed a small touring operatic company, with C. D. Hess as manager and Wetherell as assistant manager. Wetherell formed a partnership with Charles Pratt, and thereafter the firm of Pratt & Wetherell managed the company. The troupe successfully toured the United States, principally in the West, for thirteen consecutive seasons. Although Pratt & Wetherell were in charge of business matters, Abbott evidently retained full artistic control over her company, choosing repertory, ordering costumes, and hiring conductors. Her troupe was comprised mostly of young artists, sometimes numbering as many as sixty; those who were engaged were assured of a full season's work. The company's repertory included Planquette's *The Chimes of Normandy*, Massé's *Paul and Virginia*, Gounod's *Romeo and Juliet* and *Faust*, Gilbert and Sullivan's *The Mikado*, Bellini's *Norma*, Balfe's *The Bohemian Girl*, Flotow's *Martha*, Verdi's *La Traviata* (in a "cleaned-up" version) and *Ernani*, and Donizetti's *The Daughter of the Regiment*. The foreign-language operas were always sung in English translation, and many of the works were abridged.

Wetherell died suddenly in the midst of the 1888–1889 tour, and performances ceased for two weeks before Abbott took over his duties and resumed the tour. Between 1878 and 1890 the Emma Abbott English Opera Company is said to have opened some thirty-five different opera houses, primarily in the American West. The first was in Waterloo, Iowa; the final one in Ogden, Utah. Abbott died of pneumonia in Salt Lake City, Utah, during the company's 1890–1891 tour.

The Emma Abbott English Opera Company was influential in the popularization of opera in English during the postbellum period. Abbott's voice was described as a pure, clear soprano of great flexibility and volume; she evidently had a good but not an extraordinary instrument. Interpolated songs were commonplace in her opera performances. According to critic Oscar Thompson, the songs were usually chosen to display "the flexibility of her voice or the manner in which she could identify herself with the homely sentiments of the ballads of her guitar days." An example is Abbott's interpolation of Lowell Mason's popular hymn "Nearer, My God to Thee" into both Gounod's *Faust* and Bellini's *La Sonnambula*. Abbott was not popular among either the music critics or the foreign-language operatic cognoscenti. To many Americans, however, she was "the people's prima donna"; this was, in fact, her nickname. As such, she did much to promote the performance of English-language opera as an important and vital form of popular (non-elite) musical theater in the United States. Abbott was an extraordinarily well liked performer and—in part because of wise financial investments made by her husband—died a very wealthy woman.

• There apparently is no large collection of papers related to Abbott's life or career. Some of her correspondence is located in the Department of Rare Books and the Music Division of the Boston Public Library and in the Music Division of the New York Public Library. There are a number of contemporary studies that are useful, including a biographical sketch in *Illustrated American*, 24 Jan. 1891; an account of her career and life before her first European tour in 1877 in Grace Greenwood, *Emma Abbott* (1878?); and a biography by Sadie E. Martin, Abbott's close friend, *The Life and Professional Career of Emma Abbott* (1891). George Upton discusses Abbott's career in *Musical Memories* (1908), a reminiscence of the period from 1850 to 1900, during which he was a music critic; and W. S. B. Mathews includes a biographical sketch in *A Hundred Years of Music in America* (1889). There is very little modern scholarship about Abbott or her influence on musical culture in the United States. Nonetheless, Oscar Thompson discusses her career briefly in *The American Singer: A Hundred Years of Success in Opera* (1939); and Abbott's New York activities are thoroughly chronicled in George C. D. Odell, *Annals of the New York Stage*, vols. 9–14 (1937–1945).

KATHERINE K. PRESTON

ABBOTT, George (25 June 1889–31 Jan. 1995), theatrical director and producer, was born George Francis Abbott in Forestville, New York, the son of George Burwell Abbott, a tailor, town mayor, and government land agent, and May McLaury. Abbott received his early education and worked as a telegraph boy and a cowboy while moving from Wyoming to Nebraska to New York, where he earned a B.A. from the University of Rochester in 1911. Between 1911 and 1912 Abbott, who said he wanted to be a poet or journalist, was enrolled in George Pierce Baker's playwriting workshop at Harvard University. One of the short plays he wrote for Baker, *The Man in the Manhole*, won a prize which included its production at Boston's Bijou Theatre. Abbott became assistant to the Bijou's producer in 1912.

In 1913 Abbott made his New York acting debut as a drunken college boy in *The Misleading Lady*. During the play's yearlong run, Abbott married Ednah Levis. They had one child before her death in 1930. Until 1925 the tall, athletic Abbott mainly pursued a theatrical acting career, though he appeared once onscreen, as a hired man in the 1918 film *The Impostor*. Abbott's cowboy in *Zander the Great* (1923) was called one of the ten best Broadway performances of the year. In John Howard Lawson's *Processional* (1925) he played a rugged, radical labor organizer.

While working for producer John Golden beginning in 1918, Abbott was required to rewrite many scripts. His first significant play as author was *The Fall Guy* (1925), in collaboration with James Gleason. In 1926 Abbott collaborated with Philip Dunning on his first hit, *Broadway*, a fast-moving melodrama of bootlegging and show business, which also marked his directorial debut. *Coquette* (1927), Abbott's examination of southern morality, helped make Helen Hayes a star and soon afterward marked Abbott's first venture as a film producer (for Mary Pickford).

As a director Abbott became noted for lively, well-made shows. He credited Baker's workshop for his ability to bring common sense to a theatrical era in which style—"that is, artificiality"—was the norm: "Baker gave you a good sense of construction . . . [he] taught me that farce is as good as drama" (quoted in Hirsch, p. 22). According to producer-director Harold Prince, who went to work in Abbott's office next to Radio City Music Hall in 1948, Abbott "understood the trajectory of a play." He came to insist upon absolute control, which included giving readings that performers were required to follow. He wrote that he did not require interpretation, only that actors "pronounce their final syllables." If the line is funny, he added, the laughs will come.

As author, director, or producer, Abbott participated in at least 113 Broadway shows. Claiming to have invented the theatrical audition, Abbott admitted to having a "Pygmalion complex" when it came to new talent; this may first have been evident in 1927 when he gave the Yiddish-language actor Paul Muni (Muni Weisenfeld) his first English-language role in *Four Walls*, a crime drama written by Abbott and Dana Burnet that was twice adapted for film.

Between 1929 and 1932 Abbott was involved in ten films as author, adapter, or director, nearly all of them brisk melodramas of sin and redemption. These included *Half Way to Heaven* (1929), *The Saturday Night Kid* (1929, a "good-bad girl" story for Clara Bow), *Why Bring That Up?* (1929), *All Quiet on the Western Front* (1930, sharing screenplay credit with Maxwell Anderson and Del Andrews), *Manslaughter* (1930), *The Sea God* (1930, a Fay Wray tale of cannibal islanders), *The Cheat* (1931), *My Sin* (1931), *Secrets of a Secretary* (1931), *Stolen Heaven* (1931), and the Spanish-language adaptations of some of these films. Abbott's plays during this period included *Those We Love* (1930), another redemption drama adapted to film in 1932, and *Lilly Turner* (1932), written in collaboration with Dunning and adapted to a 1933 film steamy enough to be denied reissue in 1936 because it portrayed bigamy. With Leon Abrams, Abbott wrote *Heat Lightning* (1933), the 1934 film adaptation of which made the (Catholic) Legion of Decency's first list of proscribed films because of its varied seductions.

Abbott's theatrical producing career began in 1932 when he joined Dunning to present the Ben Hecht–Charles MacArthur satirical comedy *Twentieth Century*. In 1935 Abbott changed direction, co-writing (with John Cecil Holm) and directing *Three Men on a Horse* (1935), a knockabout farce about racetrack betting, which proved a long-running (812 performances), revivable hit. Another Abbott-produced and directed farce, *Boy Meets Girl* (1935), ran for nearly two years.

By now a renowned "play doctor" who knew what to change and what to leave alone (he later advised the producers of *West Side Story* not to change a thing), Abbott was called in by composer Richard Rodgers and lyricist Lorenz Hart to help with a circus tale. This first directorial stint on a musical, *Jumbo* (1935), launched Abbott into a field he dominated for the next thirty years, in part because he made sure that even the silliest plot had the internal coherence necessary to make it believable.

Abbott's next collaboration with Rodgers and Hart, *On Your Toes* (1936), grew out of his lifelong devotion to social dancing, which he regularly enjoyed at Manhattan's Roseland Ballroom and during dancing vacations in Cuba. Abbott directed and wrote the show, which was choreographed by George Balanchine and contained the first plot involving ballet to be performed on the musical stage. The Abbott-directed farce *Room Service* (1937) ran for a year and a half. Actor Keenan Wynn remembered playing in a touring version of the show, in which 264 specific laughs were noted in the script, all having to be realized lest Mister Abbott suddenly appear and find some missing.

In 1938 Abbott produced two of his Broadway hits, *Boy Meets Girl* and *Brother Rat*, for film. On Broadway he adapted Shakespeare's *Comedy of Errors* into Rodgers and Hart's *The Boys from Syracuse* (1938), subsequently proclaiming it his favorite production. Rodgers found Abbott's book "sharp, witty, fast moving and in an odd way so very much in keeping with the bawdy Shakespearean tradition" (p. 191). In 1939 Abbott directed and produced Rodgers and Hart's *Too Many Girls*, and in 1940 he produced and directed his adaptation of John O'Hara's story *Pal Joey*. This Rodgers and Hart musical broke tradition by focusing on a thoroughly unsympathetic leading character, played by Gene Kelly, another of Abbott's Galateas. Another Abbott show, *Best Foot Forward* (1941), introduced the new songwriting team of Hugh Martin and Ralph Blane.

Abbott's *Three Men on a Horse* was adapted by Arthur Miller for radio and was performed on the Theatre Guild on the Air in 1943. In 1944 Abbott directed *On the Town*, marking the musical theater debuts of composer Leonard Bernstein and lyricist-librettists Adolph Green and Betty Comden. The show, featuring Jerome Robbins's choreography, proved that dance could carry an entire musical play. Among Abbott's nonmusical credits in this era was Max Shulman's anarchic comedy, *Barefoot Boy with Cheek* (1947). In 1946 Abbott married Mary Sinclair; they were divorced in 1951.

Back on the musical stage, Abbott directed *High Button Shoes* (1947), introducing to Broadway the songwriting team of Julie Styne and Sammy Cahn. He adapted the British farce *Charley's Aunt* into the musical *Where's Charley?* (1948, with a successful 1952 filming). Composer-lyricist Frank Loesser said that Abbott had specified every point in the plot where songs were needed and that Loesser had simply carried out the plan.

In 1950 Abbott directed *Call Me Madam* for Irving Berlin and Ethel Merman. According to Lawrence Bergreen, Berlin's biographer, Abbott dealt with the show "as if he had been called in to quash a rebellion in a remote corner of the British Empire" (pp. 501–2). Abbott made a star of juvenile Russell Nype in this production by ordering him a crew haircut and horn-rimmed glasses.

In 1952 Abbott briefly experimented in television, directing the weekly United States Royal Showcase, a comedy-variety show, and acting as its host. On Broadway in 1953 he directed the Bernstein-Comden-Green *Wonderful Town*. In 1954, with Richard Bissell, he co-wrote, directed, and produced a musical comedy about labor relations, *The Pajama Game*, winning his first Antoinette Perry (Tony) Award. This production introduced Bob Fosse's choreography and the songwriting team of Richard Adler and Jerry Ross to Broadway. Abbott codirected and coproduced the film version of *The Pajama Game* with Stanley Donen in 1957. Adler later said that the show's hit song "Hey There!" resulted from Abbott's request for a number that used onstage a dictaphone, at that time a trendy business accessory.

In 1955 Abbott co-wrote, directed, and produced Adler and Ross's *Damn Yankees* (a wedding of Faust and baseball, which won another Tony); he and Donen also adapted, directed, and produced this play for film in 1958. In such shows Abbott introduced the "in one crossover," called by theatrical historian Ethan Mordden "a quick movement downstage during a major set change that pulled the plot along or threw in a cute bit, with the actors moving across the stage from wing to wing" (p. 165).

Abbott returned briefly to acting, playing George Antrobus in a 1955 television version of Thornton Wilder's *The Skin of Our Teeth*, which transferred onstage to Paris. Among his 1959 credits Abbott numbered co-writing, directing, and producing *New Girl in Town*, a musical adaptation of the work by Eugene O'Neill, which mistakenly omitted the sordidness of *Anna Christie*. In the same year Abbott shared with Sheldon Harnick, Jerry Bock, and Jerome Weidman the Pulitzer Prize for drama for *Fiorello!*, a tale of Manhattan political corruption and reform.

After another musical, *Tenderloin* (1960), Abbott directed a revival of the sentimental comedy *Never Too Late* (1962), which, at 1,007 performances, was his longest-running nonmusical. In 1962–1963 Abbott directed *A Funny Thing Happened on the Way to the Forum* in New York and London. This reworking by Burt Shevelove, Larry Gelbart, and Stephen Sondheim of the play by Plautus earned Abbott his third Tony Award. The show's effective opening song, "Comedy Tonight," developed from Abbott's need to have "something hummable." In 1965 Abbott co-wrote and directed *Anya*, a musical about Anastasia, the alleged survivor of the execution of Czar Nicholas's family. In the same year he co-wrote and directed the depression-era musical *Flora, the Red Menace*, introducing Liza Minnelli, who won a Tony for her performance. Also in 1965 a Times Square theater was named for Abbott.

For the next two decades Abbott's productivity slowed somewhat, and he generally stopped writing, though the musical *How Now, Dow Jones* (1967) was well received, and comedies such as *The Education of Hyman Kaplan* (1969) and *Norman, Is That You?* (1970) achieved respectable runs. *Music Is* (1976, Abbott and Adler's adaptation of Shakespeare's *Twelfth Night*) was a failure. The Kennedy Center Life Achievement award was presented to Abbott in 1982, and the following year, at the age of ninety-four, he married Joy Valderrama. In 1983–1984 he produced on Broadway and in London a highly successful revival of *On Your Toes*, which, using the original musical arrangements, launched the "authenticity" movement that subsequently resulted in the rediscovery of many "lost" American musicals. Abbott completely rewrote *On Your Toes*, having found his 1936 book good but out-of-date.

In 1986 Abbott directed *Tropicana*, and on the occasion of his hundredth birthday in 1987 he directed a short-lived revival of *Broadway*. In 1989 he co-wrote and codirected (with Donald Saddler) *Frankie*, an off-Broadway musical version of *Frankenstein*. Abbott assisted in the successful revival of *Damn Yankees* (1993) and was involved with a revival of *The Pajama Game* at the time of his death in Miami Beach.

A "ramrod-straight" man of great energy, impatience, and certainty who made shows of all types that "worked," Abbott virtually embodied the history of twentieth-century American theater. As discoverer and nurturer of theatrical talent and innovator of theatrical techniques that became standard practice, for eight decades Abbott regularly helped Broadway to reinvent and restore itself.

• George Abbott's autobiography is *Mister Abbott* (1963). The Billy Rose Theatre Collection at the New York Public Library for the Performing Arts, Lincoln Center, is filled with material on Abbott, as are most theatrical archives. Several theatrical biographies and autobiographies provide useful background, including Richard Rodgers, *Musical Stages* (1975), Lawrence Bergreen, *As Thousands Cheer: Irving Berlin* (1990), and Craig Zadan, *Sondheim and Co.* (1986). Foster Hirsch, *Harold Prince and the American Musical Theatre* (1989), and Ethan Mordden, *Broadway Babies* (1983), have prepared perceptive critical studies that address Abbott's work. The *American Film Institute Catalogue of Feature Films* (1958 and later) is invaluable. An excellent television documentary is Ken Howard's "Mr. Abbott's Broadway," prepared for the British Broadcasting Corporation in 1994. An obituary is in the *New York Times*, 1 Feb. 1995.

JAMES ROSS MOORE

ABBOTT, Grace (17 Nov. 1878–19 June 1939), social worker and administrator, was born in Grand Island, Nebraska, the daughter of Othman Ali Abbott, a lawyer and politician, and Elizabeth Griffin, a high school principal. The Abbott household provided an intellectually stimulating environment, emphasizing reading, discussion, and formal education for all four children. Othman Abbott encouraged both Grace and her older sister Edith to watch court proceedings and participate in political discussion. Despite unrelenting financial difficulty, Elizabeth Griffin Abbott insisted her daughters receive the best education possible. Raised as a Quaker, Elizabeth was a pacifist as well as an abolitionist. She instilled in her daughters a belief in the equality of men and women and the importance of social justice. In later life Edith Abbott remembered Grace often commenting that the Quaker influence was one of the most important influences in her life.

While the Abbott sisters romanticized their prairie childhood in later years, the harsh realities of daily life in a rural community profoundly shaped them. The continual drought that plagued Nebraska in the 1890s thwarted Othman Abbott's business investments and frustrated his children's educational pursuits. Both sisters postponed personal ambitions to help support the family. An eager and popular student, Grace was expected to follow her sister to Brownell Hall, a boarding school in Omaha, but the family could not afford to send her there. Instead Edith took a local teaching position in order to contribute to the family income; Grace attended some of her classes. She continued her education at a small Baptist college in Grand Island and, after graduating in 1898, moved to Broken Bow in Custer County to teach. There she contracted typhoid and returned to Grand Island in the spring to recover. By the fall of 1899 she was well enough to teach again and replaced her sister at the Grand Island High School.

With teaching as the main profession available to women in Grand Island and other prairie communities, the Abbott sisters constantly sought opportunities for advancement. Although family obligations and poverty kept them close to home, both Edith and Grace left Nebraska for brief periods to study. Grace attended the University of Nebraska in 1902–1903 as the only woman enrolled in law classes, but she returned to teaching in Grand Island without graduating. In 1906 Grace followed Edith to the University of Chicago, initially attending a summer session and then enrolling in a full-time program the next year.

At the University of Chicago, Grace Abbott soon came to attract the attention of her professors. Her keen interest in social welfare administration, coupled with her extraordinary understanding of law, impressed Professors Ernst Freund and Sophonisba Breckinridge, both major forces in the Progressive and social reform movements. Chiefly interested in the rights of married women in the United States, Abbott studied political economy, political science, and law in pursuit of a master of philosophy degree in political science; she earned the degree in 1909. Although she was an excellent student by all accounts, she seemed most interested in how abstract ideas could be applied in the world. Edith Abbott explained in her memoirs that Grace preferred her administrative and community work to the life of an academic.

Having arrived in Chicago at the peak of the city's Progressive reform era, Abbott quickly joined forces with leading figures in the social welfare and settlement movements. She took a position with the Juvenile Protection Association to support her studies, and while she was not particularly happy chasing children from disreputable establishments, the job did allow her to move into Jane Addams's Hull-House, one of the nation's leading settlement houses. There she was surrounded by committed social reformers, including Addams, Julia Lathrop, and Florence Kelley. When Edith returned to Chicago in 1908 and joined Grace at Hull-House, the two sisters formed an effective and complementary partnership that endured for more than thirty years.

In 1908 Breckinridge, Freund, and Judge Julian Mack founded the Immigrants' Protective League, an organization designed to assist and protect recent immigrants, and chose Grace Abbott as its first director. Believing that the law should apply equally to all urban dwellers, she worked to secure state legislation that would protect immigrants from the illegal activities of private employment agencies and fraudulent savings banks. An advocate of better legislation, wiser administration, and a keener sense of obligation in every citizen, she wrote many articles in both popular and academic publications in defense of the "new immigration" of southern and eastern Europeans. In 1912 she testified before the House Committee on Immigration and Naturalization against the proposed literacy test designed to curtail the political freedom of immigrants. Although the literacy test was passed by Congress five years later, her campaign led the Massachusetts legislature to ask her to investigate immigration in that state. Impressed with her report, the Massachusetts commission offered her a permanent position with a better salary. But Abbott turned them down to return to Chicago.

With many of her settlement house colleagues, Abbott became involved in myriad social reform projects that stemmed from the new problems of an urban industrial nation. Her work with immigrant girls and women as well as her association with Breckinridge inspired Abbott to become an active member of the Women's Trade Union League, where she supported the eight-hour day for women as well as the Saturday half-day. These reforms made it possible for working women to pursue education and recreation. She developed a state plan for the enforcement of compulsory school attendance of immigrant children; she even collected the names of school-aged children arriving at Ellis Island for the superintendents of schools. She and her helpers also visited immigrant homes to ensure that children were attending school and not working in factories. She also chaired a special Committee on Penal and Correctional Institutions in 1915, where she especially explored the treatment of women prisoners.

Abbott viewed the activities of Hull-House as both social research and social assistance. She felt that she could not understand the immigrant response to America without visiting their original homes and so took several breaks from her role as director of the Immigrants' Protective League to travel in Europe and study immigration at the source. She disseminated the fruits of the research in articles and lectures at the School of Civics and Philanthropy, which eventually became the School of Social Service at the University of Chicago. Both Edith and Grace were committed to the idea that social work followed "scientific" principles and should be taught by professional schools attached to universities. At the same time, Abbott believed that social research should inform social policy; she often criticized lawmakers for creating social and political institutions for an imaginary homogeneous people.

In 1917 Abbott published *The Immigrant and the Community*, an extended essay that merged new social science methods and policy analysis to address the "immigration problem." The culmination of eight years of work with the Immigrants' Protective League, seven years of residence in Hull-House, six months' investigation for the Massachusetts Commission on Immigration, and personal visits to some of the areas that produced the most immigrants, Abbott's book challenged the nativist thinking that dominated immigration policy and suggested state involvement in the lives of immigrants, both to protect their civil rights and to encourage their "adjustment" to American life.

Also in 1917 Abbott was offered the opportunity to direct the Industrial Division of the Federal Children's Bureau. With immigration reduced to a trickle because of the war, she welcomed the chance to engage in a new pursuit. The Children's Bureau was headed by Julia Lathrop, a close friend of the Abbotts. Lathrop eased the move to Washington, D.C., and groomed Grace Abbott for her new responsibilities as a national social welfare advocate. At the bureau, Abbott created an entirely new system for inspection, certification, and enforcement of child-labor laws and worked to ensure that the new system did not upset state practices. She returned to Illinois in 1919 to head a state immigration commission, but political maneuvering led to the elimination of the commission's funding after only two years in operation. While Abbott successfully reestablished the Immigrants' Protective League in place of the commission, she was ready to return to Washington in 1921 to succeed Lathrop as the chief of the Children's Bureau.

As the bureau's new chief, Abbott administrated the Sheppard-Towner Act of 1921, which extended the first federal grants-in-aid for social welfare purposes and authorized federal-state cooperation in promoting maternal and child health. In her thirteen years at the Children's Bureau, Abbott traveled widely and formed alliances with various women's organizations across the country; she also used the popular media to provide information for mothers. When Congress repealed the controversial act in 1929 and the Children's Bureau almost lost its health program to the Public Health Service, she mobilized support for a separate office. At the same time, she served as the official representative for the United States on the League of Nations' advisory committee on white slavery and child welfare. She was also president of the National Conference of Social Work (1923–1924) and helped to organize the first Conference of Social Work in Paris in 1928. While she resigned from the Children's Bureau in 1934, Abbott worked as a member of the President's Council on Economic Security in 1934–1935 and helped to draft the Social Security Act.

Also in 1934 Abbott returned to the University of Chicago to teach and held a professorship in the School of Social Service Administration until 1939. At the same time she edited the *Social Service Review* and published a collection of annotated documents about state responsibility in child welfare called *The Child and the State* (1938). Abbott chose never to marry and lived with her sister in Chicago until her death. Later in her life, Abbott struggled with tuberculosis and sometimes had to remove herself from official business to convalesce in Colorado. She traveled and worked virtually until the moment of her death, enjoying brief intervals of strength. She died in Chicago.

As an important member of the powerful social reform movement in Chicago at the turn of the century, Abbott greatly influenced the creation of state-sponsored social programs and increased public sensitivity to the plight of immigrants, women, and children. Following the example of her distinguished teachers, she also encouraged women to participate in public administration. Thus, Abbott was not only a pioneer in the field of social work, but also an early lobbyist. Her political savvy coupled with her formidable grasp of law and social fact made her a force to be reckoned with in Chicago as well as in the nation's capital.

• The University of Chicago library houses Abbott's personal and professional papers as well as family correspondence. Edith Abbott had hoped to publish a book about Grace's life; the unfinished manuscript is also available at the Regenstein Library at the University of Chicago. Some manuscript materials can be found in the *Survey* Papers at the Archives of Social Welfare History, University of Minnesota, and the Nebraska State Historical Society. Edith Abbott provides a rich description of Grace's ideas and achievements in "Grace Abbott: A Sister's Memories," *Social Service Review*, Sept. 1939, pp. 351–407, and the two-part "Grace Abbott and Hull-House, 1908–1921," *Social Service Review*, Sept. 1950, pp. 374–94, and Dec. 1950, pp. 493–518. For the most complete biography of her life and work, see Lela B. Costin, *Two Sisters for Social Justice: A Biography of Grace and Edith Abbott* (1983). See also Jill Conway, "Women Reformers and American Culture, 1870–1930," *Journal of Social History* 5 (Winter 1971–1972): 164–77. An obituary is in the *New York Times*, 20 June 1939.

JULIE LONGO
SANDRA VANBURKLEO

ABBOTT, Horace (29 July 1806–8 Aug. 1887), manufacturer, was born in Sudbury, Massachusetts, the son of Alpheus Abbott and Lydia Fay, farmers. His father died when Abbott was quite young, leaving the family in poverty. With little opportunity for formal education, Abbott was apprenticed to a blacksmith in Westborough, Massachusetts, in 1822. After completing his five-year term, he spent the following two years as a journeyman blacksmith. Abbott then returned to Westborough and set up his own blacksmith shop. In 1830 he married Charlotte Hapgood; they would have seven children. He remained in Westborough until 1836.

In that year, seeking greater opportunities, Abbott moved to Baltimore, Maryland, accompanied by his brother Edwin Abbott. Horace Abbott entered into a partnership with John J. Ferguson and purchased an existing spade factory in the Franklinville community of eastern Baltimore County; he then converted the factory into an ironworks. One of Abbott's most notable projects was forging a large steamship shaft for the imperial Russian frigate *Kamtschatka* at the behest of Czar Nicholas I. Weighing 26,000 pounds, the shaft attracted a great deal of attention and was exhibited in the New York Stock Exchange. By 1847 the firm was also building locomotive engines.

With the purchase of the Canton Iron Works of East Baltimore from Peter Cooper (who was eager to concentrate on his New York City enterprises) in 1847, Abbott became firmly established as a leading iron manufacturer. His company, renamed the Abbott Iron Works, produced wrought-iron axles, cranks, and shafts at its location on the corner of Boston and Hudson streets in the Canton section of Baltimore. The spreading reputation of the firm caused an increase in the demand for production capacity, and Abbott responded accordingly. A rolling mill (the largest in the nation, featuring nine-foot rolls) was erected in 1850, and a second mill (with ten-foot rolls) was added in 1857. In the latter year the firm was reorganized as Horace Abbott & Son. A third and fourth mill were added by 1861.

After the outbreak of the American Civil War, Abbott's mills proved invaluable to the Union cause. Their most notable contribution was supplying the iron plate for the USS *Monitor*. Its designer, Swedish-born John Ericsson, was under tremendous pressure to deliver his radical new design in a timely fashion. The availability of Abbott's (and several other mills') iron meant that Ericsson did not have to rely on imported English iron, as had been feared. The time saved proved to be critical in completing the *Monitor* in time for its fateful encounter with the CSS *Virginia* in Hampton Roads, Virginia. Iron from the Baltimore works was also used in the construction of other Union ironclads, including the *Roanoke*, the *Agamenticus*, and the *Monadnock*. Wartime capacity was such that in 1863 the mills rolled 250,000 pounds of iron in a 48-hour period.

The numerous accomplishments of the Abbott mills did not go unnoticed; Abbott received a commendation from Secretary of the Navy Gideon Welles for his prompt fulfillment of government contracts. So valuable was his contribution to the Union war effort that arrangements were made with Secretary of War Edwin Stanton in late 1863 to exempt Abbott employees from the draft.

Following the end of hostilities, the Abbott Iron Works was purchased by a group of businessmen and renamed the Abbott Iron Company. Abbott remained for a time as president. He had by this time become heavily involved in other enterprises, most notably the First National Bank of Maryland, organized on 16 November 1863. Abbott was a major stockholder and one of the bank's original directors, along with other leading Baltimore civic leaders, including Columbus O'Donnell and Johns Hopkins. Abbott later served the bank as vice president and also served as a director of the Second National Bank, the Baltimore Copper Company, and the Union Railroad of Baltimore.

An industrious man who, in his later years, enjoyed great wealth, Abbott spent his remaining years among other industrialists on the northern outskirts of Baltimore. His estate, "Abbottston," is now within the city limits of Baltimore and is the site of the Baltimore City College High School. He died at his estate following a long period of declining health, which included partial paralysis during the final eight years of his life. While not as well known or remembered as other "rags-to-riches" industrialists of the period, his contribution to the timely manufacturing of the *Monitor* was important, as were his early efforts on behalf of the First National Bank of Maryland, which continues in operation today.

• Abbott's papers are at the Massachusetts Historical Society, Boston, Mass. While information on Abbott's life and career is scarce, his early years in Baltimore are mentioned in William B. Marye, "Place Names of Baltimore and Harford Counties," *Maryland Historical Magazine* 53 (1958): 34–57. His later years are partially documented in J. Thomas Scharf, *History of Baltimore City and County* (1881). The information on his estate is in Karen Lewand, *North Baltimore: From Estate to Development* (1989). His obituary is in the *Baltimore Sun*, 9 Aug. 1887.

EDWARD L. LACH, JR.

ABBOTT, Jacob (14 Nov. 1803–31 Oct. 1879), educator and author, was born in Hallowell, Maine, the son of Jacob Abbot II, a merchant, and Betsey Chandler. He attended school in Brunswick, Maine, and also at the Hallowell Academy. At the age of fourteen he passed an entrance examination and was admitted into the sophomore class at Bowdoin College, from which he received an A.B. in 1820 and an A.M. in 1823. It was at Bowdoin that Abbott added the extra *t* to his family name, a practice that several of his brothers (all of whom had notable careers in their own right) adopted as well. He taught at Portland Academy in the 1820–1821 school year and the following fall began a course of study at the Andover Theological Seminary in preparation for a ministerial career in the Congregational church. He completed his training in 1824, having taught in 1823 in Beverly, Massachusetts.

In 1824 Abbott was appointed tutor in mathematics at Amherst College and the following year was named professor of mathematics and natural philosophy. While at Amherst he founded with four fellow faculty members the Pentagon, a club with the goal of examining educational policies and problems. The club investigated conditions at colleges in the United States and Europe and in 1826 presented a report to the Amherst trustees criticizing the prevailing college curriculum. Arguing that the curriculum was not "sufficiently modern and comprehensive," the report urged the establishment of a new program of study featuring more emphasis on modern history and science and the substitution of French and German for Latin and Greek. The proposed changes were implemented in the fall of 1827.

After a period of initial interest (eighteen of sixty-seven freshmen entering in 1826 registered for it), this "parallel course" soon collapsed. Faculty members lost their initial enthusiasm and also resented the increased teaching load. Additionally, Amherst College, only recently founded, lacked the resources needed to complete the experiment successfully. Abbott saw his project discontinued by the trustees in the summer of

1829 and displayed his feelings by submitting his resignation from the faculty.

Married in May 1828 to Harriet Vaughan of Hallowell, with whom he had six children, Abbott could not afford to nurse his Amherst disappointment too long. The Abbotts moved to Boston, where he opened the Mount Vernon School for Young Ladies. Founded at a time when the need for female education was still debated, the school was extremely innovative, including self-government, with students serving as jurors in disciplinary cases. All corrections were oriented to the improvement of students' behavior, which was a radical innovation in a time of near-universal corporal punishment.

After several successful years as principal of the school, Abbott felt called to the ministry (he had been licensed to preach by the Hampshire Association in 1826 and had occasionally substituted for established ministers), and he was named in 1834 as the first minister to the Eliot Congregational Church in Roxbury, Massachusetts. Ever restless, he resigned as minister the next year (turning the post over to his brother, John S. C. Abbott) and removed to Farmington, Maine, where he began to devote increasing amounts of time and effort to the field in which he was to achieve his most lasting fame, children's literature. He delayed permanent attention to literature in 1843, when he founded and maintained the Abbott Institute in New York City, a school that he ran with his brothers, John Abbott and Gorham D. Abbott. He ran this institute until 1851 (for a brief interlude he ran the short-lived [1845–1848] Mount Vernon School for Boys), after which he committed himself wholly to literary pursuits.

Abbott published his first book, *The Young Christian*, in 1832. An immediate success, it was a serial of four volumes that went through numerous editions and was translated into both Dutch and French. Writing on a wide variety of topics, Abbott concentrated on children's literature and saw his work as morally instructive. His characters generally displayed exemplary behavior—traits that Abbott hoped to inculcate through positive reinforcement in his young readers. The success of the *Young Christian* series was followed in 1834 by the *Rollo* series, which ran to twenty-eight volumes. Producing books such as *Rollo at Play; or, Safe Amusements* (1836) and *Rollo at School* (1839), Abbott achieved great popularity with works that were intended to instruct children with empathy and without condescension in both morality and everyday living. A masterful storyteller, Abbott had his character Rollo mature and deal with different themes as the series progressed.

Following the death of his first wife in 1843, Abbott married Mary Dana Woodbury in 1853. They had no children. Two of his sons from his first marriage, Benjamin Vaughn and Austin, were noted lawyers and legal authors; two other sons, Lyman and Edward, were notable for their literary and ministerial successes. Abbott died in Farmington after a quiet period of retirement.

The career of Jacob Abbott remains an example of the possibilities that were open to men of energy and innovation in the nineteenth century. Achieving success in several fields, he turned an initial disappointment in college pedagogy into an innovative school for women and also made a lasting impression on the character development of countless young people through his writings.

• The papers of Jacob Abbott are held at the Bowdoin College Library, Brunswick, Maine. The best view of Abbott's personality is provided by his son Lyman Abbott in *Silhouettes of My Contemporaries* (1921). His career at Amherst College receives mention in Claude M. Fuess, *Amherst: The Story of a New England College* (1935). An obituary is in the *New York Times*, 1 Nov. 1879.

EDWARD L. LACH, JR.

ABBOTT, Joseph Carter (15 July 1825–8 Oct. 1881), senator and journalist, was born in Concord, New Hampshire, the son of Aaron Carter Abbott, a farmer and laborer, and Nancy Badger. After graduating in 1846 from Phillips Academy in Andover, Massachusetts, Abbott studied law. He began his practice in Concord in 1852, the year he became editor and proprietor of the *Manchester Daily American*. Abbott held this position until 1857. In the meantime, in July 1855, he secured an appointment as adjutant general of New Hampshire, which allowed him to reorganize the state militia. A member of the New Hampshire State Committee of the Know Nothing party, he contributed articles to magazines on the party's philosophy. Abbott was also a member of a federal commission to negotiate the boundary between his state and Canada. His journalistic success at Concord served as a stepping stone for the editorship, from 1859 to 1861, of the *Boston Atlas and Bee*.

The Civil War offered Abbott a chance to prove himself on the field of battle. He entered the conflict as lieutenant colonel of the Seventh Regiment, New Hampshire Volunteer Infantry, in December 1861. In 1863 he became its colonel and was brevetted brigadier general of volunteers in 1865 "for gallant and meritorious services" while commanding a brigade in the capture of Fort Fisher in North Carolina. Honorably mustered out of military service in July 1865, Abbott moved to Wilmington, North Carolina.

With capital in hand, Abbott bought 3,000 acres of good timber land fifty miles from Wilmington, on the Wilmington, Charlotte, and Rutherfordton Railroad line. He built a sawmill, hired over 100 men, and turned out 100,000 board feet of lumber a month. In the process, he founded and laid out the town of Abbottsburg in Bladen County. His prosperous enterprise expanded to include a woodworking shop that manufactured molding, fences, broom handles, railroad boxcars, and window blinds, among other things. The *Wilmington Daily Journal* later described Abbott's conversion of a pine forest into a thriving town as the work of a "modern Aladdin" and a "genie of enterprise."

While pursuing his business activities, Abbott developed interests in Republican politics that stemmed primarily from the postwar situation in North Carolina. At the Republican State Convention in Raleigh in September 1867, he was nominated for permanent president of the convention, an important position for dominating the proceedings and controlling membership on the committees. Though he won black support, Abbott at first faced opposition from many delegates preferring a southern man of Union sympathies to a native northerner. A compromise was ultimately reached that allowed Abbott to continue as president with William Woods Holden, who served as Republican governor of North Carolina from 1868 to 1871, as chairman of the state executive committee. Abbott's speeches at the convention clearly demonstrated not only the soundness of his Republicanism but also his commitment to African Americans (Raleigh *Standard*, 11 Sept. 1867).

Abbott reached the pinnacle of his political prominence during the period from 1868 to 1871. He attended the state constitutional convention in 1868 and helped to write the new constitution, showing special concern over matters relating to internal improvements and opposing repudiation of the state debt. He then crisscrossed North Carolina on behalf of its adoption. In May Abbott traveled to Chicago for the Republican National Convention and endorsed Ulysses S. Grant for the presidency. In an era of greed tainted by scandal and fraud, Abbott, who had been elected to the state legislature, engaged in some questionable practices. He once accepted $20,000 from a lobbyist seeking state aid.

When North Carolina won readmission to the Union in 1868, Abbott, a successful businessman and a member of the Republican National Committee, commanded enough support among state legislators to secure election to the U.S. Senate, serving from 1868 to 1871. His political strength came primarily from African Americans, with whom he maintained a special relationship. As a carpetbagger who urged his black constituents to arm themselves for self-defense, he became unpopular with native white conservative Democrats.

Senator Abbott's votes in Congress placed him squarely on the side of federal power over the states and of political rights for the newly freed African-American constituency. On 8 February 1869, in a speech on the suffrage rights of African Americans, Abbott addressed his Senate colleagues on the subject of the proposed Fifteenth Amendment to the Constitution. He strongly supported free adult black male suffrage, contending that it was constitutional, equitable, and expedient for Congress to pass the amendment. He stated: "As there are days of storm and days of sunshine, so there are eras clouded by injustice and eras when the light of truth and equity fills the whole air. To such an era have we arrived now. . . . The moral sense of this nation now demands this amendment in obedience to the guarantees of our ancestors, as well as to a sense of justice." He emphasized the paradox of "one right for one man and one for another."

In addition to supporting black suffrage, Abbott sought federal funds to improve the Wilmington harbor, sponsored tariff protection for peanuts, and wanted a federal charter to consolidate the railroads of North Carolina and South Carolina to make them part of a southern transcontinental system. The senator also endorsed the idea of abolishing the electoral college in favor of a direct popular vote to render the election of the nation's president more democratic.

Divisions within the North Carolina Republican party and personal antagonisms undermined Abbott's political standing. When conservative Democrats took control of the state legislature in 1870, he was denied another term. Upon the expiration of his senatorial service, Abbott returned to Wilmington, where for the next decade he edited the *Wilmington Post*, a weekly Republican newspaper, and engaged in lumber manufacturing. Although he continued to attend his party's state conventions, he never again assumed a prominent role in North Carolina's political affairs. Abbott was collector of the Port of Wilmington during the last part of Grant's administration and inspector of posts along the eastern line of the southern coast as well as special agent in the U.S. Treasury Department during the first part of the presidency of Rutherford B. Hayes. Thrice married but without children, Abbott died in Wilmington, somewhat of a lonely figure within his party.

• Abbott left no personal papers. Important manuscript collections dealing with this period of North Carolina history include those of William Woods Holden and Benjamin S. Hedrick in the Perkins Library at Duke University; Thomas Settle, Kenneth Rayner, David Frank Caldwell, and David M. Carter in the Southern Historical Collection of the University of North Carolina at Chapel Hill; and Zebulon B. Vance, William A. Graham, and Calvin Cowles in the North Carolina State Division of Archives and History in Raleigh. Abbott's speeches and votes are recorded in the *Congressional Globe* (1868–1871). A sketch of his life is in the Elizabethtown *Bladen Journal*, 11 Jan. 1973. J. G. de Roulhac Hamilton, *Reconstruction in North Carolina* (1914), traces Abbott's activities during the post–Civil War period. Pertinent information on this era in North Carolina is in Marc W. Kruman, *Parties and Politics in North Carolina, 1836–1865* (1983); James L. Lancaster, "The Scalawags of North Carolina, 1850–1868" (Ph.D. diss., Princeton Univ., 1974); Richard L. Zuber, *North Carolina during Reconstruction* (1969); and William McKee Evans, *Ballots and Fence Rails: Reconstruction on the Lower Cape Fear* (1967). An obituary is in the *Wilmington Post*, 9 Oct. 1881.

LEONARD SCHLUP

ABBOTT, Lyman (18 Dec. 1835–22 Oct. 1922), Congregational clergyman and editor of the *Outlook*, was born in Roxbury, Massachusetts, the son of Jacob Abbott, a pastor and author of the "Rollo" children's books, and Harriet Vaughan. Raised in Farmington, Maine, Abbott graduated from New York University with an A.B. in 1853. He then joined his brothers' law firm, passing the bar examination in 1856. The following year he married Abby Frances Hamlin, and they settled in Brooklyn, New York. There Abbott came under the influence of the nationally renowned preacher Henry Ward Beecher. He left law practice in 1859 to tutor himself in theology at the family home in Farmington, Maine.

In March 1860 Abbott received a call to the pastorate of the Congregational church in Terre Haute, Indiana, where he served during the Civil War years. His interest in helping to create a stable postwar society led him to return to New York in 1865 to direct the American Freedmen's Union Commission, offering aid and education to both white war refugees and black freedmen.

Disillusioned with the competitiveness of aid associations, Abbott moved to Cornwall on Hudson, New York, in 1869 to build a home, raise his six children, and become a full-time writer. Within two years he became editor of the *Illustrated Christian Weekly*, a Protestant family paper published by the American Tract Society. Wishing to make the *Weekly* a broad publication with commentary on contemporary issues, Abbott chafed against the rigid orthodoxies of his publisher. Thus when Beecher invited him in 1876 to become associate editor of the *Christian Union*, Beecher's primary organ of social commentary, Abbott eagerly accepted. When Beecher resigned from the paper in 1881, Abbott assumed full editorial responsibility.

During the 1880s the *Christian Union* had a circulation of only 20,000, but Abbott's moderate Christian progressivism was evident, especially through his regular column of commentary on current affairs, which he called "The Outlook." In 1893, no longer wanting to sound so ecclesiastical, Abbott changed the publication's name to the *Outlook*. Thus ensued twenty years of growing national influence, as the magazine soared to a circulation of over 100,000.

Meanwhile, the congregation of Beecher's church, Plymouth Congregational Church in Brooklyn, also turned to Abbott, electing him pastor in 1888. As editor of the premier nonsectarian Protestant publication of the day and preacher in one of the country's most famous Protestant pulpits, Abbott was a national figure between 1890 and 1915. He knew eight American presidents and was a particularly close advisor to Theodore Roosevelt (1858–1919), who became an associate editor of the *Outlook* after his presidency. The magazine threw its full and open support behind Roosevelt's unsuccessful third-party run for the presidency in 1912, a stand that proved unpopular with many readers and was a turning point toward the publication's ultimate demise.

Abbott was an influential popularizer of Protestant progressivism. Gentle and controlled in temperament, avoiding the stiffness of orthodoxy and the heat of extremes, he was a mediator of new ideas and a persuasive advocate of moral progress. His numerous speeches and articles interpreted new scholarship such as biblical criticism or evolutionary theory for a lay public, promising that all increased knowledge was for the good of humanity and the advancement of the Kingdom of God. His most noted book, *The Evolution of Christianity* (1892), passed over the scientific hypothesis of the evolution of species, rather extending the idea of evolution to show that Christianity was the highest religion and Christendom the highest culture. Abbott rejected Darwinism's theme of survival of the fittest in favor of an irenic thesis that evolution simply described human growth toward a more ethical society. Evolution would lead to the fulfillment of Christlikeness when all humanity would become an incarnation of the divine.

Abbott shared with many Protestant contemporaries a passion for the spread of Christian civilization. He was active in the Lake Mohonk conferences (1883–1916) encouraging the full integration of Native Americans into white society. He decried isolationism and preached America's moral responsibility to intervene in such conflicts as the Spanish-American War. A moderate social reformer, he coined the term "industrial democracy" to advocate a greater share of profits and better conditions for American workers, though he abhorred the methods of labor unions.

Abbott resigned from Plymouth Church in 1899 but continued as editor of the *Outlook* with assistance from his son Ernest Hamlin Abbott. He traveled extensively, though during a family vacation in Germany in 1907, his wife died suddenly just before their fiftieth wedding anniversary. The magazine became increasingly secular, especially after World War I, eventually dropping all reference to church interests. His son assumed the editorship at Abbott's death in New York, but after various mergers and changes of ownership, the *Outlook* ceased publication in 1935.

Abbott's career exemplified the progressive period of American Protestantism. His magazine spoke for many in advancing a faith in scientific progress and growing democracy tempered by adherence to Christian ethics. Abbott and his contemporaries assumed a world that would acknowledge the moral supremacy of Christianity. When that world was shaken to its foundations by World War I, Abbott quickly lost currency as a definer of American cultural values.

• Abbott wrote not only his regular column for the *Outlook* for forty years, but also many articles in other periodicals such as *Harper's Monthly*, *Century*, and *North American Review*. His extensive speeches were collected in a number of published volumes, including most notably *Christianity and Social Problems* (1896) and *The Theology of an Evolutionist* (1897). He wrote a biography of *Henry Ward Beecher* (1903) as well as his own *Reminiscences* (1915). The latter was reissued in 1923 by Ernest Hamlin Abbott with an introduction covering the last years of Abbott's life. The major biography of Abbott is Ira V. Brown, *Lyman Abbott, Christian Evolutionist: A Study in Religious Liberalism* (1953). For a historical profile of the *Outlook*, see Charles H. Lippy, ed., *Religious Periodicals of the United States* (1986). A major obituary and editorial tribute for Abbott are in the *New York Times*, 23 Oct. 1922. Extensive tributes by political, cultural, and religious leaders are in the *Outlook*, 8 Nov. 1922.

THOMAS E. FRANK

ABBOTT, Robert Sengstacke (28 Nov. 1868–29 Feb. 1940), newspaper publisher, was born Robert Abbott in Fort Frederica, St. Simons Island, off the coast of Savannah, Georgia, the son of Thomas Abbott and Flora Butler, former slaves who operated a grocery store on St. Thomas Island. Thomas Abbott died the year after Robert was born, and his mother moved to Savannah where she eventually was remarried in 1874 to John Herman Henry Sengstacke. Sengstacke was the son of a German father and a black mother and, although born in the United States, was reared in Germany. He returned to the United States in 1869 and pursued careers in education, the clergy, and journalism. In the latter role Sengstacke became editor of the *Woodville Times*, a black community weekly newspaper that served Savannah-area residents. Abbott's admiration for his stepfather inspired him to add the name Sengstacke to his own and to attempt to become a publisher in his own right.

Abbott's first newspaper job was as a printer with the white-owned *Savannah Echo*. He soon decided to obtain a college education; after attending several other institutions, Abbott enrolled at Hampton Institute in Virginia in 1889 at the age of twenty-one. Hampton, founded by the Congregationalists and supported by northern philanthropists, was both a trade school and an academic institution for African Americans. Abbott completed training as a printer in 1893, then culminated his undergraduate career with a bachelor's degree in 1896 after nearly seven years at Hampton. His experience there included opportunities to hear two charismatic black speakers, Frederick Douglass and Ida B. Wells, who influenced him to seek a leadership role in the development of civil rights for black Americans. After graduating from Hampton, Abbott moved to Chicago where in 1899 he earned a law degree from Kent College of Law, the only black in his class of seventy students. Abbott, however, was never admitted to the bar. For the next few years he tried to establish a career as a lawyer in several midwestern cities without success; eventually he returned to Woodville to teach in a local school.

In 1905, at the age of thirty-seven, Abbott returned to Chicago and began publication of his own newspaper, the *Chicago Defender*. He chose Chicago as the base for his paper because it had a large black population of more than 30,000. At the time, the black newspaper field in Chicago was extremely crowded with three established local weeklies and the availability of two other well-respected journals, the *Indiana Freeman* and the *New York Age*. Abbott's first number of the *Defender* was virtually a one-man production operated from rented desk space in a real estate and insurance office with furnishings that included a folding card table and a borrowed kitchen chair. But with an initial investment of twenty-five cents (for paper and pencils) and the help of his landlady's teenage daughter, he was able to launch a publishing enterprise that became one of the most influential newspapers in the United States. Abbott chose the name "Defender" because it epitomized his pledge to defend his race against the ills of racism. Within ten years the *Defender* was the nation's leading black newspaper, with an estimated circulation of 230,000.

Despite his early exposure to the printing trade and newspaper publishing, Abbott was seen by many of his contemporaries as an unlikely candidate for success as a newspaperman. He was not an articulate speaker and often split verbs, confused tenses, and dropped final consonants in routine conversation. But he had a strong talent for gathering rumor, hearsay, and other information and turning them into human-interest stories. Abbott also proved a master at upstaging his competitors. Proclaiming his paper to be "the only two-cent weekly in the city" and focusing front-page coverage on sensational and crime news, Abbott steadily increased his readership. the *Defender*'s most significant contribution, however, was perhaps its crusade to encourage black migration from the former slave states of the South to Chicago and other midwestern cities.

The campaign, launched during World War I, was instrumental in bringing thousands of blacks to the North in search of better jobs, housing, and educational opportunities. For Abbott the migration was part of a plan to increase the *Defender*'s circulation and give him an opportunity to penetrate the black readership markets in the South. Several southern cities so resented the effectiveness of the *Defender*'s campaign that they banned its distribution. The *Atlanta Constitution* wrote that the migration cost the South "her best labor" force and that the region's economy suffered greatly. It has been estimated that nearly 35,000 blacks moved to Chicago from the founding of the *Defender* in 1905 to 1920, more than doubling the city's African-American population. One indirect result of the heavy influx of black migrants to Chicago was a race riot in 1919 that highlighted the tensions between whites and blacks in the city. Abbott was appointed to the Commission on Race Relations, charged with determining the causes of the riot. Although the commission's report implicated the *Defender*'s strong stance for black civil rights as a contributing factor in the riots, Abbott signed the document.

The *Defender* was a fearless champion for the cause of racial equality for African Americans. Abbott enumerated his policies as the elimination of racial prejudice in the United States, the opening of trade union membership to blacks, black representation in the president's cabinet, equal employment opportunities for blacks in the public and private sectors, and black employment in all police forces nationally. He also sought the elimination of all school segregation and the passage of federal civil rights legislation to protect against breakdowns in desegregation laws at the state level as well as to extend full voting rights to all Americans. These policies found a ready market, and the *Defender*'s growth during World War I allowed it to open and maintain branch offices in several major U.S. cities and an office in London. During the war Abbott publicly asked why blacks should fight for the United States on foreign battlefields while being denied basic rights back home. This stance provoked investigations by the federal government. In 1918, just two months short of his fiftieth birthday, Abbott married Helen Thornton Morrison; they had no children.

In the decade following World War I, the *Defender*'s circulation began to fall with the arrival of a new competitor, the *Chicago Whip*, and the onset of the depression years. The *Defender* generally supported Republican politics, although in 1928 Abbott opposed Herbert Hoover in favor of Alfred E. Smith. During the 1930s, perhaps because of the 1919 riots and the impact of the depression, the *Defender* took a more moderate stance regarding racial matters. The period also took a personal toll on Abbott, and he suffered several financial reversals. By 1935 circulation had declined to 73,000. After his mother died in 1932, Abbott began to travel extensively and attempted during the mid-1930s an ill-fated venture into magazine publishing with *Abbott's Monthly*.

Following a costly divorce from his first wife in 1932, Abbott married Edna Brown Dennison in 1934 but soon fell into ill health. In 1939 he gave control of the *Defender* to his nephew John H. Sengstacke, son of his half brother Alexander. Abbott died at his home in Chicago. He left behind a newspaper that had pioneered new territory for the black press. It had become the first national paper to have an integrated staff and to be unionized. In 1956, under Sengstacke's leadership, the *Defender* became a daily newspaper, soon to become the flagship publication of the nation's largest black newspaper chain.

• Abbott's papers are in the *Chicago Defender* Archives in Chicago. The most comprehensive biography of Abbott is Roi Ottley, *The Lonely Warrior* (1955). See also Roland E. Wolseley, *The Black Press U.S.A.* (1971; 2d ed., 1990). In periodical literature see Dewey Jones, "Chicago Claims Supremacy," *Opportunity*, Mar. 1929, pp. 92–94; Robert S. Abbott, "Looking Back," *Chicago Defender*, 4 May 1935; and Ottley, "Robert Abbott: Defender of His Race," *Ebony*, June 1955, pp. 69–75.

CLINT C. WILSON II

ABBOTT, Samuel Warren (12 June 1837–22 Oct. 1904), public health official, was born in Woburn, Massachusetts, the son of Samuel Abbott, an army captain, and Ruth Winn. He completed his secondary education at Phillips Andover Academy and received his A.B. from Brown University in 1858. He then studied medicine with Benjamin Cutter, a Woburn physician, and enrolled in Harvard Medical School, where he received his M.D. in 1862. Later that year he joined the Union navy and for the next two years served as an assistant surgeon aboard the USS *Catskill* and the USS *Niagara*. In 1864 he resigned from the navy and became an assistant surgeon in the First Massachusetts Cavalry. Also that year he married Martha W. Sullivan, with whom he had four children. For the remainder of the Civil War he participated in the Army of the Potomac's bloody but successful campaign to capture the Confederate capital.

After the war Abbott returned to Woburn, where he established a general medical practice. Relocating to Wakefield in 1869, he became president of the local medical society five years later. In 1872 he took on additional duties as Middlesex County's coroner, a court officer charged with investigating the causes of unnatural deaths. At the time coroners were not legally required to have any medical training, a deficiency that Abbott and others throughout the state worked assiduously to correct. In 1877 a state law replaced the coroner with a medical examiner, and because the new office's duties included performing autopsies on victims of suspicious circumstances, its holder had to be a licensed physician. As soon as the law went into effect, Abbott was appointed medical examiner for Middlesex, a position he held until 1884.

Abbott is best remembered for the role he played in expanding the Massachusetts state government's involvement in matters of public health. Interested in preventive medicine, he played a leadership role in the grass-roots movement that resulted in the creation of the Massachusetts State Board of Health in 1869. In 1882 he became the health officer and for the next four years oversaw the state's public health endeavors. During this period he published a list of procedural recommendations concerning the production of uncontaminated and effective smallpox vaccines and demonstrated the ill effect on the public health of so-called water gas, a substance used for illuminating homes that contained a dangerously high percentage of poisonous carbonic oxide. In 1879 the department of health had been merged because of political and financial considerations with the departments of lunacy and charity, and Abbott became a leader of the movement to revitalize the department of health so it could continue to assist the localities in achieving higher standards of public health and sanitation. In 1886, when the board of health was again made a separate entity, he became its secretary and executive officer. For the next eighteen years he played a major role in developing the board into the most effective institution of its kind in the United States.

Abbott's most significant contribution to the board's work involved his application of the techniques of demographics. In this regard he was greatly influenced by the work of William Farr, a compiler of abstracts in the British registrar general's office in the mid-1800s whose numerous statistical reports concerning illness and disease contributed significantly to the success of the British public health movement. Although the reporting of births, marriages, and deaths had been legally required in Massachusetts since 1842, relatively little use was made of these figures to shed light on evolving patterns of public health until 1883, when Abbott began publishing a weekly report. Because the board of health had become heavily involved in the construction and maintenance of improved water and sewerage systems, his report focused on the mortality figures for fourteen diseases that result from poor sanitation.

Over the next eight years Abbott conducted statistical analyses of leprosy, cholera, influenza, diphtheria, and grippe. In 1891 he developed a profile of the geographical distribution of certain causes of death in Massachusetts. Two years later he began publishing an annual report that included summaries of the weekly mortality reports, statistics concerning the outbreak and fatality rates of thirteen contagious diseases, and death reports for the various cities and towns. He edited *Registration Reports of Massachusetts* from 1886 to 1890 and *Vital Statistics of New England* from 1892 to 1904. In 1896 he compiled a forty-year summary of the state's vital statistics. These studies served as the impetus and provided a model for similar studies in other states and regions. He also wrote the first history of public health in America, *Past and Present Condition of Public Hygiene and State Medicine in the United States* (1900), a monograph presented at the Paris Exposition that outlines the public health agencies then in existence in the United States.

In 1902 Abbott moved to Newton Centre, Massachusetts, where he died. He contributed to the advance of public health in the United States through his effective, long-term administration of the Pioneering Massachusetts State Board of Health and also through his important analyses of vital statistics.

• Abbott's papers are in the Library of Congress, Manuscript Division. A biography is in George Chandler Whipple, *State Sanitation: A Review of the Work of the Massachusetts State Board of Health*, vol. 1 (1917).

CHARLES W. CAREY, JR.

ABEEL, David (12 June 1804–3 Sept. 1846), missionary, was born at New Brunswick, New Jersey, the son of Captain David Abeel, a U.S. naval officer, and Jane Hassert. At age fifteen he applied to West Point Military Academy, but, doubtful of success in the competition for places, he withdrew and began the study of medicine. Feeling a deep sense of sin, he found faith that Christ was his savior and determined to enter the ministry.

In 1823, without previous college training, Abeel entered the Dutch Reformed church seminary at New Brunswick, resolved to make "an unreserved surrender" of himself to God and to "renounce all known sin." He graduated in 1826, was ordained, and began an energetic pastorate in Athens, New York. After two and a half years, ill health, ultimately diagnosed as pulmonary tuberculosis, forced him to resign, and he spent the winter of 1828–1829 at St. John in the West Indies in search of restored health.

After reading extensively in missionary literature, Abeel determined to seek an overseas appointment. The Seaman's Friend Society appointed him as chaplain to sailors in the trading zone at Canton, the only point in China open to foreigners. The American Board of Commissioners for Foreign Missions was at the same time planning a mission to the Chinese and offered him an appointment.

In October 1829 Abeel embarked for Canton with Elijah C. Bridgman, the first American missionary to China. Abeel describes the voyage in his *Journal of a Residence in China* (1834). They arrived in February 1830, and Abeel took up his duties with the seafaring community. He also began the study of Chinese and by October had decided that his mission was to the Chinese. His appointment by the American Board to that work was confirmed.

Because access to China was limited, the American Board asked Abeel to make a voyage of exploration in Southeast Asia to discover opportunities for work there, particularly among Chinese settlers. He embarked in December 1830 on an extended journey. Arriving in Java, he went in June 1831 to Batavia, where he sought out Walter H. Medhurst, a missionary of the London Missionary Society who was working there among Chinese settlers. Abeel lived at Medhurst's house for several months and accompanied him in his work. Abeel then embarked for Singapore, the main center for producing literature to be smuggled into China, stayed there briefly, then at the direction of the American Board went to Siam to investigate possibilities for a mission there.

In Bangkok Abeel studied Chinese and Siamese, developed many contacts (including some with high ranking Siamese), preached, and distributed literature. He returned to Singapore in January 1832, and after a brief visit to Malacca in March took passage in a Chinese junk to Bangkok. His account in his journal of efforts to evangelize the Chinese crew and his fulminations against their religious rites provides a vivid picture of his missionary intensity.

At Bangkok Abeel busied himself loading Christian literature on junks sailing for China. Suffering from ill health, he returned to Singapore in November 1832, served briefly in the chaplaincy there and in May 1833 set off for America by a circuitous route. He stopped at St. Helena on the way, visited Napoleon's tomb, and arrived in London in mid-October.

Abeel's health was improved, but physicians in London advised him not to sail to America in the winter. He went to the continent, visiting France, Holland, Germany, and Switzerland, holding missionary meetings, and arousing interest in the cause. Returning to England in July 1834, he wrote "An Appeal to Christian Ladies in Behalf of Christian Education in China and Adjacent Countries" and took the initiative in founding a Society for Promoting Female Education in the East. During this European stay he also published *To the Bachelors of India, by a Bachelor* (1833).

Abeel returned to America in September 1834, spending the winter in the South on account of his health and then traveling among the Dutch Reformed churches of the North promoting the cause of missions. One of his proposals was that benevolent merchants sponsor missionary trading ships. He tried to organize a women's missionary society for the United States but was thwarted by the opposition of Rufus Anderson, chief secretary of the American Board.

Abeel planned to sail for China in October 1836 but fell sick again and spent the winter at St. Thomas in the West Indies. Returning to the United States, he undertook a strenuous schedule of speaking on missions in churches, colleges, and seminaries. He also published *The Claims of the World to the Gospel* (1838).

Finally, in October 1838 Abeel embarked for Canton, but on his arrival in February 1839 he found the Chinese-British ("Opium") War was about to break out. He left Canton for Macao, then followed American Board instructions to visit the Dutch Reformed missions in Indonesia. After two years the way was clear for his return to the China coast, and he established himself at Kolongsou, an island near Amoy under British protection. When Amoy was opened in 1842 as a treaty port, Abeel established a mission there and was pleased to receive visits from high Chinese officials and find a growing audience. In 1843 he attempted an inland visit, distributing religious literature and speaking with the people as he had opportunity. However, antiforeignism was too strong to permit a substantial stay. Two more missionaries of the Dutch Reformed church, Elijah Doty and William John Pohlman, with their wives, joined him at Amoy, and the mission flourished, becoming a major project of the Dutch Reformed church.

Illness again forced Abeel to leave for America in January 1845. After eighteen months in worsening health, he died in Albany, New York. He never married. His writings and his extensive speaking made him one of the formative figures in the early development of American foreign missions.

• Abeel's *Journal of a Residence in China and the Neighboring Countries, from 1829 to 1833* (1834) provides a detailed account of those years and communicates well Abeel's ideas and strategy. There are extensive reports by Abeel in the *Missionary Herald*, vols. 27–42 (1831–1838), and an obituary in vol. 42 (1846), p. 354. Many of his articles appear in the *Chinese Repository* for those years. Also see G. R. Williamson, *Memoir of the Rev. David Abeel* (1848), and the chapter on Abeel in J. I. Good, *Famous Missionaries of the Reformed Church* (1903).

DAVID M. STOWE

ABEL, John Jacob (19 May 1857–26 May 1938), pharmacologist, was born in Cleveland, Ohio, the son of George Abel and Mary Becker, farmers. His mother died of puerperal fever while giving birth to her eighth child when Abel was fifteen. After graduating as the top student in the Cleveland high school system, Abel enrolled at the University of Michigan in 1876. His education was interrupted at the end of his third year for financial reasons, and he spent the next three years as a teacher, principal, and then superintendent of schools in La Porte, Indiana. He met his future wife, Mary Hinman, in La Porte, where she was a high school teacher.

During his stay in La Porte, Abel made the decision to study medicine. From the beginning he was apparently more inclined toward medical research than practice. He returned to the University of Michigan in 1882 to complete his undergraduate education, spending much of his last year studying under physiological chemist Victor Vaughan and physiologist Henry Sewall in the medical school. Upon graduation in 1883, Abel married Hinman (with whom he would have three children), and they moved to Baltimore where he spent a year working in the laboratory of physiologist Henry Newall Martin at Johns Hopkins University. In 1884, lured to Germany by its growing reputation as the world center of medical research, Abel obtained a place in the laboratory of noted physiologist Carl Ludwig in Leipzig. He soon decided, however, that he lacked the necessary background to undertake sophisticated medical research, and so he enrolled at the medical school at Leipzig to enhance his knowledge of basic biomedical science. Abel spent a total of six and one-half years studying in universities in Germany, Austria, and Switzerland, obtaining his M.D. from the University of Strassburg, Germany, in 1888.

In Strassburg Abel came under the influence of Oswald Schmiedeberg, one of the key figures in the emergence of experimental pharmacology as an independent discipline. The science of pharmacology had its intellectual roots in physiology, emerging along with experimental physiology in the early nineteenth century. Its institutional roots, however, lay in materia medica, a medical school subject that placed a didactic emphasis on the description of the natural sources, physical and chemical properties, and traditional therapeutic uses of drugs. Schmiedeberg and other reformers in the Germanic universities in the second half of the nineteenth century transformed materia medica classes into courses on pharmacology, the study through experimentation of the physiological action of drugs and poisons.

Schmiedeberg also encouraged Abel's interest in the application of chemistry to medicine. Convinced of the vital importance of chemistry for medical research, Abel moved to Bern, Switzerland, in 1889 to work with biochemist Marceli Nencki. In 1891 he assumed the chair of materia medica and therapeutics at the University of Michigan. Although the traditional title was retained for the chair, Abel's appointment at Michigan must be considered the first professorship of experimental pharmacology in the United States. Abel transformed the traditional materia medica course into a course on pharmacology, which included vivisection demonstrations to illustrate his lectures. He also established a research laboratory and provided advanced students with an opportunity to undertake laboratory courses and research.

In 1893, as plans were being made for the opening of the new medical school at Johns Hopkins, Abel was offered and accepted the chair of pharmacology there. From its opening, Johns Hopkins was one of the preeminent medical schools in the country, and for the next four decades Abel's laboratory became the most important training ground for American pharmacologists. Abel was also the key figure in the establishment of a national society and a journal for the discipline. In 1908 the American Society for Pharmacology and Experimental Therapeutics was established in Baltimore with Abel as its first president. The following year Abel founded the *Journal of Pharmacology and Experi-*

mental Therapeutics, which he edited until 1932. He also played a crucial role in the founding of the *Journal of Biological Chemistry* (1905) and the American Society of Biological Chemists (1906).

Abel's most important research centered around the isolation and characterization of hormones. In 1897 he isolated in crystalline form what he believed was the active principle of the adrenal glands, a substance he called epinephrine. Jokichi Takamine proved in 1901, however, that Abel had actually isolated the hormone in the form of its benzoyl derivative. Takamine obtained the active principle, which he called adrenaline, in pure form. Adrenaline was the first hormone to be isolated.

In 1926 Abel reported that he had obtained the hormone insulin in crystalline form. His results suggested that insulin was a protein, a conclusion that was challenged by other researchers because there was considerable skepticism at the time about the ability of proteins to have the high degree of specific biological activity characteristic of hormones. Subsequent research proved Abel to be correct.

Another important research contribution of Abel's was his "vividiffusion" apparatus developed in 1913. The device allowed for the removal by dialysis of diffusible substances from the circulating blood of living animals. With this apparatus Abel and his co-workers demonstrated for the first time the presence of free amino acids in normal blood. Abel also recognized the clinical potential of the apparatus in cases of kidney failure, although a functioning artificial kidney for clinical use was not developed until the 1940s.

After his retirement from the chair of pharmacology in 1932, an autonomous Laboratory for Endocrine Research was created for Abel at Johns Hopkins so that he could continue his research as professor emeritus. Although he directed the work of the laboratory, his own research efforts in his retirement years were devoted to the study of tetanus toxin, the poison produced by the tetanus bacillus that causes the symptoms of the disease. He died in Baltimore.

Abel's work was recognized through many honors, including election to membership in the National Academy of Sciences (1912) and to the presidency of the American Association for the Advancement of Science (1932–1933). Although his contributions to scientific research were significant, Abel's most important roles were probably as a mentor to young scientists and as a builder of the discipline of pharmacology. He trained pharmacologists by taking them on as postdoctoral workers in his laboratory, teaching largely by example. His protégés appreciated his kindly disposition and were inspired by the boundless enthusiasm that he showed for laboratory work. Even serious laboratory accidents, which caused him to lose one eye and injured one of his hands, could not dampen his enthusiasm for research. He was hailed by his contemporaries and continues to be recognized by pharmacologists as the father of American pharmacology.

• The John Jacob Abel Papers at the Alan Mason Chesney Medical Archives of the Johns Hopkins Medical Institutions in Baltimore consist of about ninety linear feet of correspondence, notebooks, photographs, and other materials. The most comprehensive discussion of Abel's professional career is found in John Parascandola, *The Development of American Pharmacology: John J. Abel and the Shaping of a Discipline* (1992). *John Jacob Abel, M.D., Investigator, Teacher, Prophet, 1857–1938: A Collection of Papers by and about the Father of American Pharmacology* (1957) contains two articles about Abel and reproduces four of his papers. A special issue of *Bulletin of the Johns Hopkins Hospital* 101 (Dec. 1957) contains reminiscences of Abel from various periods of his life by seven colleagues. For information on two of Abel's major research contributions, see Jane H. Murnaghan and Paul Talalay, "John J. Abel and the Crystallization of Insulin," *Perspectives in Biology and Medicine* 10 (1967): 334–80, and Horace W. Davenport, "Epinephrin(e)," *Physiologist* 25 (1982): 76–82. The most substantial obituaries (both with bibliographies of Abel's publications) are William deBerniere MacNider, "Biographical Memoir of John Jacob Abel, 1857–1938," *Biographical Memoirs of the National Academy of Science* 24 (1947): 231–57, and Carl Voegtlin, "John Jacob Abel, 1857–1938," *Journal of Pharmacology and Experimental Therapeutics* 67 (1939): 373–406.

JOHN PARASCANDOLA

ABEL-HENDERSON, Annie Heloise (18 Feb. 1873–14 Mar. 1947), historian and author, was born in Fernhurst, Sussex, England, the daughter of George Abel and Amelia Anne Hogben. Her parents had immigrated to the United States in 1871 but had not found Kansas frontier life appealing and returned home to England. In 1884, however, they went back to Salina, Kansas, where George Abel worked as a gardener. Abel and two sisters joined their parents in 1885.

After completing her high school education Abel taught for two years before attending the University of Kansas. Upon graduation she taught high school at Colby, Kansas, for one year and then returned to receive a master's degree in history in 1900, writing a thesis, "Pessimism in Modern Thought." Dubbed brilliant by a professor who suggested she go to Cornell for a doctorate, she came home a year later, lacking sufficient funds. Once again she taught at the high school level but continued studies at the University of Kansas, learning all she could about U.S. Indian policies. A Bulkley Fellowship enabled her to attend Yale, where she earned her Ph.D. in 1905. For her work on her dissertation on Indian removal, "The History of Events Resulting in Indian Consolidation West of the Mississippi," she won the Justin Winsor Prize in 1906. Her dissertation was published in the *Annual Report* (1907) of the American Historical Association and became the standard work on the subject owing to her thorough research of Indian Office and congressional records.

Abel taught history at Wells College (1905–1906), the Woman's College of Baltimore (Goucher College) (1906–1915), where she became the department head in 1914, the Teachers College of Johns Hopkins University (1910–1915), and finally Smith College (1915–1922). At Goucher, she became president of the Maryland branch of the College Equal Suffrage League (1913–1915). During her years of teaching her skills as a researcher won her a presidential appointment as the official historian of the U.S. Bureau of Indian Affairs in 1913. Encouraged by Professor Edward Gaylord Bourne, who had published a book on California Indians and the impact of the Spanish mission system on them, Abel dug deep into the archival records at the Indian Office in Washington. Following years of research she amassed material for a paper titled "The Indians in the Civil War" and later a well-documented three-volume work titled *The Slaveholding Indians* (1915).

Between 1921 and 1922 Abel journeyed to Australia, where she studied the British government's policies toward the aborigines. At the University of Adelaide she met George Cockburn Henderson, a historian with similar interests. They were married in October 1922 after she resigned from Smith. Following the marriage, George Henderson was hospitalized after suffering from bouts of insomnia and depression, and the pair decided to separate. They had no children.

During the 1924–1925 school year Abel taught history at Sweet Briar College in Aberdeen, Washington, and then resumed extensive research in both Canada and London. Awarded the Alice Freeman Palmer traveling fellowship by the American Association of University Women in 1925, she went to England and back to Australia, where she attempted to resume her marriage to no avail. Returning home in 1927 she took the name Abel-Henderson.

In 1928 Abel-Henderson was appointed professor of history at the University of Kansas, but after only one semester she received a two-year research grant. The grant from the Social Science Research Council enabled her to travel to Canada, Washington, D.C., and St. Louis, Missouri, and to continue her studies on British policies toward the Australian aborigines. During this time she edited documents of Francis A. Chardon, a fur trader who had traveled among the American Indians on the Upper Missouri from 1834 to 1839. She also edited a manuscript on the 1803–1805 Loisel expedition, *Tabeau's Narrative of Loisel's Expedition to the Upper Missouri*, which was published in 1939.

Working with the British-American War Relief Association in Seattle, Abel-Henderson founded a chapter of the Daughters of the British Empire following the war. In 1946 the British government decorated her for her work. She died in Aberdeen, Washington. Abel-Henderson researched with relentless pursuit, and her dedication in locating primary sources led to the discovery of important historical documents such as a Lewis and Clark map, which was published in the *Geographical Review* (1916), and "The Cherokee Negotiations of 1822–23" (published in *Smith College Studies in History* 1 [July 1916]: 165–221). The discovery of these and other primary source materials has been especially important to scholars. Her investigation and subsequent writings about the relationship between government and the American Indians has proved vital to studies of the topic.

• The bulk of Abel-Henderson's research notes and her library are at Washington State University, Pullman, Wash.; a few notes are in the Library of Congress and the library of the University of British Columbia, Vancouver, Canada. Her three volumes of *The Slaveholding Indians* are titled *The American Indian as Slaveholder and Secessionist: An Omitted Chapter in the Diplomatic History of the Southern Confederacy* (1915), *The American Indian as Participant in the Civil War* (1919), and *The American Indian under Reconstruction* (1925). Her edited works based on primary sources include *The Official Correspondence of James S. Calhoun while Indian Agent at Santa Fe and Superintendent of Indian Affairs in New Mexico* (1915); *A Report from Natchitoches in 1807 by Dr. John Sibley* (1922); *A Side-light on Anglo-American Relations, 1839–1858*, with Frank J. Klingburg (1927); and *Chardon's Journal at Fort Clark, 1834–1839* (1932). A biographical sketch by George W. Martin is in *Transactions of the Kansas State Historical Society* 8 (1904). Obituaries are in Yale University, *Obituary Record of Graduates, 1946–47*, pp. 177–78, and *American Historical Review* 52 (July 1947): 833–34.

MARILYN ELIZABETH PERRY

ABELL, Arunah Sheperdson (10 Aug. 1806–19 Apr. 1888), journalist and publisher, was born in East Providence, Rhode Island, the son of Caleb Abell, a quartermaster in the War of 1812, and Elona Sheperdson. Abell left school at age fourteen and worked for two years in a shop that dealt in West Indian goods. In 1822 he was apprenticed to the *Providence Patriot* after he expressed a desire to become a printer. By age twenty-two, Abell was qualified as a master printer and began working in Boston in 1827. He moved to New York in 1828 to become a printer for the *Mercantile Advertiser*, where he worked with William M. Swain, Azariah H. Simmons, and Benjamin H. Day.

When Day told Abell and Swain about his plan to publish a daily penny newspaper in New York aimed at a mass audience, they advised against it. However, Day's *New York Sun*, first published in 1833, quickly became successful and began a boom in newspaper publishing. Inspired by Day's success, Abell, Swain, and Simmons determined to found a penny paper. Abell believed that the New York newspaper market was crowded and suggested starting one in Philadelphia, where newspapers sold for six cents an issue. On 25 March 1836 the *Philadelphia Public Ledger* appeared as a small, four-page penny newspaper with little local news other than police reports. Within a year it was paying its owners dividends.

Abell saw another opportunity in Baltimore, where the six dailies had small circulations and were aimed at a higher commercial and financial class of readers than the penny press sought. Swain and Simmons opposed the idea at first, but they relented when Abell agreed to manage the venture. Abell issued the first edition of the *Baltimore Sun* on 17 May 1837 and gave away copies to all 15,000 households in the city. By mutual agreement Swain and Simmons ran the *Public Ledger* while Abell ran the *Sun*. In 1838 Abell married Mary Fox; they had twelve children. When Simmons died in 1855 Swain became sole manager of the Philadelphia paper. In 1864 Abell sold his interest in the *Public Ledger* to George Childs. Upon Swain's death in 1868, Abell became the sole proprietor of the *Sun*.

The *Sun* published local police and court stories but avoided the trivial and personal tone of other penny papers of the day. Its first issue included an attack on banks that redeemed personal checks only in their own paper money instead of gold or silver, a policy that greatly affected the common citizens of the city. The newspaper built a reputation for accuracy and editorial independence, and by the end of the first year its daily circulation was 12,000.

Between 1837 and the Civil War, Abell's *Sun* was a national leader in gathering and disseminating news and in developing new printing technology. Abell used carrier pigeons, pony express riders, and trains to carry news reports to Baltimore and Philadelphia from Washington, D.C., Boston, New York, and Halifax. The *Sun* campaigned for congressional support for the work of Samuel F. B. Morse; when Congress granted $30,000 to construct an experimental telegraph line from Washington, D.C., to Baltimore, Abell and Swain pooled their own money to extend the line to Philadelphia. The first published account of Morse's historic telegraph message from Washington to Baltimore—"What hath God wrought?"—was a news item of eleven lines printed under "Local Matters" on page two of the *Sun* on 24 May 1844.

The *Sun*'s prestige rose during the Mexican War (1846–1848) because Abell used a relay of pony express riders from New Orleans to obtain war news thirty hours ahead of any other civilian or military news organization. The federal government often received news of the war from the *Sun* long before it arrived through official channels. In 1847 Abell established a daily pony express from New Orleans and joined several New York papers to start a cooperative telegraphic news service, a forerunner of the modern Associated Press.

The *Sun* maintained an editorial silence on the slavery debate and the election of 1860. Abell was suspected of having southern sympathies, and the paper was criticized by both proslavery and antislavery factions. During the Civil War, the newspaper steered clear of any editorial comment that might be construed as criticism of the Union, but the *Sun* was watched by federal authorities. An order to close the newspaper and arrest Abell was issued but then withdrawn before it was carried out; however, no documentation supports this story. The *Sun*, unlike most Baltimore newspapers during the war, was never suppressed.

After the war Abell supported President Andrew Johnson's reconstruction policies but led the campaign to return Democrats to power in Maryland. The *Sun* declined as a major news organization in the years after the war in part because Baltimore itself languished in slow economic growth and development. On the *Sun*'s fiftieth anniversary in 1887 Abell made his sons Edwin, George, and Walter partners, and infused new spirit into the paper. By 1900 the *Sun*'s reputation for honesty and integrity and for battling local and state political corruption had been restored.

Abell helped change newspapers from a medium of the elite to carriers of news and information to the common people. In an age of personal journalism he created a prototype of the impersonal, institutional newspaper that dominates the industry today. He died at his home in Baltimore.

• The Abell family records are held privately by the family; business records are held by the A. S. Abell Company of Baltimore, Md. The best accounts of Abell's career are histories of the *Baltimore Sun* written by former staff members: Gerald W. Johnson et al., *The Sunpapers of Baltimore* (1937), and Harold A. Williams, *The Baltimore Sun, 1837–1987* (1987). Both sources are very detailed, highly descriptive, informative, and laudatory.

JOSEPH P. MCKERNS

ABELL, George Ogden (1 Mar. 1927–7 Oct. 1983), astronomer and educator, was born in Los Angeles, California, the son of Theodore Curtis Abell, a Unitarian minister, and Annamarie Ogden. His marriage to Lois Everson in 1951, which produced two sons, ended in divorce in 1970; in 1972 he married Phyllis Fox.

Educated at the California Institute of Technology, Abell completed a Ph.D. in astronomy in 1957. While a graduate student, he made observations for the National Geographic Society–Palomar Observatory Sky Survey, a two-color photographic reference source for stars and nonstellar objects. From this material, Abell compiled a list of 2,712 rich clusters of galaxies. Previously, only a few dozen were known. The Abell Catalog of Clusters of Galaxies has become a standard reference; a particular cluster of galaxies, for example, is known as "Abell 370." At the time of his death, Abell was revising and extending his catalog to include clusters visible from the southern hemisphere.

Abell's doctoral dissertation was his most important scientific work. In addition to identifying and listing clusters of galaxies, he also studied their distribution, attempting to determine characteristics of the large-scale organization of cosmic matter. At a time when many astronomers believed that, at least on a very large scale, galaxies were scattered uniformly throughout space, Abell found indications of nonrandom distribution, suggestive of second-order clusters, that is, clusters of clusters of galaxies. Also using the Sky Survey, Abell later studied the distribution of planetary nebulae (each a large cloud of gas surrounding a star). His results confirmed other studies.

Further development of Abell's distribution study for clusters of galaxies was discouraged by a lack of many known distances. Redshifts of galaxies (indicators of distance) were being measured only very slowly because many hours of exposure time with the 200-inch telescope at Palomar were required to obtain a photographic spectrum for each galaxy. Thus it was almost impossible to obtain reliable statistical data, and other astronomers could not proceed much beyond Abell's pioneering study (which was based on distances estimated from the magnitudes of the brightest galaxies in clusters). This situation changed only with the development of electronic detectors much faster than photographic plates and multiaperture spectrographs enabling some ten to twenty galaxies in a cluster to be recorded on a single, shorter exposure.

In 1956 Abell joined the faculty of the University of California at Los Angeles, where he was a lively teacher. He wrote the first of a new generation of college astronomy textbooks, emphasizing scientific principles more than facts and the universe of galaxies more than the solar system. Over a million college students have been introduced to astronomy through his textbooks, and probably even more people saw his thirteen-part television series on relativity and cosmology. He served as chairman of the American Astronomical Society's education committee and ran a summer program for gifted high school science students.

Professional recognition and service included terms as president of the Astronomical Society of the Pacific (1968–1970) and president of the International Astronomical Union Commission 28 on Galaxies (1979–1982). Shortly before his death from a heart attack in Los Angeles, California, he was named to become editor of the *Astronomical Journal.*

Abell contributed much to general public understanding and appreciation of science. A vigorous and articulate opponent of astrology and other pseudosciences, he was a founding member in 1976 of the Committee to Scientifically Investigate Claims of Paranormal and Other Phenomena and coeditor of *Science and the Paranormal: Probing the Existence of the Supernatural* (1981). He was also one of sixty-one prominent scholars and writers to sign a Secular Humanist Declaration in 1980 calling for an emphasis on science and reason rather than on religion as a means of solving human problems.

• Abell's papers were not preserved in an archive at the time of his death. Abell's doctoral dissertation, his most important scientific publication, is "The Distribution of Rich Clusters of Galaxies," *Astrophysical Journal Supplement Series* 3, no. 321 (May 1958): 211–88. See also "Properties of Some Old Planetary Nebulae," *Astrophysical Journal* 144 (1966): 259–79. Abell was coeditor of two symposium proceedings, *Objects of High Redshift* (1980) and *Early Evolution of the Universe and Its Present Structure* (1983). Abell's primary textbook is *Exploration of the Universe* (1964; rev. 1969, 1975, 1982, 1987, and 1991, the latter two editions published posthumously and revised by coauthors). A briefer, nonmathematical version first appeared as *Exploration of the Universe: Brief Edition* (1969 and 1973) and then as *Realm of the Universe* (1976, 1980, 1984, and 1988). His *Drama of the Universe* (1978), intended for nonscience students and written in the format of a play, is organized around ideas and emphasizes the unity of concepts. See also his *Understanding Space and Time* (1980), a thirteen-part British Broadcasting Corporation television series on relativity and cosmology, in conjunction with the University of California and the British Open University. On public activities with which Abell was associated, see Boyce Rensberger, "Paranormal Phenomena Facing Scientific Study," *New York Times*, 1 May 1976, and Kenneth A. Briggs, "Secular Humanists Attack a Rise in Fundamentalism," *New York Times*, 15 Oct. 1980. Brief obituary articles are by Daniel M. Popper, "George O. Abell," *Physics Today* 37 (Feb. 1984): 76–77, and Thornton Page, "George O. Abell: 1927–83," *Sky & Telescope* 67 (Jan. 1984): 22. Donald E. Osterbrock, Abell's Ph.D. supervisor and subsequently his scientific colleague, contributed to the summary presented here of Abell's work and its influence.

NORRISS S. HETHERINGTON

ABERCROMBY, James (1706–23 Apr. 1781), British general, was born in Glassaugh, Banffshire, Scotland, the son of Alexander Abercromby, laird of Glassaugh, and Helen Meldrum. Abercromby belonged to a wealthy Scottish family; his father helped him get established in life, first by purchasing him a position in the British army, then by helping him gain the posts of commissioner of supply and justice of the peace in Banffshire. His family connections were also important in his securing election to parliament in 1734 and maintaining the seat over the years. Because of his political and military importance in his homeland, throughout his adult life he held the posts of King's Painter in Scotland and the governorship of Stirling Castle. He married Mary Duff, a third cousin, and had two children.

In 1746, after an unspectacular rise through the ranks of the British army, Abercromby was promoted colonel in the Royal Regiment of Foot, the "Royal Scots," commanded by James St. Clair. During the War of the Austrian Succession he served as quartermaster general in St. Clair's expedition against L'Orient on the French coast, and formed a friendship with David Hume. In 1747 he was wounded at Hulst. Over the next few years he became a political ally of the duke of Newcastle and a comrade of John Campbell, earl of Loudoun; in 1756, during the Seven Years' War, these connections paid off. Loudoun was appointed commander in chief of British forces in North America to replace William Shirley, successor to Edward Braddock, who was killed at Fort Duquesne. With Newcastle's encouragement, Loudoun appointed Abercromby his second officer and commander of the 44th Regiment with the rank of major general in America; "M. G. Abercromby," said Loudoun, "is a good Officer, and a very good Second Man any where." Preceding Loudoun to New York in the summer of 1756, Abercromby began preparing for an offensive militia campaign against Fort Crown Point. But when Loudoun joined him in July, the commander in chief found affairs in New York so chaotic that he quietly dropped all plans for summer operations, concentrating instead on raising and training forces for later use. The following year Abercromby accompanied Loudoun to Halifax in an abortive attempt to attack Louisbourg, then returned to New York, where because of illness he was placed in charge of Albany while Loudoun planned an expedition (which never occurred) against Fort Ticonderoga. During all these maneuvers Abercromby proved himself something of a plodder, lacking the dash to originate orders but perfectly competent to carry out someone else's. In this regard he was quite unlike the popular and daring

Brigadier General George Augustus Lord Howe, who also served under Loudoun during this time as colonel of the 55th Regiment.

On 30 December 1757 Loudoun was recalled by William Pitt and Abercromby was appointed commander in chief and colonel of the 60th (Royal American) Regiment. In the following summer Pitt instructed Abercromby to invade Canada by way of Lake Champlain. On 4 July 1758 Abercromby set off by boat down Lake George with 16,000 men. Reaching his first objective, Fort Ticonderoga, on the night of 5–6 July, he and his second in command, Lord Howe, advanced upon daunting works that the French defenders recently had erected around the fort. In a preliminary skirmish Howe was killed along with 86 other soldiers; 230 men were wounded. Now bereft of Lord Howe's wise counsel and unwilling to trust his own judgment, Abercromby turned to his officers for advice about what to do. On their encouragement he assaulted the French defenses even though an alternative might have been to emplant his cannon on Mount Defiance, an eminence that commanded the fort, and compel the French to surrender. The resulting battle on 8 July ended in horrific casualties for his forces with losses amounting to about 10 percent of all those involved. That night he withdrew to his boats and retreated southward, his army shattered, his ability to command completely destroyed by his misjudgments and the resultant carnage.

Inevitably, in the fall of 1758, Pitt recalled Abercromby as commander in chief, replacing him with Jeffery Amherst. Consequently Abercromby returned to England, missed by almost no one in America. Despite his glaring lack of military ability but because of his seniority and his "connections," he was promoted lieutenant general that same year. In 1772 he advanced to the rank of general. Continuing his parliamentary career, he went on in the 1770s to support the coercive policies of Prime Minister Frederick Lord North against the colonies. Never again holding any active military command, he lived for the remainder of his days in his native Glassaugh, where he died.

• The Abercromby and Loudoun papers, major documentary collections on Abercromby's career, are in the Henry E. Huntington Library, San Marino, Calif. Important published letters are in Gertrude Selwyn Kimball, ed., *Correspondence of William Pitt When Secretary of State with Colonial Governors and Military and Naval Commissioners in America* (2 vols., 1906); Stanley Pargellis, ed., *Military Affairs in North America, 1748–1765: Selected Documents from the Cumberland Papers in Windsor Castle* (1936); and Alfred Proctor James, ed., *Writings of General John Forbes, Relating to His Service in North America* (1938). Sources on Abercromby's Scottish background are James Grant, comp., *Records of the County of Banff, 1660–1760 . . .* (1922); Alistair and Henrietta Tayler, *The Book of the Duffs* (1914); and Joseph Foster, *Members of Parliament, Scotland . . .* (1882). For general background on Abercromby's American service, see Lawrence Henry Gipson, *The British Empire before the American Revolution*, vols. 6–7 (1946–1949); Douglas Edward Leach, *Arms for Empire: A Military History of the British Colonies in North America, 1607–1763* (1973); and Howard H. Peckham, *The Colonial Wars, 1689–1762* (1964).

PAUL DAVID NELSON

ABERNATHY, Ralph David (11 Mar. 1926–17 Apr. 1990), civil rights leader and minister, was born David Abernathy in Linden, Alabama, the son of William L. Abernathy and Louivery Valentine Bell, farmers. A sister's favorite professor was the inspiration for the nickname "Ralph David," and although Abernathy never made a legal change, the name remained with him from age twelve.

Abernathy's parents owned a 500-acre farm, one of the more successful in Marengo County. His father, a community leader, served as head deacon of the local Baptist church for nearly forty years, became the first black in the county to vote and serve on a jury, and contributed heavily to building and maintaining schools in the area, including Linden Academy, the high school Ralph attended.

From the time he was a child, Abernathy aspired to the ministry. As he related in his autobiography, "The preacher, after all, was the finest and most important person around, someone who was accorded respect wherever he went" (p. 12). But before he could pursue his calling, he was drafted into the U.S. Army in 1944. Arriving in Europe just before Germany surrendered, Abernathy, who had been named sergeant of his platoon, saw no action. A bout with rheumatic fever spared him from transfer to the Pacific theater, where all but one member of his company were killed.

Drafted prior to graduating, Abernathy had to pass a high school equivalency test before matriculating at Alabama State College (now University) in Montgomery in the fall of 1945. The GI Bill paid for his education, and he took advantage of the opportunity, making good grades, acting in drama productions, and participating in student government. As president of the student council, Abernathy organized a boycott of the school cafeteria to gain better food and better treatment for the students. The next year, while junior class president, he led a successful protest for improved housing conditions.

During the summer of 1950, having graduated in the spring, Abernathy became the first black disc jockey at a white Montgomery radio station. In the fall he enrolled in graduate school at Atlanta University (now Clark Atlanta University), where he planned to earn a sociology degree before going on to seminary. He had publicly announced his call to the ministry two years earlier, and one Sunday an Atlanta University classmate took him to hear a visiting seminary student, Martin Luther King, Jr. "I sat there burning with envy at his learning and confidence," Abernathy remembered. "Already he was a scholar; and while he didn't holler as loud as some of the more famous preachers I had heard, he could holler loud enough when he wanted to. Even then I could tell that he was a man with a special gift from God" (Abernathy, p. 89).

Completing his course work in one year, Abernathy returned to Alabama State in 1951 to become dean of men. He also accepted the pastorate of Eastern Star Baptist Church in Demopolis. That congregation met only twice a month, and on the alternate weeks Abernathy soon became the regular interim pastor at Montgomery's historic First Baptist Church. Only twenty-six years old, he "never expected to be considered" for the permanent position there, but when church leaders heard that another congregation in the city was going to call Abernathy, they quickly made their offer. By March 1952 the job was his. That August he married Juanita Odessa Jones, and although the couple's first child died as an infant, four others lived to adulthood.

Abernathy had begun to establish himself in the community by the time King took the Dexter Avenue Baptist Church pastorate in 1954. The two became immediate friends, and their families dined together nearly every night. "It was an exciting time," recalled Abernathy, as both men were looking for ways that they could start trying to change the racial situation in the area. "Martin had some general ideas about the means of attaining freedom," said Abernathy, "while I had the specific understanding of Montgomery that he lacked." Using a military analogy, he explained that while the philosophic King, who was actually three years his junior, "was talking about strategy (the broad, overall purpose of a campaign), I was thinking about tactics (how to achieve that strategy through specific action)" (Abernathy, pp. 129–30). Both felt that it would be several years before they could begin implementing their plans.

They were wrong. Rosa Parks was arrested on 1 December 1955, and organizing of the Montgomery bus boycott began, with King and Abernathy playing major roles. The parties involved formed the Montgomery Improvement Association, electing King president and Abernathy program coordinator. The boycott lasted just over a year, drawing national attention and resulting in the desegregation of the city bus system. Abernathy and King had an opportunity to test their plans of nonviolent social change, but they also learned the price that would come with it. Each man's house was bombed, as was Abernathy's church.

The bombings of Abernathy's home and church took place in January 1957, while both men were in Atlanta at the organizational meeting of the Southern Christian Leadership Conference (SCLC), the group under whose auspices they would carry out their subsequent protests. King was elected president and Abernathy secretary-treasurer.

In August 1958 Abernathy turned in his thesis, finally completing his master's degree in sociology at Atlanta University. That same month, while he was in his study at the church, a man confronted him with a pistol and hatchet, claiming that Abernathy was having an affair with his wife. "He wants to kill me!" Abernathy cried as he raced out of the office and down the street. Police arrested his pursuer, and although Abernathy did not want to press charges, the city prosecuted the embarrassing case.

King moved to Atlanta in 1960 to become copastor at his father's church, and he soon began trying to persuade Abernathy to join him. Abernathy and his wife resisted, but at the end of 1961 he accepted the call of Atlanta's West Hunter Street Baptist Church. "In retrospect," Abernathy noted, "I realize the degree to which this move defined for Martin and me the strength and importance of our friendship" (Abernathy, p. 199). "Abernathy was the glue for Martin King's soul," recalled another member of the civil rights movement, who described Abernathy as King's pastor. "He gave him counsel, he gave him solace, he gave him perspective" (Garrow, *Bearing the Cross*, p. 366).

As King led protests in Albany, Birmingham, St. Augustine, Selma, and other communities, Abernathy was usually by his side and often ended up sharing a jail cell with him. They complemented each other, with the folksy Abernathy, who became known as the pastor of the movement, able to connect with the lower and middle classes in ways that the eloquent King could not. The target areas were carefully selected. "We were always on the lookout for localities that had particularly harsh regimes," wrote Abernathy, "cities that were oppressive beyond the ordinary limits of southern society" (p. 282).

Danger was ever present, leading King to ask in early 1965 that the SCLC designate Abernathy as his heir apparent should anything happen to him. Some insisted that Abernathy was jealous of King's fame, that King made this pronouncement after winning the Nobel Prize to keep his top lieutenant from going "berserk with envy." King's wife, Coretta, while admitting that "Ralph almost forced him into putting him in this position," also pointed out that her husband felt that he had "few people he could rely on" (Garrow, *Bearing the Cross*, p. 417).

When King was shot in Memphis in April 1968, Abernathy made the ambulance ride with him and remained by his side during his last moments. Abernathy was unanimously confirmed as the new president of the SCLC and continued forward with the organization's next major undertaking, the Poor People's Campaign, a march on Washington, D.C. Its minor successes, mainly in the form of legislation, were overshadowed by the disorganization and squalor of the plyboard "Resurrection City" that the marchers built near the Lincoln Memorial and by increased bickering among the SCLC leadership. Later that summer Abernathy led a demonstration at the 1968 Republican National Convention in Miami.

In Charleston, South Carolina, in 1969 the SCLC helped to win a favorable settlement in a hospital workers strike, with Abernathy spending two weeks in jail for leading demonstrations. He was involved in planning the march from Perry, Georgia, to Atlanta in 1970 and was arrested again during a 1971 protest of the firing of three black teachers in Choctaw County, Alabama. Public interest in civil rights was waning, however, and so were contributions to the SCLC. Abernathy submitted his resignation in August 1973, criticizing blacks who "now occupy high positions made possible through our struggle . . . but [who] will not support the SCLC financially" (Fairclough, p. 397). Talked into staying, he remained SCLC president until 1977, when a bid to fill Andrew Young's vacated congressional seat offered him a graceful way out.

Abernathy lost the race, but he continued efforts to aid the poor, forming the Foundation for Economic Enterprises Development (FEED) in the early 1980s. He remained pastor of West Hunter Street Baptist Church until his death. In 1989 Abernathy published his autobiography, a widely acclaimed account of the inner workings of the civil rights movement that also generated controversy because it acknowledged King's extramarital affairs. He died in Atlanta the following year.

If he was envious of King during the heyday of the movement, Abernathy had realized by the time he wrote his memoirs that his legacy was inexorably linked to that of his best friend. "We were a team," he related, "and each of us was severely crippled without the other" (p. 478).

• The organizational records of the SCLC are at the King Center Library and Archives in Atlanta. Abernathy's *And the Walls Came Tumbling Down: An Autobiography* (1989) is selective in the civil rights ground that it covers but is the most thorough depiction of his life and his role in the movement. His master's thesis, "The Natural History of a Social Movement: The Montgomery Improvement Association" (Atlanta Univ., 1958), was published in *The Walking City: The Montgomery Bus Boycott, 1955–1956*, ed. David J. Garrow (1989). Garrow's *Bearing the Cross: Martin Luther King, Jr., and the Southern Christian Leadership Conference* (1986), Taylor Branch, *Parting the Waters: America in the King Years, 1954–63* (1988), and Stephen B. Oates, *Let the Trumpet Sound: The Life of Martin Luther King, Jr.* (1982), include numerous references. Adam Fairclough, *To Redeem the Soul of America: The Southern Christian Leadership Conference and Martin Luther King, Jr.* (1987), has a chapter called "The Abernathy Years." Henry Hampton et al., eds., *Voices of Freedom: An Oral History of the Civil Rights Movement from the 1950s through the 1980s* (1990), has several statements by Abernathy, who is mentioned, if not quoted, in the majority of works on the movement. Of particular relevance is Andrew Young, *An Easy Burden: The Civil Rights Movement and the Transformation of America* (1996). Recorded speeches include *Birmingham, Alabama, 1963: Mass Meeting* (1980) and *The Sit-in Story* (1961); notable among his interviews is his 29 Mar. 1970 appearance on CBS's "Face the Nation." Catherine Reef, *Ralph David Abernathy* (1995), is a biography for young readers. An obituary is in the *New York Times*, 18 Apr. 1990.

KENNETH H. WILLIAMS

ABERNETHY, George (7 Oct. 1807–2 May 1877), businessman and provisional governor of Oregon, was born in New York City, the son of William Abernethy, a shoemaker; the name of his mother is unknown. He attended school in New York. In 1830 he married Anne Cope, with whom he would have two children. As a young man, he entered a mercantile business and continued in it until his firm failed in the panic of 1837, an event that ruined him financially. He sold his property in Brooklyn, New York, and repaid his debts.

In 1839 Jason Lee, the superintendent of the Methodist Episcopal mission in Oregon, recruited Abernethy to return with him to the Willamette Valley and manage the mission's business affairs. Abernethy, with his wife and children, joined a group of mission workers, farmers, and artisans aboard the *Lausanne* and sailed to Oregon, arriving 1 June 1840. This party is regarded as the formal beginning of the American colonization in Oregon, then jointly occupied by the United States and Britain.

Abernethy quickly established himself as one of the leading businessmen of the Pacific Northwest. He spent several years as financial manager at the mission's headquarters, a few miles south of Salem. While there, he played a leading role in much of the activity undertaken by the *Lausanne* party. Under Abernethy's direction, this group farmed large tracts of land, built a mill, and opened an academy; they even initiated commercial activities, such as fur trading, that rivaled those of the Hudson's Bay Company. Although the Methodist mission had much influence on the secular activities of the early settlers, this influence was diminished by the arrival of Roman Catholics, who attracted the resident French Canadians and many Indians. Eventually, the Methodist mission, and the Abernethy family, moved to Oregon City. The mission closed in 1844, and Abernethy bought its store and sawmill and assumed its unpaid debts. From that time on he centered his operations in Oregon City, where he constructed the first brick building in the state. He also managed Oregon's first newspaper, promoted the burgeoning lumber and fishing industries, and formed commercial ties with California, the Atlantic Coast, and Hawaii.

Although he had a continuing interest in the political affairs of Oregon, Abernethy never showed a keen desire to run for office; however, when the provisional government was organized in 1845, he was nominated and elected governor. He was on a trip to Hawaii at the time and did not find out about his election until his return home. The most noted event during his tenure as governor was the Whitman Massacre at Waiilatpu and the ensuing war against the Cayuse Indians during 1847 and 1848. Marcus Whitman and his wife ran a medical and religious mission in the Walla Walla Valley. The Cayuse attacked the settlement on 29 November 1847, killing fourteen settlers and taking many others hostage. Some criticized Abernethy's response to the situation, saying that he was too slow to act and that he called for fewer volunteers than were necessary to hunt down the Cayuse and save the hostages. In fact, Abernethy and forty volunteers were en route to Vancouver, within one day of receiving the news of the massacre. After obtaining ammunition from the Hudson's Bay Company, Abernethy's party went to The Dalles, Oregon, where they mounted an expedition against the Indians. The expedition pursued the Indians, engaged them in battle, and defeated them, saving all the hostages. While some people criticized Abernethy for acting too slowly, the majority felt that his handling of the situation was fair and that he was intelligent and able. Thus, he remained governor until 1849, even after Oregon became a U.S. territory. When President James Polk appointed General Joseph Lane governor of Oregon, Abernethy was forced to relinquish his office, and Lane assumed its duties on 3 March 1849. Abernethy never took any of the salary granted by the legislature for his services as governor, feeling that it was a duty and a privilege to serve.

In the later years of Abernethy's life, some of his financial projects proved catastrophic, and a disastrous flood in 1861 ruined much of his property in Oregon City. He moved to Portland, where he was in business until his death there. An old Oregon pioneer wrote, "I am not seeking to make him a great man—only this: as a missionary he was consistent and conscientious; as a businessman he was honorable, enterprising and liberal; as a governor, he was patriotic efficient and unselfish." Governor George L. Curry of Oregon wrote in the *Penn Monthly* (Jan. 1875), "Gov. Abernethy, an intelligent Christian gentleman, unassuming, indisposed to court popular favor, with strong common sense, and a desire to do his duty conscientiously and quietly, was the right man for the occasion, and, whatever prejudice may assert to the contrary, it was fortunate for the colony that just such a person could be had to fill the highest and most responsible position in the pioneer government." Although Abernethy's actions were sometimes questioned by the public, he was a fair and able businessman and politician; his efforts helped to settle Oregon and to prepare the territory for statehood.

• A copy of Abernethy's letter-press book, dealing with his business affairs in the years 1847 to 1850, is in the Oregon State Historical Society Library, Salem. Abernethy's public papers are published in J. H. Brown, *Political History of Oregon* (1892); and La Fayette Grover, *Oregon Archives* (1853). See also Joseph Gaston, *Centennial History of Oregon* (1912). For information on Oregon's provisional government, see Joseph Schafer, *A History of the Pacific Northwest* (1918); and W. C. Woodward, *The Rise and Early History of Political Parties in Oregon, 1843–68* (1913). For the Methodist influence on Oregon, see Robert J. Loewenberg, *Equality and the Oregon Frontier: Jason Lee and the Methodist Mission, 1834–43* (1938). See also William Henry Gray, *A History of Oregon* (repr. 1973). For information on the Whitman Massacre and related events, see George W. Fuller, *A History of the Pacific Northwest* (1931); Marvin M. Richardson, *The Whitman Mission* (1940); and William A. Mowry, *Marcus Whitman and the Early Days of Oregon* (1901). For early Oregon history, see Malcolm Clark, Jr., *Eden Seekers: The Settlement of Oregon, 1818–1862* (1981).

KATHRYN D. SNAVELY

ABERT, John James (17 Sept. 1788–27 Jan. 1863), army engineer, was born in Frederick City, Maryland, the son of John Abert and Margarita Meng. His father is said to have emigrated to America as a soldier with Rochambeau in 1780. He entered the fledgling U.S. Military Academy at West Point, New York, in 1808, graduating in 1811. He married Ellen Matlack Stretch in 1812; they had six children. After resigning from the army, Abert was admitted to the District of Columbia bar in 1813 and the Ohio bar in 1814. Abert served his country as a private soldier in the District of Columbia Militia during the War of 1812, fighting in such engagements as the battle of Bladensburg, Maryland, on 24 August 1814.

In November 1814 Abert was reappointed to the U.S. Army as a brevet major with the Topographical Engineers. Initially constituting a branch of the Corps of Engineers, topographical engineers devoted much of their time in the early nineteenth century to surveying for purposes of national expansion and defense. In 1818 the War Department consolidated the Corps of Engineers, the Topographical Engineers, the Military Academy, and the Board of Engineers for Fortifications into one Engineering Department, headed by the senior officer of the Corps of Engineers. The Topographical Bureau was created in 1820 as a subordinate unit; its duties included surveying and scientific expeditions and internal improvements such as roads, harbors, river works, lighthouses, and railroad surveys.

From 1816 to 1818 Abert assisted in a geodetic survey project mapping the Atlantic Coast. This was followed by assignments superintending surveys of Chesapeake Bay, Narragansett Bay, New York's East River, the Fall River in Massachusetts, and the Louisville area in Kentucky, among others. In 1824 Abert was brevetted lieutenant colonel and placed in charge of surveying the Chesapeake and Ohio Canal. After superintending surveys of Maine in 1826–1827, he was appointed head of the Topographical Bureau in Washington, D.C., in March 1829, following the death of Isaac Roberdeau.

Abert's appointment as the head of the Topographical Bureau began a new era in his life, one in which he would have an impact on military affairs and help shape national policy and many facets of American culture. He quickly began applying pressure on Congress to form a Corps of Topographical Engineers separate from the Corps of Engineers, a move that increased tensions between these two engineering branches. In 1831 Abert and the Topographical Bureau acquired the duties of the recently abolished Board of Internal Improvements, and Acting Secretary of War Philip G. Randolph elevated the bureau to independent status within the War Department. Abert was named a U.S. commissioner to conduct Indian emigration to the Missouri frontier in 1832. In 1833–1834 he again served as commissioner, this time to the Creek Indians and the Wyandottes of Ohio. He last acted as an Indian commissioner in 1846.

With the Army Reorganization Act of 1838, Abert's persistence was rewarded: a separate Corps of Topographical Engineers was established. Abert was promoted to colonel and became the commander of the new corps on 7 July 1838. The corps, with Abert as their leader, played an influential part in westward expansion. Under Abert's direction, surveys were conducted as much for the collection of geographic and scientific data as for military reconnaissance, with maps, specimens, and other information returned to Washington for analysis and cataloging. Abert used the Mexican War (1846–1848) to highlight the importance of his engineers; in the corps's annual report of 1848, he stated that they were "the eyes of the commanding general . . . With these he can see the country, and can know how to direct and combine all his movements or marches, whether offensive or defensive, and without them he is literally groping in the dark." Their explorations facilitated the construction of civil and military posts and roads in the West that were "the pioneers of civilization and wealth."

Abert's continuing emphasis on exploration as a means of contributing to scientific knowledge was a reflection of his role in the emerging American scientific community. His friendship with naturalist John James Audubon and his data supporting Audubon's much-maligned research on the climbing habits of rattlesnakes cost Abert election as a member in the American Philosophical Society in 1832. (Audubon named a squirrel after Abert, the *Sciurus aberti*.) In 1840 Abert was among a small group that gathered at Secretary of War Joel Poinsett's home to form the National Institute for the Promotion of Science, which was created to oversee the collections obtained from the U.S. Exploring Expedition of 1838–1842, obtain money from the Smithson fund, and give Washington, D.C., a scientific society worthy of the nation's capital. Abert was a member of several other domestic scientific societies as well as the Geographical Society of Paris.

Abert was honorably retired from active military service in September 1861, just prior to the opening volleys of the Civil War, "having become incapacitated by long and faithful service" (Cullum, p. 102). Abert's significance to American history lies not only in the results generated from his work in topographical engineering but in the approach that he took in his work. He was instrumental in establishing the Corps of Topographical Engineers, a government body staffed by military engineers that served both military and civilian purposes, particularly in the realm of westward expansion. The goals of Abert's corps were multidimensional: surveying for military and commercial interests, construction of internal improvements, and collection of scientific data. Its overarching purpose was to create a web of communication that would solidify the Union and help the United States establish and maintain its political and commercial position. By the time of his retirement, Abert had set the United States well on its way to fulfilling these objectives through his half-century of influence in military, civilian, and scientific circles. He died in Washington.

• Abert's papers include those in the U.S. Military Academy Library Special Collections in West Point, N.Y., and among the papers of the Office of the Secretary of War, the Topographical Bureau, the Office of the Chief of Engineers, the Adjutant General's Office (1811–1863), the Office of Indian Affairs, and the Office of the Secretary of the Senate (especially vol. 3, 1836–1853), available at the National Archives in Washington, D.C. Also, see the *American State Papers, Military Affairs* (1832–1861). Letters can be found among the Daniel Parker Papers at the Historical Society of Pennsylvania and the John James Audubon Papers in the Missouri Historical Society, and by referring to Grace E. Heilman and B. S. Levins, eds., *Calendar of Joel R. Poinsett Papers in the Henry D. Gilpin Collection* (1941). The Smithsonian Archive's records of the National Institute for the Promotion of Science document Abert's involvement with that group. Works describing Abert's life and career include: G. W. Cullum, *Biographical Register of Officers and Graduates of the U.S. Military Academy*, 3d ed., vol. 1 (1891); W. H. Holcombe, "Col. John James Abert," *Professional Memoirs of the Corps of Engineers, U.S. Army*, vol. 7 (1915); Frank N. Schubert, ed., *The Nation Builders: A Sesquicentennial History of the Corps of Topographical Engineers, 1838–1863* (1988); Adrian G. Trass, *From the Golden Gate to Mexico City: The U.S. Army Topographical Engineers in the Mexican War, 1846–1848* (1993); H. P. Beers, "A History of the U.S. Topographical Engineers, 1813–1863," *Military Engineer* 34 (1942): 287–91, 348–52; William H. Goetzmann, *Army Exploration in the American West, 1803–1863* (1959); Schubert, *Vanguard of Expansion: Army Engineers in the Trans-Mississippi West, 1819–1879* (1980); and Todd Shallat, *Structures in the Stream: Water, Science, and the Rise of the U.S. Army Corps of Engineers* (1994). An obituary is in the *Daily National Intelligencer*, 28 Jan. 1863.

MARY M. THOMAS

ABRAHAM (fl. 1826–1845), also known as "Prophet," was a runaway slave who became a prominent leader among the Seminoles. Nothing is known about his parents or childhood. Fleeing his master, Abraham escaped south into Florida where he was adopted into the Seminole tribe. He enjoyed considerable status among the Seminoles, accompanying a tribal delegation to Washington, D.C., in 1826 and becoming an influential counselor to Micanopy, a leading Seminole headman. The Seminole, or Florida Indians, once were a part of the Muscogee (Creek) Nation that had been driven out of Georgia by the early English colonists, and the Oconee and Yamasee tribes that had been driven out of the Carolinas following the Yamasee uprising of 1715. They had first settled among the Lower Creeks in the Florida Panhandle and created a haven for runaway slaves. In fact, *Semino'le* is the Creek word for runaway.

In 1818 Andrew Jackson led a command of American troops into Spanish Florida partly in an attempt to capture and return the runaway slaves to their masters. After the Florida purchase of 1819 southerners increased their demands for the return of their slaves, which the Seminoles refused to do. Nonetheless fugitive slave hunters constantly raided Seminole villages and clashed violently with Indian and black warriors. Federal officials attempted to force the Seminoles to surrender the fugitives by withholding rations and annuities, but the Seminoles insisted that the blacks were their private property or had been welcomed into the tribe as full members.

In 1832, following the passage of the Indian Removal Act of 1830, Abraham was an interpreter during the negotiations between the Seminoles and James Gadsden for the Treaty of Payne's Landing. The agreement called for the removal of the tribe to Indian Territory but not before an exploration party was sent West to examine the region. Serving as the party's interpreter was Abraham. After touring Indian Territory the party signed another treaty at Fort Gibson agreeing to removal. Returning to their homeland, however, they reported that while the land was suitable the location of the tribe so close to the plains Indians was unacceptable; the tribe as a whole rejected the agreement. The federal government then dispatched troops to enforce removal. Abraham became a leader of the runaway slaves fighting alongside the Seminoles. On 3 February 1837 Abraham was induced to surrender and appeared at the camp of General Thomas S. Jesup carrying a piece of white cloth attached to a stick. Abraham entered Jesup's camp and, maintaining his dignity, walked to the general's tent where he stuck the staff into the ground and waited for Jesup to appear.

According to the *Army and Navy Chronicle*, Abraham was "a cunning negro, of good consideration with the Seminoles." Although Abraham thought that he would be hanged for his part in the Seminole rebellion, federal officials realized that he could "do more than any other" to persuade those still fighting to surrender, and they used him as a peace mediator. On 6 March 1837 he served as the chief interpreter at a meeting held at Camp Dade at which Jumper and Holahtochee agreed to stop fighting and to report to Tampa Bay for removal. Abraham continued to serve the Americans and in March 1838 was instrumental in convincing Alligator to surrender. With the end of most Seminole resistance, Abraham joined the other tribal members on their journey westward. On 25 February 1839 he, along with 195 other warriors, women, children, and former slaves, boarded the steamboat *Buckeye* for the trip to Indian Territory, where he continued to serve as an interpreter in negotiations between Seminole and U.S. officials.

Like his early life, little is known of Abraham's later years or his place of death. The Seminoles were among the more isolated of the southeastern Indians and maintained less contact with non-Indians than did other tribes; therefore, Abraham's ability to serve as a translator between the Americans and the Seminoles made him a valuable addition to the tribe.

• Records dealing with Abraham's life are sketchy. However, his activity during the Seminole removal war was recorded in vol. 4 of the *Army and Navy Chronicle*. Additional information is found in Thomas L. McKenney, *Memoirs with Sketches of Travels* (1846); Grant Foreman, *Indian Removal: The Emigration of the Five Civilized Tribes of Indians* (1932); Kenneth W. Porter, "The Negro Abraham," *Florida Historical Quarterly* 25 (1946): 1–43; and John K. Mahon, *History of the Second Seminole War, 1835–1842* (1967).

KENNY A. FRANKS

ABRAMS, Albert (8 Dec. 1863–13 Jan. 1924), physician and exponent of new theories of disease requiring treatment by unorthodox devices, was born in San Francisco, California, the son of Marcus Abrams and Rachel Leavey. He received M.D. degrees from Heidelberg University at nineteen (1882) and the next year from Cooper Medical College (later Stanford), then pursued postgraduate study in London, Berlin, Vienna, and Paris. Later he frequently returned to Europe for periods of study and earned a Master of Arts degree from Portland University in Oregon (1892). Abrams began his practice in San Francisco, gaining esteem among his peers with his numerous publications, especially a *Manual of Clinical Diagnosis* (1891) and a study of *Diseases of the Heart* (1900). His major contribution demonstrated the value of X-rays in cardiac diagnosis. Abrams was chosen president of the San Francisco Medico-Chirurgical Society, vice president of the California Medical Society, and pathology professor at Cooper (1893–1898). He built a large practice and became a prominent figure in the city, in his Van Dyke beard, pince-nez glasses, flowing tie, and derby hat, and driving his elegant carriage pulled by fast horses.

Abrams lost his position at Cooper on the charge of questionable ethics: he took fees from students for private lessons in what he had been employed to teach (Alvarez interview). Gradually his doctrines departed from prevailing orthodoxy, at first stressing a series of bodily reflexes—cardiac, lung, liver, knee, stomach, intestinal, vertebral. His theory, announced in the book *Spondylotherapy* (1910), held that stimulating reflex centers in the spine by percussion could aid in diagnosis and treatment. In 1917 Abrams fused percussion—now of the abdomen—with electricity in a system he termed the Electronic Reactions of Abrams (ERA). The electron, he argued, had superseded the cell. By charting the vibrations of the body's electrons, disease could be detected; by countering harmful vibration rates, even the direst maladies could be cured. And both discovery and therapy could occur over vast distances. "The spirit of the age," he declared, "is radio, and we can use radio in diagnosis." Abrams employed a series of devices in his regimen of diagnosing and treating. Their design was haphazard, mostly left to the ingenuity of an electrician in his employ, but to the layman the complex array was superficially impressive. A drop of a remote patient's dried blood on paper was placed in a dynamizer that was wired to a rheostatic dynamizer linked to a vibratory rheostat that was connected to a measuring rheostat from which a wire ran to an electrode on the forehead of a healthy individual, usually a young boy (but not a redhead) who was stripped to the waist and faced west in a dim light. The operator tapped the boy's abdomen, finding spots of dullness. Their location and purported ohms of resistance revealed the diseases from which the distant patient suffered, and even his religious preference. Diseases most often diagnosed were syphilis, tuberculosis, and cancer. In due course Abrams announced that an autograph would do as well as blood, permitting diagnosis of those long dead: Samuel Pepys and Edgar Allan Poe, Abrams reported, both had syphilis. Abrams further claimed that his gadgetry could determine the paternity of a child, and one such diagnosis was accepted to resolve a dispute in court.

ERA could also be harnessed to cure, although requiring another machine, the oscilloclast. Producing vibratory rates of all known diseases, the oscilloclast could destroy the ailments of sufferers no matter how far away. Abrams sold his diagnostic devices to orthodox and alternative practitioners, but he only leased the oscilloclast; the contract forbade the operator from opening the hermetically sealed box. Abrams made large sums from his sales and leases and from teaching would-be operators how to use the devices. In a period of therapeutic skepticism about drugs among elite physicians, even among the broad public, drugless healing became much in vogue, and public curiosity about electrical apparatus, especially radio, fostered the ERA craze. Abrams, moreover, gained the outspoken support of well-known figures, especially the writer Upton Sinclair. Early in 1923, some 3,500 practitioners in the nation were employing ERA devices.

Abrams also garnered severe critics. Morris Fishbein and Arthur Cramp of the American Medical Association ridiculed the claims of ERA's inventor, with Cramp adjudging him "the dean of twentieth century charlatans" (Cramp, p. 112). Many physicians sent Abrams and practitioners using his devices nonhuman blood: chicken blood brought a diagnosis of dental caries. H. L. Mencken and Paul DeKruif condemned Abrams, and the Nobel laureate physicist Robert Millikan termed the sealed boxes with their jumbled wiring the kind of gadgetry that "a ten-year-old boy would build to fool an eight-year-old" (Fishbein and Engle). *Scientific American* created a blue-ribbon panel that exposed ERA in twelve long articles, the summary judgment stated as "At best . . . ," Abrams's scheme "is an illusion. At worst, it is a colossal fraud." Abrams was scornful of his critics. He wrote to Sinclair: "I have ceased attempting to convince . . . narrow-minded individuals who call themselves scientists. And whose names are as unknown to me as Martian inhabitants. Any new discovery finds its acceptance through plaudits of the multitude" (Sinclair Manuscripts, 31 Dec. 1921). Such comments reveal that Abrams suffered from self-delusion, a transition into the irrational when his early researches did not yield the degree of fame he craved.

While the *Scientific American* series was being published, Abrams died in San Francisco. He had been twice married, in 1897 to Jeanne Irma Roth, and in 1915 to Blanche Schwabacher, but he had no children. Abrams left an estate of $2 million pledged to the perpetuation of his system. He also left a core group of followers who continued his work under the rubric of the American Association for Medico-Physical Research. Use in unorthodox practice of devices patterned on those of the master continued for decades.

• Some Abrams correspondence can be found in the Bakken Library and Museum of Electricity and Life in Minneapolis and in the Upton Sinclair Manuscripts, Lilly Library, Indiana University. The American Medical Association Historical Fraud and Alternative Medicine Collection in Chicago contains much correspondence about Abrams, some of it cited in the *Journal of the American Medical Association*, 1922–1923. Nathan Flaxman lists and analyzes Abrams's prolific publications in "A Cardiology Anomaly," *Bulletin of the History of Medicine* 27 (1953): 252–68. The *Scientific American* investigation is reported in issues published between Oct. 1923 and Sept. 1924. Appraisals of Abrams's career include Morris Fishbein, *Fads and Quackery in Healing* (1932); Arthur J. Cramp, *Nostrums and Quackery and Pseudo-Medicine* (1936); Ernest W. Page, "Portrait of a Quack," *Hygeia* 17 (Jan. 1939): 53–55, 92–93; Fishbein and William Engle, "Medical Hucksters," *American Weekly*, 1 Feb. 1948, pp. 16–17; James Harvey Young, *The Medical Messiahs* (1967); David M. Bailey, "The Rise and Fall of Albert Abrams," *Oklahoma State Medical Association Journal* 71 (Jan. 1978): 15–20; and Charles V. Pollack, Jr., "Electronic Therapeutics of Albert Abrams," *Pharmacy in History* 26 (1984): 109–13. The author held interviews with Dr. Walter Alvarez, a distinguished physician/journalist who was in California during Abrams's heyday, on 19 May 1961 and 13 Aug. 1962 (unpublished). Obituaries are in the *San Francisco Chronicle*, 14 Jan. 1923, and the *New York Times*, 15 Jan. 1923.

JAMES HARVEY YOUNG

ABRAMS, Creighton Williams, Jr. (15 Sept. 1914–4 Sept. 1974), army officer, was born in Springfield, Massachusetts, the son of Creighton W. Abrams, a railway repairman, and Nellie Randall. At the U.S. Military Academy at West Point, Abrams excelled in horsemanship, played football, and attained a mediocre academic record, finishing 185th in a class of 276. He graduated in 1936 and was commissioned a second lieutenant of cavalry. That same year he married Julia Harvey, with whom he would have six children.

Over the next five years he held a number of positions in the peacetime army. He served with the First Cavalry Division at Fort Hood, Texas, and was promoted to first lieutenant in 1939 and captain in 1940. In 1941 he went to the new Fourth Armored Division.

During World War II Abrams became a legendary figure as a tank commander. Promoted to major in February 1942 and lieutenant colonel shortly after, he was given command of the Thirty-seventh Armored Regiment. He went into action with the Thirty-seventh Tank Battalion at Normandy in July 1944 and during the next year established a reputation for fearless and aggressive leadership. His unit was the first to crack the fabled Maginot line. During the Battle of the Bulge in December 1944, it was the first to reach the embattled 101st Airborne Division at Bastogne. There he is reported to have exclaimed of the Germans, "They've got us surrounded again, the poor bastards."

Abrams's battalion was in the vanguard of General George S. Patton's drive across Europe. On one occasion his command tank destroyed a German antitank gun that was holding up the advance, an act for which he received the Distinguished Service Cross. Patton conceded him peer status among tankmen and labeled him "the world champion" of tank commanders.

Abrams held a variety of posts in the Cold War army. From 1946 to 1948 he was director of tactics at the Armored School, Fort Knox, Kentucky. During the early 1950s he commanded the Sixty-third Tank Battalion and the Second Armored Cavalry Regiment in Europe. During the Korean War he was chief of staff of I Corps, IX Corps, and X Corps and planned U.S. defenses against the last enemy offensive (July 1953).

Promoted to brigadier general in 1956 and to major general in 1960, Abrams was at numerous domestic and foreign trouble spots in the tumultuous 1960s, serving in Berlin during the crisis of 1961 and assuming command of federal troops sent to support the integration of the University of Mississippi in September 1962. He returned to Europe in July 1963 as commanding general of V Corps. Promoted to lieutenant general in 1963 and general in 1964, he was subsequently named vice chief of staff of the army.

Between May 1967 and June 1972 Abrams served in Vietnam. His first assignment was as deputy to his West Point classmate General William C. Westmoreland, commander of the U.S. Military Assistance Command, Vietnam (COMUSMACV). In that capacity Abrams assumed responsibility for the pacification program and for training the South Vietnamese Army (ARVN). During the Tet Offensive of 1968 he commanded U.S. and South Vietnamese forces in the northern provinces of South Vietnam. In June 1968 he replaced Westmoreland.

His four years as COMUSMACV involved challenges as difficult as those faced by any U.S. military leader. In the aftermath of the Tet offensive, the administration of Lyndon Johnson, responding to domestic pressures, stopped escalation of the war, made a new proposal for negotiations, and prepared to shift the military burden to the South Vietnamese. The administration of Richard Nixon went a step further, initiating a policy of phased troop withdrawals. In a military situation where any hope of victory had been abandoned, Abrams's main tasks were to cover the U.S. withdrawal from Vietnam and prepare the South Vietnamese to defend themselves.

Each posed special problems. It was very difficult to sustain morale in a no-win situation, and between 1969 and 1971 the army experienced major problems of drug and alcohol abuse, racial strife, and attacks on officers ("fragging"). Abrams kept the army together and used it as best he could under the circumstances. He shifted from Westmoreland's large-scale search-and-destroy operations to smaller unit patrols. His one-war concept ended the division of mission between U.S. and South Vietnamese forces, emphasizing combined operations and the coordination of military operations with pacification. He fought stubbornly to slow the rate of U.S. troop withdrawals to permit greater time to build up the South Vietnamese. When he departed South Vietnam at the height of the enemy Easter offensive of 1972, what remained of the U.S. Army in Vietnam was still intact, and South Vietnam still survived.

Preparing the South Vietnamese to defend themselves was an impossible task. Despite enormous U.S. aid, the ARVN remained afflicted by poor leadership, corruption, and incompetence, and there were limits to what the United States could do. Like his predecessor, Abrams never took a hard line with the Saigon government, refusing to interfere in the chronic political machinations and tolerating widespread corruption. He was keenly aware when he left Vietnam that he had not been able to carry out his mission. "We've done the best we can," he told another officer.

As army chief of staff between 1972 and 1974, Abrams presided over a major reorganization, increasing the number of combat forces while reducing costs. He helped put the new volunteer army on a solid basis. He modernized and upgraded the reserves and integrated them with regulars in a way that made it difficult to go to war again without their mobilization.

Abrams epitomized the "soldier's soldier." Rumpled in appearance and tough in demeanor, he chewed cigars and talked to soldiers in earthy, Patton-like language. He was described as a "slumbering volcano," a quiet, somewhat retiring man who could explode when angered. Yet he was deeper and more complex than the image he cultivated. Soft-spoken and compassionate, he was politically astute and skillfully handled assignments that called for restraint, finesse, and tact. Often called the "quintessential soldier," he was compared to Ulysses S. Grant for his skill in command and for the values he exemplified.

He died at Walter Reed Army Medical Center seven months before the fall of Saigon and was thus spared the agony of seeing the collapse of the army and government he had fought so hard to preserve.

• A small collection of Abrams's papers is at the U.S. Army Military History Institute, Carlisle Barracks, Pa. There is also at Carlisle Barracks a collection of oral histories called "The Abrams Story." Abrams refused even to consider writing memoirs. The only biography is Lewis Sorley, *Thunderbolt: General Creighton Abrams and the Army of His Times* (1992), an admiring but careful and scholarly study. An obituary is in the *New York Times*, 5 Sept. 1974.

GEORGE C. HERRING

ABRAMS, Harry Nathan (23 Feb. 1905–25 Nov. 1979), publisher and art collector, was born in London, England, the son of Morris Abrams, a shoe store proprietor, and Amelia Rosenberg. In 1913 the family moved from London to New York City, where Abrams studied at the National Academy of Design and at the Art Students League.

In 1926 Abrams acquired a non-salaried position with the advertising firm of Schwab and Beatty. He supported himself by working at his father's shoe store on Friday evenings and Saturdays. In 1932 Abrams married Nina Bolotoff, a bookseller; they would have two sons. Abrams became a U.S. citizen in 1936.

Through his work at Schwab and Beatty, Abrams came to the attention of Harry Scherman, who had recently founded the Book-of-the-Month Club. In 1936 Abrams became employed as the organization's art director. In this position, he oversaw the use of reproductions of artwork for the covers of the Book-of-the-Month Club's monthly bulletin. He helped to create the Random House Illustrated Modern Library in 1943 and the Grosset and Dunlap Illustrated Junior Library in 1945. Abrams also established the book club of the Grolier Society.

Determined to make high-quality art reproductions and critical commentary available to a large audience, Abrams raised $100,000 to found his own publishing company, Harry N. Abrams, Inc., in 1949. He was the first American publisher to devote himself exclusively to art books. According to Abrams, "As an art lover, I had always been interested in art books and I wanted to publish them. The $100,000 was wholly inadequate—we should have had $500,000. The only way we survived was through our friendship with suppliers, printers, and binders" (*Current Biography* [1958], p. 4). The first three books published by the company, *Renoir*, *Van Gogh*, and *El Greco*, initiated the Abrams Library of Great Painters. Each book included fifty high-quality color plates and gravure reproductions of the artists' drawings. Despite the numerous color plates, Abrams was able to sell each book for only ten dollars.

Abrams's interest in marketing and innovative publishing techniques led him to establish a relationship with Fritz Landohoff, a highly regarded European publisher, who opened a branch of Abrams's press in Amsterdam in 1953. The Abrams company became profitable in 1955 and entered the textbook market in the early 1960s. By 1958 Abrams's publications had been translated into ten languages. In addition to books, Abrams marketed booklets containing reproductions and commentary to companies such as Western Electric, Socony Mobil Oil Company, and General Motors Corporation for distribution to their employees. He also sold reproductions of artwork to recording companies to be published on record jackets and covers. Abrams explained in 1957, "I've applied merchandising techniques to what was once considered a rather esoteric field. In the past, the publication of art books in this country was limited mostly to scholarly and expensive editions put out by subsidized university presses. I wanted to offer the public as much color as possible and still keep the prices down. So I got right out into the field and made them want to buy it" (*Current Biography* [1958], p. 5; and *Newsweek*, 28 Oct. 1957, p. 101). Although the fidelity of the pictorial reproductions was of prime concern to Abrams, he also insisted on "lots of text" written by recognized scholars. In part, the success of Abrams's efforts can be attributed to the collaborators he selected in Milton Fox, as editor in chief, and Meyer Schapiro, as author and adviser.

In later years Abrams staunchly held that all his publishing ventures were tied to his own sense of what was significant. Financial success in one area of publishing permitted Abrams to publish works on less well known, contemporary artists such as Jasper Johns and Morris Louis. In a 1972 interview with Bruce Kurtz, Abrams asserted, "I only publish things that I'm interested in. And lots of people somehow wonder about why I publish certain things. I publish certain things indeed. If I'm not going to express myself, who am I going to express, a committee? I have no committee to express, nor am I going to express Clement Greenberg, who doesn't have an art book publishing business. I'll listen to Clement Greenberg, but I express what I think is important. I must" (Kurtz, p. 49).

Abrams's interest in art and particularly in contemporary American artists is apparent not only in his publishing but also in his family art collection. Abrams began collecting in the early 1930s, starting with then-contemporary American artists such as Raphael Soyer, Philip Evergood, and Jack Levine, and included other twentieth-century painters when funds permitted it. In the mid-1940s Abrams added the work of European painters to his collection, including, among others, Pablo Picasso, Henri Matisse, Claude Monet, and Georges Rouault. Abrams maintained a consistent interest in contemporary American art, and during the 1950s and 1960s he purchased work by Jasper Johns, Robert Rauschenberg, and many pop artists—Marisol, Roy Lichtenstein, and Tom Wesselmann. A 1971 portrait of Abrams by Norman Rockwell is also included in the collection. A notable omission from the paintings brought together by Abrams is work by abstract expressionist artists, whose significance Abrams could not appreciate at the time. "I understood them too late, and couldn't afford them when I finally did," he lamented (*New York Times*, 27 Nov. 1979). Abrams intended the collection to express his vision of "what this world is all about, which is a complicated world, way beyond what the human imagination can ever aspire to or even understand" (Kurtz, p. 49). The Harry N. Abrams Family Collection was exhibited at the Jewish Museum in New York during the summer of 1966. Abrams served on the board of governors of the Jewish Museum between 1959 and 1965.

In 1966 Abrams sold his publishing company, Harry N. Abrams, Inc., to the Times Mirror Corporation of Los Angeles, continuing to serve as president until 1977. At that time Abrams and his son Robert founded a new art and illustrated book publishing company, Abbeville Press. Harry Abrams headed Abbeville until his death in New York City.

With all of his varied activities, Harry Abrams made an important contribution to the world of art. As patron and board member of the Jewish Museum, Abrams supported the art of his own era. As a publisher, he effectively challenged and irrevocably changed the elite confines of art book publishing. With a broad range of publications, often available at a low cost, Abrams rendered intelligent discussion and quality reproduction of both past and present art accessible to an increasingly international audience.

• The most comprehensive biography of Abrams is in *Current Biography Yearbook* (1958), pp. 4–5. "New Publisher Goes All-Out for Art," *Art Digest* 25, no. 1 (1950): 13, provides useful commentary on the early efforts of Harry N. Abrams, Inc. Elizabeth Fowler, "Industry Has Art on Payroll Now," *New York Times*, 1 Dec. 1957, and an article in *Newsweek*, 28 Oct. 1957, provide interesting evaluations of the success of Abrams's innovative approach to publishing art books. Abrams's collection of pop art is featured in "Living with Pop Art," *Life Magazine*, 16 July 1965, pp. 56–61. A description of the Harry N. Abrams Family Collection by Sam Hunter and an interview conducted by him with Abrams were published in an exhibition catalog, *The Harry N. Abrams Family Collection*, Jewish Museum, 29 June–5 Sept. 1966. A discussion of Abrams's collecting is Christopher Finch, "Harry N. Abrams Collects," *Auction* 4, no. 2 (1970): 33–38. An important source is Bruce Kurtz, "Interview with Harry N. Abrams," *Arts Magazine* 47, no. 1 (1972): 49–51. An account of Abrams's strategies as a publisher of art books is Lee Lescaze, "Hard-Cover Art Galleries: Harry N. Abrams, Curator," *Washington Post*, 27 Nov. 1978, pp. B1 and B11. Substantial obituaries are in the *New York Times*, 27 Nov. 1979; *Publishers Weekly*, 3 Dec. 1979; and H. W. Janson, "Harry N. Abrams," *Art News* 79, no. 2 (1980): 115.

ANNE F. COLLINS

ABSHIRE, Nathan (27 June 1913–13 May 1981), Cajun musician, was born near Gueydan, Louisiana, the son of Lennis Abshire. His mother's name is unknown. From a family of accordion players, Abshire made his public dance hall debut on the accordion at the age of eight. Like many other rural French-speaking people of Louisiana during his youth, he had little schooling and never became literate in his preferred French or in English. He married Olia Boudreaux, and he and his wife adopted one son.

As a teenage accordionist, Abshire built his reputation as a dance musician at house parties and public dance halls, leading to a recording session of six sides for Bluebird in 1935 in New Orleans as "Nason Absher" with the Rayne-Bo Ramblers, a group headed by long-time Cajun guitarist and singer Leroy "Happy Fats" Leblanc. The 1930s was also an important period for Abshire's musical development through his friendships with Cajun fiddler Lionel Leleux and with the older, widely influential black Creole accordionist Amédé Ardoin. He would take turns with Ardoin playing at the latter's Saturday dance engagements and took lessons in blues styling therefrom.

As Ardoin faded from the scene in the late 1930s, the accordion itself was losing popularity in favor of the more contemporary Cajun string band sound of the Hackberry Ramblers, Leo Soileau, and Harry Choates. The new music was heavily influenced in style and repertoire by country and western music, particularly the western swing of Milton Brown and Bob Wills, and an increase in the singing of English lyrics. Abshire did not record during this period, and he was drafted into military service for a brief time during World War II.

Nathan Abshire was one of the individuals responsible for the accordion's return to the forefront of Cajun music after World War II, and a beneficiary of socioeconomic conditions that later reopened a space for the instrument in rural French Louisianian culture. Cajun folklorist Barry Jean Ancelet credits the return of Cajun war veterans with the demand for music that did more to reaffirm their sense of home than the western swing sound, which was, from a Cajun point of view, "Americanized." The first wave of this musical-ethnic sentiment surfaced in Iry Lejeune's 1948 influential 78-rpm record on the Opera label, "Love Bridge Waltz/Evangeline Special," on which the French-singing accordionist gives emotional performances in an older style. Abshire followed in 1949 on the O. T. label with "Pine Grove Blues," a French-language recording on which he sings in a plaintive baritone, addressing his woman who has come home after sunrise, while a fellow band member speaks the woman's replies. The cumulative musical effect of the recording is considerable, combining a steady danceable beat, Abshire's swinging accordion articulation, call-and-response vocals, and a blues form in text and harmony extended unpredictably over a large number of measures.

Abshire creatively molded a variety of musical sources into a Cajun dance hall style carried by his accordion, sharing melodic duties with a fiddle or steel guitar and accompanied by a strummed acoustic guitar and sometimes also drums or bass. While "Pine Grove Blues" demonstrated Abshire's ability to draw from black Creole and African-American traditions, he also adapted material from the country-western repertoire ("La Valse de Bélisaire" from Roy Acuff's "A Precious Jewel") and also composed his own songs, like "Sur Le Courtableau." Of his compositional process, he once said, "I can't read music. I can't sign my name, but I make up songs in my head. I listen to them, then practice them on the accordion until they sound like they're supposed to" (Ancelet and Morgan, p. 103).

Abshire and his wife settled in Basile, Louisiana, where at one time he was playing music seven nights a week at the Avalon Club and where eventually he took a job as guardian of the town dump. In the 1960s he made a series of classic recordings for Swallow Records and some also for Arhoolie with his group, the Pine Grove Boys, featuring Dewey Balfa on fiddle and Rodney Balfa on guitar.

Abshire's career in the late 1960s progressed from musician to cultural ambassador and celebrity partly because of his association with the Balfa Brothers, with whom he played at the 1967 Newport Folk Festival in Rhode Island. Together with Dewey Balfa's previous appearance at Newport in 1964, this experience galvanized the Balfa family to promote the value of their culture—especially the music—back home in Louisiana where it was devalued as backward, low-class, and embarrassing. Enlisting the help of Abshire and other experienced, older Cajun musicians, they played at colleges and festivals across North America and for public and school programs in their own state. Gradually, their performances succeeded in increasing interest in Cajun music among Cajuns as well as others. Their efforts coincided with and contributed to a broader positive revaluation of Louisiana French culture that began during the 1960s. Abshire's home became the site of frequent visits from those wishing to learn more about the music; among his protégés was accordionist Robert Jardell.

Abshire's widening reputation both within and outside of Louisiana brought him increased media attention during the final part of his life, with mixed results. Among numerous documentary films about Cajun culture, the unflattering ones stand out. In Les Blank's 1971 *Spend It All*, early among his many films on Louisiana cultures, Abshire seems to be presented as typifying the Cajun stereotype celebrated in the film—a hard-working, hard-playing, simple people who "spend it all" having a good time. A personal slogan of Abshire's, "The Good Times Are Killing Me," was the name of a 1975 PBS documentary on his life, in which he was made to be "the hapless antihero" (Broven, p. 241). Unfortunately, the language barrier for Abshire was real; he spoke little English and was unable to project his more articulate, confident, French-speaking persona without losing much in translation.

Abshire died in Basile, Louisiana. In contrast to the negative film images, he is now considered "one of the greatest Cajun accordion players and singers of all time" (Ancelet and Morgan, p. 102). Despite his stated wish that his music be buried with him, his recorded legacy has remained an influential one to subsequent generations of Cajun musicians who are part of a cultural renaissance that he, the Balfas, and others helped to start.

• Of the biographical sources on Abshire, John Broven, *South to Louisiana* (1983), provides the most detail. Elemore Morgan, Jr.'s full color photo portrait of Abshire comprises the cover art of Barry Jean Ancelet and Morgan, *The Makers of Cajun Music* (1984), which quotes interviews with the musician in French and English and adds some interpretive background and more color photos. His entry in Pierre V. Daigle, *Tears, Love, and Laughter*, 4th ed. (1987), contains additional information. Some of his music is transcribed in Raymond François, *Yé Yaille, Chère!* (1990). Les Blank's later film, *J'ai Été Au Bal*, gives historical overview of Cajun music similar to the one outlined here, including some footage of Abshire at the accordion. Many of his notable recordings are contained on *Cajun Fais Do-Do* (Arhoolie CD 416), *French Blues* (Arhoolie CD 373), *The Best of Nathan Abshire* (Swallow 6061), and *Pine Grove Blues* (Swallow 6014).

MARK F. DEWITT

ABT, Isaac Arthur (18 Dec. 1867–22 Nov. 1955), pediatrician, was born in Wilmington, Illinois, to Levi Abt, the owner of a general store that doubled as a post office and later, in Chicago, a partner in Hart, Abt, and Marx, a men's clothing manufacture, and Henrietta Hart. As a child Abt was indelibly affected by the agonizing deaths of other children from contagious diseases and horrible household accidents. Work in an apothecary in high school, where he ground, boiled, and filtered herbs and prepared solutions of various drugs, cemented his interest in medicine. In 1886 Abt began his formal premedical education at Johns Hopkins University. Because Johns Hopkins had no medical school until 1893, Abt left without a degree in 1889 and entered the Chicago Medical College, a department of Northwestern University, where he was a student of Frank Billings, one of Chicago's leading practitioners of internal medicine. He graduated in 1891 and served a two-year internship at Chicago's Michael Reese Hospital.

At Michael Reese Abt discovered physicians were no better able to treat diseases peculiar to children than they had been when he was a boy. Older physicians dismissed his interest in specializing, telling him that childhood illness was, and always would be, the purview of the general practitioner. Undeterred, he traveled to Europe in 1892 and spent two years there studying pediatrics. He studied in Vienna with Professor Herman Widerhofer, head of the Department of Pediatrics at the University of the St. Annen Children's Hospital. In Germany he studied with pediatric pioneer Otto Heubner. In London he attended clinics at the Children's Hospital on Great Ormond Street.

Returning to Chicago in 1894 to set up a pediatric practice, Abt attracted few patients. As the doctors at Michael Reese had predicted, mothers saw no need for a physician specializing in children's medicine. He was soon appointed district county physician, caring for the sick poor in their homes. His next job was as an inspector for the Chicago health department. There he was called on to vaccinate hundreds of people against smallpox, most of whom deeply mistrusted this preventive measure. He worked under police protection, performing what he called "shotgun vaccinations." His pioneering efforts continued. Acutely aware of diphtheria as a cause of a high death rate among children, he was not afraid to be the first physician in Chicago to administer diphtheria antitoxin in 1895 to a small boy, who recovered quickly. In 1897 he married Lina Rosenberg, a Michael Reese nurse; they had two children, one of whom, Arthur, also became a prominent pediatrician.

Abt's reputation soon brought him jobs at Chicago hospitals and medical schools in his chosen specialty. He was professor of diseases of children at Northwestern University Woman's Medical College from 1897 to 1901, associate professor of diseases of children at Rush Medical College from 1902 to 1908, and professor and head of the Department of Pediatrics at Northwestern University Medical School from 1909 to 1942. He was also a physician of diseases of children at Cook County Hospital, Sarah Morris Children's Hospital, St. Luke's Hospital, Children's Memorial Hospital, and Passavant Hospital. He joined other Progressive Era reformers when he volunteered his services to philanthropic organizations, including the West Side Dispensary, the Chicago Maternity Center, and the Chicago Children's Hospital Society and its offshoots—the Chicago Milk Commission and Chicago Infant Welfare Society, on whose boards of directors he served for twenty-five years.

The Chicago Children's Hospital Society was founded in 1902 after a small girl, stricken with diphtheria, was turned away from several hospitals as a result of a lack of beds for children. Chicago newspapers dramatized the incident: in spite of the availability of diphtheria antitoxin, she died gasping for breath in her father's arms, as her father stood weeping in the street. The incident galvanized the city's medical personnel. In 1902, with only sixty-four hospital beds for children with contagious diseases in the entire city, the Hospital Society vowed to better that statistic. Abt had a bolder vision. He wanted a children's hospital.

Abt's dream was fulfilled in 1913 when Edward Morris, of the famed Nelson Morris Chicago meatpacking family, approached him about establishing Chicago's first children's hospital as a memorial to his mother. Abt traveled throughout Europe in late 1910, studying every modern children's hospital in preparation for the building of Sarah Morris Children's Hospital. At his suggestion, it was affiliated with Michael Reese Hospital to save money. Sarah Morris, established in 1913, became a model nationwide. During his tenure there from 1913 to 1925, Abt and his colleagues brought the mortality rate of hospitalized infants down to 20 percent from 80–100 percent. He eventually regretted his decision not to make Sarah Morris a wholly independent children's hospital. As Michael Reese slowly abandoned most of the amenities Abt considered vital to a children's hospital—first the children's laundry, finally the playroom—Abt accused hospital administrators of being unresponsive to the special needs of sick children. When, in 1925, plans were announced for a pavilion designed for Michael Reese's wealthy patients that would block the view from Sarah Morris of Lake Michigan, a furious Abt resigned.

Although Abt wrote dozens of monographs published in medical journals on every phase of children's health, he had a special interest in infant feeding. He was one of the first physicians to link poor health among infants to improper diet. This led to his founding in May 1903 of the Chicago Milk Commission, which was instrumental in bringing the dairies that supplied Chicago with milk under strict legal control. Later, recognizing the importance of breast milk for sick infants, Abt insisted that wet nurses live with their own infants in a wing of Sarah Morris. There their milk was expressed and bottled for hospitalized infants whose mothers would not or could not breast-feed them. Abt was the inventor in 1921 of an electric breast pump used for decades by hospitals nationwide.

Abt edited the pediatric volume of the *Practical Medicine Series* for more than forty years. He was also the editor of the influential eight-volume *A System of Pediatrics* (1923). He was president of the Chicago Pediatric Society from 1908 to 1911, chairman of the Section on Diseases of Children of the American Medical Association in 1911–1912, member of the House of Delegates of the American Medical Association from 1919 to 1935, president of the American Association of Teachers of Diseases of Children in 1922, president of the American Pediatric Society in 1926–1927, president of the Chicago Medical Society in 1927–1928, and the first president of the American Academy of Pediatrics, in 1930–1931. Abt died in Chicago.

• The Special Collections Department of the Northwestern University Medical School Library has a small collection of Abt paraphernalia (diplomas, medals, etc.), some notes taken by a student of Abt's during one of his lectures, and all of his many published articles. The Michael Reese Hospital Papers, which include some information on the Sarah Morris Children's Hospital, are at the Jewish Archives of Spertus College in Chicago. The papers of the Chicago Milk Commission and the Chicago Infant Welfare Society, in which Abt is frequently mentioned, are at the Chicago Historical Society. Minutes of the Chicago Medical Society are also at the Chicago Historical Society, and minutes of the Chicago Pediatric Society, 1895–1929, are at the Regenstein Library, Special Collections Department, University of Chicago; Abt figured prominently in the meetings of both organizations. Abt was the author of two books: *The Baby's Food* (1917) and an autobiography, *Baby Doctor* (1944). An article-length biography of Abt is Ronald D. Greenwood, "Medical History: Isaac Arthur Abt, 1867–1955," *Journal of the Kansas Medical Society* 74 (Oct. 1973): 376–82. Obituaries are in *Pediatrics* 18 (1956): 327–35, *Journal of Pediatrics* 51 (July 1957): 107–14, and the *New York Times*, 24 Nov. 1955.

JACQUELINE H. WOLF

ACE, Goodman (15 Jan. 1899–25 Mar. 1982), and **Jane Ace** (12 Oct. 1905–11 Nov. 1974), radio entertainers of the 1930s and 1940s, were both born in Kansas City, Kansas, and broke into radio there in 1929. Goodman Ace's father was Harry Aiskowitz, a haberdasher who had emigrated from Riga, Latvia; his mother was Anna Katzen. Goodman began working in the Wormser Hat Store in Kansas City as a teenager following his father's death. At the age of twenty, however, he took a big cut in pay to become the movie and drama critic of the *Kansas City Post*, a rather raucous and even "yellow" newspaper that nonetheless provided a splendid spawning ground for the young Ace's native wit.

As a local reviewer Goodman Ace encountered a great many theatrical people, including numerous vaudevillians. He began to write some comedy routines himself and in 1927 received a telegram from Jack Benny: "Opening New York next week. Please send jokes. Will pay." Ace responded, and Benny was apparently well pleased. In the late 1920s the *Post* (now the *Journal-Post*) established a relationship with a local radio station, KMBC, and Ace, always on the lookout for ways to augment his meager income, sought part-time work on the station. He began with two fifteen-minute shows, one a chatty guide to the movies, the other a program in which he read the comic page to children. For these two programs he received an additional twenty dollars a week.

In 1922 Goodman Ace (his friends invariably called him "Goody") had married pretty, blonde, blue-eyed Jane Epstein, whose father, Jacob Epstein, was a successful Kansas City haberdasher. Jacob Epstein could not disguise his dislike of his impecunious son-in-law and continually urged him to return to the cloak and suit business where he might earn a decent living. Goody never made it back, but in a few years he would find success in radio that would far exceed the wildest expectations of his father-in-law.

One day, while finishing a movie review program, Goody waited for the signal that the following program was to go on (this program was a CBS network program with Heywood Broun), but the program never came through, so Goody had no choice but to continue talking. By chance, his wife had come into the studio so that they could leave together. He waved Jane over to the microphone, and the two of them began an amiable chat about last night's bridge game. Their chatter must have pleased the audience because, immediately thereafter, Ace got a call from a local advertising man who offered the pair a contract for a thirteen-week show sponsored by a drug store chain. Goody was to be paid twenty-five dollars a week, Jane fifteen.

Thus began the program that would later be known as "Easy Aces." It moved to Chicago and the NBC Blue network. The program grew out of Goodman Ace's highly fertile comic imagination, but Jane clearly was the star of the show, with Goody the straight man. Jane never thought of herself as an actress, but she did have a flair for reading comic dialogue as well as a memorable, whining style of delivery. The humor of the show was built around the ability of Jane, a far from beleaguered urban housewife, to outwit her apparently more intelligent and savvy husband, a harried advertising executive, by using delicious and idiotic intrigues and diversions and somehow always winding up at the top of the heap. Imbecilities would roll out of Jane's mouth, but they seemed to be cagily ordered and quite sufficient to extricate her from even the most difficult situations. Some of the malapropisms that flowed from Jane's lips became a part of the American language in the 1930s and 1940s, the best of them more than a little pointed: "time wounds all heels"; "Congress is still in season"; "living in squander"; "just explain it to me in words of one cylinder"; "in all my bored days"; "I refused to tell him who I was, I used a facetious name"; "the food in that restaurant was just abdominal"; "I've been working my head to the bone."

"Easy Aces" was a fifteen-minute program broadcast three times a week over the NBC Blue network, and in most markets it was broadcast during the dinner hour, with Goody's polished and inventive comedy writing keeping most listeners hooked. He wrote all of the programs himself and brooked no interference from sponsors. For most years the sponsor was the maker of Anacin, a headache remedy, surely an appropriate sponsor for the "Easy Aces," whose marital life was anything but easy or tranquil. Anacin dropped the program in 1944; it was later revived in a half-hour format on CBS, with an orchestra and studio audience, which neither Goody nor Jane liked. This program, called "Mr. Ace and Jane," went off the air in 1949, and Jane, not liking television, retired from show business.

In radio's last few years as a major force in the entertainment industry, Goody was the principal writer on "The Big Show," hosted by Tallulah Bankhead. He also wrote a radio show for Danny Kaye. So esteemed was he at CBS that he was named the network's supervisor of comedy. He also established in 1947, under the auspices of CBS, the School of Comedy Writers, of which he was the nominal dean. Among his students were Neil Simon, George Axelrod, Ernie Lehman, and Paddy Chayevsky.

With the decline of big-time radio, Goody moved into television, where he again became a solid success as a comedy writer. During his years as a television comedy writer, Ace was the principal writer for Milton Berle (1952–1955), Perry Como (1955–1967), and Sid Caesar (1963–1964). Ace's pace slackened somewhat after Jane's death in New York in 1974, but he continued to be known as the highest-paid comedy writer as well as one of the most highly respected. In his final years, as he approached his eighties, Goody Ace once again became a radio performer, doing short humorous sketches or monologues for PBS. He continued to follow television carefully, always aware of how much of his old material was now being recycled in new shows. "I saw something on television the other night that made me laugh," he reported to friends in his last years. "And I thought to myself, gee, I wish I'd written that. Then, about five minutes later, it occurred to me: Hey, I *did* write that."

Goodman Ace died at his home in Manhattan. For years after his death, most television comedy programs continued to echo his ingenious humor in only slightly modified forms.

• An excellent profile of Goodman Ace by Mark Singer appeared in the *New Yorker*, 4 Apr. 1977, pp. 41–80. Nearly all histories of radio have treatments of "Easy Aces." See, for example, Erik Barnouw, *A History of Broadcasting in the United States*, vol. 2, *The Golden Web, 1933 to 1953* (1968). See also John Dunning, *Tune in Yesterday: The Ultimate Encyclopedia of Old-Time Radio, 1925–1976* (1976), and Jim Harmon, *The Great Radio Comedians* (1970). Goody's obituary is in the *New York Times*, 26 Mar. 1982; Jane's is in the *New York Times*, 12 Nov. 1974.

GEORGE H. DOUGLAS

ACE, Johnny (9 June 1929–25 Dec. 1954), musician, songwriter, and rhythm and blues star, was born John Marshall Alexander, Jr., in Memphis, Tennessee, the son of John Marshall Alexander and Leslie Newsome. His father earned his living in Memphis as a packer, but his lifework was as a commuting minister to two rural Baptist churches in East Arkansas. At LaRose Grammar School in south Memphis, John, Jr., as his family called him, displayed both musical and artistic talent. He mastered the piano at home but was allowed to play only religious music there. Along with his mother and siblings, he sang in the choir at Bethel African Methodist Episcopal Church. Becoming restless at Booker T. Washington High School, he dropped out in the eleventh grade to join the navy and see the world. His sisters recall military police coming to the house in search of their brother and remember his brief period of enlistment in terms of weeks, ending in an "Undesirable Discharge" in 1947. His mother was furious. "I can't keep up with you," she scolded, "and *they* can't keep up with you."

It is possible that Alexander never had a job in the conventional sense, and he did not seek employment after his failed navy attempt. He did, however, find kindred spirits on Beale Street. Joe Hill Louis, "the Be-Bop Boy," may have started him out as a professional musician, or the credit may belong to Dwight "Gatemouth" Moore, but by 1949 he was the piano player with the Beale Street Blues Boys (later the Beale Streeters), a band that backed B. B. King when he performed live. In 1950 Alexander wooed and married Lois Jean Palmer, a ninth grader at Booker T. Washington High School, and moved her into his parents' home. A son was born to the couple that year and a daughter in 1952. Alexander's mother, who disapproved of his lifestyle and his occupation as a blues musician, embraced his wife and children but refused to let him sleep at the family home.

In 1952 David James Mattis, the program director at the Memphis all-black radio station WDIA (the "Mother Station of the Negroes"), founded Duke Records and changed Alexander's name to Johnny Ace. When Bobby "Blue" Bland could not sing a song scheduled for recording at the WDIA studio (it was subsequently revealed that Bland could not read), Mattis wrote new lyrics to an existing rhythm and blues hit, and Ace "faked out" a new melody. The result was "My Song" (Duke 102), a "blues ballad" (*Billboard* called it a "heart ballad"), which Ace sang in a vulnerable and innocent soft crooning style. Though the recording lacked professionalism in sound quality, the charm of Ace's voice made it an immediate hit with the limited audience that had access to it. "My Song" attracted the attention of Houston entrepreneur Don D. Robey, a black man who owned Peacock Records and controlled a booking agency specializing in "chitlin circuit" venues. Robey became a partner and quickly the sole owner of Duke Records, moving the entire operation to Houston. He aggressively promoted Ace's "My Song" to the top of the rhythm and blues charts and groomed him as a national headlining rhythm and blues act, carefully cultivating the kind of polished, first-class, uptown image that Berry Gordy would later emulate at Motown.

Ace's career, which lasted less than two and a half years, produced eight rhythm and blues top ten records, including three number-one hits: "My Song" (1952), "The Clock" (1953), and "Pledging My Love" (1955). Primarily he lived the nomadic life of a road musician, with no permanent home or routine beyond a string of temporary hotel stops, traveling coast to coast with a backup band and an opening act, blues singer Willie Mae "Big Mama" Thornton. In 1954 he may have performed as many as 350 one-nighters, sometimes driving as far as 800 miles between shows. According to Evelyn Johnson, the head of Buffalo Booking Agency and the closest thing to a personal manager that Ace had, the singer was shy, childlike, and unassuming. "Sweetest thing since sugar," she recalled, "but he didn't care about nuttin', honey." At a pawnshop in Florida he purchased a .22 caliber pistol to amuse himself and alleviate the boredom of the road. On Christmas night 1954, while backstage during intermission at a "Negro Christmas Dance" at Houston's City Auditorium, Ace began "snapping" his pistol at the heads of people in his dressing room. According to Thornton, he put the pistol to his own head and uttered his last words: "I'll show you that it won't shoot." Authorities ruled the cause of death to be "playing russian roulette—self inflicted."

Ace's last record, "Pledging My Love" (Duke 136), first advertised in *Billboard* on the day of his death, represented neither rhythm nor blues, but the slow ballad became a rhythm and blues triple crown hit (number one in retail sales, radio airplay, and jukebox action), the most played rhythm and blues record of 1955, and generated more than half a dozen tribute records to the romantic legend of Johnny Ace. In addition, the record crossed over to the pop charts to become a pop hit as well. For the first time in the postwar era white record buyers (primarily teens) chose this ballad by a solo black male singer signed to an independent rhythm and blues label as the unique and definitive performance of a *popular* song against which all subsequent performances were ruthlessly judged. Arguably, "Pledging My Love" represents the transitional record between rhythm and blues and rock and roll.

Johnny Ace died a rhythm and blues star and was resurrected as a rock and roll legend. He has been called rock's first "casualty," "the first fallen angel," and "the colored James Dean." For disc jockeys he remains "the Late Great Johnny Ace."

• The most complete accounts of Johnny Ace's career and contributions to American popular music may be found in James M. Salem, "Death and the Rhythm-and-Bluesman: The Life and Recordings of Johnny Ace," *American Music* (Fall 1993): 316–67, and "Johnny Ace: A Case Study in the Diffusion and Transformation of Minority Culture," *Prospects: An Annual of American Cultural Studies* 17 (1992): 211–41. In addition, Galen Gart and Roy C. Ames, *Duke/Peacock Records: An Illustrated History with Discography* (1990), provides valuable information about Ace and his relationship with record owner Don D. Robey. For an account of the beginning of his career by Duke Records founder David James Mattis, see George A. Moonoogian and Roger Meeden, "Duke Records—The Early Years: An Interview with David J. Mattis," *Whiskey, Women, and . . .* , June 1984, pp. 18–25. For overviews of Ace's life and death, see Nick Tosches, *Unsung Heroes of Rock 'n' Roll* (1984); Peter Grendysa, "Johnny Ace, the 'Ace' of Duke," *Goldmine*, 25 Sept. 1987, pp. 28 and 91; and Colin Escott, "Johnny Ace: The First Rock 'n' Roll Casualty," *Goldmine*, 21 Nov. 1986, pp. 16–17. Excellent photographs of Ace and his associates can be found in "Strange Case of Johnny Ace," *Ebony*, July 1955, pp. 63–68. The most complete and accurate discography of Ace's twenty-one recorded sides may be found in *American Music* (Fall 1993): 353–57. Useful obituaries are in the *Tri-State Defender*, 8 Jan. 1955; the *Pittsburgh Courier*, 1, 5, and 15 Jan. 1955; the *Chicago Defender*, 8 Jan. 1955; and the *Houston Informer*, 1 and 8 Jan. 1955. Newspaper coverage about his death and career is in the *Cleveland Call and Post*, 15 Jan. 1955; the *Pittsburgh Courier*, 5 Feb. 1955; and the *Tri-State Defender*, 5 Mar. 1955.

JAMES M. SALEM

ACHESON, Dean Gooderham (11 Apr. 1893–12 Oct. 1971), lawyer and secretary of state, was born in Middletown, Connecticut, the son of Edward Campion Acheson, an Episcopal minister, and Eleanor Gertrude Gooderham. He grew up in comfortable, middle-class circumstances. His mother's family wealth and his father's appointment as a bishop in 1915 attest to his family's secure place in local Connecticut society. Acheson attended Groton and then Yale University, receiving his B.A. in 1915 with an undistinguished academic record. In May 1917 he married Alice Caroline Stanley; they had three children. At Harvard Law School, he studied under Felix Frankfurter, who instilled in him a lifelong love of the law. After receiving his degree in 1918, he served briefly in the navy. The following year, thanks to Frankfurter, he was appointed law clerk for Supreme Court justice Louis Brandeis.

In 1921 Acheson joined the law firm of Covington, Burling & Rublee and began a practice that consisted largely of representing clients in the federal courts and before government agencies. He became a partner in 1926 and practiced law in Washington until 1941, except for a six-month stint as under secretary of the treasury in 1933, which ended when he resigned in protest over Franklin D. Roosevelt's gold policy.

Acheson cut a striking figure. He prided himself on his elegant appearance, always wearing tailored suits, shirts with French cuffs, and a matching handkerchief. A vigorous man, he regularly walked the fifteen blocks from his home in Georgetown to his law office in downtown Washington; after 1939 he shared this walk with Supreme Court justice Felix Frankfurter as the two men engaged in animated conversation, oblivious to their surroundings. Weekends were spent at "Harewood," an eighteenth-century farmhouse in Sandy Spring, Maryland, that Acheson bought in 1923. In later years, he found solace from the cares of office in making furniture by hand on the Maryland farm.

Acheson's strengths lay in his acute intelligence, his lively, often caustic, wit, and his insistence on getting to the heart of any matter. He became impatient with those whose minds moved more slowly, and he could not tolerate incompetence or deviousness. He was suspicious of broad generalizations and idealistic visions; he espoused a pragmatic view of public issues, striving to achieve whatever incremental progress was possible. Above all, he was a stoic. Writing of his father, he commented, "Much in life could not be affected or mitigated, and, hence, must be borne." And he added, "borne without complaint" (*Morning and Noon*, p. 18).

The events leading up to the American entry into World War II proved decisive for Acheson's career. A strong advocate for an active American role to block Hitler's domination of Europe, he wrote a key legal opinion on behalf of Roosevelt's destroyers-for-bases deal in 1940; after his reelection to a third term, FDR appointed him assistant secretary of state for economic affairs. Acheson served in this role during the war years, later focusing primarily on congressional relations. In 1945 President Harry S. Truman elevated him to the position of under secretary of state. He resigned in mid-1947, only to return as secretary of state in 1949, a position he held until Truman left office in January 1953.

Acheson's major contributions to American foreign policy began during his service as under secretary to James F. Byrnes and George C. Marshall and then reached their culmination during his own term as secretary of state. A crucial factor in his effectiveness was the cordial working relationship he established with Truman. Despite the two men's different backgrounds, they prized loyalty, honesty, and a straightforward approach to public policy. Truman admired Acheson for bringing order to a chaotic State Department and for establishing clear lines of authority and responsibility. For his part, Acheson appreciated Truman's direct style and refusal to engage in the kind of deceptive maneuvering characteristic of FDR. As a result of Truman's confidence in him, Acheson was able to conduct American foreign policy free of interference from White House aides.

Acheson, along with George F. Kennan, was one of the chief architects of the Cold War policy of containment. Unlike Kennan, who believed the contest with the Soviet Union was primarily political in nature and susceptible ultimately to a negotiated solution, Acheson stressed the military dimension. Impressed by the failure of democratic nations to halt Nazi Germany in the 1930s, most notably at Munich in 1938, Acheson advocated a policy of developing "situations of strength" before entering into negotiations with the Soviet Union. He believed the United States held a great advantage in nuclear weapons, and after the Soviet Union detonated its own atomic bomb in 1949, he played a leading role in persuading Truman to move ahead with the development of the hydrogen bomb, contrary to the advice of Kennan and Robert Oppenheimer.

Acheson played a key role in all three of the main containment initiatives in Europe adopted by the Truman administration between 1947 and 1949. When the British informed the United States in early 1947 that they could no longer support Greece and Turkey, it was Acheson who sounded the alarm in a crucial meeting with congressional leaders in late February. He warned that if the United States did not take over from the British in the eastern Mediterranean, the result would very likely be a "Soviet breakthrough" that "might open three continents to Soviet penetration." "The Soviet Union was playing one of the greatest gambles in history at minimal cost," he later declared, adding, "We and we alone were in a position to break up the play" (*Present at the Creation*, p. 219). After Republican senator Arthur Vandenberg signaled his agreement, Truman on 12 March 1947 announced his plan to give $400 million in aid to Greece and Turkey; known as the Truman Doctrine, it was intended to stem Communist advances.

Although Acheson resigned as under secretary on 30 June 1947 to return to the practice of law, he had considerable impact on the origins of the Marshall Plan, the second pillar of containment. Aware that the failure of Western Europe to recover from the ravages of World War II made it vulnerable to Communism, Acheson worked with Kennan, Marshall, and Will Clayton (the under secretary of state for economic affairs) to frame a plan to revive the European economy. Pinch-hitting for Truman in a speech to the Delta Council in Cleveland, Mississippi, in May 1947, Acheson spoke of the necessity of helping free people struggling "against totalitarian pressures." A month later, in a speech at Harvard University, George Marshall presented the plan for European economic recovery that would bear his name. After Acheson left the State Department, he took an active role in forming and co-chairing the Citizens Committee for the Marshall Plan, helping to win congressional approval in the spring of 1948.

The capstone of containment came in 1949 with the creation of the North Atlantic Treaty Organization (NATO). The early steps toward the security alliance between the United States and Western Europe were taken before Acheson became secretary of state, but he was in full agreement with the belief that American aid to Europe had to go beyond economic assistance. He presided over the final diplomatic negotiations for the North Atlantic Treaty, insisting on the inclusion of Norway and Denmark, areas vital to control of the Atlantic supply line. His greatest challenge was rebutting the isolationist objections in the U.S. Senate, especially from those who wanted to water down the key clause that an armed attack on any one member would be considered an attack against all. Carefully cultivating the cooperation of Republican senator Vandenberg, Acheson finally prevailed; the Senate ratified the North Atlantic Treaty on 21 July 1949 by an overwhelming vote of eighty-two to thirteen.

The Truman Doctrine, the Marshall Plan, and NATO achieved the primary goal of early U.S. Cold War policy—they halted Soviet expansion and laid the basis for a thriving Western Europe closely attached to the United States. During the remainder of his term as secretary of state, Acheson worked to solidify these gains, winning Senate approval for continuing the stationing of American troops in Europe and for extensive military aid to the NATO allies. He failed, however, in his larger goal of securing European approval for German rearmament, stymied by continued French opposition. Overall, however, Acheson justifiably took great pride in the way he had helped create a strong and friendly Western Europe as the bedrock of post–World War II American foreign policy.

In the minds of his critics, whatever success Acheson achieved in Europe was more than offset by a series of stunning setbacks in Asia. The first came in 1949 as Mao Zedong's Communist forces prevailed in China, forcing the American-backed Chiang Kai-shek to flee to Taiwan. Acheson angered Republicans, who called for military assistance for Chiang's nationalists, by advocating a hands-off policy; later in 1949, the State Department published a White Paper filled with diplomatic documents designed to show that the outcome in China was the result of internal forces. "Nothing that this country did or could have done within the reasonable limits of its capabilities could have changed that result," Acheson wrote in his letter of transmittal; "nothing that was left undone by this country has contributed to it" (*Present at the Creation*, p. 303).

The fury of congressional Republicans at what they considered the abandonment of China to the Communists had barely died down when North Korean forces crossed the 38th parallel on 25 June 1950 and invaded the Republic of Korea. Acheson's critics claimed that in a 12 January 1950 speech he had invited the North Korean attack by placing South Korea beyond the American "defensive perimeter" in the western Pacific; the secretary contended that he had simply said that South Korea would have to rely on the United Nations for protection. Once the war began, Acheson was a staunch defender of South Korea. In careful consultation with President Truman, he helped shape the decisions to send American forces from Japan to defend South Korea, to gain UN sanction for this effort, and to permit General Douglas MacArthur, following his decisive military victory at Inchon, to move north across the 38th parallel in an effort to unify Korea.

The tragedy that followed—the Chinese intervention in the fall of 1950, the headlong American retreat down the Korean peninsula, the firing of MacArthur and the resulting congressional outcry—sorely tested Acheson's stoic philosophy. He bore up well under these burdens, defending the policies that he and Truman had followed and gaining some measure of redemption when the Korean War settled into a stalemate. The most regrettable casualty of these events was Acheson's shrewd belief that in the long run a strong China would balance off Soviet power in Asia. After Korea, instead of waiting for the Sino-Soviet split to develop, Acheson based American policy on the false premise that Communist China was the puppet of the Soviet Union.

Acheson's tendency to see international affairs purely in European terms hampered his efforts to deal with the rising nationalism in the so-called Third World. His sympathies were with the European colonial powers rather than with the new nations emerging from imperial control. In Indochina, he sided with the French, advising Truman to make what proved to be a fatal commitment for American military assistance against Ho Chi Minh in May 1950. He tried unsuccessfully to broker an agreement in a dispute over Iranian oil, but it was clear he favored the British over the government of Mohammad Mosaddeq. He ignored Africa and Latin America almost completely, partly because neither area was yet at the forefront of the Cold War. Overall, Acheson was a man of the past rather than the future, secure in the belief that close ties to Britain and Western Europe were vital to American well being and disdainful of the forces of change that would shape the course of the second half of the twentieth century.

Contemporary critics of Acheson faulted him primarily not for being too ardent a cold warrior, but rather for not being ardent enough. He spent more and more of his time testifying before congressional committees, defending American policy, and trying, with barely concealed contempt, to explain why it was not possible to roll back Communism around the world without touching off World War III. He became a favorite target for Senator Joseph McCarthy, especially after he defended a former State Department officer with the now famous comment, "I do not intend to turn my back on Alger Hiss" (McLellan, p. 220). His relations with the press were almost as bad; he refused to curry favor with reporters, and often his biting wit was mistaken for arrogance. *Life* magazine called for his resignation in November 1950 after the Chinese intervention in Korea. But Acheson knew he could always count on public support from the one man who mattered, Harry Truman. In a December 1950 press conference, Truman set reporters straight about his secretary of state being soft on Communism by bluntly declaring that if the Communists prevailed, "Dean Acheson would be one of the first, if not the first, to be shot by the enemies of liberty and Christianity" (Smith, p. 247).

After leaving the State Department in 1953, Acheson remained a controversial and outspoken commentator on American foreign policy. Although he returned to his old law firm, now called Covington & Burling, he handled only a few high-profile cases. He became the Democratic party's leading critic of the Eisenhower-Dulles foreign policy in the 1950s, and he continued to disagree publicly with George Kennan over the essence of containment. When the Democrats returned to power in the 1960s, he became an informal adviser to both Presidents John F. Kennedy and Lyndon B. Johnson. During the Cuban missile crisis, he repeatedly urged JFK to bomb the Soviet missile sites in Cuba; on Vietnam, as one of the "wise men" LBJ consulted regularly, he advised against continuing the war after the Tet offensive in 1968. Acheson spent his last years writing a memoir of his State Department years and biographical sketches; he died peacefully at his favorite place—the desk in the study of his Maryland farmhouse.

Acheson reflects the passing of a tradition in American foreign policy. His roots go back to conservative realists such as Theodore Roosevelt and Elihu Root. He viewed the world in Eurocentric terms, striving for close relations with England, a balance of power in Europe, and support for imperial control of the remaining hinterlands. Yet despite his limited vision, he succeeded in shaping policies that helped Europe recover from the devastation of World War II and held the line in Asia. The ultimate irony is that this authentic cold warrior was so often the object of attack for the very policy he sought so hard to avoid—appeasement.

• Acheson's papers are in the Yale University Library. The Harry S. Truman Library in Independence, Mo., contains extensive documentation on Acheson's service as secretary of state. The best single source on Acheson's State Department career is his memoir, *Present at the Creation* (1969). There are two good books that describe and analyze his diplomatic achievements: Gaddis Smith, *Dean Acheson* (1972), and David McLellan, *Dean Acheson: The State Department Years* (1976). For a brief appraisal, see Robert A. Ferrell and David McLellan, "Dean Acheson," in *Makers of American Diplomacy*, ed. Frank J. Merli and Theodore A. Wilson (1974). The best accounts of his early years and his private life can be found in his *Morning and Noon* (1965), which stops in 1941, and a book by his son, David C. Acheson, *Acheson Country* (1993). Douglas Brinkley, *Dean Acheson: The Cold War Years, 1953–1971* (1992), offers thorough coverage of Acheson's activities after he left office and contains a list of the ten books he wrote. An obituary is in the *New York Times*, 13 Oct. 1971.

ROBERT A. DIVINE

ACHESON, Edward Goodrich (9 Mar. 1856–6 July 1931), inventor and industrialist, was born in Washington, Pennsylvania, the son of William Acheson, a merchant and ironworks manager, and Sarah Diana Ruple. Acheson attended the Bellefonte Academy in Centre County, Pennsylvania, for three years, concentrating his studies on surveying. In 1872, at the age of sixteen, his formal education was brought to an abrupt end by a combination of that year's financial panic and his father's declining health. Acheson went to work as a timekeeper at Monticello Furnace, an ironworks operated by his father, where he developed his first invention, a drilling machine for coal mining. This yielded him his first patent, at age seventeen, but the device was awkward to use and by no means a commercial success.

The further deterioration of the nation's economy forced the Monticello Furnace out of business in 1874. Acheson then worked as a railway ticket clerk, a chainman in a surveying party, and a tank gauger for the United Pipe Lines Company. As a tank gauger, as at the ironworks, he displayed ingenuity and scientific curiosity, making neatly written books of tables and calculations with which to estimate tank capacities.

Acheson devoted all his leisure time to the study of chemistry and electricity. Of special interest to him were electrometallurgy and the writings of Michael Faraday. Acheson's research led him to work on a dry pile battery and to build a small dynamo in 1879. He became so intent on pursuing electrical research that he left his lucrative job with the United Pipe Lines Company in September 1880 and accepted work in Thomas A. Edison's Menlo Park, New Jersey, laboratory, for one-third his former salary. Although hired as a draftsman, Acheson was soon put to work on a graphite filament for Edison's incandescent lamp. When time allowed, he investigated the decomposition of carbon compounds by electrical currents.

After ten months at Menlo Park, Edison assigned Acheson to work as an assistant engineer for his European enterprises. Acheson played a part in developing the Edison exhibit at the International Electrical Exposition in Paris. He went on to supervise the construction of the first electric light systems for Paris,

Milan, Antwerp, Amsterdam, and Brussels; he also worked for a time with alternating-current pioneer Nikola Tesla, acquainting him with Edison electric-lighting practices. After the completion of his tasks in 1883, Acheson returned to the United States, first to work again for the Edison company, and then, early in 1884, resigning to work solely on his own research. Soon he was nearly penniless, and went to work for the Consolidated Electric Light Company in New York. Margaret Cecilia Maher, a young woman from Brooklyn who supervised the factory's female workers, became Acheson's wife before the year ended. Throughout their marriage she was Acheson's closest advisor, not only in personal affairs but also in technical and business matters. They had five sons and four daughters.

In 1885 Acheson invented an anti-induction telephone wire that eliminated telephone line interference or "cross talk." In the following year he sold the patents for both the invention and its manufacturing process to the Standard Underground Cable Company. In *A Pathfinder*, Acheson wrote, "I am afraid my new riches made me reckless, but I wished my wife to be as comfortable as possible. I furnished our home as well as I thought we could afford, bought a cow, a horse and carriage, engaged a man to attend the barn and drive, all of which was beyond my means." Retained by the company as an electrician, he made time to pursue his own personal projects, most of which looked into the possibility of the direct conversion of heat into electricity.

In 1890 Acheson established a power station for electrical lighting in Monongahela, Pennsylvania. His main purpose in this venture was to acquire a source of daytime electrical power for his experiments that would, through sale of power during the night hours, pay for itself. During the winter of 1890–1891 he thought back to experiments he had performed at Menlo Park on the decomposition of carbon. After recalling another experiment that seemed to indicate that heated clay bodies increased in hardness when impregnated with carbon, Acheson attempted to dissolve carbon in fused clay, using a powerful electric current that would be converted into intense heat. By March 1891 he had succeeded in creating an abrasive second only to the diamond in hardness. He named this chemical compound "carborundum," thinking it a combination of carbon and corundum; only later did he learn that it was actually silicon and carbon. In spite of this, he insisted that its name not be changed, because it was "phonetic and of pleasing effect in print, even though a trifle lengthy." A patent for the "Production of Artificial Crystalline Carbonaceous Materials" was issued to Acheson on 28 February 1893.

In September 1891 Acheson and several other investors organized the Carborundum Company and then built a small plant in Monongahela City, Pennsylvania. Thinking it wise to "start small" in the grinding-wheel field, Acheson and his wife made 12,000 dental wheels by hand. These promotional items generated impressive sales, in one month yielding more than 90 percent of all the sales that had been made during the previous fifteen months.

By 1895 Acheson was convinced that the demand for carborundum warranted the construction of a much larger, more cost-efficient plant in Niagara Falls, New York. In the 1890s and the early 1900s, Niagara Falls was at the forefront of electrochemical and electrothermal developments. New industries flocked to Niagara, attracted by its newly available cheap, plentiful hydroelectric power. Nearly all of the Carborundum Company's directors disagreed with Acheson's line of reasoning and resigned. He responded by purchasing the stock held by the resigned directors and selecting a new directorate. The new plant, which went into production on 19 October 1895, housed the largest electrical furnace in the world. The company's product line grew to include wheels, abrasive powders, hones, slips, files, knife sharpeners, scythe stones, carborundum cloth, and rubstones. Financial problems caused by the move to Niagara Falls resulted in Acheson's losing controlling interest in the company by 1898; also during this period, the priority of Acheson's carborundum patent was threatened. Suits by the French chemist Henri Moissan and E. H. and A. H. Cowles were not decided in Acheson's favor until 1897.

In the course of Acheson's experiments, he found a form of carbon that had all of the properties of graphite. This artificial graphite was superior to naturally occurring graphite and suitable for manufacturing electrodes, lead pencils, powders for dry batteries, paints, pigments, and lubricants. On 23 July 1895 Acheson was awarded a patent for this process, receiving additional patents on 29 September 1896, 17 January 1899, and 13 March 1900. The Acheson Graphite Company was organized in January 1899 for the manufacture of graphite under these patents. Acheson went on to discover a method of producing a soft, unctuous graphite of over 90 percent purity during the summer of 1906; he obtained a patent for this process on 20 November 1906.

Over the course of his career, Acheson obtained nearly fifty patents in the United States. In 1926 the United States Patent Office selected silicon carbide (carborundum) as one of twenty-two "Important Patents That Have Influenced the World's Progress." Without silicon carbide, the manufacture of precision-ground, interchangeable metal parts, essential to economical, large-scale mass production would have been virtually impossible. Acheson died of pneumonia in the New York City home of his daughter.

• Much of the manuscript for Acheson's autobiography, including significant portions not in the published book, are in the Orrin E. Dunlap collection in the Niagara Falls, N.Y., Public Library, Local History Department. The most comprehensive work about Acheson is Raymond Szymanowitz, *Edward Goodrich Acheson: Inventor, Scientist, Industrialist—A Biography* (1971). Also insightful is Acheson's autobiography, *A Pathfinder: Discovery, Invention, and Industry* (1910). Of additional help is Edward G. Acheson, "Discovery and Invention," *Electric Journal* 3, no. 10 (1906): 554–65, and the more technical article, Edward G. Acheson, "Carborundum: Its History, Manufacture, and Uses," *Journal of the Franklin Institute*, Sept. 1893. See also Sturgis B. Rand, "Hottest Heat and Electrical Furnaces," *McClure's Magazine* 3 (1900): 213–21, which deals with Acheson's work in Niagara Falls. An obituary is in the *New York Times*, 7 July 1931.

DANIEL M. DUMYCH

ACOSTA, Bertram Blanchard (1 Jan. 1895–1 Sept. 1954), aviation pioneer, was born in San Diego, California, the son of Aphonse Ferdinand Acosta and Martha Blanche Snook, businesspeople. Acosta became enthralled with aviation at an early age, built gliders and later powered aircraft, and taught himself to fly. Because of this interest, at age sixteen his parents enrolled him in Throop Polytechnic Institute (later the California Institute of Technology) in Pasadena so that he could study aeronautical engineering, but he never graduated. Beginning in 1911 Acosta spent almost every moment not in school working for Glenn H. Curtiss, an aeronautical engineer and aviation pioneer who had established a private flying school and testing field on North Island adjacent to San Diego. At first just a mechanic's helper, Acosta soon endeared himself to Curtiss and others at the school, and they taught him what they knew about flying. The quest for speed, which was always a part of Acosta's daredevil psyche, led him both to piloting advanced aircraft and to racing automobiles. These pursuits became Acosta's main pastime for the rest of his active life.

During the years just before the U.S. entrance into World War I, Acosta traveled the nation to exhibit his aircraft and give rides to locals. In many respects he was like the postwar barnstormers, gypsy flyers who traveled the nation in search of thrills and money enough to survive and keep flying. During this time he earned a reputation as a gifted but reckless pilot, as his quest for speed outstripped his fear of death. He also worked for a time as a flight instructor to World War I–bound pilots in Toronto, Canada, and when the United States entered the war in 1917 he joined the U.S. Air Service Reserve.

When the war ended Acosta returned to southern California and went to work for Curtiss, this time as a test pilot. He became involved in aircraft racing and participated in several of the important air races that took place in the 1920s. In 1921 he took the Pulitzer silver trophy in Omaha, Nebraska, for setting a world's closed-course speed record of 176.9 miles per hour. On 14 May 1927 he was the co-pilot for Clarence D. Chamberlin during a record-setting endurance flight that circled over Roosevelt Field, New York, for 51 hours, 11 minutes, and 25 seconds. He also helped to survey the transcontinental airmail route in 1920 and flew the mail for the U.S. Postal Service for a brief time.

There was always a self-destructive streak in Acosta, and his friends worried that he was too much the carefree daredevil, the hard-drinker, and the woman-chaser for his own good. This darker side of his personality also contributed to several accidents and near misses while flying. In 1922 he had a serious accident that incapacitated him for several weeks. Acosta battled alcohol his entire life, and his drinking contributed to his divorce in 1921 from his first wife, about whom little is known except that they had two children. Not long thereafter he married Helen Belmont Pearsoll; they also had two children.

Acosta's most significant contribution to flight came in 1927 when business leader Rodman Wanamaker came to him with a scheme to make a transatlantic flight that would demonstrate the feasibility of intercontinental passenger service between the United States and France. Acosta would pilot a Fokker trimotor aircraft, christened the *America*, from New York to Paris with an illustrious crew. Richard E. Byrd, the polar explorer, was commander, while U.S. Navy lieutenant George O. Noville was flight engineer and radio operator. Noted Norwegian aviator Bernt Balchen was relief pilot, although Balchen later commented that he was specifically charged with piloting during night and in dangerous weather because Acosta had not mastered instrument flying. While this group was planning their flight, in May 1927 Charles A. Lindbergh (1902–1974) made his pathbreaking solo transatlantic flight, and in the next month Chamberlin made a flight with Charles Levine to Germany. It was anticlimactic, therefore, when on 29 June the *America* took off from New York with Acosta at the controls.

The flight was ill-fated from the beginning. The aircraft was overloaded and too heavy, and only the native skill of Acosta got it airborne in the first place. Storms and poor visibility hampered the progress of the flight, and Balchen had to fly the plane on instruments more than had been anticipated. Near the Normandy coast Acosta was at the controls when the plane entered a squall. The details of what followed are unclear, but apparently Acosta was shaken by the dangerous situation and refused to relinquish the controls to Balchen. Byrd had to force him to turn over control to the Norwegian, who could only ditch the aircraft. He did so successfully, and no one aboard was killed. Publicly Byrd praised his crew and blamed the accident on poor weather and instrument failure, but privately Acosta was blamed for having to take this extreme action. Although the flight ended with an accident, the crew members were treated as heroes, at least for a short time, both in Paris and New York City.

Acosta wanted to continue flying after 1927, but because of his less than sterling reputation fewer and fewer people were willing to back him. Reckless flying cost him his pilot's license for a time. He also invested in a succession of business deals that went bad during the 1930s. He had trouble with his ex-wife over failure to provide support, and he spent some time in jail for this as well as a series of misdemeanors. When his two daughters, now young adults, came to his assistance in the mid-1930s, he was little more than a derelict. They got him off liquor and helped rehabilitate him. He went to Spain in 1936 in a fit of idealism—although the good pay fortified that idealism—and flew combat missions against the fascists during the Spanish civil war.

When Acosta returned to the United States, essentially a fugitive for violating the Neutrality Laws, he was unable to earn a living flying. He again turned to drink and for the rest of his life drifted from menial job to menial job. He later made his way west and died of tuberculosis in the Jewish Consumptive Relief Society's sanitarium outside of Denver, Colorado.

Acosta was one of the many second-echelon pilots who operated before the Second World War. He had attained some stature with record-making flights but was never able to break into the ranks of such notable flyers as Lindbergh, Amelia Earhart, and even Roscoe Turner. Accordingly, he scraped out a living on the margins of the expanding aviation industry. He was not able to make the transition to the airline or aircraft industry, as did so many other flyers of his stature, and after his 1927 transatlantic flight he was unable to duplicate the fame he had briefly enjoyed. His self-destructive behavior also prevented him from gaining lasting respect from either the public or his fellow pilots.

• There is no formal collection of Acosta's papers. Primary material relating to him can be found in the Ernest L. Jones Collection and the Bernt Balchen Papers at the Air Force Historical Research Agency, Maxwell Air Force Base, Ala. The Jones papers have information on his military service, and the Balchen documents relate to the trans-Atlantic flight. Short sketches of his career can be found in *Who's Who in American Aeronautics* (1925) and George Carroll, "Wildest of the Early Birds," *American Mercury* 81 (Sept. 1955): 14–18. Edward V. Rickenbacker, *Rickenbacker* (1967), has a discussion of the mapping of the transcontinental airmail route. On barnstorming see K. C. Tessendorf, *Barnstormers and Daredevils* (1988). Bernt Balchen, *Come North with Me* (1958); Charles J. V. Murphy, *Struggle* (1928); and Richard E. Byrd, *Skyward* (1928), have discussions of the transatlantic flight. Acosta discussed his Spanish civil war experience in *True*, June 1937. Obituaries are in the *New York Times*, 2 Sept. 1954; *Time*, 13 Sept. 1954; and *Newsweek*, 13 Sept. 1954.

ROGER D. LAUNIUS

ACRELIUS, Israel (4 Dec. 1714–25 Apr. 1800), Lutheran clergyman and author, was born in Öster-Åker, Sweden, the son of Johan Acrelius, a pastor, and Sara Gahm. At the age of twelve he entered the University of Uppsala, where he trained for the ministry and received his ordination in 1743. Acrelius then served as a domestic chaplain until 1745, when he became the pastor of Riala, Kulla, and Norra Ljusterö.

In 1749 Acrelius was assigned by the Swedish government to serve as a missionary to the Swedish settlers along the Delaware River. He was originally assigned to serve as pastor of the parish of Racoon and Pennsneck in the colony of New Jersey, but just before his departure for America he learned that the death of the pastor of the parish of Christina (now Wilmington, Del.) had left a vacancy there. Acrelius requested that his assignment be changed to fill the new vacancy; his request was granted and he departed for Christina, reaching the province in November 1749.

Acrelius encountered a number of difficulties in Christina. Two-thirds of the parish's congregants were classified by the church as "free-holding peasants," and most were illiterate. The recently deceased pastor had been enormously popular but had not adequately trained the congregants to manage the pastorate's affairs in case of his absence. Because of this, a Quaker had taken over management of the congregation and had embezzled money and land from the uneducated church members. One of Acrelius's first actions upon his arrival in Christina was to teach the congregants to write in both Swedish and English. Five years after Acrelius's arrival, nearly 20 percent of Christina's members had knowledge of both languages. Acrelius himself mastered English in the hope of proselytizing among the non-Swedish inhabitants of the area. By 1754 Christina, with 490 members, was the largest of the seven Swedish Lutheran congregations in the Delaware Valley.

Besides tending to his own congregation, Acrelius spent a great deal of time aiding the German Lutherans of Pennsylvania. He also collected botanical, zoological, and geological specimens for study and conducted research for a history of the Swedish settlements in America. Citing poor health, Acrelius in 1754 requested that he be allowed to resign from his position and return to Sweden. After a long delay he was eventually granted his request and left America in the fall of 1756. He arrived in Stockholm in July 1757. The following year he became pastor of the Diocese of Westeras in Fellingsbro. In 1759 he published *A History of New Sweden*, a religious study and historical survey of the Delaware River region and its Swedish, Dutch, and English inhabitants. That year he also married Katarina Elisabet Strangh, the daughter of the former pastor at Fellingsbro. Acrelius died in Sweden.

Acrelius was a principal religious figure and the leading historian of the Swedish settlements in the American colonies. His historical work remained the definitive study of the Delaware River region well into the twentieth century and continues to be an essential source for historians of New Sweden.

• The best biographical study of Acrelius is in Bertil Boethius, *Svenkst Biografiskt Lexicon* (1918), a Swedish-language reference work. For English-language accounts of Acrelius's life and work, see the introduction to his *A History of New Sweden*, trans. William M. Reynolds (1874); and Gregory B. Keen, "New Sweden; or, The Swedes on the Delaware," in *Narrative and Critical History of America*, ed. Justin Winsor (1885). Demographic information on Christina can be found in Hans Norman, "The New Sweden Colony and the Continued Existence of Swedish and Finnish Ethnicity," in *New Sweden in America*, ed. Carol E. Hoffecker et al. (1995).

THADDEUS RUSSELL

ACUFF, Roy (15 Sept. 1903–23 Nov. 1992), country music singer and composer, was born Roy Claxton Acuff in Maynardsville, Tennessee, just a few miles north of Knoxville in a spur of the Great Smoky Mountains, the son of Neil Acuff, an attorney and pastor, and Ida Florence Carr. The family moved to

Fountain City, a suburb of Knoxville, when Acuff was sixteen, and he spent most of his high school years excelling in sports. After graduation he was invited to have a tryout at a major league baseball camp, but a 1929 fishing trip to Florida resulted in a severe sunstroke, and Acuff was bedridden for a number of months. During his convalescence he reawakened an early interest in music and began to hone his abilities on the fiddle. By the time he had recovered, he had given up his dreams of a baseball career and had determined to utilize his newly discovered musical talent.

Acuff apprenticed himself to a local figure named Doc Hauer, who ran an old-time traveling medicine show. Acuff provided the entertainment and drew in the crowds to hear Doc pitch his nostrums, and the experience gave Acuff a solid grounding in showmanship and traditional repertoire (a repertoire derived from old folk songs and nineteenth-century stage songs). Acuff learned to sing in a high, full-throat style and to play a variety of tunes—even to do train imitations—on the fiddle, all of which would serve him well. By the mid-1930s he had won a job on local Knoxville station WROL playing with a string band that later became known as the Crazy Tennesseans. At this point Acuff still saw himself primarily as a fiddler and front man and often left the singing to fellow band member Sam "Dynamite" Hatcher.

Sometime in 1935 Acuff heard a local gospel group sing an odd religious song, "The Great Speckle [*sic*] Bird." Although he did not know it at the time, the song had become an anthem of sorts for a popular southern religious sect, the Church of God, then headquartered in nearby Cleveland, Tennessee. Acuff paid the gospel quartet fifty cents to write down the words, and he started singing it on the air. The response was intense, and soon Acuff was known all over East Tennessee. The success of the song—the authorship of which has yet to be conclusively established—soon attracted the attention of W. R. Calaway, a talent scout for the American Record Company, then one of the nation's big three labels. He invited Acuff and his band to come to Chicago and record some twenty sides for the label, which they did in October 1936. Many of the sides languished in obscurity, but others became bestsellers: "The Great Speckle Bird," "Wabash Cannonball," "Freight Train Blues," "Steamboat Whistle Blues," and "Charming Betsy." Others ranged from gospel songs to off-color novelties, such as "When Lulu's Gone."

Like many performers in Knoxville, Acuff longed for a chance to play in the "big leagues" on Nashville's Grand Ole Opry, and in February 1938 he was finally given an audition. The response to his rendition of "Great Speckle Bird" was fast and furious: stacks of mail and phone calls poured in. Hired as a regular, he stayed with the show, except for a brief time in 1946–1947, until his death. He quickly became the lead vocal star and was selected both to appear in *Grand Ole Opry*, a 1940 Hollywood film based on the show, and to be a featured act on the NBC network part of the show, which was broadcast nationally beginning in the fall of 1939. During World War II his popularity soared even more, and soon he was one of the most-recognized American entertainers in show business. (It was widely said that Japanese soldiers taunted Marines in their foxholes by shouting, "To hell with Roosevelt! To hell with Babe Ruth! To hell with Roy Acuff!") Acuff's hit records from this period—his best-known pieces—included "Wreck on the Highway," "Low and Lonely," "Precious Jewel," "Fireball Mail," and "Wait for the Light to Shine."

Also during this time Acuff put together the Smoky Mountain Boys, a band of talented sidemen who would help define his sound and style. The senior member of the group, Pete "Bashful Brother Oswald" Kirby, was one of country music's pioneer players of a type of resonator guitar known as the Dobro. Oswald's unique playing of this instrument, his high-tenor harmony vocals, and his boisterous comedy made him a key member of the band from 1938 until Acuff's death. Two of country music's most-influential fiddlers also graced the Acuff band, Georgian Tommy Magness (famed for his "Black Mountain Rag") and Tennessean Howard "Big Howdy" Forrester. Other members included harmonica and piano player Jimmie Riddle; banjoist Rachael Veach; and guitarists Lonnie "Pap" Wilson, Jess Easterday, and Charley Collins. Many of them stayed with the band for decades.

In the 1940s Acuff and the band spent a lot of time in Hollywood, where they made a series of popular, low-budget films. In addition to *Grand Ole Opry*, these films included *Hi Neighbor* (1942), *O, My Darlin' Clementine* (1943), *Cowboy Canteen* (1944), *Sing, Neighbor, Sing* (1944), *Night Train to Memphis* (1946), and *Smoky Mountain Melody* (1948). He became so popular in Tennessee that in 1948 he made a serious run for governor on the Republican ticket, albeit unsuccessfully. Also by the late 1940s, Acuff was reaping the benefits of having established Acuff-Rose, the first modern country song–publishing company in Nashville, in October 1942. Acuff had entered into a partnership with the successful songwriter Fred Rose and founded Acuff-Rose with a cash investment of $25,000. Bolstered initially by Acuff's own popular songs, the company flourished, signing such major figures as Hank Williams and the Louvin Brothers. In addition, Rose's contacts in the pop music business enabled him to take country songs to New York and get them recorded by the great pop singers of the day, such as Tony Bennett and Rosemary Clooney. The firm's success helped to secure Nashville's status as the undisputed capital of country music.

In the 1950s, as Acuff began to have fewer hits, he founded his own record company, Hickory, and began recording for it. Like many country entertainers, he weathered hard times as rock 'n' roll began to dominate country and pop music, and for a time the band even experimented with electric guitars and steel guitars. Yet Acuff never strayed too far from his Smoky Mountains roots, and by the 1960s he had reemerged as a central figure on the Grand Ole Opry. He soon determined to stop his heavy touring schedule and to confine his performing to the Opry stage. By reaching out to a new generation of fans through his work on the 1972 crossover album *Will the Circle Be Unbroken?* and by welcoming President Richard Nixon on stage at the new Grand Ole Opry House in 1974, Acuff further solidified his role as an elder statesmen for country music, the Opry, and Nashville. His family included his long-time wife, the former Mildred Louise Douglas, who helped him run his career, and his son, Roy Neal, born in 1943, who had a successful singing career of his own in the 1960s. After Mildred Acuff died in 1981, the Opry built, near the front door to the Opry House, a cottage where he lived during his declining years.

Throughout his eighties Acuff continued to make regular appearances on the Opry and even to record; his last chart hit, in 1987, was a duet with Charlie Louvin performing Acuff's song "Precious Jewel." After his death, in Nashville, tributes poured in, attesting to Acuff's influence as a vocal stylist—on everyone from George Jones to Randy Travis—his role as a talent spotter who was responsible for giving dozens of artists their first break, and his dedication to preserving and celebrating the history of the genre. Long known as the "King of Country Music," he had been a worldwide spokesman for the music and the Opry as well as a pioneering businessman in the industry.

• At the Country Music Foundation in Nashville is the Elizabeth Schlappi Collection of tapes, posters, films, letters, and scrapbooks related to Acuff. The definitive biography is Schlappi, *Roy Acuff: The Smoky Mountain Boy*, rev. ed. (1983). General background on the Grand Ole Opry and Acuff's changing role in it is best described in Chet Hagen, *The Grand Ole Opry* (1989).

CHARLES K. WOLFE

ADAIR, James (c. 1709–c. 1783), trader and author, was born in County Antrim, Ireland. Although his parentage is not certain, he probably was a younger son of Sir Robert Adair, a scion of the "Old English" Fitzgerald family. Having noble connections, but not overburdened with wealth, Adair emigrated to South Carolina in 1735 and immediately began trading with Indians.

His first trading partners were the Overhill Cherokees whose town lay along the western reaches of the Little Tennessee River. He started trading among the Cherokees in 1736, and by 1743 he had moved on to the Catawbas. From the Catawbas he went west to join the Chickasaws in what is now northern Mississippi. These "cheerful, brave Chikkasah" were his ideal Indians, the only ones whom he did not condemn for traits stereotypically "savage," though they were no more "civilized" than the other tribes he knew. What made them different was their unwavering alliance with Adair personally and with South Carolina, which he regarded as his own country regardless of his protracted residence among Indian tribes. Extended exposure to Indian culture did not diminish his firm allegiance to his own culture. In 1759 or 1760 he led a band of Chickasaws into battle against the Cherokees and probably sold Cherokee prisoners into West Indian slavery as was standard practice among the traders of that time and place.

During the 1760s Adair wrote a history of the peoples among whom he lived. According to recent scholarship, this *History of the American Indians* is unreliable as history, but its descriptions of southeastern Indian cultures are still accepted with respect despite its arguments that the lost tribes of Israel were ancestors of American Indians. Common in Adair's time, this fallacy occupies nearly half of his book. In support of it he cites so many specific cultural traits that the historian Wilcomb E. Washburn believes that the thesis did no harm to Adair's personal perceptions. Charles Hudson, an ethnologist, thinks the thesis may actually have helped him better understand the Indians, and anthropologists generally accept the book as a valuable source.

As history of Adair's own time, however, the book has been refuted. Its assertions that Adair instigated the Choctaws to rebel against their French allies in 1746 are denied forcefully from two directions. First, Adair's petition to South Carolina's House of Commons for reimbursement of his expenses in the war was rejected on grounds of falsehood. Second, from a different direction, the ethnohistorian Richard White attributes the Choctaw uprising entirely to the war chief Red Shoes, who was intriguing to gain ascendancy over Choctaw traditional chiefs. In this interpretation, Adair was insignificant. However, Adair claimed that he risked his life by refusing a French bribe to change sides, and he went bankrupt from losses in the conflict.

The citations and quotations in Adair's *History* are evidence of wide and serious reading. He kept up the intellectual culture of an eighteenth-century gentleman, but he lacked polish in personal demeanor. In 1768 he visited Sir William Johnson, superintendent of Indian affairs, in an unsuccessful attempt to get Johnson's endorsement of his *History*. Johnson was condescending, writing to General Thomas Gage (10 Dec. 1768) that Adair's "appearance may not be much in his favor . . . but he is certainly well acquainted with the Southern Indians, and a man of Learning tho Rusticated by 30 years residence in a Wild Country."

In 1775 Adair voyaged to England to get his *History* published. Returning to America in the same year, he resumed trading in new surroundings in western Tennessee, where tradition has settled him with an anonymous Indian wife or mistress. A respected family claims descent from him, and several places bear the Adair name.

An individualist all his life, Adair was for himself first, last, and always, constantly shifting associations for advantage in South Carolina as well as among the tribesmen. He was consistent only in hostility to the French and in alliance with the Chickasaws. He was venomous in hatred for the Creeks, whose clever balancing between the French and English excited his extreme anger. He believed that Englishmen could never live in security as long as Indians were numerous and strong and that English policy should therefore be to incite the tribes to war mercilessly against each other, a precept that Adair practiced. He is notable today for his active involvement in intertribal intrigues and wars and for his record of Indian culture.

• The basic source for James Adair's life is his own book, reprinted as Adair's *History of the American Indians*, ed. Samuel Cole Williams (1930). Williams's introduction makes his edition more valuable than the first in terms of biography.

For Adair's participation in the Choctaw war, see Edmund Atkin, "Historical Account of the Revolt of the Choctaw Indians in the Late War from the French to the British Alliance and of Their Return Since to That of the French" (1753), in the Lansdowne Mss. held by the British Library (transcripts in the Library of Congress); M. Eugene Sirmans, *Colonial South Carolina: A Political History, 1663–1763* (1966); and Richard White, "Red Shoes: Warrior and Diplomat," in *Struggle and Survival in Colonial America*, ed. David G. Sweet and Gary B. Nash (1981).

For Adair's value as a reporter of southeastern Indian cultures, see Charles Hudson, "James Adair as Anthropologist," *Ethnohistory* 24, no. 4 (1977): 311–28, and Wilcomb E. Washburn, "Adair, James," in *Handbook of North American Indians* vol. 4, ed. W. E. Washburn (1990).

For background on the South Carolina traders, see Verner W. Crane, *The Southern Frontier, 1670–1732* (1929), and J. Leitch Wright, Jr., *The Only Land They Knew: The Tragic Story of the American Indians in the Old South* (1981).

FRANCIS JENNINGS

ADAIR, John (9 Jan. 1757–19 May 1840), soldier, politician, and governor of Kentucky, was born in Chester County, South Carolina, the son of Baron William Adair and Mary Moore. Little is known about his childhood. As a young man, he fought in the revolutionary war and was captured by the British. During his imprisonment he suffered many cruelties, which apparently did little to deter him from becoming a career soldier. After the war Adair traveled west, eventually settling in Mercer County, Kentucky, in 1786. In 1784 he had married Katherine Palmer; they had twelve children.

Adair was quick to realize that military glory was the precursor to political favor in the new republic. In 1791, shortly after settling in Kentucky, he joined Generals Arthur St. Clair and James Wilkinson in their initiatives against the Maumee Indians, promptly becoming a major. He is best remembered for his defeat by Little Turtle, a Maumee chief, near Fort St. Clair in 1792. Adair was commissioned, along with a troop of 100 mounted Kentuckians, to escort a train of horses to Fort Jefferson in Cincinnati, Ohio. A band of 250 Indians learned of the cavalcade and made plans to ambush the envoy upon its return. After reaching Fort Jefferson, Adair and his troops rested, returning to Fort St. Clair the next night. Ironically, the militia eventually retired "beyond the shine of their fires, on the side next to the fort" (Perrin et al., p. 258), and the Maumee mistakenly unleashed an animated attack on an empty camp. Adair's men responded by attacking the bewildered Indians, and although the Maumee gave way, they continued to drive back Adair's troop, which ultimately lost 140 horses, all its camp equipment, and six men, with an equal number wounded. Nevertheless, Adair was named lieutenant colonel in 1793, the same year he was elected to the Kentucky legislature. In 1799 he also attended the constitutional convention that fashioned Kentucky's second constitution. Frequently reelected to the legislature until 1817, he served as Speaker of the house from 1801 to 1803.

In 1805 Adair made the unfortunate mistake of entertaining the enterprises of Aaron Burr, who was traveling through the state claiming that the United States had employed him to persuade the West to wage war against Spain for the Southwest Territories. In reality, Burr had concocted a dangerous scheme in which he would engage a military force under false pretenses with the explicit purpose of usurping territory from Spain, which he would then rule as commander in chief, perhaps from New Orleans. Many westerners took Burr seriously. The question of whether Adair was a naive listener or a willing conspirator was never fully decided. When Burr was taken into custody in Frankfort, Kentucky, in 1806, Adair was implicated in the conspiracy, and there was talk of an indictment. The confusion that followed left Adair's reputation somewhat tarnished, and although he had been chosen to serve the unexpired U.S. Senate term of John Breckinridge in 1805, in November 1806 he was defeated for the full term of the office and promptly resigned.

Adair set about repairing his public image with military achievement. He volunteered to serve in the War of 1812 and quickly became a brigadier general of the state militia. Although he successfully led more than 1,000 Kentuckians at the battle of New Orleans, he came to prominence once again as the result of a public quarrel. Adair, in command on the eastern bank of the Mississippi in the absence of General Thomas, defended the honor of fellow Kentuckians on the western bank whom General Andrew Jackson had accused of "inglorious flight." After the two exchanged words, Adair wrote a full report of the events, justifying the Kentucky troop's actions. Jackson then reluctantly accepted Adair's account. Strangely, before General Thomas sent Jackson's message to Kentucky, he added a postscript stating that "the general" was "impressed" with the decision and that the regiment's "retreat was not only excusable, but absolutely justifiable" (Parton, p. 384). Absentmindedly, he forgot to sign his name, and the entire state of Kentucky believed for several years that Jackson had, in fact, written the postscript as an admission of error. In 1817 the message was printed in R. B. McAfee's *History of the War* and attributed to Jackson, who furiously insinuated that Adair had supplied McAfee with a forged paper. The confusion spread, with the *Kentucky Reporter* misprinting Jackson's words, making his assertion read that Adair himself had forged the letter. Adair and Jackson exchanged heated letters over the next two years in which the former continuously defended himself and his fellow Kentuckians.

Adair's willingness to confront Jackson greatly improved his reputation in Kentucky, and in 1820 he won the office of governor. His victory was largely the result of his sympathies with the Relief party. Earlier, the state legislature had chartered forty-six independent banks without requiring them to uphold their notes with hard currency. Paper money floated throughout the state, creating a false sense of security and a wave of speculation. By 1818 the banks were in shambles, and in 1820 the legislature relinquished their charters. The state promptly split into two factions, the Relief party and the Anti-Relief party. As a member of the former, despite compassion for his ruined constituents, Adair pressed the legislature to charter the Bank of the Commonwealth in 1820 as a relief measure. Like its predecessors, it turned out paper money whose value quickly decreased. When creditors refused to accept such money, the legislature passed a replevin law that forced creditors either to accept the paper money or to wait two years for repayment. Although this law was eventually ruled unconstitutional, Adair's time in office was characterized by his willingness virtually to bankrupt the state of Kentucky. Still, he fought for education and prison reform, while also advocating the annulment of imprisonment for debt.

By the end of his term as governor, Adair's career as a politician was largely over, although he served briefly as a member of the House of Representatives from 1831 to 1833. He died in Mercer County. Although his careers as both military leader and legislator were largely undistinguished, he earned the love of his fellow Kentuckians, who considered him an able soldier, a friend to the people, and a loyal defender of the state's honor.

• For biographical information, see the brief sketch of Adair in Lewis Collins and Richard H. Collins, *History of Kentucky* (1882). Aspects of his public life are discussed in Elizabeth Shelby Kinkead, *A History of Kentucky* (1896), which also contains a thorough discussion of the Relief and Anti-Relief parties, as well as Kentucky's financial crisis in the early nineteenth century. The circumstances of Adair's heated correspondence with Jackson are chronicled in James Parton, *Life of Andrew Jackson*, vol. 2 (1860). The conspiracy of Aaron Burr and a description of Adair's struggle at Fort St. Clair are in W. H. Perrin et al., *Kentucky: A History of the State*, 8th ed. (1888).

DONNA GREAR PARKER

ADAMIC, Louis (23 Mar. 1899–4 Sept. 1951), writer, was born in Blato, Carniola (modern-day Slovenia), the son of Anton Adamic, a peasant landholder, and Ana Adamic (a distant relative of Anton). Adamic spent four years at a local school and one at a primary school before advancing to a Gymnasium in Ljubljana. After completing two years there, his involvement in a nationalist demonstration led to his expulsion in 1913. Resisting his parents' wishes that he enter a Jesuit seminary to study for the priesthood, Adamic immigrated to the United States in December 1913. He first worked in the mail room of a Slovene American newspaper in New York and in 1916 became an editorial assistant. After the paper ceased publication later that year, Adamic had several manual labor jobs. In 1917 he enlisted in the army and the following year became a naturalized citizen. Discharged in 1920, he drifted and finally in December 1922 arrived in California, where he worked as a day laborer and then as a reporter for a Los Angeles newspaper. Unhappy with the hectic life of a journalist, he quit in June 1923, found a job as a dock worker, and then became a port pilots' clerk. The position allowed the aspiring author time to write. Adamic's early publications were primarily translations of Slavic works, but by the mid-1920s he was producing a wide range of original items for Haldeman-Julius publications. His first important recognition as a professional writer came in 1927 when H. L. Mencken published Adamic's essay "The Yugoslav Speech in America" in the *American Mercury*. By 1931 Adamic had contributed eight items to that magazine. Determined to write a book, he returned to New York in 1929.

The California years profoundly influenced Adamic's career. He met the novelist Upton Sinclair and developed a lasting friendship with the writer Carey McWilliams. His acquaintance with the Socialist Edward Adams Cantrell inspired him to investigate the 1910 bombing of the *Los Angeles Times* building. Adamic expanded his investigation beyond the Los Angeles incident, however, and the result was his first book, *Dynamite: The Story of Class Violence in America* (1931).

Following the publication of *Dynamite*, Adamic's life and career moved quickly. In 1931 he married Stella Sanders, a native-born Jewish American. They never had children. By January 1932 the autobiographical *Laughing in the Jungle* was already in galleys; he won a Guggenheim Fellowship, and in May he and Stella left for Europe. They stayed a year in Yugoslavia, where he started *The Native's Return* (1934), an analytical description of his homeland and an immigrant's introspection. Designated the February 1934 Book-of-the-Month-Club selection, the work was a bestseller for two years. Its success enhanced Adamic's reputation, and with fame came numerous invitations to speak. A 1934 lecture tour brought him in contact with old-stock Americans and recent immigrants. Adamic credited this tour, his return to Yugoslavia, and the writing of *The Native's Return* with making him more "intellectually" and "emotionally involved in the subject of immigrants and America." The immigrant saga did not particularly interest him; however, the consequences of immigration did. To demonstrate the impact of immigrants on the United States, Adamic developed a conceptual framework that emphasized the country's cultural diversity. Rejecting the notion of "America" as an Anglo-Saxon country, he argued that "America is the result . . . also of recent-immigrant groups" and that "Ellis Island is rapidly becoming as important historically as is Plymouth Rock." Identifying "diversity itself" as "the pattern of America," Adamic maintained that recognizing the contributions of all ethnic and racial groups would create "unity within diversity."

A commitment to documenting the role of recent immigrants influenced Adamic's activities for the next decade. In 1934 he joined the Foreign Language Information Service (FLIS) as a board member. In 1935 he unsuccessfully tried to convince the Federal Emergency Relief Administration to create a project to prepare an "Encyclopaedia of the Population of the United States, from the Indians to the latest immigrant group." Nevertheless, it was through books, numerous articles, and lectures that Adamic promoted his ideas. The autobiographical *My America: 1928–1938* (1938), which portrayed life during the Great Depression, also popularized Adamic's arguments about immigrants and "America." His most ambitious effort was his four-volume Nation of Nations series. Supported by a Carnegie Corporation grant, he sent thousands of questionnaires to foreign-language newspapers and appealed to immigrants for information. Using the responses and his own investigations, he produced *From Many Lands* (1940), *Two-Way Passage* (1941), *What's Your Name?* (1942), and *A Nation of Nations* (1945).

Adamic helped reorganize the Common Council for American Unity (formerly FLIS), and in 1940 he took part in establishing *Common Ground*, the council's journal dedicated to promoting respect for cultural diversity. He edited the journal's first six issues. In 1943 he accepted an invitation from the publisher J. B. Lippincott Company to become editor of its Peoples of America series, a multivolume project to produce individual histories of ethnic groups.

Throughout the 1930s and 1940s, Adamic wrote voluminously on a range of topics. In addition to producing literary items and feature articles about Yugoslavia, he covered social conditions, labor issues, and current events in the United States and Europe. His writings were often tinged with critical commentary.

In the 1940s Adamic increasingly turned his attention to the turmoil in Europe. He suggested that American ethnic groups could help reconstruct postwar Europe and establish democracy in their homelands. This idea resulted in the Adamics receiving a dinner invitation to the White House in 1942.

During the war, Adamic's efforts to shape Yugoslavia's future intensified. His hatred of Yugoslavia's government in exile caused him to lobby the American government and people to support the Partisans led by Marshal Tito. For his activities, Adamic received the Order of National Unity from Tito in 1944. Adamic's political views about his homeland, however, had long made him a controversial figure in the United States, especially among persons from Yugoslavia. An admirer of the Russian Revolution, Adamic believed that Yugoslavia's salvation rested with Russia. He altered this position when Tito split with Joseph Stalin in 1948.

After visiting Yugoslavia in 1949, Adamic began another book: a spirited defense of Tito's Yugoslavia as a democratic force resisting Soviet communism. Before he completed final revisions, he was found dead at "Mountain View Farm," his home in Milford, New Jersey. He had a gunshot wound to the head; a rifle lay across his knees; the buildings were ablaze. The unusual circumstances surrounding his death stirred widespread speculation, but, after a three-week investigation, the death was ruled a suicide. The debate, whether it was suicide or murder, has persisted. Stella Adamic oversaw the revisions and posthumous publication of *The Eagle and the Roots* (1952).

Although Adamic never embraced communism, his critical writings, disputed political views, backing of unions, and support for Henry Wallace in the 1948 presidential campaign got him branded a communist. And, while Adamic was not called to appear before the House Committee on Un-American Activities, he was mentioned several times during the committee's hearings and in its reports. Having his name cited in committee proceedings reinforced perceptions that he was a communist. After his death, especially during the McCarthy era, he remained controversial.

The ethnic revival of the 1960s brought renewed interest in Adamic, his writings, his commentary on the effects of immigration, and his observations about the United States from the 1920s into the 1940s. As a result of his pioneering work on cultural diversity, he has been viewed as a forerunner of the ethnic revival. Regardless of changing political climates and assessments of Louis Adamic's activities, his works, written by an immigrant, remain part of a unique body of American historical literature.

• Adamic manuscript materials exist in several historical archives in the United States and the former Yugoslavia, but the principal collection is in the Princeton University Library. Henry A. Christian, "A Brief Survey of Archival Sources Concerning Louis Adamic," *Spectrum* (newsletter of the Immigration History Research Center, Univ. of Minnesota) 4 (Fall 1982): 8–9, lists known American and European repositories that have Adamic materials. In addition to books cited in this article, Adamic wrote *Grandsons: A Story of American Lives* (1935), *Cradle of Life: The Story of One Man's Beginnings* (1936), *The House in Antigua: A Restoration* (1937), *My Native Land* (1943), and *Dinner at the White House* (1946). Henry A. Christian, *Louis Adamic: A Checklist* (1971), provides a bibliography of Adamic's publications and a select list of published materials about him. Although there is no standard biography, Christian offers a biographical analysis in his "Louis Adamic: Immigrant and American Liberal" (Ph.D. diss., Brown Univ., 1968). The proceedings of a 1981 international symposium on Adamic, held in Ljubljana, are available as *Louis Adamič: Simpozij Symposim* (n.d.). See also Rudolph Vecoli, "Louis Adamic and the Contemporary Search for Roots," *Ethnic Studies* 2, no. 3 (1978): 29–35. For contemporary reflections on Adamic by a friend, see Carey McWilliams, *Louis Adamic & Shadow-America* (1935), and "Louis Adamic, American," *The Nation*, 22 Dec. 1951.

JUNE GRANATIR ALEXANDER

ADAMS, Abigail (11 Nov. 1744–28 Oct. 1818), first lady and woman of intellect, was born in Weymouth, Massachusetts, the daughter of William Smith, a Congregational minister, and Elizabeth Quincy. Abigail grew up in a prominent and wealthy family, descended from Puritan leaders and successful merchants. She had no formal schooling, both because of her recurrent illnesses and the limited options available to girls. Yet neither obstacle prevented her from achieving a remarkably broad and sophisticated education. She enjoyed the family's well-stocked library, the stimulating company of educated relatives and parsonage visitors, and the attentive tutelage of her grandmother. Her studies ranged from Shakespeare to Locke, from Plato to French. She also began two lifelong habits: letter-writing to distant relatives and friends, and the practice of a deep Congregational faith.

In 1764 Abigail married John Adams, whom she had met in 1759, a fledgling lawyer from Braintree who had been a visitor at the Weymouth parsonage. The love letters exchanged during the couple's long distance courtship reveal Abigail Adams's emerging epistolary style. Taking the pen name "Diana" in the custom of the times, she wrote witty, conversational letters to her "Lysander." "I think I write to you every Day," she playfully fretted in a letter of April 1764, "Shall not I make my Letters very cheep; don't you light your pipe with them?" The couple spent their first decade of marriage living in Braintree and Boston; they had five children, one of whom died as a toddler.

Adams's life changed drastically with the onset of the American Revolution. Her husband delved ever deeper into politics and diplomacy, moving to Philadelphia for the First Continental Congress in 1774. She remained in Massachusetts with the family, and the couple lived apart for most of the next ten years. The tasks of rearing children, managing a farm, and overseeing business affairs thus fell squarely upon Adams. She met these challenges with confidence and skill: "I hope in time to have the reputation of being as good a *Farmeress* as my partner has of being a good Statesman," she wrote John in April 1776. Yet she could not always remain so optimistic. The dangers of war moved ever closer to Braintree, bringing the constant thunder of cannons before the British evacuated Boston on 17 March 1776. Disease also threatened the Adams farm, first through a dysentery epidemic and later through a smallpox scare.

These upheavals rendered Adams's letter-writing more important than ever. Her epistles were her sole connection to her absent husband, the means of exchanging business and wartime news, and the forum for her political ideas. She wrote to her extended family and to friends, like Mercy Otis Warren and Thomas Jefferson. Most often, though, she wrote to John, now signing her letters as "Portia." Her writings were steeped in her distinctive style, from their idiosyncratic spelling and punctuation to their candor and spontaneity. She moved easily between wrenching emotion, mundane farm reports, and descriptions of the political scene. Always, her keen observations shared space with her palpable longing for John, "My Much Loved Friend."

Adams was increasingly interested in politics and history, and her letters revealed a growing republican ideology. In March 1776 she remarked on the ills of slavery, suggesting that "the passion for Liberty cannot be Eaquelly Strong in the Breasts of those who have been accustomed to deprive their fellow Creatures of theirs." Later in the same letter, Adams made her most famous request to John. In creating the new government, she bade him "Remember the Ladies, and be more generous and favourable to them than your ancestors. Do not put such unlimited power into the hands of the Husbands. Remember all Men would be tyrants if they could. If perticuliar care and attention is not paid to the Laidies we are determined to foment a Rebelion, and will not hold ourselves bound by any Laws in which we have no voice, or Representation." Adams struck a delicate balance in the passage; the tone was playful, but the message was clear. She cultivated and valued traditional female virtues, but she also held dear her ideals of liberty. John responded to her request with a mixture of amusement and uneasiness, protesting a potential "Despotism of the Peticoat" and proclaiming, "Depend upon it, We know better than to repeal our Masculine systems."

With peace secured, in 1784 Adams traveled to Europe to join her husband, who had been abroad in various diplomatic positions since 1778. They spent nearly a year in Paris and three years in London. Again, Adams's writing skills served her well. In addition to directing the Braintree farm through letters, she sent home vivid descriptions of European sights and society. The luxuries of Paris initially disturbed her religious and republican sensibilities, but she gradually grew more tolerant of the French. After John Adams was appointed minister to Britain, the American couple arrived in London to a chilly reception. Adams complained to her sister in June 1785, "The Tory venom has begun to spit itself forth in the publick papers as I expected." Her view softened over the years in England, but upon leaving she wrote Jefferson that she still found her Massachusetts farm more attractive than "residing at the court of St. James's where I seldom meet with characters so innofensive as my Hens and chickings, or minds so well improved as my garden."

Adams and her family returned home in 1788; beginning in 1789 John served eight years as vice president and four years as president of the United States. Adams became increasingly involved in the world of politics and in the sharp partisan battles of her husband's presidential term. An avid Federalist and defender of John's administration, she strongly advocated the Alien and Sedition Acts. Writing to her sister about the unrelenting attacks of the anti-Federalist press, Adams fumed, "Bache has the malice & falshood of Satin [Satan], and his vile partner the Chronical is equally as bad. . . . An abused and insulted publick cannot tolerate them much longer. In short they are so criminal that they ought to be Presented by the grand jurors." Critics denounced this partisanship and alleged that she held too much influence over her husband's policies; political opponent Albert Gallatin labeled Adams "Her Majesty." During the final months of her husband's term, the couple became the first to live in the White House, still unfinished and barely inhabitable.

After 1801 Adams's life centered on the household at Braintree, now called Quincy. She continued her letter-writing, concentrating her efforts on advising her son John Quincy Adams, later the sixth president of the United States. Her faith remained deep and sustained her through the death of her daughter in 1813. Adams died in Quincy and was buried in the First Church.

Adams's intelligence, inquisitiveness, and dedication shaped her life and her writings. When her grandson Charles Francis Adams published the first volume of her letters in 1840, he sought to contribute to a history of "feeling" rather than of "action" and to glorify the bravery of revolutionary era women. This volume and subsequent fuller collections furthered the view of Adams as a patriotic maternal figure, a model of American female virtue and strength. Her letters, never intended for publication, provide a remarkable and unique portrait of a complex woman and a critical time. They give modern readers, as they gave their original recipients, a witty, unflinching look at marriage, daily life, war, and politics in early America.

• The bulk of Adams's surviving correspondence is in the Adams Family Papers at the Massachusetts Historical Society, and this collection has been made available on microfilm. Edited selections of her letters were first published by her grandson Charles Francis Adams in *Letters of Mrs. Adams, the Wife of John Adams* (1840) and *Familiar Letters of John Adams and His Wife during the Revolution* (1876). *New Letters of Abigail Adams, 1788–1801*, ed. Stewart Mitchell (1947), offers previously unpublished letters from Adams to her sister Mary Cranch. Several other collections center on specific relationships, including Lester J. Cappon, *The Adams-Jefferson Letters* (1959), and L. H. Butterfield, *The Book of Abigail and John* (1975). The most complete published collection of her letters can be found in *The Adams Papers: Adams Family Correspondence*, ed. Butterfield (4 vols., 1963–1973).

Adams's eventful life and captivating letters have inspired a number of biographies. Phyllis Levin, *Abigail Adams* (1987), provides a richly textured overview of Adams's life, largely organized around her marriage and family. Charles Akers's *Abigail Adams: An American Woman* (1980), and Lynne Withey, *Dearest Friend: A Life of Abigail Adams* (1981), are accessible, detailed portraits; both examine the status of women and situate Adams's life in the social context of her times. Several other works focus on particular facets of her story: Rosemary Keller explores Adams's experiences and accomplishments in the revolutionary decades in *Patriotism and the Female Sex* (1994), while Edith Gelles takes a critical view of the "Abigail Industry" and seeks to define Adams on her own terms in *Portia* (1992).

NANCY NEIMS PARKS

ADAMS, Andy (3 May 1859–26 Sept. 1935), writer of novels and stories about the cattle country, was born in Thornecreek Township, Indiana, the son of Andrew Adams, a farmer, and Elizabeth Elliott. His father came from Ireland and his mother's parents from Scotland. Andy called his parents' place a "stock farm," by which he meant that cattle as well as crops were raised there. Young Andy developed a special feeling for cattle, and this feeling was reinforced by his reading of the Bible with its many references to pastoral life. In his maturity Adams often said that cattle possessed "primal values": humans depended on them and felt affection for their companions "through the ages."

At the age of fifteen, Adams, who had attended school for only six years (and only three months each winter), ran away from home. After a time of drifting, he turned up in 1882 in San Antonio, working for a partnership dealing in horses and mules. Until about 1890 he trailed and shipped horses and cattle from lower Texas to northern destinations such as Caldwell and Dodge City in Kansas and the Cherokee Outlet in the Indian Territory (Oklahoma). Next, he spent three years in the feed and seed business, which he left for the mining boom in Cripple Creek, Colorado. The altitude forced him down to the lower elevation of Colorado Springs, where he continued to live except for two short periods, one in Nevada (1907–1909) and another in Kentucky (1919–1921). He joined friends in Nevada who wished to profit by the strike in Goldfield, and he acted as "treasurer" for two companies drilling for oil in Kentucky, near Frenchburg. In both states Adams continued to write fiction and communicate with his publisher, as he had since the turn of the century.

In Colorado Springs Adams had invested in mining stocks that proved to be worthless. In 1898, while watching an enthusiastically applauded farce about Texans in Washington, he conceived the idea that he could make money by writing a play about ranching people that would be "the real thing." After completing a play and finding no one to stage it, Adams turned to short stories about the West. In rejecting these stories a publisher wrote that he would welcome a coherent and inclusive account of how cowboys lived and worked. Andy began to plan and write what was to become *The Log of a Cowboy: A Narrative of the Old Trail Days* (1903). Now considered a classic of the cattle country, *The Log* has been highly praised for its truthfulness to the details of a cowboy's life and work. Adams succeeded so well in writing fiction "as convincingly as fact" that some commentators have read it as history or autobiography. *The Log* has the pattern of the performance of a group task: in 1882 a trail outfit drives a herd of cattle from the Rio Grande to the Blackfoot reservation in Montana, encountering and overcoming various obstacles along the way. This pattern permits the inclusion of stories told around the campfire.

Adams died in Colorado Springs and was buried there. Never married, he left no children. His nephew and namesake gave Adams's papers and manuscripts to the Colorado Springs Public Library and the State Historical Society of Colorado in Denver.

• Besides *The Log* (1903), Andy published *A Texas Matchmaker* (1904), *The Outlet* (1905), *Cattle Brands* (a collection of short stories published in 1906 but written before *The Log*), *Reed Anthony, Cowman: An Autobiography* (1907), *Wells Brothers: The Young Cattle Kings* (1911), and *The Ranch on the Beaver: A Sequel to Wells Brothers* (1927). The last two were written for boys. Fifty-one campfire tales from these books and a manuscript make up *Why the Chisholm Trail Forks, and Other Tales of the Cattle Country*, ed. Wilson M. Hudson (1956); this was reprinted as *Andy Adams' Campfire Tales* (1976). A critical essay by Adams, "Western Interpreters," appeared in *Southwest Review*, 10 (Oct. 1924): 70–74. J. Frank Dobie contributed several articles on Adams to Texas newspapers; for his last and most concise evaluation, see the entry in *Guide to Life and Literature of the Southwest* (1952), pp. 94–95. A full-length study was made by Wilson M. Hudson, *Andy Adams: His Life and Writings* (1964).

WILSON M. HUDSON

ADAMS, Annette Abbott (12 Mar. 1877–26 Oct. 1956), lawyer and judge, was born in Prattville, California, the daughter of Hiram Brown Abbott, a storekeeper and justice of the peace, and Annette Frances Stubbs, a teacher. Adams earned a teaching credential from Chico State Normal School in 1897 and became schoolmistress of a country school until she entered the University of California-Berkeley in 1901. After receiving her bachelor's degree in 1904, she taught high school in a rural county, serving as principal from 1907 to 1910. Encouraged by county trial judge John E. Raker, Adams entered Boalt Hall and supported herself while earning a J.D. The dean recommended her, the only woman in the class of 1912, to Western Pacific Railway for their house counsel. The company rejected her on the basis of gender, and she opened a private practice in Plumas County. She hired an instructor to learn how to change her voice from soprano to baritone to suit her masculine legal role. In 1906 she married Martin H. Adams but left him after one month. By 1914 she let others assume that she was a widow, although she and Adams never divorced. For thirty years she shared her home with her brother.

In 1912 Adams moved to San Francisco to organize Democratic women throughout the state behind Woodrow Wilson's candidacy for president. She went to Washington, D.C., for his inauguration and to ask for a patronage appointment. Continuing pressure exerted on the new administration by women's club members; party leaders; Raker, who was now in Congress; and especially by U.S. Attorney for Northern California John Preston won for her the job of assistant U.S. attorney over the opposition of Attorney General James C. McReynolds. In 1914 she was sworn in as the first woman federal prosecutor. She vigorously pursued German and Hindu defendants who were accused of conspiracy to violate the neutrality act and later American socialists accused of war crimes.

Adams's reputation as a party organizer and as a local prosecutor encouraged Attorney General A. Mitchell Palmer to invite her in 1920 to join his office in D.C. as the first woman assistant attorney general. Her initial assignment was to attend the Democratic National Convention in San Francisco and work for Palmer's candidacy among the women delegates. During her short tenure she was responsible for the prosecution of violators of the Volstead Act in all federal court districts and for the operation of the federal prisons. She was a proponent of strict law enforcement and narrowly interpreted the rights of prisoners.

With the victory of Republican presidential candidate Warren G. Harding and his choice of another woman (Mabel Walker Willebrandt) to succeed her, Adams returned to San Francisco, where she remained active in state and national party activities. She failed to win election to the board of supervisors, despite an aggressive campaign in 1923. Blaming her loss partially on women who failed to vote, she worked for the inclusion of women in the party organization and won half of the California delegate-at-large seats for women at the 1924 national convention. During Franklin D. Roosevelt's first presidential campaign, she developed Democratic clubs in northern California for the Women's Division of the Democratic National Committee. After his election she was offered the "woman's seat" on the Board of Tax Appeals, to replace the first woman incumbent, Annabel Mathews.

Adams preferred to remain on the West Coast, where she joined Preston in private practice until his appointment to the state Supreme Court. Practicing alone, she earned a respectable income by handling cases in San Francisco for a prominent Redding attorney and by serving as counsel for the state dental board. She won a celebrated case against "Painless Parker," the dentist who set up a string of inexpensive offices to serve poor clients, in 1932. She was also successful in several important public utility and water rights cases. Throughout her career she took stands that were favorable to government regulation of the economy and opposed to expansion of defendant's rights but supportive of equal opportunity for women.

Adams wanted a federal judgeship and organized support among party, legal, and women's groups for appointment to the vacancy in the Northern District in 1935. Instead, Roosevelt offered her a special counsel position in Los Angeles, working under Preston on oil and gas reserve cases. She moved to Los Angeles in 1935 and prepared the trial and appeal briefs that won for the government disputed Elk Hills Naval Oil Reserve land and more than $7 million compensation from Standard Oil Company in 1939.

The political reward of a valuable position finally came in 1942 from Governor Culbert L. Olson, who appointed her presiding justice of the state intermediate appellate court in Sacramento. To secure the position, she had to face the electorate, and in November

1942 she won a twelve-year term. In 1950 she became the first woman to serve on the state supreme court by assignment for one case. When she qualified for a pension in 1952, she retired immediately since her health prevented her from working. She died in Sacramento.

Adams watched her male colleagues receive public offices appropriate to their professional and political contributions, while her returns for great success as a litigator were always in subordinate or collegial positions. Although she was appointed by male politicians as the first woman to serve the public in the U.S. Department of Justice and the California appellate courts, she always felt that her ability, performance, and contributions to the Democratic party merited greater recognition and higher office.

• There are no Adams papers, but letters and documents that cover some aspects of her career can be found in the Jesse W. Carter, William Denman, and James Phelan collections, Bancroft Library, University of California-Berkeley. Information on her U.S. Justice Department jobs in San Francisco, Washington, D.C., and Los Angeles can be found in the records of the department, Criminal Division, at the National Archives and at the auxiliary center in Suitland, Md. Her judicial opinions appear in P2d for 1943–1952. Gladys Morgan, her court reporter, provided some information on her court years in a telephone interview, 10 July 1979. Biographical accounts include Arthur Dunn, "A Portia in the Federal Court," *Sunset Magazine*, Feb. 1915, pp. 334–37; June Hogan, "Annette Abbott Adams, Presiding Justice," the *Trident*, Oct. 1950, pp. 31–32; and Joan M. Jensen, "Annette Abbott Adams, Politician," *Pacific Historical Review* 35 (May 1966): 185–201. An obituary is in the *New York Times*, 27 Oct. 1956.

BEVERLY B. COOK

ADAMS, Ansel (20 Feb. 1902–22 Apr. 1984), photographer and environmentalist, was born in San Francisco, California, the son of Charles Hitchcock Adams, a businessman, and Olive Bray. The grandson of a wealthy timber baron, Adams grew up in a house set amid the sand dunes of the Golden Gate. When Adams was only four, an aftershock of the great earthquake and fire of 1906 threw him to the ground and badly broke his nose, distinctly marking him for life. A year later the family fortune collapsed in the financial panic of 1907, and Adams's father spent the rest of his life doggedly but fruitlessly attempting to recoup.

An only child, Adams was born when his mother was nearly forty. His relatively elderly parents, affluent family history, and the live-in presence of his mother's maiden sister and aged father all combined to create an environment that was decidedly Victorian and both socially and emotionally conservative. Adams's mother spent much of her time brooding and fretting over her husband's inability to restore the Adams fortune, leaving an ambivalent imprint on her son. Charles Adams, on the other hand, deeply and patiently influenced, encouraged, and supported his son.

Natural shyness and a certain intensity of genius, coupled with the dramatically "earthquaked" nose, caused Adams to have problems fitting in at school. In later life he noted that he might have been diagnosed as hyperactive. There is also the distinct possibility that he may have suffered from dyslexia. He was not successful in the various schools to which his parents sent him; consequently, his father and aunt tutored him at home. Ultimately, he managed to earn what he termed a "legitimizing diploma" from the Mrs. Kate M. Wilkins Private School—perhaps equivalent to having completed the eighth grade.

The most important result of Adams's somewhat solitary and unmistakably different childhood was the joy that he found in nature, as evidenced by his taking long walks in the still-wild reaches of the Golden Gate. Nearly every day found him hiking the dunes or meandering along Lobos Creek, down to Baker Beach, or out to the very edge of the American continent.

When Adams was twelve he taught himself to play the piano and read music. Soon he was taking lessons, and the ardent pursuit of music became his substitute for formal schooling. For the next dozen years the piano was Adams's primary occupation and, by 1920, his intended profession. Although he ultimately gave up music for photography, the piano brought substance, discipline, and structure to his frustrating and erratic youth. Moreover, the careful training and exacting craft required of a musician profoundly informed his visual artistry, as well as his influential writings and teachings on photography.

If Adams's love of nature was nurtured on the Golden Gate, his life was, in his words, "colored and modulated by the great earth gesture" of the Yosemite Sierra (Adams, *Yosemite and the Sierra Nevada*, p. xiv). He spent substantial time there every year from 1916 until his death. From his first visit, Adams was transfixed and transformed. He began using the Kodak No. 1 Box Brownie his parents had given him. He hiked, climbed, and explored, gaining self-esteem and self-confidence. In 1919 he joined the Sierra Club and spent the first of four summers in Yosemite Valley, as "keeper" of the club's LeConte Memorial Lodge. He became friends with many of the club's leaders, who were founders of America's nascent conservation movement. He met his wife, Virginia Best, in Yosemite; they were married in 1928. The couple had two children.

The Sierra Club was vital to Adams's early success as a photographer. His first published photographs and writings appeared in the club's 1922 *Bulletin*, and he had his first one-man exhibition in 1928 at the club's San Francisco headquarters. Each summer the club conducted a month-long High Trip, usually in the Sierra Nevada, which attracted up to two hundred members. The participants hiked each day to a new and beautiful campsite accompanied by a large contingent of pack mules, packers, cooks, and the like. As photographer for these outings, in the late 1920s Adams began to realize that he could earn enough to survive—indeed, that he was far more likely to prosper as a photographer than as a concert pianist. By 1934 Adams had been elected to the club's board of directors and was well established as both *the* artist of the Sierra Nevada and *the* defender of Yosemite.

Nineteen twenty-seven was the pivotal year of Adams's life. He made his first fully visualized photograph, *Monolith, the Face of Half Dome*, and took his first High Trip. More important, he came under the influence of Albert M. Bender, a San Francisco insurance magnate and patron of arts and artists. Literally the day after they met, Bender set in motion the preparation and publication of Adams's first portfolio, *Parmelian Prints of the High Sierras* [*sic*]. Bender's friendship, encouragement, and tactful financial support changed Adams's life dramatically. His creative energies and abilities as a photographer blossomed, and he began to have the confidence and wherewithal to pursue his dreams. Indeed, Bender's benign patronage triggered the transformation of a journeyman concert pianist into the artist whose photographs, as critic Abigail Foerstner wrote in the *Chicago Tribune* (3 Dec. 1992), "did for the national parks something comparable to what Homer's epics did for Odysseus."

Although Adams's transition from musician to photographer did not happen at once, his passion shifted rapidly after Bender came into his life, and the projects and possibilities multiplied. In addition to spending summers photographing in the Sierra Nevada, Adams made several lengthy trips to the Southwest to work with Mary Austin, grande dame of the western literati. Their magnificent, limited edition book, *Taos Pueblo*, was published in 1930. In the same year Adams met photographer Paul Strand, whose images had a powerful impact on Adams and helped to move him away from the "pictorial" style he had favored in the 1920s. Adams began to pursue "straight photography," in which the clarity of the lens was emphasized, and the final print gave no appearance of being manipulated in the camera or the darkroom. Adams was soon to become straight photography's most articulate and insistent champion.

In 1927 Adams met photographer Edward Weston. They became increasingly important to each other as friends and colleagues. The renowned Group f/64, founded in 1932, coalesced around the recognized greatness of Weston and the dynamic energy of Adams. Although loosely organized and relatively short-lived, Group f/64 brought the new West Coast vision of straight photography to national attention and influence. San Francisco's DeYoung Museum promptly gave f/64 an exhibition and, in that same year, gave Adams his first one-man museum show.

Adams's star rose rapidly in the early 1930s, propelled in part by his ability and in part by his effusive energy and activity. He made his first visit to New York in 1933, on a pilgrimage to meet photographer Alfred Stieglitz, the artist whose work and philosophy Adams most admired and whose life of commitment to the medium he consciously emulated. Their relationship was intense and their correspondence frequent, rich, and insightful. Although profoundly a man of the West, Adams spent a considerable amount of time in New York during the 1930s and 1940s, and the Stieglitz circle played a vital role in his artistic life. In 1933 the Delphic Gallery gave Adams his first New York show. His first series of technical articles was published in *Camera Craft* in 1934, and his first widely distributed book, *Making a Photograph*, appeared in 1935. Most important, in 1936 Stieglitz gave Adams a one-man show at An American Place.

Recognition, however, did not alleviate Adams's financial pressures. In a letter dated 6 August 1935 he wrote Weston, "I have been busy, but broke. Can't seem to climb over the financial fence." Adams was compelled to spend much of his time as a commercial photographer. Clients ran the gamut, including the Yosemite concessionaire, the National Park Service, Kodak, Zeiss, IBM, AT&T, a small women's college, a dried-fruit company, and *Life*, *Fortune*, and *Arizona Highways* magazines—in short, everything from portraits to catalogues to Coloramas. On 2 July 1938 he wrote to a friend David McAlpin, "I have to do something in the relatively near future to regain the right track in photography. I am literally swamped with "commercial" work—necessary for practical reasons, but very restraining to my creative work." Although Adams became an unusually skilled commercial photographer, the work was intermittent, and he constantly worried about paying the next month's bills. His financial situation remained precarious and a source of considerable stress until late in life.

Adams's technical mastery was the stuff of legend. More than any creative photographer, before or since, he reveled in the theory and practice of the medium. Weston and Strand frequently consulted him for technical advice. He served as principal photographic consultant to Polaroid and Hasselblad and, informally, to many other photographic concerns. Adams developed the famous and highly complex "zone system" of controlling and relating exposure and development, enabling photographers to creatively visualize an image and then produce a photograph that matched and expressed that visualization. He produced ten volumes of technical manuals on photography, which are the most influential books ever written on the subject.

Adams's energy and capacity for work were simply colossal. He often labored for eighteen or more hours per day, for days and weeks on end. There were no vacations, no holidays, no Sundays in Ansel Adams's life. Frequently, after an intense period of work, he would return to San Francisco or Yosemite, promptly contract the "flu," and spend several days in bed. His hyperkinetic existence was also fueled by alcohol, for which he had a particular fondness, and a constant whirl of social activity, friends, and colleagues. As Beaumont Newhall writes in his *FOCUS: Memoirs of a Life in Photography* (1993), "Ansel was a great party man and loved to entertain. He had a very dominating personality, and would always be the center of attention" (p. 235).

Adams described himself as a photographer-lecturer-writer. It would perhaps be more accurate to say that he was simply—indeed, compulsively—a communicator. He endlessly traveled the country in pursuit of both the natural beauty he revered and photographed and the audiences he required. Adams felt an intense commitment to promoting photography as a fine art and played a key role in the establishment of the first museum department of photography, at the Museum of Modern Art in New York. The work at the museum fostered the closest relationships of Adams's life, with Beaumont and Nancy Newhall, a historian and museum administrator and a writer-designer, respectively. Their partnership was arguably the most potent collaboration in twentieth-century photography. In the 1950s and 1960s Nancy Newhall and Adams created a number of books and exhibitions of historic significance, particularly the Sierra Club's *This Is the American Earth* (1960), which, with Rachel Carson's classic *Silent Spring*, played a seminal role in launching the first broad-based citizen environmental movement.

Adams was an unremitting activist for the cause of wilderness and the environment. Over the years he attended innumerable meetings and wrote thousands of letters in support of his conservation philosophy to newspaper editors, Sierra Club and Wilderness Society colleagues, government bureaucrats, and politicians. However, his great influence came from his photography. His images became the symbols, the veritable icons, of wild America. When people thought about the national parks or the Sierra Club or nature or the environment itself, they often envisioned them in terms of an Ansel Adams photograph. His black-and-white images were not "realistic" documents of nature. Instead, they sought an intensification and purification of the psychological experience of natural beauty. He created a sense of the sublime magnificence of nature that infused the viewer with the emotional equivalent of wilderness, often more powerful than the actual thing.

For Adams, the environmental issues of particular importance were Yosemite National Park, the national park system, and, above all, the preservation of wilderness. He focused on what he termed the spiritual-emotional aspect of parks and wilderness and relentlessly resisted the Park Service's "resortism," which had led to the overdevelopment of the national parks and their domination by private concessionaires. But the range of issues in which Adams involved himself was encyclopedic. He fought for new parks and wilderness areas, for the Wilderness Act, for wild Alaska and his beloved Big Sur coast of central California, for the mighty redwoods, for endangered sea lions and sea otters, and for clean air and water. An advocate of balanced, restrained use of resources, Adams also fought relentlessly against overbuilt highways, billboards, and all manner of environmental mendacity and shortsightedness. Yet he invariably treated his opponents with respect and courtesy.

Though wilderness and the environment were his grand passions, photography was his calling, his *métier*, his *raison d'être*. Adams never made a creative photograph specifically for environmental purposes. On 12 April 1977 he wrote to his publisher, Tim Hill, "I know I shall be castigated by a large group of the people of today, but I was trained to assume that art related to the elusive quality of beauty and that the purpose of art was concerned with the elevation of the spirit (horrible Victorian notion!!)." Adams was often criticized for failing to include humans or evidence of "humanity" in his landscape photographs. The great French photographer Henri Cartier-Bresson made the well-known comment that "the world is falling to pieces and all Adams and Weston photograph is rocks and trees" (quoted by Adams, Oral History, Univ. of Calif., Berkeley, p. 498). Reviewers frequently characterize Adams as a photographer of an idealized wilderness that no longer exists. On the contrary, the places that Adams photographed are, with few exceptions, precisely those wilderness and park areas that have been preserved for all time. There is a vast amount of true and truly protected wilderness in America, much of it saved because of the efforts of Adams and his colleagues.

Seen in a more traditional art history context, Adams was the last and defining figure in the romantic tradition of nineteenth-century American landscape painting and photography. Adams always claimed that he was not "influenced," but, consciously or unconsciously, he was firmly in the tradition of Thomas Cole, Frederick Church, Albert Bierstadt, Carleton Watkins, and Eadweard Muybridge. And he was the direct philosophical heir of the American Transcendentalists Ralph Waldo Emerson, Henry David Thoreau, and John Muir. He grew up in a time and place where his zeitgeist was formed by the presidency of Theodore Roosevelt and "muscular" Americanism, by the pervading sense of manifest destiny, and the notion that European civilization was being reinvented—much for the better—in the new nation and, particularly, in the new West. Adams died in Monterey, California.

As John Szarkowski states in the introduction to Adams's *Classic Images* (1985), "The love that Americans poured out for the work and person of Ansel Adams during his old age, and that they have continued to express with undiminished enthusiasm since his death, is an extraordinary phenomenon, perhaps even one unparalleled in our country's response to a visual artist" (p. 5). Why should this be so? What generated this remarkable response? Adams's subject matter, the magnificent natural beauty of the West, was absolutely, unmistakably American, and his chosen instrument, the camera, was a quintessential artifact of twentieth-century culture. He was blessed with an unusually generous, charismatic personality, and his great faith in people and human nature was amply rewarded. Adams channeled his energies in ways that served his fellow citizens, personified in his lifelong effort to preserve the American wilderness. Above all, Adams's philosophy and optimism struck a chord in the national psyche. More than any other influential American of his epoch, Adams believed in both the possibility and the probability of humankind living in harmony and balance with its environment. It is difficult to imagine Ansel Adams occurring in a European country or culture and equally difficult to conjure an artist more completely American, either in art or personality.

• Adams's vast archive of papers, memorabilia, correspondence, negatives, and many "fine" photographic prints, as well as numerous "work" or proof prints, are in the John P. Schaefer Center for Creative Photography at the University of Arizona, Tucson. A portion of his papers relating to the Sierra Club are in the Bancroft Library at the University of California, Berkeley. Adams's *Ansel Adams: An Autobiography* (1985) was unfinished at the time of his death and was subsequently completed by Mary Street Alinder, his editor. *An Autobiography* offers a somewhat rose-colored and selective view of Adams's life. A selection of correspondence, *Letters and Images* (1988), contains a small but interesting fraction of the estimated 100,000 letters and cards that Adams wrote during his lifetime. He wrote and contributed photographs to hundreds of articles and reviews from 1922 until 1984. He published eight portfolios of original photographic prints (1927, 1948, 1950, 1960, 1963, 1970, 1974, and 1976). Nearly four dozen books bear Adams's name as author and/or artist. Those not mentioned in the article include *Sierra Nevada: The John Muir Trail* (1938); *Michael and Anne in Yosemite Valley* (1941); *Born Free and Equal* (1944); *Illustrated Guide to Yosemite Valley* (1946); *Camera and Lens* (1948); *The Negative* (1948); *Yosemite and the High Sierra* (1948); *The Print* (1950); *My Camera in Yosemite Valley* (1950); *My Camera in the National Parks* (1950); *The Land of Little Rain* (1950, new ed. with Adams's photographs); *Natural Light Photography* (1952); *Death Valley* (1954); *Mission San Xavier del Bac* (1954); *The Pageant of History in Northern California* (1954); *Artificial Light Photography* (1956); *The Islands of Hawaii* (1958); *Yosemite Valley* (1959); *Death Valley and the Creek Called Furnace* (1962); *These We Inherit: The Parklands of America* (1962); *Polaroid Land Photography Manual* (1963); *An Introduction to Hawaii* (1964); *Fiat Lux: The University of California* (1967); *The Tetons and the Yellowstone* (1970); *Ansel Adams* (1972); *Singular Images* (1974); *Ansel Adams: Images 1923–1974* (1974); *Photographs of the Southwest* (1976); *The Portfolios of Ansel Adams* (1977); *Polaroid Land Photography* (1978); *Yosemite and the Range of Light* (1979); a new technical series, including *The Camera* (1980), *The Negative* (1981), and *The Print* (1983); *Examples: The Making of 40 Photographs* (1983); and, posthumously, Andrea G. Stillman, ed., *The American Wilderness* (1990); Stillman and William A. Turnage, eds., *Our National Parks* (1992); Harry M. Callahan, ed., *Ansel Adams in Color* (1993); and Stillman, ed., *Ansel Adams: Yosemite and the High Sierra* (1994). More than a decade after his death, there was still no biography covering his entire life. Nancy Newhall, *Ansel Adams: The Eloquent Light* (1963), is a relatively short and adoring biography of Adams's first thirty-six years, written with zest and insight, as well as Adams's full collaboration.

William A. Turnage

ADAMS, Brooks (24 June 1848–13 Feb. 1927), historian, was born in Quincy, Massachusetts, the son of Charles Francis Adams, a U.S. congressman and ambassador to Great Britain, and Abigail Brown Brooks. Educated in England during the American Civil War, he returned home in 1865, entered Harvard College the following year, and graduated in 1870 in spite of being convicted of plagiarism. After studying at Harvard Law School in 1870 and 1871, Adams joined his father in Geneva, Switzerland, to work on the Alabama Claims Arbitration, settling maritime claims arising from Civil War raiding. After some travel around Europe, he returned to Boston and opened a law practice. His main interest throughout the 1870s was reform politics. In Boston's Commonwealth Club and in articles for the *North American Review* and the *Atlantic Monthly*, Adams worked for numerous Liberal Republican causes, including municipal reform and tax reduction. He served on the Boston School Committee in the late 1870s and lectured at Harvard Law School in 1882 and 1883. He married Evelyn Davis on 7 September 1889; they had no children.

Adams's first major work, *The Emancipation of Massachusetts* (1887), was a self-proclaimed "new departure" in American history writing. Rejecting the traditional Puritan-centered historiography of his native state, Adams focused instead on the generation of the American Revolution. Skeptical of the religious leadership of the colonial clergy, he hailed the legacy of secular legalism dating back to his great-grandfather, John Adams. The book articulated a progressive vision of American history while also giving voice to an early form of American social Darwinism. *The Gold Standard: An Historical Study* (1894), Adams's first attempt to systematize the study of history, was an important contribution to the fierce debate over the money question. While vehemently attacking the gold standard, Adams supported a policy of moderate bimetallism, in which the value of currency is based on both gold and silver reserves.

Law of Civilization and Decay (1895), Adams's most ambitious book, was inspired by the economic collapse of 1893, the resulting wave of class conflict, and Adams's near loss of his substantial personal fortune amid the rampant speculation of the Gilded Age. Charles Beard wrote a half-century later, in an introduction to the 1943 edition, that the book represented "the first extended attempt on the part of an American thinker to reduce universal history or at least Western history to a single formula or body of formulas conceived in the spirit of modern science." Adams argued that history was an endless series of cycles, beginning with barbarism, then moving to civilization before returning to barbarism. "Decay" was the unavoidable result of the civilizing process. Influenced by John Ruskin and by his own brother Henry Adams, among others, he proclaimed the "approaching disintegration" of European civilization. Adams gave voice to a strong current of fin-de-siècle pessimism. His conservative materialism influenced Theodore Roosevelt and Henry Cabot Lodge. Between 1896 and 1898 Adams spent much time in Washington, becoming close to Roosevelt, then assistant secretary of the navy. In 1898, remarking on the Spanish-American War, Adams claimed, "Our Spanish war marked the passage of the Atlantic by the centre of force, and velocity of movement. America is now the great point toward which all movement gravitates" (letter of 12 Nov. 1899, quoted in Beringause). Adams would soon become a leading advocate of American imperialism.

America's Economic Supremacy (1900) announced the emergence of the United States as the leading world power in the new century. The work was largely influenced by Admiral Alfred Thayer Mahan's *The Interest of America in Sea Power, Present and Future* (1897). Adams called for the construction of a canal across Panama and also linked America's economic progress and future imperial possibilities to its supremacy in East Asia. All these themes came together in *The New Empire* (1902). While writing this book, Adams came to view war "as much an instrument of economic competition as trade." One result of *The New Empire* was Adams's ascendance to a position of influence in Theodore Roosevelt's White House, starting in 1903. Beginning in 1907 he also taught at the Boston University School of Law.

His last book, *Theory of Social Revolutions* (1913), was colored by Adams's growing disillusionment with the promise of the new century. His "last speech and confession" was devoted to lengthy attacks on the capitalist class in America and the politicization of the courts. Adams did not so much advocate reform as proclaim the inevitable disintegration of American civilization. Defending Theodore Roosevelt's failed 1912 presidential campaign, Adams called for the creation of a viable third party and demanded thorough judicial reform. His final public service occurred in 1917, when he was elected to the Massachusetts Constitutional Convention. His pronouncements at the convention were extreme: he argued that "democracy ought to and must perish"; in order "to carry on anything great," he asserted that America needed "to establish something close to dictatorship." In 1920 he edited a collection of his brother Henry's writings, *The Degradation of the Democratic Dogma*. His pessimism grew more and more virulent in his last years. He saw Communist conspiracies all around him, from the League of Nations to one led by Secretary of Commerce Herbert Hoover. He died in Boston.

Adams was an important voice in American culture from the Gilded Age to the end of the Progressive Era. As a prophet of American imperialism, he combined a faith in the nation's progress with a profound despair about modern society.

• Some of Adams's papers are at the Massachusetts Historical Society in Boston and at the Houghton Library, Harvard University. The most important evaluations of his career are Thornton Anderson, *Brooks Adams: Constructive Conservative* (1951); Arthur F. Beringause, *Brooks Adams: A Biography* (1955); and Timothy Paul Donovan, *Henry Adams and Brooks Adams: The Education of Two American Historians* (1961).

DAVID QUIGLEY

ADAMS, Charles (19 Dec. 1845–19 Aug. 1895), soldier and diplomat, was born Karl Adam Schwanbeck in Anclam, Pomerania, Germany, the son of Karl Heinrich Schwanbeck, a cabinetmaker, and Maria J. Markman. Adams was educated at the Gymnasium in Anclam and graduated with very high marks, especially in Greek, Hebrew, and Latin. Soon after his graduation in 1862, he moved to the United States. He had not been in the New World long before he enlisted in the Union army, serving in the Sixth Massachusetts Regiment. He fought in the Civil War for the remainder of the conflict and was wounded two times.

At the end of the war Adams enlisted in the regular army, serving in the Third U.S. Cavalry. Throughout 1868–1869 he fought the Comanche and Kiowa Indians in Texas and New Mexico. In 1870, having moved to Denver to rest his war-wounded lungs, he was appointed brigadier general of the Colorado territorial militia by Governor Edward M. McCook. In May 1872 he was appointed Ute Indian agent upon McCook's recommendation. Prior to taking this position, in 1871 Adams married Margaret Thompson Phelps, a sister of Governor McCook's wife and the mother of a son from a previous marriage. Adams's wife influenced his decision to change his name from Schwanbeck to Adams, which was accomplished by the Colorado legislature in 1871.

In June 1872, Adams arrived at the Los Pinos Agency, Colorado. At the time, the Utes maintained an uneasy balance with white Coloradans. With mining developments on the borders of their homelands, the Utes hunted in their traditional ways but were forced to accept rations from the government to supplement the increasingly scarce game. At the time Adams assumed office, the Utes were being accused of depredations, and Adams found them apprehensive and in fear of an attack. After working hard to calm their fears and gain their confidence, he undertook the task of building an infrastructure within their reservation. Adams hoped that farming would supplement their food supply. Before winter, hay was being cured, a sawmill was running, the cattle were properly tended, and a school was built and in operation. During his two years as director of the Los Pinos Agency, he cemented a personal friendship with a famous Ute chief named Ouray. This relationship, combined with his administrative activities, helped Adams to gain the respect of all of the Ute tribes. During Adams's time at the agency, mineral deposits were discovered on Ute land in the San Juan Mountains. These discoveries precipitated the Brunot Agreement, the terms of which Adams had a large responsibility in negotiating. In the agreement the Utes ceded a rectangular chunk of land out of their reservation, the San Juan country, which comprises several counties in present-day Colorado, leaving them with land along the southern and western borders of Colorado Territory. In 1874 Adams left his post at the Office of Indian Affairs to become a post office inspector of routes in Colorado and New Mexico. He was reportedly relentless in his efforts to find and punish people responsible for postal fraud and mismanagement. He achieved some measure of political influence by organizing the German vote for Governor Frederick W. Pitkin in the 1878 election; he also insisted that the state of Colorado print its laws in German in addition to English and Spanish, thus ingratiating himself with naturalized Germans.

Adams's activities as post office inspector were interrupted in October 1879 by an uprising by the Utes of White River. Nathan Meeker, the agent in charge of the White River Agency, wanted to build an agricultural paradise inhabited by Indians. The Utes, however, felt confined and oppressed by Meeker's efforts. When they started leaving the area, Meeker called for help from the army. The army's approach triggered the uprising, which resulted in Meeker and all of his employees at the White River Agency being massacred; five women and children were taken hostage. The consequence was the "Ute War" of 1879, and Secretary of the Interior Carl Schurz, on behalf of the administration of President Rutherford B. Hayes, selected Adams to lead the efforts to resolve the problem. He did not disappoint those who commissioned him; after working diligently for five months, he recovered the hostages, arrested the massacre's leaders, and negotiated a treaty with the Utes. Adams's efforts prevented the extermination of the Utes by Governor Pitkin's Colorado Militia. His relationship with Chief Ouray was seen as instrumental in his achievements. In the treaty, signed in 1880, the Utes lost all of their remaining land claims in Colorado except for a small strip of territory in the southwestern part of the state, and they conceded to move to land in Utah.

As a reward for his efforts in solving the Ute problem, Adams was named U.S. minister to Bolivia by President Hayes in 1880. At the time, Bolivia was at war with Chile; thus Adams represented the United States in the conferences held at Arica, Chile, to resolve the dispute. He resigned as minister in 1882 and returned to his position as postal inspector, where he took charge of the Colorado District. He held this position for three years, until President Grover Cleveland removed him, citing "offensive partisanship." In 1888 he became one of the founders of the Colorado City Glass Works, and he also had interests in mining and mineral water development. Adams died in an explosion at the Gumry Hotel in Denver, Colorado.

• Government records that document Adams's work include U.S. Senate, *Report of the Ute Commission of 1880*, 46th Cong., Senate executive doc. 31; the *Annual Reports* of the Departments of War and Interior for 1865–1900; and the *Annual Reports* of the Board of Indian Commissioners for 1870–1880. Sidney Jocknick, *Early Days on the Western Slope of Colorado* (1913), includes extensive material on Adams's interaction with the Utes. See also Frank Hall, *History of Colorado* (4 vols., 1889–1895). For information on the Utes and the White River massacre, see Marshall Sprague, *Massacre: The Tragedy at White River* (1957); Val J. McClellan, *This Is Our Land*, vol. 1 (1977); and Robert G. Athearn, *The Coloradans* (1976). A useful account of the history of Colo. is Carl Abbot et al., *Colorado: A History of the Centennial State* (1994). An obituary in the *Rocky Mountain News*, 20 Aug. 1895, includes a synopsis of Adams's life.

KATHRYN D. SNAVELY

ADAMS, Charles Baker (11 Jan. 1814–18 Jan. 1853), naturalist and educator, was born in Dorchester, Massachusetts, the son of Charles J. Adams, a Boston merchant, and Hannah Baker. At an early age Adams showed great interest and ability in natural history and chemistry. His parents encouraged him by setting aside a room for his rocks and fossils and the apparatus he used for chemistry experiments. He began his formal education at Boston schools and then attended Phillips Academy in Andover before entering Yale College in 1830. After a year at Yale he transferred to Amherst College, where he flourished, graduating in 1834 with highest honors. He entered the Theological Seminary at Andover with the intention of preparing for the ministry, but he left in 1836 to assist professor Edward Hitchcock of Amherst College in a geological survey of New York State. When Hitchcock resigned from the survey because of ill health, Adams also left and returned to Amherst to serve as tutor and lecturer in geology and chemistry.

Adams married Mary Holmes of New Bedford, Massachusetts, in February 1839. They had six children, one of whom died in infancy. In 1838 Adams was appointed professor of chemistry and natural history at Middlebury College in Vermont; he earned the reputation of a very able and popular teacher. During his time at Middlebury he became the state geologist of Vermont (1845). He published annual reports and collected large samples of rocks, shells, and soil while compiling a complete geological survey of the state. At the same time Adams developed an interest in tropical zoology, stimulated by the rich variety of mollusks he observed and collected during a visit to Jamaica in the winter of 1843–1844. In 1847 he gave up his position at Middlebury because the harsh Vermont climate was too taxing and he had become disenchanted with his position. Discouraged by the lack of proper funding from the state legislature of Vermont for the annual geological reports—the report for 1847 consisted of only eight pages—he abandoned his work in geology in favor of studying the taxonomy and geological distribution of mollusks.

Adams was welcomed back to Amherst College in 1847 to fill the position of professor of zoology and astronomy, created especially for him because there was no opening in natural history at the time. Amherst was happy to establish a position for Adams; in addition to his splendid record as an undergraduate, he added to the college's resources his extensive collection of shells—4,500 species—and geological specimens. He also set up a trust, the Natural History Fund, which was designed to fund and administer his original gift, ensuring its maintenance and expansion after his death. Amherst, like other elite American colleges of this period, sought competent scientists with field or laboratory experience to help build their science departments and to shift their curricula from classical education to reflect the growing interest in natural history and other sciences.

Adams became curator of the college's natural-history collections, then called its "cabinet." He spent his initial years at Amherst methodically arranging and labeling the items in the cabinet, a painstaking job which he accomplished with great skill, and teaching undergraduate chemistry and natural history. Adams was an effective and erudite instructor who wove details of the latest scientific discoveries into his teaching, in a style marked by dry, sardonic wit. When he returned to Jamaica during the winter of 1848–1849 he did further collecting, adding more specimens to the already well-stocked cabinet. In November 1850 he journeyed to Panama and was struck by its unusual variety of invertebrate animals, particularly mollusks. As a result of this expedition he collected additional material for the Amherst College Cabinet and published *Catalogue of Shells Collected at Panama with Notes on Their Synonymy, Station, and Habitat* (1852), a thorough list of the mollusks he discovered there.

Adams wrote many articles on mollusks for natural-history journals during his years at Middlebury and Amherst. Most of these papers incorporated the results of his work in Jamaica and other tropical and subtropical settings, and he became one of the most important authorities in conchology, a branch of invertebrate zoology concerned with shells. In addition to his work on the mollusks of Panama, his other significant study was *Contributions to Conchology*, published in twelve parts between 1849 and 1852.

Eager to continue his work on tropical mollusks, Adams left on another excursion to the West Indies in 1852, traveling to St. Thomas by way of Bermuda. The voyage from Bermuda to St. Thomas was stormy, and he arrived fatigued but excited by the variety of shells he had found in Bermuda (between forty and fifty new species). He was eager to start his explorations for mollusk specimens on St. Thomas, but he contracted yellow fever and died a week after his thirty-ninth birthday. Before he left on his final trip to the tropics, Adams had been asked to analyze the shells collected during the exploration of the Red River of Louisiana, under the direction of Captain Randolph B. Marcy of the U.S. Army. Adams's report on the shells appeared in the appendix to *Exploration of the Red River of Louisiana in the Year 1852* (1854); in his introduction to this work Marcy paid tribute to one of the last scientific efforts of "this distinguished conchologist."

Adams made major contributions to invertebrate taxonomy and biogeography, describing approximately 800 species of mollusks. His collection at the natural history museum at Amherst College was significant for its diversity and quantity, and it remained there for nearly ninety years until it was deposited in the Museum of Comparative Zoology at Harvard University in 1942. In addition to these specimens, his books and articles in conchology remain excellent sources of information for zoologists. His taxonomic studies of mollusks and their geographical distribution convinced him that species were not immutable, and although he rejected the Lamarckian model of evolution, his writings reveal that he would have been sympathetic to some model of evolution, perhaps one closer to Charles Darwin's theory, had he lived long enough to develop his ideas. Darwin referred to Adams's work on mollusks in a letter of February 1853 to the geologist Charles Lyell, commenting that Adams was as "heterodox" as himself. Adams's early work in geology held some promise, but his surveys of Vermont diminished in importance, and he did not follow up his initial work in the field. His lone contribution after he left Middlebury was *Elements of Geology* (1853), a text he wrote with Alonzo Gray, a classmate and professorial colleague at Amherst, and completed shortly before Adams's death. He was a member of a number of professional societies, notably the Association of American Geologists, the Boston Society of Natural History, the Philadelphia Academy of Natural Science, the Lyceum of Natural History of New York, and the American Academy of Arts and Sciences.

• A complete list of Adams's articles on mollusks is in George W. Tryon, Jr., *List of American Writers on Recent Conchology* (1861); see also W. G. Binney, "Bibliography of North American Conchology," *Smithsonian Miscellaneous Collections* 5 (1863–1864), and William T. Clench and Ruth D. Turner, "The Western Atlantic Marine Mollusks Described by C. B. Adams," *Occasional Papers on Mollusks* 1 (1950). Biographical references include Henry Baxter Adams, *History of Thomas Adams and Thomas Hastings Families of Amherst, Massachusetts* (1880); Thomas Bland, "Memoir of Charles B. Adams, Late Professor of Zoology in Amherst College, Massachusetts," *American Journal of Conchology* 1 (1865): 191–204; William H. Dall, "Some American Conchologists," *Proceedings of the Biological Society of Washington* 4 (1886–1888): 123–26; Stanley M. Guralnick, *Science and the Ante-Bellum American College* (1975); Edward Hitchcock, *Reminiscences of Amherst College, Historical, Scientific, Biographical, and Autobiographical* (1863); George P. Merrill, *The First Hundred Years of American Geology* (1924); Henry Seely, "Sketch of the Life and Work of Charles Baker Adams," *American Geologist* 32 (1903): 1–12; and William S. Tyler, *History of Amherst College during Its First Half Century* (1873).

JOEL S. SCHWARTZ

ADAMS, Charles Follen (21 Apr. 1842–8 Mar. 1918), dialect poet, was born in Dorchester, Massachusetts, the son of Ira Adams, the warden of Boston Common, and Mary Elizabeth Senter. Adams was of New England stock, a descendant of the revolutionary patriot Samuel Adams; his mother's and father's families were among the first settlers of Center Harbor and Meredith, New Hampshire, respectively. He completed his education at the age of fifteen as a graduate of the Everett School in Dorchester and began employment with a dry goods firm in Boston, where he remained for five years.

Adams's Civil War service was the first major event of his life. In August 1862 he enlisted for two years with the Thirteenth Massachusetts Infantry and served on the front lines, beginning at the second battle of Manassas. He saw action at Fredericksburg and Chancellorsville and was wounded and taken prisoner on the first day of the battle of Gettysburg. Three days later he was liberated when Union troops recaptured the town. After recovering from his wounds, he spent the final year of his enlistment serving on hospital duty in Washington, D.C.

Adams returned to Boston in 1864 and established his own successful dry goods firm. In 1870 he married

Harriet Louise Mills, the daughter of a Boston railroad official; they had two children. His literary career was primarily an avocation and began in 1872 with the publication of the German dialect poem "The Puzzled Dutchman," which appeared in *Our Young Folks*, edited by J. T. Trowbridge. His success in the genre of dialect poetry is linked in part to the appeal of Charles Godfrey Leland's "Hans Breitmann" ballads, then at the height of their popularity. This initial favorable reception paved the way for Adams's occasional contributions to Boston newspapers, *Harper's Magazine*, *Scribner's Monthly*, *Oliver's Optic Magazine*, and other popular journals. His work began to receive national recognition in 1876 with the publication of his best-known poem, "Leedle Yawcob Strauss," in the *Detroit Free Press*. The poem's instant popularity resulted in its reprinting throughout the United States and in England.

Adams's dialect poems focus on the trials, tribulations, and joys of domestic life, and they are phrased in a Germanized English reminiscent of Pennsylvania Dutch in both pronunciation and syntax. While other New Englanders, including his own distant relative John Quincy Adams, had exhibited an affinity for high German culture as early as the eighteenth century, Adams, who was named for the German patriot Charles Follen, had his initial contact with German through listening to the dialect spoken by his parents' washerwoman. Adams's knowledge of what was then generally called "scrapple English" (after the popular Pennsylvania Dutch breakfast dish) had been broadened through his service with German emigrant and Pennsylvania Dutch soldiers among his fellow Union troops.

The immense popularity of "Leedle Yawcob Strauss" created a strong demand for Adams's poetry, and, within the limits of his business obligations, he continued to turn out a steady flow of verse for such leading journals as *Harper's Magazine*. Although he wrote primarily in the evenings after devoting himself to business during the day, his efforts evoked strong encouragement from leading authors, including Henry Wadsworth Longfellow, John Greenleaf Whittier, and Oliver Wendell Holmes. In fact, Holmes wrote him "many keenly appreciative letters" encouraging his entry into the field of dialect poetry. Adams's first collection of verse was published in 1877 as *Leedle Yawcob Strauss and Other Poems*, followed by *Dialect Ballads* in 1888. A complete collection is contained in *Yawcob Strauss and Other Poems*, which appeared in 1910 and featured more than 100 illustrations attributed to Morgan J. "Boz" Sweeney.

While none of Adams's later poems reached the popularity of "Leedle Yawcob Strauss," its companion piece, "Dot Leedle Loweeza," was another favorite of the public. The two poems were perhaps inspired by Adams's son, Charles Mills Adams, and his daughter, Ella Adams Sawyer. Domestic relations also frame such other poems as "Der Oak und der Vine" and "Vas Marriage a Failure?" His parody of "The Old Oaken Bucket," titled "Dot Long-Handled Dipper," and "Der Vater Mill" were two of his better known and most successful lighthearted pieces. The best of his poems succeeded not only from his deft handling of the dialect and keen sense of both humor and pathos, but also from his use of surprising twists in the final stanza—which, as Holmes commented of "Leedle Yawcob Strauss," "moistened thousands of eyes, these old ones of mine among the rest." While his collected poems include such nondialect verse as "Sequel to the 'One-Horse Shay'" (a response to his favorite Holmes poem) and the temperance piece "John Barley Corn, My Foe," it was his dialect poetry and his dramatic readings of it that kept him, according to an obituary in the *Boston Globe*, "in constant demand as a lecturer and reader" for the last twenty years of his life. He died in Roxbury, Massachusetts.

Adams's minor but unique position in American letters is clearly owing to the popularity of his German dialect poetry with the audience of the time. The empathetic chord struck by the simple domestic themes in his verse required no translation, and his poetry retained its popularity until changing tastes in the early twentieth century led to a decline in popularity for dialect literature in general (e.g., James Whitcomb Riley, Paul Laurence Dunbar, and Joel Chandler Harris). Furthermore, the American entry into World War I made the benevolent image of the German portrayed in Adams's verse seem curiously outdated. The day after his death, the *New York Herald* published a copy of "Leedle Yawcob Strauss," noting that Adams's most famous poem "honored the German as we knew him before the days of submarine outrages, liquid fire and poison gas."

• The largest collection of Adams's correspondence, lecture notes, and manuscripts is found at the Houghton Library of Harvard University. The remainder is scattered over numerous locations, including the Boston Public Library; the American Antiquarian Society, Worcester, Mass.; the Barrett collection at the Alderman Library of the University of Virginia, Charlottesville; the Dickey manuscripts at the Lilly Library of Indiana University, Bloomington; and the Butler Library of Columbia University. Major biographical and critical sources include John C. Rand, *One of a Thousand* (1890), and Ralph Davol, "New England Humorists," *New England Magazine*, n.s., 33 (1905–1906): 675–77. Obituaries are in the *New York Herald* and the *Boston Globe*, 9 Mar. 1918.

GEOFFREY ORTH

ADAMS, Charles Francis (18 Aug. 1807–21 Nov. 1886), politician and diplomat, was born in Boston, Massachusetts, the son of John Quincy Adams (1767–1848) and Louisa Catherine Johnson. In 1827, two years after graduating from Harvard, Adams read law at the office of Daniel Webster, and in January 1829 he was admitted to the Massachusetts bar. Although he opened a law office in Boston, his primary interests were scholarly, and between 1829 and 1845 he published several extended reviews of works on British and American history in the prestigious *North American Review*. During this period he also began editing the letters of his grandmother, Abigail Adams, which he published between 1840 and 1848, commenced work on the papers of his grandfather, John Adams (1735–1826), and wrote essays on various historical topics.

In September 1829 Adams married Abigail Brooks, the daughter of a wealthy Boston merchant. The marriage allowed Adams to raise a family of six children, devote himself to literature and scholarship, and later engage in politics and diplomacy.

Adams's political career began in 1832 when he formally joined the Massachusetts Antimasonic party, which had arisen out of popular resentment of the secret and exclusive Masonic order and in 1831 had outpolled the Democrats in state elections. Adams, believing that Masonry violated traditional religious principles and threatened American society and institutions, promoted the party through newspaper articles and served as a delegate at state Antimasonic conventions in 1833 and 1834. After 1834, the Antimasons were absorbed by the Democratic party. Adams, who resented the state's elite Whig leaders' longstanding hostility toward his father and doubted their commitment to republican principles, appealed to Antimasons to vote for Democrat Martin Van Buren in the 1836 presidential election. Adams also opposed the selection of Daniel Webster, the local favorite, for the Whig nomination. Adams refused to follow his fellow Antimasons into the Democratic party and between 1838 and 1840 wrote several political essays criticizing Van Buren's policies that won the approval of Whig leaders.

Until 1835, Adams had not paid much attention to slavery, which he had regarded as a southern institution protected by the Constitution. But attempts in Massachusetts to deny free speech to abolitionists and attempts to prevent John Quincy Adams and others from presenting antislavery petitions to Congress by passage of the gag rule in 1836 convinced him that slavery threatened constitutional rights throughout the nation. When the independent Republic of Texas sought annexation to the United States in 1837, Adams became convinced that the move was part of a conspiracy by an "aggressive slavocracy." His antislavery and anti-Texas views led Whigs to urge him to run for the Massachusetts House of Representatives in 1838 and 1839. He agreed to do so only in 1840 and was easily elected. He served until 1843, when he won election to the state senate, where he served until 1845.

In the legislature, Adams quickly established himself as the leader of a small antislavery faction. In 1842 he presented a number of antislavery petitions to the legislature and sought passage of measures designed to prevent Massachusetts from participating in the seizure and extradition of runaway slaves. In 1843 he led the Whig opposition to a revived movement to annex Texas.

Adams's involvement in the anti-Texas movement in Massachusetts brought him into conflict with the Whig leadership. Initially, all Whigs opposed the annexation of Texas, but some, particularly those involved in textile manufacturing, who depended on southern cotton, preferred a restrained program that would not embarrass their southern Whig colleagues or jeopardize their economic relationships with southerners. When Congress passed a joint resolution for annexation in January 1845, conservative Whigs conceded defeat, but Adams, continuing the struggle, gathered anti-Texas petitions and promoted state resolutions against annexation. He also joined with abolitionists in an attempt to convince congressmen to reject Texas's application for statehood. The effort ended only when Congress admitted Texas to the Union in December 1845.

Adams's association with abolitionists and his separation from conservative Whigs marked the beginning of his movement out of the Whig party. From 1846 to 1848 he edited the Boston *Whig*, the organ of party dissidents who became known as the "Conscience Whigs." Adams maintained a relentless assault on "Cotton Whig" party leaders and the "aggressive slavocracy." The rift between the conservative Cotton Whigs and the Conscience Whigs widened, and in 1848, unwilling to support the Whig presidential nominee, Zachary Taylor, Adams called for a separate Conscience Whig convention.

In August 1848 the Conscience Whigs joined with other like-minded Whig and Democratic groups and abolitionists from seventeen northern states to form the Free-Soil party. Adams chaired the convention, held in Buffalo, New York, which chose Martin Van Buren and Adams as the new party's presidential and vice presidential candidates to campaign on a platform of "Free Soil, Free Speech, Free Labor, and Free Men." The Free-Soilers were soundly defeated in the election of 1848, and Adams returned to editing *The Works of John Adams*, which were published in ten volumes between 1850 and 1856.

During the 1850s, Whigs, Free-Soilers, Democrats, and the nativist American party courted Adams. Adams remained hostile to the Democrats and was not attracted to the American, or Know-Nothing, party. In 1856, however, after Free-Soilers, political abolitionists, and antislavery Whigs and Democrats joined to form the Republican party, Adams became a Republican. In 1858 the Republicans nominated him for the U.S. House of Representatives, and he was elected handily.

In Washington, Adams maintained a low profile and functioned quietly as an able exponent of Republican antislavery principles. He also formed a close political attachment to Senator William Henry Seward of New York, whose firm and principled opposition to slavery and its expansion into the territories had deeply impressed him. Seward also had been a fervent supporter of Adams's father and had delivered a powerful eulogy for him in the Albany legislature in 1848. Adams was therefore disappointed when Seward lost the Republican nomination for president to Abraham Lincoln, whom Adams thought unreliable on the slavery question and too inexperienced to be president. Nevertheless, he campaigned with Seward for the ticket in the Northwest.

When Congress convened in December, Adams was appointed to a special House committee to seek a solution to the secession crisis. Like many northerners, Adams did not believe southerners were serious, and while he was firm in opposing the extension of slave territory, he was willing to compromise in order to buy time and to prevent the secession of the border states. His moderation led to vigorous criticism from more extreme Republicans, including his former Conscience Whig ally Charles Sumner, who became Adams's chief adversary in Massachusetts.

When Lincoln offered Seward appointment as secretary of state, Adams urged him to accept. As secretary of state, Seward then secured an appointment for Adams as minister to Great Britain, a post held by his grandfather and father before him. When Adams met Lincoln shortly afterward, he was singularly unimpressed. Lincoln seemed quite unconcerned about relations with Britain, despite its likely significance should war break out with the South. Adams's opinion of Lincoln never changed.

Adams arrived in England in May 1861 and was shocked to learn that, only a few days before his arrival, Queen Victoria had issued a proclamation of neutrality recognizing Confederate belligerency. While the wisdom and legitimacy of British policy is still debated, the British action was clearly an act of diplomatic discourtesy. (France and the other nations of Europe acted with greater circumspection.) Adams presented his credentials to the queen on 16 May and had his first interview with Lord John Russell, the British foreign secretary, on 18 May. While Russell and Adams developed a deep mutual respect, their official relations were often stormy.

Adams faced an unusually difficult situation in England, and his moderation, caution, and sense of propriety were crucial to the success of his mission. The belief was widespread in Britain that the separation of the southern states could not be reversed, and British leaders thus regarded the war as pointless slaughter that could provoke a race war in the United States and certainly would imperil the British economy. Furthermore, early sympathy for the Union dissipated when the British heard Lincoln and other Federal officials insist that they sought only to preserve the Union, not to abolish slavery. Finally, Russell and many others mistrusted Seward, whose policy of bluff and bluster made Adams's task of securing Britain's benevolent neutrality all the more difficult.

Shortly after protesting Britain's recognition of Confederate belligerency, Adams received Seward's famous Dispatch No. 10 (21 May 1861), in which Seward instructed Adams to demand that British officials cease all contact with Confederate representatives. Lincoln had modified Seward's note so as to give Adams considerable discretion, and Adams wisely chose to relate to Russell only the sense of Seward's directive.

Having averted an Anglo-American crisis over Seward's note, Adams had to deal with British outrage at the illegal American seizure in international waters of Confederate diplomats James M. Mason and John Slidell from a British mail packet, the *Trent*, on 8 November 1861. The British demanded the release of Mason and Slidell and an official apology. Fearful that Anglo-American war could result, Adams remained outwardly cool in the face of popular British and American posturing throughout the controversy. When the United States released Mason and Slidell, Seward explained American policy in terms that Britain chose to accept as an apology, and the crisis passed.

Adams spent a great deal of time defending Union maritime policies and gathering evidence of Confederate attempts to build commerce raiders in British shipyards in violation of British neutrality. He initially failed to persuade Russell to seize the British-built Confederate ships, but his persistence led the British to alter their policy. When Confederate agents attempted to build two ironclad rams at the Laird shipyards in Liverpool in 1863, Adams presented Russell with documents proving that the rams were destined for the Confederacy. He demanded that the British government seize them, and when Russell hesitated, claiming that the evidence was insufficient, Adams told him that if the ships sailed, "It would be superfluous in me to point out to your lordship that this is war." In fact, Russell had decided to seize the ships before Adams's note arrived.

Problems stemming from the Confederate commerce raiders built in England occupied the bulk of Adams's time as minister from 1865 to 1868. The first claims for damages by the British-built commerce raiders, known collectively as the *Alabama* claims, were presented on 20 May 1865. Russell rejected them. He also rejected Adams's suggestion that the claims be arbitrated, proposing instead creation of a joint commission to consider some of the claims. Adams disliked the idea, and Seward ultimately rejected it. Subsequent attempts to negotiate the dispute failed when both the United States and Britain established rigid positions about what could be discussed.

Adams resigned his post on 1 April 1868 and returned to the United States. His diplomacy had been skillful and successful, and he had acquired extraordinary respect throughout Britain. British newspapers praised his services; his name drew hearty applause in the House of Commons; and leading figures wrote testimonials on his behalf.

Between 1868 and 1871 Adams lived quietly in Quincy and Boston. His open distaste for Radical Republican policies and the Radicals' continued disapproval of Adams's moderation and friendship with Seward kept him out of politics. Adams disagreed with the Radicals' "state suicide" theories and opposed both the centralization of political power and intrusion of the federal government into the states. While he supported protection for southern blacks, he opposed extending the suffrage to them so long as there remained massive opposition among white southerners. These views outraged Radical Republicans, who dominated President Ulysses S. Grant. Thus, when Britain and the United States finally agreed to create a joint commission to negotiate a settlement of the *Alabama* claims in 1870, Grant refused even to consider appointing Adams to it. Only after the vigorous intervention of Secretary of State Hamilton Fish did Grant relent and appoint Adams. The joint commission negotiated the Treaty of Washington of 1871, setting up a tribunal in Geneva, Switzerland, to arbitrate the American claims.

Because British officials thought the American claims of $2 billion exorbitant, they threatened to withdraw from the Geneva tribunal. Adams traveled to England to meet privately with cabinet officials and convinced them to continue the arbitration process. On his return to the United States, he persuaded Fish, Grant, and other members of Grant's cabinet to soften the American position. Returning once more to Europe as a member of the tribunal, Adams was instrumental in securing the final settlement, which declared unofficially that Britain was not liable for the indirect claims but officially that Britain had neglected to exercise "due diligence" in preventing the departure of the commerce raiders. The tribunal awarded the United States $15.5 million in damages.

Adams's success and national prominence led friends in the Liberal Republican movement to nominate him for president, and he was barely defeated by Horace Greeley at the party's Cincinnati convention in 1872. Adams, typically, did not promote his nomination and was not disappointed. In 1876 he was an unsuccessful candidate for governor of Massachusetts.

Adams spent his last years in retirement, highly regarded as an elder statesman and worthy exemplar of the Adams family tradition. His distinguished diplomatic career and new reputation for moderation and conservatism also earned him the respect of the old Boston elite, who gave up their former enmity and welcomed him into their social group. He delivered a few speeches, most notably a memorial address on Seward to the New York legislature in which he compared Seward favorably to Lincoln and claimed that Seward had run the Lincoln administration. Mostly, however, Adams revised his two-volume biography of John Adams and completed the *Memoirs of John Quincy Adams, Comprising Portions of his Diary from 1795 to 1848*, published in twelve volumes between 1874 and 1877. Beginning in the late 1870s, Adams's memory began to deteriorate, and he lost it entirely a few years before his death in Boston.

Although conservative by nature, Adams led a revolutionary movement in Massachusetts politics in the 1840s, and his contribution to the nation as minister to Britain during the Civil War was brilliant. Adams's political tracts and detailed diary provide valuable insights into American politics in the mid-nineteenth century, and his scholarly and edited works, although now largely superseded, are of unusually high quality.

• Adams's papers, including his letter books, his diary, his financial, literary, and legal papers, and his reminiscences of England, are in the Massachusetts Historical Society in Boston and are available in the Adams Family Papers microfilm edition. His diary is currently being edited; as of 1993, eight volumes, covering the period from January 1820 to February 1840, have appeared, edited by Aida DiPace Donald, David Donald, Marc Friedlaender, Lyman H. Butterfield, and others. An excellent biography is Martin B. Duberman, *Charles Francis Adams, 1807–1886* (1960), which supersedes the only other biography, by his son Charles Francis Adams, Jr., *Charles Francis Adams* (1900). Henry Adams, *The Education of Henry Adams* (1918), contains a perceptive analysis of his father. Examinations that place Charles Francis Adams in the context of the Adams family are James Truslow Adams, *The Adams Family* (1930), and Jack Shepherd, *The Adams Chronicles: Four Generations of Greatness* (1975).

KINLEY BRAUER

ADAMS, Charles Francis (27 May 1835–20 Mar. 1915), railroad official, civic leader, and historian, was born in Boston, Massachusetts, the son of Charles Francis Adams (1807–1886), a diplomat and politician, and Abigail Brown Brooks. He was the grandson of John Quincy Adams (1767–1848) and great-grandson of John Adams (1735–1826). His father, as minister to England from 1861 to 1868, succeeded in keeping that country neutral during the Civil War. Throughout his life the Adams name opened many doors for Charles Francis, Jr., but he found that being an insider often created envy. Adams spent his early years both in Boston and Quincy but considered Quincy his home. He left private schools at the age of thirteen to attend the Boston Latin School. He did not like the traditional curriculum of the institution, however, and left in 1851. He entered Harvard as a sophomore in 1853 and graduated in 1856. Adams finished in the lower half of his class, having concentrated on extracurricular activities. Following graduation he read law in the office of two leading Boston lawyers, Richard Henry Dana, Jr., and Francis E. Parker. He was admitted to the bar in 1858 but found that he had little interest in his new profession. His first article, "The Reign of King Cotton," appeared in the *Atlantic Monthly* in the spring of 1861.

In December 1861 Adams received a commission as first lieutenant in the First Massachusetts Cavalry and soon left with his regiment for Hilton Head and Beaufort, South Carolina. Later his regiment fought at Antietam and Gettysburg. In July 1864 Adams was given a lieutenant colonel's commission in the Fifth Massachusetts Cavalry, a Negro regiment that was stationed in Maryland. He was promoted to colonel early in 1865, and when he left the service in the summer of 1865, he had been breveted a brigadier general. Suffering from dysentery, jaundice, and malaria during 1864, he had not fully recovered at war's end. Adams felt that his war service had made a man of him, and he also believed that it had given him a new faith in democracy and mankind. In November 1865 he married Mary Hone Ogden; they had five children.

After a recuperative visit to Europe in 1865–1866, Adams returned home with his health improved but with no employment or occupation. He had no desire to return to the law, but he had recently become intrigued with American railroads. In the early postwar years the line to the Pacific was completed, railroad mileage doubled by 1873, and Wall Street speculators were busy building rail empires. Adams felt he might use his writing skills to establish himself as an advocate of railroad reform. He wrote "The Railroad System" for the *North American Review* (Apr. 1867), which was an effort to convince the American public that the expanding railways of the nation needed regulation. Later "A Chapter of Erie" (*North American Review* [July 1869]) covered in colorful detail the fight between Jay Gould and Commodore Vanderbilt for control of the Erie Railroad. When Massachusetts established a board of railroad commissioners in 1869, Adams was selected as one of the three members. He became chairman of the board in 1872 and retained that position until he left the commission in 1879. Under his leadership the commission recommended standard accounting rules for the railroads of the state and stressed measures to increase passenger safety. Rail problems in Massachusetts were quite different from those in the Midwest, and the board did not consider a "Granger" type of regulation for rail rates. The success of rail regulation in Massachusetts in the 1870s was such that other states soon sought to copy it. Advocating a railroad regulation that was moderate and not excessive, Adams was often unhappy with actions of the Interstate Commerce Commission in the 1890s. He was a member of the Board of Arbitration of the Trunk Line Association from 1879 to 1884.

In 1884 Adams was elected president of the Union Pacific Railroad. In his six years as president he faced growing labor and financial problems and a continuing dispute with Congress over the large debt that the railroad owed the government. Adams's inability to pick good subordinates, his lack of practical railroad experience, and the growing hostility of Jay Gould all contributed to his failure as a railroad president. When Gould regained control of the Union Pacific in 1890, Adams was forced to resign the presidency. During the 1870s and 1880s he wrote more than a dozen books, pamphlets, and essays on the problems and challenges facing railroads. He also found time to make extensive investments in iron and silver mines as well as railroads. He owned stock in the Union Pacific, the Burlington, the Santa Fe, and the Denver & Rio Grande. He made investments in real estate in Kansas City, Salt Lake City, Portland, and Seattle. Most of his investments were profitable, and by 1890 he had acquired a modest fortune.

Adams was an active civic leader. He and his older brother, John Quincy Adams, for twenty years served as moderators for Quincy town meetings. Charles, as a member of the school committee, initiated reforms that included a greater emphasis on reading, writing, and arithmetic plus a greater use of blackboards and more individual instruction. Known as the "Quincy System," it was widely imitated throughout the country. In 1892 Adams was appointed to a state commission to create a system of parks and open spaces for the Boston area. In 1893, when Adams moved from Quincy to Lincoln, a suburban town west of Boston, he continued his interest in town government. As a member of the Board of Overseers of Harvard University from 1882 to 1907, Adams played a leading role in reforming the college curriculum that he had earlier found distasteful. In general he favored the "elective system" introduced by Harvard president Charles W. Eliot.

Adams's interest in history was first noted when as a youth of thirteen he became absorbed in the first volume of Macauley's *England*. His career as a historian began in 1874 when the people of Weymouth, Massachusetts, invited him to present a paper on the 250th anniversary of its founding. For the next forty years Adams was a prolific historian. Much of his early writing was on the history of his own state and region. Many of these articles were published by the Massachusetts Historical Society, to which he was elected in 1875. Adams became a vice president of the society in 1890 and served as president from 1895 until his death. He wrote two major biographies, one on Richard Henry Dana, in 1890, and a second on his father, in 1900. In his last years he wrote a number of papers on the diplomatic history of the Civil War. His autobiography was published in 1916. Unlike the writing of his two younger brothers, Henry Adams and Brooks Adams, the writing of Charles Francis Adams was not pessimistic. The concluding lines of his autobiography show that he was quite content with his life.

Adams first voted as a Republican but often voted as an independent. Like several "Mugwumps," he favored civil service reform and free trade and later was opposed to the Spanish-American War and the annexation of the Philippines. He believed that most traditional practices of society and government could be improved. While often progressive in thought, he was generally conservative in action. Though his life was filled with controversy, no one questioned the honesty of Adams's convictions. He died in Washington, D.C.

• Materials relating to Adams are in the Union Pacific Railroad Company Collection, Nebraska State Museum and Archives, Lincoln, and in the Charles Adams, Jr., Papers, Massachusetts Historical Society, Boston. He reviews his own life in *Charles Francis Adams, 1835–1915: An Autobiography* (1916) but devotes three-quarters of the book to the first thirty years of his life. The volume also includes a 1915 memorial address by Henry Cabot Lodge. An excellent review of Adams's entire career is Edward Chase Kirkland, *Charles Francis Adams, Jr., 1835–1915: The Patrician at Bay* (1965). Both Maury Klein, *Union Pacific, Birth of a Railroad: 1862–1893* (1987), and Charles Edgar Ames, *Pioneering the Union Pacific* (1969), give full accounts of Adams's years with the Union Pacific.

JOHN F. STOVER

ADAMS, Charles Francis (2 Aug. 1866–11 June 1954), financier and secretary of the navy, was born in Quincy, Massachusetts, the son of John Quincy Adams II, a prominent lawyer and civic leader, and Fanny Crowninshield. His paternal grandfather, the diplomat Charles Francis Adams (1807–1886), was the son of President John Quincy Adams and the grandson of President John Adams. Public service was a family expectation, and to prepare for it Adams attended the Adams Academy in Quincy, graduated from Harvard University in 1888, and received a bachelor of laws degree from Harvard Law School in 1892. Following completion of his law degree, he made the expected grand tour of Europe and then settled into reading law in the offices of Boston attorney Sigourney Butler. In 1893 Adams was admitted to the bar and began practice, initially with Butler, then as a partner of Judge Everett Bumpus, and later on his own as a specialist in the administration of estates and trusteeships.

After the death of his father in 1894, Adams became preoccupied with repairing a family fortune that had been severely damaged by the panic of 1893; therefore, he increasingly involved himself in banking and business ventures rather than the practice of law. Through a series of shrewd investments and organizational initiatives, Adams soon became a leading figure in a number of local financial and industrial enterprises. Among the more prominent were the Boston Real Estate Trust Company, the Old Colony Trust Company, the Provident Institution for Savings, the Boston Consolidated Gas Company, the Edison Electric Illuminating Company of Boston, and the New England Gas and Coke Company. In 1899 he married Frances Lovering and moved to a home that he had built in Concord. The couple had two children. After 1900, especially after World War I, Adams's reach as an investment banker and chairman of the board of Boston's State Street Trust Company also extended to national enterprises. At the peak of his business career, Adams was on the boards of directors of some forty-three large companies, including such corporate giants as American Telephone and Telegraph, John Hancock Mutual Life Insurance, Newport News Shipbuilding, General Electric, Pan-American World Airways, and the New York, New Haven & Hartford Railroad.

While establishing himself as a financier, businessman, and family man, Adams also devoted large portions of his time and energy to three avocations. One was public service, which began with two terms on the Quincy city council from 1893 to 1895 and continued through two terms as mayor of the city in 1896 and 1897. Adams also found expression through his participation in the Massachusetts Constitutional Convention of 1917, which he attended as a Democrat, the same party to which his father belonged. But in 1920 Adams changed parties and subsequently became a supporter of the Republican policies of the 1920s. Adams's second extracurricular passion was philanthropy, expressed both in local civic work and in his thirty-one years of service beginning in 1898 as deputy treasurer and later treasurer of the Corporation of Harvard College, positions in which he played a central role in making Harvard the most heavily endowed educational institution in the United States. Still, the hobby that brought Adams early and continuing national recognition was competitive yachting. In the eyes of many, his true and most significant career was that of a yacht-racing skipper.

Adams's love of sailing began when he was a boy, his father having also been an avid yachtsman, and was developed during the summers he spent at the Glades House on Massachusetts Bay. By the 1890s Adams was achieving recognition as one of the most skilled sailors and helmsmen in the United States—one who allegedly had "perfect harmony" with the boats he raced. In 1893 he captained the yacht *Pilgrim* in its unsuccessful bid to defend America's cup, and in 1920 Adams served as helmsman of the *Resolute* in a famous sailing duel that culminated in its successful defense of the cup against the *Shamrock IV*. Over the course of his life, he would own some twenty-seven boats and would remain a standard fixture in the world of yachting and its subculture, a sportsman who was said to be readily recognizable by his standard costume of golf knickers, battered sweater, and a white canvas sailor's cap turned down over his nose.

Adams's love of sailing went hand in hand with an early and continuing interest in naval history and the development of the American navy, another passion he inherited naturally. His mother was a descendant of Benjamin Crowninshield, secretary of the navy under Presidents James Madison and James Monroe, and in 1892 his father had turned down the same position in Cleveland's cabinet. In the 1920s Adams took an interest in debates about the navy's future and made himself something of an expert on naval warfare, especially on the Battle of Jutland and the proper use of aircraft carriers. In 1929 President-elect Herbert Hoover regarded him as a logical choice for secretary of the navy, and Adams readily accepted the appointment.

As secretary of the navy, Adams was involved in negotiating the naval limitation restrictions agreed to in the London Naval Treaty of 1930, helping to secure approval of the treaty by the U.S. Senate. Adams was also forced to cope with substantial cuts in the naval budget. In administering the department and formulating policy, he developed an exceptionally close relationship with Admiral William V. Pratt, chief of naval operations from 1930 to 1933, who regarded Adams as "a seaman at heart." Unfortunately, both he and Pratt found themselves caught in the middle of growing tensions between the president and "big navy" advocates, torn by their desires to serve both the president and the interests of a revered institution. Initially, Adams followed the leadership of Hoover and Secretary of State Henry L. Stimson, especially in accepting the "yardstick" concept for measuring naval strength, working out acceptable naval ratios with Japan, and urging Senate approval of the new restrictions. But later Adams was sorely disappointed by Hoover, who quickly abandoned a naval construction program intended to build up to treaty limits. Consequently, in 1932 he argued strongly for larger naval appropriations and a greater naval presence in the Far East, firmly opposing the idea of uniting the armed forces in a department of defense. He also showed little sympathy for the nonrecognition doctrine enunciated by

Stimson in regard to Japanese action in Manchuria. At one point Adams considered resignation but was reportedly talked out of it by Admiral Pratt. Instead, he presided over a naval reorganization and contraction that decommissioned "unneeded" vessels and reduced the enlisted personnel of both the navy and the marine corps.

After 1933 Adams returned to the worlds of finance, philanthropy, and yachting, and despite his advancing years he remained an amazingly active figure until his retirement in 1952. During the 1930s he criticized New Deal reform but did well financially and subsequently became a supporter of liberal internationalism in foreign policy. He also continued to serve Harvard, both as president of the alumni association and president of its board of overseers. At the same time, he became deeply involved in community chest work, earning the title of "Boston's First Citizen" for his founding and service as president of the Greater Boston Community Fund for fourteen years. He also acted as chair of the community chests' National Mobilization for Human Needs in 1940 and helped to organize national publicity for the movement in 1946. At the age of seventy-three, Adams also led the crew of the yacht *Thisbe* to yachting's "triple crown," winning in the same year the King's, Astor, and Puritan cups.

Throughout his long life, close associates found Adams to be a curious mix of New England rectitude, aristocratic manners, eccentric idiosyncrasies, and practical good sense. Known to his friends as "the Deacon," Adams was thoroughly committed to the New England virtues of thrift, simplicity, integrity, work, duty, punctuality, personal reserve, and independence. Yet he also combined these virtues with the geniality and charm of a cultivated aristocrat, displaying both a sophisticated understanding of modern business and lovable quirks, including his refusal to learn to drive a car, his abhorrence of tobacco, and his insistence on taking lunch in the Naval Building cafeteria after standing in line and carrying his own tray. Although never an intellectual in the mold of his famous uncles—Brooks, Henry, and Charles Francis, Jr.—Adams was clearly both an educated man who understood the different worlds in which he operated and a shrewd analyzer of business, governmental, and civic situations.

As a businessman Adams achieved unusual success. But he is remembered less for his business achievements than for his philanthropic and yachting feats, his guidance of the navy through a troubled time in its history, and his success in living up to the expectations associated with the Adams name. He died in Boston.

• No collection of Adams's personal papers exists. According to one story, he destroyed them because there were already "too damned many Adams papers." However, the Hoover papers at the Hoover Presidential Library, West Branch, Iowa, do shed further light on Adams's actions as secretary of the navy. Among the most helpful biographical sketches are Charles P. Curtis, "Charles Francis Adams, 1866–1954," in *The Saturday Club*, ed. Edward Forbes and John Finely (1958); "Something Old, Something New," *Time*, 4 Nov. 1946, pp. 26–29; George C. Homans, "Sailing with Uncle Charlie," *Atlantic Monthly*, July 1965, pp. 39–45; and the account in Francis Russell, *Adams: An American Dynasty* (1976). Also useful for his actions as secretary of the navy are such works as Stephen Roskill, *Naval Policy between the Wars* (2 vols., 1968–1976); Raymond G. O'Connor, *Perilous Equilibrium: The United States and the London Naval Conference of 1930* (1962); and Gerald E. Wheeler, *Admiral William Veazie Pratt* (1974). An obituary is in the *New York Times*, 12 June 1954.

ELLIS W. HAWLEY

ADAMS, Comfort Avery (1 Nov. 1868–21 Feb. 1958), engineering professor and consulting engineer, was born in Cleveland, Ohio, the son of Comfort Avery Adams and Katherine Emily Peticolas. Although the family experienced stringent financial circumstances during Adams's youth, he entered Case Institute of Applied Science (now part of Case Western Reserve University) after attending public schools in Cleveland. At Case he was laboratory assistant to a young physicist, Albert Michelson, and helped to construct the large interferometer Michelson used in an effort to prove the existence of the ether. This project, now known as the Michelson-Morley experiment, failed in its original intention, but it later won Michelson a Nobel Prize because its results confirmed the theory of Albert Einstein. Adams learned about the importance of thoroughness in experimentation from this experience. He graduated from Case in 1890 with a B.S. in mechanical engineering.

In the summer of 1890 Adams joined an expedition to Alaska to study and measure the movement of glaciers; an ice sheet at Glacier Bay was later named for him. Upon his return to Cleveland he found his first job as assistant to the chief engineer of Brown Hoisting and Conveying Machine Company, where he assisted in the design of two cantilever cranes for Newport News Shipbuilding Company. Six months later he moved to a position at Brush Electric Company, another Cleveland firm, and worked on large direct-current generators for Rochester Electric Light Company. He also helped to design the first gearless traction motor.

In the fall of 1891 Adams was called to Harvard University as an instructor in electrical engineering; he remained on the faculty for forty-five years. He was promoted to assistant professor in 1896 and to professor in 1906. He held the title of Abbot and James Lawrence Professor of Engineering from 1914 to 1936 and was named Gordon McKay Professor of Electrical Engineering in 1936, the same year he retired as emeritus professor. Adams also served as dean of engineering in 1919.

In his early years at Harvard Adams worked steadily on the theory and design of electrical machinery. He published three important articles in *Harvard Engineering Journal* between 1902 and 1904, dealing with alternators, synchronous motors, and induction motors. These showed his ability to bring together physical principles, mathematical analysis, and practical considerations.

Adams was of the generation of engineering educators who believed that professors should keep in close contact with the real world where engineering work was performed. Adams did so through consulting work and research projects, as well as by staying active in professional engineering societies. He was a consultant to Babcock & Wilcox Company on the design of high-frequency steel-melting furnaces about 1900; he also advised American Tool and Machine Company on the production of an electric motor for sugar centrifugals. For almost fifty years he advised the Okonite Company about electrical cables, and for almost as long he helped General Electric develop electrical equipment. He also consulted on welding techniques for the Edward G. Budd Manufacturing Company, an innovative producer of railroad cars.

Adams most clearly showed his attention to real-world engineering through his longtime interest in welding technology, an application of electricity that steadily assumed greater importance after 1900. He helped Babcock and Wilcox weld boilers and pressure vessels, in the process attempting the first large-scale application of alternating current to welding. He designed the first alternating-current transformer for welding use; this equipment was later used to weld the three-inch-thick steel penstocks, which carried water to the turbines at Boulder Dam. Adams also developed an organizational base to advance knowledge of welding techniques. During World War I he chaired the Welding Committee of the Emergency Fleet Corporation, which sought to increase production and reduce costs. The American Welding Society was a direct outgrowth of this work, and Adams became its first president. He also played a large role in organizing the American Bureau of Welding after the war to promote fundamental research. In 1935 he became the first chair of the Engineering Foundation's Welding Research Council, serving until 1949.

Adams played a similar role in developing organizations to advance the implementation of technical standards in the United States. In 1910 he began a ten-year term as chair of the American Institute of Electrical Engineers standards committee, leading to his selection in 1919 as the first chair of the American Engineering Standards Committee. A year later this much-enlarged organization became the American Standards Association. Adams also promoted standards through other institutional positions. As a member of the General Engineering Committee of the Council of National Defense during World War I, he developed standard purchase specifications for fifty different bureaus in the War Department. He also served for more than twenty years on the Boiler Code Committee of the American Society of Mechanical Engineers, one of the leading standard-setting bodies in the country.

With his stature as an engineering teacher and a consultant, Adams often had the chance to work on interesting engineering puzzles. During World War I he found a method for producing heavy anchor chain, which until then had been welded one link at a time by hand. Adams proposed casting the chain interlinked, using the same steel as used for railroad couplers, and then case-hardening it. In 1949 he helped the Franklin Institute design a special motor for rotating battleship turrets.

Adams was much recognized during his career. He was elected to the National Academy of Sciences. He delivered the inaugural Adams Lecture for the American Welding Society and received its Samuel Wylie Miller Medal. In 1944 he received the American Institute of Electrical Engineer's Lamme Medal both for his work in the theory and design of alternating-current machinery and for his work in welding. Perhaps his most prestigious award was the Edison Medal in 1956 for "pioneering achievements in the development of alternating current electric machines and in electrical welding; for vision and initiative in the formation of an engineering standards organization and for eminence as an educator and consulting engineer."

Adams continued as an active consultant for almost twenty years after he left Harvard. Called the "dean of American engineers" in recognition of that longevity, he earned the esteem of his colleagues for his educational philosophy of understanding fundamentals while testing them in practice, for his alert, searching mind, and for his kind demeanor. He had married Elizabeth Chassis Parsons in 1894; they adopted two children. Adams died at home in Philadelphia.

• A collection of miscellaneous scholarly papers delivered by Adams is in the Harvard University Archives. Much information concerning Adams's life is in articles in engineering and professional journals, including "Society News," *Welding Journal* 36 (Jan. 1957): 47; "C. A. Adams to Receive the Edison Medal for 1956," *Electrical Engineering* 76 (Jan. 1957): 82; "A Grand Young Man," *Welding Journal* 36 (June 1957): 610–13; and "Comfort A. Adams, 1956 Edison Medalist," *Electrical Engineering* 76 (Mar. 1957): 224–27. A full biographical account is provided by Vannevar Bush in National Academy of Sciences, *Biographical Memoirs* 38 (1965): 1–16. Obituaries are in *Mechanical Engineering* 80 (July 1958): 156; *Electrical Engineering* 77 (May 1958): 461–62; *Welding Journal* 37 (Apr. 1958): 378–79; and the *New York Times*, 23 Feb. 1958.

BRUCE E. SEELY

ADAMS, Cyrus Cornelius (7 Jan. 1849–4 May 1928), geographer and editor, was born in Naperville, Illinois, the son of Cyrus Adams and Cornelia Stevens, farmers. He was raised by his aunt and uncle in Bloomington, Minnesota, and attended the nascent University of Minnesota for a year, continuing at the first University of Chicago. He became a reporter for the Chicago *Inter Ocean*, finally graduating from the university with an A.B. in 1876, and later joined the *New York Sun*, where he remained on the staff in one capacity or another until 1908. In 1877 he married Blanche C. Dodge; they would have a son and a daughter.

Geography became Adams's special interest, and ultimately he devoted himself almost exclusively to articles and editorials on geographical issues. A journalist by training and temperament, but a geographer at heart, he made a career acquiring and diffusing assorted geographical knowledge for the broadest possible audience. Quickly realizing how scientifically advanced the field was in central Europe, he picked up a working knowledge of German to draw on sources in that language, especially *Petermanns Geographische Mitteilungen*. In 1889 he was appointed the first president of the Department of Geography at the Brooklyn Institute of Arts & Sciences, in which capacity he created a major collection of books, maps, and other teaching aids for the field, an exhibition of which drew a combined viewership of 50,000 in Brooklyn, New York, and Boston, and which bolstered the cause for improved teaching of geography in the northeast. From 1891 to 1892 he edited the first thirteen issues of *Goldthwaite's Geographical Magazine*, the earliest popular monthly magazine devoted to geography in the United States. Although *Goldthwaite's* ceased publication in 1895, Adams's formula for content was copied in succeeding journals. His regular sections for geography teachers, innovative at the time, became the model for a later standard of the field, the *Journal of Geography*.

Such initiatives brought Adams to the attention of the professionally oriented American Geographical Society in New York, which recruited him to help publish the society's *Bulletin* in 1902. Having urged successfully that the journal be issued monthly, he became assistant editor in 1905 and editor in 1908. He guided its growth until his retirement in 1915 and its subsequent transformation into a rigorous academic periodical, the *Geographical Review*. During his stewardship of the *Bulletin*, the oldest and most respected geographical periodical in America at the time, he broadened its topical coverage and gave analytical studies more prominence in a medium otherwise long known for its descriptive and statistical reviews of foreign areas and copious accounts of exploration.

Adams was a reporter and essayist with wide geographical interests, but he wrote with particular zeal about western exploration in the Arctic and in Africa and the development of resources that followed African exploration. He formed a long association with Henry Morton Stanley and was one of the few Americans to write a biography of David Livingstone, in the *Beacon Lights of History* series. His attention to the polar exploits of Lieutenant Robert E. Peary brought personal friendship with that explorer, too, and his report of Peary's Greenland research in the *Geographical Journal* remains the standard account. As if to validate the aphorism that trade follows the flag, he published *A Text-Book of Commercial Geography* in 1901, the first American challenge to this copious British genre. It was well regarded by contemporaries, and the book, together with an abridged version, went through many editions. His varied activities on behalf of geography and his position in the American Geographical Society cast him as an important founding member of the Association of American Geographers, created in 1904, of which he became the second president in 1906. Robert Peary named Mount Adams near the Inglefield Gulf in Greenland in his honor.

Adams was a self-taught geographer, attracted by the cultural and economic implications, as well as the romance, of European and American geographical "discoveries" of the last recesses of the globe. He is significant for the role he played in establishing geography as a modern discipline in the United States. For more than twenty-five years beginning in the early 1890s he helped broaden the scope of a field long viewed in America as limited to explaining the arrangement of the purely physical features of the earth's surface. Through eclectic personal writing and editorship of geographical magazines he contributed to the rise of a human geography to balance that of the physical, and a maturation of the field by then conceived as the regional synthesis of all human interactions with the earth. Aware of the need to educate American citizens about the larger world around them, he contributed actively to the systematization of geographical knowledge in the United States in this critical period. While alert to shifts in the content and focus of geography as a formal discipline, he had neither the credentials nor the inclination to control them. In yielding what influence he had to university-trained scholars by World War I, he was ultimately a transitional figure, but one whose intellectual energy and editorial skill notably benefited American geography. He retired to Jewett, New York, and died in New York City, having seen the popular but amorphous field transformed through his writing, editing, and institutional involvement into a vibrant scientific discipline replete with specialties and methodological controversies.

• The most complete professional assessment of Adams is W. L. G. Joerg, "Memoir of Cyrus Cornelius Adams," *Annals of the Association of American Geographers* 21 (1931): 171–78. A shorter treatment is given in the *Geographical Review* 18 (1928): 496–97, and his later institutional activities receive mention in John Kirtland Wright, *Geography in the Making: The American Geographical Society, 1851–1951* (1952). An obituary is in the *New York Times*, 5 May 1928.

MICHAEL P. CONZEN

ADAMS, Edward Dean (9 Apr. 1846–20 May 1931), banker, engineer, and financier, was born in Boston, Massachusetts, the son of Adoniram Judson Adams, a businessman, and Harriet Lincoln Norton. He graduated with a B.S. degree from Norwich University, Northfield, Vermont, in 1864. After spending a year in Europe, he attended the Massachusetts Institute of Technology in 1865–1866. In 1867 he joined the Boston firm of T. J. Lee & Hill, stockbrokers, where he served as bookkeeper and cashier. In 1871 he was a founding partner of Richardson, Hill & Company of Boston, private bankers. The following year he married Frances Amelia Gutterson; the couple had three children.

Adams went to New York City in 1878 as a partner in the private banking firm of Winslow, Lanier & Company, which was then at the peak of its reputation as financier, organizer, and reorganizer of railroads and other industries. He soon became involved in the management of many enterprises in which the firm invested, while his knowledge of engineering determined the character of the companies that fell to his lot. In 1880 he became a trustee of the Missouri Pacific Railroad Company Consolidated Mortgage, a position that he held until 1920. By 1882 he was president of the Northern Pacific Terminal Company of Oregon and a trustee of the Edison Electric Light Company, which was then bringing electrical illumination to New York City. In 1883 Adams was named a vice president of the St. Paul & Northern Pacific Railroad Company, and in the same year he helped reorganize the New York, Ontario, & Western Railroad Company and the West Shore & Ontario Terminal Company. Before 1890 he was vice president of the Central & South American Telegraph Company, a director of All America Cables, Inc., and a reorganizer of the Central Railroad of New Jersey. From 1893 to 1896 he was chairman of the reorganization committee of the Northern Pacific Railroad Company.

In 1889–1890 Adams was a member of the committee that converted the American Cottonseed Oil Trust into a corporation, the American Cotton Oil Company of New Jersey. According to the *New York Times* (19 Oct. 1889), that committee "took the first step toward the abandonment of the Trust plan," which was then under attack at the state and federal levels. Adams was president and chairman of the board of the reorganized company from 1890 to 1896. At the same time he was interesting himself in the harnessing of power at Niagara Falls. In 1889 the promoters of a power plant at the falls offered a half interest to Winslow, Lanier & Company. Delegated by his firm to determine the merits of the project, Adams made a thorough study of power plants in the United States and Europe. His insistence, over opposition, on the use of alternating current at Niagara introduced an epoch in electrical power transmission. From 1890 to 1909 he was president of the Cataract Construction Company. He organized the International Niagara Commission and from 1892 to 1899 was president of the Niagara Development Company. He continued as a director of the company into the 1920s. For his contribution at Niagara Falls, Adams received the John Fritz Medal, the highest award of American engineering societies, in 1926.

Adams withdrew from Winslow, Lanier & Company in 1893 to become the American representative of the Deutsche Bank of Berlin, a position he retained until World War I. In 1895 a syndicate headed by J. P. Morgan & Company purchased with gold a large amount of U.S. bonds to counter a potentially disastrous outflow of gold from the Treasury. Adams committed the Deutsche Bank to $25 million of the loan and suggested that the bank announce the immediate shipment of gold from Europe. The action was instrumental in bolstering the U.S. currency and helped to avert a financial crisis.

A patron and benefactor of the Metropolitan Museum of Art, Adams was a trustee of the museum from 1894 to his death. In 1911 he founded the Deutsches Haus at Columbia University for the promotion of international understanding. Beginning in the same year, he was chairman of the board of the Kahn Foundation for the Foreign Travel of American Teachers. From 1918 to 1924 he was a director of the Committee for Devastated France. He belonged to and often held official positions in more than seventy other professional, scientific, historical, artistic, and civic associations. In addition to his home in New York City he owned an estate in Rumson, New Jersey. He died in New York City.

• Edward Dean Adams, *Niagara Power: History of the Niagara Falls Power Company, 1886–1918* (2 vols., 1927), is indispensable for understanding Adams's role at Niagara. Edward Everett Bartlett, *Edward Dean Adams* (1926), is an incomplete and uncritical account of Adams's career, but it includes information that is not available elsewhere. See also *New England Historical and Genealogical Register* (April 1932): 115–20, and *New York Genealogical and Biographical Record* (July 1931): 244–45. Obituaries are in the *Boston Transcript*, 20 May 1931, and the *New York Times*, 21 May 1931.

IRENE D. NEU

ADAMS, Edwin (3 Feb. 1834–28 Oct. 1877), actor, was born in Medford, Massachusetts. Little is known about his parents or childhood. He made his professional debut in 1853 in Boston, where he appeared at the National Theatre as Stephen in Sheridan Knowles's *The Hunchback*. A few months later he played a small role in *Hamlet* at the Howard Atheneum in Boston. Over the next several years he established himself in the stock companies that theaters outside New York City generally employed; stars on tour would take the leading roles while the supporting parts would be played by members of the local company.

At the Baltimore Museum theater Adams enjoyed the tutelage of the actor Joseph Jefferson, who was managing the company. Jefferson later recalled that the young actor started "almost as an apprentice," but "before we parted, he was playing the heroes of the stage with much promise." During the 1858–1859 season Adams worked as a member of the Boston Theatre Company, where he had the opportunity to play Macduff in *Macbeth* opposite the great Edwin Booth. (Descriptions of this season mention "Mrs. Edwin Adams" as a member of the company, but no additional information appears to be available about her or the number of their children, if any.) By 1860 Adams had attracted favorable notices in Philadelphia and Baltimore as well as Boston.

Adams was also beginning to make occasional appearances in New York City, starting at Burton's Theatre on 23 June 1856, when he played Antonio in a one-night production of *The Merchant of Venice*. He returned to New York in April 1862, in *The Hunchback*, this time playing Clifford opposite the popular actress Kate Bateman. As was customary, Bateman's company played in New York for a little over a month, presenting a new play each week. Adams had a part in each play. Most of his roles were second leads, although he appeared as Romeo opposite Bateman's Juliet. He joined the company for a number of performances at the new Brooklyn Academy of Music that summer and for another five-week run in Manhattan in the fall. In the winter of 1863 Adams appeared in Manhattan with Bateman in *Leah, the Forsaken*. This play lasted a month, an unusually long run for the period. Adams self-deprecatingly called himself a "war star," predicting that his new success would flicker out when the Civil War ended, but his best work lay ahead. In September 1866 he was able to carry a month-long engagement in New York himself, appearing in leading roles in *The Dead Heart*, *The Heretic*, *Romeo and Juliet*, *Wild Oats*, and *Black-Eyed Susan*. The next year he repeated several of these roles and added *The School for Scandal* and *Macbeth*.

In February 1869 Adams joined Booth's company for a four-month season to inaugurate the veteran actor's lavish new theater. The first performance, *Romeo and Juliet*, was a popular sensation. The demand for opening night seats pushed prices as high as $125, and the ten-week run ultimately earned Booth more than $60,000. Adams received excellent notices—better, indeed, than Booth's. Besides appearing opposite Booth, he played the lead in *Narcisse*, which ran on Saturday nights. This play was not financially successful, but it gave Booth some time off each week. *Othello* opened in late April, with Booth and Adams alternating as Iago and the Moor. Here the critics found Adams less successful; the *New York Times* described his Iago as "utterly deficient in subtlety and guile." Once *Othello* ended in May, Adams had a month-long engagement of his own at Booth's Theatre, appearing in five plays, one after the other. Then on 21 June he introduced the title role that would thereafter be identified with him, *Enoch Arden*, based on Tennyson's narrative poem. This melodramatic play by Julie de Margueritte ran for six weeks and established Adams as a popular star. By the following year he was able to demand the princely salary of $300 a week.

From then on Adams toured constantly, crisscrossing the country to appear in the plays for which he had become best known. In 1875 his travels took him to Australia, where he received a warm welcome, but he returned in very poor health. After playing Iago in San Francisco in May 1876, Adams never acted again. As his health and finances failed, a series of benefit performances in several cities were arranged by Adams's friends to raise funds for him and his wife. His last theatrical appearance was at one of these benefits in February 1877; too sick to perform, he sat in a chair on stage. He died in Philadelphia.

Adams never achieved critical acclaim to place him in the topmost rank of his profession, but Jefferson described him, nevertheless, as "a born actor, a child of nature if not of art, swayed by warm impulse rather than by premeditation." He delighted audiences with his vitality, charm, commanding bearing, and good looks; one admirer called his voice "the most melodious and sympathetic ever heard." He had a bravura style that moved between comedy and melodrama. Indeed, the part of Enoch Arden became so much his own that few other actors dared to undertake it. Fifty years after Adams's death, one theater critic said that *Enoch Arden* was one of the half dozen performances he could remember "as vividly as if I had seen them last season."

Adams's cheerful temper and high spirits won him a host of friends; his friend William Winter called him "a man whose smile was sunshine, from a heart full of kindness." The benefits that were organized as he lay dying testified both to the open-handed way in which he had shared his earnings and to the affection people felt for him. "Everybody loved Adams," recalled Winter. "In his day he was one of the blithest spirits in all the bright world of the stage."

• Accounts of Adams's performances appear in George C. D. Odell, *Annals of the New York Stage* (1931–1938); Eugene Tompkins, *The History of the Boston Theatre, 1854–1901* (1908); and Arthur Hornblow, *History of the Theatre in America* (1919). A biographical sketch appears in Garff B. Wilson, *A History of American Acting* (1966). For additional personal descriptions, see *Autobiography of Joseph Jefferson* (1889); William Winter, *Other Days* (1908); and Clara Morris, *A Life on the Stage* (1901).

SANDRA OPDYCKE

ADAMS, Franklin P. (15 Nov. 1881–23 Mar. 1960), newspaper columnist, humorist, and radio personality, was born Franklin Pierce Adams in Chicago, Illinois, the son of Moses Adams, a dry-goods merchant, and Clara Schlossberg, both German-Jewish immigrants. During his childhood he was an avid reader of the classics, history, nineteenth-century fiction, and light verse. He studied mathematics and science at the Armour Scientific Academy in Chicago, graduating in 1899. He attended the University of Michigan for less than a year, during which he studied literature and after which he began to earn his own living.

Adams became an insurance supply clerk and then an insurance solicitor in Chicago (1900–1902). In 1901 he met the humorist George Ade, whose seemingly easy life inspired Adams himself to become a writer. In 1903 he began a miscellaneous column in the *Chicago Journal* that contained mostly humorous verse and weather reports. His beginning salary, $25 per week, was raised the following year to $30, at which time he began to sign his work with his soon-famous initials—"F.P.A." He also contributed items to Bert Leston Taylor's *Chicago Tribune* column, "A Line o' Type or Two." In 1904 Adams married Minna Schwartze (they had no children), moved to New York City, and until 1913 wrote a *New York Evening Mail* column. Its title, "Always in Good Humor," which was suggested by the owner, bothered Adams. Meanwhile, he and O. Henry coauthored *Lo* (1909), a musical comedy. In 1911 Adams began "The Diary of Our Own Samuel Pepys," a popular feature published each Saturday in the *Evening Mail*. He started his equally famous column "The Conning Tower" for the *New York Tribune* in 1914.

During World War I, Adams was a U.S. Intelligence Service captain in France and also wrote columns for *The Stars and Stripes*, the American Expeditionary Force newspaper. After the war he resumed his *Tribune* column until 1921, then transferred it in 1922 to the *New York World*. He wrote the play *The '49ers* that same year with George S. Kaufman, Ring Lardner, and others. Having obtained a divorce in 1924, Adams married Esther Sayles Root in 1925 (the couple had four children). When the *World* went out of business in 1931, Adams moved his "Conning Tower" column to the *Herald Tribune*.

"The Conning Tower" was a mishmash of critical commentary, epigrams, parodies, poems displaying regular techniques, prose paragraphs, wild puns, summaries of his activities, and jocose translations. Masking serious literary criticism in persiflage, Adams was among the first to praise Theodore Dreiser, D. H. Lawrence, Sinclair Lewis, W. Somerset Maugham, Eugene O'Neill, Lardner, and other rising stars. Adams poked fun at psychoanalysis, once in a poem ending, "Don't tell me what you dreamt last night, / For I've been reading Freud." One parody was of a Leigh Hunt love poem, redone in an Italian accent and stressing "keeses"; another spoofed Wordsworthian sentimentality; another deflated Whitmanesque virility.

Adams got his purist points across by harmlessly chiding grammatical and typographical inaccuracies and misuse and mispronunciation of words. Not the least delightful sections of "The Conning Tower" were unpaid contributions his eager friends were allowed to print there—most memorably those of Kaufman, Dorothy Parker, and Alexander Woollcott. But it is his neo-Pepysian diary that will most likely endure. In its three or four million words Adams summarizes—in quaint seventeenth-century style—his activities (dressing, eating and drinking, reading, theatergoing, playing tennis and poker, being with important friends) and sources of concern (especially conservative and dishonest politics, at all levels of government). Thus, in many ways Adams holds up a mirror to his times, as Pepys did to his.

Back in 1920 the owner of the Algonquin Hotel in New York City made a table available in a separate room for Manhattan wits to enjoy sparkling talk over leisurely lunches. Calling their club the Round Table and the Vicious Circle, members and visitors included Adams, their prime mover, among editors Frank Crowninshield and Harold Ross; performers Tallulah Bankhead, Ethel Barrymore, Douglas Fairbanks, Lynn Fontanne, Jascha Heifetz, Alfred Lunt, Harpo Marx, and Paul Robeson; and writers Robert Benchley, Marc Connelly, Edna Ferber, Kaufman, Lardner, Parker, Robert E. Sherwood, and Woollcott. Adams's wit included one of his countless cracks, "What this country needs is a good five-cent nickel," and one of his incalculable puns, "I wish you a meretricious and a happy New Year."

Though paid $25,000 a year and syndicated in six other newspapers, Adams quit the *Herald Tribune* over a financial dispute in 1937. He continued his column in 1938 in the *New York Post* only to have the management cancel it three years later because of its overly sophisticated content. Adams soon gained national popularity of another sort. He was hired as an original panelist on "Information Please!"—the delightful radio quiz show (1938–1948) that also starred the literary critic Clifton Fadiman, the sports columnist John Kieran, and the musician Oscar Levant. Its best segments were made into movie shorts (1939–1942), and the show became a short-lived television feature (1952). In 1945 Adams began to show early symptoms of Alzheimer's disease, developed arteriosclerosis a decade later, and lived thereafter mostly in a Manhattan nursing home, where he died.

Among Adams's nineteen book titles are *The Melancholy Lute: Selected Songs of Thirty Years* (1936), his best verse; *Nods and Becks* (1944), his best newspaper pieces; and *The Diary of Our Own Samuel Pepys, 1911–1934* (1935), a two-volume abridgment. In addition, he wrote articles and introductions to books by others and edited and compiled selections of his favorite poems and quotations by others. "F.P.A." was notable in his day for two main accomplishments: his incredible wit, most dramatically wielded at the Algonquin Club, and his "Conning Tower" items, especially his neo-Pepysian diary. He was revered by all who knew him as a uniquely witty writer with a cubbyhole memory and as a rollicking friend.

• In *Our American Humorists* (1922; rev. ed., 1931), Thomas L. Masson briefly considers Adams. Carl Van Doren, "Day In and Day Out," *Century* 107 (Dec. 1923): 308–15, surveys newspaper wits of the 1920s, including Adams. Walter Blair and Hamlin Hill, *America's Humor: From Poor Richard to Doonesbury* (1978), place Adams in the long tradition of American "colyumnists." Clifton Fadiman, "The Education of Franklin P. Adams," *New Yorker*, 9 Nov. 1935, pp. 81–82, offers detailed praise of Adams's 1935 abridged *Diary of Pepys*. John Wheelwright places Adams in the tradition of comic poets in "Poet as Funnyman," *Poetry: A Magazine of Verse* 50 (July 1937): 210–15. In his anthology *The Algonquin Wits* (1968), Robert E. Drennan quotes fifty-eight arrestingly clever quips by Adams. "Notes and Comment," *New Yorker*, 2 Apr. 1960, p. 31, and Gerald W. Johnson, "No Taste for Trivia," *New Republic*, 11 Apr. 1960, p. 16, offer quick posthumous praise. Sally Ashley, *F.P.A.: The Life and Times of Franklin Pierce Adams* (1986), places Adams in his era. A detailed obituary with a portrait is in the *New York Times*, 24 Mar. 1960.

ROBERT L. GALE

ADAMS, George Burton (3 June 1851–26 May 1925), historian, was born in Fairfield, Vermont, the son of Calvin Carlton Adams, a Congregational clergyman, and Emeline Nelson. Adams attended Beloit College in Wisconsin, from which he received a B.A. in 1873. He then enrolled at Yale University, returning temporarily to teach at Beloit in 1874–1875. He earned a B.D. from Yale in 1877.

Despite having trained for the ministry, Adams accepted a position as a professor of history at newly founded Drury College in Springfield, Missouri, in 1877. In 1878 he married Ida Clarke; they had one daughter. After several years of teaching, he spent a year studying in Germany and earned a Ph.D. in history from the University of Leipzig in 1886. In 1888 Adams was called to Yale as the Larned Professor of American History. In 1890 he became simply a professor of history, teaching courses in European and medieval history until he became emeritus in 1917. One former student described him as "one of the ablest and most inspiring lecturers of his generation."

Adams was deeply involved in the development of both the undergraduate and graduate history programs at Yale, and his students there included Wallace Notestein, W. O. Ault, Albert B. White, Charles McIlwain, and George Woodbine. His interest in teaching was also reflected in the many works he published for use in the classroom, including the textbook *Civilization during the Middle Ages* (1894), his collection *Select Documents of English Constitutional History* (1901), and his editions of foreign standards.

As his reputation as a teacher and scholar grew, Adams also became a leader in the new movement to organize American historians professionally. He served on the executive council of the American Historical Association from 1891 to 1897 and from 1898 to 1901, and he served as its president in 1907–1908. In addition, he was an editor of the association's *American Historical Review* from 1895 to 1913. Adams was a fellow of the American Academy of Arts and Sciences, a member of the American Antiquarian Society, and a corresponding member of the Royal Historical Society and the Colonial Society of Massachusetts.

Adams began his work in medieval history with the study of Continental culture and feudalism. It was only after 1900 that he dedicated himself to what would be his life's work: the study of the origins of the English constitution. In an article titled "The Critical Period of English Constitutional History" (*American Historical Review* 5 [July 1900]: 643–58), Adams wrote that "it was the thorough feudalization of England which resulted from the [Norman] Conquest that made the [English] constitution possible, not by establishing a strong monarchy against which primitive Teutonic liberty reacted later, but by introducing with the strong monarchy a new conception of the relation of the king to those of his subjects who in that age constituted the nation, . . . by introducing the definite contract-idea of the feudal system." The idea that each party to a feudal contract had rights within that contract encouraged the feudal nobility to unite to force the king to recognize those rights, most momentously in the Magna Carta. When the Feudal system decayed, the survival of the Magna Carta preserved the principle that the king could be compelled to live within the law. This principle would be incorporated into the English constitution in the fact of the limited monarchy. Adams's work was an influential part of the revision of the standard nineteenth-century understanding of the English constitution, which had interpreted its representative institutions and limited monarchy as the result of a supposed Anglo-Saxon racial genius for liberty. Adams incorporated his arguments into several books, including *The Origin of the English Constitution* (1912), *An Outline Sketch of English Constitutional History* (1918), and his summary, *The Constitutional History of England* (1921). He died in New Haven, Connecticut. After his death, Yale created the George Burton Adams Professorship in English Constitutional History.

Adams was justly criticized during his lifetime for neglecting the contemporary meaning and function of the institutions he studied in his concern for their ultimate consequences. However, even those who criticized his work found it "sober," "masterly," and "judicial." A retrospective published a decade after his death called him one of the few American medieval historians whose work "will bear comparison with the best in any country." While not all elements of Adams's major argument were universally accepted, the emphasis on the importance of the Norman rather than the Anglo-Saxon contribution to the English political system that he shared with historians such as Charles Homer Haskins remained an important aspect of the study of medieval English history until the 1960s. Adams is also remembered for his 1908 presidential address to the American Historical Association, in which he urged historians to cooperate with members of newer academic disciplines—such as sociology, geography, and economics—while remaining true to the historian's primary purpose of establishing objective facts before engaging in speculation.

• Adams's papers are at the Manuscripts and Archives Division of the Yale University Library. Other important published works include his textbooks *Medieval Civilization* (1883), *The Growth of the French Nation* (1896), and *European History* (1899); his English editions of Victor Duruy's *The History of the Middle Ages* (1891) and Charles Bémont and G. Monod's *Medieval Europe from 395 to 1270* (1902); and his *History of England from the Norman Conquest to the Death of John, 1066–1216* (1905), vol. 2 of *The Political History of England*, ed. William Hunt and Reginald Poole. His final book, *Council and Courts of Anglo-Norman England* (1926), is a collection of essays published after his death. The longest biographical study of Adams is Reginald E. Rabb, "George Burton Adams," in *Some Modern Historians of Britain*, ed. Herman Ausubel (1951). Obituaries are in the *New Haven Register* and the *New Haven Journal-Courier*, 27 May 1925, and the *Yale Alumni Weekly*, 5 June 1925.

LAURA R. ROBINSON

ADAMS, Grizzly (22 Oct. 1812–25 Oct. 1860), mountain man and wild animal tamer, was born John Adams in Medway, Massachusetts, the son of Eleazar Adams and Sybil Capen. Adams apparently served an apprenticeship as a cobbler, but when he was twenty-one he began hunting and trapping animals, for showmen, in the woods of Maine, Vermont, and New Hampshire. He delighted in his work, which was cut short when he tried to control an unruly Bengal tiger.

In doing this favor for an exhibitor, Adams was badly mangled. When he recovered his health, he went back to making boots and shoes.

In 1849 Adams suddenly left Massachusetts. The exact reason for his precipitous departure is unknown, but it seems to have been neither the shock of his father's suicide nor the loss of his own savings in a speculation that year. It was probably litigation over property or debts that caused him to decamp. "I was dead broke," he told his first biographer, Theodore H. Hittell, circa 1856. "The lawyers and judges . . . contrived to rob me of everything I possessed."

Out West, Adams tried mining, trading, and ranching, but nothing seemed to work for him. He was as down on his luck in 1852 as he had been when he arrived in California in 1849. Recalling his wonderful days in the Maine woods and the Green and White mountains, he determined to live alone in the wilderness. Oddly, Adams took an alias (a common practice in gold rush California), but one that only half hid his identity. He went by James Capen Adams, his brother's name. But he was soon called Grizzly Adams or Old Adams, although he was just forty when he headed into the Sierra Nevada.

In less than eight years of almost solitary living in the wilds, Adams won wide fame in the West. His prowess in catching and taming the much-feared California grizzly—the well-named *ursus horribilis*—was unique. He became a legend in his own time. Hittell wrote a bestselling biography of him, and melodramas based on his career were staged on both coasts. Adams even played himself at Tom Maguire's Opera House in San Francisco.

Adams, who was sometimes called the Wild Yankee, was an atypical recluse. Instead of hiding in a Sierra cave, he roamed about the Coast Range, Cascades, and Sierra Nevada as if he held a roving commission. Fur trappers and market hunters were common in California, but Adams did not run a trapline for beaver and river otter, bag wild ducks and geese for restaurants, or shoot deer and elk for their skins, venison, and tallow. He took animals alive. Using a lasso as well as box traps, he captured unharmed eagles, wildcats, deer, elk, mountain lions, wolves, black bears, and grizzly bears. He penned them up, tamed and trained them, and sold them to wild animal show entrepreneurs. Often in tight spots, he more than once was injured by grizzlies.

Grizzly Adams wandered the mountains either alone or with a single companion, often an Indian. He get along well with the Indians and treated them with respect. He made pets, "watch dogs," and beasts of burden of his grizzly bears, even showing off by riding them. Although he mixed kindness with discipline, he did not spare the rod. When he was asked how he controlled such strong and ferocious animals, Adams merely remarked that he was the "hardest" of the lot.

In 1855 Adams began to tour with his wild animal menagerie and in 1856 opened his Mountaineer Museum in San Francisco, the ancestor of Woodward's Gardens and the Fleishhacker Zoo. He showed all sorts of animals, but the public came primarily to see his grizzlies, including mighty Ben Franklin, Lady Washington, and Samson. Adams became a celebrity, occupying prominent positions with his animals in civic parades such as that of 1858 celebrating the completion of the Atlantic cable.

In 1860 Adams moved his museum to New York, calling it the California Menagerie. P. T. Barnum, "the greatest American showman," bought a half-interest in it and made Adams famous in the East. Adams most likely brought eight or nine grizzlies with him, plus other "critters," including Old Neptune, Manhattan's first California sea lion.

Adams, who was suffering from the effects of many bearhugs, enjoyed his new fame only briefly. When Barnum examined Adams's head, he found his skull punctured and his brain showing. One of his grizzlies, Old Fremont, had reopened one of Adams's old head wounds. "I'm a used-up man," Adams admitted to Barnum. "I reckon I may live six months or a year, yet."

Adams was right. Although he managed to make a tour with his bears that summer, he took to his bed for the last time in October. *Harper's Weekly* (10 Nov. 1860), noting the passing of the colorful mountaineer, observed, "His tastes led him to cultivate the society of bears, which he did at great personal risk, but with remarkable success, using them as pack horses by day, as blankets by night, as companions at all times."

• The only biography of Adams since T. H. Hittell's early and incomplete work, *The Adventures of James Capen Adams, Mountaineer and Grizzly Bear Hunter of California* (1860), is Richard H. Dillon's *The Legend of Grizzly Adams* (1966; repr. 1993).

RICHARD H. DILLON

ADAMS, Hannah (2 Oct. 1755–15 Dec. 1831), historian of religions and writer, was born in Medfield, Massachusetts, the daughter of Thomas Adams, Jr., a merchant of "English goods" and books, and Elizabeth Clark. She was a distant cousin of President John Adams. Adams lost her mother when she was eleven; her father remarried and had four more children with his second wife. Using the inheritance of her grandfather's prosperous farm for capital, her father opened a store. By the time she was in her teens the business had failed and depleted the family's resources to a level of need from which they would never recover. Although her father was never able to bring to his family any financial stability, he was able to share with his daughter an avid thirst for knowledge and his love of reading. In his youth, illness had prevented him from pursuing formal education, but, driven by personal ambition, he became extremely well read and mastered an exhaustive collection of facts.

Like her father, Adams was a sickly child. Her poor health prevented her from going to school, and thus she spent much of her time at home reading. We learn from her *Memoir* that the pursuit of knowledge became her insatiable passion. She writes, "I remember that my first idea of the happiness of Heaven was of a place where we should find our thirst for knowledge fully gratified." As the family's financial problems worsened and boarders were taken for income, the tenants introduced Adams to such new areas of study as Latin, Greek, geography, and logic. One boarder suggested she read Thomas Broughton's *Dictionary of Religions*. Adams was fascinated by the discovery that a different world existed far from the old New England town of Puritan heritage in which she was raised. She began to conduct her own research and fact-gathering surveys on the world's religions. Struck by the bias that most authors imposed on their material, Adams was determined to gain a more impartial understanding of the different denominations. In her *Memoir* she described the driving forces behind her work: "As I read controversy, I suffered extremely from mental indecision, while pursuing the various and contradictory arguments adduced by men of piety and learning in defence of their respective religious systems."

While she compiled the information, her family's economic situation also required that she earn what little money she could by weaving bobbin lace during the revolutionary war and by tutoring young college-bound men. Upon the completion of her project, Adams decided to publish her work as a means of income. The result was *An Alphabetical Compendium of the Various Sects* (1784). Although the publisher received more of a profit from the book than did Adams, the publication was just the first edition of a text that would see three other printings. The second edition, titled *A View of Religions* (1791), brought her financial solvency. The vast number of sources that Adams had drawn on as well as her attempt not to be preferential in her commentaries made the book noteworthy relative to other texts of the period. After the success of *A View of Religions*, Adams published *A Summary History of New England* (1799); however, in the process of compiling data for the text she permanently damaged her eyesight. Her financial needs required that she continue to write, although as a result of her poor vision she found it difficult to read.

Adams's next project involved editing her history book into a format that could be used as a children's schoolbook. In the midst of completing her work, she discovered that two other authors, the Reverend Jedidiah Morse and the Reverend Elijiah Parish, were publishing a similar historical study. A controversy ensued. At the outset, Adams attempted to resolve the conflict on her own by contacting Morse. As the situation continued, however, she grew more concerned that the other book would infringe on her work, and she welcomed the support of Josiah Quincy, Stephen Higgenson, and William S. Shaw in settling the matter. The three men were prominent members of the liberal religious sector of Boston and came to Adams's assistance because of their appreciation of her scholarship and in reaction to their dislike of Morse's Calvinist orthodoxy. Although their participation did not bring an immediate closure to the controversy (the debate continued for a ten-year period), their support did allow Adams to return to her literary endeavors by establishing an annuity to cover her financial expenses. Finally in 1814 the rivalry was brought to a conclusion when Morse attempted to clear his name and published all the documents that had been exchanged during the conflict. According to Morse the public was to be the final judge. Meanwhile Adams had published two more books, *The Truth and Excellence of the Christian Religion Exhibited* (1804) and *History of the Jews* (1812). In 1826 *Letters on the Gospels* appeared, and her final work, *A Memoir of Miss Hannah Adams*, was published posthumously in 1832. As a tribute to her literary endeavors, Chester Harding painted her portrait, and the image was hung in the Boston Athenaeum. She died in Boston.

In assessing the literary achievements of Hannah Adams, the Reverend Samuel Willard wrote, in a review of her *Dictionary of All Religions and Religious Denominations* (1817), that he need not provide much of an introduction since "the author of this work is in such full possession of publick regard, from the benefit conferred by her writings, and the merits of her several productions are so generally known." The numerous editions of her books issued in England as well as in the United States are further testament to how widely she was read by her contemporaries. Her books are expansive compilations of data. Although she was not fully successful in achieving an objective voice as she had set out to do, Adams managed to write a far less preferential text than most other authors of the same period.

• Adams's papers are in the Schlesinger Library, Radcliffe College, and in the New England Historic Genealogical Society, Boston. Additional manuscript materials are in the Adams Family Papers at the Massachusetts Historical Society and in the Morse Family Papers at Yale University and the New York Public Library. Adams's posthumously published memoir, *A Memoir of Miss Hannah Adams, Written by Herself with Additional Notices by a Friend* (Hannah Farnham Sawyer Lee) (1832), is the most comprehensive source available. Documents pertaining to the Adams-Morse controversy—Jedidiah Morse, *An Appeal to the Public* (1814); Hannah Adams, *A Narrative of the Controversy between the Rev. Jedidiah Morse, D. D., and the Author* (1814); and Sidney E. Morse, *Remarks on the Controversy between Doctor Morse and Miss Adams* (1814)—are available on microfilm. Two modern assessments of Adams's historical role are Thomas A. Tweed, "An American Pioneer in the Study of Religion: Hannah Adams (1755–1831) and Her *Dictionary of All Religions*," *Journal of the American Academy of Religion* 60, no. 5 (1992): 437–64, and M. W. Vella, "Theology, Genre and Gender: The Precarious Place of Hannah Adams in American Literary History," *Early American Literature* 28, no. 1 (1993): 21–41. For a nineteenth-century review of her two most notable publications see Samuel Willard, "Review of *Dictionary of All Religions and Religious Denominations*, 4th ed., by Hannah Adams," *North American Review* 7 (May 1918): 86–92. On the significance of Adams's role in the study of the religious world see Gene Gleason, "A Mere Woman," *American Heritage* 24 (1972): 80–84.

CAROL BERKIN

ADAMS, Harriet Stratemeyer (11 Dec. 1892–27 Mar. 1982), author and partner in the Stratemeyer Syndicate, was born in Newark, New Jersey, the daughter of Edward Stratemeyer, an author and the founder of the Stratemeyer Literary Syndicate, and Magdalene Van Camp. Much of Adams's life was influenced by her famous father. Circa 1905 he established the Stratemeyer Literary Syndicate, whereby he developed new juvenile series, hired writers to flesh out plot outlines he created, then successfully marketed the manuscripts to publishers. Exposure to her father's career sparked an early interest in writing. Years later Adams recalled watching her father and one of his chief ghostwriters, Howard Garis, act out story ideas in the Stratemeyer living room.

Adams attended Wellesley College, where she studied English, music, and religion. Her extracurricular activities included playing piano with the college symphony orchestra, membership in the recently established Press Board, and time as a college correspondent for the *Boston Globe*.

After her graduation in 1914, Adams worked briefly for her father, editing Syndicate manuscripts at home because the conservative Stratemeyer would not permit her to work at the office. Marriage to Russell Vroom Adams, an investment broker, in 1915 ended her work at the Syndicate, for her father felt married women should not be employed outside their homes. Although Adams disagreed, she acceded to her father's wishes. For almost fifteen years she concentrated on being a wife and mother, participated in church and community activities (among them, establishing the New Jersey Wellesley Club), and confined her writing and editing to women's club and Sunday school materials.

In 1930 Edward Stratemeyer died unexpectedly, willing the Stratemeyer Syndicate—by then responsible for approximately thirty series—to his wife, an invalid. After discussing the matter with her spouse, Adams hired a nurse to care for her four children (the youngest was only five years old); relocated the Syndicate offices from New York to East Orange, New Jersey, fifteen minutes from her home; and assumed management of the Syndicate in conjunction with her younger sister, Edna Camilla Stratemeyer. Her initial duties included editing manuscripts and dealing with publishers and ghostwriters, thus allowing the continuation of popular series such as Tom Swift, Bomba the Jungle Boy, the Bobbsey Twins, the Ted Scott Flying Series, and—most importantly for the Syndicate's future—Nancy Drew and the Hardy Boys. Adams later progressed to plotting books, developing new series, and writing manuscripts.

Management by Adams and her sister brought several changes at the Syndicate. As a result of cutting costs, they soon lost some key ghostwriters; this may have prompted the decision to prune Syndicate offerings. Although Stratemeyer's forte had been variety and volume, the sisters eliminated almost half of the Syndicate's ongoing series within the first four years of their tenure and gradually narrowed the focus to juvenile mysteries. In 1934 they developed two new series, the Dana Girls and Kay Tracey, both loosely modeled on the Syndicate's popular Nancy Drew; a less successful children's series, Mary and Jerry Mystery Stories, followed a year later.

Upon their mother's death in 1935, Adams and her sister officially inherited the Syndicate, which they continued to manage jointly until Edna Stratemeyer (by then Mrs. C. Wesley Squier) retired to Florida in 1942 and became an inactive partner. The war effort (which claimed the copper plates used for printing series), the loss of a son during World War II, and Edna Stratemeyer Squier's departure may have been responsible for further reductions. By the war's end, Adams was overseeing only four series (Nancy Drew, the Hardy Boys, the Bobbsey Twins, and Honey Bunch).

Adams reversed this trend in the next decade, hiring new employees, developing series such as Tom Swift, Jr., and ultimately doubling and trebling the Syndicate's annual output. She was also writing occasional volumes, including some Bobbsey Twins titles. In 1959 she initiated a massive, sixteen-year project to revise and update the Syndicate's three longest-running series by modernizing plots, removing racial slurs, and streamlining and simplifying the prose. Although some criticized the writing and characterization in the new versions, Adams's decision brought the series a new set of readers.

The previously reticent Adams began granting more interviews after the mid-1960s and discussed the Syndicate, often focusing on her favorite series, Nancy Drew. Accounts of Adams's involvement with the series vary, and she is sometimes incorrectly touted as the author of all Nancy Drew books published before her death. In actuality she did not begin writing complete manuscripts for the series until volume 31 (1953), then penned volumes 33 through 58 (1955–1979). Additionally, Adams and/or her sister plotted and edited all of the original Nancy Drews published after 1930, and Adams wrote and/or edited all of the revised versions of the first thirty-four volumes. She also helped to shape Nancy's character, originally by modifying ghostwriter Mildred Wirt Benson's depiction of Nancy, later by redoing parts of Wirt Benson's manuscripts, and finally by writing the stories herself. Adams sometimes referred to Nancy as a "third daughter" and told interviewers she embodied Wellesley's motto, *Non ministrari, sed ministrare* (not to be ministered unto, but to minister).

During the 1960s and 1970s Adams weathered a string of personal and professional losses: her husband died in 1965; her sister, in 1974; Andrew Svenson (a Syndicate partner since 1961), in 1975. By the mid-1970s most of the Syndicate's new series had been discontinued, and even the three key series were not selling as well as expected. Again Adams prevailed. She approved a television series, *The Nancy Drew/Hardy Boys Mystery Hour* (1977–1979) and, in 1979, switched publishers so that Syndicate series could appear in an affordable and contemporary paperback format. She then testified at—and won—the subsequent lawsuit filed by her former publisher, Grosset & Dunlap. As a result, book sales increased once more.

After Adams's death at her home in Pottersville, New Jersey, her four junior partners—all longtime employees—ran the Syndicate for two years before selling it to their publisher, Simon & Schuster. By the 1980s it was estimated that Syndicate series had sold close to 200 million copies. The two fledgling series that Adams had preserved from her father's time—Nancy Drew and the Hardy Boys—were responsible for much of that total. They had been translated into Danish, Dutch, French, German, Italian, Norwegian, and other languages; had spun off into related series and merchandise; and had become a staple of American children's fiction.

• The Beinecke Rare Book and Manuscript Library, Yale University, holds a small collection of papers pertaining to the Stratemeyer Syndicate, as does the Edward Stratemeyer–Harriet Stratemeyer Adams Collection, University of Oregon, Eugene. The most extensive Syndicate archives are in the uncataloged Stratemeyer Syndicate Records at New York Public Library. For a bibliography of Stratemeyer Syndicate publications, see Deidre Johnson, *Stratemeyer Pseudonyms and Series Books: An Annotated Checklist of Stratemeyer and Stratemeyer Syndicate Publications* (1982). Harriet Adams's own brief history of the Syndicate appears in "Their Success Is No Mystery," *TV Guide*, 25 June 1977, pp. 13–16; Mildred Wirt Benson, "The Ghost of Ladora," *Books at Iowa* 19 (Nov. 1973): 24–29, describes her time as a Syndicate ghostwriter; while Ilana Nash, "The Lady and the Press: Harriet Adams Courts America," *Dime Novel Round-Up* 65 (Aug. 1996): 111–21, considers Adams in light of her interviews and public statements. Harriet Adams (writing as Carolyn Keene) comments on Nancy Drew in a chapter of *The Great Detectives*, ed. Otto Penzler (1978). The essays in Carolyn Stewart Dyer and Nancy Tillman Romalov, eds., *Rediscovering Nancy Drew* (1995), cover the creation, content, and reception of the series; a chapter in Anne Scott MacLeod, *American Childhood* (1994), explores reasons for the series' success. Nancy Drew and other series from Adams's reign are discussed in Carol Billman, *The Secret of the Stratemeyer Syndicate: Nancy Drew, the Hardy Boys, and the Million Dollar Fiction Factory* (1986), and Deidre Johnson, *Edward Stratemeyer and the Stratemeyer Syndicate* (1993). Additional sources and detailed summaries of newspaper interviews with Adams can be found in David Farah and Ilana Nash, *Series Books and the Media; or, This Isn't All!: An Annotated Bibliography of Secondary Sources* (1996). An obituary is in the *New York Times*, 29 Mar. 1982.

DEIDRE A. JOHNSON

ADAMS, Henry (16 Feb. 1838–27 Mar. 1918), historian, novelist, and critic, was born Henry Brooks Adams in Boston, Massachusetts, the son of Charles Francis Adams, a diplomat, legislator, and writer, and Abigail Brooks. He enjoyed unparalleled advantages, chief among them his famous name and many family connections: he was the great-grandson of President John Adams and the grandson of President John Quincy Adams. Henry's father was a powerful force innational and in ternational politics, serving as a congressman, a vice presidential candidate in 1848, and his country's minister to Great Britain during the American Civil War. He was also frequently mentioned as a possible presidential candidate. Presidents, high-ranking diplomats, and world leaders were thus as familiar to Adams as aunts, uncles, and grandparents are to lessfavored youth.

Although Adams later depreciated his formal education, he attended the country's best schools, including the Dixwell School, and he graduated from Harvard College in 1858. Following Harvard he spent two years in Europe on what was then called "the grand tour." During this tour he became a newspaper correspondent for the first time. His letters to the *Boston Courier* in the spring of 1860 included an interview with Italian revolutionary leader Giuseppe Garibaldi, a meeting that Adams was able to arrange through family connections.

Adams returned to the United States in the fall of 1860, in time to vote for Abraham Lincoln for president. He also began reading law in Boston but ceased his legal studies almost immediately when the newly elected Lincoln appointed his father as minister to Great Britain. When his father asked Adams to accompany him as a private secretary he accepted, no doubt relieved since he had little desire to study or practice law. During the time that he spent in England Adams added greatly to his list of acquaintances and friends, including international celebrities. Besides being presented at court to Queen Victoria, the young Adams met political luminaries such as Prime Minister Henry Palmerston, reformers John Bright and Richard Cobden, and political philosopher John Stuart Mill. His social world extended to literary giants such as Robert Browning and Charles Dickens and to Britain's foremost geologist, Sir Charles Lyell, who had recently embraced Charles Darwin's controversial theory of evolution. Indeed, Adams reviewed the tenth edition of Lyell's *Principles of Geology* (1867) for the *North American Review*. In this piece, as well as in numerous letters and published writings over the years, Adams expressed serious doubts about evolution, not because of any theological misgivings (Adams was an agnostic by this time) but because of a strong streak of personal pessimism that led him to doubt any sort of progressive theory, especially when it involved human society. It was also during the years in England that Adams made a lifelong friend in Charles Milnes Gaskell who, like his father, James Milnes Gaskell, moved in liberal circles and was well connected socially. Throughout the rest of their lives Adams and Gaskell shared a deep interest in political reform in their respective countries and conducted a fascinating transatlantic correspondence.

While in England Adams began to give a great deal of thought to what had brought the United States into a ruinous civil war and to what he and other well-placed young men of his generation might do to save the American political experiment that his own ancestors had helped launch less than a century before. His reading of Alexis de Tocqueville's *Democracy in America* (1835–1840) and several works by Mill convinced him that he and his counterparts back home could indeed play an important part in salvaging the United States. Particularly helpful in drawing such a conclusion was Mill's *Consideration on Representative Government* (1861), in which the author concluded that the masses need to be guided by a moral and intelligent elite.

In order to help guide public opinion in the United States after his return from England in 1868, Adams settled in Washington, D.C., as a freelance journalist, contributing articles to the *North American Review*, the *Nation*, and various British periodicals. Adams's most bitter attacks were aimed at President Ulysses S. Grant and at various individuals connected with the corrupt Grant administration.

In 1870, after much pressure from his family, Adams accepted a teaching position at Harvard, along with the unpaid editorship of the *North American Review*. He began teaching courses in medieval history but soon went on to develop offerings in early U.S. history. In 1872 Adams married Marian "Clover" Hooper; they had no children. Meanwhile, Adams became active in reform politics, joining the Liberal Republicans in 1872 in their unsuccessful attempt to deny Grant a second term. During the Harvard years he also continued to write a number of articles for the periodical press. Adams resigned his editorship of the *North American Review* in 1876 and his Harvard position in 1877, in part because he felt smothered by such close proximity to his family and to Boston's stiff social conventions. He also left teaching in order to concentrate his energies on researching and writing the history of the United States during the early nineteenth century—the time, he had concluded, that the American experiment had begun to unravel.

Upon leaving Harvard Adams settled in Washington, the city that he had come to prefer more than any other in the country and a place where he could make use of government archives for his ambitious historical research. He and his wife also took several trips to Europe, in part so that he could search foreign archives for material relating to American history. The principal result of these labors was his nine-volume work *The History of the United States during the Administrations of Thomas Jefferson and James Madison* (1889–1891). Throughout the work there is a note of fatalism and pessimism: the United States had failed to realize its highest ideals because the American people could not escape the bonds of human nature, and the rest of the world refused to allow the nation to pursue its noblest goals without interference. According to Adams, countries as well as their leaders—the United States included—"were bourne away by the stream, struggling, gesticulating, praying, murdering, robbing; each blind to everything but a selfish interest, and all helping more or less unconsciously to reach the new level which society was obliged to seek" (vol. 4, p. 302).

In the course of writing his history, Adams managed to publish biographies of Albert Gallatin (1879) and John Randolph (1882), both important political personalities of the Jefferson and Madison periods and both, according to Adams, brought down by forces over which they had little or no control. Adams thus finished his studies of early nineteenth-century U.S. history by concluding that his countrymen were not, as many of them seemed to believe, a chosen people under a new dispensation and thereby released from the common failings of humanity.

The years of writing history in Washington were the happiest in Adams's adult life, despite the fact that his marriage was childless. Residing across the street from the White House on Lafayette Square, the Adamses constantly entertained people of merit, distinction, and wit. Among their closest friends were diplomat and writer John Hay and naturalist Clarence King. King, Hay and his wife, Clara, and the Adamses formed an intimate circle that they dubbed the "Five of Hearts." Out of this social scene, and out of a continuing fascination with American politics, came much of the material for Adams's anonymously written novel, *Democracy* (1880), a thinly veiled account of political corruption and intrigue in the nation's capital.

Adams published a second novel, *Esther*, in 1884 (under the pseudonym Frances Snow Compton); the book grappled with the seemingly irreconcilable conflict between science and religion that troubled many well-educated men and women during the Gilded Age. Its protagonist, Esther Dudley, is forced by her lack of faith to break off her engagement to a young clergyman and is nearly driven to suicide at the end of the novel.

Many observers have connected the character and dilemmas of Esther Dudley with Adams's wife, Marian, who likewise lacked religious faith and who, unlike Esther, actually took her own life in 1885 after a period of deep depression. Marian's suicide was a terrible blow to Adams, one from which he never fully recovered. He sought distraction in an around-the-world voyage (1890–1892) with artist and friend John La Farge. His friendship with Elizabeth Sherman Cameron, the wife of U.S. senator Don Cameron from Pennsylvania, also became an important source of comfort after the suicide. This friendship—which soon turned to love, at least on Adams's part—has been the subject of intense speculation over the years, although it seems that the relationship was emotional rather than physical.

Adams interrupted his ambitious journey with La Farge with a long stay in Paris. This marked the beginning of an annual trek to France (until World War I put a halt to the peregrinations), with Adams typically spending the summer and autumn months in the French capital and the rest of the year in Washington. Using Paris as a base, he took frequent trips around France as well as to other parts of Europe, including a visit to Russia in 1901. Adams could easily afford such travel with an income, on various inheritances, of about $60,000 per year by 1900.

It was during the 1890s in France that Adams renewed his interest in French Gothic cathedrals. Out of this fascination came his book *Mont-Saint-Michel and Chartres*, privately printed in 1905 and published in 1913. Although styled as an elaborate guidebook to two of France's most magnificent works of architecture, the book is a hymn of praise for the High Middle Ages, increasingly a golden age in the past for Adams and for many other thinkers on both sides of the Atlantic who were alarmed at various trends in the "modern world." Chief among these trends was the lack of intellectual and spiritual unity in the late nineteenth and early twentieth centuries and the denial by many scientists and philosophers of either absolute truth or universal law.

This contrast between what Adams called the unity of the twelfth and thirteenth centuries (as symbolized by the Virgin of Chartres) and the multiplicity of the early twentieth century (as symbolized by the dynamo) was a recurrent theme in *The Education of Henry Adams*, privately issued in 1904 and 1906 and published in 1918. Although autobiographical in nature, Adams refers to himself in the third person and ignores many important aspects of his life, including the years of his marriage and his wife's tragic suicide. The book also conveys a strong message of personal failure that was at odds with the reality of his successful life. This persona of failure has been interpreted by readers in various ways: as a manifestation of Adams's pessimism, as evidence of his disappointment over his role in American politics, or simply as a vehicle for reflecting on the shortcomings of the modern world as a whole and American life in particular.

The Education of Henry Adams, however fascinating, must be approached with much care because of Adams's many calculated distortions. It should be read along with other writings by Adams and especially in the context of his sparkling and often brilliant personal correspondence, most of which has been collected and published. Yet even there, the tone of personal and social criticism is unmistakable. Adams's social critiques also appeared in several works that were published during his last decade, including two essays intended for historians, "The Rule of Phase Applied to History" (1909) and "A Letter to American Teachers of History" (1910). Both of these works were attempts to draw analogies between recent theories in physics, such as the "rule of phase" and the second law of thermodynamics, and social and political trends in what Adams continued to insist was an imperiled modern world. Adams saw such theories, in part, as a means of combating assertions by social evolutionists (or social Darwinists as they are often called) that progress was automatic and inexorable.

Despite his mordant views and lingering grief over his wife's death, Adams continued to enjoy a wide circle of friends during the last period of his life. Hay, who was the secretary of state from 1898 to 1905, remained a close friend and confidant until his death in 1905. Hay and Adams had built adjoining houses on Lafayette Square in Washington during the mid-1880s that were designed by their architect friend Henry Hobson Richardson. Adams and Hay often took walks in the afternoon, with Hay unburdening himself to Adams. Although Adams seldom hesitated to give advice, it remains unclear whether he had any direct influence on foreign policy. Yet he often served as an unofficial go-between, meeting with foreign envoys in his home and conveying their conversations to Hay.

In this way Adams continued to enjoy an insider's view of U.S. foreign policy. At the same time, he used his yearly stints in Paris as a window onto the European scene. He was particularly alarmed by the race for colonial spoils at the beginning of the twentieth century, and he was highly critical of his own country's decision in 1898 to annex the Philippines at the end of the Spanish-American War. Nevertheless, he grew alarmed at early signs of decline in British power, fearing that a decay of the British Empire would lead to disequilibrium and possibly war. "To anyone who has studied history," he wrote to Hay in 1900, "it is obvious that the fall of England would be paralleled by only two great convulsions in human record: the fall of the Roman Empire in the fourth century and the fall of the Roman Church in the sixteenth." Another recipe for disaster was the great potential of Russia, coupled with tremendous political and social instability in that country. As he confessed to his friend Elizabeth Cameron in 1904, "I am half crazy with fear that Russia is sailing straight into another French Revolution which may upset all Europe and us too." The outbreak of World War I in 1914 confirmed Adams's worst fears, but he was consoled by the hope that the war might lead to a great Atlantic alliance that would keep the peace for many years.

Adams's health deteriorated after he suffered a serious stroke in 1912, although he recovered enough to go about most aspects of his daily life. He died at his home in Washington, D.C. Adams was buried in Washington's Rock Creek Cemetery, beside his wife and beneath the large bronze statue of a grieving woman that Adams had commissioned from his sculptor friend Augustus Saint-Gaudens in the years just after Marian's death.

Although Adams's reputation has passed through several phases since his death, his analyses of American society and politics and his insightful criticisms of modern Western culture assures his continued relevance and importance. Adams was also a gifted writer whose prose style and use of symbolism mark him as one of the country's greatest literary figures.

• Adams's papers have been assembled in various places, but the most important repository is the Massachusetts Historical Society in Boston. These papers are part of that institution's impressive collection relating to the larger Adams family. The bulk of Adams's correspondence is in J. C. Levenson et al., eds., *The Letters of Henry Adams* (6 vols., 1983; rev. ed., 1988). The most complete biography of Adams remains the three-volume work by Ernest Samuels, *The Young Henry Adams* (1948), *Henry Adams: The Middle Years* (1958), and *Henry Adams: The Major Phase* (1964). A one-volume condensation of this trilogy, including new materials that had come to light since the earlier publications, is Samuels, *Henry Adams* (1989). Also see Edward Chalfant, *Both Sides of the Ocean:*

His First Life, 1838–1862 (1982), and Chalfant, *Better in Darkness, 1862–1891* (1994). Among the many books on various aspects of Adams's life and works are David R. Contosta, *Henry Adams and the American Experiment* (1980); William Dusenberre, *Henry Adams and the Myth of Failure* (1980); Levenson, *The Mind and Art of Henry Adams* (1957); and Brooks D. Simpson, *The Political Education of Henry Adams* (1996). A volume of essays by leading Adams scholars is Contosta and Robert Muccigrosso, eds., *Henry Adams and His World* (1993). Studies of Adams's family life include Earl N. Harbert, *The Force So Much Closer Home: Henry Adams and the Adams Family* (1977); Otto Friedrich, *Clover* (1979); and Eugenia Kaledin, *The Education of Mrs. Henry Adams* (1981). Concerning Adams's many friends see Patricia O'Toole, *The Five of Hearts: An Intimate Portrait of Henry Adams and His Friends* (1990), and Ernest Scheyer, *Circle of Henry Adams* (1970). Also very helpful in understanding Adams and his rich social connections is Harold Dean Cater's lengthy introduction to his collected Adams letters, *Henry Adams and His Friends* (1947). An exploration of the relationship between Adams and Elizabeth Cameron may be found in Arline B. Tehan, *Henry Adams in Love* (1983).

DAVID R. CONTOSTA

ADAMS, Henry Cullen (28 Nov. 1850–9 July 1906), legislator and public servant, was born in Verona, Oneida County, New York, the son of Benjamin Franklin Adams, a professor of classical languages at Hamilton College, and Caroline Shepard. His parents moved to southern Wisconsin before the Civil War, and young Henry grew up on a farm, acquiring an attachment to agriculture that would permeate the remainder of his life. He was educated in country schools, at Albion College, and then spent three years during the 1870s at the University of Wisconsin, but fragile health forced him to quit before earning a degree. Adams returned to his father's farm near Madison and in 1878 married Anne Burkley Norton, with whom he had four children.

For the next several years, Adams operated a successful dairy and fruit producing farm and became a leader in the establishment of farmers' institutes (in which practicing farmers presented lectures and demonstrations on practical topics) under the supervision of the University of Wisconsin College of Agriculture. He was president of the Wisconsin Dairymen's Association (WDA) for three years, secretary of the state horticultural society for two years (1886–1887), and a member of the state board of agriculture for eight years (1887–1895). From 1883 to 1887 he served in the state assembly, where he established himself as a champion of dairying and agriculture and of pure food laws. After a single two-year term as superintendent of public property from 1889 to 1891, Adams was appointed Wisconsin food and dairy commissioner, a post he held from 1898 to 1902. In that capacity, he campaigned vigorously for the enactment and enforcement of laws mandating high standards of purity and nutrition for the state's dairy products, positions supported by the WDA because of the damage that had been done to the reputation of their products by the production of adulterated cheese and by the competition from oleomargarine. In 1888 he was selected as a delegate-at-large to the Republican National Convention that nominated Benjamin Harrison (1833–1901) for president. In 1902 Adams and former Wisconsin governor William D. Hoard, both officials of the WDA and of the newly formed National Dairy Union, lobbied successfully over several months in support of the passage of the Grout Oleomargarine Act, which provided for the taxation and regulation of the butter substitute.

Elected to the U.S. Congress from the Second District of Wisconsin in 1902 as a supporter of Governor Robert M. La Follette, Sr. (1855–1925), and his progressive Republican movement, Adams served two distinguished and productive terms despite his rapidly deteriorating health. He proved especially adept at the art of compromise, frequently succeeding in bringing contending factions together to establish a consensus on a piece of controversial legislation. During the debate over the federal Meat Inspection Law, for example, Adams gathered together representatives of the meat packing industry, consumer advocates, and public health officials and gained their agreement, largely by convincing all present of the benefits that would accrue from federal regulation. His experience as a practical farmer and as a state inspector had firmly convinced Adams that producers and consumers shared a common interest in mandating high quality standards for food and dairy products. He shared the WDA's conviction that mandating quality would eliminate marginal operators and earn "extra prices," thus making such actions "plain business sense." After a personal tour of the New Mexico and Arizona territories convinced him that the two were too different in population and economy to form a single state, Adams spearheaded the successful effort to have each admitted to the Union separately. He also supported the Pure Food and Drug Law and took a leadership role in the enactment of a federal statute banning the interstate sale of oleomargarine; both measures were a logical outgrowth of his experience in Wisconsin. In 1905 Adams crowned his brief congressional career by securing the adoption of the act that bears his name, a measure that strengthened the Hatch Experiment Station Act of 1887 by raising the amount of funding incrementally to a maximum of $30,000 annually per state. The measure stipulated that the funds were "to be applied only to paying the necessary expenses of conducting original researches or experiments bearing directly on the agricultural industry of the United States" and gave the Department of Agriculture effective control over the administration of the fund.

So exhausted by his labors that he spent a large part of the 1905 congressional session in his sickbed, Adams died of intestinal problems in Chicago en route to his home in Wisconsin.

• Adams's speeches on the Wisconsin Primary Election Law (1901), the Philippine Tariff Bill, the Insurgents and Statehood for Arizona and New Mexico, as well as the microfilm copy of his scrapbooks for the years 1890 to 1901 are all available at the State Historical Society of Wisconsin, Madison.

Adams's career can be examined primarily in the public record. See especially the *Reports of the Wisconsin Dairy and Food Commission* (1885–1902), the *Journal of the Proceedings of the Wisconsin Legislature* (1883–1885), *U.S. Office of Experiment Stations Bulletin* 184 (1907), and *U.S. Department of Agriculture Year Book, 1906* (1906). The debates over the federal Pure Food and Drug Act and the Adams Agricultural Experiment Station Act are preserved in the *Congressional Record*, 58th Cong., 1903–1904, and 59th Cong., 1st sess., 1905. See also W. A. Henry, "Tribute to H. C. Adams," *Proceedings of the Association of American Agricultural Colleges and Experiment Stations* 20 (1906): 36–39; and Charles E. Rosenberg, "The Adams Act: Politics and the Cause of Scientific Research," *Agricultural History* 38 (1964): 3–12. An obituary is in the *Milwaukee Journal*, 9 July 1906.

JOHN D. BUENKER

ADAMS, Herbert Baxter (16 Apr. 1850–30 July 1901), historian and educator, was born in Shutesbury, Massachusetts, the son of Nathaniel Dickinson Adams, a lumber merchant, and Harriet Hastings. Adams's father died when the boy was six; as a result the family moved to nearby Amherst where his mother had relatives. There he attended local schools and later Phillips Exeter Academy.

Adams attended Amherst College from 1868 to 1872, a transitional period for the school when the classical curriculum and evangelical religious tradition were beginning to respond to newer scholarly and scientific currents. A gifted student, Adams graduated as class valedictorian. He had at first considered a career in journalism, but, influenced by Professor Julius H. Seelye, he determined to pursue postgraduate study in history instead. As the opportunity for such advanced work was then virtually nonexistent in the United States, he made plans to join the growing number of young Americans studying at one of the German universities.

In 1873, after some months of travel in Switzerland, France, and Italy, Adams reached his destination, the University of Heidelberg. With the exception of one semester spent at the University of Berlin, he studied at Heidelberg from 1874 to 1876, when he was granted the Ph.D. summa cum laude. Among the many scholars whose lectures and seminars he attended were Johann Bluntschli (political science); Bernhardt Erdmannsdörffer, Johann Droysen, and Heinrich von Treitschke (political history); Karl Knies (political economy); and Karl Stark (art history). The most important historiographical conviction he took with him was undoubtedly the so-called Teutonist thesis, according to which the institutions of modern popular government were products of Teutonic racial genius as originally embodied in the folk-assemblies of the primitive Germanic tribes.

In 1876 Adams accepted a postdoctoral fellowship in history at the new Johns Hopkins University in Baltimore, the first school in the United States established chiefly to foster graduate education and advanced research. Here he wrote *Maryland's Influence in Founding a National Commonwealth* (1877), a monograph that argued that Maryland, by insisting that state claims to western lands be surrendered to the Confederation government, was responsible for the creation of a national domain, the territorial precondition of nationhood.

In 1878 Adams was appointed to the Johns Hopkins faculty, where he soon became head of the joint department of history, politics, and economics, a post to which he brought great energy and administrative skill. During his tenure (which lasted until shortly before his death) the university came to be viewed as the center of the "New Historical School," the purpose of which was to apply the scientific (or critical) method identified especially with German historical scholarship to American historical questions. In 1882 Adams launched his graduate seminar, choosing for its motto the English historian Edward A. Freeman's dictum: "History is past Politics and Politics present History." Although the words never accurately described the scope of historical work at the university, it did express Adams's belief in the utility of historical knowledge. The seminar table in the Bluntschli Library became the weekly gathering place of such future scholars as J. Franklin Jameson, Woodrow Wilson, Charles M. Andrews, Albion W. Small, Charles H. Haskins, and Frederick Jackson Turner. As his students began to fill college and university positions around the country, Adams liked to refer to these as "colonies" of Johns Hopkins. The same year that he became director of the seminar Adams also initiated the Johns Hopkins Studies in Historical and Political Science to publicize the work of the department. This monograph series was the first of its kind in the United States and was an important incentive to historical research in the late nineteenth century.

The most distinctive feature of Adams's seminar, especially in the formative years, was its concentration on a kind of institutional history that was a direct outgrowth of his German experience. Picking up on the Teutonist thesis, he set his students to work tracing the evolution of early American local government and institutions back to what he assumed to be their prototypes in Anglo-Saxon England. He himself led the way with *The Germanic Origin of New England Towns* (1882): "The town and village life of New England is as truly the reproduction of Old English types as these again are reproductions of the village community system of the ancient Germans." Although Adams was not the first to advance this argument (popularly known as the "germ theory"), his name was most prominently identified with it. Despite its appeal to many historians, the theory was soon challenged and, by 1900, largely discarded. Nevertheless, it had served as the spur to much good research, some of which was instrumental in overturning it.

While it is as mentor to fledgling scholars that he is best remembered, Adams's services to Johns Hopkins and the historical profession were not limited to this sphere. He was a popular teacher of undergraduates, a group somewhat neglected in a setting so committed to the advancement of professional scholarship. Throughout his career Adams taught courses in ancient, medieval, and modern history that encompassed social, cultural, and economic—as well as political—considerations. He supported undergraduate extracurricular activities and established an annual prize for undergraduate debate. Not the least of Adams's services to the university was in the area of public relations. He lost no opportunity in print or on the podium to extol Johns Hopkins and its achievements. That such praise redounded to his own benefit did not detract from its sincerity. A popular public speaker, Adams could always be depended on to meet requests to address local schools, workingmen's clubs, or religious groups on historical or contemporary themes. In 1881–1882 he used his university position to good effect when he led a successful campaign to persuade the state legislature to entrust the Maryland Historical Society with the preservation and publication of the state archives, the principal repository of the state's colonial and revolutionary records.

Another institution with which Adams was closely connected was the American Historical Association. As historical research and writing became increasingly the domain of professional scholars, the desirability of a national society committed to the advancement of their goals and interests was apparent. Thus, in 1884 Adams, together with several like-minded colleagues, took the lead in the formation of such a group. Adams was chosen secretary, and from this post he guided the development of the organization for more than fifteen years. Some members came to feel that Adams's hand rested too heavily on the association, but he retained his place until ill health forced his resignation. He was thereupon named vice president, but he did not live to succeed to the presidency of the society that he had done so much to shape.

In the late 1880s Adams's commitment to American higher education led him beyond the confines of the university and the professional society. He became a strong supporter of the popular Chautauqua adult education movement; for several years he lectured at the Chautauqua summer school in upstate New York and served as director of its history curriculum. Adams's work with Chautauqua led him more or less simultaneously to a keen interest in the university extension movement, which was then enjoying considerable success in England. He is credited with introducing the idea in the United States, his plan being to forge an alliance between university extension programs and the public libraries of the country. In 1896 he traveled to Great Britain to study extension programs there on behalf of the federal Bureau of Education. In time, however, Adams became disappointed with the results of these efforts, though he never abandoned his view that the future of democracy depended on broadening the base of higher education.

During these same years, Adams took on another major project. Under the sponsorship of the Bureau of Education, he became the editor of Contributions to American Educational History (1887–1901), a series of monographs designed to examine the history and current condition of higher education in every state. Adams himself wrote the volume *Thomas Jefferson and the University of Virginia* (1888), an early study of Jefferson's educational thought. Since the undertaking was subject to the scrutiny of interested politicians, the editor had need of considerable tact.

Adams's renown as an educator brought many invitations to teaching and administrative positions at colleges and universities across the country. He was offered professorships at Smith College (where he taught during the spring semester from 1878 to 1881), the University of Pennsylvania, and the University of Michigan; he was offered the presidencies of the University of Nebraska, the University of Kansas, and the University of California, among other schools. Probably the most enticing offer came in 1891 from President William R. Harper of the University of Chicago to become head of the history department and dean of the graduate school. In each case, however, he chose to remain in Baltimore. When, in 1900, Daniel Coit Gilman resigned from the presidency of Johns Hopkins, Adams was one of those mentioned as a successor.

Adams was greatly interested in public affairs, a fact that considerably influenced his teaching. Papers on political and economic subjects were as plentiful as historical papers in his seminar, and prominent national and local figures frequently addressed the group. During his tenure the department produced as many theses in political science and political economy as it did in history. It was Adams's aim that the university send out not only academic scholars but public administrators, social workers, and journalists as well, and in this he was not disappointed.

A lifelong Republican of the mugwump reform stripe, Adams believed that the university community, both collectively and individually, ought to make itself a force for good in society. In the national arena he advocated the establishment of a "civil academy" in Washington, D.C., for the training of professional civil servants as a counterforce to the spoils system. Other typical reform positions espoused by Adams on issues before the nation included tariff reduction and hard money, revision of the public land laws in the interest of settlers, and the creation of international arbitration machinery.

But Adams recognized that local affairs provided the principal opportunities for the exercise of intelligent citizenship, and he stressed such matters. He himself was a member of the Baltimore Reform League and the Maryland Civil Service Reform Association. A firm believer in the new, so-called scientific philanthropy, he joined the Baltimore Charity Organization Society at its inception. Adams was also an admirer of the English social reformer Arnold Toynbee, whose short life served to inspire the settlement house movement. Thus, he associated himself with other civic leaders in efforts to set up university settlements. By 1900 he had come to support an increasingly active role for city government in such areas as public health, parks and recreation, and urban beautification.

In 1893 Adams published his *Life and Writings of Jared Sparks*, an authorized two-volume biography of the pioneer New England historical editor best known for his publication of the George Washington and Benjamin Franklin papers. Adams's task was laborious and almost thankless, as he was severely criticized for his too gentle handling of Sparks's disposition to bowdlerize his subjects, a common enough practice at the time. Still, the strictures were just, and Adams was sufficiently disturbed by them to react defensively.

The influence of Adams on his profession, however, is not to be measured by his publications but rather by the enduring products of his organizational skill and by the pedagogical and personal influence that he exerted upon the coming generation of historians and social scientists. Woodrow Wilson may be said to have spoken for these scholars when he wrote: "If I were to sum up my impression of Dr. Adams, I should call him a great Captain of Industry, a captain in the field of systematic and organized scholarship. . . . The thesis work done under him may fairly be said to have set the pace for university work in history throughout the United States." Adams, who was unmarried, died in Amherst, Massachusetts.

• The bulk of Adams's papers are held at the Johns Hopkins University; papers pertaining to his role as secretary of the American Historical Association are held at the Library of Congress. A representative sampling of this material may be found in *Historical Scholarship in the United States, 1876–1901: As Revealed in the Correspondence of Herbert B. Adams*, ed. W. Stull Holt (1938). A complete bibliography of Adams's publications appears in John M. Vincent, *Herbert B. Adams: Tributes of Friends; with a Bibliography of the Department of History, Politics and Economics at the Johns Hopkins University* (1902). See also Vincent, "Herbert B. Adams," in *American Masters of Social Science*, ed. Howard W. Odum (1927); Raymond J. Cunningham, "The German Historical World of Herbert Baxter Adams: 1874–1876," *Journal of American History* 68 (1981): 261–75; John Higham, "Herbert Baxter Adams and the Study of Local History," *American Historical Review* 89, no. 5 (Dec. 1984): 1225–39; and Cunningham, "'Scientia Pro Patria': Herbert Baxter Adams and Mugwump Academic Reform at Johns Hopkins, 1876–1901," *Prospects: An Annual of American Cultural Studies* 15 (1990): 109–44. Useful obituaries are by Richard T. Ely in *Herbert Baxter Adams: Tributes of Friends . . .* (1902), pp. 27–49, and by Daniel Coit Gilman in *The Outlook*, 12 Oct. 1901, pp. 370–72.

RAYMOND J. CUNNINGHAM

ADAMS, Herbert Samuel (28 Jan. 1858–21 May 1945), sculptor, was born in West Concord, Vermont, the son of Samuel Minot Adams, a machinist and patternmaker, and Nancy Ann Powers. Adams grew up in Fitchburg, Massachusetts. He studied at a technical school in Worcester and at the Massachusetts Normal Art School in Boston before traveling to Paris, where he studied with Antonin Mercié at the École des Beaux-Arts from 1885 to 1890. In 1888 he made a bronze fountain for the town of Fitchburg that features two boys playing with turtles. In 1888–1889 his work won an honorable mention at a Paris exhibition.

While in Paris Adams met Adeline Valentine Pond, whom he married in 1889; the couple had no children. His bust of her (1887, Hispanic Society of America), thrust him to the forefront of American portraiture. He followed that achievement with several distinctive polychromed and multimedia portrait and ideal busts of women, which earned him renown for their delicate and decorative qualities. These sensitively modeled busts (examples are at the Metropolitan Museum of Art, the Corcoran Gallery of Art, and the Detroit Institute of Arts) are painted naturalistically with hues that suffuse the marble, giving warmth and life to the cold stone. Adams added bronze and wooden elements as well as jewels to these sculptures. His portrait of the youthful Margaretta DuPont (sometimes Marguerite du Pont) has the head and neck made of warm-toned marble and the shoulders and base carved in French walnut. Golden fillets mask the joint and a lapis lazuli brooch completes the composition. Ernest Peixotto, writing in the *American Magazine of Art* in 1921, called these polychromed portraits "the most perfect flower of his genius." In the *History of American Sculpture* (1924), Lorado Taft said that Adams's bust of Pond "still remains, in some sense, unsurpassed by his later achievement. . . . it is of such perfect mastery that the face and neck, at least, appear plastic, as if responsive like wax to the pressure of the artist's thumb."

These busts and many of Adams's reliefs, such as *The Singing Boys* (1894, Metropolitan Museum of Art), are influenced by his study of spontaneous French modeling techniques, the work of the American sculptor Augustus Saint-Gaudens, and Florentine Renaissance art. The formal refinement, technical excellence, and delicate effect of these sculptures have earned Adams recognition equal to that which has resulted from his commissions for monumental figures and architectural sculpture.

Adams was a master at bas-relief and executed bronze doors for several buildings. He completed the doors for the Library of Congress (c. 1897) on the death of Olin Levi Warner, the original sculptor, and he made doors for St. Bartholomew's Church in New York City (c. 1901–1902), the Mariners' Museum in Newport News, Virginia, and the American Academy of Arts and Letters in New York City. He also created three-dimensional sculptures to ornament buildings and monuments. Four twelve-foot-high allegorical figures by Adams crown the cornice of the Brooklyn Museum (c. 1909). Two more heroic-scale stone figures adorn the attic of the courthouse in Cleveland, and two bronze portraits flank the steps of that building. He also modeled the Victory figures for the approaches to the temporary Dewey Arch in New York City (1898).

Like most successful sculptors of his day, Adams produced much monumental sculpture. Best known are his *William Ellery Channing* in the Public Garden, Boston (1903), and *William Cullen Bryant*, behind the New York Public Library (1911). Both are set against Renaissance revival exedrae and were designed in conjunction with the architects. Adams also created portrait figures of General Andrew A. Humphreys for the national military park in Fredericksburg, Virginia (1908), Colonel Laomi Baldwin for Woburn, Massachusetts (1918), Jerome Wheelock for Grafton, Massachusetts, and Professor Joseph Henry for the rotunda of the Library of Congress (c. 1896). His *Michigan Monument* (1916), stands in the national military park at Vicksburg, Mississippi. Other war memorials by Adams are located in Fitchburg (1917) and Winchester, Massachusetts (1927).

Throughout his long and productive career Adams exhibited widely. His work was shown at the World's Columbian Exposition in Chicago (1893), the Pan-American Exposition in Buffalo (1901), the Charleston Exposition (1902), the Louisiana Purchase Exposition in St. Louis (1904), and the Panama-Pacific Exposition in San Francisco (1915). He also exhibited at the National Academy of Design and at the National Sculpture Society.

Adams was a founder of the National Sculpture Society in 1893 and served as its president twice, from 1908 to 1910 and from 1912 to 1914; he was also its honorary president from 1933 until his death. He was a member and academician of the National Academy of Design and held the position of president from 1917 to 1920; Adams is one of only three sculptor-presidents in NAD history. He was a member of the National Academy of Arts and Letters from 1899 to 1945 and of the American Academy of Arts and Letters from 1912 to 1945.

Throughout his life, Adams's sphere of influence centered around New York. On his return from Paris in 1890, he taught at the Pratt Institute in Brooklyn until 1898. He opened a studio in Greenwich Village in the 1890s and later opened a second studio in the artist colony at Cornish, New Hampshire. Adams's career peaked about 1910. After that time the advent of abstract and nonrepresentational art diverted attention from the traditional figurative sculpture that Adams practiced. Adams was by nature a modest, sensitive, and retiring person. He was respected by fellow artists for his fine nature and firm sense of fairness. He died in New York.

• Adams's correspondence relating to the American Academy of Arts and Letters (150 items, 1912–1942), is in the library of the academy in New York. Wayne Craven, *Sculpture in America*, rev. ed. (1984), provides the fullest account of Adams's life and work. Charles Caffin, *American Masters of Sculpture*, rev. ed. (1913), devotes a chapter to Adams. Beatrice Proske, *Brookgreen Gardens Sculpture* (1943), and Lorado Taft, *History of American Sculpture*, rev. ed. (1930), are also informative. Margaret C. French, *Memories of a Sculptor's Wife* (1928), gives her impression of Adams. An obituary is in the *New York Herald Tribune*.

MICHAEL W. PANHORST

ADAMS, James Hopkins (15 Mar. 1812–13 July 1861), planter and politician, was born in Richland District, South Carolina, the son of Henry Walker Adams and Mary Goodwyn, planters. At an early age, both of his parents died and James was placed in the care of his maternal grandfather, an early settler of South Carolina from Virginia. Prosperous, his grandfather, a plantation owner, was able to raise Adams in an atmosphere of wealth and education. Shortly after his graduation from Yale in 1831, Adams married Jane Margaret Scott, with whom he had eleven children.

Settling down as a planter in Richland District, Adams took increased interest in current affairs and politics. He chose the growing Whig party as his standard, believing in a strong and progressive economy. Yet first and foremost he was a South Carolinian and rushed into the nullification crisis on the side of his state. In the South Carolina Nullification Convention, Adams departed from the Whig position in believing that nullification was a proper remedy for what he deemed as the repeated unconstitutional acts of the U.S. Congress.

Through success in this convention, Adams endeared himself to the people of his home district as an exceptional debater and speaker. As a reward, they sent him to the South Carolina House as a representative for three terms: 1834–1838, 1840–1841, 1848–1849. After the nullification crisis had passed, Adams, a supporter of the Second Bank of the United States, fought the Jacksonian independent treasury, created by President Martin Van Buren. Unfortunately for Adams, John C. Calhoun, South Carolina's political king, embraced the bank, and Adams and his associates were soundly defeated. Yet within Richland District and the state capital of Columbia, he continued to be popular.

In 1841 Adams became a trustee of the South Carolina College, a post he held until his death. Around 1840 Adams also became a brigadier general of cavalry in the South Carolina militia, bringing to prominence this arm of the service. He was known by his peers as General James Adams, a title denoting his prominence and accomplishments. During a debate over the federal banking system, as a powerful member of the South Carolina Senate from 1850–1853, Adams had tried to carry South Carolina out of the Union. Although his ploy failed, he became a Southern Democrat and staunch states' rights advocate, supporting Robert Barnwell Rhett and continually seeking to defend South Carolina and its institutions. Although the Whig party had dissolved, in large part because of sectional issues, Adams continued his interest in banking and economics when he became the director of the Exchange Bank of Columbia, a post he held from 1854 to 1861.

In December 1854 Adams was overwhelmingly elected governor by the South Carolina legislature. During his governorship, Adams advocated the reopening of the African slave trade, pursuing this goal with much earnestness, boldness, candor, and ability. As a staunch supporter of his section's institutions and fundamental beliefs, Adams believed that the African slave was inferior and was meant to hold a menial existence under the paternalistic care of the white ruling class.

By 1856 the governor brought his views to the South Carolina General Assembly. Adams proposed that the legislature take steps toward reopening the slave trade. Sent to committee, the proposal was accepted by a majority report, but heated debate on the floor eventually led to the motion being permanently tabled. When his term ended in 1856, Adams continued to push for reopening the slave trade. In the U.S. senatorial elections of 1857 and 1858, Adams was defeated after being considered too extreme in his views of the slave trade and secession. It became clear that the people of South Carolina sought conservatives and moderates to represent them in those trying times, electing former governor and moderate James Henry Hammond in 1857 and James Chesnut, a conservative states' rights supporter, in 1858.

Although he kept abreast of the states' rights fight, Adams retired to his plantation. He took only one prominent local position, in 1858 becoming the director of the Bank of Chester, a position he held until his death. Yet as the secession question grew in South Carolina after the election of Abraham Lincoln, the people of his district called Adams to be a representative at the Secession Convention in Charleston. Seeing the convention as the culmination of a fight he had waged since 1851, Adams signed the Ordinance of Secession with others on 20 December 1860. The Secession Convention and the people of South Carolina appointed Adams and two others as commissioners to President James Buchanan to obtain the return of South Carolina properties held by the U.S. government. Unsuccessful and ailing, Adams traveled to Europe to recover. After his return, his health showed little improvement, and he eventually died at his "Live Oak" plantation in Richland District.

As a plantation owner, aristocrat, and politician, Adams took an active part in defending the institutions and beliefs of his class. Unfaltering in his convictions, Adams, even in defeat, remained true to the idea of secession that he promoted for decades. True to his beloved state, Adams was forthright in his arguments and steadfast to his obligations.

• Some of Adams's papers are in the South Caroliniana Library at the University of South Carolina. One of the most thorough sketches on Adams is B. F. Perry, *Reminiscences of Public Men* (1883). Another brief outline of his private and public life can be found in Elisabeth D. English and B. M. Clark, "Richland County Economic and Social," *Bulletin of the University of South Carolina* (Jan. 1924). His political viewpoints can be found in W. J. Carnathan, "The Proposal to Reopen the Slave Trade," *South Atlantic Quarterly* 25, and Theodore D. Jervey, *The Slave Trade: Slavery and Color* (1925). Also see Carol Bleser, *Secret and Sacred: The Diaries of James Henry Hammond, a Southern Slaveholder* (1988), and Elizabeth Merritt, *James Henry Hammond 1807–1864* (1923), for the views of Adams's peers.

RONALD W. FISCHER, JR.

ADAMS, James Truslow (18 Oct. 1878–18 May 1949), historian, was born in Brooklyn, New York, the son of William Newton Adams, Jr., a disappointed stockbroker, and Elizabeth Harper Truslow. Adams attended the Brooklyn Polytechnic School for both his secondary and his college education, earning a B.A. in 1898. He was president of his class, valedictorian, and class poet. He then began graduate work in philosophy at Yale University but quit, bored, after a few months. Nevertheless, as was common then, he received an M.A. in 1900 for a fee of ten dollars.

Uncertain of his vocation, Adams worked first with his father's firm, Henderson, Lindley, and Company, and then for a railroad. In 1900 he attended the graduate history program at Columbia University for six weeks, tried to enter the publishing business, and finally returned to Wall Street. He found brokerage deadening but pledged to remain until he was thirty-five or had sufficient savings to support his nascent literary career. He sold a travel narrative to the *New York Times* in 1907 and subsequently published two small volumes on business topics: *Some Notes on the Currency Problem* (1908) and *Speculation and the Reform of the New York Stock Exchange* (1913). On his thirty-fifth birthday in 1913, he declared both parts of his pledge fulfilled and announced his retirement.

In 1912 Adams had moved with his father and sister to Bridgehampton, Long Island. The graveyard opposite their house guaranteed quiet for his studies but unexpectedly awoke in Adams a fascination with the history of his adopted area. Four years later he published privately a short narrative history, *Memorials of Old Bridgehampton*. Its favorable reception astonished and encouraged Adams. The sequel, *History of the Town of Southampton, East of Canoe Place* (1918), won critical acclaim and substantial sales. The historian Marcus W. Jernegan, in the *American Historical Review*, praised the book as a model local history.

After the outbreak of World War I, Adams worked as a cartographer for the American Geographical Society in New York, then as a captain for the Military Intelligence Division of the army in Washington, and finally for the American peace delegation in France. He returned to the United States in 1919, inspired by conversations with Europeans to write a history of the New England origins of American politics and culture.

Two years later Adams published the first volume of his New England trilogy, *The Founding of New England*. The second and third volumes followed directly, *Revolutionary New England, 1691–1776* (1923) and *New England in the Republic, 1776–1850* (1926). In these books Adams set out to upset "the old conception of New England history, according to which that section was considered to have been settled by persecuted religious refugees devoted to liberty of conscience." With fresh readings of published primary sources, Adams stressed instead historical themes similar to those of progressive historians. He detailed the Puritans' strong economic motivations, their sly dealings with the American Indians, their cruel intolerance of the Quakers, and the region's growing social stratification culminating in Shays's Rebellion. Adams also rehabilitated the Puritans' enemies, in particular the founders of Rhode Island, Roger Williams and Anne Hutchinson, crediting them with the development of New England's traditions of tolerance and self-governance.

Adams's trilogy was the high-water mark of scholarly debunking of the Puritans that had begun with Brooks Adams's (no relation) *The Emancipation of Massachusetts* (1887). He received a Pulitzer Prize for *The Founding* and election into the National Institute of Arts and Letters. Samuel Eliot Morison praised the first volume as "the best short history of New England that has appeared for a generation," even while working on a rejoinder in the Puritans' defense, *Builders of the Bay Colony* (1930). In a similar fashion, Evarts B. Greene, in the *American Historical Review*, censured Adams for unfairness to the Puritans but concluded that the volumes were "indispensable" to students of the period.

In 1927 Adams married Kathryn M. Seely, his nurse after an appendectomy in 1923. Also in 1927 he completed his contribution to the History of American Life Series: *Provincial Society, 1690–1763*. Allan Nevins, a close friend of Adams and fellow contributor in the series edited by Arthur Schlesinger, Sr., and Dixon Ryan Fox, called it "one of the best—probably the very best—of the books in the series." A host of complimentary reviews brought Adams to the peak of his historical reputation and sparked several offers of academic positions, all of which he declined. In 1930 Adams was elected to the American Academy of Arts and Letters and, shortly thereafter, a fellow of the Royal Society of Literature.

Long an Anglophile, Adams departed with his wife for England after their wedding, and a few months later they set up household in London. Adams remained equally productive there and published in 1930 a respected study of *The Adams Family* (to which he was not related). His *The Epic of America* (1931) argued that the dream of self-improvement was the motive force of American history; it became a Book-of-the-Month Club selection. He also published a popular two-volume survey of American history, *The March of Democracy* (1932–1933), and several short monographs, including an expanded essay on *Henry Adams* (1933) and a determinedly "unsectional" meditation on the Civil War, *America's Tragedy* (1934).

Along with his scholarly works, Adams developed in London a second reputation as a critical and increasingly conservative commentator on the American scene. He sent a stream of articles to *Harper's Monthly*, *Scribner's*, *Reader's Digest*, *Forum*, and other leading American magazines, the best of which were collected in two volumes: *Our Business Civilization: Some Aspects of American Culture* (1929) and *The Tempo of Modern Life* (1931). Adams compared the United States unfavorably to England's mature democracy.

Although a supporter of Franklin D. Roosevelt in 1932, Adams soon became a trenchant and highly visible critic of the president and the New Deal. After his return to the United States in 1936, he testified in Congress against the Supreme Court packing plan, warned that a third term might give "overwhelming" power to Roosevelt, and accused the New Deal of bankrupting the nation.

Adams wrote several more historical monographs from his new home in Southport, Connecticut. Among them were two on the British Empire that failed to meet his usual standards of historical research: *Building the British Empire, to the End of the First Empire* (1938) and *Empire on the Seven Seas; The British Empire, 1784–1949* (1940). Adams also wrote innumerable short essays, many of them for the *Dictionary of American Biography*. His chief accomplishment after 1936, however, came as editor of historical reference works, including the "monumental" *Dictionary of American History* (5 vols., 1940–1960), *The Atlas of American History* (1943), and *Album of American History* (5 vols., 1944–1949).

Adams died at his home in Southport. He had no children. He was a prolific and widely read historian and "critic of his country's political, economic, and social mores." He was also a principled amateur in a field increasingly dominated by university scholars, and he valued his business experience and European travels higher than any graduate training. While he shared many of the preoccupations of progressive historians, such as Charles Beard, Mary Ritter Beard, and Frederick Jackson Turner, he ultimately subscribed neither to "the economic nor any other single theory of history." He was, according to Nevins, "not a narrative and descriptive historian alone, but a philosophical historian" dedicated to the principle that human civilization had progressed and would continue to progress.

• The James Truslow Adams Papers (twenty boxes) are in the Manuscript Collection of Butler Library, Columbia University, N.Y. Adams discussed his philosophy of history in "My Methods as a Historian," *Saturday Review of Literature*, 30 June 1934, p. 778. He edited two volumes of American political thought, *Hamiltonian Principles* (1928) and *Jeffersonian Principles* (1928), and wrote, besides those works mentioned in the text, *America Looks at the British Empire*, America in a World at War, no. 1 (1940); *The American: The Making of a New Man* (1943); *Frontiers of American Culture* (1944); and *Big Business in a Democracy* (1945). A biographical essay, a bibliography, and a considerable selection of Adams's personal and professional correspondence are in Allan Nevins, *James Truslow Adams: Historian of the American Dream* (1968). Other biographical sources include Michael Kraus, *A History of American History* (1937), and a memoir by Roy F. Nichols in *American Philosophical Society Year Book* (1949). An obituary is in the *New York Times*, 19 May 1949.

CHARLES FORCEY

ADAMS, John (26 Mar. 1705–23 Jan. 1740), poet and minister, was born in Boston, Massachusetts, the son of John Adams, a shopkeeper, and Hannah Checkley. His family relocated in Annapolis Royal, Nova Scotia, several years before the young Adams matriculated at Harvard College. Adams graduated from Harvard in 1721. His connection to John Adams, the second president of the United States, is that Hugh Adams, who graduated from Harvard College in 1697, was uncle to both. In the summer of 1722, while on a journey to visit his family in Annapolis Royal, he barely escaped being captured by hostile Native Americans. The winter of 1722 found him back in New England, as he is known to have read an essay about poetry to a group of young Harvard graduates belonging to a society devoted to literary and religious studies. In the fall of 1727 Adams received an invitation to serve as assistant pastor to the Reverend Nathaniel Clap of Newport, Rhode Island, about half of whose congregation had registered objections to Clap's conservative theology. The two ministers did not see eye to eye, however, and several months later Clap, by occupying the pulpit during both Sunday services, refused to allow the younger man to preach. Many of the congregation disapproved of Clap's actions and separated from Clap's church in January 1728. John Adams was ordained over Clap's objections on 11 April 1728, marking the occasion of Adams's only printed sermon, "Jesus Christ, an Example to His Ministers." Adams's group became known as the Second Congregational Church of Newport.

Despite Adams's reputation for piety and his efforts in behalf of his congregation, he was dismissed from his post two years later, largely because of Clap's continuing animosity. After this, he returned to Harvard, where he remained for four years. By the spring of 1735 Adams was serving as an associate to Jedidiah Andrews, minister of Philadelphia's Presbyterian Church. By August 1735 Adams was back in Boston, however, where he was preaching in that town's almshouse. Not able to muster the requisite economic resources to keep Adams in its employ, the town soon let him go. After a second short tenure in Philadelphia, he returned to Boston. Adams was beset with a feverish delirium and died at Cambridge. He had never married.

While Adams's contemporaries knew him best as a minister, what is most memorable about him now is his poetry. His uncle Matthew Adams is largely responsible for John's reputation as a poet, having in 1745 gathered together enough of the younger man's verse to create a volume of 176 pages. Many of the poems, such as "The Perfection of Beauty," a paraphrase of Canticles 5:9, display a Platonic treatment of traditional Christian typology. Much of Adams's poetry is devoted to a treatment of the nature of poetic inspiration. The volume opens, for example, with a poem whose title reveals this preoccupation: "An Address to the Supreme Being, for His Assistance in My Poetical Composition." While in this poem Adams ignores the classical muses and calls directly on God to "lift my humble strains / My verse inspire," the poet unabashedly mixes classical allusions within his religious verse. For example, in a paraphrase of the entire book of Revelation, titled "The Revelation of St. John the Divine, translated," Adams depicts the movement of the moon across the evening sky in this elegant classical image: "fair Cynthia plies / Her Silver Circle thro' the gleeming skies" (p. 134).

In Adams's six translations of selections from Horace's *Odes*, however, the poet makes a marked shift from the Puritan habit of composing devotional verse toward the position that poetry should concern itself with aesthetic matters of taste. At one point in a translation of Horace's fourth ode of the first book, for example, describing how spring's promise makes one forget too easily death's ineluctable certainty, Adams renders Horace's Latin, *nec prata canis albicant pruinis* (neither are the fields made white with white frost), into this affecting, pastoral image: "And now the Fields, in native Beauty drest, / Are by the Arms of Frost no more carest" (p. 63). In such poems, Adams, along with his contemporaries Jane Turell, Mather Byles, and Joseph Green, was among the first Americans to depart from the belief that literature should serve religious conviction rather than provide pleasure.

• The manuscript of an essay by Adams on poetry may be found in the Ebenezer Parkman manuscript held by the American Antiquarian Society. See also George Duyckinck and Evert Duyckinck, *Cyclopaedia of American Literature*, vol. 1 (1875), pp. 143–45; John C. Shields, "John Adams," in *American Writers before 1800: A Biographical and Critical Dictionary*, vol. 1 (1983), pp. 13–16; and Clifford K. Shipton, *Biographical Sketches of Those Who Attended Harvard College* (1951).

JOHN C. SHIELDS

ADAMS, John (19 Oct. 1735–4 July 1826), second president of the United States, diplomat, and political theorist, was born in Braintree (now Quincy), Massachusetts, the son of John Adams (1691–1760), a shoemaker, selectman, and deacon, and Susanna Boylston. He claimed as a young man to have indulged in "a constant dissipation among amusements," such as swimming, fishing, and especially shooting, and wished to be a farmer. However, his father insisted that he follow in the footsteps of his uncle Joseph Adams, attend Harvard College, and become a clergyman. John consented, applied himself to his studies, and developed a passion for learning but refused to become a minister. He felt little love for "frigid John Calvin" and the rigid moral standards expected of New England Congregationalist ministers.

Adams was also ambitious to make more of a figure than could be expected in the local pulpits. So despite the disadvantages of becoming a lawyer, "fumbling and racking amidst the rubbish of writs . . . pleas, ejectments" and often fomenting "more quarrels than he composes," enriching "himself at the expense of impoverishing others more honest and deserving," Adams fixed on the law as an avenue to "glory" through obtaining "the more important offices of the State." Even in his youth, Adams was aware he possessed a "vanity," which he sought to sublimate in public service: "Reputation ought to be the perpetual subject of my thoughts, and the aim of my behaviour."

Adams began reading law with attorney James Putnam in Worcester immediately after graduation from Harvard College in 1755. He remained there for three years, teaching school to support himself. He disliked the job but learned from his pupils the germ of his lifelong theory that all societies create some sort of aristocracy that needs to be guarded: like the world itself, a school contained "kings, politicians, divines, . . . fops, buffoons, fiddlers, sycophants, fools, coxcombs, chimney sweepers, and every other character drawn in history or seen in the world" in miniature. After he returned to Braintree, he was presented to the Boston bar by Jeremiah Gridley and Oxenbridge Thacher in November 1758 and was sworn in as an attorney. He prepared so rigorously that he fell gravely ill in Worcester; he was cured by adhering to a diet of milk, bread, and vegetables he would turn to for the rest of his life when ill.

Adams practiced law and served in town offices in Braintree for the next several years, winning an unprecedented vote of thanks from the town for his two-year stint as selectman. He first came to wider attention during the Stamp Act crisis of 1765, when he published a number of essays in the *Boston Gazette* that were then collectively printed as *A Dissertation on the Canon and Feudal Law* (1765). He denounced these two forms of law as keeping most of humanity in "sordid ignorance and staring timidity . . . by infusing in them a religious horror of letters and knowledge." Adams stressed an educated, politically active populace such as America enjoyed as essential for the maintenance of a free government: "Liberty cannot be preserved without a general knowledge among the people, who have a right, from the frame of their nature, to knowledge."

In 1765 Adams also drafted the Braintree Resolves, which were circulated throughout Massachusetts as a model for other towns. He derived the satisfaction of having the town direct his political rival, conservative assemblyman Ebenezer Thayer, to argue that the Stamp Act "divest[ed] us of our most essential rights and liberties," since the colonies were not "in any sense" represented in the British Parliament.

In 1768 Adams moved to Boston, where his activity in the patriot cause quickened. He was selected to defend John Hancock, whose ship *Liberty* was seized for smuggling wine. Given Hancock's obvious guilt, Adams rested most of his case on the facts that Americans were not represented in the Parliaments that had passed the Acts of Trade and were tried without juries when accused of violating them. Fearful of the consequences if Hancock were convicted, the Crown attorney let the case drop. In 1769 Adams defended a seaman named Michael Corbet, who killed a lieutenant from a naval press gang in self-defense. Adams was enraged when Chief Justice Thomas Hutchinson declared Corbet innocent before he could even present the critique of impressment he had prepared. Hutchinson's "secret motives were two. 1st. to prevent me from reaping an harvest of glory; 2d. to avoid a public exhibition of the law in all its details before the people." By this date, Adams had joined his cousin Samuel Adams and other Boston leaders in thinking Hutchinson intended to destroy Massachusetts's liberties and served as the hidden hand behind British policy. He was also sure Hutchinson was personally committed to ruining his career. As he remarked when Hutchinson refused to open Massachusetts's courts in the aftermath of the Stamp Act riots, because the stamps required for legal documents had been destroyed: "I was but just getting into my gears, just getting under sail, and an embargo is laid upon the ship."

The most famous of Adams's cases was the Boston Massacre trial. In company with Josiah Quincy, he defended British captain Thomas Preston and seven soldiers accused of murder for their role in the 5 March 1770 incident. Although Adams later claimed that he lost half his practice and heard "our names execrated in the most opprobrious terms whenever we appeared in the streets of Boston," in fact the patriot leaders were happy to see the soldiers represented by two of their own: Samuel Adams even supported his cousin's successful election to the General Court in May 1770. First, Adams and Quincy could show that the resistance leaders stood up for justice even in partisan cases; and perhaps even more important, they could defend the redcoats without inquiring into whether the "massacre" was provoked by patriot leaders who had arranged for the mob to show up. Adams presented just such a defense, emphasizing that the mob was composed of "a motley rabble of saucy boys, Negroes and mulattoes, Irish teagues, and outlandish jack tars" and that the soldiers were in terror of their lives "when the multitude was shouting and hazzaing, and threatening life, the bells ringing, the mob whistling, screaming, and rending an Indian yell; the people from all quarters throwing every species of rubbish they could pick up in the street." Aided by the fact that at least some of the jurors were government sympathizers, six of the soldiers were acquitted, and two were convicted of manslaughter, for which they pleaded "benefit of clergy," were branded on the thumb, and released.

Adams suffered a severe illness or nervous breakdown for much of 1771 and 1772 and bade a temporary "farewell [to] politics" before admitting, while taking a cure at the mineral waters in Stafford Springs, Connecticut, to "grow[ing] weary of this idle, romantic jaunt." He returned to Boston in time to serve as the consultant for the Committee of the General Court, which in 1773 refuted Governor Hutchinson's speeches that no line could be drawn between the sovereignty of Parliament and the independence of the colonies. It was also Adams who suggested in 1774 that Superior Court judges willing to be paid by the Crown rather than by vote of the General Court were abrogating the Massachusetts charter and hence constitution, were guilty of high crimes and misdemeanors, and deserved to be impeached.

By the time the General Court elected him to the First Continental Congress in June 1774, Adams enjoyed a reputation as the most learned lawyer in Massachusetts who supported the patriot cause. He was already committed to independence, a position he later claimed first crossed his mind as early as the French and Indian War, when he learned of the arrogance with which British regulars treated provincial soldiers. As early as 1772 he had written in his diary that "there was no more justice left in Britain than there was in hell—that I wished for war."

Adams and his fellow New England delegates were disappointed in the First Continental Congress, which met in September 1774 and did not go beyond approving of nonimportation from Britain pending repeal of the "Coercive Acts," which closed the port of Boston, restructured the Massachusetts government, and gave the Ohio Valley to Canada. A frustrated Adams wrote, "We have been obliged to act with great delicacy and caution," given the other delegates' belief they were fanatics for independence. "We have been obliged to keep ourselves out of sight, and to feel pulses, and to sound the depths; to insinuate our sentiments, designs, and desires by means of other persons."

Beginning in December 1774, when he had returned home, Adams engaged in a protracted pamphlet controversy as "Novanglus" in refutation of Loyalist Daniel Leonard's "Massachusettensis," which ran for five months in the Boston papers. Adams insisted that Parliament had no power over the colonies, and America owed only a conditional, contractual allegiance to the king. This had always been so, he argued: "The patriots of this province desire nothing new; they wish only to keep their old privileges." Adams recounted in great detail how a new notion of absolute parliamentary sovereignty had emerged in the 1760s with Governors Francis Bernard and Hutchinson, who were abetted in their conspiracy against American liberty by an England "sunk in sloth, luxury, and corruption." Adams was unaware of the true identity of "Massachusettensis"; he believed him to be province attorney general Jonathan Sewall, his erstwhile best friend. Sewall tried to convert Adams to the royal cause in 1768 with the promise of patronage. At their final meeting in July 1774, Adams replied with the famous words, "I have passed the Rubicon; swim or sink, live or die, survive or perish with my country—that is my unalterable determination."

Adams dominated the Second Continental Congress, to which he hastened immediately after the battles of Lexington and Concord. His first great service was to nominate George Washington to command the patriot forces, a position coveted by the militarily inexperienced Hancock of Boston. Before he stepped down in November 1777, Adams served on more than ninety committees, chairing twenty-five, including the all-important Board of War, which kept the army provisioned. "Every member of Congress in 1776 acknowledged him to be first in the house," wrote fellow delegate Benjamin Rush.

Adams's most important political work of this period was *Thoughts on Government*, written early in 1776 to assist North Carolinians in framing a new constitution. While acknowledging that "virtue" was the foundation of all happy states, he went on to assail the direct democracy hinted at in Thomas Paine's recently published and wildly popular *Common Sense* (1776). Asserting his lifelong predilection for mixed government, Adams insisted that the assembly be chosen by property holders, that it select a council from among its members, and that the two houses pick a strong executive who could veto their acts. A strong, independent judiciary was also necessary. "A people cannot be long free nor ever happy whose government is in one assembly," for a "single assembly is liable to all the vices, follies, and frailties of an individual." In perhaps the first case in which he cast himself as the unique bastion of virtue and wisdom between two opposing groups, Adams commented, "In New England the *Thoughts on Government* will be disdained because they are not popular enough; in the Southern colonies, they will be despised . . . because too popular." Adams here confirmed a behavior pattern that he evinced as early as 1763 and that he would follow for the rest of his life: to "quarrel with both parties and with every individual of each, before I would subjugate my understanding, or prostitute my tongue or pen to either."

Adams's main contribution at the Second Continental Congress was, as Richard Stockton and Richard Henry Lee called him, to serve as the "Atlas" of independence. In what he considered the finest speech of his life, which unfortunately does not survive, Adams persuaded the Congress of the need for a Declaration of Independence on the practical grounds it would unite the colonies, divide England, stimulate support for the Revolution, and attract European allies to "colonies" that were acting as independent states already by waging war and forming governments. "John Adams was our Colossus on the floor," Thomas Jefferson remarked. Adams was selected for the five-man committee to frame the Declaration but yielded to Jefferson's more graceful prose style and the ever-present need to deemphasize New England's predominance. In later years he expressed some jealousy that too much attention was paid to the Declaration, "a theatrical show," where "Jefferson ran away with all the stage effect . . . and all the glory."

In November 1777 an exhausted Adams returned home to Braintree, where his wife, the former Abigail Smith, whom he had married in October 1764, waited for him with four young children. A learned and intelligent woman who capably managed the Adams farmstead during her husband's long absences, Abigail was both a dutiful wife and an intellectual equal with whom her husband corresponded on affairs of state. She is famous for asking the Congress to "remember the ladies" in planning a new commonwealth dedicated to liberty and hinted that women might "foment a rebellion, and . . . not hold ourselves bound by laws in which we have no voice or representation." John's reply, "I cannot but laugh," dismissed Abigail's argument on the grounds men "have only the name of masters." To grant women political rights "would completely subject us to the despotism of the petticoat." If the Adamses disagreed on this issue, it did not mar a loving, supportive marriage, which ended only with her death in 1818. That John recommended women receive the same classical, liberal education as men, in contrast to the emphasis on music, dancing, and household arts Benjamin Franklin and Jefferson, among others, favored, is testament to the benefits a wife so educated conferred on him personally.

Adams did not stay at home long. In February 1778 he sailed to France, accompanied by his ten-year-old son, John Quincy Adams, to replace the corrupt Silas Deane—who later turned out to be a British spy—to negotiate a treaty of alliance. His ship escaped three British cruisers and a hurricane. Finding that John Burgoyne's defeat at Saratoga the previous September had already accomplished his purpose, Adams tried to bring some order into the American mission's finances and correspondence and sought to raise money in both France and Holland for the American cause with little success. He was both attracted to yet afraid of French manners and luxury: "The politeness, the elegance, the softness, the delicacy is extreme. In short, stern and haughty republican as I am, I cannot help loving these people." He was less kind to his senior colleague Franklin, whose high living and "continual dissipation" he considered harmful to the smooth running of the mission and dangerous to the American cause, as Franklin was too friendly with the French. Nevertheless, Adams viewed himself as superfluous once the treaty was signed and requested the mission be left in Franklin's hands.

Adams returned to Massachusetts in August 1779, just in time to write the new state constitution. Unlike other state constitutions being written at the time, which rendered the governor and upper house heavily dependent on a lower house elected by a wide franchise, Adams expressed his fear of both popular enthusiasm and aristocratic intrigue by opting for a traditional mixed "government of laws, and not of men," as his preamble declared. Representatives had to be worth £100, senators £300, the governor £1,000, and voters for the senate £60. The governor appointed the militia and had an absolute veto of the actions of the other two houses. Adams justified a powerful executive on the grounds that "we have so many men of wealth, of ambitious spirits, of intrigue, of luxury and corruption that incessant factions will disturb our peace without it. . . . The executive . . . ought to be the reservoir of wisdom as the legislature is of liberty." Adams's constitution also envisioned a strong, active government furthering the public good. He took special care to mention that Harvard College would retain its support and autonomy and that "it shall be the duty of legislators and magistrates, in all future periods of the commonwealth, to cherish the interests of literature and the sciences, and all seminaries of them."

Even before his constitution was in essence adopted in 1780, Adams was off to France again, this time to negotiate peace and a commercial treaty with England. He arrived in December 1779 with his sons John Quincy and Charles Adams. Since England refused to recognize his condition for negotiations, recognition of U.S. independence, Adams remained in Paris, writing innumerable letters to Congress on diplomatic and military matters, which were barely even acknowledged, and many more missives in both the French and English press in the hopes of influencing British public opinion to side with the United States. While in Paris, he evoked the ire of the French foreign minister, Comte Charles Gravier de Vergennes, when in June 1780 Adams refused to recommend to Congress that French, unlike American holders of the U.S. debt, be paid the original value of their investment instead of depreciated currency. Adams replied that, far from being a dependent client of France, the United States was an equal partner and had benefited France by their alliance: "the flourishing state of her maritime and commerce, and the decisive influence of her councils and negotiations in Europe, which all the world will allow to be owing in a great measure to the separation of America from her inveterate enemy, and to her new connections with the United States, show that the obligations are mutual." Adams soon specified one such obligation, complaining that "the state of things in America has become really alarming, and this merely for want of a few French men-of-war upon that coast." Franklin asked to have Adams removed, putting it bluntly to Congress that they could choose between Franklin's "decency and delicacy" and Adams's "stoutness, independence, and boldness." Congress compromised by adding John Jay, Henry Laurens, Franklin himself, and Jefferson (who did not go to Europe) to its peace mission.

Unpopular in France, Adams headed for Holland, where after nearly two years of negotiations he obtained diplomatic recognition of the United States in addition to a much-needed loan. He returned to Paris for peace negotiations, which began in November 1782. With Jay he persuaded Franklin to ignore the congressional mandate that they "govern ourselves by her [France's] advice and opinions" and worked out with British envoy Richard Oswald a fait accompli that made the Mississippi River the western boundary of the United States despite the protests of France's Spanish ally. (Franklin, whose "decency and delicacy" was but one of his many masks, was delighted to go along.) Adams and his colleagues had already practiced the foreign policy that would serve the early republic so well. In Adams's words of 1780: "Let us, above all things, avoid, as much as possible, entangling ourselves with their wars or politics. Our business with them, and theirs with us, is commerce, not politics, much less war."

Adams approved in principle that American Loyalists should be compensated for property losses during the war, although the treaty clause that made reimbursement contingent on the action of individual states largely nullified it. He also compromised on the Canadian boundary and allowed that prerevolutionary debts to British merchants had to be collectible for commerce to continue. On one issue he stood fast. The "right" of New England to fish off the Grand Banks in the Atlantic Ocean he supported with massive erudition and documentation, refusing even the British willingness to write this "liberty" into the treaty: "Is there or can there be a clearer right? . . . If Heaven in the creation gave a right, it is ours at least as much as yours. If occupation, use, and possession give a right, we have it as clearly as you. If war and blood and treasure give a right, ours is as good as yours. . . . If then the right cannot be denied, why should it not be acknowledged?" This was the sort of relentless argumentation Adams used to crown the exhaustive and exhausting cases he was famous for. It also explains, as he himself well knew, why he was never as popular as conciliatory types like Franklin and Jefferson: "I have long since learned that a man may offend and still succeed." The treaty, embodying Adams's clauses on the fisheries, debts, Loyalists, and Canadian boundary, was approved on 30 November 1782 without French knowledge. Adams remained in Europe, "out of patience," in a "ridiculous state of torture," while the treaty was ratified and then signed in September 1783, and he was appointed minister to England in February 1785. Abigail Adams finally joined him after a five-year separation in the summer of 1784 at Auteuil, in the suburbs of Paris, where he lived.

Adams had lost his chance for a commercial treaty with England when the peace ministry of the earl of Shelburne was replaced by the mercantilist Tories headed by William Pitt the Younger in 1784. He could accomplish little for Americans who wanted British forts removed from New York and the old Northwest or who demanded compensation for their slaves when the states refused to compensate the Loyalists. His pay cut by 20 percent when he moved to England, Adams was unable to reciprocally entertain other ministers or British dignitaries. He and Abigail felt uncomfortable in a snobbish, aristocratic society. The most satisfying accomplishment of his years in England was the signing of a commercial treaty with Prussia in 1786.

When he heard of Shays's Rebellion in Massachusetts against the constitution he had written, Adams began writing the mammoth three-volume *Defence of the Constitutions of Government of the United States of America, against the Attack of M. Turgot . . .* (1787), which Abigail described as "an investigation into the different forms of government, both ancient and modern . . . with the purpose of demonstrating the superiority of mixed forms over simple ones," such as the unicameral legislative democracy advocated by Baron Anne Robert Jacques Turgot.

Adams returned to the United States in 1788. He was very popular, because the first volume of the *Defence* appeared just in time to provide a theoretical justification for the newly written U.S. Constitution. Adams was chosen vice president under the new government. However, he received only 34 of 69 electoral votes, and Washington received all for president. The rest scattered because Alexander Hamilton, fearing Adams would prove too independent, persuaded many of the electors to vote for other candidates in the hopes of denying him election. Adams only discovered this plot years later, when he and Hamilton had become inveterate enemies.

Although Adams wrote, "My country has in its wisdom contrived for me the most insignificant office that ever the invention of man contrived or his imagination conceived," he managed to play an important role in the first Washington administration. A firm believer that pomp, circumstance, and titles were necessary to ensure that the populace respected the government, his insistence on wearing a sword and wig to preside over the Senate led to the portly Adams being dubbed "His Rotundity." (He soon stopped appearing in this diplomatic garb.) Adams had more opportunities to break tie Senate votes than any vice president has yet had, twenty in all. His support was critical for allowing the president to remove appointees without the "advice and consent" of the Senate required to install them, and to authorize commercial retaliation against the British refusal to reopen the prerevolutionary trade with the West Indies to Americans.

Adams also wrote, in 1791, *Discourses on Davila*, which created a furor, much like Edmund Burke's *Reflections on the Revolution in France* (1790) did in England, because Adams argued that a nation such as France required a monarchy and aristocracy for political stability. Only in 1793 and 1794, with the execution of King Louis XVI and the Reign of Terror, did public opinion in both countries catch up with these conservative thinkers. Adams also made the mistake of endorsing a president for life and a hereditary upper house for the United States. Most famous in *Davila*, however, was his denial of the equality beloved by republicans in America, France, and elsewhere. In one of his most eloquent passages, Adams insisted that there was a universal passion for inequality: "Not only the poorest mechanic, but the man who lives upon common charity . . . even those who have abandoned themselves to common infamy, as pirates, highwaymen, and common thieves, court a set of admirers, and plume themselves upon that superiority which they have, or fancy they have, over some others. . . . The *passion for distinction*" lay at the root of human behavior; government was required to channel it into a constructive course.

Adams was reelected vice president in 1792, receiving 77 of the 134 electoral votes. That 50 of the votes went to New York governor George Clinton indicated the Democratic Republican party was forming in opposition to the Federalist. In 1796 Adams was chosen president over Jefferson by 71 votes to 68. Not all of Adams's electors supported the Federalist candidate for vice president, Charles Cotesworth Pinckney, so Jefferson became vice president. Once again, Hamilton schemed unsuccessfully to take votes away from Adams, to win the election for Pinckney.

Problems with France dominated the Adams administration. As soon as he took office in March 1797, he learned the Directory had dismissed the American ambassador and had begun to seize American ships trading with England and its allies in the war that raged in Europe and the West Indies in retaliation for the Jay Treaty of 1795, which signaled a rapprochement between Britain and the United States. Adams agreed with the cabinet that a special mission to France was required, but he added Elbridge Gerry, a supporter of Jefferson, to join Pinckney and John Marshall. When the envoys were not even admitted to see the Directory because they would not pay a bribe, the famous XYZ affair, they returned home. "I will never send another minister to France, without assurances that he will be received, respected, and honored, as the representative of a great, free, powerful, and independent nation," Adams told Congress.

Adams agreed with the "High Federalists" in his cabinet, who were partisans of Hamilton—Secretary of State Timothy Pickering, Secretary of War James McHenry, and Secretary of the Treasury Oliver Wolcott—that defense measures were called for. He wholeheartedly supported a navy bill that led to the construction of the USS *Constitution* ("Old Ironsides") and other frigates, which more than held their own with French warships during the Quasi-War with France fought on the high seas from 1797 to 1800. He did not endorse their plans for closer relations with Britain or support the large army Congress authorized in May 1798. Congress also passed the Alien and Sedition Acts that July in response to vituperative criticism of the administration's anti-French policy from the Democratic Republicans. These laws extended the waiting period for U.S. citizenship from five to fourteen years (most recent immigrants were Jeffersonians) and permitted the president to deport "alien enemies." The Sedition Act authorized imprisonment and fines for critics of the administration, but Adams did not enforce it vigorously. Only twenty-five cases were prosecuted, and those convicted were either pardoned or released by the incoming Jefferson administration in 1801. In 1800 Adams pardoned John Fries, who had been sentenced to death for treason for leading a 1799 tax revolt of the farmers of northeastern Pennsylvania.

Adams stunned the High Federalists, who were poised for war, by appointing the minister to Holland, William Vans Murray, a special envoy to France to negotiate differences between the nations in February 1799. This caused Hamilton and his supporters in the cabinet—whom Adams finally fired or forced to resign—to openly oppose Adams, their rancor culminating in Hamilton's "Letter Concerning the Public Conduct and Character of John Adams" of 1800. Widespread popular hostility to the standing army and the Alien and Sedition Acts led to an overwhelming defeat for the Federalists in the election of 1800. Adams, however, had managed to distance himself from the Hamiltonians and obtained 65 electoral votes to 73 for Jefferson. Had Aaron Burr, Jefferson's vice presidential candidate, not manipulated the votes in New York City, which elected the Democratic Republican legislature that cast New York's twelve votes for Jefferson, Adams would have been reelected. He left Washington a bitter and depressed man, not remaining for his successor's inauguration, after appointing as many Federalist judges as possible to stave off what he saw as the "abyss" opening before the nation. Ironically, his envoy Murray had signed a peace accord with France on the eve of the election, 30 October 1800. With the war in Europe winding down, the French did not need to seize American ships. Adams thus left his successor a prosperous nation at peace and probably saved the Union by not using the military machine Congress had provided him with to fight a full-scale war and repress dissent at home, to the disgust of the High Federalists.

For the last quarter-century of his life, Adams lived in retirement in Quincy. He wrote in support of Jefferson's embargo and vigorously opposed the Federalists who threatened disunion during the War of 1812. He also produced a notable correspondence. Beginning in 1807, he wrote a series of angry letters in response to Mercy Otis Warren's criticisms of his conduct in her history of the American Revolution. She called Adams vain, ambitious, and "corrupted" by his stay in Europe to repudiate republicanism for monarchy and aristocracy. (She did not mention that he refused to endorse her offspring, who were not very well qualified, for federal jobs.) "Madam . . . corruption is a charge that I cannot and will not bear. I challenge the whole human race, and angels and devils too, to produce an instance of it from my cradle to this hour," typifies the tone of Adams's replies. In 1814 he wrote thirty-two letters in response to John Taylor of Caroline's *An Inquiry into the Principles and Policy of the Government of the United States* (1814), which specifically criticized Adams's *Defence of the Constitutions*. Adams's most notable correspondent late in life was Jefferson, to whom Rush, their mutual friend, reconciled him in 1812. Their recollections of the events of their lifetimes and the by now gentle disagreement over whether republican America could be trusted to evolve into a moral, happy society without the traditional restraints of mixed government (Jefferson thought so, Adams did not) continued to be exchanged with decreasing frequency as they aged.

Adams retained his vigor until his late eighties—he walked three miles a day as late as 1822—but then failed. He died in Quincy during the presidency of his son John Quincy Adams, and his last words were the enigmatic, "Thomas Jefferson survives." Adams believed himself unjustly neglected and criticized by his contemporaries, as he predicted he would be by posterity. "The history of our Revolution will be one continued lie from one end to the other. The essence of the whole will be that Dr. Franklin's electrical rod smote the earth and out sprang General Washington. That Franklin electrified him with his rod—and thence forward these two conducted all the policy, negotiation, legislatures and war. . . . If this letter should be preserved and read a hundred years hence, the reader will say, 'The envy of . . . JA could not bear to think of the truth.'"

Adams had his flaws. "He is vain, irritable, and a bad calculator of the motives which govern men," Jefferson wrote in 1783, but Jefferson also wrote, "this is all the ill which can possibly be said of him." Honest, incredibly hard-working, and willing to take unpopular stands regardless of the consequences, Adams decisively shaped the fate of American history by his actions in revolutionary Boston, at the Continental Congress, in Paris as a diplomat, and in Philadelphia as president. Historians ranking the presidents almost invariably place him just below Abraham Lincoln, Washington, Jefferson, Woodrow Wilson, Theodore Roosevelt, and Franklin Roosevelt for his role in preserving the nation during a troubled time (Tim Blessing and Robert K. Murray, *Greatness in the White House*, 2d ed. [1993]). Yet he will never be a folk hero like Jefferson or Washington, as he knew well. Short, stout, blunt, and cantankerous, he told the American people truths about themselves they needed to know yet did not want to hear (Richard A. Ryerson, remark at Society of Historians of the Early American Republic Conference, July 1994). Perhaps as aristocracy and inequality become more pronounced in the United States, Adams's reputation will grow as his words of warning become increasingly relevant.

• Adams's *Works*, edited by his grandson, the statesman and historian Charles Francis Adams (10 vols., 1850–1856), are gradually being supplanted by the Adams papers project, which is appearing in various multivolume series: Lyman H. Butterfield et al., eds., *Diary and Autobiography* (4 vols., 1961), *Adams Family Correspondence* (6 vols., 1963–), and *The Papers of John Adams: General Correspondence and Other Papers* (8 vols., 1977–). Adams's *Legal Papers*, ed. L. Kinvin Wroth and Hiller B. Zobel (3 vols., 1965), form part of this series and are based on the 580-reel microfilm collection available from the Massachusetts Historical Society, which houses the papers. *The Adams-Jefferson Letters: The Complete Correspondence between Thomas Jefferson and Abigail Adams and John Adams*, ed. Lester J. Cappon (1959), is a necessary supplement. John E. Ferling has edited *John Adams: A Bibliography* (1994). The most complete biography is Page Smith, *John Adams* (2 vols., 1962–1963); the most insightful are Peter Shaw, *The Character of John Adams* (1976), Ferling, *John Adams: A Life* (1992), and Joseph J. Ellis, *Passionate Sage: The Character and Legacy of John Adams* (1993). See also Zoltan Haraszti, *John Adams and the Prophets of Progress* (1952), Ralph Adams Brown, *The Presidency of John Adams* (1975), Stephen G. Kurtz, *The Presidency of John Adams: The Collapse of Federalism* (1957), Manning J. Dauer, *The Adams Federalists* (1953), and John R. Howe, *The Changing Political Thought of John Adams* (1966). Useful material appears in two lives of Abigail Adams: Lynne Withey, *Dearest Friend: A Life of Abigail Adams* (1981), and Edith Gelles, *Portia: The World of Abigail Adams* (1992). Gordon S. Wood, *The Creation of the American Republic* (1969), and Edmund S. Morgan, *The Meaning of Independence* (1976), have good chapters on Adams. For Adams as a diplomat, see Richard B. Morris, *The Peacemakers: The Great Powers and American Independence* (1965). For aspects of his presidency, see Stanley Elkins and Eric McKitrick, *The Age of Federalism* (1993), James Morton Smith, *Freedom's Fetters: The Alien and Sedition Laws and American Civil Liberties* (1956), and Alexander DeConde, *The Quasi-War: The Politics and Diplomacy of the Undeclared War with France* (1966).

WILLIAM PENCAK

ADAMS, John (18 Sept. 1772–24 Apr. 1863), educator, was born in Canterbury, Connecticut, the son of Captain John Adams, a farmer and a veteran of the Revolution, and Mary Parker. As a boy Adams worked as a farmhand, and in his late teens his family decided, at great personal sacrifice, to send him to Yale, where he spent four years, graduating in 1795. On his return to Canterbury after graduation, Adams found his mother seriously ill and decided to teach school in town so that he could nurse her properly. During that period a woman named Elizabeth Ripley came to visit in Canterbury. Apparently it was love at first sight, and the two were married in 1798; they would have ten children. In the early 1800s he held positions at Plainfield Academy in Plainfield, Connecticut, and at Bacon Academy in Colchester, Connecticut, and successfully built up both schools. This was followed, in 1810, with his acceptance of the offer to become principal of Phillips Academy in Andover, Massachusetts.

Adams adapted easily to Andover. He was a pious Christian dedicated to the moral and religious education of his charges. Josiah Quincy the younger spoke of him as very religious but with no "literary taste." At the time of his arrival, Andover Hill was dominated by the recently founded, conservative Andover Seminary. This suited Adams to a tee. Since the seminary had been founded to combat change in religious matters, it is not surprising that Adams made almost no attempt to change the academy. The heavily weighted classical curriculum was kept almost intact while he concentrated on the development of "Christian Manhood" among the students. He was a strong supporter of revivals and prayer meetings, especially if student-inspired, and at the end of his tenure at the academy, Adams could boast that more than 150 of his students had become "hopefully pious" (i.e., converted) and that one in five had entered the ministry.

Adams also believed in corporal punishment. When he arrived he found discipline almost nonexistent, but he soon restored order. One of the features of the morning chapel service was the reading, at the end, of the names of those who were to come up and get feruled, that is, whipped by a flat piece of wood. Some of the boys took their punishment stoically; others did not. "We often yelled with the pain and shed tears at the degradation," one wrote.

During his early years at the academy Adams accomplished a lot. He restored discipline, increased the size of the student body substantially—from twenty to one hundred by 1817—and emphasized and strengthened the school's religious program. In the early 1830s, however, the school fell on hard times. Admissions dropped from eighty-two to twenty-eight over a six-year period, and morale was low. The trustees decided that a younger man was needed and in 1832 essentially forced Adams to resign. He was sixty years old, without a pension, and as a result spent the rest of his life struggling against poverty. Finally, in 1843, he became the agent of the American Sunday School Union in the Midwest. He used to drive around the countryside in his carriage and became known as "Father Adams." On a yearly salary of $400 he eventually organized 322 Sunday schools.

Throughout his life Adams was an imposing figure. One writer described him as "erect, handsome, of good presence," whereas another recalled that he had "the prestige of one born to command." His first wife died in 1829, and two years later he married Mabel Burritt, a widow from Troy, New York. At Andover, Adams is commemorated by a tablet in the chapel and a dormitory called Adams Hall. He died and was buried in Jacksonville, Illinois.

• Material on Adams can be found in the Phillips Academy Archives. A biography is M. E. Brown and H. G. Brown, *The Story of John Adams, a New England Schoolmaster* (1900). Also useful are Frederick S. Allis, Jr., *Youth from Every Quarter: A Bicentennial History of Phillips Academy, Andover* (1979), and Claude M. Fuess, *An Old New England School* (1917).

FREDERICK S. ALLIS, JR.

ADAMS, John Quincy (11 July 1767–23 Feb. 1848), secretary of state, sixth president of the United States, and U.S. congressman, was born in Braintree, Massachusetts, the son of John Adams (1735–1826), second president of the United States, and Abigail Smith Adams, noted letter writer. Adams's New England birth and his position as the eldest son in a distinguished family strongly influenced his life. His parents set perfectionist goals for him with the expectation that he would achieve distinction through strong moral commitment and assiduity in public service. Responding to these pressures, Adams was hard-driving and ambitious, introspective, and severely critical in his judgments of himself and others.

Through his father's involvement in the American Revolution and the establishment of the new nation, the boy matured in an environment committed to patriotic nationalism that transcended regional particularism. An exceptionally broad educational background promoted this perspective. When he was but ten years old, he accompanied his father to Europe on a diplomatic mission. John Quincy attended schools in France and Holland, served as secretary to Francis Dana during negotiations in Russia from 1781 to 1783, and filled the same role for his father during arrangements for the Peace of Paris, which terminated the American Revolution. Returning home in 1785, he graduated in 1787 from Harvard College, studied law, and began practice of that profession in Boston in 1790.

Young Adams found the law tedious, but in 1794 President George Washington appointed him minister to the Hague, in Holland. During an extended visit to London the following year, he met and courted Louisa Catherine Johnson, daughter of the American consul. Born in London and educated at a Roman Catholic school in France, Louisa was a talented musician and fluent in French, assets that contributed to the young couple's popularity in court circles. Married in July 1797, Adams was shortly thereafter transferred to Berlin, where the couple remained until the elder Adams's defeat in the presidential election of 1800.

With a wife and the first of three sons, John Quincy resumed practicing law in Boston. Disgusted by the "filth of faction," to which he attributed his father's political rejection, he at first foreswore politics. But within a few months he was elected to the state senate as a Federalist, and the following year he sought election to Congress in opposition to the Republican incumbent. Although then defeated, Adams was selected by his legislative colleagues as U.S. senator in 1803.

Adams's independence in voting on political issues quickly disconcerted Federalist leaders. He was one of only two Federalists to approve the purchase of Louisiana, and he supported President Thomas Jefferson's efforts to uphold neutral rights during the war between Britain and France. When he endorsed resolutions of a Republican caucus protesting the British attack upon the *Chesapeake* in 1807, he was dropped from the Federalist senatorial ranks. He thereupon published a pamphlet refuting criticism of the Jeffersonian embargo legislation and explaining his belief in independence in voting. In response, the Massachusetts legislature met in special session to select his senatorial successor nearly a year before the expiration of his term. Adams immediately resigned. His acceptance of appointment by President James Madison (1751–1836) as minister to St. Petersburg in 1809 evoked severe criticism, even from his parents. Adams defended his action, however, as one of principle against political factionalism.

He achieved some trade concessions while in Russia and served as an intermediary in Czar Alexander's effort to mediate a peace ending the War of 1812 between Britain and the United States. While the British declined Russia's intervention, they agreed to direct negotiations, in which Adams served as one of the five American commissioners. During the discussions held at Ghent, Adams argued strongly to obtain renewal of fishing privileges for Americans in the waters between Newfoundland and Labrador. When he proposed as an equivalent extending British navigation rights on the Mississippi River, quarreling within the American delegation between Adams and the Kentuckian Henry Clay nearly disrupted the negotiations. The decision to set aside both issues, as well as most of the precipitating causes of the war, satisfied neither one, but when Clay proposed rejecting the treaty, Adams subordinated his sectional interests to the more immediate national need for peace.

At this time he was transferred from the ministry at St. Petersburg to that in London. The delay caused by the move occasioned his absence during the opening of negotiations by the other commissioners for a commercial convention that was concluded in London in 1815. Thinking again of New England's interests, Adams was dissatisfied that the discussions were initiated under a stipulated omission of trading privileges with the British West Indies. Once more, however, he yielded and signed the agreement, partly because it embraced the concept of reciprocity as a fairer trading base than the more common most-favored-nation provision.

In 1817 President James Monroe named Adams as secretary of state. There his independence of judgment and the skill with which he exercised it established him among the most outstanding to have held that office. In a convention with Great Britain in 1818 he obtained the much desired privileges of fishing off Newfoundland and the Magdalen Islands and of drying and curing the catch on designated coastal areas of Newfoundland and Labrador. At the same time the northern boundary of the Louisiana Purchase was defined as extending along the forty-ninth parallel of latitude from the Lake of the Woods to the Rocky Mountains, and the parties agreed to joint occupation of the Oregon country for the next ten years. In the Adams-Onís Treaty of 1819, Spain delineated the western boundary of Louisiana and ceded the Floridas, legitimating the occupation of West Florida, which Adams with some embarrassment had defended to the Russian czar in 1810 as rightfully encompassed in the bounds of Louisiana.

The Florida negotiations markedly demonstrated Adams's diplomatic talents. He alone of Monroe's cabinet had defended General Andrew Jackson when, in pursuit of raiding Indians in 1818, Jackson occupied the town of Pensacola, captured the Spanish fort of St. Marks, and executed two British merchants for inciting Indian attacks. Arguing that the incident was the inevitable consequence of authority too weak to maintain order, Adams warned the Spanish that they must either provide a force sufficient for protection or cede the territory as "derelict." Under the resulting agreement the United States acquired the Floridas by assuming indemnity claims of American citizens against Spain amounting to $5 million and by accepting a western boundary to Louisiana based at the mouth of the Sabine River, thus relinquishing vague claims to Texas.

The latter concession again outraged Clay and his western supporters. The criticism was compounded when Adams withheld recognition of the independence of Spain's rebelling American colonies pending a long-delayed ratification of the Florida treaty. Shortly after the treaty was ratified, however, he not only extended the desired recognition but also championed the policy known as the Monroe Doctrine, enunciated in the president's annual message of 1823, which projected U.S. leadership in closing the New World to further European intervention. Once more Adams was assuming an independent course, rejecting a British proposal for a joint pronouncement that President Monroe had initially favored after consultation with Thomas Jefferson and James Madison. Adams was reluctant to tie the action of the United States to British policy considerations, and he shrewdly discounted the danger of European intervention in support of Spain's claims.

Adams was less successful in resolving the British restrictions on West Indies trade. In 1818 Congress enacted countervailing legislation in an effort to open commerce. It was effective to a degree; in 1822, under pressure from island planters, Britain authorized direct traffic of designated produce to certain ports while retaining protective duties. Although the concessions opened a market for agricultural produce from the American middle states and back country during a depression, they did not permit the importation of fish and salted provisions or the indirect shipping that primarily concerned New England. Adams's response retained discriminatory duties on British vessels unless American ships and goods were admitted to the colonial ports with no higher charges than those on British vessels and the same goods imported "from elsewhere," that is, indirectly. There the negotiations were suspended.

Throughout Monroe's second term Adams vied with Secretary of War John C. Calhoun, Secretary of the Treasury William Harris Crawford, and Speaker of the House Clay for the presidential succession. In 1822, however, General Andrew Jackson, who had previously shown little interest in civil affairs, emerged as a candidate whose military prowess held great popular appeal. By the election of 1824, old political organizations were disintegrating. When none of the candidates attained a majority of votes in the electoral college, the three leaders—Jackson, Adams, and Crawford—became the nominees for election by the House of Representatives. There, with the vote unitary by state delegations, Adams received the requisite majority of thirteen votes; Jackson won seven votes, Crawford, four. Adams carried all the New England states and had expanded his personal base by sympathetic support for the politically ostracized leadership in Illinois and assurances that in making appointments he would no longer proscribe Federalists, who were strong in Maryland and New York. But without the votes for Adams by Clay adherents who represented Kentucky, Missouri, and Ohio, his attainment of the majority would have been protracted and uncertain.

At least as early as the previous October, perhaps as early as June, Clay had voiced to friends his intention to support Adams if he were not himself a candidate. He regarded Jackson's autocratic tendencies as a menace to civil authority, and he viewed Crawford's health, following a paralytic stroke in the autumn of 1823, as too limiting for public office. Adams's revised stand in recognition of Latin American independence had, on the other hand, eliminated a major area of their disagreement. When Clay's friend Robert P. Letcher in mid-December discussed with Adams the differences arising at Ghent and learned that Adams no longer harbored ill will, there remained little basis for contention. On internal improvements, a protective tariff, and support for mercantile concerns, Adams held views that Clay had long espoused. These two leaders shared a focus on national development that differed radically from the increasingly states-rights particularism of the other candidates.

That the Kentuckian who had so frequently opposed Adams's policies extended his endorsement of the New Englander gave rise to charges of "bargain and corruption" even before the House vote. Clay immediately called for a congressional investigation. When, however, the Pennsylvania congressman George Kremer, who had first published the accusation, denied that he had meant to imply "corruption and dishonor" and refused to appear before the House committee, the inquiry was tabled.

The partisan activity embarrassed Adams, who frequently castigated himself for excessive ambition. He also recognized pragmatically that the defeated candidates would unite against his administration. Yet after long consideration and consultation with President Monroe, he offered the post of secretary of state to Clay, who accepted. Having supported Adams's election, Clay argued that he could not well refuse to serve with him, affording a sectional balance for the New Englander's administration. The decision, nevertheless, provided the basis for political attack even more destructive than that which had ended the career of Adams's father.

In his inaugural address Adams promised to continue Monroe's programs and pleaded for united support of the policy of postwar neonationalism. His "American System" called for national economic growth based on interlocking sectional diversity. Commerce, foreign and domestic, was fundamental to the approach.

Adams directed much of his attention to foreign affairs. Upholding the principle of neutral trading rights in wartime, his administration successfully supplied assistance in half-a-dozen instances where American citizens sought compensation for confiscations under the edicts of Napoleon Bonaparte and the decrees of warring Latin American states. The main body of claims for French spoliations remained unresolved, but the diplomatic pressure kept them alive and at the forefront of Franco-American relations. A convention with Great Britain in 1826 also compensated Americans for slaves and property seized by British raiders during the war years.

Following a generalized invitation opening trade on a reciprocal basis under legislation of 1824, the Adams administration negotiated more commercial treaties than any other prior to the Civil War. Direct trade under the new arrangement had already been opened with several nations before Adams assumed the presidency. It was now extended to others, and Adams gave particular emphasis to expanding the provisions to encompass indirect commerce. The latter proposal was incorporated in a revision of the general legislation of 1828, but in the meantime agreements on that basis were concluded individually with Denmark, Sweden, Norway, the Hanseatic cities, and, most notably as a model of the goals sought for commerce within the Americas, with the Central American Federation. The commercial convention with Great Britain signed originally in 1815 was extended indefinitely; trade treaties with Austria and Brazil awaited only ratification; arrangements under somewhat less favorable terms preserved commercial relations with the Netherlands and France that were threatened with disruption; and efforts to negotiate agreements with Mexico and Turkey, although remaining in abeyance, appeared promising.

But while the treaties with Scandinavian countries had opened their West Indies islands reciprocally to both direct and indirect trade by American vessels, the problem of establishing indirect or even generalized direct trade with the British West Indies continued. When the Adams administration in 1826 finally proposed resuming negotiations under instructions acceding to the British terms of 1822, it was informed that Britain had revised its policy. The British withdrew the proposal without notifying the Americans and redirected their efforts to liberalizing trading with the new Latin American states. Exports from the United States to the Caribbean continued with scant reduction by transshipment through entrepôts, but politically the episode generated severe criticism, particularly from agricultural districts, assailing the delayed negotiations.

Administration supporters attributed the new British intransigence to divisions in American congressional support made evident during the spring of 1825. Adams's decision to send ministers to Panama to participate in a congress of American states called by Simón Bolívar had provided a rallying base for opponents of the administration. Southern leaders fearful that the congress would entail recognition of the republic of Haiti, and opponents generally of the administration's Latin American interests, challenged the president's authority to make such appointments. While the mission was ultimately approved, controversy so delayed the ministers' departure that the congress adjourned before they arrived. Action that Adams had viewed as a gesture of good will had instead generated a bitter debate provoking not only the domestic embarrassment of a duel between Clay and Senator John Randolph (1773–1833) of Virginia, but also foreign outrage at the publicly voiced racial insults in reference to assembly participants. A British agent at the congress had little difficulty convincing the delegates that the contemplated U.S. participation was self-serving. The episode was one of several during the administration that made clear the limited applicability of the Monroe Doctrine.

Adams's pragmatic conception of the hemispheric relationship was made manifest in his policies toward Cuba. Under his guidance the Monroe Doctrine had cautiously renounced the intent to interfere with existing European possessions in the New World. Fearful that continuing warfare between the Latin American states and Spain might provoke an attack upon Cuba, the administration attempted both to restrain military venturism by Mexico or Colombia and to promote Spanish recognition of their independence. The first goal was amply defined in the instructions carried by the ministers to the Panama Congress. A limitation in support for winning recognition of the new Latin American states was, however, revealed by the American minister to his Spanish counterpart in Madrid when he explained that preferential trading privileges for the mother country "did not accord precisely with the President's view" as a bargaining consideration. Adams was more concerned to protect equal access for U.S. commerce with the former Spanish colonies than to assure their independence.

Much as the administration sought to expand foreign commerce, its contribution was most notable in stimulating domestic trade. Public funding, financed by tariff revenues and public land sales, was directed to a vast program of road and canal construction, harbor improvement, and removal of river snags. Adams also hoped to raise tariff levels to protect home industry, contributing to urban growth and a market for agricultural products. To facilitate the interchange, the administration would maintain sound money and credit arrangements, regulated through the operations of a national banking system.

Adams's efforts to promote internal improvements dated from 1807, when he had presented in the Senate a resolution urging preparation of a comprehensive plan for such development. Although the measure was not then approved, it led a year later to Albert Gallatin's report on "Roads and Canals" and ultimately to construction of the National Road. Under Adams's administration the Army Corps of Engineers was assigned survey and construction work to aid civil projects. The administration also provided financial support by allotting public lands in alternate sections along canal routes in several western states and by purchasing canal stock for similar undertakings in eastern areas where land grants were no longer feasible. Adams was particularly pleased that under his administration funding was finally achieved and ground broken for construction of the Chesapeake and Ohio Canal. The widespread distribution of public works was the most popular program of his presidency.

Nevertheless, particularistic interests joined in opposition to the administration. Adams's view that the public lands were a public trust to be utilized as a capital reserve ran counter to western proposals for preemption of holdings at a fixed minimum price, rather than by auction, and for gradual reduction of prices when lands remained unsold. Southerners and westerners saw his action to protect the Creek Indians from a treaty violation by Georgia authorities a restraint upon access to Indian lands elsewhere. State and local bankers criticized the administration's reliance upon the Bank of the United States in support of a national credit structure. Even efforts to lower government interest costs by refunding the public debt were opposed by the argument that the bank, as the only prospective nonforeign bidder, would liquidate its domestic loans in order to meet specie requirements in payment of the foreign bondholders. Political opponents framed tariff legislation so that administration proposals designed to protect developing industry were expanded to cover a wide range of agricultural products, thus raising costs of raw materials needed in fabrication. Cooperating in this stratagem to embarrass Adams's adherents in the upcoming presidential election, southern leaders, who generally opposed a protective tariff, rejected all moderating amendments, in the expectation that administration forces would ultimately bear the onus of repudiating their own program recommendation. When, instead, they accepted this "Tariff of Abominations," South Carolinians threatened nullification.

The outcome of the 1828 election had been foreshadowed by the administration's defeat in the congressional elections of 1827, as it lost control of both the House and Senate. Adams had refused to dismiss government appointees "without just cause" and had retained many whose political opposition was damaging to his efforts. He campaigned little for reelection. He would not even appear in celebration of the beginning of the Pennsylvania Canal, where it was thought his fluency in German might attract support. "Electioneering," he explained, ran counter to his principles. While Clay struggled to organize their followers, Adams could hold neither the expanding West nor the Ohio Valley transitional zone. Jackson electors carried all but New England, New Jersey, Delaware, and Maryland.

Adams was unhappy in retirement. His wife maintained that he had an "insatiable passion" for political office and controversy. He did not relish the art of politics, but he did enjoy the prominence of public office and fiercely resented what he called a "conspiracy of power," by which he and his father before him had been denied reelection while four Virginia presidents had served double terms. Local Republican leaders who tried to persuade him to become a congressional candidate in 1830 found that he was not reluctant to serve in the legislature, provided he were "handsomely chosen." Although his family strongly disapproved, Adams was delighted when he was elected by 71 percent of the vote. His program suited the demands of increasingly industrialized New England, and over the next seventeen years he was regularly reelected to Congress, with support levels ranging as high as 87 percent of the vote during the Jackson administrations.

During the early 1830s Adams was actively involved in the Antimasonic movement, attacking the elitism and political control identified with the fraternal order. In his view the protest represented a liberal wing of the National Republicans, opposing both the Jacksonians and the High Federalists of an earlier day. Political maverick that he was, however, he broke with the National Republican–Whig leadership to support Jackson's vigorous stand against the French delay in providing compensation for Napoleonic spoliations, and he remained publicly neutral during the presidential election of 1836.

The domestic program for which he labored remained primarily the American System of his presidency. As chairman of the Committee of Manufactures in 1832 he introduced a tariff measure that eliminated some of the more objectionable features of the 1828 tariff, notably through duty reductions on raw materials while continuing protectively high duties on cotton and woolen goods and rolled iron. He vehemently opposed the compromise tariff of 1833 with its across-the-board reductions to meet the demands of South Carolina nullifiers.

As a member of a special committee appointed by the Jacksonian Speaker of the House in 1832 to investigate the Bank of the United States, he drafted a lengthy minority report assailing the attack on the bank. He contended that the attack rested less upon traditional arguments over constitutional strict construction than upon the competitive interests of speculative and fiscally irresponsible banking rivals. When he was subsequently denied the opportunity to speak in protest of Jackson's removal of public deposits and their redistribution among politically selected "pet banks," Adams published his remarks in a pamphlet suitable for widespread dissemination.

His concern for support of large-scale public improvements remained the core of his program. He accepted the compromise Whig endorsement of a permanent preemption law for sale of public lands in 1841 but only in exchange for western support of the distribution of the treasury surplus for funding of internal improvements. When the price of southern consent to a tariff measure was a restriction upon such distribution if the tariff rose above 20 percent ad valorem, he rejected even the Whig tariff proposal of 1842.

Beginning in 1835 Adams initiated a campaign against southern political influence that was to continue the remainder of his life. On policy grounds he believed that the alliance in sectional bargaining between proponents of cheap land for the West and low tariffs for the South doomed the American System. His concern was fueled on a personal basis by conviction that the governmental dominance of southern leaders rested largely upon augmentation of their representation under the three-fifths clause of the Constitution. His decision to oppose this force was triggered primarily by a legalistic defense of constitutional democracy rather than humanitarian considerations.

Coincidentally, however, he became a leader of congressional opposition to the institution of slavery. With scathing invective he relentlessly seized every parliamentary opening for nine years to oppose application of the "gag rule" that prevented congressional acceptance of antislavery petitions. Triumphant in that stand at the session beginning in December 1844, he had also won acclaim in March 1841 when, nearly a quarter century after he had given up active legal practice, he had participated in the successful Supreme Court defense for a group of slaves taken into custody after a shipboard revolt and the seizure of the Spanish vessel *Amistad.* For yet another six years he struggled, again successfully, to block enactment of legislation counteracting the decision by compensating owners of the vessel. Meanwhile, he protested both the annexation of Texas and the U.S. war with Mexico as measures to expand southern power. His last congressional action before suffering a fatal stroke at his seat in the House of Representatives was a vote of "no," objecting to a proposal rendering thanks to various military officers for services during the Mexican conflict.

Adams, who recognized himself as "a man of reserved, cold, austere and forbidding manners," had found great satisfaction in a congressional career that brought him plaudits among slavery opponents as a popular hero, "Old Man Eloquent," "Defender of the Rights of Man." Historically, however, his reputation rests most firmly on the policies he pursued as diplomat and president. Aptly characterized by one biographer as "an Independent Man," Adams was a poor politician, unwilling to cater to popular interests and reluctant even to compromise. But sound judgment and a strong commitment to public service led him to formulate and stubbornly adhere to views of public policy that over the years have won strong approval. His primary concern was to elevate the national stature in the international community—in foreign relations, in commerce and industry, and even as a scientific and cultural contributor. The American System, translated into party platforms of the Whig and successor Republican parties, in large measure shaped the course to national maturity after 1860.

• The main body of Adams's papers, covering family manuscripts dating from 1639 to 1889, is located in the Massachusetts Historical Society, Boston, and is available in major research libraries on microfilm. The papers are in process of publication by the Belknap Press of Harvard University. Still useful is the more limited compilation, *Memoirs of John Quincy Adams, Comprising Portions of His Diary from 1795 to 1848*, ed. Charles Francis Adams (12 vols., 1874–1877).

Marie B. Hecht's biography, *John Quincy Adams: A Personal History of an Independent Man* (1972), is particularly useful for detail on Adams's early career. For narrative skill and policy analysis, despite strong bias and some inaccuracies, the two biographical volumes by Samuel Flagg Bemis, *John Quincy Adams and the Foundations of American Foreign Policy* (1949) and *John Quincy Adams and the Union* (1956), remain basic. Paul C. Nagel, *Descent from Glory: Four Generations of the John Adams Family* (1983), gives insight into the psychological and emotional pressures of Adams's family background. Studies by Mary W. M. Hargreaves, *The Presidency of John Quincy Adams* (1985), and Leonard L. Richards, *The Life and Times of Congressman John Quincy Adams* (1986), provide extensive detail on the specific phases of Adams's career.

MARY W. M. HARGREAVES

ADAMS, John Quincy (4 May 1848–3 Sept. 1922), newspaper editor and publisher, civil rights leader, and Republican party activist, was born in Louisville, Kentucky, the son of Henry Adams, a prominent minister and educator, and Margaret Corbin. Both his parents were free persons of color. Following private schooling in Wisconsin and Ohio, Adams graduated from Oberlin College. After a brief teaching stint in Louisville, in 1870 he followed his uncle, Joseph C. Corbin, to work in Arkansas in the Reconstruction. By 1874 he had risen from schoolteacher to assistant superintendent of public instruction. His lifelong activism in the Republican party began in Arkansas; there he twice served as secretary to Republican state conventions, was elected as justice of the peace on the party ticket, and held the offices of engrossing clerk of the state senate and deputy commissioner of public works. The defeat of the Arkansas Republican party in 1874 and the racial repression that followed led Adams to return to Louisville, where he again engaged in teaching.

Adams entered journalism in 1879 when he and his brother, Cyrus Field Adams, established the *Louisville Bulletin*, a weekly newspaper that served the Louisville African-American community until 1885, when it was subsumed by the *American Baptist*. In 1880 Adams helped organize the National Afro-American Press Association, which held its first annual meeting in Louisville that year. The organization elected him as its first president, and he served from 1880 to 1882.

In 1886 Adams accepted an offer to join the staff of the St. Paul, Minnesota, *Western Appeal*, a black-owned weekly. Within a year he assumed the editorship and incorporated the Northwestern Publishing Company, which supported the expansion of the newspaper to include offices in Chicago, Louisville, Indianapolis, St. Louis, Dallas, and Washington, D.C. The *Western Appeal* prospered under his leadership; it was one of only nine African-American newspapers established in the 1880s that survived until 1914. Its editorials consistently attacked racial discrimination and called for equal treatment both locally and nationally.

In 1887 Adams helped organize resistance to racial discrimination in public accommodations and in the workplace in Minnesota through the establishment of the Minnesota Protective and Industrial League, and its successor, the Afro-American League of St. Paul, in 1889. He worked with T. Thomas Fortune to found the National Afro-American League in 1890, serving on its first executive committee. The Afro-American Council, dominated by Booker T. Washington's accommodationist "Tuskegee machine," received his initial support in 1898. By 1903 the hostility of the council to civil rights activism in the North alienated Adams. Although he was not a leader in the National Association for the Advancement of Colored People, he endorsed it by 1913 and finally broke with Tuskegee accommodationism. His editorials and civic activity continued to attack racial discrimination for the remainder of his life.

The other constant in Adams's public life was loyalty to the Republican party. The *Appeal* consistently endorsed Republican candidates even as the party moved toward the establishment of a "lily-white" southern branch. Only President Warren G. Harding's acquiescence to segregation and lynching finally led Adams to question publicly his lifelong Republicanism.

Adams's influence peaked in the decade surrounding the turn of the century. By 1913 the *Appeal* had closed its offices in Dallas, St. Louis, Louisville, Chicago, and Washington and had shrunk to a local weekly. The paper and its editor remained influential in St. Paul, however, until his death. Adams was struck and killed by an automobile in St. Paul. He was survived by his wife, Ella B. Smith, whom he had married in 1892; the couple had four children.

Even as he spent his life fighting the increasing racism of the Gilded Age, Adams illustrated the possibilities that came for some African Americans in the emancipation era. His creation of a newspaper with offices in six major cities, his leadership among African-American journalists, and his advocacy of civil rights earned him a national reputation by 1900. He epitomized the African-American middle class of the urban North. Light enough in complexion to pass for white, he edited a "race journal" dependent on the African-American community for whose civil rights he fought.

• No collection of Adams's papers exists, but the Minnesota Historical Society holds copies of his newspaper. David V. Taylor, "John Quincy Adams: St. Paul Editor and Black Leader," *Minnesota History* 43 (Winter 1973): 283–96, is the most thorough biography available. See also Henry Lewis Suggs, "Democracy on Trial: The Black Press, Black Migration, and the Evolution of Culture and Community in Minnesota, 1865–1970," in *The Black Press in the Middle West, 1865–1985*, ed. Henry Lewis Suggs (1996), pp. 165–212; Willard B. Gatewood, *Aristocrats of Color: The Black Elite, 1880–1920* (1990); August Meier, *Negro Thought in America, 1880–1915* (1963); Earl Spangler, *The Negro in Minnesota* (1961); and Emma Lou Thornbrough, "American Negro Newspapers, 1880–1914," *Business History Review* 40 (Winter 1966): 467–90. Obituaries are in the St. Paul *Appeal*, 9 and 16 Sept. 1922.

WILBERT H. AHERN

ADAMS, Louisa Catherine Johnson (12 Feb. 1775–15 May 1852), first lady, was born in London, England, the daughter of Joshua Johnson, an American merchant, and Catherine Nuth (or Young). Though it is known that her father was a prominent businessman and that her uncle Thomas Johnson was the governor of Maryland, her mother's origins remain obscure. Recent scholarship has tentatively posited that her mother was born out of wedlock and that she may not have married Louisa's father until after the birth of her older children. In 1778 the family moved to Nantes, France, where Louisa began school and mastered French so thoroughly that when the Johnsons moved back to England when Louisa was eight, she had to learn her native language anew. She and her sisters received the education befitting the daughters of a fashionable London household.

In 1795 the American minister to The Hague, John Quincy Adams (1767–1848), was on a diplomatic mission in London, where he quickly became interested in twenty-year-old Louisa. Their stormy courtship began three months later, when at a ball Adams made his intentions "decidedly publick." The aloofness and ambiguity of his character often confused and irritated Louisa. In turn, he considered her to have been dreadfully spoiled by her parents. In May 1796 he left for The Hague, putatively engaged to Louisa Catherine but very vague about the future. In their first correspondence he endeavored to school his future wife on the centrality of duty in the republican way of thinking: "Every interest and every feeling inconsistent with it must disappear." Though for the most part outwardly compliant, Louisa resisted these efforts sufficiently for Adams to reprove her for such a show of "Spirit."

Eventually, after much pressure from Louisa and her family, Adams returned to London and married her at Tower Hill in July 1797. Shortly afterward her father went bankrupt. The shame of his insolvency and the suspicious timing of her marriage would become the blight of her life and "turn every sweet thing into gall." She quickly became very depressed and then fell ill, a pattern of emotional distress followed by physical collapse that recurred frequently in her life.

Suffering from the effects of her first pregnancy, Louisa sailed with her husband to Berlin, where he was posted to the Prussian court. Once on shore she miscarried the child and thus began a death-defying reproductive history that included fourteen pregnancies—nine miscarriages, four live births, and one stillbirth. When she recovered she entered court life with zest, outshining her bookish spouse. By the time her husband was recalled to America in September 1801, Louisa had given birth to the couple's first son, George Washington Adams. But even with the Adams heir in tow, she felt that she had entered a completely alien world when she arrived at the Quincy household. "Even the Church, its forms, the snuffling through the nose, the Singers, the dressing and the dinner hour were all novelties to me," she wrote. Louisa also recorded that she felt keenly the censure of her husband's family for being "a *fine* Lady" who definitely would "not suit." The only bright spot in the trip, she recalled, was old John Adams (1735–1826), "who took a fancy to *me* and he was the only one."

For two years, Louisa kept house in Boston while her husband endeavored to make a living as a lawyer. She gave birth to a second son, John Adams II, later recalling those times as the most pleasant she had enjoyed in America. In 1803 John Quincy was elected U.S. senator. For the next five years Louisa shuttled between her husband in Washington and her children in Quincy, suffering a stillbirth alone in Washington and giving birth to another son, Charles Francis Adams (1807–1886), in Boston. The rawness of Washington society both shocked and intrigued her. She immediately disliked President Thomas Jefferson (he had "a kind of sneaking greatness") and bewailed the increasing democratization of the republic.

In the summer of 1809 President James Madison (1751–1836) appointed John Quincy plenipotentiary to Russia, an event that Louisa later named as the turning point of her life. Her husband decided that she and their youngest son should go with him but that their two older sons should stay in America. Though usually deferring to him in family matters, this time Louisa fought his decision. He remained firm, however, and she sailed for St. Petersburg accompanied only by her sister Kitty and Charles Francis, whom she later described as "the only one of my children I never deserted." The family was separated for six long years, a circumstance that Louisa believed caused the early deaths of her two eldest sons. In St. Petersburg, Louisa once again shone at court, winning special regard from the emperor and his wife. She gave birth to a girl Louisa Catherine Adams, in 1811, but the child died a year later. Her husband reacted to this tragedy by retreating further into his books, while Louisa descended into a deep depression, which she attempted to alleviate by writing.

In 1814 John Quincy was called to Ghent to negotiate a peace treaty. While there he received news of a new appointment to London and sent Louisa instructions to join him in Paris. With a strength and bravado that amazed her family, she endured the forty-day carriage ride, coping with thieves, retreating armies, and an angry mob. She and her husband were reunited with all of their children in England, where they spent two idyllic years before returning to America so that John Quincy could accept the post of secretary of state under President James Monroe. Seeing her husband only a step away from the nation's highest office, but aware of his awkwardness in the kind of social situations that campaigning entailed, Louisa recognized an opportunity to exercise her hard-won political savvy and assumed almost entirely the burden of "smiling for the Presidency." She turned the task of making social calls—"the torments of my life"—into a science, in one day delivering as many as eleven such calls, covering six square miles.

When her husband was elected in 1824, her job as "campaign manager" ended, leaving her gloomy and depressed. She disliked the White House and grew tired of the "Bull Bait" of politics. When John Quincy suffered ignominious defeat in the election of 1828, she joyfully prepared to quit Washington for the peace of retirement. Her happiness was overshadowed, however, by the death of her eldest son, a possible suicide, as he was on his way to escort his parents from the White House. Five years later her second-eldest son also died after a long, wrenching battle with alcoholism. Another blow was her husband's decision to return to Washington in 1830 when called upon by district politicos to serve in Congress. Louisa, outraged by his "grasping ambition" and "insatiable passion for fame," reminded him of the price they both had paid already for his political involvement. In 1825 and 1840 she wrote "Record of My Life" and "The Adventures of a Nobody," memoirs that portray European diplomatic life and the Washington political scene and give insights into the life of an intelligent, sensitive woman in the late eighteenth and early nineteenth century.

A year after her husband's death in 1848, Louisa suffered a stroke. She died three years later in her Washington home. On the day of her funeral both houses of Congress adjourned in her memory, making her the first woman ever to receive that honor.

• The papers of Louisa Catherine Adams are on microfilm, with those of other members of the Adams family, as part of the Adams Manuscript Trust at the Massachusetts Historical Society. The late editor of the Adams papers, Lyman H. Butterfield, wrote "Tending a Dragon-Killer: Notes for the Biographer of Mrs. John Quincy Adams," *Proceedings of the American Philosophical Society* 118 (Apr. 1974): 165–78, in hopes of spurring scholarship about the person he considered "central to the Adams dynasty." Jack Shepherd provides a colorful account of Louisa Adams's life in *Cannibals of the Heart: A Personal Biography of Louisa Catherine and John Quincy Adams* (1980), and Paul Nagel covers many important aspects of her place within the Adams family in *Descent from Glory: Four Generations of the John Adams Family* (1983) and *The Adams Women: Abigail and Louisa Adams, Their Sisters and Daughters* (1987). A quick sketch of her life and several illuminating insights are in Katherine T. Corbett, "Louisa Catherine Adams: The Anguished 'Adventures of a Nobody,'" in *Woman's Being, Woman's Place: Female Identity and Vocation in American History* (1979). The person who has produced the most scholarship on the subject is Joan R. Challinor, whose "Louisa Catherine Johnson Adams: The Price of Ambition" (Ph.D. diss., American Univ., 1982), has informed much of the present work. She also wrote "'A Quarter-Taint of Maryland Blood': An Inquiry into the Anglo/Maryland Background of Mrs. John Quincy Adams," *Maryland Historical Magazine* 80 (Winter 1985): 409–19, and "The Mis-Education of Louisa Catherine Johnson," *Proceedings of the Massachusetts Historical Society* 98 (1987): 21–48, which reviews the early life of Louisa Adams in great detail.

CATHERINE A. ALLGOR

ADAMS, Marian Hooper (13 Sept. 1843–6 Dec. 1885), Washington hostess, pioneer photographer, and the wife of Henry Adams, was born in Boston to Edward Hooper, a wealthy ophthalmologist, and Ellen Sturgis, a Transcendental poet. "Clover," as she was called, grew up among an affectionate clan of community conscious relatives who offered her continuing warmth and encouragement after the death of her mother when she was just five. Her father subsequently gave up his regular practice in order to rear his three children. And he became especially close to Clover, the youngest.

Particularly important in shaping the young Clover were also her maternal grandfather, William Sturgis, an early China trader who was fluent in Native American dialects, and her aunt Caroline Sturgis (Tappan), a close friend of Margaret Fuller and Ralph Waldo Emerson. Clover's mother and aunt had both attended Fuller's Boston conversation classes designed to liberate women's minds. And Ellen Hooper published her poetry in the Transcendental magazine, the *Dial*, alongside Fuller's feminist tract, "The Great Lawsuit: Man *versus* Men, Woman *versus* Women," which was later expanded into her *Woman in the Nineteenth Century* (1845). Ellen left her writings as a heritage for her children to clarify her social and intellectual concerns. Family letters reveal that the Hoopers, unlike the Adamses, were outspoken supporters of women's rights. They were also sympathetic with many of the anti-institutional ideas of Emerson. Growing up around free thinkers made Clover independent and iconoclastic. Like many New Englanders of her time and class she never hesitated to express unpopular or critical opinions. Labeled "sharp tongued" by a number of historians who have demanded different standards of behavior for women than for men, Clover revealed her feelings honestly in weekly letters to her father. In this respect she followed the forthright tradition of other Adams women whose letters and diaries reveal inner worlds at odds with the other political successes of their husbands. Unconventional Concord and Stockbridge shaped the ideas of Clover Hooper, much as establishment Beacon Hill, Quincy, and Harvard shaped Henry Adams. Henry James, a life-long friend and admirer of her independent mind, called Clover "the genius of my beloved country." To imagine her as a model for several of his American heroines is entirely realistic.

In 1866, after working with the United States Sanitary Commission during the Civil War, Clover traveled to England, where she met Henry Adams, who was still serving his ambassador father. But it was in Cambridge, Massachusetts, when Henry returned to teach at Harvard and edit the *North American Review*, that their close relationship developed. They met often at the home of Whitman Gurney, Clover's brother-in-law and Greek tutor, another unconventional scholar who supported Clover's sister Ellen in her efforts to help found a college for women at Harvard. Both sisters understood from thorough preparatory studies at the Agassiz School for girls how important a more focused education for women was. But Clover's 1872 marriage to Henry Adams took her to Europe for a long honeymoon. And the Adamses moved to Washington for good in 1877. Letters, however, reveal Clover's ongoing, if sporadic, interest in women's education, and Henry Adams included many of her opinions in his novel, *Esther* (1884). Ideas about the power and complexity of women began to appear in Henry Adams's cultural criticism soon after their marriage.

On a second long stay in Europe in 1879–1880, Clover was able to help Henry with his historical work using her special language skills. She noted more than once in letters to her father that she was happy making good use of her brain. Back in Washington, she described her pleasure at collating materials side by side with her fastidious historian husband. Yet when he started to write there was less involvement for her. Becoming a Washington hostess was another way to be of use in the nation's capital. The salon Clover created, far from being frivolous, was designed to help selected companions thrash out political problems as well as to educate bureaucrats in moral attitudes and good taste. As "First Heart" of the Five of Hearts—the special group that included the Adamses, Mrs. and Mrs. John Hay, and the geologist Clarence King—Clover made much of the "best and brightest." If Henry James once called her a "Voltaire in Petticoats," and noted that both Adamses were rather too critical, he remembered too that she could be "the soul of wit and grace."

In her role as hostess Clover was also proud to exhibit the art collection she and Henry acquired over the years. Concern for the arts had been a significant part of her upbringing; her brother Ned remained actively involved in the establishment of the Boston Museum of Fine Arts. And Clover took the trouble to visit Augustus Saint-Gaudens's studio in New York while he was working on the great Civil War monument for her cousin Robert Gould Shaw. That she should take up photography in 1883 as still another means to express her sensibilities would not have surprised her family.

The intensity with which Clover went about her photographic studies at a time when there was no distinction between the professional and the amateur suggests the seriousness with which she devoted herself to all the possibilities open to her. The photographs she took of distinguished contemporaries created visual biographies that correspond to the literary history her husband wrote. She also captured some of her disappearing New England world. Public acclaim for Clover's work was clear. But Henry Adams discouraged broader publication of her photographs.

Henry once wrote that childless couples grow especially close. There can be little doubt that the two enjoyed marital companionship on many levels. Yet after Clover's father's death Henry could do little to dissolve her overwhelming melancholia, a characteristic of many members of her family. And he was devastated when in December 1885 (they were still living in Washington at the time) Clover finally committed suicide, taking the potassium cyanide used to develop her photographs. Although Henry would not mention Clover in recording his education, he wrote a close friend that he had had "twelve years of perfect happiness" with her, the only woman, he noted another time, who suited him exactly. The Saint-Gaudens monument that Henry Adams later erected in Rock Creek Park (Washington, D.C.) to mark their graves, continues to evoke the complexity of such gifted lives.

The character of Clover Adams was neatly summed up in a letter of condolence that John Hay sent Henry: "Is it any Consolation to remember her as she was? That bright intrepid spirit, that keen fine intellect, that lofty scorn of all that was mean, that social charm which made your house such a one as Washington never knew before, and, made hundreds of people love her as much as they admired her" (9 Dec. 1885).

• Many of Clover Adams's manuscript letters are in the Massachusetts Historical Society, available on microfilm in the collection of the Adams Papers. Her adolescent letters and papers related to her family remain in private collections. Ward Thoron's edition of *The Letters of Mrs. Henry Adams, 1865–1883* (1936) remains the most direct access to Clover Adams's adult life, along with the six volumes of *The Letters of Henry Adams, 1858–1918*, ed. J. C. Levenson et al. (1983–1988). These documents record daily activities and provide personal insights into the world of the Adamses. Eugenia Kaledin's *The Education of Mrs. Henry Adams* (1981), a scholarly biography, uses a feminist viewpoint to place Clover in a broader intellectual context. Otto Friedrich's *Clover* (1979), a popular biography, attempts to recreate her life in terms of modern sensibilities. The best general biographies of Henry Adams pay attention to Clover in relation to the events of his life. Ernest Samuel's three-volume study is thorough and clear: *Henry Adams: The Major Phase* (1964); *The Middle Years* (1958); *Young Henry Adams* (1948). Edward Chalfant's *Both Sides of the Ocean: A Biography of Henry Adams* (1982) and *Better in Darkness: A Biography of Henry Adams, His Second Life* (1993) interpret Clover more positively and offer the depth of a lifetime immersion in Henry Adams's ideas. Most successful in conveying the complexity of the Washington social world that the Henry Adamses created is Patricia O'Toole's *The Five of Hearts: An Intimate Portrait of Henry Adams and His Friends, 1880–1918* (1990).

EUGENIA KALEDIN

ADAMS, Maude (11 Nov. 1872–17 July 1953), actress, was born Maude Ewing Kiskadden in Salt Lake City, Utah, the daughter of James Henry Kiskadden, a banker, and Asenath Ann Adams, an actress. Adams's mother was raised a Mormon but married outside the church. Adams, the only surviving child, was introduced to an audience at nine months and took her first speaking role at the age of five. She used her mother's maiden name from the outset of her career. She appeared frequently in stock companies with her mother, first in Salt Lake City, then in 1874 in Virginia City, Nevada, in 1875 in San Francisco, and on tours throughout the West. Reports on Adams's schooling vary, the longest estimate being that she studied from the age of six to sixteen. According to Phyllis Robbins's biography (informed by Adams's mother and various other family members and corrected in manuscript by Adams), she had only intermittent schooling before spending her tenth and eleventh years at the Salt Lake City Collegiate Institute under her maternal grandmother's protection; formal tutoring ended when her father died and Adams was summoned to San Francisco to join her mother. They toured together until 1888, when Adams received her first engagement in a resident New York company. Several years of stock with E. H. Sothern followed before Adams made a success in 1892 in Charles Hoyt's *A Midnight Bell* and was hired by Charles Frohman, remaining in two seasons of stock then, from 1892 to 1898, appearing opposite John Drew. By this time her specialty was light comedy; her style emphasized delicacy, simplicity, and charm. In 1892 in Clyde Fitch's *The Masked Ball*, for example, she portrayed a young wife punishing her husband by pretending to be intoxicated. Instead of reeling physically or slurring her speech, she indicated her unsteadiness by the way she held a long-stemmed rose. Her ability to maintain gentility throughout this pretense brought two full minutes of applause.

In 1897 Adams essayed her first starring role, in *The Little Minister*, which J. M. Barrie adapted specifically for her. The New York run and national tour established Adams's reputation. She became a feature of Barrie productions: *Quality Street* (1901), *Peter Pan* (1905), *What Every Woman Knows* (1908), *The Legend of Leonora* (1914), *Rosalind* (1914), *The Ladies' Shakespeare* (1914), and *A Kiss for Cinderella* (1916). Though she occasionally tried serious roles, such as a production of *Romeo and Juliet* (1900) and an adaptation of Schiller's *Maid of Orleans* (1909), her forte was the sentimentally whimsical romance of Barrie or Edmond Rostand (*L'Aiglon* [1900] and *Chantecler* [1911]).

The reviews of Adams's Juliet are telling; the kindest comments emphasize Adams's injection of a sense of humor into the youthful role, suggesting that the later scenes were less than cathartic. William Winter's comment that "the personality cannot readily be described, but perhaps it may not be unfairly indicated as that of an intellectual young lady from Boston, competent in the mathematics and intent on teaching pedagogy" indicates that in tragedy Adams was beyond her depth. More specifically, "a balcony scene without passion" succinctly summarizes Adams's chief asset in comedy: spirited youthfulness completely devoid of sexuality. As Peter Pan, she exploited this trait to its fullest, though it should also be emphasized that all of Peter's band were cross-gender cast (a convention for young as well as fantastical characters), and if Adams stood out as "androgynous," she was a star precisely because of her ability to transcend the sexually infused codes of form-revealing costumes. Her "invention" of the Peter Pan ensemble (a peaked hat with feather, plain collar, and leaf-mottled knickers and tunic over pushed-up creased sleeves) may have aided the unconventionality of her seeming genderlessness. Her other predominant quality, a sexless maternity, could just as easily have suggested her for the character of Wendy, a more predictable match based on her other Barrie roles.

Adams remained in Frohman's employ until his death on the *Lusitania* in 1915. In 1918, while on tour in *A Kiss for Cinderella*, she succumbed to the flu epidemic and retired. Her subsequent appearances were limited: a tour in 1931–1932 playing Portia opposite Otis Skinner's Shylock, summer stock as Maria in *Twelfth Night* in 1934, a series of radio broadcasts in 1934 (*Peter Pan, The Little Minister, Rosemary, Secrets*, and *The Marching Song*), and in 1939 a cross-country lecture tour. None of her cinematic projects came to fruition. In 1937 she founded the Department of Drama at Stephens College in Columbia, Missouri, where she taught and directed plays for female students until 1950.

Adams was interested in electrical stage lighting and advised Frohman on replacements for the crackling and unpredictable arc lamps to improve effects at the Empire Theatre in New York. Her contributions to incandescent research in conjunction with General Electric in the early 1920s resulted in a new type of bulb for color motion picture filming. Adams was not credited with the patent and forfeited a possible fortune by not pursuing legal redress, allegedly preferring to stay out of the public spotlight.

Adams's religious views are unknown, though she endowed the Roman Catholic order of the Cenacle with her estates in Long Island (1922) and the Catskills (1949). She often stayed at the sisters' convent in New York from 1915; her initial religious retreat was to a nunnery in Tours in 1901. Adams never married and is not known to have had any romantic relationships with men. In all likelihood she was a lesbian. Her first long-term companion, Lillie Florence, died in 1902. Adams played through the winter, feeling increasingly exhausted, and did not work during the season of 1902–1903. From 1905 she was inseparable from Louise Boynton, whom the biographer Robbins calls "a friend, companion, secretary, and buffer against any unwarranted intrusion, a delightful dragon. . . . She dedicated herself to Miss Adams, and won her lifelong love." They were introduced by Adams's physician, William B. Wood, who wished to fill the gap left by Florence. Adams died at her farm in Tannersville, New York.

• Adams burned all her correspondence except letters from J. M. Barrie. Two boxes of manuscript and typescript material were deposited at the Library of Congress (including *Thumbs Up for Joy and Adventure, The Spoken Word*, manuscripts for the previously published *The First Steps in Speaking Verse* and *A Pamphlet on English Speech and English Verse*). Clippings files are held by the Billy Rose Theatre Collection of the New York Public Library for the Performing Arts, the Harvard University Theatre Collection, and the University of California at Berkeley. Installments of an autobiography appeared in the *Ladies Home Journal*, March 1926–May 1927, as "The One I Knew Least of All." Biographies include Phyllis Robbins, *The Young Maude Adams* (1959) and the authorized *Maude Adams: An Intimate Portrait* (1956); Acton Davies, *Maude Adams* (1901); Ada Patterson, *Maude Adams, A Biography* (1907); and Eileen K. Kuehnl, *Maude Adams, an American Idol* (1984). Biographic information and obituaries are listed in George B. Bryan, *Stage Deaths: A Biographical Guide to International Theatrical Obituaries, 1850 to 1990* (1991). Despite Adams's reclusive attitude toward the press, much popular journalism was composed about her, and a full bibliography can be found in Stephen Archer, *American Actors and Actresses* (1983).

TRACY C. DAVIS

ADAMS, Numa Pompilius Garfield (26 Feb. 1885–29 Aug. 1940), physician and medical educator, was born in Delaplane, Virginia. Little is known about Adams's family and early life. He attended a country school run by his uncle Robert Adams. Adams received additional instruction and inspiration from his grandmother Amanda, a midwife who shared with him the secrets of herbal medicine. When Adams was thirteen, his family moved to Steelton, Pennsylvania. Soon Adams taught himself how to read music and purchased a used cornet, which he taught himself to play, a skill that later helped him pay for his education.

After graduating from high school in 1905, Adams spent a year as a substitute teacher in Steelton and another year teaching seventh grade in Carlisle, Pennsylvania. These jobs helped him earn sufficient money to pay for his college education, and in 1907 he left Pennsylvania to enter Howard University in Washington, D.C. He soon joined the Lyric Orchestra, a dance band composed mostly of medical and dental students, which performed three to five nights a week. On other nights Adams supplemented his earnings by appearing with Louis Brown's orchestra.

Adams received his undergraduate degree magna cum laude from Howard in 1911, and the following year he earned a master's degree in chemistry from Columbia University. He moved back to Washington, D.C., to take a post as an instructor of chemistry at Howard. He remained on the faculty of Howard's chemistry department until 1919, rising through the ranks and becoming first assistant and then associate professor of chemistry. In 1918 Adams was named head of the department, but he did not find chemistry sufficiently satisfying to continue his career in it. In addition, he may have been concerned about the limited salary that a professor at that time could make; he had married Osceola Macarthy in 1915, and they had one child.

In the fall of 1919 Adams resigned the chair of the chemistry department to pursue a medical career. The following spring he moved to Chicago and entered Rush Medical College. Adams again turned to music to help finance his education, but tastes had changed, and playing the cornet was no longer a marketable skill. Adams then purchased a saxophone and within three weeks had become sufficiently expert to join the Charley Cooke Orchestra. Attending classes during the day and performing every night, Adams relegated most of his studying to the hour-and-a-half commute from Chicago to the dance hall where the orchestra played. This grueling schedule did not stop him from winning the school's Smiley scholarship nor from finishing second in his medical class. He graduated in 1924 and was elected to Alpha Omega Alpha, a medical scholastic fraternity.

After a year's internship at a city hospital in St. Louis, Adams returned to Chicago and opened a private practice; he also served as assistant medical director of the Victory Life Insurance Company. In 1927 he returned to teaching, this time as an instructor in neurology and psychiatry at Provident Hospital. In 1929 the quiet life he had established in Chicago ended when the president of Howard, Mordecai Johnson, offered him the deanship of the university's medical school.

Even before Adams agreed to become the first African-American dean of an approved medical school, he must have been aware of the difficulties that would face him. Although Howard had always been among the elite of the predominantly black medical schools, its budget was considerably less than that of many non-black institutions. Howard had no endowment and subsisted entirely on tuition fees. Ten years before, Adams's predecessors had contemplated closing the school altogether.

Despite the obstacles and the mixed greetings that he received from the standing faculty—which included many white as well as black professors—Adams set to work to chart a new path for Howard. Several of his actions in office proved controversial among the faculty. Traditionally, the faculty members had worked their teaching schedules around other paid positions. Adams put an end to this system and enforced a daytime schedule of classes that would be more convenient for the students.

In another controversial move, Adams began a campaign to bring better-trained faculty to the school. In his first years he recruited a number of new faculty with doctorates in their disciplines. When interviewing new faculty members, Adams cared little for the reputation of the schools a candidate had attended; rather, he paid particularly close attention to the candidate's course of study. Perhaps not surprisingly, given his own background, he appeared to favor those who had a background in scientific research as well as in medicine. To attract the best candidates, he offered applicants a generous starting salary of $3,500, with a $500 increase each year up to $6,000. This move drew protest from the administrators at Meharry Medical College, who argued that their school—then the only other black medical college in the country—would suffer because it could not match Howard's salaries.

Adams remained determined to provide Howard's medical students with the best possible education. Although the advent of the depression forced him to withdraw his promises of raises, he continued his quest to mold Howard into an elite institution. During his ten years as dean, he steadily raised entrance requirements in the hope of improving the caliber of the student body. This policy, however, often resulted in a decrease in eligible students; one year, the school admitted a class of only twenty-six. Critics warned of loss of tuition revenues and reduction of opportunities for blacks to enter the medical profession, but Adams's claim that this move would produce better students was proven true toward the end of his tenure as dean. Previously at least one student, and sometimes more, in each class had failed the annual board examinations, but the last four classes Adams admitted as dean all passed.

In the final years of his deanship, Adams oversaw the integration of the Freedman's Hospital with Howard University. Opened before the university, Freedman's was operated by the U.S. Department of the Interior until the late 1930s. In 1937 the secretary of the department commissioned a study on the future of the hospital. On the basis of the study's recommendation, the department concluded that Howard Medical School should take over operation of the hospital. Even this change, which Adams oversaw, was not without its detractors, but despite protests, particularly from the city's Medico-Chirurgical Society, Freedman's Hospital was transferred to Howard Medical School in 1940.

Adams died that same year in Chicago, after a long illness that many of his friends attributed at least in part to the strains of the deanship. He knew that he had antagonized many and endeared himself to few during his years as dean. Up to the end of his life, he continued to feel that his labors were unappreciated.

• The fullest sketch of Adams's life is William Montague Cobb, "Medical History," *Journal of the National Medical Association* 43 (1951): 43–52. Briefer accounts appear in the *Dictionary of American Medical Biography* (1984) and in Herbert M. Morais, *The History of the Negro in Medicine* (1967). For a short account of his years at Howard University, see Rayford Logan, *Howard University: The First Hundred Years, 1867–1967* (1969). For more information about Howard Medical School prior to Adams's deanship, see Kenneth M. Ludmerer, *Learning to Heal: The Development of American Medical Education* (1985).

SHARI RUDAVSKY

ADAMS, Pepper (8 Oct. 1930–10 Sept. 1986), jazz baritone saxophonist, was born Park Adams III in Highland Park, Michigan, the son of Park Adams, Jr., a manager of a furniture store, and Cleo Coyle. The family had been reasonably well off until the store went bankrupt in the depression, one year after Adams's birth. Adams grew up in poverty. His parents traveled to live with different relatives before settling with his grandparents in Rochester, New York.

He started playing the piano at a young age. When instruments were given out in school he tried trumpet and trombone and then found that he was better suited to reed instruments such as the clarinet and tenor and soprano saxophones. In 1941 he acquired his nickname as a result of his unfortunate resemblance to the unattractive St. Louis Browns baseball player Pepper Martin, who had just arrived in Rochester to finish out his career with the local minor league team.

Adams took lessons on tenor saxophone from Elbert "Skippy" Williams, formerly a member of Duke Ellington's band. In 1944 he began playing clarinet and tenor sax with a local band six nights per week at the E-Lite Club. The following year tenor saxophonist Coleman Hawkins performed in Rochester, and Adams subsequently imitated his style. He worked with Ben Smith, formerly a trumpeter with Jimmie Lunceford's big band.

Adams started playing baritone saxophone soon after arriving in Detroit at age sixteen. While working in a factory by day, he sat in at night with bands, and he was tutored informally by tenor saxophonists Wardell Gray and Billy Mitchell. He performed in tenor saxophonist Lucky Thompson's nine-piece band alongside pianist Tommy Flanagan late in 1947. He worked at the Paradise Club, an alcohol-free dance hall for teenagers, with trumpeter Little John (Wilson) and his Merry Men; fellow sidemen included pianist Barry Harris and tenor saxophonist Frank Foster. He also met bassist Charles Mingus in Detroit while Mingus was with vibraphonist Lionel Hampton's big band.

From 1948 to 1950 Adams attended Wayne (now Wayne State) University, majoring in English. During these years he rehearsed and worked with Gray; they often traded instruments on the job, Gray playing baritone saxophone and Adams playing tenor. In 1951 he enlisted in the U.S. Army to join the band. He discovered, by comparison with fellow bandsmen, that he was much better than he had thought, and he decided to become a professional musician. Sent to Korea in 1953, mainly to play with a Special Services show, Adams recalled going along the front lines with a carbine in one hand and an alto saxophone in the other to visit Foster in the Seventh Infantry Band.

In the summer of 1953, at the war's unofficial ending, Adams returned to Detroit and re-enrolled at Wayne. However, he then changed his mind and instead started playing at the Bluebird in Detroit, where he replaced trumpeter Thad Jones in bass player James Richardson's group with pianist Barry Harris and drummer Elvin Jones. The group accompanied visiting soloists such as Wardell Gray, alto saxophonist Sonny Stitt, and trumpeter Miles Davis. Adams stayed at the Bluebird for about a year and a half. He worked with saxophonist Yusef Lateef at Klein's Showbar; with Flanagan, Jones, and bassist Paul Chambers in guitarist Kenny Burrell's group at the West End Hotel; and with trumpeter Donald Byrd at the World Stage. "More often than not, I was the only white cat in any band I worked in," Adams told interviewer John Tynan (p. 17). Repeatedly, the most lucrative jazz jobs in town had been secured by white players who were infatuated with the cool jazz sound epitomized at that time by the playing of tenor saxophonist Stan Getz. They criticized Adams for the "old-fashioned," big-toned, almost overblown sound that he produced with the baritone instrument. He stuck with his convictions and with his African-American colleagues, and later he proudly reported that he had proved these now-forgotten musician-critics wrong.

In January 1956 Adams came to New York City with Burrell and Tommy Flanagan. Adams worked in an insurance company while awaiting his transfer into the local union. From about May 1956 through the end of the year he toured across the country with pianist Stan Kenton's big band. As his exceptional talent became apparent, he gradually took more and more solos, including a lengthy version of "My Funny Valentine" that Kenton's arranger Bill Holman had designed for alto saxophonist Charlie Parker. The tour ended at Kenton's home base, Los Angeles, where Adams remained for six months. He recorded often (including sessions as a leader) with Kenton and with West Coast jazz musicians such as trumpeter Shorty Rogers and saxophonist Dave Pell. He found little work in nightclubs.

After playing with trumpeters Maynard Ferguson and Chet Baker, Adams returned to New York, where he recorded trumpeter Lee Morgan's album *The Cooker* in September 1957. At year's end he recorded *Man Bites Harmonica* with harmonica player and guitarist Toots Thielemans (1957). At the Five Spot nightclub in the spring and summer of 1958 he led a band including Byrd, pianist Bobby Timmons, bassist Doug Watkins, and drummer Elvin Jones. They recorded his album *10 to 4 at the 5 Spot*, but the band received bad reviews, because critics did not yet appreciate Jones's innovative drumming style. That same year Adams also worked frequently at the New York nightclub Birdland. He recorded *Blue Gene* with tenor saxophonist Gene Ammons as well as a session with trombonist Jimmy Knepper, and he worked in Benny Goodman's big band. In February 1959 he recorded Charles Mingus's album *Blues and Roots*, which offers his raucous statements of the repeated opening phrase on "Moanin'" and equally gruff and characteristic bop solos on that title and on "Tensions." In the spring he was in pianist Thelonious Monk's band for a concert at Town Hall in New York, and he performed with Goodman on television before embarking on Goodman's three-week tour of the United States and Canada.

From 1959 to 1962 Adams co-led a quintet with Donald Byrd, in which first Duke Pearson and then the young Herbie Hancock served as pianist. Adams stated that it actually was Byrd's band administratively, with Adams getting a generous billing as co-leader. Their finest recording is the two-disc *At the Half Note Cafe* (1960). When an unscrupulous club owner left Byrd and Adams stranded and in debt in Kansas City, Charles Mingus helped out, hiring Adams immediately at the Five Spot. Adams spent a few further weeks with Mingus during 1962, including a stand at Birdland in October. From late 1962 into 1963 he played for four months in Lionel Hampton's big band. Further recordings include his own album of Mingus's music, under Mingus's direction (1963), and saxophonist and composer Oliver Nelson's *More Blues and the Abstract Truth* (1964).

In the mid-1960s Adams worked intermittently in a quintet with Thad Jones and drummer Mel Lewis. With Duke Pearson as pianist, they recorded the album *Mean What You Say* in 1966, and through this association Adams became a founding member of the Jones-Lewis orchestra later that year. Concurrently he played in Pearson's big band, initially co-led by Byrd. The two big bands worked so infrequently that there was no conflict. As a consequence of his exposure at Jones and Lewis's regular job on Monday nights at the Village Vanguard, Adams began working steadily in New York studios. Gradually he resumed playing jazz in clubs, as he preferred, and in the 1970s, after the demise of Pearson's band, Adams took periodic leaves from Jones and Lewis to play as a soloist with local rhythm sections, mainly in Europe and occasionally in Toronto. He left the Jones-Lewis orchestra for good late in 1976 and in that year married Claudette Nadra, becoming stepfather to her son.

While leading small groups and touring extensively, Adams recorded *Baritone Madness* with baritone saxophonist Nick Brignola (1977), pianist Don Friedman's *Hot Pepper and Knepper* (1978), and his own albums *Reflectory* (1978), *The Master* (1980), *Urban Dreams* (1981), and *Live at Fat Tuesday's* (1983). He suffered from lung cancer for nearly two years but refused to stop playing. Having appeared at the Montreal Jazz Festival in July 1986, he died two months later in New York.

Adams was among the best of those players who transferred to the baritone saxophone a fleet improvising style based on the music of bop alto saxophonist Charlie Parker. He explained that in fast passages he lightly tongued every note for clarity, rather than slurring some notes together, as would be possible were he producing a less intense tone or playing a smaller saxophone.

Bright and articulate, with a wonderful sense of humor and irony, Adams aimed to translate these qualities into sound, particularly in his oft-stated desire to mock the clichés of hard bop soloing by playing perverted versions of these clichés. But this is a subtle goal, and probably only the most experienced listeners will notice jokes buried in the context of his fast-flowing, bluesy, and hard-swinging melodies. There are times when his music takes an understated and esoteric path, including, for example, several tracks on *The Master*, but to most listeners and for much of his recorded legacy, Adams's hard bop improvising will probably sound far more conventional than he makes it out to be. Like tenor saxophonist Zoot Sims, Adams is greatly admired not as a pioneer on his instrument but for his exuberance and perfection in carrying on an established style central to jazz.

• See Adams's article "Being Unpopular Is Great Fun!" *Crescendo International* 10 (Oct. 1971): 26–27. Surveys and interviews include John Tynan, "Doctor Pepper: Valuable Detroit Internship Helped Adams Find Himself," *Down Beat* 24 (14 Nov. 1957): 17, 36; Gene Lees, "Pepper Adams," *Down Beat* 30 (23 May 1963): 18–19; Arnold Jay Smith, "Pepper Adams: The Essence of Spice," *Down Beat* 44 (3 Nov. 1977): 18–19, 40; Philip Hanson, "Pepper Adams: Detroit Roots," *Jazz Journal International* 33 (Jan. 1980): 30–31; Ekkehard Jost, *Jazzmusiker: Materielen zur Soziologie der afro-amerikanischen Musik* (1981): 109–14; Lee Jeske, "Pepper Adams," *Down Beat* 49 (Aug. 1982): 28–30; and Peter Danson, "Pepper Adams," *Coda*, no. 191 (1 Aug. 1983): 4–9. Also see Gary Carner, "The Life and Musical Times of Pepper Adams" (master's thesis, City Univ. of New York, 1985). Additional information is in Carner, "Pepper Adams: Interview Part 1," *Cadence* 12 (Jan. 1986): 13–16; "Part 2" (Feb. 1986): 5–12, 21, 29; "Part 3" (Mar. 1986): 11–17, 28, 88; and "Part 4" (Apr. 1986): 5–10, 90. For a catalog of recordings and musical analysis, see Carner, "The Discography, Bibliography, and Musical Style of Pepper Adams" (master's thesis, Tufts Univ., 1989), and Carner, "Pepper Adams's 'Rue Serpente'," *Jazzforschung* 22 (1990): 119–38. See also Brian Priestley, *Mingus: A Critical Biography* (1982), and D. Russell Connor, *Benny Goodman: Listen to His Legacy* (1988). Obituaries are in the *New York Times* and the *San Francisco Examiner*, both 11 Sept. 1986, and *Annual Obituary 1986*.

BARRY KERNFELD

ADAMS, Roger (2 Jan. 1889–6 July 1971), chemist and administrator, was born in Boston, the son of Austin W. Adams, a railroad official, and Lydia Curtis. He was related to the Adams presidential family. He completed the undergraduate course in chemistry at Harvard in three years (A.B., 1909). His Harvard Ph.D. thesis was in three parts, directed by H. A. Torrey, Latham Clark, and T. W. Richards, because Torrey, his first mentor, died in 1910. After his Ph.D. (1912), he spent the year 1912–1913 on a traveling fellowship, first in Berlin at the university and then in the new Kaiser Wilhelm Institute with Richard Willstätter. His European year contributed to his philosophy of graduate work and his ideas of how to lead a first-class department.

As instructor at Harvard (1913–1916), he was a very successful teacher of undergraduates and started his own research program with two masters candidates and one senior, Henry Gilman, who later had a distinguished chemical career. In 1916 he became assistant professor at the University of Illinois in Champaign-Urbana, which had become a promising center for graduate work in chemistry under the leadership of

William A. Noyes. He remained at Illinois for the rest of his life.

Adams plunged into chemistry undergraduate and graduate teaching at Illinois with zest. He became director of the program ("preps") for preparing organic compounds that were no longer obtainable from Germany because of World War I. The preps scheme was successful scientifically, pedagogically, and financially. After the American entry into the war, Adams joined his old friends, E. P. Kohler, J. B. Conant, and other chemists in research on chemical warfare agents at American University in Washington. As a major in the Chemical Warfare Service, Adams directed work that produced the arsenical toxic agent "adamsite."

Adams married Lucile Wheeler in 1918, and they had one child. Returning to Urbana in 1918, Adams took up the varied activities that marked the rest of his life. He directed a large group of Ph.D. students, played an important role in making Illinois one of the leading centers for graduate training in chemistry (including biochemistry and chemical engineering, which were in the chemistry department), consulted for several industrial research laboratories, particularly Abbott and DuPont, and carried on numerous public service activities in chemistry. He was head of the Illinois department from 1926 to 1954, and in this capacity he made sure that his Illinois colleagues had students and resources for developing their own research programs, so that the Illinois department functioned smoothly without rivalry between faculty members. As he said, "Students are quick to detect friction within a faculty."

Adams was the leader in establishing the annual publication *Organic Syntheses* (vol. 1 appeared in 1921), a result of the Illinois preps program and of his wartime work. This was a valuable series for students and research workers because it contained reliable procedures for making key organic compounds. Adams maintained an active interest in the series for the rest of his life, even in his crowded Washington years during World War II; fifty volumes had appeared before his death. He also started the serial *Organic Reactions* (begun in 1942), which contained exhaustive reviews of specific reactions; this was likewise a valuable publication for organic chemists, and eighteen volumes appeared during Adams's lifetime. He recruited many well-known chemists, including promising younger ones, to participate in these publications. From 1920 through 1944, Adams trained 137 Ph.D.s, about 21 percent of the Illinois department total of 641 for the same years, which was 7.7 percent of the national total in chemistry. In all, he trained 184 Ph.D.s and about 50 postdoctorates. His outgoing personality encouraged and inspired his collaborators, and he dealt with them on an informal personal basis. He followed closely their subsequent careers. Of his Ph.D. students and postdoctorates, the following, among others, may be noted for their careers in academic or industrial research: E. H. Volwiler (Abbott Laboratories), J. R. Johnson (Cornell), C. R. Noller (Stanford), S. M. McElvain (Wisconsin), W. H. Carothers (the inventor of nylon), T. L. Cairns and R. M. Joyce (DuPont), W. M. Stanley (Berkeley), R. C. Morris (Shell), W. H. Lycan (Johnson and Johnson), Allene Jeanes (USDA), N. Kornblum (Purdue), C. C. Price (Pennsylvania), N. J. Leonard (Illinois), S. J. Cristol (Colorado), and D. S. Tarbell (Vanderbilt). The success of these and many other Illinois Ph.D.s meant that Adams was a major influence on the development of both academic and industrial chemical research in this country.

Adams's first notable research accomplishment was to devise an easily prepared platinum catalyst for adding hydrogen to organic compounds; this "Adams platinum" was widely used for many years. Adams also studied stereochemistry extensively (the three-dimensional arrangement in space of atoms of organic compounds). His most valuable work was on the structure of numerous natural products, including chaulmoogric acid (used formerly in treatment of leprosy), gossypol (the yellow material in cottonseed meal), and the chemical components of marijuana. He also maintained a program on the synthesis of local anesthetics and other possible medicinals.

In 1934 Adams declined attractive offers from Harvard and MIT, receiving funds for two postdoctoral fellows from the Illinois administration as an inducement to stay at Urbana. His national standing was shown by his election as president of the American Chemical Society in 1935.

The European war, which looked particularly threatening after the fall of France, led to the formation of the National Defense Research Committee (NDRC) in June 1940, under the leadership of Vannevar Bush, J. B. Conant, K. T. Compton, and others. The object of NDRC was to concentrate American scientific research on war-related problems and to create effective liaison with the armed services; it had authority to contract for research in academic and industrial laboratories. Conant asked Adams to serve with him to organize study on chemical problems. Adams moved rapidly, assembling a group of chemists in July 1940 to discuss synthesis of new explosives. From the summer of 1940 to the end of 1941, he spent an increasing amount of time in Washington, D.C., although he was still heavily involved in his own research in Urbana, particularly on marijuana. He moved to Washington full time after Pearl Harbor, his salary being paid by the university. While overseeing research on explosives, war gases, gas masks, protective clothing, incendiaries, flamethrowers, and fluids that did not become viscous at low temperatures, he maintained his interest in graduate training and research, although he no longer had graduate students in Urbana. His responsibilities increased as Conant's deputy on NDRC when the latter became more occupied with the Manhattan Project.

The end of the war in 1945 brought the liquidation of NDRC, but Adams's return to Urbana was postponed. He served in Berlin from November 1945 to February 1946 as scientific adviser to General Lucius

Clay, deputy chief of the U.S. military government of Germany. Conditions were chaotic, but Adams and his colleagues prepared reports aimed at limiting Germany's power to make war by controlling research. Adams's most useful accomplishment was probably in helping to revive German scientific publications, in particular, the *Beilstein* and *Gmelin* compendiums, valuable for chemical research. He also improved the lot of non-Nazi scientists.

Adams returned to Urbana around 1 March 1946 and resumed his administrative and research activities, but he was called to chair a group of distinguished scientists who were to visit Japan to make recommendations about Japanese science to General Douglas MacArthur's office, which ruled Japan. During August 1947, the group visited many university and industrial laboratories and talked with many people, including MacArthur. Their report urged more democratic and open universities and the promotion of industrial research. It proposed more freedom and more general training in graduate scientific education. Adams took part in a second visit to Japan in the winter of 1948. He found that their first visit had had favorable results on Japanese science; this is supported by testimony of Japanese scientists, and Adams personally became a very popular figure in Japan. He visited Japan several times in later years and had extensive correspondence with Japanese chemists.

Adams resumed his research program after his return to Urbana, but his research was not as outstanding as it had been in the 1930s. During his absence in Washington and Berlin, organic chemistry had changed, with advances in instrumentation and in ideas about the mechanism (pathways) of organic reactions. As he realized himself, Adams never became quite at home in this changed atmosphere.

His public service activities, however, became even more significant after 1950. He chaired a committee, at the request of A. P. Sloan, Jr., that recommended that the Sloan Foundation make unrestricted grants for research to young, carefully selected people in the physical sciences. This program has been remarkably successful in helping promising young investigators develop their research capabilities; Sloan grants have become a real honor as well as a financial aid to the recipients. The program illustrates Adams's interest in individuals, rather than buildings or administrative structures. In earlier years Adams had persuaded the American Association for the Advancement of Science, of which he was president in 1950, to sponsor the Gordon Conferences, which embrace all fields of science and are held in the summer at various locations in New Hampshire and on the West Coast. The Sloan Fellowships, the Gordon Conferences, *Organic Syntheses*, and *Organic Reactions* stand, among others, as memorials to Adams's public spirit and vision in science.

Adams's retirement as head of the chemistry department in 1954 was observed by a symposium in Urbana in September 1954, attended by more than 500 students and friends. He served as research professor until 1957. After his retirement he traveled widely, spent time at his summer home in Vermont, and served as a trustee of Battelle Institute and as a member of the scientific advisory board of the Welch Foundation, among other activities. His wife died in 1964.

His scientific accomplishments and his many travels to international meetings made Adams one of the best-known American scientists in foreign countries. His voluminous correspondence with scientists of many lands emphasizes this role.

Adams's personal charm was combined with ability and an extraordinary capacity for hard, efficient work. In his younger days he was an excellent tennis player. He enjoyed poker, bridge, and stamp collecting, and he was a close follower of and investor in the stock market.

Adams received most of the scientific honors available: honorary degrees from ten universities, membership in learned academies here and abroad, medals and awards, including the Gibbs, Priestley, Richards, and Nichols awards of the American Chemical Society and the Davy Medal of the Royal Society. His career was of major significance, not only to American chemistry, but to science in general. He died in Champaign.

• About seventy boxes of Adams's papers are preserved in the archives of the University of Illinois library, Urbana. The archives of the National Academy of Sciences contain numerous documents relating to his Berlin assignment and his two trips to Japan as well as to other academy activities. The National Archives contain papers from his NDRC work between 1940 and 1945. Secondary sources include D. Stanley Tarbell and Ann Tracy Tarbell, *Roger Adams: Scientist and Statesman* (1981), Tarbell and Tarbell, *Biographical Memoirs of the National Academy of Sciences* 53 (1982): 2–48, which summarizes Adams's career and gives a complete list of his 425 research publications, and Tarbell and Tarbell, *Essays on the History of Organic Chemistry in the United States* (1986), which describes the background of Adams's work. James B. Conant's autobiography, *My Several Lives* (1970), gives information about Adams not available elsewhere. An obituary is in *Chemical Engineering News*, 12 July 1971.

D. STANLEY TARBELL

ADAMS, Samuel (27 Sept. 1722–2 Oct. 1803), revolutionary politician, signer of the Declaration of Independence, and Massachusetts governor, was born in Boston, Massachusetts, the son of Samuel Adams and Mary Fifield. Of the twelve children born to the couple, he was one of only three who survived their parents. The elder Samuel Adams was a prosperous investor in real estate and other ventures, including the ill-fated land bank of 1740–1741, and the owner of a brewery. He also held several public offices—Boston selectman, justice of the peace, and member of the provincial assembly.

Intended for the ministry, the younger Samuel Adams graduated from Harvard College in 1740. In 1743 he took a master's degree, for which he defended the auspicious if, at the time, conventional proposition that it was "lawful to resist the Supreme Magistrate, if the Commonwealth cannot otherwise be preserved."

By then he had apparently abandoned all thought of entering the ministry.

After studying law briefly, he spent a few months in the counting house of Thomas Cushing. He then went into business for himself, where he promptly lost £1,000 lent to him by his father. A man utterly uninterested in either making or possessing money, Adams was ill suited for a business career. It seems likely too that he was already distracted from the management of his affairs by what rapidly became a consuming interest in politics.

In 1741 an act of Parliament dissolved the land bank, and its directors became liable for the bank's outstanding debts. After the death of his father in 1748 and that of his mother soon thereafter, Samuel Adams successfully defended the family's estate against sale to satisfy the claims of the land bank creditors. He argued that since a fire at the Town House had destroyed records critical to the case, the proceeding was "illegal and unwarrantable." He also contributed political essays to the *Independent Advertiser*, a newspaper first issued in January 1748 and dedicated to defending the "rights and liberties of mankind." The paper was founded by a political organization known to its opponents as the "Whipping Post Club," of which Adams was a member. He seems also to have assumed his father's place in Boston's South End Caucus, which John Adams (1735–1826)—a cousin from the less distinguished Braintree, Massachusetts, branch of the family—later described as a group that met "in the Garret of Tom Dawes" and smoked until it was impossible to see from one end of the room to another, drank flip, debated various propositions, and decided who should serve as selectmen, assessors, tax collectors, and in other offices filled by vote of the town meeting. The caucus also sent committees "to wait on the Merchant's Club, and to propose and join in the choice of men and measures" (*Diary and Autobiography of John Adams*, ed. L. H. Butterfield, vol. 1 [1961], p. 235).

In 1749 Adams married Elizabeth Checkley, with whom he had two children. Seven years after her death in 1757 he married Elizabeth Wells. They had no children.

Adams served his public apprenticeship in the Boston town meeting, which at first occasionally chose him to fill minor offices such as clerk of the town market (1746–1748) or scavenger (1753). From 1756 through 1764 he was entrusted with his first important office as one of the town's tax collectors, an office he seems to have executed irresponsibly. By 1765, when he declined reelection, Adams's accounts were about £8,000 in arrears. In his defense, he argued that smallpox and other obstructions, including no doubt the town's depressed economy, had impeded his diligent efforts to fulfill his duties; but the noncollection of taxes seems to have been a perennial problem in Boston and a means by which members of the caucus consolidated support among Boston voters.

Adams's record as tax collector failed to hinder his political career, which was at best undistinguished at his fortieth birthday but developed steadily thereafter with the escalating quarrel between England and the colonies. In May 1764 and again in September 1765 he drafted Boston's instructions to its representatives in the General Court. Those documents eloquently protested British efforts to tax the colonists and called for a spirited defense of Americans' "invalueable Rights & Libertys." Over the next decade he became an increasingly prominent leader of the town meeting.

In late September 1765 the town chose Adams to fill a legislative seat opened with the death of Oxenbridge Thacher. Almost immediately the General Court drew on his literary skills. In October he wrote the house of representatives' answer to a speech by Governor Francis Bernard. That reply denied that Parliament could divest the people of "certain original inherent rights, . . . among which is the right of representative in the same body which exercises the power of taxation." Adams also drafted a set of resolutions that asserted the colonists' rights, protested recent British violations of them, rejected as impractical American representation in Parliament, and insisted that any tax imposed by a power other than the provincial general assembly violated both the colony's charter rights and the "inherent and unalienable rights" of the people (*Writings*, vol. 1, pp. 25–26).

Adams was reelected to the assembly in 1766, when he became its clerk. He held those offices continuously until 17 June 1774, when the General Court, meeting at Salem behind locked doors to prevent its being prorogued by the royal governor, included him among its five delegates to the First Continental Congress. The election of delegates was probably engineered by a Committee on the State of the Province that the assembly had appointed the previous May and of which Adams was chairman. The assembly went on to pay the delegates' expenses by assessments on the towns, denounced the purchase of goods from Britain, and called for the relief of Boston and Charlestown, many of whose people were unemployed as a result of the Boston Port Act. In 1774 Adams also presided over several critical meetings of the Boston town meeting and directed the town's "Donations" committee to receive and disperse relief, a responsibility he continued to exercise into 1775.

Soon after the First Continental Congress convened on 5 September 1774, Adams was appointed to a committee to state the rights of the colonists, list violations of them, and propose means for their restoration. He worked above all to consolidate continental support for Massachusetts, which Parliament had singled out for punishment under the Coercive Acts (1774), and where the presence of an army and popular hostility toward government under General Thomas Gage threatened war. Adams saw his objective largely accomplished on 17 September when Congress approved the "Suffolk Resolves," a set of resolutions that had been passed earlier that month by a convention of towns (including Boston) in Suffolk County, Massachusetts, and carried to Philadelphia by Paul Revere. Those "spirited" resolves called for disobedience to the Coercive Acts, endorsed military preparations to be used only for defensive purposes so long as that remained consonant with reason and self-preservation, and called for the meeting of an extralegal provincial congress. Adams opposed a plan of union proposed by Joseph Galloway of Pennsylvania that conceded parliamentary supremacy over the colonies, and supported the continental association and the program of trade restrictions it established in an effort to win redress from London.

After the dissolution of Congress in late October, Adams returned to Massachusetts, where he had been elected a Boston representative to the provincial congress. He continued to play an active role in that body until the reestablishment of constitutional state government in 1780. Adams also resumed his political leadership in Boston, where he became chairman of the committee appointed by the town meeting on 7 December 1774 to enforce the continental association. By February 1775, when Parliament declared Massachusetts to be in a state of rebellion, rumors circulated that leaders of the "rebellion," including Adams and John Hancock, would be arrested and sent to England for trial. At the urging of friends, Adams moved his family to Cambridge, where the provincial congress met until 16 February, then adjourned to Concord between 22 March and 15 April. He and Hancock were in nearby Lexington on the evening of 18 April 1775, when a body of British troops set out from Boston in an attempt to seize stores of colonial arms. Having been warned of the approaching troops, they fled the next morning before the exchange of fire at Lexington Green that became the first battle of the revolutionary war. Their fame as revolutionary leaders was firmly established on 12 June, when Gage exempted both Adams and Hancock from the pardon he offered colonists who would lay down their arms and submit to British authority.

By then Adams was in Philadelphia at the Second Continental Congress, of which he remained a hardworking member, putting in long hours on committees, including the arduous Board of War, from May 1775 until 1781. He then returned to Massachusetts, never to leave it again. But his political life was far from over: a year after returning to Massachusetts, for example, Adams was elected to the state senate, of which he became president. However, his career seemed to have peaked when he signed the Declaration of Independence, for he played his most prominent historical role, as John Eliot later put it, not in "building up a government suited to the condition of the people," but in pulling down another "becoming every day more tyrannical" (Eliot, *A Biographical Dictionary* [1807], p. 7). Adams himself seemed to share Eliot's understanding of his historic role. To his wife he affirmed a profound sense of almost religious obligation "to oppose to the utmost of my Ability the Designs of those who would enslave my country," and once suggested that he should be replaced at Congress by someone better fitted for "*founding Empires*" (*Writings*, vol. 3, pp. 349, 234–35).

Adams's importance to what became the independence movement—an importance affirmed by his enemies as well as his supporters—has served to obscure his substantial contributions to the establishment of republican constitutional government in the later 1770s and 1780s. His precise role in the American opposition to Britain has also been persistently misconstrued. Although he has often been described as the "grand incendiary" of the Revolution and a mob leader, Adams's position was in fact consistent with an English revolutionary tradition that imposed strict constraints on resistance to authority. It justified forceful opposition only against threats to the constitutional regime so serious that the "body of the people" recognized the danger and after all the peaceful means of redress had failed. Within that revolutionary tradition, resistance was essentially conservative, intended to preserve what in 1748 Adams described as "the true object" of patriotic loyalty, "a good legal constitution, which . . . condemns every instance of oppression and lawless power." It had nothing in common with sedition or rebellion, which Adams, like earlier English writers, charged to officials who sought "illegal power" (Wells, vol. 1, pp. 16–17).

Samuel Adams was not a regular member of the Loyal Nine, a club that became Boston's first Sons of Liberty. He did, however, approve of the public uprising it organized on 14 August 1765 that forced Andrew Oliver to resign his office as stamp distributor and so made execution of the Stamp Act in Massachusetts virtually impossible. Yet he and the Boston town meeting condemned the rioters who destroyed the elegant home of Thomas Hutchinson twelve days later. The riot of 26 August 1765 was provoked not by the Stamp Act but by private grievances that, the *Boston Gazette* suggested, could have been redressed through the courts. Five years later Adams served as a spokesman for the town in demanding that British troops be removed from Boston in the wake of the "Massacre," but there is no evidence that he helped set off the violence of 5 March 1770.

Adams is also often charged with inciting the Boston Tea Party, an event that occurred after Bostonians spent three weeks attempting to have the tea ships return to England with their cargoes and immediately before the tea became liable to seizure by customsmen who might release it to consignees willing to pay the execrated tea tax. The words with which Adams supposedly ended the last public "tea meeting" on 16 December 1773 and signaled local "Mohawks" to begin destroying the tea are consistent with a conviction that the peaceful means of redress had to have been tried and exhausted before forceful resistance became legitimate: "This meeting can do nothing further to save this country." Another contemporary account, however, says that Adams and others "called out to the People to stay" at the meeting despite "hideous Yelling in the Street" because "they said they had not quite done" (L. F. S. Upton, "Proceedings of Ye Body Respecting the Tea," *William and Mary Quarterly* 12 [1965]: 298).

Violence was, in fact, far from congenial to Samuel Adams's politics because it was divisive. Adams was one of the first Americans to accept the designation of "politician," a vocation that was for him as imbued with moral content as that of a clergyman, but he never made peace with party politics or with persistent political divisions of any kind. "I am no party man," he wrote in 1771, "unless a firm attachment to the cause of Liberty and Truth will denominate one such" (*Writings*, vol. 2, p. 294). Where liberty was in danger, the task of a patriot was to bring the people toward a common understanding of their plight and the best means to rectify it. That demanded firmness, a respect for popular opinion, and patience, the very foundation of Adams's politics. In late 1774 he implored his fellow Bostonians "by every thing dear and sacred to Men of Sense and Virtue to avoid Blood and Tumult" so the other colonies had time "*to think and resolve*" (*Warren-Adams Letters*, vol. 1, p. 26). The work of Congress, as he understood it, was to bring together representatives from constituencies with "different Interests & Views, to unite in Measures materially to affect them all," which was "necessarily slow." In the end, Adams took delight in the fact that Americans had accomplished their revolution "without great internal Tumults & violent Convulsions" (*Writings*, vol. 3, p. 304).

The characteristic instruments of Adams's politics were not mobs but newspapers, in which Adams published essay after essay under an array of pseudonyms such as "Vindex," "Candidus," and even "Cotton Mather"; public events designed to strengthen patriotic feelings such as the orations given in Boston to commemorate the "Massacre" of 1770; and, above all, committees, associations, and conventions that mobilized people and coordinated their efforts for the colonial cause. In 1768 Adams drafted a letter from the Massachusetts General Assembly to other colonial legislatures in an attempt to "harmonize" their efforts on behalf of American rights. Later, after Governor Francis Bernard had dissolved the assembly for refusing to rescind that "circular letter" and as British troops were about to land in Boston, Adams and Thomas Cushing, Jr., proposed an extralegal convention so town representatives could arrive at a common position in that crisis. Adams is better known as leader of the Boston Committee of Correspondence, which the town meeting established on his suggestion in November 1772 to alert townsmen throughout the province to British violations of their rights and to coordinate their responses so all would "stand firm as one man." In Congress, too, Adams sought to heal divisions and foster unity. His suggestion that the Reverend Jacob Duché, an Episcopalian, be asked to offer a prayer at the opening of the First Continental Congress effectively dispelled suspicions of New England sectarian intolerance.

Adams's preferred means for coercing the enemies of the American cause was, moreover, not violence, but personal and commercial boycotts such as those imposed under the colonial nonimportation and nonconsumption agreements between 1768 and 1770, or the rigorous "Solemn League and Covenant, respecting the disuse of British Manufactures," which the Boston Committee of Correspondence attempted to institute in June 1774. Sent to Massachusetts towns without first securing the endorsement of the Boston town meeting, the "Solemn League and Covenant" provoked heated opposition by merchants and others who charged the committee with exceeding its authority and moved that it be censured and annihilated. On 28 June 1774, after a two-day rancorous debate, the town meeting expressed its confidence in the committee "by a *Vast Majority*." The episode remains, however, the one instance in which Adams blundered badly—by violating his own counsel for patience and against acting hastily, before establishing the necessary political support.

Although Adams has frequently been described as the first advocate of American independence and a man who worked steadily but secretly toward that goal, his surviving papers, both private and public, reveal a more gradual and complex development. His writings before and during the Stamp Act crisis (1765–1766) give no indication that he expected the Americans to remain anything but "faithful and loyal Subjects" of Britain. Later, as British innovations seemed to introduce arbitrary power in America, England, and Ireland, Adams began to predict that the crisis would eventually "end in the ruin of the most glorious Empire the sun ever shone upon" (*Writings*, vol. 1, p. 387). He worked, however, to avoid that eventuality, advocating reforms that would return the "British administration and government . . . to the principles of moderation and equity" (*Writings*, vol. 3, p. 100). He understood the 1773 publication of letters written by Governor Hutchinson and other royal officials—sometimes cited as an example of his seditious politics—as a step in that direction. Those letters, which had been selected in England to suggest that Hutchinson advocated military rule and a constriction of American liberties, were sent to Massachusetts from London by Benjamin Franklin with an injunction against their publication. Adams read them to the assembly on 2 June 1773, then announced eight days later that a separate set of letters had mysteriously appeared in Boston, a ruse that allowed the assembly to bypass Franklin's restriction. Adams thought that the letters' publication, which the assembly ordered on 15 June, would demonstrate that the campaign against American freedom had begun with "a few men born & educated amongst us, & governed by Avarice & a Lust of power," and had been "adopted" in Britain. If a public outcry led to the removal of those colonists from office, there was reason to hope for the restoration of what he called "placidam sub Libertate Quietam," a peace consonant with liberty. Perhaps, however, some in England would also have to be "impeached & brot to condign punishment" (*Writings*, vol. 3, p. 44). For that purpose, he corresponded with the English radical John Wilkes and the American Wilkesite Arthur Lee, hopeful that the cooperation of patriots in the colonies and the mother country would increase their effectiveness against common enemies in London. So late as 1774 Adams discussed with Lee a possible American bill of rights that might "fix" American rights and allow the perpetuation of the empire (*Writings*, vol. 3, p. 101).

By November 1775, however, Adams had little hope that virtuous people in England could prevent a "Tyrant" from reducing the Americans to absolute obedience. In February 1776—when Thomas Paine's *Common Sense* was circulating through the colonies—Adams wrote that America was in fact independent, not by her choice, but because the administration's wanton violation of the constitution had "dissolved the dangerous tie" (*Writings*, vol. 3, pp. 241, 26). He remained, however, less eager for a declaration of independence than some of his colleagues in Boston, whom he reminded of the need for patience because "it requires Time to convince the doubting and inspire the timid." Later, after the declaration had been approved, he continued to reflect on whether it should have been adopted after the battles of Lexington and Concord. He finally decided in the negative because "the Colonies were not then all ripe for so momentous a Change" (*Writings*, vol. 3, pp. 281, 304).

Adams was no less committed to the successful establishment of American republican government than he had been to that of colonial rights. An almost instinctual egalitarian, Adams found claims to preeminence based on family objectionable and even those of gender uncongenial. Like his Old Testament namesake, the prophet Samuel, Adams understood governments free of kings and hereditary rule to be most consonant with God's will. He also welcomed the establishment of state governments founded exclusively on popular choice as an extension of the form of government long established in Massachusetts, where the relatively generous sphere of power given the people had long since been for him a source of pride. He served on the committee of Congress charged with drafting the Articles of Confederation, which he later signed. He was also a member of the Massachusetts constitutional convention of 1780 and of the committee it appointed to draft a new state constitution and declaration of rights. Although that document is often attributed to John Adams, it was a collaborative work on which Samuel Adams had a powerful influence, above all in giving the people extensive power and in formulating the statement of rights.

Once regular republican constitutional government had been established, Adams opposed extralegal political activity. Committees, conventions, or other similar embodiments of public sentiment had become illegitimate: once all officeholding depended on popular choice, the peaceful means of seeking redress for grievances could no longer be exhausted. In 1786–1787 he supported the repression of Shays's Rebellion and in 1794 forcefully condemned the Pennsylvania "Whisky Rebels" who rose against the federal excise tax.

Adams, moreover, played a crucial role in the ratification of the federal Constitution. He was at first upset by that document because it seemed to create a national government rather than a federal union of states. His opposition gave way, according to one account, after a group of Boston mechanics whose opinion he respected presented him with a set of resolutions favoring ratification. However, he himself explained his early doubts about the Constitution as the result of an incapacity to "digest every part of it as readily as some gentlemen." After he carefully studied newspaper essays on the subject and listened to debates in the Massachusetts ratifying convention, his comprehension increased and his doubts gradually gave way. When Antifederalists at the Massachusetts ratifying convention tried to cut off detailed discussions as a prelude to voting the document down, Adams intervened. He wanted "a full investigation of the subject" and said delegates should not be "stingy" with their time or the public's money "when so important an object demanded them" (Elliot, vol. 2, pp. 123, 95). In the end, he supported (and, it seems, helped formulate) a proposal presented by Hancock, the convention's president, that Massachusetts ratify the Constitution while proposing a list of amendments for adoption subsequent to its enactment. That "conciliatory proposition," he thought, would mollify the Constitution's opponents and make Americans "united in sentiment." As he predicted, its greatest effect was in states with substantial reservations about the Constitution whose conventions had not yet met. All but one of those states followed Massachusetts's example and recommended future amendments. Without that device, the Constitution might well not have been ratified.

In 1788 Adams ran for Congress, but lost to the 31-year-old Fisher Ames. The following year he was elected Massachusetts's lieutenant governor, then reelected annually until he became governor on the death of John Hancock in 1793. Voters then chose him as governor in his own right each year thereafter until January 1797, when he retired from office. Those executive positions were, however, uncharacteristic of his career: his political contributions came more often from less visible positions in legislative assemblies, where he excelled more as a committeeman than an orator, or in behind-the-scenes meetings where alternative political strategies were discussed and courses of action adopted.

The inconspicuous character of Adams's political activities was, moreover, in keeping with a more general tendency toward self-effacement. Adams had no exaggerated sense of his own talents, which he supplemented by recruiting into politics gifted younger men, including John Adams. He was inclined to yield to the views of his constituents, even when the people elected another in his place. No man, he explained, had any claims on the public; and what the people did was usually right. Nor did he long for rank and possessions: Adams disdained claims of distinction based on genealogy and took pride in his poverty. Even Loyalist Thomas Hutchinson testified to his incorruptibility. Adams left office, as he said, a poor man; were it not for claims on the federal government inherited from his son, a surgeon who died in 1788 after serving with the Continental army, he might have spent his final years as a ward of charity. Not even fame tempted him. John Adams's pleas that he preserve his papers to confirm his place in history went unheeded. Samuel Adams himself destroyed some of his correspondence while at Congress to protect others from British reprisals for their revolutionary activities. The remainder of his papers—invaluable documents that Adams described as mere "trifles"—were dissipated, often from simple neglect, both during and after his lifetime. The only objective he deemed worthy was the rectitude that came from having devoted his "utmost Exertions" to the public cause.

Samuel Adams would have died an obscure Bostonian were it not for a peculiar fit between his skills, his character, and his times. The knowledge of democratic politics he acquired in Boston took on a wider importance as the Revolution expanded the sphere of popular authority throughout the colonies. His personal austerity, rigid probity, and public commitment—which for Adams were simply the ways of his Puritan ancestors—readily identified him as a man whose person, as the marquis de Chastellux noted, corresponded exactly with his public role. But those same virtues, along with his sympathy for the French Revolution and for Jeffersonianism, and his unrelenting opposition to what he saw as the moral degeneration of Boston in the 1780s and 1790s, contributed to a sense of distance and hostility toward Adams among younger New Englanders, especially those who were Federalists. He came to seem an anachronism—"the last of the Puritans," out of place in an age more at ease with ambition, idle pleasures, and material comforts. In later times observers went further, building on discredited Loyalist charges that the American Revolution was the work of a few agitators and making a full-fledged mythic Adams, one that often reflected its creators' discomfort with revolution and their hostility toward modern urban politics.

From the start Adams's old colleagues from the independence movement warred against that tendency. None were more active in his defense than John Adams and perhaps none more moving than Thomas Jefferson. Writing in March 1801 within weeks of his inauguration as president, Jefferson expressed deep indignation at news that Samuel Adams was "avoided, insulted, frowned on." With the ship of state back on "her republican tack," he hoped for renewed harmony and "an entire oblivion of past feuds," and asked Adams for his counsel and his blessing (Wells, vol. 3, pp. 370–71). In reply, Adams protested that it was no longer in his power to offer counsel, then went ahead and counseled, as he always had, that it would take "some time" before the people once again settled "in harmony good humour and peace." But the future looked bright. Was there not, he asked in November 1801, "reason to believe, that the principles of Democratic Republicanism are already better understood than they were before"? Those principles, Adams believed, would "extend more and more" until "the proud oppressors over the Earth shall be totally broken down and those classes of Men who have hitherto been victims of their rage and cruelty shall perpetually enjoy perfect Peace and Safety till time shall be no more" (*Writings*, vol. 4, pp. 408–11).

Adams died in Boston and was buried in Boston's Granary Burying Ground, as he had requested, in a plain coffin.

• The single most important source on Adams is *The Writings of Samuel Adams*, ed. Harry Alonzo (4 vols., 1904–1908; repr. 1968), which should be supplemented by the Samuel Adams Papers in the New York Public Library. Additional items can be found in *The Warren-Adams Letters*, published in the *Massachusetts Historical Society Collections*, vols. 72 and 73 (1917–1925). The speeches Adams made in the Massachusetts ratifying convention of 1788 are available in Jonathan Elliot, ed., *The Debates in the Several State Conventions on the Adoption of the Federal Constitution*, vol. 2 (1836). William V. Wells, *The Life and Public Services of Samuel Adams* (3 vols., 1865), includes some of Adams's writings and information on his life not readily available elsewhere, and is, in many ways, still the most useful biography. John C. Miller, *Sam Adams, Pioneer in Propaganda* (1936), remains the most scholarly modern biography, but as both its title (Adams was not called "Sam" in his lifetime) and subtitle suggest, its interpretation is outdated. Steward Beach, *Samuel Adams, The Fateful Years, 1764–1776* (1965), rejects the "distortions" of earlier biographies on the basis of a careful examination of the sources, but is essentially a popular study with a bibliography but no footnotes. For a more recent analysis of both the literature on Adams and his life and politics, see Pauline Maier, "A New Englander as Revolutionary: Samuel Adams," in Maier, *The Old Revolutionaries: Political Lives in the Age of Samuel Adams* (1980), pp. 3–50. Richard D. Brown, *Revolutionary Politics in Massachusetts: The Boston Committee of Correspondence and the Towns, 1772–1774* (1970), includes considerable information on Adams. For an appreciation of his role in the ratification of the federal Constitution, see Michael Gillespie, "Massachusetts: Creating Consensus," in *Ratifying the Constitution*, ed. Gillespie and Michael Lienesh (1989), pp. 138–67.

PAULINE MAIER

ADAMS, Samuel Hopkins (26 Jan. 1871–16 Nov. 1958), muckraker and writer, was born in Dunkirk, New York, the son of Myron Adams, Jr., a minister, and Hester Rose Hopkins. He attended Hamilton College in Clinton, New York, from 1887 to 1891, with a semester at Union College. After graduation he was a devoted alumnus, serving as trustee (1905–1916), winning election to Phi Beta Kappa (1907), and receiving an honorary doctorate of humane letters in 1926.

His professional career began on the *New York Sun*, where he was a journalist from 1891 to 1900, when he joined *McClure's* magazine. He became an editorial staffer in 1904. Working with Lincoln Steffens, Ida Tarbell, and Ray Stannard Baker, he joined in exposure writing, specializing in medical reporting of public health issues, and evolved into a muckraker.

From 1904 he considered himself a freelance writer and supported himself with his writing. In 1905 he was hired by *Collier's Weekly* to prepare articles on patent medicines. In a series of articles on nostrums, in which the muckraker exposed various "remedies" and the charlatans who manufactured them, he attacked abuse and demanded legislation to label the contents. The strong public reaction and Adams's participation in preparing the bill and in lobbying helped produce the federal Pure Food and Drug Act in 1906. The articles and a second series on quack medical advisers were collected and printed under the title of the series, *The Great American Fraud* (1906), by the American Medical Association. In 1913 the AMA made Adams an associate fellow.

His marriage to Elizabeth Ruffner Noyes of Charleston, West Virginia, in 1898 ended in divorce in 1907 after they had had two daughters. In 1915 he married an actress, Jane Peyton (Jennie Van Norman) of Milwaukee.

In addition to his nonfiction writing, Adams published short stories and in 1907 wrote a novel, *The Mystery*, with Stewart Edward White. His first solo novel was another mystery, *Flying Death* (1908). A collection of detective stories in 1911 (featuring Average Jones in a book by the same name) was followed by a detective novel, *The Secret of Lonesome Cove* (1912). He combined detective work and his medical knowledge in a fictional book, *The Health Master*, in 1913. His early work was moderately successful, with reviewers kind, readership limited, and anthologists later eager to reprint his stories.

Linking his knowledge of newspapers with patent medicines, he wrote *The Clarion* (1914), which was critical of newspaper advertising practices and led to a series of consumer-protection articles in the *New York Tribune*. His service during World War I for the Committee on Public Information led to *Common Cause* (1919), a novel on a newspaper's battle against pro-Germans in Wisconsin. *Success* (1921) mirrored several articles he wrote on William Randolph Hearst, focusing on Arthur Brisbane. The three newspaper novels, although not achieving bestseller status and receiving mixed literary comment, established Adams as an author with a popular following.

He complemented his serious books with his first light fiction novel, the humorous *Little Miss Grouch*, in 1915, and he wrote regularly in that genre, which also proved popular with readers but lessened his literary reputation. Two collections of short stories, *Our Square and the People in It* (1917) and *From a Bench in Our Square* (1922), feature New York City characters.

Adams's career in the 1920s centered on a series of Jazz Age novels, beginning with *Flaming Youth* (1923), that he wrote under the pseudonym Warner Fabian. In 1927 he applied the muckraking technique in the controversial novel *Revelry*, based on the scandal-plagued Warren G. Harding administration. Creating considerable controversy at the time among politicians and literary critics, the book sold almost 100,000 copies.

While the Fabian novels provided him with income, he wrote his first biography, *The Godlike Daniel* (1929), on Daniel Webster, and the historical novel *The Gorgeous Hussy* (1934) on Peggy O'Neale Eaton. Also in the 1930s his short story "Night Bus" was adapted into the prize-winning motion picture *It Happened One Night*, one of some twenty film adaptations. *The Incredible Era: The Life and Times of Warren G. Harding* (1939) was a more scholarly look at the Teapot Dome scandals but failed to excite readers.

Adams's use of history to provide a backdrop for telling the stories of great people was not successful, and he switched to social history with *The Harvey Girls* (1942), written to accompany the motion picture. He collaborated anonymously with Frank Slaughter on two medical novels, *That None Should Die* (1941) and *Spencer Brade, M.D.* (1942). In 1942 he published anonymously a romance novel, *The Book of Ariel*, and a fourth novel, the mystery *Tambay Gold*. His versatile and prolific pen produced, in addition to his books, more than 450 short stories and articles.

An article assignment for the *New Yorker* turned him to regional history and novels on upstate New York, *Canal Town* (1944), *Banner by the Wayside* (1947), and *Sunrise to Sunset* (1950). Carefully researched, his historical novels were rich in atmospheric detail, praised by both readers and critics. He applied the same technique to a biography, *A. Woollcott, His Life and World* (1945), on fellow Hamilton alumnus Alexander Woollcott, with less success in a portrait that some reviewers found to be a dark book.

Able to support himself in elegant style during his life, he was host to a number of fellow writers at his summer home on Owasco Lake in central New York. Adams wrote a series of successful juvenile histories in the 1950s including *The Pony Express* (1950) and *The Erie Canal* (1953). Near the end of his life he turned to reminiscence in *Grandfather Stories* (1955), a Book-of-the-Month-Club selection. His fifty-sixth book, a novel about his newspaper days, *Tenderloin* (1959), was published posthumously, following his death at his winter home in Beaufort, South Carolina, and was made into a Broadway musical.

His novels were melodramatic, made of readable prose but considered of little literary merit. Considering himself always a reporter, he was a yeoman author reacting to and chronicling the changing American mores and tastes during the first half of the twentieth century.

• Adams's papers are in Arents Research Library at Syracuse University and in Burke Library at Hamilton College. Significant collections are also in Houghton Library at Harvard University and at the American Antiquarian Society in Worcester, Mass.

Other major books, not previously mentioned, are *The Unspeakable Perk* (1916), *Wanted: A Husband* (1920), *Siege* (1924), *Sailors' Wives* (1924), *The Piper's Fee* (1926), *Summer Bachelors* (1926), *Who and What: A Book of Clues for the Clever* (1927), *Unforbidden Fruit* (1928), *The Flagrant Years* (1929), *The Men in Her Life* (1930), *Week-End Girl* (1932), *Widow's Oats* (1935), *Perfect Specimen* (1936), *Maiden Effort* (1937), *The World Goes Smash* (1938), *Both over Twenty-One* (1939), *Whispers* (1940), *Plunder* (1948), *The Santa Fe Trail* (1951), *Wagons to the Wilderness* (1954), *General Brock and Niagara Falls* (1957), and *Chingo Smith of the Erie Canal* (1958).

Major biographical sketches are in Charles C. Baldwin, *The Men Who Write Our Novels* (1925); Albert Bartlett Maurice, "History of Their Books," *Bookman*, Nov. 1929, pp. 272–74; Stanley J. Kunitz and Howard Haycraft, *Twentieth Century Authors* (1942), and supplement (1955); Serrell Hillman, "Samuel Hopkins Adams: 1871–1958," *Saturday Review*, 20 Dec. 1958, pp. 15, 37; and James Stanford Bradshaw, *Biographical Dictionary of American Journalism* (1989). Bradshaw also wrote "The Journalist as Pariah: Three Muckraking Newspaper Novels by Samuel Hopkins Adams," *Journalism History* 10 (Spring–Summer 1983): 10–13. Adams's patent medicine investigations are discussed in James Young, *The Toadstool Millionaires* (1961); Stewart Holbrook, *The Golden Age of Quackery* (1959); and James H. Cassedy, "Muckraking and Medicine: Samuel Hopkins Adams," *American Quarterly* 16 (Spring 1964): 85–99. Obituaries are in the *New York Times* and the *New York Herald Tribune*, 17 Nov. 1958.

SAMUEL V. KENNEDY III

ADAMS, Sherman Llewelyn (8 Jan. 1899–27 Oct. 1986), public servant, was born in East Dover, Vermont, the son of Clyde H. Adams, a grocer, and Winnie Marion Sherman. Through his father he was descended from a collateral branch of the famous Quincy Adams clan. In 1901 the family moved to Providence, Rhode Island, but Adams's parents divorced soon thereafter. In 1916 Adams enrolled at Dartmouth College. His academic record there was solid, but he was best remembered for the gusto with which he threw himself into extracurricular activities. For Adams, physical fitness was practically a religion.

Adams's Dartmouth career was interrupted by World War I. Enlisting in the U.S. Marine Corps, Adams never saw military action, as the war ended before his division reached Europe. Consequently, he returned to Dartmouth and graduated with his class in 1920. Adams's first job out of college was as a scaler at a logging camp in northern Vermont, where he fought successfully for acceptance from a doughty crew of lumberjacks.

It was in northern New England, working for the Parker-Young Company in various capacities, that Adams earned a reputation as a tough and able lumberman. By necessity he was terse and often sharp-tongued in the woods, but at home Adams cultivated a love of history and classical music. He married Rachel Leona White of Belmont, Vermont, in July 1923. They settled in Lincoln, New Hampshire, and had four children.

Adams rose steadily through the ranks of the Parker-Young Company, and all evidence suggests that he planned to remain in the logging business. However, a devastating hurricane in 1938 changed his course. Adams joined a statewide effort to clear and salvage the fallen timber, and he was subsequently encouraged by his lumber industry associates to run for the state legislature. Elected easily in 1940 to the general assembly as a Republican in a largely Democratic town, Adams remained in public service, with one brief break, for the next eighteen years.

In the New Hampshire legislature, Adams's leadership qualities were quickly recognized. During his first term he chaired an important committee and in his second was elected Speaker. In 1944 Adams sought and won a seat in Congress. Though he opposed most New Deal domestic initiatives and emphasized the importance of free enterprise, Adams rejected the isolationism that was common among Republican backbenchers. His internationalism eventually led him into association with the Thomas E. Dewey wing of the national Republican party.

Adams remained in Congress for only one term. In 1946 he challenged incumbent governor Charles Dale in the GOP primary, losing a hotly contested race by barely 150 votes. Adams immediately promised to run again in 1948. Newspaper accounts of malfeasance and misfeasance in the state bureaucracy under Dale opened the path for Adams's reform candidacy.

Elected as perhaps the only Republican who could have won the governorship in 1948, Adams proved a vigorous and effective chief executive. He set a new tone in Concord by putting in a full work day, beginning at 7:30 A.M., and emphasizing the need for state employees to do likewise.

In the wake of the war, New Hampshire had expensive needs, notably in mental health care, road upkeep and construction, and public education, but its tax base was narrow. Adams embraced the findings of a state commission that recommended a broad-based tax. Despite lopsided Republican majorities in both houses of the legislature, however, Adams was unsuccessful in enacting either a sales or income tax. Consequently he cut state spending and undertook a comprehensive reorganization of the state bureaucracy, cutting the number of administrative departments from eighty-three to forty-three. As befit his logging background, Adams also pressed successfully for a tax on timber as it was cut, rather than on the land on which the forests stood.

By late 1951 Adams increasingly focused his attention on national politics. Fearing that Republicans would nominate Senator Robert Taft for the presidency and thereby identify the party with isolationism, Adams conferred with other politicians in New Hampshire and around the country about alternatives to Taft. He strongly preferred General Dwight D. Eisenhower, then commanding SHAEF in Europe, but it was not until early 1952 that Eisenhower publicly acknowledged his Republican leanings. Once Eisenhower announced that he would not repudiate a draft, Adams organized the Eisenhower effort in New Hampshire and campaigned vigorously for the absent candidate. And when Eisenhower triumphed decisively in the state's March preferential primary, his candidacy was launched nationwide.

Taking a leave from the governorship, Adams joined the Eisenhower campaign in 1952, first as manager of Eisenhower forces at the party's national convention and then as Eisenhower's right hand on the campaign trail in the fall. In this latter position Adams gained a reputation for his ability to make quick and canny decisions. Following Eisenhower's landslide victory in November, Adams was named assistant to the president in the new administration, a position that was modeled on Eisenhower's experiences in the military with Generals Walter Bedell Smith and Alfred M. Gruenther. Eisenhower never supplied Adams with a formal job description, but Adams understood that his essential task was to ease the burdens on the president.

As the president's de facto chief of staff from 1953 to 1958, Adams exercised more influence than any subsequent presidential assistant, until perhaps Richard M. Nixon's aide H. R. Haldeman. Adams oversaw the flow of paper in the Oval Office, ensuring that the president would not have to pore over turgid or diffuse position papers. He shielded Eisenhower from windbags and self-servers, handled innumerable requests from party leaders and special interest groups, assisted in vetting candidates for positions in the bureaucracy, and was an influential political adviser. Because his schedule was so full, Adams's penchant for terse expression was reinforced. He never said hello or goodbye on the phone, for example, a practice that upset some of his associates in the White House. When White House counsel Roemer McPhee complained to the president that Adams had hung up on him when their conversation had ended, Eisenhower told McPhee, "Don't worry about it. He even hangs up on me."

Adams soon became a celebrity in Washington, not only because he was a colorful character, but also because he was widely believed to exercise enormous influence in an administration whose chief was allegedly unable or unwilling to grapple with the details of his job. Jokes about Adams running the White House were commonplace, and savvy journalists exaggerated Adams's actual influence on policy. In fact, Adams never fully controlled access to the president (nor did he try to do so), and he rarely engaged in high-level discussions of foreign policy. He viewed himself as a facilitator for the president and, when necessary, as the president's lightning rod for criticism.

Adams's role as Eisenhower's "abominable no-man" (as one profile put it), combined with his lack of tact, won him few friends outside the White House. Moreover, his distaste for the Republican right wing was not well disguised and left him little margin of support in difficult times. In 1958, when Adams faced an unwelcome media spotlight regarding his friendship with New England textile manufacturer Bernard Goldfine, he lacked the solid support of his own party. President Eisenhower did come to Adams's defense against charges of ethical impropriety for having accepted a vicuna coat, hotel room expenses, and an oriental rug from Goldfine, who when facing troubles with the Interstate Commerce Commission had turned to Adams for help. Even though it was never proved that Adams had sought any favors for Goldfine, the drumbeat of criticism about his imprudent phone call to the ICC asking the status of Goldfine's case sullied his reputation and sapped his influence. As the 1958 elections approached it was evident that Adams was an albatross for the GOP. He reluctantly resigned his post in September 1958 and returned to his home in Lincoln.

Back in New Hampshire Adams wrote his memoirs, *First Hand Report* (1961), and occasionally taught classes at Dartmouth and other colleges and universities. He always cautioned his students against overestimating his role in the White House and underestimating the political and managerial skills of Eisenhower.

In the early 1960s, aware that the always tenuous economy in New Hampshire's North Country was facing new difficulties with the hemorrhage of manufacturing jobs, Adams saw new opportunities for the tourist industry in the Pemigewasset wilderness surrounding his home town. Adams focused his attention on Loon Montain, just outside the town borders of Lincoln, where he and his associates began building a successful ski resort in 1964.

Adams never retired from public service, despite his commitment to the Loon Mountain ski resort. He served on various state commissions, including several devoted to road building in the North Country and conservation of the state's natural resources. Adams also privately advised state and national Republican politicians. He died in Hanover, New Hampshire.

Adams's public career, though relatively brief, marked him as perhaps the most influential New Hampshire man of his era. His governorship is widely viewed as a watershed in state history, since he established the precedent of a full-time chief executive and sparked a long-lived debate about the appropriate level and means of taxing and spending in New Hampshire. Adams's White House role, moreover, has been variously a model or an example to be avoided for subsequent presidencies, with scholarly consensus holding that he was the most effective presidential chief of staff of his era, essentially defining the position. Neither a visionary nor a charismatic statesman, Adams was nonetheless a tough-talking, diligent public servant.

• Most of Adams's surviving papers are housed in the Dartmouth College Archives. Invaluable primary source material pertaining to his service in the White House (1953–1958) is in the Ann Whitman Files and other collections in the Dwight D. Eisenhower Library in Abilene, Kans. Adams was the subject of numerous profiles in the print media during his years as assistant to the president. Contemporary accounts that contain some biographical insights include Beverly Smith, "Ike's Yankee Lieutenant," *Saturday Evening Post*, 24 Jan. 1953; G. Y. Laveredge, "Mr. Eisenhower's No. 1 Man," *Providence Sunday Journal*, 24 May 1953; Robert J. Donovan, "The Man at Ike's Right Hand," *Colliers*, 14 Oct. 1955; Richard Strout, "The Administration's 'Abominable No-Man,'" *New York Times Magazine*, 3 June 1956; and [anon.], "O.K., S.A.," *Time*, 9 Jan. 1956. Two memoirs that shed light on Adams's character and modus operandi are Rachel Adams, *On the Other Hand* (1963), and Robert Keith Gray, *Eighteen Acres under Glass* (1962). Scholarly sources treating Adams in the context of White House staff operations include Louis Koenig, *The Invisible Presidency* (1960); Fred I. Greenstein, *The Hidden-Hand Presidency: Eisenhower as Leader* (1982); Phillip G. Henderson, *Managing the Presidency: The Eisenhower Legacy: From Kennedy to Reagan* (1988); and

Bradley H. Patterson, Jr., *The Ring of Power: The White House Staff and Its Expanding Role in Government* (1988). Obituaries are in the *New York Times* and the *Boston Globe*, both 28 Oct. 1986.

MICHAEL J. BIRKNER

ADAMS, Thomas (10 Sept. 1871–24 Mar. 1940), city and regional planner, was born in Edinburgh, Scotland, the son of James Adams and Margaret Johnston, dairy farmers. Educated in Edinburgh, he married Caroline Weierter in 1897; they had five children, two of whom, James Adams and Frederick Adams, also became distinguished planners. Farming, local Liberal politics, and writing were followed by the secretary-managership (1903–1906) of Letchworth, the first garden city, a new town intended to combine the advantages of town and country without the disadvantages. After a spell as Britain's first planning consultant, Adams became its first planning inspector (1910–1914) and founded the Town Planning Institute (inaugural president, 1913–1914). "Justly looked up to as the head of the profession in Britain," he served as town planning adviser (1914–1921) to the Canadian Commission of Conservation, promoting the British mode of controlling future urban development by provincial legislation, publicity, planning education, research, model communities, and the Town Planning Institute of Canada (founder-president, 1919–1921). After 1919 the collapse of Canadian progressivism compelled him to seek fresh opportunities in Britain and the United States via a transatlantic planning practice. He made numerous regional plans in the United Kingdom, introduced the American profession of landscape architecture, virtually founding the Institute of Landscape Architecture (president, 1937–1939), and remained the foremost advocate of planning in Britain.

First visiting the United States in 1911, Adams found its dominant mode of planning, the "city practical," a hard-nosed drive for civic efficiency, congenial, but his Canadian obligations restricted his contribution until 1921, when he began lecturing on planning at the Massachusetts Institute of Technology, continuing until 1936 and serving as research professor at Harvard's planning school (1930–1936). More comprehensive in his conception of planning than most contemporaries, he became its leading spokesman in America, his stature being recognized by appointment as director (1923–1929) of the Russell Sage–sponsored Regional Plan of New York, the world's grandest planning scheme. A forty-year outline plan for the 5,000-square-mile metropolitan region involving large engineering projects and control of development, much of it was carried out, though it earned the strident condemnation of Lewis Mumford. Spokesman for the social democratic Regional Plan Association of America, advocate of public-sponsored, statewide decentralization and the virtual destruction of New York City, Mumford described Adams's plan as "nothing more than the orderly dilution of New York over a 50-mile circle." Adams, a utilitarian, pragmatist, and advocate of voluntary cooperation, replied that the issue was "whether we stand still and talk ideals or move forward and get as much realization of our ideals as possible in a necessarily imperfect society, capable only of imperfect solutions to its problems" (*New Republic*, 1932).

In his last decade Adams became an elder statesman, visiting America annually to 1938 and collecting many honors. While Mumford described himself as "an insurgent," Adams was a meliorist, leading the emerging movement in professionalization, institutionalization, legislation, propaganda, education, and research, bringing planning to the brink of acceptance as a normal public function. It is arguable that between 1914 and 1940 he was the greatest figure in planning in the English-speaking world. He died at his home in Battle, Sussex, England.

• A complete bibliography of Adams's writings is in J. D. Hulchanski, *Thomas Adams: A Biographical and Bibliographic Guide* (1978), but his principal works were *Garden City and Agriculture* (1905), *Rural Planning and Development* (1917), *The Neighborhoods of Small Homes*, with R. Whitten (1931), *Recent Advances in Town Planning* (1932), *The Design of Residential Areas* (1934), and *The Outline of Town and Regional Planning* (1935). He also edited the eight volumes of *The Regional Survey of New York and Its Environs* (1927–1931) and wrote most of *The Graphic Regional Plan* (1929) and *The Building of the City* (1931). Adams's response to Mumford appears in *New Republic*, 6 July 1932. M. Simpson has an essay on Adams in G. E. Cherry, ed., *Pioneers in British Planning* (1981), and has written a full biography, *Thomas Adams and the Modern Planning Movement: Britain, Canada and the United States, 1900–1940* (1985). An obituary is in the *Times* (London), 25 Mar. 1940.

MICHAEL SIMPSON

ADAMS, Thomas, Jr. (11 Apr. 1846–4 Aug. 1926), manufacturer, was born in Brooklyn, New York, the son of Thomas Adams, a photographer and entrepreneur, and Martha Dunbar. His father, a commercial photographer who served in that capacity with the Union army during the Civil War, engaged in several small businesses after hostilities ended. When in 1866 a friend sent young Thomas a sample of chicle, a reddish-brown gum that coagulated from the sap of the Central American sapodilla tree (*Achras zapota*), his father noted its elastic properties and had the idea of converting it to a substitute for commercial rubber. Young Adams traveled to Mexico to obtain a supply, and with his father and brother Horatio he experimented with the gum for a time in the kitchen of their New York home. The experiments failed, and the material was stored in the small shop that his father was then operating in New York.

One day soon after, according to the family's recollection, someone entered the shop chewing vigorously. The customer was Rudolph Napegy, the secretary to former Mexican president Antonio López de Santa Anna, who was then living in exile in Staten Island; what he was chewing was chicle, a resin that native Mexicans had used for this purpose since before the Conquest. Thomas Adams, Sr., recalled the stock he had in his back room and, reflecting that people all over the world chewed other things besides food—betel nuts, coca leaves, tar, wax, and tobacco—he had the idea of introducing it to the American public. That night he and his two sons returned to the family kitchen and rolled their chicle into 200 marble-sized balls. He persuaded a New York drugstore to offer them to customers with each piece of candy purchased. The next day, when a small girl asked for a piece of wax to chew, the druggist handed her a ball of chicle, which had been delivered that morning by twelve-year-old Horatio. "The gum didn't come apart in the little girl's mouth as had the paraffin," according to a newspaper account of the event a century later, "and it made a resounding smack when she chewed it hard. By day's end the little girl—and her friends—were hooked" (*New York World Journal Tribune*).

The 23-year-old Thomas persuaded his father to increase production in 1869, and they formed Adams & Sons, with Thomas Adams, Sr., as president and his older son as vice president. The pioneer chewing gum company in the industry, Adams & Sons opened a small factory in Jersey City, New Jersey, with a capital of $35,000. At first the product did not find a large market among merchants, who gave it away to their customers, but when the manufacturers began adding sugar and various flavorings to the raw chicle, candy and tobacco stores were able to sell the increasingly popular confection. In 1871 Thomas Adams, Jr., married Emma Mills of Jersey City; they would have three children. In February of the next year his father obtained a patent for the process of making chewing gum, the first in the field. A much larger factory was built for Adams & Sons in Brooklyn in 1888, and when his father retired ten years later, Thomas Adams, Jr., became president.

Other firms soon started manufacturing chicle-based chewing gum, using the Adams patent, and Adams undertook to maintain the family firm's dominant position in the industry by consolidation. In 1899 he merged with the Beeman Chemical Company, W. J. White & Son of Cleveland, Ohio, S. T. Briton of Toronto, Canada, Kisme Gum of Louisville, Kentucky, and J. P. Primly of Chicago, Illinois, to form the American Chicle Company. Adams & Sons acquired a controlling interest in the company, with Thomas as president and his brother Horatio as vice president. In 1914 American Chicle bought the Sen-Sen Chiclet Company of Maine and two years later the Sterling Gum Company of Long Island City, New York. During Adams's presidency he established as subsidiaries Adams Chewing Gum Company, Limited, in London, American Chicle Company in Mexico, and Canadian Chewing Gum, Limited, in Toronto. To protect his sources of raw material, he also secured a major interest in the Chicle Development Company, which controlled the crop from 5 million acres in Mexico, Guatamala, and British Honduras.

Adams had established American Chicle's main factory in Newark, New Jersey, in 1903. By 1920 demand for the product had increased enough to necessitate the construction of a new plant in Long Island City, with a double railroad siding and a floor area of 550,000 square feet. Two years later Adams retired as the company's president, although he remained one of its largest stockholders.

A sociable gentleman, Adams was a member of several New York clubs and actively supported the Republican party. He was also a generous contributor to charity. Long a widower, he married Elizabeth Flood, his secretary and housekeeper, in December 1925. Adams died in New York City.

Thomas Adams, Jr., was a shrewd businessman who helped both invent a new product and create a worldwide market for it. Before 1900 it was reported that Eskimos preferred Adams chewing gum to blubber, and a few years later a British diplomat, kidnapped by tribesmen in Borneo, was ransomed for three cases of chewing gum. After World War II chewing gum became a dubious symbol of American civilization, but the use of the product Adams pioneered had become almost universal. In 1957 the National Health Committee announced reproachfully that the United States was spending more money on chewing gum than on medical education.

• Little has been written about the life of Thomas Adams, Jr. The history of the Adams family business is recorded in the files of the American Chicle Company, and Adams is mentioned occasionally in the press. See the *Newark News*, 25 Oct. 1953. An account of the family enterprise is given in the *New York World Journal Tribune*, 28 Mar. 1967. An obituary of Thomas Adams, Jr., is in the *New York Times*, 6 Aug. 1926. See also obituaries of Horatio Adams in the *New York Times*, 27 Jan. 1956, and the *Newark News*, 28 Jan. 1956.

DENNIS WEPMAN

ADAMS, Walter Sydney (20 Dec. 1876–11 May 1956), astronomer, was born in the Syrian village of Kessab, the son of Lucien Harper Adams and Nancy Dorrance Francis, missionaries. Upon the family's return to Derry, New Hampshire, in 1885, Adams attended public and private schools, graduating in 1894 from Phillips Academy, Andover, intent upon pursuing astronomy as a career. He trained under Edwin Frost at Dartmouth, his father's alma mater, graduating with the A.B. in 1898, and from there went to the University of Chicago, studying celestial mechanics on campus and practical astrophysical technique at Chicago's newly opened Yerkes Observatory in Williams Bay, Wisconsin, the creation of George Ellery Hale.

Under Hale, and soon Frost, who by then was also at Yerkes as a staff astronomer, Adams was exposed to modern spectroscopic and laboratory techniques in astronomy. After receiving the A.M. from the University of Chicago in 1900, Adams was encouraged to pursue the Ph.D. in Munich, following a well-established pattern. But Hale called Adams back as a Yerkes staff member within the year, mainly to work as computer and general research assistant on a large spectroscopic project comparing sunspot spectra to spectra of the redder "late-type" stars in Hale's campaign to place the evolutionary order of the stars upon a physical basis.

Adams's subsequent career, like much of American astrophysics, was largely a product of Hale's design. When Hale moved to Pasadena, California, to establish the Mount Wilson Solar Observatory in 1904, Adams went with him to build and use the larger-scale instruments that were intended to be an expansion of what they had started at Yerkes in solar and stellar spectroscopy. And as Hale became more and more involved with the organization of science on the national and international levels, Adams became his acting director, first in spirit and by 1910 in fact, since by then Hale's health was becoming unpredictable. In 1913 Adams was named assistant director, and by the onset of the First World War, Adams was managing the daily activities of the observatory, which by 1920 was by far the most powerfully equipped astronomical institution in the world, boasting 60- and 100-inch reflecting telescopes.

The early fruits of Hale's vision for how astronomy should operate can be found in Adams's first decade of work at Mount Wilson. Hale wanted to integrate diverse talents and techniques drawing not only from the observatory chamber but from the physicist's laboratory and the theorist's pen. In what would be his most important work, Adams supplied the empirical astronomical clues that others used to eventually explain, by linking laboratory evidence to modern physical theory, how and why the physical conditions in stellar atmospheres were revealed by their spectra. Between 1910 and 1914, encouraged by the visiting Dutch astronomer J. C. Kapteyn, and in collaboration with A. Kohlschütter, Adams looked for spectroscopic evidence of interstellar absorption but found instead that, for some unknown reason, the intrinsic brightnesses of stars were related directly to the appearance and character of certain absorption lines in their spectra. Adams's earlier work with Hale on sunspot spectra had helped to establish empirically that spectral appearance was related to temperature in stellar atmospheres, and Adams knew from tentative laboratory evidence that the appearance of spectral lines could also be influenced by changes in pressure. But at the time, when Bohr theory was hardly a year old, no one could explain physically why spectra could be influenced in this manner. Adams looked for guidance from the best astronomical theorists of the day, such as Arthur Stanley Eddington, but found little aid. Although he was convinced that he had detected a fundamental clue to how spectra revealed not only temperature but also pressure and density, he, along with all other astronomers of his day, was not equipped to place this knowledge on a firm, rational basis.

Nevertheless, Adams and Kohlschütter found great practical use in their discovery: it was a highly efficient way to determine distances to stars. One needed only to compare the intrinsic brightness of a star, determined by its spectrum, to its observed brightness to find its distance. The technique of spectroscopic parallaxes, as it was called, greatly extended astronomy's ability to map the structure of the local stellar system, just at a time when Henry Norris Russell and Ejnar Hertzsprung had found independently that two great classes of stars existed, what they called giants and dwarfs. The technique of spectroscopic parallaxes helped to confirm and refine this discovery about stars. For this work Adams was awarded the Gold Medal of the Royal Astronomical Society (1917) and the Draper Medal of the National Academy of Sciences (1918).

Through World War I and in its wake, Adams tended to the needs of the observatory according to policies set by Hale. Under Adams, the 100-inch reflector was completed and placed into operation and the spectroscopic laboratories Hale had created were maintained, along with Mount Wilson's battery of solar and stellar telescopes. Adams also attended to the details of administration with the Carnegie Institution of Washington, which both funded and oversaw Mount Wilson. Though administration occupied more of his life after 1920, Adams managed to participate in the ongoing research programs at first set by Hale and, by 1923 as he succeeded Hale as director, by Adams himself.

In the 1920s Adams played a role in rationalizing his technique of spectroscopic parallaxes. Starting in 1919, the Calcuttan physicist Meghnad Saha applied Bohr theory to the stars to show that, indeed, if stellar atmospheres existed in a state of ionization equilibrium, then the relative strengths of spectral absorption lines were determined by the temperature, and secondarily by the pressure, of that atmosphere. Just as Saha's papers were appearing, Hale invited the Princeton theoretical astrophysicist Henry Norris Russell to Mount Wilson on a part-time basis, and Russell immediately set about refining Saha's discoveries, using Mount Wilson resources and talent, organized by Adams. Over the next decade, Russell, working with Adams and his staff, laid the foundations for the quantitative study of stellar atmospheres using modern physical theory.

Adams as director worked on many fronts. He maintained an interest in spectroscopic radial velocity techniques, in the mid-1920s making an attempt, considered successful at the time, to detect the gravitational reddening of spectra that Eddington had predicted to exist in the dense atmospheres of white dwarf stars. With Mount Wilson staff, Adams also pursued high-dispersion spectroscopy of the planets, providing state-of-the-art estimates for their compositions throughout the 1920s and 1930s, deriving a value for the oxygen content in the Martian atmosphere that was accepted for three decades. Starting in the late 1920s, Adams also supervised the design and construction of Hale's final monument: the 200-inch telescope, which was completed two years after Adams's 1946 retirement.

Adams's first marriage, to Lillian Maud Wickham in 1910, ended with her death in 1920. He married Adeline L. Miller in 1922, and they had two children. Adams died in Pasadena, California. He is remembered as a deliberate and even-tempered researcher and administrator who deftly managed the operation of one of the world's greatest twentieth-century observatories.

• Adams's papers, consisting of some 52,000 items, including administrative, scientific, and personal correspondence from 1921 to 1956, are in the Huntington Library Manuscripts Division, San Marino, Calif. The *Finding Aid to the Papers of Walter Sydney Adams*, prepared by Helen S. Czaplicki in 1984, has been augmented by Huntington staff with the accession of the Archives of the Mount Wilson Observatory. Extensive series of Adams's earlier correspondence can be found in the George Ellery Hale Papers, of which a microfilm edition is available at the American Institute of Physics and elsewhere; in the papers of Edwin Frost, housed at the Yerkes Observatory in Williams Bay, Wisc.; and in the papers of Henry Norris Russell at Princeton, of which microfilm copies exist. Extensive listings of Adams's publications can be found in the entry by Helen Wright in the *Dictionary of Scientific Biography*, vol. 1 (1970), which includes many secondary source references, and in his entry by A. H. Joy in National Academy of Sciences, *Biographical Memoirs* 31 (1958): 1–31. Adams's role in modern spectroscopic astrophysics is covered in a three-part series of papers by David H. DeVorkin and R. Kenat, "Quantum Physics and the Stars," *Journal for the History of Astronomy* 14 (1983): 102–32, and 180–222; and 21 (1990): 157–86. An obituary is Paul W. Merrill, "Walter Sydney Adams, Observer of Sun and Stars," *Science*, 13 July 1956, p. 67.

DAVID H. DEVORKIN

ADAMS, William (25 Jan. 1807–31 Aug. 1880), minister and seminary president, was born in Colchester, Connecticut, the son of John Adams, an educator, and Elizabeth Ripley. Adams grew up in Andover, Massachusetts, where his father was the principal of Phillips Academy. He entered Yale College in 1824, where he received his A.B. in 1827. After college he returned home to study at Andover Theological Seminary and to assist his father in teaching. He completed his seminary training in 1830 and was ordained a Congregational minister. He began service as the pastor of a church in Brighton, Massachusetts, in 1831. He married Susan P. Magoun in July 1831. His wife's illness forced him to resign from the Brighton pastorate in early 1834, but following her death in May, he accepted a ministerial call to the Broome Street (later Central) Presbyterian Church in New York City. Since the Congregational and Presbyterian denominations then enjoyed a spirit of mutual respect and cooperation, Adams switched denominations and was installed as pastor in November 1834. In August 1835 he married Martha B. Magoun, the sister of his first wife.

Adams was among the group of "New School" Presbyterian clergy and lay leaders who helped found Union Theological Seminary in New York in 1836. In the early nineteenth century, the Presbyterian church in the United States was split between two rival factions: the traditionalist Old School party and the more reform-oriented New School party. Advocates of the New School, which was strongest in New York and Ohio, sought to protect their interests by establishing an educational institution reflecting their party's relatively liberal theological and social views. When the Presbyterian church officially divided in 1837 over revivalism, social reform, and antislavery ideology (all of which the New School favored and the Old School opposed), Union became the foremost seminary of the New School denomination. Adams was one of the New School's leading ministers, serving as moderator of its General Assembly in 1852. Although the coming of the Civil War split American Presbyterianism once again, this time along sectional lines, the conflict also hastened the end of the earlier schism. Adams took a prominent role in healing the breach between the Old and New School denominations in the North. He led the New School's delegation on the joint committee that discussed reunion and later chaired the whole committee itself. While Presbyterians in the South remained a separate denomination, the two northern Presbyterian churches formally reunited in 1870.

In 1853 most of Adams's congregation left the Central Presbyterian Church in downtown Manhattan and moved uptown to form the Madison Square Presbyterian Church. Adams went with them and assumed the pastorate of the new church, where he served for the next twenty years. In the early 1870s he was active in the Evangelical Alliance, an organization that fostered ecumenical cooperation between the major Protestant denominations in Great Britain and the United States. Renowned for his opposition to religious sectarianism, Adams was one of the principal speakers at the 1873 meeting of the Evangelical Alliance in New York, and he was involved with the American Board of Commissioners for Foreign Missions. Also in 1873 he became the president of Union Seminary, the third person to hold the position since the school's founding. During his presidency, he also served as the seminary's professor of sacred rhetoric. Adams proved to be an effective fundraiser, and his ability to convince affluent businessmen to demonstrate their piety by making financial contributions to the school markedly increased Union's endowment. He remained at Union until his death, which occurred at his summer home in Orange Mountain, New Jersey.

Adams provided important leadership within Presbyterianism in the Northeast during the critical middle decades of the nineteenth century. He not only helped establish one of the major Protestant seminaries in the United States, but his efforts on behalf of Presbyterian reunion also enabled his denomination to achieve stability and growth after the Civil War. Although he was not a prominent preacher or theologian, Adams greatly strengthened both the institutional and intellectual life of his church.

• The best source for studying Adams's ministerial career is the extensive collection of his manuscript papers in Burke Library at Union Theological Seminary, New York City. George Lewis Prentiss, *The Union Theological Seminary in the City of New York: Historical and Biographical Sketches of Its First Fifty Years* (1889), provides a roughly contemporary account of Adams's influence at the school. Robert T. Handy,

A History of Union Theological Seminary in New York (1987), offers a modern scholarly analysis of Adams's contributions as a Presbyterian leader.

GARDINER H. SHATTUCK, JR.

ADAMS, William Taylor (30 July 1822–27 Mar. 1897), publisher and writer of juvenile fiction, was born in Medway, Massachusetts, the son of Laban Adams, a tavern keeper, and Catherine Johnson. An honors student in the Boston and West Roxbury public schools, he also attended Able Whitney's private academy for a year after he completed his secondary schooling. He began teaching school while still in his teens but also helped his father manage the family-operated "Adams House" in Boston for a short time. As a young boy, he traveled extensively throughout the country, taking detailed notes on his journeys, many of which he used in later years in his writings. His first published work, an article in the *Social Monitor*, appeared when he was nineteen; he published several others in his early twenties. In 1846 he married Sarah Jenkins of Dorchester, and the couple had two children. Though he continued teaching in the Boston schools until 1865, he began publishing short stories and full-length novels for young readers under the pen name "Oliver Optic" as early as 1851. These books soon made him both famous and rich. Long before his death, Adams, thanks to his more than 120 novels and 1,000 articles and short stories, was one of the highest-paid writers in late nineteenth-century America, sometimes receiving as much as $5,000 for several articles. Besides his writing, he also edited a number of magazines, including *The Student and Schoolmate*, *Our Little Ones*, and his own *Oliver Optic's Magazine* (*Our Boys and Girls*), which he founded in 1867 and led until it ceased publication in 1875.

Adams's first full-length novel, *Hatchie, the Guardian Slave; or, The Heiress of Bellevue* (written as Warren T. Ashton), was published in 1853, but *The Boat Club; or The Bunkers of Rippleton*, published two years later, made him an instant success. Pitting three young teenaged friends, Frank Sedley, Charles Hardy, and Tony Weston, against a gang of local hoodlums, the book featured all those things for which Adams soon became famous: an emphasis on melodramatic but always exciting and dangerous adventures, a battle of good versus evil, the victory of morality over sin, and, ultimately, the concept of "One Big Break" by which the heroes were assured of permanent riches and preferment. *The Boat Club* was eventually followed by six other volumes in a series revolving around the original novel's characters. Each book seemed to sell better than its predecessor.

Nearly all of Adams's novels written after 1856 were parts of ongoing series ranging from five books (the Boat-Builder Series) to twelve volumes (the Young America Abroad Series). He also wrote the All-over-the-World, Army and Navy, Blue and Gray, Great Western, Lake Shore, Onward and Upward, Riverdale, Starry Flag, Woodville, and Yacht Club series. So popular were his works among young boys and girls that it did not seem strange that the year after his death his publisher, Lee and Shepard, commissioned the soon-to-be-famous Edward Stratemeyer to complete the author's last work, *An Undivided Union*, which he had left unfinished on his desk.

Adams's many books always received mixed reviews. For every reviewer who highly praised one of his novels, and there were many, there was another who literally hated it and attacked it for its supposed sensationalism. So controversial was Adams as a writer that in 1879 the American Library Association seriously debated recommending that his works be removed from the nation's library shelves. At least one library, the Fletcher Free Library of Burlington, Vermont, did just that, publicly discarding all of Optic's books the following year. Louisa May Alcott, who had gained fame with her *Little Women* only after being told by a publisher that she ought to produce a story "like Oliver Optic," openly attacked Adams in *Eight Cousins*, accusing him of writing exploitative, poor, and melodramatic works unfit for this nation's youths. He hit back in the pages of his own magazine, and for a while in 1875 the two engaged in an ongoing feud as to what was best for young readers.

Adams's writing motto was "First God, then country, then friends," and many of his stories reflected that moralizing and chauvinistic tone. At times, he could be almost pompous in his attitude toward his readers; he was also frequently sentimental if not bathetic. But millions of readers did not seem to care. They clearly agreed with a publisher's blurb that appeared in an advertisement for one of his early books: "Boys and girls have no taste for dry and tame things; they want something that will stir the blood and warm the heart [and Oliver] Optic always does this." More than 2 million copies of his books sold during his lifetime. Long after his death in Dorchester, Massachusetts, a suburb of Boston, publishers continued to reissue editions of some of his most popular volumes. *The Boat Club*, for example, went through sixty different editions. As late as the 1930s, Optic volumes were still in circulation and being read by young boys across America. John T. Dizer is quick to note that they are still widely collected and admired, if only by devotees of nineteenth-century juvenile literature. Of all of his contemporaries, only Horatio Alger, whom Adams first introduced to the American reading public when he published that author's *Ragged Dick* as a serial in *Student and Schoolmate* beginning in 1867, sold more books.

• Adams's papers are in the Houghton Library at Harvard University. Other sources of value include Dolores Blythe Jones, *An "Oliver Optic" Checklist* (1985); Peter C. Walther, *An Annotated Bibliography of the Complete Published Works of William T. Adams* (1986); Albert Johannsen, *House of Beadle and Adams and Its Dime and Nickel Novels: The Story of a Vanished Literature* (1950); Gene Gleason, "Whatever Happened to Oliver Optic?," *Wilson Library Bulletin* 49 (1975): 647–50; and John T. Dizer, "Armed with Pen and Ink: The Oliver Optic–Louisa May Alcott Feud," *Dime Novel Round-up* 56 (1987): 50–59. A brief but perhaps the most complete contemporary assessment is Carol Gay, "William Taylor Adams (Oliver Optic)," *Dictionary of Literary Biography*, vol. 42, pp. 11–18.

M. PAUL HOLSINGER

ADAMSKI, George (17 Apr. 1891–23 Apr. 1965), lecturer and writer on occult subjects and on UFOs during the 1950s' flying saucer enthusiasm, was born in Poland. His parents (names unknown) brought him to the United States when he was one or two. The family settled in Dunkirk, New York; their life was hard, and Adamski received little formal education. He joined the Thirteenth U.S. Cavalry Regiment in 1913 as an enlisted man, serving on the Mexican border, and was honorably discharged in 1916. On 25 December 1917 he married Mary A. Shimbersky (d. 1954). After leaving the army, Adamski worked as a painter in Yellowstone National Park, in a flour mill in Portland, Oregon, and by 1921 was working in a cement factory in California. He continued to live in California, reportedly supporting himself and his wife through a variety of jobs, including by the 1930s teaching and lecturing on occult subjects.

He founded the Royal Order of Tibet, headquartered at a "monastery" in Laguna Beach, California, in 1934. Under its aegis, he offered classes, radio talks, and correspondence courses on "Cosmic Law." In the forties and fifties, while continuing to lecture, Adamski and his wife also worked in a small café on the slopes of Mt. Palomar in southern California, site of the famous observatory. A growing interest in astronomy may be reflected in the delight he took in those years in a six-inch telescope given to him by his students. His home after about 1940 was, and remained until the end of his life, Valley Center, California, on the approaches of Mt. Palomar, though he devoted much time to travel and lecture tours.

The flying saucer vogue began with the June 1947 sightings of mysterious round flying objects near Mt. Rainier, Washington, by Kenneth Arnold. By October, Adamski reported seeing them as well, in the form of a fleet of no less than 184 saucers in formation above Mt. Palomar. He took many photos of what he claimed were spaceships, and began lecturing about them in March 1950. In March 1951 a story on his pictures appeared in *Fate* magazine, bringing Adamski a national audience.

It was on 20 November 1952 that Adamski and a few friends reportedly saw a UFO (unidentified flying object) land on the California desert. Proceeding alone toward the site, Adamski met Orthon, a Venusian. Adamski described his "space friend" as about five feet six inches tall, clean-shaven but with shoulder-length hair, dressed in something like a ski suit. The visitor spoke to Adamski by sign language and telepathy, telling him among other things about the space peoples' concern over nuclear testing on earth. Orthon left behind footprints, marked by enigmatic symbols, and, in a following encounter in December, a sheet of hieroglyphics. These events were detailed in *Flying Saucers Have Landed* (1953), coauthored by the English occult writer Desmond Leslie, who contributed much material on phenomena of the past comparable to the UFOs.

Further meetings with space beings, including a ride in a flying saucer, were described in Adamski's next book, *Inside the Space Ships* (1955). The book includes lengthy discourses on the "cosmic philosophy" of Adamski and his godlike extraterrestrial mentors, advancing a message of universal love, respect, and freedom. A third book, *Flying Saucers Farewell* (1961; repr. 1967 as *Behind the Flying Saucer Mystery*), centered on Adamski's 1959 world lecture tour. Though much criticized and ridiculed, Adamski and his works epitomize the quasireligious nature of the 1950s' UFO "contactee" movement, which portrayed beautiful, superior space beings, "technological angels" in the expression of C. G. Jung, addressing and befriending a troubled, divided earth. While on a lecture tour in the eastern United States, Adamski died in Takoma Park, Maryland, near Washington, D.C., of a heart attack.

• The main book-length life of Adamski is Lou Zinsstag and Timothy Good, *George Adamski: The Untold Story* (1983), an uneven and overly sympathetic but helpful source. The same can be said of Zinsstag, *UFO. . . George Adamski: Their Man on Earth* (1990), which was written prior to Zinsstag's collaboration with Good but was published afterward; the book contains pages incorporated with other material into their joint work. More concise information can be found in J. Gordon Melton, *Biographical Dictionary of American Cult and Sect Leaders* (1986), Ronald D. Story, ed., *The Encyclopedia of UFOs* (1980), and David M. Jacobs, *The UFO Controversy in America* (1975). The best critical treatment, with extensive bibliography, is Jerome Clark, *The UFO Encyclopedia, Vol. 2: The Emergence of a Phenomenon: UFOs from the Beginning through 1959* (1992), pp. 1–12. Adamski generated considerable journalistic and ephemeral writing, both his own and works pro and con by others; the best resources, in addition to Clark's *Encyclopedia*, are Richard M. Rasmussen, *The UFO Literature: A Comprehensive Annotated Bibliography of Works in English* (1985), and J. Gordon Melton and George M. Eberhart, *The Flying Saucer Contactee Movement: 1950–1990* (1990).

ROBERT S. ELLWOOD

ADAMSON, Harold Campbell (10 Dec. 1906–17 Aug. 1980), lyricist, was born in Greenville, New Jersey, the son of James H. Adamson, a building contractor, and Marion Campbell. During his childhood Adamson wrote poetry for his school newspaper and skits for school shows. While studying at the University of Kansas, he wrote songs and worked with a local professional theater company during vacations. From Kansas, Adamson moved on to Harvard University, where he wrote shows and songs for Harvard's Hasty Pudding Club. Following his graduation from Harvard in 1930, Adamson entered show business as a lyricist for both stage and screen.

Adamson attained his first success in the theater working for the celebrated producer Florenz Ziegfeld, Jr. Adamson collaborated with Mack Gordon on the lyrics to "Time on My Hands" (music by Vincent Youmans), a hit song featured in the Ziegfeld-produced musical *Smiles* (1930) that starred Fred Astaire, Adele Astaire, and Marilyn Miller. Adamson also wrote lyrics for *Earl Carroll's Vanities* in 1931.

In Hollywood Adamson found his niche. A solid craftsman who worked well within the requirements of the studio system, he successfully collaborated with an array of outstanding composers. He began his screen career working with composer Burton Lane on "Everything I Have Is Yours" for MGM's *Dancing Lady* (1933), a musical that starred Clark Gable and Joan Crawford and introduced Fred Astaire to movie audiences. Adamson also wrote both music and lyrics for Fox's *Bottoms Up* (1934) and contributed lyrics to *Kid Millions* (1934), a lavish Samuel Goldwyn production starring Eddie Cantor and Ethel Merman. Other Adamson lyrics were heard in the movies *Escapade* (1935), *Gypsy Night* (1935), *Banjo on My Knee* (1936), and *Suzy* (1936), a musical improbably starring Cary Grant and Jean Harlow, which featured Adamson's lyrics for the song "Did I Remember?" (music by Walter Donaldson), which was nominated for the Academy Award for best song (it lost to Jerome Kern and Dorothy Fields's "The Way You Look Tonight"). Adamson also wrote lyrics for "You," "You Never Looked So Beautiful," and "You Gotta Pull Strings" (all with music by Donaldson) for MGM's *The Great Ziegfeld* (1936), "When the Stars Go to Sleep" (with music by Jimmy McHugh) for Universal's *Reckless Living* (1938), and "My Own" (with music by McHugh) for Universal's *That Certain Age* (1938), starring Deanna Durbin. This last song was nominated for another Oscar. Adamson married Judy Crisfield in 1935; they had one daughter.

Returning to Broadway, Adamson contributed some lyrics to Cantor's final stage show, *Banjo Eyes* (1941), which was loosely based on *Three Men on a Horse* (1935), the hit play by John Cecil Holm and George Abbott. The show, which critic Burns Mantle described as "expansive and lavish," included Adamson's lyrics to Vernon Duke's music for "It Could Only Happen in the Movies," "Make with the Feet," and "We're Having a Baby," the last of which Cantor parlayed into a mildly popular success outside of the show. Cantor performed it in the 1944 all-star Warner Bros. film *Hollywood Canteen*. Adamson also wrote lyrics to McHugh's music for the Mike Todd production *As the Girls Go* (1948), starring Bobby Clark, and collaborated with Duke Ellington on "Manhattan Serenade."

A return to Hollywood songwriting led to two other Oscar nominations for Adamson in the best song category. These were for "Change of Heart" (music by Jule Styne) from Republic's *Hit Parade of 1943* (1943) and "I Couldn't Sleep a Wink Last Night" (music by McHugh) for RKO's *Higher and Higher* (1944), Frank Sinatra's first movie. Other screen songs in the 1940s featuring Adamson's lyrics include "Daybreak" (with music by Ferde Grofe) for MGM's *Thousands Cheer* (1943) and "It's a Most Unusual Day" (with music by Jimmy McHugh) for MGM's *A Date with Judy* (1948). Adamson also contributed lyrics to such diverse popular songs as "My Resistance Is Low" (with music by Hoagy Carmichael), "It's Been So Long" (with music by Donaldson), "The Woodpecker Song" (with music by Eldo Di Lazzaro), "Ferry-Boat Serenade" (with music by Di Lazzaro), and "It's a Wonderful World" (with music by Jan Savitt and Johnny Watson). After a divorce in 1941, Adamson married Gretchen Davidson in 1947; they had no children, although Davidson had two children from a previous marriage.

Back in Hollywood, Adamson wrote lyrics for "When Love Goes Wrong," with music by Carmichael, for 20th Century–Fox's lavish musical *Gentlemen Prefer Blondes* (1953), starring Marilyn Monroe and Jane Russell. He also contributed lyrics to the title song (with music by Victor Young) for United Artists' *Around the World in Eighty Days* (1956). A year later, Adamson wrote lyrics for the memorable 1957 tearjerking movie *An Affair to Remember*, starring Cary Grant and Deborah Kerr in a remake of *Love Affair* (1937). The title song brought another Oscar nomination for Adamson, who cowrote lyrics with the film's director Leo McCarey to music by Harry Warren. Adamson also wrote lyrics to Sammy Fain's music for several songs for the 1964 Don Knotts comedy *The Incredible Mr. Limpet*, and he contributed music to television's popular "I Love Lucy" series in 1951. Virtually every significant singer from the 1930s through the 1950s performed or recorded Adamson songs, many of which have remained popular standards. He died in Beverly Hills, California.

• For information on Adamson, see Ruth Benjamin and Arthur Rosenblatt, *Movie Song Catalog: Performers and Supporting Crew for the Songs Sung in 1460 Musical and Non-Musical Films, 1928–1988* (1993); James Fisher, *Eddie Cantor: A Bio-Bibliography* (1997); Greg Koseluk, *Eddie Cantor: A Life in Show Business* (1994); Donald J. Stubblebine, *Cinema Sheet Music: A Comprehensive Listing of Published Film Music from Squaw Man (1914) to Batman (1989)* (1991); and Richard and Paulette Ziegfeld, *The Ziegfeld Touch: The Life and Times of Florenz Ziegfeld, Jr.* (1993). An obituary is in the *New York Times*, 20 Aug. 1980.

JAMES FISHER

ADAMSON, Joy (20 Jan. 1910–3 Jan. 1980), writer and conservationist, was born Friederike Viktoria Gessner in Troppau, Austria, the daughter of Victor Gessner, a civil servant, and Traute Greipel. Before her first marriage, to automobile company official Viktor von Klarwill in 1935, Adamson studied piano and took courses in other arts, including sculpture. She made her first trip to Kenya in 1936, to investigate that country as a possible new home for herself and her husband, whose Jewish background made him eager to leave Austria at this time of Nazi advance. During this trip she became involved with Peter Bally, a Swiss botanist whom she married in 1938 after becoming divorced from von Klarwill in 1937.

While accompanying Bally on collecting expeditions around Kenya, Adamson learned from him the art of botanical illustration, at which she soon became proficient. In 1938 she accepted her first commission as an artist, to illustrate *Gardening in East Africa* (1939). It was also during her marriage to Bally that she assumed the name Joy.

Adamson was divorced from Bally after becoming involved with British game warden George Adamson, whom she married in 1944 within a few months of her divorce. While this marriage lasted until her death, it was often tense and occasionally violent, disrupted by her numerous affairs and flirtations as well as by extended periods of separation.

All of her marriages were childless. Adamson continued to practice as an illustrator, completing a series of paintings of tropical fish in 1946. She then pursued and received a commission from the Kenyan colonial government to document the traditional costumes of the many Kenyan tribes. This project required extensive and sometimes dangerous travel over the course of several years. In the end she produced more than 700 paintings as well as many photographs; selections of both were used later to illustrate her book *The Peoples of Kenya* (1967). Although the paintings tend to expose her artistic limitations, they retain some documentary value.

In 1956 Adamson and her husband began what was to be the defining project of her life: the rearing and rehabilitation of the orphaned lion cub they named Elsa. As Adamson expressed it, "George's deep love for nature, and mine, all culminated in Elsa." Around the time of Elsa's successful release, Joy Adamson began work on *Born Free* (1960), which described the process of raising Elsa and of teaching her to adapt to life as a wild lioness; the book drew extensively on George Adamson's diaries and official reports. Adamson had some difficulty finding a publisher, in part because her bad English and weak typing skills made the initial manuscript unworkable. *Born Free* was ultimately accepted by Harvill Press, whose cofounder Marjorie Villiers (along with naturalist Lord William Percy) deserves much credit for the book's final form. Once published, *Born Free*, copiously illustrated with Adamson's photographs, was an immediate bestseller.

Adamson wrote two sequels to *Born Free*: *Living Free* (1961), which chronicled Elsa's life with her cubs, and *Forever Free* (1962), about the cubs after Elsa's death. A 1966 film based on *Born Free* was commercially successful although not well received by critics. Its sequel, titled *Living Free* but including material from *Forever Free* as well, appeared in 1971.

In 1962 Adamson began a heavy international lecture schedule, speaking about her experiences with Elsa and raising money for the Elsa Wild Animal Appeal, a trust she established to support the conservation of wildlife. This trust was among the first of its kind, and it contributed greatly to conservation efforts, especially in Kenya, where it provided significant financial assistance to the Kenyan Wildlife Service and to the educational mission of the Wildlife Clubs of Kenya. The trust also made possible the acquisition of the land surrounding Adamson's final home as a National Park.

Adamson and her husband remained in contact with Elsa until the lioness's death in 1961. Adamson perceived their ongoing relationship with Elsa as "one of absolute equality." The great significance she ascribed to this continued rapport is *Born Free*'s final point: "We have achieved our aim. . . . Elsa is free; she has now lived the natural, independent life of a wild lioness for more than a year and yet retains all her affection for us."

Adamson's profound emotional attachment to Elsa was never rivaled. She did, however, repeat her experiment with two other big cats, a cheetah named Pippa and, later, a leopard called Penny. In both cases, as with Elsa, she maintained contact with the animals after successfully raising them and releasing them into the wild, where they mated and gave birth. Pippa became the subject of Adamson's first book about cheetahs, *The Spotted Sphinx* (1969); a second, *Pippa's Challenge*, followed in 1972. *Queen of Shaba* (1980) records Penny's life. During this period Adamson also published a sketchbook titled *Joy Adamson's Africa* (1972) and an autobiography, *The Searching Spirit* (1978). Her last book, *Friends from the Forest* (1981), appeared posthumously.

From the mid-1960s to the end of her life, Adamson suffered from a variety of health problems and injuries, including a smashed right hand in 1969 that severely curtailed her painting. Her demanding and temperamental personality continued to strain her relationships with both friends and employees. She was murdered outside her camp in Shaba, Kenya; a fired staff member was convicted of the crime.

Adamson's popularity as a writer has faded. Her books are unremarkable as literature and depend on the appeal of the wild animals they portray. Contemporary readers may find Adamson's books dated; in particular, her portrayals of black Kenyans may strike many as condescending. Her efforts at rehabilitating captive-raised cats have also been criticized, at first because of the large amount of wild game she and her husband killed to feed these animals, and later because of the Adamsons' unwillingness to relinquish contact with the cats after their release. As devoted observers of nature rather than biologists, the Adamsons' approach was generally not scientific.

Joy Adamson's impact as an advocate for wildlife conservation, in Africa and internationally, should not be underestimated, however. Throughout the 1960s and into the 1970s she played a significant role in raising world consciousness about the importance of protecting wild animals and their habitats, in effect helping to lay the foundation for the conservation movement.

• Caroline Cass, *Joy Adamson: Behind the Mask* (1992), is a valuable biography. Adrian House, an acquaintance of the Adamsons', wrote *The Great Safari: The Lives of George and Joy Adamson, Famous for "Born Free"* (1993), which is also a useful source and includes a helpful bibliography. Readers may also refer to George Adamson's two autobiographical books, *Bwana Game* (1968) and *My Pride and Joy* (1986). In addition to the works cited, Joy Adamson also wrote three books for children: *Elsa* (1961), *Elsa and Her Cubs* (1965), and *Pippa the Cheetah and Her Cubs* (1970). Obituaries are in the *New York Times* and *The Times* (London), 5 Jan. 1980.

EMILY A. HADDAD

ADDAMS, Charles Samuel (7 Jan. 1912–29 Sept. 1988), cartoonist, was born in Westfield, New Jersey, the son of Charles Huey Addams, the manager of a piano company, and Grace M. Spear. His father, who had studied to be an architect, encouraged young Charles to draw, and he did cartoons for the student paper at Westfield High School. Addams entered Colgate University in 1929 but transferred after a year to the University of Pennsylvania, which he left the following year (1931) to enroll in the Grand Central School of Art in New York, where he spent the next year (most of it, he once confessed, just "watching people" walk through Grand Central Terminal). Embarking on a career as an illustrator in 1932, Addams took a job as staff artist for a Macfadden true detective magazine, doing lettering, retouching of photographs, and diagrams of crime scenes for $15 a week. At the same time he started submitting cartoons to various magazines, selling his first in 1933. Soon thereafter, he was selling regularly enough to quit his job at Macfadden ("the last and only job I ever had," he said) to earn his livelihood entirely as a freelance cartoonist.

Although he sold cartoons to many magazines during the 1930s and 1940s, Addams is most closely associated with the *New Yorker*, where his macabre sense of humor became a fixture. That magazine bought its first Addams cartoon in 1935—a picture of a man standing on the ice in his stocking feet, saying, "I forgot my skates." The cartoonist's popularity, however, began with the publication (in the *New Yorker* for 13 January 1940) of a cartoon showing the parallel tracks of a skier leading directly up to a tree and then going around it, one track on either side. No caption. Addams admitted that he never quite understood the cartoon himself, but he was delighted that a Nebraska mental institution used the drawing to test the mental age of its patients. "Under a fifteen-year level, they can't tell what's wrong," Addams said.

Addams specialized in a bizarre brand of comedy founded on the inexplicable in nature and the antisocial in humanity. In one disconcerting cartoon, a skin diver comes across a giant bathtub plug (with chain) in the bottom of the ocean. In another, vultures perch in a tree at the edge of a precipice on top of which a sign reads, "Lover's Leap." Waiting in the delivery room, a cloaked and beady-eyed bald man with tiny, fanglike teeth is told by the nurse, "Congratulations—it's a baby." Addams's children often engage in fiendish amusements. In a shop class where boys are making birdhouses, one child is putting the finishing touches on a small coffin. The same boy is shown on another occasion in a bathroom, reaching up to the medicine cabinet to dip an arrow in a bottle marked "Poison." Addams's drawing style is individualistic but unassertive. His people are all a little stout and dumpy-looking. And a wash shrouds virtually every one of his pictures in somber (not to say menacing) tones of gray.

Holding up for examination all sorts of morbid and vaguely sinister curiosities, his cartoons evince the repressed violence that lurks within average people everywhere. Writer Wolcott Gibbs saw Addams's cartoons as "essentially a denial of all spiritual and physical evolution in the human race" (foreword, *Addams and Evil*). Said John Mason Brown (*Saturday Review*): "His is a goblin world of bats, spiders, broomsticks, snakes, cobwebs, and bloodletting morons in which every day is Hallowe'en." Addams maintained that he arrived at his aberrant ideas simply by observing people.

Addams's sense of humor was so distinctive that an Addams cartoon could achieve its comic effect just by being an Addams cartoon. In one such creation, a man is watching television and drinking from what seems to be an ordinary soft drink bottle. His wife, who has just returned home and is standing in the doorway to the room, has asked a question to which the man replies, "I got it out of the refrigerator. Why?" The mere fact that Addams concocted this cartoon suggests that the bottle must contain something more depraved than a soft drink.

Addams admitted to a youthful interest in drawing skeletons and in roaming cemeteries, but apart from playing an occasional practical joke, his childhood, he insisted, was normal and healthy. Once he achieved fame as a cartoonist he sometimes sought notoriety as well, appearing at costume parties in odd robes (calling himself "a defrocked ghoul") or pedaling a child's tricycle while smoking a cigar. On camping trips he drove a van that he called "the Heap," the interior of which was outfitted with dignified plush furniture, a stuffed partridge, and a stuffed grackle. It is somehow fitting that he collected medieval arms and armor, which he displayed in his home. He also enjoyed owning and driving vintage automobiles and sports cars.

During World War II, Addams served in the Army Signal Corps, illustrating manuals and making animated training films. He was married three times and divorced twice: first, to Barbara Day, a former model (1943–1951); then to Barbara Barb (1954–1956); and finally to Marilyn Matthews Miller. Their wedding in 1980 was held in a cemetery for pets. The bride wore a black dress and carried a black feather fan, saying that the groom "likes black and thought it would be nice and cheerful."

In the 1940s Addams created the family of diabolical mien for which he is most remembered. Inmates of a gloomy, gothicky Victorian pile that Gibbs called a "secret, dark and midnight manse," they include a necromantic Peter Lorre–like husband and his wife, a spindle-shanked "glamour ghoul" with lank locks and chalk-white skin in a hearse-black gown that melts into the floor; their children, an undernourished girl with six toes on one foot and a little fat boy who foments explosives and poisons with his chemistry set; a hag witch of a grandmother; and the family retainer, a looming Frankensteinian butler. In one of their most celebrated appearances, the family is on the roof of their house, poised to reward a band of Christmas carolers below by tipping onto them a caldron of what appears to be boiling oil. This ensemble became the touchstone Addams cartoon and created a pervasive image. "An Addams house, an Addams family, an Addams situation are archetypes that we see all around us," wrote *New York Times* art critic John Russell; and Addams, Russell said, was "an American landmark, one of the few by which one and all have learned to steer." Addams died in New York City.

• Addams's cartoons are reprinted in *New Yorker* anthologies of drawings and in collections: *Drawn and Quartered* (1942), *Addams and Evil* (1947), *Monster Rally* (1950), *Home Bodies* (1954), *Nightcrawlers* (1957), *Dear Dead Days* (1959), *Black Maria* (1960), *The Groaning Board* (1964), *The Charles Addams Mother Goose* (1967), *My Crowd* (1970), *Favorite Haunts* (1976), *Creature Comforts* (1982), and a posthumous compilation, *The World of Charles Addams* (1991). Most of the details of Addams's life are recapitulated in the obituary in the *New York Times*, 30 Sept. 1988. Additional information can be found in the *New York Star Magazine*, 19 Sept. 1948, p. 5; the *Saturday Review of Literature*, 11 Nov. 1950, p. 25; and Brendan Gill, *Here at the New Yorker* (1975). His famous family of lovable monsters was made into a television series, "The Addams Family," which ran from 1966 to 1968.

ROBERT C. HARVEY

ADDAMS, Jane (6 Sept. 1860–21 May 1935), social reformer and peace activist, was the daughter of John Huy Addams, a businessman and Republican politician, and Sarah Weber. Born on the eve of the Civil War in the small farming community of Cedarville, just outside Freeport, in northern Illinois, she was the youngest of five children, four of whom were girls. Her mother died during pregnancy when Jane was two years old. The Addams family was the wealthiest, most respected family in the community. Jane's father owned the local grain mill, was president of the Second National Bank of Freeport, had interests in a local railroad and a local insurance company, taught Sunday School, and was active in local Bible societies. A founding member of the Republican party and supporter of Abraham Lincoln, he was elected to the Illinois State Senate as a Republican in 1854 and served in that capacity until 1870. In 1868 John Addams married Anna Haldeman, a widow with two sons and pretensions to gentility. Under her parents' tutelage, Jane Addams acquired liberal principles regarding individual rights and republican principles regarding community responsibility, and she grew up believing that both Christian ethics and the arts were key civilizing agents.

As a student at Rockford Female Seminary between 1877 and 1881, Addams was among the first generation of college-educated women in the United States. She was an exemplary student and a charismatic campus leader, serving as class president all four years, editor of the school magazine, president of the literary society, and valedictorian. Ultimately, Addams was the first student to receive a bachelor's degree from Rockford, an event that marked the school's transition to collegiate status. Rockford's pious, missionary atmosphere only deepened Addams's own skepticism about formal Christianity and strengthened her desire for a career in community service. In the 1880s schoolteaching and missionary work were the two main occupations open to women seeking a public role, but Addams was not interested in teaching or proselytizing. For eight years after graduation in 1881, she struggled to define a secular life mission in a society with little use for educated women and in a family that expected its youngest daughter to serve at home. During those difficult years, Addams developed a close friendship with Ellen Gates Starr, a former Rockford student, traveled extensively in Europe, and gradually came to understand the tension women faced between what she would later call the "family claim" and the "social claim."

Addams's travels during the 1880s, in conjunction with her immersion in the social philosophy of John Ruskin and her exposure to London's premier settlement house, Toynbee Hall, inspired her to open a settlement house in Chicago, a city that exemplified the industrial, urban problems of the late nineteenth century. In partnership with Starr, she rented a rundown mansion that had been built in the 1850s by Charles Hull. At first, all financial support for the Hull-House settlement derived from income on the $50,000 estate Addams inherited on her father's death in 1881, but eventually Hull-House benefited from the sponsorship of wealthy women in Chicago who became Addams's allies in civic reform. Hull-House expanded over an entire square block at Halsted and Polk streets, encompassing thirteen different buildings that encircled a playground for the neighborhood's children. Hull-House was the second settlement house to open in the United States, and of the four hundred settlement houses opened around the country before World War I, it was by far the most famous, most influential, and most innovative.

The rapid expansion of programs offered at Hull-House during the 1890s mirrored the rapid development of Jane Addams's own thinking about the purpose of a settlement house. Influenced by Ruskin and Toynbee Hall and inspired by Thomas Carlyle's elitist philosophy that the rich had a duty to the lower classes, Addams and Starr originally envisioned the settlement as a place where educated women could share their knowledge of art and literature with the working poor.

Soon after opening Hull-House, however, Addams and Starr came to understand that the project's success depended less on poetry readings than on the provision of very practical social services, including a daycare center for the children of working mothers and English literacy classes for those seeking U.S. citizenship. After only three years on Halsted Street, Addams was able to describe the evolution of her mission. In two lectures, "The Subjective Necessity for Social Settlements" and "The Objective Value of the Social Settlement," she set forth her growing conviction that the value of the neighborhood settlement house lay in its "flexibility, its power of quick adaptation, its readiness to change its methods as its environment may demand." Addams saw Hull-House less as an agent of cultural uplift than as "an information and interpretation bureau." She insisted that the settlement should have a "sterner and more enduring aspect" than mere philanthropy. She saw the provision of legal services, visiting nurses, a meeting place for ethnic clubs and labor unions, a boarding house for working girls, and a group of middle-class residents ready to mediate between neighbors and the city bureaucracy as evidence that Hull-House was a "commission merchant," the middle agent uniting a cross section of Chicago residents around common civic goals.

Addams never abandoned her liberal faith in the power of the individual and never doubted her republican belief in the individual's responsibility to the community, but contact with her neighbors on Halsted Street shifted her focus from social stewardship by an elite to political and economic empowerment of all members of the community. Her interest in the contemporary philosophy of pragmatism increased with her experience; elitism, she found, was not effective in achieving social reform. "Democracy," wrote Addams in 1902, must be regarded "not merely as a sentiment . . . but as that which affords a rule of living as well as a test of faith." For this reason, she insisted, "the only cure for the ills of Democracy is more Democracy."

The depression of 1893 and the Pullman strike of 1894, coinciding with the arrival of Florence Kelley as a resident at Hull-House, served to sharpen Addams's definition of her mission. During the 1890s and 1900s, Addams encouraged Hull-House residents to expand beyond direct service to the neighborhood and to lobby the city and state for improved sanitation, factory legislation, municipal playgrounds and citywide kindergartens, a juvenile court system, and enforcement of antiprostitution and antidrug laws. In this way Hull-House participated in the Progressive Era's redefinition of the role of government in a democratic, capitalist society.

Sponsorship of *Hull-House Maps and Papers*, an innovative social survey of the conditions in the settlement's immigrant neighborhood published in 1895, was just the beginning of Addams's involvement with the era's growing enthusiasm for social science. She was closely aligned with faculty members at the University of Chicago, especially John Dewey, Sophonisba Breckenridge, and Edith Abbott, and played an active role in the founding of the School of Social Work at that institution. Addams opposed the idea that social science should only investigate, not advocate. In her view, a settlement house should not be a "sociological laboratory" in which people were studied but rather a source of "data for legislation" and a means to help "secure it."

Mediation was the keynote of both Addams's political ideology and her leadership style. From adolescence on, she insisted on cooperation and compromise in her personal and public relationships. She welded her experience as the peacemaker in a family of volatile personalities together with her reading of Leo Tolstoy, Ralph Waldo Emerson, Henry David Thoreau, and other "non-resistant" thinkers. "The most outstanding fact in the temperament of Miss Addams," said her contemporary Floyd Dell, was her "passion of conciliation." She became the first among equals in progressive circles not by argument but by consensus-building. This was as true in her writing as it was in her daily negotiations with political and business leaders. In nearly a dozen books, hundreds of articles, and thousands of speeches, Addams disarmed opponents by presuming general agreement with her views. She could be harsh in her description of social problems, but her tone changed in discussing solutions. There, her method was to ignore conflict, to assume shared principles, and to foresee a harmonious outcome. She spoke and acted as though maximum participation by all involved in any given social problem would elicit a spirit of cooperation, that a negotiated settlement would inevitably derive from the democratic climate of goodwill, and that this process would inevitably result in justice.

Addams's determination to always stake out the high ground of arbitration occasionally caused problems. In 1894 she was frozen out of attempts to end the Pullman strike when George Pullman refused all pleas for arbitration. In 1898 she naively thought she could lead a high-minded challenge to the political power of her local ward boss without becoming soiled by electoral mudslinging. As a member of the Chicago school board in the early 1900s, she alienated the city's teachers by attempting a compromise on their meager salaries. In these and similarly polarized situations, Addams's reluctance to take sides earned her more enmity than respect. In other cases, however, she was regarded by all parties as the quintessential honest broker whose commitment to fairness lent credibility to a variety of progressive efforts at civic cooperation.

At the peak of her popularity in the years between 1909 and 1915, Addams became the first woman president of the National Conference of Charities and Correction (later the National Conference of Social Work), a vice president of the National-American Woman Suffrage Association and pro-suffrage columnist for the *Ladies' Home Journal*, a founding member of the National Association for the Advancement of Colored People, and the author of six books, including her bestselling autobiography, *Twenty Years at Hull-House* (1910).

Addams made an uncharacteristically partisan foray into national politics in 1912 when she supported Theodore Roosevelt for president on the Progressive party ticket. Roosevelt endorsed the domestic platform put forth by the National Conference of Charities and Correction, and Addams agreed to deliver the seconding speech at the Progressive party convention. The campaign tested Addams's commitment to compromise because her social welfare agenda had to coexist with Roosevelt's racism, militarism, and approval of big business.

Three years later Addams and Roosevelt were bitter opponents in the national debate over U.S. participation in the Great War in Europe. Ironically, it was her firm belief in arbitration that ultimately forced Addams to take an uncompromising stand on this public issue. She was among the small handful of American intellectuals and activists who refused to support U.S. participation in World War I, disdaining what she later called the "pathetic belief in the regenerative results of war." She viewed the war as a twofold threat to human evolution: it halted progress toward civilized methods of conflict resolution and it diverted resources away from community projects and toward military spending. For the sake of pacifism, Addams sacrificed her popularity. Newspaper editors and politicians denounced her as a traitor and a fool. Teddy Roosevelt, her old ally in the Progressive party, dismissed her as a "Bull Mouse." During the war Addams chaired the Woman's Peace party and an International Congress of Women at The Hague in April 1915. Following that conference of one thousand women from twelve nations, Addams led an international delegation of women in a tour of all the warring nations, meeting with heads of state and attempting to mediate a peace. After the war Addams and her colleagues in the women's peace movement supported the League of Nations and, in 1919, formed the Women's International League for Peace and Freedom, of which Addams was the first president.

Before World War I, Addams had been the most famous and most respected American woman of her day. In 1906 the British labor leader John Burns called her "the only saint America has produced." In 1912 the *Philadelphia North American* called her "probably the most widely beloved of her sex in all the world." In 1913 the Twilight Club of New York asked three thousand "representative Americans" to name America's most socially useful Americans and Addams was listed first on over half of the ballots. That same year, the *Independent* asked its readers, "who among our contemporaries are of the most value to the community?" In that poll Addams came in second to Thomas Edison. As a result of her pacifism during the war, however, Addams's public image was transformed from saint to villain, and during the reactionary 1920s, many conservatives in the United States regarded her as a dangerous radical with suspicious ties to subversives.

During the last fifteen years of her life the criticisms of Addams darkened but did not defeat her political activism. She continued to lead Hull-House but spent increasing amounts of time and energy on international peace efforts. In her capacity as president of the Women's International League for Peace and Freedom she traveled often to Europe and Asia, meeting with a wide variety of diplomats and civic leaders and reiterating her Victorian belief in women's special mission to preserve peace. Recognition of these efforts came with a gradual thaw in the U.S. political climate, and by the late 1920s Addams had regained her stature as a beloved public figure. The culmination of this restoration came with the award of the Nobel Peace Prize to Addams in 1931. As the first U.S. woman to win the prize, Addams was applauded for her "expression of an essentially American democracy of spirit."

Age and ill health prevented Addams from playing an active role in the New Deal, but she did serve on the Chicago advisory committee of the housing division of the Public Works Administration and was one of the vice presidents of the American Association of Social Security. She was dismayed by the depression's widespread poverty but welcomed the opportunity it provided to expand public responsibility for the common welfare.

Addams died of cancer in Chicago, ten days after a banquet in Washington celebrating the Women's International League for Peace and Freedom and its founder. Thousands attended her funeral in the courtyard of Hull-House and agreed with Walter Lippmann's editorial eulogy declaring her career "the ultimate vindication of the democratic faith."

• The most extensive collection of primary materials on Addams can be found in *The Jane Addams Papers*, ed. Mary Lynn McCree Bryan (1985). These eighty-two reels of microfilm include Jane Addams's correspondence and records from her various organizational affiliations. Addams's own published works not mentioned above include *Democracy and Social Ethics* (1902), *The Spirit of Youth and the City Streets* (1909), *A New Conscience and an Ancient Evil* (1912), *The Long Road of Woman's Memory* (1916), *Peace and Bread in Time of War* (1922; repr. 1960), *The Second Twenty Years at Hull-House* (1930), *The Excellent Becomes the Permanent* (1932), and *Jane Addams: A Centennial Reader* (1960).

The best existing biography of Jane Addams is Allen F. Davis's *American Heroine: The Life and Legend of Jane Addams* (1973). The authorized biography by her nephew, James Weber Linn, *Jane Addams* (1935), contains interesting anecdotes, and John C. Farrell's *Beloved Lady* (1967) offers useful insights on Addams's political ideology. *100 Years at Hull-House*, a collection of observations and recollections of life in the settlement on Halsted Street, has been intelligently edited by Allen F. Davis and Mary Lynn McCree Bryan (1990). Christopher Lasch's observations on Addams in *The New Radicalism in America, 1889–1963: The Intellectual as Social Type* (1965) still bear consideration, as do his introductions to Addams's writings in *The Social Thought of Jane Addams* (1965). Anne Firor Scott's introduction to the 1964 reprint of Addams's *Democracy and Social Ethics* (1902) remains among the best essays on Addams's character and career.

Commentary on various aspects of Jane Addams's career can be found in Kathryn Kish Sklar, "Hull-House in the 1890's: A Community of Women Reformers," *Signs* 10 (Summer 1985); Mary Jo Deegan, *Jane Addams and the Men of the Chicago School, 1892–1918* (1988); Rivka Lissak, *Pluralism and Progressives: Hull House and the New Immigrants, 1890–1919* (1989); and Harriet Hyman Alonso, *Peace as a Women's Issue: A History of the U.S. Movement for World Peace and Women's Rights* (1993). An obituary and tributes to Addams are in the *New York Times*, 22 and 23 May 1935.

VICTORIA BISSELL BROWN

ADDERLEY, Cannonball (15 Sept. 1928–8 Aug. 1975), jazz saxophonist, was born Julian Edwin Adderley in Tampa, Florida, the son of Julian Carlyle Adderley, a high school guidance counselor and jazz cornet player, and Jessie Johnson, an elementary school teacher. The family moved to Tallahassee, where Adderley attended Florida Agricultural and Mechanical College High School from 1941 until 1944. He earned his bachelor's degree from Florida A & M in 1948, having studied reed and brass instruments with band director Leander Kirksey and forming, with Kirksey, a school jazz ensemble. He then worked as band director at Dillard High School in Fort Lauderdale, Florida, and jobbed with his own jazz group.

Adderley served in the army from 1950 until 1953, leading the 36th Army Dance Band, to which his younger brother, cornetist Nathaniel "Nat" Adderley, was also assigned. While stationed in Washington, D.C., in 1952, Adderley continued to play with his own group and furthered his musical studies at the U.S. Naval School of Music. Assigned to Fort Knox, Kentucky, he again led an army dance band. After his discharge, he returned to Fort Lauderdale to continue as the high school band director and as a jobbing musician.

Encouraged by singer and saxophonist Eddie "Cleanhead" Vinson, he moved to New York in 1955. After sitting in with Oscar Pettiford at the Cafe Bohemia, he so impressed fellow musicians that he was asked to join Pettiford's band. Almost immediately, he signed a recording contract with EmArcy. These early recordings display the influence of altoists Charlie Parker and Benny Carter. Although the bebop influence led Adderley to play long and sometimes highly chromatic solo lines, his deeply rooted interest in gospel and modern blues helped him create a distinctive voice.

In January 1956 Nat and Cannonball formed a quintet that toured nationally until 1957, when Cannonball joined the Miles Davis quintet. When tenor saxophonist John Coltrane was added, this ensemble of trumpeter Davis, Adderley, Coltrane, bassist Paul Chambers, drummer Philly Joe Jones, and both Bill Evans and Red Garland on piano, became the most influential group in jazz. The spectacular recordings where Adderley and Coltrane vie for dominance, such as 1958's "Dr. Jekyll," and the modal jazz improvisations of the *Kind of Blue* session of 1959, such as "So What?," are recognized jazz masterpieces. This latter session introduced a new style, establishing modal jazz, improvisation based on a succession of scales rather than a progression of harmonies, as one of the mainstream techniques in jazz from that time forward.

In late 1959 Adderley left Davis and re-formed a quintet with his brother, Nat. This group, with changing rhythm section personnel and the occasional addition of a second saxophonist (first Yusef Lateef and later Charles Lloyd), continued until Adderley's death and enjoyed considerable popular and critical success. Influenced by both the work of Ornette Coleman in the early 1960s and the technological advances of electronic instruments that became a part of jazz shortly thereafter, the new Adderley brothers' ensemble played a fusion of bebop, modal jazz, rock, and free jazz elements, sometimes called "Soul Jazz," that carried them on the crest of one avant-garde jazz wave of the 1960s. Their Jazz Workshop sessions, recorded live in San Francisco in 1962, display an early stage of this development, and their 1966 live album, *Mercy, Mercy, Mercy!*, which reflects this style, became one of the bestselling jazz records to that time. Their music appealed to fans of rock 'n' roll as well as to those of modern jazz, and the ensemble's tours often drew huge crowds, not only in the United States but in Japan, East and West Europe, and Great Britain. Speaking of his music, Adderley was quoted in 1966 as saying: "I'm aware that jazz is changing, and I have listened to and absorbed many influences. I feel that Ornette Coleman was a most important force. However, what I play today is a logical development of my own style."

Adderley married actress Olga James in 1962. In the late 1960s he added soprano saxophone as a regular solo instrument in his performances. His mature playing was a masterful combination of elements: lessons learned from Charlie Parker, associations with Miles Davis, John Coltrane, and keyboardist Joe Zawinul, and a natural affinity for black soul and gospel music. His solo lines and incisive sound were charged with an unerring sense of direction, a dazzling improvisatory technique, and a sense of timbral exploration married to a "down home" feel for the blues. While on tour, before his forty-seventh birthday, he suffered a stroke and died several weeks later in a hospital in Gary, Indiana.

Adderley's legacy is twofold: as a creative and compelling jazz artist of the later 1950s through the mid-1970s, and as an influential spokesperson for this music and the black community as well. He served as a committee member for the National Endowment for the Arts, was a member of the Black Academy of Arts and Letters, and also served on the jazz advisory panel of the John F. Kennedy Center for the Performing Arts. He hosted thirteen weeks of a television series, "90 Minutes"; appeared in a few motion pictures, including *Play Misty for Me* (1971), *Soul to Soul* (1971), and *Save the Children* (1973); made guest playing appearances on several television shows; and participated in many college workshops and seminars.

Among Adderley's honors are the Julian Cannonball Adderley Artist in Residence Program at Harvard University, and several *Down Beat*, *Playboy*, and *Encyclopedia of Jazz* All Star and Poll Awards. Among his important and representative recordings are *Presenting Cannonball Adderley* (1955), *Somethin' Else* (1958), Miles Davis's *Milestones* (1958) and *Kind of Blue* (1959), *Mercy, Mercy, Mercy!* (1966), *Country Preacher* (1969), and *Inside Straight* (1973). A posthumously issued recording, *Big Man* (1975), composed jointly with his brother, Nat, was based on the legend of John Henry with blues singer Joe Williams in the title role. Adderley considered this one of the major achievements of his career. Among his many jazz compositions, several have entered the repertory as standards including "Sack O' Woe," "Domination," "Sermonette," and "Them Dirty Blues."

Speaking of Adderley in 1993, Nat Adderley reflected: "I believe that a large part of what Cannonball did musically might have been missed or overlooked at the time he did it, because the concept of critical analysis of the music at that time was based more on alleged 'European concepts' than on the total impact of what the music was. So it has only been in the last few years . . . that there has been a lot more consideration, a lot more interest, in what Cannonball did as students now study the solos. It has become much more evident that Cannonball was far superior in many areas than he was originally given credit for . . . many of the critics, I think, did not understand the infusion of Southern black gospel music and blues into what they considered a hallowed European classical tradition."

• Adderley's papers, scores, and memorabilia are in the Black Archives Research Center of Florida Agricultural and Mechanical University in Tallahassee. Oral History material and recordings are preserved at the Institute of Jazz Studies of Rutgers University in Newark, N.J. Adderley's recordings are extensive, and the most complete listing of his published recordings with full discographical details may be found in W. van Eyle, "Cannonball Adderley's Discografie," *Jazz Press*, nos. 37, 38, 40, and 43 (1977). There are many interviews and popular journal articles about Adderley, and he contributed one article to the *Jazz Review* 3, no. 4 (1960), "Paying Dues: The Education of a Combo Leader." There are few critical studies to date. The best and most useful are David Baker, *The Jazz Style of Cannonball Adderley: A Musical and Historical Perspective* (1980), which includes transcriptions, and Barry Kernfeld, "Adderley, Coltrane, and Davis at the Twilight of Bebop: The Search for Melodic Coherence (1958–59)" (Ph.D. diss., Cornell Univ., 1981). An obituary is in the *New York Times*, 9 Aug. 1975.

FRANK TIRRO

ADDICKS, John Edward O'Sullivan (21 Nov. 1841–7 Aug. 1919), promoter and aspiring politician, was born in Philadelphia, Pennsylvania, the son of John Edward Addicks, a politician and civil servant, and Margaretta McLeod. Addicks's father achieved local political prominence and arranged for his son to take a job at age fifteen as a runner for a local dry goods business. Four years later Addicks took a job with a flour company and, upon reaching his twenty-first birthday, became a full partner in the business. Like many Quaker City merchants, Addicks speculated in local real estate in the booming port town, avoided service in the Civil War, and achieved a modicum of prosperity in the postwar period. He became overextended, as he would be most of his career, however, and went broke in the 1873 depression.

In 1869 he married Laura Butcher of Philadelphia, with whom he would have one child. They moved to Claymont, Delaware, where he again dabbled in the flour business and introduced Minnesota spring wheat to the local farmers. He also speculated in railroad securities and took an interest in a new industry of producing water gas, an illuminant composed of carbon monoxide and hydrogen and manufactured using steam and incandescent coke. He promoted the construction of such facilities, and as the nation emerged from the depression he built gas works in Brooklyn, Chicago, and Jersey City. He picked up the techniques of "stock jobbing" (selling stocks) and made a great deal of money through contract and stock manipulations. His gas works depended on local political support, and Addicks became adept at wending his way through the thickets of urban politics. In 1882 he created what became known as the Chicago Gas Trust, and two years later he organized and became president of the Bay State Gas Company in Boston. His shady deals, stock transactions, and high living caused a sensation in the national press, and Addicks was soon known as "Gas Addicks" and the "Napoleon of Gas." In 1886 he moved to Boston and deeded his Claymont house to his wife, who later deeded it, on his recommendation, to Mrs. Ida Carr Wilson, with whom Addicks had a romantic attachment. Six years later in 1892, Addicks bought the Brooklyn Gas Company and became its president. By the early 1890s he had an estimated worth of between $10 million and $20 million.

In the late 1880s Addicks developed a raging desire to represent Delaware in the U.S. Senate. Upon returning in 1888 from Russia, where he had speculated in that country's railroads, he read that the Delaware state legislature was deadlocked over choosing a new senator. Addicks conferred with his Boston political representative and on 1 January 1889 held a news conference at the Hotel Richardson in Dover. Addicks appeared on his inaugural outing attired in a silk high hat and a fur overcoat, raiment that occasioned a stir in the state's political circles, and announced he was a candidate for the Senate seat. Establishing his headquarters at Mrs. Wilson's house, for seventeen years he pursued his dream at a cost of an estimated $3 million. He lost the 1889 election but set about building a Republican political faction that was loyal to his cause.

Addicks approached politics as he did business; he tried to buy what he wanted. Because he could not purchase the Delaware state legislature, he worked to elect new legislators who were friendly to his interests. Delaware law stipulated that no citizen could vote without exhibiting a paid-tax receipt, and many poor citizens, who were in arrears, lost their franchise. Addicks traveled through the state and paid taxes for people in return for their promise to vote for legislators who supported his election to the senate. The poor proved a potent political force in Delaware, and Addicks soon built up a political faction, the Union Republicans, that brought him close to his goal. In 1895 he tried for the senate seat in the state legislature, and four years later he received a plurality. Unable to win, Addicks's forces prevented the election of anyone else. In the Fifty-sixth Congress from 1899 to 1901, the state had only one senator, and in the next it had no representation in the Senate at all. Addicks's ability to wreak political mischief ended in 1906 when the du

Pont family united the Republican party and captured a large majority in the state legislature; Addicks received just two votes for the Senate that year.

Addicks's fortunes began to wane in the decade of the 1890s. Henry H. Rogers of Standard Oil started a competing gas company in Boston, won the political allegiance of the city fathers, and almost bankrupted Addicks. Although Addicks retained his flamboyant lifestyle and his Claymont estate, Delaware stock farm, Philadelphia town house, New York City apartment in the Knickerbocker and suite in the Hotel Imperial, as well as his impressive steam yacht, the *Now-Then*, his resources were dwindling. Ironically, Addicks was ruined by a speculation he made with Rogers in his attempt to corner the world's copper markets with his Amalgamated Copper Company in 1899. Backed by the great Standard Oil wealth, Rogers convinced numerous rich, knowing investors, and speculators to buy into his scheme. Addicks became involved when his broker, Thomas W. Lawson, took an interest in the company. Rogers and his friends, who included William Rockefeller, made the mistake of not bringing the largest Michigan copper producer, Calumet & Hecla, into the combine, and as new copper discoveries were made in the United States, Amalgamated's share of the nation's copper industry fell. The decline in the value of the company's stocks wiped out what remained of Addicks's fortune.

Addicks's private affairs fared little better. Earlier he had married his late wife's sister, Rosalie Butcher, and in 1894 she sued him for divorce, naming Mrs. Wilson as co-respondent. Addicks contested the divorce but then withdrew his opposition and later married Mrs. Wilson. After his large losses in Amalgamated Copper, his Boston gas interests went bankrupt, and its shareholders demanded an investigation of fraud. A federal court found against Addicks in 1907 and ordered that he repay the Bay State Gas Company $4 million. He went into hiding and was later found in a dingy Hoboken tenement without heat or light. He fled again and was finally found in 1913. Taken into custody, he posted $2,000 bail and promptly forfeited it. He died in New York City.

Addicks was typical of an American breed of capitalists who rose from modest circumstances, made a great deal of money quickly through shady stock manipulations, spent lavishly and associated with other newly rich, became politically ambitious, and just as quickly disappeared from view. Addicks was a plunger, an inveterate liar, and a schemer who, through dint of his persuasive personality, reams of publicity, and a mock earnestness, bent others to do his will. Like many American businessmen in the late nineteenth century, he believed that everything in politics, business, and friendship had a price and that with money he could achieve success and happiness, a philosophy that led to his ruin.

• The major sources of information on Addicks are contemporary newspapers and periodicals. George Kennan's series, "Holding Up a State: The True Story of Addicks and Delaware," *Outlook*, 7, 14, and 21 Feb. 1903, blends Addicks's political career with a smattering of personal information. See also the progressive diatribes against Addicks in the *Nation*, 31 Aug. 1905, pp. 177–78, and 28 Mar. 1901, pp. 248–49. Obituaries are in the *New York Sun*, *New York Herald*, and the *New York Times*, 8 Aug. 1919.

JAMES A. WARD

ADE, George (9 Feb. 1866–16 May 1944), humorist, was born in Kentland, Indiana, the son of John Ade, a farmer and bank cashier who was from England, and Adaline Wardell Bush. Ade liked his village school and showed promise in composition classes, hated the farm work his parents assigned him to help with family finances, and received a partial scholarship to attend Purdue, the newly established agricultural and mechanical college in Lafayette, Indiana. His four years there (1883–1887) were both enjoyable and valuable. He studied with reasonable conscientiousness, joined a literary society and the Sigma Chi social fraternity, edited for a semester the student-run monthly literary magazine called the *Purdue*, and attended operas in Lafayette, especially delighting in Gilbert and Sullivan productions.

Armed with a B.S., Ade spent a few weeks reading for the law in a Lafayette firm, became a local newspaper reporter (1888), wrote patent-medicine ads, lost the only serious love of his life to a ministerial rival, and was persuaded by his Purdue friend John Tinney McCutcheon to join him in newspaper work in Chicago (1890). McCutcheon was a cartoonist for the *Chicago Morning News* (called the *Record* from 1893). Ade soon proved his genius at converting human-interest stories—about "shop-girls and stray dogs and cable-car conductors"—into lightly satirical humor. His exuberant vignettes of visitors to the Columbian Exposition (1893) led to a daily column called "Stories of the Streets and of the Town" (ending in 1900), illustrated by McCutcheon. Selections of these columns were issued as paperbacks beginning in 1894. Meanwhile, more dramatic assignments included Ade's reporting on the bloody Homestead steel strike near Pittsburgh and the Sullivan-Corbett prizefight in New Orleans, both in 1892.

In 1895 Ade and McCutcheon were assigned to Europe; traveling throughout the British Isles and the Continent, they mailed two illustrated, human-interest travel columns a week to the *Record*. Home again, Ade published his first two books, both outgrowths of his newspaper columns. *Artie* (1896) is about a brash Chicago office boy who sports city-slicker slang—"large juicy con talk." *Pink Marsh* (1897) stars a Chicago bootblack who calls himself a "culled lad" and is shrewd, voluble, and informative—and victimized. Although it was another Ade success, the book now seems full of dated stereotypes.

Ade began the first of his innumerable fables in slang in September 1897. Incredibly popular, these columns feature lively dialogue, deadpan clichés, on-target humor, capitalized words, and mock-serious moral tags (for example, "One cannot Rest except after steady Practice"). The moral of one of Ade's best early fables, "The Fable of the Caddy Who Hurt His Head Thinking," in which a lad contrasts rich duffers at golf with his impoverished father at his lumberyard job, is a terse "Don't try to Account for Anything." Ade returned to Europe in 1898 and later visited the Philippines, China, and Japan (1900), by which time he had published three more popular works, *Doc' Horne: A Story of the Streets and Town* (1899), *Fables in Slang* (1899), and *More Fables* (1900). Bright, bald, and white-bearded old Doc' Horne, in his cheap hotel room, spins didactic and incompletely credible yarns concerning his friends, antics, and sorrows. Ade's columns of fables went into syndication beginning in 1900. *Forty Modern Fables* soon followed (1901).

By 1900 Ade was at a crossroads. He could continue to make money by remaining slick, or he could experiment with realistic fiction, as critics such as William Dean Howells were urging him to do. Even as he continued to assemble old columns into new books, he made his choice, which was to write clever but ephemeral Broadway and on-tour hits. Of his fourteen plays, the best were his libretto for *The Sultan of Sulu* (1902, a Gilbert and Sullivan takeoff), *The County Chairman* (1903, a political satire set in what Ade called "a decidedly one-horse town"), and *The College Widow* (1904, America's first drama about college life). *The Sho-Gun* (1904, a musical comedy satirizing American social and commercial activities in the Far East), proved less successful.

But by then Ade was rich. He already owned Indiana farmland approaching $1 million in value. In 1904 he added to it by buying a 2,400-acre estate at Brook, Indiana, near Kentland. He named the place "Hazelden" and entertained lavishly, inviting as many as 8,000 guests at a time. He also continued to travel, once to Egypt (1905), and to pour out more books. One, *In Pastures New* (1906), contains travel sketches satirizing American tourists abroad in the manner of Mark Twain, who admired him enormously. Another, *The Slim Princess* (1907), his only novel, skewers mythical-principality fiction so sharply that John McCutcheon's brother George Barr McCutcheon, whose *Graustark: The Story of Love behind a Throne* (1901) started the fad, stopped attending Ade's fetes at Hazelden.

Ade was a full-time journalist for little more than a decade and a dazzling playwright for far less. In the long period following the peak of his popularity, he remained easygoing and generous and was much honored. He was a delegate to the Republican National Convention (1908), was elected to membership in the National Institute of Arts and Letters (1908), served as a Purdue trustee (1908–1915) and grand consul of Sigma Chi (1909), and was a member of the Indiana State Council of Defense (1917–1918). He wrote three movie scripts, *Our Leading Citizen* (1922), *Back Home and Broke* (1922), and *Woman Proof* (1923), and helped finance Purdue's Ross-Ade Stadium (1923–1924). In his essay "The Joys of Single Blessedness" (1922), he describes his delight in lifelong bachelorhood. An autobiographical sketch (1933) follows up with this: "My enthusiasms include golf, travel, horse-racing and the spoken drama. My antipathies are social show-offs, bigots on religion, fanatics on total abstinence, and all persons who take themselves seriously." Ade might have added that for decades he described what he saw in ways that made millions recognize themselves and laugh.

George Ade, who died at Brook, Indiana, was a vernacular storyteller of the cracker-barrel type, whose misspellings and oddly capitalized words are so tedious to modern readers that they often wrongly ignore the value of his satirical jibes. Along with other middle-American humorists, the best of whom included Finley Peter Dunne, Irvin Shrewsbury Cobb, and Will Rogers, Ade ridiculed deviations from professed American norms so gently that his readers often fail to appreciate his corrective bitterness.

• Ade's papers are widely scattered in more than fifty repositories. Most, however, are located at the Purdue University library, West Lafayette, Ind., which has more than 400 of his manuscripts, more than 1,800 of his letters, and more than 2,000 letters to him. A few manuscripts and some memorabilia may be seen at the George Ade Hazelden Home, at Brook, Ind. Dorothy Ritter Russo, *A Bibliography of George Ade, 1866–1944* (1947), lists approximately 2,500 items by Ade and countless items about him and is definitive through 1945. *Letters of George Ade* (1973) is superbly annotated by Terence Tobin. An abridgment of Ade's autobiographical sketch is in Stanley J. Kunitz, ed., *Authors Today and Yesterday: A Companion Volume to Living Authors* (1933), pp. 8–9. Jean Shepherd, ed., *The America of George Ade (1866–1944): Fables, Short Stories, Essays* (1961), and A. L. Lazarus, ed., *The Best of George Ade* (1985), contain representative works and are informatively presented. Carl Van Doren, *Many Minds* (1924), pp. 18–33, praises Ade as Indiana's Aesop and "a satirist of genius." Fred C. Kelly, *George Ade, Warmhearted Satirist* (1947), is a loving study by a friend. Lee Coyle, *George Ade* (1964), provides competent biographical details and rollicking commentary. James DeMuth, *Small Town Chicago: The Comic Perspectives of Finley Peter Dunne, George Ade, and Ring Lardner* (1979), places Ade between two peers. An obituary is in the *New York Times*, 17 May 1944.

ROBERT L. GALE

ADEE, Alvey Augustus (27 Nov. 1842–5 July 1924), diplomat, was born in Astoria, New York, the son of Augustus Adee, a surgeon with the U.S. Navy, and Amelia Kinnaird Graham. Young Alvey grew up in New York City. He lost his father at the age of two, and his mother died when he was still a teenager. A life-threatening case of scarlet fever had left him hard of hearing, an affliction that would worsen with age. Adee never attended college; however, he managed to educate himself through wide readings and extensive travel abroad, becoming an accomplished linguist and an authority on William Shakespeare. He studied for a career in engineering with an uncle, Charles Kinnaird Graham, the surveyor of the Port of New York, before entering a career in foreign affairs in 1869 as private secretary to the minister to Spain, General Daniel E. Sickles, a personal friend and client of another well-connected uncle.

In Spain Adee impressed his superiors with his intelligence, tact, and fluency in Spanish. Meanwhile, he established relationships that would serve him well in later years. Of particular importance was a close and lasting friendship with the secretary of the legation, John Hay, a former secretary to President Abraham Lincoln who would later become secretary of state under Presidents William McKinley and Theodore Roosevelt. After Hay's resignation in 1870, Adee was appointed to fill his post in Madrid. On several occasions Adee acted as chargé d'affaires on an interim basis, and he dealt diplomatically with the pompous, volatile, and indiscreet Minister Sickles. When Caleb Cushing replaced Sickles, Adee remained in his post, serving until 1877. Adee handled his government's business in Madrid with dispatch during a turbulent period in Spain's history, witnessing the downfall of Queen Isabella II, the establishment of a provisional government, a brief two-year reign by King Amadeo I, a short-lived republic, a dictatorship under Marshal Francisco Serrano, and the restoration of the Bourbon family under Alfonso XII. Adee served during the October 1873 *Virginius* affair, a diplomatic crisis that arose when officials in Cuba, then a Spanish colony, captured a ship illegally flying an American flag and executed fifty-three rebels, including three American citizens. Adee was managing the legation in 1876 when New York's William M. "Boss" Tweed, a fugitive from American justice, landed in Spain by way of Cuba under an assumed name. Although the United States had no extradition treaty with the Spanish government, Adee successfully persuaded the local authorities to hand over the notoriously corrupt politician for transport to prison in the United States.

When Adee returned to the United States in August 1877, he briefly contemplated a career in banking. However, President Rutherford B. Hayes located a clerkship for him in the Department of State's offices in Washington. Secretary of State William Evarts placed Adee in a "temporary" position drafting diplomatic correspondence, a task for which he would prove remarkably well suited. Adee soon displayed a talent for diplomacy, which enabled him to withstand the vagaries of partisan politics in a career that would span a half-century and witness six political party changes in the White House. Within a year of his appointment by Hayes, Adee became chief of the Diplomatic Bureau, and in 1882 President Chester A. Arthur named him third assistant secretary of state. In 1885, despite calls for Adee's removal by angry Democratic office seekers, President Grover Cleveland and Secretary of State Thomas F. Bayard retained him and in 1886 promoted him to second assistant secretary, a post he would hold for the next thirty-eight years. Adee deliberately avoided the limelight and worked quietly and effectively behind the scenes. However, during his remarkable tenure he served as acting secretary of state on several occasions, including a four-week period in 1898 during the war with Spain. this critical period, following Secretary of State William R. Day's departure for Paris to serve on the Peace Commission and prior to the arrival of Hay from his post as ambassador in London, proved to be the most visible of Adee's work in the State Department. Furthermore, because of his close personal relationship with Hay, Adee's influence was at its pinnacle from 1898 to 1905. Adee is credited with devising the term "administrative entity" for use by Hay in the Open Door note of 1900 that protested against the dismemberment of China by the European powers. During his long career, Adee was sent to only one overseas conference, an unanticipated assignment to fill in at a meeting in Oslo scheduled for 30 July 1914. Adee was vacationing by riding his bicycle along the byways of France at the time. The assassination of Archduke Ferdinand of Austria on 28 June 1914 by a Serbian radical led to the rapid mobilization of European armies and prevented Adee from crossing the German frontier. The stranded diplomat ended up in the U.S. legation in Copenhagen, where he assisted the anxious staff during the frantic week that preceded the outbreak of World War I.

Adee's language skills, vast knowledge of history, and solid understanding of international law made him indispensable in a State Department staffed by few professional diplomats during the critical decades of U.S. emergence from an isolationist, inward-looking nation to a world power. He wrote and edited thousands of memoranda and documents on issues such as the recognition of new states, neutrality law, most favored nation agreements, and citizenship and nationality issues. In his study, *A Digest of International Law* (1906), American legal scholar John Bassett More cited nearly three hundred documents written by Adee between 1886 and 1905. Possessing the ability to condense complex issues into clear, precise prose, Adee supervised the writing of almost all the department's outgoing dispatches and instructions until the load of diplomatic correspondence became too great for any one individual to handle during World War I. Occasionally he would complain of "a very heavy fall of diplomatic snow," but he would keep "shoveling steadily," often for long hours. The sloppy syntax and poor grammar of his staff frequently irritated Adee, and at one point he complained to Secretary Hay that "a wave of careless imbecility seems to have passed through all the bureaux, and I think I must have made at least forty corrections" (De Novo, p. 75). Adee also composed, as needed, messages of congratulations, sympathy, and condolence to foreign leaders, knowing the precise degree to which his nation's chief executive should express his nation's sadness or delight. President Theodore Roosevelt once wrote, "Always in correspondence with all the kings, princes, potentates and powers on earth . . . old Adee does that for me" (De Novo, p. 76).

Adee was far more than merely an efficient clerk. He provided an institutional memory for important procedures, protocols, and precedents. At the end of his lengthy career, the State Department files were filled with green slips of paper upon which Adee's sharp editorial comments were written in red ink. He introduced the State Department personnel to the typewriter in the 1880s and in 1906 supervised the revision of the department's cipher codes. Effective, practical, and pragmatic, he served much of his career before the Department of State became staffed with professionals. Adee's candid evaluations of American diplomats exhibited his frankness and impatience with mediocrity. Of diplomat Henry D. White he wrote, "the most valuable man in the service," while he viewed Lewis Einstein as "about the brainiest diplomatic Jew of a singularly brainy race" (De Novo, p. 74). When the famous explorer and writer Charles Chaillé-Long sought a consular post, Adee wrote, "In my heart of hearts, I regard Chaillé-Long as a blowhard" (De Novo, p. 75). Although his critics found him sharp-tempered, narrow, and hidebound, most appreciated his considerable skills and made allowances for his peculiarities. President Roosevelt responded to Senator Thomas C. Platt's calls for Adee's dismissal by writing that Secretary Hay considered "Mr. Adee, who you think could be displaced, as the most useful man he has under him" (E. E. Morison, ed., *Letters of Theodore Roosevelt*, vol. 3 [1951–1958], p. 183).

Adee never married and lived with relatives in Washington. He also visited a small farm he owned in Laurel, Maryland. During times of diplomatic crisis, he often slept on a cot in his State Department office. As hearing problems made social gatherings awkward, Adee often seemed aloof and self-centered. However, he was anything but a recluse, and his crusty disposition was offset by a keen wit. Although frail-looking, he possessed amazing stamina. He loved bicycling and spent nearly every summer riding through Europe. After several accidents, he reluctantly abandoned his bicycle in his mid-seventies, only when increased motor traffic in Washington and Europe made this form of exercise too risky. Expert in photography and proficient in the use of a microscope, Adee studied and photographed diatoms (minute, unicellular algae) and discovered several new species. He loved billiards and chess. The only book Adee ever published was an edition of *King Lear*, produced in 1890 by the Shakespeare Society of New York. He also authored literary essays and poems. His dry sense of humor was legendary in diplomatic circles. Following an important and tense meeting between Secretary of State Hay and Ambassador Woo Ting Fang of China during the Boxer uprising, Adee was asked by reporters what had passed between the two statesmen. He responded that Mr. Hay was rather Hay-zy and Mr. Woo was rather Woo-zy.

Adee was a figure of considerable influence in every administration from U. S. Grant to Woodrow Wilson, but his role in the State Department began to fade as the American diplomatic presence expanded during World War I. In addition, Adee's advanced age began to weaken him. Following his own recommendation, a special Correspondence Bureau was established in 1918 and was staffed with Adee's trainees to review mail and outgoing communications. However, the ancient and eccentric assistant secretary remained at his post until the very end. Ironically, he died in Washington just a few days after the passage on 1 July 1924 of the Rogers Act, which provided for a comprehensive reorganization and professionalization of the department he had served so faithfully.

• Adee left instructions for his personal papers to be burned after his death. Much of his extensive diplomatic correspondence is in the *Foreign Relations of the United States* for the years 1869–1924. Useful biographical sketches include "Biography of Honorable Alvey A. Adee," 25 June 1925 (File 116.3/929), General Records of the Department of State, RG 59, National Archives; E. G. Lowry, "Adee the Remarkable: Some Interesting Impressions of the Admirable Crichton of Our State Department," *Harper's Weekly*, 18 Nov. 1911, p. 9; R. Gordon Ameson, "Anchor Man of the Department: Alvey Augustus Adee," *Foreign Service Journal* 48 (Aug. 1971): 26–28; and John A. De Novo, "The Enigmatic Alvey A. Adee and American Foreign Relations, 1870–1924," *Prologue* 7 (1975): 69–80. See also Graham H. Steuart, *The Department of State: A History of Its Organization, Procedure and Personnel* (1949), and Kenton J. Clymer, *John Hay: The Gentleman as Diplomat* (1975). An obituary is in the *New York Times*, 6 July 1924, and related articles are in the *New York Times*, 7 and 13 July 1924.

MICHAEL J. DEVINE

ADGER, John Bailey (13 Dec. 1810–3 Jan. 1899), Presbyterian missionary and seminary professor, was born in Charleston, South Carolina, the son of James Adger, a merchant and banker, and Sarah Elizabeth Ellison. His father was one of Charleston's most affluent citizens. A graduate of Union College in Schenectady, New York (1828), and of Princeton Theological Seminary (1833), Adger married Elizabeth Keith Shewsbury of Charleston in June 1834. They would have eight children. Five weeks later the couple sailed to Smyrna, Asia Minor (now Izmir, Turkey), where Adger began his work as a missionary under the sponsorship of the American Board of Commissioners for Foreign Missions. Adger's primary work was among the Armenians as a translator and manager of a printing press. During the late 1830s and early 1840s he translated the New Testament, the Westminster Shorter Catechism, and *Pilgrim's Progress* into modern Armenian and Turko-Armenian. He also translated *A Catechism of Scripture Doctrine and Practice*, which was written by his Princeton classmate Charles Colcock Jones for the religious instruction of African-American slaves. In 1846, returning from Armenia because of poor health, Adger stopped in London, where he joined his brother-in-law, Thomas Smyth of Charleston, at the first meeting of the Evangelical Alliance. There he encountered the opposition of abolitionists to slaveholders' participation in the Alliance. This experience, he later wrote, revealed to him "the importance of the anti-slavery controversy" and roused within him "sympathy for my own people." On his return to Charleston, he committed himself to missionary work to the African Americans of the city.

When the Second Presbyterian Church of Charleston helped organize a separate congregation for African Americans, Adger served as the minister. While many whites in the city opposed the plan, fearing large gatherings of slaves, a church was built—largely with Adger family funds—on Anson Street. Adger retired from the work, because of failing eyesight, in 1852 but continued to be a strong supporter of his successor, John L. Girardeau, under whose leadership the church grew rapidly. In 1856, again largely with Adger family funds, the African-American congregation erected the largest church building in Charleston. They named it Zion.

In 1857 Adger became professor of ecclesiastical history and church polity at Columbia Theological Seminary in Columbia, South Carolina. He was an editor and frequent contributor to the *Southern Presbyterian Review* and a coeditor with Girardeau of *The Collected Writings of James Henley Thornwell* (4 vols., 1871–1873). In politics, like his father, he was an ardent Whig and Unionist. When war came in 1861, however, he gave himself fully to the Confederate cause. He was one of the primary shapers of the polity of the Presbyterian Church in the Confederate States of America, later known as the Southern Presbyterian church. In the 1880s Adger took the moderate side of James Woodrow when charges were brought against the latter in church courts for teaching a theistic understanding of evolution. Adger died at his country estate, "Woodburn," in Pendleton, South Carolina.

• Adger's letters and papers are in the Presbyterian Historical Foundation, Montreat, N.C.; in the Manuscript Collection of the South Caroliniana Library, University of South Carolina; and in the South Carolina Historical Society. His autobiography is *My Life and Times* (1899). See also Henry Alexander White, *Southern Presbyterian Leaders* (1911), and Ernest Trice Thompson, *Presbyterians in the South*, vols. 1 and 2 (1973).

T. ERSKINE CLARKE

ADIE, David Craig (3 Sept. 1888–23 Feb. 1943), social worker, was born in Hamilton, Scotland, the son of Lawrence Adie, a railway passenger agent, and Madeline Cooper. Raised in poverty, Adie attended school in Edinburgh but left at an early age to apprentice as a bookbinder. By the time he was twenty he had joined the Independent Labor Union and had begun working on the Clydeside as an organizer, campaigning from town to town on his bicycle. During these years he developed a rousing style of public speaking through both his union work and his service as a Methodist lay preacher. A voracious reader, Adie learned everything he could about America, and in 1913 he sailed for Canada.

Traveling alone, Adie stayed briefly in Canada and then moved on to the United States. Hearing music one night, he wandered toward it into a Minneapolis church, where he found his first American welcome. Among the people he met there was Ann Herr, whom he married in 1916; they had one child. Through Herr he obtained a job in 1914 as assistant secretary of the Minneapolis Civic and Commerce Association, where she worked. His job was to foster good relations between business and labor. With the outbreak of World War I, Adie became an adviser to the Minnesota Public Safety Commission, overseeing the recruitment and allocation of factory workers, the reorganization of the state's employment services, and the regulation of farm labor. In 1918 Adie took a position with the federal government, arbitrating labor disputes as associate secretary of the War Labor Policies Board. After becoming an American citizen in 1919, he moved to New York City, where he spent two years as impartial chair of the arbitration board for the men's and boys' clothing industry, covering about 70,000 workers in 2,000 factories.

Adie's social services work began in New York City with a brief stint at the American City Bureau, an organization that encouraged chambers of commerce to become involved in civic and social activities. Moving to Buffalo, he entered the field of social work more formally in 1921, when he became general secretary of the Charity Organization Society of Buffalo, the oldest COS in the country. Like many social workers during the 1920s, Adie came to believe that the profession's greatest potential lay not in the community reforms stressed by an earlier generation but in focused casework with individuals and families. Consistent with this priority was a strong emphasis on social workers' technical skills; in line with this concern, Adie worked with others to establish a professional school of social work at the University of Buffalo. In 1929 Adie became executive secretary of the new Buffalo Council of Social Agencies, a federation of seventy-five charitable organizations that he had helped found. Later that year Governor Franklin D. Roosevelt appointed him to the New York State Social Welfare Board. Roosevelt also appointed him to the New York State Commission for the Revision of the Public Service Law in 1930 and had him arbitrate several labor strikes in western New York while Roosevelt was governor.

In 1932 the Social Welfare Board elected Adie the state commissioner of social welfare, a position he would hold until his death. Moving to Albany, New York, as commissioner he was responsible for enforcing public welfare law in the largest state in the Union during some of the most difficult years of the depression. His duties included overseeing public assistance programs for mothers with dependent children, veterans, the aged, and the blind, as well as administering facilities for delinquent children and the disabled. He also appointed and supervised all city and county welfare heads throughout the state. In addition, Adie served as an ex-officio member on the state's Temporary Emergency Relief Administration (TERA), which since 1931 had provided both work and home relief to the unemployed. Most of TERA's work relief responsibilities were assumed by the federal Works Progress Administration in 1937; at that time TERA was disbanded, and Adie's department took over its home relief programs.

Adie believed that public welfare officials could learn from the experience of private agencies, but he was convinced that the field was essentially brand-new, posing challenges that neither private social workers nor public administrators had encountered before. "The Industrial Revolution was a pygmy compared to this revolution," he told his staff. "Our government is going to have a constructive view of humanity or it is going to smash." To carry out their new mission, he said, public administrators would need to remain closely in touch with local institutions, values, and preferences, building support among the citizenry "in very much the same way as the representatives of the people are elected, by going to the place where the people are, talking to them in homely language, and stressing human values as paramount in our concern." Foreseeing a continuing need for public assistance to vulnerable citizens even after prosperity returned, he supported federal social insurance, state and federal rehabilitation programs, and a national system of welfare administered by the states.

Besides his government responsibilities, Adie gave frequent lectures on social work and social issues, held faculty appointments at both the New York School of Social Work and Fordham University, and served on many state and national committees; he was vice president of the American Association of Social Workers, chair of the National Association of State Administrators, president of the Albany Council of Social Agencies, and a member of the executive committee of the Albany County Mental Hygiene Society. He also took a particular interest in public education, the Boy Scouts, and the problems of veterans and American Indians. He died of peritonitis in Albany.

Adie's colleagues admired him for the religious conviction that pervaded his life and for his optimism, sense of humor, insight, and empathy with the unfortunate. "He believed," said one of the speakers at his memorial service, "that selfishness would vanish from the earth; that the state exists for man and never man for the state; that government must lend its aid to the victims of injustice; that the welfare of the many must come before the profits of the few . . . that truth extinguished by tyranny's storm will burn again and light the world."

• For more about Adie's ideas on social service see his article, "Responsibility of the State in the Supervision of Public Welfare Programs," *Social Service Review* 13, no. 4 (Dec. 1939): 611–25; also helpful is Emma O. Lundberg, "Pathfinders of the Middle Years," *Social Service Review* 21, no. 1 (Mar. 1947): 31–34. See also a publication of the Charity Organization Society of Buffalo titled *Fifty Years of Family Social Work* (1927) and a publication issued by the New York State Department of Social Welfare titled *Democracy Cares: The Story behind Public Assistance in New York State* (1941). Obituaries are in *Survey Midmonthly* 79, no. 3 (Mar. 1943): 82–83, and the *New York Times*, 24 Feb. 1943.

SANDRA OPDYCKE

ADKINS, Homer Burton (16 Jan. 1892–10 Aug. 1949), organic chemist, was born near Newport, Ohio, the son of Alvin Adkins and Emily Middleswart, farmers. Adkins grew up on his parents' farm, attended local schools, and then entered Denison University, from which he received a bachelor's degree in 1915. In 1917 he married Louise Spivey, a Denison classmate and high school mathematics teacher; they had three children. In 1918 he earned a doctorate in chemistry from Ohio State University. After briefly serving as a chemist in the Department of War, he became an instructor in chemistry at Ohio State in 1918. In 1919 he began a thirty-year association with the University of Wisconsin, moving from assistant professor to associate professor in 1924 to professor in 1928.

By 1922 Adkins had found his major area of research. His third published paper was a report on metal oxides as catalysts in organic reactions. European chemists were at that time investigating the catalytic addition of hydrogen to organic compounds with carbon-carbon multiple bonds. Adkins entered the field because the existing methods for the preparation of metal oxide catalysts were unreliable. During the 1920s he developed new methods of preparation that included metal oxides with different surface structures or with trace impurities and also mixed-oxide catalysts, all of which catalyzed reactions in different ways. He discovered a major new catalyst, a copper oxide–chromium oxide mixture of great value in hydrogenation reactions. Benefiting the chemical industry, this catalyst made possible the preparation of valuable alcohols from natural acids found in vegetable oils.

From the late 1920s Adkins developed another major catalyst. In 1927 Murray Raney, a Tennessee chemist, had patented a novel method for preparing a highly active form of nickel but had never investigated its potential. Adkins made "Raney nickel" widely known throughout the world by developing improved procedures and expanding its usefulness as a catalyst. Because of its remarkable activity, Raney nickel became the most widely used hydrogenation catalyst for industrial processes by the 1940s.

Adkins studied catalytic organic reactions to the end of his career. He examined the mechanism of these reactions, disclosed new reactions, and elaborated the structures of catalysts. He also extended the value of catalysts by exploring their use at high temperatures and pressures. He popularized high pressure methods in organic chemistry, designed his own precision equipment, and made the apparatus available to others through their commercial manufacture. His studies became essential to several chemical industries, including the preparation of high octane fuels from petroleum by catalytic cracking; the synthesis of nylon, which involved a catalytic hydrogenation in its sequence of reactions; and the conversion of vegetable oils into shortenings.

By the mid-1930s Adkins was a world authority on catalysts in organic chemistry. He codified his knowledge in a major monograph, *The Reactions of Hydrogen with Organic Compounds over Copper-Chromium Oxide and Nickel Catalysts* (1937), a classic study involving many types of organic compounds with multiple bonds. His single most influential contribution, this work became a worldwide bestseller, unusual for an academic monograph. In recognition of his accomplishments, the National Academy of Sciences elected him to membership in 1942.

Adkins served the American chemistry profession in several ways. As American organic chemistry greatly expanded between the world wars it needed basic textbooks, journals, monographs, and review series. Adkins contributed to the literature of organic chemistry by writing two textbooks with Wisconsin associate Samuel McElvain: *The Practice of Organic Chemistry in the Laboratory* (1925), and *Elementary Organic Chemistry* (1928). He served on the board of editors and wrote several chapters for *Organic Syntheses* (1921), an annual volume of tested methods of preparation. He also served on the board of editors for *Organic Chemistry: An Advanced Treatise* (1938), the first American advanced textbook. Its chapters, which were written by the nation's foremost organic chemists, included two by Adkins. The first volume of the review series *Organic Reactions* appeared in 1942, and Adkins wrote articles and served in his last years on its board of editors. He also held national and regional offices in the American Chemical Society and at the time of his death was a nominee for its presidency.

Never a theorist, Adkins was an empiricist who insisted that knowledge be restricted to the facts established in the laboratory. Reinforcing his empiricism was his reading in the philosophy of science; he was especially influenced by Percy Bridgman's *The Logic of Modern Physics* and Eric Temple Bell's *The Search for Truth*.

During World War II Adkins was deeply involved in mission-oriented research. As an official investigator for the Office of Scientific Research and Development, he was in charge of research groups investigating and evaluating chemical warfare agents. He also engaged in the synthesis of potential antimalarial drugs for the government. He made dozens of classified reports on these subjects. For his wartime services, President Harry S. Truman honored him with the Presidential Medal of Merit in 1948. After the war Adkins discovered how to convert alcohols into acids having one more carbon atom by means of carbon monoxide and catalysts. This reaction led to the commercial synthesis of a new class of detergents from vegetable oils.

Adkins's main nonscientific interest was the Civil War. He not only read its history but also made several visits to its battlegrounds. He had a deep interest in current affairs and was moderately liberal on social and political matters. At Wisconsin he fought hard for democratic procedures in university affairs and was outspoken in espousing the cause of anyone at the university whom he thought to be a victim of injustice.

Adkins's heavy wartime responsibilities had an adverse effect on his health. In the late spring of 1949 he had a mild heart attack but delayed a medical checkup until after a national organic chemistry symposium in Madison, to which he devoted much time and energy. Between sessions he suffered a coronary occlusion and later died in his Madison home.

Adkins revealed what could be accomplished in organic chemistry by means of catalysts. This knowledge proved fundamental not only to the investigation and understanding of organic reactions but also to many industrial processes involving the synthesis of organic substances.

• There is no collection of Adkins papers. Farrington Daniels, a Wisconsin colleague, wrote Adkins's biography for National Academy of Sciences, *Biographical Memoirs* 27 (1952): 293–317, which includes a bibliography of books and articles by Adkins. Dean S. Tarbell and Ann T. Tarbell provide a good summary and evaluation of Adkins's achievements in catalytic hydrogenation in *Essays on the History of Organic Chemistry in the United States* (1986), pp. 169–79. Obituaries are in *Chemical and Engineering News*, 22 Aug. 1949, and the *New York Times*, 13 Aug. 1949.

ALBERT B. COSTA

ADLER, Alfred (6 Feb. 1870–28 May 1937), physician and psychological theorist, was born in Rudolfsheim, near Vienna, Austria, the son of Leopold Adler, a grain merchant, and Pauline Beer. Adler was born into a lower middle-class, religiously nonobservant, and ethnically assimilated Jewish family in Austria. The death of a close younger brother in early childhood and Adler's own near-death from illness the following year, at the age of five, seem to have inspired his interest in a medical career. A mediocre student, he attended several Viennese private schools and then began study at the University of Vienna in the fall of 1888.

Adler specialized in a premedical curriculum and received his medical degree from the University of Vienna in November 1895. During Adler's academic training, he had decided on clinical work with patients, rather than research, as his career goal in medicine. He became drawn to socialism during his student years and, though never a political leader at the University of Vienna, became active in its student socialist league.

At one of its gatherings in early 1897 Adler met Raissa Timofeivna Epstein, a Jewish-Russian feminist and socialist who had wealthy relatives in Russian lumber trade. They were married in Smolensk in November 1897 and had four children.

Adler soon set up private practice as an internist in the working-class Leopoldstadt district of Vienna. During the next few years, he developed a local reputation as a hard-working and thorough physician who had an astute diagnostic ability. In 1898 Adler issued his first professional publication, *Health Book for the Tailoring Trade*, a German-language monograph that dealt with the health problems of Austrian and German tailors. Adler's paternal uncle David had worked as a tailor and probably helped to turn his nephew's attention to this domain. The monograph evidenced a strong concern for social medicine, as it would later be called, and advocated a variety of reforms and governmental regulations to improve the working conditions of tailors. In 1902 Adler published two innovative articles dealing with social medicine, both in *Aertzliche*

Standeszeitung (Medical news bulletin). The first urged physicians to become more actively involved in disease prevention, and the second recommended that a university chair in social medicine be established to help improve public health.

In early November of that year, Adler was one of four Viennese physicians to receive an invitational postcard from psychoanalyst Sigmund Freud to meet in a weekly group for discussing topics in psychology and neurology. The other three were Max Kahane, Rudolf Reitler, and Wilhelm Stekel. How Freud and Adler had come to know each other has never been adequately documented. Adler had neither been a university student nor medical patient of Freud's and had never been part of the latter's social circle. The group of five physicians called themselves the Wednesday Psychological Society and slowly drew additional members. In 1908 the enlarged group's name was changed to that of the Vienna Psychoanalytic Society. Freud and Adler never became emotionally close but had great respect for one another professionally. Adler's conversion to Protestantism in 1904, most likely for career reasons, probably did little to endear him to the Jewish, ethnically proud Freud.

Adler's first major work, *A Study in Organ Inferiority and its Psychical Compensation: A Contribution to Clinical Medicine* (1907), set forth such concepts as compensation and over-compensation and argued that individuals with weak or "inferior" organs were likely to experience certain personality difficulties or challenges. The book also implied, but did not state explicitly, that all humans have an inborn drive for mastery and competence in the social world. *A Study of Organ Inferiority* was well received by Adler's medical colleagues in Vienna and also in Freud's own circle. But as Adler began to increasingly emphasize the striving for mastery in one's environment (which he initially called "aggression"), Freud and his supporters felt dismayed by this rival conceptualization to their overriding stress on infantile sexuality. In mid-1911 Adler and Freud decisively broke with one another and would remain bitter, implacable foes throughout their lives.

Within a year Adler had established what he called the Society for Free Psychoanalytic Study to develop psychoanalytic inquiry in a manner free from Freud's dogmatism. In 1912 he published *The Neurotic Constitution*, which contained the foundation of his entire approach to human personality and psychotherapy. In this work he presented the drive for mastery or competence as the key to human personality and our early childhood sense of inferiority as the basis for much later neurosis.

Among Adler's closest allies during these years was Dr. Carl Furtmüller, a younger, progressive educator who would later play an important role in promoting Adler's work in post–World War I Vienna. Furtmüller helped Adler edit and publish their German-language *Journal for Individual Psychology* beginning in 1914 and also coedited an anthology titled *Heilen und Bilden* (To heal and to educate) published that same year. By then, Adler had renamed his approach that of "Individual Psychology," because it emphasized each individual's tendency to develop an unconscious life-plan during early childhood that would develop into a specific lifestyle in adolescence and adulthood. In Adler's view, neurotic behavior always reflects a faulty or inappropriate effort on the part of the individual to overcome a youthful sense of inferiority.

Adler was gaining an international reputation as an innovative thinker, but the outbreak of World War I sharply limited his travel and professional activity for several years. In 1915 the University of Vienna Medical School rejected Adler's application for a junior teaching position, a decision that caused him much humiliation—especially because Freud had secured such a faculty position there nearly fifteen years earlier in his own career. The faculty committee declared Adler's work intellectually interesting but lacking empirical validation and therefore unworthy of academic recognition. He then served as a military physician, and exposure to the mass brutality and suffering of the war upset him a great deal. Unlike Freud, Adler had never supported the Austro-Hungarian Empire against the Allies. But also unlike his wife Raissa, who supported the Bolsheviks, Adler decried their use of terrorism and violence as a tactic for social change. He began to emphasize his hypothesis that all humans have an innate motivation for social feeling (*Gemeinschaftsgefühl*) and that this trait should be nurtured in family and school to avoid future wars and mass conflicts.

After the war, Adler emerged as a leading psychological figure in Austria, Central Europe, and eventually, the United States. More than Freud or Jung, his name became associated with the applied fields of child guidance, educational psychology, and social work. When the Social Democrats gained power in Vienna, they quickly pressed for massive educational and social welfare reforms. Adler's longtime friends like Furtmüller were instrumental in gaining influence for individual psychology in Vienna's schools and other public institutions.

By the mid-1920s, after the publication of his anthology *The Practice and Theory of Individual Psychology*, Adler began lecturing throughout Europe about child psychology, personality and psychotherapy, and related topics. He made his first lecture tour of the United States from late 1926 through early 1927. The following year, Adler's latest book was translated into English as *Understanding Human Nature* and became a bestseller when he toured the United States. Subsequent volumes, nearly all English translations of transcribed lectures published between 1929 and 1931 for the American/British public, included *The Case Of Miss R.: The Interpretation of a Life Story*, *Guiding the Child: On the Principles of Individual Psychology*, *Problems of Neurosis: A Book of Case Histories*, *The Science of Living*, *The Education of Children*, *The Pattern of Life*, and *What Life Should Mean to You*.

Such books emphasized the application of Adler's psychological principles to the improvement of family life and public schooling. In essence, Adler argued that the institution of the public school had a key societal role to play in promoting the emotional health of virtually all children. To help youngsters develop greater self-confidence and social feeling, he recommended that classroom teachers become better trained in psychology and that clinicians, such as counselors, social workers, psychologists, and psychiatrists, become more actively involved in educational planning and intervention. Eventually, his books met with criticism for being too moralistic and repetitious. Adler's final English-language book, *Social Interest: A Challenge to Mankind*, was published posthumously (1938).

By 1929 Adler had shifted his main focus of activity from Austria to the United States. He spoke English with a thick Viennese accent and had a warm, charismatic personality that attracted many patients and supporters. Through the financial backing of wealthy Quaker businessman-philanthropist Charles Henry Davis, Adler secured a temporary teaching position as visiting professor at Columbia University in 1929–1930 and then gained an endowed chair in medical psychology at the Long Island College of Medicine in 1932. When Austria's government turned fascist in 1934, it shut down all of Adler's thirty-odd child guidance clinics and related educational activities. He was never to build a similar movement elsewhere.

During the late 1920s and 1930s Adler was an extremely popular lecturer throughout the United States, Canada, Great Britain, and much of Europe. His main audiences were teachers, parents, and those interested in psychological self-help. In this period, Adler directly inspired such subsequent key American founders of humanistic psychology as Carl Rogers, Rollo May, and especially Abraham Maslow.

Adler died in Aberdeen, Scotland, while on a lecture tour of the British Isles. To literally his last day, he promulgated his belief to educators and the lay public that modern psychology—specifically his own system—could offer humanity the best course for social harmony and individual well-being. Ranked alongside Sigmund Freud and Carl Jung as a cofounder of modern personality study and psychotherapy, he had an optimistic and socially oriented approach. As Adler himself realized late in life, many of his most important notions became absorbed into the psychological mainstream, though often without being attributed to him.

• Adler's papers are mainly housed at the Division of Manuscripts, Library of Congress, Washington, D.C. Additional papers are in the Sanford J. Greenberger Collection, Special Collections, University of Oregon (Greenberger had been Adler's primary literary agent in the United States). Important edited anthologies of Adler's published writings include two by Heinz and Rowena Ansbacher: *The Individual Psychology of Alfred Adler: A Systematic Presentation in Selections from His Writings* (1956) and *Superiority and Social Interest: A Collection of Later Writings* (1978). The most comprehensive biographical assessment is Edward Hoffman, *The Drive for Self: Alfred Adler and the Founding of Individual Psychology* (1994). More personal and less scholarly biographies by former supporters include Phyllis Bottome, *Alfred Adler: A Portrait from Life* (1957), and Manes Sperber, *Masks of Loneliness: Alfred Adler in Perspective* (1974). An obituary is in the *New York Times*, 29 May 1937, and a more lengthy analysis of his impact is in the same publication, 31 May 1937.

EDWARD HOFFMAN

ADLER, Charles, Jr. (20 June 1899–23 Oct. 1980), engineer and inventor, was born in Baltimore, Maryland, the son of Harry Adler, a physician, and Carolyn "Carrie" Frank. At age fourteen, he patented his first invention, an electric automotive brake that he installed on his father's Packard. Following graduation from high school, which he described as "completing four years in five," Adler entered the Johns Hopkins University school of engineering. During that time he also served briefly in the Army training corps as acting corporal, being discharged in December 1918.

Adler claimed that his passion for railroads was the cause for his quitting Johns Hopkins. He obtained a job with the Maryland and Pennsylvania Railroad and by 1920 had developed an automatic highway-railroad crossing signal. The first such train-activated signal in the United States was installed the following year. Adler carried on studies of flashing and signal lights, and by the mid-1920s he was ready to experiment with a new traffic signal, this time for automobile traffic. He met and married Alene D. Steiger in 1925; they had two children.

In 1928 Adler persuaded the city of Baltimore to install an automatic, sound-activated traffic signal. The system remained green for the main artery until the sound of horns from waiting cross traffic caused it to switch for a predetermined period. This was the first traffic-actuated light in the United States. Adler's interest in traffic-light improvement persisted. In 1931 he devised a system combining shape and color to prevent confusion in colorblind drivers (at the time there was no international convention that placed red at the top and green at the bottom of a traffic light). He also developed a double-filament lamp for railroad use; a bulb could burn out but still function at half-capacity until replaced. The system, installed in 1933, was still in use on the Pennsylvania Central Railroad in the 1970s.

In 1938 Adler expanded his interest in transportation safety devices to include aviation-related mechanisms. A few years after obtaining his pilot's license, Adler had nearly collided with another aircraft in flight and decided that a better lighting system was needed on airplanes so that pilots could see each other at night. Until then aircraft had used the same lighting principles as ships, with a green light mounted on the right, a red one on the left, and a white one on the vertical tail. None of these, however, were flashing, and at night they could be confused with lights and signals coming from the ground. Adler added a red light behind the white one and made them flash in sequence; later he made the green and red wingtip lights flash too. This was probably Adler's greatest success. Despite the potential financial gains, however, he decided that in the name of safety the invention should be offered to manufacturers free of charge, so he donated his patent to the U.S. government. Further improvements and variations followed, but Adler was best known as the developer of flashing aircraft position lights.

Although Adler's specialty was lighting devices, he designed other items in the hope of saving lives. His "Spaceometer" was patented in 1958. Adler was concerned that drivers did not know how closely they could safely follow another vehicle at different speeds. For twelve years he experimented with various methods, including warning bells and flashing lights, before settling for a scale parallel to the speed indicator, showing an increasing number of car lengths in proportion to speed. Although he donated the patent to the state of Maryland and obtained informal Congressional encouragement for his idea, Adler did not see his invention installed on automobiles.

Along with his activities as an inventor, Adler served on various transportation boards in Maryland and advised the U.S. government on many issues. In 1955, while a member of Maryland's Traffic Safety Commission (1952–1980), he suggested that a federal department of transportation headed by a fully-empowered secretary be formed to monitor traffic safety. Although Adler testified before Congress the following year and had the support of Representative Samuel Fiedel (D-Md.) and Paul Burke, director of the Maryland Traffic Safety Commission, it was ten years before the new department was established. In 1961 Adler was appointed to the board of directors of Friendship International Airport, now Baltimore-Washington. He suggested in 1964 that the airport be linked to the city by rail to reduce traffic congestion. This link, the first of its kind in the United States, became reality in 1980. Ironically, on the day of the scheduled inauguration at which he was to be honored, Adler collapsed and died in Baltimore.

"If they can save lives, I want everyone to have them," said Adler of his sixty patented inventions. In that spirit he established a foundation in 1956 to help inventors in the field of safety. His selfless transfer of ten patents to the government added to his reputation as a free and eccentric spirit. Owner of a red Rolls-Royce and a mauve Maserati, he rented the apartments adjacent to his to ensure his privacy. His eccentricity, however, was overshadowed by his dedication to the public good; he applied common sense and concern for safety to his professional work. Many of his inventions were ahead of their time; even when they were not practical or adaptable, however, Adler's ideas set the tone for active research in safety issues.

• Adler's papers are at the Smithsonian Institution's National Museum of American History, Washington, D.C.; these include several scrapbooks of his writings, notably a column that appeared in the *Baltimore Beacon* in the 1970s. Several originals of Adler's patents are at New York University's Gould Memorial Library. George W. Hilton, *The MA & PA* (2d ed., 1980), p. 106, details some of Adler's contributions to railroad safety; *Popular Science Monthly*, Nov. 1931, p. 49, describes Adler's traffic light for color-blind people. See also "Plane Proximity Warning," *Skyways*, Mar. 1952, pp. 14–15; "Successor to Speedometer Found," *Traffic and Digest Review*, Mar. 1964, p. 7; and "Mr. Anti-Collision," *FAA Aviation News*, Feb. 1968, pp. 12–13. An obituary is in the *Baltimore Sun*, 24 Oct. 1980.

GUILLAUME DE SYON

ADLER, Cyrus (13 Sept. 1863–7 Apr. 1940), academic administrator and Jewish communal leader, was born in Van Buren, Arkansas, to Samuel Adler, a merchant and planter, and Sarah Sulzberger. At an early age Adler's family moved to Philadelphia and then to New York, where his father died in 1867. The family returned to Philadelphia, where his mother's brother, David Sulzberger, became head of the household and was a great influence on Adler's upbringing. As a boy, Adler received an intensive education in Judaic subjects from a consortium of Philadelphia rabbis, headed by Sabato Morais, who was influential in his intellectual and religious development. Adler attended the University of Pennsylvania, from which he received an A.B. in 1883 and an A.M. in 1886. He then pursued doctoral studies in Semitics at Johns Hopkins University and received his Ph.D. in 1887, becoming the first American-trained Ph.D. in his field.

He remained at Johns Hopkins as instructor (1887) and later associate (1890) in Semitics. His efforts to obtain a professorship, however, did not succeed, and he joined the staff of the United States National Museum, a division of the Smithsonian Institution, in 1888 as assistant curator of the department of oriental antiquities. A year later he helped found the departments of historic archaeology and religious ceremonial institutions and organized exhibitions in these fields at the United States National Museum and at expositions in Cincinnati (1889), Chicago (1893), Atlanta (1895), and St. Louis (1904). In 1890 he was appointed special commissioner of the World's Columbian Exposition by President Benjamin Harrison (1833–1901) and visited Turkey, the Middle East, and North Africa to promote these countries' participation. In 1892 he was appointed librarian of the Smithsonian and became assistant secretary in 1905. His greatest achievement at the Smithsonian was his leadership role as U.S. representative to the London conference in 1898, which established the International Catalogue of Scientific Literature. His compromise proposal created a coalition and broke the deadlock that threatened to stymie the conference. Another of his achievements at the Smithsonian was his discovery of the "Jefferson Bible," Thomas Jefferson's edition and rearrangement of the New Testament. Adler's publication of this document in 1904 created great public interest.

Starting in the 1880s, Adler took a leadership role in several initiatives within the American Jewish community. He helped found the Jewish Publication Society of America in 1888 and later chaired its publications committee. He chaired the committee of scholars that produced the society's translation of the Hebrew Bible in 1917. He was one of the principal founders of the American Jewish Historical Society (1892) and served as its president from 1898 to 1921. Recognizing the need for accurate information on American Jewry, he conceived and edited the *American Jewish Year Book* in its first years (1899–1905). In 1901 Adler joined the editorial board of the *Jewish Encyclopedia* and was instrumental in ensuring the success of that project. He was also prominent in the reorganization of the Jewish Theological Seminary of America in New York City and served as president of its board of trustees from 1902 to 1905. In 1906 Adler was a cofounder of the American Jewish Committee, an organization that sought to represent American Jewry, and became its president from 1929 to 1940. Adler married Racie Friedenwald in 1905; they had one child.

In 1908 Adler became president of Dropsie College in Philadelphia, a nonsectarian institution devoted to advanced Judaic and Semitic scholarship. Shortly thereafter, in 1910, he also became coeditor, with Solomon Schechter, of the new series of the *Jewish Quarterly Review*. Upon Schechter's death in 1915, Adler became sole editor of the journal and also succeeded Schechter as president of the Jewish Theological Seminary, while retaining his presidency of Dropsie. He served as acting president of the seminary until 1924, when he became president. He remained president of both institutions to his death. He was also influential in the United Synagogue of America, the congregational organization of Conservative Judaism, serving as its president from 1913 to 1917. Active in the intellectual life of America, Adler was chosen as president of the American Oriental Society in 1923 and was elected vice president of the American Philosophical Society in 1938. Within Philadelphia, Adler served on the board of education from 1921 to 1925, was president of the board of trustees of the Free Library of Philadelphia from 1925 to 1939, and presided over the Philadelphia *Kehilla*, or Jewish communal organization, from 1911 to 1915.

During the First World War Adler served as a leader of the American Jewish Committee in its struggle with the Zionist American Jewish Congress movement over the way in which American Jewry was to be represented. He helped found both the Jewish Welfare Board, which was designed to support Jewish servicepeople, and the American Jewish Joint Distribution Committee, which sent aid to Jews overseas who were adversely affected by war conditions. In 1919 he attended the Versailles Peace Conference as representative of the American Jewish Committee and worked, together with Louis Marshall (1856–1929), for the adoption of minority rights sections in the treaties that established the new states of Eastern Europe. Although Adler was an early opponent of political Zionism, he favored cooperation with the Zionists in the building of the Jewish National Home in Palestine that was envisaged in the Balfour Declaration of 1917. He participated in negotiations that culminated in the establishment of an enlarged Jewish Agency for Palestine in 1929, serving as president of its council and chairing its administrative committee from 1930 to 1931. In this role, he addressed a lengthy *Memorandum on the Western Wall* (1930) to the League of Nations, which defended Jewish rights of worship at the wall. He also served as a member of the board of governors of the Hebrew University of Jerusalem.

In the 1930s Adler was confronted with the economic effects of the depression on the institutions he led, the Nazi assault on German Jewry, and the worsening Arab-Jewish strife in Palestine. To the best of his ability he supported the movement of Jewish refugees from Europe and sought American governmental support for a beleaguered German Jewry. While opposing a Jewish state in Palestine, he also worked to strengthen the Jewish community in Palestine as a haven for Jewish refugees. Adler died at his home in Philadelphia.

Unifying Adler's varied activities was his conviction that active participation in the political and intellectual life of America was entirely compatible with strict adherence to the beliefs and practices of traditional Judaism. He thus opposed Reform Judaism's claim to represent the only truly "American" Judaism. This commitment led him to attempt to serve as a representative of American Jewry as well as a representative of Americanism to a Jewish community then largely made up of recent immigrants and their children.

• Major collections of Adler's papers can be found in the archives of the American Jewish Committee, New York City; American Jewish Archives, Cincinnati; American Jewish Historical Society, Waltham, Mass.; Annenberg Research Institute, Philadelphia; Jewish Theological Seminary, New York City; and Smithsonian Institution, Washington, D.C. His autobiography, *I Have Considered the Days* (1941), and Abraham Neuman, "Cyrus Adler, a Sketch," *American Jewish Year Book* (1940–1941), are the only full accounts of his life. A selection of his letters appears in Ira Robinson, ed., *Cyrus Adler: Selected Letters* (2 vols., 1985). Several articles devoted to Adler's career were published in *American Jewish History* 78 (1989): 351–98. An annotated bibliography of Adler's publications was compiled by E. D. Coleman and Joseph Reider in Adler's *Lectures, Selected Papers, Addresses* (1933). An obituary is in the *New York Times*, 8 Apr. 1940.

IRA ROBINSON

ADLER, Dankmar (3 July 1844–16 Apr. 1900), architect and engineer, was born in Stadt Lengsfeld, Germany, the son of Rabbi Liebman Adler and Sara Eliel, who died after childbirth. Economic and political pressures drove the Adler family to emigrate to the United States, where Liebman and his second wife, Zerlina Picard, settled in Detroit in 1854. Rabbi Adler occupied the pulpit of Congregation Beth El. Young Dankmar studied drawing with Julius Melchers (the father of artist Gari Melchers) and attended Ann Arbor Union High School to prepare for the University of Michigan. Having failed the entrance exam, he was variously apprenticed to Detroit architects: John J. Schaefer and then E. Willard Smith and Smith's young assistant, John Bancroft. In 1861 the family moved to Chicago.

Adler enlisted in the Union army, where he learned engineering first by "liberating books" from southern mansions (he later jokingly called this booty "unrighteous spoil") and then by joining an engineering regiment. After a brief stint with Augustus Bauer, a German-trained Chicago architect who had worked on the Crystal Palace in New York, Adler left to join a less well-known architect, O. S. Kinney, a school and church designer. After Kinney's death in 1868, Adler had a short-lived partnership with his son Ashley. In 1871 Adler became the partner of architect Edward Burling. The firm of Burling & Adler was very active in rebuilding Chicago after the great fire of 1871, putting up buildings by the mile. Adler designed several of the large commissions, among them the First National Bank (1871), the Methodist Church Block (1872–1873), the Mercantile Bank (1873), and Temple Sinai (1876). All have since been demolished.

In 1872, with a guaranteed income, Adler married Dila Kohn, the daughter of Abraham Kohn, founder of Chicago's first synagogue and a successful clothing manufacturer. He had good political connections in the Republican party, having served as city clerk. Dila and Dankmar had three children, of whom the eldest, Abraham, followed in his father's profession.

Adler left Burling in 1879 and opened his own practice, D. Adler & Company. His first solo job, and one that earned him a reputation for multipurpose projects combining performance spaces with offices and shops, was the Central Music Hall. This was at the southeast corner of State and Randolph streets and contained a large auditorium, rehearsal space, music rooms, offices, and retail stores. Adler built it simply and solidly in a modified *rundbogen* style, with strong corner blocks and a recessed central section. The project brought Adler together with Louis Sullivan, who designed the organ grilles. Sullivan joined the firm in 1881 as a draftsman and decorator; by 1883 he was a full partner.

Theater commissions were rare in this early period, and residences were Adler & Sullivan's bread and butter. Most were very competent given their small budgets, among them the Morris Selz residence and the Charles P. Kimball house, both built in 1883 and later demolished. Chicago's emerging business class and newly successful Jews provided the firm's residential clientele. Many of the same men later commissioned commercial and manufacturing structures. Among the most noteworthy of the firm's early commercial buildings were the Jewelers Building for Martin Ryerson and the Rothschild Building for Max, Emanuel, and Abram Rothschild, both 1881 and both demolished. They were strong and attractive blocks and showed a progressive integration of ornament and materials, although at this early stage the decoration tended to be Egyptoid and spiky, with lotus stalk and seed motifs and with sharply-pointed decorative elements on the facade and at the roofline.

A few early buildings showed great promise. They were larger and more coherent designs, with handsome proportions and more subtle ornament. These include the Borden Block (1880) and the Troescher Building (1884), neither extant. The Troescher was one of their earliest to incorporate structural iron and showed Adler & Sullivan to be innovative both technologically and artistically. Their talents and creativity reached an apogee in the decade from 1886 to 1895.

Adler excelled at the business of architecture—plans, schedules, budgets, materials, and the technological and managerial side of things. Sullivan was a brilliant artist. Adler, recognizing this, gave him most of the design responsibilities, but there was no doubt that Adler headed the office. Frank Lloyd Wright called him "the chief," and indeed he was, personally going over every project that came in, overseeing the transformation from two-dimensional drawing to final building. He paid the most meticulous attention to the theater and auditorium commissions and became a self-taught expert in acoustics, which earned him a national reputation. Adler consulted on the building of New York's Carnegie Hall (1889–1891).

Due to the success of the Central Music Hall and the Opera Festival Hall, the firm of Adler & Sullivan was chosen in 1886 by attorney Ferd Peck and a board of like-minded cultural elite, most of them members of the Commercial Club, to design an opera house complex for Chicago. So important was the commission that Adler was sent to Europe to examine theaters and concert halls, writing daily to his family describing the architecture and technology, which excited him greatly.

The Auditorium (1886–1889) was Adler & Sullivan's most significant commission. At $3.1 million, it was also the costliest structure of its day and the largest such building in the United States. The Romanesque revival facade was influenced by Henry Hobson Richardson in its rugged stone exterior with arched entrances, in the grouping of the windows, and in its massing and overall strength and simplicity. Within, a large and lavish opera hall boasted outstanding acoustics, gorgeous colors, and lavish decoration. It was a synthesis and a celebration of the arts, blending visual splendor with auditory magnificence. President Benjamin Harrison, who attended the grand opening, pronounced it excellent, and Wright called it "the best room in America for music—bar none" (American Institute of Architects and the Royal Architectural Institute of Canada, "Auditorium Theater Program," 25 June 1969, p. 4).

The Auditorium complex underwent several changes during construction: one story was added as was a banquet hall. From the deep foundations to the high tower, there were problems that Adler and his consultants had to surmount. Adler combined caisson foundations with a waterproofed mat, engineered sophisticated trusses for carrying the upper stories over the theater, invented a way to stabilize the tower, and installed a state-of-the-art heating and ventilation system and even a form of central air conditioning. He and his engineer, Paul Mueller, adapted the most modern of European stage technology. With the dedication of the building on 9 December 1889, Chicago's elevation from western boomtown to cultural mecca was achieved and the firm's national reputation firmly secured. Subsequently, Adler & Sullivan built a theater complex in Pueblo, Colorado (1889–1890), and designed unbuilt halls for Salt Lake City, Utah (1890), Denver, Colorado (1890), Seattle, Washington (1889), and Buffalo, New York (1894).

Their expertise was also applied to tall office buildings. One of the best was the Wainwright Building in St. Louis (1891, since remodeled). The structure has a riveted steel skeleton, a modular plan, and a terra cotta skin that served as Sullivan's canvas for efflorescent ornamentation. Adler satisfied the client by delivering a building that, at twenty-five cents per cubic foot, cost less than many inferior edifices.

Factories and warehouses, like Brunswick, Balke, Collender (1881–1891) and the Walker Warehouse (1888), both destroyed, though less flashy than the Wainwright, were similarly successful—functional, attractive, and economical to build and operate. Adler & Sullivan's landmark buildings include the Auditorium, the Wainwright Building, and the Guaranty in Buffalo, all of them still standing. Another was the Chicago Stock Exchange (1892–1893), an impressive building that employed the bay window, sometimes called the Chicago bay, in a structure with elegant proportions, brilliantly decorated with beautiful terra cotta ornament. Its demolition in 1972 was a great misfortune, although fragments now reside in museums—the entrance arch and the trading room at the Art Institute of Chicago, a staircase in the Metropolitan Museum in New York. Other outstanding auditoriums were the Schiller Theater (1891), the first to spark preservation support, albeit unsuccessfully, and Kehilat Anshe Maariv (1889–1891), built as a synagogue but now a church. These were supplemented by the firm's dozens of houses and factories and large numbers of warehouses and hotels. With these larger commissions the firm grew, and young architects were brought in to work under Adler's and Sullivan's supervision. Several of the men who trained in the office—Wright, Alfred S. Alschuler, Hugh Garden, Simeon Eisendrath, Henry Ottenheimer, and Irving Gill—became prominent architects. By 1894 the office began to contract; by 1895 there was not enough work even for the two principals.

Adler and Sullivan had been together for more than fourteen years, but Chicago was in a deep economic depression, and they parted. Their split was exacerbated by a Buffalo commission that was only partially built. The Guaranty Building was but the office block of a complex that would also have had an opera house and hotel. Apparently there was friction between the two over the credit for the office building. Although the design shows Sullivan's fine hand as an artist, Adler may have considered it overly ornamented. Whatever the reason, it was their final job. They never again collaborated. They were not, however, implacable foes. After the split, Sullivan witnessed Adler's will and was one of the executors of Adler's estate. Adler's close associates hired Sullivan as an architect and helped him in times of financial need.

In the summer of 1895, when commissions were scarce, Adler accepted an offer from the Crane Elevator Company to become sales manager and architectural consultant. But he soon returned to the practice of architecture, this time with his son Abraham, a graduate of the University of Michigan. Between 1895 and 1900 D. Adler & Company designed only five major buildings, all in Chicago. Noteworthy are Morgan Park Academy dormitories (1896–1898) and the still extant Temple Isaiah (1898). In search of new clients, Adler opened a New York office with engineer Elmer L. Corthell, but in neither New York nor Chicago did the company prosper. Nor did the firm survive Dankmar's death in Chicago following a stroke. Marshall Field, who leveled the Central Music Hall for his new retail store, gave the family a column from the demolished building to mark Adler's grave, but his less tangible monuments proved more durable than his buildings; only twenty-eight of Adler's almost two hundred commissions were still standing in 1993, some greatly altered.

Adler served his two professions, architecture and engineering, in leadership roles, often in organizations he helped to found. He was elected the first treasurer and second president of the Western Association of Architects, founded in 1884. With Adler as chair of the committee, a merger of WAA and the older, eastern-dominated American Institute of Architects (AIA) took place in 1891. Adler's skill, tact, and dedication led to his election as secretary of the AIA in 1892. He was also active in the Western Society of Engineers, which he joined in 1879 and in whose journal he published. He helped organize the International Congress of Architects at the 1893 World's Columbian Exposition, and Adler & Sullivan built the Transportation Building, which won honors and generated much enthusiasm and praise in architectural journals both in the United States and abroad.

Dankmar Adler wrote on many topics, ranging from building foundations to the canons of art to technical education, which he published in the *Inland Architect and News Record, Architectural Record*, and some engineering journals as well, largely between 1886 and 1899. At the time of his death, he was working on an article on theaters for an architectural encyclopedia. The licensing law he crafted and for which he lobbied over two decades finally passed in 1897, making Illinois the first state in the nation with any form of architectural certification. Adler was appointed the first president of the State Board of Examiners of Architects.

A modest man who fostered the talents of others, Adler had a keen sense of humor, a huge capacity for work, vast technological acumen, and a reputation for directness, probity, and fairness, as well as the determination to put both architecture and engineering on sound professional foundations. He was a fine engineer, a competent architect, an excellent mentor, and a man respected by his colleagues. Although in the literature of architectural history Adler has been overshadowed by Louis Sullivan, Adler's own accomplishments include establishing a successful architectural office, working with outstanding consultants to solve a myriad of engineering problems, unifying the two major architectural organizations, bringing together engineering and architecture, and certifying architects. His works include some of the most well-designed and accomplished structures of the nineteenth century.

• Dankmar Adler's letters, diary, autobiography, articles, and scrapbooks are in the Adler Archive, Newberry Library, Chicago, Ill. The archive also contains manuscripts of published and unpublished books and newspaper clippings. An almost complete list of his publications is in Narciso Menocal, *Architecture as Nature: The Transcendental Idea of Louis Sullivan* (1981), and a list of buildings is in Robert Twombly, *Louis Sullivan: His Life and Work* (1986). Pictures of the buildings can be found in Richard Nickel, "A Photographic Documentation of the Architecture of Adler and Sullivan" (M.A. thesis, Illinois Institute of Technology, Chicago, 1957), and in the Nickel archive (office of John Vinci, Chicago). Charles Gregersen published *Dankmar Adler: His Theatres and Auditoriums* (1990); the same subject forms the core of Charles Grimsley, "A Study of the Contributions of Dankmar Adler to the Theater Building Practices of the Late Nineteenth Century" (Ph.D. diss., Northwestern Univ., 1984). His entire oeuvre is encompassed in Rochelle S. Elstein, "The Architectural Style of Dankmar Adler" (M.A. thesis, Univ. of Chicago, 1963) and "The Architecture of Dankmar Adler," *Journal of the Society of Architectural Historians* 26 (1967): 242–49. Obituaries are in the *Chicago Tribune* and the *New York Times*, both 17 Apr. 1900.

ROCHELLE BERGER ELSTEIN

ADLER, David (3 Jan. 1882–27 Sept. 1949), architect, was born in Milwaukee, Wisconsin, the son of Isaac David Adler, a wholesale maker of men's clothing, and Therese Hyman. Adler attended the Lawrenceville School and then Princeton University, receiving his B.A. in 1904. From 1904 to 1911 Adler toured Europe while attending the Polytechnic in Munich and the École des Beaux-Arts in Paris. During his travels he collected 500 postcards and developed an extensive library which became the foundation for his eclectic approach to design.

Alder's first job was a one-year position in the office of Howard Van Doren Shaw, an eminent midwestern architect. In 1911 Adler received his first independent commission, a house built in Glencoe, Illinois, for his uncle C. A. Stonehill. The house, based on the small chateaux of the Louis XIII period, was built on a high bluff overlooking Lake Michigan; it had a great stair hall that opened to a drawing room that overlooked the lake. The plan and facade were symmetrical compositions enhanced by a long allée, or formal avenue, leading from the front entrance drive to the house and beyond to the lake, thereby dramatically connecting the house and the land. The house was later demolished to make way for the North Shore Congregation Israel. For this and other homes Adler traveled to Europe to purchase architectural artifacts, as well as the architectural elements of entire rooms to be included in the design. Adler never directly copied existing structures, but he used details from past periods to create an eclectic vision. Adler began with clear historical images that were then developed, transformed, and refined to result in complex, familiar, yet surprisingly restrained architecture. Adler often included an entire site as a key element in his concept, usually involving a strong axis linking the house with the landscape. He insisted that every detail fit into a complex whole, with nothing capricious or an afterthought; even furniture was considered part of the architectural vision.

After completing the Stonehill country home in 1912, Adler opened an office located in Orchestra Hall on Michigan Avenue in Chicago with his friend Henry C. Dangler, a schoolmate at the École des Beaux-Arts and a coworker at the Shaw office. Dangler had obtained his Illinois architectural license; Adler had not yet completed the necessary exam. The two men designed and built approximately twelve houses during their five years together, until Dangler's death in 1917. It was during this time that Dangler introduced Adler to his future wife, Katherine Keith, who had gone to Coulters School before graduating from the University of Chicago. Adler designed the clothing for their June 1916 wedding; they had no children.

One of the most interesting projects from the Adler & Dangler office was a group of four townhouses at 2700 Lake View Avenue in Chicago, designed in 1915. Based on a typical London square, Adler employed the Adam style, with characteristic red brick above a limestone street story. The Adam style, popular in the early nineteenth century, was a refinement of the Georgian style and was characterized by a lightness and delicacy into which Adler infused a grander sense of scale and proportion. The townhouses reflect Adler's sense of historical transformation, restraint, and attention to detail. Another important project was the 1913 Ralph Poole country house in Lake Bluff, Illinois, which has a low elegant appearance from its curved drive, with the mansard roof accentuating the French chateau effect. Adler's interior sensibility is evidenced by the gracious scale and flexible floor plan. After Dangler's death Adler took on Robert Work as his new technical partner; their partnership continued for eleven years.

Jobs were few for Adler and Work after World War I and consisted at first of service buildings and alterations to Lake Forest homes. Commissions later returned, with the years between 1925 and 1929 being the most prolific. For the Joseph Ryersons of Chicago in 1921 Adler designed his only townhouse in the French style. The house has a timeless urban character, with simple classical moldings and ornament. His first design in an early American style was a clubhouse for Shoreacres in Lake Bluff, his only nonresidential design, built in 1923. The long, low Tidewater Colonial building is centered by a cupola that anchors the horizontality of the building. The simplicity of the white, wooden clapboard style with its line of dormers created the gracious and welcoming style desired by the forty-seven founding members of the private club. The building derived its style from typical eighteenth-century homes, such as those in Williamsburg, Virginia, and from manor houses such as Doughoregan Manor in Howard County, Maryland. In 1983 the building burned to the ground and was rebuilt by

Booth and Hansen Architects, who demonstrated sensitivity to Adler's style in recreating the building. Beginning in 1917 Adler designed his own farmhouse in Libertyville, Illinois. The structure, though simple and informal relative to his client's homes, is graced with a sense of elegance. Adler's ability to design in a range of styles while maintaining clarity and completeness expresses his well-developed visual sensitivity. It is said that he could notice a discrepancy of as little as one-quarter inch in a molding.

Two houses from his period with Work are highlights of Adler's career: a townhouse in New York for Mr. and Mrs. Marshall Field (1925), and Castle Hill in Ipswitch, Massachusetts, for Mr. and Mrs. Richard T. Crane (1927). The townhouse stands six stories tall with the top two stories set back, breaking the plane of the facade and giving the house an elegant scale. Adler used columns in the rooms of the townhouse to modulate the scale, as the interior space is the same grand size as the facade. It was with this project that Adler began collaborating with his sister Francis Elkins, a successful interior designer; their professional relationship continued for the rest of his life. The style of the fifty-nine-room Castle Hill is reminiscent of the house he had designed for Stonehill in Glencoe. A long axis connects the landscape from the forecourt through the house to the sea. The house is in the style of British architect Christopher Wren, with the broad allée lined with statuary leading to the sea. The interior contains a gallery in the true English baroque style, sixty-three feet long with sixteen-foot-high ceilings and two fireplaces.

In 1925 Adler was elected to the board of trustees of the Art Institute of Chicago, where he was an active member serving on six committees. He became a member of the American Institute of Architects in 1926. In 1928 an Illinois architectural license was granted to Adler based on his demonstrated skill and the thirty houses he had completed. Adler then dissolved his association with Work.

In 1930 Katherine Adler was killed in a car accident in France. Adler was physically unhurt but emotionally upset by his wife's death, and his design work subsequently decreased. In 1931 he designed a house for Mr. and Mrs. Lester Armour in Lake Bluff. The center section is based on the Hammond-Harwood House in Annapolis, Maryland, with two curved arcades on either side that gather the forecourt and the guests into the house. The house continues the Adler tradition of a long axis and meticulous attention to detail. In 1935 Adler was injured in a riding accident, an incident that slowed his work even further, compounded by the fact that, as Adler himself said, the architectural era of the "great house" was ended. Nonetheless, he continued to work, designing a small white Georgian house in 1937 in Winnetka, Illinois, for Mr. and Mrs. Louis B. Kuppenheimer, Jr., and completing other small houses and a museum. He died in Libertyville, Illinois. He is buried with his wife in Graceland Cemetery under an obelisk that he designed for her after her death.

In total, Adler designed and built forty-three large houses, fourteen of which were located outside of Chicago. He is known for his elaborate "great houses," most of which are still in use today and are recognized for their grace and elegance. Adler and fellow architect Frank Lloyd Wright, a Chicago contemporary of Adler, represent diametrically opposed architectural approaches. Wright worked to create an original American architectural style not based on European models. He did not travel to Europe and declined opportunities to do so. In contrast, Adler attempted to transform the received European tradition of architecture to create a fresh American quality. He was the educated, traveled synthesizer of American country homes.

• Adler's drawings, blueprints, and other documents are in the Department of Architecture, Art Institute of Chicago. For biographical information, see Richard Pratt, *David Adler* (1970), which includes photos by Ezra Stoller that document the original condition of the buildings and their interiors. Two other sources are an unpublished biography from the David Adler Cultural Center, Libertyville, Ill., and an unpublished thesis: Stephen M. Salny, "David Adler: The Epitome of an Era" (Lake Forest College, 1977). Leonard K. Eaton, *Two Chicago Architects* (1969), a treatment of Howard van Doren Shaw and Frank Lloyd Wright, provides helpful insight into the period.

LAURENCE O. BOOTH

ADLER, Felix (13 Aug. 1851–24 Apr. 1933), religious and social reformer, was born in Alzey, Germany, the son of Henrietta Frankfurter and Samuel Adler, a rabbi. At the age of six he came with the family to the United States when his father accepted an invitation to become rabbi of the Temple Emanuel in New York City. After attending public and private schools, he entered Columbia College, graduating in 1870. Plans for him to succeed his father as rabbi sent Adler to Europe, where he studied theology, philosophy, and linguistics under the tutelage of Abraham Geiger and Heymann Steinthal at the Hochschule für die Wissenschaft des Judenthums in Berlin. Alongside that work he also attended courses on philosophy, particularly Kantian ethics, and economics, especially the questions of labor and social reform, at the University of Berlin. In 1873 he received a Ph.D. from the University of Heidelberg and returned home to take up rabbinical duties. Those plans collapsed within the year because Adler had come to reject both theism and the divine origin of Hebrew Scriptures. After an amicable parting with Temple Emanuel, Adler lectured on Hebrew and Oriental literature at Cornell University from 1874 to 1876. In 1880 he married Helen Goldmark, and the couple had a family of five children.

Adler's knowledge of historical criticism made him increasingly wary of unquestioning dependence on inherited ideas and rituals. He also thought that sectarian ideologies were obstacles to religious progress and that confessional differences impeded practical action motivated by moral force. This preference for the tangible blended with Adler's concept of spiritual evolution to yield a religious orientation characterized by "deed not creed." In this vein he turned away from ideas about a personal monotheistic God, direct revelation, and a special covenant with the Jewish people and concentrated instead on the moral good in everyone, on the possibility of realizing genuine advances in universal ethical idealism. He was convinced that an ultimate metaphysical reality existed, one that transcended both organized religions and all mundane experience in the natural world. Two sources for this synthetic higher ideology were the Hebrew prophets, who judged spiritual and social inadequacies with exemplary moral fervor, and Jesus of Nazareth, who urged people to act on the purity dwelling in each of them. Adler devoted a major portion of his life to trying to persuade others that they could improve themselves and their social setting by striving to approximate these exalted ideals.

In 1876 such action took institutional shape as the New York Society for Ethical Culture. Adler founded this organization to facilitate practical humanitarian endeavor, especially in the fields of educational and philanthropical work. As its minister he delivered regular Sunday discourses to large audiences, urging individuals to lead morally upright lives independent of theistic beliefs. He also advocated a strong social ethic wherein an entire society could rise to higher standards of behavior. Influenced to some degree by Octavius Brooks Frothingham and the precedent of the Free Religious Association, Adler wanted his group to seek more practical goals with less rationalistic theorizing behind them. Affiliated congregations in what soon came to be called the Ethical Culture Society (ECS) were begun in such cities as Chicago (1882), Philadelphia (1885), St. Louis (1886), and Boston (1920). Adler urged his followers to express their spiritual motivations through concrete action. His interests led him to address such issues as tenement slums, child labor, vice, gambling, and nationalist imperialism. He espoused causes such as racial integration, pro-labor legislation, and the League of Nations. In 1878 he was instrumental in setting up early dispensaries and nursing facilities for New York's poor. Within another two years he founded the country's first free kindergarten, a workingman's school, and a program to provide better low-income housing. By 1895 the Ethical Culture School was a pioneer in demonstrating how manual training, art, and science could both instruct students while simultaneously improving their character.

In 1902 Adler supplemented his ECS activities with a professorship in political and social ethics at Columbia University, a post he held until his death in New York City. Most adherents espoused the ECS as a religious movement, but Adler increasingly viewed it simply as a social reform agency with ethical principles. As such, its program came to resemble other humanitarian impulses, such as the Social Gospel, Christian Science, and even liberal elements of Reform Judaism. Over the years his interest in ethics, culture, spirituality, and social improvement led to many honorific positions. He was chair of the National Child Labor Commission (1904–1921), Roosevelt Exchange Professor in Berlin (1908–1909), member of the Universal Races Congress (1911), Hibbert Lecturer at Oxford (1923), participant in the International Congress for Moral Education (1926), and for several years an editor of the *International Journal of Ethics*. His life demonstrated an understanding of religion as a social utility, a principle that promoted right living based on high ideals, unrestrained by dogma.

• Most of Adler's papers, including correspondence, a diary, notes, and manuscripts, are housed in the Columbia University library system in New York City. His publications include *Creed and Deed: A Series of Discourses* (1877), *The Ethics of the Political Situation* (1884), *The Moral Instruction of Children* (1892), *The Religion of Duty* (1905), *The World Crisis and Its Meaning* (1915), *An Ethical Philosophy of Life, Presented in Its Main Outlines* (1918), and *The Reconstruction of the Spiritual Ideal* (1924). Biographical information can be found in Robert S. Guttchen, *Felix Adler* (1974); Benny Kraut, *From Reform Judaism to Ethical Culture: The Religious Evolution of Felix Adler* (1979); and Horace L. Friess, *Felix Adler and Ethical Culture: Memories and Studies* (1981). An obituary is in the *New York Times*, 26 Apr. 1933.

HENRY WARNER BOWDEN

ADLER, George J. (1821–24 Aug. 1868), philologist, was born in Leipzig, Germany, the son of John J. Adler. His mother's name is unknown. He immigrated to the United States at the age of twelve and later graduated as valedictorian of the class of 1844 at New York University. He was appointed professor of modern languages there in 1846, and by 1847 he had published two textbooks on German language.

During this period Adler labored on his monumental *Dictionary of the German and English Languages* (1849) with feverish intensity. After its publication, he was recognized as one of the great philologists of his time. Based on a thorough revision of Karl Alfred Felix Flügel's *Practical Dictionary of the English and German Languages* (1847), Adler's work offered nearly 30,000 new words as well as several hundred concise articles on synonyms. Adler's *Dictionary* remained a classic in its field for generations.

Adler worked so relentlessly on his *Dictionary* that by the time of its publication he had ruined his health. Recovering from a brush with mental illness, he sailed for Europe in the fall of 1849. George Duyckinck, a leading member of the New York literary circle, introduced Adler to Herman Melville during the embarkation, and the travelers soon became fast friends. Adler accompanied Melville's party to London and Paris, impressing the young writer with his knowledge of philosophy, particularly "the German metaphysics . . . Kant, Swedenberg [*sic*], etc." (Weaver, p. 285).

Adler returned to New York and to his work at the university in 1850, and subsequently produced a translation of Goethe's *Iphigenia in Tauris: A Drama in Five Acts* (1850) and a *Manual of German Literature* (1853). During this period his mental health continued to decline, prompting Henry Wadsworth Longfellow to note in his diary, "Poor fellow! He has overworked his brain; and has a monomania; believing himself the subject of popular persecution in New York; crowds look at him strangely in the street and voices under his window at night cry, 'Go Home! Go Home!'"

The hallucinations that plagued Adler in the summer of 1853 were followed by a violent outburst in October that resulted in his commitment to Bloomingdale Asylum. He wrote to Evert Duyckinck, brother of George, on 10 October, requesting his friends to secure his release. With grim humor, he signed the letter an "insane man at this hospital, reading, rolling ninepins, eating (what he can get), and sleeping with a better appetite than usual."

In the months that followed Adler worked on a privately printed pamphlet aptly titled *Letters of a Lunatic* (1854). Even while fighting mental illness, the remaining years of his life were far from unproductive. In addition to publishing several scholarly works on grammar and literature, he gave lectures on Goethe's *Faust*, Roman literature, and Arabian poetry. He was forced to resign his position at the university in 1854. His numerous works from this period include *Latin Grammar* (1858), a translation of Fauriel's *History of Provençal Poetry* (1860), *Notes on Certain Passages of the Agamemnon of Aeschylus* (1861), *Wilhelm von Humboldt's Linguistic Studies* (1866), and *The Poetry of the Arabs of Spain* (1867).

Adler died in Bloomingdale, New Jersey. His old friends Melville and Evert Duyckinck were among the small group of mourners present at his funeral. The *New York Times* subsequently noted, "By his death New York has lost one of her most valued citizens and literature [has lost] a faithful student and earnest teacher."

• Raymond Weaver, *Herman Melville* (1921), Merell R. Davis and William H. Gilman, *The Letters of Herman Melville* (1960), and Jay Leyda, *The Melville Log* (1969), provide valuable glimpses of Adler at the peak of his career. The few facts known about his life can be found in Evert Duyckinck and George Duyckinck's *Cyclopedia of American Literature*, rev. ed. (1875); J. L. Chamberlain, ed., *Universities and Their Sons: New York University* (1901); the *New York University General Alumni Catalogue* (1906); and Lyman R. Bradley and H. G. Wendt's sketch in the *German Quarterly* 7 (1934): 152–56. An obituary is in the *New York Times*, 25 Aug. 1868.

JAMES M. PRICHARD

ADLER, Jacob Pavlovich (12 Feb. 1855–31 Mar. 1926), actor, was born in Odessa, South Russia, the son of Feivel (Pavel) Abramovich Adler and Hessye Halperin, both of the orthodox Jewish faith. He was educated in Hebrew school, but because of his father's failure in business he was sent to work at any early age in a textile factory. His youth was dominated by a desire for pleasure that led him into bad company, but a new and all-absorbing interest in the Russian theater saved him from what he called the "grave moral danger" of this period. His enthusiasm for a leading Odessa actress came to her attention, and at her request the sixteen-year-old Adler became the leader of her clacque. In this post, which he held for several years, he saw the plays of Shakespeare, Schiller, and Ostrovsky, and the realistic acting of the Russian theater remained his ideal throughout his later life.

Adler's ambitions as an actor could not be realized by an unconverted Jew in Russia, but in 1879, learning that a Yiddish theater had come into being in Romania, his ambitions revived. Some members of the Romanian troupe performed that year in Odessa, and although he found their performances disappointing and crude, he joined them and toured Russia for several years as an actor.

In 1881, with the assassination of the liberal Alexander II, harsh anti-Jewish laws were enacted, and in 1883 all Yiddish theater was forbidden. Part of the mass Jewish migration, Adler and his troupe sailed for London. His London years were marked by poverty and by personal tragedy when his wife and three-year-old daughter died. But he grew in London as an actor, became the idol of the London ghetto, and in 1889 came to the United States as an actor of renown and a star.

Adler's success continued in New York City, but the two Yiddish theaters on the Bowery were struggling to hold an extremely small and naive public, many of whom had never seen theater before coming to America. Musicals on biblical themes were the standard fare, spectacles relying mainly on borrowed music and a strong appeal to Jewish nationalism. Adler, with no singing voice, took a lease on Poole's Theatre on Eighth Street, renamed it the Union Theater, and opened with Zolotkev's *Samson the Great*, a play Salvini had done. He followed with Scribe's *La Juive* and *Quo Vadis*, becoming the only actor to rely on purely dramatic roles from the European repertoire.

The better plays at Adler's theater had no popular success, but they interested the intelligentsia of the quarter, and Adler found another ally in the writer Jacob Gordin. He failed with Gordin's first play and again with his second. Gordin's third play *The Yiddish King Lear*, was an overwhelming success and brought the first mass audience to the Yiddish theater. A new era began, and with it, a new prosperity. Every star fought for Gordin's plays, following the trend for "better theater." In addition to performing during the next ten years in plays of Jewish life by Gordin and others, Adler also directed and starred in plays by Tolstoy, Gorki, Andreyev, Ibsen, Strindberg, Hauptmann, Hugo, Scribe, Sardou, and Shaw. By the turn of the century a number of critics and intellectuals, notable among them Lincoln Steffens, Hutchins Hapgood, and later George Jean Nathan and Stark Young, were taking a marked interest in these productions downtown.

In 1901 Adler's production of *The Merchant of Venice* caused something of a stir in New York theater circles. A number of Broadway stars came to see his performance, the critic Henry Tyrell pronounced his Shylock a revelation, and in his article, "Jacob Adler—the Bowery Garrick" (*Theatre Magazine*, Nov. 1902), compared the effect of the Yiddish actor on his audience with that of Salvini in Italy, Sonnenthal in Vienna, and Edwin Forrest in New York. Adler's name assumed a certain prominence in the wider theatrical world, and in 1903 the American producer Arthur Hopkins prevailed on him to bring his Shylock to Broadway. The play opened at the American Theatre on 25 May 1903, Adler delivering his lines in Yiddish with an English-speaking cast.

Adler's Shylock, though vindictive and avaricious, was an innovative portrayal, conveying the idea that Shylock meant to humble and humiliate Antonio but not to shed his blood. Adler was admired for his powerful acting in the trial scene and for the scornful, defiant exit in which the character expressed an indomitable pride in his people and his heritage.

Adler portrayed Shylock as the Jew of the ages, tragic but indomitable. Describing his conception of this archetypal Jew, he wrote:

> A certain grandeur, the triumph of long patience, intellect and character, has been imparted to him by the sufferings and traditions that have been his teachers. Not only can he go through life, he is *rooted* in life, and has grown strong in it. And so he has much joy, much blood, much reality in him. . . . Weighty and proud his walk, calm and conclusive his speech, a man of richest . . . national experience, a man who sees life through the glasses of eternity.

The play was revived in May 1905 and described in the *New York Herald* as "that rare experience on Broadway, the coincidence of a great play and a great actor." The production generated interest in another bilingual appearance in a historical play by Jacob Gordin. But Adler's proud, defiant Shylock had been his statement to the world as a Jew, and, having made it, he went back to his own public.

Although the American public was largely unaware of the Yiddish theater, Adler was internationally known, and in 1911 the Tolstoy estate gave him the first American rights to the posthumous play *The Living Corpse*. The play had caused a sensation at the two imperial theaters in Russia and at the Hofburg in Vienna, and Adler's premiere at the Thalia Theatre drew a glittering array of theatrical notables. Laudatory reviews appeared in the *New York Dramatic Mirror*, *Theatre Magazine*, the *New York Times*, and other publications.

In the summer of 1920 Adler suffered a paralytic stroke, and afterward he appeared only at yearly "farewell performances" that provided his only income. Al Jolson, Will Rogers, Richard Bennett, and the opera star Giovanni Martinelli were among the celebrities who took part in these events. At the end of each program Adler performed the first act of *The Yiddish King Lear*. Since that act takes place entirely around the festive table of Gordin's Yiddish "king," the paralyzed man could remain seated throughout his performance. He made his last public appearance on 17 March 1926, and two weeks later he died at his home in New York City.

Adler's funeral, on 2 April, was described in the *New York Times* as "a demonstration on the lower east side seldom equalled in the history of New York." One hundred patrolmen and a squadron of twenty-four mounted police were stationed along the route of the funeral procession, and New York newspapers estimated the mass of mourners as between 100,000 and 500,000 people. The *Daily News* and *New York Journal* both carried banner headlines of the event, articles and obituaries appeared in every New York newspaper, and an editorial in the *New York Sun* traced the history of his theatrical life. An editorial in the *New York Times* declared that with his death the heroic age of the Yiddish theater had ended.

The critic and director Harold Clurman, recollecting the Yiddish tragedian in the introduction to the biography *Bright Star of Exile*, wrote, "His charm was captivating, his dignity awesome, his wrath terrifying. When he towered as the vengeful patriarch, Shylock, or, as Uriel Acosta, raised the torch of free thought in epic loftiness, or teased as the shrewdly humorous Odessa Beggar, the *size* of the man—I do not refer to his physique—imposed a sense of peril. Grandeur always inspires a certain shudder at life's immeasurable mystery and might" (p. xiv).

While touring in Russia Adler had married the actress Sophia Solomonova Oberlander, with whom he had two children, one of whom survived. Following her death in London he married the actress Dinah Shtettin in 1887; they had one daughter, born in the United States. The marriage ended in divorce, and in 1891 he married the former Mrs. Sarah Heine, who, as Sarah Adler, would be a famous actress in her own right; they had five children. A son was born in London to Adler and the actress Jennya Kaiser.

Adler was father to a dynasty of actors who performed with distinction on both the stage and screen. Luther Adler and Stella Adler were cofounders of the Group Theater, a permanent company of the 1930s whose new approaches to acting have had a profound and lasting theatrical influence. Stella Adler's acting school, founded in 1941, was a training ground for several major American film stars. Celia Adler attained a leading position in the Yiddish Art Theater movement.

• Adler's autobiography, *Forty Years on the Stage*, was published in Yiddish in the newspaper *Die Varheit* from 30 Apr. 1916 to 3 Mar. 1919 and, under the title *My Life*, continued in *Die Neie Varheit* from 14 Mar. 1925 to 2 July 1925. Both newspapers are on microfilm at the Yiddish Institute of Research (YIVO) in New York City and in the Jewish Division of the New York Public Library. Lulla Rosenfeld's biography of Adler, *Bright Star of Exile* (1977), includes a history of the Yiddish theater from its inception in 1876; an expanded edition, titled *The Yiddish Theatre and Jacob P. Adler* (1988), includes additional material on his personal and professional life. Hutchins Hapgood, *The Spirit of the Ghetto* (1967), is an important source on Adler and other Yiddish actors and playwrights. See *Theatre Magazine* for a review of Adler's Broadway performance in *The Merchant of Venice* (July 1903) and for a review of his performance in Tolstoy's *The Power of*

Darkness (Nov. 1903). Articles in the *New York Dramatic Mirror* include a review of three plays (7 Mar. 1906) and a review of *The Living Corpse* (15 Nov. 1911); reviews of *The Living Corpse* are also in the *Morning Telegraph* (11 Nov. 1911) and the *New York Times* (5 Nov. 1911). An editorial on Adler's death appears in the *New York Times*, 3 Apr. 1926.

LULLA ROSENFELD

ADLER, Luther (4 May 1903–8 Dec. 1984), stage, film, and television actor, was born in New York City, the son of Jacob Pavlovich Adler, founder of the American Yiddish theater movement, and Sarah Levitzkaya, an actress. While all of the children acted professionally, only Luther and his sister Stella developed notable careers. Young Adler made his debut at age four in Goldfaden's *Schmendrik* at his father's Grand Street Theatre in lower Manhattan. This began a series of parts in which Adler was often unhappily required to play young female roles because of his blond ringlets. Following his parents' divorce, he was sent to Chicago where he attended the Lewis Institute.

At age ten, already a veteran of the Yiddish stage, Adler signed his first contract for a forty-week season with his mother's company at Brooklyn's Novelty Theatre. There he performed a variety of roles ranging from strapping youths to doddering old men. His repertoire included Shakespeare, Tolstoy, and other period favorites. At age seventeen Adler managed his own touring company, with his mother as leading lady, performing plays by Yiddish dramatist Jacob Gordin. Following this venture, in 1922 he was cast in his first English-speaking stage appearance in Marc Klow's touring production of *Sonya*.

In December 1921 Adler joined the famed Provincetown Players, performing in *The Stick-up* and *The Hand of the Potter*. He made his Broadway debut in February 1923 as the young violinist Leon Kantor in *Humoresque*. This led to a string of Broadway appearances that included Zizi in *The Monkey Talks* (1925), Sam Madorsky in *Money Business* (1926), Phil Levine in *We Americans* (1926), and the Old Man in *John* (1927). Early in 1927 Adler toured England and South Africa as the leading man in Harry Green's company of *The Music Master*, *Is Zat So?* and *Give and Take*. Returning to New York, he performed one season with the Yiddish Folk Theatre, playing starring roles opposite other Adler family members. In 1929 he appeared in two Theatre Guild productions, *Red Rust* and *Street Scene*, both on the Broadway stage.

In 1931 came the formation of the Group Theatre, whose pioneering mission was to produce new socially significant American dramas. The Group Theatre was based upon the Moscow Art Theatre's concept of collective ensemble acting, and its influence altered the course of American theater. It was with this company that Adler experienced his greatest professional triumphs. He had met the Group's founders, Harold Clurman, Cheryl Crawford, and Lee Strasberg, while working for the Theatre Guild; his Guild contract, however, prevented him from joining the disciples of Konstantin Stanislavski's new principles of realistic acting until March 1932, when he accepted the role of Don Fernando in *Night Over Taos*. Adler, excited with what he considered "an actor's paradise," accompanied the Group to Dover Furnace, New York, during the summer of 1932. There he was cast as Sol Ginsberg in the Group's *Success Story* (1932). "Luther Adler gave what most people agreed was 'one of the finest performances the present day theater has housed'" (Clurman, p. 101).

When *Success Story* closed, Adler left briefly to play Julian Vardaman in Katherine Cornell's production of *Alien Corn* (1933), but in September he rejoined the Group, replacing Morris Carnovsky as Dr. Gorden in *Men In White*. Adler achieved his first major success with that company when he appeared as bitter war veteran, Moe Axelrod, opposite his sister Stella, in *Awake and Sing* (1935), which critic Brooks Atkinson felt was "acted with emotional electricity." Other roles followed, establishing Adler as a first-rate character actor: Marcus Katz in *Paradise Lost* (1935), the Doctor in *The Case of Clyde Griffiths* (1936), and *Johnny Johnson* (1936).

Adler made his film debut as Schratt in *Lancer Spy* in 1937; in November of that year he returned to Broadway in the Group's *Golden Boy* as violinist turned boxer, Joe Bonaparte. Atkinson praised Adler for acting "the part of the headlong fighter with the speed and energy of an open-field runner." Opening to glowing reviews, the original *Golden Boy* cast was invited to perform at London's St. James Theatre on 21 June 1938. A *New York Times* correspondent reported that Adler "was hailed for brilliantly sensitive acting" (22 June 1938), and *(London) Times* critic James Agate commented, "The acting attains a level which is something we know nothing at all about" (quoted in Clurman, p. 225). At age thirty-five, Adler was at the zenith of his career.

In 1938 Adler married film actress Sylvia Sidney in London; they had one son. When he again returned to the New York stage, Adler played elderly bon vivant Mr. Prince in *Rocket to the Moon* (1938). His final appearance with the Group Theatre was Chatterton in *Thunder Rock* (1939). Quickly hired by the Playwright's Company, Adler went on to portray embittered theatrical producer Lawrence Ormont in *Two On An Island* (1940).

Even though he was no longer with a repertory company, Adler was rarely without work. During the 1943–1944 season he directed and costarred with his wife in a West Coast tour of *Jane Eyre*—she in the title role and he as Mr. Rochester. He later directed Broadway's *A Flag Is Born* (1946), eventually replacing Paul Muni in the role of Tevya. Although Broadway appearances diminished during the latter 1940s, Adler enjoyed increasingly more film work. From 1945 through 1950 he performed in nine films, most notably as Marcel Jarnac in *Cornered* (1945), Mayrant Sidneye in *Wake of the Red Witch* (1948), and Majak in *D.O.A.* (1950). Although his marriage to Sylvia Sydney ended in divorce in 1947, their relationship remained amicable.

During the early 1950s Adler's Hollywood career, with few exceptions, was lackluster. In the 1951 film *The Magic Face* (which Adler considered his "film triumph"), he portrayed Janus, a German actor who avenges his wife's murder by killing Hitler, impersonating his victim, and leading the Reich into destruction. That same year he appeared in a remake of *M* and was called upon to repeat his Führer impersonation in *The Desert Fox*, opposite James Mason. New York stage appearances during the decade included revivals of the City Center's productions of *Tovarich* (1952), as Commisar Corotchenco, and *The Merchant of Venice* (1953), as Shylock. Adler won renewed acclaim for his performance as Shipichelsky in the Phoenix Theatre's *A Month in the Country* (1956). "Luther Adler's cynical doctor," proclaimed *Saturday Review* critic Henry Hewes, "is a comic *tour de force*." On 14 November 1956 Adler again teamed with Sylvia Sidney in Broadway's *A Very Special Baby*. His performance as Casale earned him praise from Atkinson, who commented, "Luther Adler plays the father with tremendous force and craft" (*New York Times*, 15 Nov. 1956).

In 1957 Adler successfully directed himself as Eddie Carbone in a tour of *A View from the Bridge*. Throughout the 1950s he also appeared in a string of "B" films and television roles (such as adaptations of *Billy Budd*, *Hedda Gabler*, and *A Doll's House*). In 1959 he married Julia Roche. During the 1960s his film and television engagements dwindled; he portrayed Jacob Zion in *Cast a Giant Shadow* (1966), Dominick Bertolo in *The Brotherhood* (1968), and Imre Hyneck in television's *The Sunshine Patriot* (1968). It was primarily New York stage performances that kept him active. Adler returned to Broadway as Lenin in *The Passion of Josef D*, opposite Peter Falk's Stalin (1964), and as Chebutykin in *The Three Sisters* (1964). He replaced the vacationing Zero Mostel for two weeks as Tevye in *Fiddler on the Roof* (1965), assuming the role again the following August. After a brief tour in *The Tenth Man* (1966), Adler headed *Fiddler*'s national company (October 1967). Final stage credits included General St. Pé in *Waltz of the Toreadors* (1969) and Solomon in *The Price* (1970).

Adler worked sporadically in six minor films between 1974 and 1981, but only *The Man in the Glass Booth* (1975), *Voyage of the Damned* (1976), and *Absence of Malice* (1981) were considered notable. A master of European dialects and among the first American actors to employ the stage techniques of Stanislavsky, Adler established a reputation that reached its height during his years with the Group Theatre. "I would include playing with Luther as one of my most important influences," Stella Adler later recalled in an interview with the *Los Angeles Times* (6 Sept. 1986). "To be on stage with him was indescribable." Adler died in Kutztown, Pennsylvania.

• "Celia Adler Recalls," from Joseph C. Landis's *Memoirs of the Yiddish Stage* (1984), and David S. Lifson's *The Yiddish Theatre in America* (1965) offer useful information on Jacob P. Adler and his family. Other sources are Lulla Rosenfeld, *Bright Star of Exile: Jacob Adler and the Yiddish Theatre* (1977), and Wendy Smith, *Real Life Drama: The Group Theatre and America, 1931–1940* (1990). Harold Clurman's *The Fervent Years* (1975) traces Adler's Group Theatre years, and the Billy Rose Theatre Collection at the New York Public Library for the Performing Arts, Lincoln Center's collection of Adler's press clippings and playbills is also valuable. Other research material includes Brooks Atkinson, *Broadway* (1970); "In the Adler Tradition," *New York Times*, 2 Oct. 1932; Frances Herridge's "Luther Adler Is Frank About Love," *New York Post*, 23 Apr. 1956; and Henry Hewes's "Broadway Postscript," *Saturday Review*, 21 Apr. 1956, p. 24. An obituary is in the *New York Times*, 9 Dec. 1984.

WILLIAM SHAWN SMITH

ADLER, Morris (30 Mar. 1906–11 Mar. 1966), rabbi, was born in Slutsk, Russia, the son of Joseph Adler, a rabbi, and Jennie Resnick. Adler arrived in the United States with his mother and brother in 1913, joining his father who had settled in New York City two years earlier. A shy and bookish boy, Adler grew up on the Lower East Side, attending a Hebrew elementary school and the DeWitt Clinton High School. He studied at the Hebrew Teachers' Institute, at the Rabbi Isaac Elchanan Yeshiva (later Yeshiva University), and at the City College of New York, from which he graduated in 1928. In 1929 he married Goldie Kadish; the couple had one daughter. By this time Adler had developed a fascination with the idea of helping troubled people, and his wife recalled that he probably would have studied psychiatry if he had not entered the rabbinate. After brief service officiating at an Orthodox synagogue in St. Joseph, Missouri, he decided to enter the Jewish Theological Seminary (JTS). His father, who was the principal of an Orthodox school in Brooklyn, nevertheless supported his son's decision to seek ordination within the Conservative branch of Judaism. Adler was ordained at the JTS in June 1935.

After serving for three years at Temple Emanu-El in Buffalo, New York, Adler was hired in 1938 as assistant rabbi of Congregation Shaarey Zedek in Detroit, where he served for the rest of his life, ascending to a life term as senior rabbi in 1954. Adler was the first officially ordained Conservative rabbi in Michigan, and under his leadership Shaarey Zedek emerged as one of the most prominent Conservative synagogues in the nation, with a membership of 1,500 families by the early 1960s.

During World War II, Adler served as a chaplain, stationed in the Philippines with the Eleventh Airborne outside of Manila. He was reportedly the first American chaplain to enter Japan on the day it surrendered, and there he searched for Jewish refugees. Upon witnessing the ruins of Hiroshima, he recalled, "I felt a sense of disaster, of doom trembling over the world." This experience led him to develop a strong antiwar sentiment. In the postwar years, Rabbi Adler engaged in a flurry of activity, publishing a two-volume collection *Selected Passages of the Torah* (1947); initiating an innovative series of annual summer retreats in northern Michigan for study, prayer, and discussion of social issues (1948); and chairing the Rabbinical Assembly's Committee on Jewish Law and Standards (1948–1951), which produced a historic 1950 responsum permitting automobile travel and the use of electricity to enhance Sabbath observance.

During the 1950s and 1960s, Adler engaged in numerous organizational and publishing activities. His ecumenical and civic involvements included the chairmanship of the United Auto Workers (UAW) Public Review Board (1957–1966); the vice presidency of the Community Health Association (1958–1966); and service on the Detroit Round Table of Catholics, Protestants, and Jews, the clergy panel on moral and ethical matters for American Motors, the Michigan Fair Election Practices Commission, the State Cultural Commission, the Commission on Ethics in State Affairs, the Citizens' Advisory Committee on Equal Opportunity, the Labor-Management Citizens' Commission, the Governor's Commission on Higher Education, and the Governor's Commission on Problems of the Aging. In addition, he was an adviser and instructor in the Department of Near Eastern Languages of Wayne State University. The rabbi served various Jewish organizations and councils, with a primary commitment to adult education. From 1963 until his death, he chaired the B'nai B'rith Commission on Adult Jewish Education. Adler wrote often for the organization's quarterly *Jewish Heritage*, and he published the *Jewish Heritage Reader* (1965), an anthology of essays and articles by scholars and writers such as Salo Baron, Erich Fromm, Elie Wiesel, Leslie Fiedler, and William F. Albright. Aside from an introduction, Adler contributed to this book a concise commentary of his own on the significance of the Sh'ma, the central Hebrew proclamation of the unity of God.

Rabbi Adler's most significant book was *The World of the Talmud* (1958), which long served as one of the most accessible explanations in English of the Talmud. An example of the literary clarity that Adler's prose could attain, this compact book contains an impressively complete description of the content, style, and background of the Talmud as well as a lucid interpretation of its significance for modern people. Characteristic of postwar Jewish writing, *The World of the Talmud* emphasized the ways in which Rabbinic Judaism, which is rooted in the Talmud, offered alternatives to Christian doctrines of Original Sin, *extra ecclesiam nulla salus* (no salvation outside of the Church), and "the powers that be are ordained of God." Adler also held up the Talmudic tolerance for disagreement and respect for rationality as models for a world that had been so profoundly shaken by wanton irrationalism. Aside from its contemporary concerns, *The World of the Talmud* presents timeless evocations of the Jewish values embodied in the Oral Law.

Adler, who prided himself on his efforts to educate both adults and youth in the ways of traditional Judaism, was ironically struck down by a deranged 23-year-old congregant, who shot the rabbi in the head during Sabbath services in Detroit and then killed himself. The day of Adler's funeral, 13 March, was declared a statewide day of mourning by Governor George Romney. Many thousands of people attended the funeral, at which Romney and UAW president Walter Reuther gave eulogies.

In both his sermons and his writings, Adler focused singlemindedly on the task of maintaining the connection between contemporary Jews and the traditional rituals and ethics of Judaism. "The Hebrew tongue has no equivalent for the concept 'lost soul,'" he wrote, "for no man can move outside the orbit of God's concern and forgiveness."

• Two posthumous anthologies of Adler's writings and sermons are Goldie Adler and Lily Edelman, eds., *May I Have a Word with You?* (1967), and Jocob Chinitz, *The Voice Still Speaks: Message of the Torah for Contemporary Man* (1969). A brief biographical portrait of Adler is in Pamela Susan Nadell, ed., *Conservative Judaism in America: A Biographical Dictionary and Sourcebook* (1988). More detailed biographical information is available in T. V. LoCicero, *Murder in the Synagogue* (1970), and Nancy Savage, "The Preaching Career of Rabbi Morris Adler with Special Attention to Selected Sermons, 1958–1966" (Ph.D. diss., Wayne State Univ., 1971), which gives a lengthy analysis of Adler's religious oratory. Obituaries are in the *Detroit Free Press*, 12 Mar. 1966, and the *Detroit News*, 11 Mar. 1966.

ANDREW R. HEINZE

ADLER, Polly (16 Apr. 1900?–9 June 1962), prostitution madam and author, was born Pearl Adler in Yanow, Russia, the daughter of Morris Adler, a tailor, and Gertrude Koval (called "Isidore" and "Sarah" in her autobiography). Later in life Adler also used several aliases, including Joan Martin and Pearl Davis. When Adler was twelve, her family arranged for her to be tutored by the local rabbi in the hope that she would receive a scholarship to study at a Gymnasium in Pinsk. A year later, before learning the results of the scholarship competition, Adler's father sent his daughter to live in the United States. Traveling alone, thirteen-year-old Adler arrived in New York in December 1913.

Adler settled in Holyoke, Massachusetts, where she lived with family acquaintances and attended the local school. The escalation of World War I prevented Adler's family from joining her or sending funds for her board and schooling. After only one semester in school, she went to work in a paper factory to earn her support. Two years later she moved to Brooklyn, New York, where she lived with cousins and worked in a corset factory and then in a shirt factory, attending night school when she could.

As a vivacious and attractive urban teenager, Adler soon discovered the pleasures of dating and dance halls. She dreamed of escaping the depressing poverty of her relatives. Her hopes for a better life seemed short-lived when, at seventeen, she was raped by her factory supervisor, which resulted in a pregnancy, an abortion, and eventually the loss of her job. Following an argument with her relatives about her lifestyle, she moved to a tenement on the lower East Side of Manhattan, and after much difficulty found part-time work in another corset factory. In early 1920 a friend introduced Adler to an attractive actress on the Upper West Side. Sharing the actress's apartment, Adler was exposed to the fashionable but fast-moving world of show business, nightclubs, and bootleggers. Soon distressed with the effects of her friend's drug addiction, she accepted the offer of a bootlegger-gangster to move to a rent-free apartment, on the condition that she allow him to come there for assignations with his married mistress. Adler later commented that though she didn't focus on the implications at the time, "this was my first big step down the so-called primrose path" (*A House . . .*, p. 40). She began hiring women for other men to meet at the apartment and soon had a thriving prostitution business. After experiencing the humiliation and fear of her first arrest, however, she determined to go into a legitimate enterprise as soon as she could accumulate enough capital.

By 1922 Adler and a widowed friend had saved enough money to open "Polly's Lingerie Shop"; Adler adopted a new name for herself as well as for her business. Within a year of its opening, the shop failed, and Adler returned to managing a prostitution establishment, vowing not to retire again until she had achieved considerable financial success. Most of her clientele were gangsters and hoodlums who persuaded her to sell liquor as well as sex, a step that significantly increased her revenues. Her establishment rapidly became popular, in spite of the disruptions caused by rowdy underworld customers, corrupt police who demanded payoffs as well as hospitality, and jealous fellow madams, who periodically harassed her.

Though having to close down and relocate was a persistent inconvenience of the trade for all brothel keepers, Adler's moves became less frequent by the second half of the 1920s. She shrewdly used each move as an opportunity to reestablish her business closer to midtown Manhattan, where she hoped to attract a "higher class" of clientele. In a further effort to attract socialities, businessmen, and a theatrical crowd, Adler also opened a place in Saratoga during the racing season. When she had secured a more "respectable" clientele, Adler proudly claimed that by the late twenties "Polly's" had become "a place to meet friends, play cards, [and] arrange a dinner party . . . a club and speakeasy with a harem conveniently handy" (*A House . . .*, p. 95).

By 20 May 1929, when Adler became a U.S. citizen, she had accumulated significant assets from her business and stock investments. She sustained a considerable loss in the stock market crash of 1929, but the revenues of her house, especially the bar, continued to increase.

In November 1930 Adler received a tip that she was to be subpoenaed by the Seabury Committee, which was investigating corruption in New York City's vice and criminal justice divisions. Fearful of repercussions from both the investigators and the vice officials if she discussed her payoffs and connections with the law, Adler went into hiding for six months in New Jersey and Florida. When she believed the investigators were no longer interested in her, Adler returned to New York in May 1931. She was immediately subpoenaed to appear before the committee to answer questions concerning the nature of her relationship with vice squad officer Irwin O'Leary and the reasons she had never been convicted for operating a disorderly house—in spite of fourteen arrests. The newspapers kept Adler's name before the public from May until August of 1931, describing her as the city's most notorious vice "entrepreneuse." Although Adler refused to give any information, Officer O'Leary ultimately revealed that he and Adler were friends and had shared a joint stock account, a confession that caused his dismissal from the force. Women's Court prosecutor John C. Weston, in defending himself against charges of bribery, intimated that Adler had been free of conviction for her arrests while he was in charge because he had "feared her influence."

Although her house remained closed for a period in the aftermath of the Seabury affair, Adler felt that, on the whole, the investigation helped her business by eliminating "double-crossing Vice Squad men," frequent bribes, and "phony raids." The investigation's notoriety also "acted as a magnet for business." Adler later wrote that the publicity had "made the nation 'Polly-conscious' on a scale I had never dreamed of, and socialites and money people . . . from all over came flocking to my apartment to be entertained" (*A House . . .*, p. 227). It even became fashionable for women to go to Polly's for drinks and conversation. She did not altogether escape the rough and unruly crowd, however, because gangster Arthur "Dutch Schultz" Flegenheimer used her place as his meeting and relaxation headquarters for a period during the early 1930s.

In 1934 Adler rented one of her most prestigious Manhattan locations, an entire floor of twelve rooms on East 55th Street between Fifth Avenue and Madison. This location became a prime target of another vice clean-up campaign led by Mayor Fiorello La Guardia. In March 1935 Adler's establishment was raided. She was charged with operating a disorderly house and possessing obscene films, and three women arrested on the premises were charged with vagrancy. Adler's bail was set at approximately five times the normal level, and the federal government brought their own anti-Adler case by filing a $16,000 income tax lien against her bail money for failure to report income in the 1920s.

Although the film-possession charge was eventually dropped, Adler was convicted for operating a disorderly house, receiving a sentence of thirty days in jail and a $500 fine. She was released after twenty-four days, and tired of fighting the system, she tried once again unsuccessfully to go into a legitimate business. She found the prostitution stigma impossible to overcome and thus resolved that henceforth, if "I was a madam . . . [and] I couldn't live my reputation down . . . I'd live up to it" (*A House . . .*, p. 283).

In the post-Seabury environment, keeping a house open at a particular location for an extended period of time became increasingly difficult. When future New

York governor Thomas Dewey launched another campaign against vice in 1936, Adler took a vacation to California and tried unsuccessfully to relocate her business in Chicago. After her return to New York, her business prospered for the next eight years, flourishing during the disruptions of World War II, just as it had during the depression. Adler's last arrest occurred in 1943, when she was very ill with pleurisy. She was incarcerated in the prison ward of Bellevue Hospital for two weeks until her case was heard, and after it was dismissed, she decided it was time to retire. She moved to Los Angeles, finished her high school degree, and enrolled in a local college.

Adler never married or had children. In 1928 her parents and siblings had moved to Brooklyn, and although she visited them on occasion, the years of separation from them in her youth, as well as her fear of their disappointment if they learned of her real occupation, prevented her from ever reestablishing a close relationship with them.

Her proudest accomplishment during her final years was the completion of her autobiography, *A House Is Not a Home* (1953), a bestseller that was translated into eleven languages and made into a movie after her death. The book is a story of her public and private life, a social history of the twenties and thirties, and Adler's personal appraisal of the prostitution business. The *Atlantic Monthly* called it "a criminal version of the classic American success story" (p. 84). In spite of an upbeat veneer highlighting the positive accomplishments of her life, Adler's narrative clearly illuminates the constant stress, dangers, and obstacles of her trade, as well as her underlying disappointment, until her final years, that she was apparently unable to reassimilate into respectable society. She did not view a madam as an exploiter but as a businesswoman who had a constant supply of females working for her because she paid well and offered comfortable working conditions. She offered medical care and protection from the *real* exploiters such as pimps, crooked policemen, and corrupt sex-trade supply providers. As a businesswoman, she noted that her concerns about the trade were economic, not moral: "If I was to make my living as a madam, I could not be concerned with either the rightness or wrongness of prostitution" (*A House* . . . , p. 317)

Adler was working on a sequel to her book at the time of her death at the Cedars of Lebanon Hospital in Hollywood.

• Adler's autobiography, *A House Is Not a Home* (1953), is the best source on her life, even though she uses pseudonyms in some cases. An analysis of the role of the madam, as well as some information on Adler in the years following the publication of her autobiography, can be found in Harry Benjamin and R. E. L. Masters, *Prostitution and Morality* (1964). Information on the Seabury investigation is found in Herbert Mitgang, *The Man Who Rode the Tiger* (1963). For specific references to Adler in the *New York Times* in the years of the Seabury investigation, see 7, 21, and 24 May, 14 and 23 July, 6, 8, and 15 Aug. 1931; 6, 9, 10, 12–17, 20–23, 26, and 28 Mar., 16 and 27 Apr., 7, 11, and 12 May, 3 June, 12 and 17 July 1935. Reviews of Adler's book are Phoebe Lou Adams, "Reader's Choice," *The Atlantic Monthly*, July 1953, pp. 82–84; Lee Rogow, "The Wayside Sin," *Saturday Review*, 27 June 1953, p. 18; Meyer Berger, "Miss Adler and Guests," *New York Times*, 14 June 1953; *The New Yorker*, 13 June 1953, p. 117; and "Pollyadlery," *Newsweek*, 8 June 1953. Obituaries are in the *New York Times*, 11 June 1962, and the *Los Angeles Times*, 10 June 1962.

MARILYNN WOOD HILL

ADLER, Sara (1860?–28 Apr. 1953), actress, was born in Odessa, Ukraine, the daughter of Ellye Levitzky and Pessye (maiden name unknown), merchants. She attended a Russian school, where she made her dramatic debut at age eight in the role of Emilia in Schiller's *The Robbers*. From her early teens she performed with local amateur groups and immersed herself in dramatic literature. When she decided to join a Yiddish theater company, she was initially hampered by her lack of fluency in Yiddish; she was engaged instead as a singer of Russian songs during the divertissement offered after the play.

In her late teens Adler married Maurice Haimovitz (who later changed his name to Heine), a Yiddish actor who ran his own provincial theater troupe. In 1880 they moved to London, England, where they played under dire financial conditions. In 1883 Adler arrived in New York with her husband's troupe, the Russian Yiddish Opera Company, which was the first professional Yiddish troupe to perform in America. Their first presentation, the operetta *The Orphans* by Shomer-Shaikevitz, was given on 23 May 1884 at Turnhalle in lower Manhattan. They later moved to the Oriental Theater in the Bowery, where their musical melodramas, though crude and often ill-constructed, drew crowds of young Jewish immigrants for whom the Yiddish theater was an exciting novelty and often the only entertainment in lives spent mostly in sweatshops.

Adler was blessed with the natural attributes of a star, and she shone on stage from the start. She was often described as the most beautiful woman on the Yiddish stage, with a figure resembling a marble statue and a face that could melt one's heart. Her emotional power and electrifying voice were combined with a delicacy and truthfulness that captivated audiences for five decades.

The relationship between Haimovitz-Heine and his increasingly popular wife deteriorated. In 1887 Jacob Adler arrived from Europe and joined the Haimovitz-Heine troupe. Adler was married at the time, and Sara was the mother of two boys, but they fell in love, divorced their spouses, and married in 1891. From then on she was known professionally as Sara Adler. The Adlers had five children who all had careers on the stage and often participated in their parents' productions.

The Adlers played together in three New York Yiddish playhouses: the Thalia in the Bowery; the Grand Street Theater, which was built especially for Jacob Adler; and the Dewey Theater on East 14th Street. Jacob Adler became regarded as the greatest dramatic actor of the Yiddish stage, and Sara gave up her musical roles to devote herself to straight drama, often playing the female lead against her husband. From time to time, however, their domestic relations became explosive, and she left his company to head her own.

Sara Adler was known for her wide range of comic and tragic parts. With her husband, she introduced to the Yiddish stage a more realistic style of performance. It was estimated that her repertoire included lead roles in about 300 plays. She was particularly adept in plays of Jewish immigrant life by Jacob Gordin, Leon Kobrin, and Zalmen Libin. One of her most famous roles was in Gordin's *Homeless* (1907), in which she played a simple, unassimilated immigrant housewife who suffers from a mental breakdown as a result of her encounter with modern life in America. Though Adler did not perform much after her husband's death in 1926, she was so attached to this role that when she was in her late seventies, she staged and starred in *Homeless*, with Zvee Scooler in her late husband's role.

Adler also excelled in Yiddish adaptations of European, particularly Russian, drama. Some famous roles were Nora in Ibsen's *A Doll's House*, Okolina in Leo Tolstoy's *The Power of Darkness*, and Katusha Maslova in Tolstoy's *Resurrection*, a role she originated in America. She repeated that role in 1939 at a testimonial performance at the National Theatre on Second Avenue that celebrated her fiftieth year on the stage, a celebration in which several members of the Group Theatre, including her children Stella and Luther and daughter-in-law Sylvia Sidney, took part. Adler also acted in two silent films, *Sins of the Parents* (1914), based on the Yiddish play *God's Punishment* by Zalmen Libin, and *A Recent Confederate Victory* (1914).

At the time of her death in New York City, Adler was eulogized as the empress of the Yiddish theater in America. Always the leading lady, her life's journey paralleled and encompassed the history of Yiddish theater from its humble beginnings in eastern Europe through its heyday on Second Avenue in New York and its post–World War II decline.

• Lulla Rosenfeld, *Bright Star of Exile: Jacob Adler and the Yiddish Theater* (1977), is an important source. In English see also Nahma Sandrow, *Vagabond Stars: A World History of Yiddish Theater* (1977); David S. Lifson, *The Yiddish Theatre in America* (1963); Hutchins Hapgood, *The Spirit of the Ghetto* (1902; repr. 1967); and Irving Howe, *World of Our Fathers* (1976). In Yiddish the most important source is Zalman Zylbercwaig, *Lexicon fun yidishn teater*, vol. 1 (1931). See also Tsili Adler with Yakov Tikman, *Tsili Adler Derseylt* (1971), and B. Goren, *Di geshikte fun yidishn teater* (1923). An obituary is in the *New York Times*, 29 Apr. 1953.

EDNA NAHSHON

ADLER, Stella (10 Feb. 1901–21 Dec. 1992), actress and acting teacher, was born in New York City, the daughter of Jacob Adler, an actor, and Sara Levitsky, an actress and producer. As part of the first family of the American Yiddish theater, Adler was acting from the age of five. Like her parents and five siblings, she was in constant demand as her parents' Independent Yiddish Art Company played its ever-expanding repertory to packed houses on the city's Lower East Side. The child-actor's schedule allowed little time for formal education beyond reading and theatergoing.

Despite her success in both Yiddish and mainstream commercial theater, Adler grew dissatisfied with the unsystematic attitude toward acting that prevailed there. Seeking a more serious approach, she enrolled at the American Laboratory Theatre in 1925. The "Lab" was founded in 1923 by Richard Boleslavsky and Maria Ouspenskaya, members of the legendary Moscow Art Theater. The Lab offered study in the acting techniques developed by Konstantin Stanislavsky, cofounder and artistic director of the Moscow Art Theater, whose exercises were credited as the source of his company's lifelike performances and ensemble effects. The Lab offered classes in psychological techniques, as well as diction, voice production, movement, theater history, and art and music appreciation. The students were "flooded," in Adler's words, "with clarity and health and values" (Hirsch, p. 58). This first encounter with Stanislavskian techniques and training was to prove the springboard that propelled Adler through the rest of her life.

While training at the Lab, Adler continued to work on the commercial stage, performing more than 100 roles in Yiddish and mainstream theaters between 1927 and 1931. At the age of thirty, already a highly skilled and experienced professional, she joined the new Group Theatre. The Group was formed by Lee Strasberg (who was Adler's fellow student at the Lab), Harold Clurman, and Cheryl Crawford. These three had led a small revolution within the establishment Theatre Guild to found a new kind of American theater, one modeled on Russian and European institutions. The new theater operated with a stable nucleus of actors, directors, writers, and designers, performing plays that were relevant and meaningful to their audiences. With Clurman as intellectual leader, Strasberg as acting teacher, and Crawford as business manager, the Group would become the most respected theater company of the 1930s.

In keeping with the Group's policy against "stars," Adler played both major and minor roles. She cited her best role as that of Sarah Glassman in John Howard Lawson's *Success Story* (1932), but Adler made her greatest impression in the roles she played as a mother in Clifford Odets's *Awake and Sing!* and *Paradise Lost* (both 1935).

Adler chafed at certain aspects of her Group experience. Tall and strikingly attractive, she resented the lack of good roles for a woman of her own age and accepted the "character" roles with reluctance. More important, she disliked Strasberg's emphasis on "affective memory," that is, the use of one's own past emotional experiences to create or define emotion in a character. Adler found the experience seriously wearing on her emotional health, asserting that such rigorous self-analysis and recall made acting a kind of torture. Adler and Clurman encountered the elderly

Stanislavsky in Paris in 1934, as they returned home from a pilgrimage to the Moscow Art Theater. She told the master that his technique had made her miserable. Disturbed by this, Stanislavsky worked with Adler for a period of five weeks, sessions that Adler had recorded by a stenographer and on which she would build her own teaching technique. When she returned to the Group, she announced that Strasberg was teaching a distorted version of methods that Stanislavsky had long ago discarded. She began offering her own classes, emphasizing "given circumstances" and "actions" while disparaging affective memory. Her charges and rival training methods caused a division in the Group and precipitated a lifelong feud with Lee Strasberg, whose techniques she would later describe as "sick" and "schizophrenic."

When the Group's 1937 season was abbreviated because of lack of funds, Adler followed other Group alumni (Franchot Tone, Odets, John Garfield) to Hollywood. She returned periodically to the Group, directing the successful touring production of Odets's *Golden Boy* in 1938–1939. In 1941 she portrayed a memorable femme fatale in Metro-Goldwyn-Mayer's *Shadow of the Thin Man*.

With the dissolution of the Group in 1941 and her concurrent frustration at being considered by Hollywood executives "too Jewish" for leading film roles, Adler devoted herself to teaching. Returning to New York, from 1940 to 1942 she was one of several acting teachers in Erwin Piscator's Dramatic Workshop at the New School for Social Research. She left the Dramatic Workshop in 1949 to found the Stella Adler Theatre Studio in New York, offering a comprehensive two-year program for young actors. The syllabus included classes in scene study, voice and speech, movement, acting styles, literary study, and makeup. During the 1950s the Stella Adler Conservatory (as it was renamed) grew to a faculty of twelve, though Adler continued to teach its principal courses. She added a West Coast conservatory in 1986. In her later years, dividing her time between New York and Los Angeles, Adler continued her ambitious schedule of teaching and lecturing. In 1988 she published a book, *The Technique of Acting*, summarizing her ideas and offering specific exercises.

Adler's personal life included three marriages. She married an Englishman, Horace Elliasheff, in New York in 1922. They had her only child, a daughter, and the couple were divorced soon after Ellen was born. Adler became romantically involved with Harold Clurman in 1930, and they were married in 1943. The marriage ended in divorce in 1960. Adler later married Mitchell Wilson, a science writer and novelist, who died in 1973. Adler's teaching provided her with a comfortable though not extravagant income, allowing her to travel widely and to maintain homes in Manhattan and Los Angeles, as well as a vacation home in upstate New York. She died in Los Angeles.

Adler's approach to acting combined a close study of the text and its historical and literary context with exercises intended to stimulate and release the actor's creative imagination. She saw at its center Stanislavsky's insistence on the importance of "truth, truth in the circumstances of the play." From the 1950s onward Adler's conservatory was a major force in American theater and film, producing alumni such as Marlon Brando, who describes Adler in his autobiography as having "unerring instincts" about truth in acting, Warren Beatty, Robert De Niro, Richard Dreyfus, and Ellen Burstyn. During her long lifetime, her teaching reached successive generations of American actors, and, as Hollywood cinema came to dominate screens throughout the world, the influence of her training grew. Along with Group colleagues Lee Strasberg, Bobby Lewis, and Sanford Meisner (who founded their own training programs), Adler was central in the development of American acting technique.

• Adler's *Technique of Acting* (1988) includes an autobiographical essay and a brief sketch of Adler's life by Irene Gilbert. The world of Adler's childhood is evoked in Lulla Rosenfeld, *Bright Star of Exile: Jacob Adler and the Yiddish Theatre* (1977). A detailed picture of her activities with the Group Theatre is in Harold Clurman, *The Fervent Years: The Group Theatre and the Thirties* (1945). Additional perspectives are in Elia Kazan, *A Life* (1988), Robert Lewis, *Slings and Arrows: Theatre in My Life* (1984), and Cheryl Crawford, *One Naked Individual: My Fifty Years in the Theatre* (1977). The Dec. 1976 issue of *Educational Theatre Journal* is devoted to interviews with Adler, Strasberg, Meisner, and other Group Theatre members. Wendy Smith, *Real Life Drama: The Group Theatre and America, 1931–1940* (1990), includes additional material from interviews with Group Theatre alumni. Adler's work with students is detailed in two books on the rival Actor's Studio: David Garfield's *A Player's Place* (1980) and Foster Hirsch's *A Method to Their Madness* (1984). An unusually thorough biographical essay appears in *Contemporary Biography* (1985) and an extensive obituary in the *New York Times*, 22 Dec. 1992.

MARK FEARNOW

ADONIS, Joe (22 Nov. 1902–26 Nov. 1971), organized crime leader, was born Giuseppe Antonio Doto in Montemarano, near Naples, Italy, and illegally entered New York City as a teenager. After settling in Manhattan's Lower East Side, he adopted the surname "Adonis," believing that it reflected his good looks. He soon joined forces with other hoodlums who would become famous in organized crime—Charles "Lucky" Luciano, Albert Anastasia, Vito Genovese, and Meyer Lansky. By the mid-1920s he had become partners with Luciano and Frank Costello in bootlegging; together they controlled most of the illegal liquor flowing into mid-Manhattan.

In 1927, when the city's leading bootleggers established territories, Adonis took primary responsibility for Brooklyn, where he owned Joe's Italian Kitchen, a speakeasy that served as a meeting place for loan sharks, gamblers, and politicians. Adonis curried favor from the politicians who frequented his bar, and they protected his criminal activities. The most famous of Adonis's political allies was William O'Dwyer, who later became Brooklyn's district attorney and New York City's mayor.

In 1931 Adonis, along with Luciano, cooperated with Salvatore Maranzano against Giuseppe Masseria during the Castellammarese wars for control of New York City's Italian underworld. Various accounts indicate that in April 1931 Luciano lured Masseria to an Italian restaurant at Coney Island. After the meal, Luciano went to the men's room in order to give Adonis, Genovese, Albert Anastasia, and Benjamin "Bugsy" Siegel time to gun down Masseria. None of them was ever convicted of the murder. About six months later, with the approval of his partners including Adonis, Luciano sent Siegel and Lansky to murder Maranzano. According to underworld lore, the two posed as federal tax agents to gain access to the gangster's office where the killing took place.

The two assassinations elevated Luciano to leadership of New York's Italian crime syndicates. In 1936 prosecutor Thomas E. Dewey convicted Luciano of heading an organized prostitution racket. Before Luciano left for Dannemora prison in upstate New York, he delegated control of his businesses to Adonis and Lansky. With the end of Prohibition, Luciano focused his attention on gambling, which then became the most lucrative source of revenue for Lansky and Adonis.

Along with Costello and Lansky, Adonis was credited with controlling organized gambling on the East Coast during the 1940s and 1950s. The three men began by opening the Piping Rock Casino and Arrowhead Club in Saratoga Springs, New York. They also founded the Arrowhead Inn in Manhattan and the Beverly Country Club outside New Orleans. Later, Adonis and Lansky were partners in Florida and Havana casinos. In 1952 Adonis, Lansky, and Costello invested in the Sands Hotel in Las Vegas.

Adonis allegedly had other illegal interests, one of them a passion for jewel theft. He supposedly invested in racketeering along Brooklyn's waterfront and helped fund New York's most notorious labor racketeer, Louis "Lepke" Buchalter. Adonis was said to eliminate his foes by issuing murder contracts to Albert Anastasia. Law enforcement officials never proved any of those allegations.

With the end of Prohibition, Adonis and other former bootleggers also began investing in legitimate businesses. In the 1930s Adonis founded the Automotive Conveying Company, which transported cars from the Ford Motor Company assembly plant in Edgewater, New Jersey, to cities throughout the Northeast. He owned Kings County Buick Company, the largest Buick dealer in Brooklyn. In 1944 he moved to northern New Jersey and shifted many of his business activities there.

Adonis came to national prominence as a witness in the U.S. Senate hearings on organized crime led by Estes Kefauver in 1950 and 1951. Kefauver labeled Adonis, Costello, and Lansky as heads of organized crime in New York City. Adonis tried to avoid appearing before the committee, and when he did testify his answers were evasive. He repeatedly invoked his Fifth Amendment rights and was cited for contempt. Before he could be indicted, however, New Jersey authorities charged him with gambling. In May 1951 he pleaded no contest to the charges, admitting no guilt but offering no defense. He was fined $15,000 and served two years in prison, his first prison time since arriving in the United States.

In March 1954 a federal jury, finding that he falsely had claimed to have been born in Brooklyn, convicted Adonis of perjury. In October 1955 the U.S. Supreme Court refused his appeal, and he was deported in January 1956. After visiting relatives in Naples, Adonis settled in Milan, where he lived for the next fifteen years. In June 1971 authorities there accused him of continuing Mafia activities and exiled him to the village of Serra de Conti, where he died. His body was brought back to Jersey City for burial. Throughout his life Adonis carefully protected the privacy of his wife and four children, and little is known about his personal activities and relationships.

As with other underworld figures, Adonis's business interests included both legitimate and illegal enterprises, and he had a reputation for using violence. Although he was undoubtedly a force in the underworld, historians now believe that he and other alleged Mafia chieftains never exercised the thoroughgoing hold over crime that law enforcement officials once claimed.

• Books and articles written about Luciano and Lansky contain information about Adonis, including the unreliable books by Sid Feder and Joachim Joesten, *The Luciano Story* (1954), and Martin Gosch and Richard Hammer, *The Last Testament of Lucky Luciano* (1975). More credible evidence can be found in Robert Lacey, *Little Man: Meyer Lansky and the Gangster Life* (1991). Parts seven and eight of U.S. Senate Special Committee to Investigate Organized Crime in Interstate Commerce, Hearings, 81st Congress, contain testimony given by Adonis during the Kefauver hearings. An obituary is in the *New York Times*, 27 Nov. 1971.

MARY M. STOLBERG

ADORNO, Theodor (11 Sept. 1903–6 Aug. 1969), social and political theorist, aesthetician, and atonalist musical composer, was born Theodor Ludwig Wiesengrund in Frankfurt, Germany, the son of Oskar Wiesengrund, a wealthy wine merchant, and Maria Calvelli-Adorno, a professional singer of Corsican and Genoese origin. He adopted his mother's maiden name when his scholarly writing began to appear in 1938, perhaps reflecting his close attachment to her rather than to his remote father. His mother had borne her only child at age thirty-seven and lavished attention and resources on him, particularly with regard to "high" culture. His schooling included piano and composition training at a professional level (one teacher was Alban Berg) and philosophy with Edmund Husserl.

In 1931 Adorno became a founding member of the Frankfurt School of critical sociology and philosophy. He married Gretel Karplus (they had no children), and in 1938 he immigrated to the United States, living first in New York City and then in Los Angeles, California. He became well known to the distinguished refugee community of intelligentsia, including his neighbors in Pacific Palisades, Thomas Mann, Bruno Walter, and Arnold Schoenberg.

Adorno is best known today for his voluminous contributions to social thought, the sociology of culture (including classical music, literature, and "mass culture"), studies of prejudice and anti-Semitism (as a coauthor of *The Authoritarian Personality*, 1950), and the diagnosis of the psychopathologies of modern civilization. He created a distinctive prose style (eventually labeled "Adorno Deutsch") that featured a Hegelianized refusal to write directly or simply and a careful rhetorical effort designed to reproduce stylistically the dialectical quandaries of life and thought—a reminder to his readers that social reality is not something easily analyzed. Selected examples of Adorno's theorizing, especially *The Dialectic of Enlightenment* (written with Max Horkheimer in 1947; trans. 1972) and his masterpiece of sociophilosophical inquiry, *Negative Dialectics* (1966; trans. 1973), quite unintentionally served as the theoretical grounding of radical student movements during the 1960s in Europe and the United States. Some students, particularly in Germany, misread Adorno's suggestions and became violent, a method of resistance of which Adorno and other Frankfurt School theorists did not approve. His works, along with those of Horkheimer, Herbert Marcuse, Walter Benjamin, and to some extent Erich Fromm, were widely read and put to political-cultural use, even though Marcuse and Fromm were much more accessible than Adorno. Ironically, a humiliating public confrontation with young members of the German New Left in 1969, prompted by their belief that he had become a counterrevolutionary and elitist, preceded Adorno's death by only months and is thought to have contributed to his early demise.

Adorno's precocity would have seemed "elitist" in virtually any period of political-cultural history. He was educated in the *Buddenbrooks* atmosphere of Central European bourgeois comfort, position, and ambition that produced some of the most learned and intellectually adventurous scholars in recent Western history (for example, George Lukács, Karl Mannheim, Ernst Bloch, and Marcuse). He was simultaneously at home in the most technically arcane aspects of modern music (helping Thomas Mann with *Doktor Faustus*), philosophy, social theory, certain aspects of psychology, cultural history, and modern languages—all in a way that is virtually unimaginable today. His peers and friends, within the Frankfurt School and beyond its small circle, number among the most astute social analysts of the century, and he was more theoretically adept and broadly original than most of this august group. Perhaps only Benjamin, his close friend and sometime theoretical opponent, matched his theoretical imagination.

Adorno's principal intellectual contribution might be said to turn around his notion of "negative dialectics." Although anchored in a unique reading of Hegel and Marx and keyed to atonal musical theory, this idea held that analytical concepts that claim to subsume or "speak for" both the subject and the object in some totalistic sense are inherently false, misrepresenting both the social and cognitive worlds. Genuine, historically anchored dialectics, and the enlargement of knowledge that comes from it, had to be negative—to participate in the "Great Refusal," the popular term coined by his friend, Marcuse. Yet, apparently from the other pole, Adorno also argued against positivist/empiricist social science, which accepts as "objective" the responses of interviewees to questions which, by their nature, cannot capture what the Frankfurt School regarded as the immutably reified quality of commodifed life. In Adorno's opinion, the pressures of conformity and thoughtlessness, which are typical of "advanced" culture, leave no room for real negativity or critique, because each negative "moment" is quashed before it can develop into a real alternative to the status quo. (It was this definitive difference of opinion about social science epistemology that cut short Adorno's stay at Columbia University [1938–1940] and made his attempt to work with his fellow European Paul Lazarsfeld so fruitless.) As in all his most creative work, he refused to side with one simple position against another, insisting instead that the investigator, philosophical or sociological, resist the temptation to make apodictic assertions and instead trust in some "fearlessly passive" orientation to empirical reality. In a way Adorno would have appreciated, such a position, ironically, inflamed his readers both pro and con—making them, in sound dialectical fashion, anything but "passive."

In 1950 Adorno returned to Germany and spent his remaining years as an honored, widely read, and uniquely influential social critic, as well as a major theorist of aesthetics and serious music. He served as a professor of philosophy at Frankfurt, where since 1977 a prize in his name has been awarded annually by the city for outstanding intellectual achievement.

As one biographer wisely suggested, it was perhaps Adorno's memory of an idyllic, upper-bourgeois, prewar childhood—against which postwar European reality seemed so loathsome—that prompted his famous pessimism and dour cultural critique during the 1930s and 1940s. Thus he intentionally displaced Nietzsche's "gay science" with his own "melancholy science." Adorno has become as much an icon as a writer of well-read works, and as such he remains indispensable to an understanding of twentieth-century social analysis. He died in Visp, Switzerland.

• Adorno's German works are in Gretel Adorno and Rolf Tiedemann, eds., *Gesammelte Schriften* (20 vols. to date, 1970). His works in English translation include *Aesthetic Theory* (1983), *Aspects of Sociology* (1972), *Against Epistemology* (1983), *Alban Berg: Master of the Smallest Link* (1991), *The Culture Industry: Selected Essays on Mass Culture* (1991), *Hegel: Three Studies* (1993), *Introduction to the Sociology of Music* (1976), *The Jargon of Enlightenment* (1973), *Kierkegaard, Construction of the Aesthetic* (1989), *Mahler: A Musical Physiognomy* (1992), *Minima Moralia: Reflections from Damaged Life* (1974), *Notes to Literature* (2 vols., 1991), *Philosophy of*

Modern Music (1973), *The Positivist Dispute in German Sociology* (1976), *Prisms: Cultural Criticism and Society* (1967), and *Quasi Una Fantasia: Essays on Modern Music* (1992). Useful bibliographies of works in English include Joan Nordquist, comp., *Social Theory: A Bibliographic Series*, no. 10, *Theodor Adorno* (1988), and no. 35, *Theodor Adorno (II)* (1994). Biographical information is in Martin Jay, *Adorno* (1984); Fredric Jameson, *Marxism and Form* (1971); Gillian Rose, *The Melancholy Science* (1978); and Lambert Zuidervaart, *Adorno's Aesthetic Theory* (1991).

ALAN SICA

ADRAIN, Robert (30 Sept. 1775–10 Aug. 1843), mathematician, was born in Carrickfergus, Ireland. Neither parent's name is known; his father was a schoolteacher and a maker of mathematical instruments. Adrain was fifteen when both of his parents died. His early education, though good, had not included any mathematics beyond arithmetic. After becoming curious about algebraic notation, he began to teach himself algebra. Thus Adrain, like many of the American mathematicians with whom he would soon interact, was largely self-taught.

After his parents' death, Adrain supported himself and his four siblings as a teacher. By 1798 his prospects had improved sufficiently that he married Anna Pollock; they had seven children. During the Irish uprising of the same year, Adrain served as an officer in the insurgent forces and was severely wounded in the back by one of his own men. After being nursed back to health, Adrain and his family fled to the United States and settled in Princeton, New Jersey.

Adrain taught at the academy connected with Princeton College until 1800, when he moved to York, Pennsylvania, to become principal of the York County Academy. During this time Adrain began contributing to the *Mathematical Correspondent*, the country's first mathematical journal, founded in 1804. Perhaps his most noteworthy contribution to the journal was his article on diophantine algebra, the branch of mathematics that deals with finding integer and rational solutions to algebraic equations. It was the first article published on this topic in the United States.

In 1805 Adrain moved to Reading, Pennsylvania, to become principal of the academy there. He continued his contributions to the *Mathematical Correspondent* and succeeded George Baron as its editor. After publishing only one issue of the *Correspondent*, Adrain began in 1808 to edit his own journal, the *Analyst or Mathematical Museum*.

The material in this journal represents the best collection of mathematical work published in the United States up to that time. Adrain's own contributions to the journal, which comprise his best work, distinguish him, with Nathaniel Bowditch, as one of the first two creative mathematicians in the United States. Of particular interest, Adrain published an article on errors of observation, in which he gives two proofs of the exponential law of error. He showed that errors of measurement are distributed according to the bell-shaped, normal statistical distribution. The eminent German mathematician Carl Friedrich Gauss published his independent work on this topic a year later in 1809. Gauss nevertheless generally receives credit for the result.

There were only a few people in the United States at this time with the mathematical sophistication to appreciate the *Analyst*, and the journal ceased publication after just one year. Adrain attempted to revive the publication in 1814 but produced only one number.

In 1809 Adrain became a professor of mathematics at Rutgers (then Queen's) College in New Brunswick, New Jersey. About this time he received extensive recognition. He was awarded an honorary M.A. from Queen's College in 1810 and an honorary LL.D from Columbia University in 1818. In 1812 he was elected a fellow of the American Philosophical Society and a year later of the American Academy of Arts and Sciences. In 1813, despite Rutgers's efforts to retain him, he accepted a professorship at Columbia.

Adrain continued to make contributions to periodicals with mathematical sections until 1825, when he once again attempted to publish an American mathematical journal, the *Mathematical Diary*. With a mathematical level lower than that of the *Analyst*, the *Diary* had broader appeal in a country that lacked a substantial number of knowledgeable mathematicians. When Adrain left Columbia and New York City just one year after launching the venture, the editorship was assumed by James Ryan, who continued to publish the *Diary* until 1832.

Returning to Rutgers in 1826, Adrain left again in 1827 to accept a professorship at the University of Pennsylvania, although most of his family remained in New Brunswick. Adrain became vice provost of the University of Pennsylvania in 1828. During his last year there, Adrain had serious problems with discipline in his classes. Because the faculty saw no way to aid Adrain and feared that the disturbances would spread to other classes, the university asked for Adrain's resignation.

Although a man of wit and humor, Adrain was often irritable in the classroom. One of his students reported that whenever a student faltered in his recitation (then the principal form of classroom instruction), Adrain would terminate his efforts with a remark such as "If you cannot understand Euclid, dearie, I cannot explain it to you." Outside of the classroom, Adrain was apparently always patient and helpful.

After leaving Pennsylvania, Adrain returned to New Brunswick, where he tutored privately until 1836, when he returned to New York and taught at the Columbia College Grammar School. He retired to New Brunswick in 1840 and died there three years later.

• The University of Pennsylvania Library, Columbia University Library, the Boston Public Library, and the library of the American Philosophical Society all have small collections of manuscripts related to Adrain. The Rutgers University Library has typescripts of several manuscripts relating to Adrain that are otherwise unavailable. Extensive manuscript material held by M. J. Babb of the University of Pennsylvania was inadvertently destroyed in 1945. Babb wrote a biographical sketch of Adrain, a typescript copy of which is in the University of Pennsylvania Library. Adrain's most important papers are "A Disquisition Concerning the Motion of a Ship Which Is Steered in a Given Point of the Compass," *Mathematical Correspondent* 1 (1804): 103–14; "A View of the Diophantine Algebra," *Mathematical Correspondent* 1 (1806): 212–41, and 2 (1807): 2–17; "Research Concerning the Probabilities of the Errors Which Happen in Making Observations," *Analyst* 1 (1808): 93–109; "Research Concerning Isotomous Curves," *Analyst* 1 (1808): 56–68; and "Investigations of the Figure of the Earth and of the Gravity in Difference Latitudes," American Philosophical Society, *Transactions*, n.s., 1 (1818): 119–35; and "Research Concerning the Mean Diameter of the Earth," American Philosophical Society, *Transactions*, n.s., 1 (1818): 352–66. Biographical sketches are E. A. Brinkerhof, "Biographical Sketch of Robert Adrain, LL.D.," *Mathematical Magazine* 2 (1891): 56–58; J. L. Coolidge, "Robert Adrain and the Beginnings of American Mathematics," *American Mathematical Monthly* 33 (1926): 61–76; E. R. Hogan, "Robert Adrain: American Mathematician," *Historia Mathematica* 4 (1977): 157–172; and O. R. Seinin, "R. Adrain's Works in the Theory of Errors and Its Applications," *Istoriko-Matematicheskie Issledovaniya* 16 (1965): 325–36 (in Russian).

EDWARD R. HOGAN

AGASSIZ, Alexander (17 Dec. 1835–27 Mar. 1910), marine biologist, oceanographer, and industrial entrepreneur, was born in Neuchâtel, Switzerland, the son of Louis Agassiz, a zoologist, and Cécile Braun. Agassiz came to the United States in 1849, following the death of his mother in Germany. The domestic life of his parents had been marred by difficulties, and Alex moved to Massachusetts to join his father, who had become a professor of zoology and geology at Harvard University after a distinguished career in Europe. The American experience came at a difficult stage in Alex Agassiz's adolescence. He hardly knew his father, who had spent much time away from home on scientific projects.

The Agassiz family solidified when Louis Agassiz married Elizabeth Cabot Cary in 1850, and Alex's sisters Ida and Pauline joined the family. "Lizzie" Cary was consistently a devoted, loving, and supportive stepmother, and Agassiz was deeply devoted to her.

In 1860 Agassiz began a lifetime occupation of administering the business affairs of the Harvard museum, a task made difficult by his father's penchant for excessive collecting and expenditures. After Louis's death in 1873, Agassiz succeeded to the directorship of the museum and completed the physical plan of the building.

While a museum administrator, Agassiz was able to do significant research and publication in marine biology, especially in the study of Echinoderms (starfish, sand dollars, sea urchins, sea lilies, and related forms). *The Embryology of the Starfish* (1864) was an early mark of his capability in this new branch of science. It was followed by *Revision of the Echini* (1872–1874), a three-volume, beautifully illustrated work analyzing most known forms in Europe and America and detailing their geographical distribution, embryology, and natural history. The work remains his most distinguished contribution, and it won him many admirers in Europe and America.

The amalgamation of the Agassiz family into the rich and powerful culture of Brahmin New England was rapid and remarkable. After Louis's marriage to Cary, the daughter of a prominent family, Alex did the same by marrying Anna Russell in 1860; his best friend and fellow naturalist, Theodore Lyman, thereby became his brother-in-law. This pattern was completed when Ida and Pauline Agassiz married Henry Lee Higginson and Quincy Adams Shaw, respectively.

In 1866 Quincy Shaw persuaded Alex to go to Michigan's upper peninsula and evaluate unproductive copper properties in which he was a substantial investor. Agassiz, employing engineering and management skills, completely reorganized the enterprise. In 1871 the Calumet and Hecla Mining Company was founded with Agassiz as president, a post he held until 1901. His astute management, coupled with the fabulously rich copper deposits, made the closely held Calumet and Hecla company the richest in the world. Agassiz became a millionaire several times over, and many of the Boston elite were indebted to him for their new wealth.

Now entirely independent of the ordinary pressures of his profession, Agassiz could write and study as he pleased. He gave over a million dollars to complete the Harvard museum, fulfilling his father's dream. Conservative and devoted to order, precision, and planning, he differed from his father in manner and personality but defended him against those who attacked his views, in life and posthumously.

In 1873, after the death of his father and of his wife within a few weeks of each other, Agassiz felt as if a cloud had fallen over his life, and a severe melancholy always seemed to burden him as he raised three sons and saw to his stepmother's needs. He began to spend much time in a beautiful house he had built in Newport, Rhode Island, where the tasteful furnishings and quite natural surroundings provided relief from directing the museum and the world of business affairs.

Although he was a friend of Charles Darwin, Agassiz's relationship to the evolution concept was complicated by his strong intellectual conservatism. He abjured the dogmatic opposition of his father and held that the "theory of evolution has opened up new fields of observation in many departments of biology." Evolution did not, however, play a large role in his scientific work. He reacted negatively to the radical Darwinists of his day, urging colleagues "to wait quietly in this time of transition," avoiding the blandishments of those who would engage in "high flights" of imagination and build "castles in the air." He argued that doing "a little hard work" would be more useful than engaging in wild speculation (Agassiz, *Letters and Recollections of Alexander Agassiz*, pp. 123, 163–64). Open minded to all new evidence, yet avoiding extremes, Agassiz could not be counted as an adherent to the Darwinian doctrine.

Agassiz published more than 150 articles and books, mainly on his favorite echinoderms and related groups. In the 1870s Sir John Murray, scientific director of the world-renowned British expedition of HMS *Challenger*, asked Agassiz to describe and analyze the echini collected by *Challenger* in its exploration voyage around the world. The result, his *Report on the Echinoidea* (1881), was a primary contribution to both marine biology and knowledge of geographical distribution. Agassiz's works appeared mostly in the serial publications of the Harvard museum. As director he published without the barriers of peer review, a practice that may have dimmed his ultimate reputation, though, in Agassiz's lifetime, that reputation was unchallenged. A president of the National Academy of Sciences and active in the affairs of the American Academy of Arts and Sciences, he was admired by such naturalists as Asa Gray, James Dwight Dana, Jeffries Wyman, Darwin, and Thomas Henry Huxley. His writings and travels gave him intimate contact with naturalists all over the world. Wealth and position provided him with a determined inner rectitude in matters of science or business, another trait that was admirable yet at times verged on egoism.

The great energy Agassiz brought to all his endeavors was most evident in his oceanographic work. He pioneered in the 1870s and 1880s several highly useful technological improvements for dredging marine specimens. Murray, who was a scientific confidant and biographer of Agassiz, affirmed in 1911 that all contemporary knowledge of "the great ocean basins and their general outlines" was due to Agassiz's work and his inspiration to others (Murray, p. 148). In ships of the U.S. Coast Survey, and in private vessels he rented or bought, Agassiz traveled hundreds of thousands of miles over the oceans of the world in the period from the mid-1870s through the early 1900s, each trip planned with meticulous care.

For nearly three decades at the end of his life, Agassiz's main interest related to studies of the origin and nature of coral reefs. This interest became an obsession; by the early 1900s "he had now visited practically all the coral reef regions of the world" (Agassiz, *Letters and Recollections*, p. 395), and his vessels sailed the Great Barrier Reef, the Pacific, and the Maldives with one central purpose: to overturn the views on coral reef formation put forth by Darwin and Dana in the 1840s. According to these naturalists, coral reef and atoll development was a continuous and universal process. Corals developed on the sides of sinking volcanic islands, slowly, and then marched upward until the island ultimately subsided and disappeared, leaving a coral reef or atoll in its place. Agassiz concentrated his attack on Darwin's work, calling it "twaddle" and "nonsense" and based on incomplete observation. For Agassiz, who conducted his observations across the world and over many years, reef and atoll formation and development was the result of building up or leveling down primarily through the local and unique actions of biological, chemical, and mechanical forces continuously in operation, understandable in different ways depending on the physical and geological conditions of specific regions. Universal explanations were impossible, Agassiz urged, affirming "I am glad that I always stuck to writing what I saw in each group and explained what I saw as best I could, without trying . . . to have an all embracing theory" (Murray, p. 151).

Agassiz's opposition to "all embracing" theory was similar to his complaint that radical evolutionists built "castles in the air" with their theories. Although naturalists like Murray made use of an early Darwin work in an effort to discredit the evolutionist, Agassiz claimed no such motive. But the vituperation of Agassiz's opposition and his Ahab-like quest to prove Darwin wrong may have been spurred by an effort to use his money and ships to attack Darwin on the comfortable ground of oceanography rather than the far more complex issues of evolution. But Agassiz never produced his "coral book," which was often promised as an overview of his researches, although he did describe specific sites.

Unfortunately for Agassiz's reputation, his determination to wrest explanation from the world's coral reefs had an unhappy effect. His observations proved often unreliable, his evidence weak, and many conclusions false; later scientists proved Darwin's theory correct. Yet, in the large view, Alexander Agassiz was a notable naturalist and entrepreneur, capable of breaking the paternal grip of his father's dominance, all the while honoring his name. In Henry Adams's words, "he was the best we ever produced, and the only one of our generation I would have liked to envy" (Agassiz, *Letters and Recollections*, p. 447). He died aboard the *Adriatic* while making a transatlantic voyage.

• The Alexander Agassiz Papers are at the Museum of Comparative Zoology Archives, Harvard University. Other Agassiz materials are at the Houghton Library, Harvard University, and various collections at the Smithsonian Institutions Archives. *Letters and Recollections of Alexander Agassiz*, ed. George R. Agassiz (1913), is an important work edited by Agassiz's son. Among Agassiz's important works not mentioned in the text are *A Contribution to American Thalassography: Three Cruises of the United States Coast and Geodetic Survey Steamer "Blake" in the Gulf of Mexico, in the Caribbean Sea, and along the Atlantic Coast of the United States, from 1877 to 1880* (2 vols., 1888) and "The Coral Reefs of the Tropical Pacific," Museum of Comparative Zoology, *Memoirs*, vol. 28 (1903). A bibliography of his works is in George L. Goodale, "Biographical Memoir of Alexander Agassiz," National Academy of Sciences, *Biographical Memoirs* 7 (1912): 291–305. Sir John Murray, "Alexander Agassiz: His Life and Scientific Work," Museum of Comparative Zoology, *Bulletin* 54, no. 3 (1911): 138–58, is especially useful for Agassiz's coral reef work and his interpretations. See also David R. Stoddardt, "Alexander Agassiz and the Coral Reef Controversy" (unpublished manuscript, Berkeley, Calif.; 1992), and Mary P. Winsor, *Reading the Shape of Nature: Comparative Zoology at the Agassiz Museum* (1991), which contains useful discussions of Agassiz's scientific work and his position on evolution.

EDWARD LURIE

AGASSIZ, Elizabeth Cabot Cary (5 Dec. 1822–27 June 1907), college president, was born in Boston, Massachusetts. Her father, Thomas Graves Cary, was a businessman who became treasurer for the Hamilton and Appleton Mills in Lowell, Massachusetts, and her mother, Mary Ann Perkins, was one of the daughters of Thomas Handasyd Perkins, a wealthy citizen and leading benefactor in Boston. Raised in comfortable circumstances, she was educated at home. In 1850 she married the naturalist Louis Agassiz, who had recently been appointed professor at Harvard. Their marriage was a partnership in which Elizabeth Agassiz managed their complex household, was the devoted mother to three step-children, hostess, and assistant to her husband, who maintained that "without her I could not exist."

To ease the financial burdens of the family, Elizabeth Agassiz suggested opening a day school for girls in their home. Her husband agreed enthusiastically and recruited his Harvard colleagues James Russell Lowell, Conrad Felton, and Benjamin Peirce, among others, to teach their specialties, and himself gave a daily lecture on natural history. Elizabeth Agassiz directed the school (1855–1863), her step-son Alexander Agassiz taught mathematics, and his two sisters taught French and German. This unique day school drew seventy pupils a year from the Boston area and beyond and closed at the outbreak of the Civil War. In 1873–1874 Elizabeth Agassiz was informally involved in the administration of the Anderson School of Natural History, a coeducational summer school founded by Louis Agassiz on Penikese Island. There Louis Agassiz, and later Alexander Agassiz, provided advanced training in science to school and college teachers.

Although she had no formal training and disclaimed any technical expertise in science, Elizabeth Agassiz became a proficient scientific writer. She published two natural histories for children and with Louis Agassiz wrote *A Journey in Brazil* (1867), an account of the Nathaniel Thayer–funded expedition to the Amazon River based on her daily journals, letters home, and notes she took of Agassiz's shipboard lectures. She was official scribe of the *Hassler* expedition to South America (1871–1872) and wrote several articles about it for the *Atlantic Monthly*. After her husband's death in 1873, she compiled *Louis Agassiz: His Life and Correspondence* (1885), a graceful encomium that muted the harshness of his racist opinions.

Although a conservative on the question of women's rights, Agassiz consistently advocated higher education for women. She joined the Woman's Education Association (1872) and was a member of the committee that launched the Harvard Examinations for Women (1874). In 1879 she was invited to join the organizing committee of an experimental program for "Private Collegiate Instruction for Women" by Harvard professors, created to give women access to Harvard teaching at the undergraduate and graduate levels. The program, nicknamed the "Harvard Annex," flourished and was incorporated as the Society for the Collegiate Instruction of Women (1882). Agassiz became the first president (1882–1899) and honorary president (1900–1903). She always hoped that Harvard would absorb the Annex as a woman's department and as an inducement helped raise $100,000 for endowment. While she was unable to convince the Harvard Corporation to risk merger, because of its fear of coeducation, her tact and diplomacy helped secure an enduring relationship with Harvard. By an act of 1894 the society was incorporated as a degree-granting institution, coordinate with Harvard, and was renamed Radcliffe College (after Ann Radcliffe, the first woman donor to Harvard in 1643). The Harvard faculty provided all of Radcliffe's faculty, and Harvard's president agreed to cosign the diplomas, signifying equivalence to the Harvard diploma. To strengthen this loose institutional tie further, the Harvard Corporation served as Visitors of Radcliffe. Agassiz successfully quelled discontent among alumnae who disliked this compromise and did not wish to hurry into independence and among others who questioned Harvard's commitment to the education of women.

Agassiz was an effective fundraiser, eliciting funds from the Boston community through "parlor meetings." She purchased Fay House, the college's administrative center, and the surrounding properties that today form the Radcliffe Yard, and she acquired the land for the dormitory quadrangle, which was designed and laid out by her architect nephew, Guy Lowell. The funds for Agassiz House, the student center, were raised largely by her family as an eightieth birthday tribute in 1902.

While not the founder of the college, Agassiz was responsible, as much as any other single individual, for establishing a Harvard education for women and for putting Radcliffe on a permanent footing. At the time of her death, Charles Eliot Norton remembered her as "not a woman of genius or of specially brilliant intellectual gifts," but of judgment, character, and common sense. Said Harvard's president Charles William Eliot, "there never was in this community a more influential woman."

• Elizabeth Agassiz's personal papers, including diaries, letters from the Thayer and *Hassler* expeditions, and other correspondence, are in the Schlesinger Library, Radcliffe College. Her president's papers are in the Radcliffe College Archives. Other correspondence is in the Elizabeth Briggs Papers and other alumnae collections in the Radcliffe College Archives and in the Louis Agassiz Collection in the Museum of Comparative Zoology, Harvard University. Her works in print, in addition to those mentioned in the text, include *A First Lesson in Natural History* (1859), *Seaside Studies in Natural History* (1865) with Alexander Agassiz, and five articles published between 1866 and 1873 in the *Atlantic Monthly*. Two of the five articles described the voyage on the Amazon River and were incorporated into *A Journey In Brazil*; three described the *Hassler* expedition: "The Hassler Glacier in the Straits of Magellan, *Atlantic Monthly*, Oct. 1872, pp. 472–78; "In the Straits of Magellan," *Atlantic Monthly*, Jan. 1873, pp. 89–95; and "A Cruise through the Galapagos," *Atlantic Monthly*, May 1873, pp. 579–84. Her Radcliffe College commencement speeches are in the *Harvard Graduates' Magazine*

(1894–1899). Lucy Allen Paton, *The Life of Elizabeth Cary Agassiz: A Biography* (1919), contains many extracts from Agassiz's letters and diaries. Louise Hall Tharp, *Adventurous Alliance* (1959), is still the best biography. Sally Schwager, "Harvard Women: A History of the Founding of Radcliffe College" (Ed.D. thesis, Harvard Univ., 1982), is informative about Agassiz's role in Radcliffe's history and contains an extensive bibliography. Stephen Jay Gould, "This View of Life: Flaws in a Victorian Veil," *Natural History* 87, no. 6 (June–July 1978), discusses Elizabeth Agassiz's deletions of her husband's racist opinions. The diaries and letters of students who attended the Agassiz School are quoted in Edward Waldo Forbes, "The Agassiz School," *Cambridge Historical Society* (1954); Mrs. John D. Seaver, *Seaview Gazette* 11, no. 7 (Feb.–Mar. 1894); and Georgina Schuyler, *Radcliffe Bulletin* 10 (May 1908).

JANE S. KNOWLES

AGASSIZ, Louis (26 May 1807–14 Dec. 1873), zoologist and geologist, was born Jean Louis Rodolphe Agassiz in Motier, Switzerland, the son of Rodolphe Agassiz, a Protestant pastor, and Rose Mayor. Louis early in life spurned family pressure to become a businessman and planned to devote himself to the professional study of nature. At the age of twenty-one he predicted he would become "the first naturalist of his time, a good citizen and a good son. . . . I feel within myself the strength of a whole generation to work toward this end" (Lurie [1960], p. 31).

Such determination gained for Agassiz a superior education in the natural sciences. At the Universities of Heidelberg and Munich, and in the city of Paris, Agassiz's career was molded by contacts with leading men of science and philosophy. Naturalist Johann B. Spix allowed him in 1829 to publish a collection of the fishes of Brazil that Spix had made. Anatomist Ignaz Döllinger trained him in the use of the microscope and introduced him to the new and exciting science of embryology. Lorenz Oken's philosophy emphasized the romantic and idealistic significance of nature study.

Agassiz came to be identified with two distinct and often contradictory views of natural history, one precise and pragmatic, the other transcendental. This dualism was represented in the work of French anatomist Georges Cuvier who, knowing Agassiz in Paris, turned over to him his notable collection of fossil fish depictions and, with it, a view of nature that, while exact, also extolled the grandeur of the creative act. Geographer Alexander von Humboldt, adviser to the king of Prussia, was similarly charmed by Agassiz's intelligence and in 1832 arranged for a professorship for him at the Collège de Neuchâtel in Switzerland. In Carlsruhe Agassiz met and married in 1833 Cécile Braun. The two took residence in a small Neuchâtel apartment, soon filled by the arrival of three children.

Agassiz's Neuchâtel years were the most productive of his life, encompassing extraordinary activity in teaching, research, and instilling interest in natural history in the townsfolk. Aided by funds from European scientific societies, Agassiz spent 1832–1842 studying the fossil fish collections in museums and private holdings throughout Europe. The result was the six-volume *Poissons fossiles*, a study of more than 1,700 ancient fishes analyzed by the comparative method first taught by Cuvier. Unsurpassed in the nineteenth century, the study was the basis of Agassiz's fame and scientific fortune. It won high praise from distinguished naturalists such as Sir Charles Lyell and Richard Owen, English pioneers in geology and paleontology. The philosophy pervading these volumes was that an all-powerful deity had planned the entire range of past and present creation, making impossible any genetic connection between ancient and modern forms. Exact study, like that of the work on fossil fishes, would yield knowledge of the creative design. This view meant that Agassiz discovered many "new" species in order to prove the separate and special creation of species. Convinced his books would not be published unless he produced them himself, he established a publishing center at Neuchâtel, which employed the latest technology in photo duplication and issued the work of Agassiz and his assistants in the form of bibliographies, dictionaries, and research publications.

Between 1837 and 1843 Agassiz did remarkable work in glacial geology. In his paper "Discours pronomcé à l'overture des séances de la Société Helvétique des Sciences naturelles" (July 1837) and his book *Études sur les glaciers* (1840), he posited that a massive ice sheet had covered all of Europe and upon its retreat had left behind polished and scratched rocks and moraines to mark its path. The glacial period, or Ice Age, was cited as a gigantic catastrophe, brought about by the deity as still another demonstration of power and planning that made impossible the genetic relationship of animals and plants from one geological period to another. Although not original with Agassiz—a Swiss naturalist, Jean de Charpentier, had announced the glacial theory previously—Agassiz publicized it and applied glacial concepts to all of Europe.

Cécile Braun Agassiz left her husband and Neuchâtel in the spring of 1845. Never at home in the crude Swiss environment, she had become increasingly depressed and discomforted, especially by the seeming influence that Edward Desor, Agassiz's secretary, wielded over her husband. Overburdened with debt, Agassiz had to close the printing establishment, and, with the departure of former colleagues, friends, and wife, the scientific factory and productive environment was no more. When Agassiz's fortunes were at their lowest, however, fortuitous events intervened, a common experience in his life. Influenced by Humboldt, Friedrich Wilhelm IV of Prussia announced a grant of $3,000 to Agassiz for a two-year study comparing the flora and fauna of the United States with that of Europe. Soon thereafter, John Amory Lowell, cotton manufacturer and head of the Lowell Institute, invited Agassiz to deliver a course of lectures at the institute, the exemplar of popular culture in New England.

Agassiz took America and New England by storm from his earliest days in the New World. Naturalists were eager to show him examples of fossils, and wealthy and established New Englanders were delighted by the Swiss savant with a charming accent who spoke with such ease and enthusiasm about ancient fish, powerful ice action, and the notables of European science and culture. Benjamin Silliman, Jr., a Yale chemist, said Agassiz was "full of knowledge on all subjects of science, and imparts it in the most graceful and modest manner and has, if possible, more of *bonhomie* than of knowledge" (Lurie [1960], p. 125). Asa Gray joined in the litany of praise: "Agassiz charms all, both popular and scientific! I observed to him that there was much quite new to me in his last lecture. . . . He replied that it would be equally new in Paris, much of it" (Lurie [1960], p. 127). Commoner and Brahmin alike were pleased to hear the reverence Agassiz accorded to God's efforts to order the "plan of creation in the animal kingdom," and his lectures of this title had to be repeated, so great was the demand for them. In less than two years of lecturing in America, he was able to repay almost $20,000 in European debts. After the death of his wife in Carlsruhe in July 1848, Agassiz arranged for his children to join him in the United States, and by 1850 the family was reunited.

Provision for both family and future was guaranteed by two events that wedded Agassiz permanently to the United States. In the fall of 1847 the Harvard University Corporation appointed him professor of zoology and geology in the newly established Lawrence Scientific School. The institution was to be based on the concept that technology and applied sciences were necessary skills in the new industrial economy then transforming the nation. Agassiz's appointment, though arranged by representatives of the new industrial elite such as Lowell and Abbott Lawrence, was discordant with these aims. It was also much desired by Harvard conservatives such as Francis Bowen, Cornelius Felton, and Charles Eliot Norton, all of whom saw in Agassiz a bulwark against radical ideas in science, such as the development theory.

In 1850 yet another tie was forged when Agassiz married Elizabeth Cabot Cary. Sixteen years his junior, "Lizzie" Cary was an uncommonly intelligent, modern young woman who made Agassiz his first real home. She was also a well-connected Bostonian, with a family background in mercantile and financial enterprises. Soon the Agassiz home on Oxford Street became the center of Cambridge intellectual life for foreigners, Bostonians, and Harvard professors. Alexander Agassiz was specially grateful for his new stepmother because he found in her a solid comfort and understanding love that soothed his recent maternal loss and encouraged his early ventures in natural science.

As a professor, Agassiz badgered Harvard authorities relentlessly, seeking money for a major museum that would stimulate the love of nature, instruct the public, and serve to train advanced students. By 1859 his efforts had wrested sums totaling about $600,000 from wealthy Bostonians and the state of Massachusetts to build a fireproof museum. The building, opened in November 1859, attracted an impressive number of students who had come to Cambridge to work under Agassiz. These postgraduate students—some of them subsidized by scholarship funds—had a unique opportunity to gain firsthand knowledge of nature unrestricted by the formalities that hindered European students. The great majority of practicing naturalists active during the late nineteenth and early twentieth centuries could trace their educational lineage to Agassiz and his museum.

Agassiz believed that a modern museum should also serve as a research storehouse for international exchanges and the needs of naturalists. In philosophical terms, he planned the museum to demonstrate the master plan the deity had fashioned for the natural world, thus showing the "type plan" of various classes and emphasizing the distinct and separate creation of species. With Agassiz's mania for collecting and identifying the "entire natural kingdom all at once," the museum was soon filled to overflowing with specimens. Agassiz always wanted still more; he scoured Europe for valuable collections and, in a great burst of activity, collected vast numbers of fish "species" during an exploration he and his wife made to Brazil and the Amazon in 1864–1865. Belief in special and separate creation drove his quest to find "new" species in an effort to prove the handiwork of God.

To some colleagues Agassiz and the character of his museum seemed to add little to conceptual knowledge of natural history, and he was criticized as "species mad." His once shining reputation was tarnished by a series of Boston debates over the evolution question in which he defended his position poorly in the eyes of some students and naturalists. His continued dogmatism led those unhappy with his views to refer to him as "prince of charlatans," where once they had praised the virtues of the "prince of naturalists." In the 1850s, moreover, Agassiz's adherence to special creationism led him to support the view that the different races of man were distinct species. In the hands of some defenders of slavery this meant that the white race was scientifically superior to the black because of different origins and physical characteristics. While Agassiz did not defend racial inequality, his position lent scientific credibility to the cause of southern intellectuals and further alienated Agassiz from liberal New England scientists and philanthropists.

Sensitive to the decline in his reputation, Agassiz determined to regain his former authority. He announced in 1855 the forthcoming publication of a projected ten-volume work, *Contributions to the Natural History of the United States of America*, planned to comprise a survey of the totality of American natural history. The volumes would cost twelve dollars each, with publication to begin when 450 subscribers came forth. In total, there were more than 2,500 subscriptions, further testimony to the massive public appeal of Agassiz. Voicing his aspirations and apprehension, Agassiz told Sir Charles Lyell, "I have tried to make the most of the opportunities this continent has afforded me. Now I shall be on trial for the manner in which I have availed myself of them" (Lurie [1960], p. 196).

Despite the fanfare surrounding the volumes, only four were ever published, and two were highly technical analyses of the embryology of North American turtles. The first volume (1857) comprised the notable *Essay on Classification*, a book that encapsulated Agassiz's views on classification, the philosophy of nature, and the sanctity of the species concept.

The work drew mixed public reviews. Published just two years before Charles Darwin's epoch-making *Origin of Species* (1859), Agassiz's views were repetitions of ideas he had learned long ago from Cuvier and repeated many times in books and lectures. Agassiz saw himself as the ideal modern naturalist who, by virtue of keen observations, described and analyzed empirical evidence that led to beliefs that were above and beyond experience. This was not a unique stance for naturalists of the 1850s: Gray, James Dwight Dana, and others searched for some comfortable ground allowing at once for empiricism and faith in a higher power. It was not Agassiz's science that such naturalists found essentially discomforting; rather, it was the layer of dogmatism and rectitude that encased his ideas and his unwillingness to credit diverse approaches.

In an age of doubt about older assumptions, Agassiz's views seemed moribund. Some naturalists were frustrated by this rigidity, since it seemed to them that Agassiz, with the concept of the glacial period, had provided a mechanism for change. Moreover, his emphasis on the interplay and plasticity that shaped the stages of embryology, that is, the history of individual development recapitulating the history of a species or group as well as the geological order of succession, was another intriguing mechanism for appreciating evolution. Darwin was intrigued by the idea of phylogeny recapitulating ontogeny, but Agassiz drew away from the idea of so-called "triple parallelism" because of fear it would become a useful tool for evolutionists and because he never intended the concept to confirm the evolution hypothesis. Even though Agassiz tried to understand evolution more sympathetically by making a trip around South America, retracing Darwin's voyage, this 1872 venture did not lead him to depart from his view that the evolution idea was "a scientific mistake, untrue in its facts, unscientific in its method, and mischievous in its tendency" (Lurie [1960], p. 298). Agassiz continued to view the Harvard museum as a repository of "facts" to disprove Darwin. But his many-faceted life of lecturing, administrating, and collecting left little time for careful, reflective study. Instead, much to the dismay of his American colleagues and Darwin's friends, Agassiz turned to strident anti-Darwinian attacks in the popular press, a stance that infuriated men such as Gray and Dana.

As a result, Agassiz found himself excluded from the politics of American science. He had been one of those who spearheaded the formation of the National Academy of Sciences in 1863, but perceived dictatorial methods of membership selection resulted in a stinging electoral defeat, another measure of a decline in his status. The professional sense of Agassiz as an impediment to free inquiry and publication was heightened by the complaint of his assistant on the *Contributions*, Henry James Clark, who claimed authorship of significant parts of the volumes on turtles. Agassiz's students also felt the anguish of alleged plagiarism and domination, and by 1863 many had left the museum on their own or at Agassiz's direction. Such a condition harked back to earlier controversies with coworkers such as Karl Vogt and Edward Desor in the field of embryology, each of whom made public the same kind of complaint. Agassiz defended his position on the grounds that works commenced under his direction or intellectual impulse were in fact his "intellectual property" and could not be taken casually by another. Although no one doubted his creativity, this position, which is not unusual in modern collaborative work, nevertheless placed Agassiz in uncomfortable situations throughout his career.

For Agassiz, there was no division between research and communication, and he lived for the ability to make his ideas known to others. He made a brief attempt to reaffirm his popular standing by organizing in the summer of 1873 the Anderson School of Natural History on Penikese Island in Massachusetts, where schoolteachers could learn to "study nature, not books," a lifelong aphorism that became attributed to him.

Agassiz remained at Harvard until his death. When he died in Cambridge, Massachusetts, Americans deeply mourned his loss as if a pied piper of science had left them. The vision and image of Agassiz as a romantic, singular individual, energetically devoted solely to the study of nature remained fairly constant until recently, when more sober assessments have placed both his virtues and his faults in a more objective light.

• The Agassiz papers are in the Houghton Library, Harvard University. Agassiz manuscripts are located at the Archives of the Museum of Comparative Zoology at Harvard. The papers of James Dwight Dana at Yale University, Asa Gray at Harvard, Alexander Dallas Bache at the Library of Congress, and James Hall at the New York State Museum, Albany, also contain useful Agassiz material. Bibliographies of Agassiz's publications are in *Bibliographia zoologiae et geologiae* (4 vols., 1848–1854); Jules Marcou, *Life, Letters and Works of Louis Agassiz* (2 vols., 1895); Agassiz, *Monographies d'échinodermes vivans et fossiles . . .* (4 vols., 1838–1842), *Études sur les glaciers* (1840), and *Twelve Lectures on Comparative Embryology* (1849); and Edward Lurie, ed., *Essay on Classification by Louis Agassiz* (1962); *Geological Sketches* (1866); *Geological Sketches, Second Series* (1876). Elizabeth Cary Agassiz, ed., *Louis Agassiz: His Life and Correspondence* (2 vols., 1885), is a labor of love by Agassiz's wife, with many useful letters. Lurie, *Louis Agassiz: A Life in Science* (1960; rev. ed., 1988), is the standard interpretation. Mary P. Winsor, *Reading the Shape of Nature: Comparative Zoology at the Agassiz Museum* (1991), contains useful information and analyses of Agassiz's role and concept of museum building.

EDWARD LURIE

AGEE, James Rufus (27 Nov. 1909–16 May 1955), writer, was born in Knoxville, Tennessee, the son of Hugh James Agee, a construction company employee, and

Laura Whitman Tyler. The father's family were poorly educated mountain farmers, while the mother's were solidly middle class. Agee was profoundly affected by his father's death in a car accident in 1916. He idealized his absent father and struggled against his mother and her genteel and (he felt) cold values. "Agee's mother wanted him to be clean, chaste, and sober," the photographer Walker Evans, a close friend, observed. "So of course he was none of these things." The father's death inspired the adult Agee to spend nearly two decades, on and off, re-creating in words "my childhood and my father as they were, as well and as exactly as I can remember and represent them." The resulting manuscript, which Agee could never bring himself to finish, was published after his death as *A Death in the Family* (1957) and won the Pulitzer Prize and his greatest fame.

Emma Agee responded to her husband's death by intensifying her religious commitment. In the summer of 1918 she moved her little family (Agee had a younger sister) to St. Andrews (near Sewanee), Tennessee, to live among members of the Episcopalian monastic order of the Holy Cross. The following year she enrolled Agee in St. Andrew's School, which was run by the order. At the school Agee met Father James Harold Flye, who became his spiritual adviser and lifelong correspondent. *Letters of James Agee to Father Flye* (1962) is the best introduction to Agee the man and one of the great letter collections in American literature.

St. Andrew's was a school for farm boys from Appalachia, few of whom went on to college. More was expected from Agee, and in 1925 he entered Phillips Exeter Academy as a sophomore. He graduated three years later and enrolled in Harvard College. At these schools he wrote most of his poetry (collected in *Permit Me Voyage* in 1934) and short stories. In his senior year at Harvard he wrote a parody of *Time* magazine that appeared in the *Harvard Advocate*, of which he was president. On the strength of the parody, he was offered a job as a reporter at Time Inc.'s *Fortune* magazine.

Agee stayed with *Fortune* from 1932 until 1937, writing articles on topics as varied as steel rails, orchids, Saratoga Springs, and the Tennessee Valley Authority. Like many intellectuals during the depression, he was politically left in his sympathies (he wrote that he "felt allegiance or part-allegiance to catholicism and to the communist party"), although he was never doctrinaire or politically active. His radicalism was of the spirit: he longed to feel and communicate the pain of those on society's bottom rung.

He got his chance in the summer of 1936 when *Fortune* assigned him and Walker Evans to do an article with text and pictures on southern sharecropping. He and Evans gathered material in Alabama over two months. When they returned to New York City, Agee prepared an article that, he told Father Flye, "will be impossible in any form and length *Fortune* can use."

Rather than a typical, and typically condescending, exposé of the sharecroppers' plight, Agee wrote a piece that was a mixture of lyricism, painstaking description, scathingly personal confession, and moral outrage. *Fortune*'s editors tried reworking the article, held it for a year, then turned it down. Agee, on a small advance from Harper & Brothers, left the magazine and expanded the article into his masterpiece, *Let Us Now Praise Famous Men*, which was rejected by Harper & Brothers and was not published until 1941 by Houghton Mifflin. The book received mostly favorable reviews but sold only 600 copies. Agee never again tried to write anything so innovative.

In 1939 he joined *Time* as book reviewer, and two years later he moved to movie reviewing. His fame as a film critic rests, however, on the longer reviews he did for the *Nation* from December 1942 until July 1948. In these columns he mastered a new approach to commenting on movies—chatty, knowledgeable, opinionated, good-humored. "Of the movies I have seen lately the one I like best was *To Have and Have Not*," he wrote. "It has so little to do with Ernest Hemingway's novel that I see no point in discussing its 'faithfulness'; it is, rather, a sort of call-house version of *Going My Way*." His reviews were collected in *Agee on Film* (1958), one of the first books to present a movie reviewer's work as of permanent literary value.

By the mid-1940s Agee had been married three times (Olivia Saunders, 1933–1938; Alma Mailman, 1938–1941; and Mia Fritsch 1943–), fathered two children (two more would follow), and become a legend in New York magazine circles. A night person, an insatiable talker, he was undisciplined about everything except the writing that he had to do on deadline. He was addicted to alcohol, cigarettes, and benzedrine (his wife Mia once said his motto was "a little bit too much is just enough for me"), and he took no care of his health (movie director John Huston said Agee went to the dentist only to get teeth removed).

In the late 1940s he began to write movie and, later, television scripts. Of the scripts produced, his greatest successes were *The Quiet One* (1949), a documentary about a troubled black boy in New York City; *The African Queen* (1951), on which he collaborated with director Huston; a five-part TV series about Abraham Lincoln's early years for the prestigious "Omnibus" program (1952–1953); and *The Night of the Hunter* (1955), the only movie Charles Laughton directed. By the early fifties, though, Agee's excesses had ruined his health. He suffered a series of heart attacks and recurrent angina, which kept him from writing the end of *The African Queen* or joining its filming on location, and so weakened his work on *The Night of the Hunter* that Laughton had to rewrite the script.

In his last months Agee went back to writing about himself. He had published a short novel about his adolescent religiosity, *The Morning Watch* (1951), which provoked little interest, and he probably expected no better of his writing about his childhood and his father's death. In 1955 he died of a heart attack in a New York taxicab, with no will, no insurance, and only $450 in the bank. He considered his life a failure and a waste of talent, but the posthumous publication of *A*

Death in the Family, his film criticism, a second edition of *Let Us Now Praise Famous Men* (1960), and his letters to Father Flye earned him a reputation, which seems certain to endure, as an important and original writer.

• Most of Agee's manuscripts and letters are in the Humanities Research Center of the University of Texas at Austin. Other libraries and individuals with Agee manuscripts and letters are listed in Laurence Bergreen, *James Agee: A Life* (1984). Bergreen's biography, the most complete yet published, is unsympathetic to Agee and raised a storm of criticism when it appeared. Ross Spears, whose documentary film *Agee* (1979) contains interviews with Agee's wives and friends, points out many errors in Bergreen's book in "Fiction as Life," *Yale Review* 74 (Winter 1985): 296–306. Five of Agee's film scripts are collected in *Agee on Film*, vol. 2 (1960). *Remembering James Agee*, ed. David Madden (1974), collects essays by Agee's last wife and his important friends and co-workers. Agee's second wife, Alma Neuman, describes Agee's life while he was writing *Let Us Now Praise Famous Men* in "Thoughts of Jim: A Memoir of Frenchtown and James Agee," *Shenandoah* 33, no. 1 (1981–1982): 25–36. Richard Pells's *Radical Visions and American Dreams* (1973), and William Stott, *Documentary Expression and Thirties America* (1973) analyze *Let Us Now Praise Famous Men* and the intellectual and cultural contexts in which it was made.

WILLIAM STOTT

AGER, Milton (6 Oct. 1893–6 May 1979), songwriter, was born in Chicago, Illinois, the son of Simon Ager, a livestock dealer, and Fannie Nathan. The boy was educated first at Hull-House, Jane Addams's famed Chicago settlement house, and later at McKinley High School. When an older sister bought a second-hand piano for ten cents a week, Ager quickly taught himself to play by ear. In the summer before high school he began to help support his large family by playing piano in amusement parks and movie theaters. By 1910, his junior year, he was determined to become a composer of popular music and copyrighted his first two songs.

In 1911, when Irving Berlin's new publishing firm needed arrangers and song demonstrators, Ager's unusual musicianship won him a job. Ager, though self-taught, had already mastered the principles of theory and composition, arranging and orchestration, and he could readily transpose at sight into any key. He worked for Berlin for six years at $35 a week while trying to launch his own songwriting career. Ager was facile and versatile; he could turn out ballads, waltzes, novelties, and foxtrots with equal ease. He was also a natural-born teacher and often offered to teach his boss, who could neither read nor write music, the craft of arranging. But Berlin always refused, saying that it might distract him from "putting words and music together."

Ager admitted that Berlin was right, but his professorial bent was so strong that soon Ager was teaching orchestration to his young friend George Gershwin. Before long the orchestra leader Ben Bernie, Ager's steady golf and bridge partner and best friend, awarded the diminutive composer, who stood only 5′3″ tall, his lifelong nickname, "the Little Professor."

Ager scored his first hit in 1918 when Al Jolson introduced "Everything Is Peaches Down in Georgia" at the Winter Garden Theater. Another early hit was "I'm Nobody's Baby" (1921). Ager's first Broadway show, *What's in a Name?* opened that same year. It won critical raves but ran only thirty-eight performances. Although Ager joked that the show was "a Flop," one dainty dance number, "A Young Man's Fancy," had a tinkling, Haydn-like, contrapuntal piano arrangement that sounded like an old-fashioned music box. Ager had made it so winning (while keeping it relatively easy to play) that the tune became known as "The Music Box Song" and sold a staggering two million copies of sheet music.

Since high school Ager had been searching for a lyricist as swift and versatile as himself, and in Jack Yellen, a onetime Buffalo, New York, sportswriter, he finally found him. A nimble-witted wordsmith with an unerring ear for the vernacular, Yellen had written the 1915 hit "Are You from Dixie" and several numbers for Sophie Tucker. The first Ager-Yellen collaboration, in 1919, was a comedy number about the new federal income tax, "Don't Put a Tax on the Beautiful Girls (How Can I Live without Love?)." Yellen and Ager were a successful match professionally, a "perfect marriage" in Tin Pan Alley lingo, though personally they had little in common. Throughout the Roaring Twenties they were one of the hottest teams in the music business, turning out an astounding 130 songs, including complete scores for four Broadway shows and four movie musicals.

The team early became business as well as creative partners. They opened the music publishing firm of Ager, Yellen & Bornstein, Inc. (AY&B), in 1922 for the same reason that Irving Berlin had made himself a publisher eleven years earlier. Ben Bornstein, Ager & Yellen's "professional manager," was a brother of Sol Bornstein, who had been Berlin's professional manager, and both publishing firms had to be reorganized after both Bornsteins turned out to be mismanagers on a rather grand scale.

AY&B opened for business with an announcement in *Variety*, a total capitalization of $400, some rented furniture and pianos, and two surefire new Ager-Yellen songs: "Lovin' Sam" and the big, tearful ballad "Who Cares?" which Jolson immediately interpolated into his current hit show *Bombo*. "Lovin' Sam (The Sheik of Alabam')" had a suggestive lyric that capitalized on the 1920s passion for things Oriental, expressed in songs about Mandalay, the Shalimar, a Persian market, and "The Sheik Of Araby." The latter song was picked up at once by both Sophie Tucker and Eddie Cantor. In 1923 Ager married Cecelia Rubenstein, who became *Variety*'s first woman writer after their two daughters were born.

To the question "Which do you write first? The words or the music?" Ager always answered, "Neither! It's the *title*." For him, the title inspired a melody, and the lyric evolved from that. Yellen came up with some memorable titles, including "I Wonder What's Become of Sally?" "Hard-Hearted Hannah," "Glad Rag Doll," "Happy Feet," "Crazy Words, Crazy Tune," and, in 1927, their biggest hit to that time, "Ain't She Sweet?"

Ager and Yellen's score for Sophie Tucker's 1929 movie debut, *Honky Tonk*, contained a record-breaking five hits. But another of their musicals, *Road Show*, had such a weak plot that Metro-Goldwyn-Mayer decided to shelve the picture. Still, Ager knew that the score contained one standout song, with an exceptionally good title, and as soon as he got back to New York, he began plugging it with radio dance band leaders. Six months later, it was a hit. The song was "Happy Days Are Here Again," and when MGM chieftain Irving Thalberg first heard it, he thundered, "Goddamit! Why can't we have songs like that?" "We own it, sir," someone stammered. The studio took the movie off the shelf, rewrote and re-shot it to reprise the tune no fewer than six times, changed the title to *Chasing Rainbows*, and released the picture to resounding applause.

But also in 1929, after a bitter quarrel over funds that vanished during the stock market crash, Ager and Yellen broke up. Ager bought out his partners and, a decade later, sold the firm. Ager and Yellen never spoke to one another again. Although both went on to write hits with new partners (Ager's 1930s melodies included "West Wind," "Trust in Me," and "Auf Weidersehen, My Dear"), neither man ever again found the "perfect marriage" that Ager and Yellen had enjoyed.

Three years after it was written, "Happy Days Are Here Again" was still popular, and Franklin D. Roosevelt, the Democratic candidate for president, chose it as his theme song. Bands played it throughout each of his four presidential campaigns, after which Presidents Harry S. Truman, John F. Kennedy, and Lyndon B. Johnson also entered the White House to its stirring strains. In the 1930s, 1940s, and 1950s, "Happy Days" was also the theme song for the nation's most popular radio program, "Your Lucky Strike Hit Parade." ASCAP still rates the song among its sixteen greatest all-time favorites.

America's tastes in popular music changed radically after World War II, but the "Little Professor" remained at his piano in Los Angeles, daily revising old songs and writing new ones until his death in Inglewood, California. His last, composed at age eighty-five, was a rousing waltz for which he wrote both words and music, "Just . . . One . . . Girl at a Time."

• Ager wrote the foreword to Warren Craig's *Sweet and Lowdown: America's Popular Song Writers* (1978). A songbook is *The Great Songs of Milton Ager* (1996). Biographical information on Ager is in Shana Alexander, *Happy Days: My Mother, My Father, My Sister & Me* (1995), written by his daughter. See also David A. Jasen, *Tin Pan Alley, the Composers, the Songs, the Performers, and Their Times: The Golden Age of American Popular Music from 1886 to 1956* (1988), and David Ewen, *History of Popular Music* (1961). An obituary is in the *New York Times*, 8 May 1979.

SHANA ALEXANDER

AGNEW, Cornelius Rea (8 Aug. 1830–18 Apr. 1888), ophthalmologist and sanitarian, was born in New York City, the son of William Agnew, a prominent merchant, and Elizabeth Thomson. Agnew entered Columbia College at age fifteen and graduated in 1849. He then studied medicine with J. Kearney Rogers, a surgeon and professor of anatomy at the College of Physicians and Surgeons, and in 1852 earned his M.D. After interning at the New York Hospital, where he was also house surgeon, Agnew practiced for about a year in a village that later became Houghton, Michigan. In 1854 he was asked to be a surgeon at the New York Eye and Ear Infirmary and immediately went to Europe because his appointment was on condition that he first study there. Before returning to New York City in 1855, he studied diseases of the eye, ear, and skin as well as general medicine and surgery with some of the most renowned doctors in Dublin, London, and Paris. Back in New York Agnew took up his surgical duties at the Eye and Ear Infirmary while maintaining a general practice. In 1856 he married Mary Nash; they had eight children.

Public-spirited and a strong advocate of preventive medicine, Agnew was secretary of the first society organized in New York City for sanitary reform. He was also a member of the committee that prepared the first draft of the act that later established the nation's first Metropolitan Board of Health (1866). In 1858 he was appointed surgeon-general of the New York State Militia and in 1859 became a trustee of the New York City public schools and later was chosen president of the school board.

At the beginning of the Civil War, Agnew, the surgeon general of New York, occupied a crucial position. As states raised and equipped volunteers for the Union army, Agnew was in charge of furnishing medical supplies for all New York regiments and was appointed medical director of the state hospital for volunteers. In this work he gained valuable experience, which he put to use in June 1861 when he became a member of the U.S. Sanitary Commission that cared for sick and wounded Union soldiers, providing them with morale-boosting comforts and services.

Exhibiting the practical skill and executive ability that became his hallmark, Agnew was called the most active member of the sanitary commission. He gave generously of his time whether it was "settling the form of printed questions . . . to colonels and regimental surgeons as to the . . . precautions against disease" or briefing Secretary of War Edward M. Stanton, who was hostile to the sanitary commission. If it meant sitting in the saddle for thirty-six hours while bringing wagons to care for wounded Union soldiers "left in the field, without shelter, food, or water, from Saturday night till Wednesday morning" after the second battle of Manassas (Bull Run) that is what he did (Strong, pp. 163, 253–54). To work even more for the commission, in 1864 he resigned his position as surgeon of the New York Eye and Ear Infirmary.

Charles J. Stillé, a member of the commission and later its historian, credited Agnew with efficiently planning much of the commission's "life-saving work." Besides supervising relief work after battles, he made certain that "soldiers returning . . . from rebel prisons diseased, naked and famishing" were cared for (Atkinson, p. 486). With Wolcott Gibbs he inspected all the military hospitals in the Washington, D.C., area before planning with William H. Van Buren—who also served on the sanitary commission's executive committee—the Judiciary Square Hospital in Washington, which established the pattern for the new pavilion-hospital system, capable of caring for patients in specialized units radiating from central buildings.

In 1863 Agnew, with three others, founded the Union League Club of New York City. It raised and sponsored black regiments and worked in other ways to support the Union cause during the Civil War. The next year he assisted in organizing the School of Mines of Columbia University; in 1865 he was appointed (and twice reappointed) a manager of the New York State Hospital for the Insane at Poughkeepsie; and in 1866 he established the ophthalmic clinic at the College of Physicians and Surgeons, where in 1869 he became clinical professor of diseases of the eye and ear and remained there until his death. In 1868 Agnew brought into existence the Brooklyn Eye and Ear Hospital (which had a noted residency program and "the largest patient attendance in the country") and the following year the Manhattan Eye and Ear Hospital (Gorin, p. 231). Devoting the last thirty years of his life particularly to the diseases of the eye and ear, Agnew was one of the founders of the New York Ophthalmological Society. He served as president of the American Ophthalmological Society and the Medical Society of the State of New York (1872). From 1874 until his death Agnew was a trustee of Columbia College. President Chester Arthur, who earlier, as New York's quartermaster general, had worked closely with him, found in Agnew—a devout, but tolerant, Christian—an ideal appointee to the unpaid Protestant Board of Indian Commissioners. These men oversaw the treatment of Native Americans by the federal Indian Bureau. Agnew returned from an inspection tour of reservations with a nearly blind Native American whose sight he restored. Agnew also strongly supported educating Native Americans at the Carlisle Indian School in Pennsylvania.

Possessing great personal magnetism, Agnew made his lectures on diseases of the eye and ear simple, clear, and interesting. In his first address to a new class of medical students at the College of Physicians and Surgeons he always stressed the necessity for ophthalmologists to be observant. He illustrated the difference between seeing and observing with the story of a man who saw a ferry boat near its slip and jumped aboard, knocking down two of its passengers before observing that it was arriving not leaving.

Ranked by his colleagues in the "front of Ophthalmology in this country," Agnew made solid contributions to his specialty by inventing new instruments and operating procedures (Thomas, p. 9). Among these were an operation to correct crossed eyes and one "for thickened capsule," an important procedure that European ophthalmologists almost immediately began describing "even in their smaller manuals" (Kelly and Burrage, p. 8).

While consulting at the bedside of longtime Republican senator Roscoe Conkling, Agnew was taken ill with septic peritonitis. During the nine days before his death in New York City (on the same day Conkling died), he discussed with colleagues his hopeless medical situation and insisted that an autopsy be performed to advance science. It revealed that a ruptured appendix had caused his peritonitis. Commenting on his death, one of the city's morning papers declared, "Could every eye that Dr. Agnew cured or helped, now shed a tear, what a sea would roll over New York" (Thomas, p. 17).

• Agnew's papers, including correspondence, diaries, a scrapbook, records of patients, and the engravings he used to illustrate lectures, are in the Rare Book and Manuscript Library, Columbia University. His published contributions to ophthalmology are at the library of the New York Eye and Ear Infirmary. Among Agnew's lectures and writings are *A Method of Operating for Divergent Squint* (1866); *A Series of American Clinical Lectures*, ed. E. C. Seguin (1875); *Ophthalmic Notes: 1. Trephining the Cornea to Remove a Foreign Body; 2. A Case of Double, Extremely Minute, and Apparently Congenital Lachrymal Fistula; 3. A Contribution to the Statistics of Cataract Extraction of One Hundred and Eighteen Recent Cases* (1874); and *Canthoplasty as a Remedy in Certain Diseases of the Eye* (1875). For additional biographical information see T. Gaillard Thomas, *A Eulogy upon Cornelius Rea Agnew, Read before the New York Academy of Medicine*, 7 June 1888; William B. Atkinson, ed., *The Physicians and Surgeons of the United States* (1878); Joshua L. Chamberlain, ed., *Universities and Their Sons* (1899); Howard A. Kelly and Walter L. Burrage, eds., *Dictionary of American Medical Biography: Lives of Eminent Physicians of the United States and Canada* (1928). Numerous references to Agnew and his work for the sanitary commission are in George Templeton Strong, *Diary of the Civil War, 1860–1865*, ed. Allan Nevins (1962); *The Papers of Frederick Law Olmsted*, ed. Charles Capen McLaughlin and Charles E. Beveridge, vol. 4, *Defending the Union: The Civil War and the U.S. Sanitary Commission, 1861–1863*, ed. Jane Turner Censer (1986); William Quentin Maxwell, *Lincoln's Fifth Wheel: The Political History of the United States Sanitary Commission* (1956); Laura Wood Roper, *FLO: A Biography of Frederick Law Olmsted* (1973). See also George Gorin, *History of Ophthalmology* (1982). An obituary is in the *New York Times*, 19 Apr. 1888.

OLIVE HOOGENBOOM

AGNEW, D. Hayes (24 Nov. 1818–22 Mar. 1892), surgeon and medical educator, was born David Hayes Agnew in Nobleville (Christiana), Lancaster County, Pennsylvania, the son of Robert Agnew, a physician, and Agnes Noble. In 1833 Agnew, who grew up in a deeply religious Presbyterian household, entered Jefferson College at Cannonsburg, a stronghold of Presbyterianism in western Pennsylvania. In 1834 Agnew left Jefferson to attend Newark College, established in that year by the Delaware legislature, where his cousin, the Reverend John Holmes Agnew, was professor of languages. With other students at Newark he founded the Athenaeum Literary Society, but when his cousin left in 1835, objecting to a lottery that supported the college, Agnew left with him. After studying medicine at home under his father, Agnew entered the Medical Department of the University of Pennsylvania in 1836—one of the youngest members of the class. Agnew received his M.D. in 1838. The title of his graduating thesis was "Medical Science and the Responsibility of Medical Character."

Following graduation, Agnew returned to Nobleville to assist in his father's extensive medical practice for two years until his father moved to Maryland seeking relief from a severe asthmatic condition; Agnew continued the medical practice. In 1841 he married Margaret Creighton Irwin, the daughter of Samuel Irwin, a prosperous iron founder. The couple had three children. For unknown reasons, Agnew chose in 1843 to join his late father-in-law's firm. (Samuel Irwin died in 1842 and left his large foundry business to his children.) It was not that Agnew was dissatisfied with medical practice; he had been busily engaged in practice for five years. Later in life, at a jubilee dinner in April 1888 honoring his fiftieth anniversary in medicine, Agnew nostalgically reminisced: "Any man who has lived long in this world, and has taken a thoughtful retrospect of his life, must be forced to confess that the influences and forces which have conspired to mold his character and to shape his destiny are most mysterious indeed" (Adams, p. 59). Within three years the business, which had been declining for some time, failed, and Agnew returned to the practice of medicine, first in Cochranville in Chester County. He remained there a short time because of difficulties and bad repute related to his dissection of cadavers sent to him from Philadelphia.

Agnew's determination to become a surgeon meant he had to continue studying anatomy. In the spring of 1848 he decided to return to Philadelphia to study anatomy by dissection. "During the cholera epidemic in Philadelphia one broiling summer night, Agnew, in search of anatomical material, went to a pit in which unclaimed bodies had been dumped and injected as many as fifteen at one time in order to procure and preserve them for dissecting material. He was not above a trip to Potter's Field at midnight to resurrect a body, inject it for preservation, place it in a sack on the seat of his buggy alongside of him and drive to his dissecting school on Chant Street in Philadelphia" (Radbill, p. 255).

In 1852 Agnew purchased the private Philadelphia School of Anatomy that had opened in 1820 as the Philadelphia Anatomical Rooms. In the early nineteenth century it was the custom of well-known Philadelphia physicians to have private dissecting rooms for their office pupils so not to depend entirely on the anatomical rooms of the University of Pennsylvania. In conjunction with the Philadelphia School of Anatomy, in 1854 Agnew established the Philadelphia School of Operative Surgery. Both schools were very successful, and Agnew's reputation as both an anatomist and surgeon was immensely enhanced in the ten years he managed the schools. Also in 1854 Agnew was appointed a surgeon at the Philadelphia Hospital at Blockley, where abundant clinical surgery was available for him to do; in 1858 Henry Hollinsworth Smith of the University of Pennsylvania enlisted Agnew to lecture to his students. Agnew also served (by official appointment on 21 December 1863) as demonstrator in anatomy for Joseph Leidy, professor of anatomy at the university. By 1870 Agnew was one of the leading surgeons in America, his fame equal to that of Joseph Pancoast and Henry H. Smith, both also of the University of Pennsylvania, and Samuel D. Gross of the Jefferson Medical College.

In 1871, after Smith retired from the university, Agnew succeeded him as professor of clinical surgery and demonstrative surgery. He retained both positions until his retirement, then continued as professor emeritus until his death. In 1877 Alice Rhea Barton, widow of the famous Philadelphia Hospital surgeon, endowed the Barton Professorship of Surgery, whose first incumbent was Agnew. A great part of Agnew's surgical work was performed in the surgical wards of the various hospitals with which he was connected; first with the Philadelphia Hospital from 1854 to 1865, the Wills Eye Hospital from 1864 to 1868, the Pennsylvania Hospital from 1865 to 1871 and 1872 to 1884, the Orthopaedic Hospital from 1868 to 1871, and the University Hospital from 1873 to his death.

During the Civil War, Agnew served as surgeon in charge of the Hestonville Hospital and as consultant surgeon to the Mower General Hospital, both busy army hospitals. It was Agnew who was called in as chief consultant when President James A. Garfield was shot by Charles J. Guiteau in 1881. After the president's death, Garfield's widow praised Agnew's efforts: "Dr. Agnew's faithful attendance at the President's bedside through his days of suffering won our deepest gratitude and our entire confidence in his distinguished ability as physician and surgeon. His presence was a constant source of encouragement and comfort to General Garfield, and his ever-entertaining discourse tided my husband over many dark hours" (Adams, p. 247).

Agnew's reputation is best attested by the banquet accorded him on 6 April 1888 on the fiftieth anniversary of his graduation from the University of Pennsylvania. More than 200 physicians attended. In delivering the eulogium, Professor Jacob Mendes Da Costa of the Jefferson Medical College observed, "Your success as a surgeon of great repute must indeed have been gratifying to you; not only for the opportunities it afforded you of doing so much active work in your profession, not only because it gave a personal value to your writings, especially to your opinions expressed in your elaborate work on surgery, but because it enabled you to carry out a plan of action" (Adams, p. 303). The neurologist Weir Mitchell, distinguished as a man of letters, composed a poem read for the occasion. In 1889 the University of Pennsylvania graduating medical class commissioned the Philadelphia portraitist Thomas Eakins to paint Agnew, who was retiring that year. Eakins decided not to do a conventional portrait of Agnew but to depict him in the context of the surgical clinic. *The Agnew Clinic*, larger than life-size graphically illustrates the great change in surgery with the advent of the practice of asepsis. (Agnew had met Joseph Lister during his visit to Philadelphia in 1876 and was an early advocate of Listerian antiseptic surgery.) Eakins's painting of Agnew shows the surgeon in a clean white gown, the sterilized instruments in a covered case, and a nurse prominently in attendance. The clinic scene is transformed into a horizontal format depicting the teamwork that is more characteristic of modern surgery, all in sharp contrast to the individual heroism of *The Gross Clinic*, which Eakins had painted in 1875 showing Gross operating for the removal of dead bone from the thigh. Long suffering with coronary artery disease and angina pectoris, Agnew died in Philadelphia.

• Most of Agnew's few extant papers are at the College of Physicians of Philadelphia, with some papers and memorabilia at the Library of the School of Medicine, University of Pennsylvania. Agnew was a prolific writer. Beyond many articles for the medical journals, his chief works include *Practical Anatomy: A New Arrangement of the London Dissector* (1856; rev. ed. 1868); *Clinical Reports* (1859–1871); *Baron Larrey* (1861); *Medical History of the Philadelphia Alms House* (1862); *Vesico-Vaginal Fistula* (1867); *Laceration of the Female Peritoneum* (1868); *Lacerations of the Female Peritoneum and Vesico-Vaginal Fistula* (1873); *Biographical Sketch of Dr. John Rhea Barton* (1879); and *Principles and Practice of Surgery, Being a Treatise on Surgical Diseases and Injuries* (3 vols., 1878–1883; rev. ed. 1889). The latter is a magnum opus, whose three volumes, large octavo, comprehend some 3,000 pages and nearly two million words. Agnew, who began his surgical career before the introduction of anesthesia and asepsis, was able to record in his *Principles and Practice of Surgery* the advancement of surgery in all directions, and as such the work is an invaluable historical repository of nineteenth-century surgical technique.

The main source for Agnew's life is J. Howe Adams, *History of the Life of D. Hayes Agnew* (1892), a memorial biography commissioned by Agnew's widow. See also J. William White, "Memoir of D. Hayes Agnew," *Transactions, College of Physicians of Philadelphia* 15 (1893): 29–65, and Samuel X. Radbill, "D. Hayes Agnew, M.D. (1818–1892)," *Transactions, College of Physicians of Philadelphia* 33 (1966): 252–60. An obituary is in the *International Medical Magazine* 1 (1893): 1–8.

FRANCESCO CORDASCO

AHERN, Mary Eileen (1 Oct. 1860–22 May 1938), librarian and editor, was born on a farm southwest of Indianapolis, Indiana, to William Ahern, a farmer, and Mary O'Neill, both Irish immigrants. In 1870 the family left the farm for Spencer, Indiana, where Mary Eileen graduated from high school in 1878. Following her graduation from Central Normal College in Danville, Indiana, in 1881, she worked as a teacher in the public schools of Bloomfield, Spencer, and Peru, Indiana, for eight years.

In 1889 Ahern put herself forward for the position of state librarian, a patronage job filled by the majority party in the state legislature, at this time the Democratic party. Undeterred by being named only assistant librarian, she launched herself enthusiastically into her new career, contacting others around the country engaged in organizing public documents and calling a meeting of Indiana librarians in order to organize a state library association. She joined the American Library Association in 1891. In 1892, after organizing the Indiana Library Association, Ahern became its guiding force as secretary-treasurer, a position she held as long as she lived in Indiana. In 1893, with the support of the Democrats, she was appointed state librarian for a two-year term. She successfully lobbied legislators to remove the state library from political control, although, to gain Republican support, she had to rule herself out for reappointment.

When her term as state librarian ended in 1895, she decided to attend the recently organized Armour Institute Library School in Chicago. Formal library education was less than a decade old, but Katharine Sharp, the director, had already established a reputation for preparing students in the latest methods. Even before Ahern completed the one-year course she was offered the position that became her life work, the editorship of a new journal, *Public Libraries*, to be published in Chicago. Ahern completed the Armour course in April 1896 and produced the first issue of the new journal in May.

As editor, Ahern planned "to deal with all phases of library work in a concise, simple way, such as will give the best aid to those who need it." For one dollar, subscribers received ten issues a year, guaranteed to total at least three hundred pages. *Public Libraries* was particularly aimed at untrained librarians (almost all of them women) who staffed the new libraries opening in small midwestern towns. Ahern published articles on methods of library organization, such as the Dewey decimal system, and elementary business methods, such as "business letters, ordering correspondence, [and] how to get on with directors and trustees." She also published library news, particularly news of library organizations, which accounted for nearly a quarter of the articles. Ahern encouraged her readers to consider themselves part of a professional community imbued with "the true library spirit."

Librarians of small public libraries were not the only ones who found the journal's practical advice and library news useful. In 1926 the name of the magazine was changed to *Libraries* to reflect its broader readership. By then it was one of two generally recognized American professional library periodicals; its circulation approached three thousand, and it was distributed throughout the world. When Ahern decided to retire in 1931 because of failing eyesight, its sponsors discontinued the journal. According to one of them, "*Libraries* without its present editor is impossible."

Throughout her life Ahern devoted much of her enormous energy to organizations. She attended every American Library Association conference from 1893 to 1931, serving on its council and a variety of committees. From January to June 1919 she served as publicity coordinator for the association's Overseas Library War Service in France. Her articles describing the distribution of books to soldiers in hospitals and camps appeared in such publications as the *Chicago Daily News* and the *Christian Science Monitor*. A charter member of the selective American Library Institute, which was founded in 1905, she also served as its secretary for many years. She was elected president of the Illinois State Library Association in 1908, 1909, and 1915. With Melvil Dewey she organized the Library Department of the National Education Association in 1897 and became the department's secretary. She repeatedly urged her readers to promote the library movement by participating in library associations. Carl Milam, the longtime executive secretary of the American Library Association, gave her "a very generous share of the credit for the increased size and vigor of American library organizations." In addition to professional associations, she belonged to organizations "social, literary, civic and philanthropic, galore."

Despite memberships in the Illinois Women's Press Association, the Chicago Women's Club, and the Women's City Club of Chicago, she did not support woman suffrage. She did, however, promote the careers of many women. Her huge network of personal contacts enabled her to function as "a whole personnel bureau in herself." Ahern suffered a heart attack and died on a train outside Atlanta, Georgia.

Mary Ahern was a woman of energy, conviction, and talent. Associates spoke of her "vigor and snap and humor," her "enthusiasm and forceful personality," and her "fearless independence." She was a publicist and popularizer rather than an originator. In contrast to professionalizers who wished to improve librarians' status by increasing educational requirements and excluding volunteers, Ahern emphasized grass roots development of librarians. She made information on library methods widely available and encouraged workers in small and rural libraries to participate in professional activities. The widespread adoption of standard methods of library organization and her influence on the growth of the professional community were her proudest contributions.

• Ahern's papers are in the archives at the University of Illinois. The final issue of *Libraries* (36 Dec. 1931) was a tribute to Ahern on her retirement "by friends of the magazine and its editor." An uncritical assessment of her career may be found in Doris Cruger Dale, "Covering the Library Beat from West Baden to Great Britain: The One and Only Editor of *Public Libraries* Magazine," *American Libraries* 7 (Mar. 1976): 125. Carolyn M. Mulac's "'Librarian Militant': Mary Eileen Ahern and *Public Libraries*" (A.M. thesis, Univ. of Chicago, 1978) summarizes published information on Ahern and analyzes the content of the journal.

BARBARA B. BRAND

AHLSTROM, Sydney Eckman (16 Dec. 1919–3 July 1984), American religious historian, was born in Cokato, Minnesota, the son of Joseph T. Ahlstrom, a dentist, and Selma Eckman, a teacher. He received the B.A. from Gustavus Adolphus College in 1941. After serving as a captain in the army during World War II, he took an M.A. at the University of Minnesota in 1946 and the Ph.D. in American history at Harvard under Arthur M. Schlesinger, Jr., in 1952. In 1953 Ahlstrom married Nancy Ethel Alexander, an editor and the daughter of an Episcopal priest; together they had four children.

Ahlstrom was raised in the Swedish Lutheran tradition and remained deeply rooted and active in Lutheran affairs at the local, regional, and national level all his life. He also served on the Theological Commission on Tradition and Traditions for the Commission on Faith and Order of the World Council of Churches (1958–1963). As a scholar, however, Ahlstrom distinguished himself both by the breadth of his historical vision and by his ecumenical interest. After a brief stint of teaching at Harvard, he was appointed to the Yale faculty in 1954 and served there until his death three decades later. Ahlstrom eventually came to hold appointments in the departments of American studies, history and religious studies, as well as the divinity school, and he held various departmental administrative positions. From 1979 on he held the title of Samuel Knight Professor of American History and Modern Religious History.

During his earlier career Ahlstrom did not publish extensively; he was the author, however, of significant articles on William Ellery Channing and the Scottish "Common Sense" philosophers, and he contributed essays to *The Harvard Divinity School*, ed. George Hunston Williams (1954); *The Shaping of American Religion*, ed. James Ward Smith and A. Leland Jamison (1961); and *Calvinism and the Political Order*, ed. George L. Hunt (1965). His Beloit College Brewer Lectures were published in 1962 as *The American Protestant Encounter with World Religions*. His *Theology in America: The Major Protestant Voices from Puritanism to Neo-orthodoxy*, an anthology with an extensive introduction, was published in the Bobbs-Merrill American Heritage Series in 1967; it represented Ahlstrom's first major attempt at drawing together the threads of his broader synthetic interest in American religious thought.

The crowning achievement of Ahlstrom's scholarly career was the publication in 1972 of *A Religious History of the American People*, which ran to nearly 1,100 pages of text. Though by far the most inclusive attempt at telling the story of the religious development of the United States yet undertaken, Ahlstrom's organizing thread was his emphasis on the "Great Puritan Epoch," the 300-year period he half-humorously described as extending from the time of Elizabeth I to that of Jacqueline Kennedy, in which the Anglo-American Puritan version of the Reformed tradition profoundly influenced the development of American religion and culture. This emphasis took issue with the stress his senior contemporary, Sidney Mead, had placed on the centrality of the Enlightenment, and it evoked a review by Mead entitled "By Puritans Possessed." Ahlstrom's sense that the Puritan epoch had come to an end in his own time was expressed in his widely read essay "The Radical Turn in Theology and Ethics: Why It Occurred in the 60s," published in the *Annals of the American Academy of Political and Social Science* in January 1970. Here he argued that a sudden convergence of forces—urbanization, civil rights, scientific and technological advances, and the war in Vietnam—all brought into grave doubt the optimistic vision of mainline Christianity. Ahlstrom also devoted a considerable amount of attention to American religious thought, especially that in the Reformed tradition, which had not been taken as seriously in earlier synthetic interpretations.

Ahlstrom's *Religious History* was widely acclaimed by both the scholarly and the religious community after its publication and in 1979 was selected by the *Christian Century* as the "Decade's Most Outstanding Book on Religion." It also won the National Book Award and the Brotherhood Award of the National Council of Christians and Jews. His influence, however, was much greater than even his publications might indicate. Over the three decades of his career, Ahlstrom worked with a great number of graduate students in American studies, history, and religious studies, many of whom emerged as major scholarly voices of the succeeding generation, for example, William R. Hutchison, Clarence C. Goen, Stephen J. Stein, E. Brooks Holifield, Albert J. Raboteau, George M. Marsden, Robert A. Orsi, Anne C. Rose, Paula M. Kane, Jonathan D. Sarna, and Robert Bruce Mullin. Although his earlier students tended to pursue research in Puritanism and religious thought, a later, more pluralistic generation of students were encouraged by Ahlstrom to investigate a wide variety of traditions, including those of African Americans, Anglicans, evangelical Protestants, Jews, and Roman Catholics. Ahlstrom's irenic vision and scholarly scope thus became manifest not only in his own work but in that of a multitude of his students, many of whom pursued intellectual directions very different from his own. In 1988 the editors of the *Encyclopedia of the American Religious Experience* noted that "it is sobering for us to realize that, where we have assembled some hundred scholars for the task of synthesizing the story of religion in America, this one individual had created the previous generation's synthesis by himself."

After several years of deteriorating health, Ahlstrom died in New Haven with much work left unfinished. Two pieces were published posthumously in collaboration with others: a revision of his Harvard dissertation, *The Scientific Theist: A Life of Francis Ellingwood Abbot*, with Robert Bruce Mullin (1987), and an anthology, *An American Reformation: A Documentary History of Unitarian Christianity*, with Jonathan S. Carey (1985). Unfortunately the extensive work he had pursued on European Romantic thought while on sabbaticals in France and Germany was never shaped into publishable form.

Ahlstrom was arguably the most influential interpreter of American religion of his generation, and his *Religious History* has endured as the most comprehensive effort to address that vast subject matter in a single coherent narrative. He was recognized during his lifetime in a number of ways in addition to the awards his magnum opus received: several honorary degrees; visiting appointments or lectureships in Austria, Australia, France, Germany, Japan, and New Zealand as well as at Princeton and other American universities and the Aspen Institute of Humanistic Studies; the presidency of the American Society of Church History; and elected membership in the American Academy of Arts and Sciences.

• The Sydney Ahlstrom Papers are available at the Yale Divinity School Library under the heading "Archives and Manuscripts: Manuscript Group Number 83," compiled by Dineen K. Dowling and Martha Lund Smalley (Mar. 1990); the accompanying pamphlet includes a chronology, introduction to the papers, and extensive descriptions of the 128 folders included in the collection. One critical essay is R. Bruce Mullin, "The Contribution of Sydney Ahlstrom to the Study of American Religious History," *Proceedings of the New England Society of Lutheran Church Historians* 3 (Spring 1985): 3–5. A brief obituary notice is in the *New York Times*, 4 July 1984.

PETER W. WILLIAMS

AHN, Chang-ho (1878–10 Mar. 1938), Korean nationalist, was born near P'yŏngyang, Korea, into a well-to-do farming family. His father was An Hŭng-guk; his mother's identity is not known. Ahn reached young adulthood at the turn of the century, a time when the independence of Korea was threatened by weakness from within and aggression from without. Moving to the capital, Seoul, Ahn enrolled in a Western-style high school operated by American Presbyterian missionaries, converted to Christianity, and joined the Independence Club—a reformist organization that was active between 1896 and 1898. In 1902 Ahn left Korea and went to San Francisco, where he enrolled as an adult student in high school. Almost immediately he formed the Ch'inmokhoe (Association to Cultivate Friendship) to assist fellow Korean expatriates in finding employment and to mediate disputes within the small Korean community. In 1904 he formed the Kongnip Hyŏphoe (Cooperative Association), the first Korean political association on the U.S. mainland. After Japan established a protectorate over Korea in 1905, Ahn resolved to return to Korea and managed to do so two years later. In Korea he formed an organization called the Sinminhoe (New People's Association), a secret society dedicated to the cause of freeing Korea from Japanese control.

During this period Ahn developed his ideas about how Korea could win and keep its independence. He differed from more radical nationalist leaders in that he advocated a long-term evolutionary process, while they tended to stress military action to achieve immediate liberation. He did not believe that propaganda to win the favor of countries like the United States—the approach followed by Syngman Rhee—would be successful. Ahn's approach instead drew on the importance of education, capital accumulation, and moral uprightness to overcome what he saw as weaknesses in the Korean character. Only by overcoming these weaknesses, he felt, would Koreans be truly prepared for independence. To these ends he founded a "modern" school in Korea, established a ceramics factory that was the first all-Korean joint-stock company, and lectured extensively on the need for moral regeneration. Japanese power over Korea increased, however, culminating in annexation in 1910. The Japanese intensified pressure on Ahn's Sinminhoe, so he returned to California in 1911, settling with his wife, Helen, whom he had married in 1902, and their five children in the Los Angeles area and working as an agricultural laborer.

In 1913 Ahn founded the Hŭngsadan (Young Korean Academy), headquartered in Los Angeles, which reflected his philosophy of Korean independence. A nonpolitical organization for Koreans in the United States, its membership was restricted to an elite chosen upon clear evidence of ethical integrity and moral uprightness. It was Ahn's belief that such qualities had to be developed and nurtured to prepare future Korean leaders and to overcome the tendency toward division and bickering that was beginning to appear in the Korean nationalist movement.

When the March First movement of 1919 (a nationwide anti-Japanese demonstration) broke out in Korea, a provisional government was formed in Shanghai, and Ahn, by now a leading figure in the nationalist movement, became a key participant. He arrived in Shanghai from the United States in late 1919 and served as the provisional government's first leader while promoting his vision for an evolutionary road to eventual independence. Ahn's provisional government was weakened, however, by the existence of two other rival governments, a split with the Socialists, and personality conflicts among its own membership. Ahn was also criticized by some because he supported the controversial Rhee and because his gradualist approach seemed to acquiesce to Japanese control. Although he applied his considerable skills to mediating among the various factions, Ahn could not resolve their differences, and he resigned in 1921. After visiting Koreans resident in China and Russia, Ahn returned to California in 1924 to resume his activities in the Young Korean Academy.

Two years later Ahn returned to Shanghai, where he tried to revive the moribund provisional government. He was arrested by the Japanese in the early 1930s and sent to Korea for trial for violating the Peace Preservation Law. Convicted, he was sentenced to four years in prison, obtaining an early release in 1935. He remained in Korea giving speeches, and he died in a hospital in Seoul as he was about to be tried again by the Japanese for independence activities.

Ahn was not only a key figure in the Korean nationalist movement, whose activities took him to Russia, China, the United States, and back to Korea, but his gradualist philosophy of strengthening the mind and character of Koreans also transcended the nationalist movement to resonate with the values that even now inform Korean society. He continues to be regarded as one of the most gifted leaders in the movement to free Korea from Japanese control.

• Ahn's collected writings, both published and unpublished, have been compiled in *An Tosan Chŏnsŏ*, ed. Chu Yŏ-han (1971). The best account of the life and activities of Ahn in English is Arthur L. Gardner, "The Korean Nationalist Movement and An Ch'ang-Ho, Advocate of Gradualism" (Ph.D. diss., Univ. of Hawaii at Manoa, 1979). A broader work on Korean nationalism that contains significant details about Ahn's role in the nationalist movement is Chong-Sik Lee, *The Politics of Korean Nationalism* (1963). Other sources on Ahn include Kingsley K. Lyu, "Korean Nationalist Activities in Hawaii and the Continental U.S., 1900–1945," pt. 1 (1910–1919) and pt. 2 (1919–1945), *Amerasia Journal* 4, no. 1 (1977): 23–90, and no. 2 (1977): 53–100, and Bong-Youn Choy, *Koreans in America* (1979). Sucheng Chan, "European and Asian Immigration into the United States in Comparative Perspective, 1820s to 1920s," in *Immigration Reconsidered: History, Sociology, and Politics*, ed. Virginia Yans-McLaughlin (1990), provides a comparative perspective on immigrant nationalist movements.

WAYNE PATTERSON

AIKEN, Conrad (5 Aug. 1889–17 Aug. 1973), author and critic, was born in Savannah, Georgia, the first child of Dr. William Ford Aiken, an ophthalmological surgeon, and Anna Potter, transplanted New Englanders. Aiken's father was brilliant but unstable, hectored increasingly by bouts of paranoia in the late 1890s. The main targets of his rage during these seizures were his wife, who strove vainly to convince relatives in the North of his worsening mental condition, and his oldest son, who was often beaten for slight or imaginary wrongs. Aiken later said of this period, "I hardly ever forgot what it was to be afraid."

Dr. Aiken's internal struggle reached its climax in the dawn hours of 27 February 1901, when he shot his wife to death and then put the gun to his own head. Aiken, whose bedroom was nearby, heard the shots and found his parents' bodies. After the funeral, the children were taken north, where Aiken was parted from his sister and two brothers when they were adopted by Frederick Winslow Taylor, an affluent engineer-inventor and pioneer efficiency expert. As the eldest, Aiken was expected to carry on the family name; he became the ward of his uncle William Tillinghast, a Harvard librarian residing in Cambridge, although he never regarded his new abode as a "real home."

After graduating from a local grammar school in 1903, Aiken was sent to the Middlesex School in Concord, where he edited the school magazine, writing many of its poems and stories. Here he formed several close friendships, despite a bitter conflict with the headmaster. He entered Harvard in 1907 and immediately felt at ease. Not only had it been his father's college, but his guardian and another uncle, Alfred Potter, still worked there as librarians. More important, Harvard's intense literary atmosphere reinforced his own writing ambitions, which had been nurtured in Savannah by exposure to Edgar Allan Poe's literature and the published sermons and essays of his maternal grandfather, Rev. William James Potter, famed radical preacher. T. S. Eliot, with whom Aiken traded ideas and poems, became a permanent friend, though their relationship proved deeply ambivalent. Other class friendships destined to endure included those with Grayson McCouch, a Middlesex chum, and George Wilbur; both shared Aiken's interest in Freud's psychological theories.

The professor who had the greatest intellectual impact on Aiken was George Santayana, whose *Three Philosophical Poets* (1910) provided an epic frame for the poet's cultural task. Aiken's literary taste remained under the sway of the English Romantics, especially Keats, and the Elizabethans, always a force at Anglophilic Harvard, but he was impressed by Edwin Arlington Robinson's naturalistic verse portraits. Aiken's frequent, technically deft lyric contributions to the *Harvard Advocate*, which he helped edit, evinced a conventional 1890s stance, focusing on the self-conscious artist's function in the tradition (popular on campus) of Walter Pater's aesthete vision.

In his senior year, Aiken cut classes for two weeks to write a long poem "in the modern manner" and was put on probation for a semester, causing him to resign in a huff. As a result, he did not graduate until June 1912; he married Jessie McDonald, a graduate student from Canada, two months later. After an extended trip abroad, the couple returned to Cambridge in 1913 for the birth of their son John. Mostly supported by an inheritance from a great-great aunt, Aiken was free to pursue his literary aspirations unencumbered by a regular job. Signaled by the recent founding of Harriet Monroe's magazine, *Poetry*, the so-called poetry renaissance was in full swing, and he published widely (poetry and reviews) in various newspapers and the many small magazines sprouting in Boston, New York, and Chicago, often visiting the latter cities to make and maintain literary contacts.

Aiken's initial poetry volume, *Earth Triumphant* (1914), was heavily indebted to John Masefield's naturalistic narratives, and his second, *Turns and Movies* (1916), no less so to Edgar Lee Masters's *Spoon River Anthology*, intimating the insecurity beneath his pugnacious self-confidence that retarded the development of his own voice. This situation was not helped by the evident power and originality of Eliot's early work, including the "Love Song of J. Alfred Prufrock," which Aiken had tried to get published in England. Echoes of Eliot, in fact, abound in Aiken's fourth volume, *Nocturne of Remembered Spring (1917)*, and the symbolic impressionism of John Gould Fletcher figures strongly in much of the third, *The Jig of Forslin: A Symphony* (1916), first in a series of lush verse "symphonies" produced over the next decade in an attempt to poetically reify key aesthetic and ego dilemmas from a Freudian vantage. Protagonists in the symphonies are alter-egos who suffer from various neuroses.

Aiken was more successful in prose, particularly when evaluating contemporaries. He was an early exponent of integrating psychoanalytic tenets with more orthodox methods to forge a less subjective, not merely impressionistic, critical scale. Although he acquired a reputation for being a prickly conservative because of his campaign against imagism, he was among the few to recognize the value of Eliot, Wallace Stevens, and William Carlos Williams. His editions of *Modern American Poets* (1922), *Selected Poems of Emily Dickinson* (1924), and *American Poetry 1671–1928* (1929) helped establish the reputations of these poets and initiated a serious revaluation of Emily Dickinson and Anne Bradstreet.

Aiken moved his family to England in 1922, settling down in Rye by 1925, where Jessie gave birth to their third child. The marriage was in trouble, however; his philandering, which had been a constant from the start (unknown to his wife), was no longer sufficient to keep at bay the depression that began harrowing his days when he reached the age his father had been at the time of his death. In 1926, on a trip to America, he met and fell in love with Clarissa Lorenz, a musician and journalist, whom he would marry in 1930, after receiving a divorce from Jessie in 1929.

The period of Aiken's affair with and marriage to Lorenz, which ended in divorce in 1937, encompassed years of poisonous self-doubts and at least one attempt at suicide (in 1932). It was also, however, a time of incredible artistic achievement, marked by the publication of Aiken's two major "preludes" sequences, *Preludes for Memnon* (1931) and *Time in the Rock* (1936), which explored fundamental linguistic and epistemological problems; an autobiographical Joycean novel, *Blue Voyage* (1927); and two collections of short stories, *Costumes by Eros* (1928) and *Among the Lost People* (1934). The latter contained "Silent Snow, Secret Snow" and "Mr. Arcularis," deemed classics of the genre. In addition, his *Selected Poems* (1929) won the Pulitzer Prize for 1930.

Finances were an increasing problem after his first divorce and the stock market crash of 1929—partly instrumental in his original decision to write fiction—and Aiken ground out a "London Letter" column for the *New Yorker* under the name Samuel Jeake, Jr. (Jeake's House was his Rye home through three marriages) between 1934 and 1936. He also worked briefly for the WPA in Boston, producing four essays for that organization's *Massachusetts: A Guide* (1937). His closest friends from the late 1920s to the end of his life were artists, such as Paul Nash and Edward Burra in England, and psychiatrists or psychologists, among them his old schoolmate Wilbur, a Cape Cod neighbor from the 1940s on, and Henry Murray, at Harvard's Psychological Clinic.

Aiken's literary career continued to be an odd combination of growing public recognition, critical neglect, and poor sales—each of his five novels did worse financially than the one before. In the 1950s, for instance, he served two one-year terms as consultant in poetry at the Library of Congress (1950–1952), had a special issue of *Wake* magazine (1951) devoted to his work, saw "Mr. Arcularis" turned into a successful TV play on the *Philco Television Playhouse* (1951), and won the National Book Award (1954) for his *Collected Poems* (1953), as well as the Bollingen Prize in 1956. In the same decade, he published *Ushant: An Essay* (1952), his innovative autobiography, to generally favorable reviews, as well as several verse collections, and *A Reviewer's ABC: Collected Criticism* (1958), edited by Rufus A. Blanshard. Yet, he could justifiably claim, "Everyone thinks I'm dead."

In 1939, Aiken and his third wife, the artist Mary Augusta Hoover, had abandoned Jeake's House, which would be sold after the war. They subsequently divided their time between a house in Brewster and a tiny Manhattan flat until 1962, when they were given lifetime residency in a Savannah townhouse next to Aiken's childhood home; this became their winter retreat. Despite the painful onset of pemphigus, a skin disease, in 1962 and a heart attack in 1963, Aiken kept writing, though he now mined lighter poetic veins, completing a book of limericks and several children's books. His sole serious project was *Thee: A Poem* (1967), which addressed God directly, albeit irreverently at times. His two daughters, Jane and Joan, have written popular children's stories and adult fiction, and their brother John, a chemist, has written two science fiction novels.

Aiken died in a Savannah hospital from a second heart attack the same year Governor Jimmy Carter named him Georgia's poet laureate.

• Aiken's letters and manuscripts are at the Huntington Library in San Marino, Calif., the Harvard Archives, the Princeton University Library, and the University of Chicago's Joseph Regenstein Library. Most of his poetry is in *Collected Poems, 1916–1970* (1970), and his fiction can be found in *The Collected Novels of Conrad Aiken* (1964) and *The Collected Short Stories of Conrad Aiken* (1960). His essays and many of his reviews are in his *Collected Criticism* (1968). Joseph Killorin has edited *Selected Letters of Conrad Aiken*. Edward Butscher, *Conrad Aiken: Poet of White Horse Vale* (1988), the first part of a two-volume biography, ends in 1925. Jay Martin, *Conrad Aiken: A Life of His Art* (1962), treats the work in a biographical context. See also F. W. and F. C. Bonnell, *Conrad Aiken: A Bibliography (1902–1978)* (1982) and Ted R. Spivey and Arthur Waterman, eds., *Conrad Aiken: A Priest of Consciousness* (1989), which has a chronology, a bibliography of critical reactions, a guide to the Huntington materials, and a number of essays treating various aspects of all of Aiken's writings.

EDWARD BUTSCHER

AIKEN, D. Wyatt (17 Mar. 1828–6 Apr. 1887), agricultural editor and congressman, was born David Wyatt Aiken in Winnsboro, South Carolina, the son of David Aiken, a merchant and planter, and Nancy Kerr. Descended from an Irish family that had prospered in the United States, Aiken received an excellent education at Mount Zion Institute in his hometown and, as was common for the sons of planters, attended South Carolina College. He graduated in 1849 and taught mathematics for two years at Mount Zion. After traveling to Europe in 1851, he returned home to marry Mattie Gaillard in 1852. Before her death in 1855, they had two children. Aiken married Virginia Carolina Smith in 1857; they had eleven children. The following year he purchased a plantation from the estate of Virginia's father in Cokesbury, Abbeville District. As the proprietor of "Coronaca" plantation, he became involved in the agricultural reform movement and in states' rights politics. He fervently believed that "agriculture climbs high in the scale of science: it develops thought, matures judgment, and requires for the execution, untiring energy, perseverance, and industry." He was instrumental in the formation of the Abbeville Agricultural Society and was a member of its executive committee. In 1858 he attended the Southern Commercial Convention in Montgomery, Alabama, a meeting that quickly became a forum for disunionist politics.

In January 1861 Aiken enlisted as a private in the Secession Guards, a military company organized in Greenwood. With the outbreak of the war, Aiken's company was merged into the Seventh South Carolina Regiment, and Aiken was appointed adjutant. He fought at First Manassas (Bull Run) in July 1861 and in the spring of 1862 was elected colonel of his regiment, which had become part of the Fourth (Kershaw's) Brigade in the Army of Northern Virginia. Severely wounded at Antietam on 17 September 1862, Aiken needed several months to convalesce. After rejoining his command in June 1863, he fought in the Gettysburg campaign, but his health was so poor that he was deemed unfit for further active service. He was reassigned to a rearguard post as commander of the defenses at Macon, Georgia, and he served there until receiving a medical discharge in July 1864.

Aiken turned to politics once his military career was over. He was a representative from the Abbeville District in the South Carolina House from 1864 to 1866. The onset of Radical Reconstruction in 1867 ushered in a period of Republican dominance in South Carolina, and Aiken worked tirelessly for the restoration of the Democratic party to power. In 1868 Republicans implicated him in the murder of B. F. Randolph, a black congressman from the Third District, but the case against Aiken never came to trial. He combined his Democratic politics with a renewed commitment to the cause of agricultural reform. Believing that the Republicans were corrupt and wasteful in their fiscal policies, he argued that prosperity for South Carolina farmers could return only under Democratic rule. He was a part owner and prolific essayist for the *Rural*

Carolinian, an agricultural journal founded in Charleston in 1869. He urged farmers to diversify their crops and free themselves from excessive reliance upon cotton and the crop-lien system. Active in the National Grange, or Patrons of Husbandry, and a member of its national executive committee in 1873, he organized a state Grange in South Carolina in 1872. He hoped that the Grange would help farmers overcome their isolation and teach them the benefits of economic cooperation and progressive agricultural practices. He was the head, or master, of the South Carolina Grange from 1875 to 1877. In all of his agricultural efforts, Aiken saw himself as the champion of common white farmers against greedy merchants and an uncaring federal government.

The Democrats returned to power in South Carolina in 1876, and Aiken was elected to Congress to represent the upcountry Third District. He would serve continuously in Congress until shortly before his death. Convinced that he spoke "for those who feed the cotton-gin and the grain-thresher and walk between the plough-handles," he was one of the leading advocates for agricultural interests. Arguing that economic interest groups such as manufacturers and shippers had long been recipients of federal subsidies and protection, he demanded what he felt was only agriculture's fair share from the federal government. He favored increased mail service in rural areas and a reduction in federal taxes and tariffs so as to lighten the farmers' financial burdens. His most cherished goal was the elevation of the Department of Agriculture to full cabinet rank. Such an upgrading of agriculture's ranking in the federal bureaucracy had been a major goal of the National Grange since 1876, and Aiken led the floor fight for it in Congress during the 1880s. He achieved a posthumous victory when the Department of Agriculture was raised to cabinet status in 1889.

Apart from agriculture, Aiken was most concerned as a congressman with blocking any extension of federal power over the internal affairs of the states. He strongly opposed the Blair Bill of 1884, a measure that called for distributing federal funds to the states for public school education. In contrast with the Charleston wing of his party in South Carolina, he also opposed using any of the budget surplus that was annually being accumulated by the federal government for public works projects.

Declining health prevented Aiken from running for Congress in 1886. He died at Cokesbury, South Carolina, as a result of complications from a hip injury. He was widely acknowledged as the preeminent spokesman for the agrarian interests of the post–Civil War South.

• Aiken's papers are in the South Caroliniana Library at the University of South Carolina. His autobiography, covering his early life to 1851, is in the Southern Historical Collection at the University of North Carolina at Chapel Hill. Copies of the *Rural Carolinian*, which contain many of his agricultural essays, can be found at the South Caroliniana Library and Duke University Library. Claudius Hornby Pritchard, *Colonel D. Wyatt Aiken, 1828–1887* (1970), provides the only biographical treatment. A good source for his military career is D. A. Dickert, *History of Kershaw's Brigade* (1899).

William L. Barney

AIKEN, George David (20 Aug. 1892–19 Nov. 1984), farmer and U.S. senator, was born in Dummerston, Vermont, the son of Edward W. Aiken and Myra Cook, farmers. He attended high school in Brattleboro. In 1914 he married Beatrice M. Howard; they had four children. His first wife died in 1966, and a year later Aiken married one of his Senate aides, Lola Pierotti.

Aiken entered farming after graduating from high school in 1909. He engaged in fruit growing and the nursery business, and he later successfully experimented with marketing wildflowers. Based on his experiences, Aiken wrote *Pioneering with Wildflowers* (1933) and *Pioneering with Fruits and Berries* (1936). In 1922 he was an unsuccessful Republican candidate for the Vermont House of Representatives, but he won election in 1930, becoming the fourth generation of his family to serve in the legislature. Reelected in 1932, he was chosen Speaker of the state house the next year. In 1934 Aiken was elected lieutenant governor. He was elected governor in 1936 and reelected in 1938. Aiken established himself as an independent-minded Republican, combating special interests and condemning the "hate-Roosevelt" attitudes of so many of his fellow Republicans as counterproductive. His gubernatorial policies were often conservative and included reduction of the public debt, a pay-as-you-go plan for road construction, and state instead of federal responsibility for flood control projects.

In 1940 Aiken was elected to fill an unexpired term in the U.S. Senate and was handily reelected in 1944, 1950, 1956, 1962, and 1968. He charted an independent course in Congress, gaining esteem from the public, the press, and his fellow senators for his integrity, his decency, and his ability to rise above partisanship.

Aiken's independence was exemplified in his votes to confirm controversial Democratic appointees such as David Lilienthal as chairman of the Atomic Energy Commission and Aubrey Williams as head of the Rural Electrification Administration. An unwavering internationalist, Aiken very early in his Senate career endorsed bipartisanship in foreign policy; he also was a constant advocate of low tariffs and trade reciprocity. During the tense and partisan Cold War years, Aiken was among the few Republican senators who in 1950 and often thereafter criticized the Red-baiting tactics of Senator Joseph R. McCarthy. Indeed, in 1954 Aiken even gave up thirteen years of seniority on the Senate Labor and Public Welfare Committee to take a Republican seat on the Foreign Relations Committee that McCarthy otherwise would have received. During the 1960s, the Vermonter sat in the United Nations General Assembly and in 1963 represented President John F. Kennedy during the negotiations in Moscow over the atomic test ban treaty. A frequent critic of American intervention in Vietnam, Aiken asserted in

1966 that it would be wise to "declare the United States the winner and begin deescalation."

Despite his high-profile foreign policy positions, Aiken's major impact involved domestic policy. He was a sponsor of the Employment Act of 1946, which committed the federal government to promoting full employment and established the Council of Economic Advisers. In 1947–1948 he was chairman of the Committee on Expenditures in Executive Departments and served on the Hoover Commission, which was substantially successful in bringing greater efficiency and economy to the operation of executive branch agencies. Despite his ongoing concern with excessive federal appropriations, the Vermonter played an important role in providing federal aid to education and was a prominent champion of developing the St. Lawrence Seaway, which Congress approved in 1959. Aiken could also be counted on to back advances in civil rights legislation. His outstanding Senate committee service was on the Committee on Agriculture and Forestry, of which he was the senior Republican member during most of his career. Aiken was an unflagging supporter of rural electrification and crop insurance, and reversing his position as governor he came to support federal flood control efforts. Skeptical of farm subsidies, he was not rigid even on this matter, as was seen in his sponsorship of the Hope-Aiken Agricultural Act of 1948. Early in his Senate career, he proposed issuing food stamps for low-income families, a program which finally became law in 1965 and was probably his most significant accomplishment.

Aiken had little patience with the political preoccupations of many other lawmakers, contending that they should spend less time campaigning and more time legislating. Of course, this he could afford to do, for he was a popular representative of a relatively liberal, rock-solid Republican state. His positions, if often controversial on the national scene, were seldom looked at askance by most Vermonters. Moreover, Aiken believed that his congressional colleagues often wasted time in arriving at decisions. He exasperatedly declared, for example, concerning President Richard M. Nixon and the Watergate scandal, that Congress should "either impeach or get off his back."

Aiken declined to run for reelection in 1974, returning to Vermont, where he engaged in agricultural and civic activities. He died in Putney. His career as governor and senator amply demonstrated what an independent-minded politician of integrity could accomplish, while still being successful at the polls.

• George D. Aiken's personal papers and a lengthy oral history transcript are located in the University of Vermont; his state papers are on deposit with the secretary of state, Montpelier. Other Aiken oral history transcripts are deposited in the Dwight D. Eisenhower, Lyndon B. Johnson, and John F. Kennedy presidential libraries. For some basic material in print relating to Aiken's political career, see his *Speaking from Vermont* (1938) and *Senate Diary, January 1972–January 1975* (1976). See also Allen J. Matusow, *Farm Policies and Politics in the Truman Years* (1967). Obituaries are in the *New York Times* and the *Washington Post*, 20 Nov. 1984.

DONALD R. MCCOY

AIKEN, George L. (19 Dec. 1830–27 Apr. 1876), actor and playwright, was born in Boston, Massachusetts, the son of Lemuel G. Aiken, an actor, and Susan A. Wyatt. His "first remembrance [was] of a theater," and it was not long before his services were enlisted in children's roles at Boston's Tremont Theatre. Douglas Jerrold's *Rent Day* provided the young thespian with his debut as the "infant" son of the actress Mrs. George Barrett. These early stage experiences he wrote, "produced a natural result. I became desirous, as I grew older, of adopting the theatrical profession." Aiken and a group of like-minded boys formed an amateur theatrical society, producing plays in a rented loft they named the Sprout Shop. Aiken left school before he was age fourteen and went to work for three years in a carpet warehouse, but the dyes in the carpets began to affect his health.

Shortly before his eighteenth birthday, Aiken quit his job and moved to Providence, Rhode Island, to join his cousin, Caroline Fox, and her husband, George C. Howard, who had converted Providence's Cleveland Hall into a theater. He made his first professional stage appearance as Ferdinand in that company's 1848 production of Frederic Stanhope Hill's *Six Degrees of Crime*. Although the Howard company left Providence in 1850, Aiken appears to have stayed on, performing with his cousin George Washington Lafayette "Laff" Fox.

Aiken credited the writing of his first story to his best friend, Edward Danforth, who worked in a newspaper office. By 1851 he was trying his hand at dramatizing novels for the theater with *Orion, the Gold Beater*, which opened in New York City on 15 January and played only a few performances. His *Helos, the Helot*, a tale of a Spartan slave revolt, survived only one or two performances in June 1852.

When Howard took over management of a theater in Troy, New York, in the fall of 1851, Aiken joined his cousins in the resident acting company of what was truly a family affair. In addition to Howard and his wife, the company included Emily Fox, Howard's mother-in-law; Charles, Howard's brother-in-law; and Howard's young daughter, Cordelia. Following Cordelia's popular success in an adaptation of Dickens's *Oliver Twist*, Howard sought a vehicle for her talents. At the time Harriet Beecher Stowe's antislavery novel, *Uncle Tom's Cabin*, was immensely popular in the North. At least two other attempts to dramatize the novel had been unsuccessful, but Howard was eager to have Cordelia play the crowd-pleasing role of Little Eva. Despite Aiken's less than illustrious track record as a dramatist, Howard "entrusted the task of adaptation to cousin George Aiken . . . who could be relied upon to tailor the script to the strengths of his colleagues" with whom he had worked and with whose talents he was familiar (Senelick, p. 59). Reportedly, Aiken finished the first version of the script in a week and the play opened at the Troy Museum on 27 September 1852. Aiken played the roles of kindly slave owner George Shelby and the mulatto George Harris. The astounding success of the play, which had a run of over 100 nights in Troy, led to a production in New York City, where it opened on 18 July 1853 and played over 325 performances.

The final version of Aiken's play consists of two shorter versions, one ending with the death of Eva and the second ending with Tom's death at the hands of Simon Legree, which were melded together to form the six-act drama that is considered the definitive dramatization of the novel. Although other adaptations of the novel were written, the Aiken version was never seriously challenged by its imitators.

Despite the success of the Troy production of *Uncle Tom's Cabin*, George Aiken did not join the production in New York. He continued his acting and writing careers, staging his version of the play in Detroit in 1854. This was followed with his dramatization of Ann S. Stephens's novel *The Old Homestead* in 1856. Aiken also wrote and produced *The Ups and Downs of New York Life* in New York in 1857, *The Emerald Ring* in 1858, and *The Doom of Deville; or The Maiden's Vow* in 1859. Many of these plays were produced at Barnum's American Museum, where Aiken was resident dramatist in 1861.

Records indicate that Aiken continued both as an actor and as a dramatist, but his career appears to have taken a significant turn toward the narrative with a series of nickel-and-dime novels. *The Household Skeleton* was published in 1865, followed by *Cynthia, The Pearl of the Points* (1867); *The Young Conqueror; of Don John of Austria* (1865), a chronicle of love, intrigue and war; *Scyros the Corsair; or, the Daughter of the Sea*, subtitled a Venetian romance; *Chevalier; or the French Jack Sheppard* (1868), a historical romance. When the allure and the romance of Europe waned, Aiken turned toward the American West for local color in *A New York Boy among the Indians* and *Kit Carson's Bride*, both published in 1872.

The last play Aiken copyrighted was *Josie; or Was He a Woman?* in 1870, and he retired from acting in 1871. However, he continued writing fiction, until his death in Jersey City, New Jersey.

Aiken was an actor of little note. Although he was employed in theaters throughout the Northeast, including New York, Boston, and Philadelphia, the companies were "second string" troupes. Despite a fairly substantial number of plays and novels, his writing had little literary merit; its function was to feed the public's insatiable need for new plays and fictions that would hold their interest for a moment. It was that need for the new and novel, combined with the rising abolitionist sentiment in the North that provided the synergy for Aiken's primary claim to historical note: his popular and history-making dramatization of Stowe's *Uncle Tom's Cabin*.

• Biographical information is scattered in Aiken's brief reminiscences "Leaves from an Actor's Life" published in the *Saturday Journal*, available at the Billy Rose Theatre Collection at the New York Public Library for the Performing Arts, Lincoln Center, theatrical records of the period, and in historical accounts of *Uncle Tom's Cabin*. Harry Birdoff, *The World's Greatest Hit: Uncle Tom's Cabin* (1947), provides an interesting narrative account of the genesis of the play and Aiken's part in its writing, but the lack of documentation makes its validity somewhat suspect. Laurence Senelick's *The Age and Stage of George L. Fox 1822–1877* (1988), is a well-documented history of the Fox family and their Aiken cousins. Other accounts of the period include T. Allston Brown's *History of the American Stage* (1870), and H. P. Phelps's *Players of a Century* (1880).

JANE T. PETERSON

AIKEN, Howard Hathaway (8 Mar. 1900–14 Mar. 1973), computer pioneer, was born in Hoboken, New Jersey, the son of Daniel Aiken and Margaret Emily Mierisch. The family moved to Indianapolis, and when Howard was twelve years old, his father left home and the boy became the family breadwinner. He attended the Arsenal Technical High School during the day, working at night as a switchboard operator for the Indianapolis Light and Heat Company. Upon graduation in 1919, Aiken entered the University of Wisconsin in Madison to study electrical engineering, supporting himself and his family with a night job at the Madison Gas Company.

After receiving his electrical engineering degree in 1923, Aiken began a full-time career in industry. After about ten years, however, he changed careers, enrolling as a graduate student in physics, first at the University of Chicago (1931–1932) and then at Harvard, where he received an S. M. in 1937. At Harvard Aiken began an academic affiliation that, except for wartime service in the U.S. Navy, continued until his retirement in 1961.

At Harvard Aiken was associated with a "communications engineering" group within the physics department. His thesis topic was a study of the conductivity of vacuum tubes. He received his Ph.D. in 1939 and was appointed the equivalent of assistant professor, achieving tenure as associate professor of applied mathematics as of 1 September 1941, while on active duty as a lieutenant commander in Engineering, Special Service, U.S. Naval Reserve. He became a full professor in 1946.

Aiken's research for his thesis required many hours of tedious calculations with a desk calculator and tables; this set him to thinking about ways of mechanizing scientific calculating. By 1937, while still a graduate student, he had conceived a plan for a machine that would perform complex calculations according to a programmed sequence and yield results far more quickly and more accurately than manual calculations. This machine would solve problems in science, engineering, and the social sciences.

In April 1937 Aiken presented a formal proposal to the Monroe Calculating Company. When Monroe rejected it, he turned to the International Business Machines Corporation (IBM). He won the enthusiastic support of the noted inventor James Wares Bryce, IBM's chief engineer. After much discussion, the project was approved by Thomas J. Watson, president of IBM, and a formal agreement was made between IBM and Harvard University in which IBM agreed to design and construct a machine for Harvard according to Aiken's general specifications. The U.S. Navy did not make any financial contribution to the construction of the new machine, the total cost of which was borne by IBM.

The machine was built at the IBM plant in Endicott, New York, under the direction of Clair D. Lake, who assigned the operational development to Francis E. Hamilton and Benjamin M. Durfee. Over the next years Aiken paid regular visits to Endicott to supply the IBM engineers with specifications of the mathematical tasks the machine was to perform and to work with them on problems of design and construction. It was the job of the engineers to create a machine to achieve Aiken's purpose. They were asked to produce an electromechanical machine of a degree of complexity and accuracy they had never attempted before.

In April 1940 Aiken, a member of the naval reserve, was called to active duty and spent the next four years running the Naval Mine Warfare School at Yorktown, Virginia. For the completion of the calculating machine, Robert V. D. Campbell, an advanced graduate student in the Harvard physics department, served as Aiken's deputy. When the machine was finally completed and installed at Harvard early in 1944, Campbell was in charge, supervising the programming and running of the first problems. The navy took over the operation of the machine for the rest of the war, providing a staff consisting of naval officers and enlisted men. In spring 1944 Aiken was transferred from Yorktown to Harvard, the first naval officer in history to become commander of a computer.

Harvard University arranged an official dedication of the new machine in August 1944; the public celebration was attended by high-ranking officers of the armed forces, the governor of Massachusetts, and officers and professors in the university, as well as Watson of IBM and members of his staff. On arriving in Boston the day before the celebrations, Watson was enraged to learn that Harvard had issued a press release without consulting IBM, and that the machine was being presented to the world as the invention of Aiken alone, with IBM receiving little or no credit for the actual design and the invention. The question of who invented the new machine caused a breach between Aiken and IBM that was never healed.

Aiken's philosophy of design, as he wrote some years later in a student manual, was, "The 'design' [of a] computing machine [is] understood to consist in the outlining of its general specifications and the carrying through of a rational determination of its functions, but does not include the actual engineering design of component units." His formal proposal to IBM accords with this philosophy, specifying the combinations of mathematical operations that would be required and their sequencing, but not specifying individual components and the actual methods of linking them or of producing the programmed sequence. Aiken had set certain goals, and the IBM engineers had then designed or invented an actual machine to satisfy Aiken's requirements. It had been their job to specify the individual working parts and their mode of assembly and operation.

The new machine, officially named the IBM Automatic Sequence Controlled Calculator, became widely known as the Harvard Mark I, or simply Mark I. It was constructed with relays as its primary functioning elements and was very slow in comparison with the computers of forty years later. In the terms of the 1940s, however, the ASCC seemed unbelievably fast. It was also remarkably accurate, able to carry computations to twenty-three digits without error. More importantly, the machine could be programmed to perform its operations in a predetermined sequence. Like other early computers, the Mark I was gigantic—about fifty feet long and eight feet high, composed of more than three-quarters of a million parts and more than 500 miles of wire. During wartime, the ASCC/Mark I ran continuously; probably the most important problem it ran was a set of computations of implosion relating to the atomic bomb.

Mark I was not electronic, but it was digital and programmable. It proved to the world that a machine could be programmed to perform a series of complex mathematical operations and do so without error. Another computer pioneer, Maurice Wilkes, later recalled, "The digital computer age began when the Automatic Sequence Controlled Calculator started working in April 1944."

Aiken and his associates later constructed three other machines. Mark II, designed and built at Harvard, was installed at the Navy Proving Grounds at Dahlgren, Virginia. It was followed by Mark III, also built for the navy, and by Mark IV, built for the U.S. Air Force. Although there were a number of notable features added to these later machines, and although they did useful service, they did not represent the cutting edge of computer engineering as the Mark I did. Aiken's place in history is based not on his influence on machine design, but rather on other aspects of his career.

Aiken's most important contributions to the science and art of the computer may have been his establishing at Harvard the first full graduate program in computer science, leading to the degrees of M.A. and Ph.D. The roster of his students includes such important computer scientists as Frederick P. Brooks, Jr., Kenneth Iverson, and Anthony Oettinger. Aiken organized a series of computer conferences where the world's leading pioneers gathered to learn the latest developments in the field. He led in exploring the possible use of computers for billing purposes; he was a tireless lecturer and public advocate for the use of computers in many different areas.

Aiken's preeminence as a pioneer in the unfolding world of the computer was recognized in 1964, when the American Federation of Information Processing Societies established the Harry H. Goode award to recognize "outstanding achievement in the field of information processing." The inaugural award went to Aiken, the inventor whose giant machine had inaugurated the computer age. He received many other honors and awards, including an honorary degree from Harvard University. The computation laboratory that he founded at Harvard was named after him.

In 1960 Aiken retired from Harvard and moved to Fort Lauderdale, Florida. He founded Howard Aiken Industries and devoted his energy to taking over ailing businesses and restoring them to good health. His interest in the computer never flagged, however, and he served as a consultant to Monsanto and Lockheed. He was twice married—in 1945 to Agnes Montgomery, with whom he had one child, and after that marriage ended in divorce, in 1963 to Mary Estella McFarland Nichols. He died in St. Louis, Missouri, while on a business trip.

• Aiken's papers, including the records of the Harvard Computation Laboratory and some personal correspondence, are in the Harvard University Archives, along with a typescript of a taped oral history interview with Aiken by I. Bernard Cohen and Henry Tropp in 1970. A full-length biography is I. Bernard Cohen, *Howard Aiken: Portrait of a Computer Pioneer* (1998). Aiken's activities in the computer field are described in Cohen and Gregory W. Welch, eds., *Makin' Numbers: Howard Aiken and the Computer* (1998).

On the ASCC/Mark I, see *A Manual of Operation for the Automatic Sequence Controlled Calculator*, reprinted (1985) with foreword by Cohen and introduction by Paul Ceruzzi; Howard H. Aiken and Grace M. Hopper, "The Automatic Sequence Controlled Calculator," *Electrical Engineering* 65 (1946): 384–91, 449–54, 522–28, reprinted in *The Origins of Digital Computers: Selected Papers*, ed. Brian Randell (1975); Edmund C. Berkeley, *Giant Brains, or Machines That Think* (1949; repr. 1961), chap. 6; and Ceruzzi, *Reckoners: The Prehistory of the Digital Computer, from Relays to the Stored-Program Concept, 1935–1945* (1983), chap. 3. Manuals of operation for Aiken's other machines are available in the *Annals* of the Computation Laboratory of Harvard University. On the computer conferences organized by Aiken, see *Proceedings of a Symposium on Large-Scale Digital Computing Machinery*, 7–10 Jan. 1947.

I. BERNARD COHEN

AIKEN, William (28 Jan. 1806–6 Sept. 1887), planter and congressman, was born in Charleston, South Carolina, the son of William Aiken, Sr., an Irish immigrant, and Henrietta Wyatt. At the time of his death, the elder Aiken was president of the South Carolina Canal and Railroad Company and a wealthy merchant. Aiken attended the South Carolina College, from which he graduated in 1825. He then traveled to Europe. Upon returning to Charleston, he married Harriet Lowndes in 1831. They had one child.

Only a month after Aiken's marriage, his father was killed in an accident, and the father's large fortune and business interests devolved onto Aiken. He invested in railroads and other businesses but decided early on to devote his principal resources and energies to rice planting. Accordingly in 1833 he purchased most of 4,000-acre Jehossee Island on the South Edisto River (in Collection District), where by 1850 he had developed the South's largest rice plantation, with 1,500 acres of prime tidal rice land and 500 acres of upland suitable for growing corn and other provision crops.

Aiken practiced sophisticated scientific procedures on his plantation and amassed the greatest congregation of slaves (700) on any southern plantation. Too, he was genuinely committed to the welfare of his slaves. As was typical with antebellum rice planters, he maintained a rather ordinary residence on Jehossee Island (because of the malarial conditions on the plantation, he was there only about half the year) but resided in a sizable, three-storied mansion in Charleston with a number of adjoining dependencies and servant quarters for twenty-five slaves. Additional planting interests in Charleston District gave Aiken, in the 1850 census, 178 slaves who, when added to the 700 at Jehossee Island, made him one of the largest southern planters and slaveholders. In 1850 his Jehossee Island plantation was valued at $380,000, and the 1860 census for the city of Charleston evaluated his real and personal estates at $290,000 and $12,000 respectively. During the 1850s Aiken purchased the rest of Jehossee Island and sizably enlarged the house there, adding a colonnaded portico, an impressive avenue of live oaks, and grounds nicely laid out with urns and statuary beneath stately magnolias. His 1859 rice crop was 1.5 million pounds—an increase of 570,000 pounds over that of 1849.

In 1838 Aiken was elected as a Democrat to the South Carolina General Assembly by the Charleston parishes of St. Philips and St. Michaels and was reelected in 1840. In the South Carolina House he served on the Committees on Agriculture, the Colored Population, Privileges and Elections, and Public Buildings. In 1842 Aiken was elevated by the same constituencies to the state senate, where he was a member of the Committee on Roads and Buildings. He was elected governor of South Carolina by the legislature in 1844, and during his two-year term he encouraged economic growth, especially railroad expansion.

On 8 December 1846 Aiken retired from the governor's office to his plantation until his election to the U.S. Congress from the Charleston District in 1851. He served three terms in Congress, from 1851 to 1857. Although not given to debate, he was able to influence legislation through membership on important committees. Aiken wisely avoided either party or sectional bias and was regarded as a man of sterling character. Thus, in 1856, when the Thirty-fourth Congress could not elect a Speaker after two months of balloting, he was introduced as a suitable compromise candidate. However, while enjoying the support of Democrats and most of the southern Know Nothings, he was finally defeated on the 133d ballot by Nathaniel P.

Banks, the Republican candidate, who received 103 votes compared to 100 for Aiken and 11 for all others.

Aiken declined a fourth term in Congress and returned once again to his planting and business interests in South Carolina. He was very much opposed to disunion and regarded ultimate secession with considerable concern. However, once war came, he gave support to the southern cause by donating food and lending large sums of money. Aiken held no official Confederate or state position, either political or military. Following the war, in June 1865, he was arrested by the Federal authorities for his aid to the Confederacy and was taken to Washington, where he was quickly paroled. In the fall of 1865 he was elected by his old district to the Thirty-ninth Congress, but along with all other southern members, he was denied admission by northern Republicans.

Aiken returned to his plantation, where his benevolent treatment of his slaves had encouraged them to stay on and work for him after emancipation. While other planters were having labor problems and losing their plantations for debt, he produced in 1869 1.2 million pounds of rice, with the total value of his farm products reaching $35,000. A visitor to Jehossee Island observed that Aiken "owned the whole island and lived in style." The big house there remained unoccupied much of the year, but the workers refrained from stealing any of the china, family silver, paintings, and furniture. Apparently they took great pride in caring for it until it burned accidentally in the 1890s. Aiken died in Flat Rock, North Carolina, his summer residence.

• Most of Aiken's private papers were lost when his home on Jehossee Island burned. A few of his papers are in the South Carolina Historical Society in Charleston. See Solon Robinson, "Jehossee Island," *American Agriculturist* 9 (1850): 187–88; James M. Clifton, "Jehossee Island, the Antebellum South's Largest Rice Plantation," *Agricultural History* 59 (1985): 56–65; and Suzanne C. Linder, *Historical Atlas of the Rice Plantations of the ACE [Ashepoo, Combahee, and Edisto] River Basin, 1860* (1996). See also Chalmers Gaston Davidson, *The Last Foray: The South Carolina Planters of 1860, a Sociological Study* (1971). An obituary is in the *Charleston News and Courier*, 8 Sept. 1887.

JAMES M. CLIFTON

AILEY, Alvin (5 Jan. 1931–1 Dec. 1989), actor, dancer, and choreographer, was born in Rogers, Texas, the son of Alvin Ailey, a laborer, and Lula Elizabeth Cliff, a cotton picker and domestic. Before Ailey was a year old, his father abandoned the family, leaving them homeless for close to six years. During that time Ailey and his mother made their way, often by foot, across the unforgiving terrain of the impoverished and bitterly racist Bravos Valley in southeastern Texas to seek shelter with relatives and find work in nearby fields.

A bright, curious child, Ailey joined his mother in the cotton fields as soon as he could carry a sack. He was baptized in the black Southern Baptist faith of his heritage and reveled in the sights and sounds of the gospel choirs and traditional spirituals. Ailey also became acquainted with the less pious side of members of his congregation who spent Saturday nights dancing, drinking, and fighting in roadside black bars and dance halls where blues musicians played against the constant drone of passing trains.

Whether a result of his environment or innate ability, Ailey could read people and situations in an instant. He also had a photographic memory that allowed him to recall the body language of the people involved. In 1958 Ailey drew on his memories of Saturday nights at the roadside bars to create *Blues Suite*, which captured the parade of emotions experienced by people unable to escape the drudgery of hapless lives.

Two years later he brought the charismatic Baptist preachers, fire-and-brimstone sermons, and gospel spirituals of his church to life in his signature masterpiece, *Revelations*. Although Ailey tightened the original version, made minor adjustments, and ultimately increased the size of the cast, *Revelations* has retained the spontaneity of Ailey at his best and proven its universal appeal to audiences around the world. As a result, it remains the cornerstone of his company's outstanding repertory.

In 1937 Ailey and his mother moved to Navasato, Texas, where a distinguished, light-colored black man named Amos Alexander fell in love with Ailey's mother and took the two into his home. Alexander treated Ailey as a son and provided him with the only secure, family environment he would experience. Ailey relished the stability of living in one place, eating regularly, going to the same school, and worshiping at the True Vine Baptist Church, but he developed a deep sense of obligation to Alexander and felt inferior to his children. Ailey's 1961 *Knoxville: Summer 1915* is a moving autobiography of his life in Navasato.

In 1942 Ailey's life changed dramatically. His mother decided to move to Los Angeles. She was determined to get one of the thousands of jobs being created by West Coast aircraft factories that were gearing up to handle the demands of the impending U.S. entry into World War II. Before she was hired as a night-shift worker for Lockheed, Ailey and his mother lived in a white section of the city, where she worked as a domestic. Because of where he lived, Ailey attended a previously all-white school.

With the exception of a class field trip to see Sergei Denham's Ballet Russe de Monte Carlo in 1943, being the only black student in the school reinforced his feelings of insecurity and inferiority. He had seen vaudeville shows, revues, and theater productions, but after seeing the Ballet Russe he attended as many dance events as he could. Among them was a presentation of the Katherine Dunham company. Dunham's spectacular productions of African and Caribbean dance styles had a tremendous influence on Ailey's concept of dance, theatricality, and the unique expressionism of ethnic dance.

In 1971 in his virtuoso solo *Cry*, Ailey immortalized his reaction to attending a white school and watching his mother scrubbing floors and hanging out laundry for white families. This first significant work created for Judith Jamison was Ailey's tribute to his mother and "all black women—especially our mothers." Ailey was the first to admit that he was a product of his environment and that he created works based on his experiences from childhood to the moment at hand. Of the seventy-nine works he created during his lifetime, his least successful dealt with subjects outside the realm of human emotion.

After moving to a racially mixed section of Los Angeles, Ailey attended Jefferson High School, which drew students of black and Hispanic heritage. He excelled in foreign language studies and distinguished himself as a gymnast. Intent on becoming a foreign language teacher, he entered the University of California at Los Angeles in 1948 as a foreign language major.

By that time, however, he had started formal dance training under Lestor Horton at the urging of high school friend Carmen de Lavallade. A white man, Horton had founded the first multiracial dance company in America and developed his own modern dance technique. The breadth of movement and expression the Horton technique supported appealed to Ailey. He also was intrigued by Horton's ability to fuse elements of theater and stagecraft in his works.

Ailey made his professional debut in Horton's company in 1950. He continued working toward his college degree until a brief engagement in a nightclub act sent him to Horton as a full-time dancer and teacher of the Horton technique. Late that year, Horton died. With support from de Lavallade and veteran Horton dancers James Truitte and Joyce Trisler, Ailey took over the artistic reins of the company, ran the school, and began to choreograph.

Ailey and de Lavallade were cast in the 1955 Twentieth Century–Fox motion picture *Carmen Jones*, directed by Herbert Ross. After filming was completed in 1954, Ross paired them in the Broadway-bound Truman Capote show *House of Flowers*. Their Broadway debut catapulted Ailey and de Lavallade into the limelight, but they continued to appear with Horton's company. Ailey also remained until 1960 an integral part of the effort to keep the company alive and ensure a future for its school.

Living in New York City, Ailey studied dance with, among others, Martha Graham, Sophie Maslow, Doris Humphrey, Anna Sokolow, Donald McKayle, Karel Shook, and Charles Weidman. He also studied acting under Stella Adler. As a dancer, Ailey moved with the power and grace of a lion. His physical strength, riveting presence, and ability to make movement appear to spring from within rather than as a result of the choreography set him apart from his peers. His total immersion in the roles he performed had a profound influence on his approach to choreography and choice of dancers.

Ailey's success on Broadway as a dancer and actor garnered him a fair share of theater awards and a secure future in musicals and theater. In addition to *House of Flowers*, in 1955 Ailey appeared in *The Carefree Tree*, Harry Belafonte's 1956 production of *Sing, Man, Sing*, and Lena Horne's 1957 *Jamaica*, choreographed by Jack Cole. He also appeared off-Broadway as an actor in *Call Me by My Rightful Name*, with Robert Duvall and Joan Hackett, and *Two by Saroyan*, and he made his Broadway debut in an acting role as Claudia McNeil's son in the 1962 production of *Tiger, Tiger, Burning Bright*.

Throughout his Broadway career, Ailey never lost sight of his goal to establish a multiracial dance company with a repertoire representing the past and future of American modern dance and the unique qualities of black cultural expression. Ailey used the fees he earned on Broadway to fund his own company and recruited several Broadway dancers to join the Horton dancers he was assembling to create a concert group. At ease in the artistic environment of the theater, Ailey developed strong ties within the world of entertainment and welcomed the mentorship of those he revered, who recognized the enormity of his artistic talents.

In 1958 Ailey presented the Alvin Ailey American Dance Theater in concert at New York City's Ninety-second Street YM-YWHA. Public and critical response was excellent and inspired Ailey and his dancers to continue building the company.

To keep his dancers together, Ailey provided food and shelter when they were unable to find work between concert engagements. He also ran the company by himself, getting bookings, taking care of production details, promoting the troupe, and handling the company finances out of a shoebox.

As financially strapped as the company was, Ailey refused to limit the company and its audiences to an all-Ailey repertory. He often crossed the color line to empower those who shared his dream of establishing a dance company without racial limitations.

In 1960 the premiere of Ailey's *Revelations* created a sensation in the dance world, and the company's future began to take shape. That year, Robert Joffrey commissioned Ailey to create a work for his ballet company, which brought Ailey in touch with the company's backer, Rebekah Harkness. A dance patron of considerable wealth, Harkness established a nonprofit foundation to sponsor broadly diverse projects within the field and cooperated with the U.S. Department of State Cultural Exchange Program to generate international recognition of American cultural achievements. The success of Ailey's *Feast of Ashes*, inspired by Federico García Lorca's *The House of Bernarda Alba* and set to an original Carlos Surinach score, put him in good stead with Harkness. Impressed by Ailey's fusion of dance styles and aware of the financial gridlock his company was in, Harkness allocated foundation funds to send Ailey's company on its first foreign tour.

After Harkness severed relations with Joffrey in 1963, she established the Harkness Ballet under the artistic direction of George Skibine. Ailey was invited to restage *Feast of Ashes*, which remained the property of the new company, and he was commissioned to create a new work for the company's inaugural season. As usual, Ailey applied the fees he earned to his own company. Although Harkness's wealth reinforced Ailey's personal insecurities, his commitment to his own company enabled him to accept her largesse.

Ailey's company ran out of money during its appearance at the First World Festival of Negro Arts in Dakar, Senegal, in 1966. Ailey managed to get his dancers to Barcelona, Spain, where his *Macumba*, set to Harkness music, was scheduled to premiere. Within a few hours of their arrival in Barcelona, Ailey had arranged for his dancers to be absorbed into the Harkness Ballet for the remainder of its European tour.

Although several of Ailey's dancers immediately found jobs with other companies, several joined the Harkness company for its summer workshop in Rhode Island. Jamison and Morton "Tubby" Winston stayed on for its subsequent American tour, but only Morton remained with the ballet company after Ailey's company resumed operation following a brief period of reorganization.

Ailey's relationship with Harkness remained strong, and his company continued to receive support from her foundation despite the fact that she dissolved the original Harkness Ballet in 1969. Ailey always credited her for giving his company the opportunity to survive long enough to gain international ranking in the world of dance.

With the exception of its brief period of reorganization, the Alvin Ailey American Dance Theater continued to build audiences around the world and offer more performances a year than any other American dance company. According to Jamison, whom Ailey named his successor before his death, the company covered most of its budget from almost year-round touring engagements in the United States and abroad.

Despite Ailey's achievements and enormous contributions to the world of dance, he remained unable to put aside his insecurities and accept his success. As a result, he felt undeserving of the many honors and awards that he received during his lifetime. His most significant awards included a Dance Magazine Award in 1975, the Spingarn Medal of the National Association for the Advancement of Colored People in 1976, the Capezio Award in 1979, the United Nations Peace Medal in 1982, the Samuel H. Scripps American Dance Festival Award in 1987, and a Kennedy Center Award in 1988. The anxiety he felt over accepting awards often triggered long spells of depression and self-destructive behavior.

In 1980 Ailey was diagnosed as a severe manic-depressive during his hospitalization after he created a public disturbance. Although he continued to create significant new works for his company and others, Ailey began turning over his responsibilities for running the main company, its affiliated school, and a student repertory ensemble to others. In keeping with the active role he had taken from the outset to bring his dancers into public schools, he also developed an interactive, multidisciplinary summer workshop for inner-city children with interests in the arts.

Ailey, who never married, died in New York's Lenox Hill Hospital surrounded by his mother, Mrs. Lula Cooper; Jamison; Sylvia Waters, director of the Alvin Ailey Repertory Ensemble; and Masazumi Chaya, assistant artistic director of the Alvin Ailey American Dance Theater.

• Ailey's archive is housed at the Alvin Ailey American Dance Center in New York City. Ongoing coverage of news, reviews, and analysis is in *Dance Magazine* from 1958 to the present. Detailed references to Ailey's childhood are in *Revelations* (1995), an autobiography by Alvin Ailey, with Peter Bailey. An in-depth eyewitness view of Ailey is offered in Judith Jamison, with Howard Kaplan, *Dancing Spirit* (1993). A comprehensive research paper written by Cynthia S'thembile West, "Alvin Ailey: Signposts of an American Visionary," was published in *African American Genius in Modern Dance*, a 1993 American Dance Festival publication. An obituary is in the *New York Times*, 2 Dec. 1989, and an obituary and posthumous tribute are in *Dance Magazine*, Feb. 1990.

LILI COCKERILLE LIVINGSTON

AINSLIE, Hew (5 Apr. 1792–11 Mar. 1878), poet and construction consultant, was born at Bargeny Mains, Ayrshire, Scotland, the son of George Ainslie, an employee of some consequence on the estate of Sir Hew Dalrymple Hamilton. Ainslie paid warm homage to his mother, whose name is not known, in his writings. Originally educated by a hired "dominie" at home, wirehaired Ainslie eventually moved on to the Ballantrae parish school and finally to Ayr Academy, where he completed his formal schooling at the age of fourteen. Certainly as important as his organized education was his home background colored by his father's pride in the family's past (the model of Sir Walter Scott's "Bride of Lammermoor" was one of several notable ancestors) and his mother's "teeming repertory" of Scottish songs and lore. Another influence was his father's small personal library containing the writings of Allan Ramsay, Robert Fergusson, Robert Burns, and other Scottish classics.

In 1806, as Ainslie was beginning to achieve the tall, lanky frame (six feet, four inches; 145 pounds) he maintained for the remainder of his life, Sir Hew succumbed to the basically English fad of estate "improvement," which involved massive artificial landscape changes to conform to current ideas about "the picturesque." Thomas White, the English developer, was Sir Hew's choice for this job, which took three years as the mostly English crew moved hills, rerouted streams, created structural "follies," and planted and replanted trees and bushes, all for visual effect. Fresh from Ayr Academy, Ainslie became a part of this project, here learning some of the construction skills that would be the basis for his success in later life.

Ending a long association with Sir Hew in 1809, Ainslie's father resettled his family in Roslin, six miles south of Edinburgh. Ainslie enjoyed rambling about that historic area for a time; then he began but shortly ended the study of law in Glasgow; finally in 1810 he became an amanuensis in the Register House, Edinburgh, where he remained until 1822 except for a brief period spent in the service of Dugald Stewart.

Edinburgh in the 1820s was still in the glow of its Golden Age, and Ainslie was acquainted with most of the local literary figures, such as Alexander Campbell, Robert Jamieson, and Thomas Pringle, well known then but now consigned to literary history lists. He is reported to have contributed several pieces to Robert Chambers's *Scottish Ballads*.

In 1822 Ainslie published anonymously the book that would establish his Scottish reputation, *A Pilgrimage to the Land of Burns*. It was an account of an actual 1820 summer tour of Burns country by Ainslie and two friends, using pseudonyms borrowed from Scott's *Antiquary*. Full of flowery descriptions and poetry inspired by their experiences, it received a good review from Thomas Campbell in the *New Monthly Magazine* (Oct. 1823), but Sir Walter Scott in a private letter (quoted in Latto, p. xviii) found it wanting in originality.

By 1822 growing dissatisfaction with his prospects caused Ainslie to turn his face to the New World. In 1812 he had married his cousin, Janet Ainslie. Ten years later, leaving his wife and three children in Scotland, he sailed for America, hoping to make a better life for his family there. He bought land in Rensselaer County, New York, and tried farming for three years, but failing to achieve the level of success he sought, he moved on to Robert Owen's community, New Harmony, Indiana, where he lasted only one year.

Ainslie's success began in 1827 when he became a partner with Price and Wood, a brewery in Cincinnati. By 1829 his family was with him when he opened a branch of that company in Louisville, Kentucky. Though this brewery was destroyed by a flood and a second brewery in New Albany, Indiana, was consumed by fire, they provided Ainslie with the expertise that made him a much-sought-after, well-paid consultant on brewery and factory construction for the remainder of his working life.

The Ainslies had ten children, seven of whom were born in the United States. Apparently after his wife had died and his children had been well situated, he retired in the early 1850s and in 1855 published *Scottish Songs, Ballads, and Poems*, a collection of mostly autobiographical poems by a "weary wandering father" searching for a new and better life for "those he'd left behind him" (p. 209). Written through the years, often in heavy Scots language (*dialect* was a word he refused to recognize), the poems reflect his Americanization and his growing pride in his new country. Though the volume received scant attention outside Ainslie's circle in this country, it clearly served the purpose to express his appreciation of the advantages of his new life in America. In Scotland where his language was more easily understood, the volume enjoyed a much wider appeal.

In 1862 Ainslie returned to Scotland to unexpected acclaim. Some of his family and friends from the early years of the century had themselves experienced productive careers, even more financially successful than his, but he brought with him the *ton* of American success. He was lionized as the Scottish newspapers closely followed his activities. He expanded his trip to England, Ireland, and the Continent, finally returning to the United States by way of Scotland (and more recognition) in 1865.

A familiar long, lean figure, his now-gray hair as thick and wildly tousled as in his youth, Ainslie spent the remainder of his life in Louisville at the home of his eldest son, where he died.

More than as an individual, Ainslie is important as a representative of the thousands of nineteenth-century immigrants who became loyal citizens and contributed to the development of the United States while maintaining a heartfelt love for their native lands. His unapologetic reverence for his Scottish past and his unbridled optimism for the course he had set for the future of his descendants in the New World illustrate the melting-pot concept and the American Dream at their best.

Ainslie differs from most of his contemporaries, however, in that he enjoyed a greater reputation in his homeland than in his adopted country. The centennial of his birthday, for example, undoubtedly went unnoticed in the United States, but in Scotland it was observed in at least two locations. Suggestive of the esteem in which he was held was a poem published in the *Scotsman* (5 Apr. 1892) in which he was fondly remembered as a Scots poet and as an American success.

• The Mitchell Library, Glasgow, Scotland, has a file of newspaper clippings and other items devoted to Ainslie. The most complete biography of Ainslie is Thomas C. Latto, "A Memoir of the Author," prefixed to an edition of Ainslie's complete works, *A Pilgrimage to the Land of Burns and Poems* (1892). An earlier Scottish memoir is in Charles Rogers, *The Modern Scottish Minstrel* (1857). A piece by Thomas Wilson in the *Dictionary of National Biography* (1885) identifies Ainslie as "Scottish poet," virtually ignoring his American associations. An obituary is in the *Louisville Courier-Journal*, 13 Mar. 1878.

BEN HARRIS MCCLARY

AINSWORTH, Dorothy Sears (8 Mar. 1894–2 Dec. 1976), physical education teacher and founder of international organizations for her discipline, was born in Moline, Illinois, the daughter of Harry Ainsworth, an engineering draftsman, and Stella Davidson. Miss Ainsworth graduated with a B.A. in history from Smith College in 1916. After her undergraduate education, she taught physical education at Moline High School. In 1918 she was invited to join the first Smith College Relief Unit, founded by another Smith alumna, Harriet Boyd Hawes. While serving in Grecourt, France, Miss Ainsworth helped survivors of World War I rebuild devastated villages. In 1921 she returned to Smith College as an instructor in the Department of Hygiene and Physical Education. Teaching at Smith had convinced her to pursue physical education as a career, and she left her job at Smith to study for a master's degree in physical education, which she received from Columbia University in 1925. She was then recruited to teach at Skidmore College but stayed only a year before being offered the position as a professor and director of the physical education department at Smith in 1926. In her first three years in this position Miss Ainsworth commuted every weekend to take classes at Columbia in order to earn her doctorate. After another year of writing a thesis on the history of physical education in the twelve women's colleges, she received her doctorate in physical education in 1930. She remained at Smith until her retirement in 1960.

Miss Ainsworth's professional accomplishments at the local, national, and international level are numerous. At Smith College she increased the curriculum offerings from eleven courses in 1926 to twenty-nine in 1931, many courses straying far from the traditional gymnastics and dance offerings of that era. Soon there were tennis, track and field, baseball, and crew classes. Her philosophy was that there should be a sport for every student, and courses were designed to benefit all students, not just the superior athletes. She believed strongly in an intramural program that would serve all students at Smith. This tradition of strong intramurals has continued. She was, however, an opponent of intercollegiate competition, believing that it did not allow all students to benefit equally from the physical education budget. Her philosophy influenced the direction of sports until 1972, when Smith finally began fielding teams for intercollegiate competition. As she expanded and changed the curriculum, new positions were created in the department, and Miss Ainsworth hired faculty who specialized in particular sports and were dedicated and loyal to the department. Furthermore, she established a graduate course for training teachers in physical education at Smith College. This early graduate program for women was unique in the country and continued into the late twentieth century as a graduate program for coaching education. Consistent with her growing interests in physical education on the international level, Ainsworth actively recruited foreign students for her graduate program. She thus began a long, productive career of sharing ideas on an international level.

Miss Ainsworth involved herself wholeheartedly in various physical education associations. From 1937 to 1941 she served as president of the National Association of Physical Education for College Women. In 1950 she was elected president of the American Association for Health, Physical Education and Recreation (AAHPER), the national professional organization for men and women working in this discipline. She also served as president of the National Association of Directors of Physical Education for Women. Internationally she helped to found the International Association of Physical Education and Sports for Girls and Women (IAPESGW) to provide a format for female physical educators to share their research and information about their programs and curriculum. She served as the president of the IAPESGW, an organization that has continued to serve as an international network for women in physical education and sport. For many years Miss Ainsworth was the leading figure in international sport and physical education in the United States. She organized the First International Congress on Physical Education and Sports for Girls and Women held in Denmark in 1949, and she was the chair of the United States Joint Council on International Affairs in Health, Physical Education and Recreation, 1950–1957; organizing chair for the First International Congress on Essentials of Physical Education for Youth in the Connecticut Valley, 1954; and chair of the Committee on Physical Education in the World Confederation Organizations for the Teaching Professions in 1958.

Miss Ainsworth traveled extensively around the world to attend conferences and lectures. She demonstrated true professional leadership skills to the community around her, thereby gaining the respect of her peers. Ainsworth was recognized for her achievements by other countries, including France, Sweden, and Finland. Most notable are the Order of Merit for Sports from the French government and the Cross of Honor from the Finnish. Many of these accolades were in response to her leadership positions in the United States and around the world.

Miss Ainsworth received many awards in her field throughout her lifetime, including an honorary doctor of sciences degree from Smith College in 1956. In 1960 she was awarded the Luther A. Gulick Medal, the highest honor conferred by the AAHPER, and in 1962 the Hetherington Award from the American Academy of Physical Education. In 1968 she was honored by the National Council of Women in New York. Her character is conveyed in a letter written by a former colleague who came to Smith to teach on a Fulbright Scholarship: "Among the many attributes which I shall remember you by, will be: a vital interest in life, sound judgment, a sense of humor, generosity, and out-standing leadership in the profession of physical education" (Peterson, p. 154). Miss Ainsworth died in a nursing home in Moline, Illinois.

• Hazel Peterson's biography, *Dorothy S. Ainsworth* (1975), is the most detailed source. Obituaries are in the *Smith College Alumnae Quarterly*, Feb. 1977, and the *Smith College News*, 3 Dec. 1976.

CHRISTINE SHELTON

AINSWORTH, Fred Crayton (11 Sept. 1852–5 June 1934), military surgeon and adjutant general, was born in Woodstock, Vermont, the son of Crayton Ainsworth, a modestly prosperous businessman and machinist, and Harriet Carroll, a seamstress and Woman's Christian Temperance Union activist.

During 1869 and 1870 Ainsworth attended but did not graduate from Dartmouth College. Upon returning to Woodstock, he studied medicine for three years, then enrolled in the medical school of the City University of New York. He graduated with honors in 1874, served a brief residency on the Bellevue Hospital medical staff, and then won an appointment as an assistant surgeon in the Medical Department of the U.S. Army. In November 1874 he reported to the U.S. Military Academy at West Point for his first army assignment as a surgeon.

After an eight-month apprenticeship at West Point, Ainsworth began a succession of assignments as an army surgeon at frontier posts in the Southwest, Alaska, and the Pacific Northwest. During his western service, he spent several periods of duty in the field, including on active operations against Bannock Indians in the 1878 Bannock War in Idaho, Oregon, and Washington territories. In 1881 he married Mary Cranston; they had no children.

Ainsworth's next duty as recorder of the Army Medical Examining Board in New York City attracted the attention of the secretary of war. In 1886 he was given charge of the Record and Pension Division of the Surgeon General's Office. That division maintained Union army medical records and determined claims for pension payments—nearly $65 million annually by the mid-1880s. To reduce the growing backlog of requests (thirteen thousand) and to preserve the original records, Ainsworth had his clerks transcribe onto cards information about individual soldiers from all available medical records. The time required to respond to requests for medical information was thus decreased significantly.

Ainsworth's ability to make complicated, voluminous records more accessible had practical and political consequences. In July 1889 the Record and Pension Division of the Surgeon General's Office merged with several divisions in the Adjutant General's Office to form the Record and Pension (R and P) Office, headed by Ainsworth. By 1899 he was a brigadier general in charge of over half of all War Department employees and responsible for most army records. When the R and P Office was merged with the Adjutant General's Office in April 1904 to become the Military Secretary's Office, he headed the new organization and received promotion to major general. Because of the size of the new office and its control over large, important bodies of records affecting great segments of the population, it was a powerful position. In 1907 Congress restored the previous title of the office, and Ainsworth became the adjutant general, reflecting the power and prestige he had accrued.

As adjutant general, Ainsworth had responsibility for general administration, records keeping, and recruiting throughout the army. He worked to improve recruiting, facilitate apprehension of deserters, and raise army pay, but his brusque personality precipitated a clash with higher authority that ultimately undermined his efforts to reform army administration. Ainsworth and Leonard Wood, the army chief of staff, disagreed over several issues, from the length of the term of enlistment to the value of the army muster roll. During 1911 Wood confronted Ainsworth over matters of army paperwork. Wood's intent was to demonstrate the authority of the chief of staff and the newly created general staff over the War Department technical and administrative bureaus. Ainsworth perceived the incident as an attack on his professional prerogatives. His response was personal, intemperate, and deemed insubordinate by the secretary of war, Henry L. Stimson. Rather than face court-martial, Ainsworth retired from the army on 16 February 1912. He spent his retirement in Washington, D.C. where he died.

Ainsworth was an unusually successful military bureaucrat who promoted the adoption of modern management techniques by the army. His attempts to preserve and make accessible army records contributed to the creation in 1934 of the National Archives as the repository of all permanent records of the U.S. government.

• The Fred C. Ainsworth Papers in the Manuscript Division of the Library of Congress mostly relate to the period after his 1912 retirement from the army. The principal source of information about Ainsworth's career and contributions to army administration and records keeping are the records of the Adjutant General's Office, Record Group 94, in the National Archives. An excellent, balanced biography is Mabel E. Deutrich, *Struggle for Supremacy: The Career of General Fred C. Ainsworth* (1962). Other secondary accounts include Siert F. Riepma, "A Soldier-Archivist and His Records," *American Archivist* 4 (July 1941): 178–87.

TIMOTHY K. NENNINGER

AITKEN, Robert (22 Jan. 1735–15 July 1802), printer and publisher, was born in Dalkeith, Scotland. His parents' names are unknown. Sometime after serving a regular apprenticeship with a bookbinder in Edinburgh, he became established in Paisley, Scotland, as a binder, bookseller, and proprietor of a circulating library. From there he moved to Philadelphia in May 1771 with his wife, Janet Skeoch, and two children, the eldest of whom was seven; two more children were later born in Philadelphia. In June he opened a stationer's shop and what was soon "the largest and most valuable bookstore" in the city. With the publication in 1773 of *Aitken's General American Register, and the Gentleman's and Tradesman's Complete Annual Account Book, and Calendar . . . for the Year of Our Lord, 1773*, followed by a second edition for the next year, he became an established publisher.

In November 1774 three newspapers carried announcements of Aitken's plans to issue the *Pennsylvania Magazine; or, American Monthly Museum*, which, emphasizing "original American productions," was meant "not only to *equal*, but to *excel* every former attempt of this kind" (Richardson, p. 175). The chief contributors to the magazine were writer Thomas Paine (who edited some early numbers); statesman and satirist Francis Hopkinson; John Witherspoon, president of the College of New Jersey (now Princeton University); and Matthew Wilson, a minister, physician, and teacher of Lewes, Delaware. In his new capacity as an engraver, Aitken produced some of the first views of military operations of the Revolution. Lucky in timing, the *Pennsylvania Magazine*, which first appeared in February 1775, caught the tide of history: its monthly numbers, always on schedule, chronicled important opinions and events, ranging from hopes of reconciliation with Great Britain in early 1775 to the Declaration of Independence, which was printed in the issue of July 1776, when wartime conditions brought publication of the magazine to an end.

As printer to the Continental Congress, Aitken produced military manuals for the American troops and legislative documents. In 1777 the congress considered publication of a Bible, the war having stopped the importation of English Bibles, which had been printed exclusively under royal patent. Aitken was one of several printers who submitted bids, but no action was taken. Proceeding on his own, he issued four well-received editions of the New Testament between 1777 and 1781. These were followed in 1782 by the work for which he is best known, the first complete Bible in English under an American imprint. Despite bearing the endorsement of the First Congress as an example of American progress in the arts, the Aitken Bible was a financial failure, possibly because the price was kept too high and because imported Bibles were soon on hand again. Also, printing it had taken longer than expected, perhaps because of the great care taken to prevent typographical errors.

Aitken's meticulous work earned him the respect of fellow printers like Ebenezer Hazard, who recommended him to historian Jeremy Belknap as having "the most taste of a printer of any man in this city." The first volume of Belknap's *History of New Hampshire* (1784) was only one of Aitken's many major commissions in the postwar years; he also printed two volumes of the *Journals of Congress* (1776, 1777) and several volumes for the American Philosophical Society. Well known for his fine printing and superb bindings, he supplied services and goods to customers locally, in other cities, and in the West Indies. Aitken was active as "an Overseer of the Poor, . . . Elder of his Scots Presbyterian Church, and appraiser of estates (including [Benjamin] Franklin's)" (Spawn and Spawn, "The Aitken Shop," p. 433). Although respected for his integrity and enterprise, Aitken was in debt when he died, partly because of poor investments but chiefly because he had signed a number of notes for his deceased son-in-law Charles Campbell, who had died before his debts were repaid. Aitken had disowned his son Robert, his nominal partner from 1787 to 1797 and an undistinguished printer whom he apparently regarded as irresponsible. Aitken's creditors arranged terms for his daughter Jane, who was unmarried, to carry on her father's business in her own name while attempting to retire the debt. She sustained the Aitken reputation for excellence until her struggling business finally failed in 1814.

• Manuscript sources are in the Archives of the American Philosophical Society, the Library Company of Philadelphia, and the Historical Society of Pennsylvania. The earliest discussion of Aitken is in Isaiah Thomas, *The History of Printing in America, with a Biography of Printers, and an Account of Newspapers* (1810; rev. ed., 1874); an annotated edition of the revised edition, edited by Marcus A. McCorison (1970), contains useful information. The best account of the *Pennsylvania Magazine* is the richly detailed one in Lyon N. Richardson, *A History of Early American Magazines, 1741–1789* (1931; repr. 1966), pp. 174–96. Aitken Bibles are discussed in William H. Gaines, Jr., "The Continental Congress Considers the Publication of a Bible, 1777," *Studies in Bibliography* 3 (1950): 274–81. Aspects of Aitken's work as printer, binder, and engraver are considered in Elizabeth Carroll Reilly, *A Dictionary of Colonial American Printers' Ornaments and Illustrations* (1975); Willman Spawn and Carol Spawn, "R. Aitken: Colonial Printer of Philadelphia," *Graphic Arts Review* 24 (Jan. 1961): 11–12, 14, and (Feb. 1961): 16, 18, and "The Aitken Shop: Identification of an Eighteenth-Century Bindery and Its Tools," *Papers of the Bibliographical Society of America* 57 (1963): 422–37; Willman Spawn, "The Evolution of American Binding Styles in the Eighteenth Century," in *Bookbinding in America 1680–1910* (1983), pp. 29–36, and "Extra-Gilt Bindings of Robert Aitken, 1787–1788," *Proceedings of the American Antiquarian Society* 93 (1983): 415–17; Donald M. Stauffer, *American Engravers upon Copper and Steel* (1907; repr. 1964); and Lawrence C. Wroth, *The Colonial Printer* (1931; rev. ed., 1938; repr. 1964).

VINCENT FREIMARCK

AITKEN, Robert Grant (31 Dec. 1864–29 Oct. 1951), astronomer and fourth director of Lick Observatory, was born in Jackson, California, the son of Robert Aitken, an immigrant from Scotland and owner and operator of a meat market, and Wilhelmina Depinau. Aitken did his undergraduate work at Williams College, originally planning to become a minister. There he became interested in astronomy, under the tutelage of Truman Safford, and graduated with an A.B. in 1887. Returning to California, Aitken in 1888 married his high school classmate, Jessie L. Thomas, and that same year became head teacher at Livermore College. The couple had four children who survived to adulthood. While teaching at Livermore full time, Aitken took a three-year reading course in mathematics under Irving Stringham, head of that department at the University of California in nearby Berkeley. In 1891 Aitken became professor of mathematics and astronomy at the University of the Pacific, then located at College Park, near San Jose, California, and within sight of Lick Observatory, the University of California research institution on Mount Hamilton. The University of the Pacific had a 6-inch refracting telescope, and it broadened Aitken's horizons. He met Edward S. Holden, the director of Lick Observatory, and arranged to spend a few weeks there in the summer of 1894. Aitken met astronomer Edward E. Barnard at Mount Hamilton and, with his and Holden's encouragement, decided on a research career in astronomy. In the summer of 1895 he returned to Lick Observatory as an assistant, and when Barnard left for Yerkes Observatory, Aitken became his successor on the Lick staff. From professor at the University of the Pacific to assistant astronomer at Lick Observatory was a big step down in salary, and with several small children, it was initially a hard struggle for Aitken and his wife.

Aitken quickly became a double-star astronomer, the successor to Sherburne W. Burnham, who had left the Lick staff in 1891. The clear skies and steady atmosphere of Mount Hamilton, together with the great 36-inch refractor and the smaller but optically excellent 12-inch refractor, were ideally suited for this research program. Aitken was a steady, keen-eyed observer, with unrivaled powers of concentration, who could spend long hours at the telescope finding previously unknown close double stars and measuring the positions of their components as they slowly orbited one another through the years. He published his first papers on double-star measurements in 1895, the year he joined the Lick staff. He carried out a systematic survey of the entire sky visible from the latitude of Mount Hamilton for double stars, which his colleague William J. Hussey joined, until his departure for the University of Michigan in 1905. This survey, completed by Aitken, produced important new information on the statistics of the numbers of double and multiple stars and their orbital properties. He summarized the results in his book *The Binary Stars* (1918), which he revised in 1935 to include much additional data and the conclusions drawn from them.

Aitken collected all available measurements of double stars by observers everywhere and annotated and published them in his two-volume *New General Catalogue of Double Stars within 120° of the North Pole*, the successor to an earlier, similar catalog by Burnham. The *New General Catalogue*, universally known to astronomers as the Aitken Double Star Catalogue or ADS, remained a valuable reference source for many years.

In 1923, when W. W. Campbell, the third director of Lick Observatory, became president of the University of California, he moved to Berkeley but retained the directorship. He named Aitken associate director, in charge of operations on Mount Hamilton but still subject to Campbell's overall control, particularly on important policy issues. In this position the double-star astronomer became an administrator who in effect directed the observatory, particularly after the first few years as Campbell's time and efforts were fully devoted to his responsibilities as president. Mount Hamilton was an isolated little astronomy village, where the astronomers, the support staff members, and their families lived, and Aitken directed it as well as the scientific institution. In 1930 Campbell retired, and Aitken became the Lick director in name as well as in fact for five more years, until he himself retired in 1935. He observed double stars with the 36-inch refractor the first half of the night of 30 June 1935, then went to bed and the next day drove down to Berkeley, where he lived in retirement until his death there.

Aitken had always been active in the Astronomical Society of the Pacific, writing many of its *Leaflets*, explaining astronomical phenomena and objects in simple terms that its many amateur members could grasp. He was editor of the *Publications of the Astronomical Society of the Pacific* from 1897 to 1908 and from 1911 until his death. During his fifty-seven years as a member of the society he was twice its president, six times its vice president (all one-year terms), its secretary for thirteen years, and a director for forty-six years. Aitken was also president of the American Astronomical Society from 1937 to 1940. He gave many lectures to amateur and professional audiences alike, and from his retirement office in the Berkeley Astronomy Department on the campus he carried out a wide astronomical correspondence. Aitken was a long-time member of the First Congregational Church in Berkeley and an active figure in the Faculty Club on the university campus. Aitken was an important figure in increasing our knowledge of double stars and in directing an important astronomical research center, who at the same time was very much involved in the communities in which he lived.

• The main collection of Aitken's letters is in the Mary Lea Shane Archives of the Lick Observatory, in the University of California, Santa Cruz Library. A short autobiographical account of his astronomical career is his "Early Work on Double Stars at the Lick Observatory," *Publications of the Astronomical Society of the Pacific* 57 (1945): 138–51. See also Aitken, "The Lick Observatory, Forty Years After," *Publications of the Astronomical Society of the Pacific* 40 (1928): 151–64. Two published memorial biographies are Hamilton M. Jeffers, "Robert G. Aitken 1864–1951," *Publications of the Astronomical Society of the Pacific* 64 (1952): 5–10, and Willem H. van den Bos, "Robert Grant Aitken," National Academy of Sciences, *Biographical Memoirs* 32 (1958): 1–30. The latter contains a complete bibliography of Aitken's published scientific papers, leaflets, lectures, reviews of astronomy, and other writings. See also J. H. Moore, "Fifty Years of Research at the Lick Observatory," *Publications of the Astronomical Society of the Pacific* 50 (1938): 189–203, and Donald E. Osterbrock et al., *Eye on the Sky: Lick Observatory's First Century* (1988). Obituaries are in the *New York Times*, 30 Oct. 1951, and the *Berkeley Daily Gazette*, 29 Oct. 1951.

DONALD E. OSTERBROCK

AITKEN, Robert Ingersoll (8 May 1878–3 Jan. 1949), sculptor, was born in San Francisco, California, the son of Charles H. Aitken and Katherine A. Higgens. He received his training at the Mark Hopkins Institute of Art in San Francisco, where he studied under Arthur F. Matthews and Douglas Tilden. At the young age of nineteen Aitken opened his own studio. His first major commission, in 1902, was to create a monument to President William McKinley in St. Helena, California. The next year he created another statue of McKinley for San Francisco's Golden Gate Park. These sculptures were his first important works, and they established his reputation as a creator of public monuments. He then received further commissions, including the *Victory Monument*, a bronze allegorical figure placed atop an 83-foot-tall granite shaft, which stood in San Francisco's Union Square to commemorate Admiral George Dewey's victory at Manila Bay.

In 1904 Aitken traveled to Paris, where he worked until 1907. On his return to the United States he settled in New York City and married Laure Louise Ligny. In New York he began to receive important commissions for portrait busts. For New York University's Hall of Fame Aitken sculpted portrait busts of Thomas Jefferson, Daniel Webster, Benjamin Franklin, and Henry Clay. Other busts Aitken created include portraits of George Bellows, President William H. Taft, and Augustus Thomas. Elizabeth Semple, a contemporary writer, noted "the nameless, intangible something that gives to each and every one of

Mr. Aitken's portraits their singular and unforgettable charm" (p. 225). Aitken also continued to create public monuments, which were largely neoclassical in style. For the 1915 Panama-Pacific Exposition in San Francisco he was commissioned to create two impressive sculptural groups, *The Fountain of the Earth*, which featured a central edifice consisting of a revolving eighteen-foot glass globe surrounded by allegorical figures representing the evolution of humankind, and *The Four Elements*, in which heroic figures represented the four elements. Aitken received two medals for his sculptural work in the exposition: the gold medal of honor for sculpture from the Architectural League and the exposition's silver medal for sculpture. He also designed two $50 gold coins that were issued by the government to commemorate the exposition. Among Aitken's numerous public monuments still standing throughout the United States are the *Samuel Gompers Memorial* in Washington, D.C., which features a seated portrait figure of the labor leader with symbolic figures representing American labor, and the *G. R. Clark Monument* at the University of Virginia in Charlottesville, Virginia, for which he received the Helen Foster Barnett Prize of the National Academy of Design in 1908. His other awards include the New York Architectural League's medal of honor for sculpture in 1915 and the Elizabeth N. Watrous gold medal for sculpture from the National Academy of Design in 1921. Aitken had also distinguished himself by serving overseas during World War I as a commander captain with the machine gun company of the 306th Infantry beginning in 1917.

In addition to being famous for creating portrait busts and public monuments, Aitken was also well known for his architectural sculpture. One of his major sculptures is the *Frederick W. Schumacher Frieze* for the Columbus Gallery of Fine Arts (1937). The ten-section, two-panel frieze is a portrait series of sixty-eight significant painters and sculptors of western art, from the ancient Greek sculptor Phidias to the twentieth-century American painter George Bellows. Aitken was commissioned to create a number of sculptures for federal buildings in Washington, D.C., one of which is the western pediment of the Supreme Court Building titled *Equal Justice under Law* (1935). The neoclassical figural sculptures of the pediment serve a symbolic function as well as being portraits of prominent figures in American judicial history and individuals related to the erection of the building itself. Aitken depicted Chief Justices John Marshall, William Howard Taft, and Charles Evans Hughes, as well as the building's architect, Cass Gilbert, noted lawyer Elihu Root, and himself. In the same year Aitken created several sculptural works for the southern Pennsylvania Avenue entrance of the National Archives Building, including medallions that represented five of the twelve departments of the federal government that relinquished their records to the National Archives. For the same facade Aitken fashioned freestanding sculptures *Past* and *Future*, as well as *The Guardians of the Portal*, limestone reliefs of two armorclad figures who flank the door.

Aitken was very active in his profession, serving as an instructor of sculpture at the Mark Hopkins Institute of Art, the Art Students League, and the National Academy of Design School, where he also headed its school committee. He was the eighth president of the National Sculpture Society from 1920 until 1922, as well as vice president of both the National Academy of Design and the National Institute of Arts and Letters. Aitken was a member of many organizations including the Architectural League of New York, the American Federation of the Arts, the Union Internationale des Beaux-Arts et des Lettres, and the Institut Français aux Etats-Unis. Aitken died at home in New York, leaving behind two children from his first marriage and his second wife, Joan Louise Bruning, whom he had married in 1934 after divorcing his first wife that year.

Although Aitken's work has received little attention in art history texts since his death, he left behind a legacy of monuments and sculptures that hold a prominent place in America's buildings, countryside, and history. His sculptures are not merely dry historical records for, as Alex J. Ettl notes, "He worked in an era when connoisseurs expected sculpture to be beautiful, to this he added a vigorous force and his own brand of originality" (p. 19).

• A monograph on Aitken is available in *California Art Research* 6 (1936–1937): 60–94, a multivolume work that features monographs of artists from San Francisco. Alex J. Ettl, "Robert I. Aitken," *National Sculpture Review* 13, no. 4 (Winter 1964–1965): 19, 26, 28, provides biographical detail and a retrospective view of Aitken's sculptural production. Two important contemporary discussions of Aitken's work are Elizabeth Anna Semple, "Art of Robert Aitken, Sculptor," *Overland Monthly* 61 (Mar. 1913): 218–25, and Arthur Hoeber, "Sculpture of Robert Aitken, N.A.," *International Studio* 54, no. 213 (Nov. 1914): xv–xviii. An obituary is in the *New York Times*, 4 Jan. 1949.

KELLY WINQUIST

AKELEY, Carl Ethan (19 May 1864–17 Nov. 1926), taxidermist, naturalist, and inventor, was born near Clarendon, New York, the son of Daniel Webster Akeley and Julia Glidden, farmers. In his early teens he taught himself taxidermy. After two years at the State Normal School in Brockport, New York, he began work at the age of nineteen for Ward's Natural Science Establishment in Rochester, a company that prepared laboratory and museum specimens. One of Akeley's jobs was to skin and mount for exhibition P. T. Barnum's famous circus elephant Jumbo. For this purpose he pioneered the use of a light bentwood manikin over which the animal's hide was tacked.

In 1887 Akeley joined the staff of the Milwaukee Public Museum. Here he created the first of the lifelike habitat groups, set against painted backgrounds, for which he became famous. In 1895 he was offered a position at the Natural History Museum in London, but he instead accepted the post of chief of the department of taxidermy at the Field Columbian Museum (now the Field Museum of Natural History) in Chicago.

The following year Akeley made the first of his five expeditions to Africa to collect specimens for museum exhibits. On this trip to Somaliland he suffered the first of several animal attacks: mauled by a wounded leopard, he managed to wrestle it to death. Such anecdotes—as well as his vivid descriptions of the African landscape, which he came to love so well—enlivened his later lectures, his magazine articles, and his autobiography, *In Brightest Africa* (1923). "Ake," as he was affectionately known, did not hunt for sport; "I never shot an animal," he declared, "unless I needed it for a specimen, or had to shoot it in self-preservation" (Andrews, p. 96). He was in fact an early advocate of wildlife conservation, a charter member of the John Burroughs Memorial Association and active in the National Parks Association and the Audubon Society.

In 1902 Akeley married Delia J. Denning, who accompanied him as field assistant on several expeditions. They had no children and were divorced in 1923.

During his fourteen-year stay at Chicago Akeley developed techniques that raised taxidermy from a craft to an art and were adopted by museums around the world. He also improved on a device used to squirt liquid plaster under an animal skin after it had been applied to the manikin. His invention, the Akeley Cement Gun, first used in repairs on the walls of the Field Museum, was eventually employed in work on the Panama Canal and to reinforce reservoirs and the roofs of mines and tunnels. It won him the John Scott Legacy Medal of the Franklin Institute in 1916.

In 1908 Akeley proposed to the American Museum of Natural History (AMNH) in New York that he collect elephant specimens for them in Kenya and Uganda; he left for Africa in 1909. For the rest of his life he was associated with the AMNH, although, desiring to remain independent, he never accepted a salary; instead, he was paid retaining fees and was responsible for raising most of the money for his expeditions. The lively, informal lectures he gave all over the country attracted many influential admirers and backers. In 1911 he laid before Henry Fairfield Osborn, president of the museum, his idea for a great hall of African life: groupings of mammals mounted against faithfully represented backgrounds, which were to be painted by artists working at the actual sites. This synopsis of African fauna, flora, and topography would serve as a permanent record of fast-vanishing wildlife. Work on the hall was to begin in 1914 but was interrupted by World War I.

Meanwhile, Akeley was devising a more quickly adjustable motion picture camera specifically for the use of naturalists photographing in the wild. Patented in 1916, the Akeley Camera was used by the U.S. War Department at the front, and later as a newsreel camera; in 1926 it received the John Price Wetherill Medal of the Franklin Institute. During the war Akeley largely gave up museum work to do government research, developing searchlight reflectors and improved methods of concrete construction.

With the end of the war Akeley resumed his plans for the African hall, and in 1921 and 1922 he made his fourth safari—this time to the volcanoes around Lake Kivu to observe and collect mountain gorillas. Here he made the first motion pictures of these animals in their native state. Concerned about their threatened extinction at the hands of "sportsmen," he was instrumental in persuading King Albert of Belgium to set aside land in the Kivu area as a sanctuary. In 1925 Albert National Park (now Virunga National Park in the borderland between Uganda, Rwanda, and Zaire), the first such reserve in Africa, was established.

At this point in his career Akeley, always as much artist as craftsman, turned to sculpture and began to do small bronzes cast from the clay models he used for his mounted specimens. His first bronze, *The Wounded Comrade* (1924)—two bull elephants supporting a third—won him election to the National Sculpture Society; a copy was commissioned for his friend Theodore Roosevelt.

In 1924 Akeley married the explorer and writer Mary L. Jobe; they had no children. With her he returned to the Kivu area in 1926 to continue his gorilla studies. Exhausted and in chronic ill health, he died at his camp and was buried on Mount Mikeno. In 1927 the Field Museum dedicated its Akeley Memorial Hall in his honor. Work on the Akeley African Hall of the AMNH was completed and it was opened to the public in 1938.

In addition to the awards cited above, Akeley received the Holland Society (of New York) medal in 1922 for distinguished service in the science of exploration. He was a president of the Explorers Club and a member of the American Association for the Advancement of Science.

• Akeley's papers are in the Rush Rhees Library of the University of Rochester; the American Museum of Natural History maintains files of biographical material. Carl Akeley and Mary L. Jobe Akeley, *Lions, Gorillas and Their Neighbors* (1932), is a collection of his anecdotes, lectures, and field notes. Supplementing *In Brightest Africa*, a special issue of *The Mentor* 13, no. 12 (Jan. 1926) reprints some autobiographical notes. See also Mary L. Jobe Akeley, *The Wilderness Lives Again: Carl Akeley and the Great Adventure* (1946), which lists some of his articles; Roy Chapman Andrews, *Beyond Adventure: The Lives of Three Explorers* (1954); and Clyde Fisher, "Carl Akeley and His Work," *Scientific Monthly*, Feb. 1927, pp. 97–118. The Akeley Memorial Number of *Natural History* 27, Mar.–Apr. 1927, pp. 115–79, reprints tributes assessing Akeley's professional contributions and personal stature, read by colleagues at his memorial service at the AMNH. Akeley's field methods are described in Mary L. Jobe Akeley, *Carl Akeley's Africa: The Account of the Akeley-Eastman-Pomeroy African Hall Expedition [1926–27] of the American Museum of Natural History* (1930). An obituary is in the *New York Times*, 1 Dec. 1926.

ELEANOR F. WEDGE

AKELEY, Mary Leonore Jobe (29 Jan. 1878–19 July 1966), explorer, author, and educator, was born near Tappan, Ohio, the daughter of Richard Watson Jobe and Sarah Jane Pittis, farmers. (The year of her birth is sometimes erroneously given as 1886.) She received a Ph.B. at Scio College in Alliance, Ohio, in 1897. (Scio, a Methodist school, merged with Mount Union College in Alliance in 1911.) She took graduate courses at Bryn Mawr (1901–1903) and taught at Temple College (now Temple University). She was head of the Department of History and Civics at the New York State Normal School and Training School in Cortland, New York (1903–1906), studied history and English at Columbia University, and in 1907 began to teach American history at the Normal College of the City of New York (now Hunter College). She received her M.A. in history at Columbia in 1909.

While a student at Bryn Mawr, Akeley went on a botanical expedition to British Columbia and, while teaching at the Normal School, returned a few times to the Canadian Northwest as an expedition leader. With the Canadian government's permission, she studied Indian and Eskimo tribes in British Columbia (1913); found and mapped an undiscovered mountain north of Mount Robson, which she named Big Ice Mountain (1914); and studied and photographed the Fraser River area and Mount Sir Alexander glaciers (1915). Her companion was Donald Phillips, a trapper, mountaineer, and guide. By this time she was a well-regarded photographer, lecturer, feminist, and suffragist. She published several articles illustrated by her photographs in the *Canadian Alpine Journal*, *Harper's*, and the *Tourist*. In 1915 Akeley was elected a fellow of the Royal Geographical Society in London. In 1925 the Canadian government honored her by naming a peak in the Canadian Rockies Mount Jobe. In 1916 she discontinued teaching and established a summer camp in Mystic, Connecticut, on forty-five acres purchased two years earlier. She planned to instruct well-to-do city girls, ages eight to eighteen, in strenuous outdoor activities for purposes of holistic health, for an all-inclusive fee of $375. Effects of the Great Depression caused Camp Mystic to close in 1930.

Akeley returned to the Canadian Northwest in the winter of 1917–1918 to photograph, collect botanical specimens, and climb—sometimes with the thermometer at minus 54 degrees Fahrenheit. In 1918 or a little later, the Arctic explorer Vilhjalmur Stefansson introduced her to his friend Carl Akeley, fourteen years her senior. He was a renowned student of African wildlife, a conservationist, and an innovative taxidermist of elephants, tigers, and other animals in Uganda and Kenya for the American Museum of Natural History in New York City. He also invented the Akeley movie camera and was an expert in its use. Mary discontinued her close relationship with Phillips and was soon involved in a love affair with Akeley despite his being married to fellow explorer Delia J. Denning Reiss "Mickie" Akeley. When he was in Cape Town, South Africa, in 1921, he executed a new will disinheriting Mickie—who, he said, had deserted him three years earlier—and naming Mary the sole beneficiary of his $10,000 estate. A year after he and Mickie finalized a bitter divorce, he and Mary were married in October 1924; they had no children.

In January 1926 Mary Akeley accompanied her husband on the Akeley-Eastman-Pomeroy expedition to Africa. It was her first African venture, and his fifth. Sponsored by the American Museum of Natural History and financed by George Eastman, of the Eastman Kodak Company, and museum trustee and benefactor Daniel M. Pomeroy, a partner of J. P. Morgan and Company, the well-equipped expedition planned to film wildlife in its natural habitats, kill and stuff a variety of animals, collect samples of jungle, forest, and desert vegetation, and thereby furnish a permanent African Hall of the Natural History museum in realistic diorama style. Carl persuaded Mary to give up her independent career and become expedition secretary, safari manager, and even a driver. Initially reluctant, she soon agreed and became an enthusiastic participant. In London they completed supplying the expedition and proceeded to Belgium to make arrangements for Carl to aid King Albert's representative, zoologist Jean Marie Derscheid, in mapping a region around Parc National Albert in the Virunga mountains of the Belgian Congo (later Zaire, now the Republic of the Congo). With a huge entourage, including Eastman and Pomeroy part of the time, the Akeleys proceeded to Nairobi, where they conferred with the famous explorers Martin and Osa Johnson, and then hunted, photographed, and collected their prey in the Northern Frontier District and the Serengeti Plains in Tanganyika (now Tanzania). Carl Akeley fell ill and was hospitalized in Nairobi, but he was evidently persuaded by Mary Akeley to return to the expedition too soon. They got to the Congo in search of gorillas and in November reached Mount Mikeno, where Carl Akeley grew worse and died.

Mary Akeley supervised her husband's burial in a Mikeno slope meadow. She was highly critical of his two closest companions—Derscheid and the scene painter William R. Leigh—and quickly obtained permission from the museum to complete the expedition's work. Under difficult conditions, the group photographed gorilla habitats, reassembled an entire gorilla nest, and collected, made casts of, and otherwise preserved quantities of vegetation. Mary labored indefatigably to make her husband's dream of a gorilla diorama close to perfect. She also made a quick side trip to Kenya to photograph Lake Hannington flamingoes. She began her return to the United States in December.

From 1927 to 1938 Akeley was a special adviser and assistant for the Akeley Hall of African Mammals of the American Museum of Natural History, named for her husband. She wrote, lectured, and raised funds for the Akeley Hall, which she dedicated in 1936. Having made peace with Derscheid, Akeley collaborated with him on her husband's report concerning Parc National

Albert, for which in 1929 she was awarded the Cross of the Knight, Order of the Crown, by King Albert. Also in 1929 she became the American secretary of an international committee organized to preserve the Park, serving until 1936. She published *Carl Akeley's Africa: The Account of the Akeley-Eastman-Pomeroy African Hall Expedition of the American Museum of Natural History* (1929). She followed this long narrative with *Restless Jungle* (1936); *The Wilderness Lives Again: Carl Akeley and the Great Adventure* (1940), about exhibition plans; and *Rumble of a Distant Drum: A True Story of the Africa Hinterland* (1946), detailing how a ten-year-old Watusi lad helped her complete the 1926 expedition. She also edited Carl Akeley's notes and campfire stories. Three of her shorter works concentrate on the Belgian Congo: "Africa's Great National Park" (*Natural History*, Nov.–Dec. 1929), "Belgian Congo Sanctuaries" (*Scientific Monthly*, Oct. 1931), and "King Albert Inaugurates the Parc National Albert" (*Natural History*, Mar.–Apr. 1930).

Akeley described her 1935–1936 trip through South Africa, Swaziland, and Portuguese East Africa in *Restless Jungle* (1936). During World War II she studied Alaskan defenses and Canadian women's war work. In 1947, at the invitation of a Belgian Congo park institute, she visited her husband's grave and surveyed wildlife preserves there. In 1950 she published *Congo Eden: A Comprehensive Portrayal of the Historical Background and Scientific Aspects of the Great Game Sanctuaries of the Belgian Congo with the Story of a Six Months Pilgrimage Throughout That Most Primitive Region in the Heart of the African Continent*. Reviewers praised Akeley for vividly depicting the magical beauty of unspoiled Africa, sharing her delight in its jungle creatures, and increasing public interest in Africa. She died in Mystic, Connecticut, remembered for her unremitting crusade in books and lectures to protect primitive cultures and also species of flora and fauna facing extinction because of unbridled commercial exploitation. Her Mystic Camp, its name later changed to the Peace Sanctuary, remained a wooded retreat open to the public.

• Many of Akeley's papers are in the Mary L. Jobe Akeley Collection, Mystic River Historical Society, Mystic, Conn., and in the archives of the American Museum of Natural History, New York City. Relating to her are many of Carl Akeley's scattered papers, notably in the archives of the American Museum of Natural History; the archives of the Field Museum of Natural History, Chicago, Ill.; and the library of the University of Rochester, Rochester, N.Y. Dawn-Starr Crowther, *Mary L. Jobe Akeley* (1989), is a monograph emphasizing Akeley's verve and photographic skill. Penelope Bodry-Sanders, *Carl Akeley: Africa's Collector, Africa's Savior* (1991), contains information about Mary Akeley. Newell Yost Osborne, *A Select School: The History of Mount Union College and an Account of a Unique Educational Experiment, Scio College* (1967), discusses the merger of the two schools and mentions Akeley as "explorer and author." Obituaries are in the *New York Times*, 22 July 1966, and in the *Geographical Journal*, Dec. 1966.

ROBERT L. GALE

AKEMAN, Stringbean (17 June 1914–10 Nov. 1973), banjo player and comedian, was born David Akeman in Annville, Kentucky, the son of James Akeman and Alice (maiden name unknown). Situated halfway between Corbin and Richmond, Annville was part of a region that produced several other notable banjoists, such as Buell Kazee, B. F. Shelton, and Marion Underwood. Akeman's father planted corn and tobacco, and he played the banjo at neighborhood dances at night. Akeman had four brothers and three sisters and got his first banjo at age twelve. (Virtually all accounts of Akeman's life give the year of his birth as 1915, but his brother Dave Akeman insisted to interviewer and researcher Charles Wolfe that, based on family records, Akeman was in fact born in 1914.) He dropped out of school after the sixth grade to work with his father on the family farm. The large Akeman family was one of the first to qualify for government relief during the 1930s. Subsequently, in 1934 and 1935, Akeman worked in the Civilian Conservation Corps (CCC), continuing to play the banjo in his spare time.

Some time in 1935, Asa Martin, a local radio star and well-known singer associated with fiddler Doc Roberts, held a talent contest in McKee, the county seat of Jackson County. Akeman entered the contest and impressed Martin, who was looking for a banjo player. Akeman left the CCC camp and joined Martin's touring show. Because of his lanky appearance and his height (six feet, two inches), he was immediately dubbed "String Beans"; later, after he joined the Grand Ole Opry, his nickname was truncated to "Stringbean."

Akeman played in the old-time "clawhammer" style (predating the three-finger Earl Scruggs style that came into prominence in the late 1940s and early 1950s). He also refined his skills as a baggy-pants comedian; comedy was an integral part of country music shows at that time and would remain so until the 1950s. In addition to his work with Martin, Akeman played in a number of bands around Lexington, Kentucky, including the Lonesome Pine Fiddlers led by Cy Rogers. Akeman was often heard over WLAP as well. He refined the core of his repertoire during this time. Songs such as "Pretty Polly," "Mountain Dew," "Get Along Home, Cindy," and others would constitute the cornerstone of his show throughout his career.

Akeman was also an accomplished semiprofessional baseball player, best remembered as a pitcher, and it was this more than his instrumental skills that attracted Bill Monroe, the patriarch of bluegrass music. Monroe had organized a complete touring package that included a tent show and an exhibition baseball team. Apparently Akeman did not stay very long with Bill Monroe but in 1938 joined his older brother, Charlie Monroe, with whom he worked at WBIG in Greensboro, North Carolina. Then, for short periods between 1940 and 1942, Akeman led his own band. In July 1942 Akeman joined Bill Monroe at the Grand Ole Opry. Monroe has insisted that Akeman was the first banjo player he hired, but the instrument did not achieve much prominence in his lineup until Earl Scruggs joined Monroe's Blue Grass Boys in 1945 as Akeman's replacement.

After leaving Monroe, Akeman began a three-year partnership with Lew Childre, who was also working at the Grand Ole Opry as well as traveling with tent shows. While at the Grand Ole Opry, Akeman came under the influence of Uncle Dave Macon, and it was Akeman as much as Louis "Grandpa" Jones who would carry elements of Macon's style, both instrumental and comedic, into the post–Second World War era. Macon seemed to have no trouble taking on Akeman as a pupil, despite the fact that they were both competing for airtime on the Grand Ole Opry, and according to Charles Wolfe, Macon left Akeman his 1940 Gibson banjo that Akeman later used on several recording sessions. Akeman's early years on the Grand Ole Opry were interrupted only by six months of service in the army.

Akeman was a member of the "Prince Albert" Grand Ole Opry, the select group of musicians who performed on the thirty-minute segment sponsored by R. J. Reynolds's Prince Albert Tobacco and broadcast over the NBC network. Many of Akeman's appearances were also carried on the Armed Forces Radio Service. Red Foley hosted the Prince Albert segment, and Akeman formed a good working relationship with Foley. Later, in 1955, Foley took Akeman to Springfield, Missouri, to work on the Ozark Jubilee, a rival to the Grand Ole Opry that was networked on ABC.

It is a measure of the lack of importance placed on recordings by old-timey musicians that Akeman did not record until 1960—and, as far as is known, did not attempt to secure a recording contract until then. Starting in 1960, though, he was recorded by Starday Records, a company based in Madison, Tennessee, that specialized in recording bluegrass, old-timey, and country gospel. Starday tried to market Akeman as part of a growing folk revival craze, and the label was careful to stress the authenticity of Akeman's style. His albums included *Old Time Banjo Picking and Singing*, *More Old Time Banjo Picking and Singing*, and *Way Back in the Hills of Old Kentucky*. On an artistic level, perhaps his most successful work was his *Salute to Uncle Dave Macon*, recorded for Starday Records in the mid-1960s. Akeman also recorded several singles for Cullman Records, a Nashville-based label owned by Hal Smith of Pamper Music and Curtis Artist Attractions. Akeman's last LP released during his lifetime, recorded in 1970, was *Me and My Old Crow* on Nugget Records. A posthumous LP, recorded for Ovation Records, was released in 1976. The increasing interest that Akeman's style attracted forced him in 1962 to take on Bob Neal as a booking agent and, in 1965, led to appearances at the University of Chicago and other campus venues.

In the summer of 1969 Akeman became a charter member of "Hee Haw," broadcast nationally on CBS television. He joined Archie Campbell, Junior Samples, and Grandpa Jones. Initially he was only supposed to have a walk-on part, but producer Sam Lovullo quickly discovered that the public had a taste for Akeman's brand of humor. Akeman popularized several of the show's classic lines, such as "Lord, I feel so unnecessary." He appeared in an outfit in which his pants were belted just above the knee. This gave him a ducklike waddle when he walked onstage that proved to be durably comedic. Akeman's success on "Hee-Haw" made him a national star, and he later appeared in Las Vegas, on television talk shows, and in stage shows with Hank Williams, Jr., and Ernest Tubb. With the proceeds, Akeman and his wife, Estelle, bought a house and 143 acres in Goodlettsville, near Nashville, where they indulged their passions for hunting and fishing.

In part, the isolation of the Akemans' farmhouse as well as the rumors that they carried large sums of money on their persons accounted for their untimely deaths. After appearing on the Grand Ole Opry on 10 November 1973, Akeman and his wife returned to their house, where they surprised robbers who were lying in wait and who shot and killed them both. Their bodies were discovered the following morning by Grandpa Jones, with whom the Akemans were to go on a hunting trip to Virginia. Their deaths shocked the music community in Nashville, in part because of Akeman's peaceable nature.

After Akeman's death, Grandpa Jones became the only high-profile performer still working in the old-timey traditions. Arguably, Akeman was an anachronism by the 1970s, but the fact that he was as successful at the time of his death as he had ever been before seems to indicate that there was still a vigorous demand for the mixture of old-timey music and baggy-pants comedy that made up one of the cornerstones of the country music tradition. Akeman was often called a bluegrass performer, but his use of electric instruments onstage and his pre-Scruggs banjo style make this characterization inaccurate. His repertoire was a reliquary of old-timey music, and the obvious enthusiasm with which he performed helped to make it very much a living tradition.

• Akeman left relatively few recordings that might stoke more interest in him. As a result, the only serious attention he attracted was in the following articles: Charles Wolfe, "String," *Bluegrass Unlimited*, June 1982, pp. 45–49; Genevieve J. Waddell, "Stringbean," *Bluegrass Unlimited*, Jan. 1974, pp. 16–18; and Marshall Fallwell, "Salute to Stringbean," *Country Music*, Jan. 1974, p. 12. Akeman's enduring fame rests largely on the tragic manner of his death. The most reliable report of that is "Stringbean, Wife Found Shot to Death," UPI report from Nashville, 12 Nov. 1973.

COLIN ESCOTT

AKERMAN, Amos Tappan (23 Feb. 1821–21 Dec. 1880), attorney general of the United States, was born in Portsmouth, New Hampshire, the son of Benjamin Akerman (pronounced with a long *A*), a farmer and surveyor, and Olive Meloon. Despite straitened family circumstances, Akerman attended Phillips Exeter Academy and (with loans from friends and relatives) Dartmouth College, where he graduated Phi Beta

Kappa in 1842. Having suffered lung damage as a boy while swimming, he was advised to move to a milder climate. This he did in 1842, accepting successive school teaching assignments in North Carolina and Georgia, culminating in 1846–1848 as tutor in the Savannah home of senator and former attorney general John M. Berrien. During this time he read law in Berrien's library. After a year's sojourn in New England and Illinois, Akerman returned to Georgia, where he bought a farm near Clarkesville, thinking to improve his health through an active outdoor life. However, he gradually abandoned farming for the law. Admitted to the bar in 1850, he moved his practice to Elberton in 1856.

Although a Whig since college days, Akerman was not active politically before the Civil War. He approved of slavery, owning eleven slaves himself in 1864. Like many Georgia Whigs, he opposed secession but subsequently gave at least lukewarm support to the Confederacy. In the summer of 1863, he joined the State Guard and served off and on until the end of the war as an ordnance officer and quartermaster between Atlanta and Savannah. Akerman remained a bachelor until 1864, when he married Martha Rebecca Galloway, who was twenty years his junior. Their wedding was sudden, he leaving the next day to rejoin his regiment in Atlanta. They had seven children who survived infancy. Akerman was a regular churchgoer who put off until 1862 a formal transfer from his native Congregationalism to the Presbyterian church.

In 1867 Akerman joined the Republican party as it organized in Georgia and around the South in support of the Congressional Reconstruction policy. He remained with it for the rest of his life, at the cost of at least temporary ostracism and probably some physical danger. He explained his affiliation as one of accepting the Unionist principles that had won the war and of seeking to speed southern readmission to the Union.

Elected as a Republican to the state constitutional convention of 1867–1868, Akerman was distinctly in the conservative wing of his party. He supported a losing proposal limiting the vote to taxpayers and those who could pass an educational test. When Rufus B. Bullock, the future Republican governor, offered a motion to cancel all private debts originating before June 1865, Akerman opposed and was outvoted in committee; he similarly failed to defeat a homestead exemption from foreclosure for debt. Although Akerman did become the principal author of the constitution's judiciary section, he left the convention early on private business, announcing his overall opposition to the document because of its relief provisions on behalf of debtors.

Akerman was an active Republican campaigner and presidential elector in 1868. That, plus his prominence as a lawyer, won him an appointment by President Ulysses S. Grant as U.S. district attorney for Georgia. As he could not take the required test oath, swearing past loyalty to the United States, Akerman had to await a congressional act of December 1869 lifting his disabilities. He held the office for only six months.

Unknown nationally, Akerman became the unwitting beneficiary of a demand by southern Republicans for one of their own in the cabinet. On 8 July 1870 he took office as attorney general—the first, in fact, to serve as head of the newly created Justice Department. After organizing and staffing the new department, he addressed a mounting wave of violence in the South, particularly that created by the hooded terrorists of the Ku Klux Klan. State and local efforts to suppress the order had largely failed. Empowered by recently enacted federal legislation against the Klan, Akerman declared war on the order, employing detectives, marshals, attorneys, and even the army to discover, arrest, and prosecute offenders. He went personally to South Carolina in 1871 and was responsible for President Grant's suspension of habeas corpus to facilitate arrests in several upcountry counties. Back in Washington, Akerman called for accelerated prosecutions, offering graphic accounts of Klan atrocities. Although he met rising indifference in the cabinet, reflecting that around the country, and his prosecutions were necessarily selective, his campaign (continued by his successor) demoralized the Klan and effectively terminated it by 1872.

After only eighteen months in office, Akerman left as he had come, a victim of political pressures on the weak president. Asked to render opinions concerning the legality of certain public land claims against the government by several western railroads, Akerman ruled in favor of the government. He refused to recede when asked by railroad interests to reconsider. Grant, moreover, was losing enthusiasm for Akerman's anti-Klan campaign. This, plus pressure from the railroads, led to an almost apologetic letter from Grant in December 1871 asking for his resignation on grounds of "public sentiment." Akerman turned over the office to his successor, George Henry Williams, on 10 January 1872. He accepted his dismissal philosophically but refused the offer of a judicial or diplomatic appointment in compensation and returned to Georgia.

In 1871 Akerman moved his family to Cartersville, northwest of Atlanta. There he spent his remaining years, engaged in a busy law practice that, along with political speaking trips, occasionally took him around the country. He was again a presidential elector in 1872 and even favored Grant for a third term in 1880. Ever conservative on most issues, Akerman opposed civil service reform and paper currency inflation. He even opposed the Civil Rights Act of 1875 as too intrusive into social relations, but he condemned President Rutherford B. Hayes for abandoning the South to the Democrats in 1877.

Never in good health, Akerman died at Cartersville. For southern Republicans like Akerman, who found themselves targets of the Ku Klux Klan terror, it was more than an abstraction. The preeminent achievement of his career was to surmount growing northern indifference, if only briefly, and wage a legal campaign that vanquished the Reconstruction Klan.

• Akerman's personal papers include two letter books (1871–1876) in the Alderman Library of the University of Virginia and a discontinuous diary (1839–1880) in the library of the University of Georgia. Official correspondence is in the Justice Department records in the National Archives. The nearest approach to a biography is Lois Neal Hamilton, "Amos T. Akerman and His Role in American Politics" (master's thesis, Columbia Univ., 1939). For the circumstances behind Akerman's appointment as attorney general, see Jacob D. Cox, "How Judge Hoar Ceased to Be Attorney General," *Atlantic Monthly* 76 (Aug. 1895): 162–73. For other treatments of his life and career, see Isaac Wheeler Avery, *The History of the State of Georgia* (1881); Homer Cummings and Carl McFarland, *Federal Justice: Chapters in the History of Justice and the Federal Executive* (1937); William S. McFeely, *Grant: A Biography* (1981); McFeely, "Amos T. Akerman: The Lawyer and Racial Justice," in *Region, Race, and Reconstruction: Essays in Honor of C. Vann Woodward*, ed. J. Morgan Kousser and James M. McPherson (1982); Elizabeth Studley Nathans, *Losing the Peace: Georgia Republicans and Reconstruction, 1865–1871* (1968); Allan Nevins, *Hamilton Fish: The Inner History of the Grant Administration* (1936); Joseph Parks, *Joseph E. Brown of Georgia* (1977); and Allen W. Trelease, *White Terror: The Ku Klux Klan Conspiracy and Southern Reconstruction* (1971).

ALLEN W. TRELEASE

AKINS, Zoë (30 Oct. 1886–29 Oct. 1958), playwright and screenwriter, was born in Humansville, Missouri, the daughter of Thomas J. Akins, a postmaster, and Elizabeth Green. During Zoë's childhood, the family moved to St. Louis, where Thomas Akins was postmaster as well as a member of the Republican national committee. At age twelve, Akins was sent to Monticello Seminary in Godfrey, Illinois, and later to Hosmer Hall in St. Louis.

Akins showed an early aptitude for writing, particularly poetry. When Akins was fifteen, William Marion Reedy, editor of *Reedy's Mirror*, became her mentor. He published several of her poems and stories during the next few years as well as music and drama criticism that he asked her to write.

Acting and play-writing were other interests, and she dramatized Rudyard Kipling's "Without Benefit of Clergy" when she was fifteen years old. At eighteen, she made her acting debut as a page in *Romeo and Juliet* with the Odeon Stock Company in St. Louis, but this career ended after three weeks. Thanks to her *Mirror* assignments and to her own enthusiasm for the theater, Akins said, she saw virtually every show that came to St. Louis and frequently went backstage to read her plays to visiting stars.

In pursuit of a serious writing career, Akins went to New York City, where she eventually achieved modest success with *The Magical City*, a verse-drama in one act that the Washington Square Players produced in 1916. Her second New York production, an "amorality" play called *Papa* (1919) that satirized conventional codes of social conduct, ran for only twelve performances. Later that year, Akins offered *Déclassée*, a social melodrama about a titled English lady whose life is destroyed after she leaves her husband for a lover. Both the play and its star, Ethel Barrymore, were applauded by critics and audiences, and this encouraged Akins to write several more plays as vehicles for leading Broadway actresses. Another successful serious play that dealt with the problems of personal fulfillment versus conventional family obligations was *Daddy's Gone A-Hunting* (1921), but most of her plays had very limited runs.

In all, Akins wrote more than forty plays: original dramas, comedies, and adaptations of other literary forms and foreign plays. Her serious dramas often received negative reviews because of their romanticism and sensationalism, although the critics did recognize the power of her dialogue and characterizations. George Jean Nathan found many of her dramas overburdened with affectation, and Brooks Atkinson commented on her intense emotionalism. Alexander Woollcott wrote a satirical sketch entitled "Zowie: or the Curse of an Akins Heart," which he and his fellow critics performed in a one-night revue called *No Sirree* (30 Apr. 1922). Akins's comedies, on the other hand, were sophisticated works with a great deal of wit that generally fared well with the critics, if not the public. However, she did enjoy a major commercial success with *The Greeks Had a Word for It* (1930), a comedy about three gold-digging ex-Follies girls.

Akins was also one of the few successful women writers in Hollywood during the 1930s, where she wrote scripts for several films like *Anybody's Woman* (1930), *Camille* (1937), and *Zaza* (1939), which were designed to appeal to women. Akins often adapted her own works or the plays of others for the movies. Her philosophy was that almost all writing is adaptation, whether from another literary form, from history, or from current events, and that very little is the product of pure imagination. She boasted that she never rewrote her plays to please a producer or a star, and this quality of passionate personal integrity was often reflected in her characters, particularly her heroines, as they strove to maintain their independence in the face of societal pressures.

In 1932, Akins married Captain Hugh (Hugo) Rumbold, a British theatrical designer and director, in a ceremony at her California home. It was a short-lived marriage, for Rumbold died eight months later from complications following a minor dental operation. Akins continued to write for both stage and screen, and she won the Pulitzer Prize for *The Old Maid* (1935), her highly successful adaptation of Edith Wharton's novel. This award to an adaptation instead of an original play added to the dissatisfaction that many critics already felt about the Pulitzer Prize process, and they formed the New York Drama Critics' Circle to present their own awards.

Throughout the 1940s and 1950s, Akins worked steadily on various projects, including her memoirs, but with diminishing success. She died at her Pasadena estate, "Green Fountains."

• Most of Akins's papers (over 7,000 pieces) are in the Henry E. Huntington Library, San Marino, Calif. Smaller collections, including letters, manuscripts, and contracts, are in the library of the State University of New York at Buffalo; the Bancroft Library of the University of California at Berkeley; the University Research Library of the University of California at Los Angeles; the Lilly Library of Indiana University, Bloomington; and the Berg Collection of the New York Public Library. Akins described her approach to writing in "The Playwriting Passion," *Vanity Fair*, 8 June 1920, and "Philosophy of an Adaptation," *New York Times*, 13 Jan. 1935. The Billy Rose Theatre Collection of the New York Public Library contains files of material about Akins and the individual plays and films, including scripts, programs, photographs, and reviews.

Much personal information appears in articles in *Dictionary of American Biography*, Suppl. 6 (1980) and *Notable Women in the American Theatre* (1989). Akins's relationship with Willa Cather is commented upon in *American Women Writers: A Critical Reference Guide from Colonial Times to the Present* (1979). Her screenwriting career is covered in *Dictionary of Literary Biography*, vol. 26 (1984). See also John A. Chapman, "Zoë Akins: Experimenter in the Drama Laboratory," *Spotlight*, 24 Dec. 1921; John Van Doren, "Zoë Akins: A Playwright with Ideas," *Theatre*, Feb. 1922; Catharine Cranmer, "Little Visits with Literary Missourians," *Missouri Historical Review* 20 (Jan. 1926): 252–61; George Jean Nathan, "The Theatre," *American Mercury*, May 1928. An obituary is in the *New York Times*, 30 Oct. 1958.

DOROTHY L. SWERDLOVE

ALAMO, Susan (25 Apr. 1925–8 Apr. 1982), independent Pentecostal minister and television and radio evangelist, was born Edith Opal Horn in Dyer, Arkansas, the daughter of Edward Horn and Geneva McAlster. Edith Horn converted from Judaism to evangelical Protestantism as a child. After some high school and a brief early marriage (to Tom Brown), she moved to Hollywood to try to make a career as an actress. There she met and, around 1940, married Solomon Lipowitz, with whom she had one daughter, known as Christhaon Susan. This marriage officially ended in 1966, though the couple had separated sometime before. As Susan Lipowitz she worked sporadically as an actress but mostly traveled around the country with her daughter as an evangelical minister and tent missionary. In 1965, while working as a street evangelist in Hollywood, she met Tony Alamo (born Bernie Lazar Hoffman in 1934), a talent promoter in the music business. She soon converted Alamo, who also was born Jewish, to her strand of Protestantism, and they were married in 1966, once in Tijuana and twice in Las Vegas, to be "triple sure." It was the third marriage for both.

The Alamos developed a street ministry along the Sunset Strip among the segment of population then known as the "Jesus People," young hippies, drug addicts, and dropouts, and in 1966 founded the Tony and Susan Alamo Christian Foundation, a Pentecostal church whose members professed belief in the authority of the Bible (the King James version), expected a personal experience of the holy spirit, and adhered to a strict moral order prohibiting drugs, adultery, homosexuality, and abortion. While the church's preaching was Pentecostal in tone and message, it functioned more like a cult in that the leaders' orders were law and their interpretations of the Bible were accepted as truth. In 1969 the church moved from Los Angeles to the more rural Sargus, California, where a church compound was established. The compound eventually consisted of 160 acres of land, on which members did farm work. In 1970 the church's membership was 200, mostly disaffected middle-class dropouts.

In 1976, amid California state legal questions concerning disagreements with townspeople, Susan Alamo moved the foundation headquarters to land it had purchased in rural Crawford County, Arkansas, near the towns of Alma and Dyer, Susan's hometown. It subsequently established many foundation-owned businesses, including gas stations, restaurants, printing houses, and grocery stores, where its adherents worked, largely without pay. The organization expanded in the late 1970s to include radio shows and a syndicated religious television ministry. "The Tony and Susan Alamo Show" featured Tony singing and Susan preaching sermons and selling Tony's albums. A number of subsidiary churches were opened in other U.S. cities, including Nashville, Chicago, New York, and Miami. In association with the church in Nashville, an up-scale western clothing store sold flashy jackets designed by Tony Alamo.

In the mid-1970s Susan Alamo began to battle breast cancer. Speaking of herself as the "handmaiden of God," she sought to focus attention on the foundation by "creating a miracle," that is, using the power given to her by God to cure herself of cancer and thereby bring her message to the world. The miracle did not manifest, however, and she died from the disease at the City of Faith Hospital (an affiliate of Oral Roberts University) in Tulsa, Oklahoma, on 8 April 1982. Her body was taken back to the church's compound at Alma, and a closely guarded memorial service was held at the church in Dyer four days later. Her death, at age fifty-six, shocked the members of the sect and shook their faith in both the foundation and the leadership. Alamo had been the theological backbone as well as the stabilizing influence in the foundation, as she understood how to control the followers without pushing them too far. She also had been the primary preacher and had held the biblical authority necessary to maintain the Christian Penecostal nature of the group. Much of her notoriety came after her death in the wake of a series of events related to the foundation's subsequent decline and her husband's erratic behavior.

Tony Alamo had his wife's body embalmed and placed in a sacristy, where devotees maintained continuous, 24-hour prayer vigils in accordance with his belief that, "If anybody is doing all his works in the name of Christ, all of his works, God will honor them and he will raise the dead." Insiders maintained that as long as Tony had her body, members would feel that he also had her power. After about a year (accounts vary), during which he claimed to be organizing a program for unwed mothers, Tony announced that he had received a vision from God indicating that Susan would not come back to life. Her body was placed in a mausoleum at the Alma compound, and Tony was married again, to a Swedish clothing designer who was not a member of the church.

Also after Susan Alamo's death the foundation significantly shifted its focus and activities. The Music Square Church, which was incorporated in 1981, had replaced the Tony and Susan Alamo Christian Foundation in 1982. In 1984 controversy surrounding the foundation intensified, fueled by relatives of converts, who argued that the organization was a cult; by the Anti-Defamation League of B'nai-B'rith, primarily in reaction to the group's proselytizing among Jews; and by the Catholic church, in response to the numerous anti-Catholic tracts and leaflets that foundation members distributed across parking lots throughout the country. These leaflets charged that the Vatican, with alleged ties to the U.S. government, the "international bankers," and the media, had ordered the assassination of President John F. Kennedy and controlled all organized crime and international terrorism. In 1985 the Internal Revenue Service (IRS) revoked the foundation's tax-exempt status and began to investigate its failure to pay personal, business, and federal employee wage taxes. Alamo went into hiding in 1988, after being charged in a California child abuse case, and was declared a federal fugitive in 1989. That year the church name changed again to the Holy Alamo Christian Church Consecrated. The IRS seized the foundation's Nashville property and some in Arkansas in 1990 and began auctioning them in February 1991. On the night following the raid and seizure of the Alma compound on 13 February 1991, it was discovered that the mausoleum had been disturbed and Susan's body removed. (Tony Alamo has alternately denied any knowledge of this or has claimed that because his wife's body is rightfully his, he has stolen nothing.) Finally arrested in Tampa, Florida, in 1991, Alamo was convicted of tax evasion and sentenced to six years in federal prison. Court records stated that Alamo had "married" eight of his followers since early 1993, including minors and women already legally married. The church, though smaller in size than before, remains active in Alma. Susan Alamo's body has yet to be found.

• The church published its own pamphlet, *We're Your Neighbor* (1987), which can be obtained from the church in Alma. For outside views see Yehuda Hilewitz, "The Alamo Story," *ADL Bulletin*, Dec. 1984, pp. 10–12; and David Alexander, "Remember the Alamos," *The Humanist* Jan.–Feb. 1990, pp. 43–44. Robert S. Ellwood, Jr., *One Way: The Jesus Movement and Its Meaning* (1973), mentions the Alamos. Obituaries are in the *New York Times* and the *Nashville Tennessean*, both 10 Apr. 1982.

AMANDA CARSON BANKS

ALARCÓN, Hernando de (fl. 1540–1541), Spanish explorer, is believed to have been born in Trujillo, Spain. The names of his parents and the circumstances and year of his birth are all unknown. The only documented period of his life is 1540–1541, when he acted in response to the commands of Antonio de Mendoza, the viceroy of New Spain (Mexico). In the spring of 1540 Mendoza directed Alarcón to sail north from Acapulco, Mexico, to support the land explorations of Francisco Vázquez de Coronado, one of the best known Spanish explorers of the sixteenth century.

Alarcón left Acapulco on 9 May 1540, leading two ships northward. The *San Pedro* and *Santa Catalina* were intended to carry the heavy baggage of Coronado's expedition, but since Alarcón and his men reached the port of Aguayaval (between the Mocorito and Culiacán rivers in northwest Mexico) after Coronado and his men had left, no coordination was effected between the two groups. In that harbor Alarcón added the *San Gabriel* to his forces and sailed northward with a fleet of three ships. He was not the first Spanish leader to explore in this area. Captain Francisco de Ulloa had sailed in the same waters one year earlier.

The ships entered the Gulf of California and found it difficult to make their way. They navigated through flats and shoals and were relieved when the gulf narrowed to a breadth of five or six miles. Reaching the end of the gulf, Alarcón and his men found "a mighty river with such a furious current that we could scarcely sail against it" (Hammond and Rey, p. 126). They were certainly the first Spaniards and probably the first white men to see the mouth of the Colorado River. Alarcón chose to leave his ships at the mouth of the river. On 26 August 1540 he and twenty of his men started to ascend the river in two boats.

Alarcón's company journeyed upriver for fifteen days. They encountered many Indians and learned that their principal towns were called Quicama and Coama. Alarcón dwelled at length on the customs of the Indians in the report of the expedition: their eating habits and attitudes toward warfare and religion. One Indian told him that he was within thirty days' travel of Cíbola, which was the destination of Coronado and his men. Another Indian later told him that there were bearded men like himself at Cíbola. Alarcón was eager to send news to Coronado, but he found that only one man (a Moorish slave) volunteered to go. Seeing the lack of enthusiasm among his men, Alarcón did not press forward.

Instead, he returned with his men downriver. The current of the Colorado River (which he named the Buena Guía [Good Guide]) was such that he made the return journey in two and a half days. Historians calculate that the highest point of Alarcón's ascent of the river was just above present-day Yuma, Arizona. He went up the river again on 14 September and erected a cross, under which he buried letters for Coronado. The letters were later found by Melchior Díaz, one of Coronado's lieutenants.

Alarcón returned to his ships and journeyed back down the coast of Mexico. He made frequent landfalls, searching for Coronado, but he never made contact. He reached the port of Colima, delivered his report, and sailed away that night. On 31 May 1541 Viceroy Mendoza issued a long set of instructions to Alarcón, ordering him to return to the Buena Guía river and to make contact with Coronado, but this second expedition never set forth. Thereafter, Alarcón disappears from record; the date and place of his death are unknown.

Alarcón was a member of an adventuresome generation of Spaniards. Probably raised on stories of the exploits of Hernando Cortés and other explorers, he came to the New World and played an important, though brief, part in the Spanish exploration of the west coast of North America. Combined with the voyage of Francisco de Ulloa, Alarcón's journey proved that California was a peninsula and not an island. He brought the Colorado River into the consciousness of New Spain, and his observations of the Indians along that river were important for future explorations. Although he failed in his ostensible task (to support and assist Coronado), Alarcón paved the way for other Spaniards to follow. His exploration, undertaken seventy years before England placed a permanent colony in the New World, gave some substance to the Spanish claim by right of discovery to what would later become the southwestern part of the United States.

• Alarcón's record is in George P. Hammond and Agapito Rey, *Narratives of the Coronado Expedition 1540–1542* (1940). His career also receives treatment in Henry R. Wagner, *Spanish Voyages to the Northwest Coast of America in the Sixteenth Century* (1929); Justin H. Winsor, *Narrative and Critical History of America*, vol. 2 (1886); and Frederick W. Hodge, ed., *Spanish Explorers in the Southern United States, 1528–1543* (1907). Alarcón's report has been reprinted in Albert B. Elsasser, ed., "Explorations of Hernando Alarcon in the Lower Colorado River Region," *Journal of California and Great Basin Anthropology* 1, no. 1 (1979): 8–37.

SAMUEL WILLARD CROMPTON

ALBANY, Joe (24 Jan. 1924–12 Jan. 1988), jazz pianist, was born Joseph Albani in Atlantic City, New Jersey. His parents' names are unknown. His father was a carpenter. Raised in the Los Angeles area, Joe played accordion as a child and took up piano in high school. The family returned to Atlantic City by the summer of 1942, when he first played professionally at the Paddock, a striptease club. Immediately back in Los Angeles, Albany joined scat singer Leo Watson's group, and he also married, but details of the marriage are unknown.

He worked for a month with trumpeter Max Kaminsky at the Pied Piper in New York City (c. 1943), and then he returned to the West Coast again to join Benny Carter's big band. Carter toured to Detroit, where Albany joined Georgie Auld's big band, touring to St. Louis, where Auld disbanded. In 1944 Albany made his own way to New York City, where he shared a room and narcotics with the pioneering bop alto saxophonist Charlie Parker. He performed with Parker's group late in 1944 or early in 1945, and in the latter year he recorded "Honey" and "Stompin' at the Savoy" with Auld. He rejoined Auld for a tour back to California, and he played in Boyd Raeburn's band for five weeks. In February or March 1946 he was a member of Parker's quintet at the Club Finale in Los Angeles. That August he recorded "New Lester Leaps In" and "Lester's Bebop Boogie," with tenor saxophonist Lester Young, and around this time he worked with tenor saxophonist Stan Getz and bassist Charles Mingus, who occasionally sat in with Getz's band.

In 1947 Albany went to New York, failed to find work, and instead toured across the South and back to California. Living mainly in Los Angeles, he was in and out of jails and hospitals during the 1950s. With tenor saxophonist Warne Marsh, bassist Bob Whitlock, and a recording engineer who also played drums, Albany taped a rehearsal that proved to be perhaps his finest album, *The Right Combination* (1957), reissued as *The Legendary Joe Albany*. That year he toured England, Belgium, Denmark, and Holland. Divorced, he married Ilene (maiden name unknown), a songwriter. The album *Anita O'Day at Mr. Kelly's* includes three songs cowritten by the Albanys. Ilene died in 1959.

In the early 1960s he married Sheila (maiden name unknown); they had one daughter. He went to New York in 1963, working briefly with Mingus at the Village Gate, and joined the Russ Morgan band in 1964. From 1969 to 1971 he was again in prison, presumably for further narcotics violations. In 1972 he traveled to Europe. He married Lynn (maiden name unknown). He performed at topless bars in England and at the Montmartre Jazzhus in Copenhagen with tenor saxophonist Dexter Gordon. He also played with clarinetist Tony Scott, saxophonist Johnny Griffin, pianist Kenny Drew, and bassist Wilbur Little. He made a few albums in Europe, including *Two's Company* (1974), a duo with bassist Niels-Henning Ørsted Pedersen. By this time he was living in Amsterdam. He visited the United States briefly in the summer of 1974 and settled in Los Angeles the following spring.

In April 1979 Albany moved back to New York. He performed at the West End Cafe and the Tin Palace before securing a job as a cocktail pianist at the World Trade Center, while concurrently playing jazz at the Cookery. He made the albums *Bird Lives* (1979) and *Portrait of an Artist* (1982), and he was the subject of a documentary film by Carole Langer, *Joe Albany . . . a Jazz Life* (1980), which is notable for his playing rather than for his uninspired stories. Albany died in New York City of upper respiratory failure and a heart attack. He was survived by a son and another daughter; to which of his at least four marriages these children may be ascribed is unknown.

Like the other principal white bop pianist of the mid-1940s, Al Haig, Albany led a troubled life but survived and found himself to be somewhat of a celebrity within the modest context of the mid-1970s bop revival. Whereas Haig was an immaculately accomplished improviser, Albany was more adventuresome, quietly reharmonizing pieces in a manner that sometimes approached the clustered dissonances of free jazz piano playing and pushing rhythmic organization to the brink. Occasionally he overstepped his abilities, as during the 1957 rehearsal in a wild doubletime chorus on "Body and Soul" in which he inadvertently abridges an eight-bar phrase, losing two beats, but such slips are perhaps merely the indicator of his dazzling and audacious conception of bop melody.

• Information on Albany's life is scarce and rather inconsistent in its detail, no doubt reflecting his own disordered life and memories. The most useful sources are brief items by Ross Russell, "The Legendary Joe Albany," *Jazz Review* 2 (Apr. 1959): 18–19, 40; Ira Gitler, "Portrait of a Legend: Joe Albany," *Down Beat*, 24 Oct. 1963, pp. 20–21; "Holland—Joe Albany's Favorite," *Jazz Forum* (int'l ed.), no. 29 (June 1974): 24; J. Shaw, "Joe Albany: Out of the Wilderness," *Mainstream*, no. 1 (1974): 12; Harvey Pekar, "Joe Albany," *Coda* 12 (Mar. 1975): 10–12; Lee Jeske, "Profile: Joe Albany," *Down Beat*, June 1980, pp. 54–56; John S. Wilson, "Film: Joe Albany Story, a Jazzman's Biography," *New York Times*, 1 July 1981; and Stuart Troup, "A Keyboard Legend Returns," *Newsday*, 1 Sept. 1982. A catalog of recordings is by Don Tarrant and Chris Evans, "Joe Albany Discography," *Journal of Jazz Discography*, no. 4 (Jan. 1979): 2–7. An obituary is in the *New York Times*, 16 Jan. 1988.

BARRY KERNFELD

ALBEE, E. F. (8 Oct. 1857–11 Mar. 1930), vaudeville manager, was born Edward Franklin Albee in Machias, Maine, the son of Nathan S. Albee, a shipbuilder, and Amanda Crocker. When Albee was four years old, he moved with his family to Boston. As a child he sold newspapers, and he left school at an early age to become a cash boy at a Boston store. After seeing a performance of P. T. Barnum's circus, he joined its road tour at the age of sixteen as a "tent boy" and animal feeder. Reportedly, the unforthcoming Albee was never popular with the circus folk, although he later recalled, "I entered into the spirit of it all with the enthusiasm of a youth of 16" (*New York Times*, 23 Mar. 1930). For some years, Albee's recollection continued, "I traveled with every principal circus . . . in every State." He rose to be a road manager. His years on tour were an education, he said, that "cannot be found in any other calling; the divers experiences which one encounters in travelling with a circus—the novelty, the contact with all classes, the knowledge of the conditions of the country, its finances, its industries and its farming" (*New York Times*, 23 Mar. 1930). In 1881 he married Laura Smith; they had a son and a daughter.

In 1883 Albee returned to Boston to become the manager of the Gaiety, a struggling dime museum and theater owned by B. F. Keith, a former circus candy butcher. Albee decided to raise the tone of the house: he threw out the exhibits of the museum, tastefully redecorated the premises, and offered a cut-down version of the Gilbert and Sullivan operetta *The Mikado* for ten cents on a continuous-performance basis. Reportedly, the public response was so great that police had to be called to control the crowds of customers. In 1886 Keith was able to expand to a second Boston theater, the Bijou, and in 1887 he opened two more theaters, one in Providence and one in Philadelphia. After Keith's original partner left in 1887, Albee became the general manager of the Keith enterprises and changed their offerings from drama and musical comedy to variety acts. Mindful of the low reputation of variety theaters, he insisted that the premises be clean and inviting and that the performers avoid material that was coarse or in bad taste. He began referring to them as "artists." Instead of the terms "variety" and "music hall," he used the more elegant term "vaudeville" for the theaters' offerings. "Cleanliness, Courtesy and Comfort" became the firm's motto. Albee himself was always elegantly dressed and groomed in a conservative style.

The middle-class public responded so well to Albee's upgraded form of entertainment that in 1893 the Keith organization was able to build a splendid new vaudeville house in Boston called the Colonial. It cost more than $600,000, a staggering sum at the time, and outshone every other theater in the country for luxurious fittings and elegant decor—both in front of and behind the curtain. In 1893 the firm also took over the Union Square Theatre in New York City and converted it to vaudeville after refurbishment. The construction and decoration of increasing numbers of Keith theaters was a chief interest of Albee in years to come, and he became an art collector for his theaters, buying works by Corot and other European artists well regarded in the period.

Over time, as Keith's interest in day-to-day management waned, Albee became the de facto head of the Keith organization, although he was content to stay little known to the general public. He took note of the monopolistic "syndicate" of legitimate theater owners, booking agents, and producers formed by Marc Klaw and Abraham Erlanger in 1896. Over the next years the Keith organization began forming a similar consolidation of vaudeville theater owners and managers. The result, in 1906, was the formation of the United Booking Office of America (UBO). Functioning as a vaudeville "trust," it controlled the bookings for all eastern and midwestern vaudeville houses, which numbered in the hundreds, and was able to slash the salaries offered to acts, charge performers 5 percent commission to book them into those theaters, and blacklist any performer who did not book through the UBO. By 1912 the last manager to hold out had surrendered. That year stage journalist Robert Grau wrote, "Slowly but surely the invincible Albee has seen them fall; some have lasted longer than others; but all [have succumbed to] this prince of organizers, or else have been confronted with disaster" (Grau, p. 152).

Keith died in 1914, leaving his estate equally divided between his son, A. Paul Keith, and Albee. The two inheritors shared leadership of the B. F. Keith Corporation, with offices above the Palace Theatre in New York—the supreme showcase of vaudeville, which the firm had acquired in a takeover soon after it was built in 1913. Albee had long wished to demolish the vaudeville performers' union known as the White Rats, formed in 1900 to resist the growing power of the managers. His chance came in 1916, when the White Rats initiated a nationwide strike against the UBO because it had put a clause in its contracts requiring that vaudevillians signing the contracts not be members of the union. The strike failed after Albee and other management leaders reportedly spent up to $2 million to fight it by any and all means, including the use of "scab" performers and intimidating the opposition with the threat of force. *Variety* summed up Albee's managerial tactics: "Nothing would stop him, and he stopped at nothing" (19 Mar. 1930).

All known members of the White Rats were thereupon blacklisted, as were even those performers seen by Albee's spies going into the White Rats' clubhouse in New York. Albee immediately formed a company union, the National Vaudeville Artists (NVA), that performers were required to join.

A. Paul Keith died in 1918 and left his holdings to Albee, who became the unchallenged czar of vaudeville. Heading the B. Keith Corporation and the B. F. Keith Vaudeville Exchange (as the UBO was renamed in 1918), he had control of an entire branch of the entertainment industry. The Exchange was renamed the Keith-Albee Vaudeville Exchange in 1925 and in 1927 merged with the Orpheum vaudeville circuit of the western United States to become Keith-Albee-Orpheum. Altogether the organization Albee headed then had controlling or minority interest in 450 theaters and exclusive booking of 775 theaters nationwide.

Albee's autocratic control proved in the 1920s to be a death grip. He refused to acknowledge the appeal of newer entertainment forms such as silent pictures and radio, and he put sanctions on performers involved in them. Going against the temper of the times, he further hobbled the amusement factor of his shows by forbidding comedians not only racy material but also jokes on controversial subjects, from Prohibition to the high cost of local hotels. The time he did not devote to art collecting and large personal philanthropies went to building and decorating elaborate theaters rather than keeping vaudeville entertaining. As one vaudeville historian put it, "He never seemed to realize that it was vaudeville itself that was more important than the theaters which housed it" (Laurie, p. 347). Throughout the decade top entertainers left vaudeville for radio or silent pictures and the lavish stage shows that accompanied them. Vaudeville audiences rapidly followed them. By the time of the 1927 merger, the Keith-Albee-Orpheum circuit was far-flung but fading.

In 1928 financier Joseph P. Kennedy approached Albee with an offer to buy Albee's controlling stock in Keith-Albee-Orpheum. Kennedy and David Sarnoff, the general manager of Radio Corporation of America, wanted a chain of theaters to serve as movie houses; they were forming a motion picture producing and releasing corporation. Albee refused to sell, and a bitter takeover battle followed. Kennedy was able to gain control by buying other stock. Hard feelings were aroused in the battle, as shown by the omission of Albee's name from the new motion picture corporation's name, Radio-Keith-Orpheum (RKO). After forty-five years of building an empire, Albee by the end of 1928 was frozen out of the new company. He was left wealthy, with a fortune estimated at $25 million, but he was stripped of power. He died less than two years later at a hotel in Palm Beach, Florida.

• Materials on the life and career of Albee are in the Billy Rose Theatre Collection at the New York Public Library for the Performing Arts, Lincoln Center. Further information is in Anthony Slide, *The Encyclopedia of Vaudeville* (1994). Other views are expressed in Joe Laurie, Jr., *Vaudeville: From the Honky-Tonks to the Palace* (1953). A contemporary view of Albee as manager is in Robert Grau, *The Stage in the Twentieth Century* (1912; 2d ed., 1969). A survey of his career, quoting Albee's reminiscences, is "E. F. Albee, Co-Founder of Vaudeville," *New York Times*, 23 Mar. 1930. Information on his art collecting is in Carlyle Burrows, "Paintings Collected by Theater Man Show Popular Turn-of-Century Styles," *New York Herald Tribune*, 21 June 1959. Obituaries are in the *New York Times*, 12 Mar. 1930; the *New York Herald Tribune*, 13 Mar. 1930; and *Variety*, 19 Mar. 1930.

WILLIAM STEPHENSON

ALBEE, Ernest (8 Aug 1865–26 May 1927), philosopher and educator, was born in Langdon, New Hampshire, the son of Solon Albee and Ellen Lucillia Eames. He graduated from the University of Vermont in 1887 with a bachelor's degree. He then went to Clark University in Massachusetts, where he studied psychology. In 1892 he transferred to Cornell University, where he earned a doctorate in philosophy in 1894. He had already been made a fellow of the Sage School of Philosophy at Cornell, and in 1892 he was appointed to the faculty. Appointed a full professor in 1907, he remained at Cornell for the rest of his career. He married Emily Humphreys Manly in 1911.

Albee's main contribution to the study of philosophy was his research on the history of utilitarianism, especially English utilitarianism, an approach to morality that regards actions as right insofar as they promote happiness, which is usually defined as pleasure and absence of pain, and wrong insofar as they fail to do so. Actions are evaluated by examining their consequences and not the intentions of the moral agent. His doctoral dissertation, "The Beginnings of English Utilitarianism," was a detailed study of the movement in the eighteenth century and was published in a series of articles in Cornell's *Philosophical Review* between May 1895 and July 1897. Albee later served as coeditor of this journal (1903–1909 and 1924–1927).

In 1901 Albee published his one major work, *A History of English Utilitarianism* which was an expansion of his doctoral work to include detailed studies of nineteenth century thinkers whose ideas were influential in the philosophical progress of English utilitarianism. The book quickly became the standard study of the movement. In it Albee traces the origins of English utilitarianism to the work of Richard Cumberland, who Albee argued was the first significant influence and thinker in this tradition. He also demonstrated the importance and relevance to the history of English utilitarianism of a number of less well-known thinkers including Anthony Ashley Cooper, earl of Shaftesbury, the Irish philosopher Francis Hutcheson, and the philosophers John Gay, John Brown, and William Paley.

Albee asserted that Hume's *Inquiry Concerning the Principles of Morals*, "with all its defects and shortcomings, is the classic statement of English Utilitarianism." Unlike most scholars of utilitarianism, he did not have a very high opinion of the influence of Jeremy Bentham, who, he believed, contributed little essentially new to ethical theory. Of the various proponents of utilitarianism, including George Berkeley, David Hartley, Abraham Tucker, Herbert Spencer, and Henry Sidgwick, Albee regarded John Stuart Mill as the main authority.

Albee's style was that of the careful expositor; he was not a critical or original thinker. His study of each philosopher, however, is thorough, fair, and often insightful. His work remains indispensable for a complete understanding of the history of utilitarianism. He died in Ithaca, New York.

• *A History of English Utilitarianism* was reissued in 1962 and 1973. A facsimile of the 1901 edition was published in 1990. An obituary is in the *New York Times*, 27 May 1927.

BRENDAN SWEETMAN

ALBERS, Josef (19 Mar. 1888–25 Mar. 1976), painter, designer, and educator, was born in Bottrop, Germany, the son of Lorenz Albers, a house painter and craftsman, and Magdalena Schumacher. He graduated in 1908 from the teachers' college in Büren and went on to teach in public schools in Bottrop and neighboring Westphalian towns. In the summer of 1908 he traveled to Munich to view modern art in the galleries and the historical collections of the Pinakothek. Albers's earliest known drawing, *Stadtlohn*, a view of a church from his window, dates to 1911, and in 1913 he took a leave of absence from the Westphalian school system and enrolled in formal art studies at the Royal Art School in Berlin. He received an art teacher's certificate from the school and returned to Bottrop in 1915, now teaching art in the secondary school. At the same time he continued to take art classes at the Kunstgewerbeschule in nearby Essen and began to make prints in various media—linocuts, woodcuts, and lithographs. In 1917 Albers received his first commission, a stained-glass window for St. Michael's Church in Bottrop, which he completed in 1918 (later destroyed).

Albers returned to Munich in 1919 intent on furthering his studies, especially in the field of color. He enrolled in Franz Von Stück's master painting class at Munich's Royal Bavarian Art Academy. Stück's classes, with their traditional academic emphasis on drawing from the nude, proved a great disappointment to Albers. But Max Dörner's course in painting techniques made a lasting impression.

Seeking to move beyond the academy and valuing the craft tradition that he had grown up with, Albers was attracted by Walter Gropius's founding manifesto for the Weimar Bauhaus, which was published in April 1919. In it Gropius rejected "salon art" and called for a united effort by architects, painters, and sculptors to revitalize the visual arts through attention to craftsmanship. Albers later described to artist Neil Welliver how, in responding to Gropius's call, he "threw all my old things out the window, started once more from the bottom. That was the best step I made in my life" ("Albers on Albers," *Art News* 64 [Jan. 1966]: 48). In the autumn of 1920, at the age of thirty-two, Albers entered the Bauhaus as a student.

Albers worked more or less independently and experimentally during his early Bauhaus years, assembling fragments of colored glass into inventive pictures—abstract designs for stained-glass windows executed on the modest scale of easel paintings—and in 1922 he was appointed a journeyman in the Bauhaus glass workshop. Albers also designed and executed full-scale architectural stained-glass windows: in the Sommerfeld House in Berlin (1921–1922), one of the earliest Bauhaus collaborative works; in private Berlin residences designed by Gropius; for the Grassi Museum in Leipzig (1926–1927); and for the Ullstein Publishing House in Berlin (1926–1927). None of these works survived the Second World War.

In 1923 Albers began teaching the Bauhaus Preliminary Course (Vorkurs), a required course for every Bauhaus student. Although he initially shared this teaching with Lázló Moholy-Nagy, Albers later took over complete responsibility for the course. His emphasis on an understanding of materials and clear visual thinking, achieved by placing experiential learning and practice over theory, combined with his singular ability to inspire his students, established Albers's reputation as a unique teacher. In 1925, coinciding with the Bauhaus's move to a new home in Dessau, Albers was made a full Bauhaus master. In the same year he married Anneliese Fleischmann, a young student who was to achieve her own considerable reputation as a noted textile designer and artist under the name Anni Albers.

In Dessau from 1925 until 1932, alongside his teaching and in tune with the Bauhaus's shift from handcrafted work toward industrial production, Albers extended his work in glass to abstract geometric compositions executed by sandblasting sheets of colored laminated glass. He also designed furniture in wood, objects in glass and metal, and typefaces. In 1928 he became interested in photography and used his Leica camera to record the work of his students. Albers photographed his Bauhaus colleagues and friends and also focused his camera on aspects of nature and contemporary life. He assembled many of his photographs into unique photocollages, which were not shown publicly until 1988 at the Museum of Modern Art in New York City.

In 1933 the Bauhaus, having moved once more (from Dessau to Berlin) disbanded voluntarily under threat of a shutdown by the Nazis. After this, when the making of works in glass became too costly, Albers resumed making woodcut and linocut prints, though now in an abstract vein quite different from his work of 1917–1919. With little prospect of work or an audience for their art in Germany, in 1933 the Alberses accepted an invitation for Josef Albers to take charge of art education at the newly formed Black Mountain College near Asheville, North Carolina. When he arrived at the experimental college, where art education was central to all other studies, Albers succinctly characterized the aim of his teaching as being "to open eyes."

Josef and Anni Albers became U.S. citizens in 1939 and remained at Black Mountain College until 1949. Albers continued printmaking and renewed his interest in painting. Both in his teaching and in his own rigorously abstract paintings he increasingly investigated the behavior of color and the complexity of color relationships. During this time the Alberses also traveled widely, particularly in Central and Latin America, where their firsthand encounters with pre-Columbian art and architecture provided new inspiration for their work.

In 1950 Albers was appointed chair of the Department of Design at Yale University. Discarding the largely mimetic methods of traditional art academies that were still being followed, Albers's drawing, color, and design courses at Yale guided a new postwar generation of American students to a level of visual acuity and understanding that he often described as "thinking in situations." According to art historian George Heard Hamilton, a Yale faculty member at the time, "Albers came and shook [the art school] up. . . . It was a very exciting time."

After he retired from Yale, Albers continued to travel and teach in Latin America, Europe, and across the United States and to create new works, which were exhibited worldwide. He designed and executed at least twenty architectural projects in a variety of materials, including an abstract design incorporated into a brick wall at Harvard University's Graduate Center (1950), the formica mural *Manhattan* in the lobby of New York's Pan Am Building (1963), an architectural sculpture, *Two Supraportas*, in steel over the entrance to the Westfälisches Landesmuseum für Kunst und Kulturgeschichte in Munster, Germany (1972), and the aluminum relief mural *Wrestling* for the Mutual Life Center in Sydney, Australia (1976). Albers may be best known for his *Homage to the Square* series of paintings—searching works of intense and subtle color exploration—begun in 1950. These arrangements of solid-colored squares nested within squares occupied him for the rest of his life, and they demonstrate his goal of achieving the maximum of effect through the use of restricted means—what he frequently described as "the ratio of physical effort to psychic effect." In a review in *Arts* (Dec. 1959), artist and critic Donald Judd described how in these works "the unbounded color and the final disparity belie the apparent rigidity of the geometry and provide the central lyric and exultant ambiguity of the painting." In a 1967 letter to Josef Albers, Mexican architect Luis Barragan called the paintings "a lifelong process from which many people, now so bound to improvisation, would learn the steadiness of a profound insight." In 1971 the Metropolitan Museum of Art honored Albers with the museum's first-ever retrospective exhibition devoted to the work of a living artist. He died in New Haven, Connecticut.

Albers's legacy as an artist and teacher, perpetuated in the teaching of his own students in universities and art schools throughout the world, was commemorated in 1980 by a postage stamp, which bore the image of a *Homage to the Square* painting and the U.S. Department of Education's motto "Learning Never Ends."

• Collections of Albers's unpublished writings and papers are in the archives of the Josef and Anni Albers Foundation; the Museum of Modern Art, New York City; the Busch-Reisinger Museum, Harvard University; and the Manuscripts and Archives Collection, Sterling Memorial Library, Yale University. The largest public collection of Albers's work is in the Josef Albers Museum, Bottrop, Germany; the largest American collection is at Yale. Albers's major publications include *Despite Straight Lines* (1961), an account of the spatial complexity of his "Structural Constellation" line drawings, engravings, and prints, written in collaboration with François Boucher; the magisterial *Interaction of Color* (1963), an exhaustive investigation of the behavior of color based on Albers's teaching and illustrated with more than 100 silk-screened color plates created by students in his color course at Yale (later translated into eight languages and published in both paperback and CD-ROM editions); and *Search versus Re-search* (1965), the published version of three lectures Albers gave at Trinity College, Hartford, Conn. The most complete published accounts of Albers's life and work are Nicholas Fox Weber, *Josef Albers: A Retrospective* (1988), which includes a detailed bibliography, and Weber, *The Drawings of Josef Albers* (1984). The Solomon R. Guggenheim Museum's *Josef Albers: Glass, Color and Light* (1994), contains essays and a complete catalog of Albers's work in glass. Neal David Benezra, *The Murals and Sculpture of Josef Albers* (1985), is a detailed account of the architectural works, while John Szarkowski, *The Photography of Josef Albers: A Selection from the Collection of the Josef Albers Foundation* (1987), and Marianne Stockebrand, ed., *Josef Albers Photographien 1928–1955* (1992), document Albers's photography. For the Black Mountain period, see Martin Duberman, *Black Mountain: An Exploration in Community* (1972), and Mary Emma Harris, *The Arts at Black Mountain College* (1987). Other sources include Irving Leonard Finkelstein, *The Life and Art of Josef Albers* (1979); Jo Miller, *Josef Albers: Prints 1915–1970* (1973); Kelly Feeney, *Josef Albers: Work on Paper* (1991); and Werner Spies, *Albers* (1971).

BRENDA DANILOWITZ

ALBERT, Abraham Adrian (9 Nov. 1905–6 June 1972), mathematician, was born in Chicago, Illinois, the son of Russian Jewish immigrants Elias Albert, a retail merchant and manufacturer, and Fannie Fradkin. Elias, who had left Russia initially for England, took the last name Albert before his marriage, in deference to the British prince consort; his original family name is unknown. In 1922 Adrian, as he was called, entered the University of Chicago, from which he earned a bachelor's degree in 1926. He stayed on at Chicago for his graduate training, hardly a surprise in light of his already pronounced mathematical talents and the fact that the mathematics program there was among the best in the nation at the time. After only one year, he received an M.S. in mathematics under the guidance of America's premier algebraist, Leonard Eugene

Dickson, and in 1928 Albert was awarded a Ph.D. for his work, also under Dickson, on a certain class of associative division algebras. Albert married Frieda Davis in 1927 while engaged in his doctoral research; the couple had three children.

On the strength of the results presented in his doctoral work, Albert won a coveted National Research Council Fellowship for the 1928–1929 academic year, which he spent at Princeton University. Although the presence of Joseph H. M. Wedderburn, the father of the modern theory of algebras, had initially attracted him there, Albert's interaction with another Princeton mathematician, Solomon Lefschetz, ultimately proved more rewarding. Albert followed the postdoctoral year in Princeton with two years (1929–1931) as an instructor at Columbia University before returning to his alma mater in 1931 as an assistant professor of mathematics. At Chicago he rose through the academic ranks, becoming associate professor in 1937, professor in 1941, and Eliakim Hastings Moore Distinguished Professor in 1960; he retained the last position until his death.

Albert's first year on the Chicago faculty, however, brought with it perhaps his greatest mathematical disappointment. Having continued in the vein of his doctoral research, Albert had focused his attention on the main outstanding problem in the theory of associative algebras, namely, the determination of all finite-dimensional division algebras over the field of rational numbers. In the process Albert found himself in a mathematical race against some of the stiffest German competitors. In 1930 and 1931 he had made great headway toward the full solution of the problem, and in the fall of 1931 he wrote to one of the principal German players, Helmut Hasse, to inform him of his latest results. These, as it turned out, were extremely close to the full solution of the problem that Hasse, together with his collaborators Richard Brauer and Emmy Noether, would publish late in 1931. Seemingly because communications crossed in the post, the German mathematicians became aware of the American's independent work too late to add Albert's name as a joint author. Hasse quickly sought to remedy this situation by coauthoring with Albert an account of the history of the result's proof with due acknowledgment and recognition of Albert's work ("A Determination of All Normal Division Algebras over an Algebraic Number Field," *Transactions of the American Mathematical Society* 34 [1932]: 722–26). The result, nevertheless, continued to be referred to in the literature as the Brauer-Hasse-Noether theorem.

Fortunately for his career, Albert did not allow this setback to impede his mathematical progress for long. During Albert's year at Princeton, Lefschetz had introduced him to the concept of Riemann matrices, constructs arising in the context of algebraic geometry that could be treated from a purely algebraic point of view. The young Chicagoan had demonstrated his genius for precisely the sort of mathematics involved in such a treatment in his doctoral dissertation and proceeded to solve the key outstanding problem in the area in three papers published in *Annals of Mathematics* in 1934 and 1935. The American Mathematical Society awarded him one of its highest honors, the Cole Prize in algebra, in 1939 for this work. This year also saw the publication of his classic, *Structure of Algebras*, which introduced a generation of algebraists to the modern approach to the theory of algebras. Membership in the National Academy of Sciences followed in 1943.

With U.S. entry into World War II, Albert, like so many others in mathematics and the sciences, joined the war effort on the home front. He participated in the Applied Mathematics Group at Northwestern University, a branch of the National Defense Research Council's Applied Mathematics Panel charged with compiling mathematical tables, and served as that group's associate director in 1945. Albert also became interested in the mathematization of cryptography and gave an invited hour-address on that subject at the AMS's meeting in Manhattan, Kansas, in November 1941.

The war years also saw Albert's mathematical interests shift from the theory of associative to that of nonassociative algebras. In the latter structures, the usual associative law of multiplication $a(bc) = (ab)c$ does not hold. Particular examples of such mathematical objects had arisen in the work of the German physicist Pascual Jordan in 1932 in the context of quantum mechanics. These so-called Jordan algebras satisfy the commutative law of multiplication, $ab = ba$, but instead of the usual associative law, they obey the rule $(a^2b)a = a^2(ba)$. In 1947, in an algebraic tour de force, Albert adapted the theorems and methods of the structure theory of *associative* algebras to determine the structure theory of the *nonassociative*, Jordan algebras.

After the war, Albert continued his research in nonassociative algebras but expended increasing energies on mathematics policymaking at the national and international levels. Beginning in 1943, he served as the editor of two influential publications in the field, the *Bulletin of the AMS* and the *Transactions of the AMS*. He would hold both positions until 1949. Also in the late 1940s, he worked within the context of the AMS to set the budget for mathematics within what would become, in 1950, the National Science Foundation, and he insured that this budget did not slight mathematics at the expense of other, more costly sciences. From January 1955 to June 1957, he chaired the influential AMS Committee on a Survey of Training and Research Potential in the Mathematical Sciences, which subsequently became known as the Albert Committee. He served as AMS vice president in 1957–1958 and as its president in 1965–1966. In 1970 Albert was also elected to a four-year term as vice president of the International Mathematical Union. His death, in Chicago, prevented him from serving out the term, however.

Albert, or *A*-cubed as many mathematicians affectionately called him, was an internationally renowned mathematician who made his principal contributions to the areas of associative and nonassociative algebras and Riemann matrices. He shared his talent and enthusiasm for mathematics with twenty-nine doctoral students whom he genuinely viewed as part of his family. He also worked tirelessly to establish mathematics on an equal footing with the other sciences in a postwar era characterized by governmental and corporate funding for basic scientific research.

• The University of Chicago Archives house Albert's personal papers. His published works appear in *A. Adrian Albert: Collected Mathematical Papers*, ed. Richard E. Block et al. (2 vols., 1993), which also includes a photograph of Albert, a curriculum vitae detailing in particular his numerous awards and professional service positions, a complete list of his doctoral students, and three of his previously unpublished mathematical manuscripts, including the 1941 manuscript on cryptography. Albert's most important publications include "A Determination of All Normal Division Algebras in Sixteen Units," *Transactions of the American Mathematical Society* 31 (1929): 253–60; and, in *Annals of Mathematics*, "On the Construction of Riemann Matrices, I and II," 35 (1934): 1–28 and 36 (1935); "A Solution of the Principal Problem in the Theory of Riemann Matrices," 35 (1934): 500–515; "Nonassociative Algebras: 1, Fundamental Concepts and Isotopy," 43 (1942): 685–707; and "A Structure Theory for Jordan Algebras," 48 (1947): 546–67. On Albert's life, consult Nathan Jacobson, "Abraham Adrian Albert: 1905–1972," *Bulletin of the American Mathematical Society* 80 (1974): 1075–100; and Irving Kaplansky, "Abraham Adrian Albert: November 9, 1905–June 6, 1972," National Academy of Sciences, *Biographical Memoirs* 51 (1980): 3–22, both of which include bibliographies of Albert's works. More personal tributes are Daniel Zelinsky, "A. A. Albert," *American Mathematical Monthly* 80 (1973): 661–65; and Israel N. Herstein, "A. Adrian Albert," *Scripta Mathematica* 29 (1973).

KAREN HUNGER PARSHALL

ALBERT, Octavia Victoria Rogers (24 Dec. 1853–1890?), author and activist, was born in Oglethorpe, Georgia, the daughter of slaves. Details of her life are sketchy. Little is known of her parents or her childhood beyond the date and place of her birth and the fact that she was born into bondage; thus, it is particularly intriguing that in 1870, only five years after the Thirteenth Amendment abolished slavery and one year after Atlanta University opened, seventeen-year-old Octavia was among the 170 students enrolled at that institution. Further details of her life are equally sketchy. Most of what we know is culled from information in *The House of Bondage*, the book that made her famous. From that source we learn that in 1873 she was teaching in Montezuma, Georgia, when she met fellow teacher A. E. P. Albert. They were married in 1874 and had one daughter.

Sometime around 1877 Albert's husband was ordained a Methodist Episcopal minister, and the family moved to Houma, Louisiana, and later to New Orleans. It is not clear whether Octavia Albert ever worked professionally again. Most likely she did not because it was rare for school systems, especially in the South, to employ married women and because her husband quickly assumed a social prominence that would have discouraged her being a wage earner. A. E. P. Albert became a religious and political leader, held a degree in theology, was a trustee of New Orleans University, and served as editor of the *South-Western Christian Advocate*. As befitted her social position, Octavia Albert vacationed with her family at resorts such as the Bay St. Louis in Mississippi, attended lectures and receptions, and generally participated in the religious reform efforts deemed proper for a minister's wife. However, it is clear that she was not content with these activities, but she made her home a center of activity where people of all classes and conditions were welcome to study the Bible, learn to read and write, and discuss current events. It was from just such community involvement that the idea was born for *The House of Bondage*. Albert's sympathies and interests had been increased by the frequent conversations she had with elderly former slaves, including Charlotte Brooks, who discussed with Albert her slavery experiences in Virginia and Louisiana. Albert announced that she intended to write Charlotte Brooks's story in—as closely as possible—Brooks's own words. Years later Albert stated, "My interest in, and conversations with, Aunt Charlotte, Aunt Sallie, Uncle John Goodwin, Uncle Stephen, and the other characters represented in this story led me to interview many other people [who gave] me additional facts and incidents about the colored people, in freedom as well as in slavery."

The full title of Albert's book reveals the grandness of her project: *The House of Bondage; or, Charlotte Brooks and Other Slaves: Original and Life-Like, as They Appeared in Their Old Plantation and City Slave Life; Together with Pen-Pictures of the Peculiar Institution, with Sights and Insights into Their New Relations as Freedmen, Freemen, and Citizens*. Some months after her death, Albert's *House of Bondage* was serialized in the *South-western Christian Advocate*; it proved so popular that "letters poured in upon the editor from all directions, urging him to put it in book form." The volume was published posthumously in 1890. The scope of Albert's project, covering rural and urban slavery and using oral testimonies, distinguishes her work from other studies of the period. In the 1880s slavery had once more become a popular topic for many writers, but most were of the so-called Plantation School, which thought of the South as a place of chivalry and slavery as a benevolent, paternalistic institution. At the same time much of the contemporary media and many politicians were justifying racial discrimination and increased violence against African Americans on the grounds that former slaves harbored deep hostility and plans for revenge and were without morals, self-discipline, or ambition. Declaring that "none but those who resided in the South during the time of slavery" could testify accurately to its horror, Albert set out to set the record straight by publishing interviews with former slaves, by describing their condition since slavery, and by celebrating the achievements they and their descendants had won despite great and increasing odds.

According to historian John Blassingame, Albert was "one of the few well-trained interviewers" in the country. The stories unfold in the dialogue between Albert and the interviewees. The major narrative is that of Charlotte Brooks. The half-dozen other extended accounts and the multitude of incidents in the lives of others they knew or had heard about serve primarily to supplement or emphasize the material that Brooks provides. Albert uses poetry, songs, speeches, and other material for documentation, for context, and for texture. While she intended her work to combat negative stereotypes, Albert emphasized another goal. It was vital, she argued, that the story of those who survived slavery and those who overcame racial oppression be treasured and transmitted to "our children's children," not only to set the record straight but to inspire African Americans. Her book posits "education, property, and character" as the "trinity of power" by which African Americans could gain their rightful places in society.

• For a modern assessment of Albert see Frances Smith Foster's introduction to the 1988 edition of *The House of Bondage*. See also Monroe Majors, *Noted Negro Women* (1893), and Vivian Njeri Fisher, "Albert, Octavia Victoria Rogers," in *Black Women in America*, ed. Darlene Clark Hine (1993).

FRANCES SMITH FOSTER

ALBERTIERI, Luigi (1860–25 Aug. 1930), dancer, choreographer, and teacher, was born in Rome, Italy. Little is known of Albertieri's parents, aside from the fact that his mother was widowed when he was very young. He was adopted at the age of eight by the Italian dancer and ballet master Enrico Cecchetti and Cecchetti's wife, Giuseppina. Cecchetti had noticed Albertieri in a juvenile opera company's performance of *The Barber of Seville* in Turin, in which Albertieri sang the leading role. He displayed great talent not only as a singer but also as a dancer. Cecchetti approached Albertieri's mother who, struggling to provide for her large family, agreed to the informal adoption. Thus Luigi became "Farfa," the Cecchetti's youngest child.

For ten years Cecchetti trained Albertieri according to a strictly regimented program: initially five hours a day of intensive work at the barre, followed by carefully structured basic center floor work after the first eight months. Under Cecchetti's vigilant training regime Albertieri gradually developed a brilliant and impeccable technique that rivaled that of his teacher. Albertieri was an especially gifted turner, spinning effortless pirouettes in many different positions, and a buoyant jumper, seeming to remain airborne at the top of his leap.

In addition to careful technical training, Cecchetti prepared Albertieri as a teacher and choreographer. He noticed early on that Albertieri was a gifted choreographer with a flair for invention and began having him copy the choreographic compositions that Cecchetti was creating for his company. He then advanced Albertieri to copying the complicated graphs, verbal descriptions, and notations of large-scale spectacular ballets, such as those of Luigi Manzotti, the principal choreographer at La Scala in Milan. Cecchetti encouraged Albertieri to devise dances of his own and to note and evaluate them.

Albertieri's first public appearance in Italy took place at La Scala during a benefit performance of Manzotti's ballet *Excelsior* in 1881. At the last moment he substituted for Cecchetti in a blackface role. Cecchetti, who had feigned illness to give his young protégé the opportunity to perform, pulled Albertieri, still in costume, onstage for bows at the end of the performance. The audience, which had not been advised of the switch, roared their surprise and approval of Albertieri.

Albertieri's first engagement as a principal dancer independent of Cecchetti occurred in Brescia, Italy, in 1878. Eight years later Sir Augustus Harris, the manager at the Covent Garden Opera House in London, hired Albertieri to become his leading male dancer and the *maître de ballet*. At twenty-six, Albertieri was the youngest ballet master in the history of Covent Garden. While in London, he appeared as a principal dancer at the Empire Theatre with reigning ballerinas Katti Lanner, Malvina Cavallazzi, and Adeline Genée. On 28 December 1889 Albertieri appeared at the Empire as "Demon Avarice" in *A Dream of Wealth*, a ballet choreographed by Leopold Wenzel. He alternated performances at Covent Garden and the Empire with appearances in Drury Lane Christmas pantomimes. A press notice in the *Spy* read, "Signor Albertieri maintains his high reputation. . . . his wonderful pirouettes are greeted with deafening applause" (17 Oct. 1891).

In 1895 Maurice Grau, the manager of the Metropolitan Opera House, brought Albertieri to the United States to fill the position of *premier danseur* and, for a short time, stage manager at the newly opened theater. Until 1902 he split his time between New York and London. Albertieri continued to dance at the Metropolitan, with brief absences for engagements in Europe, for the next fourteen years.

In 1910 Albertieri officially immigrated to the United States, where he lived for the rest of his life. He served as ballet master and soloist for the Chicago Lyric Opera from 1910 to 1913, the Century Opera in New York City for a short time in 1913, and later that same year at the Metropolitan. From 1913 to 1927 he taught at the Metropolitan and staged a number of ballets, including *The Fairy Doll* and his version of *Coppélia*. In addition, Albertieri's dances for opera were seen in Mancinelli's *Ero e Leandro*, de Lara's *Messaline*, Massenet's *Le Cid*, Paderewski's *Manru*, and Wolf-Ferrari's *Jewels of the Madonna*.

In 1915 Albertieri opened his own ballet school in New York City. Many important ballet teachers and leading dancers came to study with him, including ballerina Anna Pavlova and the stars of Diaghilev's Ballets Russes, Italian ballerinas Rosina Galli and Maria Gambarelli, and American dancer-choreographers Fred Astaire and Albertina Rasch, a soloist at the Century Opera Company. Actresses Maude Adams and Emma Calvé and swimmer Annette Kellermann studied with Albertieri as well. Albertieri's advertisement in the *American Dancer* (now *Dance Magazine*) included Pavlova's statement hailing Albertieri's school as "by far the best dancing school I know of in America" (Feb. 1926). Albertieri continued to teach until the time of his death in New York City. Although the date of the marriage is unknown, he was survived by his widow, the former Abbie MacLean of St. Louis, and one daughter, who continued to manage his school.

Of the three general methods (French, Russian, and Italian) of teaching ballet employed in the United States during the late twenties, Albertieri was the acknowledged master of the Italian, founded by Carlo Blasis in the 1820s and continued by Blasis's student Cecchetti. According to Lydia Lopokova, a Diaghilev ballerina and one of Albertieri's students, Albertieri taught like Cecchetti; but unlike Cecchetti, who could often be cruel, Albertieri was kind, positive, and enthusiastic. He was said to inspire self-confidence in his students because he had such confidence in himself and his knowledge of dance. Known for his strict observance of traditional regulations and vigilance against exaggerations, mannerisms, and coquettishness, Albertieri is considered the last great exponent of nineteenth-century Italian ballet technique in the United States.

In 1931 a moving picture with sound, *The Ballet Class*, was made about Albertieri's teaching. He also wrote *The Art of Terpsichore, an Elementary, Theoretical, Physical, and Practical Treatise of Dancing* (1923), a textbook that features drawings similar to those used in Blasis's *The Code of Terpsichore* (1828). At the time of his death Albertieri was also working on an autobiography, but the whereabouts of the manuscript is unknown.

• A clipping file is available in the Dance Collection at the New York Public Library for the Performing Arts, Lincoln Center. For further information on Albertieri see Jeanne Laurent, "Luigi Albertieri Tells Stuart Palmer about Il Mio Maestro Cecchetti," *Dance Magazine*, Dec. 1929, pp. 35, 61 and Ann Barzel, "European Dance Teachers in the United States," *Dance Index* 3 (1944): 4–6. An obituary is in the *New York Times*, 27 Aug. 1930.

BARBARA BARKER

ALBERTINA, Sister. *See* Pollyblank, Ellen Albertina.

ALBERTSON, Jack (16 June 1907–25 Nov. 1981), actor, was born in Malden, Massachusetts, the son of Leo Albertson and Flora Craft, a shoe factory worker. Soon after his birth, his father abandoned his mother, and Albertson was raised by his mother and his stepfather, Alex Erlich, a barber. Albertson abandoned his formal education after a single year of high school and began working at factory jobs and as a rack boy for the local pool hall. By age eighteen he was successfully competing as a dancer in amateur talent shows and had formed his own singing group, called "The Golden Rule Four." He went to New York in 1931 in search of a job in show business. Noticed by an agent while trading steps with some of his fellow would-be hoofers in front of the Palace Theatre, Albertson was offered his first job, joining five other dancers backing a two-woman vaudeville team.

Soon after, Albertson met another aspiring performer, Phil Silvers, and the duo worked up a soft-shoe and comedy routine, with Albertson playing the straight man to comedian Silvers. After a season in the Catskills, the two signed on with Minsky's Burlesque in 1935. In future years Albertson would play "second banana" to such top comics as Milton Berle, Bert Lahr, and Jack Benny.

In 1937 Albertson went to Hollywood, where he played bit parts and secured a position as a chorus member in the Shirley Temple film *Rebecca of Sunnybrook Farm*. His Broadway debut came in 1940, when he was featured in a song-and-dance number with Eddie Johnson called "The Same Old South" in the comedy revue *Meet the People*. After several years of small parts in television (NBC's "The Hour Glass" and "The Maxwell House Coffee Show") and in the theater (*Champagne for Everybody* [1944] and *A Lady Says Yes* [1945]), Albertson got his first major break when he stepped in for the ill Eddie Foy, Jr., as Kid Conner in the revival of Victor Herbert's operetta *The Red Mill* (1945–1946). His next role was the minor part of Yasha in the revival of Blitzstein's *The Cradle Will Rock* (1947), followed by a leading role in *High Button Shoes* (1947). In 1951 he was reunited with Silvers in the hit comedy *Top Banana*, which toured nationally through 1953 and was later made into a film.

Throughout the 1950s and 1960s Albertson made a series of minor films, including *Bring Your Smile Along* (1955), *You Can't Run Away from It* (1956), and *Don't Go Near the Water* (1957), and appeared in several television series, among them "The Thin Man," "Ensign O'Toole," and "Gunsmoke." His first dramatic role on stage came in 1957, after almost forty years in show business, when he costarred as Vladimir with comedian Joey Faye in Samuel Beckett's *Waiting for Godot* in Los Angeles. The play marked the beginning of Albertson's recognition as a legitimate actor and was followed by roles in West Coast productions of *Conversation at Midnight*, *Design for Living*, *Vintage 60*, *Mother Courage*, and *The Child Buyer*. It was while Albertson was directing and playing the leading role in *Burlesque* in its 1962 stage revival that playwright Frank Gilroy asked him to do his new play, *The Subject Was Roses*.

Opening at the Royale Theatre in New York on 25 May 1964, Albertson was hailed as "brilliant" and "vibrant" in his portrayal of a tortured Irish father and husband who is unable to connect emotionally with his family. His performance won him the Antoinette Perry (Tony) Award for best supporting actor and was followed by an Oscar from the Academy of Motion Picture Arts and Sciences in 1968 for the same role in the film version. During the 1960s Albertson's films included *Days of Wine and Roses* (1963), *How to Murder Your Wife* (1965), *The Flim-Flam Man* (1967), *How to Save a Marriage and Ruin Your Life* (1968), *Changes* (1969), *Justine* (1969), *Rabbit Run* (1970), and *Willy Wonka and the Chocolate Factory* (1971).

In 1972 Albertson returned to the Broadway stage to costar with Sam Levene in Neil Simon's new play, *The Sunshine Boys*, for which he received another Tony nomination, a Drama Desk Award, and the first annual Lambs Club Award, all in 1973. Albertson's next film, the blockbuster movie *The Poseidon Adventure*, opened almost simultaneously with *The Sunshine Boys* and became one of the highest grossing movies of its time. Albertson's costarring role with Freddie Prinze in NBC's prime-time series "Chico and the Man" (1974–1976) made him a familiar face to younger audiences and won him an Emmy award in 1976, one year before Prinze's suicide. The previous year Albertson had received his first Emmy for his guest appearance on "The Cher Show."

Following the conclusion of his own TV series, Albertson continued to make guest appearances and television specials, including *The Lilac Season* (ABC), costarring Vanessa Redgrave, *Marriage Is Alive and Well* with Mary Martin (NBC), and *Grandpa Will You Run with Me* (NBC).

Albertson is one of the very few actors who have achieved the top awards in all three entertainment industries: stage, television, and film. This achievement is all the more noteworthy because he was over the age of fifty before he received this acclaim for his work. His career of over five decades encompassed a range of material from vaudeville stand-up comedy sketches to serious drama. He was a member of the Actors' Equity Association, Screen Actors Guild, American Federation of Television and Radio Artists, and American Guild of Variety Artists. He died at home in Los Angeles in the care of his wife, Wallace Thomas. They had been married since 1952; the couple had one daughter.

• A clipping file of reviews, interviews, and press releases from Albertson's career, held in the Billy Rose Theatre Collection at the New York Public Library for the Performing Arts, Lincoln Center. Additional materials can be found at the Press Department of NBC. Biographies appear in *Notable Names in the American Theatre* (1976) and *Current Biography* (1976). Reviews of his performances appear in the *New York Post*, 26 May 1964; the *Toronto Globe and Mail*, 1 June 1966; the *New York Times*, 26 May 1964, 21 Dec. 1972, and 7 Jan. 1973; the *Washington Post*, 15 Sept. 1974; and the *New York Sunday News*, 6 July 1975. Obituaries are in *Variety*, 2 Dec. 1981; the *New York Daily News*, 26 Nov. 1981; and the *New York Times*, 26 Nov. 1981.

SUSAN F. CLARK

ALBERTY, Harold Bernard (6 Oct. 1890–2 Feb. 1971), professor of curriculum design and development, was born in Lockport, New York, the son of Willard K. Alberty and Carrie L. Post. Alberty attended rural schools in northeastern Ohio and was graduated from Liverpool Township High School in Medina County, Ohio, in 1908. In 1912 Alberty was graduated from Baldwin University (now Baldwin-Wallace College) in Berea, Ohio, where he studied liberal arts and pre-law subjects. He taught eighth grade in the Berea schools during his final year of college in an effort to underwrite his tuition and continued to hold this position until 1913, when he was graduated from Cleveland Law School and was admitted to the Ohio bar. Because no law positions were then available, Alberty continued to teach, an activity that fascinated him, and he rose quickly in the county school administration, serving as assistant principal of Berea High School from 1913 to 1915; superintendent of Berea schools from 1915 to 1917; district superintendent of Cuyahoga County schools from 1917 to 1920; and assistant Cuyahoga County superintendent from 1920 to 1924. He received an A.M. in school administration from Ohio State University in 1923. Throughout this period Alberty planned to return to the practice of law. In 1916 he married Anna Hower; they had one child. Their marriage ended with her death in the latter 1940s.

In 1924, after taking a course from Ohio State University philosophy of education professor Boyd Bode, Alberty decided to devote himself to the field of education and end any thoughts of a career in law. Bode offered Alberty an assistant's position in the Department of Principles and Practices of Education at Ohio State University, where Alberty completed his doctoral studies in 1926 under Bode. "Thus began the 20 year collaboration. . . . Bode, the rumpled classic example of the absent-minded professor. . . . And Alberty, the smartly dressed, eternally young man, who would struggle to interpret, and in so doing expand and refine" the implications of Bode's work (Bullough, p. 112). Remaining at Ohio State University throughout his 35-year career, Alberty rose from instructor to professor of education and served as curriculum associate of the Progressive Education Association's Eight-Year Study from 1936 to 1938 and as director of the Ohio State University Laboratory School from 1938 to 1941. Alberty's major texts included *Supervision in the Secondary School*, with V. T. Thayer (1931); *Science in General Education*, for which he served as the unacknowledged author (1938); and, most notably, *Reorganizing the High School Curriculum* (1947), which went through three editions and made the National Education Association's List of Best Books in 1947, 1953, and 1962. In 1954 Alberty married Elsie J. Stalzer, with whom he coauthored the third edition of *Reorganizing the High School Curriculum*; they had one child.

Alberty furthered the field of educational theory and curriculum development through the development of the concepts of "core curriculum" and the "resource unit." He stressed the importance of all schools recognizing and then refining the general education component of their curriculum, which he called the "core curriculum," and he developed a conceptual framework that enabled educators to recognize the type of core curriculum embodied in their program. The framework consisted of five core "types," or approaches. Schools with a type 1, or "separate subjects approach," taught typical academic subjects (Carnegie units, the standard unit of measurement for high school course credit that was determined by a specified amount of time focused on a single academic subject) whose contents were unrelated. A type 2, "correlated," approach continued to organize material into separate subjects, yet this core sequenced knowledge in such a way that students would see relationships among the disciplines. A type 3 core, "fusion curriculum," unified two or more separate subjects and organized the curriculum around general themes or time periods. A common example would be to fuse social studies and language arts (and perhaps music), bring together the teachers and students into one block session formerly composed of two consecutive periods, and then organize the curriculum into a series of epochs such as the Colonial Period, Westward Expansion, etc. While core types 1, 2, and 3 were organized around a subjects approach to the curriculum, type 4 (problem areas core) abandoned this structure altogether. A type 4 core organized itself around broad units; these topics were determined by the psychobiological and societal needs, problems, and interests of learners. Alberty recommended this structure for secondary schools; however, he underscored the importance of subject matter and academic content as the body of knowledge from which student needs, interests, and problems were drawn. The type 5 core was based solely on teacher-student planned activities without reference to any formal structure. Alberty stated: "The argument for such a program is very simple. The teacher and students are most competent to determine the common needs of the particular group and hence to determine the learning activities best suited to meet these needs. Structuring the program in advance is just another way of imposing subject matter" (Alberty and Alberty [1962], p. 223). While type 3, 4, and 5 core programs appeared unmanageable and unstructured, the PEA's Eight-Year Study (1932 to 1940) proved that these programs better prepared students for college than did the traditional separate subjects approach (type 1). Alberty assisted the schools that participated in this study in their attempts to move to a more integrated core curriculum.

Because core curricula of the type 3 through 5 variety could not use conventional textbooks, Alberty developed and popularized the use of "resource units" for curriculum development. His general criteria for resource units required that the unit provide flexibility of content and teacher-learning procedures, be developed by a group of teachers, be published in a form that facilitates frequent and easy revision, and, lastly, include the following components: statement of philosophy, scope, suggested activities, bibliography and teaching aids, evaluation, suggestions for other units, and guides for the use of the unit. The introduction of the resource unit removed the major obstacle to the development of a more flexible and integrated core curriculum: namely, the dominance of the textbook.

Although not as well known as educators John Dewey, William Bagley, and William H. Kilpatrick, Alberty proved to be a crucial figure in the development of American curriculum from the 1920s through the 1960s. As an unacknowledged curriculum leader of the PEA's Eight-Year Study, he helped guide what is widely viewed as the most important educational experiment of the twentieth century. Equally important, Alberty served in the critical role of "middle-range" theorist by translating the educational philosophy of Progressivism into actual school practice. His writing within the PEA's publications and his curriculum text, *Reorganizing the High School Curriculum*, proved to be the most sophisticated work in the area of curriculum design and development of the mid-twentieth century.

• Few archival materials and collected papers of Alberty exist. His correspondence is included in the Ohio State University Laboratory School files of the Ohio State University Archives. Biographical portraits are by Robert V. Bullough, Jr., "Harold B. Alberty and Boyd H. Bode: Pioneers in Curriculum Theory" (Ph.D. diss., Ohio State Univ., 1976), and Victor Lawhead, "Harold Alberty, Master Teacher: A Retrospective View," in *Teaching Education* (2 vols., 1987).

CRAIG KRIDEL

ALBRIER, Frances Mary (21 Sept. 1898–21 Aug. 1987), civil rights activist and community leader, was born in Mount Vernon, New York, the daughter of Lewis Redgrey, a supervisor in a factory, and Laura (maiden name unknown), a cook. Following the death of her mother when Frances was three, she and her baby sister were reared by her paternal grandparents, Lewis Redgrey, a Blackfoot Indian, and Johanna Bowen, a freed slave, on their 55-acre farm in Tuskegee, Alabama.

Frances attended Tuskegee Institute, where she studied botany under George Washington Carver, who also advised her grandfather on productive farming techniques. In 1917 she enrolled at Howard University, studying nursing and social work. In 1920, following the death of her grandmother, she left college and moved to Berkeley, California, to join her father and stepmother. Two years later she married William Albert Jackson; they had three children. Jackson died in 1930, and in 1934 she married Willie Antoine Albrier, a Pullman Company club-car porter.

Because of precepts laid down by her grandmother and her teachers, Albrier was strongly motivated to improve the condition of black Americans. Imbued with the beliefs that education was essential in opening doors for blacks and that those fortunate enough to become educated "owed something to the race," she made education a focus of all her activities. According to an oral history conducted in the 1970s, admonished by her grandmother that "bitterness will kill you" and that she had to "fight and earn what you got . . . earn respect," Albrier "developed a sense of retaliation and fighting through the system."

Her social action began during the 1920s, when she joined Marcus Garvey's Universal Negro Improvement Association, serving with the association's Black Cross Nurses and as vice president of its women's auxiliary. From 1926 to 1931 she worked as maid and manicurist on the Pullman Company's Sunset Limited, supporting A. Philip Randolph's efforts to organize the Brotherhood of Sleeping Car Porters. During the 1930s and 1940s, as a member and then president of the American Federation of Labor's Women's Auxiliary of the Dining Car Cooks and Waiters, she actively worked to bring black men and women into the discriminatory mainstream labor unions.

In 1940, as president of the Citizens Employment Council, she led a successful "Don't Buy Where You Can't Work" movement, and in 1955, as secretary of a church-sponsored employment committee, she pushed again for black employment. From 1938 to 1943 she lobbied to hire black teachers in the Berkeley school system, first organizing the East Bay Women's Welfare Club to do research and outreach and then running for the Berkeley City Council in 1939 to publicize the color barriers in the schools and local government. In 1943 Berkeley hired its first black teacher.

During the 1930s and 1940s, Albrier assisted the East Bay Women's Welfare Club, the Association of Colored Women's Clubs, and the National Association for the Advancement of Colored People in their eventually successful effort to admit black women into the county hospitals's nurses training program and to permit them to live in dormitories. Her friendship with Mary Church Terrell and Mary McLeod Bethune, who taught her the value of black women's clubs, led to her organization of many such clubs, educating women on social and political issues and motivating them to community action.

During World War II she broke other barriers. She was a pioneer in the Red Cross, qualified to drive in the motor corps and teach first aid classes. In 1942 she became the first black woman welder allowed to work in the Richmond Kaiser shipyards without a union card. African Americans were not allowed to become members of AFL unions, and because no separate black auxiliary existed in the Kaiser yards, Albrier complained directly to the manager, who permitted her to work without a union card. After an executive order was issued barring discrimination in union membership, a segregated auxiliary was organized, and in 1943 she joined the union. Suspecting that black postal employees suffered discrimination in work assignments, promotions, and general employee relations, she left the shipyards in 1943 and went to work in the San Francisco post office. Shortly thereafter she organized the Postal Service Workers Club to deal with grievances due to discrimination.

Albrier saw Democratic party politics as another way to fight for black rights. In 1938 she was the first woman elected to the Alameda County Democratic Central Committee, a position she held until 1962. She served as delegate to state party conventions and was a member of several local Democratic party clubs, several of which she organized. She campaigned for state and national candidates, fair employment and housing legislation, and the election of black men and women to public office. Berkeley pharmacist Byron Rumford was elected to the California Assembly in 1948, and in the 1960s blacks finally won seats on the Berkeley City Council and school board.

Albrier's trip to Nigeria in 1960 to attend Nigerian independence ceremonies as a representative of the National Council of Negro Women was the crowning event of her life, symbolizing her commitment to the advancement of blacks worldwide. In line with her dedication to the acknowledgment of black achievements, in 1958 and 1965 Albrier arranged the first window displays commemorating National Negro History Week in major downtown Oakland and San Francisco department stores. During the 1960s she spoke to school children on black history, and in 1968 she was president of the East Bay Negro Historical Society.

In the 1970s Albrier turned her attention to the elderly, taking a leading role in the development of Berkeley senior centers, speaking at seminars on aging, and serving as a delegate to the 1971 White House Conference on Aging. In 1967 the mayor of Berkeley appointed her to the seven-member Committee on Aging, and in 1972 she was named to the Herrick Hospital Board of Trustees, in each case becoming the first black appointee. In 1986 she served as president of the Northern California Caucus on Black Aging.

From 1954 to 1978 Albrier received honors almost annually for her extraordinary community service, among them the NAACP West Coast Region "Fight for Freedom" Award (1954); the Woman of the Year Award (1966); the *Sun Reporter* Citizen of Merit Award (1967); a California Assembly Rules Committee commendation for battling racial discrimination (1971); the California Congress of Parents and Teachers Honorary Service Award (1971); the National Congress of Negro Women's "Outstanding Woman of Northern California" Award (1973); the City of Berkeley Community Service Award (1976); and the Greyhound Corporation's "Woman of Tomorrow" Award (1978).

Albrier died in Berkeley, California. A soft-spoken but determined leader, she pioneered the cause of civil rights and participated actively in nearly every organization aimed at encouraging African Americans to develop a sense of their own worth.

• A detailed scrapbook of Albrier's activities and other papers are in the Bancroft Library, University of California, Berkeley. An oral history conducted by Malca Chall in 1977–1978, "Determined Advocate for Racial Equality," is published in *The Black Women Oral History Project*, ed. Ruth Edmonds Hill, vol. 1 (1991), pp. 169–530. Albrier is discussed in Ruth Edmonds Hill and Judith Sedwick, *Women of Courage* (1984), and Charlotte Painter and Pamela Valois, *Gifts of Age* (1985). Obituaries are in the *Voice*, 27 Aug. 1987, and the *San Francisco Chronicle* and the *Daily Californian*, 28 Aug. 1987.

MALCA CHALL

ALBRIGHT, Fuller (12 Jan. 1900–8 Dec. 1969), endocrinologist, was born in Buffalo, New York, the son of John Joseph Albright, an industrialist and philanthropist, and Susan Fuller. Fuller Albright came from a patrician background; he attended Nichols Day School, one of two schools founded by his father. He showed himself to be a well-rounded scholar and athlete, matriculating at Harvard College at age sixteen. He volunteered to join the U.S. Army during World War I and at officer's training school contracted influenza, a likely forerunner of the postencephalitic Parkinsonism that progressively impaired his functioning in later years. He attended Harvard Medical School and began his residency training at the Massachusetts General Hospital, the institution where he remained throughout his career except for two sabbatical years, one spent in Vienna and the other at the Johns Hopkins Hospital in Baltimore. He married Claire Birge in 1933; they had two children.

With the sponsorship of James Howard Means, the chief of medicine, and under the tutelage of Joseph Aub, a pioneer clinical investigator, Albright launched a career in investigative endocrinology at a propitious time and place. Aub had just begun studies into the cause and treatment of lead poisoning, investigating live patients rather than relying on dissections at the autopsy table. The Massachusetts General Hospital saw medical research as an essential institutional goal, and Means was a strong proponent of "investigator-centered research," a conviction that research was most fruitful when a promising investigator was urged to pursue his unrestricted, individual interests.

Beyond the confluence of these favorable influences, Albright brought two additional key attributes to his work. The first was his abiding interest in human pathophysiology, the study of the mechanisms by which a healthy body becomes diseased, and the second was his willingness to engage in experiments, not only on patients but, when indicated, on human volunteers as well. Like his generation of clinical investigators, he manifested little concern for ethical niceties that loom so large in the present day. He put it bluntly: "An intelligent patient, private or otherwise, to whom you have taken the trouble to explain the nature of the investigation, makes the best laboratory animal" ("Some of the 'Do's' and 'Do-Nots' in Clinical Investigation," *Journal of Clinical Investigation* 23 [1944]: 921–26). This rough doctrine of "informed acquiescence" had merit because the modern concept of informed consent had not yet been promulgated.

Taking full advantage of the fertile setting in which he found himself, Albright embarked on an astonishingly productive career. Over a twenty-year period from 1934 to 1954 he described *de novo* or made a major contribution to the delineation of fourteen diseased states, in effect, a new disease emerging about every eighteen months.

In pursuing pathophysiological studies, Albright was preeminent in characterizing diseases of the parathyroid glands, the endocrine organs that regulate closely the level of calcium in the blood. Concurrent with these studies, he determined the cause of and offered rational treatment for a number of bone diseases including osteoporosis, a thinning of bone due to a deficiency of protein matrix. Among the disorders he described was an extraordinary disease he called, with typical whimsy, pseudohypoparathyroidism. Unlike the usual patient with hypoparathyroidism, these individuals showed no response to the administration of parathyroid hormone. Albright made the brilliant deduction that the tissues of such individuals were defective and could not respond to the hormone. This concept of "tissue resistance" was the opening wedge into the field of cell receptors, an integral construct of molecular biology.

Albright was wedded to the concept that science can make headway only when there are available some "measuring sticks," and he devised many of these with ingenuity. For example, he used, as a measure of androgen (male hormone) effect, the weighing of dried axillary hair after a local application of the hormone. Perhaps most important was his role in the development of an arduous technique known as the metabolic balance study in which the intake of food and fluids as well as the output of urine and feces of patients were carefully analyzed.

Using such techniques Albright elucidated the pathogenesis of a number of diseases of the ovaries, testes, and the adrenal cortex. In the last instance, he carried off a remarkable tour de force in defining the abnormality inherent in the disease called congenital adrenal hyperplasia, a genetic defect that results in hermaphroditism in female children and overdevelopment ("infant Hercules") in males. He adduced evidence that this disorder was due to an overproduction of an adrenocorticotrophic hormone (ACTH) of the pituitary gland, and he predicted, five years before the event, that the entire disease process would be reversed when a hormone could be found that would block the secretion of ACTH. He first administered that hormone, cortisone, to a hermaphroditic child in 1950.

Albright was a boundless source of new ideas that he felt free to disseminate, knowing full well that all of them were open to question and that many would be superseded. On occasion these hypotheses were brilliantly fulfilled. Once at a local medical conference, he suggested that a malignant tumor of the kidney was producing parathyroid hormone. This casual remark was the forerunner of a large segment of endocrinology devoted to hormone production by nonendocrine tumors.

Albright's later life was marked by tragedy. In 1936 he noted symptoms of Parkinsonism that progressed relentlessly over the years. Although his drive and creativity remained unimpaired, his speech became almost unintelligible, and he had great difficulty in controlling bodily movements. However, his disability was mitigated by the extraordinary support provided by his wife, his sons, and students and colleagues. In 1955, at his insistence, he underwent an experimental neurosurgical procedure that left him mute and mentally withdrawn for the remaining thirteen years of his life.

Quite aside from his prodigious contributions to the description and elucidation of endocrinologic diseases, Albright brought from infancy to maturity the art and science of clinical investigation. His abiding interest in pathophysiological processes provided a basis for present-day techniques indispensable for rational diagnosis and treatment not only for patients with endocrine disorders but also for human disease generally.

• Archival material relating to Albright is at the Countway Library of Medicine, Boston, Mass. Albright authored two books. The first, written with Edward Reifenstein, Jr., is the classical monograph *The Parathyroid Glands and Metabolic Bone Disease* (1946). The second, *Uncharted Seas* (1990), is a memoir written with Read Ellsworth. Published posthumously, it was edited by D. Lynn Loriaux. Lloyd Axelrod, "Bone, Stones, and Hormones," *New England Journal of Medicine* 283 (1970): 964–70, provides a short summary of Albright's life and work. A review of Albright's inimitable style, "Shaping Thought with Wit," *Harvard Medical Bulletin* (1982): 46–51, was presented by Eleanor B. Pyle. See also J. H. Means, *Ward 4: The Mallinckrodt Research Ward of the Massachusetts General Hospital* (1958); D. Lynn Loriaux, "Historical Note: Fuller Albright (1900–1969)," *Endocrinologist* 1 (1991): 212–13; and T. B. Schwartz, "Fuller Albright and His Investigatees: A Creative Collaboration," *Endocrine Practice* 1 (1995): 142–47, and "How to Learn from Patients: Fuller Albright's Exploration of Adrenocortical Function," *Annals of Internal Medicine* 123 (1995): 225–29. An informative obituary is F. Bartter, *Endocrinology* 87 (1970): 1109–12.

THEODORE B. SCHWARTZ

ALBRIGHT, Horace Marden (6 Jan. 1890–28 Mar. 1987), park service director, was born in Bishop, California, the son of George Albright, a mining engineer, and Mary Marden. He graduated from the University of California at Berkeley in 1912 with a B.A. in economics. While a law student at Berkeley, Albright worked as a reader for Professor Adolph C. Miller. In 1913, when Secretary of the Interior Franklin K. Lane selected Miller for a high post at Interior, Albright left law school and followed Miller to Washington, D.C., accepting a position as confidential clerk to the secretary of the interior. One of the duties delegated to Albright was to oversee matters for the national parks then located mostly in the West. In 1914 Albright received his LL.B. after attending night school in Washington, passed the California bar examination, and became engaged to his college sweetheart, Grace Noble, whom he married a year later. They had two children.

Also in 1914 Secretary Lane hired Stephen P. Mather, a self-made Chicago millionaire industrialist, to come to Washington to get a National Park Service Act passed by Congress, and Mather chose Albright as his assistant. Mather and Albright, working with leaders of congressional committees and park experts such as Frederick Law Olmsted, Jr., designed legislation with the dual and potentially conflicting missions of conserving national park resources while providing for their enjoyment by the public. They successfully lobbied Congress, resulting in passage of the National Park Service Act in August 1916.

At the beginning of 1917 Albright organized a national parks conference attended by congressional and national civic leaders, government officials, park superintendents, and national figures. Among them was Orville Wright, who predicted that people would soon be visiting parks by airplanes instead of horse-drawn carriages and automobiles.

When Mather suffered a nervous breakdown early in 1917 it fell to the young Albright to organize the National Park Service and run the small parks department and thirty-three park units for two years until Mather fully regained his health and returned to work. During that period Albright succeeded in getting an adequate appropriation from Congress for the parks and assembled a small staff, luring some officials away from the U.S. Geological Survey. Albright selected new superintendents for most of the parks, and his extensive annual report to Congress at the end of 1917 revealed an Albright intent on bringing historic sites and military national parks into the national park system. During World War I he succeeded in protecting the parks from natural resource developers who sought permits for logging and livestock grazing.

Using many of Mather's ideas, Albright developed a policy for national parks management and implemented it by having Secretary Lane announce the policy in a letter to Mather. The Mather-Albright management principles were that the national parks had to be maintained and protected unimpaired for the use of future generations and that the national interest should dictate all decisions concerning public or private enterprise in the parks. In addition, educational use of the parks was a high priority, private land holdings within the parks were to be eliminated through government purchase or private donation, areas adjacent to parks should be added when they would complete a park's scenic purpose, and free campsites or low-priced camps operated by concessioners should be maintained.

In 1919 Albright told Mather he planned to leave the Park Service and accept a position with a California law firm. Mather persuaded him to stay, appointing him field director of all the parks as well as the first civilian superintendent of Yellowstone National Park after the U.S. Army relinquished its management of the park.

After Mather's death late in 1928, Albright was appointed director of the National Park Service and quickly set about bringing historic sites into the national park system as well as initiating the addition of outstanding natural areas such as Grand Teton, Isle Royale, and Everglades national parks.

In 1933, while accompanying President Franklin D. Roosevelt on an auto trip to Shenandoah National Park, Albright found himself sitting directly behind the president and having Roosevelt's full attention during the long return trip to Washington. Knowing Roosevelt's deep interest in Civil War history, Albright showed the president vistas overlooking prominent battlegrounds and used the occasion to speak of the need to bring War Department parks into the national park system. At the end of the drive the president asked Albright to prepare a memo to him suggesting the transfer of Saratoga battlefield in New York and other sites to the national park system.

Roosevelt's executive order, which mandated the Park Service acquisition of thirty-three War Department historic sites and fifteen Forest Service natural areas, transformed the National Park Service from a small bureau with holdings mostly in the West into a truly national agency in charge of administering natural, historic, and archaeological sites and structures throughout the nation.

Later in 1933 Albright left the Park Service to become chief operating officer of United States Potash Company, but he continued voluntary private work in conservation for fifty more years and also served as an adviser to presidents, secretaries of the interior, and directors of the National Park Service. He died in Los Angeles.

On his departure from the National Park Service, he addressed a letter to all employees, admonishing them to be interested in the quality of park patronage, not the quantity. "We must keep elements of our crowded civilization to a minimum in our parks," Albright wrote. "We have the spirit of fighters, not as a destructive force, but as a power for good. With this spirit each of us is an integral part of the preservation of the magnificent heritage we have been given, so that centuries from now people of our world, or perhaps of other worlds, may see and understand what is unique to our earth, never changing, eternal" (*Birth of the National Park Service*, p. 311).

A tribute written to Albright by philanthropist John D. Rockefeller, Jr., stated

> The things that have been accomplished so largely through your efforts seem almost unbelievable. While relatively few people will know that it is you who have been chiefly responsible for the development of the national parks, there are hundreds and thousands, yes millions of people whose lives have been made happier, richer, better because you—their unknown friend—have opened to them nature's treasure store of beauty. This you have done at the sacrifice of your own advancement, ease, comfort, even health and other personal considerations. (Albright, pp. 311–12)

Albright's legacy to the parks continued as a granddaughter, Susan Ford Isaacson, became a National Park Service ranger and a nephew, Stanley Albright, became a park superintendent and western regional director for the National Park Service.

• There are no known repositories of Albright's personal papers. Albright left a memoir of the founding of the National Park Service, as recounted to Robert Cahn, *The Birth of the National Park Service: The Founding Years 1913–33* (1985). A useful biography is Donald C. Swain, *Wilderness Defender: Horace M. Albright and Conservation* (1970). References to Albright and his involvement with the park service appear in William C. Everhart, *The National Park Service* (1972), and Robert Shankland, *Steve Mather of the National Parks* (1951).

ROBERT CAHN

ALBRIGHT, Ivan (20 Feb. 1897–18 Nov. 1983), artist, was born in North Harvey, Illinois, the son of Adam Emory Albright, an artist, and Clara Wilson. His involvement in art began almost in infancy, as he and his identical twin brother, Malvin (who also became a professional artist), spent countless hours in early childhood posing for their father's paintings. At the age of eight the twins began to receive instruction in drawing from their father. Ivan showed considerable skill in detailed drafting, and on graduating from high school in 1915 he decided that his skills might best be put to use in architecture. Toward that end he enrolled for a year of study of architecture at Northwestern University, followed immediately by an additional year at the University of Illinois.

In 1918 Albright's study of art took a new turn, as he was drafted into the U.S. Army and served as a medical illustrator in Nantes, France. It was his unusual job to make sketches of war wounds, a practice that seems likely to have influenced the subsequent development of his art.

After the war Albright remained for a brief period in Nantes to study at the École des Beaux-Arts. Returning home in 1919, he immediately began work illustrating brain operations for a surgeon whom he had met in France. The following year he won a scholarship to study at the School of the Art Institute of Chicago. In 1923 he graduated with honors in life and portrait painting before moving on for an additional semester of art training at the Pennsylvania Academy of the Fine Arts and yet another at the National Academy of Design in New York.

Despite this extensive academic and professional preparation, Albright did not finally resolve to pursue a career as an artist until 1926. He moved the following year to Warrenville, Illinois, where he, his twin brother, and his father all set up studios in an abandoned church. In 1930 he completed *Into the World There Came a Soul Called Ida*, a painting in which most of the features characteristic of his work are prominently displayed. Albright had hired Ida Rogers, an attractive young woman of twenty, to pose for the portrait. But the finished painting depicts an aging, flabby, rather diseased-looking woman, rendered in an unsettling color scheme. Albright's virtuosity is nonetheless inescapably evident in his depiction of the woman's wrinkled flesh, in the subtle interplay of light and shadow falling upon her body, and in his precise handling of such minute details as the individual strands of hair hanging from her comb. While this painting horrified many onlookers, it also brought Albright recognition, as it won the Chicago Society of Artists' gold medal in 1931—the year of Albright's first museum exhibition, which was held at the Art Institute of Chicago.

Without ever abandoning portraiture, Albright began at this time to work on still lifes, typically depicting large and rather contrived arrangements of dozens of items, crammed closely and haphazardly together. This choice of subject matter well suited Albright's talent for rendering objects, down to the tiniest details, accurately and convincingly. More surprisingly, though these paintings typically contained very little, if any, animate matter, Albright still managed to convey through them a powerful impression of decaying flesh.

Perhaps Albright's finest painting in this genre was *That Which I Should Have Done I Did Not Do*, also known as *The Door*. He began it in 1931 and, working methodically and painstakingly, did not complete it until ten years later. It won several awards, including the Temple gold medal at the Pennsylvania Academy and the first medal at the Artists for Victory Exhibition held at the Metropolitan Museum of Art in New York. Albright himself later ranked it as his most important work.

Yet another phase of Albright's career was inaugurated in 1943, when he and his twin brother were commissioned to paint a series of portraits for the film *The Picture of Dorian Gray*. The job was tailor-made for Albright's talents, as it required the artistic depiction of the title character's moral and physical degeneration. The final portrait reportedly frequently brought horrified shrieks from movie audiences.

In 1946 Albright married Josephine Medill Patterson Reeve, the daughter of the founder of the *New York Daily News*; they had two children, and Albright also adopted his wife's children from a previous marriage.

Though Albright had by this time achieved significant success as an artist, changing fashions in the art world took him out of the limelight for several years. However, a 1964 retrospective exhibition of his work held at the Art Institute of Chicago (and at the Whitney Museum of American Art in New York the following year) was a major success, and it stimulated a renewed interest in his work. In 1965 Albright and his family moved to Woodstock, Vermont, where the artist set up his studio and continued to produce new works of art, though at his customary leisurely pace.

In 1981 Albright began a series of self-portraits. After completing eighteen of them, he suffered a stroke, but he managed to finish three more in the hospital in Woodstock before dying. These last portraits, executed when Albright was in a severely weakened condition, poignantly documented both his love of art and his fascination with death as a subject to be explored through art. In the last two portraits especially, the image of death is powerfully and inescapably present in the artist's depiction of his own face.

Albright is remembered both for his technical skill and for the uniqueness of his artistic vision. No other artist has ever pursued so relentlessly the practice of presenting people and objects in an advanced state of corruption or decrepitude. The issue of the meaning of Albright's paintings has given rise to heated debate, which Albright himself generally avoided, preferring simply to remark: "I just can't seem to paint nice things. I've tried, but it doesn't work" (Eliot, p. 248).

• The largest collection of Albright's papers is at the Ryerson and Burnham Libraries at the Art Institute of Chicago. A brief statement by Albright on his own art is included in Dorothy C. Miller and Alfred H. Barr, Jr., eds., *American Realists and Magic Realists* (1943). Albright's statement is reprinted in part in Barbara Rose, ed., *Readings in American Art 1900–1975* (1975). The most extensive and detailed monograph on Albright is Michael Croydon, *Ivan Albright* (1978). A more recent and even more comprehensive critical study is Susan F. Rossen, ed., *Ivan Albright* (1977). A brief but informative discussion of Albright's work can be found in Alexander Eliot, *Three Hundred Years of American Painting* (1957). An obituary is in the *New York Times*, 19 Nov. 1983.

DAVID DETMER

ALBRIGHT, Jacob (1 May 1759–18 May 1808), founder of the Evangelical Association, a denomination now constitutive of the United Methodist church, was born near Pottstown, Pennsylvania, in Montgomery County, the son of John Albright (German spelling Albrecht); his mother's identity is unknown. The Albrecht family were German-speaking Lutherans, and Albright was baptized and confirmed. His schooling was rudimentary. He served in the Revolution and lost a brother to the American cause. In 1785 he married Catherine Cope. They settled in Lancaster County, where Albright established a brick and tile business, a trade that he pursued even after taking up the ministry and that earned him a reputation as the "Honest Tilemaker."

The loss of several of his six children in a dysentery epidemic in 1790 led Albright in July 1791 to undergo a religious crisis, which he resolved partly with the aid of Pietists—particularly in the prayer meetings and through the counsel of a German neighbor, Adam Riegel, who was affiliated with the Pietists, just then coalescing into the German Methodism that would become known as the United Brethren. Albright also gained spiritual succor from English-speaking Methodists led by another neighbor, Isaac Davies. The conversion that he experienced drew him into the Methodist ministry.

Finding the discipline and doctrine of the Methodists congenial, Albright was licensed as an exhorter by the sect. He began itinerant preaching among Germans in 1796. Speaking wherever he could get a hearing in Lancaster, Dauphin, and Berks counties in Pennsylvania and in adjacent German areas of Virginia and Maryland, he was seen as a threat by established German denominations and aroused their opposition, even persecution. Albright nevertheless attracted converts and organized "classes," the building block of Methodism. Structuring his preaching into circuits, he brought worshipers from adjacent areas together periodically for religious festivals that among German Pietists were termed "big meetings." After he accepted a few assistants into his itinerant ministry, Albright gathered them together in 1803 as a conference; at that meeting he was ordained and elected to lead the new religious group. Later, the Evangelical Association would regard that meeting as its founding.

In 1807 the group, having elected Albright bishop, termed itself the "Newly-Formed Methodist Conference," and Albright was asked to draft the Articles of Faith and Discipline. These actions pressed the movement toward a reluctant break with established (i.e.,

English-speaking) Methodism and its declaration of being a separate denomination. Self-designations capture that hesitancy: in 1809, for instance, the conference called itself the "So-called Albright's People."

Suffering from tuberculosis and in failing health, Albright proved unable to give the movement a written creed or doctrine. He had, however, already led it to embrace Methodist discipline (law, administration, doctrine, organizational work, and procedure) and belief (e.g., entire sanctification, or Christian perfection), and others gave those commitments constitutional and creedal expression. Despite chronic sickness, Albright continued to travel. He also remained in charge of the conference, stationed the preachers (i.e., assigned them to circuits), and participated in the "big meetings." He died, on the road, at the home of a friend and associate in Kleinfeltersville, Pennsylvania.

• Albright's journal was lost, and apparently nothing else that he wrote survives. On his life, see *The Encyclopedia of World Methodism* (1974); Reuben Yeakel, *Jacob Albright and His Co-Laborers*, trans. from the German (1883); J. Bruce Behney and Paul H. Eller, *The History of the Evangelical United Brethren Church* (1979); and George Miller, *Jacob Albright*, trans. G. E. Epp (1959).

RUSSELL E. RICHEY

ALBRIGHT, William Foxwell (24 May 1891–19 Sept. 1971), biblical archaeologist, was born William Thomas Albright in Coquimbo, Chile, the son of Wilber Finley Albright and Zephine Viola Foxwell, Methodist missionaries. William and his five siblings received most of their early education from their mother. Extremely poor eyesight and a crippled right hand resulting from a farm accident curtailed William's physical activity and promoted his intellectual pursuit. At age twelve he came to Iowa and attended public school. After receiving his A.B. in 1912 from Upper Iowa University, he briefly served as the principal for a small high school in the German-speaking town of Menno, South Dakota.

In 1913 Albright moved to Baltimore, Maryland, to study at the Oriental Seminary of Johns Hopkins University under scholar Paul Haupt. At this time he also changed his middle name to Foxwell in honor of his mother. In 1916 he received his Ph.D. and remained to teach Akkadian and Arabic. With the advent of World War I, Albright was drafted in 1918 and served for a short time in the U.S. Army. In 1919 Albright went to Palestine as a Thayer fellow to pursue research at what was then the American Schools of Oriental Research (ASOR). At the end of his year of study he remained in Palestine as the acting director of the ASOR. The following year he was named its director. Albright married Ruth Norton, an expert in Sanskrit, in 1921; they had four children. He continued as the director of the ASOR until 1929, when he returned to Baltimore to become a professor of Semitic languages at Johns Hopkins University.

Beginning in 1933 Albright split his time equally between Johns Hopkins and Palestine, where he resumed his duties as the director of the ASOR. This arrangement ended in 1935, when he resigned from the ASOR to give full attention to his duties as the W. W. Spencer Chair in Semitic Languages at Johns Hopkins. Albright continued in this position until 1958, when he retired. After retiring, Albright lectured extensively and served as a visiting professor at numerous universities and seminaries.

As an Orientalist, Albright made significant contributions to a number of fields related to Near East studies, including archaeology, biblical studies, Semitic languages, and history. His leadership in Palestinian archaeology when it was still in its developmental stage earned him the informal title "dean of American biblical archaeology." He pursued archaeological fieldwork throughout the Middle East, including major excavations at Tell el-Ful and Tell Beit Mirsim. As a student he had accepted the higher critical theories taught by his mentor, Paul Haupt, but his archaeological investigations led him to reject Julius Wellhausen's theory of evolutionary development and to affirm the historical reliability of the Old Testament. This theoretical change was characteristic of Albright, who often modified his interpretations of history and religion as new evidence became available. His influence can be observed in the flexibility of modern ethnohistoriography, which attempts to marry archaeological artifacts with the ethnographic record and assumes the necessity of a new synthesis when additional data is recovered.

Albright was a humanitarian as well as a humanist. He assisted scholars fleeing Nazi persecution in finding academic positions in the United States, defended students affected by ethnic and racial quotas in educational institutions, and lobbied for equal rights for minorities.

Albright published his first scholarly article in 1913 and continued to publish throughout his busy career. From 1930 to 1968 he was the editor of the *Bulletin of the American Schools of Oriental Research*. He also served as the coeditor of the Anchor Bible. Albright was highly respected by his peers within the academic community because of his scholarly achievements and the breadth of his interests. He served as an officer of five different learned societies and actively participated in many others.

Albright received some measure of public notoriety in 1948 as a result of his role in authenticating the Dead Sea Scrolls. He was one of the first scholars to accurately date the scroll and to recognize their importance for biblical studies. A book-length bibliography of Albright's published work contains 1,083 listings. Equally impressive is the long list of Albright's students, including John Bright, Nelson Glueck, Abe Sachs, and George Ernest Wright, who have themselves become authorities within various fields of Near East studies. Many of his students adapted his methods and his systemization of Near East studies, approaches that became known as the Baltimore School. His influence continues to multiply generationally. During Albright's lifetime he received hundreds of honors and awards. In recognition of his contributions to Near East studies, the ASOR in Jerusalem was renamed the W. F. Albright Institute of Archaeological Research prior to his death in Baltimore.

• Albright's papers are at the library of the American Philosophical Society, Philadelphia, Pa., but are not currently available to researchers. He documents his work at Tell Beit Mirsim in his three-volume *The Excavation of Tell Beit Mirsim* (1932) and more briefly in the early chapters of *The Archaeology of Palestine and the Bible*, 2d ed. (1933). To explore his broad understanding of archaeology and its relation to biblical studies consult his *Archaeology and the Religion of Israel*, 3d ed. (1953). *From the Stone Age to Christianity*, rev. repr. (1957) and *Yahweh and the Gods of Canaan* (1968) lay out Albright's philosophy of Palestinian history and will be helpful for the reader interested in his opposition to the theory of unilinear evolutionary development in culture and religion. For Albright's personal reflections on his first half-century see his *History, Archaeology, and Christian Humanism* (1964), which includes an autobiographical sketch. A more extensive account of his life is David Noel Freedman and Leona Glidden Running, *William Foxwell Albright* (1975). For a critical appraisal of his work consult Gus W. Van Beek, ed., *The Scholarship of William Foxwell Albright* (1989). A complete bibliography of Albright's published works is Freedman, *The Published Works of William Foxwell Albright: A Comprehensive Bibliography* (1975). An obituary is in the *New York Times*, 20 Sept. 1971.

KEVIN E. STILLEY

ALCORN, James Lusk (4 Nov. 1816–20 Dec. 1894), governor of Mississippi and U.S. senator, was born in Golconda, Illinois, the son of James Alcorn and Hannah (maiden name unknown). Soon after his birth, Alcorn's family moved to Salem, Kentucky, where his father farmed and served as a boatman on the Ohio and Mississippi rivers. In 1836 Alcorn briefly attended Cumberland College in Princeton, Kentucky. He tried teaching in Jackson, Arkansas, but soon returned to Livingston County, Kentucky, to serve as deputy sheriff under his uncle. Alcorn also studied law and in 1838 was admitted to the Kentucky bar. In the same year he married Mary Catherine Stewart; they had four children.

After practicing law for six years in Salem, Alcorn moved his young family to Coahoma County in the rich alluvial Mississippi Delta, where he opened a law office in 1844. A fiercely competitive person with a strong interest in politics, Alcorn in 1845 was elected to the Mississippi House of Representatives as a Whig and in 1848 to the state senate, where he served until 1856, when he returned to the House. As a member of the legislature in 1850, he was a vigorous opponent of the Nashville convention that was designed to resist northern "aggression" against the South, even if it required secession. He was one of the organizers of the Union party that, in support of the Compromise of 1850, won brief control of the state in 1851.

Meanwhile, Alcorn's economic fortunes had risen. Acquiring unimproved lowland acreage, Alcorn by 1850 possessed a plantation worth $16,625 with seventeen slaves. By 1860 his property was valued at $250,000 with ninety-three slaves. His wife died in 1849, and he married Amelia Walton Glover in 1850 and built a three-story Victorian home, which he called "Mound Place." They had nine children. During the 1850s Alcorn devoted most of his time as a member of the legislature to the creation of a system of levees to protect the frequently flooded Delta counties. Due mainly to his efforts, the legislature in 1858 established the Board of Levee Commissioners, and Alcorn was chosen president. A makeshift levee was constructed, but it was washed away during the Civil War.

A partisan old Whig, Alcorn supported John Bell for president in 1860. After Abraham Lincoln won the election, Alcorn served as a Union delegate in the state convention called to debate the question of secession. When it became clear that Mississippi would leave the Union, he announced that he would vote for the secession ordinance. The convention later elected Alcorn a brigadier general to command state troops. He was denied a similar appointment in the Confederate army, however, and in January 1862, after brief service in Kentucky, he resigned and went home to spend the remainder of the war managing his plantation. He allegedly profited from the smuggling of cotton to the North.

After the war Alcorn served briefly in the state legislature which, under President Andrew Johnson's conservative plan of Reconstruction, selected Alcorn for the U.S. Senate. Congress, however, refused to seat the representatives from the former Confederate states and by early 1867 had assumed control of Reconstruction policy. Alcorn quickly adjusted to the new order of things, which included black political equality. He announced that "the colored man comes, as well as the white man within the scope" of his political thinking. "I propose to vote with him, to discuss political affairs with him, to sit if need be in political counsel with him, and from a platform acceptable alike to him, to me, and [to all citizens] to pluck our common liberty and our common prosperity out of the jaws of inevitable ruin." Alcorn admitted that such a policy was expedient to "save the people from a domestic radicalism more dangerous to both black and white than that which has triumphed in Tennessee" under William G. "Parson" Brownlow. Alcorn led in the organization of the Mississippi Republican party, and in 1869, supported overwhelmingly by black voters and a few thousand whites, he easily won the governorship.

In his inaugural address, Alcorn promised to protect black rights and to provide public education for both races. The school system that he helped establish was, however, racially segregated. His appointments to judicial positions also reflected his prejudice against not only blacks but also northern newcomers, or carpetbaggers, in the state. Most of his appointees were white southerners, usually prominent former Whigs like himself, who had resisted secession until Mississippi had left the Union. Their selection, he erroneously believed, would encourage whites to support his administration and his party. Unlike other Reconstruction governors, he warned against hasty schemes to aid economic development and reminded Mississippians that the present condition of state finances rendered inopportune "any considerable expenditure from the public treasury on internal improvements."

The greatest problem that Governor Alcorn faced was the Ku Klux Klan. Despite his administration's moderate policies, most whites remained bitterly opposed to Republican rule. Operating throughout most of Mississippi in 1870–1871, the Klan employed both intimidation and violence in an attempt to overthrow Republican rule and suppress black rights. Radical members of his party, led by U.S. senator Adelbert Ames, a carpetbagger, demanded that Alcorn seek federal intervention to put down the Klan before it engulfed the state. Alcorn, however, believed that state law enforcement resources should be fully utilized before calling on the president for federal troops. Although he had received some funds for a regular militia force, in early 1871 he asked the legislature for the authority and money to raise an elite, mobile white cavalry regiment that would be able to meet the Klan challenges wherever they might occur. Though Republicans controlled the legislature, the request was defeated by a strange combination of radicals in his party, who had no confidence in Alcorn's scheme, and conservatives, who opposed any military force controlled by "black Republicans." When terror became endemic in the South, Congress, at President Ulysses S. Grant's urging, passed legislation that suppressed the Klan by 1872 but did not end intimidation and violence against Republicans in Mississippi.

On 30 November 1871 Alcorn resigned as governor to take a seat in the U.S. Senate. His main effort in the Senate was directed toward securing federal aid for the rebuilding of the Delta levees. He failed despite almost obtaining congressional approval of a $3.4 million appropriation. When his rival Ames won the Republican nomination for governor in 1873, Alcorn returned home, bolted the regular state party, and announced that he would run as a reform Republican. Alcorn's moderate policies, designed to gain the support of conservative Democrats, who did not nominate a candidate for governor, lost him the votes of most blacks. Ames won the election by a vote of 69,870 to 50,490 for Alcorn, who only carried the predominantly white counties, where moderate Republicans and Alcorn allies controlled the local party organizations.

Alcorn continued in the Senate until March 1877. He then returned to his plantations in the Mississippi Delta, where he prospered. Though embittered by the national leadership's neglect of southern Republicans, he remained for a time loyal to the party. In 1879 President Rutherford B. Hayes briefly considered him for a cabinet position, but the post went instead to a midwesterner. In 1881 the black wing of the state Republican party, headed by John R. Lynch, offered him the nomination for governor, but Alcorn refused, explaining to a friend that he "ceased to care for the fortunes of the Republican Party."

Like many Republicans by the 1890s, Alcorn succumbed to the hardening racism of the age. In 1890 he was elected by a bipartisan vote in Coahoma County to serve as a delegate to the state constitutional convention. He supported the convention's adoption of clauses disfranchising blacks and making possible the passage of rigid segregation laws for the state. He died at "Eagle's Nest," his Delta home.

• Most of Alcorn's papers were destroyed in a fire at the home of historian John F. H. Claiborne in 1884. Claiborne's manuscript on Mississippi during the Civil War–Reconstruction era, which promised to be sympathetic to Alcorn and the state's moderate Republicans, also was destroyed. Small collections of Alcorn papers can be found in the Southern Historical Collection, University of North Carolina Library, Chapel Hill, and in the Mississippi Department of Archives and History, Jackson. The standard biography of Alcorn is Lillian A. Pereyra, *James Lusk Alcorn: Persistent Whig* (1966), although it exaggerates Alcorn's aristocratic and antidemocratic tendencies. Useful accounts of Alcorn's role in Reconstruction can be found in William C. Harris, *Presidential Reconstruction in Mississippi* (1967) and *The Day of the Carpetbagger: Republican Reconstruction in Mississippi* (1979).

WILLIAM C. HARRIS

ALCOTT, Bronson (29 Nov. 1799–4 Mar. 1888), Transcendentalist and reformer, was born Amos Bronson Alcox in Wolcott, Connecticut, the son of Joseph Chatfield Alcox and Anna Bronson, farmers. Farming the rocky Connecticut soil was not lucrative, and Alcott worked hard with his parents to help support seven younger siblings, thereby limiting his opportunities for a formal education. He attended the local district school until age ten, but thereafter his intellectual growth largely depended on his own reading and discussions with friends of a similar scholarly bent, the first being his cousin William Andrus Alcott. William later attended Yale College and established a career as a physician and popular author of health manuals, but continuing poverty prevented Bronson from obtaining a college education. At age fifteen he, like many of his young Connecticut contemporaries, began peddling small manufactured goods, first in Massachusetts and New York, then in Virginia and the Carolinas.

Several years of peddling, and a winter living with a group of North Carolina Quakers, convinced Alcott that he had no interest in the manufacture or sale of material goods nor in the industrial revolution that was uprooting the rural culture he had known. Instead, he found a growing desire to exert moral and spiritual influence over his contemporaries. His lack of an adequate formal education blocked his entrance into the ordained ministry, the traditional route to such cultural influence. Thus he began a lifelong effort to carve out a vocation outside the institutional church that would satisfy ambitions ordinarily served by the church.

Religion had exerted a powerful influence on Alcott's early life as he grew up in a Connecticut dominated by the revivalism of the Second Great Awakening. For Alcott, the revival spirit highlighted the tensions between the moral legalism of the Congregational establishment and the personal faith celebrated in John Bunyan's *Pilgrim's Progress*, and between the supernaturalism of traditional religion and the human-centered rationalism of the Scottish philosophy he read in James Burgh's *Dignity of Human Nature*. The anti-institutionalism of the Quakers he met in 1823 reinforced the doubts his own reading had raised about the efficacy of organized religion.

Beginning in 1823 Alcott initially found a vocation and an alternative religious faith in teaching. He took positions in district schools in Bristol and then in Cheshire, Connecticut. His fertile mind led him to experiment with the process of education. He abandoned corporal punishment, introduced games, storytelling, and creative writing to replace rote learning, and decorated his classroom with paintings and engravings to stimulate the children's imaginations. He found confirmation of his ideas in the *American Journal of Education* and in the educational views of European reformers such as Johann Pestalozzi and Robert Owen. Alcott quickly decided that education was the key to all human improvement and progress, whether it be moral, intellectual, or spiritual, and that he had a divine mission to promote it. The *American Journal of Education* gave him a forum to publicize his innovations, and his reading in reform literature reinforced his growing belief in the essential goodness of human nature and the infinite capacity of humans for progress. The classroom became his pulpit and reform became his theology.

The reform mission led Alcott to Boston in 1828, a fertile ground for educational experiments and a hub of many types of reforms. There he became attracted to abolitionism, pacifism, and liberal theology and in 1830 married Abigail May. In December 1830 he and Abby moved to Philadelphia, hoping to find sponsorship for experimental schools. Two such schools failed during his three years in the Philadelphia area, but he found time to read extensively on the development of the human mind and observed carefully the mental growth of his infant daughters. His obsession with the mind led him to the idealistic philosophy of Samuel Taylor Coleridge, Plato, and Immanuel Kant. By 1834 he had adopted what came to be known as Transcendentalism, a set of views that for Alcott included the Platonic concept that the physical world was but an outward symbol of an eternal spiritual essence, and an epistemology that argued that the human mind contained innate spiritual qualities that enabled it to transcend mere sense perception and to intuit eternal truths. Such ideas accorded beautifully with Alcott's faith in education and gave an even deeper religious quality to his personal mission of reform.

The Alcott family returned to Boston in the autumn of 1834, at which time Alcott established the most famous of his educational experiments, the Temple School. This school not only utilized teaching techniques that Alcott had developed earlier but also incorporated a Transcendentalist rationale that Alcott enthusiastically publicized in *Record of a School*, written by his assistant Elizabeth Peabody (1835), and *Conversations with Children on the Gospels* (1836, 1837). Human beings were born with the divine spirit within them, he argued, and it was the purpose of education or "human culture" to awaken this innate spirituality and thereby renew it and perfect it.

Alcott found reinforcement among like-minded writers and ministers such as Ralph Waldo Emerson, James Freeman Clarke, George Ripley, Frederic Henry Hedge, and Orestes Brownson, whose discussion meetings beginning in September 1836 became known as the Transcendental Club, and whose ideas convinced Alcott that the "Newness" would reshape the world. Unfortunately, the press and the established clergy panned the "conversations" and blasted Alcott for teaching heresy at the Temple School and for presuming the role of a minister. Although his Transcendentalist friends rose to Alcott's defense, enrollment at the school declined steadily and he was forced to close it in June 1838. The following year he opened a school for the poor under the patronage of some wealthy Bostonians, but that school also failed after he defied his patrons by refusing to dismiss a black student.

The loss of his schools deprived Alcott of a medium for his reformism, and he became increasingly self-righteous and bitterly angry at what he perceived to be the dogmatic intolerance of society and its institutions. Frustrated at the difficulty of relying on others to further his dreams, he retreated more and more into an extreme individualism that rejected government and organizations of any kind and asserted the sanctification of individuals as the only route to social reform. Facing destitution, Alcott and his family moved from Boston to nearby Concord in 1840, where Alcott became a subsistence farmer and day laborer.

Still interested in reform, Alcott traveled to England in the spring of 1842 to meet with correspondents who had earlier praised his educational efforts. In October he returned with renewed enthusiasm, and in June 1843 he and an English sympathizer with his ideals, Charles Lane, established Fruitlands, near Harvard, Massachusetts, where the spirit could be cultivated in isolation, untrammeled by churches, governments, and capitalistic arrangements. Unlike the congenial Transcendentalist community at Brook Farm, Alcott's utopia adopted a rigid asceticism, including an all-vegetable diet and cold water baths to cultivate the soul's purity. Few others found such self-denial attractive, and Alcott and Lane were so busy seeking converts that the hard labor of cultivating crops was left undone. The community failed after seven months, and the Alcott family was left penniless once again.

For the next fifteen years, the family struggled as Alcott continued his individualistic rebellion by refusing to take remuneration from institutions, economic or otherwise. Still searching for a vocational channel for his reformism, he turned to the public conversation, in which he adapted his Temple School teaching techniques to gatherings of adults. Conversations served two purposes for Alcott: they were an agency of reform—a way to cultivate the innate goodness in the souls of participants—and an alternative means of expression for a man whose writing style was never felicitous. He held conversations in Boston, throughout New England, and eventually in New York City, Cincinnati, and St. Louis, gaining recognition and some popularity but not enough money to support his wife and four daughters, who were forced to rely on the largess of friends and relatives for survival. Many participants praised Alcott's ability to speak beautifully on a theme such as the spiritual nature of the soul or the means of reform and to incite others to build on the theme. However, those like reformer Theodore Parker, who favored careful argument and logical analysis, found Alcott's sessions airy and insubstantial.

During the 1850s the Alcotts lived in Boston and then briefly in Walpole, New Hampshire, before returning to Concord in the autumn of 1857. By then Concordians were more accepting of reformers and iconoclasts and appointed Alcott as superintendent of schools, a position he proudly and ably held from 1859 until 1865. He introduced reforms in the classroom similar to those in his schools in Cheshire and Boston and wrote elaborate reports outlining the benefits of his changes. The position paid little but gave him recognition as an authority on education and a means of furthering his personal mission of reform. Meanwhile, the coming of the Civil War engaged his longtime abolitionist sympathies, as it did his fellow Transcendentalist Concordians Emerson and Henry David Thoreau. The onetime nonresistant praised John Brown (1800–1859) and his bloody raid and expressed regret that his age prevented his joining the march to war.

The postwar years brought success and respectability to Alcott and his family. Daughter Louisa May Alcott's books (including *Little Women*, 1868) brought financial security and helped in the publication of his own books (*Tablets*, 1868; *Concord Days*, 1872; and *Table Talk*, 1877). Between 1867 and 1882 Alcott made several westward journeys, some lasting six months or more and extending as far as central Iowa. His conversational style and his philosophical idealism were well received in the West, reinforcing his self-styled vocation as an apostle of culture and a traveling minister of reform and spirituality. His income also grew, allowing him to contribute to the family's support for the first time in decades.

The end of Alcott's career brought conflicting ideas. When he began his postwar western tours, he intended to speak once again for liberal religion and reform. He proclaimed the arrival of a new church that would shed dogma, outworn traditions, and sectarian jealousies in favor of free expression, intellectual openness, and an emphasis on personal spirituality. At first he praised the left-wing Unitarian movement called "free religion," founded by young ministers who claimed descent from Transcendentalism. But free religion, with its celebration of the scientific method and a religion of ethics, questioned any supernatural or mysterious grounds for religiosity. Faced with the logical dangers of his own religious iconoclasm, Alcott retreated to a defense of supernaturalism and increasingly found a haven in orthodox congregations and in some of the traditions that he had long abhorred. On his western travels, he increasingly combated Darwinism and religious skepticism. Concerned more and more with social stability and propriety, he spoke less of individual freedoms and rights and more of the dangers of alcohol abuse and sexual misconduct.

In 1879 Alcott and his friends in Western Platonism and Eastern Transcendentalism established the School of Philosophy and Literature at Alcott's home in Concord. The school operated with relative success each summer, even after Alcott was rendered inactive by a stroke in October 1882. The school became a monument to Alcott's self-styled career, but ironically it was also perceived by the press and participants as a bulwark against atheism and materialism, not as a hallmark of free thought and reform. The school closed shortly after Alcott died in Concord.

• The Houghton Library, Harvard University, holds most of Alcott's manuscript materials, including correspondence, scrapbooks, and the fifty-four volumes of the journal that Alcott steadfastly maintained from 1826 until 1882. Others of his published works include "Orphic Sayings" (*The Dial*, 1840), his oftentimes murky attempt to express the revelation of the spirit in verse; *Sonnets and Canzonets* (1882), a lyrical memoir of his wife and prominent friends and colleagues; and *New Connecticut* (1887), an autobiographical poem. Alcott's significant writings on education are found in *Essays on Education*, ed. Walter Harding (1960). For a comprehensive account of his life and thought, see Frederick C. Dahlstrand, *Amos Bronson Alcott: An Intellectual Biography* (1982).

FREDERICK C. DAHLSTRAND

ALCOTT, Louisa May (29 Nov. 1832–6 Mar. 1888), author, was born in Germantown, Pennsylvania, the daughter of Amos Bronson Alcott, an educator and philosopher, and Abigail May, the energetic, philanthropic daughter of a prominent liberal Boston family. Louisa grew up in Concord and Boston, suffering from poverty as a result of her selfish idealist father's inability to support his family. Bronson Alcott habitually sacrificed his wife and daughters by refusing to compromise with a venal world, most conspicuously when he subjected them to an experiment in ascetic communal living at Fruitlands farm in 1843. However, the Alcotts' intellectual environment was rich and stimulating: Louisa's parents assiduously encouraged her writing, and their friends included leaders in abolition and women's rights, including the Transcendental philosophers Ralph Waldo Emerson, Margaret Fuller, and Henry David Thoreau. Louisa took nature walks with Thoreau and had the run of Emerson's library.

By the time she had reached her teens, she felt a responsibility to help her mother and older sister provide for the family. She taught, sewed, worked as a domestic and a companion, and wrote fairy tales and romantic thrillers. When the Civil War broke out, she was eager to participate, animated by her dislike of female passivity as well as her hatred of slavery. She enlisted as a nurse and served for three weeks in an army hospital in Washington, D.C., until she contracted typhoid fever. She was treated with mercury, which permanently undermined her health. The experience did, however, provide material for her *Hospital Sketches* (1863), which vividly combines heartbreaking pathos in the death of a gentle, stoical blacksmith, indignation at (male) official callousness and mismanagement, and humorous self-portrayal as the warmhearted, hot-tempered, down-to-earth Nurse Tribulation Periwinkle. In that year, she proudly recorded in her journal, she earned almost $600 "by my writing alone," of which she "spent less than a hundred" for herself (Jan. 1864). From then on, she provided the major financial support for her family, while remaining obligated to help them with the heavy housework and nurse them when ill. She never married.

Alcott's most profitable writings at this time were sensational stories, published pseudonymously under the names Flora Fairfield and A. M. Bernard (and later denounced in *Little Women* by Professor Bhaer). These tightly plotted tales are astoundingly different from the juvenile fiction for which she is famous: typically centering on impressive angry women, they are filled with lawless passions and sensuous thrills and free of overt moralizing. The best, *Behind a Mask; or, A Woman's Power* (1866), features Jean Muir, a seemingly meek governess who brilliantly manipulates the complacent rich family she works for and ultimately triumphs by marrying its head. Meanwhile, Alcott was working on her first serious novel, *Moods,* in whose heroine, Sylvia Yule, she examines her own struggles with uncontrollable emotions and dissatisfaction with the conventional female role. Sylvia, a bright, spirited eighteen-year-old, unwisely consents to marry a man she merely likes and respects, while in fact she loves another man, an austere idealist modeled on Thoreau. The novel is Romantic in its insistence that a marriage based on anything other than intense love violates "the duty we owe ourselves" (p. 108) and that "unmated pairs" should separate rather than "trying to live their lie decorously to the end" (letter to Moncure Conway, 18 Feb. 1865). Published in 1864, the book got mixed but generally disappointing reviews; Alcott published a rewritten version in 1882.

When a publisher approached her to do a girls' book, she accepted the offer only because she needed money. The result was *Little Women* (1868; second part, 1869), one of the bestsellers of all time. Within four years it had sold 82,000 copies. The Marches are an idealized re-creation of her own family, with Bronson kept discreetly offstage: Abba May appears as warm, capable Marmee, who keeps the family together; Louisa as the hot-tempered writer Jo; and her sisters as well-conducted Meg, saintly Beth, and selfish Amy. (Abbie May, the youngest Alcott sister, was the only one who consistently asserted her wishes, an attitude Louisa sometimes resented and sometimes vicariously enjoyed.) Through fresh and honest observation, Alcott re-creates female adolescent experience that we recognize as authentic even today and makes it interesting and significant. She successfully turns into adventures such ordinary events as playacting, humiliations at school, laziness about doing minor housework, and misery resulting from a rather flat nose or tasteless clothes. She exposes the irritations of family life, as when Jo's ostentatiously boyish manners clash with Amy's affected elegance; but she also affirms its joys and consolations, as the Marches reliably support each other under setbacks from the outside world and make "a jubilee of every little household joy." The girls' moral struggles to overcome small selfish longings and to reconcile self-realization with duty to others are made significant without being inflated. The conflict is most acute for Jo, who must control her passionate temper to fit Marmee's ideal of self-repression and subdue her masculine tastes, talents, and ambitions to fit society's restrictive concept of feminine propriety. Jo's problem is dramatized hilariously in "Calls" (ch. 29), where Amy manipulates her into making the formal calls that were required of nineteenth-century ladies and vainly attempts to render her properly innocuous; while we sympathize with Jo's rational rebellion against a meaningless social ritual, we also understand Amy's exasperation at her provoking contrariness and deplore Jo's self-indulgent folly when she throws away her only chance to go to Europe by gratuitously antagonizing her aunts. As a sympathetic heroine who protests against the pressure on girls to be tactful, pleasing, and conformist, to care for dress and long for marriage as the culmination of their lives, Jo was (and is) an exhilarating model to female adolescents. And, although the book makes clear that Jo must learn to curb her impulses, it endorses her protest against reducing women to a narrow sexual-domestic role. The March girls pursue their artistic interests, struggle to correct their faults, enjoy their comradeship; they do not live to settle their destiny by marriage. Alcott pointedly refused to let Jo's friendship with Laurie develop into a conventional romance.

Most of Alcott's later books capitalized on the success of *Little Women:* they are stories about and for young people, tracing their development toward maturity and contrasting good, enlightened ways of child rearing with worldly, unnecessarily restrictive, insufficiently moral ones. *Little Men* (1871) and *Jo's Boys* (1886) continue the story of the March family. In *Little Men,* Jo and her husband preside over Plumfield, a utopian school inspired by Bronson Alcott's progressive Temple School. Jo, still a nonconformist, has become a benevolent matriarch, a broader-minded version of Marmee. In *Jo's Boys,* Plumfield has become an enlightened coeducational college, contrasting favorably with hidebound Harvard. Although constantly enlivened by humor and knowledge of young people, these books become less interesting as Alcott goes further from the authenticity of her own experience and increasingly subordinates realistic portrayal to moral teaching. Alcott herself felt the constrictions of writing the proper juvenile fiction her public demanded: near the end of her life, she made her alter ego Jo describe herself as "a literary nursery-maid who provides moral pap for the young" and acknowledged a temptation to conclude the chronicle of the March family "with an earthquake which should engulf Plumfield."

She did publish two additional adult novels. *Work: A Story of Experience* (1873) opens with Christie Devon's Declaration of Independence, her resolution to go out into the world and make her own living. Like Alcott herself, Christie progresses through most of the jobs open to women: in the first, as a maid, she works alongside a heroic black cook and demonstrates her author's admirably enlightened ideas on racial equality (which unfortunately coexisted with bigoted scorn for Irish Americans). In the end, after surmounting a crisis of suicidal loneliness, Christie becomes a leader of women workers, effective because she has been one herself, and the center of a sisterhood drawn from all ages, classes, and races. In 1877 Alcott took advantage of her publisher's "No Name Series" of anonymous novels to produce *A Modern Mephistopheles,* an absorbing tale of a young poet who sells himself for literary fame to an invalid whose only pleasure is controlling others by manipulating their passions. (It has been suggested that she was expressing her own feeling that she had sold out her talent for financial success.)

Once the cause of abolition had been won, Alcott zealously campaigned for women's rights. After 1870 she regularly contributed to the feminist *Woman's Journal* and signed her letters "Yours for Reform." She and her mother both signed a woman suffrage petition on the occasion of the national centennial in 1875, and she vigorously urged the women of Concord to use their new opportunity when they got the right to vote in school committee elections (1879). Even in her juvenile fiction, from *Little Women* on, she constantly preached the right of girls to develop their talents and pursue careers outside of marriage. Jo admits Naughty Nan to her boys' school, and in *Jo's Boys* Nan becomes a fine physician, as well as an ardent suffragist, and resolutely resists marriage. Alcott repeatedly portrayed groups of contentedly self-sufficient women, such as the young comrades in *An Old-Fashioned Girl* (1870), who support themselves in careers that interest them, each cherishing "a purpose, which seemed to ennoble her womanhood." Alcott's newspaper essay "Happy Women" (1868) describes four of her contemporaries who have found fulfillment without marriage, for whom "liberty is a better husband than love." "Transcendental Wild Oats," a hilarious and devastating exposé of her father's experiment at Fruitlands (published in the *Woman's Journal* [1874]), displays self-righteous men sacrificing women to their abstract ideals. In her unfinished novel, *Diana and Persis,* Alcott contrasts the life of a gifted woman artist who remains celibate with one who becomes a wife and mother.

Throughout her career, Alcott struggled to reconcile her Transcendentalist conviction that individuals must think independently and be true to themselves ("every soul has its own life to live and cannot hastily ignore its duties to itself without bitter suffering and loss" [*Diana and Persis*]) with the morality of submission, self-control, and self-sacrifice in which her parents trained her, a morality that was enjoined particularly on women. She sometimes evaded the conflict by preaching the supreme value of womanly, especially maternal, love, in accordance with the contemporary cult of true womanhood. She tried to resolve it by claiming that independence was compatible with traditional womanliness, that a woman can happily divide her energies among ballot box, "needle, pen, palette and broom" (*An Old-Fashioned Girl*), and even by insisting that self-denial deepens and authenticates (women's) artistic achievement. However, her assertions are less persuasive than her characters who rebel against conventionally defined female goodness—angular young Jo March, who cannot be a "little woman" and is infinitely more engaging as a tomboy, and Jean Muir, who assumes the feminine role prescribed by society only to defeat that society. Jo is a self-portrait, and Jean suggests the revealing wish fulfillment of a dutiful daughter who bitterly resents her role and consequently nurses "bad" feelings under her "good" exterior (Saxton, in Stern [1984], 257). Alcott, however, did not let her resentment surface in behavior: she constantly sacrificed her personal comfort and the artistic quality of her works to the demands of her family. She "plunged into a vortex" to write *Work* but had to stop to nurse her sister Anna through pneumonia; when she finished the book, it was "Not what it should be,—too many interruptions. Should like to do one book in peace, and see if it wouldn't be good" (*Journals,* Nov. 1872, Feb.–Mar. 1873). When her father was dying, she regularly dragged herself out to see him, although very ill herself; two days after his death, free at last of family obligations, she died in Boston.

Alcott will always be remembered for *Little Women,* the classic American story of girls growing up. In her own time, it established her reputation as a purveyor of perceptive and sympathetic, but always morally uplifting, literature for young people. The subversive, feminist element in her books has only recently been clearly recognized. We now see not so much "the Children's Friend" as a deeply conflicted woman whose work richly expresses the tensions of female lives in nineteenth-century America.

• The chief collections of Alcott manuscripts are in the Houghton Library at Harvard, the Concord Public Library, the Louisa May Alcott Association in Concord, the New-York Historical Society, the New York Public Library, and the Fruitlands restoration at Harvard, Mass. The most noteworthy of Alcott's 270 published works, other than those already mentioned, are "The Rival Prima Donnas" (1854), *Flower Fables* (1855), "Love and Self-Love" (1860), "Pauline's Passion and Punishment" (1863), "My Contraband" (1863), *Aunt Jo's Scrap-Bag* (1872), *Shawl-Straps* (1872), *Eight Cousins; or, The Aunt-Hill* (1875), *Rose in Bloom* (1876), *Under the Lilacs* (1878), *Jack and Jill: A Village Story* (1880), *Proverb Stories* (1882), and *Lulu's Library* (1886–1889). For biography, see Madelon Bedell, *The Alcotts: Biography of a Family* (1980); Joel Myerson and Daniel Shealy's editions of the *Selected Letters of Louisa May Alcott* (1987) and the *Journals of Louisa May Alcott* (1989); Madeleine Stern, *Louisa May Alcott* (1950); and Martha Saxton, *Louisa May: A Mod-*

ern Biography of Louisa May Alcott (1977). For discussion of Alcott's works, see introductions to modern editions of her fiction: Ann Douglas's and Elaine Showalter's to *Little Women* (1983, 1989); Sarah Elbert's to *Moods* (1991) and *Work* (1977); Madeleine Stern's to *Behind a Mask* (1975) and *Plots and Counterplots* (1976); and Elaine Showalter's to *Alternative Alcott* (1988). See also Nina Auerbach, *Communities of Women* (1978); Nina Baym, *Woman's Fiction: A Guide to Novels by and about Women in America* (1978); and Madeleine Stern's excellent anthology, *Critical Essays on Louisa May Alcott* (1984).

KATHARINE M. ROGERS

ALDA, Robert (26 Feb. 1914–3 May 1986), stage, motion picture, and television actor, was born Alphonso Giuseppe Giovanni Roberto d'Abruzzo in New York City, the son of Alphonso d'Abruzzo, a barber, and Frances Tumillo. After an education at the New York University Architectural School, Alda was employed as an architectural draftsman in New York from 1928 to 1931. Since he possessed an excellent singing talent, he gravitated to the stage, touring in burlesque shows such as *Charlie Ahearn and His Millionaires* (1933). As he continued in this form of popular theater, he also appeared in a number of summer stock shows from 1935 to 1940 in the Catskills. Among these were a number of famous plays of the period: *Golden Boy*, *Of Mice and Men*, *Three Men on a Horse*, *Waiting for Lefty*, *Room Service*, and *Tobacco Road*. He developed a stage name by using the first two letters of Alphonso and d'Abruzzo for his surname and by Anglicizing Roberto for his first name. In burlesque Alda played straight man and singer with Bud Abbott and Lou Costello, Rags Ragland, and Phil Silvers. Evidently he was versatile enough, as reported in the *New York Times* obituary (5 May 1986), to "portray drunks, derelicts, and juveniles" in his vaudeville period.

When Alda moved from the art of architecture to the art of burlesque, he married a New York beauty queen, Joan Browne, in 1932. They had a son, Alan, who became known for his portrait of Hawkeye Pierce in the long-playing television series "M*A*S*H," and would become as famous as his father in motion pictures. Alda's marriage to Browne ended in 1955, and in 1956 he married Flora Marino, with whom he had one son, Robert.

Alda's debut in dramatic films provided him with a leading role as the famous American composer George Gershwin in a picture titled *Rhapsody in Blue* (1945). Warner Brothers wanted the portrait of Gershwin to be portrayed by an unknown actor because the studio believed that preconceived audience views on the previous roles and personality of a star would detract from the depiction of the composer. Contemporary critics were not impressed by the stage actor's initial efforts in film. *New York Times* critic Bosley Crowther found Alda's performance wooden: "Alda plays Mr. Gershwin in an opaque, mechanical way which gives little intelligence of the character—and not much more of the way he really looks." The fledgling movie actor was chosen for an idealistic, reserved portrayal that often diminished the truthfulness of film biographies of that period. Crowther realized the shortcoming of the script in that time when a different lifestyle was whitewashed. The critic alluded to Gershwin's alleged closeted homosexuality when he stated that there were two women "who he presumably loved" (*New York Times*, 28 June 1945). Given a historical perspective, *Rhapsody in Blue* was a better total work and the skill of the lead-portrayal much stronger than contemporary critics acknowledged. Alda showed his mettle with the two works that followed the next year.

The Beast with Five Fingers and *The Man I Love* indicated the range of his suave, Latin portraits. He played a sympathetic, clever lover in the former film and a womanizing, shady nightclub owner in the latter. Under the direction of Raoul Walsh for *The Man I Love*, Alda proved he could give some dimension to a role that might merely have been interpreted as that of a melodramatic villain; instead, he underplayed the role with finesse. These two major roles indicated the variety of his acting skills but did not show how artfully he could handle comedy.

Alda's movie career faded in Hollywood as he was cast in less significant roles. However, his appearance in Italian plays and films in the 1950s offered him renewed recognition. Alda received a Golden Wing Award for the play *La Padrona di Raggio di Luna* in 1956. That same year the film *La Donna Piú Bella del Mondo* arrived in the United States in a dubbed version titled *Beautiful but Dangerous*. The American-born actor played a cad musical conductor who attempted to win the affections of "the most beautiful woman in the world," played by Gina Lollobrigida.

By far the most acclaim came to Alda before he began his career in Italy. His return to the stage in New York, when he portrayed the important character Sky Masterson in the 1946 hit musical *Guys and Dolls*, won him the most awards of his career. For his enactment of a slick gambler who took a bet that he could win the affection of a Salvation Army woman, the actor won the Tony, Donaldson, and Dramatic Circle awards. Brooks Atkinson lauded the musical for its fresh approach from the usual sentimental story line, and he praised Alda's portrayal in particular, noting, "the tall, dark and handsome gambler . . . keeps the romance enjoyable, tough and surly" (*New York Times*, 25 Nov. 1950).

The career of the New York–born actor progressed from vaudeville, to summer stock, Hollywood and Italian movies, and back to the stage while also proving he was an eclectic entertainer in television. Alda started early on the small screen when he appeared in a 1937 experimental variety show, "Alda and Henry." For over three decades, the 1950s through the 1970s, he appeared as a host for game shows, a performer in soap opera series, a guest in variety shows and in dramatic series, and an actor in three made-for-television feature-length movies. Examples of his role as emcee for game shows in the 1950s include "By Popular Demand," "Can Do," "Personality Puzzle," and "What's Your Bid?" These were half-hour, once-a-week presentations that lasted only from three to six months in a decade deluged with game shows. A more successful venture in the 1950s featured Alda in twenty-six episodes of an intrigue series, "Secret File, U.S.A.," in which he enacted the role of Major Bill Morgan, an American espionage agent. Besides many guest spots on such well-known comedy and dramatic series as "The Milton Berle Show" (1950 and 1951), "The Merv Griffin Show" (1965), "Your Story Theatre" (1951), "Ironsides" (1967, 1968, and 1969), and "Here's Lucy" (1970 and 1971), Alda appeared in two soap operas, "Love of Life" and "The Secret Storm." Of his three credits in made-for-television features during the 1970s and 1980s, the best film, *Perfect Gentleman*, which was broadcast on 14 March 1978, teamed him with Lauren Bacall, Sandy Dennis, and Ruth Gordon.

Alda left a legacy to stage, film, and TV in the person of his son Alan. He taught his son vaudeville comic skills when he was only a boy. At the Hollywood Canteen in the 1940s, Robert played Abbott to Alan's Costello, executing the famous "Who's on First?" for military personnel. The son also appeared with his father in summer stock in such comedy stage plays as *Three Men on a Horse*, *Luv*, and *Come Blow Your Horn*.

When Alda died, in Los Angeles, the *New York Times* headed its tribute to the actor by singling out two of his most famous portraits, Sky Masterson in *Guys and Dolls* and George Gershwin in *Rhapsody in Blue*. Both roles focused on music, reflecting the skill that launched Alda's stage career.

• Alda's relationship to other film actors is revealed in James Robert Parish and William T. Leonard, *Hollywood Players, The Forties* (1975). An extensive account of the actor's credits in each medium is given in editor Raymond McGill's *Notable Names in the American Theatre* (1976). Alda collaborated with Flora Marino in writing the book *99 Ways to Cook Pasta* (1980). There are two recordings of Broadway musicals featuring the actor, Decca DL-9023 *Guys and Dolls*, and Columbia KOL-6040 *What Makes Sammy Run?*

DONALD W. MCCAFFREY

ALDEN, Henry Mills (11 Nov. 1836–7 Oct. 1919), editor and author, was born in Mount Tabor, Vermont, the son of Ira Alden, a farmer, and Elizabeth Packard Moore. Alden grew up in a working-class family in rural Vermont and in the manufacturing town of Hoosick, New York, where he worked from dawn until eight o'clock at night as a "bobbin boy" in a cotton factory. With only a sporadic common school education, Alden, at the age of fourteen, decided to prepare for college by entering Ball Seminary, where he performed chores to pay for his tuition. In 1852 Alden graduated valedictorian from Ball Seminary and entered Williams College the next year.

At Williams Alden's introspection and diligent study habits earned him the nickname "Metaphysics" from fellow students, among them, James Garfield, Horace Scudder, and Washington Gladden. Alden graduated from Williams College in 1857, having supported himself by teaching in the winter at various schools in Vermont and New York and working at an assortment of summer jobs. The same year, Alden entered Andover Theological Seminary to satisfy his mother's desire that he become a member of the clergy and his own desire to study Andover's voluminous classical library. A poem Alden wrote while at Andover, "The Ancient Lady of Sorrows," attracted the attention of Harriet Beecher Stowe, the wife of faculty member Calvin Stowe. Through her auspices, two articles Alden had penned on the "Eleusinian Mysteries," were published by James Russell Lowell in the *Atlantic Monthly*. By the time he graduated from Andover in 1860, Alden was contemplating a literary rather than an ecclesiastical career. Alden served as a substitute minister at various churches but proved ill-suited for the pulpit and gained more satisfaction by writing about ancient Greek culture.

When the Civil War began, Alden was rejected for military service because of a weak heart but found work as a teacher of history and literature. In New York City he continued to pursue his own literary interests by writing occasional editorials for the *New York Times* and the *New York Evening Post*. During the summer of 1861, Alden married a young woman whom he had met at Andover, Susan Frye Foster. The couple had four children. Five years after Foster's death in 1895, Alden married Ada Foster Murray, a Virginia poet; they did not have children.

In 1862 a minor literary commission led to a major turning point in Alden's life. Harper and Brothers, one of America's leading publishing houses, released his annotated guidebook on the Central Railroad of New Jersey. Pleased with his work, the firm hired Alden the next year for its editorial staff. For the next fifty-six years, he would have no other employer. His first assignment was to collaborate with Dr. A. H. Guernsey to author *Harper's Pictorial History of the Rebellion* (1868), in addition to reading manuscripts submitted to *Harper's*.

Meanwhile, James T. Fields, the Boston Publisher and editor of the *Atlantic Monthly*, had expressed an interest in several articles on Greek culture that Alden had submitted for publication. Fields showed the essays to Lowell, Ralph Waldo Emerson, and Wendell Phillips, all of whom were impressed. Although the articles were not published in the *Atlantic* because of their narrow appeal, Fields enticed Alden to present the material at the Lowell Institute in Boston. The twelve lectures, titled "The Structure of Paganism," were delivered in the winter of 1863–1864.

Alden was appointed managing editor of *Harper's Weekly* in 1863, serving in that capacity until 1869, when he became editor of that national newspaper's sister publication, *Harper's New Monthly Magazine* (which officially changed its name to *Harper's Monthly Magazine* in 1900). Both publications were a combination of news reports and literary prose and poetry, with the *Weekly* focusing more on the former and the *Monthly* emphasizing the latter.

The mid-nineteenth century had ushered in a new era in magazine publishing. Most American magazines published in the period before 1865 were tailored to a special audience and generated only local or sectional appeal and circulation. The goal of the editorial policy that guided *Harper's Monthly*, however, was to reach a general audience by publishing what the average American would find intelligible, interesting, and useful. *Harper's Monthly* was also one of the few journals that had a genuine national circulation that included pioneer regions.

As editor, Alden selected articles for publication, wrote illustration captions, and managed daily office affairs, but Fletcher Harper made the editorial policy decisions that determined the magazine's profile. Alden gained editorial freedom upon Harper's retirement in 1875; under his direction, circulation climbed to 200,000 nationwide by 1885 and attracted 35,000 subscribers in Great Britain who found the magazine's articles on world affairs captivating and insightful. This following made *Harper's Monthly* the highest circulating publication of its kind in the United States.

Alden viewed periodicals as vehicles that could democratize literary access and elevate literary standards. He sought to showcase new American literary talents and cultivate Americans' literary tastes, while working within the confines of a general interest, family magazine as defined by the Harper vision. Alden believed that the impact of periodical literature on cultural and social development was unique in the American experience; something not shared by any other national group. By virtue of its accessibility in every region and recess of American settlement, periodical literature allowed Americans to read current novels, an opportunity that book distribution limited to the city dweller. In the modern history of periodical publishing, Alden remarked, magazine and general literature had often shared parallel development, with changes in literary form and perspective first appearing in the periodical. This greatly raised the dignity of periodical literature, which Alden considered to be the most interesting and pertinent form in literary history.

Alden's populist sentiments can also be seen in his advocacy of what he termed the "new realism" in literature. He believed that the public could best be informed and entertained through storytelling, and he chose writers with such talent. Alden exalted realistic fiction because he thought it best reflected the complexity of modern life. Instead of artificial or sentimental didactic tales, writers should represent "the common and homely things" and present the world as it was—an admixture of both good and evil (Alden, *Magazine Writing and the New Literature*, p. 148). Given Alden's enthusiasm for literary realism, he considered the popular illustrated magazine to be the real encyclopedia of American life.

Yet this diffusion of literature and elevation of literary taste was to be elite led. The new era in journalism saw the rise of editors like Alden who aimed not merely to present the news or to defend partisan positions, but rather to lead their audience—culturally, politically, and morally—to what the editors believed was a higher civilization. These editors were part of the new knowledge elite—editors, writers, professors, and other professionals—who were fully cognizant of their potential for shaping American discourse and the nation's political and cultural development. The outcome of all civilization, Alden concluded, was a "natural and therefore tolerable aristocracy" (Alden, p. 261). These editors and writers of the "new realism" were the truth tellers who would become the masters of society.

Like many late nineteenth and early twentieth-century intellectuals, Alden's worldview was influenced by dramatic revelations from the domain of natural science. He rejected the mechanistic Newtonian perspective of the Enlightenment rationalists for the organic, dynamic model of Darwin's unplanned, evolutionary universe. Science applied to imaginative literature, historical interpretation, and cultural criticism would bring forth a more realistic view of the world. Science would enlarge and emancipate the imagination and creative process.

Alden did not lose his religious faith, however, as other intellectuals of his time had when faced with the challenges presented by modern science. Alden's moral idealism and vague but deeply felt religiosity pervaded his writings throughout his life. In 1890 he anonymously published *God in His World: An Interpretation*, which impressed a number of religious thinkers and, within a year, went through four printings. A second philosophical treatise, *A Study of Death* was published in 1895, the year of his first wife's death. The book was a critical, but not a popular, success.

Alden valued urban qualities and life over rural culture, claiming that " . . . the salvation of the country has all along been the accession of urban influences" (Alden, p. 261). The advancement of science and urbanism was helping to break down the isolation of a rural society. Alden pointed out that there had been more material progress since the 1860s than in the entire history of the English race. He was convinced that the literature in periodicals was generating a new stage in world history, which he called the "psychical" age—an age of the psyche, the soul, and the mind. He perceived a revolution occurring in the transformation of human nature that would bring about peace and the abolition of poverty and would witness the greatest literature ever written.

Alden died in New York City. He was a behind-the-scenes manager and less well known to the public than other editors. Yet Alden was one of the most successful and influential editors at a time when periodical literature was perhaps more pervasive and powerful in the national culture than at any other time in American history.

• Alden's correspondence can be located in a number of repositories, including the William Dean Howells Papers at the University of Rochester; the Howells papers, Thomas Bailey Aldrich Papers, and James Parton Papers, all at the Houghton Library of Harvard University; the Walt Whitman Papers, the Richard Harding Davis Papers, and the Abbie Farwell Brown Papers (part of the Clifton Waller Barrett Library), all at the University of Virginia; the Titus Munson

Coan Papers and the Andrew Carpenter Wheeler Papers, both part of the New York Historical Society collections; the Lassiter family papers (Daniel William, Francis Rives, and Charles Trotter Lassiter) at Duke University; the Lafcadio Hearn Papers at Henry E. Huntington Library; the Mary Eleanor Wilkins Freeman Papers at Columbia University; and the manuscript collection at the American Academy of Arts and Letters Library.

An understanding of Alden's view of the important role magazine literature plays in literary and cultural development as well as insights into his general philosophy can be gained by reading his *Magazine Writing and the New Literature* (1908). An essay by Alden can be found in *In After Days: Thoughts on the Future Life* (1910). Alden collaborated with William Dean Howells to edit a number of books, including *The Heart of Childhood* (1906); *Quaint Courtships* (1906); *Their Husbands' Wives* (1906); *Under the Sunset* (1906); *Different Girls* (1906); *Life at High Tide* (1907); *Shapes That Haunt the Dusk* (1907); and *Southern Lights and Shadows* (1907). Valuable information on Alden and *Harper's Monthly* can be gleaned from Eugene Exman's *The House of Harper: One Hundred Fifty Years of Publishing* (1967); J. Henry Harper, *The House of Harper* (1912); and Frank Luther Mott, *A History of American Magazines* (5 vols., 1930–1968). An obituary written by Alden's close friend and colleague, William Dean Howells, is in *Harper's Monthly Magazine* 140 (Dec. 1919): 133–36.

ROBERT C. KENNEDY

ALDEN, James (31 Mar. 1810–6 Feb. 1877), naval officer, was born in Portland, Maine (then part of Massachusetts), the son of James Alden, a ship owner, and Elizabeth Tate. Nothing is known of his early life or education, and no information is available about his marriage or children, if any.

Alden followed his family's seafaring tradition by joining the U.S. Navy in April 1828 as a midshipman. After two years at the Boston Navy Yard, Alden cruised aboard the sloop of war *Concord* in the Mediterranean (1830–1833). He served at the Norfolk Navy Yard (1833–1834), was promoted to passed midshipman (1834), and served again at the Boston Navy Yard (1834–1835, 1836). Alden joined the U.S. Exploring Expedition (Wilkes expedition, 1838–1842) to the Pacific, the first such scientific expedition financed by the U.S. government. He served initially aboard the flagship *Vincennes* and during the cruise was promoted to lieutenant and became executive officer of the brig *Porpoise* (1841).

Alden clashed several times with the expedition's erratic and authoritarian commander, Lieutenant Charles Wilkes. Wilkes insisted that on the morning of 19 January 1840 off Antarctica, Alden sighted land, although Alden had made no journal notation, and Wilkes did not acknowledge the sighting until after learning that a competing French expedition had sighted land that afternoon. Alden initially claimed no recollection of sighting land; later he changed his mind. The discrepancy between Wilkes and Alden has never been reconciled.

At Malolo Island, Fiji Islands (July 1840), a surveying party under Alden's command precipitated a melee, in which a chief's son was taken hostage and then shot on Alden's orders while trying to escape. In turn, islanders killed two in the surveying party. Alden and his crew then recovered the bodies and destroyed the native villages. Wilkes (uncle of one of the dead Americans) called the incident avoidable, the landing unnecessary, and Alden cowardly for sending junior officers ashore while remaining aboard the *Porpoise*.

At one point Wilkes temporarily suspended Alden, and he later asserted that Alden and other officers wanted to see the expedition fail. Wilkes afterward described Alden as one of "the most deceitful and sneaking characters I had to deal with" and as one of the "busy bodies . . . who fomented discord among some of the junior officers" (*Autobiography of Wilkes*, pp. 442, 434). Alden and other officers faulted Wilkes for delaying their return with an unimportant detour to Rio and unnecessary scientific observations while the flagship proceeded home to New York. Wilkes was court-martialed for his behavior during the expedition, and many officers, including Alden, testified against him. In 1847 Alden and twelve other officers petitioned Congress to expurgate future editions of Wilkes's five-volume *Narrative* (1844) because of its critical comments about some of them. The petition was apparently unsuccessful.

After duty at the Boston Navy Yard (1843–1844), Alden took his second world cruise—to East Indian waters aboard the *Constitution* (1844–1846). During a period of general civil strife, in Zuron Bay, Cochin China (today southern Vietnam), Alden commanded a campaign that cut out several war junks from the protection of the guns of the fort. Alden served in the Home Squadron (1846–1847) during the Mexican War, participating in the capture of Veracruz, Tuxpan, and Tabasco (1846). After the war he served as inspector of provisions and clothing at the Boston Navy Yard (1847–1849). He served on the Coast Survey (1848–1860), during which time he was promoted to commander (1855), and he commanded the Coast Survey steamer *Active* (1856–1857) in military operations against American Indians on Puget Sound. His arrival at San Juan Island (1857) helped prevent an Anglo-American military clash, and the troops he helped land held the island against the threat of British attack.

In April 1861, as Virginia seceded, Secretary of the Navy Gideon Welles sent Alden to retrieve the *Merrimack* from the Norfolk Navy Yard to prevent it from falling into Confederate hands. The mission was doomed because of Commandant Charles McCauley's dithering, but Welles concluded that Alden was "timid, but patriotic when there was no danger, . . . not endowed with great oral or physical courage, . . . and no doubt really anxious to do something without encountering enemies or taking upon himself much responsibility" (*Diary of Welles*, p. 44). Had Alden been prepared to challenge McCauley's seniority, the *Merrimack* might have been saved for the Union rather than refitted as a Confederate ironclad.

In May 1861 Alden was given command of the USS *South Carolina* to participate in reinforcing Fort Pickens, Florida. Off Galveston, Texas, he engaged batteries at the rear of the city and captured thirteen cargo-laden schooners. On the morning of 3 August 1861, with his ships only three miles out, shore batteries fired on one of his tenders, which returned fire. Alden claimed he had reassured Galveston's military commandant that his ships had no intention of bombarding the city. He now waited all day for an explanation for what he believed to be a mistake. After 4:00 P.M. Alden's vessel stood toward the shore and purposely induced more fire from the batteries. Following an exchange of twelve to fifteen shots, the vessel withdrew to avoid, according to Alden, damage to the city and its innocent citizens. What Alden described as "a short but lively affair" precipitated a protest by several foreign consular officials, who decried "acts of inhumanity unrecognized in modern warfare, and meriting the condemnation of Christian and civilized nations." "Good God, gentlemen!" Alden replied. "Do you think such an act could have been deliberate or premeditated?" (*Official Records*, vol. 1, pp. 605–7). Ultimately, both Flag Officer William Mervine and the Navy Department approved Alden's actions.

In 1862 Alden took command of the sloop of war *Richmond* in the West Gulf Squadron. He participated in the capture of New Orleans (Apr. 1862) and saw action off Forts St. Philip and Jackson, below New Orleans; at Port Hudson, Louisiana; and near the Vicksburg batteries. He was officially commended several times and in January 1863 was promoted to captain.

At the battle of Mobile Bay (Aug. 1864), Alden commanded the ironclad steam sloop *Brooklyn*. With *Brooklyn* and *Tecumseh* leading the fleet in the attack, the *Tecumseh* hit a "torpedo" (a mine) and sank rapidly. Mistaking buoys for additional torpedoes, Alden indecisively and overcautiously stopped and then backed the *Brooklyn*. The ironclad turned broadside in the channel, confusing the other ships in the column and driving Admiral David Farragut, aboard the *Hartford*, to swear, "Damn the torpedoes. Go ahead!" Although there was considerable controversy later, Farragut made no issue of Alden's controversial actions, and Alden's record remained untarnished. Alden participated in the attack on Fort Fisher under Admiral David D. Porter in December 1864 and January 1865.

Following the war, Alden was commissioned commodore (1866) and assigned to special service commanding the steam sloop *Susquehanna* in the North American Squadron (1866–1867) and the frigate *Minnesota* (1867–1868). For several months in 1868–1869 he commanded the Mare Island Navy Yard. Admiral Porter recommended him for chief of the Bureau of Navigation and Detail, the navy's most influential administrative division, but Secretary Welles thought Alden, whom he called "a sycophant and courtier," would be "a mere instrument" of Porter (*Diary of Welles*, vol. 2, p. 362). However, in 1869 with a new secretary of the navy and Porter's power in the ascendancy, Alden gained the post, which he held until 1871, when he was promoted to rear admiral and given command of the European Squadron. He retired in 1872 and lived out his final years in San Francisco, where he died.

Alden's prewar and wartime careers were marked by bravery, hard and effective fighting, and generally good seamanship and professional judgment. His postwar career was distinguished but unspectacular in an era that provided officers few opportunities for spectacular achievement. Described in his day as courtly, accomplished, and of fine personal appearance and social abilities, Alden had many decent and pleasant qualities, which were widely acknowledged.

• Alden's journal is at the Mariners Museum, Newport News, Va. His official correspondence can be found in the Navy Department records at the National Archives. His official Civil War correspondence was printed in *The Official Records of the Union and Confederate Navies in the War of the Rebellion* (30 vols., 1894–1922). Howard K. Beale, ed., *Diary of Gideon Welles* (rev. ed., 1960), and William James Morgan et al., eds., *Autobiography of Rear Admiral Wilkes* (1978), provide contemporary if not always unbiased assessments. No full-length studies of Alden's life exist. Specialized studies that cover aspects of his career include William Stanton, *The Great United States Exploring Expedition of 1838–1842* (1975); David B. Tyler, *The Wilkes Expedition* (1968); and Foxhall Parker, *Battle of Mobile Bay* (1878). Obituaries are in the *New York Times*, 7 and 25 Feb. 1877, the *Army and Navy Journal*, 10 Feb. 1877, and the *New England Historical and Genealogical Register*, July 1877.

KENNETH J. BLUME

ALDEN, John (1599?–12 Sept. 1687), farmer and magistrate, was one of the original settlers of Plymouth Colony, arriving in New England on the *Mayflower* in 1620. No definite information exists about his birth, parentage, childhood, or education. In 1620 he lived at Southampton, England, where the migrating Pilgrims stopped for provisions on their way from the Netherlands to the New World. There he was hired as the ship's cooper in charge of its supply of beer and drinking water. Upon landfall, Alden joined in signing the now famous Mayflower Compact. After the colonists' arrival in Plymouth, Governor William Bradford (1590–1657) wrote that Alden, "being a hopeful young man, was much desired, but left to his own liking to go or stay when he came here; but he stayed, and married here."

Sometime between 1621 and 1623, Alden married Priscilla Mullins (or Molines), the orphaned daughter of prominent Plymouth colonists. The couple had ten or eleven children. By 1627 Alden's fortunes had advanced to the point where he could join seven of his fellow colonists as "undertakers" in assuming the debt the colony owed to its English creditors. In return, the undertakers gained control of the colony's fur trade. Land, however, was the more significant economic attraction to Plymouth's settlers, and sometime after 1627 Alden moved with his family to the nearby settlement of Duxbury, where he received a grant of 169 acres. He established himself as a farmer and in the 1650s built the house in which he lived until his death and which his descendants occupied until the early twentieth century.

The extant records of Plymouth Colony begin in 1632 and show Alden served as an "assistant," a member of the colony's advisory council to the governor, from 1632 to 1640. During the 1640s Alden was chosen as Duxbury's deputy to the lower house of Plymouth's legislature, and in 1650 he returned to the upper house as an assistant, where he remained until his death. During the 1650s he served for three years as the colony's treasurer and acted as deputy governor in 1664–1665 and 1677. He was also a frequent adviser to the colony on military affairs. In addition to these formal offices, Alden accepted a variety of lesser responsibilities, ranging from surveyor of highways to supervisor of trading stations set up by the colony along the Atlantic Coast. In 1634 the latter duty put Alden at risk, when he joined a party sent to stop illegal trading activity along the Kennebec River in present-day Maine. The ensuing confrontation resulted in two deaths, and although Alden had not taken part in the violence, he was arrested and held by Massachusetts Bay authorities in Boston until Governor Bradford dispatched Captain Myles Standish, Alden's Duxbury neighbor, "to procure Mr. Alden's release."

The known facts of Alden's life suggest that he was a significant figure in the establishment of the small Plymouth Colony, one of a number of public-spirited colonists who contributed to the success of the venture while making modest fortunes for themselves and their families. The Plymouth minister John Cotton's eulogy, *Upon the Death of That Aged, Pious, Sincere-Hearted Christian, John Alden, Esq.* (1687), outlined Alden's career as follows: "With all the governours he did assist; his name recorded is within the list of Plymouth's pillars to his dying day. . . . He set his love on God and knew his name, God therefore gives him everlasting fame." Since his death in Duxbury, Alden has enjoyed everlasting fame, but his career was no more remarkable than that of hundreds if not thousands of other early American colonists. His fame is derived not from his own actions but from the mythologies that his descendants have built on them.

In the early nineteenth century, President John Adams (1735–1826), an Alden descendant, claimed that Alden was "the stripling, who first leaped upon [Plymouth] rock," a family tradition that itself was connected to the specious idea that Plymouth Rock was the Pilgrims' original landing place in the New World. In 1814 the Reverend Timothy Alden, John Alden's great-great-grandson, first published the family legend of Alden's courtship of Priscilla Mullins in *A Collection of American Epitaphs and Inscriptions*. This legend was used by Henry Wadsworth Longfellow, yet another Alden descendant, as the basis for his wildly popular poem, *The Courtship of Miles Standish* (1858), in which Alden is depicted as the romantic suitor torn between love for Mullins and loyalty to his older friend Captain Standish, who also loves the Puritan maiden. This mythical image of the triumph of youthful American love over Old World standards and expectations has served to perpetuate Alden's name. The actual accomplishments of Alden's long and useful life have been largely obscured by the myths so often repeated in storybooks, paintings and popular legend.

• All the extant information about Alden's life can be found in William Bradford, *Of Plymouth Plantation, 1620–1647* (1952), and in Nathaniel B. Shurtleff et al., eds., *Records of the Colony of New Plymouth in New England* (1855–1861). Filiopietistic treatments of Alden include Ebenezer Alden, *Memorial of the Descendants of the Hon. John Alden* (1867), and Augustus E. Alden, *Pilgrim Alden* (1902). Justin Winsor, *History of Duxbury* (1849), describes Alden's influence in the founding of that town. More recent accounts of the Alden myth and its sources include Dorothy Wentworth, *The Alden Family in the Alden House* (1980), and Alicia Crane Williams, "John and Priscilla, We Hardly Know Ye," *American History Illustrated* 23, no. 8 (1988): 40–47.

MARK A. PETERSON

ALDEN, Joseph (4 Jan. 1807–30 Aug. 1885), president of Jefferson College and of the New York State Normal School at Albany, was born in Cairo, New York, the son of Eliab Alden, an educator who helped shape New York State's normal school system (forerunner of the State University of New York), and Mary Hathaway. Alden began teaching at age fourteen before enrolling at Brown College in 1825. He transferred to Union College and graduated in 1828. He spent the next four years in Princeton, New Jersey, first as a student at Princeton Theological Seminary, from which he received a doctor of divinity degree, and then as a tutor at the College of New Jersey (now Princeton University).

From 1832 to 1835 Alden was a clergyman and served first as pastor of the Dutch Reformed Church of Philadelphia and then of the Congregational church in Williamstown, Massachusetts. He resigned from the latter pastorate in 1835 to become a professor at Williams College. Alden devoted most of the remainder of his life to an academic career. He taught Latin, English, political economy, and history at Williams from 1835 until 1852, when he accepted a chair in mental and moral philosophy at Lafayette College in Easton, Pennsylvania. In 1857 Alden was elected president of Jefferson College (now Washington and Jefferson College) in Canonsburg, Pennsylvania. He left in 1862 and moved to the New York City area where he held several jobs, including editorship of the Presbyterian *New York Observer*.

Returning to academic life, Alden began his most important work when in 1867 he was elected the first president of the New York State Normal School in Albany (the institution's previous leaders had been designated "principal"). The position had first been offered to Edward W. Sheldon who, as principal of Oswego Normal School, was a leading national spokesman for pedagogy-based teacher training. When Sheldon declined, Alden was appointed, and Albany took a much more academic direction. Established in 1862, Albany was modeled on Sheldon's work at Oswego and offered only a two-year course that trained common school teachers. Alden immediately added a four-year classical curriculum to train high school teachers, which provided a slightly attenuated version of the standard college curriculum. The first two years were devoted to "mental discipline" and included no pedagogy courses. The emphasis throughout was on academic training, and teacher training was essentially restricted to ten weeks of practice teaching. In 1874 Alden abolished the two-year common school curriculum and committed Albany solely to training high school teachers.

Alden arrived in Albany when New York's educational system was at a critical juncture. The state had just begun to guarantee free public education and needed a system for training teachers. Albany was New York's only normal school. The state's solution was to offer funds to a handful of academies and institutes, which then were designated as state normal schools. Institutions that failed to receive state funds attacked the new system. Alden, as the head of the largest normal school and the one located in the state capital, was a central figure in the ensuing battles to preserve the fledgling normal school system's funding. Although academies continued to produce more teachers than the normal schools, Alden helped implant the idea that the latter produced the elite of the teaching corps. Under Alden's leadership, Albany became the flagship of New York's normal school system. By the time of Alden's retirement in 1882, the state had added seven other normal schools, the forerunners of today's State University of New York campuses at Brockport, Buffalo, Cortland, Fredonia, Geneseo, Oswego, and Potsdam. But during Alden's administration, Albany produced almost as many graduates as the others combined and was the only one that trained high school teachers.

Alden was also noted for promoting women's status in the teaching profession. Upon his retirement the eight female faculty at Albany presented a resolution stating that they were "deeply grateful to Dr. Alden" for his "liberal and just views as to the efficiency of women in the profession of teacher and her right to recompense, *paid for the work done* and not to the sex of the worker." The first signature was that of Kate Stoneman, who later became the first female lawyer in New York State. Immediately after retiring at the age of seventy-five, Alden married Amelia Daley, a former student who was forty years his junior. He died a few years later in New York City.

Alden was an effective teacher and pedagogical writer who was able to present subjects clearly in the classroom and in writing. He published over seventy works, many of them texts or Sunday school tracts. Although he was most at home as a teacher and writer, Alden's lasting educational accomplishment was as an administrator who helped to preserve New York State's normal school system and mold its flagship institution.

• There are relatively few materials on Alden. A 1906 fire at Albany State Normal School destroyed any papers he may have left there. An excellent unpublished history of the institution is W. Paul Vogt, "The State University of New York at Albany, 1844–1984: A Short History" (1984), in the Albany archives. Schaffer Library at Union College has a small alumni file on Alden. David D. Martin, "The Liberal Arts in the Curricula for the Preparation of Teachers at the State University of New York at Albany, 1844–1966" (Ph.D. diss., Univ. of Connecticut, 1967), examines Alden's curricular work. An obituary is in the *Princeton Theological Seminary Necrological Report* (1886).

W. BRUCE LESLIE

ALDEN, Priscilla Mullins (c. 1602–c. 1684), one of the first settlers of Plymouth Colony, was born the daughter of William Mullins, a shoemaker, and Mary (maiden name unknown). She was probably born in Dorking, Surrey, England, though there is no record of her birth. Her father's life is not well documented, but he may be the William Mollines who was brought before the Privy Council in April 1616. If so, his Puritan faith might have been the reason that he and his family joined the Separatists on their *Mayflower* voyage to the New World. Unfortunately, Priscilla was the only member of the Mullins family to survive the first brutal winter at Plymouth. William Mullins's will asked Governor John Carver to act as guardian for Priscilla, but Carver died as well. She may have moved into the common house for a while, but sometime between 1621 and 1623 she married John Alden, a cooper. Alden was not a Separatist and had been recruited by the Pilgrims to provide beer and wine casks. The marriage of Priscilla and John was one of the first marriages to occur in the colony and is the source of Priscilla's fame.

Almost no record of Priscilla Alden's life exists, but she is one of the most famous of the Plymouth settlers, indeed one of the most famous women of seventeenth-century colonial America. Her fame is the result of her appearance in a folktale that tells of her courtship by Miles Standish and John Alden and of her subsequent marriage to John. There is no documentation of the tale; it appears for the first time in print in the Reverend Timothy Alden's *Collection of American Epitaphs and Inscriptions with Original Notes* (1814). Alden wrote that the story was an "anecdote which has been carefully handed down by tradition." The story was popularized in Henry Wadsworth Longfellow's poem *The Courtship of Miles Standish* (1858). The legend tells of the desire of the widowed Miles Standish to wed Priscilla Mullins, but instead of approaching her himself he sends an emissary to plead his case. The emissary is John Alden, who also loves Priscilla. After hearing Alden put forward the case for her marrying Standish, Priscilla utters the famous question, "Why do you not speak for yourself, John?" The result is the marriage of John Alden and Priscilla Mullins, culminating in her ride to her new home on a white bull. The romantic tale captivated generations of Americans and made Priscilla, John, and Miles Standish stock characters in colonial history. However, no documentation substantiates the legend.

Little is known of Priscilla Alden after her marriage. She had eleven children, of whom nine survived to adulthood. In 1627 she and her husband were living in a house in Plymouth across from the governor, and in 1631 they moved to the new settlement of Duxbury along with Miles Standish and the woman he had married in 1623. The Aldens lived in a long narrow house that was excavated in 1960. John Alden was a leading citizen of the colony for a while, but in 1660 he had become so poor that the colony voted him a grant of £10. The last mention of Priscilla occurred on 1 December 1680, when she attended the funeral of Josiah Winslow in Marshfield. She must have died sometime between 1680 and 1687. When her husband died in 1687, she was not mentioned in his will. Nor was she one of the people who signed an affidavit claiming an interest in his estate.

Priscilla Alden probably lived as a hardworking housewife and homemaker. Her name looms large in American history, however, because she became the subject of a romantic tale of courtship that teaches two lessons: first, if you want something done well do it yourself and, second, do not trust anyone else in matters of the heart.

• Brief biographical information on Alden is in *A Genealogical Dictionary of the First Settlers of New England* (1860). The Aldens are mentioned in William Bradford, *Of Plymouth Plantation*, ed. Samuel Eliot Morison (1952). Modern genealogical works on the Alden family are based on the results of a century of research. These include Dorothy Harding, *Our Alden Ancestors* (1965), and Dorothy Wentworth, *The Alden Family in the Alden House* (1980).

ALLIDA SHUMAN MCKINLEY

ALDEN, Timothy (28 Aug. 1771–5 July 1839), clergyman and educator, was born in Yarmouth, Massachusetts, the son of Timothy Alden, a Congregational minister, and Sarah Weld. He was educated at Harvard College where he mastered Hebrew, Samaritan, Arabic, and Syriac. Following graduation in 1794, he taught in an academy at Marblehead, Massachusetts, while continuing to study theology at Harvard. In 1794 he married Elizabeth Shepherd Wormsted, the daughter of a prosperous Marblehead merchant family.

In October 1799 Alden moved to Portsmouth, New Hampshire, as assistant to the aging Reverend Dr. Samuel Haven and on 20 November 1799 was ordained to the Congregational ministry. To supplement his salary Alden opened a boarding school for girls. Haven's death brought the offer of a larger, but in Alden's mind still inadequate, salary, and in October 1805 Alden resigned and devoted himself to the operation of the school. In 1806 he aspired to a professorship of Oriental languages at Harvard and would likely have secured the post had control of the college not passed to the Unitarians the previous year.

In 1808 Alden relocated to Boston where he directed a girls' school and worked for the Massachusetts Historical Society, preparing a printed catalog of its library. He continued to support himself by operating girls' academies—in Newark, New Jersey, after 1810 and in New York City after 1812. Alden also cataloged the New-York Historical Society library, compiled two annual registers of New Jersey government and community leaders, and developed a reputation as an antiquarian with the publication of a five-volume *Collection of American Epitaphs and Inscriptions* (1814). Alden had by then moved outside traditionally Congregational territory, and he changed his denominational affiliation to Presbyterian during this period.

Alden had a longstanding interest in the American West, and in the fall of 1812 he traveled for seven weeks through western Pennsylvania and Ohio. He was impressed particularly by northwestern Pennsylvania, where his cousin Roger Alden was a land agent. After an inheritance from his mother-in-law made gainful employment unnecessary, Alden, his wife, and five children moved to Meadville, Pennsylvania, in the spring of 1815. Alden's first wife died in 1820, and in 1822 he married Sophia L. L. Mulcock, with whom he had one child.

Alden founded Allegheny College in 1815, becoming its first president and professor of Oriental languages and ecclesiastical history. His reputation drew impressive donations of books from Massachusetts, including the entire collections of clergyman and linguist William Bentley and of the Winthrop family. By 1822 the college owned 7,000 volumes, one of the nation's largest academic libraries. Alden's years at Allegheny were, however, filled with disappointments as well as successes. The number of students remained small, and finances were always precarious despite his taking no salary. Alden was particularly discouraged, even embittered, by the lack of expected support from the state government and the Presbyterian church. The withdrawal of a key local contributor who converted to Unitarianism further weakened the college's position, and Alden for the second time found his fortunes hampered by this rival denomination. He put forward various schemes, including one to attract support from eastern Pennsylvania Germans by the promise of a German professorship and another to reorganize the college according to the manual labor regimen practiced at Andover and elsewhere, but he was never able to stabilize the college's finances or enrollments. When the trustees turned to the Methodists for a solution to these difficulties, Alden resigned in August 1831. After a two-year interruption, the college reopened under Methodist leadership.

Alden went to Cincinnati in 1832 to open another girls' school, but the threat of cholera drove him back to Pittsburgh, where in 1834 he began a girls' division of East Liberty Academy. With advancing age, he took a less arduous position as stated supply pastor to the Pine Creek Presbyterian Church in nearby Sharpsburg. He died in the Pittsburgh area and was buried at the church cemetery in Sharpsburg.

Alden considered himself an heir of the Puritan tradition and was an outspoken opponent of Unitarianism. He described the new nation in millennial terms and frequently gave providential explanations for events (war, family deaths, cholera, the fortunes of his college). He wrote articles advocating family religion, and he supported revivalism, though he feared its potential for Socinianism and insisted on decorum. In 1832 he spoke with admiration of the Reverend Lyman Beecher and Lane Seminary.

Alden was politically uninvolved, although Whig in sympathy. He considered slavery a cruel but temporarily unavoidable system; he criticized most abolitionists and supported the American Colonization Society. He was an active Mason. He published, in 1827, an account of his four missionary journeys (1816–1820) to the Seneca and Munsee tribes. He made minor contributions to science by publishing observations of the effects of lightning and earthquakes.

• Alden's papers, including the typescript "Bakewell Timothy Alden Letters," are in the Allegheny College library. Other sources are Ernest A. Smith, *Allegheny, a Century of Education* (1916); *Diary of William Bentley* (1905–1914); W. B. Sprague, *Annals of the American Pulpit*, vol. 2 (1857); and Alfred Nevin, ed., *Encyclopedia of the Presbyterian Church in the United States of America* (1884).

CHARLES D. CASHDOLLAR

ALDERMAN, Edwin Anderson (15 May 1861–29 Apr. 1931), educational reformer and university president, was born in Wilmington, North Carolina, the son of James Alderman, a timber inspector, and Susan Jane Corbett. Alderman attended private schools in Wilmington before spending two years (1876–1878) at the Bethel Military Academy near Warrenton, Virginia. In 1878 he entered the University of North Carolina, from which he received a Ph.B. with honors in English and Latin. His developing mastery of the beauty and power of the spoken word was recognized when he won a medal for oratory at the 1882 commencement exercises. In 1885 he married Emma Graves; they had three children, all of whom died in early childhood.

Following graduation, Alderman taught in the newly created graded schools of Goldsboro, North Carolina. Three years later he succeeded Edward P. Moses as superintendent of the Goldsboro schools and continued in that position until 1889. He then joined forces with a college classmate, Charles D. McIver, to initiate a campaign to improve education in the state. As agents of the state board of education, they traveled throughout the state instructing teachers in improved pedagogical methods and encouraging the citizenry to increase support of public education. Their three-year campaign anticipated the educational revival that swept across the state a decade later under the administration of another classmate, Governor Charles B. Aycock.

Alderman assisted McIver in founding the Normal and Industrial School for Women (now the University of North Carolina at Greensboro). The two were the primary movers behind the legislation that established the teacher training school in February 1891. The institution opened with 200 students in October 1892 with McIver as president and Alderman as the "leading professor." Within a year, however, Alderman left this position to become professor of the history and philosophy of education at the University of North Carolina.

Alderman's career as an educational leader took on new dimensions following an address on "Higher Education in the South," presented at the Atlanta Exposition in October 1895. In this address he established himself as a spokesman for a region, not merely his home state. He proclaimed the need for a "New South" built on a solid platform of universal education and led by enlightened people dedicated to public service. "At this stage of our culture," he said, "when millions are to be impressed with the importance of knowledge, the southern scholar must forego his office of prophet and seer and become ruler and reformer."

Alderman's reputation as an educational reformer made him the unanimous choice of the trustees for the presidency of the University of North Carolina in Chapel Hill the next year. From 1896 to 1900 Alderman worked to advance the image of the university as "the mightiest single, social engine for the direction and elevation" of the new social order. His efforts to increase legislative appropriations for the university met with only limited success, but in advocating new professorships in social and political science and pharmacy, along with exciting greater support for the summer school for teachers, Alderman pushed the university in the direction of more effective public service. Although in dress and demeanor he exuded an aristocratic air, Alderman was genuinely democratic in his sympathies. During his four-year presidency, the university gained in enrollment and enjoyed a degree of popular esteem theretofore unknown.

On 5 April 1900 Alderman was elected president of Tulane University in New Orleans. At that time Tulane boasted the largest enrollment of any southern institution and a total income more than double that of UNC. Alderman clearly considered the move to Tulane an opportunity to enlarge his sphere of influence. Beginning his duties at Tulane in the fall of 1900, he endeavored there, as he had at North Carolina, to democratize the institution and connect it more closely with the public schools. Moreover, through his involvement with the Southern Education Board, which he and McIver helped to launch in 1901, and the General Education Board, with which he became associated in 1906, Alderman became deeply entrenched in the inner circle of southern reformers, northern philanthropists, and educational leaders who were directing and financing the educational crusade in the southern states and promoting university reform nationwide.

Alderman's first wife had died in 1896, and in 1904 he married New Orleanian Bessie Green Hearn, with whom he would have one child. Also in 1904, Alderman was named president of the University of Virginia. His election was precedent breaking because the university had operated since its opening in 1825 without a president. Routine administrative details had been handled by the chairman of the faculty, a position rotated among the company of scholars, while the management of corporate affairs had remained under the direction of a rector and board of visitors.

As president, Alderman departed from Thomas Jefferson's initial organizational scheme for the university, but in other respects he adhered closely to the Jeffersonian tradition during his twenty-seven years of service to the institution. Under Alderman's leadership the university emerged as the centerpiece of the state's system of public education. He persuaded the legislature to increase appropriations for both the university and the public schools of the state. On the evening of his inauguration Alderman proudly announced that a gift of $100,000 from oil magnate John D. Rockefeller had been designated for the building of a school of education to be named in honor of educational reformer J. L. M. Curry. A pledge from industrialist Andrew Carnegie of $500,000 marked the first step toward the expansion of the endowment from $350,000 to $10 million during Alderman's presidency. His administration was marked by substantial enlargement and improvement of the physical plant, reorganization and strengthening of the undergraduate programs, and the enhancement of graduate and professional education. Faculty size had increased fivefold while enrollment had quadrupled by the time the twenty-fifth anniversary of his presidency was celebrated in 1929.

Alderman continued to be in demand as a public speaker, enhancing his own and the university's reputation. He was under consideration for a diplomatic post at the time of Woodrow Wilson's election to the presidency of the United States, but his health suddenly deteriorated. On 24 November 1912, having been diagnosed as suffering from tubercular laryngitis that had affected both lungs, he became a patient at Lake Saranac, New York. Alderman's struggle to regain his health, which necessitated almost complete inactivity and silence for more than a year, marked the hardest and most crucial personal battle of his life. He was discharged from Saranac in the spring of 1914 but did not return to work until the fall.

Alderman's return to his duties brought him into controversy over a proposal to create a coordinate college for women near the university. Alderman favored the idea, but student and alumni opposition brought defeat of the measure in 1916. In 1919–1920, however, some women began to be admitted on a limited basis in the graduate and professional departments of the university. He was more successful in 1922 in fighting off an attempt to move the university's medical school to Richmond, where it would have been merged with the Medical College of Virginia, a measure proponents argued would promote both educational efficiency and economy. This victory resulted in a sizable increase in gifts to the medical school.

Alderman's acclaim as a public speaker reached its height with a memorial address on Woodrow Wilson that he delivered on 15 December 1924 to a joint session of Congress. His eulogy was acclaimed as masterful by his contemporaries and later judged by his biographer, Dumas Malone, as deserving "rank among the classics of American oratory."

En route to the University of Illinois, where he was scheduled to deliver an address, Alderman suffered a cerebral hemorrhage. He was taken from the train at Connellsville, Pennsylvania, and died at the state hospital without ever regaining consciousness. Alderman was recognized during his lifetime with numerous honors, memberships, and honorary doctorates for his role as an eloquent and ceaseless advocate for educational reform and opportunity in his native South.

• Alderman's public and private papers are housed in the main library, which now bears his name, at the University of Virginia. A comprehensive bibliography of his speeches and writings, some of which are in bound volumes, is on file there. Alderman's writings consist mainly of speeches and articles. He and Joel Chandler Harris were editors in chief of the sixteen-volume *Library of Southern Literature* (1907). With Armistead C. Gordon he coauthored *J. L. M. Curry: A Biography* (1911). A listing of Alderman's most notable writings is included in the biographical sketch in the *National Cyclopaedia of American Biography*, vol. 23 (1933). Dumas Malone, *Edwin A. Alderman: A Biography* (1940), is indispensable. Alderman's work at the University of Virginia receives attention in Philip Alexander Bruce, *History of the University of Virginia, 1819–1919*, vol. 5 (1922), and Virginius Dabney, *Mr. Jefferson's University* (1981). An obituary is in the *New York Times*, 30 Apr. 1931.

JENNINGS L. WAGONER, JR.

ALDRICH, Bess Streeter (17 Feb. 1881–3 Aug. 1954), author, was born Bess Genevra Streeter in Cedar Falls, Iowa, the daughter of James Wareham Streeter, a farmer and miller, and Mary Wilson Anderson. Aldrich was the youngest of eight children and the only one born in Cedar Falls, where her parents had moved a few years prior to her birth. Her mother and several of her brothers and sisters wrote poetry. Aldrich began writing short stories as a child; her first writing prize came at the age of fourteen when she won a camera for a children's story sent to the *Chicago Record*. Decades later, recalling that award, she said, "It was then I first tasted blood; for the intoxication of seeing my name in print was overwhelming" (*American Magazine*, Feb. 1921).

In 1901 Aldrich graduated from Iowa State Normal School (now the University of Northern Iowa) with a bachelor of didactic studies. She taught in Iowa grade schools for four years and in Salt Lake City, Utah, for one year; in the fall of 1906 she returned to her alma mater, worked for one year as assistant supervisor in the Primary Department, and in 1907 received an advanced teaching certificate. Aldrich had continued to write stories and articles through college, and as a teacher and primary grade supervisor she published several children's stories.

In 1907 she married Charles Sweetzer Aldrich, and they moved to Tipton, Iowa, where Charles worked in the bank and practiced law. In 1909 the couple moved to Elmwood, Nebraska, where Charles and his brother-in-law had purchased a local bank, and where Charles was cashier and attorney. Bess Aldrich did little writing for the next two years; then, with some 2,000 others, she entered a story contest in the *Ladies Home Journal*. Her story was one of six chosen by the magazine for publication, and from then on she was writing and publishing stories almost continually. Until 1918 she used the pseudonym Margaret Dean Stevens, a combination of her grandmothers' names. Her short stories appeared in such popular magazines as *Colliers, Saturday Evening Post, McCall's*, and other large-circulation magazines; she was one of the best-paid magazine writers of her era. Many of her articles dealt with the art of writing, for she was particularly interested in helping others enter the field she so enjoyed.

Her first book, *Mother Mason*, published in 1924, was a compilation of short stories, the first of which had appeared in 1918 in the *American Magazine*. These stories, which chronicled the doings of the fictitious Mason family, are believed to have been the first series of family stories to appear in an American magazine and also the first to portray a domestic as a family friend. In 1925, shortly before publication of Aldrich's second book, Charles Aldrich died of a cerebral hemorrhage, leaving her a widow with four children ranging in age from four to sixteen. She supported the family as a writer, including a period as a screenwriter for Paramount Studios, and as book editor for the *Christian Herald*. Through the earnings of her pen, Aldrich put all her children through college and was herself awarded an honorary doctor of letters from the University of Nebraska in 1934.

Aldrich, who sold everything she ever wrote, published well over 100 short stories and articles, nine novels, two books of short stories, a novella, and an omnibus collection. Her first novel was *Rim of the Prairie* (1925), followed in 1926 by another family series gathered from short stories, *The Cutters*. *A Lantern in Her Hand* (1928), perhaps her best-known work, was published and remained on the bestseller list for three years. *Lantern* was translated into most European languages as well as Chinese, Arabic, and Thai; in 1942 it was added to the list of classics for classroom use in the Modern Literature Series. Its sequel, *White Bird Flying* (1931), became one of the three bestsellers for that year. In 1933 *Miss Bishop* was published and in 1941 became the basis of the movie *Cheers for Miss Bishop*; Aldrich acted as adviser during the filming. *Spring Came on Forever* (1935) was followed in 1936 by a collection of her short stories bearing the title of her O. Henry Award–winning story, *The Man Who Caught the Weather*. *Song of Years* (1939) departs from her usual Nebraska setting to pay tribute to northeast Iowa, where her family settled in the 1850s. Aldrich's last novel was *The Lieutenant's Lady*, written as the diary of an army wife who, after the Civil War, followed her husband to forts far up the Missouri River and into Montana Territory. Aldrich's one novella, *The Drum Goes Dead*, another of her many Christmas stories, was originally published in *Cosmopolitan* in January 1938 and was published as a book in 1941. The omnibus *Bess Streeter Aldrich Reader* was published in 1950.

One reason for Aldrich's popularity was that she wrote about average people, particularly those found in small towns. She told Lillian Lambert in a 1928 interview that "wherever there are folks who live and work and love and die, . . . there is the stuff of which stories are made" (*Midland Schools* 42, no. 8, p. 300). Aldrich's common sense, humor, and occasional irony came through in her short stories and novels. Her themes were of life in rural towns; she understood the individuals and activities in villages, for she was a part of such life. During the period of her greatest productivity, from 1918 to 1950, young people in particular were moving in large numbers from the country to the city, and many city dwellers still had family members remaining in small towns or on farms. Her stories brought back memories of childhood and family to many of these readers.

Another of Aldrich's strengths was her sympathetic portrayal of older people. As a child she had observed elderly relatives and pioneers in her parents' home, and she drew on them for the mannerisms that made her characters so authentic. Another childhood recollection that figured in Aldrich's later writing was Christmas. As a youngster she thought that Christmas was the culmination of the year, and she carried the warmth of childhood excitement into adulthood and into her writing. She used this theme in many articles and stories and in 1949 gathered some of these stories into a book, *Journey into Christmas*. That same year she received the Iowa Authors Outstanding Contribution to Literature Award.

Aldrich was a romantic realist whose novels portrayed accurately the step-by-step process of pioneering both farms and small towns in the nineteenth-century Midwest. She wrote her novels with great accuracy because she hoped that her books would be read by later generations seeking to understand the difficulties their forebears had overcome. This hope has more than been fulfilled. Because Aldrich so thoroughly researched material for her books, her novels have been used from grade school through college for teaching history and social studies and remain relevant to the history of the nation.

Aldrich died in Lincoln, Nebraska, and was buried beside her husband and one son in Elmwood, Nebraska. Her home in Elmwood is on the National Historic Register and is a part of the Bess Streeter Aldrich Foundation holdings, which include a museum dedicated to her and to her work. In 1973 Aldrich was posthumously inducted into the Nebraska Hall of Fame.

• The museum in Elmwood contains some of Aldrich's clippings, papers, and manuscripts; still more of her notes, much of her correspondence, and some of her manuscripts may be found in the Nebraska State Historical Society archives. Other papers are housed at the University of Iowa, the University of Northern Iowa, and the Cedar Falls (Iowa) Historical Society Archives. Aldrich's daughter, Mary Aldrich Beechner, provided certain details for this article, and her son, Robert, contributed biographical information in *A Bess Streeter Aldrich Treasury* (1959). Other works about Aldrich include Annie Russell Marble, *A Daughter of Pioneers* (n.d.), and *Bess Streeter Aldrich and Her Books* (n.d.); and Amelia Mabel Meier, "Bess Streeter Aldrich: Her Life and Works" (master's thesis, Kearney State College, 1968). She has been the subject of dissertations, including Carol Jean Miles Petersen, "Bess Streeter Aldrich: A Writer's Life" (Univ. of Nebraska, 1992); Mama Hart Hawkins, "Secondary School Resource Units for Literary Study of Two Women Plains Writers and Certain of Their Works (Aldrich, Sandoz)" (Univ. of Nebraska, 1990); M. Sue Campman, "What We Must Love: Marriage in the Best-Sellers by Women during the 1930s" (Univ. of Texas at Austin, 1987); Emily Decker Lardner Jessup, "Embattled Landscapes: Regionalism and Gender in Midwestern Literature, 1915–1941" (Univ. of Michigan, 1985); William Patrick Keating, "Fulfilled Visions: The Life and Work of Bess Streeter Aldrich" (Indiana Univ. of Penn., 1985); and Ruth Jean Foreman, "The Fiction of Bess Streeter Aldrich" (D.A. thesis, Drake Univ., 1982). For a biography, see Carol Miles Petersen, *Bess Streeter Aldrich: The Dreams Are All Real* (1996). A picture of Aldrich accompanies an obituary in the *New York Times*, 4 Aug. 1954.

CAROL MILES PETERSEN

ALDRICH, Chester Holmes (4 June 1871–26 Dec. 1940), architect, was born in Providence, Rhode Island, the son of Elisha Smith Aldrich, a merchant, and Anna Elizabeth Gladding. Aldrich attended Columbia University, graduating from the recently formed (1881) department of architecture with a bachelor of philosophy in 1893. He then went to work at the New York office of John Merven Carrère and Thomas Hastings. After twelve months his employers sent him to study at the École des Beaux Arts in Paris, where he studied in the atelier Daumet-Esquié. Returning to New York to work briefly on the competition drawings for the New York Public Library in 1897, he met another young employee bound for Paris, William Adams Delano. The two were schoolmates in the ateliers of the École for the following three years. Aldrich received his diploma in 1900 and returned to the Carrère & Hastings office; following Delano's return from Paris in 1903 the two men set up their own practice on Forty-first Street, tossing a coin to determine which name would come first. Their social and educational connections immediately led to significant projects, each stewarded by the individual partner who had brought in the client. The partnership, though dominated by the more prolific Delano, was a happy collaboration lasting some thirty years.

Described by his partner as "a kind of St. Francis of Assisi," Aldrich was by all accounts a gentle, talented, altruistic man who gave his life to a balance of artistic and social causes. He never married, choosing to live with his sister Amey in New York, and often vacationing in Italy. A talented representational painter, he exhibited works at the National Academy of Design, the Fogg Art Museum, and the Rhode Island School of Design. Like his brother Richard Aldrich (1863–1937), a noted music critic, he was also a fine pianist. His devotion to social causes was widely recognized: during World War I he served as director general of the American Red Cross Commission in Italy, receiving the Order of the Crown of Italy and other medals for his work. Central among his interests was the Kips Bay Boys' Club. He designed the organization's headquarters (1930), served as president and as a trustee, and worked hard for disadvantaged youths. In fulfillment of a longtime devotion to Italian art and culture, in 1935 he was appointed director of the American Academy in Rome. He retired from practice to take the post and occupied it until his death.

Because of Aldrich's reticence and the more aggressive style of his partner, it is difficult to assess the quality of his designs, or indeed even to attribute work solely to his hand. His first major building, "Kykuit," the 1907 Pocantico house of John D. Rockefeller that forms the heart of the present mansion, was spoiled by the meddlesome client and by a clumsy design inherited from a previous architect. Institutional buildings in New York City, such as the American Red Cross Building (1931), the Chapin School (1927), and the new Colony Club (1914–1916), are somewhat stiff and conservative in comparison to Delano's designs; Aldrich was an antiquarian and more driven by academic design principles than his partner was. Of the firm's major residential projects, the 1931 Hopewell, New Jersey, house of Charles A. Lindbergh (site of the infamous kidnapping), two residences each for Dwight W. Morrow and Charles M. Chapin, and a number of smaller commissions appear to have come from Aldrich's hand. Like his partner and his mentors, Carrère & Hastings, Aldrich was a confirmed classicist who never warmed to the modernist International Style that emerged during the 1920s and 1930s.

He died in Rome and was widely eulogized by his fellow architects. His honors included fellowships in the National Academy of Design, the National Institute of Arts and Letters, and the American Institute of Architects.

• There is no full-length biography of Aldrich and no major study of the firm's work, but considerable archival sources exist. These include the Delano (1950) and McIlvaine (1986) collections of drawings, papers, and photographs in the Avery Architectural Archives at Columbia University; minor collections at the New-York Historical Society and Museum of the City of New York; the personal letters of Chester Aldrich and William A. Delano in the Yale University Libraries; and documents of the firm donated to the American Academy of Arts and Letters. Biographical sources include Mark Alan Hewitt, *The Architect and the American Country House, 1890–1940* (1990), p. 267, and a typewritten sketch by William A. Delano in the New-York Historical Society. Obituaries are in the *New York Times*, 27 Dec. 1940, and the *New York Herald Tribune*, 28 Dec. 1940.

MARK ALAN HEWITT

ALDRICH, Louis (1 Oct. 1843–17 June 1901), actor and theatrical manager, was born Louis Lyon. Aldrich led a difficult early life, though precise details about his childhood or parentage are scant. He is variously said to have been born in Germany, on a ship in passage to the United States, or in a small town in Ohio. After his father's death and his mother's subsequent remarriage, he was adopted by a Cincinnati, Ohio, family, which then moved to Cleveland. In an 1894 interview Aldrich commented that he had been on his own since childhood, touring with a manager as a child prodigy. In 1855, at age eleven, he made his stage debut performing the title role in *Richard III* at the Cleveland Academy of Music. For two years he toured the Midwest, billed as "Master Moses," "Master McCarthy," and "The Ohio Roscius," playing Shylock, Macbeth, Claude Melnotte, and various other popular melodramatic and romantic heroes. He retired briefly from the stage in 1857 and attended White Water College in Wayne County, Indiana, but in 1858 he adopted the name Louis Aldrich and joined the Robert G. Marsh troupe of juvenile players.

For the next five years Aldrich toured with the Marsh players as they traveled to Australia and the West Coast. The troupe disbanded in 1863, leaving Aldrich in San Francisco. There, in November 1863, he married Frances Clara Shropshire, also a former member of the Marsh company. They had no children. In that same year Aldrich joined the stock company at Maguire's Opera House in San Francisco, where he spent three years working with talented performers such as Frank Mayo and Junius Brutus Booth. In 1866 Aldrich signed on with the Boston Museum Theatre Company, where he remained for seven seasons. While there he established a reputation for being a "useful man" who could step into a role at a moment's notice, as he recalled in a *Dramatic Mirror* interview. In Boston Aldrich played opposite major stars such as Edwin Forrest, Edwin Booth, Charlotte Cushman, and Charles Fechter, and he supported Charles Kean in his last American performance, which was also Aldrich's New York debut. In 1873 Louisa (Mrs. John) Drew hired Aldrich to play leading men at her Arch Street Theatre in Philadelphia. The following year he starred at Wood's Museum in New York, and in 1875–1876 he worked for John Ford at his Baltimore theater. In 1876–1877 he played Salamenes in Lord Byron's *Sardanapalus* at Booth's Theatre in New York and various roles at the Eagle Theatre.

Aldrich gained instant prominence in 1877 as the Parson in McKee Rankin's production of the western drama *The Danites*, in which he toured for two years. On 16 September 1879 Aldrich starred in his own production of Bartley Campbell's *My Partner* at A. M. Palmer's Union Square Theatre in New York. The play told the story of two California mining partners—the rugged but good-hearted Joe Saunders, played by Aldrich, and the dapper but shallow Ned Singleton—who fall in love with the same woman, with the result that Joe is unjustly accused of Ned's murder. The play touched the sentimental hearts of its audience and was regarded as one of the finest American dramas ever written. The exceptional cast included Minnie Palmer, Maude Granger, Frank Mordaunt, and Charles Parsloe, who played a comic Chinese role. Aldrich toured the play for six years with occasional revivals thereafter, and it made him a wealthy man. Eventually he purchased all rights to the play, which he subsequently leased to others, and bought out Parsloe, who was his business partner in the venture. In all, he played Joe Saunders for approximately 2,000 performances. In 1888 he starred as Shoulders, a hard-drinking ruffian, in *The Kaffir Diamond*, and in 1890 he played Colonel Hawkins, a rough-hewn western newspaperman on a visit to New York, in *The Editor*, but neither play matched the success of *My Partner*. In that same year, while playing *The Editor* in Syracuse, New York, Aldrich was seriously injured in the Leland Hotel fire. For a time his injuries seemed to affect both his playing and his mental abilities.

As he performed less frequently, Aldrich devoted more of his time to the Actors' Fund, a philanthropic organization founded to assist needy performers. Aldrich served as trustee and then vice president of the Actors' Fund for eight years, from 1889 to 1897. In 1897 he became the first actor elected as president, a post he held without compensation until 1901. Aldrich increased membership, using his touring contacts to reach out to major cities beyond the East Coast. He proposed a home for indigent actors and raised large sums of money for that project through a variety of innovative fundraising techniques. Although he did not live to see it, the establishment of the original Actors' Fund Home on Staten Island in 1902 was regarded as a tribute to his arduous and incessant efforts. Aldrich also served as president of the Actors' Order of Friendship, another philanthropic group, and he worked with the Actors' Society, a forerunner of Actors Equity.

Aldrich was a large man whose most famous characterizations were burly, kind-hearted western heroes. As the *New York Clipper* noted in a 1913 retrospective, "As an actor Mr. Aldrich just escaped being great. He was talented, but was not a genius." The *Dramatic Mirror* noted at his death, "It is as a broad, generous, noble philanthropist rather than as a capable actor that he will be best remembered." He died in Kennebunkport, Maine.

• For more information on Aldrich's role in the Actors' Fund, see Louis Simon, *A History of the Actors' Fund of America* (1972). Interviews with Aldrich are in the *Boston Sunday Record*, 3 Oct. 1886, and the *New York Dramatic Mirror*, 19 June 1894. A biographical sketch, "Notable Players of the Past and Present #118," appears in the *New York Clipper*, 15 Feb. 1913. Obituaries are in the *New York Herald*, 18 June 1901, and the *Dramatic Mirror* and the *New York Clipper*, both 29 June 1901.

ROGER A. HALL

ALDRICH, Nelson Wilmarth (6 Nov. 1841–16 Apr. 1915), U.S. senator, congressman, and businessman, was born in Foster, Rhode Island, the son of Anan Aldrich and Abby Burgess, farmers. Having received a modest education in East Killingly, Connecticut, and at the East Greenwich Academy in Rhode Island, Aldrich was by age seventeen working in Providence. Eventually a large wholesale grocery firm, Waldron, Wightman & Co., hired him as a clerk and bookkeeper. His career there was briefly interrupted in 1862 by service with the Tenth Rhode Island Volunteers garrisoning Washington, D.C. After contracting typhoid that same year he returned to Providence and, by 1866, had been elevated to junior partner at Waldron, Wightman. He married Abby Chapman that year; the couple would have eleven children. His wife was of independent means, but Aldrich insisted on accumulating a fortune on his own account and gradually did so. He worked his way up to full partner at Waldron, Wightman, was a director of the Roger Williams Bank by 1872, and by 1877 was president of Providence's First National Bank. He also headed the city's Board of Trade in these years.

If Aldrich came to symbolize the marriage of government and business in the Gilded Age, that marriage, in personal terms, occurred early in his career. He had been converted to Republicanism before the Civil War and in 1869 was elected as a member of that party to the Providence common council, on which he served until 1875. Elected to the Rhode Island General Assembly in 1875, he served as its Speaker in 1876–1877. He aligned himself with the Rhode Island political machine headed by Senator Henry B. Anthony and managed in Providence by Postmaster Charles Brayton. Aldrich was elected to the U.S. House of Representatives in 1878, was reelected two years later, and sat on the District of Columbia Committee. Upon the death of Ambrose Burnside in 1881, the legislature sent Aldrich to the U.S. Senate in the late general's stead. The accommodation he would arrive at with local boss Brayton gave the latter much leeway in patronage matters and allowed Aldrich to retain his seat for almost thirty years. He was reelected by the legislature in 1886, 1892, 1898, and 1904.

Aldrich's career in the Senate exemplified his party's subordination in these years of the issues born of emancipation and black enfranchisement to a more exclusive preoccupation with building a vibrant industrial nation. Aldrich was too aloof, ironic, and, in intimate settings, charming for Richard Hofstadter's image of him as "the watchdog of the corporations" (*American Political Tradition* [1948], p. 176) to feel quite right. But the senator did, indeed, always keep an eye out for how government might best serve business. When it came to corporate regulation, he distrusted federal activism, opposing, for instance, the Interstate Commerce Act of 1887. However, he was a zealous advocate of national legislation more directly promoting the fortunes of the business sector, particularly eastern manufacturers. Accordingly, he became a master of the protective tariff, having early won a seat on the Senate Finance Committee. Excelling in committee work and floor debate though not on the stump, he participated in making the "Mongrel Tariff" of 1883; promoted a protectionist alternative to the Democrats' Mills Bill of 1888; was a key figure in ushering through that alternative's successor, the McKinley Tariff of 1890, which enforced high duties in the face of federal budget surpluses; and in 1894, when the rival party dominated Congress, struck deals with Democratic protectionists to stymie cuts in rates. The fact that he was a diehard protectionist did not mean Aldrich always sought the highest feasible rates, however. He worked, for instance, to lower or eliminate import duties on raw sugar to benefit eastern sugar refiners and attempted, in framing the Dingley Tariff of 1897, to lower rates on goods of interest to France in order to smooth the way for an international monetary agreement.

Through all these efforts, Aldrich could and did offer disinterested arguments for protection, contending that a bouyant industrial sector served both capital and labor and provided a bustling market for farm products. He sincerely believed that businesses directly affected by legislation ought to be allowed to make their cases before congressional committees. But, privately, Aldrich did not always maintain an Olympian detachment amidst the contention of competing interests. He does not seem actually to have been bribable but apparently profited by his solicitude for certain industries. In the early 1890s a sugar magnate, well served by Aldrich's tariff manipulations, advanced the money that allowed Aldrich to buy and improve streetcar lines in Providence and environs, making the senator a magnate in his own right. The United Traction and Electric Company, which Aldrich formally headed from 1893 to 1902, came to dominate the electric railway business in his native state. The millionaire senator also had interests in other utilities as well as oil, sugar, and rubber holdings. Aldrich's connections to the corporate elite were more than political and financial, however. In 1901 his daughter Abby married John D. Rockefeller, Jr. Aldrich's grandchildren thus included Nelson A. Rockefeller, David Rockefeller, and Winthrop Rockefeller.

With the Republicans dominating both houses of Congress between 1895 and 1911 and in uninterrupted control of the White House from 1897 to 1913, Aldrich became one of the true titans of the Senate. The authority accorded him by his seniority and his leadership of the Finance Committee was amplified by his power in party caucuses and his influence over congressional committee assignments and campaign contributions. He had helped hold his party firm against the cause of free silver, not by uncompromising insistence on the gold standard but, instead, by gestures toward silver interests—such as the Sherman Silver Purchase Act of 1890 and a stated willingness to embrace bimetallism if secured on a worldwide basis—that sidetracked the demand for immediate free coinage. As the strength of the silver forces faded, however, Aldrich helped pass the Gold Standard Act of 1900. Not initially party to the war fever of 1898, he nonetheless saw the advantage to American businesses of building markets in Latin America and East Asia. He helped secure both ratification of the treaty providing for acquisition of the Philippines and Puerto Rico and passage of the Platt Amendment, affirming America's right to intervene in Cuban affairs. He supported Theodore Roosevelt's Panama ventures and remained on good terms with the rambunctious president through the latter's first term. Roosevelt deferred to Aldrich and his conservative clique, Senators William Allison, Orville Platt, and John C. Spooner, on legislative matters of especial interest to them, such as the tariff. As long as Roosevelt confined himself to executive actions, Aldrich for his part did not object strenuously to the president's sallies against certain business interests, such as in the Northern Securities antitrust case and his settlement of the 1902 anthracite strike. Roosevelt acknowledged Aldrich's power, telling Lincoln Steffens: "He is a king pin in my game. Sure. I bow to Aldrich . . . ; I respect him, as he does not respect me. I'm just a president, and he has seen lots of presidents" (*The Autobiography of Lincoln Steffens* [1931], p. 506).

The Roosevelt-Aldrich relationship grew more complex after 1904. As other members of the Senate leadership died, retired, or shifted ground to accommodate a growing insurgency among their Republican constituencies, Aldrich became an increasingly lonely figure. Curiously, this most powerful of politicians remained nearly tone-deaf when it came to the voice of the people. His failure to treat with the rising forces of progressive Republicanism contributed ultimately to electoral disaster for his party and left Aldrich to be caricatured by his opponents as the embodiment of troglodyte conservatism and special interest politics. By 1906 Roosevelt sanctioned efforts to expand the authority of the Interstate Commerce Commission (ICC) by giving it power to set railroad rates (rather than simply to challenge objectionable ones) and by limiting the ability of rail companies to frustrate or undermine ICC mandates by appeals to the generally conservative courts. Aldrich's adroit maneuvering managed to rein in Roosevelt's more generous gestures toward increased federal regulatory authority. While conceding greater power to the commission in terms of rate making, Aldrich and his allies wrote into the Hepburn Act amendments confirming the courts' powers to set aside or suspend ICC rates and allowing judges themselves to determine the extent to which they might second-guess commission decisions. As it turned out, however, judicial review of ICC cases tended thereafter to be limited. In the remaining years of Roosevelt's presidency, the congressional conservatives yielded relatively little to his reform agenda.

The skill with which Aldrich wielded his power during the early years of William Howard Taft's administration ensured passage in 1909 of what became known as the Payne-Aldrich Tariff, but ultimately this proved a Pyrrhic victory. The maintenance of high rates on numerous items in face of what many understood to have been the GOP's commitment in its 1908 platform to a general reduction of the tariff and the short shrift Aldrich gave progressive Republicans in terms both of their legislative objectives and committee assignments quickened the revolt within the party against the conservative congressional leadership. Interestingly, though, one of the maneuvers Aldrich used in the tariff's passage was to offer a constitutional amendment authorizing a federal income tax, long a goal of many reformers. Taft's acquiescence in the tariff and his apparent closeness to Aldrich widened the breach, leading to the party progressives' bolt to the Bull Moose standard in 1912. More immediately, the fracas contributed to the GOP congressional setback in 1910, the same year that Aldrich, nearly seventy, declined to stand for reelection.

Aldrich had become the avatar of a standpat Old Guard, but the final phase of his public career nevertheless illustrated a distinctive quality of the conservatism of his era—the willingness to contemplate rather profound structural change in government and finance, including centralization of authority, in order to impart greater stability to a boisterous economy. The panic of 1907 had underlined the need for a more flexible money supply that might expand during economic downturns and for greater coordination within America's decentralized banking system. The Aldrich-Vreeland Act of 1908 made some effort at providing means by which, during times of contraction, national banks might issue circulating notes on the basis of securities other than federal bonds. More importantly, it established a National Monetary Commission that Aldrich would chair. After detailed investigations at home and abroad, Aldrich committed himself to the establishment of a more centralized banking system and a more elastic currency based on commercial assets. The "Aldrich Plan," which he formally presented to the commission in early 1911, proposed a National Reserve Association comprised of banks organized in regional districts. This would permit a pooling of reserves, with the association empowered to issue circulating notes on the strength of those reserves. Member banks could exchange holdings of commercial paper for these notes, thus allowing the nation's supply of currency to grow or shrink as economic circumstance warranted. Aldrich's prestige in the business community and his vigorous advocacy doubtlessly advanced the goal of fundamental banking reform in those circles. For instance, his plan was endorsed by the American Bankers' Association. Ironically, though, his reputation as an agent of the "trusts" led some important reform advocates to distance themselves from his plan in their efforts to promote the cause in Congress and among the general public. Furthermore, the disarray within Republican ranks to which Aldrich had contributed and the consequent loss of control of Congress and the presidency doomed legislation based specifically on Aldrich's recommendations. The Federal Reserve Act (1913), crafted by a Democratic Congress, provided for a national association built on regional reserve banks empowered to rediscount members' commercial and agricultural paper. Yet Aldrich seemed reluctant to acknowledge it as a stepchild, criticizing the elements of public control incorporated into the legislation. He objected to government of the system by a Federal Reserve Board made up of political appointees. Under his system, government representatives were to sit on the board, but a majority of the directors were to be chosen by member banks. He further disapproved of the currency being issued by the government itself. Little more than a year after the passage of the Federal Reserve Act and four years after his retirement from the Senate, Aldrich died in New York City.

• The Nelson Aldrich Papers are in the Library of Congress, Manuscript Division, Washington, D.C. Unfortunately, the biography by Nathaniel Wright Stephenson, *Nelson Aldrich: A Leader in American Politics* (1930), is florid and unremittingly celebratory. Sharper assessments are in three works by Jerome L. Sternstein, "Nelson W. Aldrich: The Making of the General Manager of the United States, 1841–1886" (Ph.D. diss., Brown Univ., 1968); "Corruption in the Gilded Age Senate: Nelson W. Aldrich and the Sugar Trust," *Capitol Studies* 6, no. 1 (1978):13–37; and "King Leopold II, Senator Nelson W. Aldrich, and the Strange Beginnings of American Economic Penetration of the Congo," *African Historical Studies* 2 (1969): 189–204. See also James A. Rosmond, "Nelson Aldrich, Theodore Roosevelt and the Tariff: A Study to 1905" (Ph.D. diss., Univ. of North Carolina at Chapel Hill, 1974). Aldrich is, of course, prominently featured in many histories of American politics in the late nineteenth and early twentieth centuries, including David J. Rothman, *Politics and Power: The United States Senate 1869–1901* (1966); Lewis L. Gould, *The Presidency of Theodore Roosevelt* (1991); and Gabriel Kolko, *The Triumph of Conservatism: A Reinterpretation of American History, 1900–1916* (1963). An obituary is in the *New York Times*, 17 Apr. 1915.

PATRICK G. WILLIAMS

ALDRICH, Richard (31 July 1863–2 June 1937), music critic, was born in Providence, Rhode Island, the son of Elisha Smith Aldrich, a merchant, and Anna Elizabeth Gladding. His father, who sang in the Arion Choral Society under Jules Jordan, presumably encouraged the young Aldrich to pursue his interest in music. After graduating from public high school in 1881, Aldrich was admitted to Harvard College, where, besides taking regular humanities courses, he studied music with John Knowles Paine and honed his critical and writing skills as a member of the Harvard *Crimson*. His college years were coincident with the golden musical decade in Boston that included the founding of the Boston Symphony Orchestra in 1881 and the introduction, the same year, of musical and dramatic criticism by William Foster Apthorp at the *Boston Evening Transcript*. Aldrich proved himself to be an exceptional scholar, graduating A.B., magna cum laude, in 1885.

Aldrich's initial career as a journalist began on the *Providence Journal* in 1885 and lasted, except for a year of musical study in Germany, until 1889. He then took a position as private secretary to the junior senator from Rhode Island, Nathan F. Dixon, an appointment helped by the Aldrich name and the family's distant relationship to the illustrious senior senator Nelson Aldrich. While in the nation's capital Aldrich wrote music criticism for the *Washington Star*, an activity that attracted the attention of the *New York Tribune*, where he was appointed assistant music, art, and literary critic in 1891 as a colleague of Henry E. Krehbiel, the noted music authority. When William J. Henderson left the *New York Times* to go to the *New York Sun* in 1902, he recommended Aldrich as his successor.

Aldrich married Margaret Livingston Chanler in 1906; the couple had two children. The family owned two houses, one in Manhattan and "Rokeby," a weekend and summer retreat on the Hudson River not far from Tarrytown. He was elected to the National Institute of Arts and Letters and was a member of the fashionable social clubs in New York City—University, Century, and Harvard—as well as the St. Botolph club in Boston.

Not counting military duty during World War I as an intelligence officer on the General Staff from 1918 to 1919, Aldrich served as music editor and chief music critic of the *New York Times* until his retirement in 1923. After that long service, Aldrich spent a year in London as guest critic for the *Times*, and as critic emeritus for the *New York Times* he contributed occasional editorials and book reviews. By far the greatest part of his retirement activity was spent in the building and cataloging of his music library, considered one of the finest private collections in the United States. Aldrich died in Rome while on a visit to his younger brother.

Of the two distinct groups of music critics produced by the Gilded Age, one flamboyant and opinionated, the other reserved and modest, Aldrich clearly belonged to the latter. His Yankee motto, "Praise to the face is disgrace," summed up an unshakable feeling he never abandoned. Consequently, when Aldrich lauded a performance or a composition, his readers knew that he was indeed sincere. It was said of him that he always tried to shed light, not heat, in his criticism. His opinions were backed by meticulous musical scholarship and research, and he presented his thoughts in clear and careful prose that was remembered for its "aristocratic simplicity." Aldrich's *Musical Discourse* (1928), a collection of his writing on music, is valuable for both its content and its style. Insight into his broad, exploring musical tastes may be gathered from the fact that he was, simultaneously, a champion of Brahms and a proponent of Debussy's *Pelléas et Mélisande*. Otto Kinkeldey, one of America's first musicologists, called Aldrich a critical scholar who made musical journalism a literary fine art.

• Aldrich's personal library of music and books on music was given to Harvard University; his own guide to the collection was published as *A Catalogue of Books Relating to Music in the Library of Richard Aldrich* (1931). Besides Aldrich's reviews, feuilletons, and articles in periodicals and musical dictionaries, see the posthumously published selection of his criticism, *Concert Life in New York, 1902–1923* (1941). He also wrote *A Guide to Parsifal* (1904) and *A Guide to the Ring of the Nibelungen* (1905), and he translated Lilli Lehmann's *Meine Gesangskunst* under the title *How to Sing* (1902). A discussion of Aldrich and his contemporaries is in M. Sherwin, "The Classical Age of New York Musical Criticism, 1880–1920" (M.A. thesis, City College, CUNY, 1972). See also Oscar Thompson, "An American School of Criticism," *Musical Quarterly* 23 (1937): 428. Edward Downes, "Richard Aldrich," in *Dictionary of American Biography*, supp. 2 (1940), is valuable because it was written by the son of Olin Downes, Aldrich's successor on the *New York Times*, and contains information gleaned from Olin Downes and from Aldrich family sources. Obituaries are in the *New York Times*, 3 and 6 June 1937.

VICTOR FELL YELLIN

ALDRICH, Richard (17 Aug. 1902–31 Mar. 1986), theatrical producer, manager, and author, was born in Boston, Massachusetts, the son of Edward Irving Aldrich, a rubber company executive, and Mary Pickering Joy. Both parents were members of wealthy, prominent New England families. Aldrich in childhood formed a lifelong love of the theater, which he fostered in school productions and summer student performances. He did further stage work while he attended Harvard College, both with a touring student group called the Jitney Players during summers and with the Harvard Dramatic Club, which he served as president. Though tall and well-featured, Aldrich consistently preferred to work behind the scenes as producer and business manager rather than to perform on stage. He completed his education at Harvard in 1925.

During the next two years, Aldrich served as business manager for the American Laboratory Theater of Richard Boleslavsky in New York City and in the summer of 1926 managed an early summer stock company at Woodstock, New York. Following his marriage in 1927 to New York debutante Helen Beals, Aldrich became an officer of the Guaranty Trust Company but returned to theatrical work in late 1929. Later, in a biographical press release when he was an active producer, he would express the irresistible appeal stage production had for him: "It's creation . . . taking the author's idea and making it live. Of course you hope to get your money back and show a profit, but the sense of creating something that didn't exist before is your reward, and you have it even if the play fails. And that is why you always want to try again."

Aldrich's theatrical career is characterized as much by his sheer love of the theater as by a quest for commercial success. He was as enamored of summer stock as of Broadway production and "figured prominently in the development of summer theater in America" (*New York Times*, 16 Apr. 1986). As a longtime manager of the Cape Playhouse in Dennis, Massachusetts (1935–1955), he successfully met vacationers' desires for lighthearted entertainment and close proximity to star figures of the stage. Eventually he also opened the Falmouth Playhouse at Coonamessett and the Cape Cod Melody Tent at Hyannis to entertain "straw hat" audiences. Aldrich furthered the cause of theater in his Cape Cod productions by giving stars and producers a venue for trying out possible Broadway vehicles under favorable conditions. Further, he paid his small-part summer performers the Actors Equity minimum salary, an unprecedented move, and abolished the practice of charging apprentices for the opportunity to work on his productions, believing that talented novices, however short of funds, should have the opportunity to work in a professional atmosphere.

For two years during the 1930s, Aldrich was director of Colorado's Central City Opera House Summer Festival, where he offered audiences theater of challenging artistic quality: *A Doll's House* (1937) and *Ruy Blas* (1938). In 1939, seeing that managers of summer stock theaters had problems in common no matter how different their aims, he helped to organize the Stock Managers' Association and was elected its vice president.

Aldrich had entered the ranks of Broadway producers in 1930, when he became general manager and silent partner in the production firm of Kenneth Macgowan and Joseph Verner Reed. His first personal success with the firm came in 1931. While business manager for the Millbrook Playhouse that summer, he selected and produced a play that became the comedy *Springtime for Henry* (1931), enjoyed a successful run in New York City for Macgowan and Reed, and was a touring vehicle for actors for many years.

One of Aldrich's associates at Macgowan and Reed was Alfred de Liagre, Jr. In 1933 the two formed their own production firm and brought to the New York stage several successful domestic comedies: *Three-Cornered Moon* (1933), *By Your Leave* (1934), and *Petticoat Fever* (1935). The association ended in 1936 and Aldrich became play editor and stage producer for Columbia Pictures, requiring him to travel back and forth between New York and Hollywood as he scouted scripts that had potential for film production.

A new theatrical association for Aldrich began in 1937, when he formed a production firm with Richard Myers. The new partnership first offered *Tide Rising* (1937) and scored on Broadway with a revival of *The Importance of Being Earnest* (1939), with John Barrymore's final stage appearance in *My Dear Children* (1939), and with the melodramatic thrillers *Margin for Error* (1939) and *Cue for Passion* (1940). Aldrich's first marriage had ended in divorce in 1936; the marriage produced two children. In the summer of 1939 he met Gertrude Lawrence, one of the era's most glamorous theatrical stars, when she appeared in *Skylark* at the Cape Playhouse. They wed in 1940 and did not have any children.

Aldrich volunteered for naval service immediately after Pearl Harbor, was commissioned a lieutenant, and served as a staff officer both in the United States and Europe. He was retired from active duty in 1945 with the rank of commander. He returned to civilian life as a partner in Aldrich and Myers and as the managing director of Theatre, Incorporated. For the latter organization he concentrated on bringing theatrical ensembles from around the world to the United States, including the Old Vic Theatre Company, the Dublin Gate Company, and the Habimah Players of Tel Aviv. During 1946–1947 Theatre, Incorporated, also presented revivals of distinguished plays with leading stars: these included *Pygmalion* (Gertrude Lawrence and Raymond Massey), *The Playboy of the Western World* (Burgess Meredith), and *Macbeth* (Michael Redgrave and Flora Robson). Aldrich reopened the Cape Playhouse in the summer of 1946.

On Broadway, Aldrich and Myers continued active during the 1945–1955 decade. Their successes included *Goodbye My Fancy* (1948), revivals of *Caesar and Cleopatra* (1949) and *The Devil's Disciple* (1950), *The Moon Is Blue* (1951), and *The Love of Four Colonels* (1953). In 1951, during the period of the Korean Conflict, Aldrich returned to naval service in Washington, D.C., and Europe. His wife Gertrude Lawrence died in 1952, and over the next few years, Aldrich wrote a remarkable memoir of their marriage.

Many people in the theatrical world had not expected the marriage to survive. Lawrence was an international star of the first magnitude, so completely a performer that it seemed at times there was nothing to her but the series of roles she played; Noel Coward called her "seven women under one hat." Her consistencies were only in charm, chic, and high-spirited glamor. Aldrich was an old-line New Englander of traditional values except for being incurably stagestruck, an easygoing man whose personal means allowed him to be active in the theater without losing sight of other aspects of life.

Why had they been attracted in the first place? Lawrence's biographer, Sheridan Morley, believes Lawrence met Aldrich when she was entering her forties and beginning to feel alone. After many years of affairs and romances she now wanted, in the words of a Gershwin song she had introduced in a 1920s musical, "Someone to Watch over Me." In the Cape Playhouse surroundings, she responded to Aldrich's sincere devotion to the theater and to his characteristics of steadfastness and calm control. For Aldrich, Lawrence was the epitome of theatrical glamor that had entranced him since childhood. On his wedding day Aldrich called his mother to announce the event. He blurted out to her, "Mother, I was married to Gertrude Lawrence today," like a fan whose wildest daydream has come true. His mother, whose conservative views did not include approval of the theater, was less than thrilled.

Somehow the marriage overcame such obstacles as well as five years of wartime separation. The title of Aldrich's memoir is revealing: *Gertrude Lawrence as "Mrs. A": An Intimate Biography of a Great Star*. Being "Mrs. A" was a role Lawrence could play while retaining a great deal of independence as a star. Being "Mrs. A" gave her a family, including two sons by Aldrich's first marriage, and a stable home place on the Cape instead of a succession of hotel suites. The memoir does not underplay the couple's violent disagreements when values clashed. In it Aldrich depicts the marriage as a sophisticated comedy of fencing lovers—the sort of comedy-drama beloved of summer theater audiences between the wars—complete with a subplot of how Lawrence slowly won over a mother-in-law to whom people of theatrical antecedents and habits were deeply suspect. Only in its last few pages does the book turn somber, as he chronicles their belated, reluctant realization that her illness is fatal.

For Lawrence, her periods as "Mrs. A" provided the respites needed to sustain her star qualities. She did not burn herself out by her own unabated and unrelieved intensity, as did some other flamboyant theatrical personalities of her era. She was starring triumphantly in *The King and I* when she died suddenly of cancer. Presenting Lawrence as "Mrs. A" was Aldrich's most significant achievement of theatrical management, and the one with the longest run.

His memoir, published in 1955, was widely praised at the time. With its appearance, Aldrich's career in the theater effectively came to an end. He retired as manager of the Cape Playhouse in 1955 and turned to government service. From 1955 to 1962 he was director of the Economic Aid Mission and minister of the embassy for Economic Affairs in Madrid, Spain; from 1962 to 1965 he was also American aid director to Morocco. In 1955 he was married for a third time, to Elizabeth Boyd; they had two children. In later years, he lived at his home in East Dennis, Massachusetts. He died while visiting family members in Williamsburg, Virginia. His career in the theater may be seen as a lifelong act of love for theater as an institution, and his second marriage as an act of love for a woman who embodied all that "theater" means.

• Materials on the life and career of Richard Aldrich in the Billy Rose Theatre Collection at the New York Public Library for the Performing Arts, Lincoln Center, include an extensive biographical press release (on internal evidence, written in early 1953). Further factual information on his career and productions is in *Contemporary Theatre, Film and Television*, vol. 3 (1986). Besides the information about himself that Aldrich gives in his memoir, more personal information is in the profile by Robert Lewis Taylor in the *New Yorker*, 30 July 1955, and 6 Aug. 1955. Some details of Aldrich's marriage to Lawrence are in Sheridan Morley, *Gertrude Lawrence* (1981). An obituary is in the *New York Times*, 16 Apr. 1986.

WILLIAM STEPHENSON

ALDRICH, Robert Burgess (9 Aug. 1918–5 Dec. 1983), filmmaker, was born in Cranston, Rhode Island, the son of Edward Burgess Aldrich, a leading Rhode Island newspaper publisher and Republican politician, and Lora Lawson. His grandfather was Nelson Wilmarth Aldrich, a self-made millionaire and influential U.S. senator; his aunt Abby Greene Aldrich married John D. Rockefeller, Jr., and was the mother of their six children. Aldrich attended his father's alma mater, Moses Brown School in Providence, where he excelled in football and track and was elected president of the senior class, and the University of Virginia, which he left after four years without a degree in 1941. Unwilling to follow his father in publishing and politics or to engage in the Aldrich-Rockefeller banking and investment businesses, Aldrich approached his uncle Winthrop William Aldrich, who had some minor film interests in Hollywood, and asked for an introduction to the business.

When Aldrich went to California, he effectively cut connections with his powerful family. "He really didn't have much of a past," his son William later observed, and Aldrich generally presented himself as an outsider, omitting his parents' names from his standard biographical releases. Indeed, family rumor suggested that he may not have been Lora's child, and his relationship with his conservative father was generally strained. "He had these very democratic points of view," his daughter Adell explained, "and that family was *very* Republican, right wing, almost" (Arnold and Miller, p. 4).

Aldrich began work as production clerk at RKO Studios, which was, although one of the smaller companies, also one of the more adventurous. Rejected by the Air Force Motion Picture Unit for service during World War II because of a football injury, Aldrich spent the next years working his way up from an assistant and production clerk on comedy shorts to first assistant director on feature films, supporting such important filmmakers as Edward Dmytryk, Jean Renoir, Lewis Milestone, William Wellman, Robert Rossen, and Charles Chaplin, the last of whom employed Aldrich as assistant director on *Limelight* (1952). Especially significant were the two years (1946–1948) Aldrich worked at Enterprise Studios, an independent film company with a liberal social agenda that gave directors artistic freedom to develop their own projects. Among the films he worked on were *Body and Soul* (1947) with Robert Rossen and *Force of Evil* (1948) with Abraham Polonsky, two films that, with their emphasis on moral corruption and regeneration, deeply influenced Aldrich's later work. A number of Enterprise associates were later targeted for investigation by the U.S. House Un-American Activities Committee and were compelled to testify. Aldrich was not called, but his sympathies for those who were remained strong. "One tends to forget over the years that the black list included the best and the brightest, and only very few second-class citizens, second-guessers and opportunists were ostracized," he remarked in 1982 (Arnold and Miller, p. 14).

In the early 1950s Aldrich worked in television, directing and writing for "The Doctor" (1952–1953) and "Four Star Playhouse" (1953–1954). During a break he directed his first feature film, a low-budget baseball movie for MGM called *The Big Leaguer* (1953), starring Edward G. Robinson. Returning to television, Aldrich directed episodes of the "China Smith" series starring Dan Duryea. Aldrich then used the series as the basis of his second film, *World for Ransom* (1954), which he saw as a "parody of the usual exotic espionage adventure film." Still, he later noted that "my general film themes were crystallized in this [work]," explaining that the Duryea character "is a sort of antihero in his cynicism and general attitude towards humanity, but he has a code he follows unwaveringly . . . standing for a firmer order of individual liberty and respect for humanity."

Aldrich's third film moved him into the front ranks of American directors. *Apache* (1954) was a Harold Hecht–Burt Lancaster production, and Aldrich was selected by Lancaster to direct the film, which was one of the first "pro-Indian" westerns of the 1950s. Lancaster described it as the story of the "genocide of the Indian" (Arnold and Miller, p. 24), but Aldrich considered it an indictment of racism of any sort. Lancaster and Aldrich then collaborated on another western, but one full of comedy, duplicity, and grand adventure. *Vera Cruz* (1954) stars Gary Cooper as Ben Trane, a disillusioned man of honor who finally stands against his charming but deceitful and murderous partner Joe Erin (played by Lancaster). *Vera Cruz* is now recognized as a precursor of such later revisionist westerns as *The Wild Bunch* (1969).

Both *Apache* and *Vera Cruz* brought Aldrich favorable attention, especially among French critics, but it was *Kiss Me Deadly* (1955), his satiric version of Mickey Spillane's 1952 Mike Hammer detective novel, that earned him greatest praise. Aldrich saw Hammer (played by Ralph Meeker) as a "cynical and fascistic private eye" who represents an "anti-democratic" spirit (quoted in Combs, p. 54). The film was also an attack on the Cold War mentality and ended with the strong suggestion of nuclear apocalypse. Now recognized as Aldrich's early masterpiece, *Kiss Me Deadly*, as filmmaker and critic Paul Schrader states in "Notes on *Film Noir*" (*Film Comment* 8 [Spring 1972]: 8–13), "carries *noir* to its sleaziest and most perversely erotic." It remains the essential vision of Cold War America paranoia.

In 1955 Aldrich formed his own production company, the Associates and Aldrich, inspired in part by his experiences at Enterprise. His next three films firmly established Aldrich as a director of almost anarchic energy and audacity. *The Big Knife* (1955), based on Clifford Odets's 1949 Broadway play, attacks the Hollywood studio system. *Autumn Leaves* (1956) is a Freudian soap opera starring Joan Crawford; and *Attack!* (1956) remains one of the fiercest and most unsentimental of antiwar films. With each work Aldrich invested a different film genre with his own subversive, often corrosive morality. In his book *The War Film* (1974) film historian Norman Kagan calls *Attack!* "the first postwar film to connect the new brutality of war with the confusion, corruption, and incompetence of American leadership and American motives—in this sense it is the first Cold War anti-war film." Aldrich was awarded the Silver Prize at the Venice Film Festival for *The Big Knife* in 1955, the Best Director Award at the Berlin Film Festival for *Autumn Leaves* in 1956, and, also in 1956, the Italian Critics Award at the Venice Film Festival for *Attack!*

After such a sustained period of creative activity and (largely foreign) critical acclaim, Aldrich's fortunes fell. He had signed a three-picture distribution contract with Harry Cohn at Columbia Studios in 1954; *Autumn Leaves* was the first picture made under the deal. The second film was *The Garment Jungle* (1957), an exposé of corruption in the garment industry. Aldrich considered it a pro-labor picture, but Cohn demanded that he soften the film's portrayal of racketeers. Aldrich refused and was fired, replaced by Vincent Sherman, who received final directorial credit even though Aldrich had done most of the filming. For the next eighteen months he remained tied to his contract but essentially unemployed. Frustrated, Aldrich worked outside the United States between 1958 and 1961. The films he made during this period—*Ten Seconds to Hell* (1958), *The Angry Hills* (1959), *The Last Sunset* (1961), and *Sodom and Gomorrah* (filmed in 1961, released in the United States in 1963)—did nothing to revive his faltering career.

In 1961 Aldrich bought the screen rights to Henry Farrell's novel *What Ever Happened to Baby Jane?* Starring Bette Davis and Joan Crawford, the 1962 film was an enormous success, a psychological horror story about an aging former child star and her crippled sister. Aldrich followed the movie with a throwaway film, *4 for Texas* (1963), with Frank Sinatra and Dean Martin. He then turned back to horror with the more graphic *Hush . . . Hush, Sweet Charlotte* (1964), based on another Farrell novel and again starring Davis, with Olivia DeHavilland and Joseph Cotton. His next work, *The Flight of the Phoenix* (1965), about survivors of a plane crash in the desert, was one of his finest but did little business at the box office. Aldrich's next film proved to be his biggest success. *The Dirty Dozen* (1967), led by actor Lee Marvin, is a war film that utilizes the adventure narrative to condemn the brutality of battle. By drawing his American "heroes" from convicted murderers, rapists, and criminal psychopaths, Aldrich again challenged the notion of valor and righteousness in war at the very time the United States had become involved in the military engagement in Vietnam. That *The Dirty Dozen* became the most successful and reviled film of 1967 clearly illustrates the conflicted attitudes of contemporary American society. The film received four Academy Award nominations, but Aldrich was not nominated for his directing. He was, however, named Director of the Year by the National Association of Theatre Owners.

Aldrich's next film, *The Legend of Lylah Clare* (1968), is a bizarre, outrageous satire of Hollywood. Most critics considered it a ludicrous misstep; Aldrich felt its purpose was misunderstood. Nevertheless, the huge financial success of *The Dirty Dozen* allowed Aldrich the money and influence to purchase his own studio, for which he gathered together many of the artists and craftsmen he had worked with regularly on his films. The Enterprise philosophy greatly influenced his running of Aldrich Studios, but after the successive failures of the X-rated *Killing of Sister George* (1968), the war film *Too Late the Hero* (1970), and the gangster movie *The Grissom Gang* (1971), Aldrich was forced to sell.

In debt and reduced to freelancing for other studios, Aldrich proceeded to make one of his finest films, the western *Ulzana's Raid* (1972), a reworking of *Apache* with Lancaster in the role of the army scout who must track down the renegade Indian warrior. *Emperor of the North* (1973) reunited Aldrich with Marvin in a story of hobos during the depression. Aldrich yet again found commercial success with the prison-football movie *The Longest Yard* (1974), starring Burt Reynolds and Eddie Albert. Reynolds and Albert also acted in the underrated detective film *Hustle* (1975), a moody, dark, provocative critique of the corrupt seventies.

From 1971 to 1975 Aldrich served as first national vice president of the Directors Guild of America, and in 1975 he was elected president. For the following four years he set about reforming the guild. His administration was later recognized for its unprecedented emphasis on social and economic equity for all members of the filmmaking industry.

In 1977 Aldrich released two films: the cynical, pessimistic *Twilight's Last Gleaming*, with Lancaster as a former army general and prisoner of war who takes over a nuclear missile silo and Charles Durning as the president of the United States who becomes his doomed hostage; and *The Choirboys*, the crudely comic, vulgar, but uncompromising version of Joseph Wambaugh's bestselling police novel of the same name. Wambaugh was so unhappy with Aldrich's film that he sued to have his name removed from the screenplay; *The Choirboys* brought Aldrich the worst reviews of his career. Exhausted by legal and professional battles, he next attempted a low-key comic western, *The Frisco Kid* (1979), with Gene Wilder and Harrison Ford. His final film was *. . . All the Marbles* (1981), a story of professional female wrestlers and a pointed attack against the conservative social and economic policies of the new Reagan administration.

Aldrich died at his home in Los Angeles, California. Abraham Polonsky delivered the eulogy at the memorial service held by the Directors Guild of America. Aldrich was survived by his four children, all from his 1941 marriage to Harriet Foster, whom he had divorced in 1965, and by his second wife, Sibylle Siegfried, whom he had married in 1966. In the spring of 1994 the Film Society of Lincoln Center held an Aldrich retrospective titled *Apocalypse Anytime! The Films of Robert Aldrich*. Through all of his work Aldrich remained an iconoclast of the first rank, a romantic rebel who challenged systems and subverted genres, and a fierce moralist who insisted to the end that one hold true to one's beliefs—and to one's compatriots—whatever the cost.

• Aldrich's papers, including several original unmade screenplays, are in the American Film Institute and the Directors Guild of America in Los Angeles. An important bibliographical source is Alain Silver and Elizabeth Ward, *Robert Aldrich: A Guide to References and Resources* (1979). Richard Combs, *Robert Aldrich* (1978), contains highly perceptive essays by Combs and Tom Milne and an interview with Aldrich by Combs and Chris Petit. Edwin T. Arnold and Eugene L. Miller, *The Films and Career of Robert Aldrich* (1986), and Alain Silver and James Ursini, *What Ever Happened to Robert Aldrich: His Life and His Films* (1995), provide the most comprehensive studies of Aldrich's life and works. Studies in other languages include those titled *Robert Aldrich* by Rene Micha (1957); Claver Salizzato (1983); Jean-Pierre Piton (1985); and Michel Maheo (1987). A review of the Lincoln Center retrospective is in the *New York Times*, 11 Mar. 1994. An obituary is in the *New York Times*, 7 Dec. 1983.

EDWIN T. ARNOLD

ALDRICH, Thomas Bailey (11 Nov. 1836–19 Mar. 1907), author and editor, was born in Portsmouth, New Hampshire, the son of Elias Taft Aldrich, a businessman, and Sarah Abba Bailey. Aldrich was educated in Portsmouth under Samuel De Merritt, and the Portsmouth environs furnished the background for much of his work, as did the backdrops of New York City and Boston, where he spent his adult life. Aldrich moved to New York City at age sixteen to work in his uncle's commission house. After reading Henry Wadsworth Longfellow's "The Footsteps of Angels," he became an avid Longfellow admirer and dedicated himself to writing poetry.

During the early 1850s, Aldrich published poems in the *Sunday Atlas* and in *Harper's Monthly Magazine*. His first collection of poems, "The Bells: A Collection of Chimes," was published in 1855. That same year his poem "The Ballad of Babie Bell" made him an instant popular success and helped to open his way into the literary and artistic circles of New York City. Nathaniel Parker Willis, editor of the *Home Journal*, hired him first as a junior literary critic for the *Evening Mirror*. Within a year Aldrich had been appointed subeditor of the *Home Journal*.

Aldrich's early poetry, generally lyric, often follows Romantic tendencies. His earliest verse is sentimental and, like Poe's, deals with the deaths of beautiful women and young girls. Given his early life in Portsmouth, it is not surprising to see the Romantic sense of isolation developed in his work as well. Never an innovator, he had great respect for the traditional Romanticism of Tennyson, Keats, Shelley, Longfellow, William Cullen Bryant, and Poe, and he disliked realism in poetry.

Like most writers of his time, Aldrich wrote fiction as well as poetry. He began to write prose in the middle of the 1850s, while at the *Home Journal*. Just as he disliked realism in poetry, his short stories display no glimpse into the harsh reality that other authors of his time examined. In the main, his stories are neither profound nor socially conscious. His early fiction, like his poetry, tends to be imitative and sentimental, displaying the influences of Dickens, Poe, and Nathaniel Hawthorne. His first novel, *Daisy's Necklace: And What Came of It*, was published in 1857, and his first collection of stories and sketches, *Out of His Head*, appeared in 1862.

A collected edition of Aldrich's poetry was published in New York in 1863. Titled simply *Poems*, it was noticed by many of the New England literati and drew praise from Oliver Wendell Holmes (1809–1894) and Nathaniel Hawthorne, among others. Aldrich's poetic fame was assured when his work was published in 1865 in the prestigious Blue and Gold Series of Ticknor and Fields, the leading U.S. publishers at the time.

In 1865, with his new wife, Lilian Woodman, Aldrich moved to Boston to edit *Every Saturday*, which he continued to edit until 1874. The couple had twin sons, their only children, in 1868. In 1870, *The Story of a Bad Boy* was published in book form; it had been earlier serialized in the juvenile magazine *Our Young Folks*, as well as in *Atlantic Monthly* in 1869. This semiautobiographical novel depicts an adult narrator remembering his childhood in Portsmouth. As such, it is the first realistic treatment of American boyhood. Critics claim it is an early contribution to the development of realism and that it helped to establish the tradition of treating boyhood in American fiction. The novel is considered an influence on Mark Twain's *The Adventures of Huckleberry Finn*. William Dean Howells praised the originality of the boyhood theme in the *Atlantic Monthly*. Despite this originality, Aldrich was not adept in handling longer narrative structures, and the novel's weaknesses are evident in the episodic arrangement that lacks an effective climax. Aldrich's four other popular novels are unremarkable for similar reasons.

In 1873 Aldrich published *Marjorie Daw and Other People*, which contains a number of his best stories. Howells praised the collection, claiming that Aldrich had created a species of fiction "in which character and incident constantly verge with us towards the brink of a quite precipitous surprise ending without being for a moment less delightful as character and incident, and without being less so even when we look up from the gulf into which they have plunged us" ("Recent Literature," *Atlantic Monthly* 32 [Nov. 1873]: 625; as quoted in Samuels, p. 66). The short story "Marjorie Daw" was an instant success, gained an international reputation, and was anthologized well into the second half of the twentieth century. Like most of his fiction, it is not considered great literature but is an artfully crafted, well-told tale. A few other stories in this collection utilize local color techniques, though this is not a form he admired. Gothic tales painted in fanciful touches occur in this collection as well. Aldrich's fiction shows a good deal of variety and range. The pieces are noteworthy for their light touch, their amusing wit and charm, and, particularly, their surprise endings. On the whole, Aldrich's short fiction is skillfully crafted and aimed at providing pleasure if not read too seriously.

Aldrich wrote almost exclusively for the *Atlantic Monthly* for several years, eventually serving as editor from 1881 to 1890. As an editor, Aldrich was known for literary taste, attention to form, and precise craftsmanship. During his years at the *Atlantic Monthly* he drew contributions from such major literary figures as Longfellow, Holmes, Henry James (1843–1916), and Thomas Hardy. His tenure at this position, however, was probably not the most successful in the magazine's history, in spite of its being described in a London journal as "the best edited magazine in the English language" (Greenslet, p. 147). He lacked the range of interests that both Howells and James Russell Lowell enjoyed before him, and he was more interested in the cultivated rather than the general reader; as a result, readership declined during his editorship.

Aldrich was an immensely popular poet, novelist, and editor during his lifetime. Polls taken in the 1880s and 1890s by the *Critic*, the *Harvard Crimson*, and *Literature* favorably ranked him among the most popular and significant authors of his time. Esteemed and respected as a major literary figure during the last half of the nineteenth century, Aldrich has fared less well in the eyes of twentieth-century critics who acknowledge his competence but see him as a part of the declining New England tradition. His poetry is prettily made but imitative, which makes Aldrich one of the better minor poets in American literature; his art lacks the seriousness and innovation of the first rank of writers. He died at his home in Boston.

• Aldrich's manuscripts, papers, and personal effects are somewhat scattered. Most of his papers are preserved in the Harvard College Library. Other literary effects, such as manuscripts and correspondence, are elsewhere, including Princeton University, St. John's University in New York, and the University of Virginia. His primary works, not previously mentioned, include *The Course of True Love Never Did Run Smooth* (1858), *Poems* (1863), *Prudence Palfrey, a Novel* (1874), *From Ponkapog to Pesth* (1883), *Two Bites at a Cherry, with Other Tales* (1894), *The Poems of Thomas Bailey Aldrich: The Revised and Complete Household Edition* (1897), *A Sea Turn and Other Matters* (1902), *Ponkapog Papers* (1904), and *A Book of Songs and Sonnets Selected from the Poems of Thomas Bailey Aldrich* (1906).

Ferris Greenslet's *Thomas Bailey Aldrich* (1908) is the "official" biography and contains a number of his letters. A book-length study of Aldrich's work is Charles E. Samuel's *Thomas Bailey Aldrich* (1965), which puts Aldrich and his work into historical and critical perspective. This work also has an extensive bibliography of both primary and secondary materials related to Aldrich. Of additional interest is Mrs. Thomas Bailey Aldrich's *Crowding Memories* (1920), which supplements Greenslet's biography, recounting Aldrich's social life and friendships with major literary figures of the time, such as Mark Twain and William Dean Howells. Few articles on Aldrich's work have been written recently. See Ann Beattie's "The Story of a Bad Boy," *Children's Literature* 5 (1976): 63–65, for a later assessment of Aldrich's most famous novel. A chapter-length study of Bailey's tenure as editor of *Atlantic Monthly* is presented in Ellery Sedgwick's *A History of the Atlantic Monthly 1857–1909: Yankee Humanism at High Tide and Ebb* (1994). Aldrich's boyhood home, his library, and memorabilia from his office are preserved at a memorial in Strawberry Banke, a historic preservation site in Portsmouth, N.H.

ROBERT LEE LYNCH

ALDRICH, Winthrop (2 Nov. 1885–25 Feb. 1974), lawyer, banker, and legal and political adviser, was born Winthrop Williams Aldrich in Providence, Rhode Island, the son of Nelson Wilmarth Aldrich, a U.S. senator, and Abby Chapman. Aldrich graduated from Harvard College in 1907 and Harvard Law School in 1910. Upon graduation from law school Aldrich joined the New York City law firm of Byrne, Cutcheon & Taylor, specializing in finance and commercial law. In 1916 Aldrich was named a junior partner in the firm, and in December of that year he married Harriet Alexander, the granddaughter of California railroad and banking magnate Charles Crocker. The Aldrichs had six children.

Prior to the entry of the United States into World War I, Aldrich, an ardent yachtsman, joined the U.S. Naval Reserve. While in the reserve he enrolled at Uttmark's Nautical Academy in Brooklyn, New York, for advanced navigation training. When the United States entered the war, Aldrich was called to active duty and placed in command of a training regiment for naval reservists. His repeated request for sea duty was honored in June 1918 when he was assigned as the assistant navigating and communications officer aboard the U.S.S. New Orleans for convoy duty across the Atlantic. At the conclusion of his military service, in late 1918 Aldrich resumed the practice of law with the firm of Murray, Prentice & Howland, which, by the first of January 1921, became Murray, Prentice & Aldrich.

Aldrich's life and career were closely intertwined with the Rockefeller family. His sister, Abby Aldrich, was married to John D. Rockefeller, Jr., and Aldrich devoted his career to serving the Rockefeller family's financial and political interests. In the 1920s John D. Rockefeller, Jr., expanded the family's business into finance capitalism and acquired the Equitable Trust Company, through which he conducted that business. Aldrich served as his legal counsel and confidential adviser. During the 1920s and 1930s his role in the Rockefeller family business expanded in both scope and responsibility. Among the family projects in which Aldrich played a key role were the Williamsburg Restoration project in 1927, the creation of the Rockefeller Foundation in 1929, and the building of Rockefeller Center in 1932, the largest commercial project in New York City to that time.

The Equitable Trust Company remained at the center of the Rockefeller financial empire, and Aldrich was at the center of the Equitable Trust Company. With the onset of the Great Depression he took direct control of the day-to-day operations of Equitable and was named its president in December 1929. Equitable's $1 billion in assets included the bulk of the Rockefeller family fortune, and the preservation of this fortune became Aldrich's primary duty, for which he abandoned the practice of law. In 1930 he maneuvered the merger of the Equitable Trust Company and the Chase National Bank, creating the world's largest bank. Aldrich became its president.

During the early years of the Great Depression, Aldrich consulted frequently with President Franklin D. Roosevelt on economic policy and appeared often before key congressional committees on matters of banking regulation and monetary policy. In the late fall of 1933 the Senate Banking and Currency Committee, under the aggressive direction of its chief counsel, Ferdinand Pecora, probed stock exchange practices. The investigation quickly focused on Chase Securities Corporation, a subsidiary of Chase Bank. At issue was whether Chase Securities illegally attempted to control corporations through its stock purchases or whether it was merely guiding client investments, as it claimed. While no criminal indictments resulted from the probe, Chase chairman Charles McCain resigned and was replaced by Aldrich, who immediately separated Chase's stock investments from the Chase commercial banking operation. In 1934 he was named to the Business Advisory Council of the U.S. Department of Commerce.

Aldrich's relationship with Roosevelt was cordial but guarded. Each man understood the power of the other, and they knew that ultimately their interests would diverge, but during Roosevelt's first term they sublimated personal and political differences to common interests. By 1935, however, Aldrich was speaking out against New Deal economic policies with increasing frequency. In 1936 he was one of the prime organizers of the anti-New Deal Liberty League and an early promoter of Kansas Governor Alfred M. Landon for the Republican presidential nomination.

As president of Chase, Aldrich supervised Rockefeller financial interests worldwide and established banking affiliates throughout Europe and Latin America. The rise of the Nazi party in Germany presented a special challenge to Chase interests in Europe. On 13 August 1933 Aldrich met with German Chancellor Adolf Hitler at Berchtesgaden to voice his concerns over Nazi policies, particularly the discriminatory treatment of German Jews. He was concerned about the security of approximately $35 million in Chase loans extended throughout Germany, and he feared that Hitler's policies would destabilize finance throughout Europe. Aldrich's meeting with Hitler did not resolve his concerns, and he emerged from the meeting an implacable foe of the Nazi regime.

With the onset of World War II in Europe, he became a forceful advocate for British interests within American business and political circles. He urged amendment of the Neutrality Act to provide active assistance to Britain, and he organized the American Society for British Medical and Civilian Aid. In 1940, at the height of the Battle of Britain, he organized the British-American Ambulance Corps and later that year headed an expanded Allied Relief Fund that provided food, medicine, and clothing to the battered British.

Sharing Roosevelt's interest in aiding the British cause, Aldrich suspended his criticism of the New Deal and emerged as one of the staunchest supporters of the president's foreign policy. He was one of the most vocal advocates of Roosevelt's Lend-Lease proposal in the spring of 1941. The following year Aldrich embarked on a dangerous personal tour of war-ravaged Britain and, as Roosevelt's unofficial personal emissary, met with high-ranking British officials in London. Aldrich also met with Chase Bank affiliates throughout England, and Chase business mingled freely with American interests.

With the U.S. entry into World War II, Aldrich, with Roosevelt's approval, was offered the chairmanship of the National War Fund, a civilian war relief agency that distributed massive aid to America's European allies, especially Great Britain, to bolster their ability to resist German advances. In 1943 the National War Fund under Aldrich distributed over $100 million in aid. Following the Allied victory over the Axis Powers, Aldrich took an active part in rebuilding the devastated world economy. In 1946 President Harry S. Truman appointed Aldrich to a high-level advisory committee on economic recovery; also that year he consulted on the creation of the World Bank; in 1947 he actively supported the Marshall Plan for the reconstruction of Europe.

Politically Aldrich's influence within the Republican party grew in the postwar years. As well as being a close adviser, he was a major financial benefactor of New York Governor Thomas E. Dewey, Truman's 1948 Republican challenger. Aldrich was widely believed to be the governor's choice for secretary of the treasury in a Dewey administration. Denied that opportunity by the voters, Aldrich remained active in Republican circles during Truman's second term. In 1952 the Republican party, sensing victory after twenty years of Democratic rule, was torn between General Dwight D. Eisenhower and Ohio Senator Robert A. Taft. For Aldrich the choice was clear. The elements in the party who favored Eisenhower promoted an internationalist foreign policy, one conducive to the worldwide scope of the Rockefeller financial interests; those who supported Taft advocated a less direct American involvement in the affairs of Europe and the world. For his active support for Eisenhower, which helped to shape the Republican party in the postwar decades, Aldrich was rewarded with the coveted presidential appointment to serve as ambassador to Great Britain, accepted eagerly, but only after consultation with his brother-in-law, John D. Rockefeller, Jr.

Aldrich served as U.S. ambassador to Great Britain from 1952 through 1957, when he retired from public life. His retirement years were occupied with his favorite pastime, yachting, and with charitable work for varied causes, especially service as a trustee of the Columbia Presbyterian Medical Fund. He died in New York City.

• The most comprehensive Aldrich biography is Arthur M. Johnson, *Winthrop W. Aldrich: Lawyer, Banker, Diplomat* (1968). Also useful is the essay on Aldrich in *Washington and Wall Street* (1933), an anonymously written compilation of biographical essays on thirteen prominent U.S. capitalists and financiers, as well as William H. Hillyer, "Men of Achievement: Winthrop Aldrich," *Forbes*, 15 Jan. 1948. For Aldrich's career in service to Rockefeller business and political interests, see Peter Collier and David Horowitz, *The Rockefellers: An American Dynasty* (1976). For his role as Republican party power broker in the 1940s and 1950s and as adviser and confidant to New York Governor Thomas E. Dewey, see Richard Norton Smith, *Thomas E. Dewey and His Times* (1982). Charles Higham, *Trading with The Enemy: An Exposé of The Nazi-American Money Plot, 1933–1949* (1983), is a controversial examination of Aldrich's participation, as chairman of Chase National Bank, in multinational financing of the German war effort in World War II. His pivotal role in the political and economic decisions surrounding U.S. military mobilization during the early years of the Cold War is covered in detail in Frank Kofsky, *Harry S. Truman and the War Scare of 1948* (1993). An obituary is in the *New York Times*, 26 Feb. 1974.

FREDERICK J. SIMONELLI

ALDRIDGE, Ira Frederick (24 July 1807–10 Aug. 1867), actor, was the son of Daniel Aldridge, a minister, and Lurona (maiden name unknown). Though certain historical accounts record that he was born in Senegal, Africa, the grandson of the Fulah tribal chieftain, modern biographical scholarship proves that Aldridge was born in New York City and that while Fulah ancestry is possible, his lineal descent from tribal royalty is unconfirmed. Extant evidence concerning Aldridge's life is largely sketchy, conflicting, or exaggerated, possibly due in part to the aggrandizements of theatrical publicity.

As a young boy Aldridge left home to attend the African Free School in New York. Although Aldridge's father intended for him to join the clergy, Aldridge showed an early inclination for the stage, excelling at debate and declamation. Around 1821 Aldridge tried to perform at Brown's Theatre (also known as the African Theatre), but his father forced him from the stage. English playbills state that Aldridge came via the African Theatre, New York, so Aldridge must have circumvented his father's objections before the theater was closed in 1823. Recognizing the slim prospects for an African-American actor in the United States at a time of strong prejudices against blacks, Aldridge made plans to emigrate to England.

Aldridge became a dresser to the English actor Henry Wallack, who was performing in New York. Henry Wallack's brother, James, employed Aldridge as a personal attendant while on passage to Liverpool. J. J. Sheahan, a friend of Aldridge's, wrote that James Wallack had planned to sponsor Aldridge and make money off his engagements, but when Wallack told a reporter that Aldridge was his servant, the two went their separate ways. (The often-repeated account that Aldridge became the personal attendant of Edmund Kean and accompanied him back to England has been proven false.) Aldridge arrived in England in 1824, and although he announced his return to the United States a number of times throughout his career, he never returned.

Although it has been generally accepted that Aldridge made his debut in England in 1826 as Othello, playbills show that his first major engagement in London was at the Royal Coberg Theatre on 10 October 1825 under the name Mr. Keene. Aldridge, also dubbed the "African Roscius," acted under this name until around 1832. In his debut, Aldridge played the royal slave Oroonoko in *The Revolt of Surniman*. During this engagement he also played in *The Ethiopian* and *The Libertine Defeated*. That the engagement was a success for Aldridge can be seen in a playbill announcing his appearance in *The Negro's Curse*, a play written expressly for him. His biographers suggest Aldridge rose to leading roles so quickly in part because of the novel appeal of having a "Man of Colour" in the cast. While many reviewers during the early part of his career doubted the ability of a black actor, saying, for example, "Owing to the shape of his lips it is utterly impossible for him to pronounce English in such a manner as to satisfy the unfastidious ears of the gallery" (*The Times* [London], 11 Oct. 1825), Aldridge was popular with the audience.

The prejudiced criticism demonstrated in the London press made it difficult for Aldridge, despite his popularity with the public, to establish a career in the city. He turned, therefore, to the English provinces. For the next twenty-five years he developed his craft. In his first provincial engagement at Brighton he played Oroonoko and, for the first time on record, Othello, making no great impression. He toured Sheffield, Halifax, Manchester, Newcastle, Edinburgh, Lancaster, Liverpool, and Sutherland. His repertoire consisted of *Othello*, *Oroonoko*, *The Slave*, *The Castle Spectre*, *The Padlock*, and *The Revenge*. *Othello* and *The Padlock* remained in his repertoire until his death.

In 1829 he appeared in Belfast, with Charles Kean playing Iago to Aldridge's Othello and Oroonoko to his Aboan. In 1830 Aldridge played his first "white" role, Captain Hatteraick in *Guy Mannering*, using white makeup and a wig. Afterward, Aldridge regularly played "white" roles, such as Shylock in *The Merchant of Venice* and Rob MacGregor in *Rob Roy*. In 1833 Aldridge played Dublin and for the first time crossed paths with Edmund Kean. Playing in overlapping engagements, Edmund Kean witnessed Aldridge's Othello and afterward recommended him to the Royal Theatre at Bath, a prestigious provincial theater. Within three weeks, Aldridge opened at Bath with his regular repertoire.

In 1833 Aldridge was invited to appear at the Theatre Royal Covent Garden, where he opened as Othello to Ellen Tree's Desdemona. The London press, however, was still on the whole unwilling to accept a black leading actor at its major theaters. A few critics found his performance commendable, but most agreed that the Covent Garden was no place for a "curiosity" such as Aldridge. He had been scheduled to appear in two other roles at the Covent Garden, but these performances were canceled for reasons that remain vague. It is believed the threats of critics perhaps convinced the Covent Garden manager, Pierre Laporte, the "novelty" was not worth the financial risk. Whatever the reason for the cancellation, Aldridge's achievement is recorded by his biographers, who commented that his performance at the Covent Garden "will forever be red-letter days in the history of world theatre and human progress, for . . . a lone Negro from an enslaved people challenged the great white actors in the very heart of their Empire" (Marshall and Stock, p. 135).

Rejected by London for a second time, Aldridge returned to the provinces for a number of successful years. In 1852 he began his first tour of the Continent. His success in Europe was unequaled by any other in his career. His first tour through Belgium, Hungary, Germany, Austria, and Poland lasted three years. In 1857 he toured to Sweden, and after this time he continually toured the continent, including Russia, until his death, returning to England periodically to play the provinces. It was on his first tour that he added the roles of Macbeth, King Lear, and Richard III to his repertoire and received great honors from the princes of Europe. The king of Prussia awarded him the Gold Medal of the First Class for Art and Sciences; in Vienna the emperor presented him with the Medal of Ferdinand; and he was made an honorary member of the Hungarian Dramatic Conservatoir in Hungary, the Imperial and Archducal Order of Our Lady of the Manger in Austria, and the Imperial Academy of Beaux Arts in St. Petersburg. After playing the major cities of Europe to royalty and accolades, it is no wonder that Aldridge preferred to tour Europe rather than the small provincial theaters of England. The racism in the United States and, to a lesser extent, England, was not present in other European countries at the time. As a result, Aldridge thrived in a continental Europe that judged him by his ability on the boards rather than the color of his skin. In 1858, however, Aldridge finally found success at the Lyceum Theatre and in 1863 was granted British citizenship.

His biographers credit Aldridge with being "the first to show that a black man could scale any heights in theatrical art reached by a white man—and recreate with equal artistry the greatest characters in world drama" (Marshall and Stock, p. 335). Known for his versatility, Aldridge played both the greatest tragic characters of Shakespeare as well as the melodramatic slave characters of his early career with dexterity. A physically impressive man, Aldridge was known for his strong, clear voice and a style more realistic than that used by his contemporaries—so realistic that accounts by actors mention that Aldridge caused them to forget they were on a stage and the play became "naked, shattering reality." He was known as well for personalizing his roles, especially Othello—he studied and interpreted his roles with little consideration for the traditional interpretation. When abroad, he acted in English while his supporting cast used the native language—one Russian actor who worked with Aldridge, Davydov, said that "his mimicry, gestures, were so expressive that knowledge of the English language for the understanding of his acting was not needed at all" (V. N. Davydov, *Razkaz o Proshlom* [1930], p. 98).

Aldridge was married twice, although we know very little about the women he married. His first wife, Margaret, whom he married in 1832, was an Englishwoman, and his second wife, Amanda Paulina, whom he married in 1865, was Swedish. Aldridge had four surviving children by his second wife. He died in Lodz, Poland, while on his way to perform in St. Petersburg.

• Because of the conflicting accounts of Aldridge's life, any study should begin with Herbert Marshall and Mildred Stock, *Ira Aldridge: The Negro Tragedian* (1958), and Marshall, *Further Research on Ira Aldridge: The Negro Tragedian* (1970), the only documented treatments of his life. Information in other sources should be corroborated. *Memoir and Theatrical Career of Ira Aldridge: The African Roscius* (1848) is an excellent source of reviews and correspondence; however, the information it contains is sometimes contradictory. Other sources include Mary Malone, *Actor in Exile: The Life of Ira Aldridge* (1969); Charlamae Rollins, *Famous Negro Entertainers of the Stage, Screen, and TV* (1967), a children's book; Fountain Peyton, *A Glance at the Life of Ira Frederick Aldridge* (1917); and Errol Hill, *Shakespeare in Sable* (1990). His obituary is in *The Times* (London), 18 July 1867.

MELISSA VICKERY-BAREFORD

ALEMANY, Joseph Sadoc (13 July 1814–14 Apr. 1888), first Roman Catholic archbishop of San Francisco, was born in Vich, Spain, one of twelve children of Antonio Alemany y Font, a blacksmith, and Micaela de los Santos Cunill y Saborit. Alemany entered the diocesan seminary in 1824, and six years later he entered the Dominican order. In 1835, when the secularization laws closed the religious houses in Spain as a result of the anticlerical party in power, he went to Italy to complete his studies for the priesthood. He was ordained in 1837 in Viterbo, Italy.

In 1840 Alemany emigrated to the United States to work in the "mission" territories of Ohio, Tennessee, and Kentucky. In 1848 he was named prior provincial of the Dominican order in the United States, and in 1850, he was appointed the first bishop of Monterey, Upper California. In July 1853, he was made archbishop of the newly created Metropolitan See of San Francisco.

Alemany was truly a missionary bishop. He traveled the vast reaches of his archdiocese by horse and stagecoach to visit his people and provide them with the sacrament of confirmation. Within San Francisco he lived humbly. Archbishop Herbert Vaughan wrote of Alemany, "No man is more poorly lodged in the whole city, and no man preaches the spirit of evangelical poverty" more sincerely.

Besides its missionary character, Alemany's episcopacy was characterized by the building of basic institutions. He repeatedly petitioned funds from the Society of the Propagation of the Faith in Paris and Lyons. In addition, he tried to reach a favorable settlement with the government of Mexico on the disputed Pious Fund, a missionary fund established for the church in California but confiscated by the Mexican government in the 1840s. Finally, Alemany secured legal title to all church land in his archdiocese.

Alemany also worked hard to provide the archdiocese with a sufficient supply of priests and religious men and women. Besides establishing his own seminary, St. Thomas Seminary at Mission Dolores, he repeatedly sought help from Europe, particularly graduates of All Hallows College in Dublin, Ireland. During his episcopate, several orders established houses in the archdiocese, including the Jesuits, Dominicans, the Christian Brothers, Presentation, Holy Name Sisters, the Sisters of Mercy, Notre Dame de Namur, St. Joseph of Carondolet, the Daughters of Charity, and the Ursulines. He oversaw the building of scores of churches, including San Francisco's first cathedral, St. Mary's, completed in 1854.

Alemany ministered to a diverse ethnic flock—Irish, Italian, German, French, Hispanic, Chinese—by appointing priests who spoke their languages or by establishing a national parish, which he did for the French (1856), German (1860), Spanish (1875), and

Italian (1884) communities. (A national parish had no territorial boundaries and so could be attended by anyone who was of the nationality designated.) In addition, he oversaw the building of Catholic grade schools, colleges, orphan asylums, hospitals, and other charitable and educational agencies.

In 1870 he attended the First Vatican Council in Rome, where he supported the definition of papal infallibility. In 1884 Alemany resigned the episcopacy and returned to his native Spain, where he was appointed titular archbishop of Pelusium. He died in Valencia and was buried in Vich, Spain.

• A number of Alemany's diaries and letterbooks are in the Archives of the Archdiocese of San Francisco, Menlo Park, Calif. The best biography remains John B. McGloin, S. J., *California's First Archbishop: The Life of Joseph Sadoc Alemany, 1814–1888* (1966).

JEFFREY M. BURNS

ALEXANDER, Abraham (c. 1718–23 Apr. 1786), early leader in Mecklenburg County, North Carolina, was born probably in Cecil County, Maryland, the son of Francis Alexander (mother's name unknown). Alexander was descended from one of several families bearing his surname who arrived in the middle colonies from Northern Ireland early in the eighteenth century, many of them settling in Cecil County. His grandfather, Joseph Alexander, a tanner, recorded his will in Cecil County in 1726. His father may have migrated with his wife and children, but it is more likely that Abraham was in the vanguard of younger relatives who commenced relocating in the early 1750s to the southern piedmont of North Carolina. The Alexander clan was enticed to the region by Lord George Augustus Selwyn and Arthur Dobbs, the latter a Scots-Irishman himself and royal governor, 1754–1765. These promoters and land speculators were so successful that the Scots-Irish dominated this part of North Carolina for decades.

Very little is known about Alexander's personal life. As a member of a religious denomination known to value learning, he had basic schooling and perhaps some training in an academy in Maryland. In keeping with family tradition, he may have served an apprenticeship. On the Carolina frontier, he farmed, and his land was located on Alexander's Mill Creek, a fact that may indicate he was a miller. It is likely that he did not marry until he moved south since his wife, Dorcas (maiden name unknown), was fourteen years his junior. Several of their children were born in the early 1760s and one about 1770 (total number of children is unknown).

Without doubt his public influence sprang from, and was nurtured by, his status within the Scots-Irish community. He was an elder of Sugar Creek Presbyterian Church, the oldest congregation of the region. He and his wife are buried in its graveyard. In 1771 he was one of the Presbyterians who obtained a charter from the North Carolina assembly for Queen's College. Their plans were frustrated, however, when British authorities negated the charter on the grounds they did not want a college controlled by dissenters known to be antipathetic, and increasingly antagonistic, toward English authority. Alexander remained active among trustees seeking to salvage the school by renaming it Queen's Museum and later, in 1777, obtaining a charter from the assembly designating it Liberty Hall. The college closed permanently in 1780 when British troops invaded the area.

His political career centered on local affairs. It must be presumed that his political views mirrored those of the majority of his brethren. During the 1760s, the Scots-Irish were one of the few distinguishable groups loyal to royal governors. Some historians believe that they feared disloyalty would jeopardize their land titles. Their history, going back to Ireland, taught them it was wiser to accommodate rulers than suffer retaliations for opposition. Since most other backcountry settlers resented the control exerted by royal government based at distant New Bern, they joined a loosely organized opposition known as Regulators or sympathized with them. The Scots-Irish and their neighbors often had strained relations.

Alexander's public career reflects the benefits and at least one painful result of his political stance in the 1760s. In 1762 he served briefly on Governor Dobbs's council. In that same year, when Mecklenburg County was created, he was appointed one of the first justices of the peace, a position he held for much of the balance of his life. He became chairman of the Inferior Court of Pleas and Quarter Sessions. In 1765 he and several of his relatives including John McKnitt Alexander, a cousin and surveyor, were measuring lands for Lord Selwyn when they were assaulted and beaten by squatters. In 1768 he was among trustees receiving 360 acres from Henry McCulloch, agent for Lord Selwyn, for the town of Charlotte. He was subsequently involved in laying off lots and building a courthouse. In 1769 he was elected to the North Carolina assembly.

His most consequential association was with the county militia, which he joined when it was formed in 1762. He served as an officer and remained active in its affairs at least through the 1770s. His home was one of the mustering sites. While the militia gathered to drill, contemporary accounts indicate that officers and men spent much time discussing politics. Whatever the range of opinions expressed during the 1760s, the organization never wavered openly in its support of duly constituted authority. As late as 1771, when Governor William Tryon, who had succeeded Dobbs, asked for volunteers, Mecklenburg men marched to Alamance Creek to put down the Regulators, though they arrived too late to participate in the battle.

Sometime in the early 1770s members of the militia underwent an attitudinal shift. Knowledge of happenings in other colonies had an influence, but Governor Josiah Martin, who had succeeded Tryon, provided sufficient provocations to arouse North Carolinians. In attempting to inhibit growing discontent, he dissolved the assembly in 1774. Alexander, whose term in that body had ended in 1773, was elected in 1774 to

North Carolina's first provisional assembly. Militia leaders reexamined their position in the light of threatening events. In the spring of 1775, Colonel Thomas Polk, commander, directed that every company send two delegates to Charlotte for a conference. Alexander was chosen as one of the representatives for his company.

Alexander's significance as a revolutionary leader rests on his participation in this conference. He was elected chairman, which indicates his prestige, but his role beyond that of presiding officer is clouded. Minutes of the proceedings burned in 1800, and reminiscences collected in the early nineteenth century provide the only record. From these memorials some historians conclude that the conference yielded two documents; the first, known as the Mecklenburg Declaration of Independence, was approved on 20 May. Not published until 1819, critics point to some wording strikingly similar to phrases found in the national Declaration of Independence. In fact, an aged Thomas Jefferson labeled the Mecklenburg declaration spurious. Whether authentic or not, extant reconstructed copies show Abraham Alexander and four of his kinsmen, all grandsons of Joseph Alexander, among the signers. Of the twenty-seven names affixed at least twenty are Scots-Irish. No evidence has been offered that Abraham Alexander was on the three-man committee that supposedly drafted the declaration.

Eleven days later, on 31 May, the conference produced the Mecklenburg Resolves. The validity of this document has never been challenged. The series of resolutions were intended to justify revocation of allegiance to the Crown and provide mechanisms for self-rule. In effect, the Scots-Irish and other militia released themselves from their oaths and freed themselves to espouse openly the Whig cause. No record credits Abraham Alexander as a framer of the resolves.

During the following years, a period that approximately coincides with the last ten years of his life, Alexander continued to be active locally. He was chairman of the Mecklenburg Committee of Safety, which served as a civil government until the state established a permanent county government. He continued to serve as a magistrate and an officer in the militia. He died in Mecklenburg County.

On one level, Alexander's public service indicates he retained the support of constituents because of his character, judgment, and temperament. What may never be known is whether he was merely a spokesman reflecting community values or a leader making and shaping public opinion who participated in writing significant revolutionary statements. On another level, his life is the story of the evolution of a Scots-Irish colonial who followed the royal governor in the 1760s but became a dedicated Whig by 1775, presumably convinced that independence was necessary to protect personal liberties.

• Abraham Alexander left no body of papers pertaining to his public career. Some public records mention him, but do not provide much biographical data. Alexander's ancestry and that of many of his contemporaries may be found in the suggestively titled genealogical compilations of Worth S. Ray, *The Mecklenburg Signers and Their Neighbors* (1946).

Based on the early nineteenth century recollections of what transpired in 1775, some writers have concluded that Alexander was an important revolutionary leader without offering supporting documentation for their views. A traditional interpretation, in one of the briefest sketches published in this extensive series, will be found in Samuel A. Ashe, ed., *Biographical History of North Carolina: From Colonial Times to the Present*, vol. 1 (1905), pp. 37–38. Many local histories give Alexander accolades, particularly those written years ago, such as John B. Alexander, *The History of Mecklenburg County from 1740 to 1900* (1902). More recent popular histories, an example of which is LeGette Blythe and Charles R. Brockmann, *Hornets' Nest: The Story of Charlotte and Mecklenburg County* (1961), tend to follow the evaluations of academic historians who have discounted the older view that two documents were written in 1775.

To understand the growth of the spirit of opposition to the British, see Charles R. Sellers, "Making a Revolution: The North Carolina Whigs, 1765–1775," in *Studies in Southern History*, vol. 39, ed. J. Carlyle Sitterson (1957), pp. 23–46; this author does not make Alexander a leader in the movement. An authoritative history by William S. Powell, *North Carolina through Four Centuries* (1989), confines commentary about the Mecklenburg Declaration of Independence to a footnote (p. 177, note 3), doubting that such a document was written. Powell fails to mention Alexander in either text or footnotes.

CONVERSE D. CLOWSE

ALEXANDER, Archibald (17 Apr. 1772–22 Oct. 1851), theological scholar, was born in what is today Rockbridge County, Virginia, near Lexington, the son of William Alexander and Ann Reid, farmers. Alexander's father was also a merchant. By local standards, the Alexanders enjoyed a solid affluence.

Alexander enrolled in 1781 at Liberty Academy (later Washington and Lee College). In 1788 or 1789 Alexander became private tutor in the family of General Posey in Spottsylvania County, about twelve miles west of Fredericksburg. There he underwent a spiritual crisis. Exposed to a revival among Baptists, Alexander admired their fervid evangelicalism and longed to experience a more vital piety. Yet he was also troubled by what he deemed the ignorance of the Baptist exhorters, and his wide reading made him acutely aware that many intelligent people had rejected Christianity for deism. Subsequently he found books that provided a reasoned defense of Christian faith, and this discovery marked a watershed in his life. Maintaining the unity of piety and learning would remain his enduring passion.

Alexander returned to the Lexington area to pursue theological studies with William Graham, a Presbyterian minister and the principal of Liberty Academy. Licensed as a Presbyterian minister in 1791, Alexander itinerated among many churches in Virginia and North Carolina. In 1794 he was ordained to the pastorate of the Briery and Cub Creek churches in Charlotte County, Virginia. In 1797 he assumed the presidency of Hampden-Sydney College, a position he held, except for one year, until 1806. He was elected a commissioner or delegate in 1801 to his denomination's highest governing body, the General Assembly. The assembly sent Alexander and two others as official representatives to the Congregational General Association of Connecticut. Their mission produced the Plan of Union whereby Congregationalists and Presbyterians agreed to cooperate in the formation of new churches west of the Hudson River. In 1802 Alexander married Janetta Waddel. The couple had seven children of whom two—James Waddel Alexander and Joseph Addison Alexander—eventually served as colleagues with their father at Princeton Seminary.

In 1807 Alexander became the minister of the Third (also called the Pine Street) Presbyterian Church in Philadelphia and was elected moderator of the General Assembly. In 1808 Alexander preached to the General Assembly a sermon aligning himself with a rising movement to create a theological seminary for the education of ministers, and two years later the assembly appointed him to a committee to prepare a plan for such an institution. The assembly of 1812 put the plan into effect, creating the Theological Seminary in Princeton and electing Alexander the first professor. Although he bore the entire course of instruction until the appointment of Samuel Miller (1769–1850) in 1813, Alexander's teaching responsibilities lay chiefly in the area of theology and philosophy.

Alexander's first book, *A Brief Outline of the Evidences of the Christian Religion* (1825), delineated the rational grounds for adhering to Christian faith; a revised edition in 1836 gave especial attention to demonstrating the trustworthiness of the Bible. Chastened by his encounter with religious skepticism, Alexander sought to establish theological knowledge upon scientific, objective grounds. Undergirding this stance was his commitment to the Scottish commonsense philosophy (or Scottish realism) to which he had first been exposed by William Graham.

When the Presbyterian church polarized into Old and New School factions beginning in the late 1820s, Alexander's sympathies lay with the more conservative Old School. That group called for strict adherence to the denomination's creed (the Westminster Confession), had misgivings about the growing power of extra-ecclesiastical voluntary societies, and distrusted the exuberant revivalism then common in many sectors of Protestantism, including the New School Presbyterians. The Old School saw disorder in evangelistic devices such as the anxious bench, protracted meetings, and services in which women spoke or censorious language was used. The conservatives accused the New School of teaching views that contradicted the Westminster Confession's pronouncements on Original Sin and the inability of people to contribute to their salvation. The Old School attributed many of these evils to the infiltration, via the Plan of Union, of New England Congregationalist practices and the theological revisions of Nathaniel William Taylor of Yale Divinity School. Despite his basic agreement with Old School theology, Alexander initially remained aloof from the more extreme Old School partisans for fear that their policies would divide the church. When the Old School secured a majority at the General Assembly of 1837, it abrogated the Plan of Union and expelled from the denomination a number of churches organized under the plan. The following year the New School Presbyterians established a separate church. Alexander was a commissioner to the 1837 assembly and voted, apparently with some reluctance, for portions of the Old School program. Thereafter Alexander and his colleagues at the seminary were loyal partisans of the Old School cause.

Alexander exhibited similar caution toward the slavery question. Although at least one of his early sermons contained an oblique criticism of human bondage, Alexander never condemned it per se but held an essentially romantic and paternalistic view of slavery. When abolitionism acquired notoriety after 1833, he opposed it as a fanatical and unbiblical philosophy. He continued to support the more conservative colonization movement and underscored his commitment by composing a *History of Colonization on the Western Coast of Africa* (1846).

Although Alexander's works lacked the architectonic precision displayed in the writings of his successors, he established the basic theological stance that would characterize the seminary for several generations and that his protégé Charles Hodge transformed into a massive, well-integrated theological system. That stance was marked by adherence to Reformed orthodoxy, especially as manifested in the Westminster Confession of Faith; belief that external evidences attested the veracity of Christian revelation; commitment to the Bible as the infallible authority in all theological matters; and conviction that theology was a science based on the facts of Scripture and thus was capable of rendering its conclusions as propositional truths fully consonant with the findings of other sciences. These positions made Princeton Seminary a bastion of the didactic Enlightenment and a foe of idealistic and romantic intellectual currents sweeping much of the theological world in the nineteenth century.

Despite a lifelong susceptibility to periods of melancholy, nervousness, and indigestion, Alexander fulfilled his duties with little interruption. His students regarded him as eminently approachable and frequently turned to him as a spiritual adviser. By this activity Alexander confirmed that, while diffident about his own religious experience and hostile to what he deemed the excessive emotionalism of popular revivalism, he remained deeply committed to the experiential dimensions of the Christian faith. His emphasis on the external evidences of Christianity sometimes obscured this facet of his thought, but occasionally even his published works—for example, *Thoughts on Religious Experience* (1841)—attested its existence.

Charles Hodge relieved Alexander of a portion of his teaching responsibilities in 1840, but Alexander remained an active member of the faculty until shortly before his death in Princeton.

• Many of Alexander's papers are in the Speer Library of Princeton Theological Seminary. The fullest treatment of Alexander remains James Waddel Alexander, *The Life of Archibald Alexander* (1854). See also Lefferts A. Loetscher, *Facing the Enlightenment and Pietism: Archibald Alexander and the Founding of Princeton Theological Seminary* (1983).

JAMES H. MOORHEAD

ALEXANDER, Archie Alphonso (14 May 1888–4 Jan. 1958), engineer, was born in Ottumwa, Iowa, the son of Price Alexander, a janitor and coachman, and Mary Hamilton. The Alexanders were members of a tiny African-American minority both in the town of Archie's birth and in Des Moines, Iowa, where they moved when he was eleven years old. In Ottumwa the Alexanders lived in the section of town inhabited by the poor, both black and white; in Des Moines they lived on a small farm on the outskirts of town. Since Iowa's public schools were not segregated, young Alexander attended school with whites, graduating from Des Moines's Oak Park High School in 1905. Then, uncommon for the son of a janitor, whether black or white, he went on to further study. By working hard at part-time jobs, and with some help from his parents, Alexander attended Highland Park College and the Cummins Art School, both in Des Moines, before enrolling in the College of Engineering at the University of Iowa in Iowa City (1908). He was the College of Engineering's only black student and, upon entering, allegedly was warned, bluntly but not unkindly, by one official that in the society of that day a Negro could not hope to succeed as an engineer. Continuing to support himself through a variety of part-time jobs, Alexander did well academically and also starred as the first black member of the varsity football team. It was on the gridiron as a tackle that he earned the title "Alexander the Great." He even managed to pledge a fraternity, Kappa Alpha Psi.

Upon graduation in 1912, Alexander found his adviser's gloomy warning confirmed: every construction firm in Des Moines rejected his application for employment as an engineer. So Alexander took a job, for twenty-five cents an hour, as a laborer in the steel shop of the Marsh Engineering Company. There his eagerness and his ambition would not be denied, so that when he resigned two years later to found his own engineering company he was earning $70 a week as the engineer in charge of bridge construction in Iowa and Minnesota for the March Engineering Company.

Starting modestly, often at jobs that attracted few, if any, other bidders, Alexander soon took on a white partner, George F. Higbee, with whom he had worked earlier at the Marsh Engineering Company. The partnership lasted from 1917 till 1925, when Higbee was killed in a construction accident. For the next four years Alexander ran the company alone, building mostly bridges and viaducts, his specialty, but also apartment buildings and sewage systems. He also built a new heating plant, a new power plant, and a tunnel going under the Iowa River on the campus of his alma mater in Iowa City. Not surprisingly, he occasionally ran into prejudice and even hostility, which he seems to have overcome through his unblemished record as a construction engineer and by a skin thick enough to absorb such injustices without open confrontation. Alexander was never an "Uncle Tom" or a patsy, though, and some years later he served as president of both the Des Moines chapter of the NAACP (1944) and the local Interracial Commission (1940–1941).

In 1929 Alexander took on as a junior partner a white engineer, Maurice A. Repass, a former classmate at the University of Iowa. Under the firm name of Alexander & Repass, the partners went on to complete projects in nearly every state and to build what *Ebony* magazine called the "nation's most successful interracial business." The best-known, though not the biggest, projects completed by the firm of Alexander & Repass were in the nation's capitol: the Tidal Basin Bridge and Seawall; the K Street elevated highway and underpass from Key Bridge to 27th Street, N.W.; and the Whitehurst Freeway around Georgetown.

Alexander married Audra A. Linzy of Denver in 1913. The couple had one child, who died in early childhood.

Like nearly all black Americans until the election of Franklin D. Roosevelt as president in 1932, Alexander supported the Republican party. But unlike the mass of black voters, Alexander remained a lifelong Republican, even though it might have been politically as well as economically astute for him to have supported the majority party in an era dominated by the Democratic party, especially since his engineering company did so much public work. But his politics never seemed to hurt his business, and, in fact, he was eventually rewarded for his loyalty. Alexander was not just a member of the Republican party; he was an active member who twice, in 1932 and 1940, served as assistant chairman of the Iowa Republican State Committee. In 1952 he was an early supporter of the Eisenhower-for-president movement. Alexander's long years of dedication to the party were rewarded with his appointment, in April 1954, as governor of the largely black Virgin Islands. The appointment was a disaster for all concerned, though, and it may even have hastened Alexander's death. Dogmatic, paternalistic, undemocratic, and with an openly stated contempt for the easygoing Virgin Islanders, Alexander was described as a "Midwestern Babbitt" who brought all the values of small-town America to the Caribbean. He lasted a strife-torn and acrimonious sixteen months before he was pressured into resignation in August 1955.

Alexander lived less than three more years before he died at his home in Des Moines. In his will he left a trust fund for the support of his wife, the corpus of which was to go, upon her death, to the University of Iowa, Tuskegee Institute in Alabama, and Howard University for engineering scholarships. In 1975 each of the three institutions received $105,000.

Engineer, businessman, loyal and active member of the Republican party, civil rights and interracial leader, Alexander was, ironically, a failure only in the world of state diplomacy. The one failure is ironic in that surely he had to be a diplomat in the largely white world in which he lived and worked.

• A very limited collection of Alexander's personal papers is located in the library of the University of Iowa, Iowa City, but it is of little real value. By Alexander see his, "Engineering as a Profession," *Opportunity* (Apr.–June 1946): 60–62. The most recent and complete biographical article on Alexander is Charles E. Wynes, "'Alexander the Great,' Bridge Builder," *Palimpsest* 66 (May–June 1985): 78–86. News coverage of Alexander can be found in *Ebony* magazine, Apr. and Sept. 1949; *Time*, 19 Apr. 1954; the *New York Times*, 11 Apr. 1954; 12, 13, and 18 Apr. and 18 and 19 Aug. 1955. On the Virgin Islands fiasco, see William W. Boyer, *America's Virgin Islands: A History of Human Rights and Wrongs* (1983). An obituary is in the *Des Moines Sunday Register*, 5 Jan. 1958.

CHARLES E. WYNES

ALEXANDER, De Alva Stanwood (17 July 1845–30 Jan. 1925), congressman and historian, was born in Richmond, Maine, the son of Stanwood Alexander and Priscilla Brown. When his father died in 1852, Alexander and his mother moved to Ohio, where he lived until his enlistment, at the age of sixteen, in the Ohio Volunteer Infantry during the Civil War. After the war he completed his education at the Edward Little Institute in Auburn, Maine, and graduated from Bowdoin College in 1870. He later served for several years on Bowdoin's board of overseers. In 1871 he married Alice Colby; their childless union ended with her death in 1890.

After teaching for a short time in the public schools of Fort Wayne, Indiana, Alexander edited that city's *Daily Gazette*, the leading Republican organ in the Hoosier State. In 1874 he moved to Indianapolis, where he became staff correspondent for the Cincinnati *Gazette* and secretary of the Indiana Republican State Committee. After studying law privately, he was admitted to the Indiana bar in 1877 and practiced in Indianapolis for four years, in partnership with Stanton J. Peele, who later became chief justice of the U.S. Court of Claims. His friendship with U.S. senator and later president Benjamin Harrison (1833–1901) earned Alexander an appointment as a U.S. Treasury Department auditor in 1881 and as U.S. district attorney for the Northern District of New York in 1889. He moved to Buffalo in 1885 and engaged in law practice there. During that period he also served as commander of the Department of the Potomac of the Grand Army of the Republic for one term. In 1893 Alexander was married a second time, to Anne Bliss. This marriage also did not result in children.

First elected to Congress in the Republican landslide of 1896, Alexander served seven consecutive terms in the House of Representatives, rising to the post of chairman of the Rivers and Harbors Committee. During the divisive Progressive Era battles between Republican Regulars and Insurgents, Alexander was a faithful adherent of the Regulars, generally following the leadership of fellow New Yorker Sereno E. Payne. Although a strong admirer of Theodore Roosevelt (1858–1919), Alexander eventually sided with President William Howard Taft when the latter was abandoned by his mentor in 1912. A generous patron of the port of Buffalo, for which he also secured $8.5 million in federal funds, Alexander generally was nominated for election without opposition. Renominated in 1910, Alexander lost by a single vote to his Democratic opponent, due largely to the split in the Republican party between Regulars and Progressives.

While still a U.S. representative, Alexander began writing a four-volume *Political History of the State of New York*, the first three volumes of which were published between 1906 and 1909. Asserting that "the history of a State or nation is largely the history of a few leading men," Alexander generally avoided social or economic analyses and concentrated on the activities of officeholders and party officials. The first volume examined the origins and early development of partisan politics in the Empire State between the American Revolution and the rise of the Whig party in 1834. The second focused on the evolution of the Republican party up to the outbreak of the Civil War. The third covered the politics of the Civil War and Reconstruction and the eventual resurgence of the New York Democratic party under the leadership of Grover Cleveland. In 1923, after a hiatus of fourteen years, Alexander produced the fourth volume of the history entitled *Four Famous New Yorkers: The Political Careers of Cleveland, Platt, Hill and Roosevelt*. True to his philosophy, Alexander reduced the complex socioeconomic and ethnocultural politics of New York during the Populist-Progressive Era into a personal struggle among four prominent Empire State leaders: Democratic governor and president Cleveland, Republican boss and U.S. senator Thomas Collier Platt, Democratic senator David B. Hill, and Republican governor and president Theodore Roosevelt. Several years earlier, in 1916, Alexander had drawn on his considerable experience in and knowledge of Congress to write *The History and Procedure of the House of Representatives*. Although primarily a study of the evolution of the rules and regulations governing the conduct of House business, the work also contains a number of lively biographical sketches of prominent congressmen. Alexander died in Buffalo.

• Alexander's longtime colleague Frank Hayward Severance wrote the entry on Alexander in the *Dictionary of American Biography*. Other brief sketches of his life and work can be found in the *Quarterly Journal of the New York State Historical Society* (Apr. 1925) and *The Biographical Directory of the United States Congress, 1774–1989* (1989). For critical reviews of his books see Theodore Clark Smith in the *Atlantic*, Nov. 1906; the *Nation*, 25 Oct. 1906; Charles Beard in *Political Science Quarterly* 21 (Mar. 1907); and Harold F. Gosnell in *American Political Science Review* 17 (Nov. 1923).

JOHN D. BUENKER

ALEXANDER, Dorothy (22 Apr. 1904–17 Nov. 1986), dancer, teacher, and artistic director, was born Dorothea Moses in Atlanta, Georgia, the daughter of Frank Moses, a sales executive, and Cora Mina Thibadeau. Illness first introduced Dorothy to dance. At the age of six she was forced to spend a year immobilized by osteomyelitis. Dance was recommended to accelerate her recuperation, and the remainder of her life was devoted to the art. Every summer during her early adulthood she left Atlanta in search of the best teachers. Her choices were eclectic; they included Irma Duncan, a disciple of Isadora Duncan; ballet teachers Tatiana Chamié, Michel Fokine, and Bronislava Nijinska; modern dance pioneer Hanya Holm; and ethnic artists Beaucaire Montalvo and Yeichi Nimura. She also traveled to London to study at the Royal Ballet School. And yet Alexander remained a passionate southerner, determined to develop a quality school and company in her native Atlanta.

During this period, Alexander was sought after as a concert artist, performing alone or with a partner. In 1921 she opened her own studio in Atlanta and continued to run it until 1971. Her retentive and analytical mind enabled her to synthesize the disparate elements of her training and evolve a pedagogical approach that was sensitive to the needs of the individual student. She also had a working knowledge of anatomy and kinesiology, probably acquired at college. In 1925, after graduating from the Atlanta Normal Training School, she briefly became an elementary school teacher in the Atlanta public school system and developed a dance enrichment program called "Physical Fitness through Dance." Designed for elementary school children, it was so effective that by 1927 Alexander supervised the project systemwide. She did so until 1952.

In 1926 she married architect Marion Alexander; the marriage ended in divorce the same year; they had no children. By 1929 she had formed the Dorothy Alexander Dance Art Group, which became the Atlanta Ballet. Its artists were trained in her school. She also received her bachelor's degree from Oglethorpe University in 1930, all the while continuing her independent concert career. But she remained steadfast about not pursuing the career outside of Atlanta. Instead, when touring companies like the Lucile Marsh Concert Group, the Solomonoff-Menzelli Ballet, the Hollywood Ballet, and the Edwin Strawbridge Ballet performed in Atlanta, she appeared with them as guest artist in her own repertoire. She also danced with her own company until 1947.

As a choreographer, Alexander created more than eighty works. The ballets often emphasized the human and spiritual values that informed her personal life. *Deo Gratias*, for example, dealt with the reverence of a poet (the personification of Alexander) for life and his awareness of death. *Green Altars*, which the company performed at the Jacob's Pillow summer dance festival in 1957 (it was the first regional ensemble to perform there), depicted the redemptive power of love, while *Soliloquy* evoked the uniqueness of human relationships (like mother and child, husband and wife, friends) and the ubiquity of solitude. Outstanding among her pure-dance works was *Fireworks Suite*, performed at the first American regional ballet festival in 1956. In this work, as in many of her ballets, Alexander collaborated with other Atlanta artists: composer Hugh Hodgson, scene designer Joel Reeves, and costume designer Nancy Lochridge Harrison.

In 1941 the company was renamed the Atlanta Civic Ballet; in 1967 it became the Atlanta Ballet. Its progress offered such a heartening example to other fledgling companies in the Southeast and throughout the United States that Alexander was much in demand as a consultant. At a time when there were no courses in arts administration, her broad understanding of all aspects of the craft was unusual and valuable, combining logic, human awareness, and inspiration.

In the summer of 1955, at the suggestion of Anatole Chujoy, editor of *Dance News*, she agreed to organize the nation's first regional ballet festival. It took place in April 1956, with the Atlanta Civic Ballet as host. Dance notables were invited, and there were classes for the dancers and seminars for the artistic directors and board members. Eight southeastern companies performed. The event led to the gradual formation of four more regional associations (Northeast, 1959; Southwest, 1963; Pacific, 1966; Mid-States, 1972); all relied on Alexander's guidance. A national advisory board was also formed, with Alexander as chairperson. Eventually this became the board of directors of the National Association for Regional Ballet (NARB), with Alexander as the first president. By 1972 a national office served 120 companies. Alexander's dream was taking hold.

Ill health forced her early retirement in 1962 as director of the Atlanta Ballet. She turned the company over to Robert Barnett, its principal dancer and associate director, while her teaching associate, Merrilee Smith, became director of the Atlanta School of Ballet. Alexander served as consultant to the company, the school, and the NARB. In so doing, she continued to fulfill the prophecy of a citation presented to her in 1973 by Nancy Hanks, chairperson of the National Endowment for the Arts, in commemoration of her fifty years of service to American dance. Hanks thanked her for epitomizing the artist as visionary and for having the faith that someday the people of Atlanta—and Americans everywhere—would cherish dance as a meaningful part of their lives. Alexander died in Atlanta.

• For more information on Alexander see Doris Hering, "Atlanta Civic Ballet: Company of Contrasts," *Dance Magazine*, Mar. 1959; Hering, "Tickets for the Bug Man," *Dance Magazine*, Feb. 1963; Art Harris III, "Miss Dorothy's Legacy," *Georgia Magazine*, June 1971; Helen C. Smith, "Atlanta Ballet: Fifty Golden Years," *Dance Magazine*, Nov. 1979; and Walter Terry, "Miss Dorothy's Way," *Saturday Review*, Mar. 1980.

DORIS HERING

ALEXANDER, Edward Porter (26 May 1835–28 Apr. 1910), Confederate soldier and author, was born in Washington, Georgia, the son of Adam Leopold Alexander, a planter and banker, and Sarah Hillhouse Gilbert. Educated by tutors in his wealthy family's household, Alexander entered the U.S. Military Academy in 1853 and graduated third in the class of 1857. He was commissioned a brevet second lieutenant of engineers on 1 July 1857 and was promoted to second lieutenant on 10 October 1858. Marked from the first as a promising officer, he taught at West Point immediately upon graduation, accompanied Albert Sidney Johnston's expedition against the Mormons in 1858, then returned to West Point, where during 1859–1860 he assisted Albert J. Myer in perfecting the "wigwag" system of signaling by means of flags or lanterns. In 1860 he married Bettie Mason; they had six children. The secession crisis found him stationed at Fort Steilacoom, Washington Territory. Although not a fervent secessionist, Alexander later explained, "As soon as the *right* to *secede* was denied by the North I strongly approved of its assertion & maintenance by force if necessary." He resigned his commission on 1 May 1861 and offered his services to the Confederacy.

Alexander's Confederate career embraced all the major military events in the eastern theater, from Manassas to Appomattox. Commissioned captain of Confederate engineers to date from 16 March 1861, he served as chief signal officer and chief of ordnance on the staffs of P. G. T. Beauregard, Joseph E. Johnston, and Robert E. Lee between July 1861 and September 1862. He oversaw the erection of signal stations at First Manassas, from which Confederates detected the Union flanking column; coordinated delivery of ordnance to the army during the Seven Days', Second Manassas, and Antietam campaigns; supervised the deployment of the Confederacy's only observation balloon, from which he viewed part of the battle of Gaines's Mill; and formulated plans for the organization of southern artillery into battalions. Alexander carried out various engineering and reconnaissance duties and oversaw a number of secret service functions as well. He was promoted to major of artillery on 18 April 1862 and to lieutenant colonel of artillery on 17 July 1862.

Lee understood that Alexander's most impressive military gifts related to the theoretical and practical application of artillery, and in November 1862 he selected his young lieutenant to command a battalion of guns formerly headed by Stephen D. Lee. During the reorganization of the Army of Northern Virginia's artillery into twelve battalions in the winter of 1863, incorporating many ideas put forward earlier by Alexander, Brigadier General William Nelson Pendleton, Lee's chief of artillery, stated that the army had "no more accomplished officer" than Alexander to head one of the new battalions. Alexander was rewarded with a battalion of artillery in James Longstreet's First Corps along with promotion to colonel on 3 March 1863.

Alexander spent the balance of his military service compiling an unrivaled record of excellence in the Confederate "Long Arm." To deadly effect, he chose positions for Longstreet's guns on Marye's Heights at Fredericksburg, directed the fire from Hazel Grove on 3 May at Chancellorsville that helped tip the balance in favor of Lee's attacking forces, and, in his most famous role, directed the bombardment that preceded the Pickett-Pettigrew assault on 3 July at Gettysburg. Throughout this period he acted as tactical chief of artillery in the First Corps despite the fact that Colonel James B. Walton formally headed Longstreet's artillery.

Alexander went with Longstreet's corps in September 1863 to the western theater, where he participated in the sieges of Chattanooga and Knoxville. In the winter of 1864 Joseph E. Johnston asked that Alexander be made chief of artillery in the Army of Tennessee. Lee refused to let him go, secured his promotion to brigadier general on 1 March 1864, and on 19 March approved his appointment as chief of artillery in the First Corps. Alexander was among the very few officers, noted Jefferson Davis, "whom General Lee would not give to anybody." Active service in the Overland campaign; the siege of Petersburg, during which he helped design several portions of the southern works and ended up commanding all of Lee's guns between the James and Appomattox rivers; and the Appomattox campaign ensued. After drawing the Army of Northern Virginia's last battle line at Appomattox on 9 April 1865, Alexander surrendered with the rest of Lee's army, closing a career as the most brilliant Confederate artillerist and one of the most versatile soldiers in U.S. history.

Following the war Alexander taught mathematics and engineering at the University of South Carolina from 1866 to 1869, then he headed the Columbia Oil Company, which worked with cottonseed, from 1869 to 1871. For the next two decades, he devoted himself largely to railroading, serving as superintendent or president of several small lines and as president of the Central Railroad and Banking Company of Georgia in 1882 and again between 1887 and 1892. One observer, impressed with Alexander's grasp of the business, called him "the young Napoleon of the Railways." A proponent of well-planned consolidation in the industry, Alexander published *On Various Railroad Questions* (1881) and *Railway Practice* (1887).

After his retirement from railroading, Alexander gave considerable attention to North Island and South Island, a pair of sea islands off the coast of South Carolina he owned and farmed. President Grover Cleveland, who hunted ducks on Alexander's sea island properties, appointed the former artillerist a government director of the Union Pacific Railroad (1885–1887) and an arbitrator for a boundary dispute between Nicaragua and Costa Rica (1897–1900). Alexander also served in 1882 on a board charged to investigate obstructions on the Columbia River. Widowed in 1900, he married Mary Mason, his first wife's niece, in 1901. They had no children.

Alexander's most enduring postwar legacy was a body of writings about his Confederate service. He published important essays in the popular *Battles and Leaders of the Civil War* series (4 vols., 1887–1888), the *Southern Historical Society Papers* ("The Seven Days Battle" [Jan. 1876]; "Causes of Lee's Defeat at Gettysburg" [Sept. 1877]; "Sketch of Longstreet's Division" [Oct., Nov., and Dec. 1881 and Jan.–Feb. 1882];

"The Battle of Fredericksburg" [Aug.–Sept. 1882 and Oct.–Nov. 1882]; and "Confederate Artillery Service" [Feb.–Mar. 1883]), and the 1908 *Annual Report of the American Historical Association.* While in Nicaragua, he wrote a long memoir intended for his family (published in 1989 as *Fighting for the Confederacy: The Personal Recollections of General Edward Porter Alexander*, ed. Gary W. Gallagher), which he revised heavily to produce *Military Memoirs of a Confederate: A Critical Narrative* (1907). Unmatched among the writings of ex-Confederates for their impartiality and brilliant analysis, Alexander's two reminiscences also offer splendid anecdotes about prominent individuals and famous events. Alexander died in Savannah.

• The mass of Alexander's private papers are in the Southern Historical Collection at the University of North Carolina at Chapel Hill. The Southern Historical Collection also has papers of family members and in-laws with valuable material, including the Alexander-Hillhouse Papers, Alexander R. Lawton Papers, Jeremy F. Gilmer Papers, John R. Ficklen Papers, and Louisa Porter Minis Papers. Smaller collections of importance include the Adam Alexander Papers at Duke University and the Alexander folder in the War Department Collection of Confederate Records, National Archives, Washington, D.C. An excellent selection of family correspondence is *The Alexander Letters, 1787–1900*, ed. Marion Boggs Alexander (1910; repr. 1980). A biography is Maury Klein, *Edward Porter Alexander* (1971). Also useful are a sketch by Charles L. Dufour in *Nine Men in Gray* (1963), and Jennings C. Wise, *The Long Arm of Lee; or, The History of the Artillery of the Army of Northern Virginia, with a Brief Account of the Confederate Bureau of Ordnance* (2 vols., 1915). Obituaries are in the *Savannah (Ga.) Morning News* and the *Augusta Chronicle*, both 29 Apr. 1910.

GARY W. GALLAGHER

ALEXANDER, Francis (3 Feb. 1800–17 Mar. 1880), artist, was born in Killingly, Connecticut. His parents' names are unknown. As a child he worked on the family's small farm and attended a local school. When he was seventeen he began teaching at that same school. He liked to sketch birds and other objects from nature and when he was twenty painted watercolors of fish he had caught. The pictures drew much praise from family and friends. As a result he decided to pursue a career as a painter, primarily, as he later wrote to William Dunlap, "because I thought I could make more money than by farming" (p. 427). With money he had saved form teaching, he went to New York City and took lessons from Scottish artist Alexander Robertson. After six weeks his money ran out, and he was forced to return home. There he painted landscapes on the walls of his father's house and hoped the neighbors would commission him to decorate their houses in the same way, but none did. He also painted landscapes on canvas, only two of which are known to have survived. *Ralph Wheelock's Farm* (c. 1821, National Gallery of Art) is a panoramic view of a neighbor's farm in Southbridge, Massachusetts. Farmhands in shirtsleeves are seen at work in the foreground while in the background stands the Wheelock home, surrounded by barns and other outbuildings. It is a charming view of early American farm life and has become his best-known work. Another landscape, of the part of Southbridge called Globe Village, was painted in 1822 (Jacob Edwards Library, Southbridge).

Alexander's neighbors, however, showed little interest in his landscapes, and he therefore turned to painting portraits. These the neighbors were interested in, and he received a number of commissions. He subsequently traveled from town to town seeking work. He was in Providence, Rhode Island, in 1823–1824 and in 1825 was in Boston, Massachusetts, where he sought advice from portraitist Gilbert Stuart. Stuart was very encouraging, remarking that whatever Alexander lacked in training he more than made up for in natural ability.

Stuart suggested that Alexander give up the life of an itinerant artist and settle in Boston. The younger man was agreeable to this and spent the next six years there. He received many commissions and eventually was able to charge up to $75 for a portrait. The naiveté that characterized his landscapes and early portraits now disappeared, replaced by a more academic style that owed much to the influence of Stuart. His portraits during this time generally were bust-length, well modeled, and delicately painted. In the winter of 1830 he paid a visit to Washington, D.C., where he painted portraits of President Andrew Jackson (private collection) and Secretary of State Martin Van Buren (White House Collection). The Jackson portrait is one of the least known of that chief executive but among the most striking. Dressed in black and placed against a dark background, Jackson's head—topped by a mane of white hair—emerges dramatically from the shadows, and his strong features do not yet have the careworn appearance of his later portraits. Alexander's depiction of Van Buren likewise is a handsome portrayal of the future eighth president.

By 1831 Alexander had earned enough money to take a trip to Italy. He visited Florence, Rome, and Naples with his good friend Thomas Cole and also spent seven months in Venice. He returned to Boston in 1833 and resumed his career, as popular as he was before his trip. His portraits show little if any influence from his Italian sojourn, however. In 1835 he painted perhaps his best portrait, a likeness of Daniel Webster (Dartmouth College), in which the statesman is placed off-center against a cloudy background. Webster probably sat for more artists than anyone else of his day, but few of them captured his remarkable intensity as well as Alexander.

In 1836 Alexander married Boston heiress Lucia Swett, whom he had met in Italy. They had one child, Francesca, who herself became an artist. In 1840 Alexander was named an honorary member of the National Academy of Design. Two years later he painted a portrait of Charles Dickens, who was on an American tour. The painting is a good likeness but reveals the limitations of the artist's skill. He was adept at painting head-and-shoulder likenesses, but the correct depiction of anatomy was beyond him. Dickens is shown at his desk, pen in hand, looking as if taking a momentary break from his writing. The head is well rendered, but the right arm is poorly done, and the body is not well connected to the head.

By the end of the 1840s Alexander was painting fewer portraits; he was finding it difficult to compete with the younger artists now working in Boston. With his wife and daughter he moved to Italy in 1853, settled in Florence, and stopped painting. He and his wife were able to live comfortably on her income, and he began to collect early Italian art. When asked why he gave up painting, he reportedly replied, "What's the use when I can buy a better picture for a dollar and a half than I can paint myself?" (Ball, p. 173). Apart from a short visit to America in 1868–1869, he spent the rest of his life in Italy. He died in Florence and was buried in the Protestant cemetery there.

Largely self-taught, Alexander developed beyond the limitations characteristic of the folk artist to become a good painter in the academic tradition. He was particularly successful not only in reproducing his sitters' features accurately but also in capturing their personalities, and he enjoyed much popularity during his career. Ironically, it is his earliest work—that which can be called folk art—that most appeals to the modern viewer.

• A self-portrait painted about 1830 is in the collection of the Museum of Fine Arts, Boston. Catharine W. Pierce wrote two articles on the artist, both of which were published in the periodical *Old-Time New England*: "Francis Alexander," Oct.–Dec. 1953, pp. 29–46, and "Further Notes on Francis Alexander," Oct.–Dec. 1965, pp. 35–44. An autobiographical sketch of his early years is included in William Dunlap, *A History of the Rise and Progress of the Arts of Design in the United States*, vol. 2 (1834), pp. 426–33, and an account of his later years is in Thomas Ball, *My Three Score Years and Ten* (1892), p. 173.

DAVID MESCHUTT

ALEXANDER, Franz Gabriel (22 Jan. 1891–8 Mar. 1964), psychoanalyst, was born in Budapest, Hungary, the son of Bernard Alexander, a college professor, and Regina Brössler. After receiving his B.A. from Budapest's Humanistic Gymnasium in 1908, he briefly studied archaeology and philosophy at the University of Budapest before enrolling in its medical school. In 1910 he became a research associate in physiology at the university's Institute for Experimental Pathology, where he conducted experiments correlating the work of the brain to its metabolism. In 1913 he received his M.D. and joined the university's Institute for Hygiene as a research associate in bacteriology. In 1914 he was commissioned a first lieutenant in the Austro-Hungarian army and placed in charge of a Red Cross medical unit. Three years later he took command of a bacteriological field laboratory assigned to prevent malaria on the Italian front and was awarded the Merit Cross for Distinguished Service. After World War I he returned to the university as a research and clinical associate in psychiatry and neurology in its neuropsychiatric clinic.

Although Alexander's work at the clinic involved only the purely physical aspects of the brain, such as its blood chemistry, he became increasingly interested in the psyche and in theories of psychoanalysis. Initially skeptical of these theories, he was convinced by the results a Freudian-trained psychologist colleague achieved with her patients that psychoanalysis held critical importance for the understanding of behavioral problems. In 1919 he went to Berlin, Germany, where he spent a year studying psychiatry at the newly opened Institute for Psychoanalysis; during the next year he conducted postgraduate research at the University of Berlin's psychiatric hospital. In 1921 he married Anita Venier, with whom he had two children. That same year he won the International Psychoanalytic Association's Freud Prize for his study of the formation of character in males with castration complexes; he also became a clinical associate at the institute.

In 1925, the year after he was promoted to lecturer, Alexander became interested in psychoanalyzing criminal personalities and applying the results to criminal justice. Despite the prevailing attitude among psychoanalysts that psychiatry and law did not mix, he analyzed several clients of Hugo Straub, a defense lawyer, and presented his findings before the court. He and Straub published the results of their collaboration in *Der Verbrecher und seine Richter* (1929), translated into English as *The Criminal, the Judge, and the Public* (1931), the first book ever written about forensic psychiatry. In 1929 Alexander and Straub conducted an institute seminar for attorneys and jurists on the psychodynamics of criminal behavior.

In 1930, as a visiting professor at the University of Chicago, Alexander became the first professor of psychoanalysis in the United States. He spent the next year collaborating with William Healy in a psychological study of imprisoned criminals at the Judge Baker Foundation in Boston, Massachusetts, the results of which they published in *Roots of Crime* (1935).

Alexander also developed an interest in emotional factors as contributors to medical disorders and began identifying conditions such as peptic ulcers, bronchial asthma, hypertension, rheumatoid arthritis, and hyperactivity of the thyroid gland as being caused to a large degree by specific subconscious emotional distress. In 1932 he published *The Medical Value of Psychoanalysis*, the first book to address the topic of psychosomatic medicine.

That same year, Alexander became the first director of the Chicago Institute for Psychoanalysis. In addition to serving as a training center for psychiatrists and operating the first psychoanalytic outpatient clinic in the United States, under his direction the institute also became a center for psychosomatic medicine. In 1938 he became a naturalized citizen, an attending physician at Cook County (Ill.) Psychopathic Hospital, and associate professor of psychiatry at the University of Illinois; he was promoted to clinical professor in 1943. In 1939 he cofounded the *Journal of Psychosomatic*

Medicine, serving on its editorial staff for the next ten years.

Unlike Freud, Alexander believed that neurosis resulted from dysfunctional relationships rather than from disturbed sexuality. In 1939 he and the institute's staff began working to make psychoanalysis more flexible so that it could be adapted to address a patient's specific needs. This endeavor resulted in *Psychoanalytic Therapy: Principles and Applications* (1946), coauthored with staff members of the institute, and *Fundamentals of Psychoanalysis* (1948), which he alone wrote. In 1942 Alexander addressed the psychological factors underlying the simultaneous rise of totalitarianism and democracy in the twentieth century in *Our Age of Unreason: A Study of the Irrational Forces in Social Life*.

Alexander spent the year 1955 at the Ford Foundation's Center for Advanced Study in the Behavioral Sciences in Palo Alto, California. The following year he moved permanently to Los Angeles to become director of Mt. Sinai Hospital's Psychiatric and Psychosomatic Research Institute and chief of staff of its psychiatric department. In 1957 he assumed the additional duties of clinical professor of psychiatry at the University of Southern California (USC) Medical School. Convinced that an analyst's personality significantly affects his ability to help a patient, he implemented a research project in which psychoanalysts were observed under working conditions in an effort to establish guidelines for matching therapists with patients.

Alexander served as president of the American Psychoanalytic Association in 1938 and of the American Society for Research in Psychosomatic Problems in 1947. He was a consultant to the National Advisory Mental Health Council (1947–1949), member of the National Research Council's Committee on Rheumatic Diseases (1948–1964), and chairman of the International Congress of Psychiatry's section on psychotherapy, psychoanalysis, and psychosomatic medicine (1950). He was awarded the American-Hungarian Medical Association's Semmelweiss Medal in 1957 and the Samuel Rubin Foundation Award in 1958. In 1964 USC named its chair in psychophysiology and psychosomatic medicine in his honor. He died in Palm Springs, California.

Alexander's pioneering work in understanding the degree to which the emotions contribute to cardiovascular, gastrointestinal, and endocrinological disorders made him known as the "father of psychosomatic medicine." He also pioneered the application of psychoanalytic principles and techniques to issues of criminal culpability and legal justice.

• Alexander wrote a semiautobiographical book, *The Western Mind in Transition: An Eyewitness Story* (1960). A discussion of his pioneering role in forensic psychiatry is Seymour Pollack, "Franz Alexander's Observations on Psychiatry and Law," *American Journal of Psychiatry* 121 (1964): 458–64. An obituary is in the *New York Times*, 9 Mar. 1964.

CHARLES W. CAREY, JR.

ALEXANDER, Grover Cleveland (26 Feb. 1887–4 Nov. 1950), professional baseball player, was born in Elba, Nebraska, the son of William Alexander and Margaret Cootey, farmers. Alexander seemed destined for baseball. Even as a youngster, Dode, as he was called, could bring down a wild turkey with a well-aimed rock. After graduating from high school at nearby St. Paul, he worked briefly as a telephone lineman and assiduously at pitching.

In 1909 a winning effort against a top-flight semipro team earned him a professional contract with Galesburg, Illinois, of the Illinois-Missouri League (Class D) at $100 a month. With his won-lost record at 15–8, he was injured while sliding into second base. The shortstop's relay to first hit him in the head, knocking him unconscious. Awakening two days later, he had double vision. Galesburg dealt him to Indianapolis of the American Association (Class AA) where, still seeing two of everything, he stove in three of the manager's ribs with his first pitch. The Indians sold him to Class B Syracuse (New York State League) that winter, and by spring training he had recovered normal vision. He won 29 games for the Chiefs, 15 of them shutouts, yet aroused so little interest—one scout even advising against him—that the Philadelphia Nationals got him in the 1910 draft for $750.

His freshman year was phenomenal. Working for a fourth-place club, the 24-year-old rookie led the National League with 28 wins (a rookie record), 31 complete games, 367 innings pitched, and seven shutouts. The first of a record four consecutive shutouts in September was a one-hit 1–0 victory over Cy Young, who was playing his final season.

Alexander looked and acted like the country boy he was: tall (6′1″) and lanky, sandy-haired and freckled, good-natured, easily amused, laconic, and a bit shy. Christy Mathewson, in his (ghostwritten) book, *Pitching in a Pinch*, said Alexander won "ten or a dozen games before it was fully realized he was a star."

The right-handed Alexander's delivery was effortless. He had a minimal windup, a short stride, a three-quarters overhand throw. Because his arm swung across the chest, the ball seemed to emerge from the front of his shirt, an advantage when wearing the white home uniform. He threw a fastball that broke in on right-handed batters, a sharp-breaking curve, and a screwball. He lacked a change-up but achieved the effect by varying the pace of his bread-and-butter pitches. He was adept at keeping the ball low and nicking the outside corner of the plate. His control was impressive. Warming up with his favorite catcher, "Reindeer Bill" Killefer, he once amazed bystanders by throwing ball after ball through a one-gallon tomato can with its ends cut out. On the mound Alexander was all business. His games usually were completed in an hour and a half. In 1919 he blanked the Braves in fifty-eight minutes.

The great years were with the Phils. Mathewson was a marvel, but by 1915 Pete, as Alexander was now known, was the National League's supreme pitcher. He led the league that year in wins (31), winning percentage (.756), earned run average (1.22), complete games (36), innings pitched (376⅓), strikeouts (241), and shutouts (12). He pitched four one-hitters, three of them in one month. He led the Phillies to their first pennant, and he was 1–1 in the losing World Series to the Boston Red Sox.

He bettered most of those marks in 1916, winning 33 games, pitching 16 shutouts, still a major league record, and walking only 50 batters, or only one every seven-plus innings. And with another 30 victories in 1917, he and Matty became the only hurlers of the modern era to reach that level three years in a row. All told, Alexander's 190 victories in seven seasons were one-third of the Phillies' total—a statistic the more remarkable considering that the right-field wall at Baker Bowl, his home park, was only 272 feet from the plate. Heaven for left-handed hitters.

When it appeared likely that Alexander would be drafted for World War I military service, the penurious Phillies sold him and Killefer to Chicago in December 1917 for a catcher of promise, a pitcher of modest attainments, and cash variously estimated at $50,000 to $60,000. Alexander won two and lost one in the spring of 1918, married Aimee Marie Arrants in May, then sailed for France as a sergeant in the 342d Artillery Battalion of the 89th Division, made up mostly of Kansas and Nebraska farm boys.

He returned to the Cubs in 1919, deaf in one ear from the pounding of the guns, shaken by epileptic seizures, and with his taste for whiskey—inherited, he always said, from his father and grandfather—now insatiable. The case history is imprecise. Old-time baseball was tolerant of its drinkers as long as they showed up for games and performed as expected with bat, ball, or glove. Fred Lieb, a prominent sportswriter during Alexander's era, doubted that liquor affected his pitching until late in his career, although stories persist from his earliest days of games pitched while drunk or hung over. Postwar, epilepsy accounted for at least some of his "drunken" behavior.

Although the Cubs were up and down in Alexander's time, he won 128 games for them—nearly a quarter of their total—including a league-leading 27 in 1920. His 1.72 ERA in 1919, the National League's best, remained a Cub record some seventy-five years later. In 1925 he hurled a 19-inning 2–2 tie in the postseason city series with the White Sox.

But by 1926, when Joe McCarthy came aboard as manager, the alcoholism was ungovernable. McCarthy, believing he must crack down or lose control of the club, waived his problem pitcher to the Cardinals for $4,000. Manager Rogers Hornsby handled the drinking by ignoring it as long as Alexander held his place in the rotation. His nine wins gave the Cards' pennant drive a boost, and in the World Series against the Yankees he reached a high point of his career. After complete-game victories in games two and six, he was snoozing in the bullpen at Yankee Stadium when game seven reached a crisis. With two out in the seventh inning and St. Louis leading, 3–2, New York filled the bases. Old Pete was summoned to relieve Jess Haines, whose throwing hand was blistered from too many knuckle balls. Whether or not Alexander was hung over from celebrating game six is a never-ending argument. One thing is sure, at thirty-nine no one ever looked less like a ballplayer—the uniform too big, the hat too small, the gait shambling, the face lined by hard living. But the pitching wisdom was intact. Four throws disposed of young Tony Lazzeri. A ball a bit too low; a called strike; a drive to left field, home-run length, but foul; and a swinging strike three on a knee-high curve. The last two innings were scoreless, and the Cardinals had their first world's championship.

Alexander was rewarded with a $17,500 contract in 1927, the most money he ever earned, and enjoyed a 21-win season, although the Pittsburgh Pirates won the pennant over St. Louis in a close race. In 1928 he contributed 16 wins as the Redbirds, now managed by Bill McKechnie, edged the Giants by two games to finish first. The World Series was a disaster, the Cards losing four straight to the overpowering Yankees. For Alexander, nearing age 41, the magic was gone. In five innings of work, as starter and loser in game two and reliever in game four, he was rocked for 11 earned runs on 10 hits.

After a 9–8 season in 1929 he was returned to his starting point, Philadelphia, in a trade of nonentities. He retired in 1930 after three losses, but with 90 career shutouts, a mark second only to Walter Johnson's 110, and with 373 victories, the most ever by a National League pitcher. A statistical revision, however, added one more to Christy Mathewson's total, leaving these dissimilar heroes forever tied in third place, behind Young's 511 and Johnson's 417.

Like all players with long careers, Alexander's statistics are impressive, yet his rankings in lifetime lists are not invariably high. His 438 complete games and average of 1.65 walks per nine innings, phenomenal by current standards, place him only twelfth and twenty-second, because most of those above him are iron men of the nineteenth century, when relief pitchers were unknown and walks harder to come by. Over twenty years he compiled a 2.56 ERA, had 20 or more wins nine times, and led the National League six times in strikeouts, although his high mark—241—would be unusually good but not spectacular today. Oddly, for all his shutouts and low-scoring games, he never had a no-hitter. Most of his stats put him within hailing distance, ahead or behind, of his great contemporaries, Mathewson and Johnson.

After the majors, Alexander pitched for any team that would have him, including one of the barnstorming teams of the House of David sect from Benton Harbor, Michigan, which he played for—usually a two- or three-inning stint—and managed for three seasons. He quit in 1938, the year he became the twelfth player voted into the Baseball Hall of Fame at Cooperstown, New York. He worked at a racetrack selling pari-mutuel tickets, labored in a factory, and even became a sideshow attraction at a penny arcade on New York's 42d Street. He and Aimee were divorced, remarried, and divorced. His solitary last years were buried in liquor, in a rooming house in St. Paul, Nebraska. He survived on handouts and small pensions from the league and the army, and he was a spectral guest at the Phils' 1950 World Series shortly before his death in St. Paul. In a 1952 film, *The Winning Team*, Ronald Reagan starred as Alexander.

• Specific points were established by material from the Alexander file at the National Baseball Hall of Fame library in Cooperstown, N.Y. Good summary accounts of Alexander's life and career are in Bob Broeg's *Super Stars of Baseball* (1971) and Frederick G. Lieb's obituary in the *Sporting News*, 15 Nov. 1950, although later research has outdated a number of their statistics. Biographies of the teams Alexander played for include *St. Louis Cardinals* and *Philadelphia Phillies*, by Lieb, and *Chicago Cubs*, by Warren Brown, all in a series published by G. P. Putnam's Sons in the 1940s and 1950s. Donald Honig's pages in *Baseball America* (1985) are illuminating on Alexander's personality. Jack Sher's "Grover Cleveland Alexander," in *Twelve More Sport Immortals*, ed. Ernest V. Heyn (1951), contains useful detail and a brief interview with Mrs. Alexander. Information on Alexander's 1930–1931 seasons with the House of David was given by H. Thomas Dewhirst, a surviving player of the time (telephone interview, 4 Nov. 1993). Robert Obojeski's *Bush League* (1973) is the authority on league names and classifications in any given year. Statistics are from *The Baseball Encyclopedia*, 9th ed. (1993); John Thorn and Pete Palmer, eds., *Total Baseball*, 3d ed. (1993); and Richard M. Cohen et al., *The World Series* (1979).

A. D. SUEHSDORF

ALEXANDER, Hattie Elizabeth (5 Apr. 1901–24 June 1968), microbiologist and pediatrician, was born in Baltimore, Maryland, the daughter of William Bain Alexander, a merchant, and Elsie May Townsend, both of Scottish ancestry. The family remained in Baltimore throughout Alexander's relatively happy and comfortable childhood. She attended Baltimore's Western High School for Girls prior to enrolling in Goucher College, to which she won a partial scholarship. While at Goucher, her enthusiasm for a variety of sports—hockey, baseball, basketball—exceeded that for academics, and she was an unimpressive student. Nevertheless, she exhibited marked, though largely unapplied, skill in Dr. Jessie King's bacteriology class, and fellow students in the Goucher yearbook declared that "ambition fires her; hygiene claims her; kindness portrays her."

Having earned her A.B. from Goucher in 1923, Alexander went to work as a bacteriologist for the U.S. Public Health Service laboratory in Washington, D.C., where she stayed for three years; she later worked for the Maryland Public Health Service. She was able to save money for medical school during this time, and she also acquired the necessary research experience to successfully distinguish herself among the applicants to Johns Hopkins Medical School. Now clearly focused on her work, Alexander was in all aspects an excellent student at Johns Hopkins. She secured two year-long internships upon graduation in 1930, having earned her M.D., the first was in pediatrics at the Harriet Lane Home of Johns Hopkins Hospital, and the second was at the Babies Hospital of the Columbia-Presbyterian Medical Center in New York City. In 1932 she became an instructor and began her lifelong tenure at Columbia University's Department of Pediatrics. The following year she began joint appointments at the Babies Hospital and Vanderbilt Clinic, both at the Presbyterian Hospital in New York City, where she would become professor of pediatrics at its College of Physicians and Surgeons in 1958 and where she would remain throughout her career.

Alexander saw in her early hospital work the devastating effects of bacterial meningitis, an inflammation of the membranes surrounding the brain and spinal cord that was caused by a number of virulent bacteria and was rapidly fatal to infants and young children. Her interest in this disease was to remain a lifelong passion. Following her first work on the precipitin test used to quantify the severity of infection in meningococcus meningitis patients, her attention then turned to influenzal meningitis, caused by the Type b *Hemophilus influenzae* bacterium and the most common form of bacterial meningitis. The only therapy for this disease at the time was a largely ineffective horse antiserum, the fluid component of blood containing antibodies to the capsule surrounding the bacterium. Alexander drew from the work of Kenneth Goodner and Frank Horsfall, Jr., at the Rockefeller Institute, who had produced a successful antipneumococcal serum from rabbits, and similarly developed a dramatically improved antiserum for *H. influenzae*. She earned the E. Mead Johnson Award in 1942 for her publication detailing the development of this rabbit antiserum and its considerable success in the treatment of influenzal meningitis.

Following this early success, Alexander persevered, in collaboration with immunochemist Michael Heidelberger, to improve methods for quantifying antibodies in the antiinfluenzal serum and to markedly increase its potency. Often in collaboration with Grace Leidy, also of the Babies Hospital, she developed many improvements that tailored the combination of antiserum and sulfa drugs to each patient and form of meningitis: morphological criteria that would distinguish pathogenic strains in culture; standardized techniques for assessing the severity of infection and presence of antibodies in the patient's serum; and the efficacy of various sulfa drugs against each form of bacterial meningitis. Alexander's work was extremely successful: by the mid-1940s mortality from what had been an almost invariably fatal disease was reduced to less than 25 percent.

With the rapid integration of antibiotics into medicine in the 1940s, Alexander and Leidy published in *Science* a demonstration of the antibacterial action of streptomycin against Type b *H. influenzae*. Eventually the careful use of antibiotics in combination with Alexander's rabbit antiserum and sulfa drugs would virtually eliminate fatalities from bacterial meningitis.

Even in this preliminary study, however, Alexander and Leidy noticed the rapid appearance of bacterial strains growing in the presence of more than fifty times the usual effective dosage of streptomycin; this bacterial resistance was to be the focus and inspiration for the remainder of Alexander's career. She was among the first to realize that resistance to antibiotics was a result of rare, randomly occurring mutations in the "genetic component" of bacteria, a discovery that strengthened the growing theory that DNA was the molecule that held such genetic information. The appearance of resistant strains, she deduced, simply resulted from rapid selection for those mutants within a population. She and Leidy demonstrated transformation—a procedure in which new DNA is integrated into a bacterial genome—in *H. influenzae*, separately inducing traits for bacterial resistance and pathogenicity. With others at Columbia, Alexander later applied similar techniques to change poliovirus RNA and to demonstrate its ability to infect cells in tissue culture. Late in her career she developed an ingenious method for determining the evolutionary relationship among various species of *Hemophilus* based on their relative degree of transformation. The basis of this technique—relatedness based on genetic similarity—has become widely used in constructing the phylogenies, or evolutionary histories, of organisms.

Alexander distinguished herself as a creative and determined scientist and was equally known as a gifted, perceptive teacher, excelling in the informal discourse of clinical instruction. She was particularly emphatic, even to the point of personal affront, that students exercise scientific objectivity in their clinical judgments. Alexander received numerous awards during her career. Most notably, she was the first woman to receive the Oscar B. Hunter Memorial Award for therapy of infectious diseases (1961) and to be elected president of the American Pediatric Society (1964). She also was awarded the Stevens Triennial Prize (1954), which was presented for the best essay on a medical subject, and the distinguished service medal of the Columbia-Presbyterian Medical Center in 1963 and 1967.

As in her professional work, Alexander's enthusiasm and vivacity effused her personal life. She loved to travel, jaunted around Long Island Sound in her speed boat, and cultivated many rare species of flowers in her greenhouse. She lived in Port Washington, Long Island, with her longtime companion, Elizabeth Ufford, also a physician. She remained active until her death from liver cancer in New York City.

• Dr. Edward Curnen's memorial address and Alexander's curriculum vitae (with a complete list of publications) are both available from the Health Sciences Library of Columbia University. The majority of her publications appear chronologically in the *Journal of Pediatrics*, *Pediatrics*, the *Journal of Experimental Medicine*, and the *Proceedings of the Society for Experimental Biology and Medicine*. Short biographies appear in Emily J. McMurray, ed., *Notable Twentieth-Century Scientists* (1995), and Barbara Sicherman and Carol Hurd Green, eds., *Notable American Women* (1980). Particularly insightful accounts of Alexander's work and personal attributes are Lenore Turner's "From C Student to Winning Scientist" in *Goucher Alumnae Quarterly* (Winter 1962): 18–20, and Dr. Rustin McIntosh's letter to the editor, *Pediatrics* 42 (Sept. 1968): 544, intended as an addendum to the recently published obituaries of Alexander. Obituaries are in the *New York Times*, 29 June 1968, and the *Goucher Alumnae Quarterly* (Fall 1968): 35–63, which includes a personal statement by a mother whose child was saved due to Alexander's work on bacterial meningitis.

ALLISON AYDELOTTE

ALEXANDER, James (27 May 1691–2 Apr. 1756), political leader, was born in Muthil, Perthshire, Scotland, the son of David Alexander. His mother's identity is not known. Although his grandfather was related to the first earl of Stirling, his own branch of the family did not rank among the nobility. His father provided him with a practical education as an engineer and surveyor, professions more appropriate for the middle class than the aristocracy.

Although his bitter political enemy, Governor William Cosby, later alleged that Alexander had been a Jacobite in Scotland's 1715 uprising, Alexander actually came to America that year, too early to have joined the rebels. His family's sympathies moreover lay with the Hanoverian dynasty, not with the Stuart pretenders, and his well-documented Whig political views were incompatible with the Jacobite cause. He evidently emigrated with the hope of improving his fortunes in a country short of engineering talent.

In October 1715, Alexander was appointed surveyor general of East Jersey. Within two years he obtained the same office in West Jersey and New York as well. He took full advantage of those positions to acquire valuable tracts at little cost before other speculators could patent them. Second only to land speculation in profitability was the legal profession, and in 1720 Alexander qualified to practice law in New York. He obtained New Jersey's attorney generalship in 1723 and held that post for four years.

The final advantage underpinning Alexander's financial rise was his marriage in 1721 to a wealthy widow, Maria Sprat Provost. Maria continued to manage her deceased husband's merchant affairs despite the distraction of having seven children with Alexander. His wife's large estate afforded a ready source of capital for Alexander's land speculations, and she was well connected with New York's leading families, facilitating her husband's entry into the highest echelons of the colony's elite.

Alexander established his home in New York City, where he was a vestryman of Trinity Anglican Church. He received a commission to sit on New York's royal council in 1721. At the same time, he continued to play a leading role in New Jersey, where he held extensive landholdings and belonged to the East Jersey Board of Proprietors. He became a member of New Jersey's royal council in 1722. By 1730 he ranked among the inner circle of politicians who dominated government in both provinces.

The most important period of Alexander's career occurred during William Cosby's governorship of New York. Upon taking office in 1732, Cosby sued

Councilor Rip Van Dam for half the salary Van Dam had received as interim chief executive during the previous year. Alexander and his legal partner, William Smith (1697–1769), defended Van Dam. Cosby not only blocked Van Dam's right to a jury trial, but he also took revenge on Alexander and Smith by challenging their claims to the valuable Oblong Tract in upstate New York. Cosby's vindictiveness also cost Alexander his seat on the council.

Alexander took a leading role in fomenting opposition to the governor, arguing that Cosby's arbitrary actions threatened New Yorkers' civil liberties and property rights. He and others hired printer John Peter Zenger to attack the governor in the *New York Weekly Journal*, which began publication on 5 November 1733. Alexander, not Zenger, was the paper's actual editor; he heaped scathing criticism and searing ridicule upon the governor and published essays outlining Whig political theories on the dangers of unchecked executive power.

When Cosby had Zenger prosecuted for seditious libel, Alexander and Smith served as Zenger's attorneys. They tried to use Zenger's defense as a way to indict Cosby's administration but were overruled, dismissed from the case, and ultimately barred from practicing law for two years. Alexander nevertheless assisted behind the scenes in the trial's later stages, resulting in Zenger's acquittal in 1735. Alexander's legal skills and political courage were critical in frustrating Cosby's partisan use of seditious-libel prosecutions against the press.

After Cosby's death in 1736, Alexander continued his involvement in governmental affairs but increasingly pursued cultural and scientific interests. He corresponded with members of England's Royal Society and with the Royal Observatory at Greenwich on his astronomical observations. He became one of the early supporters of the American Philosophical Society organized in Philadelphia by Benjamin Franklin (1706–1790) in 1743. In 1754 he helped found the New York Library Society, that city's earliest public book-lending service.

Alexander served as a founding trustee of King's College (now Columbia University) in New York. He objected strongly when his fellow Anglicans, who were a majority of the school's board, tried to transform King's into a denominational school affiliated with the Church of England. His opposition was instrumental in persuading the assembly to write a charter that established King's as a nonsectarian college in 1754.

With a fortune estimated at £100,000 in 1745, Alexander ranked among New York's wealthiest men. He died in New York from complications of an illness contracted while attending sessions of that colony's royal council. His only son William Alexander (1726–1783) succeeded him on the councils of both New York and New Jersey and later served as a major general in the Continental army.

• Personal manuscripts are in the James Alexander Papers at the New-York Historical Society. Alexander's letters appear in volumes 4–6 of Edmund B. O'Callaghan and Berthold Fernow, eds., *Documents Relative to the Colonial History of the State of New York* (1853–1887), and in volumes 5–7 of William A. Whitehead et al., eds., *Archives of the State of New Jersey*, 1st ser., (43 vols., 1880–1949). See also Alan Valentine, *Lord Stirling* (1969), and the collaborative entry "James Alexander," *Genealogical Magazine of New Jersey* 14 (1939): 27–29.

THOMAS L. PURVIS

ALEXANDER, James Waddell (19 Sept. 1888–23 Sept. 1971), mathematician, was born in Sea Bright, New Jersey, the son of John White Alexander, a noted artist and mural painter, and Elizabeth Alexander, the daughter of John Waddell Alexander, a president of the Equitable Life Assurance Society. Alexander received his B.S. in mathematics and physics from Princeton University in 1910 and his A.M. in 1911. He then served as an instructor at Princeton from 1911 to 1912 before continuing his studies abroad at the universities of Paris and Bologna. Upon returning to Princeton he received his Ph.D. in 1915 with a dissertation titled "Functions Which Map the Interior of the Unit Circle upon Simple Regions" and written under the direction of Thomas H. Gronwall. He remained at Princeton as an instructor (1915–1916) and a lecturer (1916–1917) before serving as a lieutenant (later as a captain) in the U.S. Army Ordnance Office at Aberdeen Proving Ground from 1917 to 1918. On 15 January 1917 Alexander married Natalia Levitzkaja; they had one son and one daughter.

After the war ended, Alexander rejoined the Princeton faculty as, successively, an assistant professor (1920–1926), an associate professor (1926–1928), and a professor (1928–1933). In 1933 he joined the Institute for Advanced Study as an original member (with Albert Einstein, John von Neumann, Oswald Veblen, and Hermann Weyl), and he remained there as a professor until his retirement in 1951. During World War II, he was a civilian with the Office of Scientific Research and Development for the U.S. Army Air Force.

Alexander's major mathematical work can be grouped into four general periods. The first period, from 1913 to 1919, included his collaboration with Oswald Veblen (1913), which showed that the topology of manifolds could be extended to polyhedra. He also established the topological invariance of the Betti numbers and torsion coefficients that had been introduced by Henri Poincaré in his early papers on algebraic topology (1915). In effect Alexander and Veblen were responsible for helping put the Poincaré theory on a firm foundation. This period also includes his work on algebraic geometry, particularly his topological derivation of the Zeuthen-Segre invariant for an algebraic surface (1914), and his proof of the Nöther theorem for Cremona transformations (1915–1916). His dissertation on univalent functions also contained results that were quoted throughout the twentieth century.

The second period of Alexander's research, from 1920 to 1926, marked his exclusive interest in topological problems. It began with an elegant proof of the Jordan curve theorem (1920), followed by a major paper on the proof and extension of the Jordan-Brouwer separation theorem, which included the celebrated Alexander Duality Theorem, and the Alexander Lemma, which addressed the topology of the n-sphere (1922). Byproducts of this work included the Alexander horned sphere (1924) and a fundamental memoir on combinatorial analysis situs (1926), which was explicitly cited in his receipt of the Bôcher Prize in 1928. The latter included a rigorous proof of the independence of homology theory from the triangulation of the simplicial complex, and homology with integer coefficients modulo *m*, where *m* is an integer. The third period, from 1927 to 1933, was largely devoted to knot theory and the combinatorial theory of complexes. Alexander was not the first to attempt to formulate a topological theory of knots, but he made fundamental contributions to the theory which include the Alexander polynomials, ideals, and invariants (1928).

Alexander's final period of work, from 1934 to 1947, began with a series of papers concerning the group-theoretic aspects of duality. It included a theory (1935), which, when subsequently generalized by Edwin H. Spanier in 1948, became known as the Alexander-Spanier cohomology theory. This also led to his simultaneous discovery (with the Russian mathematician Andrei N. Kolmogorov) of the more general notion of a cohomology theory, which was announced at the Moscow conference and published in 1936. The remainder of Alexander's mathematical papers concern various attempts to obtain more general homology theories, by generalizing the notion of a topological space, or more general systems such as lattices. His only postwar paper (1947) dealt with this question and became known as the Alexander-Cech cohomology theory.

A mathematician of unusual depth and power, Alexander was a principal figure in the American development of algebraic/combinatorial topology. In particular, with Veblen and Lefschetz, he played a major role in the founding of the Princeton school of topology. His papers were very carefully written and were very influential in the United States and abroad. Much of his work was of such a basic character that it became common knowledge in topology, with its discoverer being forgotten as a result; it was Alexander who (in his great memoir of 1926), introduced the name p-chain for the previously employed notion of a linear combination of p-cells. In person, he was an imposing figure who possessed great charm and a very "youthful" view of mathematics, being one of the first American mathematicians to fully appreciate the use of modern algebraic methods in topology. Colleagues remembered his great fondness for limericks and his passion for mountain climbing.

During his prime Alexander was a very prominent and respected member of the American mathematical community. He was a member of the council of the American Mathematical Society (1923–1925), the winner of the Bôcher Prize (1928), and its vice president (1933–1934). He addressed the International Congress of Mathematicians in Zürich (1933) and the First International Topological Congress in Moscow (1935), and during 1936 he was the Rouse Ball Lecturer at Cambridge University. He was elected a member of the National Academy of Sciences in 1930.

After World War II Alexander became more and more reclusive; following his retirement from the institute, he virtually disappeared from the American mathematical scene. He had inherited great wealth (a millionaire, he accepted no salary for his institute professorship) and held left-wing political views, which made him suspect during the McCarthy era of the 1950s. His last public appearance was his signing of a statement on 1 July 1954, along with twenty-six other prominent members of the Institute for Advanced Study, expressing his confidence in the loyalty and patriotism of J. Robert Oppenheimer upon the suspension of Oppenheimer's security clearance. Alexander died of pneumonia in the Princeton Hospital.

• Jean Dieudonné, *A History of Algebraic and Differential Topology: 1900–1960* (1989), makes extensive reference to Alexander's contributions and their subsequent influence on the development of modern algebraic topology. An obituary containing a complete list of publications is in the *Bulletin of the American Mathematical Society* 79 (Sept. 1973): 900–903. An obituary is also in the *New York Times*, 24 Sept. 1971.

JOSEPH D. ZUND

ALEXANDER, Jeff (2 July 1910–23 Dec. 1989), composer and conductor, was born Myer Alexander in Seattle, Washington, the son of Max Alexander, Jr., a salesman, and Della Goodhue, a pianist. His musical education was initiated by his mother and continued at Becker Institute of Music in Portland, Oregon, as well as under private tutors Edmund Ross in Los Angeles and Joseph Schillinger in New York. In his early teens Alexander was singing and dancing on the vaudeville circuit. By his late teens he was playing piano and writing musical arrangements for his own trio and, later, for several big bands, including that of Horace Heidt. In 1937 in Los Angeles he was creating musical arrangements for "The Hit Parade" and "The Camel Hour" radio series when he met a model, Constance Frost. The couple were married the same year and were divorced in 1967; they had one daughter.

Alexander moved to New York in 1939 and began writing musical arrangements and directing choral groups for radio shows, including "The Lucky Strike Show," often collaborating with André Kostelanetz and Leopold Stokowski at CBS radio. During World War II he wrote music for shows presented to returning soldiers. Also during the war, in 1943, he changed his name to Jeff. He moved back to Los Angeles in 1947 and that year wrote his first film arrangement. He continued to arrange and compose for films in Hollywood while also serving as musical director for the radio series "Amos 'n' Andy" and "Hollywood Star Playhouse." Some of the original film scores he composed were *The Affairs of Dobie Gillis* (1953), *Escape from Fort Bravo* (1953), *Remains to Be Seen* (1953), *Rogue Cop* (1954), *Prisoner of War* (1954), *The Tender Trap* (1955), *Ransom* (1956), *These Wilder Years* (1956), *The Great American Pastime* (1956), *Slander* (1956), *Jailhouse Rock* (1957), *The Wings of Eagles* (1957), *Gun Glory* (1957), *The High Cost of Loving* (1958), *The Law and Jake Wade* (1958), *The Sheepman* (1958), *Saddle the Wind* (1958), *Party Girl* (1958), *Ask Any Girl* (1959), *The Gazebo* (1959), *It Started with a Kiss* (1959), *The Mating Game* (1959), *All the Fine Young Cannibals* (1960), *The George Raft Story* (1961), *Kid Galahad* (1961), *The Rounders* (1965), *Double Trouble* (1967), *Clambake* (1967), *Day of the Evil Gun* (1968), *Speedway* (1968), *Support Your Local Sheriff* (1969), and *Dirty Dingus Magee* (1970). He also collaborated on several musicals for Metro-Goldwyn-Mayer, creating vocal arrangements for, among other films, *Singin' in the Rain* (1952), *Seven Brides for Seven Brothers* (1954), *It's Always Fair Weather* (1955), *Kismet* (1955), and *Gigi* (1958). The Academy Award–winning documentary *Why Man Creates* was scored by Alexander.

In the 1960s Alexander began composing music for television productions. He composed scores for series such as "Julia," the first series with a black star (Diahann Carroll), "Please Don't Eat the Daisies," "The Jimmy Stewart Show," "The Lieutenant," "The Rounders," and "Valentine's Day." He worked on "Columbo," "Barnaby Jones," "Serpico," "Doctor Kildare," "Policewoman," "Wagon Train," "Bachelor Father," "The Twilight Zone," and "My Three Sons" as well. He also scored several television movies: *The Daughters of Josh McCabe*, *Kate Bliss and the Ticker Tape Kid*, *Wild, Wild West Revisited*, and *More Wild, Wild West*, and he was the musical director of "The George Burns Special" and "The Gene Kelly Special." He also wrote music for promotional television spots and commercials for Bank of America, Ford, Chevrolet, Kawasaki, Save-On Drugstores, Union Oil, Qantas Airlines, Rainier Beer, and AT&T, among others.

Throughout his career Alexander worked with Frank Sinatra in New York, Las Vegas, and Los Angeles, and he was one of the composers Sinatra collaborated with on an album of original pieces, *Tone Poems of Color* (1958), which Sinatra conducted. The other composers on the album were Elmer Bernstein, Gordon Jenkins, Billy May, André Previn, Nelson Riddle, Alec Wilder, and Victor Young.

A co-founder around 1949 of the Composers and Lyricists Guild of America, Alexander sat on the board of governors of that organization for decades. He became a member of the American Society of Composers, Authors and Publishers in 1952, served as vice president of the Screen Composers Association, and also served on the board of governors of the Academy of Motion Picture Arts and Sciences (1974–1976, 1977–1979). He retired from films and television in 1980 and moved to Whidbey Island, Washington, to compose chamber pieces and a symphony. He composed many art songs, Divertimento for Viola and Piano, *Grass Roots—A Country Ballet*, *Ground Bass for Piano and String Quartet*, *Partage* (a ballet commissioned by the Los Angeles Ballet Association), and two preludes for flute and string quartet. At the time of his death, on Whidbey Island, he had completed a symphony, *Papa's People . . . Papa's Places*, and was reworking a musical he had begun writing in 1975 in collaboration with E. Y. "Yip" Harburg and Larry Orenstein, *What a Fine Day for a Miracle*.

• Alexander's musical scores and his papers are housed in the Special Collections of the Music Library at the University of California, Los Angeles. Brief obituaries are in *Cue Sheet* 7, no. 2 (1990) and *Variety*, 7 Feb. 1990.

JILL ALEXANDER

ALEXANDER, John White (7 Oct. 1856–31 May 1915), artist, was born in Allegheny City, Pennsylvania, the son of John Alexander and Fanny Smith. Alexander's father died soon after his birth, and his mother died when he was five years old. Sent to live with his maternal grandparents, Alexander left school at the age of twelve to work as a messenger for the Atlantic and Pacific Telegraph Company in Pittsburgh. Colonel Edward Jay Allen, an official of the firm, was impressed by a sketch done by Alexander. Allen eventually adopted Alexander.

Between odd jobs and additional high school work, Alexander continued with his sketching, hoping to become an illustrator. At age eighteen, with Allen's blessing and $300 he had saved, he moved to New York City. Hired as an office boy at Harper and Brothers, he was soon promoted to the art department, working under Charles Parsons for both *Harper's Weekly* and *Harper's New Monthly Magazine*.

Anxious for formal training, Alexander again saved his money and left for Europe in 1877, unsure whether he would study in Paris or Munich. After a brief stop in London he traveled to Paris, but he discovered that the École des Beaux-Arts was not in session. Continuing on to Munich, he was accepted by the Royal Academy, which he attended until mid-1878. Alexander left the academy and gravitated to the circle of expatriate American artists in Pölling, Germany, led by Frank Duveneck. Alexander and Duveneck became friends, and in addition to sharing a studio, they traveled together to Italy in 1879–1880. While in Venice Alexander made the acquaintance of James McNeill Whistler; they remained friends for the remainder of Whistler's life.

Alexander returned to the United States in 1881, intending to settle in New York. A shortage of funds, however, forced his return to Pittsburgh. Reestablishing contact with Parsons at Harper and Brothers, Alexander was given a number of assignments in Pittsburgh, but he was called back to New York in late 1881. For his portrait illustrations for *Harper's Weekly* and *Harper's Monthly*, Alexander began to paint the works instead of draw them for reproduction. This strategy helped him to become known as a portrait painter, and soon he received commissions for portraits of Oliver Wendell Holmes and the actor Joseph Jefferson. Though he continued his work for Harper throughout the 1880s, Alexander also did a series of illustrations for its major competitor, *Century Magazine*, beginning in 1886.

These early portraits established the style Alexander used with male subjects for the remainder of his career. He placed the figures with their sketchily depicted attire melding into the dark background. The face of the subject, often brightly lit, blazed out from the canvas with an evocative suggestion of his character. Among the male figures Alexander depicted were President Chester Arthur (1907), Samuel Clemens (c. 1902), and Thomas Hardy (date unknown). His portrait of Walt Whitman (1889) was often exhibited.

Alexander's depiction of women differed significantly, and the decorative nature of his portraits of women was noted early by critics. Often using the female figure as an element of composition, Alexander closely integrated his subject into her setting, creating a clearly recognizable style that emphasized simple arrangements, elegant lines, and harmonious color arrangements. The identity of the sitter in many of these was secondary: *Azalea (Portrait of Charlotte Colgate Abbe)* (1885), *Le Piano* (1894), *Isabella and the Pot of Basil* (1897), and *The Green Girl* (1898).

In 1882, the year following his return to New York, Alexander began a long association with the National Academy of Design when he exhibited in the academy's Fifty-seventh Annual Exhibition. Two years later he exhibited with the Society of American Artists, a group associated with the modern movement in American art.

In 1887 Alexander married Elizabeth Swan Alexander (no relation), the daughter of an insurance executive; they had one son. Traveling to Europe for health reasons, Alexander and his family arrived in Paris in 1891. Though originally planned as a short trip, their stay lasted eleven years.

After a brief foray into landscape painting, which he had first tried before leaving for Europe, Alexander returned to figure painting. Exhibiting widely in the salons of various artists' organizations, Alexander quickly formed an association with the Société Nationale des Beaux-Arts. Though actively engaged in the politics and aesthetic discussions of the Parisian art world, Alexander made frequent trips to the United States for portrait commissions, from which he earned a substantial income.

Awarded a commission for six murals on the theme of "Evolution of the Book" for the Library of Congress, in 1896 Alexander traveled to Washington, D.C., to supervise the installation of the murals. While in the United States that year he was an important source in suggesting paintings for the first international Carnegie Institute exhibition. This began his lifelong association with that event and stimulated his interest in promoting American art.

Alexander's own work continued to receive critical acclaim in Europe, as well as from American critics reviewing the Parisian salons. Exhibiting widely, he won numerous awards, culminating in his being named a chevalier of the Légion d'Honneur in 1901. Alexander's interest in encouraging American art, however, led to his permanent repatriation in New York City in late 1901.

On his return Alexander was showered with further honors and portrait commissions. His first solo exhibition was held at Durand-Ruel Galleries in New York in 1902, and he exhibited widely over the next few years. Commissioned by the Carnegie Institute in 1905 to create a large series of murals celebrating Pittsburgh, Alexander received the then extraordinary amount of $175,000. The murals, which were to cover 5,000 square feet, consumed much of his time for the next three years.

Alexander worked tirelessly to promote American art by serving on exhibition juries and as a trustee for institutions such as the Metropolitan Museum of Art, the New York Public Library, and the National Institute of Arts and Letters. In 1909 he was elected president of the National Academy of Design, a position he held until shortly before his death. Administrative duties for the academy, as well as for other organizations including the National Society of Mural Painters and the Macdowell Club, limited the amount of time he spent painting. Alexander also designed highly praised sets and costumes for actress Maude Adams, a close friend of the Alexanders. These included *Peter Pan* (1905), Rostand's *Chanticleer* (1911), and the lavish outdoor mountings of Schiller's *Joan of Arc* (1909) and *As You Like It* (1910).

Resigning his position as president of the National Academy of Design in 1915, Alexander planned to devote himself to his painting. Only two months later, however, he died in his New York home.

• Some of Alexander's works are in the collections of the National Academy of Design, N.Y.; the Metropolitan Museum of Art; the Player's Club, N.Y.; the National Portrait Gallery; the New York Public Library; and the Detroit Institute of Arts. Examples of Alexander's murals are in the Library of Congress and the Carnegie Institute, Pittsburgh, Pa. Alexander's papers are at the Archives of American Art, Smithsonian Institution. Sarah J. Moore, "John White Alexander (1856–1915): In Search of the Decorative" (1856–1915): (Ph.D. diss., City Univ. of New York, 1992), is a major source of biographical information. Mary Anne Goley, *Out of the Kitchen: The Art of Still Life by John White Alexander* (1995), is an exhibition catalog that covers this little-known aspect of his work. A few of the more useful articles include William L. Harris, "John White Alexander: His Influence on American Art and Industry," *Good Furniture* 5, no. 2 (Aug. 1915): 63–73; Arthur Hoeber, "John W. Alexander," *International Studio* 34, no. 135 (May 1908): 85–96; and Christian Brinton, "The Art of John W. Alexander," *Munsey's Magazine* 39 (Sept. 1908): 744–55. An obituary is in the *New York Times*, 2 June 1915.

MARTIN R. KALFATOVIC

ALEXANDER, Joseph Addison (24 Apr. 1809–28 Jan. 1860), Presbyterian scholar and minister, was born in Philadelphia, Pennsylvania, the son of Janetta Waddel and Archibald Alexander, a Presbyterian minister. Alexander, who was always called Addison, grew up in Princeton, New Jersey, where in 1812 his father was called to be the first professor at Princeton Theological Seminary. At an early age, Alexander displayed the ability in languages that would make him a marvel throughout his life. By the time he began formal instruction with local tutors, his father had taught him the rudiments of Latin and Greek and also introduced him to Semitic languages. By the time he graduated from the College of New Jersey as a seventeen-year old in 1826, he had read the Koran in Arabic, made considerable progress in Persian and Syriac, and begun the wide-ranging study of contemporary European languages that he never stopped. It was his habit, begun before entering college and continuing to the week of his death, to read the Bible daily in at least six languages. Alexander's nephew and biographer, Henry Carrington Alexander, concluded that he read, wrote, and spoke Latin, German, French, Italian, Spanish, and Portuguese; that he read without helps and wrote Arabic, Hebrew, Persian, Greek, Romaic, and Chaldean; that he could read Ethiopic, Dutch, Sanskrit, Syriac, Coptic, Danish, Flemish, and Norwegian; and that he knew enough Polish, Swedish, Malay, Hindustani, and Chinese to peruse works in these languages. The linguistic marvel was also a social recluse who never married and who, despite great interest in travel and world affairs, lived contentedly in Princeton as a student and professor his whole life. J. B. Adgar, who saw Alexander off and on for many years, said of him that "he had hardly any lady acquaintances. He was deep in love with books, and his communion was with the mighty dead and in outlandish tongues" (Alexander, *Life*, p. 214). An older brother, James Waddel Alexander, who was almost as brilliant but much more social, was Addison's closest companion as a youth, a constant correspondent as an adult, and his alter ego in many projects.

Alexander spent a three-year period in private reading after graduating as valedictorian of his college class, during which time he served briefly as Princeton borough clerk and wrote short essays for local newspapers. He then taught at the Edgehill Grammar School in Princeton before becoming an adjunct professor of ancient languages at the College of New Jersey in November 1830. During his time as a grammar school teacher, Alexander experienced a conversion that both provided an ideological center for his life and gave him a vocation as a minister. He taught at the college for three years while also pursuing informal theological study with the faculty of Princeton Seminary, including his father, Samuel Miller (whom he eventually replaced as professor of church history), and Charles Hodge (with whom he became fast friends). In April 1833 Alexander followed Hodge's example by taking an extended study tour of Europe, an activity not then as common for aspiring American academics as it would soon become. After short stops in England, Scotland, and France, in Halle and Berlin he enjoyed his most fruitful study with the academic leaders of German pietism—Friedrich Tholuck, Ernst Hengstenberg, and Johann Neander. In these academic preachers he found models for his own life of religious scholarship of a sort hardly found in the United States during this period. From Hengstenberg Alexander took even more, for he would later publish a lengthy commentary on the Psalms that closely followed Hengstenberg's own treatment. During his European tour, Alexander's already great admiration for the philological and historical skills of the Germans grew as rapidly as did his deepening disdain for their metaphysical preoccupations. He would later assert that "the historical literature of Germany compared with its philosophy, is gold compared with moonshine" (*Biblical Repertory and Princeton Review* 19 [1847]: 93).

Upon his return to the United States in May 1834, Alexander was appointed Hodge's assistant in Hebrew and Old Testament at Princeton Seminary. When he was later ordained to the ministry by the New Brunswick Presbytery (1838), he took over Hodge's main responsibilities in these fields as a regular professor. Later he would serve a stint as professor of biblical and ecclesiastical history (1851–1859) before returning, shortly before his death, to his first love in biblical studies as professor of Hellenistic and New Testament literature.

As a teacher, Alexander could be cutting with students who did not share his love of learning, but those with some ability who tried their best returned to praise him, often with awe, as a master instructor. Alexander was never the regular minister of a congregation but did preach widely after his ordination. Among his fellow ministers he enjoyed a lofty reputation for the capacity to preach with or without a manuscript and to adjust his style to different circumstances.

From his late adolescence, Alexander wrote regularly for the press on many subjects. For newspapers and literary journals he discussed popular literature and provided occasional poems that combined Byronic form and Christian romantic content. His most important theological writing appeared in the *Biblical Repertory and Princeton Review*, which Hodge had founded in 1825 and to which Alexander contributed at least ninety-three substantial articles (along with countless "short notices") from 1829 through 1863 (when one of his lectures was published posthumously). The range of subjects treated in these essays was vast—from the latest Continental philology and biblical commentaries to analyses of contemporary ecclesiastical affairs in Scotland, Ireland, and elsewhere. Writing for the *Princeton Review*, which he also helped to edit, gave Alexander a chance to popularize scholarship in the biblical languages, apply historical lessons to the contemporary church, and defend the Princetonians' conservative view of the Bible. The essays were written with great learning worn lightly, but also with a penchant for sarcasm that sometimes impeded his arguments. Alexander, who ranged so widely in his reading, was indifferent to philosophy. His theological forays, as a consequence, were more interesting when interacting with English or Scottish authors, who shared his disdain for metaphysics, than when addressing the proposals of German theology.

From the mid-1830s, Alexander worked steadily to publish commentaries on various books of the Bible. Of the books that resulted, his first effort, on Isaiah (1846–1847), may have been the best. It is a difficult volume, because of its dense compilation of authorities, and because Alexander's own conclusions are often frustratingly elusive. But for breadth of learning and judicious treatment of controversial passages, it remains one of the best American biblical commentaries of the precritical era. Later commentaries—*Psalms* (1850), *Acts of the Apostles* (1857), *Mark* (1858), and *Matthew* (published posthumously in 1861)—are more popular but are also marked by broad learning. His study of the gospels was exemplary in its day for breaking free from the enervating effort to harmonize details in the four accounts while attempting to clarify the distinct theological and literary purposes of the individual evangelists.

Alexander bestrode a rapidly changing theological world in which settled Protestant certainties were eroding in the face of European scholarship and American democratic individualism. Though thoroughly committed to old ways, Alexander drew enough from his contemporaries to experience substantial internal tension: between the indulgence of romantic sensibility and a great trust in science, between Enlightenment confidence in reason and romantic deference to emotion, between a full appreciation of contemporary theological insight and abiding commitment to historic Presbyterian confessions. He was too much the conservative to have an enduring influence on the main lines of American and English biblical scholarship. But for traditionalists, his biblical work has remained an example of conscientious rigor. For historians of whatever theological views, he remains a signal practitioner of serious academic scholarship in an early period of American interaction with European theology.

The death of Alexander's brother, James Waddel, in July 1859 was a blow from which Alexander never recovered. His rather rotund frame shrank noticeably in the months that followed. The last words in the diary he kept off and on throughout his life were written on 25 January 1860, three days before his death in Princeton. They spoke for his life: "Reading as usual."

• The archives of Princeton Seminary holds ten boxes of Alexander's papers, mostly notes from lectures. Besides the works mentioned in the text, a two-volume set of Alexander's sermons was published in 1860, and his *Notes on New Testament Literature and Ecclesiastical History* was also brought out posthumously in 1867. In 1993 four of Alexander's commentaries (*Isaiah, Psalms, Acts, Mark*) were still in print from Kregel Publishers, Grand Rapids, Mich. Henry Carrington Alexander, *The Life of Joseph Addison Alexander* (2 vols., 1870), is not well organized and often lapses into hagiography, but it does include much valuable primary material, especially on the relationship between Joseph Addison Alexander and James Waddel Alexander. The best short account is the unsigned biographical sketch in the *Biblical Repertory and Princeton Review: Index Volume, No. 1* (1870): 82–91. Helpful insights on Alexander's biblical scholarship are found in James H. Moorhead, "Joseph Addison Alexander: Common Sense, Romanticism and Biblical Criticism at Princeton," *Journal of Presbyterian History* 53 (1975): 51–65, and, especially, Marion Ann Taylor, *The Old Testament in the Old Princeton School, 1812–1929* (1992). On the ways in which Alexander's views of history met modern ideas halfway, see Dru A. Dodson, "Philip Schaff, Princeton, and the Idea of Church History" (M.A. thesis, Trinity Evangelical Divinity School, Deerfield, Ill., 1992).

MARK A. NOLL

ALEXANDER, Mary Spratt Provoost (17 Apr. 1693–18 Apr. 1760), merchant, was born in New York City, the daughter of John Spratt, a Scottish immigrant merchant and alderman in New York, and Maria DePeyster, an heiress of a prominent Dutch family of goldsmiths, merchants, and politicians. After John Spratt died in 1697, Maria Spratt married David Provoost, a merchant and smuggler. Alexander and her siblings lived with their maternal grandmother after their mother died in 1700. In 1711 she married Samuel Provoost, an importer and a younger brother of David Provoost, her mother's husband. The couple had three children. Alexander invested much of her inheritance in her husband's enterprises and acted as his business partner.

In 1719 or early 1720 David Provoost died. Alexander immediately assumed control of her husband's business affairs. In 1721 she married James Alexander, a descendant of the Scottish earls of Stirling and one of New York's leading attorneys and politicians. With her second husband Alexander had seven children, of whom five lived to adulthood. Her son William Alexander, who later went by the title "Lord Stirling," served as an aide and secretary to General William Shirley during the French and Indian War and as a general under George Washington during the American Revolution.

From the time of her second marriage until her death, Alexander raised her family and managed the Provoost mercantile business. She became one of the leading importers in New York City and sold the goods in her own store, which she had built along with a row of counting-house offices in front of her mansion on Broad Street. Her inventory was augmented by goods that her husband had received as payment in kind for his legal services. Alexander's house served as a meeting spot and salon for many of New York's elite politicians and businessmen, and she was reputed to be an informal adviser to many of them, including Andrew Hamilton, the attorney for John Peter Zenger. During the French and Indian War she supplied General William Shirley's Fort Niagara expedition with provisions.

Alexander died in New York City. She and her husband James were buried in the cemetery at Trinity Church in lower Manhattan.

As a leading merchant in one of the largest commercial centers on the Atlantic seaboard, Alexander was one of the most prominent and powerful women in the American colonies. In addition, she served as something of an informal power broker and adviser in some of the most important politics of the New York colony.

• Alexander's business records are deposited in the New-York Historical Society and the New Jersey Historical Society. Mrs. John King Van Rensselaer, *The Goede Vrouw of Mana-ha-ta: At Home and in Society, 1609–1760* (1898), contains considerable information on Alexander's life. See also Livingston Rutherfurd, *Family Records and Events* (1894).

THADDEUS RUSSELL

ALEXANDER, Sadie Tanner Mossell (3 Jan. 1898–1 Nov. 1989), economist and lawyer, was born in Philadelphia, Pennsylvania, the daughter of Aaron Mossell, an attorney and the first black graduate of the University of Pennsylvania Law School, and Mary Tanner. While a young girl her father abandoned the family, and she was raised by her mother with the assistance of relatives.

Alexander received her degrees from the University of Pennsylvania. With her Ph.D. in economics, awarded in 1921, she became the first African-American woman to receive a doctorate in economics and among the first three African-American women to receive a doctorate in any field in the United States. Her doctoral dissertation, "The Standard of Living among One Hundred Negro Migrant Families in Philadelphia," was a thorough social survey investigating spending patterns, from 1916 to 1918, of African-American migrant families newly arrived from the South. It was based on interviews in Philadelphia's Twenty-ninth Ward. Attentive to intraracial class distinctions, she suggested in this study, published in *The Annals of the American Academy of Political and Social Sciences* in November 1921, that the black middle class, including church leaders and professionals, should serve as an example of thrift and propriety for the masses of black people. In a 1930 article, "Negro Women in Our Economic Life," written for the National Urban League's *Opportunity* magazine, she would expand the discussion by writing that black women had an important role to play in the community and that their married lives and the lives of their children would be enhanced if they became involved in industry and business. She advised black women to produce goods that had a "price value" rather than remaining housewives and consumers who were seen as not contributing to the economic life of their families. Alexander's early interest in the role of African-American women in the larger community is further evidenced by the fact that from 1919 to 1923 she served as the first national president of Delta Sigma Theta, a black sorority and public service organization. She would later become its president emeritus.

As an African-American woman, Alexander found it difficult after earning her doctorate to find suitable employment in her field of economics. But with a minor in insurance and actuarial science, she went to Durham, North Carolina, the "Capital of the Black Middle Class," becoming an assistant actuary from 1921 to 1923 at the black-owned North Carolina Mutual Life Insurance Company. In 1923 she married Raymond Pace Alexander, a fellow economist and a Harvard Law School graduate, in Philadelphia. They had two daughters.

The year after her marriage Alexander began attending the University of Pennsylvania Law School, where she was named to the editorial board of the *Law Review*. In 1927 she became the law school's first black woman graduate and later that year the first black woman admitted to the Pennsylvania bar. After graduation she and her husband went into legal practice together; she specialized in estate and family law. She started her own practice in 1959 when her husband became a Philadelphia municipal court judge. She maintained a solo practice in domestic relations, adoption, and juvenile care until 1976, when she joined the Philadelphia law firm of Atkinson, Myers and Archie, where she remained until her retirement in 1982.

During the late 1920s and into the 1930s, Alexander served as assistant city solicitor for Philadelphia. During this period, she and Judge Alexander also became well known as civil libertarians and for their civil and human rights advocacy. They drafted laws, including the 1935 Pennsylvania Public Accommodations Act, to desegregate Philadelphia restaurants, hotels, and theaters, and they filed court cases to test the enforcement of those laws.

In 1925 the Alexanders were also instrumental in founding the National Bar Association, the association of black attorneys; Judge Alexander was one of its early presidents. Sadie Alexander wrote one of the first articles for the association's *National Bar Journal*, "Women as Practitioners of Law in the Untied States" (July 1941), and she served as the organization's national secretary from 1943 to 1947. She also drafted a section of Philadelphia's Home Rule Charter that mandated the formation of the Philadelphia Commission on Human Relations. She subsequently served as a member of its board and on occasion as its chairwoman.

In 1946 President Harry S. Truman appointed Sadie Alexander to the President's Committee on Civil Rights, and she contributed to its final report, *To Secure These Rights*, published after a series of public hearings in 1947. In 1963 President John F. Kennedy appointed her to the Lawyer's Committee for Civil Rights and Law, and President Jimmy Carter named her chair of the White House Conference on Aging in 1979.

In addition, Alexander served as a national officer on the board of the National Urban League for more than twenty-five years and was a member of the National Advisory Council of the American Civil Liberties Union and on the Philadelphia chapter's board of directors.

Alexander was significant both as an intellectual and an activist. A pioneer in social research, she became the first African-American woman to achieve a variety of personal and professional distinctions. She was a prominent and vocal member of the black middle class with a vision about the role it must play, as well as the role women working outside the home must play, in the larger African-American community. She was recognized not only for her work in Philadelphia but also nationally, with three American presidents seeking her counsel.

In her lifetime, Alexander was recognized by the academic community, where she greatly excelled, receiving a number of honorary degrees. In 1980 she received the Distinguished Service Award from the University of Pennsylvania, and in 1987 the Philadelphia Bar Association named its public service center in her honor. She died in Philadelphia.

• The papers of Sadie Tanner Mossell Alexander and her husband are located at the University of Pennsylvania. Several articles worthy of note include Marcia Greenlee, "Interview with Dr. Sadie T. M. Alexander," in *The Black Women Oral History Project*, vol. 2 (1991), pp. 70–85; Julianne Malveaux, "Missed Opportunity: Sadie Tanner Mossell Alexander and the Economics Profession," *American Economic Review* 81 (May 1991): 307–10, is an unusual account of the seminal research Alexander did for her doctoral dissertation in economics that speculates about the kind of research she might have performed and the impact she might have made had she been able to practice in the field of economics; and Theresa Snyder, "Sadie Alexander" in *Notable Black American Women*, ed. Jessie Carney Smith (1991), and V. P. Franklin, "Sadie Tanner Mossell Alexander," in *Black Women in America: An Historical Encyclopedia*, ed. Darlene Clark Hine, vol. 1 (1993). Obituaries are in the *Philadelphia Inquirer* and the *New York Times*, 3 Nov. 1989.

NANCY ELIZABETH FITCH

ALEXANDER, Stephen (1 Sept. 1806–25 June 1883), astronomer, was born in Schenectady, New York, the son of Alexander Alexander, a merchant and grist mill operator, and Maintchie (Maria) Connor. His father died when Stephen was only two, leaving a large estate in the form of property, which comfortably supported the boy, his sister, and his mother. By the time Alexander reached maturity, however, the estate had been largely squandered by its executors. He graduated from Union College in 1824, and from 1825 to 1830 he taught natural philosophy and mathematics at Yates Polytechny, a vocational school in Chittenango, New York. He had already demonstrated his interest in astronomy, and while at Yates made a variety of telescopic observations.

An important event in Alexander's life was the marriage of his younger sister, Harriet, to their first cousin, Joseph Henry. A few months after the May 1830 wedding, Alexander left Yates to reside with his sister and brother-in-law in Albany. When Henry became professor of natural philosophy at the College of New Jersey (later Princeton) in 1832, Alexander went along. He immediately enrolled as a student at the Princeton Theological Seminary. Yet it was never Alexander's intention to pursue a career as a clergyman. He attended the theological seminary solely as a way of establishing his credentials for a faculty position at the Presbyterian college. In 1833 he was appointed a tutor at Princeton. A year later he became adjunct professor of mathematics. In 1836 he was given responsibility for teaching astronomy. That same year he married Louisa Meads of Albany, with whom he had three children; she died in 1847. From 1840 until his retirement in 1876, Alexander was professor of astronomy at Princeton, holding this chair either alone, or in combination with either natural philosophy or mathematics, until his retirement in 1876. He married Caroline Forman of Princeton in 1850; they had two children.

Alexander was not a complete success either as a teacher or as a researcher. Although his lectures to the general public, which focused on the nebular hypothesis, were described as having "a lofty and poetic eloquence," he was not masterful in imparting knowledge to undergraduates. In 1846 one of his students, describing his style of lecturing, said, "He seizes upon a pin's point of Sense & wraps it up, as though he were afraid it would catch cold in these chilly days, in great muffling layers of fine words & long expletive sentences—until it is eventually lost in the overwhelming haystack of his Verbosity." Even one of his eulogizers complained that in mathematics classes, Alexander would "outrun" the students' ability to comprehend his lectures.

As an astronomer, Alexander's significance was short-lived. His early research focused on the sun, and his calculations and observations on solar eclipses were published in the *Transactions of the Albany Institute*. This was an interest he continued at Princeton, perhaps in part because of the lack of a large telescope there—the college did not begin building an observatory until 1866, and did not obtain a telescope of substantial size until 1882. None of this work was particularly profound or insightful. As Charles Young noted about the 1843 paper, "Physical Phenomena Attending Solar Eclipses," Alexander failed to provide "sufficient discrimination between the real and imaginary."

More notable to his contemporaries, and perhaps the intellectual justification for his selection in 1863 as an original member of the National Academy of Sciences, were his speculative papers applying the nebular hypothesis to a number of astronomical problems, including the comets and their origins, stellar clusters, nebulae, and the solar system. Beginning in the late 1840s Alexander spent three decades pursuing mathematical harmonies in the universe, which led to his being dubbed by critics, not always in a complimentary manner, the "American Kepler." Two major publications resulted from this work. Between March and July 1852 he published a seven-part article in the *Astronomical Journal* titled "On the Origin of the Forms and the Present Condition of Some of the Clusters of Stars and Several of the Nebulae," which argued that some of the clusters and nebulae were disintegrating stars, not stars in the process of formation, as was widely held. After years of oral presentations to the American Association for the Advancement of Science, in 1875 Alexander summed up his thoughts on the ratios of planetary distances and those of planetary satellites in "Statement and Exposition of Certain Harmonies of the Solar System."

Ironically, Alexander failed to follow up on what could have been his most important research—the relative temperature of sunspots. In 1845 he assisted Henry in the first experiments to demonstrate that sunspots were relatively cooler than the bright surface of the sun. However, for unknown reasons, he did not carry on the research after Henry abandoned it. During the late 1840s, Henry explained the technique to Angelo Secchi, an Italian astronomer at Georgetown College. Secchi subsequently received credit for the study of temperature distribution across the solar surface.

In terms of education, career, and research, Alexander was typical of those teaching the subject in American colleges during the middle third of the nineteenth century, before the coming of formal graduate education. He was neither completely preoccupied with teaching, although most of his energy was spent in the classroom, nor wholly dedicated to research, although he had, by contemporary standards, an impressive list of publications and unpublished presentations before scholarly audiences. He died in Princeton.

• Most of Alexander's surviving correspondence is in the Joseph Henry Papers, Smithsonian Institution Archives. Material dealing with his career at Princeton, including the diary of John R. Buhler, Princeton Class of 1846 is in the Princeton University Library. Select items from both depositories are being published with annotations in the *Papers of Joseph Henry*, ed. Marc Rothenberg (1972–). The Alexander publication which provides the most insight into his research objectives and methods is "Statement and Exposition of Certain Harmonies of the Solar System," *Smithsonian Contributions to Knowledge* 21 (1875). For his approach to teaching, see *Syllabus of Prof. S. Alexander's Lectures on Astronomy* (1845). No modern assessment exists. The best biographical account, although it is not entirely sympathetic, remains the memoir written by his successor at Princeton, Charles A. Young, in National Academy of Sciences *Biographical Memoirs* 2 (1886): 251–59.

MARC ROTHENBERG

ALEXANDER, William (25 Dec. 1726–15 Jan. 1783), soldier and claimant to the title of Lord Stirling, was born in New York City, the son of James Alexander, a prominent lawyer, and Mary Sprat Provoost, a merchant. He grew up in privileged circumstances, receiving an education from his father and private tutors. Although overshadowed by his rich and assertive parents, he loved them and fell into an easy working relationship with his mother in her mercantile business. In 1748 he married Sarah Livingston, daughter of Philip Livingston, and thus became connected with the rich and powerful Livingston family. The couple had two children. With such influences behind him during the Seven Years' War, it was no wonder that he became secretary to Governor William Shirley of Massachusetts. It was also no wonder that he and some business partners were hired by the governor as army contractors during the Niagara campaign of 1755–1756. But this service proved disadvantageous. When Shirley was unsuccessful in the campaign and was criticized by political enemies for supposed failings, Alexander and his partners were accused of profiteering and their bills delayed of payment. In order to defend his mentor and to secure the sums due the Niagara contractors, Alexander accompanied Shirley to England when the governor was summoned home to account for himself.

From 1757 to 1761 Alexander lived in Britain, reveling in the friendship of the landed aristocracy and imbibing the elegant style of living evinced by his new acquaintances. While rubbing elbows with the upper classes, he fought successfully for payment of his monetary claims—although, as he noted bitterly, he had actually lost money from the deal in the long run. Less successful was his defense of Shirley from calumniators, for despite his best efforts his old friend was removed from the governorship of Massachusetts. Meantime he spent a fortune pursuing the lapsed Scots earldom of Stirling, and although the Scottish lords accepted his right to the title, their English counterparts refused his petition. Undeterred that his "peers" had so rudely spurned him, he insisted that he was the sixth earl of Stirling and was so addressed by friends in Britain and America. When he returned home he abandoned his previous occupation of merchant and lived in emulation of the English country gentry. Spending money wildly in the next two decades, he squandered a fortune of more than £100,000, dabbling among other things in iron mining and land speculation. According to some of his detractors, he began drinking to excess.

Withal, he was a prominent and respected citizen, serving on the councils of New York and New Jersey and the Board of Proprietors of East Jersey, and supporting numerous organizations such as King's College. As tensions between the American provinces and Britain rose in the 1760s and 1770s, Alexander evinced pro-British attitudes, even lecturing the Board of Trade on how it might tighten enforcement of colonial mercantile and tax laws.

When the revolutionary war erupted in 1775, however, Alexander quickly asserted his support for his rebellious friends and neighbors, and he never wavered from that position. He was immediately removed from all his Royalist employments and welcomed by the rebels into the extralegal New Jersey Council of Safety and by the New Jersey militia as a colonel. Late in 1775, when Congress adopted the New Jersey forces, Alexander became senior colonel of his state's Continental line. For the next few months he commanded in his home state, and his seizure of an armed British transport on 25 January 1776 led to his promotion in March to brigadier general. Meantime he worked feverishly to put New York City into a state of defense against a threatened British assault and was happy in April to welcome General George Washington from Boston to assume this unenviable task. Finding in the proud Virginian a congenial spirit, he commenced a long and intimate association with the man.

In his first big test of battlefield leadership, at Long Island on 27 August 1776, Alexander was ordered to defend the American right wing. Through no fault of his own his brigade was seriously mauled and he was taken captive. Exchanged on 6 October, he took charge of another brigade, which fought during Washington's retreat from Manhattan in the battle of White Plains on 28 August and in the withdrawal across New Jersey. He had the pleasure on 26 December of fighting at Trenton, where Colonel Johann Räll was killed and a Hessian garrison forced to surrender; two months later he was promoted major general. On 26 June 1777, at Metuchen, he was laggard in pulling back before a superior enemy force and received a stinging check before extricating himself. Nevertheless he retained Washington's confidence and was given important roles in the battles of Brandywine on 11 September and Germantown on 4 October before going into winter encampment at Valley Forge. He accompanied Washington in June 1778 as the Continental army shadowed British forces across New Jersey, and he played a crucial role in the battle of Monmouth on 28 June. After that contest, he chaired General Charles Lee's (1731–1782) court-martial, then played a part in Major Henry Lee's (1756–1818) raid on Paulus Hook. In early 1780 he led an inconsequential raid on Staten Island and in June assisted Nathanael Greene in repulsing an enemy attack at Springfield. A year later Alexander was ordered to Albany to take charge of the Northern Department, supposedly to repel an enemy invasion of upstate New York. No such danger existed, as he soon discovered, and so his duty for the next few months was not onerous. It was just as well, for he was suffering from a fatal case of gout.

Alexander died in Albany and was mourned by his family, Washington, and a host of other Americans who felt his loss keenly. Although he was not among the best generals of the revolutionary war, he was a trustworthy and reliable soldier, and he got along well with his colleagues. He was also extraordinarily brave.

• Collections of Alexander papers are in the New-York Historical Society, New York Public Library, National Archives, and Morristown National Historical Park. The fullest assessment of Alexander's life and character is Paul David Nelson, *William Alexander, Lord Stirling* (1987). Another useful but limited biography is William Alexander Duer, *The Life of William Alexander, Earl of Stirling* . . . (1847). George H. Danforth, "The Rebel Earl" (Ph.D. diss., Columbia Univ., 1955), gives information on his nonmilitary activities. Less successful attempts to limn his life are Ludwig Schumacher, *Major-General the Earl of Stirling: An Essay in Biography* (1897); Charles A. Ditmas, *Life and Service of Major-General William Alexander* (1920); and Alan Valentine, *Lord Stirling* (1969). Thomas M. Doerflinger, "Hibernia Furnace during the Revolution," *New Jersey History* 90 (1972): 97–114, describes some of Alexander's activities in the New Jersey iron industry, and Theodore Thayer, "The Army Contractors for the Niagara Campaign, 1755–1756," *William and Mary Quarterly*, 3d ser., 14 (1957): 31–46, lucidly analyzes that vexing subject.

PAUL DAVID NELSON

ALEXANDER, William DeWitt (2 Apr. 1833–22 Feb. 1913), historian, was born in Honolulu, Hawaii (then the Sandwich Islands), the son of William Patterson Alexander and Mary Ann McKinley, Christian missionaries. His parents had joined the famous missionary Hiram Bingham the year before Alexander's birth in an attempt to convert the islanders to Christianity. Alexander received his earliest education at Punahou School in Honolulu and then was sent by his parents to his mother's birthplace, Harrisburg, Pennsylvania, to study for admission to college. In 1855 he graduated with a B.A. from Yale University and took a teaching position at Beloit College in Wisconsin. Shortly thereafter he moved to another teaching job in Vincennes, Indiana. Returning to the Hawaiian Islands in 1858, he married Abigail Charlotte Baldwin. In 1860 he became a professor of Greek at Punahou School. For the remainder of his life he pursued academic and religious interests.

Alexander's wide-ranging curiosity drew him into many scholarly and scientific pursuits. He was a student of the Hawaiian language and compiled a grammar for it. He was a charter member of the Polynesian Society of New Zealand and was active in the Royal Geographical Society and the Astronomical Society of the Pacific. For these organizations he composed many scientific papers. He was also active in the government of Hawaii, which was then a monarchy. In 1872 he assumed the lifelong post of surveyor-general; twelve years later he was appointed to the privy council, which was mostly an honorific position. Of much more importance, he became a member of the board of education and exercised a great deal of influence over the Hawaiian educational system for many years.

However useful his other activities, Alexander's greatest achievements were in the field of history. Certainly he was one of the most talented historians ever to write about Hawaii. He helped found the Hawaiian Historical Society and was one of its most active scholars for the last twenty years of his life. He wrote numerous articles for the *Papers* series of the society and also contributed to its *Annual Reports*. His essays, often cited by subsequent historians, cover topics as diverse as "Early Trading in Hawaii," "The Origins of the Polynesian Race," "Overthrow of the Ancient Tabu System in the Hawaiian Islands," "A Sketch of the Constitutional History of the Hawaiian Kingdom," and "Oahu Charity School." In addition he wrote two books. The first, *Brief History of the Hawaiian People* (1891), was designed for use as a textbook and still provides a convenient introduction to the topic of Hawaiian history. The second, *History of Later Years of the Hawaiian Monarchy and the Revolution of 1893* (1896), was an expanded version of a report that Alexander had prepared earlier for an American commissioner, James H. Blount, who had been sent to the islands in 1893 by President Grover Cleveland to investigate the results of a recent revolution against Queen Liliuokalani.

In his original report, and in his expanded history, Alexander made no pretense to scholarly objectivity, admitting that he supported the revolution that had overthrown the monarchy and established a republic. He was also strenuously in favor of American annexation of his native islands and applauded the active role that John L. Stevens, the American minister to Hawaii, had taken in support of the rebellion. Alexander was named to a five-man commission dispatched by Stevens to Washington, D.C., shortly after the revolution to negotiate a treaty of annexation to the United States. He was greatly disappointed when President Cleveland not only refused to listen to his pleas but actually tried to restore Queen Liliuokalani to her throne. In the end, however, the president was compelled to recognize the Hawaiian Republic, realizing that he would have to use military force to unseat a group of revolutionaries who were as determined as Alexander not to allow the monarchy to be reestablished in Hawaii. In 1898 Alexander was delighted when altered world circumstances finally made it possible for the U.S. Congress, by joint resolution, to approve a treaty making Hawaii "a part of the territory of the United States." He died in his native city, Honolulu, after a long and productive scholarly career.

• Alexander is listed in Anson Phelps Stokes, *Memorials of Eminent Yale Men* (2 vols., 1914). For background on his life see Hiram Bingham, *A Residence of Twenty-one Years in the Sandwich Islands* (1847); Mary Charlotte Alexander, *William Patterson Alexander in Kentucky, the Marquesas, Hawaii* (1934); Erna Ferguson, *Our Hawaii* (1942); and Laura Fish Judd, *Honolulu: Sketches of the Life, Social, Political, and Religious, in the Hawaiian Islands from 1828 to 1861* (1880; repr. 1928). An obituary is in the *Honolulu Advertiser*, 24 Feb. 1913.

PAUL DAVID NELSON

ALEXANDER, Will Winton (15 July 1884–13 Jan. 1956), leading southern liberal, expert on race relations, and member of Franklin D. Roosevelt's New Deal administration, was born near Morrisville, Missouri, the son of William Baxter Alexander, a farmer, and Arabella A. Winton, a schoolteacher. Alexander received a B.A. from Scarritt-Morrisville College in 1908 and continued his studies at Vanderbilt University, where he received a Bachelor of Divinity in 1912. Ordained a Methodist minister in 1911, Alexander held pastorates at Nashville (1911–1916) and Murfreesboro, Tennessee (1916–1917). In 1914 he married Mabelle A. Kinkead; they had three sons.

Raised in an all-white town, Alexander gained insight into the workings of the Jim Crow system when he worked as a Methodist minister with the unemployed in Nashville. In 1919, with the financial assistance of Atlanta steel manufacturer John Eagan and the Young Men's Christian Association War Work Council, Alexander formed the Commission on Interracial Co-operation in Atlanta. Alexander served as director of the commission for twenty-five years.

His primary objective was to forge an alliance of reformers like himself, educated white and black southerners, with the goal of ameliorating race relations and informing the public on the issues involved. To accomplish this goal, Alexander, or "Dr. Will" as he was called, convinced several prominent southern white sociologists, such as Howard Odum, Thomas Woofter, and Arthur Franklin Raper, to join the commission and to undertake studies documenting patterns of racial segregation in the South. Under Alexander's leadership, for example, the commission gathered information on the Ku Klux Klan and its activities in southern communities. This material provided the basis for the *New York World*'s eye-opening exposé on the Klan.

While Alexander's work with the commission helped to lay the foundation for the crumbling of the Jim Crow system, he was not a radical. Acting out of strong religious convictions, Alexander favored informing the public but opposed agitation. Looking back, Alexander wrote in 1951: "I have never lost faith by what I seemed to glimpse in the New Testament . . . I have been influenced more by this than by anything I have ever known" (Sosna, p. 173). He hoped to convince his audience that not only blacks, but also whites paid the price of segregation with poverty and government by demagogues. However, not until 1945 did Alexander take an open stand against segregation. In an article in *Harper's* Alexander wrote that "unless the problem of segregation can be solved there is no hope for any alleviation of the race problem in America" (quoted in Sosna, p. 154). In his cautious approach, Alexander served as spokesman for a growing white middle class in the South.

In addition to his work with the Commission on Interracial Cooperation, Alexander worked with several other institutions involved in interracial issues. From 1927 to 1928 he was chairman of the Advisory Commission on Race Studies of Problems and Policies Committee of the Social Science Research Council. In 1928 Alexander was honored with the Harmon Award for Service in American Peace Relations for his work as executive director of the Interracial Commission. Alexander subsequently served as member of a Commission on Minority Groups in Economic Recovery from 1934 to 1935. Through his lifelong service in numerous commissions and institutions, Alexander built a network of personal contacts and relationships that enabled him to gain the financial support of the Rockefeller, Carnegie, Rosenwald, and Stern family foundations for his work and efforts on behalf of interracial understanding.

Alexander also took a great interest in education and institutions of higher learning. He served as acting president of Dillard University in New Orleans, and he became a trustee of Antioch College. He devoted his greatest interest, however, to black colleges in and around Atlanta, where he served as trustee for Bethune-Cookman College, Atlanta University, Spelman College, and Morehouse College.

The election of Franklin D. Roosevelt and the beginning of the New Deal represented a turning point for southern Liberals like Alexander. His concern for the sufferings of southern sharecroppers brought him in contact with Roosevelt's New Deal in 1935. The New Deal was the beginning of what one historian has called a "symbiotic relationship" between southern liberals and the Democratic party (Sosna, p. 63).

Alexander influenced the New Deal's relief programs for southern sharecroppers. In 1935 Charles S. Johnson, Edwin R. Embree, and Alexander published *The Collapse of Cotton Tenancy*, which described the plight of sharecroppers and marginal tenant farmers in the South—both groups had been largely neglected by the Agricultural Adjustment Administration. In 1935 he was appointed to the post of assistant administrator of the Resettlement Administration of the U.S. Department of Agriculture, which was chaired by Rexford Guy Tugwell. As member of Roosevelt's Commission on Farm Tenancy, Alexander played an important role in the passage of the Bankhead-Jones Farm Tenancy Act (1937). The act created the Farm Security Administration (FSA) under Alexander's leadership. It was largely due to Alexander's impact that the FSA focussed on southern marginal farmers. Within the first three years of its existence, the FSA made loans to approximately 50,000 black families. In addition, under Alexander's leadership, the FSA funded filmmaker Pare Lorentz, who made *The Plow that Broke the Plains* and *The River*, and a host of photographers, such as Walker Evans, Dorothea Lange, and Gordon Parks, who documented rural blight.

It was largely due to Alexander's effort that the Farm Security Administration continued as a vital agency of the New Deal, which faced increasing opposition from the American Farm Bureau Federation and a group of Midwestern senators allied with Everett M. Dirksen of Illinois. However, Alexander resigned his position with the Farm Security Administration on 30 June 1940.

During World War II, Alexander continued his work on the problems of minorities. He worked with the labor division and the minorities branch of the Office of Production Management. In 1940 he accepted the chairmanship of the Rosenwald Fund and in December 1942 he was named director of the Race Relations Program. Until 1948 he served as vice president of the Rosenwald Fund in its efforts to provide fellowships for southern youth of both races to pursue advanced study. Upon his retirement, he settled in Chapel Hill, North Carolina.

A driving force behind southern education for minorities, a reformer in interracial issues, Alexander was one of the most influential black reformers, paving the way for future changes in southern race relations. He was "the coordinator of Southern Liberalism . . . for a generation" (Tindall, p. 199).

• For manuscript material pertaining to Alexander and his efforts, see the Will W. Alexander Papers at Dillard University, New Orleans; the Commission on Interracial Co-operation Papers at Atlanta University; the Farm Security Administration Papers in the National Archives in Washington, D.C.; and the papers of the Rosenwald Fund at Fisk University in Nashville, Tenn. A 1952 interview with Alexander is in the Oral History Collections of Columbia History. Alexander's own works include "Overcrowded Farms," United States Department of Agriculture, *Yearbook of Agriculture* (1940); "The Color Line Cracks a Little," *New Republic*, 22 Sept. 1941; "Our Conflicting Racial Policies," *Harper's*, Jan. 1945; and with Charles S. Johnson and Edwin R. Embree, *The Collapse of Cotton Tenancy* (1935). For additional biographical information on Alexander see Christina McFay Fadyen Campbell, *The Farm Bureau and the New Deal: A Study in the Making of National Farm Policy, 1933–1940* (1962); Wilma Dykeman and James Stokeley, *Seeds of Southern Change: The Life of Will Alexander* (1962); Mark Ethridge, "About Will Alexander," *New Republic*, 22 Sept. 1941; and Rexford Guy Tugwell, "The Resettlement Idea," *Agricultural History*, Oct. 1959. Alexander's life and influence on southern liberalism and race relations is also discussed in Morton Sosna, *In Search of the Silent South: Southern Liberals and the Race Issue* (1977); George Brown Tindall, *The Emergence of the New South, 1913–1945* (1967); and John Kirby, *Black Americans in the Roosevelt Era: Liberalism and Race* (1980). An obituary is in the *New York Times*, 14 Jan. 1956.

THOMAS WINTER

ALEXANDERSON, Ernst Fredrik Werner (25 Jan. 1878–14 May 1975), engineer and radio and television pioneer, was born in Uppsala, Sweden, the son of Aron Martin Alexanderson, a professor, and Amelie von Heidenstam. From an early age Alexanderson showed interest in things scientific, and so he was sent to the Royal Institute of Technology at Stockholm, where he studied engineering, graduating in 1900. The Royal Institute had no specific program in electrical engineering, which was Alexanderson's major interest, and so he spent the following year at the Königliche Technische Hochschule in Charlottenburg, Germany, then one of the best engineering schools of Europe. Here for the first time Alexanderson became acquainted with contemporary work in electromagnetics and wireless communication.

Alexanderson had given some thought to establishing his career as an engineer in his homeland, but professional opportunities were so few that in 1901 he followed numerous other educated Swedes to the United States. He visited the laboratory of Thomas A. Edison at West Orange, New Jersey, and was offered employment. Feeling that the position offered was beneath his capabilities, he did not take it. He did, however, work in several other unchallenging positions for a few months before finally accepting an offer from the General Electric Company at Schenectady, New York, in February 1902. He remained with General Electric (GE) until his retirement in 1948, becoming one of the best-known electrical engineers in the world.

For a few years Alexanderson's talents were obscured in the GE test department, but shortly the brilliant young engineer caught the attention of the company's famous scientific leader Charles P. Steinmetz, who assigned him more important projects. During his first few years, Alexanderson was involved in a number of the most important projects of the day, including that of railway electrification.

But it was another area that brought Alexanderson to the attention of the world. Reginald Aubrey Fessenden, a professor of electrical engineering, had a contract with the U.S. Weather Bureau to find ways to transmit weather information by radio and, more important, was looking for a means of broadcasting the human voice and music over the airwaves. Guglielmo Marconi's spark transmission system could send dots and dashes of Morse code, but it was not suitable for what would come to be called radiotelephony. If radio was to get out of its infancy, more elaborate technology was called for. Fessenden applied to General Electric for help, and the problem was given to Alexanderson. What was needed was a high-frequency alternator (a device that converts direct current into alternating current) so as to provide continuous radio waves. Although young, Alexanderson was chosen for the project because he had been working on alternators for several years. One of his first important patents (1906) was for a "self-exciting alternator," an achievement that had given him a certain amount of fame. He shortly began work on a 100-kHz alternator intended to provide sufficient power and the necessary continuous wave for the nascent radio industry. Over the next fifteen years Alexanderson improved his alternator, adding many advances and refinements. By 1915 he was one of the best-known radio engineers in the world: Marconi himself came to visit Alexanderson at the Schenectady laboratories, a clear admission that the Alexander alternators had made commercial broadcasting possible.

Alexanderson's contributions to electrical engineering were many and varied over the years. He was awarded more than 340 patents between 1903 and 1958, not all in communications. His resourceful mind also produced major developments in electric power transmission, radar, electric railways, ship propulsion, power conversion, and computers.

Alexanderson spent nearly all his life in Schenectady, although he made occasional trips to visit his family and friends in Sweden. He was a world-famous engineer before he was forty. Alexanderson was married three times (twice widowed) and had three daughters and a son.

When the Radio Corporation of America (RCA) was founded in 1919, Alexanderson was appointed its first chief engineer (he was on loan from GE, one of the major owners of RCA). He held this position for four years, after which he returned to GE to work in the new area of television research. Alexanderson threw himself into television and was one of the busiest individuals working in the field. He demonstrated a mechanical scanning television receiver in his own home as early as 1927, and he astonished the world in 1930 when he gave the first public exhibition of television with a system that placed the picture on a seven-foot screen suitable for theater viewing.

In the early 1930s RCA decided that it was going to do all its own television research and abandoned its contracts with GE—a severe disappointment to Alexanderson, who was forced to give up his work in the area. Before giving up entirely, however, he took out a patent for a color television set, a device that would not appear commercially for thirty years. Alexanderson then turned to numerous other things. He developed the amplidyne, a highly sophisticated control system used in factory automation and used during World War II in guiding antiaircraft guns. He was active in radar research during the war years, but many of his contributions to the war effort stemmed from work of earlier years that had been underutilized. There was, for example, a radio altimeter on which he had held patents since 1928.

Alexanderson retired from GE in 1948, but he lived another twenty-seven years, dying in Schenectady at the age of ninety-six. He was very active in retirement—a grand old man of electrical engineering—consulting for RCA, among other companies. He made important contributions to the computer field and, as his own hearing grew bad, to the technology of hearing aids. In February 1955 the *New York Times* reported that Ernst F. W. Alexanderson had taken out a patent for a color television receiver for RCA. This may have seemed like "news" to many. Everyone was getting excited about the idea of color television, a futuristic idea. But from his long career as an inventor Alexanderson might have proudly pointed out that he had already patented a primitive color television receiver in 1933—twenty-two years before! The industry was far behind him.

• Alexanderson's papers are in the Schaffer Library, Union College, Schenectady, N.Y. An excellent biography of Alexanderson is James E. Brittain, *Alexanderson: Pioneer in American Electrical Engineering* (1992). Suitable both for the specialist and the general reader, this book contains a complete list of Alexanderson's patents and a very thorough bibliography. Nearly all books on the history of early radio have accounts of Alexanderson's contributions to radio. See, for example, Gleason L. Archer, *A History of Radio to 1926* (1938); Erik Barnouw, *A History of Broadcasting in the United States*, vol. 1: *A Tower in Babel* (1966); and George H. Douglas, *The Early Days of Radio Broadcasting* (1987). An obituary is in the *New York Times*, 15 May 1975.

GEORGE H. DOUGLAS

ALFORD, Leon Pratt (3 Jan. 1877–2 Jan. 1942), engineer and publicist, was born in Simsbury, Connecticut, the son of Emerson Alford, a farmer and manufacturer, and Sarah Merriam Pratt. Alford studied at Plainville (Conn.) High School and then the Worcester Polytechnic Institute in Worcester, Massachusetts, from which he received a bachelor's degree in engineering in 1896 and, later, a master's degree (1905). He took a position in 1896 as assistant shop foreman with the McKay Metallic Fastening Association and remained with the company through a series of mergers that eventually made it a part of the United Shoe Machinery Company. In 1900 he married Grace Agnes Hutchins. The couple had one child, a son. In 1902 he helped design United Shoe's new plant in Beverly, Massachusetts, celebrated at the time as the world's largest reinforced-concrete machine shop, and in 1906, after serving as production superintendent, he became head of the company's mechanical engineering department.

In 1907 Alford left manufacturing for a long career as an engineering journalist, publicist, and educator. Beginning with an editorial position at *American Ma-*

chinist, he subsequently became that journal's editor in chief (1911–1917); the editor, in turn, of *Industrial Management*, *Management Engineering*, and *Manufacturing Industries* (1917–1928); and the vice president in charge of the Ronald Press Company's publication and promotion of a growing literature on managerial innovations and scientific management (1922–1934). Initially, his publications dealt primarily with technical machine problems, such as high-speed drilling, bearings and their lubrication, and artillery ammunition manufacture. But he also took an early interest in the scientific management schemes being promoted by such engineers as Frederick Winslow Taylor and Henry Laurence Gantt. Between 1911 and 1932 he made himself the nation's leading historian, interpreter, and codifier of the new-management theories and practices. He did this partly through the journals he edited. But also important were three surveys of management practice (1912, 1922, 1932) and one of industrial relations (1919) done for the American Society of Mechanical Engineers (ASME). He pioneered the development of management handbooks, beginning with *Management's Handbook* in 1924, and launched a much publicized effort to discern and codify managerial "laws." From the expansion of a paper given at the ASME meeting in 1926, for which he subsequently received engineering's Melville Prize, came his most influential work, *Laws of Management Applied to Manufacturing* (1928).

Alford also became deeply involved in efforts by the American Engineering Council (AEC) and Herbert Hoover's Commerce Department to promote the adoption of scientific management. He helped to produce *Waste in Industry* (1921), a study generally credited with inspiring Hoover's subsequent campaigns for waste elimination. In addition, he contributed to the AEC's publications *The Twelve-Hour Shift in Industry* (1923) and *Safety and Production in Industry* (1928), both important efforts to secure managerial reform. He also wrote the chapter on changing industrial techniques for the Hoover-sponsored study, *Recent Economic Changes* (1929).

In 1927 he helped organize the Institute of Management, hoping that it would stimulate more theoretical work in management research. In his own work, he made contributions to the theory of preferred numbers, as well as quality and cost control. He also helped devise a new system of measurement featuring the "kilo-man-hour" (the productive value of 1,000 people working one hour each) as the best measure of employment trends and productive capacity. In the early 1930s the federal government used the suggested unit in its studies of technological unemployment and census of manufactures, and for a time it was embraced by "technocracy" advocates with their visions of a planned economy run by engineers. The wide application for which Alford hoped, however, never came, and a book that he wrote on the subject, tentatively titled "Man-Hour Planning," never found a publisher.

Alford served on the AEC's Committee on the Relation of Consumption, Production, and Distribution, which studied the causes of the depression and analyzed business recovery plans, in the years from 1931 to 1936. As Alford saw it, the depression stemmed from an "imbalance" of economic forces, and the way out lay not through wage cuts or curbs on productivity but through renewed technical progress accompanied by higher wages, shorter hours, reduced prices, better coordination, and an enhanced spirit of service. And although he criticized New Deal restrictionism, he served briefly as the administration member on two code authorities created under the National Industrial Recovery Act, as chief engineer to the Silk Textile Work Assignment Board (1934), and as head of the Federal Communications Commission's Manufacturing Costs Unit during its investigation of the telephone industry (1935–1937). Meanwhile, he had also become active in the work of the Society for the Promotion of Engineering Education, especially in efforts to develop a curriculum for training engineers who could become business executives. In 1937 these interests led him to accept an appointment as head of the industrial engineering department at New York University. There he spent the last five years of his life, helping to expand the department's offerings, teaching courses that made him a student favorite (affectionately known as "The King"), writing his *Principles of Industrial Management for Engineers* (1940), and working on new handbooks and management surveys that were published after his death, in New York City.

Alford was noted for his benign countenance, infectious smile, and soft-spoken sincerity. He was a lucid thinker who had the ability to stimulate and direct others. He stands as a major figure in the history of American business management, less because of his original contributions than because of his success in organizing, interpreting, and disseminating changes in management practice.

• The Alford papers are at New York University. A biography by William J. Jaffe, which is unimaginatively written but detailed and systematically documented from the Alford papers, is *L. P. Alford and the Evolution of Modern Industrial Management* (1957). Two helpful biographical sketches are "L. P. Alford," *Mechanical Engineering* 64 (Feb. 1942): 96; and "Leon Pratt Alford," in *The Golden Book of Management: A Historical Record of the Life and Work of Seventy Pioneers*, ed. Lyndall Urwick (1956), pp. 192–95. Helpful in understanding the milieu in which Alford operated are Edwin T. Layton, Jr., *The Revolt of the Engineers: Social Responsibility and the American Engineering Profession* (1971), and John M. Jordan, *Machine-Age Ideology: Social Engineering and American Liberalism, 1911–1939* (1994). An obituary is in the *New York Times*, 3 Jan. 1942.

ELLIS W. HAWLEY

ALGER, Cyrus (11 Nov. 1781–4 Feb. 1856), inventor and manufacturer, was born in Bridgewater, Massachusetts, the son of Abiezer Alger, an iron manufacturer, and Hepsibah Keith. After several years of schooling he went to work for his father, from whom he learned the principles of iron production. Within a few years he was placed in charge of his father's Easton plant. In 1804 he married Lucy Willis, with whom he had seven children.

In 1809 Alger cofounded an iron foundry in South Boston. This foundry received large orders for military supplies during the War of 1812, particularly for cannonballs. In 1814 Alger bought out his partner, General John Winslow, and expanded the company's operations. Meanwhile he was conducting experiments that led to the first of his five patented inventions. This patent, issued on 30 March 1811, was for an improved method of making cast-iron chilled rolls, by which the part of an iron product subject to wear is given added strength. Shortly thereafter Alger introduced anthracite coal as fuel in his Boston furnaces. In 1822 he invented cylinder stoves and reversed the hearths of furnaces for melting iron, so that the molten metal would flow toward the flame. With these innovations Alger rapidly increased the capacity of his plants. In 1827 he consolidated his holdings into the South Boston Iron Company and was elected its president, a post he held until his death. The company enjoyed a remarkable reputation as a well-managed and innovative firm. Among the company's employees were several prominent leaders in the iron industry, including the manufacturer and inventor William P. Hunt.

In 1828 the South Boston Iron Company began to manufacture iron ordnance. Alger invented a method of purifying cast iron that nearly tripled the strength of ordinary iron castings. This innovation gave the firm a great advantage in making guns—especially those of large caliber. "Gun iron" was the name by which the strengthened iron came to be known, although the process was used for many kinds of castings. With this special expertise, the company increasingly focused its energies on the manufacture of ordnance and created new technology in weapons production. In 1834 the company cast and finished the first rifled cast-iron gun made in the United States, and in 1835 the firm began the manufacture of malleable iron guns, for which a patent was granted to Alger on 30 May 1837. One year later he received a patent for the use of malleable iron in the manufacture of plows.

In 1833 the South Boston Iron Company expanded its operations to include the production of bronze cannons, and Alger obtained contracts to supply these weapons to both the federal government and the state of Massachusetts. In 1842 his firm constructed the largest gun then cast in the United States—the mortar "Columbiad." He also began to focus his efforts on improving fuses and shells. Over the next two decades Alger's firm became a major supplier of ammunition to the federal government. He died in Boston.

• Little information on Alger is available. Basic sources include J. Leander Bishop, *A History of American Manufactures from 1608 to 1860*, vol. 3 (1868; repr. 1968), and the entry in the *National Cyclopaedia of American Biography*, vol. 6 (1929).

ALEC KIRBY

ALGER, Horatio, Jr. (13 Jan. 1832–18 July 1899), author, was born in Chelsea, Massachusetts, the son of Horatio Alger, a Unitarian minister and farmer, and Olive Augusta Fenno. After graduating with Phi Beta Kappa honors from Harvard College in 1852, Alger worked for several years as a teacher and journalist while contributing, sometimes pseudonymously, to such New England literary weeklies as *True Flag, Olive Branch, American Union*, and *Yankee Blade*. His first book, *Bertha's Christmas Vision: An Autumn Sheaf*, a sampler of eleven sentimental tales and eight poems, appeared to favorable notices in 1855. The Unitarian *Monthly Religious Magazine*, for example, commended the "collection of stories and verses, written in an uncommonly pure spirit and graceful style," by "a literary gentleman of high promise." Alger's next book, *Nothing to Do: A Tilt at Our Best Society* (1857), was a satirical poem of nearly three hundred lines broadly imitating William Allen Butler's *Nothing to Wear*.

Ill suited for a teaching career yet unable to earn a comfortable living by his pen, Alger entered the Harvard Divinity School in 1857 to train for the ministry. Meanwhile, he supported himself by writing sensational serial novels on moral themes, with such titles as "Manson, the Miser" and "The Mad Heiress," which appeared in the *New York Sun*. After graduating in 1860, he traveled through Europe, loitering at length in England, France, and Italy, over a period of ten months, while defraying part of his expenses by sending a series of travel letters to the *Sun* and other papers. Exempted from the Civil War draft because he was short and nearsighted, he supported the Union cause by writing unsigned patriotic fiction and verse for *Harper's Weekly*.

After he was paid only a dollar per page for an article published in the *North American Review* in 1863, Alger turned to writing juvenile fiction. He later explained that "the res angusta doni of which Horace speaks compelled me years since to forsake the higher walks of literature and devote myself to an humbler department which would pay me better." Alger's first juvenile novel, *Frank's Campaign* (1864), was designed "to show how boys can be of most effectual service in assisting to put down the Rebellion." Thomas Wentworth Higginson considered it "a good story of home life" during the war. In December 1864, Alger was ordained the minister of the Unitarian society in Brewster, Massachusetts, though he was later accused of sexually molesting boys in his congregation—a charge he did not deny—and forced to resign the position fifteen months later. Alger moved to New York in April 1866 to begin his literary career in earnest, and he soon frequented such charitable institutions as the Five Points mission, the YMCA, and the Newsboys' Lodging House of the Children's Aid Society. "I have a natural liking for boys, which has made it easy for me to win their confidence and become intimately acquainted with them," he reflected late in life. "What gratifies me most," he allowed privately in 1897, "is that boys, though strangers, seem to regard me as a personal friend." For the record, however, there is no evidence Alger repeated his earlier mistakes. After the Brewster imbroglio he was never again publicly accused of pederasty or other sexual impropriety, though by his own admission he "made friends with hundreds of urchins" over the years.

In *Ragged Dick; or, Street Life in New York with the Boot-Blacks* (1868), his most successful book and the first juvenile tale he wrote after settling in the city, Alger established the basic formula he would follow, with only minor variations, in nearly a hundred subsequent novels for boys: a young hero, inexperienced in the temptations of the city but morally armed to resist them, is unexpectedly forced to earn a livelihood. His exemplary struggle—to retain his virtue, to clear his name of accusations, to gain economic independence from the evil squires or stepmothers who seek to oppress him—this was the stuff of the standard Alger plot. In *Ragged Dick*, moreover, Alger introduced the figure of the benevolent patron, an adult who, like the author in his own relations with the street children of New York, materially aids the struggling young hero. This didactic formula would evolve over the years, to be sure, especially after Alger adapted the melodrama and episodic violence of the dime novel to it in the mid-1870s. Throughout his career, in fact, Alger negotiated a middle course between the domestic banalities of so-called Sunday school fiction and the lurid blood-and-thunder sensationalism of the *Police Gazette* and yellowback novels. Despite the persistent notion that his heroes rise "from rags to riches," moreover, only a few of Alger's characters win fabulous wealth. His young heroes normally rise not to riches, but to a secure middle-class respectability.

Never a literary lion, Alger enjoyed the middle-class social station to which most of his characters aspired. He joined the Harvard Club of New York and the historical society in his parents' hometown in Massachusetts. To supplement his income from writing, he tutored the children of some prominent local Jewish families, including E. R. A. Seligman, later a professor of political economy at Columbia University; Benjamin Cardozo, who became an associate justice of the U.S. Supreme Court; and Lewis Einstein, later a career diplomat. Alger toured Europe a second time in 1873, and he traveled by rail to the Pacific coast in 1877 and again in 1890 to gather local color for a series of juvenile novels set in the West.

However, Alger never renounced his early ambition to write for adults. A collection of his poetry, *Grand'ther Baldwin's Thanksgiving with Other Ballads and Poems*, appeared in 1875 to appreciative reviews. The *Nation* averred that his Civil War ballads in particular were "simple and direct in sentiment and expression." He collaborated *sub rosa* with his cousin William Rounseville Alger on the official biography of the actor Edwin Forrest, published in 1877. Alger experimented with a new fictional voice in his adult novella *The New Schoolma'am* (1877), which the London *Academy* called a "sparkling American tale, full of humour." He completed the manuscript of another adult novel, *Mabel Parker*, in 1878, but his publisher shelved it for financial reasons. Alger wrote a series of adult short stories that were syndicated in newspapers across the country in 1889, and under a pseudonym he published *The Disagreeable Woman* (1895), the tale of an apparently misanthropic woman who finds happiness after she is reunited with her lost lover.

Meanwhile, Alger's juvenile stories came under increasing fire from ministers and librarians, the so-called custodians of culture, for their alleged sensationalism. The *Boston Herald* editorialized that only children "raw at reading" would be attracted to the "fighting, killing, and thrilling adventures" found in Alger's novels. At the dedication of a branch of the Boston Public Library in 1877, James Freeman Clarke, a distinguished Unitarian minister and member of the Transcendental Club, denounced the "endless reams" of "drivel poured forth by Horatio Alger, Jr.," and in 1879 the Fletcher Free Library in Burlington, Vermont, became the first public library in the country known to have removed Alger's books from its shelves. Partly to disarm his critics, Alger wrote juvenile biographies of James A. Garfield, Abraham Lincoln, and Daniel Webster in the early 1880s. Some twenty thousand copies of *From Canal Boy to President*, the book on Garfield that Alger wrote in only fourteen days in the fall of 1881, were sold during the weeks of national mourning following the president's death. Nevertheless, of the hundred and forty-five libraries surveyed by the American Library Association in 1894, over a third proscribed Alger's books. In 1896, in one of the last pieces he prepared for publication, Alger sided with the genteel elite in this debate, conceding that "sensational stories, such as are found in the dime and half-dime libraries, do much harm, and are very objectionable. Better that a boy's life should be humdrum than filled with such dangerous excitement."

Though he never married, Alger informally adopted three orphan boys during his residence in New York. After retiring to Natick, Massachusetts, in 1896, he joined the local Woman's Suffrage League. He died, in declining circumstances but by no means destitute, at his sister's home in Natick after a prolonged illness. A few months earlier, he had estimated aggregate sales of his books at about 800,000 copies, with sales of the six volumes in the "Ragged Dick series" of novels nearly a fourth of this total. However, his moral tracts were selling at the rate of about one million per year in 1910 because, in their idealization of a preindustrial order, they seemed to tap the Progressive desire to reform business and government through a return to principles of equal opportunity and fair trade. The phrase "Horatio Alger hero," denoting an honest and successful entrepreneurial type, obtained popular if inflated currency in the language in the 1920s, when Alger's popularity was at its peak. Frank Luther Mott has estimated Alger's total sales at about seventeen million copies, the vast majority of them printed during the first quarter of the twentieth century. Though Alger's books largely lapsed from print during the Great Depression, the American Schools and Colleges Association, Inc., appropriated his name for the annual Horatio Alger Awards, inaugurated in 1947. The same year, the Grolier Club of New York named *Ragged Dick* one of the hundred most influential American books published before 1900.

Ironically, Alger's life has been repeatedly misrepresented by his biographers. In order to conceal his homosexuality, Alger bequeathed his private papers to his sister, with orders to destroy them after his death. Not a single letter written to him nor any personal diary in his handwriting exists. Not until the 1920s, at the height of Alger's fame, did this paucity of documentary sources become a problem. Herbert R. Mayes, Alger's first biographer, faced with the difficulty of documenting a life about which almost nothing was known, solved the problem by filling the vacuum with fabricated data. "All I had to do was come up with a fairy tale," Mayes explained in 1978. "No research required. Nothing required but a little imagination." As the title may indicate, Mayes's *Alger: A Biography without a Hero* portrays its subject as "a pathetic, quite ridiculous character." Yet in 1928, the same year as its publication, Mayes's work became the primary source for the entry on Alger in the *Dictionary of American Biography*. To this day, virtually every reference tool contains "facts" about Alger's life first concocted by Mayes. The veracity of his biography was not questioned at the time because it presented a view of Alger's vain struggle upward that was entirely attuned to the popular impression of Alger's writings. More problematically, Alger's next three biographers also relied explicitly on Mayes's "pioneering research" for their information, occasionally compounding his mistakes with fabrications of their own. Not until 1985, seven years after Mayes publicly admitted his hoax, did the first fully documented biography of Alger finally appear.

• Few of Alger's letters survive, though there are small collections at the American Antiquarian Society, Worcester, Mass.; Rare Book and Manuscript Library, Columbia University; Houghton Library, Harvard University; Seymour Library, Knox College, Galesburg, Ill.; Library of Congress; Clements Library, University of Michigan; New York Public Library; Pierpont Morgan Library; Alderman Library, University of Virginia; Beinecke Rare Book and Manuscript Library, Yale University; and the Stratemeyer Syndicate, Maplewood, N.J. By far the largest collection of letters, though it contains fewer than a hundred, is located in the Huntington Library, San Marino, Calif. Several manuscript sources about Alger's life may be found in the University Archives, Pusey Library, Harvard University. Details about Alger's dismissal from the pulpit in Brewster are available in the American Unitarian Association letter books in the Andover-Harvard Theological Library, Harvard Divinity School. The only documented biography is *The Lost Life of Horatio Alger, Jr.* (1985) by Gary Scharnhorst with Jack Bales. See also Bob Bennett, *Horatio Alger, Jr.: A Comprehensive Bibliography* (1980); and Scharnhorst and Bales, *Horatio Alger, Jr.: An Annotated Bibliography of Comment and Criticism* (1981). Obituaries appear in the *New York Tribune* and the *Boston Post*, 19 July 1899.

GARY SCHARNHORST

ALGER, Russell Alexander (27 Feb. 1836–24 Jan. 1907), businessman and politician, was born in Lafayette Township, Medina County, Ohio, the son of Russell Alger and Caroline Moulton, farmers. Orphaned at eleven years of age, he worked as a laborer and taught school before reading law in Akron, Ohio, where he was admitted to the bar in 1859. Moving to Grand Rapids, Michigan, he involved himself in the lumber industry. In 1861 he married Annette Henry; they had nine children.

When the Civil War began, Alger volunteered as a private soldier, but soon he organized a volunteer company of cavalry. Because of his connection with the Republican party he received a captaincy in the Second Michigan Volunteer Cavalry. He was promoted to major in April 1862. He gained distinction by leading a charge against a large Confederate force at Booneville, Mississippi, on 1 June 1862. He was captured but immediately escaped. Transferred to the Army of the Potomac as a lieutenant colonel in the Sixth Michigan Volunteer Cavalry, he was soon made colonel of the Fifth Michigan Cavalry, which became part of the Michigan Brigade under Brigadier General George A. Custer. He participated in many battles, including Gettysburg and the Wilderness, and later served in the Shenandoah Valley, leading a charge at Trevilian Station on 11 June 1864 that led to the capture of a large Confederate contingent. He contracted typhoid fever, which forced him to resign his commission in September 1864. Apparently through misunderstanding, Custer accused him of being absent without leave, but Alger insisted that he had been hospitalized and assigned to other duties. The matter was dropped, and on 11 June 1865 he received the brevet ranks of brigadier general and major general of volunteers.

After the war Alger settled in Detroit, Michigan, and acquired a fortune in the lumber business, gaining control of property in several states and Canada. One of his holdings, a pine forest on the banks of Lake Huron, produced 75 million feet of lumber per year, a huge amount. Following many well-known industrialists, Alger became interested in charitable organizations set up to assist orphans, and he also assisted poverty-stricken spouses of Civil War generals. A founder of the Michigan branch of the Grand Army of the Republic (GAR), Alger eventually became the national commander of the GAR in 1889. His public standing led him into politics. He was elected governor of Michigan as a Republican and served one term (1885–

1887). A favorite son of Michigan for the presidential nomination at the Republican National Convention in 1888, he later became a supporter of William McKinley. This connection led to his appointment as secretary of war in President McKinley's cabinet (1897–1899).

In 1898, when a dispute with Spain over Cuban independence led to war, Alger assumed responsibility for the mobilization of the army. Congress appropriated $50 million in March to finance prewar preparations, a means of bringing pressure to bear on the Spanish government to reach a peaceful settlement. Alger interpreted the legislation to mean that the War Department's share could be used only for defensive purposes, limiting the scope of his department's actions until the declaration of war in April. This view complicated the mobilization, but Alger's hesitancy was in part a reflection of the general assumption that the navy would play the leading role in the struggle with Spain. The War Department's decentralized bureau system was notably inefficient, although a number of competent officers made important contributions to the mobilization, particularly the adjutant general, Brigadier General Henry C. Corbin. Another administrative anomaly contributed to the confusion. Like many of his predecessors, Alger became entangled in jurisdictional disputes with the commanding general of the army, who at this time was Major General Nelson A. Miles. The secretary obtained the command of the Cuban expedition for Major General William R. Shafter of Michigan, while assigning Miles a secondary role as commander of an expedition to Puerto Rico. Despite the difficulties encountered in mounting expeditions to Cuba, Puerto Rico, and the Philippines, outbreaks of disease in training camps, equipment shortages, and inadequate food supplies, the army contributed to a complete victory after only three months. About 300,000 troops were mobilized to augment the tiny regular army of 28,000 troops.

The early difficulties, however, obscured later successes and remained in the public consciousness after the war. Critics blamed Alger for the War Department's inefficiency and mistakes. When General Miles circulated false charges that the army had been issued embalmed beef, Alger's reputation suffered further damage. A postwar investigation conducted by a commission chaired by General Grenville M. Dodge did not specifically censure Alger or the War Department but concluded, "There was lacking in the general administration of the War Department . . . that complete grasp of the situation which was essential to the highest efficiency and discipline of the Army." This judgment ignored Alger's positive contributions to the operation of the War Department, particularly in matters such as procurement where his business experience came into play.

Despite growing pressure to resign, Alger remained in office exploiting the president's reluctance to force his departure. However, Alger then interfered in a Michigan political dispute, further compromising his position in McKinley's cabinet. He finally resigned on 18 July 1899. His successor, Elihu Root, became one of the most successful secretaries of war, presiding over various administrative reforms, including the creation of a fledgling general staff in 1903, that stemmed from the desire to correct the organizational deficiencies that had caused difficulty in 1898.

In 1902 Alger returned to Washington as the junior senator from Michigan, appointed to complete the unexpired term of his predecessor. The Michigan legislature elected him to a full term in 1903, but he did not complete it. He died in Washington, D.C.

Alger's pompousness and self-absorption detracted from his evident leadership and administrative skills. Like many of his generation, he did not fully recognize the extent to which changes in the position of the United States in world affairs would affect the future role of the armed forces, but he presided over the War Department during a successful war that helped bring about an American imperial interlude in both the Pacific Ocean and the Caribbean sea.

• Alger's personal papers are in the William L. Clements Library, University of Michigan, Ann Arbor. He defended his service in the War Department in *The Spanish-American War* (1901). For his wartime activity see Graham A. Cosmas, *An Army for Empire: The United States Army in the Spanish-American War* (1971), and David F. Trask, *The War with Spain in 1898* (1981).

DAVID F. TRASK

ALGER, William Rounseville (28 Dec. 1822–7 Feb. 1905), author and religious leader, was born in Freetown, Massachusetts, the son of Catherine Sampson Rounseville and Nahum Alger, a teacher. Apprenticed at seven to a New Hampshire farmer, Alger worked at a variety of menial jobs during his hardscrabble boyhood. He earned a ministerial diploma from the Harvard Divinity School in 1847 and became pastor of All Souls' Unitarian Church in Roxbury, Massachusetts. The same year, he married Ann Langdon Lodge; they had seven children. In 1855 Alger moved to the Bulfinch Street Church in Boston, where he gained a reputation as an orator. The next year, he published *The Poetry of the East*, an anthology of Oriental verse translated from German and French sources, which went through five editions. The work was hailed upon its publication by Ralph Waldo Emerson, T. Starr King, Frederic Henry Hedge, and George William Curtis. Walt Whitman often read Alger's verse in hospitals during the Civil War. He was also well known in theological circles for his *Critical History of the Doctrine of a Future Life*, which passed through fourteen editions between 1860 and 1889.

Alger sparked nationwide controversy in 1857 when, as the Fourth of July orator in Boston, he denounced the Dred Scott decision of the U.S. Supreme Court and condemned the "complimentary flunkeyism" of local officials who had accommodated southern politicians and policies. Though the Board of Aldermen refused to pay for the subsequent publication of his address, by Alger's own estimate it was printed in some two hundred newspapers across the country. He occasionally contributed to William Lloyd Garrison's *Liberator* in these years and was one of the co-owners and editors of the *Christian Examiner*, a Unitarian quarterly, between 1864 and 1869.

When two of his children died of unrelated causes within a period of eight days in 1864, Alger's health began to fail. After a six-month tour of Europe, he resumed his ministry and enjoyed his greatest success in the late 1860s. His book *The Solitudes of Nature and of Man* (1867) received notice because of its intemperate attack on Henry David Thoreau for his paganism and misanthropy. Henry James (1843–1916), who reviewed Alger's *The Friendships of Women* (1868) for the *Nation*, later used him as a model for characters who appear in *The American* and *The Europeans*. Alger was appointed chaplain of the Massachusetts House of Representatives in 1868, the same year that he began to preach regularly in the Boston Music Hall to the largest Unitarian congregation in the United States.

In 1871, during a second tour of Europe, Alger suffered a mental breakdown from which he never fully recovered. Upon his return to America, he was hospitalized for several months in the McLean Asylum in Somerville, Massachusetts. He resigned from the Music Hall Society in 1873, though he later briefly pastored churches in New York, Denver, Portland (Maine), Newport, and New Orleans. His authorized biography of the actor Edwin Forrest was published in 1877. Alger's final years were devoted in no small part to a quixotic campaign to popularize, in lectures and such books as *The School of Life* (1881), the "aesthetic gymnastics" of the French teacher and philosopher François Delsarte. His last book, *The Sources of Consolation in Human Life* (1892), was a collection of vagrant sermons. Alger died at his Beacon Hill home in Boston.

• Letters from Alger are located in the American Unitarian Association letter books at the Andover-Harvard Theological Library, Harvard Divinity School; Houghton Library, Harvard University; Schlesinger Library, Radcliffe College; Baker Memorial Library, Dartmouth College; Massachusetts Historical Society; Boston Public Library; Essex Institute, Salem, Mass.; Princeton University Library; Beinecke Rare Book and Manuscript Library, Yale University; Huntington Library, San Marino, Calif.; Seymour Library, Knox College; Bancroft Library, University of California, Berkeley; and the New York Public Library. A sketch of his early life appears in Arthur M. Alger, *A Genealogical History of That Branch of the Alger Family Which Springs from Thomas Alger of Taunton and Bridgewater, in Massachusetts 1665–1875* (1876). The only biography is Gary Scharnhorst, *A Literary Biography of William Rounseville Alger (1822–1905)* (1990). An obituary is in the *Boston Transcript*, 8 Feb. 1905.

GARY SCHARNHORST

ALGREN, Nelson (28 Mar. 1909–9 May 1981), writer, was born Nelson Algren Abraham in Detroit, the son of Gershom (later changed to Gerson) Abraham, a machinist and factory worker, and Goldie Kalisher. When Algren was three years old, the family moved to Chicago where he attended public schools. An indifferent student and a class clown, he enjoyed city league sports, especially basketball, and gambling and carousing with his friends. He worked his way through the University of Illinois and graduated in 1931 with a journalism degree.

Unable to find a job, Algren drifted to New Orleans and Texas as a hobo and hustler, working off and on as a service station attendant, door-to-door salesman, and carnival barker. He spent four months in an Alpine, Texas, jail after he was caught stealing a typewriter. Through these experiences, he developed an affinity for life's losers and acquired material for much of his literary work. "My aspirations were middle class," Algren recalled in an interview. "I was perfectly willing to go along and stay square, but there were no jobs for me. I was made to be an outsider, and my attitude was set then."

Deciding to pursue a writing career, he sold a short story, "So Help Me," about a Texas gas station to *Story* magazine in 1933. Shortly thereafter, he received a $100 advance to write a novel, *Somebody in Boots* (1935), about a Texas family of misfit characters, but the book on publication received little notice. Nevertheless, he continued to produce short stories and poetry while employed in Chicago during the depression years with the Federal Writers' Project and in a venereal disease prevention program. He also became involved in the city's avant-garde literary left and developed a lasting friendship with the novelist Richard Wright. "A Bottle of Milk for Mother" (1941), a short story about a young murderer who confesses to his crime with the line, "I knew I'd never get to be 21 anyhow," brought Algren some recognition. It was reprinted as "Biceps" in *Best American Short Stories, 1942* and became a part of his second novel, *Never Come Morning* (1942), which, like his first, was commercially unsuccessful. From 1942 until 1945 Algren served in the U.S. Army Field Artillery and the Medical Corps, seeing combat in France and Germany, but never rising above the rank of private.

Following his army discharge, he returned to Chicago and earnestly wrote and rewrote pieces on gambling, prostitution, army life, and prizefighting. In 1947 he produced a collection of short stories, *The Neon Wilderness*, and the American Academy of Arts and Letters awarded him a $1,000 prize for *Never Come Morning*, which the judges felt had not received the recognition it deserved. Meanwhile, the Newberry Library in Chicago granted him $1,000 to complete *The Man with the Golden Arm* (1949), a novel about a drug-addicted gambler, which won the first National Book Award in 1950. Now clearly established as a leading American novelist, Algren spent a brief and unsatisfactory period in Hollywood where a successful movie of *The Man with the Golden Arm* (1955) was made by producer-director Otto Preminger. Algren was paid only $15,000 for the movie rights to his book and was ignored as a consultant. Upset with what he viewed as an effort to romanticize the central character in order to boost the acting career of Frank Sinatra, he unsuccessfully sued the producer. Algren returned to

Chicago, a city that never accepted him as it did its many other important literary figures, and produced *Chicago: City on the Make* (1951), a prose poem in which he wrote: "I never told you you smelled of anything but cheap cologne . . . anything but a loud old bag. Yet you're still the doll of the world and I'm proud to have slept in your tireless arms." In 1956 Algren, encouraged by an advance of $1,500, published his most critically acclaimed and best-known novel, *A Walk on the Wild Side*, which began as a rewrite of *Somebody in Boots*. The book tells the story of Dove Linkhorn, a young drifter, hustler, and pimp. Many literary critics viewed Algren as too sympathetic to society's outcasts, one critic, Leslie Fiedler, dismissing him as "the bard of stumblebum." But Algren was unphased by such attacks. He felt comfortable writing about people on the underside of society: "I'm confined to the black and brown world of prostitutes, drug addicts and fighters," he stated. "I'm a reporter of the black and brown world. Of people who live on the edge."

Nothing Algren produced in the final two decades of his life achieved the acclaim of his earlier works. *Who Lost an American?* (1963), a travel book about his experiences in Europe, Chicago, and New York, dedicated to the French writer Simone de Beauvoir, failed to win critical approval. Likewise, *Notes from a Sea Diary: Hemingway All the Way* (1965), about travels in the Far East, was both a commercial and literary disappointment. In 1965–1966 Algren taught writing at the University of Iowa, and in 1974 he left Chicago to live in Paterson, New Jersey, and later in Sag Harbor on Long Island, New York. There, he completed *The Devil's Stocking*, a story based on the trial of Rubin "Hurricane" Carter, a well-known black boxer convicted of a brutal triple homicide. The book was published posthumously in 1983.

Feisty, temperamental, and moody, Algren was fond of heavy drinking and high-stakes gambling. He was unconcerned about his financial affairs and never managed to earn the big royalties paid to some of his contemporaries. He was married in 1937 to Amanda Kontowicz. They were divorced in 1939 and remarried briefly in 1948 before divorcing again. His 1965 marriage to Betty Ann Jones, a young New York actress, lasted only fourteen months. Algren's longest and most notorious relationship began in 1947 when he met de Beauvoir in Chicago. There, he led her on tours of the city's slums, jails, and gambling dens while initiating a transcontinental love affair that would continue for seventeen years. In 1948 they traveled together down the Mississippi to New Orleans and on to Mexico. She visited him on several trips to the United States, and he spent time with her in Paris. She chronicled their travels and meetings together in Paris with Jean-Paul Sartre, her longtime lover, in her autobiography and in *America Day by Day* (1948); she also fictionalized their affair in *The Mandarins* (1954), which she dedicated to Algren. In 1964 she described their relationship as proof of her feminist philosophy of "contingent love" in *Harper's* magazine articles, which included excerpts from his letters to her. Following this episode, Algren never saw her again. He felt exploited and responded with a bitter essay, "The Question of Simone de Beauvoir," in which he asked, "Will she ever stop talking?"

Late in life Algren began to receive long-overdue critical recognition, and in his final year he was elected to the American Academy of Arts and Letters. He died alone and nearly broke in Sag Harbor, New York.

Considered by some literary scholars as the last in a line of great Chicago writers, Algren had the ability to shock his readers with what critic Herbert Mitgang described as "hammerblows in prose." In his works Algren depicts seedy hotels, dirty bars, and dingy police stations and jails while at the same time demonstrating a sympathy and tenderness for the pimps, whores, con men, and losers with whom he identified. Usually out of sync with most of his more critically acclaimed and commercially successful contemporaries, Algren stated, "I don't know the people [John] Updike, [Saul] Bellow, [E. L.] Doctorow, and [Kurt] Vonnegut write about. And I'm not much interested in them anyway."

• An extensive collection of Algren's papers is held in the Division of Rare Books and Manuscripts at Ohio State University. H. E. F. Donohue, ed., *Conversations with Nelson Algren* (1964), provides autobiographical material; a comprehensive listing of Algren's writings is presented in Matthew J. Bruccoli, ed., *Nelson Algren: A Descriptive Bibliography* (1989). The most complete biography of Algren is Bettina Drew, *Nelson Algren: A Life on the Wild Side* (1989). Also see Martha Heasley Cox and Wayne Chatterton, *Nelson Algren* (1975); Barbara Delatiner, "Algren Entering the East End Ring," *New York Times*, 26 Apr. 1981; and obituaries in the *New York Times* and *Chicago Tribune*, both 10 May 1981.

MICHAEL J. DEVINE

ALI, Noble Drew (8 Jan. 1886–20 July 1929), religious leader, was born and raised in poverty in rural North Carolina. The names of his parents are not known, but he grew up with the name Timothy Drew. Although he had very little formal education, he studied the teachings of Islam and claimed to have traveled in the Middle East in the early part of the twentieth century. He also said that he had been given the title "Ali" during a visit to Mecca (in modern-day Saudi Arabia). He came to prominence in 1912 when he asked President Woodrow Wilson to return the Moorish flag that he believed was hidden in a vault in Independence Hall in Philadelphia, Pennsylvania. Ali argued that black people within the United States were descendants of the Moabites of Old Testament times and that Morocco, not sub-Saharan Africa, was their homeland. Although, he believed, they had lived in freedom and practiced Islam prior to the American Revolution, they were enslaved by the Continental Congress in 1779, and the Moorish flag they had once carried was taken from them. Ali maintained that black Americans had forgotten that their true religion was Islam and as slaves had been forced to adopt Christianity instead.

Ali saw himself as a prophet of Allah whose mission was to liberate his people by helping them recognize their primordial Moorish identity. His ideas soon found acceptance within parts of the African-American community in the Northeast and Midwest, and the movement began to grow. He opened his first "Moorish Temple" in Newark, New Jersey, in 1913 and eventually established the headquarters of his organization in Chicago, Illinois, in 1925. The Moorish Temple of Science (later, the Moorish Science Temple of America) was incorporated in Illinois in 1926. The next year, Ali published *The Holy Koran*, a compilation of Moorish scientific beliefs. This book (not to be confused with the Qu'ran of orthodox Islam) contained a collection of Muslim, Christian, and Spiritualist teachings that were intended to provide black Americans with an accurate account of their origins. Ali's message of racial pride enabled him to found seventeen temples in fifteen states during the 1920s. Wearing red fezzes symbolic of their new identity, his followers soon became a familiar sight in Chicago and a number of midwestern cities in that period.

Ali, however, was unable ultimately to control the movement he created. As the religion flourished, he appointed leaders to act as his lieutenants, but many of them used the organization for their own selfish purposes. The confidence Ali engendered in his followers, moreover, sometimes led them to accost and challenge white people whom they met on the street. While these encounters were seldom marked by violence, they made police in Chicago and other cities increasingly suspicious of the Temple's activities. When Ali tried to regain power and expel his opponents, including Claude Green, the business manager of the organization, he met with severe resistance. Then, Green was murdered in March 1929 and, despite Ali's absence from the city, he was arrested for the crime. Later released on bond, Ali himself died under mysterious circumstances in Chicago a few weeks later. Some of his followers suggested that the police had beaten him to death, but it is also possible that Green's partisans were responsible for his murder. In any case, the exact cause of Ali's death was never determined.

Although the Moorish Science Temple declined as an organization after 1929, Ali was responsible for fashioning a popular movement that inspired African Americans to combine racial activism with Islamic beliefs. After his death, many of his adherents transferred their allegiance to Wallace Fard, the founder of the Nation of Islam (more commonly known as the Black Muslims) who claimed to be the reincarnation of Ali. The Moorish Temple's headquarters were moved to Baltimore in 1981, and active centers still exist in Baltimore, Washington, D.C., and Chicago.

• There is little primary source material available on Ali. Arthur Huff Fauset's *Black Gods of the Metropolis: Negro Religious Cults of the Urban North* (1944) contains an early description of Ali's movement. Another useful assessment is provided by Frank T. Simpson, "The Moorish Science Temple and Its Koran," *Moslem World* 37 (Jan. 1947): 56–61. The most complete scholarly analysis of the relationship of Islam and black nationalism is found in C. Eric Lincoln, *The Black Muslims in America* (1961; rev. eds., 1973, 1994).

GARDINER H. SHATTUCK, JR.

ALINSKY, Saul David (30 Jan. 1909–12 June 1972), community organizer, was born in Chicago, Illinois, the son of Benjamin Alinsky, a tailor, and Sarah Tannenbaum. The family lived in the predominantly Jewish Maxwell Street neighborhood when Alinsky was born, and after the age of six he grew up in the mostly pleasant West Side neighborhood of Douglas Park. His parents divorced when Saul was thirteen years old; he would visit his father in California in the summer but grew increasingly distant from him and close to the strong and contentious Sarah.

In 1930 Alinsky graduated with a degree in archaeology from the University of Chicago, where he took part in field study assignments in courses taught by Ernest W. Burgess and Robert Park in the first university sociology department in the United States. He stayed on to do graduate study in criminology from 1930 to 1932 and became increasingly interested in group dynamics, participant-observation research, and social welfare issues. In 1932 he married Helene Simon, a social worker regarded for her leadership in organizing other members of her profession. They adopted two children. He left school that year to work as a research sociologist for Clifford Shaw at the Institute for Juvenile Research, an organization that was developing an experimental antidelinquency program, the Chicago Area Project (CAP). This innovative project emphasized that the social milieu caused delinquency and that youth needed to be leaders in solving the problem, with professionals serving a supporting rather than a dominating role. From 1933 to 1936 Alinsky worked as a criminologist and member of the parole classification board at the Illinois State Penitentiary in Joliet, after which he returned to Chicago to work with Shaw.

Alinsky's experience with CAP in the 1930s helped influence his distinctive approach to community organizing. He came to value community-based citizen action and understand the need for indigenous leadership and participation in community work. During these years, two other developments contributed heavily to what would become known as the Alinsky method: the militant community action of the Communist party during its Popular Front period and the initial efforts to organize the Congress of Industrial Organizations. From the party's Unemployed Councils he borrowed the concept of organizing ordinary citizens in community efforts willing to use conflict tactics in the struggle for social change. From the CIO he developed the idea of the community organization as a "trade union" in the larger society's "factory" and realized that neighborhood people could collectively bargain, strike, struggle, and advance their interests. Alinsky was also influenced by his relationship, beginning in 1939 and 1940, with John L. Lewis, the leader of the United Mine Workers and the CIO. Alinsky was most impressed by Lewis's shrewd use of tactics and power, his tough working-class style of organizing, and his record of getting things accomplished for working people.

Sent in 1938 by CAP into the Back of the Yards neighborhood, first made famous in Upton Sinclair's *The Jungle*, Alinsky and Joseph Meegan, a neighborhood resident and community worker, organized the Back of the Yards Neighborhood Council (BYNC) by 1939. In the heated international events of the day, Alinsky began to see the BYNC as a bulwark of democracy and himself as a professional antifascist. His community work became too openly political and radical for CAP, and by 1940 he was off their payroll. Early in 1940 Alinsky established the Industrial Areas Foundation (IAF), with the support of philanthropist Marshall Field III, progressive bishop Bernard J. Sheil, and John L. Lewis's daughter Kathryn. The immediate goal was to finance the organization of more democratic community efforts. The larger vision was of a "people's movement" of grassroots, democratic organizations such as the BYNC. Nonpartisan, independent of government support, and invited into a community by local institutions that could pay for the organizing project, the early IAF trained organizers in Alinsky's method and supervised emerging organizing projects not only in Chicago but in the Chelsea neighborhood of Manhattan and packinghouse neighborhoods in South St. Paul and Kansas City.

Ideas and intellectual respectability always remained important to Alinsky. He wrote academic articles on criminology and CAP in the 1930s and offered frequent lectures as well. A month after the publication of his now-classic *Reveille for Radicals* in 1946, it made the *New York Times* bestseller list. *Reveille* was both a polemical call for a new generation of radicals and a guide to building community-based "people's organization" such as the BYNC. Throughout his life Alinsky was a defender of the downtrodden, a Jeffersonian democrat, an urban populist antagonistic to concentrated power and privilege. In 1949 he published a highly flattering biography of John L. Lewis that was excerpted in *Look* magazine. In 1947 his wife had drowned. In 1952 he married Jean Graham; the couple had no children.

Whereas Alinsky's and the IAF's efforts stalled through most of the 1950s, largely because of the reactionary Cold War politics of that era, his work took off again in the late 1950s and 1960s as the IAF, under his leadership, began to focus more on the issue of race and as the African-American struggle for equality pushed the nation to see the problems of cities and poverty as fundamentally ones of race. Groups interested in social change gravitated to Alinsky's approach as an alternative to the spontaneous disruptions of the era. Successful IAF projects in cities such as Rochester and Buffalo, New York, Kansas City, and various neighborhoods of Chicago began to draw much of their support from churches. Alinsky again became a national figure and his methods became internationally recognized through these projects, the organizing efforts of Fred Ross and Cesar Chavez in California, and the accolades of writers such as Charles Silberman, who said Alinsky's work in the Woodlawn neighborhood of Chicago was "the most important and impressive experiment affecting Negroes anywhere in the United States." In 1969 he and Jean divorced. In 1971 he married Irene McInnis; they had no children. His polemic against what he saw as the revolutionary excesses of the New Left, *Rules for Radicals*, published in 1971, counseled and scolded activists to work also with the middle classes, be pragmatic and avoid ideology, and value people's traditions. After his death in Carmel, California, the prestige of the IAF and the organizers he helped train continued to grow enormously and expanded to more than forty projects throughout the nation, most significantly in Texas, New York, and Baltimore.

Alinsky's method of community organizing both prefigured and helped direct changes in social activism after World War II—organizing in communities rather than factories, mobilizing citizens rather than workers, emphasizing democratic process, and employing politics that were consciously nonideological. His iconoclastic, independent, confident, and confrontive personal style helped suffuse these changes with dynamism. A person of many contradictions, Alinsky typified male activists of his generation: organizers were men who were clever, tough, and fearless, who kept the personal separate from the political. His writing and the ongoing work of the IAF, limited in tangible impact during Alinsky's lifetime, continued to expand his legacy after his death.

• Alinsky papers are at the University of Illinois at Chicago library, the Industrial Areas Foundation in New York, the State Historical Society of Wisconsin, and the Chicago Historical Society. A most impressive biography is Sanford D. Horwitt, *Let Them Call Me Rebel: Saul Alinsky, His Life and Legacy* (1989). Less helpful is the earlier biography by David P. Finks, *The Radical Vision of Saul Alinsky* (1984). In addition to Alinsky's own writings, see also Marion K. Sanders, *The Professional Radical: Conversations with Saul Alinsky* (1970). John Hall Fish, *Black Power/White Control: The Struggle of the Woodlawn Organization in Chicago* (1973); Charles Silberman, *Crisis in Black and White* (1964); and Robert Bailey, Jr., *Radicals in Urban Politics: The Alinsky Approach* (1974), are on Alinsky's work in Chicago in the 1960s. Joan Lancourt, *Confront or Concede: The Alinsky Citizen-Action Organizations* (1979), covers other organizing projects. For studies on Alinsky that also include IAF efforts since his death, see Robert Fisher, *Let the People Decide: Neighborhood Organizing in America* (1984; rev. ed., 1994); Harry Boyte, *Commonwealth: A Return to Citizen Politics* (1989); Peg Knoepfle, ed., *After Alinsky: Community Organizing in Illinois* (1990); Mary Beth Rogers, *Cold Anger* (1990); and Samuel Freedman, *Upon This Rock: The Miracles of a Black Church* (1993).

ROBERT FISHER

ALISON, Francis (1705–28 Nov. 1779), Presbyterian minister and educator, was born in the parish of Leck, County Donegal, in the province of Ulster in Ireland, the son of Robert Alison, a weaver. His mother's name is not known. Circumstantial evidence suggests that he was educated at one of the clandestine Presbyterian academies, probably that of Francis Hutcheson in Dublin. He received the bulk of his collegiate instruction before attending the University of Edinburgh, where he was awarded an M.A. in January 1733. He then studied divinity for two years, probably at the University of Glasgow, which awarded him a doctor of divinity degree in 1756, an honor that was usually extended only to an alumnus. Alison returned to Ireland and was licensed by the presbytery of Letterkenny in June 1735. He immediately sailed to Pennsylvania.

In 1737 Alison was ordained as the minister of the New London Presbyterian Church in New London, Pennsylvania. Soon after, he married Hannah Armitage; the couple had six children, two of whom died in infancy.

The series of revivals that became known as the Great Awakening began among Presbyterians just as Alison arrived. Initially remaining neutral, he was asked by various presbyteries to mediate conflicts that ensued when the evangelists made unauthorized intrusions into congregations and attacked their ministers. After George Whitefield arrived in 1739, the movement grew, and the revivalists launched an unsuccessful attempt to control the synod, which split in 1741 as a result. Alison was among the "Old Side" who signed a protest against the revivalists. He explained the synod's official position in the pamphlet *An Examination and Refutation of Mr. Gilbert Tennent's Remarks upon the Protestation Presented to the Synod of Philadelphia, June 1, 1741*, which was published anonymously in 1742. As leader of the Old Side, he was instrumental in effecting a reunification of the Old and New Sides in 1758, although he acknowledged that the union was "as oil and water." At the first meeting of the reunited synod, he preached "Peace and Union Recommended and Self Disclaim'd and Christ Exalted," which was the only signed piece he ever published.

By 1739 Alison had opened a school in New London where he, with the aid of one or two assistants, offered instruction through the collegiate level. Mathematics and science were left to the assistants, for these were Alison's weak areas. Generally acclaimed as the "greatest classical scholar in America," as Ezra Stiles phrased it, Alison took responsibility for the Latin school. In the collegiate or philosophy school he began with logic, progressed through metaphysics and ethics, and concluded with moral philosophy, patterning his lectures on *A Short Introduction to Moral Philosophy* by Francis Hutcheson, to whom Alison had written for advice. He later instituted the same course of study at the College of Philadelphia and at New Ark Academy. Thus, Alison was the first to introduce the Scots-Irish Enlightenment into the colonies and to offer systematic instruction in its tenets.

The New London Academy, "the most celebrated in the province" according to Thomas McKean, served as the official seminary of the (Old Side) Synod of Philadelphia from 1743 until 1752. In that year Alison left to become the rector of the academy and master of the Latin school at the newly established Academy of Philadelphia. The trustees were reluctant to employ an Irish Presbyterian, but, as Anglican trustee Richard Peters conceded, Alison's "uncommon Talents . . . skill & zeal & address in teaching Latin and Greek" left them no choice. In 1755 he joined with Scotch Anglican William Smith to add a college. He served as professor and vice provost of the College of Philadelphia until his death.

As the half-time minister to the First Presbyterian Church in Philadelphia, Alison became active in public service projects, the most notable of which was the establishment and supervision of the Presbyterian Ministers Fund, the first life insurance company in America. Alison also administered the synod's lending library for ministers and schoolmasters and supervised the fund for the German charity schools. He performed more secular services as a member and director of the Library Company, a contributing member of the Society for the Propagation of Useful Knowledge (later known as the American Philosophical Society), and a founder and manager of the Society for the Promotion of the Culture of Silk. His political activities were less public as he worked behind the scenes to defuse the explosive situation caused by the Paxton Boys and to thwart the efforts of Benjamin Franklin to rescind the charter and transform Pennsylvania into a royal colony.

In the face of a renewed threat of a colonial bishopric in 1766, Alison worked with Ezra Stiles of Rhode Island to unite the Presbyterians and Congregationalists into a General Convention that met until 1775 to oppose what they feared would become an established church. In 1768 he joined with John Dickinson and George Bryan to publish "The Centinel," a series of newspaper articles in opposition to the bishopric.

By 1766 the College of Philadelphia had acquired an elitist and Anglican tone, and, when the (New Side) College of New Jersey (later Princeton University) refused to admit any Old Side influence, Alison led his former students in expanding and chartering an academy in rural Newark, Delaware (later the University of Delaware). Under his direction as president of the board of trustees, the New Ark Academy thrived until 1777, when British troops marched through and closed the school.

When asked by Stiles in 1767 to identify his greatest achievements, Alison listed his stand against the "Enthusiasms & wild disorders" of the Great Awakening, the Presbyterian Ministers Fund, and, above all, his promotion of education. He was proud of having taught a generation of teachers who spread what a colleague termed "a happy contagion" of the Enlightenment throughout the colonies. He died in Philadelphia.

• The bulk of Alison's papers are at the Historical Society of Pennsylvania and the Presbyterian Historical Society, both in Philadelphia; the latter also houses his manuscript sermons. The longest run of correspondence is in the Ezra Stiles Papers at Yale University. The most complete contemporary assessment is Matthew Wilson, "Memorial," *Pennsylvania Journal*, 9 Apr. 1780.

The definitive biography is Elizabeth [Nybakken] Ingersoll, "Francis Alison: American Philosopher, 1705–1779" (Ph.D. diss., Univ. of Delaware, 1974). For particular facets of Alison's life, see Douglas Sloan, *The Scottish Enlightenment and the American College Ideal* (1971), and William Turner, "The College, Academy and Charitable School of Philadelphia. . . . 1740–1779" (Ph.D. diss., Univ. of Pennsylvania, 1952), for education; Alexander Mackie, *Facile Princeps: The Story of the Beginning of Life Insurance in America* (1956), for the Presbyterian Ministers Fund; Leonard J. Trinterud, *The Forming of an American Tradition: A Re-examination of Colonial Presbyterianism* (1949), and Elizabeth Nybakken, "New Light on the Old Side: Irish Influences in Colonial Presbyterianism," *Journal of American History* 68 (1982): 813–32, for religion; and Nybakken, *"The Centinel": Warnings of a Revolution* (1980), on the Anglican bishopric controversy.

ELIZABETH NYBAKKEN

ALLAN, John (14 Jan. 1746–7 Feb. 1805), revolutionary war soldier, was born in Edinburgh Castle, Edinburgh, Scotland, the son of Major William Allan, a British army officer, and Isabella Maxwell. In 1749, when Allan was only three years old, his father brought him and his mother to Nova Scotia to take part in founding the military colony of Halifax. After the dispersion of the Acadians in 1756, Allan's father retired from the army and took up a tract of former Acadian land in Nova Scotia. Soon the elder Allan was a prominent and wealthy citizen of the province. In 1762 he sent John, his eldest son, to Massachusetts to round out the latter's education. Much to his father's chagrin, John Allan imbibed the political attitudes of the New England people and thus became an advocate of the old Whig cause against Britain. Upon his return to Nova Scotia, Allan settled down as a farmer and Indian trader; his business interests flourished, and soon he was wealthy. In 1767 he married Mary Patton, with whom over the next few years he had five children. He also served in positions of honor in his home county of Cumberland: clerk of the sessions and justice of the peace. Advancing to higher ranks, he was appointed clerk of the provincial supreme court, and from 1770 to 1776 he held a seat in the Parliament of Nova Scotia.

In the summer of 1776 Allan abandoned his comfortable position in Nova Scotian society and declared in favor of his American neighbors to the south in their resistance to British "tyranny." As a member of Parliament, he learned that authorities in his province were attempting to stir up American Indians along the eastern boundary of Massachusetts (now Maine) to harass settlements there with the intention of annexing large territories to Nova Scotia. Quickly, on 19 September, he called together an Indian conference at Chediac to stymie this measure, and although he could not exact from the chiefs a promise that they would join the American cause, at least he did get them to guarantee that they would do the rebels no injury. Returning home six days later, he learned that a party of soldiers was seeking him, with orders to arrest him for treason. On 3 October he fled Nova Scotia with a small party of friends, leaving behind his family for the moment, and arrived in eastern Massachusetts eight days later. The provincial authorities proceeded to burn his houses and outbuildings, destroy his crops, and drive off his horses and cattle, inflicting $10,000 in losses. Also, they imprisoned his wife and children and offered a reward of £100 for his arrest. Finally, in September 1777, they allowed his family to join him in Massachusetts.

Meantime, Allan was being made welcome by the American revolutionaries. Arriving in Boston in late 1776, he met the governor and council and talked to John Adams (1735–1826) and James Otis about plans he had formulated for defense of Maine's eastern frontier. On their advice he proceeded to Baltimore to present his ideas to Congress, and in early 1777 that body adopted his program. He was commissioned a colonel in the Continental army and appointed superintendent of eastern Indians. He returned to Boston in March 1777 and petitioned the Massachusetts legislature to construct two forts on the St. John River to prevent enemy communication between Nova Scotia and Canada. He also requested authority to enlist 900 men from Massachusetts and Nova Scotia for service in freeing Nova Scotia from British control. Successful in his requests, even given the assistance of two naval vessels for the expedition of liberation, he commenced organizing his invasion army. But for some reason, probably paucity of war materials and too few available soldiers, the enterprise collapsed. Undaunted, Colonel Allan turned to cultivating the Indians as a support for the patriot cause. He proceeded to Machias, on the far eastern frontier of Maine, where he established his headquarters and remained for the duration of the war. An excellent Indian agent, Allan did yeoman service in keeping the natives placated and wedded to the American cause. Numbers of Indians joined him at Machias, despite the best efforts of British officials in Nova Scotia, particularly Governor Michael Francklin, to prevent them. Allan worked under extremely adverse conditions, constantly subjected to alarms and rumors of enemy attack. In August 1777 his post actually was assaulted by British troops, but he managed to repulse them. The Massachusetts General Court knew how strategically important Allan's retention of Machias was, but it was too strapped to provide him with adequate troops and supplies. Allan's life was constantly threatened by hostile Indians, and he had many narrow escapes. On one occasion, when food ran low, he was compelled to leave two of his children with the Indians as hostages while he made a personal appeal to Congress for support. On other occasions he spent his own money to purchase supplies, lest he be forced to abandon his critical post.

It is because of Allan's bulldog tenacity in occupying and holding Machias that the eastern boundary of the United States was fixed at the St. Croix River rather than the Kennebeck. In 1779 Allan wrote that the "British Government Expected to be Compelled to declare the Independency of the thirteen States, but were determined . . . to Extend their line of Territory to Kennebeck River." He was just as determined that the disputed territory would remain a part of the United States. In 1783, his duty done, Allan resigned his army commission. A year later he settled in Maine, on Allan's Island in Passamaquoddy Bay, where he became a merchant. In 1786 he retired and moved to Lubec Mills but later returned to Allan's Island, where he died and was buried. As partial compensation for his losses during the revolutionary war, Massachusetts gave him 22,000 acres of land in 1792 and Congress 2,000 acres in Ohio in 1801.

• Primary materials on Allan's revolutionary war career are in the Maine Historical Society, *Collections and Proceedings*, 2d. ser., 5, 14–20 (1894–1914), and Nova Scotia Historical Society, *Collections* 2 (1881): 11–16. Short biographies are George H. Allan, *Memoir of Colonel John Allan, an Officer of the Revolution, Born in Edinburgh Castle, Scotland, Jan. 3, 1746, Died in Lubec, Maine, Feb. 7, 1805* (1867), and "Sketch of Col. John Allan of Maine," *New-England Historical and Genealogical Register* 30 (1876): 353–59; and John F. Sprague, "Colonel John Allan," *Sprague's Journal of Maine History* 2 (1915): 233–57. Also useful are Frederic Kidder, *Military Operations in Eastern Maine and Nova Scotia during the Revolution: Chiefly Compiled from the Journals and Letters of Col. John Allan, with Notes and a Memoir of Col. John Allan* (1867), and John H. Ahlin, *Maine Rubicon: Downeast Settlers during the American Revolution* (1966).

PAUL DAVID NELSON

ALLAN, Maud (27 Aug. 1873–7 Oct. 1956), dancer, choreographer, and actress, was born Ula Maude Durrant in Toronto, Canada, the daughter of William Allan Durrant, a shoemaker, and Isa Matilda Hutchinson. In the late 1870s the family migrated from Ontario to San Francisco, where Allan grew up and, from an early age, studied piano with several teachers. San Francisco's thriving theatrical and musical environment in the late 1880s and early 1890s enabled her to see fine performances, including those by some of the best women artists, among them Adele aus der Ohe and Sarah Bernhardt. Allan's discipline, however, was piano. At age twenty-two, already musically accomplished and very beautiful, she went to Berlin for advanced piano study at the Royal High School for Music then under the direction of Joseph Joachim.

At the end of the nineteenth century, Berlin was the world capital of music. Here Allan became immersed in the city's young, vital music community. She also observed the new techniques developing in theater and movement. Experiments were occurring in set design and stage blocking, pantomime, movement ideas derived from the technique of François Delsarte, and especially new lighting concepts. Those years in Berlin are characterized by the theories of Adolphe Appia and Max Reinhardt in theater; Wagner, Strauss, Brahms, and Mahler in music. By the turn of the century, Allan had become increasingly interested in movement as a medium of expression. She also continued in piano studies, and in 1901 in Weimar she took master classes with Ferruccio Busoni, one of the finest technicians and composers of the twentieth century.

Through association with Busoni and his wife, Gerda, Allan met the Belgian writer-musician-composer Marcel Rémy. Their friendship and artistic exchanges in Berlin led directly to her dance debut in November 1903 in Vienna's Conservatory of Music. The two-hour program of ten dances titled by their scores reflected her pianist's command of the Romantic repertoire: Schubert, Schumann, Mendelssohn, and Chopin. She also employed in these early dances the music of Bach and of her contemporary Anton Rubinstein, the latter's work marking Allan's ongoing use throughout her long dance career of scores and arrangements by contemporary composers: Grieg, Brahms, Massenet, Vladimir Rebikov, Eduard Schütt, Sibelius and, most importantly, Debussy. Berlin's nurturing musical milieu was sustained in part by the efforts of Busoni, who introduced to these audiences the world's newest composers conducting their own music. Through these extraordinary experiences, Allan's dancing was distinguished by its musicality and her choreography informed by a keen awareness of the transition in music from romanticism to modernism.

On 28 December 1906, again in Vienna, Allan gave the first performance of her best-known dance, *The Vision of Salome*. Marcel Rémy, who had composed the score, died in Berlin twenty-two days before the debut and thus never saw Allan's performance of it. *The Vision of Salome* expanded the technique and comprehension evident in Allan's choreography, which to that time largely depended on her understanding of a given piano score. This change, however, was not understood because of the confusion between Allan's use of the Salome story and Oscar Wilde's play about the same biblical figure. *The Vision of Salome* became a sensational success and an abiding source of misunderstanding in Allan's performance career. It was assumed that Allan had appropriated Wilde's drama (which had been produced by Max Reinhardt in Berlin in 1902 and 1903) and, further, that the score had been taken from Richard Strauss's 1905 opera *Salomé*. In fact, Allan's scenario and Rémy's score considered the woman's inner conflict; it was a "retrospective," as Allan called her dance's approach to the familiar story.

Following more technical experiments and critical successes in other European cities—Brussels, Liége, Hamburg, Munich, Berlin, Budapest, Prague, Paris—Allan found a supportive experimental atmosphere in London, where she opened at the Palace Theatre on 8 March 1908. Later, on the event of her 250th successive performance there, Allan published, in October 1908, *My Life and Dancing*. A short, fragmented account of herself and her eight-year study of movement, *My Life and Dancing* was the first of Allan's several attempts to write or talk about her dances.

The title role of *The Vision of Salome*, which she performed at least until 1916, and others taken from familiar images of woman reveal her thoughts about a woman's experiences. Her dances were carefully costumed, lit, and musically composed, and each reflected her particular dramatic perception of the subject matter. For example, one of her earliest dances titled from its Chopin score, the *Marche Funebre* (1903), reveals Allan's conception of the medieval mourner, a concise and timeless image of woman realized through a nineteenth-century romantic score and twentieth-century electric lighting and staging. In the same way, idealized woman as madonna is evident in her rendition of Schubert's *Ave Marie* for a dance (1903) of the same name. Her Salome, accordingly, considered the responsibilities a woman must take for her own actions.

In a July 1908 concert Allan performed four separate dances from sections of Tchaikovsky's *The Nutcracker* and, the following year, another four from Ibsen's *Peer Gynt*. These dances were critical successes and reflected yet another choreographic approach: the introduction of dance images of woman first conceived in musical scores for narratives in other art forms. Artistically she continued to pursue women subjects, to employ music by contemporary composers, and to use music written specifically for dance. In 1910, for example, Allan commissioned Debussy to compose the score for the full-length dance, Allan's *Khamma* (never mounted) based on the story of an Egyptian princess. Allan's role in the early silent film *The Rugmaker's Daughter* (1915) made her dances a significant part of the plot's structure. And in 1916 she conceived, mounted, and danced in *Nair*, a love story about a slave woman that had a score composed by Enrico Belpassi. She continued to make dances using both piano and orchestral scores by other contemporary composers, such as *À Ma Bien Aimée* (1918) by Schütt and Prelude in C-sharp Minor (1923) by Rachmaninoff.

Beginning in 1908, Allan made her home in London. Her touring, however, was extensive and worldwide. She also traveled often to Los Angeles where her parents lived from 1907 until the 1920s. In 1909 Allan performed in both St. Petersburg and Moscow, then made the first of several U.S. cross-country tours. She opened in the east in Boston on 19 January 1910, went to Canada, then west, performing in San Francisco in April. In 1915 she toured the Far East and Australia. Another American tour in the spring of 1916 was interrupted by illness, then resumed again in the fall. Later tours took her to South America, Egypt, and Malta. In 1926, after an appearance at the Metropolitan Opera House in New York City, she toured across country, ending with a performance in Los Angeles. She taught master classes that summer at Berkeley, opened a studio in Los Angeles, and danced solo in the Hollywood Bowl's fifth season. That same summer, Allan danced in the recently remodeled outdoor Redlands Bowl in a program of new dances. Her compositions faithfully reflected her enduring interests and took advantage of the theater's new lighting equipment and the outdoor setting's extensive flora. Ten years later, at age sixty-three, Allan danced again at Redlands accompanied by pianist Etienne Amyot in a program that also included two new works.

Allan was cast in at least three dramatic roles. In 1918 in London she played the role of Salome in the Independent Theatre Society's production of Oscar Wilde's *Salomé*; in 1932, the role of the Abbess in Max Reinhardt's London production of *The Miracle*; and in 1934, the role of Carrie, the dancer, in Manchester Repertory's production of *The Barker*. She performed her dances in many of the world's older music theaters as well as variety and legitimate theaters and in such spaces as private studios and England's Crystal Palace. Frequent dismissals of Allan's thirty-three year performance career in histories of the development of modern dance fail to weigh more than sixty documented dances that she composed and the number of her worldwide performances to discriminating audiences.

A traffic accident in California in January 1938 resulted in injuries to Allan's spine and ribs; she was hospitalized for several months and never danced again. Following her partial recovery, she returned to her home in London, where her life became immersed in World War II. Following the London blitz, in August 1941, she made her way to Lisbon and then to Los Angeles, where she took up again long-standing interests in drawing and worked briefly as a draftsman for the Douglas Aircraft Company. Never having married, she died in Los Angeles following two years of declining health.

• Fragments of Allan's personal papers are scattered in collections throughout the world. The British Theatre Museum Library's Enthoven Collection has photographs that Allan addressed to friends as well as programs and newspaper and magazine clippings mainly of English reviews; the Dance Collection at the New York Public Library for the Performing Arts, Lincoln Center, has programs, photographs, and a newspaper and magazine clipping file that were kept by Allan's contemporary, dancer Violet Romer; Mills College Library in Oakland, Calif., has a few letters; the University Research Library, University of California, Los Angeles, has some of her books, a postcard collection that she kept in the early years in Germany, and a journal kept during her 1916 tour to the Far East; the University of British Columbia, Vancouver, has several manifestations of the Debussy *Khamma* score, one of which has notes in Allan's hand for her unrealized dance. The 1913 dance scenario that Busoni wrote for her, *Der Tanz vom Leben und vom Tode*, is in the Deutsche Staatsbibliothek, Berlin. Contemporary assessments are in Ethel L. Urlin, *Dancing: Ancient and Modern* (1911); J. T. Crawford Flitch, *Modern Dancing and Dancers* (1912); Caroline and Charles H. Caffin, *Dancing and Dancers of Today* (1912); and Samuel Morgan-Powell, *Memories That Live* (1929). Lacy McDearmon, "Maud Allan: The Public Record," *Dance Chronicle* 2, no. 2 (1978): 85–105, using primarily materials in the New York Public Library Dance Collection, first recognized her long public career and background; Elizabeth Weigand focused on Allan's California artistic associations in "*The Rugmaker's Daughter*: Maud Allan's 1915 Silent Film," *Dance Chronicle* 9, no. 2 (1986): 237–51; and Felix Cherniavsky, in *The Salome Dancer* (1991), extended his five earlier *Dance Chronicle* articles into a full study, essentially biographical, using his collection of Allan's materials.

Obituaries are in *The Times* (London) and *The Toronto Globe*, 8 Oct. 1956, the *New York Times*, 9 Oct. 1956, and *Dance News* (Nov. 1956).

ELIZABETH WEIGAND

ALLEE, Warder Clyde (5 June 1885–18 Mar. 1955), biologist, was born in Bloomingdale, Indiana, the son of John Wesley Allee, a farmer, and Mary Emily Newlin, a schoolteacher. A Quaker, Allee graduated from Earlham College in 1908 and took a three-year position as a high school teacher in Hammond, Indiana, while pursuing graduate studies during the summer months in the Department of Zoology at the University of Chicago. In the fall of 1909 he enrolled as a full-time graduate student at the university, where he came under the influence of pioneer animal ecologist Victor Ernest Shelford. Allee received a Ph.D. in 1912 for research on the physiological life histories of isopods.

That fall Allee married Marjorie June Hill, a writer of young women's novels; they had a son (who died in a tragic accident at the age of ten) and two daughters. Together, the couple ventured on a series of yearly moves from the University of Illinois–Urbana to Williams College in Massachusetts and then on to the University of Oklahoma in 1914. In 1915 Allee secured a position as professor of biology at Lake Forest College in Lake Forest, Illinois. He spent the intervening summers at the Marine Biological Laboratory (MBL) at Woods Hole, Massachusetts, an important institution for establishing a sense of professional identity and community among American biologists in the early part of the twentieth century. Allee was an instructor in the invertebrate zoology course at the MBL from 1914 to 1918 and the MBL course director from 1918 to 1921. The course provided him with abundant field material for a series of ecological investigations on the factors limiting the distribution of littoral (shoreline) invertebrates in the Woods Hole region.

At Lake Forest College, Allee became drawn into the liberal pacifist movement. In 1917 he was appointed chairman of the Quaker War Service for civilian relief in Chicago, which formed as an outgrowth of the Chicago Monthly Meeting of Friends. The Quaker War Service later became the Chicago regional committee of the American Friends Service Committee, and Allee served as either chairman or vice chairman of the regional committee from 1917 to 1950. His experiences as a pacifist during the First World War brought him into contact with social reformers and liberals of Chicago, such as Jane Addams, who shared a vision of progressive social democracy. After the war, Allee undertook scientific experiments designed to throw light on the subject of war, and he incorporated the social message of the liberal pacifist into his animal ecology research.

In 1921 Allee accepted a position as assistant professor of zoology at the University of Chicago. There he initiated a research program, outlined in his *Animal Aggregations: A Study in General Sociology* (1931), about the causes and significance of animal aggregations, on the effects group life had on individual physiology and behavior. Animal aggregations, Allee argued, helped to ameliorate the individual's struggle with harsh environmental conditions and provided physiological benefits unattainable in solitary life. In many instances, Allee argued, undercrowding had as detrimental an effect on individual survivorship as overcrowding: a phenomenon now referred to in ecology as the Allee effect. Allee hoped this research would bridge the widening gap between the laboratory and the field, between the physiological methods of individual ecology and the descriptive natural history that characterized community studies. Yet his research also served a political agenda. Through his aggregation research, Allee believed he had found both experimental evidence opposing the biological justification of war and the cornerstone of a theory of sociality centered not on the family, but on the association of individuals for cooperative purposes, as is found in the most primitive forms of life.

Over the course of the next twenty-nine years, Allee and his colleague Alfred Edwards Emerson developed a program of animal ecology that focused on the origins, development, and organization of animal societies. A series of operations for a benign spinal tumor confined Allee to a wheelchair in 1938. No longer able to endure the physical hardships of life in the field, Allee limited his research to the laboratory, particularly to social organization among the vertebrates, such as dominance hierarchies in domestic fowl, to understand the physiological and psychological mechanisms responsible for group integration. He believed that the mechanisms responsible for group integration, such as mutualism or dominance-subordination behavior, could only be explained by reference to group selection, an evolutionary view that he argued was consistent with the writings of the University of Chicago population geneticist Sewall Wright. His initial research findings in this area and their implications for human social behavior are discussed in his *The Social Life of Animals* (1938). Through his studies on the social organization of the vertebrates, Allee trained a number of students, including Nicholas G. Collins and John P. Scott, who had a significant impact on animal behavior research in the United States during the postwar years.

Allee's close friendship and interaction with Emerson and the appointment of Allee's student Thomas Park to the faculty in 1937, helped crystallize and initiate a core of ecological research at the University of Chicago on population as the fundamental unit of ecological, evolutionary, and social change. Together, Allee, Emerson, and Park, along with the Northwestern University ecologist Orlando Park and the Chicago Field Museum of Natural History herpetologist Karl Schmidt, coauthored *Principles of Animal Ecology* (1949). This work represented the first synthetic animal ecology text structured around general ecological principles and organized according to increasing levels of integration, a pattern that many ecology texts would later imitate. One year after the book's publication, Allee retired from the University of Chicago and accepted a position as head of the Department of Biology at the University of Florida in Gainesville. Following the death of his first wife in 1945, Allee married Ann Silver in 1953. He died two years later in Gainesville.

An active member in professional societies, Allee served as secretary and president of the American Society of Zoologists, president of the Ecological Society of America, vice president of the zoology section of the American Association for the Advancement of Science, and editor of the journal *Physiological Zoology*. His scientific accomplishments were recognized by his election to the American Academy of Arts and Sciences and the National Academy of Sciences. For Allee, ecology formed the basis of a scientific naturalism that functioned as both a legitimating force and prescription for his own ethical and political views of human society. In the midst of the Second World War, Allee argued that "permanent peace [was] not to be won following the precedent established by the dominance order of vertebrate animals" ("Biology and International Relations," *New Republic* 112 [1945]: 816) but was instead to be derived from humankind's drive toward cooperation, which existed "even among the Protozoa at an evolutionary level at which only vague premonitions of a possible peck-order system can be detected" (Bryson et al., p. 359). His research on animal ecology and behavior contributed to the development of professional ecology and to intellectual debates on questions of international peace and democratic order during the period of and between the First and Second World Wars.

• Allee's papers are in the Joseph Regenstein Library at the University of Chicago. Other important works by Allee include *Animal Life and Social Growth* (1932) and his translation with Karl Schmidt of Richard Hesse's *Ecological Animal Geography* (1937). For articles by Allee that discuss the implications of his biological research for human affairs, see "Cooperation among Animals," *Chicago Alumni Magazine* 20 (1928): 418–25; "Where Angels Fear to Tread: A Contribution from General Sociology to Human Ethics," *Science* 97 (1943): 517–25; and "Human Conflict and Co-operation: The Biological Background," in *Approaches to National Unity, Fifth Symposium on the Conference of Science, Philosophy, and Religion*, ed. L. Bryson et al. (1945). Karl Paterson Schmidt, "Warder Clyde Allee, 1885–1955," National Academy of Sciences, *Biographical Memoirs* 30 (1957): 3–40, is a comprehensive biography of Allee's scientific accomplishments that includes a complete bibliography of his publications. For an analysis of Allee's life and work in relation to the changing social and political landscape of biology in the United States during the first half of the twentieth century, see Gregg Mitman, *The State of Nature: Ecology, Community, and American Social Thought, 1900–1950* (1992). Allee's contributions to the field of animal behavior are discussed in Edwin M. Banks, "Warder Clyde Allee and the Chicago School of Animal Behavior," *Journal of the History of the Behavioral Sciences* 21 (1985): 345–53. See also J. Ronald Engel, *Sacred Sands: The Struggle for Community in the Indiana Dunes* (1983), on Allee's ecological research in the context of the Indiana dunes and a Midwest movement of social democratic reform; and Donald Worster, *Nature's Economy: A History of Ecological Ideas*, 2d ed. (1994), on Allee's contributions to organicist thought in ecology. An obituary is in the *New York Times*, 19 Mar. 1955.

GREGG MITMAN

ALLEN, Alexander Viets Griswold (4 May 1841–1 July 1908), Episcopal priest, theologian, and educator, was born in Otis, Massachusetts, the son of Ethan Allen, a teacher and Episcopal priest, and Lydia Child Burr. His father served churches in Massachusetts and Vermont. Both parents were strongly evangelical in the Episcopal manner of the time, emphasizing biblical authority and teaching more than sacramental theology—a conviction that produced conflict in several of the churches that Allen's father served. Their piety shaped Allen's early views, leading him to enroll at Kenyon College in Gambier, Ohio, in 1859. Kenyon was an Episcopal institution then of an evangelical stamp. An excellent student, Allen delivered the valedictory address upon graduating in 1862 and immediately entered Bexley Hall, a theological seminary in Gambier.

Highly self-directed in his education, Allen soon discovered the writings of Samuel Taylor Coleridge and theologian Frederick Denison Maurice, an encounter that produced a radical revision in his thought. Abandoning the evangelical idea of the fallibility of human institutions, Allen discovered an idealistic vision of the church. He also revised his understanding of Scripture to stress the Incarnation of Christ rather than the atoning death of Jesus. Allen left Bexley Hall after two years, transferring to Andover Theological Seminary. There he was influenced by the theologian Edwards Park, whose thought reflected the influence of Jonathan Edwards. The ideas of this early American theologian exerted a formative influence on Allen as well, and he subsequently became Edwards's major nineteenth-century expositor. Allen rescued Edwards's theology from the taint of Puritanism and retrieved his sense of historical development. He took Edwards's view of history as moving toward an ultimate salvation and blended it with Coleridge's and Maurice's vision of all things as organically interconnected; the result was a new understanding of revelation. Allen's career became devoted to promoting the conviction that Christian doctrines develop within, and must be adapted to, particular historical contexts.

Allen's intellectual odyssey did not lead him out of the church, but it did lead him on a different vocational path. On 5 July 1865 he was ordained a deacon in the Episcopal church in Boston, and on 24 June 1866, in Framingham, Massachusetts, he was ordained a priest. He then became the rector of St. John's Church in Lawrence. In 1867 he became an instructor in church history at the new Episcopal theological seminary being organized in Cambridge, adjacent to Harvard University. The position soon became full-time, and Allen left parish ministry and served the new seminary until his death. Independent of diocesan or national church oversight and committed to a combination of moderate evangelicalism with an appropriation of new biblical and historical scholarship, the seminary was an ideal match for Allen's intellectual predilections. There he achieved renown as a great teacher who regularly challenged the religious assumptions of his students. In 1872 he married Elizabeth Kent Stone. After her death, he married Paulina Cony Smith in 1907.

Allen soon became a noted author whose publications included *Jonathan Edwards* (1889), *Religious Progress* (1894), *Christian Institutions* (1897), and *Freedom in the Church* (1907). In 1900 he also published *Life and Letters of Phillips Brooks*. Brooks was the noted Episcopal preacher at Trinity Church in Boston who had become the bishop of Massachusetts shortly before his death. In this work, more clearly perhaps than in others, Allen revealed the importance of the personal examples that had shaped his thought. The work also showed that Allen's dedication to addressing intellectual issues of belief required the context of the church. Allen also delivered a memorable address in June 1900 at an event memorializing Edwards. Restating the points he had made in his popular biography of Edwards, Allen depicted him as an "American Dante" whose poetic sense lent a distinctive spirituality to American religious life. For Allen, this uniquely American outlook was a progressive sense of history and belief that led to an affirmation of the church as a divinely inspired human community and the only source of religious truth.

The most influential of Allen's works was *The Continuity of Christian Thought: A Study of Modern Theology in the Light of Its History*. Originally delivered as the Bohlen Lectures and dedicated to his friend Brooks, the book argues that "a purpose runs through the whole history of Christian thought." Allen perceived "the record of a development moving onward, in accordance with a divine law." He held that revelation is progressive, drawing Christianity toward the center of modern intellectual and social life. Suspicious of the tendency toward absolutism in creedal formulations, Allen tried to join a vision of continuity with the past and a mystical sense of the divine presence flowing from the Incarnation. An impressive sweep through the intellectual history of the church, the work won Allen critical acclaim on both sides of the Atlantic. He gained renown as one of the few American theologians pursuing the intellectual path that Europeans had pioneered. Arising out of Allen's own questions, the book proved a creative response to the search for religious foundations in a liberal and progressive age. Allen died in Boston and has been remembered as a major exponent of a new theological liberalism that rendered classical theological tenets in a revised vision that was both progressive and sacramental.

• Charles Lewis Slattery, *Alexander Viets Griswold Allen, 1841–1908* (1911), offers a detailed, admiring portrait and includes helpful biographical information. The reprinted edition of Allen's *The Continuity of Christian Thought* (1975) includes a detailed introduction to Allen and his thought by Sydney Ahlstrom. Recent treatments of Allen can be found in William Hutchison, *The Modernist Impulse in American Protestantism* (1976), and Joseph Conforti, *Jonathan Edwards, Religious Tradition, and American Culture* (1995).

WILLIAM L. SACHS

ALLEN, Arthur Augustus (28 Dec. 1885–17 Jan. 1964), ornithologist, was born in Buffalo, New York, the son of Daniel Williams Allen, a railroad and land developer, and Anna Moore. He was raised in Hamburg, New York, ten miles south of Buffalo, and he graduated from Buffalo High School in 1903. Allen then attended Cornell University, where he received an A.B. in 1907 and an M.A. in 1908. A graduate assistant in zoology from 1907 to 1911, he completed his formal training in 1911 with his doctoral dissertation, "The Red-Winged Blackbird: A Study in the Ecology of a Cattail Marsh," which was praised by leading ornithologists of the day, including Frank M. Chapman, who described it as "the best, most significant biography which has thus far been prepared of any American bird" (*Bird Lore* [1914]). Allen's dissertation was also important because it set a pattern for future monographic studies centering on detailed life histories of individual species in the context of their interaction with their environment.

Chapman was so impressed with Allen's work that he had the younger man selected to lead an American Museum of Natural History expedition to Colombia in the late summer of 1911. Though obliged to return home the following spring because he had contracted malaria, Allen's introduction to neotropical animal life proved useful in his future teaching and research.

In the fall of 1912 Allen was appointed an instructor in zoology at Cornell. Four years later he was made an assistant professor, and in 1926 he was promoted to full professor. Early in his tenure at Cornell, Allen developed the first American doctoral program in ornithology. His *Laboratory Notebook* (1927) and *The Book of Bird Life* (1930) were pioneering texts designed to facilitate study for his students and were widely used elsewhere. Allen revised the *Notebook* several times over the following two decades, and he revised *The Book of Bird Life* as late as 1961, after many reprintings. Allen's courses and his capacity for mentoring students soon began to draw substantial numbers of students to Cornell, and during his 41-year tenure some 10,000 students had taken various courses under his direction. A good many of the 100 graduate students he had sponsored initiated ornithology programs at other institutions.

One of the innovations of the Cornell program was the "Grad Lab," and weekly evening seminars were held at which Cornell faculty, students, and some distinguished scholars from other institutions discussed various ornithological research problems, observations, and projects. The close fellowship between students and faculty, particularly during the pre–World War II years, was a unique feature of Cornell's ornithology program. Labeled the "Laboratory of Ornithology," this initiative became a formal entity within the university in 1955. Two years later a separate building was constructed for the laboratory at Sapsucker Woods, some distance from the main campus, which was ideal for research and observation. It has continued as a vital part of Cornell's ornithological outreach to professionals and the general public.

Allen was a pioneer in the field of wildlife conservation in the 1930s, offering the first course on the subject at any American university. He also did extensive research and teaching in the area of game management, at a time when this field was just coming into being in the United States. He conducted investigations of ruffed grouse diseases for the American Game Association in the 1920s, determined how the birds could be raised in captivity, and was awarded the Outdoor Life Medal for his work in this area in 1924. He subsequently did groundbreaking work on sex rhythms in the ruffed grouse and a number of other species. Allen continued to do fieldwork for a number of years in various parts of the United States, including the Alaska Territory (1948). Research trips outside the country were taken to Labrador (1918 and 1945), Europe (1938), Hudson Bay (1934 and 1944), and Panama (1944–1945). A research project on jungle acoustics was carried on for the War Department's Office of Scientific Research and Development in Mexico (1946).

Almost from the beginning of his academic career, Allen began extending his appreciation of birds to the general public. For many years, beginning in 1912, he contributed pieces to *Bird Lore*, the ornithology periodical edited by Chapman, and from 1919 until 1934 he edited the school department of that publication. In this capacity he published a series of "bird autobiographies" in *Bird Lore*, several of which were reprinted in two volumes, *American Bird Biographies* (1934) and *The Golden Plover and Other Birds* (1939). Some ornithologists objected to Allen's approach to his material, arguing that it constituted a misrepresentation of the subject, but schoolteachers and students alike avidly read them.

Allen increasingly gave his time to presenting public lectures, wrote articles for a variety of general circulation periodicals and encyclopedias, and illustrated both his written and oral presentations with slides and photographs he had taken himself. Between 1934 and 1962 Allen contributed eighteen articles to *National Geographic Magazine*, many of them illustrated with his own photographs. One of these pieces, "Stalking Birds with a Color Camera" (1939), was later much expanded and developed into a book of the same title (1951; rev. ed., 1961, 1963). Allen was awarded the Burr Prize by the National Geographic Society in 1948. Allen was made a Fellow of the American Ornithologists' Union and was a founder and second president (1938–1939) of the Wildlife Society.

In 1929 Allen became interested in motion pictures and sound recordings when he assisted a visiting film crew that came to him for guidance. With the aid of Paul Kellogg, his assistant at Cornell; Albert Brand, a wealthy retired stockbroker; and others, Allen produced the first sound recording of birds and in 1935 recorded the song of endangered species in the southern and southwestern states. Other sets of recordings, "American Bird Songs" and "Voices of the Night," were produced in 1942 and 1948, respectively. All of this extracurricular activity left Allen very little time to develop the lines of original research in which he had broken ground, but he encouraged his students and others to pursue these special studies.

Allen had married Elsa Guerdrum in 1913. In addition to helping to raise their five children, she secured a Ph.D. from Cornell in her own right in 1929 and often joined her husband on field expeditions, on lecture trips, and at scientific gatherings. In 1950 colleagues, students, and friends underwrote a preretirement gift of a trip to the International Ornithological Congress in Sweden for both Allen and his wife. Allen formally retired in 1953, but he continued for some time with many of his lecture and writing projects until his death in Ithaca, New York.

• A taped interview made with Allen in 1963 is in the Carolynne H. Cline Papers at Cornell. The Ornithological Archives at Cornell contain many of Allen's correspondence, field notebooks, published articles, and other items. These materials are discussed in *Laboratory of Ornithology Newsletter*, Summer 1978. Other correspondence is in the Albert Brand, Paul Kellogg, and William Irving Myers papers at Cornell. Allen discussed "Ornithological Education in America" in *Fifty Years' Progress of American Ornithology* (1933) and construction of the building at Sapsucker Woods in "Cornell's Laboratory of Ornithology" in *The Living Bird* (1962). An excellent discussion of Allen's life and professional accomplishments is "In Memoriam: Arthur A. Allen," by his former student Olin Sewall Pettingill, Jr., in the *Auk* (1968). George Miksch Sutton, another of Allen's former students, described graduate student life in the 1930s in *Bird Student: An Autobiography* (1980). Obituaries are in the *New York Times*, 18 Jan. 1964; *Time*, 24 Jan. 1964; and *Audubon*, May 1964.

KEIR B. STERLING

ALLEN, Catherine (3 Sept. 1851–5 June 1922), Shaker eldress, was born Minnie Catherine Allen in Patriot, Indiana, the daughter of John Allen, a clergyman and reformer, and Ellen Lazarus, a reformer. Allen was born on property purchased by her mother in hopes of establishing another socialistic community like Brook Farm. When no one agreed to engage in this experiment, the family moved in 1857 to the Modern Times Colony in Brentwood, Long Island. At the request of her mother, Allen was brought as a boarder to the North Family of Shakers in Mount Lebanon, New York, on 2 February 1865. Her reception into the Shaker society was somewhat unique because the Shakers rarely accepted children if both parents were alive and neither of them planned to join the community. No doubt Allen was accepted because of her parents' long association with communities such as Brook Farm and because they were sympathetic to the Shakers.

Allen arrived at the North Family on Associate Eldress Anna White's very first day in office. One of the duties of the associate eldress was to care for the young sisters in the family. Thus Allen became White's first "girl" and "was nearer to her in a soul-to-soul relationship than to any other human being" (Taylor, p. 91). Immediately upon Allen's arrival, the Shakers were deeply impressed with her intelligence, "better suited to a scholar of 40 than a girl of 13" (*Springfield (Mass.) Homestead*, 18 May 1908). Although Allen was only supposed to stay with the Shakers for a brief time of rest and relaxation, she never left the community. Symbolic of this lifetime commitment was her name change. By 19 February 1865, less than three weeks after her arrival, Allen began to be called Catherine, her middle name, which she used for the rest of her life.

From the 1840s to the 1920s the North Family was a strong and vocal advocate of reform movements of all kinds, especially in matters of diet, health, agriculture, land distribution, peace, women's rights, and temperance. White, Allen's mentor, was one of the leaders in these liberal reform efforts. Consequently, as Allen grew into young adulthood, she was surrounded by articulate and passionate reformers who saw Shakerism as a unique way to give one's life to both God and humanity.

The few children at the North Family were sent to the district school conducted at the nearby Church Family of Shakers, where Allen enrolled at the start of the girls' term on 3 May 1865. This was to be the last of her formal education. Like other young Shaker women, Allen worked as a housekeeper, cook, and seamstress, taking her place in the rotation of jobs that was part of Shaker daily life. Unlike most of the young people who came into the society in those days, however, Allen embraced the principles of Shakerism and resolved to do all she could to support "the cause." On 12 May 1880 she signed the 1829 North Family Covenant, a legal document that bound the subscriber to a lifelong commitment without any monetary compensation.

Allen worked diligently at the tasks assigned to her by the elders. Gradually these duties included writing poems and essays for the Shaker newspaper the *Manifesto* (1871–1899). Half a dozen of her essays, mostly describing Shaker life and history, were printed for distribution among Shaker societies and throughout the world. By 1890 Allen was also in charge of receiving visitors who came to the North Family. In addition, she managed the Shaker Store, which catered to a busy trade of Shaker fancy goods, postcards, and other small tourist items. To most Shakers, Allen was only one of many bright and devoted members of the most "progressive" family of Shakerism. Since she had never been an eldress or held important office, it was a surprise when she was selected to come into the central ministry to fill the place left vacant by the death of Eldress Helen Augusta Stone in 1908. Allen's designation was the first time a regular member had been appointed directly into the ministry. At the time of her appointment, Allen was characterized as "possessing a clear, comprehensive mind, quick perception, strong conviction, and the courage of conviction, cool in judgement, but intense and persistent of purpose, with excellent business and executive abilities" (*Springfield Homestead*, 18 May 1908).

Allen was associate eldress in the central ministry from 1908 to 1914, when she took the first place, a position she held until her death. Traditionally, the duty of the central ministry was to offer spiritual guidance to the individual families in the Mount Lebanon and Watervliet communities that composed the bishopric. The ministry traveled between each community and stayed a few weeks supervising the elders. In addition, they also maintained general oversight of all of the other Shaker bishoprics. By the time Allen took office, however, it had been more than fifty years since the Shakers had received large numbers of permanent adult converts. One result of this was a severe shortage of capable people to hold the various leadership positions in the Shaker societies. For example, by the 1890s the adjacent Shaker bishopric was dissolved and the direct supervision of the two remaining communities was added to the duties of the central ministry; consequently, the single male member of the ministry went to live in this bishopric. As individual Shaker families declined, the remaining members, often either elderly or very young, were consolidated into a couple of stronger families in a particular society. When these waned, as they all did throughout Shakerdom, the whole community was then sold off. During Allen's tenure, eight of the eighteen major communities closed. With the few competent leaders already struggling to maintain the families in their own societies, the ministry had to assume the task of closing out Shaker societies from New Hampshire to Kentucky. This task, which meant months away from home and constant travel for Allen, included handling the sale and transfer of land and settling displaced Shakers into new homes.

At the same, Allen took general charge of collecting manuscripts and imprints for preservation by non-Shakers. She had always been unhappy that none of her father's papers had survived and was determined that this would not happen with the Shakers. When an individual community closed, she would make sure that local museums and libraries received artifacts and imprints. The bulk of the manuscript material was sent to Wallace H. Cathcart, president of the Western Reserve Historical Society in Cleveland. As a result, more than 10,000 items of Shaker interest were saved, and the Western Reserve collection constitutes the largest holding of Shaker manuscripts in the world. In tribute, the Western Reserve's bookplate for the Shaker Literature and Manuscript Collection bears Allen's image.

When Allen was first appointed to the ministry, an elder wrote that she "would not have accepted the place unless she expects to be able to effect some changes in time." Allen shared the views of the North Family regarding the best way to fashion a numerically declining Shaker society that would meet the needs of a rapidly changing outside world. Shaker history was seen as evolving into a "second cycle" of development.

Looking back at the organizational structure of Shaker communities, Allen wrote, "Now, no intelligent people would think of thus organizing" (*A Century of Communism*, p. 9). Instead, Shakerism would be organized into particular communities of smaller family units, all sharing a fully united interest. In an article for the *Flaming Sword*, Allen wrote that as Shakers "we are lifted up to that higher plane where we become recipients and mediators of those divine truths which constitute us the Zion of God . . . whose light and whose law shall go forth to the nations" (*Most Important Reforms*, p. 14). As a result, Shakers had a duty to "clasp hands with" those in the world "in earnest efforts for the advancement of peace and righteousness" (*Shaker Life and Ideals*, p. 3). In contrast, the surviving Shaker communities were engaged in seemingly futile efforts to preserve old structures, taking relatively little interest in Shaker efforts to reform society at large. Writing to Cathcart, Allen revealed her dissatisfaction: "Should I feel as I go from place to place that there would ever be sufficient responsiveness to my suggestions for progress . . . I would bend all the energies of being to 'labor for a gift' in Ministerial Calling—at present I see no such token." Having never been an elder, moreover, Allen did not have the years of experience offering spiritual advice and leading services from which others before her had benefited. When she failed to emphasize the religious aspects of the ministry's duties, no one else in the ministry was in a position to do so. The other female in the ministry was ninety-year-old Harriet Bullard, who lived in virtual retirement. The lone man, Joseph Holden, lived in a different Shaker community and was completely engaged in management of property and investments. For the first time, no one in the central ministry exercised religious authority, and the remaining Shaker communities had to continue as best they could in this area on their own.

Allen, for her part, longed to return to the ranks of the North Family "where there seems to be more opening for *revision* than in other places" (Allen to Cathcart). While Allen never got to return to the North Family as an ordinary member, she spent her time collecting and preserving manuscripts, handling legal matters, and caring for those who were displaced as communities closed. During her years in office, moreover, as the other members of the ministry resigned or died, Allen chose two North Family Shakers and a man who was an excellent financial manager from the community at Canterbury, New Hampshire, to replace them. This continued the complete transformation of the central ministry into a board of financial supervisors hoping to conserve what they could as Shakerism dissolved. The religious aspects of Shakerism were kept alive only in a few individual members or in some of the communities.

As plans were being made to sell the last remaining Shaker community outside of the Northeast, in South Union, Kentucky, Allen was stricken with cancer. She died at the Second House of the North Family after seven months of terrible suffering. She had been a Shaker fifty-seven years, but the philosophical stance she took regarding the future of Shakerism influenced the actions of the ministry until the 1980s.

• A complete and annotated listing of the published works of Catherine Allen can be found in Mary L. Richmond, *Shaker Literature: A Bibliography* (1977), pp. 4–5. Included are *Questions of the Day* (1888), *The Mirror of Truth: A Vision* (1890?), *A Full Century of Communism: The History of the Alethians, Formerly Called Shakers* (1897), *A Century of Communism: The History of the People Known as Shakers* (1902), *Manna: A Shakeress on the Subject* (n.d.), and *Shaker Life and Ideals* (1906). Also in 1890 Allen wrote the *Biographical Sketch of Daniel Fraser*, a memorial tribute to a Shaker brother. Copies of these imprints and of the memorial book can be found in most collections of Shaker literature. A complete run of the Shaker newspaper, the *Manifesto*, which contains many of Allen's essays and poems, is available in the Shaker Museum and Library, Old Chatham, N.Y. Allen's article "Most Important Reform" for the *Flaming Sword* is in *Fragrance from the Altar of Incense* (1892). The entire collection at the Western Reserve has been microfilmed. Seven of her poems are in a collection of North Family poems, *Mount Lebanon Cedar Boughs* (1895). Testimonies written by Allen can be found in various memorial books written for Shakers between 1890 and 1912, including *A Memorial to Eldress Anna White and Elder Daniel Offord*, comp. Leila S. Taylor (1912), pp. 91–95. Finally, references to Allen can be found in surviving letters at the western Reserve.

STEPHEN J. PATERWIC

ALLEN, Charles Elmer (4 Oct. 1872–25 June 1954), botanist, was born in Horicon, Wisconsin, the son of Charles Allen, a lawyer, and Eliza North. Having graduated from high school at age fourteen, Allen extended his secondary education by two years in order to study German and zoology. In 1888 he taught all grades in a one-room country school, then matriculated at the University of Wisconsin in 1889. His father's death that same year forced him to drop out of school, and for the next six years he supported himself, his mother, and his sister as a court reporter. In 1894 he returned to the university and received a B.S. in 1899 and a Ph.D. in botany in 1904. After graduation, he spent a year at the University of Bonn, Germany, and the Marine Biological Laboratory in Naples, Italy; his work abroad was sponsored by the Carnegie Foundation. He began his academic career as a botany instructor in 1901 while working on his doctorate, and was promoted in 1904 to assistant professor, in 1907 to associate professor, and in 1919 to professor, a position he held until his retirement from Wisconsin in 1943. He married Genevieve Sylvester in 1902; the couple had three children. He spent one semester in 1904 as a visiting professor at Columbia.

As a graduate student, Allen was primarily interested in the study of cytology, or cellular functions. His first publication addressed the tendency of a chloroplast's inner membrane to thicken during cell division before the completion of the outer wall. He also demonstrated for the first time that cell division in the zygote of the green alga *Coleochaete* is meiotic instead of mitotic—that the division results in four gametes instead of two daughter cells—raising the possibility that algae reproduce sexually. After 1905 his research combined his interest in cytology with a new-found interest in heredity, and he worked almost exclusively with the primitive, nonvascular land plants known as bryophytes, commonly known as mosses and liverworts. His first efforts investigated cellular structure, growth, and division in the male organs as well as the development of sperm cells in *Polytrichum juniperinum*, also called hair-cap moss or pigeon wheat, and resulted in a comprehensive description of spermatogenesis in mosses.

Allen next set out to study the various species of *Sphaerocarpos*, a genus of liverworts that are so small and simple that some botanists have suggested that they might have evolved from green algae, as a means to understanding plant heredity. Between 1917 and 1938 he published fourteen articles outlining the three principal discoveries resulting from this line of investigation. Most importantly, he demonstrated that this genus possesses sex chromosomes, the first such discovery in land plants. Allen found that a spore that receives an X chromosome always develops into a female plant, while the spore that receives a Y chromosome always develops into a male plant. The second discovery was that certain mutations either in the protective coverings around sex organs (the tufted character) or that resulted in profuse and irregular branching (the polycladous character) are related in some way to the sex chromosomes. Because these characters are not carried by these chromosomes, Allen concluded that the chromosomes responsible for the mutations associate in some way with the sex chromosomes while they are separating during meiosis. He discovered, however, that the character that prevents the spores of the species *S. donnellii* from adhering to one another upon reaching maturity, unlike other species of *Sphaerocarpos*, is carried by the X chromosome. The third discovery was that some gametophytes, or plants in the sexual stage, possess two sets of chromosomes, and that those gametophytes with one X and one Y chromosome grow sex organs that are partly male and partly female.

In addition to his many scholarly articles, Allen coauthored two texts on botanical studies: *A Textbook of Botany* (1917) and *A Textbook of General Botany* (1924; 2d ed., 1927). He also published two reviews of the literature on the genetics of bryophytes in *Botanical Review* in 1935 and 1945. From 1918 to 1926 he served as general editor of the *American Journal of Botany*. He was a member of the National Research Council from 1925 to 1931 and chaired its Division of Biology and Agriculture (1929–1930). He was president of the Botanical Society of America (1921); the Wisconsin Academy of Sciences, Arts, and Letters (1931–1933); the American Society of Naturalists (1936); and the American Microscopical Society (1944). In 1928 he served as vice president of the Botany Section of the American Association for the Advancement of Science. He was elected to the National Academy of Sciences in 1924. He died in Madison, Wisconsin.

Allen contributed to the advancement of botany by demonstrating the prevalence of sexual reproduction among even the lowest forms of plant life. His work with *Sphaerocarpos* also contributed significantly to a deeper understanding of genetics and heredity in plant life.

• Allen's personal papers did not survive. Gilbert M. Smith, "Charles Elmer Allen," National Academy of Sciences, *Biographical Memoirs* 29 (1956): 3–15, provides a good biographical sketch of Allen as well as a complete bibliography of his scholarly work. The importance of his work is addressed in Erick Vernon Watson, *The Structure and Life of Bryophytes* (1964).

CHARLES W. CAREY, JR.

ALLEN, Edgar (2 May 1892–3 Mar. 1943), endocrinologist and physiologist, was born in Canyon City, Colorado, the son of Asa Allen, a physician and Edith Day. In 1900 the family relocated to Providence, Rhode Island, where Allen grew up. After the death of his father, when Allen was in his early teens, his mother supported the family by working as a librarian and with the help of her children, who held a succession of odd jobs. Allen supported himself through Brown University by waiting on tables, tending furnaces, and teaching swimming among other things. Upon graduating in 1915, he entered the graduate school, from which he received an M.A. in biology with special emphasis on embryology in 1916, after which he continued on for his Ph.D. World War I intervened, however, and he left for France, where he served with a mobile unit of the Sanitary Corps. Allen married Marion Robins Pfeiffer, then a student at Pembroke, the women's college of Brown, in 1918; the couple had two daughters.

In 1919 Allen became an instructor in anatomy at Washington University, St. Louis, Missouri. While there he continued work on his Ph.D. at Brown, receiving that degree in 1921 with a dissertation titled "The Oestrous Cycle of the Mouse." While at Washington University, he entered into collaboration with Edward A. Doisy, who would later be awarded the Nobel Prize. Among other things, the two injected a crude ovarian extract into immature female rats and found that within forty-eight hours the rats went into estrus (the period during the fertility cycle when in subprimate vertebrates the female is both sexually receptive and fertile) just as if they possessed fully mature ovaries. This emphasized the importance of the endocrine glands and their hormonal products on the physiological functions of the body—in this case on sexual receptivity and fertility.

In 1923 Allen was appointed both a professor of anatomy and department chair in the medical school of the University of Missouri at Columbia. In 1930 he was promoted to dean of the medical school and director of the University Hospitals, all the time continuing his collaboration with Doisy on ovarian physiology and endocrinology. In 1929 the two managed to isolate a pure crystal female sex hormone, estrone. Once estrone—the first female hormone to be discovered and isolated—was isolated it could be produced commercially, and it first appeared on the market in 1931. Allen also collaborated with Jean Paul Pratt, a gynecologist from Detroit, and the two shared the credit for removing living ova from the human oviduct for the first time.

It was during this period that Allen both edited and wrote a chapter for the first edition of the pathbreaking *Sex and Internal Secretions* (1932), which was the first collection dealing with the new thoughts in endocrinology and helped establish endocrinology as a science. He also edited the second edition in 1939. Allen left Missouri in 1933 to become professor of anatomy at Yale, where he further studied reproductive endocrinology, setting up new laboratories to pursue his growing interest in the relationship between sex hormones and cancer. During his lifetime he produced more than 140 papers dealing with such topics as the relationship between estrogen and rapid malignant cell growth (i.e., cancer), estrogen and the onset of puberty, and mammalian ova formation. Regardless of the topic, all his publications contained methodological information of value to subsequent researchers in endocrinology. Much of his research was supported by the Committee for Research in Problems of Sex.

Allen was president in 1941–1942 of the American Society for the Study of Internal Secretions (later known as the Endocrine Society). He was also president of the American Association of Anatomists, a post he held at the time of his death. Among his prizes and awards were enrollment in the Legion of Honor in Paris in 1937 and receipt of the Baly Medal from the Royal College of Physicians in London in 1941.

Although he suffered a severe coronary occlusion in 1934, Allen returned to work after his recovery and during World War II joined the Coast Guard Auxiliary. He died of a heart attack while on duty.

Allen, with his discovery of estrogen and the hormonal mechanisms that control the female reproductive cycle, was a major figure in the development of the science of endocrinology, now one of the most significant branches of modern biology. His discoveries had practical importance, and the oral contraceptive is a natural outgrowth of his work.

• The most complete biographical account is in William C. Young, ed., *Sex and Internal Secretions*, 3d ed., vol. 1 (1961), pp. xiii–xix. A biographical account appears in *Yale Journal of Biology and Medicine* 15 (1943): 641–44; the same journal lists a bibliography of his publications in 17, pt. 1 (1944–1945): 2–12. Obituary notices include George W. Corner, C. H. Danforth, and L. S. Stone, *Anatomical Record* 87 (Aug. 1943), and W. U. Gardner, *Science* 97, no. 2521 (23 Apr. 1943): 368.

VERN L. BULLOUGH

ALLEN, Edmund Turney (4 Jan. 1896–18 Feb. 1943), test pilot, was born in Chicago, Illinois, the son of Edmund Allen, a preacher, and Abby Irene Dyer. A shy, frail-looking person, "Eddie" Allen moved around with his family before returning to Chicago, where he graduated from high school in 1913. He was initially drawn to farm work, but his mother and sister convinced him to attend the University of Illinois, which he did in 1916–1917. He then enlisted in the infantry before attending officers' training camp at Fort Sheridan, Illinois, where he became interested in aviation.

At first pessimistic about learning to fly, he nevertheless graduated and became a pilot instructor in the Signal Corps and then began to test aircraft in both the United States and England. In 1919 he became one of the first pilots for the National Advisory Committee for Aeronautics (NACA), where he remained until 1922, all the while attending courses at the University of Illinois and the Massachusetts Institute of Technology, where Edward Pearson Warner, the head of NACA, also taught engineering. From then on, Allen distinguished himself as a master test pilot, eventually reforming the popular daredevil image of test pilots into one of meticulous engineering expertise and patience. Allen's first test project for NACA, flying the Curtiss JN-4 "Jenny," demonstrated clearly that without competent and cooperative test pilots, NACA scientists would have been unable to experiment successfully with aerodynamic forms and shapes. Allen moved on to testing airplanes for the U.S. Signal Corps from 1922 to 1925. During that time he also contributed articles to *Aviation* on light planes and gliders. He then worked four years as a U.S. mail pilot for United Airlines. In 1928–1929 he enrolled at the University of Utah, where he wrote a pioneering senior thesis on pilot stress.

Eventually Allen returned to flight testing, working first for Boeing in 1930 and then as an independent test pilot and consultant for many aircraft manufacturers and airlines. In the 1930s Allen proved the correctness of his testing philosophy. By collaborating with the airplane designer, engineer, and manufacturer, the pilot could prevent technical oversights before they occurred. By the end of that decade Allen's scientific approach to flight testing had established him as the preeminent authority on the stability and control of heavy aircraft.

With such a legacy, Allen returned to Boeing in 1939 after convincing the company to establish an independent department of aerodynamics and flight research, of which he became head. His reputation by then was one of unquestioned integrity and technical expertise. That same year he was awarded the first Octave Chanute Medal, given to pilots making outstanding contributions in the aeronautical sciences. Also in 1939 he married Florence Lee Brydon; they would have two children. Soon after his marriage, Allen flight-tested the Boeing 314 hydroplane, which required directional fin modifications before it entered service. Such tests once again proved the necessity of direct interaction between testers and designers. Although engineers and airline executives were disappointed with the delays caused by the fin change, the aircraft then became one of the safest large hydroplanes built.

Allen's dedication to scientifically solving flight problems extended beyond initial flight testing. For example, he worked in 1941 to solve the problems fliers had reported on the initial bombing runs of the B-17. A year later Boeing again asked Allen to work on testing a new aircraft, the B-29 "Superfortress." Allen had warned air force officials that testing would require at least two hundred hours of flight over five months, since the aircraft was a financial and engineering gamble. His caution proved correct, as the test machines developed serious engine troubles that cost Allen his life. Allen was unable to control a fire that spread to his machine's gas tanks, causing the plane to crash in Seattle, Washington, killing all on board and several on the ground. An inquiry found quality control deficiency on the part of the engine manufacturer, which later was corrected. Unfortunately Allen's warnings were insufficient to prevent his untimely death. In tribute to him, the Boeing company named a research facility in his memory. He was also awarded posthumously the Guggenheim aeronautical medal.

Commenting on the evolution of his profession in one of his 1937 articles, Allen wrote, "Under the changing conditions of increasing knowledge, fatalistic risk-taking becomes ignorant recklessness." By applying such caution, Allen and many of his successors were able to improve markedly on the quality and safety of American aircraft production.

• The National Air and Space Museum of the Smithsonian Institution has a biographical file that contains a series of clippings as well as a partial bibliography of Allen's articles. His senior thesis, "The Problem of Operating and Navigating an Airplane under Stress," is in the Marriott Library at the University of Utah. Thomas Collison, *The Superfortress Is Born* (1945), contains valuable information on Allen's role in developing the B-29 bomber. See also Richard P. Hallion, *Test Pilots: The Frontiersmen of Flight* (1981), and G. Edward Pendray, ed., *The Guggenheim Medalists: Architects of the Age of Flight* (1964), pp. 84–85.

GUILLAUME DE SYON

ALLEN, Edward Tyson (26 Dec. 1875–27 May 1942), forester and conservationist, was born in New Haven, Connecticut, the son of Oscar Dana Allen, a professor of analytical chemistry at the Massachusetts Institute of Technology and Yale, and Fidelia Roberts Totman. Educated in the public schools and privately by his father, Allen moved with his family first to California and later to Washington State, where they lived near Mount Rainier. He began work as a reporter for the *Tacoma Ledger* in 1897.

Allen started work as a forest ranger in 1898 and entered the Bureau of Forestry (renamed the U.S. Forest Service) in 1899. He assisted Gifford Pinchot, Theodore Roosevelt's farsighted chief of the Bureau of Forestry, in the writing of a comprehensive forest reserve manual in 1902. The following year he helped determine forest reserve boundaries in the Pacific Northwest under the guidance of Pinchot. Also in 1903 Allen created a method of appraising timber value that became standard practice in the Forest Service. Through determining price, labor, equipment expense, and selling price he correctly determined that the red fir (Douglas fir) would provide the lumber industry with stable profits if harvested at maturity. This allowed younger trees to remain untouched. He served as the first California state forester in 1905 and in 1906 was put in charge of establishing and administering national forests in Oregon, Alaska, and Washington. In 1908–1910 he served as district inspector in the U.S. Forest Service and first district forester of the Pacific Northwest region.

In 1909 Allen helped organize and manage the Western Forestry and Conservation Association (WFCA) under the direction of the lumber industry. The WFCA, a regional alliance of private, state, and federal forest agencies in Montana, Idaho, California, Oregon, Alaska, and Washington, hoped to coordinate fire prevention campaigns with state governments, requiring the disposal of flammable logging slash and the protection of the Pacific Northwest's woodlands through reforestation. This type of cooperation, according to Allen, "created an unprecedented medium for advancing the science of forest protection." He advised timber owners in the western states that forest maintenance would be to their advantage. Investing in fire prevention through the WFCA resulted in more merchantable timber and less idle or cutover land. Allen served as head of the organization until his retirement in 1932.

Typical of his day, Allen believed that close cooperation between business, government, and private interests was of mutual benefit and led to effective organization. He encouraged local associations, education, and all forms of public activities in order to disseminate information on forest protection. During the First World War Allen served as a member of the Building Materials Division of the War Industries Board (later called the Lumber Division), involved in the purchase of lumber for ship and army cantonment construction. He is given much of the credit for the successful settlement of spruce production problems. Spruce was a key ingredient in the construction of aircraft. As an expert in forest taxation and economics, Allen served as counsel to the National Lumber Manufacturers Association, the U.S. Treasury Department, the Federal Trade Commission, and the Interior and Agricultural departments. In so doing he helped formulate local and national forestry policy codes stressing the importance of fire prevention, reforestation, and conservation.

Allen was particularly interested in the reforestation of deforested land in the Pacific Northwest. As these areas increased in lumber production, so would the exhaustion of forest land. Reforestation of these areas would create, in time, mature timber that would ensure a continued lumber supply into the future. In his 1911 book, *Practical Forestry*, Allen introduced the notion that "the forest is a community resource and that its wasteful destruction injures their welfare" (pp. 3–4). He laid out how forest fires, idleness, and cutover land represented costly community losses as a tax resource and in productive capacity. Forest yield taxes and cutover land taxes could be quickly recouped through reforestation of the area and close second-crop management. Allen realized that if the people of the Pacific Northwest understood the economic importance of forest management and conservation, the area would be "destined to be the Nation's great permanent wood-lot" (Allen, "Wood-lot," p. 153) and the United States would have no need to import timber supplies.

Continuing in this effort into the 1920s, Allen worked with William Greeley, head of the Forest Service, in furthering cooperative relations in forest management. He helped draft the Clarke-McNary Act of 1924, calling for some federal regulation of timber activities by creating cooperative federal, state, and private programs for fire protection, reforestation, and purchase of cutover land. Three years before his death Allen helped write the Sustained-Yield Forest Management Act of 1944. It hoped to continue cooperative arrangements in the West through responsible private ownership of timberlands. This act proved very unpopular with the Forest Service, which desired to regulate private and public timberlands against lumber companies' monopolies. Allen's ideas on forest management appear to provide a defense for timber production over forest conservation. He, however, recognized the need for compromises between private, industrial, and public needs for mutual benefit. He dedicated his life's work to this effort.

Allen married Matilda Price Riley in 1902. They had two children. After her death in 1927, he married Mildred Grudolf-Smith in 1928; the couple had no children. Allen was a charter member of the Society of American Foresters (1900). He authored many articles for journals such as *Sunset: Pacific Monthly*, *World's Work*, *Outlook*, and numerous science magazines. He retired from active forestry work a number of years before his death in Portland, Oregon.

• Allen's papers, 1903–1931, located at the Oregon Historical Society, include WFCA correspondence, poems, and a tribute by A. Whisnant. See Allen's complete entry in the *North American Forest History: Guide to Archives and Manuscripts*. Selected articles by Allen include "Method of Forestry Campaigning," *American Forestry*, Oct. 1912; "Conservation That Pays Its Way," *World's Work*, July 1913, pp. 310–15; and "Guarding the Nation's Wood-Lot," *Outlook*, 26 Jan. 1921, pp. 153–54. For a complete description of his ideas on forest management, see Allen, *Practical Forestry in the Pacific Northwest* (1911). For information about Allen's career, see J. Upham, "Organizer of the Western Forestry and Conservation Association," *Sunset: Pacific Monthly*, Sept. 1916, p. 29; Shirley Allen, "We Present E. T. Allen," *Journal of Forestry* 43 (1945): 222–23; Clyde Martin, "History and Influence of the Western Forestry and Conservation Association in Cooperative Forestry in the West," *Journal of Forestry* 43 (1945): 167–70; and Eloise Hamilton, *Forty Years of Western Forestry: A History of the Movement to Conserve Forest Resources by Cooperative Effort, 1909–1949* (1949). Allen's stint in the War Industries Board is described in Grosvenor Clarkson, *Industrial America in the World War* (1923). For more recent information about Allen's role, see Harold Steen, *The US Forest Service: A History* (1977), and David Clary, *Timber and the Forest Service* (1986). Obituaries are in the *Journal of Forestry* 40 (1942): 574–75 and the *Portland Oregonian*, 28 May 1942.

VERONICA JUNE BRUCE

ALLEN, Elisha Hunt (28 Jan. 1804–1 Jan. 1883), congressman and diplomat, was born in New Salem, Massachusetts, the son of Samuel Clesson Allen, a lawyer and later a congressman, and Mary Hunt. He graduated with honors from Williams College in 1823, studied law in his father's office, was admitted to the bar in 1825, and worked as an attorney for two years in Brattleboro, Vermont. In 1828 he married Sarah E. Fessenden; they had four children. That same year he moved to Bangor, Maine, where he formed a law partnership with John Appleton (1804–1891), who later became Maine's chief justice.

Allen was first elected to the Maine legislature in 1835, serving from 1836 to 1841 and from 1838 to 1841 as Speaker. During his tenure in the state's legislature, Allen played a prominent role in negotiating the boundary dispute between Maine and the province of New Brunswick, Canada. He was elected to Congress as a Whig in 1840 and, as a member of the House Committee on Foreign Affairs, continued to work on the northeastern boundary crisis, which was settled by the Ashburton Treaty of 1842. He was defeated for reelection in 1842 but was again elected to Maine's legislature in 1846. He moved to Boston about a year later, practiced law, was elected to the Massachusetts legislature in 1848, and in 1849 was appointed U.S. consul and diplomatic agent in Honolulu by Whig president Zachary Taylor.

Allen's move from Massachusetts to Hawaii paralleled the move of New England's whaling industry from the exhausted waters of the North Atlantic to the yet untapped Pacific, which had begun in the 1820s. The rich hunting grounds of the Central and North Pacific, high whale oil and bone prices, and Hawaii's proximity to all of the Pacific's whaling fields drew hundreds of vessels annually to the islands. At the time of Allen's arrival, American ships dominated the trade, outnumbering other foreign vessels by over 40 to 1 between 1845 and 1854, and American ships visited Honolulu and Lahaina more frequently than all other ports in the world during the 1840s and 1850s. In addition, Hawaii's independence and political future were actively contested by the Hawaiian monarchy, resident whites, and Great Britain, France, and the United States. As a result, the U.S. consular office in Honolulu was a busy place. Recognizing its strategic importance, Allen sought to secure Hawaii for the United States through annexation and later through a reciprocity treaty that would tie the island kingdom to America economically.

Allen became a naturalized citizen of Hawaii, and in 1854 he was appointed Hawaii's minister of finance during a government shake-up caused by charges of inefficiency and abuses among the king's ministers leveled by foreigners organized as the Committee of Thirteen. He supported the efforts of the Hawaiian government in 1854 to sign a treaty of annexation with the United States that was stimulated by rumors of a planned coup by the Committee of Thirteen to overthrow the monarchy and establish a white republic. Allen took the treaty of cession to Washington, but the death of Kamehameha III and the accession of a new king, Kamehameha IV, who despised Americans, ended that first annexation attempt. His first wife had died in 1845, and in 1857 Allen married Mary Harrod Hobbes; they had two children.

In 1857 Allen was appointed chief justice and chancellor of the kingdom, posts he retained for about twenty years. A fellow member of the foreign diplomatic community who was later a Hawaiian minister described Allen as "very popular and much respected, an outstanding member of the Hawaiian bench" who had "the capacity for winning the assent and sympathy even of his opposition" (de Varigny, p. 59). Allen became an intimate member of the inner circle of a succession of kings and was a leading figure in determining government policy during the 1860s. He was sent to Washington in 1856, 1864, and several times during the early 1870s to negotiate a treaty of reciprocity with the United States to open America's market to Hawaiian sugar. He described those missions that culminated with the signing on 30 January 1875 and final passage of reciprocity the following year as the most strenuous time of his life. Reciprocity boosted Hawaii's sugar industry and drew the kingdom closer to American annexation, leading to a spectacular increase in sugar production, the rapid growth of banking, shipping, and industries allied to the growing and marketing of sugar, and labor migration from Europe and Asia, which resulted in a more racially and ethnically diverse population. In 1877 Allen was appointed to Washington as Hawaii's resident minister to ensure the passage of the reciprocity treaty, which came up for renewal every seven years. At the time of his death, Allen faced a formidable opposition led by eastern refiners and southern sugar producers, who charged that free trade drained the U.S. treasury and that Hawaii's plantations employed "slave labor." Allen did not live to see the treaty's renewal in 1884 because he died suddenly at the president's New Year's reception at the White House.

As an American and a naturalized citizen of Hawaii, Allen served both of his countries effectively and faithfully in the roles of lawyer, politician, jurist, and diplomat. He favored U.S. annexation, but only insofar as agreed to by the Hawaiian monarchy. His principal accomplishment—the reciprocity treaty of 1876—led to economic growth but also unleashed forces that sealed the fate of the kingdom's independence and hastened the monarchy's demise.

• Allen's papers are in the Library of Congress, Washington, D.C., and the State Archives of Hawaii, Honolulu. For occasional references to Allen's career, see Gavan Daws, *Shoal of Time: A History of the Hawaiian Islands* (1968); Charles de Varigny, *Fourteen Years in the Sandwich Islands, 1855–1868*, trans. Alfons L. Korn (1981); and Ralph S. Kuykendall and A. Grove Day, *Hawaii: A History* (1961). The long obituary in the *Washington Post*, 2 Jan. 1883, is factually unreliable.

GARY Y. OKIHIRO

ALLEN, Elizabeth Akers (9 Oct. 1832–7 Aug. 1911), poet and journalist, was born Elizabeth Ann Chase in Strong, Maine, the second of three daughters of Thomas Chase, a carpenter and circuit preacher, and Mercy Fenno Barton. Her childhood was traumatic. A fourth sibling died accidentally, and her frail mother, whose medical treatments led Elizabeth to vow to murder the doctor, died in 1836. Her father placed his daughters separately with acquaintances until he remarried the following year. Four-year-old Elizabeth's foster parents forced her to work, whipped her, and shut her in the cellar when she failed to meet their expectations. She had some schooling at Farmington (Maine) Academy. She wrote her first verses at age twelve; these were published in a Vermont newspaper, having been submitted without her knowledge. Eager to escape a grim home, she began working at thirteen, first in a sweatshop-like bookbindery, later as a teacher.

Financial need exacerbated by men drove Elizabeth's literary career. So consistent was this pattern in her mind that in 1904 she wrote a 49-page financial memoir detailing how "nearly every man with whom I have come in business contact has seemed to see in me an easy victim, and has managed—most of them under the guise of sincere friendship—in fleecing me out of nearly every cent I had." In 1851 she married Marshall Taylor, an insurance agent, whose business she tended while he "went gunning, played ball, and rode around 'on business.'" Soon after their child was born in 1852, Taylor left for California. Elizabeth earned money writing, taking a job as assistant editor of the *Portland (Maine) Transcript* in 1855. She divorced Taylor when, around 1857, he claimed money the *San Francisco Chronicle* owed her for writing; according to law, a married woman's money legally was her husband's.

Her first book of poems, *Forest Buds, from the Woods of Maine* (1856), appeared under the pseudonym Florence Percy, which she had used since adolescence. In 1858 she met Benjamin "Paul" Akers, a talented Maine sculptor. Akers, who fancied her another Elizabeth Barrett Browning, persuaded her that a year in Europe paid for by the earnings from her book would benefit her writing. During 1859–1860 she traveled in France, Germany, and Italy with Akers and an older female companion, sending correspondence to the *Transcript* and the *Boston Evening Gazette*. While Elizabeth pennypinched, Paul wooed her and used her money to maintain appearances with fashionable friends. He was gravely ill with tuberculosis when they married in Portland in 1860; they moved to Philadelphia to escape hard winters, but he died in 1861. Their child died in infancy. Left nearly penniless, Elizabeth resumed her position at the *Transcript*, then, during the Civil War in 1863, took a clerkship with the

War Office in Washington, D.C. She was in Ford's Theater the night Abraham Lincoln was shot. Two of her strongest poems, "In the Defenses" and "Spring at the Capital," describe Washington during and after the war.

Elizabeth Akers first contributed to the *Atlantic Monthly* in 1858, and her poems appeared in leading literary journals through the remainder of her life. She sent "Rock Me to Sleep," destined to become one of the most popular American poems of the century, to the *Saturday Evening Post* from Rome in 1860. The poem's cry addressed to a dead mother seeking rest from a difficult world took hold during the Civil War. Thirty composers set it to music; thousands of copies were distributed to Union soldiers; it was sung around campfires, quoted in novels and plays, and collected in patriotic anthologies. Alexander M. W. Ball, a New Jersey legislator, contested her authorship of the poem and produced evidence that he wrote it himself, but a *New York Times* article vindicated her authorship in 1867.

In 1865 Akers married a merchant, Elijah M. Allen, whom she met in Washington, D.C., but she continued to feel "fleeced" in this marriage. She and her husband moved frequently, living in Richmond, Virginia, from 1866 to 1873, then briefly in Ridgewood, New Jersey, before returning to Maine where Allen worked as the literary editor of the *Portland Daily Advertiser* from 1874 to 1881. In 1882 they settled in Tuckahoe, New York. In her financial memoir, Allen charged that her husband mishandled the negotiation of royalties for her second book, *Poems* (1866), invested her earnings badly, and kept her on a stringent allowance. Her later verse was collected in *The Silver Bridge and Other Poems* (1886), *The High-Top Sweeting and Other Poems* (1891), and *The Sunset Song and Other Verses* (1902). Despite the apparently conventional piety of much of her verse, at her request no religious ceremony was conducted when she died in Tuckahoe.

Allen's career is representative of those nineteenth-century American women who, when they needed to support themselves, found literary work among the few middle-class occupations open to them. Whether Allen and others like her could have written more enduring poetry had financial need not pressed on them is open to debate. Later critics attacked Allen's "sing-song" style, but regular rhythm is of value when poems are sung or performed, as Allen's frequently were. Her poems were widely anthologized, and literary figures as distinguished as William Cullen Bryant, John Greenleaf Whittier, and Edmund Clarence Stedman recognized her contribution to articulating the emotional tone of the times. The cultural impact of a poem as popular as "Rock Me to Sleep" is inestimable. Allen's career spanned a half century when distinctions between high and popular poetry were forming in American literary criticism. Praised for her sweetness early in her career, she was dismissed as bathetic by the century's end. Yet, like other popular sentimental poetry, Allen's verse says much about its era and often has witty, angry, and Gothic edges.

• Allen's "History of One Woman's Financial Experiences" (1904) and other papers are held at Colby College Library. Richard Cary summarizes some of these materials in "The Misted Prism: Paul Akers and Elizabeth Akers Allen," *Colby Library Quarterly* 7, no. 5 (Mar. 1966): 193–227, with the distorting aim of psychoanalyzing her and exonerating him. Sources on the debate over authorship of "Rock Me to Sleep" are O. A. Morse, *A Vindication of the Claim of Alexander M. W. Ball* (1867), and E. W. Leavenworth, ed., *Who Wrote "Rock Me to Sleep"?* (1870). Reviews of Allen's work appear in *The Nation* 3 (1866), *Atlantic Monthly*, Mar. 1887, and the *Dial*, Jan. 1903. See also John T. Winterich's posthumous assessment, "Elizabeth Akers and the Unsubstantial Character of Fame," *Colophon* 4 (Oct. 1933). An obituary is in the *New York Times*, 9 Aug. 1911.

JANET GRAY

ALLEN, Ethan (10 Jan. 1738–12 Feb. 1789), frontier revolutionary leader and author of the first deistic work by an American, was born in Litchfield, Connecticut, the son of Joseph Allen and Mary Baker, farmers. Allen served briefly in the French and Indian War and in 1762 began operating a productive iron forge in Salisbury, Connecticut. That same year he married Mary Brownson, with whom he would have five children. But Allen's deism and aggressive personal conduct ruined his early prospects: he was warned out of Salisbury in 1765 and Northampton, Massachusetts, in 1767.

Allen turned next to hunting, at which he excelled. In 1770 he moved to the Green Mountains, then part of New York, and began investing in nearly worthless New Hampshire titles to these lands. Within a year Allen had become the leader and chief propagandist of the largely bloodless resistance to New York's jurisdiction. In 1771 he founded the Green Mountain Boys to enforce a competing group of settlers' authority in the region, calling down a £100 reward from New York for Allen's capture.

In his many newspaper articles and books, Allen argued that the land belonged to those who worked it, with or without proper legal title. The settlers were therefore entirely justified in resisting those who tried to steal that land. As Allen wrote in the *Connecticut Courant* (31 Mar. 1772), "we mean no more by that which is called the Mob, but to defend our just Rights and Properties." After four years in which he had successfully nullified New York's rule in the Green Mountains, Allen extended that reasoning to mandate the people's right to create their own state and formulate its government according to their desires. It was at this point that the British government took notice and planned to send troops to quell this frontier uprising in May 1775.

But the confrontations at Lexington and Concord interfered. On 10 May 1775 Allen led his Green Mountain Boys in a bold surprise attack on Fort Ticonderoga. Within two days Allen's forces had captured control of Lake Champlain without a single casualty. News of this first offensive victory instantly made Allen a hero, and Congress awarded him command of the Green Mountain Regiment of the Continental army. But the elderly leaders of the Green Mountain towns distrusted Allen as too radical and gave the command to his cousin Seth Warner.

Undeterred, Allen joined General Richard Montgomery's staff as a recruiter, enlisting Indians and Québecois to join the forces invading Canada. In a daring effort to capture a weakly defended Montreal with an equally small force of New Englanders and Québecois, Allen was taken prisoner by the British. Over the next two years he suffered a brutal captivity in British prisons, aboard prison ships, and in the New York City jail. Thanks to the efforts of his family, Allen's cruel treatment at the hands of the British became a cause célèbre. Finally exchanged in May 1778 for Lieutenant Colonel Archibald Campbell, Allen wrote a narrative of his captivity that lacerated the British as vindictive monsters while calling on Americans to forsake any thought of compromise. Allen's *Narrative of Colonel Ethan Allen's Captivity* (1779) was an enormous success, going through eight editions in two years, and is rated second among best-selling books of the revolutionary period after Thomas Paine's *Common Sense*.

During Allen's absence from the Green Mountains, the region had declared its independence and become the state of Vermont, though not without the continuing opposition of New York. Between 1778 and 1784 Allen operated as commander in chief of Vermont's military forces, unofficial member of its legislature, chief diplomat, adviser to Governor Thomas Chittenden, and ex officio judge of Vermont's court of confiscation. Allen devoted his energies in these years to defending his state, adopting policies that tarnished his fame as a patriot. From 1778 to 1781 Allen tried to convince Congress to accept Vermont's statehood. But twice Congress reneged on promises to admit Vermont into the Union when the government of New York threatened to abandon the revolutionary struggle. In a dangerous gambit, Allen opened negotiations with the British commander in Canada, General Frederick Haldimand, to determine possible grounds for Vermont's joining the British Empire as an autonomous province. Over the next three years Allen played back and forth between Congress and Britain, keeping each just slightly informed of his dialogue with the other, even while steering Vermont on an entirely independent course. By 1784 Allen dropped the Haldimand negotiations as passions within New York died down. In 1786 he used the upheaval of Shays's Rebellion to persuade the New York elite of Vermont's reliability, rejecting Shays's offer of leadership and keeping Vermont neutral. Within months, New York's legislature abandoned the fight to reclaim Vermont, though its governor, George Clinton (1739–1812), refused to approve Vermont's entry into the Union until 1791.

In the meantime Allen's personal life had undergone change. His first wife died in 1783, and a year later he married Frances Montresor Buchanan. There were three children by this second marriage.

Though lacking a formal education, Allen had aspirations to be accepted as an Enlightenment philosopher. From 1781 to 1785 he worked to reach these ambitions in a book, *Reason the Only Oracle of Man* (1785). One-third of this long book is devoted to showing the logical fallacies of Christianity, the other two-thirds to putting forth a deistic religion of nature. Most copies of *Reason* were destroyed in a fire, generally assumed to be intentionally set by religious opponents. Most who read *Reason* were shocked by its contents and dismissed it and its author as "atheist." This first American deistic work faded from sight, though not before destroying Allen's reputation.

Many Americans were repelled by Allen's religious heresies, agreeing with the Reverend Lemuel Hopkins's portrait of a frontier thug: "One hand is clench'd to batter noses, / While t'other scrawls 'gainst Paul and Moses." Others found his political views reprehensible. The Loyalist Peter Oliver thought Allen was "of a bad Character, & had been guilty of Actions bad enough to forfeit even a good one." But despite Allen's religious views, even many political opponents shared George Washington's estimation that "There is an original something in him that commands admiration." Allen himself gloried in the controversies he raised as what he called a "clodhopper philosopher" (letter to Crèvecoeur, 2 Mar. 1786).

Despite his disappointment with *Reason* for failing to raise more of a firestorm, Allen enjoyed his brief retirement. In 1786 he made an enormously successful journey to the Wyoming Valley of Pennsylvania that helped to secure the squatters in gaining title to the land they worked. He died near his home in Colchester, Vermont.

• Archival materials include the Ethan Allen Papers at the Vermont State Archives, Montpelier, and the Allen Family Papers in the Bailey/Howe Library at the University of Vermont, Burlington. Many other Allen papers are published in E. P. Walton, ed., *Records of the Council of Safety and Governor and Council of the State of Vermont*, vols. 1 and 2 (1873–1874), and Vermont Historical Society, *Collections of the Vermont Historical Society*, vol. 1 (1870). Works by Allen not mentioned in the text are *A Brief Narrative of the Proceedings of the Government of New York* (1774); *The Proceedings of the Convention of the Representatives of the New-Hampshire Settlers* (1775); *An Andimadversory Address to the Inhabitants of the State of Vermont* (1778); *A Vindication of the Opposition of the Inhabitants of Vermont* (1779); with Jonas Fay, *A Concise Refutation of the Claims of New-Hampshire* (1780); and with several others, *The Present State of the Controversy* (1782). A number of these works are reprinted in J. Kevin Graffagnino, *Ethan and Ira Allen: Collected Works* (3 vols., 1992). On Allen's life, see John Pell, *Ethan Allen* (1929), and Michael Bellesiles, *Revolutionary Outlaws* (1993).

MICHAEL BELLESILES

ALLEN, Florence Ellinwood (23 Mar. 1884–12 Sept. 1966), federal judge, was born in Salt Lake City, Utah, the daughter of Clarence Emir Allen, a lawyer, congressman, and mine manager, and Corinne Marie Tuckerman, a women's club leader. In 1904 she earned a bachelor's degree Phi Beta Kappa from the women's college of Western Reserve University in Cleveland. She then worked for two years in Berlin,

Germany, as a music critic. Returning to Cleveland, she taught at a private girls' school. Lacking the talent for a concert piano career and bored by teaching duties, she took a master's degree in political science from Western Reserve in 1908. The public law courses reminded her of the exciting connection between law and social reform, exemplified by her father's political career.

At first her desire to attend law school was thwarted by the sex-exclusive rule of her alma mater. In 1909, admitted to the University of Chicago law school, she felt uncomfortable as the only woman in some of her classes, and she soon discovered that Dean Roscoe Pound did not want women in the legal profession. The sexism at Chicago in addition to her lack of money for tuition and living expenses led her to move to New York City in 1910, where she lived at the Henry Street Settlement and worked at the League for the Protection of Immigrants. The next year, after discovering that Columbia University's law school only admitted women for summer sessions, she enrolled at New York University law school, where she found an environment friendly to women. She supported herself through law school by lecturing and serving as local secretary for the College Equal Suffrage Association. She received her LL.B. in 1913, second in her class.

Allen passed the Ohio bar on returning to Cleveland in 1914, started a small private practice, and provided legal services for the poor. She combined her interests in the Democratic party and women's rights by campaigning throughout Ohio and from Virginia to Montana for national suffrage and the Woodrow Wilson ticket. Her first important appellate case was before the Ohio Supreme Court, where in 1916 she argued successfully for the city charter right of women to vote in municipal elections (the county board of elections had refused to give ballots to women). She was the first woman to argue a case before the War Labor Board when she was hired by the National Women's Trade Union League in 1919 to represent female streetcar conductors who were denied membership in the all-male union and then fired by the company as former male employees returned from war.

Her career in public office began in 1919 with an appointment as assistant prosecutor by the Democratic boss of Cuyahoga County. On the adoption of the Nineteenth Amendment she ran for common pleas judge and through the efforts of civic groups and suffragists became the first woman in the nation to serve on a general jurisdiction court. The other trial judges offered her a separate division to handle family cases, but she declined such segregation and took a traditional criminal division. While on the bench she introduced innovations to improve court administration, prevent delay, and ameliorate the harsh conditions of bail and jail. She was the first woman to sentence a defendant to the death penalty, and she sent the chief judge of the Cleveland municipal court to prison.

In 1922, with the enthusiastic campaigning of members of county "Florence Allen Clubs," Allen won election as an independent to the Ohio Supreme Court. She was the first woman on a state's highest court and was reelected with minimal competition in 1928. On the court her votes in support of labor's right to picket and to receive reasonable compensation for job-related injuries followed the reform philosophy she learned from her parents. However, she failed to protect the equal right of a black woman student to residence facilities, a mistake that cost her the support of the National Association for the Advancement of Colored People at the Senate hearing on her federal court nomination. She wrote the opinions for the court in several landmark decisions, finding the progressive innovations of city manager and zoning plans constitutional. She was far ahead of her time in affirming Ohio's authority to equalize tax funding of school districts, in protecting the right to counsel and fair hearing in criminal cases, and in recognizing the legitimacy of sex harassment claims. Experience with state cases involving municipalities and power companies prepared her to handle similar issues on the federal bench.

Two unsuccessful campaigns for Congress, in the 1926 election for the Senate and in the 1932 election for the House of Representatives, where her father had served, persuaded her not to count on winning a third term to her state's highest court. Although she had served as a national committeewoman for Ohio and on the county central committee and had paid her dues campaigning for party candidates, organized Democrats gave little support to higher political ambitions. Her alternative was to win appointment to a life-tenured federal judgeship. Lobbied by national and state leaders of women's, reform, labor, and business associations, Ohio senator Robert J. Buckley agreed to support her candidacy for a vacancy on the Sixth Circuit Court of Appeals. Eleanor Roosevelt and Molly Dewson, director of the women's division at party headquarters, acted as intermediaries to the president. The Senate Judiciary Committee approved her nomination in 1934 with ill-concealed distaste, and she moved into her new office in Cincinnati.

Allen's most significant court assignment was to preside over the 1937 civil action brought by private utility companies against the Tennessee Valley Authority for unfair competition. She supervised a long and difficult trial and wrote a lengthy opinion, finding the broad powers delegated to the authority constitutional and thus establishing a favorable doctrine for other New Deal public works programs. The Supreme Court upheld her ruling (*Tennessee Electric Power Co. v. TVA*, 1939). In a 1942 case involving wheat crop controls, Allen dissented from the panel majority and supported a considerable expansion of congressional power to regulate the economy; the Supreme Court reversed, following her reasoning. However, none of the brethren in the Sixth Circuit welcomed her presence; Judge Xenophon Hicks initially refused to look at or speak to her. The male judges lunched at the exclusionary University Club; she took noon walks. Allen volunteered to write opinions in complex cases to prove her competence to her colleagues, and by the

1950s the patent bar recognized her expertise in handling patent infringement appeals. In 1955 she wrote the first federal appellate opinion approving the order to integrate public housing. Her liberalism matched her times: favorable to government regulation of the economy and government protection of basic rights and equal treatment.

Allen had the qualifications of the typical U.S. Supreme Court justice: a politically active and knowledgeable family, an elite education, and a preparatory period on the lower federal bench. Women's civic and professional associations pushed her candidacy for eleven successive associate justice vacancies on the Supreme Court from 1937 through 1949, albeit with decreasing energy. Two associations, the National Federation of Business and Professional Women and the National Association of Women Lawyers, of which she was a founding member, provided continuous nationwide support for Allen's promotion. A Committee for the Advancement of Women Lawyers to High Judicial Office, created for her in 1941, worked for her elevation, as did women judges, including Annabel Matthews of the U.S. Tax Court and Sarah Hughes, then on a Texas trial court and later on federal district court. Allen did not discourage their efforts and, in fact, her chambers and home were the heart of the campaigns. The vacancies that occurred in 1939 offered her the best opportunities, and the actions of her opponents in planting critical stories in the press indicate their serious concern over her candidacy. When India Edwards, director of the women's division of the Democratic National Committee, pressed President Harry S. Truman to appoint Allen to the Supreme Court in 1949, he asked Chief Justice Frederick Moore Vinson if the Court members would accept a woman justice. The chief reported back that they would not be comfortable with a woman in their masculine domain, and Truman quickly rejected her candidacy.

Allen's commitment to peace through world order intensified after she lost two younger brothers in the First World War. She was a major speaker at the postwar conference to outlaw war organized by Carrie Chapman Catt. She was active in the International Bar Association and the International Federation of Women Lawyers and traveled in Mexico, Europe, and Asia to speak to women in the law and the peace movement, continuing her lifelong effort to encourage women to enter law and politics.

Allen believed in exercising her body as well as her mind and routinely went walking, climbing, and swimming; her other amusements were reading and playing the piano. She lived frugally on her judicial salary, spending money on her many friends and relatives. She maintained close ties with her older sister, Esther Allen Gaw, dean of women at Ohio State University, and with another sister, and, she supported and educated a niece. Allen never married; she lived in a female household with another woman lawyer who managed her campaigns for twelve years and with a cousin who handled the domestic duties for thirty years. Allen said in 1935: "I don't cook, or sew, or shop, for the simple reason that I haven't the time or energy for these things, any more than the men judges have." In 1959 she retired to senior status after serving for one year as the first woman chief judge of a federal appellate court. She died in Cleveland.

Allen was a role model for professional and political women, appearing at hundreds of regional, national, and international meetings. She was in the mainstream of 1920s social feminism, favoring protective legislation for working women in her judicial decisions although recognizing in herself the exception who would gain more from gender-neutral equality. She was pleased that New York University created a scholarship for women students at the law school in her name, beginning in 1948. She defined her life's task as representing her sex with such distinction that men in power would be willing to choose other women to follow her. Her own talents lay more in policy making than in law application, but election to office was more difficult for women than appointment. She wrote, "I have tried with all that is in me to justify the presence of women on the courts," but in fact few women followed her into judicial careers until the 1970s. Allen believed firmly that women have the same public and private responsibilities for the human condition as men have because, she said, "Women are human beings first and women second."

• The Florence E. Allen Papers are archived with a register at the Western Reserve Historical Society, Cleveland. The large collection includes letters, diaries, drafts of opinions and speeches, clippings, and photographs. Smaller collections can be found in the manuscript division of the Library of Congress, the Schlesinger Archives at Radcliffe College, and the Sophia Smith Collection at Smith College. Her appellate opinions are in the *Ohio Reports* (1923–1928) and the *Federal Reporter* (1935–1965). The ceremony for her retirement (278 F2d 4–35 [1960]) provides information on her judicial service and relationship to colleagues.

Allen wrote an autobiography, *To Do Justly* (1965), published the year before her death, which is episodic and incomplete. Allen's other publications include two books, *This Constitution of Ours* (1940), *The Treaty as an Instrument of Legislation* (1952), and an article, "Participation of Women in Government," *Annals of the AAPSS* (May 1947): 94–103. An excellent short biography written by Jeanette E. Tuve appeared in 1984, *First Lady of the Law*. Two articles by Beverly B. Cook focus on her Supreme Court ambitions: "The First Woman Candidate for the Supreme Court," *Yearbook 1981, Supreme Court Historical Society*, pp. 19–35, and "Women as Supreme Court Candidates: From Florence Allen to Sandra O'Connor," *Judicature* 65 (Dec.–Jan. 1982): 314–26. An obituary is in the *New York Times*, 14 Sept. 1966.

BEVERLY B. COOK

ALLEN, Fred (31 May 1894–17 Mar. 1956), humorist, was born John Florence Sullivan in Somerville, Massachusetts, the son of James Henry Sullivan, a bookbinder, and Cecilia Herlihy. Allen and his younger brother were raised by their aunt Elizabeth Herlihy Lovely, following the death of their mother in 1897. The boys remained a part of their aunt's extended, working-class, Irish-American family when their brooding, alcoholic father remarried in 1909, residing in Allston and later the Dorchester section of Boston. Allen graduated from Boston's High School of Commerce in 1911 but did not seek a business career. Among James's few contributions to his son's life in comedy was the job of bookrunner that Allen filled, beginning at age fourteen, in the Boston Public Library, his father's employer. While awaiting call slips in the stacks, Allen read about comedy and practiced juggling. Fascinated with vaudeville, America's most popular live amusement in 1910, and a hanger-on in Boston's theatrical district, he appeared as a comic juggler in the library's employee talent show in the summer of 1911. Soon he was a frequent contestant in amateur vaudeville shows in the Boston area, earning sufficient prize money to encourage him to declare professional status in 1912. Although one-night stands took Allen's act as far afield as Maine and Connecticut, in September 1914 the young actor moved to New York.

Between 1914 and 1922 Allen was a "two-a-day" artist who aspired to national recognition. Billed as "Freddy James—The World's Worst Juggler" when he arrived in New York, he adopted the name Fred Allen in 1918. A William Fox Agency booking agent, Edgar Allen, created the name to conceal from the Keith-Albee vaudeville booking office Allen's performance in a competing New York theater. During his vaudeville years, Allen's act evolved into a predominantly verbal comedy presentation that used, but did not depend on, props. Although he was not, of course, preparing for radio, the jokes that Allen wrote and delivered with increasing ease, as he eliminated the juggling at which he was not adept, proved to be a good apprenticeship for his career in the sound-only broadcasting medium. A small-timer, Allen crisscrossed America on vaudeville's Poli, Sun, Pantages, and Orpheum circuits. He also toured Australia and New Zealand in 1916–1917.

In 1922 Allen joined the *Passing Show of 1922* and for the next decade earned fame as a writer-performer in a succession of Broadway revues. He experienced his greatest critical success in two "intimate revues" that appeared at decade's end: *The Little Show* (1929) and *Three's a Crowd* (1930). Allen's career benefited in several ways from his Broadway and road show experience in the 1920s. He met dancer Portland Hoffa in 1922 and began courting her in 1924. The couple married in May 1927; they had no children. Portland appeared on his radio programs from 1932 to 1949. During the first decade of her radio career Allen cast Portland as a juvenile "Dumb Dora," a simple-minded, bizarre stage persona made famous on radio by Gracie Allen of the team Burns and Allen. Portland's character matured during the 1940s. Allen gained his reputation as a stage comedian in the city that became the host of network radio broadcasts in 1926 with the birth of NBC, the National Broadcasting Company. He was, therefore, strategically located to take advantage of the employment opportunities that the New York radio industry offered while Broadway and vaudeville experienced devastating unemployment during the early depression years. Also during the 1920s Allen gained essential experience as a comedy writer, creating his own single acts and sketches for revues and vaudeville two-acts for himself and his comedy partners, one of whom was Portland. In 1926 Allen and Bert Yorke achieved the pinnacle of vaudeville success, billing at the Palace Theater in New York.

Allen made the transition to network radio comedy on 23 October 1932, when his first series, the "Linit Bath Club Revue," debuted on the Columbia Broadcasting System (CBS). From that date until his last series left NBC on 26 June 1949, Allen appeared in eight different series. His best-known, most creative series were "Town Hall Tonight" (July 1934–June 1939 on NBC Red for sponsor Bristol-Myers), "The Texaco Star Theater" (October 1940–June 1944 on CBS for Texaco), and the "Fred Allen Show" (October 1945–June 1949 on NBC for Standard Brands and the Ford Dealers of America). In the midst of changes in format and sponsorship, Allen's comic style gave continuity to his programs. In addition, throughout his radio career, Allen broadcast from and drew upon the life of New York, a city that most radio comedians had abandoned for southern California by 1938. He performed hour-long, live broadcasts before studio audiences from March 1934 to June 1942. His shows prior to and after those dates were of thirty-minute duration, still live, still acted before large studio audiences.

Although he often complained about the "treadmill" on which radio placed its creators, Allen much preferred the one-dimensional broadcasting medium to television and the movies, media in which he had much less success. "Comedy has changed with the coming of television," he lamented in his radio memoir. "There was a certain type of imaginative comedy that could be written for, and performed on, only the radio. Television comedy is mostly visual and the most successful of comedians today are disciples of slapstick" (*Treadmill to Oblivion*, p. 239). His talent for verbal comedy was wasted on the primarily visual medium of television. Allen's perspective was that of a writer, and it is as a writer, even more than as a performer, that he should be remembered. His most important work consists of scripts and letters all but inaccessible to readers today. Into his letters he poured his experience as a creator working in a complex commercial, bureaucratic, technological medium of entertainment. Encased in hundreds of forgotten radio scripts are light verse; interviews with guest celebrities and human curiosities from various walks of life; twelve-minute skits, heirs to his Broadway revue sketches, some presented by his cast of "Mighty Allen Art Players"; light banter among cast members that ranged from the tedious to the brilliantly witty; the "Allen's Alley" segments broadcast beginning on 6 December 1942, perhaps the most frequently recalled feature of Allen's radio programs; and other efforts to utilize radio as a medium of comedy entertainment.

Much of Allen's radio writing was routine and unexceptional. The need to churn out a forty-page script each week and expose it to the editorial interference of a sponsor, an ad agency, and network representatives made it so. But at its best Allen's comedy material recognized, as that of few others in the industry did, that radio was an audial medium and that its writers faced a unique creative opportunity to communicate only through sounds with a vast, undifferentiated, unseen home audience. As he wrote for this audience, Allen was well aware of British and American literary humor, and he incorporated comic personae such as the nineteenth-century tellers of tall tales and the early twentieth century's "little man" into his own art. Allen "wasn't an actor who happened to do some writing; it was the other way around," recalled Arnold Auerbach, one of the comedian's assistant authors. He "was the most gifted and prolific of Radio comedy writers" (pp. 126, ix).

Allen was a satirist, one characterized by novelist Herman Wouk as "America's greatest satiric wit in our time" (*Letters*, p. 358). Allen filled seventeen years of scripts with social commentary that gently and with a smile ridiculed the shortcomings of the American Dream. Especially knowledgeable and effective were the critical observations that he aimed at the Hollywood film industry and at broadcasting. For these powerful industries that received too little thoughtful criticism, he served as a critic from within, regularly exposing the foolish arrogance of film directors and producers, the shallow superficiality of movie stars, and the pettiness of network radio vice presidents. His scripts and letters fairly bulge with subversive and still relevant commentary on such radio institutions as celebrity guests, studio audiences, quiz programs, program ratings, sponsors, ad agency account executives—and even radio comedians and their writers. In part because of his satire, but also because of radio's hypersensitivity to individual and interest-group complaint, Allen was perhaps radio's most censored comedian. He faced problems at NBC during the 1940s in particular. In April 1947, for instance, a network vice president cut twenty-five seconds of Allen's program off the air because Allen refused to delete a humorous reference to the network. He once wrote for guest star Jack Benny the lines, "Water over the darn. . . . You know how careful we have to be in radio, Fred." His running battles with those who would reshape his art were significant beyond the news copy and script content that they provided. As a writer who happened to work in a mass medium, Allen struggled to preserve his artistic independence and freedom of expression.

Program competition, rather than censorship, ended Allen's radio career. In 1948 the quiz show genre that he deprecated as bogus entertainment gave rise to the program "Stop the Music." Appearing opposite his program on Sunday nights, this give-away show helped to erode Allen's ratings, which were high enough to have made his the top-rated program in all of radio at several points during the 1946–1947 and 1947–1948 seasons. After his retirement in June 1949, Allen made several unsuccessful attempts during the early 1950s to find a place in television. But appearances on the "Colgate Comedy Hour" and "Judge for Yourself," an amateur talent show, only exposed what Allen described as the "great problem" conforming comedians. "We don't know how to duplicate our success in radio. . . . Those things won't work in television" (John Crosby, *Out of the Blue* [1952], p. 33). A much-respected elder statesman of comedy who continued to reside in New York, Allen had published one volume of memoirs and was nearing completion of a second at the time of his death in New York City. Leading a simple, rigidly patterned existence that excluded automobiles (Allen never drove a car) and included set times for dinner at a particular restaurant, a workout at the Young Men's Christian Association (YMCA), and correspondence with old friends, the firmest commitment of this compulsive and generous man was to his wife. Humorist James Thurber, writing two years before Allen died, penned what would stand as Allen's epitaph: "You can count on a thumb of one hand the American who is at once a comedian, a humorist, a wit, and a satirist, and his name is Fred Allen" (*Letters*, p. 346).

• The Boston Public Library has the Fred Allen Papers, including all of the scripts of his radio shows and some of the shows on which he was a guest star. Scripts of Allen's programs are available on microfilm at the Manuscripts Division, Library of Congress, Washington, D.C. In 1954 Allen published an account of his radio career, *Treadmill to Oblivion*; in the year of his death appeared the unfinished autobiography of his life and career prior to radio, *Much Ado about Me*. Allen did not save copies of his voluminous correspondence, but Joe McCarthy gathered some of his letters from their recipients and published them in *Letters* (1956). The best recollection of Allen's radio career by a colleague is included in Arnold Auerbach, *Funny Men Don't Laugh* (1965). A book-length biography is Robert Taylor, *Fred Allen: His Life and Wit* (1989). A scholarly study of Allen's comic art is Alan Havig, *Fred Allen's Radio Comedy* (1990). An obituary is in the *New York Times*, 18 Mar. 1956.

ALAN HAVIG

ALLEN, Frederick Lewis (5 July 1890–13 Feb. 1954), editor and social historian, was born in Boston, Massachusetts, the son of Frederick Baylies Allen, a clergyman, and Alberta Hildegarde Lewis. Allen was educated at Groton School and Harvard University, where he received his B.A. in English in 1912 and his M.A. in 1913 in modern languages. Allen edited the literary magazine at Harvard and subsequently taught composition there for two years; he became an assistant editor at the *Atlantic Monthly* in 1914.

Allen joined the *Century* in 1915 as managing editor and in 1917 became press bureau director for the Boston Writers' Council for Patriotic Service; he moved to Washington, D.C., to serve in the same capacity for the Council of National Defense in 1918. That same year he married Dorothy Penrose Cobb; they had two children. She died in 1930, and two years later Allen married Agnes Rogers Hyde; they had no children.

Between 1919 and 1923 Allen managed publicity for Harvard; in 1923 he joined the New York publishers Harper and Bros. as an editorial assistant. Allen moved to *Harper's Magazine* in 1925 as articles editor; in 1931 he became assistant editor, and in 1941 he was named editor in chief.

Before World War II, Allen's editorial responsibilities included handling such star *Harper's* essayists as Bernard DeVoto and E. B. White. After the war he encouraged younger writers, including John Cheever, Arthur Miller, J. D. Salinger, and Truman Capote, and gained for *Harper's* a reputation of being not only a magazine with serious intentions but also one that was topical and controversial. He mulled over the influence of the mass media, encouraged debate over the morality of the atomic bomb, and during an era of strident anticommunism remained convinced that communism was not an internal threat to the United States.

Allen's memoir of his father was published in 1929, and his biography of literary agent Paul Revere Reynolds, begun in 1926, was published in 1944. While a graduate student, Allen had contributed to the British humor magazine *Punch*, and he continued to write light verse, satire, and articles during the 1920s for various magazines. Allen's 1930 meditation on the 1920s, called "The End of an Era," was published in the magazine the *Outlook and Independent*. Expanded, it became *Only Yesterday* (1931).

A portrait of the "roaring" decade drawn largely from popular culture, *Only Yesterday* went through twenty-two printings, selling more than a million copies. It was admittedly unscholarly (Allen called himself a "retrospective journalist" and confessed that he had chosen his material with an eye to its colorful qualities). It was neither unique (Mark Sullivan's *Our Times* [1926–1935] predated it) nor definitive (novelist F. Scott Fitzgerald's 1931 essay, "Echoes of the Jazz Age," has proven to be a more durable impression of the era). But it was fascinating and readable.

Only Yesterday created a pattern for Allen's subsequent books: he arranged evocative detail with dramatic effectiveness. *Only Yesterday* begins in 1919, creating an impression of "Mr. and Mrs. Smith" by listing what they wore, how their house was furnished, and what they did for entertainment. These nostalgic moments are followed by a list of the fads and follies the 1920s held in store for the Smiths: "radio broadcasting . . . the Dayton trials [teaching of Evolution], cross word puzzles, bathing-beauty contests, racketeers, Teapot Dome [the Harding administration scandal] . . . Sacco and Vanzetti [anarchists], companionate marriage, brokers' loan statistics . . . the Wall Street explosion, confession magazines . . . speakeasies . . . automatic traffic lights . . . Charles A. Lindbergh."

Such attention to the evanescence of 1920s daily life eventually caused Allen's *New York Times* obituarist to call him the "Herotodus of the Jazz Age." The book also may have enlisted a new generation of historians to the cause of writing for a broader public; Allen's influence is clearly seen in the work of Arthur Schlesinger's *The Age of Jackson* (1945) and *The Age of Roosevelt* (3 vols., 1957–1960) and Bruce Catton's Civil War trilogy: *Mr. Lincoln's Army* (1951), *Glory Road* (1952), and *A Stillness at Appomattox* (1953). Allen's next works of American popular and social history, *The American Procession* (1933) and *Metropolis* (1934), were largely pictorial, undertaken in collaboration with his wife Agnes, a photographer.

Although none of Allen's subsequent books achieved the popularity of *Only Yesterday*, they made economic history understandable to the general reader. *The Lords of Creation* (1935) examined the ups and downs of American finance since 1900. Jaunty chapter headings ("Morgan Calls the Tune," "The Seven Fat Years," "Into the Stratosphere") and set-pieces (such as the dinner at which U.S. Steel was organized) enlivened a tale of the trusts and holding companies that had moved the "center of gravity of American industrial control . . . to Wall Street" (p. 13). An admirer of President Franklin Roosevelt's measures to control and undergird the economic system, Allen blamed the financiers for the Great Depression.

Since Yesterday (1940), the continuation of *Only Yesterday* through the 1930s, was more concerned with international and economic affairs than its predecessor. Although it was not as popular, this book, too, was a bestseller. In 1947 Allen and his wife collaborated on another book, *I Remember Distinctly: A Family Album of the American People, 1918–1941*, a recapitulation of the interwar years. Among its arresting visual features was a year-by-year portrayal of corset fashions, as well as a photograph of a lonely 1930s street, captioned, "One of the strangest things about the Depression was that it was so nearly invisible to the casual eye. . . . There just didn't seem to be many people about" (p. 126).

The Great Pierpont Morgan (1949) narrowed Allen's analysis of the "Lords of Creation" to the legendary banker J. P. Morgan, a "virtual Renaissance Prince" who, directing seventy-two companies and utilities, professed powerlessness. Trusting in his own ability to "steer a true course" between Morgan's flatterers and demonizers, Allen admired him for such actions as ending the panic of 1907 by putting his fortune and reputation on the line. Men like Morgan were shown as a natural development, people who "had got a good look in their youth at competition at its most savage and unbridled worst, and had decided to try to do something about it" (p. 35).

Some of Allen's best descriptive writing was lavished upon Morgan, "rather formally dressed for a gentleman on holiday, with a wing collar, Ascot tie, and white waistcoat. He sits solidly, his weight rather forward on his two feet, his toes turned out" (p. 268). But Allen showed that people like Morgan could no longer safeguard ordinary Americans.

The Big Change: America Transforms Itself, 1900–1950 (1952), the outgrowth of a similarly named 1950 article in *Harper's*, was an optimistic summary of the American half-century, "a heartening story" of "the adjustment of capitalism to democratic ends" and the increasing interdependence of a society not split by class. Lauding America's "astonishing productive capacity combined with the widest distribution of prosperity ever witnessed in the world," Allen credited governmental action with narrowing the gap between rich and poor that had existed in 1900. But he also acknowledged the power of "monster corporations," adding that "governmental authorities have usually been amenable to pressure from people who knew exactly what they wanted—and could pay for it" (*The Lords of Creation*, p. 463).

Among Allen's last projects was a Christopher Award–winning 1952 television special (with his wife) on the changes in American life during the first half of the century. He was an overseer at Harvard (1940–1948) and a trustee of Bennington (1937–1944) and of the Ford Foundation (1952). Allen died in New York City.

Subsequent social historians, working from source material more scholarly than Allen's picked holes in the accuracy of his works. No one could deny his readability, and such late twentieth-century commentators on the American scene as Bill Bryson were still liberally quoting him.

• Allen's papers are in two locations at the Library of Congress: in his own file and in those of *Harper's*. Most of his works have remained in print. A biography is Darwin Payne, *The Man of Only Yesterday* (1975). Some information on Allen as editor can be found in *The Letters of E. B. White*, ed. Dorothy Lobrano Guth (1976). An obituary is in the *New York Times*, 14 Feb. 1954.

JAMES ROSS MOORE

ALLEN, George Herbert (29 Apr. 1918–31 Dec. 1990), college and professional football coach, was born in the Detroit, Michigan, suburb of Grosse Pointe Woods, the son of Earl Raymond Allen, an auto worker, and Loretta Hannigan. Allen attended the Lake Shore, Michigan, high school, where he earned varsity letters in football, basketball, and track. As an officer trainee in the U.S. Navy's V-12 program during World War II, Allen attended Alma College and Marquette University. He played football at both schools. In 1947 Allen received a bachelor's degree from the University of Michigan, where he also served as a part-time assistant coach for the junior varsity football team. In 1949 he earned a master's degree in physical education from Michigan. While at Michigan, the intelligent and hardworking Allen fell in love with coaching, the vocation to which he devoted his adult life.

Allen was a remarkably successful college coach. In 1948 Morningside College (Sioux City, Iowa), whose football team had not won a game in two years, hired Allen. He resurrected Morningside's football program, compiling a record of 17 wins, 11 losses, and 2 ties. In 1951 he married Etty Lumbroso, the Tunisian-born daughter of a Franco-Italian wine importer; the couple had four children. The same year he left Morningside to coach at Whittier College (Whittier, Calif.), where he revitalized another dormant football program. Under Allen's leadership, Whittier won 32, lost 22, and tied 5 between 1951 and 1956.

Allen's collegiate success attracted attention, and in 1957 he moved into the pro ranks when the National Football League's Los Angeles Rams named him assistant coach. The following year he joined the Chicago Bears, where his defensive strategies and emphasis on special-team play helped the Bears capture the NFL championship in 1963. Three years later (and one year after signing a three-year contract with Chicago) Allen left to join the Rams as head coach. His departure did not go unchallenged. George Halas, the crusty owner of the Bears, sued Allen for breach of contract; only after the courts confirmed the validity of Allen's contract with the Bears did Halas consent to release him to the Rams.

In 1966 Allen led the Rams to their first winning season in eight years. During his five years with the team the Rams won 49, lost 17, and tied 4, making Allen at the time the most successful coach in Rams history. The Rams won the NFL Western Division title in 1967 and 1969, and in both of those years Allen was named NFL Coach of the Year. Despite his success Allen was fired after the 1970 season because of disagreements with Rams owner Dan Reeves. Reeves was reported to have said that it was more fun to lose with someone else than to win with Allen.

Almost immediately after his dismissal Allen was named head coach of the Washington Redskins. In 1971 the Redskins won 9, lost 4, and tied 1, their best season in twenty-nine years. The following season the Redskins reached the Super Bowl, where they lost to the Miami Dolphins, 14–7. For his efforts Allen was named NFL Coach of the Year in 1971 and 1972. Between 1971 and 1977 Allen's Redskins had 67 wins, 30 losses, and 1 tie. Allen became the winningest coach in Redskins history to that date.

In an arrangement that was unusual at the time, the Redskins owners gave Allen almost complete control over player recruitment. Allen, who disdained the collegiate football draft and ignored young players, stocked the Redskins with aging veterans. His motto was "the future is now." So many of these old pros were acquired from the Rams that sportswriters began to refer to the Redskins as the Ramskins. Eventually, Allen's Redskins were dubbed the "Over the Hill Gang."

However, Allen knew how to get the most from his players. He built a strong sense of camaraderie among them and infused his teams with an almost fanatical "us against them" attitude. Consequently, his devoted players would do virtually anything for him. At the time of Allen's death, former player Deacon Jones said, "George was the best motivator that ever lived."

Allen was also responsible for several significant innovations that every professional football club subsequently copied. He was the first to hire an assistant coach specifically for the special teams; he was the first to employ situational substitution such as the nickel defense (five defensive backs instead of the normal four on downs when the offense could be expected to attempt a pass) and dime defense (six defensive backs); he was the first to construct a complete training facility for his football team's exclusive use (Redskin Park). Additionally, Allen wrote more than a dozen books on football training, strategy, and conditioning, including the first encyclopedia of football drills.

The quintessential workaholic, Allen seemed even more obsessed with winning than most coaches. He was once quoted as saying that "losing is like death," and after a Christmas Eve playoff loss in 1974 he said that "when you lose, there is no Christmas."

Although his football players loved him, Allen's relations with opposing coaches were often rocky because of his deviousness and duplicity in his dealings. The commissioner of football once fined him $5,000 for trading the same draft choice twice, and occasionally he hired spies to observe his opponents' practice sessions. These actions contributed to his unpopularity and, perhaps, help to explain his failure to win election to the Professional Football Hall of Fame.

Allen's relationships with his teams' owners were also less than ideal. His demand for absolute control over all his teams' operations and his spendthrift ways distressed his owners. Edward Bennett Williams, owner of the Redskins, once remarked, "George was given an unlimited budget and he exceeded it."

After the 1977 season Williams fired Allen over a contract dispute, saying, "George was given unlimited patience and he exceeded it." Allen was quickly hired to coach the Rams again, but he was mysteriously dismissed after two preseason games and never again coached in the NFL. In 1983 he coached the Chicago Blitz to a first-place finish in the short-lived U.S. Football League and repeated that accomplishment the following year with the Arizona Wranglers before retiring. In 1990 he emerged from retirement to coach the Long Beach State (Calif.) college football team. In typical Allen fashion, he revitalized the football program, winning 6 and losing 5 for a school that had lost 24 of its previous 35 games.

A physical fitness enthusiast, in 1981 Allen was named by Ronald Reagan to head the President's Council on Physical Fitness. One year later Allen founded the National Fitness Foundation, a private organization designed to promote healthy lifestyles. Allen died at his home in Rancho Palos Verdes, California. At the time of his death, former Redskins quarterback Billy Kilmer said, "All George Allen ever thought about was the next football game and the next season. He taught the Redskins and the town how to win."

• The Professional Football Hall of Fame in Canton, Ohio, maintains a George H. Allen file that contains numerous newspaper and magazine clippings on his football career and personal life. Allen wrote a number of books, including *George Allen's New Handbook of Football Drills* (1974); with Charles Maher, *Merry Christmas—You're Fired* (1982); and *Bicycling for Exercise and Pleasure* (1987), which reveal much about the man himself. His philosophy on life with its emphasis on winning as the *only* goal is explored in an interview with Joe Marshall, "A Hundred Percent Is Not Enough," *Sports Illustrated*, 9 July 1973, pp. 74–86. Allen discusses the transferability of sports leadership to business leadership in "The Attitude of a Winner," an unsigned interview in *Nation's Business*, Sept. 1975, pp. 45–52. George Frazier IV, "Portrait of the Super-Coach as a Sweetheart," *Esquire*, Sept. 1968, 116ff, details Allen's success at reviving the fortunes of the Rams, and John Underwood, "The Ice-Cream Man Cometh," *Sports Illustrated*, 25 Oct. 1971, pp. 71–77, does the same for Allen's resurrection of the Redskins. Allen's return to college football coaching at the age of seventy-two is chronicled in Douglas S. Looney, "Why, George?" *Sports Illustrated*, 24 Sept. 1990, pp. 75–77. Extensive obituaries are in the *New York Times*, the *Los Angeles Times*, and the *Washington Post*, all 1 Jan. 1991. Retrospectives were published in the *Washington Post*, 1 and 2 Jan. 1991, and the *New York Times*, 4 Jan. 1991.

FRANK W. THACKERAY

ALLEN, George Venable (3 Nov. 1903–11 July 1970), diplomat, was born in Durham, North Carolina, the son of Thomas Ellis Allen, a merchant, and Harriet Moore. He earned his B.A. in 1924 from Duke University. Between 1924 and 1928 he worked as a high school teacher and principal in Buncombe County, North Carolina, and as a newspaper reporter for the *Asheville Times* and the *Durham Herald*. He returned to school and in 1929 received an M.A. from Harvard University, winning the Charles Sumner Prize for International Relations.

Allen entered the foreign service in 1930 and undertook his first assignment as vice consul in Kingston, Jamaica. He attended foreign service school in 1930–1931 and served as vice consul in Shanghai, China (1931–1934), and in Patras, Greece (1934–1936). In 1934 he married Katherine Martin. The couple had three children. Allen was a consul in Cairo, Egypt (1936–1938), and in 1939 he went to work in the Near and Middle Eastern Division in the State Department in Washington, D.C. Within a few years he was promoted to chief of the division. He attended the Moscow Conference in 1943, the Potsdam Conference in 1945, and served in the U.S. delegation to the United Nations Conference on International Organization in San Francisco in 1945.

Allen had his greatest impact on U.S. foreign policy during the decade and a half that followed World War II. In May 1946 he became ambassador to Iran at the height of a major crisis. During the previous months the Harry Truman administration had vigorously denounced Moscow for failing to fulfill its promise to join the United States and Britain in a speedy withdrawal of allied forces from Iran. Moscow's intervention in the politics of the northwestern Iranian border province of Azerbaijan also alarmed U.S. officials.

The crisis subsided in April when Iranian prime minister Ahmad Qavam negotiated the withdrawal of Soviet troops in exchange for an oil concession and named to his cabinet several officials of Iran's Communist Tudeh party. However, Allen's arrival the following month and his intense diplomatic efforts emboldened Qavam to oust the Communist cabinet members. The following year the Iranian Majlis (parliament), whom Allen also lobbied, refused to approve the Soviet-Iranian oil agreement.

Interpreting the outcome as a Cold War victory for the United States, Ambassador Allen and the Truman administration sought to consolidate American influence by providing increased economic and military assistance to the government of the Shah Mohammed Reza Pahlavi. Allen also worked diligently to befriend the shah, going so far as to arrange weekly Saturday tennis matches with the young monarch. The policy helped safeguard U.S. economic and strategic interests at the time. In the long term, however, it wedded American fortunes to the fate of the authoritarian Pahlavi dynasty, a marriage that would continue until Iran's 1979 Islamic revolution.

Allen returned to Washington, D.C., in March 1948 to serve as assistant secretary of state for public affairs. His primary responsibility involved coordinating the growing cultural, informational, and exchange programs of the early Cold War era. He especially expanded the Voice of America radio program and U.S. participation in the United Nations Educational, Scientific, and Cultural Organization. His tenure was important historically because it helped strengthen the government's role in exporting American culture, an activity that had previously been mainly the domain of private business and philanthropic organizations.

From October 1949 through March 1953 Allen served as ambassador to Yugoslavia. U.S. officials increasingly had been impressed by the Communist dictator Josip Tito's determination to pursue policies independent of the Soviet Union. Allen counseled the Truman administration to encourage these tendencies by providing both economic and military assistance to Tito's government. The proposal won wide approval within the State Department and soon became U.S. government policy.

Sensitive to the subtleties involved, Allen also advised that the United States should not seek Tito's outright alignment with the West nor force any change in his domestic policies. Such overt pressure might provoke Soviet military intervention and diminish Yugoslavia's usefulness as an example for other nationalists within the socialist movement. Although aid to Communist Yugoslavia stirred controversy on Capitol Hill, the Truman White House and subsequent U.S. administrations persevered and bolstered Tito's posture of Cold War nonalignment.

As ambassador to India from 1953 to 1955, Allen participated in policies that ran counter to that nonaligned nation's interests. In early 1954 the administration of Dwight D. Eisenhower decided to go ahead with plans to provide India's neighbor and archrival, Pakistan, with military assistance. From Washington's perspective, the aid helped make Pakistan part of a larger, global anti-Soviet defense system. From New Delhi's, the initiative seemed to be aimed against India's foreign policy of Cold War nonalignment and represented but another example of great power domination over former colonial areas. The Indian government also protested that U.S. military aid would exacerbate religious tensions between Muslim Pakistanis and Hindu Indians and make a negotiated settlement of the ongoing dispute over the northern border territory of Kashmir more difficult to reach. While the policy had been formulated largely before his appointment, Allen advised Washington that the administration could "ride out the storm without fatal effect on U.S.-Indian relations." In February 1954 he officially informed Prime Minister Jawaharlal Nehru of the undertaking.

Although the United States continued to provide modest levels of economic assistance to New Delhi, military aid to Pakistan and that nation's subsequent membership in the Baghdad Pact and the Southeast Asia Treaty Organization badly undermined Indo-American relations. Allen returned to Washington and became in 1955 assistant secretary of state for Near Eastern, South Asian, and African affairs. The Eisenhower administration sent him to Egypt in September 1955 in a futile effort to dissuade President Gamal Abdel Nasser from proceeding with a plan to purchase Soviet arms. The subsequent breakdown in Egypt's relations with the West led in the fall of 1956 to the Suez Crisis. Then in 1956 he went to Greece as U.S. ambassador.

From November 1957 until his retirement in November 1960 Allen resumed his work in overseas cultural relations as head of the U.S. Information Agency (USIA). Under his direction, the four-year-old agency expanded its informational and propaganda activities, in part to counter Soviet gains in international prestige following the successful *Sputnik* satellite launch. Allen increased overseas English instruction, encouraged greater U.S. participation in international trade fairs, and worked to improve the journalistic reputation of Voice of America radio broadcasting. Allen played a critical role, along with U.S. ambassador Llewelyn Thompson, in planning the U.S. National Exhibition in Moscow, where the widely publicized "kitchen debates" occurred between Vice President Richard Nixon and Soviet premier Nikita Khrushchev.

Retired from public service, Allen became president of the Tobacco Institute in his home state of North Carolina and defended the industry against research that linked smoking to cancer. President Lyndon Johnson in 1966 honored Allen by giving him the title of "career diplomat" and naming him to head the Foreign Service Institute, a position that he held until 1969. He died near Bahama, North Carolina.

• Allen's papers are housed at Duke University in Durham, N.C. A copy of a chapter of his unpublished autobiography dealing with his ambassadorship in Iran is also available at the Harry S. Truman Library in Independence, Mo. Also see James A. Bill, *The Eagle and the Lion: The Tragedy of American-Iranian Relations* (1988); H. W. Brands, *The Specter of Neutralism: The United States and the Emergence of the Third World, 1947–1960* (1988); Bruce Kuniholm, *The Origins of the Cold War in the Near East* (1980); Mark Lytle, *The Origins of the Iranian-American Alliance, 1941–1953* (1987); Dennis Merrill, *Bread and the Ballot: The United States and India's Economic Development, 1947–1963* (1990); Robert J. McMahon, *The Cold War on the Periphery: The United States, India, and Pakistan* (1994). An obituary is in the *New York Times*, 12 July 1970.

DENNIS MERRILL

ALLEN, Glover Morrill (8 Dec. 1879–15 Feb. 1942), mammalogist and ornithologist, was born in Walpole, New Hampshire, the son of Nathaniel Glover Allen, a minister, and Harriet Ann Schouler. His father, who was 68 when his son was born, retired in 1885, at which time the family moved to Newton, Massachusetts. He died when his son was ten. Allen attended the local public schools and Newton High School and then entered Harvard, becoming a member of Phi Beta Kappa in his junior year and graduating magna cum laude in 1901. The early natural history interests Allen had evinced from boyhood prompted him to concentrate in botany, zoology, and foreign languages. His first major publication, *The Birds of Massachusetts*, completed with the assistance of Reginald H. Howe, Jr., was published prior to his graduation, and his monographic "List of the Birds of New Hampshire" appeared in 1903. Allen earned his M.A. at Harvard in 1903 and his Ph.D. there in 1904. His doctoral dissertation, probably the first in the field of mammalogy completed in any American graduate school, dealt with "The Heredity of Coat Color in Mice." That same year (1904) also saw the publication of Allen's "List of the Mammalia of New England."

In 1901 Allen was appointed secretary, librarian, and editor for the Boston Society of Natural History, an organization with which he spent more than twenty years of his professional career. Allen was central to the administration of the society's educational and museum programs. Combining his knowledge of the literature of ornithology and mammalogy, his foreign language skills, and his able editorial talents, he made his mark on both the various publications put out by the Society and later on the reports and journals of other organizations. For three years following the completion of his doctorate, Allen pursued postdoctoral studies in forestry at Harvard but then concluded that his real interests lay elsewhere. From 1906 until 1907 he served as editor for *The American Naturalist*. In 1907 he was hired to oversee the mammal collections at Harvard's Museum of Comparative Zoology (MCZ). He was not formally designated as curator of this collection until 1925; yet the mammal materials at Harvard had the reputation of being one of the best-organized collections anywhere, thanks to Allen's superb taxonomic skills. He retained the curatorship until his death. Allen married Sarah Moody Cushing in 1911, and they had one daughter.

Probably inspired by a desire for more time in which to conduct his own research, Allen resigned the secretaryship of the Boston Society of Natural History in 1924 and joined the faculty at Harvard as a lecturer in zoology. He was promoted to associate professor in 1928 and to full professor in 1938. Allen was not particularly interested in classroom teaching, but he did much to enthuse students concerning the study of mammals during an important period of growth in that field. Allen relinquished the librarianship and editorship he had held with the Boston Society in 1928, but he accepted his election to its vice presidency, a post he held until the end of his life.

From 1901 until 1912, with one two-year break, Allen served as secretary of the Nuttall Ornithological Club, the first American organization specifically concerned with ornithology. In 1919 he was elected president of the club, a post he held for twenty-three years until his death. During his tenure the club's membership base, previously concentrated in Cambridge, Massachusetts, was expanded, membership underwent considerable growth, and the group was incorporated. In 1919 Allen became a charter member of the American Society of Mammalogists. He was also a life member, a director, vice president, and, from 1927 until 1929, president of the Society. A longtime member of the American Ornithologists' Union, Allen was named a fellow in 1921, and served as editor of its journal, the *Auk*, from 1936 until his death.

Allen made a number of collecting expeditions abroad over a period of many years. Although he was a small man with a slight physique, he was an indefatigable field worker and collector. He visited the Bahamas in 1903, Labrador in 1906, East Africa in 1909, and various other parts of that continent in 1912; he also went to Grenada in the British West Indies in 1910. He published *Narrative of a Trip to the Bahamas* with Thomas Barbour in 1904, a paper on "The Birds of Labrador" with C. W. Townsend in 1907 and a monograph on the large West Indian shrew *Solenodon paradoxus*, which appeared in 1910. This was followed by *Mammals of the West Indies* in 1911. Allen's field work in various parts of New England and a study of specimens in the Harvard collections led to the publication of *The Whalebone Whales of New England* in 1916.

Allen did little further traveling until 1926, when he returned to Africa, visiting Liberia and the Belgian Congo. Later trips for specimen collecting were made to Brazil in 1929 and to Australia in 1931. In the main, his field work provided opportunities for collecting specimens, for observation, and reflection on various areas of current and possible future interest, but it was not generally designed to further particular projects.

Allen's books *Introduction to the Study of Birds* (1924) and *Birds and their Attributes* (1925) were followed by several major studies of bats, including *The American Bats of the Genus Pizonyx*, completed with his longtime friend and colleague G. S. Miller Jr. in 1928; and *Bats* (1939), a comprehensive text that summarized what was then known of their biology but that also delved into the folklore surrounding bats and the paleontological record. It is still regarded as one of the best introductions to the subject for general readers. Allen's years of research in Africa resulted in his *Checklist of African Mammals* (1939). Between 1938 and 1940 Allen published a detailed two-volume study, *The Mammals of China and Mongolia*, which was based in large part upon his examination of many museum specimens. Some mammalogists have regarded this as his single most impressive achievement. They have particularly commended his systematic accounts and discussion of earlier work done on the mammals of the region. Allen also translated (with E. Deichmann), Herlauf Winge's *The Interrelationships of the Mammalian Genera* (3 vols., 1941–1942) from the Danish original. Allen's final publication, which appeared after his death, was *Extinct and Vanishing Mammals of the Western Hemisphere, with Marine Species of All the World* (1942), which was reprinted thirty years later by the sponsor of the original study, the American Committee for International Wildlife Protection.

Reserved and self-effacing, but a cheerful and always courteous person, Allen was highly valued as a mentor by students and younger zoologists, and as a warm and knowledgeable friend and colleague by his peers. His knowledge of zoology extended well beyond his particular fields of specialization. Allen's published work was noted for its clearly written, direct, and accurate content. His many shorter scientific papers reflected his wide-ranging interests in paleontology, genetics, and in the comparative anatomy of vertebrates. Friends and colleagues commented on his sense of humor, as when he observed that to his mind, zoos were "museum[s] that were not yet dead." He died in Cambridge of a heart attack while recovering from surgery.

• Allen's field journals and professional correspondence are held by the archives of the Museum of Comparative Zoology at Harvard; other manuscripts are at the American Museum of Natural History in New York. A bibliography of Allen's publications is in New England Zoological Club, *Proceedings* 24 (1947): 1–81. See also the *Annual Reports* of the Museum of Comparative Zoology during Allen's tenure there. Biographical sketches are in William C. Davis, Jr., *History of the Nuttall Ornithological Club, 1873–1986* (1987), and in Elmer C. Birney and Jerry R. Choate, eds., *Seventy-Five Years of Mammalogy (1919–1994)* (1994). See also obituaries by Austin H. Clark in *Science*, 13 Mar. 1942; Winsor M. Tyler in the *Auk*, Apr. 1943; and accounts by Allen's colleagues Thomas Barbour, Barbara Lawrence, William E. Schevill, Sherwood L. Washburn, and Mary B. Cobb in *Journal of Mammalogy*, Aug. 1943.

KEIR B. STERLING

ALLEN, Gracie (26 July 1895–27 Aug. 1964), actress and comedienne, was born Grace Ethel Cecile Rosalie Allen in San Francisco, California, the daughter of George Allen, an Irish clog and minstrel dancer, and Margaret Darragh. The year of her birth has been cited as late as 1906, but the 1900 U.S. Census confirms the 1895 date. Gracie was the family's fifth child and fourth daughter. Sometime after 1900 Allen's father deserted the family, and her mother married Edward Pidgeon, a San Francisco police captain.

Allen's first stage appearance was at the age of three when, dressed in top hat and tails, she performed an Irish dance at a church social. All four Allen sisters excelled as Irish and Scottish dancers, winning many prizes and giving dance lessons at home. Gracie attended the Star of the Sea Convent School, and during school vacations she worked as a singer in local movie houses and would occasionally appear with one or more of her sisters in vaudeville theaters in the San Francisco area. For a short time the Allen sisters were known as the Four Colleens, specializing in Irish singing and dancing. They subsequently toured in vaudeville as part of an act called Larry Reilly and Company. By the time they reached the East Coast, Allen's sisters had returned to California, and Gracie had become the star attraction. Angered by Reilly's refusal to give her appropriate billing, however, she abruptly quit.

Unsuccessful in her efforts to find a suitable partner or steady bookings, Allen enrolled in secretarial school in New York. In 1923 she met George Burns, a song-and-dance man whose forgettable acts had all flopped. Burns and Allen decided to work together, with Gracie playing "straight man" to George's comedy. They made their vaudeville debut in Newark, New Jersey, in an act called "Sixty-Forty" and soon realized that audiences found Allen far funnier than Burns. Although Allen continued to sing and dance as part of their act, Burns began to rewrite their material to capitalize on her comic appeal. He reversed their roles, giving Allen the jokes and taking the straight lines for himself. Within months, Gracie Allen's distinctive stage persona had emerged: the scatterbrained innocent whose hilarious responses produced endless delight. "The character was simply the dizziest dame in the world," Burns recalled, but she differed from other "Dumb Doras" because "Gracie played her as if she were totally sane, as if her answers actually made sense" (*Gracie*, p. 48). Instead of relying on sight gags or slapstick, their act depended on Allen's "illogical logic," with the cigar-smoking Burns deftly setting up her giddy non sequiturs and cheerful inanities.

As the act and Gracie's character evolved, their salary and bookings improved. With "Dizzy" in 1925, they won their first "big time" contract for a lucrative multiweek tour on the Orpheum circuit in the western states. While introducing "Lamb Chops," a new routine in Cleveland, Ohio, Burns and Allen were married in January 1926. After successful engagements from Detroit to New York City, they signed a five-year contract for $750 a week to play the Keith-Orpheum vaudeville circuit. "We were what is termed 'hot' and from then on we got steadily hotter," Allen explained (Best, "Gracie Allen's Own Story," p. 123). By August, they had triumphed at New York's Palace Theatre, the most prestigious vaudeville house in the country. They traveled abroad in 1928 and found that the British responded with equal delight to Allen's irrepressible lunacy. Returning to England the following year for another vaudeville engagement, they were invited to perform on radio for the first time. Their debut on the British Broadcasting Corporation (BBC) was so popular that their radio program ran for several months.

In 1930 Gracie Allen and George Burns set a vaudeville record by appearing on Broadway for seventeen weeks. Soon after Eddie Cantor invited Allen to appear on his show in a routine Burns had written, Burns and Allen made their American radio debut on Rudy Vallee's popular "Fleischmann's Yeast Hour." On 15 February 1932 they joined orchestra leader Guy Lombardo on the radio show, "The Robert Burns Panatella Program," produced by the Columbia Broadcasting System (CBS). Radio introduced them to a much larger audience, and when Lombardo left for another network in 1933 CBS offered them their own show. "The Adventures of Gracie" (later called "The George Burns and Gracie Allen Show") soon became one of the most popular programs on radio.

In addition to enabling the comedy team to reach millions of listeners each week with their zany banter, radio capitalized on Allen's "dizzy" persona through wildly successful publicity stunts. Beginning in January 1933 Allen appeared unannounced on a variety of popular network programs hunting for her allegedly lost brother, George. The gimmick was followed by a one-woman show at a New York gallery of "surrealistic" paintings with madcap titles, Allen's presidential campaign as candidate of the Surprise party in 1940, and her debut at Carnegie Hall as a concert pianist playing "Concerto for One Finger."

The first movie Burns and Allen made was a nine-minute short for Paramount in 1929. In the next two years, they appeared in fourteen more short films, most of which Burns wrote. They made twelve feature films in all for Paramount, including *Six of a Kind* (1934) with W. C. Fields, *College Swing* (1938), and *Honolulu* (1939). Allen appeared without her husband in *The Gracie Allen Murder Case* (1939), in *Mr. and Mrs. North* (1941), and in *Two Girls and a Sailor* (1944), her last movie. Never enthusiastic about appearing before the camera, she preferred working on radio where she was better able to overcome her fear of performing in front of a microphone for a live audience.

Promoted as the nitwit of the networks and America's most scattered brain, Allen became the national symbol of misunderstanding and ineptitude with Burns as her loving partner. In an era when women typically played subordinate roles in the entertainment business, Allen was comfortable deferring to her husband's judgment and letting him create their scripts with the team of writers he assembled. Yet he maintained that it was her unfailing sense of comedy, natural talent, spontaneity, and brilliance as an actress that ensured their success and made her one of the most popular performers in radio history. In his words, "Gracie was the whole show" (*Gracie*, p. 246). When the show temporarily experienced a ratings decline in the early 1940s, Burns made a major format change, announcing them as the middle-aged married couple they really were. Transformed into a domestic situation comedy, the program was restored to popular favor. They continued successfully on radio until 1950 when, at Burns's urging, they brought their act to television. Although reluctant to make the transition, Allen was as uproariously funny in the new medium as she had been in the old. While her lilting, high-pitched, almost childlike voice sounded as comical on television as it had on radio, audiences had the added pleasure of watching her subtle visual antics. They could also admire the costumes she spent hours selecting each week. She often wore as many as three fashionable outfits in a single half-hour show (always with sleeves long enough to cover her left arm and shoulder, which had been badly scalded in a childhood accident).

A star for more than three decades, Allen eventually tired of the grueling routine of a weekly program and was eager to spend more time with her two adopted children and her grandchildren. Her health problems also made the rigors of a weekly television show all the more daunting. In addition to the migraine headaches she had endured for years and the stage fright she never conquered, she had had a heart attack in the early 1950s. Burns and Allen filmed the 299th and final episode of their long-running show on 4 June 1958. Burns hoped she would reconsider her decision, but Allen was adamant, and they never worked together again.

Allen spent her leisure time happily shopping and socializing. In 1961, however, she had a serious heart attack; she died three years later in Hollywood. A gifted comic artist, she was eulogized as a woman "the whole world loved" and "the smartest dumbbell in the history of show business" (Blythe and Sackett, pp. 193, 194).

• Gracie Allen's papers, part of the George Burns and Gracie Allen Collection, are in the Archives of Performing Arts at the University of Southern California. There are clipping files in the Billy Rose Theatre Collection, New York Public Library for the Performing Arts, Lincoln Center, and in the Harvard University Theatre Collection. Allen reminisced in Katharine Best, "Nitwits of the Networks," *Stage*, 1 May and 15 May 1939, and in "Gracie Allen's Own Story: 'Inside Me' as Told to Jane Kesner Morris," *Woman's Home Companion*, Mar. 1953. Her one book, *How to Become President* (1940), was actually crafted by Charles Palmer, and her column, which appeared in newspapers across the country, was also ghost-written. George Burns provides invaluable information in *Gracie: A Love Story* (1988). See also his *I Love Her, That's Why* (1955), *Living It Up; or, They Still Love Me in Altoona* (1976), *The Third Time Around* (1980), and *All My Best Friends* (1989). Shirley Staples, *Male-Female Comedy Teams in American Vaudeville, 1865–1932* (1984), has a fine chapter on Burns and Allen as well as a comprehensive bibliography. Cheryl Blythe and Susan Sackett, *Say Goodnight, Gracie!: The Story of Burns and Allen* (1986), contains several inaccuracies and no bibliography but includes an informative appendix that summarizes all 299 television episodes of "The George Burns and Gracie Allen Show." Obituaries are in the *Los Angeles Times* and the *New York Times*, 29 Aug. 1964, and in *Variety*, 2 Sept. 1964.

BARBARA W. GROSSMAN

ALLEN, Henry Justin (11 Sept. 1869–17 Jan. 1950), politician and newspaper editor, was born in Pittsfield, Pennsylvania, the son of John Allen, a farmer, and Rebecca Goodwin. In 1870 the Allens settled on a farm in Clay County, Kansas, which they lost in 1879.

The family relocated in Osage County, Kansas, where Allen graduated from Burlingame High School. Working as a barber to attend Baker University in Baldwin City, Kansas, he excelled at forensics, which led to his first newspaper job and forecast his later stature as one of America's most popular public speakers. While at Baker, he met Elsie Jane Nuzman, and they were married in 1892. Only one of their four children survived to adulthood.

Allen's 59-year newspaper career began in 1891, when he quit school to become a reporter for the *Salina Republican*, where he quickly gained a reputation for journalistic acumen and zeal. In 1894 Allen bought the *Manhattan Nationalist*, which was the first of nine Kansas newspapers that he owned and published either alone or with a partner. Buying the *Wichita Beacon* in 1907, Allen fashioned it into an outstanding and influential reform newspaper that promoted honest and efficient government. In 1928 he sold controlling interest in the *Beacon* but remained its board chairman until his death. In addition to being a highly respected newspaper executive, Allen was a prolific writer of books and syndicated news articles that ranged in content from world events to Kansas subjects.

Journalism abetted Allen's entry into politics, which he relished and played with verve. After shrewdly and successfully managing the 1898 gubernatorial campaign of Republican William E. Stanley, Allen served as his secretary between 1899 and 1901. He was a fixture in state and national politics for the next generation. Rejecting "Old Guard" political opportunism and special interest conservatism as the result of a religious conversion during Billy Sunday's evangelist crusade, Allen shifted permanently to the progressive wing of the Republican party. As chairman of the Kansas delegation at the 1912 Republican presidential convention, he gained national attention from his strenuous advocacy of Theodore Roosevelt (1858–1919). When William Howard Taft received the nomination, Allen bolted the party to support Roosevelt on the Progressive party ticket. In 1914 Allen ran as the Progressive gubernatorial candidate on a platform that endorsed a state-owned life insurance system, child-labor laws, a presidential primary, and a minimum wage law. Allen finished a dismal third in the race. Along with other Kansas Progressives, he reconciled with the Republican party two years later.

After the United States entered World War I, Allen served in France as a Red Cross officer and became embroiled in a public controversy with the military when he criticized its slowness in notifying the families of deceased and wounded soldiers. Threatened with dismissal, he transferred to the Young Men's Christian Association to stay in Europe.

Allen's war duty helped him win the 1918 Republican gubernatorial nomination, and the party campaign waged during his absence overseas resulted in his election by a record 150,000-vote margin. Reelected in 1920, he followed the Kansas precedent of not seeking a third term. Allen enjoyed little success with his moderately progressive agenda, which included a state income tax, highway improvements, workmen's compensation, and helping farm tenants buy land. His combative personality in the divisive postwar atmosphere ensured strife-filled administrations. The Non-Partisan League and the Ku Klux Klan were Allen's special nemeses, and he started litigation that eventually ousted the latter from Kansas.

Probably the fiercest controversy of Allen's administration was over the 1920 Kansas Industrial Act, passed by the legislature at his behest when a prolonged strike caused a severe coal shortage in the state. Conceived to protect the public welfare, the law forbade strikes in some industries and created a court of industrial relations with broad powers to settle labor disputes. Organized labor vehemently denounced the unpopular law, which the U.S. Supreme Court declared unconstitutional in 1923. The act was widely viewed later as a precursor to the 1947 federal Taft-Hartley Act.

Allen concentrated on business and served two years as an investigator for the Near East Relief commission between 1923 and 1929, when he was appointed to finish the unexpired U.S. Senate term of Vice President Charles Curtis (1860–1936). By defending President Herbert Hoover, Allen attained notoriety for his abrasive debating style, which prompted Thaddeus Caraway (D.-Ark.) to quip sarcastically, "The grasshopper is not the only plague to come out of Kansas." Allen was hospitalized and unable to campaign in the 1930 election, which, along with lingering animosity over the industrial court, contributed to his defeat by Democrat George McGill.

Although never again in public favor, Allen remained an active partisan. Republican national publicity director in 1928 and 1932, he participated in every presidential election campaign through 1944. Affiliated with various newspapers in later life, he was part owner and editor of the *Topeka State Journal* from 1935 to 1940. During the 1930s, he also traveled the world and wrote on international politics. In 1941 Allen served as honorary national chairman of the Save the Children Federation and visited England to observe its work firsthand.

During his lifetime, Allen generously supported charities and was a prominent Methodist layman. A civic-spirited Wichitian, he enthusiastically supported the arts. He died in Wichita after a long illness.

Allen's reputation reached national and even international levels, but his greatest influence as a politician, newspaper executive, and philanthropist was on his own state. Although not entitled to be ranked as a key national political figure, Allen's political career was significant, and it affords one of the best examples of the role of progressive Republicanism in the early twentieth century.

• Allen's personal papers are at the Library of Congress, and his official papers as governor are at the Kansas State Historical Society in Topeka. A perceptive personality profile and analysis of Allen is in W. G. Clugston, *Rascals in Democracy* (1940). Homer E. Socolofsky, *Kansas Governors* (1990), includes a biographical sketch. Important information on Allen is in the *Wichita Beacon*, 7 Apr. 1929, and his obituary, 17 Jan. 1950. He is among the politicians examined in Robert Sherman La Forte, *Leaders of Reform: Progressive Republicans in Kansas, 1900–1916* (1974). William Allen White, *The Martial Adventures of Henry and Me* (1918), humorously describes Allen's World War I activities. Domenico Gagliardo, *The Kansas Industrial Court* (1941), is a history of the controversial agency; Allen presented his view in *The Party of the Third Part: The Story of the Kansas Industrial Relations Court* (1921). Donald R. McCoy, *Landon of Kansas* (1966), often mentions Allen.

PATRICK G. O'BRIEN

ALLEN, Henry "Red" (7 Jan. 1908–17 Apr. 1967), trumpeter, was born Henry James Allen, Jr., in Algiers, Louisiana, the son of Henry James Allen, Sr., a trumpeter and leader of a brass band, and Juretta (maiden name unknown). Allen received instruction from his father and his two uncles, who were also trumpeters. Rehearsals were held at home, giving Allen the opportunity to hear New Orleans greats like Louis Armstrong, Buddy Bolden, Oscar Celestin, Bunk Johnson, King Oliver, Sam Morgan, and Kid Rena. Though surrounded by trumpet players, Allen played the violin and the alto horn before he settled on trumpet. Soon after his tenth birthday he felt secure enough on the trumpet to become a member of his father's brass band. Allen learned improvising by playing along with recordings. He varied the speed to change the key, thereby developing a keen pitch perception and knowledge of key areas in music.

In addition to playing with his father's band, Allen played riverboat gigs and freelanced until his nineteenth birthday, when he accompanied King Oliver's band to New York for a 1927 engagement at the Savoy Ballroom and recordings for RCA Victor (*King Oliver, Vols. 1 & 2*). Allen went back to New Orleans for a stint with Fate Marable's riverboat bands (1928–1929), returning to New York again in July 1929 to record *It Should Be You/Biffly Blues* (Victor 38073) and to work as sideman with Louis Armstrong on *I Ain't Got Nobody* (Okeh 8756). Allen worked in 1930 as sideman with Jelly Roll Morton on *Jelly Roll Morton and His Red Hot Peppers, 1927–1930, Vol. 1* for RCA Victor and recorded as leader on *Sugar Hill Function* (Victor 38140).

Other early recordings as lead trumpet, on such tunes as "It Should Be You," "Feeling Drowsy," "Dancing Dave," "Doctor Blues," and "Louisiana Swing," were made with members of the Luis Russell band from 1929 to 1932, which at the time included Albert Nichols, Charlie Holmes, J. C. Higginbotham and blues vocalist Victoria Spivey. Allen's work can be heard on *Luis Russell & His Louisiana Swing Orchestra* (1930, Columbia), *The Luis Russell Story* (1929, Parlophone), and *Song of the Swanee* (1930, Okeh 8780).

Allen's early improvisational style was characterized by sudden odd turns-of-phrase, asymmetrical rhythmic construction, mixing of double-time flurries, long held notes, contrasting dynamics, alternate fingerings of a single note, and a love of fast octave jumps (Schuller, pp. 618–19). Although his style was heavily influenced by Louis Armstrong, Allen's idiosyncratic rhythmic flexibility, glissandi, smears, tonguing, emotional conveyance, and technical fluency were unparalleled. Like Armstrong he challenged two and four bar phrasing, thinking more of playing through the changes. Several recordings made with Luis Russell, including "Saratoga Shout," "Doctor Blues," "Jersey Lightning," and "Song of the Swanee" on *The Luis Russell Story*, and "It Should Be You" and "Feeling Drowsy" on *Henry "Red" Allen, Vol. 1*, showcase his style.

Allen's brilliance continued with his tenure in Fletcher Henderson's band from 1932 to 1934 on tunes such as "Wrappin' It Up" and "Rug Cutter's Stomp" on *Fletcher Henderson* (1934), "Queer Notions" and "King Porter Stomp" on *The Fletcher Story, Vol. 4* (1933, Columbia), and *Wrappin' It Up* (1934, Decca 157). In 1935 Allen recorded *Ride, Red, Ride* (Columbia 30870), with the Mills Blue Rhythm Band, with whom he played from 1934 to 1937, and *Body and Soul* (Vocalion 38080). He returned to Luis Russell's band, which was then accompanying Louis Armstrong, in 1937 and found himself playing second to Roy Eldridge. Eldridge had replaced Allen in Fletcher Henderson's band as well.

Allen left Russell's band in 1940 and went on to perform and record with musicians such as Sidney Bechet (*Egyptian Fantasy*, 1941, Victor 27337), Spike Hughes (*Spike Hughes and His All American Orchestra*, London Records), Coleman Hawkins (1930–1941, CBS records), Billie Holiday (*Billie Holiday: The Golden Years, Vol. 2*, Columbia), Buster Bailey, Higginbotham, James P. Johnson, Kid Ory, and Lionel Hampton. Allen also served as leader on *Get the Mop* (1946, Victor 201808). Other releases of this period include the compilation *Henry 'Red' Allen, Vols. 1–4*. Gunther Schuller further states, "Allen's stints with Coleman Hawkins in 1957 and Kid Ory in 1959, provided evidence of his growth as a trumpet soloist. Specifically, on 'I Cover the Waterfront' and 'I Got Rhythm,' one can hear creative and contrasting ideas and a rich and singing tone" (p. 630). Allen himself describes the experience of playing his music " . . . as if somebody [is] making your lip speak, making it say things he thinks" (Balliett, p. 13). In addition to his recordings, Allen appeared in three important TV jazz specials toward the end of his life: "Chicago and All That Jazz," "The Sound of Jazz," and "Profile of the Art." His career ended with the recording of two celebrated albums, *The Henry Allen Memorial Album/Mr. Allen—Henry Red Allen* and *Feeling Good*. He died of cancer in New York City.

Like many trumpeters of his time, Allen was influenced by Louis Armstrong. Unlike most of his peers, however, he developed a personal repertoire of performance concepts and effects that freed him from the musical constraints of both the New Orleans and swing styles. That repertoire included a smooth legato articulation, a rhythm that was not tied to the fixed pulse, a wide range of dynamics, and a host of glissandi, growls, lip trills, rips, smears, and spattered notes. He thereby presaged the later avant-garde or free jazz movement, which extensively featured the performance techniques that Allen pioneered. His ability to transcend his immediate musical environment and his originality and innovativeness on his chosen instrument raised Allen to the stature of one of the best jazz performers of his era.

• Excellent materials on Allen's life and contributions can be found in Whitney Balliett's *Improvising* (1977); J. R. T. Davies and L. Wright, "The Allen Victors," *Storyville*, no. 34 (1971): 131; M. L. Hester, "Henry 'Red' Allen," *The Mississippi Rag* 12, no. 1 (1984): Gunther Schuller, *The Swing Era: The Development of Jazz, 1930–1945* (1989); and H. Allen and A. J. McCarthy, "The Early Years," *Jazz Monthly*, no. 180 (1970): 2.

EDDIE S. MEADOWS

ALLEN, Henry Tureman (13 Apr. 1859–30 Aug. 1930), soldier, was born at Sharpsburg, Kentucky, the son of Ruben Sanford Allen, a businessman, and Susannah Shumate. After a year at an academy in Georgetown, Kentucky, Allen was accepted at West Point, which he attended between 1878 and 1882. Commissioned a second lieutenant, the young officer posted at Fort Keogh in Montana Territory. In September 1884 he became aide-de-camp to General Nelson Miles, commander of the Department of Columbia in Vancouver, Washington. Miles sent Allen to Alaska to explore and survey the unknown territory surrounding the Copper, Tanana, and Koyukuk rivers. His small party of ten spent much of 1885 charting over 2,500 miles of rugged terrain. His report, published in 1887, was well received by several geographic societies.

Handsome, bright, and ambitious, Allen had a special aptitude for foreign languages and an interest in foreign travel. In July 1887 he married Jennie Dora Johnston, with whom he had three children. After the wedding, the young couple honeymooned in St. Petersburg so Allen could continue his study of Russian. His fluency in French and German earned him a teaching position in foreign languages at West Point from 1888 until 1890. He then returned to St. Petersburg as one of the first military attachés sent to Europe. Over the next seven years, Allen broadened his understanding of European politics and culture. After five years in the Russian capital, he spent two more in Berlin. With the outbreak of the Spanish-American War in 1898, Allen obtained command of Troop D of the Second Cavalry. He saw little action and spent most of his time with scouting and escort duty. Worst of all, he came down with malaria and was forced to spend several months convalescing.

Another chance to command troops came with his new assignment as commander of the Forty-third Volunteer Infantry Regiment on Samar and Leyte in the Philippines in 1900. His success in using native troops to supplement American forces in their struggle against Emilio Aguinaldo's guerrillas led to his appointment as commander of the Philippine Constabulary. The constabulary, an experimental blending of colonial military force under local civilian authority, employed American officers but used Filipino troops. Although generally successful in its mission to restore order to the islands, the constabulary was new and controversial, and Allen was criticized by some of his army colleagues for his liberal attitudes toward the Filipinos. Although a brigadier general while in command of the constabulary, this was only a temporary rank. Allen returned to the United States in 1907 as a major to command two cavalry troops in Yellowstone Park.

In 1910 Allen was appointed cavalry assistant on the General Staff in Washington under Major General Leonard Wood. This gave him the chance for the next three years to work closely with the chief of staff, whose office was directly across the hall. Of course, this also sometimes put Allen in the middle of the various controversies that swirled around General Wood. Allen's occasional brash manner did not endear him to some of the army's old guard, and although promoted to lieutenant colonel in 1912, he had little hope of rising any higher before retirement. When World War I erupted in 1914, Allen was chosen to accompany an official delegation sent to Europe to rescue more than 50,000 American civilians trapped in the war zone. While in Europe, he toured the major capitals, inspected military preparations, and observed the first battle of the Marne. Upon returning home, he submitted a twenty-page report analyzing the fighting strengths and weaknesses of the belligerents. His report was generally ignored, however, and he was assigned cavalry duty at Fort Oglethorpe, Georgia, in February 1915.

Allen became acquainted for the first time with John J. Pershing in 1916, when his cavalry unit was one of those assigned to chase Pancho Villa into Mexico. As Pershing's inspector general during the Mexican Punitive Expedition, Allen's ability impressed the future commander of the American Expeditionary Forces. With American entry into the war in April 1917, Allen was given the Ninetieth Division to organize and train and was promoted to brigadier general. The Ninetieth Division performed well in both the St.-Mihiel and Meuse-Argonne offensives in the fall of 1918. After the war Allen stayed in Europe and in July 1919 took over command of the American forces in Germany stationed along the Rhineland with headquarters in Coblenz. With 10,000 men under him, Allen was charged with maintaining order in the area during the difficult postwar years. Allen was often the senior American official, both civilian and military, in the area and was frequently thrust into the middle of simmering Franco-German tensions. He was a member of the four-power Inter-Allied Rhineland High Commission. His criticism of the French occupation of the Ruhr in early 1923 annoyed both Paris and Washington, and the American forces in Germany were soon returned to the United States. He retired from active service in April 1923 as major general.

Although retired, Allen maintained an active interest in foreign and military affairs. He wrote two books on his experiences in the Rhineland, advocated American participation in the League of Nations, and failed in his bid to be nominated as New York Governor Al Smith's running mate in the presidential campaign of 1928. His final years were spent in Washington or at his summer estate, "Charmian," in northern Maryland. He died in Buena Vista Spring, Pennsylvania.

Allen represented the new breed of army officer that came of age after the Civil War. Although his early experience on the western frontier was not unusual for his generation, his service in major European capitals set him apart from his colleagues and made him rather unique among American military professionals. Allen was a writer and a thinker, willing to share his opinions with friend and foe. He published books, wrote magazine articles, gave dozens of speeches during his career, and maintained an extensive correspondence throughout his life. His contributions to the development of the Philippine Constabulary and his postwar service in the Rhineland remain the chief legacies of his forty-one years in uniform.

• Allen's papers are at the Library of Congress. His Alaskan survey was published as *Report of an Expedition to the Copper, Tanana, and Koyukuk Rivers in the Territory of Alaska in the Year 1885* (1887). His postwar service in Germany resulted in two books, *My Rhineland Journal* (1923) and *The Rhineland Occupation* (1927). A solid biography is Heath Twichell, Jr., *Allen: The Biography of an Army Officer, 1859–1930* (1974). Robert Lee Bullard, *Fighting Generals* (1944), also contains a useful sketch of Allen's military career. An obituary is in the *New York Times*, 31 Aug. 1930.

EDWARD A. GOEDEKEN

ALLEN, Henry Watkins (29 Apr. 1820–22 Apr. 1866), Confederate soldier and governor of Louisiana, was born in Prince Edward County, Virginia, the son of Thomas Allen, a physician, and Ann Watkins. Allen and his family moved from Virginia to Ray County, Missouri, when he was thirteen. His father secured him a position working in a store, but Allen found business distasteful and enrolled in Marion College at age fifteen. At seventeen he ran away from college and traveled to Grand Gulf, Mississippi, where he became a tutor on a plantation a few miles outside of town. After tutoring for two years, Allen moved to Grand Gulf to open his own school and to study law. On 25 May 1841 he received his license to practice law in Mississippi. In 1842, when Allen was becoming an established lawyer in Mississippi, President Sam Houston of Texas called for volunteers to fight the Mexican army. Allen answered the call, was elected captain of the "Mississippi Guards," and remained in Texas for about six months. While there, he displayed an aptitude for military affairs.

Upon returning to Grand Gulf, Allen reestablished his legal practice and fell in love with Salome Crane, the daughter of a plantation owner. Her parents objected to the union, and the couple eloped in 1844. These events led to a duel, in which Allen was seriously injured by R. H. Marsteller, a physician from Grand Gulf with whom Allen had had prior difficulties. Mr. Crane eventually reconciled with the couple and provided them with a plantation in Claiborne County, Mississippi. They lived there until Salome died of tuberculosis in January 1851; they had no children. Allen left Claiborne County for Tensas Parish, Louisiana, and, because of his own illness, later moved to Cooper's Well. Upon recovering, he moved to West Baton Rouge, where he became a successful sugar planter. In 1853 he was elected to the Louisiana legislature and, in 1854, went to Harvard to further his studies in law. At this point he became very interested in the Italian struggle for independence and sailed for Europe with the intention of enlisting in Giuseppe Garibaldi's army. However, by the time he arrived the war had ended. Thus, he toured the European continent and wrote a book, *The Travels of a Sugar Planter* (1861).

While he was in Europe, Allen was reelected in 1859 to the Louisiana legislature, and upon returning home, he continued to pursue public interests. However, his political career was interrupted by the outbreak of the Civil War. Siding with the Confederacy, Allen enlisted at the very beginning of the war as a private and demonstrated a great deal of courage under fire. Soon he was elected lieutenant colonel of the Fourth Louisiana Regiment. In July 1861 he assumed command of the Fourth Regiment's activities at Ship Island, which was located off the Mississippi coast. While there, he suppressed a mutiny without bloodshed and succeeded in rebuilding the damage that was done to the fort upon its initial seizure from the Union. Because of the threat of the Union navy, the Ship Island garrison was evacuated in September 1861. Allen became colonel of the Fourth Louisiana Regiment in March 1862. On 6 April he led the regiment at Shiloh, where, although he was wounded in the face, he refused to vacate the field. He served effectively in the defense of Vicksburg and accompanied John C. Breckinridge as the commander of a Louisiana brigade in an expedition to retake Baton Rouge. In the 5 August attack on Baton Rouge, Allen fought bravely but was severely wounded, his leg being shattered by a shell fragment. Although he refused to have his leg amputated and it was eventually saved, the incident caused him extraordinary pain and suffering. Thus incapacitated from field duty, Allen was, nonetheless, promoted to brigadier general in September 1863. He was ordered to serve in the Confederate Trans-Mississippi Department, a department created to administer military affairs west of the Mississippi River. When he arrived in Shreveport to assume his duties, he was elected governor of Louisiana.

When Allen took his inaugural oath on 25 January 1864, the state of Louisiana was in desperate straits. It was overrun by Union troops, and the population west of the Mississippi River was living in extreme poverty. Faced with this seemingly impossible situation, Allen demonstrated his administrative prowess. One of his first activities was to organize a route to the Mexican border so that Louisiana could trade cotton and sugar for items that it truly needed, such as dry goods and machinery; luxuries were not imported. Furthermore, Allen established a system of state-run stores to distribute the merchandise at reasonable prices. Because he accepted Louisiana state currency at the stores, he restored its value; thus, Confederate money actually had buying power west of the Mississippi River. In addition, he built factories, mills, and a dispensary where medicines were sold inexpensively. He even manufactured some products himself, including turpentine, castor oil, and bicarbonate of soda. Having a great deal of compassion for the poor, Allen facilitated donations to them as well as to destitute war veterans. He also was responsible for the almost complete cessation of the manufacture and distribution of alcohol in the state; in fact, liquor could only be distilled in the state distillery, and then only for medicinal purposes.

When Robert E. Lee surrendered in 1865, the Trans-Mississippi Department was stronger than it had ever been. In fact, the Confederates had denied every northern attempt to enter western Louisiana and Texas and were receiving supplies consistently from Mexico. At the time the military commander of the Trans-Mississippi, General Edmund Kirby Smith, was even considering continuing the war and had drafted a letter defiantly answering the Union's demand for surrender. Allen persuaded Smith not to send the letter. Allen was selected to represent the people of Texas and Arkansas and the Confederate governor of Missouri to negotiate their surrender. It is commonly thought that, had Allen not successfully dissuaded Smith from sending his letter, Louisiana would have been destroyed by an all-out invasion of Union forces. After the war, Allen knew he could no longer stay in Louisiana and, like other Confederate officials, fled to Mexico. There he was well received by Ferdinand Maximilian and started an English newspaper, *Mexican Times*. The newspaper showed promise, but Allen's health declined rapidly, as he suffered from wounds, acute gastritis, and possibly yellow fever; he died in Mexico City.

Allen was one of the greatest administrators to serve the Confederacy. Possessing political savvy, courage, and strength of character, Allen rose to the occasion to serve his country the best way he knew.

• Information on Allen's tenure as governor is on microfilm in the U.S. Record Division, Rebel Archives, Washington, D.C. Many of his speeches as governor are located in Shreveport, La. Letters and journals are in the Andrew Jackson Grayson Papers, Bancroft Library, University of California, Berkeley, and in collections in the Louisiana State University Library at Baton Rouge, the Howard Tilton Library at Tulane University, and the Delgado Museum in New Orleans. For a chronicle of Allen, see the *Mexican Times*, which he published and edited; a complete file is at the Louisiana State University Library. Sara E. Dorsey, *Recollections of Henry Watkins Allen* (1866), is his authorized biography. Another biography, Vincent H. Cassidy and Amos E. Simpson, *Henry Watkins Allen of Louisiana* (1964), is also quite useful.

The most significant periodical articles are Henry W. Allen, "The First Railroad in Missouri," *St. Louis Western Journal and Contemporary Review* 8 (May–Aug. 1868): 35–36; John Smith Kendall, "Recollections of a Confederate Officer," *Louisiana Historical Quarterly* 29 (Oct. 1946): 1041–1228; William F. Zornow, "State Aid for Indigent Soldiers and Their Families in Louisiana, 1861–1865," *Louisiana Historical Quarterly* 39 (July 1956): 375–80; William T. Windham, "The Problem of Supply in the Trans-Mississippi Confederacy," *Journal of Southern History* 27 (May 1961): 149–68; and Barnes F. Lathrop, "Disaffection in Confederate Louisiana: The Case of William Hyman," *Journal of Southern History* 24 (Aug. 1958): 308–18. The best source for Allen's military career is *The War of the Rebellion: A Compilation of the Official Records of the Union and Confederate Armies* (128 vols., 1880–1901). Also see Robert L. Kerby, *Kirby Smith's Confederacy: The Trans-Mississippi South, 1863–1865* (1972).

KATHRYN D. SNAVELY

ALLEN, Henry Wilson, Jr. (29 Sept. 1912–26 Oct. 1991), novelist and short-story writer, was born in Kansas City, Missouri, the son of Henry Wilson Allen, Sr., a dentist and oral surgeon, and Ella Jensen, a portrait painter. Allen's father, descended from the American revolutionary war hero Ethan Allen, numbered among his charity patients Confederate veterans of the Civil War. As a child Allen read voraciously in the family library, which was well stocked with classical and popular fiction. After graduating from high school, he attended the Kansas City Polytechnic Institute (known as Kansas City Junior College) in 1930–1931, decided against following his parents' wishes that he become either a veterinarian or a journalist, and instead headed west in 1932, during the Great Depression.

In both the Southwest and the Northwest, Allen held a variety of jobs valuable for a future writer of fiction. He was a used-car caravan driver, sugar-mill operator, cowboy, sheepherder, horse wrangler, blacksmith, and gold miner. He suffered two mildly crippling accidents, one injuring a leg and the other damaging an eardrum. Settling in California, he worked as a polo-pony exerciser in Hollywood, was a journalist briefly in Santa Monica, and wrote short-subject scripts for Metro-Goldwyn-Mayer from 1938 until he was discharged in 1949 for writing his own serious fiction on company time. This caused him financial concern, because in 1937 he had married Amy Geneva Watson, a Hollywood dancer. The couple had two children. His unemployment was a blessing, however, because his first two novels, *No Survivors* (1950) and *Red Blizzard* (1951), were soon accepted for publication. His next two were *Santa Fe Passage* (1952) and *To Follow a Flag* (1953), both of which, as well as *Red Blizzard*, were sold to the movies. The Allens worked a ranch in Van Nuys then in 1955 moved permanently to Encino, California.

Allen wrote so fast and well that he decided to adopt two pen names: "Will Henry" and "Clay Fisher." Later he confessed that this was the biggest professional mistake of his life, because for decades it fragmented critical response to his work. The Clay Fisher books are often shorter, more formulaic, and simpler in characterization, while the Will Henry works are based on more historical research and follow more complex heroes over longer periods of time. Allen's production, though interrupted by occasional illness, was steady and impressive and totaled fifty-four books from 1950 through 1983 (the date of his last publication). Beginning in 1968, he tried briefly to branch out, publishing three novels under his own full name. They were *Genesis Five* (1968), a science-fiction horror novel cast in Siberia of the twenty-first century, and then *Tayopa!* (1970) and *See How They Run* (1970), both of which may be defined as traditional westerns set in contemporary times. Allen soon returned to his tried-and-true formulas. By the close of his active career, sales totaled more than 15 million copies, with numerous translations, especially into French, German, and Italian. Eight of his plots have provided the basis for successful movies, including *The Tall Men* (1955, starring Clark Gable, Jane Russell, and Robert Ryan), *Mackenna's Gold* (1968, starring Gregory Peck, Edward G. Robinson, and Telly Savalas), and *Tom Horn* (1980, starring Steve McQueen and Linda Evans). Allen was especially disappointed that *Genesis Five*, though sold to the movies, was never produced (nor were six of his other works also sold thus).

It is difficult to categorize and exemplify the striking variety of Allen's works. They include historical reconstructions featuring Indians in Red Cloud's country and in the Northwest and the Southwest, stories about horsemen and legendary gunmen, and more purely fictional works dramatizing lust for blood in wartime and for gold at all times.

Of five books by Allen about George Armstrong Custer, the best is *No Survivors*, which is elaborately narrated by a white survivor who has learned Indian ways. *The Brass Command* (1956) sympathetically presents the 1878 migration of Cheyennes led by Dull Knife and Little Wolf from Oklahoma to their old homeland. Allen's undisputed masterpiece, *From Where the Sun Now Stands* (1960), was named by the Western Writers of America as the best historical western of its year. Narrated by a pony-herd Indian lad, it details Nez Percé Chief Joseph's tragic retreat in 1877 from Idaho into Montana and his honorable surrender to the dishonorable U.S. Army. *Chiricahua* (1972), the goriest of Allen's four Apache novels, concerns raids in 1883 by real-life Chato and other Chiricahua Apaches, as well as a wily Cheyenne-Crow woman, all frustrated by army mistreatment in southern Arizona and to the north. *The Fourth Horseman* (1954) is a dark, brooding tale based on the 1880s Graham-Tewksbury feud in Arizona. *The Blue Mustang* (1956), based on a true 1876 adventure, follows a young Texan's 175-mile gallop with $25,000 in gold to save his father's ranch.

Allen usually handled historical gunmen in a revisionist fashion. Thus, the oft-romanticized Jesse James becomes a nefarious, unfeeling killer in the well-researched *Death of a Legend* (1954, retitled *The Raiders* [1956]), whereas the sometimes criticized Wyatt Earp becomes a leonine stalwart in *Who Rides with Wyatt* (1955). Unique is Allen's haunting *One More River to Cross* (1967), about real-life Isom Dart, the best-presented among an array of admirable African Americans in his fiction. *I, Tom Horn* (1975) is Allen's finest novel with a white hero. True to his formula, Allen makes a fictive hero of history's range detective, who turned killer thug and was hanged in 1903. In the novel, Horn records his own story in a personal deposition, exercises a salty sense of humor, and reveals his own ruinous dark side with confessional relief. *Journey to Shiloh* (1960), Allen's best war novel, traces the progressive disillusion of seven young Confederate soldiers. *Mackenna's Gold* (1963) derives from J. Frank Dobie's 1939 *Apache Gold & Yaqui Silver* and is a Chaucerian parable with the moral that lust for gold can turn men into beasts.

Allen also wrote more than fifty short stories, five delightful books for children, and a few hard-hitting critical essays. His plots recount elemental quests—for fun, money, love, or self-esteem—usually against a backdrop of western history and legend. His style vibrates with painterly, cinematic effects, credible and often ribald dialogue, legions of minor characters, and occasional common-sense didacticism. Loren D. Estleman, the talented novelist and critic, says in *The Wister Trace: Classic Novels of the American Frontier* (1987) that Allen "has erected a Parthenon of Western lore and scraped the dust of decades from its icons," then adds that "a Will Henry title lends integrity to any rack overstocked with Louis L'Amour's lesser work and the hackery of the 'Adult Western.'" His peers, by voting his novels and short stories at least seven separate awards in the 1960s and 1970s, regarded Allen as one of the finest frontier fiction writers who ever lived. Allen died in a Van Nuys hospital near his home.

• Many of Allen's personal papers are in the Special Collections of the University Research Library, University of California at Los Angeles. Autobiographical material by Allen may be found in Dale L. Walker, ed., *Will Henry's West* (1984). The most thorough bibliography is Keith Kroll, "Henry W. Allen (Will Henry/Clay Fisher): A Bibliography of Primary and Secondary Sources," *Bulletin of Bibliography* 44, no. 4 (Dec. 1987): 219–31. The most complete critical treatment is Robert L. Gale, *Will Henry/Clay Fisher (Henry W. Allen)* (1984). The best essay is Walker, "The Candle Has Gone Out: Remembering Will Henry (1912–1991)," *Roundup Quarterly*, n.s., 4, no. 2 (Winter 1992): 7–20. An obituary is in the *Los Angeles Times*, 31 Oct. 1991.

ROBERT L. GALE

ALLEN, Hervey (8 Dec. 1889–28 Dec. 1949), writer, was born William Hervey Allen, Jr., in Pittsburgh, Pennsylvania, the son of William Hervey Allen, Sr., an inventor and speculator, and Helen Eby Myers. Allen was reared in a middle-class environment, about which he rarely wrote or spoke. He admired his paternal grandfather, an engineer and pioneer, but was deeply critical of his father's impractical schemes, which brought the family to the brink of bankruptcy. He was also ambivalent toward industrial, urban Pittsburgh and, even as a young man, enjoyed family trips and individual excursions to the countryside.

Allen began his college education at Annapolis but sustained sports injuries there from which he never fully recovered; eventually, he transferred to the University of Pittsburgh, where he received a bachelor's degree in economics in 1915. Having no practical career objectives in that area, he instead sought to relieve his youthful indecisiveness through poetry and an interest in political Progressivism. President Woodrow Wilson's efforts to shape the Mexican Revolution to fit a constitutional pattern impressed Allen, who joined a unit of the Pennsylvania National Guard that was dispatched to El Paso in 1916. Three months after its January 1917 return, the United States declared war on Germany; Allen was recalled to active duty, given the rank of first lieutenant, and convoyed to France. His war experiences would inform his literary vision for three decades.

By the end of World War I Allen still sought a harmonious vision of existence, which had eluded him in Pittsburgh, at the Mexican border and at Château Thierry. Shell-shocked, gassed, and hospitalized at the Western Front, he wrote war poetry that was both sober and disillusioning. "The Blindman," his best-known poem in this genre, was published in the December 1919 issue of *North American Review*. It is distinguished by its sense of immediacy and its social and cultural relevance for the "lost generation" of the 1920s. Its language is relentless, cruel, and agonizing, much as the military engagements were to those who fought them. What passed for good poetry was, in fact, also good history. As a result of this publication, Allen's name became known in national poetry circles. His collected poetic war memories were included in a 1921 Yale University Press publication *Wampum and Old Gold*, and this increased his literary reputation.

During the years 1920–1924 Allen sought refuge from the sights and sounds of war in Charleston, South Carolina. While pursuing his primary occupation as a high school teacher, he spearheaded the southern literary renaissance by cofounding the Poetry Society of South Carolina and collaborating with DuBose Heyward on *Carolina Chansons*, a 1922 collection of poems that treated the South in poetry as a region of contemporary interest rather than a nostalgic anachronism. Before leaving Charleston to teach English at New York's Columbia University and Vassar College, he made the proper literary connections by obtaining two mentors: patron of the arts William Van R. Whitall, who subsidized a number of his poetic endeavors, and Amy Lowell, a poetic phenomenon in her own right who befriended Allen when he took graduate courses at Harvard University in 1919–1920.

Between 1924 and 1929 Allen gradually changed his creative vocation from poetry to prose. This transition allowed him a wider reading audience and the possibility of greater financial security. He published a war memoir, *Toward the Flame* (1925); an acclaimed biography of Edgar Allan Poe, *Israfel* (1926); and a long poetic work with a tropical, Caribbean flavor, *Sarah Simon* (1929). All of these captured the national antiwar temperament of the 1920s, characterized by an individual, spiritual search for salvation. While teaching at Vassar, Allen married one of his students, Syracuse socialite Ann Hyde Andrews, in 1927. They had three children. In twenty-two years, the family changed its residence on several occasions, as Hervey Allen sought a self-sufficient environment far removed from the urbanism and materialism he deplored. His wife fell victim to manic depression, a disorder, first diagnosed in 1937, that lent the marriage, and Allen's personal life in general, a tragic cast.

After 1929 Allen's narrative fiction became his primary occupation. His historical novel *Anthony Adverse* (1933) portrays the thoughts and feelings of his generation. Its setting is the Napoleonic period, and the main character sojourns across a half-century, three continents, a great ocean, malarial rain forests, and scorching deserts only to discover that the life connection he seeks is within his own private being. Anthony's yearning for something finer, of inestimable value in an apparently amoral, expedient collapsing world expressed the concerns of Allen, who believed that Western civilization in the 1920s was ruled by pretense and conformity. A great deal of Allen's popular success is attributable to the fact that his books told Americans what their society meant—what they thought of themselves—in terms they could understand, and without the necessity of having to probe deeply to divine the novel's interior message, they liked it. *Anthony Adverse* became a mass-market success, revolutionizing the publishing industry (by using modern marketing techniques, including product tie-ins, and by initiating fashion trends), and it demonstrated that such works could combine fine writing, intense reader interest, dynamic sales, and serious, symbolic intent. In a 1934 article he authored for the *Saturday Review of Literature*, Allen defended the historical novel against a legion of critics who thought the book shallow, plagiarized, and/or pornographic.

None of Allen's succeeding historical novels achieved the fame or popularity of *Anthony Adverse*, although they were excellent sellers by the standards of the 1930s and 1940s. Allen continued to express changing national moods. By 1941 his message was no longer antiwar, as it had been in his 1938 Civil War novel *Action at Aquila*; following Pearl Harbor, through 1948, he celebrated democratic tenacity in the face of determined opposition in his trilogy of the American frontier, *The Disinherited*. As editor of the Rivers of America series (1947), Allen's sole nonfiction undertaking, he influenced a great deal of environmentally conscious writing, including helping to focus Marjorie Stoneman Douglas on the environment of the Everglades. He died at "The Glades," his Florida home.

Whether in verse, biography, or fiction, the texture of Allen's work is poetic and its thrust is either the personal re-creation of the author's own wartime and Charleston experiences of 1916 through 1929 or the reflection, in an historical mirror, of Western civilization's travail during the apocalyptic 1930s and 1940s.

As a body, his books proclaim life's sole certainties: the passage of time and death.

• Allen's papers are located in the University of Pittsburgh Library. The best available biography is Stuart E. Knee, *Hervey Allen (1889–1949): A Literary Historian in America* (1988). Dates and titles of Allen's published works not mentioned in the text are *Ballads of the Border* (1916), *The Bride of Huitzel* (1922), *Earth Moods and Other Poems* (1925), *New Legends* (1929), *Songs for Annette* (1929), *It Was Like This* (1940), and, with Thomas Olive Mabbott, *Poe's Brother* (1926). An obituary is in the *Cazenovia (N.Y.) Republican*, 5 Jan. 1950.

STUART E. KNEE

ALLEN, Horatio (10 May 1802–31 Dec. 1889), civil engineer, was born in Schenectady, New York, the son of Benjamin Allen, a professor of mathematics, and Mary Benedict. Allen entered Columbia College, where he studied with James Renwick, a professor of natural and experimental philosophy, and graduated in 1823 with an A.B., attaining high honors in mathematics. Allen then began to study the law, but after almost one and a half years he decided he was more interested in engineering as a profession.

At the time Allen entered the engineering profession, America was embarking on a major effort to improve internal transportation. The building of the Erie Canal, begun in 1817, had set off an era of canal building. At the same time several entrepreneurs and inventors began to explore the possibility of using either horse-drawn or steam-powered railroads in conjunction with canals or as a way to compete with canals.

In 1824 Allen became resident engineer of the Chesapeake & Delaware Canal Company at St. Georges, Delaware, and in 1826 he joined the Delaware & Hudson Canal Company as assistant engineer to Benjamin Wright, whom he had met while working on the Chesapeake & Delaware Canal. Work on this project introduced Allen to railroad construction and also led to his long association with John B. Jervis, who had replaced Wright as chief engineer in 1827.

It had been decided to build a sixteen-mile steam railroad to the western end of the canal to assist with the hauling of freight. Since there were no locomotives in the United States at this time, Jervis sent Allen to England in 1828 to purchase some engines. Allen became enthusiastic about the newly invented steam locomotive, writing to Jervis that "I am at length in the land of railroads and in the atmosphere of coal smoke." He soon made contact with Robert Stephenson, one of the inventors of the steam locomotive, and purchased four engines, one from Stephenson and three from the Foster, Rastrick Works at Stourbridge.

In 1829 all four locomotives arrived in New York City, but only one engine, the *Stourbridge Lion*, arrived at the canal head in Honesdale, Pennsylvania. The other engines were used as a source of wrought iron parts. On 9 August 1829 Allen operated the locomotive on a trial run and noted that on the first commercial steam railroad in America, "I was engineer, fireman, brakeman, conductor, and passenger." Unfortunately the engine could not be put into regular use because its weight exceeded what the rails could bear. Instead it was dismantled and used as a stationary steam engine to pull freight over inclines that had been constructed to eliminate the need for locks on the steepest sections of the canal.

In September 1829 Allen became the chief engineer of the South Carolina Railroad Company, which was building a rail line from Charleston to Hamburg. At a time when other American railroads were still using horses or sail power, Allen convinced the directors of the company to use steam power. Allen contracted with the West Point Foundry in New York City to build the first commercial locomotive in the United States. When the *Best Friend of Charleston*, as the engine was named, carried 141 passengers on Christmas Day 1830, it became the first scheduled steam railroad train in America.

Allen contributed to several improvements in American railroads. During the summers of 1830 and 1831, while visiting his parents in New York state, he and Jervis, who was building the Mohawk & Hudson Railroad, consulted with each other over the problem of developing a locomotive that could maintain high speed around curves. English locomotives had rigid frames designed for travel on tracks with few curves. But the uneven terrain and long distances in the United States would require tracks that could curve down valleys and up hills. Allen's solution, an eight-wheeled, double-truck machine created by connecting together two frames, was subject to more breakdowns than Jervis's simpler swivel, or bogie, cart mounted under the front of the locomotive. Although Allen's design was not utilized, there is evidence that Jervis had benefited from Allen's advice in the development of his successful solution. Allen also began the first nighttime train travel by placing a fire on a small flatcar ahead of the locomotive.

In 1834 Allen married Mary Moncrief Simons, with whom he had four children, and resigned from the South Carolina Railroad. The next year they left for an extended stay in Europe. After returning in 1838 they settled in New York City, where Allen became a consultant to the New York & Erie Railroad. At the same time he was named principal assistant to John Jervis on the Croton Aqueduct project, which was designed to provide a healthful source of water to New York City. In assisting with the construction of the High Bridge across the Harlem River, Allen conducted some of the first experiments done in America to determine the weight that a bridge pile could support. His method of testing became an accepted standard in the field.

Allen left the Croton project in 1842 and spent much of the rest of his career as president of the Novelty Iron Works, a New York City firm that was one of the major builders of marine steam engines and boilers. As a result of his work with the company, Allen patented several improved valve mechanisms for steam engines. While president of the Novelty Iron Works, Allen continued his association with the New York & Erie Railroad, becoming its president in 1843.

Allen retired from active business in 1870 but continued as a consulting engineer for projects such as the Brooklyn Bridge and the Panama Railroad. During 1871–1873 he served as president of the American Society of Civil Engineers. Allen also became interested in the teaching of astronomy and published a book on the subject. He helped to found the Union League Club of New York City and was one of the organizers of the New York Gallery of Art. He died in East Orange, New Jersey.

Throughout his life Allen made significant contributions to America's technological development, but his major achievement must be seen as his role in developing the first railroad in the United States. The South Carolina Railroad showed that steam-powered locomotives were a practical form of transportation. Its success led to other railroad projects throughout the United States.

• Materials relating to the life of Allen are in the John B. Jervis Papers located in the Jervis Public Library in Rome, N.Y. *Astronomy in Its General Facts and Relations, Taught by Aid of Mechanical Presentation and Illustration* (1877), is Allen's only significant publication. Biographical details of Allen are in F. Daniel Larkin, "Horatio Allen," in *The Encyclopedia of American Business History and Biography: Railroads in the Nineteenth Century*, ed. Robert Frey (1988). Details of Allen's role in the Delaware & Hudson Canal project can be found in Manville Wakefield, *Coal Boats to Tidewater: The Story of the Delaware & Hudson Canal* (1965). Information on Allen's contributions to the development of American railroads is in John F. Stover, *American Railroads* (1961), and Burke Davis, *The Southern Railway* (1985).

DAVID F. CHANNELL

ALLEN, Ira (1 May 1751–15 Jan. 1814), frontier entrepreneur and Vermont political leader, was born in Cornwall, Connecticut, the son of Joseph Allen and Mary Baker, farmers. Little is known of his youth, but in 1770 he followed his five elder brothers north to the New Hampshire Grants region and joined the Yankee versus Yorker struggle, which stemmed from the 1764 Crown decree that New York rather than New Hampshire owned the area that would become Vermont. While brother Ethan was leading the Green Mountain Boys against New York's attempts to rule the disputed territory, Ira surveyed the New Hampshire–granted townships of the Champlain and Winooski river valleys on behalf of speculators from southern New England. Impressed by the Champlain Valley wilderness, he persuaded his brothers Ethan, Heman, and Zimri, along with cousin Remember Baker, to form the Onion River Land Company in January 1773 to buy discounted New Hampshire lands in what he called "the country my soul delighted in." By the start of the American Revolution, the company's partners had amassed holdings of 65,000 acres as the first step in Ira's plan for achieving personal and family wealth.

After serving as a lieutenant in the 1775 American invasion of Canada, Allen returned to the Grants in February 1776 and joined the drive for independence from New York. With brother Ethan absent until May 1778 as a British prisoner, Ira played a leading role in the series of conventions that culminated in January 1777 with the creation of the state of New Connecticut (renamed Vermont in July 1777). For the remainder of the war, Allen was a mainstay of Vermont's ruling oligarchy, working tirelessly to defend the independent republic against its many internal and external enemies. He served simultaneously as state treasurer, surveyor general, member of the Governor's Council, and secretary to Governor Thomas Chittenden; he wrote propaganda equating Vermont's struggle against New York with the national revolution against England; and he traveled widely as Vermont's ambassador-at-large to the neighboring states and Congress.

Allen's most hazardous service on revolutionary Vermont's behalf began in 1780, when the British extended overtures to the state for a separate peace. Between November 1780 and September 1781 he made three trips to Lake Champlain for clandestine discussions with representatives of General Frederick Haldimand. Initially the handful of Vermont leaders involved in the Haldimand affair conducted the talks as a necessary military strategy to forestall another British invasion from the north, but when Congress continued to withhold recognition of Vermont's independence, the Allens and their circle began to reconsider a change in allegiance. In October 1781 Haldimand sent an army south from Canada with a proclamation announcing Vermont's return to the empire, and only the news of Cornwallis's surrender at Yorktown turned Haldimand's forces around and saved the Vermont conspirators from having to make a public choice between Crown and Congress.

Following the Revolution, as an influx of newcomers replaced Vermont's pioneer leaders, Allen's political power dwindled. By 1787 he had relinquished his positions in state government and refocused his attention on the Champlain Valley. From his base at Colchester, Allen worked to attract settlers to northwestern Vermont. He had mills and shops built, roads cut, and surveys run. He also added steadily to his holdings of choice lands. In September 1789 he married 25-year-old Jerusha Enos and gave her the northern Vermont town of Irasburg as a wedding present. The couple had three children, but home and family never challenged business among Allen's priorities. Certain that his grand plans for the area could not fail, in 1791 he secured a college for the Champlain Valley with a pledge of £4,000 that persuaded the state legislature to select Burlington as the home for the newly chartered University of Vermont.

Allen's lands bordered a water system that flowed north, so trade with Canada was the key to Allen's future. He hinted to the British that independent Vermont might still rejoin the empire and collaborated with his brother Levi to ship Vermont lumber and agricultural products north in exchange for cash and European manufactured goods. The brothers had high hopes for this two-way traffic, but success proved elusive. Although Vermont's official entry into the United States in 1791 (a development Allen deplored as potentially detrimental to his trading with Canada but did not actively oppose) had little effect on their commercial operations, by the mid-1790s he and Levi were deeply in debt at Quebec and elsewhere.

In December 1795 a desperate Allen mortgaged 45,000 acres of his best lands (at the time he claimed ownership of 200,000 acres) to General William Hull for £4,000 and sailed to England. There he sought permission to build a ship canal from St. John to the St. Lawrence River just north of Montreal that would improve the Champlain Valley's access to transatlantic trade. The Pitt government hesitated, and in May 1796 Allen traveled to France and asked the directory to back a democratic revolution in British Canada. The directory agreed, and in November 1796 Allen sailed from Ostend aboard the American ship *Olive Branch* with 15,000 muskets to equip French-Canadian and American recruits. His scheme foundered, however, when a British warship captured the *Olive Branch*. During the eighteen frustrating months of litigation in London that followed, Allen published several books and pamphlets to support his claim that the guns were meant for the American state militias. Unable to convince the admiralty courts, he returned to France in 1798 to obtain additional documents, but this time the directory had him imprisoned for nearly a year, apparently on suspicion of being a British spy.

Allen returned to Vermont in May 1801 to find that creditors, taxes, and lawsuits by members of his own family had stripped him of most of his properties. Unable to shore up his fortunes, in April 1803 he fled south to avoid imprisonment for debt. He spent the last decade of his life in Philadelphia, estranged from his family, attempting to obtain compensation from England for his *Olive Branch* losses, publishing additional pamphlets, and anticipating the recovery of his lost wealth. Owner of the largest domain in Vermont during his heyday, Allen died in Philadelphia as a pauper, and his body went to an unmarked grave in the city's Free Quaker Cemetery. Yet despite his ultimate failure, in his checkered career as land speculator, leader of independent Vermont, revolutionary propagandist, and backwoods entrepreneur, Allen was northern New England's most noteworthy counterpart to William Blount, James Wilkinson, Aaron Burr, and the other American adventurers of his generation who sought wealth and power through frontier intrigue and rebellion.

• The largest collections of Allen's voluminous papers are in the Vermont State Archives, the University of Vermont Library, and the Vermont Historical Society. Most of his books and pamphlets, including his *Natural and Political History of the State of Vermont* (1798) and numerous *Olive Branch* titles, are reprinted in J. Kevin Graffagnino, ed., *Ethan and Ira Allen: Collected Works* (1992). James B. Wilbur, *Ira Allen: Founder of Vermont 1751–1814* (1928), is the only full-length biography, but its value is diminished by Wilbur's uncritical adoration of his subject. The best modern assessments of Allen's career are Graffagnino, "'Twenty Thousand Muskets!!!' Ira Allen and the *Olive Branch* Affair, 1796–1800," *William and Mary Quarterly*, 3d ser., 48 (1991): 409–31, and "'The Country My Soul Delighted In': The Onion River Land Company and the Vermont Frontier," *New England Quarterly* 65 (1992): 24–60. For background on early Vermont, see also Matt B. Jones, *Vermont in the Making 1750–1777* (1939); Charles A. Jellison, *Ethan Allen: Frontier Rebel* (1969); Michael Sherman, ed., *A More Perfect Union: Vermont Becomes a State, 1777–1816* (1991); and Chilton Williamson, *Vermont in Quandary: 1763–1825* (1949).

J. Kevin Graffagnino

ALLEN, James (25 Dec. 1697–7 Jan. 1755), merchant and politician, was born in Boston, Massachusetts, the son of Jeremiah Allen, the longtime treasurer of the province, and Mary Caball. Ranked fifth by social status in a class of seventeen at Harvard College, he graduated in 1717. Allen then entered his father's merchant business, importing dry goods from England and exchanging New England fish for West India sugar. In 1725 he married Martha Fitch, daughter of Colonel Thomas Fitch. They had no children. Allen belonged to Boston's Congregational West Church but was not a bigot: he contributed £20 to the Anglican King's Chapel for the purchase of bells.

Allen achieved both importance and notoriety as the leading "country" or opposition spokesman in Massachusetts politics between the death of Elisha Cooke in 1737 and the rise of James Otis and Samuel Adams in the 1760s. Allen entered politics after his father ran afoul of Governor Jonathan Belcher, who negatived the House of Representatives' reelection of the treasurer in 1736. Such was the ill will that the elder Allen refused to turn over his accounts; in return, the province denied him more than £7,000 he had advanced for the defense of the frontier out of his own pocket.

James Allen made his political career as one of Boston's four members of the Massachusetts House of Representatives. He was elected to this post from 1739 to 1742 and from 1747 until his death. In the late 1730s Boston faced a declining economy; chronic inflation and a shortage of hard cash that the Land and Silver Banks of 1739–1741 tried to remedy; and the hardships of King George's War (1740–1748). Young "court" politicians led by brothers-in-law Thomas Hutchinson and Andrew Oliver were chosen for the assembly along with "country" leaders such as Allen. The narrow margins that determined several of Allen's victories attest to the keen competition between his predominantly middle-class group and the more elite court faction: he won with 336 of 672 votes in 1739, 213 of 408 in 1740, 270 of 451 in 1747, and 282 of 445 in 1753, for example. One reason for Allen's less than unanimous support was his opposition to the popular Land Bank of 1740: he not only signed a remonstrance refusing to accept the bank's notes but threw people out of his shop who attempted to use them.

Allen began his career in the assembly as an opponent of Governor Belcher. In 1740 the house censured him for circulating a "false and injurious" letter, titled "A Letter to a Farmer in the Country," in which appeared "sundry base and dishonorable reflections and insinuations respecting the conduct of the house," notably that it had supported the unpopular Belcher, who was about to be replaced by William Shirley. Allen naturally supported Shirley at first, who returned the favor by appointing him judge of the vice admiralty court, the position previously held by Shirley himself.

Allen did not remain in the governor's camp for long. By 1747, having lost out to fellow merchants Thomas Hancock and Christopher Kilby for the contract to supply Massachusetts's garrison at Louisbourg, the great fortress captured from the French in 1745, Allen was at the head of Shirley's opponents. He accused the governor of trading with the enemy in November 1748; the assembly responded by suspending him until he apologized. When he refused to do so and attempted to prove the charges instead, his rival Hutchinson, serving as Speaker of the Massachusetts House of Representatives ruled him out of order and engineered his practically unprecedented expulsion on 27 December. The vote was a narrow 30 to 27, reflecting the nearly even balance between the governor's supporters and opponents as the unsuccessful King George's War ground to an expensive conclusion.

Allen did not accept his fate quietly. In his "A Letter to the Freeholders and Other Inhabitants of Massachusetts Bay" early in 1749, he targeted representatives who voted for his expulsion as well as those who approved of Hutchinson's controversial plan to use the £183,000 Britain had reimbursed Massachusetts for its expenses in conquering Louisbourg to retire the province's inflated paper currency at ten to one. In what was Massachusetts's first instance of province-wide electioneering, Allen pleaded with the voters to turn his rivals out of office.

Allen was generally unsuccessful in this attempt. Hutchinson and another key lieutenant of Governor Shirley, Robert Hale of Beverly, uncharacteristically lost their seats in the house. But eighteen of the thirty who had voted to expel Allen and twenty-six of the forty who approved the currency redemption retained their seats, both fairly normal proportions. Allen, who served in the assembly until his death, remained in opposition to Shirley for the next several years although he no longer attracted exceptional attention. He died of apoplexy in Boston.

The *Boston Evening Post* (20 Jan. 1755) eulogized Allen as "a scourge to exalted wickedness, an advocate for humble merit, an enemy to false colouring" who "dissembled nothing but his virtues. . . . Inaccessible to corruption . . . impenetrable by flattery, neither the whispers nor the clamours of the great could stifle or soften" the "independency" of a man who "abhorred the low arts of intriguing politicians." A more balanced judgment would place Allen among many mid-eighteenth-century Massachusetts political figures who shifted allegiance between Governors Belcher and Shirley and between court and country so that patriotism and personal interest nicely coincided.

• Much, albeit scattered, material on Allen for the years in which he was politically active is in the Massachusetts State Archives; the Boston Town Records, reprinted in the Boston Records Commissioners' *Reports* (1880–1902); and the House of Representatives of Massachusetts Bay, *Journals*, ed. Worthington C. Ford et al. (55 vols., 1919–1990). His two major pamphlets may be found in Clifford K. Shipton, ed., *Early American Imprints* (1959), microfilm. Allen is the subject of a sketch by Shipton in *Sibley's Harvard Graduates*, vol. 6 (1942), pp. 159–64. He figures in the political histories of eighteenth-century Massachusetts, including John A. Schutz, *William Shirley: King's Governor of Massachusetts* (1961); Robert Zemsky, *Merchants, Farmers, and River Gods* (1971); and William Pencak, *War, Politics and Revolution in Provincial Massachusetts* (1981).

WILLIAM PENCAK

ALLEN, James Lane (21 Dec. 1849–18 Feb. 1925), writer, was born on a farm near Lexington, Kentucky, the son of Richard Allen and Helen Jane Foster. The effects of the Civil War and Reconstruction depleted the family fortune but not Allen's love for the antebellum South. Almost all of his works display a tension between the idealized and the romantic, and the realistic and pragmatic. In 1872 Allen received a B.A. degree with honors from Kentucky University (later Transylvania College) after working his way through school. He later received an M.A. degree from Kentucky University (1877) and began a twelve-year teaching career that included public and private schools in Kentucky and Missouri and culminated in a professorship in Latin at Bethany College, West Virginia.

Allen's literary criticism had appeared as early as 1883—an essay on Henry James's (1843–1916) *The Portrait of a Lady*—followed by articles on John Keats and Nathaniel Hawthorne among others. After Allen published a few poems, his short story "Too Much Momentum" appeared in the April 1885 issue of *Harper's*. Allen's emphasis on a lyrical writing style and the oft-noted influence of Hawthorne can be seen in his first book, *Flute and Violin and Other Kentucky Tales and Romances* (1891). Also evident is the influence of his home state; Allen is usually classed with late nineteenth-century local color writers such as George Washington Cable and Mary Murfree. Following publication of his only book on nonfiction, *The Blue Grass Region of Kentucky and Other Kentucky Articles* (1892), Allen moved to New York City. He visited Kentucky in 1898 to receive an honorary doctor of laws from Kentucky University and then never again returned to his native state.

In 1894 Allen published *A Kentucky Cardinal* and the next year its sequel, *Aftermath*. These popular short novels, which trace the courtship and marriage of the nature-loving southern gentleman Adam Moss and the strong-willed Georgiana Cobb, demonstrate Allen's skill with the romance. Taking a different direction in *Summer in Arcady* (1896), Allen was denounced by critics for his frankness in dealing with sexual awakening. His most popular novel, *The Choir Invisible* (1897), is a return to the romantic mode of his earlier work. After 1900 Allen turned more and more to contemporary issues in his work: evolution in *The*

Reign of Law (1900), the double standard in *The Mettle of the Pasture* (1903), and marital relationships in *The Bride of the Mistletoe* (1909) and its sequel, *The Doctor's Christmas Eve* (1910). These works—both because of their subject matter and their sometimes too realistic and/or experimental style—alienated Allen's readers and the critics.

The latter part of Allen's life was hard. His own more frequent illnesses and those of his sister—for whom he had cared since their mother's death in 1889—took what little income his magazine writing was now providing. He never married. Two years after his last novel, *The Alabaster Box* (1923), was published, Allen died in New York City, in the decade that would see the rise of T. S. Eliot, Ernest Hemingway, F. Scott Fitzgerald, and William Faulkner. Within a few years, most of his work was out of print. In retrospect, however, Allen made something of a mark; in the words of Merrill Skaggs, "As fictional ground . . . Kentucky was in a real sense outlined by James Lane Allen." Allen's realistic treatment of contemporary problems is in contrast to much popular late nineteenth-century southern writing. Like Ellen Glasgow, though, he has often been dismissed as too genteel and romantic at a time when literature and its critics were rushing to embrace modernism. As a transitional writer, as one willing to attempt (too realistically for some, too romantically for others) serious literary treatment of society's problems, Allen certainly deserves another look.

• Letters of James Lane Allen are in the collections of the Kentucky Historical Society; the Filson Club of Louisville, Ky.; the Duke University Library; and the University of Kentucky Library. A brief biography, a critical review of his work, a bibliography of primary works, and an annotated bibliography of secondary works can be found in William K. Bottorff, *James Lane Allen* (1964). See also Grant C. Knight, *James Lane Allen and the Genteel Tradition* (1935), for more biographical information. Extremely brief accounts are in Merrill Skaggs, "Varieties of Local Color," in *The History of Southern Literature*, ed. Louis D. Rubin (1985), and in Charles R. Wilson and William Ferris, eds., *The Encyclopedia of Southern Culture* (1989). Memorial obituaries appear in *Outlook*, 4 Mar. 1925, and in the *American Review of Reviews*, Apr. 1925.

LEE EMLING HARDING

ALLEN, Joel Asaph (19 July 1838–29 Aug. 1921), zoologist and museum official, was born near Springfield, Massachusetts, the son of Joel Allen, a carpenter, housebuilder, and later a farmer, and Harriet Trumbull, a former schoolteacher. Allen attended the local public schools in the wintertime, but his father, a rigidly puritanical Congregationalist, insisted that he work on the family farm during good weather. From the age of about fourteen, as Allen's interest in natural history, particularly birds, increased, his interest in farming diminished. He nevertheless worked long hours for his father in a spirit of filial loyalty, possibly laying the foundation for the serious bouts of ill health that would plague him in later years. Whenever possible, he prepared study specimens of birds and animals for his own private collection. From 1858 to 1862 Allen's father supported his intermittent attendance at nearby Wilbraham Academy.

In order to reduce the financial drain on his family while continuing his education, Allen sold his painstakingly accumulated natural history specimens to the academy early in 1862. He used the proceeds to begin studying as a special student under Louis Agassiz at Harvard University's Lawrence Scientific School and its Museum of Comparative Zoology. He remained at Harvard for three years, except for one six-month period, during which a case of measles had affected his eyesight, causing him to return home. In late March 1865 Allen accompanied Agassiz to Brazil, where he assisted his mentor with specimen collecting for the museum. After returning to Cambridge early in 1866, Allen again spent some time at the family farm, recovering from another bout of ill health before undertaking a private collecting trip to the Middle West. During the winter of 1868–1869 he underwrote and led a small party on a three-month exploration of eastern Florida. His resulting monograph, *On the Mammals and Birds of East Florida* (1871), was a major systematic and biogeographical study that led to his recognition as a leading American zoologist and won him a Humboldt Scholarship at Harvard.

One of the ablest American scientists working in the fields of avian and mammalian systematics from the 1870s to the end of his life, Allen was an early advocate of the use of trinomials in zoological nomenclature. He described some 430 species and subspecies of mammals and more than 675 species and subspecies of birds during his career. A pioneering and influential biogeographer, he devoted considerable attention to the effects of climate and geography on the distribution of animals and plants in several monographs and shorter studies during the 1870s and 1880s.

Allen's tenure as curator of birds and mammals at the Museum of Comparative Zoology (1867–1885) proved to be one of his most productive periods. He made collecting trips to the Rocky Mountains (1871–1872) and the Yellowstone region (1873), the latter trip under the auspices of Spencer F. Baird, assistant secretary of the Smithsonian Institution. Following several interesting encounters with Indians on these trips, Allen remarked that he had felt very much like a collector of animal specimens in danger of being himself collected. Allen's study *The American Bisons, Living and Extinct* was published jointly by the Geological Survey of Kentucky and the Museum of Comparative Zoology in 1876. From 1876 to 1882 he was a special collaborator with the U.S. Geological and Geographical Survey, later the U.S. Geological Survey. With Dr. Elliott Coues, a government physician-naturalist, he published the substantial *Monographs of North American Rodentia* (1877) as volume eleven of the survey's *Memoir* series. His *History of North American Pinnipeds*, an 800-page monograph, appeared in 1880 as number 12 in the survey's *Miscellaneous Publications*. A massive projected study of whales and their allies was interrupted by a long illness, and only a lengthy bibliography (1882) and an account of the "North American Right Whale and Its Allies" (1908) were published. Pleurisy and a nervous breakdown compelled Allen to take an extended rest in Colorado during much of 1882, and he was never again able to withstand the rigors of fieldwork.

With William Brewster, a well-to-do independent ornithologist from Cambridge, and others, Allen was instrumental in the creation of the Nuttall Ornithological Club in 1876. He was editor of the *Bulletin* of this regional organization for seven years. In 1883 Allen, Brewster, and Coues together formed the American Ornithologists' Union, the first nationwide organization for scientists and dedicated amateurs primarily interested in the ethology, distribution, anatomy, systematics, and migration of birds. Allen was president of the union from its inception until 1891. He also served as editor of the AOU's journal the *Auk* for more than a quarter century, contributing some 643 articles, reviews, and obituaries to the journal during his tenure as its editor, and edited a number of other AOU publications. He was heavily involved in several key AOU committees concerned with nomenclaturel and classification issues for nearly thirty years. The protection of birds was also one of Allen's principal interests from 1885 onward.

Allen remained at Harvard until 1885, when as a result of fiscal stringencies placed on the Museum of Comparative Zoology, he elected to accept the position of curator of ornithology and mammalogy at the American Museum of Natural History in New York City. He remained in this position until 1907, when he was relieved of responsibilities for the ornithological collections and became curator solely of mammals. From 1887 to 1890 he also had charge of the collections in invertebrate zoology, and from 1887 to 1901, the collections of fishes and reptiles. During his thirty-eight years at the American Museum, the number of bird specimens increased from about 13,000 to more than 190,000, while the mammal collections grew from approximately 1,000 specimens to 50,000, not including skeletal material, during this same period. From the time of his arrival at the American Museum, Allen made cataloging its collections one of his principal concerns. He also edited the museum's zoological publications, including its *Bulletin* (37 vols.) and its zoological *Memoirs* (32 vols.), for more than three decades.

Allen was one of the founders of the first National Audubon Society in 1886 and helped found and direct the fortunes of the Audubon Society of New York State from 1897 to 1912. He was one of several founders of the National Association of Audubon Societies in 1905, serving as a director and member of the executive committee from 1905, and as second vice president from 1908 to 1912. From 1910 until his death, Allen served as a member of the Commission on Zoological Nomenclature of the International Congress of Zoology. When the American Society of Mammalogists was formed in 1919, its founders sought to make Allen the new organization's first president, but he declined on grounds of frail health.

A shy and retiring person, Allen was known for the meticulousness he demonstrated in his published monographs, articles, shorter notices, and reviews, which totaled roughly 1,440 titles. He rarely made public presentations, though his judgment in editorial matters and dedication to his many administrative duties were much prized by his associates.

Allen had married Mary Manning Cleveland in 1874; they had one son before her death in 1879. In 1886 he married Susan Augusta Taft; they had no children.

Allen was awarded the Walker Grand Prize by the Boston Society of Natural History in 1903 and the Gold Medal of the Linnaean Society of New York in 1916. He was a member or honorary member of some thirty scientific societies in this country and abroad. Allen died at his home in Cornwall-on-Hudson, New York.

• Some of Allen's correspondence can be found in the files of the Departments of Ornithology and Mammalogy at the American Museum of Natural History, New York City. Allen's *Autobiographical Notes and a Bibliography of the Scientific Publications of Joel Asaph Allen*, a special publication of the American Museum in 1916, includes a complete bibliography of more than 1,400 of Allen's publications to that year. This work and a number of his more important studies in the fields of speciation and biogeography were reprinted in *Selected Works of Joel Asaph Allen*, ed. K. B. Sterling (1974). Frank M. Chapman, "Biographical Memoir of Joel Asaph Allen," National Academy of Sciences, *Biographical Memoirs* 21 (1926): 1–20, brings Allen's bibliography up to date. See also Mark V. Barrow, Jr., *A Passion for Birds: American Ornithology after Audubon* (1998). An obituary by Witmer Stone is in the *Auk* 38 (1921): 490–92. A memorial by Chapman is in the *Auk* 39 (1922): 1–14.

KEIR B. STERLING

ALLEN, Levi (16 Jan. 1746–16 Dec. 1801), American Loyalist and free-trade advocate, was born in Cornwall, Connecticut, the son of Joseph Allen and Mary Baker, farmers. Though self-educated, Allen taught school in the Hudson River Valley for a year when he was eighteen. Expressing boredom with that sedentary life, he left teaching for the Indian trade in 1765. Over the next four years, Allen and his partner, Peter Pond, the prominent explorer and maker of wildly inaccurate maps, were among the first European Americans to trade in the Miami country. This experience made Allen a lifelong defender of the Native Americans. As he wrote in his autobiography, "Christians have not so much to boast over the American Indians as they Vainly attribute to themselves." After a competitor in Detroit tried to kill him, Allen moved to the Green Mountains with several of his brothers and cousins in 1771. Allen became a member of the Green Mountain Boys, the militia founded by his brother Ethan Allen to resist New York's jurisdiction.

Like every other member of his large family, Levi Allen rushed to support the patriot cause in the days after Lexington and served as a lieutenant to Ethan Allen in the capture of Ticonderoga from the British on 10 May 1775. Slated for a command in the Green Mountain Regiment of the Continental army, Levi Allen was vetoed along with Ethan by a group of senior officials who distrusted the entire family. After Ethan was taken prisoner during an attack on Montreal, Levi abandoned military duty and devoted himself for two years to obtaining his brother's release from British captivity.

In New York City, attempting to arrange his brother's release in 1776, Allen took advantage of the profits to be made supplying goods to the British army and adopted a qualified Loyalism. It seemed obvious to Allen that everyone would benefit if the Americans and British ceased their senseless fighting and devoted themselves to business. Patriot officials felt otherwise, jailing Allen for six months at New London, Connecticut, for passing counterfeit money and trading with the British.

While Allen was in jail, his brothers charged him with Loyalism, and the new state of Vermont confiscated most of his property. After his release, Allen married Nancy "Anna" Allen of New Milford, Connecticut, on 29 July 1779; the couple had one child. Allen then joined the British army in the South as a supplier and in 1781 opened a store on the St. John River in East Florida. The British government planned to make East Florida a refuge for the southern Loyalists but in 1783 betrayed its Loyalist supporters by ceding the region to Spain. Allen returned to Vermont, where, despite challenging Ethan Allen to a duel, he was welcomed back by his family and became a central character in the Haldimand Negotiations, which sought to bring Vermont into the British Empire as an autonomous province. With the failure of those efforts in 1784, Allen worked to keep Vermont out of the American Union and to effect a free-trade treaty between Vermont and Britain. As Vermont's unofficial ambassador to Canada and Britain, Allen won a number of significant trade concessions from the British. After Vermont joined the Union in 1791, Allen turned his efforts to reconciling the United States and Britain on the principles of Adam Smith and free trade, all the while speculating in frontier land titles in Vermont, New York, Quebec, Pennsylvania, and Georgia.

Levi Allen referred to himself as a citizen of no nation, but of the world. He saw free trade as the peaceful weapon that could shatter artificial barriers and archaic superstitions, and restore harmony between the United States and Britain. Though an excited proponent of the new economic theories, Allen loathed the new democratic ethos unleashed by the American Revolution. And while he despised England's traditional ways of conducting business, with its emphasis on connection and birth, he admired its wealth and stability. Not surprisingly, Allen's former allies on both sides of the Revolution remained suspicious of him. Not comfortable in Vermont, Allen settled in St. Jean, Quebec, and battled British trade restrictions. In 1797 the government of Quebec, convinced that his brother Ira Allen was behind a plot to overthrow British rule in Canada, imprisoned Levi Allen for two months in Fort St. Louis on suspicion of high treason. After his release, Allen's complicated business deals began to unravel. He died in the Burlington jail while imprisoned for unpaid debts.

Levi Allen had devoted the last twenty-five years of his life to keeping the U.S.-Canadian border open. Generally, he succeeded in these efforts, usually with the support of Vermont's government and the complicity of Canada's, and despite the opposition of the U.S. government. This advocacy of free trade had significant long-term consequences for U.S.-Canadian relations.

• Allen's papers can be found in the Levi Allen Papers in the Henry Stevens Collection at the Vermont State Archives, Montpelier; the Allen Family Papers in the Bailey/Howe Library at the University of Vermont, Burlington; and in the Colonial Series Papers at the Public Archives of Canada, Ottawa, Ontario. See James B. Wilbur, *Ira Allen: Founder of Vermont, 1751–1814* (1928), for the business activities and personal relations of the Allen family; Michael Bellesiles, "Anticipating America," in *A More Perfect Union*, ed. Michael Sherman (1991), on Allen's political views; and Bellesiles, "The Autobiography of Levi Allen," *Vermont History* 60 (1992): 77–94.

MICHAEL A. BELLESILES

ALLEN, Macon Bolling (1816–15 Oct. 1894), lawyer and judge, was born A. Macon Bolling in Indiana; the names of his parents and exact date of birth are unknown. He changed his name to Macon Bolling Allen by act of the Massachusetts legislature on 26 January 1844. Details of Allen's early life and education are sketchy and contradictory. His birth name is given in some sources as Malcolm B. Allen, and his birthplace as South Carolina. Evidence suggests that he lived in Maine and Massachusetts as a young man. Maine denied his initial application to the Maine bar because of allegations that he was not a state citizen, but he purportedly ran a Portland business before 1844. It is known that he read law in the Maine offices of two white abolitionist lawyers, Samuel E. Sewell and General Samuel Fessenden, and that the latter promoted his admission to the Maine bar in 1844.

Allen became a member of the Maine bar later in 1844 after passing the law examination required of all nonresidents. He thus became the first African American licensed to practice law in the United States. When he was admitted to the Massachusetts bar in 1845, a Boston abolitionist newspaper, the *Liberator* (9 May 1845), stated that Allen had received a classical education and that he was a brilliant and energetic young man of exceptional character and deportment. Allen never practiced law in Maine, possibly because of its small African-American population (only 1,335 in 1844); instead, after being admitted to the bar, he immediately moved (or perhaps returned) to Massachusetts.

Allen began practicing law in Massachusetts after his admission to the Suffolk County bar on 3 May

1845, making him the first African American admitted to that state's bar as well. He apparently experienced some difficulty in obtaining clients during the first year of his practice. In November 1845 Allen wrote New Yorker John Jay, Jr. (the chief justice's grandson), that New Englanders supported only famous, wealthy, or long-established attorneys; he wondered whether New York's lack of such a tradition and its large African-American population offered better opportunities for a black lawyer. Undoubtedly some of the difficulty stemmed from Boston abolitionists' public denunciation of Allen's refusal to support their petition pledging nonsupport for the government during the Mexican War. A bitter 1846 letter from Allen to radical abolitionist William Lloyd Garrison explained both his strong sympathy with enslaved African Americans and his private and independent approach to the problem.

Allen's fortunes soon changed. He was appointed a justice of the peace by Massachusetts's Whig governors in 1847 and 1854; the former event made him the nation's first appointed African-American judicial official. He remained in Charlestown, near Boston, where he practiced law and served as justice of the peace until after the Civil War.

In the late 1860s Allen joined a small cadre of northern African-American lawyers and activists who migrated South—in his case, to Charleston, South Carolina. There, in 1868, he joined Robert Brown Elliot and William J. Whipper, two African-American lawyer-politicians, in forming a law firm that attracted clients of both races. With offices at 91 Broad Street in Charleston, Whipper, Elliot, and Allen was the first known African-American law firm in the United States. The firm's combined legal talents and political influence enabled it to hire and train many other African-American lawyers. Allen never gained high political office, as his law partners did—both were elected to the South Carolina legislature, and Elliot to the U.S. Congress in 1870 and 1872—though he ran for secretary of state as a Republican in 1872 and for the same position on Martin Delaney's 1874 fusion ticket. In February 1873 the South Carolina legislature elected him a judge of the Inferior Court, to fill a vacancy left by George Lee, with whom Allen had competed for the original appointment. He was elected to probate court in 1876 and served with distinction through 1878.

Allen returned to law practice in Charleston, and little is known of his life after that. He died in Washington, D.C., leaving a widow (name unknown) and a son, Arthur W. Macon. A brief obituary appeared in the Charleston *Daily News and Courier*, 17 October 1894.

At his death, Allen left a legacy as a pioneer in African-American legal history that transcended time, space, and the tenor of the nation and placed him in the forefront of the black struggle. His accomplishments in New England and South Carolina paved the way for the generations of black lawyers and activists who followed.

• Few published materials exist about Allen's life. The best of the scattered sources are Charles S. Brown, "The Genesis of the Negro Lawyer in New England," *Negro History Bulletin* 22, pt. 1 (Apr. 1959): 147–51; J. Clay Smith, *Emancipation: The Making of the Black Lawyer, 1844–1944* (1993); G. Carter and C. Peter Ripley, *Black Abolitionist Papers, 1830–1865* (1981); W. T. Davis, *Bench and Bar of Massachusetts*, vol. 2 (1895); Paul Finkelman, "Not Only the Judge's Robes Were Black: African-American Lawyers as Social Engineers during and after Slavery," *Stanford Law Review* 47 (1994): 161–209; W. Weeks, *History of the Law, the Courts, and the Lawyers of Maine* (1863); J. O. Horton and L. E. Horton, *Black Bostonians* (1979); the *Charleston Daily Courier*, 1871 through 1874; the Boston *Daily Advertiser*, 5 May 1845; the *Daily Eastern Argus*, 15 July 1844; "Only Negro Lawyer in Maine," *Philadelphia North American*, 23 Apr. 1915; C. Ferguson, "Group Roles in American Legal History—Blacks," *Law Library Journal* 69 (1969): 470; and Wilson Armistead, *A Tribute to the Negro* (1848).

JOHNIE D. SMITH

ALLEN, Nathan (25 Apr. 1813–1 Jan. 1889), physician, social reformer, and public health advocate, was born in Princeton, Massachusetts, the son of Moses Allen and Mehitable Oliver, farmers. He spent his first seventeen years on the family farm, learning to work hard and to follow the Christian principles of his parents. He could not afford a higher education, but a friend in Leicester helped pay his tuition at Amherst Academy and then at Amherst College, where he matriculated in 1832, graduating in 1836.

Allen then served for a year as principal of the Westminster Academy, whose mode of Puritan education he extolled in "The Old Academies" (1885). In 1838 he accompanied his brother Jonathan to Philadelphia, where Jonathan studied medicine at the University of Pennsylvania. The next year Nathan entered the medical department of Pennsylvania College, graduating in 1841.

While in medical school, Allen supported himself by working as a proofreader and subeditor in the printing and publishing offices of Adam Waldie. He was involved in preparing the first three volumes (1838–1841) of Fowler and Wells's *American Phrenological Journal and Miscellany*; Allen appeared as editor of the third volume. This work brought him into contact with such distinguished men as the physiologist Charles Caldwell, the educator Horace Mann, and the Scottish phrenologist George Combe. Allen's medical thesis, "On the Connection of Mental Philosophy with Medicine," appeared in volume three of the *Journal* and was also issued separately by Waldie. Despite this experience, he appears to have had no special interest in phrenology thereafter.

In fall 1841 Allen settled in Lowell, Massachusetts, where he practiced medicine for the remainder of his life. The same year, he married Sarah Hart Spaulding; they had no children. She died in 1855, and in 1857 he married Annie A. Waters, with whom he had four children. He differed from other physicians of his day in that he believed in the use of few drugs, but those few he gave in large doses that were unpleasant to take. More importantly, he believed in the prevention of disease and the laws of health, holding that it was better to prevent disease than to cure it by medicine. In 1851 Allen published *An Essay on the Opium Trade*, in which he castigated the British for bringing the cultivation of opium to India and forcing it on the Chinese at great profit.

Early in his practice Allen's attention was drawn to the difference between the birth rates of New England women and British and European women, and by the decrease in the number of children in the New England family over a century. These observations resulted in his publication in 1868 of the first of several papers on population and human increase, based on physiological and psychological principles. He went on to a wide range of allied studies grounded on census and registration reports and vital statistics. These studies led in turn to an outpouring of often lengthy periodical and newspaper articles over the next twenty years on physical and mental culture, public health and the prevention of disease, physical degeneracy, insanity, heredity and inheritance, intemperance, longevity, pauperism and crime, state medicine and public charity, intermarriage, marriage and divorce, obstetrics and maternity, and the education of women. In 1888 Allen republished in *Physical Development, or the Laws Governing the Human System* about forty of his best articles. His works were cited widely in the United States and Europe, and several were reprinted abroad.

Allen became convinced that God, or nature, had established a general law of propagation applicable to all normal life. He envisioned a normal standard of the human system in which each organ was complete in structure and fully performed its natural functions, working symmetrically and in harmony with the others. The nearer the organization of each individual approached that standard—if the laws of propagation were strictly observed—the greater would be the number of children and the better their ability to attain the high objectives of life. If, however, the organization deviated to the extreme in either direction so that it became dominated by the nerves on one hand or resulted in a low animal nature on the other, the tendency in affected families or races would be to gradually decrease and ultimately become extinct. This explained why those enjoying the very highest civilization or others living in the lowest savage state did not multiply rapidly. This law of population thus assumed a normal standard of physiology, upon which other important principles were based. Deviations from the standard resulted in weaknesses, diseases, and feeble states that, in turn, through hereditary transmission, begat mental predispositions that produced social evils and vices.

In 1864 Allen was appointed to the Massachusetts State Board of Charities, serving for fifteen years. In 1872 he was commissioned a delegate to an international congress in London to consider reform in prisons and other correctional institutions. Allen was appointed a commissioner of lunacy for Massachusetts and was responsible for issuing an 1875 report.

In 1857 Allen was chosen by the Massachusetts legislature to be a trustee of Amherst College, serving until his death. Believing that a sound constitution was the greatest gift any human could receive, he was instrumental in establishing a department of physical education at Amherst.

Allen was a leading voice in debating the social and philosophical questions of his day and one of the most quoted American medical men of the time. He was especially prominent as an advocate of personal and public hygiene, but he was not uncontroversial. On several occasions he was deposed from the Lowell Board of Health and was never chosen its chairman, disappointments he regarded as personal insults. Nonetheless, he gave years of free service to Lowell's St. John's Hospital and to the city dispensatory.

Allen strongly advocated a "ten-hour law" to set the maximum workday, risking his professional prospects by opposing many wealthy and influential citizens. He was known as a friend to the poor, the unfortunate, and the insane and as a reformer of institutions for their care, constantly urging humane treatment. He died in Lowell as a result of a head injury suffered in a fall.

• The Francis A. Countway Library of Medicine in Boston contains, in the Edward Jarvis Papers, a dozen letters Allen wrote to Jarvis (1844–1874) and some materials documenting Allen's association with the Massachusetts Medical Society. The two most detailed and important sources on his life and works are an anonymous vignette, "Our Gallery: Nathan Allen, M.D., LL.D.," *New England Medical Monthly* 3 (1883–1884): 215–19; and a memoir by his medical preceptee, David N. Patterson, "Life and Character of Nathan Allen, M.D., LL.D.," read to the Old Residents Historical Association (later the Lowell Historical Society) on 8 May 1889 and published in its *Contributions* 4, no. 2 (1889): 151–63. Lists of Allen's published writings appear in the first and second series of the *Index Catalogue of the Library of the Surgeon General's Office of the United States Army* and in *The National Union Catalog of Pre-1956 Imprints*. His oil portrait by Thomas B. Lawson hangs in the Mead Art Museum of Amherst College.

RICHARD J. WOLFE

ALLEN, Paul (15 Feb. 1775–18 Aug. 1826), editor and poet, was born in Providence, Rhode Island, the son of Paul Allen, Sr., a Rhode Island state representative, and Polly Cooke, the daughter of a governor of that state. In 1793 he graduated from Brown University (then Rhode Island College), where he displayed talent as an orator. Several of his orations were published, the earliest being a eulogy on a classmate delivered on 22 November 1792. Allen studied law but never practiced; indeed, most sources follow John Neal in calling him unfit for that profession and labeling him "childlike, irresponsible, irresolute, and credulous." Neal had a character in his novel *Randolph* (1823) say that Allen has "a character of sluggishness, slovenly inaptitude and moroseness. . . . Yet there is not a better natured fellow on earth."

Allen's *Original Poems, Serious and Entertaining* (1801) is an uneven collection that was critically and commercially unsuccessful even though many of the poems seem to have been designed to appeal to a popular audience. Some are superficial and topical celebrations of occasions such as the Fourth of July. Several, displaying a romantic bent, seem indebted to Philip Freneau. Allen's poem "Epitaph on an Indian" concerns a man who, having followed "native conscience," will "meet his God as man would meet a friend" while "Christians turn from gospel ray" and echoes Freneau's "The Indian Burial Ground." Other poems question the pursuit of science and material wealth and praise the "Pleasures of Fancy," arguing that it is art that mellows the ferocious savage "into social man."

After moving to Philadelphia, Allen contributed to and may have served as editor for both the *United States Gazette* (also known as *Bronson's Gazette*) and the *Port Folio*. In 1814 he edited *History of the Expedition under the Command of Captains Lewis and Clark, to the Sources of the Missouri, Thence across the Rocky Mountains and down the River Columbia to the Pacific Ocean . . .* , which Nicholas Biddle had created from the original journals. Allen's contribution to this work has long been misunderstood and underappreciated. As historian Lester J. Cappon explains, Allen functioned as an editor "in so far as he 'moulded' or 'revised' the text" that Biddle had produced.

In 1811 Allen had been commissioned by Charles Brockden Brown's family to write a biography of the novelist and to finish the "Complete System of Geography" left incomplete at Brown's death in 1810. Three years after receiving his commission, Allen still had not finished the "Geography," and, though given access to Brown's papers, he had done little on the biography. Allen did have one volume of the biography printed and given to the Brown family, but most of this edition consisted of unpublished manuscripts by Brown. Allen's work was later used and acknowledged by William Dunlap in his *The Life of Charles Brockden Brown* (1815).

In 1814 Allen, at the suggestion of Thomas Howard Hill, moved to Baltimore and with him founded the *Baltimore Telegraph and Commercial Advertiser*, which in an 1816 merger became part of the *Federal Republican and Baltimore Telegraph*. In this period he also was associated with the *Portico* (1816–1818) and contributed minor pieces to works authored or edited by others. After selling his share in the *Federal Republican* in 1818, Allen became editor of the weekly *Journal of the Times* (1818–1819) and the daily *Morning Chronicle* (1819–1824). The charge that during this period Allen was impoverished and even imprisoned for debt is suspect. From 1824 until his death he managed the *Saturday Evening Herald* and published the *Morning Post*. In 1819 Allen purportedly authored a two-volume *History of the American Revolution*. Despite as much as $75,000 in advance subscriptions, Allen never finished the project. John Neal and Tobias Watkins actually wrote almost all except the preface. The work, though factually flawed, is still useful for its insights into the tendency of Allen's society to romanticize the American Revolution.

In 1821 Allen published his book-length *Noah, a Poem* (1821). He emphasized his plot's connection to its biblical subject with pages of notes, but his real concern was his own time and society. Allen's preface asserts America's special place in the scheme of divine providence, citing events such as the detection of Benedict Arnold's treachery as evidence of God's special favor toward America. The poem itself culminates in an attack on slavery and especially on the attempt by some southerners to use a portion of the story of Noah to justify enslaving blacks. While the biblical Noah curses Canaan and asks God to make him a slave, Allen's Noah tells his son Japhet to have pity on the darker races and recognize them as equals before God:

> That man who now kneels trembling by thy side
> Is still thy brother though his skin be dark,
> For him almighty mercy built the ark.

Noah foresees and laments a time when slave ships, "Arks beyond number, freighted with . . . human flesh," will cross the ocean "to find a market for immortal man." Allen died in Baltimore. He had never married.

Thomas Jefferson in a letter called Allen "one of the two best writers of America," but more typical and accurate is Neal's assessment quoted in *American Writers* (1937) that Allen "had the material for a great poet" but through lack of industry would be remembered only as "a clever . . . editor." Today Allen is noted, if at all, for his historical and biographical works, but his poetry also deserves attention. The early *Original Poems* helps our understanding of the early American Romanticism that led to William Cullen Bryant's poetry, and *Noah* is a valuable illustration of the debate about slavery in the early republic.

• Allen's correspondence with Jefferson regarding the history of the Lewis and Clark expedition is in the Jefferson papers in the Library of Congress. The best biography is in Charles E. Bennett's preface to *The Life of Charles Brockden Brown* (1975). Much of what we know about Allen and the most significant contemporaneous criticism of his work is from John Neal, *Randolph, a Novel* (1823), and his article "American Writers," *Blackwood's Magazine*, Sept. 1824, pp. 304–11, reprinted in *American Writers*, ed. Fred Lewis Pattee (1937). J. Thomas Scharf, *History of Baltimore City and County* (1881), adds information on newspapers Allen edited. Lester J. Cappon, "Who Is the Author of the *History of the Expedition*?" *William and Mary Quarterly* 19 (Apr. 1962): 257–68, explains Allen's role in editing that work and the controversies surrounding his contribution to it.

STEVEN E. KAGLE

ALLEN, Philip (1 Sept. 1785–16 Dec. 1865), manufacturer, governor, and senator, was born in Providence, Rhode Island, the son of Captain Zachariah Allen, a West Indies trader, and Nancy Crawford. Allen received his early education from tutors before attending Taunton Academy in Providence, Robert Rogers School in Newport, and Jeremiah Chaplin's Latin School in Providence. In 1799 he entered Rhode Island College (now Brown University) and graduated in 1803.

After his father's death in 1801, Allen assumed responsibility for the family business. By 1806 his colleagues had elected him to the directorate of the Providence Insurance Company, attesting to his business acumen. As an entrepreneur, he experimented widely, constructing the first steam engine built in Providence. When the difficulties with England leading to the War of 1812 interrupted trade, he established a cotton mill at Woonasquatucket (eight miles from Providence) in 1812. The town of Allenville (now Enfield) developed around the mill. Two of his brothers also enjoyed successful careers in manufacturing. As an industrialist, Allen implemented several technological innovations to improve his operations. He was the first to use, for example, the improved bobbin, fly frames, and lapping machines for cotton cards. By 1831 he had developed the capability to produce printed calico, for which his firm became widely known. He attained considerable success in manufacturing and remained an industrial leader until his retirement in 1859.

Allen served in the Rhode Island General Assembly as a representative from Providence from 1819 to 1821, politically associated with the Adams Republicans. His business and other concerns preoccupied him during the years after 1821. In 1827 Seth Wheaton, the incumbent president of the Rhode Island branch of the Bank of the United States and disbursing agent for revolutionary pensions in Rhode Island, recommended Allen as his successor to President John Quincy Adams. Adams appointed Allen to these two patronage posts, which he held until 1836. Although he became a Democrat in the 1830s, Allen unsuccessfully opposed Andrew Jackson's war on the Second Bank of the United States. When Jackson prevailed and terminated the relationship between the federal government and the bank, Allen settled the bank's affairs and turned his attention to his thriving business concerns.

During the period of agitation for suffrage reform in Rhode Island, Allen stood solidly for the maintenance of the older way. As did many of his contemporaries across the country, he had strong concerns stirred by the popular politics that accompanied the movement for a more democratic franchise. He opposed Thomas Wilson Dorr's efforts to change the government of the state without its consent in 1840–1842 and personally established and armed the Rhode Island Carbineers to defend the state against what he deemed revolution and imminent anarchy during the crisis of 1842. That year Dorr and his supporters had convened an unauthorized constitutional convention, drafted a new and quite democratic constitution, submitted it for ratification, declared it ratified by a majority of the legally qualified voters, and sought to establish a government under the new constitution. After the decisive summer of 1842, with Dorr's followers in disarray, Allen joined with like-minded Law and Order or Algerine Democrats to secure a modern constitution for the state of Rhode Island in 1843. (Dorr and his friends used the label "Algerine" to brand their opponents as autocratic despots.) Thereafter, Allen remained active in politics as a tariff Democrat, supporting Martin Van Buren for the presidency in 1848, but he did not again seek public office until 1851.

In 1851 Allen sought election as governor to prevent Dorr's erstwhile supporters from gaining political control and implementing the radical reforms introduced earlier. Following his first campaign, he won the election by only 887 votes but soon consolidated his position. His major opponent during his years as governor was Dorr, the persistent reformer. Having been convicted of treason against the state in 1844 for his reform efforts, Dorr sought in 1851 to push through the Democratically controlled general assembly a bill reversing and voiding the decision of the state supreme court convicting him of treason. Allen successfully resisted Dorr's attempt, allowing only a bill restoring Dorr's civil and political rights on the grounds of clemency. Not until 1854, after Allen left the state, did a coalition of Free Soil Democrats and Conscience Whigs finally secure passage of Dorr's resolution, reversing, annulling, and expunging the 1844 state supreme court decision from the records of the state. During the struggle in 1851, however, Allen won complete control of the Democratic party in Rhode Island. As one editorial in the *Providence Daily Journal* stated, "He *owns* it [the Democratic party]." As a result, he won reelection twice by ever larger majorities in 1852 and 1853.

In 1853, upon the death of one of the state's U.S. senators, the general assembly could not meet to elect a successor because of the split between the senate and the house under the control of the Democrats and Whigs, respectively. Allen arranged a compromise that resulted in his election to the U.S. Senate, a position he assumed in December 1853 and retained until 1859, when he retired from politics and business. During his initial four years in the Senate, he focused largely on local issues, such as pensions, relief bills, local appropriations, and the like, and served on minor committees. In general, he supported the initiatives of the Franklin Pierce administration but remained in the background.

In the years from 1853 to 1859 Allen became increasingly embroiled in the sectional and other tensions that ultimately led to the Civil War in 1861. He flirted with the Know Nothing party and actually supported the Free Soil movement for a time. However, he always returned ultimately to his traditional loyalties. Thus, he opposed the repeal of the Missouri Compromise and, although absent from the Senate during the vote, announced his opposition to the Kansas-Nebraska Act of 1854. As a tariff Democrat and a cotton manufacturer from Rhode Island, he continued to seek common ground with southern planters. By 1857 he had earned a leadership position as a loyal supporter of President James Buchanan in the national Democratic party and voted to admit Kansas as a state with the Lecompton constitution, guaranteeing slavery, in that year. As the tensions escalated and erupted into violence on the floor of the U.S. Senate and outright warfare in Kansas and Nebraska, Allen declined to run for reelection in 1859 and retired that year from all public life. Very much disillusioned by the Civil War and the resultant changes in American life, Allen lived quietly in Providence until his death and burial in that city. He was survived by his wife of twenty-one years, Phoebe Aborn, with whom he had eleven children.

• Portions of Allen's papers are in the Zachariah Allen Papers and the John Robinson Waterman Papers, both held by the Rhode Island Historical Society, Providence. Several other collections in the Historical Society contain Allen papers as well. The Dorr collection and several other collections in the John Hay Library at Brown University, Providence, have numerous letters concerning the struggle between Dorr and Allen. For the events in Rhode Island in 1842, see George M. Dennison, *The Dorr War: Republicanism on Trial, 1831–1861* (1976), and Marvin E. Gettleman, *The Dorr Rebellion: A Study in American Radicalism, 1833–1849* (1973). Allen is mentioned in A. M. Mowry, *The Dorr War* (1901); Thomas W. Bicknell, *History of the State of Rhode Island and Providence Plantations*, vol. 3 (1920); and James N. Arnold, *Vital Records of Rhode Island, 1636–1850*, vols. 13, 14, 15, and 17 (1903–1908).

GEORGE M. DENNISON

ALLEN, Phog (18 Nov. 1885–16 Sept. 1974), basketball coach, was born Forrest Clare Allen in Jamesport, Missouri, the son of William Perry Allen, a traveling salesman, and Alexine Perry. At an early age, Allen moved with his family to Independence, Missouri, where he grew up on the same block as future president Harry S. Truman. There Allen became interested in the new game of basketball; in 1904 he joined the Kansas City Athletic Club team and became an outstanding player. In 1905 Allen raised $500 as a guarantee to bring the Buffalo Germans, one of the best teams in the country, to Kansas City to play a three-game series with his team. The Kansas City A.C. won two out of the three games.

While continuing to play with the Kansas City team, Allen attended the University of Kansas, where he became a star player under Coach James A. Naismith, the inventor of basketball. He led the Jayhawks to several successful seasons and set a Kansas single-game scoring record of twenty-six points, which stood until 1939. In 1908 Naismith turned over the coaching reins at Kansas to Allen, still a student, who led the team to a 23–3 record. During the same season, Allen also coached basketball at nearby Haskell Indian School and at Baker University in Baldwin, Kansas, some fifteen miles away. In a feat unprecedented in basketball history, his three teams combined for a record of 74 wins and 10 defeats. Many years later, Naismith inscribed a photograph for Allen that read: "From the Father of Basketball to the Father of Basketball Coaches."

In 1909 Allen married Elizabeth Milton; they had six children. After graduating from Kansas that same year, he studied at the Kansas City College of Osteopathy. He received his degree in 1912. Allen never practiced full time as a physician, although he treated some prominent athletes such as Johnny Mize and George Halas. His reasons for studying medicine were simple: "After I started coaching I felt that I should learn more about a boy's body structure instead of simply what made him a good basketball player."

In 1912 Allen returned to coaching at Warrensburg (Missouri) State Teachers College. During his seven years there, he compiled a record of 107 wins and 7 defeats. Allen returned to Kansas as head basketball coach in 1919, and he remained there until his mandatory retirement in 1956. During his first nineteen years as coach, he also served as athletic director and head of the physical education department. Allen was nicknamed "Phog" by sportswriters because of his foghorn voice, which he used frequently during games. The spelling deviation remains obscure.

During his tenure at Kansas, Allen won 591 games and lost 219. His 1952 team won the National Collegiate Athletic Association (NCAA) tournament, in a championship format he had helped develop in 1939, and his 1923 and 1924 teams were judged by the Helms Athletic Foundation to have been the best in the nation. Under his direction, Kansas also won twenty-four Missouri Valley, Big Six, and Big Seven conference championships before the league became the Big Eight Conference in the 1970s. All told, his teams won 771 games while losing only 233. He held the record for most victories by a college coach until 1968, when one of his former players, Adolph Rupp of Kentucky, surpassed it.

Allen is considered one of the great innovators in college basketball. He developed a complex defense that included man-to-man and zone techniques, which he called the "Stratified Transitional Man-for-Man Defense with the Zone Principle." Later popularized by coaches Rupp and Hank Iba of Oklahoma A&M, the defense became known as the "Match-up Zone." Still widely used in the college ranks, it calls for players to use a zone defense until the offensive player with the ball enters their territory, at which point they must switch to a man-to-man defense. Allen cofounded the National Association of Basketball Coaches in 1927 and served as president from 1927 to 1929. As part of that organization, Allen campaigned successfully to include basketball on the Olympic program in 1936; he later coached the U.S. team to the 1952 Olympic Gold Medal in Helsinki, Finland. He was instrumental in the adoption of the ten-second rule, which helped speed up the game, but he failed in his attempt to have the center jump after each basket reinstated following its elimination in 1937. Allen invented the fan-shaped backboard in the late 1930s and in the late 1950s started an unsuccessful movement against the bonus-foul rule. "Only alcoholics," he quipped, "wanted two shots for one."

As a result of his medical training, Allen developed some strange but sound coaching methods. He insisted that natural body movements should be utilized to the fullest extent by basketball players and emphasized how apes used a crouched stance and rapid movement to overcome their enemies. Once a year Allen would show his players a short film, *Killing the Killer*, detailing a fight to the death between a cobra and a mongoose. He emphasized that the mongoose won the seemingly uneven battle because it had "deft movement." While some mocked Allen's animal-anatomy analogies, he continued to turn out winning teams. Before home games, he insisted that his players take an hour-long nap followed by a one-mile walk and a meal consisting of two slices of whole wheat toast, a portion of honey, half a grapefruit, and celery. He also had a phobia concerning cold feet. After the team meal, Allen led his players into a room with a large fireplace, where they were instructed to place their bare feet close to the fire. Allen explained that he never "saw a man with cold feet who wasn't nervous and jumpy."

With regard to the game itself, his views often provoked controversy. Allen was one of the first important coaches to call for the raising of the baskets from ten to twelve feet so the game would not be dominated by "goons." He also campaigned for a commissioner of college athletics to rid college sports of undesirable people and ideas. In the post–World War II era, Allen publicly warned about additional bribery scandals he believed were taking place in New York and involving games in Madison Square Garden. He placed the blame on college faculties and presidents who, he said, "have been afraid to face the facts." As he predicted, a new wave of scandals was exposed in New York in 1951.

In addition to Rupp, Allen tutored a number of players at Kansas who went on to become outstanding college basketball coaches. They include Dean Smith (North Carolina), Arthur "Dutch" Lonborg (Northwestern), Ralph Miller (Oregon State), John Bunn (Stanford), Forrest "Frosty" Cox (Colorado), and Louis Menze (Iowa State). Allen coached many outstanding players, but one of the best was Clyde Lovellette, who scored thirty-three points in the 1952 NCAA championship game won by Kansas against St. John's. He also successfully recruited but did not coach Wilt Chamberlain, one of basketball's all-time great players. Allen wrote two books, *My Basketball Bible* (1928) and *Better Basketball* (rev. ed., 1968). He was named Coach of the Year in 1950 and was elected to the Basketball Hall of Fame in 1959. Allen died in Lawrence, Kansas.

• Materials relating to Allen's career may be found in the University of Kansas Archives and the Basketball Hall of Fame in Springfield, Mass. See also Larry Fox, *Illustrated History of Basketball* (1974); Sandy Padwe, *Basketball's Hall of Fame* (1970); Neil D. Isaacs, *All the Moves* (1975); and Joe Jares, *Basketball: The American Game* (1971). An obituary is in the *New York Times*, 17 Sept. 1974.

JOHN M. CARROLL

ALLEN, Richard (14 Feb. 1760–26 Mar. 1831), American Methodist preacher and founder of the African Methodist Episcopal church, was born into slavery to parents who were the property of Benjamin Chew of Philadelphia. He and his parents and three additional children were sold in 1777 to Stokely Sturgis, who lived near Dover, Delaware. There he attended Methodist preaching and experienced a spiritual awakening. Allen, his older brother, and a sister were retained by Sturgis, but his parents and younger siblings were sold. Through the ministry of Freeborn Garretson, a Methodist itinerant, Sturgis was converted to Methodism and became convinced that slavery was wrong. Subsequently Allen and his brother were permitted to work to purchase their freedom, which they did in 1780. The next six years he worked as a wagon driver, woodcutter, and bricklayer while serving as a Methodist preacher to both blacks and whites in towns and rural areas in Maryland, Delaware, Pennsylvania, and New Jersey. At one point Bishop Francis Asbury, leader of American Methodism, invited Allen to become his traveling companion, an offer he accepted. In 1786 he preached to interracial groups of Methodists in Radnor, Pennsylvania, and at St. George's Church, Philadelphia. Assigned to preach at predawn meetings, Allen often preached four or five times a day and organized evening prayer groups. Unpaid by the church, he supported himself as a shoemaker. He married Flora (maiden name unknown) in 1791 and, after his first wife's death, married a second time in 1805 to Sarah (maiden name unknown). Allen and his second wife had six children.

By attending Methodist instructional meetings between 1777 and 1780, Allen became an exhorter and then a licentiate as early as 1780. After the American War of Independence, he traveled extensively in Delaware, Maryland, New Jersey, and Pennsylvania. In December 1784 he and Harry Hosier were the only two black preachers to attend the Christmas Conference in Baltimore, where the Methodist Episcopal church was organized. He probably saw Methodist leaders Thomas Coke, Asbury, Richard Whatcoat, and Thomas Vasey at the conference. During 1785 he traveled the Baltimore circuit with Whatcoat. By February 1786 he was in Philadelphia, where he organized a prayer-meeting society of forty-two members. Allen's concern was to find and instruct "his African brethren," few of whom attended public worship. Noting the need for a place of worship for African Americans, he, along with Absalom Jones, William White, and Dorus Ginnings, found their efforts to meet this need opposed by the leadership of St. George's Church. In November 1787, black members at St. George's Church were pulled away from prayer and asked to leave, so Allen and Jones, along with their associates, withdrew. Renting an unused store, Allen and Jones, with the help of Benjamin Rush and Robert Ralston, raised funds for a new building, which became in 1794 the St. Thomas African Episcopal Church of Philadelphia, the first independent black church in North America.

Allen remained a Methodist, purchased an abandoned blacksmith shop, moved it to Sixth Street near Lombard, and had it renovated. On 29 June 1794 Bishop Asbury dedicated the building as a church. For years Allen and his congregation thought the property called Bethel Church was theirs, only to be informed by successive elders at St. George's that Bethel Church was under their charge. In 1816, however, the Pennsylvania Supreme Court confirmed the independent existence of Bethel and official contact between the two churches ceased. Aware of friction between black and white Methodists in other places, Allen sent invitations to African churches to form an ecclesiastical organization. On 9 April 1816 sixty delegates from five black congregations met at Bethel Church and agreed to confederate. The result was the formation of the African Methodist Episcopal (AME) church. Allen, who had been ordained deacon by Bishop Asbury in 1799, was ordained elder on 10 April 1816 and the next day consecrated bishop. The first *Discipline* was published in 1817 and the first General Conference held in Philadelphia, 9 July 1820, with Bishop Allen presiding. For Allen, the Methodist emphasis on the simplicity of the gospel, expressed through discipline and community, pointed the way to freedom from sin and physical slavery as well. His life, career, and the founding of Bethel Church embodied this development and confirmed his role as a leader in the forefront of the black church movement.

Allen led and participated in the formation of a number of organizations for the betterment of his people. The Free African Society established 12 April 1787 was the first black institution with the characteristics of a benevolent and reform organization. In 1795 a day school was operational in Bethel Church, and on 26 October 1796 a First Day school or Sunday school and a night school were reported. He led in the creation of the Society for Free People of Color for Promoting the Instruction and School Education of Children of African Descent in 1804. From 1818 to 1820 he served as book steward of the Book Concern of the AME church. The creation of the Free Produce Society of Philadelphia, 20 December 1830, was also his work. He chaired the first National Negro Convention, 20 to 24 September 1830, which was held at Bethel Church. In 1831 the address to the First Annual Convention of the People of Colour, was signed by the Reverend Allen, president and senior bishop of the AME church. Allen and Jones in 1794 had been cited by the mayor of Philadelphia for their services to the sick and dying during the yellow fever epidemic in 1793. Early in 1797 Allen, Jones, and James Forten led black Philadelphians for the first time to petition the national government to revoke the Fugitive Slave Act of 1793 and to end slavery. In 1814 when it was feared Philadelphia would be attacked by the British, Allen, Jones, and Forten raised the Black Legion of 2,500 men. Although Allen did not initially oppose voluntary emigration of blacks as promoted by the American Colonization Society, formed in 1817, he came to see that a large-scale emigration of free blacks would result in the abandonment of their brethren to slavery. In *Freedom's Journal* (2 Nov. 1927), Allen declared colonization a mistake. In 1830 he presided over the first meeting of the National Negro Convention Movement, which provided a structure for black abolitionism and organized the American Society of Free Persons of Color.

Allen died in Philadelphia, but his contributions to religion, education, and culture are reflected in institutions such as the Allen Temple, Cincinnati, Ohio; Allen University, Columbia, South Carolina; and the Richard Allen Center for Culture and Art opposite Lincoln Center, New York City.

• The original published works of Allen number eight, of which the most important is *The Life, Experience and Gospel Labors of the Rt. Rev. Richard Allen* (1832?; 2d ed., 1833), to which is annexed the *Rise and Progress of the African Methodist Episcopal Church in the United States of America*. A 1960 reprint with introduction by George A. Singleton contains *A Narrative of the Yellow Fever in the Year of Our Lord 1793* and *An Address to the People of Color in the United States*. There are two *Discourses* published in 1808 and 1831, respectively, plus a few letters published in the *Journal of Negro History* 1, no. 4 (1916): 436–43. *The Doctrine and Discipline of the African Methodist Episcopal Church* (1819) and *A Collection of Hymns and Spiritual Songs* (1801), were also published in Philadelphia. Charles H. Wesley, *Richard Allen, Apostle of Freedom* (1935); Carol V. R. George, *Segregated Sabbaths: Richard Allen and the Emergence of Independent Black Churches 1760–1840* (1973); Gary B. Nash, *Forging Freedom: The Formation of Philadelphia's Black Community, 1720–1840* (1988); and Albert J. Raboteau, "Richard Allen and the African Church Movement," in *Black Leaders of the Nineteenth Century*, ed. Leon F. Litwack and August Meier (1988), are essential works. Also useful are Daniel A. Payne, *History of the African Methodist Episcopal Church* (1891), and George A. Singleton, *The Romance of African Methodism* (1952).

FREDERICK V. MILLS, SR.

ALLEN, Viola (27 Oct. 1867–9 May 1948), actress, was born Viola Emily Allen in Huntsville, Alabama, the daughter of Charles Leslie Allen, a well-known character actor (who was on tour in the South, hence his daughter's Alabama birthplace), and Sarah Jane Lyon, an actress. She attended schools in Boston, Toronto, and New York before commencing an acting career at age fourteen. Remarkably, Allen's professional stage debut came in the form of a starring role in a Broadway production when in 1882 she replaced Annie Russell in *Esmeralda*, an adaptation of a Frances Hodgson Burnett novel, at the Madison Square Theatre. The inexperienced Allen was hired at the suggestion of the play's director, who had asked her father (playing a supporting role in the play) if the beautiful fifteen-year-old daughter about whom he had been boasting could take over as an understudy for Russell. When Russell left the play, Allen assumed the role of the title character.

The next season Allen toured in *Esmeralda* (with both her parents also in the production) and was spotted by famed tragedian John McCullough, who offered the teenage actress a place in his company. Allen spent the 1883–1884 season with McCullough, the syphilis-plagued actor's final and turbulent year on the boards. Initially hired for small roles, when the leading actress suddenly left the company Allen was promoted to playing opposite McCullough in a number of

Shakespearean and classical roles. Allen's season with McCullough established her as a reliable and attractive performer. She quickly found work opposite other prominent actors such as Lawrence Barrett, with whom she appeared in *A Blot on the 'Scutcheon* in 1885, and Tommaso Salvini, in whose company Allen essayed the roles of Cordelia, Desdemona, and Juliet. Allen spent the 1888–1889 season with the stock company at the Boston Museum, where she appeared in numerous productions, most notably Bronson Howard's Civil War drama *Shenandoah*, which moved successfully to Broadway in September 1889. She left *Shenandoah* to join Joseph Jefferson, William J. Florence, and Mrs. John Drew in an all-star tour of Sheridan's *The Rivals* and other plays.

A tall woman with lustrous dark hair and eyes, Allen exhibited intelligence and good taste both onstage and off. These qualities drew the attention of the powerful theatrical manager Charles Frohman, who specialized in actresses with a reserved demeanor and a nonexotic type of beauty. Frohman sought to finally rid the theater of its tawdry image and to attract those segments of the public, especially women, who still had qualms about the propriety of theatergoing. Allen spent from 1893 to 1898 as leading lady in the stock (repertory) company at Frohman's elegant and newly built Empire Theatre, one of the few remaining stock companies in New York and the most prestigious. During her tenure at the Empire, Allen appeared in many productions, including *Liberty Hall* (1893), *Sowing the Wind* (1894), *John-a-Dreams* (1895), *Michael and His Lost Angel* (1896), *Under the Red Robe* (1896), *A Man and His Wife* (1897), and *The Conquerors* (1898). In 1895 she also played Gwendolyn Fairfax in the unsuccessful American premiere of Oscar Wilde's *The Importance of Being Earnest*. Though sometimes accused of having a chilly stage persona and limited histrionic ability, Allen proved a likable performer who developed a large following with the public. As a member of a stock company, however, she was not a star in her own right.

In 1898 the thirty-year-old Allen asked Frohman to present her as the star in a stage adaptation of Hall Caine's bestselling novel *The Christian* (the previous season Frohman had with great acclaim launched Maude Adams as a star in an adaptation of J. M. Barrie's novel *The Little Minister*). Frohman declined, and Allen took to the idea to a rival producer, Leibler and Company. *The Christian*, the florid tale of a wayward young adventuress, Glory Quayle, who is returned to the path of righteousness by a clergyman suitor, opened at Broadway's Knickerbocker Theater on 10 October 1898. "From no conceivable artistic point of view could it be called a good play," the *New York Times* critic said of the play, but added that Allen's portrayal of Quayle was "uniformly intelligent, and often charming, because of her own pleasing personality." *The Christian*, nevertheless, served effectively as a starring vehicle for Allen, and after a healthy run on Broadway she toured in the play for two seasons. She soon became one of the country's most popular performers and remained a favorite for more than a decade. Other star vehicles followed, including *In the Palace of the King* (1901), *The Eternal City* (1902), *Toast of the Town* (1905), and *The White Sister* (1909). An unsuccessful screen version of *The White Sister* for the Essanay Company in 1915 was Allen's only venture into film.

In 1905 Allen married Peter Edward Cornell Duryea, a wealthy horse breeder and sportsman several years her senior, in a secret ceremony in Louisville, Kentucky, where Duryea owned a horse farm. When the marriage was made public the following year, another actress, Sara Madden, instigated legal proceedings against Duryea. Madden claimed that Duryea had promised to marry her and that she and Duryea had lived together as husband and wife intermittently for several years. The case was quickly dropped but not before receiving considerable press attention. This brief incident was the only scandal to touch Allen's otherwise impeccable private life.

Though Shakespeare was losing luster as a popular attraction in the early twentieth century, Allen devoted much of her starring career to Shakespearean roles. These included Viola in *Twelfth Night* in 1904, both Hermione and Perdita in *The Winter's Tale* in 1905, Imogen in *Cymbeline* in 1906, and Mistress Anne Ford in *The Merry Wives of Windsor* in 1916. Also in 1916 she was Lady Macbeth to James K. Hackett's Macbeth. Allen brought to Shakespeare the same understated charm she exhibited in modern plays. Her Shakespearean work was much admired for its depth of understanding but often criticized for lacking great dramatic force.

In 1918, at age fifty-one, Allen retired from the stage. She spent the remaining three decades of her life traveling with her husband (the couple had no children) and participating in cultural and charitable activities. Allen held membership in the Episcopal Actors Guild, the Actors Fund, the Daughters of the American Revolution, the Colonial Dames of the Seventeenth Century, the Twelfth Night Club, and the Shakespeare Association of America. She died at her home on Manhattan's fashionable Park Avenue and is buried at Sleepy Hollow Cemetery in Tarrytown, New York.

• Memorabilia on the career of Viola Allen, including pictures, theater programs, and an autobiographical sketch are in the Museum of the City of New York, to which she donated these items in 1946. In "An Interview with Viola Allen," *Theatre Magazine*, Feb. 1903, pp. 44–46, and "My Beginnings," *Theatre Magazine*, Apr. 1906, pp. 93–94, viii, the actress discusses in some detail her career and general views on the theater. *Notable Women in the American Theatre: A Biographical Dictionary* (1989) offers a useful essay on Allen written by Rita M. Plotnicki, who also wrote "The Evolution of a Star: The Career of Viola Allen" (Ph.D. diss., City Univ. of New York, 1979). An obituary is in the *New York Times*, 10 May 1948.

MARY C. KALFATOVIC

ALLEN, Walter Carl (2 Nov. 1920–23 Dec. 1974), jazz scholar, was born in Flushing, New York. His parents' names are unknown. After graduating with a degree in geology from Columbia University in 1942, he served as an air corps navigator in Europe. Back from his war service, he married Anna Sowchuk; they had three children. Allen returned to Columbia for a master's degree in mineralogy. He worked for U.S. Steel in New Jersey until he tired of industrial work and entered Rutgers, the State University of New Jersey, as a doctoral student in ceramics engineering. After earning the Ph.D. in 1964, he worked as a professor in that field at Rutgers for the remainder of his life. He died in Point Pleasant, New Jersey.

Except for its emphasis on the rigorous principles of scholarly research, Allen's professional experience was irrelevant to the work for which he is best remembered, his contributions as a pioneering jazz scholar. This work began at age eighteen, when he became an avid jazz record collector. Evidently he quickly came to recognize discs as archival documents, and he began to apply a conventional scholarly apparatus to such documents whereby interviews of participants, investigations of recording company files, listening (identifying instruments and instrumentalists through familiarity with their individual musical styles), accounts in trade papers and the African-American press, and other sorts of evidence were brought to bear in answering questions related to the identification of and the relationships among recordings. He attempted to establish, among other things, basic facts about pieces of music, including the identities of the musicians, instruments, and soloists; the pieces' musical structures; and the times and places they were recorded. Perhaps not the first to bring a scholarly approach to jazz discography and biography, he was certainly the first to bring the scholarly notion of evidence to the jazz literature, documenting his sources and weighing the evidence when sources conflicted. From 1947 onward he prepared numerous listings of recordings, organized by musician or by record label; these publications are indexed in volume 2 (*Jazz*) of his son Daniel Allen's book *Bibliography of Discographies* (1981). As a by-product of his investigations into the literature, Walter Allen compiled "Allen's Poop Sheet," a listing of available jazz, blues, and ragtime books; the list circulated in fourteen issues appearing irregularly from 1955 to 1974. From 1968 to 1974 he held annual conferences on discographical research at the Institute of Jazz Studies at Rutgers; some of the conference discussions are distilled in volume 1 of *Studies in Jazz Discography* (1971), which he edited. At the end of his life he offered a basic introduction to this subfield of musical research in his article "Discographical Musicology" (*Journal of Jazz Studies* 1 [June 1974]: 27–37).

Allen's greatest scholarly achievements are his two contributions to a series of six jazz monographs he published: with Brian Rust, *King Joe Oliver* (1955), reprinted by a London publisher in 1958 and drastically revised by Laurie Wright and others—including Allen himself, up to his death—as *Walter C. Allen & Brian Rust's "King" Oliver* (1987); and as sole author, *Hendersonia: The Music of Fletcher Henderson and His Musicians: A Bio-discography* (1973). The "bio-discography" (that is, biography and discography) of Henderson set the scholarly standard and remains unsurpassed for its integration of recorded material, performance activities, contemporary reviews, musical description and attribution, biographical information, and cultural context into a single, monumental account of the life of a musician. Although some fine bio-discographers have directly followed Allen's model, his approach has nonetheless been only modestly influential on jazz literature as a whole.

• Copies of a biographical questionnaire prepared by Allen's widow are in the State College, Pennsylvania, and London files of *The New Grove Dictionary of Jazz*, ed. Barry Kernfeld (1988). See also Kernfeld and Howard Rye, "Comprehensive Discographies of Jazz, Blues, and Gospel (Part One)," *Notes: Quarterly Journal of the Music Library Association* 51 (Dec. 1994): 501–47. A belated obituary is in *I.S.A.M. Newsletter* 16 (Nov. 1986).

BARRY KERNFELD

ALLEN, William (5 Aug. 1704–6 Sept. 1780), chief justice of colonial Pennsylvania, was born in Philadelphia, Pennsylvania, the son of William Allen, a wealthy merchant. His mother's maiden name was Budd; her first name is unknown. Both parents emigrated from Dungannon, Ireland. Through close ties to William Penn, William Allen, Sr., acquired large tracts of land in the young colony while forging powerful political alliances. In 1720 he sent William to England to train for law at the Middle Temple. William received little legal training, however, preferring to spend his time touring on the very generous bills of credit given to him by his father.

In 1725, on the death of his father, Allen returned to Pennsylvania to assume control of the family's fortunes. He made important connections that aided him both politically and financially through his friendship with the Proprietary secretary, James Logan, and his marriage in 1734 to Margaret Hamilton, daughter of Andrew Hamilton, Speaker of the Pennsylvania Assembly and famed defense lawyer in the Zenger trial. The couple had nine children, six of whom reached adulthood. Allen became one of the largest land speculators in Pennsylvania; owned several iron works, copper mines, and a countinghouse; and, in war times, profited from privateering ventures as well.

Allen's wealth enabled him to emulate the life style of an English gentleman: he dressed in the English manner, sponsored dress balls, and entertained the elite and visiting dignitaries with large formal dinners. His summer house on Mount Airy, decorated with the paintings of Benjamin West, likewise reflected the influence of his years in England. Allen used his wealth and position to support charitable enterprises including the building of the statehouse and the founding of Pennsylvania Hospital and the College of Philadelphia. He also served as a patron to budding colonial talent, giving financial assistance for the European education of artists Benjamin West and John Singleton Copley, and medical doctors John Morgan and John Redman. His charitable giving and leadership of Philadelphia's social life contributed to Allen's political power as head of the Proprietary party.

Allen began his political career as a member of the Philadelphia Council in 1727. He was chosen alderman in 1730 and in the same year elected to the Pennsylvania Assembly, holding a seat in that body until 1739. In 1735 he served both as the mayor of Philadelphia and as an assemblyman. His dual role was possible because of minimal factional discord in the 1730s. None of the critical issues of the day—paper money, the establishment of courts of equity, the border dispute with Maryland, Parliament's enactment of the Molasses Act of 1733—developed into major political battles. Even the imminence of war with Spain in 1739 caused little stir in the Quaker-dominated Pennsylvania Assembly.

Yet the portents of the coming struggles were visible when both Allen and Hamilton, Speaker of the assembly and Allen's father-in-law, voluntarily gave up their positions in the legislature. Allen gave up his seat in 1739 to raise his family and to have more time for his business enterprises. When war did come (1739–1748), they were unable to regain their seats, opposed by the Quaker majority. In the political battles that ensued, Allen emerged as the leader of the Proprietary party fighting against the Quaker opposition and their inability to defend the colony from French and American Indian attacks.

In 1742 Allen campaigned for an assembly seat in the city of Philadelphia but was defeated in a riotous election that severely damaged his reputation (he was accused of creating the riot) and left the Proprietary forces in complete disarray. During the next decade Allen worked to recreate a political party to oppose the Quakers; in 1750 Governor James Hamilton, his brother-in-law, appointed him chief justice of the Pennsylvania Supreme Court. Throughout these difficult years Allen attempted to lure the talented Benjamin Franklin (1706–1790) into the Proprietary camp, extending Proprietary preference to get Franklin appointed a deputy U.S. postmaster and working with him to create a volunteer association to provide military defense for the colony. His efforts were to little avail as Franklin drifted over to the Quaker party during the 1750s.

Despite his meager legal training—he had never been called before the bar or practiced law privately—Allen held several judicial positions, all Proprietary appointments. As chief justice (1750–1774), he worked to reorganize the court and better define its powers. Most of the cases that came before him dealt with land sales that had taken place without proper legal papers or deed registration. Relying on the legal maxim *Communis Error facit Jus* (common error makes just, which means that a law long evaded or altered by its very nature becomes law), Allen upheld deviations from English law based on the conditions that existed in Pennsylvania. He likewise was a strong advocate of capital punishment, against Quaker opposition, and favored Supreme Court judges riding circuit. Throughout his tenure on the bench, he fought for an independent judiciary, upholding Pennsylvania decisions that diverged from English law.

With the outbreak of the Great War for Empire in 1754, political fighting between the Proprietary and Quaker parties entered an even more acrimonious period. Allen, representing the frontier county of Cumberland, waged a spirited defense of Proprietary rights against the Quaker party, which was now headed by Franklin.

Following the Treaty of Paris of 1763, Allen became alarmed at parliamentary efforts to raise a revenue in the colonies. In the spring of 1763 he sailed once more for England and there fought the proposed revenue act as contrary to "the right of Englishmen to be taxed by their representatives." He opposed General Jeffrey Amherst's Indian policies, which included using the army to prevent expansion beyond the Allegheny Mountains. (No white settlement in Indian Territory lowered the value of land that Allen claimed in the transmountain area.) He also proclaimed himself a supporter of John Wilkes, an Englishman jailed for his writings criticizing King George. Wilkes supported American protests and America supported him. These acts of support for colonial rights strengthened the Proprietary party in Pennsylvania and were largely responsible for the defeat of the Quaker party in the 1764 elections. Allen was now at the height of his political power, a leader in the fight against the Stamp Act and in obtaining its repeal. But as the colonial struggles with England continued and moved toward independence, Allen balked. In 1774 he retired as chief justice and tried to sit out the Revolution as a neutral, an impossible position. Three of his four sons became Loyalists, and even before Allen's death, in Philadelphia he was all but forgotten, his great contributions in building the colony and establishing its legal system unremembered, his great fortune lost in the Revolution.

• Allen's papers are in the Historical Society of Pennsylvania. A brief biography is Ruth Moser Kistler, "William Allen: Founder of Allentown, Colonial Jurist, Industrialist and Loyalist," *Proceedings of the Lehigh County Historical Society* 24 (1962): 7–58. See also Norman S. Cohen, "William Allen: Chief Justice of Pennsylvania, 1704–1780" (Ph.D. diss., Univ. of Calif., 1966) and Cohen, "The Philadelphia Election Riot of 1742," *Pennsylvania Magazine of History and Biography* 92 (1968): 306–19.

NORMAN S. COHEN

ALLEN, William (18 Dec. 1803–11 July 1879), U.S. senator and congressman and governor of Ohio, was born in Edenton, North Carolina, the son of Nathaniel Allen, a wealthy merchant and landowner, and Sarah Colburn. Allen's father had surrendered his Quaker principles to fight in the American Revolution and was a delegate to the North Carolina convention convened to consider the federal Constitution in 1788. Both parents died shortly after William's birth, and he was raised by his half sister, the wife of a Methodist Episcopal minister, the Reverend Pleasant Thurman. Although born into the gentry, the tangled genealogy of his family, owing to his father's three marriages and various legal technicalities, denied Allen any inheritance of his father's considerable assets.

As a penniless orphan, Allen apprenticed to a saddler in Lynchburg, Virginia, where the Thurmans had moved. In 1819 he traveled on foot over the Allegheny Mountains to join his half sister and brother-in-law, who had moved again, this time to Chillicothe, Ohio. Except for fourteen years in Washington, Allen spent the rest of his life in this southern Ohio town. He attended the Chillicothe Academy for two years and was also tutored at home by his half sister. In 1821 he began reading law under the supervision of two well-known local lawyers, one of whom, Edward King, was the son of the famous jurist Rufus King. In 1824 Allen was admitted to the bar, and following the circuit of county courts, he quickly rose to prominence.

Like many young men during the Jacksonian period, Allen entered politics as a Democrat, an affiliation that he maintained throughout his life. In 1832, at age twenty-nine, he earned that party's nomination for a congressional seat for Ohio's Seventh District. In a surprising result, he won by one vote against a popular Ohio governor, Duncan McArthur, whose daughter, Effie McArthur Coons, Allen married in 1840. The Allens had one daughter. He soon became known as an effective orator (later in his life he was called "Fog Horn Allen") as well as a practitioner of the new style of more active electioneering that swept over the United States. Defeated in 1834 and 1836 for Congress, Allen returned to Washington in 1837, when he was elected by the Ohio legislature to the U.S. Senate for the first of two successive terms.

A loyal Democrat and the youngest senator in both sessions, Allen vociferously defended the national program of his party, opposing a national bank, supporting the independent treasury system that President Andrew Jackson and Martin Van Buren used as the national bank's replacement, and favoring President James K. Polk's expansionist schemes in Oregon and Texas. The slogan "Fifty-four Forty or Fight," referring to the territorial designs of the United States along its northwest border, was coined by Allen in the Senate, and as the chairman of the Senate Foreign Relations Committee, he was typical of a group of young Democrats who supported Manifest Destiny and the Mexican-American War, which he saw as necessary to forestall English designs in the West. Encouraged to become an active candidate for the Democratic presidential nomination in 1848, he deferred to his friend from Michigan, Lewis Cass.

Allen's retirement from politics after the election of 1848 was not voluntary but was the result of growing divisions within the Democratic party over slavery and the emergence of new issues, such as immigration and nativism, about which he remained silent. Free Soil Democrats sent Salmon P. Chase to the Senate in his stead. From his 1,400-acre estate outside of Chillicothe called "Fruit Hill," which his wife had inherited from her father, Allen became an observer of the national turmoil, which included a split in the Democratic party, the election of Abraham Lincoln, and the Civil War. A critic of abolition, he also opposed both secession and, by 1863, what he considered Lincoln's tyrannical politics of emancipation and conscription.

In 1873 seventy-year-old Allen was nominated for the Ohio governorship in the Democratic party's effort to revive its organization through the choice of a respected proponent of states' rights. He was also attractive to the party because he had been out of politics during the war and early Reconstruction years, when so many Ohio Democrats, like Clement Vallandigham and George Pugh, had been portrayed as traitors. Referred to as "Rise up William Allen" throughout the campaign, he won by 817 votes of nearly 400,000 cast. Always sensitive to fiscal matters, Allen as governor was a prominent spokesman for the policy of monetizing greenbacks as legal tender to expand the currency. He took office just after the effects of the panic of 1873 settled on the United States and vehemently opposed any contraction of the money supply. In 1875 he failed to win reelection, but he received a final honor when he became a popular candidate for the Democratic presidential nomination eventually won by New York's Samuel Tilden.

An exemplar of a group of young midwesterners who learned politics during the Jacksonian period, Allen was a powerful man in voice and physique. He was over six feet in height, and although in later years his hair turned white, he retained his upright posture and seemed years younger than he was. A widower after his wife's death in 1847, he died at Fruit Hill.

• The bulk of the William Allen Papers are in the Library of Congress, but important materials relating to Allen are also in the Allen Thurman Collection in the Library of Congress. Other relevant manuscripts are in the John Crittenden Papers and the Thomas Ewing Papers, both in the Library of Congress. The standard secondary source is Reginald McGrane, *William Allen: A Study in Western Democracy* (1925).

JEAN H. BAKER

ALLEN, William G. (c. 1820–?), abolitionist and educator, was born in Virginia, the son of a Welshman and a free mulatto mother. After the death of both parents when he was young, Allen was adopted by a free African-American family in Fortress Monroe, Virginia. Allen soon caught the eye of the Reverend William Hall, a New Yorker who conducted a black elementary school in Norfolk. Hall wrote Gerrit Smith, the well-known philanthropist and abolitionist from Madison County, New York, asking him to sponsor Allen's education. With Smith's support, Allen studied at the Oneida Institute, an interracial and abolitionist school in Whitesboro, New York, presided over by the abolitionist Beriah Green. In a letter written to Smith, Green referred to Allen's good conduct, accomplishments on the flute, and service as clerk to Reuben Hough, the institute's superintendent and treasurer.

While attending the institute, Allen spent the summer of 1841 teaching in a school that Hiram Wilson, an Oneida Institute alumnus, had established among fugitive slaves in Upper Canada. He supported the Liberty party and the political abolitionists centered in upstate New York. Allen also participated in the black national convention movement, annual meetings organized by African Americans to discuss their common problems. Allen graduated from the Oneida Institute in 1844 and moved to Troy, New York, where he taught school and assisted Henry Highland Garnet in editing the *National Watchman*, an abolitionist and temperance paper for African Americans. Three years later he moved to Boston, where he was employed as a law clerk by Ellis Gray Loring. While in Boston Allen lectured on African-American history, writing *Wheatley, Banneker, and Horton* (1849), a collection of brief biographical sketches of African Americans, and served as secretary of the Boston Colored Citizens Association.

In 1850 Allen was appointed professor of Greek and of rhetoric and belles lettres at New York Central College in McGrawville, Cortland County. This interracial and coeducational institution, chartered in 1849 by the American Baptist Free Mission Society, was the only college in the country then employing African-American faculty. In 1852 Allen became engaged to one of the white students, Mary King, the daughter of a former trustee. The engagement incensed the residents of Fulton, New York, King's hometown, and the couple, fearing mob violence, went to New York City, where they were secretly married in 1853.

Due to the racial antagonisms their marriage had sparked, Allen resigned from the faculty of New York Central College, and he and his wife traveled to England in the spring of 1853. Allen attempted to earn a living in England by writing and lecturing on various literary and philosophical subjects. In 1854 Lady Byron engaged him to speak on behalf of the penal reform movement. Allen also advocated the moral reformatory school movement and lectured against American slavery and prejudice. In 1853 his account of the problems caused by his marriage appeared under the title, *The American Prejudice against Color: An Authentic Narrative, Showing How Easily the Nation Got into an Uproar*. Because of the warm reception he had received on a speaking trip to Ireland, Allen brought his family to Dublin in 1856, where three of his seven children were born. Here he wrote *A Short Personal Narrative* (1860).

In 1860 Allen moved his family back to London, where he continued to lecture on Africa, educational reform, and abolitionism. In 1863 he became principal of the Caledonian Training School in Islington, established by British abolitionist and philanthropist Harper Twelvetrees to meet the educational needs of the poor. The school closed after five years due to financial difficulties. Allen found it difficult to support his large family and appealed to friends of the abolitionist cause, such as Gerrit Smith, for assistance. The struggle to survive compounded the bitterness he felt toward the American prejudice exhibited at the time of his marriage. About 1878 the Allens moved back to London, living at one point in a boardinghouse in Notting Hill, dependent on the charity of friends. Little is known of the circumstances of Allen's last years or of his death.

William G. Allen belongs to that cohort of nineteenth-century African Americans who, although free of slavery's yoke, encountered many obstacles in the North. Allen used the vehicle of education, first as a student and later as an instructor, to fight against racial restrictions in the United States. After seeking exile in England he continued to attack American slavery and racism, and his personal life was beset by many difficulties. Though he never achieved the public notoriety of Frederick Douglass or was as actively involved in the American abolitionist movement as some other African-American contemporaries, Allen's most notable contribution lay in his efforts to expose the connections between the institution of slavery and American prejudice.

• Letters from Allen to Gerrit Smith are in the Smith papers, George Arents Research Library, Syracuse University. Some of Allen's letters are published in C. Peter Ripley et al., eds., *The Black Abolitionist Papers*, vol. 1 (1985). The fullest biographical treatment of Allen is R. J. M. Blackett, "William G. Allen: The Forgotten Professor," *Civil War History* 26 (Mar. 1980): 38–52.

MILTON C. SERNETT

ALLEN, William Henry (21 Oct. 1784–18 Aug. 1813), U.S. naval officer and hero of the War of 1812, was born in Providence, Rhode Island, the son of militia general William Allen, a veteran of the Revolution, and Sarah Jones, sister of William Jones, future governor of Rhode Island. William Henry's parents were prosperous members of Providence society and intended for him to follow a civilian career. His early education provided him with a good grounding in penmanship and mathematics (the latter proved useful in his naval career) and also with considerable skill as an artist. He made very competent sketches in his letters and the blank pages of his journals and did pen and ink portraits of his family. His only surviving likeness, a profile portrait, is probably based on a sketch done by Allen himself.

When Allen was twelve, in 1797, his mother died, and his father remarried the following year. At about this time, Allen decided that he wanted a more active life than had been planned for him, and he urged his parents to let him enter the navy. Senator Ray Greene (R.I.) provided an appointment as midshipman, and in May 1800 at the age of fifteen, Allen left home to join his first ship, the frigate *George Washington*. For the rest of his short life he would be near the center of action in the fledgling navy.

His first cruise, in the *George Washington* under Captain William Bainbridge, delivered a shipload of the notorious tribute to the Dey of Algiers. At Algiers, threatened by the guns of the citadel, Bainbridge was forced to carry an Algerian embassy, plus some tonnage of wild animals, slave girls, and other exotica to Constantinople, as a gift from Algiers to the sultan of the Ottoman Empire. The *George Washington* was the first U.S. naval vessel to visit Golden Horn and helped to open that area to U.S. trade. The forced voyage to Constantinople contributed to firming President Thomas Jefferson's views in favor of building up the navy in order to take a strong line against the depredations of the Barbary princes.

After Tripoli's declaration of war in May 1801, Allen made three more cruises to the Mediterranean, one as a midshipman in the frigate *Philadelphia* under Captain Samuel Barron, one in the frigate *John Adams* under Captain John Rodgers, and one as sailing master in the frigate *Congress*, again under Rodgers. During this period Allen saw much of the action in the Barbary Wars and became the protégé and friend of the irascible Rodgers. In late 1804 in the Mediterranean, Rodgers was given command of the larger frigate *Constitution* and took Allen with him, promoting him to acting lieutenant. In 1805, still in the *Constitution* with Rodgers, Allen was present in the naval expedition to Tunis, during which a treaty with the bashaw of Tunis ended the Barbary Wars.

In January 1807 Allen was ordered to the frigate *Chesapeake* as third lieutenant. The *Chesapeake* was to be sent to the Mediterranean as squadron flagship, under Commodore James Barron. Barron was the personal enemy of John Rodgers and greatly distrusted Allen, whom he knew to be a close friend of Rodgers. Among the sailors recruited for the *Chesapeake* were several deserters from the British navy. Desertion in U.S. waters was a difficult problem for the Royal Navy and Admiral Berkeley, the British commander in chief in North America, decided, without authority from his home government, to take back these deserters by force. The United States was "at peace with all the world" but as the unprepared *Chesapeake* left Norfolk, the frigate was attacked by HMS *Leopard*, a much more powerful ship, and after three destructive broadsides the *Chesapeake* surrendered. The only shot fired by the *Chesapeake* in return was fired by Allen, who took a live coal from the galley to touch off a gun in his division. After the surrender, Allen told Barron, "we have disgraced the flag," and he wrote a letter to the secretary of the navy, signed by him and the other lieutenants, recommending that Barron be court-martialed for not having prepared the ship for action. Allen came out of the *Chesapeake-Leopard* incident as its only hero.

Barron was replaced by Stephen Decatur, with whom Allen served in the *Chesapeake* until the end of 1808, when Decatur was given command of the larger frigate *United States* and took Allen with him as first lieutenant. Allen trained the gun crews to a high pitch of effectiveness, and on 25 October 1812, shortly after the beginning of the War of 1812, the *United States* met the British frigate *Macedonian* at sea, south of the Azores, and captured the vessel after a bloody, hour-long action. Allen commanded the *Macedonian* on the frigate's trip to the United States as a prize.

Decatur credited the major share of the victory to Allen's gunnery training, and in January 1813 Allen was rewarded with the command of the U.S. brig *Argus*. Allen also received a normal promotion to the rank of master-commandant later in the year.

In the late spring of 1813 the *Argus* was chosen to carry to France the Honorable William H. Crawford, the new American minister to Napoleon's court. The *Argus* sailed in mid-June 1813 and, after delivering Minister Crawford to L'Orient, Allen, in late July, took the *Argus* on a highly successful commerce-destroying cruise in the vicinity of Ireland and St. George's Channel. They had captured or destroyed twenty-two vessels when early on 14 August 1813, off the coast of Wales, they met the British brig *Pelican*, a somewhat larger and more heavily gunned vessel. The *Pelican*'s captain, John Fordyce Maples, a commander in the Royal Navy, like Allen, was very strong on gunnery training. In the first minutes of the action, Allen was struck in the left thigh by a 32-pound shot and was taken below. Several others of the *Argus* were killed or wounded, the ship's colors were brought down, and the *Argus* was taken by the *Pelican* after an action lasting about forty-five minutes.

Allen was taken ashore in Plymouth, England, where he died of his wound in the Mill Prison Hospital. He was buried in St. Andrew's churchyard with full military honors. He had never married or had children.

Allen was a young naval officer of great promise and uncompromising honor. He was part of that band of young officers in the early U.S. Navy who created the traditions that the navy still follows such as boldness and a strong sense of personal honor. His cruise with the *Argus* showed the Navy Department that the effective way to fight the then-powerful Royal Navy was to send small, nimble, heavily-gunned warships to operate against British merchant shipping, right in British home waters.

• Fifty-two of Allen's letters to his family, written between 1800 and 1813, his journal kept on board the *George Washington* (HM 250), and his journal from the *Chesapeake* (HM 564), together with a number of letters between his family members written after his death, are in the Huntington Library, San Marino, Calif. Several other letters from Allen to his family are in the Manuscripts Department, Library of Congress, Accession 4815. His journal kept on board the *John Adams* is in the G. W. Blunt White Library at the Mystic Seaport Museum, Log No. 227, "The John Rodgers Logbook." For the cruise of the *Argus* in 1813, see *Journal of an Unknown Officer* (the "Argus Log") and *The Journal of Surgeon James Inderwick*, both in the Manuscripts Division of the New York Public Library, plus *The Journal of William H. Crawford* for 4 June 1813–15 July 1813, in the Manuscripts Department, Library of Congress. There are numerous official letters from Allen to the secretary of the navy in *Letters Received by the Secretary of the Navy from Officers below the Rank of Commander, 1802–1884*, microfilm M-148, rolls 1–12 (1802–1813), RG 45, National Archives. The *Chesapeake-Leopard* affair is covered thoroughly in U.S. Navy Department, *Proceedings of the General Court Martial Convened for the Trial of Commodore James Barron, Etc.* (1822). All standard histories of the War of 1812 cover the battle of the *Argus* and the *Pelican*. The basic biosketch of Allen is in the *Port Folio* 3, no. 1 (Jan. 1814), prepared from material provided by his family just after his death.

IRA DYE

ALLEN, William Henry (25 Mar. 1808–29 Aug. 1882), educator and college president, was born at Readfield (now Manchester), near Augusta, Maine, to Jonathan Allen and Thankful Longley, farmers. He went from his parents' farm to district school, then attended Wesleyan Seminary in Maine in preparation for Bowdoin College. He graduated with an M.A. from Bowdoin in 1833. The same year Allen was appointed to teach Latin and Greek at the Oneida Methodist Conference Seminary in Cazenovia, Madison County, New York. In the spring of 1836 he became principal of the high school in Augusta, Maine, a post he held for six months.

In the autumn of 1836 Allen joined the faculty of Dickinson College, a Methodist school in Carlisle, Pennsylvania, to teach natural history and chemistry. When another professor became ill, Allen assumed additional duties teaching courses in rhetoric and logic. He earned a reputation as a devoted and inspiring instructor whose lectures were very popular with students. They nicknamed him "Bully Allen," affectionately, we may presume, because of his popular classroom demeanor, and "Corpus" because of what a former student remembered as Allen's "rotund dimensions" and "large, ruddy countenance."

While at Dickinson, Allen gave public lectures and wrote on a variety of topics, including natural history, educational reform, the temperance movement, and world peace. He published several essays in the *Methodist Quarterly Review*, including one in April 1846 on "Vestiges of Creation," which he believed attracted "some attention." However, Allen was known more for his accomplishments as an educator than as an author or scholar. In 1847, after ten years at Dickinson College, Allen began an appointment as professor of chemistry at the Philadelphia College of Medicine. He resigned after a year to return to Dickinson College, where he assumed the post of president pro tem and was appointed professor of mental philosophy and English literature.

In November 1849 Allen was elected president of the Girard College for Orphans in Philadelphia. He began his duties on 1 January 1850. Opened in 1848, Girard College was supported by a bequest from the wealthy Philadelphian Stephen Girard. Girard's will stipulated that a school be established for the academic and moral training of "poor white male orphans." Allen was the school's second president. The 500-member student body ranged in age from eight to seventeen. In September 1850 Allen issued a report that included a proposal for a Collegiate Department, which would draw its student body from the Principal School and Primary School. He was widely respected for his administrative abilities and for the personal interest he took in students. Alumni remembered him as "Father Allen." Since Girard's will also stipulated that no clergyman was to be associated with the institution, Allen was responsible for the religious as well as the administrative and educational programs of Girard College.

After nearly thirteen years of heavy administrative responsibilities, Allen resigned the presidency of Girard College and, except for occasional lectures, retired to private life on a farm along the Delaware River, not far from Philadelphia. From 1865 to 1867 he served as president of the Pennsylvania Agricultural College. In 1867, after an absence of four years and eight months, he resumed his post as head of Girard College. In 1868 he was offered but declined the presidency of Dickinson College. Allen became president of the American Bible Society in 1872. He was president of Girard College in 1882 at the time of his death.

Allen's first wife, Martha Ann Richardson, was the eldest daughter of the Reverend James Richardson, bishop of the Methodist Episcopal Church of Canada. She died in 1839. They had one daughter. His second wife was Ellen Honora, sister of Andrew G. Curtin, governor of Pennsylvania. They had four children, two of whom died in childhood. After the death of Ellen, Allen married Mary Frances Quincy of Boston. It is not known what happened to Allen's third wife, although it can be assumed that she died before 1858; that year, he married Anna Maria Dunton Gamwill, a widow. They had no children, and she survived him.

In 1853 Allen wrote that he had not yet "perpetrated a book." During the last three decades of his life, Allen devoted most of his time to administrative duties of one kind or another. A modest and self-effacing individual, Allen devoted his life to teaching and educational improvement.

• The Bowdoin College Library has a few letters written by Allen. The Dickinson College Library possesses a small collection of letters and pamphlets. Allen's published essays include *Report of the President of the Girard College to the Committee on Instruction, September 3, 1850* (1850), *Eulogy on the Character and Services of the Late Daniel Webster* (1853), *Tendencies of the Age to Peace* (1854), and *Our Country's Mission in History* (1855). Information on Allen's educational career can be gleaned from *First Fifty Years of Cazenovia Seminary, 1825–1875* (1877) and Charles Coleman Sellers, *Dickinson College: A History* (1973). A former student's recollections of Allen can be found in Moncure Daniel Conway, *Autobiography, Memories and Experiences* (1905). For a memorial tribute to Allen see "William Henry Allen," *Girard College Record* 6 (July 1887): 1–2. An obituary appears in the *Philadelphia Public Ledger*, 30 Aug.–2 Sept. 1882.

MILTON C. SERNETT

ALLEN, William McPherson (1 Sept. 1900–29 Oct. 1985), chief officer of the Boeing Company, was born in Lolo, Montana, the son of Charles Maurice Allen, a mining engineer, and Gertrude Maud Hughes, an orchardist. Following preparatory school in Missoula, Montana, he enlisted in the army for a short time during World War I. Upon his return, he went on to graduate from the University of Montana in 1922.

Later he characterized himself as a middling student who became more serious in the process of earning a law degree at Harvard.

After graduating from Harvard in 1925, Allen sought a position in the West but had no career plans. He accepted an entry-level position with a law firm (now Perkins Cole) in Seattle, Washington. As a new employee he was assigned to a small account with the Boeing Airplane Company. Good fortune, Allen later said, played a large part in his life. An early opportunity came in 1927 when the Boeing firm, which was in the business of building aircraft, asked him to draw up incorporation papers for an airline subsidiary. The airline business made Allen an expert in corporate liability and taxes, government policy issues, and the new field of aviation law. He married Dorothy Dixon, daughter of the governor of Montana, in the same year; the couple had two daughters.

After Boeing merged in 1928–1929 with the engine builder Pratt & Whitney to create United Aircraft and Transport Company (UATC), Allen became a director of several of its subsidiaries. He also continued as a legal representative of the Seattle airplane manufacturing company. After taking a special course in air law in 1931 at Northwestern University, Allen made this new field his specialty and contributed numerous articles to law journals. Through his work he became one of America's most frequent air passengers. At the same time he became a full partner in his law firm, and his influence grew at UATC.

The 1930s were turbulent years because of the government-forced breakup of UATC in 1934. The Boeing Airplane Company emerged as an independent builder of military aircraft, particularly large bombers. Starting in 1939 the buildup of U.S. air forces for World War II created a demand for more bombers, transforming Boeing into a very large company. Boeing president Philip Johnson relied heavily on Allen, who flew back and forth across the United States, often working on contractual issues. Following Johnson's sudden death in 1944, Allen was offered the presidency of Boeing. "I was amazed and laughed at [the offer]," he recalled, "I felt that I was completely unqualified for the position and told them so" (*William M. Allen: A Personal Portrait*, p. 3). However, pressured by the ending of the war, he became president on 1 September 1945, only to immediately face the cancellation of the firm's wartime contracts. In 1948 he married Mary Ellen Agen, following the death of his first wife in 1943; this second marriage was childless.

Boeing was again a much smaller firm, so Allen started rebuilding. Boeing's energies were directed toward finding applications for the newly developed jet engine in the design of large bombers. In this endeavor Boeing was so much more successful than its competitors, that it remained the dominant manufacturer of bombers into the 1960s. Its first postwar airliners did not successfully establish Boeing in the commercial market, but the firm rapidly gained experience in large jet aircraft. A jet transport for refueling the new bombers, built at company risk, succeeded because of Allen's skillful timing and the firm's strong engineering and manufacturing skills. Next, Boeing adapted the same configuration for the 707 airliner, which put the company ahead of its competitors. Boeing's next airliner designs, arriving later, faced established competitors, but under Allen the firm became the most trusted and dependable manufacturer. Its airplanes were usually chosen by customer airlines, and Boeing became the preeminent commercial builder in the world. Much of the credit for Boeing's remarkable accomplishments was attributed to the skill and teamwork of its employees, which improved markedly during the Allen years. Allen recognized that Boeing's management structure, patterned after its military customers, was not as effective for its commercial orientation. Management courses were established and careful attention was given to issues of fairness, rewards for merit, and employee communication. His subordinates found Allen approachable and engaging. His personal ethical strictness blended with tolerance and a willingness to compete freely. In most ways a conservative, he possessed a contradictory spirit that took readily to the high-risk capitalism of airplane building.

During Allen's presidency, Boeing entered its era of greatest diversification. Several inventive products failed, but the company became one of the world's leading producers of missiles, spacecraft, and helicopters. However, it was in the airliner market that Boeing saw its greatest success. In the 1960s Boeing's production of airliners surpassed its output of military equipment, and the company held the largest share of the airliner market. Allen, characteristically declining praise, said it was always easier to be a success in an expanding business. By 1968, when Allen stepped down as president and became chairman of the board, sales had grown from $13 million in 1946 to $3.3 billion. He retired in 1972. In the last years of his affiliation with Boeing, production of the huge 747 airliner, which was introduced during his administration, ushered in the era of mass worldwide air travel. He also watched Boeing experience another severe cyclic financial depression and begin its recovery.

Allen was a believer in free and competitive enterprise; he felt that this principle applied equally to those doing government work. Socialism and communism were repellent doctrines to Allen, and for a period in the 1950s he very openly opposed them. He also opposed aspects of unionization that he felt abridged individual freedom. He grew, in time, more conciliatory, as did the workers among whom he had established a reputation for fairness and concern. He died in his home in Seattle.

• The Museum of Flight, Seattle, Wash., and the Boeing Company Historical Archives, Seattle, Wash., contain materials from Allen's tenure with Boeing. Biographical materials can be found in a corporate brochure, Boeing Company, "William M. Allen: A Personal Portrait" (1991), and Harold Mansfield, *Vision: The Story of Boeing* (1966).

PAUL G. SPITZER

ALLEN, William Vincent (28 Jan. 1847–12 Jan. 1924), U.S. senator, was born in Midway, Ohio, the son of Samuel Allen, a minister who died when William was an infant, and Phoebe Pugh. His abolitionist family was actively involved in the underground railroad. In 1857 Allen's stepfather moved the family from Ohio to Fayette County, Iowa. With the outbreak of the Civil War, Allen, at the age of fourteen, tried to enlist in the army, but when his age was discovered he was sent home. The following year he became a private with the Thirty-second Iowa Volunteer Infantry and served for three years. Afterward he enrolled at Upper Iowa University in Fayette, Iowa, where he completed two or three terms before taking a job as a schoolteacher. While teaching he read law and was admitted to the bar in 1869. From 1869 until 1884 Allen practiced law in Fayette and Ackley, Iowa.

In 1870 Allen married Blanche Mott; they had four children. In 1884 he moved his family to Madison, Nebraska, where he practiced law. A longtime Republican, Allen in 1890 discovered the Farmers' Alliance, which sought political and economic reforms for farmers and which led to the creation of the Populist party in 1891. That year Allen was the Populist candidate for the Ninth District judgeship of Nebraska, and he easily won the election. During the 1893 U.S. senatorial election, the Populist candidate, John Powers, was unable to attract the necessary votes, and the Populists shifted to Allen as a fusionist alternative. In doing so, the Populists drew the needed votes from the Democratic party, and Allen was elected.

The success of fusion between the Populists and Democrats in the Allen campaign set a precedent for future cooperation between the two parties. Chairman of the Nebraska Populist State Convention, Allen was also chosen as chairman of the Populist National Convention of 1896, held in St. Louis, Missouri. The convention nominated William Jennings Bryan for president, and Allen played a controversial role in the nomination process. During the voting, Senator James K. Jones reportedly received a telegram from Bryan declining the Populist nomination, but Allen refused to yield the floor. While the delegates were voting, H. S. P. Ashby, the chairman of the Texas Populist party, repeatedly asked Allen about the rumored withdrawal of Bryan, and Allen denied knowledge of Bryan's refusal to run. Afterward the Democratic and Populist party differences contributed to the Republican election victory of 1896.

During his senate term, Allen helped investigate "sugar trust scandals," which involved illegal payments to fund political campaigns. He also fought against the repeal of the 1890 Silver Purchase Act. The fight led to a filibuster that lasted forty-six days, during which Allen set a record by holding the Senate floor for fourteen straight hours. Despite his efforts, the act was repealed. In the area of economics, Allen argued that the government should not allow national, state, and local banks to issue paper currency. As a solution to the deflationary spiral, he believed that the government should coin silver at a ratio of sixteen to one with gold. He also supported the adoption of an income tax and a gradual acquisition of telegraph and railroad lines by the government. Although he disapproved of Coxey's Army, a group of unemployed men who gathered in Washington in hopes of encouraging the Grover Cleveland administration to pass legislation relieving unemployment, he defended the marchers' right to present their complaints peacefully. He opposed the creation of a large military force and thought that imperialism was wrong. In 1899 Allen failed to gain reelection to the Senate, but when Monroe L. Hayward died before he could take office that year, Nebraska governor William A. Paynter appointed Allen to fill in. After leaving the Senate in 1901, Allen returned to private law practice.

At the Populist convention of 1904, held in Springfield, Illinois, Allen was considered a potential presidential candidate. A close race with Tom Watson of Georgia ensued until Allen gradually fell behind and withdrew. He then returned to Lincoln to practice law until 1917, when Allen was elected to the bench of the Ninth Judicial District of Nebraska, where he served until his death, which occurred in Los Angeles.

Allen was one of the most prominent spokesmen for the Populist movement of the 1890s during its brief ascendancy as a major rival to the Democratic and Republican dominance of American politics. His advocacy of fusion with the Democrats made him controversial with some Populists, but that fusion secured a number of offices for the Populist party in Nebraska and other western states. Allen's strategy helped make the Populist party one of the most successful third-party movements in American history.

• For sources on Allen's public policies see his "The Populist Program," *Independent*, 22 Feb. 1900, pp. 475–76; and Albert Shaw, "William V. Allen: Populist: A Character Sketch and Interview," *Review of Reviews* 10 (1894): 30–42. Material on Allen's record-breaking speech is in *Congressional Quarterly's Guide to Congress*, 4th ed. (1991). For information on Allen's political career see Robert W. Cherny, *Populism, Progressivism, and the Transformation of Nebraska Politics, 1885–1915* (1981), Donald R. Hickey, *Nebraska Moments: Glimpses of Nebraska's Past* (1992), and C. Vann Woodward, *Tom Watson: Agrarian Rebel* (1938). An obituary is in the *New York Times*, 13 Jan. 1924.

SCOTT STEVEN SWINGLE

ALLEN, Young John William (3 Jan. 1836–30 May 1907), missionary, educator, and journalist in China, was born in Burke County, Georgia, the son of Andrew Young John Allen and Jane Wooten. Because of the early death of both parents, Allen was raised by an aunt and uncle, Wiley and Nancy (Wooten) Hutchins, who lived in Meriwether County, Georgia. He received a sizable inheritance from his father, which financed his education at several small private schools near his home in Starrsville, Georgia, including the Baptist-run Brownwood Institute in LaGrange, Georgia, and the Morgan H. Looney schools in Palmetto, Georgia. His inheritance also allowed him to collect a personal library, which made him the envy of his classmates as early as 1850, when he was only fourteen years old. He began college work at Emory and Henry College in Virginia in 1853 but transferred to Emory College in Oxford, Georgia, in the spring of 1854. At Emory, Allen acquired the secular learning of the European tradition as well as knowledge of Christianity. His extracurricular activities included membership in a debating society and religious study groups, both of which prepared him for his subsequent careers in China.

While at Emory, Allen considered himself converted to Christianity and by his senior year decided to preach as well as to be a missionary. Upon graduation, Allen married Mary Houston in 1858; they were to have ten children, four of whom died in infancy. In December of that year both attended the Georgia Conference of the Methodist Episcopal Church, South, where they were admitted as members, and Allen volunteered for the China mission after hearing an appeal from Bishop George F. Pierce. He spent the following year soliciting funds for the southern Methodist mission in Shanghai and in the end liquidated much of his inheritance to finance the journey to China. Setting sail in December of 1859, the family, which now included a child, finally reached Shanghai in July 1860.

Within a year of his arrival, Allen found his choice of a career, his commitment to Christianity, and his place of work challenged. The American Civil War broke out in April 1861, leaving Allen and his colleagues cut off from financial support. By the end of 1861, the two seasoned missionaries, James L. Lambuth and W. G. E. Cunnyngham, had left China, leaving Allen and Marquis L. Wood (who had arrived with Allen) as the primary southern Methodist missionaries in China. Moreover, the Taiping Rebellion confined the missionaries to Shanghai.

These two civil wars forced Allen to depart from the usual pattern of missionary work in an effort to support not only his family but the mission as well. Finding work as an English teacher at the Shanghai Tongwen Guan in 1864, Allen discovered that education offered a unique opportunity to extend his missionary effort. At the same time, Allen began reading some of the basic Chinese classics, such as the *Three Character Classic* and the *Thousand Character Classic*, and found that they contained more learning than he previously had imagined. His efforts at proselytizing also were challenged as he discovered that impersonal preaching was not an effective means of introducing Christianity to China; rather, personal contact and conversation proved helpful. His own definition of Christianity expanded, and increasingly he included secular education, particularly technological and scientific subjects, in his concept of the Christian message.

Allen remained an active educator in China until 1895, teaching English in the morning at the Tongwen Guan until 1881, establishing the Shanghai Anglo-Chinese College in 1882 (of which he was president from 1884 to 1895), and, as superintendent of the southern Methodist mission in China from 1881 to 1895, overseeing the establishment of several smaller schools and educational institutions for young Chinese women, such as the Clopton School and the McTyeire Home and School for Girls. He also helped found Soochow University in 1901; the Anglo-Chinese College was merged with it in 1911.

In addition to educational work and managing the southern Methodist China mission, Allen also communicated his ideas via the written word; in fact, he was one of the most productive missionaries to convey Western ideas in the Chinese language. His translation work began in 1871 when he accepted an appointment for afternoon employment in the Kiangnan Arsenal translation bureau, a position he held until 1881. He emphasized Western history and current events, including quarterly and annual summaries of world events, but he also provided translations of pure science. In addition, he wrote three books, all of them in Chinese: *China and Her Neighbors* (1876), *The War between China and Japan* (1896), and what he considered to be his magnum opus, *Women in All Lands; or, China's Place among the Nations* (1906).

Although these works were influential, particularly *The War between China and Japan*, which went through several printings, Allen's most consistent writing career was as a journalist. As with many of his other endeavors, his journalism career began in the 1860s when he needed money to support his family. Seizing on an opportunity to edit the thrice-weekly *Shang-hai hsin-pao* in 1868 (a post he held until 1871), Allen quickly recognized journalism as a means of reaching more Chinese. Within four months, Allen started his own religious paper, the *Chiao-hui hsin-pao* (Church News) with the purpose of uniting the Protestant missions in China, but he continually added to that purpose by including current news of the West as well as information on Western science and technology. Armed with this broader definition of purpose, Allen then renamed his periodical the *Wan-kuo kung-pao* (Globe Magazine, or, A Review of the Times) in July 1874. He continued to edit the paper until 1883 when he interrupted publication while he assumed the superintendency of his mission. When the paper resumed publication in 1889, Allen was again editor, but the Society for the Diffusion of Christian and General Knowledge among the Chinese sponsored the effort. The paper continued to be published until shortly after Allen's death in Shanghai.

His journalism career is evidence of Allen's continuing focus on education as a prime means of reaching literate Chinese with his expanded Christian message. The paper was printing 2,000 copies per issue by 1874 with circulation among court members in Beijing and a readership that extended to most Chinese Christian communities. Allen's magazines provided the largest and most comprehensive body of sources of new knowledge for the Chinese in the crucial period of the 1880s and 1890s when Chinese reform thought was in gestation. The Chinese government recognized his efforts in 1876 with a Fifth Brevet Rank.

• Allen's papers are in the Robert C. Woodruff Library of Advanced Studies, Special Collections, Emory University, Atlanta, Ga. There are two biographies of Allen: Warren A. Candler, *Young J. Allen: The Man Who Seeded China* (1931), and Adrian A. Bennett, *Missionary Journalist in China: Young J. Allen and His Magazines, 1860–1883* (1983).

ADRIAN A. BENNETT

ALLEN, Zachariah (15 Sept. 1795–17 Mar. 1882), textile manufacturer, engineer, and inventor, was born in Providence, Rhode Island, the son of Zachariah Allen, a merchant, and Ann Crawford. Allen graduated from Brown University in 1813, receiving a certificate in proficiency from the newly established medical school in addition to his college degree. Although the War of 1812 frustrated his original plan to continue medical study abroad, Allen maintained a lifelong interest in science that expressed itself in practical and theoretical research and writing, principally in mechanics and the physical sciences. He joined the Rhode Island bar in 1815 after studying with James Burrill, Jr., but his career as a lawyer was brief. In 1817 he married Eliza Harriet Arnold; they had three children. Serving on the Providence town council from 1820 to 1823, Allen modernized the town's fire-fighting system and was an effective proponent of public education, two causes that he continued to espouse throughout his life.

Allen ventured into textile manufacturing in 1822 when he built a woolen mill in North Providence; he remained active in textiles until 1871, as both an owner and a manager of several factories. In addition to the initial Allendale Mill (as owner and manager, 1822–1857), he was also involved in the Phenix Mill (as co-owner and co-manager, 1835–1854), the Georgiaville Mill (as owner and manager, 1853–1871), and the Allen Printworks (as manager, c. 1857–c. 1871), all in Rhode Island. Allen epitomized the practical manufacturer who was both an owner and an active manager of his factories. In his efforts to improve his manufacturing practice he diligently monitored new developments by traveling widely in the United States, Great Britain, and Europe. He played an important role as a disseminator of new technology through both the practical example of his factories and as a lecturer and author. His most notable work, *The Science of Mechanics as Applied to the Present Improvements in the Useful Arts in Europe and in the United States* (1829), discussed the rudiments of mechanical science and their practical applications in industry and engineering.

Allen's mechanical aptitude was such that between 1829 and 1853 he registered four patents for improved textile machinery and one for a new process for weaving counterpanes that simulated the expensive hand embroidery on these popular imported bedspreads. His other inventions included a high-speed power transmission system for factories that eliminated pulleys from the belt-driven line shafting and an automatic cut-off valve for steam engines that was regulated by a flyball governor (patented in 1834). Although the cut-off valve was potentially his most important invention, it achieved only limited use before being superseded in 1849 by the slide valve developed by the engineer George Corliss.

In addition to the incremental improvements in production and power transmission systems represented by his patented inventions, Allen made significant contributions in hydraulic engineering and fire prevention. In 1822 he was instrumental in the creation of a corporation to construct reservoirs on the Woonasquatucket River for the purpose of supplying mills with water in times of drought. This systematic harnessing of a river watershed for industrial purposes appears to have been the first example in the United States of a critical technique for the expansion of water-powered manufacturing. His interest in hydraulics also led him to conduct the first scientific calculation of the volume and potential power of Niagara Falls, which was published in the *American Journal of Science and Arts* (Apr. 1844). Beginning at the Allendale Mill Allen had worked to reduce the risk of fire at his factories by adopting fire-resistant construction techniques that he and others had developed. These included roof shingles set in mortar, slow-burning heavy timber framing, metal-sheathed fire doors, and overhead sprinklers fed by rooftop cisterns. He was also one of the first to employ a water-powered rotary pump with hydrants and copper-riveted hoses as standard fire-fighting equipment.

When Allen failed to receive a reduction in rates from his insurance company despite these improvements, he organized a mutual insurance company with his fellow manufacturers. Chartered in 1835, the Manufacturers Mutual Fire Insurance Company became the prototype for the factory mutual companies that quickly proliferated over the next few decades and have continued to operate throughout the twentieth century. As conceived by Allen, the factory mutuals emphasized risk reduction through fire-preventive construction and maintenance, modern fire-fighting equipment, and annual inspections. Through these policies the factory mutuals became a major influence on industrial architecture and the practice of fire prevention. At the request of the Rhode Island Mutual Fire Insurance Company, Allen conducted a study on the explosiveness of coal oil; the study, which was published in the Smithsonian Institution's *Annual Report* for 1861, evaluated the comparative dangers of the different flammable oils and became the basis for subsequent regulations.

As an employer and a civic leader, Allen responded to the social disruptions engendered by industrialization and urbanization with a vigorous advocacy of institutions for the public welfare, especially public schools, libraries, and parks. The mill villages under his paternalistic control were popularly regarded as models of their type, characterized by high wages and educational, religious, and architectural amenities. In 1840 he succeeded in establishing public evening schools in Providence for the benefit of the working population, the first such schools in New England. He was also instrumental in founding the city's public library (chartered in 1875; opened in 1878) and in instituting successive programs of public lectures by the local learned and professional societies. The state prison, the Butler mental hospital, and the Providence waterworks also benefited from his founding efforts and early direction.

In addition to his numerous newspaper and magazine articles and addresses on public, professional, and scientific issues, Allen authored two volumes on theoretical physics, *The Philosophy of the Mechanics of Nature* (1852) and *Solar Light and Heat* (1881). A lifelong member of the Rhode Island Historical Society, he produced several essays on Rhode Island history, including *Memorial of Roger Williams* (1860), *Bicentenary of the Burning of Providence in 1676, Defense of the Rhode Island System of Treatment of the Indians, and of Civil and Religious Liberty* (1876), and *The Conditions of Life, Habits, and Customs, of the Native Indians of America and Their Treatment by the First Settlers* (1879). He died at his home in Providence.

The "love of scientific engineering and useful improvements," Allen wrote, was the motivating force in his career, which spanned a critical half-century in the country's industrial development and illustrates a key period in the emergence of the engineering profession. He brought to practical manufacturing the temperament and training of a scientist and to his civic and humanitarian efforts the desire to ameliorate the major ills of the industrial society he helped create.

• Allen's papers, including his journals and published and unpublished manuscripts, are in the Rhode Island Historical Society. Among his other major works not already mentioned in the text are "Memorial of the Woolen Manufacturers of Providence and Its Vicinity," presented to the Eighteenth Congress of the United States, 15 Dec. 1823 (repr. 1927); *Sketches of the State of the Useful Arts and of Society, Scenery &c. &c. in Great Britain, France and Holland or The Practical Tourist* (2 vols., 1835); and "The Transmission of Power from the Motor to the Machine," New England Cotton Manufacturers' Association, *Proceedings of the Sixth Annual Meeting* (1871). Amos Perry, *Memorial of Zachariah Allen, 1795–1882* (1883), includes biographical information, major newspaper obituaries, and a list of his publications. J. D. Van Slyck's sketch in *Representative Men of New England, Manufacturers*, vol. 1 (1879), draws heavily on autobiographical material provided by Allen. David Jeremy, *Transatlantic Industrial Revolution: The Diffusion of Textile Technologies between Britain and America, 1790–1830s* (1981), evaluates Allen as a disseminator of new technology. Charles and Tess Hoffmann review the controversy around the Allen steam valve in "From Watt to Allen to Corliss: One Hundred Years of Letting Off Steam," *Rhode Island History* 44, no. 1 (1985): 19–27. William Pierson, Jr., discusses the Allendale Mill in *American Buildings and Their Architects*, vol. 3, *Technology and the Picturesque; The Corporate and the Early Gothic Styles* (1980). Richard Greenwood, "Zachariah Allen and the Architecture of Industrial Paternalism," *Rhode Island History* 46, no. 4 (1988): 117–35, examines the social dimension of Allen's mill villages.

RICHARD E. GREENWOOD

ALLERTON, Isaac (c. 1586–Feb. 1659), merchant in the early years of the Plymouth colony. Little is known of Allerton's early life, and nothing is known regarding his education and religious orientation. He was a tailor in London at the time that he moved to Leiden, Holland, in 1608. When the Separatist congregation of John Robinson arrived in 1609 Allerton joined the church. In 1611 he married a fellow member, Mary Norris. In 1614 he became a citizen of the Dutch city.

When the congregation decided to emigrate to America, Allerton was one of the four members entrusted with planning the expedition, and he participated in buying and equipping the *Speedwell* on behalf of the group. He sailed with his wife and three of their four children, while their youngest daughter remained with relatives who later brought her to Plymouth. The Allertons originally sailed on the *Speedwell*, later transferring to the *Mayflower* when the older ship proved unseaworthy. Following the death of his wife in 1621 he married Fear Brewster, the daughter of Elder William Brewster. Allerton was also elected an assistant in 1621, a year after the Pilgrims' arrival in Plymouth. His duties were not spelled out, but for three years he and Governor William Bradford were the colony's only elected officials. He played a prominent role in the successful negotiations with the local Wampanoag tribe and served as one of Miles Standish's officers in the colony's defense plan. Along with Samuel Fuller and Edward Winslow, he represented Plymouth in meetings to discuss common concerns with representatives of the Massachusetts Bay Colony in the 1630s.

Allerton's greatest service to the infant colony came on two trips to England in 1626 and 1629, during which he negotiated to sever the colony's ties with the venture's English backers, thus gaining for the colonists the freedom to control their own affairs. He borrowed funds for supplies desperately needed in the colony, and he arranged terms for repayment of the colonists' existing debt owed to the merchant adventurers by organizing a group of the colony's leading citizens, known as the Undertakers, who assumed the responsibility of paying the debts in return for a monopoly of the colony's trade. Allerton was primarily responsible for securing the 1630 patent that gave the colonists title to their land and property. He also developed plans for the emigration of other members of the Leiden church who had chosen not to resettle in 1620 and induced other Englishmen to migrate to Plymouth.

In the course of these journeys, however, Allerton began to devote too much time to his own business interests and to exceed his authority in ways that lost him the support of his fellow colonists. In 1628 he engaged and sent to the colony a "Mr. Rogers" to minister to the Pilgrim church. Rogers proved "crazed" and was dispatched back to England. On a more serious level, Allerton brought goods back from England to engage in trade for private profit, mixed his own and the Undertakers' accounts, used their credit to finance his personal ventures, and involved them in enterprises that they had not approved. He also employed as his secretary Thomas Morton, whose activities at Merrymount had led to the opposition of both the Plymouth and Massachusetts authorities. Initially, Allerton was protected by the concern Bradford and the other colonists had for Allerton's father-in-law, Brewster. But in the early 1630s investigations of the business accounts of the Undertakers revealed the extent of Allerton's mismanagement, if not fraud, and he was dismissed from his posts. Though listed as a freeman of the colony until 1637, he spent little time there, especially after the death of his wife in December 1634. Their only child was a son, born in 1630.

After departing from the Pilgrim colony, Allerton maintained a trading post he had previously established at Machias, along the Maine coast, but it was destroyed by the French in 1633. He engaged in fishing ventures in the Marblehead region until 1635, when he was asked to leave by the Massachusetts authorities, who cited his religious views as the reason though they failed to specify what they specifically objected to. For most of the next decade he was a merchant in the New Netherland colony, engaged in the coastal and tobacco trades; he had a warehouse on the East River. He married his third wife, Joanna, whose maiden name and background are unknown, at about this time. Around 1646 he moved again, settling in the New Haven colony, in the town of the same name. He made but then lost a fortune in the Virginia and West Indian trade and died insolvent in New Haven. Though he made himself unwelcome in both Plymouth and Massachusetts and failed to achieve the personal fortune he strove for, Allerton's business acumen contributed to the successful transition of the early colonists to their New England environment.

• There is no collection of Allerton's papers or correspondence, nor has he been the subject of a biography. Information on him can be found in George Willison, *Saints and Strangers* (1945) George Langdon, *Pilgrim Colony* (1966), and in William Bradford's history *Of Plymouth Plantation* (1856).

FRANCIS J. BREMER

ALLERTON, Samuel Waters (26 May 1828–22 Feb. 1914), meat packer, was born in Amenia, New York, the son of Samuel Waters Allerton, Sr., a tailor and woolen mill operator, and Hannah Hurd. The youngest of nine children, he attended school for several years but received little formal education beyond that. The family experienced financial difficulties as a result of the 1837 panic and was forced to move several times, once as far west as Dubuque, Iowa, before settling on a farm in upstate New York in 1842. Eight years later Samuel and his older brother Henry rented a farm in Yates County and began raising and trading cattle and hogs. Shortly thereafter they bought a farm in Wayne County.

In 1852 Samuel quit farming and became a full-time livestock buyer and moved to Newark, New Jersey. Four years later, with money he had saved from his cattle sales, he bought a farm in Fulton County, Illinois, 100 miles southwest of Chicago. The next year he sold his first cattle in the growing Chicago livestock market. The depression of 1857 saw beef prices drop severely, and Allerton declared bankruptcy. He returned to New Jersey, where he worked in a store owned by his brother and again started saving his money.

In March 1860 Allerton returned to Chicago and went to work in the meat-packing industry as a hog shipper. By the end of the year he had made a small fortune, principally by developing a system whereby he shipped his stock directly by railroad to slaughterhouses in New York City. That same year he married Pamilla M. Thompson, whose family he had known while farming in Fulton County. They had two children, a boy and a girl. The family lived in a large house on Prairie Avenue, among Chicago's reigning elite of businessmen and bankers.

By the fall of 1863 the Allerton Packing Company was the largest shipper of hogs in the city, and Allerton became a founder and director of the city's First National Bank. Too old for the draft, he took advantage of the military's need for food to increase his income and solidify his position as one of the wealthiest citizens of Illinois. The Civil War brought great prosperity to Chicago. Meat packers benefited handsomely from lucrative army contracts. Allerton got together with the Pork Packers' Association, the nine largest railroads in the city, and former mayor John B. Sherman to establish the Union Stock Yard and Transit Company in 1865.

The company purchased thousands of acres of land on the South Side, four miles from the city's center. The yards made beef and pork easily available to railroads for shipment to the East by providing a common shipping and receiving point for all packers. It soon became the city's largest employer as by the 1880s more than a million head of cattle and a million hogs were slaughtered annually. The yards made Chicago the hog butcher to the world and the meat-packing capital of the United States. Allerton Packing continued to ship only pork and did not follow the example of Swift and Armour by diversifying its packing operations.

Allerton did, however, invest heavily in farming and purchased 20,000 acres of land in Illinois, Ohio, and Nebraska to grow feed for his hog-raising operations. He also opened in Monticello, Illinois, a 19,000-acre experimental hog farm, managed by his son Robert, which gained a national reputation for its progressive techniques. Allerton Company workers were treated well by standards of the time. The company branched out into ownership of grain elevators, seed companies, and fertilizer plants, and the Allerton State Bank became the largest in Monticello.

By 1880 Allerton Packing had branches in Pittsburgh, Baltimore, Jersey City, St. Joseph, and Omaha. Allerton continued his involvement and investment in new scientific farming techniques and wrote several pamphlets, including *Crop Rotation, Weed Controls, and Hybrid Seeds* and *On Systematic Farming: A Short Treatise on Present Farming Conditions and How to Improve Them*. He kept his eye out for new technologies in other areas, too, and in the early 1880s he brought the first street railway to Chicago after seeing the San Francisco system in operation. Allerton's wife died in 1882, and he married his sister-in-law Agnes C. Thompson the same year. The couple had no children.

A Republican, Allerton supported the reform movement in city politics and helped establish the Municipal Voters League, a group aimed at rooting out corruption from Chicago's city council. The MVL fought many battles against the forces of five-term mayor Carter H. Harrison, leader of Chicago's Democratic machine. In 1893 the Grand Old Party chose Allerton to run against the Democratic boss. Republicans wanted an upstanding businessman to lead the city during the World's Columbian Exposition, scheduled to open shortly after the election, and Allerton fit the bill precisely. He campaigned hard for civil service reform and an end to boodling in city government and advocated closing city saloons during the exposition so visitors could see Chicago at its safest and best. He lost 114,237 to 93,148 as Harrison swept to victory on the promise of keeping Chicago "a wide open town" during the exposition. The loss disheartened Allerton, and he never again sought public office.

Allerton increasingly spent much of his time at his winter home in South Pasadena, California, and turned over operation of his packing, farming, and street railway businesses to his son. He became involved in the Young Men's Christian Association's work with wayward youth, and his financial contributions helped build the St. Charles Home for Boys, a school for troubled and abandoned children located in the countryside twenty-five miles west of Chicago. There youngsters were away from the dangers of city life and learned how to work. When Allerton, Chicago's "Pork King," died in South Pasadena, the *Chicago Tribune* wrote that he had done "more work for making the greater Chicago than almost any other citizen."

Allerton's major contribution to Chicago was his development of the Union Stock Yards. Always interested in advancements in agriculture, he also contributed to modern methods of hog raising and pork production, and his major landholdings made him a key figure in the development of scientific farming in the United States.

• Allerton left no private papers, and his company left no official history or company-sponsored biography of its founder. The most important information on his life is in James S. Currey, *Chicago: Its History and Its Builders*, vol. 5 (1912). On his involvement in the founding of the stockyards and his agricultural interests, see Paul W. Gates, "Frontier Landlords and Pioneer Tenants," *Journal of the Illinois Historical Society* 38 (1945): 143–206. An obituary is in the *Chicago Tribune*, 23 Feb. 1914.

LESLIE V. TISCHAUSER

ALLIBONE, Samuel Austin (17 Apr. 1816–2 Sept. 1889), lexicographer and librarian, was born in Philadelphia, Pennsylvania. The family record is sketchy; genealogical records indicate that Allibone's parents were probably William Allibone and Mary Smith, a descendant of Pennsylvania's first English settlers. Little is known about Allibone's early years or of his education except that he was a bibliophile from an early age. He married Mary Henry, the daughter of a prominent Philadelphia merchant and philanthropist, who helped him in his library work; the couple had one child. Allibone worked in the mercantile business and then for the Insurance Company of North America in Philadelphia. His first printed work, *A Review by a Layman of a Work Entitled "New Themes for the Protestant Clergy,"* appeared in 1852. Other writings from this period included theological essays, periodical articles, and religious tracts and handbooks. In the mid-1850s and 1860s Allibone devoted most of his time to the three-volume *A Critical Dictionary of English Literature and British and American Authors* (1858, 1871). This analysis of the writings of more than 40,000 authors, with critical judgments, from earliest accounts to the latter half of the nineteenth century, established Allibone as a leading authority in his area of research. All three volumes went through several editions, and in 1896 John F. Kirk published a supplement to the dictionary.

Allibone was a devout Episcopalian with a strong interest in Sunday school work. He was twice book editor and corresponding secretary (1867–1873, 1877–1879) of the American Sunday School Union, which published his *An Alphabetical Index to the New Testament* (1868), *Explanatory Questions on the Gospels and the Acts* (1869), and *The Divine Origin of the Holy Scriptures* (1869), the first part of *The Union Bible Companion* (1871). Other works included *Poetical Quotations from Chaucer to Tennyson* (1873), *Prose Quotations from Socrates to Macaulay* (1876), and *Great Authors of All Ages* (1880).

In 1873 Allibone married Anna Bliss; they had three children. (It is not known what happened to his first wife.) In May 1879 he moved his family to New York City at the request of philanthropist James Lenox to become librarian of the Lenox Library. Established in 1870, this library consisted of about 15,000 volumes, as well as paintings and statuary, from Lenox's private collection. When the library opened in early 1877, admission was by written application only and no books circulated, a much-criticized policy. Allibone changed this policy during his tenure as librarian, allowing scholars and special students freer use of the library. In 1895 the Lenox Library was consolidated with the Tilden Trust and the Astor Library to form the New York Public Library.

At the Lenox, Allibone compiled a card catalog; contributed monographs on Bunyan, Shakespeare, Milton, and Walton to *The Contributions to a Catalogue of the Lenox Library*; and gave talks about the library's holdings to visitors. In 1886 he turned down the opportunity to join James G. Wilson and George W. Curtis in coediting *Appleton's Cyclopaedia of American Biography* but contributed several biographical articles to the project. Allibone retired from the Lenox in 1888 and traveled to Europe; he died in Lucerne, Switzerland.

In a paper to the Historical Society of Pennsylvania (8 Dec. 1890), Samuel D. McConnell, a clergyman and author, described Allibone's "beautiful face, his gracious manner, the invincible sweetness of his temper, his charm as a companion, his skill as a raconteur, his quips and jests and dainty whimsies" as "parts of the furnishing of the man." Allibone's impact on librarianship was minimal; his fame stems from his authorship of his three-volume dictionary, which, with its exceptional breadth of research, was an immense achievement for its time.

• Allibone's papers are in the Henry E. Huntington Library, San Marino, Calif. The American Library Association Archives has two signed letters (1866, 1880) in the Barbara McCrimmon Autograph Collection, along with routine material in the Annual Conference record series (Attendance Registers, 1890–1900; Cumulative Attendance Registers, 1876–1939). The Anne C. L. Botta Papers, Brown University Library, contain correspondence as does the Historical Society of Pennsylvania, in the Benson J. Lossing Papers and in the Samuel M. Felton Papers. A biographical sketch by Stebbins is in the *New England Historical and Genealogical Register* 46 (1892). See Harry M. Lydenberg, *History of the New York Public Library: Astor, Lenox and Tilden Foundations* (1923), for background on the Lenox Library and Allibone's work there. The Fine Arts Library, Harvard University, has a portrait. An obituary is in the *New York Times*, 4 Sept. 1889.

MARTIN J. MANNING

ALLIGATOR (fl. 1832–1846), Seminole war leader famous for resisting attempts of the United States to remove the Indians from Florida, had the Indian name Halpatter Tustenuggee. Nothing is known of his parents or youth except that he migrated with his parents from a Eufala town on the Tallapoosa River. Although not a hereditary chief, Alligator was connected to two important Seminole bands. He was a war leader and adviser to Micanopy, hereditary chief of the Alachua. Micanopy was a brother-in-law to Philip, hereditary leader of the Mikasukis, and Alligator generally collaborated with both Alachua and Mikasuki activities.

In the 1830s Alligator was about forty years old, well formed and strong, but only five feet tall. He was a born comedian, evoking laughter even in solemn councils. He had a prominent roman nose and an open face. Lieutenant John T. Sprague, who dealt with him, considered him the shrewdest, craftiest, and most intelligent of all the Indian leaders. Able to communicate in English and possessing fine manners, Alligator got along well with white people.

By the Treaty of Payne's Landing, 9 May 1832, the United States required a delegation of Indians to examine the land in Arkansas Territory (Oklahoma) where the government wanted the Seminoles to go. His peers chose Alligator to be one of eight examiners. His party spent January through March 1833 inspecting the designated ground, but Alligator did not like what he saw.

During the next two years white pressures goaded the Seminoles toward war. Wiley Thompson, the federal agent, demanded that the leaders sign an agreement on 24 April 1835 to migrate. When Alligator and four others refused, Thompson arrogantly struck them from the roster of headmen.

Alligator claimed that he and Osceola made plans a year ahead for the attacks on 28 December 1835 that started the war. Osceola killed Thompson and four other white men at Fort King. Fifty miles to the south, Alligator forced Micanopy to lead 180 warriors who ambushed a column of 108 men commanded by Major Francis L. Dade, marching from Fort Brooke to Fort King. All but three of the soldiers perished. Alligator later gave white listeners a rare Indian version of what took place.

Next, an army under Brigadier General Duncan L. Clinch advanced from Fort Drane to assail the foe in the cove of the Withlacoochee River. Osceola and Alligator with 250 warriors met it at the riverbank on 31 December 1835. The resulting battle was a draw, both sides withdrawing from the field.

Late in February 1836 the Seminoles trapped Major General Edmund P. Gaines's force at a bend of the Withlacoochee River. Alligator was one of the leaders of about 1,000 warriors; Gaines had the same number. After eight days of siege, Gaines's small army was in dire distress, but the Indians too were worn down. On 6 March, Alligator, Jumper, and Osceola met with a representative of General Gaines. They proposed to retire beyond the left bank of the river and remain there if the whites would not molest them. This negotiation was never completed because of the arrival of a relief party for Gaines, which opened fire.

Major General Thomas S. Jesup took command in Florida on 8 December 1836. Three months later, on 6 March 1837, he induced several chiefs to sign an agreement to leave Florida. Alligator, present but not a signer, approved. Migrants turned themselves in at detention camps established by Jesup. The war seemed to be over, but late in the night on 2 June 700 Indians followed Micanopy out of the camps. Two Seminole leaders, one of them Osceola, had given Micanopy the choice between leading the exodus or being killed.

On Christmas Day 1837 the Seminoles prepared a strong position close to the north shore of Lake Okeechobee for a rare pitched battle. Alligator commanded the center of their line with 120 warriors. Coacoochee (Wildcat) was on his left with 80, while Sam Jones (Arpeika) controlled the right with 180 men. Colonel Zachary Taylor, commanding 750 soldiers, attacked the prepared position head on. Alligator claimed that Sam Jones fled after the first fire, but eventually all the Seminoles yielded the position. Outnumbered two to one, they had killed 26 soldiers and wounded 112 with a loss of 11 killed and 14 wounded.

At the end of two and one-half years of conflict, the Florida Indians were in a desperate condition. Alligator felt that further resistance was useless. Therefore when General Jesup sent out three important chiefs, who were his prisoners, to induce holdouts to give up, Alligator listened to them. On 24 March 1838 he surrendered, bringing with him 360 warriors, women, and children. Shortly they were aboard a ship headed for a new area in the West. Alligator claimed that he would have surrendered earlier had not the Mikasukis under Sam Jones prevented it.

In 1841 Alligator made his final trip to Florida. U.S. authorities sent him from Arkansas Territory because Thlocklo Tustenuggee (Tiger Tail) was still resisting removal and insisting on conferring with Alligator before surrendering. Arriving at Fort Brooke on 14 October 1841, he went at once into the interior. He persuaded some Seminoles to surrender, but not Tiger Tail, who had to be captured later.

While Alligator was in Florida, the question arose in Arkansas Territory of moving the 1,097 persons associated with him. Zachary Taylor, in command at Fort Gibson, would not consider the issue with Alligator absent. This band was located a few miles north of Fort Gibson in Cherokee country. Their lives had been utterly disrupted. General Jesup had promised them livestock, tools, and subsistence in the West if they would leave those necessities behind in Florida. But in the spring of 1842 Alligator wrote to the War Department, "I have no gun to kill squirrels and birds with to feed my children, no axe to cut my firewood, no plow or hoes with which to till the soil for bread" and no agent to represent the Seminoles' needs. Relief was very slow in coming, and deprivation continued.

The Seminoles resisted U.S. demands for them to amalgamate with the Creeks, who oppressed them in many ways. They remained on Cherokee land, although the Cherokees wanted them out. To resolve the issue, Alligator and Wildcat led a delegation to Washington, D.C., in 1844, but not until August 1856 did the Seminoles receive their own allotment of land. Although Alligator's last years are obscure, he signed a treaty in 1845 by which the Seminoles were given some autonomy among the Creeks.

• John T. Sprague, *Origin, Progress and Conclusion of the Seminole War* (1848; facsimile ed., 1964), offers a contemporary view. Two modern accounts are John K. Mahon, *History of the Second Seminole War* (1964), and James W. Covington, *The Seminoles of Florida* (1993), both of which have reference to Alligator. For the postremoval period, see Edwin C. McReynolds, *The Seminoles* (1957).

JOHN K. MAHON

ALLINE, Henry (14 June 1748–2 Feb. 1784), itinerant evangelist, was born in Newport, Rhode Island, the son of William Alline, a miller and farmer, and Rebecca Clark. The young Alline attended a local public school, where he showed academic ability. At the age of twelve, however, he moved with his family to Nova Scotia to farm on free land offered by Governor Charles Lawrence. With over a hundred other New England "planters," the Alline family settled in the future township of Falmouth, west of Halifax. There the Allines eked out a meager existence, and Henry struggled with the isolation of frontier life.

As a young farm laborer, working hard to support his parents, Alline underwent an emotional conversion experience. Private devotional reading and the admonition of his Congregationalist parents finally bore fruit on a Sunday in the spring of 1775, when he felt his faith in God's "redeeming love" confirmed in a powerful way. This was soon followed by a perceived call to preach the gospel, but Alline's geographical isolation, his family responsibilities, and the outbreak of the Revolution in New England made ordination seem unrealistic at best. Alline brooded for months. The expectation among New England Congregationalists like his parents that clergymen be highly educated probably contributed to his doubt. He attempted to return to New England for ministerial training in the fall of 1775 but was prevented by the widening revolutionary war to the south and by family illness. Finally, after spurning a possible commission in a newly formed Nova Scotia militia unit, in April 1776 Alline decided to preach, regardless of formal theological education or ordination.

Initially, Alline's work as an itinerant evangelist took in only his village and the neighboring communities. After his ordination as an evangelist by elders from three recently organized local congregations in April 1779, he began to preach throughout the sparsely populated province. For more than seven years he toured nearly every community of any size west of Pictou, and he visited English settlements in New Brunswick several times and on Isle St. John (now Prince Edward Island) at least once. Alline traveled by horse and, in winter, by foot, though sometimes he was able to make use of coastal schooners when they could avoid U.S. privateers. On his travels, he ministered to settlers who were not being served by the Congregational or Anglican churches.

Alline's approach reflected many of the characteristics of eighteenth-century revivalism, with exhortative, extemporaneous preaching and an emotional, often confrontational style. Although his untutored sermons appear to have been highly effective among some Nova Scotians, he was not an especially successful church planter, though he did contribute to the formation of new congregations at a handful of villages. Perhaps one of the more significant was a Baptist congregation started with his assistance at Horton (now Wolfville). Like many of these congregations, however, the Horton church took a Calvinistic doctrinal stance of the kind Alline consistently criticized.

Besides these evangelistic tours, Alline also exercised an important influence through his published writings. Probably the most noted were *Two Mites on Some of the Most Important and Disputed Points of Divinity* . . . (1781) and *A Court for the Trial of Anti-Traditionalist* (1783?). His theology showed the influence of New Light thought—a pattern of ideas informed by Calvinist piety but also marked by a call for conviction of sin, a specifiable experience of conversion, and an assurance of salvation—but his reliance on his own intense religious experience coupled with his lack of formal theological training created a highly idiosyncratic product. Like other Arminians, Alline broke with a Calvinist understanding of election, but his ruminations went considerably further. He attempted to construct a theological system based on his mystical insights and limited reading in some Pietist writings. The result was an odd blend that resembled, in some respects, the mysticism of Jacob Boehme, German theosophist, mystic, and critic of Lutheran scholasticism, whose views Alline knew from the writings of William Law. In general, the biblical insight that God is love underlay Alline's perspective. Much of his youthful spiritual struggle had involved an attempt to reconcile his parents' stark conception of a judgmental God with his own experience of God's love. He came to believe that, in granting salvation, God lovingly respected human choices. Some of his writings almost imply a doctrine of universal salvation, but, unlike later Universalists, he frequently pointed to the eternally dire consequences of making the wrong choice. Besides his theological writings, Alline was also a hymnist of some note, and several of his hymns, such as "Amazing Sight, the Savior Stands," were included in popular evangelical hymnals of the nineteenth century.

Alline never married and continued to support his parents well into his adult life. He struggled with consumption for many years, and this ailment along with the draining demands of his itinerant ministry eventually took their toll. Alline died of tuberculosis while visiting a ministerial friend in North Hampton, New Hampshire.

Alline is rightly viewed as the leader in Nova Scotia of the Great Awakening, which was a genuinely popular movement. Alline's particular formulation of his evangelistic message made religious conversion an attractive alternative for the politically disfranchised settlers in Nova Scotia. His ministry served to revive a whole generation of Baptist clergy in the region. His influence is still evident in the prevalence of Baptist congregations in the Maritime Provinces and in the Protestant pietism that survives in eastern Canada in general. Indeed, some historians have argued that Alline and the Awakening gave Nova Scotians, for the first time, a strong sense of their unique calling as "a people highly favoured of God," distinct from their New England cousins and forbears. But he also influenced Free Will Baptists in the United States, especially in New England.

• Most of Alline's extant papers are in the Baptist Collection, Esther Clark Wright Archives, Acadia University. Much of this material is available in published form, including *The Life and Journal* (1806; repr. 1982). Alline's *Hymns and Spiritual Songs* (1786) may have been his best-known work. J. M. Bumstead, *Henry Alline, 1748–1784* (1971), contains a complete list of Alline's published writings. More scholarly is Gordon T. Stewart and George A. Rawlyk, *A People Highly Favoured of God: The Nova Scotia Yankees and the American Revolution* (1972). An insightful study is Rawlyk, *Ravished by the Spirit: Religious Revivals, Baptists and Henry Alline* (1984). D. G. Bell, *Henry Alline and Maritime Religion* (1993), contains a thorough listing of the secondary literature on Alline and his era.

GILLIS J. HARP

ALLINSON, Anne Crosby Emery (1 Jan. 1871–16 Aug. 1932), educator, was born in Ellsworth, Maine, the daughter of Lucilius Alonzo Emery, a lawyer, and Anne Crosby. She described her home as a literate and busy household where her parents encouraged their two children in serious study. Lucilius Emery, attorney general of Maine and later chief justice of Maine's supreme court, and Anne Emery both pushed their daughter "Nan" to "develop independence of thought and vigorous belief in the capabilities of her sex."

Emery joined a pioneering generation of American women who earned doctoral degrees just before the turn of the century. She attended Bryn Mawr College, earning the B.A. in 1892 and the Ph.D. in classical languages and literature in 1896. As an undergraduate, she was elected the first president of student government, an innovation established by M. Carey Thomas, the college's famous president known for her advocacy of rigorous classical education for women. For a year during her doctoral work, Emery served as President Thomas's secretary. A strong scholar, she won Bryn Mawr's prestigious European Fellowship, which permitted two years' graduate study in Leipzig.

Planning to head the Bryn Mawr School in Baltimore upon completing her doctorate, Emery instead was offered a post as the first dean of women at the University of Wisconsin, a job she held for three years while also an assistant professor of classical philology. The dean's job was new to higher education, generally resulting from faculty and public concern about the effects of coeducation on students. Since few coeducational schools hired academic women for teaching posts, women like Emery used the dean's position to enter academe. She fared well at Wisconsin, although she found the campus insufficiently attuned to the needs of its women students. She inaugurated student government and devoted herself to securing resources for women.

In 1900 Emery accepted the deanship of the Women's College at Brown University (later Pembroke), which she held for five years. Emery joined a venture begun eight years earlier when Brown adopted a "coordinate" plan for educating women. Unlike the full coeducation of Wisconsin or the separate education of Bryn Mawr, Brown's plan created a separate college for women students but employed the same faculty.

As the first and only woman scholar on Brown's campus, youthful and well educated, Emery left her mark on the Women's College. At a time when close, intense relationships developed between women students and faculty, she awed students and used her personal influence to guide their studies and social life. Students praised her lavishly, noting that "she so charmingly wields the scepter of Pembroke Hall that we all well nigh worship her." She organized student life, establishing self-government and various social activities. Best-loved were her "Universe meetings," Sunday gatherings at her home where students discussed contemporary issues and observed a scholarly woman at work.

Students were saddened by their dean's resignation in 1905 to marry Francis Greenleaf Allinson, a professor of classics at Brown, but they saw a model even here, explaining that her "greater task" was to prove that "college graduates make good wives." The couple raised a daughter from Francis Allinson's previous marriage. The new Mrs. Allinson remained involved with Brown, continuing her chapel talks and Universe meetings, and sitting on the college's advisory board. She served as interim dean in 1920–1921 and in 1922 when her successor took extended leaves for poor health. Although her formal career as an educator ended, Allinson was an active informal educator for the next three decades. She published widely, first on classical literature. In *Roads from Rome* (1913) she imagined the daily lives of classical writers, and in *Children of the Way* (1923) she explored the character of newly Christianizing Rome. In 1909 she coauthored *Greek Lands and Letters* with her husband.

Eventually Allinson turned to general writing, developing a career as an essayist and newspaper columnist. From 1926 to 1932 she edited the women's page of the *Providence Evening Bulletin* and contributed a daily column, "The Distaff." Her columns were literate reflections on contemporary issues, books, and personalities in which she frequently addressed educational issues. She favored a middle ground on contentious issues, and she demonstrated an appealing use of her classical training in viewing modern life. A moderate feminist, Allinson consistently advocated women's opportunities and capacities but rarely at the cost of seeming quarrelsome, noting that "the spirit of belligerency is no longer necessary."

Allinson's essays appeared in national journals, including *Yale Review*, *The Nation*, and *Atlantic Monthly*. After her death, several were gathered into *Selected Essays* (1933). Although the book was reviewed rather harshly in the *New York Times* because of its frequent sentimentality, it showcases well her educational and classical writing. In one of the essays, "The Present and the Future of Collegiate Coeducation," which she had written in 1909, she analyzes the advantages and disadvantages of various modes of women's schooling at a time when backlash against coeducation was occurring nationally. Here Allinson admonishes educators to funnel resources to the intellectual and social needs of women, else women "are never anything larger than tributary streams to the main current of university life."

Civic activism also claimed Allinson's attention. She was elected to the Providence School Committee (1925–1931) and became an active clubwoman, creating the Providence Plantations Club in 1916 and serving as its president for sixteen years. The club provided literary and social connections for Rhode Island women, sponsoring lectures and discussions on civic concerns and public welfare.

Allinson was killed in an automobile accident near her country home in Ellsworth, Maine. On her way to a favorite writing spot, she inadvertently stepped into the path of an oncoming car. Allinson was honored by the educational institutions important in her life: Wisconsin and Brown named dormitories after her, and Brown's alumnae established a fellowship in her name. A highly trained scholar in an era when few women earned the Ph.D., she helped establish the role of dean of women and influenced views of women's education. According to a colleague, as an informal educator, Allinson advanced "her sense of service" through her daily column, "as she passionately sought to extend the doctrine of women's autonomous place in a troubled world."

• Allinson left no collection of papers, but the Brown University Archives has biographical information, speeches, some clippings and scrapbooks kept by students, and references to Allinson in the Research Guide to the Christine Dunlap Farnham Archives. Allinson's additional works include *The Historical Present in Early Latin* (1897), which is a published version of her dissertation, *Friends with Life* (1924), and *Credo* (1926). After her death, some of her newspaper columns were gathered in *Selections from "The Distaff"* (1932); a fuller collection of these columns is available in two scrapbooks in the Brown University Archives. Information on the Emery family can be found in *A History of the Town of Hancock, 1828–1978* at the Hancock (Maine) Historical Society. An important biographical source is the introduction to Allinson's *Selected Essays* (1933) by her longtime friend Gertrude Taylor Slaughter. Scholarly appraisals of Allinson's work at Brown and in the community are in Grace E. Hawk, *Pembroke College in Brown University: The First Seventy-Five Years, 1891–1966* (1967); Linda Eisenmann, "Women at Brown, 1891–1930: 'Academically Identical but Socially Quite Distinct'" (Ph.D. diss., Harvard Univ., 1987); and Eisenmann, "'Freedom to Be Womanly': The Separate Culture of the Women's College," in Polly Welts Kaufman, ed., *The Search for Equity: Women at Brown University, 1891–1991* (1991). An obituary appears in the *Providence Journal*, 16 Aug. 1932.

LINDA EISENMANN

ALLIS, Edward Phelps (12 May 1824–1 Apr. 1889), manufacturer, was born in Cazevonia, New York, the son of Jere Allis, a hatter and furrier, and Mary White. Educated at Cazevonia Academy, Geneva Academy, and Union College, where he received a B.A. in 1845, Allis originally planned to practice law. In 1846, however, Allis moved to Milwaukee, Wisconsin, entering a business partnership with a college friend, William Allen, whose family had just moved its leather business there from New York. Allis and Allen opened the

Empire Leather Store in Milwaukee in May 1846, and the enterprise expanded. In 1848 Allis, Allen, and Allen's family bought a large tract of hemlock near Two Rivers, Wisconsin, and established the Mammoth Tannery to provide leather for their Milwaukee store and for shipment east. Allis served as managing director of the tannery. In 1848, as the leather business flourished, Allis married Margaret Marie Watson of Geneva, New York; they had twelve children.

In 1856, for reasons still unclear, Allis sold his interest in the leather business and spent the next five years in banking, real estate, and railroads. In 1861 he purchased the Reliance Works, a small shop that made gearing and castings to order and sawmill and flour-mill equipment, specializing in preparing and selling fine French burr millstones.

The purchase came at a fortuitous time. In the 1860s Milwaukee was the nation's milling center, and the Civil War increased orders for flour-milling equipment throughout the region. Moreover, Wisconsin and Michigan were just emerging as centers of the nation's timber industry, creating a rapidly expanding market for Allis's sawmill equipment. Edward P. Allis & Co. flourished, and in 1867 Allis moved the Reliance Works to a new and larger location on Milwaukee's south side.

In the late 1860s Allis diversified. By 1870 his firm also produced steam radiators for homes and offices, small steam engines, pile drivers, dredges, hoisting machines, fuel-saving grates, and boilers. In the early 1870s Allis went further, securing major contracts for Milwaukee's new water-supply system. This compelled Allis to erect a pipe foundry and to manufacture larger and more complex steam engines. Successful completion of these contracts established Allis as a major regional builder of first-class steam engines.

But Allis had overextended by moving into cast-iron pipes and large-scale steam engines. His philosophy of constant expansion, relying heavily on borrowed money, put him in serious jeopardy during the long business depression after the panic of 1873. By 1876 Allis was on the verge of bankruptcy. Only his excellent reputation in the local business community enabled him to reorganize the company and establish new lines of credit.

Allis's financial difficulties made him sympathetic to the Greenback party, for that party's advocacy of a flexible monetary system based on paper money and of planned inflation in times of depression to stimulate the economy favored debtors like Allis. Allis ran unsuccessfully as Greenback candidate for governor of Wisconsin in 1877 and 1881. When the Greenback party declined, Allis returned to the Republican party but played no further role in politics.

After refinancing in 1876, Edward P. Allis & Co. steadily expanded. Allis increasingly focused his efforts on the financial side of operations. For the technical end he retained the best possible experts and allowed them considerable independence. In the 1870s he hired an extraordinary triumvirate of engineers. George M. Hinkley, employed in 1873, revolutionized sawmill technology, bringing the automatically fed circular saw to new heights and introducing the first commercially practical band saw. William Dixon Gray, hired in 1877, perfected the belt-driven rotary flour mill. Under his direction, the Allis company built the first roller flour mill in America and dominated the flour-milling machinery market in its transition from millstones to rollers. Edwin Reynolds, hired in 1877 and longtime superintendent of the Reliance Works, designed and built some of the largest and most efficient reciprocating steam engines ever constructed. These engines made Allis's company a world leader in the manufacture of steam-powered blowing, pumping, rolling, and hoisting engines. By the 1880s Allis's company was selling sawmills, flour mills, and steam engines not only nationally but internationally. The firm that Allis had acquired in 1861 with twenty employees had more than 1,500 by 1889.

Allis was a paternalistic employer, who generally enjoyed good labor relations. In 1883, with his support and encouragement, his employees formed a mutual aid society to provide medical services and insurance to members in case of sickness, injury, or death. The formation of such organizations under the direction of employers was a relatively common practice in the period. But Allis matched his employees' contributions to the society's treasury, an uncommon practice. Allis also provided a reading room and meeting hall for his employees in the Reliance Works. Allis considered himself a friend of labor and was deeply perplexed when his employees joined the short-lived 1886 Knights of Labor strike for reduction of the ten-hour workday to eight hours with no reduction in daily pay.

Allis was concerned about what the fate of his firm would be after his death, especially since he continued his policy of constant expansion through borrowing. Although four of his sons worked in the firm at one time or the other, none had Allis's business acumen. To ensure his firm's survival, Allis took out a large number of life insurance policies. When he died unexpectedly in Milwaukee, Wisconsin, these policies covered both his personal debt and the firm's debt and allowed it to continue operation directed by his wife, several of his sons, and Edwin Reynolds.

Allis's contemporaries described him as modest and cultured. According to his biographer Walter F. Peterson, he was "respected rather than loved." Though active in civic affairs, Allis led a limited social life, in part because by 1870 he was hard of hearing and needed an ear trumpet. Allis had two loves outside of business: reading and art. He read extensively and, with his wife, acquired an excellent collection of paintings.

• No comprehensive collection of Allis papers survives, but the Milwaukee County Historical Society inherited the bulk of the archives of the Allis-Chalmers Company, which includes some Allis materials. The most thoroughly referenced and most detailed account of Allis's life is in the opening chapters of Walter F. Peterson, *An Industrial Heritage: Allis-Chalmers Corporation* (1978). A Wisconsin State Historical Society booklet by James I. Clark, "Edward P. Allis: Pioneer

Industrialist" (1958), presents a brief overview of Allis's career. Other accounts can be found in [Anon.], "Edward Phelps Allis, F. Am. Soc. C. E.," *Proceedings of the American Society of Civil Engineers* 25 (1889): 118–19; D. I. Nelke, ed., *The Columbian Biographical Dictionary and Portrait Gallery of the Representative Men of the United States: Wisconsin* (1895), pp. 388–95; Horatio D. Allis, *Genealogy of William Allis of Hatfield, Mass. and Descendants* (1919); William George Bruce, *History of Milwaukee City and County*, vol. 2 (1922), pp. 4–11; John G. Gregory, *History of Milwaukee, Wisconsin*, vol. 3 (1931), pp. 12–21; and Charles H. Wendel, *The Allis-Chalmers Story* (1988).

TERRY S. REYNOLDS

ALLISON, John Moore (7 Apr. 1905–28 Oct. 1978), diplomat, was born in Holton, Kansas, the son of Oscar John Allison, a furnace and stove equipment wholesaler, and Anna Belle Moore. Allison earned an A.B. in 1927 at the University of Nebraska, where he developed an interest in international relations. Rather than accepting a scholarship for graduate study, he went to Japan, where he taught conversational English for two years in programs under the supervision of the Japanese government at Odawara, Kobe, and Kyōto. In June 1929 he joined General Motors Corporation as an advertising manager tasked with opening a new sales office in Mukden (Shenyang), China. While in China, he became friends with U.S. vice consul Arthur Ringwalt and American journalists Edgar Snow and Agnes Smedley. Retrenchment at General Motors after the stock market crash cost Allison his job in March 1930. His diplomatic career started the next month, when Ringwalt helped him gain employment as a clerk at the U.S. consulate in Shanghai. Returning to Washington, Allison passed his Foreign Service oral examination in October 1931. Congress confirmed his appointment as an officer in January 1932.

Allison held various consular posts both in China and Japan during the decade before Pearl Harbor. His first appointment was clerical vice consul at Kobe late in 1931, preparatory to beginning intensive language training in Tokyo early the following year. On Christmas Day 1932 Allison arranged for Snow's wedding in his own apartment. The maid of honor was Marie-Jeannette Brooks, a French teacher at an American school in Tokyo. In 1933 Allison married Brooks. Their marriage ended in divorce. In 1934 Allison became vice consul in Tokyo, later performing consular functions in Manchuria (Dongbei) at Dairen (Dalian) and in China at Tsinan (Chinan) and Nanking (Nanjing).

In early 1938 Allison, now third secretary at the U.S. embassy in Nanking, became the focus of a diplomatic crisis. After observing and reporting extensive looting and brutality that occurred during Japan's occupation of the capital, he submitted a formal protest to Tokyo of fifteen specific illegal military entries into U.S. embassy property. On 26 January 1938, while investigating charges that a group of Japanese soldiers raped a Chinese woman who worked at Nanking University, Allison was slapped in the face by a Japanese sentry. To prevent a potential break in relations, Japan formally apologized. Allison assumed a new post as U.S. consul at Ōsaka in late December.

Following Japan's attack on Pearl Harbor in December 1941, the Japanese government interned Allison and other U.S. diplomatic personnel. Six months later these Americans left Japan aboard the *Asama Maru*. Shortly after his repatriation, Allison went to London to serve as second secretary and chief of the Far East Intelligence Section at the U.S. embassy. In late 1942 he helped prepare "Enemy Strategic Re-Inforcement through Biscay—Far East Blockade Running," a report, he wrote later, that "contributed more to the war effort than all the rest of the things on which I spent my time while in the Economic Warfare Division." In 1943–1944 Allison was U.S. observer at the International Fisheries Conference, was a delegate to the Allied Maritime Conference and the International Conference on Regulation of Whaling, and in 1944–1945 participated in the European Inland Transport Conference, which created an advisory body to expedite the movement of war supplies and to standardize tariffs. Allison's interaction with the Soviets persuaded him that Moscow had no interest in postwar cooperation. He became first secretary and vice consul at London, then returned to the United States in September 1946 to serve as adviser to the U.S. delegation at the United Nations (UN). In December Allison became assistant chief of the Division of Japanese Affairs.

A reorganization in 1947 made Allison the chief of the Division of Far Eastern Affairs, adding Korea to his responsibilities. That year the Harry Truman administration adopted Allison's plan to end the Soviet-American military occupation of Korea. The question was submitted to the UN, elections were held in South Korea alone, and the Republic of Korea was created in August 1948. By then another restructuring made Allison the director of Northeast Asian affairs. In 1948 he married Effie Bridewell Vesey. Following a brief stint as consul general in Singapore, Allison became special assistant to John Foster Dulles in 1950 to help draft a peace treaty for Japan.

When the Korean War began, Allison was in Tokyo with Dulles. The two men sent a cable to Washington urging the use of U.S. troops to defend South Korea. Despite his later denials, Allison was influential in building support in Washington for the decision to extend military operations into North Korea, arguing forcefully that reunification alone would bring lasting peace. During 1951, as counsel to the U.S. mission in Tokyo, he helped complete the Japanese peace treaty and then traveled with Dulles to India, Pakistan, and the Philippines to secure their approval prior to the signing ceremony in September. With Dulles, Allison then negotiated security pacts with Australia, New Zealand, the Philippines, and Japan. Acknowledged as "one of State's best-informed experts on the Far East" (*Time*, 4 Feb. 1952, p. 11), Allison replaced Dean Rusk in December 1951 as acting assistant secretary for Far Eastern affairs and became assistant secretary in February 1952.

Republican Dwight D. Eisenhower's election as president in November caused concern for Allison, the son of a Bryan Democrat, about his career, but his next appointment was ambassador to Japan, where from May 1953 to January 1957 he tried to persuade the reluctant Japanese to rearm. Allison completed delicate negotiations for a mutual defense assistance agreement in March 1954, providing Tokyo with $100 million in U.S. economic aid in return for its commitment of manpower, resources, and facilities to defend Japan and the "free world." Again displaying his diplomatic talent and tact, Allison arranged a payment of $2 million to resolve the case of twenty-three Japanese fishermen aboard the *Fukuryu Maru* who were burned by radioactive ashes from U.S. thermonuclear tests in March 1954 near Bikini. In April 1955 he finished work on a new mutual defense pact that reduced by $50 million Japan's commitment of support for U.S. troops while Tokyo agreed to spend the same amount to improve airfields and expand its defense forces.

Allison became ambassador to Indonesia in February 1957, beginning "the most fascinating and frustrating period in my thirty years in the Foreign Service." To avert a Communist takeover in that nation, he strongly urged that the United States press the Dutch to open negotiations for the transfer of West Irian (Irian Barat) to Indonesia and provide President Sukarno with economic and military aid. Washington ignored his advice, having decided Sukarno "was beyond redemption." Allison believed that his reassignment as ambassador to Czechoslovakia early in 1958 reflected the Eisenhower administration's belief that he had become soft on communism in East Asia. His new posting in Eastern Europe was physically and psychologically depressing, exposing him to authoritarian rule at its worst. Soon after his wife began suffering from severe emphysema, Allison retired in 1960.

In retirement, Allison, an avid collector of rare books, taught at the University of Hawaii and wrote a weekly column on foreign affairs for the *Honolulu Star-Bulletin*. In addition to serving on the State Department's advisory panel on Asia-Pacific affairs, he was elected as president of both the Pacific and Asian Affairs Council and the Japan-American Society of Hawaii. Allison also served as director of the Overseas Career Program and deputy acting chancellor of the East-West Center at the University of Hawaii.

Allison's autobiographical *Ambassador from the Prairie; or, Allison in Wonderland* (1973) is full of personal and professional anecdotes, but it also provides valuable insights about the making of U.S. policy in East Asia from 1930 to 1960. He assumed that monolithic communism was a reality, confessing, "I didn't see a Communist under every bed, but I probably did see one under every other bed." Although he characterized U.S. motives as benevolent and altruistic, he lamented that few American leaders understood "the futility of one government and people attempting to impose its methods and standards on another."

Allison's second wife died in August 1977. In 1978, just before his death in Honolulu, Hawaii, he married again, to Sue Quist. He had no children. Allison was a career diplomat in the U.S. Foreign Service who played an important but secondary role in the formulation and implementation of a series of key decisions shaping U.S. policy in East Asia for more than a decade after World War II.

• Allison's small collection of papers is at the Harry S. Truman Library, Independence, Mo. Useful information about Allison is in James I. Matray, *The Reluctant Crusade: American Foreign Policy in Korea, 1941–1950* (1985); William Stueck, *The Road to Confrontation: American Policy toward China and Korea, 1947–1950* (1981); Robert J. Donovan, *Tumultuous Years: The Presidency of Harry S. Truman, 1949–1953* (1982); and John W. Dower, *Empire and Aftermath: Yoshida Shigeru and the Japanese Experience, 1878–1954* (1979). See also *Current Biography* (1956). An obituary is in the *Department of State Newsletter*, Dec. 1978.

JAMES I. MATRAY

ALLISON, Richard (1757–22 Mar. 1816), physician, was born on a farm near Goshen, in Orange County, New York. His parents are unknown. Like most American physicians of his time, he studied his profession as an apprentice. He joined the Continental army in March 1778, serving as a surgeon's mate for the Fifth Pennsylvania Regiment. In January 1783 he was transferred to the First Pennsylvania Regiment, with which he served until the war ended later that year.

Allison was one of the few men who remained in the army after the end of the war and in 1784 became a surgeon's mate for an infantry regiment that was organized in August at Fort Harmar on the Ohio River, not far from today's Marietta, under Lieutenant Colonel Josiah Harmar. In July 1788 Allison was promoted to regimental surgeon, supervising the regiment's two surgeon's mates. Most of the men moved to the vicinity of Cincinnati in 1789, at which time Allison apparently began seeing private patients, as many army surgeons after him would do for more than a century.

In 1790, when Harmar was ordered to conduct a campaign against the American Indians in the Northwest Territory near present-day Fort Wayne, Indiana, Allison was the expedition's senior physician. Although malaria was common in much of the area in the late summer and early fall and many in Harmar's force fell ill, medicines were in short supply even before the campaign began. Those that were available, Allison maintained, were "the refuse of the druggists' shops." After Harmar's force was defeated with heavy losses in October 1790, the campaign was abandoned.

Allison was the chief surgeon for a second attempt to defeat the American Indians launched the following year under the leadership of Major General Arthur St. Clair. St. Clair was himself in poor health and suffered increasingly from gout, and his men, as one of them noted in his diary, were "badly clothed, badly paid and badly fed." Once again, medical supplies were scanty, and by the time fall was approaching the number on the sick list was high. During the battle, which took place about thirty miles from Fort Jefferson (Greenville), Ohio, on 4 November, Allison joined the officers in their attempt to rally the men, and, once defeat was inevitable, he personally helped four other men escape.

Allison did not join the third expedition to be sent against the American Indians until after the 5,000-man force, known as the Legion, had started training near Pittsburgh in the summer of 1792 under Major General Anthony Wayne. At some point, probably after joining Wayne, Allison married Rebecca Strong. Their only child died shortly after birth. As the Legion's chief surgeon, Allison struggled against high rates of disease, particularly malaria and influenza. Medical supplies were once again seriously inadequate from the outset, and as the expedition marched west, Wayne authorized Allison to buy whatever he needed wherever he could find it, regardless of price. By the time the enemy was defeated at Fallen Timbers on 20 August 1794, Allison reported that Wayne, too, was seriously ill and "in agony."

The American Indians were decisively defeated, but disease was not. The number of men falling victim to malaria continued to increase in September 1794, making it necessary once again for Allison to be authorized to buy what he needed for their care regardless of price. None of the needed supplies had arrived by the time the number of sick began to grow rapidly the next summer, more than doubling within one month's time. He had to care for patients when supplies of both opium and Peruvian bark, the raw material from which quinine was later derived, were inadequate, and he experimented with substitutes in an effort to find some way to stem the tide of fevers. Although a peace treaty with the American Indians had been signed and some of the needed medicines arrived in November 1795, by the fall of 1796 the situation was as bad as it had been the previous year, and supplies of Peruvian bark were completely exhausted. At this point, however, the Legion was dismantled, and on 1 November 1796 Allison was honorably discharged.

After leaving the military service, Allison bought property in Cincinnati and for several years continued the practice he had already started in the area. In 1799 he left Cincinnati and his practice to take up farming and real estate ventures along the Little Miami River while continuing to provide medical care for sick friends and neighbors; until 1804 he was the only physician in the area. He also served as justice of the peace in the town of Miami in 1802 but returned to Cincinnati in 1805 and resumed his practice. In 1808 he set up a joint practice with Samuel Ramsey and continued his interest in real estate. In 1814 he launched a venture to create a new town, to be called Allisonia, on the land occupied by his farm, but by the time of his death in Cincinnati he was apparently losing his interest in the project. He was buried in the Wesleyan Cemetery in nearby Comminsville, Ohio.

As the army's leading surgeon in the decade and a half following the end of the Revolution, Allison set a pattern that army surgeons after him would follow, exhibiting courage and devotion to duty under conditions of great hardship and frustration during three expeditions against the American Indians. One of those who shared this period in his life noted that "none were more brave, humane, and benevolent." In electing to remain on the frontier after leaving the army, he became the first physician to take up a permanent practice in the Cincinnati area. As a leader in the civilian community of which he had become a part, he continued throughout the rest of his life to earn the respect of those who knew him.

• Allison left no collection of papers or publications behind him; neither are there obituaries upon which to draw. Some of his letters can be found in the papers of William Lytle held by the Historical and Philosophical Society of Ohio in Cincinnati. Principal sources of information on his life are Virginius C. Hall, "Richard Allison, Pioneer Physician of Early Cincinnati Area," *Ohio Medical Journal* 50 (1954): 362; Mary C. Gillett, *The Army Medical Department, 1775–1818* (1981); and James M. Phalen, "Richard Allison—Surgeon to the Legion," *Military Surgeon* 86 (1940): 377–79.

MARY C. GILLETT

ALLISON, Samuel King (13 Nov. 1900–15 Sept. 1965), physicist, was born in Chicago, Illinois, the son of Samuel Buell Allison, a high school principal, and Caroline King. After attending the John Fiske Grammar School, Allison graduated from Hyde Park High School in 1917. He became an honors student in science and mathematics and a varsity swimmer at the University of Chicago, graduating with a B.S. in physics in 1921; he remained to earn a doctorate in physics in 1923. As a graduate student under the supervision of W. D. Harkins, he investigated X-ray spectroscopy. He published his dissertation on the absence of helium from residual gases following electrical discharges in 1924. Allison continued research in X-ray physics as a National Research Council Fellow at Harvard University from 1923 to 1925, and as a Carnegie Foundation Fellow at the Carnegie Institution in Washington, D.C., from 1925 to 1926.

In 1926 Allison joined the physics faculty at the University of California, Berkeley. He continued to investigate X-ray spectroscopy, precisely defining the widths and relative intensities of X-ray lines. Allison's research provided an experimental confirmation of P. P. Ewald and C. G. Darwin's dynamic theory of X-ray diffraction. His research also led to basic improvements in the design and use of the double-crystal X-ray spectrometer. On 28 May 1928 Allison married Helen Catherine Campbell; they had two children. In 1930 he moved to the physics faculty at the University of Chicago.

Allison continued his research on X-rays. In collaboration with Arthur H. Compton, head of the physics department at the University of Chicago, he published *X-rays in Theory and Experiment* (1935). During that year Allison also spent six months in the Cavendish Laboratory at Cambridge University in England, learning the fundamentals of nuclear physics by using the Cockcroft-Walton accelerator. On returning to

Chicago he constructed a nuclear accelerator, similar to the Cockcroft-Walton design, and expanded the laboratory of nuclear physics pioneered by his mentor W. D. Harkins. From 1935 until World War II Allison and his graduate students investigated proton-induced nuclear transformations and reactions involving heavy ions. Results of their experiments provided precise values for the masses and energy content of many light elements.

During World War II Allison joined other Manhattan Project scientists in the race to develop an atomic bomb. In 1940 he began investigating the feasibility of beryllium as a moderator for a nuclear chain reaction. In 1941 he was appointed to the S-1 Committee, formerly known as the Uranium Committee, to study the feasibility of a uranium-fueled nuclear weapon. In 1942 Compton organized the Metallurgical Laboratory at the University of Chicago to develop a reactor able to sustain a nuclear chain reaction. Compton appointed Allison as one of the coordinators of the project, along with Enrico Fermi and Eugene Wigner. Allison supervised the development of a safeguard system for the uranium-graphite reactor, which achieved history's first controlled nuclear chain reaction on 2 December 1942. Compton appointed Allison director of the Chemical Division in 1943, and director of the Metallurgical Laboratory in 1944.

Later that year J. Robert Oppenheimer, director of the Los Alamos Scientific Laboratory, appointed Allison head of the Technical and Scheduling Conference. Nicknamed the "Cowpuncher Committee," this organization established priorities, based on theoretical and experimental results, toward successful and timely completion of the atomic bomb. The committee settled on two nuclear weapon designs, one fueled by uranium and the other by plutonium. On 16 July 1945 Allison manned the countdown panel at the Trinity nuclear weapon test site; with a calm voice he counted down each five-minute interval leading to the detonation of history's first nuclear weapon.

After the war Allison returned to the University of Chicago, where he resumed his professorship in physics and became the first director of the Enrico Fermi Institute for Nuclear Studies. He was one of the most vocal spokesmen for promoting the peaceful use of nuclear energy and restoring the free exchange of scientific information concerning nuclear physics. In his famous "butterfly speech" at the press luncheon announcing the creation of the Fermi Institute, he warned that if military regulation continued to inhibit the free exchange of scientific information, "researchers in America would leave the field of atomic energy and devote themselves to studying the colors of butterfly wings." To promote intellectual freedom among nuclear physicists, in 1947 he helped to establish the *Bulletin of the Atomic Scientists*, an influential journal of science and public affairs.

In 1958, after directing the Fermi Institute for thirteen years, Allison resigned to devote time to other projects. An ambassador for nuclear energy, he visited Spain and South America as a guest lecturer and adviser in 1959. He served as a U.S. State Department visiting professor to the United Arab Republic in 1960, and as director of the Technical Assistance Field Mission to the Centro Atomico in San Carlos de Bariloche, Argentina, in 1961. A member of the National Academy of Sciences, Allison served as chairman of its Physics Section from 1960 to 1963. In 1962 he became chairman of the Committee on Nuclear Science of the National Research Council, National Academy of Sciences. In 1963 he resumed his former position as director of the Fermi Institute when his colleague Herbert L. Anderson stepped down to resume research at the Los Alamos Scientific Laboratory. Allison died in Culham, England, while attending the Plasma Physics and Controlled Nuclear Fusion Research Conference.

As a pioneer in nuclear physics, Allison represents the era in which American physicists gained their greatest global prominence. As a participant in the Manhattan Project, the top secret project that created the first nuclear weapons, he contributed to the development of a reactor capable of sustaining a nuclear chain reaction, as well as that of the nuclear weapons that ended World War II. His work on beryllium-moderated reactors saw fruition in the development of research reactors at the Atomic Energy Commission's nuclear reactor test site near Idaho Falls, Idaho. Allison, like many of his colleagues in the nuclear weapons project, later placed more value on the peaceful uses of nuclear energy and promoted the limitation and prohibition of nuclear weapons.

• The biographical file of Samuel K. Allison at the University of Chicago's Department of Special Collections contains his personal papers and articles on his career. Discussion of Allison is included in the following studies: Richard G. Hewlett and Oscar E. Anderson, Jr., *The New World: A History of the Atomic Energy Commission, 1939–1946*, vol. 1 (1962); Hewlett and Francis Duncan, *Atomic Shield: A History of the Atomic Energy Commission, 1947–1952* (1962); Rodney P. Carlisle, with Joan M. Zenzen, *Supplying the Nuclear Arsenal: American Production Reactors, 1942–1992* (1996); James W. Kunetka, *City of Fire: Los Alamos and the Atomic Age, 1943–1945*, rev. ed. (1979); Jack Holl, *Argonne National Laboratory, 1946–1996* (1997); David A. Hounsell, "Du Pont and the Management of Large Scale Research," in *Big Science: The Growth of Large Scale Research*, ed. Peter Galison and Bruce Hevly (1992); Richard Rhodes, *Making of the Atomic Bomb* (1986); and Vincent Jones, *Manhattan: The Army and the Atomic Bomb* (1985). Obituaries are in the *New York Times*, 16 Sept. 1965, and in *Nature*, 19 Feb. 1966.

ADAM R. HORNBUCKLE

ALLISON, William Boyd (2 Mar. 1829–4 Aug. 1908), U.S. senator, was born near Ashland, Ohio, the son of John Allison and Margaret Williams, farmers. After one year at Allegheny College, he taught in a country school for two years, earning enough money to enter Western Reserve College in 1850. Again he left college after only a year's residence and returned home to read law. In 1852 he opened a law office in Ashland, where over the next four years he entered into three different partnerships, none of which was successful. In 1854 he married Anna Carter, the daughter of the most prosperous farmer in the county. They had no children.

One of the major determinants in Allison's decision to enter law was his interest in politics. Following the Mexican War, the two major parties were wracked by internal divisions over the question of the extension of slavery, and Allison, like many others, was seeking new answers to old issues. For a brief time he showed interest in the Native American Know Nothing party, but after the Kansas-Nebraska Act of 1854, he was one of the first in his county to join an alliance of Free Soil Democrats and Conscience Whigs in establishing the Republican party in Ohio. He went as a delegate in 1855 to the state's first Republican convention. The following year he received the party's nomination for county attorney, but Ashland remained an island of Democratic strength in a state rapidly converting to Republicanism. Allison's crushing defeat in no way dampened his enthusiasm for his new political allegiance. It only prompted him to seek a more hospitable environment.

In 1857 Allison headed west in search of a new political base. He considered settling in either Chicago or Galena but was persuaded by his older brother Matthew Allison to join him in Dubuque. Through his brother's influence, Allison was admitted as a partner in a firm whose two senior partners represented the extremes in the political spectrum. Benjamin Samuels was a Democrat, while Dennis Cooley was an abolitionist Republican. Shortly after Allison joined the firm, the partnership was dissolved. Allison remained with Samuels, who was personally more congenial and, being a Democrat, would not be his competitor for preeminence within the Republican party. Allison realized that the smallness of the Republican field in Dubuque gave him as a newcomer an opportunity for advancement.

Advance he did. In 1860 Allison was a delegate to the Republican National Convention in Chicago. Initially supporting Salmon P. Chase of Ohio for the nomination, he wisely joined the Lincoln bandwagon before the final tally. Allison campaigned vigorously in Iowa for both Abraham Lincoln and William Vandever, the Republican candidate for Congress in his district. Vandever was running against Allison's own partner Samuels, but this apparently did not effect the two partners' relationship.

In the midst of this political activity, Allison received news in the summer of 1860 that his wife had died. She had not joined him in Iowa, so except on his rare visits to Ohio, Allison lived as a bachelor. The loss of his wife apparently made little difference in Allison's lifestyle, for he was married to politics.

The flourishing law firm of Samuels and Allison further boosted Allison's political prominence. His most important case was that of *Gelpke v. The City of Dubuque* (1862). Herman Gelpke brought suit against Dubuque for its failure to pay interest on the railroad bonds issued to promote the building of the Dubuque Pacific Railroad. The Iowa Supreme Court ruled in favor of the city on the grounds that the legislature had no authority under the Iowa constitution to delegate its power of taxation to a municipality, and consequently, the bondholders had no valid claim on the city. The U.S. Supreme Court, however, reversed that judgment. Accepting Allison's arguments, it declared that a state supreme court's interpretation of its own constitution may be subject to a higher authority and, moreover, that the impairment of contract clause could be used against state judicial as well as state legislative action. Allison's victory on behalf of the supremacy of federal constitutional law endeared him to the railroads, and he was now firmly ensconced in their camp. Since the railroads would be the most powerful force in Iowa politics for the next forty years, his political future was assured.

With the outbreak of the Civil War, Allison was appointed military aide to Governor Samuel Kirkwood with the rank of lieutenant colonel, giving him a claim to service in the Union cause, which was a sine qua non for political preferment in Iowa. Following the census of 1860, the state's representation was increased from two to six in the House of Representatives, and Allison declared his candidacy to represent his newly reorganized district. After a fierce convention fight, he received the Republican nomination and won an easy victory.

Early in his congressional career, Allison made evident his commitment to the railroad interests of his state by introducing a bill providing federal land grants for the construction of two new railroads in Iowa. He thus gave further evidence that he was precisely the man that the state Republican powers, headed by railroad builder Grenville Dodge, wanted. In return Allison asked only that he be continued in office, and he was.

No political figure was ever less of an ideologue. His political philosophy was best summarized by a statement made to a friend, "I always like to vote if I can, so as to not be called upon to explain too much at home." Even when the dictates of the Dodge machine forced him to take a stand on the controversial issues of the day—protective tariff, railroad subsidies, or sound currency—Allison was remarkably successful in remaining friendly with the opposition and finding an acceptable compromise whenever necessary. His critics often joked that Allison was the only man who could walk on piano keys from Washington to Iowa and never once strike a note.

Early in 1864 Allison joined the Radical wing of the Republican party in opposition to Lincoln's moderate plan for Reconstruction and was rewarded by being assigned to the powerful Ways and Means Committee. There he found his proper niche and in time emerged as the expert in the fields of transportation, tariff, and finance. Although Allison had from the first attached himself to the powerful Iowa senator, James W. Grimes, he occasionally differed with his mentor on specific issues. He lived with the Grimes family in Washington, D.C., and not even the bitter fight over the impeachment of President Andrew Johnson disrupted that friendship. Allison voted with the Republican majority in the House for impeachment, but unlike the other Iowa congressmen, he never raised his voice in criticism when Grimes cast the deciding vote against the conviction of the president in the Senate.

In 1870 Allison, with Grimes's blessing, became a candidate to succeed his good friend in the Senate, but his close ties with the man who had become a pariah in Iowa doomed his bid. Out of office, Allison at once began his campaign to replace Senator James Harlan (1820–1899) in 1872. Harlan, seeking his fourth term, was a formidable opponent, but Allison had the support of the railroad magnates. After one of the nastiest campaigns in Iowa history, Allison received the Republican nomination, which was tantamount to election. For the next thirty-five years, Allison was the political boss of his state. The term "boss," however, did not suit Allison's personality or his method of operating. He preferred the more benign appellation "regency," which included such powerful railroad executives as Dodge of the Union Pacific, Charles E. Perkins and Joseph Blythe of the Burlington, and Nathaniel Hubbard of the Chicago Northwestern. There was never any question, however, as to who headed this coalition of political power.

In the Senate Allison won a place on the Committee on Appropriations and later also on the Committee on Finance. From these vantage points he influenced the direction of the major domestic legislation of the day. Considering his long tenure, Allison's name appeared on few acts, the most notable being the Bland-Allison Silver Purchase Act of 1878, a masterpiece of compromise. Allison always preferred working the cloakrooms rather than shining in the limelight of the Senate floor.

Even after Grimes's death in 1872, Allison remained a member of the Grimes household in Washington. In 1873 he married Mary Neally, Grimes's wife Elizabeth's niece and the adopted daughter of the late senator. She was twenty years younger than Allison and generally regarded as one of the most beautiful and gracious women in the nation's capital, but this second marriage proved to be even more unfortunate than Allison's first. Mary Allison soon suffered a serious mental depression, necessitating constant nursing care. On 13 August 1883 she drowned herself in the Mississippi River. They had no children.

In 1888 Allison was a leading contender for the Republican presidential nomination. He was very nearly successful, but after losing the New York delegation's vote, Allison was defeated by Benjamin Harrison (1833–1901). Allison made another bid for the nomination in 1896, but again a rival candidate, William McKinley, won the prize. Allison was offered cabinet positions by Presidents James A. Garfield, Harrison, and McKinley, but he refused all offers. If he couldn't have the White House, he preferred the Senate.

In the 1890s Allison was at the apogee of his senatorial power. He, Nelson Aldrich of Rhode Island, John Spooner of Wisconsin, and Orville Platt of Connecticut comprised the Big Four of the Senate and largely determined congressional policy. Within this elite coterie, Aldrich was recognized as "the manager," Allison as "the conciliator and adjuster." Over the years Allison had ample opportunity to demonstrate his talents as repeatedly the majority party split: the Radicals and the Liberals in the 1860s and 1870s, the Stalwarts and the Half-Breeds in the 1880s, the Silverites and the Goldbugs in the 1890s, and finally the Conservatives and the Progressives at the turn of the century. Although always belonging to the conservative business interests, Allison repeatedly found ways to adjust differences over silver and tariff policies and, in his last term in the Senate, over Theodore Roosevelt's efforts to regulate railroads, which resulted in the Hepburn Act of 1906.

In 1907 Allison was in such poor health that the Progressive governor of Iowa, A. B. Cummins, challenged him for the Republican senatorial nomination. In the first primary ever held in Iowa, Allison turned back Cummins's bid. It was Allison's last hurrah. Two months after the primary, he died at his home in Dubuque. Although generally believed to be as wealthy as many of his millionaire colleagues in the Senate, Allison left only a modest estate.

• Allison's papers, consisting of 550 boxes, may be found in the Iowa Historical Archives in Des Moines. Other manuscript collections containing Allison correspondence located in the same archives are the papers of Grenville Dodge, Samuel J. Kirkwood, and Albert B. Cummins. See also the papers of Charles E. Perkins in the Newberry Library, Chicago, and the Chauncey M. Depew Papers in the Yale University library. Allison never wrote his memoirs, but there is an excellent biography, Leland L. Sage, *William Boyd Allison* (1956). Other secondary works of some value in assessing Allison's career are Dan E. Clark, *History of Senatorial Elections in Iowa* (1912); Sage, *A History of Iowa* (1974); William R. Boyd, "William Boyd Allison," *Annals of Iowa*, 3d ser., vol. 23 (1941): 118–25; Edward A. White, "A Woman Promotes the Presidential Candidacy of Senator Allison, 1888," *Iowa Journal of History and Politics* 48 (1950): 221–46; and Ethan P. Allen, "*Gelpke v. The City of Dubuque*," *Iowa Journal of History and Politics* 28 (1930): 177–93. Obituaries are in the *Des Moines Register* and the *New York Times*, both 5 Aug. 1908.

JOSEPH F. WALL

ALLMAN, Duane (20 Nov. 1946–29 Oct. 1971), blues-rock musician, was born Howard Duane Allman in Nashville, Tennessee, the son of Willis Turner Allman, a recruiter for the U.S. Army, and Geraldine Alice Robbins, a former secretary. Duane was only three years old when his father, who had moved the family to Norfolk, Virginia, in 1949, was murdered. Geraldine moved with Duane and Duane's younger brother Gregg Allman, born in 1947, back to the Allman family home in Nashville. Left to themselves much of the time, the boys grew up close to each other.

Duane and Gregg were enrolled briefly at the Castle Heights Military Academy in Lebanon, Tennessee, while Geraldine returned to school to become a certified public accountant. In 1957 the family moved to Daytona Beach, Florida. By the time Duane entered

Seabreeze High School in 1960, he and Gregg both had developed an interest in playing the guitar. Summertime visits to their grandparents in Nashville exposed the boys to the Grand Ole Opry, but it was rhythm-and-blues shows featuring B. B. King, Jackie Wilson, and other black performing stars that stoked the brothers' passion for music. Duane dropped out of high school in 1962, and shortly afterward he and Gregg began playing backup in the Houserockers, the house band at a local club.

Between 1964 and 1966 Gregg and Duane played in a number of short-lived bands, including the Escorts and the Allman Joys. In 1966 they formed Hour Glass, a quintet signed by Liberty Records in 1967. Hour Glass played the Los Angeles club circuit, opening for bands such as the Doors, but the group was unable to live up to the image of a white pop-soul group that the record company had created for them. After releasing two albums of uninspired songs that sold poorly, *Hour Glass* (1967) and *Power of Love* (1968), the band returned to Florida before breaking up in 1968.

Later that year Duane Allman accepted an invitation to serve as a sessions guitarist with the Muscle Shoals Rhythm Section, a highly respected studio ensemble that provided musical backup for a roster of distinguished pop and soul recording stars. The move to Muscle Shoals, Alabama, marked a turning point in his career. For the first time Allman was exposed on a regular basis to music professionals and, more important, to producers interested in his ideas as a musician. He developed a reputation as an inventive improviser who worked blues riffs into pop arrangements. Eventually he contributed distinguished guitar work to recordings by Clarence Carter, Aretha Franklin, King Curtis, and Wilson Pickett, most notably Pickett's cover of the Beatles hit "Hey Jude." During this time Allman also perfected slide or "bottleneck" guitar, a basic blues guitar technique that produces a softer, gliding guitar sound with near-vocal pitch.

Allman's work in Muscle Shoals brought him into contact with percussionist Jai Johanny Johanson and bass guitarist Berry Oakley, both of whom shared his musical tastes. By 1969 all three were tired of recording music written by others and decided to assemble their own band. They recruited two musicians Allman knew from the Florida music scene, guitarist Dickey Betts and drummer Butch Trucks, and asked Gregg Allman to supply vocals and keyboards for the newly formed Allman Brothers Band. Under the guidance of Phil Walden, a former manager of Otis Redding who had heard Allman's work in Muscle Shoals, the band set up residence in Macon, Georgia, to become the pioneer recording stars for Walden's new Capricorn Records, an independent label distributed by Atlantic Records.

In August 1969 Allman's common-law wife, Donna Rooseman, gave birth to their daughter (the couple were divorced in 1970). That same month the band recorded its first album, *The Allman Brothers Band*. It contained a mix of original songs written by Gregg and covers such as Muddy Waters's "Trouble No More," the first recording to capture Duane on slide guitar. "Whippin' Post," the album's anchor, featured alternating guitar solos by Duane Allman and Dickey Betts that became a band trademark. By the time the album was released in November, the band had developed a good relationship with rock impresario Bill Graham and began traveling cross-country on a grueling schedule to play on eclectic bills with blues, jazz, and rock musicians at Graham's two venues, Fillmore West in San Francisco and Fillmore East in Manhattan. Ultimately the band earned its greatest renown for live performances built on extended jams in which they freely mixed blues, jazz, country, and gospel music in a rock format.

The Allman Brothers recorded their second album, *Idlewild South*, around their touring schedule in 1970. "Midnight Rider," "In Memory of Elizabeth Reed," and other cuts showed the band developing a distinctive style, in which Duane would weave his fluid guitar sound around Gregg's keyboard or answer Dickey's guitar work in call-and-response fashion. Shortly after the recording session, Duane was introduced to Eric Clapton, former lead guitarist of the seminal British blues-rock power trio Cream. Allman was asked to play on Clapton's next album, recorded as *Layla and Other Assorted Love Songs* by Derek and the Dominoes. The album received only a lukewarm reception when released in 1971 but eventually was recognized as a landmark in rock music that married the talents of two of the best white blues guitarists of their generation. Allman contributed both lead and slide guitar to the well-known title track and several other cuts, but the album's music is so perfectly orchestrated that it is hard to tell where Clapton's work ends and Allman's begins.

In March 1971 the Allman Brothers played a three-night stand at the Fillmore East, which *Rolling Stone* magazine in 1987 rated one of the twenty best rock concerts ever performed. The music played those evenings wound up on the band's live *Fillmore East* double album, released later in 1971, and its follow-up, the *Eat a Peach* double album, in 1972. *Fillmore East* was the first album to communicate to a mass audience the excitement of the Allman Brothers' live stage jams and improvisation. Garnering almost unanimous critical acclaim, it sold well enough to give the band a respite from its relentless touring schedule that fall. Band members were planning their future when Duane Allman lost control of his motorcycle and crashed while driving back to his home in Macon. He died of massive internal injuries.

Duane Allman's death represented a major loss to popular music. Occurring within fourteen months of the deaths of Janis Joplin, Jimi Hendrix, and Jim Morrison, it added to rock's growing roster of musicians whose youthful promise was cut tragically short. Two albums spotlighting Allman's guitar work were released posthumously, *An Anthology* in 1972 and *An Anthology, Volume II* in 1974. His best work, however, remains his contributions to albums recorded by the Allman Brothers Band, especially those built from live cuts, where his sound is inextricable from the music of the band as a whole, and where that whole sounds invariably greater than the sum of its individual parts. Through the Allman Brothers Band, Allman alerted a rock music industry largely concentrated on the East and West Coasts to musical talents flourishing in the American South and influenced a generation of southern rock bands, including Lynyrd Skynyrd, the Marshall Tucker Band, and Molly Hatchet. The Allman Brothers' fusion of elements from musical idioms outside the rock mainstream reflected Allman's own wide-ranging interests and is one of the finest examples of the melting pot of ideas and influences that constituted the rock music scene of the late 1960s.

• A full account of Duane Allman's brief life and his contribution to popular music is in Scott Freeman, *Midnight Riders: The Story of the Allman Brothers Band* (1995), which grew out of articles the author began writing on the Allman Brothers for the *Macon Telegraph and News* in 1983. Freeman's book supersedes Tom Nolan, *The Allman Brothers Band: A Biography in Words and Pictures* (1976), which is nonetheless interesting for its portrait of the band's early years. Duane Allman received a front-page obituary in *Rolling Stone*, 25 Nov. 1971, the same issue that carried Grover Lewis, "Hitting the Note with the Allman Brothers Band" (pp. 52–55), a largely negative feature that portrays Allman and his fellow band members as drug-wasted poseurs hostile to journalists. More balanced assessments of Allman and the band's early years are in Cameron Crowe, "The Allman Brothers Story," *Rolling Stone*, 6 Dec. 1973, pp. 46–54, and Mikal Gilmore's feature "The Allman Brothers," *Rolling Stone*, 18 Oct. 1990, pp. 77–85, 110, 112. The band's landmark concert at the Fillmore East is briefly written up in David Fricke, "The Twenty Greatest Concerts," *Rolling Stone*, 4 June 1987, pp. 79–80, 140.

STEFAN DZIEMIANOWICZ

ALLPORT, Floyd Henry (22 Aug. 1890–15 Oct. 1978), psychologist, was born in Milwaukee, Wisconsin, the son of John Edward Allport, a small businessman and country doctor, and Nellie Edith Wise, a former schoolteacher described by her son as a rather pious woman. Allport grew up in Indiana and Ohio, where he attended many camp meetings and revivals. He received an A.B. from Harvard University in 1914 and two years later began graduate work there in anthropology, later shifting to psychology. When the country entered World War I, he joined the army. Shortly before his field artillery unit left for France in October 1917, Allport married Ethel Margaret Hudson, a nurse; the couple had three children.

Decorated with the Croix de Guerre for an adventure on a French observation balloon, Allport returned to Harvard after the war to obtain his Ph.D. in psychology in 1919. Although he found Professor H. S. Langfeld, E. B. Holt, and R. B. Perry more congenial than Hugo Muensterberg, the latter suggested a follow-up study of earlier German group experiments on schoolchildren as a dissertation topic. Developing this idea, Allport carried out an experiment on "social facilitation," which investigated the effects of others' parallel activities upon an adult individual's performance of simple tasks. This study became a classic in social psychology and was often cited as the first experiment in this new field (although strictly speaking it had precursors in Germany and America). After teaching psychology at Harvard and Radcliffe for three years, Allport moved in 1922 to the University of North Carolina where he finished his pioneering textbook, *Social Psychology* (1924). Breaking with the traditions of grand theorizing, speculative ideas such as the "group mind," and uncontrolled observations, the book's novel treatment of the field employed an experimentally oriented, behavioristic approach (though with a dose of Freudian ideas added). This orientation set the direction for the mainstream of the emerging discipline of empirical social psychology, giving it a relatively narrow emphasis on social stimuli and the individual's reactions to them while neglecting social interaction, dyadic and group dynamics, and the web of social-organizational relations surrounding the individual.

In 1924 Allport was appointed professor of social and political psychology at the new Maxwell Graduate School of Citizenship and Public Affairs at Syracuse University. This unique position, which he held until his retirement in 1956, apparently made him the first teacher of an embryonic "political" psychology. The group of graduate students who worked with him in the twenties and thirties constituted the first explicitly "social psychological" doctoral program. The program produced some seminal work on what became major topics of the future social psychology: the characteristics of political extremists; *Students' Attitudes* (with Daniel Katz, 1931) and prejudice; public versus private attitudes; and conforming behavior.

In 1933 Allport published *Institutional Behavior*, a series of essays, some of which had appeared previously in *Harper's Magazine*. The book summed up the arguments of his nominalist crusade against what he called the "institutional fallacy," the practice of reifying collectivities that, he thought, pervaded the social sciences. The mystifications produced by such habits of personalizing groups and institutional processes were exemplified in the handling of the notorious Sacco-Vanzetti murder case, which one of Allport's essays entitled "Justice Takes Its Course" criticized severely as based on evidence wholly inadequate to justify their conviction and execution. This purist position, which assigned reality only to individuals and their behavior, softened slowly over the years, however. Grappling with the problem of larger structures beyond individuals, and bypassing the recently developed General Systems Theory that aimed at unifying knowledge of organized entities from the smallest to the largest, from a single cell to an ecosystem, he began to formulate a novel theory of "event structures," which conceived of individual behaviors as components of larger repetitive and interlocking cycles of events. Several dissertations by his graduate students attempted to provide an empirical base for his developing system. In 1937 Allport and his wife divorced. In 1938 he married Helene Willey Hartley; they had no children.

After retiring from teaching in 1953, Allport expanded his subject matter beyond social psychology to include theories of perceptual processes, partly in order to attract more attention from traditional psychologists who had largely ignored his somewhat esoteric and neologistic theory. In 1955 Allport published *Theories of Perception and the Concept of Structure*, his last book. Two years later he and his wife, a professor of English and education, moved to California. There he continued his lonely work, little understood by his former colleagues, on what he called his "Structuronomic" or "enestruence" theory until his death in Palo Alto.

Allport, who had sometimes cooperated and at other times competed with his better-known brother, Harvard psychologist Gordon W. Allport, had been a more private and withdrawn individual, struggling with an occasional episode of depression. A keen observer of the public scene, he abhorred all ideas of involvement in political or social action, except for his participation in some wartime projects on rumors and civilian morale during World War II. Although by midcentury his direct influence on the rapidly expanding discipline had more or less ended, the tradition of an individualistic experimental social psychology, which his 1924 text had first established, has continued to pervade the discipline—to the satisfaction of some and the distress of others. The American Psychological Association awarded him its Distinguished Scientific Contribution Award in 1965 and the APA Foundation's Gold Medal in 1968 for his pioneering work. As much as anyone else, Floyd Allport had helped to establish the field of empirical social psychology and, beyond this, contributed to the development of the behavioral approach in the social sciences.

• The Floyd H. Allport Papers are at Syracuse University. A list of his publications to 1962 is given in *American Psychologist* 20 (1965): 1079–82. His autobiography appears in G. Lindzey, ed., *The History of Psychology in Autobiography*, vol. 6 (1974), pp. 3–29. An obituary is in *American Psychologist* 34 (1979): 351–53.

FRANZ SAMELSON

ALLPORT, Gordon Willard (11 Nov. 1897–9 Oct. 1967), psychologist, was born in Montezuma, Indiana, the son of John Edwards Allport, a physician, and Nellie Wise. He grew up in Cleveland, Ohio, and, following the example of his older brother Floyd, who also became an eminent psychologist, he attended Harvard University. As an undergraduate, he concentrated on both psychology and social ethics (the predecessor of sociology at Harvard), and he spent much of his spare time in social service during World War I. Upon his graduation in 1919, he spent a year teaching English and sociology at Robert College in Constantinople (now Boğaçızı University of Istanbul). Returning to Harvard, he continued to be influenced by his brother Floyd, then an instructor, and by Herbert Langfeld, who encouraged him to follow his own sense of direction. Allport received his Ph.D. in psychology in 1922.

He later described his next two years abroad on a traveling fellowship as "a second intellectual dawn" after his encounter with Harvard as a callow midwesterner. During a year in Germany, his mainly behavioristic orientation to psychological issues was challenged at the University of Berlin by contact with leaders of the new Gestalt school of psychology (including Wolfgang Köhler and Max Wertheimer) and with the German humanistic *Geisteswissenschaftlich* tradition in philosophy and psychology represented by Eduard Spranger. At the University of Hamburg he came to know William Stern, who studied individual differences in the context of the whole person, and Heinz Werner, who took a holistic, comparative, and structural approach to human development. The following year at Cambridge University was mainly a year of consolidation of his German experience, with scholarly courtesies extended by Frederic Bartlett. His whole subsequent career can be seen as a project to integrate the empiricism and social conscience of his American origins with the holistic, personalistic, and structural conceptions that he encountered in Germany.

In 1924 Allport returned to Harvard as instructor in the Department of Social Ethics. He married a fellow graduate student of his predoctoral days, Ada Lufkin Gould, in 1925. Their only child, a son, was born after he had moved in 1926 to an assistant professorship in psychology at Dartmouth College. After four years he returned to Harvard, where he spent the remainder of his career until his death.

Allport's primary area of contribution, the psychology of personality, was foreshadowed in the topic of his Ph.D. dissertation, "An Experimental Study of the Traits of Personality: With Special Reference to the Problem of Social Diagnosis." He later conjectured that the course he offered at Harvard in 1924 and 1925, Personality: Its Psychological and Social Aspects, was probably the first course on the subject offered in an American college. His masterwork, *Personality: A Psychological Interpretation* (1937), a scholarly treatise addressed to a broad academic audience rather than a conventional textbook, nevertheless substantially defined the field for subsequent textbooks. It focused on the normal adult personality, with special concern for criteria of maturity and good functioning. It stressed the unique patterning of individual personalities (in contrast with the variables and classifications of quantitative science, for which he also saw a place) and the "functional autonomy" of normal adult motivation (that is, its independence of infantile origins in physiological drives or in the unconscious instincts emphasized by psychoanalysis). Allport thus declared his opposition to the mechanistic view of human nature of behaviorism, then dominating mainstream American psychology, as well as to the pathology-focused doctrines of psychoanalysis, the influence of which was still rising toward its crest just after World War II. Allport therefore anticipated the "third force" of humanistic psychologists who came to prominence two decades later.

Allport's involvement with social psychology was complementary to his commitment to personality. From 1937 to 1949 he edited the *Journal of Abnormal and Social Psychology*, the most respected journal in these areas of "soft" psychology. For Allport, "attitudes" in social psychology corresponded to "traits" in personality, and he contributed a classic review of social attitudes to Carl Murchison's *Handbook of Social Psychology* (1935), which appeared at about the same time as his major work in personality.

It was in social psychology, which emerged as a vigorous subdiscipline in response to the challenges of World War II, that his strong social conscience got major expression. Just before and during the war he and his colleague Henry Murray chaired a seminar on civilian morale that produced working papers that were widely circulated. His wartime development of "rumor clinics" to expose divisive rumor mongering was followed by collaboration, with Leo Postman, in the experimentally based *Psychology of Rumor* (1947). Work with the Boston police to counteract race prejudice led to his classic examination of research and theory on it, *The Nature of Prejudice* (1954). Allport was an early (1944) president of the Society for the Psychological Study of Social Issues, which was concerned with bringing the resources of psychology to bear on human rights and social justice.

Underlying his personalistic psychology and liberal social commitments was his seriously religious orientation, uncommon among his prominent contemporaries in psychology. The "plain Protestant religion" of his childhood was succeeded in his undergraduate years by strivings toward a humanitarian religion. Soon he found this essentially Unitarian position "too arrogant" and came to regard humility and some mysticism as personally indispensable. *The Individual and His Religion* (1950), a major contribution to the psychology of religion, highlights his distinction between infantile forms of religion, which he saw as vulnerable to Sigmund Freud's atheistic critique, and the religion of maturity.

Allport was a leader in the establishment at Harvard of the Department of Social Relations in 1946, an interdisciplinary venture that combined social and clinical psychology and cultural anthropology with sociology. In his final year at Harvard he was appointed the first Richard Clarke Cabot Professor of Social Ethics, symbolically closing a circle with his first Harvard position under Cabot's supervision. Allport died in Cambridge, Massachusetts.

Altogether, Allport published more than 160 articles, two monographs, and a dozen books; there were eighteen foreign editions of his books in ten languages. He received many honors, including presidency of the American Psychological Association (1939). Although his career was spent in academic psychology, practicing clinical psychologists found his work important as it provided theoretical justification for their unavoidably greater concern with human individuality than with statistical regularities. As a teacher, he launched many contributors to psychology, including Leo Postman (experimental), Alfred Baldwin (developmental), Jerome Bruner (social and developmental), and Leonard Doob, Hadley Cantril, Gardner Lindzey, and Thomas Pettigrew (social). But he never founded a school; he had too much respect for the individuality of his students. His students remember him as open, fair-minded, and generous but somewhat austere; he was given to assuming that the hair shirt that he liked to wear would fit his students too. His disparagement of the relevance of infancy and his manifest discomfort with Freudian ideas limit the scope of his enduring contribution to the psychology of personality. But criticism of his emphasis on dispositions such as traits and attitudes, which was prevalent in the 1970s when intellectual fashion emphasized situational determinants of behavior, no longer seemed as cogent when the fashion had passed. Allport is enduringly established as a great American psychologist in the tradition of William James, whom he greatly admired.

• Allport's papers are in the Social Relations/Psychology Library at Harvard. *Personality and Social Encounter* (1960), a collection of his papers, includes a full bibliography up to its date. Edwin G. Boring and Gardner Lindzey, eds., *A History of Psychology in Autobiography*, vol. 5 (1967), contains his autobiography as a psychologist. A "Memorial Minute" appeared in the *Harvard Gazette* 64, 30 Nov. 1968. A major early empirical contribution (with Philip E. Vernon) was *Studies in Expressive Movement* (1933). In personality measurement, his main contribution was (with Vernon) *A Study of Values* (1931; rev. ed. with Vernon and Gardner Lindzey, 1951). His personality theory is summarized and evaluated in Calvin Hall and Gardner Lindzey, *Theories of Personality* (1970). His problematic relation with Freud and its impact on his theorizing is interpreted by Alan C. Elms in *Uncovering Lives: The Uneasy Alliance of Biography and Psychology* (1994). Roy de Carvalho treats his importance as a forerunner of humanistic psychology in *The Founders of Humanistic Psychology* (1991). His religious convictions are expressed in his occasional offerings for daily prayers at the Harvard chapel from 1938 to 1966, *Waiting for the Lord: Meditations on God and Man*, ed. Peter A. Bertocci (1978). An obituary is in the *New York Times*, 10 Oct. 1967.

M. BREWSTER SMITH

ALLSTON, Robert Francis Withers (21 Apr. 1801–7 Apr. 1864), planter and statesman, was born on "Hagley Plantation" in All Saints Parish (Georgetown District), South Carolina, the son of Benjamin Allston, a planter, and Charlotte Anne Allston. Allston entered the U.S. Military Academy at West Point, New York, in December 1817 and graduated tenth in his class on 1 July 1821. Appointed lieutenant in the Third Artillery and assigned to the Coast Survey, he participated in the surveying of the harbors at Plymouth and Provincetown, Massachusetts, and of the entrance to Mobile Bay. He resigned his commission on 1 February 1822 in response to his widowed mother's plea for help on their plantations and returned to South Carolina, where he remained a rice planter for the rest of his life. As a planter, however, he continued his interest in civil engineering and in 1823 was elected to the first of two terms as surveyor general of South Carolina. In 1832 he married Adele Petigru, sister of Unionist James Louis Petigru. They had eight children.

Allston proved to be one of the most successful rice planters in Georgetown District and in the entire South. Over the next thirty years he accumulated 4,000 acres of improved land and 9,500 acres of pasture, marsh, and timberland on the Pee Dee, Waccamaw, and Black rivers. These were divided into seven plantations, Chicora Wood (his residential plantation), Nightingale Hall, Exchange, Waterford, Guendalos, Pipe Down, and Rose Bank. In 1860 Allston had 637 slaves on his plantations, which produced 1.5 million pounds of rice. He had additional property in Georgetown and summer homes on Pawleys Island and at Plantersville. In 1857 he purchased the elaborate Nathaniel Russell mansion on Meeting Street in Charleston for $38,000. According to the 1860 census, his real and personal properties in the Georgetown District were valued at $150,000 and $303,000 respectively. In 1864, at the time of his death, his owned 590 slaves.

Allston was ever ready to improve his planting skills and techniques, engaging in innovative methods to increase the rice yields on his plantations and converting his mills to steam. Putting his engineering skills to use, he drained tidal swamps and constructed dikes and ditches for his rice fields. He wrote several essays on rice culture, the most important of which were *Memoir of the Introduction and Planting of Rice in South-Carolina* (1843), which became a standard on tidal cultivation of rice, and *Essay on Sea Coast Crops* (1854). He spoke frequently to agricultural groups on the subject and was regarded by his contemporaries as a scientific agriculturist of the first order.

Allston's public service began with his two terms as surveyor general. In 1828 he was elected to represent Prince George Winyah Parish in the South Carolina General Assembly, where he worked with the States' Rights party in supporting nullification. He was reelected in 1830 as a candidate of that party but was defeated by a Unionist in 1832. The next month Allston was elected to the state senate, where he served until his election as governor in 1856. In the senate he served on a number of committees, including Military; Judiciary; Agriculture; Internal Improvements; Finance; Federal Relations; and South Carolina College, Education, and Religion, and from 1847 to 1856 he was the president of the senate. On 9 December 1856 the legislature elected Allston governor for a two-year term. As governor he displayed considerable organizational talents and advocated such programs as expansion of the railroads, advancement of scientific agricultural methods, and improvements in public education in what proved to be a rather tranquil administration.

Allston's political career after retiring as governor was anything but tranquil. Early on he was committed to states' rights, strict construction of the Constitution, and nullification of federal laws. He strongly supported slavery, which he regarded as a benevolent institution with constitutional protection and secession, which he believed should be a joint venture of all the southern states. As political controversies arose between the North and South in the late 1850s, Allston adamantly supported the southern position, including secession. He was a delegate to the Nashville Convention in 1850 and served as a Confederate presidential elector in 1861. He continued to operate his plantations during the war, and his principal contribution to the Confederate effort was the production on his plantations of foodstuffs for the troops. He died at Chicora Wood Plantation near Georgetown in the midst of the war. Frequent property transactions in his last years left him heavily in debt. Emancipation brought the final blow, to the extent that his creditors found an estate worth only $60,000, a far cry from the $.5 million valuation of 1860.

• Allston's papers are in the South Carolina Historical Society in Charleston. Even though many of his papers were destroyed when he died, his rice plantation papers are massive, including some 8,000 pieces with twenty plantation account books, the cream of which have been published in J. Harold Easterby, ed., *The South Carolina Rice Plantation as Revealed in the Papers of Robert F. W. Allston* (1945). Anthony Q. Devereux, *The Life and Times of Robert F. W. Allston* (1976), purports to be a political biography and is based on Allston's political and personal correspondence. A sketch of Allston's life is in *De Bow's Review* 12 (1864): 574–75. For additional information on Allston's rice planting, see George C. Rogers, *The History of Georgetown County, South Carolina* (1970), and Chalmers Gaston Davidson, *The Last Foray: The South Carolina Planters of 1860, a Sociological Study* (1971). See Elizabeth Deas Allston, *The Allstons and Alstons of Waccamaw* (1936), for detailed information on these families. Elizabeth W. Allston, *Chronicles of Chicora Wood* (1922), is a nostalgic account by Allston's daughter. Obituaries are in the *Charleston Courier*, 12 Apr. 1864, and the *Charleston Mercury*, 23 Apr. 1864.

JAMES M. CLIFTON

ALLSTON, Washington (5 Nov. 1779–9 July 1843), painter, was born in Georgetown, South Carolina, the son of Captain William Allston, who served under General Francis Marion during the American Revolution, and Rachel Moore. After his father's death in 1781, his mother married Dr. Henry Collins Flagg of Newport, Rhode Island, who had come south in his position as chief of General Nathanael Greene's army medical staff. Allston, whose first name reflects his father's admiration for his commander, George Washington, began his education at Mrs. Calcott's school in Charleston, South Carolina. In the spring of 1787 his parents sent him to Newport for college preparation. While there, he met Edward Malbone, the future miniaturist, William Ellery Channing, future leader of the Unitarian movement, and Channing's sister Ann. In 1796 he moved to Cambridge, Massachusetts, where he entered Harvard College. While at Harvard, he began painting subjects that captured his love of the mysterious and romantic. He also avidly began reading gothic tales. He often remarked that his love for the unknown was rooted in his South Carolina childhood, where slaves delighted and frightened him with ghost stories.

After graduating from Harvard in 1800 with an A.B. with honors and as class poet, Allston briefly returned to Newport and then left for Charleston to see his family. Despite his stepfather's wish that he become a doctor, Allston secured his family's consent to sell his inheritance to finance a trip abroad to study art. He and his friend Malbone sailed for England in May 1801. In September Allston was admitted to the Royal Academy to study with American-born Benjamin West, the master of the Grand Manner of painting, a style that stressed the didactic quality of historical themes. When John Vanderlyn, another American painter, arrived in London after studying in Jacques Louis David's Paris studio, Allston saw an opportunity to travel to France. Vanderlyn planned to return to Paris to buy casts for a new academy in New York, and so the two set off together, arriving in Paris in November 1803. At the Louvre, Allston found inspiration in the works of Rubens, Titian, Tintoretto, Veronese, Poussin, and Claude. In his painting *Thunderstorm at Sea* (1804, Boston Museum of Fine Arts), Allston moved beyond the neoclassical ideals of order and reason and emphasized nature's unpredictability. While these and other early works remained popular in an England that shied away from the political implications of the neoclassical traditions, Americans were less receptive to romantic paintings that lacked the heroic didacticism of neoclassical works.

In the spring of 1804 Allston set off for Italy, making his way through the Swiss Alps to Rome, where he met Samuel Taylor Coleridge, who became a lifelong friend. After spending most of the next four years in Rome, he sailed for New York in April 1808. In 1809 he married Ann Channing; they had no children. In Boston, he used a studio previously occupied by the celebrated American painters John Smibert, John Singleton Copley, and John Trumbull and painted mostly portraits. He saw portrait painting as an opportunity to portray individual emotions and personalities in his own romantic style.

In July 1811 Allston, along with his wife and painter Samuel F. B. Morse, sailed for England, eventually settling in London. Both popular and respected in England, Allston was influenced by West. Allston's *The Dead Man Revived by Touching the Bones of the Prophet Elisha* (1811–1813, Pennsylvania Academy of Fine Arts) reflected the preference both men had for employing religious subjects to boldly portray the miraculous. Inspired by Sebastiano del Piombo's *Raising of Lazarus* (National Gallery, London), Allston employed the same biblical theme in *The Dead Man Revived* in order to portray one man's miraculous return to life. The scene is filled with emotion and sensation clearly present in the faces of the onlookers who react with disbelief and wonder. Weakened by a grueling working pace, he became ill with a stomach ailment and moved to Bristol to recover. He returned to London in the fall of 1814, when his wife became ill. She died in February 1815.

Although he suffered from depression after his wife's death, Allston continued to paint. In September 1817 he returned to Paris for a few months and focused his attention on the Venetian masters at the Louvre. This trip reaffirmed his interest in the use of color to create mood and resulted in a number of works, including his acclaimed *Elijah in the Desert* (1818, Boston Museum of Fine Arts), which represents the best of his landscapes. The scene is bleak and barren; Elijah is small and alone, dependent on the two huge ravens that feed him. In the romantic tradition, Allston excites an emotional response from his viewers by portraying the awesomeness of nature and the individual's dependence on its rhythms. Landscapes at the time were considered a lower form of art because they focused on specific places and lacked the lofty themes and messages of the Grand Manner, but with *Elijah* Allston combined the Grand Manner with landscape and created a unique and critically acclaimed canvas.

In May 1818 Allston was elected an honorary member of the American Academy of the Fine Arts in New York City. Later that year he was also elected an associate of the Royal Academy in London. While Europe treated Allston well, the artist admitted in a letter to William Dunlap that he suffered from homesickness. In October 1818 he returned to Boston. However, the return home proved fatal for his career as a monumental painter, chiefly because Americans did not appreciate his brooding romantic style.

After his return to the United States, Allston focused his creative energies on writing rather than painting. While he published romantic essays like "The Hypochondriac" and "Written in Spring" during this time, his most important work, *Lectures on Art, and Poems*, was not published until 1850, seven years after his death. Although this significant book formulated a sensual aesthetic, it remained largely unnoticed and subsequently neglected. Still, Allston remains the only nineteenth-century American artist or philosopher to formulate a detailed artistic theory.

Financial problems disrupted Allston's ability to paint, especially his *Belshazzar's Feast* (1817–1843), which he had begun in England. Because he arrived in the United States with his inheritance nearly gone, he, like most American painters at the time, was forced to paint a series of small pictures on commission. He found it nearly impossible to devote the time needed to finish *Belshazzar*, based on the Old Testament story in which Daniel predicts the end of King Belshazzar's empire and the destruction of his great city of Babylon. In an unprecedented show of patronage, however, ten Boston gentlemen purchased *Belshazzar's Feast* in advance by placing $10,000 in a trust for Allston's use as he worked on the twelve-foot by sixteen-foot canvas. Nearly two years later he unrolled the canvas and began to work again but he was uninspired. Following the advice of Gilbert Stuart, he began major revisions on the painting. These revisions, coupled with his growing preference for meditative pieces, slowed the progress on the canvas even more. And in December 1828 the barn that housed his studio was sold, and Allston was forced to move, again delaying his work.

In June 1830 Allston married Martha Remington Dana, the sister of Richard Henry Dana. Around that time the federal government began a three-year negotiation with Allston over a commission for a painting of the battle of New Orleans for the Capitol rotunda in Washington, D.C. In the end he refused, caring neither for Andrew Jackson nor for the political tone of the commission. He offered instead to paint a scene from the Bible, but the government was not interested in this proposal. Continuing to paint at a tireless pace, he exhibited forty-seven paintings at the studio of Boston painter Chester Harding in 1839. In November Allston began his final attempt to finish *Belshazzar's Feast*. In 1841 he was elected the first president of the Boston Artists' Association. Toward the end of that year he again suffered from illness and spent most of the winter in his room. He was still at work on *Belshazzar's Feast* two years later when he died in Cambridgeport, Massachusetts.

In a country that had barely moved beyond its preference for colonial portraiture to neoclassical art, Allston's radical romantic vision embodied both the promise and the failure of high ideals in a society consumed by an expanding market economy. In contrast to the attention he received in England, Allston continually found the American public uninterested in romantic idealism. When they did show an interest in art, Americans prefered the political messages embodied in the canvases of neoclassical painters and the lighthearted genre scenes of the first half of the nineteenth century. In the early nineteenth century many critics considered Allston to be one of the greatest painters produced by the United States. Nevertheless, by the end of that century his reputation was in decline, and with the triumph of artistic realism in the twentieth century, many argued that the painter's efforts to bring romantic idealism to America had failed completely. However, scholars have begun to express a new appreciation for the breadth of Allston's vision within the context of America's early republic. While Allston's art did not significantly shape his age, the artist offered his country a variety of talents that suggested possibilities well beyond his own.

• The largest collection of Allston-related manuscripts is in the Dana papers at the Massachusetts Historical Society. These contain Allston's sketchbooks, notebooks, and the most substantial group of his letters. In addition to the works mentioned, Allston's writings include a series of romantic poems about the four seasons, *The Sylphs of the Seasons, and Other Poems* (1813), and a gothic romance, *Monaldi* (1841). Nathalia Wright has edited a collection of Allston's letters, *The Correspondence of Washington Allston* (1993). The most comprehensive study of Allston's life and art remains Edgar Preston Richardson, *Washington Allston: A Study of the Romantic Artist in America* (1948). Jared Bradley Flagg, the son of Allston's half-brother, wrote a more personal and narrative biography, *The Life and Letters of Washington Allston* (1893). David Bjelajac, *Millennial Desire and the Apocalyptic Vision of Washington Allston* (1988), explores the religious foundation of both Allston's life and his art and argues for the artist's true significance as an American painter. An obituary is in the *Boston Evening Transcript*, 10 July 1843.

A. KRISTEN FOSTER

ALLYN, Robert (25 Jan. 1817–7 Jan. 1894), educator, was born near Ledyard, Connecticut, the son of Charles Allyn and Lois Gallup, farmers. The family had been among the original settlers of the eastern Connecticut region. After receiving an education in the area's district schools, Allyn attended Bacon Academy at nearby Colchester, Connecticut, in preparation for college. While a student at Bacon Academy, Allyn followed the common practice of teaching at a district school during the academy's winter quarter, teaching first at Lynne and then at Bozrah. Allyn enjoyed teaching, and he was deemed successful by the parents of schoolchildren in those districts. His dilemma, which recurred throughout his early life, was whether to be a teacher or preacher.

During the Second Great Awakening (1797–1826), the region was swept with religious enthusiasm, and camp meetings organized by Methodists, Baptists, and Presbyterians disrupted an otherwise quiet country setting. As one historian of the period wrote, "During Connecticut's Second Great Awakening great changes were wrought and new habits formed. A deep and lasting impress was made on the lives of the people of the state. Much new wine was poured into many new bottles" (Keller, p. 239). In 1835, while attending a camp meeting held by the Methodists, Allyn stepped forward to embrace the tenets of that denomination. In 1836, in keeping with his new-found faith, Allyn entered Wesleyan Academy in Wilbraham, Massachusetts. Here he prepared for Wesleyan University in Middleboro, Connecticut, which he entered in 1837. Allyn distinguished himself in the study of languages and mathematics and was admitted into Phi Beta Kappa.

After completing his college course of study at Wesleyan in 1841, Allyn returned to the Wesleyan Academy as a teacher. While there, he married Emeline H. Denison, a former classmate. Shortly thereafter, he was ordained and accepted the call of a ministry at Colchester, Connecticut, where he served from 1844 until 1845. His wife died from complications while giving birth to a daughter in 1844, leaving the young minister with two infant children.

In June 1846 Allyn married Mary Buckland Budington, and the newlyweds accepted a ministry in Thompsonville, Connecticut. After a very brief term of service, however, Allyn decided to return to education as principal at the Wesleyan Academy. In 1848 the family again relocated, to East Greenwich, Rhode Island, where Allyn became headmaster of the Providence Conference Academy, a Methodist preparatory school. Although he headed a private school, Allyn was very active in the Rhode Island Institute of Instruction, an association of public school advocates. He had become a devoted soldier in the common school crusade. Allyn believed in a God that had endowed the human creation with the power of reason. This reason, properly guided by prayer, was capable of improving life on earth through individual self-discipline and well-organized social action. Such social action was reflected in the establishment of institutions that could feed the hungry, heal the sick, reform criminals, and educate children. In this belief in the perfectibility of the species and the role of the common school as a central element, he was joined by school reformers who ran the gamut of Protestant denominational membership, from Unitarians to Baptists.

Allyn's public speaking endeavors in favor of the abolition of slavery, the spread of temperance, and the extension of tax-supported schools gave him wide public recognition, and he was elected to the state assembly in 1852 and to the post of commissioner of schools of Rhode Island in 1854. As a successor to and a devotee of Henry Barnard, Allyn continued the agenda of improving school facilities and formally preparing teachers. To this he added his own concern with the issue of absenteeism. His report for 1856 pointed out that less than half of the children enrolled attended school with any regularity. He was a frequent correspondent with both Barnard, who had moved to Connecticut to become state superintendent there, and with Horace Mann, who served as secretary to the Massachusetts Board of Education. Also while state commissioner, Allyn edited the *Rhode Island Schoolmaster*, an educational journal with subscribers throughout New England, and served as an inspector of the United States Military Academy at West Point, New York. At the end of his term of office, Allyn left Rhode Island in 1857 for Athens, Ohio, where he had been invited to accept the chair of ancient languages at Ohio University. From here, he accepted the position of headmaster of a Methodist female academy in Cincinnati in 1859.

McKendree College, a small Methodist college in Lebanon, Illinois, called Allyn to become its president in 1863. While serving as president until 1874, he continued his efforts on behalf of the Methodist church and public education and worked successfully to have McKendree open its ranks to women. He was also successful in stabilizing the college's uncertain financial condition. During his tenure the college's bulletin promised the parents of aspiring students "cheap tuition, thorough instruction, parental discipline, and a moral village."

Illinois had passed a common school law in 1855, but the normal schools at Chicago and Bloomington could not provide enough trained teachers. Seeing the need for a normal school to serve the public schools in the southern region of the state, Allyn campaigned vigorously for the establishment of such an institution. Southern Illinois Normal University was chartered by the state in 1869 and began a slow process of constructing its single building on the south side of the town of Carbondale. Just before its opening in 1874, Allyn was offered its presidency. He accepted and served in that capacity until 1892, retiring at the age of seventy-five.

As president, Allyn worked to encourage the hundreds of small rural districts to employ normal school–trained teachers and to enforce existing state laws on compulsory school attendance. In these matters, he was only partially successful. He also spoke ardently against Darwinism, a popular cause in a region committed to traditional religious views.

In the late nineteenth century, a college president in a region with limited educational opportunities was often looked to as a font of wisdom on a variety of topics. Allyn was no exception. He spoke frequently on matters as diverse as morality, current events, and ornithology. Using the occasions of required chapel exercises at the college, Sunday evening church services, graduation addresses, and the deaths of prominent Americans, such as President James A. Garfield and former president Ulysses S. Grant, Allyn exhorted students to be stalwart in their convictions, abstain from alcohol, avoid sin, seek to do good works, read the Bible, develop good personal habits, and nurture children. Graduates of the normal school remembered President Allyn as pious, demanding, and determined but not unkind. His demeanor and strength of character were greatly admired. He died in Carbondale.

• Both McKendree College and Southern Illinois University at Carbondale have presidential papers that provide an official view of Allyn as a college administrator. Student newspapers from McKendree provide an informal view of the president. Brown University has a collection of the *Rhode Island Schoolmaster* for the period when Allyn edited the journal, and official state records in Rhode Island trace his work as state commissioner. New York University houses the Henry Barnard Papers, which include some correspondence from Allyn. The biennial reports of the state superintendent of public instruction for Illinois have annual reports written by Allyn during his term of office as president of Southern Illinois Normal University. Charles R. Keller, *The Second Great Awakening in Connecticut* (1942), provides good background information on religious revivals.

WILLIAM E. EATON

ALMOND, Edward Mallory (12 Dec. 1892–11 June 1979), army general, nicknamed Ned, was born in Luray, Virginia, the son of Walter Coles Almond, a farm implement salesman, and Grace Popham. Almond earned a bachelor of science degree at Virginia Military Institute, graduating third in the class of 1915. The next year, he received his commission as a U.S. Army second lieutenant and then graduated from Fort Leavenworth Army Service School in March 1917. When the United States declared war on Germany, Almond was with the Fourth Infantry Division, commanding a machine gun company. Seven months before leaving for France, he married Margaret Crook on 4 August 1917; the couple would have two children. Almond, now a captain, commanded the Twelfth Machine Gun Battalion in the Aisne-Marne and Meuse-Argonne campaigns, sustaining a shrapnel wound at the Vesle River and receiving a Purple Heart and a Silver Star. In July 1919 he left occupation duty with the

Fourth Infantry in Germany to become a professor of military science and tactics at Marion Institute in Alabama.

Almond's career followed a conventional course during the interwar era. In 1924 he graduated from the Infantry School at Fort Benning, Georgia, remaining there as an automatic weapons instructor until 1928, when he earned promotion to major. After graduation from Command and General Staff School (1930), he joined the Forty-fifth Infantry Division in the Philippines, commanding a battalion made up of Filipino soldiers. Returning to the United States in 1933, Almond attended the Army War College and, after graduating in June 1934, went to work at the War Department General Staff in the Latin American section. After his promotion to lieutenant colonel in September 1938, he graduated from Air Corps Tactical School (1939) and the Naval War College (1940). Almond then served with the VI Corps, becoming its chief of staff one month after Pearl Harbor. In March 1942 he became assistant commander of the Ninety-third Infantry, receiving temporary promotion to brigadier and later major general.

Almond's impressive performance in training schools, staff assignments, and command resulted in his receiving the difficult assignment in September 1942 of organizing, training, and deploying the Ninety-second Infantry, the only black division slated for combat in Europe. Under extraordinary scrutiny, he commanded the unit in Italy, leading the 25,000-man force during its advance through the Serchio Valley in the fall of 1944, its assault toward Massa in February 1945, and its retreat under enemy counterattack. Shortly thereafter, Almond transformed one diversionary operation into a successful offensive that liberated Genoa and prevented German forces from demolishing port installations. In its early engagements, the Ninety-second Infantry Division fought poorly, as its soldiers often refused to attack and then retreated without orders. Army officials later attributed the soldiers' unreliability to illiteracy, lack of self-confidence, and distrust of the division's officers, most of whom were white, had below average records, and doubted the fighting ability of racial minorities. The Ninety-second Infantry Division fought effectively only after Almond had reorganized and reinforced the unit. Because its performance failed to match expectations, the unit was disbanded following the war, slowing the advancement of Almond's career. Worse, his son, a West Point graduate and captain with the Forty-fifth Infantry, was killed in March 1945 while fighting in Germany. Almond's wartime service earned him the Distinguished Service Medal, Air Medal, Bronze Star, and first Oak Leaf Cluster for the Silver Star he won for gallantry in World War I.

After World War II, Almond assumed command of the Second Infantry Division. Still ambitious, he decided in June 1946 to join General Douglas MacArthur's staff in Japan as assistant chief of staff for personnel. Six months later, he became deputy chief of staff for the Far East Command, achieving promotion to the permanent rank of major general in January 1948. Almond became MacArthur's chief of staff in February 1949. MacArthur, who disliked staff meetings, and administrative matters, came to rely heavily on Almond to implement his directives. In June 1950 Almond was considering retirement, but when the United Nations authorized U.S. military action to defend South Korea, he had a new chance to advance his career. In August 1950 MacArthur placed him in charge of planning an assault behind enemy lines that would allow the U.S. Eighth Army to break out of the Pusan Perimeter.

Under Almond's command the X Corps, a force of 70,000 men, landed at Inch'ŏn on 15 September 1950 and two weeks later liberated Seoul, South Korea's capital. Meanwhile, the Eighth Army crushed enemy forces in the south and, on 7 October, began its advance into North Korea. On 20 October the X Corps made an amphibious landing at Wŏnsan on the northeast coast and then proceeded northward to the Changjin Reservoir. On 21 November one unit reached the Yalu River. A few days later, China's massive counteroffensive forced the UN troops to retreat from North Korea, and Almond received highly favorable publicity for directing the Hungnam evacuation. His skillful coordination of sea, land, and air operations on 20 December made possible the withdrawal of 105,000 troops, 91,000 refugees, 17,500 vehicles, and 350,000 tons of equipment and supplies with only light casualties. On 26 December the Eighth Army absorbed the X Corps, but Almond, having earned a third star, remained its commander. From January to June in 1951, his forces halted the Chinese invasion at what Almond called No Name Line, resumed the advance northward, and established defensive positions forty miles north of the thirty-eighth parallel. Having earned a Distinguished Service Cross and a second Oak Leaf Cluster, Almond returned to the United States in July 1951, following President Harry S. Truman's recall of General MacArthur in April.

Almond was a controversial figure, especially during the Korean War. One fellow officer labeled him "a brilliant human dynamo," but his own chief of staff admitted that his boss "could precipitate a crisis on a desert island with nobody else around." Another colleague noted that "when it pays to be aggressive, Ned's aggressive, and when it pays to be cautious, Ned's aggressive and he wouldn't step two paces to the rear for the devil himself." His relationship with Lieutenant General Walton H. Walker, commander of the Eighth Army, was always stormy, and it became worse after the creation of the X Corps as a separate unit. Others, too, questioned the wisdom of placing an army officer in command of an amphibious operation with a force that included the First Marine Division, but MacArthur wanted to reward the sharp-spoken Almond, who had been a loyal and efficient subordinate. Almond was the only officer who had not served in the Pacific in World War II who was able to penetrate MacArthur's inner circle of confidants and earn the general's complete confidence.

Though often tactless and generally dictatorial, Almond was an effective and aggressive combat officer. His experiences in Korea persuaded him of the importance of tactical air support, which had been decisive in blunting the Chinese spring offensives of 1951. He was among the first U.S. Army officers to recognize the value in combat of helicopters, ordering studies that would lead to their widespread use later in the Vietnam War. After leaving Korea, the courtly southern soldier served as commandant of the Army War College until retirement on 1 January 1953. Thereafter, Almond became an outspoken anti-Communist, testifying to Congress that if the United States had staged an air offensive into Manchuria, it would have won the Korean War. Prior to his death in San Antonio, Texas, he worked in a public relations capacity for the Executive Life Insurance Company of Alabama. Active in many civic and charitable organizations, especially the Boy Scouts of America, Almond was a member of the board of trustees for Virginia Military Institute from 1961 to 1968, serving during the last year as president.

• Almond's papers are at the U.S. Military History Institute, Carlisle Barracks, Carlisle, Pa. The Douglas MacArthur Memorial Library in Norfolk, Va., has additional documents. Few sources focus exclusively on the life of the general, with the best information appearing in military histories of those conflicts where Almond served as a commander. These studies include Paul Goodman, *A Fragment of Victory in Italy during World War II: A Special Study* (1952), covering the operations of the Ninety-second Division; Roy E. Appleman, *South to the Naktong, North to the Yalu (June–November 1950)* (1961); James F. Schnabel, *Policy and Direction: The First Year* (1972); and Clay Blair, *The Forgotten War: America in Korea, 1950–1953* (1987). See also *Current Biography* (1951) and "'Sic 'Em, Ned,'" *Time*, 23 Oct. 1950, pp. 27–30. An obituary is in the *New York Times*, 13 June 1979.

JAMES I. MATRAY

ALMY, Mary. *See* Howe, Lois Lilley, Eleanor Manning, and Mary Almy.

ALPERN, Anne X. (c. 1903–2 Feb. 1981), attorney and judge, was born in Russia, the daughter of Joseph Alpern and Mary Leaser. (Alpern would never explain what the X in her name stood for, and it was rumored that early in her life she added it simply for fun.) The family immigrated to western Pennsylvania when she was an infant. They settled in Scenery Hill, near Washington, Pennsylvania, where her father owned a general store. Alpern attended Nicholas Elementary School and Scenery Hill High School in the town of Washington. After the family moved to Pittsburgh, she enrolled at the University of Pittsburgh, from which she graduated in 1923 with a B.A. in education. Urged by her father to study law as a result of his admiration for Clarence Darrow for defending poor and unfortunate people, Alpern matriculated at the University of Pittsburgh School of Law. While she was in her first year as a law student, her writing ability attracted the attention of a local advertising agency, and she was offered but declined an attractive position as a copyeditor at $3,000 a year. She remained in law school, graduated in 1927, and was admitted to the bar in Allegheny County that September.

Alpern joined the Pittsburgh law firm of Cunningham, Galbreath & Dickson. To quiet her entreaties to be given a court case instead of routine assignments normally reserved at that time for female attorneys, her supervisors turned over to her a "lemon"—that is, an apparently impossible case. She was to appear in court the next day and represent a client suing an awning manufacturer for defective merchandise; it seemed that his $1,000 awning had a slight rip. After researching legal precedents all night, Alpern cited them eloquently the following morning. The judge, who thought she was bluffing, ordered his clerk to provide substantiation and quickly verified Alpern's accuracy. When the defendant argued that the awning rip was small, Alpern won the case by reminding the judge that a run in a woman's stocking was never a minor one. Her firm then recommended her to assist an experienced lawyer in a huge estate case. He objected, insisted on interviewing Alpern the next morning, and was astonished when, after another all-night research stint, she was able to demonstrate mastery of all legal issues involved. He let her prepare the relevant brief, which she dictated in one all-night session to a team of stenographers.

In 1932 Alpern was appointed assistant solicitor for the city of Pittsburgh, the first woman to hold that rank. During her first six weeks she never left the building for meals, worked every evening, and often remained until the following day. Four months later she was promoted over twenty-five other lawyers to the position of first assistant city solicitor, the first woman to hold that post in any major American city. Her salary was more than doubled, to $5,000 per annum. As a member of the Democratic party, she made many friends among ordinary citizens, proconsumer organizations, and labor leaders but also not a few adversaries among Republican city moguls and civic leaders. She did so by advocating smoke control, improved public housing, reduced public transportation and utility rates, statewide standard milk prices, educational reforms, and public hospital improvements. She saved consumers millions of dollars. She also saved taxpayers tens of thousands when well-to-do companies brought unsuccessful law suits against the city. The fact that many of the decisions she won in court were later overturned on appeal did not lessen her immediate regional popularity.

In 1937 Alpern married Irwin Amdur Swiss, then an assistant U.S. attorney, and took her first vacation in years in the form of a European honeymoon. She soon returned to work, continuing to use Alpern as her professional name. The couple had one child.

In 1941 Alpern defended Cornelius Decatur Scully, a Democrat who had narrowly won election as mayor of Pittsburgh over Republican Harmar Denny, when Scully was charged with voter irregularities. She demanded the presence in court of twenty-nine wealthy Denny supporters—tycoons, bankers, presidents of institutions, and big businessmen—proved that the nullification petition they had signed against Scully contained similar irregularities, and thus persuaded the judge, a Republican, to quash the case. Alpern became famous for speeding cases through court by hiring more clerical help and by settling many cases through pragmatic compromise. In 1945, after the end of World War II, she increased her popularity by requiring the federal government to sell surplus war matériel to commonwealth of Pennsylvania agencies directly instead of through profiteering middlemen. In time, anecdotes about her were legion: she called a city light company "the Overcharge of the Light Brigade," the state Public Utility Commission "the Public Futility Commission," and a greedy local railway company "the Streetcar Named Expire." These and other bons mots may have carried little weight in court, but they augmented Alpern's ever-increasing celebrity, as did her photographic memory, impromptu oratorical skill, and flair for courtroom histrionics. Her evenhandedness is indicated by the fact that in 1946 she incurred the wrath of labor by obtaining an injunction against a union of electrical workers who briefly shut off Pittsburgh's city lights, an action she called a "man-made disaster" not to be tolerated.

In 1958 Alpern was elected judge of the Court of Common Pleas of Allegheny County. Her campaign slogans were "Mark an X for Anne X," "Anne X-alted Alpern," and "Annie, Get Your Gun." In 1959 David Leo Lawrence, former mayor of Pittsburgh and then governor of Pennsylvania, appointed her state attorney general—the first woman in the United States to serve as an attorney general. Among her achievements was the opening of the Barnes Collection (Albert C. Barnes's extraordinary collection of European art) in Merion, Pennsylvania, in exchange for its retaining its tax-exempt status. It was during this time, in 1960, that her husband was struck and killed by a truck while crossing a street near their Pittsburgh residence.

In 1961 a seat became vacant on the state supreme court, whereupon Lawrence appointed Alpern to the post—again the first woman to serve in such a position. Two months later, however, when Alpern ran for election to a full 21-year term on the court, she lost by a narrow margin to Henry X. O'Brien, another judge. Her defeat may be attributed to three main causes: she had antagonized the Philadelphia Democratic machine earlier by accusing it of voter fraud; the corporate utilities she had battled during her tenure as city solicitor in Pennsylvania mounted a heavily financed campaign against her in rural Republican areas; and she was a woman. In compensation, Lawrence named her to fill the position on the Allegheny County Pleas Court vacated by O'Brien. After retiring from the bench in 1974 she joined the Pittsburgh law firm of Berkman Ruslander Pohl Lieber & Engel.

Alpern combined her professional and personal lives in an exemplary way. Even though she was in constant demand as a speaker on what she called the "banquet circuit," she was always a devoted wife and mother. She was an inventive cook and a lively raconteur. If she liked a given dish at a restaurant, she would ask the chef for the recipe. She enjoyed the cultural life of Pittsburgh, was said to require only four hours of sleep a night, and read widely—a nonlegal book a day in her prime. She died in Pittsburgh.

Alpern greatly advanced the cause of women in various professions by her example. She once said that, whereas men "make the laws" and male judges "propound" them, it is women jurors who "actually balance the scales of justice." One of her male peers was of the opinion that she had a perfect judicial temperament, always manifesting not only a sense of legal precision but also a sympathetic attitude.

• Alpern's personal papers, professional papers, and memorabilia are in the archives of the University of Pittsburgh School of Law. The best sources of information on Alpern's career are Victor Rubin, "Portia in Pittsburgh," *Collier's*, 26 Oct. 1946; Stefan Lorant, *Pittsburgh: The Story of an American City* (1964); and Joel Fishman, *Judges of Allegheny County, Fifth Judicial District, Pennsylvania (1788–1988)* (1988). Obituaries are in the *Pittsburgh Post-Gazette* and the *Pittsburgh Press*, both 3 Feb. 1981, and the *Pittsburgh Legal Journal*, Apr. 1981.

ROBERT L. GALE
THADDEUS RUSSELL

ALSOP, George (1636–?), author of *A Character of the Province of Maryland*, was probably born in Westminster, England, the son of Peter Alsop, a tailor, and Rose (maiden name unknown). Aside from information in *A Character of the Province of Maryland*, very little is known about Alsop. His father's occupation did not provide for much education, but evidence from *A Character* suggests that he knew Latin and French and was familiar with a variety of contemporary literary forms. According to Alsop, he spent two years as an apprentice in London before emigrating to Maryland. A devout royalist, he indentured himself in 1658 for four years as a bondservant in Maryland to escape the religious and political turmoil of Cromwellian England. He was indentured to Thomas Stockett on 17 January 1659. Alsop found his duties in Maryland comfortable, claiming "had I known my yoak would have been so easie, (as I conceive it will) I would have been here long before now, rather then to have dwelt under the pressure of a Rebellious and Trayterous Government so Long as I did" (*A Character*, 1902 ed., p. 95). Thomas Stockett, also a royalist, had settled at the head of the Chesapeake near present-day Havre de Grace only a year earlier. George Alsop's name is recorded as a witness on a patent documenting Stockett's purchase of his plantation "Bourne" in June 1661. While indentured, Alsop would have benefited from Stockett's prominent social standing as a Baltimore County justice, legislator, and militia captain, and he must have had contact with the neighboring Susquehanna Indians who had to stop at Stockett's plantation to receive a traveling pass.

Alsop completed his indenture before 11 December 1662. On gaining his freedom, he had difficulties making a living and was struck by a serious illness. He remained in Maryland for only a short time, returning to England in 1663 or 1664. Alsop wrote *A Character of the Province of Maryland* in London, probably in 1665, where it was published in 1666.

Although often characterized as a rambling, overblown, or bombastic promotion tract, *A Character* is unique among colonial promotion literature. Written in a low style that capitalizes on popular literary forms, punning, innuendo, elaborate allusions, legalistic subterfuge, vulgar sayings, and sharp satire, *A Character* has properly been called "one of the most witty and scurrilous books of colonial America" (Lemay, p. 48). Despite its unique style, *A Character* generally conforms to the conventions of promotion writing, containing descriptions of plants, animals, climate, and inhabitants. Typically, colonial promotional writing exaggerated such descriptions and depicted America as an edenic paradise. Alsop's tract was no exception:

> The Trees, Plants, Fruits, Flowers, and Roots that grow here in *Mary-Land*, are only the Emblems or Hieroglyphicks of our Adamitical or Primitive situation, as well for their variety as odoriferous smells, together with their vertues, according to their several effects, kinds and properties, which still bear the Effigies of Innocency according to their original Grafts; which by their dumb vegetable Oratory, each hour speaks to the Inhabitant in silent acts, That they need not look for any other Terrestrial Paradice, to suspend or tyre their curiosity upon, while she is extant (1902 ed., p. 33).

In *A Character*, Alsop rejected stereotypical and negative depictions of indentured servitude. He appealed directly to London's lower classes to emigrate to Maryland where economic opportunity existed: "In short, touching the Servants of this Province, they live well in the time of their Service, and by their restrainment in that time, they are made capable of living much better when they come to be free" (1902 ed., p. 61).

Alsop has often been charged with grossly exaggerating the positive aspects of servant life in Maryland, yet he occasionally criticized and satirized the social and economic institutions surrounding the practice of indentured servitude on both sides of the Atlantic. By calling his promotion tracts a "character," Alsop drew general connections to the seventeenth-century character genre made popular by John Earle's *Microcosmography* (1663) and Sir Thomas Overbury and made particular connections to the national character genre as seen in Owen Felltham's *A Brief Character of the Low Countries* (1659) and John Evelyn's *A Character of England* (1659) (see Pebworth, p. 64). *A Character of the Province of Maryland* is most notable for its incorporation of various literary forms and its manipulation of the promotion genre toward witty and satirical ends.

No writings other than *A Character of the Province of Maryland* seem to have been left by Alsop. Two sermons published in England in 1669 and 1679 are by a different George Alsop. All that is known of the Maryland Alsop after his return to England and publication of *A Character* is that in 1666 he began a career as a minister in or around Westminster. George Alsop lived until sometime after 1673.

• George Alsop's *A Character of the Province of Maryland* (1666) is reprinted with notes and introduction by Newton D. Mereness (1902). The most complete biographical information is found in J. A. Leo Lemay, *Men of Letters in Colonial Maryland* (1972), pp. 48–69, and in his appendix on "The Identity of George Alsop," pp. 343–45. For criticism on Alsop see Lemay, *Men of Letters in Colonial Maryland*, pp. 48–69; Ted-Larry Pebworth, "The 'Character' of George Alsop's *Mary-Land*," *Seventeenth Century News* 34 (1976): 64–66; and Darin E. Fields, "George Alsop's Indentured Servant in *A Character of the Province of Maryland*," *Maryland Historical Magazine* 85 (1990): 221–35.

DARIN E. FIELDS

ALSOP, Joseph (11 Oct. 1910–28 Aug. 1989), journalist, was born Joseph Wright Alsop V in Avon, Connecticut, the son of Joseph Wright Alsop IV and Corinne Robinson, wealthy farmers. Both parents claimed distinguished bloodlines. Corinne Robinson Alsop's uncle was Theodore Roosevelt; her cousin was Eleanor Roosevelt. Young Alsop attended the Groton School and earned his A.B. from Harvard University in 1932. Family connections netted him a reporting position at the *New York Herald Tribune*. Quickly establishing himself an able journalist, Alsop joined the paper's Washington bureau in late 1935. Family ties and an extraordinary self-confidence gained Alsop access to the most powerful members of the federal government as well as the city's social elite. In addition to his *Herald Tribune* writing, he also began contributing political stories to the *Saturday Evening Post*. In October 1937 Alsop and fellow *Herald Tribune* reporter Robert Kintner left the paper to start a column nationally syndicated by the North American Newspaper Alliance. They also wrote for the *Saturday Evening Post* and *Life*.

Alsop ardently supported U.S. involvement in World War II. Five months before the United States entered the war, Alsop accepted an officer's commission in naval intelligence. En route to India, Alsop stopped in China and drew on his Washington connections to arrange his transfer to the American Volunteer Group, an American-staffed air force fighting for the Chinese and led by General Claire Chennault. When the British colony of Hong Kong fell to the Japanese, Alsop spent seven months as a prisoner-of-war. Out of the navy, he returned to China as head of the Lend-Lease mission in March 1942. Alsop soon became immersed in the bitter struggle for power over strategy between Chinese generalissimo Chiang Kai-shek and Lieutenant General Joseph W. Stilwell, Allied theater commander. Alsop, like Chennault, sided with Chiang and used his contacts within the Roosevelt administration to weaken Stilwell's position and secure himself an air force officer's commission in February 1944.

Returning to Washington in 1945, Alsop began a new column, "Matter of Fact," for the *Herald Tribune*, with his younger brother Stewart. Syndicated to 190 papers in the mid-1950s, the column enjoyed a national audience, perhaps second only to Walter Lippmann's column in influence. The brothers also regularly contributed to the still-popular *Saturday Evening Post*. The Alsops culled Washington sources assiduously. Adhering to what they dubbed "the rule of the feet," they asserted that each column was based on personal interviews with at least four different sources. Yet for the Alsops, especially Joe, reporting almost always meant proving a predetermined stance. Alsop "seldom allowed facts to interfere with his prejudices," one contemporary recalled. No position was more paramount to Alsop than America's supremacy. In the late 1940s he was among the earliest opinion journalists to call for massive U.S. military build-up against the Soviet Union. At the same time he consistently urged American policy-makers to oppose Communist insurgencies throughout the globe. Those lacking his ardor were likened to British leaders in the 1930s who had failed to recognize Hitler's designs on Europe. Despite his strident globalism, Alsop strongly criticized the antisubversion investigations of Senator Joseph R. McCarthy, Jr., and others. Alsop publicly supported some of those accused of being security risks, notably physicist J. Robert Oppenheimer.

In 1958 Joseph and Stewart Alsop ended their partnership. Joseph Alsop continued his column on his own, first for the *Herald Tribune* and then for the increasingly influential *Washington Post*. In 1961 he married Susan Mary Jay Patten, the widow of an old friend; they divorced in 1975.

Alsop attended most to foreign policy, manifesting what one biographer dubbed the columnist's "Chicken Little syndrome." In the late 1950s he popularized charges that the Soviet Union would soon enjoy an advantage in intercontinental missiles. Although the so-called missile gap proved nonexistent, the issue helped to elect John F. Kennedy president. Alsop greatly admired Kennedy and his administration. "I cannot recall a single broad area of policy on which I really disagreed with President Kennedy," Alsop later wrote. He frequently socialized with the president and was on similarly good terms with Kennedy's successor, Lyndon B. Johnson. To both presidents and his readers, Alsop strongly promoted U.S. support of South Vietnam, under siege from Communist guerillas. He characteristically sneered at—and attacked in print—correspondents who insisted that the South Vietnamese government was unpopular and incompetent. He applauded Johnson's decision to commit U.S. forces in Vietnam and then insisted that America was winning the war. Alsop's steadfast endorsement of U.S. involvement cost him dearly as the conflict became unpopular and split the Washington foreign policy establishment and many readers. "I cannot tell you how isolated and suddenly out of fashion I feel," he wrote in 1966. He quit his column in 1974.

Alsop devoted the remainder of his life to writing books. He died of cancer in Washington, D.C.

• The Joseph W. Alsop Papers are at the Library of Congress. Robert W. Merry, *Taking on the World: Joseph and Stewart Alsop—Guardians of the American Century* (1996), is the most complete biography. Other studies include Leann Grabavoy Almquist, *Joseph Alsop and American Foreign Policy: The Journalist as Advocate* (1993), and Edwin M. Yoder, Jr., *Joe Alsop's Cold War: A Study of Journalistic Influence and Intrigue* (1995). Alsop was the author or coauthor of nine books: with Turner Catledge, *The 168 Days* (1938); with Robert Kintner, *Men Around the President* (1939); also with Kintner, *American White Paper: The Story of American Diplomacy and the Second World War* (1940); with Stewart Alsop, *We Accuse: The Story of the Miscarriage of American Justice in the Case of J. Robert Oppenheimer* (1954); also with Stewart Alsop, *The Reporter's Trade* (1958); *From the Silent Earth: A Report on the Greek Bronze Age* (1964); *FDR, 1882–1945: A Centenary Remembrance* (1982); *The Rare Art Traditions* (1982); and with Adam Pratt, *"I've Seen the Best of It": Memoirs* (1992).

JAMES L. BAUGHMAN

ALSOP, Mary O'Hara. *See* O'Hara, Mary.

ALSOP, Stewart (17 May 1914–26 May 1974), political columnist, was born Stewart Johonnot Oliver Alsop in Avon, Connecticut, the son of Joseph Wright Alsop, an insurance executive, and Corinne Douglas Robinson. His father was a member of the Connecticut legislature for many terms and a public official. His mother, a niece of Theodore Roosevelt, was very active in Republican politics and was one of the first women elected to the state senate. Alsop grew up on the family's comfortable dairy and tobacco farm, where political argument was a daily occurrence.

As a child, Alsop was afflicted with eczema and then asthma so bad that he would turn blue during attacks. Agnes Guthrie, a Scottish nurse, was hired to watch over him throughout his childhood and became a second mother. He recovered his health enough to attend Groton School, in Groton, Massachusetts, which he disliked, but there he became associate editor of the *Grotonian* and a member of the drama society. Alsop received his A.B. from Yale in 1936 and then became a junior editor for Doubleday Doran & Co. with Ted Roosevelt, Theodore Roosevelt's son, as his boss. The first professional article Alsop wrote appeared in the *Atlantic Monthly* in 1941. In it he described himself as a Marxist liberal, but in reality he was, as he later described himself, a "very square New Deal liberal."

In 1941, even before the Japanese attack on Pearl Harbor, Alsop tried to enlist in all three military services but was rejected on medical grounds because of his asthma and high blood pressure. He went to Britain and enlisted as a private in the Sixtieth Regiment, King's Royal Rifle Corps. In 1942 he was commissioned second lieutenant and two years later was promoted to captain. He then transferred to the U.S. Army to become a parachutist with the Office of Strategic Services (OSS). After D-Day he parachuted into France to join the French underground resistance. He was awarded the French Croix de Guerre with palm.

Alsop was strongly affected by the war. He became a lifelong admirer of Winston Churchill, made close lifelong friends, and said he benefited from having the chance to face death when young. In 1945 he resigned his commission and in 1946 published, with Thomas Braden, *Sub Rosa*, which described the achievements and failures of the OSS. The book was praised as exciting reading in portraying "sweating, frightened men doing a job" (as Lewis Gannett said in the *New York Herald Tribune*) but criticized for its limitations as a history of the OSS.

In 1944 Alsop married Patricia Hankey, an Englishwoman who, unknown to him, had been working for British Secret Intelligence Service. They had six children.

In December 1945, Alsop went to Washington to join his brother Joseph in writing political columns four times a week under the title "Matter of Fact" for the Herald Tribune Syndicate. They wrote together in the great days of Washington columnists such as Walter Lippman, Arthur Krock, and James (Scotty) Reston. Their first column was, according to Alsop's brother, a "nondescript and embarrassingly dismissive assessment of Harry Truman." They gathered their information by telephone, interviews of forty-some people per week, and trips throughout the world. Their typical practice was to have one brother travel and report international news while the other stayed in Washington to report national developments. They had a rule that they would never write about a country or its rulers unless they had first gone there.

Although his brother had previously written columns with Robert Kintner, Alsop had difficulty adapting to column writing. His brother advised him to write as plainly as possible with an absolute minimum of adjectives, ornaments, and images. The point of the column was to increase information and improve the average reader's understanding of national affairs. The simple approach proved effective. By 1950, 137 papers were carrying their column.

As Washington prognosticators, the Alsop brothers were sometimes prescient, sometimes not. They gave Truman little credit for the achievements of his first administration and thought Dewey unbeatable. They felt that Truman was a simple, average man with severe limitations and that he could not lead America's transition from war to peace. They particularly resented his business-minded cronies. Joseph Alsop in 1965 apologized to Truman for underestimating him. The Alsops did become good friends with many high-ranking officials in the Truman administration, with the exception of Secretary of Defense Lewis Johnson, whom they had criticized for heavily cutting defense. They covered Robert Taft's 1950 Ohio senate race and briefly had high hopes for Adlai Stevenson as successor to Truman. They blamed Douglas MacArthur for the defeat of Lieutenant General Walton H. Walker's Eighth Army by the Chinese in Korea and were highly critical of Eisenhower for meeting with U.S. senator Joseph McCarthy in Milwaukee and giving legitimacy to McCarthy's attacks on General George Marshall. They later criticized Eisenhower for overprudence in defense spending. They believed strongly in the importance of balance of power and felt military security was the best way of preventing war.

The Alsops' columns brought them attention and criticism. In 1950 and 1952 they were cited by the Overseas Press Club for "best interpretation of foreign news." On the other hand, they were investigated by the Federal Bureau of Investigation when Alsop broke the story that the Soviets had decided to use ballistic missiles to drive satellites. They were denounced by Soviet Foreign Minister Andrei Vishinsky before the United Nations General Assembly for advocating U.S. air bases in northern India, the Middle East, and North Africa.

In the early 1950s the Alsops first began imitating the practice of and sometimes canvassing with professional pollsters. They went from house to house asking questions, easiest first, in a no-nonsense tone of voice. Alsop later wrote that from this polling he learned that political journalists write for not more than 5 percent of the population: "the other 95% don't give a damn."

Strident in their demands for a strong military and strong foreign policy, the Alsops defended civil liberties in domestic policy. They became most famous for their attacks on Senator McCarthy and their support of Robert Oppenheimer. The Alsops wrote that "a miasma of neurotic fear and internal suspicion" had engulfed the capital "like some noxious effluvium from the marshy Potomac." McCarthy grew so irritated with their repeated public attacks that he accused them of being communists. Another source of friction was the controversy surrounding Robert Oppenheimer, founder and director of the Los Alamos laboratory that first developed the atomic bomb, who had in 1949 opposed development of the hydrogen bomb. In 1953, the Atomic Energy Commission began to remove classified material from his custody and then conducted a secret inquiry into his security clearance. The commission ruled that Oppenheimer had allowed personal relationships and convictions to interfere with national security. When the case against Oppenheimer became public knowledge in 1954, the Alsops wrote many outraged columns about the misjudgments of Oppenheimer and finally produced a book entitled *We Accuse!* about them. The book was unsuccessful although it provoked strong reaction. Nevertheless, the Alsops received the 1955 Authors Guild prize for contributing to civil liberties.

In 1958 the brothers' partnership broke up in what Alsop called an "amicable divorce." The brothers had always held strong views and were often combative. Alsop subsequently became a full-time columnist for the *Saturday Evening Post* at a substantially higher salary.

In 1960 Alsop published *Nixon & Rockefeller: A Double Portrait*, which had grown out of long articles about both. Alsop claimed that, after the Eisenhower periods of adjustment and stabilization following the enormous changes of the New Deal and World War II, the time was ripe for "fertility, inventiveness and a willingness to experiment." Both men, Alsop wrote, were remarkable, interesting, and unusual, and either might be the next president, a prediction that proved to be wrong.

In 1962 Alsop became contributing editor for national affairs for the *Saturday Evening Post* and then in 1966 its Washington editor. When the *Post* was going to cease publication (a new series began in 1971), he moved in 1968 to *Newsweek*, for which he wrote a weekly column located on the last page, dateline Washington, and printed between two red streamers.

In the 1960s Alsop covered important topics such as race, drugs, and subcultures within American society. Shortly after the 1965 Watts riot, he went to Los Angeles and wrote that the racial problem in the United States "is wholly insoluble," that is "like some incurable disease, with which both whites and Negroes must learn to live in pain." He visited the Ku Klux Klan in North Carolina, black militant leaders in Harlem, and a heroin speakeasy near Central Park. He also began two-week lecture tours during which he tried to learn what the American public was interested in.

The main political topic that engaged Alsop at this time was the Vietnam War. He and his brother foresaw as early as 1953 that after the final settlement in Korea, U.S. attention would turn to Vietnam. Alsop once told an interviewer that "from the start I was dubious about the Vietnam war, where Joe wasn't. But once we made the decision, I, too, felt we could not just sneak out." Later he wrote of antiwar protestors that "there's something going on here our generation will never understand." While his brother remained a "hawk," Alsop in 1971 wrote, "It is not practical to try to continue to fight a war that has no popular support at all." He traced America's heavy involvement in Vietnam to John F. Kennedy's desire after the Bay of Pigs and diplomatic loss in Laos to preserve America's reputation as protector of world peace.

In July 1971 Alsop was diagnosed with a rare form of leukemia, which he battled for three years. During this time he wrote *Stay of Execution: A Sort of Memoir* (1973) about the experience of having inoperable cancer. He wrote that the American system was falling apart, that we are a "failed nation, a failed people." Watergate he called "a peculiarly depressing way to say farewell to all our greatness." But personally he came to terms with death, and the book was praised for its candor and humor. Alsop was admired for living gracefully, courageously, and productively. He died in Bethesda, Maryland. Alsop's importance lies in his honest and intelligent coverage of the United States from post–World War II through the Vietnam War, coverage that expressed American ideals and influenced the public's view of postwar communism, national defense, McCarthyism, and foreign policy.

• Stewart and Joseph Alsop's papers and correspondence are in the Library of Congress. In addition, Alsop donated his own papers from 1958 to 1967 to the Boston University libraries. Other works by Alsop not previously mentioned include *The Reporter's Trade* (with Joseph Alsop, 1958) and *The Center: People and Power in Political Washington* (1968). Biographical sources include his own memoir, *Stay of Execution* (1973); his brother Joseph Alsop's autobiography, *I've Seen the Best of It* (1992); Edwin M. Yoder, Jr., *Joe Alsop's Cold War: A Study of Journalistic Influence and Intrigue* (1995); early biographical information is in *Current Biography Yearbook* (1952). A recent biography is Robert W. Merry, *Taking on the World: Joseph and Stewart Alsop—Guardians of the American Century* (1996). Obituaries are in the *New York Times*, 27 May 1974, and *Newsweek*, 3 June 1974.

ANN W. ENGAR

ALSTON, Joseph (1779–10 Sept. 1816), planter and statesman, was born in All Saints Parish (Georgetown District), South Carolina, the son of Colonel William Alston, a rice planter, and Mary Ashe. He attended the College of Charleston from 1793 to 1794, then entered Princeton in 1795, his junior year, but he withdrew without graduating. He read law in the office of Edward Rutledge, a signer of the Declaration of Independence, and was admitted to the bar before age twenty (probably in 1799).

Aiken spent 1800 traveling the United States. He returned to South Carolina to become a rice planter. Alston's grandfather Joseph Alston had been one of the largest planters in All Saints Parish with thousands of acres of land and over 500 slaves and had bequeathed to Alston the "Oaks Plantation," which comprised 1,300 acres on the Waccamaw River, and 100 slaves. Alston's father gave him "Hagley Plantation," also on the Waccamaw in All Saints Parish, later as a wedding present. Alston acquired an additional 2,000 acres in land grants in All Saints and land in Greenville District, where he built a summer home. He enjoyed considerable success as a planter, practicing careful and skilled management on his plantations, and he eventually owned about 300 slaves.

In 1801 Alston married Theodosia Burr, daughter of Aaron Burr and Theodosia Prevost. He had met her on his travels in New York. Doubtless his father-in-law had a great influence on Alston entering politics. A Democratic-Republican, he was elected to the South Carolina General Assembly from Christ Church Parish in 1802. He chose not to serve in the session of 1804, instead devoting his time exclusively to planting. He made the Oaks Plantation his principal residence. In 1805 he returned to the assembly from Prince George Winyah Parish, serving until 1812. From 1805 to 1809 he was Speaker of the South Carolina House.

Alston was associated with Aaron Burr's western conspiracy in 1806. Although no evidence suggests that he was involved in any plot to separate the West from the Union, Thomas Jefferson thought Alston was guilty because he had backed the scheme financially and traveled in the western territories with Burr, Alston made great efforts to distance himself from his father-in-law following Burr's arrest. He had good reason to suspect Burr of deceiving him, but later he helped greatly in Burr's efforts to establish his innocence. Harman Blennerhassett, who lost his fortune in Burr's scheme, claimed Alston had guaranteed him against losses and threatened to make a public disclosure unless Alston paid him $50,000. Alston did not submit to the blackmail, but he did ultimately give Blennerhassett $12,000.

In 1812, following a caustic campaign, Alston was elected governor, serving from 1812 to 1814. His administration was characterized primarily by strong support for the War of 1812 against England, manifested in the building of forts and the arming of merchant seamen. Following his term as governor, Alston was elected from All Saints Parish to the state senate in the place of his father, who did not file for office.

Alston's last years were shadowed by a series of personal tragedies. His only child died at Pawleys Island on 30 June 1812 from fever, and his wife was lost at sea in January 1813 on her way to visit her father in New York. This proved to be the death knell of Alston's political career, for no longer would he be able to go to her for assurances of sympathy and support as he had done in every emotional crisis, generally of political origin, during their marriage. When Burr asked for his political aid in behalf of Andrew Jackson, Alston responded in a letter on 16 February 1816 that showed the level of despair to which he had sunk. He agreed "in sentiment; but the spirit, the energy, the health necessary to give practical effect to sentiment, are all gone. I feel too much alone, too entirely unconnected with the world, to take much interest in anything." A few months later Alston died in Charleston.

• Alston's papers have not survived. However, a good short account is in Anthony Q. Devereux, *The Rice Princes: A Rice Epoch Revisited* (1973). For additional information, especially on his marriage and his relations with Aaron Burr, see George C. Rogers, *The History of Georgetown County, South Carolina* (1970). See also Elizabeth Deas Allston, *The Allstons and Alstons of Waccamaw* (1936), and Joseph A. Groves, *The Alstons and Allstons of North and South Carolina* (1901). An obituary is in the *Charleston Courier*, 11 Sept. 1816.

JAMES M. CLIFTON

ALSTON, Melvin Ovenus (7 Oct. 1911–30 Dec. 1985), educator, was born in Norfolk, Virginia, the son of William Henry "Sonnie" Alston, a drayman, and Mary Elizabeth "Lizzie" Smith, a laundress. Of middle-class background in terms of an African-American family in the urban South in the 1920s, he grew up in a house that his family owned, free of any mortgage. After attending Norfolk's segregated black public schools and graduating from Booker T. Washington High School, he graduated from Virginia State College (B.S., 1935), honored for his debating and for excellence in scholarship, and began teaching math at Booker T. Washington High School in 1935. Beginning in 1937 he served as president of the Norfolk Teachers Association, and he also held local leadership positions in the Young Men's Christian Association and the First Calvary Baptist Church.

Alston played a key role in an effort by black teachers in the Norfolk city public schools to challenge the racial discrimination in their salaries. In 1937 the Virginia Teachers Association (VTA) and its local branch, the Norfolk Teachers Association, representing black teachers in the public schools, joined forces with the National Association for the Advancement of Colored People (NAACP) to organize a joint committee to pursue salary equalization—by which they meant that all teachers would be paid according to the white teachers' salary schedule rather than the lower, black teachers' schedule. The NAACP supplied legal assistance, and the VTA established a $1,000 fund to indemnify the lost salary of any teacher who was fired in retaliation for serving as plaintiff in a court case. In 1939 Alston's colleague Aline Elizabeth Black initiated but lost a case in state court to achieve salary equalization. Before her case could be appealed to the Virginia Supreme Court of Appeals, the school board declined to renew her contract, and when she lost her job, her lawyers concluded that she no longer had standing to sue. The joint committee paid Black her salary for the school year, and she went to New York, where she taught school and took classes toward a doctorate at New York University. With some reluctance Alston took her place in the litigation, guaranteed a similar indemnity of a year's salary if he lost his job as a consequence.

Alston's lawyers were the NAACP's big guns—Thurgood Marshall, Leon A. Ransom, and William H. Hastie—together with Virginia attorneys Oliver W. Hill and J. Thomas Hewin, Jr. As a teacher Alston sought a permanent injunction against the school board's discrimination in its salary schedule on racial grounds, and as a taxpayer he also challenged the city's discriminatory allocation of the state school fund. He and his attorneys lost the case in February 1940 in federal district court, but in June they won on appeal in the Fourth Circuit Court of Appeals, *Alston v. Board of Education of the City of Norfolk*. Pending a final resolution of the case, the court directed the school board not to distribute contracts for the coming year until July, so Alston could not be denied his job and no teachers could be required to waive their rights for that year.

The appeals court determined that the Norfolk School Board had denied equal protection of the laws by paying black teachers lower salaries than white teachers solely on the basis of race. The court rejected the school board's contention that teachers, having signed contracts for the year, could not contest the terms to which they had agreed and, if they failed to sign, had no standing to sue. The court ruled that such waivers could not extend beyond the single year of the contract. Moreover, the appeals court overruled the district judge in the matter of whether the case concerned only Alston; rather, it was a class action suit that affected all black teachers in the Norfolk system.

In October 1940 the U.S. Supreme Court let the decision stand. Alston's case proved one of the NAACP's more important victories in its campaign in the courts for equalization of salaries, as it supplied a powerful precedent, both in law and in strategy, for similar suits in Virginia and in other southern states over the next ten years. The NAACP immediately altered its approach to a case then in progress in Florida, for example, and an out-of-court settlement in Richmond, Virginia, reached in 1942, called for salary equalization in five annual increments. The Alston case led to litigation designed to achieve progress on other fronts, too—equal busing, equal facilities, and equal curricula—in the public schools of the South, and black Virginians achieved victories regarding each of those in the 1940s.

After two years away and no longer a litigant, Black retrieved her old job in 1941, while Alston undertook graduate work at Columbia University. He earned an M.S. in mathematics education in 1942 and an Ed.D. in the same field in 1945 with a dissertation on "Vitalized Verbal Problem Material in Algebra." During 1945–1946 Alston was perhaps the only teacher in the Virginia public schools, black or white, with a doctoral degree. In 1945 he married Doris Ruby Newsome. They had five birth children and an adoptive daughter.

In 1946 Alston moved to Tallahassee to take a position as professor of mathematics and head of the math department at Florida's black land-grant school, Florida Agricultural and Mechanical College. People who knew him there recalled him with great respect as someone with prodigious industry; his wife remembered him as a "workaholic." He served as college registrar in 1947–1948 and as dean of the School of Education from 1948 to 1953. Reflecting its new status as a university, the school changed its name in 1953 to Florida Agricultural and Mechanical University and reorganized its divisions into eight colleges. Alston served for a time as acting dean of the Graduate School, and he was dean of the College of Education from its establishment in 1953 until he retired in 1969.

Alston then took a position at Southern Illinois University. From 1969 to 1974 he taught courses in secondary education and conducted research in local school systems. In declining health, he retired again and returned to Tallahassee, where he died.

• The NAACP Papers in the Library of Congress include letters to and from Alston as well as other materials on his court case. Other sources that illuminate his life and times are *Who's Who in Colored America*, 6th ed. (1942); Mark V. Tushnet, *The NAACP's Legal Strategy against Segregated Education, 1925–1950* (1987); Eric Lewis, *In Their Own Interests: Race, Class, and Power in Twentieth-Century Norfolk, Virginia* (1991); Leedel W. Neyland and John W. Riley, *The History of Florida Agricultural and Mechanical University* (1963); and the *Norfolk Journal and Guide*, 10 June 1939, 17 Feb. 1940, 15 Feb. 1941. An obituary is in the *Tallahassee Democrat*, 1 Jan. 1986.

PETER WALLENSTEIN

ALSTON, Theodosia Burr. *See* Burr, Theodosia.

ALSTON, Walter Emmons (1 Dec. 1911–1 Oct. 1984), baseball manager, was born on a farm near Venice, Ohio, the son of William Emmons Alston and Lenora Neanover. After losing his farm in bankruptcy in 1923, the elder Alston took a job at a Ford Motor Company plant, moving the family to Darrtown, Ohio. Alston's interest in sports was encouraged by his father, with whom he played semipro baseball. Nicknamed "Smokey," Alston enrolled at Miami University in Ohio in 1929, but he dropped out the following year to marry his high school sweetheart, Lela Vaughn Alexander. A daughter was born of this union. Returning to Miami University in 1932, Alston worked his way through college, starring in baseball and basketball, and graduated in 1935 with a degree in education.

Alston began his career by signing to play minor league baseball for the St. Louis Cardinals' organization. In 1936 the 6′ 2″ right-handed batting first baseman played at Huntington, West Virginia, and led the Middle Atlantic League in home runs. Called up by the Cardinals that September, he played in one game and struck out in his only major league plate appearance. He spent most of his 13-year playing career in low-level leagues because he was unable to hit top-level pitching. His baseball income was augmented by 14 years of high school teaching and coaching.

Although Alston's playing failed to impress Cardinals' general manager Branch Rickey, his knowledge of the game prompted Rickey to name him playing manager at Portsmouth, Ohio, in the Middle Atlantic League in 1940. It was the start of Alston's minor league managerial career that saw him manage seven different teams over 13 seasons.

In 1944 when Rickey became general manager of the Brooklyn Dodgers, Alston joined that organization as a minor league manager. While managing Nashua, New Hampshire, in the New England League in 1946, Alston impressed Rickey with his sympathetic handling of Roy Campanella and Don Newcombe, the first black players in that league. In 1948 Rickey promoted Alston to St. Paul of the American Association, and after his team won the 1949 championship, he was named manager at Montreal of the International League. In four seasons as manager of the Dodgers' top minor league franchise, Alston's teams won two pennants, one Junior World Series against the American Association titlist, and twice finished second.

At the close of the 1953 season Alston was the surprising choice of Dodgers' owner Walter F. O'Malley to replace the popular and successful Charley Dressen as manager. A contract dispute prompted Dressen's firing, but O'Malley's choice of Alston, a protégé of Rickey who had earlier been ousted, puzzled New York sportswriters, and they ridiculed the appointment of the little-known Alston. O'Malley had been impressed by Alston's loyalty to the organization and by his demonstrated competence in helping to develop many players on the Dodgers' roster. Alston signed the first of 23 single-year contracts that by his retirement ranked him third behind Connie Mack and John J. McGraw among managers with the longest tenure with a single team.

Alston started out inauspiciously. Expected to win the 1954 championship, the Dodgers finished second to the rival New York Giants. However, Alston's 1955 team dominated its National League opponents and defeated the New York Yankees in the World Series, giving Brooklyn its first world championship. Alston's Dodgers repeated as pennant winners in 1956, but this was Brooklyn's last pennant; the team became the Los Angeles Dodgers in 1958. In their first West Coast season, the aging, injury-ridden Dodgers fell to seventh place. It was Alston's worst year as manager, but after belatedly receiving a new contract he drove his revamped 1959 team to a first-place tie with Milwaukee. In the playoff series the Dodgers won the pennant and went on to defeat the Chicago White Sox in the World Series. The victory silenced his critics and established the quiet, competent Alston as one of baseball's foremost managers. His style was to concentrate on winning each game, but never at the team's longer-run expense. A quiet, seemingly unemotional manager, he imposed few rules, which were applied fairly, and in return demanded honesty and maximum performance from his players and coaches. He was effective in developing young players (including Sandy Koufax, whom he persuaded the team to sign as a bonus player) and was generally deemed a good tactician.

Over the next two seasons Alston transformed the Dodgers from a slugging team to one that stressed pitching, defense, and speed on the bases. In 1962 the team occupied newly built Dodger Stadium and ended the season in a first-place tie with the San Francisco Giants, who defeated them in a three-game playoff. But the following year the Dodgers won the pennant and defeated the New York Yankees in the World Series.

Bolstered by the league's best pitching, the light-hitting Dodgers won consecutive pennants in 1965 and 1966, with the 1965 team winning the World Series. It was the fourth and last world championship for Alston, who lost the services of his great pitcher Koufax following the 1966 season. Over the next seven seasons Alston rebuilt the team, which in 1974 won the expanded National League's Western Division title. The Dodgers defeated Pittsburgh to win a seventh league championship under Alston but lost in the World Series to the Oakland Athletics.

Retirement at 62 ended Alston's managerial career in 1976, when his record of 2,040 wins and 1,613 losses ranked him the fifth most successful manager in major league history. Alston won major league manager of the year honors in 1955, 1959, and 1963. During his tenure, the Dodgers became baseball's most prosperous franchise. In 1983 he was voted into the Baseball Hall of Fame. He spent his last years in retirement in Darrtown and died in nearby Oxford, Ohio.

• The National Baseball Library at Cooperstown, N.Y., has an extensive file of newspaper articles on Alston's career. Two ghosted autobiographies, Walter Alston with Si Burick, *Alston and the Dodgers* (1966), and the more complete Walter Alston with Jack Tobin, *A Year at a Time* (1976), provide intimate, well-illustrated accounts. Donald Honig, *The Man in the Dugout* (1977), compares Alston with 14 other major league managers. Stanley Cohen, *Dodgers! The First 100 Years* (1990), and Neil Sullivan, *The Dodgers Move West* (1987), describe Alston in the perspective of Dodgers' history, and David Q. Voigt, *American Baseball* vol. 3 (1983), places his Dodgers' teams in the context of post–World War II major league baseball's history. See also Bob Broeg, "Alston Ages Gracefully as Dodger," *Sporting News*, 3 July 1976; *The Sporting News Hall of Fame Fact Book* (1983); John Thorn and Pete Palmer, eds., *Total Baseball* (1991). A comprehensive obituary appears in the *New York Times*, 2 Oct. 1984.

DAVID QUENTIN VOIGT

ALSTON, William (1757–26 June 1839), planter and legislator, was born in All Saints Parish (Georgetown District), South Carolina, the son of Joseph Allston and Charlotte Rothmaler, planters. He became the first of the Allston family to spell his surname with a single *l*, making the change about 1790 to avoid being mistaken for his cousin William Allston of Brookgreen. In February 1777 Alston married Mary Ashe, with whom he had five children. After the death of his first wife in 1789, he married Mary Motte in 1791. They had six children.

With only academy training (his formal education was curtailed by the American Revolution, in which he served as a captain in Francis Marion's brigade), Alston began his rice planting at Fairfield Plantation on the Waccamaw River with about 100 slaves inherited from his father. He added so abundantly to this inheritance over the years that he became the greatest rice planter of his day in South Carolina. Eventually he would possess about 30,000 acres and 723 slaves, the largest land- and slaveholding of that period. This great acreage constituted seven rice plantations on the Waccamaw: Fairfield, Weehawka, Claremont, Midway, Crabhall, Strawberry Hill, and Clifton, where he lived in baronial style and lavishly entertained President George Washington on his southern tour in April 1791.

Alston was a most successful planter, ever ready to adopt new planting methods and techniques on his plantations. He also constructed the finest of facilities; as early as 1787 he had a rice mill built at Fairfield (which became his residence sometime between 1803 and 1810, after the elaborate home at Clifton was burned). He was renowned for fair treatment of his slaves, combining humanity with enlightened self-interest. Alston maintained several summer residences, most important of which was "The Castle" on Pawleys Island, where his daughter-in-law Theodosia Burr Alston, spent a number of summers and where his grandson Aaron Burr Alston died in 1812. As the result of his second marriage, he also acquired the distinguished Miles Brewton House on King Street in Charleston.

Of great social prominence, Alston often engaged in his first love, horse racing. Accordingly, he served as member and steward of the Jockey Club and helped to organize the fourth South Carolina Jockey Club. Alston was also able to produce a fine strain of thoroughbreds, with which he won a number of races. His inlaws humorously claimed that his holiday plans were generally determined by his wanting "to be in the neighborhood of Race-horses and Democrats, two species of animals, you know, he is very fond of." Because of his great race horses and material wealth, Alston was given the label of "King Billy." Inventories at his death in 1839 showed a combined estate of $573,232, which included, in addition to land and slaves, 600 shares in the Pennsylvania Bank of the United States, 88 shares in the Bank of Charleston, a library of 250 books, and various other plantation and household items.

Alston's political career began with his election from All Saints Parish to the second General Assembly (1776–1778). He won reelection to the third, fourth, fifth, and sixth General Assemblies (1779–1786) but declined to serve in the sixth. In 1786 he was elevated to the senate for All Saints and Prince George Winyah parishes; he served in that body for the next twenty-eight years. Alston in May 1788 represented Prince George Winyah Parish at the state convention, where he voted to ratify the federal constitution.

In addition to Alston's legislative and agricultural careers, he also served as a presidential elector in both 1800 and 1812, voting first for Thomas Jefferson and then for James Madison. Along the way he also held a number of local offices and memberships, such as tax inquirer and collector for All Saints, founding member of the Georgetown Library Society, and member of the vestry for All Saints. Alston died in Charleston and was buried at "The Oaks," plantation of his deceased son, Joseph Alston.

• For a brief biographical account of Alston, see Anthony Q. Devereux, *The Rice Princes: A Rice Epoch Revisited* (1973). A good deal of information on Alston is given in George C. Rogers, *The History of Georgetown County, South Carolina* (1970). See also Elizabeth Deas Allston, *The Allstons and Alstons of Waccamaw* (1936), and Joseph A. Groves, *The Alstons and Allstons of North and South Carolina* (1901). For fond remembrances of Alston by his grandson, see Arney R. Childs, ed., *Rice Planter and Sportsman: The Recollections of J. Motte Alston* (1953). For Alston's involvement in horse racing, see John B. Irving, *The South Carolina Jockey Club* (1857), and Fairfax Harrison, *The John's Island Stud, 1750–1788* (1931). Obituaries are in the *Charleston Courier* and the *Charleston Mercury*, both 28 June 1839.

JAMES M. CLIFTON

ALTER, Karl J. (18 Aug. 1885–23 Aug. 1977), archbishop, was born Karl Joseph Alter in Toledo, Ohio, the son of John P. Alter, a cigar manufacturer and liquor dealer, and Elizabeth Kuttner. He attended St. John's College in Toledo and St. Mary's Seminary in Cleveland prior to his ordination to the priesthood on 4 June 1910 in the newly established diocese of Toledo. After two brief parish assignments in Ohio, he served the diocese for fifteen years as the first director of Catholic Charities, gradually linking the various charitable agencies into a unified system while also providing them with approved contemporary methods and standards of social welfare work. Alter was also a lecturer in sociology at Mary Manse College in Toledo, and in 1929 he was named director of the National School of Social Service in Washington, D.C., which was sponsored by the National Catholic Welfare Conference. On 22 April 1931 he was named the third bishop of Toledo, succeeding Samuel Stritch who had been appointed the fifth archbishop of Milwaukee.

As Alter entered the cathedral for his episcopal consecration, newspapers were announcing the closing of the first of five Toledo banks that would eventually fail during the Great Depression. Within two years parish income had dropped by 50 percent. Parishes were no longer able to pay their assessments to support the diocesan offices or to complete the monumental Spanish plateresque cathedral built by Bishop Stritch.

The improvements that Alter had made earlier in the diocesan charitable agencies made their services more effective during those troubled times, and his careful management of his limited financial resources enabled the monumental new cathedral to be completed and solemnly dedicated on 1 October 1941. Alter also established a diocesan newspaper, the *Catholic Chronicle*, in 1934 and convened the first diocesan synod in 1941, which enacted 426 statutes that clarified diocesan policies concerning liturgy, temporal affairs, and the life of the clergy.

On 21 June 1950 Alter was appointed archbishop of Cincinnati, succeeding John Timothy McNicholas. Under his administration there were over 130 major building projects, the most ambitious being the expansion of St. Gregory's College Seminary, which soon closed because of declining enrollments, and the restoration of the historic St.-Peter-in-Chains Cathedral. Alter also helped build seven high schools, an orphanage, and a home for the aged, as well as a number of churches, elementary schools, and parish halls. In 1952–1953 he reorganized the Archdiocesan Councils of Men and of Women in order to involve laypersons more actively in liturgy, religious education, social action, and family life, eventually merging these two groups into the Archdiocesan Council of the Laity in 1969.

From 1952 to 1955 Alter served as the chairman of the administrative board of the National Catholic Welfare Council, then the permanent secretariat of the American bishops. During his tenure he began to associate himself with the growing support among some bishops, notably Cardinals Samuel Stritch and Edward Mooney, for the Jesuit theologian John Courtney Murray, who urged universal Catholic acceptance of religious liberty. During his tenure Alter also declined to give active support to Cardinal Francis J. Spellman's campaign to establish American diplomatic relations with the Vatican.

In 1960 Pope John XXIII appointed Alter to the Preparatory Commission of Vatican II, and in 1966 Pope Paul VI named him to the post-conciliar Commission for Bishops and the Government of Dioceses, which was to guide the practical implementation of the council's decrees. As a member of the preparatory commission, Alter became the first American bishop to request that the council include religious liberty on its agenda.

Although Alter was not an initiator of structural changes in the church, he was eager to implement policies on which the college of bishops had reached a consensus. After Vatican II, therefore, he quickly established in the archdiocese of Cincinnati a senate of priests and an archdiocesan pastoral council, also suggesting that a council be established in every parish. In the area of social justice and social welfare, Alter exercised even more initiative, establishing an active poverty commission, a human relations commission, and a planning and budget commission, which gave attention to racial tensions, urban ghettos, and other critical problems of the cities. On 23 July 1969 Alter retired and was succeeded by Paul F. Leibold. He died in Cincinnati.

Alter was a cautiously progressive leader in rather turbulent times. He frequently said that his archdiocese would be neither the first nor the last to introduce the more dramatic changes proposed in the wake of Vatican II. His regal self-confidence, combined with his innate courtesy, enabled him to lead his archdiocese through the unsettled post–Vatican II period in the Catholic church with a minimum of disquiet. His fellow bishops welcomed his leadership and valued his advice.

• Alter's papers are in the Archives of the Archdiocese of Cincinnati. Lawrence A. Mossing, *The Bishop Alter Years in the Diocese of Toledo* (1989), has a comprehensive account of his earlier years. Some of his lectures and sermons can be found in Maurice E. Reardon, *The Mind of an Archbishop* (1960).

M. EDMUND HUSSEY

ALTGELD, John Peter (30 Dec. 1847–12 Mar. 1902), governor of Illinois and leader of midwestern reform forces in the 1890s, was born in Nieder Selters in Nassau, Germany, the son of John Peter Altgeld, a wagon maker and farmer, and Mary (maiden name unknown). He was three months old when he and his parents immigrated to the United States and settled in Newville or Mansfield, Ohio. Raised in poverty by a stern and parochial father who saw no benefit in education, Altgeld received instruction only in a few terms of public school and Methodist Sunday school. Seeking to escape his father's control, in 1864 he joined the Ohio Home Guards for a 100-day stint. This experience confirmed his desire for advancement, but he also contracted a disease, probably malaria, which recurred throughout his life.

Returning home, Altgeld left the farm and attended secondary school, after which he taught for two years. In 1869 he went west, working as a laborer, but he became very ill and nearly died. He recovered and settled in Savannah, Missouri, where he read law and in 1871 was admitted to the bar. He moved immediately into public office, serving as city attorney from 1872 to 1873 and winning election in 1874 as county prosecutor on a Democratic-Granger ticket. In the fall of 1875 he resigned.

Moving to Chicago, Altgeld quickly achieved financial and personal success. By 1877 he had a reasonable income from his legal work, and in 1879 he began investing in real estate. The considerable profits from these activities were far exceeded when he began constructing and selling buildings, and by the late 1880s he was quite wealthy. In 1877 he married Emma Ford, who was a painter and musician and who in 1887 published a novel, *Sarah's Choice; or, The Norton Family*. They had one child, who was stillborn.

In 1884 Altgeld renewed his interest in politics. That year he published *Our Penal Machinery and Its Victims*, which argued that the legal system discriminated against the poor and advocated speedy trial, indeterminate sentencing, and rehabilitation. Altgeld expanded the book's impact by buying and distributing many of the copies, and it did influence numerous people, including Clarence Darrow, who soon moved to Chicago and became Altgeld's law partner. Altgeld also began seeking public office, losing in an 1884 bid for Congress, failing to win as a compromise candidate for the Democratic nomination for the U.S. Senate in 1885, and winning election in 1886 to the Superior Court of Cook County as a Democrat also endorsed by the Union Labor party. In 1889 he financed and assisted a successful Democratic antimachine candidate for mayor of Chicago. Altgeld became chief justice of the superior court in 1890 but left the bench in 1891 to devote attention to his investments and to continue his political pursuits. In 1891 he again unsuccessfully sought the Democratic Senate nomination, and in 1892 he became the Democratic nominee for governor. His success in this latter effort was aided by his ability to spend money on the campaign, reportedly $100,000. During the campaign he justified supporting labor unions as a necessary counterbalance to the inevitable formation of large corporations. He also denounced the McKinley Tariff; the state's Edwards Act, which called for state inspection of parochial schools and required that all instruction be in English; and the Lodge Force Bill, which concerned federal intervention in southern elections.

As governor, Altgeld won labor legislation for women and children, including factory inspectors; improved conditions in state institutions; and reforms in the legal system. Like his wife, who was a member of the Executive Committee of the Illinois Equal Suffrage Association, Altgeld strongly favored women's rights, including equal opportunity and pay. He endorsed protective labor legislation, and he appointed women to important state boards, commissions, and institutions. He also supported the University of Illinois and greatly increased its budget. Although his appointments went to Democrats, he won reformers' support by choosing able and reform-minded persons and by his efforts to reduce corruption in state and municipal governments. Even after Republicans recaptured the state legislature in 1894, Altgeld remained an activist governor, though his role was largely negative. He vetoed numerous bills, most notably several that would have assisted gas and streetcar monopolies.

Altgeld was best known, however, for actions concerning two labor-related issues. Three of the men convicted in connection with the infamous Haymarket bombing of 4 May 1886 remained in prison in 1893 and had become a cause célèbre for labor and reformers. After careful study Altgeld concluded that the jury was packed, that the jury and judge were biased, and that the case was unproved. In pardoning the men, Altgeld unleashed a firestorm of attacks upon himself. In 1894 he resisted demands from employers to intervene in the Pullman railroad strike and strongly protested when President Grover Cleveland sent in federal troops. These actions, his criticism of the Supreme Court's overturning of the income tax, and his support for free silver made him a great favorite of reformers and a leading figure in the transformation of the Democratic party in 1896. Indeed, had he been born in the United States, he would have been a leading candidate for the presidential nomination. Instead, he ran for reelection and, like most Illinois Democrats, lost.

Besides electoral defeat and severe personal attacks, Altgeld also experienced financial disaster. The economic depression of the 1890s caught him overcommitted on a building project, which failed in 1900 and eliminated virtually his entire estate. However, his law practice provided some income, and many loyalists continued to admire him for his courageous actions. He also remained committed to politics. After supporting Carter Harrison, Jr., for mayor in 1897, Altgeld ran in 1899 against him as an Independent candidate, basing his campaign on municipal ownership of streetcars. Starting in 1898 he was also a vocal opponent of imperialism, speaking out against America's acquisition of colonies and the British war against the Boers. He had just spoken on this subject on 11 March 1902 when he died of a cerebral hemorrhage in Joliet, Illinois. Though vilified by his opponents, he was loved by his supporters and made famous by Vachel Lindsay's poem "The Eagle That Is Forgotten."

• Altgeld's official papers are in the Illinois State Archives. He apparently destroyed his personal papers, though some materials survive at the Illinois Historical Library in the Waldo Browne, George Shilling, and Emma Ford Altgeld collections. His book mentioned above was reprinted with other essays in *Live Questions, Including Our Penal Machinery and Its Victims* (1890). His other writings include *Oratory: Its Requirements and Rewards* (1901) and *The Cost of Something for Nothing* (1904). His *Reasons for Pardoning Fielden, Neebe & Schwab, the Haymarket Anarchists* (1986) has been published with a memorial address by Clarence Darrow and an introduction by Leon M. Despres. Also useful is Henry M. Christman, ed., *The Mind and Spirit of John Peter Altgeld; Selected Writings and Addresses* (1960). The most complete biography is Harry Barnard, *"Eagle Forgotten": The Life of John Peter Altgeld* (1938), but Ray Ginger, *Altgeld's America: The Lincoln Ideal versus Changing Realities* (1958), provides information in a larger context. Thomas R. Pegram, *Partisans and Progressives: Private Interest and Public Policy in Illinois, 1870–1922* (1992), includes an analysis of Altgeld and the transformation of policy making in the state. See also David Falcone, "John Peter Altgeld: Progressive Apologist for Social Justice" (Ph.D. diss., St. Louis Univ., 1989); and Sandra O. Harmon, "Altgeld the Suffragist," *Chicago History* 16 (1987): 14–25.

PHILIP RAY VANDERMEER

ALTHAM, John (1589–5 Nov. 1640), Jesuit priest and missionary who accompanied the first colonists to Maryland in 1634. Few sources exist through which a biography might be constructed. His parents are unknown and his schooling obscure. He entered the Society of Jesus (the Jesuits) in 1623 at the age of thirty-two and was ordained to the priesthood after an apparently perfunctory course of studies in philosophy and theology for which he showed, it seems, little aptitude. Laboring in Devonshire and the district of London, he earned a reputation as a zealous and hardworking missionary, which recommended him for the Maryland enterprise.

Upon the colonists' arrival in Maryland, Altham accompanied Governor Leonard Calvert on a reconnaissance of the Potomac River and its environs in search of a permanent settlement site. During this trip he preached with some success to native Piscataway through an interpreter. After the selection of the site of St. Mary's, Maryland's first capital, Altham and his fellow Jesuit missionary Andrew White negotiated the use of an Indian longhouse as the first Catholic chapel in the province. Initial efforts at missionary outreach to the Indians proved unsatisfactory. The Jesuits had at first to depend on Protestant interpreters, whom they regarded as untrustworthy, and English fears of Indian intentions likewise hampered their missionary efforts. Nonetheless, Altham seems to have rapidly gained a favorable reputation with the local Indians. A Jesuit correspondent in Maryland reported to his English superiors that Altham had developed "many noble freyndes and allies who have sent him since our coming large signes of their love." By 1639 this reputation had won him an important position within the province on Kent Island.

Contained within the Maryland patent, Kent Island had been settled in 1631 by William Claiborne (c. 1587–c. 1677), a Virginia colonist and trader. Claiborne had hoped to establish a trading outpost there to win a portion of the lucrative fur and skin trade from the French. Angered by the donation of his fledgling trading empire to Lord Baltimore, Claiborne sought for decades to undo Baltimore's charter and to stir up the local Indians and English settlers there against him. Claiborne's early success at developing a trading network centered on the island made it a promising base for missionary work to the English and Indians who frequented it. However, Altham's missionary work there undoubtedly had several larger purposes: to strengthen Baltimore's claim to the island through the presence of a Jesuit priest, to win the Indians' allegiance, and to proselytize among the English settlers in hopes of winning them to Baltimore's side by converting them to Catholicism. Given Baltimore's ongoing problems with Kent Islands, it may be presumed that these efforts met with scant success.

Altham's prominence as an Indian missionary is further witnessed by his presence at a large ceremony in July 1640, during which he assisted Andrew White in receiving into the Roman Catholic church a number of the Piscataway, including Chief Kittamaquund and his wife, in a ritual attended by Governor Calvert. Altham and White became ill shortly afterward. White soon recovered, but Altham continued to decline, eventually losing the use of his feet because of an abscess. He died at St. Mary's.

• There is no biography of Altham. The historical context for his life and work can be found in Clayton Colman Hall, *Narratives of Early Maryland, 1633–1684* (1910); Thomas Hughes, *The History of the Society of Jesus in North America*, part 1 (1908); and William P. Treacy, *Old Catholic Maryland and Its Early Jesuit Missionaries* (1889).

MICHAEL GRAHAM

ALTMAN, Benjamin (12 July 1840–7 Oct. 1913), merchant and art collector, was born in New York, New York, the son of Philip Altman, a dry goods merchant, and Cecilia (maiden name unknown). His father, a Jewish immigrant from Bavaria who had come to the United States in 1835, operated a small dry goods store named Altman & Co. on Third Avenue near Tenth Street. Young Altman worked with his brother Morris in his father's shop in the afternoons. He left school at the age of twelve to work there full time and later held a variety of sales jobs with other dry goods shops in New York City and in Newark, New Jersey. When his father died in 1854, Altman and his brother took over the store, changing its name to Altman Bros. The business prospered, and by 1865 they moved to Third Avenue and Tenth Street; they moved again to a larger building on Sixth Avenue between Eighteenth and Nineteenth Streets in 1870. Morris left the business but remained a partner, and when he died in 1876, Altman became sole owner, later changing the name of the firm to B. Altman & Co.

The store on Sixth Avenue grew rapidly and became one of the leading retail establishments in the city, but Altman cherished a dream of moving uptown. In 1895 he purchased his first parcel of land on Fifth Avenue between Thirty-fourth and Thirty-fifth streets, and for nearly a decade he continued buying connected properties until he had what the *New York Herald* called "an ideal site for an ideal store in an ideal shopping district" (8 Oct. 1913). He closed the Sixth Avenue store on 15 October 1906 and, with his partner and vice president Michael Friedsam, became a pioneer in the uptown movement of mercantile trade by reopening in the block bounded by Fifth and Madison avenues and Thirty-fourth and Thirty-fifth streets. Repeatedly enlarged, the imposing granite structure became one of the architectural landmarks of New York City. The interior was equally splendid. Lit by crystal chandeliers, its center aisle was said to be wide enough to drive through with a coach and six horses. The cost of the land and the twelve-story Italian Renaissance edifice was estimated at close to $12 million.

Altman was known for the personal concern he felt for the welfare of his employees, whom he provided with excellent working conditions and medical care. He was also exceptionally generous to his customers; he allowed many to run up large bills, and some even withdrew cash from his store and charged it to their accounts during the panic of 1907. A very private person, he never married and belonged to no clubs, although he was said by his close friends to be warm and sociable personally. He avoided publicity, declined interviews, and never permitted his name to be used in connection with his many philanthropic activities, but he consented to serve as a director of the Astor Trust Company and the Bank of the Metropolis and as a trustee of the Garfield Safe Deposit Company.

Apart from his business, Altman's chief interest lay in art collecting; he had developed his eye for fine art since his teens. His first preference was for Chinese enamels, which he began to purchase in 1882, building what was generally considered the foremost collection in the world. During the next few years his range of artistic interests grew, and he acquired fine examples of Oriental rugs, pottery, medieval European gold and silver sculptures (including the famous Rospigliosi Coupe by Cellini), sixteenth-century Italian and German rock crystals mounted in gold, terra cotta statuary by Della Robbia and Donatello, and more than fifty paintings by Dutch, Flemish, Italian, German, and Spanish masters. From 1888 to 1909 he made a series of trips to Europe, the first vacations he had ever allowed himself from his store, and purchased numerous rare and choice works. Although he consulted professional experts in his acquisitions, he ultimately depended on his own excellent discernment, and the collection he assembled ranked among the finest in the world. It included thirteen paintings by Rembrandt, the greatest number in private hands, as well as works by Vermeer, Hals, Van Dyck, Mantegna, Botticelli, Velázquez, Holbein, Dürer, and Memling. The entire collection, along with $150,000 for its care and maintenance and Altman's superb library of art books, was bequeathed to the Metropolitan Museum of Art in New York, the most valuable bequest that institution had ever received. Altman also left $150,000 to the National Academy of Design, as well as sizable sums to several New York hospitals.

The bulk of Altman's estate, estimated to be between $35 million and $45 million was left to a foundation he established and incorporated in the same year that he died at his home on Fifth Avenue in New York City. The Altman Foundation provided for the welfare of all his employees as well as for charitable and philanthropic work, with a special focus on the arts, early childhood education, hospitals and health care, housing and shelter, aging, and the economically disadvantaged. When the seven B. Altman department stores were sold in 1985 to the L. J. Hooker Corp., the $86 million in proceeds went to the foundation, the assets of which were reported in 1993 to amount to over $144 million.

Benjamin Altman was a model of American enterprise and social responsibility. Described by the eminent department store founder John Wanamaker as the foremost merchant in America, Altman dedicated himself not only to building a great business, a great fortune, and a great collection of art, but to service to his community. A marble plaque in the New York Public Library bears the words that attest to his gifts and his generosity: "The sagacity of a great merchant was joined to an ardent and discriminating love of art—and a noble public spirit dedicated his cherished collection to the benefit of mankind."

• Little has been published about the personal life of Benjamin Altman, but his business activities were widely reported in the contemporary press. For a brief discussion of Altman's career and business philosophy, see David A. Brown, "Yesterday, Today, Tomorrow—the Altman Tradition: A Sacred Trust," *The American Hebrew*, 25 Mar. 1932, pp. 477–78. Long obituaries appeared in all major New York newspapers on 8 Oct. 1913, and his will was printed in the *New York Times*, 15 Oct. 1913. Tributes, descriptions of his art collection, and reports of his legacy appeared over a period of several months. See especially the *New York Times*, 15 Nov. 1913, 27 Jan. 1914, 28 Jan. 1914, 6 Feb. 1914, and 29 Mar. 1914.

DENNIS WEPMAN

ALTMEYER, Arthur Joseph (8 May 1891–17 Oct. 1972), first Social Security commissioner, was born in De Pere, Wisconsin, the son of John G. Altmeyer and Carrie Smith. While sorting mail as an office boy in his uncle's law firm, Altmeyer came across a pamphlet describing Wisconsin's landmark Workmen's Compensation Act, the first of its kind legislated in this country. In retrospect, Altmeyer claimed that this incident sparked his lifelong interest in social welfare and labor legislation. On entering the University of Wisconsin, he took courses from John R. Commons, the dean of American labor economists. Commons stressed the "Wisconsin Idea," the belief that members of the academy should play an active role in policymaking. Altmeyer received his B.A. and Phi Beta Kappa key in 1914. He taught high school for two years and then, after marrying Ethel M. Thomas in 1916, served two years as a high school principal.

Altmeyer returned to the University of Wisconsin in 1918. While serving as Commons's research assistant, he coauthored a report, "The Health Insurance Movement in the United States," which greatly influenced the deliberations of the Illinois Health Insurance Commission and the Ohio Health and Old Age Insurance Commission. In 1920 Altmeyer became chief statistician of the Wisconsin Industrial Commission. In this capacity he launched a monthly publication, *Wisconsin Labor Market*, which became a prototype for employment indices in the nation. In 1922 he became the secretary of the Wisconsin Industrial Commission, a post he held for eleven years. In this period, he managed to earn both his M.A. and Ph.D. (1931) from the University of Wisconsin; he also took a six-month leave in 1927 to serve as deputy commissioner for the United States Employees' Compensation Commission for the Great Lakes region to put into effect the Longshoremen's and Harbor Workers' Compensation Act. The highlight of his tenure as secretary of the WIC was the enactment in January 1932 of the Wisconsin Unemployment Reserves and Compensation Act, which was the first unemployment insurance law passed in the United States.

Altmeyer's academic and administrative background caught the attention of New Deal architects, some of whom hoped to model federal social welfare and labor legislation on progressive Wisconsin laws. On the recommendation of Senator Robert La Follette, Jr., Frances Perkins, the secretary of labor, invited Altmeyer in 1933 to come to Washington to assist in the development of working relationships with state labor departments. During the next year, while on leave from the Wisconsin Industrial Commission, he served as director of the Labor Compliance Division of the National Recovery Administration and helped organize the Federal Emergency Relief Administration and the Civil Works Administration. In May 1934 Altmeyer became second assistant secretary of labor and was charged with reorganizing the department. A month later he was asked to chair the technical board advising the president's Cabinet Committee on Economic Security.

Altmeyer drew on his University of Wisconsin connections. He recruited Edwin Witte to be his staff director; Witte, in turn, brought along one of his recent graduates, Wilbur J. Cohen. Altmeyer worked closely with Thomas Eliot (who drafted the enabling legislation) and other federal officials in creating an omnibus bill that provided relief for the elderly poor, the blind, and families with dependent children; collected money from employers and employees to underwrite old-age insurance; coordinated a federal-state unemployment system; and played a role in developing public health services, especially in rural areas. After signing the Social Security Act into law on 14 August 1935, President Franklin Delano Roosevelt named Altmeyer to the three-member Social Security Board, assigned "the duty of studying and making recommendations as to the most effective methods of providing economic security through social insurance, and as to legislation and matters of administrative policy concerning old-age pensions, unemployment compensation, accident compensation, and related subjects." Altmeyer became chairman of the board in 1937. In this capacity, he was instrumental in securing the enactment of the 1939 Social Security amendments, which expanded coverage for old-age insurance. "Social legislation," Altmeyer wrote at the time, "requires the development of new [governmental] techniques, calling for resourcefulness and imagination of a high order. Its success lies entirely in its administration."

During World War II dreams of expanding Social Security were put on hold, but Altmeyer resisted pressure from Congress and the president to scale down operations. He ridiculed the idea of finding "steel for the turrets of the Ship of State by prying a few plates off the bottom." Like other top officials, he took on additional tasks. Altmeyer became executive director of the War Manpower Commission from 1942 to 1945. Beginning in 1942 he chaired the American delegation to the first five biennial inter-American conferences on Social Security. After the United Nations was chartered, he served for seven years as a consultant on social welfare legislation.

In 1946 Altmeyer became the first commissioner of Social Security, when his growing bureaucracy was transferred to the Federal Security Agency. For the next seven years he staved off attacks by conservatives, who still hoped to rely on private initiatives and state-level schemes to provide a safety net for senior citizens and other beneficiaries. The passage of the 1950 Social Security amendments was Altmeyer's greatest legislative victory: Harry S. Truman approved a 77 percent increase in old-age insurance benefits. But his greatest achievement was probably the recruitment and retention of a cadre of men and women who would dedicate their careers to advancing social security in the United States by expanding coverage and liberalizing programs and benefits in an incremental manner.

Upon retiring from government in 1953, Altmeyer was lauded by friends and colleagues for his "remarkable gifts of patience and wisdom and understanding of human problems." Remaining active, he served as president of the National Conference on Social Work (1954–1955). He advised the governments of Iran and Turkey on social welfare matters and advised private agencies in Colombia, Peru, and Pakistan. At the time of his death, Altmeyer was serving on the board of the National Industrial Group Pension Plan and was chief appeals officer of the International Ladies' Garment Workers Union National Retirement Fund. The new Social Security Administration offices in Baltimore were named in his honor. He died in Madison, Wisconsin.

• Altmeyer traces his early career in his preface to *The Formative Years of Social Security: A Chronicle of Social Security Legislation and Administration, 1934–1954* (1966; rev. ed. 1968). The best biographical sources are the accounts in *Who Was Who in America*, vol. 5 (1973), p. 12, and *Current Biography* (1946), p. 14. Valuable insights can be gleaned from Martha Derthick, *Policymaking for Social Security* (1979), Carolyn Weaver, *The Crisis of Social Security: Economic and Political Origins* (1982), and W. Andrew Achenbaum, *Social Security: Visions and Revisions* (1986). Obituaries are in the *New York Times* and the *Washington Post*, both 18 Oct. 1972.

W. ANDREW ACHENBAUM

ALTSHELER, Joseph Alexander (29 Apr. 1862–5 June 1919), author of juvenile fiction, was born in Three Springs, Hart County, Kentucky, the son of Joseph Altsheler and Louise Snoddy, farmers. He attended Liberty College, Glasgow, Kentucky, and Vanderbilt University but graduated from neither school. He married Sarah Boles in 1888; they had one child. He began work as a newspaperman for the *Louisville Evening Post* in 1885 but soon moved to the *Louisville Courier-Journal*, serving as that paper's drama critic, assistant city editor, commercial editor, and, eventually, editorial paper writer. He remained there until 1892 when he accepted a position as a feature writer for the New York *World*. He continued on the staff of the *World* until his death, serving for many years as editor of that newspaper's "Thrice-a-Week Magazine."

In 1918 Altsheler was voted by the nation's public librarians the most popular author of boys' books in the United States. His recognition still rests in that area. As a young boy, he had enjoyed reading about the colonial frontier and listening to the stories about the Civil War from Union and Confederate veterans in his native Kentucky. Needing a short story one day to complete an edition of his magazine section but distressed by the then extremely popular Horatio Alger stories for young boys, he wrote his own, using some of the tales he had first heard a generation earlier. It was well received, and Altsheler never looked back. In 1896 he published his first full-length novel, *The Hidden Mine*. It was quickly followed by *The Rainbow of Gold* (1896), *A Soldier of Manhattan, and His Adventures at Ticonderoga and Quebec* (1897), *The Sun of Saratoga: A Romance of Burgoyne's Surrender* (1897), and *A Herald of the West: An American Story of 1811–1815* (1898). During the Spanish-American War, Altsheler served as his newspaper's Honolulu correspondent, but after his return to New York, his writing of juvenile books began again in earnest. Between 1900 and 1919 he wrote and published forty-two new novels for boys. He attempted only one adult work of fiction, a novel titled *The Candidate: A Political Romance* (1905). It was poorly received.

Altsheler is best known for six separate series of books that he authored: the French and Indian War Series, the Great West Series, the Young Trailers Series, the Texas Series, the Civil War Series, and the World War Series. Reviewers were always full of praise for his realistic portrayals of "the smell of powder and the crack of the rifle," which, one critic noted, "every good American enjoys." Probably his most popular books, and the ones most intimately connected with him during his life, are the eight volumes of the Young Trailer Series: *The Young Trailers: A Story of Early Kentucky* (1907), *The Forest Runners: A Story of the Great War Trail in Early Kentucky* (1908), *The Free Rangers: A Story of Early Days along the Mississippi* (1909), *The Riflemen of the Ohio: A Story of Early Days along "The Beautiful River"* (1910), *The Scouts of the Valley: A Story of Wyoming and the Chemung* (1911), *The Border Watch: A Story of the Great Chief's Last Stand* (1912), *The Keepers of the Trail: A Story of the Great Woods* (1916), and *The Eyes of the Woods: A Story of the Ancient Wilderness* (1917). These books, their facts carefully authenticated, feature young Henry Ware, the quintessential American frontiersman, and a number of his companions as they travel west, first into Kentucky and then, ultimately, throughout most of the Indian-dominated frontier. Believing, as he noted in the introduction to *The Border Watch*, that "the conquest of the North American continent at a vast expense of life and suffering is in reality one of the world's greatest epics," Altsheler painted an exciting but honest picture of frontier life, one filled with immense hardships and danger. Epic pioneer heroes, cruel Indians, and renegade villains appear in every novel, but all were based closely on thoughtful research. The weak, stereotypical figures so often seen in other juvenile books of the era never appear. It was what a generation of young American boys, especially those who had never experienced rural life, desired. Millions of America's urban youngsters such as Saul Bellow had their ideas of the West shaped by Altsheler's vision of the wilderness as a place where a boy could live in harmony with nature, overcome its challenges courageously, and find, in so doing, both "glamour and reality."

At the beginning of World War I in the summer of 1914, Altsheler and his family, traveling in Europe, were trapped in Germany. His experiences near the front lines during the next few months provided him with material for such uncharacteristically grim volumes as *The Forest of Swords: A Story of Paris and the Marne* (1915) or *The Guns of Europe* (1915), but the ordeal broke his health, and he never fully recovered. He died in New York City.

Altsheler was a natural storyteller. During his peak years, he wrote no fewer than two full-length novels per year; in 1915 he published five. Many, especially those dealing with the trans-Appalachian frontier and the Civil War, remained popular long after his death, being reprinted by Appleton-Century-Crofts as many as twenty different times, the last as recently as 1967. Today, however, all are out of print. Virtually no libraries possess copies, and though his reputation as an important writer for boys remains, few young readers are aware of his exciting and often excellent work.

• There are no collections of Altsheler's personal papers. A brief, yet dated, biographical sketch is in Annie Carroll Moore, *Joseph A. Altsheler and American History* (1919). A thoughtful analysis of his Young Trailer Series is William H. Slavick, "Joseph Altsheler's Kentucky Frontier Epic: Manifest Destiny and the Hero Ollie Gatsby Isn't," *Consumable Goods II* (1988), pp. 327–37. His forty-eight novels are chronologically listed in George Kelley, "Joseph A(lexander) Altsheler," *Twentieth Century Children's Writers* (1989), pp. 23–24. An obituary is in the *New York Times*, 7 June 1919.

M. PAUL HOLSINGER

ALVAREZ, Francisco Sanchez (29 Nov. 1928–31 Mar. 1980), chemist, was born in Jalapa, Veracruz, Mexico. Little is known of his childhood, including the names of his parents. He prepared for college studies at Christopher Columbus College, then received his B.S. in chemistry in 1948 at the National University of Mexico in Mexico City. In 1953, while working toward a Chem.D. at the same institution, he joined the chemical firm of Syntex (Mexico) as a research assistant. The following year he married Yolanda Dragonne, with whom he would have four children. In 1955, after earning his doctorate, Alvarez moved to Cambridge, Massachusetts, where he remained for two years, first as a research fellow working for the noted Harvard chemist Louis Fieser (1955–1956) and then as a Camille Dreyfus fellow (1956–1957). On his return to Mexico Syntex made him a group leader, organic chemistry, a position he held from 1957 to 1960, when he became a department head. In 1964 Alvarez moved to Palo Alto, California, the site of the central research facility of Syntex (now Roche Laboratories). Initially a senior research chemist, he became a group leader, organic chemistry, in 1967 and a department head in 1968, remaining in that capacity until his death. He also was named principal scientist in 1973.

Alvarez was peripherally associated with the research efforts of Carl Djerassi, noted for his development of chemical methods of birth control ("the pill"). Alvarez was named co-inventor in a number of the production patents for Norethindrone, a steroid component of birth control pills marketed by a half-dozen or more pharmaceutical companies. His name is associated also with the fluorinated glucocorticoid Synalar, which is used as a topical anti-inflammatory and antipruritic. His other research interests included prostaglandins, the fatty acid–derived compounds that display hormonal activity in the body; nonsteroidal anti-inflammatory and antiarthritic drugs; anabolic and antiandrogenic compounds; and large-scale drug production methods. He was named as co-inventor in some eighty drug patents; he produced fifteen research papers published in the chemical literature; and he was a member of the American Chemical Society.

Alvarez lived in Sunnyvale, California, but he was found dead in a hotel room in nearby Mountain View. The Santa Clara County Medical Examiner's Office ruled the death a suicide by cyanide poisoning.

• Material on Francisco "Pancho" Alvarez is thin. He is featured in the twelfth edition only of *American Men and Women of Science*. Nearly identical thumbnail sketches appear in Matt S. Meier and Feliciano Rivera, eds., *Dictionary of Mexican American History* (1981), and in Meier, *Mexican American Biographies: A Historical Dictionary, 1836–1987* (1988); these add little to *American Men and Women of Science*. An obituary and death notice are in the *San Jose Mercury News*, 2 Apr. 1980; these too provide little additional information other than to identify his children and relatives by name.

ROBERT M. HAWTHORNE JR.

ALVAREZ, Luis Walter (13 June 1911–1 Sept. 1988), physicist and inventor, was born in San Francisco, California, the son of Walter Clement Alvarez, a physician, and Harriet Smyth, a teacher. Alvarez attended the University of Chicago from 1928 to 1936, earning his bachelor of science degree in physics in 1932, his master of science in 1934, and his Ph.D. in 1936. Alvarez married Geraldine Smithwick on 15 April 1936. He had two children with her, including the geologist Walter Alvarez. The marriage ended in divorce. Alvarez married Janet Lucile Landis in 1958 and had two children with her. Alvarez held forty patents for inventions in radar, optics, and electronics. For his work with liquid hydrogen bubble chambers he was awarded the Nobel Prize in physics in 1968.

Alvarez made his first important discovery, the "east-west effect" in cosmic rays, as a graduate student under the direction of Arthur Compton. Using a pair of Geiger counters, Alvarez detected more cosmic rays in the western sky than in the east, demonstrating that most cosmic rays are positively charged. This work was more notable than his dissertation, "A Study of the Diffraction Grating at Grazing Incidence."

Upon receiving his doctorate from Chicago, Alvarez took a position under Ernest Lawrence at the Lawrence Radiation Laboratory at the University of California at Berkeley. He started as a research associate in 1936, advancing to the rank of instructor in 1938, assistant professor in 1939, associate professor in 1941, and professor in 1946. His first four years at the lab were extremely productive, resulting in a series of fundamental discoveries. During this time he made the first experimental demonstration of K-electron capture by nuclei, developed a technique for producing a beam of slow neutrons, discovered the isotopes hydrogen 3 and helium 3, and made the first measurement of the magnetic moment of the neutron. During these years, Alvarez honed his expertise not just in nuclear physics but also in the collaborative approach to science and the utilization of industrial-scale equipment and commensurate monetary resources in science, as pioneered by Lawrence in Berkeley.

Alvarez took leave from Lawrence's lab to work on military projects in the Radar Research and Development section of the Radiation Laboratory at the Massachusetts Institute of Technology (MIT) from 1940 to 1943. There he was responsible for the development of several important radar systems. The Ground Controlled Approach (GCA) system is the best known of these: a "blind" landing system designed to allow military aircraft to land in conditions of low visibility, GCA made Allied aerial bombing of Germany feasible in weather conditions previously unsuitable for flight. The system was adapted after the war to make civilian air travel safer as well. Alvarez also invented VIXEN, an airborne radar system that allowed air patrols to detect German submarines on the surface without alerting the submarine radar operator that they were under surveillance. Submarines in World War II spent most of their time on the surface, submerging only to hide from air patrols or to approach enemy ships. The Germans had learned to submerge and hide from an approaching radar signal; VIXEN was designed so that the signal received by the target became weaker as VIXEN got closer. In addition to developing these systems, Alvarez also promoted their use and demonstrated the prototypes to military authorities in the United States and England.

While Alvarez was working on radar systems at MIT, many of America's physicists were developing the first atomic bomb. Alvarez's mentor Lawrence adapted his cyclotrons to the problem of separating isotopes of uranium and provided a constant link between Alvarez and the bomb project. In 1943 Alvarez left the Radiation Laboratory at MIT for the University of Chicago Metallurgical Laboratory, where he worked under Enrico Fermi on instrumentation for the first nuclear reactor. Six months later, Alvarez was transferred to the explosives division at Los Alamos, New Mexico, to work on the timing mechanism that synchronized the detonation of the explosives that start the nuclear reaction in the plutonium bomb.

Alvarez also worked on the problem of yield assessment. He designed, tested, and operated the systems that measured the power of the atomic bombs and flew as a scientific observer on the Hiroshima mission. At the end of World War II, Alvarez returned to the University of California and turned his attention back to the construction of progressively larger particle accelerators. By building larger accelerators, more energetic nuclear collisions could be arranged, facilitating a better understanding of the physics of subatomic particles. He was responsible for the design and construction of the forty-foot proton accelerator built in Berkeley in 1947.

Alvarez's career took a major turn in 1953 when he met Donald Glaser, the inventor of the bubble chamber. The bubble chamber is an instrument used to detect and record the paths of subatomic particles. The chamber contains a liquid very near the state where it will boil and become a gas. When a subatomic particle passes through the chamber, small bubbles of vapor form where the particle passed through, leaving a trail of bubbles behind as evidence of the journey. A magnetic field of known intensity is placed near the chamber so that charged particles will be deflected. The direction of this deflection will indicate the charge, and the amount of deflection will indicate the mass. By photographing these bubble trails and analyzing the photographs, physicists can then infer the speed, charge, and mass of the particles that left the trails.

Alvarez and his group made dramatic improvements to all three components of the bubble-chamber detection system—the chamber itself, the devices for recording and measuring tracks, and the computerized data analysis system—allowing them to study effectively the particle collisions created by the world's largest accelerators.

Where Glaser's bubble chambers contained ether and were characteristically one or two inches in diameter, Alvarez envisioned a much larger instrument. He used liquid hydrogen, which simplified the nuclear reactions that occurred within the chamber, and, in the spirit of his mentor Lawrence, started making progressively larger instruments. His first chamber was a cylinder 1.5 inches in diameter. He followed this with chambers of 2.5, 3, and 4 inches in diameter. He then built a rectangular chamber 72 inches in length. The smaller chambers started producing results in 1957; the 72-inch chamber began operation in 1959.

Alvarez also automated the analysis of the photographs, developing equipment to record data from the tracks and store them on punched cards for analysis by computers. The computers were programmed to make use of the laws of conservation of momentum and energy to deduce the missing information in the interactions. For fifteen years Alvarez developed the techniques and equipment used in bubble-chamber photography, analyzing millions of photographs each year in search of rare and short-lived subatomic particles. The Alvarez group discovered a large number of fundamental particles, including both mesons and hyperons. These particles had been unexpected by theorists and led to the theory of quarks. The tools and techniques that Alvarez developed were adopted by physics labs around the world, including the Rutherford Lab in England and CERN in Switzerland.

Alvarez applied his expertise in nuclear physics and particle detection to a variety of other problems, most notably his work from 1964 to 1969 on the Second Pyramid at Giza. Archaeologists had discovered three chambers in the Great Pyramid of Cheops and two chambers in the Pyramid of Sneferu, but no chamber was known to exist in Chephren's Pyramid at Giza. Alvarez proposed that they "X-ray" the pyramid, measuring the resistance that it presented to cosmic ray muons going through it. By setting muon detectors in a chamber under the pyramid, Alvarez and the Joint UAR-USA Pyramid Project were able to demonstrate that the Second Pyramid is solid.

In 1979, collaborating with his son, the geologist Walter Alvarez, Alvarez produced a theory regarding the extinction of the dinosaurs. Walter had discovered that a thin layer of rocks separating Cretaceous and Tertiary rocks contained a much higher than normal level of one isotope of iridium. Luis hypothesized that the iridium was the scattered remains of a huge asteroid that had struck the earth 65 million years ago. He argued that the dust thrown into the air after the impact blocked so much sunlight that photosynthesis by plants was virtually halted, leaving large animals such as the dinosaurs with an insufficient food supply. The correlation of the iridium layer with the impact of a large comet or asteroid was accepted by paleontologists, but Alvarez's conclusions about the resulting mass extinction remained controversial long after his death in Berkeley.

Alvarez built a career in physics by embracing the best parts of his colleagues' instruments, improving them in dramatic fashion, and exploiting the power of large-scale efforts in large laboratories. Though he later expressed disdain for this committee approach to science, he was a master of collaborative research. He was best known among physicists for his work in particle physics and among scientists in general for his impact theory of dinosaur extinction. His career exemplified the culmination of the trend toward big science that was initiated in the United States by the work of Ernest Lawrence and accelerated by the rush to build the atomic bomb.

• Alvarez's papers are in RG 326 and 434 of the Pacific Science Regional Archives, National Archives and Records Administration, San Bruno, Calif. His autobiography is *Alvarez: Adventures of a Physicist* (1987). W. Peter Trower, ed., *Discovering Alvarez: Selected Works of Luis W. Alvarez, with Commentary by His Students and Colleagues* (1987), is a collection of 21 of Alvarez's scientific papers. Appendices list 169 articles and 40 patents. The transcript of an interview conducted in February 1967, a year and a half before the announcement of his Nobel Prize, is on file at the Niels Bohr Library of the American Institute of Physics. An extensive obituary by two of his collaborators, Gerson Goldhaber and Wolfgang Panofsky, is in *Physics Today* (June 1989).

CRAIG SEAN MCCONNELL

ALVAREZ, Manuel (1794–5 July 1856), merchant and U.S. consul, was born in Abelgas, León, Spain, the son of Don José Alvarez and Doña María Antonia Arias. Alvarez spent his childhood in his native village in the Cantabrian Mountains. Under the care of his parents, he became proficient in both French and Spanish. As a youth he wanted to become a writer. An avid reader, he was familiar with the writings of Thomas Carlyle, Sir Walter Raleigh, and Benjamin Franklin. His private notebooks reflect his interest in history; he wrote on the American Revolution and on Hernán Cortés's conquest of Mexico. In 1818 Alvarez left for Mexico in search of adventure. In 1823 he went to Havana, Cuba, where he received a U.S. passport. Within a year he sailed to New York, then traveled to Missouri.

From the trappers and traders who congregated in St. Louis, Alvarez learned about the recently opened Santa Fe Trail and the business opportunities available in Mexico's northern department, New Mexico. On 30 September 1824 he and eleven companions began the journey across the plains for New Mexico. They arrived in Taos in late November. In Santa Fe Alvarez opened a store, which he built into one of the major mercantile enterprises in the Southwest. Mexico denied Alvarez's application for citizenship because the passport papers Missouri's governor Alexander McNair had written referred to him as a U.S. citizen. Alvarez stayed in New Mexico and became a landowner by allowing the Mexican officials to believe he was a naturalized citizen.

From 1828 to 1833 Alvarez worked as a fur trader in the central Rockies. He was one of the discoverers of the natural wonders of present-day Yellowstone National Park. In 1839 the Americans in New Mexico petitioned successfully to have Alvarez named U.S. consul to Mexico. He served in this capacity until 1846, overseeing the rights of American citizens who came into Mexico's northern settlements. Most of them were merchants or trappers who complained of Mexico's methods in imposing taxes. Despite his impatience with governmental red tape, Alvarez liked and admired the Mexican people.

In September 1841 Mexican authorities captured the Santa Fe expedition, a detachment of Texans who expected to be welcomed by New Mexicans anxious to join the Republic of Texas. Among those taken prisoner were several Americans, including George Wilkens Kendall, editor of the *New Orleans Picayune*, who had used the expedition to get to Santa Fe as a journalist. Alvarez protested that to imprison American citizens, along with the Texans, was to disgrace the U.S. government, and because of his stance, he suffered theft, physical assault, and attempted murder at the hands of the local Mexican officials. He met with Charles Bent, later governor of New Mexico, and James Magoffin, an experienced trader, to discuss extralegal means of freeing Kendall. They raised $3,000 and offered it to Governor Manuel Armijo for the release of Kendall and former Mexican senator Antonio Navarro, to show that they were not wholly partial to the Americans. Armijo rejected the offer and withheld passports from Alvarez and fifteen Americans until 25 October 1841.

By February 1842 Alvarez was in Washington, D.C., protesting to Secretary of State Daniel Webster about the injuries suffered by American citizens in New Mexico. He presented a 32-page memorial, carefully footnoted, with over sixty letters substantiating its text. The State Department replied that the new minister to Mexico, Waddy Thompson, would make proper representations to that government. Two weeks later Alvarez petitioned on his own behalf. He told of the attempt on his life, claiming that, although the Mexican government had recognized him as the U.S. consul, the local authorities had given neither reparations nor an apology. For this and for losses incurred on the trail, he asked for a total indemnity of $22,700. Webster replied that he could not request compensations from the Mexican government because Alvarez was not a U.S. citizen. Disgusted with Webster's attitude, Alvarez became a naturalized citizen on 9 April 1842 in St. Louis. Witnesses Theodore Papin and Pascal L. Cerri lied on his behalf, certifying that he had resided in the United States for at least five years and in the state of Missouri at least one year.

On his return trip to New Mexico, Alvarez found Texans seeking to disrupt the Santa Fe trade. At the Arkansas crossing, he met Colonel Jacob Snively and 180 men waiting to ambush a westbound caravan under the protection of Captain Philip St. George Cooke of the U.S. Army. Alvarez feared that such plunder would alienate all Santa Fe Trail merchants. Therefore he and Bent had dinner with Captain Cooke on 16 June 1843 and informed him that both the Texans and Governor Armijo planned to attack the caravan. Cooke, anxious to avoid an international dispute, took his guests' information very seriously. When he met Snively and his force, he disarmed them and announced that the Union wished to protect its trade routes.

From summer 1843 to spring 1844 Alvarez traveled throughout the United States and Europe on personal merchandising business. He returned in 1844 to Santa Fe, where he sold textiles and other goods from New York and London. In 1847 he was elected as a representative to the legislative general assembly of New Mexico during American occupation.

In 1848 Mexico ceded most of New Mexico to the United States in the Treaty of Guadalupe Hidalgo. Alvarez led the new territory's first statehood party, a group made up primarily of Hispanic people, who petitioned Congress for statehood. He was elected lieutenant governor in the unsuccessful bid for statehood in 1850. In 1851 he was appointed a brigadier general in the New Mexico militia. He served on the Public Building Commission from 1853 to 1854.

In the early 1850s Alvarez became aware of the potential profits from herding sheep and mules to the California minefields. He played an integral role in the New Mexico–California sheep industry, helping to raise capital and to buy sheep for three major drives.

By 1854 Alvarez had retired from public life, but he kept up with current affairs. He supported southern New Mexico's attempt to become a separate territory, suggesting it be named Cibola. He also continued to work as a business agent for others.

Alvarez traveled to Europe in 1855, perhaps to see his family. He was unable to correspond because of painful rheumatism. It is not known whether he traveled to Spain. After coming home in the late fall, he continued operating his store as usual. On 26 February 1856 Judge Miguel F. Pino named him to the Santa Fe County Board of Education.

Alvarez died in Santa Fe. He never married. Alvarez's mercantile and diplomatic activities contributed to the economic growth and political development of the southwestern United States before the Civil War. His life and career still challenge those who would restrict immigration and foreign trade.

• Papers of Alvarez are in the Mexican Archives of New Mexico, New Mexico State Records Center and Archives, Santa Fe. Additional material is in Dispatches from U.S. Consuls in Santa Fe, Mexico, Manuel Alvarez, 1839–1846, RG 59, National Archives, Washington, D.C. The History Library of the Palace of the Governors, Santa Fe, has a copy of the dispatches. Thomas E. Chávez, ed., *Conflict and Acculturation: Manuel Alvarez's 1842 Memorial* (1989), is a good example of the consul's lucid prose. Chávez is the primary authority on Alvarez, and his works include "The Life and Times of Manuel Alvarez 1794–1856" (Ph.D. diss., Univ. of New Mexico, 1980), *Manuel Alvarez 1794–1856: A Southwestern Biography* (1990), and "Manuel Alvarez and the Santa Fe Trail: Beyond Geographical Circumstances," *La Gaceta* 9, no. 2. El Corral de Santa Fe Westerners (1985). George Kendall, *Narrative of the Texan–Santa Fe Expedition* (1844), portrays Alvarez as a hero.

DIANNE JENNINGS WALKER

ALVAREZ, Walter Clement (22 July 1884–16 June 1978), physician, medical researcher, and medical columnist, was born in San Francisco, California, the son of Luis Fernandez Alvarez, a physician, and Clementina Schuetze. When Alvarez was three, his family moved to Hawaii, where his father was a government physician in two isolated Oahu villages. Alvarez was eleven when his father established a Honolulu hospital for lepers and attempted to develop a serum to combat the disease. While assisting his father, Alvarez resolved to become a physician.

In 1901 Alvarez entered Cooper Medical College (forerunner of Stanford University Medical School), from which he earned an M.D. in 1905. As an intern at San Francisco City and County Hospital between

1905 and 1906, Alvarez treated the injured of the famous 1906 earthquake. During his internship, he confirmed Fritz Richard Schaudinn's discovery of the *Spirochaeta pallida* (the microorganism that causes syphilis) and reported it in *Journal of the American Medical Association* (46 [1906]: 1687), in the first of hundreds of medical publications from his prolific pen. Between 1906 and 1907, he was a clinical pathology instructor in the Cooper College wards of the hospital.

In 1907 Alvarez moved to the Cananea mining camp in Sonora, Mexico, as a replacement for his retiring father. Over the next three years he cared for the area's impoverished people, while learning folklore to reinforce treatment and developing the ability to recognize hysteria; the latter helped him to focus his deep interest in psychosomatic medicine. He married Harriet Skidmore Smyth in 1907; they had four children, of whom one, Luis Walter Alvarez, became a Nobel prize winner in physics.

At the invitation of his former professor Emile Schmoll, Alvarez returned to assist Schmoll in San Francisco in January 1910. Under Schmoll's tutelage, Alvarez acquired internal medicine training and was introduced to the new science of dietetics, through Schmoll's use of low-calorie reducing diets. Alvarez also became proficient at conducting, for area physicians, the new diagnostic test for syphilis that was developed by German bacteriologist August Paul von Wassermann. He became Schmoll's partner and held medical assistantships in San Francisco Polyclinic in 1910 and Stanford University School of Medicine from 1911 to 1912.

In early 1913 Alvarez spent a few months with pioneer Harvard physiologist Walter B. Cannon, who had generously offered his laboratory for the study of flatulence. While conducting this research, Alvarez stumbled onto a more interesting phenomenon—the differences in the progress of waves in the walls of the intestines. Encouraged by Cannon, Alvarez spent much of his early career researching the gradients of these movements in the intestines and the stomach.

Between 1913 and 1925 Alvarez practiced internal medicine in San Francisco, initially sharing an office with Carl L. Hoag, a young surgeon. With only a minimal laboratory, Alvarez was elated when the University of California at San Francisco established the George Williams Hooper Foundation for Medical Research, at which he was offered a physiology laboratory plus a research medicine appointment in 1915. During the next decade Alvarez worked mornings at Hooper, gathering intestinal gradient data in animals and some humans while seeing patients in the afternoons. He became the first to record electrogastrograms—records of electrical changes occurring in the stomach muscles during their contraction—in humans. His investigations were reported in some forty scientific papers and a 1922 book, *The Mechanics of the Digestive Tract*, which went through four editions. Also, between 1918 and 1919, Alvarez studied statistical methods and published an analysis of some 16,000 blood-pressure readings in young people.

At the university, Alvarez became associate professor of research medicine in 1924. The success of his investigations brought election to membership in a number of prestigious research societies, including the Association of American Physicians in 1924. In 1920 he gave the first Caldwell Lecture of the American Roentgen Ray Society. Alvarez's presidency of the American Gastroenterological Association in 1928 began his acquisition of a series of honors and professional association memberships in the United States and abroad.

In the 1920s an increase in Alvarez's number of patients had begun to limit his research opportunities. He began seeking a balance. By chance, William J. Mayo, co-founder of the Mayo Clinic, America's pioneer private group practice of medicine, learned of his situation. As a result, Alvarez was appointed a Mayo consultant in medicine and an associate professor of medicine in the Mayo Foundation for Medical Education and Research (later the Mayo Graduate School of Medicine). Arriving in Rochester, Minnesota, on 1 February 1926, he started a 25-year career at Mayo. He later became head of a section of medicine, and in 1934, a professor of medicine.

Initially, Alvarez worked mornings in his laboratory and in the afternoons saw clinic patients with stomach complaints. In the laboratory, his collaboration with Arnold Zimmerman produced the first movies of digestive tract movement in anesthetized rabbits. Produced in 1926, the unique film was widely shown to the profession. Afterwards, between 1926 and 1930, George Little, a Mayo mechanic, helped him design and construct an X-ray motion picture machine that recorded digestive tract movements. Besides his laboratory interests, Alvarez promoted the development of Mayo's medical statistics department and recruited the first statisticians. In 1935 he helped inaugurate Mayo's Museum of Hygiene and Medicine, which featured educational exhibits for the general public.

In clinic consultations, Alvarez primarily saw patients with gastric complaints who suffered digestive neuroses, stomach pains for which no abdominal cause had been found. Diagnosis of their complex problems was taxing, but Alvarez's care in history taking and interpretation solved many of his patients' complaints. As patient numbers grew, Alvarez became caught up in writing on gastrointestinal neuroses, food allergy, constitutional inadequacy, and migraine. In 1930 his *Nervous Indigestion*, a volume written for the layperson, was a sellout. Other works followed, some directed to the professional, and others, the general reader.

A colorful, direct speaker and writer, Alvarez held strong opinions on a number of issues. He opposed the practice of "decebrate" (unthinking) medicine, full of routine but lacking in a good medical history. He particularly disliked psychoanalysis and its "unintelligible gobbledegook." In addition, he favored treating the dying patient with frankness, indulgence, and generous drugs to dull the pain.

Alvarez's affinity for medical exposition led to editorial appointments with *American Journal of Digestive Diseases and Nutrition* (1938–1942), *Gastroenterology* (1943–1950), *General Practitioner* (1950), *Modern Medicine* (1951–1975), and *Geriatrics* (1952–1975). Following his retirement from Mayo in 1950, Alvarez settled in Chicago, where he continued editing and publishing works, including special-interest booklets for lay readers, many of which later appeared in several languages. *How to Live with Your Nerves* (1950) was translated into nine languages and read worldwide. In 1952 Alvarez produced a new medical column that appeared four times weekly in the New York *Herald-Tribune* and was syndicated in more than eighty papers with a readership of some twelve million. In 1975 he retired from his Chicago activities and returned to San Francisco, where he died.

• A collection of fifty-three annual diaries kept by Alvarez is at the Lane Medical Library, Stanford University. Alvarez's extensive correspondence with Walter B. Cannon between 1913 and Cannon's death is in the Papers of Walter B. Cannon, Countway Medical Library, Harvard University. Alvarez's two autobiographies are *Incurable Physician: An Autobiography* (1963) and *Alvarez on Alvarez* (1977). Among the most significant of Alvarez's hundreds of publications are *Nervousness, Indigestion, and Pain* (1943); *The Neuroses: Diagnosis and Management of Functional Disorders and Minor Psychoses* (1951); *Danger Signals: Warnings of Serious Diseases* (1953); *Minds that Came Back* (1961); and *Little Strokes* (1966). Biographical sources include R. C. Pruitt, "Walter C. Alvarez," *Transactions of the Association of American Physicians* 95 (1982): xcii–xcv; and F. G. Lloyd, "Medicine's Mark Twain," *Today's Health*, May 1969, pp. 52–55. An obituary is in the *New York Times*, 20 June 1978.

CLARK W. NELSON

ÁLVAREZ DE PINEDA, Alonso (?–1520), ship captain and explorer, is presumed to have been born in Spain, although neither his place of birth nor the names of his parents are known. In the spring of 1519 Álvarez de Pineda was commissioned by Francisco de Garay, Spanish governor of Jamaica, to explore the still unknown northern Gulf Coast between the discoveries of Juan Ponce de León in Florida and those made on behalf of Diego Velázquez in the southern gulf. The stated purpose of the voyage was to search for a strait to the Pacific Ocean. Probably in late March of that year, Álvarez sailed from Jamaica with four ships and 270 men, about six weeks after Hernán Cortés left Cuba on the expedition that led to the Mexican Conquest.

Approaching the coast of western Florida, Álvarez sailed east, then south. He thus proved Florida a part of the mainland and not an island as Ponce de León had supposed. He continued until contrary wind and current forced him to turn back and then ran the coast from the Florida Keys to Villa Rica de la Vera Cruz, Cortés's nascent settlement on the Mexican coast. While sailing west on or about the day of Pentecost—2 June 1519 by the Julian calendar—he perceived the mighty outflow of the Mississippi River and named it, for the holy day, Río del Espíritu Santo (River of the Holy Ghost).

Anchored off Villa Rica, some thirty-five miles up the coast from the present Mexican city of Veracruz, Álvarez sent six men ashore to treat with Cortés. The conqueror-to-be seized the emissaries and employed trickery to get the captain to come ashore. Álvarez, suspecting the treachery, weighed anchor and sailed north in late July or early August 1519.

A witness to these proceedings was Bernal Díaz del Castillo, historian of the Mexican Conquest, the only source to identify Álvarez de Pineda by name. Díaz relates that Álvarez had established a settlement on a river "thirty leagues" north of Almería, or Nautla. The river afterward was shown to be the Río Pánuco. Neither this information nor the captain's name was revealed by Garay when, a few months later, he petitioned the Spanish Crown for permission to establish a settlement on the basis of Álvarez's discoveries.

The ships returned to Jamaica in late fall 1519. Circumstantial evidence suggests that Álvarez himself and a number of his companions remained on the Río Pánuco to continue the work of establishing a settlement among the Huastecs. In January 1520 a ship commanded by Diego de Camargo sailed from Jamaica with supplies for the Pánuco colony. Soon after Camargo arrived the settlement was besieged by the Huastecs. Álvarez de Pineda and all the colonists were slain, Díaz del Castillo relates (vol. 2, p. 104), except about sixty who were evacuated by Camargo and sailed south to join Cortés's army of conquest.

Garay's actual petition for colonization rights to the region discovered by Álvarez is not known. The few known details of the voyage come from the royal patent, whereby Garay was granted the concession he sought. Although it fails to acknowledge that settlement already had begun on the Río Pánuco, the document relates that on the return voyage Álvarez had sailed six leagues up a large and fluent river; remaining there for forty days, he careened his ships. Regional historians have been wont to identify this river as the Río de las Palmas (the colonial name for the Río Soto la Marina in the Mexican state of Tamaulipas), the Rio Grande, or even the Mississippi. Bernal Díaz, however, clearly shows it to have been the Río Pánuco.

The map of the gulf attributed to Álvarez or his pilots was found in the Spanish archives, attached to the royal patent, which attributes it to the voyage. It survives today in the Archive of the Indies in Seville. The patent, referring to the territory explored as the "province of Amichel," describes a healthful and fruitful land with accessible ports and rivers yielding fine gold. The precious metal, it is said, was evidenced by "affectionate" natives who adorned themselves with gold jewelry. The document also tells of a diversity of peoples, including giants more than seven feet tall and dwarfs attaining a height of scarcely four. Thus the Álvarez voyage seems certainly to have been responsible for some of the place names on the 1529 map by Diogo Ribeiro, a Portuguese cosmographer in the service of

Spain. The Álvarez map sketch is devoid of toponyms between the Río del Espíritu Santo (Mississippi) and the Río Pánuco, yet there was no other voyage from which Ribeiro might have heard of a "River of Gold" and a "River of Giants."

After the disastrous failure of the colony Álvarez had begun, Garay himself sought to renew the effort in 1523. But the royal tide had changed; his authority, superseded. Garay and his sizable fleet reached the Río Pánuco to find Cortés forces in charge. His own force, seduced by tales of Aztec riches, dwindled rapidly by defection. Garay, going to the City of Mexico to treat personally with Cortés, became ill and died there, probably of pneumonia.

Álvarez de Pineda's discovery of the northern Gulf of Mexico coast ended in personal tragedy for both himself and his patron. Yet his map and word descriptions provided insight for European cartographers and cosmographers as they pieced together an image of the New World. He gave shape to the Gulf of Mexico, the existence of which was scarcely known a decade previously. Written histories of all the southern states west of Florida as well as of Tamaulipas may yet begin with the statement, "The first European to glimpse these shores was Alonso Álvarez de Pineda."

• The map attributed to Álvarez de Pineda, "Traza de las costas de Tierra Firme y de las Tierras Nuevas," is preserved in the Archivo General de Indias, Seville, Spain. Bernal Díaz del Castillo, *Historia verdadera de la conquista de la Nueva España* (1955), identifies Alonso Álvarez de Pineda as captain of the four ships sent out by Francisco de Garay and names Álvarez as the head of the settlement on the Río Pánuco. Sources that have to do with the voyage and the settlement but fail to identify the leader include the royal patent to Garay, "Real cédula dando facultad a Francisco de Garay para poblar la provincia de Amichel," in Martín Fernández de Navarrete, *Colección de los viages y descubrimientos que hicieron por mar los españoles* (1955), vol. 3, pp. 147–53, and the "Probanza de méritos y servicios" of Alonso García Bravo, in the Archivo General de Indias. More recent works that treat Álvarez de Pineda and his voyage in proper context include Donald E. Chipman, *Nuño de Guzmán and the Province of Pánuco in New Spain, 1518–1533* (1967), pp. 47–51, and Robert S. Weddle, *Spanish Sea: The Gulf of Mexico in North American Discovery, 1500–1685* (1985), pp. 94–108. The influence that the Álvarez voyage had on Gulf Coast cartography and toponymy is discussed in Weddle, "Exploration of the Texas Coast: Álvarez de Pineda to La Salle," *Gulf Coast Historical Review* 8 (Fall 1992): 31–41.

ROBERT S. WEDDLE

ALVORD, Clarence Walworth (21 May 1868–24 Jan. 1928), historian, was born in Greenfield, Massachusetts, the son of Daniel Wells, a lawyer, and Caroline Betts Dewey. He attended the schools of Northampton, Massachusetts, and Phillips Academy, Andover, and graduated from Williams College in 1891. From 1891 to 1893 he taught at Milton Academy in Massachusetts. He was married in 1893 to Jennie Kettell Blanchard Parrott. From 1893 to 1895 he did graduate work in history at Friedrich Wilhelm University in Berlin. For part of the following year, Alvord studied European history at the University of Chicago, concentrating on the Italian Renaissance. He became an instructor in the preparatory school of the University of Illinois in 1897 and in 1901 began teaching European history in the university proper. There he would stay until 1920, receiving a Ph.D. in 1908 and becoming a full professor in 1913.

In 1905 Alvord discovered the records of the French settlements of Cahokia and Kaskaskia in Illinois, long believed lost, in the town of Belleville, Illinois. This important discovery led to his appointment by the State Historical Library as general editor of the *Illinois Historical Collections*, despite his lack of editorial experience. He edited fourteen volumes of the *Collections*, which made available a large number of original documents relating not only to Illinois history, but also to the history of the upper Mississippi Valley region. His introduction to the *Cahokia Records* (1907) provides a concise, insightful overview of the County of Illinois created by Virginia in 1778. In 1909 Alvord was appointed director of the Illinois Historical Survey, created within the University of Illinois as a research bureau and clearinghouse for historical materials on Illinois and the Mississippi Valley. Alvord became a specialist in midwestern history who emphasized development of the West as the key to understanding national history and was determined uncover sources on midwestern and Illinois history. His research into the early years of the Midwest and the British role in its development culminated in *The First Exploration of the Trans-Allegheny Regions by Virginians, 1650–1674*, published in 1912 in collaboration with Lee Bidgood.

Alvord's first wife had died in 1911, and in 1913 he married Idress Head. In 1913 the Illinois Centennial Commission appointed Alvord editor of the five-volume *Centennial History of Illinois*. He wrote the first volume, *The Illinois Country, 1673–1818* (1920), which became an invaluable contribution to the historical record of the Midwest.

Known for his editorial and organizational skills, Alvord juggled many projects at once, yet was able to give his attention to all equally. His best-known individual achievement is *Mississippi Valley in British Politics* (1917), a two-volume work that covered the period from 1763 to 1774 in the Illinois region during the American Revolution. This work was recognized by scholars in America and abroad as an outstanding contribution to English history, to the study of the causes of the American Revolution, and to the history of the Mississippi Valley. Alvord's use of rare English political pamphlets and other previously unused sources gave his work even more importance, opening study into new areas of Mississippi Valley history. In 1918 the book received the Loubat prize for the best work on American history published in five years, a rare public acknowledgment of Alvord's writing ability and scholarship.

One of Alvord's most lasting achievements was his role in founding the Mississippi Valley Historical Association in 1907 (renamed the Organization of American Historians in 1965). His efforts to ensure the scholarly intent of the organization kept it from becoming a loose group of historical societies. Instead Alvord urged that the association should consist of individual scholars, amateur and professional, who were interested in the history of the Mississippi Valley region. He realized the association needed to focus on further research and study of the entire region of the West. His goal was to discover the crucial links between the history of the West and Midwest and the history of the nation. To this end, in 1914 he advocated the association's establishment of a quarterly magazine, the *Mississippi Valley Historical Review*, which he edited for nine years. His tireless efforts to publish the highest-quality articles soon earned the review a reputation as the most important scholarly journal devoted to American history; this led to the renaming of the review to the Journal of American History in 1964.

In 1920 Alvord resigned his teaching, editing, and administrative positions at the University of Illinois and became professor of history at the University of Minnesota, where he was able to get better compensation. In 1923 he left the University of Minnesota to spend his time researching and writing, intending to write a history of the American Revolution that focused on events in the West. He went to England to conduct his research, but soon found himself busy with numerous projects that kept him from his work on the American Revolution. In 1925 he delivered the annual Raleigh lecture before the British Academy, speaking on the motives and influences behind the peace negotiations at the end of the American Revolution. In 1926 he became the first American chosen to deliver the Creighton lecture at the University of London, taking as his subject the politics of King George III. During the later years of his life, these projects, along with periods of illness, prevented him from completing his work on the American Revolution. He died on the Italian Riviera, at Diano Marina.

Known primarily for his work in midwestern history, Alvord was a genuine sectional historian, whose work helped open new avenues of research. He understood the importance of strong institutional backing for state and sectional historical research and favored such aid in helping historians uncover the history of the Mississippi Valley.

• The Alvord papers are at the Minnesota Historical Society in St. Paul. Solon J. Buck, "Clarence Walworth Alvord: Historian," *Mississippi Valley Historical Review* 15 (1928–1929): 309–20, 385–90, provides a good biography as well as an extensive bibliography. For a critical assessment of Alvord's work and impact on western historiography, see Marion Dargan, Jr., "Clarence Walworth Alvord" in *The Marcus W. Jernegan Essays in American Historiography*, ed. William Hutchinson (1937). For an account of Alvord's work in Illinois, see Dixon Ryan Fox, "State History II," *Political Science Quarterly* 37 (1922): 99–118.

DOMINIC F. ABRAM

ALVORD, John Watson (18 Apr. 1807–14 Jan. 1880), Congregational minister and antislavery reformer, was born in East Hampton, Connecticut, the son of James Hall Alvord, a saddle maker, and Lucy Cook. His father was an active Whig and a deacon in the local Congregational church; his mother was the daughter of Richard Cook, a revolutionary soldier. Alvord attended the common schools of Winsted, Connecticut, and upon leaving school in 1828 he worked for a prominent merchant in Hartford, Connecticut. He went to Lane Theological Seminary in Cincinnati, Ohio, where his interest in the antislavery movement began. He left Lane in 1834 because of his participation in the Lane antislavery rebellion of that year, and he received his degree from Oberlin College in 1836. Upon his graduation Alvord continued his antislavery activism and also began training to be a missionary in Africa. An illness prevented his going, and instead he preached to slaves in Florida while recovering his health.

When Alvord returned to the North, he pursued his ministerial career. He preached for two years at Barkhamstead, Connecticut, and then became associate pastor of the First Congregational Church in Stamford, Connecticut. In 1845 he married Myrtilla Mead Peck of Greenwich, Connecticut; they had eight children, five of whom died in childhood. In 1846 Alvord accepted a calling to preach at Phillips Church in Boston, Massachusetts. Although he was involved in the antislavery movement, he probably did not support William Lloyd Garrison's radical American Anti-Slavery Society; more likely he supported Lewis Tappan's American and Foreign Anti-Slavery Society. In 1852 Alvord resigned from Phillips Church because of ill health and became secretary of the American Tract Society.

The advent of the Civil War allowed Alvord to continue his ministerial and antislavery commitments. He distributed religious tracts to soldiers at the front, worked with the Sanitary and Christian Commissions, and organized schools for freedmen, becoming friends with General O. O. Howard, later commissioner of the Bureau of Refugees, Freedmen, and Abandoned Lands, also known as the Freedmen's Bureau.

In 1865 Alvord became general superintendent of education for the Freedmen's Bureau and remained in this position until 1872. During this time he worked to establish a systematic and efficient network of freedmen's schools. One of his assistants at the Freedmen's Bureau was S. Willard Saxton, brother of General Rufus Saxton, who had implemented General William Tecumseh Sherman's Field Order 15 calling for the settlement of freedmen on abandoned Confederate lands in South Carolina. Alvord and others were interested in setting up a system of schools for blacks and whites modeled on the northern common school. To facilitate this, he instituted standard examinations for both teachers and students and asked for monthly reports from his local superintendents. He also supported the establishment of normal schools for black teachers. Like many other reformers, he felt that education was the key to reconstructing the South and elevating the condition of former slaves. For Alvord, an efficient school system was the surest means to achieve progress. As he wrote in his *Fourth Semi-Annual Report*, dated 1 July 1867, "We desire that the development of this oppressed race shall prove to be a living permanent reality; and for this end these schools should be perfected in all their details."

Alvord helped establish the Freedmen's Savings Bank, becoming its president in 1868. The reform-minded founders intended the bank to teach former slaves to be frugal. However, the Freedmen's Savings Bank was in financial trouble by 1870 due to bad investments and corrupt management. In March 1874 the trustees replaced Alvord with Frederick Douglass, hoping to restore confidence in the bank by appointing a black man as president. The Freedmen's Savings Bank failed in July 1874, losing the savings of thousands of former slaves. Owing to his own financial ignorance, Alvord did not knowingly defraud the freedmen. In an attempt to recover their money, he became president of the Seneca Stone Company, one of the bank's bad investments. After the failure of the Freedmen's Savings Bank, Alvord discontinued his involvement in social reform. He died in Denver, Colorado.

Alvord was a member of a generation of activists who looked to the federal government and to voluntary reform efforts to solve the problems of the nation after the success of the antislavery movement and the Civil War. Alvord had hoped that the Freedmen's Bureau and the Freedmen's Savings Bank would allow the national government to guide the slaves' transition to freedom with the help of interested citizen reformers, but when business interests replaced the idealism of the Civil War era, he, like many reformers, retreated from public activism.

Alvord contributed to the failure of the Freedmen's Savings Bank through his lack of financial knowledge and thereby assisted one of the greatest betrayals of the freedpeople's confidence during Reconstruction. However, as superintendent of education for the Freedmen's Bureau, Alvord directed fragmented benevolent efforts to educate freedpeople. His leadership centered a movement that otherwise would have become intensely factional, and as a result education became the bureau's most important legacy to former slaves.

• Alvord's correspondence can be found in the Records of the Education Division of the Bureau of Refugees, Freedmen, and Abandoned Lands, RG 105, National Archives. His published writings on freedmen's education can be found in his *Semi-Annual Reports* (1866–1870) for the Freedmen's Bureau; see also his *Letters from the South Relating to the Condition of the Freedmen* (1870). Some description of Alvord's participation in the Lane Rebellion can be found in Lawrence Thomas Lesick, *The Lane Rebels: Evangelicalism and Antislavery in Antebellum America* (1980). For information on Alvord's time at the Freedmen's Bureau see James Anderson, *The Education of Blacks in the South, 1860–1935* (1988), and the papers of S. Willard Saxton and Rufus Saxton at Yale University. Useful histories of the Freedmen's Savings Bank are Carl R. Osthaus, *Freedmen, Philanthropy, and Fraud: A History of the Freedmen's Savings Bank* (1976), and Walter L. Fleming, *The Freedmen's Savings Bank: A Chapter in the Economic History of the Negro Race* (1927).

CAROL FAULKNER

AMBERG, George (28 Dec. 1901–27 July 1971), professor of film and dance critic, was born Hans Aschaffenburg in Halle, Germany, the son of Gustav Aschaffenburg, a prominent Jewish psychiatrist, and Maja Nebel. He was educated in Davos, Switzerland, from 1916 to 1918, at a fashionable boys' private high school where the kaiser sent his children, and also in Cologne, Munich, and Kiel. In 1923 he founded Cassette, the avant-garde theater in Cologne, and was also a stage director there. From 1924 to 1928 he worked in theatrical festivals with noted German director Gustav Hurtung, first as a dramaturge and play director at the Cologne Theater, then in 1926 at the Heidelberg Theater Festival, and thereafter in 1927–1928 as director in the Darmstadt Theater. Amberg earned his doctorate in December 1930 from the University of Cologne on the German novelist Theodor Fontane as critic. He was also a lecturer and member of the drama department at the university. From 1930 to 1933 Amberg helped to organize the University of Cologne's theater museum and also established and directed its film library and institute. His published writings from this period concerned the subject of dance. He was a contributing editor on dance to the Ullstein and Herder encyclopedias. Amberg also gave visiting lectures in Berlin, Frankfurt, Zurich, and Basel. He established a cabaret as well, which was usually considered a low-class entertainment venue, but his was experimental theater that included all of the arts.

In 1933 Amberg fled Hitler's Germany using the name de Spina, an old French Huguenot name in his mother's family. He worked as a photographer in Paris. The Vichy government gave him the choice of joining the French Foreign Legion or going back to Germany. He chose the Foreign Legion, which was demobilized shortly before France's surrender. Amberg immigrated to the United States in 1941 and became a citizen in 1946.

From 1943 to 1948 Amberg served as curator of the Dance Archives, later called the Department of Dance and Theatre Design, at the Museum of Modern Art in New York City. In the January 1944 *Museum of Modern Art Bulletin* his appointment was deemed "a post unique in American museums," and he oversaw the largest dance archives in the United States, made up in part of the Lincoln Kirstein Dance Archives, photographic slides, microfilm and books (now all housed in the Dance Collection of the New York Public Library for the Performing Arts). In documenting and analyzing the growth of ballet in the United States, Amberg met many of its rising star dancers, choreographers, and directors.

Amberg's experiences resulted in *Ballet in America* (1949), the first full-length book describing the history of ballet in the United States as well as its new personalities and trends. Amberg was also the first to pay detailed attention to American choreographers such as Agnes de Mille and Jerome Robbins. He was fascinated with their uniquely American adaptations of the classic dance form of ballet and printed their original ballet libretti in his book. The work is the only source for Robbins's *Fancy Free* and de Mille's "Laurie Makes Up Her Mind" ballet from *Oklahoma!* Also listed are the repertories of eleven ballet companies and a chronology of dance in the United States from 1767 to 1948. These elements and his insights afford important resources to readers and researchers of American dance.

Amberg's portfolio-size book *Art in Modern Ballet* (1946), which features designs for ballets, provides more examples of his viewpoints. In it he discussed the newest ballet designs, giving them a forum and a setting and showing the importance not only of the European artists but of the new American artists as well. In his introduction he wrote that while "so vast and varied a subject calls ideally for comprehensive treatment, physical limitations and wartime restrictions compelled a severe selection. . . . Rather than compromise in a hopeless attempt to please everybody, the editor endeavored to offer a truly representative survey of contemporary trends and achievements." Through his explanations, Amberg's books introduced countless readers to the magic of how the arts were combined in the ballet.

In 1946 Amberg married Gisela Engle. They had no children. He began to champion cinematography and became a leader in promoting the idea that film was a legitimate course in academic study. From 1948 to 1952 he lectured in the general education division of New York University (NYU). He then moved to Minneapolis, Minnesota, to head the Humanities Program at the University of Minnesota from 1952 to 1966, developing courses in cinema. From 1966 until his death in New York City, Amberg served as professor and chairman of the Department of Cinema at NYU, the first department in the United States authorized to award both masters and doctorate degrees in the study of cinema.

Following Amberg's death his wife, who shared his passion for the arts, helped with the reissuing, in 1983, of his pioneering book on American ballet, and she made provisions in her estate for the Department of Cinema at NYU to administer the Amberg Dissertation Award. This award, a scholarship to complete a dissertation on film, is given to a deserving doctoral student each year. Also memorializing Amberg is the George Amberg Memorial Study Center, which consists of the video/film, book, and periodical library at NYU. Amberg willed his own extensive collection of books to the library.

Amberg, an erudite and urbane man, had a paradoxical sense of history and the avant-garde. Despite the collapse of the world he knew owing to the Nazis and the difficulties of establishing himself as a spokesman for the arts in a new language and a new country, Amberg consistently championed dance, film, and avant-garde theater throughout his life. While continuing his own artistic activities he also organized departments and institutions and wrote and taught, turning his insightful mind to areas of the arts sometimes considered undeserving. These included American comics and film; the latter he felt had "radically changed the way we live, the way we perceive and the way we comprehend," as he wrote in the introduction to his volume of selected *New York Times* film reviews from 1913 to 1970. "The realization that the cinema is a total and unique art form in its own right dawned very gradually and very late, in the world at large as well as in the newspaper community implying the recognition that film is neither literature nor drama, but a complex composite of many arts and crafts."

Amberg knew that life could be very unpredictable, politically volatile, and dangerous, perhaps explaining why he loved how movement, in contrast, could be beautifully resolved in drawing, film, and dance. With the zeal of a new citizen, he loved the energy and creativity he found in the United States, and he hoped that by analyzing and helping to define and capture its creativity, he could improve it and give it depth and longevity. He particularly devoted himself to the art of cinema through his writing, teaching, and his establishment of academic institutions.

• Amberg's papers are in the George Amberg Memorial Study Center of the Department of Cinema at New York University. Books written by Amberg not mentioned in the text include *Jean Cocteau as Film Maker* (1967) and *Ambivalence of Realism* (1960). He also edited *Hound and Horn: Essays on Cinema* (1972) and *The Art of the Cinema* (1972). Amberg contributed an important catalog of dance films to *Dance Index* in 1945 as well as an educational pamphlet for New York City public school teachers, called *Elements of Design* (n.d.), published by the Museum of Modern Art. His published articles include "Design For Theatre," *Theatre Arts Magazine*, Apr. 1948; "Tributary Theatre Design," *Theatre Arts Magazine*, June 1948; and "Art, Film, and Art Films," *Magazine of Arts*, Mar. 1952, and he occasionally wrote reviews, for example, "Flood of Film Books," *Saturday Review*, 24 Dec. 1960. An obituary is in *Ballet Review* 4, no. 1 (1971): 73–76.

JUDITH BRIN INGBER

AMBLER, James Markham Marshall (30 Dec. 1848–30 Oct. 1881), naval surgeon and explorer, was born in Markham, Virginia, the son of Richard Cary Ambler, a physician, and Susan Marshall. At age sixteen Ambler became a volunteer in the Twelfth Virginia Cavalry. He studied a premedicine curriculum at Washington College in 1865–1867 and then entered the University of Maryland. After acquiring a medical degree in 1870, he practiced in Baltimore until his appointment as an assistant surgeon in the U.S. Navy. During 1874–1875, he was stationed in the North Atlantic. In 1877 he joined the staff of the Naval Hospital at Norfolk, Virginia.

Ambler's life took a decided turn in 1879 when, after consultation with his mother, he reluctantly agreed to join Lieutenant George W. De Long's arctic expedition on the *Jeannette* (July 1879–Oct. 1881). He believed it was his duty to serve his nation at a time when world explorers were competing to discover the North

Pole. Promoter James Gordon Bennett, who had sponsored Henry Morton Stanley's expedition into Africa, funded the arctic venture, which was launched from San Francisco on 8 July 1879.

The physician's primary goal was to ensure a healthy crew. Despite the harsh natural conditions, the young doctor maintained a cheerful countenance and an eagerness to attend the sick, personal characteristics that proved to be great assets, especially after the ship was grounded in ice on 6 September 1879; for the next twenty-one months the *Jeannette* was icebound. To prevent disease, Ambler vigilantly rationed the lime juice to prevent scurvy and performed monthly checkups on the men. He also administered subtle psychological treatment on the sick and sometimes depressed seamen.

As Ambler noted in his journal, the doctor also executed intricate surgical procedures. Operations on Lieutenant John D. Danenhower's eye, in particular, revealed Ambler's special skills. Anesthetizing the patient with brandy and opium, he probed the officer's eye with a knife and then performed a "paracentesis corneal and let out a lot of turbid fluid." In his diary, Commander De Long described Ambler's lengthy operation, under a magnifying glass with candle illumination, as "beautifully performed . . . and borne with heroic endurance." Ambler saved the crew from sure death when he discovered that canned tomatoes were causing lead poisoning; he successfully treated the afflicted men for severe stomach cramps and other symptoms. He also massaged cramped muscles, applied skin ointment, and prescribed diarrheal medicines.

On 12 June 1881 the *Jeannette* sank. The crew then began a grueling journey of more than 300 miles pulling boats across the moving ice-covered landscape in search of leads of open sea, the ultimate goal being the delta of the Lena River of Siberia. Their position was desperate, the nearest Russian town more than 1,800 miles away. Ambler found the going especially difficult because of his multiple roles as physician, psychologist, and roadmaster (cutting sea paths into the hummocks of ice). The doctor soon found his own health suffering, noting in his journal that he was "sleeping in wet clothes in a wet bag on wet ice [which] makes every bone & separate muscle ache."

After discovering and naming three islands (Bennett, Henrietta, and Jeannette), the weakening explorers traveled to the New Siberian Islands, finally encountering open seas at the end of August 1881. On 12 September a gale separated their three boats. De Long's first cutter, with Ambler aboard, was blown to the west and landed at the northern point of the Lena Delta; Lieutenant George W. Melville's whaleboat was hurled south and landed nearest the main course of the river; Lieutenant Charles W. Chipp's cutter and crew were lost forever.

Ambler survived the storm and wrote that "we became a wreck, taking in water, wallowing in the trough of the sea the whole night, the next day and until morning. . . . There was no sleep for 36 hrs." The next six weeks proved ill-fated. Inaccurate maps, blizzards, and a lack of adequate nutrition weakened the travelers, who now found themselves stranded on land. Ambler did what he could for the frostbite victims, at one point taking on the gruesome task of amputating the blackened, frostbitten toes (and later feet) of one crewman, who was the first to perish.

On 8 October 1881 De Long announced that he could forge on no longer, not knowing that a Tungus village was only a day or two away. Command passed to Ambler, who was given the decision to stay or leave. He acted decisively: "no one should leave him [De Long] as long as I was alive." They made a final camp and waited for a rescue team or death by starvation. On 20 October Ambler made a final entry in his journal, a letter to his brother. He was resigned to his own death after almost two weeks without food. "I have myself now very little hope of surviving. . . . I . . . bow my head in submission to the Divine Will." Melville found Ambler and the other frozen victims on 23 March 1882, symbolically ending the *Jeannette*'s polar expedition. On 20 February 1884 Ambler's body was returned to Markham for final interment. He was never married.

Ambler sacrificed his life in the name of science and adventure despite his own misgivings about the expedition. His diligent service ensured a healthy crew—the first arctic journey without a single case of scurvy—until the elements and starvation took their toll. Because of his efforts, later expedition teams used the account of the *Jeannette* expedition to prove that a warm Gulf undercurrent did not rise to open the seas in the north polar cap as had been previously believed. This information facilitated future arctic ventures including Norwegian Fridtjof Nansen's expedition in the 1880s and Lieutenant Robert E. Peary's discovery of the North Pole in 1909.

• Ambler's original journal, along with letters, is housed at the Virginia Historical Society. The largest collection of primary documents on the *Jeannette* are at the National Archives, Office of Naval Records and Library. The U.S. Naval Academy Museum and the U.S. Naval Historical Center house photographs, maps, and drawings of the expedition, and the U.S. Naval Medical Command Archives has photographs of Ambler. The *Records of the Proceedings of Courts of Inquiry Boards of Investigation and Inquest, May 1866–Dec. 1940* (1953), contain the inquest papers concerning the officers' conduct during the expedition. James Markham Ambler, *The Private Journal of James Markham Ambler, M.D.* (12 June–18 Oct. 1881), is the physician's account of the final months of the De Long expedition. John Cropper Wise, *James Markham Marshall Ambler, A Sketch* (1906), and William Taylor Thom, *A Notable Beta of Yesterday* (1921), are the most useful published biographical sketches of Ambler. Firsthand accounts of the *Jeannette* expedition include George W. De Long, *The Voyage of the Jeannette: The Ship and Ice Journals of George W. De Long* (1883), ed. Emma De Long; and George W. Melville, *In the Lena Delta* (1884). The best secondary accounts of the expedition that discuss Ambler's role are Adolph A. Hoehling, *The Jeannette Expedition:*

An Ill-Fated Journey to the Arctic (1969), and Leonard F. Guttridge, *Icebound: The Jeannette Expedition's Quest for the North Pole* (1986).

CHRISTOPHER J. HUGGARD

AMECHE, Don (31 May 1908–6 Dec. 1993), actor, was born Dominic Felix Ameche in Kenosha, Wisconsin, the son of Felix Ameche, a saloon operator, and Barbara Hertle. Ameche's father, a native of Italy, had changed the spelling of his name from "Amici" to "Ameche" when he immigrated to the United States. Ameche, one of eight children—his brother Jim Ameche became a popular radio personality—studied at Columbia Academy, a Roman Catholic preparatory school in Dubuque, Iowa, for four years beginning at age fourteen. He then entered Columbia College (also in Dubuque) but left in 1928 in order to study law, taking courses at Marquette University in Milwaukee, then at Georgetown University in Washington, D.C., and finally at the University of Wisconsin in Madison. He never received a degree. Ameche had performed in plays in high school, and while he was at the University of Wisconsin he performed in a Madison stock company. This interest led him, in 1929, to again change course and pursue a professional acting career. That same year he landed his first Broadway role, as the butler in *Jerry-for-Short*. His entrée on stage was short-lived, however. He would not return to Broadway until 1955.

Ameche then toured the vaudeville circuit with Texas Guinan until the early 1930s, when he got his start in radio. His smooth, baritone voice was well suited for the medium, and he starred in radio well into the late 1940s, appearing on noted shows such as "The First Nighter," "Grand Hotel," and "The Chase and Sanborn Hour." Ameche achieved his greatest popularity in late 1946 and early 1947 when he performed opposite Frances Langford in a series of stereotypically funny husband-and-wife sketches called "The Bickersons" on "The Drene Show" on NBC. Ameche reprised his portrayal of the beleaguered John Bickerson on television in 1960 in a sketch on "The Frances Langford Show" on NBC.

Ameche's success in radio caught the attention of Hollywood studios. Following an unsuccessful screen test with Metro-Goldwyn-Mayer, he was signed to a $1,500-a-week contract by 20th Century–Fox head Darryl Zanuck. Ameche's film debut, in *Sins of Man* (1936), was unexceptional, but he soon registered with audiences as a romantic lead playing opposite Loretta Young in *Ramona* (1936). From the mid-1930s to the mid-1940s Ameche starred in a long line of films for Fox, mostly period pieces or comedies. His most memorable role from this period was the lead in *The Story of Alexander Graham Bell* (1939), a fictionalized account of the life of the inventor of the telephone. Ameche played other historical figures as well, such as songwriter Stephen Foster in *Swanee River* (1939) and Sir Hiram Stevens Maxim, inventor of the automatic rifle, in *So Goes My Love* (1946). These portrayals served to cement Ameche's reputation as a dramatic lead when in fact he was more adept in comedies and musicals. Films such as *Heaven Can Wait* (1943) and *Alexander's Ragtime Band* (1938) demonstrated his versatility as a performer, one who was quite comfortable in roles that demanded both a comedic and dramatic touch.

After his contract with Fox ended in 1946, Ameche freelanced for several studios but became increasingly disenchanted with the film roles he was being offered. In 1950 he moved to New York, where he concentrated on television and radio and, in 1955, returned to Broadway, starring in the musical comedy *Silk Stockings*, which ran from February 1955 until April 1956. The play, based on the 1939 film *Ninotchka*, starring Greta Garbo, was warmly received by critics and audiences, as was Ameche himself. *New York Herald Tribune* critic Walter Kerr wrote, "Mr. Ameche is a decided find. . . . possessed of a penetrating show-baritone, . . . an easy-going authority . . . and great good humor" (25 Feb. 1955). Ameche subsequently starred in three other Broadway shows, *Holiday for Lovers* (1957), *Goldilocks* (1959), and *13 Daughters* (1961), all less successful than *Silk Stockings*, though Ameche continued to garner favorable reviews.

While starring on Broadway, Ameche also broke into television, appearing in several specials such as "High Button Shoes," "Woodrow Wilson and the Unknown Soldier," "General Motor's Fiftieth Anniversary Show," and "Climax," and on the game show "To Tell the Truth." Then, in the fall of 1961 he became the host of "International Showtime," a weekly program on NBC that showcased circuses, water shows, ice shows, and other performing troupes from around the world. The program ran from 1961 through the 1964–1965 seasons, and because every show was taped on location, Ameche spent much of those four years crisscrossing the globe. Also during this period and into the early 1970s he starred in a few minor motion pictures and television movies, such as *Picture Mommy Dead* (1966), *Suppose They Gave a War and Nobody Came* (1970), and *Gidget Gets Married* (1972).

Following a decade-long hiatus from the entertainment industry, mostly brought about by a dearth of character parts, Ameche returned to motion pictures, starring opposite Ralph Bellamy in the Eddie Murphy hit comedy *Trading Places* (1983). In the film, both Ameche and Bellamy are delightfully animated in their comic roles as two conniving brothers who are blinded by money and power but who, in the end, are foiled by their own greed and insensitivity. *Trading Places* led to several more roles, including his portrayal of a rejuvenated senior citizen in *Cocoon* (1985), which won Ameche his one and only Academy Award, for best supporting actor. In his twilight years, Ameche's zany antics in *Cocoon*, including performing diving stunts in one scene and dancing gracefully in another, demonstrated once again his versatility and appeal as a comic actor. He continued to appear in films for the rest of his life, exuding his special brand of suave, sophisticated charm even under the most strenuous of circumstances.

Ameche's death in Scottsdale, Arizona, brought a varied, sixty-year career in the entertainment business to an end. He had been preceded in death by his wife, high school sweetheart Honore Prendergast, whom he had married in 1932 and with whom he had raised six children.

• Biographical sources include "Interview with Don Ameche" in the SMU Oral History Project on the Performing Arts (microfiche no. 113), and an interview in *Advertising Age*, 18 June 1990. See also Robert Carringer's *Ernst Lubitsch* (1978), specifically the bibliographic notes to *Heaven Can Wait*. Other information is contained in articles in *TV Guide*, 22 Dec. 1962, the *Celebrity Register* (1963), and the *International Motion Picture Almanac* (1964). A full filmography is in the Internet Movie Database on the World Wide Web. An obituary is in *Variety*, 20 Dec. 1993.

PATRICK BJORK

AMERICAN, Sadie (3 Mar. 1862–3 May 1944), social welfare activist and educator, was born in Chicago, Illinois, the daughter of German-Jewish immigrant Oscar L. American and Amelia Smith. Little is known of her childhood, but she was educated in Chicago public schools.

American became a founder in 1893 and later executive secretary of the philanthropic, middle-class reform organization the National Council of Jewish Women (NCJW). In her early thirties she held positions in dozens of social welfare, charitable, and educational institutions from 1893 to 1904, including that of president of the New York Section of the NCJW and of the Consumers' League of New York State (1893–1894). She also directed the Woman's Municipal League in New York City and was chair of its Tenement House Committee (1893–1894).

In 1894 American returned to Chicago, where she served as a teacher at Rabbi Emil G. Hirsch's Temple Sinai Sunday School (1894–1899). In 1896 she became president of the League for Religious Fellowship in Chicago, where she also served as a director of the Cook County League of Women's Clubs. She was interested in promoting general education as well as Jewish education, and in 1897–1898 she served on the executive committee of the Committee of One Hundred to revise laws regulating education in Illinois and during 1899–1903 on the Public Education Association's Committee on Night School and Social Centres.

American was a speaker and delegate representing the NCJW at the Atlanta Exposition in 1896 and at the International Congress of Women in London in 1899 and in Berlin in 1904. She was a frequent lecturer, mostly on civic and educational subjects, at clubs and conventions, and in synagogues and churches. She also helped organize the Union of Jewish Women Workers in England in the 1900s and assisted in the formation of the Judischer Frauenbund in Berlin in 1904.

American's most important work, beginning in 1903, helped protect immigrant women and girls arriving in the United States. In a letter to the Baron de Hirsch Fund asking for financial assistance, she wrote, "Many girls are misled into immoral lives, and others are subjected to great dangers . . . at Ellis Island." She asked for support to establish a "complete chain of protection" for "our immigrant sisters," including the posting of women agents at the port of entry. Her efforts enabled the NCJW to extend aid to tens of thousands of immigrant women and children. Council workers were hired to help women avoid financial and sexual exploitation and to help with translation and directions. They also searched for lost baggage, sent telegrams and letters to locate relatives, and found appropriate lodgings for women who had no relatives waiting to receive them. These efforts were followed by home visits to assure "successful adjustment." The NCJW, led by President Hannah G. Solomon and Executive Secretary Sadie American, also developed programs for vocational training and established night schools and residential hotels for women as well as social clubs to ensure "wholesome recreation."

Sadie American's concern for immigrant women might now be seen as over-protective, but patronization was inherent in the general social work of the day. More important, there appeared to be a growing incidence of prostitution in the immigrant Jewish community and an increasing focus by critics on Jewish participation, as perpetrators and victims, in the "white slave trade." Worried about anti-Semitism, American tried to counter these exaggerated charges, but she also tried to suppress Jewish involvement on both ends of the "evil enterprise" so as to protect its women victims. She was the U.S. delegate to the Jewish International Conference on the Suppression of Traffic in Girls and Women in London in 1910 and to the International White Slave Traffic Conference, also held in 1910 in Madrid. American was granted an audience with the king and queen of Spain, who praised her and the work of the NCJW.

The head of the European delegation to the Madrid conference, Claude Montefiore, a prominent British Jew, also recognized American's contribution, saying that her work was to be commended because it helped check anti-Semitism and promoted the decline of Jewish involvement in white slavery. American called for protective education, as well as vigilance and safeguards against potential abductors, at the ports of embarkation. At the international conferences and in dozens of addresses and letters to editors in subsequent years, she also attacked the double sexual standard and advocated treating the "whole question of prostitution differently" by emphasizing the poverty of the prostitutes and by holding their male patrons accountable. In 1913 she became a founder and for a short time the president of the Lakeview Home for Girls on Staten Island, which had the goal of "reclaiming" young women first offenders.

Most Jewish philanthropic organizations were controlled by men, but Sadie American and the other women of the NCJW, despite occasional resistance from male leaders, took greater responsibility for the welfare of Jewish women immigrants and their children. For more than two decades American was indefatigable in her drive for funding on behalf of the NCJW's Immigrant Aid Department and championed the council's volunteer women workers. She was representative of the German-Jewish middle-class women reformers who were aware of, and welcomed, the challenge they presented to the stereotype of the "lady." American insisted that "for a woman to give . . . publicly . . . of the wisdom of her experience to make life fuller and better for others, is quite as womanly as to sing operatic arias . . . [or] to execute Sonatas . . . all of which meet with general approval" (Baum, p. 49).

American had great confidence in her ability and would not accept exclusion from leadership easily. Men, she commented, "have not such immense faith in the women's ability; in fact, they fear that the women will make a mistake and hurt all the Jews." But American not only helped the less fortunate, she also found useful and rewarding work for herself and helped redefine acceptable behavior for women. She made her mark in Jewish philanthropy and social work in the early twentieth century.

Sadie American never married. After being forced out of the NCJW in 1914 for the "self-righteous defense" of her "controversial" positions, she virtually disappeared from historical records except for a term of service on New York governor Franklin D. Roosevelt's Conference on Child Welfare in the late 1920s. She died alone in a hotel room in Morristown, New Jersey.

• American's reports and miscellaneous writings can be found in the *Proceedings of the National Council of Jewish Women* (1897–1923), in the papers of the NCJW at the American Jewish Historical Society in Waltham, Mass., and in the papers of the NCJW, New York City. Information about her is available in *The American Jewish Yearbook, 1905–1906*; Charlotte Baum et al., *The Jewish Woman in America* (1976); Jacob Rader Marcus, *The American Jewish Woman, 1654–1980* (1981); June Sochen, *Consecrate Every Day: The Public Lives of Jewish American Women, 1880–1980* (1981); and Faith Rogow, *"Gone to Another Meeting": The National Council of Jewish Women, 1893–1993* (1993). An obituary is in the *New York Times*, 4 May 1944.

GERALD SORIN

AMERICAN HORSE (1840?–16 Dec. 1908), Oglala Lakota leader known to his people as Waśiču Taśunka, was the son of Sitting Bear, an Oglala chief, and an unknown mother. His birthplace is not known.

The name *American Horse* carries a complex history. In addition to two unrelated Oglala leaders who lived during the same era, Sitting Bear may also have been called by the name, as was at least one Cheyenne. American Horse the elder, known to Oglalas as Iron Shield or Iron Plume, was born around 1830 and established a reputation as a warrior and leader, probably participating in George Armstrong Custer's defeat before getting killed at the battle of Slim Buttes on 9 September 1876. American Horse the younger, the man considered here and the most widely known bearer of the name, will hereafter be referred to by his Lakota name.

Waśiču Taśunka first appears in most historical records fighting with Crazy Horse in the William Judd Fetterman massacre near Fort Phil Kearny, Wyoming, in 1866. Waśiču Taśunka claimed to have killed Fetterman personally. Ten years later, however, he and other Oglala leaders favoring peaceful relations with the United States tried to persuade Crazy Horse to end his resistance in the aftermath of their victory at the Little Bighorn. In 1878, with other Lakota and Cheyenne scouts, Waśiču Taśunka helped lead soldiers from Fort Robinson, Nebraska, to find Dull Knife's Cheyennes on their return trek from Indian Territory to their homelands in the Yellowstone country. He pursued peaceful relations with the United States for the remainder of his life, earning the enmity of Lakotas favoring resistance and contributing to political factionalism among Lakotas.

As a son-in-law and lieutenant to Red Cloud (Maȟpiyaluta), the premier Oglala chief of the era, Waśiču Taśunka played an active role in the early years of the Pine Ridge reservation. After helping choose the site for the Red Cloud agency in South Dakota, he lived there continually from 1871 through 1879. He accompanied Red Cloud and other Lakota leaders to Washington, D.C., in 1875 to discuss Lakota grievances stemming from white incursions into the Black Hills, accompanied Red Cloud on another diplomatic mission to Washington in 1877, and represented Oglala interests with other Lakota leaders in Red Cloud's absence in subsequent Washington trips in 1888 and 1889.

The U.S. government sponsored the 1888 trip to get Lakota approval of that year's Sioux bill, which called for a reduction in Lakota landholdings. Aware of Red Cloud's opposition to the act, the government kept him on the reservation while bringing lesser leaders to Washington in hopes of securing their approval. The delegation, however, rejected the act. When a commission from Washington traveled to Pine Ridge in 1889 to present a revised bill more favorable to the Sioux, Waśiču Taśunka supported it. In what has been called one of the great oratories in Indian diplomatic history, Waśiču Taśunka spoke in favor of the bill for nearly three days to an assemblage of Oglalas and Washington officials. Following the conference, U.S. officials contemplated recognizing Waśiču Taśunka, instead of Red Cloud, as chief of the Oglalas but abandoned the plan. They did, however, choose him to lead the Pine Ridge delegation to Washington in December 1889 for a final conference on the Sioux bill, which he signed.

Waśiču Taśunka and the others who signed the treaty produced a split in the Lakota community. Many who disagreed with the Sioux bill became adherents of the Ghost Dance religion, which anticipated the elimination of whites and the restoration of the land to Indian peoples. Waśiču Taśunka became embittered with the U.S. government when it failed to deliver the commodities it had promised in exchange for his signature on the Sioux bill. Despite this sentiment, Waśiču Taśunka did not participate in the Ghost Dance religion. During the height of Ghost Dance activity in 1890, Waśiču Taśunka advocated assimilation at least to the extent of Indians taking land in severalty and Indian children attending the government boarding school for Indians at Carlisle, Pennsylvania. His views placed him in danger from his own people and demonstrate the degree of intratribal friction of the day. Ghost Dancers reportedly attacked his followers, ransacked his house, and stole his livestock. Less than one month before the Wounded Knee massacre, he wrote, "I am trying to advance these Indians, but instead they are growing worse and some of them hate me so that they say they would shoot me, if they should have an opportunity." Nevertheless, in December 1890 U.S. officials sent him and other Lakotas to convince Ghost Dancers to stop dancing and to return to the Pine Ridge agency. Waśiču Taśunka and his party persuaded Kicking Bear and Short Bull to bring their followers to the Catholic mission near Pine Ridge, where they escaped violent conflict with the army.

Shortly after the Wounded Knee massacre, Waśiču Taśunka traveled with Lakota delegates to Washington to testify in government investigations. He reiterated his disappointment in the government for its duplicity and brutality despite continued loyalty from himself and other Lakotas. The Lakota delegation's Washington visit improved government administration of Sioux affairs, obtaining compensation for horse confiscations made during the summer of 1876 and gaining increased rations during 1891.

Waśiču Taśunka acted as a key source of Lakota religious knowledge for U.S. ethnographers and historians. Among other things, Waśiču Taśunka related details of the Ghost Dance religion.

In 1897 Waśiču Taśunka again traveled with a Lakota delegation to Washington to present, without avail, a list of grievances concerning government handling of Sioux affairs. In perhaps his final moment as a diplomat, Waśiču Taśunka joined other Lakota leaders in complaining of the government's taking of the Black Hills and in seeking to change the treaty by which the United States claimed the hills. They also testified before the Senate Committee on Indian Affairs. Their pleas fell on deaf ears, however, and the United States refused to discuss the issue. Waśiču Taśunka died at Pine Ridge, South Dakota.

Waśiču Taśunka stood among those Native Americans who advocated wholesale cultural change to adapt to the conditions imposed on his people by the United States. The policy he chose and the resistance it engendered reflect the diversity of opinions among Lakotas on how to address significant threats to their culture. His experiences also call attention to the record of the U.S. government in Indian affairs.

• Waśiču Taśunka's papers, including correspondence and an extensive portfolio of art on ledger paper depicting Oglala life, reside in the Western Americana Collection, Beinecke Rare Book and Manuscript Library, Yale University. Since material on Waśiču Taśunka is rare, readers must be satisfied reading about him in works on other subjects. Some of the best include George E. Hyde, *Red Cloud's Folk: A History of the Oglala Sioux Indians* (1937); Robert M. Utley, *The Last Days of the Sioux Nation* (1963); James C. Olson, *Red Cloud and the Sioux Problem* (1965); and Dee Brown, *Bury My Heart at Wounded Knee: An Indian History of the American West* (1970). Mari Sandoz's works *Crazy Horse: The Strange Man of the Oglalas* (1942) and *Cheyenne Autumn* (1953; repr. 1975) are particularly helpful in sorting out the various Indians called American Horse. James R. Walker, *Lakota Belief and Ritual*, ed. Raymond J. DeMallie and Elaine A. Jahner (1980; repr. 1991), and James Mooney, *Fourteenth Annual Report of the Bureau of Ethnology, 1892–93*, pt. 2 (1896), also contain important information.

TODD M. KERSTETTER

AMERINGER, Oscar (4 Aug. 1870–5 Nov. 1943), humorist and socialist editor, was born in a Swabian village in Germany, the son of August Ameringer, a cabinetmaker. His mother's maiden name was Hoffman, and she was the previously widowed owner of a twelve-acre farm. Relocated to Laupheim, Ameringer grew up in the relative comfort of the lower middle class, yet he despised the religiosity and anti-Semitism of his Lutheran schooling. An instinctive antimonarchist, storyteller, and musician, he seized his first opportunity, at age sixteen, to flee to the United States. There he would become the "Mark Twain of American socialism," a famed literary comedian, stage entertainer, and labor and political organizer.

A skilled woodworker and unionist during his first years in the United States, Ameringer was swept up, in Cincinnati, in the strikes of 1886 for an eight-hour day. Blacklisted for his activity, he became a traveling musician and portrait painter. His keenly developed sense of humor and his search for a livelihood drew him to writing. Striving to improve his English, he read Mark Twain and sold a satirical story of his own, "The Duke and His Dog," to *Puck* magazine. On the verge of an American literary career, he was drawn back to Germany by news of his mother's illness. There he attended art classes and was converted to the ideas of socialism.

On his return to the United States, Ameringer drifted into a labor career. Editor of a labor weekly in the first five years of the new century, he moved on to organizing New Orleans workers, advocating interracial collaboration. Relocating again to Oklahoma City in 1907, Ameringer found his constituency and his métier. The rapidly growing socialist movement of that state, unimpeachably grassroots in character, adored his homespun way of explaining complex ideas perhaps even more than they did his moral dedication to setting coal miners and sharecroppers free from the demeaning conditions of their labor. Pamphlets such as *Socialism for the Farmer Who Farms the Farm* jokingly explained rural capitalism in terms of insect pests and cajoled the reader to give up his conservative voting habits. His paper, the *Oklahoma Leader*, spread the faith and gained Ameringer avid readers across the Southwest.

Ameringer's virtuoso performances at week-long socialist "encampments," telling stories and playing music, best demonstrated his continuing stage presence. Ameringer took this show on the road regularly as a socialist agitator for more than a decade. Poet Carl Sandburg wrote that he had seen the comic "in Milwaukee and Chicago, taking the platform in a crowded, smoke-filled hall, facing rows of somber and sober-faced working men, talking to them about their troubles . . . soon bringing smiles to the faces and finally roars of laughter."

Ameringer's major literary contribution, a comic history of the United States titled *Life and Deeds of Uncle Sam: A Little History for Big Children*, sold a half-million copies in fifteen languages through many editions from 1912 through the 1930s. He turned his editorial talents to the *Milwaukee Leader* during World War I and in the 1920s to the *Illinois Miner*, then closed his career with a remarkably personal paper, the Oklahoma-based weekly *American Guardian* (1932–1942). He remained an avid socialist until the end of his life, penning one of the most popular radical autobiographies of the time, *If You Don't Weaken*.

• No Oscar Ameringer papers exist, but the humor editor's autobiography, *If You Don't Weaken* (1940), is an invaluable source. The 1983 edition contains an introduction by James R. Green, which is one of the best surveys of Ameringer's life and significance. Green's *Grass-Roots Socialism* (1978) also treats Ameringer and his milieu at length. Among related studies, Garin Burbank, *When Farmers Voted Red: The Gospel of Socialism in the Oklahoma Countryside, 1910–1924* (1976), is the most comprehensive. On the nature and significance of Ameringer's literary humor style, see Paul Buhle's introduction to the 1985 edition of *Life and Deeds of Uncle Sam*.

PAUL BUHLE

AMES, Adelbert (31 Oct. 1835–13 Apr. 1933), soldier and politician, was born in Rockland, Maine, the son of Jesse Ames, a sea captain, and Martha B. Tolman. After spending some time at sea as a teenager, Ames entered the U.S. Military Academy, graduating in 1861. He was commissioned a second lieutenant and assigned to the Fifth Artillery. During the Civil War he was wounded at First Bull Run (First Manassas) on 21 July, and he later received the Congressional Medal of Honor for his heroism there in refusing to leave his post despite the wound. He served with the Army of the Potomac during the Peninsula campaign of 1862, and for his actions at Malvern Hill he was brevetted lieutenant colonel. On 8 August 1862 he was named colonel in command of the Twentieth Maine Volunteer Infantry, with Joshua L. Chamberlain as his lieutenant colonel. Ames proved to be a strict disciplinarian. The regiment was present at Antietam but engaged in its first combat at Shepherdstown, Virginia (19 Sept. 1862). In 1863 Ames secured a position on the staff of Fifth Corps commander George G. Meade, and on 20 May he was promoted to brigadier general of volunteers with command of a brigade in the Eleventh Corps. At Gettysburg, Ames succeeded the wounded Francis C. Barlow as division commander. Soon afterward he joined the Army of the James and participated in the Petersburg campaign and the assault on Fort Fisher as a division commander.

When the war ended, Ames remained in the South with the occupation forces, heading the Western District of South Carolina. In 1866 he was commissioned a lieutenant colonel of the Twenty-fourth Infantry in the regular army. After his return from an excursion in Europe in 1867, he was assigned to duty in Mississippi, where the persistence and scope of antiblack violence eroded his earlier reservations about Reconstruction and black suffrage. On 15 June 1868 he became provisional governor of Mississippi, replacing Benjamin G. Humphreys, and in March 1869 President Ulysses S. Grant named Ames to head the Fourth Military District. Originally comprising Arkansas and Mississippi, the district was coterminous with Mississippi after Congress recognized Arkansas's compliance (in 1868) with the Reconstruction Acts. Mississippi voters, who in 1868 had failed to ratify a new state constitution, did so under Ames in 1869. Critics accused Ames, not without justification, of aiding the Republican cause in the elections for governor and the state legislature. The following January the Republican majority in the state legislature elected Ames to the U.S. Senate. He took his seat only after defending his claim that he was indeed a resident of the state, a questionable assertion. It would have been more accurate to say that he had a tour of duty there.

In 1870, during Ames's short senatorial career, he married Blanche Butler, daughter of Benjamin F. Butler, a powerful Republican congressman; the couple had six children. As a senator, Ames advocated measures providing for federal protection of black voters, at times battling his colleague from Mississippi, James L. Alcorn. Among Mississippi Republicans, Alcorn had the support of native whites ("scalawags"), while blacks and northern-born whites ("carpetbaggers") backed Ames. In 1873 Ames defeated Alcorn in a contest for governor and took office on 22 January 1874.

Ames's tenure as governor proved difficult. Many whites who had once supported conservative Republicans such as Alcorn either dropped out of politics or shifted to the Democratic opposition, polarizing Mississippi politics along racial lines. Racial strife overshadowed Ames's commitment to cutting taxes and spending less and his actions against railroads, including the taxation of their property. However, his opposition to debtor relief angered farmers hard hit by economic depression following the panic of 1873; they also resented financing public education for blacks as well as whites. State Democrats resorted to a campaign of intimidation and violence in the effort to regain political power, adopting the motto of the so-called "Mississippi Plan," which was to triumph "peacefully if we can, forcibly if we must." The level of violence was calibrated not to spark federal intervention, and the Democrats' tactics were successful in Vicksburg in August 1874. However, in the aftermath of an outbreak of violence the following December, President Grant dispatched soldiers to that city. When Democrats applied their tactics of voter intimidation and fraud in the 1875 state elections, Ames requested federal troops. Grant's reply, carefully edited to satisfy Attorney General Edwards Pierrepont's distaste for intervention, argued that Ames had not exhausted all means of state action to quell violence and that the northern public would no longer support intervention. Grant's decision was influenced by advice from Ohio Republicans that intervention in Mississippi might well cost the Republicans a victory in Ohio and by reassurances from some Mississippi Democrats that they would curb violent activities. After the Democrats triumphed in the election, the new state legislature impeached Ames, who resigned rather than face a trial with a preordained outcome.

Ames left Mississippi to seek his fortune. First he joined his father's flour-milling business in Northfield, Minnesota; then he moved to Tewksbury, Massachusetts, where he invested in textile mills and real estate. He displayed a talent for inventing mechanical devices, from pencil sharpeners to ladders for fire engines. Accumulating a sizable fortune, he counted among his associates John D. Rockefeller. In 1898, when the Spanish-American War began, Ames returned to military service as a brigadier general of volunteers and participated in the siege of Santiago and the battle of San Juan Hill. At the time of his death in Ormond, Florida, sixty-eight years after the surrender at Appomattox, Ames was celebrated as the last surviving Civil War general.

• Ames's correspondence and other personal papers are at Smith College. Many of them are reprinted in Blanche Ames Ames, *Adelbert Ames, 1835–1933: General, Senator, Governor* (1964), and Blanche Butler Ames, comp., *Chronicles from the Nineteenth Century: Family Letters of Blanche Butler and Adelbert Ames* (1957). Richard N. Current, *Those Terrible Carpetbaggers* (1988), discusses Ames and nine of his fellow carpetbaggers. Obituaries are in the *New York Times* and the Jackson, Miss., *Daily Clarion-Leader*, 14 Apr. 1933.

BROOKS D. SIMPSON

AMES, Blanche Ames (18 Feb. 1878–1 Mar. 1969), artist and women's rights activist, was born in Lowell, Massachusetts, the daughter of Adelbert Ames, a Civil War general and governor of Mississippi during Reconstruction, and Blanche Butler, whose father was a general and governor of Massachusetts. The younger Blanche graduated from Smith College in 1899 with diplomas from both the College and the School of Art.

In 1900 she married Oakes Ames (1874–1950), a Harvard instructor in botany from North Easton, Massachusetts; although they had the same surname, they were not related. Between 1901 and 1910 they had four children. In 1911 they built "Borderland," a large house surrounded by 1,200 acres in North Easton.

Blanche began to illustrate orchids for her husband, who was later the director of the Botanical Museum at Harvard, and over the next fifty years she produced hundreds of outstanding drawings and watercolors of orchids. For a course Oakes taught in economic botany, she illustrated four wall charts depicting plants useful to humans. The "Ames Charts of Economic Plants" are still in use. Her orchid drawings illustrated at least twenty books and countless articles over the years.

Blanche Ames was also a portrait painter. She was particularly concerned with accurate color representation, and with her brother, Adelbert, she developed a system of notations for 4,000 color variations. For more than half a century she accepted commissions from prominent men and women whose portraits are displayed in New England, New York, and Mississippi.

In addition to her family commitments and her art, she was a concerned feminist. She was an active member of the Easton Equal Suffrage League, as was Oakes Ames, and in 1914 she became an officer in the state league. The following year she began a series of popular suffragist cartoons that were published nationally.

Among other reforms, she saw the need for women to have control over the size of their families. In 1916 she cofounded the Birth Control League of Massachusetts and was its first president. Disseminating birth control was illegal, so the only immediate solution was self-help. Blanche ingeniously developed a formula for spermicide and found a way to use a baby's teething ring or a canning jar sealing ring as a diaphragm. She continued her dedication to helping women and gave years of service to the New England Hospital for Women and Children, which in recognition of her devotion has established a fund in her name for the medical education of women.

Blanche's active imagination and scientific methods, developed over years of studying orchids, produced three patents. The first was in 1939 for a hexagonal lumber cutter; the next in 1945 was for a system for ensnaring low-flying aircraft; and in 1968 she developed an antipollution device for toilets.

In 1964 she published a biography of her father, General Adelbert Ames. Irate over a statement in John F. Kennedy's *Profiles in Courage* that under her father's administration "no state suffered more from carpetbag rule than Mississippi," she resolved to set history straight. She was proud of her father, a West Point graduate who was the youngest major general in the Civil War. Her book is a spirited defense of his tenure as military governor, and later governor, of Mississippi.

Blanche Ames died at Borderland.

• Most of the papers of Blanche Ames Ames are in the Sophia Smith Collection at Smith College; some are at the Schlesinger Library, Radcliffe College. Smith's papers include details of the publishing history of her orchid drawings as well as original paintings and suffrage cartoons. There are no full-length biographies; her daughter Pauline Ames Plimpton wrote *Oakes Ames: Jottings of a Harvard Botanist* (1979), which includes information about Blanche. Plimpton also edited *Orchids at Christmas: Oakes and Blanche Ames* (1975), *The Ancestry of Blanche Butler Ames and Adelbert Ames* (1977), and *Ramblings about Borderland* (1987). Richard Evans Schultes printed *Blanche Ames Ames, 1878–1969: An Appreci-*

ation, in Botanical Museum Leaflets, Harvard (1969), and Bonnie L. Crane prepared an excellent catalog for an exhibit at the Brockton Art Museum/Fuller Memorial in 1982, *Blanche Ames Ames: Artist and Activist*. Borderland was sold to the Commonwealth of Massachusetts after Blanche's death. The estate is now Borderland State Park and is open to the public. Obituaries are in the *Boston Globe* and the *New York Times*, 3 Mar. 1969.

JACQUELINE VAN VORIS

AMES, Edward Scribner (21 Apr. 1870–29 June 1958), theologian and Disciples of Christ minister, was born in Eau Claire, Wisconsin, the son of Lucius Bowles Ames, a Disciples minister and farmer, and Adaline Scribner, a housekeeper. Ames was educated at Drake University, receiving a B.A. in 1889 and an M.A. in 1891. He then studied at Yale, where he received a B.D. in 1892. He completed his Ph.D. at the University of Chicago in 1895. After teaching at Butler College in Indianapolis from 1897 to 1900, Ames moved to Chicago as pastor of the Hyde Park (later University) Church, Disciples of Christ, serving until 1940. In 1893 he married Mabel Van Meter; they had four children. Ames began teaching philosophy at the University of Chicago in 1900. He later edited the *Scroll*, a liberal Disciples theological journal (1925–1951), and served as dean of the Disciples Divinity House (1927–1945).

As a theologian and philosopher, Ames was a leader of the so-called Chicago School, which tried to bring empirical rigor to theology. While studying philosophy at Yale and Chicago, he had read widely in pragmatism, especially the works of William James and John Dewey. He also became convinced that religion, like other aspects of human life, had evolved from relatively simple beginnings to more complicated forms. For him, the study of the psychology of religion was the best way to explore the meaning of religion and theology and to investigate the implications of pragmatism and evolutionary thought for religious faith.

In his *Psychology of Religious Experience* (1910) and *Religion* (1929), Ames analyzed the interaction between the individual and the group in religious life. He traced the evolution of religion from primitive to modern times. He contended that religious psychology differed in the various stages of human development, although some early styles and traits continued in successive ages. According to Ames, the religious psychology of children, adolescents, and adults differed. He also analyzed such phenomena as conversion, religious genius, and the religion of criminals.

Ames's theology reflected his psychology. For him, metaphysical statements about the world did not constitute religion. Instead, religion was one way in which human beings adjusted to their environment. Religious statements were not so much true or false as they were functional or dysfunctional. Good religion enhanced a person's basic humanity and enabled that person to mature intellectually and socially; bad religion hindered human development. For instance, statements ostensibly about God really referred to the human ideas of fellowship, love, and hope.

Ames's commitment to a functional understanding of religion informed his commitment to the social gospel. He believed that the old apologetic attempts to establish the truth of Christianity by rational argument were not useful in the modern world. According to him, contemporaries wanted to know whether Christianity inspired people to "open schools in India, hospitals in China . . . [and create] institutions of learning, of health, of comradeship, and of hope."

Ames's leadership was a major factor in the transformation of the Disciples of Christ into a mainline denomination. A perceptive Disciples historian, he studied the writings of Alexander Campbell and other early Disciples leaders and found traces of the influence of the seventeenth-century philosopher John Locke. What Disciples needed, Ames believed, was for the movement to follow the deeper meaning of this earlier example and be as open and responsive to modern democratic idealism as earlier Disciples were to the social idealism of their day.

Ames made his Hyde Park pastorate a model of a modern Disciples congregation, experimenting with new forms of liturgy, worship, and mission. For example, Hyde Park accepted members from other churches without requiring that those persons be baptized by immersion ("open membership"). When controversy over the practice arose, Ames used his considerable theological skills to lead other ministers in the same direction, and as editor of the *Scroll*, he also contributed to a more liberal atmosphere in the denomination.

When Ames entered the ministry, few Disciples ministers had received a theological education and the denomination had little funds to establish seminaries. His work at the Disciples Divinity House allowed Disciples students to attend the University of Chicago Divinity School, one of the nation's best, while living, studying, and worshiping together. He erected a building for the House, recruited able students, and collected an important library of early Disciples materials.

As a theologian and church leader, Ames made significant contributions to both his academic discipline and his denomination. Teachers in other theological seminaries frequently assigned his works, especially *The Psychology of Religious Experience*. The Disciples eventually adopted almost all of the reforms he advocated and consider him one of the parents of the modern denomination.

• Ames frequently reflected on his own career. He contributed an early bibliographical essay, "Theology in Practice," to *Contemporary American Theology*, ed. Vergilius Ferm (2 vols., 1932–1933). Shortly after his death, his son Van Meter Ames edited his autobiography, *Beyond Theology* (1959). The most valuable work for understanding the context of Ames's theology is Kenneth Cauthen, *The Impact of American Religious Liberalism* (1962). A sound discussion of the relationship between Ames's thought and that of his colleagues is found in Charles Harvey Arnold, "A School That Walks the Earth: Edward Scribner Ames and the Chicago School of Theology," *Encounter* 30 (Fall 1969): 314–39. An invaluable source for changes in the Disciples denomination is D. Newell Williams, ed., *A Case Study of Mainstream Protestantism: The Disciples' Relationship to American Culture, 1880–1989* (1991).

GLENN T. MILLER

AMES, Ezra (5 May 1768–23 Feb. 1836), painter, engraver, and gilder, was born Ezra Emes in Framingham, Massachusetts, the son of Jesse Emes, a soldier and farmer, and Betty Bent. Ames's mother died when he was seven. Nothing is known of his education; he may have been educated at home. In 1790 his father, who had remarried, moved the family to Staatsburg, New York. By that time Ezra had chosen to spell his surname Ames and was working as a journeyman painter and craftsman in Worcester, Massachusetts. In 1793 he settled in Albany, New York, which was his home for the rest of his life. In October 1794 he married Zipporah Wood of Uxbridge, Massachusetts, and returned with her to Albany, where their three children were born.

A self-educated artist, he sought from the outset to achieve competence in both the fine and the decorative arts. His advertisements in the Albany newspapers indicated this range in 1793, offering "Portrait and Sign Painting, Gilding and Limning, Miniatures and Hair Devices" and ornament of "Signs, Coaches, Chaises and Sleighs." In 1799 design of Masonic regalia and engraving were added to his list of specialties: "Freemasons aprons, sashed and ornamental paintings in general . . . Seals, . . . Mason's medal, & C. Engraved neatly and elegantly." His account books from 1790 to 1834 document prolific, varied phases of his career. Even after 1812, when Ames began to achieve national prominence as a portraitist, he continued on occasion to accept lucrative craft commissions. He recorded payments for 162 shop signs painted between 1791 and 1820; two of his signs for tobacconists were illustrated in contemporary woodcuts (engraver/artist unknown) in the *Albany Gazette* on 11 November 1818 and 3 June 1819. None of his signs are known to have survived.

Ames sold four miniatures to four Worcester patrons in 1790, an event that initiated his miniature production on ivory through the first decade of the nineteenth century. He attracted the patronage of the wife of the governor of New York, Mrs. George Clinton, for whom he did a portrait miniature (unlocated) given to the governor in 1794. The pair of portrait miniatures of Mrs. Abraham Van Santvoort (1805, National Museum of American Art) and of her husband (private collection) are characteristically meticulous and direct. Commissions for miniatures were sometimes accompanied by orders for hairwork, which were fashioned from a lock of the subject's hair and were usually enclosed in a glass aperture in the back of the case. A few mourning themes in miniature attributed to Ames (Albany Institute of History and Art) are memorial pictures of grieving figures on ivory painted in watercolors, with chopped hair added to the pigments.

Though styles of miniatures changed with the times, Ames stayed in tune with fashion. His portrait of his daughter Marcia Ames (c. 1820, private collection) abandoned the oval shape for a newer rectangular format suggestive of full-scale painting, emphasized by the half-length pose of a seated figure in an interior. His late miniatures were frequently on paper: for example, *Dr. James Wade* (1822, private collection) and *Mrs. John Hills* (1831, private collection).

Ames approached portraiture in oils as he had the miniature, by joining an aptitude for technique with an assiduous study of the works of other painters, notably Gilbert Stuart, John Singleton Copley, and John Wesley Jarvis. His excellent copy of *Elkanah Waston* (c. 1809, Albany Institute of History and Art) after Copley's portrait of 1782 demonstrated his progress from a primitive to a professional painter. At age forty-five, he experienced his first critical and popular success with the portrait *Vice-President George Clinton* (1812, versions owned by the New-York Historical Society and the Albany Institute of History and Art), when it was shown at the second annual exhibition of the Pennsylvania Academy of the Fine Arts in Philadelphia.

The New York state legislature commissioned a full-length portrait of Clinton (New York State Capitol, Albany), followed by portraits of the current governor, George Clinton's nephew, DeWitt Clinton (1818), and of several former governors, including John Jay, copied from Gilbert Stuart's 1794 painting (both Ames portraits are in the Albany Institute of History and Art). DeWitt Clinton became Ames's most significant patron, commissioning several portraits of himself, a copy of a portrait of his first wife, Maria Franklin Clinton (c. 1810, Henry Ford Museum); a portrait of his second wife, Catherine Jones Clinton (1820, Brooklyn Historical Society); and portraits of two sons (dates unknown). At DeWitt Clinton's request, Ames painted one of his few known landscapes, a handsome scene of Lake George (c. 1812, Albany Institute of History and Art). Judging from his account books, he seems to have perceived his paintings and "burnished gilt" frames as an ensemble. He priced these accordingly, often charging, for example, fifty dollars for a frame of his design and manufacture.

In 1818–1819 Ames painted several portraits of American statesmen for Joseph Delaplaine's gallery of distinguished Americans, including a bust-length version of his earlier portrait of George Clinton (Frances Tavern Museum, New York City). His portrait of Congressman Benjamin Tallmadge (1826, Litchfield Historical Society, one of three versions) was engraved by George Parker for a similar project, James B. Longacre and James Herring's multivolume series of illustrated biographies, *The National Gallery of Distinguished Americans* (1833–1839).

Ames received further national recognition by being elected in 1824 to the American Academy of the Fine Arts in New York. However, it was the Albany community that was most responsive to his work. A former seventeenth-century Dutch colony, Albany became a city of major significance with the opening of the Erie

Canal, an inland waterway creating a gateway to the Northwest Territory. The dedication of the canal on 25 November 1825 was locally celebrated by, among other displays, a large transparency representing the "Genius of America" supporting one of Ames's images of Governor Clinton and an image of the inventor Robert Fulton.

Ames's scrupulous and methodical record-keeping, which has shed light on his career, was a characteristic that also commended him to the board of the Farmers and Mechanics Bank, of which he had become a member in 1814. Ames gave to the bank that year a *Self-Portrait* (now owned by the Albany Institute of History and Art). He was elected president of the Farmers and Mechanics Bank in 1834. Ames had arrived impecunious and unknown in Albany in 1793, and he died there a prosperous, respected member of the community.

Ames's artistic versatility is the most striking aspect of his career. Best known for his large and miniature portraits, he also investigated landscape and still life, the latter mainly as studies of details in larger paintings. He remained an adept craftsman long after he rose to prominence in portraiture. His self-taught, diverse accomplishments are as quintessentially American as the distinguished subjects he painted in the early nineteenth century.

• All of the likenesses of Ezra Ames are self-portraits, and almost all of them (covering the years c. 1790–1814) belong to the Albany Institute of History and Art. The New-York Historical Society also owns a self-portrait. Two of Ames's account books (1790–1797 and 1797) are at the New-York Historical Society. Another account book (1804–1834) is at the Albany Institute of History and Art, which also owns the largest collection of the artist's paintings and miniatures. Comprehensive studies of his life and work are Theodore Bolton and Irwin F. Cortelyou, *Ezra Ames of Albany: Portrait Painter, Craftsman, Royal Arch Mason, Banker, 1768–1836* (1955), and Cortelyou, *A Supplement to the Catalogue of Pictures by Ezra Ames of Albany* (1957). A biographical sketch is in the Metropolitan Museum's *Catalog of American Paintings*, vol. 1 (1994). For Ames's miniatures in context, see Robin Bolton-Smith, *Portrait Miniatures in the National Museum of American Art* (1984).

ANNE HIRSHORN

AMES, Fanny Baker (14 June 1840–21 Aug. 1931), charity organizer and women's rights advocate, was born Julia Frances Baker in Canandaigua, New York, the daughter of Increase Baker, a coal measurer, and Julia Canfield. In 1857 she completed a one-term preparatory course in teaching at Antioch College in Ohio. She taught for five years in the Cincinnati public school system before volunteering in military hospitals during the Civil War.

On 25 June 1863 Ames joined the Reverend Charles G. Ames, a Unitarian minister, in a marriage devoted to social reform. They lived in Albany, New York, with a son from his first marriage and two daughters of their own. A third child died in infancy after their 1866 move to California. In 1869 Ames and her husband attended a conference in Cleveland at which the American Woman Suffrage Association (AWSA) was founded. When they returned to California, they helped organize what would be California's first state suffrage society. Pressure from within led to affiliation with the National Woman Suffrage Association, a rival of the AWSA. Subsequently, Ames and her husband withdrew their support.

The Ameses moved in 1872 to Philadelphia where Charles held a Unitarian pastorate in Germantown. When an industrial depression struck the city the following year, Ames and her husband spearheaded the charity movement in the United States by founding the Germantown Relief Society. Following the guidelines of the Elberfeld system for the poor, Germantown was divided into eight divisions, each appointing a visiting committee of volunteers that encouraged cooperation among families in need. Money and material charity were provided only in the most dire cases.

When her husband took a job as editor of Boston's *Christian Register*, Ames dedicated herself to the advancement of women through denominational work. At the 1878 National Conference of Unitarian and Other Christian Churches in Saratoga, New York, Ames proposed the formation of an auxiliary organization dedicated to women's issues. In 1880 the Women's Auxiliary Conference of the Unitarian Church was founded with Ames as vice president. The Unitarian women pledged to make use of their "unused power" at home, "to stimulate denominational faith and work and to spread abroad a knowledge of the distinctive view by which [they strove] to live" (Fifield, p. 8). In 1889 women's auxiliary organizations from 125 branches united to become an independent body, the National Alliance of Unitarian and Other Liberal Christian Women. Ames was chosen to help draft the constitution and was elected a national leader and branch president. She continued to play an influential role in the alliance as a counselor to other women until shortly before her death.

Following the success of the Germantown Relief Society, Ames remained committed to reform in Philadelphia and in 1877 was a founding member and later president (1887–1888) of what perhaps would become the most prestigious women's reform organization of the nineteenth century, the New Century Club. Ames and her husband founded the Philadelphia Society for Organizing Charity in 1878. Following their move to Philadelphia in 1880, Ames took a particular interest in the city's poor children and the institutions that took responsibility for them. In 1883 she contributed to the founding (and was later president) of the Children's Aid Society and Bureau of Information of Pennsylvania. Under state authority, she traveled throughout Pennsylvania for five years, assisting in the organization of county branches, inspecting public institutions or almshouses, and raising money to place almshouse children with private families under the supervision of local volunteer women. After observing those methods that proved beneficial and those that proved fruitless and even abusive, Ames reported her findings to the Board of State Charities. In 1891 she delivered a paper, "The Care of Defective Children," before the National Council of Women. She was selected by Governor Russell as the first female factory inspector of Massachusetts in the same year.

After making a final move back to Boston in 1888, Ames devoted herself to educational causes while her husband was a minister at the Unitarian Church of the Disciples. From 1896 to 1899 Ames was a member of the Boston School Committee. Because of her prominence in the field of charitable and philanthropic organizations, she was chosen in 1899 as one of the first women to serve on the original board of trustees of Simmons Female College, the first New England school committed to the utilitarian education of women. Simmons was erected in honor of the seamstresses who sewed by hand the clothing that built the fortune of the late John Simmons, the school's benefactor. Ames held various offices in Massachusetts and New England suffrage associations, including presidency of the Boston Equal Suffrage Association for Good Government. Though no longer an active member, Ames expressed in a 1917 letter to the organization her pride in the active women members for their continuing work to ensure a place for women in American democracy.

Ames died at Barnstable, Massachusetts, of a heart ailment and nephritis. A devoted member of Boston's Unitarian Church of the Disciple for more than forty years, Ames was praised at her memorial service for her allegiance to Unitarianism and the advancement of women's rights, for her contribution to the church as a teacher and organizer, and as an inspiration to other women.

• For Ames's involvement with the suffrage movement see the Fanny Baker Ames Papers (Woman's Rights Collection) at Schlesinger Library, Radcliffe College, which includes the eight-page address read at Ames's memorial service on 3 Oct. 1931. Elizabeth C. Stanton et al., eds., *History of Woman Suffrage* vol. 3 (1887), makes brief mention of Ames's contribution in California. For Ames's involvement in Unitarianism and the National Alliance of Unitarian Women, see Emily A. Fifield's *A History of Alliance* (1945) and Charles Ames's *Spiritual Autobiography* (1913). Frances E. Willard and Mary A. Livermore include a sketch of Ames in their *A Woman of the Century* (1893), detailing her charity work in Philadelphia. For Ames's contribution to the founding of the Children's Aid Society see Mary Lesley Ames's *Life and Letters of Peter and Susan Lesley*, vol. 2 (1909); Frank D. Watson's *The Charity Organization Movement in the U.S.* (1922); and Children's Aid Society and Bureau of Information of Pennsylvania, *First Annual Report* (1882–1883). The New Century Club's 1899 pamphlet, *New Century Club History*, makes reference to Ames's contribution. Kenneth L. Mark outlines the founding of Simmons with reference to Ames in *Delayed by Fire, Being the Early History of Simmons College* (1945).

BARBARA L. CICCARELLI

AMES, Fisher (9 Apr. 1758–4 July 1808), Federalist party leader, member of Congress, essayist, and renowned orator, was born in Dedham, Massachusetts, the son of Nathaniel Ames, Sr., a physician, tavern keeper, and almanac writer, and Deborah Fisher. Intellectually honed, Ames was admitted to Harvard at twelve. Steeped in the classics, he excelled in elocution and participated in a debating club, the Institute of 1770. Graduating in 1774, he served with the Dedham militia at the time of the battle of Bunker Hill but did not see combat. At home he pursued his scholarly interests, reading widely in classical literature and history. He also occasionally taught school. Under the tutelage of the prominent William Tudor, Ames studied law. He was admitted to practice before the Court of Common Pleas and by 1784 before the Supreme Judicial Court in Boston. He never enjoyed his profession, preferring the stimulus of active politics.

Ames first became a public figure in 1786, responding to Shays's Rebellion with the publication of his political essay, "Lucius Junius Brutus," in the Boston *Independent Chronicle*. He roused civic concern that, "when the pillars of government are shaken" by such a revolt, the Commonwealth is in jeopardy (Seth Ames, vol. 1, p. 92). In his three "Camillus" essays of 1787, he detailed the instability of the Confederation government, contending that only a supreme federal government could revive public credit, protect the Republic, and provide "the greatest permanent happiness of the greatest number of people" (Seth Ames, vol. 2, p. 108). Through his forceful style as an essayist and the clarity of his argumentation, he soon came to the attention of men of wealth, education, and civic power.

Ames was elected in 1788 to the Massachusetts convention for ratifying the federal Constitution. His cogent analysis of the advantages of biennial congressional elections combined with his marked skill as an orator deflected anti-Federalist fears that the Constitution would subvert liberty. Opposing the popular Samuel Adams on representation and the structure of the Senate, he endorsed proposed amendments that won ratification in Massachusetts. As a supporter of the federal Constitution, Ames was elected to a term in the state legislature, and in 1788 he successfully challenged Adams for a seat in the First federal Congress.

With the opening of Congress in March 1789, Ames plunged into the process of forming the new government, serving on some sixteen committees between 1789 and 1791. His numerous legislative activities in the First Congress included shaping legislation on the American Indian trade, Indian treaties, the post office, and the permanent seat of the government. He also endeavored to maximize jurisdiction for federal courts in the Federal Judiciary Act of 1789. As an idealist, Ames became disillusioned that Congress did not reflect the virtues of the Roman Senate nor concentrate on establishing a stable, efficient government. Instead congressmen revealed narrowly local and regional interests.

In the House of Representatives Ames engaged in heated debates with James Madison, whom he respected but regarded as "very much Frenchified in his politics" (Seth Ames, vol. 1, p. 35) and "more troublesome than a declared foe" ("Memoir of Tudor," *Massachusetts Historical Society Collections*, 2d ser., vol. 8 [1819], p. 322). Ames's own dualism in politics soon surfaced. He promoted national interests and argued against encroachments upon the federal government by powerful states. Yet he fought tenaciously to defeat tariff duties and anti-British trade policies injurious to New England merchants.

Greatly impressed by Alexander Hamilton's "First Report on the Public Credit," which was presented to the House of Representatives in January 1790, Ames became the champion spokesman in the House for the secretary of the treasury's financial system, supporting funding the national debt and the assumption by the federal government of the states' revolutionary debts. He contended that since the debts of the national government were a public contract, the government could not legislate against such a contract and scale down the sum to be funded. Ames emphatically opposed Madison's compromise proposal to differentiate between the original and current holders of revolutionary securities. Under Madison's plan present speculators would be paid only at the highest market price (about 50 percent) while original holders were to receive the balance. Effective in defeating the proposed "discrimination," Ames only garnered strong public condemnation. Yet he continued to insist, "Without a firm basis for public credit, I can scarcely expect that government will last long" (Seth Ames, vol. 1, p. 79). In a powerful speech on 26 February 1790, Ames supported assumption, arguing that defending common liberty during the war was a common charge and that only the federal government could pay the debts. Despite his valiant efforts, he was unable to prevent the initial defeat of assumption.

An independent-minded Ames, however, rejected the bargaining in 1790 for proassumption votes in return for establishing the permanent capital on the Potomac. Disgusted that clear reasoning was subverted by scheming, he insisted, "The world ought to despise our public conduct" (Seth Ames, vol. 1, p. 83). Ames vigorously refuted Madison's objections to establishing a national bank, contending that Congress, with certain reservations, could do "what is necessary to the end for which the Constitution was adopted" (Joseph Gales, ed., *The Debates and Proceedings in the Congress of the United States . . .*, vol. 2 [42 vols., 1834–1856], p. 1955). His stand foreshadowed Hamilton's exposition of the doctrine of implied powers. Privately he wrote to Hamilton, "All the influence of the moneyed men ought to be wrap'd up in the union and in one Bank" (H. Syrett, ed., *The Papers of Alexander Hamilton*, vol. 8 [27 vols., 1961–1987], p. 591).

Increasing political partisanship in Congress led Ames to observe that "tranquility has smoothed the surface. But . . . faction glows within." He lashed out at southern opponents of a forceful national government, taking the position that "a debt-compelling government" is no solution for men with land and slaves "and debts and luxury" who are not really industrious (Seth Ames, vol. 1, pp. 104–5). Irritated by Ames's influence in Congress, Thomas Jefferson dismissed the Massachusetts representative as "the colossus of the monocrats and paper men," castigating him for alleged monarchical leanings and for his unsubstantiated financial speculations in the revolutionary debt.

As repercussions of the French Revolution engulfed American politics, Federalists frequently turned to this forceful orator and advocate of their cause. Urbane and erudite, Ames went to the heart of an issue, often presenting his ideas with colorful imagery near the end of a House debate. Though of moderate stature, he entranced his audience with the rapidity of his thinking and the balance he struck between reasoning and pathos. He became the exemplar of brilliant public speaking for later prominent leaders. In 1792 he married Frances Worthington, a daughter of John Worthington, one of Springfield's "River Gods." The couple had seven children.

Deteriorating relations with Great Britain over the confiscation of American vessels and issues stemming from the Revolution brought the United States to the brink of war in 1794. In an especially forceful speech on 27 January 1794, Ames rejected Madison's proposal to have Congress initiate a commercial war against Great Britain. Republican opposition to the Federalist position increased to the point that a pro-French mob in Charleston burned Ames and South Carolina representative William Loughton Smith in effigy. To Ames, John Jay's diplomatic mission to London and the resulting treaty were the only way a ruinous war with Great Britain could be avoided.

A severe illness in the spring of 1795, diagnosed as "lung fever" and possibly a precursor of Ames's later tubercular condition, fundamentally altered the representative's political career. Unable to return to Congress until early 1796, he remained a bystander during much of the bitter strife over the Jay Treaty. Federalists, anxious for rapprochement with Great Britain, pushed ratification through the Senate but encountered intense opposition in the House from Republicans, who wanted to block the treaty by denying funds to carry out its provisions. Convinced that "we dance upon the edge of the pit . . . [and] it is but a little way to the bottom," an infirm Ames rallied his strength on 28 April 1796 to defend the British treaty.

Ames gave one of the most eloquent and persuasive speeches ever heard in Congress. Dramatic and incisive, it alternated between rational argument and emotional appeal. He denounced the Republican refusal to vote appropriations since the House did not share in the treaty-making power with the president and the Senate, then he presented the grim consequences of rejection. National honor was at stake; Britain would retain control of frontier posts and unleash a devastating Indian war, which Ames portrayed in vivid terms. Spellbound, Supreme Court justice James Iredell exclaimed to Vice President John Adams, "My God, how great he is." Ames's famous speech had a decided impact on the final favorable vote to provide funds for the Jay Treaty.

Although Ames had been elected to the first four Congresses by substantial majorities, he retired to his home in Dedham in 1797 at age thirty-nine because of chronic ill health. No longer a gladiator, he dourly endeavored to counter the increasing influence of the Jeffersonian Republicans. He encouraged a strong anti-French stand during the XYZ crisis of 1798, reaping censure in the Republican press for his continued pro-British position. Undaunted, Ames advocated an undeclared naval war with France. In his view, only the Federalists could rescue the Republic from extreme democracy and anarchy, which he feared would soon engulf the United States. "The struggle with our Jacobins," he declared, "is like the good Christian's with the evil one" (Seth Ames, vol. 1, p. 245). Ames approved the restrictive Alien and Sedition Acts, yet he aided a Dedham neighbor who had run afoul of the laws. As tensions fragmented the Federalists, Ames turned against the president in 1799, when Adams on his own volition nominated William Vans Murray as minister to France to carry out a peace mission, totally undermining Federalist foreign policy. Ames did not retreat from politics, but his only remaining allies were the extremist High Federalists, known as the "Essex Junto."

As the sage of New England Federalists after 1800, Ames strove to rally resistance against the "invidious" influences of the Jeffersonian revolution. With faith in the power of the press to convince the public of the correctness of Federalist concepts, he wrote more than fifty essays, many of which were published in the Boston *Repertory* and the *New England Palladium*. In them he combated the "Jacobins" for undermining popular liberties and condemned the "ignorant rabble" who gloried in Napoléon's triumphs. Underlying Ames's direful prognostications was a fundamental distrust of the common person, who, he believed, was prone to violence and endangered the survival of the state. Reviewing the posthumous *Works of Fisher Ames* (1809) in 1809, John Quincy Adams, starkly and not entirely accurately, asserted that Ames had engaged in a "reasoning frenzy," admiring England, abhorring France, and condemning his own country.

Ames, however, was neither a misanthrope nor a hysteric. Instead, he was an engaging person, enjoying a wide circle of prominent political friends who were profoundly impressed by his intellectual brilliance. In his relationships with his neighbors he was amiable, witty, and hospitable—anything but undemocratic. His relationship with his brother, Dr. Nathaniel Ames, a resolute Jeffersonian Republican, was complicated by conflicts over inheritance, landownership, and religious affiliation that frequently led to intense clashes. But Fisher Ames never broke off contact, turning to his brother for family medical help. The needs of his growing family led Ames to resume his legal work and to invest, successfully, in the burgeoning India trade. "Squire Ames" also promoted new domestic activities through his experimental dairy farm and orchard and in support for building the Norfolk and Bristol Turnpike between Boston and Rhode Island.

Elected president of Harvard College in 1805, Ames declined the office because of his poor health. His zest for politics never abated. Though some High Federalists fostered a plan for the secession of New England from the Union, he rejected this scheme as a solution to political problems. Toward the end of his life he asserted that "rather than . . . the Union should be endangered, every sacrifice . . . should be made. . . . For his own part . . . he would stand by the ship to the last—he would pump so long as a single plank could be kept above water" (Fisher Ames Papers, Dedham Historical Society). Ravaged by "consumption," Ames died in Dedham. A public funeral in Boston became a Federalist political spectacle.

In his congressional career Ames became an influential proponent of a cohesive, enduring federal government. His genius for vivid verbal expression and trenchant thought made him an outstanding spokesman of the emerging Federalist party. In a period when the structure of the embryonic Republic was being determined, he resisted the centrifugal forces of sovereign state governments, assiduously strengthened the federal government, and supported the Hamiltonian system as the keystone of national security. After retirement, a disheartened Ames observed the spread of Jeffersonian Republicanism. Ultimately he recommended to party leaders that New England state governments become bastions for the dwindling Federalist party. Condemned by the opposition as an arch antidemocratic elitist with a dismal view of America's future, he also was extolled by Federalists for his adamant if futile defense of an idealized Republic directed by the wealthy and intelligent few. Ames has become one of the most quotable voices of the extreme Federalist position through his iconoclastic, epigrammatic observations.

• The main collection of Ames manuscripts is at the Dedham Historical Society, Dedham, Mass. Other family papers are at Stanford University, Stanford, Calif. Letters from Ames are in numerous collections, such as the Theodore Sedgwick Papers and the Timothy Pickering Papers at the Massachusetts Historical Society, Boston. Still others are at the Houghton Library, Harvard University; the Connecticut Historical Society, Hartford; the New-York Historical Society; and the Library of Congress. Ames's letters, speeches, and essays have not been published in their entirety. *Works of Fisher Ames* (1809) contains a selection of his essays and fourteen letters, while Seth Ames, ed., *Works of Fisher Ames* (2 vols., 1854), reprints numerous letters, though with deletions, and a large number of essays. A recent edition edited by W. B. Allen, *Works of Fisher Ames, as Published by Seth Ames* (2 vols., 1983), adds other letters and essays but is not comprehensive. A full-length biography of Ames is Winfred E. A. Bernhard, *Fisher Ames: Federalist and Statesman, 1758–1808* (1965). It may be supplemented by Samuel Eliot Morison, "Squire Ames and Doctor Ames," *New England Quarterly* 1 (1928): 5–31, and "The India Ventures of Fisher Ames, 1794–1804," *American Antiquarian Society Proceedings*, new ser., 37 (1927): 14–23. See also Elisha P. Douglass, "Fisher Ames, Spokesman for New England Federalism," *American Philosophical Society Proceedings* 103 (1959): 693–715; and James M. Farrell, "Fisher Ames and Political Judgment: Reason, Passion, and Vehement Style in the Jay Treaty Speech," *Quarterly Journal of Speech* 76 (1990): 415–34. Early biographical sketches are "Fisher Ames," *Port Folio*, 3d ser., 1 (1813): 2–21; and "Biographical and Critical Sketch of Fisher Ames," *Analectic Magazine* 3 (1814): 309–33.

WINFRED E. A. BERNHARD

AMES, James Barr (22 June 1846–8 Jan. 1910), dean of Harvard Law School, was born in Boston, Massachusetts, the son of Samuel Tarbell Ames, a merchant, and Mary Hartwell Barr. Ames attended the Brimmer School and the Boston Latin School. He enrolled at Harvard College in 1863, receiving an A.B. in 1868. During the next two years he taught at a private school and toured Europe.

Upon his return he studied at Harvard, earned an A.M. (1872), tutored in French and German, and lectured in medieval history. Meanwhile he studied at the Law School.

After receiving the LL.B. in 1872, Ames was asked to join the Law School faculty; his appointment was a sharp departure from the custom of hiring practicing lawyers to teach. To justify the appointment Christopher Columbus Langdell, dean of the Law School, cited Ames's excellent record as a teacher and his remarkable legal mind. He was appointed full professor in 1877, Bussey Professor of Law in 1879, and Dane Professor of Law in 1903. In 1880 he married Sarah Russell; they had two children. He became dean of the Law School in 1895 and held that position until shortly before his death.

Under Ames's deanship, legal education at Harvard became more rigorous. Breaking from the standard practice among law schools of admitting students on the basis of character and some degree of secondary education, Ames increased the requirements for admission, continuation, and graduation and doubled the length of the residency requirement to three years. A bachelor's degree became a prerequisite for a law degree, making legal education a graduate level course of study. Despite these more exacting requirements for students, the Law School witnessed unprecedented growth in enrollment.

Another significant innovation associated with Langdell and Ames concerned the method of legal instruction. Convinced that law was a science that should be studied inductively, Langdell developed the case method of instruction. The success of the case method, however, was largely due to Ames. An engaging teacher, he overcame early resistance from fellow faculty members and students who favored the traditional textbook-lecture method and helped popularize the case method by publishing nine casebooks.

The reforms introduced at Harvard Law School initially garnered widespread criticism. Many claimed that raising requirements for admission constituted a form of elitism antithetical to the egalitarian nature of the legal profession. The case method also drew criticism. Nonetheless, the reforms implemented at Harvard Law School proved ineluctable, and by the early twentieth century several major law schools had emulated Harvard's admissions policies and adopted the case method of instruction, and within a few decades Harvard's practices became the norm in legal education. Moreover, by the 1920s even business schools began using the case method.

Ames also made several noteworthy contributions to legal scholarship. In the late 1880s he played an important role in founding the highly influential and respected *Harvard Law Review* that became the standard for student-edited law reviews. In later years, he was a regular contributor. As dean, Ames helped transform the Law School library into a world-class collection. His scholarly interests included the history of common law and he published several important essays in the field. His most important works were published posthumously in *Lectures on Legal History and Miscellaneous Legal Essays* (1913). He also served as the chairman of the American Bar Association's legal education division (1904). Ames died in Wilton, New Hampshire.

• Harvard Law School and Harvard University Archives has some of Ames's papers connected with his work as dean. Ames's role in legal education is discussed in William P. LaPiana, *Logic and Experience: The Origin of Modern American Legal Education* (1994), as well as histories of Harvard Law School, including *The Centennial History of the Harvard Law School, 1817–1917* (1918); Arthur E. Sutherland, *The Law at Harvard: A History of Ideas and Men, 1817–1967* (1967); and Charles Warren, *History of the Harvard Law School and of Early Legal Conditions in America*, vol. 2 (1908). A lengthy obituary is in the *Harvard Law Review* 23, no. 5 (1910). Obituaries are also in the *New York Times*, the *Boston Globe*, and the *Boston Herald*, all 9 Jan. 1910.

KATHLEEN A. MAHONEY

AMES, Jessie Daniel (2 Nov. 1883–21 Feb. 1972), antiracism reformer and suffragist, was born Jessie Harriet Daniel in Palestine, Texas, the daughter of James Malcolm Daniel, a train dispatcher and telegraph operator, and Laura Maria Leonard, a teacher. James and Laura Daniel were pious parents who stressed the importance of education but showed little affection for their children. They openly preferred their younger daughter, Lulu, and Jessie suffered deeply from a lack of self-confidence. When Jessie was four, the family moved to Georgetown, Texas, an impoverished and often violent community. There Jessie attended local schools and, later, Southwestern University.

Fearful of spinsterhood, Jessie married Roger Post Ames in 1905. Roger Ames, a friend of Jessie's father, was a U.S. Public Health Service physician. The marriage was not a happy one; the couple were sexually incompatible, and the Ames family felt Roger had married "beneath" him. Rather than face pressure from his family, Roger pursued medical research in South America, deserting his wife for most of their marriage. With the exception of several trips to South America, Jessie lived with her wealthy married sister in Tennessee. In 1914 Roger Ames died of blackwater fever, leaving Jessie with the care of their two children and with a third on the way.

At age thirty-one Jessie Daniel Ames began her public career to support herself and her children. She and her mother ran a local telephone company. As Ames grew more confident, she developed an interest in social justice issues and began to work for woman suffrage. She was elected treasurer of the Texas Equal Suffrage Association in 1918 and worked to secure suffrage for women in primary elections. In an effort to organize woman voters, Ames became founding president of the Texas League of Women Voters and served as a delegate to the national Democratic party conventions from 1920 to 1928. By working in organizations such as the Federation of Women's Clubs and the American Association of University Women, Ames sought to further women's participation in the reform movement.

Through her participation in woman suffrage, Ames discovered the limitations of the reform movement. She grew increasingly sensitive to the contradictions of a movement that served a predominately white constituency in a South dominated by the Ku Klux Klan. To educate herself on racial issues, Ames enrolled in courses at the University of Chicago and began to address racial concerns. Her work against racial injustice began in 1922, when she became the director of women's work for the Commission on Interracial Cooperation (CIC) in Atlanta, where she held various positions until the 1940s.

By 1930 Ames was alienated from suffragist colleagues and began to concentrate on antiracism work. In that same year she founded the Association of Southern Women for the Prevention of Lynching (ASWPL), as a volunteer organization within the CIC, though the ASWPL eventually outgrew its parent organization. The ASWPL grew out of Ames's belief that lynching was the most visible symbol of black oppression within southern society. As a means of social control over blacks, whites used the threat of lynching as a form of coercion for enforcing labor contracts. Ames believed that the fear of violence against white women by black men allowed the justification for lynching as a means to protect white women. The goal of the ASWPL was the eradication of mob violence by whites against blacks within southern society, through educational efforts that attacked the justification for lynching and through encouraging women to refute the stereotype of themselves as vulnerable creatures in need of protection. The cornerstone of Ames's educational campaign was statistics from her own research stating that of 204 lynchings over an eight-year period, only 29 percent of the victims were accused of crimes against white women.

Ames traveled extensively throughout the South as the chief organizer for the ASWPL and formed local chapters by working mainly through Protestant women's missionary societies. She also formed alliances with Jewish women's groups, the Young Women's Christian Association, and organizations such as the Parent-Teachers Association. The ASWPL gained support from both the white and the African-American press. "The daughters of the South are not content with hurling denunciations," wrote one newspaper, "they are militantly marching out to make war upon the barbarism that has flourished in their name" (Hall [1979], p. 164).

To her contemporaries Ames appeared "animated, positive, and full of determination" (Hall [1979], p. 262). Her chief contributions were her dedication as a single-minded reformer and her genius as an organizational founder. Ultimately Ames's desire to preserve her autonomy within the ASWPL prevented the organization from working more effectively with other organizations on related causes. Though outraged by racially motivated violence, Ames failed to collaborate with black reformers or to significantly include blacks within the ASWPL. Though quick to respond to persons less fortunate than herself, Ames was unresponsive to the issues raised by blacks themselves. Ames became increasingly alienated from the emergent liberalism of the late 1930s and early 1940s, and as the number of lynchings decreased the ASWPL itself dissolved in 1942. Ames's attempts to reinvigorate the organization failed, and she was forced to retire from the reform movement.

In retirement, Ames moved to Tryon, North Carolina, and from 1944 to 1968 devoted her energies to local Democratic politics. Always busy, the loss of her life's work took its toll, and her old feelings of insecurity returned. In addition to the rigors of her public career, Ames faced personal trials most of her life. Her youngest daughter contracted polio in 1920. Money was always a problem, and the situation worsened when her mother's resources were wiped out in the depression. Influenced by her own experience, Ames ensured that all her children were educated and were financially independent. Severe arthritis eventually forced Ames to return to Texas to be near her daughter. Jessie Daniel Ames died in Austin, Texas.

• The Jessie Daniel Ames Papers are in the Southern Historical Collection at the University of North Carolina, Chapel Hill, and contain materials related to her personal and public life. The CIC papers, 1919–1944, and the ASWPL papers, 1930–1942, are at the Atlanta University Carter Woodruff Library and are also available through University Microfilms, Ann Arbor, Mich. The Texas State Library, Austin, holds Ames's papers related to the League of Women Voters and the Texas Equal Suffrage Association. Papers related to her suffrage work are in the Dallas Historical Society. An interview with Ames, c. 1965/1966, is in the Southern Regional Council Papers, Southern Oral History Program, University of North Carolina, Chapel Hill. Ames's publications include *Cast Down Your Bucket Where You Are* (1932) and *The Changing Character of Lynching* (1942), both published by the CIC, and *Southern Women Look at Lynching* (1937), published by the ASWPL. For additional information, see Jacqueline Dowd Hall, *Revolt against Chivalry: Jessie Daniel Ames and the Women's Campaign against Lynching* (1979) and her "Second Thoughts on Jessie Daniel Ames," in *The Challenge of Feminist Biography: Writing the Lives of Modern American Women*, ed. Sarah Alpen (1992).

SHERYL A. KUJAWA

AMES, Mary Clemmer (6 May 1831?–18 Aug. 1884), journalist and author, was born Mary Clemmer in Utica, New York, the daughter of Abraham Clemmer, a merchant, and Margaret Kneale. Her father came from an Alsatian Huguenot family that had settled in this country before the American Revolution, and her mother had emigrated from the British Isle of Man in 1827. She received her formal education at the Westfield Academy in Westfield, Massachusetts, where the family moved about 1847; she attended the academy probably until 1850. A poem that she wrote at the academy was published in the *Springfield* (Mass.) *Republican*, a well-known newspaper whose editor, Samuel Bowles III (1826–1878), later helped her career.

Mary Clemmer's father was a failure as a merchant; this put such financial pressures on the family that in 1851 she entered an unfortunate marriage to Daniel Ames, a Presbyterian minister, with whom she moved to Knowlesville, New York, and later to Winona, Minnesota, where he held pastorates. They had no children. After serving as principal of a boys' school in Jersey City, New Jersey, her husband obtained a federal job as a storekeeper in Harpers Ferry, Virginia (now West Virginia), at the start of the Civil War. There Mary Ames observed the surrender of the town to Confederate forces and was taken prisoner briefly. Her novel, *Eirene; or, A Woman's Right* (1871), drew on these experiences and received acclaim. She served as a nurse in Union hospitals in Washington, D.C., during the war and formed friendships with political figures, including Representative Portus Baxter and Senator Justin S. Morrill, both of Vermont, who later became sources of news for her columns.

Eager to earn her own living, in 1859, before the war started, Ames contributed letters from New York City, where she was living temporarily, to the *Utica Morning Herald* and the *Springfield Republican*. In New York she was befriended by the sisters Alice and Phoebe Cary, authors who introduced her to literary circles. She later wrote an acclaimed tribute to them, *Memorial of Alice and Phoebe Cary* (1873).

Ames was so unhappy during her marriage that she considered suicide. But instead she separated from her husband in 1865 after the publication of her first novel, *Victoire* (1864), and embarked on her successful journalistic career from the nation's capital. The couple was finally divorced in 1874, and she resumed her maiden name but referred to herself as "Mrs. Clemmer."

Ames's widely read column, "A Woman's Letter from Washington," began in 1866; it ran in the *Independent*, a New York religious weekly with a Radical Republican orientation, until her death. The column ranged over politics, personalities, and women's roles, with Ames condemning political leaders for morally questionable conduct. Unlike other Washington women correspondents of the day, she prided herself on not covering society news. Viewing Congress from the ladies' galleries, she claimed that she had no need to compete directly with male journalists by entering the congressional press galleries. For example, in her column of 24 March 1870 she wrote, "Because a woman is a public correspondent it does not make it at all necessary that she as an individual should be conspicuously public—that she should run about with pencils in her mouth and pens in her ears; that she should invade the Reporters' Galleries, crowded with men; that she should go anywhere as a mere reporter where she would not be received as a lady." Her prose, although often sentimental and verbose in the style of the era, could be biting. Of Representative Roscoe Conkling of New York, she said in the column of 3 May 1866: "The trouble with 'Roscoe' is that he is as arrogant as he is able. . . . It was the misfortune of Roscoe Conkling to have been considered very early a rising great man at home." Commenting on the death of President James A. Garfield, who was shot by a disappointed office seeker, she wrote in her 29 September 1881 column: "Heaven was kind to his fame to take him when it did."

During the 1870s Ames worked at a feverish pace, publishing books as well as doing newspaper work. From 1869 to 1872 she wrote for the *Brooklyn Union*, owned by Henry C. Bowen, who also was publisher of the *Independent*, churning out columns, book reviews, and other assignments. In 1872 she earned $5,000 annually, believed to be the highest salary paid to an American newspaperwoman to that time. After her contract with the *Union* ended, she became a correspondent for the *Cincinnati Commercial*.

In the mid-1870s severe headaches resulting from overwork began to cause her discomfort. Her hard-earned income, however, permitted her to buy a mansion on Capitol Hill in 1876 and to bring her parents there to live with her. In 1878 she fractured her skull when she panicked and jumped from a carriage because the horses bolted. She never fully recovered, and her literary output declined. In 1883 she married Edmund Hudson, a Washington journalist who edited the *Army and Navy Register*. The couple took a wedding trip to Europe hoping to restore her health, but after she returned later that year she was stricken with paralysis and died in her Washington home of a cerebral hemorrhage.

Ames's significance as a Washington correspondent lay in the skill with which she operated in the male world of politics and journalism by trading on the Victorian mystique that women were morally superior to men. Although an advocate of suffrage, she did not work for it publicly. Instead, appearing to be a personally timid individual, she positioned herself as a political observer whose nature as a "true woman" gave her a religious responsibility to criticize the corruption of male political leaders.

• A small collection of Ames's papers, mainly letters written to her and a file of her columns, are at the Rutherford B. Hayes Library, Fremont, Ohio. Her books include a third novel, *His Two Wives* (1875); two collections of her columns, *Outlines of Men, Women and Things* (1873) and *Ten Years in Washington: Life and Scenes in the National Capital as a Woman Sees Them* (1875); a second memorial tribute, *Memorial Sketch of Elizabeth Emerson Atwater: Written for Her Friends* (1879); and *Poems of Life & Nature* (1883). A letter she wrote in support of woman suffrage can be found in Elizabeth Cady Stanton et al., eds., *History of Woman Suffrage* (1886). Biographical accounts are by Lilian Whiting, "Mary Clemmer," in *Our Famous Women: An Authorized Record* (1884), and Edmund Hudson in *An American Woman's Life and Work: A Memorial of Mary Clemmer* (1886). A modern assessment is Maurine H. Beasley, "Mary Clemmer Ames: A Victorian Woman Journalist," *Hayes Historical Journal* 2 (Spring 1978): 57–63. Obituaries are in the *New York Times* and the *Washington* (D.C.) *Evening Star*, both 19 Aug. 1884, and the *Literary News*, Sept. 1884.

MAURINE H. BEASLEY

AMES, Nathaniel (22 July 1708–11 July 1764), almanac maker, physician, and innkeeper, was born in Bridgewater, Massachusetts, the son of Captain Nathaniel Ames, Sr., an astronomer and mathematician, and Susannah Howard. Probably after an apprenticeship with a country doctor, Ames became a doctor. With the likely assistance of his father, in 1725 Ames produced the first almanac to carry his name, though he was a youth of only seventeen. The almanac soon became well known and remained a staple product in New England, appearing annually for a half century.

In 1732 Ames moved to Dedham, outside Boston. In September 1735 he married Mary Fisher, and in October 1737, the couple had a son, Fisher Ames. The son died less than a year later but survived his mother, who had died in November 1737. Her death led to an important colonial lawsuit in which Ames claimed his wife's residuary interest in property. He won the case, thereby establishing that the estate interest passed to the father as next of kin to his now-deceased son; the decision upheld province law but was contrary to the English common law tradition of the rules of inheritance.

In 1740 Ames married Deborah Fisher, the daughter of Jeremiah Fisher, whose family appears to have been unrelated to that of his first wife. The couple had five children; the eldest, Nathaniel Ames III, succeeded his father as an almanac maker and physician and later became a Jeffersonian Democrat. The third son, Fisher Ames, was a lawyer, a conservative intellectual, and a Federalist congressman. Nathaniel Ames also was proprietor of the Inn at the Sign of the Sun in Dedham, which he managed until his death.

Ames claims historical importance as publisher of his almanac. His first almanac (published in late 1725 for 1726) predated James Franklin's almanac by three years and *Poor Richard's Almanack*, published in Philadelphia by Franklin's brother, Benjamin Franklin, by eight years. Printed by Bartholomew Green, Jr., until around 1733 and then by Green's brother-in-law John Draper from 1736 to 1763, Ames's almanac was a single folded sheet, made up in sixteen pages, from 1725 until 1759, when it was increased by a half sheet to twenty-four pages. The almanac contained accurate astronomical observations (Ames, probably trained by his father, was a talented astronomer) and included weather predictions, principally derived from astrology, interspersed with wit, wisdom, predictions, and maxims, plus epigrams, farming information, and medical advice. Entries for November 1754, for example, note that "More die by Gluttony, than perish by the Sword," "Now some light Heads and sharp Wits invent smooth Lies, to the prejudice of honest Men," and "The Herd that Graze, the barren Fields, complain and shrink and shiver with the beating Rain."

Poetry, written by Ames and of a somewhat higher quality than that found in other almanacs of the period, short articles, and extracts from English poets such as John Milton, Alexander Pope, Sir Richard Blackmore, and John Dryden graced the pages of the almanac as well. Ames also provided practical information such as interest tables, the values of selected currencies, and lists of post roads and road houses, always including his own tavern. In later years, there was more information on history and politics, especially relating to the colonial wars between Great Britain and France and the emerging fiscal crisis in the American colonies. Ames was a partisan of the colonials in the political conflicts that erupted, and in 1758 he predicted the future greatness of British America and the spread of its arts and sciences to the Pacific Ocean. In late June 1764 Ames took ill in Dedham and died there shortly after. The almanac was continued for some ten years after Ames's death by his equally able son, Nathaniel Ames III, who enlisted its pages in the service of the Boston patriots as the Revolution approached.

Ames's almanac conveyed large quantities of information and entertainment for the public, in prose and verse, from history and literature; the absurd consorted amiably with the wise, and amusing anecdotes followed essays on scientific themes. But the main purpose of the almanac was to provide practical information in a readily accessible format and secondarily, to entertain through literature and other information in a variety of formats. By mid-century historical and political topics had also found their way into Ames's annual. Ames's almanac was said eventually to have achieved sales of more than 60,000 copies annually throughout New England (in later years there were also several pirated versions), and literary historian Moses Coit Tyler regarded Ames's almanac as superior to that of *Poor Richard*, noting that "Ames's almanac was . . . , probably, the most pleasing representative we have of a form of literature that furnished so much entertainment to our ancestors, and that preserves for us so many characteristic tints of their life and thought" (*A History of American Literature, 1607–1765* [1949], p. 365).

• The principal source of information for the career of Nathaniel Ames remains Samuel Briggs, *The Essays, Humor, and Poems of Nathaniel Ames* (1891), which publishes in chronological order much of the contents of *Ames' Almanack*. Useful references are still to be found in J. H. Tuttle, "The Two Nathaniel Ames," Colonial Society of Massachusetts, *Publications* 19 (1916–1917): 259–65; George Lyman Kittredge, *The Old Farmer and His Almanack* (1904); and Fisher Ames, *A Bit of Ames Genealogy* (1898). A monograph useful for setting the context of Ames's work is John T. Kelly, *Practical Astronomy during the Seventeenth Century: Almanac-Makers in America and England* (1991), while other estimates are found in David D. Denker, "American Almanacs in the Eighteenth Century," *Journal of the Rutgers University Li-*

brary 18 (1954): 12–25, and Robb Sagendorph, *America and Her Almanacs* (1970). Milton Drake, *Almanacs of the United States* (1962), is a comprehensive bibliography and location list.

WILLIAM L. JOYCE

AMES, Nathaniel (9 Oct. 1741–20 July 1822), almanac writer, physician, and political activist, was born in Dedham, Massachusetts, the son of Nathaniel Ames, Sr., and Deborah Fisher. Nathaniel, Sr., strongly influenced his son with his deep interest in the "new science" of Isaac Newton and his activities as a physician, tavern proprietor, and compiler of a notable almanac. At sixteen Nathaniel, Jr., entered Harvard College and in January 1758 began to keep a diary. His lively, absorptive mind responded to new ideas, particularly Professor John Winthrop's lectures on physics or "natural philosophy." Whether making rockets, engaging in "much deviltry," or taking part in forbidden plays, such as James Thomson's *Tancred and Sigismunda*, "for which we are like to be prosecuted," Ames was an eager participant (Ames Diary, 13 June, 9 Sept. 1760, Nathaniel Ames, Jr., Papers).

Despite his Harvard-engendered resistance to authority, Ames was close to his father and, after graduation, assisted him in his medical practice. In August 1761 he noted, "Begun the Practice of Phy[sician] by bleeding a Taylor in the Foot." On 11 July 1764 he poignantly wrote, "My Father's noble and generous soul took his flight into the region of spirits." Encouraged by friends to continue the almanacs, Ames ran the family tavern and maintained his practice while fending off intruding medical "quacks" and rival almanac makers. As eldest, Ames was expected to assume responsibility in a family where his brother Fisher Ames was only six. Ames testily asserted, "I was deeply engaged in calculating for an Almanack for 1767 and broke off by the importunity of my mother, to settle the estate" (Ames Diary, 4 Sept. 1766).

Until the outbreak of the American Revolution, Ames continued publication of the almanac, *An Astronomical Diary; or, Almanack*. Extremely popular throughout New England, it had an annual circulation of approximately 60,000. The almanacs contained a potpourri of useful information and skillfully written essays on politics, literature, and science, interspersed with humorous and trenchant observations. In his writings, he promoted colonial self-sufficiency through agriculture, discussed the frequency of eclipses, or reminded readers that "ignorance among the common people is the very basis . . . of tyranny and oppression" (Briggs, p. 382).

Responding to the escalating colonial crisis, Ames expressed radical opposition to British policies in his almanacs and diary. In 1765 he noted, "The country incens'd against the Stamp Distributors and begin to hang them in effigy" (Ames Diary, Aug. 1765). Honoring William Pitt for his role in Parliament's repeal of the hated Stamp Act, Ames and local Sons of Liberty erected a bust of Pitt on a "Pillar of Liberty" on Dedham Common. In January 1775 Ames turned from political to personal affairs when he married Meletiah Shuttleworth. They had no children, but they took guardianship of Meletiah's young, orphaned sister. Ames served as surgeon with the outbreak of fighting in April 1775, marching to Concord with Dedham's 242 militiamen. Forty years later he reminisced, "I went arm'd to Conc[or]d fight extracted a ball from J. Everet's arm. Dead men and horses strew'd along Road" (Ames Diary, 19 Apr. 1815).

Recurrent smallpox epidemics during the Revolution led Ames to practice inoculation with "Variolus Matter," a risky procedure used before cowpox vaccine was adopted. With patients from Dedham, Newport, and Providence, he was licensed to practice, but a fearful town meeting curbed him. He commented ruefully, "Court suspend my Hospital & turn many Guineas out of my pocket" (Ames Diary, 3 Sept. 1776). He continued inoculating in Marblehead, returning to Dedham in June 1777 with "More than 50 in my Hospital" (Ames Diary, 11 June 1777). Although midwives were preferred, Ames served as physician in numerous births until he was nearly eighty. Constantly called on for his medical services, he even reached patients on snowshoes or by skating on the Charles River. As an outspoken advocate of medical education and physicians' organizations to protect "this noble science," he joined the Massachusetts Medical Society and in 1811 promoted the Massachusetts College of Physicians.

Opinionated, overtly critical of his townsmen, and outspoken in his reactions against his brilliant Federalist brother Fisher Ames, Nathaniel Ames nevertheless was charitable to the unfortunate. During the Revolution he helped release Dedham's Anglican minister from a Boston prison ship. Siding with Shays's rebels in 1786–1787, he was sensitive to the "many oppressions" of the common people while "all property [was] accumulating . . . into a few people's hands" (Ames Diary, 21 Jan. 1787).

Ames's political development led to unswerving support of Jeffersonian Republicanism. Hostile to lawyers and Federalists, he championed government "not by the terror of power but by the pen and tongue of reason" (Ames Diary, addendum, 1794). He rejoiced in French revolutionary successes and denounced President George Washington for signing the pro-British Jay Treaty, regarding it as the "highest insult" to Americans. When Republican opposition intensified, he exulted, "The spirit of '75 is not evaporated," but made no comment about Fisher's famous congressional speech supporting the treaty. In 1799 Ames was brought before the U.S. Circuit Court in Boston, accused of contempt of court for refusing to testify about a "Liberty Pole" set up in Dedham in defiance of the Sedition Act. Furious at being fined, he stormed, "I was set among pickpocks at the Bar, and was spunged of 8 dollars" (Ames Diary, 22 Oct. 1799).

To Ames, Jefferson's election to the presidency signified "the irresistible propagation of the Rights of Man," while to Fisher Ames it was the nadir of Federalism. As a Yankee Republican, Ames considered Jefferson sacrosanct and condemned Alexander Hamilton, when he visited Dedham, as the "high Adulterer." In contrast to many New Englanders, Ames strongly advocated the Embargo of 1807 and gloried in American victories in the War of 1812. During the Missouri crisis of 1820, he was incensed that a Republican Congress did nothing to "combat Slave holding States who speculate on breeding slaves" (Ames Diary, 8 Mar. 1820).

Content to remain active locally rather than seeking a national political forum, Ames was influential in helping create Norfolk County and, as county chairman, rousing support for Democratic-Republican candidates. He was appointed a justice of the peace in 1790. In 1793 Governor John Hancock appointed him clerk of the Court of General Sessions and Common Pleas, where he roused Federalist antipathy. In 1797 he noted, "Am persecuted by the Hedgehogs [Federalists]—yield Clerk's office . . . to one of the Order" (Ames Diary, 21 Aug. 1797). Yet he resumed his clerkship subsequently and served as justice of the peace as late as 1812.

Often at odds, the Ames brothers even clashed publicly over political philosophy and party policies as well as over fence lines and farming. Fisher supported appointing a new Congregational minister in 1802, while an irate Nathaniel refused to agree and joined the Episcopal church. Despite the altercation, Fisher likewise transferred his membership a few years later. Yet Nathaniel was not merely a curmudgeon; he was colorful, bright-minded, and emotionally dedicated to the common people. His intellectual reach encompassed science, Ricardian economics, French literature, and ecclesiastical history, and he vigorously encouraged new modes of transportation and "factory enterprize." In many ways he was atypical, combining unique practical and professional talents in his role as a major figure of his community. His diary of sixty-three years with pungent and witty commentaries is a superb source of information on life in a rural community within the orbit of Boston. Ames died in Dedham.

• The papers of Nathaniel Ames, Jr., at the Dedham Historical Society include Ames's diaries, his medical and legal papers, and a file of the Ames almanacs. The society also has papers of Nathaniel Ames, Sr., papers of Fisher Ames, and Dedham newspapers of the period: *Columbian Minerva*, *Dedham Minerva*, and the *Dedham Gazette*. Materials relating to Dedham are at the Massachusetts Historical Society, Boston, and at the American Antiquarian Society, Worcester. In the 1890s extracts from Ames's diaries were published in "Extracts from the Diary of Dr. Nathaniel Ames," ed. Sarah B. Baker et al., Dedham Historical Society, *Register* 1 (1890) through 14 (1904). Charles Warren, *Jacobin and Junto; or, Early American Politics as Viewed in the Diary of Dr. Nathaniel Ames, 1758–1822* (1931), published extensive passages from the diaries. The Ames almanacs were reprinted chronologically in *The Essays, Humor, and Poems of Nathaniel Ames, Father and Son . . . from Their Almanacks, 1726–1775*, comp. Samuel Briggs (1891). Clifford Shipton's essay on Ames in *Sibley's Harvard Graduates*, vol. 15 (1970), contains interesting biographical data. Details on the interaction of the politically opposite brothers are in Winfred E. A. Bernhard, *Fisher Ames, Federalist and Stateman, 1758–1808* (1965). Samuel Eliot Morison, "Squire Ames and Dr. Ames," *New England Quarterly* 1 (1928): 5–31, subjectively presents the contrast between Nathaniel and Fisher Ames. "Nathaniel Ames's Correspondence with Nathaniel Ames, Jr., 1758," ed. Julius H. Tuttle, Colonial Society of Massachusetts, *Proceedings* 19 (1917): 259–65, illuminates the relationship of father and son.

WINFRED E. A. BERNHARD

AMES, Nathan Peabody (1 Sept. 1803–3 Apr. 1847), manufacturer and entrepreneur, was born in Dracut (now Lowell), Massachusetts, the son of Nathan Peabody Ames, a cutlery and edge toolmaker, and Phoebe Tyler. Nathan served an apprenticeship with his father and then joined the prosperous family business. In 1829 Ames met Edmund Dwight, who offered him four years of rent-free use of property in Cabotville, Massachusetts, if he would move himself and his business to that location (Cabotville was incorporated as Chicopee in 1848). Ames agreed to the condition and he, his father, and his younger brother, James Tyler Ames, moved to Cabotville the same year.

At that time the manufacturing industry in western Massachusetts was underdeveloped, and the Connecticut river had not yet been used for industrial purposes. The Ames family set up shop in Cabotville, and Nathan Ames devoted most of his time to making swords. He was fortunate that at that time there was an increased demand for swords and that the man who had previously made most of the swords for the federal government (Nathan Starr of Middletown, Connecticut) had ceased production. During the 1830s Ames made thousands of swords for elite volunteer militia companies in Massachusetts and throughout New England. In June 1832 he received a contract from the federal government to produce 2,000 artillery swords. This was only the first of many contracts he would receive from the U.S. government. By the late 1830s Ames was also producing swords for the newly created Republic of Texas. He went on to receive more contracts for the production of dragoon sabres and swords for both the U.S. Army and the U.S. Navy. Branching out into the artillery department, he cast his first bronze cannon at Cabotville in 1836.

Ames and his brother consolidated their activities in 1834 with the incorporation of the Ames Manufacturing Company, founded with a capitalization of $30,000. This sum grew substantially during the 1830s as the brothers expanded into the making of leather belting, military accoutrements, bells, and various other ornamental fixtures. By around 1840 the company had a total capitalization of $250,000.

In spite of this success, Ames was worried as the 1840s began by the knowledge that the United States government had sent a commission of ordnance officers abroad to examine weaponry made in Europe. In 1840 Ames went to Europe himself to determine the extent of his competition. He returned to Massachusetts in 1841 and participated in the takeover of the Chicopee Falls Company, which bolstered the fortunes of the Ames Manufacturing Company.

While his business fortunes continued to flourish, Ames's health began to deteriorate. His physical problems had begun in the spring of 1840, during his trip to England, when he had dental work done in London. An amalgam paste—probably of silver and mercury—was used, and Ames soon developed a form of spleen cancer. His condition was discovered soon after his return to the United States, and he was placed under a doctor's care in 1841. Since there was some hope for his recovery, he married Mary C. Bailey of Newburyport, Massachusetts, in October 1842; the couple had no children. Ames struggled against his illness for a number of years before he succumbed in Chicopee. His net worth at the time of his death was $40,174.52, a surprisingly low sum given the extent of his manufacturing activities. A devout Congregationalist, he was a quiet but active philanthropist and had given half of his fortune for the building of the Third Congregational church in Cabotville in 1834.

Ames was a remarkable craftsman and manufacturer. His work in the area of sword production had no rival during the 1830s and 1840s, and the business that he and his brother created remained the primary furnisher of swords for the U.S. government for more than a generation after his death. Both as a craftsman and a businessman, Ames exemplified the virtues that were extolled in early nineteenth-century New England: hard work, thrift, and success followed by local philanthropy. What was most unusual about his manufacuring career was the extent to which he dominated a market. Swords made by "N. P. Ames/Cutler/Springfield" were used by militia units, U.S. Army and naval units, and the army of the Republic of Texas during his lifetime.

• The best single source for Ames's life and career is John D. Hamilton, *The Ames Sword Company 1829–1935* (1983). There is an important article on the Ames company in the *Springfield Republican*, 15 Jan. 1899. Other helpful sources are Louise Johnson, *Chicopee Illustrated* (1896), and Clifton Johnson, *Hampden County, 1636–1936* (1936).

SAMUEL WILLARD CROMPTON

AMES, Oakes (10 Jan. 1804–8 May 1873), businessman and politician, was born in North Easton, Massachusetts, the son of Oliver Ames, a manufacturer, and Susanna Angier. He was educated in local schools and, for a few months, at Dighton Academy. At the age of sixteen, he entered his father's shovel factory as an apprentice, rising quickly to become the works superintendent and then his father's assistant. In 1827 he married Evelina Orvile Gilmore, and for the next three decades lived with her and their four children in one wing of his father's house opposite the factory.

In 1844 Ames's father turned over two-thirds of the business to Oakes and his younger brother Oliver, Jr. The gold rush and railroad development combined to create a dynamic market for competitively priced, lightweight shovels. Ames was frugal and industrious but also showed a readiness to grasp new opportunities and take risks. Under his management profits grew rapidly and by 1855 he had accrued sufficient spare capital to begin speculating in land and railroads in the West. Sensing the future business opportunities of a transcontinental railroad, he promoted railroads in Iowa, two of which would later bring much of the Union Pacific traffic through to the East.

As sectional tensions rose in the 1850s, Ames was drawn into politics, supporting the establishment of the Republican party. He contributed $10,000 to the Emigrant Aid Society during the conflict between Free Soil and proslavery forces in Kansas, and in 1860 he was elected to the Massachusetts executive council. During the Civil War he was involved in the mobilization of state government resources and he personally raised and equipped two regiments for service. In 1862 he ran for the U.S. Congress and, in the most Republican state in the Union, was returned for the second district with a comfortable majority of 3,364. As a congressman, Ames was neither ambitious nor publicly prominent, rarely making an intervention on the floor of the House. But he was a valued working member of several committees, the most important of which was the House Committee on the Pacific Railroad. In this latter capacity he was intimately involved in legislation to promote and regulate western rail routes. He also developed a good personal relationship with President Abraham Lincoln and made a substantial financial contribution to the president's reelection campaign in 1864. Ames was a taciturn man, but friends regarded him as unpretentious and honest. He was much respected in Congress for his business expertise.

In 1865 Ames and his brother were approached by Thomas Durant, vice president and chief promoter of the Union Pacific Railroad, who wanted their reputations and capital to breathe life into a struggling project. Although the Union Pacific had been endowed by an act of 1864 with $54 million of public credit and a grant of twenty acres of land per mile of track, the notion of building a railroad across hundreds of miles of unsettled territory had not presented an attractive risk for capital investment. Consequently, Durant had sought a means of limiting his liability for investors while at the same time exploiting government subsidies in order to make quick profits. Resorting to a strategy employed by other promoters of railroads at this time, Durant became president of his own finance company, the Crédit Mobilier of America, and contracted with himself at an inflated price to build the road. While ensuring that backers would receive a return on their investment during the construction stage of the project, this arrangement artificially inflated costs and concentrated the resulting profits among a small clique of stockholders. In August 1865 Ames bought a major stake in the Crédit Mobilier, motivated by profit, the need to invest spare capital, and the desire, he later said, to connect his name publicly with "the greatest public work of the present century" (*Memoir*, p. 113).

Construction proceeded slowly, hampered by materials of poor quality and a growing feud between Durant and the Ameses over control of policy. In 1867

Durant was ejected from the vice presidency of the Crédit Mobilier, but through his continuing influence as a stockholder, and in his capacity as vice president of the Union Pacific, he succeeded in preventing the Crédit Mobilier from securing any future contracts from the Union Pacific. Although not at this stage a director of either company, Ames broke the impasse by devising a scheme by which he contracted as an individual with the railroad to build 667 miles of track. He then assigned his contract to a board of seven trustees, all of whom were directors and principal stockholders of the Crédit Mobilier, in which capacity they would receive the profits. Under the Ames contract, the total price, to be paid in bonds and stock of the railroad at par, worked out at an average of more than $70,000 per mile. This was despite the fact that 138 miles of the contracted road had already been built at a cost of only $27,000 per mile. Ames was now the most powerful figure in the project, and the extent of his responsibilities meant that he was playing for high stakes.

In late 1867 Ames actively sought buyers for Crédit Mobilier stock. Later confessing to a desire for "capital and influence," he approached several congressmen. He wished to create, he wrote, a "general favorable feeling" since "if the community had confidence in our ultimate success, that success was insured" (*Poland Report*, p. 16). Ames thought this a legitimate means of securing federal support for the enterprise, which, after all, was of "incalculable benefit to the government" (*Memoir*, p. 124). A shady tone was given to these transactions, however, because Ames did not record his deals systematically, and because the stock he sold, which the holder was in several cases to pay for from the first dividend rather than when it was issued, remained in his name. This last provision was in part a means of shielding the congressmen from the possible implications of a brewing legal storm that was eventually to shatter Ames's reputation for honesty. In November 1868 Henry S. McComb, a leading stockholder in the Crédit Mobilier, began a long battle to claim ownership of the shares being sold to congressmen. McComb alleged that Ames was distributing the stock to congressmen at a rate below the market price and that in effect he was therefore bribing them with preferential rates on shares that were rightfully not even his to sell. McComb intended to substantiate these charges with three injudicious letters written by Ames in which, discussing his efforts to distribute Crédit Mobilier stock among congressmen, Ames commented that he would "put them where they would do most good to us." Arguing that "we want more friends in this congress" in order to ensure that "we shall not be interfered with," Ames observed that it was difficult to get men committed enough to support the railroad "unless they have an interest to do so" (*Poland Report*, pp. 5–7). From this evidence Ames appeared to be intent on using the shares to buy political influence among his congressional colleagues. McComb had at first attempted to use the letters to extort a personal settlement from Ames. When that failed he released them to the court.

In the midst of the presidential campaign of 1872, the *New York Sun* published the letters together with a series of wild allegations about the "most damaging exhibition of official and private villainy ever laid bare to the gaze of the world" (4 Sept. 1872). Only $16,000 worth of shares had been sold to nine representatives and two senators. But the campaign was already dominated by the issue of "reform," and politicians reacted to the dramatic "revelations" with panic. Most of those who had taken stock denied their involvement, while those who were genuinely uninvolved rushed to condemn their colleagues. Ames was not a candidate for reelection, but to his horror he suddenly found himself at the center of a major political scandal implicating, among others, Vice President Schuyler Colfax and Vice President–elect Henry Wilson.

In December 1872 Congress appointed two committees of inquiry whose open hearings aroused great public excitement. One, chaired by representative Luke P. Poland, investigated the bribery allegations. It concluded that Ames had sold stock at much below its true value, payment for some of which was to come only from future dividends, with the intention of influencing the votes of members of Congress. His expulsion from the House was recommended even though the Republican-dominated committee exonerated all but one congressman, the Democrat James Brooks, from complicity in the "bribery." Meanwhile the other committee, under the chairmanship of Jeremiah M. Wilson, concluded on the basis of more than 800 pages of confused and contradictory evidence that the Crédit Mobilier had defrauded the government. Ames responded to these charges in a well-argued and dignified speech. He insisted that the stock had not been worth more than par when he sold it. "I have risked reputation, fortune, everything," he pleaded, in an enterprise "from which the capital of the world shrank" (*Memoir*, p. 124). In the end, expulsion was felt to be too severe a penalty for misdemeanors committed so long previously, but congressmen bowed to the pressure of public opinion and overwhelmingly passed a resolution condemning Ames's conduct.

The principal problem with the financing of the Union Pacific railroad was not that it was ruined by rapacious promoters but that the system established by Congress burdened the company with a bonded debt exceeding the cost of construction, nominally reducing the amount of private equity capital needed to finance the road, but fatally increasing the risk to that capital. Ames was not the only capitalist of his generation to have exploited government largesse in order to make personal profits, but the high profile of the Union Pacific ensured that public anxiety about the moral and political consequences of the untrammeled rise of big business focused for a time on Ames to the lasting damage of his reputation. The financial markets were panicked by the scandal, and for a while leading investors in London boycotted American bonds.

In the sale of shares to congressmen Ames had been insensitive to the political implications and somewhat cavalier about the ethical questions involved. But his own conscience was clear and he was deeply wounded by the avalanche of public criticism. Returning dispirited to North Easton in March 1873, Ames was received in his hometown with great warmth and respect. But the strain of the scandal and the public exposure had proved too much. Two months after his return from Washington, Ames suffered a stroke and, four days later, he died at his home in North Easton. Although he ended his career under a cloud of public obloquy, Ames was a public-spirited man and an inventive entrepreneur who must take much of the credit for the building of the Union Pacific railroad.

• The Ames/Union Pacific Railroad Collection, in the Baker Library at the Harvard Business School, contains correspondence between Ames and his brother, as well as Ames's account books. Letters from Ames appear in several collections, most notably the *John A. Andrew Papers* at the Massachusetts Historical Society and the *Abraham Lincoln Papers* at the Library of Congress. Information on Ames's early life and family is in Winthrop Ames, *The Ames Family of Easton, Massachusetts* (1938). Works that stoutly defend Ames include Charles E. Ames, *Pioneering the Union Pacific* (1969), and Jay Boyd Crawford, *The Crédit Mobilier of America: Its Origin and History* (1880). See also John Hoyt Williams, *A Great and Shining Road* (1988), a good general study of the building of the Union Pacific; Logan Douglas Trent, *The Crédit Mobilier* (1981), a short study of Ames's role in the financing of the project; and Arthur M. Johnson and Barry E. Supple, *Boston Capitalists and Western Railroads* (1967), which puts Ames into a broader context. After Ames's death, his sons strenuously sought to rehabilitate his reputation. Oakes A. Ames published *Oakes Ames and the Crédit Mobilier* (1880), and the family compiled *Oakes Ames: A Memoir* (1883). The Poland Committee report is in 42d Cong., 3d sess., H. Doc. 77 and 78, and the Wilson Committee report is in 42d Cong., 3d sess., S. Rept. 519. An obituary is in the *Boston Weekly Transcript*, 13 May 1873.

ADAM I. P. SMITH

AMES, Oakes (26 Sept. 1874–28 Apr. 1950), botanist, was born in North Easton (near Boston), Massachusetts, the son of Oliver Ames, a wealthy financier and former governor of Massachusetts, and Anna Coffin Ray. Named after his grandfather, one of the builders of the Union Pacific Railroad, Oakes developed his lifelong interest in botany early on, when as a young boy he collected plants of the local flora of North Easton using a tin cookie box as a makeshift vasculum. He attended Noble and Greenough school in Boston and later Harvard College, where he studied botany and received an A.B. degree in 1898 followed by an A.M. degree in 1899. From 1900 to 1910 he served as instructor of botany at Harvard and became assistant professor of botany in 1915. In 1926 he was appointed professor of botany by President A. Lawrence Lowell and served as Arnold Professor of Botany from 1932 until 1935, when he became research professor of botany. He retired in 1941 as research professor emeritus and held this title until his death. For the more than fifty years that he was associated with Harvard, Ames distinguished himself as an international authority on orchids, a pioneer and promoter of economic botany, and one of the foremost administrators in Harvard's history.

Ames's interest in orchids began when, as a child, he first glimpsed two beautiful specimens of *Dendrobium nobile* in his father's study. Nathaniel L. Britton of the New York Botanical Garden later encouraged Ames to pursue the study of orchids seriously because Ames had not only the interest and ability but also the time and the personal wealth that would be required to work with orchids. Taking Britton's suggestions seriously, Ames began what would become his life's study. Largely as a result of Ames's efforts, the Orchidaceae are the most well-studied plant family. Relying on personal resources, Ames collected living materials from around the world and grew them in his home at North Easton. He eventually donated the living specimens to the New York Botanical Garden. Along with his extensive orchid library (all donated to Harvard Botanical Museum in 1941), Ames's contributions to the Ames Orchid Herbarium at Harvard helped create a collection that outnumbered all orchid collections in the new world and rivaled great European collections. Ames named some 1,000 species himself, and his collection numbered some 64,000 specimens. Ames's early interest in the orchids of the Philippines eventually expanded to include the Caribbean, South America, and other regions of the world. He was especially well acquainted with the orchids of Florida, where he spent the winter months. Many of his contemporaries considered him the leading orchidologist of his day.

Ames's secondary scientific interest in economic botany grew out of his extensive travel and association with George Lincoln Goodale, whose course in economic botany Ames took over teaching in 1909–1910. He also developed a related interest in tropical medicine. Pursuing these interests, Ames amassed well over 14,000 herbarium sheets, a library of 16,000 books, and other unique plant products useful in agriculture, medicine, or anthropology from all parts of the world, all of which he also donated to Harvard. His interest in economic botany culminated in the 1930s with the reform of Harvard's "general education" program to include economic botany and with the publication of a landmark book, *Economic Annuals and Human Cultures* (1939).

Ames also led a remarkably distinguished administrative career in numerous posts at Harvard. These included director of the Botanic Garden from 1909 to 1922; curator of the Botanical Museum from 1923 to 1927; chairman of the Division of Biology from 1926 to 1935; chairman of the Council of Botanical Collections and supervisor of the Biological Laboratory and Botanic Garden at Cuba, and of the Arnold Arboretum from 1927 to 1935; director of the Botanical Museum from 1937 to 1945 and then associate director of the museum from 1945 to 1950. He had a lasting effect on the Arnold Arboretum, where he helped to increase not only the endowment but also the scope of the institution's mission by including a plant pathologist on the staff who would be able to both study and combat plant diseases on ornamental plants (most experts on plant diseases had concentrated on agricultural plants) and a plant breeder to help produce better varieties. At his death, his administrative talents were noted by his staff and co-workers.

Among Ames's many honors were the Gold Medal of the American Orchid Society in 1924 and the Centennial Medal of the Massachusetts Horticultural Society in 1929. He was elected Fellow of the Linnean Society of London, the American Academy of Arts and Sciences, and the American Association for the Advancement of Science; he also belonged to Sigma Xi and numerous other honor societies.

Ames had married Blanche Ames (no relation) of Lowell, Massachusetts, in 1900; they had four children. A skilled illustrator and artist, Blanche Ames frequently accompanied her husband on his trips and drew many of the illustrations accompanying his descriptions. His donated collections included many of her splendid drawings. In 1906 the couple established "Borderland," their celebrated home estate. A reserved yet well-liked man of refined tastes and interests, Ames was a lifelong member of the Unitarian church. He died in his winter home in Ormond, Florida. He is remembered for his extensive work in orchids and for his effective administration of several botanical institutions at Harvard.

• Ames's papers are scattered across several botanical libraries and archives, including the Arnold Arboretum Archives and the University Archives of Harvard University. Some of his personal papers are housed with those of Blanche Ames at the Schlesinger Library at Radcliffe College. A selection of his voluminous writings (from diaries, journals and letters), compiled and edited by his daughter Pauline Ames Plimpton, is *Jottings of a Harvard Botanist (1874–1950)* (1979). See also Richard Evans Schultes, "Oakes Ames, 1874–1950," *Rhodora* 53 (1951): 66–79; and Karl Sax, "Oakes Ames, 1874–1950," *Journal of the Arnold Arboretum* 31 (1950): 334–49, which includes a full bibliography. An obituary by Schultes is in the *Proceedings of the Linnean Society* 162 (1951): 223–28.

VASSILIKI BETTY SMOCOVITIS

AMES, Oliver (5 Nov. 1807–9 Mar. 1877), manufacturer and railroad promoter and official, was born in Plymouth, Massachusetts, the son of Oliver Ames, a pioneer manufacturer, and Susanna Angier. Early in his childhood the family returned to their home in North Easton, twenty miles south of Boston. Ames attended the local schools and also became an adept worker in his father's shovel works. At the age of twenty-one, having been temporarily disabled by a severe fall, he entered Franklin Academy at North Andover, Massachusetts. He was interested in debating clubs and intended to ultimately study law.

Ames spent eighteen months at the academy and a period as a law student in an attorney's office in West Bridgewater. He had fully regained his health but found that he actually did not like to work in an office. With the family business prospering, Ames decided to join his father and elder brother, Oakes, in the Ames Shovel Works. In 1833 Oliver Ames married Sarah Lothrop of Easton, a second cousin of his brother's wife. As a wedding gift his father built them a house on Main Street, not far from the parents' home. The couple had two children.

The Ames brothers both entered their father's factory at the bottom, joining several dozen Irish employees who worked a ten-hour day, six days a week. The water-powered plant produced several types of tools but chiefly manufactured shovels. The Ames Shovel Works weathered the depression of 1837, and by the early 1840s both brothers had moved up to positions of management. In 1844 their father retired, and the firm was reorganized as Oliver Ames & Sons, with the brothers as co-presidents.

The brothers were quite different from each other. Oliver was friendly, gentle, and modest; tall and handsome, he was less rugged than Oakes, but robust enough to have been the wrestling champion of North Easton. In contrast, Oakes was a broad-shouldered giant of 200 pounds, a man of few words, abrupt action, and great self-reliance. In spite of their differences, together they built up the shovel business. The thousands of new western farms settled each year, the California gold rush of 1849, and the extensive railroad building of the 1850s all increased the demand for Ames shovels. By mid-century an Ames shovel was often accepted as legal tender in much of the Mississippi Valley. The firm was valued at $4 million by 1860.

In 1852 Oliver Ames, a Whig, was appointed to the Massachusetts State Senate, and in 1857 he was elected to the same office by popular vote. He was an effective speaker in the senate, but his interest in politics declined, and he did not stand for reelection. In the late 1850s he did take a lively interest in the newly formed Republican party.

In 1855 the brothers built the four-mile Easton Branch Railroad from the shovel works to Stoughton, where it connected with a line to Boston. Later Oliver was a director of the Old Colony and Newport Railroad, which took over control of the Easton Branch line. In the 1850s Oakes made several investments in railroads in Iowa, but Oliver's interest in the projected lines was modest. The Civil War years brought large government contracts for shovels, swords, and other war equipment. By 1865 the firm had risen to a value of $8 million (two years later the Ameses sold one million shovels, one in every two produced in the nation), and the brothers had new money available for investment.

In 1865 Oliver Ames became interested in the Union Pacific Railroad, which was generously supported by the Pacific Railroad Acts of 1862 and 1864. The Union Pacific was managed by Dr. Thomas C. Durant, a railway promoter known better for his skill in stock manipulation than for his practice of medicine. Early in 1864 Durant acquired the Crédit Mobilier, a false-front construction company that would provide owners of the Union Pacific an extra profit for constructing the road. Building railroads beyond the frontier, facing American Indians, mountains, and deserts was a risky business, and many western lines devised comparable "construction" companies.

Early in 1865 both Oliver and Oakes made major purchases of the Union Pacific Crédit Mobilier stock. Durant needed the reputation of the Ames name to attract additional investors. Other businessmen, mostly in Boston, were soon buying the stock. Before long the Durant group was in conflict with the Boston investors—Durant was looking for a quick profit, while the Ames group sought a construction profit and the long-term value of a completed road. Soon the Boston investors owned more stock than the Durant faction, and Oliver Ames was placed on the Union Pacific board of directors. He was made acting president of the road from 1866 to 1868, and president, succeeding General John A. Dix, from 1868 to 1871. During the five years Oliver was in office, four-fifths of the road was built, and the line was completed in May 1869. Oliver was never directly involved in the congressional Crédit Mobilier scandals of 1872–1873, when it was revealed that Oakes had sold or given shares to several U.S. congressmen in 1867–1868, but his rather indecisive presidential leadership occasionally did contribute to various problems faced by the Union Pacific. He remained a director of the line until his death.

After leaving the presidency of the Union Pacific, Oliver turned his full attention to the shovel works, which was facing bankruptcy because of its earlier large financing of the Union Pacific. He obtained an extension of time from the major creditors, and the affairs of the business were soon in order. In his last years Oliver held many positions of responsibility beyond those with the Union Pacific. He was a director of several railways, including the Chicago & North-Western, Colorado Central, Denver Pacific, Kansas Pacific, and Sioux City & Pacific. He also was a director of several banks in Boston and North Easton. Before the Civil War Oliver had been an active financial supporter of the Emigrant Aid Society of Boston, which sent Free Soilers to Kansas. He was a longtime vice president of the Massachusetts Total Abstinence Society, which he had supported since the age of nineteen. In the mid-1870s Oliver, a devout Unitarian, built a substantial new Unity church and parsonage in North Easton. He also provided the building site for a Catholic church and a meetinghouse for the Methodists in the same town, where he later died. His will provided funds for the library, public schools, and local roads in North Easton. He was commemorated with a huge stone monument built by the Union Pacific Railroad in 1881–1882 along the Union Pacific tracks near Sherman, Wyoming, and dedicated to Oakes and Oliver Ames.

• Archival materials on Ames are in the Charles E. Ames Papers, Baker Library, Harvard Business School, and the Union Pacific Railroad Records, Union Pacific offices, Omaha, Nebr. Other material on his life and career is in Charles Edgar Ames, *Pioneering the Union Pacific: A Reappraisal of the Building of the Railroad* (1969). The best account of the building of the line is Maury Klein, *Union Pacific: The Birth of a Railroad, 1862–1893* (1987). Additional views on the financing of western railroads are Arthur M. Johnson and Barry E. Supple, *Boston Capitalists and Western Railroads* (1967), and Robert W. Fogel, *The Union Pacific Railroad* (1960). An obituary is in the *Boston Transcript*, 13 Mar. 1877.

JOHN F. STOVER

AMES, Oliver (4 Feb. 1831–22 Oct. 1895), industrialist and governor of Massachusetts, was born in North Easton, Massachusetts, the son of Oakes Ames (1804–1873), a manufacturer and congressman, and Evelyn Gilmore. Ames came from a long line of Massachusetts capitalists. The family gained notoriety in 1872, when the House of Representatives censured Oliver's father because of his part in the Credit Mobilier scandal. Oliver was to fight throughout his life to clear his father's besmirched image.

Ames went to the public schools of Easton, and he attended several nearby academies. At the age of fifteen he began a five-year apprenticeship in the family business of shovel manufacturing, after which he went to Brown University for one year of study. He then returned to the family business and became a partner in 1863. In 1859 Ames was elected to the Easton School Committee. He served on that board for twelve years, during which time he was also treasurer and chairman of the Easton Republican Committee. In 1860 Ames married Anna Coffin Ray; they had six children. He was active in the state militia, rising to the rank of lieutenant colonel, but resigned just before the Civil War began. During the war Ames paid for a substitute, and this action was to haunt his later political ambitions.

When his father died in 1873, Ames served as executor and found that not only was the family name blemished, but the family finances were in debt. Ames was determined to restore both. In 1880 Ames and his two brothers, Oakes Angier Ames and Frank Ames, published a book to vindicate their father's honor, stating, "This man was made a scapegoat for the manifold sins of American political life, and his name was unjustly tarnished" (Ames, p. 19). To commemorate the memory of their father, in 1881 the brothers donated a building, the Oakes Ames Memorial Hall, to their hometown of Easton.

Ames resolved the family's financial problems by carving out a great fortune through railroad building, stock speculation, finance, and manufacturing. Just after his father's death in 1873 he traveled to Kansas to build the Central Branch of the Union Pacific Railroad. "I traveled in stage coaches all along the proposed route of the road, secured right-of-way grants and got town aid. . . . It was all done in three years, and I had made myself independent. That was my greatest business success" (*Boston Globe*, 22 Oct. 1895). Ames also served as president of the Sioux City and Pacific Railroad and on the board of directors of over twenty railroads, several savings companies, banks, and coal, water power, and land corporations.

He speculated on the stock market and at one point bested the canny railroad magnate Jay Gould in a deal that netted Ames over a million dollars. By 1892 Ames's net worth was well over $8 million.

Well before that year Ames began to use his enormous wealth as a lever to enter politics in a serious manner. He gave generously to his party's war chest, and the Republicans rewarded him with a safe seat in the Massachusetts Senate, where he served from 1881 to 1883. From 1883 to 1887 he held office as lieutenant governor. It was the norm for lieutenant governors automatically to become candidates for governor. Ames ran in 1886 and defeated Democrat John Andrew by a meager 9,463 votes, having been hurt at the polls by his failure to serve in the Civil War and by popular resentment of his wealth. The issue of his poor war record also came up during his reelection bid in 1887. Ames won, nevertheless, and he won again in 1888.

Ames's record during his three terms was lackluster, and he prided himself that his major act as governor was the construction of a new state house extension. Two of his pet reforms—severing the connection of state banks with national banks that resulted in fiscal irregularities, and transferring claims against the state from the legislature to the courts—were passed by the legislature. He supported the improvement of public schools and was a capable administrator. The *New York Times* (23 Oct. 1895) characterized his governorship as "careful, conservative and dignified. . . . He made few attempts to outline a personal policy or to lead his party." Bulkley Griffin, a noted Republican editor and journalist, summed up Ames, "Amiable, rather dull, with no gifts for public life, [he] is entitled to remembrance because in advance of the coming of the automobile age, he inaugurated the building of permanent roads by the state" (Griffin, p. 260). Ames's lack of distinction in office may be traceable in part to his motivation for entering politics. His ultimate goal—never realized—was to be elected to Congress and to efface the record of his father's censure.

In 1890 Ames retired from politics because of ill health and became involved in philanthropy. His philanthropic efforts were typical of the paternal capitalist of the day, providing funds for school and library buildings and acting as chair for artistic and charitable societies. As befitted a financial mogul, he lived out his retirement as a semi-invalid in baronial splendor, dividing his time between grand residences in Boston, Martha's Vineyard, and Easton. Besides his charity work and travel abroad, he bought rare books and old masters for his private collection. He died in North Easton, Massachusetts.

Ames, like his father, was a typical "industrial statesman" or "robber baron" of the Gilded Age. Using inherited wealth, he took advantage of the tremendous capitalist opportunities available at a time of soaring industrialization. Unfettered by government regulation and imbued with an ethical climate predicated on Andrew Carnegie's "gospel of wealth" philosophy, men like Ames became the main protagonists in the drama of the unfolding industrial revolution.

• No known collections of papers are available for Ames, and no biographies, critical studies, or scholarly articles yet exist. Ames and his brothers defended their father in a privately published book, Oakes Angier Ames et al., *Oakes Ames and the Credit Mobilier* (1880). Among the many reference works that mention Ames, the best source is Edwin Bacon, ed., *Men of Progress: 1,000 Biographical Sketches of Massachusetts Men* (1896). Ames is mentioned in Geoffrey Blodgett's analysis of the Mugwump Republicans' transformation into Democrats, *The Gentle Reformers: Massachusetts Democrats in the Cleveland Era* (1966). For a discussion of Republican party problems, see Richard Harmon, "Troubles of Massachusetts Republicans during the 1880s," *Mid-America* 56 (1974): 85–99; and Solomon Bulkley Griffin, *People and Politics: Observed by a Massachusetts Editor* (1923). To find out about Ames's and his brothers' financial activities in western railroads, see Arthur M. Johnson and Barry E. Supple, *Boston Capitalists and Western Railroads: A Study in the Nineteenth-Century Railroad Investment Process* (1967). The major sources of information are the obituaries in the *Springfield Republican*, 23 Oct. 1895, the *Boston Globe*, 22 Oct. 1895, the *New York Times*, 23 Oct. 1895, and the *Boston Transcript*, 22 Oct. 1895.

JACK TAGER

AMES, Van Meter (9 July 1898–5 Nov. 1985), professor of philosophy, was born in De Soto, Iowa, the son of Edward Scribner Ames, a minister, and Mabel Van Meter. He received his Ph.D. in philosophy from the University of Chicago in 1924 and took a position in the philosophy department at the University of Cincinnati the following year. He was married in 1930 to Betty Catherine Breneman, with whom he had three children. During his career Ames held a number of visiting appointments at other American universities, including Cornell, Texas, Hawaii, and Columbia, and abroad, on a Rockefeller grant to France and a Fulbright Fellowship to Japan.

Aesthetics was Ames's chief academic interest, and he wrote some 200 articles and a number of books about art in all its forms. Two of his earlier books were general treatments of aesthetics: *Aesthetics of the Novel* (1928) and *Introduction to Beauty* (1931). These were followed by works on more particular aspects of art, including a book on the writer André Gide. One of his more important books was *Proust and Santayana: The Aesthetic Way of Life*. "Proust and Santayana," he says, "belong, with Schopenhauer, to the great tradition that puts contemplation above action." This first appeared in 1937, at which time it was widely reviewed, and reappeared in 1966. Following World War II, he began to take a serious interest in oriental thought, especially in Zen Buddhism; on this subject he wrote numerous papers and his book *Zen and American Thought* (1962), and he co-authored *Japan and Zen*.

The early text on aesthetics, *Introduction to Beauty*, is divided into three parts: the first deals with aesthetic theory; the second is titled "Fine Arts" and contains chapters on the movies, the theater, painting and sculpture, music, dancing, architecture, literature, and printing; and the last part relates art to life and has as its final chapter "The Art of Life." The book closes with the lines,

Because life is desperate there is hope in art. Because life is ugly there is belief in beauty. Art is life aspiring to beauty through human ingenuity and effort. Life does not always achieve the values which are contemplated in beauty; art does not always surmount the difficulties that give it birth. Success shines against a background of failure, but, despite all discouragement, as long as there is life there is art.

Throughout his career Ames focused on the importance of art to a good life and, indeed, the treatment of the good life itself as an artistic endeavor. This is reflected in the literary figures about whom he wrote, who tended not to be social activists but, rather, devoted themselves to reflection, contemplation, and the creation of art. He took a particular interest in the French authors Gide, with his reflective diaries, and Proust, with his long, multivolume, probing novel. For several reasons, Ames was especially interested in the writings and life of George Santayana. Ames's *Introduction to Beauty* was in many ways similar to Santayana's first book, *The Sense of Beauty*. Santayana's *The Life of Reason* was treated by Ames as a major contribution toward his theme of the art of living, showing how reason can figure in the many aspects of contemporary life. Ames was also interested in Santayana's later life devoted to contemplation and writing, following Santayana's resignation from Harvard in mid-career. Ames's later fascination with Zen Buddhism is tied to the same lifelong concern with a way of life independent of arbitrary social pressures.

Ames remained at the University of Cincinnati until his retirement in 1966, having been departmental chair for the previous seven years. He became professor emeritus, and in 1976 he was named by the American Humanist Association as Humanist Fellow for Outstanding Contributions to Humanist Thought in Ethics. He died in Cincinnati.

Contemporary philosophical writings on aesthetics in English tend to specialize on a particular aspect of the arts and are normally written from the point of view of the analytic or linguistic philosopher. Although there has been a retreat from hard analytic philosophy, wide-ranging works in nontechnical language, like those of Ames and of Santayana before him, have not so far come into academic favor. This is no doubt one reason that the name Van Meter Ames is not well known among late twentieth-century philosophers.

• Ames wrote volumes of poetry and edited two religious works by his father, *Beyond Theology* and *Prayers and Meditation*. Two notable papers among the many he wrote are "The Zenith as Ideal," *Journal of Philosophy* (1952), and "A Humanist at Heaven's Gate," *Humanist* (1963). An obituary is in *Philosophy East and West* 36 (1986): 195.

ANGUS KERR-LAWSON

AMES, Winthrop (25 Nov. 1870–3 Nov. 1937), theatrical producer and theater owner, was born in North Easton, Massachusetts, the son of Oakes Angier Ames, a manufacturer, and Catherine Hobart. The Ames family was wealthy and socially prominent. Ames concluded his education at Harvard with a postgraduate year of dramatic studies. He had long been interested in the theater but, because of family opposition to a career in that field, he joined a Boston publishing firm, for which he founded two monthly magazines, *Masters in Music* and *Masters in Art*, and edited the *Architectural Review*.

In 1904 Ames resumed his interest in theater. He joined another wealthy young man to take over the management of a Boston stock company, the Castle Square Players. Having traveled in Europe and seen there the break away from stale conventions of theatrical staging toward greater artistic freedom, the new artistic stirrings in theater there, Ames was ambitious to offer more than the standard line of stage entertainments of the day. He added new plays, revivals of literary classics, Shakespeare, and some children's theater. The public resisted the unfamiliar offerings, and the company lost money its last two years. The venture ended in 1907, with Ames the poorer in pocket but richer in the practical experience of producing a play a week under less than ideal conditions.

Ames had thoughts of building his own "perfect" theater in Boston, one that would meet all his requirements. First he went to Europe in 1907, traveling through England, France, Germany, and Austria, to make an intensive study of theaters and theatrical production there. But the theater in Boston never materialized. In 1908 he received an irresistible invitation to preside over the New Theatre, the United States' first repertory theater, in New York City.

The New Theatre was an ambitious project started by a consortium of wealthy patrons of the arts. Where theater in the United States had been entirely a commercial venture, the New Theatre was meant to reflect the state-supported theaters and opera houses of Europe and to lead the way in raising theater to an art. In truth, the project was foredoomed by the size of the New Theatre building, too large for effective production of anything but opera and erected at an out-of-the-way location. Other possible directors had turned the position down before Ames was approached. He was willing to take on the assignment, even knowing that he faced difficulties that might be insuperable. Indeed, the undertaking did fail in 1911, although by then Ames had mounted distinguished productions of plays by Shakespeare, Maeterlinck, Galsworthy, Pinero, and Sheldon. His mastery of lighting effects and his use of a revolving stage and other devices of stage machinery at the New Theatre were particularly noted by reviewers. Also in 1911 Ames married Mrs. Lucy Fuller Cabot; they had two children.

In 1912 Ames began building New York's smallest theater, the 299-seat Little Theatre, where a small, intelligent segment of the theatergoing public could enjoy plays and subtleties of acting that were lost in the reaches of the New Theatre. Meanwhile he imported to Broadway Max Reinhardt's Deutsches Theater production of *Sumurun* (1912), a pantomime play of Oriental romance. With its stylized settings, emotive lighting effects, and entrances by actors running down a ramp, Gerald Bordman commented that "the production alerted Broadway to the ferment rising on European stages and signaled that the day of the scene painter and the careful realism of his flats was about to give way to the more imaginative architecture and lighting of the set designer" (p. 703). By October 1912 the Little Theatre was open and presenting *The Affairs of Anatol*, by the Viennese playwright Artur Schnitzler, with John Barrymore as Anatol. Concurrently, at matinees, Ames presented a highly successful play for children, *Snow White and the Seven Dwarfs*, with a spectacular onstage metamorphosis of the wicked queen into a shabby hag when she learns she is no longer the fairest of them all. In 1913 Ames opened a somewhat larger but similarly beautiful and well-designed playhouse, the Booth. His productions were noted for their visual appeal. Marc Connelly, coauthor of *Beggar on Horseback* (1924), which Ames produced, said that the appeal rose from "his insistence on genuine pictorial beauty rather than mere opulence" (*New York Times*, 4 Nov. 1937).

For years to come, Ames continued to produce Broadway plays that he deemed a contribution to the art of theater. Using his own money, he mounted each handsomely, often at greater expense than other producers would have used. Brock Pemberton, himself a producer, recalled the uniqueness of Ames's methods. "His fancy ran to drawing room comedy and to plays with serious themes. The great majority of his productions was made up of foreign plays . . . And because this was a fertile field he dealt chiefly in finished plays which had either been already produced abroad . . . or were delivered complete by their authors. He thus avoided the hectic throes of rewriting, which have become so much a part of current production" (*New York Times*, 7 Nov. 1937). Ames did present American plays at times, notably *Beggar on Horseback* by Connelly and George Kaufman and *Minick* (1924) by Kaufman and Edna Ferber. Most often, however, the authors were English.

Pemberton says voices were never raised during the staging of a play by Ames. "He directed his own plays and his rehearsals were models of smoothness. His method of direction was to work out in advance of rehearsal all business and movement with little dolls representing the characters." Then came several days of reading with the actors, followed by "directions in minutest detail" (*New York Times*, 7 Nov. 1937).

Ames preferred not to work with stars but with the most appropriate talent available for a part. One exception was the star George Arliss, with whom Ames had two of his greatest successes: *The Green Goddess* (1921), and *Old English* (1924). In *On the Stage: An Autobiography* (1928), Arliss recalled how Ames strengthened *The Green Goddess*: "The last act of the play in its original form was admittedly weak . . . Ames is a past master in the art of stage lighting and when we came to the final rehearsals he decided that this whole scene must be relighted." The outcome was lighting with "a weird, uncanny suggestion of impending catastrophe that resulted in maintaining the interest to the fall of the curtain." The play ran for two years. After Ames thought of casting Arliss against type in the leading role of *Old English*, the actor said with glee that the play "proved the greatest financial success I have ever had" (p. 325).

As might be supposed, producers from the commercial theater looked on Ames as one from another sphere. He was European and patrician in his tastes, not even an inveterate playgoer who went to see what else was succeeding on Broadway. Yet he made himself available in his offices at the Little Theatre to anyone of the theater who wished to see him and treated all with courtesy. Furthermore, says a *New York Times* editorial, "along the Rialto his reputation was so high that whenever the theater wanted to put the best face on a sorry business [such as the 1927 public outcry against salacious material in some productions, where he served as chairman of a committee of producers to set acceptable standards, lest official censorship of productions be imposed], instinctively it turned to him for assistance" (4 Nov. 1937).

Ames's last productions at the Booth were revivals of *Iolanthe*, *The Pirates of Penzance*, and *The Mikado*, 1926–1929. The editorial writer called them "the most magnificent productions of Gilbert and Sullivan New York had seen. . . . thoroughly fresh and beguiling in casting and mounting . . . the crown of his series of masterworks" (*New York Times*, 4 Nov. 1937). Then in 1929 Ames retired, ending twenty-five years of theatrical endeavor. Broadway was in sad shape because of the competition of the movies, especially the new talkies supplying the mass audience with traditional fare from melodrama to musicals. With perhaps ironic optimism he told an interviewer that movies might be the salvation of good theater: "With the advent of sound and dialogue pictures, the thinking audience, which is growing larger all the time, is led back even more inevitably to the spoken stage" (*New York Herald Tribune*, 6 Oct. 1929). He was not at all sure commercial Broadway could rebound.

The remaining years of Ames's life were spent in travel, writing, and enjoyment of his home in North Easton. His final theatrical activity was to help organize the Cambridge School of Drama. He died in Boston of pneumonia. He died virtually bankrupt, it was later revealed, having spent his personal fortune to give the American public theatrical productions of true distinction.

Ames was described by Allen Churchill in *The Great White Way* (1962) as "tall, fastidious, formal, aloof—and somehow warm and kindly. His physical person as well as his productions carried the stamp of quality, and with varying degrees of approval he was called the first gentleman among producers" (p. 249). His enduring significance in American theatrical history is the groundbreaking work he did in introducing the new movements of the twentieth-century European theater to the United States. John H. Jennings noted that it is a "mistaken notion" to "think of the art theater movement [i.e., following European styles of drama and staging] as the work of amateurs almost exclusively." Instead, "it was on the professional stage of New York that the earliest and most significant European innovations were introduced . . . [and] Winthrop Ames was chiefly responsible for inaugurating European theatre practices in America, and through the work of Ames the influence of European ideas upon American theater building and management [as well as] stage production is clearly traceable" (Jennings, p. 9).

• Materials on the life and career of Ames are in the Billy Rose Theatre Collection at the New York Public Library for the Performing Arts, Lincoln Center. A list of his productions is in *Who Was Who in the Theatre: 1912–1976* (1978). Brief descriptions of some of his productions are in Gerald Bordman, *The American Theatre: 1869–1914* (1994) and *The American Theatre: 1914–1930* (1995). John H. Jennings, "Winthrop Ames's Notes for the Perfect Theatre," *Educational Theatre Journal* 12 (Mar. 1960): 9–15, analyzes in detail the 85-page notebook Ames kept during his 1907 theatrical tour of Europe and relates its notations to effects Ames achieved at the New Theatre. Weldon Durham, *American Theatre Companies: 1888–1930* (1987), describes the strengths and weaknesses of the Castle Square Players during Ames's time. Obituaries and editorial comment on Ames's contributions to American theater are in the *New York Times* and the *New York Herald-Tribune*, both 4 Nov. 1937.

WILLIAM STEPHENSON

AMHERST, Jeffery (29 Jan. 1717–3 Aug. 1797), British soldier and first baron Amherst, was born at Riverhead, Kent, England, the son of Jeffery Amherst, a barrister, and Elizabeth Kerrill. The family had close connections to the duke of Dorset, whom Jeffery served as a page at age twelve, and whose influence procured for him an ensign's commission in the First Regiment of Foot Guards in 1731. His active service began in 1735 with the cavalry regiment of Sir John Ligonier, perhaps the ablest general in the British army. Serving as Ligonier's aide-de-camp in the War of the Austrian Succession, Amherst saw action at the battles of Dettingen (1743) and Fontenoy (1745), became a lieutenant colonel in 1745, and was appointed aide-de-camp to the duke of Cumberland, commander in chief of allied forces in Europe.

At the beginning of the Seven Years' War Amherst was colonel of the Fifteenth Regiment of Foot, on detached duty with Britain's Hessian allies in Germany. In that capacity he was present at the disastrous battle of Hastenbeck (1757), which destroyed the military reputation of his patron, the duke of Cumberland. Fortunately for Amherst, Cumberland's successor as commander in chief of the British army was his other patron, Ligonier, who needed capable officers to send to North America, where the war effort had been sunk in inertia and defeat since 1755. In early March 1758, Amherst, with the temporary rank of "major general in America," was given command of an expedition against the French fortress of Louisbourg on Cape Breton Island, the strategic key to Canada.

The successful Louisbourg campaign (2 June–26 July) marked the beginning of Amherst's rise to celebrity. By the end of 1758 he was commander in chief of British forces in America. Two other recent victories—the taking of Fort Frontenac on Lake Ontario and of Fort Duquesne at the forks of the Ohio—had paved the way for the invasion of New France, which the British forces undertook in 1759 by two routes. Amherst himself headed an 11,000-man expedition northward from Albany against the French forts on Lake Champlain at Ticonderoga and Crown Point, which guarded the main southern approach to Canada. Brigadier General James Wolfe, more impetuous than Amherst and a hero of the Louisbourg siege, commanded a simultaneous expedition up the St. Lawrence River. Wolfe succeeded, at the cost of his life, in taking Québec; Amherst proceeded more methodically against the French forts on Lake Champlain. Had he moved quickly, Amherst might have reached Montréal before the close of the campaigning season and brought an early end to the war. Instead he paused to repair the French forts at Ticonderoga and Crown Point, to build gunboats to protect his troop transports on the lake, and to construct a supply road from the upper Connecticut Valley to Crown Point. Thus by the end of 1759, thanks to Amherst's cautious, systematic approach, the heartland of New France remained under French control; but the British army was so well positioned that the successful outcome of the next year's campaign was virtually certain.

The triple assault on Canada of 1760—with Amherst leading an expedition down the St. Lawrence from Lake Ontario, Brigadier General William Haviland moving northward along the Lake Champlain corridor from Crown Point, and Brigadier General James Murray ascending the St. Lawrence from Québec—trapped the last French forces at Montréal. This remarkable achievement would have been impossible without Amherst's planning and attention to detail. His victories were rewarded with the sinecure governorship of Virginia and a permanent promotion to major general (1759), the colonelcy in chief of the Royal American (Sixtieth) Regiment, and promotion to the rank of lieutenant general and a knighthood in the Order of the Bath (1761).

Amherst had neither liked nor trusted Indians during the war and had never understood the importance of subsidizing tribes with arms and other supplies. When hostilities ended he cut back drastically on Indian gifts and insofar as possible denied them access to arms and ammunition. This economizing policy, disastrous for the Indians who needed subsidies to sustain themselves, helped precipitate the Indian uprisings known as Pontiac's Rebellion, which lasted from 1763 to 1766. Amherst left for Britain late in 1763, before it was clear that most of the rebellious tribes were prepared to negotiate a peace in return for liberalized trade relations. His successor, Major General Thomas Gage, adhered to Amherst's intention to punish the Indians militarily and thereby prolonged hostilities for at least a year.

Amherst's return to England was clouded by the madness of his wife, Jane Dalyson (also Dallison), whom he had married in 1753. She died in 1765. Two years later he married an heiress, Elizabeth Cary, and devoted himself to completing "Montreal," his country estate in Kent. He took no part in the British government's attempts to assert control over the fractious Americans, resigning his governorship of Virginia in 1768 rather than return to the colonies; when George III offered him command of the forces in America in 1775 he refused. It was not sympathy for the colonists that made him decline, but the conviction that only an economic blockade rather than direct military action could make them submit.

Despite his reluctance to serve, Amherst was the nation's most distinguished military officer and therefore important to the government, which rewarded him with a peerage (as Baron Amherst of Holmesdale) in 1776. With the outbreak of war between Britain and France in 1778, he finally accepted promotion to the rank of general and the command in chief of Britain's land forces. In this capacity he was responsible for organizing home defenses, including the disposition of the militia, duties that made him the target of the parliamentary opposition. His suppression of the Gordon riots (1780) restored order when London seemed on the verge of revolution, but this did little to secure him permanent popularity. Following the resignation of Lord North's ministry in 1782, Amherst was stripped of his military offices. Thereafter he remained inactive until early 1793 when he was recalled as commander in chief in anticipation of war with France. Despite his advanced age he continued to serve until early 1795, when he retired to his estate in Kent. On 30 July 1796 he received the final honor of being named Field Marshal. One year later he died at his estate, Montreal.

Neither of Amherst's marriages produced children, and although he fathered an illegitimate son, whom he acknowledged and supported from the time of the child's birth in 1752, he sought to maintain the family name and the succession to his title by adopting his niece and nephew. Several years before his death the king renewed Amherst's patent of nobility as Baron Amherst of Montreal. Upon his death the title passed to his adopted son, William Pitt Amherst. Both the town of Amherst, Massachusetts, and Amherst College were named in his honor.

During his lifetime Amherst's reputation fluctuated dramatically. His aloof manner, which made Americans think he was polite (unlike previous commanders in chief), served him well in the colonies but eventually helped destroy his popularity in England. Horace Walpole, who described him in 1763 as "circumspect," "provident, methodic, conciliating, and cool," and "possessed [of] the whole system of war," two decades later wrote that Amherst had proven himself "a man of incapacity," "determined to bury his deficiency in obstinate silence"; an incompetent who, when "reproached in Parliament with his negligence and insufficiency, . . . confirmed them by the sullen and inadequate brevity of his reply." He was in fact a competent officer who excelled at organizational tasks but who never acquired acute political sensibilities. The leading historian of the British army, Sir John Fortescue, accurately characterized him as England's "greatest military administrator" between Marlborough and Wellington.

• Copies of Amherst's official correspondence and journals can be found in the Public Record Office, London; the Library of Congress; the Public Archives of Canada, Ottawa; and the Library of Amherst College, Amherst, Mass. There are two biographies of Amherst, neither recent and neither entirely satisfactory: Lawrence Shaw Mayo, *Jeffery Amherst: A Biography* (1916), and John Cuthbert Long, *Lord Jeffery Amherst: A Soldier of the King* (1933). Mayo wrote before the discovery of Amherst's private correspondence in 1925, but Long, who had first access to these papers, was almost entirely uncritical in his use of them. See also John Clarence Webster, ed., *The Journal of Jeffery Amherst* (1931) and *The Journal of William Amherst in America, 1758–1760* (1927). A fine Ph.D. dissertation by Daniel John Beattie, "General Jeffery Amherst and the Conquest of Canada, 1758–1760" (Duke Univ., 1975), examines Amherst as a military administrator and situates his American career in the contexts of the contemporary British army and colonial warfare. Secondary sources that address aspects of Amherst's career include Lawrence Henry Gipson, *The British Empire before the American Revolution*, vol. 7 (1949) and vol. 8 (1954); John Shy, *Toward Lexington* (1965); and John W. Fortescue, *A History of the British Army*, vol. 2 (1910).

FRED ANDERSON

AMIDON, Charles Fremont (17 Aug. 1856–26 Dec. 1937), federal judge, was born in Chautauqua County, New York, the son of the Reverend John Smith Amidon and Charlotte Ann Curtis. Raised in rural poverty, he worked his way through high school and Hamilton College, from which he graduated in 1882 with honors. He then moved to Fargo, Dakota Territory, as the principal and sole teacher in the city's newly established high school but soon gave up teaching to read law. Admitted to the bar in 1886, Amidon established himself as a successful lawyer and civic reformer in the growing frontier city. In 1892 he married Beulah Richardson McHenry, who, in addition to caring for their five children, became a prominent civic reformer and feminist.

An active Democrat, Amidon was appointed to the federal district judgeship in the recently admitted state of North Dakota in 1896 by President Grover Cleveland, but early in the twentieth century he became an avid supporter of Theodore Roosevelt's (1858–1919) brand of Republican progressivism. Roosevelt wrote to ask Amidon for a copy of his speech on judicial reform delivered at the American Bar Association meeting in 1907, beginning their long correspondence. By 1910 it had grown in frequency and intimacy as Amidon's reformist views and proposals found great favor with the former president, and they visited each other several times. During his Bull Moose campaign for the presidency in 1912, Roosevelt regularly included substantial portions of Amidon's letters in his speeches and articles, occasionally crediting them merely to a "wise judge." Amidon was also influential in persuading Roosevelt to advocate recall of judicial decisions in his 1912 platform, a proposal that proved highly controversial in the campaign.

Their epistolary intimacy cooled, however, as Roosevelt grew increasingly intolerant of opposition to America's intervention in the war in Europe, and they finally parted company on the question of what constituted permissible dissent when the nation joined the Allied effort in early 1917. Amidon's judicial district of North Dakota saw more federal prosecutions per capita under the Espionage and Sedition Acts than any other state, largely because of the strength of the farmers' Nonpartisan League, which was pragmatically socialist as well as anti-interventionist, but also because of the sizable German-American population. As a judge, Amidon interpreted the sedition laws narrowly, resulting in few convictions. Consequently he was vilified by the conservative press and by business interests opposed to the Nonpartisan League. Civil libertarians, by contrast, recognized him as a courageous defender of free speech.

In leading cases after the war Amidon upheld the constitutionality of the Nonpartisan League's socialist industrial program for North Dakota. He issued a novel labor injunction in the national railway shopmen's strike in 1922, placing restraints on the plaintiff railroads as well as on the union, something no judge had done before. His advocacy of the rights of labor later led to his selection as national chairman of the American Civil Liberties Union's anti-injunction committee, which contributed to the Norris–La Guardia Anti-Injunction Act of 1932. Amidon died while wintering in Arizona and was buried in Fargo.

• A collection of Amidon papers is in the University of North Dakota library. The only full-length biography is Kenneth Smemo, *Against the Tide: The Life and Times of Federal Judge Charles F. Amidon, North Dakota Progressive* (1986). See also an article by Amidon's daughter, Beulah F. Ratliff, "Charles Fremont Amidon, 1856–1937," *North Dakota History* 8 (Jan. 1941): 3–20. An obituary is in the *New York Times*, 28 Dec. 1937.

KENNETH SMEMO

AMMANN, Othmar Hermann (26 Mar. 1879–22 Sept. 1965), civil engineer, was born in Schaffhausen, Switzerland, the son of Emanuel C. Ammann, a manufacturer, and Emilie R. Labhardt. He attended the Swiss Federal Polytechnic Institute and graduated with a degree in civil engineering in 1902.

Upon leaving school, Ammann worked in Brugg, Switzerland, as a structural draftsman for the firm of Wartmann and Valette. He relocated to Frankfurt am Main, Germany, in 1903, as a design engineer for Buchheim and Heister, where he designed reinforced concrete structures. On the suggestion of one of his former professors, Ammann immigrated to the United States in 1904 and secured a position in the New York office of Joseph Mayer, a consulting engineer. At the same time that Ammann acted as Mayer's chief engineer, chief draftsman, tracer, and general factotum, he found time to work on railroad bridge design. It was while in Mayer's employ that he first became cognizant of the physical and technical challenges facing anyone who proposed to bridge the Hudson River at or near New York City.

Ammann returned briefly to Switzerland in 1905 to marry Lilly Selma Wehrli. The couple had three children. That same year he returned to the United States to work for the bridge department of the Pennsylvania Steel Company at Steelton, Pennsylvania. There Ammann worked under the supervision of engineer Frederic C. Kunz. He gained valuable practical experience in the position, for it involved him in a broad spectrum of activities associated with the manufacture and construction of several types of bridges. Ammann's knowledge and experience were further broadened in 1906 when he won a position designing steel bridges in the Chicago office of consulting engineer Ralph Modjeski.

Ammann gained valuable knowledge about building large bridges in general and of cantilever construction in particular in examining the 1907 collapse of the Quebec cantilever bridge. He volunteered to assist engineer Charles C. Schneider, a former vice president of the American Bridge Company, asked by the Canadian government to conduct an inquiry into the failure. Ammann became the de facto investigator, and the fine quality of the report (completed in 1908) garnered respect for him throughout the profession. This was followed by a position, which he assumed in 1909, with the Philadelphia office of engineers Kunz & Schneider. While working for the firm, Ammann progressed from draftsman to designer and ultimately to chief engineer on projects such as the St. Johns, New Brunswick, arch bridge and a proposed replacement for the failed Quebec Bridge.

Gustav Lindenthal, one of the nation's leading bridge designers, hired Ammann in 1912. He served as Lindenthal's principal assistant, as well as the assistant chief engineer of the East River Bridge Division of the New York Connecting Railroad. In August 1914 Ammann temporarily left his engineering position and returned to Switzerland to help prepare for the threat of invasion by the German army. While serving in the military, he used his engineering skills in building fortifications. He remained abroad until late 1914, when he returned to the United States and Lindenthal's engineering office.

Ammann was promoted to the position of deputy chief engineer and put in charge of the design and construction of the Hell Gate arch bridge across the East River. The four-track railroad bridge created a direct rail link between New York City and the New England states. While work progressed on it, he was engaged in a number of other projects, including studies for a Hudson River crossing at 57th Street and the design and construction of the Chesapeake & Ohio Bridge at Sciotoville; it and the Hell Gate both opened in 1917. That same year Lindenthal faced a dearth of work and suggested that Ammann seek temporary employment elsewhere.

With little bridge work to be found, in 1917 Ammann accepted a management position at a New Jersey clay works in which Lindenthal had a financial interest. By 1920 Ammann's careful guidance had returned the nearly bankrupt works to solvency. Later that same year, he was once again in Lindenthal's engineering office as assistant chief engineer of the Hudson River Bridge Company. The company was formed to promote a massive suspension bridge across the Hudson River at 57th Street. The bridge, designed to carry both highway and rapid transit traffic, would be a direct link between the heart of Manhattan and New Jersey. As president and chief engineer, Lindenthal pushed forward plans that he had formulated over many years.

Ammann held serious reservations about Lindenthal's projected schedule, the huge scope of the plan, and finances. These concerns, coupled with the elder engineer's refusal to modify his proposal in any way, brought their association to an end in 1923, and Ammann opened his own office as a consulting engineer. He too had come to believe in the need for a Hudson River span, but one more modest than that proposed by Lindenthal. Ammann developed his own preliminary designs and plans and lobbied vigorously for a suspension bridge that was eventually built across the Hudson at 179th Street. During this time, in 1924, he became a U.S. citizen.

In 1925 final approval came from the federal government and the states of New York and New Jersey for the construction of a Hudson River bridge. Authority was given to the recently formed Port of New York Authority to build the George Washington Bridge across the river between Washington Heights on the east shore and Fort Lee on the west. The authority hired Ammann as chief bridge engineer. Ground was broken for the bridge in September 1927 with Ammann in charge of its design. Under his direction the bridge was completed ahead of schedule in October 1931. As construction progressed on the Hudson span, the Goethals and Bayonne bridges were being built. Less than a month after the Hudson bridge was completed, the Bayonne arch bridge across the Kill-van-Kull, connecting Staten Island, New York, to New Jersey, opened to traffic.

Ammann served as chief engineer of the authority from 1930 to 1937 and as director of engineering from 1937 to 1939. While he was there, in 1933, his first wife died, and in 1935 he married Kläry Vogt Nötzli; they had no children. During his tenure, he supervised the planning for Manhattan's second subaqueous vehicular crossing, the Lincoln Tunnel, which opened in 1937. Despite his busy schedule around New York City, Ammann served from 1929 to 1937 on the board of engineers that reviewed the plans and construction of San Francisco's Golden Gate Bridge designed by Joseph B. Strauss. From 1934 to 1939 he also held the position of chief engineer of the Triborough Bridge and Tunnel Authority, which was charged with building several East River highway crossings. He was responsible for the plans and construction of both the Triborough suspension bridge in 1936 and the Bronx-Whitestone suspension bridge in 1939.

Ammann retired from the Port of New York Authority in 1939 and again went into private practice. Because of his reputation for large suspension bridges he received contracts to perform studies for several more large bridges, including those planned for Wilmington, Delaware; Philadelphia, Pennsylvania; Yorktown, Virginia; and the Mackinac Straits in Michigan. In November 1940 Ammann, Theodor von Kármán, and Glenn B. Woodruff were appointed to a board of engineers charged to investigate the collapse of the recently completed Tacoma Narrows suspension bridge near Seattle, Washington. Their results were published in April 1941 in a lengthy and highly praised report to the Federal Works Administration. Although Ammann specialized in suspension bridges, his office was open to all engineering work, and he produced plans for the New York–New Jersey Palisades Parkway and several modern highways in New York City.

In 1946 Ammann joined with consulting engineer Charles S. Whitney to form the engineering firm of Ammann & Whitney. Their professional association dated from the years when both worked for Lindenthal on the Hell Gate Bridge. In addition to the staple of bridge work, Whitney's expertise in reinforced concrete led the firm into the design and construction of other large structures. Generally these were buildings that encompassed expansive unobstructed spaces such as airport hangars and auditoriums. The association was prosperous and international in scope; employing a staff of nearly 500 workers, it had offices in several cities around the country. Ammann's final project was perhaps his most ambitious. Because of studies he produced, the firm was selected in 1954 to produce plans and then oversee construction of the Verrazano-Narrows Suspension Bridge that joined Staten Island and Brooklyn. When the bridge opened to traffic in November 1964, it was the world's longest suspension span, measuring more than 4,200 feet.

Ammann belonged to several professional organizations. He was an honorary member and director (1934–1936) of the American Society of Civil Engineers. He held memberships in the American Institute of Consulting Engineers, American Railway Engineering Association, American Society for Testing and Materials, New York Academy of Sciences, and the Engineer's Club of New York. He died at his home in Rye, New York.

Ammann stands as a leading figure in twentieth-century suspension bridge design. In and around New York City he produced structures of monumental proportions. Scientifically sound and artistically graceful, his bridges are timeless and should stand for many generations. Exquisitely prepared technically for the tasks he undertook, Ammann superimposed his guiding principles of simplicity and truthfulness that produced a timelessness in the final designs he produced. He was to comment "Mere size and proportion are not the outstanding merit of a bridge; a bridge should be handed down to posterity as a truly monumental structure which will cast credit on the aesthetic sense of present generations."

• Information on Ammann's various projects can be obtained from his many detailed technical articles and reports, some in book form. Ammann recounted the construction of the Hell Gate Bridge and its approaches in the *Transactions* of the American Society of Civil Engineers (1918). In "Brobdingnagian Bridges," *Technology Review* 33, no. 9 (July 1931), Ammann presented a popular account of the progress of large bridge construction as of that date. The closest thing to a biography of him is Edward Cohen, *The Engineer and His Works: A Tribute to Othmar Hermann Ammann* (1967); the author, a partner in the firm of Ammann & Whitney, provides a lengthy list of technical papers and addresses by Ammann. An obituary is in the *New York Times International Edition*, 24 Sept. 1965.

WILLIAM E. WORTHINGTON, JR.

AMMEN, Daniel (16 May 1819–11 July 1898), naval officer, author, and inventor, was born in Brown County, Ohio, the son of David Ammen and Sally Houtz, farmers. While still a boy, Ammen exerted an unanticipated influence on later national affairs when he pulled his friend and schoolmate Ulysses S. Grant from a swollen stream into which Grant had fallen while the two boys were fishing. Grant wrote later in life that this act saved him from certain drowning. Ammen and Grant remained personal and professional intimates throughout their lives.

Ammen began his naval career at the age of seventeen, when he received an appointment as a midshipman in the U.S. Navy. Prior to the Civil War, from 1838 to 1860, Ammen's sea service took him on extended cruises of exploration and mapping in areas of the world including the Gulf of Mexico, the West Indies, Labrador, the Mediterranean, Japan, China, and South America. His most notable performance during these cruises was as ship's navigator on several vessels and in surveying duties on missions of coastal mapping. While a midshipman, Ammen spent several months of special study at the military academy at West Point, at the time without equal as an engineering school, and he became an accomplished engineer.

During the Civil War, Ammen participated in or commanded assaults in several important engagements. He began the war as a lieutenant and served as executive officer on the frigate *Roanoke*, conducting blockade duties around southern ports in 1861. He received his own command, the *Seneca*, later in the same year. As commander of the *Seneca*, Ammen took part in the attack on Forts Walker and Beauregard at Port Royal, South Carolina (7 Nov. 1861). Also aboard the *Seneca*, he was engaged in the battle for Tybee Island (Dec. 1861) and commanded the forces assaulting Port Royal Ferry (1 Jan. 1862). He was promoted to commander on 21 February 1863 and was given command of the monitor vessel *Patapsco*. With this vessel he participated in the attacks on Forts McAllister, Georgia (3 Mar. 1863), and Sumter (7 Apr. 1863). In May 1864 Ammen, commanding naval recruits aboard the passenger steamer *Ocean Queen* bound for Panama, suppressed a mutinous uprising. He physically confronted two leaders of the mutiny, shot one dead, and put down the mutiny. Associate Justice Stephen J. Field of the U.S. Supreme Court was aboard the vessel as a passenger, and he took statements from passengers that were later presented as evidence in Ammen's court-martial. Ammen was acquitted of the charges of murder and exonerated professionally. He saw further action in the winter of 1864–1865 commanding the steam-powered sloop *Mohican* in attacks on Fort Fisher, North Carolina.

After the Civil War, Ammen was appointed director of the Bureau of Yards and Docks (1868–1871) and then director of the Bureau of Navigation (1871–1878), where he initiated notable improvements in naval procedures and technology, including methods for signaling and deep-sea sounding. He was promoted to commodore on 1 April 1872. Also during this period, Ammen served as secretary of the Isthmian Canal Commission (1872–1876) and represented the United States at the Interoceanic Canal Congress in Paris in 1879. Along with Grant, he was a proponent of building a canal across Central America. Ammen authored seven pamphlets in support of this idea and was in charge of conducting a survey of the isthmus to determine the feasibility and best route for the proposed waterway. President Grant displayed considerable confidence in Ammen. For instance, upon Ammen's appointment to the Paris Congress, Grant wrote, "I do not believe there is another American who understands the relative advantages of the one feasible route over all others, nor who can state the advantages and obstacles . . . as clearly as you can" (Ammen, "Recollections and Letters of Grant," vol. 348, p. 424). In addition Ammen designed the *Katahdin*, a twin-screwed ramming vessel that attracted significant interest from naval engineering experts, and a prototype for lifeboats to be used aboard naval vessels.

Ammen was promoted to rear admiral on 11 December 1877. After about 1870 and upon his retirement in 1878, he lived on his estate "Ammendale," northeast of Washington, D.C. His elder brother, Jacob Ammen, likewise a Civil War military officer, had also retired near there, and the area still bears the name Ammendale. During his retirement, Ammen wrote several books, including *The Atlantic Coast* (1883), which comprised one volume of a thirteen-volume official history of *The Army in the Civil War*. Other works by Ammen are *Country Homes and Their Improvement* (1885) and *The Old Navy and the New* (1891), a recounting of his travels as well as the changes in naval operations over the course of his career. Upon his death in Washington, D.C., the *New York Times* devoted a full-column story to his life, calling him "one of the heroes of the civil war," who saw "active service of the most serious kind" (12 July 1885).

Details of Ammen's personal life are somewhat sparse, and his writings do not discuss his marriages. He married twice, first to Mary Jackson (date unavailable), then in 1866 to Zoe Atoche, with whom he had five children. A contemporary wrote in 1898 that Ammen was twice a widower, although a later biographical account states that his second wife survived him. Contemporaneous accounts or recollections of Ammen tend to be respectful, describing him as a skilled naval officer dedicated to bringing about technological and procedural improvements in naval operations and "distinguished . . . for his tact in the handling of men" under his command (Belknap, p. 270).

• The largest single collection of Ammen's personal papers is at the Special Collections Library of the University of California at Los Angeles. Official papers and correspondence, including vessel deck logs, are at the National Archives in Washington, D.C. Some of Ammen's personal letters are at the Rutherford B. Hayes Presidential Library in Fremont, Ohio, and in the manuscript collections of Salmon P. Chase, George Belknap, and John Lowe at the Library of Congress. A small biographical file is at the Operational Archives Branch of the Naval Historical Center at the Navy Yard in Washington, D.C. Ammen, very much dedicated to the defensive of Grant, authored "Recollections and Letters of Grant," *North American Review* 347 (Oct. 1885): 361–73, and 348 (Nov. 1885): 421–30. Material regarding Ammen is also available in *The Official Records of the Union and Confederate Navies in the War of the Rebellion* (1894–1922) and *Civil War Naval Chronology, 1861–1865* (1971). A biographical sketch of Ammen by a contemporary is George E. Belknap, "Rear Admiral Daniel Ammen, U.S.N.: A Biographical Sketch," *Cassier's Magazine* 14, no. 3 (July 1898): 267–73. A related article examining Ammen's ram *Katahdin* is William Ledyard Cathcart, "The Ram in Modern War Fleets," *Cassier's Magazine* 14, no. 3 (July 1898): 215–33. Obituaries are in the *New York Times*, 12 July 1898, and the *Army and Navy Journal* and the *Army and Navy Register*, 16 July 1898.

MICHAEL HAUSENFLECK

AMMONS, Albert C. (23 Sept. 1907–2 Dec. 1949), jazz pianist, was born in Chicago. His parents' names are unknown; both were pianists. Ammons was a teenage friend of Meade Lux Lewis. The two learned to play by following the key action of player pianos and by imitating more experienced musicians, including Hersal Thomas and Jimmy Yancey. Ammons, having access to his parents' instrument, developed his skills faster than Lewis. Both men were particularly influenced by a tune called "The Fives," a blues involving strong, repetitive, percussive patterns in the left hand, set against equally strong and percussive but less rigorously repetitive counterrhythmic patterns in the right; this piano blues style came to be known as boogie-woogie.

In 1924 Ammons joined a band in South Bend, Indiana. He married around this time, although details about his wife are unknown; his ultimately more famous and talented son, the tenor saxophonist Gene Ammons, was born in 1925. At some point Ammons left for Chicago and then returned to South Bend to play in a big band at a whorehouse, the Paradise Inn. By 1927 he was playing in Detroit and then back in Chicago. He continued to perform regularly while working as a driver at the Silver Taxi Cab company, where Lewis also was employed; they lived in the same rooming house as fellow pianist Pine Top Smith, who taught Ammons "Pine Top's Boogie Woogie," the piece that named the style.

At some unspecified point Ammons led a band at the Dusty Bottom club in Chicago. He joined François Moseley's Louisiana Stompers in the summer of 1929 and William Barbee and His Headquarters from 1930 until 1931. Barbee, also a pianist, gave him valuable lessons that expanded his stylistic range, and he became somewhat comfortable playing in swing groups in the 1930s, although his repertoire remained limited by comparison with many jazz pianists. He joined drummer Louis P. Banks's Chesterfield Orchestra from 1931 until 1934 in clubs in Chicago and then on a theatrical tour. He led a five-piece band, including trumpeter Punch Miller, which played for weekend excursions to the South on the Illinois Central Railroad. In 1934, Ammons formed his Rhythm Kings, which toward year's end began a two-year stand at the Club DeLisa. The group made recordings in February 1936, including "Nagasaki," which finds Ammons breaking away from the boogie-woogie style, and "Boogie Woogie Stomp," an arrangement of "Pine Top's Boogie Woogie," without Smith's vocal chatter and with the six-piece group rather than piano alone. In April 1936 the Rhythm Kings' bassist Israel Crosby left to join the Fletcher Henderson band. When soon thereafter the Club DeLisa began to present more complicated floor shows and the music proved too difficult for Ammons, he was fired and the job given to his saxophonist Delbert Bright.

Ammons played alone at the It Club, and in 1938 he led a band at the Claremont Club before traveling to New York to take part in the "Spirituals to Swing" concert at Carnegie Hall on 23 December. There he accompanied Big Bill Broonzy on two numbers, including "Louise, Louise," and he formed a boogie-woogie piano trio with Lewis and Pete Johnson. Their enthusiastic reception furthered the public's developing passion for the boogie-woogie style, and the three pianists were catapulted to fame. With Big Joe Turner, the trio worked at Café Society in New York and the Hotel Sherman in Chicago and broadcast nationally. He remained at the uptown location of Café Society in a duo with Johnson until 1942, when the two men began touring together.

In 1939 Ammons recorded a solo version of "Boogie Woogie Stomp" and his finest solo, "Shout for Joy," which critic Jimmy Hopes recommends for the rhythmic power of Ammons's left hand, his sense of structure, and the unusual final choruses, which are surprising within the context of the often predictable boogie-woogie style. A recording session that same year with the Port of Harlem Jazzmen, including trumpeter Frankie Newton, produced "Port of Harlem Blues," which finds Ammons improvising an uncharacteristically delicate, high-pitched, tuneful, and nonpercussive blues melody. In 1941 he recorded with Johnson and drummer Jimmy Hoskins, and he performed in the movie short *Boogie Woogie Dream*. The following year he recorded "Suitcase Blues," in memory of his early influence Hersal Thomas, who had recorded a version of it in 1925. "Bass Goin' Crazy," a playful performance also recorded in 1941, was equally percussive but altogether freer and more dissonant than Ammons's usual boogie-woogie style. Although he revived the name Rhythm Kings for 1944 recordings that featured eminent swing musicians, the results were dull.

Sometime in the mid-1940s Ammons suffered a temporary paralysis of both hands. He resumed playing, mainly in Chicago, and in 1947 he recorded under the leadership of his saxophonist son. Ammons joined Lionel Hampton at the beginning of 1949 and recorded "Chicken Shack Boogie," but having long suffered from alcoholism, he died in Chicago before year's end. His death date is commonly given as 2 December, but the brief and not necessarily reliable *Chicago Tribune* obituary of 4 December reports his death "yesterday."

Ammons was a somewhat more versatile pianist than his close friend Lewis and hence able to work regularly with jazz groups, but he was never more than competent in this area and no match for their colleague Johnson. His specific significance lies within the confines of the boogie-woogie piano style, in which Lewis and he are rated as the finest practitioners after Yancey. Later and indirectly, his music reached a vast audience when the rhythm-and-blues, urban blues, and rock-and-roll styles adopted boogie-woogie piano patterns as part of their basic vocabulary.

• Essays on Ammons's career are by Sharon A. Pease, "'Pine Top' Smith Influenced Early Piano Style of Swingin' Ammons," *Down Beat*, July 1937, pp. 28–29, including a notated musical excerpt from "Boogie Woogie Stomp"; Jimmy Hopes, "Boogie Woogie Man: A Bio-discography of Albert Ammons," *Jazz & Blues* 1, no. 6 (1971): 4–7, including a full list of recordings; Stanley Dance, liner notes to the Ammonses' album *Boogie Woogie and the Blues* (1980); and Leonard Feather, "Piano Giants of Jazz: Albert Ammons," *Contemporary Keyboard*, Feb. 1981, pp. 70–71, which also includes a musical excerpt, "The First Two Choruses of Albert Ammons' 'The Boogie Rocks,'" notated by Jim Aikin. Eli H. Newberger, "Archetypes and Antecedents of Piano Blues and Boogie Woogie Style," *Journal of Jazz Studies*, Fall 1976, pp. 84–109, includes a notated music example and discussion of an excerpt from Ammons's "Woo Woo." Singer Tommy Brookins describes the engagement at the Dusty Bottom in Nat Shapiro and Nat Hentoff, eds., *Hear Me Talkin' to Ya: The Story of Jazz as Told by the Men Who Made It* (1955), pp. 112–13. Other information about Ammons's groups in Chicago appears in Dempsey J. Travis, *An Autobiography of Black Jazz* (1983), pp. 127–28, 390; included are photos of the Club DeLisa and the Rhythm Kings.

Ammons figures prominently in surveys of his chosen style: William Russell, "Boogie Woogie," in *Jazzmen*, ed. Frederic Ramsey, Jr., and Charles Edward Smith (1939), pp. 183–205; Ernest Borneman, "Boogie Woogie," in *Just Jazz*, vol. 1, ed. Sinclair Traill and Gerald Lascelles (1957); Max Harrison, "Boogie Woogie," in *Jazz*, ed. Nat Hentoff and Albert J. McCarthy (1959), pp. 105–35; Martin Williams, "Cuttin' the Boogie," in *Jazz Heritage* (1985), pp. 160–72; and Mike Rowe, "Piano Blues and Boogie-Woogie," in *The Blackwell Guide to Blues Records*, ed. Paul Oliver (1989), pp. 112–38. See also the unsigned article "Meade Lux Lewis: A Blues Man's Story," *Down Beat*, 19 Feb. 1959, pp. 16–17; and Don Hill, "Meade Lux Lewis," *Cadence* 13 (Oct. 1987): 16–28.

BARRY KERNFELD

AMMONS, Gene (14 Apr. 1925–6 Aug. 1974), jazz tenor saxophonist, was born Eugene Ammons in Chicago, Illinois, the son of Albert Ammons, a boogie-woogie pianist; his mother's name is unknown. Like several other prominent jazzmen, Ammons studied music at Du Sable High School under Captain Walter Dyett. Initially he idolized Lester Young's improvising and even imitated Young's manner of playing with head and horn at a grotesquely tilted angle. During his third year in high school he began playing locally with trumpeter King Kolax's band. At the semester's end he embarked on a cross-country tour with Kolax that included performances at the Savoy Ballroom in New York.

In 1944 singer Billy Eckstine formed a big band that included tenor saxophonist Charlie Rouse and alto saxophonist Charlie Parker. According to the group's pianist, John Malachi, Rouse was so smitten by Parker's playing that he was unable to concentrate on his own parts. Around August 1944 Rouse was fired. Ammons took Rouse's place on the recommendation of a friend, Eckstine trumpeter Gail Brockman, who would later participate in Ammons's early recordings as a leader. The group mainly recorded ballads featuring Eckstine's romantic voice, but it was also known as the first bop big band. That aspect of its musical personality is best preserved on two takes of "Blowin' the Blues Away," in which Ammons engages with tenor saxophonist Dexter Gordon in a magnificent battle of fast-paced blues improvisation. (Both men win.) Playing such as this exemplified Ammons's (and Gordon's) ability to draw a perfect balance between smooth tunefulness, a heady linear expression of harmony, and earthy honking and riffing.

While with Eckstine, Ammons acquired his nickname, "Jug." Evidently he had difficulty finding a straw hat big enough to fit, and the singer said, "You've got a head like a jug." From late 1944 onward Ammons was the principal instrumental soloist in a band teeming with up-and-coming bop musicians. He is featured on several records, including "I Love the Rhythm in a Riff" (1945), "Second Balcony Jump," "Cool Breeze," and "Oop Bop Sh'bam" (all from 1946), and in the movie *Rhythm in a Riff* (also 1946).

In Chicago in the first part of 1947, Ammons was featured alongside trumpeter Miles Davis and alto saxophonist Sonny Stitt in jam sessions at the Jumptown Club, and he played in Stitt's octet at the Twin Terrace Café in March. Around May 1947, if not a couple of months sooner, the Eckstine group disbanded. Ammons led small groups from mid-1947 onward. He had immediate success with the tuneful blues "Red Top" (1947), which had a second life when it was rereleased with lyrics overdubbed in 1953, but apart from this title his recordings of the late 1940s, including a session with his father on piano, are not among his best.

Ammons interrupted his bandleading in late March or early April 1949 to replace Stan Getz in Woody Herman's Second Herd, with which he figured most prominently on "More Moon." He left Herman at the beginning of September 1949, his place taken by tenor saxophonist Billy Mitchell. Following directly in the tradition of "Blowin' the Blues Away," Ammons then formalized the saxophone battle in a quintet co-led by Stitt, who was now focusing on tenor as well as alto saxophone. They worked mainly at Birdland in New York from 1950 to 1951. Their finest recordings, made for the Prestige label, are two takes of "You Can Depend on Me" and three of "Blues Up and Down" (1950). The group continued intermittently until 1955. Around 1955 he married Geraldine (maiden name unknown). They had two children. From 1955 to 1958 he led a number of ad hoc all-star blues and bop sessions for Prestige, one of which resulted in the outstanding album *Blue Gene* (1958).

Ammons has been rumored to be the composer of the blues theme "Walkin'," popularized by Miles Davis in 1954. Legally, "Walkin'" is credited to Ammons's manager, Richard Carpenter. There is no firm evidence that Carpenter appropriated it (although such actions have been commonplace in jazz). In any event, Ammons was not a significant jazz composer.

Ammons started using heroin sometime in the early 1950s (by his own account) and perhaps before that time; several of Herman's sidemen were notorious junkies. In 1958 he was convicted for possession of narcotics and sent to the Statesville Penitentiary near Joliet, Illinois. Paroled in June 1960, he recorded the album *Boss Tenor* but was then returned to prison for violation of the condition of his parole that forbade him to perform in nightclubs. He served out the remainder of his sentence and in January 1961 resumed his career, recording the album *Boss Tenors* as co-leader with Stitt in August of that year. For engagements at McKie's Lounge in Chicago Ammons was joined by Gordon in September and by Stitt and saxophonist James Moody from late that year into February 1962.

During this period, 1960 to 1962, Ammons modified his style, placing less emphasis on his abilities as a bop improviser and instead focusing on African-American gospel-influenced melodic gestures that were becoming popular in soul music. This reorientation led to a few modest hit singles, including his soulful instrumental rendering of the songs "Canadian Sunset" (from the Prestige *Boss Tenor* disc) and "Ca' Purange" (from the 1962 LP issued as *Bad! Bossa Nova* and also as *Jungle Soul*).

In June 1962 he began using narcotics again, and in September he was arrested. For this second conviction he spent seven years in Statesville, where, as previously, he kept his career alive by directing the prison band and playing every day; meanwhile Bob Weinstock of Prestige, having recorded many sessions with Ammons in 1961–1962, released these gradually throughout the decade, effectively keeping Ammons's name before the public. He was paroled in October 1969 and resumed his career with an engagement at the Plugged Nickel in Chicago, with Kolax playing trumpet. The following month a two-day recording session yielded two new albums, *The Boss Is Back* and *Brother Jug!*, the latter including a new hit single, Ammons's romantic instrumental rendering of "Didn't We." In March 1970 the New York State Liquor Board ruled against his performing in New York City, but he was able to work elsewhere and held a noted engagement in Chicago with tenor saxophonists Don Byas and Gordon in September 1970. He worked alongside Eddie "Lockjaw" Davis in Chicago in May 1973. Ammons performed at the Ahus Jazz Festival in Sweden on 14 July 1974. Nine days later he entered Michael Reese Hospital in Chicago, where he died of bone cancer and pneumonia.

• Leonard Feather interviews Ammons in "The Rebirth of Gene Ammons," *Down Beat*, 25 June 1970, pp. 12–13, 31. Jim Burns surveys his career and recordings to 1955 in "Gene Ammons," *Jazz Journal* 23 (Apr. 1970): 22–24. See also Alun Morgan, "Woody's Tenors," *Jazz Monthly* 6 (Sept. 1960): 5; Brooks Johnson, "Forum for Three: Gene Ammons, Bennie Green, and Dexter Gordon," *Metronome* 78 (Dec. 1961): 12–14; Marc Crawford, "Jug Ain't Changed," *Down Beat*, 17 Aug. 1962, pp. 24, 42; Jim Burns, "The Billy Eckstine Band," *Jazz Monthly* 13 (Jan. 1968): 6–10; "Gene Ammons Back; Opening Night a Gas," *Down Beat*, 27 Nov. 1969, p. 8; and Dan Morgenstern, "Gene Ammons: Here to Stay," *Down Beat*, 9 Mar. 1970, p. 12. Catalogs of recordings include Bob Porter and Frank Gibson, "Gene Ammons: A Discography," *Discographical Forum* 6 (May 1968): 11–14 and 7 (July 1968): 10–12; Malcolm Walker and Tony Williams, "Private Recordings," *Discographical Forum* 5 (Mar. 1968): 11–12, 13 (July 1969): 2, and 16 (Jan. 1970): 2; James A. Treichel, *Keeper of the Flame: Woody Herman and the Second Herd, 1947–1949* (1978), and Dieter Salemann et al., *Sonny Stitt: Solography, Discographical Informations, Band Routes, Engagements in Chronological Order* (1986). Obituaries are in the *Chicago Tribune*, 7 Aug. 1974, *New York Times*, 8 Aug. 1974, *Chicago Defender*, 10 Aug. 1974, and *Down Beat*, 10 Oct. 1974, p. 11.

BARRY KERNFELD

ANAGNOS, Michael (7 Nov. 1837–29 June 1906), educator of the blind, was born in the remote village of Papingo in the Epirus region of northwestern Greece, the son of a peasant named Demetrios Anagnostopoulos, whose family held a prominent position within the community; his mother's name is not known. He attended high school in the city of Ioannina and in 1856 entered the National University of Athens, where he took courses in Greek, Latin, French, and philosophy. Shortly after graduating from the university he went to work for *Ethnophylax*, one of the first daily newspapers in Athens, and within a short time he became the editor in chief. At some time during this period he was married to a young woman from his village. Little is known of his wife or the marriage except that the couple had a son and eventually divorced.

In 1867 Anagnos was employed by Dr. Samuel Gridley Howe, an American who had served in the

Greek War of Independence (1825–1830) and had become the first director of what is now known as the Perkins School for the Blind in Boston, Massachusetts (the oldest school for the blind in the United States). Howe's wife, Julia Ward Howe, was the social reformer, writer and author off "The Battle Hymn of the Republic." Howe had continued to take an interest in Greece and in 1867, along with his eldest daughter Julia Romana, carried relief to Cretan refugees in Athens. At the same time he made plans to visit and examine schools for the deaf and institutions for the mentally retarded and, in order to assist him, hired Anagnos as his secretary. Howe then urged Anagnos to return with him to the United States so that he could "learn the manners of the country so as to be of greater services to his countrymen on his return to Greece." In 1868 Anagnos arrived in Boston, where Howe hired him to teach some of his blind students Greek and Latin. During the next few years Anagnos's role in the administration of the school increased, and by 1870 he had become Howe's secretary and general assistant. In December 1870 he married Julia Romana Howe and, shortly after, officially shortened his name to Anagnos. Howe's increasingly poor health led Anagnos to take over more and more responsibility for the running of Perkins School, and on the death of Howe in 1876, he became the director. Anagnos's wife, like him, had a great love of children although they had none of their own. She took a great interest in her husband's work, especially in his efforts to establish a kindergarten for the blind. She died in 1886, and the following year he founded the first kindergarten in the world for blind children; this was to be his most notable achievement.

Anagnos brought about many changes in Perkins School, including the establishment in 1880 of a print library and museum on the history of the education of the blind. In 1881 he established the Howe Memorial Press to increase the number of embossed books that were available to the blind. These books were in Boston Line Type, a raised type system developed by Howe in 1835, which continued to be used at Perkins and by many blind persons even after braille came to the United States.

Anagnos continued to emphasize the education of deaf-blind children, which had been started in 1837 when Howe began to educate Laura Bridgman, a seven-year-old deaf-blind child from Hanover, New Hampshire. By 1886 several other deaf-blind children came to Perkins to be educated. The work of educating deaf-blind children became known to many, including Alexander Graham Bell. At the suggesting of Bell, Captain Arthur Keller wrote Anagnos in late 1886 to request the name of a person to work with his daughter Helen. Helen, who was born in June 1880, had become deaf-blind at the age of nineteen months as the result of an unknown illness. Anagnos recommended to Captain Keller a young woman, Anne Mansfield Sullivan, a recent graduate of Perkins. Sullivan was herself partially sighted and had learned while at Perkins to communicate with the deaf-blind. Prior to entering Keller's employment in Tuscumbia, Alabama, she studied Howe's methods of instruction. Sullivan arrived in Tuscumbia on 3 March 1887, a day that Helen Keller would later refer to as her "soul's birth day," the most important day in her life. Sullivan opened the door of communication that for so long had been closed to her pupil. Sullivan and Keller spent the years 1889 to 1893 as guests of Anagnos at Perkins. The widespread interest in Keller and her teacher brought Anagnos to the attention of the general public.

In his thirty years as director of Perkins, Anagnos was tireless in his efforts to improve the quality of life of both students and staff in areas ranging from academic curriculum to housing and health. In education he organized courses of instruction and tests that made it possible for Perkins students in 1880 to be awarded diplomas. He stressed nonacademic subjects, such as physical education, in which he firmly believed, and vocational training, so that departing students could earn a living. While visiting the 1893 World's Fair in Chicago, he saw the Sloyd System of manual training being demonstrated and persuaded the Finnish teacher to come to work at Perkins. According to Perkins staff member Anna Gardner Fish, Anagnos's "life was one of Spartan simplicity, and he required no self-sacrifice on the part of his teachers that he was not willing to share. His industry was tireless. He ate sparingly, as his health demanded. His own nobility of character and his lofty ideas were apparent in his dealings, as too were his wisdom and soundness of principles. He made his living and his profession one." Since Perkins was a private school, Anagnos worked hard to establish its financial base through his fundraising efforts. He raised enough funds that by 1892 a new building could be built to house a library of embossed books, a music library, and a tactual museum. The library was open to both Perkins students and to all blind adults in New England.

In keeping with his position as a leader in the field of education of the blind, Anagnos was a member of such organizations as the American Association of Workers for Blind and attended many conferences and conventions both in the United States and Europe. He made it a point to visit other schools and agencies for the blind to keep abreast of new developments in the education and welfare of the blind.

Anagnos also sought to improve the conditions of the immigrant Greek community in New England. He was a true father to all Greeks, and many sought him for advice on a diversity of problems. At one time he served as president of the National Union of Greeks. He was a major contributor to the Greek Orthodox church in Boston and elsewhere. He made three visits to Greece between 1889 and 1906 and never lost his love and interest in his homeland, especially the region from which he came and to which he gave financial contributions for education. On his last visit in 1906 he created an endowment of £5,000 for the maintenance of two primary schools in his village of Papingo. He died while visiting family and friends in Turn Severin, Romania, where his son had lived since childhood. Anagnos left most of his savings for the establishment of a school in Konista, Greece, which he hoped would educate the young people of the region so that they would not leave. In 1938 his remains were moved from Romania to Konista and were buried on the grounds of the Anagnos School.

• The largest collection of material by and about Anagnos is in the archives of the Samuel P. Hayes Research Library, Perkins School for the Blind, Watertown, Mass. This material deals in large part with his years as director of Perkins School for the Blind and includes his writings, *Education of the Blind, Historical Sketch of its Origin and Progress* (1882); *Helen Keller, a Second Laura Bridgman* (1896); and *Schools and Workshops for the Blind. Their Scope and Limitations* (1905). Franklin Benjamin Sanborn, a lifelong friend, wrote *Michael Anagnos 1837–1906* (1907), a record of what was said at the time of Anagnos death, which was revised from the 75th Annual Report of the Perkins Institution and Massachusetts School for the Blind. Anna Gardner Fish wrote an eighteen-page work, *Michael Anagnos 1837–1906, on the Occasion of the Centenary of Michael Anagnos and the Semi-centennial of the Kindergarten for the Blind* (1937).

KENNETH A. STUCKEY

ANDERS, Glenn (1 Sept. 1889–26 Oct. 1981), actor, was born Charles Glenn Anders in Los Angeles, California, the son of Charles Gustave, a contractor, and Etta Arvilla Slade. His father was born in Sweden, and his mother, whose ancestors were Scotch-Irish, was born in Vermont. Both parents were strict Methodists and initially opposed his intention to become an actor. After Anders graduated from Los Angeles High School in 1908, his mother persuaded his father to let him attend the local Wallace Dramatic School. His first professional stage appearance came in a bit part in the Los Angeles Stock Company's production of *Macbeth* in 1910. When Sarah Bernhardt came to San Francisco in 1912 on one of her "final" tours, Anders appeared as an extra in two of her productions. That same year he toured with Sothern and Marlowe's Shakespearean Company. He also worked in vaudeville as a sketch artist on the Keith-Orpheum circuit from 1913 to 1915.

Because Anders wanted a career in the legitimate theater, he was advised to go to New York City. He had made several previous appearances there while on tour, but his first significant role came in *Just Around the Corner* on Broadway in 1919. For the next two years he played supporting roles in one lightweight comedy after another. During the day he attended classes at Columbia University, although he never graduated.

The turning point in Anders's career came when he was chosen to play Andy Lowry, a roughneck Appalachian farm boy, in *Hell-Bent Fer Heaven* in 1924. His impressive performance led to his being cast as Joe, an IWW farmhand who fathers the unmarried heroine's child in Sidney Howard's *They Knew What They Wanted* that same year. The play, which starred Pauline Lord, was an enormous popular success, in part because of its sensational theme and language. Anders was asked to repeat his role in a 1926 London production with Tallulah Bankhead, whom he later described as too beautiful to evoke pity for the character she played. In 1928 he played the role of Dr. Edmund Darrell in the premiere of Eugene O'Neill's *Strange Interlude*. All three plays won a Pulitzer Prize for drama. That Anders created principal roles in these three plays in a four-year period was a tribute to his dramatic abilities and to his growing reputation. Further recognition came when Eugene O'Neill himself cast Anders opposite Claudette Colbert in the premiere of his *Dynamo* in 1929. Anders played the role of Reuben Light, a worshiper of modern technology.

By the late 1920s Anders had gained a reputation as a talented, versatile actor of considerable range. Critics praised him for his "casual naturalness" and comic delivery, yet he was also able to play serious parts in realistic dramas. Unlike some Broadway actors of his generation, he was never histrionic. Producers and directors did not cast him solely for his recognized dramatic abilities, however. Tall, handsome, and striking in profile, he was a matinee idol of the 1920s and for much of the 1930s. Using his expressive face, he projected a magnetic charm, wit, and romantic appeal across the footlights. Fifty years later Helen Hayes remembered him as "very romantic, a great wit and full of laughter." Despite these attractive qualities, he never married.

From the 1920s through the 1940s Anders appeared annually in one or more Broadway productions as well as doing tours and summer stock. He costarred with almost all the leading dramatic actresses of the period, including Judith Anderson, Lynn Fontanne, Ruth Gordon, Helen Hayes, and Gertrude Lawrence. The range of his characterizations was astonishing. In 1934 he appeared in a Theatre Guild production of *Moor Born* as Branwell Bronte. He costarred with Kitty Carlisle in *Three Waltzes* (1937), playing a European aristocrat. He played opposite Gertrude Lawrence in the 1939 hit *Skylark*. In 1944 he played Alexander Craig, a detached observer of his contemporaries in *Soldier's Wife*. In 1948 he starred in Moss Hart's *Light Up the Sky* as Carleton Fitzgerald, an effeminate director. One of his last major roles came as Lord Hector, a foolish aristocrat, in a 1957 production of Jean Anouilh's fastasy, *Time Remembered*, which costarred Richard Burton, Susan Strasberg, and the only leading lady of the American theater of his generation with whom he had not previously acted, Helen Hayes. His final stage appearance came as Professor Muller in a 1960 production of Friedrich Duerrenmatt's *The Visit*, which starred Lynne Fontanne and Alfred Lunt. He also toured in the part.

Anders had a limited career in Hollywood, appearing in only eight films from 1930 to the early 1950s, usually as a villain. His first film was *Laughter* (1930) in which he portrayed Frederic March's rival for Nancy Carroll's affection. His best role came as Grisby, the sinister lawyer, in Orson Welles's *Lady from Shanghai* (1948), starring Welles's wife Rita Hayworth. He died at the Actor's Fund Home in Englewood, New Jersey.

• Most encyclopedias and dictionaries of the American theater contain information about Anders. Robert L. Daniels, "Glenn Anders: He Knew What He Wanted," *After Dark*, Nov. 1977, pp. 52–56, is partly based on an interview. Walter Rigdon, *The Biographical Encyclopedia and Who's Who of the American Theatre* (1966), contains a complete list of his theatrical performances after 1919. An obituary is in the *New York Times*, 27 Oct. 1981.

G. F. GOODWIN

ANDERSEN, Arthur Edward (30 May 1885–10 Jan. 1947), certified public accountant, was born in Plano, Illinois, the son of John William Andersen, a foundry foreman, and Mary Aabye. Shortly after his birth the Andersen family returned to their native Norway, where they lived for several years before immigrating again to the United States and taking up residence in Chicago. After the deaths of his mother (1896) and his father (1901), Andersen began his working career as an office boy at the Fraser & Chalmers Company in Chicago (later Allis-Chalmers Manufacturing Company), his father's employer. In 1906 he married Emma Barnes Arnold of Chicago, with whom he had three children. Andersen decided to become an accountant in 1907 when as assistant to Allis-Chalmer's controller he was given the responsibility of aiding the firm's independent auditors. That year he joined Price Waterhouse & Company in Chicago, where he remained until 1911.

Andersen pursued his education through night study, as was common then for those interested in accounting careers. He was granted a certified public accountant's (CPA) license in Illinois in 1908. That same year he enrolled as an evening student in Northwestern University's School of Commerce, where he was later engaged in 1909 to serve as an adjunct lecturer in accounting because he held a professional license. In 1912, two years before completing his bachelor's degree in business administration, Andersen was asked by the university's administration to take charge of the program after the department chairman, Seymour Walton, abruptly resigned to form a proprietary accounting school.

Andersen's educational affiliation bolstered his image of authority in accounting. In 1917, for example, he published his instructional materials as a textbook titled *Complete Accounting Course*. This work, whose subsequent editions were revised with the assistance of David Himmelblau and Eric L. Kohler of the Northwestern faculty, established Andersen's reputation as a leader in professional education. Andersen also served for a time as the chairman of the Illinois board of Certified Public Accounting Examiners. Although he gave up teaching in 1922 because of the demands of his private practice, Andersen remained active at Northwestern, serving on its board of trustees beginning in 1927 and as president of the board between 1930 and 1932.

These educational pursuits paralleled Andersen's primary commitment to the practice of public accounting. Although he withdrew from practice after joining the Jos. Schlitz Brewing Company in Milwaukee as its controller in 1911, it was only for a short period. Andersen reentered public accountancy in 1913 by purchasing with Clarence M. DeLany the Audit Company of Illinois from the estate of its founder, Clarence W. Knisely. Known initially as Andersen, DeLany & Co., the new firm adopted the name Arthur Andersen & Co. in 1918 after the withdrawal of its cofounder.

Andersen became identified with the electrical utility industry after acquiring the Audit Company of Illinois, which had served the Consumers Power Company and the Louisville Gas and Electric Company. Soon Iowa Electric Power and Light Company (1915), Southern Indiana Gas and Electric Co. (1918), and International Telephone and Telegraph Corporation (1920) were added to the client list. Andersen enhanced his reputation in utility accounting by writing a pamphlet titled *The Accounting Treatment of Overhead Construction Costs in Public Utilities* (1917). Later his firm achieved national prominence when it was engaged by a bankers' consortium from 1932 to 1935 to monitor the financial rehabilitation of the electrical utility empire created by Samuel Insull. Success in this assignment led to the firm's appointment as auditors to many of the utility companies that formerly composed the Insull group.

Many of the earliest partners who joined Andersen, a liberal Republican, had been associated with progressive political regimes that had used accounting as a mechanism for controlling economic affairs, especially the activities of natural monopolies such as railroads and public utilities. Three of his partners in the 1920s, Grant Chandler, John Jirgal, and John C. Reyer, either had formed connections with Senator Robert M. La Follette of Wisconsin or had served in regulatory authorities in that state. The firm later collaborated with the New Deal administration of President Franklin D. Roosevelt. The first chief accountant of the Securities and Exchange Commission, Carman G. Blough, joined Andersen's firm as a partner in 1938.

Andersen shaped the character of his firm in important ways during his tenure as managing partner (1913–1947). He differentiated his practice from many of the profession's leaders through the strong emphasis he placed on consulting services beginning in the 1920s. Andersen saw that the largest corporations generally would turn to better-established firms for their audits and that income from audits would be seasonal because many corporations used 31 December as the end of the fiscal year. Moreover, Andersen recognized from his experience as a corporate controller that managements of medium-sized businesses needed financial experts to prepare specialized studies that could inform decisions about plants, products, markets, and organization. Aware of how these opportunities were being successfully addressed by emergent, Chicago-based, management-consulting firms such as McKinsey & Company and Cresap, Moore and McCormick, Andersen began to define a new service role in consulting for public accountants in his pamphlet *Financial and Industrial Investigations* (1924). These engagements became a major source of growth that, besides satisfying corporate managements, were found to be useful to investment bankers in planning mergers and in underwriting the securities of companies going public.

A second dimension of the development of consulting services involved the establishment of capacities for tax compliance and planning. These activities became important during World War I with the promulgation of the excess profits tax. Assisted by his younger brother Walter, Andersen first won recognition for his firm's tax competency by organizing special training at Northwestern that was attended by prominent local bankers, businessmen, and lawyers. By 1927 his growing reputation in this field led to his engagement as an expert witness in the celebrated Ford Motor Company tax case.

Andersen's successful practice-development strategies led the firm to open branch offices to serve a growing client list. By 1947 the firm managed sixteen offices in the United States and had representatives in Europe, South America, and Asia. The firm was also a pioneer in the recruitment of college-educated employees, especially from prestigious middle western universities such as Northwestern, Illinois, Michigan, and Wisconsin that had established rigorous accounting programs. In 1940 Andersen established a central training facility in Chicago to assure a uniformly high level of competent and diligent performance throughout his firm.

Andersen's educational experience contributed to his reputation as an expert in accounting theory—an identification that was particularly valuable in the 1920s when no formal institutional focus for the standardization of accounting principles existed. He played an active role in the early efforts of the national representative organization for public accountancy, American Institute of Accountants (AIA), to address the criticisms leveled by skeptics such as William Z. Ripley of Harvard University. In a celebrated series of articles appearing in *Atlantic Monthly* in 1926 (published in book form in 1927 as *Wall Street and Main Street*), Ripley had called into question many contemporary financial accounting practices. One element of this was the confusion of techniques employed to adjust equity accounts, a key performance measure for the growing body of common stock owners that had emerged in the United States after World War I.

Also in 1927 Andersen chaired the AIA's committee on the definition of earned surplus available for dividends to discover by means of a mail survey whether consensus existed among practitioners about what constituted "generally accepted accounting principles" for these transactions. The responses reflected a wide diversity of opinion that underscored the need for the establishment of a formal standards-setting authority. The slowness of the profession to respond decisively to this problem led to a second wave of criticism. Kohler, for example, who might have been reflecting some of Andersen's personal views, castigated the profession for its reluctance to standardize financial accounting in editorials in *Accounting Review*, the official publication of the American Association of University Instructors in Accounting (now the American Accounting Association). The AIA, however, did not take the initiative in these matters in a sustained way until 1939, after the Securities and Exchange Commission threatened to intervene by exercising its authority to prescribe accounting rules as had been done earlier by other federal agencies for the interstate railroads, pipelines, telephone and telegraph, and power companies.

Andersen was active in many professional, scholarly, civic, and social associations. He served as president of both the Illinois Society of Certified Public Accountants (1918–1919) and the Norwegian-American Historical Society (1936–1942). After the outbreak of war in Europe in 1939 this latter involvement and a lifelong strong personal identification with the country of his forbears led the Norwegian government to make Andersen a knight commander of the Royal Order of St. Olaf. He died in Chicago.

Arthur Andersen's crowning achievement lies in the founding of his national public accounting practice, which grew to become one of the world's largest professional services enterprises.

• No public collection of Arthur Andersen's personal papers and correspondence exists. Information about his career can be found in three books published posthumously by his firm: the most comprehensive, *The First Sixty Years, 1913–1973* (1974), chronicles the achievements of Andersen and other leaders in the practice he founded; *Behind the Figures* (1970) is an assemblage of Andersen's basic writings about the purposes of a professional service; he is discussed tangentially in *The Growth of Arthur Andersen & Co., 1928–1973: An Oral History by Leonard Spacek* (1989). His ideas about management and consulting services were laid out in *Duties and Responsibilities of the Comptroller* (1934), and his thinking about the reordering of economic affairs in light of the Great Depression was presented in *Major Problems Created by the Machine Age* (1931), *The Future of Our Economic System* (1934), and *A Layman Speaks* (1941). His notable writing about accounting technical problems was offered in *Present Day Problems Affecting the Presentation and Interpretation of Financial Statements* (1935). Andersen's involvement in the committee on the definition of earned surplus available for dividends is summarized in *The American Institute of Accountants Annual Yearbook for 1927* (1928), pp. 169–71, and in John L. Carey, *The Rise of the Public Accounting Profession* (2 vols., 1969–1970), especially vol. 1, pp. 158–59. Andersen and his firm are mentioned in other standard histories of the accounting profession, including James Don Edwards, *History of Public Accounting in America* (1960); Paul J. Miranti, Jr., *Accounting Comes of Age: The Development of an American Profession, 1886–1940* (1990); and Gary John Previts and Barbara Dubis Merino, *A History of Accounting in America: An Historical Interpretation of the Cultural Significance of Accounting* (1979). An obituary is in the *New York Times*, 11 Jan. 1947.

PAUL J. MIRANTI, JR.

ANDERSEN, Dorothy Hansine (15 May 1901–3 Mar. 1963), pediatrician and pathologist, was born in Asheville, North Carolina, the only child of Hans Peter Andersen, a secretary for the YMCA, and Mary Louise Mason. Andersen's father died in 1914, leaving her alone to care for her invalid mother. The two moved to Saint Johnsbury, Vermont, where Louise Andersen died six years later. At the age of nineteen Andersen, with no close relatives, became fully responsible for her own upbringing.

Andersen supported herself financially while attending Mount Holyoke College, studying zoology and chemistry (B.A., 1922), and Johns Hopkins Medical School (M.D., 1926). Her research at Johns Hopkins was the source of two papers in *Contributions to Embryology* describing the lymphatic and blood vessels of the female pig's reproductive organs. Following graduation from Johns Hopkins, Andersen served a one-year teaching assistantship in anatomy at the Rochester School of Medicine and then interned in surgery at the Strong Memorial Hospital, also in Rochester, New York. She was denied a residency in surgery at Strong Memorial Hospital upon completion of her internship—because she was a woman, according to her biographer Libby Machol—so she instead focused her efforts on research.

In 1929 Andersen moved to New York City to begin work as assistant in pathology at Columbia University's College of Physicians and Surgeons. The following year she became instructor in pathology at Columbia Medical School and began studies at Columbia University toward an advanced degree in endocrinology, examining the influence of endocrine glands on the onset and rate of sexual maturation in rats. She received her doctorate in medical science in 1935 and became assistant pathologist at Babies Hospital at the Columbia Presbyterian Medical Center, where she would remain for the duration of her career. She eventually held appointments as both pathologist and pediatrician, becoming chief of pathology in 1952 and full professor at the College of Physicians and Surgeons in 1958.

Throughout her career Andersen was especially thorough and meticulous in her examination of case histories. With this skill and discipline she noticed an important anomaly in the pathology of celiac disease, a disorder of infants and young children characterized by severe malnutrition and frequently resulting from insufficient pancreatic function. Andersen noted a distinct fibrosis—and thus malfunction—of the pancreas in a patient who had died of celiac disease but was thought to have normal pancreatic function. On subsequent examination of all postmortem data available for celiac disease, Andersen recognized that such fibrosis of the pancreas was a disease entity, separate from other disorders forming the clinical picture of celiac disease. In 1938 she published these findings in the *American Journal of Diseases of Children*, terming the disorder "cystic fibrosis of the pancreas"; it is now known simply as cystic fibrosis because of the myriad pathological manifestations subsequently discovered. She was awarded the E. Mead Johnson Award and remains best known for her recognition of this disease.

Andersen continued to work on cystic fibrosis and, though unsuccessful in finding a cure, contributed greatly to its diagnosis and treatment. She developed the first reliable diagnostic test for cystic fibrosis in 1942; later, with Paul di Sant'Agnese, also at Babies Hospital, she determined the effectiveness of various antibiotics in relieving the respiratory-tract infections that were the main cause of death from cystic fibrosis. The American Academy of Pediatrics in 1948 awarded Andersen the Borden Bronze Plaque for her successful work on dietary therapy for cystic fibrosis and celiac disease patients. Andersen also became interested in the source of cystic fibrosis; after performing extensive surveys on its familial occurrence, she correctly deduced that it was a recessively inherited disease. In addition, she was among the first to document the sweat electrolyte abnormalities characteristic of this disease and to develop the corresponding diagnostic test for cystic fibrosis, still widely used today. Late in her career, in 1958, Andersen noted in the *Journal of Chronic Diseases* that what had once been a fatal disease of early infancy now saw many patients surviving until early adulthood. Certainly as a result of its complexity, determination of the actual cause of cystic fibrosis—a single mutation causing incomplete synthesis of a transmembrane protein, resulting in thick, clogging secretions mainly in the pancreas and respiratory tract—eluded Andersen and other researchers and was not made until the early 1980s.

Andersen's lesser-known contributions were on the pathology of glycogen storage diseases and congenital heart defects. From her first years at Babies Hospital she maintained a collection of specimens of different cardiac abnormalities that was later used by surgeons in the development of open-heart surgery. She also conducted numerous training seminars on the anatomy and physiology of cardiovascular abnormalities; her expertise was so highly regarded that all cardiologists at Babies Hospital were required to complete her seminar before performing surgery. For her fruitful work in these disparate areas of medicine, she was posthumously awarded the distinguished service medal of the Columbia Presbyterian Medical Center.

Andersen's professional success was not easily achieved. She remained a controversial figure throughout her career, encountering resistance from colleagues for reasons ranging from professional etiquette to physical appearance. She persevered beyond her expertise in pathology to learn the clinical skills needed to diagnose and treat cystic fibrosis and celiac disease. Though characterized as reticent and self-sufficient, she was at times outspoken in her support of women's rights. Perhaps most notably, Andersen and her laboratory were constantly unkempt. She further distinguished herself by "unladylike" hobbies such as woodworking, stonemasonry, and "anything in the woods." Despite condemnation from some, however, she had as many ardent supporters, who described her as generous and unconditionally loyal. Though Andersen was generally solitary, perhaps even lonely, numerous colleagues joined her for weekends at her rustic upstate New York farm—her chief hobby—for cooking and conversation and enjoying the outdoors, even participating in the many building projects Andersen had in various stages of completion. Andersen, a heavy smoker, underwent surgery for lung cancer in 1962 and died of the disease early the following year in New York City.

• Most of Andersen's research is published in the *Journal of Physiology, American Journal of Physiology, American Journal of Diseases of Children*, and *Pediatrics*. A curriculum vitae and list of her publications are available at the Columbia University College of Physicians and Surgeons, and scattered autobiographical information is available from Mount Holyoke College. See also the biography of Andersen by Libby Machol in *Notable American Women: The Modern Period*, ed. Barbara Sicherman and Carol Hurd Green (1980). A list of her appointments and professional affiliations appeared in *Journal of the American Medical Association* 184 (May 1963): 670. An obituary focusing on her professional work is in the *Stethoscope*, Apr. 1963, and a more personal eulogy by Douglas A. Damrosch, a colleague at Columbia University, is in *Journal of Pediatrics* 65 (Oct. 1964): 477–79.

ALLISON AYDELOTTE

ANDERSON, Alexander (21 Apr. 1775–17 Jan. 1870), engraver, was born in New York city, the son of John Anderson, a printer and publisher, and Sarah Lockwood. By 1790 the Andersons were living on Wall Street; they were Episcopalians, of moderate means, with varied interests and social contacts. The family was close-knit and affectionate.

As a boy Anderson was fascinated by illustration, particularly Hogarth's work, and he imitated line engravings by copying them in India ink. His first graver was the sharpened backspring of a pocket knife used on pewter or rolled-out copper pennies. He found instructions on engraving by reading Chambers's *Cyclopaedia*, and he watched silversmiths at work. He may have learned from the copperplate engraver Peter Rushton Maverick, whom he knew.

Denigrating his interest in art but noting that he drew from anatomical engravings in medical books, Anderson's parents apprenticed him soon after his fourteenth birthday to the physician Joseph Young. He obtained his license in 1795, that year working at Bellevue Hospital during the yellow fever epidemic. His efforts were publicly praised, and he was given the chance, which he refused, to apply for a position at the New York Dispensary. He attended Columbia College, graduated in medicine in 1796, and began to practice.

In 1797 Anderson married Ann Van Vleck, the daughter of a Moravian tax collector of the city. Anderson's wife, their infant son, his parents, and his brother died during a yellow fever epidemic the following summer. Their deaths released him from parental and family pressures. Despite his obvious grief, and perhaps partly due to his inability to save the family he loved, he quickly abandoned medicine to pursue full time his first and enduring interest, engraving.

Anderson's first signed relief engraving, on type metal, was a frontispiece for Thomas Dilworth's *A New Guide to the English Tongue* (1791). At seventeen he contributed the first two of his seven copperplates for William Durell's edition of Maynard's *Josephus* (1792–1794). By 1793 Anderson was etching his copperplates and describing his relief and intaglio engraving in his diary, 1793 to mid-1799. He executed simple designs on boxwood as early as 1793; of importance were his illustrations begun in 1794, at first on type metal and completed on boxwood, for Arnaud Berquin's *Looking-Glass for the Mind* (1795).

In 1797 Anderson opened a short-lived bookshop in New York City that may have been the first in America to sell only children's books; four of them were illustrated with his own wood engravings. Notable among his early work were an engraving on wood of a skeleton (1798) after Albinus and the line etching of a male anatomical figure (1799) after Gautier d'Agoty, both over three feet tall.

Inspired by the English wood engraver Thomas Bewick, whose *General History of Quadrupeds* he had seen in 1795, Anderson adopted the white-line method of engraving on wood and, chiefly in the first decade of his career, copied many of Bewick's designs. He illustrated editions of Thomson's *Seasons*, beginning in 1802, Webster's spellers (1804?–1857), Langhorne's *Fables of Flora* (1804), an edition of Thomas Bewick's *Quadrupeds* (1804), Irving's *Salmagundi* (1807–1808, 1814). Countless children's books published in New York by Samuel Wood and by Mahlon Day, the Babcocks in New Haven, and Munroe and Francis in Boston and New York used his work. He illustrated the American Tract Society's adult and juvenile publications as well as publications in many other fields. His two large, bold wood engravings, *Waterfowl* (1817) after Teniers and *Returning from the Boar Hunt* (c. 1818?) after Ridinger, were considered masterpieces of the art of wood engraving by the English wood engraver William J. Linton. Conforming to the change in taste, by the 1840s Anderson often adapted to a sketchier line but with less success artistically. Garret Lansing, William P. Morgan, John H. Hall, and Anderson's daughter Ann were his pupils.

By about 1820 Anderson had turned to engraving exclusively on wood. Although he favored the Bewick-school style through much of his career and copied illustrations from English publications, a demand perhaps dictated by his publishers, he developed his own designs and expression, marked by a distinctive, vigorous line, and a strong, telling contrast of light and dark. His work is detailed and usually well drawn, perhaps owing to his study of anatomy. His engravings of children display a freshness and joy, sense of humor, and gentle caricature. At times he also revealed an unfashionable interest in the grotesque. Anderson also depicted the isolation and sadness inherent in humanity, emotions perhaps reinforced by the anguish he experienced as a young man on the death of his family. His work is best seen in his surviving scrapbooks of over ten thousand well-printed proofs of his wood engravings. His biographer, Benson Lossing, wood engraver and historian, describes Anderson's modesty, integrity, and gentleness. Anderson's diary and a group of letters to his daughter Julia (1836–1869) show his enthusiasm, pride as an artist, dislike of conflict and hypocrisy, devout but unspecified religious beliefs, and, in later life, an anxious, gloomy hypochondria associated with a fatalistic acceptance of adversity.

In 1800 Anderson married his first wife's sister, Jane. She died in 1815, leaving him with five daughters and a son. He continued his career as an engraver in New York City until 1866, when he moved to his daughter Jane and son-in-law Edwin Lewis's house in Jersey City, where he died. He cut his last wood engraving for publication two years before his death.

Anderson's woodblocks for the 1795 *Looking-Glass for the Mind* were the first documented book illustrations engraved on end-grain boxwood in America. He introduced a medium that was relatively inexpensive to print and that used a durable material with ample potential for artistic expression. Until the 1840s Anderson was the major American illustrator of books using wood engravings. He was elected to the precursor of the Pennsylvania Academy of Fine Arts (1810), to the American Academy of Fine Arts in New York (1816), exhibiting in both institutions. He was elected to the National Academy of Design at its founding in 1826. Stereotypes of many of his woodblocks were included in type foundry specimen books from 1809 to the 1850s, diffusing his work throughout the country.

Anderson has been called the father of wood engraving in America, an epithet engraved on his tombstone. Few children could have avoided seeing his work. An incomplete bibliography of books illustrated by Anderson contains more than two thousand titles.

• Anderson's manuscript diary, 1793–1799, is at Columbia University; a typescript version in the same location is unreliable. A handwritten copy, as well as a large collection of his papers, including letters to his daughter Julia (1836–1869), are in the New-York Historical Society. Additional papers are in the New York Public Library. Seventeen of Anderson's proofbooks, plus two more collections, are in the Print Room, New York Public Library. More are located in the New-York Historical Society, where his miniatures and a large collection of his woodblocks can be found. A scrapbook in the Boston Athenaeum contains proofs executed mostly for the American Tract Society. Benson J. Lossing, *A Memorial of Alexander Anderson, M.D., the First Engraver on Wood in America* (1872), is the most detailed biography. Frederic M. Burr, *Life and Works of Alexander Anderson, M.D., the First American Wood Engraver* (1893), prints excerpts from Anderson's diary. Both include his short autobiography. *A Brief Catalogue of Books Illustrated with Engravings by Dr. Alexander Anderson with a Biographical Sketch of the Artist* (1885) was compiled after Anderson's death by Evert A. Duyckinck, according to a note by Benson Lossing accompanying the biographical sketch; it provides a partial and not always accurate listing. See also Jane R. Pomeroy, "Alexander Anderson's Life and Engravings before 1800, with a Checklist of Publications Drawn from His Diary," *Proceedings of the American Antiquarian Society*, pt. 1 (1990). Pomeroy has compiled the incomplete bibliography mentioned at the end of the text above.

JANE R. POMEROY

ANDERSON, Benjamin McAlester (1 May 1886–19 Jan. 1949), economist, was born in Columbia, Missouri, the son of Benjamin McLean Anderson, a businessman and politician, and Mary Frances Bowling. Anderson entered the University of Missouri in Columbia in 1902 and earned an A.B. in 1906. He was appointed professor of political economy and sociology at Missouri Valley College in Marshall in 1906 and was named as the head of the Department of History and Political Economy at the State Normal School at Springfield the following year. He married Margaret Louise Crenshaw in 1909; they had four children.

Anderson earned his A.M. in 1910 from the University of Illinois in Urbana and his Ph.D. in economics from Columbia University in 1911. The prestigious Hart, Schaffner & Marx prize in economics was awarded to him in 1910 for part of his dissertation that was published in 1911 as *Social Value: A Study in Economic Theory, Critical and Constructive*. The book was an important contribution to the development of economic thought and method in which Anderson developed a "truly organic doctrine of social value." He criticized cost theories of value as a "blind thing" and other theories of social value as normative or mechanical. He criticized the Austrian school's theory of individual marginal utility by emphasizing the importance of what author and business editor Henry Hazlitt called the essential "social conditions which go to form both the individual's marginal valuations and prices in the market" (foreword to Anderson's *Economics and the Public Welfare*). Subsequent Austrian economists were quick to point out the heterogeneous influences on an individual's marginal valuations, a view that has become the hallmark of scientific economics.

Anderson served on the economics faculty of Columbia University from 1911 to 1913 and then on Harvard's economics faculty from 1913 to 1918. In 1917 he published *The Value of Money*, a devastating critique of leading American economist Irving Fisher's quantity theory of money, which used a mechanical approach common in the neoclassical school of economics. Building on his concept of social value, Anderson constructed a "psychological" theory of money that emphasized the quality and the quantity of money and credit. Hazlitt labeled the book "one of the classics of American economic writings."

In 1918 Anderson joined the National Bank of Commerce in New York City as an economic adviser. His book *Effects of the War on Money, Credit, and Banking in France and the U.S.* was published in 1919 and recorded the significant economic and financial developments of World War I, focusing on the issues of money, credit, and banking. Chase National Bank hired Anderson in 1920 as economist and editor of the influential *Chase Economic Bulletin*. There he wrote a stream of learned articles critical of progressive policy in such diverse areas as money, credit, international economic policy, agriculture, taxation, war, government debt, and economic planning. He was a leading opponent of the New Deal and an enthusiastic supporter of a free market gold standard. He served as president of the Economists National Committee on Monetary Policy in 1948 and often testified before Congress on matters of monetary and economic policy.

Anderson's talents and abilities are underscored by his status as a world-class chess player. He wrote a brilliant preface to world chess champion José Capablanca's book *A Primer on Chess* (1935). In 1939 he became professor of economics at the University of California at Los Angeles and was named the Connell Professor of Banking in 1946. He died in Santa Monica, California, just before the publication of his magnum opus, *Economics and the Public Welfare: A Financial and Economic History of the United States, 1914–1946*.

Ludwig von Mises, the foremost economist of the Austrian school, called *Economics and the Public Welfare* a "great book." It covered a period that Anderson had intensely studied and examined using his highly advanced economic theory. His history was a warning for future generations about the dangers of "progressive" government intervention in the economy, such as income taxation, price controls, and protectionism. Writing near the end of World War II, Anderson recommended a return to free markets, sound money, and balanced budgets while dismissing the popular Keynesian notion that the end of the war would bring economic ruin without massive government intervention.

Anderson was a pariah in the community of academic economists. His unwillingness to suppress his views or soften his crushing criticisms of fashionable policies made him very unpopular among most economists and politicians. He was deprecated by progressives as old-fashioned and reactionary. History, however, seems to have vindicated his theoretical contributions and pronouncements on public policy. Ludwig von Mises, who was often a target of Anderson's criticisms, called him "one of the outstanding characters in this age of the supremacy of time-servers."

• Anderson wrote regularly for the National Bank of Commerce's *Commerce Monthly* (1919–1920) and Chase National Bank's *Chase Economic Bulletin* (1920–1937). His articles in other economic and financial periodicals include, in the Capital Research Company's *Economic Bulletin*, "Economic Aspects of the War . . . Contrasts and Resemblances 1914 and 1939," 1, no. 1 (12 Oct. 1939): 1–28, "Postwar Stabilization of Foreign Exchange, the Keynes-Morgenthau Plan Condemned, Outline of a Fundamental Solution," 4, no. 1 (11 May 1943): 3–36, and "Inflation, the Rate of Interest and the Management of the Public Debt," 5, no. 1 (27 May 1947): 3–23; and, in the *Commercial and Financial Chronicle*, "Equilibrium Creates Purchasing Power" (25 Jan. 1945), and "Has New Deal Planning Been a Success?" (31 Oct. 1946). See also his contributions to Jacob H. Hollander, ed., *Economic Essays Contributed in Honor of John Bates Clark* (1927), and Paul Homan and Fritz Machlup, eds., *Financing American Prosperity: A Symposium of Economists* (1945). An obituary is in the *New York Times*, 20 Jan. 1949.

MARK THORNTON

ANDERSON, Broncho Billy (21 Mar. 1882–20 Jan. 1971), the first western film hero, was born Max Aronson in Little Rock, Arkansas, but little else is known of his background, including the identity of his parents. While in his late teens Aronson became a traveling salesman, a job that brought him into the company of actors and a resulting interest in the theater. He moved to New York, where he changed his name to Gilbert Anderson and found work as a fashion model, posing in illustrations for publications such as the *Saturday Evening Post*. His first appearance in a film, at the salary of fifty cents an hour, came in 1902, but his career was seriously launched by his role in Edwin S. Porter's *The Great Train Robbery* (1903). This one-reeler, made at the Edison Studios in New Jersey, capitalized on the notoriety of Butch Cassidy's last train robbery in 1901. Anderson got the part by assuring Porter that his "western birth" had made him a horseman, a boast disproved when Anderson fell off his horse on camera.

Following that appearance, Anderson moved to Vitagraph, a film studio in New York, where he directed one-reel pictures at a salary of $25 per week. He directed *Raffles, the Amateur Cracksman* (1905) and conceived the idea for a character that audiences could follow from film to film. In this era of American cinema, producers sold their films to exhibitors rather than renting them, and some exhibitors decided to produce their own pictures. John Harris and Harry Davis brought Anderson to Pittsburgh in 1906 to produce their films; the following year he moved to Chicago and affiliated with William Selig, with whom he made several westerns. Selig and Anderson differed over production philosophy, however—Anderson wanted to film in Colorado for authenticity, but Selig objected because of the expense.

By 1908 Anderson had ended his association with Selig and begun a partnership with George K. Spoor. Together they established Essanay, creating the name from their initials—S and A. Anderson began the Broncho Billy series of one- and later two-reel films featuring the continuing character that became the screen's first western hero. Although Anderson had conceived the idea of the series before reading Peter B. Kyne's story in the *Saturday Evening Post* featuring the Broncho Billy character, he obtained the name from that source. Anderson intended to produce and direct the series, but when he was unable to find an actor who satisfied him, he decided to play the part himself. Because of its better climate, he chose to make the films in California, where he and Spoor obtained facilities at Niles, near San Francisco.

In 1907 Anderson produced and directed *The Bandit Makes Good*, and then in 1910 *Broncho Billy's Redemption*, in which the character was established as a "good badman," the sort of protagonist who might even be an outlaw, but who always displayed positive traits. At first, only one-reel films were produced, which were extremely profitable; for an investment of $800, Essanay often realized a gross of $50,000. Essanay produced approximately 375 Broncho Billy films before 1915, most of which are lost because of decomposition of the film stock. Eventually, Anderson expanded his films to two reels, and noting the success of five-reel features produced at other studios with William S. Hart and Tom Mix in starring roles, he wanted to expand further. His partner, however, did not see the need since their existing operation was so lucrative.

This disagreement led to Spoor's buying Anderson out of the company in 1915. The sales contract called for Anderson to take no part in film production for a period of two years. During that time the public shifted its loyalty to Hart, Mix, Buck Jones, and other rising western stars. Essanay also lost stature when its other major star, Charlie Chaplin, moved to the Mutual Film Corporation in 1916.

During his two-year hiatus from films, Anderson and a new partner, H. H. Frazee, acquired the Longacre Theatre in New York, where they produced several plays. In 1917 Anderson returned to films in a new Broncho Billy series produced by L. Lawrence Weber at Golden West Photoplay Company. These films did not prove profitable, and Anderson ceased making them after 1918. He continued to produce films for a time, including comedies starring Stan Laurel, but retired following a disagreement with Louis B. Mayer. He dropped out of the industry until 1957, when he was awarded a special Oscar for his pioneering role in film.

Anderson appeared in a cameo role as Broncho Billy one last time in *The Bounty Killer* (1965) and spent his final years at the Motion Picture Country Home in Woodland Hills, California. Obituaries indicate that Anderson was married and had a daughter, but neither wife nor child is named. He died in South Pasadena, California.

• The best account of Anderson's contribution to the development of westerns is Jon Tuska, *The Filming of the West* (1976); see also Rita Parks, *The Western Hero in Film and Television: Mass Media Mythology* (1982), and his obituary in *Variety*, 27 Jan., 1971.

ARCHIE P. MCDONALD

ANDERSON, Carl David (3 Sept. 1905–11 Jan. 1991), physicist, was born in New York City, the son of Carl David Anderson and Emma Adolfina Ajaxson. In 1912 the family moved to Los Angeles, where the elder Anderson managed a small restaurant business. Carl Anderson graduated from Los Angeles Polytechnic High School in 1923. The following fall he entered the California Institute of Technology (Caltech) in Pasadena, intending to study electrical engineering. In his sophomore year, during a course with Ira Bowen, a protégé of Robert Millikan, Anderson changed his major to physics, receiving his B.S. in 1927. He stayed at Caltech for graduate and postgraduate work, eventually becoming assistant (1933), associate (1937), and finally full professor (1939).

For his graduate work, Anderson was drawn directly into Millikan's orbit. The most prominent American physicist of his day, Millikan won the Nobel Prize for physics in 1923 for measuring the charge on the electron and for verifying experimentally Einstein's interpretation of the photoelectric effect, the release of electrons from a substance through the effect of radiation. Anderson's doctoral thesis on the photoelectric effect of X-rays, completed in 1930, was titled "Space-Distribution of X-ray Photoelectrons Ejected from the K and L Atomic Energy-Levels." The experimental apparatus he used included a cloud chamber, in which charged particles, such as electrons, pass through moist air—the "cloud"—leaving characteristic trails. Invited by Millikan to continue his experiments, Anderson stayed at Caltech as a research fellow and conducted his most famous experiment; it would lead to the discovery of a new subatomic particle, the positron. At this time scientists had only identified two elementary particles of matter, the electron and the proton. However, in 1928 Paul Dirac posited the existence of another particle, comparable in mass to the negatively charged electron but with a positive charge.

Millikan wanted Anderson to use a cloud chamber in a strong electromagnetic field to measure the energy of cosmic rays. This form of penetrating radiation from outer space was not well understood then, but Millikan held it to be the product of atom-building reactions in space. To carry out the cosmic-ray experiment, Anderson designed and constructed a giant electromagnet wrapped around a cloud chamber. An arc-lit camera was focused on the chamber's window to record the vapor trails of electrons or other charged particles passing through. The magnet cloud chamber was put into operation in October 1931. Anderson looked at thousands of photographs taken in the new cloud chamber, showing equal numbers of high-energy positive and negative particles. To lessen the particles' energy and to clarify the direction of their motion (negatively charged particles moved downward), he inserted a lead plate into the middle of the cloud chamber. On 2 August 1932, viewing a very clear photograph of an upward-moving particle with mass similar to the electron, he knew he had discovered the "positive electron" predicted by Dirac.

Anderson published his research in *Science* on 9 September 1932. At first his results were met with skepticism. Ultimately they were confirmed by experimenters, initially in 1933 at the Cavendish Laboratory in Cambridge, England, by Patrick M. S. Blackett and G. P. S. Occhialini. Anderson's work earned him the Nobel Prize in 1936; he was only thirty-one. In 1935 Anderson and his first graduate student, Seth Neddermeyer, discovered another subatomic particle, which they named the mesotron (later called the μ meson or muon). The muon discovery grew out of experimental work on cosmic rays done at around 14,000 feet altitude on Pikes Peak, Colorado.

During World War II Anderson was closely associated with the Caltech rocket research and development effort, led by Charles C. Lauritsen and funded by the U.S. Office of Scientific Research and Development (OSRD). Anderson spent his time working on problems associated with the launching of rockets from airplanes. For his wartime work he received the Presidential Certificate of Merit in 1945. In 1946 Anderson married Lorraine Bergman; they had two sons.

After the war Anderson returned to his work on cosmic rays. He and his graduate students continued to take cloud-chamber photographs at high altitudes, now using a B-29 aircraft; they also measured variations in cosmic-ray effects at selected latitudes on the Earth's surface. They painstakingly accumulated further evidence of the existence of more subatomic particles, the so-called "strange particles," thus confirming the underlying complexity of the structure of matter. Anderson became chairman of Caltech's Division of Physics, Mathematics and Astronomy in 1962, a position he held until 1970. He retired from Caltech in 1976 with the title Board of Trustees Professor of Physics, Emeritus.

In addition to the Nobel Prize, Anderson was the recipient of many other awards: the Gold Medal of the American Institute of the City of New York (1935), the Elliott Cresson Medal of the Franklin Institute (1937), and the John Erikson Medal of the American Society of Swedish Engineers (1960). He was elected to the National Academy of Sciences in 1936 and to the American Academy of Arts and Sciences in 1954. Anderson died in San Marino, California.

Anderson's fundamental contribution to science sprang from two sources—his skill as an experimentalist and the originality of his approach. Well suited to the experimental physics of the 1920s and 1930s, which was based on naturally occurring, high-energy particles, Anderson was less comfortable with the large manmade accelerators that dominated particle physics in the postwar period. He nonetheless played a major role in answering the urgent questions of his day about the structure of the atomic nucleus, opening the door to better understanding of the fundamental properties of matter.

• A collection of papers and artifacts given by Anderson to the Archives of the California Institute of Technology in 1988 includes lecture and technical notes, plates and prints of cloud-chamber photos, and portions of the apparatus used by Anderson in his discoveries of the positron and the muon. An oral-history interview conducted by the Caltech Archives in 1981 provides a good survey of his life and work. A biographical essay by W. A. Fowler and E. W. Cowan appeared in *Proceedings of the American Philosophical Society* 136, no. 2 (1992): 275–78. On the fiftieth anniversary of the discovery of the positron, the Caltech magazine, *Engineering and Science*, published a special issue (Nov. 1982) devoted to Anderson and his work. An account of the discovery is in Daniel Kevles, *The Physicists* (1978). Obituaries are in the *New York Times* and the *Los Angeles Times*, both 12 Jan. 1991, and in *Engineering and Science* (Spring 1991): 37–38.

CHARLOTTE E. ERWIN

ANDERSON, Cat (12 Sept. 1916–29 Apr. 1981), jazz trumpeter, was born William Alonzo Anderson, Jr., in Greenville, South Carolina. Nothing is known of his parents, who died when he was four. Anderson grew up in Jenkins' Orphanage in Charleston, where as a boy he received the nickname "Cat" after scratching and tearing in a fight with a bully. He played in the orphanage's renowned bands, beginning on trombone and playing other brass and percussion instruments before taking up trumpet. From 1929 onward he participated in orphanage band tours, and in Florida in 1933 he formed the cooperative Carolina Cotton Pickers with fellow orphanage musicians. Returning to Charleston in 1934, they continued playing as the Carolina Cotton Pickers and then resumed touring.

Independent of the orphanage, Anderson held his first lasting affiliation with the Sunset Royals (c. 1936–1942). From 1942 to 1944 he worked in the big bands of Lucky Millinder; trumpeter Erskine Hawkins, from which Anderson was quickly dismissed for upstaging Hawkins with his high-note trumpeting; Lionel Hampton; Sabby Lewis (1943); and Hampton again. In September 1944 Anderson joined Duke Ellington's orchestra. He followed in the path of established trumpeting roles in that group, contributing an intense but understated and muted solo on his own composition "Teardrops in the Rain" (1945) and a vocalized plunger-muted solo on "A Gatherin' in a Clearin'" (1946), but his personal trademark was his ability to play in an unbelievably high range, of which the finest example is certainly "Trumpet No End" (also 1946).

Leaving Ellington in February 1947, Anderson led his own band until rejoining Lewis briefly in 1949 and Ellington in December 1950. Apart from a long absence in 1951, he remained with Ellington until November 1959. Notable recordings from this period include a plunger-muted solo on his own blues composition "Cat Walk" (1951), with a septet, the Coronets, spun off from the big band; an improvised trumpet battle with Clark Terry and Willie Cook on "Duke's Jam" on alto saxophonist Johnny Hodges's album *Ellingtonia '56* (1956); and Anderson's featured solo on "Madness in Great Ones" on Ellington's album *Such Sweet Thunder* (1957).

After leading another band and freelancing in Philadelphia, Anderson rejoined Ellington once again in April 1961. He may be seen and heard in the film short *Duke Ellington and His Orchestra* (1962). In 1967 Ellington held a lengthy engagement at the Rainbow Grill in New York City with an eight-piece band that afforded Anderson an opportunity to demonstrate much more versatile trumpeting skills than his role as a high-note player normally allowed. Anderson remained in the orchestra until January 1971.

In 1971, finally tiring of incessant touring, Anderson became a freelancer on the West Coast, where he worked extensively as a studio musician. But he continued playing with jazz bands. He was a guest soloist with bassist Charles Mingus's group at the Newport Jazz Festival in July 1972 and on a European tour in the fall; Mingus featured Anderson in lengthy, plunger-muted solos on "Perdido." Anderson later played with trumpeter Bill Berry's big band, and he participated in a few reunions with Ellington's band and with Hampton's, including the album *Lionel Hampton and His Jazz Giants '77* (1977) and some European tours with Hampton to 1979. Anderson also recorded his own album *Cat Speaks* (1977). He died of cancer in Norwalk, California. He was survived by his wife, Dorothy; the marriage date and her maiden name are unknown.

Before Canadian trumpeter Maynard Ferguson emerged during the 1950s, Anderson was the undisputed master of freakish high-note trumpeting. Many Ellington aficionados prefer his stylistically derivative work, after the manner of Louis Armstrong, Cootie Williams, and others, to his personalized high-note displays, which were often sloppy, out-of-tune, and tasteless (for example, numerous versions of "Jam with Sam"). But on those occasions when it worked, as in the last minute of "Trumpet No End," Anderson's exhilarating trumpeting was nothing short of spectacular.

• An interview of Anderson appears in Stanley Dance, *The World of Duke Ellington* (1970; repr. 1981), and details of his upbringing and early career are in John Chilton, *A Jazz Nursery: The Story of the Jenkins' Orphanage Bands of Charleston, South Carolina* (1980). Further details of his career may be pieced together from Duke Ellington, *Music Is My Mistress* (1973); Albert McCarthy, *Big Band Jazz* (1974); Brian Priestley, *Mingus: A Critical Biography* (1982); and Mark Tucker, ed., *The Duke Ellington Reader* (1993). For a survey of his work as a soloist, see Eddie Lambert, "Cat Anderson: A Résumé of His Recorded Work," *Jazz Journal International* 35 (June 1982): 16–18 and 35 (July 1982): 10–11. Obituaries are in the *New York Times*, 2 May 1981, and *Jazz Journal International* 34 (July 1981): 15.

BARRY KERNFELD

ANDERSON, Charles William (28 Apr. 1866–28 Jan. 1938), politician and public official, was born in Oxford, Ohio, the son of Charles W. Anderson and Serena (maiden name unknown). After a public school education in his hometown and in Middletown, Ohio, he studied at Spencerian Business College in Cleveland and the Berlitz School of Languages in Worcester, Massachusetts. His schooling continued informally, as Anderson matured into an intellectually accomplished and engaging man. His friend James Weldon Johnson noted his versatility, which included acute powers of observation and an ability to converse on many subjects, including "the English poets, the Irish patriots, [and] the contemporary leaders of the British Parliament" (Johnson, p. 219).

Anderson put these talents to good use after moving to New York City in 1886. He grasped at what opportunities Republican party politics offered ambitious black men and developed a ward heeler's capacity for keeping close track of voters, loaves, and fishes. By 1890 he had entered upon a succession of party employment and patronage positions that would keep him busy through much of the rest of his life. That year he became president of the Young Men's Colored Republican Club of New York County and was appointed a gauger in the Internal Revenue Service. He served in this capacity until 1893, when he became private secretary to the New York state treasurer. In 1895 he was named chief clerk of the state treasury and in 1898 became supervisor of accounts for the state racing commission, holding that position until 1905. In 1904 Anderson organized the New York City Colored Republican Club and worked for the reelection of Theodore Roosevelt. By this time he had married Emma Lee Bonaparte.

Anderson's rise through the ranks seems to have been due not simply to party loyalty and personal charisma but also to the fact that he performed his jobs quite well. Theodore Roosevelt, one-time governor of New York, praised the "splendid efficiency" of Anderson's work for the racing commission and, in 1905, named him collector of internal revenue for the Second New York District. Explaining Anderson's appointment to this most visible position, Booker T. Washington contended that, given the widespread resistance to black officeholding, Roosevelt was "determined to set the example by placing a coloured man in a high office in his own home city, so that the country might see that he did not want other parts of the country to accept that which he himself was not willing to receive" (Harlan and Smock, eds., vol. 1, p. 442). But the collectorship was not a position that could have been well served by any mere token appointee. The Second District included the financial heart of New York (and, consequently, of the nation) as well as the Manhattan docks. Anderson had charge of scores of deputy collectors, inspectors, and clerks and annually collected millions of dollars in revenue, eventually including income taxes. By all accounts, he did good work, earning considerable support among the Wall Street elite. During this and his second collectorship, Anderson always kept his eye out for openings that might be filled by African Americans in the Internal Revenue Service, in other federal, state, and municipal agencies, and in the Republican party. For instance, he helped arrange James Weldon Johnson's appointment to the consular service.

Though he had a hand in the passage of a state civil rights statute in 1895, Anderson's interest in developing practical opportunity and material reward for African Americans, rather than in more forthrightly agitating for racial justice, put him in sympathy with Booker T. Washington. The two were close allies as well as ideological soulmates. Washington helped secure the collectorship for Anderson, and Anderson became one of the most important cogs in the "Tuskegee Machine," the vehicle of patronage and discrete influence that Washington operated from his Alabama base, even as he counseled African Americans to put aside politics. As the machine's man in New York, Anderson traded political intelligence, gossip, and favors with Washington, who periodically forwarded an opossum from Alabama for Anderson's dinner table.

Anderson egged Washington on in his struggles with critics like W. E. B. Du Bois, recommending he administer "a good thrashing" to "these young upstarts" (Harlan, p. 78). Indeed, Anderson did what he could to have Washington's adversaries dismissed from federal jobs, monitored the progress of the National Association for the Advancement of Colored People (NAACP), and even played dirty tricks on NAACP supporters, such as planting stories of race mixing in white newspapers.

Anderson's excellent reputation as collector, which moved even Du Bois to recommend him for a diplomatic post, and his strong ties to the New York business community apparently kept him from immediately falling victim to Woodrow Wilson's hostility to black Republican officeholders. He was not required to step down until March 1915, two years into Wilson's term as president. Anderson thereupon returned to state and party employ to wait out the interregnum. In 1915 he went to work for the state agriculture department, supervising inspectors and marketing operations in New York City. In 1916 and 1920 he was active among black voters during the GOP national campaigns. He returned to the higher reaches of federal patronage in 1923, when he was appointed collector of internal revenue for the newly created Third New York District. The district included his own neighborhood of Harlem. By 1928 the ailing Anderson had become less active in the day-to-day operations of the collectorship. He retired in 1934 and died in New York City.

Anderson was the first important black politician in New York City and was certainly among the most powerful African-American officeholders anywhere in the United States in the first decades of the twentieth century. His influence illustrated the growing importance of northern city dwellers in black politics, as African Americans migrated out of the South and those that remained were marginalized by disfranchisement and the rise of "lily white" Republicanism. His career symbolizes, too, the significance in that era of the federal government and the Republican party to African Americans not simply as guarantors, though inconstant, of civil rights but as providers of professional opportunity.

• No distinct collection of Anderson papers exists, but many letters from him are in the Booker T. Washington Papers, Library of Congress, Manuscripts Division, Washington, D.C. A good deal of this correspondence is printed in *The Booker T. Washington Papers*, ed. Louis Harlan and Raymond Smock (14 vols., 1972–1989). The Schomburg collection of the New York Public Library holds an Anderson clipping file. For James Weldon Johnson's description, see *Along This Way: The Autobiography of James Weldon Johnson* (1933). An informative discussion of Anderson's career is in Gilbert Osofsky, *Harlem: The Making of a Ghetto* (1966), and considerable material is in Harlan, *Booker T. Washington: The Wizard of Tuskegee, 1901–1915* (1983). See also August Meier, *Negro Thought in America, 1880–1915: Racial Ideologies in the Age of Booker T. Washington* (1963). An obituary is in the *New York Times*, 29 Jan. 1938.

PATRICK G. WILLIAMS

ANDERSON, Clinton Presba (23 Oct. 1895–11 Nov. 1975), secretary of agriculture and U.S. senator, was born in Centerville, South Dakota, the son of Andrew Jay Anderson and Hattie Belle Presba, farmers. His childhood was spent in Mitchell, South Dakota, where his family had to work hard to make a living from the stubborn land. The experience made his father an activist in Populist party politics. This childhood and his struggle for health as a young adult made Anderson sensitive to the varied hardships faced by many people. In 1915, after two years at Dakota Wesleyan University in Mitchell, Anderson transferred to the University of Michigan. At Ann Arbor, Anderson was a successful student editor of the school newspaper while he worked at several odd jobs. When his father suffered a major injury, Anderson returned to Mitchell. He never completed his college degree.

Anderson worked for the newspaper in Mitchell, which supported the Democratic party. For a while he enjoyed life in the small South Dakota community. Unfortunately, for several years Anderson had experienced increasing difficulty breathing. Because he had tuberculosis, in 1917 the selective service rejected him. His condition worsened, and in October 1917, with his small savings and a loan from his parents, Anderson moved to Albuquerque, New Mexico. According to his autobiography, Anderson was near death as he waited in a reception room of the Albuquerque sanatorium for a patient to die and make a bed available. By 1919 Anderson's health had greatly improved. That year his sister who also had tuberculosis, joined him in New Mexico. Not as fortunate as her brother, she later died from the disease. In his autobiography Anderson includes the tragic event in an argument for a national health insurance program.

Anderson worked for the *Albuquerque Herald* from 1918 to 1919, when, with his health improved, he wanted to return to Mitchell and marry Henrietta McCartney, whom he had courted via the mail, but a case of smallpox prevented him from going. Within two years he was working for the *Albuquerque Journal,* and when he quit the *Journal* in 1922 he was editor of the paper. Other events continued to keep Anderson from returning to Mitchell, but by 1921 he had convinced Henrietta's family that Albuquerque was a respectable place, and they married in June. They had two children.

Over the next twenty years Anderson was active in the civic and political life of New Mexico. He worked with the New Mexico Tuberculosis Association and the New Mexico Public Health Association as a volunteer in public relations and fundraising. His work in the Rotary International resulted in his election as international president of that organization. Along with his activities in service organizations, his experience as a journalist would in time help his political career. He was active in local and state Democratic politics, holding various party positions. His work to include Hispanics in the Democratic party as candidates and members marked him as a reformer. These years were also filled with many private and business activities. For example, from 1922 to 1924 he was manager of the insurance department of the New Mexico Loan and Mortgage Company, which he bought in 1925. By 1937, as a result of several business deals, he was owner and president of the Mountain States Mutual Casualty Company, a position he held for the remainder of his life.

Politics became a larger part of his life by 1930. Within three years he was appointed treasurer of the state of New Mexico. Through his service he created an effective and honest government agency. In 1935 and 1936 he was chief administer of the New Mexico Relief Administration. As a New Deal politician, and through his friendship with Harry Hopkins, Anderson represented New Mexico interests effectively. From 1936 to 1938 he was chairman and executive director of the state Unemployment Compensation Commission. During the last two years of the decade he was managing director of the United States Coronado Exposition Commission.

By 1940 Anderson had moved to the national political stage. He was elected to the House of Representatives as a Democrat. In his slightly more than four years in the House (he was elected to a third term but resigned a few months into it), Anderson particularly defended the agricultural and public land interests of New Mexico. Generally his record and reputation were New Deal in philosophy and policy.

After President Harry Truman reorganized his cabinet, Anderson became secretary of agriculture on 30 June 1945. While the Truman farm policies drew much criticism, Anderson was a key spokesman and policymaker for the Truman administration. He supported an adequate price structure for farm products, and his department's regulations conserved wheat and reduced available grain for livestock feed. With such a program Anderson's agency gathered food stocks for export, and the Department of Agriculture met the record world food requirements as stated by President Truman's Nine Point Famine Relief Program. Anderson resigned in May 1948.

After his resignation, Anderson was elected U.S. senator from New Mexico. He was reelected in 1954, 1960, and 1966 and retired in 1972 undefeated. As a reforming Democrat he was a major player in several areas. In 1957 he was an effective leader for a stronger civil rights bill against the weaker bill endorsed by the Dwight D. Eisenhower administration. By May 1959 Anderson had successfully led the fight to deny confirmation of Lewis Strauss as secretary of commerce. The admiral's behavior as chairman of the Atomic Energy Commission upset Anderson, who believed in civilian control of the atomic program, and Strauss's apparent disregard of New Mexico's interests and concerns in the program further annoyed Anderson. Anderson was also upset about Strauss's repudiation of J. Robert Oppenheimer. As chairman of the Joint Committee on Atomic Energy, Anderson provided strong leadership.

During the John F. Kennedy and Lyndon B. Johnson presidencies he generally supported the New Frontier and Great Society programs, and he worked to advance the reform agenda of the 1960s. This agenda often fit well with New Mexico interests, particularly in the areas of land conservation and general environmental concerns, and with his continued fight on behalf of his state's Hispanics. Also as senator, Anderson generally supported the Cold War foreign policy of containment. To that degree Anderson's career was a good historical example of post–World War II liberalism that combined domestic reform and an internationalist foreign policy. It was significant that by 1970 he publicly expressed concern about U.S. policy regarding Vietnam.

Because of health problems and age, Anderson retired from the Senate in 1972; he died three years later in Albuquerque. As the historian James L. Forsythe observed, "Throughout his career he never abandoned his major guideposts as a businessman and a dedicated Democratic politician."

• The Clinton P. Anderson Papers are on deposit at the Library of Congress. Anderson also provided oral history interviews for the Kennedy and Johnson presidential libraries. The senator tells his own story in Clinton P. Anderson, *Outsider in the Senate: Senator Clinton Anderson's Memoirs* (1970). Richard A. Baker, *Conservation Politics: The Senate Career Of Clinton P. Anderson* (1985), is informative and solid. A bit more critical is James L. Forsythe's article, "Clinton P. Anderson: Agricultural Policymaker and Southwesterner," in *Southwestern Agriculture: Pre-Columbian to Modern*, ed. Henry C. Dethloff and Irvin M. May, Jr. (1982). Another evaluation is James L. Forsythe, "Clinton P. Anderson: Politician and Business Man as Truman's Secretary of Agriculture" (Ph.D. diss., Univ. of New Mexico, 1970). Forsythe also wrote the entry on Anderson in *The Harry S. Truman Encyclopedia*, ed. Richard S. Kirkendall (1989). Allen J. Matusow, *Farm Policies and Politics in the Truman Years* (1967), provides a solid context for understanding Anderson's contributions as secretary of agriculture. An obituary is in the *New York Times*, 13 Nov. 1975.

DONALD K. PICKENS

ANDERSON, David Lawrence (4 Feb. 1850–16 Mar. 1911), China missionary and first president of Suzhou University, was born in Summerhill, South Carolina, the son of James Harkins Anderson and Mary Margaret Adams. For two years he attended Washington and Lee University, at that time under the presidency of Robert E. Lee. The university would later confer on him an honorary doctor of divinity degree. After working briefly as a bookkeeper with the *Atlanta Constitution*, which his father had founded, Anderson entered the ministry, probably in 1869. He served with the North Georgia Conference of the Methodist Episcopal Church, South, becoming a presiding elder of the Dahlonega District. In 1879 he married Mary Garland Thomson, a trained musician as well as a church worker; they had at least four children.

Anderson volunteered for foreign service, and in 1882 he and his wife departed for China under the auspices of the southern Methodist mission society. Following a year as an evangelist at a small station near Shanghai, Anderson was transferred to Suzhou, where he would spend the remainder of his 27-year career as a China missionary. He was initially a pastor at the Kung Hang (Gong hang) chapel and then became a presiding elder of the Methodist mission district.

In 1895 Anderson turned to education. The year was a crucial one for China; China had been defeated in the Sino-Japanese War of 1894–1895, and a number of Chinese literati had initiated a movement to strengthen China through institutional change. Reformers advocated adding Western learning to traditional Chinese study of the Confucian classics. One day in late 1895, when Anderson was preaching in his Kung Hang chapel, several young scholars in long gowns entered and then remained after the conclusion of the service. Surprised by this seeming interest in Christianity on the part of educated Chinese, Anderson invited the group into his office and inquired what he could do for them. Their answer: teach us English. They explained that they had been convinced by the writings of the reformers that China must follow Japan's example and learn from the West in order to become strong. They desired, therefore, to learn English so that they could read Western books. Anderson agreed to teach the youths if they could recruit a class of twenty-five students. Soon three members of the Anderson family were offering English instruction. Courses in mathematics, science, Western geography and history, and the Christian religion were quickly added. Out of these beginnings, Kung Hang School came into existence.

Two other secondary educational institutions were simultaneously being maintained in China by the southern Methodists: Buffington Institute in Suzhou and Anglo-Chinese College in Shanghai. In 1899 the China mission of the Methodist Episcopal Church, South, voted to coordinate all their educational work into one system capped by a university in Suzhou. Local Chinese officials and the general conference of the denomination in the United States both enthusiastically endorsed the proposal and contributed funds for the university. Anderson was named its first president and spent 1900 in the United States raising money for buildings and equipment. In 1901 students and teachers from the three institutions came together on the Buffington campus to found Suzhou University.

The Chinese name of the institution, Tung Wu (Dong Wu), derived from a letter by the local Chinese viceroy promising to facilitate purchase of land for the school: "In days to come your school's graduates will be the peaches and pears [i.e., the choice products] of Tung Wu" (Lutz, p. 112). The choice of Tung Wu, the ancient name for the Suzhou region, denoted Anderson's insistence that the new institution should ensure that Chinese students master their own language as well as study English, Western learning, and Christianity. Anderson's son Roy taught English at the school for eight years, during which time he experimented with a direct method of instruction without employing any Chinese. Students learned oral English through the teacher's use of pantomime and their memorization of complete English sentences. All of the entering students in 1901 were below college level; it was not until 1907 that the school awarded its first bachelor's degree. In that year there were still only seven college students, the majority of the pupils being enrolled in the attached middle school.

Anderson devoted his presidency to expanding the institution and raising its academic level. Not only was he in charge of administration, but he taught courses in history and religion and was responsible for fundraising among southern Methodists in the United States. Just as Robert E. Lee had expected every Washington and Lee student to conduct himself as a gentleman, so Anderson challenged his students to act in accord with Confucian ideal of *junzi* (gentleman). On several occasions Anderson represented the China mission at the General Conference of the Methodist Episcopal Church, South, in the United States. At the time of his death in Suzhou, a new college building was under construction, financed by donations he had solicited while in the United States on furlough. It was named Anderson Hall in his memory, and devoted students persuaded his family to inter him on the university campus. His former students and Chinese friends raised money for a bronze statue of Anderson on campus and named March 16, the date of his death, University Day.

Though Suzhou University was only a fledgling institution when Anderson died, it eventually became an institution of higher education in fact as well as name. Notable for its strengths in commerce and business and in science, it also boasted a pioneering school of comparative law, located in Shanghai. Successor schools are national Suzhou University on the mainland and Suzhou University on Taiwan, the latter founded by teachers and alumni of the Christian institution. Both are distinguished in many of the same fields in which the original Suzhou University had made a special contribution.

• One folder of correspondence by Anderson and the journals of the China Mission Annual Conference, Methodist Episcopal Church, South, 1887–1896, 1901–1908, 1910–1940, are in the Archives of Drew University, Madison, N.J. A missionary colleague, Alvin P. Parker, wrote, "In Memoriam, Dr. D. L. Anderson," *Chinese Recorder* 43 (May 1911): 294–95. Minutes of the China Mission Conference for 1890, 1892, 1894–1895 and the fiftieth anniversary report of the China annual conference, 1886–1935, contain data on Anderson and the founding and history of Suzhou University; they are located in the Union Theological Seminary Library, New York City. Information on Anderson's tenure as president of Suzhou University is in Walter B. Nance, *Soochow University* (1956), and Jessie G. Lutz, *China and the Christian Colleges,*

1850–1950 (1971). The *Missionary Voice* published obituaries and eulogies of Anderson in its issues of May 1911, pp. 7–9, and Aug. 1911, pp. 32–34.

JESSIE GREGORY LUTZ

ANDERSON, Eddie (18 Sept. 1905–28 Feb. 1977), radio and movie actor, known as Rochester, was born Edward Lincoln Anderson in Oakland, California. Anderson was from a show business family; his father, "Big Ed" Anderson, was a vaudevillian, and his mother, Ella Mae (maiden name unknown), was a circus tightrope walker. As a youngster Eddie sold newspapers on the streets of Oakland, which, according to his own account, injured his voice and gave it the rasping quality that was long his trademark on radio.

Between 1923 and 1933 Anderson's older brother Cornelius had a career in vaudeville as a song and dance man, and Eddie, who had little formal education, joined him occasionally. With vaudeville dying, however, Anderson drifted toward Hollywood. In the depths of the depression, pickings were slim. His first movie appearance was in 1932 in *What Price Hollywood?* For a few years he only had bit parts, but then he secured a major role in the movie *Green Pastures* (1936), playing the part of Noah, an old southern preacher. *Green Pastures* was a movie adaptation of a Marc Connelly play from stories by Roark Bradford. A rather lavish version of a simple Negro interpretation of the Bible, with heaven a giant "fish fry," the movie was considered to be the first film since *Hallelujah 29* to treat sympathetically issues of concern to blacks.

After his performance in *Green Pastures* Anderson was continually employed in Hollywood and made a great many pictures. Very often he was in minor roles, usually black stereotypes, but there were enough of them to provide a handsome living. For example, he had minor roles in *Show Boat* (1936) and *Gone with the Wind* (1939) in which he was so elaborately made up that few people recognized him. His talent for both comic and serious roles was readily apparent to the movie industry; in the year 1937 alone he appeared in six movies.

Anderson's rise to fame and stardom came through the role of Rochester on the "Jack Benny Show." This radio program had been on the air since 1932, and Benny had tried numerous comic personae—always purporting to be himself and not a fictional character—before settling on "the 39-year old skinflint." Anderson joined the show in 1937. According to numerous scripts of later years Benny "found" Rochester working as a Pullman porter and hired him as his personal valet. The truth was slightly different. Anderson was engaged for one show in which he played a train porter, and the sketch was so successful that five weeks later Benny decided to put in another porter scene featuring Rochester. These two shows worked so well that Benny decided to make Rochester a permanent part of his radio team. Rochester became his butler, valet, and general factotum.

By the early 1940s Anderson was earning more than $100,000 a year, making him the highest paid African American in show business until Sidney Poitier arrived on the scene in the 1950s. A superb comic actor with exquisite timing, Anderson owed much of his success to his highly distinctive voice, often described as rasping or wheezing. Whatever the description, it was one of the classic voices of radio, instantly recognizable after two words—perhaps even one syllable. Someone once suggested to Anderson that he have an operation to remove the "frog" in his throat. His response was that if he had a frog in his throat he had no intention of having it operated on since it was a "gold-plated frog."

Because all the characters played themselves on the Benny show, many listeners came to believe that Rochester (as he was now called by everyone, even members of his own family) really was Benny's much-harried servant. Several listeners wrote in to complain about the low wages that Rochester was receiving and the other intolerable burdens that he had to endure. Benny was forced to write to many of these people and tell them that Rochester was really a well-paid actor named Eddie Anderson. During these years Anderson and his family lived in a mansion with a ballroom and were waited on by servants of their own. (He had married Mamie Sophie Wiggins in 1932; they had three children.) Anderson collected custom-built sports cars and raised thoroughbred horses. One of these ran in the Kentucky Derby in 1945.

Benny was actually sensitive to the problem of using a "stock colored butler character" and its racial implications. In the early forties he made an effort to eliminate any of Rochester's traits or habits that might appear to be racial stereotypes. For example, he removed all references to Rochester's eating watermelon or drinking gin. The racial issue was seldom raised in these years, least of all by Eddie Anderson, probably in part because it was always Benny, and not Rochester, who was the butt of all the jokes.

Anderson stayed with the Benny radio program until it ended in 1955. He also appeared on Benny's television show until it came to a close in 1965; but in Benny's later television specials he was not a regular. By this time feelings were running high against black stereotypes. When asked in a 1970 television appearance to recreate his old role as butler he said, "Massa Benny, we don' do dat no mo" (Leslie Halliwell, *The Filmgoer's Companion* [4th ed., 1974] p. 22).

All throughout the radio years and beyond, Anderson continued his film appearances. In 1943 he had the lead in the successful movie version of the Harold Arlen and E. Y. Harburg stage musical "Cabin in the Sky," which also included Ethel Waters and Louis Armstrong. Directed by Vincent Minnelli, this film was considered notable for its humanized version of black American life. Anderson continued to have movie roles in the 1960s and had a splendid part as a taxi driver in Stanley Kramer's visual farce *It's a Mad, Mad, Mad, Mad World* (1963). On television he had a role in "Bachelor Father" (1962) and "Love American

Style" (1969). He also did a cartoon voice for the Harlem Globetrotters's television program.

Anderson's first wife died in 1954; his second marriage was to Eva Simon, but it ended in divorce. He died in Los Angeles.

• A good account of Anderson's career is in Donald Bogle, *Blacks in American Films and Television: An Encyclopedia* (1988). See also Eileen Landy, *Black Film Stars* (1973), and Mel Watkins, *On the Real Side: Laughing, Lying, and Signifying* (1994). For a treatment of Anderson's role on the "Jack Benny Show," see Jack Benny and his daughter Joan's *Sunday Nights at Seven: The Jack Benny Story* (1990); the account by one of Benny's principal writers, Milt Josefsberg, *The Jack Benny Show* (1977); and Jim Harmon, *The Great Radio Comedians* (1970). An obituary is in the *New York Times*, 1 Mar. 1977.

GEORGE H. DOUGLAS

ANDERSON, Edgar (9 Nov. 1897–18 June 1969), botanist, was born in Forestville, New York, the son of A. Crosby Anderson, an educational administrator, and Inez Evora Shannon, a pianist. When Anderson was three, his family moved to East Lansing, Michigan, where his father accepted the position of instructor of dairy husbandry at Michigan Agricultural College and then became professor of dairy science.

From a very early age, Anderson demonstrated an unusual level of curiosity and interest in plants. He appears to have been comfortable in an academic atmosphere and did well in school. In 1914 he entered Michigan Agricultural College, where he hoped to study botany and horticulture. Shortly after graduation he joined the Naval Reserve, where he became gunner's mate second class. In 1919 he left for Boston when he was accepted for graduate work at the Bussey Institution of Harvard University. Under the supervision of agricultural geneticist, Edward Murray East, Anderson undertook research on the genetics of self-incompatibility in *Nicotiana*, the tobacco plant. As part of his training he interacted closely with other Harvard botanists, notably Oakes Ames, and was especially fond of visiting the Harvard-affiliated Arnold Arboretum to study cultivated plants. He received a master's degree in 1920 and a doctor of science degree in agricultural genetics in 1922.

Shortly after graduation, Anderson accepted a position as geneticist at the Missouri Botanical Garden and at the same time was appointed assistant professor of botany at Washington University in St. Louis. He also worked at reestablishing the Henry Shaw School for Gardening, also in St. Louis, by serving as its director. Much of his research at this time was spent on developing novel methods to study geographic variation in plant populations of the common blue flag, *Iris versicolor*. In 1929 he left the garden on a National Research Fellowship to study at Britain's John Innes Horticultural Institution. During this time he studied cytogenetics with C. D. Darlington, statistics with R. A. Fisher, and botanical genetics with J. B. S. Haldane. Among his projects was a study following the pleitropic effects of genes as expressed in growth process in the plant *Primula sinensis*.

At the end of his fellowship year in 1931 Anderson accepted the position of arborist at the Arnold Arboretum, where he was to stay until 1935. Much of his subsequent research was with geneticist Karl Sax, who eventually became the director of the Arnold Arboretum, and Anderson's former student Robert Woodson, on the cytogenetics of meiosis and pollen development in the plant species *Tradescantia*. The results of this research facilitated Anderson's understanding of hybridization patterns leading to evolution. In 1935 he returned to the Missouri Botanical Garden with the title of full professor, receiving the Engelmann Professorship at Washington University in 1937. In 1954 he took on the administrative task of director of the Missouri Botanical Garden but rapidly found this work onerous. He resigned this position and resumed his teaching and research career in 1957, taking on the title of curator of useful plants. He retired officially in 1967, retaining the title of Engelmann Professor of Botany, emeritus, at Washington University.

Anderson was recognized for the development of novel visual and quantitative techniques to measure variation, among which the best known were "ideograms." A product of diverse intellectual traditions, Anderson was able to synthesize newer developments in genetics and ecology to help solve older problems of botanical systematics. In his contributions to understanding processes of evolutionary change, he is best known for his articulation of the concept of "introgressive hybridization," a process by which new genetic material is introduced through hybridization and backcrossing of unlike individuals. His book *Introgressive Hybridization* appeared in 1949 and was immediately recognized as an original and important contribution to botanical genetics. His study on geographic speciation on *Iris* in the Mississippi Delta, and on the species *Aster anomalus*, received much recognition. In the early 1940s Anderson turned to classification and genetic problems of maize, inspired by the work of Paul C. Manglesdorf. At this time he also turned to economic botany, no doubt as a result of the initial influence of Oakes Ames. In 1952 he wrote the very popular *Plants, Man, and Life*, a semi-autobiographical account of plants in the service of humans. He was also known for his extensive public activities, such as the promotion of botanical practices and the development of new economically useful cultivars. His editorship of the *Bulletin of the Missouri Botanical Garden* was effective in informing public audiences of the usefulness of plants.

Anderson was a talented individual with a strong personality. He was frequently called a showman and was known for his theatrical nature. Despite his charismatic and forceful personality, Anderson was plagued by emotional problems that stemmed from fundamental insecurities. In the later years of his life, beginning especially in the late 1950s, Anderson was diagnosed and institutionalized with breakdowns that required extensive hospitalization and seem to have stemmed from manic-depressive illness. Though he had a largely successful marriage to Dorothy Moore, a fellow botanist who received her training from Wellesley whom he married in 1923, he appears to have experienced some family problems especially following the birth of his only child, who suffered from cerebral palsy. Through much of this stressful period, Anderson sought solace in the Society of Friends, of which he was an active and cherished member.

Despite the setbacks, which interfered greatly with his work (many of his projects were never completed and colleagues frequently complained of his inability to meet deadlines), Anderson was honored with many awards, prizes, and fellowships. Among these was the invitation to give the prestigious Jesup Lectures at Columbia University with avian systematist Ernst Mayr in 1941. Anderson was to provide the plant side of the new systematics. Though he gave the lectures, he failed to produce a promised manuscript of his lectures for publication. The completion of this manuscript would have placed Anderson within the circle of architects of the Neo-Darwinian synthetic theory of evolution, the leaders of twentieth-century evolutionary biology. He was eventually elected to the National Academy of Sciences and the American Academy of Arts and Sciences; he received the Darwin-Wallace Medal of the Linnean Society. He was president of the Botanical Society of America, the Society for the Study of Evolution, and the Herb Society (which he had helped to found). Other important administrative activities included serving on the Committee for Common Problems of Genetics and Paleontology, a precursor to the Society for the Study of Evolution (Anderson was a charter member). He continued to travel widely for the purposes of collecting field data and understanding the practices of economic botany, but also in serving as visitor to key botanical institutions in the 1940s and 1950s. In 1943 he received a Rockefeller grant to work with Carl Sauer, the distinguished geographer at the University of California. This was followed by a Guggenheim Fellowship that took him to Mexico. Never very far from the center of intellectual activity, he was visiting fellow at Princeton University, Stanford University, and Wesleyan University. He was generally regarded as a creative, and in fact, brilliant scientist whose extreme theatrical and eccentric nature was generally viewed with fondness. He died suddenly of a heart attack in his home, the Cleveland Avenue Gatehouse, located on the grounds of the Missouri Botanical Garden.

• Anderson's papers are in the archives of the Missouri Botanical Garden. A psychological profile of Anderson is in the Library of the American Philosophical Society, with Anne Roe Simpson's research papers for *The Making of a Scientist* (1952). By far the best biographical source is G. Ledyard Stebbins, "Edgar Anderson," National Academy of Sciences, *Biographical Memoirs* 49 (1978): 3–23. A special issue of the *Annals of the Missouri Botanical Garden* 59 (1972)], introduced by Duncan M. Porter, includes a suite of essays on Anderson, many of which grew out of the Missouri Botanical Garden's Seventeenth Annual Systematics Symposium dedicated in his honor; see especially John J. Finan, "Edgar Anderson (1897–1969)," pp. 325–45, and Erna R. Eisendrath, "The Publications of Edgar Anderson," pp. 346–61. Other contributors include Charles B. Heiser, Jr., and G. Ledyard Stebbins and an introductory statement republished from the *Society of Friends Journal*, 1 Aug. 1969, p. 419. Biographical sketches that appeared in the *Missouri Botanical Garden Bulletin* are Hugh Cutler, "Plants, Man, Life and Edgar Anderson," 55 (1967): 8–11, and David Gates, "Edgar Anderson, 1897–1969," 57 (1969): 3–5. See also Anonymous, "Edgar Anderson: Some Biographical Notes," *Boxwood Bulletin* 24 (1984): 35–40.

VASSILIKI BETTY SMOCOVITIS

ANDERSON, Edwin Hatfield (27 Sept. 1861–29 Apr. 1947), librarian, was born in Zionsville, Indiana, the son of Philander Anderson, a physician, and Emma A. Duzan. In his youth the family, a large one reared by the strict Presbyterian standards of his father, moved to south Kansas, where his father took up banking. From 1879 to 1883 Anderson attended Wabash College in Crawfordsville, Indiana, graduating with an A.B. degree. After trying various occupations—reading law, writing for newspapers, and teaching school in Chicago—he embarked on the new profession of librarianship. From October 1890 to May 1891 he was a student at the New York State Library School at Albany and in June 1891 began work as a cataloger at the new Newberry Library in Chicago. The following December he married Frances R. Plummer; they adopted two French girls after World War I.

The 1890s proved to be an opportune time for an attractive, affable young man of vigor and intelligence such as Anderson to rise in the library world. A modern library movement was under way in the United States, a trend that would be accelerated by the widespread library philanthropy of Andrew Carnegie. Libraries were proliferating, with urban libraries beginning to offer varied, community-based services in multibranch systems, and librarianship was becoming professionalized. In May 1892 Anderson became director of an early Carnegie benefaction, the Carnegie Free Library in Braddock, Pennsylvania, and in 1895 he was named director of the newly built Carnegie Library of Pittsburgh. With Carnegie's financial help, Anderson organized a model institution in Pittsburgh. He recruited an outstanding staff, created a distinguished collection, produced important library catalogs, initiated pioneering children's services, and established a department of technology, the first special collection and service unit in that subject in an American public library. Anderson also supervised the design and construction of a new central library wing and neighborhood branches, and to train children's librarians he inaugurated a school, the progenitor of the Carnegie Library School of the Carnegie Institute of Technology. These undertakings exemplified Anderson's belief in the public library's mission to foster popular enlightenment through providing convenient access to good books. He also believed it was the library's role to support scholarship, science, and technology by making scholarly publications and specialized information readily available—all achieved through the work of expert, community-oriented librarians.

At the end of 1904 Anderson, wishing to try his hand in the business world and feeling the need to work in the open air, resigned his position at Pittsburgh and went into lead and zinc mining in southwestern Missouri. In January 1906 he resumed his professional career as the controversial Melvil Dewey's successor as director of the New York State Library and the New York State Library School. In his two years in Albany, Anderson managed to revitalize these preeminent institutions and to accomplish important planning and reorganization of them.

In June 1908 Anderson made a move that would take him to the acme of his career: he became assistant director of the New York Public Library. There Anderson's executive ability and experience—organizing and directing a public library in a populous, multicultural industrial center, planning library buildings, developing professional personnel, and working with trustees, donors, and public officials—would all be brought into play on a very large scale. The New York Public Library, founded in 1895, combined under one management a privately financed central research library and a publicly supported circulating library network in three of the city's five boroughs—Manhattan, the Bronx, and Richmond (now Staten Island). The aging director, John Shaw Billings, needed help in administering a multifaceted enterprise and overseeing its expansion. The City of New York was constructing a majestic central building in Manhattan (to open in 1911), and twenty-five new branch buildings had recently opened, with fifteen more in progress (all the branches but one were built with Carnegie's money). Anderson served as assistant director for five years. On 14 May 1913, soon after Billings's death, he was appointed director, a position for which he was qualified not only by his background and experience but also by his strong character, genial manner, and commitment to providing library service of wide scope and prime quality and usefulness.

Anderson presided until 1934 over the largest and most-used public library system in the world, during a time of growth and change in response to demographic trends, economic and political conditions, and community interests. Between 1913 and 1934 the research holdings doubled to more than two million volumes, and branch library holdings rose nearly 75 percent; total staff increased by a third. Central building attendance also doubled, to more than four million visitors a year, and 11.5 million books were lent in the nearly fifty branches existing by 1934. New units and services established during Anderson's administration included a municipal reference library, the manuscript division, picture and theater collections, readers advisory and young adult services, a division of Negro history, literature, and prints (later the Schomburg Collection), an important circulating music library, and bookmobiles in outlying districts. There also were services and collections for new immigrants and experiments in adult education.

To operate this complex organization Anderson assembled a distinguished staff with extraordinary loyalty to the New York Public Library and gave them opportunities for professional growth and leadership. He began his notable staff development work when, as assistant director, he persuaded Carnegie to underwrite the New York Public Library School, which opened in 1911 and quickly rose to prominence. Many librarians at the New York Public Library and elsewhere were trained there until 1926, when the school merged with the New York State Library School to form the School of Library Service of Columbia University. Anderson was instrumental in this move, which manifested the shift of professional library education to academic settings.

Anderson resigned from the New York Public Library on 1 November 1934 at the age of seventy-three and was named director emeritus. He died in Evanston, Illinois.

Active in professional circles, Anderson served as president of the American Library Association and of local library associations. He received several honorary doctorates and, in appreciation of the New York Public Library's services to ethnic groups, was decorated by the governments of Rumania and Czechoslovakia. Apart from official communications, he wrote little for publication. A charming, sharply humorous conversationalist in congenial company, Anderson was a very private man, by conviction as well as inclination; he believed in quiet accomplishment. He was an outstanding leader of his generation of librarians who developed collections and services to meet a modernizing society's needs for information, education, amusement, and scholarship.

• The archives at the New York Public Library contain Anderson correspondence and other documents, including some biographical and genealogical material; the minutes of the board of trustees and its committees contain material about his administration; the Harry M. Lydenberg Papers have Anderson folders. The annual reports and other publications of the various institutions Anderson directed also are sources of information about his work.

A biographical assessment of Anderson is Phyllis Dain, "Anderson, Edwin Hatfield," in *Dictionary of American Library Biography* (1978). On the history of the New York Public Library during part of Anderson's tenure, see Dain, *The New York Public Library: A History of Its Founding and Early Years* (1972), and Harry Miller Lydenberg, *History of the New York Public Library, Astor, Lenox and Tilden Foundations* (1923). Keyes D. Metcalf, *Random Recollections of an Anachronism; or, Seventy-Five Years of Library Work* (1980), includes reminiscences of the Anderson years at the New York Public Library. A personality sketch of Anderson is in the *New Yorker*, 21 Dec. 1929, p. 19. Obituaries include Franklin F. Hopper, "Edwin Hatfield Anderson," *Bulletin of the New York Public Library* 51 (1947): 389–90, and the *New York Times*, 1 May 1947.

PHYLLIS DAIN

ANDERSON, Garland (1886–31 May 1939), playwright and minister, was born in Wichita, Kansas. Little is known about his parents, although his mother is said to have been an active reformer and a poet. Garland completed four years of school (the only formal education he ever received) before his father moved his family to California to take a job as a janitor in the post office. The following year Garland's mother died, and at age twelve he left home to become a newsboy, selling the *Telegraph Press* on the corner of Third and Market streets in San Francisco.

After working as a porter on the railroad, for the next fifteen years Anderson worked as a bellhop in various San Francisco hotels. During this period he also became a temporary convert to Christian Science. One afternoon in 1924 he saw a performance of Channing Pollack's moralistic drama *The Fool* and knew immediately that he had found the medium for his message to the world. He would write a play.

Later he wrote, "At first the idea seemed absurd. . . . No one realized more than myself that though I wanted to write this play, I had no training in the technique of dramatic construction; but I also realized that to shirk what I wanted to do could be likened to the outer shell of the acorn after it was planted in the ground saying to the inner stir of life for expression, 'What are you stirring for? Surely you don't expect to become a great oak tree?' With this firm conviction I determined to write a play" (*From Newsboy and Bellhop to Playwright*).

In three weeks of writing, between phone calls summoning him at the hotel where he worked, he completed *Don't Judge by Appearances* (later shortened to *Appearances*), the story of a black bellhop falsely accused of rape by a white woman, a bold topic in 1924 for a black author. At the play's denouement, however, the woman is revealed to be a mulatto who has been passing as white, the only possible resolution in the year that riots had threatened the Provincetown Playhouse in New York City because the black actor Paul Robeson had kissed onstage the hand of a white actress playing his wife in Eugene O'Neill's drama *All God's Chillun Got Wings*.

With the encouragement of the residents at the hotel where he worked, Anderson sent his play to the popular performer Al Jolson, who provided Anderson with the means to travel to New York City to seek his fortune. At a backers' audition at the Waldorf-Astoria Hotel, 600 guests applauded the reading of the play by actor Richard B. Harrison, but they donated only $140 toward the production of *Appearances*.

Believing that "you can have what you want if you want it hard enough," Anderson wrote President Calvin Coolidge and persuaded his secretary to grant him an appointment at the White House. Possibly as a result of the publicity surrounding that meeting, producer Lester W. Sagar took over the script in June 1925 and put the play into rehearsal with three African Americans in the cast of seventeen. Immediately, the white actress Nedda Harrigan resigned, refusing to perform on the same stage with a black actor (in previous Broadway shows, the black characters had been played by whites in blackface). Nevertheless, on 13 October 1925 at the Frolic Theater, *Appearances* opened. It was the first full-length play by a black playwright to be presented on the Broadway stage and the first Broadway play to incorporate both black and white cast members. Although it received tepid notices, the reviewers praised Anderson's entrepreneurial spirit. The drama ran for twenty-three performances, then toured major American cities until on 1 April 1929 it returned to the Hudson Theatre in New York City to prepare for its opening at the Royale Theatre in London the following March.

In London, the play became a *succès de curiosité*. Apparently Anderson's impeccable manners coupled with his unrelenting optimism attracted the British press, and he became somewhat of a celebrity. He was introduced to Queen Mary and was invited by author John Galsworthy to speak at a meeting of PEN, the most prestigious literary club in London. He also undertook a business venture, with the backing of a British industrialist, by establishing a chain of milk bars called Andy's Nu-Snack, thus introducing to Londoners the cold malted milk. During his stay in England, he met a white English woman named Doris (maiden name unknown), whom he married in 1935 in Vancouver, Washington, one of the few states at that time to allow racially mixed marriages. She later published, under the name Doris Garland Anderson, her own account of the interracial marriage, the provocatively titled *Nigger Lover* (1938).

Although Anderson is said to have written two or three other plays, none was produced, and in his middle years he turned his energies to religion. In 1933 he published *Uncommon Sense: The Law of Life in Action*, a text extolling the virtues of religious faith. In 1935 he became a minister in the New Thought movement, at the Seattle Center of Constructive Thinking. During the last five years of his life, he toured the United States, Canada, and England, lecturing on the topic, "You Can Do What You Want to Do If You Believe You Can Do It." Following his free lecture in the optimistic tradition of Elbert Hubbard, and later Dale Carnegie, he offered a series of eight lessons (for $15) on how faith in self and God can lead to good fortune. In 1936 a newspaper in Regina, Canada, observed: "He is the first Negro since Booker T. Washington to tour the country speaking to white people only. Seldom, he admitted, does a Negro ever appear to hear him. 'They are not interested,' he said rather sadly." He died in New York City.

Anderson sold a second script entitled *Extortion* to David Belasco in 1929, but it was never produced. Nor was his first play ever produced again. According to James Weldon Johnson, *Appearances* "may not be an altogether convincing argument for the theories it advances, but the author himself is." Nonetheless, Anderson left his stamp on the Broadway stage. Because no New York critic complained about black and white actors appearing together on stage, within four months of the opening of Anderson's most notable play, Belasco produced *Lulu Belle* (1926), with ninety-seven black actors and seventeen white actors. Hence the production of *Appearances* marked the beginning of an integrated Broadway stage.

• No collection of Anderson's papers is known to exist. He published a small pamphlet entitled *From Newsboy and Bellhop to Playwright* (1929), a copy of which is in the Hatch-Billops Collection, an archive of African-American cultural history in New York City. The little available information about Anderson may be found in the following works: Doris Abramson, *Negro Playwrights in the American Theatre, 1925–1959* (1969); James V. Hatch, *Black Theatre USA* (1974) and *Black Playwrights, 1823–1977* (1977); Bernard L. Peterson, Jr., *Early Black American Playwrights and Dramatic Writers* (1990); and Allen Woll, *Dictionary of the Black Theatre* (1983).

JAMES V. HATCH

ANDERSON, George Thomas (3 Feb. 1824–4 Apr. 1901), Confederate brigadier general, was born in Covington, Newton County, Georgia, the son of Joseph Stewart and Lucy Cunningham Anderson. Although his family was in comfortable circumstances, he early became accustomed to the hard work of farm life. After attending Emory College near his home, he served in the Mexican War from 1847 to 1848. Joining the Georgia Mounted Volunteers as a second lieutenant in 1847, Anderson participated in the fighting around Mexico City and served under Major General Stephen W. Kearny in the occupations of Veracruz and Mexico City. Mustered out of the army in 1848, he settled in Walton County, Georgia, where he was a farmer and railroad agent. In 1855 he was commissioned a captain in the First Cavalry Regiment, of which Joseph E. Johnston was lieutenant colonel. Resigning his commission in 1858, he returned to Walton County, where he owned considerable property in land and slaves.

At the outbreak of the Civil War in 1861, Anderson was elected captain of the Walton Infantry, which became Company H of the Eleventh Regiment of Georgia Volunteer Infantry. When the regiment was organized and received into the Confederate service in Atlanta on 2 July 1861, Captain Anderson, because of his previous military service, was elected colonel. The regiment was immediately sent to Virginia and assigned to the Army of the Shenandoah under General Johnston, Anderson's former commander. Although the Eleventh Georgia reached the scene too late to fight in the battle of First Manassas on 21 July, Anderson became a temporary commander of his brigade after Francis S. Bartow was killed in that engagement. Remaining in northern Virginia during the winter of 1861–1862, Anderson again served as a temporary brigade commander when Brigadier General Samuel Jones was reassigned.

In the spring of 1862 Anderson's regiment was assigned to the brigade of David Rumph Jones and was sent to relieve General John B. Magruder's forces in the lower Virginia Peninsula. When Jones was named to the command of a division, Anderson was placed in charge of the brigade, which he commanded during the Seven Days' battles around Richmond. At the beginning of the campaign, Anderson's brigade rendered valuable service by guarding bridges and fighting rearguard actions to the east of Richmond. When the brigade was ordered to attack the Federal forces on Malvern Hill, he led his men across open fields and up the slopes. Although the Confederates were repulsed, Anderson succeeded in keeping his brigade intact and retreated in good order. After the Seven Days', he remained in temporary command of the brigade when it was assigned to the First Corps of General James Longstreet in General Robert E. Lee's reorganization of the Army of Northern Virginia in July 1862.

Continuing to act as brigade commander at Second Manassas and Sharpsburg, Anderson was not commissioned as brigadier general until 1 November 1862. His brigade led the vanguard of Longstreet's corps through Thoroughfare Gap to join Thomas "Stonewall" Jackson's forces for the battle of Second Manassas. While the brigade was exposed to a "murderous fire," Anderson demonstrated his fighting spirit by leading his men on foot when his horse was shot from under him. Because of heavy losses at Second Manassas, Anderson's brigade served only as a tactical reserve at Sharpsburg and did not play a major role in that battle. While General Anderson witnessed the battle of Fredericksburg in December 1862, his brigade saw little action. Assigned to General John B. Hood's division of Longstreet's corps in early 1863, his brigade was sent in the spring to besiege Suffolk in the Virginia Southside and missed fighting at Chancellorsville. His brigade, however, returned to northern Virginia in time for Lee's invasion of Pennsylvania in June 1863. Leading the brigade at the battle of Gettysburg, Anderson fought valiantly at Devil's Den and Little Round Top and was severely wounded.

Out of action for several months, by September Anderson had recovered sufficiently to rejoin his brigade, which was temporarily detached from Longstreet in the fall of 1863 to reinforce the defenses of Charleston. The brigade rejoined Longstreet's forces in eastern Tennessee later that year and participated in the siege of Knoxville. Anderson's brigade returned with Longstreet to the Army of Northern Virginia in the spring of 1864. In the battle of the Wilderness, his brigade marched at the head of Longstreet's column and was one of the units deployed to attack the Federal left flank in the heaviest fighting of that engagement. Although Anderson's brigade fought at Spotsylvania and Cold Harbor, it was not in the main action of those battles. Engaged in the Petersburg campaign from the beginning, Anderson's brigade at various times served both north and south of the James River in defending the eastern approaches to Richmond and the vital Richmond-Petersburg railroad. When Lee surrendered at Appomattox in April 1865, Anderson was present with his decimated brigade.

Anderson's nickname "Tige" was an apt characterization, for he was an intrepid fighter. While he was considered to be a steady, dependable, and competent officer, his military career was not spectacular in advancement or promotion. He acted as a brigadier general for more than a year before he was commissioned, and he never rose beyond the brigadier rank despite his aspirations to become a major general. His not being a West Point graduate may have been an obstacle, even though he had served in the regular army. It is also known that he and General Hood, who became his divisional commander in 1863, were not on good terms. Neither he nor General Longstreet shared the high regard for the younger Hood held by Generals Lee and Jackson. Moreover, Anderson had resented Hood's threat during the Suffolk campaign to arrest him when he objected to Hood's criticism of one of his captains. There is ample evidence, however, that "Tige" Anderson was held in high and affectionate regard by his men, one of whom described him as being a "kind, generous and brave" leader who never ordered his men to go where he would not go himself (Adams, p. 6). Another wrote that he had "the air of one blessed with a spirit born to rule" and that "no difficulties could shake the force and power of his resolution" (Warren, p. 41).

After Appomattox, General Anderson returned to Georgia and was freight agent of the Georgia Railroad in Atlanta for several years. In 1877 he was named city marshal and chief of police. He moved to Tuscaloosa, Alabama, in 1881 and was a merchant there until he removed to Anniston, Alabama, in 1889. In Anniston, where he lived until his death in 1901, he served first as city clerk and chief of police and then as tax collector of Calhoun County.

General Anderson married Elizabeth Bush Ramey in 1848. After her death in 1867, he married Linda Spiller in 1881. There were no children by his first marriage, but there were a son and daughter by the second.

• There is no full-length biography of Anderson, though Francis B. Heitman, *Historical Register and Dictionary of the United States Army* (2 vols., 1903), provides useful information. Also informative are Ezra J. Warner, *Generals in Gray, Lives of the Confederate Commanders* (1959); Stewart Sifakis, *Who Was Who in the Civil War* (1988); and Clement A. Evans, *Confederate Military History*, extended ed., vols. 7 and 8 (1987). The most important source for the history of Anderson's brigade is John David Wilson, "George Thomas Anderson's Rebel Brigade: A Military History, 1861–1865" (Ph.D. diss., Emory Univ., 1977). Accounts by Anderson's comrades are found in Kittrell J. Warren, *Muster Roll and History of the Eleventh Regiment, Georgia Volunteers* (1863); W. T. Laseter, "Co. H, 11th Regt. Ga. Inf.," in *Roster of the Confederate Soldiers of Georgia, 1861–1865*, vol. 2, ed. Lillian Henderson (1959); Anita B. Sams, ed., *With Unabated Trust: Major Henry McDaniel's . . . Letters from Confederate Battlefields* (1977); and John J. Adams, "History of the Quitman Grays, Co. I, 11th Ga. Regiment" (n.d.), in the Georgia Department of Archives and History.

MALCOLM LESTER

ANDERSON, Herbert Lawrence (24 May 1914–16 July 1988), physicist, was born in New York City, the son of Joseph Anderson; his mother's name is not recorded. After graduating from New York City public schools in 1932, he entered Columbia University, graduating with a bachelor of arts degree in 1935 and a bachelor of science degree in electrical engineering in 1936. As a graduate student in physics at Columbia under the direction of John R. Dunning, Anderson assisted in the construction of a 37-inch cyclotron, which led to a lifelong interest in nuclear physics. In 1939 he began working closely with Nobel laureate Enrico Fermi, who had immigrated to the United States to escape Benito Mussolini's Fascist regime. After learning of the fissioning of uranium by Lise Meitner and Otto Frisch from Danish physicist Neils Bohr, Anderson, Fermi, and Dunning successfully fissioned the element themselves in the Columbia cyclotron and in an ionization chamber built by Anderson. Anderson, who earned a doctorate in physics from Columbia in 1940, postponed the publication of his doctoral dissertation on the resonant absorption of neutrons by uranium until after World War II as part of the self-imposed secrecy of scientists investigating nuclear physics during the war.

After completing his doctoral studies Anderson became involved in the U.S. government's top-secret Manhattan Project to develop an atomic bomb. Working closely with Fermi, he studied different pile, or nuclear reactor, designs at Columbia. In 1942 Anderson accompanied Fermi to the University of Chicago, where Fermi had been selected to develop a reactor capable of sustaining a nuclear chain reaction. Fermi placed Anderson in charge of the team to build the reactor, known as CP-1, in which the world's first nuclear chain reaction occurred on 2 December 1942. For the next eighteen months Anderson led the construction of CP-2, the Metallurgical Laboratory's second nuclear reactor, which measured the cross sections of various nuclei and other reactor properties. Working with the Du Pont Company in 1944, he participated in the design of the plutonium production reactors at the Manhattan Project's remote facility in Hanford, Washington.

In 1944 Anderson joined Fermi at the Manhattan Project's weapons laboratory at Los Alamos, New Mexico. As leader of the Los Alamos Scientific Laboratory's newly formed F Division, he spearheaded the development of techniques to measure the explosive yield of the first experimental nuclear weapon. Anderson proposed a measurement technique that compared the amount of fissioned to unfissioned material in a soil sample taken from the explosion test site. After the 16 July 1945 nuclear explosion at Alamogordo, New Mexico, Anderson descended into the crater in a Sherman tank and successfully retrieved the valuable soil sample. After World War II his method of studying fission products to determine the yield of the Trinity test was used to analyze atmospheric samples to detect nuclear weapon tests conducted by foreign powers.

Anderson continued to work at the Los Alamos Scientific Laboratory until 1946, when he joined the physics faculty of the University of Chicago as an assistant professor. Also appointed to Chicago's Institute for Nuclear Studies, he directed the construction of a

460-Mev proton synchrocyclotron, which ranked then as the world's largest particle accelerator. Anderson, in collaboration with Fermi, used the powerful instrument to investigate pion-hydrogen scattering, studies that culminated in the discovery of the delta particle. Promoted to associate professor in 1947, he reached the rank of full professor in 1950.

Anderson renewed his association with the Los Alamos Scientific Laboratory as a consultant in 1954. A Guggenheim fellow in 1955, he served as a Fulbright lecturer in Italy from 1956 to 1957. While serving as director of the Enrico Fermi Institute from 1958 to 1962, Anderson entered the hospital for treatment of berylliosis, a respiratory disease he had acquired by inhaling beryllium dust during his early work on pile development. After the Chicago cyclotron was decommissioned and its huge magnet transferred to the Fermi National Accelerator Laboratory (Fermilab) in Batavia, Illinois, Anderson in 1962 transferred his interest to that facility and to the Argonne National Laboratory South of Chicago. The magnet became the heart of the muon spectrometer that Anderson designed for studying deep inelastic muon scattering.

In 1978 Anderson returned to the Los Alamos National Laboratory, where he began a program of research on rare and normal muon decays. At Los Alamos he acquired a new interest in biophysics and developed a method of reading gel electrophoresis patterns that proved valuable in the study of protein distribution during stages of cell development in bacteria. In 1981 the Los Alamos National Laboratory appointed Anderson a distinguished senior fellow, and in 1982 the University of Chicago appointed him a distinguished service professor emeritus. In 1982 the U.S. Department of Energy presented him the Enrico Fermi Award for his lifelong achievements in nuclear physics. Anderson died in Santa Fe, New Mexico, from berylliosis, while he was studying human molecular biology.

A pioneer in the development of nuclear physics, Anderson participated in the invention of the nuclear reactor. His collaboration with Fermi, first at Columbia and then at Chicago, led to the construction of a uranium-graphite reactor that conducted history's first nuclear chain reaction and became the archetype from which future reactors would evolve for the production of plutonium and tritium for nuclear weapons, for the propulsion of submarines and surface ships, and for the generation of electrical power. The nuclear reactor not only revolutionized the study of physical phenomena but also shifted the center of physics research from Europe to the United States. After World War II Anderson turned his attention to basic nuclear physics research and made significant contributions to understanding the behavior of many atomic particles.

• Some of Anderson's papers are at the Los Alamos National Laboratory Archives. A biographical file on him is at the University of Chicago's Department of Special Collections. For Anderson's contributions to the development of the nuclear reactor, see Rodney P. Carlisle and Joan M. Zenzen, *Supplying the Nuclear Arsenal: American Production Reactors, 1942–1952* (1996). Consult James W. Kunetka, *City of Fire: Los Alamos and the Atomic Age, 1943–1945* (1979), for Anderson's work on the Manhattan Project at Hanford and Los Alamos. For his contributions to the development of physics and a history of American physics in general, see Daniel J. Kevles, *The Physicists: The History of Scientific Community in Modern America* (1978). Obituaries are in the *New York Times* and the *Chicago Tribune*, both 17 July 1988.

ADAM R. HORNBUCKLE

ANDERSON, Ivie (10 July 1905–27 or 28 Dec. 1949), jazz singer, was born in Gilroy, California, the daughter of Jobe Smith. Her mother's name is unknown. Anderson's given name is sometimes spelled "Ivy." She studied voice at St. Mary's Convent from age nine to age thirteen, and she sang in the glee club and choral society at Gilroy grammar and high school. While spending two years at the Nunnie H. Burroughs Institution in Washington, D.C., she studied voice under Sara Ritt.

She performed in Los Angeles, California, around 1921, and in 1922 or 1923 she joined a touring version of the pioneering African-American musical revue *Shuffle Along*, which brought her to New York City. She performed in Cuba in 1924, at the Cotton Club in New York City in 1925, and then in Los Angeles, where she was accompanied by the bands of Paul Howard, Curtis Mosby, and Sonny Clay. In 1928 she sang with Clay's group in Australia. She starred at Frank Sebastian's Cotton Club in Los Angeles in April 1928 and then toured the United States as a solo singer.

Anderson spent twenty weeks with pianist Earl Hines's big band at the Grand Terrace in Chicago, Illinois, from 1930 into early 1931. In February 1931 she joined Duke Ellington's orchestra, and during the next dozen years her career followed Ellington's incessant touring, mainly in America, but also for his first appearance in Europe in 1933. With Ellington she recorded "It Don't Mean a Thing (If It Ain't Got That Swing)" (1932), "Raisin' the Rent," "Stormy Weather," and "I'm Satisfied" (all 1933), and in 1933 she also performed "Stormy Weather" in a film short, *Bundle of Blues*. In 1937 she sang "All God's Chillun Got Rhythm" in the Marx Brothers' movie *A Day at the Races* (1937). Further significant recordings with Ellington include vocal versions of his instrumental themes "Solitude" and "Mood Indigo" (both 1940), "I Got It Bad and That Ain't Good" (1941)—also on a soundie (a film short for a video jukebox) of the same name, released in 1943—and "Rocks in My Bed" (1941). She left Ellington's band in 1942.

Anderson married Marque Neal, with whom she opened Ivie's Chicken Shack in Los Angeles. After divorcing Neal and selling the business she married Walter Collins. The dates of the marriages are unknown; she had no children. Having suffered for years from asthma, she died in Los Angeles. In what is evidently the most detailed and earliest obituary (its source unidentified), her date of death is given as 27 December 1949; all other sources give 28 December.

Anderson was probably Ellington's most versatile singer and perhaps, after the extraordinary Swedish vocalist Alice Babs, his finest as well. She was a scat singer who imitated instrumental sounds, including the growling, trumpet-like vocalizations that Adelaide Hall had earlier introduced into Ellington's repertoire; she sang lively pop tunes, clearly enunciating lyrics that she delivered in a piercingly bright voice; and she sang ballads, in which setting her voice became full-bodied and took on a sultry quality. With her joyful delivery of "It Don't Mean a Thing," Anderson gave the forthcoming swing era its name and rhythmic spirit. Her affiliation with Ellington is also remembered especially for her understated but emotionally powerful rendition of the ballad "I Got It Bad and That Ain't Good." Ellington wrote of Anderson in his *Music Is My Mistress* (1973),

> Although Ivie was not well known at that time [early 1930s], I soon found that she was really an extraordinary artist and an extraordinary person as well. She had great dignity, and she was greatly admired by everybody everywhere we went, at home and abroad. . . . She stopped the show cold at the Palladium in London in 1933. Her routine normally consisted of four songs, but while she was singing "Stormy Weather," the audience and all the management brass broke down crying and applauding. (p. 124)

• Anderson's career is featured in Herbert E. Walker, "Ivy Anderson Quit Typing to Sing; She's a Star Now," *Chicago Defender*, 9 Feb. 1935; and Paul Eduard Miller, "Ivie Joined the Duke for Four Weeks, Stays with Band for 12 Years," *Down Beat*, 15 July 1942, p. 31, repr. in *The Duke Ellington Reader*, ed. Mark Tucker (1993). More information about Anderson appears in Sally Placksin, *American Women in Jazz: 1900 to the Present: Their Words, Lives, and Music* (1982); James Lincoln Collier, *Duke Ellington* (1987); Gunther Schuller, *The Swing Era: The Development of Jazz, 1930–1945* (1989); and Robert P. Crease, "Divine Frivolity: Hollywood Representations of the Lindy Hop, 1937–1942," in *Representing Jazz*, ed. Krin Gabbard (1995). A detailed but unidentified newspaper obituary, hand-dated 29 Dec. 1949, is in the files of the Institute of Jazz Studies, Newark, N.J. Other obituaries are in the *New York Times*, 30 Dec. 1949, the *Pittsburgh Courier*, 7 Jan. 1950, and *Metronome* 66 (Feb. 1950): 13.

BARRY KERNFELD

ANDERSON, John August (7 Aug. 1876–2 Dec. 1959), physicist, was born in Rollag, Minnesota, the son of Brede Anderson and Ellen Martha Berg, farmers. Anderson received his B.S. in 1900 from Valparaiso College, Indiana, and entered Johns Hopkins University in 1904 for graduate work in physics. He received his Ph.D. in 1907, doing research in laboratory spectroscopy under Joseph Sweetman Ames. After a brief period at the Rouss Physical Laboratory of the University of Virginia, Anderson returned to Johns Hopkins in 1908 as an instructor, eventually becoming associate professor in 1911. During his time in Baltimore Anderson married Josephine Virginia Barron in 1909; they had no children.

Johns Hopkins became a leading center for spectroscopy at the end of the nineteenth century because of the work of Henry Augustus Rowland. Rowland had perfected a machine (the "ruling engine") that could produce outstanding reflection diffraction gratings. These gratings, mirrors cut by a diamond with fifteen to twenty thousand grooves per inch, were necessary to produce the high-dispersion spectra needed for the study of complicated spectra of the sun and the heavier elements. Work with the gratings suffered after Rowland's death in 1901, and in 1909 Anderson was put in charge of the ruling machines. He thoroughly rebuilt two of Rowland's engines and was once again able to produce world-class gratings with them. Anderson's success with the Rowland ruling engines led George Ellery Hale, director of the Carnegie Institution of Washington's Mount Wilson Observatory, to ask for his assistance in constructing an engine for the observatory. Hale's plan was to build a ruling engine that would produce larger gratings than any other (gratings up to forty by sixty centimeters square) in order to make the best use of the large telescopes on Mount Wilson. Anderson spent part of 1912 and 1913 at the observatory's offices in Pasadena, California, supervising the construction of the ruling engine (eventually known as the "A" ruling engine) before returning to Baltimore. By 1916, however, Hale was convinced that he needed Anderson on his staff in order to ensure the proper completion and operation of the engine. Anderson joined the observatory staff in July 1916 and promptly went to work on the Mount Wilson ruling engine. When completed, however, the engine was never able to produce the large gratings that Hale had wanted. The large size of the engine created problems because of its lack of stability, initial start-up friction, and deformities in the oversized screw. As a result, although Anderson supervised the production of many excellent smaller gratings, he could never obtain any of the large high-quality gratings that the engine was designed to produce.

During the First World War Anderson designed and tested micrometers for the Bureau of Standards and did research on submarine detection devices for the navy. After the war, Anderson worked briefly with Albert Abraham Michelson's interferometer on the Mount Wilson 100-inch telescope in order to determine the separation of the two components of the star Capella. But Anderson's most significant work during the 1920s was at the observatory's physical laboratory, where he pioneered the use of exploding wires to briefly achieve temperatures comparable to those found at the surfaces of stars. Anderson, with the assistance of Sinclair Smith, also developed a rotating mirror camera to take the very fast (about one microsecond) exposures necessary to study the rapidly dissipating shell of gas caused by the exploding wire. During the 1920s Anderson collaborated with Harry Oscar Wood at the California Institute of Technology in developing the theory behind and the construction of a torsion seismograph. This new seismograph was significant in that contemporary seismometers were not very useful for studying nearby earthquakes.

In 1928 George Ellery Hale secured a grant from the Rockefeller Foundation's International Education Board to the California Institute of Technology for the construction of a 200-inch telescope, twice the size of the existing largest telescope in the world. Anderson was selected to be the executive officer of the Observatory Council for the 200-inch. As executive officer, Anderson would oversee the details of the project and serve as de facto chair on the committees formed to select the observatory site, the mirror design, the mounting and construction of the telescope, and the design of the auxiliary instruments. The success of the 200-inch telescope depended on Anderson's ability to manage the project, and he would often take personal charge of several aspects of the telescope's development. One problem he faced was in assembling a team of opticians who could take on the grinding and figuring of the large 200-inch glass disk. No one was experienced in working on mirrors of that size, and so Anderson had to hire relatively untrained men and teach them the procedures required to make a perfect mirror. Anderson, with the aid of Frank Elmore Ross, also determined a method for testing the figure of the 200-inch mirror without the use of an equivalent-sized flat test mirror. Anderson also took great pains in making sure that a battery of exceptional instruments would be produced that would take full advantage of the increased light-gathering power of the 200-inch telescope.

Anderson developed heart problems in 1940 and was forced to slow down his pace. He could only be on site for half a day, the rest of the day being spent lying down at home, immersing himself in the problems encountered during the completion of the 200-inch telescope. The telescope was placed on hold during the Second World War, however, and Anderson spent part of his time doing war research. His main contribution was his work with Ira Sprague Bowen on the development and improvement of optical range finders from 1941 to 1943. Anderson officially retired from the Mount Wilson Observatory on 1 September 1943 and thereafter concentrated solely on the completion of the 200-inch telescope. In the spring of 1948, with the 200-inch mirror finally at the observatory site on Palomar Mountain and with final tests underway, Anderson retired as executive officer of the Observatory Council. He withdrew completely from scientific research and lived quietly until his death in Altadena, California.

In the field of scientific research, Anderson's strength was in the development and construction of scientific instruments. His success with diverse instruments such as ruling engines, seismographs, and high-speed cameras gave Hale confidence that Anderson could organize the intricate details, make the right decisions, and see to completion the 200-inch telescope project.

• Anderson's papers are in the Archives of the California Institute of Technology, but the majority of the collection only deals with his work on the 200-inch telescope project. Of additional interest is Anderson's own article, written with Russell W. Porter, "The 200-inch Telescope," *Telescope* 7 (1940): 29–39. The best source of information about Anderson, along with a complete bibliography of his publications, is Ira S. Bowen, "John August Anderson, 1876–1959," National Academy of Sciences, *Biographical Memoirs* 36 (1962): 1–18. More information on Anderson's work with ruling engines is in Horace W. Babcock, "Diffraction Gratings at the Mount Wilson Observatory," *Physics Today* 39 (July 1986): 34–42. Anderson's involvement in the 200-inch telescope project is mentioned in Helen Wright, *Palomar, the World's Largest Telescope* (1952).

RONALD S. BRASHEAR

ANDERSON, Joseph Inslee (5 Nov. 1757–17 Apr. 1837), jurist, U.S. senator, and Treasury official, was born near Philadelphia, Pennsylvania, the son of William Anderson and Elizabeth Inslee (occupations unknown). When not yet twenty, Anderson enlisted in the Continental army as a private and rose to the rank of major by the war's end. He was regimental paymaster during much of the war, and his experience in that capacity served him well in positions he held later. He was with George Washington at Valley Forge and was at Yorktown when the British surrendered in October 1781. Anderson was separated from the service in 1781 and practiced law in Delaware for much of the next decade. He was married in 1797 to fifteen-year-old Only Patience Outlaw, daughter of Colonel Alexander Outlaw of North Carolina. After the war, Outlaw had taken up land claims in what later became Tennessee. The couple settled on a large tract of land in Jefferson County given to them by Colonel Outlaw and had seven children.

The Territory of the United States South of the River Ohio had been created in 1790, and six years later it became the state of Tennessee. William Blount of North Carolina was named territorial governor. It is quite possible that Anderson had known both Washington and Blount as soldiers during the Revolution, and in 1790 Anderson was appointed one of three territorial judges after another appointee had refused to serve. Blount, in describing the young jurist to James Robertson of Nashville, wrote of him in laudatory terms.

Anderson entered upon his duties with characteristic vigor. In at least one address, he urged white inhabitants to obey the laws of the territory and avoid trouble with the Cherokee Indians by respecting treaty provisions. He presided over a number of cases, including one involving a Creek leader named Abongpohigo, upon whom he pronounced a death sentence after the Indian was convicted of the murder of a white settler near Knoxville.

By 1795 a census taken in the territory revealed a population sufficient under the Northwest Ordinance for the territory to be considered for statehood. Anderson became a delegate to the constitutional convention held the following January in Knoxville. Joined by

Outlaw, soon to become his father-in-law, Anderson mustered strong opposition to those who supported a bicameral general assembly. He opposed both Blount and Andrew Jackson on the matter and spoke for a unicameral legislature like that which his native state retained until 1790. He also believed the powers given legislators were excessive, and he played a role in drafting a bill of rights, which ultimately became the state constitution's first article. He and Outlaw exhibited a defiant attitude in a resolution they drafted stating that in the event Congress should not accept the territory as a new state, its leaders should declare their independence and operate as a separate and independent state. Jackson, although a close friend of Anderson, believed the jurist was overly influenced in his defiance by Outlaw, and he informed Blount that both men were trying to "weaken" the constitution. Jackson believed that both had "detracted from their popularity" and damaged their chances of political advancement in the future.

Tennessee was admitted as the sixteenth state on 1 June 1796. Anderson became a candidate for a U.S. Senate seat but soon withdrew, and Blount and William Cocke became Tennessee's first senators, the former being chosen for four years and the latter two, under the Senate's staggered plan. Blount, however, was expelled on 8 July 1797, and Anderson succeeded him and served until 12 December 1798. In the meantime, Cocke's term had expired, and Jackson was elected for a full six-year term in 1797. After six months, however, Jackson resigned, and the governor then appointed Daniel Smith to serve until the legislature could convene and select his successor. On 12 December 1798 legislators met and filled both Senate seats. In the balloting they ignored the candidacy of Smith and others and elected Cocke to the former Blount seat and Anderson to the former Cocke seat; both took office on 4 March 1799. Anderson's term expired in 1803, and when Smith challenged him again, he defeated the former territorial official by one vote after they were tied at 18-all throughout most of a day of balloting. Six years later in a bid for reelection he defeated the popular six-term governor John Sevier and served until 1815.

During his long tenure in the Senate, Anderson served on various committees and briefly was president pro tempore of the body after Aaron Burr resigned as vice president. He entered readily into the debates and, in his early years in the Senate, was heard frequently on the floor eloquently defending the western people's claim to a right of deposit at the mouth of the Mississippi River. He spoke frequently regarding troubles with England and France during the years leading to the War of 1812. Once war began, he supported a move to invade and annex parts of Canada. Anderson did not seek another term in 1815 but soon was appointed by President James Madison as Comptroller of the Treasury—a position he filled ably until 1836, at which time he retired from public service.

Anderson County, Tennessee, was created in 1801 and named for him. He was a trustee of Washington College and also of Blount College, which ultimately became the University of Tennessee. Anderson died at the home of his son in Washington, D.C. His public service, including eight years as a soldier in the Revolution, encompassed fifty-three years.

• Some Anderson letters are in the John Overton Papers in the Southern Historical Collection, University of North Carolina at Chapel Hill. All of the standard works on Tennessee mention Anderson. Occasional reference also is made to him in letters of prominent men of the day, such as Andrew Jackson, James Robertson, John Sevier, and Daniel Smith. Most of the Jackson papers have been published or are in the process of publication by the University of Tennessee at Knoxville. Papers of others mentioned are found in the State Library and Archives at Nashville.

Fay McMillan, "A Biographical Sketch of Joseph Anderson," *East Tennessee Historical Society's Publications* 2 (1930): 81–93, surveys his public life. Mrs. Charles Fairfax Henley provides interesting information about his forebears and his descendants in "The Hon. Joseph Anderson and Some of his Distinguished Relatives and Descendants," *American Historical Magazine* 3 (1898): 240–99. Sketches of his life are found in several accounts, particularly, Joshua W. Caldwell, *Sketches of the Bench and Bar of Tennessee* (1898). Helpful data on his senatorial elections and service are in Robert H. White, *Messages of the Governors*, vol. 1 (1952), Walter T. Durham, *Before Tennessee: The Southwest Territory, 1790–1796* (1990), and Durham, *Daniel Smith: Frontier Statesman* (1976).

ROBERT E. CORLEW

ANDERSON, Joseph Reid (16 Feb. 1813–7 Sept. 1892), industrialist and Confederate soldier, was born in Botetourt County in the Shenandoah Valley of Virginia, the son of William Anderson and Anna Thomas, farmers. Anderson received his early education in the local schools. After having been rejected twice, he entered the U.S. Military Academy in 1832 at age nineteen. Graduating fourth of forty-nine in 1836, he preferred a post in the elite Corps of Engineers but was commissioned a second lieutenant in the Third Artillery. Soon he was assigned to Fort Monroe, where he met his first wife, Sally Archer, daughter of the post physician, Dr. Robert Archer. They were married in the spring of 1837 and eventually had five children.

Chances of promotion in the regular army being few, Anderson reentered civilian life when Colonel Claude Crozet, then supervising the construction of the Valley Turnpike, offered him a position as assistant state engineer. Anderson accepted, and in September 1837 he and Sally settled in Staunton, Virginia. He remained with Crozet until 1841.

A Whig by temperament, Anderson believed that the state should invest in internal improvements. His enthusiasm led him to join the commercial convention movement, in which he met the officials of the ailing Tredegar Iron Works. Each saw opportunity in the other, and after negotiations, Anderson was appointed commercial agent in 1841.

As a result of the panic of 1837, the demand for railroad iron had declined and with it the fortunes of the company. Anderson looked to the federal government and the Department of Ordnance in particular for contracts. This sound business decision kept the company alive. By 1848 Anderson had borrowed $125,000, bought out the old owners, formed new partnerships, and was named head of the Tredegar. From then on the Tredegar Iron Works was also referred to as J. R. Anderson and Company.

Anderson cut costs where he could. One way, or so he thought, was to hire slaves. This practice did not result in a substantial savings, but it pricked the ire of white workers, who walked out on strike in 1847. Anderson fired the lot, stating that these men were stabbing a knife into the heart of the slave system. All of Richmond supported him, and the strike ended with the white workers defeated.

Even though Anderson maintained a complementary relationship with the navy and war departments, he refused to accept some of the latest technology offered. The Rodman method for casting heavy ordnance, for example, he rejected out of hand, resulting in the loss of a $20,000 government contract in 1859. In addition to having doubts about the procedure, his company would have to invest heavily in retooling in order to produce the weapons now demanded by Secretary of War John B. Floyd. Anderson held to this position until 1864, when, though too late to help the Confederacy, he reluctantly began to cast heavy ordnance with this method.

Anderson was a businessman above all else, and his company had customers throughout the country. The antislavery movement, though, poisoned his hopes for sectional peace. He began to view everything outside the South as corrupt, and by the time the states began to secede, he was a passionate supporter of the cause. Passion or not, he willingly sold ordnance to the federal government as well as making a handsome profit by selling shot and shell to the recently seceded state of South Carolina. Anderson could see that his company had much to gain from an independent South.

After the states of the upper South left the Union and joined the Confederacy, Anderson offered his services to the new nation. In August 1861 he requested a commission as a brigadier general from Secretary of War Leroy Pope Walker. Noting that three of his former classmates, Montgomery C. Meigs, John W. Phelps, and William T. Sherman, had been commissioned brigadiers in the "Army of the Enemy," he surmised that it would be proper for him to receive the same consideration in the Confederate army. Besides, he had raised a battalion among the workers at the Tredegar and had offered its services to the government. He was commissioned, placed in command of the District of the Cape Fear, and stationed in Wilmington, North Carolina. For a short time he was commander of the Department of North Carolina.

During the Peninsula campaign, Anderson's command was ordered to the defenses of Richmond. During the Seven Days battles, he saw action at Beaver Dam Creek and Frayser's Farm, where he received a head wound that put him out of action for a few days. On 19 July 1862 Anderson, now fully recovered, tendered his resignation to Adjutant and Inspector General Samuel Cooper (1798–1876). It was not the wound that forced his resignation, however, but the conditions at the Tredegar.

The contributions of J. R. Anderson and Company to the Confederacy were immense. The company was the largest supplier of cannon and other war matériel to the Confederate government. Between 1861 and 1865 Tredegar produced over 1,000 cannon for the army and virtually all of the armor plate for Confederate ironclads. The production of siege and field seacoast ordnance continued throughout the war. The Confederate government was not the only customer though, for with the war came increased demands on the South's railroads. Once again Anderson and Company began to make rails. It sold more than $300,000 (Confederate) worth of rails to the Virginia Central Railroad alone.

At Anderson's request, the Confederate War Department willingly assigned soldiers who had experience in iron work to the company, and even though the government and Anderson disagreed over prices, he usually received a profit of between 20 and 25 percent of the cost of production. The first year of the war saw Anderson and Company earn a profit of 100 percent and in 1862 70 percent. Reasoning that a diversification of investment in additional profit-making enterprises was needed, Anderson invested in cotton and blockade running. The profits from these ventures remained in England. The commodities Anderson acquired for import were not ones designed to improve either production or quality at the Tredegar, for he imported consumer goods designed for quick sale and fat profit. He reasoned that the continued success of his company was inextricably joined with that of the Confederacy, and therefore, the profits from blockade running did not negate his patriotism.

After Richmond fell to the Union army, Anderson quickly requested a meeting with President Lincoln. On 4 April 1865 he asked the president for a pardon, stating that he headed a committee whose purpose it was to bring Virginia back into the Union. After Lee surrendered, however, this movement lost its momentum. Anderson's request was not without motive. The Federals had confiscated his property, and he feared that they would not return it. Help came when Major General Henry Halleck pressed the Ordnance Department to allow the Tredegar to repair damaged ordnance, and in May 1865 the company was once again operating.

Anderson petitioned the less conciliatory Andrew Johnson for amnesty in June 1865. Realizing that he would have to make a good case for himself, Anderson denied that he had anything to do with Virginia seceding. Further, he indicated that he had been "called" into the army and stayed only a few months and that he had not held an office in the Confederate government. The facts were distorted, but with the aid of Governor Francis H. Pierpont, Anderson was given amnesty and had his property restored. With the assets from his blockade-running enterprises, Anderson resumed business.

The Tredegar Iron Works continued to do well until the panic of 1873. With its resources seriously depleted and with the advent of steel as the new building material, the company could no longer compete on the national level. It continued to make iron for a smaller market, however. After the death of his first wife, Anderson married Mary Evans Pegram, sister of General John Pegram. (The date of his second marriage is unknown.) He died at Isles of Shoals, New Hampshire, where he had gone to restore his health.

• Manuscript sources related to Anderson may be consulted among the holdings of the National Archives and Records Administration. Record group 94, Records of the Adjutant General's Office, contains Anderson's application to the U.S. Military Academy and his amnesty petition. The scope of involvement of Anderson and the Tredegar Iron Works with the Confederate government lies in record group 109, War Department Collection of Confederate Records, including letters received by the secretary of war as well as letters received by the adjutant and inspector general. In addition, Anderson's brief career as a Confederate general is capsuled in record group 109, Compiled Military Service Records, General and Staff Officers. The best study of Anderson and the Tredegar Iron Works is Charles B. Dew, *Ironmaker to the Confederacy: Joseph R. Anderson and the Tredegar Iron Works* (1966). James I. Robertson, "The Boy Artillerist, Letters of Colonel William Pegram, C.S.A.," *Virginia Magazine of History and Biography* 98 (Apr. 1990): 221–60, corrects the longheld belief that Anderson married Pegram's daughter. An obituary is in the *Richmond Dispatch*, 8 Sept. 1892.

MICHAEL T. MEIER

ANDERSON, Larz (15 Aug. 1866–13 Apr. 1937), diplomat and philanthropist, was born in Paris, France, the son of Nicholas Longworth Anderson, a highly decorated Civil War officer, and Elizabeth Coles Kilgour. Anderson grew up in a socially prominent and public-spirited Virginia and Ohio family known primarily for its military exploits and philanthropy. His notable forebears included soldier George Rogers Clark; explorer William Clark (1770–1838); Nicholas Longworth (1782–1863), the first millionaire in the Northwest Territory; and Robert Anderson, who surrendered Fort Sumter, South Carolina, in the opening skirmish of the Civil War. Larz Anderson spent his early years in Cincinnati, Europe, and Washington, D.C. He prepared for college at Phillips Exeter Academy in Exeter, New Hampshire, and in 1888 received his A.B. from Harvard College.

After graduation, Anderson and a friend celebrated with a trip around the world. On his return to the United States, in the winter of 1889–1890 he worked briefly in the office of a New York East India trader before entering Harvard Law School. He had barely completed his first year there when one of his father's friends, Robert Todd Lincoln, the American minister to the Court of St. James, requested that young Anderson come to London and take the post of second secretary of the U.S. legation. As second secretary, Anderson assisted with the daily business of the legation. Handsome and impeccably mannered, he also was required to attend a dizzying array of social events and to mingle regularly with England's governing class and literati.

After Democrat Grover Cleveland became president in 1893, he named former secretary of state Thomas F. Bayard as the first U.S. ambassador to Great Britain and kept Anderson on as second secretary of the American embassy. A year later Anderson was posted to Rome as first secretary under Ambassador Wayne MacVeagh. In addition to his administrative and social functions, Anderson sought to bolster MacVeagh's effort to maintain good relations with Italy after a spate of lynchings of Italians in the state of Louisiana. In 1896, after a mob killed three Italians awaiting trial for murder in Holmesville, Louisiana, Anderson took part in delicate negotiations that led to the payment of a $6,000 indemnity to the Italian government. Following MacVeagh's resignation in early 1897, Anderson acted as chargé d'affaires at the American embassy for more than two months until the arrival of the new ambassador. Anderson then left immediately for home to marry Isabel Weld Perkins, who had inherited a fortune of $17 million from her maternal grandfather, William Fletcher Weld, a shipping magnate. The couple had no children.

In the spring of 1898 Anderson volunteered for service in the Spanish-American War. He turned down an army commission as major, which he believed inappropriate for one without prior military experience, and accepted the lower rank of captain. He was also made assistant adjutant general and ultimately acting adjutant general on the staff of General George W. Davis, commander of the Second Division of the Second Army Corps at Fort Alger, Virginia. After three months of intense training under difficult conditions, Anderson was demobilized when the war ended.

Anderson and his wife spent most of the rest of their lives traveling the world, attending the charity balls and formal dinners of high society in Boston and Washington, and hosting many events themselves at "Weld," their Brookline, Massachusetts, country house, where they summered, and at the Florentine villa they built at 2118 Massachusetts Avenue in the nation's capital, where they often spent their winters. In their travels they collected much valuable art for their homes and flora for their extensive gardens.

Anderson, who had contributed financially to the successful presidential campaign of William Howard Taft in 1908, commenced a brief return to the world of diplomacy in 1910. He and his wife accompanied Secretary of War Jacob McGavock Dickinson and General Clarence Edwards on an official tour of the Philippines that also took in China and Japan. In 1911 Taft offered Anderson a return to the foreign service as ambassador to Germany. Out of a personal disdain for German militarism and authoritarianism, Anderson turned down the post in Berlin and instead replaced Charles Page Bryan as minister to Belgium. In Brussels he utilized some of the many international contacts he had made over the years to convince the Belgian State Railways to end discrimination against American crude oil in violation of a Belgian-American tariff agreement.

In the fall of 1912 Taft appointed Anderson ambassador to Japan. However, Taft's defeat by Democrat Woodrow Wilson in the presidential election caused Anderson's stay in Tokyo to end after only three months. Upon the change of administration, Anderson resigned and returned to his life of leisure, which was interrupted in 1914 by the coming of World War I. He soon immersed himself in relief activities in Washington and Boston. He served as honorary chairman of the New England Belgian Relief Committee and was a member and officer of the National Belgian Relief Committee, the New England Italian Relief Committee, and the Red Cross Council of the District of Columbia. His wife was even more heavily involved with relief chores, working in the Red Cross canteen in France and in hospitals on the Belgian and French fronts in 1917. The Anderson home in Washington became the Belgian mission in the United States, housed French officers, and was often given over for use by the Red Cross and the Belgian relief effort.

Beyond diplomacy and their energetic participation in the social scene, the Andersons were best known for their philanthropy. Phillips Exeter, Harvard, and Boston University were regular recipients of Anderson donations. Their largest single gift was a contribution of $200,000 to Harvard for the construction of the Nicholas Longworth Anderson Bridge connecting the university's Cambridge campus with its playing fields across the Charles River in Boston. The Andersons' Washington home ultimately became the headquarters of the national Society of the Cincinnati, and Weld, which garaged the Andersons' thirty-one cars (dating back to 1898), became an auto museum.

Anderson's personal papers, edited by his wife (an accomplished author of travel books and works for children) and published in 1940 as *Larz Anderson: Letters and Journals of a Diplomat*, are a chronicle of a bygone age of aristocratic pomp and diplomatic civility. Pleasant descriptions of balls, receptions, and hobnobbing with royalty in Europe and Japan take up most of the volume's pages. References to diplomatic intrigue and high politics are scarce. Though not a major figure of his generation, Anderson was charming, efficient, patriotic, and generous. His contemporary William Cameron Forbes characterized Anderson as "the finished and polished product of what was best in our civilization." Anderson died in White Sulphur Springs, West Virginia.

• In addition to Anderson's published letters and journals, short autobiographical articles can be found in the periodic *Reports* of the Harvard class of 1888. Anderson's communications with the State Department from Belgium are in *Foreign Relations of the United States, 1912* (1919). The Quinquennial File in the Harvard University Archives has newspaper clippings on Anderson's life and career. Edgar Erskine Hume, *Captain Larz Anderson, Minister to Belgium and Ambassador to Japan, 1866–1937* (1938), is a memoir reprinted by the Society of the Cincinnati of Virginia from its *Minutes* of 1937. Obituaries are in the *Boston Herald* and the *New York Times*, both 14 Apr. 1937.

RICHARD H. GENTILE

ANDERSON, Leroy (29 June 1908–18 May 1975), composer, was born in Cambridge, Massachusetts, the son of Brewer Anton Anderson, a postal employee and amateur mandolin player, and Anna Margareta Johnson, a church organist. Both parents had immigrated to the United States from Sweden as young children. Leroy picked up Swedish by listening to his parents speak at home, and he learned to play the organ and piano while sitting in his mother's lap. Although he studied organ with Henry Gideon, his principal instrument was the double bass, which he studied with the Boston Symphony's Gaston Dufresne.

In the fall of 1925 Anderson entered Harvard University as a music major, where he studied composition with Walter Piston and briefly with visiting professor George Enescu. In later life, Anderson credited Piston with teaching him "how to be objective" and Enescu with teaching him "craftsmanship." While at Harvard, Anderson played trombone in and eventually directed the Harvard University Marching Band. Anderson graduated from Harvard magna cum laude and Phi Beta Kappa in 1929 and earned an M.A. in music in 1930. After two unsuccessful attempts to secure a Paine Traveling Fellowship in order to study with Nadia Boulanger in Paris, he began work on a Ph.D. in Harvard's German Department, majoring in Scandinavian languages.

While pursuing his doctorate in the early 1930s, Anderson supported himself as a freelance musician, conductor, and arranger, most notably for dance bands under Ruby Newman's management. In 1936 he wrote the *Harvard Fantasy*, an arrangement of Harvard songs for Arthur Fiedler, the conductor of the Boston Pops. At Fiedler's request Anderson subsequently submitted an original composition intended as "a little encore number, à la Fiedler," *Jazz Pizzicato* (1938) for pizzicato string orchestra. Anderson himself conducted the work's premiere on 23 May 1938. Its successful reception encouraged Fiedler to commission a companion piece, *Jazz Legato* (1939), so that he could record both numbers on one side of a 78-rpm record.

By this time Anderson had given up work on his doctorate, devoting himself full time to composition and arranging. In 1942 he married Eleanor Jane Firke; they had four children. Anderson served in the military from 1942 to 1946, first as a translator and interpreter in Iceland, then as chief of the Scandinavian Desk in Washington, D.C. From 1946 to 1949 the Andersons lived in Brooklyn, New York, and in 1949 they settled permanently in Woodbury, Connecticut.

Even during World War II Anderson continued to compose. In response to a request from Fiedler for music for a Boston Pops' Army Night on 28 May 1945, he wrote *Promenade* and *The Syncopated Clock*. After the war Anderson became a principal arranger for the Boston Pops, arranging medleys from *South Pacific*,

Annie Get Your Gun, and other Broadway shows. In 1955 he arranged three *Suites of Carols* for brass choir, string orchestra, and woodwind ensemble, respectively. Anderson also provided the Pops with a steady supply of two-to-four-minute original compositions, including *Fiddle-Faddle* (1947) for strings, *Saraband* (1948), *Sleigh Ride* (1948), *A Trumpeter's Lullaby* (1949), *The Typewriter* (1950), *The Waltzing Cat* (1950), and *Blue Tango*, *China Doll*, *Horse and Buggy*, *Belle of the Ball*, *The Penny-Whistle Song*, and *Plink, Plank, Plunk!* (all 1951).

Two events catapulted Anderson to national acclaim in the early 1950s: in 1950 WCBS–New York selected *Syncopated Clock* as the theme song to *The Late Show*; and in 1951 his recording of *Blue Tango* sold over a million copies and became the first instrumental work to make it to the top of the Hit Parade. Reflecting on the success of *Blue Tango*, Anderson said, "The whole thing was completely unbelievable to me, because the kind of music I write was not popular music, it was concert music." The concurrent growth of pops concerts around the nation furthered Anderson's popularity, and a 1953 study revealed him as the American composer whose works were most frequently performed by American orchestras, ahead of George Gershwin, Aaron Copland, and Samuel Barber.

In 1951 Anderson returned to active duty to aid intelligence in the Korean War. After his release in 1952 he continued to write miniatures for the Boston Pops, including *The Sandpaper Ballet* and *Bugler's Holiday* (both 1954). In 1953 Anderson composed his only large orchestral work: the three-movement Concerto in C for Piano and Orchestra, premiered in Chicago on 18 July 1953 by Eugene List and the Grant Park Symphony, with Anderson conducting. Dissatisfied with the concerto, Anderson withdrew the work after a few performances. After his death, however, his family allowed it to be revived, and the concerto was reintroduced in 1989 in Toronto by conductor Erich Kunzel and pianist William Tritt.

On 11 October 1958 Anderson's one musical comedy, *Goldilocks* (book by Walter and Jean Kerr; lyrics by the Kerrs with Joan Ford), opened at New York's Lunt-Fontanne Theatre. The show was directed by Walter Kerr and choreographed by Agnes de Mille. In contrast to most Broadway composers, Anderson orchestrated some of the music himself. Set in New York in 1913, motion picture director Max Grady (played by Don Ameche) forces Broadway star Maggie Harris (played by Elaine Stritch) to honor a contractual agreement to star in one of his films before she retires and marries wealthy George Randolph Brown (played by Russell Nype). Grady and Harris gradually fall in love, leaving Brown to be consoled by a chorus girl named Lois Lee (played by Pat Stanley). *Goldilocks* ran a disappointing 161 performances, closing on 23 February 1959. However, six of the show's numbers arranged by Anderson, including the romantic ballads "Save a Kiss" and "Shall I Take My Heart and Go," had continued success, as did the original cast album.

The popularity and tunefulness of Anderson's orchestral works prompted his publisher, Mills, to adapt some of them as songs, and in the early 1950s Anderson did so in collaboration with the well-known lyricist Mitchell Parrish. Most successful was their 1950 rendition of "Sleigh Ride," which became a Christmas favorite, though Anderson intended it simply as a winter landscape. Anderson especially liked the lyrics for "The Waltzing Cat," and his favorite performance was jazz singer Sarah Vaughan's rendition of "Serenata." He was posthumously inducted into the Songwriters Hall of Fame in New York in 1988.

In 1962 Anderson produced his final miniatures: *Arietta*, *Balladette*, *The Golden Years*, *Clarinet Candy*, *Home Stretch*, and *The Captains and the Kings*. By and large this later music had much less success than his earlier, more picturesque scores. Anderson's last work was a 1974 arrangement of music from Gershwin's *Girl Crazy*. He died in Woodbury.

Distinguished by fine workmanship, rhythmic verve, and a sweet, ingratiating humor, Anderson's style derived largely from that of Gershwin, Richard Rodgers, and other popular American song composers, but it also showed the influence of Piston's elegant wit. Anderson's colorful orchestrations (for example his use of the whip, sleigh bells, and trumpet "horse whinny" in "Sleigh Ride") often suggest vivid pictures. On two occasions he used nontraditional instruments for such purposes: a typewriter in *The Typewriter* and sandpaper in *The Sandpaper Ballet*.

Anderson essentially created a new genre: the popular contemporary orchestral miniature. He himself described his music as "concert music with a pop quality." His work was featured not only in pops concerts but also in radio, television, and Muzak, making his music very familiar to millions of people who would not have recognized his name. As a master of light classical music, Anderson played a role in twentieth-century America somewhat comparable to that of Johann Strauss, Jr., in late nineteenth-century Austria and Germany. This comparison would hardly have troubled him: on the contrary, he recognized that Strauss stood alongside Johannes Brahms and Richard Wagner as one of the best-remembered musicians of that epoch.

• Anderson's papers and scores, including taped interviews, are at Yale University. The most extended published piece on Anderson is the chapter "Songs without Words: The Orchestral Miniatures of Leroy Anderson" in Howard Pollack, *Harvard Composers: Walter Piston and His Students, from Elliott Carter to Frederic Rzewski* (1992). See also Eliot Spalding, "Leroy Anderson," *Harvard Magazine*, July–Aug. 1993, p. 38. For information on *Goldilocks* see the *Goldilocks* files of the Theater Department, New York Public Library at Lincoln Center; and George Wright Briggs, Jr., "Leroy Anderson on Broadway: Behind-the-Scene Accounts of the Musical *Goldilocks*," *American Music* 3, no. 3 (1985): 329–36.

HOWARD POLLACK

ANDERSON, Margaret (24 Nov. 1886–19 Oct. 1973), editor and author, was born Margaret Carolyn Anderson in Indianapolis, Indiana, the daughter of Arthur Aubrey Anderson and Jessie Shortridge. Anderson's father was a railway executive who provided a comfortable middle-class existence for his wife and three daughters. Anderson, whose chief interest as a young woman was music and literature, was soon regarded as the rebel of the family. After three years at Western College for Women in Ohio, she dropped out and made her way to Chicago, hoping to find work as a writer. After various stints as a bookstore clerk, print assistant, and part-time critic, Anderson decided to start her own literary journal. With little money but a great deal of enthusiasm and support from friends, Anderson founded the avant-garde *Little Review* in March 1914.

The *Little Review* was established at a critical moment in the cultural history of Chicago. The city was undergoing a literary revival known as the Chicago Renaissance. Writers such as Sherwood Anderson, Floyd Dell, Theodore Dreiser, Maxwell Bodenheim, and Ben Hecht were creating works designed to attack the dominance that nineteenth-century conservatism still had in art, politics, and moral values. Friends of Anderson, these writers joined her in making Chicago the vortex of early twentieth-century modernism.

Because of her interest in political radicalism, Anderson published articles by anarchist Emma Goldman as well as critiques of Victorian views of gender and sexuality. Her 1915 article, "Mrs. Ellis's Failure," criticized Edith Ellis, the wife of sexologist Havelock Ellis, for not addressing and defending modern views on homosexuality. Anderson's article has been cited as the "earliest defense of homosexuality by a lesbian in the United States" (Jonathan Katz, *Gay/Lesbian Almanac* [1983]).

Two years after launching the *Little Review*, Anderson met Jane Heap, known in Chicago's art circles for her short hair, men's clothing, and provocative comments. Heap became coeditor of the *Little Review*. A native of Kansas, she taught art and was involved in Maurice Browne's Little Theater. Upon meeting Heap, Anderson was instantly mesmerized. "Here," she wrote later in *My Thirty Years War* (1930), "was my obsession—the special human being."

In 1917 Anderson and Heap moved the *Little Review* to New York City to make the journal, in Anderson's words, "an international concern." The pair were tremendously successful; their new foreign editor, Ezra Pound, provided much material from artists abroad, including Ford Maddox Ford, Wyndham Lewis, and James Joyce. Beginning in 1918 Anderson and Heap published installments of Joyce's new novel, *Ulysses*. After three years of struggle with the U.S. Post Office the two women were charged with obscenity and convicted in 1921. They were fined $100 and released on the guarantee they would stop publishing excerpts from the novel. Their attorney, John Quinn, defended Anderson and Heap, although his personal correspondence revealed disgust with their lesbianism.

After the trial the *Little Review* was published sporadically, often appearing as a quarterly, and by the late 1920s less frequently. Financial problems, new interests, and the unraveling of the relationship between Anderson and Heap all contributed to the journal's demise in 1929. Anderson, in the meantime, became involved with Georgette Leblanc, a Parisian opera singer and the former mistress of Belgian poet and playwright Maurice Maeterlinck.

Anderson's life took a dramatic turn when she was introduced to the theosophy of Russian mystic George Gurdjieff. Gurdjieff's system of the "Fourth Way" maintains that all human beings are in a state of sleep and can only achieve true consciousness through a series of exercises, disciplines, and shocks. Anderson became an enthusiastic student of Gurdjieff. She traveled to France to study at Gurdjieff's Harmonious Institute for the Development of Man near Fontainebleau. Anderson later wrote about her spiritual quest in *The Unknowable Gurdjieff* (1962). Anderson spent the next years writing three autobiographies: *My Thirty Years War* (1930), *The Fiery Fountains* (1951), and *The Strange Necessity* (1969), along with *The Little Review Anthology* (1953) and an autobiographical lesbian novel, "This Thing Called Love," which could not find a publisher until 1996, when it was released by Naiad Press as *Forbidden Fires*.

Anderson lived with Leblanc in Le Cannet, France, until the latter's death of breast cancer in 1941. Anderson returned to the United States in 1942 and became involved in a long-term relationship with Dorothy Caruso, widow of Enrico, until Caruso's death, also of cancer, in 1955. Anderson returned to Le Cannet, where she spent her remaining years writing her last books and keeping up a voluminous correspondence. Her close friends in France during this period included Janet Flanner and her partner, Solita Solano, who edited Anderson's books. Anderson died in Cannes.

Anderson was an important figure in the advent of literary modernism in the twentieth century. She not only advanced the work of innovative Americans but exposed the United States to the latest in European art and letters. Besides Joyce and Pound, she published Gertrude Stein, Djuna Barnes, Hart Crane, Amy Lowell, H.D., William Carlos Williams, and T. S. Eliot. Her uncompromising stance in both her career as an editor and her life as a feminist and lesbian has led to a renewed scholarly interest in her.

• Anderson's letters are in the Allen Tanner Collection, University of Texas, Austin; the Flanner-Solano Collection, Library of Congress; the *Little Review* Archive, University of Wisconsin, Milwaukee; the Amy Lowell Collection, Houghton Library, Harvard; and the Florence Reynolds–Jane Heap Collection, University of Delaware. Her three autobiographies give us the best insight to the enthusiastic nature of her personality. *Beyond My Imagining*, a short documentary film about Anderson's career, was nominated for an Academy Award in 1993. Two dissertations provide in-depth studies of her career as an editor: Jackson Bryer, "A Trial-Track for Racers: Margaret C. Anderson and the *Little Review*" (Ph.D. diss., Univ. of Wisconsin, Milwaukee, 1965); and Holly Baggett, "Aloof from Natural Laws: Margaret C. Anderson and the *Little Review*, 1914–1929" (Ph.D. diss., Univ. of Delaware, 1992). For a history of literary Chicago in Anderson's time, see Robert M. Crunden, *American Salons: Encounters with European Modernism, 1885–1917* (1993). Her obituary appears in the *New York Times*, 20 Oct. 1973.

HOLLY A. BAGGETT

ANDERSON, Marian (17 Feb. 1897–8 Apr. 1993), contralto, was born in Philadelphia, Pennsylvania, the daughter of John Berkeley Anderson, a refrigerator room employee at the Reading Terminal Market, an ice and coal dealer, and a barber, and Anne (also seen as "Annie" and "Anna," maiden name unknown), a former schoolteacher. John Anderson's various jobs provided only a meager income, and after his death, before Marian was a teenager, her mother's income as a laundress and laborer at Wannamaker Department Store was even less. Yet, as Anderson later recalled, neither she nor her two younger sisters thought of themselves as poor. When Marian was about eight her father purchased a piano from his brother; she proceeded to teach herself how to play it and became good enough to accompany herself. Also as a youngster, having seen a violin in a pawn shop window, she became determined to purchase it and earned the requisite $4 by scrubbing her neighbors' steps. She attempted to teach herself the violin as well but discovered that she had little aptitude for the instrument.

Anderson joined the children's choir of Union Baptist Church at age six. Noticing her beautiful voice and her ability to sing all the parts, the choir director selected her to sing a duet for Sunday school and later at the regular morning service; this was her first public appearance. Later she joined the senior choir and her high school chorus, where occasionally she was given a solo.

While she was still in high school, Anderson attempted to enroll at a local music school but was rejected with the curt statement, "We don't take Colored." She applied and was accepted to the Yale University School of Music, but a lack of finances prevented her from enrolling. Although she was not the product of a conservatory, Anderson was vocally prepared by Mary Saunders Patterson, Agnes Reifsnyder, Giuseppe Boghetti, and Frank La Forge. Over the years she was coached by Michael Raucheisen and Raimond von zur Mühlen, and she also worked briefly (in London) with Amanda Aldridge, daughter of the famous black Shakespearean actor Ira F. Aldridge. Boghetti, however, had the greatest pedagogical influence.

Anderson's accompanists (with whom she enjoyed excellent relationships) were African Americans Marie Holland and William "Billy" King (who for a period doubled as her agent), Finnish pianist Kosti Vehanen, and German pianist Franz Rupp. Between 1932 and 1935 she was represented by the Arthur Judson Agency; from 1935 through the remainder of her professional life, the great impresario Sol Hurok.

One of the happiest days of Anderson's life was when she called Wannamaker to notify her mother's supervisor that Anne Anderson would not be returning to work. On another very happy occasion, in the late 1920s, she was able to assist in purchasing a little house for her mother in Philadelphia. Her sister Alyce shared the house; her other sister, Ethel, lived next door with her son James DePreist, who became a distinguished conductor.

For many, including critics, an accurate description of Anderson's singing voice presented challenges. Because it was nontraditional, many simply resorted to the narrowly descriptive "Negroid sound." Others, however, tried to be more precise. Rosalyn Story, for example, has described Anderson's voice as "earthy darkness at the bottom . . . clarinet-like purity in the middle, and . . . piercing vibrancy at the top. Her range was expansive—from a full-bodied D in the bass clef to a brilliant high C" (p. 38). Kosti Vehanen, recalling the first time he heard Anderson's "mysterious" voice, wrote, "It was as though the room had begun to vibrate, as though the sound came from under the earth. . . . The sound I heard swelled to majestic power, the flower opened its petals to full brilliance; and I was enthralled by one of nature's rare wonders" (p. 22). Reacting to his first encounter with the voice Sol Hurok wrote, "Chills danced up my spine . . . I was shaken to my very shoes" (Story, p. 47).

In 1921 Anderson, who was already a well-known singer at church-related events, won the National Association of Negro Musicians (NANM) competition. Believing that she was ready for greater public exposure she made her Town Hall (New York City) debut in 1924. Disappointed by the poor attendance and by her own performance, she considered giving up her aspirations for a professional career. The following year, however, she outcompeted 300 other singers to win the National Music League competition, earning a solo appearance with the New York Philharmonic at Lewisohn Stadium.

In 1926, with financial assistance from the Julius Rosenwald Fund, Anderson departed for Europe for further musical study. After returning to the United States, she gave her first Carnegie Hall concert in 1930. That same year she gave her first European concert, in Berlin, and toured Scandinavia. In 1931 alone she gave twenty-six concerts in fifteen states. Between 1933 and 1935 she toured Europe; one of her appearances was at the Mozarteum in Salzburg, where the renowned conductor Arturo Toscanini uttered the memorable line, "Yours is a voice such as one hears once in a hundred years" (*My Lord, What a Morning*, p. 158). Another exciting experience took place in the home of noted composer Jean Sibelius in Finland. After hearing Anderson sing, he uttered, "My roof is too low for you," then canceled the previously ordered coffee and requested champagne. Sibelius also honored Anderson by dedicating his composition *Solitude* to her.

Anderson's second Town Hall concert, arranged by Hurok and performed on 30 December 1935, was a huge success. A one-month tour of the Soviet Union was planned for the following year but ended up lasting for three months. She was a box office sensation as well in Europe, Africa, and South America.

Anderson's seventy U.S. concerts in 1938 continues as the longest and most-extensive tour in concert history for a singer. Between November 1939 and June 1940 she appeared in more than seventy cities, giving ninety-two concerts. Her native Philadelphia presented her with the Bok Award in 1941, accompanied by $10,000. She used the funds to establish the Marian Anderson Award, which sponsors "young talented men and women in pursuit of their musical and educational goals."

During 1943, a very special year, Anderson made her eighth transcontinental tour and married architect Orpheus H. Fisher of Wilmington, Delaware. The marriage was childless. In 1944 she appeared at the Hollywood Bowl, where she broke a ten-year attendance record. In 1946, 600 editors in the United States and Canada, polled by *Musical America*, named Anderson radio's foremost woman singer for the sixth consecutive year. Anderson completed a South American tour in 1951 and made her television debut on the "Ed Sullivan Show" the following year. Her first tour of Japan was completed in 1953, the same year that she also toured the Caribbean, Central America, Israel, Morocco, Tunisia, France, and Spain.

Anderson sang the national anthem at the inauguration of President Dwight D. Eisenhower in 1957, and between 14 September and 2 December of that year she traveled 39,000 miles in Asia, performing twenty-four concerts under the auspices of the American National Theater and Academy and the U.S. State Department. Accompanying Anderson was journalist Edward R. Murrow, who filmed the trip for his "See It Now" television series. The program, which aired on 30 December, was released by RCA Records under the title *The Lady from Philadelphia*. In 1958 Anderson served as a member of the U.S. delegation to the General Assembly of the United Nations. Three years later she sang the national anthem at the inauguration of President John F. Kennedy, appeared in the new State Department auditorium, and gave another concert tour of Europe. Her first tour of Australia was a highlight of 1962.

In early 1964 Hurok announced Marian Anderson's Farewell Tour, beginning at Constitution Hall on 24 October 1964 and ending on Easter Sunday 1965 at Carnegie Hall. The momentousness of the event was reflected in Hurok's publicity: "In any century only a handful of extraordinary men and women are known to countless millions around the globe as great artists and great persons. . . . In our time there is Marian Anderson." After the tour she made several appearances as narrator of Aaron Copland's *A Lincoln Portrait*, often with her nephew James DePreist at the podium.

Although in her own lifetime Anderson was described as one of the world's greatest living contraltos, her career was nonetheless hindered by the limitations placed on it because of racial prejudice. Two events in particular that illustrate the pervasiveness of white exclusiveness and African-American exclusion—even when it came to someone of Anderson's renown—serve as historical markers not only of her vocal contributions but also of the magnificence of her bearing, which in both instances turned two potential negatives into resounding positives.

In 1938, following her numerous international and national successes, Hurok believed it was time for Anderson to appear in the nation's capital, at a major hall. She had previously appeared in Washington, D.C., at churches, schools, civic organization meetings, and at Howard University, but she had not appeared at the district's premiere auditorium, Constitution Hall. At that time, when negotiations began for a Marian Anderson concert to be given in 1939 at the Daughters of the American Revolution–owned hall, a clause appeared in all contracts that restricted the hall to "a concert by white artists only, and for no other purpose." Thus in February 1939 the American who had represented her country with honor across the globe was denied the right to sing at Constitution Hall simply because she was not white.

A great furor ensued, and thanks to the efforts of First Lady Eleanor Roosevelt and Secretary of the Interior Harold Ickes, the great contralto appeared the following Easter Sunday (9 Apr. 1939) on the steps of the Lincoln Memorial before an appreciative audience of 75,000. She began the concert by singing "America" and then proceeded to sing an Italian aria, Schubert's *Ave Maria*, and three Negro spirituals, "Gospel Train," "'Trampin,'" and "My Soul Is Anchored in the Lord." Notably, she also sang "Nobody Knows the Trouble I've Seen." Commemorating the 1939 Lincoln Memorial concert is a mural at the Interior Department; it was formally presented in 1943, the year that Anderson made her first appearance in Constitution Hall, by invitation of the Daughters of the American Revolution and benefiting United China Relief.

The second history-making event came on 7 January 1955, when Anderson made her debut at the Metropolitan Opera House in New York, becoming the first black American to appear there. Opera had always interested Anderson, who tells the story in her autobiography of a visit with the noted African-American baritone Harry T. Burleigh, during which she was introduced to and sang for an Italian gentleman. When she climbed the scale to high C, the man said to Burleigh, "Why sure she can do Aida," a traditionally black role. On her first trip to England, Anderson had visited a teacher who suggested that she study with her, guaranteeing that she would have her singing Aida within six months. "But I was not interested in singing Aida," Anderson wrote. "I knew perfectly well that I was a contralto, not a soprano. Why Aida?"

Anderson's pending debut at the Met was announced by the international press in October 1954. As educator-composer Wallace Cheatham later noted, the occasion called for the most excellent pioneer, "an artist with impeccable international credentials, someone highly respected and admired by all segments of the music community" (p. 6). At the time there was only one such individual, Marian Anderson. About Anderson's debut, as Ulrica in Verdi's *Un Ballo in Maschera* (The masked ball), *Time* magazine (17 Jan.

1955) reported that there were eight curtain calls. "She acted with the dignity and reserve that she has always presented to the public. . . . Her unique voice—black velvet that can be at once soft and dramatic, menacing and mourning—stirring the heart as always."

In addition to her other awards and honors, Anderson was a recipient of the Spingarn Medal (NAACP), the Handel Medallion (New York City), the Page One Award (Philadelphia Newspaper Guild), and the Brotherhood Award (National Conference of Christians and Jews), and she was awarded twenty-four honorary doctorates. She was cited by the governments of France, Finland, Japan, Liberia, Haiti, Sweden, and the Philippines. She was a member of the National Council on the Arts, was a recipient of the National Medal of Arts, and in 1978 was among the first five performers to receive the Kennedy Center Honors.

Several tributes were held in the last years of Anderson's life. In February 1977 the musical world turned out to recognize Anderson's seventy-fifth (actually her eightieth) birthday at Carnegie Hall. On 13 August 1989 a gala celebration concert took place in Danbury, Connecticut, to benefit the Marian Anderson Award. The concert featured recitalist and Metropolitan Opera star Jessye Norman, violinist Isaac Stern, and maestro Julius Rudel conducting the Ives Symphony Orchestra. Because Anderson's residence, "Marianna," was just two miles from the Charles Ives Center, where the concert was held, the 92-year-old grand "lady from Philadelphia" was in attendance. Educational television station WETA prepared a one-hour documentary, "Marian Anderson," which aired nationally on PBS on 8 May 1991. She died two years later in Portland, Oregon, where she had recently moved to live with her nephew, her only living relative.

Many actions were taken posthumously to keep Anderson's memory alive and to memorialize her many accomplishments. The 750-seat theater in the Aaron Davis Arts Complex at City College of New York was named in her honor on 3 February 1994. The University of Pennsylvania, as the recipient of her papers and memorabilia, created the Marian Anderson Music Study Center at the Van Pelt–Dietrich Library. Of course, the greatest legacy are the ones who came after. As concert and opera soprano Leontyne Price, one of the many beneficiaries of Anderson's efforts, said after her death, "Her example of professionalism, uncompromising standards, overcoming obstacles, persistence, resiliency and undaunted spirit inspired me to believe that I could achieve goals that otherwise would have been unthought of" (*New York Times*, 9 April 1993).

• Anderson's papers and memorabilia are housed at the Van Pelt–Dietrich Library at the University of Pennsylvania. Shortly before her death a birth certificate was located, verifying her year of birth as 1897 rather than the 1902, 1903, or 190? listed in various biographical sources. Her autobiography is *My Lord, What a Morning* (1956); several of her life philosophies are shared in Brian Lanker, *I Dream a World* (1989). Very complete entries are included in the *Biographical Dictionary of Afro-American and African Musicians*, ed. Eileen Southern (1982); *Black Women in America: An Historical Encyclopedia*, ed. Darlene Clark Hines et al. (1993); Donald Bogle, *Brown Sugar: Eighty Years of America's Black Female Superstars* (1980); Rosalyn Story, *And So I Sing* (1990); and Southern, *The Music of Black Americans: A History*, 2d ed. (1983). Of tremendous value is the biography by her early accompanist Kosti Vehanen, *Marian Anderson: A Portrait* (1941; repr. 1970). As a valuable reference, see Janet Sims, *Marian Anderson: An Annotated Bibliography and Discography* (1981). Wallace Cheatham's comments about Anderson's debut at the Metropolitan Opera House are included in his "Black Male Singers at the Metropolitan Opera," *Black Perspective in Music* 16, no. 1 (Spring 1988): 3–19. An excellent, front-page obituary is in the *New York Times*, 9 Apr. 1993. See also the appreciation by Joseph McLellan, "The Voice That Tumbled Walls," *Washington Post*, 9 Apr. 1993.

D. ANTOINETTE HANDY

ANDERSON, Martin Brewer (12 Feb. 1815–26 Feb. 1890), college president, was born in Brunswick, Maine, the son of Martin Anderson, a shipwright and schoolteacher, and Jane Brewer. During his youth, Anderson labored in a shipyard to augment the small family income and to save money for his education. His mother infused him with Baptist piety. Inspired by personal religious experience at age eighteen, Anderson went to the Baptist college in Waterville (now Colby College) in 1836, where he worked in various jobs to pay his way while studying the conventional, antebellum curriculum to prepare for the ministry. Upon graduating in 1840 with an A.B., he entered Newton Theological Institution in Massachusetts, but finding it a "dull, lonesome" place, he left after a year. Returning to his alma mater, Anderson served as an instructor from 1841 to 1843 and professor of rhetoric until 1850. Meanwhile, he met Elizabeth Gilbert, a woman from a prominent family in New York, and the two were married in 1848. They had no children.

Two years later Anderson became part-owner and editor of the *New York Recorder*, a Baptist weekly that soon gained influence in the denomination. The paper supported a group seeking to remove Madison University, a Baptist institution, from Hamilton to Rochester, New York. Madison (renamed Colgate University in 1890) remained in Hamilton despite these efforts. However, in 1850 a new institution was provisionally chartered and opened for instruction as the University of Rochester. A majority of Rochester's trustees, as well as five professors and some sixty students, had "emigrated" from Madison. By 1853 the enrollment exceeded 100, making the University of Rochester the second largest Baptist college in the country after Brown University. At that point, the three-year search to find a president ended with the appointment of Anderson, who agreed to leave his comfortable editorship provided that he would not be responsible for the finances of the university. With a president and healthy enrollments, the University of Rochester was permanently chartered in 1861.

Meanwhile, President Anderson molded the young institution in the form of an antebellum liberal arts college. By 1853 the émigré faculty from Madison University had set aside a progressive curriculum, offering electives and advanced scientific courses, that the trustees had laid out in 1850. The faculty's lead was then confirmed and extended by Anderson; as a typical "old-time" college president, he taught practically every course in the traditional required curriculum at some point and steadfastly opposed elective courses. In response to Ezra Cornell's famous 1868 proclamation that his new university would be a place "where any person can find instruction in any study," Anderson commented, "To attempt to make [an American college] a place where any man can pursue any course of study is to destroy its organization and defeat its real object." Like his views on curriculum, Anderson's approach to students was traditional. He felt that the president should have a personal relationship with each undergraduate. Of Harvard's reforming president Charles W. Eliot, Anderson observed with disapproval, "He never teaches the students and has not the least formative control over their minds or characters. He is really a sort of general manager with duties analogous to those of a superintendent or president of a railroad."

Anderson remained at the University of Rochester for thirty-five years, publishing numerous essays and the texts of his public lectures and lecture courses for undergraduates. During his long and successful tenure, he declined the presidencies of Cincinnati, Brown, Union, Michigan, and the original University of Chicago, as well as overtures about the presidencies of Vassar, Harvard, and the future New York University. Eventually, he became worn down by the load of teaching and especially the burden of alleviating the "pecuniary embarrassment" of the university, which he shouldered soon after his appointment notwithstanding the promise that the trustees would bear responsibility for finances. He also continued his denominational activity, serving as president of the American Baptist Home Mission Society in 1864 and president of the American Baptist Missionary Union from 1869 to 1872.

He became ill in 1877, but continued in office through 1888 by reducing his workload and taking vacations in Florida. In 1889 he and his wife retired to Lake Helen, Florida, where he died.

• Anderson's papers and lectures were compiled into William C. Morey, ed., *The Papers and Addresses of Martin B. Anderson, LL.D.* (2 vols., 1895). The best biographical treatment is Asahel C. Kendrick, *Martin B. Anderson, LL.D.: A Biography* (1895). This is supplemented by Arthur J. May, *A History of the University of Rochester 1850–1962* (1977), which is an abridged and undocumented version of the original, carefully annotated manuscript held in the library at the University of Rochester, where there is a collection of Anderson's papers.

BRUCE A. KIMBALL

ANDERSON, Mary (28 July 1859–29 May 1940), actress, was born Marie Antoinette Henry in Sacramento, California, the daughter of Charles Henry, an English gentleman, and Antonia Leugers, a Philadelphian of German descent. While Anderson was an infant, she moved with her family to Louisville, Kentucky, where her uncle, Father Anthony Müller, a Franciscan, lived. Her father enlisted as an officer in the Confederate army and rose to the rank of general before he was killed near Mobile, Alabama, in 1863. Four years later her mother married Dr. Hamilton Griffin.

Reared a steadfast Roman Catholic, Anderson attended the Ursuline Convent and the Academy of the Presentation Nuns. She was a poor student, however, and left school at age fourteen. Her stepfather, an amateur actor, encouraged her interest in acting and took her to see a performance by noted actor Edwin Booth. Although her mother disapproved, Griffin, through actor Henry Wouds, arranged for Anderson to meet the famous actress Charlotte Cushman, who advised the teenager to start "at the top." Impressed with Anderson's dramatic ability, Cushman suggested that she study with noted drama critic and teacher George Vandenhoff in New York City. On her return to Louisville, Anderson refused an offer to play Lady Anne in John McCullough's production of *Richard III*, preferring to wait for leading roles.

For over two years Anderson studied drama, especially Shakespeare's plays, and memorized possible roles. At the age of sixteen she was offered the leading role in a benefit performance of *Romeo and Juliet* at Macauley Theater in Louisville after the leading actress became ill. Her 27 November 1875 debut impressed the audience, the critics, and the management, who later offered her a week's engagement. She toured in the title role of Richard Lalor Sheil's *Evadne*, as Julia in *The Hunchback*, as Bianca in *Fazio*, and as Pauline in *The Lady of Lyons*. She barnstormed to St. Louis and New Orleans, where she gave such a triumphant performance as Meg Merrilies in *Guy Mannering* that an enthusiastic crowd of thousands escorted her to the railroad station. After performing in San Francisco and in several southern cities, she made her New York City debut on 12 November 1877 at the Fifth Avenue Theater, reprising her role in *The Lady of Lyons*. One of her most popular roles on the tour, Parthenia in Mrs. Lovell's *Ingomar*, also proved welcome in New York City. Despite a small setback in *Macbeth* at the National Theater in Washington, D.C. (1877)—she was considered too young for the role of Lady Macbeth—Anderson enjoyed unqualified success both on tour and in New York City over the next six years, including her Galatea in Sir William Sullivan's *Pygmalion and Galatea*.

Anderson debuted in London on 3 September 1883 in *Ingomar*, having been advised by American critic William Winter against competing with renowned and beloved English actresses in roles like that of Juliet. Winter assured her that London critics would praise her attempts to humanize Parthenia. His assessment proved accurate; her performance was highly acclaimed, and the play ran for ten months. Thereafter offered her choice of roles, she not only played Juliet, but also Galatea and later fulfilled a personal goal by performing at Stratford-upon-Avon as Rosalind in *As You Like It*. Anderson also created the role of Clarice in *Comedy and Tragedy*, a play written for her by Sir William S. Gilbert.

After another successful American tour in 1885, Anderson returned to London to star in dual roles—Hermione and Perdita in *The Winter's Tale*. Her portrayal of both the noble, womanly, tragic Hermione and the winsome, bright, youthful Perdita was a tour de force that impressed both fans and critics. The love scene between Perdita and Florizel was praised as the high point of the play. After a run of 166 performances, Anderson brought the production to the United States, where it was warmly received. The tour ended in 1889, however, in Washington, D.C., during the festivities accompanying the inauguration of President Benjamin Harrison (1833–1901), when Anderson collapsed onstage from exhaustion. She returned to London to rest. Retiring from the stage, in 1890 in Holly Hill, Hampstead, she married American attorney Antonio de Navarro; they had three children, one of whom died shortly after birth. During the next fifty-one years, she became a renowned hostess, entertaining notables such as Sir Edward Elgar, Sir James Barry, and Sir William Gilbert at her home in Broadway, Worcestershire.

Anderson interrupted her retirement during World War I to perform in benefits, reviving Clarice, Juliet, and Galatea to the delight of critics and fans in Manchester, Birmingham, Dublin, and Edinburgh. In 1911 she collaborated with Robert S. Hichens on a dramatization of his novel *The Garden of Allah* and brought her family to New York City for its opening, her final visit to the United States. She wrote two memoirs, *A Few Memories* (1896) and *A Few More Memories* (1936), before her death at home in Broadway, Worcestershire.

Anderson's classic beauty, great charm, superb acting ability, and rich contralto voice inspired such affection in her American fans that she was always referred to as "Our Mary" despite her long years abroad. Conservative in her choice of vehicles, she lent vivacity to the old-fashioned plays that consistently captivated her audiences. She remained a devoted Roman Catholic throughout her lifetime, returning in later years to musical interests inspired during her childhood in Louisville by her Franciscan uncle.

• For further information, see the Robinson Locke Collection of Dramatic Scrapbooks and Clippings, Lincoln Center Theater Collection, New York Public Library; Lewis C. Strang, *Famous Actresses of the Day in America* (1902); Henry Williams, *The "Queen of the Drama": Mary Anderson, Her Life on and off the Stage* (1885); Frederic Edward McKay and Charles Wingate, *Famous American Actors of Today* (1896); William Winter, *The Stage Life of Mary Anderson* (1886) and *Other Days* (1908); Phyllis Hartnoll, ed., *Oxford Companion to the Theater* (1967); and Lloyd Morris, *Curtain Time: The Story of the American Theater* (1953). An obituary is in the *New York Times*, 30 May 1940.

ELIZABETH R. NELSON

ANDERSON, Mary (27 Aug. 1872–29 Jan. 1964), labor leader and federal administrator, was born in Lidköping, Sweden, the daughter of Magnus Anderson and Matilda Johnson, farmers. She received her only formal education at a local Lutheran school. Inspired by letters from her older sister Anna who had moved to the United States, Mary and her sister Hilda traveled to Ludington, Michigan, in 1889. Sixteen years old when she arrived in America, Anderson struggled to learn English while she worked as a dishwasher and cook in a boardinghouse for lumber workers.

In 1892 Anderson moved to West Pullman near Chicago, Illinois, to live with her sister Anna and her husband. Unenthusiastic about housework but intent on finding job security and good wages, Anderson sought factory work. She worked briefly in a garment factory but became aware of the trade union movement only when she took a job as a stitcher at Schwab's, a large shoe factory, in 1894. Within months she became convinced that trade unionism was the only way to ensure fair treatment of labor. A few years later she joined the International Boot and Shoe Workers Union. A year after becoming a member she was elected president of the women stitchers' Local 94. Anderson was the only woman to sit on the executive board of the International Boot and Shoe Workers' Union and traveled to Boston twice a year to represent the women of the union; she was the only unpaid board member. Her local also elected her a delegate to the Chicago Federation of Labor, an organization she remained affiliated with for fifteen years.

After Schwab's went out of business, Anderson found that her work was never secure; frequently unjustly fired, she was underemployed or mistreated. Often in the face of management hostility, Anderson worked endlessly to ensure safe working conditions and fair practices in the shoemaking industry. As president of the Boot and Shoe Workers Union and a delegate to the Chicago Federation of Labor, Anderson traveled widely, forming alliances with other labor leaders and social reformers such as Jane Addams. As a result of her contacts she joined the Chicago branch of the Women's Trade Union League (WTUL) in 1905 and quickly devoted her efforts to organizing women workers.

The 1910 Chicago garment workers brought an end to Anderson's stitching career. The WTUL had worked with the striking women to secure the right to collective bargaining; in 1911 the firm of Hart, Schaffner & Marx agreed to establish an arbitration process. Asked to create the organization's new arbitration framework, WTUL's president, Margaret Dreier Robins, offered Anderson a full-time, salaried position organizing the women at the company's numerous locations and acting as a facilitator in the grievance process. She never regretted her decision to leave the factory to work for the WTUL, and she viewed her work on the Hart, Schaffner & Marx agreement as her greatest accomplishment.

For the next four years Anderson worked with the WTUL in many capacities, both nationally and in Chicago. Encouraged by reports that Illinois would grant suffrage to women, Anderson took her citizenship examination in 1915. At the same time, she traveled to mining districts to report on strikes and working conditions at the mines. Her reports attracted the attention of the United Mine Workers Union and further enhanced her reputation in the masculine world of the American labor movement. In 1916 she worked for the creation of a division for women in the Department of Labor; and although her articulate appeals to the Federation of Labor attracted the support of labor leader Samuel Gompers, the organization never openly supported the idea. Support from Gompers in his role as labor representative to the Committee on National Defense, however, combined with the increasing number of women in the wartime work force by 1918, led to the creation of the Women in Industry Service. Anderson was appointed assistant director of the service headed by Mary Van Kleeck.

In that position Anderson worked to establish labor standards for working women, including the enforcement of an eight-hour workday with a forty-hour week, no night work, and equal pay for men and women. Although these standards were not adopted before the war, they later became the official mandate of the Women's Bureau under Anderson. In 1919 Anderson and WTUL colleague Rose Schneiderman represented the National Women's Trade Union League at the labor meetings in conjunction with the Paris Peace Conference. The only women representing labor at the conference, their presence inspired the inclusion of women in future international labor discussions.

When Mary Van Kleeck resigned in 1919, Anderson became director of the Women in Industry Service. A year later the service was converted into a permanent division in the Department of Labor called the Women's Bureau, which (like the service) investigated working conditions for women and ensured that employers adhered to fair work standards. The establishment of a permanent division, in turn, ensured that the problems of working women would be addressed and cemented Anderson's growing reputation as an administrator.

Anderson enjoyed the support of women's organizations as well as the two Republican secretaries of labor in the 1920s, but the Women's Bureau came to be sharply challenged by an increasingly diverse women's movement. The appointment of Frances Perkins to secretary of labor in 1933 marked a change in the relationship between the department and the Women's Bureau that reflected personality conflicts as well as new ideas about labor law. Wrestling to keep the bureau's financial affairs separate from the department and trying to accommodate Perkins's new recruits, Anderson sensed a loss of ground. Yet she enjoyed the support of Franklin and Eleanor Roosevelt; the president appointed her chief of the U.S. delegation to the International Labor Organization in 1933 and then in 1937 adviser to the U.S. government delegate to the Technical Tripartite Conference on the textile industry.

World War II brought new responsibilities to the Women's Bureau. Although Anderson continued to conduct investigations and create standards, she soon found herself working closely with employers to ease the transition of women into the work force. She staunchly supported equal pay for equal work and protective legislation for women workers, and therefore she opposed the efforts of the National Women's party to affect an Equal Rights Amendment.

Anderson never married, explaining that marriage could not provide the security she needed. She saw the trade union movement as a way to arm working women with the means to achieve greater individual security. After she retired from the Women's Bureau in 1944, she continued to work for equal pay for equal work into the 1950s. She died in Washington, D.C. Directly responsible for the inclusion of women in trade union meetings and international conferences, Mary Anderson paved a path for modern American women in the labor movement and in government.

• Anderson's papers are in the Schlesinger Library, Radcliffe College. Her autobiography, *Woman at Work: The Autobiography of Mary Anderson as Told to Mary N. Winslow* (1951), richly evokes her ideas and achievements. For additional biographical information see Sister John Marie Daly, "Mary Anderson, Pioneer Labor Leader" (Ph.D. diss., Georgetown Univ., 1968), and Cecyle S. Neidle, *America's Immigrant Women* (1975). Cynthia Harrison, *On Account of Sex* (1988), explores the final years of Anderson's work at the Women's Bureau. An obituary is in the *New York Times*, 30 Jan. 1964.

JULIE LONGO
SANDRA VANBURKLEO

ANDERSON, Matthew (25 Jan. 1845–11 Jan. 1928), Presbyterian pastor, educator, and social reformer, was born in Greencastle, Pennsylvania, the son of Timothy Anderson and Mary Croog. One of fourteen children, he was raised in the comforts of a rural, middle-class home, less than thirty miles from historic Gettysburg. On a typical day of his youth, he faced the physical demands of farm life and experienced the movement back and forth between two cultures. One, dominated by commerce and materialism, was uncharacteristically open to the Andersons, who owned lumber mills and real estate at a time when most black Americans were dehumanized and disenfranchised by chattel slavery. The other was a culture defined by close family ties and Presbyterian piety. At home Matthew heard Bible stories and dramatic tales of runaway slaves; indeed, religious piety and the pursuit of racial freedom were dominant themes in his life. These early experiences inspired Anderson so deeply that, by the time he left Greencastle in 1863, he had decided on the ministry as his vocation. Study at Oberlin College was the first step toward serving his religious faith, his racial group, and his vision of social justice.

After graduation from Oberlin in 1874, Anderson entered Princeton Theological Seminary the same year. He became the institution's first African American in residence by refusing to live off-campus, which at that time was the custom for black American seminarians. This refusal to accommodate himself to segregationist practices was the first of many assertive acts against unjust social and church practices. Anderson completed his theological studies in 1877 and then spent two years in part-time pastoral assignments in New Haven, Connecticut, where he took courses at Yale Divinity School. It marked the end of his "supply" (temporary) work and formal academic training.

While traveling to the South to do missionary work in October 1879, Anderson stopped in Philadelphia to visit friends. It was, however, to be a permanent stop. On 17 August 1880 he married Caroline Virginia Still Wiley, daughter of civic leader William Still and later the mother of their two children. Caroline, known as "Carrie" to friends, distinguished herself professionally by becoming one of the first black women to graduate from the Women's Medical College of Philadelphia in 1878. Together, Matthew and Caroline raised a family, were active in church and civic affairs, and collaborated on many programs until she died in 1919. Anderson was remarried the following year to Blanche Williams, a long-time associate.

In 1880 Anderson founded the Berean Presbyterian Church; in 1884 he established the Berean Building and Loan Association, a bank that has never—not even during the 1929 stock market crash—closed its doors; and in 1899 he opened the Berean Manual Training and Industrial School. Each institution grew out of a need to provide services, skills, and support systems for the black community of Philadelphia during Reconstruction, when the country was being transformed from a slave-holding nation to a more pluralistic one. In addition, each institution bore the imprint of Caroline Anderson's medical training, whether in prenatal and vocational classes for women or in the establishment of nurseries she supervised within the Berean complex. Each of these institutions continued to thrive throughout the twentieth century.

Through the "Berean enterprise," his general name for the complex of institutions he established, Anderson continued a clergy tradition of activism within the African-American community in Philadelphia that had been established by African Methodist Episcopal bishop Richard Allen and Reverend Absalom Jones in the late eighteenth century. Like them, Anderson formulated ideas and plans for improving the lives of blacks in particular but without excluding others. The name Berean represented two known references in Anderson's life and work. One came from studying Christian history and the early importance of the ancient city of Berea in northern Syria. The other reference was to Berea, Ohio, where in 1872 Anderson, then an uncredentialed but self-proclaimed evangelist, was confronted by church people who rejected his spiritual enthusiasm. Anderson was also known for his civic and intellectual leadership, for example, as an active member from 1901 to 1910 in the Universal Peace Movement, a Quaker organization opposed to slavery and war, and in the Afro-American Presbyterian Council, an organization started in 1893 for social fellowship and inspiration among black Presbyterians.

Anderson's Berean enterprise stood out like a signpost at a time when the course of Reconstruction presented the most savage attacks on black Americans. In this setting, Anderson's initiatives bore added significance because they were taken at a time when the social order was undeniably antiblack and fervently racist. Moreover, the struggle for freedom, as Anderson saw it, was not simply removing sinful barriers of racial discrimination; it also meant replacing them with the pieties of religious, specifically Presbyterian, devotions. This was the ideal for Anderson, and the title of his only published book, *Presbyterianism: Its Relation to the Negro* (1899), symbolized his view of the interrelatedness of self and religion, in particular, the racial "self" as it defined the experiences of the black American. In the book's preface, Anderson outlined his work as a goal that would benefit all. He saw the doctrines of Presbyterianism as leading the oppressed black person into a state of "independence and decision of character necessary to enable him to act nobly and well his part as a man and a citizen of our great republic."

Another important illustration of his views is to be found in "A Private Investigation of Prevalent Conditions on the Panama Canal Zone," a report written in his seventy-fifth year in which Anderson continued to make personal statements about life events that, dominated by racial bigotry, contradicted positive (Presbyterian, he would say) human values. Anderson wrote the report while visiting the Canal Zone and traveling through much of the West Indies and Latin America in 1921. It was addressed to his Princeton seminary classmate and lifetime friend, the Reverend Francis Grimké, informing him of the pattern of color prejudice that he saw in the zone. Anderson characterized these discriminatory policies as a "prodigious blunder" that diminished the great technical achievement of the Panama Canal. It was not always secular prejudice, however, that Anderson witnessed and protested against.

Anderson became increasingly involved in the Presbyterian church's struggle to remain united after the Civil War, when some church policies toward the freed person threatened to divide blacks and whites, particularly in the church's debate over whether the Board of Home Missions and the Freedman's Board should remain separate organizations. Anderson believed that not enough money was being given to the Freedman's Board, and he eventually concluded that the two boards should be merged. Anderson's account of his role in this struggle is preserved in his book, in which he presents a record of his service as chairman of the Philadelphia Council of the Freedman's Board (1889–1890). This account describes how Anderson continually tried to raise the consciousness of the church's power structure not just once, but over a period of time, through written appeals and involvement in the church's regional and national meetings. Several subsequent publications funded by the Presbyterian church offer additional examples of Anderson's writing as the regional leader of Presbyterian clergy, most of whom were serving predominantly black congregations. By that time, Anderson was no longer just a local leader; he was spokesman for the protest against a national Presbyterian church policy that he and others believed violated the principles of the church's mission to the poor and diminished its potential for closing the gap between the races. He died in Philadelphia.

Through the development of the Berean Presbyterian Church, the Berean Bank, and the Berean School, and through other reform activities, Matthew Anderson, defender of his Presbyterian faith and an articulate witness for social justice, created a legacy of hope and opportunity while leaving a permanent mark on community development in Philadelphia and the nation.

• Few original materials of Anderson's exist. Princeton Theological Seminary, the Schomburg Center for Research in Black Culture, and the Blockson Collection of Temple University hold most of Anderson's publications. *Presbyterianism: Its Relation to the Negro* remains the most reliable source of information about Anderson's life and achievements. C. James Trotman's essays on Anderson in *American Presbyterians* 66, no. 1 (1988): 11–21, and in the *Princeton Seminary Bulletin* 9, no. 2 (1988): 143–155, discuss his life and work. An obituary is in the *Crisis* 35, no. 4 (Apr. 1928): 117.

C. JAMES TROTMAN

ANDERSON, Maxwell (15 Dec. 1888–28 Feb. 1959), playwright, was born James Maxwell Anderson on a farm near Atlantic, Pennsylvania, the son of William Lincoln Anderson, a lumberman and later a railroad fireman and Baptist preacher, and Charlotte Perrimela Stephenson. His restless parents moved the family to Andover, Ohio, in 1890; to Richmond Center and then Townville, Pennsylvania; and in 1895 to Edinboro, Pennsylvania, where Anderson first went to school. They lived in McKeesport, New Brighton, and Harrisburg, Pennsylvania; moved to Jefferson, Ohio, in 1901; then to Algona, Iowa; and in 1904 to New Hampton, Iowa, where Anderson first attended high school. In 1907 they moved again, to Jamestown, North Dakota. A year later Anderson graduated from high school and entered the University of North Dakota at Grand Forks, graduating in 1911. That same year he married Margaret Ethel Haskett; the couple had three children.

After teaching high school in Minnewauken, North Dakota, for two years, Anderson attended graduate school at Stanford University in 1913 and 1914, writing his master's thesis on William Shakespeare. He taught in a San Francisco high school until 1917 and wrote editorials for the *Bulletin* and poetry for the *New Republic*. He was a professor of English and department chairman at Whittier College in Whittier, California, in 1917 and 1918 until his dismissal for pacifist comments.

Anderson then began a three-year residence in New York City, where he was an editor and writer for the *New Republic*, the *Globe and Commercial Advertiser*, and the *New York World*. In 1921 he bought a farmhouse north of New York City near the Hudson River in New City, and made it—and a bigger house he built there later—his summer residence until 1952. He continued to publish traditionally styled poems—reprinted in *You Who Have Dreams* (1925)—and founded and edited *Measure* (1921–1926), which published poetry by newcomers, including Robert Frost, Langston Hughes, John Crowe Ransom, Wallace Stevens, Elinor Wylie, and Conrad Aiken (Anderson's favorite among contemporaries). Anderson's first produced play, *White Desert* (1923), about repressed lives in lonely North Dakota, was in verse and failed. His second play, the realistic, ribald, bitter antiwar drama *What Price Glory?* (1924), coauthored with Laurence Stallings, was such a critical and financial success that Anderson resigned from the *World* and became a full-time playwright. His literary fecundity is legendary. In all, thirty-three of his plays were produced on stage and three of his radio plays were broadcast between 1923 and 1958. He drafted many others, only some of which he published, and wrote or coauthored eight screenplays, including *Rain* (1932), *Death Takes a Holiday* (1934), *So Red the Rose* (1935), and *Joan of Arc* (1948, based on his 1946 *Joan of Lorraine*), and numerous critical essays.

Anderson's *Elizabeth the Queen* (1930), featuring Queen Elizabeth I and Essex, is a drama about love and power. In sinewy blank verse, it exemplifies Anderson's consuming creative passion: to provide the modern theater with dramas combining serious themes and lofty, terse poetic language and thus inspire audiences—by rhythmic dialogue studded with apt imagery—to view playgoing as a religious experience. In time, Anderson completed a poetic Tudor trilogy, with *Mary of Scotland* (1933), which violates history by contrasting a noble Mary with an unscrupulous Elizabeth, and *Anne of the Thousand Days* (1948), which presents memories of tragically flawed Anne Boleyn concerning Henry VIII in incremental flashbacks.

Anderson's wife died of a stroke-induced car accident in 1931. Two years later, he married Gertrude Maynard, an actress fifteen years his junior. The couple had one child. Anderson's *Night over Taos* (1932) is a pro-Spanish, anti-American critique of the nineteenth-century U.S. occupation of Taos. *Both Your Houses* (1933), a prose exposé of U.S. congressional corruption, won the Pulitzer Prize. *Winterset* (1935), in sonorous verse, is clearly Anderson's masterpiece. It was inspired by the controversial case of anarchist-immigrants Nicola Sacco and Bartolomeo Vanzetti, executed in 1927 on a 1920 Massachusetts murder charge. The play details not only the tragic efforts of a self-doubting man to prove the innocence of his father, an Italian radical wrongly executed for murder, but also the effects of a guilty conscience on the judge who helped frame him. Anderson's poetic tragedy is daringly contemporary in setting. In *High Tor* (1937) he dramatized in compelling verse one man's losing battle to protect a beautiful mountain from being turned into a gravel mine.

In 1938 Anderson, together with lawyer John F. Wharton and fellow playwrights Samuel Nathaniel Behrman, Sidney Howard, Elmer Rice, and Robert Sherwood, founded the Playwrights' Producing Company in order to gain artistic and financial control over their work. That year the company produced *Knickerbocker's Holiday*, a musical comedy that blended Anderson's words with his close friend Kurt Weill's score to satirize President Franklin D. Roosevelt's New Deal policies. In 1939 Anderson abrasively refused to apply for a Social Security card. A year later he supported Wendell Willkie, Roosevelt's unsuccessful opponent for the presidency. In 1942 he helped purchase the real High Tor, a basaltic mountain above Haverstraw, New York, to make it a state park. He also visited a U.S. Army base in North Carolina to gather material for *The Eve of St. Mark* (1942), a smash hit now regarded as too idealistic and sentimental, about an American soldier's self-sacrificial heroism against the Japanese. Anderson so mismanaged the $300,000 he was paid for movie rights to it that he had trouble with the Internal Revenue Service for the rest of his life.

By now no longer a pacifist, Anderson loathed fascism and feared the spread of communism, and in 1943 he went to England and North Africa as a war correspondent. He was outraged when the 1944 production of *Storm Operation*, his play about the Allies in North Africa, was censored by the War Department to tone down the sexual looseness of the Australian nurse and other elements of possible offense to the Allies and to delete frank language and unflattering depictions of North Africans. Anderson succeeded with his *Joan of Lorraine* (1946), which combines an intriguing play-within-a-play structure and the theme of faith—and compromise—in politically debased times. He negotiated with Ingrid Bergman to star in it on stage and in the movie adaptation.

In 1953 Anderson's wife Gertrude, who had grown depressed and lonely, and then was unfaithful, committed suicide. A year later, Anderson married Gilda Romano Hazard, a divorced actress (also known professionally as Gilda Oakleaf and Gilda Storm), and began a happy residence with her in Stamford, Connecticut. In addition to *Anne of the Thousand Days*, of Anderson's last plays only *Barefoot in Athens* (1951) and *Bad Seed* (1954) are notable. *Barefoot in Athens* shows how Socrates's undeviating search for truth costs him his friends and how his lofty arguments fatally offend his jurors. Anderson's depiction of Athens (which he had visited in 1947) as democratic and Sparta as communist owed much to the fact that *Barefoot* was produced during the time of Senator Joseph McCarthy's infamous anticommunist witchhunting. *Bad Seed* is a spellbinding adaptation of William March's 1954 novel of the same name, about an attractive eight-year-old girl who is condemned by her genes to kill and kill again.

Anderson was active until his death in Stamford, Connecticut. He was an immensely talented, productive, and versatile author. His favorite authors were Aristotle, Shakespeare, and John Keats. His rivals among contemporary playwrights were Clifford Odets, Eugene O'Neill, and T. S. Eliot. His most enduring accomplishment was in the realm of richly charged verse drama, which he felt—anachronistically, it would seem, in the light of later popular theater, movie, and television developments—ought to be enlisted to aid humankind in achieving its spiritual and artistic potential.

• An enormous collection of Anderson papers is in the Humanities Research Center of the University of Texas. Smaller collections are in the Library of Congress, the American Academy of Arts and Letters in New York, and libraries at Columbia University and Yale University. Noteworthy are Anderson's *The Essence of Tragedy and Other Footnotes and Papers* (1939) and the following plays: *Gods of the Lightning* (1928), based on the Sacco-Vanzetti case; his patriotic but suspenseless *Valley Forge* (1934); and *Lost in the Stars* (1949, with Kurt Weill), a tragic musical based on Alan Paton's novel *Cry, the Beloved Country* (1948). Alfred S. Shivers, *Maxwell Anderson: An Annotated Bibliography of Primary and Secondary Works* (1985), is a compilation of Anderson's published and unpublished works and written and oral secondary sources. Barbara Lee Horn, *Maxwell Anderson: A Research and Production Sourcebook* (1996), contains not only a bibliography of Anderson's plays, theatrical criticism, articles, and essays but also plot summaries of the plays, productions and credits, critical overviews, and lists of reviews. Laurence G. Avery, *Dramatist in America: Letters of Maxwell Anderson, 1912–1958* (1977), is well annotated and contains short biographies of Anderson family members and the main recipients of his letters. Shivers, *The Life of Maxwell Anderson* (1983), is a detailed biography. Mabel Driscoll Bailey, *Maxwell Anderson: The Playwright as Prophet* (1957), is analytically critical. Nancy J. Doran Hazelton and Kenneth Krauss, eds., *Maxwell Anderson and the New York Stage* (1991), assemble essays by others. Abe Laufe, *The Wicked Stage: A History of Theater Censorship and Harassment in the United States* (1978), considers Anderson's problems with would-be censors of *What Price Glory?* and *The Masque of Kings*, his 1937 romantic tragedy about Austrian Prince Rudolph at Mayerling. An obituary is in the *New York Times*, 1 Mar. 1959.

ROBERT L. GALE

ANDERSON, Patton (16 Feb. 1822–20 Sept. 1872), Confederate soldier, was born James Patton Anderson in Winchester, Franklin County, Tennessee, the son of William Preston Anderson, a soldier and U.S. district attorney, and Margaret L. Adair. His father died in 1831. Patton Anderson attended common school in Tennessee and Kentucky and in October 1836 entered Jefferson College in Canonsburg, Pennsylvania. His stepfather, J. N. Bybee, suffered financial reversals that led to Anderson's withdrawal from college in 1837. In the autumn of 1838 Anderson accompanied his stepfather and the family to Mississippi, where they settled at Hernando, in De Soto County. Anderson reentered Jefferson College in April 1839 and graduated in 1840.

Anderson returned to Hernando, read law in the office of Buckner & Delafield, and was admitted to the Mississippi bar in 1843. He became deputy sheriff of De Soto County, a position he held until 1846, when the economic situation improved and "the prospect seemed favorable to commence the practice of law." In the winter of 1846–1847 he entered into partnership with R. B. Mayes.

Anderson commanded a volunteer battalion in the Mexican War, but his unit saw no action. After the war he resumed his partnership with Mayes and in November 1849 was elected to represent De Soto County in the Mississippi House of Representatives, starting his term in 1850. He supported Senator Jefferson Davis and Governor John Quitman in their bitter feud with U.S. senator Henry S. Foote over the latter's support of the Compromise of 1850. In the election of 1851, the electorate supported Foote, and Anderson lost his fight for reelection.

In March 1853, with the backing of Secretary of War Davis, Anderson was named by President Franklin Pierce to be U.S. marshal for Washington Territory. Before leaving for the Pacific Coast, Anderson married Henrietta Buford Adair, a cousin. They had several children, but the exact number is unknown. His first task on reaching Olympia on 4 June 1853 was to take a census of the new territory's population. In November 1855 Anderson, a Democrat, was elected territorial delegate to the Thirty-fourth Congress. When he left Congress in March 1857, he relocated to his aunt's plantation, "Casa Bianca," near Monticello, Florida.

On 10 December 1860 Anderson was elected captain of the Jefferson Rifles, and he briefly serviced as officer in charge of the battalion posted at the Chattahoochee Arsenal. Supporting states' rights, he was elected as a Jefferson County delegate to the convention called by Governor Milton S. Perry that assembled in Tallahassee on 1 January 1861. On 10 January the convention passed a secession ordinance strongly endorsed by Anderson. He was one of three delegates named by Governor Perry to represent Florida at the Montgomery convention that adopted a provisional constitution and elected Davis provisional president of the Confederacy.

On 27 March, at the Chattahoochee Arsenal, Anderson was elected colonel of the First Florida Infantry and was mustered into Confederate service. Ordered to Pensacola, Anderson reported to Major General Braxton Bragg. On 12 April the regiment went into camp, and Anderson "commenced drilling and exercising his soldiers."

Anderson first led troops into combat on the night of 7–8 October 1861, when he landed on Santa Rosa Island and, with other Confederates, raided and routed the Sixth New York Zouaves from their camp. Promoted to brigadier general on 10 February 1862, he reported to Bragg at Jackson, Tennessee, on 20 March. From there he traveled to Corinth, Mississippi, to take command of a brigade in Brigadier General Daniel Ruggles's division, one of the two divisions constituting Bragg's corps.

Anderson and his brigade saw desperate fighting at Shiloh on 6–7 April. Of his service, Bragg wrote, "Brig. Gen. Patton Anderson was among the foremost where the fighting was hardest, and never failed to overcome whatever resistance was opposed to him. With a brigade composed of raw troops his personal gallantry and soldierly bearing supplied the place of instruction and discipline."

In mid-April Anderson found himself leading a division as senior brigadier. As such, he participated in the siege and evacuation of Corinth and the retreat to Tupelo. At Clear Creek, Mississippi, he was taken ill, and a newcomer to the Army of the Mississippi, Major General Samuel Jones replaced him as division commander. On 1 September, following Jones's reassignment, Anderson again found himself in charge of the division, which he led during Bragg's Kentucky campaign. Anderson and his troops next met the enemy at Perryville (8 Oct.). In mid-December, while posted at Eagleville, Tennessee, Anderson's division was disbanded, and on 27 December he was assigned to lead Brigadier General Edward C. Walthall's brigade of Mississippians in Major General Leonidas Polk's corps, Jones Withers's division. Walthall had become violently ill.

The battle of Stones River began the next morning. Anderson saw bitter fighting the last day of 1862, when his brigade was called on to take three Union batteries "at any cost" and succeeded, according to Bragg, under his "cool steadfast and skillful leadership." He crossed Stones River on 2 January and helped rally Major General John C. Breckinridge's troops, who had suffered a disastrous repulse.

Soon after the Confederate retreat to Tullahoma, Withers became sick, and Anderson, as senior officer, commanded the division for more than a month. On Withers's return to duty, Anderson was given command of the Mississippi infantry brigade formerly led by James R. Chalmers. He and his brigade participated in the Tullahoma campaign (23 June–4 July) and Bragg's retreat across the Tennessee River. Anderson and the Mississippians, an element of Major General Thomas C. Hindman's division, were heavily engaged at Chickamauga on 20 September, first crossing the La Fayette Road and shattering Jefferson C. Davis's division and then at Snodgrass Hill.

In mid-October General Hindman was placed under arrest by General Bragg, and command of his division devolved on Anderson, who led the division at Missionary Ridge. In his autobiography Anderson recalled that on the morning of 25 November he "protested against the disposition which had been made of the troops . . . which was the worst I have ever seen. The line was in two ranks, the front rank at the foot of the hill and rear rank on the top!!" When the Union late-afternoon attack came, Anderson's division "made no fight at all, but broke and ran," the first of

Breckinridge's corps to do so as Union battle lines swept forward and scaled the ridge.

On 9 February 1864 Anderson was promoted to major general and assigned to the division formerly led by Breckinridge. At the battle of Jonesboro (31 Aug.), he was badly wounded and returned to his Monticello home to recuperate. Ignoring the advice of his doctors, Anderson rejoined the Army of Tennessee at Smithfield, North Carolina, on 8 April 1865 and, as time was running out for the Confederacy, assumed command of Major General William Taliaferro's division. A bitter-ender, Anderson opposed General Joseph E. Johnston's decision to surrender the forces constituting his command at Durham Station, 26 April 1865. Along with his troops, Anderson was paroled at Greensboro, 2 May 1865.

Anderson did not return to Florida but relocated to Memphis, where he edited and published a paper devoted to agrarian interests and was collector of state taxes in Shelby County. He died in Memphis.

Anderson was a commander who, although never long associated with any command, led his men into action rather than ordering them in. A stern disciplinarian, he did not hesitate to execute deserters. Unlike many of the Army of Tennessee's generals, he was loyal to Braxton Bragg, their mutual admiration dating to their Pensacola days. He stood by Bragg again and again during the controversies that clouded Bragg's leadership of the army. He opposed Major General Patrick R. Cleburne's January 1864 proposal to enlist slaves in the Confederate army.

• There is no known collection of Anderson papers. He wrote "Autobiography of Gen. Patton Anderson, C.S.A.," *Southern Historical Society, Papers* 24 (1896): 57–70. A biographical sketch is in *Biographical Dictionary of the American Congress, 1777–1989* (1989). See also *Compiled Service Records of Confederate General & Staff Officers & Nonregimental Enlisted Men*, National Archives, M-331; Etta Anderson, "General Anderson's Different Commands during the War," *Southern Historical Society, Papers* 24 (1896): 71–72; John J. Dickison, *Confederate Military History Extended Edition: Florida*, vol. 16 (1899); and Ezra J. Warner, *Generals in Gray: Lives of the Confederate Commanders* (1959).

E. C. BEARSS

ANDERSON, Paul Y. (29 Aug. 1893–6 Dec. 1938), journalist, was born near Knoxville, Tennessee, the son of William Holston Anderson, a stonecutter, and Elizabeth Dill Haynes, a schoolteacher. Anderson was three years old when his father died in an accident, and his mother was left as sole support for him and his two young sisters. He worked his way through high school, and in 1911, at the age of eighteen, he began his career in journalism when he joined the staff of the *Knoxville Journal*. A year later Anderson moved to St. Louis, Missouri, where he reported for a succession of newspapers, beginning with the *St. Louis Times*. In 1913 he joined the *St. Louis Star* and the next year moved to the *St. Louis Post-Dispatch*, where he came under the direction of noted managing editor O. K. Bovard.

Anderson's reporting and writing skills brought him early recognition. He achieved national attention in 1917 when he testified before a congressional committee investigating a race riot in East St. Louis, Illinois, on which Anderson had reported for the *Post-Dispatch*. The committee commended Anderson's reporting, pointing out that he had defied powerful public officials and risked assassination to expose the circumstances leading to the riot. While continuing to report for the *Post-Dispatch*, Anderson attended Washington University in St. Louis from 1920 to 1922, although he never received a diploma. During his tenure from 1921 to 1923 as a *Post-Dispatch* editorial writer Anderson investigated the plight of political prisoners jailed in the United States during and after World War I, providing the grist for the paper's successful crusade that ended in the release of those unjustly imprisoned.

Like most of the earlier muckrakers, Anderson embraced progressivism and was influenced by a leading Progressive politician, Senator Robert La Follette, Sr. Throughout his career Anderson disdained industry barons and championed labor's causes.

In 1923 Anderson left the *Post-Dispatch*, which refused to assign him to its Washington, D.C., bureau, to be a freelance reporter in Washington. With the encouragement of La Follette, he focused his penetrating reportage on the scandal-plagued administrations of Warren G. Harding and Calvin Coolidge. Anderson's early work in Washington, published in a variety of newspapers including the *Post-Dispatch*, the *Omaha World-Herald*, and the *Raleigh News and Observer*, drew attention to Senate hearings investigating the Teapot Dome scandal, a complex bribery scheme involving the leasing of public land oil rights in Wyoming and California.

The hearings concluded in early 1924. However, Anderson, who had since rejoined the *Post-Dispatch*, continued to pursue the case. Prodded by Bovard and advised behind the scenes by the politically insightful La Follette, Anderson, through his reporting, convinced the Senate to hold new hearings under the chairmanship of his friend, Senator George W. Norris of Nebraska. The Senate investigation, which Anderson actively aided, resulted in the imprisonment of Albert B. Fall, secretary of the interior, and oil magnate Harry Sinclair and led to the government's recouping $6 million from principals in the bribery scheme. In reporting on the Teapot Dome scandal, Anderson "dug facts from available records; he interviewed responsible officials. He kept the story alive in ways that were legitimate until the inevitable time came when it could no longer be ignored," observed his contemporary, Lowell Mellett, editor of the *Washington Daily News*. In recognition of his work Anderson was awarded the Pulitzer Prize in 1928.

Anderson covered some of the biggest stories of the time: the notorious Loeb-Leopold kidnapping and murder trial, the Scopes monkey trial that forced the nation to confront the theory of evolution, and the army's attack on protesting World War I veterans in

Washington during the Bonus Army march in 1932. In 1926 Anderson's crusading led to the resignation of an Illinois federal judge, the rejection of Supreme Court nominee John J. Parker of North Carolina because of antilabor and racist attitudes, and the exposure of ties between the Ku Klux Klan and Senator James E. Watson of Indiana. Between 1929 and 1934, and again in 1938, Anderson supplemented his reporting with a political column in the *Nation*, in which he editorialized against government corruption and misdeeds and frequently criticized the nation's press for failing to challenge the government. In 1973 *Nation* editor Carey McWilliams wrote that had the magazine done nothing more than publish Anderson's work during the 1920s and 1930s, it still would have made "a significant contribution to the continuance of the muckraking tradition" in the United States. In 1937 Anderson was awarded a gold medal by the Headliner's Club, which cited his reportage on a Senate committee's investigation of civil liberties as "the best series of news stories on a subject of great public interest."

Anderson was involved in the founding of the American Newspaper Guild when he represented the newspaper industry's Washington correspondents during a congressional hearing in 1933, arguing for the inclusion of journalists in the workweek and wage regulations of the National Recovery Act. This hearing provided the impetus for the guild's formation later that year.

While Anderson's work brought him fame, his personal life was often unhappy. His first marriage was in 1914 to Beatrice Wright. They had two children but divorced in 1919. His second marriage, to Anna Alberta Fritschle, lasted from 1928 to 1936, when they too divorced. His third marriage, in 1937 to entertainer Katherine Lane, was marred by a legal separation. In addition to damaging his personal relations (he had few close friends), alcoholism also interfered with his career. The *Post-Dispatch* fired him for reasons related to his excessive drinking in January 1938. He joined the Washington bureau of the *St. Louis Star-Times* and resumed his column for the *Nation*, but in December, after leaving a note declaring that his "usefulness was at an end," Anderson committed suicide at his Washington home by taking an overdose of sleeping pills.

Journalists Heywood Broun and H. L. Mencken called Anderson one of the finest journalists of his time. Historians praise Anderson's work for its wit, its evidence of aggressive digging for facts, its insider Washington knowledge, and its vivid, impressionistic writing. His coverage of William Jennings Bryan's funeral was included in *A Treasury of Great Reporting* (1949). Nevertheless, Anderson's participatory style countered journalism's more mainstream tradition of objectivity, and some commentators have criticized him for getting too involved in the stories he covered. Richard Strout of the *Christian Science Monitor* and the *New Republic* admired Anderson but criticized him for having a "prosecutorial complex." Some have attacked him for working closely with congressional committees, when he would feed questions to investigators during their interrogations of witnesses, testify himself, and supply the committee with whatever evidence he had collected. However, a respected investigative reporter, Clark Mollenhoff, who often worked with government investigators to expose corruption and mismanagement during the 1950s, admired Anderson's cooperation with authorities and credited him with setting a worthwhile precedent for modern investigative reporters, who, Mollenhoff argued, should not only expose social problems but work to correct them as well.

• Anderson's private papers are in the possession of his relatives. Facts about Anderson may be found in his article, "Many Obstacles Met in Discovering Disposition of Continental Bonds," *Editor & Publisher*, 18 May 1929, pp. 10–11. The most authoritative writing on Anderson's life is in two articles by Edmund B. Lambeth, "The Lost Career of Paul Y. Anderson," *Journalism Quarterly* 60, no. 3 (Aug. 1983): 401–6; and "Paul Y. Anderson," *Dictionary of Literary Biography* 29 (1984). Lambeth's research benefits from his access to Anderson's papers and interviews with his relatives. Some details of Anderson's relationship with Bovard and the *Post-Dispatch* are in Daniel W. Pfaff, *Joseph Pulitzer II and the Post-Dispatch: A Newspaperman's Life* (1991). Anderson's colleagues pay tribute to him in *Where Is There Another? A Memorial to Paul Y. Anderson* (1939). Former *Nation* editor Carey McWilliams notes Anderson's contributions to muckraking in *Muckraking: Past, Present and Future*, ed. John M. Harrison and Harry H. Stein (1973). Anderson's role in the founding of the newspaper guild is noted in Daniel J. Leab, *A Union of Individuals: The Formation of the American Newspaper Guild, 1933–1936* (1970). Other facts about Anderson are found in Heywood Broun, "Roundsman of the Lord," the *New Republic*, 4 Jan. 1939, pp. 257–58; Fred Freed, "Paul Y. Anderson," *Esquire*, Mar. 1948, p. 101; and Clark Mollenhoff, *Investigative Reporting* (1981). Obituaries are in the *New York Times*, 7 Dec. 1938, and the *St. Louis Post-Dispatch*, 6 Dec. 1938.

JAMES L. AUCOIN

ANDERSON, Richard Clough, Jr. (4 Aug. 1788–24 July 1826), congressman and diplomat, was born in Louisville, Kentucky, the son of Richard Clough Anderson, Sr., a revolutionary war soldier, and Elizabeth Clark, sister of frontiersman George Rogers Clark. His father had come to Kentucky in 1783 to become surveyor of the Virginia Land District in Louisville. In 1789 the family moved to "Soldiers' Retreat," a farm ten miles east of the city, where young Anderson grew up. Tutors instructed him until 1800, when he went to a private school in Virginia. In November 1802 he enrolled at the College of William and Mary. After graduating, Anderson left Williamsburg in July 1806 and arrived at his father's home in September. In February of the following year he moved to Frankfort, Kentucky, to study law under John Allen. He stayed in Frankfort about a year, then lived briefly at his father's house before returning to William and Mary in September 1808 to complete his legal training. Returning to Kentucky by way of Washington, D.C., where he witnessed the inauguration of President James Madison, Anderson settled in Frankfort for a few months, then in October 1809 moved to Louisville to begin the practice of law.

In December 1810 Anderson married his first cousin, Elizabeth Gwathmey; they had eight children, of whom three survived the parents. Because of his family's prominence, Anderson appears to have assumed that he was expected to follow a career in politics. Although he practiced law due to financial necessity, he found it uninteresting and was increasingly caught up in the speculative mania of the day. The losses that he, his father, father-in-law, and other relatives experienced in land speculation often placed the family in economic jeopardy, but he never lost his belief that such activity should be the true occupation of a gentleman.

Anderson's first foray into public life came with his election to the Kentucky House of Representatives in 1812. After serving one term, he declined to become a candidate at the next election, but in 1814 he returned to the Kentucky house for the 1814–1815 and 1815–1816 sessions. He then was elected to the Fifteenth and Sixteenth Congresses of the United States, serving from 1817 to 1821. An excellent orator, Anderson spoke during the Fifteenth Congress in opposition to a resolution of censure against Andrew Jackson for his execution of two Englishmen in Florida. During the next Congress, Anderson served on the Committee on Public Lands. His longest speech was one in which he advocated the admission of Missouri to the Union as a slave state. Since he did not particularly like serving in Congress, Anderson decided not to stand for reelection. Instead, in 1821 he returned to the Kentucky house, where he served as Speaker for the 1822–1823 session.

Anderson's losses from land speculation during the depression that followed the panic of 1819 caused him considerable disquiet. He began to pursue a political appointment from his friends, President James Monroe and Secretary of State John Quincy Adams. Finally, in 1823 he was named minister plenipotentiary to La Gran Colombia, Simón Bolívar's short-lived union of Ecuador, Venezuela, and New Granada (Colombia). He sailed with his family for La Guayra on 17 June 1823, arrived there three weeks later, and began the overland trip to Bogotá, which they reached on 10 December. Although he disliked Colombia, which he found to be unhealthy and uncomfortable for himself and his family, he planned to stay until he was out of debt and had some money saved. He struggled with the language but was able to negotiate successfully a treaty of commerce with Colombia, which was signed on 3 October 1824. The treaty, the first concluded by the United States with any of the South American republics, was ratified by the U.S. Senate the following spring. On 16 March 1825 he also concluded a claims convention relating to reparations for the seizures of U.S. vessels by Venezuelan squadrons during the South American revolutionary actions from 1817 to 1820. While in Colombia, Anderson wrote an article, which appeared in the *North American Review* in 1826, comparing Colombia's constitution to that of the United States.

In January 1825 Anderson's wife died after giving birth prematurely to a son, who did not survive. This tragedy caused Anderson to leave Colombia in March to take his three surviving children back home. They arrived in the United States in May and reached Louisville on 21 June. The children went to stay with their mother's family.

Before his departure for Colombia on 16 October, Anderson learned that he was President John Quincy Adams's choice as a delegate to the Panama Congress, which was to meet the following year. Due to developing political opposition to the Adams administration, Senate approval of the nomination was delayed, but Anderson finally was confirmed in March 1826 by a vote of 27 to 17. He was to proceed to Porto Bello, where he would meet John Sergeant, the other delegate, so that they could travel together to Panama. Sergeant, afraid of going to Panama in the sickly tropical season, resigned from the mission, but Anderson set out for the congress, leaving Bogotá for Cartagena on 12 June 1826. When he arrived in Turbaco, a jungle village near Cartagena, on 11 July, he was advised to stay there because of the fever-ridden condition of the port. According to his final journal entry of 12 July, however, Anderson was planning to proceed to Cartagena. On 26 July John M. Macpherson, U.S. consul at Cartagena, wrote Secretary of State Henry Clay that Anderson had reached Cartagena on the fourteenth; suffering from fever, he had died there ten days later. Anderson was buried in Cartagena but was later reinterred in the family cemetery at Soldiers' Retreat in Jefferson County, Kentucky.

• A small group of Richard C. Anderson, Jr., papers, including the original diary and journal, are included in a much larger collection of Richard C. Anderson, Sr., and Anderson family papers at the Filson Club in Louisville, Ky. The most important source for Anderson is Alfred Tischendorf and E. Taylor Parks, eds., *The Diary and Journal of Richard Clough Anderson, Jr., 1814–1826* (1964), which includes an introductory overview of Anderson's life. For a discussion of the family home and biographical sketches of notable members of the family, see Kitty Anderson, "Soldiers' Retreat, a Historical House and Its Famous People," *Register of the Kentucky Historical Society* 17 (1919): 67–77. Substantial information about Anderson's diplomatic career, including reprints of manuscript material from the National Archives diplomatic collection, may be found in James F. Hopkins et al., eds., *The Papers of Henry Clay*, vols. 3, 4, and 5 (1963, 1972, 1973). See also Richard C. Anderson, Jr., "Constitution of Colombia," *North American Review* 23 (1826): 314–49.

MELBA PORTER HAY

ANDERSON, Richard Heron (7 Oct. 1821–26 June 1879), Confederate general, was born at "Hill Crest," near Statesburg, in Sumter District, South Carolina, the son of William Wallace Anderson, an eminent surgeon, and Mary Mackenzie. His grandfather, Richard Anderson, served in the revolutionary war as an officer in the Maryland Line. Anderson's early schooling was at Edge Hill Academy in Sumter District. At age seventeen he entered the U.S. Military Academy, from which he graduated number forty of a class of fifty-six in 1842. He was appointed a brevet second lieutenant in the First Dragoons.

In 1843, following training at the cavalry school in Carlisle, Pennsylvania, Anderson was ordered to Little Rock, Arkansas, for service on the frontier. During the war with Mexico he served in Winfield Scott's column and saw action in several engagements, including the battles of Contreras and Molino del Ray. He won a brevet to first lieutenant for gallant and meritorious service at a skirmish at St. Augustine, Mexico. Following the war, Anderson was assigned to recruiting service and later to the cavalry school. He married Sarah Gibson, the daughter of Pennsylvania chief justice John B. Gibson, in 1850. Their marriage produced two children. In 1852 Anderson was posted to Texas to serve with the Second Dragoons. He was at various posts in Texas, New Mexico, and Kansas until 1857, when he returned to the cavalry school as an instructor. In 1858 he conducted recruits across the nation to participate in the 1858–1859 Utah expedition against the Mormons. He was subsequently assigned to Fort Kearney, Nebraska, where he remained until the outbreak of the Civil War.

The approach of the war found Anderson's family divided over the issue of slavery. His father was an ardent supporter of states' rights and a defender of the institution of slavery. Anderson was not as impassioned, and he attempted to remain neutral on the emotional issues. Privately he objected to slavery. The pressures of his father and his state forced him to take a stand when the war came, and on 15 February 1861 he resigned his commission in the U.S. Army. He was commissioned colonel of the First South Carolina Regular Regiment, which he commanded until 27 May 1861, when he relieved General P. G. T. Beauregard as commander of South Carolina forces and defenses. On 19 July 1861 he was promoted to brigadier general and in August was ordered to report to General Braxton Bragg at Pensacola, Florida. On 9 October 1861 Anderson led a force of about eleven hundred troops in a partially successful night assault upon Santa Rosa Island, near Fort Pickens, where he was wounded in the arm. In February 1862 he was ordered north to Virginia to take command of a South Carolina brigade in the division of his former West Point classmate James Longstreet. During the Confederate retreat from Yorktown, Anderson skillfully directed the operations of seven brigades in the battle of Williamsburg on 5 May 1862, which checked the Union pursuit. During the action, Anderson's younger brother, Mackenzie, was killed. Anderson wrote that his brother's death "was the most agonizing moment of my life."

Anderson distinguished himself again at Seven Pines on 31 May 1862, when his brigade made the deepest penetration of the battle into Union lines. Longstreet reported Anderson's advance "decided the day in our favor." During the Seven Days' battles Anderson continued to distinguish himself. On 14 July 1862 he was commissioned major general and assigned to command Benjamin Huger's division. On 20 August his division was ordered north to join the army in operations in northern Virginia. Anderson arrived on 30 August and took part in the Confederate counterattack that drove the Federal army from the field at Second Manassas. The invasion of Maryland followed, and Anderson's division participated in the operations that resulted in the capture of the Union garrison at Harpers Ferry, Virginia, then made a forced march to Sharpsburg, where on 17 September 1862 it took part in the battle of Antietam. While attempting to reinforce the Confederate position at the "Bloody Lane," Anderson was severely wounded in the thigh and forced to relinquish command. He returned to duty by the time of the battle of Fredericksburg (13 Dec. 1862), where his division was only lightly engaged. At Chancellorsville (1–5 May 1863), with three of his brigades, he delayed the initial advance of Joseph Hooker's Army of the Potomac, then participated in the bloody fighting that defeated Hooker's main body. Anderson's division marched with Lafayette McLaws's division to confront the Union Sixth Corps, which had broken the Confederate line at Fredericksburg. The combined Confederate attack drove these Federal troops back, securing a complete southern victory.

Following Chancellorsville, Robert E. Lee reorganized his army and assigned Anderson's division to General A. P. Hill's Third Corps. At Gettysburg Anderson's command was heavily engaged on both 2 and 3 July in unsuccessful attacks. Anderson's performance drew criticism from within his own command. General Cadmus Wilcox complained, "I am quite certain that Genl A. never saw a foot of ground on which his three brigades fought on the 2d July. . . . I always believed he was too indifferent to his duties at Gettysburg." Major G. Moxley Sorrel, who served on Longstreet's staff, offered some explanation for Anderson's inertia: "His [Anderson's] courage was of the highest order, but he was indolent. His capacity and intelligence excellent, but it was hard to get him to use them. Longstreet knew him well and could get a good deal out of him, more than any one else."

During the battle of the Wilderness, on 6 May 1864, General Longstreet was severely wounded and Anderson was temporarily placed in command of the First Corps. His rapid march of the corps from the Wilderness battlefield to Spotsylvania Court House on the night of 7 May prevented the Union army from cutting Lee's army off from Richmond. Anderson commanded the First Corps until Longstreet's return in the fall of 1864. On 31 May 1864 he was promoted to lieutenant general. His tenure as corps commander, apart from his night march to Spotsylvania, was not particularly distinguished. Richard Sommers, in *Richmond Redeemed*, wrote, "Despite a promising debut at Spotsylvania, his subsequent record was disappointedly marred by lack of initiative, of boldness, and of capacity to co-ordinate large bodies of men."

When Longstreet returned to the army in October, Anderson was placed in command of a newly organized corps of two divisions, but one division was detached before the corps became operational. His reduced responsibilities coupled with the deteriorating situation in the South left him discouraged and depressed. After the Confederate defeat at Five Forks, Anderson's command joined in the general retreat from the Petersburg and Richmond lines. On 6 April 1865 Anderson's command was overwhelmed at Saylor's Creek. One day later Lee relieved him of command.

Following the war, Anderson attempted to work his family's plantation. His efforts failed, and he was left nearly destitute. He took a job as a common laborer with the South Carolina Railroad in Camden, South Carolina, and was forced to live in a boardinghouse. He eventually became an agent for the railroad but lost his position for reasons never satisfactorily explained. His wife died in 1872, and in 1874 he married Martha Mellette. In 1875 he was named the state phosphate agent for South Carolina, which afforded Anderson some relief from his poverty and a brief period of happiness until his death in Beaufort of apoplexy.

Anderson was a simple, devout man and was exceptionally modest. As a soldier, Confederate General John Bratton wrote of him, "In an army unsurpassed in chivalric courage, and in the dash and skill of its officers, it was this modest soldier who won for himself the sobriquet of 'Fighting Dick Anderson.'"

• Anderson's papers are scattered and are not extensive. His letter book of official correspondence from 29 Jan. 1854 to 23 Aug. 1863 is at the Confederate Museum in Richmond. Some of Anderson's Civil War reports and correspondence are in *The War of the Rebellion: A Compilation of the Official Records of the Union and Confederate Armies* (128 vols., 1880–1901). An early and dated biography is C. Irvine Walker, *The Life of Lt. Gen. R. H. Anderson* (1917). Joseph C. Elliott, *Lieutenant General Richard H. Anderson: Lee's Noble Soldier* (1985), is a thoroughly researched and sympathetic biography. For Anderson's U.S. Army military record, see G. W. Cullum, *Biographical Register of the Officers and Graduates of the U.S. Military Academy*, 3d ed., vol. 2 (1891). Edward N. Thurston provided a sketch of his career in "Memoir of Richard H. Anderson, C.S.A.," *Southern Historical Society Papers*, vol. 39, pp. 146–52. G. Moxley Sorrel, *Recollections of a Confederate Staff Officer* (1958), offers a perspective of Anderson from the viewpoint of one of Longstreet's staff. Anderson's performance at Gettysburg is well covered in Edwin Coddington, *The Gettysburg Campaign* (1984). For a perspective on Anderson as a corps commander, see William D. Matter, *If It Takes All Summer: The Battle of Spotsylvania* (1988), and Richard Sommers, *Richmond Redeemed: The Siege at Petersburg* (1981). Anderson's death was reported in the *Columbia Daily Record* (Columbia, S.C.), 29 June 1879.

D. SCOTT HARTWIG

ANDERSON, Robert (14 June 1805–26 Oct. 1871), soldier and hero of Fort Sumter, was born in Jefferson County, Kentucky, at "Soldier's Retreat," the family plantation. His father, Richard Clough Anderson, an officer of the Continental Line, moved to Kentucky after the Revolution; his mother, Sarah Marshall Anderson, was Richard's second wife. Robert graduated from West Point in 1825, fifteenth in a class of thirty-seven. Commissioned a second lieutenant in the Third Artillery, he served for a time as secretary to his half-brother Richard Clough Anderson, Jr., who was minister to Colombia. In 1832 he saw action in the Black Hawk War, and in 1837–1838 he fought in the Seminole War. He was said to have sworn in Abraham Lincoln, who saw brief service during the Black Hawk War.

Promoted to first lieutenant in 1833, Anderson was a brevet captain when he served as assistant adjutant general in the Eastern Department from 1838 to 1841. He became a captain in the Third Artillery in 1841. During the Mexican War he served under General Winfield Scott, a personal friend. Wounded at the battle of Molino del Rey, Anderson was brevetted major for his services. His letters written while on campaign to his wife, Elizabeth Bayard Clinch, whom he had married in 1845 and by whom he would have four children, were later published.

Although sometimes dismayed by the slowness of promotion, Anderson remained in the army after the war. He relieved boredom by translating some French works on artillery and preparing a textbook on that subject, and he lobbied successfully for the creation of a home for old soldiers. Promotion to major finally came in 1857.

A compact figure with courteous manners and a deep religious faith, Anderson was a competent, conscientious officer who held routine assignments for most of his career. A kinsman declared of him, "The Ten Commandments, the Constitution of the United States, and the Army Regulations are his guides in life."

As the nation became increasingly divided by sectional interests, Anderson, who until 1860 owned a few slaves in his wife's native state of Georgia, wrote, "In this controversy between the North and the South, my sympathies are entirely with the South." Although he believed that in the long run secession was probably inevitable, Anderson was devoted to the Union, and he opposed immediate demands for separation and what he saw as extremism on both sides. This combination of southern sympathies and Union loyalty led to Anderson's being assigned in November 1860 to command the three Federal forts at Charleston, South Carolina, where cautious tactfulness was needed. Aware that Fort Moultrie, at which he was headquartered, was indefensible, he vainly sought reinforcements and specific orders from the Buchanan administration, which was strongly influenced by southerners. South Carolina's secession on 20 December convinced Anderson that he should move to Fort Sumter, an incomplete but stronger post on an island in Charleston Harbor. He did so secretly on 26 December and then rejected all demands that he evacuate the fort.

While the outgoing Buchanan administration and then the incoming Lincoln administration debated what action should be taken, Anderson tried to cope with dwindling supplies, a blockade of his post, and the fear that he might be held responsible for starting a war. Determined to give no excuse for war, Anderson did not respond when southerners fired on a supply ship, the *Star of the West*, on 9 January 1861. His situation worsened, and Anderson informed southern emissaries that he would have to surrender by 15 April unless resupplied. Fort Sumter had become a symbol for both the North and South, and when Lincoln notified South Carolina governor Francis W. Pickens of his intention to supply Sumter with provisions, Confederate general Pierre Beauregard demanded the fort's surrender. Anderson refused, and bombardment of Fort Sumter began at 4:30 A.M. on 12 April. His 127 officers and men, including 43 civilian workers, defended the fort under great disadvantages until 14 April, when Anderson surrendered with full honors of war.

The Union's first hero of the war, Anderson was promoted to brigadier general in the regular army on 15 May. Assigned to command the Department of the Cumberland, which gave way to the Department of Kentucky and Tennessee on 15 August 1861, his Kentucky connection was expected to help hold that border state in the Union. When Kentucky's strained neutrality ended in early September, Anderson moved his headquarters from Cincinnati to Louisville.

Exhausted, physically and mentally, by his ordeal, Anderson was warned by physicians not to take a field command. On 7 October he requested to be relieved of his assignment, and the next day he was replaced by William T. Sherman. Anderson retired on 27 October 1863. Brevetted major general of volunteers, he returned to Fort Sumter on 14 April 1865 to raise the flag he had lowered there four years earlier.

An inadequate income and a futile effort to regain his health took Anderson and his wife and children to Europe, where living costs were lower than in the United States. He died in Nice, France, and was buried at West Point.

• Some 5,000 items are in the Robert Anderson papers in the Library of Congress. Anderson's Mexican War letters to his wife are in *An Artillery Officer in the Mexican War, 1846–7: Letters of Robert Anderson*, which includes an introduction by his daughter Eba Anderson Lawton (1911). W. A. Swanberg, *First Blood: The Story of Fort Sumter* (1957), should be supplemented by *The War of the Rebellion: A Compilation of the Official Records of the Union and Confederate Armies* (128 vols., 1880–1901), especially ser. 1, vol. 1. Anderson's military record is outlined in Francis B. Heitman, *Historical Register and Dictionary of the United States Army* (2 vols., 1903), and Ezra J. Warner, *Generals in Blue* (1964). His brief command in Kentucky is discussed in Thomas B. Van Horne, *History of the Army of the Cumberland* (2 vols., 1875).

LOWELL H. HARRISON

ANDERSON, Rufus (17 Aug. 1796–30 May 1880), mission administrator and theologian, was born in North Yarmouth, Maine, the son of Rufus Anderson, a Congregational minister, and Hannah Parsons. His mother died when he was seven, and Anderson moved to Wenham, Massachusetts, after his father remarried. He grew up in the midst of the evangelical Protestant Christianity of the churches and other religious organizations in which his father was a leader and attended the 1812 ordination of the first Protestant foreign missionaries sent to India from the United States by the American Board of Commissioners for Foreign Missions. Anderson attended Bowdoin College (A.B., 1818), where he experienced the conversion expected in his religious tradition and decided to be a missionary. He graduated from Andover Theological Seminary in 1822.

While in seminary Anderson began working as an assistant to Jeremiah Evarts, corresponding secretary of the American Board. In 1823 he volunteered for foreign missionary service but was assigned instead to the board's Boston office, where he served as assistant secretary until 1832. He was ordained in 1826, one of the first Congregationalists ordained for service outside of a local church. He married Eliza Hill in 1827. She hosted annually in their home hundreds of departing, visiting, and returning missionaries, raised their five children, and was active in her later years in women's missionary organizations.

As a board secretary, Anderson corresponded with missionaries overseas, attended the meetings of the board's Prudential Committee (its executive body), and published official board position papers, magazine articles, instructions to missionaries, and devotional pieces. He was sent to the Mediterranean in 1828 to investigate missionary conditions and opportunities and published his findings as *Observations upon the Peloponnesus and Greek Islands* (1830).

It was as foreign corresponding secretary, from 1832 to 1866, that Anderson most influenced both the American Board and the wider missionary movement. He was responsible for the board's relations with its personnel overseas—almost 400 lay and clerical missionaries and spouses in 1854—and by virtue of his longevity and skill in the position as well as his ability to bring together existing elements of evangelical thought into a cogent theology of missions became the board's most prominent officer and theorist.

Anderson's theology of missions centered around a "three-self" formula, articulated simultaneously by English mission administrator Henry Venn and widely accepted in late nineteenth- and twentieth-century Protestant missiology. This formula defined the goal of missions as the conversion of individuals and their subsequent gathering into self-supporting, self-governing, and self-propagating congregations. Building on the evangelical emphasis on the transforming power of the Christian gospel, Anderson insisted on distinguishing both the mission from the missionary and Christianity from Western culture. The evangelist was to preach the gospel, help converts organize into churches, and then move on, leaving the newly planted faith to develop its own indigenous forms. The tendency of Western missionaries to become involved in education, publishing, social reform, and other forms of cultural transformation seemed to Anderson a diversion from their primary task of carrying a religious message.

Anderson's views were expressed through various official board reports, missionary ordination sermons—most notably "The Theory of Missions to the Heathen" (1845)—and instructions to missionaries. They were reinforced by his observations on a second tour of the Mediterranean missions in 1843–1844 and gradually were implemented in various board policies and actions. In 1848, when the Prudential Committee began phasing out the board's most highly publicized and overtly successful mission, the missionaries in Hawaii were offered the chance to either return home or, if they agreed to continue evangelizing Hawaii as "native" Christians, settle in the islands on a share of former mission property. Although the offer took almost twenty years to implement and was compromised by American cultural and economic imperialism in Hawaii, it was consistent with Anderson's theory of missions. He traveled to the islands himself in 1863 to facilitate and accelerate the transition from foreign to local church government and outreach. Christianity had been successfully "planted" in Hawaii, he claimed in reports to the board and in his books *The Hawaiian Islands: Their Progress and Condition under Missionary Labors* (1864) and *A Heathen Nation Evangelized: History of the Sandwich Islands Mission* (1870), and would now expand and mature from within.

A decade before he went to Hawaii, the same missionary ideals motivated an 1854–1855 deputation to the board's missions in Sri Lanka, India, and the Mediterranean. Accompanied by a Prudential Committee member, Anderson forcefully presented what was now Prudential Committee policy to the missionaries in their various stations, leading some missions to close schools, ordain native pastors, and endorse indigenous forms of church government. Others, however, protested to the board at home. Valuing education and American forms of church government more highly than did the Prudential Committee, these missionaries claimed to have been coerced or intimidated by the deputation members into implementing a theory of missions that they did not support. After a thorough investigation, which revealed both widespread respect for Anderson and the variety of understandings of mission work held by missionaries and mission activists, the board exonerated the deputation of any wrongdoing and formally adopted most of Anderson's principles. The one change the board made was to adopt a position of official neutrality with regard to mission church organization, a retreat from Anderson's emphasis on indigenous development. This adjustment was necessitated by the increasing denominational consciousness of American Presbyterian and Reformed supporters of the board, a focus that led each group to insist on the formation of its own kind of churches in mission fields. Dissatisfaction with the board's nondenominational approach to foreign missions persisted after the 1856 change and contributed to the decisions of the Dutch Reformed in 1857 and New School Presbyterians in 1869 to transfer their support from the American Board to denominational mission organizations.

Anderson retired as corresponding secretary in 1866 and served as an active member of the Prudential Committee until 1875. He published extensive histories of the board's mission fields and used the lectures on missions he gave at Andover, Bangor, Hartford, Auburn, and Union seminaries as the basis for the major statement of his mature theory of missions, *Foreign Missions: Their Relations and Claims* (1869). Anderson continued to attend Prudential Committee meetings as an emeritus member until shortly before his death at his home in Roxbury, Massachusetts.

• Anderson's extensive professional correspondence and most of his surviving personal papers are in the archives of the American Board preserved in Harvard University's Houghton Library. R. Pierce Beaver, *To Advance the Gospel: Selections from the Writings of Rufus Anderson* (1967), is the standard scholarly work on Anderson. It consists of a brief biography, an analysis of Anderson's theory of missions, an extensive bibliography, and selections from many of Anderson's most significant publications. Among those publications were other histories of the American Board, *Memorial Volume of the First Fifty Years of the American Board of Commissioners for Foreign Missions* (1861), and its missions, *History of the Missions of the American Board of Commissioners for Foreign Missions to the Oriental Churches* (1872–1873) and *History of the Missions of the American Board of Commissioners for Foreign Missions in India* (1874). For his life see Augustus Charles Thompson, *Discourse Commemorative of Rev. Rufus Anderson, D.D., LL.D., Late Corresponding Secretary of the American Board of Commissioners for Foreign Missions* (1880). Anderson's place in the development of American Protestant missionary ideology is explained most clearly in William R. Hutchison, *Errand to the World: American Protestant Thought and Foreign Missions* (1987).

ROBERT A. SCHNEIDER

ANDERSON, Sherwood (13 Sept. 1876–8 Mar. 1941), writer, was born in Camden, Ohio, the son of Irwin McClain Anderson, a harnessmaker, and Emma Jane Smith. For the first thirty-five years of his life, Anderson made himself into just the man that the culture considered ideal. His father was a wayward man, barely able to support his wife and seven children. When Anderson was nineteen his long-suffering mother died, after which, having tried so hard to earn money in Clyde, Ohio, where the family had settled, he became known as "Jobby," and having completed less than a year of high school in the process, he set out for Chicago in search of his fortune.

Failing to find it as a common laborer, Anderson enlisted to fight in the Spanish-American War but arrived in Cuba only after the armistice was signed in August 1898. He attended Wittenberg Academy in Springfield, Ohio, for a year (1898–1899) and then returned to Chicago where he finally succeeded in becoming an advertising solicitor and copywriter. In 1904 he married Cornelia Platt Lane, of a well-to-do Toledo, Ohio, family, and with her had three children. From advertising he moved on to the mail-order business. By 1907 he was president of his own company, the Anderson Manufacturing Company, specializing in Roof-Fix, in Elyria, Ohio. As a youth in Clyde he had been told "money made the mare go"; in 1911 he was riding high.

But starting in 1912, Anderson remade himself into a very different kind of American man. He entered a midlife crisis that became legendary. In late November he walked out of his office and wandered through the countryside in a "fugue state," coming to his senses four days later in a Cleveland hospital. For several years he had been trying to write—at night, in a room he kept locked—trying to imagine a less material existence for himself in writing. In 1913 he left his family for good and returned to Chicago once more, joining a group of young artists and writers in what he later called its "robin's egg renaissance." The next year he published his first story. Two years later, he published his first novel, *Windy McPherson's Son* (1916), which tells of a man's escape from the world of business and commerce and his search for truth. *Seven Arts* considered it a clear sign of "emerging greatness." Anderson's stories, especially "Hands" (which became the first of those collected in *Winesburg, Ohio*), influenced and encouraged the young intellectuals in the East, to whose magazines he sent them. Van Wyck Brooks considered Anderson's writing "the most beautiful prose fiction of our time" and his famous flight "the symbol of an epoch." In *Our America* (1919), Waldo Frank said that "what happened to Sherwood Anderson and turned him from the traveled American part of money-making is of vast significance: not as regards the life of Anderson alone, but in the life of the United States."

Anderson's second novel, *Marching Men* (1917), was ostensibly more political than his first, but in urging workers to protest against the life imposed on them by industrial America, his hero had no program for them. They had only to march. That Anderson was more inclined to exhort men to realize the ideals of democracy within themselves than societally is evident from the pale imitations of Walt Whitman that constitute his next volume, *Mid-American Chants* (1918).

Anderson's best and most famous work, *Winesburg, Ohio* (1919), is a collection of stories or, as he preferred to call them, tales, held together by the pervasive presences of a young reporter, to whom many of the protagonists confess, and of the older narrator intent upon evoking sympathy for them. They are what Anderson called "grotesques," figures whose lives have become misshapen because each has taken one of the truths of the world, "the truth of virginity and the truth of passion, the truth of wealth and of poverty, of thrift and profligacy, of carelessness and abandon . . . called it his truth, and tried to live his life by it." They inhabit a small town that resembles Anderson's native Clyde, but they were modeled after people he knew in his Chicago boardinghouse. He meant them to mirror the condition of contemporary American culture generally.

Drawing again on his midwestern heritage, this time as it was filtered through Mark Twain, Anderson rendered in *Poor White* (1920) the interconnections between men's drive toward worldly success and their failures as sexual partners and as husbands. Once again he envisioned salvation for them in a relatively ill-defined creative or "poetic" life. In 1921 and 1923 he published collections of tales he titled *Triumph of the Egg* and *Horses and Men*. In the better known among them—"I'm a Fool" and "I Want to Know Why"—Anderson used a vernacular style modeled on Twain's to explore the typical American boy's emergence into manhood. Anderson's quest for liberation was, characteristically, personal, often sexual. (Those who took "the truth of passion" as their truth in *Winesburg, Ohio* had made him notorious as well as famous.) As his second marriage to Tennessee Mitchell ended and a third to Elizabeth Prall began, Anderson wrote *Many Marriages* (1923) on his hopes for a union that would leave him free. In *Dark Laughter* (1925) he experimented with Joycean techniques and borrowed from credos of D. H. Lawrence in his effort to explore new sexual territory. It was the only volume of his to enjoy commercial success, in part because, as the title indicates, it coincided with a particularly intense period of exploitation of African-American culture for that purpose.

In 1921 Anderson received the first *Dial* award for service rendered to American letters (subsequent winners included T. S. Eliot and Ezra Pound); in the December 1926 issue of *Vanity Fair*, H. L. Mencken described him as "America's most distinctive novelist." But at the same time, Anderson's powers of invention were beginning to fail him. He went back over his life in *A Story Teller's Tale* (1924) and then again in *Tar: A Midwestern Childhood* (1926), and he collected some of his essays and reflections in *Sherwood Anderson's Notebook* (1926). Abandoning fiction altogether, in 1927 he bought two weekly newspapers—one Democratic, the other Republican—in southwest Virginia, where he had recently built a country house. After two years he turned his newspapers over to his oldest son and collected his editorials, articles, and sketches in *Hello Towns!* (1929).

Through Eleanor Copenhaver, head of the Industrial Division of the YWCA (and, in 1933, his fourth wife), Anderson discovered the lives of the men and women who worked in the mills and in the mines of Kentucky, Tennessee, and Virginia. "The woman had poked me with a stick. She had forced me to crawl out from under my bush," he wrote in *Perhaps Women* (1931). He was still inclined to focus his attention on the opposite sex and on sex. It was still machinery, the making and worship of things, he thought, that was emasculating men ("perhaps women" would save them), but now he had a clearer vision of what men might become. He observed firsthand the effects of the depression, and in journalistic pieces, many of which were published in Raymond Moley's *Today*, he celebrated the decency and courage of those who were struggling, and he explained and supported New Deal programs (the Civilian Conservation Corps and the TVA, especially) that were designed to assist them. His growing interest in politics and his flirtations with radical causes found expression in another novel, *Beyond Desire* (1932).

In the mid-1930s Anderson became interested in the theater, in a dramatization of *Winesburg, Ohio* in particular, but it was the small town itself that occupied him in his final years. His last work was a long essay, published with numerous photographs from the files of the Farm Security Administration, titled *Home Town* (1940). His last journey was to South America, where he intended to discover the virtues of another culture's ordinary citizenry. But having swallowed a toothpick before his departure, he was afflicted with peritonitis onboard ship and died in a hospital in Colon, in the Panama Canal Zone.

Anderson's colloquial style and his themes, as well as his own colorful life, did much to put "middle America" on the cultural map. He was generous in his support of greater writers who were to succeed him, most notably William Faulkner and Ernest Hemingway, and he had some influence on their literary manners and choice of subject matter. Erskine Caldwell, James T. Farrell, William Saroyan, John Steinbeck, Thomas Wolfe, and, more recently, Raymond Carver also have been inspired by Anderson's commitment to the craft of writing as a means of exploring common men's lives openly and sympathetically.

• Almost all of the documents, letters, and memorabilia that bear on Anderson's life as a writer are in the Newberry Library in Chicago. His *Complete Works* have been edited by Kichinosuke Ohashi (1982). Howard Mumford Jones and Walter Rideout edited a large selection of his letters in 1953; Charles Modlin published a supplementary edition of them in 1984. Published in 1942, *Sherwood Anderson's Memoirs* is an important if not wholly reliable resource. William A. Sutton, *The Road to Winesburg* (1972), documents Anderson's life up through 1919. James Schevill published *Sherwood Anderson: His Life and Work* in 1951; Kim Townsend, *Sherwood Anderson: A Biography* (1987), has many years of subsequent research to draw on. Irving Howe, *Sherwood Anderson* (1951), is still provocative, as are critical essays in Paul P. Appel, ed., *Homage to Sherwood Anderson* (1970). Eugene P. Sheehy and Kenneth A. Lohf, *Sherwood Anderson: A Bibliography* (1960), and Ray Lewis White, ed., *Sherwood Anderson: A Reference Guide* (1977), provide further references.

KIM TOWNSEND

ANDERSON, Willie (1878?–25 Oct. 1910), golfer, was born William Anderson in North Berwick, Scotland, the son of Tom Anderson, a golf greenskeeper. (His mother's name is unknown.) His birth year has appeared as 1878 and 1880; most obituaries list his age as 30 at his death. Anderson grew up in North Berwick, spending much of his youth on the golf course of the club where his father was employed. He never worked as a caddie but focused on playing golf and learning the required skills. He came to the United States in 1894 when golf was being introduced as a recreation and sport. In his first tournament, the U.S. Open in 1897, he finished one stroke behind the winner, Joe Lloyd. He also fared well in the 1898 and 1899 opens, finishing third and fifth.

In 1901 the U.S. Open, regarded at the time as the national golf championship, was held at the Myopia Hunt Club in Hamilton, Massachusetts. In those years, the sport was viewed as an elite pastime, and professional golfers were regarded by club members as less than socially acceptable. Amateur participants that year were welcome in the clubhouse dining room, but professionals were excluded. Anderson and other professionals protested the discrimination, and a compromise of sorts resulted in their being served in a tent.

Anderson won his first U.S. Open title that year. At the end of regulation play, which had been extended to 72 holes in 1898, he was tied for low score with his close friend Alex Smith. Both recorded totals of 331 strokes, the worst mark ever posted for a first-place finish in the Open. In an 18-hole playoff match, Anderson defeated Smith by one stroke, 85 to 86.

The next year Anderson finished fifth, 11 strokes behind the winner. He then accomplished a feat still unmatched by winning the U.S. Open three consecutive years (1903–1905). In 1903 he again won in a playoff, defeating David Brown, a former British Open titleholder, 82 to 84. Anderson's 73 in the opening round set a new low score in U.S. Open play. The following year he won decisively by five strokes over his nearest competitor, Gil Nicolls, his total score of 303 the best up to that time. In Anderson's final U.S. Open victory in 1905, he again defeated Smith, this time by 314 to 316. It appeared that Anderson would win the Open in 1906 when he was tied for the lead after the first round. But a dismal final round of 84 put him out of contention, and he never again was a threat to win the U.S. Open.

The second most prestigious tournament during Anderson's career was the Western Open, which he won four times (1902, 1904, 1908, and 1909). His 71–73–72–72 scores in the 1909 Western set a record for low total score (288) over a lengthy course. Two years earlier, in 1907, he had won the North Florida Open with an unprecedented 138 for 36 holes. He shot 67 for 18 holes, including a remarkable 32 on one of the nines, to win $100.

Anderson's personality showed signs of instability. From the age of 16, he was employed at 10 different golf clubs from New York to Illinois. Although well liked by his fellow professionals, he was seen as melancholy. Some golf historians believe he was disappointed at not being appreciated by the public. On the golf course, he was all business. He was even-tempered, and no one could tell from his appearance during play whether he was winning or losing.

Anderson was 5′10″ and weighed 165 pounds, with broad shoulders and large hands. Although he did not hit long drives, his forte was accuracy off the tee. Some reports describe his straight drives and ability to avoid bunkers around the greens. His swing was smooth and deliberate with a full pivot, which extended through his whole body, effectively disguising his power. Photographs of Anderson show a flat swing with his left arm bent, the standard technique for his time. His golfing style was not graceful by modern standards.

Anderson adapted well to changes in the golf ball during the early twentieth century. The earlier ball consisted of gutta-percha, a hard rubber substance, which was replaced by the so-called Haskell ball, consisting of a rubber core with elastic wound around it and enclosed in a gutta-percha cover. Of the two, the Haskell ball was livelier and more responsive. Some professionals were reluctant to switch to the new ball, but Anderson became the only player to win the U.S. Open using the "gutty" and the Haskell.

Anderson died unexpectedly in Philadelphia. The cause of his death was recorded as arteriosclerosis, but he was rumored to have died of acute alcoholism. According to many accounts of American golf's early days, professional players were heavy drinkers. Nonetheless, his death at such a young age came as a shock. Only a week before, he had played several 36-hole exhibition matches in Pittsburgh. He was survived by his wife.

Charles Price, in *The World of Golf* (1962), claims that some of Anderson's contemporaries considered him a better golfer than Bobby Jones and Ben Hogan. But Peter Aliss, in *The Who's Who of Golf* (1983), writes that many others believe Anderson could not have been their equal. Anderson belongs to that group of immigrant Scotsmen who influenced the early history of American golf. He ranks as the best of the early Scotch champions whose game was formed in the United States. Robert Sommers writes in *The U.S. Open: Golf's Ultimate Challenge* (1987) that Anderson was a complete golfer, skilled in every phase of the game.

• A brief account of Anderson's career and accomplishments appears in Ross Goodner, *Golf's Greatest: The Legendary World Golf Hall of Famers* (1978). For additional information, see Donald Steel and Peter Ryde, eds., *The Encyclopedia of Golf* (1975), and Herbert Warren Wind, *The Story of American Golf: Its Champions and Its Championships* (1956). George Peper and the editors of *Golf Magazine* rank Anderson the best golfer of the first decade of the twentieth century in *Golf in America: The First One Hundred Years* (1988).

LEWIS H. CROCE

ANDRÉ, John (2 May 1750–2 Oct. 1780), British officer and spy, was born in London, England, the son of Anthony André, a merchant, and Marie Louise Girardot. His early schooling was with a tutor, the Reverend Thomas Newcomb, and he may have attended St. Paul's School. In his teens André studied mathematics and military drawing at the University of Geneva, giving vent to his romantic temperament by dreaming of a military career. He was rudely brought back to reality by his merchant father when he was called home to work in the countinghouse before he completed a degree. Despising the family business, he nevertheless labored at it manfully for a number of years. After his father died on 14 April 1769, he felt a particular obligation as the eldest son to continue the business, even though his father had left him financially independent, with a small fortune of £5,000. In the summer of 1769 he joined a Lichfield literary group presided over by Anna Seward, a poet. The group included a young lady named Honora Sneyd, for whom he developed a passion. They became engaged and courted for a year and a half before she suddenly rejected him for another man at a Christmas party in 1770. Shattered by this betrayal, André revived his earlier ambition to become a soldier and in early 1771 bought a second lieutenant's commission in the 23d Regiment, Royal Welsh Fusiliers. Later he purchased a first lieutenancy in the same regiment.

Becoming bored with the peacetime routine of the British army, André secured a leave of absence in early 1772 to travel with George Rodney, the famous admiral's son, to Göttingen. There he enrolled at the university to study mathematics and joined another literary society, the Hain, to pursue his love of poetry. Ordered in the summer of 1774 to rejoin his regiment at Quebec, he made his way leisurely to that city, arriving just before the winter freeze. In the spring of 1775 he was sent to St. Johns on the Sorel River, where the British were constructing fortifications to halt an impending American attack against Canada. On 3 November he and his comrades were taken prisoner. Held captive in Lancaster and Carlisle, Pennsylvania, until 28 November 1776, he was then released in a prisoner exchange. He spent a quiet winter in New York, accomplishing little except promotion to captain in the Twenty-sixth Regiment and commencing a journal. In June 1777 his fortunes changed. On 3 June Major General Charles Grey sailed into New York and, upon the recommendation of William Howe, British commander in chief, chose André as an aide-de-camp. Learning that the hard-fighting general agreed with him that warfare against American rebels should be harsh, André found Grey a congenial commanding officer. In June 1777 André campaigned with Grey in New Jersey and in July sailed with him southward toward the Chesapeake Bay. André was at the battles of the Brandywine (11 Sept.), Paoli (20–21 Sept.), Germantown (4 Oct.), and Whitemarsh (4 Dec.). During the British occupation of Philadelphia in the winter of 1777–1778, he staged amateur theatricals and was largely responsible for designing the stage scenery and costumes for what he called the Mischianza, an extravagant "variety of entertainments" presented on 18 May 1778 in honor of General Howe when he resigned his command. André also became a favorite of Philadelphia's young Tory ladies, particularly Elizabeth "Peggy" Shippen, who would later marry General Benedict Arnold.

On 18 June 1778 André was with Howe's replacement as commander in chief, Sir Henry Clinton, when Clinton abandoned Philadelphia and marched across New Jersey toward New York. He was at the battle of Monmouth ten days later, and during 4–6 September he assisted Grey in raiding New Haven and Fair Haven, Connecticut, on Long Island Sound. In the early hours of 28 September he and Grey surprised Lieutenant Colonel George Baylor's Third Continental Light

Dragoons at Old Tappan, New York, and annihilated that unit as a fighting force. Praising André to Clinton after he had returned to England in November 1778, Grey declared, "I do not think a better principled young man exists." Agreeing, Clinton chose André to be one of his aides. During the winter of 1778–1779 in New York, André wrote and staged plays and recited poetry at parties. He suffered a financial blow in July 1779 when his extensive estates on the West Indian island of Grenada fell into French hands. Thereafter, he and his family had to alter "their mode of life." On 23 October 1779 Clinton appointed him deputy adjutant general of the army, "with all the duties of the principal of the department," and with the rank of major. In this new capacity André accompanied Clinton southward in early 1780 for operations against Charleston, and after that city fell on 12 May he returned with Clinton to New York. In the summer of 1780 he published a long poem in the *Royal Gazette* titled "The Cow Chace," bitingly satirizing American generals Anthony Wayne, Henry Lee, and William Alexander as cowboys, cowards, and drunkards.

As part of his duties on Clinton's staff, André was in charge of correspondence between the commander in chief and British secret agents in America. In that capacity he became enmeshed in Benedict Arnold's treasonous correspondence with Clinton in May 1779. On 20 September 1780, as part of his clandestine negotiations with Arnold for the surrender of West Point, he sailed up the Hudson River in the sloop *Vulture* to meet Arnold at Haverstraw, New York. After the meeting in the early morning of 22 September he was unable to return to the *Vulture* because it had been compelled by American fire to sail southward. Trapped behind enemy lines but bearing a pass from Arnold, he spent the night of 22 September with a friendly farmer, then changed from his uniform into civilian clothes in order to make his way back to British lines near Tarrytown. At nine o'clock in the morning on 23 September, within sight of his own comrades, he was detained by three American militiamen, whom he had mistaken for British soldiers. Identifying himself as a British officer rather than producing Arnold's pass, he was immediately searched, and incriminating military documents that Arnold had given him were found in his boots. He was arrested, despite his vain attempts to bribe his captors, and taken to a local command post. There he was almost turned over to Arnold before a suspicious Major Benjamin Tallmadge intervened to hold him, while forwarding the captured documents to General George Washington. Arnold, learning of André's seizure, fled to the British lines.

André was conveyed to Tappan, New York, where on 29 September Washington convened a military tribunal of high ranking officers to try him as a spy. He was found guilty and sentenced to death by hanging. Although he petitioned Washington to be shot as a soldier, Washington refused on the ground that to do so would imply that André's conviction was unjust. Clinton desperately tried everything in his power to save his young protégé, save the one thing to which Washington would have consented: exchanging Arnold for André. On 2 October André was executed, dying calmly, and mourned not only by the English officers but also by the Americans, who had come to admire him in the short time they had been in his company. He was honored in Britain by a monument in Westminster Abbey, to which his remains were removed in 1821. He was remembered for his nobility of character, manners, military abilities, and varied talents as an actor, playwright, stage and costume designer, sketch artist, and satirical poet.

• Considerable André material is in the Sir Henry Clinton Papers, William L. Clements Library, University of Michigan. His journal is *André's Journal: An Authentic record of the Movements and Engagements of the British Army in America from June 1777 to November 1778*, ed. Henry Cabot Lodge (2 vols., 1903). Clinton's views are in *The American Rebellion: Sir Henry Clinton's Narrative of His Campaigns, 1775–1782*, ed. William B. Willcox (1954). Three of André's letters are in Anna Seward, *Monody on Major André: Who was Executed at Tappan, November—1780* (1788). The best biographies are Winthrop Sargent, *The Life and Career of Major John André, Adjutant-General of the British Army in America*, ed. William Abbott (1902); and Harry S. Tillotson, *The Beloved Spy: The Life and Loves of Major John André* (1948). Other biographies are Henry Pleasants, *John André: Spy Extraordinary* (1939), Adele Nathan, *Major John André: Gentleman Spy* (1969), Lois Duncan, *Major André: Brave Enemy* (1969), and Robert M. Hatch, *Major John André: A Gallant in Spy's Clothing* (1986). Accounts of André's spy role are Benson J. Lossing, *The Two Spies: Nathan Hale and John André* (1886), Carl Van Doren, *Secret History of the American Revolution* (1941), James T. Flexner, *The Traitor and the Spy: Benedict Arnold and John André* (1953), and John E. Bakeless, *Turncoats, Traitors, and Heroes* (1959). Good biographies of Arnold are Willard M. Wallace, *Traitorous Hero: The Life and Fortunes of Benedict Arnold* (1954), and Clare Brandt, *The Man in the Mirror: A Life of Benedict Arnold* (1994). Clinton's biographer is William B. Willcox, *Portrait of a General: Sir Henry Clinton in the War of American Independence* (1962). For Grey's role, see Paul David Nelson, *Sir Charles Grey, First Earl Grey: Royal Soldier, Family Patriarch* (1996). John W. Jackson, *With the British Army in Philadelphia, 1777–1778* (1979), discusses André's activities there.

PAUL DAVID NELSON

ANDREI, Giovanni (1770–21 Oct. 1824), sculptor, was born in Carrara, Italy. His parents' names and occupations are unknown. His earliest known work was the creation of the balustrade of the high altar at Santa Maria Novella in Florence. In 1805 Benjamin Henry Latrobe, then architect of the U.S. Capitol in Washington, D.C., wrote to President Thomas Jefferson's friend in Italy, Philip Mazzei, to ask the latter to find two sculptors who would execute the decorative work for the Capitol and send them to the United States. There were then only carvers of wooden shop signs and ships' figureheads active in America, for the art of sculpture wrought in stone was hardly known. Andrei, accompanied by his pupil and brother-in-law, Giuseppe Franzoni, arrived in Baltimore in February 1806, and soon proceeded to Washington. (The name of Andrei's wife is unknown.) Andrei and Franzoni set up a sculptors' lodge on the Capitol grounds and were charged with hiring and training apprentices while they were creating the architectural ornaments for the rising building.

Because of financial constraints brought about by Jefferson's trade embargo, Andrei and Franzoni had little work to do in 1808 and so were "loaned" to the architect Maximilian Godefroy, who was then erecting St. Mary's Chapel in Baltimore. They executed many of the interior adornments in that early Gothic revival building. While in Baltimore the two Italian sculptors also created a large pediment (now at the Peale Museum) for Union Bank, representing Neptune and Ceres in the prevailing neoclassical style.

Back in Washington, Andrei modeled the twenty-four large capitals for the columns in the House of Representatives chamber, but these were destroyed when the British burned the Capitol in August 1814. The next year Andrei was sent to Italy to execute another set of Corinthian capitals for the Capitol. His partner Franzoni having died that same year, Andrei was also commissioned to hire two more sculptors to bring back with him; he chose Carlo Franzoni, brother of Giuseppe, and Francesco Iardella, both of whom worked for many years at the Capitol site.

Andrei remained in charge of the sculptural work at the Capitol until his death in Washington, D.C., becoming respected both for his character and for his talent as an artist. Latrobe once referred to Andrei and Franzoni as "very skillful sculptors." Charles Bulfinch, Latrobe's successor as architect of the Capitol, paid Andrei a fine tribute soon after the carver's death when he wrote the following in a report to Joseph Elgar, the commissioner of public buildings, under date of 8 December 1826:

> His ability and refined taste are fully evidenced in the ornamental parts of the Capitol, modelled by him and executed under his inspection; while all, who have been officially connected with him, can bear witness to his fidelity and persevering industry, and to the urbanity and correctness of his deportment. In expressing my respect for the character of Mr. Andrei, and regret at his loss, I hope it will not be considered improper to make this mention of him, in a report on a work which his talents have so much contributed to improve. (*Documentary History of the Construction and Development of the United States Capitol Building and Grounds* [1904], p. 266)

Andrei's widow was enabled to return to her native Italy through a special appropriation of $400 by act of Congress on 22 May 1826; a Perpetua and a Maddalena Andrei were listed as administrators of the sculptor's estate. While more of a sculptor of architectural decorations than of figures or portrait busts, Andrei occupies a special place in the history of American sculpture as one of the earliest of the European sculptors to implant in the United States the concept of that previously little known art form.

• Giovanni Andrei left no papers. References to him in Congressional records are found in Charles Fairman, *Art and Artists of the Capitol of the United States of America* (1927). See also Richard R. Borneman, "Franzoni and Andrei: Italian Sculptors in Baltimore, 1808," *William and Mary Quarterly*, 3d ser., 10, no. 1 (1953): 108–11. For an overview of the influence of Italian immigrant sculptors and Andrei's and Franzoni's historical position see Wayne Craven, *Sculpture in America* (1984). A brief obituary for Andrei appears in the *National Intelligencer*, 22 Oct. 1824.

WAYNE CRAVEN

ANDREW, James Osgood (3 May 1794–2 Mar. 1871), Methodist Episcopal bishop, was born in Wilkes County, Georgia, the son of the Reverend John Andrew and Mary Cosby. In 1789 John Andrew became the first native Georgian to enter the itinerant ministry of the Methodist Episcopal Church. James was educated in country schools and through his own personal reading. About 1809, Andrew recalled, he "attended a camp meeting and was powerfully awakened." Shortly thereafter he became a member of the Asbury Chapel on the Broad River Circuit. In 1812 he was licensed to preach and admitted on trial to the South Carolina Annual Conference of the Methodist Episcopal Church.

Andrew's pastorates included Charleston, South Carolina; Wilmington, North Carolina; Columbia, South Carolina; Augusta, Georgia; Savannah, Georgia; Greensboro, North Carolina; and Athens, Georgia. During these pastorates he gained a reputation as a leader and preacher. In 1820, 1824, 1828, and 1832 he was a delegate to the denomination's General Conference. The 1832 General Conference elected him a bishop of the church. His episcopal assignments included most of the Annual Conferences in the South as well as Ohio, Kentucky, and Missouri. His episcopal residence was in Georgia.

Bishop Andrew became one of the most controversial figures in Methodism, because he was both a bishop and a slaveholder. An acquaintance had bequeathed him in trust a young female slave who was to be sent to Liberia when she was nineteen years of age or, if she refused, was to be freed as the laws of Georgia permitted. Additionally, Andrew married three times and acquired slaves from two of his wives. In 1816 he married Ann Amelia McFarlane, with whom he had four children. When his wife died in 1842, she left him a young male slave. In 1844 he married a widow, Leonora Greenwood, who was also a slave owner. Soon after her death in 1854, Andrew married another widow, Emily Sims Childers.

At the 1844 General Conference of the Methodist Episcopal Church, Andrew was attacked by northern Methodist abolitionist delegates for his slaveholding. He responded that he had never personally bought or sold a slave and that he had attempted to free himself from any slaveholding. The female slave he acquired in trust refused to go to Liberia, and the laws of Georgia prohibited her emancipation; the young male slave was not yet old enough to provide for himself, and Georgia laws prohibited owners from emancipating slaves if freedmen were to remain in the state. Andrew also disclaimed any legal right to or responsibility for the slaves owned by his second wife.

The antislavery delegates were unconvinced by Andrew's defense. They adopted a resolution, over southern opposition, that suspended him from the exercise of his episcopal position as long as he continued to own slaves. Although he offered to resign his office, southern supporters persuaded him to remain at his post. The protest of the southern delegates to the action against Andrew led to their drawing up a Plan of Separation, which resulted in the formation of a new Methodist denomination that would not oppose slavery. In May 1845 the Methodist Episcopal Church, South was created in Louisville, Kentucky, with Andrew as one of its bishops.

Andrew was the author of numerous articles in the periodicals of his denomination. He also published a number of pamphlets and books including *Family Government* (1847) and *Miscellanies* (1855). In 1866 he retired from the active ministry of the church. He died in New Orleans, Louisiana.

• Andrew's name appears prominently in histories of American Methodism such as Emory S. Bucke, ed., *The History of American Methodism* (1964), and Gross Alexander, *A History of the Methodist Episcopal Church, South* (1894). See also George G. Smith, *The Life and Letters of James Osgood Andrew* (1882).

CHARLES YRIGOYEN, JR.

ANDREW, John Albion (31 May 1818–30 Oct. 1867), reformer, antislavery advocate, and Civil War governor of Massachusetts, was born in Windham, Maine, the son of Jonathan Andrew, a farmer and general store owner, and Nancy Green Pierce, a schoolteacher. Educated at private academies and then at Bowdoin College, from which he graduated in 1837, Andrews learned early about the evils of slavery and the religious necessity to oppose it. One of his contemporaries at Bowdoin was John Russwurm, Bowdoin's first African-American graduate who was soon to become an influential abolitionist. The college supported a vigorous antislavery society, to which Andrew belonged. From the first, his political and religious outlook was shaped by a hostility to slavery.

Moving to Boston in 1837 to read law at the offices of Fuller and Washburn, Andrew found himself in a setting that deepened his antislavery convictions. He was active in the local Unitarian church, a denomination well known in Boston for its reforming spirit and its antislavery-minded ministers. He also joined the Boston Port Society, an organization dedicated to assisting impoverished common seafarers, and after being admitted to the bar in 1840, he began visiting the Boston jail, offering free legal assistance to indigent prisoners.

State and local politics, not the sweeping radicalism of abolitionists William Lloyd Garrison and Wendell Phillips, began to engage young Andrew in antislavery activism. During the early and mid-1840s, the national issue of slavery's westward expansion and local controversies over the return of fugitive slaves created divisions within Massachusetts's Whig party. "Conscience Whigs," including Andrew, began pressing their party's established leadership to take forthright antislavery positions on these and related questions. Opposing their efforts to commit the state's Whig party to antislavery principles were some of Massachusetts's wealthiest manufacturers and businessmen, who were known as "Cotton Whigs." In 1846 open disagreements between these two factions gave Andrew his first opportunity to engage in antislavery politics. When Conscience Whigs held a meeting in Faneuil Hall to object to the return of fugitive slaves, Andrew took the lead by framing and reading resolutions of protest that condemned the Cotton Whigs for their subserviency to southern interests. When the Whig party nominated slaveholding Zachary Taylor for the presidency in 1848, Andrew declared his allegiance to the new Free Soil party. As a Free Soiler, Andrew embarked on a career of insurgency that a decade later would make him one of the most powerful politicians in Massachusetts. In 1848 he married Eliza Jones, with whom he had four children.

The 1850s in Massachusetts witnessed complicated political upheavals, from which the state's Republican party finally emerged. On specific antislavery and general egalitarian grounds, Andrew vigorously opposed the anti-Cathlolic, anti-Irish Know Nothing party. In recognition of his strong antislavery credentials, he was elected as a Republican to the state legislature, where he began building a reputation for eloquent speaking and energetic leadership.

The individual who suddenly catapulted Andrew to the forefront of Massachusetts politics was John Brown, whose 1959 raid on Harpers Ferry and subsequent trial and execution inspired Andrew to action. While the captured insurrectionist awaited his fate, Andrew spoke boldly in defense of Brown's actions, raised funds for his legal defense, and worked zealously to support Brown's family. So fervent was his espousal of Brown's cause that he was suspected of having conspired with Brown. His testimony before a congressional investigative committee was eloquent and was favorably reported in Massachusetts. Consequently Andrew was easily selected as chairman of the state delegation to the Republican National Convention.

In a closely contested nomination struggle, Andrew gave essential support to Abraham Lincoln, whose nomination put the resources of the national Republican organization at Andrew's disposal while greatly increasing his political stature. Andrew easily captured the gubernatorial nomination on the first ballot and then secured an unprecedentedly large majority in the general election. At age forty-two, Andrew had become Massachusetts's most powerful politician and one of the president's most stalwart allies in facing the impending crisis of the Civil War.

Massachusetts, under Andrew's vigorous direction, quickly assumed leadership in the North's military mobilization. Wealthy manufacturers and financiers in the state added their private resources to Andrew's successful legislative campaign to secure a $100,000 appropriation to support Massachusetts militia units. Hence, when war commenced, Massachusetts was already well prepared to send a full regiment to the defense of Washington, D.C., in April 1861.

While Andrew continued to keep Massachusetts on a war footing, he also began stressing that the purpose of the fighting must be to emancipate the slaves. When, for example, in 1861 Lincoln countermanded General John C. Frémont's order that escaped slaves be freed as "contraband of war," Andrew protested loudly against the president's decision. When Lincoln issued his Emancipation Proclamation, Andrew applauded its goals but criticized its timid approach, remarking that it was "a poor *document* but a mighty *act*."

Andrew sensed that beyond the process of emancipation lay the larger problems of racial inequality and the transition from slavery to citizenship. For this reason, in 1862 he became active in the cause of freedpeople's education, serving as president of the Boston Education Commission, which supported "the industrial, social, intellectual, social, moral and religious education of persons released from slavery in the course of the War for the Union." Concurrent with his efforts for aid for freedpeople, Andrew took the lead in the experiment in racial egalitarianism for which he is most famous, the mobilization of African-American soldiers.

Andrew was the politician best situated to transform into military policy the demands of black activists that African Americans be allowed to achieve their own equality through combat. In January 1863, after several months of vigorous lobbying, Andrew obtained authorization from Secretary of War Edwin Stanton to recruit an African-American regiment in Massachusetts, but only with the proviso that all commissioned officers be white. Swallowing his objections to this stipulation, Andrew organized the Fifty-fourth Massachusetts Volunteers. Recruitment proved difficult, however. Free African Americans resented the "whites only" policy regarding commissioned officers and feared, correctly as it turned out, that they would be paid less than white soldiers. Pamphlets like Frederick Douglass's stirring *Colored Men, To Arms!* with Andrew's political assistance made it possible in May 1863 to add the Fifty-fifth Regiment to the already assembled Fifty-fourth. Immortalized by their courageous attempt to storm Fort Wagner outside Charleston, South Carolina, the Fifty-fourth Massachusetts Volunteers represented Andrew's finest contribution to the struggle for racial equality.

In 1864 Andrew was reelected governor, but he had lost much of his national political stature because of his support for Salmon P. Chase over Lincoln as the Republican presidential nominee. While still committed to equal rights for freedpeople, he also advocated lenient treatment for secessionists as the process of Reconstruction began, a position that put him in direct conflict with Massachusetts's leading radical, U.S. senator Charles Sumner. He retired from the governorship in 1866. Though only forty-eight years of age, he was clearly exhausted and his political career was over. He died in Boston after a brief illness.

In the estimation of historians, Andrew was an unusually effective Civil War governor. His administrative and political achievements earned him particular distinction because of their effectiveness in advancing the causes of emancipation and racial equality.

• Andrew's papers are at the Massachusetts Historical Society. Henry Greenleaf Pearson, *The Life of John Andrew* (1904), is an old but standard biography, and Richard H. Abbott, *Cotton and Capitalism: Boston Merchants and Antislavery Reform, 1854–1868* (1991), provides useful information and contexts bearing on Andrew's career.

JAMES BREWER STEWART

ANDREWS, Alexander Boyd (23 July 1841–17 Apr. 1915), railroad executive, was born near Franklinton, North Carolina, the son of William J. Andrews, a small planter and merchant, and Virginia Hawkins. The family soon moved to Henderson, North Carolina. After the death of his mother in 1852 and his father the next year, young Andrews passed into the care of his mother's family. In 1859, not yet eighteen years old, he left the Henderson Male Academy to work for his uncle Philemon B. Hawkins, who had a construction contract on the Blue Ridge Railroad in South Carolina. In short order he was promoted to superintendent, paymaster, and purchasing agent of his uncle's operation.

At the outbreak of the Civil War Andrews enlisted as a private in what would soon become the First North Carolina Cavalry. By July 1862 he had reached captain. That month, while patrolling along the Roanoke River, his company intercepted three lightly armed Federal gunboats ascending the river to destroy two strategic railroad bridges. In what may have been the first case of a cavalry–naval vessel engagement, the rifle fire of Andrews's men forced the gunboats to retreat back down the river. The regiment was later attached to Robert E. Lee's Army of Northern Virginia and fought several campaigns under J. E. B. Stuart, including the battle of Antietam (Sharpsburg) and Stuart's second ride around George B. McClellan. On 22 September 1863, in a skirmish at Jack's Shop, Virginia, Andrews was shot through the lung, ending his military service.

In July 1865, needing employment, Andrews borrowed $100 to lease and operate a ferry across the Roanoke at Gaston, North Carolina, where one of those same two bridges now lay in ruins. Early in 1866 he took a job in Henderson, North Carolina, with the Raleigh and Gaston Railroad, of which William J. Hawkins (another uncle) was president. He was promoted in July 1867 to superintendent (or operations manager) and soon added the same position on the related Chatham Railroad. He repaired wartime damage and built new mileage, an activity that would occupy much of his time into the 1890s. In 1869 Andrews married Julia Martha Johnston, daughter of Charlotte railroad president William Johnston; they had five children.

Andrews developed a reputation for efficiency and business acumen. In 1875 he moved to the larger Richmond & Danville Railroad, then an agent of northern railroad expansion in the Southeast, as superintendent of its operations between Goldsboro and Charlotte, North Carolina. In a few years he was supervising all R&D operations in the state.

In 1881 (still working for the R&D) Andrews assumed the presidency of the Western North Carolina Railroad, which had been struggling for years to reach the Tennessee line at both Paint Rock near Asheville and Murphy in the western tip of the state. Using outside capital and convict labor, he reached these points in 1882 and 1890, respectively. (The town of Andrews, near Murphy, was named for him, as was the Andrews Geyser, a 100-foot fountain and once-popular train stop near Swannanoa Gap.)

Andrews continued to rise in the management of the R&D and, after 1894, its successor, the Southern Railway. At different times he was also president of some two dozen dependent railroads in the Southeast, adding trackage and making them profitable to the parent road. For the last twenty years of his life, he was first vice president of the Southern and chief of its operations in North Carolina.

North Carolina had its textile and tobacco barons; Andrews was its nearest approach to a railroad baron. He lived and acted the part. Townspeople of Raleigh were awed by his open carriage and span of white horses. From his office, his private car, and his handsome home near the governor's mansion and the capitol, he courted the road's friends and punished its enemies. When editor Josephus Daniels and other advocates of railroad regulation characterized him as the state's leading corruptor of public officials, Andrews subsidized rival newspapers. "If a man puts his money in a railroad," he was quoted as saying, "it is his railroad and he has a right to run it as he damn pleases."

Andrews had a variety of subordinate civic and business interests. He was a director and official of several banking, insurance, and other corporations, centering in North Carolina and the South; an active Episcopalian; a founder and president of the Home for Confederate Veterans in Raleigh; a longtime trustee of the University of North Carolina; and an alderman in Henderson and Raleigh. His customary title of "Colonel" derived from largely honorific service on the staffs of two governors. A lifelong southern Democrat, he nevertheless supported William McKinley over William Jennings Bryan in 1896.

As a builder and operator of railroads, Andrews was credited with laying more miles of track in North Carolina than any other person. Rising in the ranks, he became increasingly involved in railroad finance and lobbying. During his last twenty-five years, he was the most visible and powerful railroad man in the state, a major force in its business and political affairs. He died at his home in Raleigh.

• The large collection of Andrews's papers in the Southern Historical Collection, Wilson Library, University of North Carolina, Chapel Hill, deals mainly with railroad matters prior to his move to the Richmond & Danville in 1875. His later business papers were turned over to the Southern Railway, whose archives (including records of the R&D, the Western North Carolina, and other subordinate roads) are in the Newman Library, Virginia Polytechnic Institute and State University, Blacksburg.

Andrews's military career is discussed in Walter Clark, ed., *Histories of the Several Regiments and Battalions from North Carolina in the Great War*, vol. 1 (1901), pp. 417–87; and "Additional Sketches Illustrating the Services of Officers and Privates and Patriotic Citizens of North Carolina," *Confederate Military History* 4 (1899): 359–61.

Margaret W. Morris, "The Completion of the Western North Carolina Railroad," *North Carolina Historical Review* 52 (1975): 256–82, is the fullest treatment of that subject. Andrews receives very critical treatment from Josephus Daniels in his autobiographical *Tar Heel Editor* (1939) and *Editor in Politics* (1941) and from Jeffrey J. Crow and Robert F. Durden in their biography of Governor Daniel L. Russell, *Maverick Republican in the Old North State* (1977). For favorable, even adulatory treatments, see the sketches by Samuel A. Ashe in his *Biographical History of North Carolina*, vol. 1 (8 vols., 1905–1917), pp. 45–59; and in Archibald Henderson, *North Carolina: The Old North State and the New*, vol. 3 (1941), pp. 17–19. Andrews's obituary and a related editorial are in the *Raleigh News and Observer*, 18 Apr. 1915.

ALLEN W. TRELEASE

ANDREWS, Charles McLean (22 Feb. 1863–9 Sept. 1943), historian, was born in Wethersfield, Connecticut, the son of the Reverend William Watson Andrews and Elizabeth Williams. Andrews was a remarkably normal New England boy: mischievous (his elementary school teacher in Wethersfield predicted that her pupil would "come to some bad end"); unstudious (graduating from Hartford High School in 1879, "he took no prizes and had no honor standing"); uncertain (as a sophomore at Trinity College, Andrews wanted to drop out and "go to work"); and parochial (he went no further than the West Hartford High School for a job, becoming principal there on his graduation from Trinity in 1884). It was only because he disliked disruptive students in large numbers that Andrews turned to a new option for the unfocused: graduate school. There he found a profession with which he could mature.

The cardinal dates of Andrews's career coincided with the milestones of the new historical profession. In 1884, the founding year of the American Historical Association, Andrews had graduated from Trinity College in Hartford, Connecticut. In 1886 Andrews matriculated at the pioneering center of graduate study, the Johns Hopkins University. This was the initial year of the *Political Science Quarterly*, the first organ of the new learning. Andrews's contemporaries at Hopkins included John Dewey, Richard T. Ely, Frederick Jackson Turner, and Woodrow Wilson. In 1889 Andrews published his doctoral dissertation as *The River Towns of Connecticut* and was appointed to teach history at Bryn Mawr.

In 1895 Andrews married Evangeline Walker, a graduate of Bryn Mawr; they had two children. She became the editor of all of her husband's future work, including his scholarly articles and professional addresses in the *American Historical Review,* inaugurated in this year. In 1898 Andrews joined the leading colonial historian, Herbert Osgood, on the program of the American Historical Association. They divided the early American field between them. As the senior scholar, Osgood claimed "empire building and the imperial as well as the colonial side of the subject" for his own. Andrews was left to point to the archives of the commercial regulatory agencies in the Public Record Office of Great Britain as the central source of colonial history. Six years later, he completed the first round of archival searches that underlay his famous *Guides* to American materials in the Public Record Office, the British Museum, the lesser London repositories, and the libraries of Oxford and Cambridge. Published by the Carnegie Institution in 1908, 1912, and 1914, the *Guides* gave a bureaucratic and metropolitan cast to generations of subsequent work on Anglo-American governance. "If my name lives," Andrews said, "it is because I was the author of those *Guides.*"

The first fruits of Andrews's archival research, entitled *Colonial Self-Government, 1652–1689,* had appeared in 1904, part of the 28-volume *American Nation.* Andrews's work elaborated his characteristic and perennial bureaucratic concerns—its first chapter was "Navigation Acts and Colonial Trade," its last "Commercial and Economic Conditions in the Colonies." But the work was overshadowed by the simultaneous publication of the first two of Osgood's three-volume *The American Colonies in the Seventeenth Century.* Nonetheless, in 1907 Andrews succeeded Herbert Baxter Adams, the founder of graduate study in history, at Johns Hopkins. In 1910 Andrews became the Farnham Professor of American History at Yale and editor of the Yale Historical Publications. For the next twenty-one years he concentrated on graduate instruction and on the work of the committees and councils of the American Historical Association.

In 1924 Andrews published a set of interpretative essays entitled *The Colonial Background of the American Revolution,* a scholarly rejoinder to the fulminations of popular anglophobe writers. *The Colonial Background* also revealed the personal roots of Andrews's historical interpretation of the Anglo-American connection. Profoundly offended by isolationism, Andrews considered most Gilded Age Americans to be mindless and materialistic and American foreign policy to be a replication of British mercantilism. Finding the origins of present ills in the historical past, he declared that England's colonial objectives in America were "commercial," that is, "mercantilistic." He then went on to argue that mercantilism

> was a doctrine of exclusiveness and self-sufficiency, opposed to cosmopolitan coöperation and to any form of international control. It has its counterpart in the American nationalistic and self-protective policy of the nineteenth and twentieth centuries, the chief characteristics of which are isolation, high protective tariffs, and the subordination of dependencies with their miscellany of governors, some indifferent, others worse, appointed by the president of the United States with the advice of party leaders.

Andrews became in the 1920s not only the premier interpreter of the colonial period but also the chief spokesman of the historical profession. The death of Woodrow Wilson in 1924 led to Andrews's appointment as acting president of the American Historical Association. In his presidential address to the association's fortieth anniversary meeting, Andrews proclaimed the creed of that new professional, the scientific historian. The principle of objectivity, he argued, was the distinctive characteristic of the historian; its application had been the great accomplishment of this first professional generation. "Objectivity is merely the historian's insistence that history must be true and that the truth of history should be the only end sought," Andrews explained. Scholars could discover the truth by letting primary source materials dictate their interpretations. They could further avoid partisanship by studying history "for its own sake and not primarily for the sake of interesting or benefiting society." And historians were not to think too much about the structure of their discipline "for all interpretations couched in terms of philosophy are proving vague and unsubstantial." Any dicta save the "laws of impermanence," any lesson save "the need of readjustment to new conditions," were but the empty effusions of prophets, philosophers, and popularizers.

The historical test of the laws of impermanence and readjustment, declared Andrews in his 1925 address to the AHA, was that British failure to observe them had led to the American Revolution. Far from being actively oppressive, "English habits of thought and methods of administration . . . had reached a state of immobility" on the eve of the Revolution. The American colonists, however, "in closest touch with nature and characterized by growth and change" had progressively eliminated feudal law, proprietary property, and royal prerogative. In their stead Americans had instituted ideals of self-government and institutionalized those ideals in representative assemblies. While "the American revolutionaries," Andrews concluded, "had an 'ideal of living;' it can hardly be said that, in 1776, the Englishmen of the ruling classes were governed in their colonial relations by any ideals that were destined to be of service to the human race."

But in 1931, when Andrews retired from Yale, both his institutional and political approaches and his vision of the historian as objective scientist were under attack. Carl Becker's 1931 presidential address, "Everyman His Own Historian," rejected Andrews's 1924 denunciation of "those who decry the work of the historical specialist, believing that every man can be his own historian." Class-conscious and economic interpretations of early America now prevailed ("maintained only by a system of clever, ingenious, and seemingly plausible but really superficial manipulations of fact and logic in the interest of a preconceived theory," Andrews grumbled).

Yet his last decade was not only Andrews's most productive period, it was also his most influential. In 1934 he published the first volume of the first part of *The Colonial Period of American History*. It received the Pulitzer Prize in 1935. In 1936 the second and in 1937 the third volume completed Andrews' account of *The Settlements*. Many of these descriptions of the fundamental institutions in the formative American polities have yet to be equaled. In December 1937 Andrews sent to his publisher *England's Commercial and Colonial Policy,* the fourth volume of *The Colonial Period,* but he fell ill when the volume was in galley proof. He could never return to the great work. Andrews died in East Dover, Connecticut, leaving behind his plan for the uncompleted summa, "On the Writing Of Colonial History."

Published in January 1944, in the inaugural issue of the third series of the *William and Mary Quarterly,* Andrews's last testament appeared together with a moving memoir by his successor at Yale, Leonard W. Labaree, and a bibliography of Andrews's 102 articles, essays, and books. Canonized in the scripture of a revived early American history, Andrews's "commercial and colonial interpretation," first formulated in 1898 and fully defined by 1904, became in 1944 the founding truth, "the system of our limitations," for the third and fourth generations of early American historians. Not until another thirty years had passed did early American historians look to a different past than that of Charles M. Andrews to explain a different present.

• Extensive collections of Andrews's papers are in the possession of his family. A perceptive study, with full references to the manuscript sources, is A. S. Eisenstadt, *Charles McLean Andrews: A Study in American Historical Writing* (1956). It is reviewed in an evocative essay by Bernard Bailyn, "Becker, Andrews, and the Image of Colonial Origins," *New England Quarterly* 29 (1956): 522–34. Leonard W. Labaree's eulogy heads the *William and Mary Quarterly,* 3d. ser., 1, no. 1 (Jan. 1944): 3–13. This is followed by Andrews's bibliography (pp. 15–26) and his valedictory, "On the Writing of Colonial History" (pp. 27–46). Andrews's place in the revived and widened "imperial" history is authoritatively treated by Richard R. Johnson, "Charles McLean Andrews and the Invention of American Colonial History," *William and Mary Quarterly* 43 (1988): 519–41.

STEPHEN SAUNDERS WEBB

ANDREWS, Edward Deming (6 Mar. 1894–6 June 1964), educator, collector, and Shaker scholar, was born in Pittsfield, Massachusetts, the son of Selden Deming Andrews, a hardware store owner, and Caroline Althea Volk. Andrews received a B.A. from Amherst College in 1916 and a Ph.D. in education from Yale University in 1930. He taught in secondary schools for seven years in Connecticut and Massachusetts while completing his graduate studies. His doctoral dissertation, "The Academies and County Grammar Schools of Vermont," was an analysis of the rise of the public high school system. He married Faith Young in 1921, and they had two children.

Andrews and his wife pursued their hobby of collecting and selling colonial and post-colonial artifacts as early as the 1920s while engaging in teaching and graduate study. According to his recollections, in September 1923 they purchased their first Shaker artifact, a chair, at the Hancock, Massachusetts, Shaker village. Andrews identified that purchase as the first step in what became a lifelong personal and professional preoccupation. His first effort at interpretation of Shaker furniture was published in the August 1928 issue of *Antiques* at the encouragement of Homer Eaton Keyes, founding editor of the publication. This text marked the beginning of an astonishingly productive career as a historian of Shakerism and as an interpreter of the material and cultural legacy of the Shakers.

From 1931 to 1933 Andrews served as curator of history at the New York State Museum in Albany. In 1933 he published his first major work: *The Community Industries of the Shakers*, a handbook to accompany an exhibition of Shaker agricultural and manufacturing items, including objects such as oval boxes, chairs, and baskets. The book portrays the Shakers as "progressive" entrepreneurs whose material success was the product of their spiritual sense and practical techniques. In later years he was responsible for organizing and curating numerous exhibitions on the Shakers at several leading museums.

In 1937 Andrews published a second major study, *Shaker Furniture: The Craftsmanship of an American Communal Sect*. Illustrated with photographs by William F. Winter, the volume reinforces the theme that Shaker objects reflect the sect's religious values. In that same year Andrews and his wife purchased a rundown farmhouse in Richmond, Massachusetts, which they eventually restored and lived in, first during the summers and later permanently. In 1937 Andrews also was awarded a Guggenheim fellowship in support of his research.

In 1940 Andrews published *The Gift to Be Simple*, the first significant scholarly effort to collect, describe, and analyze the vast body of Shaker songs, dances, and rituals. A sizable portion of the book was devoted to the publication of the texts and tunes he had gathered. These artifacts, according to Andrews, gave voice to the "mystic afflatus" within the society, thus serving as authentic expressions of "gospel simplicity" and evidence of the close association between Shakerism and primitive Christianity.

From 1941 to 1956 Andrews taught at Scarborough School in Scarborough-on-Hudson, New York, where he served as dean of students and chair of the history department. While there he published *The People Called Shakers: A Search for the Perfect Society* (1953), a narrative history and cultural analysis of Shaker life. This volume, which gave a detailed account of Shakerism from its English origins to the closing decades of the nineteenth century, represented Andrews's mature scholarly judgments concerning the Shakers. His account was sympathetic to the Shakers; he admired both their physical artifacts and spiritual legacy, judging their record to be one of "truth, and beauty, and light." Andrews's volume became the standard introduction to the Shakers for more than forty years and played a major role in the renaissance of interest in the Shakers during the second half of the twentieth century.

In 1956 Andrews resigned from Scarborough School, accepting a position at Yale as consultant on Shaker culture and history in conjunction with a plan to donate his collection of Shaker artifacts, books, and manuscripts to the university. This effort to preserve his collection intact and to make the university a center for Shaker studies was aborted, however, when personnel changes at Yale resulted in new plans unacceptable to Andrews, and the next year he withdrew his gift.

From 1961 to 1963 Andrews served as curator and program consultant for the historic restoration effort in Hancock, Massachusetts, the site of a former Shaker village. He also donated a substantial number of items from his collection to the undertaking. A disagreement with the trustees at the site led to his resignation. Andrews died in Pittsfield, Massachusetts.

Andrews's research and writing had been carried out in close collaboration with his wife. Following his death several additional publications by him appeared, including *Religion in Wood: A Book of Shaker Furniture* (1966) and *Visions of the Heavenly Sphere: A Study in Shaker Religious Art* (1969). In 1969 the Andrews collection of manuscripts and published materials concerning Shakerism was transferred to the Henry Francis du Pont Winterthur Museum. In 1975 *Fruits of the Shaker Tree of Life: Memoirs of Fifty Years of Collecting and Research* appeared under the names of both Edward and Faith Andrews.

Mark Van Doren captured the significance of Andrews's career when he wrote, "THE WORD AUTHORITY, often loosely used to mean one who knows more than most people about some subject, regains its dignity as soon as we consider Edward Deming Andrews. He knew more about the Shakers than anyone ever has, and I am quite certain that his knowledge of them will never be surpassed." Andrews was a leading force in the revival of interest in the Shakers and deserves to be recognized as the most significant Shaker scholar of the twentieth century.

• Andrews's papers are located at the Henry Francis du Pont Winterthur Museum. Correspondence can also be found in a variety of repositories containing Shaker materials. For additional references to publications by Andrews, including essays in various periodicals, see "Publications of Edward Deming Andrews and Faith Andrews: A Select Chronological List," in A. D. Emerich, comp., *Shaker Furniture and Objects from the Faith and Edward Deming Andrews Collections Commemorating the Bicentenary of the American Shakers* (1973); Mary L. Richmond, *Shaker Literature: A Bibliography* (2 vols., 1977); and E. Richard McKinstry, comp., *The Edward Deming Andrews Memorial Shaker Collection* (1987). Obituaries appear in the *Shaker Quarterly* 4, no. 3 (1964): 105–6, and in the *New York Times*, 13 June 1964.

STEPHEN J. STEIN

ANDREWS, Elisha Benjamin (10 Jan. 1844–30 Oct. 1917), clergyman and college president, was born in Hinsdale, New Hampshire, the son of Erastus Andrews, a Baptist minister and politician, and Almira Bartlett, a schoolteacher. When Benjamin (as he was always known) was six months old, his father accepted a new pastorate in Sanderland, Massachusetts, and relocated the family to Montague, Massachusetts, where Andrews attended local schools and was occasionally tutored by his mother before the family moved yet again in 1858 to Suffield, Connecticut. In Suffield his father presided over the First Baptist Church and took advantage of the nearby Connecticut Literary Institute, also a Baptist institution, for the education of his children. Shortly after their move to Suffield, Andrews seriously injured his left foot; after a slow and painful recovery that prevented his attendance at school until 1860, he resumed his education at the Literary Institute.

Andrews's formal instruction took a detour when, following the outbreak of the Civil War, he abruptly enlisted in the Union army. Entering the service in May 1861 as a private with the Fourth Connecticut Volunteer Infantry Regiment (later the First Connecticut Heavy Artillery Regiment), Andrews served with distinction despite the near-constant pain from his old foot injury and was soon appointed squad leader. Andrews's regiment participated in all the major engagements of the Army of the Potomac, including Hanover Court House, Gaines's Mill, and Malvern Hill, and he was successively promoted to corporal in April 1862 and sergeant in January 1863. In the summer of 1864 Andrews, by now a second lieutenant, was serving with his unit in the siege of Petersburg, Virginia. He survived the Battle of the Crater only to fall, badly wounded, during a Confederate attack in late August. As a result of his wounds, Andrews lost the sight in his left eye and was discharged from the army in late October.

Returning home, Andrews resumed his education at the Powers Institute in Bernardston, Massachusetts, although he left the school after less than a year, finishing his preparatory education at the Wesleyan Academy in Wilbraham, Massachusetts. Having decided to follow in both his father's and his grandfather's footsteps, Andrews enrolled at Brown University in the fall of 1866 with the goal of entering the Baptist ministry. As an undergraduate he contributed to the student literary magazine and was elected to membership in Phi Beta Kappa. In line with his career goals, Andrews also taught Sunday school and supplied local pulpits with substitute preaching. Upon graduation in 1870 he took a temporary professional detour, returning in the position of principal to the Connecticut Literary Institute, where he also taught classes. In November 1870 Andrews married Ella Allen; the couple eventually had two children. Andrews continued to serve as principal of the Literary Institute until 1872, when he resigned to enter the Newton Theological Institution. Upon completing his studies in the summer of 1874, he accepted a position as pastor of the Baptist congregation in Beverly, Massachusetts.

Following his ordination in July 1874, Andrews remained at Beverly for fourteen months. Although successful in his ministry, he could never resist the challenge of a new position. Believing that his leadership was badly needed and that Baptist influence could be greatly enhanced by a quality institution of higher education in the West, in August 1875 Andrews accepted a position as president of Denison University in Granville, Ohio. Like so many of its church-affiliated educational brethren, Denison had struggled financially for years, and the effects of the panic of 1873 only added to its woes. Andrews held the chair of moral and intellectual philosophy in addition to his teaching duties, and during his four years as president he effected numerous changes in the campus. Construction began on a new library building, and a system of elective coursework was initiated. Andrews also hired a young, non-Baptist instructor in Latin and Greek, William Rainey Harper, who became not only his lifelong friend but a prominent educator in his own right. Additionally, Andrews gained the friendship of John D. Rockefeller, then serving on the university's board of trustees. Although his relationship with Rockefeller was sound, as a sold proponent of the newly emerging "social gospel," Andrews often clashed with other trustees who, according to Andrews, held conservative theological views that often stifled the free exchange of ideas within academia. Frustrated also by the lack of forthcoming funding for his expansion plans, Andrews resigned as president in May 1879 and returned to Massachusetts, where he became professor of homiletics and pastoral theology at the Newton Theological Institution.

Andrews remained at Newton until 1882. During that year he also taught philosophy at Colby College in Waterville, Maine, substituting for the ailing president, Henry Robins. In the same year, missing the diversified environment of the college campus, he accepted the post of professor of political economy and history at Brown. Before assuming his new post at his alma mater, Andrews traveled to Germany and spent the academic year of 1882–1883 studying history and political economy at the Universities of Berlin and Munich. In the latter year, Andrews returned to the United States and took up his duties at Brown, where he remained until 1888. His personal scholarship flourished during this period, and he published a memoir, *A Private's Reminiscences of the First Year of the War* (1886), as well as *Brief Institutes of General History* (1887) and *Brief Institutes of Our Constitutional History, English and American* (1887), both historical outlines.

Andrews left for Cornell in 1888, and after serving for a year as professor of political economy and finance he returned to Brown as its new president in 1889. His administration was one of remarkable growth, and it was largely through Andrews's efforts that the graduate school was founded. Likewise, undergraduate enrollment increased from 176 to 641, graduate enrollment went from three students to 117, and the number of courses offered went from fewer than 100 to more than 250. The faculty also increased from twenty-two to eighty; included among the ranks of the new additions were Charles Foster Kent, Hammond Lamont, and John Matthew Manly. Perhaps Andrews's greatest contribution was the founding of what later became Pembroke College in 1928. Women first attended classes at Brown in October 1891, with student fees and out-of-pocket contributions from Andrews initially serving as the sole means of financial support until the University Corporation assumed responsibility for the "Women's College" in June 1896.

The aggressive course of expansion charted by Andrews clashed, however, with both the University Corporation's intransigence and a lack of funding. Although in his report of 1891–1892 Andrews had called for "a million dollars within a year, and two million more in ten years," fundraising results, for numerous reasons, including economic slowdowns, fell far short. Additional issues, such as Andrews's outspokenness on a variety of political and social issues, also rankled the corporation members. Andrews had long favored international bimetallism, and by 1896 he had even advocated that the United States take the initiative on the issue, with the idea that other nations would soon follow. The issue was a hot topic in 1896 (a presidential election year), and Andrews's position gathered little support in the Northeast; it was equally unpopular among potential financial donors to the university. Andrews had spoken out regularly on the subject while a professor, but he had forborne discussion of the issue while president for those very reasons. The corporation based its actions solely on a few pieces of Andrews's correspondence that had been published without his permission and in at least one case without his knowledge. Exhausted from his duties, Andrews traveled to Europe in 1896 and spent a year's leave of absence abroad. Just prior to his return to Providence in June 1897, the corporation met to discuss Andrews's professional future. With financial concerns paramount and the controversy over the issue of free coinage of silver still simmering from the previous year's election, the corporation drafted a statement asking Andrews to refrain from advancing his views on the issue.

The corporation's request was presented to Andrews in July 1897; Andrews resigned the following day, believing that he could no longer effectively serve in his post. A huge controversy ensued, with petitions urging the corporation to reject Andrews's resignation arriving from Brown alumni and faculty members as well as from other noted figures in higher education such as Daniel Coit Gilman, Charles W. Eliot, and William Jewett Tucker. After a summer of controversy, the corporation drafted a statement asking Andrews to withdraw his resignation.

Following the withdrawal of his resignation, Andrews remained at Brown for another year; he resigned in July 1898 and assumed the post of superintendent of schools in Chicago. In that equally volatile post, Andrews succeeded in establishing kindergartens within the system, as well as regular health examinations for students; he also established special programs for physically challenged children. Blocked in his attempts to promote a centralized administration and merit promotions for teachers, he resigned in April 1900 and became the chancellor of the University of Nebraska. During his eight-year tenure, schools of medicine, education, and law were established, enrollment increased by 1,355 students, faculty size doubled, additional buildings were erected, an experimental farm was created for the benefit of an enlarged agricultural department, and, perhaps most important, appropriations almost trebled.

Declining health eventually forced Andrews to resign his last academic position in December 1908. A two-year world trip failed to restore his vigor, and by 1912 he and his wife had relocated to West Palm Beach, Florida. They moved to Interlachen, Florida, during the following year, but Andrews's strength continued to decline; he eventually became a complete invalid prior to his death in Interlachen.

Following conspicuous service during the Civil War, Andrews contributed significantly to the development of three institutions of higher learning and the school system of a major American city. He is best remembered, however, for the controversy of 1897, which forced the issue of academic freedom to the front pages of newspapers across the globe.

• While no collection of Andrews's papers has survived, the Brown University Archives in Providence, R.I., maintains scrapbook collections and a set of reminiscences by individuals who knew Andrews. Similar collections are held at the University of Nebraska's Lincoln Library and the Denison University Library in Granville, Ohio. Scattered correspondence can also be located within the Charles W. Eliot Papers, Harvard University Archives; the Seth Low Papers, Columbia University Library; the Daniel Coit Gilman Papers, Johns Hopkins University Library; the William Rainey Harper Papers, University of Chicago Archives; the John Franklin Jamison Papers, Library of Congress; and the John D. Rockefeller Papers, Rockefeller Archives. In addition to publications cited in the text, Andrews also wrote *An Honest Dollar* (1889), *Institutes of Economics* (1889), *The Economic Law of Monopoly* (1890), *Syllabus of Lectures . . . upon the Rise and Growth of the Government of the United States* (1891), *The Duty of a Public Spirit* (1892), *Wealth and Moral Law* (1894), *Eternal Words and Other Sermons* (1894), and *The Sin of Schism* (1896). Andrews was the subject of "Gallant, Stalwart Bennie: Elisha Benjamin Andrews (1844–1917), an Educator's Odyssey" (Ph.D. diss., Univ. of Denver, 1969). Dated but still useful is Walter C. Bronson, *The History of Brown University, 1764–1914* (1914). An obituary is in the *New York Times*, 31 Oct. 1917.

EDWARD L. LACH, JR.

ANDREWS, Eliza Frances (10 Aug. 1840–21 Jan. 1931), author and educator, was born at Haywood Plantation near Washington, Georgia, the daughter of Garnett Andrews, a judge and planter, and Annulet Ball. After attending the Ladies' Seminary in Washington, Georgia, Andrews, often known as "Fanny," was, in 1857, one of the first students to receive an A.B. degree at LaGrange Female College in LaGrange, Georgia.

Although both her parents were determined Unionists throughout the Civil War, Andrews sided with her three older brothers who joined the Confederate army. At the time of secession, she and her sister secretly sewed the first Confederate flag to hang above the Washington, Georgia, courthouse. In late 1864 their father sent them to stay with relatives in southwest Georgia where there was less danger from invading Union troops. The diary that Andrews published decades later covered her days as a Civil War refugee and the early days of Reconstruction back on her father's plantation.

In 1865, at her father's suggestion, Andrews sent an article, "A Romance of Robbery," to the *New York World* describing, as if she were a Union officer, the mistreatment of some family friends by Reconstruction officials. She followed the success of this first publication with letters to the *New York World* on topics such as distinctions between the "intelligent and cultivated whites" and the "low white people." At some point she adopted the pseudonym, Elzey Hay, that she would use for over a decade when publishing articles and poems. She published an article in *Godey's Lady's Book* (July 1866) on the difficulties "rebel women" had experienced while trying to dress fashionably under the constraints of the wartime blockade.

An article by Andrews on Eli Whitney and the cotton gin first appeared in the early 1870s. Reprinted in 1910 in *The Library of Southern Literature*, her work has been considered the basis for the popular version of Whitney's noted invention. It took many years, however, for professional historians to follow her lead in acknowledging the role played by Catherine Greene Miller when she gave Whitney the idea of including a machine part similar to a clothes brush that allowed the gin to be a true success.

After Andrews's mother died in 1872 and her father in 1873, the family fortune suffered from some bad investments made by a family adviser, forcing the sale of the family home and the need for Andrews to earn more money. Andrews secretly edited the *Washington Gazette* in her hometown until, after six months, the publisher discovered her sex and announced that newspaper editing was not proper work for a female. Her subsequent decision to become a teacher and school principal was one she made more by necessity than by choice. She did not, however, allow her school jobs to end her literary career.

Andrews's first school job, in 1873, was as principal of the girls' high school in Yazoo, Mississippi, where one of her brothers was practicing law. She reportedly did not like having to work for a black superintendent of education and in 1874 returned to her old school in Washington, Georgia, as its principal. While teaching there, Andrews published two novels, *A Family Secret* (1876), about the concerns of postbellum southern society, and *A Mere Adventurer* (1879), about a young woman's attempts to lead an independent life.

Andrews became so ill in the early 1880s that she had to give up school administration for several years. She did, however, prop herself up in bed to write another novel, *Prince Hal, or The Romance of a Rich Man* (1882), a tale of antebellum plantation life. While recuperating in Florida, she served as a special correspondent for the *Augusta Chronicle*.

From 1886 to 1896 Andrews taught French and literature at Wesleyan Female College in Macon, Georgia. In 1898 she returned to Washington, Georgia, as a teacher of French and botany in the public high school, where she remained until 1903. By 1906 she was teaching in Montgomery, Alabama, where she served as the historian for the United Daughters of the Confederacy and as a member of the Civic Improvement League. By 1912 she had retired to Rome, Georgia, where she remained until she died.

Andrews's output after 1882 includes mainly a combination of fictional and nonfictional contributions to journals such as *Cosmopolitan*, *Arena*, the *Nation*, the *Chautauquan*, and *Popular Science Monthly*. Her novels and short stories blend social commentary with melodramatic plot twists such as the discovery that an overseer's son in "A Colonial Christmas in the Red Hills of Georgia" (*Chautauquan*, Dec. 1895) was actually the son of a gentleman and therefore a proper mate for the planter's daughter who had always loved him. In both her fiction and her essays, she wrote forcefully about the right of single women to earn their living in new ways, but she also suggested in "Education and the Employment of Children" in *Popular Science Monthly* (June 1888) that it would be better to encourage working-class children to take factory jobs than to have their mothers working outside of the home. In the *Arena* (Dec. 1897), she published "A Political Deal," about a poor teacher who committed suicide when she lost her job as a result of a political deal by a corrupt candidate. The *Women's Who's Who of America* of 1914–1915 listed her as a suffragist, but she was not a prominent suffrage leader in Georgia and she had opposed women voting in the postbellum decades.

In 1908 Andrews published an abridged version of her early diary as *The War-Time Journal of a Georgia Girl*. In her editorial commentary, scattered throughout the volume, she explained that she had already destroyed a number of the more embarrassing pages as she had reread them over the years and that she had edited out other personal material before publication. The diary still includes, however, many scenes of social visits, picnics, and dances, as well as tales of hardships she and her family experienced during the war.

Andrews had been a strong supporter of slavery when she first wrote the diary, but by the time she published it she was ambivalent about antebellum southern society, considering it an anachronism doomed to give way to the more advanced but still flawed "wage-slavery." In her introduction to *The War-Time Journal* she was, nevertheless, nostalgic for the "wholesome, happy, and joyous life" of "the privileged 4,000" who "stood for gentle courtesy, for knightly honor, for generous hospitality," and "for lofty scorn of cunning greed and ill-gotten gain."

Andrews's analysis of antebellum society was influenced by her interest in Fabian socialism. From 1899 to 1918, she listed herself as a socialist in *Who's Who in America*. She even wrote an article for the *International Socialist Review* (July 1916) entitled "Socialism in the Plant World." She interpreted Marx's theory of economic determinism and contemporary ideas of Social Darwinism, however, so as to reinforce her belief in a clear separation of the races. In *Century Magazine* (April 1907) she declared in "Where the Race Problem Has Solved Itself" that her hometown of Washington, Georgia, with the timely help of the Ku Klux Klan, had overcome the "race problem" by honoring "Nature's plan" of preserving "the color-line," with "the Anglo-Saxon on top."

As the twentieth century progressed, Andrews focused primarily on activities and articles connected to biological science. Her two botany textbooks, *Botany All the Year Round* (1903) and *A Practical Course in Botany* (1911), rivaled *The War-Time Journal* in popularity, with the second book becoming a basic text in France. In 1926 the International Academy of Science in Italy made Andrews their first female American member. At her death, Andrews, who had never married, gave the city of Rome, Georgia, the rights to the royalties from her botany texts to be used to create a public woodland.

The life and writings of Andrews illustrate in numerous ways a blending of the beliefs and ideals of the antebellum planter society of her youth with newer ideas about the role of women. Although she was one of countless southern women who spent decades working in schools, she also succeeded in developing a regional, national, and international reputation as a writer and a botanist.

• No major collection of papers for Eliza Frances Andrews is available, but a few letters and a scrapbook including some of her early articles and poems can be found in the Garnett Andrews Papers at the Southern Historical Collection, the University of North Carolina, Chapel Hill. It is not known if any of the original diary exists and Andrews implied that she destroyed the segments that she edited out of the published version. In addition to the writings mentioned in the text, Andrews published a number of other stories and essays in various journals. Key articles in *Popular Science Monthly* include "Will the Coming Woman Lose Her Hair?" (Jan. 1893). Among her short stories in the *Chautauquan* are "The Story of an Ugly Girl" (Jan. 1895) and "In the Pine Lands of Georgia" (July and Aug. 1895); the same journal also published, among other essays, "Cracker English" (Apr. 1896). She published "Rudimentary Suggestions for Beginners in Story Writing" in *Cosmopolitan*, Feb. 1897. Articles on botany appeared in several journals including "Relation Between Age and Area in the Distribution of Plants" in *Science* (8 Feb. 1918). One of her last publications was "Biology in the Public Schools" in *Education* (Mar. 1925). There is no full-length biography. The 1960 edition of *The War-Time Journal* includes an introductory essay by Spencer Bidwell King, Jr. An obituary is in the *New York Times*, 23 Jan. 1931.

CITA COOK

ANDREWS, Fannie Fern Phillips (25 Sept. 1867–23 Jan. 1950), pacifist and educational reformer was born in Margaretville, Nova Scotia, the daughter of William Wallace Phillips, a shoemaker, and Anna Maria Brown, a church activist. Andrews grew up in Lynn, Massachusetts; she graduated from Salem Normal School in 1884 and taught school in Lynn between 1884 and 1890. In 1890 she married Edwin G. Andrews, a salesman in Lynn; they had no children. In 1895–1896 Andrews resumed her studies, at the Harvard summer school, and in 1902 she received her A.B. from Radcliffe in education and psychology.

Andrews supported woman suffrage, but her major reform interest at this time was education. In 1907 she founded the Boston Home and School Association to encourage parents' interest in their children's education. She served first as the organization's secretary (1907–1914) and then its president (1914–1918). Melding her interest in education with a growing enthusiasm for peace work, she formed the American School Peace League in 1908, serving as secretary and head. The league was founded, with the support of the U.S. Commission of Education, to aid teachers in educating for peace and international understanding. Andrews compiled suggestions for the "promotion of peace" in schools, including an observation of peace day and the performance of peace songs, poems, and speeches. Andrews traveled throughout the United States, encouraging others to join the movement to increase world peace through education; by 1915 there were league branches in forty states. In 1918 the league became the American School Citizenship League, and that organization continued until 1950. Andrews also helped start similar leagues in Great Britain and Germany.

When World War I broke out, Andrews threw herself wholeheartedly into the campaign for peace. She joined the League to Enforce Peace, which developed school programs to disseminate information on peace. Andrews also became involved in the Central Organisation for a Durable Peace, a "study group" based in The Hague; she was on its international executive committee and in 1917 helped from the U.S. branch. Andrews was appointed by President Woodrow Wilson to represent the United States at the International Conference on Education at The Hague in 1914, and in 1915 she served as a U.S. delegate at the Hague Peace Conference. Andrews supported the conference's call for a league of nations for the "pacific settlement of international conflicts" and tirelessly campaigned for such a league. In 1917 she wrote a monograph, *The Freedom of the Seas*, outlining one component of a peaceful world. She helped organize the League for Permanent Peace in 1918 and attended the Paris Peace Conference as a representative for both the U.S. Bureau of Education and the League for Permanent Peace. Andrews tried to establish an education bureau under league auspices and finally succeeded in the 1920s, serving as one of the delegates appointed by President Franklin D. Roosevelt in the 1930s. Andrews was thus able yet again to combine her two major reform interests of education and international peace.

After attending the Paris Peace Conference, Andrews realized she wanted to know more about the workings of international diplomacy. She began graduate study in international affairs at Radcliffe, receiving her Ph.D. in international law and diplomacy in 1923. Her dissertation, "The Mandatory System after the World War," led to further exploration of the mandate system. In 1925 she and her husband began travelling throughout the Middle East, gathering information for her two-volume study, *The Holy Land under Mandate* (1931). This work made her one of the few women scholars recognized as an expert in the field of international diplomacy. The study is very detailed, including numerous interviews and statistical analyses. She regarded the project as a "dramatic and inspiring" investigation, and unlike most scholarly works, it reads like a fascinating travelogue of the "mysterious land of the East." Andrews's balanced study is hopeful for peace: "The world longs for a pacified Holy Land!" After completing her study of the Middle East, she was active as a Radcliffe trustee (1927–1933), in the American Association of University Women and Phi Beta Kappa, and as an organizer of the Harvard-Radcliffe Research Bureau of international law. Andrews died in Somerville, Massachusetts, leaving an unfinished study of European diplomacy.

• Andrews's manuscript collection is in the Schlesinger Library of Radcliffe College, including pamphlets, articles, and published writings, with materials like bulletins from the U.S. Bureau of Education. Her autobiography is *Memory Pages of My Life* (1948). Additional biographical material appears in *Lucia Ames Mead: Memorial Meeting* (1937); Madeleine Doty, *The Central Organisation for a Durable Peace (1915–1918)* (1945); and Merle Curti, *Peace or War: The American Struggle, 1636–1936* (1936).

LINDA G. FORD

ANDREWS, Frank Maxwell (3 Feb. 1884–3 May 1943), army officer and airman, was born in Nashville, Tennessee, the son of James David Andrews, a newspaper reporter, and Louise Adeline Maxwell. He graduated from the Montgomery Bell Academy in 1901 and the following year gained admittance to the U.S. Military Academy at West Point. Graduating in 1906, Andrews was commissioned a second lieutenant in the cavalry. He spent the next eleven years drawing routine assignments in the American West, Hawaii, and the Philippines. In 1914 he married Jeanette Allen, the daughter of Major General Henry T. Allen. They had three children.

Following U.S. entry into World War I, Andrews transferred to the Air Section of the Signal Corps in August 1917 and subsequently received flight training at Rockwell Field in San Diego, California. An adept flier, he was appointed commander of Carlstrom and Dorr fields in Florida. In October 1918 Andrews advanced to supervisor of the Southeastern Air Service District, headquartered in Montgomery, Alabama, and received temporary promotion to lieutenant colonel. He functioned in this capacity until March 1919, when he was transferred to Washington, D.C., as part of the War Plans Division of the General Staff.

Andrews remained at the War Department until August 1920, when he ventured to Germany as part of the army of occupation and replaced William "Billy" Mitchell as air service officer. Returning to the United States in 1923, he was billeted at Kelly Field, Texas, as executive officer. Andrews assumed control of the Tenth School Group in July 1925, rising to commandant of the Advanced Flying School by June 1927. He began his grooming for higher command functions by attending the Air Corps Tactical School in 1927–1928, the Army Command and General Staff School in 1928–1929, and the Army War College in 1932–1933. That summer Andrews assumed control of the First Pursuit Group at Selfridge Field, Michigan, where he broke several speed and distance records. In October 1934 he again returned to the General Staff in Washington, D.C., where reorganization of the Air Corps was underway.

Andrews had long advocated the creation of a General Headquarters (GHQ) Air Force, a unified, strategic bomber force under the army's senior command. His excellent reputation held him in good stead, and on 1 March 1935 General Douglas MacArthur appointed him to head the newly organized GHQ force with the temporary rank of brigadier general. During his tenure Andrews made an indelible impression upon future Army Air Force policy and doctrine. He believed in the strategic potential of bomber aircraft in modern war and agitated for a large, modern air force without actually demanding autonomy. He also played a role in developing and acquiring strategic weapons like the Boeing B-17 Flying Fortress. Andrews's confidence in heavy bombers for national defense was amply rewarded in May 1938, when three B-17s navigated by Lieutenant Curtis E. LeMay successfully intercepted the Italian liner *Rex* seven hundred miles at sea. However, his strident advocacy of air power and hints at air force independence unsettled a conservative-minded General Staff. Hence, when Andrews's tenure at GHQ expired in February 1939, he was demoted to his permanent rank of colonel and assigned to a minor field in Texas. many contemporaries viewed this rotation as punishment for promoting change.

Andrews's exile was of short duration. In August 1939 Army Chief of Staff George C. Marshall recalled him to Washington to serve as assistant chief of staff for training and operations (G-3); he was the first airman so honored. In November 1940, through the personal recommendations of both Marshall and President Franklin D. Roosevelt, he was brevetted major general and given command of the new Panama Canal Air Force. Promoted to temporary lieutenant general in September 1941, he was directed to lead the Caribbean Defense Command, becoming the first airman entrusted with a theater command. Andrews promptly shored up the slim resources allotted to defend what was considered the Achilles heel of American hemispheric defenses. He subsequently completed several sensitive missions to Argentina and Brazil to promote American interests and was well received in diplomatic circles.

Andrews presided over Caribbean affairs until 30 October 1942, when he was ordered to Cairo, Egypt, as commander of U.S. forces in the Middle East. The following January he attended the Casablanca Conference and successfully argued for a unified, strategic air offense against Germany. In February 1943 Andrews succeeded General Dwight D. Eisenhower as supreme commander of American forces in Europe and commenced organizational groundwork for Operation Overlord, the cross-Channel invasion of Europe. He also conferred regularly with British prime minister Winston Churchill over air matters, and voiced his support for American precision daylight bombing over nighttime saturation bombing as practiced by the Royal Air Force. On 3 May 1943 Andrews departed England on an inspection tour of Icelandic defenses. He died near Meek Field, Kelflavik, when his plane crashed in bad weather.

Andrews was a forceful advocate of strategic bombing and a tactful supporter of air force autonomy. While not entirely successful in these roles, he was instrumental in originating the World War II air power doctrine of decisively attacking an enemy's industrial heartland. His principle contribution was in transforming the small GHQ air force into an efficient armada, thereby demonstrating the viability of strategic aircraft. Andrews's untimely death cut short a promising career. In 1949 the newly independent U.S. Air Force acknowledged its debt to him by naming Andrews Air Force Base, Maryland, in his honor.

• Collections of Andrews's papers are at the Air Force Academy Library, Colorado Springs, Colo.; the George C. Marshall Foundation, Lexington, Va.; the Manuscripts Division, Library of Congress; and the Tennessee State Library and Archives, Nashville. Official correspondence is in the ETOUSA Files, RG 338, Modern History Field Branch of the National Archives, College Park, Md. For biographical sketches, consult three works by S. Copp DeWitt: *A Few Great Captains* (1980); *Forged in Fire* (1982); and "Andrews: Marshall's Airman," in *Makers of the United States Air Force*, ed. John L. Frisbee (1987). For his contributions to the development of American air power, see Wesley F. Craven and James L. Cate, eds., *The Army Air Forces in World War II* (7 vols., 1948–1958); Robert F. Futrell, *Ideas, Concepts, Doctrine* (1974); and R. Earl McClendon, *Autonomy of the Air Arm* (1954). A detailed obituary is in the *New York Times*, 5 and 7 May 1943.

JOHN C. FREDRIKSEN

ANDREWS, George Leonard (31 Aug. 1828–4 Apr. 1899), soldier, engineer, and educator, was born in Bridgewater, Massachusetts, the son of Manasseh Andrews and Harriet Leonard. After attending the state normal school at Bridgewater, he was accepted as a candidate at the U.S. Military Academy at West Point. He graduated at the head of the class of 1851 and was appointed second lieutenant of engineers. His first duty after graduation was in his home state, participating in the construction of Fort Warren in Boston Harbor. He then returned to the academy as an assistant professor.

Andrews resigned his commission in 1855 and, until the 1861 outbreak of the American Civil War, pursued a career as a civil engineer. Siding with the Union, he obtained a commission as a lieutenant colonel in the Second Massachusetts Infantry Regiment. Since the regiment's colonel was often absent, serving at a higher level, effective command of the unit devolved on Andrews, and he proved equal to the task. Under his command, the Second Massachusetts gained a reputation for discipline and competence in battle. He led the regiment during the Shenandoah Valley campaign of 1862 and was promoted to colonel in June of that year. After the battles of Cedar Mountain and Antietam in the same year, he was promoted to brigadier general of volunteers on 10 November.

General Andrews's most notable military service in the Civil War was as a member of the Federal expedition to Louisiana, beginning in late 1862. Initially he supervised the port of embarkation, ensuring that troops and supplies were properly dispatched to Louisiana. On arrival in Louisiana, he was elevated to the position of chief of staff to General Nathaniel Banks, the commander of the expedition. In that role, he became familiar with the overall Federal strategy, an attempt to sever the Confederacy into east and west segments along a Union-controlled Mississippi River.

Andrews played a prominent role in the 1863 campaigns that severed the Confederacy. When General U. S. Grant's forces defeated southern general John C. Pemberton's defenders at Vicksburg, Mississippi, on 3 July, Union forces were laying siege to another Confederate Mississippi River bastion at Port Hudson, Louisiana, 135 miles above New Orleans. There, about 20,000 Federal troops had been facing 6,300 rebels, 20 or more heavy guns, and 31 field pieces since late May. On 7 July, when news of Grant's success came to Port Hudson, the Confederate commander, Major General Frank Gardner, decided to surrender his starving garrison. Negotiations ensued, and Andrews was chosen to consummate the victory. On 9 July, at the head of eight regiments, with flags flying and a band playing, he rode into Port Hudson. The Confederate forces stacked their arms. Andrews directed that the U.S. flag be hoisted, and at the direction of General Banks, he accepted, then courteously returned General Gardner's sword, an act signifying an honorable surrender. The Mississippi River was open, and the Confederacy was split.

Subsequently, Andrews was appointed as the Baton Rouge territorial district commander and later joined in the battle of Mobile, 5 August 1864. In the latter part of the war, General Andrews was a key officer in the Union's program to recruit, train, and employ black troops. This effort placed the Confederacy, already short of sufficient manpower, at a distinct disadvantage, and it also allowed Federal forces to control large areas of the South. The resulting organization was first known as the Corps d'Afrique, but it later became institutionalized within the normal order of battle for the U.S. Army. Black units were then simply designated as numbered regiments of colored troops. Andrews's recruiting activities were centered in the lower Mississippi River basin. Mostly, these troops were engaged under Andrews's command in occupation duties in the same areas from which they were recruited. Andrews remained in uniform a few months after the war's end, leaving the army as a brevet major general in August 1865.

Andrews's postwar life involved varied occupations. At first he remained in the South, becoming a planter in Mississippi, but in 1867 he returned north to Massachusetts. He was appointed U.S. marshal and served in that capacity until 1871, when he returned to the U.S. Military Academy as a language professor.

Andrews established a reputation as a sound educator for the Corps of Cadets. When West Point's curriculum was revised in 1882, the academic departments were reorganized. Andrews was selected to head the new Department of Modern Languages, and he was department head and professor until his retirement ten years later.

Andrews married Sara Bridge, but the date of the marriage is not known. They had three children. Andrews spent his retirement years in Brookline, Massachusetts, where he died. In his professional life, he was never noted for a particularly warm personality, but his straightforward, fair dealings and his conduct and personal bearing inspired respect. He was a well-read, serious officer and educator who had few intimate friends. Among his contemporaries, he was best remembered as the Union officer who managed the dignified, correct surrender ceremony at Port Hudson.

• Andrews's military career is detailed in George W. Cullum, *Biographical Register of the Officers and Graduates of the U.S. Military Academy*, 3d ed., vol. 2 (1891–1950). Andrews's role in the surrender of Port Hudson is detailed in Richard B. Irwin, "The Capture of Port Hudson," in *Battles and Leaders of the Civil War*, vol. 3, ed. Robert U. Johnson and Clarence C. Buel (1887). An obituary is in the *Bulletin of the Association of Graduates of the Military Academy* (1900): 21–28.

ROD PASCHALL

ANDREWS, Israel DeWolf (May 1813?–17 Feb. 1871), diplomat and politician, was born either in Eastport, Maine, or on Campobello Island, New Brunswick, the son of Israel Andrews and Elizabeth DeWolf. His paternal grandfather had emigrated to Nova Scotia from Danvers, Massachusetts, in 1738. By the time Andrews was four, his family lived in Eastport. Thomas Keefer reported that Andrews was a frontier trader, mostly of contraband, as a young man and that experience sparked his interest in reciprocal trade between the provinces and the United States. His schooling is unknown, but he was a clear, persuasive writer at ease with statistical data, and he moved easily in the journalistic, commercial, and political circles of his time.

Andrews petitioned the Department of State to be appointed U.S. consul in St. John, New Brunswick, and received the appointment in March 1843. By 1845 he regularly urged Secretary of State James Buchanan to lower tariffs and other barriers to trade with the provinces. He used his consular appointments to promote formal American-provincial commercial ties, which he believed would hasten provincial independence from Britain and eventual union with the United States. He deluged secretaries of state from Daniel Webster to Lewis Cass with commercial and political intelligence about British North America, advocating reciprocal trade, and it seems clear that these officials used him as their source on provincial affairs.

In 1849 Andrews was appointed consul to New Brunswick and Canada and worked out of Halifax, St. John, and Montreal. In addition, John M. Clayton appointed him a special agent to collect commercial intelligence on British North America. That same year a group of Montreal businessmen formed a movement for provincial annexation to the United States as a way to restore prosperity lost because of the British repeal of trade and navigation laws (Corn Laws) that had favored the provinces. As Andrews collected data, the idea of eventual provincial-American union captured his imagination, and he collaborated with provincial public servants, such as Keefer, who between November 1851 and February 1852 traveled to Boston and New York to help with the first of Andrews's reports on provincial commercial affairs. By 1853 Webster and other American officials recognized Andrews as an expert on virtually all aspects of British North America.

Andrews's voluminous reports reached the files of the secretary of the Treasury as well as the Department of State and shaped the negotiations and terms of what became the Reciprocity Treaty of 1854. This treaty provided lower tariffs on coal, grains, and other products as well as U.S. access to navigation on the St. Lawrence and St. John rivers and the North Atlantic fisheries. Once the treaty had been drafted and negotiated with British representatives, Andrews promoted ratification in Washington and among manufacturers, merchants, and politicians in Boston and New York. He conducted a skillful campaign, using such contacts as Henry Poor of the *Railroad Journal* and writers for the *North American Review*, *Hunt's Merchant's Magazine*, and *De Bow's Review* to place articles favorable to reciprocity. He reportedly entertained lavishly and spent freely, both with funds from the U.S. government and on credit from commercial interests that anticipated benefits from freer trade with the provinces. Contemporaries credited him with collecting the votes that passed the Reciprocity Treaty in the Senate. Despite his own belief in an eventual provincial-American merger, he persuaded southern senators, such as Virginia's James M. Mason, that reciprocity would not produce provincial annexation and the addition of more nonslave territory to the Union.

Andrews also lobbied provincial politicians and may have purchased votes with funds advanced by provincial and perhaps even British officials. Contemporaries credited him with smoothing provincial objections and constructing local majorities to ratify the treaty, but he exposed himself to later charges of profiteering. He seemed to collect from all sides and afterward petitioned Congress for yet more money to meet expenses he claimed to have incurred in his campaign to insure passage of the Reciprocity Treaty.

The Reciprocity Treaty of 1854 has been variously viewed, but it at the least recognized and regularized portions of a large American-provincial trade that had developed over the preceding two decades. It generated the first direct provincial-American discussions around the recurring theme of trade and commerce in Canadian-American relations. Andrews was also the first American to develop, articulate, and promote a coherent U.S. policy toward Canada and was a forerunner of the commercial expansionists and the Anglo-Saxon Union movement of the latter half of the nineteenth century.

In 1855, after the Reciprocity Treaty came into effect, Andrews was appointed consul general of the United States to Canada but henceforth spent little time there. His campaign for reimbursement of the expenses he incurred to that point began to preoccupy him, and he developed a reputation as a shady manipulator. Even so, he advocated enlarging the terms of this treaty and increasingly saw provincial-American interchange as part of the "high destiny of the North American continent."

Andrews supported John C. Frémont's bid for the Republican presidential nomination in 1855, and rumors circulated about a scheme he had concocted to line his own pockets with Maine campaign funds. This image made him a liability when he supported Nathaniel P. Banks to be Speaker of the House of Representatives. Andrews was jailed at least once and was held on bail several times because of his debts. His health declined from drinking. Friends and contacts came to his partial rescue, and in 1856 a committee of the Boston Board of Trade collected funds and petitioned the president to have Congress defray his claimed expenses above the more than $132,000 public and private sources had given. Andrews's illness persisted, and he was increasingly absorbed by his financial woes. President Buchanan removed him as a consul for failing to discharge his duties, and Andrews receded from public life.

In 1858 the Senate requested that the secretary of state review Andrews's accounts and reimburse his expenses, but no money emerged. By 1862 Andrews identified personally with every attack against reciprocity, and he remained deeply in debt until he died in alcoholic poverty in Boston's City Hospital.

• Pieces of Andrews's correspondence are in the papers of Lord Elgin (Public Archives of Canada), William Marcy, and James Buchanan (both in the Library of Congress). His ideas are expressed in his *Report on the Trade and Commerce of the British North American Colonies with the United States and Other Countries Embracing Full and Complete Tabular State-*

ments from 1820–1850 (1851), *Report upon the Trade and Commerce of the British North American Colonies and upon the Trade of the Great Lakes and Rivers* (1854), and *Report upon the Mines, Minerals, and Quarries of the British North American Colonies*, in Senate Exec. Docs., no. 23, 6 Feb. 1851. See also Department of State, Despatches from United States Consuls, National Archives, RG 59, T485 (St. John), T222 (Montreal); and Letters and Reports Received by the Secretary of the Treasury from Special Agents 1854–1861, National Archives, RG 36, M177. Thomas C. Keefer discusses Andrews in *A Sketch of the Rise and Progress of the Reciprocity Treaty* (1863). Thomas Le Duc, "I. D. Andrews and the Reciprocity Treaty of 1854," *Canadian Historical Review* 15 (Dec. 1934): 437–38; Donald C. Masters, "A Further Word on I. D. Andrews and the Reciprocity Treaty of 1854," *Canadian Historical Review* 17 (June 1936): 159–67; and William D. Overman, "I. D. Andrews and Reciprocity in 1854: An Episode in Dollar Diplomacy," *Canadian Historical Review* 15 (Dec. 1934): 248–63, assess his career.

REGINALD C. STUART

ANDREWS, Jane (1 Dec. 1833–15 July 1887), educator and writer of children's books, was born in Newburyport, Massachusetts, the daughter of John Andrews, a bookseller and later a cashier, and Margaret Demmon Rand. Andrews was educated at Newburyport's new Putnam Free School, an academy that quickly attained a reputation for high standards. She also took part in a small writing group (with Harriet Prescott Spofford and Louisa Parsons Stone Hopkins) led by Thomas Wentworth Higginson, a Unitarian church pastor. Higginson also organized a free evening school for cotton-mill workers; Andrews taught in this school during the winter of 1850–1851. She attended the State Normal School at West Newton, Massachusetts, in the spring of 1851 and graduated in July 1853 as valedictorian of her class. One of her fellow students was Elizabeth Peabody, whose brother-in-law, Horace Mann, was in the process of establishing a new college, Antioch, in Ohio. Andrews was the first student to enroll in the fall of 1853, and she evidently helped in the preparatory classes and in tutoring. However, the college was unfinished, and the living conditions were less than satisfactory. Overwork and illness forced Andrews to leave Antioch within the first year and return to Newburyport.

After Antioch, Andrews spent the greater part of six years recovering from a disorder called "spinal affection." By 1860 she had recovered sufficiently to start a small primary school in her home. She ran the school for the next twenty-five years and employed teaching methods in it that were far ahead of her times. What particularly characterized her teaching methods was direct observation rather than a rigorous attention to textbooks alone in nature study, geography, and other subjects. Lessons were based on current national and local issues. The pupils were stimulated to take responsibility and be creative in a society of interrelation and equality. Andrews translated many of Horace Mann's educational ideas into reality. She, like Mann, believed in active participation on the part of the pupils in contrast to the prevailing rote learning and relying on textbooks. For example, she developed simple experiments and wrote games and plays, enabling children to learn by doing. Several geography games and plays were published by Lee and Shepard as separate booklets; in them Andrews stated her purpose and gave suggestions for their use in the classroom. Geography included human life, and nature study was built on direct observation. Lessons were also based on political events and the town shipping news. Her pupils included Ethel Parton, author; Alice Stone Blackwell, editor and suffragist; and J. Lewis Howe, chemist and educational leader.

Six of Jane Andrews's books were conceived as she worked in the school. First she told them informally to the children; then later she wrote them down and read and retold them to her audience before they were actually printed. In schools they were used as supplementary readers. Her first book was a collection of stories used to supplement geography lessons, *Seven Little Sisters Who Live on the Round Ball That Floats in the Air* (1861). The book includes seven tales of happy girls, each living in a different place on the earth but all members of God's human family. It also appeared in German, Chinese, and Japanese. A companion volume, *Each and All; or; How the Seven Little Sisters Who Live on the Round Ball That Floats in the Air Prove Their Sisterhood* (1885), contained an additional incident about each little girl. In order not to show favoritism for girls through the two *Little Sisters* books, Andrews also wrote a book especially for boys. Essentially a survey of the social history of Western civilization, *Ten Boys Who Lived on the Road from Long Ago to Now* (1886) is probably her greatest achievement. The book ties together the stories of ten boys in ten different historical periods, combining scholarly detail with a fresh conversational tone. An additional book, *The Stories Mother Nature Told Her Children*, appeared more than a year after her death. This book did not use all of the nature stories, however, and in 1900 Ginn and Co. published *The Stories of My Four Friends*.

Ill health forced Andrews, who had never married, to close her school in 1885. She died of what may have been meningitis in Newburyport.

Andrews's greatest contribution to education was her transformation of Mann's ideas into practice and the publications she wrote disseminating those ideas. She stressed the importance of equality and individual responsibility to society, in contrast to the popular McGuffey Readers, which tended to stress virtue from the personal point of view. Her intuitive understanding of children led her to interpret reality through entertaining narrative based on observation. Characteristic of her stories is the idea of the earth as one world. Published by Ginn and Co. after 1893, the six "Andrews books" enjoyed a wide reading in elementary schools for more than fifty years after the author's death. *Seven Little Sisters* paid royalties for ninety years; it appeared in a new edition sixty-three years after its publication and may have sold up to a half million copies.

• Information on Andrews can be found in the papers of Ticknor & Fields, James Parton, and Thomas Wentworth Higginson at Houghton Library, Harvard University; and the records of State Teachers College, Framingham, Mass.; of Antioch College; and of Ginn and Co., Boston. Norma Kidd Green, *A Forgotten Chapter in American Education: Jane Andrews of Newburyport* (1961), remains the authoritative biography. Other sources of information are Louisa Parsons Stone Hopkins, "Memorial of Miss Jane Andrews," in the 1887 edition of *Seven Little Sisters*; and Harriet Prescott Spofford, *A Little Book of Friends* (1916). Also helpful are John J. Currier, *History of Newburyport, Mass.* (2 vols., 1906–1909). An obituary is in the *Woman's Journal*, 23 July 1887.

JON D. ORTEN

ANDREWS, John Bertram (2 Aug. 1880–4 Jan. 1943), leader in the social insurance movement, was born in South Wayne, Wisconsin, the son of Philo Edmund Andrews and Sarah Jane Maddrell, farmers. He entered the University of Wisconsin in 1900, graduating with a B.A. in 1904. After receiving an M.A. in economics at Dartmouth in 1905, Andrews returned to Wisconsin to continue his studies under the economist and social activist John R. Commons. He received a Ph.D. in political economy and history in 1908; the subject of his dissertion was the history of the American labor movement from 1863 to 1873.

Commons and several other social scientists, including Richard T. Ely of Wisconsin and Henry T. Farman of Yale, founded the American Association for Labor Legislation (AALL) in 1906. This marked the emergence of an organized effort by social scientists to encourage and shape social legislation and signaled the beginning of the American social insurance movement. The movement's founders sought to insure industrial workers against the loss of earnings resulting from unemployment, illness, injury, and old age. This would be achieved through programs mandated by government and financed by contributions from employers and employees.

Commons arranged for the appointment of Andrews as executive secretary of the AALL in 1908. Another former Commons student, Irene Osgood, was appointed assistant secretary. Andrews and Osgood were married in 1910; they had one son.

The AALL social insurance philosophy combined the American tradition of self-reliance with a belief in the effectiveness of the profit motive as a means of achieving reform. Properly drafted legislation could incorporate into law economic incentives to induce desired changes in the social environment, particularly in the workplace. To promote the association's reform agenda, Andrews founded the *American Labor Legislation Review* in 1911 and edited it until his death, when it ceased publication.

Andrews's initial efforts were directed at prevention of work-related illnesses and industrial accidents. He campaigned in various states for passage of compulsory workers' compensation laws. Under tort law, workers injured on the job collected compensation only if they could demonstrate the employer's negligence. The AALL drafted model legislation creating no-fault compensation for injured workers through employer-financed insurance. Because premiums would be related to claims, each employer had an incentive to create a safer work environment. The campaign for compulsory workers' compensation led to passage of legislation in a number of states, beginning in 1911. Andrews also was instrumental in gaining passage in 1912 of federal legislation outlawing the use of poisonous white phosphorus in the manufacture of matches. He is credited with focusing attention on work-related illnesses, although his efforts to extend workers' compensation coverage to such illnesses was only partially successful.

Another initiative by Andrews involved the AALL in a campaign to introduce compulsory health insurance for wage earners. In 1913 he appointed a commission to draft a proposal for compulsory health insurance for industrial workers, to be financed by contributions from employers and employees, augmented by a subsidy from general tax revenues. The proposal, modeled after programs operating in England and Germany, aroused strong opposition from insurance companies concerned with competition from government insurance and from organized medicine. The medical profession feared government intrusion into billing procedures and doctor-patient relations. Opponents attacked the European roots of the AALL proposal, an effective tactic in the anti-German and xenophobic atmosphere of 1917–1920. Legislatures in California and New York rejected legislation drafted by the AALL. Following these defeats, Andrews and his associates abandoned the campaign for health insurance, and the bitterness of this confrontation appears to have contributed to Andrews's subsequent reluctance to adopt redistributionist European models of social insurance in the United States.

Andrews is also recognized as a pioneer in inducing states to introduce compulsory unemployment insurance for industrial workers. This effort began in 1912 and continued for more than two decades before it enjoyed any success. Andrews and Commons favored unemployment insurance patterned after workers' compensation. Each employer would be required to assume the cost of insuring its own employees, creating the financial incentive to smooth out seasonal and even cyclical variations in employment. Andrews proposed employment exchanges that would match workers seeking jobs with potential employers, and he suggested that governments should be prepared to activate a backlog of emergency public works projects to provide jobs during economic downturns.

During the prosperous 1920s, all efforts to advance the cause of social insurance were rebuffed by the conservative forces that controlled federal and state governments. The movement was also weakened by a bitter dispute between the AALL, led by Andrews, and the social reformer Isaac Rubinow, a former ally. Rubinow rejected Andrews's approach, which gave each employer responsibility for the security of its workers; he favored a more generous program that would guarantee adequate living standards for the unemployed and the disabled. Rubinow emphasized social adequacy; Andrews emphasized economic incentives and feared that the guarantees favored by Rubinow would discourage people from working.

Opposition to social insurance weakened during the 1930s as the onset of the Great Depression altered the political climate. In 1932 Wisconsin became the first state to introduce compulsory unemployment insurance, under a law requiring each employer to fund benefits to its own unemployed workers, as proposed by Andrews.

Andrews was not formally associated with the Committee on Economic Security, appointed by President Franklin D. Roosevelt in 1934 to lay the groundwork for the Social Security Act of 1935. He was, however, invited to consult with the committee, and once its proposal was forwarded to Congress, he was enlisted to lobby members of Congress and to organize outside support for the legislation. The 1935 act introduced a national system of old-age insurance and created a joint federal-state welfare system. It also introduced a nationwide system of unemployment insurance, to be administered by the states under federal supervision and to be financed by a payroll tax on employers. It did not provide for individual employer accounts, but it contained an experience-rating formula that reduced tax rates for employers who maintain stable levels of employment. Experience rating reflects the enduring influence of Andrews and the AALL philosophy.

Although Andrews was primarily a social activist, he maintained a lifelong commitment to scholarship. He taught classes on labor legislation at Columbia University and wrote several books, including *Administrative Labor Legislation* (1936), *Labor Laws in Action* (1938), and *The Townsend Crusade* (1938). *Principles of Labor Legislation* (1916 and subsequent editions), coauthored with John R. Commons, became a standard reference.

Andrews was one of a small group of activist social scientists who encouraged and helped shape legislation advancing worker safety and security during the three decades ending in 1940. He served as executive secretary of the AALL until his death in New York City.

• John B. Andrews Papers are deposited at Cornell University. Other sources of information include Jerry R. Cates, *Insuring Inequality* (1983); Roy Lubove, *The Struggle for Social Security, 1900–1935* (1968); and Carolyn L. Weaver, *The Crisis in Social Security* (1982). Obituaries are in the *New York Times*, 5 Jan. 1943, and the *South Wayne (Wis.) Homestead*, 28 Jan. 1943.

CHARLES W. MEYER

ANDREWS, Lorin (1 Apr. 1819–18 Sept. 1861), educator, was born in Uniontown (now Ashland), Ohio, the son of Alanson Andrews and Sally Needham, farmers. Little is known about Andrews's early life except that at age seventeen his July Fourth speech was recorded in a local newspaper. The next year he attended a preparatory grammar school for Kenyon College. Enrollment in the college followed, but in 1840 he withdrew, apparently for lack of funds.

Andrews's public career began as a teacher at Ashland Academy in 1840. Three years later he married Sarah Gates of Worcester, Massachusetts. They had three children. In 1847 Andrews was admitted to the bar, but he never opened a law office. In the same year he was appointed superintendent of the Massillon, Ohio, schools and assumed that role as well as that of a teacher in the high school in 1848. At the same time Andrews became active in Masonry. He helped to organize the lodge in Ashland and became master of the Clinton Lodge, number forty-seven, in 1850. In 1854–1855 he was appointed grand orator by the grand master of Ohio.

Andrews became a leader in the formation of the Ohio State Teachers' Association, serving on its executive committee in 1848 and chairing the same in 1851. During 1854 and 1855 he was president of the association. By 1851 Andrews had a reputation as a champion of the common schools, and word of his efforts to improve the quality of teaching through the establishment of teacher institutes was widespread. The educational reformer Henry Barnard wrote to Andrews on 20 December 1851 saying, "You have done a noble work this fall, and your Association is setting the teachers of the whole country a noble example."

In the fall of 1853 Andrews was the favorite of Ohio teachers for the new, elected position of state commissioner of common schools. Politics intervened, however, in the form of a "democratic hurricane" that toppled Andrews and many Whig candidates. Among Andrews's few remaining letters are several dealing with the "injustice" of the outcome.

Notwithstanding the defeat, Andrews was named the first lay president of Kenyon College in Gambier, Ohio, in 1853. The 1853–1854 Kenyon College catalog records that he was "President and Professor of Mental and Moral Philosophy, Political Economy, etc." It may be that Andrews's conversion and baptism in 1839 under Bishop Charles Pettit McIlvaine, while the former was a student at Kenyon and the latter president of the college, influenced McIlvaine and the trustees to hire Andrews. Certainly he was known for his intense religious beliefs. It is more likely, however, that Andrews's efforts and leadership on behalf of public education, his rhetorical skills, and his training in law convinced McIlvaine and others of his executive ability. McIlvaine later recounted that in 1853 "no name was so universally known in this State . . . and none so influential" (address at funeral).

Under Andrews's presidency, Kenyon's enrollment grew rapidly and its financial condition was stabilized. The religious climate of the college also grew more intense, and Andrews attempted to meet with all his students for prayer during the great revival of the winter of 1858–1859. Other aspects of campus life also flourished, including the reactivation of debating and literary clubs.

When the Civil War began Andrews was quick to volunteer. He raised a company in Knox County for the Fourth Regiment Ohio Volunteer Infantry and was elected and commissioned colonel. Shortly after the regiment arrived in West Virginia, he contracted "camp fever" (probably typhoid) and was forced to return to Gambier on 26 August 1861, where he died from the effects of the fever.

• The largest number of letters to Andrews are in the Ohio Historical Society, Columbus. Two letters as well as numerous memorials, obituaries, and sermons about Andrews are in Olin Library, Kenyon College. A small file is also in Massillon Museum, Massillon, Ohio. Biographical sketches appear in William B. Bodine, *The Kenyon Book* (2d vols., 1891), and James Burns, *Educational History of Ohio* (1905). See also Alfred Andrews, *Geneological History of John and Mary Andrews* (1872). The *History and Proceeding* (1851) of the Ohio State Teachers' Association and the *Ohio Journal of Education* help document the activities of Andrews in that association.

EDWARD W. STEVENS, JR.

ANDREWS, Lorrin (29 Apr. 1795–29 Sept. 1868), missionary and educator, was born in East Windsor (now Vernon), Connecticut, the son of Samuel Andrews and his wife, whose name is unknown. Andrews grew up on the frontier in Kentucky and Ohio and later attended Jefferson College in Pennsylvania. After graduation he studied at Princeton Theological Seminary in New Jersey, where he graduated in 1825. He worked as a mechanic and printer while in school, and later as a teacher. On 26 April 1827 he volunteered his services to the American Board of Commissioners for Foreign Missions (ABCFM) and was accepted for work in the Sandwich Islands, as Hawaii was then called. His various job experiences and his life in rough pioneer country where hard work was valued prepared him well for his missionary tasks.

In keeping with Board policy that all missionaries be married, Andrews wed Mary Ann Wilson of Washington, Kentucky, in 1827. They had seven children, and their grandson, Lorrin Andrews Thurston, later became a leader in the 1893 overthrow of the Hawaiian monarchy. On 21 September 1827, soon after his marriage, Andrews was ordained, and on 3 November of that year he and his bride sailed on the *Parthian* with the Third Company of missionaries to Hawaii. Arriving on 30 March 1828, they became part of a small community of forty-four missionaries. "We have . . . set our feet on heathen shores," Andrews wrote home soon after his arrival, "for the purpose as we hope of making known the plan of Salvation to those that have long abode in ignorance."

The missionaries lived and worked in seventeen stations scattered among the five islands. Andrews was sent to Lahaina, on the southwest coast of the island of Maui. A bustling seaport where whaling ships docked for repairs and supplies, Lahaina was then the capital of the kingdom.

Three years after Andrews's arrival and nine years after the missionaries began teaching basic literacy in schools throughout the islands, they decided to open an institution of higher learning to train native Hawaiians as schoolteachers and assistant preachers. Established in 1831, Lahainaluna was the first school of higher learning west of the Rocky Mountains, a remarkable undertaking considering that the first high school in the United States had been established in Boston only ten years earlier. The missionaries selected Andrews as the school's first principal and sole instructor. Situated on the mountainside, just above the town of Lahaina, Lahainaluna opened with twenty-five students, all men, who brought their wives and children. Students had to raise their own food, build their own homes and schoolhouse, and print their reading materials using the printing press Andrews had set up. In February 1834 Andrews began publishing the island's first newspaper, which was also the first newspaper west of the Missouri River. Written in Hawaiian, *Ka Lama Hawaii* (The Hawaiian Luminary) provided students with an outlet for their writing as well as material to read. Andrews developed a course of studies that was ahead of its time, including not only academic subjects but also practical trades like farming, animal husbandry, carpentry, printing, and engraving.

To supply students with maps and illustrations, Andrews taught himself the technique of copper-plate engraving from books. Collecting copper sheets and pieces from the shipmasters, he taught his students the process, and together they printed numerous illustrations. In 1834 another missionary joined Andrews. In 1836 the school began admitting boys instead of men, assuming that youths could more easily learn Christian habits; it later became a boarding school for boys.

On 1 April 1842, after eleven years at Lahainaluna, Andrews resigned his post as missionary. Among his reasons for resigning were his disagreement with the ABCFM's management of its missionaries; his desire to devote some time teaching his own children, who had no school to attend; and his discovery that slaveholders were contributing funds to the mission. A strong opponent of slavery, Andrews realized that he could not continue to take money, no matter how little, that came from slavery.

After one year as Seamen's Chaplain at Lahaina, Andrews moved to Honolulu in 1845, where the king appointed him judge for cases involving foreigners. Although not formally trained in law, his fairness and integrity led to his appointment as appellate judge the next year and in 1848 as associate justice of the Superior Court, which functioned as a supreme court. From 1850 until 1859 he served as secretary of the king's Privy (private) Council, keeping records in both Hawaiian and English. In 1852 he became the first associate justice of the Supreme Court. He left this position in 1854 to become judge of a newly formed probate court. He resigned as probate court judge in 1855.

In order to transform the islands into an "elevated state of Christian civilization," the missionaries had given the Hawaiian language a written form and taught the Hawaiians to read and write. From the

1820s to the 1860s, missionaries wrote and published about 200 works in Hawaiian, including thousands of copies of the Bible, hymnals, and sermons. They also published textbooks as well as books on science, history, literature, government, and other general interest works.

Andrews played a key role in this effort to spread literacy. In 1836 he published a 6,000-word vocabulary of Hawaiian words, which was used as the principal vocabulary book until 1865, when he published his monumental *Dictionary of the Hawaiian Language*. In 1854 he authored a Hawaiian grammar book. He also wrote other textbooks in Hawaiian and translated numerous works from English to Hawaiian.

Andrew had a superior command of the Hawaiian language, and his study of Hawaiian literature and *meles* (chants) was more extensive than any other American missionary. He collected and published a number of *meles* in Hawaiian and English, preserving them for posterity. Shy and retiring, yet well respected as a scholar, Andrews died in Honolulu.

• Andrews's papers, including his letters and journal, as well as secondary accounts, are in the Mission Houses Museum Library, Honolulu. See also Ralph S. Kuykendall, *The Hawaiian Kingdom*, vol. 1, *1778–1854* (1938; repr. 1968), and Hiram Bingham, *A Residence of Twenty-one Years in the Sandwich Islands* (1847), for Andrews's work in the context of missionary efforts; Hawaiian Mission Children's Society, *Missionary Album* (1969), for biographical sketches of Andrews and other American Protestant missionaries; Rufus Anderson, *History of the Sandwich Islands Mission* (1870), for further biographical information, and *The Hawaiian Islands: Their Progress and Condition under Missionary Labors* (1864), for a short discussion of Andrews; and Rev. and Mrs. Orramel H. Gulick, *The Pilgrims of Hawaii* (1918), for selections of Andrews's letters. An obituary is in *The Friend*, Oct. 1868, p. 84.

EILEEN H. TAMURA

ANDREWS, Ludie (1875–1943?), black nursing educator, was born in Milledgeville, Georgia, the daughter of a poor family. Little is known about Andrews's parents or early years, though something clearly happened to inspire in her a desire to become a nurse. In 1901 Andrews applied to Spelman College's MacVicar Hospital School of Nursing. On her application, she asked for financial assistance, explaining that her family could not help her pay. Her mother had a large family to support and "an old flicted husband," who was not Andrews's father. Andrews also said that she had been married but did not currently live with her husband and expected no support from him. Letters praising Andrews and talking about her "good moral character" that came from the pillars of Milledgeville society proved instrumental in securing Andrews's admission.

In 1906 Andrews received her diploma from Spelman and set upon her life's work. During her training she resolved "that I wanted to work for my people, how or where this was to be done I did not know." She did not have to wait long to find out. After caring for only two private cases—the bread and butter of black nurses in that time period—Andrews was offered the position of superintendent of Lula Grove Hospital and Training School for Colored Nurses and Patients.

Located in Atlanta, the school was run by a group of white physicians who served on the faculty of the Atlanta School of Medicine and was one of the few health facilities in the area for blacks. Andrews quickly developed a reputation for excellence both in administration and on the surgical floor. Howard Kelly, an internationally known surgeon and professor from Johns Hopkins University, helped cement that reputation after Andrews assisted him on an operation. At the end of the procedure, he proclaimed, "I have never been better served even by nurses that I myself have trained."

Believing that white and black nurses had equal skills, Andrews in 1909 started a crusade to allow black nurses to take the same state medical exam as white nurses. Some proposed that black nurses take a different test than their white counterparts. Andrews did not accept that suggestion, pointing out that this scenario would make it difficult for graduates of black nursing schools in Georgia to find jobs in other states. The state board then offered to issue her a license. Again Andrews refused, saying she wanted that opportunity for all black nurses. When the state board refused to change its policy, Andrews instituted legal proceedings, a case she would eventually win.

When the city of Atlanta opened the 250-bed Grady Hospital in 1914, Andrews seemed a natural choice to serve as superintendent of colored nurses of the facility. Always cognizant of opportunities for women like herself, Andrews spearheaded the organization and opening of that hospital's Municipal Training School for Colored Nurses in 1917. Grady had had a nursing school, founded in 1892, but that institution allowed only white women to apply. Once more, she earned kudos from her physician colleagues. One doctor, W. B. Symmerall, said of her, "Her services were of the highest character; she showed ability in organization and in administration. I always found her thoroughly devoted to her duties; she had high ideals in regard to the work of her people and the nursing profession."

In 1920 Andrews not only won her case against the state medical board, but she received one of the more coveted positions in black nursing, the superintendency of Morehouse College's infirmary. As a faculty member, Andrews also taught home and community hygiene in the summer program for teachers and the social work school. She did not restrict her message to students enrolled at Morehouse. A frequent lecturer in public health throughout the community, Andrews delivered a variant on that lecture in the Neighborhood Union. Her efforts in public health went beyond the theoretical. She served on the Tuberculosis Association, chairing its relief committee and helping to raise money for patients. She also was a member of an interracial committee that worked with troubled women who had ended up in prisons or in medical wards with social diseases.

Andrews continued to champion the cause of black nurses throughout her life. She served on a committee of several nursing organizations as a representative of the National Association of Colored Graduate Nurses. In that capacity she argued before representatives from the American Nursing Association, the National League of Nursing Education, and the National Organization for Public Health Nursing that black nurses should have the same opportunities as white nurses. In 1926 Andrews suggested to the American Nursing Association that it allow black nurses who could not join their local chapters because of discrimination to join the national group. Her lifetime of hard work for black nurses made Andrews a natural choice for the colored nursing association's Mary Mahoney Award in 1943, given shortly before she died.

• Accounts of Andrews's life appear in Adah B. Thoms, *Pathfinders: A History of the Progress of Colored Graduate Nurses* (1985); Mary Elizabeth Carnegie, *The Path We Tread: Blacks in Nursing Worldwide, 1854–1994* (1995); Darlene Clark Hine, *Black Women in White: Racial Conflict and Cooperation in the Nursing Profession, 1890–1950* (1989); and Mabel Keaton Staupers, *No Time for Prejudice: A Story of the Integration of Negroes in Nursing in the United States* (1961).

SHARI RUDAVSKY

ANDREWS, Mary Raymond Shipman (2 Apr. 1860–2 Aug. 1936), novelist and short story writer, was born in Mobile, Alabama, the daughter of the Right Reverend Jacob Shaw Shipman, an Episcopal minister, and Anna Louise Johns. In 1861 the family moved to Lexington, Kentucky, where she learned to appreciate outdoor activities, particularly riding. Mary's father later served as bishop in Fond du Lac, Wisconsin, and then at Christ Church in New York City, where the family settled in 1877. After graduating from high school, Mary studied with her father and later with her husband, William Shankland Andrews, an attorney whom she married in 1884. They had one child.

Andrews's best-known work is *The Perfect Tribute* (1905), based on an imaginary story about Abraham Lincoln and a dying Confederate soldier, in which President Lincoln learns that his Gettysburg Address had not fallen on deaf ears, as he had thought, but had made a profound impression on the man and others. Published in *Scribner's Magazine*, the story sold more than 600,000 copies in book form.

Although sources differ about when her works were copyrighted and published, Andrews's output was prodigious. Her works include *Kidnapped Colony* (1903), *Bob and the Guides* (1906), *The Militants* (1907), *The Enchanted Forest* (1909), *Courage of the Commonplace* (1911), *Counsel Assigned* (1912), *Marshal* (1912), *The Eternal Masculine* (1913), *Three Things* (1915), *The Eternal Feminine, and Other Stories* (1916), *Her Country* (1918), *Joy in the Morning* (1919), *His Soul Goes Marching* (1922), *Yellow Butterflies* (1922), and *A Lost Commander: Florence Nightingale* (1929).

In many of her earliest stories, written for children, Andrews's love of the outdoors is evident. In an autobiographical sketch published in *The Junior Book of Authors* (Stanley J. Kunitz and Howard Haycraft, eds.; 1940), she cites with pride having won a silver cup in a horse show, having caught a five-and-three-quarter-pound trout, and having shot some deer and caribou. Andrews also claimed to know how to host dinners, how to swim, and how to paddle a canoe: the last, she noted, was one of the few things she did really well.

Andrews's family spent their summers at a family camp in Canada, 100 miles from Quebec; there she did most of her writing. She loved dogs and wrote about them in "The Everlasting Bow-Wows," published in *Colliers* (1921). In 1928 Andrews achieved the status of a big-game hunter by killing three caribou, two moose, and seven deer.

Andrews explored feminist issues in several of her works. In her short story "The Fling," published in *The Eternal Feminine, and Other Stories*, she wrote that her heroine found "it was pleasant to have this stranger look at her as he was looking—as though she were a person." The woman's daughter pictured her mother staying home and sewing upstairs, when in reality her mother wanted to reject her traditional female role, "to live and do things, worthwhile things." In "A Play to the Gallery," published in the same collection, the female protagonist focuses the man in the story on the subject that interests him the most—"himself"—thereby underscoring male self-centeredness. In another story, a mayor stresses the need for girls to be educated when he tells a young girl to "stick to your book and mind your lessons."

Many of Andrews's short books, poems, articles, and stories appeared in *Scribners Magazine, McClure's Magazine, Harper's Monthly Magazine, Colliers*, and *Ladies' Home Journal*. Her work has been variously described as well written, humorous, tender, patriotic, and dramatically conceived. She wrote on romantic themes and often used the traditional sentimental plot, causing some reviewers to criticize her work as overly sentimental. Nevertheless, her writings are accurate reflections of her time. Andrews died in Syracuse, New York.

• Additional novels by Andrews not mentioned in the text include *Vive l'Empereur* (1902), *A Good Samaritan* (1906), *Better Treasure* (1908), *The Lifted Bandage* (1910), *August First* (with R. I. Murray, 1915), *Old Glory* (1916), *Crosses of War* (1918), and *Pontifex Maximus* (1925). See Lina Mainiero, ed., *American Women Writers* (1979), for some insight into Andrews's complexity, and Norma Olin Ireland, ed., *Index to Women* (1970), which lists Andrews's works. Obituaries are in the *New York Times*, 3 Aug. 1936, and *Newsweek*, 15 Aug. 1936.

MARY ADELAIDE GARDNER

ANDREWS, Philip (31 Mar. 1866–18 Dec. 1935), naval officer, was born in New York City, the son of Phoebe D. Andrews, a Jersey City schoolteacher (father's name unknown). Andrews completed his U.S. Naval Academy course in 1886 and entered the navy in the early stage of conversion from wood and sail to steel and steam-powered warships. About this same time he married Clara Fuller; they had one child. During the 1890s Andrews served on a number of these new steel men-of-war, including the armored cruiser *Chicago* and the cruisers *Newark* and *Baltimore*, and on the gunboats *Petrel* and *Castine* on the Asiatic Station between 1900 and 1901. He helped develop the rifled ordnance and armor plate for this "new American navy" of steel and steam warships while serving in the Bureau of Ordnance, Washington, D.C., between 1893 and 1895 and as an inspector of ordnance at the South Bethlehem, Pennsylvania, plant of the Bethlehem Steel Company in 1898. Andrews's ordnance duty culminated in 1907 at the New York shipbuilding yard in Camden, New Jersey, where he inspected the final fitting out of the new 16,000-ton battleship *Kansas*. He then made a world cruise as lieutenant commander in the *Kansas* between 1908 and 1909 as part of the "Great White Fleet."

Andrews's early naval career coincided with the emergence of the Naval War College in Newport, Rhode Island, the Naval Institute in Annapolis, and the General Board of the Navy in Washington, D.C., as instruments of professionalization and reform. He attended the war college course in 1891, 1904, and 1916; served on the General Board in 1904 and 1913; and participated in the discussions organized by the Naval Institute. Each influenced his interest in naval reorganization and modernization and brought him into intimate contact with insurgent officers, such as William S. Sims, who advocated radical naval reforms, including creation of a navy general staff system. Andrews's lifelong friendship with Sims deeply influenced his own ideas. "I think that the individual ship is pretty well organized, and that it is in fleet and squadron administration that we are behind the times," Andrews told the Naval Institute in 1909. The general staff system centralized planning and fleet operations in a professional naval staff, taking away power from old navy bureau officers and their civilian political allies. Secretary of the Navy Josephus Daniels and more conservative bureau chiefs saw the general staff movement as an attempt to "Prussianize" the navy by removing civilian control.

Andrews had an opportunity to influence naval organization as Secretary of the Navy George von Lengerke Meyer's naval aide, 1909–1911, and as the chief of the Bureau of Navigation, 1911–1913. Meyer's administrative innovations included the creation of a system of four top aides to run the naval side of the department and the complete reorganization of the navy yards and stations. The aide system created a corporate management structure for operations, material, inspection, and personnel and replaced the inefficient navy bureau organization. Meyer also sought to close outdated navy yards, consolidate functions, modernize drydocks and engineering facilities, and adopt efficient business accounting methods. Andrews accompanied Meyer on inspection trips to naval yards and advised him on other changes in departmental business. Though Andrews remained behind the scenes, Meyer's successor, Josephus Daniels, an opponent of the navy general staff idea, claimed that Andrews had performed all "Meyer's dirty work."

When Daniels replaced Meyer as secretary of the navy under Woodrow Wilson's administration in 1913, he immediately removed Andrews as the chief of the Bureau of Navigation. Daniels suspected that Andrews used his authority to give officers who supported the navy general staff system assignments that put them in positions to affect naval policy and organization. After his abrupt departure from shore duty, Andrews commanded the *Montana* in 1913 and the *Maryland* in 1914. Between 1916 and 1917 Andrews commanded the Naval Training Station in San Francisco and served on the staff of the commandant of the Fifth Naval District, Norfolk, Virginia. From 1918 to early 1919 Andrews commanded the battleship *Mississippi* with additional duty as commander of the U.S. Naval Base, Cardiff, Wales.

Andrews received his most difficult assignment on 22 March 1919, when he took command of U.S. naval forces in the eastern Mediterranean and became commander of the U.S. naval detachment in the Adriatic in August 1920. In this capacity, Andrews landed U.S. Marines from his flagship, the *Olympia* (later the *Pittsburgh*), to prevent a clash between Italians and Serbs at Trogir (Traù) on the Dalmatian coast. After returning from the eastern Mediterranean command, Andrews became commandant of the Norfolk Navy Yard in 1921 and the Fifth Naval District in 1923. He commanded U.S. naval forces in Europe in 1923–1925, returning to the Boston Navy Yard and command of the First Naval District. Andrews experienced constant problems with Prohibitionists, who accused the navy of promoting drunkenness in the Boston vicinity. He also spent time until his retirement from active duty in 1930 working to restore the historic USS *Constitution*. He continued to promote naval modernization and reorganization after his retirement. However, Andrews caused a public stir in 1927, when he announced that Charles Lindbergh's solo flight across the Atlantic was mostly luck by contrast with his son-in-law Carlton C. Champion's record-setting flight in a navy seaplane that same year, because he saw publicity about Lindbergh as a threat to developing naval air power doctrine. Andrews died at the Naval Hospital, San Diego.

Andrews's career spanned the most exciting period of technological and organizational innovation in U.S. Navy history. He participated actively (although largely behind the scenes) in most of the changes and reforms that shaped the modern American navy.

• Little has been written about Andrews, and his only personal correspondence lies in the papers of other naval officers, including those of William S. Sims, Mark L. Bristol, William S. Benson, and Samuel McGowan, all located in the Manuscript Division, Library of Congress. Although Andrews was one of Sims's closest comrades, he is barely mentioned in Elting E. Morison, *Admiral Sims and the Modern American Navy* (1942); and although he was Meyer's closest aide, he is mentioned only once in Mark A. DeWolfe

Howe, *George von Lengerke Meyer* (1919). Andrews's trouble with Daniels is documented in E. David Cronon, ed., *The Cabinet Diaries of Josephus Daniels, 1913–1921* (1963).

JEFFERY M. DORWART

ANDREWS, Roy Chapman (26 Jan. 1884–11 Mar. 1960), explorer and zoologist, was born in Beloit, Wisconsin, the son of Charles Ezra Andrews, a wholesale druggist, and Cora May Chapman. As a young boy Andrews resolved "to be an explorer, to work in a natural history museum, and to live out of doors" (*Under a Lucky Star* [1943]). His pastimes included hunting and fishing, and he taught himself taxidermy. He attended Beloit College, where he studied physiology and anatomy and worked as a taxidermist under the direction of Dr. George Collie, curator of the Logan Museum of Anthropology. After receiving a B.A. degree in 1906, Andrews went directly to the American Museum of Natural History in New York. He presented himself, without introductions, to director Hermon C. Bumpus and offered to work at any job for the opportunity to be employed by the museum. Impressed with his persistence and singleness of purpose, Bumpus hired him to assist James L. Clark with model preparation in the Department of Taxidermy.

For the next six years the primary focus of Andrews's work was on cetaceans, an order whose life histories were poorly known. Along with Clark, he devised a method to construct a scale model of a 76-foot blue whale, which was exhibited until the 1950s. The two men also met the challenges of retrieving the entire skeleton of a beached *Balaena glacialis* (right whale), whose anatomy Andrews described in his first scientific monograph (1908). As museum naturalist, he pursued cetaceans on expeditions to Alaska (1908); British Columbia (1909); Japan, China, the Philippines, Borneo, and the Celebes Islands (USS *Albatross* expedition, 1909–1910); and Korea (1911, 1912). On the 1912 expedition, Andrews discovered that the Korean "devilfish" that flourished off the coast of east Asia was synonymous with the California gray whale, a species thought to be extinct. This discovery formed the basis of his thesis at Columbia University, where he graduated with an M.S. degree in 1913. In 1914 he married Yvette Borup; they had two sons.

Although Andrews had become a leading authority on whales, he did no research of his own after the age of thirty. Instead he turned his attention to leading the museum's Asian expeditions, on which his wife served as photographer. His first expedition was to Burma and the Yunnan province of China in 1916–1917. In 1918 he worked for U.S. Naval Intelligence in Mongolia and China, and in 1918–1919 he led the second expedition to northern China and Outer Mongolia. These first small-scale ventures were primarily for hunting specimens for the museum's exhibit and research collections. However, in 1919, while traveling along the edge of the Gobi in the badlands of southeast Mongolia, Andrews noticed exposed sedimentary beds and realized their potential for fossils. He thus proposed to mount an expedition to test the theory posited by Henry Fairfield Osborn (then museum director), William Diller Matthew, and William K. Gregory that the Northern Hemisphere, particularly central Asia, was the probable source of mammalian life, including human ancestors. Osborn approved the plan, and Andrews prepared to lead his third and most significant expedition into the Central Asian Plateau between 1922 and 1930.

Believing that adventure-seeking was the mark of incompetence, Andrews carefully planned for every physical, scientific, and economic contingency. The vast distances and severe climatic conditions combined to drastically shorten the field season. Andrews overcame these logistical concerns by transporting explorers by automobile—then an untried innovation in the desert—and bulk supplies by camel caravan. This approach allowed researchers to accomplish ten years of work in a single season. A major scientific problem was that to successfully test Osborne's theory, data would need to be correlated from fields as disparate as topography, ichthyology, and anthropology. Andrews was the first expedition leader to conceive of assembling a multidisciplinary team to collaborate in the field on a single, broad scientific issue. Among these were paleontologist Walter Granger, geologists Charles Berkey and George Olson, archeologists Nels Nelson and Pierre Teilhard de Chardin, and cinematographer James B. Shakleford. The total cost of Andrews's ambitious expedition, which swelled to forty people, seven cars, and 125 camels in 1925, was about $700,000. Andrews raised most of these funds himself through lecturing, writing popular articles, and contacting financiers such as John D. Rockefeller, Jr., Cleveland Dodge, and J. P. Morgan.

The Central Asiatic Expedition began in 1922 with a reconnaissance loop through the Gobi that served to orient subsequent forays in 1923, 1925, 1928, and 1930. At the very first stop in 1922, Granger discovered dinosaur bones, an unexpected find that immediately added 80 million years to the Gobi's known historical record. Sites all along the route proved to be rich in their number and diversity of fossils, from dinosaurs to early humans, and every field season yielded major scientific finds. One of the most important discoveries, in terms of the expedition's chief purpose, was complete skulls of the ancient shrewlike *Zalambdalestes*, which indicated that mammals shared the earth with dinosaurs. Other notable finds included dinosaur nests with eggs, which captured the popular imagination and gained Andrews worldwide renown; skulls of a *Baluchitherium* (*Indricatherium*), the largest terrestrial mammal, and of *Andrewsarchus mongoliensis* ("Chief Andrews"), the largest terrestrial predatory mammal; fossil arrays complete enough to reconstruct entire life cycles of Protoceratops and Platybelodons; and artifacts of the "Dune Dwellers," people of the Stone Age. By the end of the expedition, more than 10,000 specimens had been collected and 3,000 miles had been mapped. Andrews's popular account of the Central Asiatic Expedition, *On the Trail of Ancient Man* (1926), was a bestselling book.

Mounting political tensions in the Far East and economic depression at home brought Andrews's exploring days to a close. Although he was named the museum's vice director in 1931 and director in 1935, he found himself unsuited to routine administration. Also in 1935 he married Wilhelmina Anderson Christmas. (He and his first wife had divorced in 1931.) In 1941 he retired to his country home in Connecticut, where he wrote several popular books about his explorations. He received honors from the National Geographic Society, the American Geographical Society, and the Royal Swedish Society for Anthropology and Geography. He died in Carmel, California.

Often depicted with field glasses in his hand and a revolver at his side, Andrews is a romantic figure once rumored to be the model for movie legend Indiana Jones. But Andrews was no mere adventurer. His carefully planned route through the Gobi, particularly the site of Flaming Cliffs (Shabarakh Usu), oriented subsequent Gobi expeditions of Soviet, Polish, Mongolian, Swedish, Canadian, Chinese, and American scientists from the 1940s until the 1990s. In its 1994 celebration of 125 years of exploration, the museum exhibited the sandblasted American flag carried by Andrews's team to symbolize "the quest for knowledge, insight, and understanding that is the impetus for all expeditions."

• Most of Andrews's papers, including his journals and his correspondence with museum officials, are at the American Museum of Natural History. Andrews wrote more than twenty popular accounts of his life and work including *Whale Hunting with Gun and Camera* (1916), *Camps and Trails in China* (with photographs by Yvette Borup, 1918), *Ends of the Earth* (1929), *The New Conquest of Asia* (1932), *Under a Lucky Star* (1943), and *An Explorer Comes Home* (1947), as well as books for young people, such as *Meet Your Ancestors* (1945). In his lecture, "Explorations in Mongolia: A Review of the Central Asiatic Expeditions of the American Museum of Natural History," published in the *Geographical Journal* (Jan. 1927), Andrews discusses his rationale and methodology for the Central Asiatic Expedition from a scientific perspective.

A good biographical article is James Chapin Ahern et al., "Roy Chapman Andrews: Born under a Lucky Star" (guide to the Roy Chapman Andrews exhibit at Beloit College, 1991); a popular book-length biography is Jules Archer, *From Whales to Dinosaurs* (1976). The overall significance of his Asiatic explorations is evaluated in "The Gobi: Men of the Dragon Bones," in *American Museum of Natural History: 125 Years of Exploration* (1995). See also John M. Kennedy, "Philanthropy and Science in New York City: The American Museum of Natural History, 1868–1968" (Ph.D. diss., Yale Univ., 1968). Obituaries are in the *New York Times* and *New York Herald-Tribune*, 12 Mar. 1960.

JAN S. BALLARD

ANDREWS, Stephen Pearl (22 Mar. 1812–21 May 1886), eccentric philosopher and reformer, was born in Templeton, Massachusetts, the son of Elisha Andrews, a Baptist clergyman, and Wealthy Ann Lathrop. He attended the village school and, after the family moved to Hinsdale, New Hampshire, in 1816, was taught at home by his father. In 1828 and 1829 he studied in the classical department of Amherst Academy, where he was influenced by Professor Edward Hitchcock to seek connections among all thought systems.

In 1830 Andrews taught in the Jackson Female Seminary, founded by his deceased brother Elisha and the latter's wife, in Jackson, Louisiana, and the next year he tutored in Latin at the College of Louisiana. Two months later he settled in Clinton, Louisiana, where he studied law in his brother Thomas's firm, Andrews and Lawson. In 1833 he was admitted to the practice of law in Louisiana. Subsequently he joined his brother's firm, then renamed T. L. and S. P. Andrews.

In 1835 Andrews delivered the Fourth of July oration near Clinton, which, a year later, became his first published work. The oration, given in the heart of a slave state, did not hesitate to condemn slavery. In the fall his partnership with his brother was dissolved, and Andrews moved to New Orleans. There in 1835 he married Mary Ann Gordon, with whom he had three sons. Practicing law independently, he regarded the law courts as "admirable schools for the study of humanity." Among his cases was that of Myra Clark Whitney (later Gaines) whose successful claim to her father's estate became a prolonged cause célèbre.

Andrews and his wife moved to the Republic of Texas in 1839, when free land was available. In Houston he opened a law office, later taking as partner William W. Swain in the firm of Andrews and Swain. Andrews's belief in individual sovereignty convinced him that slavery was a demoralizing form of human oppression and led him to devise a plan whereby it might be eradicated in Texas. He proposed selling Texas lands to British immigrants who would then free the slaves. To implement this scheme he traveled to London in 1843 with abolitionist Lewis Tappan, hoping to negotiate loans to emancipate Texas slaves. The project failed partly through fear of British influence in Texas, and Andrews resolved not to resume residence there.

By November 1843 the family was settled in Boston, where Andrews became absorbed in Isaac Pitman's phonography, or shorthand, a phonetic writing system that he viewed as a rapid method of increasing literacy and instructing illiterate blacks. Accordingly, he founded a phonographic institution, issued phonographic manuals and journals, taught classes in shorthand, and in 1845 formed the American Phonographic Society.

Andrews and his family relocated to New York in 1848. As he had once abandoned the legal profession to advocate abolition, he now relinquished the phonographic crusade for another reform, the Equitable Commerce preached by Josiah Warren, an American anarchist who also upheld the principle of "Cost the Limit of Price." Opposed as he was to government interference with individual rights, Andrews advocated the sovereignty of the individual in society, stipulated that the best government was the government that governed least, and held that the best commerce was that regulated by individual laborers.

In 1853 Andrews and Warren applied their beliefs practically in the community of Modern Times, which they established in the township of Islip, Suffolk County, Long Island, New York. The same year Andrews published his *Love, Marriage, and Divorce, and the Sovereignty of the Individual*, an outcome of a debate in the *New York Tribune* with Henry James, Sr., and Horace Greeley. Andrews's views on marriage were also aired and applied at Modern Times with the result that the community was branded a society of free lovers and forced to dissolve.

Andrews's wife died in 1855, and the next year he married Esther Hussey Bartlet Jones; they had no children. At this time Andrews established in New York a small community, the Unitary Home, where the cost principle, along with individual sovereignty, was practiced. There in 1860 Andrews formulated the constitution of his Pantarchy, "a new spiritual Government for the world." He spent most of the Civil War years writing essays, most of them unpublished, on the slavery question, the Pantarchy, women's rights, and a universal language that he devised and called "Alwato." Seeking connections among all reforms and envisioning unity in diversity, he produced his exegesis *The Primary Synopsis of Universology and Alwato* in 1871, the year his second wife died.

The colorful and notorious feminist Victoria Claflin Woodhull entered Andrews's life in 1870. With her sister Tennessee Claflin, Woodhull launched *Woodhull & Claflin's Weekly* in May of that year, and by August the paper declared itself the "Organ of Universal Science . . . Universal Government . . . Universal Religion . . . The Universal Language . . . and of all the Unities." It was also the organ of Andrews, who expressed his views and explained his purposes in its pages. By May 1871 he supplied it with a "Weekly Bulletin of the Pantarchy," and the next year he endorsed the candidacy of Victoria Woodhull for the presidency of the United States.

Andrews devoted much of his time to preparation of his longest and most involved tome, *The Basic Outline of Universology*, published by subscription in 1872. In it he elaborated cosmic analogues, attempting to relate all the sciences, arts, and philosophies. The same year he chartered the Normal University of the Pantarchy, where he taught integralism to some twenty students and enlarged the vocabulary of his universal language, Alwato. He also appeared in 1875 as a witness in the Henry Ward Beecher–Samuel Tilton trial occasioned by a sexual scandal first exposed in *Woodhull & Claflin's Weekly*.

In 1877 Andrews found a new organ for his ideas in *The Radical Review*, published by Benjamin R. Tucker, an American anarchist. He spoke before the Manhattan Liberal Club, chaired meetings of the Union Reform League, contributed to the *Truth Seeker*, and organized the Colloquium, a club of freethinkers that became his final podium. As his life neared its close, he dictated ideas for his pamphlets to a devoted student and amanuensis, Theodora Freeman Spencer, or wrote Andrusian tracts on universal themes. When he died in New York City he was still at work on his dictionary of Alwato.

Many causes—the abolition of slavery, the role of women in government, the rights of the individual, equity in commerce, free love, phonography as an instrument of literacy, and a universal language—engaged Andrews's attention at various stages of his career. He perceived all these diverse causes as related, interconnected aspects of the unity he sought. His efforts failed more often than they succeeded, and at his death one commentator noted, "The world at large is unable to determine whether he was a crank or the founder of a great system of philosophy."

• A collection of Stephen Pearl Andrews Papers is deposited in the State Historical Society of Wisconsin. A full-length biography is Madeleine B. Stern, *The Pantarch: A Biography of Stephen Pearl Andrews* (1968). Other sources include Sidney Ditzion, *Marriage Morals and Sex in America* (1953); Stewart Hall Holbrook, *Dreamers of the American Dream* (1957); George Everett Hussey Macdonald, *Fifty Years of Freethought* (1929); and James J. Martin, *Men against the State* (1957). "Death of the Only Pantarch" is an unidentified newspaper clipping in the collection of Elfa H. Streeter, Hinsdale, N.H. Obituaries are in the *New York Times*, *New-York Daily Tribune*, and *New York Herald*, 23 May 1886.

MADELEINE STERN

ANDREWS, V. C. (6 June 1923?–19 Dec. 1986), novelist, was born Virginia Cleo Andrews in Portsmouth, Virginia, the daughter of William Henry Andrews, a retired serviceman who owned a tool-and-die business, and Lillian Lilnora Parker, a telephone operator. Little is known about her personal life, and she sought to keep her exact age a secret. Andrews spent her childhood in Portsmouth and later in Rochester, New York. She was a gifted artist from an early age, and her talents were encouraged. Andrews also expressed a great desire to act. By her own account, she lived a life of the imagination, reading a great deal (Alexander Dumas and Edgar Allan Poe were childhood favorites). Her dream of a career on the stage ended in her late teens, when she injured her hip in a fall down some stairs. Arthritis resulted from the injury, and after a failed attempt to correct her condition with surgery she was largely confined to a wheelchair.

Andrews worked as an illustrator and portrait painter before earning a living from writing. Bored with painting, she began to write full time in 1972 while living in Apache Junction, Arizona. Her first novel, which was never published, was a science-fantasy work, "The Gods of the Green Mountain." Nine novels and twenty short stories later Andrews sold her first novel, *Flowers in the Attic*. She claimed to have written a ninety-page version of the book in one evening. Pocket Books purchased a longer, revised version in 1978. *Flowers* was released in 1979 as a paperback original, and it remained on the *New York Times* bestseller list for fourteen weeks. In 1980 the book's sequel, *Petals on the Wind*, was released and also took its place on the bestseller lists. Before a third installment was published, *Flowers* and *Petals* together had sold more than 7 million copies in paperback, vaulting Andrews from obscurity to fame in the world of paperback fiction and earning her a reputation as the "fastest-selling writer of any kind of fiction" during the 1980s (Winter, pp. 163–64). Her dominance in the field was made more notable by the fact that she was one of the few women writing horror fiction at the time. In a rare interview, she acknowledged that her editors decided to publish her fiction under her initials so that her gender could not be recognized. She admitted, "Without the initials, I think it's very likely that I would be discriminated against as a woman in a man's field" (Winter, p. 175).

Flowers in the Attic established the characters for many of Andrews's novels and set the tone for all of them. Themes of incest, rape, greed, revenge, voyeurism, dark family secrets, hidden passageways, and attic prisons, among others, set her books squarely within the Gothic tradition. *Flowers* involves three generations of the Dollanganger family. The four children learn that their mother is married to her half-uncle. When he dies, the mother moves the family to "Foxworth Hall," her parents' house, seeking a reconciliation with her father, who had disowned her when she married a blood relative. For the reconciliation to work, she must hide the children from her father, which she does in the attic, biding time until her sick father dies so that she can inherit his money. Her father lives much longer than anticipated, and the children grow up in the darkness of the attic, where they are treated cruelly by their grandmother, who is in on the secret. The children turn to each other for emotional and physical support. The rest of the Dollanganger novels involve the children's escape from Foxworth Hall and their lives as adults, as they face more tragic events and the revelation of other family secrets. From this brief account, it is easy to imagine why Andrews's editor, Ann Patty, described Andrews as a "very romantic woman schooled on fairy tales and soap operas who has a little hint of Bette Davis lurking around" (*New York Times Book Review*, 14 June 1981).

Andrews said that her childhood experiences did not produce the nightmares that the Dollanganger children endure. She told Douglas Winter, her interviewer, "I didn't have a terrible childhood. The most terrible things about my childhood were those that I created in my mind, because my childhood was so ordinary, and I wanted it to be more exciting" (p. 165). However, she did feel that the illness and injuries that confined her to a wheelchair influenced the fictional worlds she created. She said, "Suddenly, you are not in control anymore. You are made helpless by circumstances that you don't have any say about. . . . When I wrote *Flowers in the Attic*, all of Cathy's [the character of the oldest daughter] feelings about being in prison were my feelings. So that, when I read them now, I cry" (Winter, p. 169).

Having never married, Andrews was living with her widowed mother at the time of her death in Virginia Beach, Virginia. She is primarily known for the remarkable rate at which her books sold (more than 30 million copies by her death). After her death another writer of the horror genre, Andrew Neiderman, a former high school teacher in New York state, was enlisted to reconstruct the notes she left behind and to fill in missing material. It was not until the fifth posthumous book was published that the ghostwriting was revealed, although even then Neiderman was not named. The sales of novels written by him were as strong as those by Andrews (Neiderman said that by the fifth work he was creating entirely new material for the books). By 1997 nineteen novels had appeared with Andrews's name on the cover.

Andrews's phenomenal success with her readers was in contrast to her lack of success with critics, whose reviews tended toward the pejorative. But in a book-length study of Andrews's work, E. D. Huntley examines the ways in which Andrews pushed the boundaries of the female Gothic tradition and offers a variety of critical assessments of her novels. In *V. C. Andrews: A Critical Companion* (1996), Huntley credits the appeal of Andrews's work to "her ability to reproduce in fiction the powerful and unnameable emotions universal to young people who stand, frightened and uncertain, on the verge of adulthood" (p. 15) and states that Andrews "fulfills a need that has not been addressed by any other popular writer of Gothic fiction" (p. 8).

• Other works by Andrews not mentioned in the text include *If There Be Thorns* (1981), *My Sweet Audrina* (1982), *Seeds of Yesterday* (1984), *Heaven* (1985), and *Dark Angel* (1986). Novels published after her death that are said to be reconstructions of material she left behind are *Garden of Shadows* (1987), *Fallen Hearts* (1988), *Gates of Paradise* (1989), and *Web of Dreams* (1990). Few sources of information exist about Andrews. However, she did grant an interview to Douglas Winter for his collection of interviews with horror writers, *Faces of Fear: Encounters with the Creators of Modern Horror* (1985). A lengthy article by David Streitfeld, "A Novelist's Tales from the Crypt," *Washington Post*, 7 May 1993, quotes Winter's book on the legal battles between Andrews's estate and the Internal Revenue Service and discusses the matter of Neiderman's ghostwriting efforts. See also Cosette Kies, *Presenting Young Adult Horror Fiction* (1993), which contains a discussion of Andrews's work. Obituaries are in Patricia Burgess, ed., *Annual Obituary 1986*; the *Washington Post*, the *Los Angeles Times*, and the *New York Times*, all 21 Dec. 1986; and the *Chicago Tribune*, 22 Dec. 1986.

SCOTT ANDREWS

ANDREWS SISTERS, singers, were born in Minneapolis, Minnesota, the daughters of Peter Andrews, a restaurant owner, and Ollie Sollie. The three sisters were La Verne (6 July 1915–8 May 1967), Maxene (3 Jan. 1918–21 Oct. 1995), and Patty (Patricia; 16 Feb. 1920–). Word spread in jazz-age Minneapolis that a local sister team might get Americans to forget the Boswells. On infant radio and scratchy Victor Records LaVerne, Maxene, and Patty Andrews had listened to

Connee, Martha, and Helvetia Boswell and as adolescents imitated their vocal style. None of the girls could read music. In school musical productions and on local amateur shows, the girls built their musical reputation. Patty sang the lead; Maxene was high soprano; and LaVerne took the alto part. The girls took first prize in an amateur contest at Minneapolis's Orpheum Theatre, beating out Edgar Bergen and his dummy Charlie McCarthy. They graduated to juvenile musical reviews, and in 1931, when the depression wrecked their father's restaurant business, they dropped out of school and joined the vaudeville circuit full-time with Larry Rich and his orchestra. They remained with Rich for eighteen months.

Chaperoned by their Norwegian mother and Greek father, while living out of the backseat of a 1929 Buick, the girls joined Joe E. Howard's vaudeville act in 1933 and then sang in relative obscurity in the mid-1930s with the Ted Mack Band. Their first recordings came after Leon Belasco spotted the act in a Chicago nightclub and signed the sisters to a contract in 1937. The girls then toured in their father's 1931 Packard, and on 18 March 1937 they recorded "There's a Lull in My Life," "Wake Up and Live," "Turn off the Moon," and "Jammin'" with Belasco's band. Their energetic harmonizing won them a radio job singing at New York City's Hotel Edison at $15 a week and brought them to the attention of Lou Levy, who soon became their manager.

Levy taught the sisters the words to an old Yiddish song, "Bei Mir Bist Du Shoen," and tried to sell the idea to Decca Records. Decca gave the song a workover with Sammy Cahn doing the lyrics and Sholom Secunda the music. The girls recorded the reworked song on 24 November 1937. George Gershwin's "Nice Work If You Can Get It" was on the flip side. The sisters were paid $50 by Decca and no royalties. "Bei Mir" sold more than 1 million copies and climbed to the top of the radio program "Your Hit Parade," and after ten years of hard work the Andrews Sisters were an overnight sensation.

A string of hits quickly followed, many of them celebrating ethnicity and nostalgia, in a world sliding into war. "Oh, Johnny, Oh, Johnny, Oh" had been written in 1916. "Beer Barrel Polka" was a Czechoslovakian tune from 1934. The success of "Hold Tight, Hold Tight" and "Well, All Right" allowed the sisters to negotiate a new contract with Decca that paid them five cents a copy for every record sold. By 1941 *Time* was reporting "the Juke Box Divas" had sales of 8 million records. A contract with Universal had the women appearing in four films in two years. *Argentine Nights* (1940) produced the hit "Rhumboogie" and *Buck Privates* (1941) featured "Boogie Woogie Bugle Boy from Company B," the song that became the act's signature theme. *In The Navy* (1941) and *Hold That Ghost* (1941) may not have been great motion pictures, but, starring Abbott and Costello, the films cleaned up at the box office. Maxene married Levy in 1941; they had two children. Peter Andrews, confident that his daughters had finally made it, bought a 1939 Buick.

The Andrews Sisters reached the peak of their popularity during World War II. They made nine movies at Universal and a tenth at Warner Bros. based on their war work at the Stage Door and in Hollywood canteens, where movie stars boosted war morale by meeting soldiers. Recordings by the Andrews Sisters were at the top of the pop music charts with those of Bing Crosby and Glenn Miller. War bond rallies, featuring the sisters, Crosby, Bob Hope, and Irving Berlin, among others, made millions of dollars for the government. In 1941, when the sisters appeared at New York's Paramount Theatre, they broke all attendance records. A weekly radio show, "Club Fifteen," which ran for five years, allowed the act to introduce "Don't Sit under the Apple Tree with Anyone Else but Me," "Beat Me, Daddy, Eight to the Bar," "Shoo-Shoo Baby," "Pistol Packin' Mama," and "Pennsylvania Polka." United Service Organizations tours to Italy and North Africa further ingratiated the sisters to American servicemen and servicewomen. The Andrews Sisters were regulars on "Command Performance," which was broadcast on the new Armed Forces Radio Service. They recorded frequently with Crosby, including Harold Arlen and Johnny Mercer's "Accentuate the Positive" and Cole Porter's "Don't Fence Me In."

Cultural commentators pointed out that during the war the swinging voice of the Andrews Sisters became as recognized as that of President Franklin Roosevelt. When 14,500 troops arrived home on 28 September 1945 aboard the *Queen Mary*, the singing Andrews Sisters were at the New York docks to greet them. Years later the sisters would be repeatedly asked to sing the songs that had made the home front home to millions. These postwar years brought a gradual ebbing of the group's popularity in the face of internal quarreling and a shift in musical tastes. "You Don't Have to Know the Language," sung in a shipboard scene with Crosby in *The Road to Rio* (Paramount, 1947), was a sudden success. But it was more of an end to their career than a beginning. The sisters began to go their separate ways after Patty married Marty Melcher in 1947. The death of their parents in 1948 accelerated the breakup, as did the wedding of LaVerne to Lou Rogers the same year. LaVerne and Lou had no children.

Maxene and Patty were divorced from their husbands in 1950 and 1951, respectively. Maxene's illness and subsequent surgery made Patty and LaVerne a duet, until Patty married the group's arranger, Walter Wescheler, and began a solo act. A suit by Patty in 1954 over their mother's estate deepened divisions. Maxene took an overdose of sleeping pills in December of that year but later denied it was a suicide attempt. A television guest appearance in 1956 reunited the sisters briefly, but rock-and-roll was beginning to rule the musical world. The early 1960s saw the sisters embroiled in a tax dispute with the federal government. LaVerne died of cancer in Los Angeles, and Maxene became the dean of women at a Nevada community college in 1968. In 1973, when Bette Midler sang the sisters' "Boogie Woogie Bugle Boy," they were again in demand, and Patty and Maxene teamed for *Over Here!*, a 1974 Broadway musical saluting the sisters' songs that were popular during the war. After the final curtain each night Patty would ask the audience, "Do you want to hear some of the old ones?" and amid thunderous applause she and Maxene would sing encore after encore.

Maxene had quadruple bypass surgery in 1982 and joined Patty when the Andrews Sisters star was unveiled on the Hollywood Walk of Fame in 1987. Maxene recorded her first and only solo album when she was seventy-two. In 1992 she performed "America the Beautiful" for thousands of veterans in Honolulu on the fiftieth anniversary of V-J Day and received the Pentagon's highest civilian honor, the Medal for Distinguished Public Service. Maxene was preparing to rejoin the New York cast of *Swingtime Canteen* when she died in Hyannis, Massachusetts. The Andrews Sisters sold more than 100 million copies of nearly 900 recordings and earned nineteen gold records. Maxene Andrews's death marked the end of a cherished American institution that had inspired the members of the country's armed forces at a time of national anxiety and peril at the midpoint of the twentieth century.

• A lengthy biographical file on the Andrews Sisters is maintained at the Minnesota Historical Society in St. Paul. Maxene Andrews co-wrote with Bill Gilbert *Over Here, Over There: The Andrews Sisters and the USO Stars in World War II* (1993). An excellent biographical sketch, "The Andrews Sisters," is found in James Robert Parish and Lennard DeCarl, *Hollywood Players: The Forties* (1976). See also Andrew Smith, "The Andrews Sisters," *Harper's Bazaar*, Apr. 1974, pp. 89, 110–11; the *New York Times*, 28 Apr. 1974; the *New Yorker*, 11 Nov. 1991, pp. 33–35; and Ron Ross's liner notes to *Boogie Woogie Bugle Girls: The Andrews Sisters* (Paramount Records, PAS 6075. MCA-27082).

For important context, see Sigmund Spaeth, *A History of Popular Music in America* (1948); Roger D. Kinkle, *The Complete Encyclopedia of Popular Music and Jazz, 1900–1950* (1974); Henry Pleasants, *The Great American Popular Singers* (1974); Charles Hamm, *Yesterdays: Popular Song in America* (1979); and Gene Lees, *Singers and the Song* (1987). An obituary for LaVerne is in the *New York Times*, 9 May 1967. An obituary for Maxene is in the *New York Times*, 23 Oct. 1995.

BRUCE J. EVENSEN

ANDROS, Edmund (6 Dec. 1637–19 Feb. 1714), imperial administrator, was born in London, England, the son of Amias Andros, seigneur of Sausmarez, Guernsey, and master of the ceremonies to King Charles I, and Elizabeth Stone, the sister of Sir Robert Stone, cupbearer to Queen Elizabeth of Bohemia. Raised with royalty, Edmund Andros suffered with the Stuarts. He went into exile in October 1643 when his father took up a command in the besieged Castle Cornet, Guernsey. The last place in Europe to hold out for the Stuarts, the castle was not surrendered until 15 December 1651. The Andros family took refuge at the court of Elizabeth of Bohemia in The Hague. There, in April 1656, "Mun" Andros was commissioned in the cuirassier troop of his uncle Sir Robert Stone and fought in Denmark from 1655 to 1658. Andros was then named gentleman-in-waiting to Queen Elizabeth and also served her nephews, the exiled Charles II of England and the prince of Orange, later William III.

In 1661, following King Charles's restoration, Andros accompanied Queen Elizabeth to London. After the queen's death, Andros, now an ensign in the First Guards, helped repress the Derwentdale plot in 1663. During the second Dutch War Andros defended the Isle of Wight in 1665, organized privateers in 1666, and in 1667 was commissioned major of the first royal regiment raised for American service, the "Barbados" Regiment.

Andros's regiment prevented civil war in Barbados, was decimated trying to recapture St. Kitts from the French, and pacified the Caribs (Andros negotiated the final treaty). He sailed home in August 1668 as the regimental agent. He also represented Barbados sugar and Guernsey wool manufacturers. In 1671 Andros reorganized the Barbados Regiment as dragoons and joined the household of James Stuart, duke of York and heir to the imperial throne. In February 1672 Andros married Marie Craven, niece of the earl of Craven. Her dowry included 48,000 acres of land in Carolina, a province of which the earl was a proprietor. In April 1672 Andros took command of Yarmouth, site of the camp of the army designed to invade the Netherlands during the third Dutch war. His military staff accompanied Andros to New York when the king and duke sent him out to recover it from the Dutch following the peace of Westminster, 9 February 1674.

Andros arrived in New York on 22 October 1674, with his wife, their household, a staff of thirteen officers plus supernumeraries, a group of English merchants, and a hundred soldiers. The duke of York's proprietary government included Maine, the offshore islands, Connecticut west of the river, Long Island, Manhattan, Staten Island, the Hudson valley to Albany, the Jersies (the land was held by proprietors), and the Delaware settlements. To all of these areas, Andros introduced English law and government, supplanting what were to him, as a royalist, the republican regimes of the Dutch, the Puritans, and the proprietors. Capitalizing on his experience with the Caribs, Andros agreed with the Lenni Lenape (Delaware) and the Five Nations (Iroquois) about their respective jurisdictions, legal and territorial. In each region of the duke's multiethnic dominion, Andros built anglicized administrative elites.

Andros remodeled New York City politically, largely with the aid of Dutch collaborators; he also transformed it physically. He ordered the construction of new docks, warehouses, customs offices, a mercantile exchange, public privies, slaughterhouses, and a new city wall. Within the wall (now Wall Street) he filled in the stagnant canals of the Dutch era, making New York's first paved streets. He had new mills built. Then he regulated the wheat trade with the West Indies, the foundation of New York's new prosperity. He reordered New York's staple, the fur trade, which depended on the good will of the Iroquois. In 1675 Andros began to negotiate with the senior sachem of the Iroquois, Garacontie, what became the "Covenant Chain" treaties. These treaties defined the first American frontier between natives and colonists. The Covenant Chain was New York's greatest security until 1760 and was the primary diplomatic vehicle of Anglo-American expansion in North America until 1794.

As a reward for his achievements in New York, in 1678 Andros was knighted, but his identification with the duke of York led to his recall at the height of the transatlantic campaign to exclude James from the imperial throne. Andros left New York in January 1681. In December he was effectively absolved from the charges of embezzlement, extortion, and oppression brought by Jacob Milbourne. Milbourne, his brother-in-law Jacob Liesler, and other New Yorkers were alienated from the liberal and erastian Dutch Reformed and Church of England denominations patronized by Andros. The dissidents were economically excluded from the trading privileges Andros extended to his anglicized supporters and were politically resentful of Andros's autocratic regime. (Andros's repeated requests for a representative assembly had been refused by the duke.)

Andros's exoneration in English courts was quickly followed by his restoration to royal office and then by his return to American command. In May 1682 King Charles named Andros a gentleman of his bedchamber. The accession of King James provoked James Scott, duke of Monmouth's rebellion in 1685. Andros rode west to repress it and was promoted to lieutenant colonel of cavalry. Then on 30 July 1685 he was commissioned governor-general of the new Dominion of New England. The consolidation of the colonies, first of Plymouth, Massachusetts Bay, New Hampshire, and Maine, to which were added Connecticut, Rhode Island, and all of greater "New York," was largely the result of Andros's recommendations for a consolidated colonial defense, regional economic rationalization, and administrative uniformity. Characteristically, King James exaggerated his aide's centralizing suggestions. The king not only consolidated the administrations of England's northern colonies, he also eliminated their representative assemblies. The king intended his American experiment in absolutism to be a model for southern and West Indian dominions.

On 20 December 1686 the governor-general of the Dominion of New England landed in Boston, with Lady Andros, his second in command Captain Francis Nicholson, and two hundred soldiers. They would govern the new dominion with the assistance of the professional staff Andros summoned to Boston from the dominion's second city, New York, and a royally appointed council composed of Crown officials, such as Secretary Edward Randolph, and local bigwigs, including most prominently President Joseph Dudley, who later became Massachusetts's governor-general. By 7 April 1688 the territory under Andros's command extended from the border with New France to the Delaware River.

Andros applied to the dominion the programs that he had tested in New York and met the same objections. Religious toleration and an Anglican presence offended Puritans. Administrative ordinances regulated land sales, enforced customs regulations, and reorganized the military. Each reform offended some special interest, but all were imposed by Andros without much consultation. He and his council levied the necessary taxes without representative consent. Because the governor-general acted for a Catholic and absolutist king, James Stuart, the ordinances of the dominion were the more suspect, religiously and politically, and the king's Francophilia made his legate's patriotism suspect also. Yet Andros's imposition of English county government, of English property law, and of English military institutions made the Puritan provinces "New England" indeed. The brief interlude of the dominion made possible New England's and New York's integration into the imperial wars against France; led to the social, cultural, and legal anglicization of northern elites; and laid lasting institutional and attitudinal foundations throughout the vast territories of the Dominion of New England.

Word of the November 1688 invasion of England by William of Orange reached Andros, at the head of the dominion army pursuing the Eastern Abenaki on the Maine frontier, on 1 January 1689. On 16 March he learned that the Congregational clergy of Boston were circulating the prince of Orange's propaganda. Andros took ship for the dominion capital. In his absence the provincial army in Maine mutinied, returned home, and on 18 and 19 April 1689 seized Boston and jailed the governor-general. In February 1690 the revolutionary government sent Sir Edmund Andros home to judgment; Lady Andros had died during the crisis, ostracized and heartbroken. On 17 April 1690, however, the privy council endorsed Andros's administration. King William welcomed the companion of his youth to his royal court and offered Andros a choice of American commands, New England or Virginia.

Andros landed at Jamestown on 13 September 1692 with his new wife, Elizabeth Crispe (whom he had married in August 1691), and was met by the lieutenant governor, Colonel Nicholson, who had been transferred to the old dominion from New York after the Leisler and Milbourne coup in that colony. Although Andros immediately summoned an assembly, he administered Virginia through the royally appointed council of English officials and English-born magnates. The latter, as judges, militia colonels, presiding justices, and vestry wardens, "being only instruments of his arbitrary power," so the Scots cleric James Blair complained, "the Government is more arbitrary than if it were lodged in him alone, without any Council" (*A Short Character*, p. 14). Blair, Virginia commissary of the bishop of London, protested that the governor-general gave too little support to Blair's new foundation, the College of William and Mary. Instead, Andros, fearing that his command was "wholly open and Exposed to all Enemies Especially Indians" (letter to privy council, 5 Jan. 1693), invested in the provincial army. In part to rationalize the militia basis of that army, Andros made county jurisdictions uniform. He established the first central register of Virginia land titles, making possible the accumulation of quit-rents and thus creating a fund to help finance the war against France elsewhere in America. Finally, Andros strengthened the Crown's control of the assembly, then bullied the legislators into making grants to defend New York and strengthen the Iroquoian alliance.

In 1697 the peace of Rijswijk worked a ministerial change in England that left Andros vulnerable to the complaints of "the College Faction," headed by Nicholson and Blair, that the governor-general neglected clerical concerns. English church authorities held hearings about Andros's administration in December. During the same period, Andros "burst himself" in a fall from his horse in Virginia. Immobilized, he fell prey to recurrent malaria in March 1698 and asked the king's leave to come home for recovery of his health. This was granted on 20 July 1698, and in December Andros was succeeded by Nicholson.

Andros's American career was over. It had begun at the moment in 1667 when, having consolidated its authority in England, the Crown could turn to America, imposing royal authority first in the West Indies, and then, at the end of the Dutch wars in 1674, on the mainland. Andros's administration of New York laid down the imperial doctrines of regulated commerce, prerogative politics, and military defense. Andros's alliance of English imperialism with the imperialism of the League of the Iroquois was the cardinal diplomatic and military act of the century. His administration of the Dominion of New England has been esteemed as "the most important piece of constructive statesmanship in the field of British colonial policy" (Barnes, p. 277) before the Dominion of Canada.

Andros retired to Guernsey where, after 5 July 1704 he served as lieutenant governor. He married a third time, to Elizabeth Fitz-Herbert. In 1714, the year of peace with France, Andros died in Guernsey, sitting in his father's seigneurial chair. He was without issue, save for the imperial legacy of his service to five Stuart sovereigns.

• The destruction of the Andros manor house eliminated Sir Edmund's personal papers. His official dispatches are in the Colonial Office Group, British Public Record Office, Kew. Orders for Andros's commissions are entered in the State Papers Office Group, and for the coup in Boston, see the log of the *Rose* in Admiralty 51/3955, both also at Kew. Andros is frequently mentioned in two classes of British Library manuscripts, the Egerton manuscripts and Additional manuscripts 28076, 29533, 29554, and 29577. The church hearings on his Virginia administration are in the Fulham Palace Papers, Lambeth Palace Library, London. Printed materials on Andros's early career include Edith F. Carey, "Amias Andros and Sir Edmund His Son," *Transactions of the Guernsey Society of Natural Science and Local Research* 7 (1913–1916); Ferdinand Brock Tupper, *Chronicles of Castle Cornet* (1851); and Vincent T. Harlow, *A History of Barbados 1625–1685* (1925). On his New York administration, see Robert C. Ritchie, *The Duke's Province* (1977); Peter R. Christoph and Florence A. Christoph, eds., *The Andros Papers* (3 vols., 1989–1991), trans. Charles T. Ghering; and John Romelyn Brodhead, ed., *Documents Relative to the Colonial History of the State of New York* (1853). On the dominion, the standard study remains Viola Florence Barnes, *The Dominion of New England* (1923; repr. 1960). See also Richard R. Johnson, *Adjustment to Empire* (1981); W. H. Whitmore, ed., *The Andros Tracts* (1868–1874); and T. S. Goodrick and R. N. Toppan, eds., *Edward Randolph: Including His Letters and Official Papers . . . 1676–1703* (1898). There is no biography of Andros, but see Jeanne Gould Bloom, "Sir Edmund Andros: A Study in Seventeenth-Century Colonial Administration" (Ph.D. diss., Yale Univ., 1962), and Stephen Saunders Webb, *The Governors-General* (1979; repr. 1987). Andros's career through 1689 is treated in an imperial context in Webb, *1676: The End of American Independence* (1984; repr. 1995), which details Andros's New York administration; Webb, "The Trials of Sir Edmund Andros," in *The Human Dimensions of Nation Making*, ed. James Kirby Martin (1976), pp. 23–53, which summarizes the criticisms of Andros through 1689; and Webb, *Lord Churchill's Coup: The Anglo-American Empire and the Glorious Revolution Reconsidered* (1995), which analyzes the fall of the dominion.

STEPHEN SAUNDERS WEBB

ANDRUS, Ethel Percy (21 Sept. 1884–13 July 1967), educator and founder of the National Retired Teachers Association and the American Association of Retired Persons, was born in San Francisco, California, the daughter of George Wallace Andrus, a lawyer, and Lucretia Frances Duke. After the births of Ethel and her sister Maud, the family moved to Illinois to enable her father to study advanced law at the University of Chicago. Influenced by her parents, Ethel developed a love and respect for learning that would mark both stages of her career.

Andrus graduated from Austin High School in 1900. She took a Ph.B. degree from the University of Chicago in 1903 and began teaching English and German at Lewis Institute (later the Illinois Institute of Technology). She also worked at two settlement houses, the Chicago Commons and Hull-House. Andrus resumed her study while at the Lewis Institute, which led to a B.S. from that institution in 1918. Returning to California in 1910, she accepted a teaching position at Santa Paula High School. From 1911 to 1916 she taught at the Manual Arts High School in Los Angeles, serving as acting principal for one year. In February 1916 she became vice principal of Abraham Lincoln High School in Los Angeles and in June, was named principal, becoming the first female high school principal in California. She maintained this position until her retirement in 1944.

While Andrus was developing her career at Lincoln High School, she engaged in further academic study at the University of Southern California, where she earned an M.A. in 1928 and a Ph.D. in 1930. She wrote her doctoral dissertation on educational programs for adolescent girls. During the summers from 1930 to 1940 Andrus taught courses in guidance, educational philosophy, and school administration at USC, Stanford University, and the University of California at Los Angeles. As principal of Lincoln High

School, she established the Opportunity School for Adults, an evening school for immigrants in the district. In 1940 the Educational Policies Commission of the National Education Association selected Lincoln High School as a case study for a new textbook, *Learning the Ways of Democracy*.

Andrus was an educator who reflected the liberal views of the early decades of the twentieth century. Earlier work with Jane Addams, no doubt, influenced her activities at Lincoln. The 2,500 students came from families that spoke thirty-two different languages and included Latino, southern European, and Asian children. Andrus set a goal for her students that set her apart from many of her colleagues—"To bring to each a sense of his own worth by treating him with dignity and respect, by honoring his racial background, not as a picturesque oddity, but as a valued contribution to the rich tapestry of American life" (*Modern Maturity*, Jan. 1968, p. 25). The driving concern at Lincoln under the administration of Andrus, in both curricular and extracurricular arenas, was the creation of community spirit. Andrus's philosophy was illustrated in a core curriculum that was developed in the 1930s for "underprivileged" youth. She described the core curriculum as "our answer to the legislative enactment of compulsory school attendance" (*California Journal of Secondary Education*, Jan. 1937, p. 19). The curriculum included two hours of social living (the development of social skills, such as communication, literacy, and understanding of the self and one's environment), one hour of health, one hour of science, and two hours of electives from the fields of fine arts, commerce, foreign language, mathematics, practical and vocational arts, and music. Like other educators of her day, Andrus considered the "spirit of democracy—the spirit of strenuous effort, the spirit of loyal and united support" the paramount goal of the public school (*Modern Maturity*, Jan. 1968, p. 17).

In 1944 Andrus retired, leaving her administrative position at Lincoln High School in order to care for her ailing mother. Although her financial situation was not based solely on her school pension, the small sum of approximately sixty dollars per month introduced Andrus to the economic plight of other retired educators. As welfare director of the southern section of the California Retired Teachers Association, she mounted a protest in the California legislature, rallied former teachers, and traveled to other states to compare pension programs. Providing organizational support for the elderly became Andrus's second career. Believing that older persons could attain goals of personal dignity and social usefulness by recognizing their own individual worth in a crusade for service, she became the prototype for her philosophy. In 1947 Andrus founded the National Retired Teachers Association (NRTA). In 1954 the organization opened the first national teachers' retirement residence, Grey Gables, in Ojai, California. The success of the NRTA, which offered access to low-cost medicine and affordable insurance programs for its members, brought demands for a more inclusive retirement organization: the American Association of Retired Persons (AARP) was established in 1958 with Andrus as its first president. She also edited a number of journals that were connected with these organizations, including *Modern Maturity, Journal of the Association of Retired Persons International*, and *Dynamic Maturity*.

In addition to her administrative duties and the publication of journals, Andrus worked to enact legislation. She actively promoted the Retirement Income Amendment to the Internal Revenue Code and liberalization of the Social Security law, and she monitored developments pertaining to Medicare. She crusaded against mandatory retirement laws and urged industry and the government to develop preretirement plans. As a member of the board of the National Council for Accreditation of Nursing Homes and the American Nursing Home Association, Andrus testified before committees in Congress and state legislatures, drew plans for facilities, and persuaded builders to adopt improvements, such as wheelchair ramps.

In 1961 Andrus served as a delegate to the White House Conference on Aging, which had resulted, in part, from her membership on President Dwight D. Eisenhower's National Advisory Committee. The influence of the national retirement organizations continued to grow, and in 1963 Andrus formed and served as president of the Association of Retired Persons International. In 1963 she established the Institute of Lifetime Learning, an adult education center, which offered a seminar and lecture forum for older persons. In 1964–1965 the Dynamic Maturity Pavilion provided a showcase for the work and philosophy of AARP and its related organizations at the New York World's Fair. This, too, was the vision of Andrus.

From her initial retirement in 1944 through the end of her life, Andrus was an active spokesperson for older people. The themes of service and community that had permeated her educational philosophy became the essence of her message to retired individuals. She taught that aging was "an achievement. The later years have meaning and purpose. Activity is life, and work is one's salvation" (*Readers' Digest*, Jan. 1964, p. 200). She died in Long Beach, California.

• Andrus's published articles in the *California Journal of Secondary Education* include "An Experiment in Social Living," 10 (Jan. 1935): 82–87; "Core Curriculum at the Lincoln High School," 12 (Jan. 1937): 17–19; and "Social Living Classes for the Underprivileged," 14 (Nov. 1939): 414–17. She also wrote "What the Girl of Today Asks of the School," *Journal of American Association of University Women* 25 (Apr. 1932): 146–48, and "Retirement Readiness," *NEA Journal* 41 (Apr. 1952): 233–34. The Jan. 1968 issue of *Modern Maturity* is dedicated to Andrus and provides a substantial body of information on her work. The AARP headquarters contains an unpublished autobiographical sketch. Other sources include Dorothy Crippen, ed., *The Wisdom of Ethel Percy Andrus* (1968), and Jean L. Brock, "Dynamic Retirement Is Their Goal," *Reader's Digest*, Jan. 1964, pp. 195–200. An obituary is in the *New York Times*, 15 July 1967.

KAREN L. GRAVES

ANGEL, John Lawrence (21 Mar. 1915–3 Nov. 1986), physical anthropologist, was born in London, England, the son of John Angel, a sculptor, and Elizabeth Day Seymour, a classicist. After attending elementary school in England at Ovingdean School in Sussex, Angel traveled to the United States at the age of thirteen. He attended Choate School in Wallingford, Connecticut, and graduated from Harvard College in 1936 with an A.B. degree, magna cum laude, Phi Beta Kappa. For graduate work, Angel went to Harvard University, working primarily under Earnest Hooton. At Harvard he studied physical anthropology within the broader program of anthropology, specializing in human skeletal anatomy and the geographic area of the Near East. In 1937 he married Margaret Seymour Richardson, a student at Radcliffe; they had three children. While still a graduate student, he taught at Harvard from 1939 to 1941 and at the University of California at Berkeley from 1941 to 1942 with a dissertation on biocultural associations (correlation of data gleaned from the study of human skeletal remains with cultural information derived from archaeological study) in ancient Greece.

From 1941 to 1942 Angel taught anthropology at the University of Minnesota and subsequently (1943–1962) taught anatomy at the Daniel Baugh Institute of Anatomy of the Jefferson Medical College in Philadelphia. From 1946 to 1962 he was a research associate at the University Museum of the University of Pennsylvania. From 1957 to 1962 he also served as consultant in surgical anatomy to the United States Naval Hospital in Philadelphia. Seeking more opportunity for research and fieldwork, in 1962 he became curator of physical anthropology of the National Museum of Natural History of the Smithsonian Institution in Washington, D.C., where he remained until his death at a Washington hospital. He continued teaching through annual courses in physical anthropology at George Washington University and in forensic anthropology at the Smithsonian. The latter course was offered primarily for forensic pathologists.

Through fieldwork, publication, and lecturing, Angel maintained his career interest in human skeletal anatomy and in the human skeletal biology of the Near East. He conducted seven major research expeditions to Greece and Turkey. He regularly presented research papers at the annual meetings of the Archaeological Institute of America, the International Congress of Anthropological and Ethnological Sciences, the American Association for the Advancement of Science, the American Anthropological Association, the American Academy of Forensic Sciences, the Paleopathology Association, and the American Association of Physical Anthropology. Throughout his career, Angel was active in these organizations, serving on their committees and publishing in their journals.

Angel's research covered a broad spectrum of topics within physical anthropology but primarily focused on new methodology to extract information from the human skeleton and topics in forensic anthropology. His record in forensic anthropology began in 1962 upon his arrival at the Smithsonian. At that time he assumed the role of primary consultant to the FBI, succeeding T. Dale Stewart, who had assumed major administrative responsibilities. According to Stewart (pp. 512–13) "Because of his anatomical background, Larry took to forensic anthropology, as the saying goes, like a duck to water." His caseload grew rapidly from an initial six cases in 1962 to a career high of sixty-six in 1976, totaling 565 by 1986. In 1977 the Smithsonian's D. H. Ubelaker assumed responsibility for the FBI consulting, but Angel continued to study and testify on cases from the District of Columbia, Maryland, Virginia, and other areas. Angel was certified a diplomate (fully qualified to practice forensic anthropology) by the American Board of Forensic Anthropology in 1978. He served as president of the American Board of Forensic Anthropology from 1979 to 1984 and received the Physical Anthropology Section award for outstanding service in 1984. In his honor, and in recognition of his outstanding teaching in forensic anthropology, the physical anthropology section of the American Academy of Forensic Sciences offers an annual award, "The J. Lawrence Angel Award," to the best student paper delivered at the annual meeting.

In order of decreasing frequency, Angel's publications focused on descriptive osteology, social biology (the interaction of human biology and culture, especially involving the human skeleton), paleopathology, paleodemography, general physical anthropology, biological distance studies, forensic anthropology, obesity, and dental anthropology. Regionally, his work in Greece and the eastern Mediterranean is most frequently cited. Topically, most citations focus on his descriptive osteology papers, followed closely by those in paleodemography and paleopathology.

Working from a long-standing admiration of ancient Greek civilization, Angel rapidly became a leader in the physical anthropology of the eastern Mediterranean, and his work established a foothold for scientific research in this area. Angel's pioneer analysis of human remains from Bronze Age Troy in northwestern Turkey established a pattern for himself and others to follow for decades. Encouraging archaeologists to recover all aspects of the skeleton, Angel assembled a large sample of well-documented human remains. His research focused on the disease history of the area, the evidence for migration and other population shifts, and the complex interaction of biology and culture through time. Largely through his work in the Near East, Angel explored the relationship between culture and disease. In particular, he interpreted data from many disciplines to trace the development of thalassemia and other diseases prevalent in the Near East and demonstrate their cultural and environmental contexts. The large samples of human remains he worked with allowed him to extract population-based vital statistics. Such research made him a pioneer in the fields of paleodemography and paleoepidemiology. Along with Hooton, his Harvard mentor, Angel championed the "population" approach to disease, working to assemble large samples that would yield frequency data. Although Angel remained interested in differential diagnosis and the history of particular diseases, he especially valued viewing disease in a broad cultural, anthropological context.

Angel's work documents the activity of an innovative thinker with enormous energy. His lasting contributions include the hypothesis that obesity has a genetic component, coining the term "porotic hyperostosis" for a skeletal condition frequently studied in anemia research, and detecting individual patterns of activity from skeletal evidence of degenerative joint disease. Angel pioneered the population approach and interdisciplinary research in human skeletal biology and inaugurated interest in the analysis of human remains from the historic period, producing the first broad comparative data from eastern colonial America. Angel championed using detailed knowledge of skeletal anatomy in a broad population within an interdisciplinary framework.

• For Angel's work in the eastern Mediterranean, see "Greek Teeth: Ancient and Modern," *Human Biology* 16 (1944): 283–97; "A Racial Analysis of the Ancient Greeks: An Essay on the Use of Morphological Types," *American Journal of Physical Anthropology* 2 (1944): 329–76; "Skeletal Change in Ancient Greece," *American Journal of Physical Anthropology* 4 (1946): 69–97; "The Length of Life in Ancient Greece," *Journal of Gerontology* 2 (1947): 18–24; *Troy: The Human Remains* (1951); "Porotic Hyperostosis, Anemias, Malarias, and Marshes in the Prehistoric Eastern Mediterrance," *Science* 153 (1966): 760–63; "Porotic Hyperostosis or Osteoporosis Symmetrica," in *Diseases in Antiquity: A Survey of the Diseases, Injuries, and Surgery of Early Populations*, ed. A. T. Sandison and Don Brothwell (1967); and *The People of Lerna: Analysis of a Prehistoric Aegean Population* (1971). For his work in palaeodemography in particular, see "Ecological Aspects of Palaeodemography," in *The Skeletal Biology of Earlier Human Populations*, ed. D. R. Brothwell (1968); "The Bases of Palaeodemography," *American Journal of Physical Anthropology* 30 (1969): 427–37; "Palaeodemography and Evolution," *American Journal of Physical Anthropology* 31 (1969): 343–53; "Paleoecology, Paleodemography and Health," in *Population, Ecology and Social Evolution*, ed. Steven Polgar (1975); and "History and Development of Paleopathology," *American Journal of Physical Anthropology* 56 (1981): 509–15. For his other areas of interest see "Constitution in Female Obesity," *American Journal of Physical Anthropology* 7 (1949): 433–71; "Osteoporosis: Thalassemia?" *American Journal of Physical Anthropology* 22 (1964): 369–74; "The Reaction Area of the Femoral Neck," *Clinical Orthopaedics* 32 (1964): 130–42; "Colonial to Modern Skeletal Change in the U.S.A.," *American Journal of Physical Anthropology* 45 (1976): 723–35; and, with Michael R. Zimmerman, eds., *Dating and Age Determination of Biological Materials* (1986). A festschrift is Jane E. Buikstra, ed., *A Life in Science: Papers in Honor of J. Lawrence Angel* (1990). Also see the biographical sketches by T. D. Stewart, *American Journal of Physical Anthropology* 51 (1979): 509–16, and by D. H. Ubelaker, *American Antiquity* 54, no. 1 (1989): 5–8. An obituary by L. E. St. Hoyme is in the *American Journal of Physical Anthropology* 75 (1988): 291–301.

D. H. UBELAKER

ANGELA (21 Feb. 1824–4 Mar. 1887), educator and religious sister, was born Eliza Marie Gillespie in Brownsville, Pennsylvania, the daughter of John Purcell Gillespie, an attorney, and Mary Madeleine Miers. After the death of her father the family moved to Lancaster, Ohio, in 1838. Eliza was educated by Dominican nuns in Somerset and later attended the Ladies' Academy of the Visitation in the Georgetown section of Washington, D.C.

In the fall of 1851 she accepted a teaching position at St. Mary's Seminary, an Episcopal school, in St. Mary's, Maryland. She excelled in her work and was offered the post of principal despite a rule that only an Episcopalian could hold the office. However, wanting a life of service, she decided to become a sister of Mercy.

While en route to Chicago, Illinois, to enter the Mercy Convent, she stopped to visit her younger brother, Neal, who was studying for the priesthood with the Holy Cross fathers at the University of Notre Dame. There she encountered Father Edward Sorin, founder of Notre Dame, who, with the help of her brother, prevailed on Eliza to enter the Marianites of Holy Cross, a religious community of women like the Sisters of Mercy. She received the habit on 17 April 1853 and was given the religious name Sister Mary of St. Angela. She was promptly sent to Caen, France, for her novitiate under the direction of the Bon Secours sisters. She made her profession on 24 December 1853 at the Holy Cross motherhouse in LeMans, France.

Upon her return to the United States, Angela was assigned as director of studies at St. Mary's Academy in Bertrand, Michigan, a post she held until 1870. From 1857 to 1860 she also served as provincial superior of her community. She stressed liberal education with emphasis on modern languages and classical literature. Her belief that religious women should be trained as educators led her to require that her sisters take summer school classes to improve their academic skills. In 1855 the academy moved south to Indiana to a location one mile west of Notre Dame, where she supervised the construction of Bertrand Hall.

In 1869 the sisters at St. Mary's became autonomous from France, and Angela was elected mother superior for the Sisters of the Holy Cross, serving in this capacity until 1882. She visited sisters working in various missions and made two journeys to Europe to recruit women for the congregation. In her travels she founded several schools for women, including institutions in Morris, Illinois; Woodland, California; Austin, Texas; Washington, D.C.; Salt Lake City, Utah, and in 1875 St. Catherine's Normal Institute for the education of girls in Baltimore, Maryland. Exercising her belief that women should be educated to their highest level of intellectual ability, she initiated a postgraduate program in arts and classical studies at St. Mary's in 1870. This program developed into Saint Mary's College in Notre Dame, Indiana.

Dissatisfied with the poor quality of textbooks in Catholic schools, Mother Angela edited a series of Metropolitan Readers, published by Sadlier Company and a second group of Excelsior Readers. These texts were used in Catholic schools until the late nineteenth century. She applied her skills to Catholic journalism as well. In 1865 she joined Sorin in the foundation of *Ave Maria* magazine, which became (along with the *Catholic World* started the same year) the first successful Catholic periodical in the United States. Besides editing and writing for the magazine, she helped print it. She also prevailed on Orestes Brownson, a noted writer and intellectual of the period and Catholic convert, to contribute to the magazine.

When the Civil War began Angela was asked by the governor of Indiana to enlist Holy Cross sisters for service as nurses. During the war, while still engaged at Saint Mary's, she founded military hospitals at Mound City, Illinois; Memphis, Tennessee; and Paducah and Louisville, Kentucky, for the Union forces under the command of Ulysses S. Grant, serving at several hospitals but principally at Mound City. After the war Angela was responsible for permanent hospital foundations at Cairo, Illinois; Salt Lake City, Utah; and Columbus, Ohio.

Mother Angela's work was consistent with the progressive or Americanist approach in American Catholic history. Influenced by Sorin, who divorced himself from his French roots, Angela adapted her method to the American ideals of freedom and democracy. (She opted to support American foundations over those of France, where the Holy Cross community was born in 1837.) She believed that Europeans, including the Holy Cross founder, Father Basil Moreau, did not understand America and its unique system of government. Angela's progressive attitude toward education for women as well as her insistence that sisters be trained to teach, an idea that foreshadowed the Sister Formation Movement of the Catholic renaissance of the 1950s, illustrate her progressive ideas. She died in Notre Dame, Indiana.

• The archives of the Sisters of the Holy Cross at Saint Mary's, Notre Dame, Ind., holds numerous manuscripts that describe various aspects of Mother Angela's family and life. Anna Shannon McAllister, *Flame in the Wilderness* (1944), is a noncritical chronicle of Angela's life. Sisters of the Holy Cross, *A Story of Fifty Years, 1855–1905* (1956?), gives information about her years as a religious superior. More scholarly sources are Mary Georgia Costin, ed., *Fruits of the Tree* (2 vols., 1988), a series of essays, one of which, "Americanization" by M. Campion Kuhn, demonstrates how Angela's Americanism and that of her family influenced the congregation of the Sisters of the Holy Cross. Costin, *Priceless Spirit: A History of the Sisters of the Holy Cross 1841–1893* (1994), describes Angela's accomplishments within the context of the history of the Sisters of the Holy Cross. Arthur Hope, *Notre Dame: One Hundred Years* (1943), gives some information on Angela's family and her initial meeting with Sorin.

RICHARD GRIBBLE

ANGELL, Israel (24 Aug. 1740–4 May 1832), revolutionary soldier, was born in Providence, Rhode Island, the son of Oliver Angell, a cooper, and Naomi Smith. A descendant of Thomas Angell, one of the original settlers of Rhode Island, Angell received a good education, developing especially an interest in science. He followed his father into the position of cooper and settled in Johnston, Rhode Island. He married Martha Angell, a second cousin, in 1765; the couple had eleven children prior to her death in 1793.

At the start of the revolutionary war, Angell was commissioned as major of Colonel Daniel Hitchcock's Rhode Island regiment. He served at the siege of Boston and accepted the rank of major in the Eleventh Continental Regiment in January 1776. Promoted to lieutenant colonel (1 Jan. 1777) and then to full colonel (13 Jan. 1777) of the Second Rhode Island Regiment, Angell led his men at the battles of Brandywine and Monmouth and won special notice for the skillful fighting of his men at Red Bank, New Jersey, in October 1777. The heaviest test of Angell and his soldiers came on 23 June 1780 at the battle of Springfield, New Jersey.

American commander General Nathanael Greene deployed approximately 1,000 Continental troops and militia in an effort to stop the advance of 5,000 British and Hessian troops led by General Wilhelm von Knyphausen, the highest ranking Hessian soldier in North America. A significant element of General Greene's battle plan was to hold two bridges over the Rahway River. Angell's Second Rhode Island Regiment guarded the Galloping Hill Road bridge, while Major Henry "Light Horse Harry" Lee and his men defended the Vauxhall bridge. After a sharp but fierce engagement, both sets of American defenders were forced to withdraw, but they had inflicted significant casualties on their foes. The British and Hessians burned the town of Springfield that afternoon but then withdrew, having accomplished very little given the size and strength of their force. Colonel Angell and his men were singled out for bravery and skill under fire. The American commander in chief, George Washington (who had not been present at the battle), wrote to Major General Robert Howe: "The bridge at Springfield was pretty obstinately defended by Colonel Angel's [*sic*] regiment nor was it gained by the enemy till near a contest of forty minutes. This Regt. had about 40 killed and wounded. Our whole loss during the day does not rise much higher but from all the accounts which we have been yet able to collect, the enemy's has been very superior" (Fitzpatrick, p. 66). Historians have gone as far as to label Springfield one of the forgotten American victories during the revolutionary war.

Angell retired from the army in January 1781 when two Rhode Island regiments were combined under the command of one colonel. He returned to Johnston, Rhode Island, where he remained a cooper and married for a second time, to Susanna Wright, with whom he had six children. Following her death in 1824 he married again, this time to Sarah Wood in 1826. They had no children. He moved to the neighboring town of Smithfield, Rhode Island, where he died.

Angell was one of the many American patriots who emerged from obscurity in 1775 and dwelled for a brief time in the spotlight of revolutionary history. Little is known of his personality, but he was probably an adroit and courageous military leader. Like many another "Cincinnatus" of the American Revolution, he returned to his former life and trade and was fortunate enough to live a long life. Angell's story reveals more about his times than it does about the man himself. It was a period when farmers, carpenters, coopers, and masons banded together to form an army that, by 1780, was good enough to withstand the best of its British and Hessian opponents.

• Primary sources are Edward Field, ed., *Further Reading: Diary of Colonel Israel Angell . . . 1778–1781* (1899; repr. 1971), and Louise Lewis Lovell, *Israel Angell: Colonel of the 2nd Rhode Island Regiment* (1921). See also Francis B. Heitman, *Historical Register of Officers of the Continental Army* (1914), and John C. Fitzpatrick, ed., *The Writings of George Washington*, vol. 19: *12 June 1780–5 Sept. 1780* (1937). Angell's most important battle is covered in detail in M. C. Diedrich, *The Battle of Springfield* (1955); Thomas Fleming, *The Forgotten Victory: The Battle for New Jersey, 1780* (1973); and Fleming, *The Battle of Springfield* (1975).

SAMUEL WILLARD CROMPTON

ANGELL, James Burrill (7 Jan. 1829–1 Apr. 1916), educator and diplomat, was born near Scituate, Rhode Island, the son of Andrew Aldrich Angell and Amy Aldrich, farmers and tavernkeepers. He was educated in local schools and at Brown University, where he received an A.B. in 1849 and was significantly influenced by President Francis Wayland (1796–1865). From October 1850 until May 1851 Angell traveled throughout the South with his college friend Rowland Hazard. The trip provided them with the opportunity to observe slavery and the plantation system on a first-hand basis. Later, Angell's pro-Union editorials in the Providence *Journal* reflected the impact of this trip on his thinking. Angell and Hazard studied French and German in Europe from December 1851 to June 1852, when Hazard returned. Angell continued to travel and study for another year, returning home to become an assistant professor of modern languages at Brown. In 1855 he married Sarah Swope Caswell, the daughter of Dr. Alexis Caswell, who later became president of Brown. They had three children, including James Rowland Angell, president of Yale University from 1921 to 1937.

From 1860 to 1866 Angell was editor of the Providence *Journal*, and his editorials gave strong support to President Abraham Lincoln during the Civil War. In 1866 he was named president of the University of Vermont, where for five years he worked to obtain public approval for an agricultural school that was favored by the trustees while teaching German, history, rhetoric, and international law. In 1871, after two years of hesitation and negotiation, Angell left Vermont to assume the presidency of the University of Michigan. He remained in this post for thirty-eight years and became one of a generation of university presidents whose personal identification with his institution was strong and prominent, such as Charles W. Eliot of Harvard and Andrew Dickson White of Cornell.

For the first twenty years of his tenure at Michigan, Angell was personally involved in university life. Until the early 1890s he answered his own mail in longhand, taught courses in international law and the history of treaties, and resisted bureaucratic growth. Until 1895 he personally conducted morning chapel services and gave the baccalaureate sermon on the Sunday that preceded commencement. During these years, enrollment increased from 1,110 to 2,420 students, of whom 445 were women and about half were Michigan residents. Angell prided himself in knowing the names of virtually every student in the Literary (Arts and Sciences) Department. The faculty increased from 36 to 103 (including 11 "non-residents"), and the annual budget quadrupled from the 1871 figure of $100,000. Eight major new buildings graced the campus, and several others were enlarged. The number of courses offered increased more than sixfold, and during the 1870s alone new programs in dental surgery, homeopathic medicine, pharmacy, and education were initiated.

With a few notable exceptions, Angell's tenure was free of major controversy. By all accounts he enjoyed the support of the faculty and the board of regents, and he developed a good rapport with the student body, tempering some of its youthful excesses early in his tenure but tolerating active fraternity and athletic programs.

The most serious difficulty of Angell's early years at Ann Arbor was the Rose-Douglas controversy. In 1875 chemistry department chairman Silas H. Douglas accused assistant professor Preston Rose of withholding a portion of monies that had been collected during the previous six years from students for chemicals and other laboratory supplies. An investigation by the regents revealed a shortfall of nearly $7,000, which led to Rose's firing. Rose was a prominent member of the Methodist church, while Douglas was an Episcopalian. Methodist leaders in the community, including the editor of the *Ann Arbor Courier*, came to Rose's defense. In 1877 a state legislature investigation put Douglas's liability at $4,477 and Rose's at only $497, which caused the regents to dismiss Douglas. Finally, in 1879, the regents reappointed Rose as an assistant professor of chemistry; Douglas's case ended in 1881 when the state supreme court ruled in his favor, but the regents never restored him to his faculty position. The controversy was so bitter that at one point, the president of Cornell offered Angell sanctuary at his university if the political climate at Michigan became unbearable.

Another problem that clouded university affairs during Angell's tenure was a conflict between the scientific medical school and the homeopathic school. Angell believed that both could and should be allowed to offer their differing theories and methods of diagnosis and treatment, and between 1875 and 1895 both schools existed side by side, although not comfortably. In 1895, the entire homeopathic faculty resigned because of problems within their own field; a new faculty was appointed, but gradually the two fields came closer together, and homeopathy was formally disbanded as a separate school in 1922.

After the mid-1890s Angell became more of a full-time university administrator, spending his days raising funds, making budgets, dealing with the legislature, and articulating the goals of the institution. Enrollment continued to grow and passed 3,300 in 1900. In 1901 Angell headed a successful move to introduce a new A.B. degree, which consolidated several specific degrees in the Literary Department and no longer required proficiency in Greek and Latin. In 1905 college football came under attack across the country, both for the injuries and deaths that the violent style of play produced and for the seeming overemphasis on sport as opposed to academic pursuits. Angell called a special meeting of representatives of the Western Intercollegiate Conference (later the Big Ten) in 1906 to discuss the role of football in university life. Several recommendations came out of this meeting, including one that specified that athletes also be students in good standing. But the controversy continued for several more years, until faculty control of intercollegiate athletics was firmly established. In early 1909, shortly after his eightieth birthday, Angell resigned. He was made president emeritus and was allowed to continue to live in the president's house during his retirement.

During his long tenure as president of the University of Michigan, Angell was called to diplomatic duty on four occasions. In 1880 he was named minister to China, with instructions to negotiate a new immigration treaty that would replace the Burlingame Treaty (1868) and limit, but not prohibit, Chinese immigration into the United States. Working on a delegation with diplomats John F. Swift and William H. Trescot, Angell was successful in his talks with the Chinese, obtaining in November 1880 not only the immigration treaty, but also a commercial treaty that prohibited opium trade with the United States. Although Angell was not an expert on China or Chinese affairs, his status as an educational leader and his moderation in discussion won the respect of his Chinese counterparts and contributed to the success of his mission. The treaties were ratified in May 1881 and led to the Chinese Exclusion Act (1882), which suspended the immigration of Chinese laborers for ten years.

In 1887–1888 Angell, along with Secretary of State Thomas F. Bayard and William L. Putnam of Maine, represented the Grover Cleveland administration on the Anglo-American Northeastern Fisheries Commission, which negotiated a treaty settling a long-standing dispute over fishing rights in the north Atlantic. Although the treaty was rejected by the U.S. Senate, a *modus vivendi* was worked out that implemented the terms of the treaty and stayed in effect for many years. In 1896–1897 Angell sat on the Canadian-American Deep Waterways Commission, along with John E. Russell of Massachusetts and Lyman E. Cooley of Illinois. This binational body investigated and reported that deep water communication was feasible between the Atlantic Ocean and the Great Lakes, but no action was taken on the recommendations, and it became one of several studies done before the building of the St. Lawrence Seaway in the 1950s.

Angell's final and most difficult diplomatic mission was as minister to Turkey in 1897–1898. In this capacity he worked to maintain Turkish neutrality in the Spanish-American War. He successfully obtained an official apology after a U.S. ship was fired upon when it unwittingly sailed into a harbor that was customarily closed at night. More frustrating to Angell was Turkish unresponsiveness to his complaints regarding the treatment of American mission schools and hospitals in Turkey. There had been substantial damage to American property during a revolt by Armenians. At times Turkish troops had damaged and looted American property, while at other times they had simply failed to provide adequate protection. Angell always believed that because the United States, then involved in the Spanish-American War, was unable to back him up by sending gunboats to lurk off the Turkish coast, the government was unwilling to meet his demands for an indemnity. He left Turkey after just a year at the post. In his retirement he continued to teach courses on international law and treaties and wrote his *Reminiscences* (1911). He died at his Ann Arbor residence.

Angell's reputation as an educator and diplomat rests not only on the brilliance of his intellect and the flamboyance of his personality, but, of more importance, on the calm and competent methods he employed to attain his objectives. Attuned to the changing society of late nineteenth-century America, he worked quietly but effectively to enhance the university's share of state funding, develop closer ties with the state public school system, modernize the curriculum, and encourage coeducation. A man of unimposing physical stature and voice, he was still a highly effective speaker, both in public and in diplomatic circles.

• Angell's papers are at the University of Michigan. His correspondence during the years he was being courted by the University of Michigan have been edited by Wilfrid B. Shaw, *From Vermont to Michigan: The Correspondence of James Burrill Angell, 1869–1871* (1936). The only full biography is Shirley W. Smith, *James Burrill Angell: An American Influence* (1954). The most recent history of the University of Michigan that treats Angell's years there is Howard H. Peckham, *The Making of the University of Michigan, 1817–1967* (1967). For details of Angell's diplomatic work, see his *Reminiscences* (1912) as well as Earl D. Babst and Lewis G. Vander Velde, *Michigan and the Cleveland Era* (1948), and David L. Anderson, *Imperialism and Idealism* (1985).

JOHN E. FINDLING

ANGELL, James Rowland (8 May 1869–4 Mar. 1949), academic psychologist and fourteenth president of Yale University, was born in Burlington, Vermont, the son of James Burrill Angell, president of the University of Vermont and later the president of the University of Michigan, and Sarah Swope Caswell, daughter of Alexis Caswell, president of Brown University. The youngest of three, Angell spent much of his childhood alone, mostly in Ann Arbor, Michigan, where his father served the state university. Bouts with scarlet fever and malaria left him partially deaf and, he recalled, "somewhat timid and unassertive" as a child. Poor vision turned him away from medicine, though his hearing loss likely spurred his later interest in evaluation of biological aspects of psychology, particularly the body's response to affective stimuli and the localization of sound.

Except for a year in Beijing at age eleven when his father was minister to China, Angell attended public schools in Ann Arbor. A distinct preference for athletics turned to an interest in intellectual pursuits after he read John Dewey's textbook on psychology soon after its publication in 1886. Angell received an A.B. from Michigan in 1890 and an A.M. in 1891. A graduate seminar that he took with Dewey that year introduced him to William James's *Principles of Psychology*, a book that he characterized as affecting his thinking "more profoundly than any other" for the next twenty years. After a year at Harvard studying philosophy and psychology with William James and Josiah Royce, Angell received a second master's degree and ventured to Germany for further study. His doctoral thesis on freedom in Kant's philosophy was never accepted by the university at Halle because of his difficulty with written German. Nevertheless, his academic reputation was sufficiently enhanced to result in an instructorship in philosophy at the University of Minnesota in 1893. By this time his father, jesting that Angell might follow in his footsteps, encouraged him to be cognizant of the ways of university administration. In 1894 he married Marion Isabel Watrous, a college classmate; they had two children.

Brought to the University of Chicago by Dewey, Angell was assistant professor of philosophy and director of the psychology laboratory there between 1894 and 1901. Angell achieved recognition through his advocacy of the Chicago movement of psychology, which was dubbed "functionalism." Though it would not survive as a vital intellectual movement, functionalism marked a milestone in the history of American psychology by calling upon psychologists to look not just at the structure of constructs, but also at their purpose. Angell hoped to employ a biological viewpoint in order to characterize the process by which the mind aids in the adjustment of the psychophysical person to his or her environment. In so doing, he provided a rationale for the dominant American psychology of his era.

Angell received his first promotion at Chicago in 1901, when he began to get competing offers from other campuses. His popular textbook *Psychology* was published in 1904. That year he became a full professor, and the following year he became department chairman. As a professor he supervised fifty dissertations, thereby training many leaders in American psychology. In 1906 he was elected president of the American Psychological Association. Rejecting the presidency of Dartmouth College in 1908, Angell became dean of the Senior College at Chicago that year. In 1911 he was appointed dean of the university faculties—a position second only to that of the university president. Following service on two army committees during World War I, he became acting president at Chicago in 1918. His Congregationalist background conflicted with Chicago's requirement for a Baptist president, however, and the return of university president Harry Pratt Judson interfered with any opportunity for him to continue to occupy the post. Angell accepted the chairmanship of the National Research Council in 1919–1920 and moved to New York City in 1920 to become president of the Carnegie Corporation.

In 1921 Angell was invited to become the president of Yale University. Pulled between the knowledge that he would be the first non-Yale graduate to lead the university in almost two centuries and the possible feeling of obligation to carry on his familial professional legacy, Angell was convinced to accept the Yale offer. The marriage between Angell and a community that was protective of tradition and sometimes wary of scholarship was polite, but cold. The generous donation by alumnus Edward S. Harkness that founded (along with those at Harvard) the first residential colleges among America's great universities, and the unparalleled endowment left by John W. Sterling allowed Angell to remake Yale in mortar and in scholarship at the most impressive scale in its first three centuries. Under his stewardship a great college became a great university. His success, however, perhaps owed more to his good fortune in presiding over a period of unprecedented income than to his leadership. A reluctance to take a stand left him a bystander to many great educational issues of his campus and his day. Wry humor and mastery "of an easy, shimmering eloquence" (Pierson, p. 180) allowed him to express his mind, but he could rarely bring himself to challenge the status quo. His difficulty in forging a sense of collegiality with the Yale College faculty left him as much an outsider as a leader at Yale. In 1931 Angell's first wife died, and he married Katharine Cramer Woodman the following year. Retiring as Yale's president in 1937, Angell became a full-time educational consultant to the National Broadcasting Company. He died at home in the New Haven suburb of Hamden, Connecticut.

Angell's stature in psychology remains undiminished seventy-five years after his contributions were made: he was an administrative hero who greatly encouraged growth of the field in America. The functionalism he advocated is now considered the bridge between mentalism and behavioralism in the history of American psychology. The accomplishments during his stewardship of Yale may never be equaled, but his contemporaries and biographers have asked if someone else might have marshaled the same resources and achieved more.

• Angell's extensive presidential papers are in the Yale Manuscripts and Archives Library. The influence of Angell's father on his life may be gleaned from his father's letters to him in the presidential papers. Personal papers may be found in his father's papers at the University of Michigan, the President's Papers at the University of Chicago, and in the William James Papers at Harvard. Angell's *The Relations of Structural and Functional Psychology to Philosophy* (1903); "The Province of Functional Psychology," *Psychological Review* 14 (1907): 61–91; and *Chapters from Modern Psychology* (1912) outline his program on functionalism. Essays on general issues in education appear in his *American Education: Addresses and Articles* (1937). The personal character and professional achievement of Angell as Yale president are the core of George Wilson Pierson, *Yale: The University College 1921–1937* (1955). Also on his Yale years, see Maynard Mack, "James Rowland Angell," *Yale Literary Magazine* 97 (1931): 38–46, and Archibald MacLeish, "New Yale," *Fortune* 9 (1934): 70–81, 148–58.

A brief autobiography dwelling largely on Angell's pre-Yale years appears in Carl Murchison, *History of Psychology in Autobiography* (1936). His earlier publications are listed in Carl Murchison, *Psychological Register*, vol. 3 (1932), pp. 11–12. His career in psychology is detailed in *National Academy of Sciences Biographical Memoirs* 26 (1951): 191–208; Darnell Rucker, *The Chicago Pragmatists* (1991); Robert I. Watson and Rand B. Evans, *The Great Psychologists* (1991); David Hothersall, *History of Psychology* (1990); and Thomas Leahey, *A History of Modern Psychology* (1991). Obituaries are in the *New York Times*, 5 Mar. 1949, and the *Yale Alumni Magazine*, Apr. 1949. He was memorialized in Walter Miles, "James Rowland Angell, 1869–1949, Psychologist Educator," *Science* 110 (1949): 1–4.

DAN A. OREN

ANGELL, Joseph Kinnicutt (30 Apr. 1794–1 May 1857), legal writer, was born in Providence, Rhode Island, the son of Nathan Angell, a storekeeper, and Amy Kinnicutt. Angell entered Brown University in 1809 at the age of fifteen and graduated in 1813 with a B.A. He immediately began a three-year preparation for the bar, first at Tapping Reeve and James Gould's famous Litchfield, Connecticut, law school, followed by a period of reading law in the Providence office of Thomas Burgess, a noted counselor and probate judge. Angell was admitted to the Rhode Island bar in 1816.

Preferring the role of counselor to that of advocate, Angell soon established a reputation as a sound theoretical lawyer and developed a practice advising Providence's merchant community. His career took a brief detour in February 1820, however, when he pursued a claim to a large family estate in England before the chancery courts; he remained there until 1822, aside from a brief trip back to Providence in the fall of 1820. Unfortunately for Angell, the court of equity ultimately decided against him on a technicality, and in 1822 he returned to Providence empty-handed, except for the learning and culture he had absorbed while visiting the courts at Westminster Hall, the theater, and the libraries of Oxford University.

Upon returning to Providence, Angell pursued a career as a law writer. Rhode Island was at that time undergoing a transformation from a commercial to an industrial economy, based on a burgeoning textile industry. There was accordingly a growing demand for the legal system to meet this dramatic change, a demand that Angell recognized. His first book, *Treatise on the Common Law in Relation to Watercourses* (1824), responded to the requirements of industry by providing a source of law relating to watercourses and their use as a source of power. Of this work and Angell's *Right of Property in Tide Water and in the Soil and Shores Thereof* (1826), James Kent of New York, a leading authority in nineteenth-century law, asserted, "No intelligent lawyer could well practice without them" (Rider, p. xiv).

These works set the pattern for all of Angell's subsequent books. After 1826 he produced a steady stream of treatises, the topics of which reflected the effects on the law of changes in American industry, business organization, and methods of transportation. The books were designed to provide in one volume a history and summary of both the cases and the points of law they decided in particular branches of the law. In *Watercourses* Angell had summarized the traditional law on the subject and asserted that upstream mill owners did not possess the right to adversely affect downstream users by damming the flow of the watercourse. In 1837 his *Adverse Enjoyment* reflected changes in American law that permitted such development when it was of "valuable use" to the public. In *Essay on the Right of a State to Tax a Body Corporate* (1837) and the *Treatise on the Law of Private Corporations Aggregate* (1832), which he wrote with Samuel Ames, Angell examined the legal implications of "the infinite number of corporations" in the United States. His *Law of Carriers of Goods and Passengers by Land and Water* (1849) and *Treatise on the Law of Highways* (1857) examined the law concerning transportation companies in an age of rapidly expanding commerce, while his *Treatise on the Law of Fire and Life Insurance* (1854) reflected the rise of the insurance industry in the United States.

At the same time that he sought to systematize and summarize the law in his books, Angell also sought to make legal knowledge more accessible by producing a monthly publication. The *United States Law Intelligencer and Review*, initially printed in Providence and later in Philadelphia, was intended to provide "a synopsis or abridged record of the changes and progress of the Law" (Rider, p. xv). Angell oversaw publication of the first volume in 1829 and remained the editor for two years following the magazine's removal to Philadelphia; however, only three volumes were published before the venture failed in 1831.

In 1842 popular demand for reform of a narrow suffrage and an outdated apportionment reached a peak in Rhode Island. Angell was among those who signed an article titled "The Right of the People to Form a Constitution," otherwise known as the "Nine Lawyers' Opinion" (*Providence Daily Express*, 16 Mar. 1842). The article argued that "the power to prescribe the form of government rested with the people; that the legislature was the creature of the people, and was not superior to its creator" (Rider, p. xix). In the opinion of these lawyers, the present constitution of the state had been a product of the general assembly, while the amended "Peoples' Constitution" was a product of the people themselves, "and therefore rested on the firmest possible basis" (Rider, p. xx).

In the March term of 1845, Angell was appointed as the reporter for the Supreme Court of Rhode Island. The first decisions appeared in pamphlet form in July 1847 and consisted of cases dating from as early as 1828. Angell also prepared a second pamphlet before resigning his position as reporter in the September term of 1849.

Angell, who never married, died suddenly in Boston, where he had traveled on business.

Angell's work as a legal writer represented parallel developments in nineteenth-century American law. His books met the perceived need of a growing nation for a clear summary of current law as well as the necessity of selecting and featuring the most important cases from the rapidly growing number of adjudged cases and state reports. The success of Angell's books was due in large part to his simple and direct style, which admirably met those requirements.

• Correspondence from Angell can be found in the papers of Richard James Arnold at the Rhode Island Historical Society in Providence. His other works include *Treatise on the Limitations of Actions at Law and Suits in Equity* (1829; 2d ed., 1846) and *Practical Summary of the Law of Assignments in Trust for the Benefit of Creditors* (1835). The most useful biographical account is Sydney S. Rider, "Memoir of Joseph K. Angell," *Rhode Island Reports* 1 (1847): v–xx. The "Nine Lawyers' Opinion" was reproduced with the memoir in *Rhode Island Historical Tracts* 11 (1880). Incidental references to Angell can be found in Abraham Payne, *Reminiscences of the Rhode Island Bar* (1885), and Avery F. Angell, *Genealogy of the Descendants of Thomas Angell* (1872). See also Morton J. Horwitz, *The Transformation of American Law, 1780–1860* (1977).

MARK WARREN BAILEY

ANGLE, Paul McClelland (25 Dec. 1900–11 May 1975), historian and museum director, was born in Mansfield, Ohio, the son of John Elmer Angle, a grocer, and Nellie Laverne McClelland. After spending his freshman year at Oberlin College, he transferred to Miami University at Ohio and graduated magna cum laude and Phi Beta Kappa in 1922. Two years later, he received an M.A. in history from the University of Illinois at Urbana-Champaign. He then took a job with the American Book Company selling textbooks and in 1925 accepted the secretaryship of a little-known historical society in Springfield, Illinois, the Abraham Lincoln Centennial Association. In 1926 he married Vesta Verne Magee, a fellow student at Miami; they had two children.

While at the Lincoln Association, Angle became well known for his refutation of the spurious correspondence between Lincoln and Ann Rutledge that Wilma Frances Minor had published from December 1928 to February 1929 in the *Atlantic Monthly*. Angle's rebuttal in the April 1929 issue was publicly supported by Worthington C. Ford, editor of the Massachusetts Historical Society, among others. A year later Angle published an edition of *Herndon's Life of Lincoln* and *New Letters and Papers of Lincoln*. In 1932 he collaborated with the poet Carl Sandburg on *Mary Lincoln, Wife and Widow*, which included a narrative by Sandburg and documents compiled by Angle. Sandburg, who had initially opposed Angle's position on the Lincoln-Rutledge letters, reversed his position after seeing Angle's evidence. Angle's career continued to advance; in 1932 he was appointed executive secretary of the Illinois State Historical Society and librarian at the Illinois Historical Library.

In 1945 Angle moved upstate to run the Chicago Historical Society. His twenty-year directorship resulted in a major improvement and expansion of the society's activities. He developed the society's collection of old books into an up-to-date research library; he increased funding by enlisting the interest and financial support of the city's prominent businessmen; he instituted an educational outreach program; and he built up the society's membership, which rose from 1516 in June 1947 to 2210 in June 1963. As a way of attracting members and of disseminating knowledge about the Civil War era and the history of the city and the state, he established, and authored every article of, a quarterly magazine, *Chicago History*. Between 1945 and 1969 he edited and wrote ninety-six issues, which were richly illustrated with contemporary photographs and reproductions. Under Angle's leadership, the Chicago Historical Society became a significant cultural and intellectual institution in the city.

During this period Angle produced numerous edited collections of historical documents that related to Lincoln. In 1946 he published *A Shelf of Lincoln Books*. The *Lincoln Reader*, a compilation of assessments by historians and contemporaries, was a Book of the Month Club selection in 1947. These were followed by a volume of Lincoln's autobiographical writings (1948), *Abraham Lincoln: By Some Men Who Knew Him* (1950), *The Living Lincoln* (1955), and Lincoln's speeches and letters in two volumes (1957). He also published several collections of documents (1959, 1960) and one pictorial history (1967) on the Civil War and edited the Lincoln-Douglas debates of 1858 (*Created Equal?* [1958]). Among his anthologies of eyewitness accounts were descriptions of the Great Chicago Fire of 1871 (1946) and first impressions of the state of Illinois (1968). He also compiled anthologies on American culture, which included *The American Reader* (1958), *The American Family* (1963), *American Culture* (1961), *By These Words: Great Documents of American Liberty* (1954), and *Books: The Image of America and Doorways to American Culture* (1958). Most of these publications were coedited with Earl Schenck Miers, also an authority on Lincoln and the Civil War. Angle was most proud of *Bloody William-*

son: A Chapter in American Lawlessness (1952), a grim study of a notoriously violent coal-mining county in southern Illinois from 1901 to 1922, which was one of the few historical narratives that he wrote.

For the most part, Angle was an editor and compiler of collections of historical documents, the raw data and actual text of history, which he hoped to make accessible to a wide audience. In his view, it was the task of historians to bring history to the citizenry, either in its documentary and immediate form, or through narratives that were well written, told a story, and were factually accurate. He believed that academic historians, by contrast, made history unappealing and inaccessible to most people and, consequently, was quite disdainful of them. "I fear we live in two different worlds," he once wrote. For Angle, Francis Parkman was the greatest American historian, while, among his own contemporaries, he most admired Allan Nevins and Bruce Catton. As one of the most productive popularizers of American history in the mid-twentieth century, Angle considered history to be a literary enterprise and the job of a historian a civic responsibility.

After retiring as director of the Chicago Historical Society in 1965, he continued to edit and write *Chicago History* for four more years. In the year before he died, he published a short life of Phillip K. Wrigley, one of the society's major benefactors, and *On a Variety of Subjects*, a collection of essays and reminiscences, which demonstrates his eclecticism as well as his views about history and historians. He died in Chicago.

• Angle's papers are in the Chicago Historical Society. They cover most of his directorship and contain a record of the controversy over the Lincoln-Rutledge letters and his correspondence with Sandberg. There is also a small file of clippings and obituaries. A discussion of Angle's role in the Lincoln-Rutledge matter can be found in Don E. Fehrenbacher, "The Minor Affair: An Adventure in Forgery and Deception," in his *Lincoln in Text and Context* (1987). Details about Angle's directorship of the Chicago Historical Society were derived from a phone interview on 12 May 1993 with Teresa Krutz, who was registrar of the society under Angle. An appreciation of Angle is Irving Dilliard, "Paul M. Angle: Warm Recollections and Clear Impressions," *Journal of the Illinois State Historical Society* 68 (Nov. 1975): 435–43. Obituaries are in the *Chicago Tribune* and *Chicago Sun-Times*, 12 May 1975.

MICHAEL PERMAN

ANGLETON, James Jesus (9 Dec. 1917–11 May 1987), counterintelligence official, was born in Boise, Idaho, the son of James Hugh Angleton, a cavalry officer and later a businessman, and Carmen Mercedes Moreno. His father's business took the family to Italy during Angleton's teenage years, and Angleton attended preparatory school in England. In 1937 he enrolled at Yale University, where he majored in English and was regarded as a highly intelligent student, though he neglected his academic studies in favor of literary pursuits. He wrote poetry and cofounded a first-rate literary magazine, *Furioso*, to which Ezra Pound and E. E. Cummings contributed. Although graduating in 1941 in the bottom quarter of his class, Angleton went to Harvard Law School, but he completed only one year of studies before being drafted into the army. In July 1943, while undergoing army training, he married Cicely d'Autremont, with whom he had three children.

Angleton was assigned to the military's intelligence agency, the Office of Strategic Services, where he joined the counterintelligence unit (X-2). He spent the war years first in London and later in Italy, where he rose in March 1945 to become chief of X-2 for all Italy. With his keen memory, obvious talent, and intense commitment to his work, he quickly developed a reputation as a brilliant intelligence officer. When the Central Intelligence Agency (CIA) was formed in 1947, he joined it, continuing to work in counterintelligence. In 1954, under the patronage of Director of Central Intelligence Allen Dulles, Angleton was appointed the first chief of the newly created Counterintelligence Staff, a position he held for two decades.

Angleton became known as one of the most fascinating and controversial figures in the history of the CIA. He was credited with several major successes, including obtaining a copy of Nikita Khrushchev's "secret speech" of 1956, in which the new Soviet premier denounced his predecessor, Joseph Stalin. During his tenure at the CIA, Angleton developed an aura of mystique, which, together with his reclusiveness, his sometimes eccentric behavior, and his charismatic ability to inspire devotion among his subordinates, earned him the status of a "living legend" within the intelligence community. His various nicknames included "Slim Jim," "the Fisherman," "the Gray Ghost," and "the Poet."

Angleton's primary responsibilities were to prevent and to detect penetration or subversion of the CIA and other government agencies by the KGB, the Soviet Union's intelligence arm. He and his staff scrutinized CIA operations for possible spies and disinformation planted by the KGB. As Angleton saw it, the Soviet Union used a vast array of deceptions to mislead and weaken the West, creating a pattern of illusions he once referred to as "a wilderness of mirrors" (a phrase from T. S. Eliot's poem "Gerontion"). It was Angleton's job to navigate the "wilderness of mirrors," discerning reality from illusion and truth from deception. In retrospect, however, many of his CIA colleagues concluded that Angleton lost his way in this wilderness in the 1960s, when he launched an extensive and eventually damaging hunt for Soviet spies (or "moles") within the CIA.

Angleton launched the mole hunt after a relatively low-level KGB officer, Anatoly Mikhailovich Golitsyn, defected to the United States in 1961. Golitsyn claimed that the KGB had placed spies at high levels in the CIA and other government agencies as part of a huge and highly sophisticated plan to deceive the West. According to Golitsyn, the Sino-Soviet split that had recently become evident was a complete fabrication, designed to lure the West into providing aid to China. Although Golitsyn was diagnosed as paranoid and prone to self-aggrandizement, his elaborate theories found a receptive audience in Angleton, who shared Golitsyn's conspiratorial mindset. Angleton was convinced that Golitsyn's tales of a massive KGB conspiracy were true, and in a highly unusual move he allowed the defector access to secret CIA files to help identify possible spies.

In the "Great Mole Hunt" that ensued, Angleton and his staff investigated scores of officers in the CIA's Soviet Division. No moles were ever found, but the investigation ruined the careers of several loyal officers who fell under suspicion. Golitsyn's claims also led Angleton to press for disruptive investigations in the British, French, and Finnish intelligence services, which strained relations between the CIA and its Allied counterparts. Moreover, Angleton's suspicions caused him to doubt the authenticity of many Soviet agents recruited by the CIA's Soviet Division and hampered the division's efforts to obtain information from the Soviet bloc. He also viewed most Soviet defectors, except for Golitsyn, as "provocations," deliberately sent by the KGB to mislead the West.

When Yuri Ivanovich Nosenko, a KGB officer with high-level connections, defected in 1964, Angleton decided that Nosenko was a Soviet disinformation agent who had been sent to discredit Golitsyn's testimony. Nosenko's view of the KGB—particularly his assertion that the KGB had played no role in Lee Harvey Oswald's assassination of President John F. Kennedy—differed markedly from the grandiose conspiracy claims advanced by Golitsyn. On the basis of inconsistencies in Nosenko's testimony, the Soviet Division, with Angleton's acquiescence, imprisoned the defector for over three years in an unsuccessful effort to induce him to confess that he was a KGB plant. A CIA report subsequently established that Nosenko was a genuine defector, but the questions about his reliability had delayed action on several spy cases he revealed.

In retrospect, Angleton's vigilance seems excessive and even paranoid, but his mole hunt took place during a period when fear of the KGB was widespread. Revelations that Soviet spies had deeply penetrated the British intelligence service (especially the exposure of Kim Philby in 1963) and the arrest in 1962 of an important CIA agent in Soviet military intelligence, Colonel Oleg Penkovskii, among other circumstances, made it seem plausible that the KGB had penetrated the CIA.

Angleton was respected and trusted by the directors of Central Intelligence under whom he served until 1973, when William E. Colby was appointed director of Central Intelligence. Colby did not sympathize with Angleton's conspiracy theories and considered Angleton's methods harmful and extreme. In 1974, when the *New York Times* discovered illegal domestic surveillance and mail-opening operations that had been directed by Angleton, Colby used the unfavorable publicity as a pretext to force Angleton into retirement. Angleton's top deputies were also removed, and the Counterintelligence Staff was reduced and reorganized following a report by the CIA's inspector general that criticized Angleton's management practices.

After Angleton's dismissal, his previously secret role in counterintelligence became publicly known. The press seized on the tall, gaunt, and mysterious figure as an emblem of America's Cold War struggle against the Soviet Union. He was called "America's legendary master spy," and characters in dozens of spy thrillers were modeled after him. Angleton's hobbies—orchid growing, fly fishing, and jewelry work—occupied much of his time during retirement, but he occasionally granted interviews to journalists, in which he continued to promote his conspiracy theories. He died in Washington, D.C., but the controversy over his achievements continued, with his defenders noting that no proven penetration of the CIA occurred under his watch and his detractors arguing that his mole hunt had devastated and paralyzed the CIA's Soviet operations.

• Assessments of Angleton's career have been contentious and provisional because much of the record of his tenure at the CIA remains classified. Most studies of Angleton are based largely on interviews with former CIA officers. Tom Mangold's biography, *Cold Warrior: James Jesus Angleton; The CIA's Master Spy Hunter* (1991), paints an unflattering portrait of its subject. David C. Martin's earlier biography, *Wilderness of Mirrors* (1980), presents a more balanced view. A thorough sketch of Angleton's character and counterintelligence methodology is in Robin Winks, *Cloak and Gown: Scholars in America's Secret War*, chap. 6, "The Theorist: James Jesus Angleton" (1987). Angleton's search for a Soviet mole is described in David Wise, *Molehunt: The Secret Search for Traitors That Shattered the CIA* (1992). Edward Jay Epstein, *Deception: The Invisible War between the KGB and the CIA* (1989), defends Angleton's vision of a vast KGB conspiracy directed against the CIA. The best account of the Nosenko affair is "Nosenko: Five Paths to Justice," in *Inside CIA's Private World*, ed. H. Bradford Westerfield (1995). For a general history of the CIA, see John Ranelagh, *The Agency: The Rise and Decline of the CIA* (1986). An obituary appeared in the *New York Times*, 12 May 1987.

BARBARA J. KEYS

ANGLIN, Jack (13 May 1916–7 Mar. 1963), country musician, was born in Franklin, Tennessee, the son of John Benjamin Anglin and Lue Tucker, tenant farmers who moved often. Anglin grew up on farms near small towns in the Nashville area, including Shelbyville, Fayetteville, Columbia, and then near Athens, Alabama. He began playing music with two of his brothers, Van Lear (or "Red") and Jim. Their parents gave them a solid grounding in traditional folk forms, and in 1935 the three brothers moved to Nashville to perform on WSIX radio. They were billed as "The Anglin Brothers—A Vocal and String Trio." They also worked on other southern stations, including WMC in Memphis, WWL in New Orleans, WAPI in Birmingham, and WSB in Atlanta. On 5 November 1937 the Anglin Brothers made twenty recordings for Art Satherley of Columbia Records. The following November, Satherley made fourteen more recordings with them. On the latter occasion, they were billed as the Anglin Twins and Red.

In 1936 Anglin met Johnnie Wright. Wright was singing then as part of Johnnie Wright and the Harmony Girls. Wright and Anglin would later team up to form the duet Johnnie and Jack, although on their first appearance together, as part of a benefit show for the victims of the 1938 Ohio River floods, they called themselves the Backwater Boys. They later changed the name to the Tennessee Mountain Boys.

In 1938 Anglin married Louise Wright; they had one child. About that same year the Anglin brothers group broke up, and Anglin moved to Nashville to work for the Selig Hosiery Company. He and Wright began performing together on WSIX as Johnnie Wright and the Happy Roving Cowboys. Wright and Anglin tried repeatedly to gain a spot on the Grand Ole Opry but were turned away. In the winter of 1940–1941, Wright, Anglin, and Wright's wife, Kitty Wells, moved to station WBIG in Greensboro, North Carolina, and then on to WCHS in Charleston, West Virginia, doubling on WHIS, in Bluefield, West Virginia. The act broke up because of wartime gasoline rationing, and Anglin briefly played with Roy Acuff before being inducted into the Army Medical Corps in July 1943. He remained in the service until January 1946.

After he returned to the Nashville area, Anglin rejoined Wright and Wells, who were then performing in Raleigh, North Carolina. They joined the Grand Ole Opry in January 1947 and on 25 March of that year began recording for Apollo Records in New York. In January 1948 they moved to Shreveport, Louisiana, and, that April, became one of the first acts on the newly formed Louisiana Hayride, broadcast over KWKH. That same year, Johnnie and Jack were signed to RCA Victor Records. Their first RCA session was held on 31 January 1949.

Johnnie and Jack's first hit was "Poison Love," an innovative record that incorporated a Latin beat carried by bassist Ernie Newton and guitarist Eddie Hill. The Latin beat would become Johnnie and Jack's trademark for several years. The duo also recorded many songs from the pen of Jim Anglin, who became one of the most accomplished songwriters in country music during the late 1940s and early 1950s. Earlier, he had written two songs, "(Beneath That) Lonely Mound of Clay" and "As Long As I Live," that Roy Acuff had purchased in 1941, although Anglin's estate later reclaimed them.

After the success of "Poison Love," Johnnie and Jack left KWKH and began touring the South, working at many small radio stations. They were invited to rejoin the Grand Ole Opry in January 1952 and remained there until Jack Anglin's death. Their repertoire included a mixture of sacred and secular songs, most featuring the trademark "brother harmony" sound. They covered several rhythm and blues hits for the country market, including "Goodnight Sweetheart Goodnight," but they remain best known for a string of country songs, many delivered with a Latin rhythm.

The advent of rock 'n' roll in the mid-1950s led to Johnnie and Jack's sales tailing off. Like many other country artists in a similar predicament, they tried recording rock 'n' roll, but the results were unsatisfactory on both an aesthetic and commercial level. Their last major hit was "Stop the World (and Let Me Off)" in 1958. In 1961 Johnnie and Jack were signed to Decca Records, the label that Wells recorded for. They recorded six sessions for Decca and scored one minor hit, "Slow Poison," in 1962.

Wright and Anglin were still good draws on the road, due in some measure to the fact that they worked as a double act with Wells, who was then one of the bestselling female vocalists in country music. They had returned from an extended engagement at the Flame Club in Minneapolis when they received the news that Patsy Cline, Hawkshaw Hawkins, and Cowboy Copas had been killed in a plane crash. Anglin died in Nashville when his car spun out of control on the way to a memorial service for the performers.

Anglin's career can only be considered in conjunction with Johnnie Wright's. He and Wright attempted to bring the primordial "brother harmony" sound into contemporary times by introducing new elements, such as Latin rhythms and a broader repertoire.

• Anglin's career is covered in Walt Trott, *The Honky Tonk Angels: The Kitty Wells and Johnnie & Jack Story* (1993), and in the booklet by Eddie Stubbs and Walt Trott accompanying the CD *Johnnie and Jack: The Tennessee Mountain Boys* (1992).

COLIN ESCOTT

ANGLIN, Margaret (3 Apr. 1876–7 Jan. 1958), actress, was born Mary Margaret Anglin in Ottawa, Canada, the daughter of Timothy Warren Anglin, Speaker of the House of Commons, and Ellen A. McTavish. Born a Roman Catholic, she was educated at the Convent of the Sacred Heart in Montreal until she left school at fifteen to pursue a career as a concert reader. Despite her father's disapproval, her mother supported her choice and enabled Margaret to go to New York to study elocution when she was seventeen.

Anglin enrolled at Nelson Wheatcroft's Empire Dramatic School and, renamed Margaret Moore, became one of the students selected by Charles Frohman for places in his company. She made her professional stage debut in his production of Bronson Howard's *Shenandoah* in 1894. Frustrated by being ignored by Frohman, Anglin barnstormed with a Buffalo stock company to portray "the girl" in Richard Mansfield's production of *Dr. Jekyll and Mr. Hyde* and Mrs. Linde in Ibsen's *A Doll's House*. She traveled through the Midwest in 1896, playing Nadia in *Michael Strogoff* and the lead in David Belasco's *The Girl I Left Behind Me*.

An audition for James O'Neill's company won her female leads in five plays for the 1896–1897 season, including Ophelia in *Hamlet*. O'Neill persuaded her to return to her own name and encouraged her to perform in Shakespeare's plays. She left O'Neill when she was invited to act in and direct a Maritime tour of *As You Like It* in the summer of 1897. She also played in

W. S. Gilbert's *Comedy and Tragedy* and his *Pygmalion and Galatea*, as Meg in *Lord Chumley*, Belasco's domestic drama, and in the starring role in the Anthony Hope comedy, *The Adventure of Lady Ursula*. At the end of 1898 she met Richard Mansfield, who cast her as Roxane in Edmond Rostand's *Cyrano de Bergerac*, making her the first American actress to create the role and catapulting her into immediate fame.

In 1900 Anglin returned to the Frohman company as a leading lady, creating the title role in Henry Arthur Jones's *Mrs. Dane's Defence*, a role so sympathetic that fans would importune her for advice on personal problems and so popular that it was often revived. This triumph was followed by another, the role of Dora in Victorien Sardou's *Diplomacy* (1901). She created a whimsical Gwendolyn Fairfax for Oscar Wilde's *The Importance of Being Earnest* (1902). During the summer of 1903, in San Francisco and on tour, Anglin starred opposite Henry Miller (1860–1926), as a member of his stock company, in George Bernard Shaw's *The Devil's Disciple* and in *Camille*, the hit of the season but a failure on its New York opening in 1904. Her featherbrained darling in the title role of H. H. Davies's *Cynthia* in Toronto in 1903 highlighted her "naturalness" as an actress. In 1904 she produced as well as acted in *The Eternal Feminine*, for which she earned an inappropriate association with feminism. After the failure of a new drama by George Middleton, *A Wife's Strategy* (1905), which was marred by her revisions, Anglin joined the Shubert organization (1905–1906) for an adaptation of Wilkie Collins's *The New Magdalen*, now titled *Zira*, in which Anglin played the title role.

By accepting the role of Ruth Jordan in William Vaughan Moody's *The Sabine Woman* and starring with Henry Miller in the new version, entitled *The Great Divide* (1906), Anglin was drawn into the realist movement in American theater and away from the heavily melodramatic vehicles of the nineteenth century. Moody's play, though still tinged with what Brooks Atkinson called "hokum," is one of the landmarks of American drama. It attacked theatrical provincialism and rebelled against authority and convention, linking it with the modern drama being shaped by Eugene O'Neill in Provincetown. The play ran for two years and was followed by an extensive tour; Anglin was acclaimed for her excellent acting and emotional intensity. Despite the popularity of *The Great Divide*, melodramas still flourished, and Anglin's ability to project strong emotion was well suited to the genre. With a damp handkerchief as one of her chief props, Anglin became the "first practitioner of anguish," and it was said that she could "wring emotion from a keg of nails."

Anglin capped her nationwide success in *The Great Divide* by a 25-week tour of Australia (1908), introducing *The Taming of the Shrew* and *Twelfth Night*, appearing in seven plays, and repeating the lead roles 166 times. She returned to the United States to star in a reliable tearjerker, *The Awakening of Helena Richie* (1909), but used the summer of 1909 to study Greek drama. On 30 June 1910 Anglin made her debut in Greek tragedy in the title role of *Antigone* at the Hearst Greek Theater in Berkeley, California. During her preoccupation with Greek drama and American melodrama, Anglin made headlines by declaring that she wanted to appear in comedies. More than 400 scripts were forwarded to her, and *Green Stockings* (1911) was the most successful comedy that emerged from them. In May 1911 Anglin married playwright Howard Hull, who had played Haemon in her production of *Antigone*. He died in 1937.

For the next twenty years, Anglin's attention was fixed on the classics, acting in or producing Greek drama, using new translations when possible, sometimes producing or directing such works as *Antigone, Hippolytus, Iphigenia in Aulis*, or *Medea*, usually in summer outdoor performances, mainly in Berkeley but also in Kalamazoo, Ann Arbor, and Providence. Her 1927 *Electra* at the Metropolitan Opera House in New York City was the greatest single success in her career. Anglin created a distinguished Clytemnestra in *Iphigenia in Aulis* (1921) at the Manhattan Opera House, accompanied by Walter Damrosch conducting his original music. She also brought productions of Shakespeare's plays from the West Coast through Canada to the Atlantic. In 1913–1914, with stops at sixty-five cities, Anglin presented *The Taming of the Shrew, Twelfth Night, As You Like It*, and *Anthony and Cleopatra*, with comic relief from *Lady Windermere's Fan*.

Anglin did not entirely abandon melodrama, however, and she triumphed as Vivian Hunt in *The Woman of Bronze* (1920)—her longest-running and most financially successful property—and, inspired by her devotion to the saint, excelled in the title role of *The Trial of Joan of Arc* (1921). She used box-office successes such as *Beverly's Balance* (1915), *The Vein of Gold* (1916; renamed *The Lioness* a year later), Somerset Maugham's *Caroline* (1916), *Lonely Soldiers* (1917), and several revivals of *The Woman of Bronze* to finance her own productions, especially of the classics. Other productions during the 1920s were *The Open Fire* (1921), *The Sea Woman* (1923), *Candida* (1926), *Gypsy April* (1927), a revised *Diplomacy* (1928), and *Security* (1929). With Paul Kewster she produced *The Great Lady Deadlock*, appearing in a dual role as Lady Deadlock and Hortense, her maid, in an adaptation of Dickens's *Bleak House* (1923). The tour de force was mildly successful on the West Coast and on tour but failed at the Ambassador in New York City (1929). Officially retired from Broadway with Ivor Novello's *Fresh Fields* (1934–1936), Anglin still appeared in *Retreat from Folly* (1937) and *Marriage Royal* (1937) in upstate New York and in Dennis, Massachusetts. In Chicago she replaced Mary Boland as Mrs. Malaprop in Sheridan's *The Rivals*. She made her last stage appearance in her late sixties, when she took part in a road-company production of Lillian Hellman's *Watch on the Rhine* (1943).

During Anglin's last years, ill health and the lack of suitable projects confined her to coaching and readings, although she was constantly devising new projects, such as Jean Giraudoux's *The Madwoman of Chaillot* in 1948. With few financial resources at her disposal, she returned in 1953 to family and friends in Toronto, where she died.

Anglin's rich, golden voice, flair for evoking emotions, and fierce independence and integrity mark her as one of the most important turn-of-the-century American actresses. When proposed plays did not suit her, she coauthored, produced, and acted in her own. She did not hesitate to stop performing when audiences were unruly or to defy the Actors' Equity strike (1919) by joining the rival Actors' Fidelity League. Her opposition to unions cost her roles in plays and lockouts for her productions. Her most significant contribution to the American theater, however, was her staging of Greek drama when there seemed no audience for it.

• Archival material on Anglin is in the Robinson Locke Collection of Dramatic Scrapbooks and Clippings, New York Public Library Theater Collection, Lincoln Center. See also the biography by John LeVay, *Margaret Anglin: A Stage Life* (1989); Lewis Strang, *Famous Actresses of the Day in America* (1902); Thoda Cocroft (Anglin's friend and publicist), *Great Names and How They Are Made* (1941); Lloyd Morris, *Curtain Time: The Story of the American Theater* (1953); Anthony Slide, ed., *Selected Theatre Criticism*, vol. 1 (1985); and Brooks Atkinson, *Broadway* (1970). An obituary is in the *New York Times*, 8 Jan. 1958.

ELIZABETH R. NELSON

ANGOFF, Charles (22 Apr. 1902–3 May 1979), editor and author, was born in Minsk, Russia, the son of Jacob Joseph Angoff, an unskilled laborer, and Anna Pollack. Young Angoff grew up in the Jewish immigrant neighborhoods of Boston, where his family moved in 1909 and which he later used as a backdrop for his fiction. Entering Harvard University on scholarship in 1919, Angoff studied philosophy with Harry Wolfson and was much in awe of the writings of H. L. Mencken. According to his later portrayal of his fictional surrogate, David Polonsky, Angoff was stung by the anti-Semitism of the faculty and his fellow students and appalled at the intellectual shallowness of many of his teachers.

Following his graduation in 1923, Angoff began a less than promising career in local journalism as a one-person staff for a suburban weekly. In 1925, however, his search for a better position brought Angoff to the notice of Mencken himself, then looking for a "slave," as he put it, to help run the already notorious *American Mercury* without his longtime coeditor George Jean Nathan. Within a few days of meeting Mencken in New York, Angoff was hired to take up the duties of assistant editor, charged with reviewing and rejecting manuscripts, checking copy, sending the magazine to press, and dealing with whatever else happened in the small office in New York while Mencken pursued his life in Baltimore. Promoted to managing editor in 1931, Angoff also served as frequent dining and drinking companion to the "sage of Batimore" and contributed articles and features to the magazine both anonymously and pseudonymously. His days with Mencken were marked by frequent disagreements over literary and social matters, according to Angoff's later account, but their unlikely relationship continued through the early 1930s, the remainder of the *Mercury*'s heyday. In Mencken's view, Angoff was the "best managing editor" in America. In turn, Angoff, despite his disagreements with Mencken, absorbed the Menckenesque manner of iconoclasm, a quality that marked his first major book, *A Literary History of the American People* (1931), an ambitious chronicle that some reviewers found "jaunty, up-to-the-minute, vivacious, sometimes amusing" (*The Nation*, 25 Mar. 1931), but which others found "pretentious . . . immature . . . cluttered with dubious judgments delivered in a Messianic manner" (H. S. Commager, *Forum*, June 1931, p. 85). Angoff's calling Benjamin Franklin the ancestor of Babbitt is typical of the tone of the work. Only the first two of the projected four volumes were published.

As the *Mercury* lost circulation during the depression, Mencken was impervious to suggestions about how to save the magazine. In 1933 he finally relinquished the editorship, but Angoff was passed over as successor by Alfred Knopf, the magazine's publisher, in favor of Henry Hazlitt. Angoff succeeded Hazlitt in 1934, however. His editorial policy, in Mencken's view, took the *Mercury* too far to the left, a reason perhaps for Knopf's finally deciding to sell the magazine to Paul Palmer and Lawrence Spivak in January 1935, a sale kept secret from Angoff. Although offered the opportunity to stay on under Palmer, Angoff decided to quit, joining the editorial board of *The Nation* and then serving as editor of the *American Spectator* from October 1935 to September 1936. In his year at the *Spectator*, Angoff tried to recapture the tone of the 1920s *Mercury* with articles seemingly designed to shock, such as "Is the Audubon Society a Racket?" The *Spectator* folded in 1937. After holding a number of other editorial positions in the late 1930s, Angoff returned to the *Mercury* in 1943, the same year as his marriage to Sara Freedman; the couple had one daughter. As literary and managing editor under Spivack, Angoff remained at the *Mercury* and served as executive editor of Mercury Publications (including *Ellery Queen's Mystery Magazine*) until Spivack sold out in 1951. Never quite happy with the *Mercury*'s direction in these years, Angoff ventured out on his own literary career during the 1940s, publishing some books on classical music and a handbook on libel law, attempting playwriting, and beginning his fictional account of his life with a collection of short stories, *When I Was a Boy in Boston* (1947), and the first volume of the Polonsky saga with *Journey to the Dawn* (1951).

Originally projected as a trilogy but eventually comprising eleven volumes with a twelfth nearly complete at the time of Angoff's death, the Polonsky novels found a warm initial reception, twice receiving prizes from the Jewish Book Council. Later volumes, however, were neglected by reviewers. Filled with details drawn from Angoff's life (or embroidered from it) and with myriad characters occupying center stage, the saga often meanders and loses sight of its eponymous hero, and in later volumes there are inconsistencies in chronology. (In *Mid-Century* [1974], for example, David Polonsky appears to be ten years younger than he should be.) Nonetheless, there is a wealth of incident and a rich tapestry of American Jewish social life packed into the series. The early volumes are especially poignant in their account of the assimilation of David's family and their failures and heartbreaks against a background of labor unrest, economic depression, and changing social mores.

In 1954 Angoff entered a new career, as a college professor, joining the faculty of Fairleigh Dickinson University in New Jersey. Although lacking the conventional professorial credentials and often acerbically anti-academic in his attitudes, Angoff flourished in his new life, cofounding a quarterly with his colleague Clarence Decker (*Literary Review*) in 1957 and launching the Fairleigh Dickinson University Press in 1967. During his years at Fairleigh Dickinson, Angoff continued the Polonsky novels, wrote a controversial memoir of his days with Mencken in 1956 and other memoirs of the 1920s (*Tone of the Twenties* [1966]), edited several volumes of material from the writings of George Jean Nathan, lectured frequently at writers' conferences and other venues, and maintained an active life well after his retirement in 1977. He died in New York City, his longtime home.

• Angoff's personal papers are in the Boston University Library. Angoff's account of his first meeting with Mencken and his subsequent career on the *Mercury* is found in his memoir, *H. L. Mencken: A Portrait from Memory* (1956), which at the time of publication was severely criticized for its portrayal of Mencken as an anti-Semite and boor. A commemorative account of his life and work forms the introduction to a collection of his writings edited by his longtime publisher Thomas Yoseloff, *The Man from the Mercury: A Charles Angoff Memorial Reader* (1986). Angoff's contribution to the *Mercury* is treated critically in M. K. Singleton, *H. L. Mencken and the American Mercury Adventure* (1962), and more positively by Harriet Helms Wagniere in an essay in a Festschrift for Angoff, *The New Century and the Old*, ed. Alfred Rosa (1978). An obituary is in the *New York Times*, 4 May 1979.

MARTIN GREEN

ANN (fl. 1706–1718), queen of Pamunkey, may have ruled as late as 1723. The Pamunkey people of Virginia were part of the larger grouping that had once been known as Powhatan's confederacy. In the century after the arrival of the Europeans not only had the larger tribal polity declined but also the population had diminished and the land base had dwindled. The collapse of the confederacy had presented leadership challenges to the several tribes. One crisis that emerged was the death of tribal leaders in intertribal wars, struggles largely precipitated by their support of the English colonial governments. The best-known example of this, the death of Totopotomoy in 1656 in battle with the Rickohokans, brought his widow Cockacoeske to the position of queen of the Pamunkeys, a role she played for almost thirty years. Following in this tradition were two more Pamunkey queens, Betty and Ann, whose leadership was exercised early in the eighteenth century. By that time, moreover, their ascendance to leadership may also have been a function of declining population that left women of prominent families as the only choice to lead the tribe.

When Queen Ann became tribal leader about 1706, she immediately addressed the tribe's long-standing difficulties in dealing with the Virginians. She knew that survival for the Pamunkeys meant retention of land base, a goal all the more difficult in light of constant pressure from the colonials, who always wanted more land. Holding on to tribal territory was a challenge, since land was the only marketable commodity exchangeable for cash in times of economic crisis. Queen Ann insisted to the Virginia authorities that following a transaction, land surveyors could not show up unannounced to start surveying, nor would she allow them to survey more land than had actually been sold. In an effort to retain lands for the tribe and thereby put a stop to unauthorized sales, Queen Ann requested that the colony approve a plan whereby no more Pamunkey territory would be sold; tracts could be leased only. The queen also was confronted by that other longtime nemesis of native peoples, excessive sales of liquor to the Pamunkeys. Archival sources reflect her complaints to Virginia's authorities.

Another source of difficulty arose from the annual tribute the tribe was supposed to pay Virginia's government. What had seemed a minor amount in the more prosperous seventeenth century had become onerous. Queen Ann sought relief from this yearly payment, pleading her tribe's poverty and asking the Virginians to forgo it. Since the Virginians wished to keep some means of control over the Pamunkeys, despite the relatively insignificant tribal population, the colony's governor proposed that the tribute could be forgiven if the queen would send her son to be educated at the College of William and Mary. The Pamunkey leader responded by agreeing to enroll both her son and another Pamunkey youth at the college. Like her predecessors, Queen Ann sought to preserve the integrity of her people's heritage, culture, and land. Flexibility seemed the watchword of her efforts as she worked to fend off the never-ceasing demands for land, attempts to undermine her people with liquor sales, and almost total disregard of Pamunkey rights. The continued existence of a remnant of Pamunkey into the late twentieth century suggests that her struggle was not in vain.

• The limited information about Queen Ann may be found in Valerie S. Mathes, "A New Look at the Role of Women in Indian Society," *American Indian Quarterly* 2 (1975): 131–39; Martha W. McCartney, "Cockacoeske, Queen of Pamunkey, Diplomat and Suzeraine," in *Powhatan's Mantle: Indians in the Colonial Southeast*, ed. Peter Wood et al. (1989); Nono Minor, "The American Indian: Famous Indian Women in Early America," *Real West*, Mar. 1971, pp. 35, 78; Helen C.

Rountree, ed., *Powhatan Foreign Relations, 1500–1722* (1993); and Rountree, *Pocahontas's People: The Powhatan Indians of Virginia through Four Centuries* (1990).

JAMES H. O'DONNELL III

ANNEKE, Mathilde Franziska Giesler (3 Apr. 1817–25 Nov. 1884), suffragist, author, and educator, was born in Lerchenhausen, Westphalia, Germany, the daughter of Karl Giesler, a Catholic landlord and mine owner, and Elisabeth Hülswitt. She grew up comfortably and was well educated, more through learned company than tutors and schools. In fact, as a teacher in later years she would read "Fridjhoff's saga to her pupils and recite from memory the translation she had read when eleven years old," given to her by a prince (Heinzen, p. 3).

Mathilde Giesler was an avid reader; she also composed two prayer books of prose and verse, edited for several newspapers, and translated English novels under the name "Mathilde Franziska." At nineteen this "beautiful, blooming girl . . . nearly six feet tall," of combined "gentleness and determination," married Alfred von Tabouillot, a French wine merchant. The marriage lasted a year and a half before it was annulled. To support herself, in 1840 she published a collection of poems by Petrarch, Byron, Ferdinand Freiligrath, and others (including herself). This was followed two years later by a second collection, *Ladies Almanac*, and then her operatic play, *Oithono, or the Consecration of the Temple* in 1844.

Giesler's estrangement from her religion and class began with her divorce and fight for custody of her daughter and became complete as she developed her ideas on the rights of women. Influenced by her reading in 1846 of Theodor Gottlieb von Hippel's *About the Rights and Status of Women*, Giesler defended the poetess and free thinker Luise Aston in a pamphlet she titled *Woman in Conflict with Social Conditions* (1847). Her literary and political efforts brought her into contact with Karl Marx (in whose letters she is mentioned), Friedrich Engels, Gottfried Kinkel, and husband-to-be Fritz Anneke, who wrote to Freiligrath of the "young author who read poetry aloud with a rare dramatic effect differing greatly from the theatrical pathos then in vogue" (Heinzen, p. 8).

They married on 3 June 1847. Fritz Anneke, an idealist "equally ready with sword and pen," gave up a promising career in the Prussian army to found the Cologne Workers Association, join the Democratic party, and coedit the working-class *Neue Kölnische Zeitung*. When in June 1848 her husband was imprisoned for conspiracy to overthrow the government, Anneke, in addition to giving birth to their son, "united rare idealism with practical insight" by turning her parlor into a printing operation in order to take over publication. The government repressed the paper in September 1848, leading Anneke to publish her first *Frauenzeitung* in support of women's rights.

Upon her husband's release in May 1849, Anneke joined Fritz (now a lieutenant-colonel in the Palatinate People's Army) as his mounted orderly in Baden. The revolution failed, and the couple fled to France, Switzerland, and finally, in September, to the largely German Milwaukee, Wisconsin, where they settled. The next year, in addition to lecturing on the German Revolution, Anneke spoke on literature and women's rights. In March 1852 she began a suffragist paper, *Deutsche Frauenzeitung*, which was typeset by women compositors, including her daughter Fanny. Other printers, threatened by a woman's success, charged her as an "unauthorized interloper" and forced the paper's closing. In order to raise funds to establish her own press, Anneke lectured in several major U.S. cities on women's right to vote and work.

The tour's success not only enabled Anneke to move with her husband to Newark, New Jersey, purchase a press to resume her *Frauenzeitung*, and establish the equally radical *Newarkerzeitung*, but it prompted Susan B. Anthony to invite her to speak at the Broadway Tabernacle Woman's Rights Convention on 7 September 1853. Described by Wendell Phillips as "a noble woman who stood . . . in the battle-fields of Hungary" and "faced the cannon of Francis Joseph of Austria, for the rights of the people," Anneke addressed an unruly mob in German, translated by fellow suffragist, Ernestine Rose: "Our sisters in Germany have long desired freedom, but there the desire is repressed as well in man as in woman. . . . The only hope in our country for freedom of speech and action, is directed to this country for illustration and example" (quoted in Stanton, vol. 1, p. 570).

In 1858 smallpox took Anneke's oldest son and two daughters. Subsequently, the Annekes sold their home and business and returned to Milwaukee with two surviving children. Fritz went to Europe as a war correspondent in June 1859, and Anneke soon followed. They settled in Switzerland where they fought off poverty, because publishers failed to pay for their articles. When Fritz left in September 1861 to join the Union army, Anneke depended on European friends for moral and financial support. She returned to Milwaukee in February 1865 and, with Cecilie Kapp, established a girls' day and boarding school first called Maedchen-Erziehungs Anstalt von Cecilie Kapp, then later Milwaukee Töchter Institut. In addition to running the school and household, "Madam Anneke" taught mythology, German, literature, geography, geology, writing, and aesthetics. She also wrote articles and sold insurance to keep up with school expenses.

Anneke remained idealistic and active until her death, lecturing on German literature, working for the German theater (in the United States), writing suffrage articles, and fighting for humanitarian causes. In May 1869 she gave a speech at the National Association of American Equal Rights Association in New York, attacking religion, the Bible, nativism, and temperance, and she was afterward described by Elizabeth Cady Stanton as "a German lady of majestic presence and liberal culture." At an 1870 convention, where Anneke represented Wisconsin's support of a bill franchising women in Washington, D.C., her "presence, gestures, oratory, were simply magnificent." She became active in the newly founded Radical Society in 1874, and, because of her efforts the Freethinkers' Society took an active part in the suffrage movement. In 1876 she wrote a speech (accompanied by thousands of signatures and presented at Philadelphia's Independence Hall by Stanton), protesting against an anniversary celebration of the Declaration of Independence because half of the citizens of the United States were disenfranchised. When a scratch to her right hand in July 1876 developed into blood poisoning and its eventual disability, her daughter Hertha acted as her amanuensis so that she could continue her social work until her death. Anneke's feminist efforts were posthumously rewarded by inclusion in the *History of Woman Suffrage* and by placement on the honor roll of suffrage leaders in 1933 by the National League of Women Voters.

• The most detailed portrayal of Anneke is Henriette M. Heinzen's 1940 "Biographical Notes in Commemoration of Fritz Anneke and Mathilde Franziska Anneke," written in collaboration with Hertha Anneke Sanne (Anneke's daughter) and held at the Wisconsin Historical Society, Madison. The biography includes numerous translated letters passed between Anneke and her husband, suffragists, and literary persons in America and Germany. Elizabeth C. Stanton et al., eds., *History of Woman Suffrage* (6 vols., 1887), names her as one of the first women in newspapers and includes her translated speech at the 1853 New York women's rights convention. See also Lillian Krueger's "Madame Mathilda Franziska Anneke: An Early Wisconsin Journalist," *Wisconsin Magazine of History* 21, no. 2 (Dec. 1937): 160–67; Bruce Levine's *The Spirit of 1848: German Immigrants, Labor Conflict and the Coming of the Civil War* (1992); and Robert Henry Billigmeier's *Minorities in American Life: Americans from Germany: A Study in Cultural Diversity* (1974).

BARBARA L. CICCARELLI

ANNENBERG, Moses Louis (11 Feb. 1878–20 July 1942), publisher and race wire operator, called by contemporaries "Moe," was born in Kalwichen, East Prussia, the son of Tobias Annenberg, a storekeeper, and Sarah Greenberg, who were Orthodox Jews. In 1882 Tobias Annenberg moved to the United States, opening a store in "the Patch," a tough neighborhood and breeding ground for criminals in Chicago. He saved enough money to send for his wife and children in 1885.

Moe Annenberg had little formal education, picking up much of his knowledge from the streets in a city notorious for its brothels and gambling dens. In 1899 Annenberg was working as a bartender when he married twenty-year-old Sadie Cecelia Friedman, the daughter of a retail shoe salesman; they would have seven children, one of whom, Walter Hubert Annenberg, would become a powerful newspaper publisher, friend of Richard Nixon, and ambassador to the Court of St. James. The turning point in Annenberg's life came when he followed his brother Max into the brutal newspaper circulation business. William Randolph Hearst's *Evening American* was pushing its way into the city, and other newspapers fought back. At the heart of the battles were unscrupulous men who were not afraid to use their fists, set fire to rivals' papers, or dump them in the river. The deal newspapers made with circulation men was simple: "Sell 'em or eat 'em." By the time a truce was declared years later, at least twenty-seven newsdealers had been killed.

Moses advanced in the business, as did his brother Max, who later became head of circulation for the New York *Daily News*. He also looked for other opportunities. In 1907 he pawned $700 worth of his wife's jewelry and borrowed another $1,500 to establish a news agency in Milwaukee. The agency was successful, and he invested in liquor stores, dry cleaners, and bowling alleys and built the largest parking lot in Milwaukee.

In 1917 Annenberg became publisher of the *Wisconsin News*, which was owned by Hearst columnist Arthur Brisbane. Brisbane brought Annenberg together with Hearst, who placed Annenberg in charge of his half-dozen magazines, including *Cosmopolitan* and *Harper's Bazaar*, and the circulation of his nineteen newspapers. Hearst also made him publisher of the *New York Daily Mirror*, which Annenberg accepted with relish because it put him into competition with his brother Max at the *Daily News*. (The brothers, who were constantly trying to show up one another, had become enemies. On Max's fiftieth birthday, Moe sent him a funeral wreath.)

While looking out for Hearst's interests, Annenberg still looked for his own opportunities. In 1922 he bought the *Racing Form* for $400,000 from Frank Bruenell, a former sports editor of the *Chicago Tribune*, who had started the paper in 1894. Under Annenberg, the *Form* became not one but seven papers, coming out in New York, Chicago, Miami, Houston, Los Angeles, Seattle, and Toronto. The paper grew by Annenberg's relying on old tactics. Rivals were terrorized; the tires of their delivery trucks were slashed, and their plants were sabotaged and firebombed.

The *Form* also led Annenberg into a related business that made him even more vulnerable to the law than he had been in the past. This was the General News Bureau, a Chicago operation that used telephone lines to relay horse-racing information primarily to bookies. The "race wire," as it was known, was the brainstorm of John Payne, a former telegraph operator. Payne placed a man at a racetrack who used a mirror to flash results to a telegrapher in a nearby building. The telegrapher relayed the information instantaneously to bookies. Payne was pushed out of the business by a Chicago hoodlum. Annenberg bought the majority interest in the company. His partners were Chicago gamblers and gangsters. They set about bribing police and politicians to keep the business going. Through threats, intimidation, and the smashing of rivals, the race wire went not just nationwide but spread across Canada, Mexico, and Cuba. In the underworld, Annenberg and his wire became known as "the Trust."

Annenberg continued buying newspapers, including the *Miami Tribune* (1934) and the *Philadelphia Inquirer* (1936). The way he chose to run the *Inquirer* was as unwise as it was effective. Annenberg made himself a Republican kingmaker, using the newspaper to promote his candidates, demolish rivals, and attack the New Deal in Washington. He had his men elected to local and state offices, including governor, but he made enemies of prominent Democrats, including President Franklin D. Roosevelt.

The federal government first tried to retaliate through the race wire. Since customers were bookies, the government asked AT&T to cut off service. AT&T refused. After all, the wire was its fifth largest customer. Then the government began building an income tax evasion case against Annenberg. In 1939 the U.S. attorney general presented his findings to a grand jury. Annenberg tried to negotiate his way out of the charges but failed; he even severed ties with the race wire, but that had no effect either. In April 1940 he went on trial; the presiding judge was James H. Wilkerson, who had sentenced Al Capone to prison in a similar income tax trial. Annenberg was given a four-year sentence and fined $9.5 million in penalties and interest. He had achieved the distinction of becoming the biggest tax cheat convicted in the United States.

Annenberg served his time at the federal penitentiary at Lewisburg, Pennsylvania. He had suffered migraines during the trial, and in prison his health deteriorated. He was paroled on 11 June 1942. Testing at the Mayo Clinic in Rochester, Minnesota, revealed he had a brain tumor. He was taken to St. Mary's Hospital in Rochester, where he died.

• For additional information on Annenberg in the context of newspaper publishing, see Edwin Emery, *The Press and America* (1954); Emile Gauvreau, *My Last Million Readers* (1941); Paul G. Jeans, *Tropical Disturbance: The Story of the Making of the Miami Tribune* (1937); Thomas M. Nickel, *Click: Innovation or Imitation* (1976); Harold L. Ickes, *America's House of Lords* (1939); George Seldes, *Lords of the Press* (1938); Nixon Smiley, *Knights of the Fourth Estate* (1974); and J. David Stern, *Memoirs of a Maverick Publisher* (1962). For information on Annenberg in the context of organized crime, see Wayne Andrews, *Battle for Chicago* (1946); Gordon L. Hosteter and Thomas Quinn Beesley, *It's a Racket* (1929); Elmer L. Irey, *The Tax Dodgers* (1948); Hank Messick, *Secret File* (1969); George Murray, *The Madhouse on Madison Street* (1965); and Virgil W. Peterson, *Barbarians in Our Midst* (1952). Annenberg is featured in Oliner Carlson, *Brisbane: A Candid Biography* (1937); John Cooney, *The Annenbergs: The Salvaging of a Tainted Dynasty* (1982); and the unpublished diaries of Henry Morganthau, Jr., books 94, 149, 154, 165, 169, 170, 177, 181, and 189, Franklin D. Roosevelt Library, Hyde Park, N.Y.

JOHN COONEY

ANSHUTZ, Thomas Pollock (5 Oct. 1851–16 June 1912), artist and art teacher, was born in Newport, Kentucky, the son of Jacob Anshutz and Jane Abigail Pollock. Very little information survives about his parents or his youth, though he seems to have received an early education in Newport. In 1871 Anshutz moved to Brooklyn, New York, to study art. There he lived with an uncle who had been favorably impressed by the young man's drawings of boats on the Ohio River. Enrolling in 1873 at the prestigious National Academy of Design in New York City, Anshutz took cast- and life-drawing classes, principally with Lemuel Everett Wilmarth.

After two years of study Anshutz moved to Philadelphia and enrolled in the Philadelphia Sketch Club's life class, taught by Thomas Eakins. In the fall of 1876 Anshutz took classes in life drawing, anatomy, and painting at the newly reopened Pennsylvania Academy of the Fine Arts in Philadelphia. His classes at the PAFA were taught by Christian Schussele, William W. Keen, and Eakins.

In 1878 and 1879 Anshutz acted as Eakins's assistant, helping to teach anatomy classes. Strongly impressed by Eakins's art and teaching, Anshutz began to emulate his supervisor's approach to painting, specifically Eakins's emphases on anatomy, on unidealized, "factual" representations of nature, and on capturing the essential sculptural mass of the objects depicted.

At this time Anshutz painted several scenes based on summer trips to Wheeling, West Virginia, his mother's hometown. Agricultural images like *A Farmer and His Son at Harvesting* (1879, Berry Hill Gallery) and *The Cabbage Patch* (1879, Metropolitan Museum of Art) demonstrate Anshutz's emulation of both Eakins and Winslow Homer. Inherently nostalgic though the themes are, these pictures also present an appearance of unvarnished naturalism. This kind of unidealized realism is also present in the artist's best-known image, *The Ironworkers' Noontime* (1880, Fine Arts Museums of San Francisco). Begun on one of his trips to Wheeling, this painting shows a group of ironworkers on their midday break and offers a unique record of late nineteenth-century American industrial life. Although other postbellum factory scenes were produced, such as John Ferguson Weir's *Forging the Shaft* (1877, Metropolitan Museum of Art), they are anomalous and—unlike *The Ironworkers' Noontime*—portray men actually working. Focusing on the men as individuals, Anshutz's depiction rejects the customary mythologization of his subject. He consciously ignored popular stereotypes of ironworkers, undercutting their inherent melodrama. His almost photographic recording of this mundane activity also serves to remove the scene from the realm of the romantic or mythical. The total image pays homage to Eakins and his artistic vision.

In 1881 Anshutz became a full-time instructor at the Pennsylvania Academy of the Fine Arts. He taught cast- and life-drawing classes. Over the next ten years he spent far more time teaching than painting. In the summer of 1884 Anshutz assisted Eakins and Eadweard Muybridge in a series of photographic motion studies. Anshutz, like Eakins, continued to take photographs until the end of his life, employing many of them as studies for paintings. But Anshutz exhibited nothing publicly between 1886 and 1892. By 1885 he and other junior academy faculty members had come to resent Eakins, the school's director, for what they perceived as his dogmatic approach to teaching and an unwillingness to vary course curriculum. They also believed that Eakins had committed serious ethical transgressions, which, however, have never been proven. Anshutz took a leading role in Eakins's ouster from the academy in 1886. Yet he continued many of his former teacher's approaches to instruction. While rejecting Eakins's "scientific" method, with its emphasis on dissection, photographic motion studies, and perspective, Anshutz continued to propagate Eakins's emphasis on the empirical study of nature. Believing that art schools were in the business of teaching not art, but rather fundamental skills and knowledge, he encouraged his students to develop their own artistic visions. In class assignments and numerous after-class discussions, the tall, lanky, and somewhat shy Anshutz emphasized the necessity for artistic change, experimentation, and the questioning of accepted conventions. During this period Anshutz produced several Dutch-inspired interior genre scenes, including *In a Garret* (1891, Pennsylvania Academy of the Fine Arts), a rare example of an American treatment of death and a woman.

In 1892 Anshutz married Effie Shriver Russell; they had one child. Immediately after the wedding, Anshutz and his wife left for Paris, where he enrolled in the well-known art school, the Académie Julian, taking classes taught by Lucien Doucet and William Adolphe Bouguereau. After a decade of teaching, Anshutz had decided to concentrate exclusively on his painting and followed in the footsteps of the majority of other celebrated late nineteenth-century American painters, who had studied in Europe. However, Anshutz, who quickly grew bored with the Paris institution's many drawing classes, left the school after only six months. During the spring he traveled through Europe, visiting various museums and, in Paris, viewing the art of the French impressionists and postimpressionists. Impressionist painting inspired him to produce a series of bright plein-air watercolors of Paris street scenes.

After his return to Philadelphia in the late spring of 1893, Anshutz once more took up his teaching position at the PAFA. He spent that summer in Holly Beach, New Jersey, where he continued painting plein-air watercolors. The following summer he produced a group of vibrant watercolors and pastels of boys along the New Jersey coast, including *Two Boys by a Boat* (c. 1894, Carnegie Museum of Art). Among his most elegant and luminous images, they include no extraneous detail, describing only the general masses of the bodies and revealing the painter's continuing interest in an artistic distillation of nature. From 1895 through 1900 Anshutz painted many plein-air landscapes of New Jersey and Pennsylvania scenes, and in the summer of 1897 he produced a group of oil paintings of sailing ships based on a trip down the Delaware River. For example, *The Lumber Boat* (c. 1897, private collection), rendered in a new impressionist-inspired style, effectively conveys the atmospheric effects of a rainy, breezy day.

Between 1893 and 1910 Anshutz created more than one hundred charcoal drawings, based on his work as a teacher of cast-drawing classes. These are some of the most accomplished American cast drawings of the period. Anshutz was able to rethink the tradition-bound genre, and he succeeded in infusing into the drawings a new sense of drama and creativity. In the best of these works, through use of strong chiaroscuro and distillation of form, the casts appear animated and coursing with life.

During this same period, from 1896 to 1910, Anshutz painted several postimpressionist-inspired watercolors, gouaches, and oils. These were a product of his earlier exposure to modern art in Paris and also a response to the bright impressionist paintings of Hugh Breckenridge. In 1899 Breckenridge and Anshutz founded a summer art school in the rural southeastern Pennsylvania community of Darby. The art school was later moved to Fort Washington, Pennsylvania. Many of Anshutz's undated landscape sketches, which range from delicate pointillist-inspired watercolors to brilliantly colored, highly abstracted fauvelike oils, derive from walking trips around Fort Washington. Some of these sketches are among the most daring produced in Philadelphia before the Armory Show of 1913. Of all of Anshutz's landscapes, only two combine bright non-naturalistic color and a high level of abstraction. Both are titled simply *Landscape*. One of these works (c. 1911–1912, Pennsylvania Academy of the Fine Arts) is a Nabis-inspired watercolor; the other (c. 1911–1912, private collection) is reminiscent of Van Gogh and Maurice Vlaminck.

The most ambitious of Anshutz's modernist pictures is his oil painting *Steamboat on the Ohio* (c. 1896–1907, Carnegie Institute). Based on his photographs of Wheeling, it depicts a group of men and boys on the shore of the Ohio River watching a majestic white steamboat pass an orange-red factory on the far shore. Probably one of the earliest Nabis-inspired images painted in America, the picture strangely conflates conservative Gauguin and Mark Twain. It offered the viewer the vicarious pleasure of escaping into a nostalgic world. Despite its modern style, *Steamboat on the Ohio* is essentially an adaptation of popular artistic conventions that juxtaposed the rural and the industrial, the past and the present. Yet Anshutz made it his own. By adopting a modern artistic style, he was able to reinvigorate an older iconographic tradition.

Anshutz's modernist paintings undercut traditional notions about the development of early American modernism concerning the separation between realist and modernist, conservative and avant-garde. This is not, however, to argue that Anshutz was a major modernist: he painted only a small number of modernist works, and they were never exhibited publicly. Moreover, Anshutz was an artist clearly rooted in the nineteenth century, of the generation and training of Eakins and Homer. It was this artistic and cultural milieu that forged his outlook and made his forays into modern painting unusual.

Beginning in 1902 Anshutz again exhibited paintings on a regular basis, a sign of the artist's newly won confidence and ambition and of his growing enthusiasm for portraiture. He regarded that genre as a demanding and rewarding artistic challenge and said that it allowed him to explore the temperament and intellect of his sitters. His finest portraits, such as *Portrait of Mrs. Anshutz* (1893, Pennsylvania Academy of the Fine Arts), *Portrait of Margaret Perot* (c. 1908, Hirshhorn Museum and Sculpture Garden), *Portrait of Emily Fairchild Pollock* (c. 1900, private collection), *A Rose* (1908, Metropolitan Museum of Art), and *Self Portrait* (c. 1909, National Academy of Design), endow their subjects with dignity and strength of character. The artist's portrait style brings together the dry naturalism of Eakins with the painterly brushwork of Robert Henri and William Merritt Chase. Late in his life, Anshutz also produced some very fine brightly colored pastel portraits based on the pastels of the French artist Albert Besnard.

Portraiture provided Anshutz his first widespread recognition as a painter. In 1909 he won the Pennsylvania Academy's Walter Lippincott Prize for his figure study *The Tanagra* (1909, Pennsylvania Academy of the Fine Arts). Some of his other awards include a silver medal at the Saint Louis annual, a gold medal from the Pennsylvania Academy in 1909, and a gold medal at the Buenos Aires International Exposition in 1911. As his artistic reputation increased, so did his stature in art organizations. In 1909 he became director of the Pennsylvania Academy and a year later president of the Philadelphia Sketch Club. Also in 1910 he was made a member of the National Academy of Design.

At the time Anshutz finally began to receive national and international recognition he was becoming increasingly ill. Already suffering the effects of terminal heart disease by late 1909, he had to quit teaching at the PAFA by the fall of 1910. In the summer of 1911 he visited London, Paris, and Bad Nauheim, Germany, where for six weeks he was hospitalized for curative treatment. He returned in the fall to Philadelphia, where he died.

Anshutz left a greater legacy as a teacher than as an artist. He rarely achieved a truly distinctive artistic vision and produced only a few paintings that are currently well known, including *The Ironworkers' Noontime* and *The Girl in White* (1908, Hirshhorn Museum and Sculpture Garden). Yet as a teacher he was as influential as Benjamin West and Robert Henri. With important artists among his students such as Henri, Breckenridge, John Sloan, William Glackens, George Luks, Charles Demuth, Arthur B. Carles, and John Marin, Anshutz acted both as a nexus between Eakins and the group of New York realist painters known as the Eight of 1908 and as a catalyst for the beginnings of early American modernism in Philadelphia. His former students have written that they respected his insight, openness, and honesty.

• Anshutz's papers are in the Pennsylvania Academy of the Fine Arts and the Archives of American Art. The most complete assessment of his work is Randall C. Griffin, *Thomas Anshutz: Artist and Teacher* (1994). See also Griffin, "Thomas Anshutz: A Contextual Study of His Art and Teaching" (Ph.D. diss., Univ. of Delaware, 1994). Other important sources are Sandra Lee Denney, "Thomas Anshutz: His Life, Art, and Teachings" (master's thesis, Univ. of Delaware, 1969), and Ruth Bowman, "Thomas Pollock Anshutz: 1851–1912" (master's thesis, New York Univ., 1971). See also Francis J. Ziegler, "An Unassuming Painter—Thomas P. Anshutz," *Brush and Pencil* 4 (Sept. 1899): 277–84. For a discussion of *The Ironworkers' Noontime*, see Griffin, "Thomas Anshutz's *The Ironworkers' Noontime*: Remythologizing the Industrial Worker," *Smithsonian Studies in American Art* (Summer–Fall 1990): 128–43.

RANDALL C. GRIFFIN

ANSLINGER, Harry Jacob (20 May 1892–14 Nov. 1975), U.S. commissioner of narcotics, was born in Altoona, Pennsylvania, the son of Robert J. Anslinger, a barber, and Christiana Fladtt. After attending Altoona Business College and a two-year program at Pennsylvania State University, Anslinger worked as a silent-movie pianist, railroad policeman, and state police administrator before serving as an ordnance inspector and earning a commission in the Ordnance Reserve during World War I. In 1918 he joined the U.S. Diplomatic Corps, serving in Germany and Holland (where he acted as liaison with the deposed kaiser's staff) until 1923, when he was posted as consul to La Guaira, Venezuela, and, in 1926, to Nassau. In 1923 he married Martha Denniston, a relative of the Mellon banking family. Anslinger adopted her son from a previous marriage; they had no children of their own.

World War I and the succeeding new era substantially changed the federal government's law-enforcement responsibilities concerning use of alcoholic beverages and illicit drugs. Enforcement of the Volstead Act, implementing the Eighteenth Amendment's ban on liquor, and the earlier Harrison Narcotics Act, banning drugs, both being tax measures, were assigned to a new Prohibition Bureau in the Treasury Department, which undertook reckless and aggressive campaigns against both liquor drinkers and drug users. Consul Anslinger soon came to the notice of senior Treasury officials as a result of his success in persuading British authorities to cooperate in curbing the flow of bootleg liquor through the Bahamas. In mid-1926 these officials borrowed Anslinger from the diplomatic service to arrange similar cooperation in other problem spots. By 1930 he won promotion to assistant commissioner in the Prohibition Bureau, and when enforcement of the Harrison Act was shifted to the new Bureau of Narcotics, President Herbert Hoover named him to head it as commissioner of narcotics. Also in 1930 Anslinger earned a law degree from Washington College of Law.

Under the original Harrison Act, only opiates and cocaine were regulated by an identifying tax. These narcotics, although relatively harmless compared to alcohol and tobacco, had become a subject of public concern only after the turn of the century. In World War I propaganda they were demonized as poison used by German agents to make "heroin maniacs" of schoolchildren, and during the 1920s they were blamed for armies of dangerous "dope fiends" roaming the streets. By the time Commissioner Anslinger took office, the act had been interpreted to prohibit doctors and public health authorities from ministering to "addicts," who were now supplied by underworld peddlers, mostly Chinese tongs and the Mafia.

Anslinger fully exploited this situation. Estimates of the nearly invisible addict population had ranged from millions to tens of thousands, but Anslinger stabilized the figure in the 60,000 range, an evil population held at bay by his small force of agents (never more than 300, with annual budgets never exceeding $6 million). He discouraged research relating to drug use and dependency on the grounds that such study would encourage "experimentation." The bureau instead pressed for punitive laws against addicts and traffickers and encouraged state lawmakers to follow suit. In 1932 state legislatures began to adopt a Uniform State Narcotic Drug Act providing for stiff criminal penalties. In 1937 Congress passed the Marijuana Tax Act, adding this relatively harmless weed to the prohibition pattern.

In 1952, responding to recently publicized charges that judges were "coddling" drug offenders, Congress passed the Boggs Act, with extreme mandatory minimum sentences, and many states followed. In 1956 the Narcotic Control Act further increased penalties, by adding mandatory life sentences and, in some instances, the death penalty. These laws effected expansion of Anslinger's responsibility and authority.

Anslinger's influence was not confined to the American scene. When he became commissioner in 1930, the patterns of international control had also been set, with the United States urging stringent repression and, in contrast, most of the rest of the world indifferent or resistant to such policies. The basic Hague Opium Convention of 1912 would never have been ratified by more than a few nations had the United States not insisted on its inclusion in the World War I peace treaties, which created the League of Nations in 1921. Though the United States never joined the league, U.S. representatives nonetheless retained a voice in drug matters. At the outbreak of World War II Anslinger invited the entire League of Nations drug-enforcement bureaucracy to branch offices in Washington, where they survived as most other league agencies disappeared. He also accused the Japanese of using opium to undermine the targets of their conquests, and he forced U.S. allies to adopt repressive measures to protect American occupation troops from contamination by drug-using Asian cultures. Anslinger dominated international deliberations, leading U.S. delegations to league and United Nations drug-control agencies even after his resignation as U.S. commissioner. He was the leading proponent of the Single Convention on Narcotic Drugs, which in 1961 incorporated much of the U.S. repressive policy in an international instrument. Though widely ratified, many adherents ignored its requirements, and lacking enforcement sanctions, it had small effect.

Anslinger's long reign as commissioner ended in 1962, when John F. Kennedy and Robert Francis Kennedy elevated drug issues to Oval Office importance, seeking to exploit public concern. After his retirement Anslinger remained active as U.S. delegate to the United Nations and other international agencies, and he continued to influence U.S. drug policies as a chief proponent of severe repressive measures. Anslinger's sincerity as a relentless drug-prohibition advocate and enforcer has never been questioned, but his skillful bureaucratic empire building inspired much of the "war" on drugs that has gripped the nation and nurtured the gigantic U.S. drug-war establishment ever since. He died in Holidaysburg, Pennsylvania.

• Anslinger's papers are in the Pattee Library, Pennsylvania State University. His writings include *The Traffic in Narcotics* (1953) and, with Will Oursler, *The Murderers: The Story of the Narcotics Gangs* (1961). On his career at the bureau, see John C. McWilliams, *The Protectors: Harry J. Anslinger and the Federal Bureau of Narcotics* (1990); and Edward Jay Epstein, *Agency of Fear: Opiates and Political Power in America* (1977). The best general work is Rufus King, *The Drug Hang-Up: America's Fifty-Year Folly*, 2d ed. (1974). See also Edward M. Brecher et al., *Licit and Illicit Drugs: The Consumers Union Report* (1972); Alfred R. Lindesmith, *The Addict and the Law* (1965); and David F. Musto, *The American Disease: Origins of Narcotics Control* (1973).

RUFUS KING

ANSLOW, Gladys Amelia (22 May 1892–31 Mar. 1969), physicist, educator, and spectroscopist, was born in Springfield, Massachusetts, the daughter of John Anslow, a textile colorist, lay preacher, and insurance agent, and Ella Iola Leonard, an art and music teacher. In 1909 she entered Smith College in nearby Northampton. Her first science course there was Frank Waterman's sophomore physics, which she found thrilling. In her junior year she took laboratory physics, using Waterman's text, and in her senior year she took courses in mechanics, electricity, and magnetism from Waterman.

Anslow received an A.B. in 1914 from Smith and worked there as a demonstrator while she continued to study physics, including a course in spectroscopy from Janet Howell of Mount Wilson Observatory. Using a Rowland grating spectrograph recently purchased by Smith, Anslow obtained emission spectra of radium. She reported these results in her thesis, "Spectroscopic Evidence for the Electron Theory of Matter," and in a research paper (Howell and Anslow, *Proceedings of the National Academy of Science* 3 [1917]: 409–12). Anslow received an A.M. in 1917 and was promoted to instructor.

Encouraged by chemist Mary Louise Foster, one of her thesis readers, Anslow took graduate courses during the summer of 1921 at the University of Chicago. She was also encouraged by Alan Waterman, son of Frank Waterman, who had become a member of the

Yale physics faculty in 1919 and was influential in Anslow's decision to enter a doctoral program there in 1922. Smith College supported this graduate work by awarding her a fellowship for her studies at Yale. After Anslow received a Ph.D. in physics from Yale in 1924, she returned to Smith to become assistant professor of physics.

Sharing a home with her father and three sisters in Northampton, Anslow remained free of household duties throughout her professional life. She thus was able to establish herself as an independent person supported by the strong personalities of her youth, including her family and Frank Waterman. Meanwhile, she continued to collaborate with her mentor Mary Louise Foster, and she maintained contacts made at Yale with Alan Waterman and Ernest Lawrence (Nobel laureate 1939). She became associate professor at Smith in 1930.

Foster and Anslow began research on the chemistry and absorption spectra of amino acids. Specialized optical equipment was borrowed from the National Bureau of Standards (NBS) via Fred Mohler, physicist at NBS and brother of Nora Mohler, one of Anslow's graduate students who taught at Smith. Anslow and Foster also collaborated on several publications in the *Journal of Biological Chemistry* and the *Physical Review*.

After Foster's 1933 retirement, Anslow returned to high-energy physics. Lawrence had moved from Yale to the University of California at Berkeley, where his laboratory held unique opportunities for extending her experiments, and he invited her to join him there as a research fellow. As the first woman to work with his eight-million-volt cyclotron, she explored ionization resulting from the newly discovered neutrons and collaborated with Paul Aebersold in neutron bombardment for cancer therapy. While at Berkeley, Anslow noted the advantages of focused group research, and she was impressed by Lawrence's success in obtaining research funding.

Meanwhile, Anslow continued to advance professionally. In 1936 she became professor and, in 1948, Gates Professor at Smith. She was elected a fellow of the American Academy of Arts and Sciences, the American Association for the Advancement of Science, and the American Physical Society. The director of graduate study at Smith from 1941 to 1959, she supervised the research of about twenty graduate students. Anslow, who had been elected to the scientific research society Sigma Xi at Yale, was also instrumental in beginning a chapter at Smith in 1935; it was the first Sigma Xi chapter ever to be installed at a woman's college, and she served as the first chapter president.

Anslow imported the Berkeley model of group research to Smith, creating a research team there with Douglas Ewing, who had experience with a cyclotron at Rochester; Nora Mohler, who had similar experience at Cambridge, England; and James Koehler, who had looked for mesotrons in cosmic rays at Cal Tech. A Van de Graaff generator was built and demonstrated at the American Physical Society meeting in Northampton on 11 October 1941. However, when the United States entered World War II just a few weeks later, plans changed, and Ewing, Koehler, and Mohler joined MIT laboratories to develop warfare devices.

New combat technologies were introduced in World War II, and modifications of equipment under field conditions were often needed. Alan Waterman, who had left Yale in 1942 to join the Office of Scientific Research and Development, saw urgent needs for providing reliable and timely technical field assistance. In order to meet these needs, he appointed Anslow as chief of the Communications and Information Section to make information available to specialists internationally. For this service, Anslow was one of two women awarded the Presidential Certificate of Merit by Harry Truman.

When the dislocations of war thwarted Anslow's 1930s plan for a Smith College high-energy research center, she turned her attention to a new project. She knew from her work with Foster that absorption spectra produced important chemical information. With this knowledge in mind, Anslow seized an opportunity to form a pioneer research program, contracting with the Office of Naval Research—thus obtaining Smith's first research grant—for a prototype infrared recording spectrometer designed to utilize wartime technology for automated data collection. The building-block pattern of the instrument permitted Anslow to modify it, greatly increasing its usefulness.

A five-room laboratory was created in 1951 for research by Anslow and crystallographer Dorothy Wrinch. Wrinch came to Smith College in 1943 and collaborated with Anslow for over twenty years on spectral explorations of amino-acid protein subunits, polymers of amino acids, and hemoglobin and insulin. Although Alan Waterman, who in 1951 became the first director of the National Science Foundation, may have been reluctant to support his father's department, after Frank Waterman's 1958 death, Anslow received three NSF grants that funded her research until her death.

Anslow was named the 1950 Woman in Science by Sigma Delta Epsilon. She retired from teaching in 1960 but continued active experimental research. She died in Brookline, Massachusetts.

• Photographs, news clippings, and copies of Anslow's publications are in the Smith College Archives. A biography with a list of her publications is in Louise S. Grinstein et al., *Women in Chemistry and Physics: A Biobibliographic Sourcebook* (1993). An obituary is in the *Daily Hampshire Gazette*, 1 Apr. 1969.

GEORGE FLECK

ANSON, Cap (17 Apr. 1852–14 Apr. 1922), professional baseball player and manager, was born Adrian Constantine Anson in Marshalltown, Iowa, the son of Henry Anson, a land developer, town founder, and mayor, and Jeannette Rice. By his young adult years, Anson was tall and well built at 6′ and 227 pounds. He often was referred to as "the Swede" because of his square shoulders and wavy blonde hair, but, in fact, his parents were of English-Irish extraction. Anson was taught to play baseball and invited to join his father and older brother who formed the nucleus of the Marshalltown team, an amateur club of great repute. While in his teens, he attracted attention as an outstanding hitter and all-around athlete. Local residents dubbed him the "Marshalltown Infant."

Anson began college at the University of Iowa, but he transferred to Notre Dame in 1869. While attending classes at South Bend, he organized the first varsity baseball team and played second and third base. However, he left college to sign his first professional contract as a catcher with the Forest City club of Rockford, Illinois, then managed by 21-year-old Albert Goodwill Spalding. Slow afoot, and uncomfortable behind the plate, Anson was moved to third base midway through the season.

When the financially strapped Forest City club was disbanded in 1872, Anson signed with the Philadelphia Athletics of the National Association of Professional Baseball Players. In Philadelphia he established himself as a star of the emerging professional game and as an eagle-eyed hitter who fashioned his own bats out of yellow poplar. Each year he would have the wood cut in the shape of a bat and would hang the pieces in the chimney of his home to dry. After a suitable time, he would drill a hole at the end, weight the bat, replug the hole with cork, and apply a coat of paint. Until the National League implemented and standardized rules governing playing equipment in the mid-1880s, the "Anson Special" was regarded as baseball's most potent bat.

The National Association ceased operation in 1875, and in 1876 Anson accepted an invitation from Spalding to play for the Chicago White Stockings of the newly christened National League. So began a mostly fruitful, 22-year association between Anson and the White Stockings, a team he elevated to legendary status. He batted a robust .356 and helped Chicago to its first pennant in the inaugural season. During the offseason he married Virginia Fiegel of Philadelphia, with whom he had seven children. His wife persuaded him to give up alcoholic spirits, starchy foods, and other intemperate habits. A roughhousing, drinking man before marriage, he became a staunch temperance advocate and an early proponent of rigorous physical conditioning.

Anson took over as manager of Chicago on 1 May, 1879, and immediately the sagging fortunes of the franchise began to improve. The next year, his White Stockings won the pennant on the strength of an awesome 67–17 showing. Anson is generally credited with originating spring training after taking his team to Hot Springs, Arkansas, in 1886 to "boil out" the players' bad habits and excess fat accumulated over the winter.

These were truly the glory days of early Chicago baseball when Anson guided the team to league championships in 1880, 1881, 1882, 1885, and 1886, with a supporting cast that included Mike J. "King" Kelly, Jimmy Ryan, John G. Clarkson, and Silver Flint. "Cap" (or "Captain" as he was called by his players) earned a reputation as a firebrand who never backed down from speaking his mind to an umpire or a player who challenged his authority.

As a first baseman, Anson's range was limited, and his fielding skills were only adequate. But certain baseball historians credit him, rather than Charles A. Comiskey, with being the first player to position himself off the bag as opposed to maintaining a rigid stance directly on top of the base. Anson was conservative in his thinking and a baseball purist. This much was evident in 1886, a watershed year for him; that season saw his club pitted against Comiskey's upstart St. Louis Browns of the American Association in a postseason championship series.

The series was important for two reasons. St. Louis was representative of the "inside game," which was just coming into vogue. Comiskey's willingness to employ new tactics like the sacrifice bunt, the hit and run, and perfectly coordinated play between outfielders and infielders spelled defeat for the White Stockings in a six-game series. The publicity attending the 1886 showdown further solidified baseball's role in the new American culture at a time when Anson's star began its long, slow descent.

In 1892 James A. Hart succeeded Spalding as president of the Chicago club. Anson fumed at the repeated intrusions of the meddlesome Hart, who, according to the Chicago *Tribune*, undermined his authority by attempting to stir up dissension among the players. The White Stockings slipped to seventh place in 1892. The press began calling Anson "Pop" and suggested that the time had come for him to retire as a player. Anson answered his detractors with four straight .300-plus seasons. On 18 July 1897 he had his 3,000th career hit, thus becoming the first professional player to accomplish the feat. The same year he inveigled Chicago *Inter-Ocean* columnist Hughie Fullerton to run the following item: "Capt. A. C. Anson desires me to announce in black type at the head of this column that the Chicago club is composed of a bunch of drunkards and loafers who are throwing him down."

Hart finally had enough. On 1 February 1898 Anson was released from his duties as player-manager after twenty-two years, 2,276 games as a player, batting titles in 1881 and 1888, and a cumulative average of .329. While he managed the White Stockings (now called "Orphans," and after 1902 "Colts," then finally "Cubs"), his teams won 1,283 games and lost 932.

Anson was a proud, exceedingly vain man who bristled at Hart's insistence that he was in arrears to the club for the trifling sum of $200; later, he refused Spalding's offer to organize a nationwide benefit aimed at raising $50,000 for his needs. If he required help, Anson stormed, he would seek it from the county welfare office. On that sad note Anson parted ways with Spalding and moved to New York where he accepted Andrew Freedman's offer to manage the Giants in 1898. After just twenty-two games, however, a disgusted Anson walked off the job, citing irreconcilable differences.

During the last two decades of his life Anson desperately tried to hang on to his fleeting fame. In 1900 his name was used by promoters of a second professional league that collapsed for lack of revenue. Four years later he organized a bowling team that won the American Bowling Congress championship. That same year he parlayed a lifelong interest in politics by winning election as city clerk under the Democratic administration. He served one undistinguished term before turning to the vaudeville stage. "Cap Anson and Daughters" toured the vaudeville circuit for several years, appearing before bemused audiences who came to see the old man reprise his role as one of baseball's premier sluggers. He would invite members of the audience to pitch him papier-mâché balls, which he would swat into the crowd. In his declining years, he staged billiard tournaments at his Madison Street parlor; he then was invited into any number of frivolous money-making schemes, including a toboggan slide, an ice skating rink, and a ginger beer distributorship.

The day before he was stricken with a fatal glandular disorder, the ebullient Anson ran into Alexander Spink, publisher of the *Sporting News* and one of the backers of the ill-fated 1900 league that Anson had agreed to front. When Spink said that he would turn seventy within a few months, Anson replied in characteristic fashion: "I will be seventy this April, and I am good for another twenty years." Not so. He died in Chicago a short time later.

Comiskey and other old-timers considered Anson to be the greatest player of his era. Arguably, he was professional baseball's first great "star." Comiskey eulogized him as "the greatest batter that ever walked up to hit at a baseball thrown from a pitcher." Anson was elected to baseball's Hall of Fame in 1939.

• The Baseball Hall of Fame at Cooperstown, N.Y., has a newspaper file of Anson clippings, magazine articles, and fact sheets. There is no full-scale biography of Anson, but a volume of his reminiscences, *A Ballplayer's Career*, was published in 1900. Among noteworthy anthologies containing biographical sketches are *Baseball's Greatest Managers*, by Edwin Pope (1960); Ira L. Smith's *Baseball's Famous First Basemen* (1956); and *Great Baseball Managers*, by Charles B. Cleveland (1950). Former Hall of Fame historian Lee Allen and coauthor Thomas Meany profiled Anson in *Kings of the Diamond* (1965). For his career statistics, see Macmillan's *Baseball Encyclopedia*, 9th ed. (1993), and John Thorn and Peter Palmer, eds., *Total Baseball*, 3d ed. (1993), the reference consulted for this biography. Magazine articles include "Interview with an Old Timer," *Baseball Magazine*, June 1918; "Cap Anson, One Baseball Idol Who Never Fell," *Literary Digest*, 17 Mar. 1928; "Cap Anson Passes On," by William A. Phelon, *Baseball Magazine*, June 1922; and former National League President John K. Tener's observations in *Baseball Magazine*, "The Greatest Batter of All Time," March 1917. Also valuable are obituaries appearing in Chicago newspapers—the *Daily News*, the *Herald and Examiner*, and the *Tribune*, all 15 Apr. 1922.

RICHARD C. LINDBERG

ANTHEIL, George (8 July 1900–12 Feb. 1959), composer and writer, was born Georg Johann Carl Antheil in Trenton, New Jersey, the son of Henry William Antheil, a merchant, and Wilhelmina Huse. Antheil's parents were German immigrants who had done well enough to be able to afford him an economically secure childhood in Trenton. His musical training included private study in piano with Constantin von Sternberg in Philadelphia and from 1919 to 1921 with Ernest Bloch in New York. He was also trained in composition.

Antheil decided to pursue a career as a concert pianist and embarked on a European tour in 1922. His performances revealed his ability to appeal to the sensibilities of audiences. He often concluded his recitals of works from the standard classical repertory with adventuresome encores, including compositions of his own and harmonically dissonant pieces by such modern composers as Igor Stravinsky and Arnold Schoenberg. He would also play fragments of the new musical rage from America—jazz. Even though performances of modernistic compositions engendered public protests and caustic comments from some critics, Antheil's concerts were popular. Less conservative critics glossed over his "adequate" treatment of the traditional piano literature and expressed delight with his encores. Sensing his potential success as a composer, Antheil began to perform less in order to have time to compose music.

Wishing to be part of the artistic avant-garde of the era, Antheil settled in Paris's Left Bank district and took a flat above Sylvia Beach's famous bookshop, Shakespeare & Co. He befriended many distinguished artists of the time, including James Joyce and Stravinsky, and soon won considerable public attention. During the mid-1920s the music-listening public in the United States considered Antheil one of the nation's best-known composers, on a par with George Gershwin and Irving Berlin and ranked ahead of Aaron Copland and Charles Ives.

Amidst the cultural hubbub of the 1920s Antheil capitalized on the public desire for audacious, shocking art. He desired fame as an avant-gardist and succeeded for a short time. His famous works of the time incorporated the sounds of American jazz, modern industrial machinery, and harmonic dissonance. Most notorious was his *Ballet mécanique* (1925), scored for pianos, an array of percussion instruments, two electric doorbells, and two airplane engines (propellors optional). Premiered at a private party in Paris, the work enjoyed immense social *éclat*, and Antheil later recalled with pleasure the audience's shock. The deafening music combined with the heat from the airplane engines prompted many guests to drink a great deal of champagne, resulting in a debauch. At the work's New York premiere, one member of the audience began waving a handkerchief from his walking stick. Ezra Pound, the decade's self-appointed arbiter of modern aesthetics, proclaimed that Antheil's compositions constituted the cutting edge of artistic expression. Although elements of futurism and surrealism were present in some of Antheil's works, the key to his reputation lay in the scandalous qualities of his music rather than in its musicality.

The ephemeral nature of Antheil's success, however, illustrates what can happen to an artistic celebrity whose work lacks genuine substance. Nothing loses its luster more rapidly than novelty designed to shock, and Antheil's musical vision quickly grew passé. By the late 1920s contemporaries like Copland and Virgil Thomson began to show audiences how fragments of American popular music could be cast in substantive, rather than merely sensational, musical languages. Meanwhile, Antheil was running out of ideas. He attempted to write an opera based on James Joyce's *Ulysses* but gave up. Stravinsky fell out with him, calling him a "four-flusher." As new musical ideas came forth, Antheil seemed unable to grasp them. He became more a curiosity than an artist, and his compositions seemed increasingly tame. Thomson later reflected that "the self-proclaimed 'bad boy of music' merely grew up to be a good boy."

Antheil had grown comfortable in Paris. He knew many luminaries. In 1925 he married Elizabeth "Böski" Marcus (they had no children). He left Paris in 1928, dividing his time for the next six years between Vienna, Frankfurt, and New York. In these years his fame as an avant-gardist faded. With Hitler's rise, Antheil returned to the United States and lived in Los Angeles and New York. William L. Shirer, who had witnessed much of the hubbub of Parisian life during the 1920s, recalled encountering the composer's name in the 1930s when Antheil was working for a West Coast newspaper, writing a trashy advice column for the lovelorn. "Was this the Antheil of Paris?" Shirer wondered: "I could hardly believe it." Antheil continued as a journalist and composed largely tepid, sometimes pompous music for films, ballets, and opera. In 1945 he published an entertaining autobiography, *Bad Boy of Music*. In the 1950s he wrote several Hollywood filmscores and the theme music for CBS's television program "The Twentieth Century," which proved to be Antheil's best-known work among the general public. He died in New York City.

• Antheil's *Bad Boy of Music* and Linda Witesitt's "The Life and Music of George Antheil" (Ph.D. diss., Univ. of Maryland, 1981) provide thorough accounts of the composer's life and music. Many histories of Parisian cultural life in the 1920s, however, refer to Antheil. He is the subject of lengthy treatment in Ezra Pound, *Antheil and the Treatise on Harmony* (1927); Bravig Imbs, *Confessions of Another Young Man* (1936); and Hugh Ford, *Four Lives in Paris* (1987). Those three books consider only the compositions written during his years in Paris; they should be read for what they reveal about the sense people had for Antheil in his heydey, as well as for their view of Parisian cultural life in the ebullient 1920s. Several journal articles capture the same mood: Aaron Copland, "George Antheil," *League of Composers Review* 2, no. 1 (1925): 26; Copland, "America's Young Men of Promise," *Modern Music* 3, no. 3 (1926): 13; and Ezra Pound, "Antheil, 1924–1926," *New Criterion* 4 (1926): 695. Virgil Thomson's *American Music since 1910* (1970) provides the most insightful perspectives on Antheil's value as an artist and his role in American musical culture.

Alan H. Levy

ANTHON, Charles (17 Nov. 1797–29 July 1867), professor of Greek and Latin, was born in New York City, the son of Dr. George Christian Anthon, a surgeon of German ancestry, and his French wife Genevieve Judot. A conspicuously brilliant student at Columbia College (1811–1815), Anthon opted for the legal profession and was admitted to the bar of the Supreme Court of New York State. He practiced little, however, for in 1820 he was called to Columbia, where he was to spend his entire professional life. He rose from adjunct professor of Greek and Latin (1820–1830) to become John Jay Professor of Greek Language and Literature, a post he held from 1830 to his death. From 1830 to 1864 he was also rector of the grammar school attached to Columbia, where he was a harsh taskmaster whom the students nicknamed "Bull." An exacting teacher, he was assiduously devoted to his academic duties at Columbia College, rarely leaving his native city. Intensely reclusive, he never married and seldom even communicated with other scholars in his field.

Anthon's professional career spans the decades of the groping transition in American classical studies from the centuries-old traditional learning to the foundations of native critical scholarship under German influence in the 1870s. Anthon felt the need to combat the sterility of American liberal education and the superficiality of its classical scholarship. The curriculum emphasized study of the Latin language, and teachers who were poorly trained were little more than drillmasters. Equipped with boundless energy and excellent German, Anthon devoted most of his career to the preparation of textbooks in the classics for college students, producing about fifty volumes. Under contract with Harper & Bros., from 1830 on he ground out at least one volume a year, becoming the leading and most popular American author of classical textbooks. Methodically culling his material mostly from German editions, he produced, besides numerous critical and profusely annotated school editions of Greek and Latin authors, books on ancient geography, classical antiquities, Latin and Greek prose composition, grammar, and prosody as well as classical dictionaries and a Latin-English/English-Latin lexicon. Among his works was the first American edition of Lemprière's famous *Classical Dictionary* (1833), which, substantially revised, was published in 1841 as *Anthon's Dictionary of Greek and Roman Antiquities*. His textbooks were severely criticized as largely unoriginal and too copious for the needs of college students.

Anthon's claim to fame rests mainly on his being the first American systematically to attempt to introduce the advances of German philology to America. Few of his works, however, survived the progress of American classical scholarship; an exception is his *Classical Dictionary*, which was superseded only in 1949, with the publication of the *Oxford Classical Dictionary*. Yet, for his generation, Anthon, together with Cornelius Conway Felton at Harvard, raised the level of classical education in America before the advent of critical scholarship ushered in by Basil Lanneau Gildersleeve.

Anthon was honored by his alma mater with the LL.D. degree in 1831. He died in New York City, still devoted to his lifework, and his memory is enshrined today at Columbia University in the Anthon Professorship of Latin.

• For details of Anthon's career and publications see the eulogy by his best student and successor, Henry Drisler, *Charles Anthon, LL.D., Late Jay-Professor of Greek Language and Literature in Columbia College: A Commemorative Discourse* (1868). An appreciation of Anthon's achievements as a scholar can be found in Stephen Newmyer, "Charles Anthon: Knickerbocker Scholar," *Classical Outlook* 59 (1981–1982): 41–44.

MEYER REINHOLD

ANTHONY, Sister (15 Aug. 1814–8 Dec. 1897), member of the Sisters of Charity and Civil War nurse, was born Mary O'Connell in Limerick, Ireland, the daughter of William O'Connell and Catherine Murphy. After her mother's death in about 1825, Mary and a sister emigrated to the United States, where they lived with an aunt in Maine. While still quite young, both girls were enrolled in the Ursuline convent in Charlestown, Massachusetts.

Under the guidance of Father William Tyler, Mary entered the Sisters of Charity community in Emmitsburg, Maryland, on 25 June 1835. Here, in a community founded by Mother Seton in 1809, Mary became a novice and received the name Sister Anthony. Two years later, on 3 March 1837, Sister Anthony was sent to Cincinnati, where the influx of Catholic immigrants encouraged creation of a new Catholic see. "Among the many needs of the newly created see" wrote one chronicler, "(if one may speak of many needs where everything was needed) not the least urgent were Catholic education for the daughters of the poor, and adequate protection and training for orphan girls" (Cincinnati *Times-Star*, 25 Apr. 1940). Sister Anthony worked in the St. Peter's Orphanage until the 1850s, frequently asking for contributions of food from local merchants to meet the needs of her charges.

In 1852 the Cincinnati Sisters of Charity became independent of Mother Seton's order and began plans to expand their mission. Sister Anthony was one of the seven founding members of the new order. In that same year she took charge of the new St. Joseph Orphanage for Boys in Cumminsville, Ohio. Also in 1852, the Cincinnati Sisters of Charity purchased an old French Catholic institution, the Hotel for Invalids, and reopened it under the name St. John's Hospital and Hotel for Invalids. The Catholics and other religious groups pioneered in the founding of hospitals and other social services for poor immigrants of their own religious affiliation. This was especially necessary in the case of Irish Catholics, since prejudice from the Protestant community made it difficult for Catholics to find jobs or safe places to live and worship.

Archbishop John B. Purcell of Cincinnati encouraged the sisters to improve their nursing skills, and Sister Anthony was among those who began training as a nurse in 1854, under the direction of Dr. George Curtis Blackman. The many medical schools in Cincinnati before the Civil War made the city a leader in medical and nursing education. Some women received nursing training in order to earn a living, but the religious orders provided nursing services free of charge.

A year later, in 1855, Sister Anthony was put in charge of St. John's Hospital and was elected procuratrix of the Cincinnati Sisters of Charity. Her long years of work in Cincinnati and her successes in aiding the indigent made her a well-known figure in the Catholic community. The hospital gained an excellent reputation as one of the first Catholic teaching hospitals in the country, staffed by professors from Miami Medical College and Ohio Medical College.

With the outbreak of the Civil War in April 1861, Sister Anthony and five other Sisters of Charity proceeded to Camp Dennison, a Union military encampment fifteen miles from Cincinnati, where they helped treat an outbreak of measles. Subsequently thirty-eight to forty other Sisters from the Cincinnati order joined them in the field, following the footsteps of the Ohio regiments in the Army of the Cumberland, the Army of the Tennessee, and the Army of the Ohio.

The battle of Shiloh, 6 and 7 April 1862, established the reputation of Sister Anthony as a remarkable battlefield nurse, known as the "Angel of the Battlefield." Robert Murray, the medical director of the Army of the Ohio, wrote that after one day of fighting there were "six or seven thousand wounded to be provided for, with literally no accommodations or comfort, not even the necessaries of life, no bedding, no cooking utensils or table furniture, not even cups, spoons, or knives or forks, no vegetables and no fresh beef" (Emmanuel, p. 11).

Sister Anthony braved the rain, filth, and blood to carry "cordials," bandages, and comfort to wounded survivors, as the numbers of unburied dead multiplied around her. When the medical interns assisting Dr. Blackman temporarily abandoned their duties, Sister Anthony assisted her old mentor with the surgery in such a way that, as the Sister recorded in her diary, "He expressed himself well pleased" (Emmanuel, p. 11). She also helped put the wounded aboard steamships that had been converted to hospital ships and transfer them to St. John's and other hospitals on the Ohio River. Sister Anthony and about 570 other Sisters of various communities worked under the overall authority of Dorothea Dix, the superintendent of women nurses for the army. Sister Anthony served in battle at Stone River, Murfreesboro, Culpeper Court House, Harpers Ferry, Winchester, and Richmond (Ky.). For twenty-eight months she served in General Hospital #14, an army field hospital in Nashville, Tennessee.

Sister Anthony's nursing work brought her into contact with General William T. Sherman (whose children she cared for briefly), Ulysses S. Grant, and William S. Rosecrans, from whom she obtained a pardon for a young Confederate who strayed across enemy lines. She also knew Jefferson Davis personally and dined with him on many occasions during the war.

Discharged on 31 July 1865, Sister Anthony returned to St. John's Hospital in Cincinnati and immediately began seeking funds for a larger building. She received a donation from two Protestant gentlemen, Joseph C. Butler and Louis Worthington, who enabled the hospital to relocate in a new building under the name Good Samaritan Hospital and to open it to patients of all faiths. From these same donors she also received funds to establish St. Joseph Infant and Maternity Home, a shelter for unwed mothers, in 1873. Despite much criticism regarding its mission, the maternity home also flourished, and Sister Anthony served as supervisor of both institutions until her retirement in 1880. She died in Cincinnati and is buried at Mount Saint Joseph Cemetery, at the motherhouse of the Sisters of Charity.

Sister Anthony and other Sisters of Charity who brought nursing care to the battlefields also brought some measure of reconciliation between the Catholics and Protestants of the Midwest, who had been at violent odds before the Civil War. One historian writes that "soldiers who had never before known a Catholic, much less a nun, jeered 'Pious Maria' when first the staunch . . . figure passed them" (Emmanuel, p. 10). Dorothea Dix herself had specified that she wanted only Protestant nurses but accepted the services of the Catholics. Later generations were able to describe Sister Anthony as "reverenced alike by the Blue and the Gray, by Protestant and Catholic" (*Times-Star*, p. 23).

• Sister Anthony's diaries and a number of short articles concerning her work may be found at the motherhouse of the Sisters of Charity in Mount St. Joseph, Ohio. Among these articles are Sister Marie Emmanuel, SC, "Angel of the Battlefield," *Saint Anthony Messenger*, Apr. 1962, pp. 8, 10–12, and "Sisters of Charity Have Been Angels of Mercy in Cincinnati," *Cincinnati Times-Star*, 25 Apr. 1940, p. 23. References to her work may be found in Ursula Stepsis, CSA, and Dolores Liptak, RSM, eds., *Pioneer Healers: The History of Women Religious in American Health Care* (1989).

SARAH H. GORDON

ANTHONY, Harold Elmer (5 Apr. 1890–29 Mar. 1970), mammalogist, museum curator, and author, was born in Beaverton, Oregon, the son of Alfred Webster Anthony and Anabel Klink. His father, a mining engineer and amateur ornithologist and collector, encouraged the boy's interests in natural history. Anthony was an avid hunter, as were other lads in his community, but he early evinced an interest in preserving small mammal and bird skins for further study. Educated in the local public schools of Portland, Oregon, Anthony attended Pacific University in Forest Grove, Oregon, for one year (1910–1911).

Anthony began his career in the spring of 1910 as a field collector for the U.S. Biological Survey (part of the Department of Agriculture) in North Dakota and Montana and was again employed by the survey in Wyoming during the summer of 1911. That same year he was engaged by the American Museum of Natural History as a naturalist in Lower California, collecting albatrosses for the museum's collections. He moved to New York in the fall of 1911 and, in the capacity of cataloger and general handyman in mammalogy and ornithology, began an association with the American Museum of Natural History that would continue for nearly fifty-five years. His service to the museum was briefly interrupted during World War I, in which he served as a first lieutenant and later captain of field artillery. He saw some action in France and was discharged in 1919. His first wife, Edith Irwin Demerel, whom he had married in 1916, died in 1918, following the birth of their son. In 1922 he married Margaret Feldt; they had a daughter and a son.

Anthony acquired both a B.S. (1915) and M.A. (1920) from Columbia University while at the same time he rose swiftly in the museum administration. He was named assistant curator of mammals in 1919 and became curator of mammals in 1926, holding that post for more than three decades, until his initial retirement in 1958. He was chairman of the Department of Mammals from 1942 to 1958, deputy director of the museum from 1952 to 1958, honorary curator of the Department of Conservation and General Ecology from 1953 to 1956, and dean of the scientific staff of the museum for most of the period from 1942 to 1956. Well versed in financial matters, he served from 1926 to 1958 as a member of the museum's Pension Board, where he played a major role in establishing a pension plan and credit union for museum employees. A contemporary museum employee newsletter reported that Anthony "knew that a bear market wasn't always a place where grizzlies and kodiaks were sold, and that there are two kinds of bulls." Following his retirement from the Mammalogy Department at the museum in 1958, Anthony was associated with the Frick Laboratory, an independently administered fossil research facility (after 1968 an integral part of the museum's Department of Vertebrate Paleontology), from 1958 to 1966.

Anthony did much to meet the needs of the museum-going public at the American Museum, playing a major role in the creation of the Hall of North American Mammals, the Akeley Hall of African Mammals, and the Hall of South Asiatic Mammals.

A dedicated and enthusiastic field worker, Anthony participated in and led a number of museum expeditions to various parts of the world, including the western United States, Alaska, Canada, Africa, and southeast Asia. He ultimately visited every continent except Australia. By 1939, he estimated that he had traveled some 200,000 miles on museum business. Though primarily a mammalogist, Anthony collected a wide range of organisms, including amphibians naturally occurring without legs and unusual edible orchids from Nyasaland (now Malawi), the rare black barking deer from Burma (now Myanmar), and a species of leaf-eared mice from the Grand Canyon. He was an authority on extinct mammal species of the West Indies and made comparisons between them and their living relatives in the Americas.

Anthony was the author of a number of professional papers in mammalogy and paleontology. These included several studies (1916 and 1918) on the mammals of Puerto Rico, culminating in the two-volume *Mammals of Porto Rico, Living and Extinct* (1925–1926). In an effort to meet the needs of laypersons interested in identifying and collecting what they observed, he served as scientific editor of *Mammals of America* (1917, several times reprinted) and *Mammals of Other Lands* (1941), and consulting editor for the section on mammals in the *Wonder Book of Knowledge* (1926). His *Field Book of North American Mammals* (1928) was the first publication designed to aid individuals attempting to identify all species and subspecies in the field; it was the only available publication of its kind for two decades. His American Museum booklet, *The Capture and Preservation of Small Mammals for Study* (1925), was a well-known and practical aid for collectors in the field and went through several editions.

A charter member of the American Society of Mammalogists (1919), Anthony served the society as vice president and later as president (1935–1937). He was also active in a number of other professional organizations, serving as treasurer of the New York Academy of Sciences and as a director of the National Audubon Society and of the Explorers Club.

Anthony was a dedicated gardener from boyhood and was especially noted for his cultivation of orchids. He served as treasurer of the American Orchid Society, which awarded him a gold medal for his contributions to that organization and to orchid culture, and as president of the Greater New York Orchid Society.

Anthony died of a heart attack while on a family outing in Paradise, California.

• Anthony's collected papers for the years 1913–1929 are at the Northern (Calif.) Regional Library Facility, University of California, and some correspondence is in the files of the Department of Mammalogy, American Museum of Natural History, N.Y. A taped interview with Anthony done by the author in 1965 focuses on his work with the Biological Survey. Biographical sources include "Harold Anthony Retires," *Grapevine* (in-house newsletter of the American Museum) 15, no. 7 (1 Apr. 1958), and a sketch in Elmer C. Birney and Jerry R. Choate, eds., *Seventy-five Years of Mammalogy (1919–1994)* (1994). An obituary is in the *New York Times*, 31 Mar. 1970.

KEIR B. STERLING

ANTHONY, Henry Bowen (1 Apr. 1815–2 Sept. 1884), newspaper editor and U.S. senator, was born in Coventry, Rhode Island, the son of William Anthony, a cotton manufacturer, and Mary Kinnicutt Greene. Preparatory school in Providence preceded Anthony's entrance into Brown University. He graduated in 1833, fifth in a class of twenty. His lifelong regard for literature and Brown University culminated in the bequest of an exceptional collection of poetry volumes.

Following graduation, Anthony worked as a broker in his brother's cotton goods business for five years, residing some of the time in Savannah, Georgia. Anthony disliked daily involvement in the family concern, but he invested in the business following his father's death in 1845. His investment in this mill and other manufacturing ventures greatly increased his personal wealth.

In 1838 Anthony married Sarah Aborn Rhodes, daughter of another old Rhode Island family. She died in 1854. The couple had no children, and the widower did not remarry. After his wife's death, Anthony moved from her home town of Pawtuxet to Providence.

During his married years, Anthony established himself as editor of the *Providence Journal* and a leader in the state Whig party. He had written for the *Journal* previously, but his formal association began with a temporary assignment as editor in 1838. Anthony displayed remarkable aptitude, and in July 1840 he became a member of the firm controlling the newspaper and never relinquished a financial interest.

Circumstances accelerated Anthony's rise in Rhode Island. Agitation for constitutional reform and broadened suffrage, led by Thomas W. Dorr, reached crisis proportions between 1841 and 1843. Anthony positioned the *Journal* with the "law and order" party, seeking to retain a property requirement for voting and checks on the political power of foreign immigrants. His regular columns and mock heroic poem, "The Dorriad" (1843), derided Dorrites, satirized their abortive military attempts to overthrow the state government, and helped dissuade wavering Rhode Islanders and the federal government from siding with the insurgents. A new state constitution continued restrictive suffrage and signaled a conservative victory.

Dorr's Democratic antecedents and Anthony's own tastes turned the *Journal* into a Whig party organ. Anthony obtained information and nurtured relationships during a weekly gathering at his offices that gained the name "*Journal* Sunday school." This convocation, originally a forum welcoming various opinions, came to focus almost exclusively on Anthony's political fortunes and lasted until its founder's death.

Despite his growing eminence among Rhode Island Whigs, Anthony's nomination for governor provoked dissension. He disarmed the opposition enough to win election in 1849 and the following year won reelection without concerted resistance. While governor, he downplayed the volatile fugitive slave issue as an unnecessary aggravation of sectional disagreements and frustrated measures to ensure a secret ballot. Anthony advocated open balloting as the surest guarantee of honest elections and believed secret ballots fostered corruption.

After declining a third nomination for governor, Anthony accepted the chairmanship of the Whig State Committee. Although he conveyed political intelligence to William Henry Seward in May 1852, Anthony supported Winfield Scott as the presidential nominee because he stood the best chance of election. While the Whig party unraveled in Rhode Island during late 1855, Anthony traveled through Europe and sent letters to the *Journal* with unflattering observations of European people, politics, religion, and business habits. On his return, Anthony backed the Know Nothing movement and placed the *Journal* behind the American party.

The American party in Rhode Island merged with the Republican party, and in 1858 Anthony first sought a seat in the U.S. Senate as an "American-Republican." He orchestrated a second Providence city convention to nominate state representatives after the original convention selected men opposed to his senatorial candidacy. This maneuver supplanted the original nominees and led to an agitated party caucus in May 1858, which settled on Anthony by one vote on the third ballot. He then secured near unanimous election in the legislature. Besides the influential columns of the *Journal*, Anthony employed political legerdemain and bribery in his subsequent reelections. After 1865 Charles R. Brayton, a notoriously effective political lieutenant, helped Anthony subdue rival Republican factions and partisan opponents.

Anthony's manner and willingness to compromise with secessionists during his first year in the nation's capital prompted Henry B. Adams to characterize the novice senator as "very fishy and weak-kneed" (J. C. Levenson et al., eds., *The Letters of Henry Adams*, vol. 1 [1982], p. 205). Anthony earnestly supported President Abraham Lincoln for his determination to preserve the Union and gravitated toward the Radical Republicans following the start of the Civil War. He favored President Andrew Johnson until this former Democrat directed Rhode Island patronage to Anthony's political enemies, and his vote to impeach Johnson when it was hoped that he would vote to acquit may have been retaliation. President Ulysses S. Grant liked Anthony, and he promoted the senator's reelection in 1870. Senate colleagues acknowledged Anthony's stature by multiple elections as president pro tempore.

Conscientious committee work and solicitude for his conservative Rhode Island constituency of wealthy manufacturers and landed residents distinguished Anthony's four full terms in the Senate. As chairman of the Committee on Printing for more than two decades, he ended expensive contracting practices and founded the Government Printing Office. As a member of the Committee on Naval Affairs, Anthony strove unsuccessfully during the Civil War to make permanent the relocation of the U.S. Naval Academy to Newport, Rhode Island. His spirited oratorical defenses of Rhode Island's history, reputation, and political institutions on the Senate floor when slighted by Jefferson Davis in 1860, assaulted by William Sprague in 1869, and probed by a congressional committee between 1879 and 1881 won acclaim. He achieved additional acclaim for eloquent eulogies, especially those for Stephen Douglas, Charles Sumner, and Henry Wilson (1812–1875). His final memorial address, for Ambrose E. Burnside, was a passionate expression of friendship.

Kidney disease limited Anthony's activities after 1882, and he died at his home in Providence. Eulogized by a former governor of Rhode Island as the personification of "a sound old-fashioned conservatism," Anthony parlayed a ready pen, xenophobic views, and political adroitness into a career that greatly influenced the state.

• Anthony's papers evidently have not survived in a body. *Catalogue of the Library and Autographs of the Late Senator Henry B. Anthony . . . to Be Sold at Auction . . . George A. Leavitt & Co., Auctioneers* (1885) suggests their fate. A scattering of his correspondence may be found in the papers of Abraham Lincoln, Andrew Johnson, Justin S. Morrill, James F. Simmons, Thomas A. Jenckes, and Nelson W. Aldrich, Library of Congress; William Henry Seward, Rush Rhees Library, University of Rochester, Rochester, N.Y.; Henry S. Sanford, General Sanford Memorial Library, Sanford, Fla.; Benjamin Perley Poore, Haverhill Historical Society, Haverhill, Mass.; and Beverly Wilson Palmer, ed., *Papers of Charles Sumner* (1988), microfilm. The *Providence Journal* and the records of the U.S. Senate in the *Congressional Globe* and *Congressional Record* are the essential primary sources on Anthony's career. Many of his most notable speeches and addresses were published as pamphlets. The only sustained biographical treatment, William B. Thornton, "Henry Bowen Anthony: Journalist, Governor, and Senator" (master's thesis, Univ. of Rhode Island, 1960), is helpful for its research in Rhode Island newspapers and archives. Rhode Island General Assembly, *Henry Bowen Anthony: A Memorial* (1885), contains eulogies that reveal none of the complexities or frictions of Anthony's life. Henry R. Davis, *Half a Century with the Providence Journal* (1904), offers sympathetic glimpses into Anthony's editorial activities. Obituaries are in the *New York Tribune* and the *Chicago Tribune*, both 3 Sept. 1884.

WILLIAM M. FERRARO

ANTHONY, John Gould (17 May 1804–16 Oct. 1877), conchologist, was born in Providence, Rhode Island, the son of Joseph Anthony and Mary Gould. As a child he became interested in natural history, particularly in marine mollusks, the study of which absorbed him all his life and led to his appointment as first curator of conchology in the Museum of Comparative Zoology at Harvard. Before that he was an accountant by profession and a collector at heart.

Details of Anthony's years in Providence are scanty, but family accounts indicate that he left school at the age of twelve, probably to clerk in a mercantile office (all his life he wrote in the classic clerk's or copperplate hand), and that in 1832 he married Anna Whiting Rhodes of Providence, with whom he had nine children. In 1834 John and Anna joined other members of the Rhodes family in Cincinnati, Ohio, where Anthony first appears in the historical record as a member of the Western Academy of Natural Sciences of Cincinnati, and of the firm of Allen, Rhodes & Co., manufacturers of silver plate. City directories later list him as an independent accountant (1840) and as a partner in Derby Bradley & Co. (1844), subsequently Bradley & Anthony, Booksellers and Publishers (1849).

Although Anthony began to exchange specimens with other conchologists before arriving in Cincinnati, it was there that he gained national prominence as an expert on the terrestrial and fluviatile shells of the western United States, and as the collector and distributor of thousands of specimens each year to correspondents all over the world. As a collector, he could ignore the issue of the relationship of fossil mollusks to contemporary mollusks, which in a pre-Darwinian age brought systematic malacology to a virtual standstill. Nonetheless, through his collections he became an inadvertent contributor to the emergence of invertebrate palaeontology as a distinct discipline. His reputation was due at least in part to his advantage of collecting around Cincinnati, where fossil mollusks are both numerous and easily found. In addition, he received support and stimulation from the Western Academy, an association of serious amateurs that Anthony joined in 1835, serving as secretary for a decade from 1837. Finally, he benefited from the relatively low status of malacology, then seen as merely the data-gathering part of mineralogy and economic geology; palaeontology meant big bones and bird tracks, and geology itself was an abstruse science grappling with concepts of Creation and Deluge.

In this context Anthony, the diligent and careful amateur collector, could find a niche and make a contribution. His career thus marks the transition from an age when natural science was the province and product of entrepreneurs and adepts, to the modern age of specialization and professionalism dominated by natural history museums and then by universities. It also marks the redirection of natural history from its traditional justification as useful training for the mind or a mode of assessing the habitability of a region, and its traditional focus on the odd and unfamiliar (the opossum, the moose, the humbug), to a new legitimacy and a new concern with the characteristics and distribution of forms and species.

In the absence of any nationally recognized forum for the establishment of species discovery, Anthony proposed in April 1837 that descriptions be submitted to and promulgated by such public bodies as the Western Academy, upon which he presented a list of species he had identified. He also submitted species for publication in the new national journals of science after 1840 and himself published two catalogs of shells found in the Cincinnati area. In 1847 he contracted scarlet fever, which left him virtually blind for two years and ailing for almost a decade. He continued his conchological labors during this period, however: a suite of sixteen fossil species sent to A. A. Gould for publication in 1849 included at least one that Anthony had "determined by touch alone while I was blind." In 1853, still with limited eyesight, he made an extensive walking tour of Kentucky, Tennessee, and Georgia to collect specimens and probably also to aid in the restoration of his health. When money became scarce, Anthony began selling parts of his collection.

By 1856 Anthony was a partner in the firm of Taylor & Anthony, General Insurance Agents, complaining that his conchological activities could no longer pay his expenses. He wished for a full-time professional position in one of the new museums. In 1863 he wrote to Louis Agassiz about the possibility of appointment as an assistant at Harvard's Museum of Comparative Zoology; Agassiz had just written to Anthony offering a job, and their letters crossed in the mail. Anthony arrived in Cambridge in August 1863 and settled his family in Cambridgeport. In 1865–1866 he was one of the paid naturalists accompanying Agassiz on his collecting expedition to Brazil, but Anthony's principal duties at the museum consisted of sorting specimens and pasting them on slate, glass, or wooden plaques. By the time of his death, in Cambridgeport, he had mounted several hundred thousand specimens, all of which, in light of later curatorial practices, had to be removed from their backing and often reorganized according to more modern systems of classification. Many of Anthony's identifications also had to be corrected. But his reputation stands on the fact of the collections he made and maintained, first as an individual, then as agent of the museum, and on the legitimacy of data-collecting as a scientific endeavor during the nineteenth century.

• Anthony's papers and his extensive collections of shells, including numerous type specimens, were deposited with the Museum of Comparative Zoology at Harvard; the shells have been merged with the museum's conchological collections, and the papers are in the Harvard University Archives. Much correspondence between Anthony and other scientists, largely on conchology or on the politics of American science (including the issue of priority), is in the papers of individuals and institutions. His holographic minutes as secretary of the Western Academy are in the Cincinnati Historical Society library, along with Anthony's printed "List of Land and Fresh-Water Shells, Found Chiefly in the Vicinity of Cincinnati" (1840?), revised and expanded as "Catalogue of the Terrestrial and Fluviatile Shells of Ohio. Second Edition, Cincinnati, January 1, 1843."

The fullest account of Anthony's life and contributions is Ruth D. Turner, "John Gould Anthony, with a Bibliography and Catalogue of His Species," *Occasional Papers on Mollusks*, no. 8 (1946), based in part on a memoir by Anthony's granddaughter, Fanny Garrison (typescript in Harvard University Archives). For Anthony's role in Cincinnati science, see Henry D. Shapiro, "The Western Academy of Natural Sciences of Cincinnati and the Structure of Science in the Ohio Valley," in *The Pursuit of Knowledge in the Early American Republic*, ed. Alexandra Oleson and S. B. Brown (1976).

HENRY D. SHAPIRO

ANTHONY, Katharine Susan (27 Nov. 1877–20 Nov. 1965), author, was born in Roseville, Arkansas, the daughter of Ernest A. Anthony and Susan Jane Cathey. Her father was a distant relative of suffrage activist Susan B. Anthony, and her mother was an energetic suffragist. Anthony's life work reflected a keen interest in women's issues that undoubtedly flowed from her family circumstances.

After graduating from high school, Anthony left Arkansas at age eighteen to begin a ten-year educational odyssey. From 1895 to 1897 she attended Peabody Normal College in Nashville, Tennessee. She spent the next few years teaching until she went to Europe to resume her studies at the Universities of Heidelberg and Freiburg in 1901–1902. She studied German, philosophy, and the emerging field of Freudian psychology. Anthony then returned to the United States to attend the University of Chicago, and in 1905 she received a bachelor of philosophy degree from that institution. In 1907–1908 she accepted a position teaching English at Wellesley College, but her interest in writing moved her to relocate to New York City where she assumed a position as researcher and editor at the Russell Sage Foundation in 1909. Anthony remained at the Sage Foundation until she resigned in 1913 to pursue writing full time.

Anthony belonged to a new generation of educated women trained in the ideas and methods of the emerging social sciences, and all of her writing bore this stamp. Although she credited her experience at the Sage Foundation with teaching her how to arrange statistical data into readable prose, her studies in Germany and at the University of Chicago provided the intellectual underpinning to all her writing. Her first book, *Mothers Who Must Earn,* published in 1914 with funding from the Sage Foundation, was an investigation of the lives of 370 working mothers residing in tenement housing. In *Feminism in Germany and Scandinavia* (1915), Anthony set the tone for the remainder of her writing about the lives of women from a feminist perspective. In this work she used her proficiency in German to translate for the first time into English several essays and monographs written by European feminists and to compare their theories with those of major American feminists. Anthony argued that "the emancipation of woman as a personality" was the fundamental aim of feminism. The purpose of the feminist movement, she claimed, was to secure both individual freedom and self-respect for women. In order to do so, the feminist movement needed to change the existing dependent relationship of women to the state to one wherein society recognized maternity "as a service to the state" deserving of government support. Anthony believed that recognizing women's contribution to the state in this way would elevate the economic status of women to a par with that of men and simultaneously eliminate women's economic dependency on husbands or the fathers of their children.

After publishing two books, Anthony turned her attention to examining women's personality and freedom in a series of biographies of influential women. The first biography, a profile of Margaret Fuller, appeared in 1920. Anthony wrote eight biographies in all. Other subjects included Catherine the Great, Louisa May Alcott, Dolley Madison, Queen Elizabeth I, Susan B. Anthony, and the British writers Charles and Mary Lamb. Anthony's last book, published in 1958, was a biography of Mercy Otis Warren, a playwright and historian at the time of the American Revolution. In all her biographies Anthony continued to utilize her early training in the social sciences and languages. She translated and published the diaries and letters of Catherine the Great. Although her strong psychological profile of Margaret Fuller earned much praise for its innovative technique, it was also criticized for what some deemed her excessive reliance on Freudian psychology.

At various times in her life, Anthony participated in a variety of feminist causes. In 1917, at the request of the Consumers' League, she compiled a handbook of the labor laws of New York State. She belonged to the Women's Trade Union League, campaigned against involuntary conscription during World War I, and in 1932 rode in the massive Chicago peace parade. Anthony also belonged to a circle of feminists in New York City called the Heterodoxy, a group that began in 1912 and lasted until the late 1930s or early 1940s. The aim of the Heterodoxy was to discuss and act upon a wide range of political and social innovations. Its emphasis on fostering women's self-development meshed neatly with Anthony's own ideas about women. She never considered herself a political activist but confessed to regarding Eleanor Roosevelt and New York Mayor Fiorello La Guardia as her personal heroes. She gave her political allegiance, she once said, to whichever political party seemed to be working "in the most practical way" to advance "the cause of civilization for most of the people."

Anthony never married, but she lived much of her adult life with her companion Elisabeth Irwin, the progressive educator who founded the Little Red Schoolhouse. When she and Irwin informally adopted several children, she put into practice her belief in women's freedom and autonomy that was so clearly reflected in her writings and in her membership in the Heterodoxy. Anthony died in New York City.

• Some correspondence between Anthony and Ethel Sturgis Dummer survives in the Dummer Collection, Arthur and Elizabeth Schlesinger Library on the History of Women in America, Radcliffe College, Cambridge, Mass. The clearest explanation of Anthony's ideas is found in her books, especially in *Feminism in Germany and Scandinavia.* There are no biographies of Katharine Anthony. Beyond her own work, information on Anthony can be found in diverse works on feminism. Judith Schwarz, *The Radical Feminists of Heterodoxy* (1982), discusses her participation in this circle. Nancy F. Cott, *The Grounding of Modern Feminism* (1987), analyzes her feminist ideas in the context of the 1920s. Additional information can be found in her obituary in the *New York Times,* 22 Nov. 1965.

MAUREEN A. FLANAGAN

ANTHONY, Susan B. (15 Feb. 1820–13 Mar. 1906), reformer and organizer for woman suffrage, was born Susan Brownell Anthony in Adams, Massachusetts, the daughter of Daniel Anthony and Lucy Read. Her father built the town's first cotton mill. When Susan, the second of eight children, was six, the family moved to Battenville, New York, north of Albany, where Daniel prospered as manager of a larger mill and could send Susan and her sister to a Friends' seminary near Philadelphia. His good fortune, however, collapsed with the financial crisis of 1837; the mill closed, Susan left boarding school, the family lost its house, and for nearly a decade the family squeaked by, assisted by Susan's wages as a teacher. Looking for a new start in 1845, Daniel moved to a farm near Rochester, the city that would be Susan's permanent address for the rest of her life.

Susan taught for ten years in district schools, private academies, and families, concluding her career as head of the female department in the academy at Canajoharie, New York, from 1846 to 1849. This work had a lasting effect on her ideas as a reformer and on her views about equality. Having experienced women's unequal wages, she gave primacy, in later years, to their need for economic equality; "Woman Wants Bread, Not the Ballot" was the title of her best-known and favorite lecture about woman suffrage. She approached working women not as a philanthropist curious about their plight but as a veteran of their tribulations.

When she quit teaching in 1849 to run her father's farm, Anthony had already moved tentatively into the arena of women's reform. At Canajoharie she delivered her first speech to a meeting of the Daughters of Temperance. At home, however, her family introduced her to their new friends—including Frederick Douglass, Isaac and Amy Post, and others—who formed the core of Rochester's antislavery and women's rights radicals. These members of the Western New York Anti-Slavery Society and participants in the women's rights convention at Rochester in 1848 conducted their private, religious, and political lives by a code of sexual equality that presented Anthony with unimagined alternatives for her own life.

In 1851 Anthony met Elizabeth Cady Stanton, and over the next year the two women discovered the sort of liberating partnership they could forge. Their ideas were converging. Anthony had found women welcome in the temperance movement as long as they confined themselves to a separate sphere and did not expect an equal role with men, while Stanton had focused her attention on the need for women to reform law in their own interests, both to improve their conditions and to challenge the "maleness" of current law. In 1852 Anthony and Stanton founded the Women's New York State Temperance Society, which, even in its name, claimed an equality with the leading male society and featured women's right to vote on the temperance question and to divorce drunken husbands. Beginning as an agent for this society, Anthony became a full-time reformer.

Through the 1850s Anthony and Stanton made New York State the nation's showpiece of women's rights agitation. To the struggle for equality in the increasingly political temperance movement, they added campaigns for coeducation, modeled "Bloomers," a costume that freed women from the constraints of fashionable dress, and, through their New York State Woman's Rights Committee, presented the legislature with demands for suffrage, married women's property rights, mothers' custody rights, liberalized divorce laws, and rights associated with specific jobs performed by women.

Anthony proved to be an effective organizer and fell into a style of life centered on the demands of reform politics. On the road most of each year for the next four decades, she avoided keeping house and supported herself by work for her political causes. This willingness to live in perpetual motion made her a perfect partner in the 1850s for Stanton, whose children and household tied her down. Anthony supplied legs and voice for Stanton's ideas, or in Stanton's phrase, "I forged the thunderbolts and she fired them" (*Eighty Years and More*, p. 165). Anthony's persistence as a traveler and organizer was legendary; William Henry Channing dubbed her the movement's Napoleon. In an 1855 tour for women's rights she met her goal of lecturing at least once in every one of New York's sixty-two counties. (At age seventy-four, she insisted on repeating that feat in the service of a suffrage amendment to the state constitution.) Recognizing her talents, the American Anti-Slavery Society signed her up as its principal agent in New York State from 1856 until the Civil War.

The political methods that Anthony worked out in New York set the pattern she would follow nationally for the rest of her life. Her objectives were to change laws, and she took her arguments to the public through lectures, pamphlets, subscription newspapers, and personal appeals for signatures on petitions. Each year had its cycle: fieldwork with education and petitions paced to produce an annual presentation of opinion to the legislature. At Albany she would schedule the best speakers in a large meeting to coincide with the start of the legislative session in order to attract politicians and the press. As the movement gained importance, she could schedule hearings as well. When she left a town, she sought to leave behind some "wide-awake" individuals who would carry on the education. She did not, however, build organizations or solicit memberships.

With the start of the Civil War, advocates of women's rights put their cause on hold and devoted their time to abolitionism. In 1863 Anthony, again with Stanton, founded the Women's Loyal National League to engage women in the political debates prompted by war, and for a year and a half Anthony circulated a national petition that urged Congress to abolish slavery by constitutional amendment. Employing a loose network of individuals and soldiers' aid and antislavery societies, the league gathered petitions with 400,000 signatures, which were presented to Congress by Senator Charles Sumner. This effort marked Anthony's debut as a national reformer and was also the advent of a focus on the federal government for women's rights. The Thirteenth Amendment and subsequent debate about securing citizenship for freed slaves introduced Anthony and her co-workers to the potential for sweeping change through amendment to the national Constitution.

Anthony spent much of 1865 in Leavenworth, Kansas, at work on her brother's newspaper. Carefully following congressional debates, she became convinced that universal suffrage was the only just solution to the challenges of Reconstruction, yet Congress intended to limit rights by introducing the word "male" into the Fourteenth Amendment. With a lecture on universal suffrage, she worked her way east. By year's end, the core of women's rights activists in the Northeast had reassembled to launch their first national campaign for woman suffrage, petitioning Congress for an amendment to "prohibit the several States from disfranchising any of their citizens on the ground of sex" (Stanton et al., *History of Woman Suffrage*, vol. 2, p. 91).

Hopes for universal suffrage from Congress bound former abolitionists together in the American Equal Rights Association, established in 1866. As its corresponding secretary Anthony oversaw petitions to Congress and coordinated several campaigns to amend state constitutions. She divided her time in 1867 between campaigns in New York and Kansas. Kansas voters defeated proposals for African-American and woman suffrage, but the campaign itself exposed profound differences within the equal rights coalition and drove a wedge among woman suffragists that would divide them until the end of the century. Republican party leaders and the reformers they influenced withdrew support for the woman suffrage amendment midway through the campaign, aligning the party's stance in Kansas with its national advocacy of suffrage for black males. Grasping for any support, Anthony accepted the assistance of George Francis Train, showman, financier, Democrat, and blatant racist, to complete the tour of Kansas. Moreover, while traveling home with Train, she and Stanton accepted his offer of capital to launch a newspaper. The *Revolution*, published in New York City by Anthony and edited by Stanton and Parker Pillsbury, appeared in January 1868.

In one sense, Anthony simply separated her cause from dependence on Republican leadership to test its political appeal. She signaled the same intention with an approach to the Democratic party's 1868 convention for an endorsement of suffrage. But she and Stanton crafted their move in terms that pitted the rights of women against the rights of freedmen and claimed a higher right for themselves.

Though the *Revolution* preserves the worst pronouncements of Anthony and Stanton in this period—opposing the Fifteenth Amendment and casting the enfranchisement of freedmen as a threat to the safety of white women—it also captures their excitement about women's potential and their growing rebelliousness. The paper attracted good poets, short story writers, and journalists; its columns reported grass-roots activism in California, Nevada, South Carolina, Wisconsin, and the District of Columbia; and thorough reports about women's rights in Geneva, Paris, and London appeared regularly.

Their convictions about an independent movement led Anthony and Stanton to form the National Woman Suffrage Association (NWSA) in 1869, distinct from the equal rights movement. Henry Blackwell and his wife, Lucy Stone, set up the rival American Woman Suffrage Association (AWSA), which took a more predictable and Republican line by calling for suffrage by state, rather than federal, law. Until their merger in 1890, the two associations rarely agreed on strategy and competed for suffragists' loyalty.

Although Anthony advocated a sixteenth amendment for woman suffrage as early as 1868, the strategy of the NWSA remained uncertain and subject to change until 1875. National suffragists sought legislative and judicial tests of the theory that the Fourteenth and Fifteenth Amendments together had, in fact, granted women the right to vote by linking citizenship—which women enjoyed—to the franchise. Through direct action in local elections dozens of women created test cases, and, on the initiative of Victoria Woodhull, the NWSA petitioned for an act of Congress to implement what the amendments had established in principle.

Anthony lectured and wrote about this "new departure," but she did not try to vote herself until 1872, when she joined a group (that included two of her sisters) to cast ballots on election day in Rochester. Within weeks she was arrested for violating federal law. Convicted by the judge, without a poll of the jury that heard her case, and fined, Anthony was not ordered to jail and thus could not take her case to the Supreme Court on a writ of habeas corpus. She never paid the fine. In another case, *Minor v. Happersett* (1874), the Court ruled that under the Constitution the states still could determine the political rights of women. In response to this ruling, Anthony revived the proposal for a constitutional amendment in 1876 and sustained a national campaign for the next decade.

By a cruel twist of fate, women's interest in their enfranchisement was mounting while politicians' willingness to assert federal authority over the states was waning. Floods of petitions produced modest gains among congressmen, and suffragists' best efforts could not produce a majority, or even a solid bloc, of legislative support. When an amendment finally reached the Senate floor in 1886, it lost decisively. From that point until after Anthony's death, supporters of the federal amendment went through the motions of petitions and hearings without much hope of sympathy from a Congress dominated by advocates of states' rights.

Women's support for suffrage came from constituencies that Anthony cultivated with her grueling schedule. From October through December and from February until the planting season, Anthony stayed on the lecture circuit, booked into towns and cities of every size. In January she convened her followers in Washington to make their case to Congress. Never comfortable as a lecturer, she labored hard to become adequate in the job, and eventually her reputation drew audiences that her style might not.

Anthony's dedication to the cause made her a celebrity whose speeches earned serious comment, and she gave hundreds of interviews to local newspapers. She came to personify the demand for woman suffrage to most Americans. As her fame mounted, Anthony used the power it gave her to link suffragists with groups of women organized for other purposes. By befriending Frances Willard, she slowly won the permission of the conservative Woman's Christian Temperance Union to speak about voting rights at their meetings. She put together the International Council of Women and its affiliate, the National Council of Women, in 1888. Neither group endorsed suffrage, but in both suffragists collaborated with groups seeking to enhance women's opportunities. By the 1890s Anthony had access to the platform of any women's organization in the country.

Two years of acrimonious negotiations with Lucy Stone's representatives from the AWSA succeeded in merging the rival associations as the National-American Woman Suffrage Association (NAWSA) in 1890. Stanton presided over the new organization from 1890 to 1892, when Anthony replaced her. Anthony served until her eightieth birthday in 1900. Anthony cultivated the new talent coming up—people like Alice Stone Blackwell, Carrie Chapman Catt, Laura Clay, and Anna Howard Shaw—but none was ready to lead.

Without diminishing the contribution she continued to make toward public acceptance of suffrage, it is fair to say that by the 1890s Anthony was not up to meeting the challenges arising among suffragists themselves. Growth and merger had introduced new political cultures into the movement, often more conservative and more wedded to building strong state suffrage societies primed for local action. Pressure for campaigns to win suffrage by state legislation or referendum escalated after 1890, straining resources and diverting attention from the federal amendment. Serious conflicts about basic values threatened the goal of sustaining a single national organization for the cause. Veneration of Susan B. Anthony held the NAWSA together during some of its worst years.

Expecting to settle down, she had arranged with her sister to share housekeeping at Mary's house in Rochester, beginning in 1890. For the first time in her life she entertained, taking great pleasure in hosting friends with whom she had stayed across the country. But she did not really give up travel: South Dakota for seven months in 1890; Chicago for four months in 1893; the South for two months in 1895 and again in 1903; California in 1895, most of 1896, and then again in 1905; London in 1899; Berlin in 1904; Washington every year; and plenty of short trips in between. She was on the road until a month before her death in Rochester, having insisted on rising from her sickbed to attend the NAWSA's annual convention in Baltimore and proceeding to Washington for a birthday party at the Corcoran Gallery.

In 1902 Anthony wrote a public letter in advance of Stanton's birthday, not knowing that her friend would die before its publication. She conceded that neither she nor Stanton had expected in "the hope and buoyancy of youth" to leave their life's work for another generation, but she harbored "not a shadow of doubt that they will carry our cause to victory." The old pioneers would have to settle for "the next sphere of existence . . . where women will be welcomed on a plane of perfect intellectual and spiritual equality." When Anthony died, she left an enormous legacy to those other generations. Her image, words, and standards of work permeated the struggle for what women called the "Susan B. Anthony amendment." So thoroughly had she become the embodiment of women's aspirations for political equality that suffragists fought long after their victory in 1920 over their competing claims to be her true political descendants.

Another legacy lasted still longer; Anthony made certain that the movement's history survived. In the middle 1870s, with contributions to *Johnson's New Universal Cyclopaedia* (1879), she began a series of projects to ensure recognition of eminent individuals and documentation of critical events. Between 1881 and 1886, working alongside Stanton and Matilda Joslyn Gage, she produced three volumes of the *History of Woman Suffrage*, corralling contributors from each state and tracking down sources. In 1897 she brought Ida Husted Harper to live with her in Rochester to prepare two volumes of the *Life and Work of Susan B. Anthony* (1898), based on massive archives that had accumulated in the attic. With Harper she then produced a fourth volume of the *History* (1902). Anthony donated her books and scrapbooks to the Library of Congress and personally shipped thousands of volumes of the *History* and the biography to academic and public libraries.

• Anthony's papers, compiled from archives and printed sources, are microfilmed and indexed as the *Papers of Elizabeth Cady Stanton and Susan B. Anthony*, ed. Patricia G. Holland and Ann D. Gordon (1991). Not included there in their entirety are scrapbooks at the Library of Congress, a remarkable record of lifetime attention to political and social issues. The *History of Woman Suffrage* still provides the best record of Anthony's movement. A valuable selection of documents appears in Ellen C. DuBois, ed., *Elizabeth Cady Stanton, Susan B. Anthony: Correspondence, Writings, Speeches* (rev. ed., 1992). Stanton wrote several biographical chapters on Anthony in *Eminent Women of the Age* (1868), the *History of Woman Suffrage*, vol. 2 (1882), and *Eighty Years and More* (1898). Ida Husted Harper added vol. 3 to her *Life and Work of Susan B. Anthony* in 1908, and the principal biographies since then are by Rheta Childe Dorr (1928), Katherine Anthony (1954), Alma Lutz (1959), and Kathleen Barry (1988). Eleanor Flexner's *Century of Struggle* (1959; rev. ed., 1975) offers the best interpretative treatment of suffragism. For Anthony's campaigns in the immediate postwar years, Ellen C. DuBois, *Feminism and Suffrage* (1978), is the basic work. Nancy A. Hewitt's work defines the context for Anthony's conversion to women's rights: *Women's Activism and Social Change: Rochester, New York* (1984). Though obituaries appeared in hundreds of papers, the principal ones are those from Rochester, New York, 13 Mar. 1906, in the *Rochester Democrat and Chronicle*, the *Rochester Herald*, the *Post Express*, and the *Evening Times*.

ANN D. GORDON

ANTIN, Mary (13 June 1881–15 May 1949), author, was born in Polotzk, Russia, the daughter of Israel Antin, a scholar and unsuccessful shopkeeper, and Esther Weltman. The assassination of Czar Alexander II three months before her birth unleashed a series of brutal pogroms and increased restrictions on the employment, residency, and education of Jews. These events formed the background of Antin's childhood, a world she recalled as divided in two, between Polotzk and Russia, Jews and Gentiles, with the constant presence of anti-Semitism.

In 1891 Israel Antin left the Pale of Settlement for the United States; his wife and children followed three years later. Mary Antin immortalized the 9,000-mile journey in *From Plotzk [Polotzk] to Boston*, a series of letters she wrote in Yiddish to her Uncle Moses in Russia, which she translated into English. Due to the intervention of Jewish philanthropist Lina Hecht, whom Mary befriended in Boston, the letters were published in *American Hebrew* and in 1899, when Antin was eighteen, as a separate volume, with an introduction by English author Israel Zangwill.

Antin's early literary success was indicative of her easy assimilation into American society. Just thirteen when she arrived in the United States, Antin quickly shed her name (originally, she was called Mashke) as well as other Old World accoutrements. Within six months, she had completed the first five grades of school and become a published author; her essay, "Snow," was published in *Primary Education* in 1894.

In spite of her family's declining economic fortunes, the success of *From Plotzk to Boston* ensured that Antin's education would continue at Boston Latin School, the public preparatory school for Radcliffe College. Her older sister Fetchke (renamed Frieda in America) was never allowed an education, since like both parents she had to work to support the family. As their income decreased, Israel Antin grew disillusioned with the once golden promise of America. Yet to conform to its ways, he violently rejected "everything old," casting aside traditional religion. Embracing the patriot gods of her country, Mary Antin also abandoned Judaism. Later she would write that in its stead her family found only "chaos" and "disintegration."

Yet Mary Antin's faith in America was not extinguished. In high school, where she was one of only a few Jews, she was fully accepted by her schoolmates. She became active at Hale House, a neighborhood settlement established by one of Boston's most distinguished literary figures, Edward Everett Hale. At Hale House's Natural History Club, Antin met Amadeus William Grabau, a geologist eleven years her senior then completing a doctorate at the Massachusetts Institute of Technology. Instead of entering Radcliffe College, Antin married Grabau, the son of a German-born Lutheran minister, in October 1901 and moved with him to New York, where he was to teach at Columbia University. Antin enrolled at Barnard College, but because of ill health she became a special student. She later transferred to Teachers College but did not complete a degree.

Antin's only child, a daughter, Josephine Esther, named after the writer Josephine Lazarus and Antin's mother, was born in 1907. Lazarus encouraged Antin to begin her literary career in earnest by writing a full account of her experiences in America. After Lazarus's unexpected death in 1910, Antin fulfilled her friend's wish by publishing stories and essays. "Malinke's Atonement," a short story about an impoverished Russian Jewish girl who yearned for education, appeared in the *Atlantic Monthly* in 1911; the magazine published several other stories and essays that became the basis of Antin's major work, *The Promised Land* (1912).

Widely hailed in its own day, *The Promised Land* is considered one of the first great works of American Jewish literature as well as a classic tale of assimilation. During Antin's lifetime, the book went through thirty-four printings and sold nearly 85,000 copies. In the autobiographical account, Antin tells of being reborn and "made over" on American soil, where freedom and opportunity replaced the rigidity of ancient customs. Although celebratory in tone, in its sober account of her father's denial of heritage and the frank admission of the bleakness of her mother's and sister's lives, the book hinted at the emotional costs of the immigrant's journey.

Antin's own literary success proved a mixed reward: she became a popular and well-paid lecturer, speaking on subjects such as Jews in the shtetl, problems of immigration, and American citizenship, and was a minor celebrity, known to many notable Americans, including Theodore Roosevelt. Yet many coreligionists found Antin distant, elitist, and embarrassed by her own past. She published only one other volume, *They Who Knock at Our Gates: A Complete Gospel of Immigration* (1914), a passionate plea for the continuation of unrestricted admission for newcomers.

Although Antin's eloquent patriotism did not diminish her support of policies favorable to Jews, her marriage to a Gentile and her renunciation of formal ties with Judaism offended many coreligionists. She never tempered her support of assimilation, arguing that in the United States, where cultural tolerance, social equality, and individual freedom of choice held sway, more narrowly based ethnic and national group identities were throwbacks to an archaic age. By the end of World War I, however, Antin was convinced that American Jews needed to support an independent Jewish state, and she insisted that Zionism was in no way contradictory to assimilation.

In her personal life, Antin had more difficulty maintaining her universalist ethics. The agonies of World War I split the Grabau household, with Antin lecturing around the country on behalf of the Allies and Grabau supporting Germany. The Grabaus separated in 1918, and their daughter was sent to boarding school. Left alone, cut off from the Jewish community, and despondent about the zenophobic trend of American life and her own misfortunes, Antin suffered a nervous breakdown from which she never recovered. Recuperating at various rehabilitative facilities, she wound up at the Gould Farm in Great Barrington, Massachusetts, as a follower of "Brother Will" Gould and his wife, Agnes, who preached the gospel of Christian love. Though Antin would write only a few essays in the remaining quarter century of her life, she collected a vast amount of material for a proposed book on Gould, intending to relate his life and work to the story of Jesus and Christian community through the ages.

Antin continued to celebrate America for the freedom it gave her to follow her "inborn drive" for religious exploration without reference to Judaism. "For decades I lived cut off from Jewish life and thought, heart-free and mind-free to weave other bonds," she wrote without regret in her last essay, "House of One Father" (*Common Ground* [1941], p. 41). Although the rise of Fascism caused Antin to publicly reclaim her Jewish identity, she refused to allow anti-Semitism to draw her back into Jewish particularism—what she called a "ghetto without walls." She spent her last years at Gould Farm, surrounded by her daughter and her loyal sisters, but the nervous illnesses never abated, nor did the productivity of earlier times return. She died in a nursing home in Suffern, New York.

In her early writings, Antin gave public voice to the aspirations of millions of immigrants who came to the United States during the mass migration of the late nineteenth and early twentieth centuries. One of the first to write as a representative American, a Jew, and a woman, she expressed the multiple identities that characterized many immigrant daughters. Her work stands as a chronicle of the bittersweet experiences of that generation.

• There is no known collection of Antin papers. Her essays include "A Woman to Her Fellow Citizens," *Outlook*, Nov. 1912; "A Zionist's Confession of Faith," *Maccabean*, Feb. 1917; "The Zionists' Bit," *Maccabean*, Feb. 1918; and "The Soundless Trumpet," *Atlantic Monthly*, May 1937. Her stories include "The Amulet," *Atlantic Monthly*, Jan. 1913, and "The Lie," *Atlantic Monthly*, Aug. 1913. "Malinke's Atonement" was reprinted in *America and I: Short Stories by American Jewish Women Writers*, ed. Joyce Antler (1990).

Critical essays on *The Promised Land* include Sarah Blacher Cohen, "Mary Antin's *The Promised Land*: A Breach of Promise," *Studies in American Jewish Literature* 3 (1977–1978): 28–35; William A. Proefriedt, "The Education of Mary Antin," *Journal of Ethnic Studies* 17 (1990): 81–100; Steven J. Rubin, "Style and Meaning in Mary Antin's *The Promised Land*: A Reevaluation," *Studies in American Jewish Literature* 5 (1986): 35–43; and Richard Tuerk, "The Youngest of America's Children in *The Promised Land*," *Studies in American Jewish Literature* 5 (1986): 29–34.

The best biographical material is Oscar Handlin's introduction to *The Promised Land* (1969; repr. 1985). For an imaginative treatment, see Sam Bass Warner's "Listening for the Dead," *Public Historian* 5 (Fall 1983): 63–70. An obituary is in the *New York Times*, 18 May 1949.

JOYCE ANTLER

ANTOINE (18 Nov. 1748–19 Jan. 1829), Roman Catholic priest, was born Francisco Antonio Ildefonso Moreno y Arze at Sedella, in Granada, Spain, the son of Pedro Moreno and Ana de Arze. As a young man he entered the Capuchin branch of the Franciscans, a segment of the Franciscan order established by Matteo di Bassi of Urbano, Italy, in 1525. Antonio de Sedella studied with and received his spiritual formation under the Capuchins of the Spanish province of Castile and during that period apparently earned a doctorate in theology. After spending a few years in Central America and then teaching theology back in Sedella, in 1779 he responded to a request from the bishop of Santiago de Cuba, who then held ecclesiastical jurisdiction over Louisiana, for missionary priests for Louisiana. Antonio de Sedella served as a Capuchin priest in New Orleans from January 1781, at the age of thirty-two, until his death forty-eight years later. Thus, although he was an Andalusian Spaniard, he is most prominently known for his labors among the city's predominantly French-Catholic population, and for that reason, his French appellation, Père Antoine, has prevailed in the historical record.

Virtually upon his disembarkation at New Orleans Antoine was assigned to the parish church of St. Louis, located in what is now Jackson Square, on the edge of the French Quarter that abuts the Mississippi River, which had been built and established as a parish back in 1720. (Many decades later, after the great fire of 1788 and another conflagration that destroyed much of the city of St. Louis in 1794, St. Louis Church was elevated to the status of a cathedral church.) On 15 June 1782 Antoine was named administrator and director of the Charity Hospital of San Carlos, another Catholic institution he had been serving since his arrival in New Orleans eighteen months earlier. In 1785 he was named temporary pastor of St. Louis Church, a position that was made permanent on 4 July 1787 by Santiago José de Echevarría, the bishop of Santiago de Cuba.

Earlier, on 12 June 1787, Antoine had announced publicly, as well as to his confreres and other church officials, that he had accepted a commission from the Cartagena Tribunal of the Holy Inquisition, thereby becoming the local commissioner for the Inquisition in Louisiana. This appointment brought to a head a confrontation between him and the auxiliary bishop of Santiago-Havana, Cirilo de Barcelona, who though assigned to oversee Louisiana, did not enjoy ordinary authority over the jurisdiction. Joining Cirilo in his struggle with Antoine was the Spanish governor of Louisiana, Esteban Miró, who feared a negative reaction from his many and varied colonists to the presence of a commissioner of the Inquisition in Louisiana. The followers of Cirilo and Miró viewed Antoine as a self-serving, insubordinate cleric who could no longer be tolerated, and even though he made no attempt to start up the Inquisition in New Orleans, the bishop and the governor conspired to have him deported to Spain in April 1790. Antoine had his own supporters, however, and when the ecclesiastical and royal authorities in Spain reviewed the case against him, Antoine was exonerated of all charges. He returned to New Orleans as pastor of St. Louis Church in 1795.

Turmoil continued to plague Antoine after his return. Many of his difficulties seem to have been rooted in historic dissimilarities between Spain, France, and the United States, such as their varying jurisdictions for church and state, but there were also political differences—secular as well as ecclesiastical—and personality conflicts. The situation was complicated and exacerbated after the United States purchased Louisiana from France in 1803 and the American Church hierarchy took over episcopal control of the region. One result of the purchase was that Antoine had to struggle to retain his position as pastor of St. Louis Church. The benefice was conferred upon him by the first bishop of Louisiana, Luis Ignacio María de Peñalver y Cárdenas, assisted by an Irish priest, Father Patrick Walsh, vicar general of the Diocese of Louisiana. Another serious battle, which consumed fifteen years of his life, was Antoine's confrontation with Louis-Guillaume DuBourg, a French Sulpician whom American bishop John Carroll had sent to administer Louisiana in 1812 and who in 1815 became bishop of the diocese. Antoine and DuBourg disagreed over who held ecclesiastical authority in New Orleans, especially in regard to pastoring the cathedral. Their conflict was so serious that DuBourg chose to reside in St. Louis instead of New Orleans after he returned from his consecration in Rome. Initially very suspicious and distrustful of Antoine, DuBourg seems to have softened his attitude toward the Cupuchin priest as the years passed. What seems to have existed at the heart of Antoine's struggles was his concern that legitimate ecclesiastical authority be respected. In his time, there were too many years during which it was unclear who held such jurisdiction in New Orleans.

At his death in New Orleans, Antoine had been castigated by many in the church throughout the United States and other countries, but he was viewed as a saint in New Orleans. He was buried from St. Louis Cathedral on 22 January after an impressive funeral.

• Primary sources on Père Antoine can be found in the Antoine Blanc Memorial Archives, Archdiocese of New Orleans. Also see Roger Baudier, *The Catholic Church in Louisiana* (1939), and Charles Edwards O'Neill, S.J., "A Quarter Marked by Sundry Peculiarities: New Orleans, Lay Trustees, and Père Antoine," *Catholic Historical Review* 76 (Apr. 1990): 235–77. Antoine is covered in Glenn R. Conrad et al., *Cross, Crozier, and Crucible: A Volume Celebrating the Bicentennial of a Catholic Diocese in Louisiana* (1993).

PATRICK FOLEY

ANTONY, Milton (7 Aug. 1789–19 Sept. 1839), physician and educator, was born presumably in Henry County, Virginia, the son of James Antony, Sr., a military officer, and Ann Tate. At sixteen, he became an apprentice under physician Joel Abbott of Monticello, Georgia. At nineteen he enrolled in the University of Pennsylvania School of Medicine but, owing to economic circumstances, had to leave without a diploma. He married Nancy Godwin in 1809. They had eleven children.

After practicing medicine in Monticello and New Orleans, Louisiana, Antony settled in Augusta, Georgia, in 1819. He achieved notoriety for, among other things, performing in 1821 the world's first thoracotomy, or surgical opening of the thorax, to treat what was later interpreted as possibly having been a case of pulmonary hemangiopericytoma (a giant malignant tumor subject to bursting during removal). Antony performed the operation on a seventeen-year-old boy who had been injured to the right side of the abdomen and had fractured his fifth and sixth ribs after a fall from his horse a few years earlier. At the time Antony visited, the patient was in extreme pain, had a fever, and was having breathing difficulties. He had a tumefaction that extended "from the sternum to the anterior edge of the latissimus dorsi." After incision and removal of "a kind of grume," Antony proceeded to remove bone fragments and to saw the fractured ribs (which by then had become cascous) with cutting forceps. He also had to remove a portion of the right lung that had been destroyed in the accident. Once the wound was cleaned, he closed it but not without leaving a small opening for discharge of pus. The patient's health started improving a few days after surgery, but the problem relapsed several times, and he had to have more "disorganized parenchyma of the lungs" removed. About four months later the patient died, apparently from the measles and, against Antony's prescription of absolute rest, after having walked for several miles. Antony published the results of this first thoracotomy in "Case of Extensive Caries of the Fifth and Sixth Ribs, and Disorganization of the Greater Part of the Right Lobe of Lungs, with a Description of the Operation for the Same," in *Philadelphia Journal of Medical and Physical Sciences* (6 [1823]: 108–18).

A new treatment for fractures of the thigh recommended by physician William C. Daniell of Savannah, Georgia, in 1829 was adopted by Antony, who in 1836 published the results of his own successful experience with its application. This new method was supposed to avoid the contraction of the muscles, which had the tendency to shorten the fractured limb. Antony selected a small group of patients representative of a variety of circumstances, ages, weights, and temperaments. He reported that the traditional treatment, which juxtaposed heavy extension and counter-extension, was extremely uncomfortable, painful (it could produce excoriations and ulcerations), and inevitably provoked deformations of the limbs. The new treatment, which consisted of using gentle traction with splints to secure the straight position of the limb and body weight as counter-extension, allowed for the fracture to heal without displacing the bone or damaging the muscles, thus keeping the proportionate size and original shape and function of the limb. This technique only became standard procedure in surgery after its publication in 1861 by Dr. Gurdon Buck, and it later became known as "Buck's extension."

Also a gynecologist, Antony in 1836 argued that the use in childbirth of substances such as ergot was unappreciated and undervalued. Instead of contributing, as was thought, to the death of the fetus, he defended its use in the acceleration of labor, which nevertheless had to be complemented with manual assistance and the selection of the best position for the woman to give birth. He also defended, following the examples of contemporary physicians Laennec, Gherard, and Bigelow, the importance of performing physical examinations such as auscultation and percussion, especially on the thorax and the abdomen, since they often allowed for precise diagnosis of internal conditions by touch.

The role of Antony in the organization of the Richmond County Medical Society in 1822 was pivotal. According to him, the criteria for admission into the medical profession was not demanding enough. He believed that course requirements should be extended in both duration and diversity of fields covered, that there was a need for more practical training, and that individual medical societies should be established. Antony also advocated the dissemination of medical information through medical journals and annual conventions. Eventually, his biggest projects became the regulation, extension, and improvement of the medical curriculum. His request to the state legislature to appoint a State Board of Medical Examiners was granted in 1825, and he was elected its first president. Only those who were examined and given licenses by the board could practice within the state. The other purpose of the board was to eliminate "Thomsonianism" (a type of alternative medicine that used plants in the treatment of all types of diseases), at the time considered by many to be the dominant healing system. Three years later, with other physicians from Augusta, Antony applied again to the legislature for a charter to organize the Medical Academy of Georgia, which was finally founded in 1828. Also in 1825 the Medical College of South Carolina gave him an honorary medical degree.

The Medical Academy of Georgia was authorized to confer, after one year of courses, the degree of bachelor of medicine. Antony in 1829 was elected a member of its executive committee, and from 1832 to 1839 he served as professor of institutes and practice of medicine and of midwifery and diseases of women and children. In 1829 he succeeded at having the charter extended to authorize, after two years of courses, the granting of the M.D. The academy had its name changed to Medical Institute of Georgia and, in 1832, to Medical College of Georgia. In 1835 Antony was appointed vice president of its board of trustees.

In 1836 Antony became the founding editor of the *Southern Medical and Surgical Journal*, considered by many as one of the best medical journals of the antebellum south. Its purpose was to facilitate the diffusion of concise, practical medical information, including the treatment of diseases specific to the southern climates as well as "history of epidemics, reports of cases, the application of new remedies, and all interesting medical facts and experiments." He remained editor of the journal until he died in Augusta, Georgia, a victim of the yellow fever epidemic.

In 1837 the *Southern Medical and Surgical Journal* (2 [Aug. 1837]) reprinted a letter that Antony and Lewis D. Ford, the dean of the Medical College of Georgia, had circulated to all medical schools, pressing for a reform of medical education in the United States. This reform, which had been tried at the Medical College of Georgia, was meant to expand the curriculum and lengthen the term from three or four months to eleven or twelve. The reform also would have included the founding of a "National College, which *alone* should confer the *Doctorate*; all other institutions subsidiary; limited in their honors to the first degree" (p. 53). The suggestion that the University of Pennsylvania, the oldest and most prestigious medical school, take the lead in supporting a national meeting in Washington, D.C., to discuss these matters was rejected, and the medical college had to reduce the curriculum to its traditional size. Antony's letter calling for educational reform is considered nevertheless to have been crucial to the later establishment of the American Medical Association.

• Biographical accounts of the life and work of Antony are in W. H. Goodrich, *The History of the Medical Department of the University of Georgia* (1928); Russell R. Mores, "Exegit Monumentum Aere Perennius," *Richmond County History* 9 (1977): 10–17; and Martin Dalton and Samuel Connally, "Milton Antony: Pioneering Surgeon and Medical Educator," *Journal of the Medical Association of Georgia* 83 (1994): 79–82. For the history of the early years of the Medical College of Georgia, see Evelyn Ward Gay, *The Medical Profession in Georgia: 1733–1883* (1983) and Phinizy Spalding, *The History of the Medical College of Georgia* (1987). For an appreciation of how Antony's treatment of thigh fractures was influenced by the work of William Daniell, see Daniell, "Method of Treating Fracture of the Thigh Bone," *Boston Medical and Surgical Journal* 4 (1829): 330–33. Antony's paper on his application of this method to a selection of his own patients can be found in "Case of Fracture of the Os Femoris—Adjustment by Weight and Fulcrum," *Southern Medical and Surgical Journal* 1 (Oct. 1836): 281–87. This method became widely used after the publication of Gurdon Buck, "An Improved Method of Treating Fractures of the Thigh," *Transactions of the New York Academy of Medicine* 2 (1861): 232–50. For the objectives of Antony's medical journal for southern physicians, see his introduction in *Southern Medical and Surgical Journal* 1 (June 1836): 1–4.

TERESA CASTELÃO-LAWLESS

ANZA, Juan Bautista de (7 July 1736–19 Dec. 1788), military commander, explorer, and governor, was born in the presidio of Fronteras, Sonora, Mexico, the son of Juan Bautista de Anza, commandant of the post since 1719, and María Rafaela Becerra Nieto; his grandfather was commandant of Janos presidio, Chihuahua. Anza's father was killed in combat in 1739, but Anza continued in the family tradition, and on 1 December 1752 entered the militia at Fronteras. On 1 July 1755 he was promoted to lieutenant at Fronteras, and, after participating in Indian campaigns in

Sonora, he rose in 1760 to the rank of captain and commander of the presidio at Tubac (in present-day Arizona). On 24 June 1761 he married Ana María Pérez Serrano of Arizpe, Sonora, but no children were born of the union.

Anza led five expeditions against the rebellious Seri and in 1767 was one of the officers charged with removal of Jesuit missionaries from Sonora under the decree of King Charles III expelling the order from Spanish domains because of political intrigues. With reports of Russian and English advances toward Spanish settlements in California, Viceroy Antonio María Bucareli ordered the opening of an overland trail from Sonora to California for the movement of settlers and supplies. On 17 September 1773 Anza was ordered to explore for a route, and on 8 January 1774, with twenty soldiers, three Franciscan missionaries, and eleven muleteers, he left Tubac, crossed the Colorado River, and arrived on the Pacific Coast at San Gabriel near present-day Los Angeles on 22 March. Although the weather was relatively cool, the expedition had traversed the most arid region of North America. Men and livestock relied on the infrequent oases and natural cisterns, and after a month of trial and error they opened a trail from the Colorado River across the barren Imperial and Mexicali valleys to the San Jacinto mountains. After a brief rest, on 18 April Anza reached the presidio of Monterey, by 5 May he was again at San Gabriel, and on 28 May he completed the return trek to Tubac.

Anza reported to Bucareli in Mexico City and delivered his diaries. He was promoted to lieutenant colonel and on 24 November was ordered by Bucareli to return to California with a group of colonists and twenty-eight soldiers to found a new mission and presidio on the bay of San Francisco. Some 136 settlers were enlisted, and, with two Franciscans, two officers, ten soldiers, and thirty-one muleteers, on 23 October 1775 the expedition left Tubac on the route established the preceding year. They reached San Gabriel on 4 January 1776 and followed the coast northward, sighting the bay of San Francisco on 28 March. Although several earlier expeditions had explored the region, no appropriate site for settlement had yet been determined, and so Anza reconnoitered the northern end of the San Francisco peninsula. He recommended a mesa overlooking the entrance to the bay as the location of the projected presidio and the area of Arroyo de los Dolores on the interior of the bay for the mission. His task accomplished, Anza returned to Monterey on 4 April and arrived at the presidio of San Miguel de Horcasitas in Sonora on 1 June.

In February 1777 Anza delivered his reports and diaries to Bucareli, and on 24 August he received appointment as governor of New Mexico, a post he held until 10 November 1787. During his term, he oversaw the preparation of a map of the province by Bernardo de Miera, led an expedition against Comanches near Pike's Peak (1779), explored the Hopi pueblos (1780), and again in 1780 opened the trail from Santa Fe to Sonora.

In 1782 Anza was promoted to colonel, but in 1784, because of political conflicts with Felipe de Neve, commandant of the Provincias Internas, Anza was suspended from government, charged with misinformation and incompetent judgment in the massacre by Yuman Indians on the Colorado River of Fernando de Rivera y Moncada, four Franciscan missionaries, and over thirty settlers in July of 1781. The successor to Anza's post did not arrive until the end of 1787, and at that point Anza returned to Tubac where, on 1 October 1788, he was reappointed commandant, a post he held until his sudden death after a brief illness at the town of Arizpe, where he was interred in the church of Nuestra Señora de la Asunción. His remains were identified and ceremonially reinterred in 1963.

In addition to his active life as a military commander, explorer, Indian agent, and governor, Anza was one of a very few Spaniards native to the frontier to achieve fame. Energetic, ambitious, and proud of having risen from the ranks, he was known to have been sensitive and easily offended, probably due to his lower social status relative to his Spanish-born superiors.

• Extensive manuscript material relative to Anza and his commands, administration, and explorations can be found in the Archivo General de la Nación, Mexico City, Mexico, in the *ramo* Provincias Internas and *ramo* Californias. Principal published sources include Herbert Eugene Bolton, *Anza's California Expeditions* (5 vols., 1930; repr. 1966), J. N. Bowman and Robert F. Heizer, *Anza and the Northwest Frontier of New Spain* (1967); Mario Hernández Sánchez-Barba, *Juan Bautista de Anza: un hombre de fronteras* (1962); and Alfred B. Thomas, *Forgotten Frontiers* (1932).

W. MICHAEL MATHES

APESS, William (31 Jan. 1798–Apr. or May 1839), writer, Methodist minister, and Native-American activist, was born in Colrain, Franklin County, Massachusetts, the son of William Apes, a shoemaker and laborer, and Candace (surname unknown), probably a slave or indentured servant in the house of Captain Joseph Taylor of Colchester, Connecticut. According to Apess's autobiographical accounts, his father was part Anglo-American and part Pequot and his mother "a female of the [same] tribe, in whose veins a single drop of the white man's blood never flowed," although some evidence indicates that she may have been part African American. Only in myth do such beginnings spawn great achievements. At age three, abandoned by his parents, he was nearly beaten to death by his maternal grandmother while she was in a drunken rage, a rage that Apess later understood as an effect of the theft by whites of Native American lands, culture, and pride. Bound out at four, he spent his youth as an indentured servant in three different white households in Connecticut and as an infantryman in a New York State militia company during the War of 1812. He received his only formal education, six winter terms of school, between the ages of six and eleven.

Treated as inferior because he was an Indian, Apess turned early and repeatedly to the more egalitarian evangelical churches of his day. He could thus make contact with others who were considered "lowly": poor whites, Native Americans, African Americans, and peoples of mixed racial heritage. These religious communities enabled Apess to convert the desolation and trauma of his upbringing not only into spiritual fervor, but also into an affirmative identification with the Pequots, to whose culture he belonged by birth. He became a baptized Methodist in December 1818 in Bozra, Connecticut, an occasion of much significance to him.

In 1819 Apess felt the call to preach and began to lead Methodist prayer meetings. Like many Americans of his class, and many Native Americans in the Northeast, Apess moved frequently in search of work. Among his many different jobs were a day laborer on a number of farms, a barkeep in a tavern, a cook on a boat, an itinerant book peddlar; all his life he supported himself with such ordinary transitory jobs. This itineracy, as well as the oral nature of Native American cultural forms, intersected nicely with the practice of Methodist circuit riding. Apess traveled widely, preaching throughout southern New England and eastern New York, mostly to the same kinds of outsider communities that had nurtured him. He emphasized a Christ who came to save "all people" and who was himself a man of color devoted to the poor and despised. During these journeys he met his wife, Mary Wood, of Salem, Connecticut, herself of mixed parentage. They were married in Salem in 1821. They are known to have had at least three children.

Licensed as an exhorter by the Methodist Episcopal church, Apess sought to obtain his license as a preacher from the conference of the church. Impatient with several denials and reasonably suspecting that the church was reluctant to allow "an Indian" such standing and independence, he broke with the Methodist Episcopal church in April 1829 and joined a new, antiepiscopal and more democratic church, the Protestant Methodists, also known as the Methodist Society, which ordained him sometime later in 1829 or in early 1830.

A Son of the Forest: The Experience of William Apes, a Native of the Forest, his first book and the first published book by a Native American, appeared in July 1829. Although Apess may have begun his autobiography to fulfill a church requirement that he account for his life and his conversion, the final work also serves as a justification of Native Americans as equal to Euro-Americans before God, a call for fair and civil treatment, and a compilation history of Native Americans.

Apess's autobiography marks the beginning of nine years of an intense and increasingly controversial public life. His preaching continued and included a special mission to the Pequots. Three more books and a sermon were published, documenting Apess's movement toward a direct challenge of both Euro-American assumptions of racial superiority and the exploitation of Christianity as an agent of Euro-American imperialism and the humiliation of Native Americans. He achieved widest public notice when, in 1833–1834, he took up the cause of the Mashpees, inhabitants of the one sizable surviving Indian town in Massachusetts. Long governed by appointed overseers and ministered to by a man not of their choosing who regarded them as children, the Mashpees found in Apess a new leader. He quickly displayed a genius for gaining public attention by helping the Mashpees write a "Nullification Proclamation" that declared their grievances and requested their rights as equal citizens to govern themselves. For a brief moment, the "Mashpee Revolt," as it was called, gained national attention and sufficiently frightened the governor of the state, Levi Lincoln (1782–1868), that he hysterically threatened to call out the militia to quell what he believed was major civil unrest. Throughout the conflict, Apess so skillfully assisted the Mashpees through his writings and his testimony to the Massachusetts legislature that they gained most of their ends.

Apess's last-known public appearance was in Boston in 1836, when he delivered his *Eulogy on King Philip*, a wily and brilliant revision of American historical mythology. He proposed the by-then obscure King Philip as a hero and patriot equal in stature to George Washington and the cause of Indian independence as grand and noble as the American Revolution. The eulogy was a reminder that Native Americans remained in the United States and that their history should be an integral part of the narrative of the whole culture.

A series of lawsuits brought by creditors against Apess in 1836, 1837, and 1838, perhaps continuations of the harassment he had earlier experienced from white authorities for his role in the Mashpee Revolt, resulted in his losing all his property, including his house in Mashpee. He moved to New York City and suffered a return of his earlier struggles with alcoholism. One can only speculate about the causes, but his drinking increased so that he lost all credibility. He died in late April or early May 1839 of "apoplexy," according to the autopsy, an attack apparently brought on by effects of alcoholism. In his writings he had identified alcohol as perhaps the most insidious weapon that Europeans wielded against Native Americans. Its power he recognized as depending on the ways Indian peoples felt shame and loss. In his death could be read defeat—and defeat of a kind there surely was—but to read it so wholly would be to mistake his life and achievements. His determined affirmation of the cause of his people and his remarkable eloquence live on.

• There is no known collection of Apess's papers. His own publications, in addition to those mentioned above, include a second autobiography, "The Experience of the Missionary," in *The Experiences of Five Christian Indians of the Pequot Tribe* (1833), most of which was probably written before *A Son of the Forest*, as well as *The Increase of the Kingdom of Christ* and *The Ten Lost Tribes* (1831) and *Indian Nullification of the Unconstitutional Laws of Massachusetts Relative to the Marshpee Tribe; or, The Pretended Riot Explained* (1835). *On Our Own Ground: The Complete Writings of William Apess, a Pequot*, edited and with an introduction by Barry O'Connell (1992), provides the first modern edition of his writings and also the most detailed biographical and critical study to date.

Apess received little notice from historians or from literary critics until Kim McQuaid's important essay, "William Apes, a Pequot: An Indian Reformer in the Jackson Era," *American Quarterly* 50 (1977): 605–25. Donald M. Nielsen, "The Mashpee Indian Revolt of 1833," *New England Quarterly* 58 (1985): 400–20, is thus far the definitive historical account of the episode that brought Apess brief national prominence and regional notoriety. Arnold Krupat, *For Those Who Come After: A Study of Native American Autobiography* (1985) and *The Voice in the Margin: Native American Literature and the Canon* (1989), the latter containing extensive commentary on Apess, are indispensable for anyone interested in Apess or in Native American literature. See also Krupat, "Native American Autobiography and the Synecdochic Self," in *American Autobiography: Retrospect and Prospect*, ed. Paul John Eakin (1991). David Murray, *Forked Tongues: Speech, Writing, and Representation in North American Indian Texts* (1991), is equally valuable on Apess and on the literary context. See also A. LaVonne Brown Ruoff, "Three Nineteenth-Century American Indian Autobiographers," in *Redefining American Literary History*, ed. Ruoff and Jerry W. Ward, Jr. (1990).

BARRY O'CONNELL

APGAR, Virginia (7 June 1909–7 Aug. 1974), physician, anesthesiologist, and teratologist, was born in Westfield, New Jersey, the daughter of Charles Emory Apgar, an insurance executive, and Helen May Clarke. She had two brothers, one of whom died of tuberculosis at age three. Apgar's father conducted amateur experiments in electricity and astronomy, which stimulated her interest in science and medicine. After schooling in Westfield, Apgar attended Mount Holyoke College, obtaining her A.B. degree in 1929. She completed her M.D. at Columbia University College of Physicians and Surgeons, New York City, in 1933. Then followed two brilliant years in surgery at Columbia-Presbyterian Medical Center, but the department chairman, Alan Whipple, discouraged her from surgical practice. He cited the depression and financial insecurities experienced by his previous female trainees and urged her instead to consider anesthesia, not yet a medical specialty but often done by women nurse practitioners. Apgar spent six months in anesthesia training at the University of Wisconsin, Madison, and six months at Bellevue Hospital in New York City before returning to Columbia-Presbyterian in 1938 as director of the Division of Anesthesiology; she was the first woman to head a medical division in that institution.

Apgar continued in this capacity as a busy practitioner, engaged teacher, and researcher for eleven years. She worked to resolve problems of remuneration for anesthetists. When her division became a department in 1949, she expected to become chair, but the position was given to a male colleague. She was, however, appointed full professor, once again the first woman at Columbia to hold that rank. Then she withdrew from administration to pursue research in obstetrical anesthesia.

During this period Apgar developed a standard scale to assess the health status of newborn children. The method is based on an ingeniously simple scoring system that takes into account heart rate, respiration, movement, color, and irritability. Apgar's inspiration came in answer to a question from a medical student over breakfast in the hospital cafeteria. She presented the method in September 1952 at the Twenty-seventh Annual Congress of Anesthetists in Virginia Beach, Virginia, and published it the following year. Through the next four decades, this classic paper has been the most frequently cited of her publications, and the "Apgar score" has remained the world's standard assessment of newborns. With L. Stanley James, Apgar correlated the score with the physical condition of infants and the effects of maternal anesthesia in a series of elegant studies, using innovative catheterization of the umbilical vessels and the newborn heart.

In 1959 Apgar took a sabbatical to complete her master's of public health degree at Johns Hopkins University. She intended to study statistics and return to anesthesia; however, she began to promote research on the causes of birth defects (teratology) and on improving care for the disabled. This transition was marked by her review of congenital abnormalities, presented at the American Medical Association meeting on 15 June 1960 and published the following year. Her new interest in genetics led to her appointment to several executive positions in the National Foundation–March of Dimes, from 1959 to her death; she was an energetic advocate and fundraiser. Her subsequent professional appointments reflected these same concerns: as lecturer (1965–1971) and then clinical professor (1971–1973) of pediatrics (teratology), Cornell University Medical College; and as lecturer in medical genetics, Johns Hopkins University School of Hygiene and Public Health, 1973. At Cornell she held the first American faculty position devoted to the subspecialty of congenital disorders.

Apgar was a gifted and enthusiastic teacher who spoke quickly and was fond of surprising demonstrations: she had students feel her own coccyx as an example of pelvic variation. According to her friend and colleague, Mary Ellen Avery, Apgar was pleased to discover her name in lower case letters in a dictionary, and she like to greet strangers by saying, "My name is Apgar; I bet you thought I was a thing." Her commitment to the welfare of children and their families combined with her love of teaching in her book, coauthored with Joan Beck, *Is My Baby All Right? A Guide to Birth Defects* (1972). Each chapter tells the story of a typical patient with a congenital disorder and lucidly explains what science could and could not do to assuage parental fears.

Apgar was also a talented musician; she played in symphony orchestras and built her own viola and cello. She enjoyed fishing, golfing, gardening, and stamp-collecting, and colleagues remember her passion for fast driving and flying airplanes, which she took up after age fifty. She never married and avoided women's associations. In public she was reserved about the limitations imposed on women, but her frustrations can be read in her diary and correspondence. In her final illness with cirrhosis of the liver, she refused to allow friends to visit her in Columbia-Presbyterian hospital, where she had trained and worked for many years, and where she died.

Apgar was the recipient of a number of awards and distinctions: the Alumni Gold Medal for Distinguished Achievement in Medicine, Columbia University College of Physicians and Surgeons; the *Ladies' Home Journal* Woman of the Year in Science and Research; and the Ralph M. Waters Award of the American Society of Anesthesiologists. A twenty-cent stamp depicting her was issued in 1994, and she was inducted into the Women's Hall of Fame in Seneca Falls, New York, in 1995. Apgar achieved a number of firsts for medical women, but her accomplishments should also be recognized as milestones in the emerging professions of anesthesiology and teratology.

• Apgar's papers are at Mount Holyoke College, South Hadley, Mass. Her classic articles include "A Proposal for a New Method of Evaluation of the Newborn Infant," *Current Researches in Anesthesia and Analgesia* 32 (Jul.–Aug. 1953): 260–67, and "Human Congenital Abnormalities: Present Status of Knowledge," *AMA Journal of Diseases of Children* 101 (1961): 249–54.

A short biography based on Apgar's diaries and correspondence is Selma Harrison Calmes, "Virginia Apgar: A Woman Physician's Career in a Developing Specialty," *Journal of the American Medical Women's Association* 39 (1984): 184–88. For a tribute by an associate, see L. Stanley James, "Fond Memories of Virginia Apgar," *Pediatrics* 55 (1975): 1–4. An obituary is in the *New York Times*, 8 Aug. 1974.

JACALYN DUFFIN

APPEL, Benjamin (13 Sept. 1907–3 Apr. 1977), novelist and short story writer, was born in New York City, the son of Louis Appel, a successful real estate businessman, and Bessie Mikofsky, both Polish émigrés from once-wealthy families. He grew up in a largely immigrant section of Hell's Kitchen on the West Side of Manhattan, and his parents did their best to shield their son from the deprivation and periodic violence that often plagued their neighborhood. Such concerns form much of the substance of Appel's early novels.

As a teenager Appel liked to spend time with his father's driver, "Red." Appel's father regularly held large poker games at the office, attracting wealthy businessmen and politicians. Appel's association with Red ended when the driver was implicated in two holdups at the office on days when the poker pot was particularly high.

Appel was a student at DeWitt Clinton High School near Fifty-ninth Street and Tenth Avenue, and he attended the University of Pennsylvania in 1925–1926. In 1926 he transferred as a sophomore to New York University and concentrated on developing his talents in football, rowing, and athletics. Gradually, writing became his primary interest, and in 1927 Appel gave up sports (with the exception of fishing) and transferred yet again, this time to Lafayette College in Easton, Pennsylvania. He graduated with a B.S. in 1929. By that time he had already published a collection of poetry, *Mixed Vintage* (1929), and he soon began to achieve limited recognition for the short stories he was publishing in literary magazines. Nevertheless, as a young writer Appel struggled to make ends meet, supporting himself during the depression years with stints as a factory worker, bank clerk, farmer, lumberjack, and tenement house inspector. In 1936 he married Sophie Marshak, with whom he had three daughters.

Appel's first three novels, *Brain Guy* (1934), *Four Roads to Death* (1935), and *Runaround* (1937), as well as thirty or more short stories, deal with the world of the poor and the relationship between poverty and crime that he had observed so closely throughout his youth. His experience in Hell's Kitchen had taught him that neither crime nor West Side politics were particularly glamorous and, furthermore, that they were not infrequently related. In his early explorations of the relationships between petty crime, mob violence, racial tension, racketeering, and local politics, Appel attempted to explain the values and aspirations of his human subjects, ordinary people whose lives were seldom reflected in novels. While his approach distinguished him from many writers of the time, it also initially prevented him from achieving success in popular magazines, publications for which he was required to write according to an established pattern, something he said he was unable to do. *Brain Guy* was the first novel in a trilogy, followed by *The Power House* (1939) and *The Dark Stain* (1943). In this series Appel follows the rise of Bill Trent, a college student from a good family who, driven by greed, becomes a small-time hoodlum, a gangster, and finally a fascist agent committed to union-busting and stirring up racial hatred. For Appel, Trent is a potential American Everyman, a figure who has sold his social and moral values for capitalistic gain. As a whole, the trilogy presents a significant exploration of the divisiveness of American racism and the rise of international fascism in the years leading up to World War II. Significantly, Appel demonstrates how the legal, social, and religious institutions of 1930s America forged unholy alliances with both bigots and fascists.

In *The People Talk* (1940) Appel expressed his interest in the ordinary citizens of the United States. This, his first nonfiction book and a significant early oral history, presents the results of eight months of research that he conducted while he and his wife traveled the country, joining working people in their daily lives in fields and factories. Appel recorded the people's thoughts—mostly about the current hard times—and the ways in which their various regional accents and idioms expressed the texture of a diverse America.

In 1941 Appel was severely burned and came close to death as the result of an explosion. He moved to Long Island, New York, and after making a complete recovery went to work as an aviation mechanic. Six months later he moved again, this time to Washington, D.C., where he wrote speeches and articles for the Office of Civilian Defense and later for Paul V. McNutt, the chairperson of the War Manpower Commission. In 1944 McNutt was made U.S. high commissioner to the Philippines, and Appel joined him in 1945 as special assistant, bearing the titular military rank of colonel. This trip furnished Appel with the experience that inspired the critically acclaimed *Fortress in the Rice* (1951), a panoramic novel about the Philippines under Japanese occupation during the war years. Appel later adapted the work for the screen as *Cry of Battle* (1963), starring Van Heflin and Rita Moreno. Appel returned to Washington in 1946 and found work in the Office of War Mobilization, moving to Roosevelt, New Jersey, in 1947. When Congress dissolved the office later that year, he devoted himself to full-time fiction writing.

From then on Appel turned his attention in his novels from the urban poor to the middle class, which he began to envisage as the future backbone of America. In 1959 he published *The Funhouse*, a science fiction satire concerning a nuclear threat to a future America. In the mid-1950s, after preliminary research had taught him that American children knew very little about the peoples of the world, and that what they did know was often skewed by alarmingly bizarre fallacies, Appel devoted much of his energy to publishing educational works for young people. Two such works, *Why the Russians Are the Way They Are* (1966) and *Why the Chinese Are the Way They Are* (1968), won New Jersey Authors awards.

Appel died in Princeton, New Jersey. In his works Appel charted the bitterness and disillusionment of hard-working Americans ruined by the depression. He also described a trend in the national character toward a tolerance of violence as a means to success. Yet even in his darkest moments, such as those in which he exposes the "kill the union idea" (*The Powerhouse*, 1939) as the moral conscience of America caves in to fascist demagoguery, his fiction remains dramatic rather than didactic. Appel's characters always have a choice: their actions, for good or evil, always spring from a clearly chosen course of action. This warning is perhaps Appel's most enduring legacy.

• There is a collection of Appel papers, including manuscripts and some correspondence, at the University of Oregon in Eugene, Or. An extensive bibliography of his writings appears in Ann Evory, ed., *Contemporary Authors*, New Revision Series, vol. 6 (1982). A profile of Appel is in the *New York Times Book Review*, 16 June 1940; this piece is reprinted in Robert Van Gelder, *Writers and Writing* (1946). An obituary is in the *New York Times*, 4 Apr. 1977.

PETER E. MORGAN

APPLEBY, John Francis (23 May 1840–8 Nov. 1917), inventor, was born in Westmoreland, New York, the son of James Appleby and Jane (maiden name unknown), farmers and recent immigrants from England. When he was five his parents moved to a farm in Walworth County, Wisconsin. In 1857 Appleby worked for a farmer near Whitewater, who had purchased a reaper. The implement's performance impressed Appleby, but he believed that a mechanical harvester could be designed both to cut the stalks of grain and bind them into sheaves. He applied himself to this problem and soon carved a knotting device in the shape of a bird's bill from wood. In 1858 he crafted a similar knotter from steel at a gunshop in Beloit, but he did not believe that it merited the expense of patenting. His service from 1861 to 1865 in the Twenty-third Wisconsin Infantry during the Civil War interrupted this work. During the war years he served in the battle of Vicksburg and invented a magazine and automatic cartridge-feeding mechanism, which he patented. The sale of this patent supported his work on a binder after the war. In 1867 Appleby married a woman whose name is unknown; they had three children.

After the Civil War, Appleby returned to the task of inventing a grain harvester that would mechanically tie the sheaves. In 1867 he experimented with wire and demonstrated a harvester that wrapped a band around a sheaf and deposited it on the ground. Appleby patented this binder in 1869 and improved it in his Beloit shop, where in 1872 he attracted the financial support of businessmen Charles H. Parker and Gustavus Stone. This binder worked efficiently, but farmers soon feared that the wire would foul threshing machines and that cattle would ingest pieces of it in their hay and feed. They also had difficulty disposing of the wire. Millers worried that bits of wire might accidentally pass through the threshing machine into the grain and damage their burrs.

As a result of these problems, Appleby began work in 1874 to develop a twine binder that was based on the tying mechanism that he had designed in 1858. After considerable experimentation trying to attach a knotting mechanism to a harvester, Appleby solved the problem in 1875. By 1877 he had several twine-binding mechanisms attached to Marsh harvesters. In May 1878 Appleby shipped his twine binder to Travis County, Texas, for demonstration and testing. He patented this implement and improvements on 8 July 1878 and 18 February 1879. After its successful demonstration in Travis County, Appleby soon manufactured more than a hundred binders. His implement proved so successful during field tests that the company of Gammon and Deering purchased a license to manufacture it in 1878 and placed the binder on the market the following year. Deering's substitution of Appleby's twine for a wire-tying mechanism began the large-scale production of his invention and the general adoption of twine binders. In 1880 the Deering Harvester Company built 3,000 twine binders based on Appleby's design. Appleby also manufactured twine binders as demonstration models for other agricultural implement firms and sold licenses that returned six dollars on each machine built. Appleby licensed his knotting mechanism to the companies of Esterly (1880), Excelsior (1880), McCormick (1881), Buckeye (1882), Champion (1882), Osborne (1883), and Wood (1892). McCormick paid Appleby $35,000 for the right to manufacture his twine binder and in 1884 sold 15,000 of these implements. By the turn of the twentieth century, approximately 90 percent of the twine binders manufactured in the United States used Appleby's tying mechanism.

The invention of the twine binder enabled farmers to harvest their small grain crops by combining the processes of cutting and tying the sheaves. By so doing, the binder eliminated the need for workers to follow the reaper and tie the sheaves before setting them in small upright stacks called shocks for pick up by wagon at threshing time. Although the machine did not increase the amount of acreage that could be harvested in one day, it did contribute to the total reduction in the amount of time required to produce a bushel of wheat from three hours and forty minutes in 1830 to ten minutes in 1880. By reducing the number of hands required to harvest the crop, the farmer saved time and money. This implement also eased the burden on the farmer's wife, who cooked meals for the harvest crew. Appleby's twine-binding mechanism remained unsurpassed until combines increasingly eliminated the need for binders during the first half of the twentieth century. During the late twentieth century, however, the manufacturers of hay balers still used Appleby's bill-hook knotter on their implements.

Appleby died in Chicago, Illinois.

• F. B. Swingle, "The Invention of the Twine Binder," *Wisconsin Magazine of History* 10 (1926): 36–41, is based on an interview with Appleby. For a general discussion of agricultural inventions that include the twine binder see R. L. Ardrey, *American Agricultural Implements* (1894); R. Douglas Hurt, *American Farm Tools: From Hand Power to Steam Power* (1982); and Graeme R. Quick and Wesley F. Buchele, *The Grain Harvesters* (1978). An obituary is in the *Chicago Tribune*, 9 Nov. 1917.

R. DOUGLAS HURT

APPLEGATE, Jesse (5 July 1811–22 Apr. 1888), Oregon pioneer and publicist, was born in Kentucky, the son of Daniel Applegate, a veteran of the revolutionary war, and Rachel Lindsay. When he was ten his family moved to Missouri, where his father was the village schoolmaster and deputy surveyor general. In 1827 and 1828 Applegate attended Rock Spring Seminary in Shiloh, Illinois, where he showed talent in mathematics and surveying. Later he continued private study of these subjects while teaching school. He then secured a position clerking for the surveyor general's office in St. Louis and was promoted quickly to deputy surveyor general; he spent much of his time surveying in the western part of Missouri. In 1832 he married Cynthia Parker and settled on a farm in Osage Valley, where the couple lived for twelve years and had several children.

Applegate became increasingly interested in the western migration, especially when he learned that Oregon was an ideal site for raising cattle. This interest, combined with a poor economy and the growing presence of slavery in Missouri, spurred Applegate to join the westward movement to Oregon in 1843. He and a thousand other pioneers from Missouri and other midwestern states gathered near Independence, Missouri. When the travelers reached the Kansas River, there was a dispute over the responsibilities of guarding and tending to the cattle, and the settlers without cattle split from the cattle owners. The latter formed the "cow column," over which Jesse Applegate was chosen to be captain.

When Applegate's party reached Oregon, he settled in the Willamette Valley, Dallas, and established a farm and a mill. He also worked as a surveyor. In 1844 the legislature appointed him surveyor general of the colony.

At that time the United States and Great Britain maintained joint occupation of Oregon, and there was an ongoing dispute over which nation had dominion over the territory. As a result, the settlers had to devise their own government and organic laws. Although Applegate was not politically inclined, he thought that it was his duty to try to calm the unrest. He therefore ran and was elected delegate to the provisional government in 1845. Serving as a member of the legislature representing the Yamhill District, he became a powerful figure in reconciling contending British and U.S. nationals. At his suggestion, the Oregon oath of office was amended to read, "I do solemnly swear that I will support the organic laws of the Provisional Government as far as said organic laws are consistent with my duties as a citizen of the United States, or a subject of Great Britain." Applegate led the legislative effort to reassert U.S. rights over the entire territory of Oregon, not just the area south of the Columbia River. He secured the support of the British inhabitants north of the river, most of whom preferred that the territory be maintained intact rather than permanently divided.

After completing the rugged journey to Oregon, Applegate became convinced that there must be an easier route to the Willamette Valley better suited for wagon trains. Therefore, he explored and eventually helped to open a southern route to Oregon by way of Fort Hall, Idaho, through Nevada and northern California. While exploring this route, he noticed the fertile land and navigable river in the Umpqua Valley in western central Oregon. When Oregon was made a U.S. territory on 13 August 1848, Applegate moved his family to the Umpqua Valley and settled at Yoncalla. There he raised cattle, which he sold in California.

Applegate was a Whig, a Union party supporter, and adamantly opposed to slavery. He stated, "Whoever is against the extension of slavery is of my party." Because of his beliefs and his reputation as an educated and principled man, he was elected a delegate of Oregon's Constitutional Convention in 1857. His effort to outlaw slavery in Oregon failed, however, and he left the convention in disgust before it ended. In addition to these activities, he was a representative on the board appointed to settle the trade disputes with Britain's Hudson's Bay Company.

Applegate continued to exert political influence on his community from his Yoncalla ranch. A notably well-read pioneer, he wrote essays on politics and topics of general interest. One of his best-known works is a series of essays on the problems presented by Reconstruction in the post–Civil War South, published in the Oregon *State Journal*. He also wrote letters to the territorial newspapers and to many of Oregon's prominent political figures.

Applegate was a determined, passionate, and honorable man who figured prominently in Oregon's territorial history. While many people considered him talented in the political arena, his independence prevented him from turning to powerful friends who might have furthered his political career. He died at his ranch in the Yoncalla Valley.

• Major collections of Applegate's papers are in the Western Americana Collection at the Yale University Library; the Bancroft Library, University of California, Berkeley; the library of the Oregon Historical Society; and the University of Oregon Library, Eugene. For information on the political turmoil and the settlers' effort to establish a government, see W. C. Woodward, *The Rise and Early History of Political Parties in Oregon, 1843–68* (1913). See also William Henry Gray, *A History of Oregon* (repr. 1973); George W. Fuller, *A History of the Pacific Northwest* (1931); Gustavus Hines, *Oregon: Its History, Condition, and Prospects* (repr. 1973); and Malcolm Clark, Jr., *Eden Seekers: The Settlement of Oregon, 1818–1862* (1981). For Applegate's journey to Oregon, see "The South Road: Jesse Applegate's Infamous Emigrant Trail," *Real West* 25, no. 182 (Jan. 1982), pp. 30–34.

KATHRYN D. SNAVELY

APPLESEED, Johnny. *See* Chapman, John.

APPLETON, Daniel (10 Dec. 1785–27 Mar. 1849), publisher, was born in Haverhill, Massachusetts, the son of Daniel Appleton and Lydia Ela. He grew up in modest circumstances, but he seems to have formed a talent for organization at an early age. He opened a general store in Haverhill in 1813. That same year he married Hannah Adams of Andover, Massachusetts; the couple eventually had six sons and two daughters. Appleton moved both his business and family to Boston in 1817, where he opened a wholesale dry goods store on 21 Broad Street, featuring "English goods."

In 1825 Appleton moved to New York City. He, his wife, and their children moved into a home at 102 Houston Street, while he opened a store at 15 Water Street, in the heart of the fashionable retail district. Much of his store was allocated to the sale of books. From 1826 through 1830 Appleton's brother-in-law, Jonathan Leavitt, handled the bookselling part of the business. After his departure Appleton sold his remaining stock of dry goods and rented a new place of business (No. 3 Beekman Street), where he decided to sell books exclusively. Appleton's demeanor and his style of dress led many of his customers to comment that he resembled Daniel Webster, a similarity that perhaps enhanced his reputation as a serious man of literature. In any event, New Yorkers of note, such as diarist George Templeton Strong, frequented his store.

Appleton became a publisher almost by accident. In 1821 he published his first book, *Crumbs from the Master's Table*, a selection of Biblical texts compiled by W. Mason. This was followed by *Gospel Seeds* (1831) and *The Refuge: The Righteous Man's Habitation in the Time of Plague and Pestilence* (1832), which sought to address the fear created by a sweep of cholera through New York in that year. The success of these first books prompted Appleton to continue publishing. He brought out a one-volume edition of the complete works of the preacher Jonathan Edwards in 1834 and continued to publish religious tracts. He chose to avoid the publication of fiction.

Appleton weathered the financial crisis that swept the United States in 1837, and in May 1838 he, his wife, and their daughter Maria Louisa traveled to Europe. He established a branch office of his company at 16 Little Britain in London. This, the first office of an American publisher in England, was maintained for over 100 years. On 27 January 1838 Appleton took his son William Henry Appleton into partnership, changing the name of the firm to D. Appleton & Co. In the same year Appleton moved his store to 200 Broadway, which provided the larger space needed for the growing volume and scope of his publishing and bookselling.

Appleton diversified his business in the 1840s. He brought out his first book for children, Harriet Martineau's *The Crofton Boys*, in 1841. The success of this book led to the development of a juvenile department in the firm. Around 1845 Appleton entered an entirely new market for American publishers, Latin America. He took a large risk in sending books to Buenos Aires without having established any firm contact person there; however, the risk paid off handsomely in that Latin America, having recently won its independence from Spain, was eager for books. Thus began the long and profitable association of D. Appleton & Co. with Latin America. It was said that by the late nineteenth century Latin American schoolchildren were as familiar with the name of Appleton as their North American counterparts were with the names of Webster and McGuffey. The company also entered the field of travel literature, bringing out Wellington Williams's *Appleton's Railroad and Steamboat Companion* in 1847.

Appleton retired from the business in 1848. He died in New York City after a short illness. Appleton exemplified the Yankee shopkeeper who found a workable idea and used it to maximum advantage. It was perhaps no more than good fortune that enabled him to rise from Haverhill to Boston to the peak of success in New York City. What makes him stand out from many of his fellows is that he was perhaps the first American publisher to emerge from a largely unrelated field (the selling of dry goods). In an era before the modern corporation he established a business that thrived and remained solidly within the hands of the family.

• Most of the early Appleton business papers disappeared through fire or negligence. The best sources are Grant Overton, *Portrait of a Publisher* (1925); Samuel Claggett Chew, *Fruit Among the Leaves* (1950); and Gerard R. Wolfe, *The House of Appleton* (1981). See also Charles A. Madison, *Book Publishing in America* (1966), and Allan Nevins and Milton Halsey Thomas, eds., *The Diary of George Templeton Strong* (4 vols., 1952).

SAMUEL WILLARD CROMPTON

APPLETON, John (12 July 1804–7 Feb. 1891), lawyer and judge, was born in New Ipswich, New Hampshire, the son of John Appleton and Elizabeth Peabody, farmers. After graduating from Bowdoin College in 1822, Appleton taught school briefly, then studied law in the offices of George F. Farley of Massachusetts and Nathan Dane Appleton, a relative and prominent attorney in Maine.

From 1826 until 1832, Appleton practiced law successfully in Dixmont and Sebec, Maine, and in the latter town served for a time as justice of the peace and town treasurer. During this period he wrote four articles for *The Yankee*, a weekly newspaper published by John Neal. The first three articles, on lotteries, usury laws, and the balance of trade, marked Appleton as a rationalist and laissez-faire individualist; the fourth, on the testimony of atheists in court, launched him on a career as a legal reformer.

In 1832 Appleton moved to Bangor, where he formed partnerships at various times with Elisha H. Allen, John B. Hill, and his cousin Moses Appleton. All three were Whig politicians, and although Appleton displayed strong Democratic proclivities on such matters as free trade, banking, and law reform, he remained a Whig until that party disintegrated in the 1850s. In 1834 he married Sarah Newcombe Allen, Elisha Allen's sister. The couple had five children.

Appleton had a large and varied practice in Bangor. During Edward Kent's second brief tenure as Whig governor of Maine in 1841, Appleton also served as reporter of decisions for the Supreme Judicial Court. The legal profession received his reports favorably, but the Democrats replaced him with one of their own after their return to power in 1841.

In 1850 Appleton was appointed to a commission to study the problems of delay and expense that plagued Maine's judicial system and to recommend solutions. His report, submitted to the legislature in 1852, denounced the existing state of affairs as "a denial of justice to the poor." His proposed reorganization of the state judiciary included, among other things, the abolition of the intermediate district court and the transfer of its jurisdiction to an expanded supreme court. The proposal generated considerable controversy, but the legislature adopted it with only slight modifications. In 1883 Appleton looked back on the reform with great satisfaction.

During his years in private practice and then as a judge, Appleton continued his campaign, begun with his fourth *Yankee* article, to overhaul the law of evidence. In a series of articles published anonymously in leading law journals, Appleton assailed the common law of evidence for its absurdity and inconsistency. He especially objected to those rules that prevented witnesses from testifying on the ground that they might be unreliable. Cases could not be decided in the dark, said Appleton; the jury should be allowed to hear the evidence and decide for itself the issue of credibility.

While Appleton objected to the exclusion as witnesses of atheists, felons, spouses of parties, and parties themselves, he gained his greatest fame from his long and ultimately successful campaign to make the criminal defendant competent to testify. The most serious objection to allowing the defendant to testify was that it would dilute the constitutional privilege against self-incrimination; a defendant who had the right to testify but refused to do so would necessarily look guilty to the jury. Appleton, however, could not believe that an innocent person accused of crime would refuse to clear himself on the stand. If the defendant is innocent, Appleton wrote, "he will regard the privilege of testifying as a boon justly conceded. If guilty, it is optional with the accused to testify or not, and he cannot complain of the election he may make."

In 1864, under Appleton's prodding, Maine became the first jurisdiction in the common-law world to grant testimonial competency to all criminal defendants. By the 1880s most states had followed suit. However, Appleton's victory opened a protracted constitutional debate over the right of prosecutors and judges to comment to the jury on the refusal of a defendant to testify. In *State v. Cleaves* (1871), Judge Appleton argued that the defendant's silence was "a fact patent in the case," to be treated the same as any other evidence. Appleton's opinion in *Cleaves* figured prominently in debates on the issue until well into the twentieth century. Ultimately, however, legislatures and courts came to the conclusion that while defendants ought to have the option to testify, their exercise of the constitutional right to refuse should not be the subject of comment or adverse inference.

In 1852 Governor John Hubbard, a Democrat, appointed Appleton to the Maine supreme court. As a trial judge, he worked diligently and quickly, and while most observers commended his efficiency, some were affronted by his hasty rulings and tendency to take sides. His vigorous and often erudite opinions on appeal, however, quickly restored some of the Maine court's sagging prestige.

In 1854, in the wake of violent nativist activity in Maine, Appleton ruled in *Donahoe v. Richards* that school boards could constitutionally require the use of the King James Bible for instruction in reading and morals. As a broad-minded Unitarian, Appleton sympathized with the Catholic victims of Know Nothing agitators, but he saw nothing unconstitutional in the use of the King James version as long as sectarian doctrine was not taught; redress for unwise laws, he maintained, must come from the electorate and not the courts. *Donahoe* remained the country's leading case on Bible-reading in the public schools during the nineteenth century.

In 1857, following the *Dred Scott* decision, the Maine Senate asked the state's high court for its opinion on whether blacks could be United States citizens. Appleton, an early Republican and a firm believer in equality, responded with a lengthy, learned disquisition in favor of black citizenship. In 1860 he appended to his collection of articles on evidence, published as *The Rules of Evidence Stated and Discussed*, a chapter denouncing laws that disqualified witnesses from testifying on the basis of race. The next year Appleton vigorously dissented when a majority of the state supreme court found Maine's personal liberty law, which would have prevented state officers from assisting in the recapture of runaway slaves, unconstitutional, and during the Civil War and Reconstruction he corresponded often with leading Republican senators Charles Sumner and William Pitt Fessenden on legal, political, and military matters, usually taking a Radical Republican position.

From 1862 until 1883, when he retired, Appleton served as chief justice of Maine. His most notable postbellum opinions, *Allen v. Jay* and *Brewer Brick Company v. Brewer*, have been seen by some historians as classic expressions of the "laissez-faire constitutionalism" that arose after the Civil War. In these cases, Appleton and his brethren struck down laws intended to aid private enterprises through subsidies and tax exemptions. At one time scholars tended to view laissez-faire jurisprudence as a conscious effort on the part of judges to protect business from governmental regulation. However, while Appleton believed in laissez-faire economic principles, he generally upheld regulatory laws. What he and other so-called laissez-faire jurists objected to was legislation designed to aid some categories of citizens at the expense of others.

Appleton's first wife died in 1874, and in 1876 he married Anne V. Greeley, who survived him. Appleton died in Bangor. He was, in the words of twentieth-century chief justice of Maine Leslie Cornish, "a legal reformer in the best sense" and the man who had "made the greatest impress upon the jurisprudence of this State." His opinions on Bible-reading in the schools and on public aid to private enterprise were widely influential, and he was largely responsible for some of the most significant nineteenth-century reforms in the law of evidence.

• Most of Appleton's articles on evidence were collectively published as *The Rules of Evidence Stated and Discussed* (1860). His judicial opinions may be found in vols. 34 through 76 of the *Maine Reports*. The most significant manuscript collections containing Appleton correspondence are the William Pitt Fessenden Papers (Western Reserve Historical Society), the Charles Sumner Papers (Houghton Library, Harvard University), and the Willard Phillips Papers (Massachusetts Historical Society). The best accounts of Appleton's life and work by contemporaries are Charles Hamlin, "John Appleton," in *Great American Lawyers*, vol. 5 (1908), pp. 41–79, and *Proceedings of the Penobscot Bar in Relation to the Death of the Honorable John Appleton*, 83 Maine 587 (1891). For a full-length treatment, see David M. Gold, *The Shaping of Nineteenth-Century Law: John Appleton and Responsible Individualism* (1990). An obituary is in the *Bangor Daily Whig and Courier*, 9 Feb. 1891.

DAVID M. GOLD

APPLETON, Moses (17 Mar. 1773–5 May 1849), physician, was born in New Ipswich, New Hampshire, the son of Isaac Appleton and Mary Adams. Nothing is known of his early life except that he graduated Phi Beta Kappa from Dartmouth College with an A.B. in 1791. He then taught school in Medford, Massachusetts, until 1793 when he entered Harvard Medical School. Appleton graduated after two years with a B.M. (the only medical degree awarded by Harvard at that time), and following a preceptorship with Dr. John Brooks (later a governor of Massachusetts) and an examination by a committee from the Massachusetts Medical Society he received a diploma and medical license from that group in 1796. That same year he began to practice in Ticonic (now Waterville) in the province of Maine, then part of the state of Massachusetts, where he practiced medicine until his death. In 1801 he married Ann Clarke, with whom he had four children.

Ticonic, located at the junction of the Kennebec and Sebasticook rivers, was strategically important during the eighteenth century as a key location on the route between Maine and Quebec. Fort Halifax had been built there in 1754 to help control depredations by the Indians, last fought at the fort in 1757. When Appleton began practicing in the village about 1,000 townspeople lived mostly in log cabins. He soon became a revered figure and the most prominent physician in the area. "A skilful physician, kind and courteous in manner, he was always welcome by his patients as a friend as well as a physician" (Whittemore, p. 126). He was best known during his life as a pioneer physician, for many years the only physician in the community.

It was common in those days for physicians to assume civic responsibilities and to eke out their income with a variety of other pursuits, and in these efforts Appleton was quite successful. He had the first apothecary shop in town as part of his practice, owned and operated a distillery making whiskey from potatoes, and helped establish the first bank in Ticonic. In addition, Appleton was an incorporator of the first Ticonic Bridge, and his real estate ventures resulted in considerable profit. He was chairman of the school committee and headed a committee to observe the semicentennial of the Declaration of Independence.

Appleton is of greater than just regional importance because of his personal journals. These include lecture notes from his anatomy and chemistry classes at Harvard Medical School and offer a fascinating picture of the state of medical education in the United States at that time. Also included are his examinations from all three of the Harvard faculty, and a list of the operations he performed while in practice (almost all either fractures or dislocations). Of great epidemiologic interest is his list of the causes of death of his patients from 1807 to 1837 ("July, 1808, child of Rev. D. Loring, dysentery, 1½ years" and "Daniel Dudley, Jun., drowned, 24 years"). As the only physician in the area during most of those years, Appleton's list fairly reflects the overall death rate; tuberculosis (phthisis) was the cause of almost one-quarter of the deaths due to illness, mainly striking young adults in their twenties.

• The Appleton papers are in the Francis A. Countway Library of Medicine in Boston, and they were described by Frederick T. Hill, "Medicine in Colonial Maine," *Journal of the Maine Medical Association* 54 (1963): 27–31, and by Alton

S. Pope and Raymond S. Patterson, "M. Appleton, 1800, Chronicler of Colonial Medicine," *Harvard Medical Alumni Bulletin* (Spring 1962): 18–23. References to his life are included in Edwin C. Whittemore's chapter in *Centennial History of Waterville* (1902); James A. Spalding, *Maine Physicians of 1820* (1928); Howard A. Kelly and Walter L. Burrage, *American Medical Biographies* (1920); and Ernest Marriner, *Kennebec Yesterdays* (1954).

PAUL G. DYMENT

APPLETON, Thomas Gold (31 Mar. 1812–17 Apr. 1884), writer and artist, was born in Boston, Massachusetts, the son of Nathan Appleton, a merchant, and Maria Theresa Gold. Nathan Appleton, whose family had settled in New England in 1635, helped develop Lowell, Massachusetts, into an industrial center and amassed a fortune that made it possible for Thomas to pursue his interests freely. After a year at the Boston Latin School and three at the Round Hill School conducted by Joseph Green Cogswell and George Bancroft in Northampton, Appleton was admitted to Harvard College as a sophomore in 1828. After graduation in 1831, he remained in Cambridge through 1832 studying law to please his father, but he had no liking for the profession.

In 1833 he went to Europe for the first of many trips, some of which were years long, throughout his bachelor life as essayist, poet, painter, connoisseur of the arts, traveler, and conversationalist, welcome everywhere for his warmth and wit. Eleven years later, aware that without a fixed occupation he seemed a mere idler, he explained himself to his father as "a man improving his character and mind" in order to try "to do good and find the truth and speak it" (Hale, p. 253). He read widely and wrote many letters to friends and relatives over a long period but published most of his books of poems, essays, and travels in later life. Impromptu poems in his letters are more interesting than his formal efforts. Although their merit varies, his essays show the breadth of his interests, which ranged from the positive influence of Japanese thought on the Western mind in "The Flowering of a Nation" (1871) to the changing nature of the "New England conscience" in an 1875 essay by that title, which was evidently the first appearance of the term in print, predating by four years its use by Henry James (1843–1916) in his short novel *Confidence*.

Appleton studied painting in Paris and copied masterpieces there and in Florence, activities important to him as a serious amateur painter and as a founder and benefactor of the Boston Museum, which he passionately believed was of great value to the public. He befriended many artists and was at home in the studios of Frederick Edwin Church, F. O. C. Darley, and John Frederick Kensett. Appleton also served as trustee of the Boston Athenaeum and the Public Library and was deeply committed to promoting civic improvement. During the Civil War, he provided Governor John Andrew with public and financial support. Many-sided as he was, it was for his talk that Appleton was most valued by friends, who in journals, letters, and memoirs lamented that its quality could not be reproduced in any written record. Thomas Wentworth Higginson recalled "a tête-à-tête dinner . . . when for two hours he mainly sustained the conversation and seemed at the end to have passed in review, in the most brilliant way, half the celebrities of Europe" and rated him "a more brilliant talker than either Holmes or Lowell," their fellow members of the Saturday Club (Higginson, p. 89). Appleton maintained a lifelong friendship with his brother-in-law Henry Wadsworth Longfellow, with whom he shared evenings at the Saturday Club in Boston and family summers at Nahant. After a cruise on the Nile in 1874 and travels in Syria in the company of the artist Eugene Benson, his wife, and her daughter (Appleton had met Benson in a Florence gallery and with characteristic generosity invited them to be his guests on the expedition), Appleton settled down in his new home in Boston, surrounded by his paintings and books, hosting dinners for his many friends, and talking almost to the end. Returning from a customary spring visit to Washington, D.C., Appleton fell ill en route and died of pneumonia in New York City.

• Various manuscripts and letters can be found at Harvard University, the Boston Public Library, Haverford College, Yale University, the Historical Society of Pennsylvania, the Library Company of Philadelphia, and the Massachusetts Historical Society. Appleton's essay "The Flowering of a Nation" appeared in the *Atlantic Monthly*, Sept. 1871, pp. 316–19. "The New England Conscience" was published in his collection *A Sheaf of Papers* (1875) and is discussed in Volker Bischoff, "The 'New England Conscience,' Thomas Gold Appleton, and Mrs. Vivian," *New England Quarterly* 53 (June 1980): 222–25. Appleton's other works include his poetry collections, *Faded Leaves* (1872) and *Fresh Leaves* (1874); *A Nile Journal* (1876); *Syrian Sunshine* (1877); *The Boston Museum of Fine Arts: A Companion to the Catalogue* (1877); and his essay collections, *Windfalls* (1878) and *Chequer-Work* (1879). An uneven biography is Susan Hale, *Life and Letters of Thomas Gold Appleton* (1885). Hale, a friend, used her access to Appleton's letters to his father to cover much of his activity abroad. Biographical sketches are in Thomas Wentworth Higginson, *Old Cambridge* (1899); Edward Waldo Emerson, *The Early Years of the Saturday Club, 1855–1870* (1918); and M. A. DeWolfe Howe, *Memories of a Hostess . . . Drawn Chiefly from the Diaries of Mrs. James T. Fields* (1922). For additional information, see *The Letters of Henry Wadsworth Longfellow*, ed. Andrew Hilen (4 vols., 1966–1972). An obituary by Oliver Wendell Holmes (1809–1894) is in the *Atlantic Monthly*, June 1884, pp. 848–50.

VINCENT FREIMARCK

APPLETON, William Henry (27 Jan. 1814–19 Oct. 1899), publisher, was born in Haverhill, Massachusetts, the son of Daniel Appleton, a store owner and publisher, and Hannah Adams. He ended his schooling at the age of sixteen and entered his father's store in New York City (the family had moved to Boston in 1817, then to New York in 1825). Appleton came of age at a time when his father was just giving up his store to become a bookseller and publisher.

In 1835 Appleton went abroad to buy books and to develop contacts for his father's business. In London, he soon gained the friendship and confidence of William Longman, a prominent British publisher. He made friends as well with the Irish poet Thomas Moore. Passing on to the Continent, he made the acquaintance of the German publisher Baron Tauchnitz in Leipzig and developed what became a lifelong friendship in Paris with William Makepeace Thackeray. By the time of his return to New York in 1836, Appleton had accomplished things that no other American sales representative of his time period had done.

In 1837 he made a second trip to Europe to purchase books and reprint rights. Hearing hints of a financial crisis at home, he returned quickly to the United States, where he was welcomed with great approval by his father, who was alarmed by the panic of 1837. Perhaps as a reward, his father made Appleton a full partner in the firm, which was renamed D. Appleton & Co. on 27 January 1838.

From this point, Appleton's rise was rapid. He kept a watchful eye on the business while his father went to Europe in 1838, and by 1840 Appleton was making important business decisions for the firm. During the 1840s D. Appleton & Co. expanded into the Latin American market and published books in the travel field. After the retirement of his father in 1848, Appleton became the president of the company, with two of his younger brothers as partners (two others entered later). He had married Mary Worthen of Lowell, Massachusetts, in 1844; the couple had four children, one of whom, William Worthen Appleton, sought to carry on the family business.

Thus began one of the most dramatic expansions of any American publishing concern during the nineteenth century. Whereas his father had been careful in his business pursuits, Appleton was dynamic and willing to take chances. During the next forty years, he oversaw the business that developed into the leading American publisher overall, with several distinct specialty areas. First came the travel books, such as *Appleton's Northern and Eastern Traveller's Guide* (1850). Then came the entry into the area of popular reference, heralded by the publication of the *New American Cyclopaedia* (1857–1683) and followed much later by *Appleton's Cyclopaedia of Biography* (1887–1889). Poetry and fiction soon followed as well. The Appletons published a two-volume edition of the poetry of William Cullen Bryant in 1854, starting what became a long association with the poet and editor (he later wrote the introduction to *Picturesque America; or, The Land We Live In* [2 vols., 1872, 1874]). The Appletons published much of the fiction of Emma Dorothy Eliza Nevitte Southworth as well.

Science was brought to the attention of average Americans by the Appleton company. A long association between Appleton and Edward Livingston Youmans led to the Appleton company becoming the first American publisher to bring out editions of the groundbreaking works of Charles Darwin and Herbert Spencer on evolution.

Following the conclusion of the Civil War, Appleton turned to the remembrance of that conflict. The Appleton firm brought out the *Military History of Ulysses S. Grant* (1868–1881) and biographies of Generals Philip Sheridan and William T. Sherman. They also published Jefferson Davis's *The Rise and Fall of the Confederate Government* (1881). Appleton did not neglect younger readers and soon brought out the first American edition of *Alice's Adventures in Wonderland* (1866) and George Catlin's *Life amongst the Indians: A Book for Youths* (1857).

Appleton clearly had a solid business acumen in addition to a love of literature. During his long tenure as president of the company (1848–1894), D. Appleton & Co. moved its location several times, always to a more upscale part of Manhattan. In 1867 the company developed a printing plant of its own in Brooklyn, New York; this concern alone had more than 600 employees. In 1866 Appleton bought a summer house and estate in Riverdale, New York. This property, "Wave Hill," was soon converted from Greek revival style to a Victorian villa, decorated in the popular Second Empire fashion.

In his later years Appleton devoted himself to the passage of an international agreement concerning copyright law. He resigned as president of the firm in 1894 and retired to Wave Hill, where he spent a peaceful five years before his death in Riverdale, New York.

Appleton was one of the great American publishers of the nineteenth century. In a league with Charles Scribner and other publishers, he had great success in his career as both a businessman and a sponsor of the arts. The success of the Appleton firm during his period as president laid the foundations for a distinctly American approach to the dissemination of knowledge. Although he began his career by courting European publishers and authors, Appleton clearly geared his publishing toward the area of mass production. In doing so, he helped to create a generation of truly literate Americans, citizens who had few rivals in the world in terms of their understanding of science, travel, fiction, and popular reference.

• Most of the early Appleton business papers disappeared as a result of fire or negligence. The best sources are Grant Overton, *Portrait of a Publisher* (1925), Samuel Claggett Chew, ed., *Fruit among the Leaves* (1950), and Gerard R. Wolfe, *The House of Appleton* (1981). Also see Charles A. Madison, *Book Publishing in America* (1966), and *The Diary of George Templeton Strong*, ed. Allan Nevins and Milton Halsey Thomas (4 vols., 1952). An obituary is in the *New York Herald*, 20 Oct. 1899.

SAMUEL WILLARD CROMPTON

APPLETON, William Sumner (29 May 1874–24 Nov. 1947), preservationist, was born in Boston, Massachusetts, the son of William Sumner Appleton, a numismatist and genealogist, and Edith Stuart Appleton (Appleton was both her maiden and married name). Appleton grew up in the materially and culturally privileged world of Boston's Beacon Hill. His family's involvement in the formation of several historical and cultural organizations dedicated to preserving some aspect of their Puritan heritage influenced him. His grandfather, the industrialist and banker Nathan Appleton, one of the wealthiest and most influential men in Massachusetts, was an organizer of the Boston Athenaeum. His father had no need to pursue any gainful employment and wrote many works on numismatics and genealogy. He was also a founder of the Bostonian Society, the Boston Numismatic Society, and the American Historical Society.

Appleton spent his childhood in a house on Beacon Street, Boston, designed for his grandfather by the well-known architect Alexander Parris, and attended Hopkinson's School. In 1886 he and his family departed for an extended stay in Europe. Returning to America, he enrolled at St. Paul's School in Concord, New Hampshire. In 1892 he entered Harvard University, where he came under the influence of Charles Eliot Norton, professor of the history of art, and was no doubt exposed to the theories of William Morris and John Ruskin. Appleton wrote later that he considered attendance at Norton's lectures, which were "nominally on the fine arts, but actually on anything," a privilege and an honor. After his graduation from Harvard in 1896, he embarked on a six-month grand tour of England and the European continent. Upon his return he entered an unsuccessful business venture as a real estate and investment broker and subsequently suffered a nervous breakdown, which he attributed to hypermetropic astigmatism.

Appleton spent the next ten years working on a number of projects and pursuing interests that would ultimately prepare him for his life's work. He was elected to membership in several patriotic, historical, and antiquarian organizations, including the Massachusetts Society of the Sons of the Revolution. It was through his association with the Sons of the Revolution that he took his first active role in the preservation movement. In 1905, as secretary of the Paul Revere Memorial Association, he successfully spearheaded the drive to save the home of the patriot, which also happened to be the oldest surviving structure in Boston, from threatened demolition. In 1906 he fought the plans of the Boston Transit Commission to significantly alter Boston's Old State House by expanding the subway. A compromise was reached whereby the upper floors became a museum and the lower level was used for a subway station.

Simultaneously with his preservation efforts Appleton undertook graduate work at Harvard, including Denman Ross's course on architecture in the Graduate School of Arts and Sciences. In addition, he worked on the "Boston-1915 Movement," the goal of which was to create a single citywide improvement plan. His involvement included serving as chair of the executive committee of the civic organization conference. In 1909 he spent several months in England and Europe, where he observed the preservation efforts of organizations such as the Commission des Monuments Historiques in France and the Society for the Protection of Ancient Buildings in England. The theories of the arts and crafts movement and the principles articulated and followed by the European preservationists were assimilated by Appleton and became evident in his own theory of preservation and later work.

In 1910 Appleton's growing dismay over what he perceived to be the rapid disappearance of New England antiquities and his outrage over alterations to the Jonathan Harrington House in Lexington, Massachusetts, caused him to found the Society for the Preservation of New England Antiquities (SPNEA). Drawing on his educational background and travel experiences, his work with nonprofit organizations, and his knowledge of real estate, he was able to formulate a well-thought-out and coherent plan for the first regional preservation organization in the United States. For the next thirty-seven years, Appleton was the corresponding secretary and the driving force behind the organization. Able to live on the income from his trust fund, he worked without a salary. According to Charles B. Hosmer, Jr., in *Preservation Comes of Age*, Appleton was the first full-time preservationist in twentieth-century America.

Appleton envisioned a strong, aggressive society that would be able to act instantly whenever a building or historic site was in need of preservation. His goals for the society were unique. He described them as "to own for purposes of preservation, appropriate old houses throughout New England, or else to take such steps, by means of advice or financial assistance, as may lead other societies to undertake the work of such ownership and preservation" ("Destruction and Preservation of Old Buildings in New England," p. 164). In this statement Appleton articulated his strong commitment to private ownership of sites and to a spirit of cooperation and coordination among organizations concerned with preservation. In addition to acquiring properties, Appleton established a New England Museum for smaller antiquities, such as household objects, relics, and models, and a library of views of New England.

In his appreciation of a building, Appleton differed from many of the earlier preservationists, for whom a building's only significance was its historic or patriotic associations. For him the most interesting buildings were those with intrinsic architectural and aesthetic merit as well as historic significance. In describing the Bowler-Vernon House in Newport, Rhode Island, Appleton wrote, "This building, which would have been worth preserving on account of its own artistic merits alone, is even more valued as the headquarters of Rochambeau" ("Destruction and Preservation of Old Buildings in New England," p. 160).

Appleton was also an innovator in his approach to building preservation. The principles that guided him and the methodology that he employed remained current for many decades after his death. He believed in preserving the evidence of different periods when it was possible and in keeping the amount of new work to a minimum. He was opposed to any attempt to prettify a house simply to make it more appealing to a lay audience. He articulated his philosophy when he wrote in 1930 about the Coffin House (c. 1654) in Newbury, Massachusetts:

The more I work on these old houses the more I feel that the less of W. S. Appleton I put into them, the better it is. I am perfectly certain that 999 [*sic*] restorers out of 100 working on [the Coffin House] would have made all sorts of changes that I didn't make. . . . I left there a perfectly good classic porch and door of about 1850. On opening this you are faced with the staircase built not in 1651 but at the time that the chimney and stairs were altered, . . . whereas the doors from the entry into the rooms on each side are of goodness only knows what dates, and so it goes throughout the house. It shows the process of evolution during 280 years and it seemed to me that it should be continued to show this process which was of infinitely more interest than a restoration of the old appearance of any part of the building could have been. (to W. W. Cordingley, 26 July 1930)

Appleton also stressed the importance of hiring experienced professionals to do the work on a building and of thoroughly documenting the work by means of photographic and written records. His work on the Abraham Browne house (c. 1698) in Watertown, Massachusetts, which began in 1919 and included the creation of copious written records and annotated photographs, was arguably the first modern scientific restoration.

In 1944 Appleton received the Trustees of Public Reservations' Award for Distinguished Service for Conservation in 1943. He was again honored in 1946, when he was awarded the George McAneny Medal by the American Scenic and Historic Preservation Society. The citation for this award describes him as a "diligent preserver in tangible form of the traditions, the manners and customs and the ancient habitations of New England." It goes on, "You have met success and frustration with even mind, but victory for preservation has been so often on your side that historians of the nation revere you." Only a year after receiving this award, Appleton died of a stroke in Lawrence, Massachusetts. He had never married.

Under Appleton's guidance, SPNEA grew from a small group of committed incorporators to an organization of regional and national importance. At the time of his death, SPNEA owned fifty-one properties throughout New England and a collection of thousands of three-dimensional and archival objects. Appleton was an omnivorous, and often indiscriminate, collector. It fell to his successors, always guided by his principles, to better define the strengths of SPNEA's collections and to add to them. Today SPNEA's collections are critical to the understanding of three centuries of New England architecture and daily life.

• Appleton's voluminous professional papers from his 37-year tenure as corresponding secretary of the Society for the Preservation of New England Antiquities are in the library and archives of SPNEA. SPNEA's holdings also include a collection of diaries (1906–1910, 1936–1940, 1947) and personal correspondence. Thirty oversized scrapbooks compiled by Appleton from 1893 to 1919 clearly document his social activities and his political, artistic, and organizational interests (twenty-four of the scrapbooks are in the SPNEA collection; six are in the collection of the Massachusetts Historical Society). The majority of Appleton's published works are articles and reports that appear in the *Bulletin of the Society for the Preservation of New England Antiquities*, which was renamed *Old-Time New England* in 1920. Appleton outlined his philosophy of preservation in "Destruction and Preservation of Old Buildings in New England," a lengthy article that appeared in *Art and Archaeology* 8, no. 3 (May–June 1919): 131–83. His autobiographical entries for the successive editions of *Harvard University Class of 1896* (1899 et seq.) provide useful information about his life. Charles B. Hosmer, Jr., *Presence of the Past* (1965) and *Preservation Comes of Age* (1981), are two important sources that document Appleton's and SPNEA's role in the history of the preservation movement in the United States. The most recent critical studies include James M. Lindgren, *Preserving Historic New England: Preservation, Progressivism, and the Remaking of Memory* (1995), and Michael Holleran, *Boston's 'Changeful Times': Origins of Preservation and Planning in America* (1998). See also Bertram K. Little, "William Sumner Appleton," in *Keepers of the Past*, ed. Clifford L. Lord (1965); Katharine H. Rich, "Beacon," in *Old-Time New England* 66, nos. 3–4 (Winter–Spring 1976): 43–60; and Louise Hall Tharp, *The Appletons of Beacon Hill* (1973). The magazine *Antiques* devoted its May 1960 and Mar. 1986 issues entirely to SPNEA, marking the fiftieth and seventy-fifth anniversaries of the organization. See also Jane Brown Gillette, "Appleton's Legacy," in *Historic Preservation* 46, no. 4 (July–Aug. 1994): 32–39, 95–97.

LORNA CONDON

APTHORP, William Foster (24 Oct. 1848–19 Feb. 1913), music critic and writer, was born in Boston, Massachusetts, the son of Robert Apthorp and Eliza Hunt. Since before the American Revolution, Apthorp's ancestors had participated in the mercantile and intellectual life of Boston. After studying languages, art, and music for four years in France, Germany, and Italy, Apthorp returned with his family to Boston in 1860. Deciding upon a career in music rather than in art, he entered Harvard College and studied piano, theory, and counterpoint with John Knowles Paine until Paine's departure for Europe in 1867. Apthorp graduated in 1869 from Harvard College, where he had been conductor of the Pierian Sodality in his senior year. He also studied piano with B. J. Lang for several years.

Apthorp taught piano and theory at the National College of Music from 1872 to 1873, then taught piano, theory, counterpoint and fugue at the New England Conservatory from 1873 to 1886. He also held classes in aesthetics and the history of music in the College of Music of Boston University until 1886. In 1876 Apthorp married Octavie Loir Iasigi.

It was as music critic and writer that Apthorp achieved national distinction and influence. His most important positions in this area were as music editor and critic of the *Atlantic Monthly* from 1872 to 1877, music and drama critic of the *Boston Evening Transcript* from 1881 to 1903, and annotator and editor of the Boston Symphony Orchestra concert programs from 1892 to 1901. He also lectured in Boston, New York, and Baltimore; co-edited, with John Denison Champlin, Scribner's *Cyclopedia of Music and Musicians* (1888–1890); and contributed articles to diverse publications, including *Dwight's Journal of Music* and *Scribner's Magazine*. He published a prodigious body of work in books, translations, and editions from 1875 to 1903, the year of his retirement. Thereafter, he lived in Vevey, Switzerland, until his death there.

An issue of considerable cultural significance in the later nineteenth century was the extent to which European "new music" would be supported by the American public. Apthorp's writings reveal, with few exceptions, his active leadership in fostering its acceptance. He wrote perceptively not only about compositions by Bach and Beethoven, but also about the contributions of more recent and then controversial composers including Berlioz, Liszt, and Wagner. As compiler of an annotated list of Richard Wagner's published works (1875), translator of selected letters and writings of Hector Berlioz (1879), editor of the songs of Robert Franz (1903), and as an annotator who clarified the large-scale structures or instrumental resources of unfamiliar works with reference to the musical scores, Apthorp performed a vital service by disseminating to American readers source material and musically informed commentary. His broad musical knowledge and experience also enabled him to assist the cause of American music through respectful treatment of works by contemporary American composers. Apthorp's proud advocacy of the "new spirit in music" may have contributed, however, to his exaggerated view of Mendelssohn's stylistic, and John S. Dwight's later critical, conservatism.

Apthorp wrote valuable historical and descriptive notes for the *Boston Symphony Orchestra Programmes* from 1892 to 1901; in the "Entr'acte" section of the program books, he penned short essays of general interest, some of which were reprinted in two volumes about music and musicians entitled *By the Way* (1898). In one of these pieces, on form, Apthorp described his particular admiration for the organic structural principles underlying the fugue and the sonata, but he avowed an open spirit in greeting newer compositional approaches. In *Musicians and Music-Lovers* (1894), Apthorp explained his individual conception of the music critic's role: he was not to judge but rather "to raise the standard of musical performance and popular musical appreciation." Citing his admiration for the French style of subjective critical advocacy appearing with the critic's signature, which he called "personal criticism," Apthorp expressed his hope to "set people thinking" by mediating as interpreter between the composer, or performer, and the public. He believed that the critic's highest function should be to let the public "listen to music with his ears."

Boston's active concert life assured Apthorp of ready access to instrumental music, about which he wrote more persuasively than he did about opera. In *The Opera Past and Present: An Historical Sketch* (1901), Apthorp noted a connection between the dramatic aims of the Florentine Camerata and Wagner and stressed Gluck's musicodramatic individuality, but he focused too exclusively on the prominence of the supernatural in German Romanticism to the detriment of other stylistic features.

In general, Apthorp's tendency to simplify complexities, disadvantageous in his historical essays, may have been a decisive factor in furthering his successful communication with the general public. He filled a constructive critical and educational role in his era by guiding readers toward greater understanding of unfamiliar musical works. Apthorp's writings encouraged recognition in American society for art music and musicians.

• According to D. W. Krummel et al., *Resources of American Music History: A Directory of Source Material from Colonial Times to World War II*, Apthorp's miscellaneous letters and papers are located in the Rare Books and Manuscripts Division of the Boston Public Library and at the Isabella Stewart Gardner Museum in Boston; additionally, research files pertaining to a biographical study are in the collection of Joseph Mussulman. Works by Apthorp not mentioned by title in the text include "A List of the Published Works of Richard Wagner," in *Art Life and Theories of Richard Wagner*, selected and trans. by Edward L. Burlingame (1875); *Hector Berlioz: Selections from His Letters, and Aesthetic, Humorous, and Satirical Writings*, trans. with a bio. sketch by William F. Apthorp (1879); and Robert Franz, *Fifty Songs*, ed. William Foster Apthorp (1903). See also the entry by Richard Aldrich in *The New Grove Dictionary of American Music*, ed. H. Wiley Hitchcock and Stanley Sadie, vol. 1 (1986), p. 62. Obituaries are in the *Boston Herald*, 22 Feb. 1913, and the *Boston Transcript*, 20 Feb. 1913.

ORA FRISHBERG SALOMAN

ARAGÓN, José Rafael (c. 1796–1862), religious artist, was the son of Juan Andres Aragón and Juana Dominguez Mascareñas. His birthplace is unknown, but in 1815, when he married María Josefa Lucero, he was living in the barrio of San Francisco in Santa Fe, New Mexico. He was still living there in 1833, when he described himself as an *escultor* (sculptor) on the census. At that time he and María Josefa had three children. María Josefa died in 1832, and in 1834 Aragon married María Josefa Córdova of Pueblo Quemado (now Córdova, Rio Arriba County, New Mexico) and moved to that town. He and his second wife had at least five children, one of whom, José Miguel, also became a religious artist, or *santero*.

Aragón was the major decorator of northern New Mexico's Roman Catholic churches after 1825. He made painted *bultos* (three-dimensional carved figures), *retablos* (paintings on boards), and *reredos* (altar backings containing both *bultos* and *retablos*). His work was installed in the church at Santa Cruz de la Cañada, the Sanctuary of Nuestro Señor de Esquipulas at Chimayó, the chapel of San Buenaventura at Chimayó, the chapel of San José de Chama at Hernandez, the church of Nuestra Señora de Guadalupe at Pojoaque, the chapel of San Antonio at Córdova, the chapel of San Miguel at El Valle, the chapel of San Lorenzo at Picurís pueblo, the chapel of Nuestra Señora de Talpa at Ranchos de Taos, and the chapel of San Antonio at Llano Quemado. The most accessible examples of his work in situ today are the *reredos* behind the side altars at the Sanctuary of Nuestro Señor de Esquipulas in Chimayó. The *reredos* and a number of *bultos* from the chapel of Nuestra Señora de Talpa are now at the Taylor Museum of the Colorado Springs Fine Arts Center in Colorado Springs, Colorado. The *reredos* is a brightly painted representation of three different manifestations of the Virgin Mary, Jesus Christ, St. Francis of Assisi, and the Holy Trinity, with each figure surrounded by painted draperies or geometric designs and the whole surmounted by a dove representing the Holy Spirit. The painted *bultos* are carved from cottonwood, and they include an articulated figure of Christ that can be removed from its cross and placed in a wooden coffin, as well as numerous images representing various aspects of the Christian ideals of penance and mercy. Taken together they represent, according to art historian William Wroth, "the finest and best documented collection of work by a New Mexico *santero* to have survived intact from the nineteenth century." Examples of Aragón's work are also at the Museum of New Mexico in Santa Fe and the Smithsonian Institution's National Museum of American History.

Aragón was one of the most prolific santeros of northern New Mexico. Although he has been described as a folk artist, Aragón's work is closely derived from academic European models available to him from printed sources. It is executed with a skill that indicates that he had formal training, probably as an apprentice to an unknown *santero* in Santa Fe. His artistic achievement lies in his sure technical sense of color and line and in his remarkable naturalism. His figures, unlike those of other *santeros*, are carefully drawn in proper human proportions and with expressive facial features. His work has provided inspiration and spiritual guidance to generations of New Mexican Catholics, and he is regarded by art historians as the most accomplished of the nineteenth-century New Mexico *santeros*. Aragón died in Pueblo Quemado.

• The most complete biographical information about Aragon and the most thorough analysis of his work can be found in William Wroth, *Christian Images in New Mexico* (1982). See also Jose Edmundo Espinosa, *Saints in the Valleys: Christian Sacred Images in the History, Life, and Folk Art of Spanish New Mexico* (1967); E. Boyd, *Popular Arts of Spanish New Mexico* (1974); and William Wroth, *The Chapel of Our Lady of Talpa* (1979).

LONN TAYLOR

ARAPOOSH (1789/1794?–1834), Crow Indian chief whose name is Eelápuash in modern Crow language orthography or Sore Belly (often mistranslated in historical accounts as Rotten Belly) in English, was a River Crow chief well known to early white trappers and traders. Many details of his life are unknown. Described as a fine tall man, Arapoosh as a youth had fasted in the Crazy Mountains in what is now Montana, where he received his medicine (spiritual power), the thunder. The Thunderbird appeared to him in a vision and showed him how to lead a war party as well as how to make war medicine so his trail would be clear. It may have been after this vision that he made his shield, or he may have been given the shield during a vision of the moon on another fast. This shield is said to have had powers of prophecy that aided him in battle. It was used long after his death, even into the reservation period. Eventually it was purchased and placed in a Chicago museum.

Arapoosh used his medicine power effectively in war. He became an outstanding and brave war party leader. Privately and quietly he prayed without any public show of his medicine. He seems to have been a man of decision and action, not words. When he did speak, people listened. Beginning his war career as a young man—probably first accompanying war parties between the ages of twelve and fifteen and most likely leading them before he was twenty—he brought back large numbers of captured horses while returning safely with his men. He seems to have been a very methodical and calculating war leader. He always handpicked his men, checked their weapons, and made sure his war parties took a route whereby they could retreat to a place of safety if attacked. Arapoosh's followers claimed he had powers of prophecy and often foresaw what would happen in battle. On at least two occasions, for example, he is said to have accurately predicted that horses of a certain description or condition would be found and captured.

As Arapoosh rose within the ranks of the chiefs, he was successful not only in war but also in leading his camp to areas where game (especially buffalo) was plentiful, where grass grew well for the horses, and where the camp could be easily defended. This further increased his standing among his people. In addition, he looked to their welfare through emphasizing trade for guns and ammunition and by ensuring that there were always guards and lookouts posted around the village both day and night. His road to the head chieftainship of the River Crows by the time he was thirty years old was also aided by the fact that he had many wealthy relatives.

In the summer of 1825 the United States negotiated peace and friendship treaties with several tribes on the northern plains in an effort to facilitate or resume good trade relations. The Crows had good relations with the whites and met with the government representatives, who were escorted by soldiers at a Mandan village in what is now North Dakota. The council was attended by the River Crows under Arapoosh and the Mountain Crows under Red Plume at the Temple (also known as Long Hair). Red Plume signed the treaty, but Arapoosh did not. During the council an incident occurred in which a Crow chief was pistol-whipped by a U.S. representative. There are several versions of the causes and events of this incident. Regardless, the argument that ensued after Chief Does Not Rain was hit nearly resulted in a battle between the warriors and the soldiers. After calm was restored, Arapoosh refused to sign the treaty and was so angry that it was said he used his medicine powers to bring down a storm that destroyed the earthen lodges and crops of the Mandans. The Mandans brought him gifts to stop the storm.

Regardless of the details of this particular incident, both Arapoosh and Red Plume had reputations for being great friends of the whites, whom they treated with great hospitality in their lodges. Many of the whites at this time were fur trappers and traders with whom the Crows traded. The Crows allowed many of them to trap and trade in Crow country. Arapoosh made a famous speech in about 1832 or 1833 to Robert Campbell of the Rocky Mountain Fur Company about the virtues of Crow country. As recounted in Washington Irving's *The Adventures of Captain Bonneville* (1843), Arapoosh told them, "The Crow country . . . is a good country. The Great Spirit has put it exactly in the right place; . . . whenever you go out of it, whichever way you travel, you fare worse. . . . It has snowy mountains and sunny plains; all kinds of climates, and good things for every season. . . . There is no country like the Crow country."

As his standing increased within the tribe, Arapoosh began to lead large war parties that sometimes struck deep into enemy territory. In about 1832 or 1833 he destroyed eighty lodges of Blackfeet on the Musselshell River (Montana) and defeated a Cheyenne village on the Arkansas River (Colorado). Angry at white traders for trading guns and ammunition to the enemy Blackfeet tribe, he led an expedition against Fort McKenzie (Montana) in 1834. Arapoosh and his men surrounded the fort and attempted to starve the traders out, but the siege was lifted by the arrival of a force of Blackfeet. Soon after, he led a war party against the Blackfeet. The Crows found a small party of the enemy and killed them all, but Arapoosh was also killed in the attack. Three sources tell us that he was killed near Fort Benton (Montana). However, tribal leader and patriarch Robert Yellowtail, who died in 1988 at age 100, wrote that he was killed and buried near what is now Dayton, Wyoming.

In a time of change, Arapoosh led his people through the challenges posed by both traditional tribal enemies and the white newcomers. He helped to preserve his beloved Crow country for the Crow people.

• Robert Summers Yellowtail's notes on Crow chiefs are in the Little Big Horn College Archives, Crow Agency, Mont. Accounts of Arapoosh are in James H. Bradley, "Historical Sketch of the Crows," in *Contributions to the Historical Society of Montana*, vol. 2 (1896; repr. 1966); Bradley, "Affairs at Fort Benton," in *Contributions to the Historical Society of Montana*, vol. 3 (1900; repr. 1966); Bradley, "Arrapooash," in *Contributions to the Historical Society of Montana*, vol. 9 (1923; repr. 1966); and Joseph Medicine Crow, "All Time Great Chieftains of the Crow Indians, 1600–1904," in *Absaraka, Crow Tribal Treaty Centennial Issue*, ed. Eloise Pease (1968). See also Edward S. Curtis, *The North American Indian*, vol. 4 (1909; repr. 1980), and Edwin Thompson Denig, *Five Indian Tribes of the Upper Missouri: Siouxs, Arickaras, Assiniboines, Crees, Crows* (1950–1953; repr. 1961).

TIM BERNARDIS

ARBUS, Diane (14 Mar. 1923–26 July 1971), photographer, was born Diane Nemerov in New York City, the daughter of David Nemerov and Gertrude Russek. Her parents were the children of Jewish émigrés from Eastern Europe who had arrived penniless in the United States; they acquired wealth as successful furriers, becoming part-owners of Russeks Fifth Avenue, the New York fur and gown showplace established in the 1890s by Arbus's maternal grandfather. One of three children (her brother Howard Nemerov would win the Pulitzer Prize in poetry), Arbus was raised by a German nanny, sent to Ethical Culture School on the West Side, and then enrolled at Fieldston School in Riverdale, where at age thirteen she fell in love with Allan Frank Arbus. She continued to meet him through the rest of her course at Fieldston and one summer at Cummington School of the Arts. After graduating from high school in 1940, she decided not to proceed to college but rather to persuade her father to let her marry Allan, whom she had been furtively meeting. With David Nemerov's consent, Diane and Allan were married in 1941. They had two children.

During World War II Allan Arbus attended the U.S. Army Photographic School. When he returned home in the evening, he passed on what he had learned to his wife. After the war they began to work as a team, mostly making fashion pictures and portraits in the studio for magazines such as *Glamour*, *Harper's Bazaar*, and *Vogue*. Their collaboration was at first total: models reported that with both Arbuses under the view-camera's cloth, they couldn't tell who snapped the shutter. Later, Diane Arbus stayed on the sidelines, limiting herself to "styling" the models, doing their hair and accessorizing their outfits. She let Allan take the pictures. Ultimately she drifted away from the Diane and Allan Arbus firm because she had become interested in what she photographed with her rogue Leica on long expeditions in the streets at night and in the early morning. Once a friend saw her huddled on Fifty-sixth Street with her camera poised and asked her to take his picture, "but she refused—with a smile. 'It would take five hundred exposures before I'd get you without your mask.'"

Around 1957 Arbus enrolled in a photography course with Alexey Brodovitch, art director for *Harper's Bazaar*. Later she studied with Lisette Model, whose grainy, even grotesque, images she had long admired. She was also influenced by the photography of Richard Avedon (who started out in fashion photography) and Robert Frank, although the stylistic differences between her work and Frank's are more instructive than are their apparent similarities.

A career breakthrough came for Arbus with two assignments, one for *Esquire* (Oct. 1959) and the other for *Harper's Bazaar* (Nov. 1961). Interior space, grotesque human forms, and night photography had come together in her pictures to yield something like Weegee's quasi-journalistic night world. She had taken pictures of corpses in a morgue, female impersonators, nudist camps, giants, public lunatic asylums, and the wealthy. Disparate subject matter was unified in her distinctive visual style. "To Diane the real world was always a fantasy," said a friend. Arbus added, "I could learn things, but they never seemed to be my own experience."

She was working out personal problems in her work, combating severe bouts of depression by taking fevered night forays into an alternative world, tirelessly applying a frenzied energy to the subjects her style made a part of our imagination: another New York, a world as clearly separate from the familiar New York as that of Lewis Hine and Berenice Abbott. Unlike theirs, however, Diane Arbus's New York is a world out of kilter, slightly off-center, weirdly parallel to the commonplace lives of her viewers. "There's some thrill going to sideshows," Arbus remarked. "I felt a mixture of shame and awe." Arbus's photographs made sideshows of what might, but for her style, have been banal: the rich boy in Central Park throwing a hand grenade at the viewer, the Jewish giant stooping to avoid the ceiling as he greets the parents he dwarfs, the sawed-off Christmas tree sitting squeezed into a corner in a creepy, untenanted room on Long Island.

In 1965 three of Arbus's pictures were included in a recent acquisitions show at the Museum of Modern Art, and in the fall of that year she taught a course in photography at the Parsons School of Design. She continued to teach small courses; she had a profound influence on her students and on almost everyone she met. Arbus had an arresting physical presence, sometimes sexy and sometimes painfully intense. At times she seemed like a wraith, appearing and disappearing at large public gatherings, silently staring. At other times she was aggressive, confrontational about everything.

In March 1967 John Szarkowski of the Museum of Modern Art included thirty of her prints in a show called "New Documents": it made her career. Her pictures had reached critical mass, so the group was large enough to allow a viewer to judge her staggering proficiency and almost overwhelming subject matter. One critic said, "Diane Arbus is the wizard of odds." She went to the show and then returned to the museum again and again to stare at her work, eavesdrop on its viewers, and revel in the way the work looked in this bastion of the "Establishment."

In 1971, still subject to melancholic depression, she returned her friends' letters to them, called her mother to ask how she had gotten through depressions in her own life, and then threw herself on her friends, trying to nest in their lives. "My work doesn't do it for me any more," she said. On 26 or 27 July 1971 (the body was discovered later), she slit her wrists in a bathtub in her apartment. At her funeral Richard Avedon said to Frederic Eberstadt, "Oh, I wish I could be an artist like Diane!" Eberstadt said, "Oh, no you don't."

The year after Arbus's death, the Museum of Modern Art held a retrospective exhibition of her work. That work has been compared by some to "a horror show," her subjects termed "grotesques" and misfits. But in her photographs the viewer sees something beyond the lunatic asylum inmates, reactionary patriots, wealthy matrons, kings and queens of the ball, and nudists—something closer to home. If her photographs present a horror show, then the America of her time was a horror show. Her brother Howard Nemerov addressed her in a poem as one who runs on and on, evidently tormented by what she sees, yet "you don't look down / Nor ever jump because you fear to fall." Her influence on other photographers was profound.

• The best biography is Patricia Bosworth, *Diane Arbus: A Biography* (1984). Doon Arbus and Marvin Israel, *Diane Arbus* (1972), is useful because one of its authors is Arbus's daughter; Israel and Doon Arbus also published *Diane Arbus, Magazine Work* (1984), which contains some of her important commercial work.

There are a number of interesting articles dealing with Arbus's work, including "Playing Games with Magazines: 3. The Moving Finger Writes and Having Writ Moves On," *Print*, July–Aug. 1970, pp. 43–51, and Alan Levy, "Working with Diane Arbus," *Artnews*, Summer 1973, pp. 80–81. John Szarkowski, "Photography and the Mass Media," originally in *Dot Zero*, Spring 1967, and reprinted in *Creative Camera*, Feb. 1969, pp. 62–63, is more analytical. Arbus's work is prominently mentioned in Leonard Wallace Robinson's "Discussion" with Harold Hayes, Gay Talese, and Tom Wolfe in *Writer's Digest*, Jan. 1970, pp. 32–35.

JOSEPH W. REED

ARBUTHNOT, May Hill (27 Aug. 1884–2 Oct. 1969), educator and children's literature specialist, was born in Mason City, Iowa, the daughter of Frank Hill and Mary Elizabeth Seville. May's childhood was reminiscent of the quality of family life she advocated throughout her professional life—hers was a family in which it was "as unnatural not to read as not to eat." Arbuthnot later said that her mother, whose "joy in books and people never failed," guided May and her brother to "the Alcott books and swung us into Dickens and the Waverley novels at an early age." Her father read aloud classics such as *Robinson Crusoe*, *The Swiss Family Robinson*, and *The Adventures of Tom Sawyer*. *The Book of Common Prayer* instilled in May "a sensitivity to the beauty and power of words." The Hill family spent several years in Newburyport, Massachusetts, and moved frequently throughout May's childhood. She was enrolled in schools in Minneapolis and Chicago and graduated from Hyde Park High School in Chicago.

Arbuthnot earned a kindergarten-primary supervisor's certificate from the University of Chicago in 1913, ultimately receiving the Ph.B. degree from Chicago with honors in education and Phi Beta Kappa in 1922. Family finances had necessitated the delay in attaining her undergraduate degree; in the interim, she taught kindergarten, served as the kindergarten director at the Superior, Wisconsin, State Teacher's College (1912–1917), and taught in the teacher training program at the Ethical Culture School in New York City (1918–1921). Additionally, she taught children's literature courses at the University of Chicago during nine summer sessions (1913–1922). She earned an M.A. from Columbia University in 1924.

In 1922 Arbuthnot was hired as the principal of the Cleveland Kindergarten-Primary Training School, which in 1927 was annexed by the Western Reserve University (later Case Western Reserve University) Department of Nursery-Kindergarten-Primary Education. She was named director of the school and associate professor of education, holding the latter position until her retirement.

Arbuthnot established the University Nursery School, a laboratory school on the Case Western Reserve campus, in the fall of 1929. She often reminded the constituents of the laboratory school—the faculty, student teachers, and parents—that, "The child and his needs come first." Arbuthnot taught courses entitled "Principles of Teaching," "Psychology of Childhood," and "Parental Education." For these and other endeavors, she received national attention: from 1927 to 1929 she was national vice president of the International Kindergarten Union (later known as the Association for Childhood Education); in 1930 she was invited to serve on President Herbert Hoover's White House Conference on Children; and in 1933 she was tapped for membership on a national committee charged with the creation of emergency nursery schools during the depression.

In 1932 she married a genial, respected colleague from Case Western Reserve University, Charles Crisswell Arbuthnot, a professor of economics. Their marriage was a satisfying and joyful partnership. Lifelong Republicans, both May and Charles Arbuthnot were well known for their support of liberal causes, chief among them human rights.

The years following her marriage were the most productive of Arbuthnot's career. She was named review editor of children's books for *Childhood Education* (1933–1943) and later served as review editor for *Elementary English* (1948–1950). These reviews were distinguished not only by the author's passion for literature, but by her sensitivity to the needs of all children—especially the children of segregation and poverty. Arbuthnot coauthored the widely used, sometimes disparaged Scott Foresman *Basic Readers* (1940), known as the "Dick and Jane" readers, with William S. Gray, a University of Chicago faculty member. Her most critically acclaimed work was *Children and Books* (1947), an anthology of children's literature that quickly became and long remained the compulsory text for students of children's literature. She also published *The Arbuthnot Anthology* (1953), a compilation of earlier titles intended for use in reading instruction, including *Time for Poetry* (1951), *Time for Fairy Tales, Old and New* (1952), and *Time for True Tales* (1953). The author of more than 100 articles in a variety of publications, Arbuthnot was also a popular speaker across the country.

Arbuthnot's retirement in 1950 from Case Western Reserve was the beginning of a period of sustained attention to her writing and increased national recognition of her work. During this time the Arbuthnots maintained homes in Pasadena, California, and Cleveland. She was the recipient of the Constance Lindsay Skinner Medal from the Women's National Book Association in 1959 for distinguished contributions to the field of books and the Regina Medal of the Catholic Library Association in 1964 for distinguished contributions to the field of children's literature. Although Case Western Reserve University awarded her the honorary degree doctor of humane letters in 1961—recognizing her contributions as an "inspiring teacher, gifted scholar, popular lecturer, and lucid writer"—Arbuthnot confessed to feeling frustrated and disappointed that she failed to win a promotion during her 23-year tenure at the University. After her husband's death in 1963, Arbuthnot's own health deteriorated. At the age of eighty-three, when life threatening hip surgery was recommended, she consented, explaining stoically, "It's bad enough I'm losing my eyes, I will not be assigned to a wheelchair also." Four months after Scott Foresman created the May Hill Arbuthnot Lectureship in her honor, Arbuthnot died of cancer in a Cleveland nursing home.

In one of the many accessible, lively articles Arbuthnot wrote for parents, she suggested that reading was essential to children's development because it "increase[s] what Albert Schweitzer calls 'a reverence for life.'" Perhaps the reverence for life inculcated in her as a child led to Arbuthnot's significant accomplishments as a teacher, professor, and prolific writer. All that she effected—increased attention to the importance of early childhood education, rapprochement between librarians and teachers that enabled both to be stewards of children's literature, and recognition of children's literature as an area of scholarship—is testament to a life well lived.

• The Case Western Reserve University Archives has a file on Arbuthnot, which includes Mary C. Austin, "May Hill Arbuthnot: Teacher, Author, Friend," the *Alumnae Folio*, Mar. 1951, and Gladys S. Blue, "Biographical Essay on May Hill Arbuthnot" (unpublished ms., Spring 1976). Also available in the archives is Arbuthnot "Western Reserve Nursery School" (unpublished ms., 9 Sept. 1936) Articles about Arbuthnot include "May Hill Arbuthnot," *Education*, Mar. 1958, pp. 446–47, and Marie C. Corrigan and Adeline Corrigan, "May Hill Arbuthnot," *Catholic Library World*, Feb. 1964, pp. 337–39. The *Notable American Women* entry on Arbuthnot is helpful because Zena Sutherland, her former coauthor, wrote the article. Obituaries are in the *Cleveland Plain Dealer*, 3 Oct. 1969, and the *Library Journal*, 15 Nov. 1969.

SUSAN BERTRAM EISNER

ARCHBOLD, John Dustin (26 July 1848–5 Dec. 1916), oil industry executive and philanthropist, was born in Leesburg, Ohio, the son of Israel Archbold, a minister, and Frances Dana. His education at local schools ended when his father died. Not yet in his teens, Archbold took a clerking position in 1859 at a country store in Salem, Ohio, to help support his family. In that same year he noted the excitement surrounding the discovery of oil in nearby Titusville, Pennsylvania. After several years of hard work, he journeyed to the oil fields of western Pennsylvania with $100 in savings.

Upon arriving in Titusville, Archbold obtained a position in the office of William H. Abbott, one of the leading oilmen in the fast-growing region. He used every moment not spent in the performance of his duties to study and was soon familiar with oil refinement, transportation, brokering, and production. Recognition of his ability came in the form of a partnership in the firm before he reached the age of nineteen. Archbold's efforts, however, failed to save the badly overextended firm from collapse in 1869. Undaunted, he scraped together additional savings and became a partner in the local refining firm of Porter, Moreland & Company. In 1870 he married Annie Mills of Titusville; the couple had four children. By the early 1870s Archbold also established a sales office in New York City, where he sold oil on behalf of his own firm and outside producers as well.

Although by 1872 the firm of Porter, Moreland was refining 25,000 barrels of oil per month (more than any other refiner in the region), trouble loomed ahead. A group of refiners from Cleveland, led by John D. Rockefeller and operating as the South Improvement Company, had achieved a dominant position in their local market by the use of persuasion, price-cutting, and railroad rebates. In early 1872 South Improvement sought to force competing independent refiners from the oil regions surrounding Titusville to join the company. With the refining industry plagued by excess capacity and falling prices, South Improvement's threat to run out of business any competitor that failed to take advantage of their offer seemed very real. Nevertheless, the refiners and producers, led by Archbold, fought back. A key figure in the formation of the Petroleum Producers' Association, Archbold and his allies succeeded in forcing the South Improvement Company to back down, and the state of Pennsylvania subsequently revoked the company's charter.

The joy felt by refiners in the oil region was short-lived. Excess capacity continued to plague the fledgling industry, and the effects of the panic of 1873 only worsened matters. Given a chance to operate with his peers as an equal, Archbold led Porter, Moreland into the newly created (Oct. 1874) Standard Oil alliance. Technically operating under the direction of the Central Refiners' Association, his firm soon provided the nucleus of the Acme Oil Company. Ostensibly acting on its own, the new company proceeded to acquire most of the remaining independent refiners in the oil region. Having received a directorship in Standard Oil upon joining the firm, Archbold acquired the last of his area's competitors in June 1879, remarking at the time that they had all "retired from the business gloriously" (Nevins, p. 488).

Archbold played a leading role in the continuing development of Standard Oil. Assuming the duties of vice president shortly after joining the firm, he continued to hold that position after the formal incorporation of the Standard Oil Trust in 1882. With the Trust under constant scrutiny from both the public and the government in an era of progressive politics and muckraking journalism, Archbold often assumed the duty of company spokesperson. Bright, witty, and outgoing as well as completely versed in company operations, he proved invaluable to the firm in his testimony before numerous investigations and legislative hearings. Rockefeller, as head of Standard Oil, fully appreciated Archbold, noting well his "Enthusiasm, his energy, and his splendid power over men" (Nevins, 479).

Archbold continued as vice president of Standard Oil following the "technical" dissolution of the Trust in 1892. After 1896 Rockefeller, suffering declining health, virtually retired from an active management role, and Archbold served as de facto president of the firm. Under his direction Standard Oil expanded its operations overseas, increased product sales, and implemented an improved product distribution system that resulted in an increasingly efficient operation. In addition to his duties at Standard Oil, he served as either president or director of a host of smaller oil companies and was heavily involved with philanthropy. The primary object of his charity was Syracuse University, which he also served as trustee president from 1893 until his death. During his lifetime, Archbold donated $2 million to the school, part of which went to build a football stadium that bore his name. He gave the school an additional $500,000 in his will and also provided a new headquarters for the New York Kindergarten Association.

Despite the formal breakup of the Trust, few of its critics remained satisfied with the arrangement. Archbold himself added fuel to the fire when letters were stolen from his office and published by William Randolph Hearst in 1908. Although several of the letters were subsequently shown to be forgeries, the correspondence (written to several United States Senators including Matthew Quay, Boise Penrose, and Joseph Foraker) appeared to illustrate the undue influence and power that many critics attributed to Standard Oil. The existing firm was dissolved by a Supreme Court decision in 1911, and with the formal retirement of Rockefeller in that same year, Archbold served as the president of the newly formed Standard Oil of New Jersey. He held that position until his death at Tarrytown, New York.

The life and career of John Archbold was typical of many self-made industrialists of the nineteenth century. He rose from less than modest beginnings to leadership in one of the great business organizations of his time by hard work, thorough knowledge, and a not inconsiderable amount of charm. The Exxon Corporation stands as his (and the other leaders of Standard Oil) legacy.

• The papers of Archbold are held at the Syracuse University library in Syracuse, New York. His career was the subject of a Ph.D. dissertation by Austin L. Moore titled, "John D. Archbold and the Early Development of Standard Oil" (Columbia Univ., 1948). Standard secondary sources include, Allan Nevins, *John D. Rockefeller: The Heroic Age of American Enterprise* (2 vols., 1940); Ralph W. Hidy and Muriel E. Hidy, *History of Standard Oil Company (New Jersey): Pioneering in Big Business, 1882–1911* (vol. 1, 1955); and George

Sweet Gibb and Evelyn H. Knowlton, *History of Standard Oil (New Jersey): The Resurgent Years, 1911–1927* (vol. 2, 1956). A critical study is Ida Tarbell, *History of the Standard Oil Company* (2 vols., 1904). Obituaries appeared in the *New York Times* following his death, 6, 8, 19, and 30 Dec. 1916.

EDWARD L. LACH, JR.

ARCHDALE, John (c. 5 May 1642–c. 4 July 1717), colonial governor and a proprietor of Carolina, was born in Chipping Wycombe, Buckinghamshire, England, the son of Thomas Archdale, the local squire, and Mary Nevill. His grandfather Richard Archdale, a London merchant, had earlier purchased "Loakes" and "Temple Wycombe" manors and joined the county gentry. Although relatives had attended Wadham College, Oxford, John Archdale apparently was self-educated.

He was drawn into a lifelong involvement in colonial affairs through the patronage of his brother-in-law Ferdinando Gorges, grandson of the Elizabethan adventurer Sir Ferdinando Gorges, who had secured a proprietorship of Maine. In 1652, during the Commonwealth, Massachusetts Bay Colony had annexed Maine, but after the Restoration under Charles II the Gorges family sought to reassert their proprietary claim. Serving as a commissioner for the Gorges family, Archdale journeyed to New England in 1664 to reestablish proprietary government but soon found himself in a bewildering confrontation with the Massachusetts Bay authorities and a royal commission. For a brief period in Maine, Archdale appointed local officials for the proprietor and served as colonel of militia, ending his tenure and returning to England in 1665 in deference to royal commissioners.

Over the next decade Archdale assumed his role as "chief gentleman of the village." After his marriage in December 1673 to Anne Dobson Cary, a widow with a son, Thomas Cary, who later became deputy governor of the northern colony, Archdale settled into country life. The couple later had four more children. Prior to 1674 Archdale came in contact with George Fox, founder of the Society of Friends (Quakers), and was convinced to join that sect. This change in faith had a profound impact on his life and his later public role. The persecution of the Quakers eventually led their leaders, most notably William Penn, to seek a haven in the colonies. While Penn and others were acquiring proprietary rights to New Jersey and Penn was pursuing the Pennsylvania grant, Archdale in 1678 purchased the Carolina proprietary share of John, Lord Berkeley of Stratton, in trust for his young son, Thomas. From this point on, in both England and Carolina, Archdale worked to develop the colony by settling members of his family there, nurturing the fledgling Quaker community, reinforcing the proprietary policy of religious toleration, and recruiting colonists, especially among dissenters. Archdale was appointed chief justice of Carolina by the proprietors on 13 June 1680. Because there is no evidence of his serving in this position, the appointment may have lapsed by the time he got to the colony in 1683. Acting as a proprietor for his minor son, Archdale also accepted appointment as collector of quitrents in 1682 and the following year went to Albemarle County in northern Carolina, remaining there three years. Several times in this period and throughout 1685 when Governor Seth Sothel was absent, Archdale, as a proprietor, served as acting governor. When he returned to England he again was involved in the Gorges New England enterprise as a commissioner, and there is evidence that he was appointed proprietary governor of Maine in 1691.

Years of unrest and rebellion in both of the Carolina colonies finally led to the proposal that a proprietor assume the governorship. Archdale's previous residence in the northern colony, his proven administrative ability, and his reputation (partly stemming from his being a Quaker) as a just, tolerant, and wise man, made him the logical choice, and on 31 August 1694 he was commissioned governor of Carolina. He also received the title of landgrave, the highest rank in the Carolina nobility, entitling him to a barony of 48,000 acres. Accompanied by his son, Thomas, Archdale landed in Maine early in 1695 and then traveled south overland through all the colonies, arriving in June in the Albemarle settlement where his daughter Anne and her husband Emmanuel Lowe were living. There Archdale examined and approved the administration of the acting deputy governor, Thomas Harvey. Archdale arrived in Charles Towne in August and confirmed his nephew Joseph Blake as deputy governor of the southern colony. His stepson, Thomas Cary, was named secretary of the council. Knowing that the colony had been torn by political and ethnic strife, Archdale, with the backing of the assembly majority, addressed the colony's tensions in a comprehensive series of acts that became known as "Archdale's Laws." These touched on the broad spectrum of problems, including regulation of the Indian trade and liquor traffic, quitrents, land policy, a more humane Indian policy, a slave code, and a poor law. Although Archdale was obligated by the proprietors to support the political rights of the beleaguered Huguenots, he realized pragmatically that in order to govern he would have to acquiesce to a reduction of their political representation in order to gain the support of the English majority. He revealed his tolerance through enlightened diplomacy that improved relations with the Spanish in Florida and the various frontier Indian tribes. Leaving the government in Blake's capable hands, Archdale returned after a year to England through Albemarle. Blake immediately purchased the proprietary share of Thomas Archdale. Both assemblies in the Carolina colonies passed unprecedented addresses of appreciation to the governor praising his "wisdom, discretion, patience, and labour."

Archdale arrived in England in 1696, and in 1698 was elected to Parliament from Chipping Wycombe. As a Quaker, however, he conscientiously refused to take an oath of office and was denied a seat; thereupon his brother Thomas went to Parliament. Archdale retained his interest in Carolina by recruiting prospective colonists, and in 1705 he purchased the Sir William Berkeley share, which he held until 1708 when he conveyed it to his daughter Mary and her husband John Danson. He published in London in 1707 a promotional narrative, *A New Description of that Fertile and Pleasant Province of Carolina: With a Brief Account of Its Discovery, Settling and the Government Thereof to This Time. With Several Remarkable Passages of Divine Providence during My Time.*

His last years were spent at the family manor. An earlier biographer, Stephen B. Weeks, who had characterized Archdale as "sagacious, prudent, and moderate," wrote that "no other man exerted as much influence for good on the development and growth" of the Carolina colonies. Archdale's peaceful interlude there laid a foundation for a decade of stable government that enabled the settlements to weather renewed turmoil in the eighteenth century.

• Archdale's papers are found in the manuscript collections of the Library of Congress; in the Charles Roberts Collection of Haverford College; in William L. Saunders, ed., *The Colonial Records of North Carolina*, vols. 1–2 (1886–1887); and in Bartholemew R. Carroll, ed., *Historical Collection of South Carolina*, vol. 1 (1836). An excellent source for his attitudes and administration is his *A New Description of that Fertile and Pleasant Province of Carolina . . .* (1707), reprinted in Alexander S. Salley, Jr., ed., *Narratives of Early Carolina, 1650–1708* (1911; repr. 1959). Secondary studies of value are Henry G. Hood, Jr., *The Public Career of John Archdale, 1642–1717* (1976); Rufus Jones, *The Quakers in the American Colonies* (1911); William S. Powell, *The Proprietors of Carolina* (1963); Edward McReady, *South Carolina under Proprietary Government* (1897); M. Eugene Sirmans, *Colonial South Carolina: A Political History 1663–1763* (1966); and two articles by Stephen B. Weeks, "John Archdale and Some of His Descendants," *Magazine of American History*, Feb. 1893, pp. 157–62, and "John Archdale," in *Biographical History of North Carolina*, ed. Samuel A. Ashe, vol. 1 (1905), pp. 61–65.

LINDLEY S. BUTLER

ARCHER, James Jay (19 Dec. 1817–24 Oct. 1864), Confederate brigadier general, was born at Stafford in Harford County, Maryland, the fourth son of physician James Archer and Ann Stump. The early career of James Archer is often confused with that of kinsman John Archer, who graduated from West Point. James Archer graduated from Princeton in 1835, obtained an engineering degree in 1838 from Bacon College, studied law under an older brother, and was admitted to the Maryland bar. Though he never married, as a young man Archer was so attractive that his friends called him "Sallie." He entered the U.S. Army during the Mexican War as a captain of infantry and earned brevet promotion to major for gallantry at the 1847 battle of Chapultepec. He resigned from the army and practiced law until 1855, when he reentered the service. Archer was in command of a post on the Pacific coast at the outbreak of civil war. He resigned from the army and handed over command of his station to Lieutenant Philip H. Sheridan. Archer made his way across the continent to Richmond and accepted a captaincy in the Confederate army.

On 26 September 1861 Archer was promoted to colonel and given command of the Fifth Texas Infantry Regiment. He saw duty along the Potomac River fortifications until 3 June 1862, when he was promoted to brigadier general and assigned to lead the Tennessee brigade in Robert E. Lee's army. It took Archer several months to gain the respect of his regiments. Slightly built and heavily bearded, he was a humorless, no-nonsense officer. One Tennessee soldier recalled: "So cold was his manner that we thought him at first a Martinet. Very non-communicative, and the bearing and extreme reserve of an old army officer made him for a time, one of the most intensely hated of men."

The Tennessee brigade was part of A. P. Hill's celebrated division, and Archer became one of the most reliable field commanders in an army known for outstanding leadership. He and Hill were not close friends, but this had no effect on Archer's battlefield performance. He was conspicuous at Mechanicsville, Gaines' Mill, and Cedar Mountain. He led a furious counter-attack on 29 August at Second Manassas and had a horse killed under him during the action. At the 17 September battle of Antietam, Archer was so ill (probably from diarrhea) that he arrived on the field in an ambulance. He barely kept in the saddle as he directed his troops throughout that day's bloody fighting. The following May, at Chancellorsville, Archer played a key role when his brigade seized Hazel Grove, the artillery emplacement that was the key to the entire battlefield. By then, the stern Marylander had acquired the reputation and nickname of "The Little Gamecock."

On 1 July 1863 Archer's troops were the van of Lee's army when it met Union forces at Gettysburg and initiated the most famous battle of the Civil War. Archer was near exhaustion when Federal troops overran his lines, routed his brigade, and took him prisoner. A year's confinement followed at the military prison on Johnson's Island in Ohio. The ordeal permanently shattered Archer's health. Exchanged in the summer of 1864, he rejoined his command in the trenches at Petersburg. Yet debilitation forced him from the ranks, and he died that autumn in Richmond. Archer was a soldier who pursued his duties with no room for distractions. Because he did not broadcast his own deeds, his accomplishments have remained obscure in Civil War history.

• Archer's papers are at the Maryland Historical Society in Baltimore. No biography has yet been written of the brigadier. An article on his pre–Civil War years is in the *Maryland Historical Magazine* (Dec. 1959). The more important items in Archer's wartime correspondence have been printed in two installments. See C. A. Porter Hopkins, ed., "The James J. Archer Letters," *Maryland Historical Magazine* (Mar. and June 1961).

JAMES I. ROBERTSON, JR.

ARCHER, John (5 May 1741–28 Sept. 1810), physician, patriot, and public official, was born in Maryland, either near Brinckley's Mills, Cecil County, or near the present town of Churchville, Harford County, the son of Thomas Archer, a farmer and ironworks agent, and Elizabeth Stevenson. Archer attended the West Nottingham Academy in Cecil County and the College of New Jersey (Princeton), from which he received the A.B. degree in 1760 and the M.A. in 1763. Thereafter he taught school in Baltimore and studied theology. However, after a second examination by the Presbytery of New Castle, in 1764, the presbytery decided that it "cannot encourage him to prosecute his tryals for the Gospel ministry any further," and he turned his attention to medicine. He became a pupil of Dr. John Morgan and attended the new Philadelphia College of Medicine that was established in 1765. He received his B.M. degree in 1768, alphabetically the first of the first ten recipients of a medical degree from an American medical school. He had begun to practice medicine in New Castle, Delaware, in 1767 even before he received his degree, and in 1769 he returned to Maryland, where he practiced medicine, with interruptions due to his public service, for about forty years.

An early and prominent Whig, Archer was chosen a member of Harford County's Committee of Correspondence and of the Committee on Observation in 1774. In December 1774, having been largely responsible for raising a company of militia, the first in the county, mainly from among his patients, he was commissioned its captain. He drilled his men himself, using a trumpet because of a chronic throat ailment that persisted throughout his adult life. In 1776 he was promoted to major.

In August 1776 Archer was a member of the state convention that framed a constitution and bill of rights for Maryland. He was counted among the "radical segment" of the convention, a group that sought, for example, wider suffrage. He was active in state and local politics thereafter. In 1777 and again in 1779–1780, he represented Harford County in the lower house of the state legislature. In 1777 he was appointed commissioner of peace for Harford County (the commissioners constituted the county court), and he held that post for at least thirteen years. He was justice of the Orphans' Court of Harford from 1779 to 1784 or later. In 1779 he served as subscription officer of the Continental Loan Office for Harford County, and in 1786 he was appointed judge of the Harford County Court of Appeals for Tax Assessment. In 1796 he was elected to the electoral college from Maryland as an avowed Jeffersonian. From 1801 to 1807 he was a member of the House of Representatives. A robust and imposing figure, he made no speeches because of the problems with his voice. He voted the straight Republican (Jeffersonian) party line.

Archer's medical practice in Harford County was extensive, and about 1785 he undertook a career as a medical educator. Renaming his house "Medical Hall," he trained at least fifty young men in medicine, including five of his own sons. In 1797 his students formed what has been named the Harford Medical Society, at which papers were read and discussed. In 1799 he and his son Dr. Thomas Archer were charter members of the Medical and Chirurgical Faculty of Maryland. He became an examiner for the faculty and in 1802–1803 was a member of its executive committee.

Archer did contribute a few communications to the *Medical Repository*. He is credited with having "perfected" a method of administering Peruvian bark in intermittent fevers, with having recommended vaccination in the early stages of whooping cough to render the disease virtually harmless, and with having introduced senega snakeroot as a remedy for croup. The last of these earned Archer recognition in medical circles.

Archer had married Catherine Harris in 1766. They had ten children, four of whom died in childhood. Of six sons who reached adulthood, four became physicians, one died while studying medicine, and the youngest, Stevenson Archer, became an attorney and eventually chief justice of Maryland. John Archer died at Medical Hall, survived by his wife and five sons. At his death his personal wealth amounted to about $60,000. Estimates of the size of his home plantation vary from 700 to over 800 acres, and he owned an additional 260 acres in Harford County. He provided also for the eventual manumission of his slaves, of whom he had seven or eight at various times.

James Thacher, in his 1828 *American Medical Biography*, characterized Archer as "a gentlemen of much professional respectability, though of eccentric memory." The eccentricity is not explained.

• There are Archer family papers, including medical ledgers, at the Maryland Historical Society. The chief biographical accounts include an article by one of his descendants, [George W. Archer], "A Biographical Sketch of John Archer, M.B.," *Bulletin of the Johns Hopkins Hospital* 10 (1899): 141–47; as well as E. C. Papenfuse et al., *A Biographical Dictionary of the Maryland Legislature*, vol. 1 (1979), pp. 107–8; J. McLachlan, *Princetonians: 1748–1768, a Biographical Dictionary* (1976), pp. 300–302 (note that this volume confuses two John Archers); and E. F. Cordell, *The Medical Annals of Maryland 1799–1899* (1903), pp. 746–52.

DAVID L. COWEN

ARCHEY, Jimmy (12 Oct. 1902–16 Nov. 1967), jazz trombonist, was born James H. Archey in Norfolk, Virginia. Nothing is known of his parents. He started playing the trombone in 1912 and from 1915 to 1919 studied music at Hampton Institute, spending his summers playing in a band led by pianist Lillian Jones. After working in Quentin Redd's band on the Atlantic City boardwalk around 1922, Archey moved to New York City in 1923 and played with trumpeter Lionel Howard's band at the Saratoga Club and the Capitol Palace. The next year he worked at Ed Small's and from 1925 to mid-1926 spent a year touring with the Lucky Sambo Revue and another few months with the Tan Town Topics. Starting in late 1926 he worked with the bands of John C. Smith and Arthur Gibbs and began a residency at the Bamboo Inn with Ed Campbell. In 1927 he played in pianist Edgar Hayes's pit band at the Alhambra Theater, briefly toured with King Oliver in early June, and continued working at the Bamboo Inn with Campbell and then Henri Saparo. In 1928 pianist Joe Steele took over leadership of the Bamboo Inn band, and Archey remained with him into 1929. After leaving Steele he filled out the remainder of the year working with the bands of Charlie Skeete and Bill Benford. In April 1930 he once again toured with Oliver and in June joined Luis Russell's band for long engagements at the Saratoga Club, Connie's Inn, the Arcadia Ballroom, and other venues.

In early 1931 Archey worked for six months with Bingie Madison at the Broadway Danceland. But then he rejoined and remained with Russell's band, from Oct. 1935 under the leadership of Louis Armstrong, until early 1937, at which time he joined singer Willie Bryant for regular appearances at the Apollo Theater. Archey stayed with Bryant until March 1939, when he left to begin a long residency at the Savoy Ballroom with Benny Carter. Carter's band was a favorite at the Savoy, but it occasionally played at other locations as well, among them the Apollo, Roseland Ballroom, Howard Theater, and Golden Gate Ballroom. In June 1940 Archey left Carter to work in the bands of Ella Fitzgerald and Coleman Hawkins at the Savoy, but he was back with Carter in late January 1941 for a monthlong engagement at Nick's in Greenwich Village. After a series of tours, from March through September, Carter disbanded, and Archey began a three-year period of freelancing, during which time he occasionally worked with Cab Calloway and Duke Ellington. In 1944 and 1945 he was at the Zanzibar with Claude Hopkins, and from 1946 through 1948 he played sporadically at Billy Rose's Diamond Horseshoe with Noble Sissle.

For almost twenty years Archey had found regular employment in big bands, usually playing lead trombone but rarely having the opportunity to establish a reputation as a jazz soloist. All that changed, however, in June 1947 when Rudi Blesh, producer of the "This Is Jazz" radio series, hired him as a permanent replacement for George Brunies. The half-hour broadcasts were aired weekly through 7 October, and Archey appeared on all the shows alongside widely respected jazzmen such as Wild Bill Davison, Albert Nicholas, Sidney Bechet, James P. Johnson, Danny Barker, Pops Foster, and Baby Dodds. For part of the summer of 1947 Archey also took part in "Jazz on the River," Blesh's weekend chartered boat trips up the Hudson. In February 1948 Archey made his first trip to Europe to play at the Nice Jazz Festival with Mezz Mezzrow in a band that also included trumpeter Henry Goodwin, pianist Sammy Price, Foster, Dodds, and a young disciple of Bechet, clarinetist and soprano saxophonist Bob Wilber. After they returned home, Wilber decided to build a band of his own around Goodwin and Archey. In December 1948 Archey, Goodwin, and Foster, along with young stride pianist Dick Wellstood and drummer Tommy Benford, joined Wilber at the Savoy Café in Boston. Playing in a style associated with Bechet's New Orleans Feetwarmers, the personnel of Wilber's band remained intact until April 1950, when Wilber himself left the group to form another band to open George Wein's new Storyville Club in Boston.

The leadership of the Savoy band was turned over to Archey, who replaced Wilber with veteran Harlem clarinetist and saxophonist Benny Waters, whom both Archey and Goodwin had known since the 1920s. After their departure from the Savoy, the Archey band began a residency at Jimmy Ryan's on Fifty-second Street, where they remained until the spring of 1952, alternating with Wilbur De Paris's recently formed Rampart Street Paraders. After leaving Ryan's, Archey's band embarked on a European tour, but when that folded because of poor management, the band broke up. The men returned home, but Archey stayed on to play with Earl Hines's sextet, which was then also on tour. Back in New York, he resumed freelancing, frequently appearing at the Central Plaza, where, with Jimmy McPartland, Pee Wee Russell, and others, he was in the 1954 documentary film *Jazz Dance*. From late 1954 to early 1955 Archey toured Europe again, this time as a sideman with Mezzrow, and from September 1955 through December 1962 he played with an all-star sextet under the alternate leadership of Muggsy Spanier and Hines. In 1963 he led his own bands on dates in the United States and Canada, and in February 1966 he toured Europe once more with the New Orleans All Stars, a stellar group assembled by British trumpeter Keith Smith. Archey remained active professionally until his death in Amityville, New York.

Even from the beginning of his recording career, Archey was considered a reliable and forthright soloist, as is evidenced by the space accorded him by King Oliver, Fats Waller, Joe Steele, James P. Johnson, and Henry "Red" Allen on recordings made between 1927 and 1929. On the earlier of these his brash, blues-intoned style reflects that of Kid Ory, whom he replaced in Oliver's band, but by late 1929 he had come under the influence of the more technically assured, rhythmically propulsive J. C. Higginbotham, then the trombonist with Luis Russell's exciting new orchestra. Though lacking Higginbotham's inventiveness, Archey continued to play with a sprightly, robust earthiness for the remainder of his career. Between 1934 and 1939 he recorded with the Russell/Armstrong orchestra, Willie Bryant, and Benny Carter but almost exclusively in the capacity of a sectionman. Starting in 1947, though, he was heard to advantage on small-band sessions led by Mutt Carey, Wild Bill Davison, Punch Miller, and Tony Parenti and from 1949 through 1953 as a sideman with Sidney Bechet, Bob Wilber, Sidney De Paris, George Wettling, and Willie "the Lion" Smith. Between 1954 and 1961 he worked and recorded with Muggsy Spanier and Earl Hines at Los Angeles clubs such as the Hangover and the Crescendo and in 1966 appeared on several albums by the touring New Orleans All Stars. Additionally, a number of his band's weekly radio broadcasts from Jimmy

Ryan's in 1952 have since appeared on record as well as on audio checks of Blesh's "This Is Jazz" series.

Nothing can be ascertained about Archey's private life, including whether he ever married or had children.

• Something of Archey's background can be learned from Walter C. Allen and Brian Rust, *King Oliver*, ed. Laurie Wright (1987); Albert McCarthy, *Big Band Jazz* (1974); Max Jones and John Chilton, *Louis: The Louis Armstrong Story* (1971); James Lincoln Collier, *Louis Armstrong: An American Genius* (1983); and Chilton, *Sidney Bechet: The Wizard of Jazz* (1987). For a more general understanding of the Harlem jazz scene of the 1920s and 1930s, see Morroe Berger et al., *Benny Carter: A Life in American Music* (2 vols., 1982); Clyde E. B. Bernhardt, *I Remember: Eighty Years of Black Entertainment, Big Bands, and the Blues*, as told to Sheldon Harris (1986); and Benny Waters, *The Key to a Jazzy Life* (1985). An abbreviated biographical entry of Archey is in Chilton, *Who's Who of Jazz* (1982), and a very short 1949 interview with him is summarized in *Storyville* 147 (1 Sept. 1991): 89–90. Discographical listings are in Rust, *Jazz Records, 1897–1942* (1982), and Walter Bruyninckx, *Traditional Jazz Discography, 1897–1988* (6 vols., 1985–1988) and *Swing Discography, 1920–1988* (12 vols., 1986–1989).

JACK SOHMER

ARCHIPENKO, Alexander Porfirevich (30 May 1887–25 Feb. 1964), sculptor, was born in Kiev, Ukraine, the son of Porfiry Antonovich Archipenko, a mechanical engineer, inventor, and professor of engineering, and Poroskovia Wassilevna Machova. Archipenko decided early on a career in art and attended art school in Kiev from 1902 to 1905. The next year he left for Moscow, where he worked and participated in different group shows. In 1908 he left his native land for Paris.

The decade that followed was his most creative and original period. In the stimulating artistic atmosphere of Paris in the heyday of cubism, he made a number of important innovations in sculpture.

The years 1913 and 1914 stand out as the creative highpoint of his early period. His most successful and important sculptures, among them some unqualified masterpieces, like *Carrousel Pierrot*, *Médrano II*, and *Boxing (Boxers)* (all three are in the collection of the Guggenheim Museum in New York), were created in these two years. Incorporated into these works are all of the significant sculptural innovations that earned Archipenko a position among the handful of pioneers of modern sculpture.

Archipenko's contributions were threefold. He presented an alternative to the traditional notion of the monolithic sculpture that merely displaces space by designing pieces that surround and enclose space. He reintroduced color into sculpture, both overall, unified color that minimizes the role of representation and establishes the sculpture's self-sufficiency as an object as well as color used for optical effects or as a means of clarifying structure. Finally, he explored the use of planar materials like sheet metal and plywood, which required a new schematic, rather than descriptive, approach to sculptural mass.

Archipenko was a born tinkerer who created a medium of his own, the sculpto-painting, which may well constitute his most original body of work. Its unique quality is the unexpected passage from one medium to the next—from projecting volume to pictorial surface. Although in subject matter and style the sculpto-paintings (1914 to early 1920s) rely on cubist paintings—for example, *Woman with Fan* (1914) and *Bather* (1915)—the compositions are conceived with a greater spontaneity and imagination and are entirely free of aesthetic constraints. Their most striking feature is dazzling, dissonant color. Quite casually Archipenko introduced into sculpture a number of novelties like transparent glass, reflective metals and mirrors, a photograph, inscribed words, movable parts. A man of intuitive sensibility and idiosyncratic talent, he was seemingly unencumbered by aesthetic doctrines or formal strictures. His commitment to innovation, and what appears to have been a certain intellectual restlessness, constantly propelled him on; he did not stay long with an idea or, as it turned out, remain in one place for any length of time; but in the fertile artistic environment of Paris, under the aegis of cubism, Archipenko was always among the first to perceive a new possibility in sculpture and initiate its development.

After World War I, which he spent in Nice, Archipenko resumed his busy exhibition schedule. In 1920 he was honored with a retrospective at the Venice Biennale, which at the time was the most prestigious art event in the world. Hailed by critics and art historians for his revolutionary approach to form, materials, and color, he was considered by many to be the greatest living sculptor. His works were exhibited in New York under the auspices of Katherine S. Dreier's organization, Société Anonyme, Inc., in 1921. That same year Archipenko moved to Berlin, married the expressionist sculptor Gela Forster (whose real name was Angelica Schmitz), opened a highly successful art school, and exhibited with Der Sturm, the avant-garde art gallery of Herwarth Walden, publisher of the cultural weekly of the same name. A measure of his great popularity in Europe in these years is the amount of literary attention he received: six monographs on his work were published between the years 1921 and 1924. Coinciding with his marriage and move to Berlin came a sudden stylistic change in Archipenko's work. He abandoned his bold, innovative experiments of the previous decade and assumed a mannered naturalistic style. Although the langorously posed sleek female figures corresponded to the local taste, Archipenko's new work did not meet with much critical favor. Barely two years after his arrival in Berlin, in October 1923, Archipenko left for the United States. Perhaps he felt that his reputation was waning, but the principal reason, it seems, was to escape the economic and social crisis in Europe.

In the United States, Archipenko was never able to regain the fame he had enjoyed in Europe. He continued to sculpt and exhibit, bought land near Woodstock, New York, became an American citizen (1929), lived in Los Angeles (1935) and in Chicago

(1937 and 1946–1947), founded art schools in all three places, and taught for brief periods at institutions across the country. In 1936 he was represented by six sculptures in Alfred Barr's historic exhibition, *Cubism and Abstract Art*, at the Museum of Modern Art in New York. This was followed by an acrimonious correspondence between Barr and Archipenko that focused on two important issues that have clouded Archipenko's career and reputation: replication and antedating. Archipenko's position is spelled out in his *Archipenko, Fifty Creative Years* (1960):

> Sometimes I sculpt a new version of the same statue after a considerable time has elapsed. Of course, in modelling the same problem the forms are not as mathematically exact as if they were cast from the same mold. However, in all versions I prefer to keep the date of the first, since I want to conserve the chronology of the idea. The particular stylistic and creative approach I use equally in all versions unless changes are purposely made (caption to pl. 141).

Archipenko later remade about thirty early works from photographs and from memory. These resulted in bronze editions, many of which were begun in the mid-1950s. In some cases there is more than one edition of a work, and sometimes there are editions of the same sculpture in different sizes or in different materials. In every case the works were assigned the dates of their original creation.

The type of figure most commonly identified with Archipenko today is the female torso with a flowing arabesque contour. Repeatedly throughout his career, Archipenko returned to this universally pleasing motif, first conceived in the elegant, streamlined *Flat Torso* (1914). Whether vertical or horizontal, or merely suggested by an S-shaped outline in his sculpto-paintings, the curvilinear female torso is the formal *idée fixe* in Archipenko's work. These figures, cast in bronze editions, continue to appear frequently in auction sales.

After the death of his first wife in 1957, Archipenko married Frances Gray in 1960. Both marriages were childless. When he died in New York City, his reputation rested chiefly on his brief, intensely creative interlude of the 1910s. Although the formal innovations of his early work outlined above are recognized by scholars as important contributions to modern art, the work itself is not well known. The largest concentration of his works is to be found, by an accident of history, in the Tel Aviv Museum, where they have been since 1933, when the German collector Erich Goeritz sent them there for safekeeping. Three important early works are at the Guggenheim Museum in New York, with isolated examples in various other museums in the United States and Europe.

• Archipenko's papers are in the Archives of American Art, Smithsonian Institution, Washington, D.C. *Archipenko, Fifty Creative Years* is by far the most complete source of illustrations of Archipenko's sculpture. The text provides little factual information, although the appendix includes a brief biographical chronology, exhibitions, teaching positions, owners of works, and a bibliography. Among the monographs of the 1920s, Hans Hildebrandt's, published in Berlin in 1923 in English, French, Spanish, and Ukrainian editions, deserves to be singled out. More recent publications are Donald H. Karshan, *Archipenko, the Sculpture and Graphic Art* (1974), and Katherine Jánszky Michaelsen, *Archipenko, a Study of the Early Works* (1977); the latter established a chronology of the early work, redated a number of works, and eliminated some inconsistencies of dating. Noteworthy exhibition catalogs are *Archipenko: International Visionary* (National Collection of Fine Arts, Washington, D.C., 1969), *Archipenko, the Early Works: 1910–1921* (Tel Aviv Museum, 1981), and *Alexander Archipenko, a Centennial Tribute* (National Gallery of Art, Washington, D.C., 1986–1987). An obituary is in the *New York Times*, 26 Feb. 1964.

KATHERINE JÁNSZKY MICHAELSEN

ARDEN, Elizabeth (31 Dec. 1878?–18 Oct. 1966), businesswoman, was born Florence Nightingale Graham (her legal name throughout life) in Woodbridge, near Toronto, Canada, the daughter of William Graham and Susan Tadd, farmers. Florence would remain a citizen of Canada until she married an American, Thomas Jenkins Lewis, in 1915. Her mother died when Florence was a small child. Unable to finish high school because of her straitened finances, she entered nursing but found that she disliked working with sick people. She moved quickly through jobs as dental assistant, stenographer, and cashier and finally followed her brother William to New York City. By then she was about thirty, although her youthful complexion made her look about twenty. In 1908, as a cashier in a New York beauty salon, she persuaded her employer, Eleanor Adair, to teach her how to give facials, and she quickly mastered this "art of the healing hands."

After a short, unsatisfactory partnership in a beauty salon with Elizabeth Hubbard at 509 Fifth Avenue in New York City, Florence Graham took over the business in 1909. She assumed a new name by scraping "Hubbard" off the front door and substituting "Arden," a name she remembered, she said, from Alfred, Lord Tennyson's poem *Enoch Arden*. Her slim capital was augmented by a loan of $6,000 from her brother. Except for one short-term bank loan (she met her first husband while applying for it), this was all the outside financing she would ever need.

Elizabeth Arden believed in elegant surroundings, including antiques and oriental carpets, and her embellishments paid off handsomely. Her red door would become famous as the trademark of hundreds of Elizabeth Arden salons in the United States and Europe. Despite the outbreak of World War I in 1914, she traveled to Paris to see how facials were done in the city's beauty salons (except that of her arch rival, Helena Rubinstein) and discovered the value of cosmetics, such as mascara, eye shadow, rouge, and lipstick. With their adept use, she could make women in the United States look as stylish as Parisian women.

Elizabeth Arden the enterprise moved triumphantly up Fifth Avenue, to no. 673 in 1915 and no. 691 in 1930. The rich profits from cosmetics subsidized the salons and made such growth possible; yet without the salons, the Elizabeth Arden name would not have acquired its cachet. Arden gave close attention to product research. Her most successful product, developed by chemist A. Fabian Swanson, was Amoretta, a fluffy, nongreasy face cream. Arden also gave her clients advice on proper diet and offered an exercise salon once exercising became popular. Apart from her natural youthfulness, freshness, and elegance, her profound practical knowledge of female psychology was her greatest asset.

Arden and Rubinstein shared many talents, but because only one could sit atop the beauty culture pyramid, they remained bitter enemies. "That woman," Arden called Rubinstein, who gave as good as she got. After hearing that Arden had lost the tip of the index finger of her right hand to a horse's bite, Rubinstein is said to have asked, "What happened to the horse?"

Arden's one deep interest, apart from her business, was breeding and training racehorses, at which she was so successful that in 1946 she was featured on the cover of *Time* magazine as the owner of a stable. The next year, one of the horses, Jet Pilot, won the Kentucky Derby. Her marriage to Lewis, who had filled a subordinate post in the company for years, ended in 1934, and her 1942 marriage to a Russian émigré, Prince Michael Evlanoff, resulted in divorce in 1944. She had no children from either marriage.

Arden advertised extensively in slick magazines, lecturing her advertising agency on the right way to promote her salons, but her best investment in advertising, she said, was her charity balls, which were always featured prominently on the society pages. Her message to all women remained, "Hold fast to life and youth." Eventually she had annual sales of $60 million and a net worth that, although never disclosed, must have reached well into the eight figures.

Arden owned every share of stock in her company and consistently rejected her advisers' urgings to make provision for the continuation of the company in its same legal form after her death, which would have saved millions in tax liabilities. Arden, who loved horses, travel, and big parties, remained in firm control of her business virtually to the day she died in New York City. Apart from substantial legacies to her sister, Gladys, who had managed the Arden salon in Paris, and a loyal niece, Patricia Young, her estate was liquidated by taxes. To take care of death duties, the business was sold for $37.5 million to Eli Lilly & Company.

• No papers of Elizabeth Arden, the person or the business, are publicly available. Arden's birth year is not substantiated; there is no record in the Office of the Registrar General in Toronto. There is a biography, *Miss Elizabeth Arden* (1972), by Alfred Allen Lewis and Constance Woodworth, in the writing of which the authors had the cooperation of former Arden employees and relatives, but the book is rather superficial. Articles on Elizabeth Arden are Margaret Case Harriman, "Glamour, Inc.," *New Yorker*, 6 Apr. 1935, pp. 24ff.; "I Am a Famous Woman in This Industry," *Fortune*, Oct. 1938; the *Time* cover story, "Lady's Day in Louisville," 6 May 1946, pp. 57–63; and Hambla Bauer, "High Priestess of Beauty," *Saturday Evening Post*, 24 Apr. 1948, pp. 26–27, 189–90. See also obituaries in the *New York Times*, 19 Oct. 1966, and in *Time*, *Life*, and *Newsweek*, 28 Oct. 1966.

ALBRO MARTIN

ARDEN, Eve (30 Apr. 1912?–12 Nov. 1990), stage, film, radio, and television actress, was born Eunice Quedens in Mill Valley, California, the daughter of Lucille Frank. Her parents divorced when she was two because of her father's inveterate gambling. As a single parent, her mother made a living as a milliner, work that accounts in part for the headpieces Arden was noted for in her Hollywood days. She was raised by her mother in San Francisco and by her aunt in Mill Valley, inland from Sausalito. Success in a high school play led her to begin acting professionally at age sixteen with the Henry Duffy company in San Francisco. Soon after, she toured West Coast resorts and hotels ("the citrus circuit") with the Bandbox Repertory Theater, a "superstock" company. Both allowed her to develop her acting skills. An appearance in a Leonard Sillman revue, *Lo and Behold*, at the Pasadena Playhouse led to Lee Shubert hiring her for the *Ziegfeld Follies of 1934*, supporting Fanny Brice. The next year she appeared successfully in a revue, *Parade*, singing "Send for the Militia," leading to a return engagement with the *Follies* in 1936, again with Fanny Brice and with Bob Hope. According to Arden, when Shubert asked her to shorten and simplify her name, she chose the heroine of the current book she was reading, Eve, and the manufacturer of the cosmetics she was using, Elizabeth Arden.

After several early screen appearances—*Song of Love* (1929), *Dancing Lady* (1933)—her film career began in earnest at Universal with *Oh Doctor* (1937). The same year she was memorable in RKO's all-star *Stage Door* as the actress in a theatrical boardinghouse with a cat named Henry draped around her neck. She worked steadily as a supporting player, making eight films in the next two years, including *At the Circus* (1939) with the Marx Brothers. She returned to the theater, which remained her first love, in Jerome Kern's short-lived *Very Warm for May* (1939) but was hired immediately after for the revue *Two for the Show* (1940). She returned to Hollywood, appearing in four films in 1940, her best opportunity occurring as Clark Gable's journalist pal in *Comrade X*. She made eleven films in 1941, among them *Ziegfeld Girl*, uncharacteristically as a gold-digging showgirl; *Manpower*, with Marlene Dietrich; and *Whistling in the Dark*, with Red Skelton. She returned to Broadway with Danny Kaye in a Cole Porter musical, *Let's Face It* (1941), repeating her role in the film version (1943), which reunited her with Kaye's film counterpart, Bob Hope. As a fashion editor, she provided acid commentary on the action in *Cover Girl* (1944), at one point accidentally tearing the top of an expensive billiard table and exiting deadpan. As a rifle-toting Russian war heroine in wartime Washington in *The Doughgirls* (1944), she roused enough laughter to merit a seven-year contract at Warner Bros.

For the film that followed, *Mildred Pierce* (1945), starring Joan Crawford, she was nominated for an Academy Award as Ida, Mildred's sharp-tongued best friend, who has the film's most memorable line. Speaking of Mildred's unappreciative daughter, Ida observes, "Alligators have the right idea, they eat their young." In the next few years, Arden established her screen persona, usually as the heroine's best friend. In his *Halliwell's Filmgoers Companion* (1988), Leslie Halliwell credited her with "patenting the comic image of the cool, sophisticated but usually manless career woman." In David Shipman's words, Arden created "an appreciative buzz" in audiences at her first appearance. "Her slightest glance," he adds, "was treasured more than all the star's vaporings." Sometimes Arden was the best thing in a film, the only reason to see it, as she was, for instance, as Yvonne de Carlo's dizzy mother in *Song of Scheherazade* (1947). "She saved many a movie with her biting sarcasm and caustic wit," according to Sol Chaneles and Albert Wolsky in *The Movie Makers* (1974). One of her best parts was with Eleanor Parker and Ronald Reagan in *The Voice of the Turtle* (1947), the Hollywood version of a three-character play that had been a long-running hit on Broadway. She made thirteen other films—good, poor, or indifferent—between 1945 and 1951, at Warners or on loan, as in Universal's *One Touch of Venus* (1948), ending, again with Joan Crawford, in *Goodbye, My Fancy*, as a wisecracking secretary, played on the stage by Shirley Booth. The casting of Arden in the film was inevitable because such a role, then as now, was known as "an Eve Arden part."

In her personal life, as in her career, Arden was generally fortunate. She married Edward Bergen, whose business was providing insurance for people in theater and in film, in 1939, but the marriage was dissolved amicably in 1947. The Bergens adopted a child, and as a single parent Arden adopted a second. In 1950 she starred in stock in New England in Ruth Gordon's *Over Twenty-One*, and in 1951 she married her leading man in that production, Brooks West. The marriage lasted happily until his death in 1984; they had one child and adopted another. The Wests bought a ranch in the San Fernando Valley once owned by Ronald Colman, which they renamed "Westhaven"; the good years there were in large part the subject of her autobiography.

Arden began work in radio in 1947 ("The Sealtest Village Store") and found her niche the following year in "Our Miss Brooks," the high school teacher Connie Brooks becoming her best-known characterization. Teachers throughout the country welcomed her portrayal of a lively, witty, and warmhearted woman both in and out of the classroom. In 1952 she was named woman of the year in radio, and in the same year she took the nation's favorite teacher to television, where the program ran for three years. Arden won an Emmy for her TV work in 1953. She starred in a film version in 1956.

Arden remained busy despite the decline of the studio system. "The Eve Arden Show" existed briefly on television (1957–1958), but she performed *Auntie Mame* to great acclaim on West Coast stages in 1958 and returned to film as James Stewart's secretary in *Anatomy of a Murder* (1959). She also had a serious role as Dorothy Mcguire's sister in *The Dark at the Top of the Stairs* (1960). She played the lead in *Hello, Dolly!* in Chicago in 1967 and won that city's Sarah Siddons award for distinguished work in the theater. Then for two years (1967–1969) she costarred with Kaye Ballard in "The Mothers-in-Law" on television. She starred as the mother in *Butterflies Are Free* (1970) and toured in stock in several plays with her husband.

Arden's later films include *Sergeant Deadhead* (1965); *Grease* (1978), the popular version of the stage hit in which she delighted audiences playing a high school principal; *Under the Rainbow* (1981); and *Grease II* (1982). Back on Broadway, she withdrew from a disastrous play, *Moose Murders* (1983), which ran for one performance starring her replacement. She was scheduled to appear in a film by Woody Allen, who admired her greatly, but she withdrew because of her husband's terminal illness. Arden died in Los Angeles.

• Eve Arden's autobiography is humorously titled *Three Phases of Eve* (1985). It is woefully vague on dates but is filled with stories of her family, particularly of their travels in Europe. An appreciation of her career that includes titles and dates of all her films is in David Shipman, *The Great Movie Stars: The International Years* (1972). Also appreciative is the assessment of Mary Unterbrink in *Funny Women: American Comediennes, 1860–1985* (1987). A summary of Arden's career at the time of her radio and television success in "Our Miss Brooks" is in *Current Biography*, Sept. 1953. See also Larry Langman, *Encyclopedia of American Film Comedy* (1987).

JAMES VAN DYCK CARD

ARDREY, Robert (16 Oct. 1908–14 Jan. 1980), anthropologist, playwright, and novelist, was born and raised in Chicago, Illinois, the son of Robert Lesley Ardrey, an editor and publisher, and Marie Haswell. Ardrey earned a Ph.D. in the natural and social sciences from the University of Chicago in 1930. After taking a writing course taught by Thornton Wilder, he abandoned anthropology and zoology in favor of playwriting, in the meantime earning a living as a jazz pianist and civil service test writer. His first play, *Star Spangled*, a comedy about Poles in Chicago, opened on Broadway in 1936 but closed after twenty-three performances. After obtaining a Guggenheim Fellowship, Ardrey toured the United States by bus. In 1938 two of his plays, *How to Get Tough about It* and *Casey Jones*, were also flops. That same year he married Helen Johnson; they had two children. He worked at MGM Studios in Hollywood for three months and then went to Nantucket to write *Thunder Rock*, an anti-Fascist play. It opened on Broadway in 1939 but closed after three weeks. In Europe, however, the play was very popular. It was made into a successful British film and also into a BBC television drama.

During the war years Ardrey worked for the Office of War Information in New York City, meanwhile writing screenplays and a novel, *Worlds Beginning* (1944). The films were more successful than the book. Discouraged by still another theatrical failure, the play *Jeb* (1946), Ardrey returned to Hollywood to write screenplays, including, for MGM, *The Three Musketeers* (1947) and *Madame Bovary* (1948). His second novel, a thriller called *Brotherhood of Fear* (1952), elicited some favorable reviews. In October 1954 his play *Sing Me No Lullaby*, an anti-McCarthyist satire, opened in New York. It too was not a success. During the next twelve years Ardrey continued to write screenplays, including *Quentin Durand* (1955), *The Power and the Prize* (1956), *The Wonderful Country* (1959), *The Four Horsemen of the Apocalypse* (1962), and *Khartoum* (1966), which was nominated for an Academy Award.

In 1955, on assignment for the periodical *The Reporter*, Ardrey met Dr. Raymond Dart, who had excavated fossils of early human predecessors, in South Africa. He soon was fascinated by Dart's views on the violent behavior of these *Australopithecines* ("southern apes"), as Dart had dubbed his finds, and Ardrey's latent interest in anthropology resurged. In a series of papers published between 1949 and 1965, Dart reviewed the archaeological evidence of these alleged human ancestors found at Makapansgat, South Africa. On the basis of fractured skulls and bone fragments, Dart concluded that *Australopithecus* was not only a carnivorous hunter and scavenger but also a cannibalistic killer of members of its own kind, in spite of the fact that its brains were still relatively small. "The loathsome cruelty of mankind to man," Dart asserted, "is explicable only in terms of his cannibalistic origins." This was, as Edward Wilson (*Sociobiology* [1975]) commented, "very dubious anthropology, ethology, and genetics," but Dart's theories inspired the first of Ardrey's series of speculations on the nature of man, *African Genesis*.

During studies at the London Museum of Natural History, where he gathered material for his book, Ardrey managed to write another play, on the Hungarian uprising of 1956, *Shadow of Heroes: A Play in Five Acts from the Hungarian Passion*. This was his last attempt at playwriting. Dissatisfied and disappointed in its lack of success, he turned to science for good. In 1960 Ardrey divorced his wife and married Berdine Grunewald, an actress and artist who later illustrated Ardrey's nonfiction books.

In 1961 *African Genesis: A Personal Investigation into the Animal Origins and Nature of Man* was published. Its basic argument is that humans originated in Africa and that contemporary humans are descendants of a race of predatory and cannibalistic "killer apes." This, Ardrey submits, explains the aggressiveness and warlikeness of modern humans. Ardrey speculated that the African ancestor of *Homo sapiens* was a primitive primate (Dart's *Australopithecus*) who, not being equipped by nature with claws, fangs, hooves, horns, or particular agility, began to use weapons. Tools, weapons, culture—these are all the result of man's predatory nature. "[W]e are born of risen apes, not fallen angels, and the apes were armed killers besides," he wrote. "The miracle of man is not how far he has sunk, but how magnificently he has risen. We are known among the stars by our poems, not our corpses." Ardrey's ideas about the evolutionary roots and instinctive nature of human violence stirred the scientific community to vehement and sometimes acrimonious debates. Critics deplored his sensationalism, his simplistic analogizing, and his general amateurism, though many reviewers praised his audacity, eloquence, and writing skill. Ardrey's views of the violent inheritance of humanity apparently meshed with those of ethologist Konrad Lorenz (*On Aggression* [1963]), anthropologist Robert Bigelow (*The Dawn Warriors* [1969]), other scientists, and even some novelists, such as William Golding (*Lord of the Flies* [1955]).

In his next book, *The Territorial Imperative: A Personal Inquiry into the Animal Origins of Property and Nations* (1966), Ardrey claimed that attachment to territory and property is instinctive, a general evolved characteristic of organisms, expressing itself as hostility toward territorial neighbors. He attributed even greater importance to the drive to acquire or protect a territory than to the sex drive. "[I]t may come to us as the strangest of thoughts that the bond between a man and the soil he walks on should be more powerful than his bond with the woman he sleeps with. Even so, in a rough preliminary way we may test the supposition with a single question: 'How many men have you known in your lifetime who died for their country? And how many for a woman?'"

In the last of his books on the evolutionary inheritance of mankind, *The Social Contract: A Personal Inquiry into the Evolutionary Sources of Order and Disorder* (1970) and *The Hunting Hypothesis* (1976), Ardrey furnished evidence for some of the themes introduced in *African Genesis*. The common denominator is still humanity's allegedly inherited aggressive instinct and its persistent influence on contemporary social problems. The aura of novelty had dimmed somewhat by then, and these books had far less impact than his earlier ones.

Ardrey lived in Rome from 1963 to 1978. He then moved to Kalk Bay, Cape Province, South Africa, where he died.

As a playwright, novelist, and screenwriter, Ardrey was more critically praised (he received several awards) than commercially successful, despite his sense of the humorous, his social commitment, and his dramaturgical and literary talents. It was his four controversial books on the evolutionary roots of human behavior in general, and human violence in particular, that brought him acclaim and wide recognition but also opposition and vilification. One of Ardrey's most ardent opponents, anthropologist Ashley Montagu (*Man and Aggression* [1968]), regarded Ardrey's doctrine as "original sin revisited" and "the myth of innate depravity."

It has since become apparent that Dart and Ardrey's sanguinary and phantasmagoric imaginings have more qualities related to the genre of literary horror stories than to science. If such biological freaks as killer apes had ever existed, they would, in all probability, have exterminated each other long before they would have given rise to modern man. Whatever the merits or faults of Ardrey's evolutionary speculations, however, he forced his critics to phrase their objections carefully and clearly and both his opponents and supporters to state explicitly their implicit assumptions about the nature of *Homo sapiens*. Indeed, many of the themes that Ardrey touched on were later elaborated on in sociobiology, Darwinian psychology, and evolutionary anthropology. Ardrey was convinced that our legacy from prehistoric times included not only an instinctively based capacity for violence but also a counterbalancing capacity for simple human decency, equally rooted in our animal past. "If there is hope for man," he wrote, "it is because we are animals."

• The main source for biographical details is Janet Podell and Sybil Pincus, *The Annual Obituary 1980* (1981), pp. 31–33. Raymond Dart's article in which he formulates the "killer ape" hypothesis adopted by Ardrey is "The Predatory Transition from Ape to Man," *International Anthropological and Linguistic Review* 1, no. 4 (1953): 201–13.

J. M. G. VAN DER DENNEN

ARENAS, Reinaldo (16 July 1943–7 Dec. 1990), novelist and political activist, was born in Holguín, a town in rural eastern Cuba, the son of Oneida Fuentes, a poor peasant woman, and a peasant father who abandoned his unborn child. Barely sixteen years old at the time of the Cuban Revolution, Arenas received excellent instruction during the Campaigns against Illiteracy conducted by volunteers sympathetic to Fidel Castro's ideals. Such an opportunity for self-improvement was unheard of during the regime of the deposed leader, Fulgencio Batista. In 1960 Arenas received a scholarship so that he might pursue a career in accounting in Havana.

Arenas began to write while working at the National Library from 1963 to 1968. In 1965 his first novel, *Celestino antes del alba*, received a literary prize from the Casa del Autor Cubano (the Cuban Writers' Guild), and in 1969 it won the French Prix Medici for the best foreign novel. The book did not attract much attention from Cuban critics, however, when it was published in Cuba in 1967. In 1966 his second novel, *El mundo alucinante*, was awarded a literary prize by the Cuban Writers' Guild. The book was never published in Cuba.

Eventually Arenas's enthusiasm for the revolution faded as he confronted the socialist doctrinaire norms. His work came to be viewed as counterrevolutionary, and its liberal approach to sex and its lack of political activism provoked legal persecution. Although his works were published in several foreign languages, the Cuban government denied him permission to travel abroad at the invitation of academic institutions. In 1977 he was forced to work in a labor camp despite his stature as a well-known novelist.

Persecution of Arenas had begun in 1965, when he was expelled from the University of Havana for having "dubious morality and ideological frames." Many of his friends disappeared from their homes, punished for their deviations from the "proper" socialist moral code. Their crimes included violations of the dress code (wearing tight clothes or blue jeans and having long hair or Afros) and refusal to comply with civilian responsibilities like the obligatory military service. These young men were taken into work camps that combined physical labor, mostly agricultural, with indoctrination of Communist teachings. For a time Arenas escaped work in the camps by going underground. Eventually, however, he had to return to the visible world because he lacked the mandatory official identification card; the inability to show an ID during random police inspections constituted a violation punishable by jail sentences.

In 1974 Arenas was imprisoned, accused of corrupting a minor and of violating national copyright laws when he published abroad without official permission. The guards' failure to lock his cell allowed him to escape, and for forty-five days he pleaded, without result, for help from such international peace groups as the United Nations, UNESCO, and the Red Cross. Later, as Arenas had feared, the police captured him and forced him to write letters stating his satisfaction with the Cuban system. In jail Arenas staged a symbol of his own death by placing flowers in a funeral tribute near one of his photographs. After his 1976 release he tried unsuccessfully to leave his country legally or illegally. Finally, on 5 May 1980, he escaped to Key West, Florida, among perhaps 150,000 Cuban exiles who arrived in the Mariel boat lift.

Upon settling in the United States, Arenas became Castro's most vocal opponent as he claimed that, like thousands of other homosexuals, he had suffered persecution and torture in Cuban jails. His verbal accusations took shape in *Necesidad de libertad* (1986), a collection of personal essays and legal documents that set forth his case against the Cuban government. His rejection of the Cuban government's charge of improper conduct added fuel to the escalating controversy about Castro's violations of human rights. Arenas presented firsthand testimony of persecution of Cuban homosexuals, including himself, because of their sexual orientation.

Further homosexual activism came in 1984 when he took part in a documentary film, "Improper Conduct," produced by Néstor Almendros and Orlando Jiménez Leal, expatriate Cuban movie directors who had experienced political oppression by Cuban authorities. Arenas's statements on the already heated issue of Cuba's persecution of homosexuals provoked controversial opinions among both advocates of Cuban policies and counterrevolutionaries. On the one hand, political activists against Castro's regime did not validate the plight of homosexuals and their charges against the Cuban Revolution, preferring other orthodox political agendas, such as the mistreatment of political prisoners. On the other hand, American and Cuban homosexual groups never found a common ground to assess these charges against Castro, and many, of the right and of the left, believed that the alleged violations had been overrepresented by witnesses like Arenas.

Nevertheless, Reinaldo Arenas continued his international campaign against Castro. In 1990 he drafted a letter to Fidel Castro asking him for a plebiscite to allow Cubans to decide their political destiny. The document, published by important newspapers around the world, was signed by distinguished intellectuals, including presidents and Nobel Prize winners.

Along with his political activities, Arenas continued his literary production. In a significant phase he developed some homosexual themes in *El portero* (1989), a novel inspired by his experiences in New York City. A much stronger and more overt treatment appeared in his posthumously published autobiography, *Antes que anochezca* (1992), which describes the homosexual underground world that he witnessed as a student, as a writer, as a prisoner, and as an underground vagrant. The latter book, unique in contemporary Latin American letters, promotes the incorporation of the homosexual experience as a valid literary motif.

A victim of AIDS, Reinaldo Arenas committed suicide in his New York City apartment. With his early death Latin America lost one of its most significant representatives of the neobaroque, a highly sophisticated and experimental literary style. His departure was not in silence; his last political declaration was his suicide note, in which he charged that Fidel Castro, alone, was responsible for his death.

• On his arrival in the United States, the impoverished Arenas sold a considerable amount of personal writings to the Princeton University Library. This special collection consists of published and unpublished literary manuscripts and correspondence. In addition to the works mentioned above, Arenas's production includes *Con los ojos cerrados* (1972), *El palacio de las blanquísimas mofetas* (1980), *La vieja Rosa* (1980), *El central* (1981), *Cantando en el pozo* (1982), *Otra vez el mar* (1981), *Termina el desfile* (1981), *Arturo, la estrella más brillante* (1984), *Persecución* (1986), *La loma del angel* (1987), *Voluntad de vivir manifestándose* (1989), and *Viaje a La Habana* (1990). Since his arrival in the United States in 1980, almost all of his works have been translated into English: *Hallucinations* (1971), *Central: A Cuban Sugar Mill* (1984), *Farewell to the Sea* (1986), *The Graveyard of the Angels* (1987), *Singing from the Well* (1987), *The Doorman* (1991), and *Before Night Falls* (1993).

A number of literary critics have produced books on his works, including Perla Rozencvaig, *Reinaldo Arenas: Narrativa de la transgresión* (1986); Eduardo Béjar, *La textualidad de Reinaldo Arenas: Juegos de la escritura posmoderna* (1987); and Julio Hernández-Miyares and Perla Rozencvaig, eds., *Reinaldo Arenas: Alucinaciones, fantasías y realidad* (1990). His works have been the subject of doctoral dissertations. An obituary is in the *New York Times*, 9 Dec. 1990.

RAFAEL OCASIO

ARENDS, Leslie Cornelius (27 Sept. 1895–16 July 1985), businessman and politician, was born in Melvin, Illinois, the son of George Teis Arends, a businessman and farmer, and Talea Weiss. After graduating from Melvin High School in 1912, he attended Oberlin College for two years and then briefly attended Illinois Wesleyan University. He enlisted in the navy during World War I. Following his discharge in 1919 he returned to Melvin to work in the grain business and in the small Commercial State Bank founded by his father. A tall, easygoing, and likable young veteran, Arends enjoyed success in business and was elected district commander of the American Legion. In 1935 he became a member of the Ford County (Ill.) Farm Bureau and in 1938 joined the Board of Trustees of Illinois Wesleyan University.

In 1934 Arends won election to the U.S. House of Representatives, the only Republican to unseat a Democrat that year, and the conservative voters of his rural East-central Illinois district returned him to Congress in each of the following nineteen elections. During his 1934 election campaign he walked to nearly every village and farm in the district and later recalled that his principal attribute for office was a pair of long legs. His House Republican colleagues elected him party whip in 1943, and he held that post until 1973. For most of that time his party was in the minority, but from 1947 to 1949 and from 1953 to 1955 he served as majority whip. In 1946 he married Betty Tychon; they had one daughter. A genial and popular politician, he was one of President Dwight D. Eisenhower's favorite golfing companions. Arends was also a highly effective vote counter on upcoming legislation who ensured that his fellow Republicans were present on important roll calls and was known for his encyclopedic knowledge of each member's voting record. He served as ranking Republican on the House Armed Services Committee, voted consistently for increased military expenditures through the Cold War era, and attended carefully to the concerns of his constituents in rural Illinois, particularly the selection of small-town postmasters. In addition, he vigorously fought off several efforts to close Chanute Technical Training Center at the air force base in Rantoul, Illinois.

"I was brought up right," Arends once said, "as a Republican." During his forty-year career in the U.S. House of Representatives, his party loyalty never wavered. First elected to Congress during the depths of the Great Depression, when House Republicans were a small minority, Arends immediately allied with his party's conservative members in attacking the social and economic programs of Democratic administrations and Democratic Congresses. Following the landslide victory of Lyndon B. Johnson in the presidential election of 1964, House Republicans were outnumbered by 2 to 1. A group of "Young Turks" headed by Representative Gerald R. Ford of Michigan challenged the conservative leaders of their party's "Old Guard," but Arends remained loyal to the incumbent conservative minority leader Representative Charles Halleck of Indiana in a tough fight for party leadership. "We're going to beat you badly," Arends told Ford on 4 January 1965 as the two entered the House chambers for the vote to decide minority leadership. For one of the few times in his career, Arends's numbers were wrong. Ford emerged with a narrow victory, but his winning coalition was so fragile that he was unable to replace Arends as whip with the more liberal Charles Goodell of New York. Nonetheless, Arends served Ford with the same loyalty he had given past Republican House leaders.

Throughout the Watergate crisis of 1973–1974, Arends fought until the very end to save the presidency of Richard M. Nixon, laboring to maintain solid support for the president among House Republicans. In 1973 Arends joined Ford in an unsuccessful effort to have House Speaker Carl Albert initiate impeachment proceedings against Vice President Spiro Agnew, a legal maneuver intended to allow Agnew to delay criminal prosecution, which would force his immediate resignation. When Agnew was forced to resign in October 1973 after pleading no contest to criminal charges, Ford was named vice president, and Representative John J. Rhodes of Arizona succeeded him as minority leader. By this time Arends, whose Seventeenth House District had been redrawn, had already announced that he would not seek reelection in 1974. "Now more than ever we need unity, not division in the Republican ranks and in the Republican leadership in Congress," he stated. During Arends's final year in office, he and Rhodes desperately advised their Republican colleagues to "keep their own counsel" on the Watergate affair until all the evidence was in. Following Nixon's forced resignation in August 1974, Arends advised President Ford to refuse the Democrats' call that he testify before a House committee looking into his pardon of former president Nixon. Ford ignored Arends's advice and testified in the fall of 1974 before the House committee. Furthermore, the president apparently ignored Arends's recommendations when selecting liberal Republican Nelson A. Rockefeller as his vice president. Of the Watergate affair, which led to disastrous losses for his beloved party in the 1974 elections, the ever-optimistic Arends stated, "Regrettable as it was—and as perplexing and puzzling as the entire matter may have been to many of us—the nation withstood the test and emerged with a sense of confidence in our Constitution." He resigned his House seat on 31 December 1974. In 1976 President Ford appointed him to serve on the Foreign Intelligence Advisory Board, created to overhaul the Central Intelligence Agency and other foreign intelligence gathering agencies. Despite this appointment, Arends's public career was largely ended. In retirement, he maintained homes in Washington, D.C., and Naples, Florida, where he died.

Arends's four decades in the House were not marked by important legislative achievements. His party was almost always in the minority, and as whip he devoted his time to mustering votes for his party's agenda. His conservative ideals also put him out of step with the direction the federal government was moving during his many years of public service. "What we have seen since the 1930's and with increasing momentum in the 1960's, is an alarming trend toward imbalance in the federal system," he said in 1974. "In the last forty years we have had the New Deal, the Fair Deal, the New Frontier, and the Great Society—all of which have added up to a raw deal for state government [and] . . . more power on the Potomac." While he believed that Strategic Arms Limitation Talks (SALT) agreements on atomic weapons with the Soviet Union in the mid-1970s offered "much encouragement," he consistently advocated continued military expansion "as long as the Godless men of the Kremlin and those who share their doctrines threaten the peace of the world and our own security." However, in Arends's view, military strength alone would not ensure the nation's survival. "We must return to the faith of our Fathers," he contended while vigorously denouncing Supreme Court rulings that prohibited Bible reading and prayer in public schools, activities he felt were necessary to maintain the nation's moral fiber.

• Arends's political papers are in the library of Illinois Wesleyan University in Bloomington. Also see *Blue Book of the State of Illinois* (1936–1974); *Biographical Directory of the United States Congress, 1774–1989, Bicentennial Edition* (1989); and Gerald R. Ford, *A Time to Heal: The Autobiography of Gerald R. Ford* (1979). Obituaries are in the *New York Times* and the *Chicago Sun-Times*, both 17 July 1985; and the *Ford County Press*, 18 July 1985, which printed a related article on 25 July.

MICHAEL J. DEVINE

ARENDT, Hannah (14 Oct. 1906–4 Dec. 1975), political theorist and philosopher, was born in Hanover, Germany, the daughter of Paul Arendt, an engineer, and Martha Cohn. She was raised in her parents' hometown, Königsberg, East Prussia, where the family moved when Paul Arendt became seriously ill with syphilis. He died in 1913. The years during World War I were especially difficult for the family; their safety was often threatened by the nearby battles of the Prussian and Russian armies. After the war, Arendt's mother became a German Social Democrat and a follower of Rosa Luxemburg, whose writings later had a great influence on Arendt's thought. In 1920 her mother married Martin Beerwald, who provided the family a renewed measure of security and Arendt with two older stepsisters.

A precocious student, Arendt studied philosophy at the University of Marburg, where she met Martin Heidegger, her mentor and, briefly, her lover. She finished her Ph.D. under the supervision of Karl Jaspers at Heidelberg in 1929. Her dissertation was entitled "St. Augustine's Concept of Love."

In 1929 Arendt married Gunther Stern, an author whose pen name was Gunther Anders. While living in Berlin with Stern, she wrote a biography of a famous eighteenth-century Jewish salon hostess, *Rahel Varnhagen* (1957), and affiliated herself informally with the German Zionist Organization. She was doing research for the organization's president, Kurt Blumenfeld, when she was arrested in 1933 by the Gestapo. After her release, she joined the migration of German Jews and Communists seeking refuge in Paris from Hitler's totalitarian regime.

Arendt lived in France from 1933 to 1941. During that time she developed a close relationship with the remarkable, autodidactic Berlin Communist Heinrich Blücher. After divorcing Stern, Arendt married Blücher in 1940. While in France, she belonged to a group of fellow émigré antifascist intellectuals—Arendt called them "the tribe"—that included the essayist Walter Benjamin and the novelist Hermann Broch. She worked for Youth Aliyah, an organization that trained young people for life in Palestine, until the German occupation of France resulted in her internment. She and Blücher, also an internee, soon escaped, however, and eventually made their way to the United States.

After arriving in New York in 1941, Arendt learned English and began working in émigré publishing. She wrote articles advocating the creation of a binational Jewish-Arab state in Palestine for the newspaper *Aufbau*, as well as articles on European history for such journals as *Politics*, *Partisan Review*, *Review of Politics*, and the *Nation*. As World War II drew to a close, she began to assemble the material for what would become her major treatise, *The Origins of Totalitarianism* (1951). The book established Arendt's reputation as a leading political theorist and triggered an intense debate—which persisted throughout the Cold War—about the true nature of totalitarianism.

Arendt's analyses of anti-Semitism, imperialism, and totalitarianism—the three main sections of *Origins*—convey a complex and dynamic image: European nation-states declining, supranationalist movements arising, political anti-Semitism becoming the key ideology of the Nazis, and traditional class structures crumbling, replaced by masses of alienated, déclassé proto-totalitarians. While many felt Arendt clearly analyzed Nazism, some critics believed she was less successful in identifying the development of Stalinism, which in Arendt's view was a horrible new form of one-party dictatorship, or totalitarianism.

The debate that engulfed *The Origins of Totalitarianism* prompted Arendt to write *The Human Condition* (1958), a number of important essays later collected in *Between Past and Future* (1961), and *On Revolution* (1963). These works examine the history of modern revolutions and, in particular, Marxism and its distortion into Stalinism. Claiming that action and speech are the basic ingredients of political life, Arendt sought to demonstrate how these are distinguished from the focus of Marx's theories, labor and work. She looked at political affairs in the light of social arrangements and analyzed modern shifts in technological conditions and intellectual habits. Concepts that had been staples of the European political philosophical tradition since Plato—freedom, authority, forms of government, revolution, violence—received her close attention, especially councils. Councils attracted Arendt's admiration because she believed them to be the essential ingredient of a democratic republic. She therefore attempted to establish a "new science of politics" by envisioning the democratic forms most likely to prevent a reappearance of totalitarianism.

Arendt's study of Nazi totalitarianism gained a new focus when she attended the trial of the infamous Nazi criminal Adolf Eichmann in Israel in 1961. Her account of that trial—published serially in the *New Yorker* (1963) and then as *Eichmann in Jerusalem: A Report on the Banality of Evil* (1964)—aroused tremendous controversy. Critics argued that she mistakenly stressed the role of the European Jewish councils (*Judenräte*) in the Nazis' Final Solution; that her portrait of Eichmann as an unthinking, banal human being rather than a sociopathic monster was overly generous; and that her analysis of the inadequacy of Israeli or international laws to address "crimes against humanity" was mistaken. Even though Arendt's key phrase in describing Eichmann—"the banality of evil"—has passed into common parlance and no longer raises a storm of protest, her underlying theses about the character of evil continue to be debated.

Believing that she had raised more questions than she had answered with her portrait of Eichmann, Arendt set out to explore philosophically his thoughtlessness and banality. From this quest came a posthumously published two-volume work, *The Life of the Mind* (1977, 1978). While she was again working on philosophy, her "first amour," she became deeply concerned about the moral and political condition of the United States, her second homeland. She published articles on the assassination of John F. Kennedy, the civil rights movement, the Vietnam War, and the consuming violence that had erupted in the nation's cities and on college campuses. Her essays, including "On Violence," are collected in *Crises of the Republic* (1972).

During the tumultuous 1960s, Arendt depended upon the companionship of her husband Blücher, her old émigré friends from "the tribe," and a group of new American friends, including the novelist Mary McCarthy. Arendt taught at the University of California–Berkeley and the University of Chicago from 1957 to 1967 and at the New School in New York City after 1968. Blücher's death in 1970 left her without her "thinking partner," the person who shared most deeply her passion to understand and explain the twentieth century, of which they had what she liked to call "a pariah's perspective." Arendt died in New York City.

Among the important twentieth-century American political theorists, Hannah Arendt probably has had the least effect on public policy, as her work did not translate into the mainstream of either liberal or conservative politics. But her oeuvre stands unequaled as a model of historical range and philosophical depth.

• Arendt's papers are housed in the Library of Congress. The main parts of her German correspondence are in the German Literary Archive, Marbach, Germany. The extensive correspondence with Jaspers, who was a key figure in her intellectual development and a close friend until his death in 1969, was published in German in 1985 and in an English translation in 1992: *Hannah Arendt/Karl Jaspers Correspondence, 1926–1969*, ed. Lotte Kohler and Hans Saner. Elisabeth Young-Bruehl, *Hannah Arendt: For Love of the World* (1982), is a detailed biography that includes a complete bibliography. Collections of essays on Arendt's work are numerous and include an issue of *Social Research* (1990). See also Margaret Canovan's major study, *Hannah Arendt: A Reinterpretation of Her Political Thought* (1992).

ELISABETH YOUNG-BRUEHL

ARENSBERG, Walter Conrad (4 Apr. 1878–29 Jan. 1954), art collector, poet, and writer, was born in Pittsburgh, Pennsylvania, the son of Conrad Christian Arensberg, an industrialist, and his second wife, Flora Belle Covert. Arensberg attended Harvard University, receiving his B.A. in 1900 with the accolade of class poet. While at Harvard he was an editor of the *Harvard Monthly* (1898–1900). Following graduation Arensberg spent more than a year in Europe, primarily Italy. When he returned to Harvard for graduate work in English (1903–1904), he began a lifelong study of cryptography, ciphers, codes, and the theories positing that Francis Bacon was the author of the plays and poems generally attributed to William Shakespeare. Arensberg reported on various issues for the *New York Evening Post* (1904–1906) and wrote articles and art reviews, a few of which appeared in the *Craftsman* (1905) and *Burlington Magazine* (1907).

After his marriage in 1907 to Mary Louise Stevens, an accomplished amateur pianist and bel canto singer whose family established prosperous textile mills in Massachusetts, the couple moved to Boston and then to New York City. The childless couple returned to the Boston area in 1912. Having ceased newspaper reporting and writing reviews for magazines shortly before his marriage, Arensberg concentrated on composing poetry and translating poems by French and German authors. These works, combined with poems and translations published in the *Harvard Monthly* and magazines such as *Trend*, *Others*, and *Rogue*—the latter two financially supported by Arensberg—were subsequently gathered in *Poems* (1914) and *Idols* (1916).

At this time Arensberg's writing style and aesthetic interests were somewhat progressive, betraying a European bias that continued throughout his literary career and art patronage. His poems were primarily influenced by symbolist poets; his art collection consisted of inherited pieces of early Americana from the Stevens family and contemporary works by European and American expatriate artists such as Legros and James Abbott McNeill Whistler.

The Armory Show (1913), which traveled from New York to Boston and Chicago, was crucial to the radicalization of Arensberg's interests in art. Under the guidance of one of the show's organizers, American artist and critic Walter Pach, Arensberg's tenuous inclinations toward modernism were quickly transformed into enthusiastic support. He acquired his first avant-garde work from the exhibition (Jacques Villon's *Sketch for "Puteaux: Smoke and Trees in Bloom," No. 2* of 1912), later adding to his and his wife's collection several others, most of which had received considerable publicity, including the show's cause célèbre, Marcel Duchamp's *Nude Descending a Staircase, No. 2*.

Arensberg won his renown largely for amassing the largest contemporary holding of Duchamp's work. Arensberg viewed the French artist's works as encapsulating the newest aesthetic, both in theory and in practice, which questioned the very definition of art and artistic production, including artistic originality and intentionality. Moreover, Duchamp's hermetic visual and textual language, his use of chance as a manipulative aesthetic tool, and no less devotion to chess paralleled Arensberg's investigations in cryptographic and other linguistic structures, his interest in physiological and psychological theories, and acumen at the game.

Upon Duchamp's first trip to the United States in 1915, Arensberg immediately befriended him, offering living quarters in the Arensbergs' New York apartment building (their residence since 1914) in exchange for the artist's work in progress, *The Bride Stripped Bare by the Bachelors, Even (Large Glass)*. At the Arensbergs' apartment Duchamp joined other émigrés such as Francis Picabia, Albert Gleizes, and Jean Crotti, and a diverse group of American artists, writers, and intelligentsia that included William Carlos Williams for almost nightly soirées. During its heyday in the mid- to late 1910s, the Arensbergs' salon was a center for New York dada and other avant-garde and literary activities. Arensberg fully partook in the collaborative undertakings of the salon members and their associates, including founding or sponsoring magazines devoted to experimental poetry and avant-garde art (such as *Others*, the *Blind Man*, and *Rong Wrong*), galleries that showed European and other modernist art, and the Society of Independent Artists.

In this milieu, Arensberg's poetry became decidely enigmatic and abstract. Only a handful of these dada texts, such as "Arithmetical Progression of the Verb 'To Be,'" and "Vacuum Tires: A Formula for the Digestion of Figments *à la la*," were published in sympathetic magazines of salon members like *391* (1917) and *TNT* (1919). Guided by Duchamp, the Arensbergs greatly altered their collection in these years, both in quantity and aesthetic interest, acquiring more than forty modern and avant-garde works, most notably European-based or cubist-inspired works dating from 1912–1913 and sculptures by Constantin Brancusi.

Arensberg's promotional efforts and active participation in various dada events as well as his financial support of the émigrés through art purchases and other means caused Picabia to bestow on him the title of "le vrai dada de New York" and to include the patron in one chart of dada published in *391* (Feb. 1919). Arensberg did not write "Dada est américain," a manifesto that Picabia ascribed to him in an issue of *Littérature* devoted to dada (May 1920).

These activities ceased in 1921, when the Arensbergs decided to vacation and eventually relocate to Los Angeles, California (1927), where they lived until their deaths. Throughout the 1920s Arensberg was preoccupied with publishing his findings on Bacon, Shakespeare, and the Baconian theory, which was generally dismissed by his contemporaries. (Arensberg himself would discover in the 1940s that his numerological calculations were in error, although he steadfastly believed that cryptographic methodology would prove the Baconian thesis of authorship.) Only in the 1930s did the couple renew art purchases. With added vigor, expanded preferences, and almost limitless funds from Louise Arensberg, they acquired works by surrealist and other contemporary artists in addition to pre-Columbian and other indigenous American artifacts. While the couple's aesthetic predilections were wide ranging, displaying their inclinations toward formal and symbolic affinities, the central focus of their collection remained Duchamp's works, these nearly all acquired directly from the artist. Duchamp was also the source for most of the Arensbergs' modern art purchases.

In 1937 the Arensbergs incorporated the Francis Bacon Foundation, a nonprofit research and educational private entity, to ensure the continuity of Arensberg's Baconian studies. The foundation was also designated the legal holder of their collection. For more than a decade beginning in the late 1930s, the Arensbergs sought an appropriate institution to which they could bequeath their diverse collection. With Duchamp's assistance as the Arensbergs' negotiator, the collection was eventually donated to the Philadelphia Museum of Art in 1950. Twenty-two galleries in a specially designated wing of the museum were opened to the public in 1954.

Arensberg died in Hollywood. He was one of a handful of collectors and patrons who were instrumental in fostering and promoting European-based avant-garde and modern art in the United States subsequent to the Armory Show, as well as the aesthetic implications and cultural importance of pre-Columbian and other indigenous artifacts.

• Arensberg's papers are in the Arensberg Archives, Philadelphia Museum of Art, and the Manuscript Department, Henry E. Huntington Library, San Marino, Calif. His journal writings, art reviews, and poetry are in the *Harvard Monthly* (Mar. 1898–Apr. 1900); "Jacob A. Riis: Practical Philanthropist," *Craftsman* 8 (1905): 174–89; *Burlington Magazine* 10 (Jan.–Feb. 1907); *Trend* (sporadically Apr. 1914–Dec. 1914); *Rogue* (1915 and 1916); *Others* 1 (1915): 53–54; *Blind Man* (2 May 1917): 8–9; *391* (June and Aug. 1917); and *TNT* (Mar. 1919). *Mr. Pennell's Etchings of London* (1906), first published as a gallery review in the *New York Evening Post*, was reprinted for the Frederick Keppel Gallery. Kenneth Fields, "Past Masters: Walter Conrad Arensberg and Donald Evans," *Southern Review* 6 (1970): 317–39, gives an overview of Arensberg's early poetry. Only three of eight published works on cryptography and the Shakespeare authorship controversy were printed by established presses: *The Cryptography of Dante* (1921); *The Cryptography of Shakespeare: Part One* (1922; additional parts never appeared); and *The Secret Grave of Francis Bacon at Lichfield* (1923). The most comprehensive appraisals of the Arensbergs' New York salon are by Francis M. Naumann: "Walter Conrad Arensberg: Poet, Patron, and Participant in the New York Avant-Garde, 1915–20," *Philadelphia Museum of Art Bulletin* 76 (Spring 1980): 2–32, and "Cryptography and the Arensberg Circle," *Arts Magazine* 51 (May 1977): 127–33. The relationship between the Arensbergs and Duchamp is examined by Katharine Kuh, an eyewitness to their interaction during the late 1940s, in "Walter Arensberg and Marcel Duchamp," in Kuh's *The Open Eye: In Pursuit of Art* (1971); and Naomi Sawelson-Gorse, "The Art Institute of Chicago and the Arensberg Collection," *Art Institute of Chicago Museum Studies* 19 (1993): 81–101, 107–11; Sawelson-Gorse, "Hollywood Conversations: Duchamp and the Arensbergs," *West Coast Duchamp*, ed. Bonnie Clearwater (1991); and Molly Nesbit and Sawelson-Gorse, "*Concept of Nothing*: New Notes by Marcel Duchamp and Walter Conrad Arensberg," in *The Duchamp Effect*, ed. Martha Buskirk and Mignon Nixon (1996). See also Fiske Kimball, "Cubism and the Arensbergs," *Art News* 53 (1954): 117–22, 174–78, for biographical information gleaned from the Arensbergs' friends. The Art Institute of Chicago's exhibition catalog *20th Century Art from the Louise and Walter Arensberg Collection* (1949) has the most inclusive listing of the Arensbergs' modern holdings; and the Philadelphia Museum of Art's two-volume *The Louise and Walter Arensberg Collection* (1954) contains partial listings and reproductions of the modern and pre-Columbian works.

NAOMI SAWELSON-GORSE

ARGALL, Samuel (1580–24? Jan. 1626), English explorer and colonial leader in early Virginia, was baptized at East Sutton, Kent, England, on 4 December 1580, the son of Richard Argall, a gentry landowner, and Mary Scott, daughter of a wealthy knight. As the eighth son and twelfth child of a prominent family, Argall had neither the luxury of living as a landed gentleman nor the necessity of forging a career without influential kin connections in Kent and London.

Argall gained military experience and navigational training in continental warfare and in 1609 received command of an expedition to America from Sir Thomas Smythe, a relative who was director of the Virginia Company of London. His 69-day voyage set a record as the shortest to Virginia, and in 1612 he made the crossing in the unprecedented time of fifty-seven days. Argall's navigational skills enabled another relative, Sir Thomas West, Baron De La Warr, to arrive in Virginia on 8 June 1610, just in time to save the struggling, starving colony from abandonment. Argall immediately sailed off in search of provisions, and before returning to Jamestown, he explored much of the Atlantic Coast southward from Cape Cod and on 27 August named Delaware Bay.

Appointed captain of a fifty-man company of colonial militia, Argall raided Indian villages along the James River in 1610–1611 as part of the first Anglo-Powhatan war. More significantly, he was a frequent trader and accomplished diplomat among the Patawomekes, the dominant Algonquian tribe on the Potomac River. He obtained a large quantity of maize and furs on his first visit in December 1610 and spent the winter of 1612–1613 living at their villages and exploring the upper Chesapeake Bay and the falls near present-day Washington, D.C. His friendship with Werowance (or chief) Japazaws (Iapassus) led to the capture of Pocahontas, who was visiting the Patawomekes, in April 1613.

Argall was most influential in ending England's first Indian war in 1614. His diplomacy succeeded in alienating key tribes from the Powhatan alliance. After a year as a hostage at Jamestown, a Christianized Pocahontas married colonist John Rolfe to symbolize the end of hostilities. More important, the Patawomekes remained English allies for several decades, as did the Accomacs and Accohannocs of the Eastern Shore, because, as Samuel Purchas quotes Argall's relatives, "they had received good reports" from the Potomac River tribes of Argall's "courteous usage of them."

Argall was not so courteous to French "interlopers" along Virginia's northernmost charter territories. Between July and November 1613 he raided René Le Coq de la Saussaye's Saint-Sauveur settlement on Mount Desert Island in present-day Maine, claiming it for James I. Argall devastated similar bases at Sainte-Croix and Port Royal, Acadia (now Nova Scotia). Before returning to Jamestown with French prisoners, he also paid a hostile visit to the "pretended Dutch governor" at Manhattan.

Argall's military expertise, Indian experience, and mastery of both negotiation and intimidation made him a logical choice as deputy governor of the Virginia Colony during the difficult and controversial period between 15 May 1617 and 10 April 1619. While trying to encourage profitable free enterprise without totally sacrificing the order and security that the colony had known during the previous seven years of martial law, Governor Argall was criticized from all sides. The charges of extortion and theft, and both harshness and laxness in enforcing martial law and military preparedness, cannot be objectively evaluated, since the animosity between the Virginia Company faction led by Sir Edwin Sandys and the one led by the earl of Warwick, Argall's patron and business partner, taints surviving evidence. Argall was probably no more aggressive, vengeful, or greedy than others who served as governor in the unruly colony. The leading historian of the Virginia Company, Wesley Frank Craven, concluded that "the records are so few and contradictory that it is impossible to pass a satisfactory judgment on the man" (p. 36).

In the context of later developments, Argall was an important leader in early American history. His explorations of Chesapeake Bay and the northern Atlantic coastline were as significant as Captain John Smith's more publicized voyages, and during Argall's tenure as transitional governor, black indentured servants and slaves and private tobacco plantations were introduced into Virginia. Moreover, Argall's administration anticipated the shift of political control from the Virginia Company to local planter-merchant oligarchs who merged private entrepreneurship and public policy.

Returning to England in the spring of 1619, Argall successfully defended himself against the accusations of his corporate critics and set about refurbishing his reputation. He commanded a 24-gun ship in an attack on Algiers in 1620, was appointed "Admiral of New England" and a member of the council for New England, and was knighted on 26 June 1622. In 1624 he served on the Mandeville Commission, which oversaw the reorganization of the Virginia Colony after the demise of the Virginia Company, and he unsuccessfully bid to be appointed the new governor at Jamestown. Active to the end, Argall was one of the commanders in a large English fleet that successfully plundered several Spanish vessels and made an abortive attack on Cadiz in the fall of 1625. The exact location is unknown, but he died, probably as a result of this expedition, on or about 24 January 1626. There is no record of a marriage or children.

Although less well known than his Virginia contemporaries John Smith and John Rolfe, Sir Samuel Argall should be remembered for the circumstances that also linked his life to the legendary Pocahontas. He was responsible for her capture, which ultimately led to her Anglicization, and in 1617 he commanded the ship that was to take Pocahontas back to her Virginia homeland, when she sickened and died along the Kentish shore at Gravesend. Argall's legacy continued to influence developments in Virginia long after his demise. Throughout the 1620s and 1630s fellow Kentishmen followed his precedents in fur trading, Indian diplomacy, military campaigning, and economic exploitation of the northern Chesapeake Bay and Eastern Shore, which his voyages and policies had opened to the colonists.

• The most important primary sources for Argall's career are Samuel Purchas, *Hakluytus Posthumus, or Purchas His Pilgrimes* (1625; repr. in 20 vols., 1906), see, especially, vol. 19, pp. 90–95, 106, 120, and 213–16; Ralph Hamor, *A True Discourse of the Present Estate of Virginia* (1615), which is available in a modern edition, ed. A. L. Rowse (1957); Susan Myra Kingsbury, ed., *Records of the Virginia Company of London* (4 vols., 1906–1935); and Philip L. Barbour, ed., *The Complete Works of Captain John Smith* (3 vols., 1986). Among secondary sources, the most reliable details on Argall are found in Barbour, *Pocahontas and Her World* (1969), and Wesley Frank Craven, *Dissolution of the Virginia Company* (1932). Less reliable and contradictory are several now dated entries in various standard reference works, as well as Seymour V. Connor, "Sir Samuel Argall: A Biographical Sketch," *Virginia Magazine of History and Biography* (1951).

J. FREDERICK FAUSZ

ARISS, John (fl. 1750–1775), architectural designer and builder, was active in colonial Virginia. The circumstances of his birth and education are uncertain. Ariss (the name is also recorded as "Ayres") has some renown today because Thomas Tileston Waterman in his landmark publication *Mansions of Virginia, 1706–1776* (1946) attributed to him, on circumstantial evidence, a dozen Virginia mid-Georgian mansion houses, including such famous structures as "Mount Vernon" and "Mount Airy." Waterman even credited Ariss with introducing and adapting the English Palladian style to the colony. In actuality, Ariss achieved considerably less. He did possess several architectural skills. He was a builder of modest accomplishments who worked locally in at least four Virginia counties; he was capable of estimating building expenses and on occasion did so; and he was a draftsman who was influenced by the mid-century wave of British architectural books to produce designs of some sophistication, though only two of those designs can be identified. Those books sparked a new awareness of classical architecture in the colony at a time of prosperity and growth: Ariss was active in Virginia at a propitious moment for a designer.

Ariss was but one of several hundred men engaged in the building profession in colonial Virginia. He merits less attention than more active builders like Larkin Chew, Lewis Deloney, or Major Harry Gaines, who completed numerous commissions far and wide and commanded large work forces. Ariss is different in having a command of English Palladianism and in his ability to create original designs and put them on paper. In a peculiar way, his unusual combination of various architectural talents is characteristic of the inconsistency and complexity of the manner that patronage, design, undertaking (contracting), and craftsmanship unfolded in colonial Virginia in innumerable commissions.

The facts about Ariss are few and far between. At mid-century he advertised his services as a builder, designer, estimator, and architectural draftsman. His announcement was placed in the *Maryland Gazette* from 22 May through 19 June 1751:

> By the subscriber (lately from Great Britain), Buildings of all Sorts & Dimensions are undertaken and performed in the neatest Manner (& at the cheapest Rates), either of the Ancient or Modern Order of *Gibb's* Architect & if any Gentleman should want Plans, Bills of Scantling, or Bills of Charges, for any Fabric, or Public Edifice, may have them by applying to the Subscriber at Maj. John Bushrods at Westmoreland County, Virginia, where may be seen a great Variety, & sundry Draughts of Buildings in Miniature, & also some Buildings near finished, after the Modern Taste. John Ariss.

Ariss apparently remained in Westmoreland County a few more years, for in 1752 he was appointed there to serve on a committee to inspect the construction of a church in Cople Parish. By 1762 he was in neighboring Richmond County. In 1766 Ariss provided a "plan and estimate" for Payne's Church, in Fairfax County. In 1772 he was appointed a commissioner to "ascertain the value of certain churches and chapels" in Frederick County. A year later in the same region (near what is now the Virginia–West Virginia border), he presented "a plan of a church to be erected . . . at a place called Carney's Spring . . . together with proposals for building the same." Although the church was never built, due to conflict within the vestry as to its location, it was to have been of stone and thirty by fifty feet in size. Also in 1773 Ariss was one of eighteen men appointed by the governor as justices for Berkeley County (now West Virginia). Presumably the "John Ariss" cited in these various references was the same person, who over three decades simply migrated westward toward the colony's frontier in search of opportunity.

Payne's Church is Ariss's only known design. The exterior survives in a photograph of 1861 taken before the building was destroyed; the interior is described in the Truro Parish vestry book. It was a handsome, one-story, brick Virginia Palladian design akin to the extant taller structures of Falls Church and Pohick Church, also in Fairfax County and constructed at virtually the same time. As with those buildings, Payne's Church was distinguished by understatement, good proportioning, and a skillful use of arched windows and rubbed and gauged brick details. For the interior Ariss designed "an Altar Piece sixteen feet high & twelve feet wide, and done with wainscot after the Ionic order," a "Pulpit, Canopy and reading Desks . . . Wainscoted with proper Cornish," and a "Gallery . . . supported by Collums turned & fluted." At both Payne's Church and Carney's Spring Church, the commission to undertake construction was awarded to a builder other than Ariss. That separation of design and contracting was unusual in colonial Virginia but not unique. For designing Payne's Church, Ariss was awarded forty shillings (two pounds), the same sum paid to James Wren for his design of Christ Church, Alexandria.

The important questions of who Ariss was and how he entered the building profession remain unanswered. Was he a Virginian who received some degree of education or training in architecture in England, or was he English-born? And was he a craftsman who expanded his skills to include contracting, estimating, and draftsmanship, or did he begin his career as an undertaker and draftsman? The questions are related. Some historians have assumed that he was English, because Ariss states in the newspaper announcement that he is "lately from Great Britain." Waterman, however, presumes that this was the John Ariss born in Westmoreland County around 1725, a man whose family on his mother's side had been prominent in the county and in Cople Parish since Nicolas Spencer had immigrated there in 1657. Waterman's argument cannot be dismissed because the *Maryland Gazette* notice and other records place Ariss in Westmoreland County at the start of his career and because there is little evidence that architectural designers left England for Virginia in the way that we know craftsmen did. There is no evidence that Ariss worked as a craftsman. Ariss's mention in 1751 of "some Buildings near finished" points to at least a small body of domestic work for which he was responsible but which has yet to be documented through references in private papers of the period. The question of that domestic work is a final Ariss problem yet to be resolved.

• The actual historical figure of John Ariss must be reconstructed from Virginia county and parish records, a number of which are reproduced in Elizabeth Brand Monroe, "William Buckland in the Northern Neck" (master's thesis, Univ. of Virginia, 1975), Philip Slaughter, *The History of Truro Parish in Virginia* (1908), William Waller Hening, *The Statutes at Large* (1810–1823), and Benjamin Duvall Chambers, *Old Chapel and the Parish in Clarke County, Virginia* (1932). Thomas Tileston Waterman, in *Mansions of Virginia, 1706–1776* (1946), pp. 243–48, discusses Ariss's career, but the account is flawed. Dell Upton, *Holy Things and Profane: Anglican Parish Churches in Colonial Virginia* (1986), provides facts about design and building in colonial Virginia when Ariss was active there.

WILLIAM M. S. RASMUSSEN

ARLEN, Harold (15 Feb. 1905–23 Apr. 1986), songwriter, was born Hyman Arluck in Buffalo, New York, the son of Samuel Arluck, a cantor. His mother's name is not known. Arlen began his singing career performing in his father's synagogue's choir. His musical performing career began at age fifteen when, as a ragtime pianist, he formed the local Snappy Trio, which performed at small clubs and parties and on scenic cruises of Lake Erie. The trio grew into the Yankee Six and then into the larger Buffalodians. With this enlarged band Arlen traveled in the mid-1920s to New York, where he soon found work as a singer-pianist on radio and record. He also wrote a few arrangements for the popular Fletcher Henderson dance band.

In 1929 Arlen met lyricist Ted Koehler, and the two began writing songs, hoping to place them in a popular Broadway revue. Their first success came with "Get Happy," performed by the singer Ruth Etting in the 1930s show *9:15 Revue*. Arlen was sympathetic to both blues and jazz and was at home writing on African-American themes, as was shown by his second major hit, "Stormy Weather," pouplarized by blues singer Ethel Waters at Harlem's Cotton Club, where Arlen and Koehler worked as house writers from 1930 to 1934.

In 1934 Arlen contributed melodies to E. Y. "Yip" Harburg's lyrics for the revue *Life Begins at 8:40*. He also traveled to Hollywood, where he soon began composing entire scores and individual numbers for films, often working with lyricists Harburg, Ira Gershwin, or Johnny Mercer. In 1937 Harburg and Arlen collaborated on the Broadway show *Hooray for What!* and two years later, on the classic movie musical *The Wizard of Oz*, featuring the young Judy Garland. This was among the few Hollywood musicals that used songs to advance the plot, in the manner of a Broadway show, rather than merely as dropped-in diversions or introductions to big chorus numbers.

In 1941 Arlen began a prolific collaboration with pop lyricist Johnny Mercer, turning out a series of hits over four years that included "That Old Black Magic" and "Accentuate the Positive," primarily as featured numbers in films. Arlen returned to Broadway in 1944 with *Bloomer Girl*, again in collaboration with Harburg, and two years later he collaborated on the bluesy *St. Louis Woman*, written with Mercer.

The 1950s brought perhaps Arlen's most sophisticated Broadway shows, all with African-American themes: *House of Flowers* (1954), written with the young author Truman Capote, and introducing dancer Alvin Ailey to Broadway; *Jamaica* (1957), written with Harburg; and *Saratoga* (1959), with Mercer. Perhaps because of their themes, and also because they lacked strong books, these shows were less successful for Arlen and spawned fewer hits. His major success of this time was the 1954 film, *A Star is Born*, to which he contributed the classic "The Man That Got Away," again for Judy Garland, with lyrics by Ira Gershwin, among other songs.

Arlen retired from music making in the 1960s, as his style faded in popularity with the ascendency of rock and other popular forms. However, he enjoyed a second career as an interpreter of his own material, recording several albums of his hit numbers. He died after battling Parkinson's disease in New York City.

• A definitive biography of Arlen is Edward Jablonski, *Happy with the Blues* (1961; 2d ed., 1985). Arlen's contribution to songwriting is discussed in many standard texts, including Alec Wilder, *American Popular Songs: The Great Innovators, 1900–1950* (1972; 2d ed., 1990). An obituary is in the *New York Times*, 24 Apr. 1986.

RICHARD CARLIN

ARLEN, Michael (16 Nov. 1895–23 June 1956), writer, was born Dikran Kouyoumdjian in Ruse, Bulgaria, the son of Sarkis Kouyoumdjian, an Armenian importer. His mother's name is unknown. In 1901 the family emigrated to Manchester, England. In 1913, after having attended Malvern College in Worcestershire and, briefly, the University of Edinburgh, Arlen settled in London. He began contributing articles to *Ararat: A Searchlight on Armenia*, a militant expatriate journal devoted mainly to publicizing the plight of Armenians suffering from the Turkish deportations and massacres of 1915. Some of his pieces were earnestly nationalistic; others, more characteristic of his later style, were in the vein of personal observation and social commentary. He also contributed to A. R. Orage's journal *New Age* a series of fictional conversations about romance between a sympathetic male listener and various upper-class women. These rueful fictions were collected in his first book, the somewhat autobiographical *London Venture* (1920). In the preface he announced that he was changing his name to Michael Arlen in order, as he put it, to deprive his readers "of their last excuse for my obscurity."

In the wake of the book's commercial success, Arlen produced the short story collections *The Romantic Lady* (1921) and *These Charming People* (1923) and the novel *Piracy* (1922), all works that successfully wedded romance and social satire. His next book, *The Green Hat* (1924), became an enormous bestseller in large part because of its dashing and enigmatic heroine, Iris March. Iris, condemned as a reckless wanton by society, is, in the tragic conclusion, revealed to be the guardian of her husband's reputation, which she has saved by preserving his shameful secret but in the process sacrificing her own reputation and chances for personal happiness. In 1925 Arlen wrote a play version of *The Green Hat*; the London production that year starred Tallulah Bankhead, the New York production Katherine Cornell, and the 1926 Los Angeles production featured Ruth Chatterton. Though generally derided by serious critics as overheated melodrama, as the novel had been, the play proved a tremendous commercial success, as partially evidenced by Cornell's U.S. tour of the production. Film versions followed, including *A Woman of Affairs* (1928), directed by Clarence Brown with a scenario by Bess Meredyth and starring Greta Garbo and John Gilbert; and *Outcast Lady* (1934), directed by Robert Z. Leonard with a screenplay by Zoë Akins and starring Constance Bennett and Herbert Marshall. In both films, the plot of the original story was altered to avoid the issue of venereal disease.

In March 1925 Arlen traveled to the United States to publicize *The Green Hat*, to hobnob with the New York literati, and to test the commercial waters. He left New York for Hollywood in October to accept a high-paying position with the Famous Players–Lasky Corporation, which became Paramount Studios in 1927. His primary duty was to rescue the floundering career of film star Pola Negri, a task that proved largely unsuccessful. Nonetheless, Arlen sold a few projects while in Hollywood, among them *The Age of Cads* (1926), starring Adolphe Menjou. In 1926 Arlen returned to Europe, where he was plagued by ill health and bitterness toward the fickle critical establishment that dismissed him as a has-been after having lionized him as a literary genius. D. H. Lawrence portrayed Arlen as the Irish playwright Michaelis in *Lady Chatterley's Lover* (1927). In 1928 Arlen married Atalanta Mercati, a Greek countess, in Cannes, France; they had two children.

Extending his literary range in the aftermath of *The Green Hat*, Arlen wrote a novel of disillusionment, *Young Men in Love* (1927), followed by a novel about a misunderstood but inwardly noble woman, *Lily Christine* (1928). Both works were credited by reviewers as being more mature and serious than *The Green Hat*, but neither had the same success; nonetheless, a film version of *Lily Christine* appeared in 1932, directed by Paul Stein and starring Corinne Griffith and Colin Clive. Arlen returned to the genre of social comedy in the short story collection *Babes in the Wood* (1929), the play *Good Losers* (1931), and the novel *Men Dislike Women* (1931). His futuristic novel *Man's Morality* (1933), a melodramatic but creditable effort at political commentary, was followed by a silly gothic yarn, *Hell! Said the Duchess* (1934); the short story collection *The Crooked Coronet* (1937), comprised of pieces that had appeared in the popular English magazine the *Strand*; and his last novel, *The Flying Dutchman* (1939), a sloppy political thriller derided by most critics and by Arlen himself, who described it as "terrible." With the outbreak of World War II, Arlen moved in 1939 from Cannes to England, where from November 1939 to May 1940 he wrote a regular column of witty social commentary in the London magazine the *Tatler*.

After having been appointed public relations officer for the western midland region of England in November 1940, Arlen had to resign in 1941 after a question was raised in Parliament about the suitability of giving the post to a Bulgarian by birth. Arlen subsequently moved to Hollywood to join his family, who had emigrated earlier the same year; his time there proved relatively unproductive. While there, however, he wrote the screenplay for the film *The Heavenly Body* (1944) in collaboration with Walter Reisch, and he sold his roguish short story character Gay Falcon to RKO for a successful series of "B" films (none of which he wrote) starring George Sanders and, later, Tom Conway. In 1945 Arlen moved with his family to New York, where in 1950 he appeared for a brief and unsuccessful stint as a television personality. His time in New York, although characterized by his friend Alec Waugh as a comfortable round of gracious lunches with old friends at the St. Regis Hotel, was described by his son Michael J. Arlen as a period of frustration and disappointment as Arlen strove, without success, to revive his career.

Arlen's own self-effacing summary of his career well conveys his personal stance and style: "I was a flash in the pan in my twenties. I had a hell of a good time being flashy and there was, by the grace of God, a good deal of gold dust in the pan" (*New Yorker*, 9 Apr. 1949, p. 25). His is a just remark: although some of his works have historical interest and have been reprinted in modern editions—*The London Venture* in 1968 and *The Green Hat* in 1983—Arlen's literary reputation did not survive his age. He died in New York City.

• Arlen's correspondence, which is in the possession of his son Michael J. Arlen, has never been published. The primary biographical account is a memoir by Michael J. Arlen, *Exiles* (1970). The only full-length study of his writing is Harry Keyishian, *Michael Arlen* (1975). Other sources containing biographical information include Tallulah Bankhead, *Tallulah* (1952), Anne Chisholm, *Nancy Cunard* (1979), Katherine Cornell, *I Wanted to Be an Actress* (1979), Noël Coward, *Present Indicative* (1937), Daphne Fielding, *Those Remarkable Cunards* (1968), and Alec Waugh, *My Brother Evelyn and Other Portraits* (1967).

HARRY KEYISHIAN

ARLEN, Richard (1 Sept. 1898–28 Mar. 1976), film actor, was born Cornelius Van Mattimore in Charlottesville, Virginia, the son of James Mattimore, a lawyer, judge, and grain broker, and Mary Van. Arlen's childhood was spent primarily in the St. Paul, Minnesota, area, where sports and the outdoor life more than formal schooling engaged his attention. Paramount Pictures would later invent an academic career at the University of Pennsylvania for him, but in fact he attended St. Thomas College near his boyhood home, and that only briefly. In 1917 he left school to join the Royal Canadian Air Force. Although he never saw World War I combat, he learned to fly, eventually rose to the rank of lieutenant, and developed a love of aviation that would last through life.

Arlen tried a number of careers after the war, including oil field worker, swimming coach, and sports reporter. He was trying to find a job in California in the fledgling commercial aviation industry when he entered motion pictures. Working temporarily as a film laboratory messenger, he was struck by a car on the Paramount lot and taken to the studio hospital; there he was "discovered" by a Paramount executive.

Arlen entered motion pictures as an extra, but it was not until a small role in *Vengeance of the Deep* (1923) that his career really began. Billing himself as Van Mattimore, he played supporting parts for several years. Director William Wellman, like Arlen an avid pilot, offered him the costarring role in an aviation film that Wellman was soon to begin, *Wings* (1927), the film that won the first Academy Award. With its mixture of high drama and daredevil adventure, as well as its startling aerial footage, this tale of young combat pilots overseas remains one of the finest aviation films of its era. In 1969, when Arlen talked about his costarring role in the film, he said that Wellman occasionally asked more of him and his costar Charles "Buddy" Rogers than just acting ability: "We were using the first motor-driven cameras which were mounted in front of the cockpit. The 400-foot reels . . . gave us only a little more than four minutes of picture. Bill Wellman would tell us on the ground what he wanted us to do in the air. We would waggle our wings when ready and then take over as producer, director, and actor. . . . That was why Wellman wanted actors for *Wings* who could fly. 'Buddy' couldn't, but he learned damned quick." *Wings* solidified the career of Rogers, made director Wellman a force to be reckoned with, boosted the career of Gary Cooper through a bit part, and seemed about to elevate the good-looking Arlen to the status of matinee idol. Yet that sort of success always eluded him.

Perhaps the timing was simply off. The industry was in a state of confusion. Talkies were on their way in, silents on their way out. By the time the transition was complete, Arlen had become typecast, identified at Paramount with journeyman work, primarily significant roles in insignificant action films. For example, he played a wild mustang hunter in *Gun Smoke* (1931), one of the studio's first sound westerns; he played one of the shipwrecked sailors in the Charles Laughton horror classic *Island of Lost Souls* (1933); he was a gangster in *Song of the Eagle* (1933); a farmer struggling against union corruption and economic collapse during the depression in *Golden Harvest* (1933); a straight man in *College Humor* (1933), which starred Bing Crosby, George Burns, and Gracie Allen.

Arlen's most obvious asset—how he looked—may have worked against him, for his broad-shouldered, all-American appeal was generic, somehow nondescript. It was an appeal that was masculine without being specific to Arlen, and the same might be said about the parts he went on to play until the last years of his career. Primarily, Arlen played "he-men" in "he-man" movies, stories in which the action was more important than the characters.

As the United States prepared for possible entry into World War II, Arlen was still being offered starring roles in such low-budget air action films as *Flying Blind, Forced Landing*, and *Power Dive* (all 1941). Those parts, as well as the business he had begun, the Arlen-Probert Aviation Corporation at Van Nuys airport, made him a lightning rod for the war effort. His company became a gathering place on weekends for Robert Taylor, James Stewart, Andy Devine, Roscoe Ates, Barton MacLane, Wallace Beery, Robert Cummings (Bob Cummings), Wayne Morris, and other Hollywood celebrities, many of whom would go on to military flying during World War II. Arlen himself served as an adviser to the government in creating flight instruction programs for air crew trainees.

In May 1947 during closed hearings of the House Committee on Un-American Activities on possible Communist influence in Hollywood, Arlen appeared as a friendly witness and denounced "groups of parlor pinks" that "we would be better off without." Arlen was profoundly patriotic and reportedly proudest of his military service rather than his roles in movies. His willingness to testify may have sprung from his unwillingness to abide what he saw as any threat to American ideals.

As Hollywood lost some of its audience to television at the start of the 1950s, Arlen guest-starred on such TV series as "Lawman," "Yancy Derringer," "Bat Masterson," and "Wanted: Dead or Alive," where he found himself being offered the same roles as he was playing in films. In movies he now appeared as older authority figures, often sheriffs or senior military officers, including supporting parts in *Kansas Raiders* (1950), *Sabre Jet* (1953), *Hidden Guns* (1956), *Warlock* (1959), *The Last Time I Saw Archie* (1961), *Waco* (1966), and *Hostile Guns* (1967).

Arlen was married three times, each time to an actress, first in the early 1920s to Ruth Austin, with whom he had one daughter. They divorced, and in 1927 he married his costar in *Wings*, Jobyna Ralston; they had one son and later divorced. In 1945 he married Margaret Kinsella, who survived him. Arlen died in North Hollywood.

• The most complete single collection of material on Arlen is in the Academy Library, Academy of Motion Picture Arts and Sciences, Los Angeles. Biographical information and Arlen's filmography can be found in such reference sources as *The American Movies Reference Book: The Sound Era* (1969), *The Film Encyclopedia* (1979), *Forty Years of Screen Credits, 1929–1969* (1970), and *Who Was Who on the Screen* (1984). The most complete list of his television credits is to be found in *The Complete Actors' Television Credits, 1948–1988* (1989). Among the best scholarly work on Arlen is an article in *Films in Review* (June/July 1979). Arlen's experiences during the making of *Wings* are most fully recounted in an interview, "Box Office Ace," in *Air Classics*, Feb. 1969. Much of this interview was reprinted in James H. Farmer's *Celluloid Wings* (1984), a book that also addresses Arlen's importance as an aviator and his contributions during World War II. An obituary is in the *New York Times*, 29 Mar. 1976.

JAY BOYER

ARLISS, George (10 Apr. 1868–5 Feb. 1946), actor, was born in London, England, the son of William Arliss-Andrews, a printer and publisher. His mother's name is unknown. He grew up in literate, cultured, and somewhat bohemian surroundings. The family home in Bloomsbury was close to the British Museum, and his father was patron of a circle of writers and eccentrics who frequented it. Privately educated, he became stagestruck at age twelve when introduced to amateur theatricals by Joseph and Henry Soutar, two sons of an acting family who also became actors.

Through the Soutars, Arliss was hired at eighteen to play walks-ons and extras at a suburban London theater, where he first appeared on the stage in 1886. Arliss learned stage craft and art in the following years through work in stock, repertory, and touring companies. After gaining better roles in road productions, he came to London's West End, playing a small role in a successful production, *On and Off* (1898). While still on tour, he wrote a farce, *There and Back*, which was performed by stock and amateur companies for years thereafter. Through the years he continued to write, without notable success. In September 1899 Arliss married actress Florence Montgomery; they had no children.

Arliss joined the company of prominent actress Mrs. Patrick Campbell, playing in productions of two of her starring vehicles, *The Notorious Mrs. Ebbsmith* and *The Second Mrs. Tanqueray*, in the 1900–1901 season. In 1901 he went with her company to present the plays in New York. "I was quite unprepared for what followed," he said in an interview for *Windsor Magazine* (Aug. 1932). After excellent notices, Arliss found himself "quite amazed when these were followed, by next post, by offers of engagements from American managers." He signed with David Belasco and appeared as the sinister Japanese official Zakkuri in *The Darling of the Gods* (1902) to widespread acclaim. He became a member of Minnie Maddern Fiske's outstanding company in 1904 and remained with it in New York and on tour through 1907, playing important character roles. It soon became evident that Arliss had star quality: a Chicago reviewer of his performance as a callous English aristocrat in *The New York Idea* wrote, "George Arliss . . . was exceptionally entertaining. His own personality is so vivid and attractive and his art so polished that his own skill and individuality carried rather an absurd part to classical distinction. He was welcomed with almost as much sincere enthusiasm as was the star" (*Chicago News*, 16 Oct. 1906).

Arliss arrived at stardom playing a Mephistophelean character in a comedy, *The Devil* (1908). Two productions of the play were presented at the same time because two producers both claimed to have rights to it. Arliss's performance was found superior by the public and carried the day. The *New York Evening Journal* (20 Aug. 1908) wrote, "His curious intonation, his mordant emphasis, his angular grace, went into the part a perfect fit. Never had we seen this kind of Satan—so brilliantly impertinent, so fashionably bad-mannered, so witty, so casual, and yet so deadly." His star status was confirmed permanently when he appeared in the title role of *Disraeli* (1911). A *New York Times* reviewer (19 Sept. 1911) predicted that "Mr. Arliss's highly interesting and skillfully contrived performance . . . will be chiefly responsible for the success of [the] play." It ran in New York and on tour until 1915.

Later stage successes came in the title role of *Alexander Hamilton* (1917), which he co-wrote, as the evil rajah in *The Green Goddess* (1921), and as the swaggering old shipowner in *Old English* (1924). His stage career ended with semisuccess in his only attempt at Shakespeare, playing Shylock in *The Merchant of Venice* (1928). Ultimately, he turned to talking pictures because he disliked the rigors of touring plays and thought playwrights of the 1920s had turned to bad or vulgar writing, which made it increasingly difficult for him to find suitable parts.

Arliss had been a stage star for twenty years because he had mastered the secret of remaining a star: giving the public a variety of roles that still showed off a consistently attractive and recognizable personality underneath. Arliss considered himself basically a character actor. His apprentice years had given him the ability to play many sorts of character roles. As a star, he specialized in three types of roles: historic figures, villains, and still-vital older gentlemen. To find plays for himself, he spent a great deal of time reading scripts, poring through hundreds. "He *knows*," reported *Strand Magazine* (Apr. 1932), "He knows with as much certainty as there is in this uncertain world whether a play is a George Arliss play. Since he was in a position to choose plays for himself, he has never chosen a failure." His starring roles always presented Arliss as a man of power, an autocrat who dominated others with the power of his mind. His forte was subtlety and finesse of movement and intonation. He could not convincingly play parts that demanded emotional abandon, a point that some critics of his Shylock noted. Arliss further remained recognizable by adapting the historical appearance of his famous men to his own distinctive face and physique.

Speaking of Arliss's character, once an interviewer wrote, "He confesses to his share of the actor's vanity—boasts of it, in fact, says that it is inherent to the profession" (*Pearson's*, Feb. 1910). Yet offstage Arliss shunned public attention. He was devoted to his wife, a chief adviser who also played all of his stage and screen wives. She and his longtime theater dresser, Jenner, made sure his every need was met. Arliss ate vegetarian meals, walked every day, and faithfully returned home to England for three months every summer after performing nine months in the United States. His manner was quiet, studious, and cultured. He displayed both wit and humor in conversation and in his autobiography, which was written near the end of his stage career and titled *Up the Years from Bloomsbury* (1927). His long, thin, bony face with its beaky nose gained added distinctiveness by his lifelong use of a monocle offstage.

Arliss had begun making silent films in 1921, mainly repeating his major stage roles and in the process learning what acting for the camera required. With the arrival of talking pictures, he went seriously into film work at age sixty. "Harry Warner told me," he recalled, "that when he decided to do *Disraeli* he did not expect it to pay, but he was using me as an expensive bait to hook people into the cinema who had never been there before" (*New York Times*, 6 Feb. 1946). Instead, the film was an international smash hit, winning Arliss an Academy Award as best actor for the 1929–1930 season.

Having appeared successfully in his historic-figure persona, Arliss went on to his villain, in *The Green Goddess* (1930), and his grand old man, in *Old English* (1930). He remade two other silent films as talkies: *The Ruling Passion* (1922) became *The Millionaire* (1931), and *The Man Who Played God* (1922) retained its title for the 1932 version. By now, Arliss's box office power was such that he could demand run-through rehearsals of each production before camera work started. Two *Photoplay* articles (May 1931 and June 1933) show that he had control over the script, the choice of director, even the costumes and the actors' diction. In effect, he was a star who was the *auteur* of his own films. After making three comedies and *Voltaire* (1933), he reached the height of his film career in *The House of Rothschild* (1934), where he played both Mayer and Nathan Rothschild. According to the *New York Times* (15 Mar. 1934), "Mr. Arliss outshines any performance he has contributed to the screen, not excepting . . . Disraeli."

Later Hollywood films did not prove as successful. Arliss wound down his motion picture years back in England. His last appearance on screen was in a storybook comedy of eighteenth-century smuggling, *Dr. Syn* (1937). He played a pirate who has supposedly been hanged but who reappears as the parson of an English village, helping it prosper by directing its thriving smuggling enterprises, "a sort of maritime Robin Hood," according to the *New York Times* (15 Nov. 1937). Nevertheless, Arliss retired when his wife lost her eyesight. In 1940 he published a further part of his autobiography, *My Ten Years in the Studios*. He died at his home in Maida Hill, London.

Arliss claims a place in theatrical and film history for his fifty-year career as a character actor who attained and kept star status by his ability to give brilliant performances in roles he had chosen carefully to display his abilities and obscure his limitations and by his ability to dominate any production through the power of his personality.

• Materials on his life and career are in the Billy Rose Theatre Collection at the New York Public Library for the Performing Arts, Lincoln Center. Besides the books mentioned earlier, Arliss wrote an introduction to *On the Stage* (1928). Quotations of Arliss's own views on the stage and himself, along with theatrical criticisms of his work, are in William C. Young, *Famous Actors and Actresses of the American Stage* (2 vols., 1975). Articles about Arliss include W. P. Dodge, "The Actor in the Street," *Theatre*, Dec. 1909; B. N. Wilson, "The Autocrat of the Stage," *Theatre*, Oct. 1925; Harry Lang, "His Two Bosses," *Photoplay*, May 1931; John Gliddon, "The Art of George Arliss," *Strand Magazine*, Apr. 1932; W. S. Meadmore, "George Arliss Speaks," *Windsor Magazine*, Aug. 1932; Ruth Biery, "Arliss Puts His Foot Down," *Photoplay*, June 1933; and Ken Hanke, "George Arliss Reappraised," *Films in Review*, Nov. 1985. All articles include portraits and production stills. An obituary is in the *New York Times*, 6 Feb. 1946.

WILLIAM STEPHENSON

ARMIJO, Manuel (1793?–9 Dec. 1853), governor of New Mexico, was born at Plaza San Antonio within present-day Albuquerque, New Mexico, the son of Vicente Ferrer Armijo, a landowner and stockraiser, and Bárbara Chávez. In 1819 Armijo married María Trinidad Gabaldón; the marriage was childless.

As a landowner, Armijo was eligible to hold local political and militia offices. In 1822 and again in 1824 he was alcalde (mayor-judge) of Albuquerque and a lieutenant in the militia. During a battle with Apaches he received a leg wound that caused him frequent pain and forced him to curtail several of his terms of office. In the spring of 1827 he was appointed governor of New Mexico and moved to Santa Fe. New Mexico was then a territory of fewer than 60,000 people encompassing present-day Arizona, southern Colorado, and the town of El Paso within its loosely defined limits. As governor, Armijo became a liberal advocate of public schools and prompt pay for soldiers and civil servants. He also took strong measures against Americans who trapped without licenses and traded without paying customs duties. In 1828 he resigned and returned to Albuquerque, where he served as alcalde and elector of territorial officers and made a small fortune selling sheep and blankets in the interior of Mexico. He was called back to Santa Fe in 1836 as subcomisario (territorial revenue officer) but was unable to leave Albuquerque because of his painful leg wound.

In 1837 citizens and Indians of the settlements of Rio Arriba (northern New Mexico) raised a rebellion against the new governor, Albino Pérez, a haughty outsider appointed to establish centralism and new taxes. The rebels murdered Governor Pérez and officers of his government and marched to Santa Fe, where they elected one of their leaders as governor. A month later the new governor was ousted by Armijo, who was commanding a citizen army from Rio Abajo (southern New Mexico). Armijo persuaded the rebels to disband, then assumed the governorship and was confirmed in this office by a grateful central government.

Armijo's second term as governor (1838–1844) was characterized by a series of controversial land grants to naturalized foreigners and by conflict with Americans, particularly with American traders who brought wagonloads of goods from Missouri to Santa Fe. The duties collected on their goods at the Santa Fe customhouse supported the local government and presidial troops. The 1837 rebellion had discouraged American traders, and in 1838 customs duties dwindled and left the territory in financial straits. To increase trade, Armijo discharged dishonest customs officers, set customs fees for American traders at a low $500 per wagon, and favored Mexican traders with even lower duties on their imported goods. By 1840 both American and Mexican traders were thriving. Over half the traders were now Mexicans, and Americans' stranglehold on the New Mexican economy had been broken.

Americans in New Mexico, armed with superior weapons and contemptuous of the poorly armed and organized Mexican soldiers, were often lawless and violent. After Armijo had crushed the 1837 rebellion, an American at Taos, James Kirker, threatened to organize an army to continue it; no sooner had Armijo sent the militia against the Navajos than he heard of North American adventurers who had joined with Apaches to support a Texan invasion of New Mexico.

As soon as the new Republic of Texas was formed in 1836, Texas announced its claim to New Mexico east of the Rio Grande. In 1840 the president of Texas, Mirabeau B. Lamar, enlisted Americans in Taos to aid him in annexing New Mexico. In the summer of 1841 more than 300 fully armed Texans marched to assert their claim or at least to open a trade between the two countries. Governor Armijo surprised the army in eastern New Mexico on 17 September, disarmed and arrested them, and sent them to Mexico City under guard. Armijo became a national hero and was awarded the Cross of Honor and the military command of New Mexico, but his glory was brief.

In May 1843 Armijo and 100 militia marched to the Arkansas River crossing of the Santa Fe Trail to escort a caravan, largely of Mexican traders, to Santa Fe. Lying in wait at the crossing was a party of vengeful Texans, who attacked and routed Armijo's vanguard of Taos Indians. Armijo promptly retreated all the way to Santa Fe, where he dismissed the militia and sent the presidial troops to El Paso. His resignation as commanding general was quickly accepted, and his actions were called unpatriotic and dishonorable. Soon after, he resigned as civil governor and returned to Albuquerque in March 1844.

In the summer of 1845, after a series of inexperienced or incompetent governors had served, Armijo was again appointed governor. In May 1846 the United States declared war on Mexico; in St. Louis Colonel Stephen W. Kearny collected about 1,700 officers and men, 1,350 of them raw volunteers, and marched toward New Mexico. As Kearny's Army of the West drew closer, Armijo wrote his government for military aid and called a meeting of leaders who decided to resist the Americans in spite of the overpowering size of Kearny's well-armed force. Armijo issued a tepid proclamation calling on his people to prepare for battle and victory if possible but noting "no one can do the impossible." To Armijo's surprise, the people gathered by the thousands at Apache Canyon to fight the Americans. On 18 August, with the oncoming troops nearly upon them, Armijo sent the people back to their homes. Then he fled with his presidial troops to meet federal troops from Chihuahua, who did not arrive as promised. As Armijo and his troops proceeded south, Kearny's volunteers took Santa Fe without firing a shot.

Charges against Armijo for cowardice and bribery were filed in Mexico City, but a grand jury found insufficient evidence for an indictment. Armijo returned to live in New Mexico and died in the village of Limitar (now Lemitar).

Perhaps no figure in New Mexico's history is as contradictory in personality and reputation as Manuel Armijo or has attracted so much invective in so many books. Two famous American accounts, by a Santa Fe trader (Josiah Gregg, *Commerce of the Prairies*) and a Texan (George Wilkins Kendall, *Narrative of the Texan Santa Fe Expedition*), both published in 1844 and long in print, describe him as a monster, murderer, bloodthirsty tyrant, cowardly braggart, corrupt official, and abuser of women, among other things. Both of these writers had personal and political reasons for vilifying Armijo, who never bothered to challenge their lurid overstatements. W. H. H. Davis in *El Gringo; or, New Mexico and Her People* (1857) calls Armijo "the most distinguished man that New Mexico ever produced," probably another overstatement. It is enough to say that Armijo was New Mexico's most important political figure of that era.

• The Mexican archives of New Mexico containing a wealth of material on Armijo are available in manuscript and on microfilm at the New Mexico Records Center and Archives in Santa Fe. Transcripts of documents from the Mexican archives in Mexico City relating to Armijo are in the Bancroft Library, Berkeley, Calif. A full-length biography has yet to be published. The fullest short biography is Janet Lecompte, "Manuel Armijo and the Americans," *Journal of the West* 19 (1980): 51–63. Viewpoints of American traders are contained in the three major contemporary sources cited in the text as well as in reprints of contemporary American accounts in the first seven volumes of the Southwest Historical Series, ed. Ralph P. Bieber (1931–1938).

JANET LECOMPTE

ARMISTEAD, George (10 Apr. 1780–25 Apr. 1818), soldier, was born on the Baylor estate of "Newmarket" in Caroline County, Virginia, the son of John Armistead and Lucy Baylor, farmers. Details of his early life remain vague. Commissioned an ensign in the Seventh Infantry Regiment in January 1799, by May 1800 he had been promoted to first lieutenant. He was given an honorable discharge on 15 June 1800, however, because of reductions in the military establishment.

Rapid reductions in the army created a shortage of officers, allowing Armistead to be recommissioned in February 1801 as a second lieutenant in the Second Regiment Artillery and Engineers. The following September he was ordered to Fort Niagara, New York, to assume command of an artillery company. While stationed on the Great Lakes frontier, Armistead became a captain in the Second Regiment Artillery and Engineers. In addition to serving as an artillery officer, he also doubled as assistant military agent; he remained at Fort Niagara until 1807.

From 1807 to 1812 Armistead served at Baltimore's Fort McHenry as acting military agent. Being second in command of that bastion provided him with connections within the community. In 1810, at the Otterbein Church in Baltimore, he married Louisa Hughes, sister of Christopher Hughes, Jr., a militia officer at the fort and later U.S. chargé d'affaires in Denmark, Norway, and Sweden. The couple had four children.

With the commencement of war with Britain Armistead returned to Fort Niagara, where in early March 1813 he was promoted to major and transferred to the Third Regiment of Artillery. Less than three months later Armistead participated in the American attack on Fort George, located on the Canadian side of the Niagara River. The joint army-navy operation, commanded by General Winfield Scott and Commodore Oliver H. Perry, began in early May 1813 with the concentration of 4,500 troops near the enemy position. On 24 May American artillery units started firing on Newark, a small town near Fort George that housed British forces. Three days later naval vessels laid down a barrage to cover troop landings west of the fort. As the British withdrew from the bastion to meet the invaders, it became apparent they were outnumbered. They evacuated the fort and fled south. During the operation Armistead distinguished himself and was given the honor of carrying the captured British flags to Washington, D.C., for President James Madison.

While in Washington, during late June 1813, Armistead assumed command of Fort McHenry and its dependencies: Forts Severn and Madison in Annapolis; Fort Washington on the Potomac River; and all federal defenses in Baltimore. During the next several months he secured additional cannon to bolster McHenry, oversaw the construction of new batteries near the fort, and obtained troops to reinforce the detachment. Soon after his appointment as commander, Armistead suggested that a large ceremonial flag be provided for the fort. Soon thereafter a military committee commissioned Mary Pickersgill to make the flag (42 feet by 30 feet); the major received it in mid-August 1813.

Armistead worked diligently over the next year to improve Baltimore's defenses and was rewarded for his persistence on 30 March 1814, when his commission in the Third Artillery Regiment was transferred to the newly created U.S. Corps of Artillery, composed of the three former regiments. He became involved in the controversy that arose between U.S. senator and major general Samuel Smith, who commanded the Maryland militia, and General William H. Winder, of the U.S. Army, concerning jurisdiction over Baltimore's defense. While Armistead belonged to the regular army, he nonetheless supported Smith's claim for jurisdiction. After the British burned Washington in late August 1814, Winder became Armistead's commanding officer, since all regular troops in Baltimore had been placed under Winder's command.

When the British forces approached Baltimore in early September, Armistead's garrison at Fort McHenry consisted of 1,000 troops. British general Robert Ross landed 4,500 troops on North Point to assault the city by land. Meanwhile Admiral Alexander Cochrane's ships proceeded up the Chesapeake Bay to engage Fort McHenry.

Armistead saw sails of frigates and ships-of-the-line as well as smaller craft moving toward his position on 12 September. Cochrane intended to reduce the fort so his ships could bombard the city and provide artillery support to the troops under Ross. Armistead ordered that the large ceremonial flag be hoisted as the British ships approached. Early on the morning of 13 September Cochrane moved sixteen ships within two miles of Fort McHenry and opened fire. Armistead's cannon returned fire, driving the English ships back a half mile where they continued their barrage. While American guns did not have the same range, Armistead ordered his men to remain huddled in shelters while occasionally firing their guns to notify the city of the fort's determination. For twenty-five hours during a driving rain on 13–14 September 1814, British ships fired more than 1,500 shells at Fort McHenry with about 400 striking their mark. Throughout the barrage, Armistead knew that the fort's powder magazine was not bombproof and should a shell strike that building the entire bastion would be destroyed. The fort, however, received only minor damage and suffered light casualties (four killed and twenty-four wounded). The combined British army-navy expedition, failing to break the defenses of the city from land or sea, discontinued their attack and withdrew in the early morning hours of 14 September; the events surrounding the battle provided the setting for Francis Scott Key's famous poem, the "Star Spangled Banner."

Immediately after the battle, the major, exhausted by weeks of preparations, became bedridden with fever. After he recovered, the citizens of Baltimore presented him with gifts (a silver bowl shaped like a bombshell, a salver, and a set of goblets) for his service to the city. The historic flag, the "Star Spangled Banner," that flew over the fort during the battle and now hangs in the Smithsonian Institution, was also given to him. President Madison promoted him to brevet lieutenant colonel for his service to the nation. He remained as commander of Fort McHenry until he died in Baltimore of a heart condition less than three years later. He was buried in St. Paul's Cemetery, Baltimore.

Armistead's fame is based largely on his command of Fort McHenry during the British attack on Baltimore. His bravery at Fort George earlier in the War of 1812 should also be remembered.

• The most complete source of information on Armistead is a collection of official documents contained in the George Armistead Collection, Fort McHenry Library, Baltimore, Md. Armistead's official report concerning the battle of Baltimore is recorded in *Niles' Weekly Register* 7 (Oct. 1814): 40. A book-length study of Armistead's life has yet to be written because the materials are so scarce. Virginia Armistead Garber, *The Armistead Family, 1635–1910* (1910), provides limited information on the family, but very little on George Armistead outside of his service at the battle of Baltimore. Francis B. Heitman, *Historical Register and Dictionary of the United*

States Army (1903), provides a detailed account of his military career. The most detailed account of Armistead's service at Fort McHenry before the battle is Scott S. Sheads, *The Rockets' Red Glare: The Maritime Defense of Baltimore in 1814* (1986). There are several other sources that provide complementary information about Armistead's service at Baltimore including Ralph Robinson, "Controversy over the Command at Baltimore, in the War of 1812," *Maryland Historical Magazine* 39 (Sept. 1944): 177–98; and Frank A. Cassell, "Response to Crisis: Baltimore in 1814," *Maryland Historical Magazine* 66 (Fall 1971): 261–87.

GENE A. SMITH

ARMISTEAD, James. *See* Lafayette, James.

ARMISTEAD, Lewis Addison (18 Feb. 1817–4 July 1863), Confederate general, was born in New Bern, North Carolina, the son of Brigadier General Walker Keith Armistead of the U.S. Army and Elizabeth Stanley. George Armistead, Lewis's uncle, commanded Fort McHenry near Baltimore during its famous defense in 1814. Lewis entered West Point in 1834, finding nothing but trouble there. He barely passed academically in his first year and remained in deep disciplinary difficulties until forced to resign in February 1836 for "imprudence" and "disorderly conduct." Tradition has it that the final straw came when Armistead broke a mess-hall plate on the head of fellow cadet Jubal A. Early. Despite this affair, Armistead received a commission as second lieutenant in the Sixth Infantry in 1839 and served in the U.S. Army until 1861, winning two brevets for gallantry during the Mexican War. He married Cecilia L. Love about 1844; they had two children, one of whom survived to adulthood.

When the Civil War began, Armistead sent in his resignation from California in May 1861 and headed east in the company of Albert Sidney Johnston. He reached Richmond on 15 September and at once received a Confederate commission at his old rank of major. Later that month he was promoted to colonel and given command of the Fifty-seventh Virginia Infantry. After a quiet winter in that role, Armistead became a brigadier general on 1 April 1862. He led his brigade at Seven Pines (31 May–1 June), where his horse was killed under him, and through the Seven Days' campaign. At Malvern Hill (1 July), Armistead's brigade had the misfortune to be included in the hopeless and costly assaults. Armistead spent the night after that fiasco with a remnant of his troops close to the enemy lines. A Georgian who "was behind the same poplar tree that he was behind" that night wrote that Armistead's "long pull" from a brandy bottle won him the affectionate nom de guerre of "Poplar" Armistead, "which clung to him" the rest of his life.

General Robert E. Lee assigned Armistead to serve as provost marshal general of the Army of Northern Virginia during the summer of 1862. At the end of September, Armistead returned to line command with his brigade of five Virginia infantry regiments as part of George Edward Pickett's division. Neither Armistead nor the division was engaged at Fredericksburg, and they were absent with James Longstreet's foraging expedition at the time of Chancellorsville. The division likewise missed the first two days of the battle of Gettysburg, but on the third day Pickett and his men stood at center stage during one of the most famous episodes in American military history. Pickett's Charge, as Virginians called the desperately brave assault on 3 July 1863, included Armistead's command as one of three brigades of Pickett's division that charged into the teeth of the Federal might on Cemetery Ridge. Armistead led his doomed men from in front, his hat on the tip of his raised sword, until he was hit by a Federal volley in the midst of the northern position. He lived long enough for a brief encounter with his antebellum friend General Winfield Scott Hancock, via Hancock's aide Henry H. Bingham, and died just beyond what has often been called the High Water Mark of the Confederacy.

• No body of Armistead manuscripts survives. A brief sketch of his life is James E. Poindexter, *Address on the Life and Services of Gen. Lewis A. Armistead* (1909). See also Virginia Armistead Garber, *The Armistead Family* (1910); Mary Selden Kennedy, *Seldens of Virginia and Allied Families* (1911); and Armistead's Compiled Service Record in National Archives Microcopy M331, Roll 9. More literature exists on the general's death than on his life, much of it fatuous nonsense about a supposed deathbed recantation of his Confederate service.

ROBERT K. KRICK

ARMITAGE, Merle (13 Feb. 1893–15 Mar. 1975), book designer, author, and impresario, was born near Mason City, Iowa, the son of Elmer Ellsworth Armitage and Lulu Jacobs. He claimed 12 February as his birth date in honor of Abraham Lincoln. Armitage grew up in Texas and spent his youth in the West, where he lived on a number of ranches. Primarily self-educated as a civil engineer, he worked for the Kansas City, Mexico & Orient Railroad (later the Atchison, Topeka & Santa Fe Railway Company). He claims to have abandoned that career because of severe eyestrain. He then worked in the publicity department of the Packard Motor Company, where it is thought he learned graphic design. He also became interested in stage design and worked in New York City. He served in World War I as an instructor in mechanical engineering.

Both before and after his military service Armitage was a concert promoter. He became acquainted with the impresario Charles L. Wagner, who was later his partner. Wagner and Armitage arranged performances for Mary Garden, Feodor Chaliapin, John Charles Thomas, Rosa Ponselle, Anna Pavlova, and Ruth St. Denis. In the early 1920s he moved from New York to Los Angeles, where he was cofounder of the Los Angeles Grand Opera Association and its general manager. In 1932–1933 he was director of the "Public Works of Art" program for the Works Progress Administration in southern California. From 1933 to 1939 he was manager of the Philharmonic Auditorium in Los Angeles. Armitage befriended Igor Stravinsky, Martha Graham, Leopold Stokowski, and George

Gershwin and presented them on the West Coast. In 1938 he was responsible for the West Coast production of Gershwin's *Porgy and Bess.*

As a diversion from his "arduous duties" as impresario, Armitage began to write and design books—work that could be done as he traveled. It was, he said, "an ideal solution." His first book design was for a work of his own, *The Aristocracy of Art* (1929), published by Jake Zeitlin in Los Angeles. During the 1930s he wrote and designed a number of books, primarily about his interests in art, music (Schoenberg, Stravinsky, and Gershwin), modern dance (Martha Graham), and cooking. His designs were often selected by the American Institute of Graphic Arts for their "Fifty Books of the Year" competitions. In 1936 he was married to Elise Cavanna, who illustrated some of his books.

In World War II Armitage joined the Army Air Force; promoted to lieutenant colonel, he was awarded the Legion of Merit. During the war years he continued to write and design books. Although not an admirer of Armitage's style, George Macy commissioned him to design an edition of Edward Bellamy's *Looking Backward* for the Limited Edition's Club in 1941. In the announcement for the book Macy referred to him as "that bull-in-our-china-shop, that man Merle Armitage." E. Weyhe published Armitage's first book of memoirs, *Accent on America*, in 1944. The year before, after having divorced, he was married to Elsa Stuart, with whom he had one child; it cannot be determined how this second marriage for Armitage eventually came to an end.

After the war Armitage began to publish with and design for Duell, Sloan and Pearce. In 1946–1947 he also designed film titles for Metro-Goldwyn-Mayer, which seems to have inspired his book design, especially in his "cinematic" treatment of the opening pages. The books he designed during the late 1940s were often about southwestern subjects, such as the work he did for the Laboratory of Anthropology at the University of New Mexico. In 1949 he was invited by Gardner Cowles to be art director and member of the editorial board of *Look* Magazine. He redesigned that magazine (winning awards for his work) and other Cowles publications. In 1950–1951 he was president of the American Institute of Graphic Arts. He was by then one of the best-known designers of books, and with Marshall Lee he organized the influential exhibition "Books for Our Time" (1951).

In 1953 Armitage was married to his third wife, Isabelle Heymann, with whom he worked on a number of projects, including the cookbook *Fit for a Queen* (1958). They were to divorce in 1965.

Armitage retired from the Cowles organization in 1954 and went to live at his Manzanita Ranch in Yucca Valley, California. There he designed and produced books for his Manzanita Press as well as for Duell and other publishers. He also did design for *Western Family* magazine. Armitage's fourth and final marriage—to an Austrian artist, Marlinde von Ruhs—took place in 1966 and lasted no more than two months and perhaps as briefly as two weeks; it was annulled.

During Armitage's lifetime there were thirteen exhibitions of his work, the last in 1963 at the Harry Ransom Humanities Research Center at the University of Texas in Austin, which has a collection of his books and letters. A bibliography compiled by Robert Marks lists over ninety titles designed by Armitage, many of which he also wrote. In his second book of memoirs, *Accent on Life* (1965), he records having told Henry Miller, "I write books so that I will be able to design them" (p. 276).

Armitage's design work was notable for its exuberant typography. He was an anathema to his more conventional peers because he felt that books should reflect their own time and place rather than be subject to the traditional typographic conventions of "timeless" and "neutral" design that sought only to make books legible. In his *Rendezvous with the Book* (1949), he contends that "there are no formulas or rules for design . . . each book presents special and particular problems . . . and provides ample and exciting opportunities." In Armitage's view, "looking backward forsakes adventure, experimentation, research, and the opportunity to make new and significant statements allied to our particular time. It is a basic menace to the growth, the health and the potentialities of design, typography, and the graphic arts generally." The catalog to the 1963 exhibition at the University of Texas includes his own assessment of his work's impact:

> Naturally what I did stirred violent criticism. I became, in certain circles, the destroyer of book tradition, the bad boy of typography, the usurper of the placid pools of bookmaking. But through the years some of my most criticized inventions have been quietly adopted, i.e., use of the endsheets, double-page title pages, large readable type, generous margins, etc. . . . The books speak for themselves, and good or bad, they certainly are not indifferent.

Armitage died in Yucca Valley, California.

• The text above benefited from information provided by Isabelle Armitage and Dick Higgins. Higgins's *Merle Armitage and the Modern Book* (n.d.) is a well-illustrated and extensive study of Armitage as book designer. A partial list of his work can be found in Robert Marks, *Merle Armitage Bibliography* (1956). Robert M. Purcell, *Merle Armitage Was Here!: A Retrospective of a 20th Century Renaissance Man* (1981), is a personal recollection. An obituary is in the *New York Times*, 18 Mar. 1975.

RICHARD HENDEL

ARMOUR, Norman (14 Oct. 1887–27 Sept. 1982), career diplomat, was born in Brighton, England, while his parents, George Allison Armour and Harriette Foote, were vacationing there. Armour earned his B.A. in 1909 from Princeton University, and following his graduation four years later from Harvard Law School, he was admitted to the New Jersey bar. In

1915, the same year he earned an M.A. from Princeton, Armour passed the State Department's Foreign Service examination.

Armour served as an attaché to the French government at Paris for a year until his 1916 appointment as third secretary of the U.S. embassy in Petrograd, where he remained until 1919. While witness to the Bolshevik revolution and Russia's withdrawal from World War I, Armour's most noteworthy act was the assistance given to a young princess, Myra Koudacheff, in fleeing to Sweden, for which he was detained for a month by the revolutionary government. He escaped, reportedly disguised as a Norwegian courier. In 1919 he married the princess; they had one son.

Throughout the 1920s Armour held positions at U.S. embassies in Brussels, The Hague, Montevideo, Rome, Tokyo, and Paris. In 1932 President Herbert Hoover (1874–1964) appointed him minister to Haiti, where he negotiated the 1933 executive agreement that spelled out the details of the U.S. Marines' withdrawal, which brought to an end nineteen years of U.S. presence in the island nation. Completed in 1935, the withdrawal demonstrated President Franklin D. Roosevelt's "Good Neighbor Policy," which renounced U.S. interference in the internal political affairs of Caribbean and Central American nations.

Following a three-year stint in Canada, Armour was promoted to the rank of ambassador and posted in 1938 to Chile, where he encountered a leftist coalition government headed by President Pedro Aguirre Cerda and a country ravaged by an earthquake. Aguirre Cerda supported increased government activism, higher export taxes on the copper produced by the American-owned companies, and a $100 million U.S. loan to promote the nation's economic and social development. Armour favored the loan, but the State Department resisted because of the Chilean government's threat to tax the U.S. companies and its increased role in the economy. For the moment, Washington provided only aid for earthquake reconstruction.

In 1939 Armour became ambassador to Argentina, where he served until June 1944. He had hoped that the Roberto Ortiz administration would take a pro-Allied position once war engulfed Europe, but the hope faded after Vice President Ramón S. Castillo took over the government in July 1940. Despite Castillo's professions of neutrality, Armour's reports portrayed Castillo as an obstacle to hemispheric solidarity with ever-increasing expressions of pro-Axis sentiments. When Castillo was ousted in June 1943, Armour initially looked favorably on the junta headed by General Edelmiro Farrell, because Farrell's rhetoric indicated a change in wartime policy and a restoration of democracy. Neither occurred, and as Armour expressed his disillusionment, the Farrell administration distanced itself from the ambassador. Differences between the U.S. and Argentine governments hardened to the point that the State Department instructed Armour to reject an Argentine government proposal that he meet privately with the war minister, Colonel Juan Perón, in March 1944 in an effort to reconcile differences between Buenos Aires and Washington.

Frustrated by Argentina's refusal to join the Allied wartime coalition, Washington recalled Armour in June 1944. He replaced Laurence Duggan as assistant secretary of state for Latin American affairs. In that position Armour worked for the implementation of the Dumbarton Oaks Agreements, which provided for the establishment of the United Nations. In March 1945 Armour was appointed ambassador to the fascist regime of General Francisco Franco in Spain, but disenchanted with Franco's refusal to democratize the Spanish government, Armour withdrew from Madrid ten months later and retired from diplomatic service.

In 1947 President Harry S. Truman recalled Armour from retirement to become assistant secretary of state for political affairs, an administrative position in which Armour coordinated the State Department's four geographical divisions and centralized the Foreign Service operations. He also continued to call for greater U.S. economic and social assistance to Latin America, not only to enhance economic development and to correct social disparities but also to improve the U.S. image and relations throughout the hemisphere. Influenced by Armour, Secretary of State George C. Marshall assured the 1948 Inter-American Conference at Bogotá that Latin America was not a forgotten region.

Following the Bogotá conference, Armour again retired, only to return in 1950 as ambassador to Venezuela. During his year-long stint in Caracas, Armour played a significant role in the development of contracts for the exploitation by foreign companies of the oil reserves in eastern Venezuela. When President-elect Dwight D. Eisenhower's nominee for the ambassadorship to the Soviet Union, Charles E. Bohlen, came under attack by the supporters of Senator Joseph R. McCarthy because of his links to Truman's foreign policy, Armour joined with four other career diplomats to publicly deplore McCarthy's "sinister" and "flimsy" attacks on the Foreign Service.

Armour returned to service in 1954, when he was appointed ambassador to Guatemala following the U.S. Central Intelligence Agency's directed overthrow of the Jacobo Arbenz Guzmán government. For a year he administered the vast quantities of U.S. economic assistance to the rightist government for the restoration and development of the economy. In 1955 Armour again retired from the diplomatic corps.

In October 1956 Senator J. William Fulbright had Armour appointed chair of a special task force to assess the impact of U.S. assistance in Greece, Turkey, and Iran. The task force reported in 1957 that U.S. security interests remained threatened in the region and recommended additional assistance because of Turkey's inadequate military capabilities, Greece's unsettled relations with Cyprus, and an anticipated long-term threat to Iran from the Soviet Union. As a result of the task force's report and other Soviet actions in the Middle East, the United States increased military assistance to the Persian Gulf States. At the conclusion of this fact-finding mission, Armour retired permanently from public life, spending his remaining years lecturing and serving as a consultant to the government and private interest groups. He died in New York City.

• There is no known repository of Armour's papers, but his reports from the various diplomatic missions are in the National Archives, RG 59. Scattered correspondence is in the papers of other diplomats to Central America. Information on Armour is included in Randall B. Woods, *The Roosevelt Foreign Policy Establishment and the "Good Neighbor"* (1979); William F. Sater, *Chile and the United States: Empires in Conflict* (1990); Joseph F. Tulchin, *Argentina and the United States: A Conflicted Relationship* (1990); Michael J. Francis, *The Limits of Hegemony: United States Relations with Argentina and Chile during World War II* (1977); and George S. Harris, *Troubled Alliance: Turkish-American Problems in Historical Perspective, 1945–1971* (1972). An obituary is in the *New York Times*, 29 Sept. 1982.

THOMAS M. LEONARD

ARMOUR, Philip Danforth (16 May 1832–6 Jan. 1901), meat packer, was born in Stockbridge, New York, the son of Danforth Armour and Juliana Brooks, farmers. One of eight children, five of whom became involved in packing and grain dealing, he was educated at the Cazenovia Academy. In 1852 Armour left the farm to mine gold in California and returned in 1856 several thousand dollars richer. Not long after, he went to Milwaukee, where he started a soap factory that burned to the ground. By this time, one of his brothers, Herman Ossian, had already started H. O. Armour & Company, dealing in grain and provisions. After a couple of years of hide sales in St. Paul, Armour himself went into the provision business with Frederick B. Miles in Milwaukee in 1859. He married Malvina Belle Ogden of Cincinnati in 1862; they had three sons, two of whom worked in the family business.

After the partnership with Miles ended, Armour formed Plankinton, Armour & Company in 1863 in Milwaukee with John Plankinton, a grain dealer and meat packer. The most important business coup of Armour's early career occurred near the end of the Civil War when he predicted heavy Confederate losses and thus the dropping of pork prices. As a consequence, he made contracts with buyers at $40 per barrel before prices plummeted to $18 when the war ended in a Union victory. This deal netted him a profit of $22 per barrel or an alleged total of $1 million to $2 million. Before Plankinton retired in 1877, Armour had already proved himself to be a worthy junior partner with the additions that he made to the Milwaukee plant, including an ice house and a curing house, and the extension of operations to Kansas City.

In the meantime, four of Armour's brothers were also involving themselves in the grain and packing businesses and playing their respective roles in the establishment of the "House of Armour." Armour left for Chicago in 1875 after he became convinced that the city would soon replace Cincinnati as the meat packing capital of the country. After all, Chicago had many advantages over Cincinnati, including its accessibility by water, its fast-growing rail system, and its proximity to hog and cattle farms in the Midwest. Eventually, much of Armour's interests became grouped in Chicago.

To Armour goes credit for many innovations in the meat packing industry though he had no butchering skills himself. He was one of the first users of refrigerated cars and a conveyor system on the killing floors. Also, he was one of the first to use all parts of an animal in manufacturing. Thus, out of meat packing came auxiliary industries such as glue, fertilizer, margarine, lard, gelatin, and isinglass. It is said that Armour sometimes checked sewers himself to make certain that no parts were wasted, not even a trace of fat that could have been used somehow. Competition was close when Gustavus Swift, dubbed the "dressed beef king," entered pork packing and Armour entered the area of dressed beef. Yet, in financial terms, Swift was bested by Armour, who in 1893 claimed an overall sales total of $110 million, while his competitor claimed in 1892 $90 million. Both, however, are credited with being two of the first developers of an efficient assembly-line technique. The two also did much to expand the reach of their products, including the opening of sales offices in the East, some of which had their own cold storage; extending their domestic and foreign markets by establishing plants outside Chicago; and opening overseas sales offices.

In the 1890s Armour made his mark on a couple of events that occurred on the financial scene. The panic of 1893 saw him coming to the rescue of Chicago banks when he bought $500,000 in European gold to endorse people's checks. In 1897 Armour broke the threat of Joseph Leiter's near corner in wheat. Yet, all of these victories became overshadowed by the "embalmed beef" scandals of 1898–1899 when it was claimed that the meat fed to troops from certain packing houses was tainted with chemicals. However, the court of inquiry appointed to investigate these complaints found no evidence of such contamination. Consequently, Armour and his fellow packers were charged with "fixing" the results of the panel's report. Armour refuted these accusations of bribery fervently.

Indeed, this scandal obscured some of the positive things that Armour did earlier for his community, such as the creation of the Armour Mission and the Armour Institute. The former was started on behalf of his brother Joseph who passed away in 1881. It was essentially a resource center that included a medical dispensary, day nursery, kindergarten, library, and classrooms. Around it were the Armour Flats, housing for workers and their families. The institute, which opened in 1893, offered to young men and women a relatively inexpensive education and career training in technical fields like engineering and architecture.

Having started from the bottom himself, Armour empathized with others in his previous situation and respected any person who could rise up the corporate ladder by dint of hard work. Industry and honesty were the qualities in a worker most valued by him. At the same time that he sympathized with the workers, he also patronized them and disapproved of the organization of labor. Personally, he was short-tempered but fought to control himself and did not drink. His lifestyle was comparatively simple, and he enjoyed working long hours. He once said, "I have no other interest in life but my business . . . I do not love the money. What I do love is the getting of it." At the time of his death in Chicago, Illinois, it is reported that he had amassed a fortune of $50 million. Throughout history, Armour is regarded both positively for his charitable deeds, hard work, and solid values and negatively for his sometimes questionable business practices. It is certain, however, that he was a leader in his field. He changed the way meat was packed. His ideas and innovation set a precedent for others to follow.

• Some records of Armour & Co. may be found in the Greyhound Tower, Phoenix. The only extant biography of Armour is Harper Leech and John C. Carroll, *Armour and His Times* (1938). Other works about the subject are Arthur Warren, "Philip D. Armour," *McClure's*, Feb. 1894; Frank W. Gunsaulus, "Philip D. Armour: A Character Sketch," *Review of Reviews*, Feb. 1901; and H. I. Cleveland, "Philip Armour, Merchant," *World's Work*, Mar. 1901. For works about the Armour family, consult Cora Lillian Davenport, "The Rise of the Armours: An American Industrial Family," (M.A. thesis, Univ. of Chicago, 1930), and Edwin D. Shutt, "The Saga of the Armour Family in Kansas City, 1870–1900," *Heritage of the Great Plains* 23 (1990): 25–42. Other sources dealing with the company are *Armour Magazine* and *Armour Engineer and Alumnus Magazine*, published by the Armour Institute. See also Clifford L. Snowden, "The Armour Institute of Technology," *New England Magazine* 16 (May 1897). Primary sources include J. Ogden Armour, *The Packers, the Private Car Lines and the People* (1906), and Philip D. Armour, "The Packing Industry," in *One Hundred Years of American Commerce*, ed. Chauncey M. Depew (1895). Obituaries are in the *New York Times*, the *New York Tribune*, and the *Chicago Tribune*, all 7 Jan. 1901.

DEBORAH S. ING

ARMOUR, Richard Willard (15 July 1906–28 Feb. 1989), educator and satirist, was born in San Pedro, California, the son of Harry Willard Armour, a drugstore owner, and Sue Wheelock. He earned a B.A. degree from Pomona College in 1927 and an M.A. from Harvard in 1928. In 1932 he married Kathleen Fauntleroy Stevens, with whom he had two children.

After receiving his Ph.D. in literature from Harvard in 1933, Armour embarked on an academic career that lasted more than fifty years. Starting at the Main University campus of the University of Texas (now the University of Texas at Austin), he served as an instructor in English in 1928 and 1929. During 1930 and 1931 he was an instructor in English at Northwestern University in Evanston, Illinois, and in 1932, at the College of the Ozarks in Clarksville, Arkansas, he accepted his first professorship in English. From here Armour moved to Germany, where he was American lecturer at the University of Freiburg during 1933 and 1934. In 1934 he accepted a professorship in English at Wells College in Aurora, New York. Armour served in the Army Antiaircraft Artillery corps from 1942 to 1946. In 1945 he accepted a professorship closer to home at Scripps College in Claremont, California, where he served as professor of English until 1963 and as dean of faculty between 1961 and 1963. From 1964 to 1970 he traveled in Europe and Asia as a lecturer for the U.S. State Department. During this time he was also professor of English at the Claremont Graduate School and, between 1966 and 1989, dean and professor emeritus. In addition to these duties Armour was Carnegie Visiting Professor at the University of Hawaii in 1957, Stanford University author of the year in 1965, writer in residence at the University of Redlands in 1974, visiting professor at Whittier College in 1975, trustee of the Claremont Men's College between 1968 and 1989, and California State Universities and Colleges Chancellor's Lecturer between 1964 and 1989.

In addition to his career as a scholar whose primary field was Chaucer and the Romantic poets, Armour wrote or edited over sixty books, primarily light verse and satire. In these Armour pokes gentle fun at topics ranging from scholarship and pedagogy to parenting. He also wrote a number of books for children; penned an autobiography, titled *Drug Store Days: My Youth among the Pills and Potions* (1959); and contributed over 6,000 light verse and prose works to magazines in the United States and England. His best-known works are a series of humorous quasi-historical studies of subjects from medicine and education to art, communism, and war. A noteworthy feature of these "histories," along with their relish for wordplay and generally irreverent attitude toward pedagogues and pedants, is their long, discursive titles, which offer an initial indication of the seriousness with which the author approaches his work. An example is *It All Started with Columbus: Being an Unexpurgated, Unabridged, and Unlikely History of the United States from Christopher Columbus to John F. Kennedy for Those Who, Having Perused a Volume of History in School, Swore They Would Never Read Another* (1953). (In the bibliography that follows, short titles are used wherever appropriate.)

Reviewers of Armour's work regularly groan at his insistent punning, but the word is one Armour found disagreeable. "I prefer the more descriptive word, wordplay. . . . In some of my books there is much wordplay, perhaps too much. But in others, such as *Drug Store Days*, my favorite of my books, there is none at all."

In 1971 an animated film was produced based on one of Armour's several works directed primarily at students, *On Your Marks: A Package of Punctuation*, and in 1976 a musical version of his *Going around in Academic Circles* was produced for the stage. Armour was a member of PEN, the Modern Language Association, the California Writers Guild, and the American Association of University Professors. He died in Claremont.

• Most of Armour's papers, including the manuscripts of some books, correspondence with his publishers, and some educational films, are at the Denison Library, Scripps College. A smaller collection is at Boston University. Though primarily an author of light verse and prose, Armour began his career as a writer with the publication of *Barry Cornwall: A Biography of Bryan Waller Procter* (1935), followed by *The Literary Recollections of Barry Cornwall* (1936). In 1940, in collaboration with Raymond Howes, he edited *Coleridge the Talker: A Series of Contemporary Descriptions and Comments.* He served as editor also of *Young Voices: A Book of Wells College Verse* (1941). Armour's first book of light verse, *Yours for the Asking*, appeared in 1942, and in 1943 he and Bown Adams co-wrote *To These Dark Steps*, a play published by the New York Institute for the Education of the Blind. *Private's Lives* also appeared in 1943. In 1946 came *Golf Bawls* and *Leading with My Left*; in 1947, *Writing Light Verse.* Another book of verse, *For Partly Proud Parents*, was published in 1950, and in 1953 the first of Armour's satirical histories, *It All Started with Columbus.* At this point Armour's books of verse and prose began appearing at the rate of nearly one a year until 1983 and include works about pedagogy such as *American Lit Relit* (1964) and *It All Started with Freshman English* (1973); examinations of marriage and sexual relations such as *My Life with Women: Confessions of a Domesticated Male* (1968) and *A Short History of Sex* (1970); and thoughts on parenting such as *Through Darkest Adolescence* (1963) and *Educated Guesses: Light-Serious Suggestions for Parents and Teachers* (1983). Armour also wrote a number of children's books, including *The Year Santa Went Modern* (1964), *All Sizes and Shapes of Monkeys and Apes* (1970), and *Have You Ever Wished You Were Something Else?* (1983). Biographical information is available in Everett S. Allen, *Famous American Humorous Poets* (1968). Obituaries are in the *Los Angeles Times*, 1 Mar. 1989; the *New York Times* and the *Washington Post*, 2 Mar. 1989; and *Writer*, June 1989.

DAVID LAWRENCE ARNOLD

ARMOUR, Tommy (24 Sept. 1895–11 Sept. 1968), professional golfer, was born Thomas Dickson Armour in Edinburgh, Scotland, the son of George Armour, a confectioner. His mother's name is unknown. His father died when Armour was four. Armour's older brother, Sandy, took the young child to a golf course adjacent to their house and introduced him to the game of golf. As an adolescent, Armour caddied for Sandy as he won the Scottish Amateur championship. After entering Stewart's College in Edinburgh, Armour graduated from the University of Edinburgh in 1914.

Although Armour was considered a promising young amateur golfer in Scotland during his years at the university, he enlisted in the Black Watch Regiment in the latter part of 1914, thus thrusting him into World War I. During the war Armour established a reputation as being one of the fastest and deadliest machine gunners in his entire regiment. In 1918 Armour transferred to the newly established Tank Corps; in June of that year his tank was shelled by enemy fire, and he was one of only two survivors. Before the end of the war Armour fell victim to a mustard gas attack, resulting in a heavily wounded left arm and temporary blindness in both eyes. Although the arm would eventually heal (yet remain in a weakened condition), he permanently lost sight in his left eye.

In 1920, the year after his marriage to Consuelo Carrera (the couple would have two children), Armour came to the United States and found work as a traveling salesman. Still an amateur golfer, he won three amateur events that year, including the French Amateur championship. In 1921 Armour competed in an international amateur golf competition between Great Britain and the United States. This event, which Armour helped win for Great Britain, would be recognized as the precursor to the inauguration of the biannual Walker Cup matches one year later. In 1922 Armour became a citizen of the United States, and in 1925 he renounced his amateur status and joined the American professional golf tour. Armour also accepted a position as club professional at the prestigious Congressional Country Club in Washington, D.C., in 1926 after briefly serving as secretary at the Westchester-Biltmore Country Club.

Although the "Silver Scot," so nicknamed for the color of his hair, had one victory on the professional tour in 1925, few expected the incredible success Armour enjoyed in 1927. He broke the single season record for tour victories, including one in the highly competitive Canadian Open. However, Armour's greatest victory that year occurred at the Oakmont Country Club in Pennsylvania, as he captured the U.S. Open. Armour, who throughout his career had a penchant for making seemingly impossible comebacks, birdied the final hole of regulation play to tie Harry Cooper with a score of 301, after holing a one-iron shot from the fairway; the following day Armour defeated Cooper by three strokes on the way to his first major championship. Later that year Armour participated in the first official Ryder Cup match, held at Worcester Country Club in Massachusetts and won convincingly by the American team.

Armour's life could best be described as a roller-coaster ride during the next few years. In 1928 he dominated the professional tour by winning four more tournaments. Yet in 1930 Armour underwent a highly publicized divorce from his wife, which was settled in April. Armour, who had fallen in love with Estelle Andrews, suffered substantial financial damages in the proceedings. (Armour and Andrews later married, and they would have one son.) However, later that year Armour defeated Gene Sarazen 1-up at Fresh Meadow in Flushing, New York, to win the PGA (Professional Golfers' Association) championship. In 1931 Armour composed another improbable comeback, making up a five-stroke deficit in the final round and defeating Argentine Jose Jurado by one stroke to win the last of his major championships, the British Open at Carnoustie, Scotland.

Although Armour remained highly competitive on the professional tour for another five years, at this point in his life he established himself as one of the most respected (and highly priced) golf instructors in the world. Armour held the position of golf instructor at the Boca Raton Club in Florida for almost twenty-five years, teaching and correcting the swings of noted golfers such as Babe Didrikson Zaharias and Lawson Little. In 1940 he was elected to the PGA Hall of Fame. In the 1950s Armour frequented Winged Foot Country Club in Mamaroneck, New York, while authoring instruction manuals and arguing for the importance of a dominant right hand throughout the swing. He also designed golf clubs for the Crawford, McGregor and Canby Company. Armour died in Larchmont, New York.

Although his professional career was relatively short, the legacy Armour left on the game of golf will never be forgotten. Although he was not considered to be the most congenial person on the tour, he was deeply admired for his unyielding determination to win (or in the case of battle, to survive and recover). Few were his equal as a golf instructor, and his books have remained influential. And there is no doubt that Armour will always be remembered for his uncanny ability to come back. In the process Armour changed the game of golf and molded generations of successful players.

• Armour wrote three books: *How to Play Your Best Golf All the Time* (1953), *A Round of Golf with Tommy Armour* (1959), and *Tommy Armour's ABC's of Golf* (1967). For more information on Armour, consult Charles Price, *The World of Golf: A Panorama of Six Centuries of the Game's History* (1962), and Herbert Warren Wind, *The Story of American Golf: Its Champions and Its Championships* (1956). An obituary is in the *New York Times*, 14 Sept. 1968.

JASON W. PARKER

ARMS, John Taylor (19 Apr. 1887–13 Oct. 1953), architectural etcher, was born in Washington, D.C., the son of John Taylor Arms, a real estate broker, and Kate Watkins. Born into a long line of businessmen, clergymen, and teachers descended from a seventeenth-century Massachusetts stocking-knitter, Arms was the first in his family to become an artist.

Arms drew devotedly from his early boyhood onward and was fascinated by French artists who specialized in architecture, such as Aimé-Edmond Dellemagne. He attended the Lawrenceville School in Lawrenceville, New Jersey (1904–1905), and then, following his father's wishes, enrolled in pre-law studies at Princeton University. In 1907, however, he transferred to MIT's school of architecture. His most influential professor at MIT was Desiré Despradelle, head of the department of design. Arms earned his B.S. in architecture in 1911 and an M.S. in 1912.

Arms moved to New York City, where he worked first as an architectural draftsman for the firm of Jean Carrière and Thomas Hastings, which designed houses and buildings in the late Victorian Roman, Gothic, and Italian revival styles. Among the designs Arms helped to develop were those for Henry Clay Frick's Fifth Avenue mansion in New York, now the Frick Museum.

In 1913 Arms married Dorothy Frothingham Noyes, a gifted writer who virtually abandoned her own career to be her husband's helpmate. The couple would have three children, all born between 1914 and 1918. Shortly after their wedding, Dorothy gave Arms a small hobbyist's etching kit for Christmas. Despite his lack of training in any form of printmaking, Arms took to the medium at once and was almost entirely self-taught. His first published plate, "Sunlight and Shadow"—which was only his fifth print—appeared in 1915. At about the same time, he bought the first of what would eventually become an enormous personal collection of prints, an Ernest Lumsden scene of Benares, India. Arms also made a comprehensive study of the entire history of etching; Meryon, Whistler, and Millet were probably his deepest influences.

In 1914 Arms left his employer to form a partnership with Cameron Clark, designing houses in the Colonial Revival style. He quickly tired of routine office work, however, and spent more and more time drawing architectural subjects for pleasure. In 1916 he joined the U.S. Navy as an ensign, eventually becoming a navigation officer on the destroyer USS *Montgomery*, which searched for submarines off the Atlantic coast. After his discharge from the navy in 1919, Arms quit the firm he had founded to devote his life to etching. He had already begun to win prizes for his work and received his first commission in 1919.

From the beginning of his career, Arms organized his work in thematic series, some of which preoccupied him only briefly, while others stretched over decades. His earliest published prints, the Gable Series (1915–1916 and 1921–1922) depict the gables, doorways, and half-timbered storefronts of fifteenth- and sixteenth-century houses in the villages of Normandy, especially Lisieux, rendered in a manner that relies heavily on the romantic, impressionist style of Whistler's etchings of two generations earlier. The Gable Series shows Arms's confident draftsmanship and his still somewhat tentative handling of the etcher's needle. Though he made great, rapid strides as a technician in subsequent series, the notions of the quaint and the picturesque that dominated these early prints continued to inform much of his work throughout his life.

Arms experimented in style, subject matter, and technique through the 1920s, his most prolific decade, in which he produced 186 of his lifetime output of 448 prints. Experiments with mezzotint and lithography proved abortive; the indistinct outlines of mezzotint in particular were inimical to Arm's reflexive precisionism. He had greater success with aquatint (mainly in combination with etching), which he virtually revived as a serious medium. Inspired by seventeenth- and eighteenth-century French and English masters, he tried to go beyond the flat, posterlike style to which the neglected art of aquatint had been confined by his own day, since its eclipse by commercial lithography, half-tone, and photogravure. In his aquatints he also tried to emulate the subtle color of hand-tinted eighteenth- and nineteenth-century French and English etchings. The rich veils of subtly graded wash that render sky and water in his Aquatint Series (1919–1925), especially in several prints of solitary boats skimming over calm mountain lakes, reveal Arms's command of the process. Despite his success with the color medium, Arms abandoned it, feeling that it distracted him from his true vocation as an etcher.

With the Gargoyle Series (1920–1924, plus two additional prints dated 1929 and 1947), Arms made an important and original innovation, devising a meticulous stipple technique that allowed him to capture the nuances of texture in weathered stone—an approach that he quickly raised to a level of exquisite refinement and used throughout his career. (Stipple textures are usually associated with the coarser means of engraving, not with etching; Arms drew his every dot individually with his needles.) In the gargoyle prints he also began to approach the subject that would obsess him for the rest of his life: Gothic architecture.

Starting in 1923, Arms—accompanied by his family—made extended annual pilgrimages to draw the cathedrals of Europe. The etchings that resulted from these trips constitute his main artistic achievement: the French Churches (1924–1953) and Spanish Churches (1923–1950); the Italian Series (1925–1935), which includes churches, street scenes, hill-town panoramas, and several remarkable images of Venice; and the English Series (1937–1952), which pictures the modest village churches of Hertfordshire, Berkshire, and Buckinghamshire.

During the 1930s and 1940s, when travel to Europe was often impossible, Arms went on several trips to sketch Mayan and Aztec ruins, which resulted in his Mexico and Yucatan series. With the outbreak of World War II he attempted to reenlist but was turned down because of his age. Instead, he organized several wartime print exhibitions and made four monumental etchings in his U.S. Navy Ships Series (1943–1947). While he lavished his usual skill on the Mexican prints, he eventually abandoned these series and resumed his yearly trips to Europe at war's end.

Arms always drew on site, spending as many as ten to fourteen days on a single sketch. In his studio he sometimes augmented his sketches and memory with photographs. Using transfer, he would trace only the main lines of a composition onto the grounded, smoked copper plate and draw the mass of detail directly into the ground. Although Arms assiduously collected a tremendous arsenal of etching tools, he never used them but drew instead with ordinary sewing needles set in a small wooden handle. Early in his career he denied that he ever used magnification (his much-greater-than-normal visual acuity was several times confirmed by medical testing), yet he was to admit that for some of his later plates he needed as many as three lenses in series. He often worked from dawn to midnight, hardly pausing to eat; some of his later prints required 2,000 hours of work or more—each step carefully logged to the quarter hour in a notebook.

Without question one of the leading etchers of his day, Arms was an eloquent and indefatigable evangelist for his art. He developed an extraordinary form of lecture-demonstration, in which he delivered a stentorian discourse on the history, methods, and aesthetics of etching, all the while drawing ambidextrously, demonstrating every stage of the etching process from sketch to pulled proof. Between 1920 and 1953 Arms gave some 150 such performances to groups at colleges, libraries, museums, art associations, and business and industrial exhibitions.

Losing no opportunity to spread the gospel of etching, Arms also contributed more than fifty articles on printmaking and printmakers to such journals as *Hobbies* (1931), *Prints* (1932–1937), *Print* (1940–1952), *Print Collector's Quarterly* (1941 and 1948–50), and *Art Digest* (1948). His *Handbook on Print Making and Print Makers* (1934), though poorly illustrated, remained a standard text for many years.

Ever eager to advance the work of his peers, Arms chaired the selection juries for exhibitions of American graphic art that traveled to the Bibliothèque Nationale in 1928 and to London's Victoria and Albert Museum in 1929. He was secretary and then president (1920–1953) of the Society of American Etchers (originally the Brooklyn Society of Etchers); president of the American Society of Graphic Arts; president and cofounder of the National Committee of Engraving; and a member of the Pennel Fund committee (1937–1953), which approved purchases of prints for the Library of Congress.

During his lifetime Arms's work entered the collections of the Bibliothèque Nationale, the British Museum, the Victoria and Albert Museum, and the Museum of Fine Arts in Boston as well as numerous smaller private and public collections throughout the United States, Canada, and Europe. Widely honored, he received some 109 etching and printmaking awards—most in competitions and exhibitions in the United States—including a gold medal at the 1937 Paris International Exposition.

Extravagant claims have sometimes been made for Arms's work, especially by his wife, who, in her *John Taylor Arms: Modern Medievalist* (1941), called his Gothic images "not slavish imitations of existing structures" but rather "spiritual reconstructions in which are embodied all the faith or aspirations or thoughts of a far-away age." Even in his prime, however, some critics found his work, with its fanatical factuality and obsessive detail, to be cold, calculated, or pedantic. Arms himself confessed in the mid-1940s that much of his career had been absorbed in problems of technique; however, he believed that in his last years he transcended this preoccupation and was able to concentrate solely on thought, emotion, and mood. In truth, there is little discernible development in Arms's oeuvre after 1930, and the mood of all his prints is a monotonously timeless, Apollonian tranquillity. There is light in Arms's etchings but no weather, and there are almost no people (which Arms could not draw well), animals, or movement. He was driven purely by his love of buildings.

Affable and optimistic; humble (elaborately so in print), private, and devout; deliberate, persistent, and restrained; a studied perfectionist almost entirely lacking in spontaneity—Arms the man and his work were one. He saw himself as a craftsman in the medieval tradition (Albert Reese called him "an apostle of the bitten line"). He never doubted the Beaux-Arts aesthetic in which he had been trained or questioned his faith in Gothic architecture as representing the apex of human artistry. Of all the upheavals that shook the art world in his lifetime—fauvism, cubism, surrealism, abstraction—there is in his work not a trace.

For most of his married life Arms maintained studios at two homes, his "Stone House" in Happy Valley near North Pomfret, Vermont, and "Millstones" at Greenfield Hill near Fairfield, Connecticut. Arms died in New York of Hodgkin's disease. Though his work was almost forgotten soon after his death, it was shown in some fifteen retrospective exhibitions from 1975 to 1988.

• The standard catalog of Arm's work used by dealers and auction houses is the manuscript prepared after his death by his secretaries, Mary Bradshaw Hays and Marie Probsfield, for the New York Public Library Prints and Drawings Division, despite a number of misspellings and errors regarding sizes, colors, and editions. The 1970 listing of Arms's collection A, his own private collection of his work deposited in the Library of Congress, includes a number of similar errors. Dorothy N. Arms, *The Published Plates of John Taylor Arms*, prepared for the Pequot Library in Southport, Conn., is largely reliable. William Dolan Fletcher, *John Taylor Arms: A Man for All Time* (1982), is a catalogue raisonné of Arms's entire output, which—confusingly—uses a numbering system different from the New York Public Library listing. The Library of Congress owns the largest collection of his work (527 prints); other major collections are held by the Prints and Drawings Division of the New York Public Library, the Boston Public Library, the Metropolitan Museum of Art, the Princeton University Art Museum, the Davison Art Center at Wesleyan University, the Hobart College Library, the Dartmouth College Museum, and the Bibliothèque Nationale in Paris.

The three-part article "John Taylor Arms Tells How He Makes an Etching," *American Artist*, Dec. 1940–Feb. 1941, explains the technical minutiae of his approach. He published two major retrospective essays on his career: "Self Estimate," in *Twenty-One Years of Drawing: A Retrospective Exhibition of the Work of John Taylor Arms* (1937), and "Credo," in *Selected Examples from Thirty Years of Etching by John Taylor Arms* (1946). Elizabeth M. Whitmore, *Notes on the Development of an American Etcher* (1925), offers an insightful analysis of style and technique in Arms's early prints. Ben L. Bassham, *John Taylor Arms, American Etcher* (1975), is a thorough evaluation of Arms's entire output in the context of the late-nineteenth-century revival of etching.

CHRISTOPHER CAINES

ARMSBY, Henry Prentiss (21 Sept. 1853–19 Oct. 1921), agricultural chemist, was born in Northbridge, Massachusetts, the son of Lewis Armsby, an artisan and cabinetmaker, and Mary A. Prentiss. He attended the common schools of Whitinsville and Millbury and was interested in chemical experiments from an early age. Armsby graduated in 1871 with a B.S. from Worcester County Free Institute of Industrial Science (later Worcester Polytechnic Institute), where he was subsequently an instructor in chemistry from 1871 to 1872. As a postgraduate he specialized in analytical chemistry and spent two periods at Yale's Sheffield Scientific School, from which he received a Ph.B. in 1874 and a Ph.D. in 1879. In the meantime, and after a year as a teacher at Fitchburg High School in Massachusetts, he had gone to Germany in 1875 to study animal nutrition with the University of Leipzig's leading agricultural scientists and with Julius Kühn and his colleagues at nearby Möckern Agricultural Experiment Station, Germany's oldest agricultural experiment station. It was there that Emil von Wolff had begun his pioneering research into agricultural chemistry in 1851.

In 1877, after a year as a chemistry assistant at Rutgers College (later University), Armsby was employed as a chemist by the Connecticut Agricultural Experiment Station, two years after its establishment as the country's first state-funded station. Except for 1881–1883, when he was vice president and professor of agricultural chemistry at Storrs Agricultural School in Connecticut, Armsby dedicated the rest of his life to the service of state experiment stations. He married Lucy Atwood Harding in 1878. The couple had five children.

In 1880 Armsby published his *Manual of Cattle Feeding: A Treatise on the Laws of Animal Nutrition and the Chemistry of Feeding Stuffs*. It was based loosely on the outline of von Wolff's *Die landwirthschaftliche Fütterungslehre und die theorie der menschlichen Ernährung* (1861). Adapting it to American conditions, Armsby made considerable changes from the original method employed by von Wolff and also by Kühn, making it the first book of its kind in the United States. Armsby's work went through several editions and served a generation of students as a textbook.

In 1883 Armsby joined the newly established Wisconsin Agricultural Experiment Station. It had been organized by the University of Wisconsin and was funded by the state legislature under the joint direction of Armsby, William A. Henry, and William Trelease. In 1886 Henry became director, and Armsby was named associate director after Trelease's resignation. Armsby also was employed as the station's chemist and the university's professor of agricultural chemistry from 1883 to 1887.

While at the Wisconsin station Armsby was one of the participants invited to a convention organized in July 1885 by Norman J. Colman, federal commissioner of agriculture, to consider among other matters the future of agricultural experiment stations in the United States. The convention led to the establishment in October 1887 of what was to become the Association of American Agricultural Colleges and Experiment Stations. Armsby played a prominent role in the association, serving as a member of its executive committee and various other subcommittees, and he was elected secretary in 1890 and president in 1898–1899.

Armsby also oversaw the agricultural science sections of *Science*, the journal of professional science that had been founded in 1883. Through this journal he argued that agricultural scientists should publish the results of their experiments in *Science* instead of in the unscientific agricultural newspapers, whose audience typically comprised practical farmers. Armsby also advocated the installation of a technical expert, rather than a politician, to the post of federal commissioner of agriculture. Through the pages of *Science* he also proposed the professionalization of the work of the experiment stations and recommended that they be divided into stations that concentrated on scientific work and farms that provided practical assistance to farmers.

In 1887, with the passage of the Hatch Act, which provided federal funding for the state experiment stations, Armsby was called to Pennsylvania State College to organize the station in that state, serving as its director from 1887 until 1907. Following the reorganization of the college into schools in 1900, he also served as dean of the school of agriculture from 1900 to 1904. In 1907 he was relieved of his administrative duties to become the first director of the station's new Institute of Animal Nutrition, a position in which he was able to focus all of his attention on research.

Armsby had become one of the country's leading authorities on animal nutrition. Hence, in cooperation with the Pennsylvania station in 1898 the Federal Bureau of Animal Industry began a series of investigations supervised by Armsby into the fundamental principles of nutrition. This cooperative arrangement continued until 1920, when federal funding was withdrawn as a result of budget cuts. Armsby subsequently succeeded in obtaining temporary funding from the Rockefeller Institute for Medical Research to continue with his research.

Also in 1898 Armsby began the construction of a modified version of the Atwater-Rosa respiration calorimeter, with which experiments could be made with cattle and later other large farm animals. With this machine experiments were first conducted with a steer to study the available energy of timothy hay and subsequently of red clover hay and maize meal. As a result of his experiments Armsby concluded that cattle utilize food for tissue replacement rather than the production of heat, and, therefore, the maintenance value of a given feeding stuff depends on the availability of its energy. Armsby's research showed that feeding vegetable materials to livestock was extremely inefficient, and he believed it was wasteful to feed livestock any vegetable material that could be consumed directly by human beings. For example, only 14 to 61 percent of the energy of grains consumed by animals is recovered when they are processed into meat. Armsby argued that the adjustment of human and animal food supplies provided the basis for food conservation and a national policy.

Armsby served as a member of the Commission on Agricultural Research from 1906 to 1908. In 1908 he was a founding member of the American Society of Animal Nutrition (later the American Society of Animal Production) and served as its first president from 1908 to 1911. From 1914 to 1919 he was a member of the editorial board of the *Journal of Agricultural Research*, which had been founded by the federal Department of Agriculture in 1913.

During World War I Armsby broadened his research to apply the principles of animal nutrition to human beings. After the formation of the National Research Council by the National Academy of Sciences in 1916 to support the war effort, Armsby became a founding member of its agricultural committee in 1917. In 1919 this committee was reorganized as the Division of Biology and Agriculture, and Armsby became a member of its Committee on Food and Nutrition. It was in this role that he proposed in July 1921, shortly before his death in State College, Pennsylvania, the foundation of a well-funded National Institute of Nutrition to establish the food requirements of different classes of Americans.

Armsby made a major contribution to the development of information on animal and human nutrition. He also played a major role in the development of government-funded agricultural experiment stations in the United States. He believed they should not limit their activities to providing practical assistance to farmers but should also specialize in pure scientific research. Armsby's vision of the mission of experiment stations remains controversial, but his work laid the cornerstone for the discourse.

• Letters from Armsby are in the George W. Atherton Papers, Special Collections Department, Pennsylvania State University, University Park. The Pennsylvania State University Archives also has a manuscript by Henry Horton Armsby, "Henry Prentiss Armsby: A Personal Appraisal by His Son" (1966). The results of Armsby's research using the respiration calorimeter were published in the bulletins of the Bureau of Animal Industry, other publications of the Department of Agriculture, and articles in scientific journals. His *Principles of Animal Nutrition* (1903) was based on a series of lectures he gave at the first session of Ohio State University's graduate school of agriculture in 1902, and *The Nutrition of Farm Animals* (1917), a comprehensive survey of the fundamental principles of successful stock feeding, was written for the student rather than for the farmer. In *The Conservation of Food Energy* (1918) Armsby summarized the most important results and principles of his research that was relevant to the wartime food situation. Another book, in collaboration with C. Robert Moulton, *The Animal as a Converter of Matter and Energy: A Study of the Role of Livestock in Food Production* (1925), was published posthumously. A short biography is in T. I. Mairs, *Some Pennsylvania Pioneers in Agricultural Science* (1928). Alfred Charles True, *A History of Agricultural Experimentation and Research in the United States, 1607–1925* (1937), places Armsby's career in context, while Alan I. Marcus, *Agricultural Science and the Quest for Legitimacy: Farmers, Agricultural Colleges, and Experiment Stations, 1870–1890* (1985), provides a modern assessment of Armsby's contribution to the development of agricultural science in the early part of his career. Also see Raymond W. Swift, "Henry Prentiss Armsby," *Journal of Nutrition* 54, no. 1 (1954): 3–16. An obituary is in the U.S. Department of Agriculture's *Experiment Station Record* 45 (1921): 601–9.

RICHARD A. HAWKINS

ARMSTRONG, Barbara Nachtrieb (4 Aug. 1890–18 Jan. 1976), law professor, was born in San Francisco, California, the daughter of John Jacob Nachtrieb and Anne Day. Barbara grew up in San Francisco, traveling with her family every summer to their camp in the woods on Lake Tahoe. She received her degrees from the University of California at Berkeley (A.B. 1913; J.D. 1915; Ph.D. 1921) and taught briefly in a one-room country school between completing her bachelor's degree and entering law school.

After earning her J.D., Armstrong practiced law for a few years with a classmate, Louise Cleveland. She also served as an assistant in Berkeley's Department of Economics from 1914 to 1919 and as executive secretary of the California Social Insurance Commission from 1915 through 1919. Her experience as secretary of the commission and her interest in the relationship between law and the economy led to her doctoral work in the Department of Economics under Jessica B. Peixotto, Ira B. Cross, and Felix Flugel. She focused on social economics, social legislation, and labor. The university appointed her lecturer in law and economics in 1919. When she finished her Ph.D., she was promoted to instructor of law and economics in 1921 and then to assistant professor of economics and law in 1924. In 1928 she moved fully to the law school and was promoted to associate professor in 1929 and professor in 1935. Armstrong was the first woman appointed to the faculty of a major law school in the United States. In 1926 she had married Ian Alastair Armstrong, an importer, and they had one child. Her success in maintaining both domestic and professional commitments was manifest in her strong and loving marriage, her continued devotion to her daughter, and her impressive record of lifelong teaching and scholarship at the University of California.

Armstrong taught the history of economics, the economic history of Europe, social insurance, and crime as a social problem, and then developed graduate courses exploring the relationship between economics and family law, child labor law, and labor relations. At the university she was respected as both a gifted teacher and an excellent scholar. Her students found her passionate about the law and the people affected by the law. By expressing forthrightly her views on legal problems, she created an invigorating climate in the classroom that encouraged her students to read, discuss, and understand the law and legal scholarship, particularly in the areas affecting both professional and personal issues in their lives.

From the start of her work at the university, Armstrong was an outspoken feminist, committed to research into government policies and programs for workers and their families. During the 1910s and 1920s she produced a steady stream of articles on topics including unemployment insurance, health insurance, protective labor laws, minimum wage, and the rights of women in family law. This series of articles laid the groundwork for the areas to which she devoted the remainder of her scholarly career. Her massive study, *Insuring the Essentials: Social Insurance and Minimum Wage in Theory and Practice* (1932), was important to the field of economics and to public policy as a timely, major contribution to the debates over both minimum wage and social insurance legislation in the United States.

Armstrong's study compared U.S. minimum wage and social insurance policies with those in countries in Asia, Africa, the South Pacific, South America, North America, and Europe. She concluded that except in provisions for industrial accidents, the United States was the most backward of all the developed nations in ensuring that workers were protected from the abuses of industry or the cyclical nature of capitalist economies. In her plea to see all economic activity as part of a global economy, she defined the essentials as those programs that provided economic security to workers in the wage system of modern industry. Minimum wage and social insurance were the linchpins of an adequate government social economic program, she argued. In the United States, minimum wage protection and workmen's compensation legislation had been enacted on a state-by-state basis, leaving many individuals and families dependent on a private charity system woefully inadequate to meet their needs, particularly during economic depression. Armstrong suggested that the federal government provide constitutional protection of minimum wage legislation for women workers, who were significantly underpaid in comparison with men and without access to organized labor for help. She hoped such protection would lead eventually to acceptance of the principle of minimum wage for male workers. Her publications earned Armstrong a national reputation. In 1934 she was appointed to President Franklin D. Roosevelt's committee on economic security, directing the old-age security study and working with others to design the collection of laws that became the Social Security Act of 1935. She was disappointed then that the committee failed to provide for health insurance in the act.

Armstrong spent the 1940s and early 1950s working on the most significant study of family law in California by mid-century, *California Family Law: Persons and Domestic Relations; The Community Property System* (2 vols., 1953), which not only analyzed case and statute law in that state but also recommended numerous changes in the laws, many of which guided subsequent legal reforms. In recognition of this work and her earlier publications in the area of social insurance, Armstrong was appointed to a number of public service positions. She led an unsuccessful campaign to enact state health insurance in California in the 1940s and was part of the successful campaign to do so in the 1960s. She served in the U.S. Office of Price Administration during World War II as a vigorous and effective chief of rent enforcement for the San Francisco district. In 1959 she acted as the U.S. representative to the International Conference on Social Security and Labor Law held in Belgium. And in 1961 she was appointed consultant to the White House Conference on the Aged and Aging.

Despite this success and her obvious contributions to the law school at the University of California, Armstrong's salary was never on a par with that of her male colleagues, including those in junior positions. She received support from other women faculty in the university to redress this disparity and eventually obtained increases from the administration. But such discriminatory treatment did not inhibit her devotion to the university and to Boalt Hall. Her male colleagues perceived her as a vital member of the faculty; she devoted considerable resources to improving the climate for students and staff. Her colleagues counted on her to confront them over serious issues, to insist on open and honest discussion, and to take clear stands on principle. They also delighted in her sense of humor and admired her persistence. The university honored her with the A. F. and May T. Morrison Chair of Law in 1955. She remained a committed feminist and insisted that the university appoint more women, which was done after she retired in 1957. She continued to teach law until 1966, when she was attacked, beaten, robbed, and left for dead by two unknown assailants on the street in Berkeley in 1970. The perpetrators were never caught.

Armstrong was a woman of great strength. Despite suffering permanent physical disabilities that kept her bedridden and precluded her returning to regular teaching and from completing her planned revision of *California Family Law*, she continued to advise and encourage colleagues and former students in the law school until her death in Berkeley.

• Biographical materials on Armstrong are located in the Presidents' Papers and Personnel Files in the University Archives, Bancroft Library, University of California, Berkeley. In addition to the works mentioned above, she published numerous articles in the *California Law Review* from the 1920s through the 1960s. See also her "The Nature and Purpose of Social Insurance" and "Trends in Workmen's Compensation Legislation," *Annals of the American Academy of Political and Social Science* 170 (Nov. 1933): 1–6 and 18–20; "Workmen's Compensation," *Encyclopedia of Social Science* (1934); "Rational Old Age Security System," in *Essays in Social Economics in Honor of Jessica Blanche Peixotto* (1935); "Federal Social Security Act," *American Bar Association Journal* 21 (Dec. 1935): 792–97; and "Old Age Security Abroad: The Background of Titles II and VII of the Social Security Act," *Law and Contemporary Problems* 3 (Apr. 1936). Other sources include "Barbara Nachtrieb Armstrong, 1890–1976," *University of California in Memoriam, 1977–79* (1979); Roger J. Traynor et al., "Barbara Nachtrieb Armstrong," *California Law Review* 65 (1977): 920–36; Sandra P. Epstein, "Women and Legal Education: The Case of Boalt Hall," *Pacific Historian* 28 (Fall 1984): 4–22; Mary Cookingham, "Social Economists and Reform: Berkeley, 1906–1961," *History of Political Economy* 19 (1987): 47–65; and Edwin E. Witte, *The Development of the Social Security Act* (1962). An obituary is in the *New York Times*, 21 Jan. 1976.

MARY ANN DZUBACK

ARMSTRONG, Edwin Howard (18 Dec. 1890–31 Jan. 1954), electrical engineer and inventor, was born in New York City, the son of John Armstrong, a publisher, and Emily Smith, a teacher. Armstrong attended public schools in New York City and in Yonkers, New York, where the family moved in 1900. Fascinated by machinery, he enjoyed repairing broken toys for friends and later learned to repair automobiles. In his teens he was impressed by *The Boy's Book of Inventions* (1899) by Ray Stannard Baker and *Stories of Inventors* (1905) by Russell Doubleday, especially the chapters on Guglielmo Marconi and his invention of radiotelegraphy.

During high school Armstrong accumulated equipment for wireless communication with nearby enthusiasts. An uncle introduced him to Charles Underhill, who had invented a version of the teletype machine and who taught the boy a great deal about electricity and electromagnetic waves. Armstrong built a receiver using a piece of crystal from Underhill, and at night he could at times receive signals from as far as two thousand miles.

Armstrong entered the School of Mines, Engineering, and Chemistry at Columbia University in 1909. During his college years he devoted much of his time to wireless telegraphy and was not an outstanding student, except in courses that keenly interested him. In 1910 he built a radio antenna 125 feet tall on his parents' property in Yonkers overlooking the Hudson River.

The crystal was the primary signal detector used by early wireless telegraphers. Coming into use was an early version of the three-element (triode) vacuum tube developed in 1906 by Lee de Forest, who called it the "audion" and admitted that he could not explain its action. At the engineering school in the laboratory of professor John H. Morecroft, Armstrong in 1912 set out to understand the device. He found that the plate current oscillated steadily; he then created a circuit that used feedback to the grid circuit to amplify the signal from the antenna. This technique, called regeneration, enormously amplified the sound. With that improvement, signals from several thousand miles away could be heard clearly, without the customary use of earphones. Armstrong's design of regeneration is considered basic to all modern electronics.

After noting a hissing at the greatest amplification of the regenerated sound, Armstrong measured the sound and concluded that the equipment was itself putting out radio waves. During his last year of college he modified the circuit to behave as a transmitter. He preferred to work in isolation and to be secretive about his results, but colleagues were becoming aware of his accomplishments.

In 1913 Armstrong graduated in electrical engineering from Columbia. His professor, Michael Idvorsky Pupin, appointed him as assistant to teach wireless communication to navy personnel. After a demonstration of techniques at his home, Armstrong, at the urging of Professor Morton Arendt, filed for a patent in October 1913 for "new and useful improvements in wireless receiving systems." Apparently because he preferred secrecy, he failed to include in it any reference to the transmission of electromagnetic waves, which he included rather in his second patent application in December 1913. That same month Armstrong demonstrated his equipment to David Sarnoff and engineers of the American Marconi Company, who were highly impressed by the quality of signal from distant stations.

After receiving a patent for his first application in October 1914, Armstrong demonstrated his equipment to several companies and licensed it to Telefunken Company of Germany for $100 a month from 1915 until the United States entered World War I in April 1917. In 1916 he licensed it to the American Marconi Company for $500 a month. In 1915 de Forest applied for a patent that included regeneration, maintaining that he had discovered it accidentally in 1912. Pupin aided Armstrong in fighting de Forest's application by lending him money and by arranging for his further appointment as an assistant in the laboratory of the engineering school. Action on the patent dispute was delayed by a federal moratorium until the end of World War I, so as to ensure ample production of radio equipment for the war.

In early 1917 Armstrong volunteered in the U.S. Army Signal Corps as a captain. He was assigned to Paris, France, to find and solve problems of wireless communications of Allied services in Europe. In Paris he built improved equipment for the military forces, and he installed radio sets in airplanes, thoroughly enjoying the test flights. He became concerned with the question of whether the Germans were sending messages by way of very high frequency waves, in the range of five hundred thousand to three million cycles instead of the range of ten thousand to one hundred thousand cycles of Allied equipment. Working with Sergeant Harry W. Houck, he developed a concept discovered earlier by Reginald Aubrey Fessenden, who called it the "heterodyne principle." The researchers created a new circuit with an eight-tube receiver that transformed high frequency waves to an intermediate frequency that passed through an amplifier and a regenerative circuit to a speaker. In tests from the Eiffel Tower they received and amplified weak signals. Armstrong called his technique the superheterodyne circuit, and he filed for a patent in France in 1918 and in the United States in 1919. This equipment became basic to the tuners of all modern radio and television equipment.

Armstrong received the French Legion of Honor and a promotion to major. He continued in the Signal Corps until the fall of 1919. In his absence, in 1918 the Institute of Radio Engineers had made its first award of the Medal of Honor to Armstrong for his development of the regenerative circuit. Upon his discharge from the army, he returned to the engineering laboratory of Columbia University to continue his research.

The use of radio increased greatly after the war, and companies were vying to enter the field. In 1920 Armstrong sold his patents for regeneration and the superheterodyne circuit to Westinghouse Electric and Manufacturing Company for $335,000. The next year he developed a circuit to quench the oscillation squeal that occurred when a regeneration amplifier was set for too high a gain. He called the system superregeneration. For the rights to this system, in negotiations with Sarnoff at Radio Corporation of America (RCA, formerly the American Marconi Company), Armstrong in 1922 obtained $200,000 and 60,000 shares of RCA stock. This was accompanied by an agreement with RCA for first refusal on Armstrong inventions. When in 1923 RCA found it difficult to mass produce radios with complex circuits, Armstrong and his earlier colleague Houck worked out a technique to reduce the controls simply to two for tuning and one for volume. A wealthy man, Armstrong married Marion MacInnis, who had been Sarnoff's secretary, in 1923; they had no children.

The patent litigation with de Forest from 1915 over regeneration included American Telephone and Telegraph Company (AT&T), to whom de Forest had sold his rights. Thirteen court cases followed, which were finally ended by the Supreme Court in 1934 in favor of AT&T. It was a severe blow to Armstrong. The Institute of Radio Engineers that year refused to let him return the Medal of Honor, and members of the profession acknowledged his priority of invention. He advanced to professor of electrical engineering at Columbia University in 1934.

In continued researches Armstrong concentrated on developing a radio that would not be affected by static from electrical storms. From 1930 to 1933 he took out five basic patents on such a system. It had required extensive changes in the radio transmitter by varying the frequency rather than the amplitude of the transmitted signal and then a modification of the receiver to clip off noise spikes and recover the original audio signal. He called the result frequency-modulated, now known as FM. Armstrong set up a station using frequency modulation in 1940. The next year the Franklin Institute awarded him its Franklin Medal, primarily for his early work on regeneration.

During World War II the U.S. military used FM radio communication extensively. Armstrong did research for the U.S. Signal Corps on long-range radar, which led to the demonstration in 1946 of a radio signal reflected from the moon, the first proof that FM waves could penetrate the ionosphere. As FM came into commercial use after World War II, Armstrong was frustrated by actions of the Federal Communications Commission over new station frequencies, which made earlier radio equipment obsolete and were opposed by radio manufacturers but were to the advantage of the television industry. In 1948 he sued RCA for their use of his patents on FM. In 1953 he and John Bose developed a method for multiplexing radio signals, which made stereo broadcasting possible.

In 1948 Armstrong filed lawsuits against several companies on charges of infringing his FM patents. In the next few years he realized that multiple lawsuits would continue for a long time, deliberately delayed by large companies while he remained a lone individual in the battle. Frustrated and in declining health, he took his own life by jumping from his apartment window in New York City. His widow eventually won twenty-one patent infringement suits and $10 million in damages.

Armstrong's pioneering developments led to faultless clarity of sound in radio, television, and space communications.

• Armstrong's archival records are in the Armstrong Memorial Research Foundation of Columbia University. Some of his papers on his inventions are "Some Recent Developments in the Audion Receiver," *Proceedings of the Institute of Radio Engineers* 3 (Sept. 1915): 215–46; "A New Method of Receiving Weak Signals for Short Waves," *Proceedings of the Radio Club of America* (Dec. 1919); "The Super-Heterodyne: Its Origin, Development, and Some Recent Improvements," *Proceedings of the Institute of Radio Engineers* 12 (1924): 539–52; "A Method of Reducing Disturbances in Radio Signaling by a System of Frequency Modulation," *Proceedings of the Institute of Radio Engineers* 24 (1936): 689–740; and "Frequency Modulation and Its Future Uses," *Annals of the Academy of Political and Social Science* (Jan. 1941): 153–59. Biographical material on Armstrong and on the development of radio is in Tom Lewis, *Empire of the Air: The Men Who Made Radio* (1991). An account of Armstrong's accomplishments is in Thomas S. W. Lewis, "Radio Revolutionary," *American Heritage of Invention and Technology* 1 (Fall 1985): 34–41. A discussion of the use of frequency modulation is in Don V. Erickson, *Armstrong's Fight for FM Broadcasting* (1973). An obituary is in the *New York Times*, 2 Feb. 1954.

ELIZABETH NOBLE SHOR

ARMSTRONG, George Dod (15 Sept. 1813–11 May 1899), minister and author, was born in Morris County, New Jersey, the son of Amzi Armstrong, a minister, and Polly Dod. After graduating from Princeton College in 1832, Armstrong taught school for three and a half years. Following graduation from Union Theological Seminary in Prince Edward County, Virginia, in 1837, he served as professor of general and agricultural chemistry and geology at Washington College (now Washington and Lee University) in Lexington, Virginia, from 1838 to 1851. For the next forty-eight years he pastored the First Presbyterian Church of Norfolk, Virginia. While conducting this long and effective ministry in Norfolk, Armstrong wrote on a wide variety of topics. His more than twenty books, published sermons, and addresses influenced southern opinion about many aspects of Christian theology and experience in the late nineteenth century.

During the 1850s Armstrong helped battle a yellow fever epidemic, which in 1855 took the lives of many residents of Norfolk including Armstrong's first wife (name unknown) and oldest child. He worked long hours aiding the afflicted and almost died from the disease; his *The Summer of the Pestilence* (1856) describes the devastating effects of the epidemic. In *The Christian Doctrine of Slavery* (1857) he argued in response to the writings of Albert Barnes (?–1870), a Presbyterian pastor in Philadelphia, that slavery was not evil, but rather a positive good. Armstrong contended that the Bible did not denounce owning slaves as a sin; that the apostles received slaveholders into the church without instructing them to release their slaves; that Paul sent a fugitive slave, Onesimus, back to serve his Christian master; and that the apostles repeatedly taught the proper duties of both masters and slaves and instructed other church leaders to do the same. The book provoked a controversy that led to the publication the next year of *A Discussion of Slaveholding; Three Letters to a Conservative by George D. Armstrong, D.D. of Virginia, and Three Conservative Replies by C. Van Rensselaer, D.D., of New Jersey*. The controversy over biblical teaching on slavery that is reflected in these works contributed to the split of the Old School Presbyterian church into northern and southern branches in 1857. In 1858 he married Lucretia Reid.

During the Civil War Armstrong remained in Norfolk, preaching wholeheartedly on behalf of the southern cause. His published sermon, "The Good Hand of Our God upon Us; a Thanksgiving Sermon, Preached on the Occasion of the Victory of Manassas" (1861), expressed his conviction that God was with the Confederacy in its fight for independence. When southern forces evacuated Norfolk during the war, he chose to remain behind. He took the loyalty oath required by the federal government, but his refusal to use his pulpit to support the government led to his being forced to do menial labor and to a period of solitary confinement at Fort Hatteras.

Armstrong wrote several theological works that helped to shape and explain southern Presbyterian views. Especially significant were *The Theology of Christian Experience* (1858) and *The Sacraments of the New Testament as Instituted by Christ* (1880). The first book is a traditional Reformed discussion of humanity's religious nature; the nature of faith, sin and the Fall, the Atonement, regeneration, conversion, and the Christian life. The second book defends a Calvinist understanding of the sacraments as opposed to Baptist and Roman Catholic views.

During the second half of the nineteenth century Armstrong was the most highly respected authority within the Presbyterian church in the United States on the relationship between theology and science. He argued in numerous lectures and papers and most importantly in *The Two Books of Nature and Revelation Collated* (1886) that evolution was an atheistic hypothesis that could not be reconciled with the Bible. In this book he attacked the theories of Herbert Spencer, Charles Darwin, Thomas Huxley, and James Woodrow of Columbia Theological Seminary. He defended Mosaic cosmogony, arguing that the first two chapters of Genesis were actual history and that God had directly created Adam and Eve. Accepting evolutionary theory, he contended, would undermine belief in the inspiration of the Bible and lead to the denial of the doctrine of the Fall. He presented the majority report of the 1886 Southern Presbyterian General Assembly, which repudiated Woodrow's theistic evolution position.

During his many years of service to Washington College, the First Presbyterian Church of Norfolk, and the Presbyterian church in the United States, Armstrong displayed a strong dedication to duty and great perseverance. Never one to shrink from a battle, he staunchly and passionately defended what he loved—the South and classic Reformed theology. He died in Norfolk.

• Another characteristic work by Armstrong is "The Pentateuchal Story of Creation," *Presbyterian Quarterly* 2 (Oct. 1888): 344–68. For further information on Armstrong see Alfred Nevin, *Encyclopedia of the Presbyterian Church in the United States of America* (1884); Gary Scott Smith, *The Seeds of Secularization: Calvinism, Culture and Pluralism in America, 1870–1915* (1985); and Ernest Trice Thompson, *Presbyterians in the South*, vol 2: *1861–1890* (1973).

GARY SCOTT SMITH

ARMSTRONG, Hamilton Fish (7 Apr. 1893–24 Apr. 1973), editor, was born in New York City, the son of David Maitland Armstrong, an artist and diplomat, and Helen Neilson. Reared in New York City, Armstrong attended the Gilman Country School, Baltimore, Maryland. He entered Princeton University, from which he received his B.A. in 1916. For part of 1916 and 1917 he directed publicity for the *New Republic* and in 1918 published *The Book of New York Verse*.

When, in 1917, the United States entered World War I, Armstrong received a commission in the regular army. Later that year he was made an aide to the Serbian War Mission in the United States, a group seeking equipment and volunteers. In December 1918 he was appointed acting military attaché to the American Legation in Belgrade, a post he held until July 1919. Also in 1918 he married Helen MacGregor Byrne, with whom he had one child. In 1920 he joined the editorial staff of the *New York Evening Post*, then served for a year as the *Post*'s special correspondent in Eastern Europe.

In 1921, when the Council on Foreign Relations (CFR) was founded, Armstrong became executive director, holding the post until 1928. From 1944 to 1958 he was also its president. Thanks in part to Armstrong's influence, the CFR was a moderate body, drawing on an elite membership of establishment political, business, and academic leaders and seeking to promote a "middle-of-the-road" internationalism, one that seldom involved schemes for universal pacifism or world government. Always a Wilsonian in his worldview, in 1923 he was made a trustee of the Woodrow Wilson Foundation, after which he became vice president (1928–1930) and president (1935–1937).

Also in 1922 Armstrong became the first managing editor of the CFR quarterly journal *Foreign Affairs*. In January 1928, after the death of the editor, Harvard historian Archibald Cary Coolidge, Armstrong became editor, a position he held until 1972. Under his leadership the journal achieved preeminence as a platform for world leaders and as a forum for a great variety of American policymakers, including Elihu Root, George F. Kennan, and Henry Kissinger.

Armstrong himself contributed forty-nine articles to the journal and wrote several books as well. A frequent traveler overseas and possessing many friends among Europe's rulers, he often drew upon firsthand observations. In *The New Balkans* (1926) and *Where the East Begins* (1929), he summarized postwar developments in southeastern Europe. His *Hitler's Reich—the First Phase* (1933) began with the words, "A people has disappeared." Armstrong had just been the first American ever to interview Hitler. *Europe between Wars?* (1934) and *We or They: Two Worlds in Conflict* (1936) discussed circumstances that could lead to another major conflict, such as the Dollfuss regime in Austria and totalitarianism in Germany and Italy.

In 1927 he warned against an overreliance on the Kellogg-Briand Pact outlawing war, claiming that it could not replace serious grappling with the underlying causes of war. In the early 1930s he found the world depression rooted in economic nationalism and called for the gradual lowering of U.S. tariffs. In 1936, with international lawyer Allen W. Dulles, he wrote *Can We Be Neutral?*, in which the authors traced the evolution of current U.S. neutrality policy as reflected in the Neutrality Act of 1935 and then made a series of recommendations concerning the ideal neutral legislation: restricting American travel on belligerent ships and on any ships entering a war zone; forbidding foreign powers to float loans in the United States; giving the president discretion to impose embargoes on shipments of goods useful in war; permitting other trade at the risk of the shipper. The United States, wrote the authors, must be in a position where it could "use its influence on specific occasions to turn the balance in favor of peace." In 1939, in *Can America Stay Neutral?*, the authors updated the work, adding a summary of neutrality legislation enacted since 1936.

In 1938 Armstrong divorced his wife; he married author Carmen Barnes in 1945 and, after another divorce, wed Christa von Tippelskirch in 1951. In the late 1930s, as Europe moved toward war, he wrote two journalistic accounts. *When There Is No Peace* (1939) offered an account of the Czech crisis and the subsequent Nazi putsch. *Chronology of Failure: The Last Days of the French Republic* (1940) described the conquest of France in light of Armstrong's personal observations made shortly before Paris fell. Three months after World War II broke out he launched a major CFR project, War and Peace Studies, which eventually produced some 250 memoranda analyzing the conflict and its possible aftermath.

From 1942 to 1944 Armstrong was a member of the State Department Advisory Committee on Post-War Foreign Problems. On 23 September 1944 he was appointed special assistant to Ambassador John G. Winant in London, possessing ministerial rank and serving as adviser on matters relating to the European Advisory Commission. Late that December he was appointed a special adviser to Secretary of State Edward R. Stettinius, Jr. In 1945 he was adviser to the U.S. delegation at the San Francisco conference establishing the United Nations.

In 1947 Armstrong's book *The Calculated Risk* was published. In it he called for prompt adoption of the Marshall Plan for European recovery, seeking an immediate allocation to cover four years rather than annual installments, and endorsed mandatory rationing for Americans. The United States, he continued, should renounce its right to veto any collective action desired by the United Nations. Other powers, he maintained, would follow suit though there was a "calculated risk" that such action would bitterly antagonize the Soviets. Four years later, in *Tito and Goliath*, Armstrong called for the continuation of Western overtures to the Yugoslav dictator; his comments were based on a trip to that nation the previous year as well as personal contact with Tito himself.

In his later years Armstrong wrote memoirs of his New York boyhood (*Those Days* [1963]) and of his life in the 1920s (*Peace and Counterpeace: From Wilson to Hitler* [1971]), and he edited a fiftieth-anniversary anthology of *Foreign Affairs* articles (*Fifty Years of Foreign Affairs* [1972]). In 1968 he opposed continued involvement in the Vietnam War, a conflict that, he said, wasted American manpower and isolated the United States from other nations. He died in New York City.

A man of easygoing charm, Armstrong bore a commanding appearance. Bushy eyebrows, thick brown hair, riveting eyes, and a broad moustache conveyed a tone of distinction. A quintessential member of the foreign policy establishment, he used the CFR and *Foreign Affairs* to convey the establishment's views to the attentive public. While not an original theorist of international relations, Armstrong was an articulate and powerful proponent of mainstream internationalism for over fifty years.

• Although there are no Armstrong papers per se, there is much Armstrong correspondence in the papers of the Council of Foreign Relations, in possession of the CFR in New York City. A full-length biography has yet to be published; however, for Armstrong's life and views, see the books cited in the text, especially *Those Days* and *Peace and Counterpeace*. Material on Armstrong is in Robert D. Schulzinger, *The Wise Men of Foreign Affairs: The History of the Council on Foreign Relations* (1984). An obituary is in the *New York Times*, 25 Apr. 1973.

JUSTUS D. DOENECKE

ARMSTRONG, Harry (22 July 1879–28 Feb. 1951), vaudeville performer, pianist, and popular composer, was born Henry Worthington Armstrong in Somerville, Massachusetts, the son of Henry Armstrong, a piano salesman, and Elizabeth Stuart. Armstrong competed as a professional boxer before joining a street corner vocal quartet in Boston in 1896. He moved to New York in 1898 and played piano in a restaurant in Coney Island and later at the Sans Souci Music Hall in Manhattan. He composed and performed his own songs, many of which were published by the firm of M. Witmark, where Armstrong worked as a rehearsal pianist.

Armstrong's most famous composition, "Sweet Adeline," was rejected by Boston publishers under its original title, "My Old New England Home." After he had moved to New York, Armstrong searched for a lyricist to set new words to the melody, but he had little success at first. Charles Lawlor, who wrote "The Sidewalks of New York," failed to produce suitable words, as did future mayor Jimmy Walker, with whom Armstrong composed "Goodbye, Eyes of Blue" for the vaudeville stage. Richard Gerard Husch then proposed his lyric "Sweet Rosalie," but the combination was rejected by several publishers, including Witmark. Finally, Armstrong and Husch hit upon the idea of using the name Adeline in the lyrics (after the opera singer Adelina Patti), and Witmark published the song in 1903. "Sweet Adeline" received many vaudeville performances and was turned into a hit by such groups as the Quaker City Four, who performed it at Oscar Hammerstein's Victoria Theatre in New York. The song later boosted the 1906 and 1910 campaigns of John F. "Honey Fitz" Fitzgerald, who ran successfully for mayor of Boston. "Sweet Adeline," which had sold more than two million sheet-music copies by the middle of the twentieth century, has been included in numerous films and has remained a mainstay of the barbershop quartet repertory. Despite the association implied in the title, *Sweet Adeline*, the 1929 operetta by Jerome Kern that starred Helen Morgan, does not include Armstrong's song.

Although "Sweet Adeline" remains Armstrong's most popular sentimental ballad, he was also known for "The Frisco Rag," "I Love You Just the Same, Sweet Adeline," "The Little Grand Daughter of Sweet Adeline," and "Nellie Dean," which was popular on the British music hall circuit. Armstrong continued to perform as a vaudeville singer in the United States and Canada as part of the team of Armstrong & Clark, which popularized the Harry Von Tilzer song "I Love, I Love, I Love My Wife, But Oh, You Kid!" During World War I, Armstrong sang and played for troops at camps and hospitals and also performed for the merchant marine.

In 1937, after his performing career ended, Armstrong joined forces with Frank Sherman at the Broadway booking agency United Entertainment Productions, where he worked from 1937 to 1949. His contribution to popular music was recognized with his election to membership in the American Society of Composers, Authors, and Publishers (ASCAP) in 1929. Armstrong married Addie Harris Russey in 1943. He died in New York City.

Armstrong was a popularizer rather than an innovator in the sentimental ballad genre. While his music broke no stylistic ground, his songs were loved for their wide audience appeal.

• For information on Armstrong's life and music, see Nicholas Tawa, *The Way to Tin Pan Alley, American Popular Song, 1866–1910* (1990); David A. Jasen, *Tin Pan Alley: The Composers, the Songs, the Performers, and Their Times* (1988); Isidore Witmark and Isaac Goldberg, *From Ragtime to Swingtime* (1939); Douglas Gilbert, *Lost Chords* (1942); and Sigmund Spaeth, *A History of Popular Music in America* (1948). See also the *ASCAP Biographical Dictionary*, the files in the ASCAP Collection in New York, and the obituary in the *New York Times*.

BARBARA TISCHLER

ARMSTRONG, Henry (12 Dec. 1912–22 Oct. 1988), boxer, was born Henry Jackson, Jr., near Columbus, Mississippi, the son of Henry Jackson. His mother, whose name is unknown, was a full-blooded Iroquois, and his father was of mixed Indian, Irish, and black ancestry. He was the eleventh child in a family of sharecroppers. When he was four years old his family moved to St. Louis, Missouri, where his father and oldest brothers worked in the food-processing industry. His mother died a few years later, after which he was reared by his paternal grandmother. He graduated from Toussaint L'Ouverture Grammar School and Vashon High School, working during his school years as a pinboy at a bowling alley and becoming interalley bowling champion in midtown St. Louis. He gained his first boxing experience by winning a competition among the pinboys.

Lacking funds to attend college, Armstrong worked at a series of unskilled jobs. At the "colored" Young Men's Christian Association, he came under the tutelage of a former boxer, Harry Armstrong, who gave him the ring name of "Melody Jackson" after hearing him singing in the shower. He had several amateur fights in St. Louis and then left with Harry Armstrong for Pittsburgh, where he trained to become a professional. Ill-nourished and badly trained, he was knocked out in his first professional fight in July 1931 but won his second on points. He returned to St. Louis and then with Armstrong went (probably in the fall of 1931) to Los Angeles, where he fought as an amateur boxer, using the name "Henry Armstrong."

Managed by Tom Cox, Henry Armstrong had almost a hundred amateur fights in California and won nearly all. Meanwhile, he set up a shoeshine stand and from 1931 to 1934 mainly earned his living by shining shoes. In 1932 Cox sold Armstrong's contract to Wirt Ross; the boxer became a professional again, losing his first two battles on points before becoming a consistent winner. A 5′5½″ featherweight, he fought mostly in Los Angeles, with occasional trips to other California cities. In November 1934 Armstrong had his first major fight, losing a close decision in Mexico City to Baby Arizmendi, who claimed the world featherweight championship. In January 1935 he fought Arizmendi for the California-Mexico version of the featherweight title but lost. Later that year he beat former flyweight champion Midget Wolgast in Oakland, California, and in August 1936 he defeated Arizmendi to claim the featherweight title. Armstrong won his last twelve fights in 1936, including a victory over Mike Belloise, another featherweight contender. Late that year Ross sold his contract to New York manager Eddie Mead; the actual cash for the sale was supplied by entertainers Al Jolson and George Raft.

In 1937 Armstrong had twenty-seven fights and won them all, twenty-six by knockout, including several matches in New York City. On 29 October he knocked out Petey Sarron to win the world featherweight title at Madison Square Garden. This remarkable series of victories was followed in 1938 by fourteen consecutive wins, ten by knockout, and the acquisition of two more world titles. Armstrong challenged lightweight champion Lou Ambers to a title fight, but Ambers's manager refused the match. Then, in an audacious move, Armstrong challenged welterweight champion Barney Ross, and they met in Long Island City on 31 May. Armstrong severely trounced Ross on points in fifteen rounds and won the world welterweight title although weighing only 133½ pounds (less than the lightweight division limit). On 17 August at Madison Square Garden he defeated Ambers in fifteen rounds and won the lightweight title. Armstrong held the championship of three divisions until November, when he voluntarily relinquished the featherweight title, which he had never defended. He successfully defended his welterweight title twice that year against Ceferino Garcia and Al Manfredo.

Armstrong's manner of fighting was aptly described by sportswriter and cartoonist Ted Carroll: "Armstrong's hurricane style . . . has amazed veteran ring observers for many reasons. Although he is forever pressing forward, he sheds punches with a peculiar movement of head and shoulders like the proverbial duck sheds water. His energy and endurance seem limitless as he . . . forces his opponents to break ground with a ceaseless barrage of punches tossed with power and precision from all angles." Armstrong's style invariably resulted in action-filled, exciting fights.

Armstrong frequently was handicapped by the loss of points or rounds due to fouling. His head-down windmill style often resulted in low blows, butts, and other infractions. This problem cost him the lightweight title in his second fight with Ambers at Yankee Stadium on 22 August 1939, when referee Arthur Donovan deducted five rounds for fouls. However, Armstrong successfully defended his welterweight title eleven times in 1939, including victories over Arizmendi, Davey Day, Lew Feldman, and Ernie Roderick.

Armstrong's amazing series of successes continued in 1940, including six more successful defenses of the welterweight title. Furthermore, he fought a draw with Ceferino Garcia for the middleweight title, 160 pounds weight limit, in Los Angeles on 1 March, although weighing only 142 pounds. Had he not been penalized two rounds by referee George Blake for "rough tactics," Armstrong would have held a fourth world title.

At last, on 4 October 1941 at Madison Square Garden, Fritzie Zivic found the answer to overcoming Armstrong's style and captured the welterweight title. Zivic won decisively by throwing right uppercuts as Armstrong advanced, dramatically flooring the champion at the final bell, as the arena lights suddenly failed. In a return match on 17 January 1941, before a record crowd at the Garden, Zivic pummeled Armstrong even worse, stopping him in twelve rounds. Armstrong made a financially successful comeback in 1942 and continued boxing until 1945; although winning many fights, he was never again a serious title contender.

Armstrong lost his earnings to high living and excessive generosity. He served a brief stint in the army near the end of World War II and managed other fighters. Then he began to drink excessively before experiencing a religious conversion in 1949 and becoming a Baptist minister shortly afterward. He spent the remaining years of his life as an evangelist and founded and directed the Henry Armstrong Youth Foundation in Los Angeles. He had married Willa Mae Shandy in 1934 and the couple had one child. Later, he married a second time, but his wife's name and the date of their marriage are unrecorded. In his later years he suffered from many medical problems, some of them boxing-related, such as cataracts and mental impairment. He died in Los Angeles. He was an inaugural inductee into the International Boxing Hall of Fame in 1990.

• The main source of information on Armstrong's life is his *Gloves, Glory and God: An Autobiography* (1956). Similar information is presented in Nat Fleischer, *Black Dynamite*, vol. 2 (1938). His record is available in the 1986–1987 edition of Herbert Goldman, ed., *The Ring Record Book.* Fleischer's accounts of Armstrong's most important fights are in the *Ring* magazine, particularly his fights with Barney Ross (Aug. 1938), Lou Ambers (Oct. 1938 and Nov. 1939), and Fritzie Zivic (Dec. 1940 and Apr. 1941). Ted Carroll, "New Terror of the Ring," *Ring*, Oct. 1937, pp. 26–27, includes an excellent description of his boxing style. An obituary appears in the *New York Times*, 25 Oct. 1988.

LUCKETT V. DAVIS

ARMSTRONG, John (13 Oct. 1717–9 Mar. 1795), soldier, surveyor, and member of the Continental Congress, was born in County Fermanagh, Ulster, Ireland. The identities of his Scotch-Irish parents and circumstances of his youth are unclear, but his father may have been named James. A trained surveyor, John Armstrong evidently received some education fairly early in life. Sometime in the mid-1740s Armstrong immigrated to America, settling initially in Delaware and then in Pennsylvania, where he worked as a surveyor. It was probably at some point after his arrival in America that he married Rebeckah Armstrong. The couple had two sons (the younger, also named John, with whom the elder Armstrong is sometimes confused, served as secretary of war under James Madison). In 1749 Armstrong was elected to represent York County in the Pennsylvania Assembly.

As a legislator, Armstrong came to the attention of the province's proprietors, the Penn family, and would subsequently play a leading role in the development of western Pennsylvania. He became the Penns' surveyor and agent in the sizable portion of the province west of the Susquehanna River. He moved to the frontier town of Carlisle, surveyed large tracts for the proprietors, and in turn received land grants of his own. Elected in 1751 to represent recently formed Cumberland County in the assembly, Armstrong saw to it that other men friendly to the Penns followed him to the legislature. He also served as magistrate, justice of the peace, and—by 1757—judge of the court of common pleas, being for a time the sole judicial authority on his side of the Susquehanna. In 1754 he represented Pennsylvania in its dealings with Connecticut regarding the intrusion of settlers from that colony into the Wyoming Valley region of Pennsylvania. A Presbyterian elder in Carlisle, Armstrong was in 1773 a founding trustee of an academy that became Dickinson College. In the absence of John Dickinson, he served as president pro tempore of that institution.

Beyond Cumberland County, Armstrong would become best known as a soldier, owing largely to the role he played in operations against the French and American Indians in western Pennsylvania. In 1755 he helped survey and cut supply routes across the mountains for British general Edward Braddock. The same year he persuaded the Quaker colony to establish its first chain of frontier forts, stretching from the Maryland border to the Susquehanna. As commander of provincial forces west of that river, Armstrong in the summer of 1756 planned and executed the first offensive action against the Indians following Braddock's defeat near Fort Duquesne. Marching 250 men to Kittanning, a major Delaware Indian stronghold on the Allegheny River north of Fort Duquesne, Armstrong on 8 September launched a dawn attack, burning the town, destroying stockpiled ammunition, and killing the Delaware war leader "Captain Jacobs." The defeat prompted another Indian leader, Teedyuscung, to sue for peace, thus ending—for a time—Indian assaults on the white frontier. Armstrong, who lost seventeen men and was himself wounded, received the formal thanks of the city of Philadelphia for his victory. In 1758 he led Pennsylvania troops in General John Forbes's advance on Fort Duquesne. Armstrong himself raised the flag over the fort after the French had abandoned it. Five years later, during the renewal of Indian warfare known as Pontiac's Rebellion, Armstrong again commanded Pennsylvania troops, leading 300 men north against Indian settlements on the western branch of the Susquehanna. While fighting no pitched battles, they put the Indians to flight and put their villages and provisions to the torch. Early in 1764 Armstrong served as a mediator between provincial officials and the so-called Paxton Boys, backcountry settlers enraged that the province was not doing more to fight Indians.

At the same time as antiproprietary forces were gaining strength in Pennsylvania in the 1760s, Armstrong's status started to slip with the Penns. Officials began to question the quality and propriety of some of his surveys. Armstrong left the Penns' service in 1770. By 1774, though not a radical, Armstrong supported resistance to British imperial policy. That year he was appointed to the Cumberland County Committee of Correspondence by a meeting called in support of the citizens of Boston. As a member of that body, he proposed that his protégé James Wilson represent Pennsylvania in Congress. With the outbreak of war, Armstrong went back into uniform, initially as commander of county forces, then, in March 1776, as the first brigadier general commissioned by Congress. He commanded some of the Continental troops defending

Charleston, South Carolina, then returned to Pennsylvania to recruit. After a number of his fellow officers were promoted to major general, Armstrong resigned his command in April 1777 and was immediately appointed a brigadier general of the Pennsylvania militia. Armstrong's leadership of Pennsylvania troops against British regulars did not win him the same sort of acclaim that he had enjoyed as an Indian fighter. On the far left of George Washington's line at Brandywine, his troops saw no action. At Germantown in October 1777, Armstrong's militia men were to feint at the British left flank to divert attention from Washington's main attack, but they were held back by a line of Hessians and had to withdraw from the field without accomplishing that objective. By the time of the Valley Forge encampment of 1777–1778 Armstrong had been promoted to major general of state militia.

In 1778 Armstrong was elected to the Continental Congress, where he served from February 1779 until August 1780. Citing the "Pride, Ambition & intrigue" and "annimossitys, divisions & destruction of time," Armstrong told Horatio Gates that "compared to Congress in its present attitude, I call the Army a Bed of ease, a Pillow of Down" (Smith, vol. 12, p. 280). Known as a radical within the Pennsylvania delegation, Armstrong was an outspoken proponent of price controls, opposed the recall of diplomat Arthur Lee, and thought exemplary punishment ought to be dealt out to "the more attrocious" Tories (Brunhouse, p. 50). By the mid-1780s, however, he was willing to support revision of the state constitution that drove Pennsylvania conservatives to distraction, and he also backed the adoption of the federal Constitution. Armstrong, who had persuaded Congress to establish the army's principal ordnance and commissary installation at Carlisle, died there at age seventy-seven.

A power to be reckoned with in the Pennsylvania backcountry and a military leader in three conflicts, Armstrong was praised by George Washington for his spirit, his courage, and his "enterprize against the Indians" (Stradley, p. 119).

• There are Armstrong letters at the Historical Society of Pennsylvania in Philadelphia; the Dickinson College Library in Carlisle; and the private Rokeby Collection in Barrytown, N.Y. Some of his correspondence is reproduced in Paul H. Smith, ed., *Letters of Delegates to Congress, 1774–1789*, vols. 12–16 (1985–1989). An Armstrong letter describing his attack on Kittanning is reproduced as "Col. John Armstrong's Account of Expedition against Kittanning, 1756," *Pennsylvania Archives*, vol. 2 (1856), pp. 767–73. There are also useful documents in *The Papers of Henry Bouquet*, ed. S. K. Stevens et al. (1951–1972) and *The Susquehanna Company Papers*, vols. 1–2, ed. Julian P. Boyd (1930). Robert Grant Crist, "John Armstrong: Proprietors' Man" (Ph.D. diss., Pennsylvania State Univ., 1981), covers his career through 1774. See also Milton Flower, *John Armstrong: First Citizen of Carlisle* (1971); William Darlington, "Major-General John Armstrong," *Pennsylvania Magazine of History and Biography* 1 (1877): 183–87; Wilson Stradley, "General John Armstrong," *Valley Forge Journal* 5 (1990): 117–28; C. Edward Skeen, *John Armstrong, Jr., 1758–1843: A Biography* (1981); and Robert Brunhouse, *The Counter-Revolution in Pennsylvania 1776–1790* (1942).

ROBERT GRANT CRIST
PATRICK G. WILLIAMS

ARMSTRONG, John (20 Apr. 1755–4 Feb. 1816), soldier, was born in New Jersey, the son of Thomas Armstrong and Jane Hamilton. Little is known about his early life and education. He joined the Continental army on 11 September 1777 and served as an officer in the twelfth and third Pennsylvania regiments.

Armstrong commanded the outpost at Wyoming, Pennsylvania, in 1784 and then moved west to Fort Pitt in 1785–1786. During the conflict between the United States and the Native American tribes in the Old Northwest, Armstrong, then an ensign, was part of the force patrolling the Ohio River. As settlers clamored for more and more western land, Armstrong was one of the army officers assigned to discourage violation of treaties with the Ohio tribes. In April of 1785 he led a detachment down the Ohio and found the frontier farmers crossing the river in utter disregard of all agreements. For the next five years he was stationed at several outposts along the Ohio from Fort Pitt to Louisville, as the thinly stretched western army sought to deal with conflicts between the Indians and the western settlers.

The army to which Armstrong belonged suffered a lack of accurate, firsthand information about the western frontier. In 1790 General Josiah Harmar, the commander, sought to fill that gap by sending Armstrong on a tour of the west. Apparently Armstrong and two Native American guides went down the Ohio and for a distance up the Missouri, into Spanish territory, before French trappers urged them to turn back or risk death at the hands of hostile tribes. On the return journey, Armstrong, then a captain, explored briefly in Illinois and Indiana before rejoining General Harmar.

Armstrong's military experience was needed in the summer of 1790 as an expedition was being planned to move northwest from Fort Washington toward present-day Fort Wayne, Indiana, to destroy the Miami villages. In a sense the army was caught in a double bind. On the one hand they were responsible for patrolling the sievelike frontier to prevent violations of existing land and boundary agreements; on the other they were looked to for protection when such incursions prompted raids against the settlements. Soldiers had been insulted by the settlers and attacked by Indian raiders. At the same time the federal troops in the west were treated poorly by the national government, which not only had cut their pay but also had allowed unscrupulous contractors to cheat on provision contracts. Despite all this, the army was willing to fight, but because the number of regulars was relatively small, the expedition had to rely on several hundred militia from Kentucky. The training and leadership of frontier militia worried veterans like Armstrong, who understood the discipline necessary to carry out a successful military campaign. Unfortunately, all that

Armstrong feared came true. On 18 October 1790, Armstrong and thirty of his men were detached to accompany a unit of 150 Kentucky militia under Colonel John Hardin in an attack against an Indian settlement on the Eel River. When the native warriors ambushed their pursuers, "from the dastardly conduct of the militia, the troops were obliged to retreat." As Armstrong explained: "Many of the militia [including the commander] threw away their arms without firing a shot, ran through the federal troops and threw them in disorder." This disastrous action cost Armstrong his sergeant and twenty-one of the thirty men he had taken on this expedition. When Armstrong and the remnant were forced to flee for their lives, Armstrong at first hid beneath a fallen tree, then took refuge in the middle of an icy pond for seven hours, and finally slipped far enough away from the enemy camp to build a fire and dry. Only after several days of circuitous movement was he able to rejoin the badly dispirited expedition. Despite this personal military disaster, Armstrong did not blame the expedition's failure on his commander, General Harmar. When Armstrong was called on to testify during Harmar's court-martial in 1791, he attributed his predicament to the collapse of the militia and the military incompetence of Harmar's subordinates.

After spending some time recruiting in the East during 1791, Armstrong returned to the Ohio Valley, where he served as the commandant at Fort Hamilton until 1793. His new commander was James Wilkinson, to whom Armstrong wrote in 1792 about continuing difficulties with the tribes living along the Wabash. Life in the army remained demanding and dangerous, and, given these rigors, it is not surprising that the next year Armstrong resigned his commission.

In 1793 Armstrong married the daughter of Judge William Goforth, an influential Ohio pioneer, and settled near Cincinnati. Thanks to his loyal service to the nation during the Ohio Indian wars, he was named treasurer of the Northwest Territory in 1796. He also served as a judge in Hamilton County, Ohio, and as a magistrate in Columbia, Ohio, from 1796 until 1814. The last two years of his life were spent on a farm in Clark County, Indiana, where he died.

• Details regarding Armstrong's life and career can be found in *American State Papers, Class V, Military Affairs*, vol. 1 (1832); James McBride, *Pioneer Biography*, vol. 1 (1869); and Charles Cist, *The Cincinnati Miscellany; or, Antiquities of the West*, vol. 1 (1845). A useful discussion of Indian policy in the late eighteenth century is Wiley Sword, *President Washington's Indian War: The Struggle for the Old Northwest, 1790–1795* (1985).

JAMES H. O'DONNELL III

ARMSTRONG, John, Jr. (25 Nov. 1758–1 Apr. 1843), soldier and politician, was born in Carlisle, Pennsylvania, the son of John Armstrong and Rebecca Lyon. His father, a surveyor and a prominent figure on the Pennsylvania frontier, achieved fame as the "Hero of Kittanning" during the Seven Years' War when he destroyed a particularly troublesome Indian village; he later served as an officer in the revolutionary war. Armstrong attended the College of New Jersey (later Princeton) for two years but left in 1776 to join the Continental army. He served successively as aide-de-camp to Brigadier General Hugh Mercer and Major General Horatio Gates with the rank of major, and he participated in the battles of Princeton, Trenton, and Saratoga.

Near the end of the war, in the camp at Newburgh, New York, Armstrong, encouraged by members of Gates's staff, penned anonymously the controversial "Newburgh Addresses," intended to pressure Congress into redressing the army's grievances, particularly the lack of pay. These writings were widely interpreted as challenging General George Washington's authority and inciting the army to insurrection against Congress. Washington intervened to quash a supposed conspiracy. Although he eventually understood Armstrong's motive and forgave him, the onus attached to Armstrong's authorship was detrimental to his future career. It was raised against him on several occasions when he came before Congress for confirmation to office.

Following the war, Armstrong became secretary of the Pennsylvania Supreme Executive Council, an important position in the state government. In 1784, he became embroiled in the so-called Pennamite War with Connecticut settlers who claimed the Wyoming Valley of Pennsylvania. Now adjutant general of Pennsylvania, Armstrong favored a policy of repression that only exacerbated the situation; it was not settled until much later, generally in favor of the Connecticut claimants. His political career, however, was not affected. He was selected as a delegate to the Annapolis Convention of 1786; in 1787 he served as a representative to the Confederation Congress.

Armstrong was chosen as one of the three judges of the newly created Northwest Territory, but he declined, in part because he had met and become engaged to Alida Livingston, sister of Chancellor Robert R. Livingston (1746–1813) of New York. Armstrong married Alida Livingston in 1789, thereby coming into possession of approximately 25,000 acres along the Hudson River, where he settled among the Livingston family as a gentleman farmer. His connection to the Livingston family, he believed, barred his selection as a delegate to the Constitutional Convention and later his election as a senator from Pennsylvania.

Armstrong retained his interest in politics and formed a strong friendship with Ambrose Spencer, a rising force in New York politics. Spencer's influence and the Livingston family connection led Armstrong to join the Republican party and were instrumental in his selection to the U.S. Senate in 1800. Armstrong also had denounced the Federalist party by writing an anonymous pamphlet attacking the Alien and Sedition Acts.

Armstrong's Senate career was undistinguished. He resigned in 1802 but then accepted reappointment in late 1803. In 1804, when Chancellor Livingston asked to be relieved as minister to France, President Thomas Jefferson chose Armstrong as his successor. Armstrong's six-year tenure as minister to France proved controversial. He was involved in numerous pamphlet wars with American merchants in Paris and their supporters in America who criticized his supposed partiality in handling claims arising under the Louisiana Purchase treaty. Armstrong also vigorously attacked French measures harmful to America's neutral trade, and he frequently urged the U.S. government to take stronger retaliatory measures. He viewed the 1810 Cadore letter, in which France ostensibly withdrew its offending anti-neutral policies, as attributable in part to his vigorous attacks, and he returned home in 1810 in triumph.

Armstrong was snubbed by President James Madison's (1751–1836) government on his return, but he supported the administration because of its movement toward war with Great Britain. He also strongly supported Madison against De Witt Clinton in the 1812 presidential election. As a reward, Armstrong was appointed brigadier general and assigned the defense of New York harbor. When William Eustis resigned as secretary of war, Madison reluctantly appointed Armstrong, whose appointment was confirmed in February 1813. Armstrong's reputed military knowledge and Madison's need for a sectional balance in his cabinet outweighed Armstrong's well-known irascible temperament.

Armstrong infused new energy into the Department of War, recruiting new staff officers to cope with the myriad problems of administration. However, Armstrong treated his officers imperiously and interfered far too often in matters more properly belonging to the commanders, such as sending orders directly to field officers and bypassing their superior officer. He even went to the northern front in the fall of 1813, but his presence did not advance the campaign and was resented by Major General James Wilkinson. Armstrong also failed to coordinate with Major General Wade Hampton (1752–1835), which contributed to the failure of the campaign against Montreal. Perhaps Armstrong's most significant contribution was advancing junior officers of merit. As a consequence, by 1814, a new generation of officers, such as Jacob Brown, Andrew Jackson, Winfield Scott, and Edmund P. Gaines, gave a better account of American arms. They influenced the American military establishment to the Civil War.

Armstrong feuded with Secretary of State James Monroe, who resented Armstrong and viewed him as a potential rival for the presidency. By the summer of 1814, Armstrong's relations with President Madison had also deteriorated because of his failure to coordinate his activities with the president. The British defeat of American militia at Bladensburg that resulted in the burning of Washington, D.C., brought the simmering dispute to a head. The people of the district blamed Armstrong for his seeming indifference to their defense, which he felt was too insignificant militarily to warrant a British attack. When Madison responded equivocally to demands for Armstrong's dismissal, Armstrong resigned in September 1814 in disgust. Many saw his resignation as a tacit admission of failure, however, and Armstrong's career was ruined. He never again held political office.

Armstrong devoted the remaining years of his life to agriculture and writing. He wrote several pamphlets attacking his old enemies Wilkinson and Monroe. He also wrote a treatise on agriculture and several works on history, the most important being his two-volume *Notices of the War of 1812* (1836, 1840), which has some useful analysis of the campaigns but reveals little about the author's involvement in these events.

Armstrong's wife died in 1822. They had six sons and one daughter, Margaret, who married William B. Astor. Armstrong died in Red Hook, New York. One of the best writers of his generation, Armstrong used his talents primarily for polemical purposes. Despite many enemies who worked to undermine his efforts, he achieved several eminent positions and made important contributions to his country.

• The largest collection of Armstrong papers is the William Astor Chanler Collection of photostats in the New-York Historical Society, which are copies of a private collection held at "Rokeby" (Armstrong's old estate), near Red Hook, New York. The only biography of Armstrong is C. Edward Skeen, *John Armstrong, Jr., 1758–1843: A Biography* (1981). Armstrong contributed two thinly researched essays on Richard Montgomery and Anthony Wayne to the *Library of American Biography* series, ed. Jared Sparks, vols. 1 and 4 (1834).

C. EDWARD SKEEN

ARMSTRONG, Lil (3 Feb. 1898–27 Aug. 1971), jazz pianist, composer, and singer, was born Lillian Hardin in Memphis, Tennessee. Nothing is known of her father, but her mother, Dempsey Hardin, was a strict, churchgoing woman who disapproved of blues music. At age six, Lil began playing organ at home, and at eight she started studying piano. In 1914 she enrolled in the music school of Fisk University in Nashville, taking academic courses and studying piano and music theory. After earning her diploma, around 1917 she joined her mother in Chicago, where she found work demonstrating songs in Jones' Music Store. Prompted by her employer, in 1918 Hardin auditioned for clarinetist Lawrence Duhé's band at Bill Bottoms's Dreamland Ballroom, where she played with cornetist "Sugar Johnny" Smith, trombonist Roy Palmer, and other New Orleans musicians. When Smith became too ill to continue working, he was replaced by first Freddie Keppard and then Joe Oliver. Hardin remained on as house pianist. Still a minor, her mother picked her up every night after work.

In January 1920 Hardin joined a second Oliver-led band comprising clarinetist Johnny Dodds, trombonist Honore Dutrey, bassist Ed Garland, and drummer Minor Hall. In late May 1921 she went to San Francisco with Oliver's Creole Jazz Band for a six-month job at the Pergola Dance Pavilion. Around November, though, when Oliver chose to remain in California to pursue other engagements, Hardin went back to Chicago and a job at the Dreamland. After the Oliver band returned to Chicago, Hardin resumed her former position in the summer of 1922. In late August Oliver wired Louis Armstrong to come up from New Orleans to join his group as second cornetist. Shortly thereafter Armstrong and Hardin began courting. However, while working at the Dreamland, she had married a singer named Jimmie Johnson, whose infidelities soon proved grounds for divorce. Eager to help free Armstrong from his own ill-advised first marriage, Hardin arranged divorces for both of them in 1923, and they were married in February 1924. They had no children. Between April and December 1923 King Oliver's Creole Jazz Band recorded thirty-seven performances, on which the pianist was limited to a strictly subordinate role in the rhythm section, although the other members of the front line were occasionally heard in solos.

Even before they were married, Lil had begun trying to make Louis more sophisticated in his manners and dress, as well as urging him to leave Oliver, his childhood mentor and role model. Louis, however, remained adamantly loyal to Oliver until mid-1924, when the band broke up following a long midwestern tour. Months of Lil's prodding had finally taken their toll, and, now convinced that he should seek better avenues to showcase his own talent and reap its reward, he gave Oliver notice in late June and tried out for a job in Sammy Stewart's society band. Stewart ignored him, but in September he was offered a featured position in Fletcher Henderson's orchestra at the Roseland Ballroom in New York. In October Lil followed her husband east but soon returned to Chicago to lead her own band at the Dreamland. By virtue of his nightly appearances with Henderson's top-ranking band and his many recordings during this period, Louis Armstrong's reputation grew far beyond what it had been in Chicago, but by early November 1925 he was ready to leave, primarily because Lil wanted him to come home. By this time she was enjoying a successful run with her Dreamland Syncopators and encouraged the owners to pay a higher salary than usual to bring in Louis as a featured attraction. By December Louis was working at both the Dreamland and in Erskine Tate's large pit orchestra at the Vendome Theater.

Between 12 November 1925 and 13 December 1927, Lil Armstrong appeared on all of the Louis Armstrong Hot Five and Hot Seven recordings, forty-four titles in all, as well as leading one Hot Five date under her own name (as Lill's Hot Shots) in May 1926 and participating, along with Louis, on sessions with Butterbeans and Susie, Alberta Hunter, and the Red Onion Jazz Babies. In July 1926 she also recorded with the New Orleans Bootblacks and the New Orleans Wanderers—actually the Hot Five personnel of Dodds, trombonist Kid Ory, and banjoist Johnny St. Cyr, but with the addition of a saxophone player and the substitution of cornetist George Mitchell for Armstrong. In January and February 1929 she recorded with Dodds in both trio and sextet settings.

Although her command of the piano was marred by limited technique, swift, unswinging time, and a paucity of melodic ideas, Lil Armstrong was nevertheless a highly productive composer of jazz songs. It is difficult, though, to ascertain exactly which songs were written by her independent of Louis Armstrong, but it may be assumed that she played an important role in transcribing and arranging certain melodic themes that he invented. Among those Hot Five and Hot Seven numbers for which she is given full or partial credit are "I'm Gonna Gitcha," "Droppin' Shucks," "King of the Zulus," "Jazz Lips," "Struttin' with Some Barbecue," "Hotter than That," and "Knee Drops." She also contributed "Gate Mouth," "Too Tight Blues," "I Can't Say," "Perdido Street Blues," "Papa Dip," and "Mixed Salad" to the 1926 Bootblacks and Wanderers sessions as well as "Pencil Papa," "Heah Me Talkin'," and "Goober Dance" to Dodds's 1929 dates. However, it must be said that her own contributions on piano, whether as soloist or accompanist, are invariably the least interesting elements of these recordings.

During the late 1920s Lil bought an eleven-room home in Chicago as well as real estate on Lake Michigan's Idlewild resort, properties she retained throughout her life. However, Louis, who had started philandering while in New York, was beginning to tire of her constant jealousy and pressure for him to better himself commercially. Perhaps due to the many arguments they were having, he began getting serious with another woman, Alpha Smith, around 1928. When Lil's job at the Dreamland ended in the spring of 1926, Louis joined Carroll Dickerson's orchestra at the Sunset Café while Lil worked in Hugh Swift's band and later toured with Freddie Keppard. During this time she also had been studying at the Chicago Musical College, and after earning a degree in teaching she studied at the New York College of Music, where she received her postgraduate degree in 1929. After numerous arguments with her now successful husband, she finally sued for legal separation in August 1931, retaining her properties and receiving a considerable cash allowance. In 1938 she finally granted him a divorce, as well as winning a suit against him for the rights to the songs they had cocomposed. Lil never remarried, and she kept all relevant Louis Armstrong memorabilia, including letters, photos, and his old cornet, until her death.

Through the mid-1930s Lil Armstrong led both all-female and all-male bands of varying sizes in the Midwest, sometimes under the billing of Mrs. Louis Armstrong and Her Orchestra. She also broadcast regularly and appeared as a soloist in the *Hot Chocolates* and *Shuffle Along* revues. From 1936 Armstrong lived in New York and worked as a house pianist for Decca Records, between October 1936 and March 1940 leading small jazz groups with such featured sidemen as Joe Thomas, J. C. Higginbotham, Buster Bailey, and Chu Berry. She also provided the accompaniments for singers Blue Lu Barker, Rosetta Howard, Alberta Hunter, Frankie "Half Pint" Jaxon, Helen Proctor, Johnny Temple, Peetie Wheatstraw, and Georgia

White, as well as participating in jazz dates under the leadership of Red Allen, Johnny Dodds, and Zutty Singleton. She emerges as a vivacious and entertaining singer on her own Decca recordings of 1936–1940. Among her compositions from this period are "My Hi-De-Ho Man," "Brown Gal," "Just for a Thrill," "Born to Swing," "Let's Get Happy Together," and "Everything's Wrong, Ain't Nothing Right." In late 1940 Armstrong returned to Chicago, where she worked throughout the next decade as a soloist in many local venues.

In early 1952 Armstrong went to Paris, where she recorded in a trio with Sidney Bechet and Zutty Singleton and also under her own name in 1953 and 1954. She worked primarily as a soloist in Paris but also spent some time in London before returning in the late 1950s to Chicago, where she played many engagements in and around town. In December 1960 she recorded with Franz Jackson's band and in September 1961 led her own group for an album in the Riverside label's *Chicago: The Living Legends* series. In late October 1961 she participated in the telecast of *Chicago and All That Jazz*, an all-star jazz concert segment of NBC's "Dupont Show of the Week." Little is known of Armstrong's activities after this point, but she probably continued appearing in clubs in Chicago and environs. Following Louis Armstrong's death in July 1971, a memorial concert was staged in his honor on 27 August at Chicago's Civic Center, and it was during her performance at this event that Lil Armstrong suffered a massive coronary. She died in Chicago.

• Lil Armstrong's career is discussed in Linda Dahl, *Stormy Weather* (1984); Sally Placksin, *American Women in Jazz* (1982); and Mary Unterbrink, *Jazz Women at the Keyboard* (1983). For insight into Armstrong's role in King Oliver's Creole Jazz Band and her romantic and working relationship with Louis Armstrong, Walter C. Allen and Brian Rust, *King Oliver*, ed. Laurie Wright (1987); Max Jones and John Chilton, *Louis: The Louis Armstrong Story* (1971); James Lincoln Collier, *Louis Armstrong: An American Genius* (1983); and Gary Giddins, *Satchmo* (1988) are essential reading. In 1960 or 1961 an oral interview with Lil Armstrong titled *Satchmo And Me* was released as Riverside RLP12-120, and it is this source that provides the foundation for the relevant material in the works cited above. Complete discographical listings are in Brian Rust, *Jazz Records, 1897–1942* (1982), and Walter Bruyninckx, *Swing Discography, 1920–1988* (12 vols., 1985–1989). An obituary is in the *New York Times*, 28 Aug. 1971.

JACK SOHMER

ARMSTRONG, Louis (4 Aug. 1901–6 July 1971), jazz trumpeter and singer, known universally as "Satchmo" and later as "Pops," was born in New Orleans, Louisiana, the illegitimate son of William Armstrong, a boiler stoker in a turpentine plant, and Mary Est "Mayann" Albert, a laundress. Abandoned by his father shortly after birth, Armstrong was raised by his paternal grandmother, Josephine, until he was returned to his mother's care at age five. Mother and son moved from Jane Alley, in a violence-torn slum, to an only slightly better area, Franklyn and Perdido streets, where nearby cheap cabarets gave the boy his first introduction to the new kind of music, jazz, that was developing in New Orleans. Although Armstrong claims to have heard the early jazz cornetist Buddy Bolden around age five, this incident may be apocryphal. As a child he worked odd jobs, sang in a vocal quartet, and around 1911 bought a used cornet with his savings. He dropped out of school, got into trouble, and in 1913 was placed in the New Orleans Colored Waifs' Home for Boys, where Peter Davis, the music instructor, gave Armstrong his first formal music instruction. He left the home in June 1914. Although remanded to the custody of his father, he soon moved to live with his mother and younger sister, Beatrice, whom Armstrong affectionately called Mama Lucy.

As a teenager Armstrong played street parades, associated with the older musicians, and held various day jobs, including delivering coal with a mule-drawn coal wagon. In his second autobiography, *My Life in New Orleans*, he relates the importance of these years in his development, particularly the influence of Joe "King" Oliver:

> At that time I did not know the other great musicians such as Jelly Roll Morton, Freddy Keppard, . . . and Eddy Atkins. All of them had left New Orleans long before the red-light district was closed by the Navy and the law [1917]. Of course I met most of them in later years, but Papa Joe Oliver, God bless him, was my man. I often did errands for Stella Oliver, his wife, and Joe would give me lessons for my pay. I could not have asked for anything I wanted more. It was my ambition to play as he did. I still think that if it had not been for Joe Oliver jazz would not be what it is today. (p. 99)

In 1918 Armstrong married Daisy Parker and began his life as a professional musician. Between November 1918 and August 1922 he played cornet at Tom Anderson's club as well as in the Tuxedo Brass Band, in Fate Marable's band on Mississippi River excursion paddle-wheel steamers and incidentally in several New Orleans cabarets. His musical associates during these years were Oliver, Warren "Baby" Dodds, Johnny Dodds, Johnny St. Cyr, Honoré Dutrey, George "Pops" Foster, and Edward "Kid" Ory.

Armstrong's rise to prominence began with his move to Chicago in August 1922 when Oliver invited him to come to the Lincoln Garden's Cafe as second cornet in Oliver's Creole Jazz Band. This group defined jazz for the local Chicago musicians and stimulated the development of this music in profound ways. Armstrong's first recordings were made with Oliver in 1923–1924; "Riverside Blues," "Snake Rag," "Mabel's Dream," "Chattanooga Stomp," and "Dipper Mouth Blues" are some of the performances that preserve and display his early mature work.

In 1924 Armstrong divorced his first wife and that same year married the pianist in Oliver's band, Lillian Hardin. She encouraged him to accept an invitation to play with the Fletcher Henderson orchestra at the Roseland Ballroom in New York City. Armstrong's impact on this prominent name band was phenomenal. His solo style brought to the East a tonal power, creative virtuosity, and rhythmic drive that had not been a regular aspect of the Henderson band's performance practice. Armstrong's influence on Henderson, himself an arranger and pianist, and two of his fellow band members, in particular the arranger and saxophonist Don Redman and saxophone virtuoso Coleman Hawkins, was partially responsible for the development of a new jazz idiom or style—swing. During his fourteen months with Henderson, Armstrong participated in more than twenty recording sessions and left memorable solos on "One of These Days," "Copenhagen," and "Everybody Loves My Baby," on which he cut his first, brief, vocal chorus. While in New York, Armstrong also recorded with Clarence Williams's Blue Five, a small combo that included the already famous saxophonist Sidney Bechet, and with the star blues singers Ma Rainey and Bessie Smith. With Henderson, Armstrong played trumpet, but in these small-group sessions he returned to cornet. For another two years he continued to use both instruments but finally retired his cornet for the brighter, more-focused sound of the trumpet.

In spite of his growing stature among the jazz community, Armstrong was still but a sideman when he returned to Chicago in 1925. He immediately became the star of his wife's band at the Dreamland Cafe and soon joined Erskine Tate's orchestra at the Vendome Theater. In November 1925 he made his first recordings as a leader with a pickup group of old associates he called the "Hot Five"—his wife, Lil, on piano, Kid Ory on trombone, Johnny Dodds on clarinet, and St. Cyr on banjo. These recordings of the Hot Five and the Hot Seven (with the addition of bass and drums) are towering monuments of traditional jazz. "Cornet Chop," "Gut Bucket Blues," "Heebie Jeebies," "Skid-Dat-De-Dat," "Big Butter and Egg Man," "Struttin' with Some Barbecue," "Hotter Than That," and several others are numbered among the classics of this style, have entered the standard repertory, and continue to be studied and performed regularly. In these recordings Armstrong established his eminence as a cornet and trumpet virtuoso, unparalleled improviser, composer, and jazz vocalist. Melrose Brothers published notated transcriptions of some of his solos in 1927 immediately after the appearance of these recordings; these may be the first transcriptions from recorded performances ever published. The significance of this series of recordings is summarized by Gunther Schuller in his study *Early Jazz*:

The smooth rhythms of the earlier improvisations give way to stronger, contrasting, harder swinging rhythms. Double-time breaks abound. Melodic line and rhythm combine to produce more striking contours. This was, of course, the result not only of Armstrong's increasing technical skill, but also of his maturing musicality, which saw the jazz solo in terms not of a pop-tune more or less embellished, but of a chord progression generating a maximum of creative originality. . . . His later solos all but ignored the original tune and started with only the chord changes given. (pp. 102–3)

Armstrong's association with Earl Hines in 1927 led to another series of pathbreaking recordings in 1928, most notably "West End Blues," with a reconstituted Hot Five, and "Weather Bird," a trumpet and piano duet. In "West End Blues" Armstrong not only achieves an unprecedented level of virtuosity but displays the beginnings of motivic development in jazz solos. In "Weather Bird" Hines and Armstrong partake in a rapid exchange of antecedent-consequent improvised phrases that set a pattern for future jazz improvisers who "trade fours and twos."

In 1929 Armstrong moved with his band from Chicago to New York for an engagement at Connie's Inn in Harlem. The floor show used a score by Fats Waller that became a Broadway success as *Hot Chocolates* and featured an onstage Armstrong trumpet solo on "Ain't Misbehavin'." He also pursued many other endeavors, going into the recording studio to front his own band with Jack Teagarden and playing and singing in Luis Russell's group, which also featured the Chicago banjoist and guitar player Eddie Condon. Armstrong's singing style was unique in American popular music, especially when it was first presented to listeners on a broad scale through recordings of the 1920s. One of his first vocal accomplishments was to introduce an improvisatory vocal-instrumental mode of singing called "scat singing" in his recordings of "Heebie Jeebies" and "Gully Low Blues" of 1926 and 1927, respectively. Although this method of singing nonsense syllables was common in New Orleans and had been used by others before, it was Armstrong's recordings that were credited with the invention of this new device and that influenced hosts of later jazz singers. Contrasting with the classically oriented popular-song vocalists of the day, also with the shouting-and-dancing stage singers of ragtime and minstrelsy, as well as with the loud and lusty belters of the classic blues, Armstrong's natural technique brought a relaxed but exuberant jazz style and a gravelly personal tone to popular singing. His 1929 recordings of "I Can't Give You Anything but Love" and "Ain't Misbehavin'" achieved great popular success. Armstrong continued to sing throughout his career and reached a pinnacle of popular success in 1964 when his recording of "Hello Dolly" became the bestselling record in America, moving to number one on the popular music charts.

From 1930 to the mid-1940s Armstrong was usually featured with a big band. In 1935 he joined forces with Joe Glaser, a tough-minded businessman who guided his career until 1969. Also in 1935 Armstrong divorced Lil Hardin; he married Alpha Smith in 1938. He later divorced her and was married a fourth and final time in 1942 to Lucille Wilson. He had no children with any of his wives. After World War II Armstrong returned to performing with a small ensemble and played a concert in New York's Town Hall, with Peanuts Hucko (clarinet), Bobby Hackett (trumpet),

Jack Teagarden (trombone), Dick Cary (piano), Bob Haggart (bass), and Sid Catlett (drums), that inaugurated a new phase in his career. After the success of this "formal concert," Armstrong began to tour with a band labeled his "All Stars," ensembles of approximately the same size but with varying personnel selected from the ranks of established, well-known jazz musicians. Through Glaser's efforts, Armstrong and his All Stars became the highest-paid jazz band in the world. They toured successfully, sparked a renewed interest in Armstrong's recordings, and earned him a place on the cover of *Time* magazine on 21 February 1949.

Throughout his long career Armstrong, as trumpeter, remained the leading figure among classic jazz musicians and rode many waves of public and financial success, but his historical impact as a jazz instrumentalist lessened as new styles developed and younger musicians looked elsewhere for leadership. Still, his solo trumpet playing remained superlative while other phases of his career, such as singing, acting, writing, and enjoying the fruits of his celebrity, gained prominence as time passed. Between 1932 and 1965 he appeared in almost fifty motion pictures, including *Rhapsody in Black and Blue* (1932), *Pennies from Heaven* (1936), *Every Day's a Holiday* (1937), *Doctor Rhythm* (1938), *Jam Session* (1944), *New Orleans* (1946), *The Strip* (1951), *High Society* (1956), *Satchmo the Great* (1957), *The Beat Generation* (1959), *When the Boys Meet the Girls* (1965), and *Hello Dolly* (1969). Beginning with broadcasts in April 1937, he was the first black performer to be featured in a network radio series, and he appeared as a guest on dozens of television shows starting in the 1950s.

Often unjustly criticized for pandering to the racist attitudes that prevailed in the venues where he performed, Armstrong was, in fact, a significant leader in the struggle for racial equality in America. He was a black artist whose work blossomed contemporaneously with the other artistic and intellectual achievements of the Harlem Renaissance, an important personage who spoke publicly in protest and canceled a State Department tour in 1957 when Governor Orval Faubus of Arkansas refused to let black children attend a public school. Armstrong firmly believed in equal opportunity as a right and in personal merit as the only measure of worth, and he was one of the first black jazz musicians to perform and record with white musicians (Hoagy Carmichael, Tommy Dorsey, Jack Teagarden, Bud Freeman, and Bing Crosby, among others). His artistry was such that he became a role model not only for black musicians but also for numerous aspiring young white musicians, most notably Bix Beiderbecke, Jimmy McPartland, Bobby Hackett, and Gil Evans. Informally he became known as an "Ambassador of Goodwill," and Ambassador "Satch" toured Europe and Africa under the sponsorship of the Department of State during the 1950s. Armstrong amassed many honors in his lifetime—medals, stamps in his honor from foreign countries, invitations by royalty and heads of state, and critical awards such as the annual *Down Beat* Musicians Poll—but none seemed to hold greater significance for him personally than returning to his birthplace, New Orleans, in 1949 as King of the Zulus for the annual Mardi Gras celebration.

Even though ill health seized him in his last few years, Armstrong continued to work, appearing on television and playing an engagement at the Waldorf-Astoria Hotel in New York City during the last year of his life. He died in his home in Corona, Queens, New York.

Louis Armstrong and but three or four others are preeminent in the history of jazz. His importance in the development of this art form has gained greater, almost universal, recognition in the years since his death as scholars and musicians reevaluate his contributions as a soloist, composer, band leader, and role model. The measure of his impact on the social history of twentieth-century America also seems to be greater now as he gains recognition for his contributions to the Harlem Renaissance, for his actions as a thoughtful spokesman for black Americans, as a significant writer of autobiography, as an entertainer of stature, and as a singer responsible for the development of major trends in American popular and jazz singing. His most accomplished biographer, Gary Giddins, wrote in *Satchmo*:

> Genius is the transforming agent. Nothing else can explain Louis Armstrong's ascendancy. He had no formal training, yet he alchemized the cabaret music of an outcast minority into an art that has expanded in ever-widening orbits for sixty-five years, with no sign of collapse. (p. 26)

• The papers of Louis Armstrong are preserved in the Louis Armstrong Archive at Queens College of the City University of New York, and virtually all of his recordings, some oral history material, and other related documents are at the Institute of Jazz Studies at Rutgers University in Newark, N.J. Armstrong's most important publications, of course, are his recordings, and an extensive listing of his published recordings with full discographical details can be found in Hans Westerberg, *Boy from New Orleans: A Discography of Louis "Satchmo" Armstrong* (1981). Armstrong wrote two autobiographies, *Swing That Music* (1936) and *Satchmo: My Life in New Orleans* (1954). Several critical studies of the trumpeter have been written, including the biography by Max Jones and John Chilton, *Louis: The Louis Armstrong Story 1900–1971* (1971, rev. ed., 1988), a carefully researched and documented study. In some ways it has been superseded by Gary Giddins, *Satchmo* (1988), which corrects birth information and contains a useful select list of long-playing records and compact discs available in 1988 but unfortunately suffers from the lack of an index. A controversial study by James Lincoln Collier, *Louis Armstrong: An American Genius* (1983), is important, but it should be read in the light of some criticism (see Dan Morgenstern's book review, "Louis Armstrong: An American Genius," *Annual Review of Jazz Studies* 3 [1985]: 193–98). The best analytical study of Armstrong's music may be found in Gunther Schuller's two books, *Early Jazz: Its Roots and Musical Development* (1968) and *The Swing Era: The Development of Jazz 1930–1945* (1989); two worthy earlier studies are Albert McCarthy, *Louis Armstrong* (1959), and Hugues Panassié, *Louis Armstrong* (1971). Beginning studies of Armstrong, the singer, are Leslie Gourse, *Louis' Children: American Jazz Singers* (1984), and Will Friedwald, *Jazz Singing: America's Great Voices from Bessie Smith to Bebop and Beyond* (1990). An obituary is in the *New York Times*, 7 July 1971.

FRANK TIRRO

ARMSTRONG, Paul (25 Apr. 1869–30 Aug. 1915), playwright, was born in Kidder, Missouri, the son of Richard Armstrong, a steamship businessman, and Harriet Scott. Armstrong's family settled in Bay City, Michigan, where he finished high school. By the age of twenty-one he had become a licensed master of steam vessels on the Great Lakes. He eventually became the purser of a steamship.

In the mid-1890s, after attempting different occupations, Armstrong became a journalist, working on newspapers in Buffalo, Chicago, and New York. While in New York he worked for the Hearst organization as a sports reporter. He wrote under the name of "Right Cross" because he occasionally covered boxing events. While still working as a reporter, he began writing plays. In July 1899 Armstrong married Rella Abell in London; the couple had three children. It was Armstrong's second marriage, as an obscure marriage in his youth had ended in divorce.

In 1904 Armstrong left newspaper reporting and tried to devote himself fully to playwriting. His early attempts were mostly unsuccessful. These failures included *St. Ann*, which he attempted to produce himself. Reportedly, on opening night Armstrong physically fought one actor and was forced to fire two others. Not surprisingly, the production was a failure. In 1905 Armstrong finally enjoyed his first successful production, *The Heir to the Hoorah*. In 1907 Armstrong announced he was returning to the role of manager with the intention of producing his own play, *The Renegade*. In 1908 he not only became the manager of the Liberty Theatre, but he enjoyed further success with the melodrama *Via Wireless* (written with Winchell Smith). In 1909, with managers becoming increasingly antagonistic toward critics, Armstrong also became embroiled in the controversy. In *Everybody's Magazine*, he charged that a number of critics were "incompetent" and "dishonest" (July 1909, p. 121).

In January 1910 Armstrong achieved his greatest playwriting success when *Alias Jimmy Valentine*, based on an O. Henry story, was produced to critical and popular acclaim. H. B. Warner, who played the title role, colorfully defined the play and Armstrong's playwriting style as "gripping melodrama, that makes the women gasp and the men clench their hands" (*New York Times*, 30 Jan. 1910). Warner also claimed that Armstrong wrote the play in five days, with the production opening after six days of rehearsal. The production was also noteworthy for featuring Laurette Taylor in a supporting role. In March 1910 the play was staged in London. It also received a production at San Quentin prison.

Alias Jimmy Valentine reflects Armstrong's fascination with criminals and the judicial system. He gained notoriety for personally attempting to reform people with criminal histories. In some instances he gave troubled individuals jobs as extras in his productions. One of his attempts at criminal reform became a publicized failure. The playwright convinced a judge to parole a convicted burglar to his supervision so he could observe the man. Armstrong claimed, "It's my business to study them." The paroled man was given an extra's role in Armstrong's *A Romance of the Underworld* (1911), which concerned the fate of a burglar. Unfortunately, a few months later the parolee was arrested again and was sentenced to two and a half years at Sing Sing.

In 1911 Armstrong's marriage received public scrutiny as Rella Armstrong initiated a series of suits for divorce. A few days after the divorce was finalized in 1913, Armstrong married Catherine "Kittie" Cassidy in New Haven. Cassidy was better known by her stage name, Catherine Calvert. Under that name, she had starred in two Armstrong successes, *A Romance of the Underworld* and *Deep Purple* (1910), the latter written with Wilson Mizner. The couple had one child.

In addition to the divorce actions, Armstrong encountered other personal difficulties. In June 1912 a jury fined the playwright $5,000 for assaulting the actor James Young. Also, in April 1914 Marc Klaw and Abraham L. Erlanger took Armstrong to court, demanding the return of a $1,000 advance royalty. The court ruled that Armstrong could keep the disputed money. In April 1915 he entered Johns Hopkins hospital for treatment of an enlarged heart. Late that summer he suffered a heart attack while riding in his automobile in Central Park in New York City. He was rushed to his home and died shortly thereafter.

Armstrong was one of the most commercially successful playwrights of his time. He specialized in creating light comedies and suspenseful melodramas. H. L. Mencken wrote of Armstrong, "He was a curious man, and had some talent. His plays, to be sure, were mainly trash, but nevertheless they were very adroitly constructed, and he made success after success, some of them record-breaking" (*Newspaper Days*, p. 117). Within some of his commercial plays, such as *The Escape* (1913), which dealt with a woman trying to flee the slums, Armstrong attempted to address certain social ills. The artistic credit given to Armstrong by scholars, however, has been limited to his popularizing the "crook play" genre of his era.

Despite the popularity his work enjoyed, Armstrong's plays have not often been revived in the years since his death, although some of his plays were adapted for film, including *Alias Jimmy Valentine* in 1915. Cinema scholars have credited it with being an early prototype of the "gangster film." In 1918 Catherine Calvert appeared in a movie version of *A Romance of the Underworld*. Another of Armstrong's plays was reworked in 1945 for *Hold That Blonde!* which starred Eddie Bracken and Veronica Lake.

• An informative recollection about Armstrong is provided by H. L. Mencken in his book *Newspaper Days* (1941). A chapter in Alexander Woollcott's *Shouts and Murmurs* (1922) includes an account of Armstrong's method of writing *Alias Jimmy Valentine*. A lengthy interview with Armstrong about his interest and theories regarding criminals, which inform some of his plays, can be found in the *New York Times*, 23 Apr. 1911. Obituaries are in the *New York Times*, 31 Aug. 1915, and the *New York Dramatic Mirror*, 8 Sept. 1915.

MICHAEL SOLOMONSON

ARMSTRONG, Samuel Chapman (30 Jan. 1839–11 May 1893), educator, was born in East Wailuku on the island of Maui, Hawaii, the son of Richard Armstrong and Clarissa Chapman, Protestant missionaries in the Hawaiian Islands. As a boy Armstrong attended Punahou, a combined high school and experimental two-year college (Oahu College) established for the sons of the Hawaiian missionaries. In 1857, when he was eighteen, he helped found the Hawaiian Mission Children's Society, otherwise known as the "Cousins' Society," becoming its first president and in later years its most faithful foreign correspondent. When he was a sophomore at Oahu College in 1859–1860, Armstrong served as chief clerk in the Office of Public Instruction of the Royal Hawaiian Government; his father had been minister of public instruction since 1847.

During 1859–1860, while his father was absent in the United States, Armstrong received his first real introduction to the public school system of Hawaii. From the perspective of his job as chief clerk, he was able to observe the first principles of agricultural and industrial training at schools like the Lahainaluna Seminary on Maui and the Hilo Boarding School on Hawaii. This kind of education was not just practical; it was "wise missionary work," endowing native Hawaiians not only with the work skills they would need to survive in a market society but with the moral and spiritual values that made work itself more than a mere necessity, an act of redemption.

After his father's sudden death in 1860, Armstrong decided to leave the islands to complete his education at Williams College in Massachusetts, graduating with honors in 1862. Seeing in the plight of black slaves a cause worthy of the high moral idealism spoon-fed to him as a child, Armstrong joined the Union army with a captain's commission, moving quickly up the ranks from lieutenant colonel to colonel of the Eighth and Ninth regiments of the U.S. Colored Troops. To Armstrong the war of abolition also was an outlet for the desire for Christian martyrdom and sacrifice that was the trademark of his generation. He was often at pains to point out that it was not for something so temporal as preservation of the Union that he fought and risked his life in the Civil War. "I see no great principle involved in it," he wrote to his mother during a truce in the campaign at Big Bottom. "I see only 4,000,000 slaves, and for and with them I fight."

Armstrong left the war a brevet brigadier general, but, instead of returning to Hawaii or to New England, he remained in the South, taking a job as the Freedmen's Bureau officer in charge of ten counties of eastern Virginia, with headquarters at Hampton. Under the leadership of General O. O. Howard and with the assistance of the American Missionary Association (AMA), the Freedmen's Bureau began the work of ensuring former slaves their rights under the Fourteenth Amendment, not simply by guaranteeing their political equality, but also by locating them on confiscated lands and providing rudimentary job-training assistance and free schooling. Emphasis was on moral and spiritual uplift as well as on material well-being.

Already persuaded of the benefits of manual training through his Hawaiian experience and convinced through his war experience of the "excellent qualities and capacities" of the freedmen, Armstrong approached the AMA about supporting a manual training school for blacks—"an industrial system, not only for the sake of self-support and intelligent labor, but for the sake of character," he wrote. Through Armstrong's efforts, the Hampton Normal and Agricultural Institute, the first black vocational school in the South, opened its doors in 1868 and was chartered by the state of Virginia in 1870.

From its start Hampton was devoted to demonstrating learning by doing, under the belief that the salvation of the black race would have to "be won out of the ground," Armstrong, the school's president, wrote in the annual report for 1872. "Skillful agriculturalists and mechanics are needed rather than poets and orators." Armstrong's most famous student at Hampton, Booker T. Washington, would go on to enshrine these sentiments at his own manual training school in Tuskegee, Tennessee, and in his famous 1895 Atlanta Compromise message to black Americans to "cast down your bucket where you are." Washington beseeched blacks to develop first and foremost their economic prospects, realizing that "there is as much dignity in tilling a field as in writing a poem." Armstrong and Washington maintained close personal ties throughout their lives; Armstrong helped to provide the much-needed publicity and financial contacts for Tuskegee's success.

In 1869 Armstrong married Emma Dean Walker of Stockbridge, Massachusetts, with whom he had two children before she died in 1878. In 1890 he married Mary Alice Ford of Lisbon, New Hampshire, and had two more children. Between 1868 and his death from heart disease in Hampton, Armstrong gave his life to pushing the Hampton-Tuskegee idea, the model of black industrial and missionary education that formed so large a part of the liberal-progressive response to the so-called "Negro problem," the question of how to meet growing black demands for equal education and for greater political and economic recognition.

In Hampton's first brochure Armstrong stated the general aims of the institution: "In the Home or the Farm, and in the Schoolroom, the students have the opportunity to learn the three great lessons in life—how to live, how to labor, and how to teach others." The three-year course of study offered, in addition to ordinary common school curriculum, lectures on agriculture and agricultural chemistry (with analysis of soils and experiments by pupils) and instruction in bookkeeping and other practical business methods. It also offered a course in political economy, decrying "communism" and stressing "the utmost amity" and "the most intimate reciprocal relations" between capital and labor, and a "Daily Order of Exercises," beginning with a full military-style inspection at 5:45 A.M. followed by a regimen of prayer, field and shop work, and study ending at 9:00 P.M. Students also were trained at Hampton to go out into the rural country schools of the South as industrial supervising teachers to help introduce work such as cooking, sewing, manual training, agriculture, basketmaking, bricklaying, and tinsmithing.

More representative of white than black educational thought in the nineteenth century, Hampton's influence extended far beyond the South, generally wending its way from Africa to India to British New Guinea to "the aboriginal race of Japan." Borrowing from the examples of the Lahainaluna and Hilo schools, where students were kept in school and in the fields from dawn to dusk, raising crops and reciting the catechism, Armstrong instituted at Hampton a kind of Christian penal colony in which the moral lessons of hard labor combined with conservative Christian values would drive home what he called "the one great lesson of the Hawaiian mission": the lack of sustained attention to a race only at the beginning of its prospects—weak, vulnerable, and prey to all the blandishments of a corrupt material civilization.

In the South and elsewhere, Armstrong's educational policies nevertheless had deleterious effects, restricting the future political and economic roles of indigenous peoples, consigning students to a life of menial labor, robbing them of the benefits of higher education, and enforcing the values of a dominant white middle-class culture. W. E. B. Du Bois, just one among many black educators of the time who was an outspoken critic of the school, said Hampton was at the center of an "underground and silent intrigue" to keep the former slave "a docile peasant and peon, without political rights or social standing." But the impact of Hampton and Armstrong's educational ideas extended beyond blacks and other oppressed groups—Native Americans and Hawaiians, for example—most directly affected by the system. Combining the rhetoric of uplift, a salvational message concerning the "dignity of labor," and the most nihilistic industrial values and assumptions, the Hampton-Tuskegee idea became the model for an international Christian educational system that presumed to "save" everyone, white and black, rich and poor alike.

• The Samuel Chapman Armstrong Papers are at Hampton University and Williams College. Papers and correspondence of the Cousins' Society are located at the Hawaiian Mission Children's Society Library, Honolulu. For Armstrong's description of the influence of Hawaiian upbringing on his later educational philosophy, see his "Lessons from the Hawaiian Islands," *Journal of Christian Philosophy* 3 (Jan. 1884): 201–29. Armstrong's posthumously published *Education for Life* (1914) is a collection of quotations from his writings on the education of head, hand, and heart, the pedagogy for which Armstrong became famous. Helen Ludlow's comprehensive biography is unpublished and largely appreciative; the manuscript is available through the Hampton University Archives. The Ludlow manuscript reproduces whole passages from Armstrong's diaries and letters, many of which no longer survive in the original. For a published account of his life, see Edith Talbot, *Samuel Chapman Armstrong: A Biographical Study* (1904). For assessments of his education philosophy and the effect of his Hawaiian experience on it, see Henry Allen Bullock, *A History of Negro Education in the South from 1619 to the Present* (1967); Ronald E. Butchart, *Northern Schools, Southern Blacks, and Reconstruction: Freedmen's Education, 1862–1875* (1980); James D. Anderson, *The Education of Blacks in the South, 1860–1935* (1988); Robert F. Engs, *Freedom's First Generation: Black Hampton, Virginia, 1861–1890* (1979); and J. M. Heffron, "The Ecology of Contact: The Life and Times of Samuel Chapman Armstrong, Yankee Islander in the South" (conference paper, 1992 History of Education Society Meeting).

J. M. HEFFRON

ARNAZ, Desi (2 Mar. 1917–2 Dec. 1986), bandleader, actor, and television producer, was born Desiderio Alberto Arnaz y Acha III in Santiago de Cuba, Cuba, the son of Desiderio Arnaz II, a landowner and politician, and heiress Dolores "Lolita" de Acha. His early youth was privileged, but the revolution of 1932 broke up his secure home. His father was jailed briefly, and the family ended up in Miami with very little money.

In 1936, after graduating from high school and working at odd jobs, Arnaz began singing for a living. On a trip through Miami, Xavier Cugat invited the singer to tour the United States with his prestigious orchestra. In December 1937 Arnaz returned to Miami as a bandleader and introduced the conga to the United States; both musician and music proved to be immediate successes.

In 1938 Arnaz moved his orchestra to New York. The next year producer George Abbott and the songwriting team of Rodgers and Hart chose him to perform in their musical comedy *Too Many Girls*. Arnaz enjoyed acting and went to Hollywood to work on the film version of the show in 1940. There he fell in love with Lucille Ball, who portrayed the picture's ingenue. The pair married in November of that year. They had two children.

The promise Arnaz showed in *Too Many Girls* led to few other film roles, and he concentrated on band engagements in the early 1940s, although he garnered excellent reviews as a dying soldier in Metro-Goldwyn-Mayer's *Bataan* (1943). Drafted in 1943, Arnaz never went overseas. Instead he organized schooling for illiterate soldiers and entertainment for wounded veterans. His association with the showgirls who put on the entertainments led to frequent quarrels with Ball. She filed for divorce in 1944, although the couple reconciled before the divorce was finalized.

At the war's end the brief inroad Arnaz had made in films before being drafted had been forgotten by the film industry. Ball found him work doing music for Bob Hope's radio show during the 1946–1947 season, and she lobbied with CBS starting in 1950 to have Arnaz cast as her co-star when her radio situation comedy, "My Favorite Husband," moved to the new medium of television. CBS made Arnaz the host of a radio game show "Your Tropical Trip," but the network expressed reluctance to let the Cuban co-star in his Anglo wife's television program.

Ball and Arnaz toured the country with a vaudeville show to prove that they could work together. Its success enabled them to negotiate with the network to produce and star in a situation comedy titled "I Love Lucy," under the auspices of a family production company called Desilu.

Arnaz and Ball chose to plan and execute the program in ways that were new to television but would soon, thanks to their example, become standard practice. CBS expected them to move to New York, the center of American television production. The couple chose to stay on the West Coast. The network protested that live production in Los Angeles would prove impractical. The time difference between coasts would necessitate airing low-quality kinescopes in the East, where most television-viewing homes were located. Arnaz and Ball suggested producing the show on film in order to dispense with kinescopes altogether. Together with cinematographer Karl Freund, the pair came up with a way to light and shoot a weekly staged performance. Shooting on film would cost more than shooting the program live, so the stars agreed to take a cut in their weekly salary. In exchange, CBS granted them full ownership of the filmed shows after their first season. This gamble would make Ball and Arnaz rich within a few years.

Ball spent most of the next few months resting at home; she gave birth to a daughter in the summer of 1951. Meanwhile, Arnaz threw himself into arrangements for the show. "I Love Lucy," which focused on a Cuban bandleader and his stagestruck American wife, debuted in October 1951 and was an immediate hit. Arnaz enjoyed producing it and running Desilu and began expanding the production company almost immediately—working out deals to shoot more weekly situation comedies à la "I Love Lucy."

Desilu expanded into feature-film production as well in the summer of 1953, when Arnaz and Ball produced and starred in the popular movie *The Long, Long Trailer*. Despite the picture's success, Desilu remained dedicated to television throughout the 1950s, mushrooming in size and the number of programs produced as the decade progressed.

Arnaz hit his zenith as leader of Desilu—and perhaps of American television production as a whole—after purchasing RKO's movie studio in 1957. Desilu produced 270 hours of television in 1958. In that same year, the company went public.

Years later, American readers were to learn that Arnaz drank heavily in the late 1950s. His alcoholism contributed to his flagging health; in 1957 he underwent a colostomy and then rushed back to work. These problems did not come to public notice at the time—although Arnaz's arrest for fighting in 1958 did make it into several newspapers, as did an arrest for public drunkenness in 1959. Nor did reporters generally dwell on the rifts in the Arnaz marriage. The pair were divorced in 1960, shortly after winding up a final "I Love Lucy" special.

Arnaz apparently had neither the heart nor the health to continue running Desilu for long. In 1962 he sold his shares in the company to his ex-wife. In 1963 he married Edith Mack Hirsch. He briefly resurfaced on the television landscape to produce "The Mothers-in-Law" in 1967. The series died after two seasons, however, and future efforts at pilots also failed.

In 1976 Arnaz published his memoirs, which he titled *A Book*. He made sporadic television appearances in his later years, including a guest stint on "Saturday Night Live." After his death in Del Mar, California, he was honored as the television pioneer he was—a pathbreaker in shooting programs on film and, to some extent, the inventor of the rerun.

• The Billy Rose Theatre Collection of the New York Public Library for the Performing Arts, Lincoln Center, has extensive clipping files on Arnaz's life and career. In addition to his memoirs, helpful sources include two biographies that treat him along with Ball, Warren G. Harris, *Lucy and Desi* (1991), and Coyne Steven Sanders and Tom Gilbert, *Desilu* (1993). "I Love Lucy" and the Desilu company receive analysis in Bart Andrews, *Lucy and Ricky and Fred and Ethel* (1976), and Thomas Schatz, "Desilu, *I Love Lucy*, and the Rise of Network TV," in *Making Television*, ed. Robert J. Thompson and Gary Burns (1990).

TINKY "DAKOTA" WEISBLAT

ARNETT, Benjamin William (6 Mar. 1838–9 Oct. 1906), African-American religious, educational, and political leader, was born in Brownsville, Pennsylvania, the son of Samuel G. Arnett and Mary Louisa (maiden name unknown). Arnett was a man of "mixed Irish, Indian, Scots, and African ancestry" (Wright, p. 79). He was educated in a one-room schoolhouse in Bridgeport, Pennsylvania. Arnett worked as a longshoreman along the Ohio and Mississippi rivers and briefly as a hotel waiter. His career as a longshoreman and waiter ended abruptly when a cancerous tumor necessitated amputation of his left leg in 1858. He turned to teaching and was granted a teaching certificate on 19 December 1863. At that time, he was the only African-American schoolteacher licensed in Fayette County, Pennsylvania. For ten months during the academic year 1884–1885, Arnett served as a school principal in Washington, D.C. He returned to Brownsville in 1885, teaching there until 1887. Although largely self-educated, he attended classes at Lane Theological Seminary in Cincinnati. A man of many interests, he was an occasional lecturer in ethics and psychology at the Payne Theological Seminary at Wilberforce University, served as a historian of the AME church, was a trustee of the Archaeological and Historical Society of Ohio, served as a member of the Executive Committee of the National Sociological Society, and was statistical secretary of the Ecumenical Conference of Methodism for the western section from 1891 to 1901.

Arnett's formal association with the AME church began in February 1856. He was licensed to preach on 30 March 1865 and was ordained a deacon on 30 April 1868 in Columbus, Ohio. He became an elder on 12 May 1870 in Xenia, Ohio. As a delegate from the Ohio Annual Conference, Arnett attended the General AME Conference in 1872. He was appointed assistant secretary of the General Conference in 1876 and became general secretary in 1880. He was elected financial secretary of the General Conference in 1880 and again in 1884. As financial secretary, he had primary responsibility for the publication of the annual *Budget* of the AME church. Arnett's budgets contain not only detailed financial records but personal observations and historical information as well. He continued as an editor of the AME *Budget* until 1904.

At the General Conference of 1888, Arnett was elected a bishop of the AME church; he was the church's seventeenth bishop. He served the Seventh Episcopal District (South Carolina and Florida) from 1888 to 1892; the Fourth Episcopal District (Indiana, Illinois, and Iowa) from 1892 to 1900; the Third Episcopal District (Ohio, California, and Pittsburgh) from 1900 to 1904; and the First Episcopal District (Philadelphia, New York, and New England) from 1904 to 1906.

An ardent Republican and active in party politics, he was chaplain to the Ohio legislature in 1879 and to the Republican State Convention in Ohio in 1880. His most notable political accomplishment was his election (by eight votes) to the Ohio legislature to represent predominantly white Greene County in 1886. Arnett was the first African-American legislator in Ohio to represent a predominantly white constituency. During his term in office, he drafted a bill to abolish Ohio's "Black Laws" and introduced bills to secure state funding for Wilberforce University, which at that time was near bankruptcy. While in the Ohio legislature, he also established an enduring friendship with William McKinley, Jr. Arnett, on behalf of the AME church, presented McKinley with the Bible used when he took the oath of office of the presidency in 1897. Arnett maintained close ties with McKinley and is said to have exerted considerable influence in Washington during the McKinley administration (1897–1901). He served as chaplain to the Republican National Convention in St. Louis in 1896.

Arnett enjoyed considerable and deserved reputation as a public speaker and parliamentarian. He addressed the Republican State Convention in Denver in 1886 and the Centennial Celebration of the First Settlement of the Northwest Territory in Mariti, Ohio, in 1888; was invited to give commencement addresses at Wilberforce University in 1887 and at Claflin College (South Carolina) in 1889; and presented the keynote address at the meeting of the Grand Army of the Republic in Chicago in 1900. He presided at the Parliament of Religion held at Chicago (Sept. 1893) and at the Ecumenical Conference of Methodists held in London (Sept. 1901). He was vice president of the Anti-Saloon League of America and an active member of Frederick Douglass's National Equal Rights League. Arnett was also active in the Masons and worked diligently on behalf of the Young Men's Christian Association.

He married Mary Louise Gordon in 1858. The couple had seven children. Two of his sons, Benjamin William Arnett, Jr., and Henry Y. Arnett, became ministers in the AME tradition. Benjamin W. Arnett, Jr., became president of Edward Waters College and Allen University. Henry Y. Arnett became a pastor and presiding elder in the Philadelphia and Delaware Conferences.

During Arnett's term in the Third Episcopal District (1900–1904), he established a ten-acre estate, "Tawawa Chimney Corner," near Wilberforce University, where he hosted numerous visitors and amassed a large collection of African-American literature. A number of volumes from Arnett's personal library were later acquired by W. E. B. DuBois; other volumes from Arnett's library are now a part of the Arthur A. Schomburg collection. Arnett died of uremia in Wilberforce, Ohio.

Richard R. Wright, Jr., in *Eighty-seven Years behind the Black Curtain* describes his initial encounter with Arnett: "I was greatly impressed. Bishop Arnett, a handsome, clean-shaven man, was Northern born, very intelligent, unusually witty, an expert in church financing, author of half a dozen books and pamphlets, a distinguished and convincing orator, and a 'soul-stirring' preacher" (pp. 92–94). This assessment was echoed by many of Arnett's contemporaries.

Arnett served as a bishop for more than eighteen years and had considerable impact on church affairs. Perhaps his greatest contributions stem from his ability to mediate among various factions within the church and his successful transgression of racial, ethnic, and class boundaries. His published lectures, notably his 1888 centennial address "The Northwest Territory," evidence careful scholarship and a keen intellect.

• Arnett's papers are in the Carnegie Library, Wilburforce University. Of Arnett's own writings *The Budget*, which he edited between 1881 and 1904, provides considerable insight into his personality as well as details on the inner workings of the church. His annual *Budgets* also preserve valuable materials of the history of the denomination. His speech "The Northwest Territory" was reprinted in *Ohio Archaeological and Historical Quarterly* 8 (1900): 433–64. Arnett served as editor and chief for the first collaborative editing project by African Americans titled *Duplicate Copy of the Souvenir from the Afro-American League of Tennessee to Hon. James M. Ashley of Ohio* (1894). This volume contains speeches and writings of the radical Republican leader in the U.S. House of Representatives. Arnett also played a key role in editing the addresses and papers published as *The World's Congress of Religions* (1894), which were delivered before the World's Columbian Exposition in Chicago in 1893. Sources on Arnett's life include a brief sketch in *The Bishops of the African Methodist Episcopal Church* (1963), by Richard R. Wright, Jr. Wright also includes some personal reminiscences of Arnett in *Eighty-seven Years behind the Black Curtain* (1965). Arnett's role in securing state support for Wilberforce University is covered in Frederick A. McGinnis, *A History and an Interpretation of Wilberforce University* (1941). Arnett's relations with other members of the church hierarchy are described in Stephen Ward Angell, *Bishop Henry McNeal Turner and African-American Religion in the South* (1992), and Dorothy E. Hoover, *A Layman Looks with Love at Her Church* (1970). Lucretia H. Newman Coleman's biography, *Poor Ben: A Study of Real Life* (1890), gives a highly impressionistic account of Arnett's life and times. An obituary is in the *New York Times*, 9 Oct. 1906.

STEPHEN D. GLAZIER

ARNO, Peter (8 Jan. 1904–22 Feb. 1968), cartoonist, was born Curtis Arnoux Peters, Jr., in New York City, the son of Curtis Arnoux Peters, a New York Supreme Court justice, and Edith Theresa Haynes. As scion of a prominent family, Curt (as he was called then) was sent to Hotchkiss School in Lakeville, Connecticut, and then to Yale College, where he indulged his interest in music and art instead of preparing for the career as a banker or a lawyer that his father planned for him. He drew cartoons for the *Yale Record* and formed a nine-piece band called the Yale Collegians, playing piano, banjo, and accordian as needed. With young Rudy Vallee as lead singer, the group performed at Gilda Gray's Rendezvous, one of Manhattan's first postwar nightclubs. Quickly succumbing to the taste of the era for nightlife, Peters was virtually a prototype of the Jazz Age's young man about town: rich and debonair, he was tall, urbane, impeccably dressed, and multitalented, and he had the jutting-jaw good looks of a model in the popular Arrow shirt ads of the day.

In 1923 he moved from Yale to Greenwich Village and changed his name to Peter Arno in order to separate his identity from his father's. He wrote music, played in his band, painted murals in cafés and restaurants, and submitted drawings, without selling many, to the venerable humor magazines *Judge* and *Life*. He was about to abandon his ambition to be an artist for a musical career with a band in Chicago when he received a check for a drawing that he had submitted to a new humor magazine. With the publication of this spot illustration in the 20 June 1925 issue of the *New Yorker*, Arno began a 43-year association with Harold Ross's journal, his single-panel cartoons helping to shape significantly the magazine's sophisticated, irreverent personality.

Arno's first success in the magazine was with a series of cartoons about two tipsy, middle-aged shrews who were probably charwomen on their night off, which they spent gadding about town in feathered hats, long formal gowns, and muffs, punctuating their incongruously earthy observations of life around them with spirited cries of "Whoops!" Christened the "Whoops Sisters," this bibulous pair of dowdy rowdies appeared three times a month for three years and stimulated newsstand sales of the magazine.

It was with his next creations, however, that Arno contributed most vitally to the character of the *New Yorker*. The first of these was an aristocratically mustached old gent in white tie and tails, whose eyes, as Somerset Maugham observed, "gleamed with concupiscence when they fell upon the grapefruit breasts of the blonde and blue-eyed cuties" whom he avidly pursued. These same voluptuous damsels kept company with another regular member of Arno's ensemble—a thin, bald, albeit youngish man with a wispy walrus mustache, a razor-sharp nose, and an ethereally placid expression who was often seen simply lying in bed beside an empty-headed ingenue with an overflowing nightgown. The other regular was a ponderous dowager, stern of visage and impressive of chest, whose imposing presence proclaimed her right to rule. This trio was joined by an assortment of rich, predatory satyrs in top hats, crones, precocious moppets (one of whom was forever chancing upon his shapely aunt when she was naked), tycoons, curmudgeonly clubmen, fuddy-duddies, and barflies of all description—in short, the probable population of all of New York's café society. This Manhattan menagerie Arno subjected to merciless scrutiny from his position within the pale, and he found something ridiculous and therefore valuable in everyone from roué to cabdriver. Arno's cartoons juxtaposed the seeming urbanity of his cast against their underlying earthiness. He showed again and again that humankind is just a little larcenous and lecherous, and trivial in its passions and pursuits, social decorum to the contrary notwithstanding.

Arno did not invent the single-speaker, or one-line, caption cartoon that by the end of the decade had replaced its historic predecessor, the illustrated comic dialogue, in which the humor resided entirely in the verbal exchange between several speakers that was printed beneath a picture. The one-line caption had been used occasionally for years, but Arno deployed it consistently (thereby doing much to establish the form) because he valued the astonishing and therefore risible economy of its interdependent elements: neither words nor picture made any sense alone, but together they blended unexpectedly to create comedy.

An admirer of Honoré Daumier and Georges Rouault, Arno showed in his earliest drawings, with their simple outlines and grease-crayon shading, the influence of the former; before long, however, the Rouault line began to assert itself. Eventually, Arno employed a broad brush stroke to delineate his subject with the fewest lines possible, holding the compositions together with a wash of varying gray tones. He worked hard to give his drawings the look of spontaneity. "It must be done rapidly, with careless care," he once wrote, "so it doesn't look like work." A dedicated craftsman, he customarily rendered a single cartoon scores of times until the combination of artful design and accidental execution felt right.

Arno devised a leisurely way of life: he worked only about two days a week, making rough sketches of cartoon ideas and sending them to the *New Yorker* for review. He produced the final drawings in batches, several at a sitting, working twenty-four or thirty-six hours at a stretch. Sometimes he grew worn with the expenditure of nervous energy his method required, and he would take several months or a year off to travel.

On 12 August 1927 Arno married Lois Long, who as a writer for the *New Yorker* used the pen name Lipstick; they had a daughter and then divorced by Reno decree on 29 June 1931. Arno's second wife was a glamorous debutante named Mary "Timmie" Livingston Lansing, whom he married in August 1935 and divorced in July 1939.

By the late 1930s, Arno had lost the ambivalence he doubtless felt as an insider satirizing café society: no longer a devotee of its rituals, he became disgusted with "fatuous ridiculous people," and his anger, he said, "gave my stuff punch and made it live." He soon gave up his duplex apartment on West 54th Street in Manhattan and moved to a farm near Harrison, New York. He spent his last years luxuriating in idyllic seclusion, enjoying music, guns, sport cars, and drawing, and making contact with the outside world only once a week when he telephoned the art director of the magazine. Despite his isolation, his subject (and his bemused scorn of it) remained the same as ever. Ill with emphysema, he continued to contribute regularly, and his last cartoon was published the week of his death. The *New York Times* printed his obituary on the front page, signifying perhaps that in his person and in his work, he had been the archetypal New Yorker.

• In addition to his cartooning, Arno wrote a modestly successful song, "My Heart Is on My Sleeve," in the 1920s and a novel based upon his first cartoon characters, *Whoops Dearie!* (1927), and he coauthored a Broadway musical satire, *Here Comes the Bride* (1931). Several collections of his cartoons have been published: *Peter Arno's Parade* (1929); *Peter Arno's Hullabaloo* (1930); *Peter Arno's Circus* (1930); *Peter Arno's Favorites* (1931); *Peter Arno's Bride for a Night* (1934); *For Members Only* (1935); *Peter Arno's Cartoon Revue*, with an introduction by Somerset Maugham (1941); *Peter Arno's Man in the Shower* (1944); *Peter Arno's Pocket Book* (1946); *Peter Arno's Sizzling Platter* (1949); *Peter Arno's Ladies and Gentlemen*, which includes introductory matter by Arno in which he describes his methods and answers questions about his work (1951); and *Peter Arno's Hell of a Way to Run a Railroad* (1956). Information about Arno's life can be found in the *New York Times* obituary, 23 Feb. 1968. Arno's relationship with Harold Ross and his place in the history of the *New Yorker* is briefly discussed in Dale Kramer, *Ross and the New Yorker* (1951); James Thurber, *The Years with Ross* (1959); and Brendan Gill, *Here at the New Yorker* (1975).

ROBERT C. HARVEY

ARNOLD, Benedict (14 Jan. 1741–14 June 1801), revolutionary war general and traitor, was born in Norwich, Connecticut, the son of Benedict Arnold III, a merchant, and Hannah Waterman King. Of his mother's eleven children, only he and a younger sister survived. At age eleven he was sent away to grammar school, but he left two years later when his alcoholic father lost the family's fortune. Apprenticed to his mother's cousin, an apothecary in Norwich, he volunteered in three campaigns (1757–1759) of the French and Indian War, deserting finally to be with his dying mother. His father died soon after, leaving little except debts, but his generous master paid the debts and set Arnold up in business when he decided to move to New Haven in 1762.

Arnold showed the qualities that later brought him success and, eventually, ruin. Not tall, but strongly built, he welcomed tests of his manhood; he was quick to lead and quick to find trouble. A small circle of indulgent women—his mother, his master's wife, and his sister Hannah—did little to curb his impulsiveness and aggressiveness. Later he confessed that he had been a coward until he was fifteen.

In New Haven Arnold used the business skills learned as an apprentice to become a successful merchant–sea captain, trading mainly in horses and other livestock with Canada and the West Indies. Early in 1766 he emerged in local politics, leading the New Haven Sons of Liberty against a former crewman who had informed against him for smuggling. At least twice during voyages he fought duels, and at home he earned a reputation as a free-spending roughneck. In 1767 he married Margaret Mansfield, daughter of the New Haven sheriff; by 1772 they had three children. His sister lived with them, and there is strong evidence that his passive, sickly wife, dominated by her sister-in-law, failed to satisfy his emotional needs; soon he was being denounced for infidelity as well as smuggling.

Late in 1774, as the imperial crisis peaked, Arnold joined an elite company of New Haven militia, who soon elected him captain. At the news of war, he seized powder and shot from the town magazine, marching his men without orders to Boston. In earlier travels to Canada, Arnold had seen the weakness of the British forts on Lake Champlain at Ticonderoga and Crown Point, and he soon persuaded the Massachusetts Committee of Safety to order him, with the rank of colonel, to capture the forts and bring their badly needed cannon to Boston. Although empowered to lead 400 men, Arnold set out ahead of his men and en route met two rival parties—one from Connecticut and another, large contingent of "Green Mountain Boys" led by Ethan Allen—with the same idea.

Arnold bullied his way into cocommanding the ragged force that surprised the small garrison of Fort Ticonderoga at dawn on 11 May 1775, but he soon lost any control of the mutinous, drunken victors. When his own recruits arrived, Arnold used them to seize a schooner at the south end of the lake, renamed it *Liberty*, armed it with cannon from the fort, and sailed north to attack the British post at St.-Jean, where he captured the small garrison and a sloop-of-war. Back at Ticonderoga, he began to build a navy to hold the lake and to prepare for an invasion of Canada. Unsupported by Massachusetts, however, which had agreed to let Connecticut direct the campaign against Canada, Arnold resigned his command in late June and headed for New Haven, where his wife had just died.

By early August he was again in Boston, leaving his sons under the care of his sister and offering his services to George Washington, the new commander of the

Continental army. Convinced that only seizure of the St. Lawrence Valley could prevent the British from using it as a base to attack the exposed American frontier, Arnold persuaded Washington to let him lead an expedition through the Maine wilderness against Quebec. A larger force, under Philip Schuyler of New York, was already preparing to move down Lake Champlain against Montreal, and Arnold's attack through Maine was expected to draw British forces away from Schuyler's front.

The thousand men led by Arnold up the Kennebec River, over the ill-mapped and almost impassable "Height of Land" and down the rapid Chaudière River, arrived exhausted, hungry, and sick opposite Quebec city in early November. It was one of the great marches of military history. Nothing but Arnold's stamina and driving leadership kept the men going. Arnold joined with part of Schuyler's force under Richard Montgomery to lead a night assault on 31 December against the fortified city, where the British governor had concentrated all his forces. The assault failed: Montgomery was killed, and Arnold was badly wounded in the leg. Arnold and his army were able to hang on through the winter, but when the ice melted in May and British reinforcements sailed up to Quebec, the Americans, ravaged by smallpox, withdrew from Montreal to Crown Point.

Under Schuyler's command, Arnold threw himself into the task of building a navy to resist the expected British advance from Canada toward Ticonderoga and the upper Hudson Valley. Even as he worked to assemble a fleet of galleys and sailing gondolas around the nucleus of ships captured on the lake in 1775, he was caught in the middle of a growing conflict between Schuyler and General Horatio Gates, who Congress had sent to take command at Ticonderoga. He also faced a court-martial for plundering enemy property during the confused retreat from Canada. He still managed to complete his navy by early August. Almost a year later Congress exonerated him from the charge of illegal plundering.

He sailed north with ten ships in late August under orders to block a British advance. The British fleet was far stronger, and in a bloody, day-long battle on 11 October 1776 Arnold's fleet took a severe beating. In the dark he managed to slip away and fight his way to Ticonderoga. He lost all but four ships and a few hundred men. Despite defeat and heavy losses, Arnold had delayed the British advance for about a month, making a farther move southward impossible as winter came on.

On the way to Philadelphia to answer in Congress a variety of charges lodged against him by officers he had antagonized, and to protest the promotion of other officers to major general, Arnold had stopped at his New Haven home in late April 1777 when a British expedition from New York landed on the Connecticut shore, heading inland for Danbury, a major American supply base. After burning much of Danbury, the retreating British force met 400 militia under Arnold blocking the road near Ridgefield. The Americans inflicted heavy casualties, and when reports reached Congress Arnold got his promotion.

After a long evening with Arnold, Congressman John Adams (1735–1826) concluded that the general had been "basely slandered and libelled." But still faced with a tangled set of accusations, ranging from venality to treachery, and by the reluctance of Congress to restore his seniority of rank, Arnold submitted his resignation in July 1777. He withdrew it almost immediately on learning of a large British invasion on Lake Champlain and of Washington's request that Congress send him "an active, spirited officer" at the head of militia reinforcements.

When he arrived, Ticonderoga had already fallen, and Schuyler and Gates were vying for chief command. Both men had supported Arnold in the past, but Arnold sided with Schuyler. Schuyler sent him into the Mohawk Valley to block a secondary British advance from the westward. Arnold succeeded in doing so, but when he returned to the main army, Gates, now his enemy, was in command.

The exact role Arnold played in the two battles of Saratoga that led to the surrender of a British field army and the formal alliance of France with the United States is unclear. In the first battle, Gates let him command part of the American left wing in a spoiling attack on the advancing British force. Fearing a British trap and counterattack, Gates rejected his plea for more troops to exploit early success and ordered him back to headquarters. In the aftermath Arnold exploded, and Gates relieved him of command, but Arnold stayed in camp. When the British advanced again in early October, he rushed to the front and led several assaults on fortified positions into which enemy forces had retreated. Always at the front, he was wounded, hit by a bullet in the same leg wounded at Quebec.

Crippled and still in pain, Arnold reported to Washington at Valley Forge in May 1778, when the occupying British army was clearly preparing to evacuate Philadelphia. Washington then made one of the worst decisions of his career, appointing Arnold as military governor of the rich, politically divided city.

No one could have been less qualified for the position. Arnold had amply demonstrated his tendency to become embroiled in disputes, as well as his lack of political sense. Above all, he needed tact, patience, and fairness in dealing with a people deeply marked by months of enemy occupation.

He began by living and entertaining on a lavish scale, financed by private business deals that, if not strictly illegal, clearly involved the use of his power as military governor. He was soon caught in the middle of a fight between the radical state government, eager to punish Tories who had collaborated with the enemy, and Congress, from whose authority Arnold derived his own power. At the same time he was courting Margaret Shippen, youngest daughter of one of the city's leading families, itself suspected of Toryism.

In February 1779 Pennsylvania authorities charged him with corruption and abuse of power. Embarrassed by its agent, Congress took cognizance of these charges and in effect made a bargain with the state at Arnold's expense. In March a congressional committee exonerated him of some charges but referred others to Washington for court-martial; Arnold then resigned his Philadelphia command. In May, shortly after he married Peggy Shippen, the same congressional committee rejected Arnold's request for papers relevant to his pending court-martial.

From this period began the plot that would end, eighteen months later, with Arnold's defection to the British side. Through his new wife's family and friends, as well as his own staff, he had ready channels of communication to British headquarters in New York City. He used those channels to inform General Henry Clinton, commanding the British army, that he was ready to serve the Crown. He explained to Clinton that he had lost faith in the revolutionary cause when the United States allied itself with France. No evidence before May 1779 supports this claim.

Clinton was cautious but interested in the chance that Arnold might betray a key point in American defenses. He left the matter in the hands of young staff officer, John André. By July Arnold had named his minimum price—£10,000—and André had drawn his attention to the strategic American post at West Point. But the matter languished as the campaigning season ended, and Arnold awaited his postponed court-martial while trying to settle his tangled public accounts. In January 1780, after hearing his flamboyant defense, the court acquitted Arnold of fraud but convicted him of conduct "imprudent and improper" and sentenced him to a reprimand, which Washington worded as gently as possible.

Arnold used his New York connections to angle for the sedentary command at West Point, claiming to be too lame and ill to take the active field command that Washington planned for him. In early August Arnold got the West Point assignment and firm British agreement to his final terms: £10,000 for defection and £20,000 for the delivery of West Point and 3,000 rebel troops. Excited by the prospect of catching a large part of the American army along with a strategic post and a dangerous enemy general, Clinton planned a major operation up the Hudson and sent André to make direct contact with Arnold. But the mission misfired: André was caught in civilian dress with compromising documents and was later hanged. Leaving his wife to convince Washington that she knew nothing of the plot, Arnold fled downriver.

News of Arnold's treason, along with stunning military defeats in the South, shocked supporters of the faltering American cause. Peggy Arnold soon joined her husband in New York City, where British officers shunned him as a traitor. Although he got only part of the promised £10,000, the Arnolds got a pension, and Clinton sent him, as a British brigadier general, with an expeditionary force at the end of 1780 to raid the Chesapeake. Arnold's force routed the Virginia militia, burned ships, munitions, and tobacco, and forced Governor Thomas Jefferson into humiliating flight. In mid-1781 he led a raiding party into Connecticut, sacking and burning New London, butchering the garrison of its fort in one of the ugliest incidents of the war. But surrender of the British army at Yorktown in October ended the active war. The Arnolds sailed for England at the end of the year.

Snubbed even by American Loyalist exiles, Arnold pushed a variety of schemes to revive his career. In 1785 he sailed alone to St. John, New Brunswick. Commercial ventures did well enough in a troubled economy for his wife and their children to join him in 1787, but in 1788 fire wiped out his business. The insurers refused to pay, suspecting that he himself had ordered the blaze. In 1791 the Arnolds returned to England.

The outbreak of the French revolutionary war offered fresh opportunity. By 1794 Arnold was a privateer in the West Indies. Arrested by the French as a British spy, he escaped and later helped British planters on Martinique put down a slave uprising. But back in England he learned that the government had no use for his services in the war. Depressed and ill, he died in London.

More than any commander on either side of the conflict, Benedict Arnold had a genius for war. His performances reveal a shrewdly calculating mind as well as a recklessly combative personality. His energy and confidence inspired the men who followed him but often alienated colleagues and superiors. By turns outrageous and obsequious in dealing with problems caused largely by his own behavior, he must be reckoned a disaster in dealing with the nonmilitary side of his life. His painful wounds, which shattered his left leg above and below the knee, giving him a permanent limp, doubtless contributed to his defection in 1780, but the move itself, gambling that he could succeed and later convince the world that he had done the right thing, was consistent with the amoral boldness characteristic of his whole life.

• Important collections of Arnold material are in the Library of Congress, the William L. Clements Library at the University of Michigan, the New-York Historical Society, and the Historical Society of Pennsylvania. Published collections of importance are Kenneth Roberts, ed. *March to Quebec* (1938); P. H. Smith et al., eds., *Letters of Delegates to Congress, 1774–1789* (1976–); *The Writings of George Washington*, ed. J. C. Fitzpatrick (1931–1944); *The Diaries of George Washington*, ed. D. D. Jackson and D. Twohig (6 vols., 1976–1979); *The Papers of George Washington*, ed. W. W. Abbot et al. (1976–); and W. B. Clark et al., eds., *Naval Documents of the American Revolution* (1964–1986), vols. 3–7.

Willard Sterne Randall, *Benedict Arnold: Patriot and Traitor* (1990), is the most complete of many biographies; it is sympathetic but sensible. Isaac N. Arnold (no relation), *The Life of Benedict Arnold* (1880), is still valuable, especially for its extensive quotation from sources. James T. Flexner, *The Traitor and the Spy: Benedict Arnold and John André* (1953; new ed., 1975), is more critical and has a valuable discussion of the evidence. Carl Van Doren, *Secret History of the American Revolution* (1941), is indispensable on Arnold's treason, and for the British documents it reprints, while Charles Royster, *A Revolutionary People at War: The Continental Army and American Characters, 1775–1783* (1979), Chap. 6, ably describes the context and impact of his treason. A useful brief sketch by another biographer is Willard M. Wallace, "Benedict Arnold: Traitorous Patriot," in *George Washington's Generals*, ed. G. A. Billias (1964), 163–92.

JOHN SHY

ARNOLD, Elliott (13 Sept. 1912–13 May 1980), writer, was born in Brooklyn, New York, the son of Jack Arnold, a singer with the Metropolitan Opera, and Gertrude Frank. Arnold was raised and educated in New York City. He graduated from New York University in 1934. Before college, when he was only fifteen years old, he had started his first career, as a newspaper reporter for the *Brooklyn Daily Times*. After graduating from college he was a feature writer and rewriteman for the *New York World Telegram* until he joined the army air corps in 1942.

While employed as a reporter for the newspaper, Arnold was also working on his own writing. His first novel, *Two Loves*, was published in 1934. Arnold said it "was a mistake." He wrote two more novels: *Personal Combat* (1936) and *Only the Young* (1939), which, like the first, as Arnold admitted, "almost nobody read." It was during this time that Arnold decided to try his hand at books for young people. While on a trip to Europe, he visited the home of Finnish composer Jan Sibelius. *Finlandia: The Life of Sibelius* (1942) was the result. As an author of books for young readers, Arnold said that he wrote for children for "a selfish reason . . . to improve my writing." Writing for children, he felt, was a way of "going into a kind of artistic retreat, refinding the truths." With young readers as his audience, Arnold honed his writing skills, omitting wordiness, realizing that "excesses and indulgences" won't hold the interest of children. "You can't fake with those minds," he once remarked.

Previous to his service in World War II, Arnold had an idea for a book concerned with commando operations being planned in England to be implemented in enemy territories. With the technical information provided by a commando who was en route to Canada to train troops, Arnold started the book, which "almost wrote itself." Written just before the attack on Pearl Harbor, *The Commandos* (1942) was widely read, and in 1943 it was produced by Columbia as the film *First Comes Courage*, starring Merle Oberon and Brian Aherne.

Although Arnold enlisted as a private in the army air corps he was commissioned and trained as an intelligence officer. He was sent first to North Africa and then to Italy. Lieutenant General Ira C. Eaker, "air boss" of the Mediterranean, ordered Arnold to write an official air history of the Mediterranean theater in collaboration with Major Richard Thruelson. *Mediterranean Sweep: Air Stories from El Alamein to Rome* was published in 1944. A similar history on the South Pacific air war, *Big Distance* (1945), was written with Captain Donald Hough. In addition to these writing "duties," Arnold managed to write the novel *Tomorrow Will Sing* (1945). For his service during the war, Arnold was awarded the Bronze Star. He left the air force in 1945 with the rank of captain.

During the war he married Helen Emmons. They had his only two children before they divorced in 1957. He married Julie Kennedy in 1958; they divorced in January 1961. A month later he married Jacqueline Harris Stephens; they divorced in 1963. In 1964 Arnold married actress Glynis Johns; they divorced in 1973. He married Joanne Shwam in 1980.

As an author, Elliott Arnold admired heroism, and his novels reflect his examination of what it meant to be a hero. Two novels, in particular, with this theme were based on actual events: *Blood Brother* (1947) and *A Night of Watching* (1967). *Blood Brother* was based on a short article Arnold had read about Thomas J. Jeffords, an Indian agent, who had learned to speak Apache and became a close friend of Cochise, chief of the Chiricahua tribe of Apache. Arnold traveled to Arizona and spoke to many tribal members before writing his "scrupulously accurate" account of this friendship. Ethnological detail was interspersed with invented conversation, and although Cochise was somewhat romanticized, and Jeffords was given an Apache bride, the book sold well and was reprinted eight times in thirteen years. Arnold was awarded a silver medal in 1948 by the Commonwealth Club of California for the novel.

In 1950 the film *Broken Arrow*, based on the novel, was released by 20th–Century Fox. Starring Jeff Chandler as Cochise and James Stewart as Tom Jeffords, it represented the first major studio film to depict Native Americans sympathetically. Deborah Paget played the role of Jeffords's fictional wife, Sonseeahray. Arnold, with Michael Blankfort, wrote the screenplay, which was awarded the Screenwriters' Guild prize in 1951. He also wrote an abridged juvenile edition, *Broken Arrow* (1951), as well as the scripts for the television series of the same name that aired on ABC from 1956 through 1958.

Arnold's second important novel dealing with actual heroism was *A Night of Watching*. Although the major characters were fictional, the events were based on the fact that the Danish Underground, with the aid of the Danish people, was able to smuggle 8,000 Jews to Sweden during a two-week period in 1943. When the Germans acted to round up the Jewish residents of Denmark to send them to concentration camps, they only found 460 people. All but sixty survived the camps. In 1968 the book was awarded a silver medal by the Commonwealth Club of California and a Brotherhood Award by the National Conference of Christians and Jews. This bestselling novel was a Literary Guild selection and was later filmed as a television documentary.

Arnold also won a Commonwealth Club of California medal in 1960 for *Flight from Ashiya* (1959). Set in Japan, the novel is about the rescue of Japanese women and children from a lifeboat by American servicemen. In addition to being the story of a thrilling air-sea rescue, the novel is also about unresolved Japanese-American issues some years after World War II. The novel was filmed by United Artists in 1963 and starred Yul Brynner, Richard Widmark, and Shirley Knight. Arnold and Waldo Salt wrote the screenplay. The William Allen White Children's Book Award for best juvenile fiction of 1958 was awarded to *White Falcon*, the true story of John Tanner, who was kidnapped from his Kentucky frontier home in the late 1700s by Indians and taken to Canada. There, living with the Chippewa, he tried to win their friendship by becoming a good Indian. After acquitting himself with distinction in battle with the Sioux, he was honored with the name of "White Falcon" and became a leader of his adopted people.

Another Arnold work, his biography of Sigmund Romberg, *Deep in My Heart* (1949), was filmed by MGM with an all-star cast, including Gene Kelly, Ann Miller, and Helen Traubel. Jose Ferrer played the title role. In addition to books and screenplays, he wrote short stories and articles for publications such as *Cosmopolitan*, the *Saturday Evening Post*, the *Atlantic Monthly*, and *Reader's Digest*.

Sympathetic to the plight of Native Americans, Arnold joined the editorial staff of the *American Indian* in 1948. Arnold died in New York City.

• For a complete list of Arnold's writing, see *Contemporary Authors*, new rev. ser., vol. 24 (1988). A studio biography of Arnold is available at the Margaret Herrick Library of the Academy of Motion Picture Arts and Sciences in Beverly Hills, Calif. Additional information can be found in *Twentieth Century Authors* 1st supp. (1955) and *Something about the Author* (1973). Background information concerning *Broken Arrow* is in Larry Ceplair, "Who Wrote What???" *Cineaste* 18 (1991): 18–21. An obituary is in the *New York Times*, 14 May 1980.

MARCIA B. DINNEEN

ARNOLD, Harold DeForest (3 Sept. 1883–10 July 1933), physicist, was born in Woodstock, Connecticut, the son of Calvin Arnold and Audra Allen. Arnold attended Wesleyan University in Middletown, Connecticut, from which he received a bachelor of philosophy degree in 1906. The following year he earned an M.S. in physics from the same institution. In 1911 he received a Ph.D. in physics from the University of Chicago, where he had studied under the future Nobel laureate Robert A. Millikan. During the 1906–1907 academic year, Arnold was an assistant in physics at Wesleyan University and was first a fellow in physics and then an assistant in physics at the University of Chicago between 1907 and 1909. He was professor of physics at Mount Allison University in Sackville, New Brunswick, Canada, during the 1909–1910 academic year and was again appointed assistant in physics at the University of Chicago in the later part of 1910. He married Leila Berman in 1908; they had two daughters.

Millikan recommended Arnold highly to Frank B. Jewett of the Western Electric Company when Jewett wrote to Millikan seeking someone to develop electron-discharge "repeaters" (amplifiers) to overcome the weakening of the signals that occurs in long-distance telephony. As the result of his work under Millikan, Arnold already had demonstrated a high level of expertise on the topic of electric discharges in gases. Beginning work in the Engineering Department of Western Electric, the manufacturing branch of the Bell Telephone System, under the supervision of Edwin H. Colpitts in January 1911, Arnold had, by July 1912, developed a repeater element that utilized a mercury arc discharge. Soon after this development, however, Arnold's attention was directed to Lee de Forest's (no relation to Arnold) gaseous triode "audion," to which the American Telephone and Telegraph Company had recently purchased the patent rights. Although the audion in its original form was incapable of satisfactory use as an amplifier for long-distance telephone use, Arnold had immediately recognized its potential for that purpose.

Having already demonstrated outstanding ability in both research and development at Western Electric, Arnold was put in charge of the project to investigate and develop the audion's capabilities. By 1914 Arnold's personal scientific work together with his leadership of the project team resulted in the transformation of the audion into a sensitive, three-element, high-vacuum thermionic tube, which was extremely well suited for use in telephone repeaters. Arnold made the principal contributions to the development of the triode vacuum by 1) recognizing the need to operate the device at a very high vacuum together with developing the technology for producing that vacuum during manufacture; 2) identifying the existence and importance of the various physical phenomena involved in the triode's operation; 3) determining mathematical formulas to predict the operation of the triode device when used in an electronic circuit; and 4) suggesting and overseeing the development of an oxide-coated filament that enabled the tube to function better and longer. Almost totally as a result of Arnold's vacuum tube work, nationwide long-distance telephone communication was made possible, as evidenced by the establishment of New York to San Francisco commercial telephone service in January 1915. Arnold's continued research in vacuum-tube operation also made possible the first radiotelephone transmission between Arlington, Virginia, and Paris, France, in October 1915.

Beginning in late 1915, Arnold's interests became focused on his new experimental research efforts to increase knowledge of the physics of speech and hearing. Arnold had the scientific vision to realize that the vacuum tube amplifier would be an indispensable tool in this work. This research, for which Arnold provided valuable leadership, ultimately made possible, either directly or indirectly, significant improvements in the audio quality of phonographic recording and reproduction, "talking" motion pictures, and radio broadcasts. In addition to these benefits for audio entertainment media, the research group that Arnold headed developed the instrument, now known as the "audiometer," which can accurately measure the degree to which the hearing ability of a person is impaired. Knowledge obtained by Arnold's research team also made possible the development of electronic devices to aid persons with hearing impairments. Together with Irving B. Crandall and Edward C. Wente, Arnold developed the "thermophone" in 1917, which provided a precision source of sound for laboratory experiments.

Arnold was commissioned a captain in the U.S. Army Signal Corps in World War I. During this time, he continued his work in the laboratories of Western Electric, where he designed equipment used for the detection of submarines and directed the work of some of his colleagues on other war-related research topics.

Following World War I, in 1923, Arnold collaborated with Gustav W. Elmen in the development, analysis, and application of the extremely important family of magnetic alloys known as "permalloy," which increased by five-fold the ability of undersea cables to carry telephone messages and resulted in reduced distortion when used in sound-reproducing equipment. This collaboration between Arnold and Elmen also resulted in 1927 in the development of the magnetic alloy "perminvar," which has been widely used in the cores of telephone circuit loading coils.

Arnold was appointed director of research of the Western Electric Company in 1917 and served in that capacity until the end of 1924, when the research departments of Western Electric and of the American Telephone and Telegraph Company were combined to form the Bell Telephone Laboratories. From 1925 until his death, Arnold served as the director of research at Bell Labs.

Arnold was awarded membership in several honorary and scholarly societies, including Phi Beta Kappa and Sigma Xi. A fellow of the American Institute of Electrical Engineers, he served that organization as a member of its electrophysics committee from 1917 to 1922 and as a member of its research committee from 1927 until his death. In addition, Arnold was a fellow of the American Physical Society, the Acoustical Society of America, and the American Association for the Advancement of Science as well as a member of the Franklin Institute and the American Chemical Society. He died following a heart attack at his home in Summit, New Jersey.

Arnold is best remembered for his recognition and development of the potential of the triode audion tube. The resulting triode vacuum tube, together with the other forms of vacuum tubes that subsequently evolved from it, were the most important electronic devices of the first half of the twentieth century. In recognition of his extensive work in developing the three-electrode thermionic vacuum tube, the City of Philadelphia awarded Arnold the John Scott Medal in 1928.

• Arnold's laboratory notebooks and reports are in the American Telephone and Telegraph Company Archives in Warren, N.J. Obituaries are in *Bell Laboratories Record* (1933): 351–60; *Electrical Engineering* (1933): 589; and the *New York Times*, 11 July 1933.

JAMES P. RYBAK

ARNOLD, Henry Harley (25 June 1886–15 Jan. 1950), airman, was born in Gladwyne, Pennsylvania, the son of Herbert Alonzo Arnold, a physician, and Anna Louise Harley. Arnold received a public education and in 1903 entered the U.S. Military Academy at West Point. A mediocre student, he graduated in the middle of his class in 1907 and was commissioned a second lieutenant of infantry. He served four years with the Twenty-ninth Regiment in the Philippines and New York before volunteering for flight training with the Aviation Section of the Signal Corps. In April 1911 Arnold reported to Dayton, Ohio, and received instruction from the Wright brothers. Two months later he joined the army's first cadre of military aviators. Arnold subsequently transferred to College Park, Maryland, as a flight instructor and on 1 June 1912 established a world altitude record of 6,540 feet. This act garnered him the first-ever Mackay trophy.

Arnold proved himself to be a natural flier who distinguished himself in a number of capacities. He helped pioneer aerial reconnaissance in December 1912 by becoming the first pilot to report his observations by radio. In September 1913 he married Eleanor A. Pool; they had four children. Following some near accidents and the loss of several friends, Arnold quit flying for three years to accept reassignment with the Thirteenth Infantry in the Philippines. He resumed flying in October 1916 and joined the Aviation Section at Rockwell Field in San Diego, California.

By 1917 Arnold headed the Seventh Aero Squadron in the Panama Canal Zone. Following American entry into World War I, he transferred back to Washington, D.C., where on 21 May 1918 he was promoted to brevet colonel. Arnold actively sought a combat assignment but was retained at home as assistant executive officer of the newly formed Office of Military Aeronautics. By February 1918 he was assistant director. Arnold finally arrived in France shortly after the armistice and spent several months inspecting and evaluating aerial facilities.

The interwar years were a period of growth and controversy for military aviation, and Arnold was at the forefront of events. He received numerous assignments along the Pacific Coast, where he pioneered air patrolling of forests for the Conservation Corps and inflight refueling of aircraft. Arnold then expanded his technical acumen between 1925 and 1926 by attending the Army Industrial College and, from 1928 to 1929, the Command and General Staff School. Following a brief tour as chief of the Information Division, Office of the Chief of the Air Corps, he rose to lieutenant colonel in February 1931 and then served as commander of March Field, Riverside, California. Mindful of technological trends, Arnold deliberately cultivated close personal ties with the scientific faculty at the nearby California Institute of Technology. Seeking to expand public awareness of military aviation, he also cooperated closely with the Hollywood film establishment on a number of aerial productions. Convinced of the potential of aircraft in modern war, he authored or coauthored with Ira C. Eaker five books on the subject for young and general audiences.

Arnold's subsequent military activities attracted nationwide attention. A disciple of General William "Billy" Mitchell, Arnold testified on his behalf during Mitchell's celebrated court-martial. He also oversaw the unsuccessful army attempt to deliver mail in the western air mail zone in 1934, which failed on account of inferior equipment and inadequately trained personnel. Though the nominal commander, Arnold was absolved of any blame and continued flying. Between 19 July and 20 August of that year he conducted a spectacular flight of ten Martin B-10 bombers on a 5,290-mile roundtrip flight from Washington to Fairbanks, Alaska, demonstrating the potential for strategic bombing. For this feat he received his second Mackay trophy.

In recognition of his accomplishments, Arnold was promoted to temporary brigadier in February 1935 and appointed to command the First Wing of the newly created General Headquarters (GHQ) Air Force at March Field. In January 1936 he was recalled to Washington as assistant chief of the Air Corps. He served in this capacity until September 1938, when he rose to major general to succeed General Oscar Westover, who had died in a crash, as chief. His title changed to chief of the Army Air Force in July 1941, and in this capacity he was a spokesman for army aviation at the Atlantic Charter Conference, Argentia, Newfoundland, in August, 1941. He rose to lieutenant general in December 1941.

U.S. entry into World War II was marked by dramatic expansion of the size, mission, and capabilities of army air power. Arnold, by virtue of his technological expertise and industry wide contacts, was ideally positioned to orchestrate production increases. Under his aegis the Army Air Forces mushroomed from 22,000 men and 3,900 aircraft to 2.5 million personnel and 63,715 planes arrayed in 243 combat groups. He also addressed and resolved issues of close-air support, long-range escort fighters, and creation of a worldwide air transport net. Furthermore, as these assets were deployed, Arnold strove tirelessly to ensure they were utilized effectively. In May 1942 he flew to London to confer with high-ranking British airmen to develop and coordinate air offensive strategy against Germany. Foremost among his concerns was retention of daylight, precision bombing for American forces instead of less costly but less accurate nighttime air bombing, as practiced by the Royal Air Force. For the next three years Arnold represented American air interests at all major Allied conferences with the exceptions of Washington in 1943 and Yalta in 1945, when he was sidelined by heart ailments.

Arnold joined the Joint Chiefs of Staff in March 1942 as air member but, despite his work load, he would not be chained to a desk. In September 1942, following a tour of the Pacific war zone, he completed a record-breaking flight from Brisbane, Australia, to San Francisco. In 1943 he rose to four-star general and concluded a 35,000-mile tour of North Africa, the Middle East, India and China. Promoted to five-star general of the army in December 1944, Arnold also directed B-29 operations of the Twentieth Air Force from his Pentagon office, culminating in the atomic bombings of Hiroshima and Nagasaki. Although he suffered intermittent heart problems brought about by stress, he strove tirelessly to ensure that American air power was a vital contribution to the Allied victory.

Poor health necessitated Arnold's retirement in March 1946. He withdrew to his ranch home in the Valley of the Moon, near Sonoma, California, where he penned his memoirs, *Global Mission*, in 1949. That year a special act of Congress made him the first general of the Air Force, which had become a separate entity in 1947. Arnold died at his home.

More than any other individual, Arnold's career closely paralleled the growth, fortunes, and ultimate triumph of American air power. Personally contributing many of its milestones, he was the most technologically astute airman of his generation and worked closely with scientists such as Theodore von Kármán to ensure American supremacy in aviation. Furthermore, like his mentor Mitchell, Arnold realized the importance of air power in modern warfare; but unlike Mitchell, he had the perspicacity not to antagonize conservatively minded superiors in that quest. Consequently, the tactful Arnold functioned with a near-autonomy that presaged the creation of an independent air force. Neither a great strategist nor organizer, his greatest contribution was in orchestrating the creation of the world's largest air force and leading it to victory.

• Major collections of Arnold's papers are at the Air Force Historical Research Center, Maxwell Air Force Base, Montgomery, Ala.; the Manuscripts Division, Library of Congress; and the Air Force Academy Library, Colorado Springs, Colo. Smaller collections are with the Arnold Air Society, Texas Tech University, Lubbock; and the Oral History Collection, Columbia University, New York. A complete listing is in the index to Cloyd D. Gull and Charles L. Smith, *A Directory of Sources for Air and Space History* (1989). Arnold's own writings include *Airmen and Aircraft* (1926); *This Flying Game*, with Ira C. Eaker (1936); *Winged Warrior* (1941); and *Army Flyer* (1942). The best biographical treatment is Thomas M. Coffey, *Hap: The Story of the U.S. Air Force and the Men Who Built It* (1982). Informative sketches are in DeWitt S. Copp, *A Few Great Captains* (1980); Edgar Puryear, *Stars in Flight* (1981); John W. Hutson, "The Wartime Leadership of Hap Arnold," in *Air Power and Warfare*, ed. Alfred F. Hurley and Robert C. Ehrhart; David MacIsaac, "Leadership in the Old Air Force," in *Harmon Memorial Lectures in Military History, 1959–1987* (1988). The best overviews of Arnold's accomplishments in peace and war are Maurer Maurer, *Aviation in the U.S. Army, 1919–1939* (1987); Robert F. Futrell, *Ideas, Concepts, Doctrine* (1971);

and Wesley F. Craven and James L. Cate, ed., *The Army Air Forces in World War II* (7 vols., 1948–1958). Technological concerns are addressed in Dik A. Daso, "Architects of Air Supremacy: General Hap Arnold and Dr. Theodore Von Kármán," (Ph.D. diss., Univ. of South Carolina, 1996). More popular accounts include John F. Wukovitz, "Nothing Is Impossible," *American History Illustrated* 19 (1984): 56–63; Lawrence S. Kuter, "How Hap Arnold Built the Air Force," *Air Force Magazine* 56 (1973): 88–93; and Murray Green, "Hap Arnold, Man on the Go," *Air Power History* 37 (1990): 29–36. A useful obituary is in a series of articles appearing in the *New York Times*, 16–20 Jan. 1950.

JOHN C. FREDRIKSEN

ARNOLD, Isaac Newton (30 Nov. 1815–24 Apr. 1884), congressman and biographer, was born in Hartwick, Otsego County, New York, the son of George Washington Arnold, a doctor, and Sophia Mason. His parents, natives of Rhode Island, had moved to Otsego County around 1800. Isaac attended local schools, including Hartwick Seminary. Between 1832 and 1835 he taught school and studied law, and in 1835 he was admitted to the bar. After practicing in Cooperstown for about a year, he moved in the fall of 1836 to Chicago, where he entered a partnership. In 1837 he was elected city clerk, a post he resigned in order to attend to his expanding practice.

A Democrat, Arnold became increasingly interested in politics, winning a seat in the state house of representatives in 1842. As a legislator he fought repudiation of the state debt incurred in building the Illinois and Michigan Canal, and as chairman of the Finance Committee he assisted in freeing the state from debt. In 1844, though preferring the candidacy of Martin Van Buren, he reluctantly served as a presidential elector for the expansionist James K. Polk, and he himself was reelected to the legislature.

In 1848 Arnold abandoned the Democratic party, became a delegate to the Free Soil National Convention, and helped organize the latter party in Illinois. (The Free Soilers opposed expansion of slavery in the territories and southern resistance to internal improvements and free homesteads.) His growing antislavery convictions found him in 1850 a member of the Chicago committee that protested against the Fugitive Slave Law enacted that year. He served in the state house of representatives as a Free Soiler in 1855–1856, and he was elected to the U.S. House of Representatives as a Republican in 1860 and 1862. During the Lincoln administration, Arnold was a strong supporter of the president, whom he had known in the practice of law.

Arnold's years in Congress were characterized by his interest in the defense and economy of the Northwest, his ardent opposition to slavery, and his strong support of confiscation. In his second term the party gave Arnold the chairmanship of the Roads and Canals Committee. His bill to enlarge the Illinois and Michigan Canal to connect the Great Lakes and the Mississippi River, for both military and economic advantages, won Lincoln's endorsement in his annual message of 1863. Arnold's bill passed the House but failed in the Senate. Supporting the project in an eloquent speech, he argued its importance in case of war with the British in Canada and in growing foodstuffs for the North. "Cotton is dethroned," he declaimed, corn is king.

When Congress debated the second Confiscation Bill, proposing a sweeping exercise of federal power over the property of rebels, including slaves, Arnold gave a learned defense of the legal and constitutional right to confiscate in wartime. Figuring importantly in emancipation, he introduced in March 1862 a bill "to render freedom national and slavery sectional." Amended to apply only to territories, it became law on 19 June 1862. On 15 February 1864 he moved that the Constitution be amended to abolish slavery. In a congressional speech, "The Power, Duty and Necessity of Destroying Slavery in the Rebel States," given on 15 June 1864, he unsuccessfully pleaded, "We can have no permanent peace while slavery lives." Failing to pass in June, the bill was renewed after Lincoln's reelection and passed in January 1865.

In December 1863, by executive proclamation, Lincoln took into his hands Reconstruction of the Union. When debate began over whether the president or the Congress had the power to govern the rebel portion of the Union, Arnold argued, "In the absence of the action of Congress, [the president] may do all that is necessary to restore the Union" (*Congressional Globe*, 38th Cong., 1st sess., 1864, pp. 1198–99). Reporting to Lincoln, Arnold said that speech, which was printed as a campaign document, enjoyed "greater demand than any other document published" by the congressional campaign committee. When Congress passed the Wade-Davis Bill, spelling out a congressional plan of Reconstruction, Arnold voted for it. His vote was consistent with his earlier declarations about constitutional authority to reconstruct and did not mean a parting of the ways between Lincoln and Arnold. Responding to a Radical Republican effort in 1864 to shoulder Lincoln aside by postponing the national nominating convention, Arnold penned an influential letter to the press opposing delay.

Against Arnold's protest, Lincoln in 1861 had appointed John L. Scripps, his 1860 campaign biographer, as postmaster of Chicago. In 1864 Scripps determined to win Arnold's seat in Congress. He held the advantage of influencing the vote of his postal employees, and Arnold suffered from a charge that he had influenced Lincoln's decision to rescind a military order to suspend publication of the "copperhead" *Chicago Times*. Arnold secured the president's support, but feeling the weight of opposition to him, in late August he withdrew from the race, not wanting his party to lose control of his district. He then sought a presidential appointment, and Lincoln offered him the position of auditor in the Treasury Department. Arnold served in that post from 29 April 1865 to 29 September 1866.

Arnold had asked for the appointment in order to write a history of the Lincoln administration. He devoted his postcongressional years to practicing law, writing biography and history, and fostering history. Hastily written, heavy with historical detail, and laudatory in tone, his book, *The History of Abraham Lincoln*, came out in 1866. The candor and criticism of the president by his law partner and intimate Ward Hill Lamon, in a book published in 1872, shocked Arnold. "Do I not owe it to the memory of the dead to vindicate him?" Arnold asked Lincoln's friend O. H. Browning. Arnold conducted a wide correspondence about Lincoln, kept in touch with Lincoln's widow and son Robert Todd Lincoln, and drew on his own extended acquaintance with his subject. In 1885 he published *The Life of Abraham Lincoln*, assailing what Arnold believed to be many misconceptions. Focusing more closely on the man, it contained valuable firsthand accounts, and, written in Arnold's clear style with his flair for craftsmanship, it stood for years as the best one-volume life.

Arnold also wrote a *Life of Benedict Arnold* (no relation) in 1880, wrote some works of piety, and gave many addresses. He dedicated the building of the Chicago Historical Society, whose charter he had secured when he served in the state legislature. He was elected its president in 1876.

Arnold married twice. His first wife was Catherine E. Dorrance, with whom he had one son. She died in 1839. His second wife was Catherine's sister, Harriet Augusta Dorrance, with whom he had nine children. He died in Chicago.

As a member of the Civil War Congress, Arnold contributed significantly to the emancipation of the slaves. An ardent admirer of Lincoln, he supported the president in nearly all particulars. Though considered by his colleagues to be a Lincoln man, he differed from the president in favoring prompter action against slavery and in congressional control of Reconstruction. His *Life of Lincoln* has continued to be a source for biographers.

• Arnold's papers, mainly dealing with the period after the Chicago fire of 1871, are in the Chicago Historical Society. They include a volume, *In Memoriam*, which contains a brief biographical sketch and various tributes. The principal printed sources are the *Congressional Globe*, 1861–1865, and Roy P. Basler, ed., *The Collected Works of Abraham Lincoln* (9 vols. and supps., 1953–1990). An obituary is in the *Chicago Tribune*, 24 Apr. 1884.

JAMES A. RAWLEY

ARNOLD, Jonathan (3 Dec. 1741–1 Feb. 1793), political leader of the revolutionary period, was born in Providence, Rhode Island, the son of Josiah Arnold and Amy Phillips, occupations unknown. Though he did not attend college, Arnold studied medicine and opened his own practice in Providence in the late 1760s. An early supporter of the revolutionary cause, Arnold commanded a company of volunteer grenadiers in Providence in the alarm following Lexington and Concord in 1775. Elected to represent Providence in the Rhode Island Assembly in 1776 and reelected the following year, Arnold wrote the statute, approved on 4 May 1776, repealing the oath of allegiance to Great Britain required of all public officials. That same year he organized the Revolutionary Hospital of Rhode Island and was appointed its chief surgeon by the governor, a position he held until 1781. He gained a reputation as an innovative doctor and an efficient administrator. In 1781 he was elected assistant to the governor of Rhode Island, largely in honor of his wartime service.

In 1782 the Rhode Island Assembly selected Arnold as a delegate to the Confederation Congress. Arnold's two years in Congress were marked by controversy. He and Rhode Island's other delegate, David Howell, led the opposition to the impost amendment authorizing Congress to place a 5 percent duty on all imported goods as well as to every other effort to strengthen the Articles of Confederation. Convinced that granting such taxing power to Congress was the first step to a powerful central government, Arnold and Howell sent copies of secret congressional dispatches on foreign loans to the Rhode Island Assembly, where they quickly became public knowledge. The congressional leadership vilified Arnold and Howell, threatening them with expulsion. The Rhode Island Assembly responded by voting its approval of its representatives' actions and by reelecting Arnold later that year.

At the same time, in early 1783 Arnold was charged by the Continental army with warning two Vermont Loyalists, Luke Knowlton and Samuel Wells, of their impending arrest, thus aiding their escape from justice. Arnold, who opposed punishing Loyalists, defended himself vigorously before Congress and General George Washington, though he was unable to produce any of the evidence he promised in his behalf. James Madison reported that most of his colleagues believed Arnold guilty but were unwilling to proceed further in such a messy affair.

While serving in Congress from 1782 to 1784, Arnold acted as Vermont's chief advocate; he argued consistently against New York's claims to the Green Mountain region and in favor of Vermont's admission to the Union. This ardent support for Vermont may be connected to Arnold's heavy investment in Vermont land titles. Between 1780 and 1782 Arnold headed up a group of Rhode Islanders who purchased three complete townships in Vermont, two of which, Lyndon and Billymead, were named for Arnold's sons.

In late 1784 Arnold suddenly quit Rhode Island politics and moved to Vermont. Arnold led a group of twenty-three families that founded and settled the Vermont town of St. Johnsbury, named for St. John de Crèvecoeur, in 1786. From the start, Arnold was the town's largest landowner and most active citizen, taking personal charge of even mundane tasks such as the construction of the meeting house and the laying out of roads.

Though busy with the numerous tasks necessary for the establishment of a frontier town, Arnold moved quickly to the center of Vermont politics. The Vermont Assembly, impressed with his previous experience in Congress—a positive impression his former congressional colleagues did not share—chose Arnold without opposition as its representative to appear before Congress in 1788 and 1789. The following year

Arnold was elected to the governor's council, a position to which he was twice reelected by large majorities, and he was appointed a trustee of the planned University of Vermont. Though he had long opposed granting the federal government increased powers, he understood that ratification of the Constitution was the only route by which Vermont could enter the Union, and he took the federalist side at the Vermont Constitutional Convention in 1791. Shortly afterward the Vermont Assembly selected Arnold as one of the special councillors charged with negotiating with Congress for Vermont's admission to the Union.

With Vermont finally part of the United States, Arnold returned to St. Johnsbury, where he had been elected to the Orange County court. After only a year on the bench, Arnold developed a serious lung infection that led to his death at his home in St. Johnsbury. Arnold had been married three times, to Molly Burr of Providence, with whom he had seven children; to Alice Crawford; and to Cynthia Hastings of Charlestown, New Hampshire, with whom he had one son, Lemuel Hastings Arnold, a future governor of Rhode Island. The dates of his marriages are unknown.

• Arnold's papers are at the Vermont State Archives, Montpelier. A biography of Arnold has yet to be published. On his congressional service see Paul H. Smith, ed., *Letters of the Delegates to Congress, 1774–1789*, vol. 19 (1992), and Worthington C. Ford, ed., *Journals of the Continental Congress, 1774–1789*, vols. 22–25 (1904–1937). Irwin H. Polishook, "Rhode Island and the Union, 1774–1790" (Ph.D. diss., Northwestern Univ., 1961), includes many references to Arnold. On Arnold's last years in Vermont, see Edward T. Fairbanks, *Town of St. Johnsbury, Vermont* (1914).

MICHAEL A. BELLESILES

ARNOLD, Richard Dennis (19 Aug. 1808–10 July 1876), physician, was born in Savannah, Georgia, the son of Joseph Arnold and Eliza Dennis, occupations unknown. Despite hardships accompanying the deaths of both parents during childhood, Arnold, who had been an only child, received an excellent preliminary education and graduated with distinction from Princeton in 1826. He immediately began a medical apprenticeship under William R. Waring, a distinguished preceptor and member of an illustrious Charleston and Savannah family of physicians. After receiving his M.D. from the University of Pennsylvania in 1830, Arnold served for two years as a resident house officer in Philadelphia's old Blockley Hospital before returning to Savannah where in 1833 he married Margaret Baugh Stirk. Their only child, Eleanor, born the next year, became the lifelong object of her father's loving solicitude following her mother's untimely death from pulmonary tuberculosis in 1850.

Antebellum southern culture afforded numerous opportunities for able and energetic young men to contribute to community life far beyond the requirements and duties of a profession or vocation. Thus, while still in his mid-twenties, along with the vicissitudes of beginning medical practice Arnold entered on the various activities of an ever-widening public career that filled his lifetime. In 1833 he bought half interest in the Savannah *Daily Georgian*, and although he sold it two years later the editorial venture exercised his literary talents and whetted his interest in politics and public service. An ardent Jackson Democrat, he served in both houses of the state legislature, 1839–1843, was first elected a city alderman in 1842, and in 1843 began the first of four nonconsecutive terms as mayor of Savannah. His efforts for public improvement also included sponsorship of a state vital statistics registration law, support for sanitary reforms in Savannah, and service on the boards of health, water, and education, both state and local. He was also a founder in 1839 of the Georgia Historical Society.

As sectional tensions mounted in the wake of the Mexican War, Arnold repudiated the fire-eating southern secessionists as he had John C. Calhoun during the earlier nullification crisis. Taking his stand as a Union Democrat (he was many times a delegate to national party conventions), he supported Henry Clay's Compromise of 1850 and subsequently backed for the presidency Franklin Pierce and James Buchanan, conservatives in whose hands he believed the nation would weather the storms of conflict. Although he held abolitionists and freesoilers in contempt, Arnold was widely acquainted and highly regarded in both medical and political circles in Philadelphia, New York, and Boston, where he was a frequent visitor and welcome guest. Yet he would finally conclude, in an oft-quoted letter to his daughter on 23 June 1854, that "the only good thing for which we are indebted to the North is Ice, a fit emblem of their hearts and manners" (Shryock, *Letters*, p. 67). It is ironic that he had close Jewish friends and was a harsh critic of anti-Semitism, yet, as a slaveholder, he firmly believed that blacks constituted an inferior race, even though he regarded individual African Americans with respect and affection. In the crisis of secession, like many a southern nationalist, Arnold's ultimate loyalty was to his homeland.

As mayor of Savannah during the war, Arnold fought the community's losing battles against inflation, scarcity, and demoralization while serving as director of the Confederate hospital there. Finally, in December 1864, following the fall of Atlanta and the "march to the sea," Arnold surrendered the beleaguered city to General William T. Sherman, who presented it to President Abraham Lincoln as a Christmas gift. Shortly afterward, in early 1865, with Savannah overrun by starving refugees and business at a standstill, Arnold appealed for relief to his friends in northern cities. They responded generously with clothing, food, and money, thereby averting disaster, even before the war had ended. He was severely criticized for this, as he was for claiming the protection of federal law under military occupation and as he was for offering memorial resolutions for a fallen president. But he opposed "radical" Republicanism in Georgia and in 1868 led a successful movement against it in Chatham County. Advancing in years and in diminished circumstances and health Arnold rested from his political labors when the Democratic party returned to power.

Looking back, he wrote to a physician friend on 28 March 1868, "Although I have taken a part in local politics, as I think every educated man ought to do, my profession has ever been my guiding star" (Shryock, *Letters*, p. 137). Having started out by caring for slaves on nearby plantations, Arnold had been appointed physician to the Savannah Poor House and Hospital in 1835, a position he held for more than thirty years. Known to be kind and sympathetic in ministering to the sick of all classes, he had built a flourishing and lucrative practice. A founder of the Medical Society of the State of Georgia in 1849 and its president in 1851, he was also present at the founding of the American Medical Association (AMA) in 1846, subsequently serving as a secretary and vice president. His interest in elevating the standards of medical education led to the establishment of the Savannah Medical College in 1850, a reputable proprietary school, where he was professor of principles and practice. Between 1857 and 1860 his professional standing and position as mayor of Savannah made him a major figure in the four National Quarantine and Sanitary conventions held during those years. Elected vice president at the Boston convention in 1860, he gave the president's address on behalf of the elderly and enfeebled Jacob Bigelow, a gracious gesture that reflected Arnold's character.

Arnold was known and respected by the leading physicians of his day, both North and South. He was an adherent of anticontagionist etiological thought and therefore supported a wide range of sanitary reforms. In practice he followed the lancet-and-calomel school of therapeutics with moderation, although traditional theory and its methods were even then being challenged both within the profession and without. On a variety of questions and issues he made significant contributions to medical literature, particularly to the *Savannah Medical Journal*, which he edited for a time. His principal interest was in yellow fever and the severe Savannah epidemic of 1854, during which he served heroically.

An epicure and devotee of gastronomy, a connoisseur of Madeira whom gout in June 1872 "reduced . . . to cold water rations" (Shryock, *Letters*, p. 157), Arnold was described the following year in the *Savannah Morning News* as "genial, vivacious, and true hearted still" and as "one of the best read men in the state" (Shryock, "A Doctor in Public Life," p. 301). He died in the same room of the house in which he was born.

• The Arnold papers are held in the Perkins Library, Duke University. Another valuable source is Richard H. Shryock, ed., *Letters of Richard D. Arnold, M.D., 1808–1876* (1929). Arnold's medical writings are primarily in issues of the *Savannah Medical Journal* and the *Charleston Medical Journal and Review* of the 1850s. Pieces that represent his main professional interests include "The Dengue, or Break-Bone Fever, as It Appeared in Savannah in the Summer and Fall of 1850," *Charleston Medical Journal and Review* 6 (1851): 323–40; "Medical Education," *Savannah Medical Journal* 2 (1859–1860): 54–59; *The Reciprocal Duty of Physicians and the Public toward Each Other* (1851), president's address to the Medical Society of the State of Georgia; and *An Essay upon the Relation of Bilious and Yellow Fever* (1856), read before the Medical Society of the State of Georgia. Contemporary appraisals may be found in Joseph M. Toner, "Report on American Medical Necrology, 1878," AMA *Transactions* 29 (1878): 615–18; Charles C. Jones et al., *History of Savannah* (1890), pp. 439–41; and Adelaide Wilson, *Historic and Picturesque Savannah* (1889), pp. 128, 153, 158. Primary materials that display his role in major medical events include Nathan Smith Davis, *History of the American Medical Association, from Its Organization Up to January, 1855* (1855), and *Minutes and Proceedings from the First, Second, Third, and Fourth National Quarantine and Sanitary Conventions* (1857–1860). Among important secondary background materials are Shryock, *Georgia and the Union in 1850* (1926), C. Stephen Gurr, "Social Leadership and the Medical Profession in Antebellum Georgia" (Ph.D. diss., Univ. of Georgia, 1973), and Shryock, "A Doctor in Public Life: Richard D. Arnold of Savannah (1808–1876)," in *Medicine, Science, and Culture*, ed. Lloyd G. Stevenson and Robert P. Multhauf (1968). An obituary is in the *Savannah Morning News*, 11–12 July 1876.

JOHN H. ELLIS

ARNOLD, Thurman (2 June 1891–7 Nov. 1969), lawyer, social and economic theorist, and government official, was born Thurman Wesley Arnold in Laramie, Wyoming, the son of Constantine Peter Arnold, a prominent attorney and rancher, and Annie Brockway. After spending his youth in what he would later remember "as a time that Tom Sawyer would have envied," Arnold enrolled, for one year, at Wabash College in Crawfordsville, Indiana, in 1907. After a college career characterized by loneliness, he graduated from Princeton University, Phi Beta Kappa, with a B.A. in 1911. Arnold received his LL.D. from Harvard Law School in 1914 and then entered legal practice in Chicago with the firm of Adams, Follansbee, Hawley, and Shorey. In 1916 he established the firm of O'Bryan, Waite, and Arnold. Eight months later his artillery battery of the Illinois National Guard was mobilized for duty with General J. J. Pershing's expedition against Pancho Villa into Mexico. On 4 September 1917 Arnold was called up for World War I duty. On 11 September, four days after he married Frances Longan of Sedalia, Missouri (with whom he would have two children), he embarked for Europe.

Arnold always recalled the war as one of the bleakest periods of his life. After the armistice, with few economic prospects in Chicago, he returned to Laramie to join his father's law practice. Soon he became immersed in a three-tiered life of Laramie society, the practice of law, and local and state political affairs. Arnold won election to the lower house of the Wyoming state legislature as the lone Democrat in 1921. A year later he was elected mayor of Laramie on what amounted to a Progressive platform. Always acutely aware of the impact of eastern domince over western land, Arnold became a fervent opponent of vested economic interests as espoused by jurist Louis Brandeis. Bouncing from one political opportunity to another,

Arnold ran for county prosecutor in 1924 but was defeated.

Through the efforts of a Harvard classmate Arnold was appointed dean of the West Virginia University Law School in 1927. Two interests that became challenges confronted the new dean: one, upgrading the law school; two, procedural reform of the West Virginia courts. In his three years as dean, Arnold revolutionized the antiquated court system of West Virginia, efforts that won him the attention of Charles Clark of the Yale Law School. Soon Clark was lecturing at West Virginia, and Arnold was appearing before Yale classes.

In 1930, energetic and restless, Arnold accepted Clark's invitation to join the faculty at Yale, then an intellectual hot bed of legal realism. Characterized by an all-pervasive skepticism of rules, facts, and precedents, legal realism was debated, with fervor, by a brilliant faculty that included, among others, William O. Douglas, Walton Hamilton, Wesley Sturges, Arthur Corbin, and Underhill Moore. Arnold's classroom style—iconoclastic, witty, innovative, unconventional, and above all loud, even raucous—became the talk of the campus. In common with many legal realists, Arnold scorned case book instructional methodology. Hence one of his singular contributions to the Yale Law School was the introduction of the moot court, wherein students were trained to be lawyers through practical courtroom practice.

Also during the Yale years, Arnold wrote two influential books, *The Symbols of Government* (1935) and *The Folklore of Capitalism* (1937), which catapulted him to the forefront of the national intellectual arena. In *Symbols*, Arnold argued that laws were not collections of immutable truths but rather mental representations of symbolic thinking. Arnold refashioned that argument and carried it a step further in *Folklore*, wherein he asserted that social progress was possible only through a pragmatic (rather than experimental) approach to government. Reassuring the nervous brokers on Wall Street that his was essentially a conservative diagnosis of America's economic and social ills were Arnold's assurances that there was no reason to root out capitalism; what civilization needed was fresh folklore for the common man and new vitalized myths. Some readers recognized that Arnold had deviated from legal realism by maintaining that myths were often as prescriptive as facts and that for all its emancipating self-discipline, legal realism did not provide the philosophical foundation for a vital civilization.

The Yale years ultimately were transformed into the Washington years as Arnold routinely accepted, from the administration of Franklin Roosevelt, one special assignment after another. In the spring of 1937, the foes of monopoly succeeded in their campaign to gain President Roosevelt's favor. One such adviser, Attorney General Robert Jackson, a good friend, recommended Arnold for the post of assistant attorney general for the antitrust division. Perceiving his role, first and foremost, as an enforcer of existing antitrust statutes, Arnold shunned the promotion of additional antitrust legislation and thereby bypassed a role as policy maker. Instead he moved quickly to implement his antitrust program, which pivoted around three essential points: a well-publicized, uniform policy; the creation of an effective, viable antitrust division; and the elimination of partisan politics from within the division.

As Arnold crisscrossed the country, preaching his antitrust philosophy with missionary zeal, his implementation of antitrust enforcement veered in two directions. First, accepting the Sherman Antitrust Act as flawed but workable legislation, he refashioned and revived the consent decree such that any indictment issued would be dropped provided that fundamental remedial practices were undertaken by the industry; second, he dramatically increased criminal prosecutions. These tactics were amazingly successful. Within two years Arnold's staff had skyrocketed from forty-eight to just over three hundred attorneys. In all, the division initiated 93 suits and launched 215 investigations into virtually every sector of the economy, from cinema to fertilizer to the petroleum industries. Neither labor nor the American Medical Association were exempted from Arnold's nonpartisan and highly publicized scrutiny. Many historians and commentators have referred to Arnold's tenure at Justice as the most effective of antitrust enforcement in U.S. history.

As clouds foreboding World War II gathered over Washington, Roosevelt's attention became increasingly diverted from domestic issues to foreign policy. When Arnold realized that monopolists were being enlisted without prejudice in mobilizing the war effort, he became disillusioned and made no secret of it. His resignation a seeming inevitability, in March 1943 Roosevelt appointed Arnold a judge of the U.S. Court of Appeals for the District of Columbia. In his two-plus years as an appellate court judge, Arnold wrote sixty-seven opinions, and in two areas, insanity and obscenity, his words made legal history. Intellectually and temperamentally, though, Arnold was ill-suited for a judicial role. Later, when asked why he left the bench, Arnold would quote his friend George Wharton Pepper, "I would rather make my living talking to a bunch of damn fools than listening to a bunch of damn fools."

In the summer of 1945 Arnold left the court and formed a law firm with Arne Wiprud, a specialist in transportation law. A merger of dissimilar temperaments and talents, the firm was dissolved within a year. On 18 April 1946 Arnold joined forces with Abe Fortas, recently undersecretary of agriculture. Although he was never comfortable being a corporate attorney, Arnold brought to Arnold, Fortas and Porter an uncanny ability to perceive the complexities of a case as well as the Arnold mystique of genius.

Every bit of Arnold's optimism, brilliance and courage was tested during the early 1950s, a period of national panic driven by fears of communist infiltration of the government as vociferously alleged by Wisconsin senator Joseph R. McCarthy. For Arnold, the gauntlet was dropped in the form of a client, Dorothy Bailey, a government employee who was being called before the House Un-American Activities Committee. One of Arnold's three most highly publicized cases during the McCarthy era, it was lost on legal technicalities and not constitutional grounds. The second well-known case, which was a victory, was that of Dr. John Peters, a faculty member at the Yale Medical School and consultant for the U.S. Public Health Service. His disloyalty was questioned, and after a three-year period of hearings and investigations he was cleared. The charges in the third case, involving scholar Owen Lattimore, were dismissed on the basis of being too vague.

With the censuring of McCarthy in December 1954, Arnold returned to his corporate practice. Subsequently, however, he lost much of his aura as a champion of civil liberties. A hawk on the war in Vietnam, Arnold considered the campus riots, the disruption of the draft, and the general civil disobedience of the 1960s as bordering on treason. He died at his home in Alexandria, Virginia.

• The Arnold papers are in the American Heritage Center, University of Wyoming. Arnold wrote prolifically; among his many books are *Report on West Virginia Procedure and Legal Reform* (1927), *Cases on Trials, Judgments, and Appeals* (1936), *Bottlenecks of Business* (1940), *Democracy and Free Enterprise* (1942), *Cartels or Free Enterprise?* (1945), and *The Future of Democratic Capitalism* (1950). His autobiography is *Fair Fights and Foul* (1965). See also *Voltaire and the Cowboy: The Letters of Thurman Arnold*, ed. Gene M. Gressley (1977). Biographical sketches and career analyses abound. The following have varying degrees of usefulness: Joseph Alsop and Robert Kinter, "Trust Buster—The Folklore of Thurman Arnold," *Saturday Evening Post*, 12 Aug. 1939; Warren Hill, "Psychological Realism of Thurman Arnold," *University of Chicago Law Review* 22 (Winter 1955): 5–11; Abe Fortas, "Thurman Arnold and the Theatre of Law," *Yale Law Journal* 79 (1970): 566–76; Richard L. Strout, "The Folklore of Thurman Arnold," *Christian Science Monitor*, 11 May 1940, pp. 8–12; Corwin Edwards, "Thurman Arnold and the Antitrust Laws," *Political Science Quarterly* 42 (Sept. 1943): 143–55; Gene M. Gressley, "Thurman Arnold, Antitrust, and the New Deal," *Business History Review* 38 (Summer 1964): 214–31; Edward N. Kearny, *Thurman Arnold, Social Critic* (1970); Ellis W. Hawley, *The New Deal and the Problem of Monopoly* (1966); Wilfrid E. Rumble, Jr., *American Legal Realism* (1968); and Laura Kalman, *Legal Realism at Yale* (1986) and *Abe Fortas* (1990). An obituary is in the *New York Times*, 8 Nov. 1969.

GENE M. GRESSLEY

ARNOW, Harriette Simpson (7 July 1908–21 Mar. 1986), writer, was born in Wayne County, Kentucky, the daughter of Elias Simpson, a schoolteacher and bookkeeper, and Mollie Jane Denney, a schoolteacher. Arnow's early life was spent in Burnside, Kentucky, a lumbering center known as Head of Navigation of the Cumberland River, and the Cumberland area maintained a strong hold on her, inspiring a number of her books and stories. Following her graduation from Burnside High School, Harriette enrolled at Berea College, a school that stressed a Christian life and maintained strict regulations regarding students' work, dress, and social activities. Although she thrived on the academic challenges of Berea, she found it difficult to accept all of the restrictive aspects of the school. She was forced to leave after her freshman year for financial reasons, and although only eighteen years old, she found a teaching position in a remote part of her home county and set out on her first career.

She soon decided that if she were to be a good teacher she would need more education. Moving to Louisville, she enrolled at the university there, eventually receiving her degree in 1930. From 1931 to 1934 she taught and served as principal in a small rural high school in Pulaski, Kentucky, and taught at a junior high school in Louisville. Her interests, however, were moving toward writing, ultimately leading her to move to Cincinnati, where she supported herself by working as a waitress. It was here that she published stories in little magazines and began work on *Mountain Path*, her first novel, which was published in 1936.

The story of a young schoolteacher, Louisa Sheridan, *Mountain Path* appears on the surface to be just another melodramatic story of the mountains, complete with suspense, violence, and romance. But in fact it offers a penetrating view of mountain life and a sensitive treatment of those caught up in its harsh conditions. Although *Mountain Path* was well received by reviewers, it was criticized by Harriette's relatives, who thought that she should have written about "nicer people."

In 1938 Harriette met Harold Arnow, a newspaperman from Chicago who was looking for work in Cincinnati. Their common interest in writing first drew them together, and they were married in 1939. With romantic thoughts of life in the country, the couple bought a picturesque piece of land on Little Indian Creek in Kentucky. Life there was anything but romantic, however, and after the birth of their first child in 1941, the Arnows decided to leave their rural home. In 1945 Harold Arnow took a position with the *Detroit Times*, and the family moved to a housing project in Detroit. Shortly after, their second child was born.

In Detroit Arnow finished her novel *Hunter's Horn* (1949), the story of a Kentucky fox hunter consumed by the desire to kill King Devil, a fox that he is convinced is evil. What *Mountain Path* began, this novel brings to fruition. *Hunter's Horn* analyzes the need for love and compassion amid a life of unrelenting hardship.

Following the publication of *Hunter's Horn*, Arnow turned to Detroit as the setting for her next major effort, *The Dollmaker* (1954), which focuses on people who came to Detroit from the South during the war to work in automobile factories. The protagonist is a strong Kentucky woman who tries desperately to keep her family together in a setting that she finds strange disorienting, and destructive. Her source of strength is a giant block of wood out of which she hopes to carve a figure of Christ. Unable to find the right face for her figure, she finally destroys it by splitting it, understanding that there can be no single face for Christ.

With a husband and two children to care for, Arnow was pressed to find time for writing. Undaunted, however, she carried out considerable research on the Cumberland area that resulted in two excellent books of social history, *Seedtime on the Cumberland* (1960) and *Flowering of the Cumberland* (1963). Both are rich in the detail of the history of the region and of the people who settled it.

By this time the Arnows were living on the outskirts of Ann Arbor, Michigan. Surrounded by a growing urban sprawl, their ramshackle house was another version of their home on Little Indian Creek. It became the setting for *The Weedkiller's Daughter* (1970). The tale of a teenage girl, it does not reach the creative level of Arnow's previous fiction but touches sensitively on the generation gap between the protagonist, a child of the 1960s, and the adults of her world. In 1974 Arnow published her last novel, *The Kentucky Trace*, which presents a gallery of Kentucky characters caught up in the turmoil of the American Revolution. She died in Ann Arbor.

Although Harriette Arnow cannot be rated as one of the great modern American fiction writers, she has certainly earned a place in the American literary chronicle. Her work expresses an ironic yet realistic faith in humankind and its future. Rejecting the experimental and the complex, she chose to present her artistic vision with a simplicity that gives her writing considerable stature. Focusing on character more than on plot, Arnow peopled her novels and stories with characters who are often circumscribed by restrictive and environmental forces that dictate their lives but also provide some opportunity for hope and creativity. Whether her characters live in Detroit or in the hills of Kentucky, whether they are kind or cruel, iconoclast or preacher, they are real.

• Harriette Arnow's entire collection of papers and manuscripts is in the University of Kentucky Library, Special Collections. Wilton Eckley, *Harriette Arnow* (1974), presents a critical study of her works up to *The Kentucky Trace*, along with biographical material. Arnow is also featured in an essay by Joyce Carol Oates in her *New Heaven, New Earth: The Visionary Experience in Literature* (1974).

WILTON ECKLEY

ARNSTEIN, Margaret (27 Oct. 1904–8 Oct. 1972), public health nurse and educator, was born Margaret Gene Arnstein in New York City, the daughter of Leo Arnstein, a successful businessman, and Elsie Nathan, a volunteer social worker. She was exposed to public health nursing at an early age by her parents, both second-generation Jewish Americans of German heritage, who were involved with Lillian Wald's famous Henry Street settlement house and had a strong commitment to helping the poor. Her father later applied his Progressive beliefs as welfare commissioner of New York City. Inspired by Wald, a close family friend and a nurse herself, Arnstein knew even before she graduated from the Ethical Culture School in 1921 that she would pursue a career in nursing.

Upon graduating from Smith College in 1925, Arnstein entered the New York Presbyterian Hospital School of Nursing. She received her nurse's cap and diploma in 1928 and spent the following year studying for an A.M. in public health nursing at Teachers College. Arnstein then moved to White Plains, New York, to become a staff nurse at Westchester County Hospital. By the close of a five-year stint there she was promoted to supervisor, but Arnstein realized that hospital nursing did not satisfy her desire to make a difference in public health.

In order to qualify as a public health nurse, Arnstein next went to Johns Hopkins University, where in 1934 she earned a master's in public health. Armed with her new knowledge, she returned to New York City to start work as a consultant nurse in New York State's Department of Health's Communicable Disease Division. Three years later she moved on again, when the University of Minnesota offered her a job as director of its nursing course and as a professor of health and nursing in its Department of Preventive Medicine.

Once more, Arnstein found that she wanted to play a greater role when it came to policy making. She felt that nurses should be encouraged to participate in the analysis of health care because they have "an intuitive grasp of the ways in which their patient might fare better." Practicing what she preached, in 1940 Arnstein returned to New York to take a job as a consultant nurse to the Department of Health. She devoted a large portion of her time to designing field studies to poll nurses for suggestions on how to modernize the field. In 1941 she coauthored with Gaylord Anderson a text entitled *Communicable Disease Control*.

During World War II Arnstein served from 1943 to 1945 as a chief nurse for the United Nations Relief and Rehabilitation Administration in the Balkans. Her experience there brought her to the attention of the Public Health Service, and at the close of the war she accepted a job in Washington, D.C., as assistant to the chief of the nursing division. In 1949 she was promoted to chief of the division of nursing resources, and by 1960 she had risen to chief of public health nursing. She continued her field research in this new post; in 1953 she played a role in the publication of the World Health Organization's *Guide for National Studies of Nursing Resources*, and in 1956 she organized the first International Conference on Nursing Studies.

Always balancing her twin interests in public health and education, Arnstein in 1958 took a leave from the Public Health Service to spend a year teaching at Yale's Nursing School. Public service lured her out of the classroom two years later and back to the Public Health Service, where she was promoted to chief of nursing. In this post she continued her longstanding interest in international welfare and public health. In 1964 she moved to the Office of International Health, where, funded by the Rockefeller Foundation and the Agency for International Development, she began studying what health services developing countries needed. A research trip to India persuaded her to enlist local midwives and nurses in an education campaign for preventive medicine.

In 1965 Arnstein was named the first senior nursing adviser for international health in the surgeon general's office. That same year she became the first woman ever to receive the Rockefeller Public Service Award, which came with a monetary award of $10,000. Five years later she received the Sedgwick Memorial Medal from the American Public Health Association. An avid tennis player and theatergoer, Arnstein was considered an indefatigable worker. Although she never married, she had many friends, both professional and social.

In 1966 Arnstein ended her Public Health Service career for good, accepting a position as a professor at the University of Michigan's Nursing School. Later on a friend of hers who was then at Michigan took full credit for recruiting her to Ann Arbor. He explained, "I wanted the best in the world and she was it." The Yale School of Nursing agreed, and in 1967 she was appointed dean of the school. She died five years later from cancer at her home in New Haven, Connecticut.

• The Margaret Arnstein Papers are in the National Nursing Archives, Mugar Library, Boston University. See also Myron Wegman, "A Tribute to Margaret Arnstein," *American Journal of Public Health* 63 (Feb. 1973): 97. An obituary is in the *New York Times*, 9 Oct. 1972.

SHARI RUDAVSKY

ARONSON, Boris (Oct. 1900–16 Nov. 1980), scene and costume designer, was born in Kiev, Russia, the son of Solomon Aronson, the chief rabbi of Kiev, and Deborah Turfsky. By the age of eight he was exhibiting astonishing artistic talent and went on to study art in Kiev, Moscow, and Paris.

This was an exciting time of artistic experimentation in Russia, and Aronson served his design apprenticeship in the world of Russian Jewish theater. There was a growing movement in Yiddish theater, and the Vilna Troupe (founded in 1916) was developing subsidiary companies in a number of countries, including the United States. The troupe's success led to the founding in 1917 of the Jewish Theater in Moscow, where Aronson was strongly influenced by theater sets in the cubist-fantastic style developed by Marc Chagall and Nathan Altman. In 1923 Aronson emigrated to New York, where he designed scenery for two Yiddish theater groups, the Unser Theater and Maurice Schwartz's Yiddish Art Theatre.

Aronson's first important Broadway assignment came in 1932 with S. J. Perelman's *Walk a Little Faster*. By the mid-1930s Aronson became identified with the liberal-left artists of the Group Theatre who were revolting against the glitter and extravagance of the typical Broadway fare. The most important dramatist discovered by the Group was Clifford Odets, and Aronson captured the mood of his play *Awake and Sing* (1935) in form and color. Aronson's sets conveyed the genteel shabbiness to which Odets's characters clung in their struggle to keep from sliding into abject poverty. His work on the Group productions *Paradise Lost* (1935) and *Gentle People* (1939) was equally effective. Aronson continued to work on Broadway as well, most notably designing the successful farce *Three Men on a Horse* (1935) and Thornton Wilder's *The Merchant of Yonkers* (1938).

Perhaps Aronson's most influential work was the development of "projected scenery." The use of light to enhance and exploit the three-dimensionality of the stage had been advocated by Adolph Appia and Edward Gordon Craig, leaders of the European theater design revolution, as early as the 1890s, experimented with all over Europe in the first half of the century, and popularized by demonstrations such as Thomas Wilfred's *Color Organ*. Aronson, building on these developments, designed a complete stage set consisting of basic permanent units of interrelated abstract shapes. These set units were covered in neutral grey gauze that enabled them to be "painted" any hue, saturation, and tint by the way in which colored light was directed on them. The wide variety of directions from which each light could be projected on the gauze, the number of lighting instruments used, and the flexibility of the intensity of each light made the visual effects infinitely variable. Stage lighting was becoming a separate design area, and one of the innovators in this field, Jean Rosenthal, worked with Aronson early in her career.

The projected scenery method proved especially useful for the enormously decorative scenery needed for ballet and opera. Aronson first used this style of scenic design in the production of *The Great American Goof* (1940), a ballet-play by Eugene Loring and William Saroyan. His designs were so artistically stimulating that in 1947 Aronson was asked to exhibit his projected scenery works at the Museum of Modern Art. The exhibition, titled *Painting with Lights*, displayed examples of stage sets created with colored lights. He continued to do more conventional theatrical work as well. *Detective Story* (1949), for instance, was marked by the stark realism of Aronson's set. In 1945 Aronson married Lisa Jalowertz, who assisted him in his artistic enterprises. They had one child.

Aronson earned an Antoinette Perry (Tony) Award, the theater's most prestigious award, for his design for Tennessee Williams's *The Rose Tattoo* (1951). Aronson's use of color, light, and texture enabled him to highlight qualities unique to each production. He became a much sought after designer for opera and ballet. Among other operas, Aronson designed sets for Marvin David Levy's *Mourning Becomes Electra* and Beethoven's *Fidelio*. His opera and ballet work in no way diminished his increasing number of Broadway and other productions, including *The Country Girl* (1950), by Odets; *I Am a Camera* (1951); *The Diary of Anne Frank* and *Bus Stop* (both 1955); Archibald MacLeish's *J.B.* (1958); and *Coriolanus* in Stratford-upon-Avon, England (1959). Aronson also began a long association with the productions of Arthur Miller when he designed *The Crucible* (1953) and *A View from the*

Bridge (1955). Constantly working, he turned down more design opportunities than he was able to take. Among Aronson's designs during the 1960s were Miller's *Incident at Vichy* (1964) and *The Price* (1968) and the musicals *Fiddler on the Roof* (1964), *Cabaret* (1966), and *Zorba* (1968). He earned two more Tonys for *Cabaret* and *Zorba*.

Even when he was in his seventies, Aronson continued to be sought after as a musical comedy designer. He created innovative, unique, Tony-winning designs for the Stephen Sondheim musicals *Company* (1970), *Follies* (1971), *A Little Night Music* (1973), and *Pacific Overtures* (1976).

Aronson died in a hospital near his home in Nyack, New York. His enormous body of work had a lasting influence on the development of theatrical design in the United States. He mastered the use of light and texture to convey the essence of a work. Aronson is among the great American stage designers of the twentieth century.

• The most useful account of Aronson's career is Frank Rich with Lisa Aronson, *The Theatre Art of Boris Aronson* (1987), which includes a bibliography. Works on Aronson's exhibitions include *Art in the Theatre* (1927, Anderson Galleries, New York City); a retrospective of all his stage work, *Boris Aronson: From His Theatre Work* (1981, Vincent Gallery, New York Public Library for the Performing Arts, Lincoln Center); and *Boris Aronson: Stage Design as Visual Metaphor* (1989, Katonah Gallery, Harvard Theatre Collection). Frank Rich, the chief drama critic for the *New York Times* reviewed the Katonah exhibition in *Theatre Design & Technology* 25 (Fall 1989): 8. Waldemar-George [pseud.], *Boris Aronson et l'art du theatre* (1928), in the *Maitres de l'art etranger* series, contains thirty-two leaves of plates. Only 315 copies were printed. See also Lore Lindenfeld, "Boris Aronson: Setting the Stage for Theatrical Invention," *Surface Design Journal* 14 (Spring 1990): 19. An obituary is in the *New York Times*, 17 Nov. 1980.

CARY CLASZ

ARONSON, Rudolph (8 Apr. 1856–4 Feb. 1919), theatrical impresario and composer, was born in New York City to German immigrant parents (names and occupations unknown). When he was six, his music-loving parents arranged for him to have instruction on the piano. Recognizing in Aronson a definite musical precocity, his teacher, Leopold Meyer, persuaded Aronson's parents to allow the child to be trained for a musical career and introduced Aronson to the violin and the theory of music. At age fourteen Aronson attended a concert featuring musical stars under the direction of Patrick S. Gilmore at the New York Academy of Music. Included in the program was the waltz king himself, Johann Strauss, who conducted several of his own compositions. So impressed was Aronson with Strauss and his music that he decided to follow in Strauss's footsteps. When he was sixteen he wrote his first waltz, the "Arcadian," which was presented the same year at the Arcadian Club in New York. The waltz was published in September 1873 and was played professionally at the Central Park Garden shortly thereafter. Encouraged by the work's success, Aronson left New York, accompanied by his three sisters, to study in Europe.

Arriving in Paris in 1874, Aronson became the pupil of Émile Durand of the Conservatoire National, and for three years he studied harmony, counterpoint, and instrumentation. His education was augmented by attendance at most of the major concerts, operas, and theatrical presentations that Paris had to offer. He was present at some debuts of works by composers such as Charles Gounod, Camille Saint-Saëns, and Georges Bizet. In August 1876 he traveled to Bayreuth in Germany for the first Wagner Festival and reported his experience in the 19 August issue of the *American Register* of Paris.

After completing his studies in Europe, Aronson returned to the United States and immediately began pursuing a career as a composer of waltzes and orchestral works. His first waltzes were introduced by Gilmore in New York. Aronson's friends persuaded him to lease the Madison Square Garden on Sunday evenings for a series of popular concerts in 1877, but he found himself in competition with Barnum's Circus and the sounds of the menagerie. Consequently, he decided to find another hall. With the help of influential friends and patrons, Aronson organized the Metropolitan Concert Company the following year and was able to build the 3,000-seat Metropolitan Concert Hall in 1880, where he established himself as the conductor of a fifty-member orchestra and where he introduced many of his own compositions. The hall, which stood on the corner of Broadway and Forty-first Street, was modeled after concert resorts in Vienna and Berlin and provided refreshments with the entertainment, both at reasonable prices. The venture was, however, not the success Aronson had envisioned, and he relinquished the hall to other management in 1881.

Aronson returned to Europe in 1881 seeking a fresh outlet for his musical ambitions. After revisiting the famous concert halls of Europe, he returned to the United States intent on erecting a building that would include a roof garden and amenities such as a ballroom, a reading room, and a restaurant, in addition to a theater for concerts and musical entertainment. He began raising money for his venture in 1881, naming it the Casino Theatre. While the theater was being built, Aronson returned to Europe to line up attractions for his new musical venue. He had arranged to open the theater with the famous singer Madame Theo and a season of French opera, but the Casino was not completed in time, and he was forced to book another theater for Theo's engagement. Although his theater was not quite finished, the undaunted Aronson presented Strauss's *The Queen's Lace Handerkerchief* as the theater's opening attraction on 21 October 1882. The run was interrupted while the construction of the theater continued to completion. It resumed on 30 December and played a total of 234 performances, a notable success for the time. Of more interest to New Yorkers was the opening of the Casino Roof Garden on 7 July 1883. It offered after-theater entertainment and light refreshments in an open-air setting on the roof of the building during the months of mild weather. The garden became the prototype for a spate of other roof gardens in New York and, more important, a precursor of the twentieth-century nightclub. Aronson's name is indelibly associated with the creation of the roof garden, which became a Gay Nineties institution.

During his sixteen-year stewardship of the Casino, the theater, an imposing Moorish-style presence at the corner of Broadway and Thirty-ninth Street, became New York's premiere light and comic opera house. Aronson set new standards of production, providing lavish costumes and scenery and employing the finest talent available. Under his aegis, the Casino developed the talents of Lillian Russell, Francis Wilson, Della Fox, DeWolf Hopper, and Jefferson de Angelis, all of whom in their time became stars of the American stage. Aronson produced a succession of operettas by Strauss, Jacques Offenbach, Gilbert and Sullivan, and other popular composers. His greatest triumph was a 1,256-performance run in 1886 of *Erminie* (1886), an operetta by Henry Paulton and Edward Jakobowski. Aronson's popularization of the operetta and comic opera became one of the foundation blocks for the later emergence of American musical comedy.

For a while during the 1880s Aronson managed the Bijou Theatre, which also featured light opera, but he eventually left theatrical production to become an impresario and agent around the turn of the century. As a successful impresario and entrepreneur, he established offices in London, Paris, and Milan, always seeking musical talent and works that he could book into theaters in the United States. During his various activities, Aronson continued composing, producing approximately 150 works, including waltzes, orchestral pieces, and a few light operas. Aronson married Alma D'Alma, (the stage name of Ann Chandler), a member of the Casino chorus, in 1889; the couple subsequently divorced in 1896. The number of their children, if any, is unknown. During his final years Aronson built and managed hotels in New York and Puerto Rico. He died at the home of his sisters in New York.

• Aronson's autobiography, which is somewhat self-congratulatory, was published in 1913 as *Theatrical and Musical Memoirs*. The book was based on a multipart series titled "Memoirs of a Musician" published in the *Saturday Evening Post*, beginning on 6 Apr. 1912. His activities were reported in *Musical America*, 11 Aug. 1906. See also George C. D. Odell, *Annals of the New York Stage*, vols. 14 (1942) and 15 (1949), and the clipping file on Aronson at the New York Performing Arts Library. Obituaries appeared in many newspapers throughout the United States.

MARY C. HENDERSON

ARP, Bill. *See* Smith, Charles Henry.

ARRINGTON, Alfred W. (17 Sept. 1810–31 Dec. 1867), minister, author, and judge, was born in Iredell County, North Carolina, the son of H. Archibald Arrington, a Methodist minister. (His mother's maiden name was Moore; her first name is not known.) Arrington passed his childhood amid the picturesque scenery of the Blue Ridge Mountains. His early education consisted solely of reading from the Bible, until a family with a small library moved into the area and he was able to read more widely.

When his father moved to Arkansas, then almost a wilderness, Arrington himself became a Methodist preacher at the age of eighteen. He preached for several years and during that time also contributed articles to *Southern Magazine*. In "Travels through Arkansas," he commented on the great proliferation of whiskey in that state and satirically expressed his desire for a little water. Arrington eventually lost his faith and abandoned the ministry. In 1835 he was admitted to the bar in Missouri and for twelve years practiced law in Missouri, Arkansas, and Texas. He became a member of the Arkansas legislature and also published a number of pamphlets, one dealing with the execution of a number of persons at Cane Hill. These literary endeavors were incorporated into his later works.

In 1847 Arrington traveled east, visiting Boston and New York. He wrote *Sketches of the South and South-West*, which was printed in several newspapers. During this period, under the pseudonym of Charles Summerfield, he published *The Desperadoes of the South-West* (1847), which described "deadly combats, desperate duels, and bloody assassinations, the mere recollection of which chills the blood in my veins, and excites an involuntary shudder of horror." A second volume of *Desperadoes* titled *Duelists and Duelling in the South-West* (1847) was also published and included sketches of southern life. Arrington also wrote an essay titled "The Mathematical Harmonies of the Universe," which was later translated into both French and German.

Two years later, in 1849, Arrington moved to Brownsville, Texas, where in 1850 he was elected a judge of the Twelfth Judicial District. He held the office for five years. In 1856 he resigned because of ill health and moved to New York City, where he completed a work on logic that was never published and also wrote the novel *The Rangers and Regulators of the Tanaha* (1956). Similar to his first compilation, *The Rangers* was written under the pseudonym of Charles Summerfield. The subject matter, also similar to his earlier works, dealt with the rough, forceful, and often deadly forms of justice encountered in the then pioneer state of Texas.

In 1857 Arrington moved to Chicago, where he again engaged in the practice of law. A highly respected lawyer in both state and federal courts, he handled various high-profile cases and became well known for his oratorical skills. He was even credited by a contemporary as "having a very large brain—as large, if not larger, than that of Daniel Webster" (Linder). Not abandoning his literary pursuits, Arrington wrote poetry in his spare time. These poems were collected and published posthumously by his wife, Leora, in 1869. The verses in *Poems* address his affection for his wife and daughter, include a eulogy to General William Tecumseh Sherman, and deal at great length with both spiritual and religious subjects. Prior to his death, Arrington returned to his Christain faith and received baptism in the Catholic church. He died in Chicago.

Arrington, a restless individual, successful minister, gifted orator, and respected attorney, is best remembered for his literary pursuits. His objective insight concerning the administration of pioneer justice in fledgling southern and western states provides an accurate account of frontier history. Concerning the subject of his works, Arrington wrote:

> I might have chosen a much more facile course; and dealt in bitter denunciations [of frontier justice]; and whetted barbed satires dipped in gall; for it is much easier to rail than to reason; and the very lowest flight of genius is truculent tirade. But I could not make up my mind to do so, for I am a man myself, and an erring one too; and neither an ascetic or a fiend. I chronicle the deeds of men; and neither perfect good nor perfect evil, appertains to human nature or any of its acts. (*The Desperadoes of the South-West*)

• Secondary sources about Arrington include Usher F. Linder, *Reminiscenes of the Early Bench and Bar of Illinois* (1879), and John M. Parker, *The Bench and Bar of Illinois, Historical and Reminiscent*, vol. 2 (1899). Valuable information may also be found in the preface to his *Poems* (1869). An obituary is in the *Chicago Tribune*, 1 Jan. 1868.

JASON B. SHAW

ARTHUR, Chester Alan (5 Oct. 1829–18 Nov. 1886), twenty-first president of the United States, was born in Fairfield, Vermont, of Irish and English descent, the son of William Arthur, a teacher and Baptist minister, and Malvina Stone. During his youth he and his family experienced considerable economic insecurity. Still, "Chet," as friends called him, was given a solid classical education, and he graduated from Union College in Schenectady, New York, in 1848. At eighteen, Arthur was a tall, good-looking, charming, somewhat romantic young man who enjoyed debating and writing and who shared his father's abolitionist beliefs.

After teaching school in upstate New York and studying law privately, Arthur went to New York City in 1853 to work in a law office. He was admitted to the bar in May 1854, became a partner in a law firm, and soon was involved in two cases that significantly expanded the rights of blacks.

Arthur was an early member of the new Republican party. He made friends with the powerful politician Thurlow Weed and with the merchant Edwin D. Morgan, who was elected governor in 1858. Morgan named Arthur engineer in chief (an unpaid and largely ceremonial position) on his general staff. At thirty, Arthur seemed to have an extremely promising future in New York politics.

On 25 October 1859 Arthur married Ellen Lewis Herndon, the only child of the Amazon explorer and naval captain William Lewis Herndon. Ellen, attractive and ambitious, was an upper-class Virginian who had spent most of her life in Washington, D.C. The Arthurs had three children, one of whom died at an early age.

Shortly after the Civil War broke out, Governor Morgan made Arthur a brigadier general and then named him acting assistant quartermaster general. He was given the complex task of feeding, housing, clothing, and equipping thousands of troops pouring into New York City on their way to combat. By all accounts, he handled the assignment effectively. He also lobbied in Albany for wartime legislation, such as the state militia law, and inspected forts and defenses in various parts of New York State. The closest he came to battle was during the spring of 1862 when he made a brief tour into the South to inspect New York troops.

Promotions came rapidly. In February 1862 Arthur was appointed inspector general, and in July of the same year he was commissioned quartermaster general. While at this rank, he supervised the enlistment and preparedness of more than 200,000 enlistees, receiving widespread praise for his energy, integrity, and organizational skills.

Morgan and his staff lost their commissions on 1 January 1863 when a new Democratic governor took office. Arthur did not reenlist, in part because of the prosouthern sentiments of his wife and her relatives. During the remainder of the war, he devoted himself to politics, law, and money-making. The Arthurs soon purchased a handsome two-story brownstone home in New York City and traveled in high social circles.

In 1864 Arthur became a close friend of the wealthy and unscrupulous New York hatter Thomas Murphy. Both were members of the conservative wing of New York's Republican party and supported Andrew Johnson of Tennessee for their party's vice presidential nomination. The two also collected assessments from political appointees during the campaign and solicited donations from affluent army contractor friends. Increasingly, Arthur abandoned the idealism of his youth and accepted ideas and methods embraced by some of the era's shadiest politicos.

Arthur moved up rapidly within the state GOP machinery. In the late 1860s he allied himself with New York senator Roscoe Conkling. Both men labored intensively in 1868 for Republican presidential candidate Ulysses S. Grant, Arthur serving as chairman of the Central Grant Club of New York as well as a member of the Republican State Committee. From 1869 to 1870 Arthur served as counsel to the New York City tax commission, a position controlled by corrupt Tammany Hall boss William Marcy Tweed. In late 1871 Arthur succeeded scandal-plagued Murphy as collector of the New York customhouse. His appointment was widely understood to be a triumph for Conkling and his supporters.

The New York customhouse was the largest single federal office in the nation and the country's richest source of political patronage. (About 75 percent of the nation's customs receipts were collected there; by 1872 the customhouse payroll was approximately $1.8 million annually.) The spoils system had long flourished at the customhouse, where roughly 1,000 political associates were given jobs regardless of qualifications and then assessed a portion of their salaries. By

1866, according to one study, corruption and inefficiency in the customhouse were costing the government between $12 million and $25 million annually. When Arthur took office, he became the country's highest-paid employee.

Arthur used his authority as collector in large part to benefit the Conkling faction of his party. Despite new civil service rules, the corruption, inefficiency, and waste that had flourished under Murphy continued. Reformers, who wanted appointments based on merit and sought an end to political assessments, had hoped for better things from Arthur. Still, the collector was popular with businessmen and subordinates. His sophistication, tact, appearance, education, and good manners made him appear a cut above the crude politicos with whom he associated and earned him the nickname "Gentleman Boss."

Arthur played a highly active role in politics while serving as collector. He attended state and national party conventions, encouraged political assessments (illegal after October 1872), and paid careful attention to appointments on all levels. He also transmitted funds to GOP candidates across the country. By 1873 Conkling and his allies in other states, who were labeled the "Stalwarts," were in command of the Grant administration, leading it through one of the most corrupt periods in American history. But by 1876 Conkling's power was waning, in large part due to the public's disapproval of the second Grant administration. The senator failed badly in an effort, supported by Arthur, to win the Republican presidential nomination.

In April 1877 the successful candidate, Ohio governor Rutherford B. Hayes, with the backing of businessmen and reformers, launched an investigation of the New York customhouse. After a thorough probe, a commission issued three reports that criticized the customhouse and its leadership and called for an end to partisan control. When Arthur resisted recommendations for reform, the president, following a bitter struggle that included a temporary victory by Conkling in the Senate and a second customhouse investigation, dismissed him in July 1878. The customhouse battle, which reflected a struggle between GOP factions as well as a desire for civil service reform, concluded in February 1879 with an administration victory.

Arthur, insisting that he had done nothing wrong, joined Conkling and other Stalwarts in all-out efforts to restore their power. They won important victories in state elections in 1879 but were unable to secure the GOP presidential nomination for Grant in the following year. The nomination went instead to Senator James A. Garfield of Ohio. In order to balance the ticket geographically and placate the Stalwarts, the Republicans gave the vice presidential nomination to Arthur, who had sought the position despite Conkling's disapproval. A place on the national ticket, Arthur believed, would repair his reputation, which had been damaged during the customhouse row. Arthur was the central figure in New York's Republican campaign. Among other things, he quietly raised large sums of money by assessing government workers. New York turned out to be the pivotal state in an extremely close presidential election.

Soon after the GOP victory, Garfield and the Conklingites began to quarrel. The battle was initiated by the new president's failure to live up to alleged campaign promises regarding patronage. Moreover, it was clear that Garfield had allied himself with his secretary of state, James G. Blaine, who despised Conkling and his allies and was determined to undermine their power. Arthur received much bad publicity for openly siding with Conkling.

Garfield was wounded by an assassin's bullet in July 1881 and died as a result of his wound on 19 September. On 20 September Arthur took the oath of office as president. Arthur's reputation as a spoilsman and political manipulator did not inspire confidence, and many thought that Conkling would now control the White House. But the new chief executive quickly made it clear that he would not be Conkling's puppet. Faced with a crisis that shocked and sobered him, Arthur rose above his shady past.

The Arthur administration won considerable praise during its first several months. The president's appointments were sound, and his recommendations, including an endorsement of civil service reform, were encouraging. Arthur redecorated the White House and entertained lavishly. His wife had died of pneumonia in January 1880, so Arthur's youngest sister, Mary Arthur McElroy, assumed the role of first lady. The president's fine clothing and polished manners prompted him to be called "a veritable Chesterfield." Still, Arthur was unhappy as president. He chafed at the responsibilities and deplored the lack of personal privacy. He had very little influence with Congress and restricted his role in legislative matters to delivering annual messages and issuing vetoes.

In 1882 Arthur vetoed a bill backed by a coalition of Democrats and western Republicans that would have suspended Chinese immigration for twenty years and placed restrictions on Chinese already in the country. The president thought the bill was in conflict with a treaty obligation, and he condemned its harsh treatment of the Chinese. Soon, however, Arthur signed a similar bill, favored overwhelmingly in Congress and throughout the nation, that reduced the term of exclusion to ten years. The Chinese Exclusion Law marked a sharp departure in the country's willingness to open its doors to all peoples.

That same year Arthur won widespread praise for vetoing a "River and Harbor" bill that was thought to be extravagant—appropriating almost $19 million—if not altogether unnecessary. But Congress passed the bill over the veto almost immediately. On the whole, Congress was committed to local over national goals and was keenly interested in rewarding political supporters with federal funds.

Nevertheless—but still with an eye to political advantage—in late 1882 Congress passed the Pendleton Act, a landmark civil service bill. The popular legislation created the Civil Service Commission and reformed a number of long-standing abuses. Arthur, who had backed the bill from the start, won applause for signing it, appointing reformers to the commission, and administering the act effectively.

Arthur was less successful in prosecuting leaders of the Star Route frauds, former political allies who had plundered the Post Office of millions of dollars. Although the president ordered a thorough investigation and threw the full weight of his office behind government attorneys, two juries acquitted the defendants. Opponents within both parties blamed the administration for the verdicts, and Arthur's popularity plummeted.

In foreign affairs, the president and his new secretary of state, Frederick T. Frelinghuysen, reversed the aggressive Latin American policy of Blaine, who had continued to serve as secretary of state under Arthur until mid-December 1881. To bolster his reputation and his chances for the presidency in 1884, Blaine had boldly entangled the nation in the isthmian canal question, the War of the Pacific (a struggle between Chile, Peru, and Bolivia), and a boundary dispute between Mexico and Guatemala. He had also called for an inter-American peace congress in Washington, the first such proposal ever made by the United States. When the administration abandoned this controversial posture, Blaine and his allies attacked Arthur furiously in the press.

The president, however, was not uninterested in foreign affairs. He strongly endorsed the creation of a modern navy and signed two bills authorizing construction of the nation's first steel ships. During the last nine months of the administration, Arthur and Frelinghuysen proposed a treaty with Nicaragua for the construction of an interoceanic canal, forged a system of reciprocity treaties in Latin America, and expressed a strong interest in trade with the Belgian Congo. For a variety of reasons, however, none of these initiatives was acceptable to Congress.

Arthur's work habits were affected throughout his presidency by illness. In 1882 he discovered he had Bright's Disease, an almost inevitably fatal kidney affliction in adults that produces spasmodic nausea, mental depression, and indolence. He suffered greatly, choosing, out of pride and fortitude, to keep his mortal illness private. Excursions to Florida and Yellowstone Park failed to ease his misery.

In 1884 Arthur quietly informed close political associates that under no circumstances would he seek reelection. This was a significant factor in the Republican party's decision to award the nomination to Blaine. Even if he had been healthy and interested in the nomination, Arthur might not have captured it. He had failed to satisfy the warring GOP factions with patronage, and not all independents were convinced of his integrity. Moreover, many Republicans feared that defeats they had suffered in the elections of 1882 would be repeated with Arthur heading the ticket.

The president did almost nothing to assist Blaine during the campaign. The election was the closest in U.S. history, and the Democratic candidate, Grover Cleveland, won by a plurality of about thirty thousand votes. Arthur's home state of New York gave the Democrats the victory margin, and Blaine was bitterly critical of the administration for its inactivity.

Arthur's health declined rapidly after his departure from the White House. He died of a massive cerebral hemorrhage in New York City. Highly sensitive about his personal reputation, Arthur had ordered the destruction of his personal papers and records shortly before his death. At funeral services throughout the nation, eulogists lauded Arthur's able handling of his presidential duties. Few chose to mention his many years as the "Gentleman Boss."

• Arthur papers are in the Library of Congress and the New-York Historical Society; administration scrapbooks are at Columbia University. See also Arthur's personnel file in the general records of the Treasury Department at the National Archives and the microfilmed Mrs. Charles Spicka Collection at the Wyoming State Historical Society. The standard biography is Thomas C. Reeves, *Gentleman Boss: The Life of Chester Alan Arthur* (1975). See also Justus Doenecke, *The Presidencies of James A. Garfield and Chester A. Arthur* (1981); John G. Sproat, *"The Best Men": Liberal Reformers in the Gilded Age* (1968); Charles E. Rosenberg, *The Trial of the Assassin Guiteau: Psychiatry and Law in the Gilded Age* (1968); David M. Pletcher, *The Awkward Years: American Foreign Relations under Garfield and Arthur* (1962); and H. Wayne Morgan, *From Hayes to McKinley* (1969).

THOMAS C. REEVES

ARTHUR, Joseph Charles (11 Jan. 1850–30 Apr. 1942), botanist and plant pathologist, was born in Lowville, New York, the son of Charles Arthur and Ann Allen. When Arthur was six, his parents moved first to Stirling, Illinois, then to Charles City, Iowa; and several years later, they finally settled in Spirit Lake, Iowa. Growing up on a farm environment, he attended the country schools of Floyd County, Iowa, and then completed high school at Charles City High School.

Arthur's apparent early interest in botany matured during his undergraduate education at the newly established Iowa State College at Ames. There Arthur studied botany with Charles E. Bessey, the country's foremost teacher of the "New Botany," a new approach imported from Germany that stressed the microscopic, laboratory-oriented study of plants. A new acquisition to the faculty, Bessey proved to be an inspiring teacher, and he encouraged Arthur, whom he called his "first botanical son," to study botany full time. Jobs in botanical research were scarce at the time, and after earning a B.S. in 1872, Arthur returned to teach at country schools while he continued to earn a graduate degree from Iowa State. In 1877 he received the first M.S. in botany given by Iowa State College, for a study of the anatomy of *Echinocystis lobata* (the wild-cucumber vine). During this time, he also prepared an award-winning exhibit (for which he received a bronze medal) for the Philadelphia Centennial Exposition of 1876 on the flora of Iowa. In 1879 he was appointed instructor of botany at the University of Wisconsin. A chance visit to Baltimore and meeting with the president of Johns Hopkins University, Daniel Coit Gilman, resulted in a small fellowship ($100) from the university. This allowed him to study for three months at Johns Hopkins, during which time Arthur attended the lectures of the noted Harvard University cryptogamic botanist William Gilson Farlow.

Arthur spent the following summer at Harvard, where he worked with Farlow and other noted botanists, including George Lincoln Goodale and Asa Gray. There he also formed a lasting partnership with two other students, John Merle Coulter and Charles R. Barnes, with whom he cowrote the *Handbook for Plant Dissection* in 1881. Published in 1887, the handbook became known as the "ABC" because of its introductory and inclusive character.

In 1884 Arthur was offered a research position as botanist in the newly formed Agricultural Experiment Station at Geneva, New York. He quickly accepted this position, the first of its kind in the country, and began to pursue full-time research on a devastating disease of orchard pears, fire-blight, while he was enrolled as a graduate student at Cornell University. He earned a D.Sc. from Cornell in 1886 for his work on fire-blight. In 1887 he moved to Purdue University in West Lafayette, Indiana, where he became professor of botany and professor of vegetable physiology and pathology while also serving as botanist at the Indiana Agricultural Experiment Station.

Although he began his scientific career in floristic botany, publishing his first major study on the flora of Iowa ("Double Flowers of *Ranunculus rhomboideus*," *American Naturalist* 6 [1872]: 427), Arthur ultimately gained his scientific reputation in the study of plant diseases, or plant pathology, a field which was only then becoming recognized in the United States. His work on fire-blight, which proved that bacteria could serve as causal agents of plant disease, earned him wide attention in the new field. Arthur also distinguished himself through his detailed examinations of the biology of the complex Rust-fungi, members of the fungal order the Uredinales. In 1883 he published the first of a series of papers on the Uredinales. In addition to sorting and naming this problematic group of economically destructive fungi—a process that occupied him until the end of his career—he also worked on the anatomy and life-cycle of the rust fungus, whose especially unusual alternation of parasite-host interaction often used intermediary hosts for different stages of the parasitic life-cycle. Over the years, Arthur made over 2,400 collections and approximately 3,750 greenhouse cultures on the rusts. He published "A New Classification of the Uredinales," *Journal of Mycology* 12 (1906): 188–91, followed by a complete study of the North American rusts in 1907. In later years he studied the rusts of the Philippines, New Zealand, and the Himalayas as well as other distant regions of the world, although he never personally traveled to these places. He married Emily Stiles Potter of Lafayette, Indiana, in 1901.

Arthur's honors included membership in the American Academy of Arts and Sciences, the American Philosophical Society, the Academy of Natural Sciences of Philadelphia, the American Society of Naturalists, the Torrey Botanical Club, and the Mycological Society of America and Sigma Xi, and presidencies of the Indiana Academy of Sciences, in 1893; the Botanical Society of America, in 1902 and 1919; and the American Phytopathological Society, in 1933.

He died in Brook, Indiana. Arthur is now generally recognized as a pioneer in the field of plant pathology, and his work on the rust-fungi has formed the foundation of all subsequent work on the rusts.

• Many of Arthur's papers are in the Purdue University Archives. The most complete biographical essays are by F. D. Kern, "Joseph Charles Arthur," *Phytopathology* 32 (1942): 833–44, which includes a complete bibliography, and by E. B. Mains in *Mycologia* 34 (1942): 601–15. See also W. E. Edington, "Joseph Charles Arthur," *Proceedings of the Indiana Academy of Sciences* 52 (1943): 1–3. Arthur is included in Harry Baker Humphrey, *Makers of North American Botany* (1961). For an overview of Arthur and his role in American botany and plant pathology, see Joseph Evan, ed., *A Short History of Botany in the United States* (1969). An obituary by F. D. Kern is in *Science* 95 (1942): 617–19.

VASSILIKI BETTY SMOCOVITIS

ARTHUR, Julia (3 May 1869–29 Mar. 1950), actress, was born Ida Lewis in Hamilton, Ontario, Canada, the daughter of Thomas J. Lewis, a cigar manufacturer, and Hannah Arthur. One of sixteen children, she took after her mother, an accomplished Shakespearean reader, spending her young years learning and reciting the best of Shakespeare's heroines. At the age of eleven she performed the role of Zamora in *The Honeymoon* for a local dramatic club that gave private performances in her father's home, and at fourteen she joined Daniel E. Bandmann's Shakespearean company, touring with the group for three seasons (as Ida Lewis) and playing, as Chicago critic Amy Leslie put it, "everywhere and everything," including Juliet, Portia, Ophelia, and Lady Anne from *Richard III* as well as non-Shakespearean roles, like Lady Teazle in *The School for Scandal*. George C. D. Odell chronicles a week of the group's performances in 1886 in which Arthur played Nerissa in *The Merchant of Venice* on Tuesday, the Nurse in *Romeo and Juliet* on Thursday, and Queen Elizabeth in *Richard III* on Saturday. Odell believed it to be the "youngest representation of Juliet's nurse ever seen on [the American] stage" (vol. 14, p. 579).

After a year of study in Europe in 1887 Arthur went to San Francisco, joining Kate Forsyth's repertory company. Taking the leads in numerous plays, including *The Colleen Bawn*, *The Galley Slave*, *The Two Orphans*, and *Divorce*, she gained experience in more contemporary plays. For the next four years she played with companies in Nova Scotia and in 1891 appeared as Julia Arthur (taking her mother's maiden name), playing Elinore Fordham in *The Still Alarm* in New York. In August of that year she scored her first real success as Queen Fortunetta in the Union Square Theatre's production of *The Black Masque*, followed by another success in September in *The Marquis' Wife*, by Sidney Bowkett. The *New York Herald* reported that the last-named play was saved by her excellent acting.

Her success in these roles led to her employment as a leading woman in A. M. Palmer's New York stock company, a very successful and respected group. In her first appearance with the company she played Jeanne in *The Broken Seal* (1892), followed by Letty Fletcher in *Saints and Sinners* and Lady Windermere in the American premiere of Oscar Wilde's *Lady Windermere's Fan* (1893), playing opposite Maurice Barrymore's Lord Darlington. Following her success in Thomas Bailey Aldrich's *Mercedes* (1893), the author allegedly presented Arthur with the complete rights for the play, and she continued to play the role periodically throughout her career.

In 1895 Arthur accepted an offer from Sir Henry Irving to join his company at the Lyceum Theatre as leading lady and understudy to Ellen Terry. With Irving's company she played Elaine in *King Arthur*, Sophia in *Olivia*, Rosamond in *Becket*, Lady Anne in *Richard III*, and Imogen in *Cymbeline* as they played London and toured the United States. Critics of the time believed Imogen to be one of her finest characterizations.

According to Leslie, once "Sir Henry Irving recognized her beauty and gifts, and Miss Terry petted her, America woke up, lit its pipe and asked her to star" (p. 315). Whether Irving's approval made her career or not, by 1897 she had gained enough popularity in the United States that she decided to start her own company, opening with *A Lady of Quality*, by Stephen Townsend and Frances Hodgson Burnett, at Wallack's Theatre. The play, adapted from Burnett's novel with Arthur in mind, quickly became associated with the actress. Her portrayal of Clorinda Wildairs garnered good reviews, and at least one critic felt her performance rose above the tediousness of the script. Over the next year she produced and starred in the company's productions of *Ingomar*, *As You Like It*, and *Pygmalion and Galatea*. Theater historian and critic Lewis Strang called her portrayal of Rosalind a "strikingly original conception" (p. 170), some critics comparing it to the performance of Adelaide Neilson. Indeed, many conceded it to be the finest portrayal of Rosalind yet seen on the American stage.

After Arthur's marriage in 1898 to Boston financier Benjamin Pierce Cheney, Jr., her husband financed several of these productions. Two years after her marriage Arthur retired from the stage. The couple had no children. Her husband suffered severe financial losses, however, and in 1915 she returned to the stage to star in *The Eternal Magdalene* at the 48th Street Theatre in New York. In 1917 she starred in and directed *Seremonda* and in 1918 was selected as a member of the all-star cast of *Out There*. During the 1920–1921 season she played Lady Cheveley in Wilde's *The Ideal Husband* and Lady Macbeth.

During World War I Arthur helped the war effort by volunteering with the Red Cross and organizing benefit productions. Before finally retiring from the stage in 1924 she toured in the title role of *St. Joan* and made her only film appearance as Edith Cavell in *The Woman the Germans Shot* (1918). Arthur died in Boston; her ashes were scattered at sea.

Just prior to her first retirement, Strang wrote that the most distinguishing characteristic of her acting was her "power to burn into the memory of the person that sees her in any role whatsoever, an impression that never wholly fades away" (p. 162). While Strang and other critics recognized her talent and potential, they concede that she never really developed it. Strang did not consider Arthur a great actress; however, his regard was evident when he placed her among the "three or four persons in this country who are actually—and at some personal sacrifice, too—accomplishing something for the drama as an art" (p. 162).

• Arthur donated scrapbooks, boxes of clippings, programs, and pictures to the Harvard Theatre Collection. Other documents concerning her career can be found in the Player's Collection at the Player's Club and in the Robinson Locke Dramatic Scrapbooks in the Theatre Collection of the New York Public Library for the Performing Arts. Arthur published a series of articles in *Heart's Magazine* (Mar.–July 1919) titled "My Career," which covers especially her early work. John Clark, *The Julia Arthur Book* (1899), is a collection of pictures with a review of her career prior to her first retirement in 1900. Her New York performances are chronicled in George C. D. Odell, *Annals of the New York Stage*, vols. 14 and 15 (1970). She is also featured in Lewis Strang, *Famous Actresses of the Day in America*, 1st ser. (1899), and Amy Leslie, *Some Players: Personal Sketches* (1899). Her participation in *Out There* is noted with detail in Laurette Taylor, *"The Greatest of These": A Diary with Portraits of the Patriotic All-Star Cast of "Out There"* (1918), which is one of the few commentaries on her later career. An obituary is in the *New York Times*, 30 Mar. 1950.

MELISSA VICKERY-BAREFORD

ARTHUR, Peter M. (1831–17 July 1903), labor leader, was born in Paisley, Scotland. Although he was born Peter McArthur, a payroll error later in his life listed him as Peter M. Arthur and he used that name thereafter. Little is known about his parents or early boyhood, but in 1842 he immigrated to the United States, where he settled on his uncle's farm in New York state. After dropping out of school early, he worked for his uncle, then for another farmer, and later he tried unsuccessfully to establish himself in the carting business in Schenectady. In 1849 he went to work for a railroad line that soon merged with the New York Central Railroad; after a brief period as an engine wiper, a maintenance position, he was promoted to locomotive engineer.

Arthur became active in the engineers' union, holding several offices in his local. In 1863 he helped found the Brotherhood of Locomotive Engineers (BLE, initially called the Brotherhood of the Footboard). The BLE began primarily as a benevolent society bound by the principles of "Sobriety, Truth, Justice & Morality." The key to improving working conditions, members believed, was to win their employers' respect by improving their own characters. Despite this philosophy some BLE members became increasingly assertive during the early 1870s, and when the union's grand chief engineer denounced a strike they had organized, Arthur was elected in 1874 to replace him. Although he entered office as an insurgent, Arthur shared his predecessor's belief that the interests of capital and labor were fundamentally harmonious. "Most men of thrifty and industrious habits are capitalists," he observed; the worker of today might well turn out to be the capitalist of tomorrow.

Arthur preferred negotiation and arbitration, but he reluctantly ordered strikes in 1876 and 1877. Both failed, as did the Great Railroad Strike of 1877 (in which the BLE did not officially participate). Arthur responded by expelling BLE members who had joined the Great Railroad Strike, condemning them for their "hasty, ill-advised, unwarranted actions." For the next decade he rejected all "entangling alliances with other classes of labor," pursued a conciliatory policy with management, and concentrated on building the BLE as a conservative benevolent association of skilled workers. He even opposed the eight-hour day, arguing that working two hours less would only allow more time for drinking and "loafing about the corners."

The BLE's policies drew scorn from leaders like Eugene V. Debs, who claimed that the trade exclusivity and conservatism of such unions set them apart as the "Aristocrats of Labor." But many workers admired the brotherhood's stability and prosperity. Furthermore, Arthur's accommodating policies plus the soaring demand for railroad workers made company officials more inclined to deal with him. The BLE was therefore able to negotiate raises and improved work conditions on a number of lines during the early 1880s. By 1886 it had 20,000 members and had become one of the strongest unions in the country.

Despite its history of independence and despite a running dispute with the Brotherhood of Locomotive Firemen over membership, the BLE joined the firemen in several successful strikes during the mid-1880s. In February 1888 they launched a strike against the Chicago, Burlington, and Quincy Railroad (CB&Q). The walkout began successfully, and within a week it had broadened to include a boycott against CB&Q cars hauled by other railroad lines. The strike rapidly lost its momentum, however, and the reasons illuminate both the difficulties faced by labor during this period and the problems caused by Arthur's own policies. The CB&Q managers persuaded a federal judge to issue an injunction against the boycott. Faced with the threat of a contempt citation, Arthur told the strike committee that he "would not go to jail twenty-four hours for your whole Brotherhood" and pulled the BLE out of the boycott; the firemen's chief soon followed suit. Meanwhile, the two brotherhoods' history of ignoring strikes by the Knights of Labor was repaid by the knights, who provided the struck railroad with replacement workers. During the course of the summer, Arthur put increasing distance between himself and the waning strike; that fall he ended BLE's participation without even notifying the firemen in advance.

Although the failure of the 1888 strike persuaded many unionists that railroad workers must cooperate more closely in the future, it strengthened Arthur's conviction that the BLE must go its own way. He therefore continued to keep the BLE out of the Knights of Labor, the American Federation of Labor, and a new federation of railroad unions organized by Debs. He was even more opposed to Debs's next step, the formation in 1892 of a single union—the American Railway Union (ARU)—open to all railroad trades. The ARU had some early success, but it collapsed in 1894, destroyed by its involvement in the failed Pullman strike. Arthur contributed to the failure by encouraging his members to fill in as replacement workers and by urging railroad officials to fire any engineer who refused to cooperate with them; for this Debs called him a "traitor to organized labor." With the demise of the ARU, Arthur resumed his conciliatory policies toward management. One expression of his conviction that workers had no distinct class interests was his decision to join the labor division of the National Civic Federation, which was organized in 1899 to promote cooperation between capital and labor.

Arthur served as grand chief engineer of the BLE until his death, but during his later years he began a very profitable second career, speculating in Cleveland real estate. He never married. He died suddenly of a heart attack just as he was accepting a floral tribute at a labor convention in Winnipeg, Canada. Having started as an impoverished immigrant, he had risen to become one of the most powerful labor leaders in the country. The most problematic feature of his career was his lifelong reluctance to make common cause with other labor organizations and his readiness to combine with employers against them. His greatest achievement was the BLE itself, an organization that lasted longer and did more for its members' dignity and prosperity than most other unions of the day.

• Arthur wrote the article on railroad organizing in *The Labor Movement: The Problem of Today* (1887, prepared under the direction of George E. McNeill; Arthur also served as an associate editor of the project). His career is discussed in Melvyn Dubofsky and Warren Van Tine, eds., *Labor Leaders in America* (1987); Gary Fink, ed., *Labor Unions* (1977); Philip S. Foner, *History of the Labor Movement in the United States*, vol. 2 (1955; repr. 1975); Shelton Stromquist, *A Generation of Boomers: The Pattern of Railroad Labor Conflict in Nineteenth-century America* (1987); and Philip Taft, *Organized Labor in American History* (1964). His interactions with Debs are discussed in Ray Ginger, *The Bending Cross: A Biography of Eugene V. Debs* (1949), and Nick Salvatore, *Eugene V. Debs: Citizen and Socialist* (1982). Obituaries appear in *Literary Digest*, 1 Aug. 1903, *Outlook*, 25 July 1903, *Independent*, 23 July 1903, and *Locomotive Engineers Monthly Journal*, Aug. 1903 and Sept. 1903.

SANDRA OPDYCKE

ARTHUR, Timothy Shay (6 June 1809–6 Mar. 1885), editor, temperance crusader, and novelist, was born in Orange County, New York, the son of William Arthur and Anna Shay, occupations unknown. He was named for his maternal grandfather, Timothy Shay, an officer in the revolutionary war. By his mid-twenties, Arthur had yet to identify a profession or receive an education. In the 1830s, however, he began an intense program of self-education as well as a writing career as a journalist in Baltimore, where he quickly became a well-known and articulate champion of numerous social causes including temperance, Swedenborgianism, feminism, and socialism. In 1836 he married Eliza Alden; they had seven children.

Arthur turned to fiction in the 1840s, ultimately publishing a total of 150 novels and short-story collections. He was not only the most published American fiction writer in the century; his sales of more than a million copies indicate that he was also one of the most popular American authors of his time.

Arthur's intense interest in one of the most energetic social movements of his day provided the message for much of his work, including his most famous work, *Ten Nights in a Bar-Room, and What I Saw There* (1854). His work was not the exploitation of a popular cause; for some years he had been an active participant in temperance societies and was widely known as a reporter and fiction writer who believed in the cause of prohibition of alcohol. As in the case of the temperance play *The Drunkard*, it was as a play that Arthur's story endured, bringing new audiences into the theater, which had long been condemned for encouraging the use of alcohol by selling it on the premises. Many a tale of the downfall of a young man begins with his consumption of alcohol in the theater. Ironically, then, Arthur's greatest influence on American culture may have been on its theater, for the play produced from his novel was performed routinely on the New York stages and by companies traveling throughout the United States; its presence on the boards, like that of *The Drunkard* and *Uncle Tom's Cabin*, somewhat mitigated the low regard in which religious people held the theater.

If Arthur's name survives in the twentieth century chiefly as the author of a work of fiction that generated one of the longest-running plays in theatrical history, Americans of his day knew him as a popular writer of fiction, and the student of the nineteenth century finds a rich picture of social life in his works. Not only did the reading public clamor for his temperance fiction, of which *Ten Nights in a Bar-Room* was only one example; it could go to Arthur's work for a discussion of many other hotly debated topics of the day: mesmerism in *Agnes; or, The Possessed. A Revelation of Mesmerism* (1848); financial speculation in *The Debtor's Daughter; or, Life and Its Changes* (1850); divorce in *The Hand but Not the Heart; or, The Life-Trials of Jessie Loring* (1858); and feminism in *Woman to the Rescue* (1874). Swedenborgianism and labor relations also were current topics that Arthur explored in his fiction.

Arthur's career as editor began in Baltimore, where he was part of a literary circle that included Edgar Allan Poe. The magazines he edited there include the *Baltimore Athenaeum and Young Men's Paper*, the *Baltimore Literary Monument*, the *Baltimore Saturday Visitor*, and the *Baltimore Merchant*. In 1850 Arthur began editing and publishing what would become a long-lived magazine with a large readership. Through *Arthur's Home Gazette*, later *Arthur's Home Magazine*, he was not only able to present to a large reading public discussions of the social issues that were most important to him; he was also able to interact with most of the prominent literary figures of his day. To the publishing of this journal he added both a magazine for children, the *Children's Hour*, in 1867, and, in 1869, *Workingman*, which was aimed at a working-class audience. Though his eyesight had begun to fail, up until his death in Philadelphia he was still active as a magazine editor in Baltimore and Philadelphia.

Although Timothy Arthur's reputation in the twentieth century rests solely on *Ten Nights in a Bar-Room*, his influence as an editor-publisher in the nineteenth century was formidable. His popularity, productivity, and recognition as a prolific fiction writer far exceeded that of the literary men and women of his day who are now anthologized as major American authors.

• Arthur's other works include *Six Nights with the Washingtonians: A Series of Original Temperance Tales* (1842), *Fanny Dale; or, The First Year of Marriage* (1843), *The Seamstress: A Tale of the Times* (1843), *The Tailor's Apprentice: A Story of Cruelty and Oppression* (1843), *Trials of a Needlewoman* (1853), *The Angel and the Demon: A Tale of Modern Spiritualism* (1858), *Three Years in a Man-Trap* (1872), and *Danger; or, Wounded in the House of a Friend* (1875). Four biographical and critical works on Arthur are a four-page autobiographical statement in *The Lights and Shadows of Real Life* (1851); *T. S. Arthur: His Life and Works by One Who Knows Him* (1873); Donald A. Koch, "The Life and Times of Timothy Shay Arthur" (Ph.D. diss., Case Western Reserve Univ., 1954); and "Godey's Portrait Gallery, No. 1: T. S. Arthur," *Godey's Lady's Book* 29 (Nov. 1844): 193–94.

CLAUDIA DURST JOHNSON

ARTIN, Emil (3 Mar. 1898–20 Dec. 1962), mathematician, was born in Vienna, Austria, the son of Emil Artin, an art dealer, and Emma Laura (maiden name unknown), an opera singer. After his father died, his mother remarried and moved with her children to Reichenberg, Bohemia (now Liberec, Czech Republic), southeast of Dresden. Artin returned to Vienna for his university studies but was drafted into the Austrian army after only one semester. Following World War I he did not return to Vienna but went to the University of Leipzig, where he studied chemistry and mathematics, the latter primarily with Gustav Herglotz. There his thesis for the Ph.D., which he earned in 1921, was devoted to quadratic extensions of the field of rational functions (of one variable) over finite constant fields.

From Leipzig Artin went to the University of Göttingen. After a year there, he accepted a position at the University of Hamburg, where he directed the Mathematical Seminar with Erich Hecke and Wilhelm Blaschke. He married one of his former students, Natalie Jasny, in 1929, and the Artins had three children; two were born before the family immigrated to the United States in 1937. After a year at the University of Notre Dame, Artin taught for several years at Indiana University in Bloomington, where his classic book, an introduction to the theory of gamma functions, was the outcome of courses he taught there before accepting a position at Princeton, where he remained from 1946 until 1958. It was during this twenty-year period, beginning in 1937, that he exercised a significant influence upon the development of mathematics in the United States.

In 1956 Artin was invited back to Germany, to spend a semester as the prestigious Gauß Professor at Göttingen, after which he spent another term at the University of Hamburg. This convinced him, after one last year in the United States, to accept a permanent professorship at Hamburg, whereupon he returned to Germany in 1958. Unfortunately, Artin died four years later of heart failure in Hamburg. Earlier that same year, on the occasion of the tercentenary of the death of Blaise Pascal, he was awarded an honorary doctorate by the University of Clermont-Ferrant. Among his most prominent students were Max Zorn, Shôkichi Iyanaga, George Whaples, Robert Thrall, Serge Lang, and Tim O'Meara, as well as Claude Chevalley and John Tate, who made major contributions to the development of cohomology theory in algebra.

Equally well known was Artin's collaboration with Otto Schreier, which led to a solution of Hilbert's Seventeenth Problem related to decomposition of positive definite functions into sums of squares of rational functions. By characterizing formally real fields as fields in which -1 is *not* the sum of squares, they were able to show the existence of an algebraic ordering of such fields—an advance that may be taken as the beginning of real algebra, linking algebra and analysis. However, the Artin-Schreier theorem was a pure existence theorem and did not actually construct or otherwise exhibit the ordering in question.

Subsequently, Artin was able to show that Hilbert's assumption that every ideal of a field is a principal ideal of its absolute class field (a term Artin also introduced). Later, in the 1950s Hans Zassenhaus asked Artin about more recent developments of class field theory, especially the results Georg Kreisel and Abraham Robinson achieved showing that indeed Artin's solution of the Hilbert problem could be turned into a construction. He reacted, Zassenhaus noted, with "philosophical calmness" and actually preferred his own existence proof "to a construction that required ${}_2 2^{100}$ steps" (Zassenhaus, p. 4).

Artin's best-known works are his contributions to class field theory. By the 1930s Galois theory was a well-developed field, and Artin was anxious to simplify it. Drawing on work of Dirichlet, Frobenius, and Takagi on Abelian fields, Artin investigated prime ideals in Galois fields. This eventually led him to formulate a "general law of reciprocity," including not only Gaussian reciprocity but reciprocity in general, which subsequently became one of the main theorems of class field theory. All of this was conveniently summarized in a book he wrote on the subject with his son-in-law John Tate in 1961. (Tate married Artin's daughter, Karin, in 1956).

No matter how abstract the subject, Artin was always partial to the old school of German mathematics in that he always liked to give examples. Thanks to his wide-ranging interests as a mathematician, he had plenty of good examples at hand, all of which were intended to give students a graphic idea of basic concepts, however abstract. When it came to teaching, Artin would often say, "I want you to see this concept in your mind in full clarity (as a group, ring, field or ideal)" (Zassenhaus, p. 3). In fact, Artin devoted a considerable amount of time to teaching undergraduates. At Princeton he gave honors courses to freshmen, and in Hamburg he took an active part in developing mathematical curricula at the high school level. Artin also became involved in several secondary school projects elsewhere in Germany, and in India as well.

In 1933 Artin produced a set of seminar notes on the structure of semi-simple Lie algebras over the complex field; this set the stage for work that took over a decade to work out. Although his notes have not been published, the prominent number theorist Hans Zassenhaus admits that they were especially influential on him as a student in Hamburg (as they were on Walter Landherr and others who studied there as well). In topology, Artin introduced the notion of braids, which he first developed in a paper of 1926, and to which he returned again in 1947. In group theory, he studied the order of the known finite simple groups (the alternating groups, the five Mathieu groups, and the Lie groups of normal type). In two papers of 1955 he showed that these could indeed be characterized by their order (with only a few exceptions). He also conjectured that the structure of simple groups could be determined from their order (something John G. Thompson later verified in part for minimal simple groups). Artin also wrote two papers in 1927 on the theory of hypercomplex numbers, which along with his student Käthe Hey's dissertation on the subject inaugurated the extension of algebraic number theory to noncommutative rings.

Artin was a mathematician of broad interests. In Hamburg he taught general mechanics and relativity theory (and discussed not only the theory itself but the decisive experiments that led up to or helped to confirm it as well). He enjoyed working with instruments, was adept at using his own telescope and microscopes. His expertise was wide ranging, and he was knowledgeable on diverse subjects from the best recipe for cooking rice to tuning a cembalo or building an organ. He also had a special interest in the bearing of medical research on psychoanalysis. But it was his emphasis on the unity of mathematics, especially the connections between algebra and number theory, that left his mark on some of the great works of this century, including those by B. L. van der Waerden on algebra, Zassenhaus on group theory, and Tim O'Meara on quadratic forms. Above all, Artin's general spirit of abstraction proved especially influential on the Bourbaki group that was so influential at first in France and then much more widely beginning in the 1940s.

• Artin's works are easily available as *The Collected Papers of Emil Artin*, ed. Serge Lang and John T. Tate (1965). His most important books include *Galois Theory* (1942); *Geometric Algebra* (1957); and, with John T. Tate, *Class Field Theory* (1961). For comprehensive biographical studies by colleagues who knew Artin and his works well, consult Richard Brauer, "Emil Artin," *Bulletin of the American Mathematical Society* 73 (1967): 27–43; Henri Cartan, "Emil Artin," *Abhandlungen aus dem Mathematischen Seminar der Hamburgischen Universität* 28 (1965): 1–6; Claude Chevalley, "Emil Artin," *Bulletin de la Société mathématique de France* 92 (1964): 1–10; Bruno Schoeneberg, "Emil Artin zum Gedächtnis," *Mathematisch-physikalische Semesterberichte* 10 (1963): 1–10; and Hans Zassenhaus, "Emil Artin and His Work," *Notre Dame Journal of Formal Logic* 5 (1964): 1–9. This latter work includes a list of Artin's books and articles, as well as the names of eleven students (and their dissertations) who studied with Artin at Hamburg, along with twenty more who took their Ph.D.s with him in the United States.

For studies of Artin and his important collaboration with Otto Schreier, see Hourya Sinaceur, "La théorie d'Artin et Schreier et l'analyse non standard d'Abraham Robinson," *Archive for History of Exact Sciences* 34 (1985): 257–64, and Sinaceur, *Corps et modèles. Essai sur l'histoire de l'algèbre réelle* (1991); on the specific contributions of Robinson and Kreisel, consult Joseph W. Dauben, *Abraham Robinson. The Creation of Nonstandard Analysis, a Personal and Mathematical Odyssey* (1995). For a description of Hilbert's Seventeenth Problem and an overview of its significance, refer to Albrecht Pfister, "Hilbert's Seventeenth Problem and Related Problems on Definite Forms," in *Mathematical Developments Arising from Hilbert Problems*, ed. Felix E. Browder (1976), pp. 483–89.

JOSEPH W. DAUBEN

ARVEY, Jacob Meyer (3 Nov. 1895–25 Aug. 1977), lawyer and Democratic leader, was born in Chicago, Illinois, the son of Israel Arvey, a businessman, and Bertha Eisenberg. His parents were Jewish Lithuanian immigrants. Arvey, known as "Jack," married Edith Freeman in 1915; they had three children. After earning a degree at the John Marshall School of Law, he opened a law practice in Chicago in 1916.

Best remembered for the major role he played for over four decades in Chicago and Illinois Democratic politics, Arvey first became active in politics in 1914, before he was even old enough to vote. He served as assistant state's attorney in Cook County from 1918 to 1920. In 1923 he became the first alderman elected in the newly created, mostly Jewish Twenty-fourth Ward, a position he held until 1941. During the 1920s Arvey was closely associated with Anton J. Cermak, and he was active in Cermak's successful campaign for mayor in 1931. After Cermak was killed in the attempted assassination of President-elect Franklin D. Roosevelt in 1933, Arvey continued to exercise a powerful role in Chicago politics under the leadership of Patrick A. Nash and Cermak's successor, Edward J. Kelly, Chicago's mayor from 1933 to 1947.

World War II interrupted Arvey's political career. He resigned his position as alderman in 1941 to join the Thirty-third Infantry Division of the Illinois National Guard as a judge advocate general and civil affairs officer. He served in the Pacific theater as a lieutenant colonel and was awarded the Bronze Star and the Legion of Merit.

Soon after Arvey's return to Chicago at war's end, Mayor Kelly appointed him chair of the Cook County Democratic Central Committee. The Democratic party had suffered severe losses both nationally and in Cook County in 1946, and opponents of Mayor Kelly seemed poised to elect a Republican mayor in 1947 for the first time since the 1920s. Convinced that Kelly could not be reelected, Arvey persuaded party leaders to nominate Martin F. Kennelly, an outsider who was a respectable businessman and civil leader with little political experience, to offset the negative image of the Democratic organization. Kennelly was subsequently elected mayor.

A year later Arvey extended his efforts to improve the Democratic party's image in statewide offices by engineering the nomination and election of Adlai E. Stevenson II for governor and Paul H. Douglas for U.S. senator. Thus, by the selection of outstanding candidates, in merely two years Arvey strengthened the Democratic party in Chicago and Illinois and helped gain the support of Cook County and Illinois in 1948 for the Democratic presidential candidate, Harry Truman. He was also a major figure in the successful campaign of powerful Illinois and national Democratic leaders to nominate Stevenson for president on the Democratic ticket in 1952 and 1956.

Arvey's successful efforts to promote the political careers of Kennelly, Stevenson, and Douglas established his reputation as an enlightened "boss." However, in 1950 he backed a candidate for Cook County sheriff who lost after it became known that he had become wealthy using inside information to invest in the grain and stock markets. Soon afterward Arvey stepped down as chair of the Cook County Democratic Central Committee, a post claimed by Richard J. Daley in 1953. Arvey then accepted a position on the Democratic National Committee, serving on the committee until 1972. He also continued to exercise the role of elder statesman in Cook County politics for many years.

As his influence in Chicago Democratic politics declined after 1950, Arvey devoted more of his energies to Jewish and other philanthropic causes. He was deeply committed to the welfare of the state of Israel and in 1964 won the first National Man of the Year Award presented by the State of Israel Bond Organization. Arvey died in Chicago. He was buried in Shalom Memorial Park, Palatine, Illinois.

Jacob Arvey's career in the Chicago Democratic organization led many of his critics to perceive him as a typical "machine boss," a stereotype he did fit in some ways. For example, during the Great Depression as ward committeeman Arvey provided his constituents with jobs and legal advice, fixed parking tickets, and distributed food on Passover and Christmas. Using the traditional methods of the "boss," Arvey played a major role in the massive shift of Chicago voters into the Democratic party. In 1936 he won the personal congratulations of President Roosevelt after he swept Arvey's ward with over 95 percent of the vote. Arvey was also loyal to the Democratic organization. In the 1936 primary election, when the Kelly-Nash organization opposed the renomination of Democrat Henry Horner as governor, even though Horner was the first Jewish governor of Illinois and Arvey's personal friend, Arvey carried his ward overwhelmingly against the governor. Horner won reelection despite the opposition of the Chicago Democratic organization, and later Arvey called his opposition to Horner "my greatest blunder politically."

In other ways, Arvey was not a typical "machine boss." He avoided scandal or corruption, and he distinguished himself by rising above the parochial concerns of Chicago politics to help elect outstanding men like Stevenson and Douglas to high office. The *Chicago Tribune*, not noted for its sympathy with Cook County Democratic politicians, on the occasion of Arvey's death recalled that although he "was often criticized as a symbol of backroom big city politics, . . . there have been far worse forms of backroom politics than those practiced under Mr. Arvey. In general, he served his party well—and in doing so, he served the city well" (27 Aug. 1977).

• Papers related to Arvey's early career are in the Archives and Manuscripts Department, Chicago Historical Society. Several Arvey items are in the Harry S. Truman Library, Independence, Mo., and some of Arvey's recollections are preserved in "The Adlai E. Stevenson Project: Oral History Collection, 1966–1970," Columbia University Library, New York. Arvey's essay, "A Gold Nugget in Your Backyard," is published in *As We Knew Adlai: The Stevenson Story by Twenty-Two Friends*, ed. Edward P. Doyle (1966), pp. 50–65. Useful articles about Arvey are Stanley Frankel and Holmes Alexander, "Arvey of Illinois: New Style Political Boss," *Colliers*, 23 July 1949, pp. 9–11, 65–67; Donald M. Schwartz, "Jack Arvey: The Man Behind the Name," *Chicago Sun-Times*, 13 Dec. 1964; and Joe Mathewson, "Jacob Arvey, Boss Emeritus," *Chicago Tribune Magazine*, 18 Mar. 1973. Obituaries are in the *Chicago Sun-Times* and the *Chicago Tribune*, 26 Aug. 1977.

HOWARD W. ALLEN

ARVIN, Newton (23 Aug. 1900–22 Mar. 1963), literary critic and educator, was born Frederick Newton Arvin, Jr., in Valparaiso, Indiana, the son of Frederick Newton Arvin, Sr., an insurance agent often away on business, and Jessie Hawkins. Arvin was rather dominated by his mother, grandmother, and four sisters, and was unfortunately regarded by his jeering father as weak and effeminate. After graduating from his local high school, he attended Harvard University (where he was greatly influenced by Van Wyck Brooks), from which he obtained his B.A., summa cum laude, in 1921. He taught for a year at a private school for boys in Valparaiso and then became a member of the English department at Smith College, first as an instructor (1922–1925, 1926–1929) and then as an assistant professor (1929–1933). He took a leave of absence from Smith in 1925 and 1926 to go to New York City and coedit *Living Age*, a weekly magazine that was mainly a repository of material from foreign publications.

Arvin married Mary Jordan Garrison, a former Smith student, in 1932. Espousing the cause of Marxism, he signed a pledge to vote for Communist candidates (1932) and also worked for the American Federation of Teachers and joined the National Committee for the Defense of Political Prisoners. He was promoted to the rank of associate professor at Smith in 1933 and was a full professor from 1941 to 1961. As a member of the League of American Writers, he signed a 1937 letter to Congress deploring Spanish fascism. Arvin and his wife, who had succumbed to a nervous disorder in 1938, were divorced in 1940 because of his homosexual tendencies. The couple had no children. Having already tried on three occasions to commit suicide, Arvin in 1940 suffered a nervous breakdown and entered a sanatorium for a period of months the following year.

Beginning in 1930 and continuing into the 1940s, Arvin summered at the Yaddo colony of writers and artists, near Saratoga Springs, New York. Among others he met there, including Malcolm Cowley, Granville Hicks, Louis Kronenberger, Carson McCullers, and Katherine Anne Porter, was Truman Capote, whom Arvin first encountered in 1946. The two soon began a three-year homosexual relationship, memorialized by Capote's dedicating his first book, *Other Voices, Other Rooms* (1948), to Arvin.

Arvin taught and wrote steadily. In September 1960 his progress was interrupted, however, when police raided his home, seized his collection of gay pornography, and arrested him for possession of obscene and lewd pictures intended for exhibition. He was convicted, fined, and given a one-year sentence, which was suspended partly because he informed on other collectors of pornography. He was also forced to retire from Smith, with a small annual stipend. Embarrassment and humiliation caused another breakdown requiring hospitalization. Not long after his release he died in Northampton.

Arvin published often in his career, beginning with book reviews in the *Freeman* while he was still at Harvard. Substantial articles, usually on American authors, appeared in the 1920s and later in the *Atlantic Monthly*, the *Independent*, the *Nation*, the *Hudson Review*, the *New Republic*, the *New York Herald Tribune*, and the *Partisan Review*. He edited a selection of Nathaniel Hawthorne's journals (1929), short stories (1946), his novel *The Scarlet Letter* (1950), Herman Melville's *Moby-Dick* (1948), a selection of Henry Adams's letters (1951), and George Washington Cable's *The Grandissimes* (1957). But his most valuable contributions to literary scholarship were his four critical biographies: *Hawthorne* (1929), *Whitman* (1938), *Herman Melville* (1950), and *Longfellow: His Life and*

Work (1963). Death prevented his completing several projects, notably a four-volume "History of Literary Ideas in America." Daniel Aaron and Sylvan Schendler assembled twenty-nine of Arvin's reviews of books in the field of American literature (1830–1900) in a posthumous collection entitled *American Pantheon* (1966).

In his four book-length studies, Arvin combined sociohistorical and depth-psychological criticism. He displayed an awareness of and sympathy for each writer's position in the frequently decivilizing society of his times and verified each writer's consequent loneliness in his search for idealistic values and abiding truths. In doing so, he discovered that the artist affirmed the dignity of the human spirit. Arvin also brilliantly analyzed various elements of each subject's artistry. His own writing is notable for erudition, care, clarity, distinction, and grace. In *Hawthorne*, Arvin both deplored Nathaniel Hawthorne's aloofness from humanity and admired his honest recognition of it. Hawthorne, in Arvin's view, envied the simple joys of ordinary people even while depicting, in lights and darks together, their seemingly inevitable estrangements and consequent guilt. In *Whitman*, Arvin presented Walt Whitman as a socialistic poet of great value to his times and Arvin's own because of his liberal positions on economics, politics, and science. In *Herman Melville*, Arvin cavalierly dismissed too much of Melville, including *Pierre*, "Benito Cereno," several other short stories, and his poetry. His chapter on *Moby-Dick*, however, is nothing short of hypnotic, especially for its fresh reading of Ahab as an egocentric, self-destructive neurotic, and for its analysis of the symbolism and figurative language in the novel, its uniquely Melvillean diction, and its levels of meaning. (If Arvin could have written in a more modern, freer academic air, he would have addressed homosexuality in Whitman and Melville less tangentially.) In *Longfellow*, his simplest study, Arvin did not defend Henry Wadsworth Longfellow's frequent sentimental moralizing but did demonstrate that his poetry was often artistically and thematically varied and appealing.

In his autobiography, Van Wyck Brooks called Arvin a "quiet man with a violent mind" who "would gladly have stood against a wall and faced a fusillade for his convictions" (p. 564). Edmund Wilson declared that among critics of American writers only Brooks and Arvin can be defined as great writers themselves. Arvin is of permanent worth for his elegantly expressed hope that the humane values of America's nineteenth century—spiritual integrity, individual worth, respect for artist and laborer alike—can survive the corrosive effects of twentieth-century industrialism. Despite his timidity in addressing problems of human sexuality and the dated quality of his Marxist inclinations, Newton Arvin is of abiding value as one of the premier literary critics of his era.

• Arvin's letters to his friend David Lilienthal are at the Princeton University Library. His letters to Van Wyck Brooks are at the University of Pennsylvania Library. His unpublished lecture notes, diaries, and autobiography are currently in private hands. Arvin's *American Pantheon* (1966) includes introductory essays by Daniel Aaron and Louis Kronenberger, two of Arvin's closest friends. Van Wyck Brooks, *An Autobiography* (1965), mentions Arvin briefly. Raymond Nelson, *Van Wyck Brooks: A Writer's Life* (1981), narrates the Brooks-Arvin friendship in detail. Gerald Clarke, *Capote: A Biography* (1988), discusses Arvin's love affair with Truman Capote. Jonathan Ned Katz, *Gay American History: Lesbians and Gay Men in the U.S.A.: A Documentary History* (1976; rev. ed., 1992), presents the pornography case against Arvin. Granville Hicks, "A Critic to Remember," *Saturday Review*, 13 July 1963, pp. 21–22, summarizes Arvin's accomplishments as a critic. Edmund Wilson, "Arvin's Longfellow and New York State's Geology," *New Yorker*, 23 Mar. 1963, 174–81, accords Arvin unique praise. Arnold Goldman, "The Tragic Sense of Newton Arvin," *Massachusetts Review* 7 (Autumn 1966): 823–27, stresses Arvin's pro-proletarian stance. A brief, belated obituary of Arvin is in the *New York Times*, 1 Apr. 1963.

ROBERT L. GALE

ARZNER, Dorothy (3 Jan. 1897–1 Oct. 1979), film director, was born in San Francisco, California, the daughter of Louis Arzner, a restaurateur. Her mother's name is unknown. After moving the family to Los Angeles, her father managed the Hoffman Café, a popular establishment frequented by movie people, including a number of directors. Arzner graduated from Westlake School for Girls, then enrolled in the University of Southern California with the hope of becoming a physician. With the outbreak of World War I she volunteered for service with the Los Angeles Emergency Ambulance Corps. At the end of her stint with the corps Arzner realized she did not want to continue pursuing a career in medicine. Determined to become financially independent from her father, she sought a job in the movie industry.

Arzner started as a studio typist in 1919 and rapidly moved into positions of responsibility. Her jobs, however, remained of the type frequently held by women during this era. She became a manuscript reader, "script girl," scenario writer, and film editor ("cutter") for Famous Players–Lasky (later Paramount Pictures). Her work as editor on Fred Niblo's *Blood and Sand* (1922) brought her acclaim, and she went on to edit prestigious productions for director James Cruze, including *The Covered Wagon* (1923), *Ruggles of Red Gap* (1923), and *Old Ironsides* (1926); she also coscripted *Old Ironsides*. In 1927 Arzner was allowed by Paramount to direct a silent film, but only after she threatened to quit for a job directing films at Columbia, a "poverty row" studio.

The film Arzner had to fight for, *Fashions for Women*, exploited built-in appeal to the style-conscious female portion of the audience. In a *New York Times* interview some years later, Arzner noted that she could see only logic in her desire to be a director because "the greater part of the motion-picture audience is feminine. Box-office appeal is thought of largely in terms of the women lined up at the ticket window. If there are no women directors there ought to be" (27 Sept. 1936). Also in 1927 the debut of *The Jazz Singer* marked the industry's entry into an awkward period of transition to sound technology. There were several women directors during the silent era, but after World War I those numbers began to diminish, and in the late 1920s, as the industry nervously grappled with new technological demands, fewer and fewer women were allowed to direct.

For Arzner, however, other directorial assignments quickly followed, and she proved herself to be an able director of sound productions, often in a sophisticated "modern" vein. Films such as *Sarah and Son* (1930) and *Merrily We Go to Hell* (1932) were not only popular successes but also demonstrated Arzner's talent for drawing out natural and winning performances, especially from women. This talent is particularly evident in *The Wild Party* (1929), the first "talkie" feature for Clara Bow, who starred as a college coed. Bow's friendships with her female classmates are more vividly represented than her love affair with a young professor (Fredric March).

Like *The Wild Party*, many of Arzner's other films also focused on strong-willed women protagonists, among them *Christopher Strong* (1933), starring Katharine Hepburn as an aviatrix whose unexpected pregnancy leads to tragedy, and *First Comes Courage* (1943). Over the course of her career, Arzner showed a marked sensitivity in delineating complex relationships between women, to which another of her best known films, *Dance, Girl, Dance* (1940), attests. The nonstereotypical quality of female friendships (and rivalries) drew praise for Arzner's work from feminist film scholars in the 1970s.

After the advent of sound Arzner became the only woman directing on a regular basis until Ida Lupino assumed that mantle after Arzner's retirement. During the 1930s Arzner gained a reputation as a soft-spoken, competent professional given neither to temperamental outbursts nor radical experimentation. Her unique status in the industry may have necessitated her carefully controlled demeanor and her apparently conservative filmmaking style. She once suggested that if she failed to make a financially successful film she believed that she would not have the kind of support the male fraternity provided one another. Perhaps because of this fraternity her films reveal that Arzner was not always working with the best scripts nor was she always offered established stars. On the contrary, she frequently directed actors who were in their first starring roles or who took their assignments with some reluctance. Arzner claimed she had to coax Rosalind Russell to play against type in *Craig's Wife* (1936), in a role Russell supposedly thought so unsympathetic that she desperately attempted to be released from her obligation to portray the title character. Yet Russell's performance in the production earned the young actress an Academy Award nomination. Arzner's pride in her ability to "make" stars is apparent in several interviews. She also claimed to have rescued Hepburn from a jungle production to cast her as the protofeminist heroine of *Christopher Strong*, but whether such claims are valid is uncertain.

What is certain is Arzner's devotion to the art of filmmaking. In the 1936 *New York Times* interview, she told a reporter that she followed her own system of directing, one in which she worked "on every phase of the picture" to make it "an Arzner production throughout." She frequently worked with other women, including editor Viola Lawrence and Pulitzer Prize–winning writer Zoë Akins. Nevertheless, as many of Arzner's statements suggest, the difficulties of working within an overwhelmingly male-dominated system must have been ever-present.

Prompted in part by ill health, Arzner retired in 1943 after having directed seventeen films. She volunteered to teach film at the Pasadena Playhouse, then taught filmmaking at the University of California at Los Angeles in the 1960s. She also directed training films for the Women's Army Corps during World War II and fifty television commercials for Pepsi-Cola at the request of Joan Crawford, who had starred in Arzner's *The Bride Wore Red* (1937) and who was now married to Pepsi's chair of the board. In 1975 the Director's Guild of America Committee of Women Members honored Arzner with a formal tribute to her work, even as her films began to be screened within the context of women's film festivals and revivals.

Recent scholarly interest has focused on the female camaraderie and woman-centered themes that are readily apparent in Arzner's films, but interest in her filmmaking has expanded to consider how her films resist male domination in more subtle ways. Some argue that her film style is deceptive in its simplicity and that, in fact, her films visibly undermine the "male gaze" of Hollywood filmmaking that makes women into objects for male sexual looking.

Little is known of Arzner's private life, but recent research suggests she was a lesbian, a fact long assumed from the sensuality with which female friendships are handled in her films, from her own penchant for mannish suits and haircuts, and from her unmarried status. When she died at her home in La Quinta in the California desert, Arzner left no survivors. Longtime companion Marion Morgan had died in 1971. In keeping with the unsentimental edge that characterizes many of her best films, Arzner requested that no funeral be held.

• Significant critical and theoretical discussions of Arzner's work include Judith Mayne, *Directed by Dorothy Arzner* (1975); Claire Johnston, *The Work of Dorothy Arzner: Towards a Feminist Cinema* (1975); Beverle Houston, "Missing in Action: Notes on Dorothy Arzner," *Wide Angle* 6, no. 3 (1984): 24–31; and Jacquelyn Suter, "Feminine Discourse in *Christopher Strong*," *Camera Obscura* 3–4 (Summer 1979): 135–50. Critical overviews of Arzner's career are in Louise Heck-Rabi, *Women Filmmakers: A Critical Reception* (1984), and Ally Acker, *Reel Women: Pioneers of the Cinema, 1896 to the Present* (1991). For a contemporary discussion of Arzner's status as Hollywood's only female director, see the *New York Times*, 27 Sept. 1936. An interesting fan magazine discussion of Arzner as a fledgling director is in Ivan St. Johns, "Goodbye to Another Tradition," *Photoplay*, Mar. 1927, pp. 20–41, 142. The lengthiest interview with Arzner is in Gerald Peary and Karyn Kay, "Interview with Dorothy Arzner," *Cinéma* 34 (1974): 9–25. Obituaries are in the *New York Times*, 12 Oct. 1979, and the *Los Angeles Times*, 3 Oct. 1979 and 8 Oct. 1979.

GAYLYN STUDLAR

ASBOTH, Alexander Sandor (18 Dec. 1811–21 Jan. 1868), Union officer, was born in Keszthely, county of Zala, Hungary. His parents' names are unknown. His father was a professor at the Lyceum of Kesmark and the director of the Georgikon at Keszthely. Educated at the academy at Selmecbanya, Asboth later passed a course of legal studies at Presburg. He also trained as an engineer and was employed by the Austrian government on various hydraulic works in the Banat region of present-day Romania. Asboth participated in the Hungarian uprising of 1848 under the leadership of Lajos Kossuth, serving as the Hungarian leader's adjutant. When the uprising failed, he accompanied Kossuth into exile and shared his imprisonment at Kutaiah (Kütahya) in Turkey. Upon their release in 1851, the two came to the United States, and Asboth became an American citizen. He worked first as an architect for a firm in Syracuse, New York, but later went west as a mining engineer. Returning to New York City, he opened a small steel foundry and was later employed by the city planning commission, in which capacity he played a prominent role in planning Washington Heights and Central Park.

At the outbreak of the Civil War, Asboth unsuccessfully attempted to organize a regiment in New York. Based on his Hungarian military experience, was then appointed chief of staff with General John C. Frémont, commanding the Department of the West at St. Louis, with the rank of brigadier general of volunteers, although the latter was not officially confirmed by Congress until 21 March 1862. He participated in Frémont's campaign in southwestern Missouri in the fall of 1861. After Frémont's removal from the western command in November 1861, Asboth remained on the staff of General David Hunter and later commanded the Second Division of Franz Sigel's corps under General Samuel R. Curtis at the battle of Pea Ridge in March 1862, during which Asboth was wounded in the arm. In spite of his wound, he continued to direct his men while suffering great pain. He became apprehensive about the army's success, however, and urged Curtis to retreat. Curtis declined and the next day turned the tide of battle in his favor.

Thereafter Asboth and his division were assigned to General John Pope's (1822–1892) Army of the Mississippi and participated in the skirmishes accompanying the abandonment of Corinth, Mississippi, by Confederate general P. G. T. Beauregard at the end of May 1862. In January 1863 Asboth was given command of the Federal post at Columbus, Kentucky, serving there until early August. Ordered to report to General William T. Sherman at Vicksburg, he took command of the Third Division of the Fifteenth Corps.

Within a month, however, Sherman determined that Asboth would be better suited to a more "fixed command," and in October the Hungarian became commander of the District of West Florida, headquartered at Fort Pickens. There Asboth sought to recruit regiments from among the pro-Union whites and freedmen of the area. Badly wounded during a reconnaissance near Marianna, Florida, in September 1864, his left arm and cheekbone were shattered. Among those fighting under his command at the time were three of Kossuth's nephews. He left his post to seek medical assistance in New Orleans and did not return to active duty until the following February. A fellow officer reported at the time, "He is full of valor and energy, and seems very desirous of going into the field, but it appears to me he is too feeble" (*War of the Rebellion*, ser. 1, vol. 49, pt. 1, p. 790). Asboth remained at his post, nevertheless, until he resigned his military commission in August 1865, having been brevetted major general in March.

President Andrew Johnson appointed Asboth minister resident to the Argentine Republic in March 1866. Still suffering from the bullet wound to his face, Asboth traveled first to Paris in the hope of finding surgeons who could remove the bullet that remained lodged in his neck. Several operations proved unsuccessful. He arrived in Buenos Aires on 14 October 1866 to assume his ministerial duties. There he became involved, with his American counterparts in Brazil and Paraguay, in diplomatic negotiations to mediate an end to the Paraguayan War, which proved unsuccessful. His painful wound continued to plague him, however, and finally produced his death in Buenos Aires. Asboth never married.

• No body of Asboth papers is known. The best biographical sketch of Asboth is Earl J. Hess, "Alexander Asboth: One of Lincoln's Hungarian Heroes?" *Lincoln Herald* 84 (Fall 1982): 181–91. For other accounts of Asboth, see Eugene Pivaney, *Hungarians in the American Civil War* (1913), and Edmund Vasvary, *Lincoln's Hungarian Heroes: The Participation of Hungarians in the Civil War, 1861–1865* (1939). Brief sketches also appear in F. B. Heitman, *Historical Register and Dictionary of the U.S. Army* (1903), and Marcus Wright, *Battles and Commanders of the Civil War* (1902). Obituaries are in *Appleton's Annual Cyclopedia* (1868) and the *New York Times*, 6 Mar. 1868.

WILLIAM E. PARRISH

ASBURY, Francis (20 Aug. 1745–31 Mar. 1816), missionary, bishop, and founder of the Methodist Episcopal Church, was born in Staffordshire, England, the son of Joseph Asbury and Elizabeth Rogers, farmers. His parents encouraged him early in his education, and he was reading the Bible by the age of seven. At twelve, however, he dropped out of school after being harshly treated by the schoolmaster and never returned to formal education.

For the next six and a half years Asbury was employed as an apprentice, possibly in the making of either saddles or buckles, but his mind was occupied by spiritual matters. His mother was deeply pious and took him he was brought to many prayer meetings, often led by fervent Methodists; these followers of John

Wesley advocated a personal relationship to God. In the summer of 1760, after one such meeting, Asbury realized a "sense of his own sinfulness and helplessness" and dedicated himself to the work of the Lord and of Methodism. He soon began to lead the prayer meetings he attended with his mother.

At the age of eighteen Asbury became a local preacher. In 1766 he began to travel through Staffordshire and Worcestershire to preach in the place of a traveling minister. The next year he was appointed, though not ordained, as an itinerant minister and preacher. For the next five years his appointment as a circuit rider was renewed, and Asbury honed his oratory throughout Bedfordshire, Colchester, and Wiltshire. At a conference at Bristol in 1771, John Wesley called for volunteers to journey to the American colonies. Asbury accepted the call and left England to preach on the circuit of America in the fall of 1771. The first official Methodist service held in America had been in 1766; only five years later, Asbury became a part of the first wave of Methodists in the New World.

One of the most significant events of Asbury's early years there was the American War of Independence. He had come not as an immigrant but as a missionary; his loyalties lay with his friends and family in England. Although he could sympathize with the plight of the colonists, he did not involve himself in the politics of the day. In fact, events such as Bunker Hill and the Declaration of Independence did not even warrant entries in his journal. More than anything, he considered himself a citizen of heaven, and he cared little for the allegiances those around him might claim.

In England, however, the Methodists were quite vocal in their denunciation of the rebellion in the colonies. Wesley himself published a treatise to try to reason with the colonists. Although all but one of the Methodist missionaries sent from England returned either before or during the war, Asbury wrote to Wesley, "It would be to the eternal dishonor to the Methodists that we should all leave the three thousand souls who desire to commit themselves to our care; neither is it the part of the Good Shepard to leave his flock in time of danger . . . let the consequence be what they may." Asbury's decision to remain in America left him surrounded by many who considered him an enemy of the Revolution.

Because of the position taken by Wesley and others, Methodists in America were seen as spies and Tory sympathizers. In 1777 Asbury had to take refuge in Delaware when he refused to take the Maryland state oath. Even though Methodists were oppressed during the Revolution, their numbers grew enormously. During his two-year exile in Delaware, Asbury realized that the growing church in America could not remain under the same command as the Methodists in England. At the conference of 1779 in Fluvanna County, Virginia, all the Methodist leaders in attendance recognized Asbury as the leader of Methodism in America.

The formal split of the American Methodists from British Wesleyan societies was made official at the Christmas Conference of 1784 in Baltimore. The split was not a contentious one, as it was sanctioned in part by Wesley. Both American and English Methodists recognized the different issues that had to be addressed by the church in the newly independent United States. By the beginning of 1785 the Methodist Episcopal Church was a distinct entity from its parent church in England. Asbury, who until this time had not been ordained or administered sacraments, became Bishop Asbury, the superintendent of the Methodist Episcopal Church.

Although Asbury was now the leader of all American Methodists, he continued and even expanded his preaching circuit. His rounds took him from New York and Massachusetts all the way through Kentucky, Tennessee, and Georgia. Each year he visited almost every state in the union, frequently covering 5,000 or 6,000 miles a year; it has been estimated that in his travels he preached more than 17,000 sermons of one to two hours.

In 1784, the year of the Christmas Conference, there were approximately eighty preachers and 15,000 members in the Methodist Church, residing in a narrow strip along the East Coast from New York to North Carolina. Over the next thirty-two years, under the direct control of Asbury, the church grew to encompass more than 2,500 preachers serving 140,000 parishioners, from Canada to the Gulf of Mexico, into the Midwest, beyond the Mississippi, and into the Louisiana Territory.

Asbury's travels wore down his health. By the end of his life he had logged about 275,000 miles, often traveling and preaching despite pain and sickness. By 1814 he was unable to ride on horseback, so he took to a carriage, not moderating his wearisome schedule. During the next two years his health continued to deteriorate. Asbury anticipated his death and called his friends to his room in George Arnold's home in Spotsylvania, Virginia, to sing hymns during his last moments.

Asbury lived to a great extent in the public arena. He was not well educated; he considered his life and experiences to be his classroom, and God and the scriptures his professors. He never married because he felt it unfair to ask a woman to make the sacrifices he thought necessary to his mission. He had no place to call home and rarely stayed more than a few days in one town. He never became a citizen of the United States, but he never returned to England. He lived his life as he had intended, "to live to God and bring others to do so." After his death a close friend said, "Bishop Asbury possessed more deadness to the world, more of a self-sacrificing spirit, more of the spirit of prayer, of Christian enterprise, of labor, and of benevolence, than any other man I ever knew; he was the most unselfish being I was ever acquainted with." The Methodist Episcopal Church became the United Methodist Church in 1968 after mergers with several other denominations. Entities named for Asbury include Asbury College and Asbury Theological Seminary, both in Wilmore, Kentucky; and the town of Asbury Park, New Jersey.

• Among the most valuable sources on Asbury are the three volumes of his *Journal* (1852), and the collection of his papers accumulated by Robert Emory, now held in the Emory Collection at Drew Theological Seminary. Asbury's own publications include *The Causes, Evils and Cures of Heart and Church Divisions, Extracted from the Works of Mr. Jeremiah Burroughs and Mr. Richard Baxter* (1792), and *Extracts of Letters Containing Some Account of the Work of God since the Year 1800; Written by the Preachers and Members of the Methodist Episcopal Church to Their Bishops* (1805). Significant biographies include William Peter Strickland, *The Pioneer Bishop* (1858); George P. Mains, *Francis Asbury* (1909); Ezra Squire Tipple, *Francis Asbury: The Prophet of the Long Road* (1916); L. C. Rudolph, *Francis Asbury* (1966); and Charles Ludwig, *Francis Asbury: God's Circuit Rider* (1984). Also of note is Norman Nygaard's biographical novel, *Bishop on Horseback* (1962).

JAMES D. STAROS

ASBURY, Herbert (1 Sept. 1891–24 Feb. 1963), journalist and popular historian, was born in Farmington, Missouri, the son of Samuel Lester Asbury, a surveyor and city clerk, and Ellen N. Prichard. His grandfather and great-grandfather were Methodist ministers. Asbury claimed that his great-great uncle was Francis Asbury, the first bishop of the Methodist church in America. Asbury rejected the religiosity that dominated his youth, later proclaiming "contempt for the church, and disgust for the forms of religion." "I abandoned the traditional faith of the Asburys and, in the eyes of Methodists at least, disgraced my name," he recalled, "because when I was a boy religion was poured down my throat in doses that strangled me and made me sick of soul. There was simply too much of it."

Asbury was educated at Baptist College and Carleton College in Farmington, after graduation beginning his newspaper career on the Farmington *Times*. He reported for the Quincy, Illinois, *Journal* (1910–1912) and the Peoria *Journal* (1912–1913) before moving to William Randolph Hearst's Atlanta *Georgian*, a sensationalistic newspaper that "burst upon Atlanta like a bomb" and upon its stodgy competitors "like the crack of doom." Asbury did "gum shoe work" for the *Georgian*'s successful campaign to reform the state's child labor laws. "What can be said of a God who employs a Hearst newspaper as His instrument in a project involving the welfare of His Little Ones?" Asbury quipped. In 1915 he went to New York City to work for the *Press* (1915–1916), the *Tribune* (1916), and the *Sun* (1916–1917).

On 8 December 1917 he entered the U.S. Army as a private in the 306th Machine Gun Battalion in World War I. He was promoted to sergeant in the 2d Army Corps and then to second lieutenant, infantry, before the war's end. After being wounded in France, he was honorably discharged in January 1919. He rejoined the New York *Sun*, then moved to the New York *Herald* (1920–1924) and the merged *Herald Tribune* (1924–1928). He married fellow *Herald Tribune* staff member Helen Hahn in 1928; they divorced sixteen years later.

In April 1926 H. L. Mencken's *American Mercury* published Asbury's sketch, "Hatrack," about a prostitute who plied her trade in his hometown's Catholic and Masonic cemeteries. Boston's Watch and Ward Society deemed the article obscene and got sales of the *American Mercury* banned in that city. Asbury later commented that "Hatrack" also was "construed as an attack upon religion . . . with the cry of blasphemy and sacrilege." Mencken challenged the ban, selling a copy of the offending issue to a Watch and Ward Society official on the Boston Common to engineer his own arrest. The case went to court, Mencken prevailed, and the ban was lifted.

Asbury's first book, *Up from Methodism* (1926), was an autobiographical account that a reviewer called "the epic of an apostate pilgrim's progress through the stultifying valley of Farmington Methodism and final triumph of his sinfulness." Another reviewer complained of the "ill humor of many passages and animus which frequently leers through the pages." Critical response to his biography of Francis Asbury, *A Methodist Saint* (1927), ranged from "a masterpiece" to "a complete dud."

Asbury's popular, informal histories of crime, corruption, and underworld vice were widely read and appreciated for their brisk, impersonal, journalistic style and compelling narrative. *The Gangs of New York* (1928) was hailed for being written by "a newspaperman who does not mind denying himself the pleasure of melodrama." *The Barbary Coast: An Informal History of the San Francisco Underworld* (1933) won praise because its author "has not been abashed by the gruesome or intimidated by the vicious." In a similar work, *The French Quarter: An Informal History of the New Orleans Underworld* (1936), Asbury "skimmed the scum from the history of this fantastic pageant of saints and sinners," a critic wrote, and produced "a lusty, bawdy, and Rabelaisian book." *Sucker's Progress: An Informal History of Gambling in America from the Colonies to Canfield* (1938) prompted a reviewer to notice Asbury's lack of "moral indignation" and "spontaneous admiration for rascality." *Gem of the Prairie: An Informal History of the Chicago Underworld* (1940) was called "a gaudy, bawdy, uproarious, sad shocking job." Asbury's "sure eye for the preposterous, the tragic, the heroic, or merely the witless in American life and times," a critic noted, made *The Golden Flood: An Informal History of America's First Oil Field* (1942) a lively companion to scholarly works on the subject. The *American Historical Review* (Oct. 1942) called *The Golden Flood* a "familiar" and "informal" history, "insofar as it is historical. . . . Sin among the derricks is the real theme, and how the author does revel in all the details!" His final book, *The Great Illusion: An Informal History of Prohibition* (1950), a critic wrote, served as a warning to a younger generation about the futility of legislating morality. The *American Historical Review* (July 1951) called it a "significant and fascinating study" and noted that "Herbert Asbury is ideally qualified to write this book."

The *New York Times* called Asbury "this country's chief chronicler of sin for many years. . . . He thought gang fights and rum running and murders and prostitution were a gaudy show. With one of the fastest typewriters in the United States, he made the most of it." Asbury also contributed to magazines, writing for *Cosmopolitan*, the *New Yorker*, and *Popular Science* as well as serving as an editor at *Collier's Weekly* (1942–1948).

He married Edith S. Evans in 1945; the marriage ended in separation. Neither of his marriages produced children. Asbury died in New York.

• Asbury's first article for the *American Mercury*, "Up from Methodism" (Feb. 1925), describes his religious upbringing and subsequent hostile rejection of it. His experiences on the Atlanta *Georgian* are detailed in "Hearst Comes to Atlanta," *American Mercury*, Jan. 1926, and his reminiscence of Mencken and "Hatrack" appear in "The Day Mencken Broke the Law," *American Mercury*, Oct. 1951. Asbury's other books are *The Devil of Pei-Ling* (1927), *Carry Nation* (1929), *Ye Olde Fire Laddies* (1930), and *All Around the Town* (1934). His obituary appears in the *New York Times*, 25 Feb. 1963.

A. J. KAUL

ASCH, Moses (2 Dec. 1905–19 Oct. 1986), sound engineer and record company executive, was born in Warsaw, Poland, the son of Sholem Asch, a world-renowned Yiddish novelist and playwright, and Matilda Spiro. Since Asch's father acquired literary fame early in life, the family lived in material comfort. But they moved frequently, and Asch often was left in the care of others, notably his mother's sister Basha, a Social Democrat and revolutionary. Additionally, although a prominent figure in international Jewish intellectual circles, Asch's father was an iconoclast by nature, and as a consequence Asch was never bar mitzvahed. In 1912 the persecution of Jews in Poland rendered life intolerable for the Asches, and they moved to a villa in the suburbs of Paris. When in 1915 war's violence engulfed France as well, the family resettled in New York City.

Young Asch developed an interest in radio electronics while still in high school, and when his parents resettled in various parts of France in 1923 he was sent to a technical *Hochschule* in Koblenz, Germany. Although he completed neither high school in New York nor an engineering degree in Germany, he did acquire two substantive years of training in sound electronics, which enabled him to return to New York in 1926 and begin a career in radio electronics. Initially he worked for both the fledgling Radio Corporation of America and the mercurial inventor Lee de Forest, and later he supported himself as a radio repairman. But he had aspirations to be an inventor, and in 1930 he began his own shop, Radio Laboratories of Brooklyn. In 1928 he married Frances Ungar; they had one child.

Financial circumstances forced Asch to merge his company in 1934 with another that specialized in public address systems. This merger enabled him to branch into other areas of sound electronics. Capitalizing on his father's connections with New York's Yiddish theaters, Asch found work wiring burlesque houses and other establishments for sound. A more propitious event occurred in 1938 when his father's employer, the *Jewish Daily Forward*, commissioned Radio Labs to construct a transmitter for its Yiddish-language radio station, WEVD. From this project Asch recognized a market for recorded Yiddish music, both sacred and secular, and for both the retail market and radio airplay. In 1940 Radio Laboratories was dissolved; in its place he established Asch Recordings. From that point on, Asch was immersed in the recording, manufacture, and sale of phonograph records.

In the early 1940s he primarily recorded cantorials—Jewish liturgical music. However, early exceptions prefigured the direction that his recording ultimately took. In 1941 he began to record the southern African-American folk singer and ex-convict Huddie Ledbetter (Lead Belly). During this era the enthusiasm for folk music came primarily from political leftists, and specifically from the mid-1930s' initiative of the Communist Party U.S.A., known as the Popular Front, which celebrated American (and particularly African-American) folk culture as the expression of the proletarian will. Through World War II, Asch recorded most of the premier American folk musicians of that time, including Josh White, Burl Ives, and Sonny Terry; many of the musicians were not overtly political themselves, although they were pleased to attract a leftist audience. Starting in 1944, however, with the first recordings of Woody Guthrie and Pete Seeger, Asch was recording musicians who sought to deliberately use folk music as a vehicle for promoting assorted progressive agendas, particularly the cause of labor, racial harmony, and (after the war) international peace. Asch's own political sympathies were often ambiguous, and he avoided party affiliation (particularly with the Communists); still, he did at times describe himself as an "anarchist" (in the tradition of his aunt Basha) and often lent his resources and those of his company to leftist causes.

Asch's early commercial successes came not with folk musicians, but with such major jazz figures as Mary Lou Williams, James P. Johnson, Stuff Smith, Art Tatum, and Coleman Hawkins. At the close of the war, to get out from under a partnership he had entered into with Stinson Records, Asch formed the Disc Company of America. Through Disc, Asch continued to release folk and jazz records, avant-garde symphonic music, and, with the assistance of Harold Courlander, a series of ethnic recordings that featured traditional musics from around the world. The most lucrative part of his operation in the Disc years was a collaboration with jazz impresario Norman Granz who, through his Jazz at the Philharmonic series, made popular the recording of improvised jazz in concert settings. But this association also caused Asch to overextend himself financially, and in 1948 he declared bankruptcy.

Late that same year Asch was able to resurrect his recording business by having his secretary, Marian

Distler, purchase his assets and establish a new recording company, Folkways Records, in her own name. Although nominally a "consultant" to Folkways in the early years, Asch ran the company from its formation until his death. By concentrating on folk music, historical and political documentaries, children's, and spoken-word recordings, he was able to create an immense catalog of titles (almost 2,200 at his death), which had a modest but dependable market, particularly among music educators and school librarians. His most unambiguous political convictions received expression in the many recordings of African-American folk music, blues, documentary history, poetry, and, in several magnificent collections, songs of the civil rights period. When the "folk revival" began in the 1950s, the Folkways catalog provided much of the impetus and inspiration. Although most of the bigger names of the folk revival recorded with more commercial labels, they depended on the material available in Asch's catalog—as well as on the example he had set by recording seminal figures in the 1940s.

Over the years Folkways became a repository for the field recordings of anthropologists and others who brought Asch the traditional musics of the world. Asch often was accused of compensating musicians and field recorders meagerly, but most of them were pleased that he kept the material available to the public—nothing ever was deleted from the catalog. Additionally, he gave artists and collectors free reign in album production and encouraged them to include printed material that provided social and historical context. He died in New York City.

Long before most others, Asch recognized the value of folk music in helping people understand who they are in all their cultural complexity. Neil Alan Marks wrote in the *New York Times* (2 Nov. 1980): "Folkways Records was for folklorists and musicians the talmudic source for much primary material. Its founder, Moses Asch, may have more to do with the preservation of folk music than any single person in this country."

• Asch's papers as well as the entire Folkways collection (and the rights to it) are deposited in a special archive within the Smithsonian Institution. Several useful articles about Asch appeared during his lifetime, notably Robert Shelton, "Folkways in Sound . . . or the Remarkable Enterprises of Mr. Moe Asch," *High Fidelity*, June 1960, pp. 42–44, 102–3; and Israel Young, "Moses Asch, Twentieth Century Man, Parts I & II," *Sing Out!* 26, no. 1 (1977), pp. 2–6, and no. 2 (1977), pp. 25–29. See also Tony Sherman's generally accurate article, published a year after Asch's death, "The Remarkable Recordings of Moses Asch," *Smithsonian*, Aug. 1987, pp. 110–21; and Robbie Lieberman's *My Song Is My Weapon: People's Songs, American Communism, and the Politics of Culture, 1930–1950* (1989), a thoughtful book about the political uses of folk song during two critical decades. The most complete obituaries are in the *New York Times*, 21 Oct. 1986, and *Sing Out!* 32, no. 3 (1987).

PETER GOLDSMITH

ASCH, Nathan (10 July 1902–23 Dec. 1964), novelist, was born in Warsaw, Poland, the son of Sholem Asch, a well-known Yiddish writer, and Mathilda Spira. The Asch family moved from Warsaw to Paris in 1912 and then to Switzerland at the outbreak of World War I. They settled permanently in the United States, on Staten Island, in 1915. Asch completed public schooling in Brooklyn, New York, and then attended Syracuse and Columbia universities. He never received a degree, deciding instead to leave school and to devote his energies to learning the craft of writing.

Asch supported himself during his first years out of school by working on Wall Street, where he developed a keen eye for urban life that played a prominent role in his early novels. Like many young American writers of the age, Asch traveled to France in 1923 with the goal of pursuing his art more seriously. Once there he made friends among others in the exile community in Paris, including Malcolm Cowley and Ernest Hemingway. Asch and Hemingway became friends, although Asch later complained that Hemingway tended to be condescending toward his work. Nevertheless, Asch admired Hemingway, who proved to be a great stylistic influence on Asch.

Asch also made the acquaintance of Ford Madox Ford, who in 1924 published Asch's first story in the *Transatlantic Review* and helped to have his first novel, *The Office*, published in 1925. Asch followed this work in 1927 with *Love in Chartres*, a semi-autobiographical novel that records the early stages of his love affair with his first wife, Liesl Ingwersen, whom he had met in France. The couple returned to the United States after their marriage in 1926, making their home in Connecticut and then in New Jersey over the next several years; they had one child. Asch set his third novel, *Pay Day* (1930), in the turbulent days surrounding the Sacco-Vanzetti execution. Though at the time it was nearly suppressed for its candid sexual content, it has become his most highly regarded work.

Asch supplemented his income in the early 1930s by writing numerous book reviews for the *New Republic*. But increasing financial pressures prompted him to move to Hollywood in the middle of the decade to work on scripts for the film studios. He also continued to write, publishing *The Valley* in 1935 and a non-fictional piece two years later titled *The Road: In Search of America*, which chronicled a bus trip he had taken across the United States before arriving in California. From 1937 to 1939 Asch worked in the education program at the Works Progress Administration. Asch and his wife Liesl had divorced in 1930. In 1939 Asch married Caroline Tasker Miles, who often supported him financially while he attempted to find a publisher for his work; they had no children.

Soon after the outbreak of the Second World War, Asch enlisted in the U.S. Army Air Force as a journalist. He lived in London from 1942 to 1945, and then he was sent to Paris as a member of the Allied occupation forces rather than as an aspiring novelist. For his military service Asch received the Air Medal and the Bronze Star. Despite his wartime efforts, Asch came to be investigated by the House Un-American Activities Committee during the McCarthy era. Asch most likely came to the committee's attention because of the sympathy he expressed toward Sacco and Vanzetti in his novel *Pay Day*, and because he had explored the problem of rural poverty in *The Valley*.

After the war Asch moved to Mill Valley, California, and continued to publish short fiction. He also worked on what he considered to be his best novel, *Paris Is Home*, a description of life in postwar Paris that he completed in the late 1940s. The book failed, however, to be accepted for publication, and Asch apparently quit working on it in the early 1950s. He was ultimately unable to publish any of the longer fiction he wrote after the war. In the last years of his life Asch built furniture and conducted writing workshops out of his home in Mill Valley. He never, however, gave up writing or the effort to get his longer works published. He died in California.

His father had gained renown as an author whose writing was steeped in the traditions of the past, but Asch's sensibilities were wholly modern. In novels such as *The Office* and *Pay Day*, Asch depicted the stark realities of everyday urban life. He was, moreover, a close observer of the modern spiritual condition, and his works are suffused with a pervasive sense of humanity's rootlessness. The sense of displacement in his fiction seems to have grown out of the conditions of his own life. As Asch himself put it in a 1936 proposal for a Guggenheim Fellowship that he never received:

> Most writers, like most persons, have within them the memory of a home—physical: they spent their childhood in one house, went to one school, grew up, played, fought in one neighborhood—a spiritual home: they relax in one language, one region, one country. . . . There seems to be, there seems always to have been, a quality to being native. It is a quality the writer of this statement does not possess.

Perhaps because Asch was so culturally unmoored, his longer fiction tends to be overly episodic, lacking in cohesion and unity. It is principally for this reason that Asch, a fine, even lyrical writer, had difficulty finding readers—and, later in life, publishers as well.

• Asch's papers are located in the Winthrop College Library Archives in Rock Hill, S.C. His letters to Malcolm Cowley are in the Cowley papers at the Newberry Library in Chicago. Although Asch never found a publisher for *Paris Is Home*, a section of this work can be found under the title "The 1920's: An Interior," *Paris Review* 6 (Summer 1954): 82–101; Cowley offered a brief foreword to the piece. For a fascinating study of Asch's love-hate relationship with Hemingway, see Eva B. Mills, "Ernest Hemingway and Nathan Asch: An Ambivalent Relationship," *Hemingway Review* 2 (1983): 48–51. Walter Berthoff includes some biographical information and an insightful discussion of Asch's chief themes in his introduction to a reissue of *Pay Day* for the Proletarian Literature Series (1990). An obituary is in the *New York Times*, 25 Dec. 1964.

KEVIN R. RAHIMZADEH

ASCH, Sholem (1 Nov. 1880–10 July 1957), Yiddish novelist, dramatist, and short story writer, was born in Kutno, Poland, a small town near Warsaw, the son of Moishe Asch, a cattle dealer and innkeeper, and Malka Wydawski. Asch was raised in a small town and was essentially self-educated. His father taught him the alphabet from the Bible, which was, as Asch later noted, "the first book that I ever held in my hand" (Siegel, p. 3). The Bible served as his grammar, geography, and history textbooks, as well as a storybook of sorts; later the Scriptures became a source of continual literary inspiration. As an adult Asch became a serious collector of rare biblical editions. He attended local schools to train for the rabbinate, studying the Talmud but also reading German classics and Shakespeare. Finally, against his family's wishes, Asch made up his mind to become a writer.

In 1896 Asch sent his first "ungrammatical effusions" to Reuben Brainin, and the publisher rejected them as "immature reflections." At age seventeen Asch, whose growing secular outlook distressed his family, was sent to a nearby village as a Hebrew teacher for young children. After some months Asch went to Wloclawek, a Vistula River port and industrial center, where he would stay for two years. While there he held a variety of jobs, including one writing letters for people who could not write, a task that gave Asch an increased insight into life's "hidden corners" and served as his "higher schooling."

During this period Asch also began writing his own short stories and sketches about the people and customs in the small towns he knew so well. In 1899 he went to Warsaw with a folder of these tales, written in Hebrew; they became the foundation of his writing career. In Warsaw he sought out Isaac Leib Peretz, one of the "fathers" of modern Yiddish literature, who encouraged Asch and suggested that he write the stories in Yiddish. Asch later said that Peretz freed him from the "chains of Hebrew." In 1900 his first stories, "Little Moses" and "On the Way," were published. In 1901 Asch married Mathilda (Madja) Spira. They had four children.

Living in Warsaw, Asch continued to take Peretz's advice, writing his sketches in both Hebrew and Yiddish. *Dos shtetl* (The little town), which celebrates Jewish life and community in the small towns (*shtetls*) far from the mainstream of European culture, was Asch's first novel. Published in 1904, the text established his reputation as a major Yiddish writer. That same year Asch wrote his first play titled *The Return* (later retitled *Downstream*), a two-act drama that was produced in Polish in Cracow.

This drama and his subsequent plays gave Asch recognition on the Polish and Russian stage, but it was the powerful *God of Vengeance* (1907) that climaxed his career as a dramatist and brought him world renown, as well as severe criticism. When Asch first read the play to a group of Jewish writers and intellectuals, the reaction was not favorable. His mentor Peretz even advised Asch to "burn it." The play depicts a man attempting to bargain with God to preserve his daughter's moral purity. Unwilling to change his life as owner of a brothel, the hero's "moral degradation" is inevitably inflicted on the daughter. The play was first produced in St. Petersburg by the Russian actress W. P. Komisarjevsky and was a success. Max Reinhardt, the German producer, also had the play translated into German and produced it two years later in his Berlin theater. Although the play was withdrawn after eighteen performances, it provoked much discussion and spread Asch's name across Western Europe, winning him his first large non-Yiddish audience. The play would eventually be produced in other large cities, including New York in 1923 where the subject matter and brothel scenes almost caused a riot. It was shut down by the police, and the star, Rudolpf Schildkraut, was jailed.

The play's initial success in Russia enabled Asch to make his first trip to Palestine in 1908. That was also the year his short stories were first published in America by Abraham Cahan in the *Jewish Morning Journal*, introducing Asch to American readers. The following year Asch made his first trip to New York, a trip which resulted in a series of articles contrasting the natural beauty of America with the cruel, seamy side of Jewish immigrant life. His novel *America* (published in Yiddish in 1911; translated into English in 1918) was the first to be serialized by Cahan.

In 1912 Asch moved his family to Paris for two years, and in 1914 they moved once again to New York City, living first in the Bronx and finally, for ten years, on Staten Island. During this period Asch wrote continuously; for example in 1913 he wrote a book of children's stories, a prose poem, three plays, and the novel *Reb Shloyme nogid* (Wealthy reb Shlome), yet another successful portrayal of the fading *shtetl* world. It was the humor and characters of his novel *Mottke the Thief* (1916), however, that made Asch a household name among American Jews. Although different in tone, the more serious *The Sanctification of the Name* (1919) was similarly described as an "enduring masterpiece of Yiddish literature." This novel details Jewish life in Poland during a decade of persecution in the seventeenth century, a decade that was almost as devastating as the Holocaust would someday be.

Asch became a United States citizen in 1920. The following year his collected works were published in Yiddish; they amounted to twelve volumes. Within a decade or so Asch had written what became known as his "city" novels: *Petersburg* (1929), *Warsaw* (1930), and *Moscow* (1931). In 1933 the books were published as the trilogy *Three Cities*, and Asch was nominated for a Nobel Prize. He also traveled during this period to Warsaw, Paris, Palestine, and Vienna. Asch moved to Nice in 1932, and by 1936 his fame was so widespread that Ludwig Lewisohn grouped him with Einstein, Freud, Henri Bergson, and Martin Buber in his list of the "World's Greatest Living Jews." Three years later Asch was hated by many of his former Jewish admirers.

For years Asch had been fascinated by the New Testament. Consequently, he had begun gathering material for a novel about Jesus during his first visit to Palestine. *The Nazarene* (1939) was a huge success with non-Jewish readers and was ninth on the annual bestseller list, but it provoked vicious attacks from Asch's Jewish fans. The previous year Abraham Cahan, who had serialized most of Asch's previous fiction in his newspaper, had urged him not to complete the novel. Many accused Asch of distorting the Jewish tradition in order to make it conform to Christian dogma about Jesus, and in doing so, they felt Asch had betrayed his heritage. What made Jewish reaction even more severe was the timing of the publication: Asch had published the novel during the Holocaust, a time when Jews were being slaughtered in Europe.

Undaunted, Asch published two more "christological novels:" *The Apostle* (1943), a text about St. Paul, and *Mary* (1949). Both were on the annual bestseller lists. Another novel titled *East River* (1946), a story about the love between a Jewish boy and a Roman Catholic girl, was again popular with his Christian readers but not with his Jewish audience. The success of these novels made Asch "the most debated Jewish writer of his time" yet "filled his last years with acrimony" (Siegel, p. 8).

Asch had been living in Stamford, Connecticut, since 1940, but he left the New York area for Miami Beach in 1951. These were difficult years for Asch. Not only had Cahan refused to publish any more of Asch's work, but he also convinced other Yiddish newspapers to boycott Asch. Only the Marxist paper the *Morning Freiheit* would publish his work, an arrangement that resulted in Asch being called before Senator Joseph McCarthy and the House Un-American Activities Committee. Asch's *Freiheit* connection suggested that Asch, who ironically had attacked Marxism for a decade in his writing, was a Communist. Attacks against him and his writing continued, and in 1953 Chaim Lieberman's vitriolic *The Christianity of Sholem Asch* took Asch apart, book by book, line by line.

After being mugged by Yiddish extremists in Miami, Asch had had enough. He stated, "I am returning to England with a broken heart. Intolerance among my own race has been too much of a handicap for me to work" (Siegel, p. 198). By 1956 Asch had settled in Bat Yam, Israel, and was writing a new novel, *Jacob and Rachel*, when he suffered a stroke. The novel was never finished, and the following year he died in London while visiting his daughter.

Asch introduced Yiddish literature to mainstream European and American culture. He has been described as the Yiddish Dickens because of his characters and as a Maupassant because of the sexual frankness of his stories. Although persecuted by some because of his New Testament novels, he was read and beloved by many. Of particular value to Asch was the reaction to his novel *Song of the Valley* (1938), written about Israel. After World War II Asch received a tattered copy of the book from a concentration camp survivor. The novel had secretly passed through the hands of hundreds of Jewish prisoners, giving them hope that they might survive to go to that holy land described by Asch.

• Asch's manuscripts and letters are at the Yale University Library. A smaller collection can be found in the Gelman Library at George Washington University. A list of Asch's principal works is in *Twentieth Century Literary Criticism*, vol. 3 (1980). Ben Siegel, *The Controversial Sholem Asch: An Introduction to His Fiction* (1976), is a basic source and includes biographical information. An extremely negative assessment of Asch and his work is Chaim Lieberman, *The Christianity of Sholem Asch: An Appraisal from the Jewish Viewpoint* (1953). For positive discussions of Asch's work see Charles A. Madison, *Yiddish Literature: Its Scope and Major Writers* (1968), and Sol Liptzin, *The Flowering of Yiddish Literature* (1963). Gloria L. Cronin et al., *Jewish American Fiction Writers: An Annotated Bibliography* (1991), contains both primary and secondary sources. Oscar Cargill, "Sholem Asch: Still Immigrant and Alien," *The English Journal* 39 (Nov. 1950): 483–90, is both biographical and critical. Recent articles include Stanley Brodwin, "History and Martyrological Tragedy: The Jewish Experience in Sholem Asch and Andre Schwartz-Bart," *Twentieth Century Literature* 40 (Spring 1994): 72–91, and Amy Alexander, "The Jews of *East River*: Americans Yet Forever Jews," *Studies in American Jewish Literature* 5 (1986): 54–60. See also Cheryl Amy Alexander, "Major Themes in Selected American Novels by Sholem Asch" (Ph.D. diss., East Texas State Univ., 1984). An obituary is in the *New York Times*, 11 July 1957.

MARCIA B. DINNEEN

ASCOLI, Max (25 Jun. 1898–1 Jan. 1978), political philosopher, editor, and publisher, was born in Ferrara, Italy, the son of Enrico Ascoli, a coal merchant, and Adriana Finzi. Despite serious problems with his eyesight, which were to plague him much of his life, Ascoli earned his LL.D. at the University of Ferrara in 1920 and his Ph.D. in philosophy at the University of Rome in 1928. His first book, a study of the radical French thinker and writer Georges Sorel, appeared in 1921. An opponent of fascism from its beginnings, Ascoli wrote articles for *Rivoluzione Liberale* and other antifascist journals before being arrested in 1928 and jailed briefly. For refusing to join the Fascist party, which he later described as "a totalitarian system tempered by sloppiness," he was kept under police surveillance for the next three years.

In 1931 he came to the United States on a Rockefeller Foundation fellowship, and in 1933, along with several refugees from Nazi Germany, he was appointed to the newly established graduate faculty of political and social science—known as the University in Exile—at the New School for Social Research in New York City. There he wrote frequently for the quarterly that was published by the graduate faculty, *Social Research*, and contributed to *Atlantic Monthly, Survey Graphic, Foreign Affairs*, and the *Nation*. His first book in English, *Intelligence in Politics*, appeared in 1936. The following year he and Fritz Lehmann edited a collection of articles by their colleagues, *Political and Economic Democracy*, and in 1938 he and another colleague, Arthur Feiler, coauthored *Fascism for Whom?* In 1939 Ascoli became an American citizen, and in 1940 he married Marion Rosenwald; they had one child.

From 1940 to 1943 Ascoli served as the first president of the Mazzini Society, an Italian-American group founded to oppose fascism, and in 1944 he founded a nonprofit organization to help revive the handicraft industries in Italy that had been destroyed by the war. His experience traveling in Latin America in the early 1940s for the wartime government Office of the Coordinator of Inter-American Affairs, together with his continuing activity as a writer on politics for various journals, led him to feel the need for a new kind of political journalism. The result was the establishment of the *Reporter*, which was financed largely by Ascoli and his wife. Its masthead identified the magazine as "A Fortnightly of Facts and Ideas," and the prospectus in its first issue (26 Apr. 1949) described it as "a magazine for the citizen and not just the reader." The basic theme of the magazine, Ascoli told his staff, could be found in a book that he published in 1949, *The Power of Freedom*, in which he insists that citizens in a democracy must be independent enough to think intelligently and to act responsibly. In practical terms this meant that the *Reporter*, although consistently describing itself as a "liberal magazine," never hesitated to advocate its own distinctive version of liberalism, a practice that sometimes disconcerted conservatives and liberals alike.

As editor during the *Reporter*'s entire nineteen years, Ascoli wrote nearly all of the editorials at the front of the magazine, and he usually handled the major articles. A man of passionate convictions who suffered from recurrent health problems, Ascoli conceded that he was a difficult man to work for, but his staff respected his brilliance as an editor. His senior editors over the years included Philip Horton, Robert Bingham, and Harlan Cleveland. Among the more prominent staff writers were Douglass Cater, Meg Greenfield, George Bailey, and Claire Sterling. In addition, the *Reporter* published the work of some seventeen hundred outside contributors, including several hundred prominent political, journalistic, or academic figures such as Adolf Berle, Isaac Deutscher, John Kenneth Galbraith, Alfred Kazin, Henry Kissinger, Hilton Kramer, Eric Sevareid, and George Steiner. Although the *Reporter* did not attain a circulation of 200,000 until its final two years, it was highly regarded by Washington journalists for its fairness and reliability, and it received thirty-two journalistic awards for excellence. It probably had its greatest influence in the 1950s and early 1960s; in 1966 its paid subscribers included the president and vice president of the United States, seven members of the cabinet, and one-third of the Senate.

The *Reporter* was the first national magazine to devote a special issue (6 June 1950) to the dangers of McCarthyism, and later it ran articles by several of Joseph R. McCarthy's victims. Its strong defense of civil liberties and civil rights bolstered its reputation as a leading liberal magazine; some conservatives even attacked it as procommunist. Ascoli, however, opposed communism as uncompromisingly as he opposed fascism, writing on one occasion that "Communism is hell endured for the sake of a sham heaven. Fascism is hell for the hell of it." By the early 1960s his outspoken editorials opposing Castro, criticizing Khrushchev's visit to America, and attacking the Kennedy administration's apparent acquiescence in the building of the Berlin Wall were drawing strong reactions from some of his readers. And as the *Reporter* after 1965 continued to give strong support to U.S. policy in Vietnam, it found itself more and more estranged from many in the liberal community. Concerned about this estrangement, about the approach of his seventieth birthday, and about his failure to find a suitable successor as editor, Ascoli felt increasingly that the *Reporter* was approaching its end. Shortly after President Lyndon Johnson's announcement at the end of March 1968 that he would not seek reelection, Ascoli announced that the *Reporter* would cease publication with the issue of 13 June 1968.

Although Ascoli described the *Reporter* as a liberal magazine, he admitted that he himself was a liberal "in the old European tradition." Consequently, he was sometimes at odds with American liberals, remaining as critical of big government as of big business. As a political philosopher he insisted on the limitations of politics, writing in an editorial in 1955, "For a liberal, approximately only half of a man is a political animal—Caesar's half." Freedom was at the heart of his political beliefs, but that was a term he found difficult to define, probably because it stemmed directly from his religious beliefs, about which he was most reluctant to write except in his annual Christmas editorials. Though ethnically a Jew, Ascoli held beliefs that could best be described as Catholic, and in 1970 he received the Catholic rite of baptism.

After the *Reporter* ceased publication, Ascoli kept busy for several years with a number of writing projects, but increasingly fragile health prevented his completing most of them before his death at his home in New York City. A courageous and vigorously independent thinker, Ascoli made the *Reporter* a forum for the expression of acts and ideas that would call Americans to understand and fulfill their intellectual and ethical responsibilities in the world. During its nineteen years of existence, his magazine provided a distinctive, respected, and influential liberal voice in American journalism.

• The papers of Ascoli, which include both his personal papers and the files of the *Reporter*, are in the Special Collections of the Boston University Library. In addition to the works listed above, Ascoli edited three books: *The Fall of Mussolini: His Own Story by Benito Mussolini* (1948), *The Reporter Reader* (1956), and *Our Times: The Best from the Reporter* (1960). He also contributed the introduction to Beatrice Bishop Berle and Travis Beal Jacobs, eds., *Navigating the Rapids 1918–1971* (1973), a selection from the papers of his longtime friend Adolf A. Berle. The most complete published assessment of Ascoli and the *Reporter* is Martin K. Doudna, *Concerned about the Planet: The Reporter Magazine and American Liberalism 1949–1968* (1977), which draws heavily on interviews with Ascoli and several members of the *Reporter* staff. For a personal reminiscence by a staff member who worked closely with him, see Douglass Cater, "Max Ascoli, of *The Reporter*," *Encounter* 50 (Apr. 1978): 49–52. Theodore H. White, *In Search of History* (1978), gives a brief account of his relationship with Ascoli during the several years he contributed to the *Reporter*. An obituary is in the *New York Times*, 2 Jan. 1978.

MARTIN K. DOUDNA

ASHBRIDGE, Elizabeth (1713–16 May 1755), Quaker minister and autobiographer, was born Elizabeth Sampson in Middlewich, Cheshire, England, the daughter of Thomas Sampson, a ship's surgeon, and Mary (maiden name unknown). What little is known about Ashbridge's life is elicited almost entirely from her brief but compelling autobiography, *Some Account of the Fore Part of the Life of Elizabeth Ashbridge*, written shortly before her death and first published in 1774. The *Account* is a fine example of the genre of spiritual autobiography and an illuminating record of the life of a woman and Quaker convert in colonial America.

Ashbridge's early life is rendered with poignancy and emotional power in her memoir. Her impetuous first marriage (husband's name unknown), at age fourteen, caused an estrangement from her father that haunted her for the rest of her life. An authoritative and unforgiving man, her father refused to take her back into his home following the untimely death of her husband, even against the pleadings of his wife, and in 1728 Ashbridge was forced to seek the support of relatives in Ireland, where she lived for five years. Ashbridge had been raised an Anglican and from an early age had shown an intense religious sensibility. The hardships of the tragic marriage and the separation from her family left her in spiritual anguish, and so began a lifelong pattern of religious questing. She found little consolation in the church of her upbringing, and the faith of her Quaker relatives in Ireland seemed alien with its doctrinal emphasis on Inner Light and its practice of lay ministry. Her exploration of other denominations, including Catholicism, left her ungratified.

In 1732 Ashbridge booked passage on a vessel bound for the American colonies, determined to start a new life far away from her past unhappiness. The autobiography describes how she was tricked into signing an indenture to the captain of the ship in exchange for her passage and the three years of abusive servitude she endured under an unnamed master who purchased her indenture after her arrival in New York City. Her master "would not suffer me to have Clothes to be Decent in, having to go barefoot in his Service in the Snowey Weather & the Meanest drudgery, wherein I Suffered the Utmost Hardship that my Body was able to Bear." This newest round of afflictions, imposed on her by a man who purported to be a "Very Religious Man," prompted a crisis for Ashbridge, who saw her victimization as punishment for her own faithlessness. Spiritual solace, however, continued to elude her.

During her period of indenture, the *Account* relates, Ashbridge fleetingly nursed dreams of a career in the theater, but though a gifted singer and dancer, she turned to a more practical vocation, employing herself as a seamstress to buy her freedom. Her musical abilities attracted a schoolteacher named Sullivan, whom she married in 1736. Their volatile union constitutes much of the focus of the autobiography and offers a provocative look at marital politics in early America. The divisions between husband and wife were considerable: he had been drawn to a woman whose musical predilections made her seem mirthful and worldly and so felt disaffected by her religious searching; she resented his imperious temperament, excessive drinking, and failure to secure a stable position in a settled community. She seems, however, to have willed herself to love him, praying "that my Affections might be in a right manner set upon my husband, and . . . in a little time my Love was Sincere to him."

Ashbridge's hunger for spiritual fulfillment persisted, impelling her continued search for a fulfilling religious affiliation. During a stay with relatives in Pennsylvania in 1738, she was again brought in contact with practicing Quakers, and this time she was profoundly moved by her exposure to the faith. Convinced of the truth of Quaker teachings, she became an impassioned convert to a belief system and way of life that divided her even more from her husband. He shared the mainstream culture's suspicions and prejudices about Quakers, particularly the disdain for female preachers, whose public proclamations violated firmly held notions of womanly propriety.

The autobiography traces the marital strife occasioned by Ashbridge's newfound religious piety, what she refers to as "the Tryal of my faith," and follows her futile efforts to secure her husband's support. Sullivan's response to his wife was alternately to shun and harangue her. He tried various strategies to quash her conversion, including humiliating her publicly, striking her, forbidding her to associate with fellow Quakers, and depriving her of a horse, thus forcing her to walk miles to meetings. Ashbridge held her ground, however, and continued to attempt to win him over to the faith. Remarkably, despite his cruelty, Ashbridge maintained an affection for her husband.

Ultimately, the memoir tells us, Sullivan experienced a conversion, though it did not result in the kind of personal reformation that Ashbridge had hoped for. Following a drinking spree, he enlisted impulsively in the British army, but refusing, as a principled Quaker, to take up arms, he was beaten as punishment and eventually died of his wounds in a London hospital in 1741. Significantly, the *Account* ends at this point.

The remaining fourteen years of Ashbridge's life were productive and happy. An active member of the Quaker society in Goshen, Pennsylvania, she gained recognition as a Public Friend (a traveling Quaker preacher). In 1746 she married Aaron Ashbridge, an affluent landowner and prominent member of the local religious community. Like her other marriages, this one remained childless. Their relationship was, by his accounting, "dear and agreeable," and he countenanced his wife's sermonizing. When in 1753 she applied to the Goshen meeting for permission to travel overseas to spread her ministry, he endorsed her petition though it meant a lengthy separation. Taken sick during the difficult Atlantic crossing, Ashbridge experienced declining health during the two years she spent abroad. She managed to follow an extensive itinerary in England and Ireland but died in Kilnock, County Carlow, Ireland, before she could reunite with her husband.

Elizabeth Ashbridge is remembered chiefly for the autobiographical account of her earlier life, which shows her to have been both a remarkable woman and a gifted writer. Her narrative provides crucial insights into the gender and religious politics of early American life and affords a compelling portrait of an individual's personal trials and spiritual odyssey. Ashbridge's story demonstrates the efficacy of conscience and integrity; as a woman and Quaker, she claimed authority over her own life against pervasive cultural constraints, turning her marginalized status into an instrument of power.

• Copies of various manuscript versions of Ashbridge's autobiography are located at the Boston Public Library, the Friends Historical Library at Swarthmore College, the Quaker Collection of the Haverford College Library, the Friends Library at Swanbrook House in Dublin, the Bevan-Naish Library at the Woodbrooke Quaker Study Centre in Birmingham, England, and the Library of the Society of Friends in London. Several edited versions of the autobiography are available in print. The most authoritative is Daniel Shea's edition, *Some Account of the Fore Part of the Life of Elizabeth Ashbridge, . . . Written by Her Own Hand Many Years Ago*, in *Journeys in New Worlds: Early American Women's Narratives*, ed. William L. Andrews et al. (1990); Shea provides a notably substantive introduction. For significant biographical and critical material on Ashbridge, see Cristine Levenduski, "Elizabeth Ashbridge's 'Remarkable Experiences': Creating the Self in a Quaker Personal Narrative" (Ph.D. diss., Univ. of Minnesota, 1989). Shea, *Spiritual Autobiography in Early America* (1968), examines Ashbridge's *Account* in the context of its genre and period. See also Carol Edkins, "Quest for Community: Spiritual Autobiographies of Eighteenth-Century Quaker and Puritan Women in America," in *Women's Autobiography: Essays in Criticism*, ed. Estelle C. Jelinek (1980), and Luella M. Wright, *The Literary Life of the Early Friends, 1650–1725* (1932). Several studies of Quaker culture are useful, including Margaret Hope Bacon, *Mothers of Feminism: The Story of Quaker Women in America* (1986); Mary Dunn Maples, "Saints and Sinners: Congregational and Quaker Women in the Early Colonial Period," in *Women in American Religion*, ed. Janet Wilson James (1980); Jack D. Marietta, *The Reformation of American Quakerism, 1748–1783* (1984); and Frederick B. Tolles, *Meeting House and Counting House: The Quaker Merchants of Colonial Philadelphia, 1682–1763* (1948).

LIAHNA BABENER

ASHBROOK, John Milan (21 Sept. 1928–24 Apr. 1982), congressman, was born in Johnstown, Ohio, the son of William Albert Ashbrook, a U.S. congressman and businessman, and Marie Swank. He joined the U.S. Navy in 1946, after graduating from high school, and served until 1948. He was a member of Admiral Richard E. Byrd's final Antarctic expedition. In 1948 he married Joan Needles; they had three children and divorced in 1971. He received an A.B. with honors from Harvard University in 1952 and a J.D. from Ohio State University Law School in 1955. Ashbrook did not practice law. Instead in 1953 he had become publisher of the *Johnstown Independent*, a weekly newspaper founded by his father in 1884. Even after he had been in Congress for many years, he still considered himself first and foremost a publisher. When asked about his often precarious political existence, he claimed not to worry because he "would rather be a printer" anyway.

Ashbrook's newspaper career ensured him wide public exposure, and in 1956 he was elected as a Republican to the Ohio General Assembly where he served two terms. A vacancy led him to seek election to Congress from the Seventeenth District in 1960. During that campaign he warned his constituents against "unbridled national power with a resultant loss of individual freedom and local autonomy." He won what was a safe Republican seat and served without interruption for twenty-two years. He served on the House Internal Security Committee (formerly the House Committee on Un-American Activities) and on the Education and Labor Committee. An ardent conservative and one of the most articulate anti-Communists in Congress, Ashbrook used his committee assignments to oppose the expansion of federal aid to education and other New Deal and Great Society programs. Throughout his political life he acquired a nationwide reputation as an intelligent, candid, and persuasive champion of the conservative cause. By the end of Richard Nixon's first term as president, Ashbrook had established himself as a national political leader with impeccable conservative credentials, and he contributed energetically to the national conservative movement. He had been chairman of the Young Republican National Federation from 1957 to 1959; one of the founders of the American Conservative Union, serving as chairman from 1966 to 1971; and on the Steering Committee of the Committee of One Million against the Admission of Communist China to the United Nations, whose campaign began in 1953.

Although Ashbrook was one of the founders of the draft Barry Goldwater movement in 1963 and supported Goldwater's presidential candidacy in 1964, he supported Nixon's bid for the Republican presidential nomination in 1968. He urged fellow conservatives not to bolt to the third-party candidacy of Alabama governor George Wallace, arguing that Nixon's election would provide a unique opportunity to build a nationwide conservative coalition. By December 1971 Ashbrook publicly broke with the Nixon administration, criticizing "the presentation of liberal policies in the verbal trappings of conservatism." He especially opposed the president's budget deficits, wage and price controls, and recent rapprochement with China. New Deal policies, he claimed, "have not been changed but extended and refined" under the Nixon presidency.

At the end of 1971 Ashbrook announced his intention to oppose Nixon's renomination in a number of Republican primaries. In justifying his candidacy, he denounced the Nixon administration for squandering an opportunity to build a conservative coalition to govern the country: "The result of such leadership could well have been a period of conservative and Republican ascendancy to match the Democratic era that followed upon the victory of Franklin Roosevelt. Instead, the net result of this administration may be to frustrate for years to come the emergence of the conservative majority."

Ashbrook denied that his purpose was either personal ambition or the expectation of success, rather offering his candidacy as the "rallying point" for those Americans who wanted to remind Nixon of his campaign promises of 1968. Adopting the motto "No Left Turn," he called his campaign in New Hampshire "a small Paul Revere ride." Although he received only 9.6 percent of the vote in the Republican primary in New Hampshire, he pushed on to Florida, where he got less than 9 percent. The campaign was chaotically run and always in financial difficulties, and his 10 percent showing in California persuaded him to withdraw from the presidential contest. He supported Nixon's reelection campaign in 1972 "with great reluctance." In 1974 Ashbrook married Jean Spencer.

Although unsuccessful in shaping congressional policy substantially, Ashbrook's conservative challenge to an incumbent Republican president paved the way for Ronald Reagan's challenge to Gerald Ford's nomination in 1976. That challenge fell short, but it cleared the way for Reagan's successful nomination and election in 1980. Reagan became the beneficiary of a new conservative majority that Ashbrook had helped create.

In 1982 Ashbrook announced that he would seek the Republican nomination to oppose the incumbent Democratic senator Howard Metzenbaum, and most political observers thought that he would win the GOP nomination. However, while campaigning in March, he collapsed in Mansfield, Ohio, and died a month later in his office in Johnstown.

• The Ashbrook papers are in the Ashbrook Center at Ashland University, Ashland, Ohio. The collection spans the years 1950 to 1982 and consists of 309 linear feet of predominantly congressional papers with some personal and business files. See also John M. Ashbrook and Randy McNutt, *No Left Turns: A Handbook for Conservatives Based on the Writings of John M. Ashbrook* (1986); Charles A. Moser, *Promise and Hope: The Ashbrook Presidential Campaign of 1972* (1985); and U.S. Congress, *Memorial Services Held in the House of Representatives and Senate of the United States, Together with Tributes Presented in Eulogy of John M. Ashbrook, Late a Representative from Ohio*, 97th Cong., 2d sess., 1982. Obituaries are in the *New York Times* and the *Washington Post*, 25 Apr. 1982.

PETER W. SCHRAMM

ASHBURNER, Charles Albert (9 Feb. 1854–24 Dec. 1889), geologist and mining engineer, was born in Philadelphia, Pennsylvania, the son of Algernon Eyre Ashburner, a shipbuilder, and Sarah Blakiston. Charles Ashburner obtained his college education at the Towne Scientific School of the University of Pennsylvania and ultimately was granted a total of three baccalaureate and advanced degrees by his alma mater. In June 1874 he received his B.S. degree in civil engineering and graduated valedictorian of his class. Three years later he was awarded an M.S. degree in geology. Upon recommendation of the faculty, in recognition of his outstanding career and accomplishments, Ashburner became the first member of the alumni to receive an honorary D.Sc. degree, in June 1889.

As an upperclassman, Ashburner was taught geology by J. Peter Lesley, then professor of geology at the university and later state geologist of the Second Geological Survey of Pennsylvania (1874–1895). Lesley became mentor to Ashburner and profoundly influenced the direction and development of his career. Ashburner's college years marked the beginning of a close personal and professional relationship between the two that lasted all of their lives.

Ashburner was a man of nervous temperament and restless energy. Yet he was genial and cordial, not arrogant as some people believed. He was a meticulous, systematic, and persevering worker, practical by nature. He "was not what is called a 'magnetic man'; there were many who did not like him, though generally recognizing his ability; his self-confidence was not always flattering to the self-esteem of others; yet his versatility and information on a wide range of topics made him a most entertaining companion" (Winslow, p. 72). According to Lesley, Ashburner's chief passion "was the desire of fame; he loved above all things to be correctly understood and well and widely esteemed," but never at the expense of his integrity ("Obituary Notice," p. 54).

After graduation Ashburner worked briefly for the U.S. Lighthouse Service Survey, which was responsible for the construction and maintenance of the nation's lighthouses. However, shortly after the Second Geological Survey of Pennsylvania was established, he resigned his position and volunteered to serve as an unpaid worker for the Second Survey. Lesley, then state geologist, accepted Ashburner's offer but before long hired him as a geologic aide. Thus Ashburner abandoned his fledgling career in civil engineering for one in geology. Although Lesley abhorred favoritism and Ashburner had to prove himself, Lesley's choice of assignments for Ashburner was undoubtedly influenced by their deep friendship and by Lesley's particular interests.

Ashburner, along with another aide who was a former classmate, was first assigned to help an assistant geologist who was studying the iron-ore deposits of central Pennsylvania. During 1874 and early 1875, Ashburner conducted several topographic and geologic field investigations that clearly demonstrated his superior scientific aptitude and abilities. Later in the second year, he was promoted to assistant geologist and assigned to study a separate district, which included the eastern portion of the Broad Top coal field.

In 1876 Ashburner was commissioned to survey a four-county region or district that was considered one of the most geologically significant and challenging in the state. Situated in north-central Pennsylvania, the district included the Bradford oil field, then becoming famous for its productivity. Although the primary focus and success of Ashburner's work were related to coal, he also contributed much to the understanding of the oil-and-gas and other geology of the region. During this time, perhaps more than any other geologist of the Second Survey, he made extensive use of the aneroid altimeter in his fieldwork to determine elevations accurately, and he repeatedly demonstrated the value of the instrument to help quantify geologic relationships.

In the summer of 1880, Ashburner was directed to undertake a geologic reconnaissance of the anthracite coal fields in eastern Pennsylvania and the following year was appointed geologist in charge of the newly approved anthracite survey. His ability to plan, organize, and carry out the geological survey of the anthracite region was his greatest achievement and led to international acclaim for the Second Survey. At the time, anthracite coal was one of the largest and most important mining industries in the United States.

Ashburner's methods for conducting the anthracite survey were thorough and meticulous. He hired qualified staff, set up field offices throughout the region, made numerous contacts with requisite coal and railroad companies, and established an organized system of mapping, colleague review, and publication. The anthracite survey produced a wealth of detailed graphical and descriptive information and represented the first large-scale, systematic effort at quantitative geologic mapping, an approach in which Ashburner applied innovative techniques for portraying the geology with mathematical precision (e.g., use of structure contours, which are lines of equal elevation on some defined geologic datum). This mapping was of great value to geologists and mining engineers alike and, among its many uses, permitted better mine planning and estimates of the region's coal resources.

While planning the anthracite survey, Ashburner married Roberta Mercer John of Pottsville, Pennsylvania, in 1881; they had two children.

In 1885 Ashburner was also appointed first assistant geologist and given the added responsibilities of general supervision of all Second Geological Survey activities. This position was created to allow time for the state geologist to begin writing a comprehensive final report on the geology of Pennsylvania.

Reluctantly, Ashburner formally resigned from the Second Survey a year later (although he agreed to continue working half time until the summer of 1887) to accept a more lucrative position as mining engineer and geologist with George Westinghouse, Jr.'s Fuel Gas and Manufacturing Company in Pittsburgh. Thereafter Ashburner became an independent consultant but continued to receive much work from Westinghouse. Sadly, he died unexpectedly from Bright's disease in Pittsburgh at the age of thirty-five, shortly after returning home prematurely, because of illness, from a business trip to Arizona.

Despite his heavy workload, Ashburner actively participated in many professional organizations. He was a member of the American Association for the Advancement of Science, American Institute of Mining Engineers (in which he was a manager from 1885 to 1888), American Philosophical Society, Geological Society of America (as an original fellow), Philadelphia Academy of Natural Sciences, and many others.

Ashburner was a superb field geologist and administrator and was one of the most distinguished and productive members of the Second Geological Survey of Pennsylvania. He received accolades from the geologic and mining communities for setting new standards of geologic precision and quantitative geologic mapping. He was a recognized expert on the geology of coal, petroleum, and natural gas. As such he contributed greatly to our knowledge and understanding of the economic geology and mineral resources of Pennsylvania during an age of great industrial expansion.

• There is no known formal collection of Ashburner papers. However, scattered correspondence, financial records, and other items pertaining to his years with the Second Geological Survey of Pennsylvania can be found at the State Archives, Pennsylvania Historical and Museum Commission, Harrisburg, and among the J. Peter Lesley Papers, American Philosophical Society, Philadelphia. The most complete modern treatment of Ashburner's life is Clifford H. Dodge, "The Geologic Genius of Charles Albert Ashburner," *Northeastern Geology* 3 (1981): 86–93. On his life, career, and publications, see also J. Peter Lesley, "Obituary Notice of Charles Albert Ashburner," *American Philosophical Society Proceedings* 28 (1890): 53–59; Lesley, "Biographical Notice of Charles A. Ashburner," *American Institute of Mining Engineers Transactions* 18 (1890): 365–70; and Arthur Winslow, "Charles Albert Ashburner," *American Geologist* 6 (1890): 68–78. On his contribution to the geological survey of the anthracite coal fields, see Clifford H. Dodge, "The Second Geological Survey of the Anthracite Region of Eastern Pennsylvania—an Early Endeavor of Quantitative Geological Mapping," *Field Conference of Pennsylvania Geologists Guidebook* 53 (1988): 88–103. An obituary is in the *New York Times*, 26 Dec. 1889.

CLIFFORD H. DODGE

ASHBY, Irving C. (29 Dec. 1920–22 Apr. 1987), jazz guitarist, was born in Somerville, Massachusetts, the son of an apartment superintendent. His parents' names are unknown. The family was musical and closely in touch with the world of entertainment: "Fats Waller used to come by the house all the time," Ashby told writer James Haskins (p. 57). Ashby taught himself to play guitar. At age fifteen he joined a band that played sophisticated arrangements for college dances, and, deeply embarrassed by his inability to read music, he began to learn chordal notation. He performed at a nightclub at Revere Beach while attending Roxbury Memorial High School. Ashby's abilities as a classical guitarist won him a scholarship at an open audition for the New England Conservatory of Music in Boston, but the school had no guitar teacher and thus the award went to the runner-up: "So that's the extent of my conservatory background—in and out the same day," he told writer Harvey Siders (p. 10). Having made his own ukulele at age twelve, Ashby helped to manufacture guitars at the Stromberg factory in Boston during a period when he was performing on a radio show on station WNAC.

When guitarist Charlie Christian came to prominence in 1939, he became the strongest influence on Ashby, who memorized all of Christian's recorded solos. While performing in Providencetown, Massachusetts, and planning to enter Boston University to study art and writing, Ashby received an offer to join Lionel Hampton's band in California in fall 1940. Late in life Ashby regretted the move. He needed the money, but music was not his first choice for a career, and he felt—correctly, despite his considerable talent—that he never ranked with the greatest jazz guitarists. His recordings with Hampton include "Altitude" and "Fiddle-dee-dee," both from 1941. Sometime before the middle of that year he had an opportunity to play informally with Christian when the Hampton and Benny Goodman bands were staying at the same hotel in Chicago. He left Hampton's band in 1942.

In Hollywood in January 1943 Ashby played in the group that accompanied Waller in the celebrated film *Stormy Weather*. Drafted, he served in an army band. In 1946 he returned to Los Angeles, where he worked with pianist Eddie Beal and participated in recording sessions as a sideman with tenor saxophonist Lester Young; pianist André Previn (toward the start of Previn's career in jazz); bassist Charles Mingus; and singers Ivie Anderson, Lena Horne, and Helen Humes; and also as a leader. Around this time Ashby married Pauline (maiden name unknown), a school teacher; they had two daughters. He performed with pianist Erroll Garner and tenor saxophonist Wardell Gray at Gene Norman's Just Jazz concert in Hollywood in April 1947.

On 27 September 1947 Ashby replaced Oscar Moore in singer and pianist Nat King Cole's trio. After enjoying over a year of touring, he encountered musical and personal problems early in 1949, when conga and bongo player Jack Constanzo joined Cole's group. Ashby's best known recording, "Bop Kick," is from this period, but unfortunately Costanzo's incongruous playing and Cole's new fascination with bop—a style to which Cole was unsuited—made this performance unsatisfying. Ashby nonetheless continued greatly to admire Cole's talent, and he stayed in the quartet through a European tour and the making of the film short *King Cole and His Trio*, both in 1950. Finally, around March 1951, Cole's gambling and tax problems provoked Ashby's resignation.

He joined bassist Ray Brown in pianist Oscar Peterson's trio for live performances, but Barney Kessel—who would soon replace Ashby in the trio—made studio recordings with Peterson late in 1951. Ashby recorded only a single session as Peterson's guitarist in January 1952. Among his work from this date is a solo on "Blue Moon." The highlight of his career came later the same year, when he joined Peterson, Young,

Ella Fitzgerald, and other stars for a European tour with Jazz at the Philharmonic: "That's what spoiled me; that's what ruined all other music for me" (Siders, p. 30).

Ashby then dropped out of the international and national jazz scene, with the exception of intermittent recordings, including sessions with tenor saxophonist Illinois Jacquet (1955), alto saxophonists Earl Bostic (1957) and Willie Smith (1965), Peterson (1972), pianist Count Basie and singer Joe Turner (1973), and guitarist Mundell Lowe (1974), and his own album *Memoirs* (1976). He taught guitar in the Los Angeles area, worked in landscape design, and after moving to Perris, California, in 1969, delivered newspapers. His *Guitar Work Book* was self-published sometime in the early 1970s. He died at home in Perris.

Despite his doubts about his career, Ashby was a significant jazz guitarist who closely adhered to the model of Christian's innovative, single-note improvisational style, while, unlike Christian, he also excelled as a chordal, rhythmic player.

• Additional information on Ashby can be found in Harvey Siders, "Irving Ashby: Playing with the Greats," *Guitar Player* 8 (Sept. 1974): 10, 27, 29–30. Other sources on Ashby and jazz music generally include James Haskins with Kathleen Benson, *Nat King Cole* (1984); Leonard Feather, *The Encyclopedia of Jazz*, rev. and enlarged ed. (1960); Feather, *The Encyclopedia of Jazz in the Sixties* (1966); and Feather and Ira Gitler, *The Encyclopedia of Jazz in the Seventies* (1976). An obituary is in the *Los Angeles Times*, 2 May 1987.

BARRY KERNFELD

ASHBY, Turner (23 Oct. 1828–6 June 1862), Confederate cavalry leader, was born on the family farm in Fauquier County, Virginia, the son of Turner Ashby (Sr.) and Dorothea Green. He was the grandson of noted revolutionary war soldier Captain "Jack" Ashby. Educated privately, Turner Ashby spent the pre–Civil War years in farming and operating a mercantile business in the village of Markham. In October 1859 abolitionist John Brown raided nearby Harpers Ferry. Ashby responded by calling together a volunteer cavalry company, to which his reputation as a horseman and community leader attracted a large, enthusiastic following. The unit was not needed; but eighteen months later, at Virginia's secession, Ashby helped to plan the state's seizure of Harpers Ferry. (He had fought secession sentiment to the end before casting his lot with the Confederacy.)

He and his company became part of Colonel Angus McDonald's Seventh Virginia Cavalry Regiment. Late in the spring of 1861, with Federal forces poised on the north bank of the Potomac River, Ashby demonstrated the daring for which he became famous. The Confederate officer disguised himself as an itinerant horse-doctor and traveled as far as Chambersburg, Pennsylvania, to get information on Union troops, positions, and planned movements. On 25 June Colonel McDonald urged his promotion and called Captain Ashby "one of the best partisan leaders in the service." The next day, Ashby's younger brother Richard was on a patrol when he was ambushed by a hostile force. When Turner Ashby found the body, all indications were that Richard had been stabbed several times after he fell to the ground. Thenceforth, Turner Ashby became a grim avenger against all Yankees. In November, Ashby became colonel of the Seventh Virginia Cavalry. He was a well-proportioned man, with eyes, hair, and long beard as black as a raven. His personality contained neither humor nor banter. Yet Ashby possessed polished manners, piety, and the aura of a dedicated warrior who inspired total allegiance from his troops.

Ashby commanded the various cavalry units attached to General Stonewall Jackson in the 1862 Shenandoah Valley campaign. Controversy still surrounds his overall performance. Ashby covered the Confederate right at Kernstown, screened Jackson's movements well on the secret march to Front Royal, and burned four vital bridges in the face of Union fire during Jackson's withdrawal toward Harrisonburg. However, although a devoted combat officer, Ashby gave too little attention to organization and administration. Discipline among his cavalry was loose; the units too often operated in small, disjointed bands rather than as a single powerful force. At Winchester, for example, his men fell to plundering abandoned Union stores rather than continuing to pursue the broken Federal army. Confederate General D. H. Hill once remarked that Ashby "never had his equal in a charge, but he never had his men in hand." A member of Jackson's staff added that Ashby's "service to the army was invaluable, but had he been as full of discipline as he was of leadership his successes would have been more fruitful and his reputation still greater." On 23 May 1862 Ashby received promotion to brigadier general. Two weeks later, he was killed in a skirmish near Harrisonburg.

• No collections of Ashby papers exist, although some of his letters are scattered among several manuscript holdings, including the Chicago Historical Society and the Virginia Historical Society in Richmond. His Civil War career barely spanned a year. Hence, biographical treatments of him are few. James B. Avirett, *The Memoirs of Turner Ashby and His Compeers* (1867), is a collection of personal reminiscences that is still the best source on the cavalryman. Thomas A. Ashby, *Life of Turner Ashby* (1914), is a eulogistic and superficial account. Two popularly written studies have been done in recent years: Frank Cunningham, *Knight of the Confederacy, General Turner Ashby* (1960), and Millard K. Bushong, *General Turner Ashby and Stonewall's Valley Campaign* (1980).

JAMES I. ROBERTSON, JR.

ASHE, Arthur (10 July 1943–6 Feb. 1993), tennis player, author, and political activist, was born Arthur Robert Ashe, Jr., in Richmond, Virginia, the son of Arthur Ashe, Sr., a police officer, and Mattie Cunnigham. Tall and slim as a young boy, Ashe was forbidden by his father from playing football; he took up tennis instead on the segregated playground courts at Brookfield Park, near his home. By the time he was ten he came under the tutelage of a local tennis fan and physician from Lynchburg, Walter Johnson. Johnson had previously nurtured Althea Gibson, who would become the first African American to win Wimbeldon, in 1957 and 1958, and his second protégé would prove no less successful.

Johnson was an exacting coach; he had his charges practice hitting tennis balls with broom handles to develop their hand-eye coordination. But his lessons extended beyond tennis; he also helped the young Ashe navigate an often hostile, segregated South. Johnson and Ashe's father (his mother died when he was six) instructed Arthur in the manners, discipline, and grace that would mark his carriage within and without the nearly all-white tennis world. When Arthur was fifteen, Johnson tried to enter him in an all-white junior tournament sponsored by the Middle Atlantic Lawn Tennis Association and held at Richmond's Country Club of Virginia, but the club refused his application. As a result, Ashe, who was ranked fifth in his age group in the country, was unable to earn a ranking from his own region.

In 1958, Ashe reached the semifinals in the under-15 division of the junior national championships. Soon afterward a tennis coach from St. Louis, Richard Hudlin, offered to take Ashe under his wing, and after completing his junior year in high school in Richmond, Ashe accepted. He moved in with Hudlin and his family and completed his schooling at Sumner High School in St. Louis, the alma mater of African-American comedian and activist Dick Gregory. In 1960 and 1961 Ashe won the U.S. junior indoor singles title.

After graduating from high school, Ashe accepted a tennis scholarship to the University of California at Los Angeles (UCLA), where he became an All-American, led his college team to the NCAA national championship, won the U.S. Hard Court Championship, and was named to the U.S. Davis Cup team. While at UCLA he also spent time training with tennis legends Pancho Segura and Pancho Gonzalez, who helped him develop the powerful serve and volley game that would become, along with his sheer athleticism, Ashe's trademark.

In 1965, while still in college, Ashe was ranked third in the world, and he beat Australian Roy Emerson in five sets to win the Queensland championships at Brisbane, Australia. Graduating from UCLA in 1966 with a degree in business administration, he entered a Reserve Officer Training Corps camp and finished second in his platoon for overall achievement at the end of the six-week course. He attained the rank of first lieutenant, serving in the military from 1967 to 1969. During this time he continued playing tennis, winning the U.S. Clay Court Championships in 1967. In 1968, while still an amateur and still in the U.S. Army, he defeated Tom Okker to win the first U.S. Open, one of the two most prestigious tennis tournaments in the world, and with this victory he became ranked first in the world. Numerous titles would follow, including his place on three victorious Davis Cup teams, the World Championships of Tennis in 1975 (a year in which he again became the world's highest ranked player), and two additional Grand Slam championships—the Australian Open in 1970 and Wimbledon in 1975, where he became the first African American male to win at the All-England Club, beating Jimmy Connors. He also won the doubles titles at the French, Australian, and Wimbledon championships.

John McPhee, whose book *Levels of the Game* (1969) chronicled Ashe's match with Clark Graebner, his opponent in the semifinal of the 1968 U.S. Open, considered Ashe a competitive genius. "Even in very tight moments, other players thought he was toying with them," McPhee wrote later in an appreciation piece in the *New Yorker* after Ashe's death.

> They rarely knew what he was thinking. They could not tell if he was angry. It was maddening, sometimes, to play against him. Never less than candid, he said that what he liked best about himself on a tennis court was his demeanor: 'What it is is controlled cool, in a way. Always have the situation under control, even if losing. Never betray an inward sense of defeat.' And of course he never did—not in the height of his athletic power, not in the statesmanship of the years that followed, and not in the endgame of his existence.

Over the course of his career Ashe earned more than \$1.5 million, becoming the sport's first black millionaire and one of his era's most visible African-American athletes. He was hired by several companies, including Coca-Cola and Philip Morris, to promote their products, and he worked for ABC television and Home Box Office as a sports commentator. Ashe married Jeanne Marie Moutoussamy in 1977, and they had one daughter, Camera Elizabeth. In 1979, at the age of thirty-six, Ashe suffered a myocardial infarction, which forced him to undergo bypass surgery and retire from playing competitive tennis. However, one year after his operation he became the first and only African American to be named captain of the U.S. Davis Cup team, a position he held until 1985. Under his leadership the team won the international competition in 1981. In 1985 he became the first African American male elected to the International Tennis Hall of Fame.

Throughout his career and afterward Ashe spent considerable time and energy working for civil and human rights. He wrote eloquently about his complex position as a world-renowned success in a field dominated by whites; even as his moderation appealed to whites, he was occasionally criticized by more vocal black activists. "There were times, in fact, when I felt a burning sense of shame that I was not with other blacks—and whites—standing up to the fire hoses and the police dogs, the truncheons, bullets and bombs that cut down such martyrs as Chaney, Schwerner, and Goodman, Viola Liuzzo, Martin Luther King, Jr., Medgar Evers and the little girls in that bombed church in Birmingham, Ala.," he was quoted as saying in *The Black 100: A Ranking of the Most Influential African-Americans, Past and Present* ([1993], p. 363). "As my fame increased, so did my anguish. I knew that many blacks were proud of my accomplishments on the tennis court. But I also knew that many others, especially many of my own age or younger, did not bother to hide their indifference to me and my trophies or even their disdain and contempt for me."

In 1973, after three years of trying, Ashe had received an invitation to play in the previously all-white South African Open; twelve years later the longtime friend of the still-imprisoned Nelson Mandela was arrested in South Africa for protesting apartheid. In 1992 he joined a group of protesters who were arrested in Washington, D.C., for objecting to the George Bush administration's treatment of Haitian refugees.

Always a bookish, thoughtful man, Ashe cultivated a second career as a writer and sports historian; through his research, he managed to trace his own roots back ten generations on his father's side to a woman who in 1735 was brought from West Africa to Yorktown, Virginia, on the slave ship *Doddington*. Ashe's benchmark three-volume history of black athletes in America, *A Hard Road to Glory*, was published in 1988.

Ashe's concern for fairness and human dignity also extended beyond race. In 1974 he helped found the Association of Tennis Professionals, a player's union, and served as president until 1979. He later became a board member of the United States Tennis Association; chairman of the American Heart Association; and a board member for the National Foundation for Infectious Diseases.

Ashe suffered a number of serious health problems that ended his playing career but barely seemed to slow him down. He had a heart attack in 1979, one bypass surgery six months later, and a second in 1983. He had emergency brain surgery in 1988, and after this operation rumors about his infection with HIV, the virus that causes AIDS, began to spread. Although he kept his illness secret for nearly a decade, Ashe was forced to admit his diagnosis publicly when on 7 April 1992 the newspaper *USA Today* threatened to print the story as soon as it could be confirmed. Because Ashe did not officially confirm his illness himself, he was able to put off publication of the story for a day and to personally inform friends, family members, and health officials of his condition. The day after *USA Today*'s initial phone call on 8 April, Ashe held a press conference to break the news himself, reporting that the virus had been transmitted during blood transfusions associated with his second heart operation in 1983. The event prompted both a worldwide outpouring of grief and a squall of commentary about the conflict between the press's responsibility to report the news and an individual's right to privacy. That year he helped raise $15 million for the Arthur Ashe Foundation for the Defeat of AIDS, and in part for this work he was named "Sportsman of the Year" by *Sports Illustrated*.

Ashe's death in New York City provoked a sense of loss that extended far beyond boundaries of the tennis world or the borders of the United States. A memorial service held at the Richmond governor's mansion of Douglas Wilder, the first African-American governor of Virginia, attracted thousands of admirers from around the world. Wilder said that Ashe's "leadership may not be confined to athletics and sports alone, for he was totally committed to improving the lives of those yet to enjoy the full fruition of rights and opportunities in this country" (*New York Times*, 7 Feb. 1993).

Ashe's passing, like his life, was mourned by many who saw in his example an unusual dignity and elegance, even in the face of a terrible disease. "Why, when we knew Arthur Ashe's health was precarious, did the news of his death from pneumonia last Saturday hit us like a ball peen hammer between the eyes?" wrote Kenny Moore in a cover story in *Sports Illustrated*. "Why did the announcement of this gentle man's passing force even the raucous Madison Square Garden crowd at the Riddick Bowe–Michael Dokes fight into unwonted reflection, never quite to return to the fray? In part, surely, we reel because, even with AIDS and a history of heart attacks, Ashe didn't seem to be sick. He, of all men, hid things well. His gentility shielded us from appreciating his risk" (15 Feb. 1993, p. 12).

• Ashe also wrote *Arthur Ashe: Portrait in Motion*, with Frank Deford (1975); *Off the Court*, with Neil Amdur (1981); and an autobiography, *Days of Grace*, with Arnold Rampersad (1993). Useful source material on Ashe can be found in any number of trade tennis magazines published during his lifetime, including *Tennis* and *World Tennis*.

McKAY JENKINS

ASHE, John (1720?–24 Oct. 1781), colonial politician and military officer, was born in the Albemarle Sound region of North Carolina, the son of John Baptista Ashe, an assemblyman, and Elizabeth Swann. In late 1727 the elder Ashe moved south from Beaufort County and purchased a 640-acre plantation near the Cape Fear River. There, John Ashe was tutored in Latin, Greek, and French. Entering Harvard as a member of the class of 1746, he proved to be a rebellious student, continually chafing against authority and chronically absenting himself from class.

Returning home without his degree, Ashe settled on the northeast Cape Fear River at a plantation that he named "Green Hill." Some time after his return, Ashe married his cousin Rebecca Moore, the daughter of politician and planter Maurice Moore. They had seven children. The restlessness exhibited at Harvard disappeared as he adapted to the roles that he would play throughout his adult life—military officer and politician. In 1752 Ashe launched his legislative career; he was elected to fill the seat in the lower house of the assembly vacated by his uncle, John Swann, who had been appointed to the governor's council. Within months of his legislative debut, Ashe was serving on the Committee on Public Accounts and Claims. In 1762 he rose to the speakership of the assembly and held this position for the following three years. Ultimately Ashe enjoyed a 23-year legislative career, remaining in the lower house until 1775. As an assemblyman, he was known for his rousing eloquence and strong will.

Ashe's reputation for doggedness gained strength when coupled with the rebellious disposition of his New Hanover neighbors. In May 1765 Ashe privately warned North Carolina's royal governor, William Tryon, that the Stamp Act would be resisted, perhaps even to the death. His prophecy proved only partially correct when stamped paper arrived in Wilmington the following fall. On 28 November, in a fortunately bloodless demonstration, Ashe led an armed mob that prevented the cargo from being landed. By the beginning of the following year he was encouraging New Hanover's citizens to organize themselves into a loose, semimilitary organization, the Sons of Liberty, to fight the Stamp Act. Resistance climaxed on 19–20 February 1766, when a mob led by Ashe unsuccessfully attempted to seize Wilmington's port comptroller in hopes of forcing him to relinquish his office.

Discontent with British authority in North Carolina simmered for the following two years, eventually boiling over in the revolt known as the War of the Regulation. Between 1768 and 1771 backcountry residents sought to correct the suffering that they had endured at the hands of corrupt local officials appointed by a legislature dominated by unsympathetic easterners. When the easterners, who were separated from the western Regulators by social, political, and economic differences, rejected the backwoodsmen's requests for reform, lower taxes, and an equal share in political power, the colony came apart along geographic lines. During this crisis, Ashe sided, as did many of his eastern counterparts, with Tryon as the governor sought to restore order. On 16 May 1771 he was an officer in the army that defeated the backcountry insurgents at the battle of Alamance.

In January 1775 Ashe joined the New Hanover Committee of Safety and began an aggressive campaign against violations of the Continental Congress's boycott of British trade by Wilmington's Scottish merchants. During the spring of 1775, at the head of a mob, Ashe attempted to bully the town's shopkeepers into signing the patriots' nonimportation agreement. His threat of military execution produced the result desired by the committee as the recalcitrant Scots signed the boycott pledge but, at the same time, hardened support for royal authority among Cape Fear's trading community. Tensions between the Whigs and the Crown's supporters escalated that summer as rumors surfaced that Josiah Martin, North Carolina's royal governor, intended to reinforce Fort Johnston (below Wilmington). On 17 July Ashe launched a preemptive strike and destroyed this outpost of British authority.

Despite his past military experience, Ashe failed to secure the colonelcy of North Carolina's First Continental Regiment, a position that he coveted. On 15 September 1775 that honor went instead to his brother-in-law, James Moore, who was chosen over Ashe by a one vote margin. Momentarily blocked in his quest for a command, he raised an independent body of rangers that soon took the field against the Scottish Loyalists of the upper Cape Fear. On 9 February 1776 he and his rangers were part of the army that defeated the Tories at Moore's Creek Bridge. In reward for his services, a thankful assembly appointed Ashe brigadier general for the Wilmington Military District. By the end of 1778 he had risen to the position of major general. Early the following year he was sent to Charleston, South Carolina, with a large body of North Carolina militia to reinforce Major General Benjamin Lincoln's southern army. This set in motion events that would end Ashe's military career in defeat and disgrace.

In February 1779 his command crossed the Savannah River and encamped at Briar Creek, forty-five miles below Augusta. The 1,670 Carolinians and Georgia Continentals that Ashe led were inadequately armed, poorly positioned, and lacking in vigilance. On 3 March a British force approached the rear of the American troops, taking them by surprise. In the ensuing battle, the Georgians stood their ground until overwhelmed while the North Carolinians broke and ran, some without having fired a shot. Ashe's defeat dashed the hopes of Lincoln and other patriots to recover Georgia and left the state firmly in British hands. In the aftermath of the disaster, a court martial exonerated Ashe on charges of cowardice, which resulted from his attempt to head off the flight of panicky troops while the Georgians continued the fight. He was, however, censured for his failure to take the precautions necessary to secure his camp and obtain timely intelligence of the movements of the British.

A depressed and dispirited Ashe returned to North Carolina where he found his military services were no longer needed. By the spring of 1781, with Wilmington in the hands of the British, as were two of Ashe's sons, Ashe was hiding in the swamps bordering the northeast Cape Fear River. Betrayed to the enemy by a slave, the aged patriot was wounded in the leg as he attempted to escape. While imprisoned at Wilmington he contracted smallpox. Paroled because of his illness, he was so weakened by these experiences that he died en route to Hillsborough, North Carolina, where his family was living as refugees, and was buried in an unmarked grave in Sampson County.

• The most complete biographies of John Ashe can be found in Samuel A'Court Ashe, *Biographical History of North Carolina* (1906); William S. Powell, ed., *Dictionary of North Carolina Biography*, vol. 1 (1979); and Clifford K. Shipton, *Sibley's Harvard Graduates*, vol. 12 (1962). An unpublished biography by Archibald Maclaine Hooper containing an account of Ashe's court-martial after the battle of Briar Creek is housed at the Southern Historical Collection, University of North Carolina, Chapel Hill. Papers relating to Ashe's political and military careers are included in Powell et al., eds., *The Regulators in North Carolina: A Documentary History, 1759–1776* (1971), and William L. Saunders et al., eds., *The Colonial and State Records of North Carolina* (1886–1914).

JOSHUA L. MCKAUGHAN

ASHE, John Baptista (1748–27 Nov. 1802), member of the Continental Congress and U.S. Congress, soldier, and state politician, was born in Rocky Point, New Hanover County, North Carolina, the son of Samuel Ashe, a jurist, and Mary Porter. His grandfather John Baptista Ashe, for whom he was named, served on His Majesty's Council of North Carolina; his father was assistant attorney for the Crown, the first judge for the state of North Carolina, and later governor. Ashe, who grew up on "The Neck," his father's tobacco plantation, learned about tobacco cultivation and received his education from a private tutor. There is no indication that he pursued a college education.

Ashe's first military service came in May 1771, during the Regulator insurrection. Regulators were residents of several backcountry (western) counties who worked to end corruption among local officials between 1766 and 1771. Having lost faith that the colonial government in the East would address their grievances, backcountry residents worked to "regulate" the conduct of local government officials themselves. Regulators refused to pay taxes, disrupted courts, and used violence to redress their grievances against corrupt officials. Ashe served as a lieutenant in the New Hanover militia and was captured and beaten by the Regulators. The Regulator movement ended when Governor William Tryon sent 1,185 colonial militia and defeated a Regulator force of more than 2,000 at Alamance on 16 May 1771. At the beginning of the Revolution Ashe fought with Colonel Alexander Lillington's militia during the patriot victory at Moore's Creek, North Carolina, on 27 February 1776. On 16 April 1776 he was promoted to captain of the Sixth Regiment, North Carolina Continental Line. By early 1777 he had achieved the rank of major and served at Valley Forge during the agonizing winter of 1777–1778. In June 1778 the Sixth Regiment merged with the First Regiment. The following year Ashe married Elizabeth Montfort, daughter of Joseph Montfort, former North American grand master of Masons. They had one child. In 1780 Ashe's regiment surrendered at Charleston to the British forces under General Cornwallis. Fortunately, Ashe was not with the unit at the time.

In January 1780 Ashe was promoted to lieutenant colonel and served in Wilmington, North Carolina, acquiring supplies for the troops. With 300 soldiers under his command, he was detached to South Carolina in July 1781 to join the forces of Major General Nathanael Greene. As commander of a battalion he fought at the battle of Eutaw Springs on 8 September 1781; his unit's severe mauling of a British regiment drew the praise of General Greene.

Shortly before Cornwallis's surrender at Yorktown, Ashe resigned from the Continental army and accepted 4,457 acres of land for his sixty-five months of military service. He served in the North Carolina Society of Cincinnati and later became its president. His career in politics began when he served in the North Carolina House of Commons for three terms (1784–1786); he was chosen Speaker of the House of Commons in 1786.

On 16 December 1786 Ashe was elected for a one-year term to the Continental Congress, which he attended from 28 March to 10 May and from 13 August to 29 October 1787. His correspondence with Governor Richard Caswell of North Carolina highlighted his concerns and those of his fellow North Carolina delegates to Congress. Writing for the delegation in a letter dated 18 April 1787, Ashe communicated their concern for navigation on the Mississippi, a request from the North Carolina legislature for Congress to send troops to Davidson County to quell Indian troubles, and the "infractions of the Treaty of peace with Great Britain," which included the British refusal to abandon forts in the northwest territory and to return slaves confiscated by their troops during the revolutionary war. Ashe sought to protect North Carolina's land claims in the West. In a letter to the governor dated 16 August 1787, Ashe wrote of his and William Blount's attempt in Congress to correct the Hopewell Treaty. This treaty granted land claimed by the state of North Carolina to the Indians for a hunting ground. On 25 April both Blount and Ashe presented their case for North Carolina's ownership of the disputed land; however, Congress judged their claim insufficient. Ashe believed that the forfeit of the state's claim would be "flagrantly abusive in its consequences." Though reelected to the Continental Congress beginning in November 1788, Ashe declined to serve.

Ashe served as a member of the North Carolina convention, which met in Fayetteville in November 1789 to consider ratification of the Constitution. He served as chairman of the Committee of the Whole and voted with the majority for ratification. In 1789 he served in the state senate as Speaker pro tempore and chairman of the Finance Committee.

After North Carolina joined the union, Ashe was elected to represent Halifax County in the First and Second Congresses, which met in New York and Philadelphia, respectively. A Democratic-Republican, he opposed the financial plans of Alexander Hamilton, President George Washington's secretary of the treasury. Hamilton sought to restore the credit of the new nation and gain the loyalty of creditors through the federal government's assumption of state debts, funding the national debt through the selling of government securities, raising revenue with an excise tax on liquor to pay on the debt, and the creation of a national bank to hold federal funds and expand credit. Ashe, along with Fellow Democratic-Republicans, believed that Hamilton's financial programs greatly expanded the power of the federal government beyond its role authorized by the Constitution. In addition, Ashe opposed assumption because North Carolina was well on its way to paying off its wartime debt and assumption would seem to reward states that had a large debt remaining. Ashe served on committees that dealt with the merchants of Portsmouth, New Hampshire, the Quakers of North Carolina, and navigation. He served in Congress from 24 March 1790 through 3 March 1793.

Following his congressional service, Ashe returned to his farm and family in Halifax. Two years later the Halifax electorate returned him to the North Carolina House of Commons. His final elective office was the governorship, to which he was elected on 20 November 1802. Ill at the time of his election, he died at his Halifax home before he took office.

Ashe was a planter of some means. His slave holdings increased from forty-eight in 1785 to sixty-three in the year of the federal census of 1790. In recognition and honor of the important contributions made by the Ashe family, the towns of Asheville and Asheboro, along with Ashe County, North Carolina, were named for Samuel Ashe, and Ashe's Island, offshore in Onslow County, North Carolina, was named for John Baptista Ashe.

• There exists no collection of John Baptista Ashe's papers. His surviving correspondence is scattered among the William Blount Papers at the North Carolina State Achives in Raleigh and the Richard Caswell Papers at the Southern Historical Collection at the University of North Carolina at Chapel Hill. For Ashe's work with the Society of Cincinnati, see the General Society of Cincinnati Archives, Library of Congress, North Carolina folder. Some correspondence is in *Letters of Members of the Continental Congress*, ed. Edmund C. Burnett, vol. 8 (1936). Some general sketches of Ashe appear in W. C. Allen, *History of Halifax County* (1918); Samuel A. Ashe, ed., *Biographical History of North Carolina*, vol. 8 (1917); and John Hill Wheeler, *Historical Sketches of North Carolina from 1584 to 1851* (1851). For Ashe's military service, see Walker Clark, ed., *Colonial and State Records of North Carolina*, vols. 17–21 (1889–1903), and C. L. Davis and H. H. Bellas, *A Brief History of the North Carolina Troops . . . in the War of the Revolution* (1896). Ashe's work in the First Congress is recorded in the *Documentary History of the First Federal Congress of the United States of America, 1789–1791*, vol. 3: *House of Representative Journal*, ed. Linda Grant Depauw (1977). Ashe's obituary is in the *Raleigh Register*, 30 Nov. 1802.

TIM VANDERBURG

ASHE, Samuel (1725–22 Jan. 1813), judge and governor, was born in Beaufort County, North Carolina, the son of John Baptista Ashe and Elizabeth Swann. His father, Beaufort's representative in the lower house of the assembly and its Speaker at the time of Samuel's birth, was allied through marriage to a clique of planters who hoped to open the Cape Fear River to white settlement. In 1727 the elder Ashe moved his family of two sons, John Ashe and Samuel, and one daughter southward to a plantation on the lower reaches of that river. Following their father's death in 1734, the Ashe children were reared by their uncle and guardian, Samuel Swann, who was the Speaker of North Carolina's lower house.

At the urging of his uncle, Ashe was sent to Harvard to begin a legal education later completed in North Carolina under Swann's tutelage. Ashe was married by 1748 to his cousin Mary Porter, with whom he had three children. By the 1770s he was serving as the assistant attorney for the Crown. His allegiance to British authority was none too strong, however, and by 1774 he was regarded as a staunch patriot. That July he helped draft an appeal asking the people of North Carolina to send delegates to a meeting at Johnston Court House. This extralegal meeting, however, was quickly moved to the colonial capital of New Bern; Ashe represented his New Hanover neighbors. Between 25 and 28 August, under the very nose of the royal governor, the assembly elected representatives for the Continental Congress slated to meet the following month in Philadelphia—the first act of the American Revolution in North Carolina. Ashe's revolutionary activities increased during the next two years. In 1775 he, along with his brother John, joined the New Hanover Committee of Safety. The following year he was appointed as one of thirteen members of the Council of Safety, which enjoyed virtually dictatorial powers over North Carolina's military and civil affairs. By that August, he had risen to the presidency of this body. Ashe's integrity and freedom from influence as a member of this assembly earned him rare praise from the colony's last royal governor, Josiah Martin, a bitter critic of his Whig adversaries. Ashe shone above the lawyers in the council castigated by Martin for lacking "good principles or character, and some of them are despicable to the last degree" (Saunders et al., vol. 10, p. 269). Indeed, Ashe's guiding principle, as he later explained, was to remain "independent in person, and in purse, and neither court love [from those of influence], nor fear their enmity" (McRee, *Life and Correspondence*, vol. 2, p. 601). Following the death of his first wife in 1767, Ashe married Elizabeth Jones Merrick. The total number of their children is unknown, but only one child survived to maturity.

From 1775 to 1778 Ashe represented his county in the Provincial Congress. As a member of this body, he was one of twenty-four legislators chosen in November 1776 to frame North Carolina's constitution. Ashe's fortunes continued to rise as he became the first Speaker of the state senate in April 1777 and was elected presiding judge of the new state supreme court, a position he held until 1795. His most noteworthy decision during his tenure as judge established the precedent of judicial review of a legislative decree. Ashe's verdict in *Bayard v. Singleton* (1785) declared a recently passed law that prohibited courts from hearing suits for the recovery of confiscated Loyalist possessions invalid under North Carolina's constitution, which guaranteed the right to a jury trial in all matters concerning property.

In principle, however, Ashe opposed the return of assets to North Carolina's former Tories. The 1780s found him at loggerheads with a body of attorneys, led by Archibald Maclaine, that hoped to profit from suits launched by these disaffected Carolinians. Egged on by visions of large legal fees exacted from their clients, this clique sought to depose Ashe and his fellow justices and replace them with more agreeable men. The matter came to a head in November 1786 when one of Maclaine's allies in the house, John Hay, charged the state's three supreme court justices with misconduct and negligence in their duty to the public. An indignant Ashe condemned Hay's actions and called on the legislature to reject it, which it did.

In 1795, at the age of seventy, Ashe was elected governor and served the constitutional limit of three one-year terms. During his second term he became embroiled in a scandal that involved the sale of forged warrants for lands in Tennessee by North Carolina secretary of state James Glasgow. Presenting the legislature with evidence supplied by Andrew Jackson that implicated Glasgow, Ashe announced that "an Angel hath fallen" (Powell, vol. 2, p. 304) and called for an investigation. A series of trials confirmed the secretary of state's guilt and led to his departure from both public office and the state. While governor, Ashe also served as president of the University of North Carolina's Board of Trustees.

During the first decade of the nineteenth century Ashe found himself pitted against his son Samuel, who joined the Federalist party. The elder Ashe was an ardent supporter of states' rights. He could, however, restrain these views in times of national crisis as evidenced by his support for President John Adams's policies during the 1798 quasi war with France. The emergency over, Ashe again fiercely opposed the Federalists. In the election of 1800 he ardently campaigned for the Republican candidate Thomas Jefferson.

By the time of his death at "Rocky Point" in present-day Pender County, North Carolina, Ashe owned at least 1,390 acres of land scattered across North Carolina and Tennessee, including his home located at the Neck on the northeast Cape Fear River. One of his contemporaries described Ashe as being "of stalwart frame, endowed with practical good sense, [and] a profound knowledge of human nature" (McRee, *Life and Correspondence* vol. 1, p. 194).

• The North Carolina State Department of Archives and History, Raleigh, and the Southern Historical Collection, University of North Carolina, Chapel Hill, contain letters and other documents by Samuel Ashe. The most complete accounts of Ashe's life appear in Samuel A'Court Ashe, *Biographical History of North Carolina* (1917), and William S. Powell, ed., *Dictionary of North Carolina Biography*, vol. 1 (1979). Powell's work also contains a useful account of the Glasgow land scandal that occurred during Ashe's second term as governor. Additional biographical information can be gleaned from Griffith J. McRee, *Life and Correspondence of James Iredell* (1858) and *Cyclopaedia of Eminent and Successful Men of the Carolinas in the 19th Century* (1892). Papers relating to Ashe's career are in William L. Saunders et al., eds., *The Colonial and State Records of North Carolina* (1886–1914). An obituary appears in the Raleigh *Star*, 5 Feb. 1813.

JOSHUA L. MCKAUGHAN

ASHE, Thomas Samuel (19 July 1812–4 Feb. 1887), jurist and congressman, was born at "the Hawfields," Orange County, North Carolina, the home of his maternal grandfather, where his parents regularly spent the summer. He was the son of Pasquale Paoli Ashe, the owner of a plantation in coastal New Hanover County, North Carolina, and a coal mine in Alabama, and Elizabeth Jane Strudwick. His father lost his entire fortune about 1829 as surety for the debts of a friend.

The Ashe family moved to Perry County, Alabama, when Thomas was about twelve, but he returned to North Carolina to attend the Bingham School and the University of North Carolina, from which he graduated in 1832, third in his class. He lived in Hillsborough with the family of Chief Justice Thomas Ruffin, with whom he read law. After being licensed, he began his practice in Wadesboro in 1836. The following year he married Caroline Athelia Burgwin; the couple had seven children.

A member of the Whig party, Ashe represented Anson County in the North Carolina House of Commons in 1842–1843. In 1842 he also became a trustee of the University of North Carolina, where he served until 1868 and again during the years 1877–1883. He was appointed by the legislature to be solicitor of the judicial district in which he resided from 1848 to 1852, and he was a state senator in 1854–1855. He was nominated for Congress in 1858 but declined to be a candidate.

On the eve of the Civil War Ashe expressed Union sentiments. In February 1861 he was elected as a Unionist delegate to a proposed state constitutional convention, yet at the same time voters of the state rejected the referendum for such a convention. After Abraham Lincoln's call for troops to coerce the seceded states back into the Union in April 1861, Ashe favored secession. As a member of the Confederate House of Representatives from February 1862 to May 1864, he was a member of the Committee on the Judiciary and consistently opposed efforts to increase the power of the central government at the expense of the states or individuals. Defeated by a peace candidate in a bid for a second term, he was nevertheless elected to the Confederate Senate in December 1864, but the Confederate government ceased to exist before his term began.

Highly regarded by many of his contemporaries, Ashe was elected by the North Carolina General Assembly to a seat on the Council of State, an advisory executive committee created by the constitution of 1776. The membership was elected by the general assembly, and Ashe served from 10 December 1866 until 26 March 1867. In 1868, the first year in which blacks voted, the Democratic-Conservative convention tried without success in two instances to persuade men to become candidates for governor. Both declined, and the convention appealed to Ashe to become the party's candidate. At considerable personal sacrifice he consented, even though, during the current military occupation of the state under terms of the Reconstruction Act and the Fourteenth Amendment, he was denied the suffrage himself because he had been an antebellum officeholder who had supported the Confederacy. He conducted a vigorous campaign, opposing the ratification of the new state constitution, but he was defeated by the Republican candidate, William W. Holden, by a vote of 92,235 to 73,600. After the readmission of his state to the Union, Ashe continued to affiliate with the Conservative party in its opposition to the new state constitution and was twice elected to Congress, where he served from 1 December 1873 to 3 March 1877. During his second term he was a member of the Committee on the Judiciary and participated in drawing up impeachment charges against Secretary of War W. W. Belknap. He also helped prepare the resolution calling for an electoral commission to decide the disputed election of 1876. While in Washington Ashe took part in the investigation of James G. Blaine in the Mulligan letters scandal.

In 1878 Ashe was nominated by the Democratic party and elected an associate justice of the North Carolina Supreme Court. Reelected in 1886, he was described as "learned and patient and faithful" on the bench. The courtesy with which he, as attorney, legislator, or judge, treated all who came before him was universally acclaimed. The long hours of diligent attention to his work gradually sapped his strength, and finally indigestion resulted in a month's serious decline. He died at his home in Wadesboro. From many generations of Episcopalians, he was a vestryman of Calvary Church in Wadesboro for thirty-two years.

• An autobiography by Ashe is in the Personal Collections at the North Carolina Division of Archives and History, and a few letters, largely on his law practice, are in miscellaneous papers in the Southern Historical Collection, University of North Carolina Library, Chapel Hill. The sketch of Ashe by Peter M. Wilson, chief clerk of the U.S. Senate, in *Biographical History of North Carolina*, vol. 8, ed. Samuel A. Ashe (1917), is drawn largely from personal information. An appraisal of his role in the state by persons who knew him with the comments of his associates is in the N.C. Supreme Court's *North Carolina Reports*, vol. 96 (1909). A careful account of his life by W. Buck Yearns is in *Dictionary of North Carolina Biography*, vol. 1, ed. William S. Powell (1979). See also Kemp P. Battle, *History of the University of North Carolina* (2 vols., 1907, 1912); John L. Cheney, Jr., *North Carolina Government, 1585–1979* (1981); and Daniel L. Grant, *Alumni History of the University of North Carolina* (1924). An obituary, a lengthy editorial tribute, and an account of his life are in the Raleigh *News and Observer*, 5 Feb. 1887.

WILLIAM S. POWELL

ASHFORD, Emmett Littleton (23 Nov. 1914–1 Mar. 1980), baseball umpire, was born in Los Angeles, California, the son of Littleton Ashford, a truck driver, and Adele Bain. Ashford was two or three years old when his father abandoned the family, so he grew up under the strong influence of his mother, a secretary for the *California Eagle*, an African-American newspaper published in Los Angeles. As a youth, Ashford exhibited the traits that marked him in adult life as a gregarious extrovert whose behavior possibly masked deep feelings of inadequacy and insecurity. At Jefferson High School he was a sprinter on the track team, a member of the scholastic honor society, and the first black to serve as president of the student body and editor of the school newspaper. He graduated from Los Angeles City College and later attended Chapman College in nearby Orange (1940–1941). From 1944 until 1947 he served in the U.S. Navy.

Ashford began his umpiring career in 1941 by working recreation league, high school, college, and semiprofessional games. While in the navy in 1946, he first thought about an umpiring career and the possibility of reaching the major leagues after hearing that Jackie Robinson had broken the modern color line in organized baseball. After the war Ashford added softball to his umpiring schedule and twice worked the National Softball Congress World Tournament for women. After the 1948 tournament, in which the team from Georgia initially opposed his presence on racial grounds but wound up insisting that he umpire the plate in the final game, he decided give up his administrative job in the payroll and finance division of the Los Angeles post office to explore professional umpiring. With the assistance of major league scout Rosey Gilhousen and after a four-game tryout in Mexico, Ashford was hired in July 1951 by the Class C Southwest International League, thereby becoming the first African-American umpire in minor league baseball. He spent two seasons in Class C, advanced in 1953 to the Class A Western International League, and in 1954 reached the Class AAA Pacific Coast League, thanks to the support of league president Clarence "Pants" Rowland, a former major league manager. Ashford spent twelve years in the PCL, three as umpire-in-chief (1963–1965), quickly becoming a favorite with fans because of his effervescent personality and flamboyant style. During the off-season he became the first black to referee high school and college football and basketball games in southern California. He also conducted an umpiring clinic in Japan in 1958 under the auspices of the U.S. Air Force, and he umpired in the Dominican Republic winter league in 1959 and 1964.

After fifteen years in the minors, Ashford reached the major leagues at age fifty-one when he was hired by the American League in September 1965 for the following season. During a brief career terminated by the league's mandatory retirement of umpires at age fifty-five, he umpired the 1967 All-Star game and the 1970 World Series. He retired in 1970, but he continued umpiring activities by working Pacific Coast Conference college games, serving as commissioner and umpire-in-chief of the professional-amateur Alaskan League, and conducting clinics in Canada, Europe, and Korea. He also served from his retirement until his death as a special assistant to the commissioner of baseball, Bowie Kuhn, performing public relations duties on the West Coast. Married four times (1937, 1950, 1966, 1979) and detached from his three children, he never experienced the family intimacy he missed as a child.

Controversy dogged Ashford throughout his major league career. As the first African-American to reach the major leagues in a capacity other than a player, he received numerous threats and endured racial epithets. In addition, some fellow umpires criticized his flamboyant officiating style and resented his popularity with fans and sportswriters. Ashford's jocularity, booming voice, and exaggerated motions when making calls led many people to regard him as a "clown" who sacrificed judgment and accuracy for self-promoting showmanship. Others, especially blacks, considered his "showboating" to be a manifestation of a degrading Stepin Fetchit behavior that perpetuated negative stereotypes. Still others considered his elegant use of language, cultural interest in the arts and opera, and fashionable wardrobe (he wore cufflinks when umpiring) to be affectations intended to impress whites. Most pervasive were the charges that Ashford was a poor umpire who reached the majors solely to satisfy civil rights advocates who championed his promotion.

The criticisms of Ashford, while not unfounded, were exaggerated. By the time he reached the majors his umpiring skills had diminished, particularly when he called balls and strikes and when he followed batted balls into the outfield. But as some fellow umpires and Dewey Soriano, president of the PCL who had urged Ashford's promotion, argued, he was a hard-working, competent, thorough professional who was neither the best nor the worst in the league. Ashford's jovial demeanor, especially pronounced during arguments with players and managers, occasionally called to mind uncomplimentary racial stereotypes, but his personality was authentic, and his wit and charm facilitated acceptance as a racial pioneer in sports officiating. His unconventional style clashed with the traditional conservative demeanor of veteran umpires, but it was natural rather than deliberate and presaged the more aggressive bearing and emphatic gestures that soon became the norm. Political pressures and the exigencies of the civil rights movement did boost his promotion, but his hiring had been long delayed by racist attitudes.

When asked why he gave up fifteen years of seniority with the U.S. Post Office to become the first black umpire in minor and major league baseball, Ashford replied simply: "How many men go to their graves without ever doing what's in their hearts?" He was a courageous and determined man whose pioneering achievements spurred the racial integration of sports officiating at all levels of athletic competition. Even after his death in Los Angeles, Ashford, who always considered himself "an *umpire*, not a black umpire," achieved a historic first: his was the initial burial in the section of a cemetery in Cooperstown, New York, owned by the National Baseball Hall of Fame. In 1982 a Little League field in Los Angeles was named in his honor.

• A file of clippings on Ashford is in the National Baseball Library, Cooperstown, N.Y. A revealing autobiography is "Emmett Ashford" in Larry R. Gerlach, *The Men in Blue: Conversations with Umpires* (1980), pp. 265–87. Biographical accounts include Art Rust, Jr., *"Get That Nigger Off The Field!"* (1976), pp. 88–92, and Alan Margulies, "The Entertainer," *Referee*, Sept. 1992, pp. 44–48. See also Art Rosenbaum, "Colored Umpire with Color," *Baseball Digest*, Dec. 1965, pp. 57–59; Joe Falls, "Ump GETS This Decision," *Baseball Digest*, July 1966, pp. 84–86; and Joe McGuff, "Emmett Ashford: The Majors' Pioneer Black Umpire," *Baseball Digest*, July 1980, pp. 65–66ff. The most important obituaries are in the *Los Angeles Sentinel*, 6 Mar. 1980; the *Los Angeles Times*, 7 Mar. 1980; and the *New York Times*, 4 Mar. 1980.

LARRY R. GERLACH

ASHLEY, Clifford Warren (18 Dec. 1881–18 Sept. 1947), artist and author, was born in New Bedford, Massachusetts, the son of A. (which stood for Abiel) Davis Ashley, a grocer, and Caroline Morse. As a youth, growing up in New Bedford, Ashley witnessed the long decline of the once prosperous whale fishery that had brought fame and great fortune to New Bedford before the Civil War. The waterfront, with its wharves, derelict hulks, support facilities, and few remaining active vessels became his favorite playground and made a lasting impression on him. While a student at New Bedford High School, Ashley took an interest in art, which he subsequently pursued in Boston at the Eric Pape School. During the summer of 1901 he and his friends N. C. Wyeth and Henry J. Peck studied at Annisquam, Massachusetts, with George Noyes, and that fall Ashley moved to Wilmington, Delaware, to join Howard Pyle's school, at that time the best place to learn the techniques of illustration. The life of a Pyle student was vigorous, characterized by hard work at the drawing board and easel, hikes, sleigh rides, sporting events, costume parties, and practical jokes. To provide financial assistance for his students, Pyle secured commissions for them to produce illustrations for various publications. Ashley's early work included frontispieces for the publisher Peter F. Collier and illustrations for articles that appeared in *Delineator, Leslies, McClure's*, and *Success*.

It was not long before Ashley's interest in whaling appeared in his work. In 1904 he secured a commission from *Harper's Monthly Magazine* to write and illustrate a two-part article on whaling. Although he had a good knowledge of the vessels from his observations around New Bedford harbor, the only place he could become fully acquainted with the details of the whale fishery was at sea. Accordingly, in August of 1904 he set sail aboard the bark *Sunbeam*. During the six weeks he remained aboard, three sperm whales were taken, enabling Ashley to witness the chase, capture, and processing of whales as well as the use of whaling gear. The resulting article brought high praise from *Sunbeam*'s master, Benjamin A. Higgins: "I think it is the best whale story I ever read. . . . The illustrations are so true to life even the Old Barnacles here cannot find fault with them."

Ashley worked principally at painting and illustration for the next decade, spending summers in New Bedford and winters in Wilmington. In 1913 he put aside illustration to concentrate on painting out of doors. A successful exhibit in New Bedford the next year was followed by the three most prolific years of his career, concentrating on the New Bedford waterfront, including the trades that supported the whale fishery and scenes around the shores of Buzzards Bay. He hoped for the opportunity to paint a series of murals to record the whaling industry. The focus on whaling suggests a sense of mission that Ashley articulated in a newspaper interview: He wanted to "pitch in and do for my native place something that would make a race of heroes live" (New Bedford *Sunday Standard*, 9 Mar. 1916). He believed that he combined to a greater degree than any contemporary the skills of the artist and the knowledge of the whaleman, which would enable him to "perpetuate whaling as it is . . . to combine technical excellence and realism . . . to be able to face the sailor critic and the artist critic." His perpetuation of the whale fishery eventually came not in a series of murals, but in a book, *The Yankee Whaler*, published in 1926. In addition to his experience aboard *Sunbeam*, this volume includes a historical account of the whale fishery, descriptions of the vessels and all related equipment, one of the first descriptive evaluations of the whaleman's folk art of scrimshaw, and a glossary of whaling terms, illustrated with 105 of Ashley's paintings and drawings. It has remained one of the most useful and readable books on the subject.

Following publication of *The Yankee Whaler*, Ashley began to devote himself increasingly to other pursuits. His marriage to Sarah Scudder Clark in 1932 provided the occasion for him to remodel a farmhouse in Westport, Massachusetts, which he finished with antique mantels and paneling to provide a suitable setting for his extensive collection of country furniture. The marriage produced two children, and Ashley adopted his wife's oldest daughter from a previous marriage. Historic preservation was a major concern of his; in that same 1916 interview he urged the people of New Bedford to hold on to as much of their past as possible: "It should not be sacrificed heedlessly and without need." Of all his accomplishments, none is more widely known than *The Ashley Book of Knots*, published in 1944. This great compendium containing descriptions and illustrations of 3,854 knots with historical notes, practical evaluations, and supplementary illustrations remains one of the most distinguished works on the subject. It has been continually in print and has been translated for publication in France, Italy, and Germany.

Those who knew Ashley spoke of him affectionately as someone who brought out the best in those around him, loved a joke, and lived his life with energy and enthusiasm. His two major books have made lasting contributions to their respective subjects, and of the more than 300 paintings he is known to have produced, a good number of the best have found their way into museums. He died in Westport, Massachusetts.

• The principal public collections of Ashley's work are at the Old Dartmouth Historical Society and the Free Public Library, both in New Bedford, Mass. The Archives of American Art, Smithsonian Institution, Washington, D.C., has microfilmed a quantity of his papers. In addition to the books and articles mentioned above, he published another volume in 1929, *Whaleships of New Bedford*, which contains a group of drawings of whaling vessels and scenes. In 1973 the Old Dartmouth Historical Society and the Brandywine River Museum, Chadds Ford, Penn., collaborated on an exhibition of Ashley's paintings, for which a fully illustrated catalog with an introductory essay was published entitled *Whalers, Wharves, and Waterways*. In 1982 the Old Dartmouth Historical Society published *Sperm Whaling from New Bedford* by Elton W. Hall, a book containing photographs taken by Ashley aboard *Sunbeam* together with his "Blubber Hunters" articles and the glossary from *The Yankee Whaler*. Obituaries are in the New Bedford *Standard Times* and the *New York Times*, 20 Sept. 1947.

ELTON W. HALL

ASHLEY, James Mitchell (14 Nov. 1824–16 Sept. 1896), congressman, was born in Allegheny County, Pennsylvania, the son of John Clinton Ashley, an itinerant Campbellite minister, and Mary Ann Kirkpatrick. Although he grew up mainly in Portsmouth, Ohio, Ashley spent much of his youth traveling with his father through Ohio, Kentucky, and western Virginia. It was probably during these early trips that he first witnessed the practice of slavery, an institution he came to despise. He received no formal education.

At age fourteen, Ashley left Portsmouth for Cincinnati, where he worked as a steamboat cabin boy. By the age of seventeen, Ashley, a Democrat, had become involved in political life in Scioto County, Ohio, and was working for a number of newspapers, including the *Scioto Valley Republican*. In 1848 he became co-owner and editor of the Portsmouth, Ohio, *Democrat*. During his years with these and various other newspapers, Ashley studied law under Ohio attorney Charles O. Tracy and was admitted to the bar in 1849. Always active in the antislavery movement, Ashley was a part of the so-called Underground Railroad between 1839 and 1841. In 1851 he married Emma J. Smith; they had four children. That same year he was forced to leave Portsmouth when it was discovered that he had helped some slaves escape from Kentucky. He moved to Toledo, where he and a partner opened a general store, but he soon sold this enterprise and opened his own store. In 1858 he sold the business to his brother Eli Ashley and turned his full attention to politics.

Ashley had become increasingly visible in party politics since the early 1850s. In 1853 he broke with the Democrats over their stand against temperance and supported a slate of protemperance, independent Democratic candidates. A year later Ashley joined with other antislavery Democrats to oppose Senator Stephen A. Douglas's Kansas-Nebraska Act. From 1854 on Ashley was active in anti-Nebraska and Republican politics, although he had a very brief affiliation with the state Know Nothing party. In 1855 he helped secure the election of Salmon P. Chase as Ohio governor on an anti-Nebraska ticket, and in 1856, as a member of the Republican National Convention, he tried to secure the presidential nomination for Chase. When the movement for Chase foundered, Ashley, following Chase's orders, backed John C. Frémont, the eventual Republican candidate. In 1858 Ashley ran as the Republican candidate for Congress from the Ohio Fifth District and won by 189 votes out of 3,303 cast. As a former Democrat in the Republican party, he was more moderate on issues like tariff reform and internal improvements than were many of his Republican colleagues, and he favored hard money. He also favored the referendum and recall, desegregation of schools, and voting rights for minorities and women long before those issues were embraced by his party.

As a first-term congressman, Ashley spent most of his time trying to win the 1860 Republican presidential nomination for Chase. After Chase was denied the nomination in favor of Abraham Lincoln, Ashley worked assiduously for the election of Lincoln, whom he had known since 1858. After Ashley's reelection in 1860, he fought against all compromise measures with the seceding states, and once the Civil War began, he advocated an aggressive policy of confiscation and emancipation. He also helped draft the bill for the abolition of slavery in Washington, D.C., which, under his leadership, passed in April 1862. As early as December 1861 Ashley, acting as chairman of the Committee on Territories, drafted a radical plan of Reconstruction that called for the Federal government to abolish slavery, to set up "territorial" governments in the seceded states, to distribute confiscated lands to loyal citizens of any color, and to establish universal male suffrage. After President Lincoln offered his own outline for Reconstruction in December 1863, Ashley drafted a bill that conformed to the president's "10 percent" plan, under which a loyal tenth of a state's citizenry of 1860 could create a new state government, but Ashley included in his bill a provision allowing blacks and whites to vote as equals. This provision was unacceptable to moderates and conservatives, and it was dropped from the Wade-Davis Bill, which replaced Ashley's bill and was pocket-vetoed by Lincoln in July 1864.

After winning reelection in 1864, Ashley scored his greatest success by steering through the House of Representatives the bill for a constitutional ban on slavery that became the Thirteenth Amendment. In June 1864 Democrats in Congress who objected to the amendment as a violation of states' rights and a danger to the white race had marshaled a successful opposition. There had been sixty-five votes against the bill and ninety-three for, so it had failed to receive the requisite two-thirds majority required for passage. During the first vote Ashley voted against the bill so that, by legislative procedure, he could bring up the measure later. In the second session of the Thirty-eighth Congress, fifteen Democrats who had opposed the amendment changed their vote, either because of a newfound conviction against slavery or because Ashley, Lincoln, and Secretary of State William H. Seward led them to believe that they might receive political favors in exchange for a positive vote. The amendment was adopted by the House on 31 January 1865, by a vote of 119 to 56. During the last months of the Civil War, Ashley continued to press for some version of his Reconstruction plan, but none of the bills he proposed or supported passed.

During the first year of Andrew Johnson's presidency, Ashley compromised on his stance in favor of black voting rights and proposed a plan of "impartial suffrage," under which the vote would be granted to white and black men who could read, who had served in the military, or who had paid taxes. This plan was blocked by Johnson, who opposed the proposed legislation of Ashley's Radical faction and eventually campaigned against the reelection of Ashley and his allies. Ashley did win reelection in 1866, and in January 1867 he introduced articles of impeachment against President Johnson. During the long impeachment debate, Ashley at times became obsessed with Johnson's villainy, even suggesting that Johnson was in some way responsible for Lincoln's assassination. This unfounded accusation was joined by Ashley's equally bizarre claim that William Henry Harrison and Zachary Taylor also had died because of the actions of their vice presidents. Statements such as these, combined with Ashley's sometimes brash style, damaged his reputation among his contemporaries and generations of historians. He was also forever haunted by the story that in 1861 he had used his office to speculate illegally in land in Colorado and to secure positions for his two brothers in the surveyor's office there. Ashley was exonerated of these charges by a congressional committee in 1863, but his political opponents never stopped using the stories against him. In 1868 he was defeated for reelection, but a year later President Ulysses S. Grant appointed him territorial governor of Montana. Grant, however, refused to renew Ashley's appointment, perhaps because Ashley had denounced Grant to some associates. The former congressman responded in 1871 by joining the Liberal Republican movement opposed to Grant.

In 1875 Ashley moved to Ann Arbor, Michigan, where in 1877 he purchased the Toledo and Ann Arbor Railroad. He returned to Toledo in the 1880s, and during that decade the railroad expanded to become the Toledo, Ann Arbor and Northern Michigan Railroad. In part because of the financial panic of 1893, Ashley was forced to sell the railroad in that year. Ashley ran unsuccessfully for Congress in his old district in 1890 and 1892. While visiting in Michigan, he died in Ann Arbor.

Throughout his career, Ashley was a champion of individual liberties and expansive political rights. As Frederick Douglass wrote of him, "He makes his pleas for the protection of the weak against the combinations of capital, and with eloquence and power he denounces the spirit of caste and all special legislation for the benefit of any one class at the expense of labor and the rights of humanity" (Arnett, p. 6).

• Ashley's papers were destroyed during his lifetime, but he wrote a brief "Memoir" that is in the University of Toledo Library. The most comprehensive collection of his speeches and other public documents is Benjamin W. Arnett, ed., *Duplicate Copy of the Souvenir from the Afro-American League of Tennessee to Hon. James M. Ashley of Ohio* (1894), but also relevant is Ashley's article, "Abraham Lincoln," *Magazine of Western History* 14 (1891): 23–36. The best biography is Robert J. Horowitz, *The Great Impeacher: A Political Biography of James M. Ashley* (1979). W. Sherman Jackson, "Representative James M. Ashley and the Midwestern Origins of Amendment Thirteen," *Lincoln Herald* 80 (1978): 83–95, also contains insights. Other works with discussions of Ashley include James G. Blaine, *Twenty Years of Congress* (2 vols., 1884–1886); Herman Belz, *Reconstructing the Union: Theory and Policy during the Civil War* (1969); and two books by Michael Les Benedict, *The Impeachment and Trial of Andrew Johnson* (1973) and *A Compromise of Principle: Congressional Republicans and Reconstruction, 1863–1869* (1974). An obituary is in the *New York Tribune*, 17 Sept. 1896.

MICHAEL VORENBERG

ASHLEY, Thomas Clarence (29 Sept. 1895–2 June 1967), folk singer and instrumentalist, was born Clarence Earl McCurry in Bristol, Virginia, the son of George McCurry, a bartender, and Rosie Belle Ashley. Shortly before he was born, his father, who was locally known as an old-time fiddler, revealed that he had a second family and left to be with them; it was only years later that the young singer met him. The boy took the name of his mother's family and moved with them to Ashe County, North Carolina, about 1896. In this remote mountain area he grew up, learning folk songs and the old clawhammer style of banjo-playing. By 1907 he had received his first guitar, an instrument only then becoming popular in the mountains, and by the time he was a teenager he was gaining his first professional experience by traveling with Doc White Cloud's medicine show. Such shows, common in the rural South through the 1930s, featured a self-styled doctor who sold patent nostrums to the public; to attract an audience, the doctors hired musicians to play on a makeshift stage. Ashley played off and on in such shows for about twenty years, often portraying a traditional blackface comic character called "Rastus" in addition to making music. Later he helped train another young singer in the show, Roy Acuff.

In 1914 Ashley married Hettie Osborne; they had four children, but only two survived infancy. He struggled to find a way to make music and provide for his family; he began traveling through the mountain hamlets, playing music with the fiddler G. B. Grayson and the banjoist Hobart Smith, among others. Their venues ranged from square dances to streetcorners and courthouse lawns, and their wages were whatever the audience tossed in their hat. By the late 1920s record companies were scouring the mountains looking for talent to feed the burgeoning country record market, and Ashley decided to try his luck. In 1928 he embarked on an intense period of recording, and over the next five years he appeared as either leader or band member on about seventy recordings.

After an unsuccessful attempt to record as a soloist for the Starr Piano Company (Gennett Records) in February 1928, Ashley joined forces with the singer and banjoist Dock Walsh and the harmonica player Garley Foster to form a band, the Carolina Tar Heels. Recording for the Victor Talking Machine Company (later RCA Victor), the nation's largest, they created a number of popular and lucrative records, including "Peg and Awl" (1928), an early song about technological unemployment; "My Home's across the Blue Ridge Mountains" (1929), later revived by bluegrass bands; and "Somebody's Tall and Handsome" (1929), one of country music's earliest love songs. In later years Ashley recorded and performed with Byrd Moore's Hot Shots (1929), the Haywood County Ramblers (1931), the Blue Ridge Mountain Entertainers (1931), and Ashley and Foster (1933).

In 1929 and 1930 Ashley recorded a series of solos for Columbia, and it is on these that his later reputation rested. Using the unorthodox "sawmill" tuning on the banjo, he preserved classic versions of old British ballads like "The House Carpenter" and "The Coo-Coo Bird," as well as definitive readings of American ballads such as "John Hardy" and "Poor Omie," and eerie white blues like "Dark Hollow." Although the depression curtailed sales of these records in 1929 and 1930, they were often reissued in the 1960s and 1970s and became emblematic of mountain singing.

After the depression, Ashley played music less and less; for a time he worked in the coalfields of West Virginia, and he ran his own trucking company. An accident to his finger made him think he could no longer play an instrument, so he confined his performing to blackface comedy with bluegrass groups, including Charlie Monroe and the Stanley Brothers. He also purchased a large farm near Shouns, Tennessee, and began to work it.

In 1960 Ashley met a young musician and folk music researcher, Ralph Rinzler, who was amazed that Ashley was still alive and playing. Rinzler persuaded him to come north to perform at folk clubs in Greenwich Village, and even to make some new recordings. During the next seven years Ashley traveled across the country, appearing at numerous folk festivals, often with Doc Watson, Fred Price, Clint Howard, Tex Isley, and others. *Old Time Music at Clarence Ashley's* was the first of five successful LPs he recorded for the Folkways label.

Ashley's high, keening singing style and his use of unusual minor chords, which had made him a favorite with his original mountain audience, endeared him to the new generation of folk-music fans. Although he never achieved the fame of Acuff and Watson, he was a powerful influence on revivalist performers.

• The most detailed account of Ashley's life is Ambrose Manning and Minnie Miller, "Tom Ashley," in *Tom Ashley, Sam McGee, Bukka White: Tennessee Traditional Singers*, ed. Thomas G. Burton (1981); the volume also includes a complete discography of Ashley's recordings. The recordings themselves have been frequently reissued; the Smithsonian-Folkways CD, *Doc Watson and Clarence Ashley: The Original Folkways Recordings, 1960–1962*, repackages two LPs originally issued as *Old Time Music at Clarence Ashley's*, and contains a booklet by Ralph Rinzler. Some of the 1929–1930 solo recordings are reproduced on *Mountain Ballads* (County CD).

CHARLES K. WOLFE

ASHLEY, William Henry (1778–26 Mar. 1838), fur trader and politician, was born in Chesterfield County, Virginia. His parents are unknown, and there is no definitive record of his early years. In 1798 Ashley moved west to Kentucky. Four years later he crossed the Mississippi and took up residence in the lead-mining community of St. Genevieve (now in Missouri). From that time until his death, Ashley energetically and successfully pursued profits and power in the fluid frontier society.

Ashley's first commercial venture was in the local lead trade. By 1809 he had extended his lead-trading ventures to New Orleans and New York. But the economy was unpredictable, and his debts were heavy, so by 1812 Ashley was penniless. Always resourceful, Ashley regained his capital in the gunpowder business during the War of 1812 and by speculating on rising land values in Missouri. He was also active in the Missouri militia, and he cultivated connections with influential politicians like William Clark, governor of Missouri Territory. This patronage brought Ashley a number of political appointments, including that of surveyor of the public domain from 1816 to 1822.

By 1819 Ashley's ambitions had outgrown St. Genevieve, and he moved his operations north to the nascent metropolis of St. Louis. From 1819 to 1821 he expanded his real estate operations, amassing almost 21,000 acres of land, and he continued to nurture his political connections. In 1820 he was elected lieutenant governor of the new state of Missouri, serving until 1824 when he ran unsuccessfully for governor. But this was all just prelude to his entry into the fur trade, a move that made him a crucial figure in the American settlement of the West.

In 1822 Ashley, in partnership with his old lead-trading partner Andrew Henry, launched a fur trading and trapping expedition to the upper Missouri. Henry was the field partner; Ashley organized the capital, credit, and supply of the operation. Their strategy was to combine direct trapping of beaver at the headwaters of the Missouri and Yellowstone rivers with trading for furs at the Indian villages along the Missouri. By the late summer of 1822 Henry and his trappers had built a post at the mouth of the Yellowstone. In October Ashley brought them supplies and then immediately returned to St. Louis to arrange the next year's outfit, leaving Henry and his men to trap and trade through the winter.

In March 1823 Ashley started up the Missouri with supplies. On 2 June his party was attacked at the Arikara villages and was forced to withdraw downriver. Ashley improvised by dispatching a small party of his best men, led by Jedediah Smith, overland from Fort Lookout on a direct route to the Rocky Mountains. In the winter of 1824 Ashley's men made the official American discovery of South Pass. In the course of the next two years, Ashley devised a successful method of getting beaver pelts from the Rocky Mountains to St. Louis, based on leaving American trappers in the field year round, the rendezvous trade fair, and the Platte overland supply route through South Pass.

Ashley himself took supplies to the Rocky Mountains in 1825 (during which expedition he explored the Green River) and 1826. He returned with hundreds of packs of pelts. His perseverance and resourcefulness made him a wealthy man. But Ashley preferred the comforts of St. Louis to the hazards of the mountains, and at the 1826 rendezvous he sold his interest in the trapping side of the business to Smith and his partners and contracted to act as their sole supplier. In doing so, he reduced his risks and increased the potential for profits. Ashley never returned to the Rocky Mountains.

For Ashley the fur trade was only a means to an end, another opportunity to make money and gain power. After 1828, for the last ten years of his life, he concentrated on politics. He was elected to the U.S. House of Representatives in 1831 and reelected in 1832 and 1834. At first he was aligned to Jacksonian policies, and he drew his support from frontier farmers in the west, north, and south of Missouri. Gradually, however, in the 1830s he took a more probusiness stance favoring the St. Louis elite. During his years in Congress he was particularly active in opposing Indian removal to the "permanent Indian frontier" to the west of Missouri, believing that their presence was a threat to frontier security and a waste of good land.

Ashley's years in Washington were the happiest of his life—he had achieved the wealth and fame he had long sought. Nevertheless, in 1836 he relinquished his seat in Congress and ran again for the position of governor of Missouri. He lost by a wide margin, largely because he had alienated the Jacksonians. He fell back on making money in real estate, but his health rapidly deteriorated. He died of pneumonia.

Ashley was married three times and widowed twice. He married Mary Able, the daughter of the owner of a large Spanish land grant, in 1806. Mary, always of fragile constitution, died in 1821. In 1825 Ashley married Eliza Christy, who came from a prominent St. Louis family. Eliza died in 1830. Ashley married Elizabeth Moss Wilcox of Missouri in 1832. They adopted two girls in 1833. When he died at his country home on the Missouri River, Ashley left his family an estate valued at $52,000.

Although Ashley found success in many walks of life—as merchant, manufacturer, speculator, politician, and socialite—his place in history was earned by his achievements in the fur trade. He initiated a successful strategy for taking furs from the Rocky Mountains, and he was one of the few men who ever made profits in that risky business. In the process, he forged the Platte overland trail, later to become the way to Oregon and California.

• Ashley's papers are housed in the Missouri Historical Society in St. Louis. For many years, the essential source for Ashley was Dale L. Morgan, ed., *The West of William H. Ashley, 1822–1838* (1964); this remains the best source on Ashley's role in the fur trade. A more recent and comprehensive account of Ashley's life is presented in Richard M. Clokey, *William H. Ashley: Enterprise and Politics in the Trans-Mississippi West* (1980). Shorter biographical essays are by Harvey L. Carter, "William H. Ashley," in *The Mountain Men and the Fur Trade of the Far West*, ed. Leroy R. Hafen, vol. 7 (1969), pp. 23–32, and in Dale L. Morgan and Eleanor Towles Harris, eds., *The Rocky Mountain Journals of William Marshall*

Anderson: The West in 1834 (1967), pp. 251–52. Ashley and the trapping system he devised are also featured prominently in David J. Wishart, *The Fur Trade of the American West, 1807–1840* (1992).

DAVID J. WISHART

ASHMUN, George (25 Dec. 1804–17 July 1870), congressman, was born in Blandford, Massachusetts, the son of Eli Porter Ashmun, an attorney, politician, and, later, U.S. senator, and Lucy Hooker. Ashmun graduated from Yale in 1823 and subsequently read law. By 1828 he had established a legal practice in Springfield, Massachusetts, and that year he married Martha E. Hall. The couple had two daughters.

While continuing to practice law in Springfield, Ashmun entered politics. First elected to the Massachusetts House of Representatives in 1833, he served there until being elevated to the state senate in 1838. He returned to the lower house in 1841, serving in this final term as Speaker. Ashmun was elected to the U.S. House of Representatives in 1844, just as the nation's attention was beginning to focus on its manifest destiny and the status of slavery in areas acquired in the course of expansion. A northern Whig, Ashmun looked dimly upon both territorial acquisition and slavery's extension. Opposing the Mexican War as unconstitutional and unnecessary, he went further than a great many Whigs who similarly denounced the venture but continued to vote for military appropriations. In May 1846 Ashmun joined John Quincy Adams, Joshua Giddings, and a handful of others in the House in voting against an important army supply bill.

While he made common cause with the likes of Adams and Giddings, Ashmun at the same time distanced himself from "Conscience Whigs," who placed antislavery principles over party loyalty. He accused leaders of this faction of self-interested ambition, and one of them, in turn, termed him "skillful and unscrupulous" (Gatell, p. 140). He submitted to his party's nomination of a southern slaveholder and Mexican War hero, Zachary Taylor, for president in 1848, though he had supported Daniel Webster's claims to the honor. This loyalty to Webster was ultimately Ashmun's political lodestar. Samuel Bowles (d. 1878), to whose newspaper, the *Springfield Republican*, Ashmun contributed, went so far as to say that "this strong man, before whom and to whom all others yielded, surrendered himself almost completely" to Webster (Merriam, vol. 1, p. 41). On a number of occasions Ashmun doggedly took to the House floor to defend Webster against charges that, during his several stints as secretary of state, he had misused official funds or accepted gratuities from parties materially interested in government business. After Webster proposed, during the momentous debates of 1850, that slavery need not be formally banned from the southwestern territories, he found Ashmun to be one of his few allies left among the state's congressional delegation. Yet the Springfield congressman was not as quick as the Massachusetts senator to shrug off the Wilmot Proviso, and Ashmun's loyalty knew certain bounds. While defending Webster against the attacks of more zealously antislavery colleagues, Ashmun did not actually vote for the Compromise of 1850's component parts except banning the slave trade in the District of Columbia. Still, the disenchantment in certain quarters with Webster dimmed Ashmun's fortunes as well. He was not a candidate for reelection later that year but instead continued the practice of law.

In 1852 Ashmun again worked to secure the Whig presidential nomination for Webster. At the party's national convention he headed the committee that drew up a platform embracing the Compromise of 1850, including the Fugitive Slave Law. Unlike a number of Webster loyalists, he refused to endorse an independent bid when the nomination went to Winfield Scott instead. Webster died shortly thereafter, and in the years following Ashmun, though often in Washington, D.C., generally stayed away from politics. "I have had too much of public life for my own good . . . ," he groused, "[but] not enough to be of any service to any one else" (Merriam, vol. 1, p. 39).

By 1860 Ashmun had cast his lot with the Republican party. He presided with aplomb over the party's national convention and was subsequently a member of the committee that traveled to Springfield, Illinois, to give Abraham Lincoln formal notice of his nomination. Upon Fort Sumter's surrender the following spring, he arranged for Stephen Douglas to confer with his old rival Lincoln, yielding a statement of support from the Illinois Democrat for the president's efforts to save the Union. Ashmun was not rewarded with a federal appointment until fairly late in Lincoln's administration, when the president named him as one of the government's representatives on the Union Pacific Railroad board of directors, where he served until 1869. Apparently counted as a conservative within Republican ranks, Ashmun was elected to attend the National Union Convention, which was called in 1866 to support Andrew Johnson in his struggle with Congress over Reconstruction. He chose not to participate. Ashmun had gained some reputation as a determined opponent of the Mexican War and a prominent disciple of Webster, yet his death in Springfield left even his admirer Bowles feeling that he might have made better use of his opportunities and his talents.

• Bowles's memoir of Ashmun is excerpted in George S. Merriam, *The Life and Times of Samuel Bowles* (1885). Brief discussions of aspects of Ashmun's career are in Kinley Brauer, *Cotton versus Conscience: Massachusetts Whig Politics and Southwestern Expansion 1843–1848* (1967); Frank Gatell, *John Gorham Palfrey and the New England Conscience* (1963); John Schroeder, *Mr. Polk's War: American Opposition and Dissent, 1846–1848* (1973); and Charles E. Ames, *Pioneering the Union Pacific: A Reappraisal of the Builders of the Railroad* (1969). A number of studies of Webster make mention of Ashmun, including Maurice G. Baxter, *One and Inseparable: Daniel Webster and the Union* (1984), and Robert Dalzell, Jr., *Daniel Webster and the Trial of American Nationalism 1843–1852* (1973). An obituary is in the *Springfield Republican*, 18 July 1870.

PATRICK G. WILLIAMS

ASHMUN, Jehudi (21 Apr. 1794–25 Aug. 1828), colonial agent and missionary in West Africa, was born in Champlain, New York, the son of Samuel Ashmun, a justice of the peace, and Parthenia (maiden name unknown). An intensely devout Christian from the age of sixteen, Ashmun studied theology and classics at Vermont's Middlebury College and the University of Vermont in Burlington. Following his graduation from the latter in 1816, he was appointed principal and instructor at the Maine Charity School, a Congregationalist college in Hampden, Maine. In 1818 he married Catherine Gray; it is not known if they had any children.

Ashmun's early career was marked by frustration and controversy. In 1819, discredited by rumors of romantic indiscretions, he resigned his post at the Maine Charity School and moved to Baltimore, Maryland. Following a failed attempt to publish a weekly missionary journal there, he proceeded to Washington, D.C., where he joined the Episcopalian church and edited the *Theological Repertory*, an Episcopalian monthly. In 1821 Ashmun's application to enter the Episcopalian ministry was denied, apparently because he was unwilling to give up his literary activities. Meanwhile, his secretive management of the *Repertory*'s finances aroused the opposition of his colleagues, prompting him to leave the journal in early 1822.

While at the *Repertory*, Ashmun first publicly associated himself with the American Colonization Society (ACS) and its program of resettling freed American blacks in West Africa. Here, too, his efforts initially faltered. In 1820 ACS managers cautiously underwrote his proposal to edit a monthly journal publicizing the society's projects. Owing to lack of public support, however, the managers withdrew their backing after only one issue. In 1821, facing financial difficulty, Ashmun published his laudatory *Memoir of the Life and Character of the Rev. Samuel Bacon*, a biography of a former ACS agent who had perished on a failed 1820 mission to colonize West Africa, but the book sold poorly, leaving the author with a heavy printer's bill. Partly in search of commercial opportunities that might resolve his financial difficulties, and partly in fulfillment of long-standing missionary aspirations, Ashmun in 1822 contracted with the ACS to make an inspection tour of the society's newly established colony in Cape Mesurado, in present-day Liberia. He also agreed to serve for the duration of his tour as the U.S. government's agent in West Africa, charged with resettling freed captives from intercepted slave vessels. (In 1819 Congress had authorized the United States to maintain a station in Africa for this purpose.) In May 1822, accompanied by his wife and fifty-two black settlers, Ashmun sailed for West Africa.

Arriving in Cape Mesurado on 8 August 1822, Ashmun found the American colony in a desperate state—leaderless, hungry, racked with disease, and vulnerable to attack by the Cape's native inhabitants. Setting aside his commercial ambitions, he assumed the position of ACS agent, which he had been authorized to do in the event he found that post vacant. Placing the colony under martial law, he enhanced its defenses by building fortifications and organizing military drills. Such precautions, taken amid a fever epidemic that killed Mrs. Ashmun and severely weakened her husband, were vindicated in November 1822, when the colony's defenders, thirty-five men and boys, repulsed an attacking native force of about 800 warriors. This victory and another in December ensured the colony's survival and set the stage for its later development.

Ashmun's next major challenge was gaining the confidence of the ACS managers, who resented his profligacy with society funds, and of the black settlers, who chafed under his strict discipline. In the spring of 1823 Ashmun was relieved as ACS agent, only to regain de facto authority when disease and settlers' hostility drove his replacement from the continent. In April 1824 a settler insurrection forced Ashmun himself into exile on the Cape Verde Islands. Provisionally reinstated in August 1824, he began a new policy of conciliation and public works that finally won him the settlers' loyalty. Impressed by the transformation, in 1825 the ACS appointed him its permanent colonial agent in Cape Mesurado. In 1826 Ashmun wrote *History of the American Colony in Liberia, from December, 1821, to 1823* (1826), which celebrated the establishment of the Cape colony as an act of "heroic virtue" by the black settlers, an achievement made all the more remarkable by their humble status.

As permanent agent, Ashmun aggressively promoted the interests of the ACS colony. By establishing trading posts beyond the colony's borders, he strengthened trade relations between settlers and neighboring tribes. His continuing role as U.S. government agent also gave him access to federal funds, which he used for purchasing and leasing adjacent territories, thereby enlarging the colony. He occasionally acquired land by force, arguing that such encroachments were necessary to protect the colony's trade routes and factories from native plundering. He also improved the fortifications around his Monrovia base, from which he sometimes attacked nearby slave factories operated by Spanish and French traders. Less successful were his efforts to promote agriculture among the settlers, who found commerce more attractive. Still, by 1828 Cape Mesurado had become a relatively stable and prosperous colony whose population of American blacks, well under a hundred in 1822, was now about 1,200.

Ashmun, who never fully recovered his health after his first bout with fever in Africa, fell gravely ill in early 1828. On 26 March he left Cape Mesurado, seeking relief in the temperate climate of the West Indies. When this proved unavailing, he sailed for New Haven, Connecticut, where he died shortly after his arrival.

Ashmun was a solitary, bold, and impulsive man who, for all his ritual professions of self-doubt, had a vast practical faith in his own abilities and judgment that occasionally prompted him to act without consulting others. Although such headstrong independence served him ill in the collegial confines of academia and publishing, it distinguished him in Cape Mesurado, where the precariousness of life placed a premium on decisive leadership and where black settlers generally lacked the status to take offense at his presumptions. Unconstrained by jealous peers, concerned with starker questions of physical survival and security, Ashmun served the Cape colony with courage and initiative, laying a solid foundation for the future Liberian state.

• The papers of the American Colonization Society, at the Library of Congress, contain some of Ashmun's letters, as well as much information about the ACS generally. The fullest treatment of Ashmun's life is Ralph Randolph Gurley, *Life of Jehudi Ashmun* (1835). Briefer modern accounts are in Philip J. Staudenraus, *The African Colonization Movement, 1816–1865* (1961), and Richard West, *Back to Africa: A History of Sierra Leone and Liberia* (1970). For a contemporary assessment, see Leonard Bacon, *Discourse Preached in the Center Church, in New Haven, August 27, 1828, at the Funeral of Jehudi Ashmun, Esq*. (1828).

SALIM YAQUB

ASHURST, Henry Fountain (13 Sept. 1874–31 May 1962), U.S. senator, was born in Winnemucca, Nevada, the son of William Henry Ashurst, a sheep rancher, and Sarah Elizabeth Bogard. In 1875 he moved with his family to northwestern Arizona and in 1877 settled in the vicinity of present-day Flagstaff. The second of ten children, Henry dropped out of school at age thirteen to work for his father as a cowboy, and at nineteen he took a job as a jailer in Flagstaff. While working as a jailer, he developed his interest in oratory and law by reading Sir William Blackstone's *Commentaries on the Laws of England* (1765–1769) and declaiming to the surrounding desert as many five-syllable words as he could find. "I could throw 56-pound words clear across the Grand Canyon. As a matter of course I went into politics."

Ashurst studied law at night and took courses in stenography at the Stockton (Calif.) Business College. In 1896 he was appointed justice of the peace in Williams, Arizona, near Flagstaff, and won a seat in the house of representatives of the Arizona Territorial Legislature. He served in that body during 1897 and 1899, holding the post of Speaker in the latter year, and in 1903 he served a year in the territorial senate. During this period Ashurst read widely and polished his natural talents as a public speaker, memorizing classical American orations and poetry. In 1903 he entered the University of Michigan for a final year of legal training. When he returned to Arizona the following year, he married Elizabeth McEvoy Renoe, a widow, who remained actively engaged in his career as a political adviser until her death in 1939. The union produced no offspring, although Elizabeth had four children from her previous marriage.

In 1905 Ashurst became district attorney of his native Coconino County, which helped to establish his political base. He served as a delegate to the Democratic Territorial Conventions of 1906 and 1908. After four years, he resigned as district attorney and in 1909 moved his law practice to Prescott, his official residence for the remainder of his public life.

Near the end of 1911, on the eve of Arizona's admission to statehood, Ashurst won the Democratic primary and general elections for a seat in the U.S. Senate, a victory that the state legislature unanimously confirmed on 27 March 1912. He was reelected to the Senate in 1916, 1922, 1928, and 1934. In the Senate Ashurst loyally supported President Woodrow Wilson and chaired the Committee on Indian Affairs from 1914 to 1919. When his party lost control of the Senate in 1919 and the White House during the 1920s, Ashurst emerged as a persistent critic of Republican leaders and programs. With the Democrats back in command in 1933, he became chairman of the Senate Judiciary Committee, a post he held until he left the Senate nearly eight years later.

Ashurst failed to attain significant legislative influence in the Senate, despite his Judiciary Committee chairmanship. His Arizona congressional colleague Carl Hayden once categorized senators as "work horses and show horses." The reserved Hayden perhaps had the eloquent and dramatic Ashurst in mind for the latter breed and himself for the former. While Hayden mastered behind-the-scenes legislative detail, the tall and charming Ashurst performed for the galleries and ultimately for an admiring constituency garbed in his signature morning coat, striped trousers, winged collar, and tortoise-shell pince-nez eyeglasses. One newspaper described him as looking "like something left over in Washington by a visiting Shakespearean stock company." Another praised him as a "swashbuckling orator who wielded words like a dueling sword." Hayden observed that, with the election of Ashurst to the Senate, "no longer could it be suggested that erudition and wisdom, urbanity and wit could not be found west of the Alleghenies."

Ashurst was one of a very few senators to win an oratorical duel with the boisterous and profane Senator Huey Long. In a celebrated encounter on 15 June 1935, Ashurst observed, "In these agitated and distressful days, we must expect to encounter whimsical, droll, eccentric, and erratic persons who occupy the stage for a time, and they, at least, divert us, interest us, entertain us, and, I am bound in fairness to add, they sometimes instruct us." Long said he did not understand a word of the speech but confessed that he could not help admiring it.

Ashurst claimed to be proud of his legislative inconsistency. "I always use sweet words because it is easier to swallow them." He voted on a soldiers' bonus bill four times, twice in support and twice in opposition; he supported both the Prohibition amendment and its appeal. As chairman of the Senate Judiciary Committee, he labeled as "a prelude to tyranny" President Franklin Roosevelt's rumored plan to "pack" the Supreme Court with friendly justices to curb the High Court's assault on New Deal legislation. When Roosevelt actually introduced the plan, the Arizona senator said, "I'm for it. It's a step in the right direction." Then he earned Roosevelt's wrath by delaying hearings. "No haste, no hurry, no waste, no worry—that is the motto of this committee," he advised a presidential aide. During the Court-packing debate, Ashurst again changed his mind and engineered the measure's defeat. "Never have I let what I said yesterday bind me today. No Senator can change his mind quicker than I."

On 17 June 1910 Ashurst began a diary that he kept faithfully until 27 July 1937. That quotable document's final sentence suggests its flavor. "It is comforting assurance that nothing in this diary will cause pain to any living person or bring reproach to the memory of anyone who is dead."

Saddened by the death of his wife, who had been a driving force in his life, Ashurst lost his zeal for electoral politics and neglected to return home to campaign for the 1940 Democratic primary. Many believed he had lost touch with his constituency. His opposition to a military draft as war engulfed Europe weakened his traditional support and led to his defeat by Ernest McFarland, a county judge.

After leaving the Senate, Ashurst served from 1941 to 1943 on the Board of Immigration Appeals in the U.S. Department of Justice. He then retired, devoting himself to public speaking and classical poetry. At the age of eighty-seven, he relished his cameo role as a befuddled senator in the 1962 film version of Allen Drury's *Advise and Consent* (1959). Reporting on his death in Washington, D.C., the *Washington Post* commented that Ashurst had come to be "a living symbol of the Senate on its best behavior."

• Many of Ashurst's papers are believed to have been destroyed. Small collections are available at the Arizona Historical Society and the University of Arizona. George F. Sparks edited *A Many-Colored Toga: The Diary of Henry Fountain Ashurst* (1962), and Senator Barry Goldwater selected fourteen significant addresses in *The Speeches of Henry Fountain Ashurst* (1953). Two academic theses provide biographical details: Robert Earl Cognac, "The Senatorial Career of Henry Fountain Ashurst" (M.A. thesis, Arizona State Univ., 1953), and George F. Sparks, "The Speaking of Henry Fountain Ashurst" (Ph.D. diss., Univ. of Utah, 1953). See also Alva Johnston, "The Dean of Inconsistency," *Saturday Evening Post*, 25 Dec. 1937; George Creel, "Coconino Cloudburst," *Collier's*, 13 Nov. 1937; and *Time*, 23 Sept. 1940 and 8 June 1962. Obituaries are in the *Washington Post* and the *New York Times*, 1 June 1962, and the *Washington Evening Star*, 31 May 1962.

RICHARD ALLAN BAKER

ASIMOV, Isaac (2 Jan. 1920–6 Apr. 1992), writer, was born in Petrovichi, USSR, the son of Judah Asimov, a merchant, and Anna Rachel Berman. Asimov's Russian-Jewish father and mother emigrated to New York City in 1923. After a number of years working odd jobs, they bought a candy store in Brooklyn in 1926, the first of many in that borough that Asimov would help run until he was twenty-two years old. Working long hours in the candy store left Asimov's parents with little time to raise their children. His mother was especially hard on him, frequently hitting him when she lost her temper and reminding him that he was responsible for their hand-to-mouth existence. Asimov was a precocious child who taught himself to read before he was five, and he read omnivorously thereafter. At seven he taught his younger sister to read, "somewhat against her will," he confesses in his memoir, *I. Asimov* (p. 10). He also admitted that he was self-confident and arrogant about his knowledge and that his lack of social skills estranged him from his schoolmates and teachers. Nevertheless, he skipped several grades and received his high school diploma when he was fifteen years old.

The long hours working in the candy store established Asimov's working habits throughout his life. It was also where he read the pulp magazines his father sold, particularly science fiction titles like *Science Wonder Stories* and *Amazing Stories*. They sparked his interest in science and in writing and heavily influenced his early writing style. He started writing stories at the age of eleven, mostly imitations of dime novels such as the Rover Boys and pulp stories that relied heavily on action and overwrought writing. His first published work was a humorous essay for his high school literary magazine, which the teacher told him he accepted because it was the only one of its type submitted. The teacher even appended a note to the top of the essay virtually apologizing for its appearance. Nearly six decades later, Asimov still resented the teacher.

To fulfill his father's dream of a professional career for his son, Asimov took classes at Columbia College, earning a B.S. in chemistry in 1939. Without much enthusiasm, he tried to enter medical school, but he was rejected because of his grades and his personality. He stayed at Columbia, earning an M.A. in 1941 and a Ph.D. in 1948, both in chemistry. Asimov had little interest in his work, but he did not feel he could make a living as a writer.

In 1938 Asimov met John W. Campbell, Jr., the editor of *Astounding Science Fiction* magazine and Asimov's first mentor. At first Campbell rejected his stories, but he offered editorial advice that resulted in the publication elsewhere of "Marooned Off Vesta" later that year. It was Asimov's first professional sale. In 1940 they conceived the Three Laws of Robotics, three simple rules with which robots were programmed in Asimov's fiction. They are "1. A robot may not injure a human being or, through inaction, allow a human being to come to harm. 2. A robot must obey the orders given it by human beings except where such orders would conflict with the First Law. 3. A robot must protect its own existence as long as such protection does not conflict with the First or Second Law." The stories became the foundation of at least two dozen short stories and three novels and are one source of Asimov's popularity in science fiction. In 1941 Campbell's magazine published "Nightfall." This short story, written when Asimov was twenty-one years old, was based on a quotation by Ralph Waldo Emerson ("If the stars should appear one night in a thousand years, how would men believe and adore and preserve for many generations the remembrance of the city of God"). Three decades later the story was voted the best science fiction short story ever written by the Science Fiction Writers of America.

From 1942 to 1945, while working at the Naval Air Experimental Station in Philadelphia, Asimov wrote several stories that were to form the highly popular Foundation series. Inspired by Gibbon's *The Decline and Fall of the Roman Empire*, the three books, *Foundation* (1951), *Foundation and Empire* (1952), and *Second Foundation* (1953), told the story of the decline and fall of the Galactic Empire, the Dark Ages that followed, and the rise of the Second Galactic Empire, all of which were predicted by the invented science of "psychohistory," the ability to predict the mass currents of future events.

Asimov married Gertrude Blugerman in 1942, and they had two children. The marriage was long but not happy. He pressured her into marrying, she did not love him, and despite realizing how incompatible they were, they decided to remain married until their children were grown. They were divorced in 1973, and Asimov married Janet Opal Jeppson, a longtime friend, two weeks later.

In 1949, with a Ph.D. in chemistry, Asimov joined the Boston University School of Medicine to teach biochemistry. "I didn't feel impelled to tell them that I'd never had any biochemistry," he writes in *I. Asimov*. "By 1951 I was writing a textbook on biochemistry, and I finally realized the only thing I really wanted to be was a writer."

In 1950 Asimov published his first novel, *Pebble in the Sky*, the first of sixteen he would publish in that decade. He also wrote many textbooks and general science books during that time, on biochemistry, the atom, and biology.

Meanwhile, Asimov discovered that he did not like academic life or living in Boston. His reputation outside the university grew as a writer of science fiction and as an explainer of scientific subjects to general readers, and he was popular with students as a lecturer, but he hated research and was unable to get along with his immediate superior or most of his fellow professors. The dean of the school liked him enough to promote Asimov to associate professor in 1955, granting him tenure, but when the dean retired, his replacement fired Asimov in 1957. Although the school could refuse to pay Asimov and take away his lectures, his tenured position meant he could keep his academic title. His pride stung, Asimov refused to be forced out, and he continued to visit the school to pick up his mail and perform small jobs. He was promoted to full professor in 1979.

At the end of the 1950s Asimov stopped writing science fiction, convinced that he had said all he wanted, and turned to nonfiction. His fame in the science fiction community, however, continued to grow because of the popularity of his earlier writings and his regular column in the *Magazine of Fantasy and Science Fiction*, where his ability to make complicated scientific subjects understandable to the general reader won him a wide renown.

Once Asimov became a full-time writer, he established the routine, acquired in his early years, that he would follow for the rest of his life. He worked what he called "candy store" hours. He would awaken at 6 A.M.—he prided himself on never needing an alarm clock. He would be at his typewriter by 7:30 A.M. and work steadily until 10 P.M. He disliked traveling except for sea cruises, his acrophobia kept him out of airplanes, and above all else, he preferred to write. In this fashion, he wrote and edited nearly five hundred books, marking his hundredth book in 1969, his two hundredth in 1979, and his three hundredth in 1984. He wrote science fiction and mystery short stories and novels and edited more than a hundred anthologies. His nonfiction subjects included general science, mathematics, astronomy, earth sciences, chemistry, biochemistry, physics, biology, history, the Bible, literature, humor and satire, and autobiography. In *I. Asimov*, he explained the driving force behind his productivity: "No one ever acclaimed me as a great literary light. . . . Yet we all want recognition, we all want to be known for something, and I was beginning to see that there would be a good chance that if for nothing else, I would be known for the vast number of books I would publish and for the range of subjects I wrote about."

During the 1960s and 1970s Asimov wrote only a handful of science fiction stories and two novels. Nevertheless, one of the novels, *The Gods Themselves* (1972), and the short story " The Bicentennial Man" (1975) each won a Hugo and a Nebula award, and his novelization of the film *Fantastic Voyage* became one of his biggest sellers. In 1982 he returned to the Foundation series that he had left in 1953. The highly anticipated *Foundation's Edge* became his first bestseller, and he followed it with a sequel to his robotic series, *The Robots of Dawn* (1983). He united the two series with *Robots and Empire* (1985) and *Foundation and Earth* (1986). He died in New York City.

Asimov is considered alongside Robert Heinlein and A. E. Van Vogt as one of the three greatest writers of science fiction in the mid-twentieth century. He was a pioneer in elevating science fiction from pulp-magazine adventure to a genre that dealt with sociology, history, mathematics, and science. He was also one of science fiction's most popular writers, a noted raconteur and wit, and an engaging public speaker. His nonfiction made complex subjects understandable and inspiring to the general reader and even inspired some to pursue a career in the sciences. In an interview with the *New York Times*, Asimov said that his talent lay in the fact that he "can read a dozen dull books and make one interesting book out of them."

• Asimov's papers are housed at Boston University. It is not surprising for a man who wrote nearly 500 books that his memoirs are the best source of biographical information; see the two-part *In Memory Yet Green* (1979) and *In Joy Still Felt* (1980), as well as *I. Asimov* (1994). The last book also contains a complete bibliography of his book-length works that runs to ten pages. He also frequently wrote about his life in his nonfiction essays. Other Asimov novels are *I, Robot*

(1950), *The Caves of Steel* (1954), and *The Naked Sun* (1957). His nonfiction books include *Asimov's Guide to the Bible* (1968, 1969) and *Asimov's Guide to Shakespeare* (1970). An obituary is in the *New York Times*, 7 Apr. 1992.

BILL PESCHEL

ASPINWALL, William (1605–?), tract writer and public figure, was born in Manchester, Lancashire, England, the son of William Aspinwall and Marie (maiden name unknown), and was christened on 10 December 1605 at Burnley. Aspinwall probably grew up in Toxeth Park near Liverpool. He entered Brasenose College at Oxford University on 2 November 1621 and graduated with a bachelor of arts degree on 25 February 1625. In 1627 he married Elizabeth Goodier or Goodyear; they had four children.

After sailing with the Winthrop fleet to New England, Aspinwall first settled at Shawmut on the Charles River, where, on 27 July 1630, he was installed as a deacon in the first Boston church. He then moved to Boston and actively participated in early Boston life. In 1635 the General Court appointed him to survey, fix boundary lands, and help distribute land to the early settlers. In 1636 and 1637 the town chose him as a selectman and in 1637 as a deputy to the General Court.

He assumed a leading role in the antinomian controversy with Anne Hutchinson. John Winthrop (1588–1649) labeled Aspinwall as the author of a petition to the General Court that supported the minister John Wheelwright, who lectured that the Holy Spirit united with the soul and revealed to the believer his or her own salvation. In this petition, Aspinwall denied the General Court's charges of sedition against Wheelwright. Confessing his involvement in the Wheelwright petition, Aspinwall disputed with the General Court, arguing the antinomian cause and claiming a right to petition. Because of his contemptuous behavior, the court dismissed him as a deputy, disenfranchised him, and banished him from the Massachusetts Bay Colony on 20 November 1637 for seditious behavior.

Although the details of his life from this time are sketchy, scraps of records reveal his involvement in the shifting political and religious disputes of the future Rhode Island. Before he left for Rhode Island, in the spring of 1638 he wrote a manuscript copy of the political covenant of Rhode Island. In Boston, he also was elected secretary of the new plantation on 7 March 1638.

Aspinwall continued his political activity in Rhode Island. However, for whatever reasons, for the next several years he disagreed with his former associates from Boston. On 13 May he was not present at the general meeting in Rhode Island. An entry in the Portsmouth meeting record of 2 February 1638 addresses his behavior: "To deale wth Wm Aspinwall Concerning his defaults." Although the exact reasons are unknown, on 7 February the authorities accused him of sedition and stopped the building of his boat. During factional disagreements in the area, Aspinwall apparently sided with Samuel Gorton and Anne and William Hutchinson at Pocasset, a group opposing William Coddington. However, in 1639, at a meeting with Boston church members, Aspinwall, now living apart from the Hutchinsons at Aquidneck, realized his mistakes in the antinomian affair, according to John Cotton. But Aspinwall continued to wander before returning to Boston. He appeared in New Haven on 2 March 1641 to testify against the accused at a trial involving a case of bestiality.

Returning to Boston, he soon achieved prominence in civic affairs. On 18 May 1642 the General Court restored him to his former status, and on 27 March he confessed his past mistakes to the Boston congregation. With other merchants, he founded in March 1644 a trading company to search for beaver pelts but was stymied when the Dutch and Swedes would not let the party proceed up the Delaware River. In 1643 and 1644 he was appointed as clerk of the writs for Boston, recorder, and public notary. He began his notarial records on 13 November 1644. He also compiled his *Book of Possessions*, a record of land and houses in Boston. Appointed by the Boston church, he participated in the Cambridge Synod of 1648.

Two legal cases led to his return to England. In a suit beginning in 1648, a ship owner charged that Aspinwall had peculated money from a ship sold to pay back wages. After much litigation, the General Court in 1653 decided that Aspinwall had acted correctly in the matter. In another case, following a suit over a gristmill, the General Court found that Aspinwall had abused his public offices when, as the court recorder, he misled the jury, tampered with evidence, and tried to stop the court proceedings against him. On 23 October 1651 the General Court suspended him from the office of recorder and clerk of the writs. The court on 19 October 1652 replaced Aspinwall with a new public notary. He left New England permanently after these events.

Aspinwall wrote religious and political pamphlets positing for England a Christian, millenarian utopia. In Boston, on 12 March 1652, he finished *Speculum Chronologicum*, an abstruse tract outlining millenarian events based on biblical and astronomical ideas. In England, he published in 1653 *A Brief Description of the Fifth Monarchy* and on 3 November 1653 *An Explication and Application of the Seventh Chapter of Daniel.* In 1654 *A Premonition of Sundry Sad Calamities Yet to Come* appeared and was reissued in 1655 as *Thunder from Heaven*. In 1655 he wrote the preface to *An Abstract of Laws and Government*, a presentation of John Cotton's legal code. He wrote in 1655 *The Work of the Age* and in 1656 *The Legislative Power Is Christ's Peculiar Prerogative*. He issued in 1657 *The Abrogation of the Jewish Sabbath*. Generally, he outlined in his Fifth Monarchy tracts the dates of a Christian utopia ruled by Christ's saints. Rather than calling for armed insurrection against the state, Aspinwall was a moderate Fifth Monarchist, advocating passivity and dreaming of a holy commonwealth in his sectarian writings. In

England Aspinwall's pamphlets were read widely enough to elicit several responses to his works.

Joining other ministers in attempting to puritanize Ireland, he served as minister at Kilcullen about 1655 but was removed with the Restoration on 7 April 1660. A letter dated 13 April 1662 by Aspinwall from Chester, England, to Boston survives. The date and place of his death are unknown.

Besides his prominence in Massachusetts Bay Colony and Rhode Island history, Aspinwall is an important early American and English writer of sectarian tracts. His tracts provide a glimpse of millenarian thinking in England and Massachusetts Bay in the mid-seventeenth century.

• Manuscripts relating to Aspinwall are in the Archives of the Commonwealth and at the Massachusetts Historical Society in Boston. His pamphlets are in the British Library in London, and his *Speculum Chronologicum* is in the Bodleian Library in Oxford. His biography and an explication of his works can be found in Stephen L. Robbins, "Manifold Afflictions: The Life and Writings of William Aspinwall, 1605–1662" (Ph.D. diss., Oklahoma State Univ., 1988).

STEPHEN L. ROBBINS

ASPINWALL, William (23 May 1743–16 Apr. 1823), physician, was born in Brookline, Massachusetts, the son of Lieutenant Thomas Aspinwall and Joanna Gardner. His loss of an eye from an archery accident in youth threatened a promising career, but earning a bachelor's degree from Harvard College in 1764 and teaching in local schools gave him courage. He resolved to study medicine in 1767 and apprenticed himself to Dr. Benjamin Gale of Killingworth, Connecticut. A year later his father underwrote expenses to attend the lectures at the Pennsylvania Hospital in Philadelphia, where he completed his medical studies in 1769.

Returning to Brookline he became the town's first resident physician and remained in active practice there for over forty years. Aspinwall's practice, compared with prescribed English remedies and techniques, was therapeutically mild. Like his counterparts in New England, he bled and purged less than the published authorities advised. He practiced midwifery but did not perform major surgery such as lithotomy or amputation. Records reveal long trips on horseback to visit patients and a well-deserved reputation as a comforting healer.

The routines of practice were broken by the battle of Lexington on 19 April 1775. That morning he joined Major Issac Gardner's company of Minutemen and soon found himself taking his commander's lifeless body back to Brookline. He first sought a military commission, but during the siege of Boston he accepted appointments as brigade surgeon and deputy director of the resistance army hospitals first in Jamaica Plain and later in Roxbury. Shortly before the end of the siege in April 1776, he returned to Brookline and soon wed Susanna Gardner, the late major's daughter. Their happy life together brought them seven children.

In March 1776, with a smallpox epidemic threatening, Aspinwall and some colleagues had developed a plan for mass inoculations at quarantine hospitals in Brookline and Cambridge. The procedure required that a healthy patient be infected with matter from lesions on a victim with active disease. He was not without some preparation for such a bold venture; his mentor, Dr. Gale, had written a practical treatise on the technique. The initial reaction of the people was hostile. Ever since the great Boston epidemic in 1721, New England's practitioners, public officials, and the general populace had known of inoculation. The treatment, introduced to America by Dr. Zabdiel Boylston and Rev. Cotton Mather in Boston, seriously threatened the community because some patients were sent home while still infectious, and the epidemic spread. Nevertheless, the procedure did produce much lower mortality levels in those inoculated. Aspinwall neutralized the opposition by erecting the quarantine hospital some distance from the town. By October 1776 the facility at Brookline housed 100 inoculated patients. With the hospital running smoothly, he returned to the medical department of the Continental army as surgeon in the Rhode Island campaign of 1778.

After the war his reputation grew, and his private practice flourished. In 1788 he opened another inoculation hospital that provided good care. In 1800 he invited Dr. Benjamin Waterhouse to demonstrate the English-derived technique of vaccination that required the use of matter from a patient with cowpox, not smallpox. The demonstrable immunity to smallpox conferred by the new and virtually risk-free procedure impressed him greatly. He abandoned inoculation and dismantled the hospital. Aspinwall's reputation and his enthusiasm for vaccination contributed to the growing acceptance of this preventive measure.

His therapeutics may have been nominal for the region, but Aspinwall was not the typical medical practitioner. He was a college graduate with both apprenticeship training and knowledge gained from formal hospital lectures. Only about one-third of the state's medical practitioners shared these educational advantages. From this group a smaller number that included Aspinwall were permitted to operate inoculation facilities. Other events placing him squarely within the profession's elite include his receiving an honorary M.D. from Harvard College in 1808 and his election to membership in the Massachusetts Medical Society in 1812.

Over the years Aspinwall served Brookline as town warden, surveyor, treasurer, representative to the legislature, justice of the peace, state senator, and member of the governor's council. A generous supporter of education, he also served on the Harvard Board of Overseers. His medical practice and community service ended abruptly only a few years after the death of his wife in 1814; a cataract operation on his remaining eye took the last of his sight. He died in Brookline.

• Using information based on a meticulous analysis of record books, J. Worth Estes discusses Aspinwall's medical practice in "Therapeutic Practice in Colonial New England," in *Medicine in Colonial Massachusetts, 1620–1820*, ed. Philip J. Cash et al. (1980). Most of Aspinwall's military environment is explored in Philip J. Cash, *Medical Men at the Siege of Boston, April, 1775–April, 1776: Problems of the Massachusetts and Continental Armies* (1973). Providing a regional context for appraising Aspinwall's training and career is Eric H. Christianson, "Medicine in New England," in *Medicine in the New World: New Spain, New France, and New England*, ed. Ronald L. Numbers (1987). The standard biographical sketch is in Clifford K. Shipton, *Sibley's Harvard Graduates*, vol. 16 (1972).

ERIC HOWARD CHRISTIANSON

ASPINWALL, William Henry (16 Dec. 1807–18 Jan. 1875), merchant, was born in New York City, the son of John Aspinwall, an importer of dry goods and a commission merchant, and Susan Howland. A member of a prominent family with strong ties to the sea, Aspinwall was schooled in New York City, where he gained fluency in Spanish and French. In 1830 he married Anna Lloyd Breck, with whom he had four children.

In 1832 Aspinwall and his cousin William Edgar Howland joined the firm of G. G. and S. Howland, importers and commission merchants who traded with the Mediterranean, the Caribbean, and Britain. The firm, established in 1816 by Aspinwall's uncles, Gardiner Greene Howland and Samuel Shaw Howland, was one of many founded after the War of 1812, a time when New York began its ascent as principal port in the United States. After learning the business, Aspinwall and William Edgar Howland assumed the daily operation of G. G. and S. Howland. The firm's name was changed to Howland & Aspinwall in 1834. In 1837 the two senior partners retired, leaving Aspinwall and his cousin in control.

The firm withstood a fire (16 Dec. 1835) that devastated New York and burned out its offices as well as the panic of 1837. By 1845 it had a fleet of vessels actively engaged in regular trade to the ports of London, Liverpool, Havana, Tampico, Callao and Valparaiso, Hong Kong, Canton, and to others in the West Indies and East Indies, South America, the Mediterranean, Europe, and China. Aspinwall's role as vice consul for the Grand Duchy of Tuscany probably aided the company as did a friendship with President José Antonio Paez of Venezuela. Paez granted Howland and Aspinwall an exclusive right to trade with Venezuela.

Aspinwall, despite a conservative demeanor, was a risk-taker when it came to business. He convinced his directors to undertake the construction of a radical new ship designed by John W. Griffiths. Named *Rainbow*, the vessel embodied the clipper form with extremely sharp lines forward and a heavy rig with six courses of sail on the masts and a low freeboard. Launched in January 1845, *Rainbow* promptly set a new record for a round trip to China and netted twice its cost in profits on the maiden voyage. The firm built another clipper, *Sea Witch*, which in 1849 set an unsurpassed record for a sailing vessel of seventy-nine days from China to New York. Howland and Aspinwall's success with their clippers inspired others, paving the way for over a decade of clipper ship domination of the American deepwater trade.

Aspinwall's second risky venture was his purchase in November 1847 of a contract to carry mail between Panama, San Francisco, and Oregon by steamship. Authorized and subsidized by Congress, the mail contract required that three steamers carry the U.S. mail from Panama to the Pacific Coast, commencing in October 1848. In April 1848 Aspinwall chartered a new company, the Pacific Mail Steamship Company, with himself as president, and with he and Howland acting as the new firm's agents. Three steamships were built for the company—*California*, *Panama*, and *Oregon*. The Mexican War had resulted in the American acquisition of much of the Pacific Coast, and on 6 October 1848, just weeks before the peace treaty was signed with Mexico, the *California* departed for the Pacific.

The steamer sailed with only seven passengers, despite reports that gold had been discovered in California. By the time *California* reached Panama in mid-January 1849, some 1,500 would-be passengers awaited the steamer and passage to San Francisco. The California gold rush had begun, and the Pacific Mail's steamers were swept into the rush. The overcrowded fleet of three steamers was augmented by others that were chartered, purchased, and then built for the Pacific Mail. Aspinwall's potential folly reaped a fortune.

By 1851 the Pacific Mail boasted a fleet of nine steamers and had negotiated a deal to merge with its competitor on the Atlantic, the United States Mail Steamship Company. Aspinwall now presided over a company that linked both coasts. The Panama route blossomed with Aspinwall's steamers and, beginning in 1848, with his establishment of the Panama Railroad Company. The narrow isthmus of Panama was crossed by steamer passengers and others who took mules and canoes across jungle streams, rivers, and mountains to reach the Pacific. To rectify this, and to speed up the transit of passengers, mail, baggage, and specie, Aspinwall lobbied Congress and the government of New Grenada for favorable concessions for a railroad across the isthmus.

Work to build the railroad began in May 1850 and continued for five years. On 28 January 1855, just hours after the last track was laid, the first locomotive rolled into Panama City. The 65-mile span of track, from sea to sea, was the first transcontinental railroad in the Americas. Firmly commanding American transcoastal trade, both the Panama Railroad and the Pacific Mail prospered; by 1869, when the transcontinental railroad linked both coasts of the United States, more than 596,000 people and over $710 million in gold had crossed the Panama route. Aspinwall had become one of the nation's richest men; in its first seven years of operation, the railroad alone netted about $6 million in profits.

Aspinwall began to withdraw from business as early as 1850, when he retired as an active partner in Howland & Aspinwall, turning the company's operations over to his younger brother, John Lloyd Aspinwall. Aspinwall retired from both the Panama Railroad and the Pacific Mail in 1856, although he continued to sit as a director on the boards of several companies and organizations in which he had been a principal.

A staunch Unionist, Aspinwall helped found the Union League Club in New York in 1863, supported the establishment of the Sanitary Commission, and regularly consulted with and advised the government. In 1863 Secretary of the Treasury Salmon P. Chase and Secretary of the Navy Gideon Welles sent Aspinwall and John M. Forbes of Boston on a secret mission to Great Britain. Entrusted with a million pounds sterling, Aspinwall was ordered to buy any cruisers or ironclads then being built for Confederate use by a sympathetic Britain. The two men scouted British shipyards and sent a detailed report back to Washington but were unable to stop any ships from passing into Confederate hands.

After the Civil War, Aspinwall devoted more of his time to philanthropic pursuits. He helped found the Society for the Prevention of Cruelty to Animals in 1866, the Metropolitan Museum of Art in 1869, and in 1870 the Lenox Library, which would later merge with other institutions to form the New York Public Library. Entertaining at "Rockwood," his Hudson River estate in Tarrytown, and occasional travel also occupied his time.

Aspinwall died in New York City. His obituary in the *New York Times* praised him as "a modest, retiring, liberal gentleman, with as reputation for probity and honour second to none in the business community." His legacies included the Panama Railroad, which continues to operate, and the Pacific Mail, which when it ceased operations in 1942 was one of the nation's longest-lasting steamship lines. The eastern terminus of the railroad, named Aspinwall in his honor and today known as Colón, remains the Caribbean entrance to the Panama Canal.

• Most of Aspinwall's business papers were destroyed. Some of the records of the Pacific Mail Steamship Company are in the Henry E. Huntington Library, San Marino, Calif., and a letter book of Aspinwall's containing correspondence largely between him, Samuel Comstock, and Alfred Robinson pertaining to the company's business is in the Bancroft Library, University of California, Berkeley, where it is identified as the Robinson Letterbook. There is one biography, Duncan S. Somerville, *The Aspinwall Empire* (1983). See also John Haskell Kemble, *The Panama Route: 1848–1869* (1943). The railroad's story is told in Fessenden N. Otis, *Illustrated History of the Panama Railroad* (1861; repr. 1971).

JAMES P. DELGADO

ASTAIRE, Adele (10 Sept. 1898–25 Jan. 1981), musical theater dancer, was born Adele Marie Austerlitz in Omaha, Nebraska, the daughter of Frederick Austerlitz, a brewer from Vienna, and Ann Geilus. As children, Adele and her younger brother, Fred Astaire, showed promise as entertainers, performing in local amateur theatricals. Around 1904 their parents took them to New York where they studied at the the Metropolitan Ballet School and the Claude Alvienne School of Dance. They also trained with Ned Wayburn, a well-known director and choreographer, who groomed them as a juvenile vaudeville act. Because of Gerry Society restrictions (for the protection of youth), the team was forced to perform outside New York until they came of age professionally. From 1906 through 1916 Adele and Fred danced in cities on the Keith-Orpheum circuit in Wayburn-produced vaudeville acts. They essayed a variety of skits, including one in which they imitated "adult life," usually accompanied by exhibition ballroom numbers such as the "Tongo Dance" and the "Picture Waltz." Critics embraced this new, lively duo.

Adult success came swiftly. After a successful tour on the Orpheum circuit, they were spotted by the Shubert brothers, who engaged them for their first Broadway revue, *Over the Top* (1917). The up-and-coming team appeared in another Shubert revue, *The Passing Show of 1918*, but it was in the Charles Dillingham production of *Apple Blossoms* in 1919 (with music by violinist Fritz Kreisler) that they scored their first hit. Adele and Fred drew on their eclectic training in ballet, exhibition ballroom, and eccentric dance to perform a combination of athletic numbers with interpolated ballroom routines. The *New York Evening Post* noted: "Adele and Fred Astaire in eccentric dancing were graceful in the extreme even in seemingly . . . impossible stunts."

Throughout the twenties the Astaires appeared in a succession of musical comedies that brought them acclaim in the United States and abroad. In 1922 they were featured in *For Goodness Sake*, with music by George Gershwin; and in the 1922 musical comedy, *The Bunch and Judy*, composed by Jerome Kern, they provided the principal romantic interest. The following year, *For Goodness Sake* was transported to London where it reopened as *Stop Flirting*, and the Astaires became the darlings of British high society. The London production ran for one and a half years.

During their heyday Adele and Fred became associated with several well-known composers and lyricists, such as George and Ira Gershwin in 1924's *Lady, Be Good!* The musical comedy provided numerous comic turns for them and augmented their status to that of musical theater stars. Their stylish delivery and dancing captured the ebullience and wit of the Gershwins' lyrics and songs. The show is also remembered for Adele's solo rendition of "Fascinating Rhythm." In 1927 the Astaires once again were featured performers in the George Gershwin musical *Funny Face*, prompting Brooks Atkinson of the *New York Times* to note: "They have not only humor but intelligence; not only spirit but good taste; not only poise but modesty; and they are not only expert eccentric dancers but they never make an ungraceful movement."

Adele's final performances were in the highly celebrated 1931 musical revue *The Band Wagon*, by George S. Kaufman and Howard Dietz, with music by Arthur Schwartz. The production boasted spectacular dance numbers and featured Adele and Fred performing atop a revolving stage. Adele once again received accolades for her comic abilities, particularly her "hoops" number, in which she and her brother, impersonating unruly French children, roll hoops in a park and perform other antics.

In 1932 Adele retired from the stage and married Lord Charles Cavendish, the second son of the ninth Duke of Devonshire. She lived in Lismore Castle in County Waterford, Ireland. Although she remained relatively secluded, she made some fleeting forays back into show business, including a program of songs for an RCA radio broadcast in 1936. She also accepted an invitation to appear with the British stage and screen actor Jack Buchanan in a light, comedic film directed by René Clair.

Adele's retirement years were marked by several tragedies. In 1933 her first child died at birth, and in 1935 she gave birth to premature twins who also died. In 1944 her husband died after a protracted illness. She remarried in 1947, to Kingman Douglass, an investment broker and former assistant director of the U.S. Central Intelligence Agency. While her retirement from the stage disappointed her many followers, her place in musical theater history was secure. She died in Phoenix, Arizona. As Fred Astaire said of his sister, "She was a great artist and inimitable."

• For her life and career, see the Adele Astaire clipping file and the Fred and Adele Astaire clipping file at the Billy Rose Theatre Collection of the New York Public Library for the Performing Arts at Lincoln Center. For programs, reviews, and other memorabilia, consult the Fred and Adele Astaire scrapbook in the same collection. In addition, see Ray Harper, "Funny Feet," *Dance Magazine*, 28 Apr. 1928; Hugh Leamy, "The Ascending Astaires," *Collier's*, 31 Mar. 1928; and Isaac Goldberg, "The Astaires: Early, Late, and All the Way Between," *Boston Transcript*, 23 Jan. 1922. Notable reviews include Percy Hammond, "The Theaters" (review of *The Bunch and Judy*), *New York Tribune*, 29 Nov. 1922; Heywood Broun, "At the Globe Theatre, *The Bunch and Judy*," *New York World*, 29 Nov. 1922; "Mr. Hornblow Goes to the Play" (review of *Lady, Be Good!*), *Theatre Magazine*, Feb. 1925; Brooks Atkinson, "The Play" (review of *Funny Face*), *New York Times*, 23 Nov. 1927, and Wilella Waldorf, "The Play" (review of *The Band Wagon*), *New York Evening Post*, 4 June 1931. Obituaries appear in the *New York Times*, 26 Jan. 1981; *Variety*, 28 Jan. 1981; and *Dancing Times*, Apr. 1981.

JULIE MALNIG

ASTAIRE, Fred (10 May 1899–22 June 1987), dancer, film star, and choreographer, was born in Omaha, Nebraska, the son of Frederick Austerlitz, an immigrant Austrian brewery employee, and Ann Geilus. Astaire's sister, Adele, showed unusual talent in early dancing school recitals and was taken to New York in 1904 by her mother for professional training. Her brother, younger by a year and a half, was enrolled in dancing school with her. In 1906, when Fred was only seven, the two children began performing successfully in vaudeville.

In a few years they outgrew their material and could no longer get bookings. For two years they stayed out of show business, attending regular school sessions in Highwood Park, New Jersey. But they soon returned to vaudeville, and with the advice of vaudeville dancer Aurelio Coccia, whom Astaire considered the most influential person in his dancing career, they developed a show-stopping act. By their last season in vaudeville, still in their mid-teens, they had become featured performers earning $350 a week.

In 1917 they moved up to the musical stage. From then until 1932 they appeared in ten musical productions on Broadway and in London. A few flops were among these, but most were hugely successful, particularly two musical comedies with songs by George Gershwin and Ira Gershwin (*Lady, Be Good!* in 1924 and *Funny Face* in 1927) and a revue with songs by Arthur Schwartz and Howard Dietz (*The Band Wagon* in 1931). Astaire tended to be self-effacing around his talented sister, whom he adored, but his own gifts did not go unnoticed.

As his stage career progressed, Astaire became increasingly involved with the choreography for the routines. Beginning with *Lady, Be Good!*, he performed solo numbers, which he mostly devised himself.

When his sister retired from show business in 1932 to marry a British aristocrat, Astaire sought to reshape his career. He performed the lead role in *Gay Divorce*, a "musical play" with songs by Cole Porter. The show was important not only because it proved that Astaire could flourish without his sister, but because it helped establish the pattern of most of his coming film musicals: a light, unsentimental comedy, largely uncluttered by subplot, built around a love story for Astaire and his partner (in this case, dancer Claire Luce) that was airy and amusing, but essentially serious—particularly when the pair danced together. To the show's hit song, "Night and Day," he fashioned his first great romantic duet. However, he never saw himself as a true romantic lead and had an antipathy to "mushy" dialogue.

In 1933 Astaire married Phyllis Livingston Potter, who came from one of Boston's most aristocratic families and who had never seen him on the stage. They had two children.

Shortly after his marriage, Astaire ventured to Hollywood. He worked a few days at MGM where he had a dancing bit in *Dancing Lady* (1933), and then, over at the financially shaky RKO, where he was under contract, he was fifth-billed in the exuberant, fluttery *Flying Down to Rio* (1933), in which he mostly repeated the juvenile characterization he had used on Broadway. *Flying Down to Rio* was a hit, and it was obvious that Astaire's performance was a major reason for its success. The most perceptive trumpeting of his potential came in a *Variety* review: "He's assuredly a bet after this one, for he's distinctly likeable on the screen, the mike is kind to his voice and as a dancer he remains in a class by himself" (26 Dec. 1933). To Hollywood, the message was clear: the thin, balding, self-conscious, romantically unimpressive tap dancer from New York was a moneymaker.

Joining him was Ginger Rogers, a contract player at RKO, who had performed opposite him in *Flying Down to Rio* as comedy foil more than anything else. *The Gay Divorcee* (1934), a film version of *Gay Divorce*, was the first of the Astaire-Rogers pictures, and it scored even better than *Flying Down to Rio*. Although Astaire had reservations about being tied into another partnership, the new team was an almost overnight success.

Roberta (1935) followed, firmly establishing Astaire and Rogers as king and queen of the RKO lot. Moreover, in this film they reached their full development as a team—the breathless high spirits, the emotional richness, the bubbling sense of comedy, the romantic compatibility are all there. Six more films followed to make them one of the legendary partnerships in the history of dance: *Top Hat* (1935), *Follow the Fleet* (1936), *Swing Time* (1936), *Shall We Dance* (1937), *Carefree* (1938), and *The Story of Vernon and Irene Castle* (1939). For these films Astaire created a series of romantic and playful duets as well as an array of dazzling and imaginative solos for himself. Although the films' plot lines sometimes lurch improbably, Astaire was concerned from the beginning with giving his numbers a motivation in the script. Playing off the feisty, yet arrestingly vulnerable Rogers, his screen persona developed more depth, sexual definition and security, and, eventually, maturity.

Astaire was in an excellent bargaining position, both creatively and financially. The directors of his films were instructed to give him complete freedom on the dances and as much rehearsal time as he wanted, and he had little difficulty convincing the studio powers to accept his requests for higher fees.

Astaire's lone effort without Rogers during this period, *A Damsel in Distress* (1937), was his first film to lose money. By the end of the 1930s the revenues of his films with Rogers were also beginning to fall. After a disagreement over fees with the studio, Astaire left, dissolving his partnership with Rogers for the time being.

The next years were nomadic ones for Astaire. He wandered from studio to studio, appeared with a variety of partners, and prospered both financially and artistically. Between 1940 and 1946 he made three films at MGM, two at Columbia, three at Paramount, and one back at RKO: *Broadway Melody of 1940* (1940) with Eleanor Powell, *Second Chorus* (1941) with Paulette Goddard, *You'll Never Get Rich* (1941) and *You Were Never Lovelier* (1942) with Rita Hayworth, *Holiday Inn* (1942) with Virginia Dale and Bing Crosby, *The Sky's the Limit* (1943) with Joan Leslie, *Yolanda and the Thief* (1945) and *Ziegfeld Follies* (1945–1946) with Lucille Bremer, and *Blue Skies* (1946) with Joan Caulfield and Crosby.

All of these films are comedies, and the first few mostly seek to emulate the zany insouciance of the pictures with Rogers. But other approaches are tried. *The Sky's the Limit* is a dark comedy about the impact of World War II on life and love. *Ziegfeld Follies* presents a sumptuous (if sometimes overcalculated) opulence, and most of its numbers have an arrestingly hard edge.

By 1946 Astaire had decided to retire from motion pictures. His films had created a boom in the dancing school business, and at his wife's urging and in response to many letters he hoped to cash in by establishing his own chain of schools. The venture proved successful but only after considerable difficulty.

In 1947 he returned to the movies. Of the ten Astaire films released between 1948 and 1957, seven were made at MGM, and six of these were produced by Arthur Freed, the dominant figure in Hollywood musicals in that era.

Easter Parade (1948), with Judy Garland, was a major hit. Because of Garland's illness, she was replaced in Astaire's next film, *The Barkleys of Broadway* (1949), by Rogers. Most of Astaire's other partners in these later musicals were ballet-trained: Vera-Ellen in *Three Little Words* (1950) and *The Belle of New York* (1952), Cyd Charisse in *The Band Wagon* (1953) and *Silk Stockings* (1957), Leslie Caron in *Daddy Long Legs* (1955), and Audrey Hepburn in *Funny Face* (1957). For variety, there was Jane Powell, a singer-actress, in *Royal Wedding* (1951), and Betty Hutton, a bombastic comedienne, in *Let's Dance* (1950).

This period was marked by a personal tragedy for Astaire. In 1954 his wife died from cancer at the age of forty-six.

By the late 1950s the era of the classic Hollywood musical as Astaire had experienced it—indeed, defined it—was coming to an end. Revenues were declining, costs were rising, the studio system was becoming superseded, competition with television was growing, and popular music had entered the age of rock-and-roll. Undaunted, Astaire moved into other fields. He was highly successful in television, where he appeared on many shows as host or performer and where he produced four carefully crafted, award-winning musical specials from 1958 through 1968. His partner in them was Barrie Chase, a limber young dancer who had appeared briefly in two of his films in the 1950s.

In 1968 Astaire appeared in one more musical film, as the gnarled, dotty title character in *Finian's Rainbow*. In the 1970s he helped host two MGM compilation films called *That's Entertainment* to salute the studio's by-then vanished golden age of musicals. He also explored other fields. Shattering Hollywood tradition, he wrote his autobiography himself (in longhand). And he tried his hand at straight acting roles with considerable success. In films he played a misanthropic scientist in *On the Beach* (1959), a debonair playboy in *The Pleasure of His Company* (1961), a diplomat in *The Notorious Landlady* (1962), a British secret agent in *The Midas Run* (1969), con men in *The Towering Inferno* (1975) and *The Amazing Dobermans* (1976), a country doctor in *The Purple Taxi* (1977), and a conscience-stricken murderer in *Ghost Story* (1982). On television he played a number of characters, usually suave ones, in dramatic specials and series.

As he entered his eighties, Astaire, a lifelong thoroughbred horse racing enthusiast, romanced Robyn Smith, a successful, 37-year-old jockey who had not seen him in films. They were married in 1980. Astaire died in Beverly Hills, California.

During his long performing career Astaire achieved admiring recognition not only from his peers in the entertainment world but from major figures in ballet and modern dance such as Serge Diaghilev, George Balanchine, Margot Fonteyn, Merce Cunningham, and Mikhail Baryshnikov. In quantity and especially in quality Astaire's contribution is unrivaled in films and, indeed, has few parallels in the history of dance. And, since he worked mainly in film, Astaire is that great rarity: a master choreographer the vast majority of whose works are precisely preserved.

Although the creation of many of Astaire's dances involved a degree of collaboration with another choreographer, dance director, or dance assistant—the most important of whom was Hermes Pan—the guiding creative hand and the final authority on his solos and duets was Astaire himself. His choreography is notable for its inventiveness, wit, musicality, and economy. Each dance characteristically takes two or three central ideas that might derive from a step, the music, the lyric, his partner's qualities, or a plot situation and carefully presents and develops them.

A perfectionist who was obsessed with not repeating himself, Astaire spent weeks working out his choreography. His courtesy, professionalism, and tireless struggle for improvement earned him the devoted admiration of his co-workers. From the start Astaire focused his attention on the problems and prospects in the filming of dance, and he soon settled on an approach that he was to follow throughout his career and one that dominated Hollywood musicals for a generation: both camerawork and editing are fashioned to enhance the flow and continuity of the dances, not to undercut or overshadow them.

Astaire made an impact in many ways. He helped enormously to define and develop a film genre, he brought out the best in some of the era's leading composers and lyricists, he influenced a generation of filmmakers and choreographers, and he inspired many people to take up dance. He also activated the fancies and fantasies of millions in his audiences, and he will continue to do so as long as films are shown.

• Astaire's autobiography is *Steps in Time* (1959). Books focusing on his dancing, effect, and choreography are Arlene Croce, *The Fred Astaire & Ginger Rogers Book* (1972), and John Mueller, *Astaire Dancing: The Musical Films* (1985), which includes an extensive bibliography and filmography. See also Bill Davidson, *The Real and the Unreal* (1961); Stanley Green, *Starring Fred Astaire* (1973); and Stephen Harvey, *Fred Astaire* (1975). For a lively commentary on Astaire by his sister, see Adele Astaire, "He Worries, Poor Boy," *Variety*, 18 Mar. 1936. Useful interviews with Astaire are found in Morton Eustis, *Players at Work* (1937) and *Inter/View*, June 1973. An obituary is in the *New York Times*, 23 June 1987.

JOHN MUELLER

ASTOR, Caroline (22 Sept. 1830–30 Oct. 1908), society leader, was born Caroline Webster Schermerhorn in New York City, the daughter of Abraham Schermerhorn, a wealthy co-owner of a ship chandlery firm, and Helen White. Related to many prominent New York City families, Caroline grew up proud of her aristocratic background and social standing. After finishing her education in Europe, she married William Backhouse Astor, a son of one of America's richest families, in 1853. The couple had five children.

Following the Civil War a financial boom produced a market for industrial stocks and created many millionaires who flocked to New York City, where the greatest stock exchange was located. Caroline Astor believed that money alone did not determine one's place in society and saw the nouveau riche as people who would degrade the high standards that the well-bred had maintained for generations. In the early 1870s, as her four daughters were about to debut in society, Astor initiated preparations to have them introduced to the most prominent and established families. Although Astor was a capable organizer, she employed Ward McAllister following their meeting in 1872. McAllister circulated among New York's elite and was noted for his ideas on producing successful functions. Together the pair held balls and parties at which the invited guests, all of whom came from the highest echelon of society, were approved by Astor and McAllister. Astor soon became society's leader, a position she retained for decades.

The first social occasions were called subscription parties, and Astor's ball held every January at her mansion on Fifth Avenue created the greatest sensation. Her guest list was limited to four hundred people, the number that fit into her ballroom. By the end of the decade a regular column appeared in the *New York Journal* titled "Mrs. Astor's 400." Astor earned the nicknames "The Queen" and "Mystic Rose," and McAllister became known as her "Prime Minister."

Requirements for invited guests were wealth, a family history that included three generations of Americans, and the social graces. At the ball Astor alone greeted her guests as she stood beneath a portrait of herself. She sat on a red damask divan called her "throne" that could accommodate six other women. Many people aspired to be invited to the ball, which eased their way into English society and gave them access to British titles.

During an era known as the "Gilded Age," Caroline Astor and "The Four Hundred" epitomized society life. Dressing in extravagant gowns dotted with pearls and diamonds and wearing a fortune in jewels, including a diamond stomacher and a large tiara, Astor became the icon of style, and millions of American women wanted to copy her clothing. The garment industry began to imitate and mass-produce her dresses seen in newspapers and copied onto woodcuts. High-button shoes became fashionable, as did gloves, parasols, and feathered hats.

Astor set the tone for society and carefully scripted its movements. In winter she traveled to Europe, in summer she stayed in Newport, Rhode Island, and during the first week of October she returned to Manhattan. Twice a week she attended the opera, a practice previously considered snobbish. All turned out to watch "Mrs. Astor" arrive late, receive visitors in her box during the second intermission, and leave before the end of the performance. Other social gatherings included frequent receptions, teas, and dinner parties at her home where lavish oil paintings adorned the walls, crystal candelabras and Tiffany lamps bathed the rooms in light, and Oriental rugs graced the parlors. Those with lesser means purchased look-alike Oriental rugs from Belgium, Sears, Roebuck sold dining-room furniture that resembled hers, and her wallpaper patterns were copied and sold to the public. Clothes and home furnishings were labeled "The Fifth Avenue Set" and "The Society Set." Astor was an example of social grace, good manners, and attention to personal conduct and practices that encouraged proper etiquette and cleanliness for many Americans.

Astor's husband was absent from most of her social functions. He spent only a few weeks at home and much of the rest of the time on his yacht, but she never complained or said a harsh word about him. She had only praise for him, as was proper deportment for a wife in a well-mannered society. However, when her daughter Charlotte divorced in 1896 after being caught in an adulterous relationship, Caroline Astor stood by her daughter. Astor's stance helped to bring acceptance of divorce not only to the upper strata of society but to others as well.

In the early 1890s the mansion on Fifth Avenue was torn down to make way for a hotel, and Astor built a new palatial home overlooking Central Park. As the decade passed, both her husband and McAllister died. Astor's influence started to wane as other families surpassed the Astor wealth, and a new breed of society leaders gained recognition. By the turn of the century her prominence gave way to a host of other women establishing positions for themselves. Astor's last January ball was held in 1905. The next year a fall confined her to a wheelchair, and she canceled the ball. She lived in near seclusion until her death at her home in New York City.

Often criticized by the newspapers for her lavish displays, Astor never defended her position or lost her temper because a lady shrank from "notoriety." Said to be kind and reserved, she always remained loyal to friends. A contributor to many charities, particularly New York hospitals, Astor also encouraged other leading members of society to endorse the building of museums and galleries. She supported efforts to bring about reform in sweatshops but never promoted public speaking for women to voice these views. Described as "maternal" and "matriarchal," Caroline Astor helped change some of society's crude behavior by creating standards for the cultured rich. In doing so she unknowingly set an example for millions of less fortunate Americans who copied the styles and traditions of the wealthy.

• Details of Astor's life are in Ward McAllister, *Society as I Have Found It* (1890); R. Burnham Moffat, *The Barclays of New York* (1904); Richard Schermerhorn, Jr., *Schermerhorn Genealogy and Family Chronicles* (1914); Elizabeth Eliot, *Heiresses and Coronets: The Story of Lovely Ladies and Noble Men* (1959); Kate Simon, *Fifth Avenue: A Very Social History* (1978); Virginia Cowles, *The Astors* (1979); Stephen Longstreet, *The Queen Bees: The Women Who Shaped America* (1979); W. A. Swanberg, *Whitney Father, Whitney Heiress* (1980); John D. Gates, *The Astor Family* (1981); Stephen Birmingham, *The Grandes Dames* (1982); David Sinclair, *Dynasty: The Astors and Their Times* (1984); Clarice Stasz, *The Vanderbilt Women: Dynasty of Wealth, Glamour, and Tragedy* (1991); and Derek Wilson, *The Astors, 1763–1992: Landscape with Millionaires* (1993). Issues of *Town Topics* between 1885 and 1895 followed society events; see also the *New York Evening Post*, 13 July 1901. Obituaries appear in the *New York World*, 30 and 31 Oct. and 3 Nov. 1908, and in the *New York Times*, 30 and 31 Oct. 1908.

MARILYN ELIZABETH PERRY

ASTOR, John Jacob (17 July 1763–29 Mar. 1848), fur trader and financier, was born in Waldorf, duchy of Baden, Germany, the son of Jacob Astor, a butcher, and Maria Magdalena Vorfelder, who died when John was about three. His family was of the artisan class, and few records survive from his youth. Due in large part to a fine town schoolmaster, Astor's education seems to have been better than average. It ended at age thirteen with his confirmation in the Lutheran church. At an age when many contemporaries became apprentices, Astor spent two years as an assistant in his father's butcher shop but had little interest in learning the business.

When Astor decided to leave Waldorf in 1779, his primary options were to join brothers in either London or America. With the latter area consumed in revolution, he chose London, where his eldest brother, George, made musical instruments. John joined him in that pursuit. Soon after the Treaty of Paris ending the American Revolution was signed in 1783, Astor decided to journey to the United States, both to renew contact with his brother Henry and to scout the market potential for musical instruments. With several of these and some sheet music he boarded the *North Carolina* in November 1783 and reached the Chesapeake Bay two months later. Less than a day from port, the vessel froze in the bay and did not reach Baltimore until 24 or 25 March. By mid-April Astor arrived in New York City.

Astor saw the instruments as a way to raise capital for the business in which he was more interested—fur trading. He apparently already had the idea before he left London, and it crystalized during conversations with a German-American trader during the Atlantic passage. Achieving some success implementing his plans, he sailed for London in June or July 1784 with furs. There he made arrangements with a fur merchant, and also with a leading piano manufacturer, then returned to New York at the end of the year. He married Sarah Todd, with whom he had eight children, in September 1785 and set up an instrument importing business in a building owned by his mother-in-law. It is probable that his wife ran the music shop, as Astor was soon heavily involved in fur trading.

Among his first business contacts were New York merchants Robert Bowne and William Backhouse. Some accounts state that Astor worked for Bowne, but it is more likely that Bowne and Backhouse simply provided Astor the opportunity to sell his furs through their establishments. He began making buying trips to the vicinity of Albany, a regional fur trade outlet, and in 1787 journeyed to Montreal, the center of fur trading in North America, where he rented a warehouse and began making agreements with traders.

The logistics of exporting furs from Montreal were not simple, as British law prohibited direct trade between Canada and the United States. Furs had to be shipped to London and then New York, or transported overland while risking seizure by the British. Astor employed both methods, with an increasing reliance on overland transport as he built a network of agents along the routes. By the early 1790s Astor had established himself as the leading American fur trader in both the Montreal and London markets, a reputation that led the Montreal-based North West Company to send its furs through Astor's New York operation when it attempted to circumvent the all-trade-through-London requirement for Canadian firms by shipping directly to China in 1792–1794. With several middlemen like Astor involved in the shipments, the North West Company lost money on the venture, but Astor profited handsomely, especially on the sale of return cargoes such as teas and silk, and became convinced of the potential of the Chinese market.

Astor expanded his operations slowly and cautiously, in a manner similar to methods employed by tycoons later in the nineteenth century. "Tho desirous to make some business," he wrote an agent, "I am equally so to avoid risks—some I know must be run, but let [them] be as little as possible" (Haeger, p. 148). Astor did not incur the expense of enlisting and equipping his own fur suppliers but instead cultivated relationships with many different suppliers and companies, allowing him to obtain his choice of furs at the best prices. As the Jay Treaty (1794) and the European wars opened more ports to American shipping, Astor traveled to England and Continental Europe in 1795–1796 and established contacts with merchants willing to purchase his furs or sell them on commission. At home his primary customers remained hat and clothing manufacturers.

In 1796–1797 Astor began to cultivate the China market. Employing his usual cautious approach, he first bought space on ships, later expanding to become the primary backer of voyages. About 1803 he purchased the first vessels for his own fleet. In addition to furs, which could be sold at twice the U.S. value, most expeditions carried large quantities of ginseng, which brought six times the U.S. price in Canton. The proceeds were invested in the extremely profitable return cargoes of teas, silk, and nankeen.

From the beginning of his American business enterprises, Astor invested his profits in real estate, buying his first tract in New York City in 1789. From 1800 to 1848 it is estimated that he spent over $2 million in land deals, acquiring both urban and agricultural properties. By the 1820s he was collecting more than $100,000 a year in rent payments. Banks, canals, railroads, and numerous public bond issues also attracted Astor's money, and he regularly made loans to finance housing and hotel construction, often on his property.

By 1807 Astor was a millionaire and firmly established as the leading U.S. fur trader, but he was not satisfied with the many remaining limitations to his operations. He complained to New York Mayor De-Witt Clinton in early 1908 that "we are obliged to draw 34 of our furs for home consumption from Canada I suppose annually to an amount of $400,000" (Haeger, p. 100). To begin rectifying the imbalance, Astor proposed to exploit the route charted through the Louisiana Purchase to the Pacific by Meriwether Lewis and William Clark, allowing furs to be shipped from the Pacific Northwest. With Clinton's support he secured a charter from the New York legislature in April 1808 for the American Fur Company, under whose auspices Astor implemented his quest for a shipping base on the Pacific. He also sought backing from the federal government, contacting his friend Albert Gallatin, who was treasury secretary, and President Thomas Jefferson. (Astor also befriended James Monroe, Henry Clay, and John C. Calhoun, among many others, at times providing loans for some of his political allies, including Monroe and Clay.)

After months of planning, two Astor-backed expeditions departed for the mouth of the Columbia River in mid-1810, one overland from Montreal, and another sailing aboard the *Tonquin* from New York. For two years Astor heard nothing of either party. In the meantime he continued negotiations with the two leading Canadian fur firms, the North West Company and the Michilimackinac Company, in an attempt to avoid conflict and direct competition at a West Coast port. In January 1811 he signed an agreement with them, forming the South West Company and eliciting the word of the Canadian firms that they would not continue procurement in the United States except through Astor's company. Soon thereafter the *Tonquin* reached the mouth of the Columbia, where its passengers established the settlement of Astoria in March 1911. The *Tonquin* sailed inland and never returned, reportedly blowing up during a fight with Native Americans. The starving remnants of the overland expedition staggered into Astoria during the first two months of 1812.

Astor, meanwhile, had been informed by friends in the government that war with the British was imminent, and he was desperately trying to get furs he had already purchased out of Canada. His dealings with Canadians did not cease when the conflict began, though, as he managed to export $250,000 in furs during 1812–1813. During the latter year Gallatin called on Astor to mobilize East Coast capitalists to help raise $10 million in government bonds. Astor invested heavily in these, and when military reverses in 1814 caused a drop in their prices, he became a major proponent for the reestablishment of a national bank in order to help protect his investment.

He also sought military support for another venture—Astoria. In March 1813 Astor received word that the North West Company was sending a ship outfitted with troops to take the outpost. That September an overland expedition from the same company, supported by British soldiers, reached the encampment. After peaceful negotiations, the agent in charge of Astoria turned the settlement and its furs and provisions over to the North West Company for $58,290. Astor, who failed to convince officials in Washington to send a force to protect his investment, lamented that "in peace we should have done well, [but] in war we can do nothing" (Haeger, p. 160). He tried to get government support after the war for forcibly retaking the settlement, but with no success. In the 1830s he hired his friend Washington Irving to write a history of the venture.

The War of 1812 had cut off the China trade, but as the conflict drew to a close in 1815, Astor put his fleet of eight ships back into operation. Soon his vessels were making regular stops in China, Europe, Latin America, and Hawaii and along the American Pacific Coast. Astor continually studied world markets, shifting emphases as prices rose and fell. By 1827 he decided that it would be more cost-effective for him to sell his ships. He also ended regular trade with China during that period.

Soon after the war Astor gave up on the idea of an outlet for furs on the Pacific Coast and concentrated his efforts on the Great Lakes region. Contrary to many reports, the American Fur Company never held a monopoly in any area. Astor did prefer to reach agreements with established companies as American Fur moved into new territories, however, as he felt heated competition was detrimental to all. When Canadian firms were forced to scale back operations in U.S. territory in the late 1810s, Astor purchased many of their posts, including the facilities on Mackinac Island, which became the center of his Great Lakes operations. He cautiously moved into the highly competitive St. Louis–Missouri River region, and through a series of deals with area companies, he was firmly established there by the early 1820s.

In the postwar period Astor also became involved with the second Bank of the United States (BUS), which was created in April 1816. Astor was chosen for the board of directors by James Madison, and he was named president of the New York branch and put in charge of organizing it. Astor and fellow board member Stephen Girard argued that the BUS should follow a fiscally conservative plan, but they were outvoted by a contingent of Baltimore capitalists whose liberal loan and interest rate policies led to rapid inflation and ultimately a depression in 1819.

By that time Astor was no longer heavily involved with the BUS, or in the everyday operations of his company. The drowning death of seven-year-old grandson John Jacob Bentzon in February 1818 sent Astor into deep depression, or "Low Spirits" as he described it, and in 1819 he turned the fur company over to his partners and son William and sailed for Europe with daughter Eliza and mentally ill son John. He lived and traveled on the Continent for the next fifteen years, purchasing a home on the shores of Lake Geneva in 1824. Despite his detachment, Astor received regular reports on his businesses and continued to make the major decisions, returning to the United States periodically to finalize deals.

In 1834 Astor decided to move back to the United States and to sell the company. Furs were no longer as profitable, for a variety of reasons. Machines were allowing manufacturers to make clothes for much less than they could be produced from furs. Western expansion brought greater competition for American Fur in the Rocky Mountains and the Far West and deprived it of the cheap labor of Native-American fur traders, whose tribes ceded their lands and relocated to reservations. Soon after his arrival in New York in April 1834, Astor completed the two-part deal that transferred the northern part of his operation to a syndicate headed by longtime partner Ramsay Crooks (who borrowed the majority of the money for the purchase from Astor), and the western part to St. Louis–based Pratte, Chouteau, and Company, which had been working in that area in cooperation with American Fur since 1826.

Astor already had another major project to occupy his attention, as the hotel that had been conceived in 1831 began to rise in 1834. Astor House (originally Park Hotel), which cost over $400,000, opened in New York in 1836 and quickly became the nation's most famous hotel. Not all of Astor's endeavors bore fruit, however, as his financing and name were not enough to make the settlement of Astor a success. Begun in 1835, it was combined with another township three years later to form Green Bay, Wisconsin.

Astor's death, in New York City, received extensive press coverage, as many believed that he was the richest man in the United States. The exaggerated accounts placed his net worth at $20 million, at least twice the actual amount. At the time many criticized him for not leaving a large bequest to philanthropic causes, although $400,000 went toward the completion of his last major project, the Astor Library, which opened in 1854 (its resources became a substantial part of the consolidated New York Public Library in 1895).

Although he did not transform the way business was conducted, Astor was one of the most proficient practitioners of the craft that his era produced. Through shrewd evalution of the world marketplace, an efficiently organized and run company, and aggressive exploitation of any opportunity with which he was presented, he rose from humble origins to become the most prominent businessman of his age.

• There are collections of Astor's papers at Baker Library, Harvard University; Beinecke Library, Yale University; New York Public Library; Historical Society of Pennsylvania, Philadelphia; New-York Historical Society, New York City; and Missouri Historical Society, St. Louis. American Fur Company papers are also collected at several repositories, with the most substantial set at Clarke Historical Library, Central Michigan University, Mount Pleasant. Kenneth W. Porter, *John Jacob Astor: Business Man* (2 vols., 1931), is a detailed biography and prints nearly 400 pages of documents, including Astor's will. John D. Haeger, *Business and Finance in the Early Republic* (1991), places Astor in the context of his times and includes a bibliography and a discussion of earlier works on him. Also of note is Washington Irving, *Astoria; or, Anecdotes of an Enterprise Beyond the Rocky Mountains* (1836), which Astor commissioned.

KENNETH H. WILLIAMS

ASTOR, John Jacob, III (10 June 1822–22 Feb. 1890), capitalist and philanthropist, was born in New York City, the son of William Backhouse Astor and Margaret Rebecca Armstrong. The family was noted for great wealth and public charity. Astor graduated from Columbia College in 1839, and after studying at the University of Göttingen for a short time and traveling through Europe he earned a law degree at Harvard in 1842. He practiced briefly as an attorney specializing in commercial transactions and then entered his father's burgeoning real estate office. In 1846 Astor married the socially prominent Charlotte Augusta Gibbes of South Carolina. They had one child, William Waldorf Astor, who eventually became a naturalized British citizen, a member of Parliament, and the first Viscount Astor.

In contrast to his father, who supported the Democrats prior to the Civil War because of the family's economic ties to the South, Astor backed the Republicans in 1860. When the Civil War broke out he became a volunteer aide-de-camp with the rank of colonel on Major General George B. McClellan's (1826–1885) staff, where he served in the Peninsula Campaign to capture Richmond. On July 11, 1862, shortly after the climactic battle at Seven Pines, he resigned his commission and lashed out at what he called Secretary of War Edwin M. Stanton's deliberate interference in McClellan's strategy. Even so, Astor remembered his military experience as the happiest time of his life. He remained loyal to McClellan, supported and bankrolled his presidential candidacy in 1864, and became his benefactor when he left the military, helping to purchase for him a four-story brick house in New York City and seeking to have him named president of the New Jersey Railroad.

After leaving the army, Astor returned to the family's real estate business. When his father died in 1875, Astor and his brother, William Backhouse Astor, Jr., inherited equal shares of his fortune, estimated at about $20 million each. As the eldest son, Astor took over his father's position as the head of the Astor family estate, which included the administration, purchase, and construction of office buildings, hotels, private homes, warehouses, and tenements. In addition, Astor was a trustee or director of the Union Trust Company, the Western Union Telegraph Company, the Farmers' Loan and Trust Company, and a major stockholder in numerous New York banks. Over the next fifteen years, he bought a great deal of prime New York real estate, seldom selling any of it. He parlayed his inherited fortune into one that contemporary newspapers guessed was worth between $75 million and $100 million.

Tall, slender, and aristocratic, Astor was a man of towering contradictions. To critics, he seemed vain, imperious, conceited, pompous, parsimonious, hypocritical, and the classic slum landlord. A man of limited social sympathies who grew even richer by exploiting the poor in an era when municipal authorities rarely enforced building codes, Astor owned scandalously ramshackle tenements. He constructed new ones out of flimsy material and rarely improved the inadequate living conditions of those he purchased. Astor habitually protected his property by relying on political influence. He was on good terms with prominent Tammany Hall leaders. His relationship with "Boss" William M. Tweed, however, proved embarrassing. In 1871, shortly before revelations about Tweed's corruption made his name synonymous with municipal thievery, Astor joined five other prominent businessmen in inspecting the ledgers of Comptroller Richard B. Connolly, one of Tweed's close associates, and pronounced them honest and above suspicion.

Supporters drew a more favorable picture of Astor. They argued that he had a high sense of social responsibility and religious obligation. Both he and his wife gave large sums to charitable institutions such as the Children's Aid Society, the New York Cancer Society, and the Metropolitan Museum of Art. Astor also was for years a vestryman at Trinity Church and a large contributor to its building and maintenance funds. Even more, he carried on his family's commitment to the Astor Library, founded by the first John Jacob Astor (1763–1848). He deeded the library three city lots, built an addition costing $250,000, and left the library $400,000 in his will.

Astor was secure enough to ignore his critics. Unlike his brother's wife, the gregarious Caroline Schermerhorn Astor, who sought to make herself the social arbiter of New York society, Astor avoided ostentation. However, he and his wife spent lavish sums on quiet entertainments, furniture, books, paintings, and vacations in Newport, Rhode Island, and in Europe. Astor imported a French chef and became a noted connoisseur of vintage wines and cigars. He died in New York City.

• Although Astor left no personal papers, relevant material may be found in contemporary newspapers. There are some useful studies of the Astor family. Three in particular provide glimpses of his career: Virginia Cowles, *The Astors* (1979); Lucy Kavaler, *The Astors: An American Legend* (1968); and Harvey O'Connor, *The Astors* (1941). See also Ward McAllister, *Society as I have Found It* (1890); Lloyd Morris, *Incredible New York* (1951); and Gustavus Myers, *The History of the Great American Fortunes* (1910). A short obituary is in the *New York Times*, 23 Feb. 1890.

JEROME MUSHKAT

ASTOR, John Jacob, IV (13 July 1864–15 Apr. 1912), businessman, was born at "Ferncliff," his father's estate at Rinebeck-on-Hudson, New York, the son of William Backhouse Astor, Jr., and Caroline Webster Schermerhorn. As the great-grandson and namesake of fur trade magnate John Jacob Astor, he grew up in a household that possessed both enormous wealth and social prominence. After completing his secondary education at St. Paul's School in Concord, New Hampshire, Astor entered Harvard College. He graduated with a B.S. in 1888 and spent the following two years traveling throughout Europe and South America. Upon returning to the United States, Astor assumed the management of his family's New York City real estate holdings and married Ava Lowle Willing of Philadelphia in 1891. They had two children.

Astor's great-grandfather, having created the family fortune through his activities in the fur trapping and shipping industries, solidified his holdings through a long series of real estate investments in the New York City area. He assiduously followed a policy of buying cheap raw land and then holding on to it as its value rose in response to the expansion of the city; as a result the family's wealth grew to enormous proportions. Much of the Astor land was subsequently rented out to subcontractors who built poorly constructed and badly overcrowded tenement buildings. Despite often horrific conditions, there was no shortage of prospective tenants among New York's immigrants. Following family tradition, Astor ignored conditions within his properties and focused on the financial management of his varied holdings. He not only maintained profitability among existing Astor properties but created new properties that proved equally remunerative. He built a number of apartment and office buildings, including the Schermerhorn building, the Putnam building, the Apthorpe apartments, and the Exchange Court. His first love, however, was hotels: he built the St. Regis and Knickerbocker hotels in 1904 and 1906, respectively, but the highlight of his career was building the Astoria section of the Waldorf-Astoria Hotel in 1897. In addition to managing the family properties, Astor served on the boards of numerous outside firms as well, including the Illinois Central Railroad, the Morton Trust Company, Western Union Telegraph Company, Niagara Falls Power Company, the Delaware and Hudson Railroad, and the New York Life Insurance Company.

Although successful in business, Astor never gained a total sense of fulfillment from his work. Hence, he dabbled in a variety of outside activities with widely varying results. He tried his hand at literature, producing the little-noticed *Journey in Other Worlds*, a science-fiction novel, in 1894. Astor also devoted considerable attention to mechanical inventions. His efforts resulted in a new type of brake for solid-tired bicycles, a "Pneumatic Road Improver" that removed dirt from road surfaces (and won first prize at Chicago's World Columbian Exhibition in 1893), and suction cups for ocean liner deck chairs that prevented sliding in rough weather. He also patented a marine turbine engine but disobeyed a traditional Astor edict—"never give something away for free"—when he assigned the patent to the public.

Astor's most notable contribution came in the field of military activity. Urged by sense of duty (possibly mixed with boredom), he served on the staff of New York governor Levi P. Morton from 1895 to 1896. With the outbreak of the Spanish-American War in 1898, Astor seized the opportunity for additional service. He immediately placed his sumptuous yacht *Nourmahal* (Light of the Harem) at the service of the Navy Department and also contributed $100,000 toward the outfitting of an artillery battery, which subsequently saw service in the Philippines. Volunteering for duty himself, Astor gained a commission as a lieutenant-colonel. Following a stint as army camp inspector at Camp Chickamauga in Tennessee under Major General Joseph C. Breckinridge, he later joined the staff of Major General William R. Shafter. Under Shafter's command Astor took part in the landing of American forces at Santiago and saw additional combat during the fighting at El Paso Hill. At the close of the war he received a brevet promotion to the rank of colonel and a commendation "for faithful and meritorious service."

Never happy in his first marriage, which ended in divorce in November 1909, Astor subsequently married Madeline Talmadge Force of New York City in Newport, Rhode Island, in 1911. Following a trip to Europe, the couple (expecting their first child together) booked return passage on the newly launched *Titanic*. Madeline Astor escaped the sinking ship in a lifeboat and gave birth to a son some time later. Astor died the night of the disaster, and his body was later recovered with $2,500 in his pockets. In the terms of his will he violated yet another Astor precept—that of leaving estates to grandchildren—by leaving the bulk of his wealth to his son from his first marriage, Vincent Astor, in fee simple. This act greatly facilitated the later transference of Astor wealth from real estate to stock holdings.

Although widely mourned, Astor did not earn the place in history suggested by the laudatory attributes given at the time of his death. In the heart of the Progressive Era he refused to ameliorate or even acknowledge the often horrific conditions under which tenants on Astor-owned land were forced to live. Nevertheless, he does deserve credit for the successful maintenance of his family's wealth, as well as for the foresight and drive that created the original Waldorf-Astoria Hotel.

• The papers of the Astor family are held at the New-York Historical Society. The best secondary sources on Astor's life and career are two books by Lucy Kavaler, *The Astors: A Family Chronicle of Pomp and Power* (1966) and *Astors: An American Legend* (1968). See also Derek A. Wilson, *The Astors, 1763–1992: Landscape with Millionaires* (1993). Obituaries are in the *New York Times*, 16 Apr. 1912, and the *New York Sun*, 17 Apr. 1912.

EDWARD L. LACH, JR.

ASTOR, Mary (3 May 1906–25 Sept. 1987), actress, was born Lucile Vasconcellos Langhanke in Quincy, Illinois, the daughter of Otto Ludwig Wilhelm Langhanke and Helen Vasconcellos, both teachers. Astor was the product—and she considered herself just that—of an ambitious German immigrant father who had worked at teaching, chicken farming, and window dressing with varying degrees of success before getting what Astor would later call the "Great Idea." "My father decided I should become an actress," she wrote, "and my father had never been wrong."

Astor attended the Kenwood-Loring School for Girls in Illinois and later received her high school diploma through the Horace Mann correspondence course. At age eleven she sent her picture to a "Fame and Fortune" beauty contest. After she was a runner-up in the contest for two years in a row, the family moved to New York, lured by a mass film test of fifty "Fame and Fortune" contestants. Astor did not win the contest but made an important contact in photographer Charles Albin. He saw a "Madonna" quality in the girl and in 1920 asked her to model for him. Among Albin's portrait clients was actress Lillian Gish, who saw Albin's photographs of Astor and arranged for a screen test with her boss, director D. W. Griffith. The test came to nothing after Griffith met Astor's overbearing father, whom he labeled a "walking cash register." Months later in 1920, however, Famous Players–Lasky gave her a contract and a new name. "Mary Astor," part Madonna, part blueblood, was credited to the triumvirate of Jesse Lasky, Louella Parsons, and Walter Wanger. When her contract ended after six months, Astor had performed in (and been edited out of) *Sentimental Tommy* and had had a small part in *Bullets or Ballots*, an unreleased propaganda film.

Her break came in a two-reel silent art film called *The Beggar Maid* (1921). The film was called "a little gem" by one critic, and the exposure led to six more two-reelers and then, in 1922, to the feature *John Smith*. After completing ten films in the next two years, she was cast opposite John Barrymore in *Beau Brummel* (1924). Barrymore, a married actor nearly a quarter-century older than she was, soon became her acting coach and secret lover. Barrymore wanted Astor to play Lady Anne in his London production of *Richard III*, but her father, who had grown comfortable on the $2,500 a week his daughter earned, turned the offer down, calling it "impractical." By 1926, when Barrymore made *Don Juan* with Astor, their personal relationship had ended.

In 1927 Astor played a princess in the Oscar-winning comedy *Two Arabian Knights*. The next year brought her first "bad girl" role, in *Dressed to Kill*, and marriage to film director Kenneth Hawks. Later in 1928, as part of a contract negotiation, she took a Movietone sound test to judge the suitability of her voice for talking pictures. The test, she wrote, was "indescribably bad." Her voice was called hollow, dark, and almost masculine. The studio offered to renew her contract with a 50 percent salary cut. Her father turned down the offer, and she received no others. After ten months and no film work, she took a part in a Los Angeles stage production of *Among the Married*. The uniformly good reviews were responsible for five different film offers within a week. Her first talking picture was *Ladies Love Brutes* (1930), followed by films such as *Holiday* (1930) and the classic *Red Dust* (1932), opposite Clark Gable and Jean Harlow.

While she played supporting parts in most of her 1930s films, her private life made her a tabloid star. In 1931 Kenneth Hawks was killed in an airplane crash while filming a movie. The couple had no children. Later that year Astor married her doctor, Franklyn Thorpe, and in 1932 they had a daughter. At age twenty-six, Astor was supporting five people and still giving the lion's share of her earnings to her parents. Between 1920 and 1930 she made $485,000, of which her parents kept $461,000. In 1934, at the urging of her husband, she put them on an allowance, and they sued her for nonsupport. She agreed to pay them $100 a month, and the suit was dropped. Astor divorced Thorpe the same year, giving him custody of their daughter as well as a settlement of $60,000. In 1936 she sued Thorpe for custody of their child, a move that led to one of the biggest Hollywood scandals up to that time. Thorpe produced a diary Astor had written in purple ink (she claimed the color was "Aztec Brown"), which he alleged detailed sexual adventures with a number of Hollywood leading men and included "box scores" of their abilities. Printed excerpts from the diary, which Astor later claimed were forgeries, detailed her relationship with playwright George S. Kaufman, christened "Public Lover Number One" by the press. Astor admitted the affair on the stand, but the diary, having been tampered with by Thorpe, was inadmissible in court. Judge Goodwin Knight impounded the diary, and sixteen years later it was burned. Astor was awarded custody of their daughter for nine months of each year.

Just months after the trial, one of Astor's best films was released. *Dodsworth*, based on Sinclair Lewis's novel, starred Walter Huston. Astor played Edith Cortright, the widow Dodsworth comes to after he is abandoned by his wife. In addition to good reviews, Astor was actually cheered by some of the film's audiences. Her career unscathed, Astor continued to freelance and appeared in films such as *The Prisoner of Zenda* (1937); *The Hurricane* (1937), codirected by John Ford; *Midnight* (1939), with Claudette Colbert, Don Ameche, and John Barrymore; and *Brigham Young, Frontiersman* (1940). In 1941 she starred with Bette Davis in *The Great Lie*. She played Sandra, a bitchy concert pianist described by director Edmund Goulding as a woman who loved "a piano, brandy and men—in that order." She won the best supporting actress Oscar for the role. Her next film was the classic *The Maltese Falcon* (1941), with Humphrey Bogart. Astor was not director/writer John Huston's first choice to play Dashiell Hammett's amoral heroine Brigid O'Shaunnessy. After Geraldine Fitzgerald turned down the part, Astor stepped in, with memorable results. Bosley Crowther of the *New York Times* called her "well nigh perfect as the beautiful woman whose cupidity is forever to be suspect."

As her film career soared, Astor moonlighted in radio, hosting the Hollywood Showcase, and, during World War II, recruiting WAVES (women to serve in the navy). She volunteered with the Red Cross, and as a licensed pilot, she joined the Civil Air Patrol. In 1944 she signed a contract with MGM and soon settled into a string of "mother" roles. Between 1944 and 1949 she parented stars such as Judy Garland and Elizabeth Taylor in films such as *Meet Me in St. Louis*, *Cynthia*, and *Little Women*. In 1949, bored and ill, she ended her contract, left MGM, and spent time in a sanitarium for alcoholics.

By 1952 Astor was working again, in the road company of *The Time of the Cuckoo*. She went to Broadway with the short-lived *The Starcross Story* and toured with the second company of *Don Juan in Hell*. She also performed in a number of television plays. In 1959 she published *My Story*, her bestselling autobiography that she had written as part of a course of psychotherapy. The book discussed Astor's love affairs, four marriages (her marriage in 1937 with Del Campo, which produced a son, ended in 1942; a 1945 marriage to businessman Thomas Wheelock lasted until 1955), alcoholism, illnesses, and rumored suicide attempt. A year later Astor published *The Incredible Charlie Carewe*, which the *New York Herald Tribune* called "an exceptional first novel." *The Image of Kate* was released in 1962 to mixed reviews. Other fictional works included *The O'Connors* (1964), *Goodbye Darling, Be Happy* (1965), and *A Place Called Saturday* (1969).

Astor's film work dwindled in the 1960s. In 1964 she took a final cameo role in the southern Gothic film *Hush, Hush Sweet Charlotte*, starring her *Great Lie* costar, Bette Davis. After 109 features she turned in her actors' union cards and retired to Mexico to write. In 1971 she completed a second volume of memoirs, *A Life on Film*. The *New York Times Book Review* called it "stimulating, disillusioned and caustic, dealing courageously with a largely wasted career." Astor herself wrote, "I was never totally involved in movies. I was making someone else's dream come true."

In 1974 she retired to the Motion Picture Country Home in Woodland Hills, California, where she died.

• Mary Astor provided fairly comprehensive documentation of both her personal and professional lives in her autobiographies. Other sources are Scott Siegel, *The Encyclopedia of Hollywood* (1990); Ephraim Katz, *The Film Encyclopedia* (1994); David Thompson, *A Biographical Dictionary of Film* (1994); *Current Biography* 1961; and *Contemporary Authors*, new rev. ser., vol. 3 (1981). Obituaries are in the *Los Angeles Times* and the *New York Times*, 26 Sept. 1987.

DIANA MOORE

ASTOR, William Waldorf (31 Mar. 1848–18 Oct. 1919), businessman and philanthropist, was born in New York City, the son of John Jacob Astor, a businessman, and Charlotte Gibbes. Astor received his education at home under private tutors and studied law at Columbia University. He worked at law for a short while but found his first real calling in Republican politics. He served a term as a New York State assemblyman beginning in 1877, and two years later he was elected to the state senate. Twice he ran for the U.S. House of Representatives, but he was defeated each time. The press and his political enemies found Astor's inherited wealth an easy target for excoriation, and the public humiliation he suffered at their hands was the first step on the path toward his alienation from everything American. By all accounts Astor was extremely sensitive and simply could not endure criticism. Nor did he find satisfaction in his 1878 marriage to Mary Dahlgren Paul, although the union produced four children. The marriage suffered as shy Mary Astor was forced into a contest with her husband's Aunt Caroline for the position of most important society matron in New York's upper crust—the famous "Four Hundred Families." In addition, the Astors were concerned for the safety of their children, whom they feared might become victims of a kidnapping for ransom.

In 1882 President Chester Arthur rewarded Astor's service to the Republican party with an appointment as minister to Italy. During the three years he was there, he added to his art collection and cultivated a growing love for European culture. Astor also began to write fiction while in Italy, an activity he continued until 1900. His works include *Valentino: An Historical Romance of the Sixteenth Century in Italy* (1885), *Sforza: A Story of Milan* (1889), and *Pharaoh's Daughter and Other Stories* (1900). His favorite subjects for study were said to be Napoleon Bonaparte and Cesare Borgia.

Astor's father died in 1890, and he spent a few desultory months trying to administer the estate that left him the richest man in America. The press that had discredited Astor the politician continued to vilify Astor the businessman and philanthropist, and by September 1890, William Astor had had enough. Leaving his business interests in the hands of an administrator and bequeathing the Waldorf section of what would be the Waldorf-Astoria hotel as his one legacy to America, Astor took his family to England, where he spent the rest of his life. Newspapers of the day quoted Astor as saying "America is not a fit place for a gentleman to live."

Once in England, Astor occupied his time with several pursuits. He first tried publishing, buying several newspapers—the *Pall Mall Gazette*, *The Budget*, and *The Observer*—and a periodical called the *Pall Mall Magazine*. He remained interested in publishing for only a short time, seldom going into the offices and contributing only occasional, usually anti-American, editorials. In 1915 he disposed of all these holdings after years of neglect.

Astor was far more interested in being accepted as an equal by the British upper class than in working, and he began acquiring large estates, London houses, and all the other trappings of British high society. He even educated his sons at Eton and Oxford. Wealth and ostentation, along with participation in the activities that highbrow society thought important, were his guarantee of acceptance. In 1894 Astor achieved British citizenship, and in 1916 he became a peer—Baron Astor of Hever Castle. In 1917 he was made a viscount. But he never was quite able to let go of his concern for what Americans thought of him, even though he had turned his back on the United States. One of the most bizarre episodes in his life occurred in 1892, when Astor sent false reports of his death to American newspapers in hopes of finding out what the United States thought of him as he was eulogized by the press. The ruse was discovered before any paper printed the story, and Astor found himself left with a not undeserved reputation for peculiarity.

Having achieved all he wanted in England, Astor retured to his estates and London houses in quiet seclusion. He was a widower during his last few years, and by all accounts he became increasingly eccentric. Paranoid about security, he booby-trapped his house with dozens of odd contrivances to repel intruders. He kept loaded pistols in his bed stand, allowed almost no visitors unless he expressly invited them, and marked out his life by a rigid schedule, allowing a prescribed amount of time for each activity. Astor died alone in his Brighton house.

Looking at the life of William Waldorf Astor is difficult because the real man is all but hidden beneath the trappings of wealth and the peculiarities of his own personality. He seems a caricature of the upper-class dilettante with inherited wealth who could never find an identity or a purpose of his own. Perhaps his tragedy is that his life so closely mirrored the stereotype.

• There is no single repository for papers and publications concerning the life of William Waldorf Astor. Most of the available information is in the newspapers and periodicals of his time, particularly obituaries from *The Times* (London), *New York Times*, *New York World*, and *New York Sun*, all published on 20 Oct. 1919. Two histories of the Astor family, Lucy Kavaler, *The Astors: A Family Chronicle of Pomp and Power* (1966), and Virginia Cowles, *The Astors* (1979), offer the reader material from interviews with family members, as well as historical data, family trees, and photographs.

BONNIE MARIE SYKES

ASTWOOD, Edwin Bennett (29 Dec. 1909–17 Feb. 1976), physiologist and endocrinologist, was born in Hamilton, Bermuda, the son of Earnest Millard Astwood, a jeweler, watchmaker, and optometrist, and Imogene Doe. Astwood spent his childhood and received his early education in Bermuda, where his family had a longstanding business interest. Because of his family's religious ties, Astwood was sent to Washington Missionary College in Ohio. Deciding to study medicine after receiving his college degree in 1929, Astwood attended the Medical College of Evangelists at Loma Linda University in Loma Linda, California.

Two years of conflict between his family and their religious ideas and a desire for personal freedom made Astwood leave Loma Linda and complete his medical education at McGill University in Montreal, Quebec, Canada, from which he received an M.D. and a C.M. in 1934. He spent the next year as house officer at the Royal Victoria Hospital in Montreal, where his interest in science was stimulated by a talented group of investigators: J. S. L. Browne, Eleanor Venning, and Hans Selye. Astwood then obtained a position in surgical pathology at the Johns Hopkins Surgical Pathology Laboratory and worked with Charles Geschicter from 1935 until 1937, when he received a Rockefeller Fellowship and was accepted for graduate study in biology at Harvard University. There he worked with Professor Frederick L. Hisaw, a pioneer in endocrinological research. In 1937 Astwood had married Sarah Ruth Merritt, a nurse at Johns Hopkins; they had two children.

After obtaining his Ph.D. from Harvard in 1939, Astwood returned to Johns Hopkins and worked with GeorgeAnna Seegar Jones in obstetrics. Astwood's work resulted in an improved method for measuring pregnandiol in urine as well as describing a third gonadotropin, which he named luteotropin (later shown to be prolactin). In 1941 Soma Weiss lured Astwood back to Boston by offering him a joint appointment as associate in medicine at the Peter Bent Brigham Hospital and assistant professor of pharmacology in Otto Krayer's department at the Harvard Medical School. In 1945 Astwood accepted a position at Tufts University School of Medicine and the New England Medical Center. Here Astwood was given the opportunity to establish one of the world's most eminent endocrine research laboratories. Astwood was promoted to professor of medicine at Tufts University School of Medicine in 1952.

Astwood's first important scientific contribution was the discovery that pituitary extracts induced a pigment change in the fish *Phoxinus laevis*, and that the active factor causing the pigment change was intermedin, a substance previously discovered by Bernard Zondek and H. Krohn. Astwood furthered the knowledge of this subtance by showing that it was the same factor present in the blood of patients with advanced malignant melanomas. At about this time Astwood and Geschicter began a study of the hormonal control of the mammary gland, which demonstrated that removal of the hypophysis resulted in regression of breast tissue growth while administration of the pituitary growth hormone produced a breast characteristic of pregnancy. Their studies on uterine weight demonstrated that weight changes were due to retention of water and normal cell growth, which were enhanced by administration of progesterone and suppressed by testosterone. Astwood's investigation of the question of whether the placenta excreted a factor necessary for maintaining pregnancy resulted in the discovery that the placenta secreted a luteal-stimulating factor that differed from any known gonadotropin. Astwood also contributed to the development of the contraceptive pill by following up the work of A. W. Makepeace, George Weinstein, and Maurice Friedman. Astwood's experiment showed that injecting immature rats simultaneously with progesterone and follicle-stimulating hormone for ten days prevented luteinization, whereas with omission of progesterone, luteinization occurred after the fourth day of administration of follicle-stimulating hormone. This confirmed that progesterone prevented the release of luteinizing hormone from the pituitary.

Astwood's work on thyroid physiology revolutionized the treatment of thyroid disease. While at Johns Hopkins, Astwood learned that two compounds, sulfaguanidine (used to inhibit bacterial growth in the intestine) and phenylthiourea (a rat poison), caused thyroid hypertrophy. Through a series of exhaustive studies, Astwood and his group demonstrated that these compounds inhibited thyroid hormone synthesis by interfering with the binding of iodine in the thyroid. This inability to bind iodine decreased the circulating thyroid hormone concentration, which, through negative feedback, stimulated the pituitary to release thyrotropin, which stimulated thyroid hypertrophy. Astwood's discovery of the antithyroid compounds resulted in the introduction of thyrouracil and propylthyrouracil for the clinical treatment of thyrotoxicosis, a medical treatment that replaced the more dangerous surgical management.

When radioisotopes became available after World War II, Astwood mastered their use and developed more accurate methods for assaying thyroid function that not only became significant clinically but also yielded a better understanding of the thyroid. Astwood reintroduced the use of thyroxine to treat nontoxic "simple" goiter and single thyroid nodules (those not the result of iodine deficiency), another medical treatment that reduced the necessity for surgical intervention. Astwood and R. Tyslowitz made another important contribution in 1940, when they found that corticotropin (ACTH) could be extracted from pituitary extracts by hot glacial acetic acid and purified fortyfold by chromatography with oxycellulose. This led to the purification of corticotropin and the determination of its structure.

Astwood retired in 1972 as senior physician at the New England Medical Center. He returned to Bermuda, where he spent the remainder of his life. He died in Hamilton, Bermuda.

• There is no known collection of Astwood's papers. A biographical account is Roy O. Greep and Mont A. Greer, National Academy of Sciences, *Biographical Memoirs* 55 (1985): 2–42.

DAVID Y. COOPER

ATCHISON, David Rice (11 Aug. 1807–26 Jan. 1886), lawyer and U.S. senator, was born in Frogtown, in the Bluegrass region of Kentucky, the son of William Atchison and Catherine Allen, farmers. Educated at Transylvania University, he studied law and was admitted to the bar in 1827. After practicing for three years in Carlisle, Kentucky, he moved to Liberty in western Missouri.

Shortly thereafter, Atchison was retained by ousted Mormons to assist them in regaining their lost homes and property in Jackson County. Unsuccessful in this, he assisted them in resettling in Clay County, where they helped elect him to the state legislature in the fall of 1834. When renewed difficulties between the Mormons and their neighbors led to full-scale warfare in western Missouri in 1838, Atchison found himself in the uncomfortable position of being the Mormons' lawyer while also serving as militia commander. He sought unsuccessfully to mediate but the Mormons were driven from the state under orders from Governor Lillburn W. Boggs.

The general assembly created the Twelfth Judicial Circuit from the Platte Purchase acquired in 1837, and Atchison was appointed its first judge in 1841. Following the death of U.S. Senator Lewis F. Linn two years later, Atchison was chosen to fill the position. He was reelected without difficulty in 1849. In the Senate, Atchison long held the chairmanship of the Committee on Indian Affairs. With many of his constituents from western Missouri going west to Oregon, he strongly supported protection for them along the Oregon Trail and the extension of United States jurisdiction over the region. When the final Oregon treaty was presented to the Senate in June 1846, he voted against it, not wishing to compromise at the forty-ninth parallel.

First elected president pro tempore of the Senate in August 1846, Atchison received that honor from his colleagues sixteen times in eight years. This placed him next in line for the presidency behind the vice president and gave him considerable power in the appointment of Senate committees. Some have asserted that Atchison became president of the United States for one day when 4 March 1849 fell on Sunday and President-elect Zachary Taylor refused to take the oath of office until the following day. Atchison later joked about the matter, claiming that he had slept throughout his term because the Senate had not adjourned until the early morning hours of 4 March.

In the controversies over slavery following the Mexican War, Atchison increasingly allied himself with John C. Calhoun and the southern ultras, thereby reflecting the views of his western Missouri constituency where slavery was strongly entrenched. When his colleague Senator Thomas Hart Benton (1782–1858) refused to take a stand against the Free Soil movement, Atchison helped engineer "Old Bullion's" reelection defeat in 1850 in a move that left the Missouri Democratic party bitterly divided over the issue of slavery extension.

With the death of Vice President William R. King early in the Franklin Pierce administration, Atchison's position as president pro tempore became increasingly important. Forming a strong alliance with several other prominent southern senators who occupied key Senate committee chairmanships, he played a significant behind-the-scenes role in securing President Pierce's support for the repeal of the Missouri Compromise as a part of the Kansas-Nebraska Act of 1854, thus allowing his proslavery Missouri River constituency equal access to the new territories.

Over the next three years Atchison worked diligently to secure the new Kansas Territory for slavery. He toured the South appealing for immigrants with some success, and the proslavery town of Atchison in northeastern Kansas was named for him. He organized groups of western Missourians, known as the "border ruffians," to cross into the territory and influence territorial elections at the ballot box, claiming that the Kansas-Nebraska Act had made no provision for a residency requirement for voting. These forays resulted in the election of a proslavery territorial legislature and a proslavery delegate to Congress. They were denounced by Free State leaders, who organized a separate legislature, and open warfare quickly broke out on the Kansas plains. It reached its climax when Atchison and other proslavery leaders led a raid on the Free State town of Lawrence on 21 May 1856, which led to a retaliation by John Brown (1800–1859) against proslavery settlers at Pottawatomie Creek three days later.

The continued split in the Missouri Democratic party cost Atchison his Senate seat in 1855 as a badly divided legislature could not reach agreement, and the seat remained vacant for two years. Atchison did not participate in the Lecompton constitution imbroglio over Kansas's admission as a slave state, but retired to his farm in Clinton County, Missouri, in 1857. When the Civil War broke out, he supported the pro-Confederate government of Governor Claiborne Fox Jackson, which was driven into exile by the Union military. He accompanied Jackson to Richmond where they secured the promise of aid from Atchison's longtime friend and former Senate colleague, Jefferson Davis. Atchison was present at the battle of Pea Ridge, Arkansas, in March 1862 but thereafter withdrew to Texas where he remained until the end of the war. He returned to his Clinton County farm in 1867 where he lived quietly until his death. Atchison never married.

• There is a small collection of Atchison papers in the Western Historical Manuscripts Collection at the University of Missouri–Columbia. William E. Parrish, *David Rice Atchison: Border Politician* (1961), is the only biography. Atchison's view of his presumed presidency for one day is discussed in Walter B. Stevens, "A Day and Night with 'Old Davy': David R. Atchison," *Missouri Historical Review* 31 (Jan. 1937): 129–39.

WILLIAM E. PARRISH

ATHERTON, Charles Gordon (4 July 1804–15 Nov. 1853), U.S. representative and senator, was born in Amherst, Hillsborough County, New Hampshire, the son of Charles Humphrey Atherton, a politician and lawyer, and Mary Ann Toppan. Atherton graduated in 1822 from Harvard College, where he received a classical education, and he then studied law under the tutelage of his father, a former Federalist politician and one of the most distinguished attorneys in the state. The bar admitted Atherton in 1825, and he established practice in Dunstable (now Nashua). He continued to practice law for the rest of his life. He married Ann (Nancy) Barnard Clark in 1828; they had no children.

It is not clear when Atherton first became involved in politics, but by 1829 he had joined the Democratic party. Although loosely allied with Senator Levi Woodbury in his patronage dispute with party cofounder Isaac Hill (part of a larger controversy between Martin Van Buren, whom Hill supported, and John C. Calhoun, whom Woodbury favored), Atherton remained in good graces with most party officials. In 1830 Atherton became Hillsborough County's representative on the party's state central committee, and Dunstable elected him to the state house of representatives. Afterward, he held the clerkship of the state senate for two years. Elected again as a representative in 1833, he served four consecutive annual terms, the last three of those as Speaker of the state house.

In 1837 Atherton won election to the U.S. House of Representatives, where he remained until 1843. In 1838 he introduced the so-called "gag rule"—the annual resolution by which the House tabled, automatically and without debate, petitions relating to the abolition of slavery in the District of Columbia. The following year New Hampshire's legislature endorsed Atherton's view when it adopted, by a party vote in which nearly all Democrats voted in the affirmative, a resolution that maintained that the gag rule did not violate the right of petition. Atherton supported Van Buren's proposal creating the independent treasury system, whereby the federal government accepted payments only in specie or bank notes backed by specie reserves, and he voted against the Whig economic package of a national bank, high protective tariffs, and the distribution of the proceeds of land sales to the state. Atherton's support of an inactive federal government matched the ideological propensities of the Democratic party in New Hampshire, which in the late 1830s and early 1840s opposed both the chartering of any business corporations (including banks) and the granting of eminent domain powers to prospective railroad companies.

In 1843 the legislature elected Atherton to the U.S. Senate, where he supported the annexation of Texas, the Mexican War, and President James K. Polk's economic program of low tariffs and an independent treasury. As a senator, Atherton served on the Roads and Canals, Finance, and Printing committees, chairing the latter in the Twenty-ninth Congress. Atherton supported, though he had earlier advised against, the ouster of Congressman John P. Hale from the state party when Hale refused to support the annexation of Texas. Abolitionists and Free Soil politicians considered Atherton a "doughface" because of his opposition to abolitionism.

In 1846 Atherton first opposed and then in 1847 reluctantly supported the party's position in favor of the Wilmot Proviso, the amendment to an army appropriations bill that prohibited slavery in any territories gained from Mexico. In 1848 he favored the doctrine of popular sovereignty, which prescribed that the settlers of territories decide for themselves the status of slavery therein. Although Democrats endorsed popular sovereignty in the presidential election, the following year northern Democrats again took a position favorable to the proviso, and Atherton's earlier lack of enthusiasm for it helped defeat his efforts to win a second term as senator.

In 1850 Atherton served as a delegate to a convention that revised the state constitution by eliminating the property qualification for holding office. After Democrats rallied in support of the sectional compromise measures of 1850, which incorporated the principle of popular sovereignty in the Utah and New Mexico territories, Atherton's political fortunes fully revived. He was a delegate to the Democratic National Convention that nominated his friend Franklin Pierce for president, and in November 1852, with Pierce's endorsement, the Democratic-controlled legislature chose Atherton to replace Hale as senator. Yet as president, Pierce would never have the benefit of Atherton's counsel. While preparing for a case in a Manchester, New Hampshire, courthouse on 10 November 1853 (less than one month before the beginning of the Thirty-third Congress), Atherton suffered a paralytic seizure and died there five days later. He was buried in Nashua Cemetery in Nashua.

• Small collections of the Charles Gordon Atherton Papers are in the New Hampshire Historical Society (Concord) and in the American Antiquarian Society (Worcester, Mass.), most of which deal with political matters. Atherton's role in New Hampshire politics can be gleaned from Roy F. Nichols, *Franklin Pierce: Young Hickory of the Granite Hills* (1931); Donald B. Cole, *Jacksonian Democracy in New Hampshire, 1800–1851* (1970); and Charles H. Bell, *The Bench and Bar of New Hampshire* (1894). On Atherton's death, see "Obituary Addresses on the Occasion of the Death of Hon. Charles G. Atherton," *Congressional Globe*, 19 Dec. 1853.

LEX RENDA

ATHERTON, George Washington (20 June 1837–24 July 1906), college president, was born in Boxford, Massachusetts, the son of Hiram Atherton and Almira Gardner. Atherton endured a Spartan childhood. His father died in 1849, and the twelve-year-old boy went to work in a cotton mill and on a farm to support his mother and two sisters. He also managed to secure an education sufficient for teaching and tutoring and in 1855 left home for his first teaching post. In 1856 he enrolled in Philips Exeter Academy in Exeter, New Hampshire, graduating with the class of 1858. He then worked as a teacher of Latin and Greek at the Albany (N.Y.) Boys' Academy until 1860, when, at age twenty-three, he enrolled in the sophomore class at Yale.

In his junior year of college Atherton joined the Union army, serving as first lieutenant in the Tenth Connecticut Volunteers. He took part in the Burnside expedition against North Carolina but suffered a near-fatal illness and resigned his commission in the spring of 1863. Later that year he married Frances Washburn, with whom he had nine children. He returned to his teaching post at Albany and simultaneously studied for his examinations at Yale, which he passed in July 1864 (he was ranked as a graduate in the class of 1863). In 1866–1867 he accepted a professorship at St. John's College in Annapolis, Maryland, and in 1868 he was hired as one of the two original faculty members of Illinois Industrial University (now the University of Illinois at Urbana-Champaign), where he taught history. In 1869 Atherton was appointed to the endowed Vorhees Professorship of History, Political Economy, and Constitutional Law at Rutgers, where he remained for thirteen years.

At Rutgers, Atherton began his lifelong advocacy of federal support for land-grant colleges and forged a professional relationship with U.S. senator Justin S. Morrill of Vermont. Morrill's congressional legislation of 1862 directed each state to establish a college, endowed by the sale of public lands given to the states for this purpose, "where the leading object shall be, without excluding other scientific and classical studies, and including military tactics, to teach such branches of learning as are related to agriculture and the mechanic arts . . . to promote the liberal and professional education of the industrial classes." Despite this auspicious start, land-grant colleges across the nation struggled mightily during their first quarter century. Most found their endowment insufficient to support educational programs. Appropriations from their sponsoring states were slim if forthcoming at all. Public support was negligible in an era when most students attended small local private colleges.

Atherton's grand strategy for addressing the plight of land-grant colleges was to argue that in establishing the schools the federal government had incurred a continuing obligation to support them. He thus countered the strong bias against a federal role in education that was held by many congressmen and the presidents of leading endowed colleges such as Harvard and Princeton. In 1873 Atherton received wide attention for his speech advocating federal support at the meeting of the National Education Association:

The nation as a nation must educate. There is no argument to prove the duty of the state governments in this respect which does not apply with at least equal force to the national government. If the welfare of the individual citizen is the welfare of the particular commonwealth in which he happens to reside, much more is it the welfare of the entire nation . . . Education alone may not make a free country; but there can be no such thing as a free country without education. The question whether a free country has a right to educate its citizens is no other than the question whether it has a right to live, as a free country.

In 1882 Atherton was named president of the Pennsylvania State College, a land-grant institution that was on the verge of closing its doors because of financial stress, dwindling enrollments, and political strife with the legislature, the Grange, and its own trustees. Atherton in effect became the second founder of the institution. Over his 24-year tenure the student body grew from eighty-seven to 800, the ranks of faculty increased from seventeen to sixty-six, and the physical plant grew from a single building to twelve major ones. The technical courses—especially engineering—were expanded considerably, the liberal arts curriculum was developed, and private fundraising was begun. By the early 1900s Penn State was at last on solid footing.

But the eventual success of this single institution—and all other land-grant colleges—was more firmly rooted in Atherton's work on the federal level. Shortly after his arrival at Penn State he became the prime mover of the 1887 Hatch Act, which encouraged the establishment of agricultural experiment stations at land-grant colleges and provided an annual appropriation of $15,000 for each station's work. He rewrote a bill originally drafted in 1882, oversaw its introduction and reintroduction—the bill was slightly reworked at least four times—in Congress, testified in its behalf, and with a few collaborators lobbied Congress hard for its passage. The Hatch Act marked the first instance of federal support for research associated with colleges and universities and had a profound effect on American agricultural productivity in the years that followed.

Atherton was also the prime mover in what eventually became the Morrill Act of 1890. This was, in fact, the culmination of a series of land-grant college aid bills that Atherton had cowritten with Senator Morrill and that had been introduced unsuccessfully in Congress beginning in 1873. The 1890 Morrill Act provided annual federal appropriations from general revenues for a broad range of educational programs, from English to engineering, and became the broad financial underpinning the colleges had always needed. It also created the first black land-grant institutions. Moreover, the act encouraged the states to begin providing a dependable flow of annual funding. By decade's end, aggregate state support for the land-grant colleges exceeded total federal support.

The success of both the Hatch Act and the Morrill Act stemmed from the tight network of land-grant college presidents and agricultural scientists, which became formalized in 1887 as the Association of American Agricultural Colleges and Experiment Stations, the first association of peer colleges and universities in the nation. Atherton played a leading role in the early years of the organization. He wrote its charter and led its legislative committee. In recognition of his work with the Hatch Act, Atherton was elected the association's founding president in 1887, serving two terms through 1889.

Informally, Atherton served as the association's chief legislative architect and emissary to Congress, working in concert with other association leaders such as Henry E. Alvord, the president of Maryland Agricultural College, and Henry H. Goodell, the president of Massachusetts Agricultural College. Atherton involved himself in association work on a variety of fronts such as relationships with the federal cabinet departments of interior (which housed the Bureau of Education), agriculture, and war. He helped to resolve common issues about how land-grant colleges should reform the undergraduate curriculum, implement graduate education, adopt uniform entrance and graduation requirements, and address military instruction and the new discipline of mining engineering. Through the association Atherton and his colleagues attempted to forge their vision of the land-grant college as a comprehensive institution attending to the liberal and scientific education of the whole person, rather than simply as a training ground for technicians. He was still president of Penn State at the time of his death in State College, Pennsylvania.

American land-grant colleges began to pull out of their period of struggle to begin an era of growth and relative stability in the years around 1890. This happened because certain land-grant college presidents resolved to use the political process to sustain these schools. No one was more prominent in this work than George W. Atherton.

• The Atherton papers are located in the Pennsylvania State University archives. Atherton's work on behalf of the land-grant college movement is detailed in Roger L. Williams, *The Origins of Federal Support for Higher Education: George W. Atherton and the Land-Grant College Movement* (1991), and his presidency at Penn State is covered in Wayland F. Dunaway, *History of the Pennsylvania State College* (1946), and Michael Bezilla, *Penn State: An Illustrated History* (1985). Obituaries are in the *Philadelphia Public Ledger*, 25 July 1906, and the *Bellefonte* (Pa.) *Democratic Watchman*, 27 July 1906.

ROGER L. WILLIAMS

ATHERTON, Gertrude Franklin (30 Oct. 1857–14 June 1948), author, biographer, and historian, was born Gertrude Franklin Horn in San Francisco, California, the daughter of Thomas Horn, a businessman, and Gertrude Franklin. Her maternal grandfather, a grandnephew of Benjamin Franklin, was a banker and editor of one of San Francisco's first newspapers. Gertrude lived with him when her parents were divorced after three years of marriage. Although she was well read, her formal education was sporadic—while she was attending the Sayre Institute in Lexington, Kentucky, she contracted tuberculosis. After twice becoming engaged, she eventually eloped in 1876 with George H. Bowen Atherton, a former suitor of her mother's. They had a daughter and a son who died at the age of six.

Gertrude Atherton had decided to become an author when she was fourteen, and at that age she had produced several stories that were mostly unfinished. In 1882 *The Randolphs of the Redwoods* was published anonymously as a serial in the San Francisco *Argonaut*. This "erotic" work was considered to be scandalous and was, in fact, the first of many of her works that defied all conventions. Despite the disapproval of her husband and her Spanish, aristocratic mother-in-law, Atherton continued to write. When her husband died in 1887, she left California to live in New York and travel in England and France. In England Atherton's work received the praise that it had been denied in America, although *Hermia Suydam*, published in London in 1889, was denounced as being immoral. Atherton's heroines were ahead of their times; they were unconventional because they thought for themselves and they expressed sexual desire. While in France, Atherton finished her first Californian novel, *Los Cerritos* (1890). She also completed her research on Spanish missions and published the novels *Before the Gringo Came* (1894) and *The Doomswoman* (1893).

Atherton moved to England in 1895, and there her first major novel, *Patience Sparhawk and Her Times*, was published in 1897. She followed this success with *American Wives and English Husbands* (1898), which contrasts the values of the two cultures. Much of Atherton's work has been classified as romantic-realism; it would frequently explore the nineteenth-century argument regarding the effect of environment and heredity or nature versus nurture. Atherton would take a character who appears to be doomed by the circumstances of one environment and transfer the character to a different environment to investigate the changes that occur.

Atherton had the ability to take the facts of a person's life and transform them into novels. She saw these facts as "stimulants: each opens up a new vista." The year 1900 saw the beginning of her series of biographical novels: *Senator North* (1900), based on Eugene Hall of Maine; *The Conqueror* (1902), based on Alexander Hamilton; and *The Gorgeous Isle* (1908), which presents the West Indian romance of a poet who was based on Swinburne.

Atherton was interested in the developing woman suffrage movement and wrote *Julia France and Her Times* (1912), featuring a heroine who is a suffrage campaigner in England. When World War I started in Europe in 1914, Atherton played an active part by helping in hospital relief. She later earned three decorations from the French government, including the Legion d'Honneur, for this work. Her wartime experiences enabled her to write essays on women's war work in *The Living Present* (1917); in *The White Morning* (1918) she predicted that the women of Germany would overthrow their government in order to bring peace. During this period Atherton was also editing *The American Women's Magazine*, which ran for ten months.

In 1923 Atherton published her biggest bestseller, *Black Oxen*, a story based on the true experiences of a woman who underwent the Steinach treatment—stimulation of the sex glands by X-ray for the purpose of rejuvenation. Atherton herself had taken the treatment under Dr. Harry Benjamin and said that "she had implicit faith in the treatments." Many women wrote to her asking for details of the treatment.

Atherton went on to write books about women's lives in the ancient world. She read 200 books in order to write about the female philosopher Aspasia (*The Immortal Marriage*, 1927), about Alcibiades (*The Jealous Gods*, 1928), and about Dido (*Dido, Queen of Hearts*, 1929).

In 1932 Atherton returned to San Francisco. She had developed a reputation as a Californian author, for which she received several honorary degrees as well as headed the list of California's thirteen most distinguished women. She published two memoirs, *Adventures of a Novelist* (1932) and *My San Francisco* (1946), a book of mingled history and reminiscence, which appeared in her ninetieth year. Atherton climaxed a career that had spanned two world wars with novels depicting the "new woman" in San Francisco, *The House of Lee* (1940) and *The Horn of Life* (1942). She died in San Francisco.

Gertrude Atherton, who also wrote under the names Asmodeus and Frank Lin, produced thirty-four novels, seven short fiction collections, six history-based books and essays, and many newspaper and magazine articles on feminism, politics, war, and other contemporary issues. By fictionally portraying the "new woman" at the threshold of the twentieth century, she highlighted the psychological problems facing women in changing societies in both America and Europe. Atherton's work concerns subjects similar to those of authors such as Mary Wilkins Freeman, Edith Wharton, Ellen Glasgow, and Willa Cather, although her work is richer in variety of theme and background.

• Atherton's papers are in the Library of Congress and the University of California, Berkeley. Her other published works include *What Dreams May Come* (1888), *A Question of Time* (1891), *A Whirl Asunder* (1895), *The Californians* (1898, rev. 1935), *The Aristocrats* (1901), *A Few of Hamilton's Letters* (1903), *Mrs. Pendleton's Four-in-Hand* (1903), *Ruler of Kings* (1904), *Rezanov* (1906), *Ancestors* (1907), *Tower of Ivory* (1910), *California: An Intimate History* (1914), *Perch of the Devil* (1914), *Mrs. Balfame* (1916), *Life in the War Zone* (1916), *The Living Present* (1917), *The White Morning* (1918), *The Avalanche* (1919), *Transplanted* (1919), *The Sisters-in-Law* (1921), *Sleeping Fires* (1922), *The Crystal Cup* (1925), *The Sophisticates* (1931), *The Foghorn* (1934), *Golden Peacock* (1936), *Dona Concha* (1937), *Can Women Be Gentlemen?* (1938), *The Horn of Life* (1942), and *Golden Gate Country* (1945).

Biographical information dealing with Atherton can be found in *Current Biography Yearbook*, 1940; Charlotte S. McClure, *Gertrude Atherton* (1976); McClure, *Gertrude Atherton* (1979); Virginia Blain, *Feminist Companion to Literature in English* (1990); and Emily Leider, *California's Daughter: Gertrude Atherton and Her Times* (1991).

ELAINE OSWALD

ATHERTON, Joshua (20 June 1737–3 Apr. 1809), attorney general of New Hampshire, was born in Harvard, Massachusetts, the son of Peter Atherton, a blacksmith who also served on the General Court, and Experience Wright. Atherton attended Harvard College and graduated in 1762. He taught school in Bolton, read law with both James Putnam and Abel Willard, and in 1765 was admitted to the bar. That same year he married Abigail Goss, with whom he had fourteen children, seven of whom died in infancy. Soon thereafter Atherton moved to New Hampshire where in 1773 he became the register of probate in newly formed Hillsborough County. He settled in Amherst and resided there the rest of his life as one of the town's most prestigious and controversial inhabitants.

The prestige came from Atherton's success as a lawyer, an extensive record of public service, and conviviality. As an attorney Atherton was knowledgeable, hard working, and an effective courtroom debater. His track record gained him clients throughout southern New Hampshire and eventually led to appointment in

1793 as the state's attorney general. Both town and state benefited from Atherton's public service. He helped found a social library and an academy in Amherst, chaired numerous local committees, and in 1792 represented the community in the General Court. He sat as Amherst's delegate in the state constitutional convention held in 1792 as well as the convention held to ratify the proposed federal constitution. He also served briefly as state senator in 1792–1793. Atherton's legal and political careers were bolstered by his reputation as a generous host. Ministers, lawyers, judges, and any other country gentlemen in the area felt welcome at the Atherton homestead.

The controversy stemmed largely from Atherton's consistent opposition to governmental change. He opposed resistance to British authority and so infuriated inhabitants in neighboring towns that a mob threatened to destroy his home. Later Atherton refused to sign New Hampshire's revolutionary oath of allegiance. Open loyalism soon led to accusations of cooperation with British counterfeiters. Atherton was arrested and spent over a year in various jails before being found innocent. After the battle of Saratoga he decided that independence was inevitable and supported the revolutionary government.

Atherton's mental set also made him leery of constitutional change. He opposed most of the many efforts to reform the state constitution in the years 1778–1792. He argued successfully in town meeting that Amherst should vote against the federal constitution, became the leader of anti-Federalist forces in the convention itself, and corresponded with other anti-Federalists in the Northeast. In 1827 someone—possibly his son Charles—published an abolitionist speech Atherton supposedly gave at the ratifying convention, but there is no contemporary evidence any such speech was made or that Atherton ever criticized slavery.

In the 1790s Atherton once again courted controversy. An outspoken Federalist and critic of both France and Thomas Jefferson, he agreed to assess local property for federal tax purposes. An arsonist torched his barns, and he was hung in effigy. Partisanship and failing health eventually cost Atherton the attorney-generalship. In 1800 he resigned after the General Court eliminated his salary.

Atherton died at the Amherst family homestead. His son Charles Humphrey Atherton and grandson Charles Gordon Atherton became leading state politicians.

• Few Atherton papers have survived: the largest collections are in the Charles G. Atherton Papers in the New Hampshire Historical Society and the John Lamb Papers at the New-York Historical Society. Biographical treatments include Charles H. Atherton, *Memoir of the Honorable Joshua Atherton* (1852); Anne M. Means, *Amherst and Our Family Tree* (1921), pp. 7–58; and Clifford K. Shipton, *Biographical Sketches of Those Who Attended Harvard College*, vol. 15 (1970), pp. 167–72. See also Jere R. Daniell, *Experiment in Republicanism: New Hampshire Politics and the American Revolution* (1970); Daniel F. Secomb, *History of Amherst 1728–1882* (1883); and Lynn W. Turner, *The Ninth State: New Hampshire's Formative Years* (1983).

JERE R. DANIELL

ATKINS, Mary (7 July 1819–14 Sept. 1882), educator, was born in Jefferson, Ohio, the daughter of Quintus Flaminius Atkins and Sarah Wright. Her father, an ardent abolitionist, worked as an auditor, a sheriff, and then as a judge. She began teaching at sixteen, entered Oberlin College while teaching, and graduated with honors in 1845. Two years later she returned to serve as assistant principal in the "Ladies' Department."

After teaching and serving as school principal in Columbus and in Cincinnati, in 1854 she traveled, by way of Panama, to California, where she became principal of the Young Ladies' Seminary at Benicia, California. In January 1855 she purchased the academy and was its sole proprietor until 1866. She increased enrollment to more than one hundred, purchased additional land, and enlarged the school's facilities. She traveled by mule to recruit students from the rough mining towns of California.

Somewhat egalitarian for her time, Atkins diversified her school to include the daughters of bankers, merchants, ship captains, miners, and ranchers. She accepted Spanish-speaking students and was especially pleased when a Native American student did well in her school. Although Atkins was ardently pro-Union and antislavery, her students included girls with both southern and northern sympathies. During the Civil War tensions were high at the school and conversation was often "at swords' points."

Some of Atkins's pedagogical requirements may have stemmed from her own experiences of strictures against women in the academic and professional worlds. At the time of her graduation from Oberlin, women students were not permitted to make public presentations at commencement exercises. Their graduation theses were read, instead, by male teachers or students. Atkins purposefully held public graduation ceremonies at Benicia to which the community and press from the greater San Francisco Bay area were invited. Each student was required to both present and defend her work in this public forum.

Atkins had traveled to California wearing "bloomers," the early equivalent of trousers for women. On board ship, she had been warned that wearing such garments would make it impossible for her to succeed in her career plans. After purchasing the academy, Atkins required all students to wear bloomers during physical exercise classes. The dress was the cause of much comment in the Benicia area.

Atkins's academy grew in the midst of the pioneer environment of early California. Violence was commonplace, and Atkins once stood up to the threat of one parent to kill everyone in the school "except the littlest children." At another time she shot a pistol at a would-be intruder, chasing him from the school. One of her pupils reported passing the bodies of soldiers, killed during a Native American uprising, while traveling from her home to the academy.

In spite of, or, more likely, because of, the rough-and-ready quality of California life, Atkins set high standards of behavior for her students. The girls were required to learn and practice "polite behavior," not necessarily found in the mining camps and ranch houses from which they had come. They were taught music, dancing, and table manners in addition to academic subjects.

In 1863, restless and tired of the daily responsibilities of the school, she placed a colleague in charge of the academy for one year and sailed to Shanghai, the lone woman on a sailing ship. Her journal of the voyage was published posthumously in 1937. Attendance declined during her absence to approximately half the previous enrollment. By 1865 the school was not earning enough to meet its expenses. She sold the establishment to Cyrus and Susan Mills, missionaries and educators whom she had met in the Hawaiian Islands during her sabbatical trip to China.

Freed from the burdens of ownership, Atkins traveled in Europe and England, visiting school systems and briefly studying under Thomas Huxley. She then returned to Ohio and became a teacher at Cleveland High School. In 1869, at the age of fifty, Atkins married John Lynch, a former public school supervisor and officer in the U.S. Army during the Civil War. Lynch was a prominent figure in Reconstruction Louisiana, and the couple lived in New Orleans for six years before moving to Philadelphia and then to California. In 1879 she and her husband purchased the Benicia Academy, the core of which had been moved to Oakland to become the Mills Seminary (later Mills College). She ran the school until her death in Benicia.

• Letters and a diary are in the Mary Atkins Papers in the Mills College Library, and family letters are in the Bancroft Library, University of California, Berkeley. For the account of her travels, see *The Diary of Mary Atkins: A Sabbatical in the 1860's* (1937). For biographical information, see "Reminiscences of Young Ladies' Seminary at Benicia," a collection of eighteen typed memories and tributes, bound by Mills College Library, undated. See also E. O. James, *The Story of Susan and Cyrus Mills* (1953), and Rosalind Keep, *Fourscore Years: A History of Mills College* (1931). Anecdotal material is in Clara Wittenmyer, ed., *The Susan Lincoln Mills Memory Book* (1915).

MARGARET MISKELLY THOMAS

ATKINSON, Brooks (28 Nov. 1894–13 Jan. 1984), drama critic, was born Justin Brooks Atkinson in Melrose, Massachusetts, the son of Jonathan Henry Atkinson and Garafelia Taylor. His father was a Boston newspaperman, and when he was in primary school young Brooks decided that he would also be a journalist. At the age of eight he "printed" with rubber type a home newspaper called *The Watchout*; four years later he joined the National Amateur Press Association and printed another newspaper, *The Puritan*, this time in lead type.

Atkinson majored in English at Harvard University and during his senior year worked as a reporter for the *Springfield* (Mass.) *Daily News*. After receiving a B.A. in 1917, he joined the English department faculty at Dartmouth College as an instructor. After a year of teaching, he returned to newspaper work as a reporter and an assistant to the drama critic at the *Boston Transcript*, where his father had also been employed. Atkinson remained at the *Transcript* for four years, taking a leave of absence in 1918 to serve for several months as a corporal in the U.S. Army at Camp Upton on Long Island. From 1920 to 1922 he was also employed as associate editor of the *Harvard Alumni Bulletin*.

In 1922 Atkinson joined the staff of the *New York Times* as a book reviewer; two years later he became editor of the paper's Sunday *Book Review*. Atkinson gave up this position in 1925 to become a full-time drama critic for the *New York Times*. During the following decade he established a reputation as an influential reviewer whose opinions could determine the success or failure of a production. He used J. Brooks Atkinson as his byline until 1932, when he dropped the *J*.

Beginning in the mid-1920s Atkinson published a series of nonfiction books. His first, *Skyline Promenades* (1925), was about mountain climbing. This was followed by *Henry Thoreau: The Cosmic Yankee* (1927), a biography; *East of the Hudson* (1931), a collection of essays about New York City; *Cingalese Prince* (1934), a travel book; and *Cleo for Short* (1940), a memorial to his dog. A collection of Atkinson's *Times* drama reviews, *Broadway Scrapbook*, was published in 1947. His other books included four collections of his essays and articles: *Once Around the Sun* (1951), *Tuesdays and Fridays* (1963), *Brief Chronicles* (1966), and *This Bright Land* (1972); *Broadway* (1970), a theater history; and, with illustrator Al Hirschfield, *The Lively Years: Reviews and Drawings of the Most Significant Plays since 1920* (1973). Atkinson also edited collections of essays by Henry David Thoreau and Ralph Waldo Emerson.

During World War II Atkinson served as a *New York Times* news correspondent overseas, reporting on the conflict in the Far East from his base in Chungking, China. In 1945–1946 he served as a *Times* correspondent in Moscow. Following his return to New York in July 1946, Atkinson wrote a series of articles on Russia that were published in the *Times* and won him the Pulitzer Prize in journalism in 1947.

In fall 1946 Atkinson resumed his position as the chief drama critic of the *New York Times*; he served in that capacity for fourteen years. During this period Atkinson's influence became even greater in the world of the theater than it had been before the war. He was known for being fair and objective—it was public knowledge, for example, that he never read the out-of-town reviews of a play before attending a New York performance, and he refused to encourage personal relationships with actors and directors—and his opinions were widely quoted by a broad spectrum of the public, from ordinary playgoers to theater historians and scholars. Praised for his high standards as well as his commonsensical approach, Atkinson claimed that he judged every play he saw by one overriding criterion: did it provide enjoyment to the audience? A staunch supporter of Off Broadway theater as it developed in the 1950s, Atkinson lamented the simultaneous decline in quality of Broadway plays as a consequence of increasing production costs.

In 1960, following his retirement as full-time drama critic of the *Times*, Atkinson was honored by having a Broadway theater named for him—the first New York drama critic to be so honored. For the next five years he contributed a twice-weekly column, "Critic at Large," to the *Times*. His subjects included not only the theater but other aspects of culture, including books, music, and television as well as environmental issues and the world of nature. Atkinson received additional honors in 1972 when he was among the first inductees into the newly founded Theatre Hall of Fame.

An amateur ornithologist, Atkinson was an ardent birdwatcher for most of his life. He pursued his hobby not only in and around New York City but also at his country home, a farm in Durham, New York, that he shared with his wife, Oriana A. Torrey MacIlveen, whom he had married in 1926, and a stepson. In 1981 Atkinson and his wife moved to Huntsville, Alabama, to be near their son and his family. Atkinson died in a Huntsville hospital.

During his lifetime Atkinson frequently claimed that he was primarily a newspaperman and only secondarily a theater critic, but his preeminent influence on the American stage was long acknowledged not only by playwrights, producers, and actors but also by fellow critics. At the time of his death dramatist Arthur Miller paid tribute to Atkinson as the only critic who ever "presided over Broadway"; Arthur Gelb, a colleague at the *New York Times*, characterized Atkinson as nothing less than "the conscience of the theater."

• An account of Atkinson's life and career can be found in the *New York Times Magazine*, 24 Mar. 1940. *Over at Uncle Joe's* (1947), a bestselling memoir of the Atkinsons' ten-month sojourn in the Soviet Union written by Oriana Atkinson, also includes biographical information. An obituary, together with excerpts from Atkinson's theater reviews, is in the *New York Times*, 14 Jan. 1984.

ANN T. KEENE

ATKINSON, Edward (10 Feb. 1827–11 Dec. 1905), businessman and reformer, was born in Brookline, Massachusetts, the son of Amos Atkinson II, a merchant, and Anna Greenleaf Sawyer. He was educated in private schools in both Brookline and Boston, but the family's financial distress prevented him from attending Harvard as planned and propelled him instead at age fifteen into the world of business. After rising to the accounting department of a Boston dry goods firm, Atkinson in 1851 was appointed treasurer and agent of the textile company Ogden Mills.

Like many northerners Atkinson was convinced that the North's free-labor system best promoted industrious self-advancement and hence economic progress. Consequently Atkinson vigorously opposed southern slavery and its extension. Spurning compromise with the South, he left the Whig for the Free Soil party in 1850 and then joined the new Republican party, which was organized in 1854. Following passage of the Kansas-Nebraska Act in 1854, he played a leading part in the New England Emigrant Aid Company, an effort of antislavery Massachusetts businessmen to establish free-labor settlements in Kansas. In 1855 he married Mary Caroline Heath of Brookline. They had nine children.

Once the Civil War began, Atkinson contributed to the cause of emancipation by working to persuade his fellow northern textile manufacturers that slavery's destruction would boost rather than harm cotton production in the South. In *Cheap Cotton by Free Labor* (1861), he argued that southern cotton could be grown more efficiently with free labor and that producing enough of it to satisfy world demand necessitated using such labor. Despite his private admission that "I am not very fond of negroes as such" (Abbott, p. 223), Atkinson, especially during early Reconstruction but also late in his life, pressed for civil and political rights for free blacks. Black equality, he believed, was not simply a matter of justice but was also essential to building a prosperous, free-labor New South. Throughout his life he continually espoused the notion that "commerce rests on liberty and law" (Abbott, p. 231). His vision of the former slaves as primarily cotton-growing wage laborers, however, led him to oppose all Radical Republican talk of confiscating plantation land for division among them.

In 1878 Atkinson embarked on a new career as president and treasurer of the Boston Manufacturers' Mutual Fire Insurance Company. With characteristic intensity and some success, he campaigned to maximize the fire safety of factories and public buildings through improved construction and the installation of automatic sprinklers.

By this time Atkinson had assumed his role as longstanding prominent publicist for Gilded Age liberalism. In an outpouring of letters, articles, pamphlets, and books written between the late 1860s and early 1900s, he argued for free trade over protectionism, for the gold standard over government-issued paper money and unrestricted silver coinage, and for "higher" economic laws based on competition and supply and demand over legislated reforms, such as laws regulating railroads and hours of labor. Atkinson's arguments combined extensive statistical evidence with the unflagging faith in progress that characterized American exponents of laissez-faire classical economics like himself. His approach to the problem of economic inequality in industrial America particularly exuded rosy liberalism. In *Addresses upon the Labor Question* (1886), for example, he affirmed his belief "in competition as a beneficent and constructive force, gradually but surely promoting greater equality in the division of the increasing annual product, upon which human welfare depends."

Atkinson's sincere, if naive, concern for the welfare of American workers prompted his invention of the Aladdin Oven. Designed to allow the slow and efficient stewing of inexpensive cuts of meat, it would, he maintained, save workers money while also improving the nutritional value of their food. The oven, however, never caught on; difficult to use, it also attracted the wrath of labor spokesmen who, mindful of Atkinson's opposition to unions, denounced it as a callous attempt to lower workers' standard of living. Atkinson developed his ideas about the oven's benefits and dietary reform in *The Science of Nutrition* (1896).

Politically, during the Gilded Age, Atkinson aligned himself with reform-minded independent Republicans, or "Mugwumps" (a label he proudly embraced), who supported Democrat Grover Cleveland for president in 1884. In 1898, with significant help from the Mugwumps, he helped to organize the Anti-Imperialist League as part of the movement to block America's expansion overseas following the Spanish-American War. He reserved his fiercest opposition for the annexation of the Philippine Islands and subsequent military suppression of the Filipino independence movement, actions he denounced as both economically ill advised and heinous. "Every life destroyed in the Philippine Islands by the troops of the United States . . . is an act of murder," Atkinson wrote to Massachusetts senator George F. Hoar in 1900; "every dwelling or village destroyed is an act of arson; every piece of property taken an act of robbery."

Energetic, ambitious, intellectual, and public-spirited, Atkinson made his mark as an expert on cotton and cotton manufacturing, as a prolific economic writer whose works illuminated late nineteenth-century industrialization and economic growth while trumpeting liberal axioms, and as a genteel businessman and reformer who figured, often prominently, in a remarkable range of causes during his lifetime. He was, Charles Francis Adams tartly observed, "always in evidence" (Beisner, p. 89). If Atkinson was also, as the *New York Times* said, "sometimes too vehement in argument and advocacy," he clearly remained true to his belief, articulated in a letter at age twenty-one, that "it is not for himself alone that [a man] is to labor, he must remember that 'mankind is the true man' and that the real progress of his own nature is indissolubly connected with the progress of his fellow men." Atkinson died in Brookline.

• Atkinson's papers are in the Massachusetts Historical Society. His many publications include *On Cotton* (1866); *The Cotton Manufacturers of the United States* (1876); *Labor and Capital Allies, Not Enemies* (1879); *Address in Atlanta for the Promotion of an International Cotton Exhibition* (1880); *The Distribution of Products* (1885); and *The Industrial Progress of the Nation* (1890). The fullest treatment of his life and economic thought is Harold Francis Williamson, *Edward Atkinson: The Biography of an American Liberal* (1934). See also Richard Abbott, *Cotton & Capital: Boston Businessmen and Antislavery Reform, 1854–1868* (1991), on his efforts to end slavery and secure equal rights for the freedmen; Daniel Horowitz, "Genteel Observers: New England Economic Writers and Industrialization," *New England Quarterly* 48 (Mar. 1975): 65–83, on the significance of his economic writings; Harvey Levenstein, "The New England Kitchen and the Origins of Modern American Eating Habits," *American Quarterly* 32 (Fall 1980): 369–86, on his involvement in diet reform; and Robert L. Beisner, *Twelve Against Empire: The Anti-Imperialists, 1898–1900* (1968), and Joseph S. Tulchin, "The Reformer Who Would Not Succeed: The Aberrant Behavior of Edward Atkinson and the Anti-Imperialist League," *Essex Institute Historical Collections* 105 (1969): 75–95, on his anti-imperialism. An obituary is in the *New York Times*, 12 Dec. 1905.

GREGORY KASTER

ATKINSON, George Francis (26 Jan. 1854–15 Nov. 1918), botanist, was born in Raisinville, Monroe County, Michigan, the son of Joseph Atkinson and Josephine Fish. Little is known about his family or about his early life. Although reticent, Atkinson later told some of his graduate students that he had run away from home when he was thirteen, had never entered high school, had handled grain on a Mississippi River boat, and had driven a stagecoach in the Black Hills of Dakota. The latter occupation was revealed decades later when he shocked his students by driving a four-horse team at breakneck speed on a field trip to Enfield Gorge, New York. His boyhood offered only poor country-school studies, with no information about higher education, and he remarked that he was a man before he realized that he must have an education to be anything other than a crude laborer. A sister with whom he kept in touch inspired him to attend her alma mater, Olivet College in Olivet, Michigan. There he took preparatory classes from 1878 to 1880 and a regular program until 1883, when he transferred to Cornell University. He proved an avid student and received a bachelor of philosophy degree from Cornell in 1885. There is no record of his having received any further academic instruction.

After graduation Atkinson was appointed assistant professor, and in 1886, associate professor, of entomology and zoology at the University of North Carolina at Chapel Hill. He married Elizabeth S. Kerr. In 1888 he became a professor of botany and zoology and botanist to the experiment station at the University of South Carolina at Columbia. He moved in 1889 to the Alabama Polytechnical Institute, where, as a professor of biology and botany and botanist to the experiment station for three years, he published a remarkable twenty-five papers in these fields. In 1892 he returned to Cornell as assistant professor of cryptogamic botany (plants without true flowers and seeds). A year later he was promoted to associate professor, and in 1896 he became professor and head of the botany department. He was also in charge of the botanical research conducted by the Cornell University Experiment Station from 1896 to 1906. Many students and colleagues apparently found him a difficult and socially awkward man, but others valued his breadth of knowledge and dedication to biology. His only interest outside of his work appeared to be his three-acre tract of land, called "Laurelton," north of Fall Creek (now Cornell Heights), New York, where he planned a "pretentious home site," according to his former student Charles Thom. Thom remembered grand plans but little action, and Atkinson's wife prudently bought them a house across from her husband's laboratory. Eventually she left Ithaca without him, and he moved into his one-story "shack" on the tract.

Atkinson was editor of the *Botanical Gazette*, the *Botanisches Centralblatt*, the *Centralblatt für Bacteriologie und Parasitenkunde*, and *The New Systematic Botany of North America*. He was recognized for his botanical work by becoming chairman of Section G (botany) of the American Association for the Advancement of Science in 1897. He was a delegate to the International Botanical Congress in Vienna in 1905, and in Brussels in 1910. In 1907 he became the first president of the Botanical Society of America and in 1918 was elected to the National Academy of Sciences, having written over 180 scientific papers.

Although Atkinson began his career as a zoologist, with early papers on birds, spiders, and parasitic animals such as the nematode *Heterodera radicicola* (an important pest of field crops), most of his papers were on various crop diseases. The change in the titles of his academic positions reflected his shift in emphasis from zoology to botany, but he maintained an applied focus. With the turn in his attention to parasitic plants, he became one of the most proficient mycologists in the country. His early mycological work began as a survey of the fungi of the high mountains of North Carolina but rapidly broadened into a study of the physiology, systematic class, evolutionary relationships, and economic importance of fungi. He was the first botanist to pay close attention to fungi's early life stages, as he applied the common theory that embryology mirrored the life stages of evolution. He followed his natural history study, *Biology of Ferns* (1893), with *Studies of American Fungi* (1900), the first book on the higher fungi to appeal to both scientific and popular audiences.

A painstaking botanist, Atkinson standardized and built the botanical type collections at Cornell by carefully using nomenclature verified with complete descriptions and photographs. He made many far-ranging collecting trips for fungi in Sweden, England, France, and the United States. A summer collecting expedition in 1918 to the Pacific Northwest was his last. After his students and assistants had returned to their other duties, Atkinson had continued his collecting into the bad weather of autumn. Caught by a storm on the slopes of Mount Rainier, he returned to camp in a state of exhaustion and was taken to a hospital in Tacoma, Washington. He suffered influenza, then pneumonia, and as he lay dying he desperately tried to dictate his last mycological observations to his nurse. On receiving the shocking news of his death in Tacoma, his students rushed there to care for his valuable field notes and specimens.

• Some of Atkinson's correspondence and academic records are in the Cornell University archives. Charles Thom, a former student of Atkinson's, has written the most thorough obituary of him for the National Academy of Sciences, *Biographical Memoirs* 29 (1956): 16–44. It includes an explanation of Atkinson's loss of teaching responsibility and a full bibliography of his work. Harry B. Humphrey, *Makers of North American Botany* (1961), presents Atkinson's role in establishing Cornell's biology curriculum and summer short courses, while *Science* 49 (1919): 230 presents the Cornell faculty resolution on his death.

SARA F. TJOSSEM

ATKINSON, Henry (1782–14 June 1842), army officer, was born in Person County, North Carolina, the son of John Atkinson, a plantation owner and local politician. Nothing is known of his mother, who died shortly after his birth. Little is known of his youth or education, but as the youngest child in a reasonably wealthy family he presumably received whatever education was available. While a young man he worked on the family plantation. Then on 1 July 1808 he received an appointment in the newly enlarged U.S. Army. For the rest of his life he remained on active duty serving on the Gulf Coast, on the Canadian border in New York, and as far west as Montana.

Atkinson entered the army as a captain in the Third Infantry, which was then being formed as a part of President Thomas Jefferson's response to continuing diplomatic difficulties with France and Britain. With his unit Atkinson served in and around New Orleans until the War of 1812. In early 1813 he participated in General James Wilkinson's seizure of Mobile, Alabama, from Spain. Soon after that he was reassigned as a staff officer for General Wade Hampton on the New York–Upper Canada border. There he became an inspector general and was promoted to the rank of colonel. During early 1814 he became the commanding officer of the Forty-fifth Infantry and then of the Thirty-seventh Infantry. With both of these units he spent time guarding the border and carrying out routine duties as the war drew to a close. After the Treaty of Ghent ended the war the federal government cut the army drastically; Atkinson helped direct the demobilization of troops in the northeast. Despite his modest command experience, he retained his rank and received command of the Sixth Infantry as a part of the ongoing army reductions.

During the years immediately following the end of the war the federal government strove to extend American influence west beyond the Mississippi River. By 1818 Secretary of War John C. Calhoun planned to have the army establish a series of forts as far west as the Rocky Mountains to impress the American Indians and to exclude British fur trading companies from American territory. As part of that effort the War Department ordered Atkinson to prepare his regiment for a move west. By 1819 the Sixth Infantry had traveled to St. Louis, where they were to board steamboats and ascend the Missouri River to eastern Montana. Difficulties with the boats plagued the army repeatedly, and the soldiers never reached their goal, the Yellowstone River. Instead, they halted at Council Bluffs (near present-day Omaha) where the troops built what became Fort Atkinson.

From his new headquarters in St. Louis, Atkinson came to direct activities in much of the early West. At the end of 1819 he received command of the Ninth Military Department, which included the states of Kentucky, Tennessee, and Illinois as well as the region beyond the Mississippi River and north to Canada. His duties included supervising the construction of the new military garrisons that Calhoun had envisioned, as well as keeping pioneers and Indians apart. In 1820 Atkinson became commander of the right wing of the western department of the army and was promoted to his highest rank, brigadier general. However, in the 1821 reorganization and reduction of the army he lost that rank, being reduced to colonel and again getting the command of the Sixth Infantry. He retained that position for the rest of his career, as well as the brevet rank of brigadier general, which meant that if required he could temporarily serve as a general. For most of the 1820s he remained occupied chiefly with administering the supply and movement of troops in the area beyond the Mississippi River and with trying to prevent warfare between whites and Indians on the frontier. Because of the fort-building activities carried out under his command the tribes of the region called him the "White Beaver."

As American traders extended their activities into the Missouri Valley and the Rocky Mountains, armed clashes with the Indians increased, prompting the War Department to plan an expedition up the Missouri to negotiate treaties of peace and friendship with tribes near that river. In the summer of 1824 President James Monroe appointed Atkinson and Benjamin O'Fallon as the peace commissioners to the Indians, but not early enough for them to organize the expedition that summer. It was not until May 1825 that the 450-man military escort for the commissioners boarded keelboats and the Yellowstone expedition began. That summer Atkinson and O'Fallon negotiated treaties with sixteen tribes and bands of Indians along the Missouri River between Omaha and eastern Montana. Their findings also dispelled the myth that British fur traders had any significant influence among the tribes of the region. The expedition made one other contribution to American expansion when Atkinson reported the location of South Pass, "an easy passage across the Rocky Mountains . . . indeed so gentle in ascent as to admit of wagons being taken over."

The following summer, 1826, Atkinson located a site on the bluffs about ten miles south of St. Louis and supervised the construction of Jefferson Barracks, the first army infantry school. Also in 1826, at age forty-four, Atkinson married Mary Ann Bullitt, the daughter of a prominent family in Louisville, Kentucky. They spent most of their married life at Jefferson Barracks, Missouri, where they had three children, only one of whom survived to adulthood.

The next summer Atkinson led troops north to Wisconsin and helped prevent a war between elements of the Winnebago tribe and the pioneer miners who had invaded the Indians' lands. Although successful at preventing war with the Winnebago, Atkinson failed in dealing with another frontier crisis five years later. In early 1832, just a few months after having been ordered to stay west of the Mississippi River, the Sauk warrior Black Hawk led the "British Band," some 2,000 Sac and Mesquakie people, east from Iowa into Illinois. The Illinois governor cried invasion and threatened to exterminate the Indians, so federal authorities ordered Atkinson to intervene. He moved hundreds of troops to Illinois and sent messengers to overtake the Sauks, hoping to persuade them to return to Iowa. Negotiations failed and when an Illinois militia unit fired on Black Hawk's unarmed negotiators, war began. At the end of a frustrating summer spent chasing them across Illinois and Wisconsin, the troops caught and destroyed most of the British Band. The Black Hawk War happened by accident and leaders on all sides received much criticism for their roles in the conflict.

During most of the last decade of his life Atkinson remained at Jefferson Barracks, supervising troop movements and dealing with Indian-related issues. With the federal government busily moving tribal people west beyond the Mississippi he faced objections from frontier citizens that the eastern tribes were being located too close to the settlements. To facilitate rapid troop movements needed to keep peace between tribal people and the pioneers near the frontier, the War Department ordered a new road built to connect army garrisons. It stretched from Green Bay in Wisconsin southwest across Iowa to Omaha and then south along the western borders of Missouri and Arkansas. The soldiers almost never got to where they were needed in time, so the road failed. While the road work continued Atkinson supervised efforts to remove the Potawatomi from western Missouri. To his surprise, on 12 June 1838 President Martin Van Buren appointed him governor of the new Iowa Territory. Atkinson declined the position. Two years later, in 1840, he directed the removal of the Winnebago people from Wisconsin to Iowa. He died suddenly while still on active duty at Jefferson Barracks.

Like many officers who served in the first half of the nineteenth century, Atkinson experienced long periods of administrative work interspersed with short bursts of travel, heavy building activity, and only isolated combat circumstances. He served on the frontier during the era of rapid population growth, American ascendency over the British, and the domination and removal of the Indians. While he left no stirring record of military victories, his work helped American pioneers move into frontier areas with a reasonable expectation of safety. At the same time he worked to keep peace with the Indians and did what he could to limit their exploitation and suffering by helping them to resettle beyond the reach of most frontier troublemakers.

• Most of Atkinson's papers were destroyed in the 1871 Chicago fire, although the Missouri Historical Society, St. Louis, has a small collection. His official correspondence is available at the National Archives. Roger L. Nichols, *General Henry Atkinson: A Western Military Career* (1965), is the only full treatment of his life to date. *The Missouri Expedition, 1818–1820* (1969), edited by Nichols, provides a look at his leadership skills. Francis P. Prucha, *The Sword of the Republic: The United States Army on the Frontier, 1783–1846* (1969), places Atkinson's experiences in the general military context of the time. Two earlier studies, Henry P. Beers, *The Western Military Frontier, 1815–1846* (1935), and Edgar B. Wesley, *Guarding the Frontier: A Study of Frontier Defense from 1815–1825* (1935), focus on related issues and events.

ROGER L. NICHOLS

ATKINSON, Juliette Paxton (15 Apr. 1873–12 Jan. 1944), tennis player, was born at Rahway, New Jersey, and grew up in Brooklyn, New York, the daughter of Jerome Gill Atkinson, a physician, and Kate McDonald. She and her younger sister, Kathleen, taught themselves to play lawn tennis at Fort Greene Park in Brooklyn. They carried their own net, poles, stakes, rackets, and balls, erecting and dismantling their court each trip. For social reasons, they joined the Kings County Tennis Club about 1891. Club tournaments soon roused their competitive instincts. "Julie" first entered open tournaments during 1893, winning two of three handicap events in the New York City area and losing in the first round of the Middle States Championship at Mountain Station, New Jersey. Atkinson and Helen Hellwig, the club's best women players, entered the 1894 National Championship at Wissahickon, Pennsylvania, and won the women's doubles, while Atkinson and Eddie Fischer captured the mixed doubles title. In the singles, Atkinson lost a close struggle in the semifinals to Bertha Townsend Toulmin, the champion of 1888 and 1889. Hellwig, however, defeated Toulmin in the all-comers final and then vanquished Aline Terry, the defending titleholder, in a five-set challenge round to become U.S. champion. (Customarily women's matches were the best of three sets, but from 1891 through 1901 their finals and challenge rounds were the best of five sets.) Later, Atkinson bested Hellwig in five sets to win the 1894 Middle States crown.

The following year, the Atkinson-Hellwig and Atkinson-Fischer duos retained their U.S. doubles titles. Atkinson defeated her sister, Kathleen, in the singles and Bessie Moore in the all-comers final before easily conquering Hellwig to win the championship. She then lost the title in 1896. During the 1896 Middle States final against Moore, she sprained an ankle previously injured in a horse show accident and defaulted. The next week at Wissahickon, with her ankle heavily taped, she proved no match for Moore in the challenge round. Atkinson and Moore won the women's doubles, and Atkinson and Fischer scored their third consecutive mixed doubles triumph. Thereafter, Atkinson wore flat, rubber-soled shoes only on dirt courts and donned a pair with spikes attached for play on turf.

During 1896 Atkinson, fully recovered, won the Canadian and Canadian International singles championships, both held at Niagara-on-the-Lake, Ontario, downing Moore in the former and Kathleen Atkinson in the latter. She recaptured the U.S. singles title in 1897, again defeating Kathleen and surviving a five-set challenge match with Moore. The Atkinson sisters won the women's doubles title. Subsequently Atkinson successfully defended her two Canadian singles titles. Her 1897 season record was marred only by a straight set loss in the Western Championship final to Louise Pound, later renowned as a scholar, educator, and author.

The Atkinson sisters repeated as U.S. women's doubles champions in 1898, but Julie barely retained the singles title. She survived two match points against challenger Marion Jones; Jones lost one match point because Atkinson's return struck a spare ball lying within Jones's court. With Jones visibly weakening in the extreme heat, Atkinson salvaged the set and match, 7–5. This third singles victory gave her permanent possession of the Wissahickon Prize, a cup donated by the Wissahickon Inn in 1887 when the women's championships began. In 1942 she donated the cup to the West Side Tennis Club in Forest Hills, New York. Fifty years later, the cup was presented to the International Tennis Hall of Fame at Newport, Rhode Island.

Atkinson concluded 1898 with additional triumphs in the Canadian, the Canadian International, and the Western, overcoming Pound in straight sets in the latter. The Brooklyn Citizen Savings Bank Hall Board awarded her its trophy as the North American Athlete of the Year for 1898. Atkinson played in only two 1899 tournaments, defending her Western Championship title against Myrtle McAteer and losing the Cincinnati Open to the same player. After staying out of competition in 1900, Atkinson played in the 1901 and 1902 U.S. nationals. She won the doubles both years, first with McAteer and then with Jones, but she lost in singles semifinals to Moore and Carrie Neely. During these final years of tournament play, her only singles victory was in the 1901 Middle States Championship.

Atkinson married George B. Buxton in 1918; the couple had no children. They resided at Norwalk, Connecticut, and Cranford, New Jersey, and were employed by the Indian Refining Company. About 1925 the company transferred them to Lawrenceville, Illinois. After they retired from that business, they opened a grocery store at Lawrenceville. Atkinson died at a sanitarium in nearby Olney, Illinois. An obituary in the *Lawrence County News* stated that she had been a trained musician, performed opera in New York, continued her singing in Lawrenceville, and "had some ability as a writer." No further details about these activities are available.

Exactly five feet tall, Atkinson probably was the shortest of all U.S. singles champions, smaller by a fraction of an inch than Ellen Roosevelt, the 1890 winner, and Hazel Hotchkiss Wightman, the 1909, 1910, 1911, and 1919 victor. A natural all-around athlete, Atkinson competed in those sports open to women.

She won medals for skating and ribbons for riding, excelled at swimming, played basketball and golf, bowled, and cycled. Self-taught at tennis, she profited from instruction by her mixed doubles partners, William Frazer and Eddie Fischer, and, more important, from J. Parmly Paret, whose coaching also helped Moore and Jones to win championships.

The slender, right-handed Atkinson, extremely mobile on the court, hit accurate, softly paced groundstrokes and excelled in the forecourt, where she remained far superior to her rivals. She smashed lobs surely and volleyed crisply and effectively. Considered one of the most intelligent players of her time, male or female, she maintained an even match temperament, imperturbable demeanor, and seemingly limitless endurance. She won every important five-set singles match she played. Wallis Merrihew, editor of *American Lawn Tennis* for thirty-five years, named Atkinson as the greatest nineteenth-century American woman player. Her thirteen U.S., seven Canadian, four Western, and four Middle States titles attest to her dominance. She was elected to the International (then National Lawn) Tennis Hall of Fame in 1974.

• A biography of Atkinson has yet to be published. "A Girl Tennis Champion: Miss Juliette Atkinson, Her Games, Her Trophies, and What She Wears," *New York Times*, 10 July 1898, provides information obtained by a personal interview. Obituaries are in the *Lawrence County News*, 13 Jan. 1944, and *American Lawn Tennis*, June 1944, pp. 18–19.

FRANK V. PHELPS

ATKINSON, Theodore (20 Dec. 1697–22 Sept. 1779), chief justice of New Hampshire, was born in New Castle, New Hampshire, the son of Theodore Atkinson, a provincial councilor, and Mary (maiden name unknown). He was the fourth of five linearly descended Theodore Atkinsons and as long as his father lived was known as Theodore Atkinson, Jr. After graduating from Harvard College in 1718 he returned to New Castle and succeeded his father, who died the following year, in several minor public offices. Atkinson also traded, gained election to the General Court, and used his position as clerk of common pleas to learn law. In 1731 he was admitted to the New Hampshire bar.

Both before and after admission to the bar Atkinson's political fortunes were tied closely to those of the Wentworth family. Lieutenant Governor John Wentworth, who had been a close associate of his father, not only appointed young Atkinson to numerous offices (including, in 1728, that of provincial sheriff) but gave him diplomatic experience by appointing him provincial agent to negotiate with Indians on the northern frontier. After Lieutenant Governor Wentworth died in 1730, his son Benning Wentworth assumed responsibility for maintaining the family's power. Atkinson married Benning's widowed sister, Hannah Plaisted, in 1732, was appointed councilor with Wentworth's sponsorship, served on the boundary commission that increased New Hampshire's size at the expense of Massachusetts, and helped finance Wentworth's successful campaign to become governor of the newly enlarged and now independent province.

Atkinson thrived from 1741 to 1767, the years Wentworth held office. He became clerk of the council, provincial secretary, and a colonel in the militia. After representing New Hampshire at the Albany Conference in 1754, he was appointed chief justice of the superior court by the governor. Atkinson also became an active land developer. He invested in and helped manage the Masonian Proprietorship, a corporation owning all the ungranted land within sixty miles of New Hampshire's coast; in addition, Atkinson owned dozens of rights in towns erected beyond the proprietorship.

At the same time, Atkinson became a leading participant in the area's social life. In the mid-1730s he moved to Portsmouth, erected a large house, helped found an Anglican church known as Queen's Chapel, and became warden of the Masonic Order. He raced sulkies, owned the fanciest carriage in town, loved fishing, and in general enjoyed the perquisites of his privileged position. Undoubtedly, Atkinson took special pride in the fact that his only son, Theodore, was placed first when entering Harvard's class of 1757.

The last decade of Atkinson's life brought disappointment. Benning Wentworth was forced from office in 1767, and although his nephew John Wentworth (1737–1820) replaced him, the Wentworths' fortunes began to wane. Both his wife Hannah and son Theodore, whom he had groomed to succeed him in his various offices, died in 1769. The coming of the Revolution not only destroyed Atkinson's authority but violated his sense of dignity and order. Having no descendants—his two daughters had died early—concerned him so much that when his health began to fail he willed much of what he owned to a distant cousin, George King, on condition that King change his name to Atkinson. Theodore Atkinson died soon thereafter in Portsmouth.

• Unpublished primary material is scattered among collections in several repositories, including the New Hampshire Historical Society, the Dartmouth College Archives, the Huntington Library, and the Library of Congress. The bulk of Atkinson's published correspondence is in vols. 4–8 and 18 of the *New Hampshire Provincial and State Papers* (1870–1890) and the *Massachusetts Historical Society Collections*, 6th ser., vols. 6 and 7 (1893–1894). Clifford K. Shipton, *Biographical Sketches of Those Who Attended Harvard College*, vol. 6 (1942), pp. 221–31, is the longest biographical treatment. For Atkinson's political career see Jere R. Daniell, *Experiment in Republicanism: New Hampshire Politics and the American Revolution, 1741–1794* (1970), and William H. Fry, *New Hampshire as a Royal Province* (1908). David E. Van Deventer, *The Emergence of Provincial New Hampshire, 1623–1741* (1976), provides essential background information on Atkinson.

JERE R. DANIELL

ATKINSON, William Biddle (21 June 1832–23 Nov. 1909), obstetrician and medical biographer, was born in Haverford, Pennsylvania, the son of Isaac Sleeper Atkinson and Mary Reese Biddle. Atkinson began his medical studies in 1850 under the preceptorship of Samuel McClellan, who was probably influential in Atkinson's choice of a medical specialty and certainly influential in his later appointment to the Pennsylvania Medical College. Atkinson completed his medical training in 1853 after three courses of lectures at the Jefferson Medical College. For several years after graduation he devoted part of his time to teaching classics and mathematics in Philadelphia and part to his medical practice. It was during this period that Atkinson began a lifelong involvement as the correspondent or editor of various medical periodicals.

In 1857 Atkinson began to lecture independently on obstetrics, and in 1859 he was appointed assistant professor of obstetrics and diseases of women and children at the Pennsylvania Medical College. When this institution folded in 1861, Atkinson was appointed to the department of obstetrics and diseases of women at the Howard Hospital in Philadelphia. His obstetrical career was interrupted by service as an acting assistant surgeon in the U.S. Army during the Civil War (1862–1864).

In 1877 Atkinson was made lecturer on the diseases of children at the Jefferson Medical College. He held this position until 1887, when he was appointed professor of sanitary science and pediatrics at the Medico-Chirurgical College in Philadelphia. He held this appointment until 1891.

Atkinson was a fairly productive author. His *Hints in the Obstetric Procedure*, originally delivered as an address when he retired as president of the Philadelphia County Medical Society, appeared in three editions between 1874 and 1879. *The Therapeutics of Gynecology and Obstetrics* was published in two editions (1880, 1881).

Atkinson is best remembered, however, as compiler of *The Physicians and Surgeons of the United States* (1878), a biographical dictionary containing entries for 2,607 of his medical contemporaries. "The selections were made," Atkinson wrote in the preface, "to include all professors, hospital physicians and surgeons, officers of the more important medical societies and authors, together with those who by length of service or success in the profession had become of eminence." It remains an invaluable source of biographical data on American physicians who were prominent late in the nineteenth century, many of whom are now obscure. A second and somewhat enlarged edition was published in 1880 under the title *A Biographical Dictionary of Contemporary American Physicians and Surgeons*.

Atkinson was able to compile a work of this scope through extensive contacts made through active membership in local, regional, and national medical societies. In 1854 he became a member of the Philadelphia County Medical Society, in which he held many offices, including the presidency (1873). In 1858 he joined the Medical Society of the State of Pennsylvania, becoming permanent secretary in 1863 and editor of its *Transactions*. He joined the American Medical Association (AMA) in 1859 and was made permanent secretary and editor of its *Transactions* in 1863. Atkinson had served in this office thirty-one years when William Osler rose at the 1895 AMA meeting in Baltimore to declare, "I stand here and say plainly and honestly before Dr. Atkinson what I and many other members have said behind his back, that he is not an efficient secretary of this Association, and that we have not found him so." Although Osler's remarks were greeted with hisses and a motion was immediately carried to retain Atkinson in office, the association's constitution was amended to assure that future permanent secretaries would be elected annually. Atkinson remained in office until June 1899.

Atkinson also served as medical inspector of the Pennsylvania State Board of Health (1886) and was appointed to the State Associated Health Authorities of Pennsylvania, of which he was secretary from 1894.

For most of his career Atkinson was active in editing medical periodicals. In 1858 he coedited the *Medical and Surgical Reporter* with Samuel Worcester Butler. His association with this publication was severed in 1859 when Atkinson became obstetrical editor for the *North American Medico-Chirurgical Review*, which was under the editorship of Samuel David Gross until it ceased publication in 1861. In 1882 Atkinson was secretary of the AMA publications committee that recommended "journalizing" its annual *Transactions*. Through this committee's recommendations, the *Journal of the American Medical Association* began publication in 1883. Atkinson also edited at least three editions of the *Philadelphia Medical Register and Directory* (1878–1884) and the 1890 edition of *The Medical and Dental Register-Directory and Intelligencer of Pennsylvania and Delaware*.

Atkinson was twice married. In 1867 he married Philadelphian Jennie R. Patterson, who died in 1871 and with whom he had one child. His second marriage was to S. J. Hutchinson, also of Philadelphia, with whom he had two children. Atkinson died at his home in Philadelphia.

• Biographical sources on Atkinson are few. He included an article on himself in both editions of his own *Physicians and Surgeons of the United States* (1878, 1880). The best sources remain the articles in I. A. Watson, *Physicians and Surgeons of America* (1896), and Howard A. Kelly and Walter L. Burrage, *Dictionary of American Medical Biography* (1928).

CHRISTOPHER HOOLIHAN

ATKINSON, William Walker (5 Dec. 1862–22 Nov. 1932), New Thought writer and popularizer of Eastern ideas, was born in Baltimore, Maryland, the son of William C. Atkinson and Emma L. Mittnacht. Atkinson is a relatively obscure figure. In particular, little is known of his early life, except that he attended public schools. In 1889, approaching his twenty-seventh birthday, he married Margaret Foster Black. The couple had two children. Following an initial path that was much like those taken by Henry Wood, Charles Brodie Patterson, Ralph Waldo Trine, and other male New Thought contemporaries, Atkinson seemed destined to spend his life as a mainstream professional, first as a businessman and then, beginning in 1895 when he was admitted to the Pennsylvania bar, as a lawyer. Yet also much like Wood and Patterson, he was unable to cope with the mundane pressures of everyday life, and within a few years of becoming a lawyer, he had suffered an emotional breakdown. Atkinson had already dabbled in metaphysical ideas and alternative religious beliefs—his essay "Mental Science Catechism" had been the lead article in the sixth issue of the magazine *Modern Thought* 1, no. 6 (1889)—and after failing to find spiritual relief elsewhere, he turned to New Thought. In doing so, he found his calling. He moved to Chicago, where he would become an influential exponent of the variegated, therapeutic religious beliefs that constituted the New Thought movement, with its emphasis on the self as a vessel of divine truth dispensing good health and improvement. Atkinson did not entirely abandon his legal career—he was admitted to the Illinois bar in 1903—but New Thought offered him a way to make his own life more fulfilling as well as a calling to disseminate, through books and lectures, a message that others would appreciate—and pay for.

Atkinson's early article in *Modern Thought* was the first in what would be a long series of ultimately futile efforts to define fully and clearly New Thought. His first widely read contribution to the literature was an influential 1899 pamphlet titled *The Secret of the I AM*. As New Thought drew in more adherents around the turn of the century, Atkinson became fairly well known). Hundreds of magazines and periodicals espousing New Thought ideas sprang up in this period. One of them, *Suggestion: A Magazine of the New Psychology*, named Atkinson its associate editor in 1900. Around this same time, Atkinson came into contact with publisher Sydney Flower, a promoter of the burgeoning business of self-help texts. Flower engaged Atkinson to write for and, from 1901 to 1905, serve as editor of his journal *New Thought*. Flower apparently introduced Atkinson to New Thought publisher and writer Elizabeth Towne, who published some of his work and promoted Atkinson and his writing in her extremely popular journal, the *Nautilus*. Towne also published a popular short work, apparently written by Atkinson under the pseudonym Theodore Sheldon, called *Vim Culture* (1913), an inspirational tract emphasizing the effectiveness of living "the active life," as exemplified most clearly by Theodore Roosevelt.

In addition to New Thought, Atkinson helped to popularize Hinduism at the turn of the century. For his more explicitly Hindu, and clearly less capitalistic or Christian writings, Atkinson wrote under the pseudonym Yogi Ramacharaka. Out of his Yogi Publication Society in Chicago he published about a dozen books, most between 1903 and 1910, that did much to make Eastern philosophies, including yoga, accessible to Americans. Taking on the persona of a Hindu guru called Yogi, Atkinson revealed himself to be a distinctively American pragmatist. In the preface to *Science of Psychic Healing* (1909), he warned readers that although the text might sound dogmatic, he, like all true thinkers, based truth on the workability test and held no belief that he was not "willing to throw away when a better one presents itself." Atkinson's appropriation of an Eastern spiritual guide did not philosophically contradict his New Thought involvement. New Thought borrowed heavily but selectively from Eastern concepts, in particular, the idea that one's life is a continuous unfolding of truth—a concept that found easy acceptance in the Progressive Era, when there was a virtually unqualified confidence in human progress. At the same time, New Thought proponents incorporated aspects of the new psychology of William James, of the genetics research of Luther Burbank, and of other scientific and technological advances, particularly in communication and photography, as clear evidence that humanity was evolving toward a higher state.

New Thought: Its History and Principles (1915) was Atkinson's fullest attempt to clarify and define the popular phenomenon. His thoughtful analysis focused on both the philosophical roots of the movement, which he identified as a "strange mingling of the Orient and Ancient Greece [Platonism]," and the development of New Thought itself, which began with Ralph Waldo Emerson and which during the course of Atkinson's career had changed from emphasizing healing illnesses to focusing on "self-help and character-building." This shift was reflected in Atkinson's own work, as he began, in the 1910s, to publish texts with titles such as the *Psychology of Salesmanship*. Also in this period Atkinson became active in formulating an associational structure for the movement. In 1916 he was named an honorary president of the International New Thought Alliance (INTA), which had been formed in 1915. In 1917, however, he took a firm anticreedal stance at the INTA meeting in St. Louis, where he asserted, among other things, that any attempt to institutionalize the movement would end up "dwarfing and stultifying it" because the basis of the movement was an "Infinite Presence-Power" that could not be defined as a particular set of beliefs. By 1916 Atkinson had a sounding board for his positions, the editorship of the journal *Advanced Thought*, which he held through 1919.

At some point in the early 1920s, as the New Thought movement was fading in popularity, Atkinson moved to California, where he teamed up with writer Edward E. Beals to write several self-help works, including *Character Power; or, Positive Individuality* (1922). He died in Los Angeles.

Atkinson's writings would have a profound influence on brothers Fenwicke and Ernest Holmes, founders in Los Angeles of the New Thought–inspired Religious Science, one of the most successful churchlike bodies to grow out of New Thought in the second half of the twentieth century. More generally, Atkinson contributed to the growing fascination among Americans with Eastern religious philosophies.

• An overview of Atkinson's life and career and a partial bibliography of his writings is in Gordon Melton, ed., *Religious Leaders in America* (1991). Charles Braden, *Spirits in Rebel-*

tion (1963), includes significant material on Atkinson's role in the INTA creed controversy in 1917 as well as other aspects of his career; Braden also includes a useful bibliography. Donald Meyer is much less sympathetic to Atkinson and the New Thought phenomenon in *The Positive Thinkers: Religion as Pop Psychology from Mary Baker Eddy to Oral Roberts* (1980).

CLAY BAILEY

ATLAS, Charles (30 Oct. 1893–23 Dec. 1972), physical culturist, was born Angelo Siciliano near Acri in the Calabria province of Italy, the son of farmers. (The parents' names cannot be ascertained.) He emigrated to the United States with his mother in 1904 and settled in Brooklyn. After leaving school at fifteen, he worked in a women's pocketbook factory; his future seemed unpromising. Like most "pedlars" from this era, Siciliano was psycho-asthenic and of foreign extraction. Anemic and lacking confidence, Siciliano was subjected to beatings from a neighborhood bully and from an uncle. These humiliations provided an impetus for his lifelong struggle to overcome weakness. Statues of Hercules and other mythological heroes he saw at the Brooklyn Museum inspired him to build his body. Realizing that such beautifully proportioned physiques came from exercise, young Siciliano began reading *Physical Culture*, published by Bernarr Macfadden, and he practiced every conceivable form of resistance training. Too poor to buy barbells, he made a set from a stick and two stones weighing twenty-five pounds each. Spectacular results eventually came from a system, originally featured by Macfadden, that pitted one muscle group against another and was popularized later as "dynamic tension." Neighborhood friends likened his impressive physique to a statue of Atlas on a local bank. Combining this epithet with his old nickname of "Charley" led to the nom de plume of Charles Atlas.

With his newfound muscles, Atlas acquired a series of strongman jobs. The first involved demonstrating chest developers in a Broadway shop window at age nineteen. He then joined the circus-vaudeville circuit, where he posed and performed such feats as pounding nails bare-handed, bending railroad spikes, and tearing telephone books in half. While working at a Coney Island sideshow, Atlas met Margaret Cassano. They were married in 1918 and lived happily together for forty-seven years, bringing up two children. In 1918 Atlas encountered sculptor Arthur Lee, who used him to model for a statue of Abraham Lincoln. He subsequently posed for nearly seventy-five statues of classic American heroes: among them, Alexander Hamilton (1755–1804) at the U.S. Treasury Building in Washington D.C., George Washington in Manhattan's Washington Square, and *Energy in Repose* at the Federal Reserve Bank in Cleveland. Sculptors dubbed Atlas "the Greek god." The climax to his bodybuilding exploits came when he won the titles of "Most Beautiful Man in America" (1921) and "America's Most Perfectly Developed Man" (1922) as well as cash awards totaling $2,000 in contests staged by *Physical Culture*. Later, he triumphed over 750 bodybuilders in a much-publicized exhibition at Madison Square Garden.

Atlas's first commercial association came at the end of World War I when he worked with Earle Liederman, whose bodybuilding courses dominated the mail-order market in the 1920s. Atlas launched a similar venture in 1922 in collaboration with an English naturopath, Frederick Tilney. Drawing from Atlas's dynamic tension principles, Hindu muscle-control exercises, and Walter Camp's ideas on calisthenics, Tilney devised a course of thirteen bodybuilding lessons. Offered by mail order, the enterprise was only moderately successful until Atlas entered a partnership in 1928 with a young businessman named Charles Roman. Roman conducted a brilliant merchandising campaign. Advertising slogans like "I'll add five inches to your chest" and "YOU, too, can have a body like mine," accompanied by pictures of Atlas in leopard breechclouts, soon made his name synonymous with health, strength, and manliness. Even more successful was the image of the ninety-seven-pound weakling who has sand kicked in his face by the beach bully; after building a herculean physique, the new strongman trounces the bully and wins his girlfriend's admiration. This mail-order advertisement, considered a classic, attracted thousands of converts to "dynamic tension." To prove the method's efficacy, Atlas once pulled six automobiles a mile through Brooklyn, and in 1936 he tugged a 145,000-pound locomotive 112 feet. Atlas always denied detractors' claims that he had built his muscles with weights. By 1942 he had sold his courses to more than 400,000 pupils; his offices occupied an entire floor of a Manhattan office building; and twenty-seven secretaries answered the daily correspondence.

Charles Atlas, via scores of pulp magazine advertisements, remained a celebrity the rest of his life. But he never abandoned his roots. A devout Catholic with an Old World accent and manner, he enjoyed the simple pleasures of family life. Even into his seventies, he exercised regularly, maintained a healthy diet, and abstained from tobacco, alcohol, and stimulants. "Naive and sincere," one observer's assessment, best describes his personality. By the time of his death, Atlas courses were still being sold in seven languages to 70,000 people yearly for $30, the same price he had charged a half-century earlier.

• There are no known manuscripts or correspondence files on Charles Atlas. His only publication is the *The Complete Charles Atlas Dynamic-Tension Training Course* (1960). The only book-length treatment of him is a pictorial biography, *Yours in Perfect Manhood, Charles Atlas* (1982), composed by Charles Gaines and George Butler, and based on the recollections of Charles P. Roman, his business partner. Otherwise, Maurice Zolotow, "You, Too, Can Be a New Man," in the *Saturday Evening Post*, 7 Feb. 1942, contains the fullest account of his life. Also see Robert Lewis Taylor, "I Was Once a 97-Pound Weakling," in the *New Yorker*, 3 Jan. 1942; Robert Ernst, *Weakness Is a Crime: The Life of Bernarr Macfadden* (1991); David Webster, *Barbells + Beefcake: An Illustrated History of Bodybuilding* (1979); and "The Big Muscle Boys,

The Apotheosis of Brawn as a Goal of Health," *Hygeia*, Apr. 1925. An obituary appeared in the *New York Times*, 24 Dec. 1972.

JOHN D. FAIR

ATLEE, John Light (2 Nov. 1799–1 Oct. 1885), physician and surgeon, was born in Lancaster, Pennsylvania, the son of Colonel William Pitt Atlee and Sarah Light. With the exception of the winter of 1813–1814, when he attended Gray and Wylie's Academy in Philadelphia, he received his early schooling in Lancaster. In 1815 he began the study of medicine under Samuel Humes, continuing there while attending the medical department of the University of Pennsylvania; he received his M.D. in 1820. He returned to Lancaster to establish himself in practice and remained there for the rest of his life. In 1822 he married Sarah Howell Franklin, daughter of Judge Walter Franklin of Lancaster County; they had three children.

Early in his career, Atlee supervised the initial medical training of his younger brother, Washington Lemuel Atlee, who studied in Atlee's office before matriculating at Jefferson Medical School. John Atlee built a successful general practice in Lancaster, but he was known primarily for his public service and for his success as a surgeon.

Atlee's interest in public service may have begun while he was studying with Humes, who was an attending physician to the Lancaster County Hospital. The hospital was connected to the Lancaster County Almshouse, and several prominent physicians attended its inmates. Atlee began attending the paupers in 1822 and was active as one of two or three attending physicians at the hospital from 1824 to 1854, in addition to maintaining his private practice.

Atlee's most dramatic moment in attendance to the pauper patients came just after he had surrendered his position as attending physician to his son, John Atlee, Jr., in the summer of 1854. That August cholera broke out in Lancaster and Columbia; most of the deaths in Lancaster were confined to the almshouse and hospital, and the management of the outbreak in the institutions was entrusted to Atlee. In addition, he was a member of the sanitary commission formed by the county to combat the disease. Atlee's 1855 report on the subject, to the Committee on Epidemics of the Lancaster City and County Medical Society, is a valuable source both for understanding contemporary thinking about the disease and for describing the specific measures taken to contain the epidemic within the institutions. In addition, the report makes clear that Atlee was among the earliest practitioners to employ microscopic analysis of his patients' discharges in studying the cause and transmission of cholera.

Atlee was praised by contemporaries for his high success rate in a wide variety of surgeries, including amputations, trephining, tracheotomies, and operations for hernias and eye problems. His fame as a surgeon, however, rests primarily on his revival in 1843 of the operation of ovariotomy. This procedure was not unknown in the United States, but most surgeons considered it to be too risky because of the difficulty of correctly diagnosing ovarian tumors and the high mortality rate. In 1843 Atlee performed the procedure successfully for the first time since 1813, removing both ovaries from a patient who survived the operation. Accounts of Atlee's life credit him with performing ovariotomy seventy-eight times between 1843 and 1883, with sixty-four surviving patients.

Atlee was deeply interested in medical organizations. Among those he helped to found were the Lancaster County Medical Society (1844), the Pennsylvania Medical Society (1848), and the American Medical Association (1847). He served as president of the Lancaster City and County Medical Society (1848), as president of the Pennsylvania Medical Society in 1857, and as both vice president (1865) and president (1882) of the American Medical Association. In addition, he was a professor of anatomy and physiology at Franklin and Marshall College and a trustee of the college. His honors included election to the College of Physicians as an associate fellow in 1847, and election as an honorary fellow of the American Gynecological Society in 1877.

Atlee's involvement with charitable institutions continued after he resigned as attending physician to the Lancaster County Hospital. He was a trustee of the Bishop Bowman Church Home in Lancaster. He also served terms as president of the board of trustees for the State Lunatic Hospital in Harrisburg, and for the Friendless Children's Home in Lancaster. A proponent of free public education, he served on the school board in Lancaster County for about forty years. Atlee remained active in professional organizations and as a physician until shortly before his death in Lancaster.

Atlee was immensely popular among his colleagues, praised as much for his service to the profession and to his community as for his medical skill. He was one of a growing number of physicians who recognized early in the nineteenth century that organization and the application of scientific research to medicine were vital to improving both the status of the profession and basic medical care. His advocacy of ovariotomy in cases of life-threatening disease, and his comparatively high success rate in performing it, helped to advance both public and professional acceptance of gynecological surgery.

• For Atlee's accounts of his cases, see *A Case of Successful Peritoneal Section for Removal of Two Diseased Ovaria Complicated with Ascites* (1844); *Hydrocephalus acutus* (M.S. thesis, Univ. of Pennsylvania, 1820); and *Address Delivered before the Medical Society of the State of Pennsylvania* (1858). Informative memoirs of Atlee include D. Hayes Agnew, "Memoir of John Light Atlee, M.D., LL.D.," *Transactions and Studies of the College of Physicians of Philadelphia*, 3d ser., 8, no. 1 (1886): xxxv–xliii; *Proceedings of the Lancaster City and County Medical Society Relative to the Death of John Light Atlee, M.D., LL.D., and an Address in His Memory Delivered before Them, November Fourth, 1885, by J. L. Zeigler, A.M., M.D.* (1885); and B. H. Detwiler, "Personal Recollections of Doctors John L. and Washington Atlee," *Pennsylvania Medical Journal* 8, no. 2 (1904): 16–18. For Atlee's achievements in gynecological surgery, see Richard Leonardo, *History of Gynecology* (1944).

Atlee's report on the cholera outbreak is reprinted in the *Journal of the Lancaster County Historical Society* 62, no. 2 (1958): 109–46, with the report of T. Heber Jackson, the physician who handled the cases in Columbia, a collection of contemporary views on cholera, and a discussion of modern understanding of the disease.

MONIQUE BOURQUE

ATLEE, Washington Lemuel (22 Feb. 1808–6 Sept. 1878), physician and surgeon, was born in Lancaster, Pennsylvania, the son of Colonel William Pitt Atlee and Sarah Light. After an unsuccessful apprenticeship in a dry-goods store, he went at age sixteen to study medicine with his brother, John Light Atlee. He received his M.D. degree from Jefferson Medical College in 1829. He settled in Mount Joy, a village about twelve miles from Lancaster, and established himself in private practice. Sometime around 1830 he married Ann Eliza Hoff; they had ten children.

During Atlee's medical apprenticeship he worked in the Lancaster County Hospital, a charitable hospital attached to the Lancaster County Almshouse, where his brother John Light Atlee was attending physician for much of the second quarter of the century. After four years in Mount Joy, Washington Lemuel Atlee returned to Lancaster, where he continued to serve as attending physician to the Lancaster County Hospital between 1837 and 1838, and again from 1840 to 1845.

In Mount Joy Atlee became involved in the active pursuit of natural history and in reform organizations, interests that persisted all his life. He began to collect botanical specimens (he later donated a collection of specimens to Pennsylvania College at Gettysburg) and to deliver public lectures on both reform and scientific subjects—temperance, astronomy, and botany. In the mid-1840s Atlee was offered the chair in medical chemistry in the medical department of the College of Philadelphia (later the University of Pennsylvania). He relocated his family to Philadelphia, where they remained until Atlee's death.

Atlee was known throughout his career as a man who was unafraid of controversy. In 1839 he was one of a team of physicians—including George McClellan and John Light Atlee—who, with their students, conducted a series of electrical experiments on the body of an executed criminal before dissecting the corpse and taking extensive phrenological measurements. Atlee authored most of the report on the experiments. The case received a great deal of public attention, and some censure.

Atlee was well known for his espousal of ovariotomy, and for the frequency with which he successfully performed the operation. Ovariotomy was not a new procedure when Atlee began performing it; however, the procedure was generally avoided because it was too risky in the absence of either anesthesia or asepsis, and because it was difficult to establish the existence and location of ovarian tumors or cysts.

After attending John Light Atlee's famous demonstration of ovariotomy in 1843, generally regarded as the first successful removal of both ovaries, Washington Lemuel Atlee began a special study of the procedure. He performed his first ovariotomy in 1844—an unsuccessful operation—and his next two in 1844 (successful) and 1849. In 1853 he resigned the chair of medical chemistry at the College of Philadelphia to devote himself to private practice, and by the mid-1850s he was known primarily as a gynecological surgeon. Atlee's "Table of All the Known Operations of Ovariotomy," published in the *American Journal of the Medical Sciences* (1845), and in updated form in the *Transactions of the American Medical Association* (1851), was regarded as a pioneering work. Atlee persisted in defending the validity of the procedure in the face of harsh criticism from colleagues, and contemporary accounts attribute about 378 ovariotomies to him between 1844 and 1878.

The controversy surrounding Atlee in Philadelphia in the early 1850s involved many of the country's most prominent physicians. Atlee was supported in public and in print by such luminaries as Samuel D. Gross, Nathan Chapman, Thomas M. Drysdale, and George McClellan (whose special student he had been while working toward his degree); he was reviled in the same arenas by Thomas Dent Mütter, Charles D. Meigs, and John Livingston Ludlow. Atlee countered his critics by inviting them to attend performances of the operation and by continuing to perform the procedure when he judged it appropriate. The controversy gradually subsided as ovariotomy became more widespread; by the mid-1870s Atlee was as well known for considerably less controversial surgeries for uterine fibroid tumors as he was for ovariotomy.

Atlee was active in a variety of medical organizations at both the local and national levels. With his brother John, he was a founder of the Lancaster City and County Medical Society in 1844. He was elected a fellow of the College of Physicians of Philadelphia in 1846. He served as president of the Philadelphia County Medical Society in 1874, as president of the Pennsylvania State Medical Society in 1875, and as vice president of the American Medical Association in 1875. He was among the founders of the American Gynecological Society, and of the Lancaster Conservatory of Arts and Sciences.

While John Light Atlee was credited with reviving the operation of ovariotomy, Washington Lemuel Atlee was instrumental in gaining widespread acceptance for the procedure. His success at removing ovarian and uterine tumors was an important contribution to the advancement of gynecological surgery in general, and his methods played an important role in the increasing sophistication of tumor diagnosis.

• Memoirs of Atlee include Thomas Murray Drysdale, *Biographical Memoir of Washington Lemuel Atlee, M.D.* (1879); and "Personal Recollections of Doctors John L. and Washington Atlee," *Pennsylvania Medical Journal* 8, no. 2 (1904): 16–18. For a general biography see R. French Stone, ed., *Biography of Eminent American Physicians and Surgeons* (1894).

For the controversy over ovariotomy, see John Livingston Ludlow, *Reply by John Livingston Ludlow, M.D., to a Pam-*

phlet Entitled "Corrections of the Erroneous Statements of Henry H. Smith, M.D., Published in the Medical Examiner, January, 1855, in Relation to a Case of Gastrotomy Which Occurred in the Practice of Washington L. Atlee, M.D. (1855). Atlee's own account is *A Retrospect of the Struggles and Triumphs of Ovariotomy in Philadelphia* (1875).

Atlee's addresses to medical schools and organizations, published as pamphlets, illuminate his views. See, for example, *Physical Education: The Only Solid Foundation of Moral and Intellectual Culture and Development* (1851); *Lecture Introductory to the Course of Medical Chemistry in the Medical Department of Pennsylvania College, Philadelphia, for the Session 1844–45* (1844); and *Valedictory Address to the Graduates of the Medical Department of Pennsylvania College, Session of 1846–47* (1847). Atlee's major work on gynecological surgery is *General and Differential Diagnosis of Ovarian Tumors with Specific Reference to the Operation of Ovariotomy* (1872).

MONIQUE BOURQUE

ATSIDI, Sani (c. 1830–c. 1917), Navajo silversmith, was born in Navajo country in present-day Arizona near Canyon de Chelly, a member of the Dibelizhini (Black Sheep) clan. His parents' names and occupations are unknown. Given the era, it is safe to assume that his parents were typical members of Navajo society who raised sheep and farmed. As a young man, Atsidi Sani, or Old Smith in English, learned ironwork from a Mexican in the Mount Taylor area of western New Mexico. Nakai Tsosi (Thin Mexican), as the Navajos called him, apparently became friends with Atsidi Sani despite the frequent conflict between their two peoples during this period. Atsidi Sani's initial efforts with ironwork concentrated in a commercially profitable endeavor: he learned to make bridles. Navajos who previously had been compelled to purchase bridles for their horses from Mexican ironworkers could now turn to a local source.

From ironwork, Atsidi Sani turned eventually to silversmithing. The date of this transition is debated, with some writers insisting on a time prior to the Navajo incarceration at Fort Sumner (or Bosque Redondo) in east central New Mexico from 1864 to 1868. Others, including those who interviewed prominent Navajos such as Chee Dodge, contend that Atsidi Sani did not begin to practice silversmithing until after he and other members of the Navajo tribe returned to a portion of their homeland, following the signing of the treaty with the United States in the summer of 1868. Atsidi Sani by that time had risen to a position of political influence and was one of the signatories to the treaty.

In any event, there is no disagreement about his role in initiating and promoting the art of silversmithing for which the Navajos (or Dine, as they call themselves in their own language) would become internationally famous. In addition to bridles, Atsidi Sani also fashioned jewelry. His early work in silver included the making of bracelets and ornamental round or oval pieces, or conchas, used for belts. Photographs taken before the turn of the century illustrate the rapid development of the art form, with Navajos wearing magnificent squash blossom necklaces, bracelets, and concha belts.

According to one Navajo man whose name in English was Grey Moustache, Atsidi Sani's significance came as much from teaching as from his own work. Grey Moustache said that Atsidi Sani had four sons to whom he taught both ironwork and silversmithing. These men—Big Black, Red Smith, Little Smith, and Burnt Whiskers—in all likelihood passed their knowledge along to others. Atsidi Sani taught silversmithing to Grey Moustache as well as to Smith Who Walks Around, Big Smith, and Crying Smith, whom Grey Moustache labeled as great craftsmen. A younger brother of Atsidi Sani, Slender Maker of Silver, also gained renown for his excellent work in silver. Prior to the turn of the century, he introduced new designs and ideas. Improved tools, often brought in by the growing number of traders at the posts in Navajo country, allowed for more intricate and consistent products. Initially made for internal consumption, Navajo silver soon became publicized throughout the rapidly expanding tourist market in the Southwest. The arrival of the Santa Fe Railroad and the Fred Harvey hotels and shops that accompanied it quickly transformed Navajo silver into a commodity. By the time of Atsidi Sani's death, hundreds of craftsmen and craftswomen practiced the art.

Although not too many details are known about other dimensions of Atsidi Sani's life, he was also highly regarded as a ceremonial leader. He learned how to perform the ceremony known as the Mountain Top Way, one of the great Navajo curing rites that takes days to carry out and years to learn how to conduct properly and thus effectively. The ability to conduct the Mountain Top Way alone would have marked Atsidi Sani as a man to be admired in Navajo society, given the difficulty of mastering the intricate ceremony and the significance that the Navajos gave to maintaining balance and harmony in their lives, in part through proper religious observance.

• This brief account is based primarily on the authoritative book by John Adair, *The Navajo and Pueblo Silversmiths* (1944). See also Arthur Woodward, *A Brief History of Navajo Silversmithing* (1938), and Frederick J. Dockstader, *Great American Indians: Profiles in Life and Leadership* (1977).

PETER IVERSON

ATTAKULLAKULLA (c. 1705–c. 1780), Cherokee chief known to whites as Little Carpenter, was raised in the Cherokee towns along the Little Tennessee and Hiwassee rivers called the Overhill towns because they lay across the mountains from the Cherokee villages in the Carolinas. Nothing is known of Attakullakulla before 1730, the year in which he was among seven Cherokees who went to London with Sir Alexander Cuming, an adventurer with no official connection to the Crown or any colony. In London the Cherokees were presented to George II, an honor Attakullakulla flaunted throughout his life. Attakullakulla was impressed by Great Britain's power, but after his return he was captured by the pro-French Ottowas and held in honorable captivity in Canada (c. 1742–1748).

Upon his return he decided to promote competition between Britain and France for Cherokee trade, but this proved impractical because of France's chronic inability to supply goods. He resolved instead to engender competition between two English colonies—Virginia and South Carolina.

By the late 1740s Attakullakulla's power derived from his position as principal deputy to his maternal uncle Connecorte, the Chota Uku or Beloved Man of Chota, whom whites called Old Hop. He was unsuccessful, however, in breaking South Carolina's monopoly of Cherokee trade until the outbreak of the French and Indian War. After General Edward Braddock's defeat at the hands of French and Indian troops in 1755, Virginia's desperation for Indian allies caused it to agree to open trade with the Cherokees and to build a fort in the Overhills to protect Cherokee women and children while the warriors were away fighting the French. A small fort was built, called the Virginia fort, but, having ascertained that Virginia did not plan to garrison it, Attakullakulla persuaded South Carolina to erect and garrison a larger fort (called Fort Loudoun) on the Little Tennessee River, opposite the Virginia fort, in exchange for formal acknowledgment of George II's sovereignty over the Cherokee nation. Attakullakulla made his promise to send warriors to the Virginia and Pennsylvania frontiers contingent on the Overhill towns having exclusive control over the distribution of British gifts and supplies within the Cherokee nation.

Fort Loudoun was completed in 1757, the same year in which Attakullakulla organized five war parties against the pro-French Choctaws on the lower Mississippi and the Twightwees of the Illinois country. The party he led killed six French soldiers and took two prisoners.

In January 1758 Attakullakulla was feted regally in Charleston. He agreed to assist General John Forbes in his expedition against the French at Fort Duquesne, but once the chief joined Forbes in the field they argued over the presents Britain's Indian allies should receive. Attakullakulla left Forbes's camp, and the general accused him of desertion. Attakullakulla replied that Virginia's governor Robert Dinwiddie had asked him to negotiate peace between Cherokee warriors and backcountry settlers with whom they clashed passing to and from the war front in Pennsylvania. Some Cherokees stole horses, occasionally killed settlers, and were killed in return. The Cherokee code of blood called for retaliation for every loss, so the cycle of violence escalated. In May 1759 fifteen settlers along the Yadkin and Catawba rivers in the Carolinas were killed, and despite Attakullakulla's efforts, which included a successful war party in the Illinois country, South Carolina forbade trade with the Cherokees. Soon the Cherokee War of 1760 began. Oconostota, the Cherokee war leader, ambushed Lieutenant Richard Coytmore at Fort Prince George in upper South Carolina, whereupon fifteen Cherokee hostages in the fort were killed. The Cherokees besieged Fort Loudoun on 4 March 1760. Attakullakulla moved into the British fort and contrived to smuggle in food. On 2 June 1760 he left the fort, was expelled from the Cherokee Council, and went into the woods to live, finding it impolitic to be found among either the vanquished or the victors. The fort capitulated on 7 August, and two days later many of the survivors were massacred. At great expense Attakullakulla ransomed Captain John Stuart, the only British officer to survive the massacre, and they escaped to Virginia.

In June 1761 a punitive British expedition dispatched by General Jeffrey Amherst and commanded by Colonel James Grant ravaged the Cherokee towns in the Carolinas and was poised to march against the Overhills. Having failed to secure French support, the Cherokees recalled Attakullakulla to the council to negotiate peace with the British. Having done so, he also influenced the selection of John Stuart as superintendent of southern Indian affairs.

Connecorte having died, Attakullakulla, the diplomat, and Oconostota, the war leader, shared power and led the Cherokees for a generation. In 1767 they traveled to Johnson Hall in upstate New York to negotiate peace with the Iroquois Confederacy, which contested many Cherokee hunting grounds.

After 1763, despite the Royal Proclamation line, settlers poured across the Appalachians. In 1772 Attakullakulla reluctantly agreed to lease lands to the Watauga Association, an ad hoc government formed by settlers in what is now the upper eastern corner of Tennessee. In 1775 he favored the so-called Transylvania Purchase by which North Carolina colonel Richard Henderson bought twenty million acres in Kentucky and Middle Tennessee, reasoning that the whites would take the land anyway and hoping to divert settlement away from the Overhills. A leading critic of the transaction was Dragging Canoe, said to be Attakullakulla's son.

At the outset of the American Revolution, Attakullakulla favored the British, who were not the threat to Cherokee lands that the Americans were. He was not anxious to fight either, however, but he was overruled, and the Cherokees launched largely unsuccessful offensives against the Americans in 1776. When American expeditions from Virginia and North and South Carolina were poised to march against the Cherokees, Attakullakulla's influence rose (as in 1761), and he helped negotiate the Treaty of Long Island in July 1777. The last reference to him alive was in February 1778. His death was remarked upon at the Treaty of Hopewell in 1785.

A small, slender man, Attakullakulla knew some English but was not fluent. However, he was considered the most gifted Cherokee orator. The conventional dichotomy of Attakullakulla as a man of peace and Oconostota as a man of war is overdrawn. Attakullakulla led many successful war parties and seldom failed to present French scalps before a negotiation in Charleston. It was, indeed, to masterful diplomacy that he owed his power—and he considered war an extension of diplomacy. Decentralized power among the Cherokees made it difficult, however, to consistently follow any policy. He was often reduced to expedients but nonetheless had underlying principles. One, ultimately achieved, was to break South Carolina's trade monopoly. Another, also successful, was to ensure acceptance of the Overhill towns as the national leadership of the Cherokee nation. Still another was to avoid fighting the British. He was temporarily unsuccessful but, had he not kept the Cherokees from joining the French early in the French and Indian War, the fate of the trans-Appalachian West might have been different. The young frontiersman Felix Walker aptly called him "the most celebrated and influential Indian among the tribes then known."

• The most detailed study, copiously noted, is James C. Kelly, "Attakullakulla," *Journal of Cherokee Studies* 3 (Winter 1978): 2–34; see also his "Oconostota," *Journal of Cherokee Studies* 3 (Fall 1978): 221–38. Also, Attakullakulla is frequently mentioned in John R. Alden, *John Stuart and the Southern Colonial Frontier* (1944). Good general accounts of Cherokee affairs, and of Attakullakulla's role, are found in John P. Brown, *Old Frontier* (1938); David Corkran, *The Cherokee Frontier: Conflict and Survival, 1740–1762* (1962); and in editor William MacDowell's introduction to *Colonial Records of South Carolina*, ser. 2, *Documents Relating to Indian Affairs, 1754–1765* (1962), the last of which is the largest single source of documents concerning Attakullakulla.

JAMES C. KELLY

ATTELL, Abe (22 Feb. 1884–6 Feb. 1970), featherweight boxer, was born Albert Knoehr in San Francisco, California, the son of Mark Knoehr and Annie (maiden name unknown), Russian Jewish immigrants. His father owned a small jewelry store in a predominately Irish neighborhood south of Market Street. As a youth, Attell sold newspapers in front of the Mechanics' Pavilion at Eighth and Market Streets, and he engaged in many street battles to protect his territory. By 1900, he had already assumed the name "Abe Attell," by which he would be known for the rest of his life. Two of his brothers, Monte and Caesar, followed him into boxing and also assumed the name of "Attell."

Attell ran up a string of victories in San Francisco rings, after which the first of his many managers, Jack McKenna, took him to Denver, Colorado, where his successes continued. In Colorado, he twice fought former bantamweight champion George Dixon to draws, and he learned from Dixon that clever boxing was a superior strategy to the reckless slugging that he had previously practiced. When they met for a third time, in St. Louis on 28 October 1901, Attell gained his first major victory by outpointing Dixon. Despite two losses in St. Louis, on points to Harry Forbes and by a knockout to Benny Yanger, Attell gained further respect by knocking out the famous Mexican knockout specialist Aurelio Herrera in 1902. On 3 September 1903 he gained recognition as featherweight champion by outpointing Johnny Reagan in 20 rounds, again in St. Louis.

In 1904 Attell defended his title twice in St. Louis, first against Forbes, whom he knocked out in five rounds, and then against Reagan, whom he outpointed in 20 rounds. On 13 October, also in St. Louis, he was defeated by Tommy Sullivan, who floored Attell with a seemingly low blow in the fifth round, but the match was made at 124 pounds, two above the 122-pound limit of that time, and Attell retained his title. In nontitle fights in 1904 and 1905, Attell greatly increased his reputation with many stellar performances, including a victory by newspaper decision over future lightweight champion Battling Nelson in Philadelphia.

On 22 February 1906 Attell retained the featherweight championship by decisively outpointing Jimmy Walsh in Chelsea, Massachusetts, in 15 rounds. That year he defended his title six more times, against Tony Moran, Kid Herman (although held to a draw), Frankie Neil, Harry Baker, Billy DeCoursey, and Walsh. Attell became renowned for his great foot speed, quick reflexes, intelligent defense, and splendid two-fisted boxing ability. Although not regarded as a heavy puncher, he would often stop his opponents by hitting them so frequently with sharp punches that they were finally rendered defenseless.

Attell's successes continued in 1907 with successful featherweight title defenses against Baker, Kid Solomon, and Freddie Weeks. On 1 January 1908 he was held to a 25-round draw by the equally clever Welshman, Owen Moran, in San Francisco. This was followed by successful defenses against Frankie Neil and Eddie Kelly, a nontitle draw with Battling Nelson, and another winning defense against Tommy Sullivan, whom Attell knocked out in four rounds. On 7 September Attell fought a 23-round rematch with Moran in San Francisco, resulting in another draw after an epic battle of lightning movements and hot exchanges. Later in the year, Attell lost on points to one future lightweight champion (Freddie Welsh) and bested another (Ad Wolgast). In 1909 Attell retained his title in two more defenses, against Freddie Weeks and Eddie Kelly, and then fought another Welshman, Jem Driscoll, in a nontitle fight in New York City. This fight, on 19 February, created a sensation because Attell at last found himself outboxed by a more skillful opponent, one who was able to avoid most of Attell's blows. Attell then won a long series of nontitle bouts over the next year, with Moran and famous lightweights Harlem Tommy Murphy and Charley White among his victims. He then retained his featherweight title in defenses against Eddie Marino and Billy Lauder, both in Canada, and Johnny Kilbane at Kansas City and Frankie Conley in New Orleans.

In 1911 Attell's abilities began to wane. Although he did not defend his featherweight title, he was adjudged the unofficial loser in several no-decision bouts. His last defense came in a rematch against Kilbane in Vernon, California (now a part of Los Angeles), on 22 February 1912, in which Attell was decisively beaten. He continued to fight until 1917 with decreasing success, although boxing two important 20-round battles with Harlem Tommy Murphy and outpointing the famous knockout specialist, George Chaney. In 171 fights, he was defeated only 19 times, including unofficial decision losses rendered by newspaper reporters.

Attell's dominance of the featherweight division was so great during the years 1906 to 1911 that he was sometimes accused of faking on the relatively few occasions when an opponent made a good showing against him in a nontitle fight. It was claimed that he tried to make opponents look good for the purpose of engaging them later in more lucrative matches, but it is difficult to substantiate this claim on the basis of his record. Indeed, in retrospect he appears to have been remarkably consistent, although he sometimes took no-decision, nontitle fights rather lightly.

Attell enjoyed gambling during his boxing career, and after his retirement he became an assistant to Arnold Rothstein, a wealthy New York City gambler. In 1919 he was prominently involved in the notorious fixing of the outcome of the World Series, the "Black Sox" scandal. Attell's role in this affair was as a liaison between eight players of the Chicago White Sox, who were favored to win the World Series, and Rothstein, who supplied the payoff money to the ball players which Attell actually dispensed. In September 1920, as the details of the fix became known, Attell fled to Montréal, Québec, Canada, to escape possible arrest. Eventually he returned to New York City, where he was indicted and charged with conspiracy but not convicted. Together with the other gamblers involved in the devious fix proceedings, he never received a prison sentence.

Attell was garrulous and friendly, and his loose talk played a role in the revelation of the Black Sox plot. He liked to be referred to as "The Little Champ," dressed fastidiously, and evidently saw himself as a clever manipulator of other persons. He could never be relied upon to give a true account of his experiences, which undoubtedly deterred the writing of his biography. Not until 1961 did he finally make a public statement about his involvement in the Black Sox scandal.

For the remaining years of his life, Attell lived in New York City. There, he operated taverns, engaged in ticket speculation, gambled, and made a living in various other ways. Attell married twice: his first marriage to Elizabeth Margaret Egan ended in divorce, and his second wife, Mae O'Brien, shrewdly managed the tavern that he opened in 1939 and made it a success. Attell had no children of his own, but he helped raise three stepdaughters. For many years he attended all of the major fights in the New York City area, and he was often seen at ringside.

Attell was an inaugural inductee to the International Boxing Hall of Fame in 1989. He died in a nursing home at Libertyville, New York.

• Attell's complete record as a boxer is in Herbert G. Goldman, ed., *The Ring Record Book and Boxing Encyclopedia*, 1986–1987 ed. (1987). A brief biography is in Ken Blady, *The Jewish Boxers Hall of Fame* (1988). Attell's role in the Black Sox scandal is explained fully in Eliot Asinof, *Eight Men Out* (1987); and Harold Seymour, *Baseball: The Golden Age* (1971). His fights with Owen Moran and Jem Driscoll are described in two articles by Dan Daniel in *The Ring*: "Attell and Moran in Classic Draw," Mar. 1945, and "Driscoll vs. Attell: Battle of Giants," Jan. 1946. See also Jersey Jones, "Controversial Abe Attell Dead at 85; Held Feather Title 12 Years," *The Ring*, May 1970. An obituary, by Mark Hawthorne, is in the *New York Times*, 7 Feb. 1970.

LUCKETT V. DAVIS

ATTERBURY, William Wallace (31 Jan. 1866–20 Sept. 1935), railroad executive, was born in New Albany, Indiana, the son of John G. Atterbury, an attorney and Presbyterian home missionary, and Catherine Larned. After graduating from Yale's Sheffield Scientific School in 1886, Atterbury entered the mechanical engineering department of the Pennsylvania Railroad (PRR) as an apprentice in the Altoona, Pennsylvania, shops. In 1889, he was named road foreman of engines and in 1892 was promoted to assistant engineer of motive power for PRR Lines West (of Pittsburgh). Three years later he became master mechanic of the road's Fort Wayne, Indiana, shops—the second-largest on the system, after Altoona. In 1896 Atterbury returned to Altoona as superintendent of motive power for PRR Lines East and five years later became general superintendent of motive power for the entire PRR, then the nation's largest railroad by nearly every measure.

As a college-trained engineer and former apprentice, Atterbury was rare for that era in that he possessed both a theoretical and practical understanding of steam locomotives. He subsequently helped to implement a system of standard designs that became the hallmark of PRR motive power. The railroad produced hundreds of engines based on a relative handful of similar designs, thus exploiting efficiencies inherent in interchangeable parts and mass production. In 1902 Atterbury left the engineering ranks for the operating department which had broad responsibilities for actually running trains and, where there were more possibilities for advancement. He became general manager of Lines East, with an office in the road's Philadelphia corporate headquarters. He reached the company's highest operating position, fifth vice president, in 1909 and was made vice president of operations in 1912 when the practice of numbering vice presidencies was discontinued. Widely known as an energetic manager who was familiar with virtually all aspects of railroading and who preferred an informal "shirtsleeves" approach to problem solving, Atterbury was elected to a three-year term as president of the American Railway Association in 1916.

Soon after the United States entered World War I in April 1917, President Woodrow Wilson named Atterbury director general of transportation for the American Expeditionary Force. The appointment came in response to General John Joseph Pershing's request to be sent "the best railroad man in the U.S." Atterbury oversaw the part of the French railway that supplied American troops and brought order and efficiency to a previously chaotic situation. For his efforts he won medals from six nations and forever after preferred the title "General."

Atterbury returned to the PRR as vice president of operations in 1920. However, president Samuel Rea soon assigned him the task of ridding the company of its shopcraft unions, which were affiliated with the American Federation of Labor. They had won collective bargaining rights and substantial wage increases during the war, when the railroad industry had come under federal control, but the PRR was traditionally opposed to dealing with national unions. Although Atterbury had risen through the ranks and enjoyed the admiration of PRR employees at all levels, he moved forcefully to exterminate the unions. With the sanction of the U.S. Railroad Labor Board, newly created by Congress to oversee the volatile rail labor situation nationwide, he arbitrarily imposed company unions and terminated AFL contracts. Thousands of employees were permanently discharged, as a result both of a postwar reduction in staff and of contract terminations. There was practically no violence, however, and even as the PRR was gaining an anti-labor reputation that would last for generations, it also was recording record net income, which reached $51.5 million in 1923. Atterbury's success in ousting the AFL secured his place as Rea's heir apparent, and he was elected president on 1 Oct. 1925.

Atterbury anticipated later trends in the railroad industry by trying to remake the Pennsylvania into a total transportation enterprise. The PRR invested in Greyhound Bus Lines, Trans World Airlines, and a number of trucking companies and experimented with containerized and piggyback truck shipments on railroad flatcars. Federal regulatory constraints and a shrinking traffic base during the Great Depression caused most of these ventures to be shortlived. Atterbury also was a leading advocate of consolidation as a means of rationalizing the nation's overbuilt rail network. He established a holding company, the Pennroad Corporation, to buy stock in the Wabash, Lehigh Valley, New Haven, and several smaller roads. The acquisitions were a first step toward grouping the multitude of rail lines into seven large regional carriers—a scheme that bore a remarkable resemblance to the nation's rail systems of the 1980s and 1990s. Again, the depression intervened to thwart his plans. Consolidation became moot as most railroads fought for their economic lives, and the actual worth of the Pennroad acquisitions proved to be far less than the purchase price.

It was in the field of electric traction that Atterbury left his most enduring legacy. Steam railroads had long been reluctant to adopt this new form of motive power. Few could afford electrification's high installation costs, and fewer still had the traffic density that was required if electricity's many advantages over steam were to be fully realized. But the PRR had both the financial resources and the traffic base, and on 1 November 1928, Atterbury announced that the railroad intended to electrify its 245-mile multitrack main line between New York and Washington. Along with related terminal improvements, such as Philadelphia's Thirtieth Street Station, the project cost more than $250 million. Upon its completion in 1935, it ranked as the largest capital improvement project ever undertaken by an American railroad. The Pennsylvania reaped many benefits from electrification, including faster schedules, increased equipment reliability, decreased labor costs, and less terminal congestion. During World War II, electrification also helped prevent a recurrence of the kind of traffic jam that in World War I had nearly brought the railroad to a standstill. Today Amtrak continues to make use of the electrified system as part of its Northeast corridor route.

Hard hit by the depression, the railroad completed the electrification project only with the help of loans from the Public Works Administration. Atterbury secured this aid as a last resort, since as a fervid Republican he loathed most of President Franklin Roosevelt's New Deal programs. He was a power behind the scenes in Pennsylvania Republican politics, allying himself with Philadelphia's Vare machine against the liberal Republicans led by the populist governor, Gifford Pinchot. He also served on the Republican National Committee.

Atterbury retired in July 1934 after he suffered what were eventually fatal complications from gallstone surgery. He was survived by his second wife, the former Arminia Rosengarten MacLeod, whom he had married in 1915. They had one child, and he had adopted her three children from a previous marriage. His 1895 marriage to Matilda Hoffman, which ended with her death in 1910, was childless.

In the tradition of the PRR's up-from-the-ranks executives, and in contrast to many of his counterparts on other railroads, Atterbury put the advancement of the company before personal gain. He shunned public attention and lived without ostentation, his chief luxury being a small yacht that he sailed along the East Coast. He also was an inveterate mechanical tinkerer and had both the yacht and his home outfitted with machine shops. However, his unpretentious nature and years of shirtsleeve experience in railroad workshops belied an overweening hatred of labor unions—perhaps his only serious managerial flaw.

• The Hagley Museum and Library in Wilmington, Del., holds voluminous presidential correspondence and related executive records from Atterbury's administration. The Pennsylvania Historical and Museum Commission holds records from the PRR engineering department. Some personal papers are held by Atterbury's descendants. *Railway Age*, 3 Oct. 1935, pp. 625–27, and *American Magazine*, Mar. 1920, pp. 36–37 and 105–23, offer good biographical profiles. Obituaries are in the *New York Times*, 21 Sept. 1935, and *Transactions of the American Society of Civil Engineers* 101 (1936): 1518–24.

MICHAEL BEZILLA

ATTERIDGE, Harold Richard (9 July 1886–19 Jan. 1938), librettist and lyricist, was born in Lake Forest, Illinois, the son of Richard H. Atteridge and Anna T. O'Neill. He attended the University of Chicago, graduating in 1907 with a bachelor's degree in philosophy (Ph.B). While at the university, Atteridge joined the

Phi Kappa Psi fraternity and began writing skits and revues, including two musical comedies, *A Winning Miss* (1905) and *The Girl in the Kimono* (1907). Immediately after college, Atteridge signed on with a song publishing company in Chicago. Encouraged by the acceptance of two of his song lyrics for the show *Madame Sherry*, and carrying a letter of introduction and a single suitcase, Atteridge arrived in New York City in 1910.

Within a week of his arrival, an interview with J. J. Shubert marked the beginning of a professional relationship that would last most of Atteridge's life. Shubert immediately bought several of Atteridge's song lyrics for the then-running *Revue of Revues* and offered him a contract. Atteridge's first Winter Garden revue, *Vera Violetta* (1911), featured Gaby Deslys and Al Jolson. Within a few years, Atteridge had become the poet laureate of the Winter Garden, and the primary lyricist, script writer, and "show doctor" for the largest producing organization in New York, the Shuberts.

Atteridge was responsible for creating the annual *Passing Shows*, which were intended to compete with the rival Ziegfeld *Follies*. As the lyricist working with composer Louis Hirsch on the *Passing Show* of 1912, Atteridge helped to develop the format that would be used in all the succeeding *Passing Shows* through 1924. Beginning in 1914, Atteridge wrote both dialogue and lyrics for the shows. Though the *Passing Shows* were topical in nature, satirizing current events or other popular legitimate shows, the primary attraction was the scantily clothed chorus girls who appeared in abundance. Atteridge is credited with introducing the famous runway to the Winter Garden Theatre, borrowed from Max Reinhardt's exotic production of *Sumurun*, down which many an aspiring actress made her first bare-legged New York appearance. Though not noted for their literary quality, the *Passing Shows* were the "bread and butter" of the Shubert organization.

Atteridge, a "rapid-fire librettist," stated that it took him "between thirty minutes and an hour" to write the lyrics for a song. He took his inspiration for dialogue from "everyday life—on the subway, in restaurants, on the street . . . most any place where ordinary people are to be seen." Though most of his scripts have long ceased to be performed, the audiences who made Atteridge one of the best-paid librettists in the theatrical world of his day were amused to find their own lives, issues, and concerns amidst the beautiful girls and the opulent surroundings of the Winter Garden Theatre.

In addition to the *Passing Shows*, Atteridge wrote the book and lyrics for musical comedies and other revues, many of them designed to highlight the talents of a particular star, most frequently Al Jolson. In addition to being featured in *Vera Violetta* (1911), Jolson also appeared or starred in seven other Atteridge shows: *The Whirl of Society* (1912), *The Honeymoon Express* (1913), *Dancing Around* (1914), *Robinson Crusoe, Jr.* (1916), *Sinbad* (1918), *Bombo* (1921), and *Big Boy* (1925). Atteridge adapted the story lines to accommodate the Jolson blackface character and used interpolated songs, such as "Swanee," that made the performer the most popular box-office attraction in New York City. *Sky High* (1925) was created for Willie Howard, and *Make It Snappy* (1922) was molded to Eddie Cantor's talents. Cantor and Atteridge collaborated to create the Ziegfeld *Follies* in 1927.

His musical collaborators were many, including: Louis Hirsch, Jean Schwartz, Sigmund Romberg, Rida Johnson Young and Victor Herbert, Henry Wagstaff, Harry Carroll, Captain Harry Graham, and Irving Berlin. Rarely the creator of an original plot, Atteridge took the inspiration for his shows from other well-known plays (resulting in frequent litigation), folk stories, contemporary themes, and popular French and German plays. Besides those already mentioned, other show titles include: *The Whirl of the World* (1914), *The Last Waltz* (1921), *The Rose of Stamboul* (1922), *Lady in Ermine* (1922), *The Dancing Girl* (1923), *Innocent Eyes* (1924), *Gay Paree* (1925), *Princess Flavia* (1925), *A Night in Spain* (1927), *The Duchess of Chicago* (1928), *A Night in Venice* (1929), *Pleasure Bound* (1929), *Broadway Nights* (1929), *Everybody's Welcome* (1931), and *Fredericka* (1937).

When the *Passing Shows* of 1923 and 1924 failed to please audiences, the Shuberts and Atteridge began a new series of revues titled *Artists and Models* (started in 1923), followed by the *Greenwich Village Follies* (started in 1925). Though continuing to write for the Shubert Organization, Atteridge engaged in acrimonious correspondence with J. J. Shubert when Atteridge contracted his services to other producing companies, including Ziegfeld's. In 1933 Atteridge moved to Hollywood to pursue a more active involvement with the motion picture industry and radio.

Atteridge was married in 1923 to Mary Teresa Corless, who had been a chorus girl in *The Dancing Girl* using the stage name Jean Thomas. His wife was often his first audience as he read his completed scripts to her in the early morning light. Atteridge died from cirrhosis at their Long Island home.

Though he rarely received top billing for his role in creating a show or the fame that came to other writers, from the early days of his career until his death, not a single year went by when an Atteridge show was not playing somewhere in the country. With the additional royalties accrued from the sale of sheet music (published by Leo Feist, T. B. Harms, and Jerome Schwartz Publishing Company), phonograph recordings, and, later, movies, Atteridge was reputed to be the wealthiest writer in the theater. Atteridge penned the lyrics to over 1,500 songs and completed over 100 librettos or revues. It was through the vehicle of Atteridge shows that performers such as Al Jolson, Eddie Cantor, Ed Wynn, and Fred and Adele Astaire got their introductions to stardom.

• Many of the Atteridge papers are in three separate New York libraries or archives: the Shubert Archives at the Lyceum Theatre contains contracts, correspondence, reviews, and Shubert-produced librettos; the rare book and manuscript room at the New York Public Library, Main Branch, holds six folders, including his account books from 1909 to 1928 and royalty agreements with producers other than the Shuberts; the Billy Rose Theatre Collection at the New York Public Library for the Performing Arts, Lincoln Center, maintains a clipping file and Atteridge's scrapbook, as well as the Harold Atteridge Collection of scripts, which contains musical plays or revues produced primarily outside of New York. Both Jerry Stagg's *The Brothers Shubert* (1968) and Brooks McNamara's *The Shuberts of Broadway* (1990) give additional information about the chronology and circumstances of individual shows. Obituaries are in the *New York Times*, 17 Jan. 1938, and *Variety*, 19 Jan. 1938.

SUSAN F. CLARK

ATTUCKS, Crispus (c. 1723–5 Mar. 1770), probably a sailor, was the first to be killed in the Boston Massacre of 5 March 1770. Generally regarded to have been of mixed ancestry (African, Indian, and white), Attucks seems to have hailed from a Natick Indian settlement, Mashpee (incorporated as a district in 1763, near Framingham, Massachusetts).

While Attucks's life and background before the tragic event are uncertain, two reasonable conjectures stand out. First, he was a descendant of those Natick Indians converted to Christianity in the seventeenth century. One tribesman, John Attuck, was hanged on 22 June 1676 for allegedly conspiring with the Indian insurrection of that year. Second, it appears that Attucks may have once been a slave. The *Boston Gazette* of 2 October 1750 printed this notice: "Ran away from his Master, William Brown of Framingham on the 30th of September last, a mulatto Fellow, about twenty-seven years of age, named Crispus, 6 feet 2 inches high, short curled hair, his knees nearer together than common . . . "

J. B. Fisher, who argues that Attucks had Indian blood, also claims that he became a crewman on a Nantucket whaler, owned by a Captain Folger, which was docked at the time of the Massacre in Boston harbor. A sailor, James Bailey, testified that the assaulting group, which Attucks headed, "appeared to be sailors." John Adams (1735–1826) said that Attucks "was seen about eight minutes before the firing at the head of twenty or thirty sailors in Cornhill. . . . He was a stout fellow, whose very looks were enough to terrify any person. . . . He was about forty-seven years old."

The Bostonians' wrath had long been building against the stationing of the Fourteenth and Twenty-ninth British regiments in the town. In the evening of 5 March, Attucks dined at Thomas Symmonds's victualing house and, learning of the commotion taking place at the customshouse on King Street, joined a group headed in that direction. It is said that he and others had earlier threatened British soldiers at Murray's barracks. Attucks and his gang gathered cordwood sticks and wooden pieces from butchers' stalls, carrying these makeshift weapons over their heads as they approached the scene of the disturbance. John Adams, in remarks before the jury that tried the British soldiers for their role in the Massacre, stated that "Attucks appears to have undertaken to be the hero of the night, and to lead this army with banners." In his summation, Adams also said that "it is in this manner, this town has been often treated; a Carr from Ireland, and an Attucks from Framingham, happening to be here" to "sally out upon their thoughtless enterprises, at the head of such a rabble of negroes, &c., as they can collect together . . . " Testimony at the soldiers' trial differed over whether Attucks had grabbed for the bayonet of Private Hugh Montgomery, causing a struggle that resulted in the shooting. John Adams tried to portray Attucks as the instigator, "to whose mad behavior, in all probability, the dreadful carnage of that night is chiefly ascribed." Adams added that Attucks's group was a "mob whistling, screaming, and rending like an Indian yell." Some witnesses, however, testified that Attucks was killed while leaning on his cordwood stick. Two shots to his breast caused the fatality.

After the massacre, the bodies of Attucks and James Caldwell, the two nonresident victims, were brought to Faneuil Hall. On 8 March, a funeral procession of ten to twelve thousand people and numerous coaches accompanied the hearses of Attucks and three other victims to Granary burial ground, where all four coffins were buried in one grave.

Captain Thomas Preston, the British officer of the day who commanded the squad that fired upon the civilians, and eight soldiers were tried before the Suffolk Superior Court in Boston from 27 November to 5 December 1770. Preston and six of his men were acquitted, including William Warren, who was charged specifically with killing Attucks; two others were found guilty of manslaughter and were branded on the thumb after pleading benefit of clergy.

Crispus Attucks, apparently of African and Indian ancestry, was the first martyr of the American Revolution. Later, black military companies were named for him. In 1888 the city of Boston and the state of Massachusetts erected on Boston Common a memorial to Attucks and other victims of the massacre.

• Different perspectives on whether Attucks was African American or Indian are in J. B. Fisher, "Who Was Crispus Attucks?" *American Historical Record* 1 (1872): 531–33, and Benjamin Quarles, *The Negro in the American Revolution* (1961). For the legal documents and trial record pertaining to the Boston Massacre with substantial mention of Crispus Attucks, see L. Kinvin Wroth and Hiller B. Zobel, eds., *Legal Papers of John Adams* (3 vols., 1965). A comprehensive treatment of the Massacre is Hiller B. Zobel, *The Boston Massacre* (1970). Josiah H. Temple, *History of Framingham, Massachusetts, 1640–1885* (1887), offers background information on Attucks. Of interest also is *A Memorial of Crispus Attucks, Samuel Maverick, James Caldwell, Samuel Gray, and Patrick Carr, from the City of Boston* (1889).

HARRY M. WARD

ATWATER, Caleb (25 Dec. 1778–13 Mar. 1867), author and politician, was born in North Adams, Massachusetts, the son of Ebenezer Atwater, a carpenter, and Rachel Parker. He was distantly related to other

Atwaters who would become prominent in Ohio, including a Captain Caleb Atwater, founder of Atwater Township in Portage County. Atwater was raised by a guardian, a Mr. Jones of North Adams, Massachusetts, after the death of Atwater's mother when he was five years old. At the age of eighteen he was sent to Williams College, where he received both a B.A. and an M.A. in 1804.

Following his graduation, Atwater opened a school for young ladies in New York City but soon gave this up in order to study theology. Although he became a Presbyterian minister, ill health forced him to abandon this career following the death of his first wife, Diana Lawrence, with whom he had one child. He then studied law with a Judge Smiley of Marcellus, New York, and was admitted to the bar. In 1811 he married Belinda Butler, the daughter of a local judge; they had nine children. Rather than practicing law after admission to the bar, Atwater immediately entered into a business affair that soon bankrupted him, foreshadowing the penury that would follow him throughout his life.

This business failure contributed to his decision to move in 1815 to Circleville, Ohio, a burgeoning frontier town that traded in local farm produce and manufactured products. Here he divided his time between the law and an interest in the local antiquities and earthworks. The latter interest led to the publication by the American Antiquarian Society of his *Descriptions of the Antiquities Discovered in the State of Ohio and Other Western States* (1820). He maintained memberships in both the Antiquarian Society and the Lyceum of Natural History.

In 1821 Atwater was elected to represent the Pickaway-Hocking District of the Ohio state legislature, where his politics would reflect an eclecticism present in his larger life. While his legislative activity conformed to National Republican and, later, Whig ideology (he, in fact, named two of his sons DeWitt Clinton and Henry Clay Atwater), he was an ardent Jacksonian Democrat. In the legislature Atwater early opposed the temporary abandonment of the road tax as penurious and damaging to the state's long-term interests. An active advocate of internal improvements, he also supported legislation in favor of the Ohio and Erie canal, which was eventually completed in 1832. His procanal editorials in the Circleville newspaper were published under a Latin pseudonym.

Atwater's most important legislative contribution, however, was in the promotion of common schools through taxation and the efficient use of school lands. After his election to the legislature, he soon began to agitate over the wasteful and corrupt dispensation of government land allocated for the support of schools by the provisions of the Northwest Ordinance and six other federally sponsored land grants. Atwater complained that these lands were leased for long terms at unrealistically low prices as rewards for corrupt politicians and their friends. He further argued that valuable timber was frequently plundered and legally required improvements avoided. Much of Ohio's legislative activity between 1802 and 1820 revolved around complex schemes to distribute or retain these lands.

In December 1821 a committee of five legislators including Atwater was formed to examine the issue. On the committee's recommendation, Governor Allen Trimble appointed in May 1822 a seven-member commission to deal with both the school lands problem and the larger issue of common school legislation, with Atwater as the chairman. One commissioner was responsible for reporting on each of the seven land categories: congressional lands, especially the sixteenth section specified in the Northwest Ordinance of 1787; Virginia Military Land reserved by Virginia in 1783; U.S. Military Land reserved by the U.S. government in 1796; Symmes's Purchase, 311,000 acres bought by John Cleve Symmes in 1787; the Ohio Company's purchase of 1787; the Refugee Lands extending from Columbus to Zanesville and including the Rupee, Moravian, Trent, Dohmore, and Zane's grants; and the Connecticut Western Reserve Fund purchased by Connecticut in 1784. In addition swamp lands and salt lands were to be used to supplement school funds. At his own expense, Atwater sent out 500 letters to various individuals involved in the use of these lands and incorporated the data into three pamphlets: one described the present state of school lands, another proposed legislation for these properties, and the third proposed that a statewide school system be created by the prospective funds. These pamphlets were then used to garner popular support for school legislation.

Although Atwater was to be reimbursed for the expenses incurred by the commission, opponents in the legislature managed to divert much of this money, leaving him with a personal net loss. Atwater was not a member of the subsequent session of the state legislature, having instead campaigned unsuccessfully for election to the U.S. Congress in 1822. Consequently, he was able to devote his entire, uncompensated time to the commission. Although the proposed legislation was not passed in 1823, the October election of 1824 brought in a more congenial group of politicians who in 1825 passed legislation providing for the mandatory establishment of township schools, a county tax to support these schools, and the certification of teachers by a county board of examiners. This legislation resulted from a compromise between canal and school supporters that called for the sale of school lands with the proceeds used for canal bonds. Atwater thereby helped promote canals and schools simultaneously.

In 1824 Atwater began editing in Chillicothe his own paper, *Friend of Freedom*, dedicated to the promotion of internal improvements and education in Ohio. This enterprise soon failed, however, leaving him at the mercy of creditors. President Andrew Jackson, whom Atwater visited at the "Hermitage," appointed him in 1829 one of three commissioners to conduct treaty negotiations with the Winnebago Indians at Prairie du Chien in Wisconsin. Atwater used the experience as the basis for his *Remarks Made on a Tour to Prairie du Chien* (1831). His solution to the "Indian problem" involved the acculturation of American Indians through manual training in schools to be established for that purpose. Atwater deplored the past treatment of Indians and suggested that future historians would condemn the nation for its practices with regard to this population. Both *Remarks Made on a Tour to Prairie du Chien* and his *History of the State of Ohio* (1838) received scathing criticism. The former contained substantially plagiarized and often inaccurate information; the latter presented antislavery views. He also wrote *Mysteries of Washington City during Several Months of the Session of the Twenty-eighth Congress* (1844), warning citizens to keep a wary eye on their national politicians, and *An Essay on Education* (1841), in which he called for the further expansion of schooling, better pay for teachers, and the same education for women as for men. None of his writings sold well, providing him with little income with which to supplement his scant earnings from his law practice.

In many ways Atwater was representative of the spirit of antebellum America: he was antislavery, an avid promoter of education and science, a believer in progress and utilitarianism, and an egalitarian. While personally detesting slavery, he advocated a pragmatic approach. Atwater maintained that by not pressing for abolition Ohio would benefit relative to the slave-holding states, which would deteriorate from the inefficiencies and negative aspects of the institution. Ohio simultaneously would flourish as a magnet for enterprising free citizens.

Described by a contemporary as an unhappy, disappointed man and a "queer talker," Atwater, through his personal trials, mirrored the effects of a wider tension in these years between individual ambition and an almost religious civic-mindedness. In spite of his literary and political contributions and his good standing in the community, Atwater's death in Circleville received only brief mention in the local newspaper, and he died in virtual obscurity.

• The largest collection of Atwater's manuscripts is in the archives of the American Antiquarian Society in Worcester, Mass. Additional manuscripts can be found in the Burton Historical Collection of the Detroit Public Library. The best accounts of his life are in Clement L. Martzolff, "Caleb Atwater," *Ohio Archaeological and Historical Society Publications* 14 (1905): 247–71, and Henry Howe, *Historical Collections of Ohio*, vol. 2 (1902). Thematically conflicting versions of common school formation in Ohio by Kenneth W. Lottich, *New England Transplanted* (1964), and William McAlpine, "The Origin of Public Education in Ohio," *Ohio Archaeological and Historical Society Publications* 38 (1929): 409–47, provide good accounts of the context in which Atwater acted. Also useful is Amory D. Mayo, "Education in the Northwest during the First Half Century of the Republic, 1790–1840," *Report of the United States Commissioner of Education, 1894–1895*, vol. 2 (1896): 1513–50. The complex history of common school funding is examined in Fletcher H. Swift, *A history of Public Permanent Common School Funds in the United States, 1795–1905* (1911).

TED D. STAHLY

ATWATER, Helen Woodard (29 May 1876–26 June 1947), home economist, was born in Somerville, Massachusetts, the daughter of Wilbur Olin Atwater, an agricultural and food chemistry pioneer and expert in physiology and scientific administration, and Marcia Woodard. She grew up in Middletown, Connecticut, where her father was a professor at Wesleyan University. Beginning when she was six, her family lived in Europe several times. Her father had done postdoctoral work in chemistry at Leipzig and Berlin, and he returned in the 1880s to carry on research in nutrition and calorimetry (the energy-producing values of foods). While in Europe, Atwater attended school, becoming fluent in both German and French; she entered Smith College in 1894 and was keenly interested in studies and experiments in human nutrition. She graduated from Smith in 1897 with a bachelor's degree in literature.

By this time, Atwater's father had been serving for three years as head of the new U.S. Department of Agriculture's (USDA) Office of Experiment Stations, an innovation he inspired and inaugurated in Connecticut in 1875. In 1896 he had come out with the first tables ever made on the composition of familiar foods, and after Atwater graduated she worked with him on the first popular presentation of these facts in the *USDA's Farmers' Bulletin 142*. Her strength was interpreting scientific findings and putting them into language that the general public could understand. She returned to Middletown to help her father write his calorimetry papers and to write and edit the USDA's popular and technical bulletins and their nutrition investigations. After her father's death in 1907, Atwater stayed on in Middletown, working on her father's papers and preparing a bibliography of his extensive writings.

In 1909 Atwater moved to Washington, D.C., to join the staff of her father's former USDA department, the Office of Home Economics. Atwater brought scientific and editorial expertise to the USDA, for which she both wrote and edited articles for the department's *Farmers' Bulletin* series (nos. 817 and 824) and wrote the "Home Economics" entry for the 1921 *Yearbook of Agriculture*. While head of editorial work for this department, she also authored articles for such other publications as the *Journal of Home Economics* and the *Annals of the Academy of Political and Social Science*. Atwater's book, *Home Economics: The Art and Science of Homemaking*, was published in 1929. During her fourteen years with the USDA, Atwater's extensive writings focused on food preparation and on the nutritive values of foods—work that continued her father's commitment to using food science to bring a low-cost, nutritious diet to working-class and rural homes.

After fourteen years at the USDA, Atwater accepted an offer from the American Home Economics Association (AHEA) to become the first full-time editor of its publication, the *Journal of Home Economics*. Published since 1909, when the AHEA was established, the journal provided Atwater an excellent opportunity to continue influencing the still very young and developing field of home economics. She brought her wide reading in current scientific research to her selection and editing of articles for the journal and incorporated new scientific information on nutrition and food preparation into her editorials and articles. Lita Bane, a former president of the American Home Economics Association, commenting on Atwater's contributions as editor of the *Journal of Home Economics*, remarked that her "insight and clear thinking . . . her sound sense of values and active imagination . . . enabled her to make the *Journal* . . . a stimulating leader of thought in a rapidly developing educational field" (*Journal of Home Economics* 33 [Nov. 1941]).

Along with her editorial skills and ability to interpret new food science findings for the journal's readers, Atwater brought to the journal and to the AHEA her network of associations from the extensive committee and agency work she had been doing since going to Washington in 1909. During World War I, she was the USDA's liaison officer to the Council for National Defense, and she served as executive chair of the food production and home economics department of the Women's Committee of the council.

From 1923 until 1943, Atwater was a member of the Women's Joint Congressional Committee, a group of delegated Washington representatives of women's organizations that worked on Capitol Hill on behalf of social welfare legislation; she served as its chair from 1926 to 1928. She worked on the committee for the White House Conference on Child Health and Protection (1930) and took part in the President's Conference on Home Building and Home Ownership (1931). A member of the American Public Health Association, she served as chair of its committee on housing hygiene in 1942. Atwater was also a fellow of the American Association for the Advancement of Science. She regularly attended, organized sessions, and presented papers at national and international meetings, and she encouraged an international outlook among her colleagues at the AHEA and the *Journal of Home Economics* as well. Atwater was an organizer of international conferences on human welfare and served as a consultant for the Associated Countrywomen of the World, headquartered in London. The AHEA recognized her international commitment when they honored her memory by establishing the Atwater International Fellowship Award in 1948.

Atwater's notable contributions to science and home economics were as an editor who was familiar and conversant with the science of nutrition research and who could translate that science into the lay person's language. She was dedicated to grounding the young field of home economics firmly on science, and her strong backgrounds in science and in editing, coupled with her broad reading in food and nutrition science, allowed her to continue this focus during her entire career. As an administrator, Atwater excelled. Her warm sense of humor could always be depended upon "to enliven even the most sober committee meeting" (*Journal of Home Economics* 33 [Nov. 1941]) and her keen analytic skills and dependable good judgment made her a constant source of counsel among her wide array of colleagues. Atwater died in Washington, D.C., having never married. She was buried in the Indian Hill Cemetery in Middletown, Connecticut.

• For additional information on Atwater, see Lita Bane et al., "Saluting Helen W. Atwater: First Full-Time Editor of the *Journal of Home Economics*," *Journal of Home Economics* 33 (Nov. 1941): 223–26. See also *American Men of Science*, vols. 3 and 4 (1906–1968), and *American Women of Science*, ed. Martha J. Bailey (1994). Obituaries are in the *New York Times*, 27 June 1947, and the *Smith Alumnae Bulletin* (Nov. 1947).

JANET CARLISLE BOGDAN

ATWATER, Lyman Hotchkiss (23 Feb. 1813–17 Feb. 1883), minister and professor, was born in New Haven, Connecticut, the son of Lyman Atwater and Clarissa Hotchkiss, farmers. Raised in New Haven, where he attended First (Congregational) Church pastored by Nathaniel W. Taylor, one of the outstanding theologians of the era, Atwater began his studies at Yale at the age of fourteen. During the winter of 1831 a religious awakening swept the campus, and Atwater underwent a life-changing conversion experience. That spring he graduated second in a class that included Noah Porter (who later served as Yale's president), a future U.S. senator, and two men who became Episcopal bishops. After teaching classics for a year at Mount Hope Seminary in Baltimore, Atwater began study for the ministry at Yale Divinity School, where Taylor had become a professor of theology. During his last two years at the seminary, Atwater also served as a tutor of mathematics at the college.

After being licensed to preach in 1834, Atwater was ordained and installed as the pastor of the First Congregational Church of Fairfield, Connecticut, on 29 July 1835. He diligently served this congregation, which was one of the oldest and most influential in the state, for nineteen years. During these years he opposed Taylor's New Divinity views and denounced the excesses of revivalism. While pastoring at Fairfield, Atwater also contributed many articles to the *Literary and Theological Review*, the *Biblical Repository*, the *Princeton Review*, and other journals. In 1835 he married Susan Sanford of New Haven, with whom he had five children.

His reputation as a scholar, a Calvinist, and a political and social conservative led Princeton to invite him in 1854 to take its chair in mental and moral philosophy. After seven years in this position, Atwater taught courses at Princeton on the relationship between revealed religion and metaphysics from 1861 to 1867. For most of the 1868–1869 academic year he served as the interim president of the college. When James McCosh became Princeton's president in 1869, Atwater was appointed professor of logic, metaphysics, ethics, economics, and politics, a position he held until his death.

Atwater served his college and the Presbyterian Church, U.S.A. (PCUSA), which operated Princeton, faithfully and effectively. His broad knowledge, personal character, concern for students, and ability to present ideas clearly and to stimulate thinking made him an outstanding teacher. He conceived and conducted a campaign in 1862 that raised $140,000 as an endowment, which was necessitated by Princeton's financial troubles caused by the withdrawal of its southern students. In 1869 he served on the committee that devised a basis of reunion between the Old School and New School branches of the PCUSA, which had divided in 1837. In 1880 he chaired the PCUSA Judicial Committee. From 1858 to 1863 he regularly taught courses at Princeton Theological Seminary on philosophy and ethics. He was a member of the seminary's board of trustees from 1860 until his death, and for the last six years of his life he served as its vice president.

Atwater's primary contribution, however, was his many publications. He wrote one book, *Manual of Elementary Logic* (1867), which for many years was widely used in American college classrooms. From 1869 to 1878 Atwater served as the coeditor of the *Princeton Review* (called the *Presbyterian Quarterly and Princeton Review* from 1872 to 1878), first with Charles Hodge and then with Henry B. Smith. Between 1840 and 1883 Atwater published more than 110 articles in the *Review* on many subjects, including theological issues, apologetics, spirituality, history, education, philosophy, ethics, politics, economics, and financial questions. His first article in the *Review*, "The Power of Contrary Choice" (Oct. 1840), defended Old School Calvinism, which Atwater championed until his death, against the theory of personal responsibility espoused by his former pastor and professor Nathaniel Taylor. In "Calvinism in Doctrine and Life" (Jan. 1875), Atwater defended Reformed theology against its many detractors, who he believed often misconceived and misrepresented its tenets.

Many of Atwater's essays in the *Review* dealt with economic and financial topics. He insisted in "The Late Commercial Crisis" (Jan. 1874) that the panic of 1873 reaffirmed "the warnings of Scripture" against covetousness, extravagance, and luxury. The panic reminded Americans of the importance of "industry, frugality, economy, prudence, [and] reasonable provision for the future," and it summoned everyone, especially the rich, "to feed the hungry, clothe the naked, shelter the homeless, . . . and above all to support the great evangelistic enterprises of the church" (p. 124). Atwater defended the private ownership of property, promoted "benevolent" capitalism, and objected to many practices of labor unions. He charged that socialism would destroy people's incentive to work hard, be frugal, and save and would therefore thwart both the capital formation and the productivity so important to economic development ("Our Industrial and Financial Situation," *Princeton Review* [July 1875]). Atwater insisted that the key to solving America's industrial problems was cooperation between management and labor, and he praised profit sharing as a way to increase productivity, prosperity, and worker satisfaction.

Atwater contended that the United States had a responsibility to be a Christian nation, as evidenced in its "origin, history, tradition, institutions, [and] in the whole drift" of its "social and national life" ("Taxation of Churches, Colleges and Charitable Institutions," *Princeton Review* [Apr. 1874]: 347). In several articles Atwater argued that the second table of the Ten Commandments should underlie and control all legislation. He called on the state to punish adultery and slander, prohibit obscene literature, restrain vagrancy and idleness, and enforce contracts.

Through his nearly two decades of ministry and almost three decades of teaching at Princeton, as well as his service to the PCUSA and his numerous publications, Atwater significantly influenced the views of the Reformed community in the United States, especially on economic and industrial issues, during the middle decades of the nineteenth century. Listened to "with the profoundest respect" at his presbytery, synod, and the General Assembly, this "quiet and unassuming" professor was a "diligent student of the past" and "a close observer" of his own era (*Presbyterian Banner*, 21 Feb. 1883, p. 1). Atwater "delighted" in "criticism and debate" and at times used "vehement . . . invective" (Porter, pp. 19, 21), but he always accurately presented the arguments of his opponents. Along with Charles Hodge, Atwater was the most able and prolific defender of Old School Calvinism during the mid-nineteenth century. He died in Princeton.

• In addition to the works by Atwater cited in the biography, other important articles he published in the *Princeton Review* include "Revivals" (Jan. 1842): 1–45; "The True Progress of Society" (Jan. 1852): 16–38; "The Matter of Preaching" (Oct. 1856): 655–88; "The Manner of Preaching" (Apr. 1863): 177–206; "Herbert Spencer's Philosophy" (Apr. 1865): 243–70; "The Labor Question in Its Economic and Christian Aspects" (July 1872): 468–95; "Civil Government and Religion" (Apr. 1876): 195–235; "The Higher Life and Christian Perfection" (July 1877): 389–419; "Morality, Religion, and Education in the State" (Mar. 1878): 395–422; "Horace Bushnell" (Jan. 1881): 114–44; "Christian Morality, Expediency and Liberty" (Jan. 1881): 61–82; and "Proposed Reforms in Collegiate Education" (July 1882): 100–120. Another of Atwater's significant essays is "Religion and Politics" in *Proceedings of the Second General Council of the World Alliance of Reformed Churches* (1880).

In *Addresses Delivered at the Funeral of Lyman Hotchkiss Atwater* (1883), Noah Porter et al. provide important information about Atwater's life and contribution. Also useful are Francis Atwater, *Atwater History* (1901), and *Princeton University General Catalog* (1906). Gary Scott Smith, *The Seeds of Secularization: Calvinism, Culture and Pluralism, 1870–1915*, discusses Atwater's views on political, economic, social, and ethical issues. A lengthy obituary is in the *Presbyterian Banner*, 21 Feb. 1883.

GARY SCOTT SMITH

ATWATER, Wilbur Olin (3 May 1844–22 Sept. 1907), nutritionist and professor of chemistry, was born in Johnsburg, New York, the son of William Warren Atwater, a methodist clergyman, and Elizabeth Barnes. The family moved from place to place within New England during his childhood. He attended the University of Vermont for two years but graduated in 1865 from Wesleyan University in Middletown, Connecticut. After three years of teaching school, he moved to Yale's Sheffield Scientific School as a graduate student in agricultural chemistry under Professor Samuel Johnson and received a Ph.D. degree in 1869. Atwater spent two further years studying in Leipzig and Berlin and visiting German agricultural experiment stations. On his return to the United States he spent two years teaching at East Tennessee University (later the University of Tennessee), then was able to obtain a position at Wesleyan, first as instructor and in 1874 as its first professor of chemistry. In 1873 Atwater had married Marcia Woodard; they were to make their home in Middletown for the rest of his life and to have two children.

Atwater's ambition was to establish the first agricultural experiment station in the country. With the support of Orange Judd, a wealthy publisher who had already given Wesleyan a new science building, he persuaded the Connecticut legislature to give money for a temporary station that would be under his direction. He persuaded local farmers to cooperate in fertilizers trials and also tested fertilizers in pot trials at Wesleyan. The legislature then decided to establish a permanent station, but at New Haven, in conjunction with the Sheffield School facilities.

Atwater, determined to continue research despite this political setback, began to concentrate on questions of human nutrition and the composition of foods, beginning with a grant from the U.S. Commission of Fish and Fisheries. He published his first research paper, on the determination of the fat content of foods, at age thirty-four, and for the next decade organized systematic work by a team of assistants. In 1882 he spent several months in Munich studying the techniques being used by Carl Voit, including nitrogen balance trials and respiration calorimetry, and also the German method of calculating the economic value of different foods.

Atwater was then asked to assess the adequacy of workers' diets, from food consumption data collected by the Massachusetts Bureau of Statistics and Labor. He assumed that men engaged in moderate labor needed 125 grams of protein per day, since that was roughly what was consumed by those able to afford it. In general, the workers appeared to have been adequately fed, but at the expenditure of 50 percent or more of their income. He was convinced that they could eat more cheaply and thus have more income left for housing, clothing, and other necessities if they would choose more economical sources of protein and fat—cheese, beans, and margarine for example, in place of steaks and butter.

To demonstrate and publicize his ideas, Atwater wrote five articles for the *Century Magazine* on the chemistry of foods and nutrition that gave him a national reputation and significant income. He expressed there his belief that "if we care for men's souls most effectively, we must care for their bodies also," so that his was a work of charity in the true Christian tradition of feeding the poor. This was, in part, a response to the president of Wesleyan, a clergyman, who at one time had said that Atwater's work was "not in consonance with the intellectual dignity of a university."

In 1887 the Hatch Act was passed, authorizing federal funding for an agricultural experiment station in each state. For Connecticut the funds were divided between the existing New Haven station and a new one, under Atwater's direction, at Storrs, a few miles from Wesleyan. Atwater was also invited to assume a new position in the U.S. Department of Agriculture (USDA) as director of the Office of Experiment Stations. He did this for nearly three years by staying eight months of each year in Washington, D.C., and having deputies act for him at Wesleyan and Storrs. He set up the *Experiment Station Record* as a central point of publication for the main findings from each station and established the principle that each station should concentrate its work in a few areas in which it could "conduct . . . investigations on such a scale and . . . accuracy as to secure results of permanent value." He also organized the collection and tabulation of data for food composition and the results of balance trials on both animals and humans from all over the world.

In 1890 he returned to Europe to learn more about the techniques of calorimetry. His ambition was to build the first respiration calorimeter in the United States that would be able to hold human subjects. With the help of his colleague Edward Rosa, professor of physics at Wesleyan, the complicated equipment was gradually designed, constructed, and put in working order by 1896, ultimately requiring a team of altogether sixteen people to keep it in operation day and night.

The heat emitted from complete combustion of fats and carbohydrates is the usual measure of their energy values—roughly nine and four kilocalories per gram respectively. Atwater's team was able to confirm that for human subjects a kilocalorie from one source was as effective as a kilocalorie from the other, both in maintaining resting metabolism and for muscular work. They also demonstrated that ethanol (the alcohol in fermented beverages) provided usable calories. This finding was promoted by the liquor industry and caused an outcry from temperance advocates who had been teaching that alcohol at any level was a poison.

During this period Atwater was appointed by the USDA to coordinate the nutrition research in progress at sixteen of the experiment stations nationwide. Some stations studied the chemical composition of particular classes of food (e.g., nuts, meats, and wheat flours milled in different ways) and others the composition of the diets consumed by contrasting groups such as low-income workers in different parts of the country, university professors, athletes, Chinese immigrants, and vegetarians. In Europe, Atwater collected further records of food consumption and studied the procedures being used there for nutritional research.

In November 1904 Atwater suffered a disabling stroke and lay at his home in Middletown until his death there three years later. In that period his assistant, Francis Benedict, published most of the results that had been obtained with the human calorimeter in their joint names.

Wilbur Atwater has been called "the father of nutritional science in the U.S.A." He was one of a group of young men who went to Germany for postgraduate study in the mid-1800s and returned with the burning ambition to see science similarly developed in their own country and put to practical use. He was a man of great energy and had the administrative ability to get things done. He certainly was a pioneer in attempting to make his science a quantitative one, but his dietary recommendations were already under attack in his last years. Russell Chittenden at Yale was showing that men could remain healthy and vigorous with one half of the protein intake recommended by Atwater and the German school. Atwater had also written that fruits and green vegetables were an unnecessary luxury because they were uneconomic sources of the nutrients recognized at the time. After his death, with the discovery of vitamins, it was realized how wrong this had been. However, much of the pioneering work on vitamins was done at the Wisconsin and New Haven Agricultural Experiment Stations under the government-financed programs of basic nutritional research that Atwater had worked so hard to establish.

• Atwater's papers and a large collection of his letters are available at the archives at Olin Library, Wesleyan University, Middletown, Conn. Much of his scientific work is summarized in his *Methods and Results of Investigations on the Chemistry and Economy of Foods*, bulletin no. 21 of the U.S. Department of Agriculture's Office of Experiment Stations (1895). The articles that made him well known to the public had the general title "The Chemistry of Foods and Nutrition," *Century Magazine* 34 (1877): 59–74, 397–405. See also L. A. Maynard, "Wilbur O. Atwater—A Biographical Sketch," *Journal of Nutrition* 78 (1962): 2–9, and K. J. Carpenter, "The Life and Times of W. O. Atwater (1844–1907)," *Journal of Nutrition* 124 (1994): 1707S–14S. A family memoir by his granddaughter is Catherine Atwater Galbraith, "Wilbur Olin Atwater," *Journal of Nutrition* 124 (1994): 1715S–17S.

KENNETH J. CARPENTER

ATWILL, Lionel (1 Mar. 1885–22 Apr. 1946), actor, was born in Croydon, England, the son of Alfred Atwill and Ada Emily Dace. He was educated at Mercer's School in London as an architect and surveyor. In 1904 he decided to pursue a career as an actor, playing a footman in a play called *The Walls of Jericho*. Atwill then toured the provinces with H. V. Neilson's company, specializing in such Ibsen roles as Captain Horster in *Enemy of the People*, Johann Tönnesen in *Pillars of Society*, and Rank in *A Doll's House*. From 1910 to 1912 Atwill toured Australia, and in 1914 he acted in Maeterlinck's *Monna Vanna* with the Horniman Players in Manchester. His major breakthrough came earlier, in 1912, when he played Arthur Preece, the leading role in a play called *Milestones*; that play had a successful two-year run with over 600 London performances. In 1913 he married Phyllis Relph; they had one child.

In 1915 Atwill was persuaded to join Lillie Langtry in an American tour of a play called *Mrs. Thompson*. Although it was unsuccessful, Atwill decided to remain in America, acting a season with George Foster Platt's company in Milwaukee, Wisconsin. In 1917 he produced and starred in a successful murder mystery called *The Lodger*. A year later he had leading roles in no fewer than five New York openings, including the male leads opposite Alla Nazimova in Arthur Hopkins's revivals of Ibsen's *Hedda Gabler* and *A Doll's House*, as well as in the Hopkins-directed American premiere of *The Wild Duck*. In *The Wild Duck*, Atwill initially played Ekdal, but when the play was later revived by Hopkins, he played Werle and was praised in both performances for adding a comic flair to productions that were otherwise criticized for an overly solemn approach. In 1918 Atwill scored another success as the politician Clive Cooper in a play called *Tiger! Tiger!* Atwill divorced his first wife in 1919. A year later he married the actress Elsie Mackay, with whom he had one child.

Late in 1920 Atwill played the title role in David Belasco's production of Sacha Guitry's bittersweet comedy *Deburau*. Belasco and Atwill followed with productions of two other Guitry adaptations, *The Grand Duke* (1921) and *The Comedian* (1923). In 1924 Atwill starred in Dorothy Brandon's *The Outsider* with Katharine Cornell; the play was successful financially but closed after three months because of a union dispute. Four years later Atwill revived the play with Isobel Elsom in the Cornell role. In 1925 he performed with Helen Hayes in Shaw's *Caesar and Cleopatra*. That same year Atwill was involved in a minor scandal when he publicly announced that he was suing Mackay for divorce after she left America for Liverpool with her lover, the actor Max Montesole. Mackay and Atwill later reconciled briefly, finally divorcing in 1928.

Atwill remained a popular actor until 1932, although he never acted in a play as successful as those earlier in his career. In 1928 he once again became a figure of controversy after the failure of *Napoleon*, in which Atwill played the title role. On the closing night of that production, Atwill used a curtain speech to castigate New York theater critics, accusing one of "leaving in the middle of the second act and writing his review as though he had seen all the play." A *New York Times* editorial responded by defending critics in general, blaming the play's unpopularity on the fact that it was unfashionably conservative. In 1930 Atwill remarried, this time to Louise Cromwell Brooks MacArthur, the former wife of General Douglas MacArthur.

In 1932 Atwill appeared in his first motion picture, a screen adaptation of the play *The Silent Witness*, in which he had previously appeared in New York. Later that same year, Atwill appeared in the film *Dr. X*. In an interview, he said, "I'm one of those few stage actors who really like the films, and admit it." He continued, "The motion pictures have a future I wish to share," to provide "adult entertainment with adventure and sophistication" (*New York Times*, 14 Aug. 1932).

Atwill moved to Hollywood in 1933, spending the remainder of his career in the motion picture industry. His films included *Mystery of the Wax Museum*, *Nana*, *The Firebird*, *Captain Blood*, *Son of Frankenstein*, *The Three Musketeers*, *Hound of the Baskervilles*, and many others. He particularly became known as a popular film villain, specializing in horror and suspense films.

In 1941 Atwill suffered a personal tragedy when his son from his second marriage, a pilot in the RAF, was killed in the Battle of Britain. Two years later he was indicted for perjury for false testimony given to a grand jury regarding pornographic films shown at a private party in his Hollywood home. He was given five years probation after admitting he had "lied like a gentleman" to protect the reputations of friends at the party. In 1943 his third wife filed for divorce. In 1944 he married Mary Paula Pruter Shelstone, known professionally as Paula Pruter, in Las Vegas. They had one child. Atwill died at his home in Pacific Palisades, California.

Atwill was a sophisticated actor with superb comic timing. Although he was mostly known as a film actor at the time of his death, his earlier stage work seems, in retrospect, far more significant. Atwill was an important dramatic actor of the early twentieth-century American theater, working repeatedly with such major figures as Lillie Langtry, Arthur Hopkins, Alla Nazimova, David Belasco, Katharine Cornell, and Helen Hayes. He was also one of the first important stage actors to see the potential of film as an art form and to voluntarily give up stage acting for a film career.

• The *New York Times*, 14 Apr. 1918, contains a profile, "The Rise of Lionel Atwill," that is useful in documenting his career in Great Britain. Otherwise, his career must be pieced together through play reviews and other newspaper accounts taken mostly from the *New York Times*, *The Times* (London), and *Variety*. For a detailed description of Atwill's American stage and film careers see his obituaries in the *New York Times*, 23 Apr. 1946, and *Variety*, 24 Apr. 1946, although neither source is entirely reliable.

ERIC SAMUELSEN

ATWOOD, Charles Bowler (18 May 1849–19 Dec. 1895), architect, was born in Charlestown, Massachusetts, the son of David Atwood, a banker, and Lucy Bowler. Atwood took an early interest in the architectural profession, applying for instruction in drawing to the office of Worcester architect Elbridge Boyden, where his talent was quickly identified and his tuition remitted. The youth assisted Boyden in his competition entry for the state capitol at Albany, New York, one of five premiated designs. He continued his formal education at the Lawrence Scientific School of Harvard University in 1868–1870, and his practical education with the Boston firm of Ware & Van Brunt, architects of Harvard's High Victorian Gothic Memorial Hall and among the most highly regarded professionals of the era. Atwood remained with the firm until 1872, when he established his own office in Boston, executing works primarily in Worcester.

In 1875 Atwood was employed by Christian Herter of the notable New York interior design firm of Herter Brothers, best known for their elaborately inlaid and carved furniture. As the head of their architectural department, Atwood was responsible for realizing Herter's ideas for the twin Vanderbilt mansions on Fifth Avenue, between Fifty-first and Fifty-second streets. During his tenure at Herter Brothers, his most notable commission was for work on the Mrs. Mark Hopkins house in Great Barrington, Massachusetts, where he spent two years (1886–1888) before returning to private practice in New York. Throughout his career, Atwood seemed to prefer designing monumental architecture to domestic, and in pursuit of such commissions the entered numerous competitions. His greatest success in this arena before his move to Chicago was the 1884 competition for the Boston Public Library, for which he won first prize for a classically inspired building with a high basement, arcaded and pedimented *piano nobile*, and a dome on each corner. Despite securing the prize, Atwood's design was never executed.

Atwood's career became one of national historical significance following the premature death of Chicago architect John W. Root in 1891, which left his partner Daniel H. Burnham in need of assistance as sole proprietor of their private practice and as chief of construction for the World's Columbian Exposition to be held in Chicago in 1893 to celebrate the quartercentenary of Columbus's arrival in the New World. Upon a recommendation from Atwood's former mentor Ware, Burnham hired Atwood as designer in chief for the exposition staff. The replacement of Root with Atwood signaled an important change in the design conception of the fair from Root's modified Richardsonian Romanesque to a beaux-arts–inspired classicism advocated by Burnham after Root's death. The central group of buildings at the fair, the Court of Honor, was designed in grand classical style by the most prominent architects of the time, including Richard Morris Hunt and the firm of McKim, Mead & White. Atwood contributed not only the fair's classical Fine Arts Palace but also provided the Court of Honor with a grand milieu of terraces, bridges, balustrades, and incidental buildings. As Burnham said of him, "More of the actual beauty of the Fair was due to him . . . than to any one else." In all, Atwood designed more than 100 structures for the fair, including the dairy, forestry, and anthropological buildings; the peristyle framing the end of the Court of Honor; the casino; the music hall; the railroad terminal station; and a wide variety of such miscellaneous structures as sheds, warehouses, shops, public restrooms, barns, flagstaffs, and entryways. It was, however, the Fine Arts Palace, containing the international art exhibitions at the fair, that secured Atwood's reputation among his peers and provided one of the showpieces of a famously showy event. The Fine Arts Palace was a bilaterally symmetrical building with pedimented porticoes on the two main facades, blind colonnades on the long wings, and a low saucer dome crowning the central crossing. Like many architects of his era, Atwood culled elements from a variety of sources for his structure, from the Porch of the Maidens on the Erechtheum to student work from the École des Beaux-Arts in Paris. Regarding this historicist approach, Atwood claimed, "My design is as original as anything in architecture can be and a great deal more original than some architectural work. The difference between me and some other architects is that I know what to take and what to leave and know how to combine things that come from different sources" (*Chicago Tribune*, 15 Jan. 1893). The result of this approach was a highly influential structure that received accolades from fellow artists and architects who claimed, as sculptor Augustus Saint-Gaudens did, that it was the finest building since the Parthenon, and from which elements were copied in such buildings as the Milwaukee Public Library and the Brooklyn Museum. Indeed, the building was reproduced wholesale in the 1924 Field Museum of Natural History in Chicago; and the beloved but temporary Palace was itself restored and made permanent between 1926 and 1940 and now serves as the Museum of Science and Industry.

After the fair, Burnham incorporated Atwood as an important member of the renamed D. H. Burnham & Co., under whose auspices Atwood participated in the design of the Ellicut Building in Buffalo and the upper stories of the Reliance Building in Chicago (originally designed by Root), as well as work on the Chicago lakefront development that served as a precursor to Burnham's groundbreaking 1907 work *Plan of Chicago*. Atwood, however, appears to have been an erratic personality, frequently late, often unreliable, and, according to an unpublished interview with Burnham, a drug user. Only two years passed from the close of the World's Columbian Exposition until Atwood's death in Chicago from "a complication of nervous and brain disorders," attributed to overwork at the fair. A small scandal erupted in Chicago and New York newspapers after Atwood's death, whereupon a "comic opera artist" named Marion Singer claimed to be Atwood's widow and heir to his $600,000 estate. According to the reports, records in White Plains, New York, showed that Atwood had married Singer in August 1881; that the two had had a son who had died in infancy; that they separated after 1884; and that Atwood's wife sued for divorce in 1891, but her application was denied.

Despite the relatively small output of Atwood's career, the huge success of his Fine Arts Palace and his influence on the overall appearance of the World's Columbian Exposition guarantee him a significant role in the shaping of American architectural history. The initial popularity of the beaux-arts look of the 1893 fair caused its buildings to serve as an architectural starting point and sourcebook for decades of important public buildings constructed in the United States, from government buildings at every level to libraries, museums, and schools. Although the style fell into disrepute with the onset of the international style in the 1920s, it enjoyed a revival of stature with postmodern architects and a reassessment by historians. The imposing classical appearance of buildings in many cities across the United States is indebted to the imaginative conception of classicism at the fair of which Atwood was so integral a part.

• Little material remains in connection with Atwood's life or work, but the best source of original information is certainly that contained in the Daniel H. Burnham Collection, Ryerson and Burnham Libraries, Art Institute of Chicago. Much information on Atwood can be gleaned from Thomas S. Hines, *Burnham of Chicago: Architect and Planner* (1974), and the older but useful Charles H. Moore, *Daniel H. Burnham: Architect, Planner of Cities* (1921). A great deal has been written about the World's Columbian Exposition; see especially Reid Badger, *The Great American Fair: The World's Columbian Exposition and American Culture* (1979), and David F. Burg, *Chicago's White City of 1893* (1976). An in-depth analysis of the architecture of the fair is contained in Titus Marion Karlowicz, "The Architecture of the World's Columbian Exposition" (Ph.D. diss., Northwestern Univ., 1965). Burnham wrote a lengthy professional obituary, "Charles Bowler Atwood," *Inland Architect and News Record* 26 (Jan. 1896): 56–57; shorter obituaries may be found in the *Chicago Tribune*, 21 Dec. 1895, and the *New York Herald*, 20 Dec. 1895.

INGRID A. STEFFENSEN-BRUCE

ATWOOD, Wallace Walter (1 Oct. 1872–24 July 1949), geomorphologist and geographer, was born in Chicago, Illinois, the son of Thomas Greene Atwood, a builder and planing mill operator, and Adelaide Adelia Richards. After graduating from West Division High School, Atwood enrolled in the new University of Chicago in 1892. There he studied under the geographer-geologist Rollin D. Salisbury, who took him on the university's first summer field-camp in geology to the Devil's Lake region near Baraboo, Wisconsin. Not only did the experience provide Atwood with the data for his first publication, "Drift Phenomena in the Vicinity of Devil's Lake and Baraboo, Wisconsin," written jointly with Salisbury (*Journal of Geology* 5 [1897]: pp. 131–47), but it also inspired his developing view of nature as a living laboratory. Years later, he wrote of the summer field-camp, "We were like chemists working in a laboratory with unknowns. But what a laboratory! The whole out-of-doors, with sunshine, winds, clouds, rain and people . . . Here was a laboratory which served as the stage setting of real human dramas" (Mather, p. 107). This experience gave rise to his consequent primary emphasis on fieldwork in research and teaching and convinced him that the study of geomorphology (then called physiography) was essential to understanding human geography.

In 1897, after earning his S.B. degree that year, Atwood entered the graduate program in geology at the University of Chicago. Meanwhile, he served as Salisbury's junior assistant on the New Jersey Geological Survey in 1897 and on the Wisconsin Natural History Survey in 1898–1899. The next year, Atwood married Harriet Towle Bradley, a laboratory teacher at the university; they would have four children. In 1901 Atwood became an assistant geologist under the U.S. Geological Survey (USGS). Eight years later he was promoted to geologist and remained an active member of the survey until his death.

Atwood secured an appointment as instructor in geology at the University of Chicago two years before his dissertation, *Glaciation of the Uinta Mountains*, was published in 1903, the same year he received his Ph.D. from Chicago. By 1910 he had risen to the rank of associate professor. Three years later he left Chicago to become the professor of physiography at Harvard University, where he remained until 1920.

During these years Atwood conducted the fieldwork in the United States and the rest of the world that underlay his principal publications. It was in the Rocky Mountains, however, that he concentrated his energies. Working initially with the USGS in the San Francisco Mountains of Arizona and the Uintas and the Wasatch of Utah, he soon focused on the San Juan Mountains in Southwest Colorado. As a result of conducting twenty-five intensive explorations of the Rockies covering more than 1,300 miles of terrain—during which he was often accompanied by his wife and children—Atwood became one of the leading authorities on the geomorphology, glacial geology, and recent history of the region. From data collected during these trips, he published numerous technical papers and his major monograph, coauthored with K. F. Mather, *Physiography and Quaternary Geology of the San Juan Mountains*, USGS Professional Paper 166 (1932).

In 1920 Atwood accepted an appointment as president of Clark University in Worcester, Massachusetts. Simultaneously hired as the head of its School of Geography, he also was authorized to establish a graduate studies program in that discipline, only the second fully staffed graduate program that could confer Ph.D.s in geography in the United States, thereby advancing significantly the status and dissemination of geographical knowledge through its training. Soon, however, he became embroiled in controversy, having exceeded his budget in his first year by 40 percent and then eliminating unilaterally several other graduate programs to cover the shortfall and facilitate the new program. This action led many professors to resign in protest. Atwood's tumultuous presidency was also marked by controversies over such issues as academic freedom and administrative disorders in several departments. Despite these difficulties, Atwood nevertheless greatly increased the size of the university's faculty and physical plant. At the same time, Clark was able to boast of possessing one of the most prominent geography departments in North America, whose members included O. E. Baker, C. F. Brooks, C. F. Jones, C. F. Marbut, E. C. Semple, and H. L. Shantz. When Atwood retired in 1946, the university's board of trustees proclaimed that he "left it in every respect a far better institution than it was when he came to it" (Mather, p. 108).

Atwood's greatest contributions to geography and geology came from his activities as an educator, promoter, and popularizer of those sciences. His first teaching experiences at Chicago placed him under the direct supervision of two of the most famous educational reformers of the day, Colonel Francis W. Parker and John Dewey. He also developed a reputation as an extremely popular lecturer and unwavering proponent of fieldwork, offering courses in both the classroom and the field. While at Harvard, however, he fell out of favor with President A. Lawrence Lowell over Atwood's tendency toward grade-inflation and a controversial field trip to Mount Monadnock.

Atwood nevertheless inspired a generation of aspiring geographers and geologists by his teaching excellence and delivered numerous lectures on scientific topics to popular audiences. He contributed similarly to the diffusion of knowledge through his activities with local museums. As the secretary and director of the Chicago Academy of Sciences, starting in 1908, he was responsible for arranging numerous public exhibits. He was especially proud of his role in starting the Children's Museum in Cambridge, Massachusetts, later boasting that "literally thousands of the public school children came [there] to receive lessons that . . . became an integral part of their school work" (Van Valkenburg, p. 676).

Contributing to his self-conceived role as a popularizer, Atwood wrote textbooks in geomorphology and geography for all educational levels, including the college textbook *The Physiographical Provinces of North America* (1940). In 1916 he contracted with Ginn and Company to author a series of educational works designed to revise and continue the geographical series started by Alexis E. Frye, a task he would continue for the rest of his life. In each work Atwood stressed the regional approach to studying geography, arguing that geomorphology was fundamental to the study of human geography because people did not conquer nature but were controlled by it and forced to adapt to their surroundings. What he hoped to accomplish was an expanded and diffused knowledge of geography that would allow people to "discover the laws of nature and accomplish better and better adjustments to natural conditions on this earth" (Koelsch, p. 14). For this reason, his textbooks were designed to build on the previous year's education in a manner consistent with his view of child development, derived from the influences of Parker and Dewey. He also directly supervised the production of numerous geographical and political maps that were used in classrooms throughout North America for years to come. In addition, Atwood penned numerous articles and books on scientific subjects, such as *The Rocky Mountains* (1945), directed toward a lay audience. Some of his works, such as *The Protection of Nature in the Americas* (1940), which epitomized his lifelong interest in the conservation of natural resources, were translated into other languages and distributed throughout the Western Hemisphere. Finally, in 1925 he founded the widely circulated magazine *Economic Geography*, and during his twilight years he became involved in the production of educational films in geography and geology. Of Atwood's publishing successes, fellow geographer George B. Cressey commented in 1949 that "few authors in any field have written more prolifically or had such a wide audience. Thirty thousand schools have used his elementary textbooks, and the sales have run into the millions" (p. 298).

Atwood also was able to exert an influence on the development, status, and dissemination of scientific knowledge through his activities with various congresses and societies. An active member of numerous professional organizations, including the Geological Society of America, he rose through their ranks to positions of prominence in many of them, becoming, for example, the president of the National Council of Geography Teachers in 1921 and receiving its Distinguished Service Award in 1944. He also held the presidency of the National Parks Association (1929–1933), of the Pan American Congress of Geography and History (1932–1935), and of the Association of American Geographers in 1934. He regularly attended conferences, including the Pacific Science Congresses of 1926 and 1948, and the International Geographical Congresses of 1927 and 1929. Furthermore, his concerns with the conservation of nature impelled him to be an active member in the National Park movement, the American Forestry Association, and the Save the Redwoods League. His honors and awards include a medal from the University of Chicago in 1941 and the Helen Culver Gold Medal from the Geographical Society of Chicago in 1948. Atwood died at his summer retreat in Anisquam, Massachusetts.

• Atwood's papers and manuscripts are in the Clark University Department of Rare Books and Special Collections, the American Geographical Society (New York City), the Association of American Geographers (Washington, D.C.), the University of Chicago, and Harvard University. Brief, informative biographies include William A. Koelsch, "Wallace Walter Atwood 1872–1949," *Geographers Biobibliographical Studies* 3 (1979): 13–18, and Kirtley F. Mather's memorial in *Proceedings of the Geological Society of America* (Annual Report for 1949): 107–12. George B. Cressey's memorial in *Annals of the Association of American Geographers* 39 (1949): 296–306 is useful for its nine-page bibliography of Atwood's works. Other memorials include those by S. Van Valkenburg in *Geographical Review* 39 (1949): 675–77; C. S. Brigham in the *Proceedings of the American Antiquarian Society* 59 (1949): 174–76; and *Memorial Service Honoring Wallace Walter Atwood* (1950).

TRENT A. MITCHELL

AUB, Joseph Charles (13 May 1890–30 Dec. 1973), physician and medical researcher, was born in Cincinnati, Ohio, the son of Samuel Aub and Clara Shohl. His father died when he was eleven. Having attended the Franklin School, a private preparatory school in Cincinnati, he went to Boston to attend Harvard College, where he received an A.B. in biology in 1911. He then went to Harvard Medical School and received the M.D. in 1916.

Aub was interested not only in practicing medicine but also in doing medical research, which in this period was typically done by doctors as an adjunct to practice. As a first-year medical student, Aub conducted a project on the effects of nicotine on the secretion of adrenalin, working under Walter Cannon, an eminent physiologist. His career as a clinician began in 1914 with an internship at Massachusetts General Hospital (MGH), where David Linn Edsall, professor of medicine at Harvard and at MGH, was building a medical research tradition. Edsall sent young Aub to Eugene DuBois and Graham Lusk at Bellevue Hospital in New York, where he spent a year studying the emerging field of basal metabolism and calorimetry. When he returned to Boston in 1916, he became the second resident in the program of residency that Edsall had started at MGH.

During World War I (from 1917) Aub served at a base hospital in France as part of the MGH unit. Later he joined Cannon's study of wound shock at the front. After returning from the war, he rejoined Cannon in the Department of Physiology at Harvard to study the metabolism of traumatic shock.

After that time Aub spent most of his life in the Harvard Medical School community. He became assistant professor of physiology (1920–1924), assistant professor of medicine (1924–1928), associate professor of medicine (1928–1943), and professor of research medicine (1943–1956). The Harvard Cancer Commission also appointed him physician in chief (1928–1943) and director of medical laboratories (1943–1956) at Huntington Memorial Hospital. In 1925 he married Elizabeth Francis Cope; they had three daughters.

Aub's major contribution to medical research lies in the areas of industrial lead poisoning, endocrinology, and cancer, which were all connected to his interest in metabolism. In 1921, encouraged by Edsall's interest in industrial hygiene, Aub took charge of a project on lead poisoning that was funded for three years by the National Lead Institute, a group of white-lead manufacturers. He and his colleagues traced the absorption, storage, and excretion of lead from the approach of chemical physiology. They found that lead in the bloodstream induced symptoms of lead poisoning, whereas lead stored in the bones did not. Under certain conditions, however, lead was released from the bones and the symptoms developed. Aub's group found that calcium and lead were deposited and released from the bones via a similar pathway. Based on these studies, they developed treatments for lead poisoning. Acute cases of lead poisoning could be treated by the administration of calcium salts to induce the storage of the dissolved lead in the bones; chronic cases could be cured by the "de-leading" process, in which a low-calcium diet induced lead to move from the bones into the bloodstream. In 1926 Aub and his colleagues published a monograph, *Lead Poisoning*, which was long known as the best source of knowledge about the subject.

In 1925, when J. B. Collip discovered that the extract of parathyroid glands was related to the level of blood calcium, Aub saw a possibility that this new extract might help to remove lead from bones. Although it was later shown that humans developed a tolerance for the extract, this interest led Aub into research on endocrinology. He turned to studying the parathyroid gland and its diseases. He also investigated the effects of endocrine secretions on metabolic processes involving organic and inorganic compounds, the endocrinology of adolescence, and the hormonal therapy of breast cancer.

In 1928, at a time when cancer research was not a promising field, Aub accepted an appointment by the Harvard Cancer Commission at Huntington Hospital. He thought that cancer could be better understood if it were seen as a disease of growth—that is, an aberration in the control of the normal growth mechanism.

As a member of the second generation of laboratory medical researchers in the United States, Aub promoted a new style of medical research. He witnessed the important transition from the days when "laboratory work was little more than blood counts and urinalyses" (Aub and Hapgood, p. 150) to large-scale, often publicly funded, medical research in hospital laboratories. He also was a pioneer in cancer research, pursuing it before it was a widespread area of interest in the medical field.

Aub was president of the Society for Endocrinology (1931–1932) and the American Association for Cancer Research (1945–1946). He received many honors, including membership in the National Academy of Sciences, the Bertner Award for his cancer research in 1956, and the Kober Medal of the Association of American Physicians for his scientific contribution in 1966. He retired from the laboratory in 1964 and died in Belmont, Massachusetts, several years later.

• The Joseph Aub Papers are at the Countway Library, Harvard Medical School. Another important source is "The Reminiscences of Joseph Aub," Oral History Collection, Oral History Research Office, Columbia University. The biography of Edsall written by Aub and Ruth K. Hapgood, *Pioneer in Modern Medicine: David Linn Edsall of Harvard* (1970), provides glimpses of Aub's days at Harvard and his view of medical research. For a discussion of his research on lead poisoning and its impact on industrial medicine, see Christopher Clare Sellers, "Manufacturing Disease: Experts and the Ailing American Worker" (Ph.D. diss., Yale Univ., 1992). Aub's research is described in detail in James Means, *Ward 4* (1958), a history of the metabolic research unit. Obituaries are in the *Boston Globe*, Jan. 1974; the *Harvard University Gazette*, 13 Dec. 1974; *Endocrinology* 96 (1975): i–ii; and *Transactions of the Association of American Physicians* 87 (1974): 12–14.

YOUNGRAN JO

AUCHMUTY, Robert (1687–28 Apr. 1750), lawyer and Massachusetts vice admiralty judge, was born in Newtown Flood, County Longford, Ireland, of a Scottish family of noble lineage. He was the son of Captain John Auchmuty, a member of Parliament, and Isabella Stirling.

Auchmuty received his legal training in London at the Middle Temple beginning in 1705 and was called to the bar in 1711. He emigrated to Massachusetts in 1716, apparently as a protégé of the new royal governor, Samuel Shute, and soon established himself as one of the foremost trial lawyers in the province. On occasion he acted as attorney general. His son Robert Auchmuty and a number of other distinguished lawyers, including William Bollan, John Overing, and Benjamin Prat, are said to have studied with him.

In 1733 Auchmuty was commissioned judge of the royal Court of Vice Admiralty in Massachusetts, with jurisdiction also over Rhode Island and New Hampshire. He had previously served as advocate general of the court and had gained a reputation as a strict enforcer of the British Acts of Trade and Navigation and an expert on admiralty law and practice. During his tenure as judge, the court had a busy docket of maritime cases, the great majority of which concerned the compensation or conduct of seamen or forfeitures for violations of the Acts of Trade. As was customary at the time, he continued to practice before other courts.

Auchmuty and his court were extensively involved in provincial and imperial politics. His appointment in 1733 reflected the support of Governor Jonathan Belcher. Auchmuty was, however, a close associate of William Shirley, another English-trained lawyer, who succeeded him as advocate general. Shirley in 1736 began a campaign to use his English connections to oust Belcher and gain his own appointment as governor. In 1737 Auchmuty represented Belcher and Massachusetts before royal commissioners appointed to decide a boundary dispute with New Hampshire. Soon, however, Belcher began to complain of Shirley's lax prosecution of forfeiture actions in Auchmuty's court; the decline in enforcement of the laws was also reducing the fees that Belcher was entitled to receive. Thus, in 1739 Belcher exclaimed, "The Irish Judge is a villain and the Advocate a greater." Later, declaring Auchmuty a "man of most scandalous, abandon'd character," Belcher sought to have him removed from office (*Belcher Papers*, vol. 2, pp. 203, 532). In 1741, however, Shirley succeeded in obtaining appointment as governor, and Auchmuty's position was saved.

Meanwhile, Auchmuty had been one of the most prominent directors of the Land Bank of 1740, a paper currency scheme that Belcher had opposed and Parliament had suppressed just prior to Belcher's downfall. Auchmuty now assisted Governor Shirley's successful efforts to heal political wounds by liquidating the bank, and the vice admiralty court again became a hospitable forum for forfeiture actions. From 1742 through 1744 Auchmuty represented Massachusetts in another boundary dispute—this time with Rhode Island before the Privy Council in London. There he also, at Shirley's request, presented lengthy memorials urging stricter enforcement of the Acts of Trade. The political reaction in Massachusetts to Auchmuty's views on enforcement ultimately caused Shirley to withdraw support. Auchmuty was not continued as London agent, and in 1747 Shirley secured the appointment of Chambers Russell, a well-connected member of the Massachusetts establishment who was untainted by prior involvement with trade enforcement issues, as vice admiralty judge.

While in London in 1744 Auchmuty had also presented a memorial on the economic and strategic benefits to be derived from the capture of the French fortress of Louisbourg at Cape Breton, Canada, together with a plan for a joint Anglo-American naval and military operation. The document was published in 1745 as a pamphlet titled *The Importance of Cape Breton to the British Nation*. His efforts helped to put before the British authorities the possibilities for this attack, which Shirley successfully executed in 1745. Auchmuty later represented Shirley in litigation over military accounts arising out of the Louisbourg expedition.

Auchmuty lived on a substantial estate in Roxbury from 1733 until his death there and was long a vestryman of King's Chapel, Boston. Little is known of Auchmuty's personal life. By his third wife, Mary Julianna (maiden name unknown), he had five children. Samuel Auchmuty was rector of Trinity Church, New York, and a leading Loyalist spokesman for Anglican views. Robert Auchmuty became a prominent Massachusetts lawyer and vice admiralty judge.

Auchmuty, described as "an eminent Attorney at Law" in his obituary in the *Boston Gazette* and other newspapers, was highly regarded by his contemporaries. An examination of his surviving pleadings and other professional writings bears out this evaluation. Coming from the formal background of the Inns of Court, he was a leader in the first group of trained lawyers in Massachusetts. As Emory Washburn wrote in his *Sketches of the Judicial History of Massachusetts* (1840), "[T]he profession owed much to his character and efforts for the elevated stand it was beginning to assume, and the system and order which now began to distinguish its forms of practice." A more nearly contemporary—and human—assessment is John Adams's 1774 diary entry comparing a leading New York lawyer to "old Mr. Auchmuty. Set up all Night at his Bottle. Yet argue to Admiration the next Day. An admirable Speaker."

• Auchmuty's judicial and legal career is documented in "Court of Admiralty Records 1740 to 1745," vol. 5 in the Massachusetts State Archives; in Dorothy S. Towle, ed., *Records of the Vice Admiralty Court of Rhode Island, 1716–1752* (1936); and in the Massachusetts Superior Court records, 1716–1750, Massachusetts State Archives. For the 1744 memorial, see Massachusetts Historical Society, *Collections*, 1st ser., 5 (1798), pp. 202–5. His only other surviving printed work is *The Copy of Some Queries Put to Mr. Auchmuty, Judge of the Admiralty, and His Opinion and Answer Thereto* (1734). The most complete biographical sketch is Annette Townsend, *The Auchmuty Family of Scotland and America* (1932), pp. 1–23, which also contains genealogical data and two portraits, one by Joseph Badger. It also contains a reproduction of Auchmuty's pamphlet on Louisbourg on pp. 8–12. See also David H. Flaherty, "Criminal Practice in Provincial Massachusetts," in his *Law in Colonial Massachusetts, 1630–1800* (1984), pp. 194–202, 210–15. For contemporary views of Auchmuty's activities, see M. Halsey Thomas, ed., *The Diary of Samuel Sewall, 1674–1729*, vol. 2 (1973), pp. 836–1046; *The Belcher Papers*, Massachusetts Historical Society, *Collections*, 6th ser., vols. 6–7 (1893–1894). For specific episodes, see John A. Schutz, *William Shirley: King's Governor of Massachusetts* (1961); George A. Rawlyk, *Yankees at Louisbourg* (1967), pp. 30–32; and Joseph H. Smith, *Appeals to the Privy Council from the American Plantations* (1950), pp. 442–53. For an unflattering portrayal, see M. H. Smith, *The Writs of Assistance Case* (1978), pp. 67–94.

L. Kinvin Wroth

AUCHMUTY, Robert, Jr. (1725–11 Dec. 1788), lawyer and Loyalist, was born in Boston, Massachusetts, the son of Scottish-born Robert Auchmuty, a judge of admiralty in Massachusetts, and Mary Julianna. As a youth Robert attended Boston Latin School and was admitted to Harvard, class of 1746, but never matriculated. He benefited from growing up in an upper-class family and learned law from his father. In 1762 he became a barrister, and many considered him the third best lawyer in Massachusetts, just behind James Otis, Jr., and Oxenbridge Thacher.

Auchmuty often found himself as counsel for Loyalists and government officials in opposition to Otis and John Adams (1735–1826), who served as lawyers for patriots. A good example was *Gill v. Mein* (1768–1769), in which Auchmuty defended John Mein, the Scottish editor of the Loyalist newspaper the *Boston Chronicle*, who had caned John Gill, rival editor of the patriot newspaper the *Boston Gazette*. However, Auchmuty also served alongside Adams and Josiah Quincy, Jr., as defense lawyer for Captain Thomas Preston at the famous 1770 Boston Massacre trial. Fellow Loyalists felt that Auchmuty's spirited defense of the British captain caused much "prejudice" against Auchmuty. As a lawyer Auchmuty was noted for his "mellifluous" tongue, but he continually "scolded and rail'd about the lowness" of lawyers' fees. Adams, who disliked Auchmuty for his "air of reserve, design, and cunning," recalled Auchmuty's oratory as "repeated volubility" and a "nauseous eloquence." In contrast, Governor Francis Bernard asserted that Auchmuty was "learned and eloquent in his arguments."

Under the influence of his older brother Samuel Auchmuty, the Episcopal rector of Trinity Church in New York City, Auchmuty actively took the Crown's side in political issues. Such loyalty was expensive as he spurned patriot offers of salaries ten times larger than his salary from the Crown. In a Boston town meeting following the Stamp Act riots, he spoke out against mob violence. As a reward for this and previous pro-British stances, Auchmuty collected appointive plums in Massachusetts: advocate general in the Court of Admiralty, 1762–1767; judge of vice admiralty for the Northern District, which included Massachusetts, New Hampshire, and Rhode Island, 1767–1776 (salary £600 per annum); judge of the Boston District Court of Admiralty, 1768–1776 (held simultaneously with judgeship of vice admiralty); justice of the peace and of the quorum, 1769; one of five commissioners on the Gaspée Affair, 1772. As the king's advocate, without additional legal assistance, he prepared briefs and argued cases of libel against the king, breaches of the laws of trade, and cases involving preservation of the king's masts.

As judge of admiralty, Auchmuty's rulings indicate he possessed a bright, incisive mind and rendered clear judgments in many complex cases. In 1768 he presided over a famous case against the merchant John Hancock on charges that Hancock's sloop *Liberty* smuggled 100 pipes of Madeira wine (*Sewall v. Hancock*, 1768–1769). There were two cases involved, one for confiscation of the vessel and the other a £9,000 (treble value penalty) suit against Hancock. In the first case Auchmuty declared the *Liberty* forfeited. The second trial lasted five months, but, after an eloquent defense by John Adams, the advocate general, Jonathan Sewall, dropped the case. Both cases received heavy newspaper coverage, with patriots using the occasion to turn popular opinion against the British customs system, the juryless vice admiralty courts, and Auchmuty, who was labeled a "base American" who would "sacrifice" his country by taking a salary six times larger than ever before paid an American judge.

In 1761 Auchmuty was wealthy enough to build a mansion on six acres of land at the corner of Cliff and Washington streets in Roxbury, hire servants, and own an African-American slave. In this home in 1772 he discussed with other Loyalist leaders (Governor Bernard, Thomas Hutchinson, Benjamin Hallowell, and Charles Paxton) plans to revoke the charter of Massachusetts and sent letters to officials in London complaining of the rising tide of disloyalty. In 1773, when Benjamin Franklin obtained these letters and sent them to Massachusetts, they caused a storm of protest against the Loyalist establishment. For patriots these letters proved that Auchmuty and Hutchinson were animated by a spirit of "revenge" and "ambition." In the spring of 1776 Auchmuty sailed to Halifax to obtain tools and supplies for the British army on Long Island; instead, he was captured by the Americans.

After he was exchanged, Auchmuty sailed to England and became a charter member of the New England Club of Loyalists. In exile he turned his brilliant legal mind to writing endless petitions to the British Treasury for stipends or pensions for Loyalist refugees. While in exile, Auchmuty's earlier zealous support of the Crown made him a target for revenge by the patriot party. In 1778 the Massachusetts legislature named him in the Banishment Act. In 1779 the legislature singled out twenty-nine Loyalists, including Auchmuty, as "notorious conspirators," and immediately forfeited all property they held, without a hearing or trial. The twenty-nine conspirators in exile in England selected Auchmuty to draft a collective petition to the Crown on their behalf.

Under the 1779 Conspirators Act, Auchmuty's mansion in Roxbury was auctioned off and purchased by Increase Sumner, later governor of Massachusetts. In 1784 his confiscated library was sold at auction. In addition, eighteen citizens filed for payment of false debts against the absent Auchmuty, and the judge of probate for Suffolk County awarded them £467. Auchmuty hired William Pynchon of Salem as his attorney to counter these false claims, but a 1784 Massachusetts law specifically exempted conspirators like Auchmuty from returning or recovering debts. Auchmuty then hired William Tudor as his attorney; Tudor used the threat of a lawsuit to recover Auchmuty's debt from Curtis. When the Massachusetts supreme court learned of this action it ordered Tudor to pay the recovered money not to Auchmuty, but to Massachusetts. Not all of his possessions went on the auction block. The committee of sequestration gave some of his goods to his mother-in-law, Mary Cradock. Auchmuty filed claims with the Crown totaling £3,075 for the loss of his mansion in Roxbury, a distillery house, and various debts. The commissioners on American Loyalists, appointed by Parliament to recompense Loyalists, allowed him £1,775, as well as a one-time payment of £600 for loss of his legal income during the war and an annual pension of £300. When he died in London, his wife, Deborah Cradock of Boston, survived him and also petitioned for a pension. Auchmuty left no known children.

• Some of Auchmuty's papers, especially his correspondence with Thomas Hutchinson, are in the British Museum. His claims for losses suffered are in American Loyalists Claims, Public Record Office, Audit Office 12 and 13, AO 13/43: 224–77, in London. Valuable family information and his portrait are in Annette Townsend, *The Auchmuty Family of Scotland and America* (1932). Two short biographies are in James H. Stark, *The Loyalists of Massachusetts and the Other Side of the American Revolution* (1907), and E. Alfred Jones, *The Loyalists of Massachusetts: Their Memorials, Petitions and Claims* (1930). Fellow lawyer John Adams made numerous assessments of Auchmuty; for these see *The Adams Papers: Diary and Autobiography of John Adams*, ed. Lyman Butterfield (3 vols., 1961–1962). For samples of Auchmuty's legal arguments see *The Adams Papers: Legal Papers of John Adams*, ed. L. Kinvin Wroth and Hiller B. Zobel (3 vols., 1965). Valuable primary sources include Oliver Dickerson, *Boston under Military Rule* (1936).

DAVID E. MAAS

AUCHMUTY, Samuel (16 Jan. 1722–4 Mar. 1777), Episcopal minister and Loyalist, was born in Boston, Massachusetts, the son of Scottish-born Robert Auchmuty, a judge of admiralty in Massachusetts, and Mary Julianna. He would have been a graduate in the Harvard class of 1742 but dropped out during his junior year. At the encouragement of his uncle, James Auchmuty, dean of Armagh, Samuel prepared for holy orders by reading under the direction of the Reverend Alexander Malcolm of St. Michael's Church in Marblehead and the Reverend Benjamin Bradstreet of Gloucester. Based on the recommendation of these two ministers as to Samuel's character and learning, Harvard awarded him his B.A. in 1745 and his M.A. in 1746.

Auchmuty was ordained an Episcopal minister in 1747 by the bishop of London and appointed as a missionary by the Society for the Propagation of the Gospel (SPG). For the next sixteen years he served as assistant minister of Trinity Church in New York City and as catechist in its African-American school. In December 1749 he married Mary Tucker, the widow of Captain Thomas Tucker. They had seven children. Auchmuty felt socially superior to the majority of his parishioners, whom he described as "of no consequence" and whom he planned to keep at "a proper distance." He was intolerant of other religious sects. He frowned on his parishioners who participated in George Whitefield's revivals, called the Dutch in the city "Loggerheads," and wrote against the Presbyterians' attempts to obtain a charter of incorporation for a church in New York City.

Auchmuty took an active role in the founding of King's College (present-day Columbia) in 1754 and from 1759 to 1764 served as governor of King's College. After 1764 he recruited teachers, interviewed potential students, and conducted baccalaureate services for graduates. In September 1764, following the death of the rector, Henry Barclay, the vestry unanimously selected Auchmuty as the new rector of Trinity Church. He moved into the recently remodeled parsonage, with a comfortable yearly salary of £250, New York currency, and stocked the house with "liquors in large quantities." A close friend and frequent correspondent, Samuel Johnson, president of King's College, exercised his influence and obtained for Auchmuty an honorary doctorate from Oxford in 1766 and a second doctorate in 1767 from King's College.

Auchmuty's political, family, and social contacts all leaned toward the Crown. He preached sermons on the induction of governors into office and funeral orations on their deaths. All royal governors of New York attended Trinity Church and became staunch friends and admirers of Auchmuty. Governor William Tryon gave "a complete set of rich and elegant hangings of crimson damask for the pulpit, reading desk, and communion table" at St. George's Chapel (*Boston News-Letter*, 21 Jan. 1773, quoted in Sibley, p. 123). During the Stamp Act crisis in 1765 Auchmuty sincerely believed that only Anglicans were loyal to the Crown and claimed all non-Anglicans were "republicans" and "rebellious."

As part of his efforts to promote Anglicanism, Auchmuty organized in 1766 a convention of Anglican clergy from Connecticut, New York, and New Jersey. In 1767 he formed a corporation for the relief of the widows and orphans of the clergy of the Church of England. In 1770 he acted as president of a convention of clergy that argued for the necessity of an American Episcopate. In correspondence he constantly lobbied politicians and SPG officials for the appointment of a bishop for America. Such advice prompted John Trumbull in his satirical poem "Mc Fingal" to suggest that "high-church clergyman" Auchmuty was really hoping the Crown would make him the first American bishop.

In 1775, to Auchmuty's political embarrassment, patriots intercepted and published some of his correspondence with the Reverend Samuel Peters of Connecticut and a British officer, Captain John Montresor. In these letters Auchmuty candidly denounced New Yorkers as a "rascally Whig mob," stated New York officials had "not the spirit of a louse," and characterized the Continental Congress as "rebellious followers." Patriot editors upon printing these letters labeled Auchmuty a "servile wretch," "a Tory Clergyman," "vermin," and a "parricide" who sacrificed his conscience for "ambition and avarice." Attendance dropped at his church, and he felt so threatened that in the summer of 1775 he burned most of his letters. Still his seventy manuscript sermons (three published) reveal a pious and scholarly mind, which drew arguments from the Bible, old Catholic Fathers, and Divines of the Church of England. Although he favored deistic phrases, he believed in a God who intervened in history. During the American Revolution from the pulpit he advocated nonresistance and passive obedience.

Auchmuty's parish ministry included genuine and humane service to criminals and the poor. He once obtained a week's stay of execution for four condemned criminals so he could educate them spiritually. In 1774, when destitute and starving Scottish immigrants arrived on the *Nancy*, Auchmuty led in raising £120 from his parishioners for their relief.

After the American army occupied New York City in 1777, Auchmuty was warned by American general Lord William Earl Sterling not to read the traditional prayer for the king at the next Sunday service. He felt that his ordination vows required such a prayer and when he commenced reading the traditional prayers, Sterling marched into the church with soldiers to the tune of Yankee Doodle. Auchmuty finished the prayer, but after this service locked up the church until he could again perform the traditional liturgy. He moved with his family into his son-in-law's home in New Brunswick, New Jersey, a town occupied by the British. When the British relinquished the town to Continentals, Auchmuty asked for permission to return to New York City, now under British control. When his request was denied, he tenaciously bypassed American lines, spent a week on foot sleeping in the woods, and arrived ill in New York City. His misery was compounded when he discovered that fires set by unkown incendiaries, upon the retreat of the American army had destroyed Trinity Church and 493 houses, including his own home. He estimated the loss of his house at £2,500 sterling and his total personal loss at $12,000.

Auchmuty briefly carried on services at nearby St. Paul's, and a raid by British soldiers into New Jersey liberated his family and brought them back to New York City. Auchmuty's spirits now revived, but he caught a cold and died in the city only weeks after his return to his parish. His widow filed a claim with the British Treasury for £7,075 sterling and received £1,580 sterling and an annual pension of £80.

Auchmuty deserves respect for his consistency and courage in supporting the Crown when the majority of New Yorkers took a different course. He should be honored for standing by his oath and conscience, for his hard work in Trinity Parish, and for his compassion, but condemned for his narrow spirit of bigotry.

• A number of his papers are in the New-York Historical Society and in the Archives of the SPG. Valuable family information and portraits are in Annette Townsend, *The Auchmu-*

ty Family of Scotland and America* (1932). Short biographies are in James H. Stark, *The Loyalists of Massachusetts and the Other Side of the American Revolution* (1907); E. Alfred Jones, *The Loyalists of Massachusetts: Their Memorials, Petitions and Claims* (1930); (1903); William Sprague, *Annals of the American Pulpit*, vol. 5 (1859), pp. 127–28; and Clifford Shipton, *Sibley's Harvard Graduates*, vol. 11 (1963), pp. 108–27. For his service at the parish of Trinity Church and extracts of sermons consult Morgan Dix, *A History of the Parish of Trinity Church in the City of New York* (1898). For full citations on his three published sermons see "Eighteenth-Century Short Title Catalog" (1992), CD-ROM. For his wife's Loyalist's claim see American Loyalists Claims, Public Record Office, Audit Office 12/24/112; AO 12/24/264; AO 12/99/65; AO 12/109/74; in London.

DAVID E. MAAS

AUDEN, W. H. (21 Feb. 1907–29 Sept. 1973), poet, was born Wystan Hugh Auden in York, England, the son of George Augustus Auden, a physician and public health officer, and Constance Rosalie Bicknell, a nurse. Both his grandfathers were Church of England clergymen. His father was originally in private medical practice; when Auden was eighteen months old, the senior Auden became school medical officer for the city of Birmingham. Thus Auden grew up in a large industrial town and in a family that was comfortably off, though no more than that. His father's intellectual interests were broad and included history, archeology, and philosophy; his mother was devoutly religious and loved music. Both parents' interests were reflected in Auden's later life.

Auden was educated in boarding schools and at Oxford University, where he began by studying biology and then switched to English. (English was a new subject at Oxford at that time—1926—and switching was unusual and difficult.) Almost immediately after his graduation in 1928, he became recognized as the most talented of his generation of British poets, indeed as the voice of a new generation. Besides his precocious gifts as a versifier and phrasemaker in many forms and idioms, Auden gave voice to the deepest themes of his generation: concern over political and economic crises, suspicion of aestheticism, Marxist and Freudian understandings of self and society, and distrust of established authority, whether in literary, political, religious, or personal life. Bourgeois society was in its death throes, he believed, its fatal illness manifest in psychosomatic ailments, failed relations, and decaying institutions. The job of the artist was to help pave the way for a revolution that would destroy the old order and would free individuals for rebirth.

This, at least, was the message many readers heard in Auden's earliest works, *Poems* (1930), *The Orators* (1932), and several plays coauthored with Christopher Isherwood. With such messages, they also found a poet of stunning talent. The writer and critic Clive James asks, "Was there ever a more capacious young talent? It goes beyond precocity." He continues:

> The plainest statement he could make seemed to come out as poetry. . . . It was a Shakespearean gift, not just in magnitude but in its unsettling . . . characteristic of making anything said sound truer than true. In all of English poetry it is difficult to think of any other poet who turned out permanent work so early—and whose work seemed so tense with the obligation to be permanent. (*Times Literary Supplement*, 12 Jan. 1973, p. 25)

Immediately after leaving Oxford, Auden spent a year in Weimar Germany and then returned to England as a teacher and, later, a documentary film writer. In 1935, his homosexuality notwithstanding, he married Erika Mann, daughter of the German novelist Thomas Mann. She, an actress and journalist, was a vehement anti-Nazi, and the marriage was solely for the purpose of obtaining British citizenship for her.

Auden also traveled a great deal during the 1930s, writing travel books—hodgepodges of verse, journalism, photographs, and personal reflections—about his trips to Iceland (with the poet Louis MacNeice) and (with Isherwood) to China, where he observed the war resulting from Japan's invasion of Manchuria. Like other European artists and intellectuals, he spent some time in Spain during the civil war there and wrote one famous and controversial poem about it, "Spain 1937." Although Auden was highly esteemed by the British left, his attitude toward politics, and particularly toward Communist politics, was becoming more and more skeptical.

As general war in Europe approached, Auden, to the amazement of many people, emigrated to the United States (with Isherwood). Some saw this act as desertion of the home country at the time of its greatest peril. A great deal was happening to Auden personally, spiritually, and intellectually at this time, and to his poetry. Despite his status as a spokesman for rebelliousness against all forms of authority, Auden had been for several years moving toward a religious conversion, a process that was completed during his first two years in the United States: for the rest of his life he was regular and devout in his worship. Unlike T. S. Eliot, however, who had also gone through a conversion, Auden did not become a respectable churchman but retained his generally eccentric and bohemian style of life.

At about the same time, Auden fell in love with a young college student, Chester Kallman. It was a lifelong attachment, both profound and troubling for Auden. Auden was devoted to Kallman; Kallman, less so to Auden. For the next thirty and more years the attachment continued, and for much of the period the two lived together.

In America Auden turned again to teaching, as well as to lecturing, reviewing, and editing. He taught at various institutions, his longest stint being at Swarthmore College. During the 1940s he published several long poems, including *The Double Man* (1941), *For the Time Being* (1944), and *The Age of Anxiety* (1947). In 1945 *The Collected Poetry of W. H. Auden* appeared, fixing his reputation as a major poet. It also created controversy, for several reasons. Most noticeably, his poems were arranged not in chronological order but alphabetically by first lines and by categories. He omitted some early poems, drastically changed a few others, and made many minor emendations. Poems that were originally published without titles—as was his practice in the thirties—now received them, and some of the titles seemed to undercut political messages of the originals. All in all, a number of critics and other readers felt that Auden had marred some of his best early work, as well as blurring the lines of his own development.

Perhaps the most notorious example involved a poem from Auden's first year in the United States. At the time of the German invasion of Poland, he wrote "September 1, 1939." As time went on, however, not only in the *Collected Poetry* of 1945 but in later collections, he first tinkered with some of the most stirring lines of the poem, then excluded a whole stanza ("All I have is a voice . . . "). Finally he stopped including the poem at all (although the original version is now included in posthumously published volumes). Auden's stated reason for its exclusion was that the whole poem, but particularly the line "We must love one another or die" was "infected by an incurable dishonesty and must be scrapped."

The poetry written by the American Auden disappointed some of the most avid admirers of the English Auden. With at least some justice, they saw the poet whose early gifts could be described as Shakespearean becoming more cerebral, more traditional, more formal and less experimental, more predictable, more rhetorical, and more abstract. Nonetheless, Auden quickly became not only one of the most widely read poets in America but an influential cultural presence. For years he selected the winner of the Yale Younger Poets award, which gave him the opportunity to boost the careers of poets with a dedication to craft and to the careful use of language. He lectured widely; he was one of the judges (along with two Columbia University professors, Lionel Trilling and Jacques Barzun) of an important intellectual book club (the Reader's Subscription, subsequently the Mid-Century Book Society); and he reviewed regularly for influential publications, such as the *New Republic*, *Encounter*, and the *New York Review of Books*.

At the end of World War II Auden returned to Europe (somewhat improbably with the rank and uniform of army major, though he was still a civilian), participating in the U.S. Strategic Bombing Survey. In 1946 he became a U.S. citizen. By the time of his return from Europe, he was able to live off his literary work and did no more full-time teaching. He was established not only as a poet but as a person resembling an old-fashioned man of letters, whose taste and reading, as well as whose writing, helped shape American culture at a time of enormous growth in the institutions of culture: literary reviews, publishing houses, book clubs, and the academic study of literature.

Auden was still in many ways a European, however; he referred to himself as "not an American, but a New Yorker," and his existence was clearly cosmopolitan and international. Beginning in 1948 Auden spent summers on the island of Ischia, near Naples, Italy; from 1957 until his death he frequently went to Kirchstetten, near Vienna, Austria, where he owned a house (celebrated in a series of poems published in 1965, "Thanksgiving for a Habitat") and where he died. From 1956 until 1961 he was professor of poetry at Oxford University (an elected position carrying honor and some duties, but not a full-time commitment).

What did he contribute to American history in the period of his residence, from 1939 to 1973, from the beginning of World War II until almost the end of the war in Vietnam? First, he had an enormous range of interests: history; philosophy; psychology; literature in many languages, both classical and modern; music (he wrote librettos for operas by Igor Stravinsky and Benjamin Britten); cooking; medicine; and almost anything else. Second, he contributed a quick intelligence that expressed itself equally in memorable verse and in witty, unencumbered prose. Third, at a time when the dominant assumptions of American criticism emphasized a severe separation between literature and personal life, literature and history, and literature and politics, Auden—though he partially agreed with these assumptions—brought a sense of the existence of literature in social and cultural history, and thus an image of a poet not simply as a craftsperson of artifacts but also a humane thinker and commentator.

As a poet, as a critic, and as a man of letters, Auden affected British and American poetry by pulling the experimentalism and difficulty dominant in early twentieth-century modernism (in the poetry, for example, of Ezra Pound, T. S. Eliot, and Wallace Stevens) toward a kind of traditionalism and formalism. In this his influence was enormous. A subtler but even more important effect comes from the fact that Auden was both British and, in his tastes and reading and many of his friendships, broadly European. The tradition that Auden fostered in American poetry (not without many countermovements in reaction to it) was large and inclusive, not merely British or American, but international. Whatever his intentions in emigrating, he left England as it was losing its position of preeminent world power and came to the United States as it was beginning its period of undisputed preeminence in the world. Auden's time in America was also a time in which American intellectual, cultural, and scientific life was enriched by an extraordinary infusion of European talent. Though much of this emigration was from Germany and Central Europe, Auden was part of the flow and gave voice to an enlarged cultural understanding. Many of his closest friends and collaborators—Stravinsky, the philosopher Hannah Arendt, the psychologist Wolfgang Köhler, the Mann family, his close friend Elizabeth Mayer, and countless others—were part of this massive demographic movement. Auden did not so much become an American as bring to America, and synthesize in his verse, a broadly European culture, which was cosmopolitan and shaped by the darkened vision of Nazism, Stalinism, and World War II.

Perhaps one of the best—certainly one of the most generous—assessments of Auden comes from the Russian poet Joseph Brodsky, who learned English partly by reading Auden's poems while imprisoned in Siberia, and whose first stop upon being exiled from the Soviet Union was Auden's house in Austria. Brodsky talks of "the man whom I consider the greatest mind of the twentieth century: Wystan Hugh Auden" and writes of him:

> Whatever the reasons for which [Auden] crossed the Atlantic and became an American, the result was that he fused both idioms of English and became—to paraphrase one of his own lines—our transatlantic Horace. One way or another, all the journeys he took—through lands, caves of the psyche, doctrines, creeds—served not so much to improve his argument but expand his diction. (*Less Than One*, p. 382)

The reference to Horace is carefully considered. During the early days of the Roman Empire, while Virgil celebrated its imperial power and Ovid explored its old myths from his place of exile, Horace retired to his farm to write carefully fashioned lyrics that enriched the language. This is what Brodsky refers to when he talks of Auden's journey serving to expand his diction. Auden's foremost goal—and what many, like Brodsky, would consider his enduring legacy—was to be, as Auden says of W. B. Yeats in his famous elegy for that poet, "one by whom language lives."

• The most extensive collection of Auden's papers is in the Berg Collection at the New York Public Library. There are other manuscripts and papers at Swarthmore College; the Bodleian Library of Oxford University; the British Museum; the Lockwood Memorial Library, Buffalo, New York; and the Humanities Research Center, University of Texas. B. C. Bloomfield and Edward Mendelson, *W. H. Auden: A Bibliography, 1924–1969*, 2d ed. (1972), is authoritative. Humphrey Carpenter's *W. H. Auden: A Biography* (1981) is the best biography. *The Complete Poetry of W. H. Auden*, ed. Edward Mendelson (1976), is the best edition of the poems. Mendelson also edited *The English Auden* (1977) and *Plays and Other Dramatic Writings by W. H. Auden, 1928–1938* (1988), and is the author of *Early Auden* (1981), a critical study. The best work on Auden's English years is Samuel Hynes's *The Auden Generation* (1977). Auden's critical prose is collected in *The Dyer's Hand* (1962) and *Forewords and Afterwords* (1973). Monroe Spears's *The Poetry of W. H. Auden* (1963) is the most useful general study of Auden's work. Two early essays by the poet and critic Randall Jarrell, reprinted in his *The Third Book of Criticism* (1969), are important. John Fuller's *Reader's Guide to W. H. Auden* (1970) is useful. Critical studies include John G. Blair, *The Poetic Art of W. H. Auden* (1965); Herbert Greenberg, *Quest for the Necessary* (1968); George Bahlke, *The Later Auden* (1970); Richard Johnson, *Man's Place: An Essay on Auden* (1973); Edward Callan, *Auden: A Carnival of Intellect* (1983); Lucy McDiarmid, *Auden's Apologies for Poetry* (1990); John Boly, *Reading Auden* (1991); and Anthony Hecht, *The Hidden Law: The Poetry of W. H. Auden* (1993). George Bahlke, ed., *Critical Essays on W. H. Auden* (1991), reprints a number of critical essays on Auden. John Haffenden, *W. H. Auden: The Critical Heritage* (1983), collects a wide range of reviews and other comments on Auden's work. Hilton Kramer wrote the obituary that appears in the *New York Times*, 30 Sept. 1973.

RICHARD JOHNSON

AUDUBON, John James (26 Apr. 1785–27 Jan. 1851), naturalist and artist, was born Jean Rabin Fougere in Les Cayes, Santo Domingo, the son of Captain Jean Audubon, a French sea captain, planter, and slave dealer, and Jeanne Rabin (or Rabine), a young Frenchwoman employed as a chambermaid on the island. The traditional view, that Mlle Rabin was a Creole woman native to Santo Domingo, has been disproved. Audubon's mother died before he was seven months old, and the child was cared for by another mistress of the father's with whom he had several children. In 1791, fearing worsening conditions in Santo Domingo, Captain Audubon arranged for his son and a younger daughter by his mistress Catherine "Sanitte" Bouffard to be taken to France. There both were well cared for by Captain Audubon's legal spouse, Anne Moynet Audubon, who had no children of her own. Both children were formally adopted by the couple in 1794, as was required if they were legally to inherit Captain Audubon's name and property, and were baptized in 1800. At this time the boy received the name Jean-Jacques Fougere Audubon.

Audubon revered his stepmother, who doted on the child, providing him with the rudiments of an education at home. He attended Rochefort-sur-Mer Naval Academy between 1796 and 1800 but intensely disliked the training regimen there, and his father permitted him to develop his artistic talents. For the remainder of his life Audubon found it difficult to express himself in writing, either in his native tongue or in English. Audubon's claim to have studied in Paris with the painter Jacques-Louis David in the years 1802–1803 has since been discounted.

Captain Audubon had become increasingly concerned about his son's chances of surviving young manhood in light of the Napoleonic wars then raging in Europe. He had owned "Mill Grove," a farm outside of Philadelphia, Pennsylvania, for several years. To protect the younger man from forced military conscription, the senior Audubon sent his son, then eighteen, to manage the property in 1803. There young Audubon first became acquainted with American birds and conducted the earliest known experiments in bird banding in 1804. In that year he met his future wife, Lucy Bakewell, daughter of a neighboring landowner. They were married in 1808 and had two sons, who later actively supported their father's artistic and publishing endeavors, and two daughters, both of whom died in infancy. Audubon was briefly a partner with Ferdinand Rozier, son of a friend of his father's, in managing Mill Grove and the mining of lead deposits on the property. The two young men found it increasingly difficult to work with Francis da Costa, a Nantes-born Frenchman employed by Captain Audubon as his son's guardian, who had purchased a half-interest in Mill Grove. On the captain's instructions, da Costa objected to the younger Audubon's projected marriage, but the son returned to France and obtained his father's consent. Back in Philadelphia, young Audubon and Rozier, frustrated at every turn by da Costa in the management of Mill Grove, sold their half-interest to him and briefly went into business, Audubon in New York City, Rozier with a French importing firm in Philadelphia.

In 1807 both men left their jobs to begin a general store in Louisville, Kentucky, where Rozier felt they might prosper. Rozier did most of the work while Audubon sketched birds and tramped about the surrounding countryside. Audubon did, however, make trips to New York and Philadelphia for stock. Lucy Bakewell Audubon's father and uncle invested heavily in the Louisville enterprise, which moved several times, first to St. Genevieve, Missouri, and later to Henderson, Kentucky, before it was finally dissolved in 1809. Audubon and Rozier decided to go their separate ways, and Audubon continued to operate the business independently with the aid of clerks. Between 1811 and 1821 Audubon was a partner with his brother-in-law Thomas W. Bakewell in a commission merchandising enterprise based in New Orleans, Louisiana, with a branch in Henderson. For a time, the partners operated a sawmill and gristmill there and had a part-interest in a steamboat. These enterprises ultimately failed, in part because of the panic of 1819. Audubon suffered other reverses in these years, several hundred drawings having been destroyed by rats during one of his absences from home. Audubon's father died in 1818, and four French cousins contested the will, which had left his remaining property to his widow. Captain Audubon's adulteries and their reflection on the Audubon family's honor appear to have been central to the dispute. His stepmother was in financial difficulties and hoped for his aid, but Audubon was himself in no position to return to France and defend his stepmother's interests. By 1819 Audubon's store in Henderson had failed, and he was briefly jailed for debt.

Admitting bankruptcy, Audubon took up portrait painting and teaching. He was briefly employed as a taxidermist for the Western Museum Society in Cincinnati, the only formal scientific position he ever held. The proprietor, Dr. Daniel Drake, soon found it difficult to meet his payroll and, with regret, discharged Audubon. During the next five years, until 1825, Audubon taught art, dancing, fencing, and French in Kentucky and Louisiana, while working at various short-term jobs and perfecting his artistic abilities. His wife raised their children, taught school, and welcomed her husband home at intervals from his collecting trips and periodic employment. During this difficult period Audubon managed to publish several scientific papers in the *Annals of the Lyceum of Natural History* in New York and received a few free lessons in painting from Thomas Sully. He would subsequently (after 1826) publish nearly a dozen other papers, having primarily to do with birds and mammals he encountered, his travels, and his methods of drawing, in various other journals, notably the *Edinburgh New Philosophical Journal*, the *Edinburgh Journal of Science*, and the *Proceedings of the Academy of Natural Sciences of Philadelphia*.

The genesis of Audubon's career as a painter may be said to have taken place in 1810, when the Scots-American ornithologist Alexander Wilson stopped in Henderson to seek subscriptions for his *American Ornithology*. Audubon was approving of Wilson's efforts and was prepared to subscribe when his partner Rozier intervened. Rozier pointed out that the partners lacked the discretionary funds for such an investment and also suggested that Audubon was much the superior artist. Wilson departed without the hoped-for subscription. Not until 1820, however, when he was thirty-five and after years of disappointment in business, did Audubon conclude that he wanted to publish an ambitious folio of all American birds. Accompanying him on the first of several collecting and painting trips was young Joseph Mason, the first of several associates who later would paint at least fifty backgrounds for Audubon's bird plates. Following this trip, Audubon spent some months in New Orleans making a modest living sketching portraits and then as tutor to Eliza Pirrie at the plantation owned by the latter's father on Bayou Sara. Throughout, he gradually began accumulating his bird pictures.

A trip to Philadelphia in 1824 to look into the possibilities of publication and other support was a disaster. Audubon foolishly antagonized the artist Titian Peale and the engraver Alexander Lawson, who were preparing illustrations for Charles Lucien Bonaparte's *American Ornithology; or, The Natural History of Birds Inhabiting the United States, Not Given by Wilson*. With his criticisms of Wilson's artistry, he also infuriated the Philadelphia businessman and naturalist George Ord, Wilson's friend, editor, biographer, and champion, who became Audubon's lifelong enemy and did whatever he could to block Audubon's success in the United States. Following Ord's lead, most Philadelphia naturalists and engravers refused to assist Audubon with his project. Audubon now concluded that he had no choice but to go to Europe to seek out engravers and printers, and this he did with money he and Lucy earned from teaching the children of the Percy family of Beechwood Plantation near New Orleans in 1825 and early 1826.

Arriving in Liverpool, England, in July 1826, Audubon soon found the support and fame that had so long eluded him in the United States. He went on to Manchester, where the response to his work was tepid, and then to Edinburgh, Scotland, where he found not only more support but William H. Lizars, the engraver he had been looking for. There he matured his ideas concerning his project and decided on an elephant folio on a subscription basis. He took time to fulfill a longtime ambition by meeting Sir Walter Scott in January 1827. He was much impressed, as was the Scots author with his visitor's artistic talents. With the engraving of his paintings well under way, Audubon went to London in the spring of 1827. Soon after his arrival, he was informed that the men coloring his engravings at Lizars's firm in Edinburgh had gone on strike.

Fortunately, he soon was put in touch with the London engraver Robert Havell, Jr., who was to be Audubon's valued collaborator on the four-volume Elephant Folio project for the next eleven years (1827–1838). When his money ran low, Audubon raised what was needed to pay his engravers with portrait sketches, and he painted portraits in oil and watercolor animal scenes. He also solicited subscriptions in England and in France, where he met Baron Georges Cuvier, the leading French zoologist of the time, who was both gracious and supportive.

Audubon did more collecting of specimens and painting in the United States in 1829, then returned to England in 1830, this time with his wife. He engaged the young Scots naturalist William MacGillivray to correct the infelicities in his grammar and to supply the necessary zoological detail for his *Ornithological Biography*. Some English observers, notably Charles Waterton, an eccentric naturalist friend of George Ord's, were critical of this arrangement, but the first volume was published to considerable acclaim in 1831. Between 1831 and 1834 Audubon made additional trips for collections and painting to Florida, South Carolina, and Labrador. George Lehman, a Pennsylvania landscape painter, was now engaged to complete many of the background details in Audubon's watercolors. Much of 1834 and 1835 was spent in England, during which additional volumes of the *Birds of America* and the *Ornithological Biography* were published.

Audubon's final trip to England began in the summer of 1837. He remained for two years and oversaw the completion of both publication projects. A total of 435 "double elephant" aquatints had been produced. Only a relative few of the copper plates for these engravings exist today. Some were destroyed by fire in 1845, and others were sold years later as scrap. *A Synopsis of the Birds of America*, a one-volume index to both the folio edition of the *Birds of America* and the *Ornithological Biography*, was published in London in 1839, principally for folio subscribers. A smaller octavo edition of the *Birds*, combining engravings on a smaller scale and the text of the *Ornithological Biography*, was published between 1840 and 1844 and sold extremely well.

In 1839 Audubon and his family settled in New York City, and in 1842 they built their first permanent home there, which Audubon named "Minnie's Land." Audubon now turned to a new project, *The Viviparous Quadrupeds of North America*, with a new collaborator, the Reverend John Bachman, a New York–born Lutheran clergyman long resident in Charleston, South Carolina. Audubon and Bachman had first met in Charleston when Audubon visited there in 1831. The two agreed to collaborate on the mammal project after the *Birds* had been completed. Their two families became increasingly close, and John Woodhouse Audubon married Bachman's daughter Maria in 1837, and his brother Victor married her sister Eliza in 1839. Tragically, both young women died of consumption, Maria in 1840 and Eliza a year later. Both sons subsequently remarried.

Work on the *Quadrupeds* began in 1840, with Bachman, an able and experienced student of mammalogy, writing much of the scientific text, which supplemented observations drawn from Audubon's journals. Relations between the two men were often strained because Audubon frequently neglected to forward the necessary specimens and books Bachman needed. Audubon undertook a final expedition up the Missouri River to secure additional specimens from March to September 1843. The scientific results of this trip were minimal, however, though Audubon did some sketching with Edward Harris, a naturalist and gentleman farmer from New Jersey, who accompanied him on the trip. Audubon became disillusioned about the sad state of the Indians he encountered and rarely ventured far from their vessel, the *Omega*, which reached Fort Union near the mouth of the Yellowstone River before turning about. Bachman was greatly disappointed by Audubon's failure to bring back the many new specimens he had anticipated.

Audubon returned east to paint and to resume periodic trips, during which he solicited subscriptions. By the mid-1840s the increasingly weary naturalist turned many details of the preparation and merchandising of the *Quadrupeds* over to his sons. John Woodhouse Audubon's marked artistic talents had manifested themselves at an early age, and he made some artistic contributions to the *Birds of America*. His work on the *Quadrupeds* was substantial; he completed half of the 150 plates, and later critics admitted that it was difficult to tell the difference between the work done by father and son. Victor Audubon, less talented as an artist, proved to be a competent editor and business manager. John Woodhouse was dispatched to Europe to draw some of the American mammal specimens located in museum collections there. By 1846 Audubon's eyesight was rapidly failing; soon his mental faculties began to slip. The decision was made to abandon any coverage of bats and marine mammals in the *Quadrupeds*. Bachman's sister-in-law Maria, who for twenty years had drawn flowers and insects for the bird and mammal portraits, became Bachman's second wife several years following the death of her sister. Audubon had a stroke in the spring of 1847, and his sons, with Bachman's aid, completed and published the final volume of the *Quadrupeds* the following year. The younger Audubons kept the fact of their father's retreat into senility as quiet as possible during his final years; to do otherwise might have had a negative effect on the hoped-for success of the *Quadrupeds* for both the Audubons and Bachmans.

Since Audubon's death, there has been considerable debate concerning his artistry. He almost always used recently killed specimens as his models, but these were sometimes posed in anatomically improbable positions. Yet his pictures helped to create the earliest public appreciation of American nature, and he has consistently enjoyed a place of preeminence among American painters of birds and animals. Of his early bird art, he once wrote, "My pencil gave birth to a family of cripples. So maimed were most of them that they resembled the mangled corpses on a field of battle." He veered between scrupulous scientific accuracy and impressionistic action paintings, thus inevitably disconcerting both his artistic and scientific audiences. At times he worked under enormous pressure, owing to constraints of both time and money, and these had their effect on some of his work. Some of the later bird portraits in the Elephant Folio, for example, were excessively crowded with several dissimilar species, and this was done in part to save the costs of engraving and coloring.

Subsequent to his death, Audubon's sons completed publication of the text of the *Quadrupeds* and several other projects based on their father's work, but they later suffered serious business reverses and died in 1860 and 1862, respectively, leaving their widows and fifteen children. Lucy Audubon, once more in financial straits, sold Minnie's Land and then, in 1863, the original drawings from which the plates of the *Birds of America* had been prepared to the New York Historical Society for $4,000. Obliged to resume teaching in her seventies, she subsequently went blind and died at the home of a grandchild in Louisville in 1874.

Audubon had a proud and sensitive personality, in part on account of the circumstances of his birth. Much confusion arose over the years because he told conflicting stories about his origins and his place of birth, clearly out of a desire to disguise the fact of his illegitimacy. Some of these tales adumbrated materials in *Audubon and His Journals*, a two-volume work published by Maria R. Audubon, a daughter of John Woodhouse Audubon, in 1897. One enduring fiction to which these obfuscations gave rise was that John James Audubon had been the lost dauphin of France, a son of Louis XVI and Marie-Antoinette.

Audubon was at times insensitive and thoughtless of others, most especially his long-suffering wife and sons. His name is associated today with the conservation of wildlife, yet during his lifetime he was an enthusiastic hunter of birds and mammals. Toward the end of his life, however, he seems to have realized that the indiscriminate killing of wildlife must eventually lead to its extinction.

Audubon died at his home in New York City.

• The literature on Audubon is enormous. The major manuscript collections, consisting primarily of correspondence and manuscripts for the *Ornithological Biography*, are at the American Museum of Natural History, New York; the American Philosophical Society, Philadelphia; the Audubon Memorial Museum, Henderson, Ky.; the Houghton Library, Harvard University; Princeton University Library; and Yale University Library. The original paintings for the Elephant Folio are at the New-York Historical Society, New York City. Some of the copper plates used in the production of the Elephant Folio are at the American Museum of Natural History, New York. Edited versions of Audubon's letters and journals include Maria R. Audubon, ed., *Audubon and His Journals* (2 vols., 1897), much of which is badly bowdlerized and unreliable; J. W. Audubon, ed., *Audubon's Western Journal, 1849–1850* (1906); Howard Corning, ed., *Journal of John James Audubon Made during His Trip to New Orleans in 1820–1821* (1930) and *The Letters of John James Audubon, 1826–1840* (1930); and Alice Ford, ed., *The 1826 Journal of John James Audubon* (1967). The principal biographies include Francis H. Herrick, *Audubon the Naturalist*, rev. ed. (2 vols., 1938); Alice Ford, *John James Audubon* (1964); Alexander B. Adams, *John James Audubon: A Biography* (1966); and Shirley Streshinsky, *Audubon: Life and Art in the American Wilderness* (1993). Other useful studies include Carolyn DeLatte, *Lucy Audubon: A Biography* (1982), and Jay Shuler, *Had I the Wings: The Friendship of Bachman and Audubon* (1995). See also Waldemar Fries, *The Double Elephant Folio: The Story of Audubon's Birds of America* (1973); Susanne M. Low, *An Index and Guide to Audubon's "Birds of America"* (1988); John F. McDermott, ed., *Up the Missouri with Audubon: The Journal of Edward Harris* (1951); Robert Cushman Murphy, "John James Audubon (1785–1851): An Evaluation of the Man and His Work," *New-York Historical Society Quarterly* (Oct. 1956); Margaret C. Welch, "John James Audubon and His American Audience: Art, Science, and Nature, 1830–1860" (Ph.D. diss., Univ. of Pennsylvania, 1988); Charlie M. Simon, *Joe Mason, Apprentice to Audubon* (1946); Thomas W. Bakewell, "Audubon and Bakewell, Partners; Sketches of the Life of Thomas Woodhouse Bakewell . . . by Himself," *The Cardinal*, vol. 4, no. 2 (1935). A number of complete and selective editions of the *Birds of America* and of the *Viviparous Quadrupeds* have been published over the last 150 years.

KEIR B. STERLING

AUER, John (30 Mar. 1875–30 Apr. 1948), pharmacologist and physiologist, was born in Rochester, New York, the son of Henry Auer, a German-born brewer, and Luise Hummel. After secondary education in church and public schools in Chicago, he received his B.S. from the University of Michigan in 1898 and his M.D. from Johns Hopkins University in 1902. He spent a year as a medical house officer (intern) at the Johns Hopkins Hospital, and in 1903 he moved to the brand new Rockefeller Institute for Medical Research, which became Rockefeller University in 1965.

Auer began as a fellow at the Rockefeller Institute. He married the physiologist Samuel J. Meltzer's daughter Clara (also a fellow at the Rockefeller) in 1903; they had three children. In 1905 he became an assistant in Meltzer's laboratory; here he rose through the ranks of the institute to become an associate member. In 1906–1907 the institute sent him to Harvard for advanced study in physiology; while there he instructed in the same subject. During World War I the Institute was made a U.S. Auxiliary Laboratory, and Auer was set to work on poison gases, with no notable result except for a major's commission in the Medical Reserve Corps. In 1920 Meltzer died and his laboratory was disbanded. The next year Auer moved to St. Louis as professor and director of the department of pharmacology. In 1924 he became pharmacologist to the St. Mary's group of hospitals operated by the university. He held all of these positions until his death.

Auer's research began in 1906 while he was still at the Johns Hopkins Hospital, where he detected previously unobserved inclusions in the lymphocytes (a variety of white blood cell) of a patient with acute leukemia. These came to be called "Auer bodies." At the Rockefeller he worked closely with Meltzer for his eighteen years there, contributing a rare experimental skill in Meltzer's ongoing research program while adding important contributions of his own. Their first major collaboration produced some twenty-five papers on the use of magnesium sulfate as an anesthetic and muscle relaxant, particularly useful in the spasmodic muscular seizures of tetanus, eclampsia, and the like. Efforts to use magnesium ion for surgical anesthesia were forestalled by its depression of the respiratory centers in the brain, which could result in death. The solution to this problem opened a new area of surgical technique: the lungs could be oxygenated without the breathing action of the chest by blowing a stream of air into them through a tube inserted into the trachea, a procedure called insufflation. Thoracic surgery that was formerly impossible now became routine with this method.

Auer's major research dealt with anaphylaxis, the systemic reaction to foreign proteins in the bloodstream that produces capillary dilation and loss of fluids, edema, loss of consciousness, and sometimes death, usually from cardiac failure. He showed in guinea pigs and rabbits that anaphylaxis was preceded by asphyxia caused by contraction of bronchial muscles and that heart stoppage was the result of direct interference with ventricular action. Auer also investigated the workings of the gastrointestinal tract, discovering in the process a previously unknown part of the rabbit's colon that dehydrated material passing into the descending colon. In other research he examined the function of kidneys, liver, gall bladder, and connective tissue, and the physiological action of various drugs.

When Auer, then in his late forties, went to St. Louis he was plunged into teaching and administrative duties, and for eleven years his research fell by the wayside. He devoted himself with characteristic energy to building his own courses and those of the pharmacology department, and gradually establishing the department as a research group. When he returned to his own research, with the help of his junior staff he studied the motor functions of the digestive and urinary systems, but his findings were not as important as his earlier work. His teaching efforts were rewarded by his students in the establishment in 1944 of the John Auer Lectureship by the medical fraternity Phi Beta Pi.

Auer's importance in pharmacology and medical physiology lies partly in his research in the latter, which has taken its place among the unsung advances of medical understanding, but mainly in building a strong department in a university that was moving toward international prominence. He belonged to a number of professional societies and helped to organize the American Society of Pharmacology and Experimental Therapeutics, serving as its secretary (1912–1916), vice president (1917–1918), and president (1924–1928). He was an amateur painter and read French, German, and Latin literature. Auer died in St. Louis.

• A collection of reprints of Auer's papers on experimental medicine is at the John Crerar Library, Chicago, Ill. A smaller collection of his papers in physiology (1902–1917) is at the National Library of Medicine, Washington, D.C. Scattered references to Auer may be found in George W. Corner, *A History of the Rockefeller Institute, 1901–1953* (1964), which also lists his scientific papers up to 1921. His lifetime output of more than 140 research papers is not gathered in any single publication but is in the volumes of the *Index Medicus*, 1906–1948. An obituary is in the *New York Times*, 2 May 1948. Obituary memoirs of Auer in professional journals include George B. Roth, "John Auer, 1875–1948," *Journal of Pharmacology and Experimental Therapeutics* 95 (1949): 285–86; and Ralph Kinsella, *Transactions of the Association of American Physicians* 61 (1948): 5ff.

ROBERT M. HAWTHORNE JR.

AUGUR, Christopher Colon (10 July 1821–16 Jan. 1898), soldier, was born in Kendall, New York, the son of Ammon Augur and Annis Wellman. Ammon Augur died within a year of Christopher's birth, and the widow and son soon moved to Michigan.

Christopher was appointed to the U.S. Military Academy from Michigan and reported for duty at West Point as a plebe in July 1839. He stood sixteenth in the class that graduated on 1 July 1843. In the class of 1843 were thirteen young men, besides Augur, who would become general officers during the Civil War, including Ulysses S. Grant. Commissioned a brevet second lieutenant, Augur was assigned to the Second U.S. Infantry, then posted at Fort Ontario, New York. In 1844, while stationed there, he took leave to marry Jane Elizabeth Arnold; they had eleven children, ten of whom lived to adulthood. Ordered to Corpus Christi, Texas, in the summer of 1845, he was promoted to second lieutenant in the Fourth U.S. Infantry and soldiered with Lieutenant Grant.

Augur participated in the battles of Palo Alto and Resaca de la Palma, fought on successive days in May 1846. Soon after the occupation of Matamoros, Augur, having taken sick, returned to the United States on recruiting service. Promoted to first lieutenant on 16 February 1847, he served as aide-de-camp first to Brigadier General Enos Hopping and then to Brigadier General Caleb Cushing.

The years following the Mexican-American War found Augur pulling garrison duty at East Pascagoula, Mississippi, and Forts Niagara and Columbus, New York. Ordered to the Pacific Coast in 1852, he was posted to Benicia Barracks, California, and was promoted to captain to rank from 1 August 1852. From 1852 until the spring of 1861 he and his company served in the Northwest at Fort Vancouver (1852–1854, 1855–1856), Forts Dalles and Yakima (1855), Fort Orford (1856), and Fort Hoskins (1856–1861).

Augur was promoted to major of the newly constituted Thirteenth U.S. Infantry on 4 May 1861 and reported to the U.S. Military Academy as commandant of cadets and instructor of tactics on 26 August 1861.

Promoted to brigadier general of volunteers on 12 November 1861, he was ordered to Washington, D.C., where he was placed in charge of the city's advance defenses. The spring of 1862 found Augur commanding a brigade in Brigadier General Rufus King's division of Major General Irvin McDowell's corps, which was detached to guard the Virginia approaches to Washington when George McClellan began his Peninsula campaign. On 25 May, as a result of Thomas "Stonewall" Jackson's victories in the Shenandoah Valley, Augur and his troops rushed to the valley but reached Front Royal too late to forestall Jackson's retrograde up the Valley Pike.

The organization of the Army of Virginia by Major General John Pope in late June 1862 benefited Augur's career. Major General Franz Sigel was named to lead the army's First Corps, and in mid-July Augur succeeded Sigel as commander of one of the two divisions in Major General Nathaniel Banks's corps, then posted at Little Washington. On 9 August Banks's corps attacked Major General Jackson's three-division corps at Cedar Mountain. After having his horse shot from under him, Augur, whose small division was on Banks's left, was severely wounded in his right hip and had to leave the field. General Pope, in his after-action report, called attention to Augur's "conspicuous gallantry." The War Department, in recognition of his conduct at Cedar Mountain, made Augur a brevet colonel and promoted him to major general of volunteers to rank from 9 August.

On limited duty because of his wound, Augur in September and October served on the commission to investigate the surrender of Harpers Ferry. On 4 November General McClellan, learning that Augur was again fit for duty, called him to Rectortown and placed him in command of the Army of the Potomac's First Corps. McClellan was sacked on 7 November, and Augur's stay with the First Corps was brief. Three days later Augur was ordered to Washington to report to Banks, who was outfitting a force to accompany him to New Orleans, where Banks was to assume command of the Department of the Gulf. Banks had requested Augur to be his second in command.

Augur reached New Orleans in mid-December and in mid-January 1863 assumed command of a three-brigade division that was to be concentrated in and around Baton Rouge. On 26 February he was named commander of the Baton Rouge forces, 17,000 strong. Augur and his division constituted Banks's reserve in mid-March, when the army advanced from Baton Rouge against the Port Hudson perimeter to cover Rear Admiral David G. Farragut's passage of the Port Hudson river batteries on the night of 14–15 March.

Augur and his command held the Baton Rouge enclave in April and the first three weeks of May, as Banks's columns struck north from Brashear City to Alexandria, crossed the Mississippi, and closed on Port Hudson from the northwest. With 3,000 men, Augur advanced from Baton Rouge and, at Plains Store on 21 May, beat the Confederates. On 27 May Augur's command participated in the failed assault on Port Hudson, attacking the Confederate center. The 14 June assault, likewise repulsed, found Augur feigning an attack in the center. On 15 July, one week after Major General Franklin Gardner, his West Point classmate, surrendered Port Hudson, Augur, weakened by diarrhea and dysentery, departed Louisiana on sick leave.

On 14 October Augur relieved Major General Samuel P. Heintzelman as commander of the Department of Washington and the Twenty-second Corps. In mid-May 1864 Augur culled the Washington defenses and rushed reinforcements to the Army of the Potomac to replace the thousands of casualties suffered in Grant's Overland campaign. Jubal Early's 4–14 July raid north of the Potomac to the gates of Washington created a crisis. Augur called out the Provisional Division and deployed units from the Sixth and Nineteenth corps to bolster the forces in the forts guarding the northern approaches to the city, causing the Confederates to return to Virginia.

To facilitate the transfer of the Sixth and Nineteenth corps of Philip Sheridan's Army of the Shenandoah from the valley to Alexandria, General Augur, on 6 October, took personal charge of reconstruction of the Manassas Gap Railroad westward to Piedmont and warded off the attacks of Colonel John S. Mosby and his partisans. During the last six months of the war, Augur spent much energy coordinating operations to suppress the partisan activities led by Mosby in the northern Virginia counties. Between 14 and 26 April his attention was engrossed by successful efforts to hunt down John Wilkes Booth and the Abraham Lincoln assassination conspirators.

On 13 August 1866 Augur was relieved as commander of the Department of Washington, and on 1 September he was mustered out of the volunteer service, reverting to his rank as colonel of the Twelfth U.S. Infantry, to which he had been named on 15 March 1866. From 16 August 1866 to 2 June 1867 he served as a member of the army's promotion board. From 15 January 1867 to 13 November 1871 he commanded the Department of the Platte, where his responsibilities were increased by the building of the Union Pacific Railroad, the westward migration of thousands of homesteaders, and the wars that resulted as the Indians sought to defend their hunting grounds.

On 4 March 1869 Augur was promoted to brigadier general to fill a billet created by Grant's inauguration as the eighteenth president. Augur commanded the Department of Texas from 29 January 1872 to March 1875, and while there he served as lay delegate from Texas to the General Convention of the Protestant Episcopal Church held in New York City in 1874. He headed the Department of the Gulf, 27 March 1875 to 1 July 1878, during the disputed election of 1876, when opposing factions threatened civil war. In 1880 he sat on the Gouverneur Kemble Warren court of inquiry. His final duty was as commander of the Department of the Missouri. On 10 July 1885, having reached his sixty-fourth birthday, he retired from the army. Augur died in Georgetown, District of Columbia.

• For further information on Augur, see Letters Received by the Commission Branch of the Adjutant General's Office, M-1064, National Archives; John C. Ropes et al., comps., *Papers of the Military Historical Society of Massachusetts*, vol. 2 (1905); *The War of the Rebellion: A Compilation of the Official Records of the Union and Confederate Armies* (128 vols., 1880–1901); George W. Cullum, *Biographical Register of the Officers and Graduates of the U.S. Military Academy*, 3d ed., vol. 2 (3 vols., 1891); Edwin P. Augur, *Family History and Genealogy of the Descendants of Robert Augur* (1904); and Ezra J. Warner, *Generals in Blue: Lives of the Union Commanders* (1964).

E. C. BEARSS

AUGUR, Hezekiah (21 Feb. 1791–10 Jan. 1858), sculptor, was born in New Haven, Connecticut, the son of Hezekiah Augur, Sr., a carpenter, and his second wife, Lydia Atwater. The boy early on learned to use his father's tools and even tinkered with making machinery. In a letter written when he was eight years old, Hezekiah noted that he "preferred the confines of the shop to fighting schoolfellows" (French, p. 47). His father, however, apprenticed him at the age of nine to a grocer; Augur, Sr., apparently wanted his son to aspire to more than a manual trade, even though young Hezekiah seemed quite happy carving wood. One of his duties in the grocery was to fix and make shoes. He was more adept at the awl than the record book, however, and upon finishing his apprenticeship seems to have been regarded as "an abominably poor grocer, but a proficient cobbler" (French, p. 47).

Augur's early dabblings in carpentry, invention, and cobbling would later stand him in good stead, but at around the age of fourteen he endeavored to learn to be an apothecary. Toward this end, he was required to study anatomy. This experience too would later find application in a profession other than that for which it was originally intended. The apothecary trade did not hold Augur's attention, so, at sixteen, he began work as a clerk in a mercantile house. The next several years saw him succeed fairly well in several business concerns (contrary to his earlier inadequacies as a grocer), helped initially by some financial backing from his father. This culminated in a position as both partner and manager of a dry goods business in New Haven. Financial disaster blindsided Augur in December 1816 when his business partner not only dissolved their partnership but also informed Augur of an indebtedness amounting to several thousand dollars. At the age of twenty-five Augur found himself bankrupt and jobless. His father and some relatives assumed his debts for him. After a few probably embarrassing months of working for his father, he borrowed enough money to open a cigar and fruit stand, while continuing to live at home with his parents and sister.

During all his ventures Augur had always kept up his wood carving and continued to do so as a fruit vendor. One of his carved works was a frame case for a harp. The cabinetmaker to whom he took it to be varnished expressed such regard for his work that Augur was encouraged to give up selling fruits and cigars and set up shop as a woodcarver. The inventiveness of his youth had not left him. His creation of the first bracket saw and a machine for making worsted lace and epaulets (and the income gained therefrom) allowed him to pursue his dream. Also, in 1818 his father died. It is possible that, with his father's death, Augur finally allowed himself to follow his own goals, which he began to do with marked success. At the time, though, Augur noted, "With a life-blot behind me, my only ambition is to drown memory and reflection in a pleasant pastime" (French, p. 48).

Augur's carving business, which produced decorative architectural pieces and furniture legs, expanded. By 1823 he had paid off all his debts to his relatives and finally settled with his former dry goods partner. This bulk payout, however, again put Augur in a difficult financial situation, which might have turned dire if not for his serendipitous encounter with painter and inventor Samuel F. B. Morse. Morse, a resident of New Haven, urged Augur to try carving in marble, not just wood, and suggested attempting a copy of the Apollo Bellevedere.

The meeting with Morse and the completion of the marble bust of Apollo a year later, in 1824, marked the start of Augur's true career. Augur's Apollo (which he had carved directly into the marble, essentially "freehand") received great critical praise at its exhibition in 1825 at the New York Academy of Arts. He called it his "first essay in marble" when it was shown again in 1831 at the Pennsylvania Academy. Augur also carved a Sappho and a bust of George Washington. In 1827 Augur completed his commemorative bust of Yale mathematics professor Alexander M. Fisher, which had been commissioned by the professor's class, and it was presented to the college. And in 1834 he was commissioned to carve the bust of Oliver Ellsworth, chief justice of the U.S. Supreme Court (Supreme Court Room, U.S. Capitol). Augur, unschooled and self-taught, had a natural, native talent for carving in marble that was quickly recognized. There was a physical and emotional vibrancy to his style that was apparent in all his work and was unusual for the time.

In the early 1830s Augur carved a pair of marble statuettes, *Jephthah and His Daughter* (Yale Art School), which became his most celebrated work. Augur did not use live models for the work, drawing instead on illustrations, small porcelains, and his own imagination, an unusual approach for creating three-dimensional artwork. The figure of Jephthah's daughter seems to have intimations of the delicacy and fluidity of Cellini. The figures are about one-half life-sized, seemingly quick-frozen in motion, and the deft carving of the folds of their drapery reflects their creator's origins in skillful woodcarving. This father and daughter group—Augur's "marble people" as Ralph Waldo Emerson called them—also demonstrated Augur's artistic ambition to move beyond mere "portraits" in marble.

Accolades followed Augur with regularity. Without the imprimatur of formal training, he was elected a member of the National Academy of Design. His hometown of New Haven took pride not only in him but in the fame he was bringing to the city. The *Literary Tablet* of 1 November 1832, writing about the traveling exhibition of *Jephthah and His Daughter*, reported: "Mr. Augur, whose skill and taste as a sculptor are contributing so largely to the reputation, not only of our city, but of this nation, has gone to New York with his beautiful group of statuary. . . . Mr. Augur intends to visit Philadelphia, Baltimore, and Washington—thus affording a fine opportunity for the admirers of American genius to evince their approbation of this exquisite speciman [*sic*] of art, by solid testimony" (Craven, p. 93). In 1833 Yale College conferred upon him the honorary degree of master of arts.

All the praise, however, did not translate into lucrative income. The majority of his work was done by private commission or under his own volition. The strikingly executed bust of Chief Justice Ellsworth, finished in 1837, was one of his rare public works. Augur did get enough work to sustain him modestly, and, following the death of his mother in 1837, he moved out of the family home and into separate quarters. He designed the bronze medals commemorating the 200th anniversary of New Haven's settlement and in 1840, according to his diary, carved a monument for a Miss Ogden of New Haven. But by 1845 artistic aspiration had to give in to financial necessity, and Augur sold his belongings at auction, including the Apollo bust, heads of George Washington and Benjamin Franklin, and a "sleeping Cupid" figure, all now lost.

This last conflict between money and art seems to have ultimately undermined Augur's creative will. He did manage one final, recorded burst of innovation—what he referred to as the "single ray of light" in what he saw now as a darkened creative existence—his invention of a machine for carving marble. He patented the machine in 1849; it reconfirmed him as a mechanical genius and was still in general use more than thirty years after its invention. The carving machine was a solid success, and Augur linked up with the company that promoted its sale in New England, thereby assuring himself some steady income. But as far as can be determined, from 1840 until his death in New Haven, Augur never carved in marble again.

Augur's was not an assertive or self-promoting personality; indeed, he was rather retiring and unpretentious, except for an inclination to dress well (which he was not often able to indulge). His clear and genuine skill as a sculptor was recognized and hailed, it seems, almost in spite of himself. But he was recognized and he was praised; and, contrary to the type of life that had been mapped for him, his passive but dogged determination resulted in remarkable works of decoration, art, and invention. Augur never married and fathered no children. He formed no atelier and had no disciples, students, or acolytes to learn and build on his style of carving (his nature may not have lent itself comfortably to that anyway). The subjects and themes of his sculptures were generally of his own choosing and preference, which might partly explain why his career was not more profitable. Although he did not influence any particular artistic style, he did make a small, singular, and precise contribution to early American sculpture, both as artist and as technician. And he was, on his own and by his own study, one of the first successful American sculptors. Without benefit of education, training, paternal approval, money, or special patronage, a shy young man went from being a grocer's apprentice, cobbler, and fruit vendor to a sculptor of rank and reputation solely by virtue of talent. Augur, and his work, were completely self-made.

• Augur is discussed briefly in various nineteenth- and twentieth-century biographical listings of American sculptors. (Mantle Fielding's *Dictionary of American Painters, Sculptors and Engravers* [1983] incorrectly lists Augur's father as a shoemaker, rather than a carpenter, probably confusing Augur's cobbling duties as an apprentice grocer with the work of his father.) The best sources of information on Augur and his contributions to American sculpture are H. W. French, *Art and Artists of Connecticut* (1879; repr. 1970); Lorado Taft, *The History of American Sculpture* (1903; repr. 1924); G. H. Hamilton, "New Haven Sculptors," *Bulletin of the Associates in Fine Arts at Yale University* 8 (June 1938): 70–72; and Wayne Craven, *Sculpture in America* (1968; repr. 1984). See also Edwin P. Augur, *Family History and Genealogy of the Descendants of Robert Augur* (1904); William Dunlap, *A History of the Rise and Progress of the Arts of Design in the United States* (1918); Albert TenEyck Gardner, *Yankee Stonecutters: The First American School of Sculpture, 1800–1850* (1945); Oliver Larkin, "Early American Sculpture: A Craft Becomes an Art," *Magazine Antiques* 56 (Sept. 1949): 176–78; and Tom Armstrong et al., *Two Hundred Years of American Sculpture* (1976). An obituary is in the *New Haven Register*, Jan. 1858.

E. D. LLOYD-KIMBREL

AUGUSTA, Alexander Thomas (8 Mar. 1825–21 Dec. 1890), physician and medical educator, was born a free African American in Norfolk, Virginia, to parents whose names and occupations are unknown. Augusta received his early education from a Bishop Payne, defying a law that forbade African Americans to read or write. He continued to improve his reading skills while working as an apprentice to a barber. His interest in medicine led him to relocate to Baltimore, Maryland, where he studied with private tutors. Eventually, Augusta moved to Philadelphia, Pennsylvania, to serve an apprenticeship. Although he was denied entry to the University of Pennsylvania, Augusta caught the attention of Professor William Gibson, who allowed the young man to study in his office.

In January 1847 Augusta married Mary O. Burgoin in Baltimore, Maryland. They lived in California for three years before returning to the East Coast so that Augusta could pursue a medical degree. Denied access, despite his prior training in the medical field, to the medical schools in both Philadelphia and Chicago, he applied to study in Canada. He was accepted by Trinity Medical College in Toronto, Ontario, from which he graduated in 1856 with a bachelor of medicine degree. While studying in Toronto, he supported himself and his wife by operating a store that offered services, such as cupping and bleeding, and medicines. Mary worked as a much-sought-after dressmaker.

Augusta's records for the years between 1856 and 1861 are incomplete. He apparently ran the City Hospital and acted as a physician at Toronto's "poor house," while possibly managing a private practice. There is further speculation that he was in charge of an industrial school for two years. He may also have spent some of this period in the West Indies, eventually returning to Canada.

With the onset of the Civil War, Augusta was eager to utilize his talents. In 1862 he journeyed to Washington, D.C., to take the examination for the volunteer medical service. Impatience prompted him to petition both President Abraham Lincoln and Secretary of War Edwin M. Stanton on 7 January 1863 with respect to a surgical appointment. In March he received an unfavorable reply from the Army Medical Board denying his petition on the grounds that, first, he was of African descent, and second, accepting him into the service would be a direct violation of Queen Victoria's Proclamation of Neutrality because, as a Canadian resident, he was "an alien and a British subject." In a letter to Lincoln and the Army Medical Board dated 30 March 1863, Augusta argued that the officials had misinterpreted his case. He explained that he had expected to serve the colored regiments, and that he was still a U.S. citizen despite having obtained his medical credentials in Canada.

On 1 April 1863 the board overturned its decision, finding Augusta "qualified for the position of surgeon in the Negro regiment now being raised." On 14 April 1863 Augusta was appointed a surgeon with the Seventh U.S. Colored Infantry, making him the first African American to receive a medical commission in the U.S. Army. Only seven other African Americans were to receive such an appointment during the Civil War.

Serving from 1863 to 1864 as chief executive officer of Freedmen's Hospital, formerly called "Camp Barker," Augusta was the first African American to head a U.S. hospital. In February 1864 several white physicians of the hospital petitioned the president to have him permanently reassigned, as they refused to be subordinate to an African American. Augusta was then assigned to a recruiting office in Baltimore, Maryland. When the Seventh U.S. Colored Troops were sent to Beaufort, South Carolina, Augusta went with them. He remained there until the end of the war.

Throughout most of Augusta's war service, the army paid him at the level of an enlisted Negro soldier, despite the fact that he held the rank of major. This insult continued until Senator Henry Wilson of Massachusetts intervened on Augusta's behalf. The indignities that Augusta suffered during the war were not limited to the military, however. Average citizens were enraged at the sight of an African American in an officer's uniform. While journeying to Baltimore at one point during the war, Augusta was assaulted by a group of men and had to be rescued by police. When Augusta and his protégé, Anderson Ruffin Abbott, attended the White House Levee of 1863–1864, Abbott recorded that in full dress regalia the two were "the synosure of all eyes."

Augusta's obstinacy scored a major victory for all African Americans residing in Washington, D.C., however. On his way to testify in a court-martial case on 1 February 1864, he was ejected from a street car when he refused to sit in the "Negroes Only" section. When he was forced to give an explanation for his tardiness to the judge advocate, the incident drew the attention of the Senate and became the subject of a debate resulting in the integration of all Washington street cars.

On 13 March 1865 Augusta was brevetted lieutenant colonel in the U.S. Volunteer Corps "for meritorious and faithful service." He was the first African American to be awarded such rank. Following the war his services were retained by the medical division of the Bureau of Refugees, Freedmen, and Abandoned Lands, where he served as an assistant surgeon responsible for the Freedmen's Hospital in Savannah, Georgia.

Augusta, the highest ranking African American to serve in the U.S. Civil War, mustered out of the army on 13 October 1866, returning to Washington, where he opened a medical practice. On 21 September 1868 he was appointed demonstrator of anatomy at the newly formed medical department at Howard University, making him the first African American to hold a faculty position at a U.S. medical school. While at Howard, Augusta held several different professorships in anatomy. He was one of three faculty members to remain in their positions in the medical department, despite severe salary cuts, when the nation and the university faced financial collapse in 1873. In 1877, after the medical faculty recommended to the trustees that Augusta switch positions with Dr. Daniel Lamb and become chair of materia medica rather than anatomy, Augusta resigned and returned to private practice.

In 1869 Augusta and two other African-American doctors were denied membership in the Medical Society of the District of Columbia, an association responsible for licensing and professional development. Frustrated with racist admission policies, Augusta helped found the Medical-Chirurgical Society of D.C. in 1884, the first African-American medical society in the United States.

In 1870 Augusta became the attending physician at a smallpox hospital in Washington, also renewing his involvement with Freedmen's Hospital. By this time the hospital had become the teaching facility for Howard University's medical department. From 1870 to 1875 he served as a staff physician for the Urino-Genital Diseases Division, and from October 1875 to July 1877 he was the ward physician at the hospital. In 1888 he assumed the position of Clinical Lecturer on Diseases of the Skin. Augusta died in Washington, D.C.

• Firsthand accounts of Augusta appear in the scrapbooks of his protégé, Anderson Ruffin Abbott, in the Abbott Collection, Metropolitan Toronto Reference Library. Biographical sketches include William Montague Cobb, "Medical History: Alexander Thomas Augusta," *Journal of the National Medical Association* 44, no. 4 (July 1952): 327–29, the most complete; Daniel Smith Lamb, "Alexander Thomas Augusta, A.M., M.D.," in *Howard University Medical Department Washington D.C.: A Historical, Biographical and Statistical Souvenir* (1971); and Robert Ewell Greene, "Alexander T. Augusta," in *Black Defenders of America, 1775–1973: A Reference and Pictorial History* (1974). Reference to Augusta is also in Daniel G. Hill, *The Freedom-Seekers: Blacks in Early Canada* (1981). For Augusta's military service, see Herbert M. Morais, *The History of the Negro in Medicine* (1967), p. 37; Ira Berlin, *Freedom A Documentary History of Emancipation 1861–1867: Selected from the Holdings of the National Archives of the United States, Series II: The Black Military Experience* (1982), pp. 354–58, which extrapolates information from Augusta's personal files; and Edwin S. Redkey, ed., *A Grand Army of Black Men: Letters from African-American Soldiers in the Union Army, 1861–1865* (1992), pp. 252–56. Two excellent sources on Howard University and Freedmen's Hospital are William Montague Cobb, "Original Communication: A Short History of Freedmen's Hospital," *Journal of the National Medical Association* 54, no. 3 (May 1962): 271–87; and Rayford W. Logan, *Howard University: The First Hundred Years 1867–1967* (1969).

DALYCE NEWBY

AUSLANDER, Joseph (11 Oct. 1897–22 June 1965), poet, editor, and translator, was born in Philadelphia, Pennsylvania, the son of Louis Auslander and Martha Asyueck. He attended Columbia University from 1914 to 1915, then transferred to Harvard, receiving his B.A. in 1917. In 1919 he became an instructor in English at Harvard. He pursued graduate studies there until 1924, with the interruption of one year (1921–1922) at the Sorbonne in Paris, where he went on a Parker Traveling Fellowship. His poetry began to appear in national magazines in 1919, and his first volume, *Sunrise Trumpets*, with an introduction by Padraic Colum, was published in 1924. For a first publication, the book received outstanding reviews; critics praised Auslander's "astonishing use of color and striking image" (H. S. Gorman, *Bookman*, p. 468) and "beautifully chiselled verse" (Malcolm Vaughan, *Boston Transcript*, p. 5). Two years later came the collection *Cyclops' Eye*, and on the basis of these two volumes John Drinkwater included him in his anthology, *Twentieth Century Poetry* (1930), praising his "stark narratives."

Auslander collaborated with Frank Ernest Hill in writing *The Winged Horse*, a popular history of traditional western poetry, in 1927, and the following year they edited *The Winged Horse Anthology*, a collection of poetry complementing the first, though limiting itself to selections from English and American poetry. Both were widely used as textbooks in primary and secondary schools over the years. These marked the beginning of his attempts to establish poetry in American popular culture. In 1929 he published two new volumes of his poetry, *Hell in Harness* and *Letters to Women*. The latter, his tribute to women, contained letters to eight women, from Sappho to Elinor Wylie, including a "Letter to Emily Dickinson," which won the *Palms* magazine award for that year.

From 1929 to 1937 he served as a lecturer in poetry at Columbia. In 1930 and 1931 he published three books of translations, *The Fables of La Fontaine: Books 1–6*, *The Vigil of Venus*, and *The Sonnets of Petrarch*, all of which appealed to a wide audience. In May 1930 he married Svanhild Kreutz, but less than a year later she died, leaving a daughter. In May 1933 he married the poet, Audrey Wurdemann, winner of the 1935 Pulitzer Prize for her second volume of poetry, *Bright Ambush*. During the 1930s he published four more collections of his poetry; *No Traveler Returns* appeared in 1935. The first half of the book deals with his grief over the death of his first wife and his attempts to come to terms with it; the second half is dedicated to his new wife, and it is this portion that was published later the same year as a separate volume titled *Green World*. *More than Bread* appeared in 1936, and *Riders at the Gate* in 1939. In addition he edited a new printing of the sonnets of Shakespeare, published in 1931, and also wrote a book on Shakespeare for young people, which appeared in 1934.

Auslander served as poetry editor of the *North American Review* from 1936 until its demise in 1939. In 1937 he became the first consultant in poetry at the Library of Congress, Washington, D.C., serving in that capacity and later as gift officer until 1944. During his tenure there he set up a Poetry Room that sponsored a series of readings by prominent American poets, beginning in the spring of 1941. Following those appointments he returned to his former position of lecturer in poetry at Columbia University. A year before his return to Columbia he wrote, with the help of his second wife, a series of poems on World War II published as *The Unconquerables*, a feeling memorial to the victims of war.

Several of Auslander's poems have been adapted for chorus, piano, and solo, notably by Carlisle Floyd for the Brown University Glee Club. Auslander's poem "Marriage Anniversary" appeared in *The Best Poems of 1942*, and *Life* magazine featured a series of his war poems in its 18 September 1944 issue. In 1948, with his second wife, he wrote the novel *My Uncle Jan*, a rollicking story of Czech immigrants in southeastern Wisconsin. They also wrote together the novel *Islanders* (1951), a poetic prose tale about an immigrant Greek family adapting to life in Florida. Audrey Wurdemann died in May 1960, in Miami, where the Auslanders had retired. Auslander died five years later in the same city. Shortly before his death he received the Robert Frost prize for poetry.

Auslander read deeply in Greek and Roman literature, translating both classical writing as well as Italian and French. His poetry tended toward the traditional—rhyme, rhythm, and stanza patterns—and he wrote with remarkable ease and facility. He is, however, less remembered for his own poetry than for his work in popularizing poetry. Even so, there are certain poems ("Steel" and the free verse "Letter to Amy Lowell") and certain collections (*Letters to Women* and *No Traveler Returns*) that show Auslander as a fine and memorable craftsman with the voice of a "troubadour," as Patrick Colum characterized him.

• The Virginia Wilson Lachicotte Papers at the University of South Carolina contain some correspondence of Auslander, and the original sound discs of Auslander recitations from the 1930s are in Columbia University's Brander Matthews Dramatic Museum Collection. Obituaries are in the *New York Times*, 23 June 1965, *Newsweek*, 5 July 1965, and *Publishers Weekly*, 19 July 1965.

RICHARD BOUDREAU

AUSTELL, Alfred (14 Jan. 1814–7 Dec. 1881), businessman and financier, was born in Dandridge, Tennessee, the son of William Austell and Jane Wilkins, farmers. Austell was reared in the East Tennessee foothills and received little formal education. At the age of seventeen he left Tennessee to join his older brother William's cotton business in Spartanburg, South Carolina. The business was heavily encumbered by debts, but Austell and his brother were able to turn it into a success and pay off their $20,000 liability in just three years.

Austell became enamored of the business world during his stay in South Carolina, and that interest led him to travel to New York in 1835 to take advantage of opportunities in that northern city. After only a year, however, Austell returned to his native region, and settled in the small northern Georgia town of Campbellton. There he again entered into a business partnership with his brother William, but this time they concentrated on becoming merchants. The brothers' mercantile business boomed, but William did not live to enjoy it; he died in 1836 and left Alfred to settle his affairs and to continue running the firm.

Austell's mercantile business flourished during the late 1830s and 1840s. His growing prosperity enabled him to expand his investments to include both land and slaves. As a result, by the 1850s, Austell had the reputation of being one of North Georgia's most enterprising businessmen; he also ranked among the wealthiest landowners and slaveholders. In this way he typified many southerners of middle-class status who successfully made the transition into the slaveholding elite. It was while he worked in Campbellton that he met and married Francina Cameron of LaGrange, Georgia, in 1853. They had four children.

In 1858 Austell decided to move his business interests to Georgia's boomtown, Atlanta, where he grew even more successful. Indeed, it was in Atlanta that Austell branched out his business interests again by becoming in 1859 the owner, cashier, and director of the Bank of Fulton, one of the city's strongest. It remained a key fixture of Atlanta's commercial community until it suspended operations after Union forces captured the town in 1864.

Austell bitterly opposed secession along with most of Atlanta's leading businessmen, who denounced disunion because they feared its effects on commercial transactions. An additional reason for Austell's opposition may be traced to his East Tennessee birthplace, a region long noted for its fierce Unionist sentiments. Austell spoke openly about the industrial and financial disadvantages the Confederacy faced and urged that southern interests be pursued and protected within the federal Union. Once Georgia's secession became an established fact, Austell joined a group of other outspoken antisecessionist Atlantans who met secretly during the war in the city's Union Club. While Atlantans widely criticized other prominent members of the Union Club, Austell seems to have escaped censure. Perhaps this was because Austell reportedly aided local Confederate officials in financial and commercial dealings during the war, and joined the Georgia homeguard unit that was called out to defend against Sherman's advance in 1864. Those actions seem to indicate that Austell came to embrace, albeit reluctantly, the southern cause. (Typically referred to as "General Austell," he acquired the nominal rank before the war during his service with the state militia.)

When the war ended in 1865, most of Atlanta was in ruins—including Austell's Bank of Fulton. Like others in the city, however, he immediately engaged in rebuilding, and in September 1865, Austell organized the Atlanta National Bank, the first national bank in the post–Civil War South. Established under the auspices of the National Banking Act of 1863, the Atlanta National Bank opened with capital stock of $100,000. Credit reporters considered bank president Austell and his directors "wealthy men & respectable in every way." The Atlanta National Bank figured prominently in the dramatic rebuilding and resurgence of Atlanta after the war, remaining a keystone of the city's financial rebirth.

After the war Austell remained one of Atlanta's foremost businessmen and demonstrated a great diversity in his dealings. He was a founding partner of one of the South's premier cotton firms, Austell, Inman, and Swann (later Inman, Swann and Company). Austell also manifested a great interest in railroad development. Correctly perceiving the advantages rail connections would have for his city and region, Austell became an ardent booster of the Georgia Air Line Railroad. This project dated back to the antebellum era when local businessmen envisioned a direct link between Atlanta and Washington, D.C., via the Carolina piedmont. Working in conjunction with A. S. Buford of the Richmond & Danville Railroad, Austell oversaw the management of the Atlanta and Richmond Air Line in 1871. Later he became a director and stockholder in two other major railroad projects, the Georgia Pacific, which connected Birmingham, Alabama, with Atlanta, and the East Tennessee, Virginia, and Georgia Railroad, which ran from Atlanta to Rome, Georgia. In addition to his banking and railroad interests, Austell was an active member of the Atlanta Board of Trade and its successor, the Atlanta Chamber of Commerce.

Austell was also active in state politics. He was one of several prominent city leaders who signed resolutions accepting Reconstruction policies and urging Atlantans and other Georgians to abide by the new laws. Although President Andrew Johnson encouraged him to become provisional governor immediately after the war, Austell declined. He chose instead to promote conciliation and acceptance of federal policies on a more informal basis. Austell was in the minority, but he recognized better than most of his peers that Georgia and the South's future was linked to following Republican policies to benefit from Republican largess.

As many of his partners in Atlanta's business community, Austell was generous with the fortune he made. Most of his contributions went to his church, the First Presbyterian Church of Atlanta, but contemporaries also commented on the assistance he extended to other congregations throughout the city. His obituary in the *Atlanta Constitution* (7 Dec. 1881) noted that Austell was a frequent benefactor of the African-American congregations in the city.

Austell died in Atlanta. He was eulogized by the *Atlanta Constitution* as "wise, prudent, and sagacious. . . . General Austell died in the fullness of integrity, without a blot on his career, leaving to his children the legacy of an honest and stainless name." Perhaps more importantly, he left a solid financial foundation and transportation network that would enable his adopted hometown to become one of the preeminent cities of the New South.

• Austell's business career may be traced through the R. G. Dun & Company ledgers, Baker Library, Harvard University Graduate School of Business Administration. Other papers may be found at the Atlanta Historical Society. For other references to Austell's life and career, see Franklin M. Garrett, *Atlanta and Environs: A Chronicle of Its People and Events* (2 vols., 1954); William J. Northen, ed., *Men of Mark of Georgia*, vol. 3 (1911), pp. 357–65; James Michael Russell, *Atlanta, 1847–1890: City Building in the Old South and the New* (1988); and Don H. Doyle, *New Men, New Cities, New South: Atlanta, Nashville, Charleston, Mobile, 1860–1910* (1990).

MARY A. DECREDICO

AUSTEN, Peter Townsend (10 Sept. 1852–30 Dec. 1907), chemist, was born in Clifton (later Rosebank), Staten Island, New York, the son of John H. Austen, a dry-goods auctioneer, and Elizabeth A. Townsend. Austen was educated at the Isaac Holden School before attending the School of Mines of Columbia University. He studied in the chemical course, winning the Torry Prize for best qualitative analysis work, and graduated with the Bachelor of Philosophy degree in 1872. He continued his studies in postgraduate programs, first at the University of Berlin and then at the University of Zurich, obtaining his Ph.D. in 1876.

Austen began his academic career as an instructor of chemistry at Dartmouth College in New Hampshire. He remained there from 1876 until 1878, the year in which he was married to Ellen Middleton Munroe; the couple had three children. Austen then became an assistant professor in the department of chemistry at Rutgers College and at the New Jersey State Scientific School, both part of Rutgers University in New Brunswick, New Jersey. He quickly rose through the ranks, becoming professor of analytical and applied chemistry in 1880; his title was changed to professor of general and applied chemistry in 1882. Austen was particularly noteworthy as the first chemistry professor at Rutgers who devoted his full time to the teaching of chemistry. He also assumed administrative duties as a division officer of the college and was responsible for the system of student attendance. A local journalist wrote, "The name of Dr. P. T. Austen is more before the public perhaps than that of any other professor connected with [Rutgers College], and almost every newspaper . . . contains complimentary allusions to the good work he has done . . . in the cause of science" (*Rutgers Targum*, 15 Mar. 1889).

Austen resigned his position in 1891 because of increasing demands on his time from his private consulting practice, but when Rutgers decided to begin university extension courses the following year, Austen was asked to introduce the program. Throughout the New Jersey and New York area he gave a series of well-attended popular lectures on chemistry, illustrated with simple experiments, which he carried with him in a handbag. The YMCA in Paterson was several times so crowded that people had to be turned away from his programs. Austen conducted these lectures from 1892 to 1893. His love of teaching brought him back to the classroom, and in 1893 he accepted the position of professor of chemistry in a newly created department at the Polytechnic Institute of Brooklyn, New York. In 1896 he retired from academia to devote his energies to consulting and expert chemical work.

As president of the Austen Chemical Research Company, Austen was a nationally known consulting chemist, particularly regarding the analysis of municipal water supplies. At various times throughout his career he was a chemist for the boards of health for Richmond County, New York, and Newark and New Brunswick, New Jersey, as well as the New Jersey State Board of Agriculture and the Newark Aqueduct Board. He testified as an expert witness for the complainant in a suit brought by Newark against Passaic in 1889. He asserted, based on his experimental measurements, that the pollution of the Passaic River would extend from Passaic to Newark. In the face of political pressure, he condemned the Passaic River as a water supply for Newark and successfully convinced the city to seek another water source. Austen was also called as an expert chemist in numerous court cases involving patent and technical litigation. He was an inventor of various manufacturing processes and a long-time consultant to the National Starch Company.

Austen was an author of more than fifty articles in scientific and technical journals. He also translated and revised *Pinner's Organic Chemistry* (1893) and wrote *Notes for Chemical Students* (1897) and *Occurrence of Aluminum in Nature* (with C. F. Langworthy, 1904). He was a member of the American, English, French, German, and Russian chemical societies, the New York Academy of Science, the American Association for the Advancement of Science, and other professional organizations. For three years he served as presiding officer of the New York section of the American Chemical Society.

In addition to his professional affiliations, Austen was active in several professional lodges and social clubs. An avid musician, he organized and led the choir of the Second Reformed Church of New Brunswick and the New Brunswick Choral Association. He died after a short illness in New York City.

Despite the brevity of his life, Austen made contributions in both the academic and the industrial spheres of chemistry. He tried to balance his commitment to teaching and research with his desire to provide sound scientific advice to the progressively urbanized society in which he lived; his most lasting contribution was to improve the quality of drinking water for New York and New Jersey residents at the turn of the century.

• A collection of biographical material, letters, and reprints of Austen's published articles are held at the Rutgers University Special Collections and Archives, New Brunswick, N.J. A biographical sketch, including testimonials from his colleagues, was published in the *University Magazine*, Nov. 1893. Obituaries are in the *New York Times*, 31 Dec. 1907, and the *Rutgers Targum*, 15 Jan. 1908.

DAVID S. GOTTFRIED

AUSTIN, Benjamin (18 Nov. 1752–4 May 1820), polemicist and Democratic-Republican leader, was born in Boston, Massachusetts, the son of Benjamin Austin, a merchant and provincial councilor, and Elizabeth Waldo. He attended Boston Latin School but did not go on to college. In 1779 he was elected a clerk of the market by the Boston Town Meeting. Austin visited England in 1783 and following his return joined with his brother, Jonathan Loring Austin, in an ongoing business partnership. They termed themselves merchants but also developed active interests in ropewalks, shipping, and local real estate. Austin also shared a pew in the First Church of Boston with his brother and later served the church on its standing committee and as moderator. The two brothers married sisters, the daughters of James Ivers, a local sugar refiner, and nieces of Barlow Trecothick, a wealthy merchant and sometime lord mayor of London. Benjamin Austin's 1785 marriage to Jane Ivers produced five children.

Much of Austin's reputation rests on some of his earliest political work, the series of thirteen letters he published in Boston's *Independent Chronicle* between 9 March and 22 June 1786. Signing himself "Honestus," Austin attacked the growing power of lawyers, arguing that this "order" grew to the detriment of the citizens. He went so far as to suggest that for "the welfare and security of the Commonwealth . . . this 'order' of men should be ANNIHILATED." Austin's main goal, however, was the simplification of the legal process. He promoted the use of binding arbitration, a legal code that could be easily understood by every citizen, a direct relationship between the judiciary and the contesting parties without the intervention of lawyers, and the appointment of an advocate general to represent defendants against charges prosecuted by the state's attorney general. The first ten articles were later reprinted in a pamphlet, *Observations on the Pernicious Practice of the Law* (1814). Despite the pseudonym, the writer's identity was widely known.

Throughout his career Austin identified himself with the artisans of Boston and became their leading exponent, expressing his populist concerns in public meetings as well as in the press. Although he himself was an early industrial elite, Austin saw his opposition as the "aristocratic" elite of inherited fortunes. A much-cited town meeting incident in 1792 concerning a proposed police force was captured for posterity by John Quincy Adams, who reported Austin's claim that such a body would "destroy the liberties of the people; it was a resignation of the *sovereignty* of the town; it was a link in the chain of aristocratic influence; it was intended in its operation to throw the whole burden of taxation upon the poor." Supporting Austin with their votes were "seven hundred men, who looked as if they had been collected from all the jails on the continent, with Ben. Austin like another Jack Cade at their head" (*Writings of John Quincy Adams*, ed. Worthington C. Ford, vol. 1 [1913], p. 113).

Austin represented Boston in the state senate in 1787 and again from 1789 to 1794, with one final term in 1796. Despite his highly partisan politics, Austin was also entrusted with nonpartisan matters as a manager of the state and Harvard College lotteries.

Under the name "Old South," Austin helped to define Jeffersonianism for the urban artisan population in the *Boston Chronicle* in a series of seventy-five articles later published as *Constitutional Republicanism, in Opposition to Fallacious Federalism* (1803). By holding the Constitution as "the polar star" (*Constitutional Republicanism*, p. 148), Austin justified every innovation of the Jefferson administration and railed against every aspect of Federalism through attacks on John Adams (1735–1826) and the elitist Essex Junto. He advocated a full range of reforms, ranging from rotation of offices to expunging the national debt. Austin himself benefited from the concept of rotation of offices when Thomas Jefferson appointed him commissioner of loans for Boston in 1803.

In 1806, however, Austin's outspokenness led to a personal tragedy. Following a misunderstanding about a public Fourth of July celebration, Austin accused a local Federalist lawyer, Thomas Oliver Selfridge, of instigating a damage suit for his own benefit. Selfridge demanded that Austin retract his statement, and after learning the full facts Austin did so, although not to Selfridge's satisfaction. In the *Boston Gazette* of 4 August, Selfridge posted a notice accusing Austin of being "a Coward, a Liar and a Scoundrel." Austin retaliated with a milder notice in the *Independent Chronicle*. However, Austin's eighteen-year-old son Charles, a Harvard student, met the affront with a physical attack on Selfridge and was shot and killed in the ensuing scuffle. Austin's reaction to news of his son's death was "Good God! Is this the work of federalism?" The resulting trial proved politically divisive, but Selfridge was acquitted on the charge of manslaughter.

During his later years Austin continued his calls for strengthening the economic base of the United States and wrote to Thomas Jefferson to promote the concept of congressional efforts "to bring forward the Agricultural and Manufacturing interests of the United States." His letter and Jefferson's response were published in 1816 as a broadside (*National Utility in Opposition to Political Controversy*) to local acclaim and were validated by the enactment of the tariff in 1816.

In its announcement of Austin's death (in Boston), the *Independent Chronicle* (6 May 1820) proclaimed him "a steadfast, undeviating Republican." He would have chosen a like epitaph himself. Best known in his own time for his partisan politics, Austin is better remembered today through his "Honestus" articles as an advocate of a simpler legal system relying on judge and jury without the interference of lawyers.

• There is no significant collection of Austin papers. He has been little studied as an individual. Placing him in the context of party politics in Massachusetts are Paul Goodman, *The Democratic-Republicans of Massachusetts: Politics in a Young Republic* (1964), and Ronald P. Formisano, *The Transformation of Political Culture: Massachusetts Parties, 1790s–1840s* (1983). Frederic D. Grant, Jr., published two articles on the antilawyer sentiments of "Honestus," "Benjamin Austin, Jr.'s Struggle with the Lawyers," *Boston Bar Journal* 25 (1981): 19–29, and "Observations on the Pernicious Practice of the Law," *American Bar Association Journal* 68 (1982): 580–82. Austin's portrait by Ethan Allen Greenwood (c. 1820) is at the Bostonian Society with another version owned by the city of Boston.

EDWARD W. HANSON

AUSTIN, David (19 Mar. 1759–5 Feb. 1831), Congregational clergyman, was born in New Haven, Connecticut, the eldest son of David Austin and Rebecca Lines Mix. His father was a deacon in the White Haven Church pastored by the younger Jonathan Edwards (1745–1801), under whose ministry Austin was deeply influenced by the New Divinity. As a restatement of Calvinism in its most provocative forms, the New Divinity took its inspiration from the revivalism of the Great Awakening and from the teaching of Samuel Hopkins, Joseph Bellamy, and the younger Edwards. After graduating from Yale College in 1779, Austin studied with Bellamy in order to prepare for the ministry. He was licensed to preach by the New Haven East Association, with Edwards as one of the examiners, on 30 May 1780. But when no call to a congregation was forthcoming, Austin instead embarked on a tour of England and the Low Countries from 1781 until 1782. He married Lydia Lathrop of Norwich, Connecticut, in June 1783; they had no children.

Austin evidently fell into a period of religious indifference, for he made no further attempts to find a parish, and he allowed his preaching license to lapse in May 1784. But in 1787 he was awakened "from his worldly lethargy and aroused to the service of God." He was re-licensed by the New Haven East Association on 16 October 1787, and the following spring Edwards was able to promote Austin as a candidate for the Presbyterian church in Elizabethtown, New Jersey. He preached at Elizabethtown for the first time in April 1788 and was formally called by the Elizabethtown church in May. He was examined by the Presbytery of New York and ordained for the Elizabethtown pastorate in September 1788.

In addition to his preaching ministry in Elizabethtown, Austin struggled to organize a series of religious publishing ventures, beginning with the short-lived *Christian's, Scholar's, and Farmer's Magazine* from 1789 until 1791. That year he launched a more ambitious magazine, the *American Preacher*, which anthologized sermons from prominent American preachers. Austin hoped, by showing the common themes in the evangelical preaching of the various Reformed denominations, to demonstrate how Americans could "unite the different denominations of professing Christians into one bond of Christian fellowship and ministerial communion." To that end, he solicited sermon manuscripts from a wide variety of preachers: James Dana and Moses Mather (Old Calvinist Congregational), Benjamin Moore (Episcopalian), David Linn (Dutch Reformed), Samuel Stanhope Smith (Old School Presbyterian), and Charles Backus, Edwards, and Samuel Spring (New Divinity Congregationalist). But the project proved cumbersome and the contributors unreliable, and the *American Preacher* folded after its fourth volume in 1793.

In promoting Christian unity, Austin also planned to resurrect Jonathan Edwards's (1703–1758) "concert of prayer" proposal, and he circulated "a sketch" among the ministers attending the 1794 Yale Commencement for a common Tuesday of prayer, once a month, through 1795. To support the "concert," he also planned a new magazine, the *Christian Herald*, but "a difference of opinion in respect to the leading features of the magazine" forced Austin to change the magazine's name to the *United States Christian Magazine*, and then he killed it after only a few issues.

Like many of the New Divinity, Austin was caught up in a resurgence of millennial speculation in the 1790s, especially with upheavals in France signaling unprecedented turnovers in world political affairs. Samuel Hopkins published his famous *Treatise on the Millennium* in 1793, and Austin followed him in 1794 with *The Millennium; or, the Thousand Years of Prosperity Promised to the Church of God*, which reprinted an early work by Joseph Bellamy, Edwards's original "concert" proposal, and a millennialist sermon by Austin, "The Downfall of Mystical Babylon." Austin portrayed the papacy in conventional Protestant millennialist terms as "mystical Babylon" and applauded the Jacobins as "well-chosen instruments" for the overthrow of papal authority. But he departed from convention by insisting that Christ would inaugurate the millennium (rather than conclude it) by his own descent from heaven, thus identifying Austin as a premillennialist when prevailing millennialist thinking leaned heavily toward a postmillennial eschatology. He added an even more unconventional element (possibly borrowed from the elder Edwards's *Some Thoughts on the Revival*) by interpreting the founding of the American republic as a signal for Christ's imminent return.

Austin became so obsessed with these themes that on 5 February 1796 he fell "prostrate upon the carpet in the parlour" of his parsonage in Elizabethtown and received a revelation from "the Author of my existence," which informed Austin that "the THEOCRACY of Moses, or of the Sinai dispensation, is again to be set up, or rather to be renewed" by the return of Christ. "The month of May [1796] will probably not go over without putting the question out of doubt," Austin disclosed in a hurriedly published booklet, *The Voice of God to the People of These United States*, and he was certain that "these United States will be found to be the favored spot," since "common sense seems . . . to declare, that this *first-born* of nations to the enjoyment of natural and civil liberty, must also, by analogy of providence, be the *first-born* of the nations in the favors of grace." Austin began frantically preaching about the nearness of Christ's return as many as three times a day; when the month of May passed without any great event, Austin's exasperated congregation appealed to the Presbytery of New York to dissolve the pastoral relation. But Austin relieved the presbytery of the awkward responsibility himself by renouncing the presbytery's jurisdiction in May 1797.

He returned to New Haven, where his millennial enthusiasms raged unabated. During the presidential election of 1800, he attacked the Old Calvinist ministerial coalition of Timothy Dwight (1752–1817) and Jedidiah Morse as tools of the antichrist and addressed open letters to the king of England, the pope, and the peoples of Europe and America to explain how the millennial temple in Jerusalem would really be erected upon a "Washingtonian" base in the American republic. He beggared himself in New Haven building houses and docks, which he announced were for the use of the Jews en route to Palestine to set the stage for the millennial kingdom. In 1807 the death of his father-in-law opened up a substantial inheritance to him, which allowed Austin and his wife to live in comfort in Norwich, Connecticut, for the rest of their lives. By this time his fanaticism on millennial themes had substantially receded, and the New Haven Association agreed to re-license him for preaching. In 1815 he was called as pastor of a small Congregational church in neighboring Bozrah, where he served "with great acceptance and success" until his death.

Austin contributed little in the way of substantial theological reasoning to American speculations on the millennial kingdom, and his published writings on the millennium are wordy, disjointed, and sometimes incoherent. But he offers a colorful example of how confident some Americans were that their new republic represented an abrupt departure from the old European system, so abrupt that the future of the nation had to be closely identified with God's millennial purposes for the world.

• No substantial body of papers or manuscripts by Austin seems to have survived apart from a scattering of letters in such collections as the Matthew Carey Papers at the Historical Society of Pennsylvania and the Roger Sherman Papers at the Beinecke Rare Book and Manuscript Library, Yale University. Austin's *The Voice of God to the People . . .* (1796) supplies important details about his revelation of that year, while F. B. Dexter's *Biographical Sketches of the Graduates of Yale College*, vol. 4 (1907), and W. B. Sprague's *Annals of the American Pulpit*, vol. 2 (1856), offer more comprehensive reviews of his ministerial career. Austin continued to publish sermons and booklets on millennialist themes, including *A Prophetic Leaf* (1798), *The Millennial Door Thrown Open* (1799), and *The Dawn of Day* (1800). Austin's peculiar premillennialism is discussed in Ernest Lee Tuveson, *Redeemer Nation: The Idea of America's Millennial Role* (1968), and James W. Davidson, "Searching for the Millennium," *New England Quarterly* 45 (1972): 241–61.

ALLEN C. GUELZO

AUSTIN, Harriet N. (1825–1891), hydropathic physician and health and dress reformer, was born in Connecticut but raised in Moravia, New York. Little is known about her parentage or early life. At age twenty-six she enrolled in the first class of the coeducational American Hydropathic Institute operated by Mary S. Gove Nichols and Thomas Low Nichols in Manhattan. She completed the three-month course in December 1851 and received a medical diploma. In 1854–1855 she also attended the winter session of the Eclectic Medical Institute of Cincinnati.

In July 1852 Austin joined the staff of James Caleb Jackson's Glen Haven Water Cure, a hydropathic institution on Skaneateles Lake near Scott, New York. A "kind, gentle, genial woman" as well as a "skillful and accomplished Physician," she proved to be an asset for the fledgling establishment. Glen Haven's advertisements soon featured her prominently. In 1855 Jackson, married and the father of two sons, adopted her. As his "Beloved Daughter and Friend" Austin continued her medical partnership with Jackson for nearly forty years.

In 1858 Austin moved with the Jacksons to Dansville, New York, where in partnership with F. Wilson Hurd and Giles E. Jackson she cofounded the water cure establishment known as "Our Home on the Hillside," later known as the Jackson Health Resort. There Austin's professional life blossomed. She won kudos from patients and grudging admiration for the local populace unaccustomed to independent, self-confident, assertive women physicians.

Trained in hydropathy, a nineteenth-century reform medical sect, Austin posited that internal consumption and external application of "pure" (i.e., not mineral) water, when combined with fresh air, exercise, simplified diet, and the elimination of the "artificial habits" of urbanizing life could "cure" diseases and prevent illness. Influenced by Jackson she rejected blood-letting and all "heroic" drug-oriented therapeutics, substituting localized baths, wet-sheet "packing" to induce sudorific action, and daily ingestion of large quantities of water.

For Austin, health reform in its various aspects became a moral imperative. Strict obedience to the "Laws of Life and Health" were for her a necessary prerequisite for the regeneration of American society. Writing to her "Sick Sisters," she insisted that they could hope "to stand on an equality with [men] in every department of life" only after they had learned how to take care of their own health and that of their dependents. Self-reliance and self-confidence were attainable only in combination with woman's "most urgent right" to sound health and stamina.

In the interest of preserving Victorian canons of modesty and delicacy, antebellum women physicians usually limited their practice to women and children. Austin, however, rejected this gender-specific concept, treating female complaints and attending to general heart, kidney, and lung ailments for both sexes.

A prolific writer, Austin was a regular contributor to the *Water-Cure Journal*, hydropathy's leading periodical. In 1858 she and Jackson cofounded the *Letter Box*. As editor of this reform periodical she publicized Our Home, kept in contact with former patients, printed their testimonials to water cure, and furnished rules for healthful living. Remaining as editor of the journal, renamed the *Laws of Life and Health* in 1860, Austin kept the message of health reform before the public for many years.

Austin was also one of the nation's most prominent and enduring dress reformers. Taking up the cry against tight lacing and confining clothing, she experimented throughout the 1850s with short-dress alternatives to the wide-trousered reform "bloomer" introduced by Elizabeth Smith Miller and briefly popular among some women's rights advocates. Eventually dress reform became for Austin "one of the MAIN SPRINGS" that moved her. The *Syracuse Journal* credited her with designing the "American Costume," which featured narrow trousers suspended from the shoulders and worn beneath a knee-length jacket or skirt. Emphasizing that the point of dress reform was to "release [women] from the tyranny of fashion," she experimented with various fabrics and designs, rejecting the idea of a single model for all.

Austin was a founding member of the National Dress Reform Association, which held its first annual meeting at Glen Haven in June 1855. She served as the organization's president as well as corresponding secretary and board member. Throughout the 1850s and early 1860s she attended most dress reform conventions, lecturing about and appearing in the American Costume. Among the Dansville patients influenced by Austin's campaign were Seventh-day Adventist founder Ellen G. White and Clara Barton, founder of the American Red Cross. In an address in 1880 Barton praised Austin's unremitting dedication to dress reform, observing that it was she who had "trod the pioneer paths with bleeding feet in order that others might walk on flowers." At the time of her death in North Adams, Massachusetts, Austin had established a wide reputation in reform circles. She had never married.

• There is no known collection of Austin papers. Austin authored one book, *Baths and How to Take Them* (1861). Her many articles in the *Water-Cure Journal* include "An Extraordinary Community," 29 (Mar. 1860): 37–38; "The Reform Dress," 23 (Jan. 1857): 3–4; "Thoughts in Spare Minutes," 23 (May 1857): 103–4; "To My Sick Sisters," 17 (Apr. 1854): 75; and "What Is the American Costume?" *Laws of Life* 10 (Aug. 1867): 10. A full-length biography has yet to be published, but some useful sources are Susan E. Cayleff, *Wash and Be Healed: The Water Cure Movement and Women's Health* (1987); William D. Conklin, *The Jackson Health Resort* (privately printed, 1971); Jane B. Donegan, *"Hydropathic Highway to Health": Women and Water Cure in Antebellum America* (1986); Regina Markell Morantz, "Nineteenth Century Health Reform and Women: A Program of Self-Help," in *Medicine without Doctors: Home Health Care in American History*, ed. Guenter B. Risse et al. (1977); Ronald L. Numbers, *Prophetess of Health: Ellen G. White and the Origins of Seventh-day Adventist Health Reform*, rev. ed. (1992); and Henry B. Weiss and Howard R. Kemble, *The Great American Water-Cure Craze: A History of Hydropathy in the United States* (1967).

JANE B. DONEGAN

AUSTIN, Henry (4 Dec. 1804–17 Dec. 1891), architect, was born in the Mount Carmel section of Hamden, Connecticut, the son of Daniel Austin and Adah Dorman. At an early age he was apprenticed to a carpenter and advanced in this occupation to become a builder, working for the renowned architect Ithiel Town. The latter had assembled the largest architectural library in the country; in his future career, Austin found the library's resources invaluable.

In 1828 Austin married Harriet Hooker; they had six children, of whom only two survived childhood. Harriet Austin died in 1835 during the birth of twins. With Town's support, Austin opened an architectural office in New Haven on 7 January 1837, the year of the beginning of the financial panic and a very unfortunate time to open a business. That same year Austin married Jane Hempsted; three of their five children survived childhood.

Austin's first known buildings were Greek Revival residences. In 1840 Austin moved his office to Hartford to rebuild the tower of Ithiel Town's Christ Church Cathedral. He returned to New Haven the next year and began work on three major commissions that were awarded to him through Town's influence. Austin collaborated with the firm of Town and Davis on the Gothic Wadsworth Atheneum of 1842–1844 in Hartford. A Gothic library for Yale College was begun in 1842. A massive Egyptian Revival sandstone gate for New Haven's Grove Street Cemetery was built in 1845–1848. All three of these structures have survived. With Town's death in 1844, Austin took advantage of the opportunity to become Connecticut's leading architect.

In the late 1840s Austin became entranced with architectural detailing from India. To the cubical, monitor-topped Italianate villas in vogue, he introduced exotic columns copied after those in the Buddhist rock-cut caves at Ellora, India. One such existing residence of this style was built in 1848 for Yale geology professor James Dwight Dana; it is a National Historic Landmark. Austin also used Mughal-style decorative elements on his villas. In keeping with his eclectic styles, Austin designed in New Haven in 1848 a 300-foot-long railroad station that combined Italianate arcading with two soaring towers topped with features of Buddhist origin. It was destroyed by fire in 1894.

In the 1850s Austin designed such diverse structures as churches, libraries, hotels, theaters, schools, banks, stores, and an octagon house. Most of his buildings were in New Haven County, but during his many years of practice his work extended to New Jersey, New York, Massachusetts, and Maine.

Austin designed three outstanding projects before the onset of the Civil War. In 1859 work was started on an elaborate towered Italian villa–style mansion in Portland, Maine, for Ruggles Morse, a New Orleans hotelier. It remains open as a museum containing much of its original Victorian decorative opulence. In 1860 the former home and library of Ithiel Town was completely renovated by Austin in the Italian villa–style for Joseph Earl Sheffield, benefactor of the Yale Scientific School. This historic building was demolished by Yale in 1957. The third prewar project was the New Haven City Hall (1861–1862). It was the first major High Victorian Gothic building to be completed in this country; others were started earlier but were delayed by the Civil War. The interior of the city hall was modeled after the Morse House, and the exterior was based on an exhibition design at London's Royal Academy by Sir Ernest George. Much of this building has been demolished, but the facade with its bell tower proudly overlooks the New Haven Green.

Shortly after the Civil War, Austin designed two massive adjacent residences in New Haven for gun manufacturer Oliver O. Winchester and his partner in a shirt business, John M. Davies. The Winchester house was a French villa and featured ornate carved gable decorations, numerous balconies and canopies, a large conservatory, and many greenhouses. The Davies mansion was a well-sited, monumental example of the French Second Empire style. The Winchester house was demolished by an heir in 1902, and the Davies mansion was ravaged by fire in 1990.

The last creative phase of the aging architect was the design in the 1870s of large wooden summer homes on the Connecticut shore at West Haven and Branford. These houses of the Stick style featured broad verandas, soaring towers, and a proliferation of straight and turned wooden decorative elements.

Over the years, many architects had trained in Austin's office, and his influence continued to be felt after his death in New Haven. Austin's life had touched all the decades of the century. Through his creativity, diversity, and longevity, he had embellished the landscape of New Haven, its environs, and beyond.

• Two albums of Austin designs are in the Henry Austin Papers, Manuscripts and Archives, Yale University Library. Published plans and elevations are in Chester Hills, *The Builder's Guide* (1845), and L. C. Tuthil, *History of Architecture* (1848). See the Austin entry and bibliography in *Macmillan Encyclopedia of Architects* (1982). An obituary is in the *New Haven Evening Register*, 17 Dec. 1891.

JOHN B. KIRBY, JR.

AUSTIN, Jane Goodwin (25 Feb. 1831–30 Mar. 1894), historical novelist and juvenile writer, was born Mary Jane Goodwin in Worcester, Massachusetts, the daughter of Isaac Goodwin, a lawyer, antiquarian, and authority on Pilgrim history, and Elizabeth Hammatt, a poet and songwriter. After her father's death in 1832, the family moved to Boston, where Jane was educated in private schools. As a young girl she began to cultivate her lifelong interest in family genealogy and her Pilgrim ancestors, writing stories about their lives for her own and her family's amusement. Some of these stories were eventually published under various pen names in contemporary periodicals. Her brother, the Honorable John Abbot Goodwin, was also inspired by their heritage and wrote a history of Plymouth settlement, *The Pilgrim Republic* (1888). Jane could trace her lineage to the Pilgrims in at least eight distinct lines from her parents, who also shared a common ancestor, Francis LeBaron, a figure featured in her novel, *The Nameless Nobleman* (1881).

In 1850 she married Loring Henry Austin, an architect, and they had three children. Jane Goodwin Austin took up writing again some years later and began to submit her stories to the leading magazines of the day. Her work appeared in *Harper's Magazine*, *Atlantic Monthly*, and *Putnam's Magazine*, as well as others. Her last volume, *David Alden's Daughters and Other Stories* (1892), was a collection of many of these stories. In addition to her short stories she was the author of at least fifteen books. The bulk of her writing was in the popular children and young adult reading genre of romance and adventure. Her early works were originally published as serials in such periodicals as *Galaxy* and *Emerson's Magazine* and were later issued in book form. These works were well received, *Cipher: A Romance* (1869) and *Moonfolk* (1874) being the best known.

Of her many literary works, however, Austin is perhaps best remembered for her series of Pilgrim books for young adults, which cover the period from the landing of the Pilgrims at Plymouth in 1620 until the Revolution in 1775. Their titles are *A Nameless Nobleman*, *Standish of Standish* (1889), *Dr. LeBaron and His Daughters* (1890), and *Betty Alden* (1891). She was at work on the fifth and final novel of the series at the time of her death. This work, tentatively entitled "Next Door to Betty," was to have followed *Betty Alden* in the Pilgrim sequence, detailing the adventures of Captain Benjamin Church and the Indian Wars.

With the exception of a short stay in Concord, her summers in Plymouth doing research, and her final years in Roxbury, Austin lived most of her life in Boston along with other Mayflower descendants. During her stay in Concord she developed lasting friendships with Louisa Mae Alcott, the Hawthornes, and the Emersons. She died in Roxbury, near Boston, at the home of a daughter.

Austin's literary output was large, even by modern standards, and represents the early years of a book market directed exclusively toward children and young adult readers. She was popular with her reading public and was well received by publishers and reviewers alike. Perhaps most significant in her writing was her ability to package history in an attractive and exciting manner, portraying the atmosphere, customs, and characteristics of early American history for leisure reading by children. Copies of her works can occasionally be found in collections of local public libraries.

• There is no standing collection of Austin's personal papers and manuscripts, although a few photographs and papers are housed at Harvard University Portrait Collection of Prints and Photographs. Austin's principal literary output was in the historical fiction genre, which concerned the early life of the Pilgrims in America. However she wrote a number of other works in the romance/adventure genre, including *Fairy Dream* (1859), *The Novice* (1865), *Dora Darling: The Daughter of the Regiment* (1865), *The Tailor Boy* (1869), *The Shadow of Moloch Mountain* (1870), *Outpost* (1867), *Mrs. Beauchamp Brown* (1880), *Nantucket Scraps* (1883), *It Never Did Run Smooth* (1892), *Queen Tempest* (1892), and *The Twelve Great Diamonds* (1892). A genealogical assessment of the Austin family is found in Mary LeBaron Stockwell, *Descendants of Francis LeBaron of Plymouth* (1904). While general accounts of Austin's life and work are limited, the numerous obituaries appearing after her death contain information about her literary contributions and mention memorable events from her life; among these are *Book Buyer*, May 1894; *Literary World*, 7 Apr. 1894; the *Boston Transcript*, 30 Mar. 1894; and the *Boston Herald* and *Boston Journal*, 31 Mar. 1894.

AMANDA CARSON BANKS

AUSTIN, Johnny (23 Dec. 1910–14 Feb. 1983), musician, was born John A. Augustine in Vineland, New Jersey, the son of Samuel Augustine and Henrietta Labriola, occupations unknown. Little is known about his early years, and it is not known when he began using the name "Austin" professionally. Originally a student of the violin, he took up drums and played in his high school band and, later, with dance bands in the greater Philadelphia area. In one of these combos was a trumpeter whose playing Austin found unusually exciting. When the trumpeter left to join another band, Austin obtained a horn of his own and did his best to emulate the man's style. He matured rapidly as a trumpeter and began to build a local reputation as a forceful performer on the instrument. On occasion, to please and impress audiences, he would play trumpet and drums simultaneously.

In April 1938 Austin was hired to play the jazz trumpet solos with the new band of Glenn Miller, the first of many swing orchestras in which he would fill that role. With Miller he performed in ballrooms, hotels, clubs, and colleges throughout the eastern states and also made his first recordings, soloing on "Sold American," "By the Waters of Minnetonka," and "King Porter Stomp." In a review for *Metronome* (June 1938), George Simon, a leading critic of the day, praised Austin as the orchestra's outstanding soloist, describing him as "one of the most inspiring hot trumpeters to hit dancebandom in a long, long time." Simon added, "Few white men have ever played with such thrilling abandon."

Austin parted ways with Miller at the end of January 1939 with the intention of resuming his trumpet studies in Philadelphia. However, he joined the orchestra of Jan Savitt, becoming the most compelling soloist in a band that included several excellent jazzmen. His volatile, hard-driving choruses earned him favorable comparisons with Harry James, the brilliant trumpet star of the Benny Goodman band, who only recently had launched an orchestra of his own. (Austin sat in with Goodman one night and received an offer of a regular chair in the brass section. He decided, however, to remain with Savitt.)

Austin won sufficient acclaim during this period to warrant the printing of his picture in *Down Beat* (1 Nov. 1939), foremost among musicians' trade papers. The caption characterized him as a "powerhouse hot man" whose "gutty" style was among the factors "that caused the term 'out of this world' to be introduced into Americans' vocabularies." In both 1939 and 1940 he placed in the top ten in the trumpets category of the *Down Beat* annual poll and in the hot trumpet category of the *Metronome* poll. Austin married in the late 1930s and divorced in the late 1940s; the name of his wife and the number of their children, if any, are unknown.

Austin left Savitt in 1940. In early 1941 he was featured on both trumpet and drums with the Lincolnaires, a five-man combo that served as the house band at the Hotel Lincoln in New York City. In February of that year he returned to the big-band scene, joining Larry Clinton for a tenure of several months. His solo trumpet sparked many of the recordings the orchestra made for Victor/Bluebird. In April 1942, following a brief stay with the band organized by Ben Pollack for Chico Marx, Austin went to work for Teddy Powell. A review of the Powell band in *Metronome* (May 1942) observed that Austin was "a man with a mountainous wallop, who plays upper register jazz with great facility and remarkable good taste [and] carries the up tempo assignments wonderfully." In 1943, after stints with Abe Lyman and Van Alexander, he joined the studio orchestra of the Columbia Broadcasting System in New York City, playing for various radio shows, including that of Arthur Godfrey.

About 1945 Austin settled in Vineland, New Jersey. He opened a music store and taught trumpet privately but devoted most of his energies to organizing and directing a big band of local musicians. On drums was his brother Ernie Austin, formerly a sideman with the great Jack Teagarden. In 1947–1949 the orchestra operated as the house band at the Sunset Beach Ballroom in Almonesson, New Jersey, playing each weekend from fall through spring. Eventually hookups with the CBS network and Armed Forces Radio carried the music to listeners across the nation and overseas. While on leave from the ballroom during the summer months, the band fulfilled engagements in Philadelphia, Trenton, and on the Jersey shore. In September 1949 Austin and his men had a falling out with the ballroom's manager over pay. He immediately disbanded and put together a new orchestra.

Austin remained active as a leader for the rest of his life. He enjoyed considerable popularity on the ballroom circuit that included locations in Pennsylvania, New Jersey, and New York City. With the decline of the ballroom era he was compelled to head small combos of various sizes, putting together a big band only for one-night stands and special engagements. He billed himself as the "Man of All Horns" and performed on trumpet, flugelhorn, French horn, valve trombone, and midget trumpet. Sometimes Austin played two horns at once or did scat singing to enhance his group's commercial appeal. He spent his last few years working mostly with a trio in local night clubs. At the time of his death in Camden, New Jersey, Austin was married to Josephine C. Filipponi; the date of their marriage and the number of their children, if any, are unknown.

Austin was one of the truly dynamic trumpeters of the big-band era. While not of the stature, in terms of overall artistic excellence and impact on other performers, of contemporaries such as Bunny Berigan, Roy Eldridge, or Cootie Williams, he was capable of playing brilliantly in the established swing idiom. His exuberant, often brash, improvisatory flights, especially those he played on recordings with the Savitt band, represent some of the most exciting trumpet work of the period.

• There are no published books or articles on Austin. This biography is based on a variety of sources, including *Down Beat* and *Metronome* magazines, Austin's death certificate, publicity materials provided by his widow, correspondence with other jazz researchers, and telephone interviews with musicians who were personally acquainted with him, including Van Alexander, Butch Stone, Paul Tanner, Rolly Bundock, and Johnny Best.

Some of Austin's best solos with Savitt can be heard on a Decca album, *Jan Savitt and His Orchestra/"The Top Hatters" (1939–1941)*. (Not all the choruses attributed to Austin in the liner notes are actually his. Some were recorded after he had left the band.) His trumpet is also featured on *Teddy Powell and His Orchestra (1942–1943)*, released by First Time Records.

STEVEN M. KANE

AUSTIN, Jonathan Loring (2 Jan. 1748–10 May 1826), government agent and state official, was born in Boston, Massachusetts, the son of Benjamin Austin, a merchant and politician, and Elizabeth Waldo. Austin graduated from Harvard College in 1766 and soon began a merchant career in Portsmouth, New Hampshire, and neighboring Kittery, Maine.

At the outbreak of the Revolution, Austin already owned a six-gun privateer, the *McClarey*, and served as a major in the home guards of Governor John Langdon of New Hampshire. Soon he returned to Massachusetts as an aide to General John Sullivan and on 21 November 1776 became the secretary to the Massachusetts Board of War. The following autumn, the Massachusetts Council selected Austin as its official messenger to inform the American commissioners in Paris of the surrender of General John Burgoyne at Saratoga. Austin sailed for France on 31 October 1777 with a letter of introduction from his father to Benjamin Franklin and arrived at Passy on 4 December. Franklin was impressed by young Austin and sent him on a secret mission to London as an unofficial spokesman. Austin was received into the highest circles: he was introduced to Lord Shelburne and the Prince of Wales, attended the debates in Parliament, and generally attempted to provide information on America for the Opposition leaders. He remained in London until March 1778, when news of the Franco-American treaty became known and communications with the Continent became threatened. After a few more months in Paris engaging in secretarial work for the commissioners, Austin returned to Boston, traveling through St. Eustatius in the Dutch Indies on a trading venture and stopping off in Philadelphia, where the Continental Congress compensated him for his expenses.

In January 1780 the Massachusetts legislature appointed Austin as its agent to negotiate a £150,000 loan in Europe. He sailed aboard the continental packet *Zepher*, which was captured by a Jersey privateer, and Austin was taken to England as a prisoner. Fortunately his former contacts arranged his release, and by early May he was in Holland. He met with John Adams and Francis Dana in Paris but was unsuccessful in obtaining a loan on the Continent. He was able to obtain £3,000 worth of clothing for the army from deNeufville & Sons in Amsterdam but did not succeed in his major goal before returning to Boston in 1781.

Back in Boston Austin began a long series of business ventures with his brother Benjamin, concentrating on real estate transactions, with a particular interest in the ropewalks from which the family fortune originated. In 1782 he married Hannah Ivers, the niece of Anglo-American merchant Barlow Trecothick, from whom she had received a substantial inheritance. The couple had three sons, two of whom survived infancy.

Austin's business interests now tied him to Boston, where he became a director of the Union Bank and served the town from 1784 to 1802 as an overseer of the poor. He was a longtime member of Boston's First Church, serving as a member of the standing committee from 1795 to 1804 and following that congregation into Unitarianism.

Never matching his brother's Republican rancor, Austin nonetheless served the party cause as a legislator: he was elected to the state senate from Boston in 1801, and, upon his removal across the river to Cambridge, to the state house of representatives from that town in 1803 and 1806. In the latter year Austin became more personally allied to the Democratic-Republican cause when his son James married the daughter of future governor Elbridge Gerry. Austin served as secretary of the commonwealth (1806–1808) under Governor James Sullivan and as treasurer (1811–1812) under Governor Gerry.

Austin continued to develop real estate out of his Cambridge holdings and the former ropewalk property on Beacon Hill in Boston. When he returned to Boston and statewide office, he also began an active membership in the Massachusetts Humane Society and the Massachusetts Charitable Society, of which he was president from 1807 to 1810. He died in Boston, leaving a much depleted estate, which consisted almost exclusively of a $10,000 promissory note against his son James and a few shares in the West Boston Bridge.

The polished manners that Austin acquired during his youthful excursions to Europe, combined with his ability to quote long passages from Virgil and Homer well into old age, stamped him as a true gentleman. However, the high expectations created by his early activities were never fully met, and the balance of his career was spent as a capable follower rather than a leader.

• Austin's only published work was *An Oration, Delivered July 4, 1786, at the Request of the Inhabitants of the Town of Boston, in Celebration of the Anniversary of American Independence* (1786). Portions of his diary were printed in E. E. Hale, Jr., *Franklin in France*, vol. 1 (1887), and in the *Collector* 21 (1908): 123–25, and 22 (1909): 3–5. A biographical sketch of Austin, probably by his son James T. Austin, is "Memoir of Jonathan Loring Austin," *Boston Monthly Magazine* 2 (July 1826): 57–66; another is in James Spear Loring, *The Hundred Boston Orators* (1852). A more recent sketch is in Clifford K. Shipton, *Sibley's Harvard Graduates*, vol. 16 (1972), pp. 303–8.

EDWARD W. HANSON

AUSTIN, Lovie (19 Sept. 1887–10 July 1972), pioneer jazzwoman, was born Cora Calhoun, in Chattanooga, Tennessee. Little is known about Austin's personal life. She studied music theory and piano at Roger Williams University in Nashville and Knoxville College in Knoxville. Her musical contributions were nearly overlooked until the revived interest in women in jazz in the 1970s. The reacquaintance with Austin can be attributed to the publication of three books on women in the early days of jazz.

The pianist/composer/arranger Mary Lou Williams throughout her career consistently recalled her impression of an early exposure to Austin's genius. Williams indicated that as a child she visited a Pittsburgh theater and was fascinated and inspired by the female at the keyboard, Austin, who was writing down music with her right hand while accompanying the performance with her swinging left. Austin had done all of the orchestrations for the show. Behind schedule, she was at the same time arranging the music for the next act. (Quoted in Nat Shapiro and Nat Hentoff's *Hear Me Talkin' to Ya*, 1955.) In a later interview Williams recalled: "During this period, we didn't have very many readers and this woman was a master reader. I haven't seen a man yet that can compare with that woman" (*The Black Perspective in Music*, Fall 1980).

In a feature article on Austin, the journalist George Hoefer wrote that "Lovie" was a nickname given to Austin by her grandmother. He further claimed that Lovie's grandmother "also brought up another little girl a few years younger than Lovie. Her name was Bessie Smith, and the two little playmates were parted before either of them began to get the blues" (*Down Beat*, 16 June 1950).

Austin's career was launched in 1912 when she began touring the vaudeville circuit. Austin's first marriage, at about this same time, was to a Detroit movie house operator, which lasted briefly. She then married vaudeville performer Austin of the team Austin and Delaney. She worked the vaudeville circuit as piano accompanist of her husband's act. She then traveled with Irving Miller's "Blue Babies" revue. Other revues with which she was associated as director/producer were "The Sunflower Girls" and "The Lovie Austin Revue." The latter had a long and successful run at New York City's Club Alabam. The former was a part of her experiences with the Theater Owners Booking Association (TOBA), a group of influential theater owners organized in 1920.

Austin settled in Chicago in the early 1920s, where she remained until the end of her life. She worked as house pianist for Paramount Records, accompanying such classic blues singers as Ida Cox, Ma Rainey, Alberta Hunter, and Ethel Waters. She was the pianist on Cox's first record and Rainey's first release. Other blues singers with whom she performed and/or recorded were Bessie Smith, Bertha "Chippie" Hill, Edmonia Henderson, Edna Hicks, Hattie McDaniel, Priscilla Stewart, Viola Bartlette, and Ozzie McPherson. As for her collaborating instrumentalists, the list includes trumpeters Louis Armstrong, Lee Collins, and Tommy Ladnier; saxophonist William "Buster" Bailey; clarinetist Johnny Dodds; trombonist Kid Ory; and drummer Warren "Baby" Dodds. She also recorded under her own name, Lovie Austin and Her Blues Serenaders. Her accompaniments were described as "sturdy and even-pulsed, yet rolling and rhythmic."

During the twenties, the piano was a vital rhythm accompaniment instrument. Not a solo improviser, Austin believed in collective improvisation. Although she often led small supporting ensembles (generally three members) for accompaniments, there was always a fullness of sound. Of her individual playing, a *Chicago Defender* journalist wrote, "percussive, pushing the beat along, filling in the bass parts with her right hand maintaining a steady flow of counter/melody." Austin's distinguishing features were "considerable skill and musical sophistication." Her many recordings with the Blues Serenaders are currently classics.

Austin worked as musical director for the Monogram Theater in Chicago, where the leading black performers appeared. She remained in the post for twenty years and accompanied acts by Ethel Waters, Hattie McDaniel, Bill "Bojangles" Robinson, and others.

Subsequently she worked in a similar capacity at both the Gem and Joy theaters. Austin shared composition credits with Alberta Hunter on "Nobody Knows You When You're Down and Out" and "Down Hearted Blues." Other Austin compositions included "Bad Luck Blues," "Barrel House Blues," "Travelin' Blues," "Steppin' on the Blues," and "Frog Tongue Stomp." But there was little copyright protection and she was deprived of many royalties.

As her New Orleans-style playing fell out of vogue, she worked as a security inspector at a naval defense plant during World War II. When Hoefer wrote his 1950 feature article on Austin, she was pianist for the Penthouse studios at the Jimmy Payne School of Dance in Chicago. She recorded with Hill for Capitol Records in 1946 and with Hunter for Riverside Records in 1961, although her longest recording association was with the Paramount label. She officially retired in 1962. An excellent band pianist, accompanist, composer, arranger, musical director, and occasional singer, Lovie Austin died in Chicago.

• The most extensive coverage of Lovie Austin is to be found in *Black Women in America: An Historical Encyclopedia* (1993). Austin's place in the history of blues and early jazz is well covered in D. Antoinette Handy, *Black Women in American Bands and Orchestras* (1981); Sally Placksin, *American Women in Jazz: 1900 to the Present* (1982); George Hoefer, "Lovie Austin Still Active as a Pianist in Chicago," *Down Beat*, 16 June 1950, p. 11; and Linda Dahl, *Stormy Weather* (1984). Obituaries appear in the *Chicago Tribune*, 9 July 1972, *Living Blues* (Summer 1972), and *Down Beat* (12 Oct. 1972).

D. ANTOINETTE HANDY

AUSTIN, Mary Hunter (9 Sept. 1868–13 Aug. 1934), writer, was born in Carlinville, Illinois, the daughter of George Hunter, an attorney, and Susannah Savilla Graham. Throughout her earliest years, Austin's father, who was her sole source of literary and personal support, suffered from ill health owing to a malarial fever contracted during his Civil War service. After the deaths of her father and sister, which occurred when she was ten years old, Austin led a lonely life in a home where her mother's emotional energy was devoted to her eldest son. Writing became the solitary child's means of expression. She studied art and majored in science at Blackburn College, receiving her B.S. in 1888. Although her first twenty years were spent in the Midwest, Austin dedicated much of her life as a writer to the culture and landscape of the Southwest. In 1888 she moved with her mother and siblings to California's San Joaquin Valley, where the family established a desert homestead and she taught school. In 1891 she married Stafford Wallace Austin; they had a daughter the following year. Her daughter was severely retarded, and Austin was eventually forced to commit her to an institution, where she died in 1918.

The years of her marriage exposed Austin to life in a number of small desert towns, where she taught, while her chronically dissatisfied and unstable husband worked first as manager of a failed irrigation project and then as a county superintendent of schools. It was this experience that provided the background for her first book, *The Land of Little Rain* (1903), a collection of fourteen sketches about the natural world of the desert and the people and beliefs it nurtured. Austin separated from her husband the year the book was published, and they divorced in 1914. Although the Southwest she loved remained her base, she was free to travel, study, write, and lecture wherever she chose.

In the years immediately following her divorce, Austin lived and participated in the artists' communities in Carmel, California, Greenwich Village, and London. Most of her writing from this period continued to center on western and southwestern themes. Notable among the books she published at this time are *The Basket Woman: A Book of Fantastical Tales for Children* (1904), *Isidro* (1905), *The Flock* (1906), and *Lost Borders* (1909). Austin's approach to the Southwest and particularly to Native American culture reflected her passion for nature and her embrace of native religion based on natural forces.

Austin's own religion brought together mystical elements from both Native American and Christian sources. When she was diagnosed with incurable breast cancer in 1912, she went to Italy to die and later linked the spontaneous remission of her tumor to prayer, in which she had engaged, under Catholic tutelage. Her books *Christ in Italy: Being the Adventures of a Maverick among Masterpieces* (1912) and *The Man Jesus: Being a Brief Account of the Life and Teachings of the Prophet of Nazareth* (1915), later revised and enlarged as *A Small Town Man* (1925), reflect the Christian dimension of her faith. The Native American aspects are present, in one sense or another, throughout her writings about the Southwest.

The other dominant theme in Austin's writings, particularly in her novels, is the status of women in modern society. Her narratives often focus on the conflict between a woman's independent identity, particularly her creative life, and the institution of marriage. *A Woman of Genius* (1912), Austin's best novel, attacks her society's dominant hypocritical values about gender and sexuality as the means by which women's creative gifts are stifled. *Love and the Soul-Maker* (1914) is a feminist *roman à thèse* about the nature and purpose of marriage.

Earth Horizon (1932), Austin's third-person autobiography, is the only book in which she successfully links her feminist concerns and her involvement with the Southwest; she is able to do so in this volume precisely because it is the story of her own life, where these themes and the experiences that informed them actually intertwined. The memoir not only recounts events in Austin's life and explains the texts she produced, but it also expounds the philosophical positions that derived from her experience and that she attempted to embody in her writing. Although her philosophy is mystical, it has room for both the material appreciation of nature and the social struggle against the institutionalized oppression of women and Native Americans.

Austin's main contribution to social reform was made through her writing. There is a difference, however, between the more general way she treats feminist issues in her novels and the advocacy of specific policies entailed in much of her writing about southwestern Indian life and environmental conservation. For the last twenty years of her life, Austin alternated periods of writing with periods of lecturing. Her lectures, as well as other forms of activism, did much to introduce academic audiences and the general public to the culture and conditions of Native Americans in the Southwest.

The most mature of Austin's collections of essays about the Southwest is *The Land of Journey's Ending* (1924). That "land" is New Mexico, where Austin lived for the last decade of her life and found the quintessence of everything she loved about the region. In Santa Fe, she lived in a Spanish adobe house, "Casa Querida," and added Spanish colonial art to her studies of regional culture. She died at home, and her ashes were buried in a natural mountain crypt overlooking Santa Fe.

• Austin's extensive collection of papers is housed at the Huntington Library in San Marino, Calif. There is also a small collection of "Austiniana" in the Coronado Room of the Main Library at the University of New Mexico, Albuquerque. Major works not already mentioned include *Santa Lucia: A Common Story* (1908), *Outland* (published under the pseudonym Gordon Stairs, 1910), *The Arrow-Maker: A Drama in Three Acts* (1911), *The Lovely Lady* (1913), *California: The Land of the Sun* (1914; revised as *The Lands of the Sun*, 1927), *The Ford* (1917), *The Trail Book* (1918), *No. 26 Jayne Street* (1920), *The American Rhythm* (1923; revised as *The American Rhythm: Studies and Reexpressions of Amerindian Songs*, 1930), *Everyman's Genius* (1925), *The Children Sing in the Far West* (1928), *Taos Pueblo* (1930), *Starry Adventure* (1931), *Experiences Facing Death* (1931), *One-Smoke Stories* (1934), *Can Prayer Be Answered?* (1934), *Mother of Felipe and Other Early Stories*, ed. Franklin Walker (1950), *One Hundred Miles on Horseback*, ed. Donald P. Ringler (1963), and *The Man Who Didn't Believe in Christmas* (1969). Austin's letters have been published as *Literary America, 1903–1934: The Mary Austin Letters* (1979). Biographies of Austin include Ringler, *Mary Austin: Kern County Days* (1963), Esther Stineman, *Mary Austin: Song of a Maverick* (1989), Peggy Pond Church, *Wind's Trail: The Early Life of Mary Austin* (1990), and Augusta Fink, *I-Mary: A Biography of Mary Austin* (1983). For memoirs by two of Austin's friends, see Helen M. Doyle, *Mary Austin: Woman of Genius* (1939), and Thomas M. Pearce, *The Beloved House* (1940).

LILLIAN S. ROBINSON

AUSTIN, Moses (4 Oct. 1761–10 June 1821), industrialist, was born in Durham, Connecticut, the son of Elias Austin, a tailor and tavernkeeper, and Eunice Phelps. Little is known of Austin's early life until the age of twenty-one, when he entered the dry-goods business in Middletown, Connecticut, with a brother-in-law and then moved to Philadelphia, Pennsylvania, in 1783 to join his brother, Stephen, in a similar enterprise. In Philadelphia, Austin met and in 1785 married Mary "Maria" Brown, with whom he had five children.

Austin extended the dry-goods partnership to Richmond, Virginia, where he established Moses Austin and Company. In 1789 he secured a contract to roof the new Virginia capitol in lead, and, since the state promised to pay 5 percent above market price if the contractor used Virginia lead, Austin, again in partnership with Stephen, gained control of Virginia's richest lead deposit. Austin brought experienced miners and smelterers from England to improve the efficiency of his operation, and the resulting expertise and industry he introduced into the lead business created the American lead industry. He established Austinville (Wythe County) at the lead mines in 1792 after he moved to the mines.

When Austin encountered problems in roofing the capitol and in financing his enterprise, he looked for relief to the rumored lead deposits in Spanish Upper Louisiana. After visiting the mines during the winter of 1796–1797, he sought and obtained a grant to part of Mine à Breton (at modern Potosi, Missouri), where in 1798 he established the first Anglo-American settlement in Missouri. Imbued with the New England Calvinist belief that to those most able to manage resources should go the lion's share of the assets, Austin sought aggressively to expand his holdings. Using the efficient reverberatory furnace, the design of which he had learned from the English smelterers, he soon controlled virtually all smelting in the region and amassed a wealth of $190,000. The second period in the history of the American lead industry is known as the Moses Austin period, and Austin's contributions characterized the lead industry until heavy machinery revolutionized mining and smelting after the Civil War.

Seeking to dominate the mine area economically, politically, and socially, Austin struggled inconclusively for nearly a decade with John Smith T for supremacy in the mines, a contest that kept the region in perpetual turmoil. Consistently he courted the friendship of men in prominent positions. Governor William Henry Harrison appointed him a justice on the Court of Common Pleas and Quarter Sessions for the Ste. Genevieve District. And to provide a suitable seat for his operations, Austin built, in the style of a southern mansion, an imposing home that he called "Durham Hall."

With sales lost because of the disruption resulting from the Aaron Burr conspiracy, the War of 1812, and subsequent depressed conditions, Austin joined a group of prominent businessmen seeking to increase the money supply in circulation by founding the Bank of St. Louis, the first bank west of the Mississippi River. The bank's failure in 1819 severely compromised Moses's already weak financial condition. Austin had already, in 1816, relinquished the Potosi mine to his son Stephen F. Austin and moved to Herculaneum, Missouri, a town he had established in 1808 as a river shipping point for his lead, where he returned to merchandising.

Unsuccessful in escaping debt through traditional business pursuits, Austin in 1819 developed a plan for settling an American colony in Spanish Texas. Characteristically he took an aggressive tack in times that conventional wisdom dubbed best for holding the line. After the Adams-Onis Treaty clarified Spanish title to Texas, he traveled to San Antonio, arriving on 23 December 1820, and sought permission to bring a colony of Anglo-American settlers. Spurned by Governor Antonio María Martínez, he chanced to meet the Baron de Bastrop in one of the most famous turns of history in Texas. Austin and Bastrop had chanced to meet nineteen years earlier when in New Orleans on unrelated trips and had had no contact during the interim. Nevertheless, the two recognized each other. After Bastrop, a resident of San Antonio, heard the enthusiasm with which Austin spoke of his colonization plan, Bastrop returned with him to the governor's office to request permission to establish the colony. On 26 December 1820 Governor Martínez endorsed the plan and forwarded it to his superiors.

On the trip out of Texas, Austin contracted pneumonia from exposure during four weeks of cold, wet weather, the last week subsisting on roots and berries. Shortly after he reached home, he learned that permission had been granted, which caused him to neglect his health and devote all his energies to the "Texas venture." Austin lived barely two months more. Two days before he died, he called his wife to his bed and told her to tell their son Stephen, who to that time had not shared his father's enthusiasm for the Texas venture, that Moses's last request was for Stephen to establish the colony in Texas. As a result of the work he did in carrying out his father's request, Stephen is known as "The Father of Texas." Moses Austin died at his daughter's home in Missouri.

• The Austin papers are at the Center for American History, University of Texas at Austin. A full biography is David B. Gracy II, *Moses Austin: His Life* (1987).

DAVID B. GRACY II

AUSTIN, Stephen Fuller (3 Nov. 1793–27 Dec. 1836), founder of Anglo-Texas, was born in Wythe County, Virginia, the son of Moses Austin, an entrepreneur in lead mining, and Maria Brown. At age five Austin moved with his family to Potosi, Missouri, a town founded by his father. Moses Austin sent his son to various schools in Connecticut (1804–1808) and to Transylvania University (1809–1810) in Lexington, Kentucky. Stephen joined his father's business ventures in the spring of 1810, managing the lead-mining operation as well as working in the family store.

Austin obtained prominence in public affairs in Missouri, serving in the territorial legislature from 1814 to 1820, and in 1815 Governor William Clark appointed him adjutant of a militia battalion. In 1818 he became director of the Bank of St. Louis, in which his father had invested heavily, but after the bank collapsed as a result of the panic of 1819, Austin went to Arkansas. Governor John Miller appointed him circuit judge of the first judicial district of Arkansas in 1820, despite his lack of legal experience. Austin took the oath of office in July 1820, but he probably never held court, for he went to New Orleans in August and joined in a mercantile partnership with Joseph H. Hawkins, who later helped finance the first Texas colonization venture. Austin studied law with Hawkins and in early 1821 wrote for the New Orleans paper, the *Louisiana Advertiser*.

Moses Austin, who had witnessed a decline in lead mining with the end of the War of 1812, suffered further reversals of fortune when the Bank of St. Louis collapsed. In December 1820 Moses went to San Antonio de Bexar seeking a grant from the Spanish Crown to settle 300 families in Texas. He received notice in March 1821 that the Spanish had approved his grant, but the trip back to Missouri had weakened his already frail health, and he died in June. Stephen Austin reluctantly decided to support his father's colonization venture. When news of Moses' death reached him, partially out of loyalty to his father's memory, Stephen went to San Antonio in August 1821 and negotiated with Governor August Maria Martinez for the right to continue the venture. He returned to New Orleans and advertised for settlers, purchased the schooner *The Lively*, sent it on to Texas with supplies and a few settlers, and then he left for Texas.

Austin arrived in December 1821 to find a few settlers already in the area around Washington on the Brazos between the Brazos and Colorado rivers. He failed to make contact with *The Lively*, and, somewhat discouraged, he journeyed to San Antonio in March 1822 to report to Governor Martinez. The governor told him that the provisional government of the newly independent Mexico had refused to recognize the Spanish grant. Austin left for Mexico City to plead his case, arriving there in April 1822. While in Mexico City, Austin learned Spanish, acquired some skills in political dealings, and secured his grant through the Imperial Colonization Law of 1823. Austin was the only *empresario*, or contractor, who received land for colonization under this law. Austin returned to Texas to issue land titles in August 1823, and by 1824 the exact boundaries of the first grant were defined. Those 300 settlers chose lands along the Brazos, Colorado, and Bernard rivers in an area roughly bounded by the present towns of Navasota, Brenham, and La Grange with a corridor to the coast. Austin located his home at San Felipe and from there conducted the governing of the grant.

The Mexican congress passed the National Colonization Law in August 1824, and, acting within its guidelines in 1825, the state legislature of Coahuila y Tejas authorized further settlement by *empresarios* in the state. Under the provisions of this law, Austin received three more grants (1825, 1827, 1828) to settle 900 families in areas adjacent to his original colony. One grant allowed him to issue land claims between the Brazos and Colorado as far north and east as present day Bryan, another authorized settlers on the east bank of the Colorado River, with Bastrop becoming the major community, and another grant extended ultimately as far south as the coastal areas bounded by the Lavaca and San Jacinto rivers. The *empresario* earned five *sitos* (approximately 22,140 acres) of grazing land and five *labors* (approximately 885 acres) of farm land for each 100 families settled in the geographic area authorized by a colonization grant. Although Austin originally intended to charge 12.5 cents an acre for the land meted to each settler, disputes over the validity of such charges and the refusal of settlers to pay led to a survey charge to each settler of around $30. Austin, along with his secretary Samuel M. Williams, received permission in 1831 to take over the grant of the Texas Association of Nashville and settle 800 families in Northwest Texas. Disputes over this grant between Austin and Sterling C. Robertson led to protracted appeals to Mexican authorities and litigation in Texas courts that were not settled until 1847 in Robertson's favor. Austin was the most successful of the *empresarios*, locating more than 1,500 families in Texas. He wrote a few years before his death that he envisioned Texas as a land of prosperous settlers, if not in Mexico then as a nation, and it was to this end that he sacrificed all hope of family or personal wealth. He never married. He evidently thought of Texas eventually becoming much like the mixed economy of the United States but with an availability of free land to attract industrious settlers.

The *empresario* issued land titles and governed the colony until the terms of the grant were fulfilled. The specific obligations of the *empresarios* to mediate between settlers and the Mexican authorities were not clear. From 1824 to 1827 Austin exercised almost complete civil and military authority in his four grants. He authorized local settlers to elect militia officers and *alcaldes*—a Spanish word for mayors but literally a head man whose duties would be similar to a judge, mayor, and sheriff. He wrote a simple civil and criminal code for the colonies and established an appellate court. As commander of the militia, he undertook punitive expeditions against the Karankawas and the Tonkawas, who were accused of raiding nearby settlements. In November 1827, when Mexico approved of the constitution for Coahuila y Tejas, Austin encouraged the rapid organization of *ayuntamientos*, or governing bodies of a municipality, to replace his delegated authority. He believed that productive citizens would soon have a stake and affection for a region that they themselves governed. His importance and influence remained. Other *empresarios* sought his advice, and he mediated among Mexican authorities, settlers, and state officials seeking compromise over issues of trade, slavery, and taxes, for example.

Austin saw his major political role as that of mediator. He argued that the colonists would succeed if they maintained harmonious relationships with state and federal authorities. He urged the settlers to remember the bountiful land provisions that the Mexican government had bestowed upon them. He led the militia from his colony in 1826 to help Mexico thwart the Fredonian Revolt, where Benjamin Edwards and some thirty colonists, disgruntled over a conflict between the *empresario* Hayden Edwards and Mexican authorities, rode into Nacogdoches and declared East Texas to be the free state of Fredonia. He helped assuage settler discontent with the sometimes awkward government regulations and in turn assured authorities of the loyalty of Anglo settlers and of their willingness to obey federal and state laws and regulations. He was always somewhat ambivalent about the institution of slavery but nevertheless saw it as necessary for the economic development of the region. He accepted the duplicity of Anglo settlers' classification of African Americans as indentured servants to avoid Mexican law, which outlawed slavery. His eminent reputation allowed him to secure exemptions from the law of 6 April 1830, which eliminated further immigration from the United States to Mexico, for the colonies of both himself and fellow-*empresario* Green DeWitt, who had—as had Austin—nearly fulfilled his contract. Austin thus secured a window of entry that allowed some continued immigration from the United States into Texas.

Meanwhile the law of 6 April 1830, which recognized existing African-American slavery but prohibited the further introduction of slaves, and arguments in the spring of 1832 over the tariff had led to conflicts between some Anglo settlers and Mexican authorities at Anahuac. The resulting battle of Velasco in June increased tensions in Texas, and consequently the *ayuntamiento* of San Felipe called on the other municipalities to send delegates to a convention to meet in October in San Felipe. Austin was at Saltillo, serving as a member of the legislature of Coahuila y Tejas, when the call was issued. He returned to San Felipe and served as the president of the Convention of 1832. He called for moderation at the convention, and the body pledged loyalty to Mexico and asked for some administrative reforms and repeal of the 1830 legislation. For a variety of reasons the petition was never forwarded to Mexico City. The weaknesses of the Convention of 1832, plus the apparent victory of Antonio López de Santa Anna as a liberal in the Mexican presidential election of 1833, led the central committee on safety, created at the Convention of 1832, to call for the meeting of the Convention of 1833 in April at San Felipe. This convention, less moderate than its predecessor, dispatched Austin to Mexico City to present the colonists' demands to President Santa Anna.

Austin reached the capital that summer. He negotiated the repeal of the 1830 law and some other concessions for Texas. He did not, however, succeed in persuading Santa Anna to agree to a separate state government for Texas. Austin left for home in December. At Saltillo in January, Mexican authorities intercepted him and charged him with inciting a revolution in Texas. The charges stemmed from an unfortunate letter he had written much earlier to the *ayuntamiento* in San Antonio urging the Hispanic leaders of the city to take the lead in acquiring statehood status for Texas. Austin was returned to Mexico City and imprisoned. He was incarcerated until December 1834 and remained under house arrest until freed by a general amnesty law in July 1835.

The twenty-eight months that Austin was away from Texas damaged his reputation with fellow colonists. The migration that increased from 1833 to 1835, partially through his efforts, brought into Texas settlers who, as far as they knew, owed nothing to Austin. Moreover, many Anglo-Texans faulted his post-1830 conciliatory policies toward Mexico. Even after his return to Texas and his endorsement at Brazoria for war against Mexico and the need for the Consultation called for September 1835 at San Felipe, he seemed to many of his fellow Texans, already committed to independence from Mexico, to be too cautious and possibly willing to compromise any movement for independence for concessions that would allow Texas to remain as a state within the Republic of Mexico. He was elected, nonetheless, at Gonzales in October to command the troops at the siege of San Antonio. In November, however, the Consultation selected him as one of three commissioners to go to the United States and solicit money, arms, and men for the revolution. Although an excellent choice, Austin spent the desperate months from December 1835 to June 1836 out of Texas, and he returned to find Sam Houston and others now the heroes of independence. Austin agreed, nevertheless, to run for the presidency in September 1836 and placed a distant third. President Houston appointed him secretary of state. Austin served at that post until his death, described by his friends as from overwork and exposure, at Columbia, Texas, at the end of the year.

The presidential campaign of 1836 represented the nadir of Austin's reputation. He was charged with both being soft on Mexico and a land speculator. Austin had indeed acquired well over 100,000 acres of land from various *empresario* contracts. Moreover, the legal battles after his death between his company and Sterling Robertson and the defunct Nashville company added to the image of land speculator. As time distanced revolutionary controversies, Austin's reputation as the "father of Texas" resurfaced. The monumental biography of Austin in 1925 by the Texas historian Eugene C. Barker placed Austin in the pantheon of Anglo-Texas heroes, a mythic figure second only, perhaps, to Sam Houston. That historical image of Austin has endured, but historians have begun the work of revising and creating a more judicious depiction of him. Whatever new revisions of Austin emerge, the final accounts will probably still portray him as a dedicated pioneer, who profited not very much from his endeavors and who led in the creating of Anglo-Texas.

• Austin's papers are available in *The Austin Papers*, ed. Eugene C. Barker (3 vols.). The two-part vol. 1 was published as vol. 2 of the *Annual Report of the American Historical Association for 1919* (1924); vol. 2 was published as vol. 2 of the *Annual Report of the American Historical Association for 1922* (1928); and the final volume was published by the University of Texas in 1928. The standard biography is Barker, *The Life of Stephen F. Austin: Founder of Texas* (1925), but also see David B. Gracy, *Moses Austin: His Life* (1987). For a historiographical survey and a comprehensive bibliography of Austin and the revolution see Paul D. Lack, "In the Long Shadow of Eugene C. Barker: The Revolution and the Republic," in *Texas through Time*, ed. Walter L. Buenger and Robert A. Calvert (1991).

ROBERT A. CALVERT

AUSTIN, Warren Robinson (12 Nov. 1877–25 Dec. 1962), U.S. senator and ambassador, was born in the rural community of Highgate Center, Vermont, near the Canadian border, the son of Chauncey Goodrich Austin, a successful country lawyer, and Anne Robinson. He attended the University of Vermont, receiving his Ph.B. in 1899. He married Mildred Lucas in 1901, and they had two children.

After graduating Austin read law in his father's firm, which had been moved to St. Albans, the county seat. He passed the Vermont bar exam in 1902 and began practice in the firm. Becoming active in local politics, in 1904 he ran successfully for state's attorney for Franklin County and in 1909 for mayor of St. Albans, and he was a U.S. commissioner from 1907 to 1915. An effective public speaker, Austin worked hard for the Republican party and, gaining recognition, was chosen in 1908 as chair of the state convention. In 1912, as a progressive in the party, he lost the Republican nomination for Congress. Nonetheless, while a number of Vermont Republicans joined Theodore Roosevelt's (1858–1919) new progressive "Bull Moose" party, Austin campaigned for the party regulars.

Austin concentrated on advancing his legal career and interests. In 1914 the U.S. Supreme Court admitted him to practice, and in 1916 he received an offer from the American International Corporation (AIC), recently established by some of the nation's prominent financial and manufacturing leaders. Led by New York's National City Bank, AIC proposed to expand vigorously American investments abroad. Austin went to Peking (Beijing), China, as legal representative in negotiations for financing and building railroads and the development of the Shantung province Grand Canal. In an example of dollar diplomacy and the "Open Door," he wrote contracts for some $130 million worth of American loans. He believed, furthermore, in the efforts of the Protestant missionaries. Although he foresaw other financial opportunities in China, when he completed his work in 1917 he returned to the United States and opened his own firm in Burlington, Vermont's major city.

Austin's law practice, meanwhile, grew, and he attracted considerable attention throughout the state. During the 1920s he won a record settlement in an alienation-of-affection case, and he successfully represented the state of Vermont in a boundary dispute with New Hampshire before the U.S. Supreme Court. His clients included some of the major interests in the state, and while participating in numerous community activities, he once again became active in Republican party politics.

In 1930 Austin entered the U.S. Senate race to fill the unexpired term of the late Frank L. Greene. He showed his political skill by winning a difficult primary contest the following March, emphasizing local issues and personalities and straddling the issue of Prohibition. In the special election three weeks later he easily defeated his Democratic opponent. In Washington, D.C., he expressed his and his state's conservatism, and he lamented President Herbert Hoover's (1874–1964) defeat in 1932. With his concepts of small government, frugality, and individualism he became concerned about President Franklin D. Roosevelt's use of executive power during the Hundred Days. Austin's consistent opposition to the New Deal gave Vermont Democrats, with active national support, the opportunity to wage a strenuous campaign against him in 1934 by stressing what the administration had done for Vermont during the depression. The New Deal became the major issue, and Austin's emphasis on conservatism and individualism enabled him to survive an extremely close election. Not surprisingly, his legal thinking and political beliefs prompted him to oppose ardently Roosevelt's unsuccessful Supreme Court proposal in 1937.

This anti–New Deal Republican senator, however, did not share his party's isolationist position on the restrictive neutrality legislation during the 1930s. Instead, he supported "limited internationalism." As historian George Mazuzan has shown, for years Austin had held a "moral-legal" view that saw "law as the only rational solution to problems among men and nations," leading later to his belief in the necessity of a postwar international organization. In 1938, as the totalitarian challenge in Europe and Asia grew, he insisted that "isolationism was dead." He advocated a flexible foreign policy that meant, in 1939, neutrality revision and a stronger defense program, particularly after the start of the European war. In 1940 he easily won reelection; however, his support of the administration's foreign policy, from the destroyers-for-bases deal to lend-lease, increasingly separated him from his Republican colleagues.

After the Pearl Harbor attack, Austin's internationalism led Secretary of State Cordell Hull to choose him to be a charter member of the congressional foreign policy advisory group for the State Department; later, as one of the leading senators endorsing a postwar organization, he was on its Committee of Eight. However, as Austin tried to lead his party to internationalism and support for postwar cooperation among nations, the Republican isolationist leadership removed him as assistant minority leader, a position he had gained in 1933 for his conservatism, and kept him off the Senate Foreign Relations Committee until late in the war.

As the war ended, Austin served as an adviser at the Inter-American Conference at Mexico City on the problems of war and peace, and he recognized the important role of the economy in rehabilitation and peace. He believed that foreign economic aid would be vital for recovery, and he argued for America's leadership role in the United Nations with his "missionary zeal." His work on behalf of internationalism and a postwar role for the United States highlighted his Senate career.

To further bipartisan support for the UN, President Harry S. Truman named Austin the country's first ambassador to the UN on 5 June 1946, although a provision of the Constitution prevented him from assuming the title until after that session of Congress ended. He idealistically carried to the UN his faith in legal rules and reason, and he believed that the UN would be a vital force for world peace under U.S. leadership. This universalism would be sorely tested during the late 1940s with the emerging Cold War and Washington's strategy of containment of Communism.

The administration seldom consulted with Austin on the formulation of policy, and none of the secretaries of state under Truman shared Austin's faith in the UN. Thus, Austin became primarily a spokesman for the United States. Reconciling his views with the increasingly unilateral and anti-Soviet position of his government, he defended publicly those policies and convinced himself that they supported the growth of the UN. The Communist defiance of the UN during the Korean War completed his conversion to a cold warrior, and the *New York Times* wrote that the ambassador constantly "ridiculed the Soviet Union for talking peace while carrying on aggression." When Truman fired General Douglas MacArthur as UN commander, the ambassador, even though he was the most prominent Republican in the administration, repeatedly endorsed the decision and the UN's limited war. As the *New York Times* recalled, "Combining Yankee shrewdness in bargaining with a forceful mode of expression, he made an eloquent protagonist for the American viewpoint in world affairs," and in doing so he provided a valuable service for his government.

After Republican Dwight D. Eisenhower won the presidency in 1952, the 75-year-old Austin, whose health had been failing, asked to be relieved. A few months after Austin returned to Burlington, his longstanding heart condition caused a cerebral attack. He made a remarkable recovery and indulged his lifelong interest in growing apple trees, and he accepted an honorary chairmanship of the Committee of One Million to keep the People's Republic of China out of the UN. He died at home.

• Austin's papers are in the Bailey Library at the University of Vermont, with the exception of some Austin material on the 1937 federal judiciary reorganization at Yale University. For his ambassadorship, State Department material at the National Archives should be consulted, as well as the appropriate volumes in the Foreign Relations of the United States series. Austin's published writings are few. George T. Mazuzan, *Warren R. Austin at the UN, 1946–1953* (1977), has a long opening chapter on Austin's earlier career. See also Henry W. Berger, "Warren R. Austin in China, 1916–1917," *Vermont History* (Autumn 1972): 246–61; Mazuzan, "Vermont's Traditional Republicanism vs. the New Deal: Warren R. Austin and the Election of 1934," *Vermont History* (Spring 1971): 129–41; Mazuzan, "'Our New Gold Goes Adventuring': The American International Corporation in China," *Pa-*

cific Historical Review (May 1974): 212–32; David Porter, "Warren R. Austin and the Neutrality Act of 1939," *Vermont History* (Summer 1974): 228–38; and Mazuzan, "America's U.N. Commitment, 1945–1953," *Historian* (Feb. 1978): 309–30. Obituaries are in the *New York Times* and the *Burlington Free Press*, both 26 Dec. 1962.

TRAVIS BEAL JACOBS

AUSTIN, William (2 Mar. 1778–27 June 1841), writer and lawyer, was born in Lunenberg, Massachusetts, the son of Nathaniel Austin, a pewterer and enterprising dealer in real estate, and Margaret Rand. Austin was raised in Charlestown, Massachusetts, which had been the family home for five generations. He received an A.B. from Harvard in 1798. The following year Austin obtained an appointment as both a schoolmaster and chaplain in the U.S. Navy. He sailed on the historic frigate *Constitution* and had the distinction of being the first chaplain in the navy appointed by government commission. A short naval career gave Austin the means to pursue legal studies at Lincoln's Inn, London, which he completed in 1803. For the rest of his life, Austin practiced law but devoted time to political and literary activities as well.

While studying law in England, Austin prepared his first noteworthy literary work, *Letters from London* (1804). These letters presented sketches of both the English national character and individual Englishmen, and they developed moral and political themes, while often comparing the English and American systems of government.

Austin returned to the United States in 1803 and began, at the age of twenty-five, a quite successful law practice in Charlestown. But the promising life of the young writer and lawyer was endangered when he fought a duel with James Henderson Elliot in 1806. The duel's cause reflects Austin's lifelong political allegiance and sense of justice. Austin, a staunch Democrat, verbally attacked Elliot's father, a Federalist major general, in an article published in the *Independent Chronicle* (17 Mar. 1806). Writing an open letter under the pseudonym of "Decius," Austin accused General Elliot of having unjustly prolonged, for strictly partisan motives, the imprisonment of Captain Joseph Loring, Jr., himself a Democrat, who had been acquitted by a court-martial of disobeying orders. To defend the general's honor, the younger Elliot challenged Austin, who had willingly revealed the identity of "Decius." Because dueling had been outlawed in Massachusetts, the young men fought with pistols at sunrise in Providence, Rhode Island. Austin was hit in the neck and thigh; neither wound was serious. Elliot was not injured.

Austin, the father of fourteen children, married twice. In June 1806 he married Charlotte Williams. After Charlotte died in December 1820, Austin wedded Lucy Jones in October 1822.

Austin was first elected to public office in 1811 as a representative from Charlestown, Massachusetts, to the General Court. His popularity, public spirit, education, and oratorical ability (he had delivered a well-received Bunker Hill anniversary speech in 1801) prompted his community to elect him as their representative four more times (1812, 1816, 1827, 1834) and to send him three times (1821, 1822, 1823) to the Massachusetts Senate as a member for the county of Middlesex. Austin was never once defeated for elective office. Austin was also chosen by his neighbors to be the delegate from Charlestown at the convention held in 1820 for revising the Massachusetts constitution.

Austin published "Peter Rugg, the Missing Man" as a serial in the *New England Galaxy* from September 1824 to September 1826. "Peter Rugg," Austin's most popular work, is the story of a man who, apparently as punishment for a rash temper, must wander the countryside for years and years, pulled along by a strange black horse in a carriage, continually followed by storm clouds, seeking his Boston home. The story bears resemblance to the work of Washington Irving and Nathaniel Hawthorne, and its literary merit gives it a place in the early history of the American short story. "Peter Rugg" most probably influenced the fictional technique of Hawthorne, who alludes to Austin's story in his sketch "A Virtuoso's Collection" (1842). In the following passage from "Peter Rugg," Austin's narrator, Jonathan Dunwell, who is conversing with a stagecoach driver, describes a mysterious scene and comments upon its ambiguous interpretation:

> And now the successive flashes of chain lightning caused the whole cloud to appear like a sort of irregular network, and displayed a thousand fantastic images. The driver bespoke my attention to a remarkable configuration in the cloud. He said every flash of lightning near its centre discovered to him, distinctly, the form of a man sitting in an open carriage drawn by a black horse. But in truth I saw no such thing; the man's fancy was doubtless at fault. It is a very common thing for the imagination to paint for the senses, both in the visible and the invisible world.

Austin published only six stories, however, the last being "Martha Gardner; or Moral Reaction," which appeared in the *American Monthly Magazine* (Dec. 1837).

After a protracted illness, Austin died at his lifelong home in Charlestown, Massachusetts, respected for his life of public service and literary achievement.

• Important works by William Austin not cited above are *Strictures on Harvard University* (1798); *Oration before the Artillery Company, Charlestown, June 17, 1801* (1801); *Essay on the Human Character of Jesus Christ* (1807); "The Sufferings of a Country Schoolmaster," *New England Galaxy*, 8 July 1825, pp. 1–2; "The Late Joseph Natterstrom," *New England Magazine*, July 1831, pp. 11–19; "The Origin of Chemistry: A Manuscript Recently Found in an Old Trunk," *New England Magazine*, Jan. 1834, pp. 13–18; and "The Man with the Cloaks: A Vermont Legend," *American Monthly Magazine*, Jan. 1836, pp. 331–42. A biographical sketch of Austin by his son appears in James Walker Austin, *The Literary Papers of William Austin* (1890), and a detailed biography, as well as a collection of his short stories, is by his grandson Walter Austin, *William Austin: The Creator of Peter Rugg* (1925).

CHARLES ZAROBILA

AVERELL, William Woods (5 Nov. 1832–3 Feb. 1900), Union general and businessman, was born in Cameron (Steuben County), New York, the son of Hiram Averell and Huldah Hemenway, farmers. Averell attended the U.S. Military Academy, graduating in 1855, twenty-sixth in a class of thirty-four, only excelling in horsemanship. He then served with the cavalry in the Southwest and was seriously wounded during a fight against the Navajos at Canyon de Chelly, New Mexico Territory (1858). He was in New York on convalescent leave when the Civil War began.

Averell traveled to Washington and presented himself to Winfield Scott, commanding general of the U.S. Army. Averell's first assignment was to warn the isolated garrison at Fort Arbuckle, Indian Territory, that the war had begun. In June 1861, Averell was sent to Elmira, New York, to help muster volunteers, but his background made him contemptuous of the untrained recruits. He soon joined the staff of Brigadier General Irvin McDowell, who commanded the Union army at the first battle of Manassas (Bull Run). Averell was appalled at the disorganized rout that followed the battle and was critical of the Lincoln administration, which he thought had encouraged premature military action.

In October 1861, Averell was assigned to command the Third Pennsylvania Cavalry, an unruly group that was widely dispersed from Georgetown, District of Columbia, to Alexandria, Virginia. Averell ordered the regiment to assemble in one camp, where he instructed officers in the manual of arms and told them to teach their men what they had learned. In March 1862, the Third Pennsylvania was transferred to southern Virginia. They were put on the left flank of the Union army and participated in the Seven Days' battles. Their position kept them out of most of the action.

Shortly after the campaign, Averell was promoted to brigadier general and given command of a brigade of cavalry. Malaria kept him from further military action until February 1863, when Major General Joseph Hooker reorganized the Army of the Potomac and created a separate cavalry corps. Averell was given command of one of the three divisions in the new corps. On 25 February 1863, a West Point classmate of his, Confederate brigadier general Fitzhugh Lee, captured 150 of Averell's cavalrymen. Three weeks later (17 Mar.) Averell crossed the Rappahannock River at Kelly's Ford and awaited Lee. Although Lee was outnumbered more than 3 to 1, he put on a spirited attack. After three clashes, Lee left the field in Averell's hands, permitting him to declare the battle a victory. Averell's success at Kelly's Ford won him undeserved praise from Washington.

Hooker, however, was not so pleased. He knew that Averell had missed the chance to destroy Fitzhugh Lee's cavalry and win a complete victory. Hooker sent his cavalry commander, Major General George Stoneman, and most of the cavalry in the Army of the Potomac, including Averell's division, on a raid behind Confederate lines, hoping to distract Robert E. Lee's attention from the Union army's movement around the Confederate left flank prior to Chancellorsville. Stoneman's raid fooled no one. Averell returned to the main army on 3 May with thirty-one prisoners and a few barrels of food. Hooker ordered Averell to find a suitable field for a cavalry fight on his right flank. When Averell reported that he could not find one, Hooker removed him from command.

Averell was reassigned to West Virginia, where he commanded another scattered brigade. Again, Averell proved his organizational skills, forging 3,000 West Virginia volunteers into a military force. He then began a series of raids directed at Confederate strongholds in the Shenandoah Valley. On 6 November 1863, Averell's brigade defeated the last major Confederate force in West Virginia at Droop Mountain. Averell's cavalry raid against the Virginia and Tennessee Railroad depot in Salem, Virginia (Dec. 1863), was his most successful venture in the war. With small loss to his own force, Averell's troopers captured 200 prisoners and 150 horses and destroyed a large quantity of enemy supplies.

When the Department of West Virginia was reorganized in March 1864, Averell was given command over half the cavalry in the state. He spent much of that spring fretting over supplies, at times complaining to Ulysses S. Grant, the commanding general, that he did not have enough horses or weapons.

In September 1864, Major General Philip H. Sheridan, the new Union commander in the Shenandoah Valley, made it clear to Averell that he expected decision and ruthlessness. "I do not want you to let the enemy bluff you or your command," Sheridan warned. "I do not advise recklessness, but I do desire resolution and actual fighting with necessary casualties, before you retire." On 22 September 1864, Sheridan's forces drove the Confederates off Fisher's Hill. When Sheridan learned that Averell's cavalry had gone into camp that night instead of supporting the infantry's fifteen-mile chase, Sheridan summarily dismissed Averell. Averell would struggle for the rest of his life to refute Sheridan by gathering evidence to prove his contention that his removal was politically motivated.

Averell sat out the rest of the war recuperating from severe dysentery, malaria, a head wound, and a seriously damaged ego. On 13 March 1865, Averell was given the rank of brevet major general of volunteers; two months later (18 May 1865), he resigned.

While soldiering in West Virginia, Averell sought profitable investments. He was especially interested in coal, iron ore, and petroleum. In the summer of 1865, Averell joined a coal and oil company and helped survey coal lands, build a railroad to access deposits, and find necessary manpower and machines. Despite Averell's efforts, the company soon failed.

On 2 October 1866, Averell was appointed counsel general to British North America in Montreal. He served in that post until 1 June 1869, when President Grant appointed a Republican to replace him.

By the fall of 1870, Averell had become interested in asphalt; the rapid urbanization of the Northeast had created a market for cheap but reliable street-paving material. Averell headed the Gramfamite Asphalt Paving Company, but by the time the company had received a patent for an improved process in 1878, the throes of the financial panic of 1873 had caused it to fail.

Averell was a lifelong Democrat, but he opposed Tammany Hall, which not only blocked some of his paving contracts but also prevented him from gaining the 1878 Democratic nomination as congressional candidate from New York's Eighth District. On 24 September 1885, Averell married an English widow, Kezia Hayward Browning. They had no children.

In 1888 Averell was reinstated in the army by special act of Congress and placed upon the retired list. This act was the culmination of a dogged, continuous effort by Averell to achieve some degree of vindication—at least, as he viewed it—for being relieved of his command by Sheridan twenty-four years earlier. The act made Averell assistant inspector general of soldiers' homes. He evaluated conditions for the care and treatment of veterans and lobbied for congressional appropriations. Averell resigned this post in 1898. He died in Bath, New York.

Averell was just what the army needed early in the Civil War—disciplined, capable, and cautious. As colonel of the Third Pennsylvania Cavalry, he found a role that suited his temperament and abilities. By 1864, however, the army needed decision and resolution. Averell, only thirty-one, had risen too high, too fast. He was unable to adapt his background and training to the changed nature of the war. In his postwar career, Averell was energetic and diligent but was never able to become a "captain of industry." He was an intelligent, farsighted person, but his character lacked the ruthlessness required to succeed in modern business and the military.

• Averell's personal and professional papers (tens of thousands of them) are in the New York State Library in Albany. The *Official Records of the Union and Confederate Armies* (128 vols., 1880–1901) is the foremost primary source for military material about the Civil War. The State Department papers covering Averell's service in Montreal as consular general are on three reels of microfilm in the Diplomatic Section of the National Archives. In *Ten Years in the Saddle* (1978), Edward K. Eckert and Nicholas J. Amato have written an extended introduction and epilogue to Averell's unfinished and previously unpublished memoirs and Averell's article on the Third Pennsylvania Cavalry, which he wrote for *Century Magazine*'s *Battles and Leaders* series. Robert B. Boehm's "The Unfortunate Averell," which Boehm describes as "a personality profile," is in *Civil War Times Illustrated*, Aug. 1966, pp. 30–36, and gives an objective assessment of Averell's wartime activities.

EDWARD K. ECKERT

AVERILL, Earl (21 May 1902–16 Aug. 1983), baseball outfielder, was born Howard Earl Averill in Snohomish, Washington, the son of logger Joseph Averill and Annie Maddox. Reared in the big timber country of the Cascade Mountains near Seattle, young Earl knew hard work in the lumber mills. Although never a big man, his body hardened, and he developed the biceps of a blacksmith.

Averill began his professional career with San Francisco in the Pacific Coast League in 1926 as an outfielder. A solid hitter, he enjoyed three successful seasons and was sold to the Cleveland Indians of the American League. Their general manager, Billy Evans, had scouted Averill: "There was something about the nonchalant Averill that won you over. I guess it was the easy, steady manner in which he did his work, without any great show." In his first time at bat in the majors (16 Apr. 1929), Averill hit a home run; he was the first Hall of Famer to accomplish that feat. His season's average was .332, and his eighteen homers topped Tris Speaker's seventeen for the Indians' club record. Averill was an immediate star.

Through the 1930s Averill, often called "Rock" and the "Earl of Snohomish," established himself as a complete ball player. Playing center field, batting left-handed and throwing right, he stood 5′9″ and weighed 172 pounds. Devoted to his work ethic during the depression years, he hit above .300 in his first five consecutive seasons. Altogether, he batted over .300 eight times and once finished at .299. In 1931 he drove in 143 runs. In three seasons he produced better than thirty homers, and he hit four in one doubleheader for eleven runs batted in. During his greatest season (1936) he finished at .378 with 232 hits, one short of the Indians' club record set by "Shoeless Joe" Jackson in 1911. Averill made the first six All-Star teams from 1933 through 1938, the first major leaguer to do so. His career batting average was an excellent .318, comparable to the .320 average of such Hall of Famers as Charlie Gehringer, Chuck Klein, and Mickey Cochrane, and to Arky Vaughan's .318. Averill's lifetime average ranks fiftieth among major leaguers. He played in 673 consecutive games (1931–1935), one of the longest stretches in major league history.

Averill found smaller League Park (where the Indians played on weekdays) more to his liking than Cleveland's expansive Municipal Stadium. Although generally cordial by nature, Averill could be outspoken. Sportswriter John P. Carmichael told of Averill's dispute with Indians' manager Roger Peckinpaugh, who once complained of his throwing arm. After making a circus catch to end a game, Averill threw the ball into the grandstand, shouting: "Now do you think there's anything wrong with my arm?"

Averill's success can be attributed to his standing forward in the batter's box and making solid contact with pitches. Using a forty-two-ounce bat (heaviest in the league after Babe Ruth's), he crowded the plate, seeking to drive the ball through the center of the diamond. One time his shot struck the foot of pitcher Dizzy Dean, breaking Dean's toe during the All-Star Game of 1937, which injury helped to curtail Dean's career. That same year Averill severely strained his back, shortening his own playing days. "My back affected my swing," he said. Traded to Detroit, he appeared in his only World Series in 1940. The following season, the last of his thirteen-year career, he spent with the Boston Braves (National League) and the Seattle Rainiers (Pacific Coast League). Retiring to Snohomish (1941), he opened a floral business and later a motel.

One of his sons, Earl Douglas Averill, reached the majors as a catcher with several teams between 1956 and 1963. His father urged him to work hard: "You've got two hours to play in. When you go home you might as well feel you have earned your money." In 1969 Averill joined Speaker and Jackson in being selected by sportswriters to Cleveland's all-time outfield. Being named to the National Baseball Hall of Fame at Cooperstown was the highest reward for his dedication. Averill, however, was bitter at having to wait thirty-four years for the honor. In his induction address (18 Aug. 1975) he criticized the committee that had chosen him. "There is no meaning to this honor if you're not alive," he declared, and he named other deserving stars who had been forced to wait too long.

Averill died in Everett, Washington. A long-time teammate, pitcher Mel Harder, called him "a true Hall of Famer." Sports historian Douglas G. Simpson said that Averill "had earned his place among the royalty of baseball's rich history." Earl Torgeson, a former major-league first baseman from Averill's hometown, had been named for him. To his many fans, however, Averill remained the only "Earl of Snohomish."

• Earl Averill files can be found in the libraries of the National Baseball Hall of Fame, Cooperstown, N.Y., and the *Sporting News*, St. Louis, Mo. In lieu of an authoritative biography, sketches and official records appear in John Thorn and Pete Palmer, eds., *Total Baseball*, 3d ed. (1993), and in Lowell Reidenbaugh, *Cooperstown: Where Baseball Legends Live Forever* (1983). Essays in greater depth may be found in David L. Porter, ed., *Biographical Dictionary of American Sports: Baseball* (1987), and in Douglas G. Simpson, "The Earl of Snohomish," *Baseball Research Journal* 11 (1982): 156–61. Also, Averill's son's recollections of his father appear in Rick Hines, "Earl Averill, Jr., Former Big Leaguer, Recalls Career," *Sports Collectors Digest*, 22 Mar. 1991, pp. 200–201. Likewise, the following newspaper articles are especially significant for Averill's stormy entry into the Hall of Fame: Bob Broeg, "Averill Out of Line with Blast," *Sporting News*, 13 Sept. 1975; Joseph Durso, "Old Timers Harris, Herman, and Averill Gain Hall of Fame," *New York Times*, 4 Feb. 1975; and Michael Strauss, "Averill Assails Hall of Fame Selectors," *New York Times*, 19 Aug. 1975. Obituaries appear in the *New York Times*, 18 Aug. 1983, the *Sporting News*, 29 Aug. 1983, and *Sports Collectors Digest*, 14 Oct. 1983.

WILLIAM J. MILLER

AVERY, Giles Bushnell (3 Nov. 1815–27 Dec. 1890), Shaker elder, was born in Saybrook, Connecticut, the son of Gilbert Avery and Sophia Bushnell. Avery's family converted to Shakerism, a celibate religious communal movement, in 1817 and moved to the New Lebanon, New York, Shaker community in 1819. Only four years old, Avery first lived with his mother in a gathering family designed for those first setting out to become Shakers. In 1821 he moved to the Church family, the most spiritually advanced order, where he remained until 1859.

Avery's was a typical Shaker boyhood. He received a basic education in the Shaker school and as he grew older was given a variety of work assignments from teaching school to running the family farm. When he was twenty-five he entered the ranks of the Church family leadership, where he served for twenty years, first as elder brother and then as elder. Even as elder his labor did not cease. A partial list of his occupations—plastering, stone masonry, copying music, plumbing, cabinetmaking, and grafting trees—indicates the breadth of his skills. Avery did not begrudge the constant work, however, recognizing "how similar to colonization in a new country, communal association necessarily is; that members of a community should be willing to turn a hand in any needed direction, in order to render their best service in building up and sustaining the cause" (*Autobiography*, p. 6).

In October 1859 Avery was appointed elder brother in the Central Ministry, the ruling body of the Shaker movement, and divided his time between New Lebanon and the Watervliet, New York, Shaker community. He remained in this position until his death, and it was there that he developed the intellectual and theological abilities that made him a respected leader. Freed from much of the manual labor expected of him as a family elder, Avery now spent his time addressing the spiritual and organizational problems of Shaker society at large. One of his primary concerns was providing the non-Shaker public with information on Shaker theology. He made no apologies for those doctrines that many of the world found repugnant, but he did take great pains to present the ideas in a way that the world could understand. In *Sketches of "Shakers and Shakerism": Synopsis of Theology of United Society of Believers in Christ's Second Appearing*, published in 1883 and in a somewhat longer version in 1884, Avery laid out twenty-three basic Shaker precepts, including the Shakers' denial of Jesus' divinity, of vicarious atonement for sin, and of the resurrection of the body. Being a Shaker, concluded Avery, required only three steps: confessing one's sins, adopting the celibate life, and dedicating one's body and soul to "Christ's Kingdom."

Avery played an important role in the Central Ministry, acting as a counterbalance to a growing trend toward liberalization within the Shaker communities. By the mid-nineteenth century, some Shakers were advocating a more open and ecumenical relationship with the world and the adoption of new theological ideas. Avery and Central Ministry elder Daniel Boler, however, believed that the Shakers should not abandon their principle of sectarianism. Avery was concerned with preserving the sharp contrast between the Shakers and the world that their founder, Ann Lee, had instituted. In 1888, in an effort to revive Lee's message, Avery re-edited and reissued the 1816 edition of the *Testimonies of the Life, Character, Revelations and Doctrines of Our Ever Blessed Mother Ann Lee, and the Elders with Her* (originally edited by Rufus Bishop and Seth Y. Wells), a collection of stories and traditions about Lee gathered from the Shakers who had known her personally. Avery made some editorial and language changes, but he did not tamper with Lee's basic message of celibacy and renunciation of the world.

In his lifetime, Avery witnessed many changes within the Shaker movement. Ecumenism continued to gain ground, while the Shaker population declined numerically. Yet Avery's faith in the triumph of Shakerism remained firm and is best expressed in his article, "Are the Shakers Dying Out?" published in the June 1879 issue of the *Shaker Manifesto*. While acknowledging that the Shakers were experiencing a decrease in numbers, he claimed that their religious principles had actually gained an ascendancy in the modern world. "Shakerism," he concluded, "is not '*dying out*,' nor preparing to die; and, were . . . the entire numbers who profess its faith, to be swept from the earth at once, the mental and spiritual light and truth in vigorous operation, would, phoenix-like, suddenly raise it again into immortal glory, prosperity and renown. *Shakerism never can 'die out!'*" (p. 125).

To ensure that Shakerism did not die out, Avery spent a great deal of time instructing communities with problems, and he traveled widely for the society during the last ten years of his life. He visited the eastern villages several times and made two trips to the western communities in Ohio and Kentucky. Some visits were more painful than others. In 1889 he presided over the dissolution of the North Union, Ohio, community.

Traveling and emotional strain took a toll on Avery's health, and when he died at Watervliet, his loss was felt both within and without the Shaker community. Elder Frederick Evans, a well-known leader of the progressive Shaker faction, put aside his own theological differences to write Avery's obituary. A non-Shaker friend sent her condolences, mourning the loss of "a noble, true type of manhood" (*Autobiography*, p. 32).

Avery had spent almost his entire life as a Shaker, working tirelessly to strengthen the bonds of community, and he became one of the most respected and well-loved leaders of the late nineteenth century. But his influence extended beyond his own surroundings. His life was a model of Shakerism for the world, and, despite his sectarian outlook, Avery's promotion of Shaker principles among the public made him an important intellectual link between the Shakers and the outside world.

• Many of Avery's unpublished writings are in the Shaker Collection of the Western Reserve Historical Society, Cleveland, Ohio. The journals that he kept during his tenure in the Central Ministry are located at the New York Public Library, New York City. Other papers are scattered among the various smaller Shaker archives. For names and addresses of these collections, see Edward R. Horgan, *The Shaker Holy Land: A Community Portrait* (1982), pp. 192–98.

Avery's major published works include his *Autobiography*, written in 1880 and published posthumously in 1891. His edition of the 1816 *Testimonies* was published under the almost identical title *Testimonies of the Life, Character, Revelations and Doctrines of Mother Ann Lee, and the Elders with Her* (1888). He was also a frequent contributor to the *Shaker Manifesto* and other journals, such as *Mind and Matter*, *Progressive Thinker*, and *Truthseeker*. For a complete list of Avery's publications, see Mary L. Richmond, *Shaker Literature: A Bibliography* (2 vols., 1977). For a discussion of Avery's role in Shakerism, see Stephen J. Stein, *The Shaker Experience* (1992).

Evans's obituary of Avery was published in Avery's autobiography and also appeared separately as *Obituary: Death of a Prominent Shaker in the Community at Watervliet, N.Y.* (1891). A short tribute to Avery is in Aurelia Gay Mace, *The Alethia: Spirit of Truth* (1899).

SUZANNE R. THURMAN

AVERY, John (18 Sept. 1837–1 Sept. 1887), linguist, was born in Conway, Massachusetts, the son of Joseph Avery and Sylvia Clary. Early in life he struck out on his own, attended Williston Seminary, and graduated from Amherst College in 1861. He taught at Leicester Academy and from 1862 to 1863 tutored at Amherst. The college awarded him an M.A. in 1864.

In 1863 Avery entered a four-year course in philology at Yale University under Professor William Dwight Whitney, America's leading Oriental scholar of the nineteenth century. While at Yale, Avery served as a tutor in physics at Sheffield Scientific School. Though he found physics distasteful, teaching it enabled him to support his linguistic studies. In New Haven he married Cornelia M. Curtiss of that city in 1866; they had one child.

Following the path of Whitney and many other renowned linguistic scholars of the nineteenth century, Avery traveled to Germany and studied Sanskrit and other subjects at Berlin and Tübingen in 1867–1868. Through his program at Yale and studies in Germany, Avery's scholarly interests were fixed on the languages and peoples of India for the rest of his life.

In 1870 he was elected to the American Oriental Society based in Boston. Founded in 1842, the society was the main scholarly organization in the United States devoted to studying Asia. The society met annually in the Northeast, and Avery presented papers at its meetings and published articles or notes in almost every issue of its journal until his death. In 1875 he became assistant editor of the *American Antiquarian and Oriental Journal*. He was also admitted to the Royal Asiatic Society, London.

From 1870 to 1871 Avery served as professor of Latin and then from 1871 to 1877 as professor of Greek at Iowa College in Grinnell, Iowa. From Iowa he moved to Bowdoin College in Maine, where he was professor of Greek from 1877 to 1887. Avery was known as a conscientious teacher whose awe-inspiring scholarship involving the knowledge of some twenty languages was often beyond his college students. Avery retired in 1887 and planned to write a book on the aboriginal tribes of India. He contracted a disease while nursing his son, however, and died later that same year, probably in Brunswick, Maine. The book was never finished.

Avery's two major published articles appeared in the *Journal of the American Oriental Society*, "Contributions to the History of Verb-Inflection in Sanskrit" (vol. 10 [1880]) and "The Unaugmented Verb-Forms of the Rig- and Atharva-Vedas" (vol. 11 [1884]). As a careful, methodical scholar, Avery determined in the first of these articles to trace the changes in verb inflection in Sanskrit by examining every instance of verb usage in a sequence of texts including one of the Vedas, one of the Brahmanas, the *Bhagavadgītā*, and *Nala*, the last two from the epic poem the *Mahābhārata*. He then classified and counted these usages and by elementary statistical methods showed the different percentages of usages in what he called the three stages of the development of the Sanskrit language: "the Vedic, or stage of unsettled linguistic usage"; "the Brahmanic, or stage of transition"; and, "the Epic or classical stage, when further change was debarred by inflexible grammatical laws." Avery described his field as "modern linguistic science" and contrasted his methods with those of ancient Indian Sanskrit grammarians. Through his investigations of Sanskrit morphology and his systemic approach, Avery wanted to show the evolutionary stages of ancient Indian linguistic development. Using terms common in nineteenth-century evolutionary thought, he referred frequently to the rude barbarian tribes gradually replaced by peoples at a higher level of development. As one of those nineteenth-century orientalists who thought Aryans in the West had raised science and civilization to a high level, he saw the Sanskrit-using Aryans of India as distant cousins but members of the same family.

In addition to his interest in the Aryans and the changes in the Sanskrit language, Avery had a keen desire to understand the aboriginal tribes of the northeast frontier area of India, mainly in Assam. Many of his research notes, which appeared annually between 1875 and 1887, were devoted to the rudimentary analysis of the languages of these tribes as reported by missionaries in the field. Thus he wrote about the Garos and the Khasis and also the Lepchas of Nepal. He was attracted by the great diversity of these tribes linguistically, their long-term resistance to incorporation into the Great Sanskritic Tradition of India, and the fact that they were just beginning to be studied. As an armchair linguist-anthropologist, Avery had to rely on reports by missionaries who had braved numerous difficulties in traveling to these remote areas and making contact with these tribes. His unfulfilled hope was to use these early reports as a basis for a book on the aboriginal tribes and their non-Indo-European languages.

One of the few scholars Whitney acknowledged in his fundamental work, *Sanskrit Grammar* (1879), Avery is remembered as a pioneer American scholar of Asian languages and a member of the small international fraternity of nineteenth-century scholars of Asia.

• Information about Avery can be found in the *Journal of the American Oriental Society*, where his scholarly reports, notes, and articles were published from 1870 to 1887. Nathaniel Schmidt, "Early Oriental Studies in Europe and the Work of the American Oriental Society, 1842–1922," in the 1923 volume briefly mentions Avery. An excellent book on nineteenth-century American interest in Asia (which also mentions Avery) is Carl T. Jackson, *The Oriental Religions and American Thought* (1981). Two important works on studies of ancient India in the nineteenth century are Raymond Schwab, *The Oriental Renaissance: Europe's Rediscovery of India and the East 1680–1880* (1984), and Nirad C. Chaudhuri, *Scholar Extraordinary: The Life of Professor the Rt. Hon. Friedrich Max Müller, P.C.* (1974).

LEONARD A. GORDON

AVERY, Martha Gallison Moore (6 Apr. 1851–8 Aug. 1929), lecturer and lay Catholic preacher, was born in Steuben, Maine, the daughter of Albion King Paris Moore, a house builder, and Katharine Leighton. She was educated in the village public school and then in a private dame school. When Martha was thirteen years old her mother died and she went to live with her grandfather, Samuel Moore, who was active in local and state politics. This atmosphere may have contributed to Martha's future political interest. As a young woman she carried on a millinery business in Ellsworth, Maine, where she joined a Unitarian congregation. It was there that she met Millard Avery, a fellow church member. They were married in March 1880; they had one daughter. In 1888 Avery and her daughter moved to Boston to be closer to her husband, who was working as a traveling salesman. That year she joined the newly organized First Nationalist Club of Boston and wrote articles for its publication, *The Nationalist*. She also lectured for the movement and held several elected offices. In 1890 her husband died.

Avery became disenchanted with nationalism, and in 1891 she joined the Socialist Labor party, working in the election campaign of that year. She served on the State Central Committee of the party from 1892 until 1895. By the mid-1890s she was regarded as one of the most active lecturers in the party, earning a living through speaking engagement fees. In 1897 she ran as the Socialist Labor party's candidate for state treasurer, the first woman to run on a state ticket in Massachusetts, but lost by a large margin.

In 1890 Avery founded the Karl Marx Class, a weekly lecture and discussion series to explore Marx's writings, as she felt too many socialists did not understand the theories. She was the director and chief lecturer. The secretary of the class was David Goldstein, a fellow socialist, who was to play a very important role in the rest of Avery's life. In 1901 the name of the class was changed to the Boston School of Political Economy.

In 1899, when her daughter Katherine graduated from high school, Avery sent her to a school in Quebec that was run by the Sisters of the Congregation de Notre Dame. A few months after arriving at the school, Katherine announced that she had decided to become

Catholic. She wrote Avery about the decision and in 1900 was baptized a Catholic. Katherine and Avery continued to correspond about Catholicism, with Katherine sending literature to explain her Catholic beliefs. A few years later Katherine entered the congregation as Sister St. Mary Martha.

At the same time that Avery began to learn more about Catholicism, she was becoming increasingly unhappy in the socialist movement. She became concerned that there was widespread atheism and immorality inherent in socialism. She took steps to try to curb these problems. At the party's state convention in 1902, she and some others introduced a motion that would have disqualified socialist speakers who attacked religion or who advocated violence or free love. The motion failed. After this, Avery began to criticize the party strongly, and in April 1903 was suspended by the Central Committee. At that point, she left the socialist movement.

Avery began to lecture and write against socialism, even working within the American Federation of Labor to oppose socialist ideas. In 1903 she and Goldstein, who had renounced socialism with her, authored *Socialism: The Nation of Fatherless Children*, which criticized socialism, saying it was atheistic and would destroy the family and society. The book sold quite well, and even received praise from Theodore Roosevelt.

In 1904 Avery converted to Catholicism and began to speak against socialism in Catholic forums. She spoke for social justice based on the principles enunciated by Pope Leo XIII in his encyclical *Rerum Novarum* (1891). In 1912 the Common Cause Society was founded by a group of Boston Catholic laymen. The society's purpose fit well with Avery's beliefs in social justice. She took part in the weekly question and answer forums, wrote articles for the magazine *Common Cause*, and served as president of the society from 1922 until her death.

In 1916 Avery, with Goldstein, who had also converted to Catholicism and had been lecturing on the Catholic faith and touring for the Knights of Columbus, decided to try using the street-corner propaganda methods of the socialists to preach Catholicism. In 1917 Avery and Goldstein founded the Catholic Truth Guild to explain Catholic beliefs, as well as to create a more favorable opinion of the church. With Avery as president and Goldstein as secretary, the guild held open-air meetings from a custom-made auto van painted yellow and white (papal flag colors) and equipped with a sounding board. They would distribute Catholic literature and begin the meetings with a lecture, concluding with a question and answer session. The meetings were well attended. Sixty-six years old when the guild was founded, Avery confined her lecturing to the Boston area and managed the business aspects, while Goldstein toured the country. She served as president until her death in Medford, Massachusetts.

After her conversion, Avery embraced the Catholic church's traditional position on the role of women, even speaking against woman suffrage. Although the American Catholic church did not formally take a stand against woman suffrage, many local church leaders openly opposed it. She spoke of the role of women as being in the home and offered the example of the Blessed Virgin Mary and other women who ministered to Jesus as models. In one article she spoke of the demand for equal rights as a "rebellious attempt to undo God's plan." Despite this attitude, Avery did show signs of being disturbed by the church's dim view toward women taking a leadership role. In one particular instance she seemed to chafe under some of the restrictions of Cardinal William O'Connell of Boston, reporting to Goldstein that "The Cardinal laid down the law . . . If . . . there are women who mean to work on their own will, they are not wanted." (Campbell, 1983, p. 109). It is also interesting to note that, although Avery and Goldstein had both been giving public lectures on Catholicism, it was Goldstein who was asked by Cardinal O'Connell in 1914 to travel and lecture for the Knights of Columbus, although Avery would liked to have done this. In addition, even though Avery and Goldstein had both planned the lay street preaching concept, it was Goldstein alone who, in 1916, approached the Cardinal for permission to proceed. Ironically, while Avery was Goldstein's mentor, and much of what they did was collaborative, he has probably had more written about him than she. Avery was nevertheless one of the foremost lay Catholic preachers of her time. In his autobiography Goldstein spoke of "the beauty of her intonation . . . even though her language and profound line of reasoning were . . . far above the power of her hearers to appreciate" (p. 7).

• Avery's papers are in the Beaton Institute at the University College of Cape Breton, Sydney, Nova Scotia, Canada. Other materials are in the David Goldstein-Martha Moore Avery Collection at Boston College. Avery wrote many articles and several other publications. In addition to *Socialism: The Nation of Fatherless Children* (1903), she and Goldstein coauthored two other books: *Bolshevism: Its Cure* (1919) and *Campaigning for Christ* (1924). Her series of six articles on woman suffrage in *America* ran from 9 Oct. 1915 until 13 Nov. 1915 and was reprinted in *Catholic Mind* 13 (8 Dec. 1915): 625–54. Biographies include Goldstein, *Autobiography of a Campaigner for Christ* (1936), and D. Owen Carrigan, *Martha Moore Avery: The Career of a Crusader* (1966). Other useful sources are Henry F. Bedford, *Socialism and the Workers in Massachusetts, 1886–1912* (1966) and Debra Campbell, *David Goldstein and the Lay Catholic Street Apostolate, 1917–1941* (1982). Articles include two by Carrigan, "Martha Moore Avery: Crusader for Social Justice," *Catholic Historical Review* 54 (Apr. 1968): 17–38, and "A Forgotten Yankee Marxist," *New England Quarterly* 42 (Mar. 1969): 23–43; and two by Campbell, "'I Can't Imagine Our Lady on an Outdoor Platform': Women in the Catholic Street Propaganda Movement," *U.S. Catholic Historian* 3 (Spring/Summer 1983): 103–14, and "A Catholic Salvation Army: David Goldstein, Pioneer Lay Evangelist," *Church History* 52, no. 3 (1983): 322–32. Obituaries are in the *New York Times*, 9 Aug. 1929, and the *Boston Globe*, 8 Aug. 1929.

CONNIE L. PHELPS

AVERY, Milton Clark (7 Mar. 1885–3 Jan. 1965), artist, was born in Sand Bank (later Altmar), New York, the son of Russell N. Avery, a tanner, and Esther March. In 1898 Avery moved to Wilson Station, Connecticut, where he worked in factories, as a file clerk, and at other occupations. Sometime between 1905 and 1911 Avery registered at the Connecticut League of Art Students with the intent of becoming a commercial artist, but when the lettering class closed, he joined the life drawing class. His interest piqued in fine art, Avery pursued this course of study under Charles Noel Flagg, the league's director, until 1918, when he enrolled at the School of the Art Society of Hartford. He studied at that institution until the age of thirty-four, probably because he worked instead of attending full-time. (Avery lived with and supported an extended family until he married.) Avery also attended the Art Students' League in New York City from 1926 to 1938, a circumstance that suggests that he viewed his education as a continuous process.

Avery moved to New York City in May 1925 in order to be with Sally Michel, a woman whom he had met in Gloucester, Massachusetts, during the summer of 1924. The two married in 1926, when Avery was forty and Michel was in her early twenties; they had one daughter. The family lived frugally in New York City during the winters, hosting informal gatherings for artist friends, and they spent the summers at the beach or in the country. The Averys returned to Gloucester several times and also sojourned in Jamaica and Rawsonville, Vermont; Provincetown, Massachusetts; Maitland, Florida; and other resort areas. Avery toured London, Paris, and the French Riviera in 1952.

Chronologies of Avery's personal life and accounts of his views on art are thin because he was exceptionally reticent and even disliked to write. As art historian Barbara Haskell puts it, "Milton Avery lived and worked as if to avoid biography. He left no significant autobiographical remnants. He wrote virtually nothing; participated in no organizations, and spoke with such reticence that scant oral testimony was recorded" (Haskell, p. 13). Art, it seems, was Avery's primary form of expression, an attitude that is summed up by his statement, "Why talk when you can paint?" (Haskell, p. 13).

Avery's career would not have succeeded without his wife's support. Also an artist, Sally Michel abandoned a career as a painter and worked as an illustrator in various capacities, including at Macy's Department Store, in order to allow her husband to develop his art. After marrying Michel, Avery never held a job again. He did not even teach, as many artists did even when financial gain was not an object. Michel firmly believed that any activity other than painting was a waste of Avery's time and would impede his growth.

Avery committed himself to a career as a painter in 1911, when he listed his occupation as an artist in the *Hartford City Directories*. Over the years he developed a modernist approach that stood out in its focus on formalism, especially the elements of shape and color, and in its lyrical mood. Formalism engaged Avery more so than portraying objects naturalistically or conveying political or philosophical messages. As he explained, "If I have left out the bridles or any other detail that is supposed to go with horses, trees or the human figure, the only reason for the omissions is that not only are these details unnecessary to the design but their insertion would disorganize space in the canvas already filled by some color or line" (Hobbs, p. 51). These latter goals interested many other artists at the time, however. Grant Wood, Ben Shahn, Thomas Hart Benton, and the dominant movement called "American Scene" painting rejected modernism in favor of depicting subject matter with ideological content.

Avery's modernism was probably inspired in part by the French painter Henri Matisse. Avery particularly admired Matisse's fauve works, which utilized bright colors and joyful themes. These traits influenced Avery's palette of rich pastels and his whimsical subject matter. In his early years Avery's approach was so in tune with Matisse's that critics dubbed him the "American Matisse" (Hobbs, p. 225).

Indigenous movements inspired Avery as well. His preference for pastel colors, for example, also derives from American impressionism, a movement that peaked in the early 1900s just as he was coming into his own. Additionally, exhibitions of American folk art were an added influence on the lyrical or "untutored" look of his subject matter. During the 1930s, when critics sought to posit a unique American aesthetic, folk art was highly esteemed.

In general, abstracted landscapes, seascapes, still lifes, and figure studies dominate Avery's *oeuvre*. He simplifies objects by reducing them to their basic forms, and does not attempt to render nature realistically. Avery flattens most volumes to the extent that he often causes them to appear parallel to the two-dimensional picture surface, and he all but eliminates perspectival cues. He omits most detail, choosing instead to describe a few key elements, often scratching these details into the paint in order to create thin lines that expose the white canvas beneath.

A good example of Avery's mature style is *Seated Girl with Dog* (1944, Collection of Mr. and Mrs. Roy R. Neuberger). The piece portrays, in abstract terms, a young girl holding her pet in her lap. The girl is a mass of solid shapes of color, including blue, lavender, pinks, and neutrals, and the dog is a bulky black shape. The only shadow, and thus the only attempt at volume, is found in the girl's featureless face, which is bisected by a shadow. The rest of the forms are flat, including the broad expanses of gray forming the wall behind the figure and the orange that makes up the building in the background. Details consisting of a few lines scratched onto the canvas describe windows and a fire escape in the distance.

A typical landscape by Avery is *White Sea* (1947, private collection, New York). In this piece, three craggy rock shapes punctuate a field of white that symbolizes a sea. A thin, horizontal strip of green covers the top eighth of the canvas to stand for an expanse of sky. Again, all shapes are flat and suggest nature rather than present it realistically.

One sees Avery's influence in the work of several younger painters. The color field artists Mark Rothko and Adolph Gottlieb, who knew Avery personally, especially benefited from their association with him. Both painters and their families vacationed with the Averys during summers away from New York City. Rothko incorporated Avery's broad fields of color into his paintings, while Gottlieb profited from his whimsical manner of representing shape.

Avery is distinguished for his foray into abstraction at a time when to paint in such a mode was unfashionable. Unlike most nontraditional artists, who wait for acknowledgment their entire careers, Avery received recognition for this approach soon after he was engaged in painting full time. His output was prodigious from that point onward. Only heart disease slowed Avery's production in his later years. The artist survived major heart attacks in 1949 and 1960 but succumbed during a third episode. He died in New York.

• The major archival resource is the Milton Avery Papers collection at the Archives of American Art, Smithsonian Institution. Avery's paintings are represented in most major American museums, including the Museum of Fine Arts, Boston; the Whitney Museum of American Art, the Museum of Modern Art, and the Metropolitan Museum of Art, New York; and the National Museum of American Art, the Phillips Collection, and the Hirshhorn Museum and Sculpture Garden, Washington, D.C. For information on his career, see Barbara Haskell, *Milton Avery* (1982), and Robert Hobbs, *Milton Avery* (1990). See also "The Reminiscences of Sally Michel Avery: Interviews with Louis Schaeffer," Oral History Research Office, Columbia University.

CATHERINE MCNICKLE CHASTAIN

AVERY, Oswald Theodore (21 Oct. 1877–20 Feb. 1955), bacteriologist, was born in Halifax, Nova Scotia, Canada, the son of Joseph Francis Avery, a Baptist minister, and Elizabeth Crowdy. Avery's family moved in 1887 to New York City, where he attended New York Male Grammar School. He received his diploma from that institution in 1893 and continued his education at the Colgate Academy. In 1896 he entered Colgate University, from which he received a B.S. in 1900. He then began the study of medicine at Columbia University's College of Physicians and Surgeons and received an M.D. in 1904. After completing his medical studies, Avery joined the clinical practice of a group of surgeons in New York City. He related well to patients, but because clinical work did not satisfy him intellectually or emotionally, he left the practice around 1907 and worked for a time with the New York City Board of Health and then the Sheffield Dairy Company in Brooklyn as a milk bacteriologist. Later in 1907 he became a bacteriologist at the Hoagland Laboratories in Brooklyn, where director Benjamin White became so impressed with Avery that within a short time he appointed him chief of the division. Avery's work on bacteria and their relationship to infectious disease attracted the attention of Rufus Cole, director of the hospital of the Rockefeller Institute (now University) of New York City, who invited him to become a member of its staff. Avery joined the institute in 1913 and became a full member there in 1923.

In his first fifteen years at the institute, Avery developed his knowledge of the pneumococcus with the assistance of a number of colleagues, including Karl G. Dernby, Glen E. Cullen, Theodore Thjotta, Hugh J. Morgan, and James M. Neill. His most significant early work began in 1916 when he joined with Alphonse R. Dochez, who had just discovered a specific chemical substance produced by pneumococci that was precipitated by antigen prepared against the same organism. A study of the material's chemical, which they named the specific soluble substance (SSS), showed it was not a degradation product but a true chemical produced by pneumococci. They also demonstrated that in acute pneumonia, pneumococci release this material into the bloodstream, and it passes into the urine. Further work in the early 1920s with Michael Heidelberger proved the SSS was a capsular polysaccharide specific for each pneumococcus.

The studies of organic chemist Walter Goebel, who joined Avery in 1924, demonstrated that the Friedlander bacillus (*Klebsiella pneumonia*) capsular polysaccharide not only bestowed immunologic specificity, but it also bore a close chemical resemblance to the type II pneumococcus polysaccharide. Even more significant was the demonstration that mice infected with type II pneumococci could be protected from pneumonia with serum from rabbits vaccinated with the encapsulated Friedlander bacilli. Furthermore, mice infected with Friedlander bacilli could be protected with pneumococci type II serum. These impressive findings demonstrated that immunity was not bestowed through biological direction but by the chemical configuration of the capsular substance.

In the late 1920s Frederick Griffith demonstrated that type II smooth (S) virulent pneumococci could be isolated from the blood of mice inoculated with large doses of nonvirulent pneumococci type I with a rough capsule (R) if they were injected at appropriate intervals prior to sacrifice with killed type II (S) pneumococci. Impressed with these findings, Avery encouraged Martin H. Dawson, a young Canadian scientist, to investigate the conditions most favorable for producing the transformation of the pneumococci from the rough to the smooth form. Dawson confirmed and extended Griffith's findings. Research physician James L. Alloway added to these studies by finding that the transformation could be brought about with a soluble fraction prepared from S pneumococci made by dissolving the cells in sodium deoxycholate and removing the cell fragments by filtration (Berkefeld filter). In 1935 Avery's colleague Colin MacLeod improved the method by killing the bacteria that produced the destructive enzyme before subjecting the material to solubilization with sodium deoxycholate. MacLeod's replacement, Maclyn McCarty, an investigator with a background in biological chemistry, advanced the understanding by showing the transforming substance of the viscous fraction was deoxyribonucleic acid (DNA). Avery, MacLeod, and McCarty published their classic paper "Transformation of Pneumococcal Types Induced by a Deoxyribonucleic Acid Fraction Isolated from Pneumococcus Type III" in the *Journal of Experimental Medicine* in 1944, disclosing that DNA was the hereditary substance. Although this paper initiated the genetic revolution, in it, Avery and his collaborators expressed the relevance of their work in muted tones. Despite the fact that these investigators made every effort to free their DNA preparation from contaminating protein and carbohydrate, other scientists continued to maintain that the transformation was produced by small amounts of contaminants bound to DNA. Because of this objection, total acceptance of DNA as the hereditary substance did not occur until 1952, when Alfred Hershey and Margaret Chase demonstrated, with double-labeled phage, that DNA alone was the hereditary substance.

Called "Fess" by his friends, Avery was a slender man, always neatly dressed, who warmly interacted with friends and colleagues. He had the ability to transform a conversation into a playful performance with gestures, mimicry, and vivid analysis. During his early years at the institute, he spent his summers by the sea in Gloucester, Massachusetts, where he developed a love for sailing. Through his friend Allen Chesney, he was introduced to Deer Island, Maine, where he spent the remaining summers of his life. He never married. Avery retired in 1948 and moved to be with his brother in Nashville, Tennessee, where he died.

• A few of Avery's papers are preserved in the archives of Rockefeller University, New York City, and the Tennessee State Library and Archives in Nashville. The development of Avery's scientific career can be followed in his published papers, the detailed annual reports he submitted to the board of directors of the Rockefeller Institute, and the reports to the trustees submitted by the director of the Rockefeller Hospital. Biographical accounts include Alphonse R. Dochez, "Oswald T. Avery," National Academy of Sciences, *Biographical Memoirs* 32 (1958): 32–49, and Rene J. Dubos, "Oswald Theodore Avery, 1877–1955," *Biographical Memoirs of Fellows of the Royal Society* 2 (1958): 35–48. See also Dubos, *The Professor, the Institute, and DNA* (1976). An obituary is in the *New York Times*, 21 Feb. 1955.

DAVID Y. COOPER

AVERY, Rachel G. Foster (30 Dec. 1858–26 Oct. 1919), suffragist, was born in Pittsburgh, Pennsylvania, the daughter of J. Heron Foster, the founder and editor of the *Pittsburgh Dispatch*, and Julia Manuel, an early advocate of women's rights. Both of her parents were members of the Society of Friends (Quakers); her father's pacifist religion, however, did not prevent him from serving as a colonel in the Union army during the Civil War. Her parents also strongly opposed slavery and were active in the abolitionist movement. Her mother, a native of Johnstown, Pennsylvania, was a friend of Elizabeth Cady Stanton, also of Johnstown, and hosted some of the earliest suffrage meetings in the Foster home.

Rachel's father died when she was ten. Left financially secure, her mother moved the family to Philadelphia, Pennsylvania, where Rachel and her sister studied in private schools and became active in Lucretia Mott's Citizens' Suffrage Association. In the late 1870s Julia Foster took her daughters to Europe where they traveled for several months.

At the National Woman Suffrage Association (NWSA) meeting in Washington, D.C., in 1879, Rachel met Susan B. Anthony, who immediately took a liking to the young, enthusiastic suffragist. Anthony later called Rachel "one of my girls" and "my adopted niece." The following year Rachel was named secretary of the NWSA. Part of her duties included organizing suffrage meetings in the Midwest and New England in 1879–1880. In 1882 she was in charge of efforts in Nebraska to pass a woman suffrage amendment to the state constitution.

Rachel, who was independently wealthy, made generous monetary contributions to the suffrage cause, and in 1883 she invited Anthony, whom she called "Aunt Susan," to accompany her to Europe. During this excursion, while visiting England, Rachel was presented at the Court of St. James. For the next two decades she acted as a counselor to Anthony as well as an organizer of Anthony's lecture tours. In 1885 Rachel attended the University of Zurich in Switzerland, where she studied political science. After returning to the United States, in November 1888 she married Cyrus Miller Avery, a manufacturer's representative and the son of Rosa Miller, a leader of the suffrage movement in Chicago. They had three children—two of their own, and one whom Rachel had adopted the year before—and made their home in Chicago. Threatened by Rachel's marriage—she was jealous of sharing her intimate friend with another—Anthony, who was unmarried, also feared that Avery might lose interest in the women's rights movement and in feminism itself as a result of the marriage. In time Anthony acquiesced to Avery's marriage, especially because the latter remained constant in her work and in her friendship with Anthony. Avery eventually arranged to provide financial security for Anthony in her old age, by soliciting donations and contributing her own money to purchase an annuity for Anthony.

Avery helped plan and finance the suffrage campaign in Kansas in 1887 and again in 1892. Along with May Wright Sewall, Frances Perkins of the Women's Christian Temperance Union, and Anthony, she organized the 1888 meeting in Washington, D. C., that established the International Council of Women, sending 10,000 invitations worldwide. She was corresponding secretary of the council from 1888 to 1893 and for its American branch, the National Council of Women, from 1891 to 1894.

Avery worked diligently over the years to unite the National Woman Suffrage Association, of which she was secretary, and the American Woman Suffrage Association, which eschewed the radicalism of Anthony's moral and social philosophy and favored a grassroots campaign for suffrage on the local and state levels.

(Anthony and the NWSA wanted change at the federal level with an amendment to the Constitution.) She achieved her goal in February 1890 when the NWSA and the AWSA, under Alice Stone Blackwell, the daughter of Lucy Stone and Henry Blackwell, overcame more than twenty years of acrimony and merged, becoming the National American Woman Suffrage Association. Avery served as corresponding secretary of the newly united association until 1906. Following the passage of the Nineteenth Amendment in 1920, which gave women the right to vote, the NAWSA became the League of Women Voters.

Avery helped organize the World's Congress of Representative Women in Chicago in 1893, which was held in conjunction with the Columbian Exposition. Three years later another major controversy beset the now united suffrage movement and threatened the friendship between Avery and Anthony. The year before Elizabeth Cady Stanton had published *The Woman's Bible*, a feminist commentary on the Old Testament. The book used isigesis as its method of interpretation, whereby each commentator (all women) evaluated passages according to whether the passage supported or contradicted her own opinion or ideology. The wholly subjective book lacked any critical investigation of the Scriptures, relying solely on the commentator's bias. At the NAWSA convention in Washington, D.C., Avery denounced the book in her annual report as "without either scholarship or literary value, set forth in a spirit which is neither that of reverence or inquiry" (DuBois, p. 189). Anthony defended Stanton, but to no avail. Avery and a majority at the convention supported a resolution declaring that the NAWSA was nonsectarian and disavowing any connection with Stanton's book. Avery and Anthony disagreed bitterly on the issue, but in time they were reconciled.

After retiring as secretary of NAWSA in 1901, Avery moved to Philadelphia and then lived in Switzerland until 1907. She was secretary of the International Woman Suffrage Alliance from its 1904 founding in Berlin, Germany, until 1909. After returning to the United States she became NAWSA's first vice president, serving from 1907 to 1910; in the latter year she and several other officers resigned because of a disagreement with Anna Howard Shaw, the president. Between 1908 and 1910 Avery was president of the Pennsylvania Woman Suffrage Association. In this capacity she persuaded the state chapter of the Federation of Labor to endorse woman suffrage.

Avery died of pneumonia in Philadelphia, a year before the ratification and enactment of the Nineteenth Amendment. An important and steadfast figure in securing the vote for women, she was recognized for her organizational skills, keen political judgment, and business acumen.

• For a survey of the women's rights movement in the nineteenth century, see Miriam Gurko, *The Ladies of Seneca Falls: The Birth of the Woman's Rights Movement* (1974). There are references to Avery in Ellen Carol DuBois, *Elizabeth Cady Stanton and Susan B. Anthony: Correspondence, Writings, Speeches* (1981), and Ida H. Harper, *The Life and Work of Susan B. Anthony* (3 vols., 1898–1908). See also Alma Lutz, *Susan B. Anthony* (1959), and Eleanor Flexner, *Century of Struggle* (1959).

GEOFFREY GNEUHS

AVERY, Samuel Putnam (17 Mar. 1822–11 Aug. 1904), wood engraver, art dealer, and rare book and print collector, was born in New York City, the son of Samuel Avery and Hannah Parke. His father, variously listed as a shoe maker and a leather merchant, died of cholera in 1832. Through an apprenticeship in a banknote company, Avery was able to learn the essentials of the wood-engraving trade. Officially recorded as an engraver in the 1842 New York City directory, he earned a living by engraving labels and making handbills for local merchants. At the same time he began a long involvement with the publishing trade, working for periodicals such as *Appleton's*, *Harper's*, and the *New York Herald*. In 1844 Avery married Mary Ann Ogden; they had six children.

By 1847 Avery was able to hire an assistant, Isaac G. Pesoa. Pesoa became skilled enough to take over routine work, which freed Avery to illustrate several anthologies, including *The American Joe Miller* (1853), *Laughing Gas: An Encyclopedia of Wit, Wisdom and Wind by Sam Slick, Jr.* (1854), and *The Harp of a Thousand Strings* (1858).

Another of Avery's activities was the publishing of line engravings and photographs of American paintings. Both publishing and engraving careers brought him into contact with local artists working as illustrators to supplement their incomes. He bought modest samples of their work, as well as books of art, and invited those interested in the visual arts to "artist's evenings" at his home in Brooklyn.

Avery's career took a new direction when a Baltimore businessman, William T. Walters, began to collect American paintings. Walters needed the help of an agent in New York to commission pictures and ship the finished work to him. When Walters moved to Paris during the Civil War, Avery continued to assist him. He began working in collaboration with George A. Lucas, a Paris-based art agent from Baltimore who was recommended by Walters. Avery turned the engraving business over to Pesoa, and in December 1864 Avery opened an establishment on the corner of Broadway and Fourth Street in New York City for the purpose of selling engravings, fine oil paintings, and art objects. He received the endorsement of forty-eight American artists and with Lucas's help began to import modern European art. In addition to running his gallery, Avery also managed a series of annual art auctions over a period of sixteen years.

In 1867, when American artists were invited to exhibit their work at the Universal Exhibition in Paris, Avery was officially appointed commissioner to supervise assembling, packing, and hanging work for the American section. Before leaving New York he liquidated his collection of American art in order to be able to buy work abroad. During the six months Avery spent in Europe, with Lucas's assistance he was able to meet and familiarize himself with the work of prominent French artists such as William-Adolphe Bougereau, Jules Breton, Jean-Léon Gérôme, and Ernest Meissonier, as well as German artist Ludwig Knaus. Avery also learned about the intricacies of coping with foreign bankers, shipping agents, and arcane export and import procedures.

During the 1870s Avery made annual buying trips to Europe. Some of his acquisitions were sold at his gallery, but he also commissioned art for specific clients, including William Henry Vanderbilt, Edwin Dennison Morgan, William W. Corcoran, and James Jerome Hill. As secretary of the art committee of the Union League Club, Avery was at the meeting that resulted in the founding of the Metropolitan Museum of Art. He later became a lifelong trustee of the institution.

By the end of the 1880s Avery spent less of his time in the gallery. His son Samuel P. Avery, Jr., assisted in the daily running of the business and established his own gallery in 1888. As president of the Grolier Club, founded in 1884 for the purpose of "literary study and promotion of the arts pertaining to the production of books," Avery, Sr., was able to devote more time and energy to his interest in rare books and exceptional bindings. He was an influential print collector, and with the collaboration of George Lucas he amassed an outstanding collection of nineteenth-century prints. He was instrumental in establishing a separate print room at the New York Public Library, and he installed its first keeper of prints, Frank Weitenkampf, in December 1899. In 1900 Samuel Avery presented the library with a gift of 19,000 prints.

A pioneer in the field of selling both American and European art in New York, Avery reveals in his correspondence the extent to which his opinions and wisdom were appreciated by artists, collectors, and other art dealers. Avery's business interests, his involvement with social reform, and his support of the arts moved him to join a great many social clubs and associations. He founded the Avery Architectural Library at Columbia College, New York, in memory of his son Henry Ogden Avery, an architect who died in April 1890. Samuel Avery died in New York City.

• Diaries, correspondence, scrapbooks, and samples of Avery's wood engravings are collected at the Metropolitan Museum of Art. Microfilms of some of this material is available through the Archives of American Art. Avery's writings include "Progress of the Fine Arts in New York during the Last Fifty Years," in *Lossing's History of New York City, 1830–1880*, ed., Benson J. Lossing (1884). See also *The Diaries 1871–1882 of Samuel P. Avery, Art Dealer*, ed. M. Fidell-Beaufort et al. (1979). Biographical information is in R. Sieben-Morgan, *Samuel P. Avery (1822–1904) Engraver on Wood: A Biographical Study* (1940; rev. ed., 1942). Other worthwhile sources are Fidell-Beaufort, "A Measure of Taste: Samuel P. Avery's Art Auctions, 1864–1880," *Gazette des Beaux-Arts*, Sept. 1982, pp. 87–89; Fidell-Beaufort and J. K. Welcher, "Some Views of Art Buying in New York in the 1870s and 1880s," *Oxford Art Journal* 5 (1982): 48–55; and Fidell-Beaufort, "Brooklyn Art Gatherings in the 1850s," *Confrontation* (1983): 90–95. An obituary is in the *New York Times*, 13 Aug. 1904.

MADELINE FIDELL-BEAUFORT

AVERY, Sewell Lee (4 Nov. 1874–31 Oct. 1960), business executive, was born in Saginaw, Michigan, the son of Waldo Allard Avery, a prosperous lumberman, and Ellen Lee. He attended Michigan Military Academy and the University of Michigan Law School, where he received his LL.B. in 1894. After graduation he worked as manager of the Western Plaster Works plant in Alabaster, Michigan, a position he secured through his father, who was part owner of the plant. In 1899 he married Hortense Lenore Wisner, with whom he had four children.

In 1901, when Western Plaster Works merged with a large number of other midwestern companies to form the United States Gypsum Company, Avery assumed control of the new firm's Buffalo, New York, office. Next he became the sales manager for a large Ohio district headquartered in Cleveland. In 1905, after bitter rivalry within the company had twice brought about its reorganization, Avery, who along with his brother Waldo owned most of the company stock, became its president. He served in that capacity until 1937; he was chairman until 1951.

Avery was responsible for turning U.S. Gypsum into the country's chief supplier of building materials. In September 1929, in anticipation of the stock market crash and subsequent depression, he reduced his work force by 50 percent. During the 1930s, as many of his competitors went out of business, Avery was able to use his firm's retained earnings to expand. The company showed a large profit during the depression, and although employees might have bemoaned his methods, stockholders were pleased. Acclaimed for his extraordinary organizational abilities, he was invited to join the boards of numerous major American companies. He was also named a trustee of the University of Chicago.

In 1931 Henry P. Davison, a partner in J. P. Morgan and Co., asked Avery to take charge of Montgomery Ward and Co., which at the time was the country's second largest mail-order firm but whose success was threatened as a result of poor management during the 1920s. Avery at first declined the offer, but in November he accepted the position of chief executive officer in return for stock options, whose value stood to increase dramatically should he succeed in turning Ward's around.

While maintaining his position at U.S. Gypsum, Avery worked to save Ward, transforming it from a strictly mail-order operation to one that included retail outlets. He revised its catalog, discontinued unprofitable lines, centralized its management, and hired new managers. He also kept a close eye on the performance of his 35,000 employees, 22,000 of whom had left the firm by 1934. That same year the company had become so profitable that Avery's stock options were worth $1.8 million.

Although Montgomery Ward benefited from New Deal agricultural programs that improved the rural economy and allowed farmers—major customers of Ward's—to afford to purchase items from its catalog, Avery did not support New Deal measures. When World War II began he became involved in a long dispute with the War Labor Board, which, in its effort to prevent work stoppages during the war, supported the inclusion of a "maintenance of membership" clause in labor contracts. Avery opposed the clause, without which union organization of Ward's sales staff would be hindered.

When Avery rejected a contract containing the clause in April 1944, the government took over his firm (under the authority of the 1943 Smith-Connally Act). Avery refused to leave his office and was carried out by soldiers. A photograph of his eviction appeared on front pages throughout the nation, and opinion polls showed that 61 percent of respondents sided with Avery. The matter went to court, Avery testified before Congress, and troops took over his plants again in December 1944 and October 1945. Avery continued to oppose the "maintenance of membership" clause and remained a national symbol of opposition to government regulation of business.

After the war Avery experienced new problems. While other merchandisers expanded, Ward's opened no new stores and carried no surplus inventory. In expectation of another depression, Avery built up Ward's cash reserves, which in 1954 almost equaled Ward's annual sales. But Avery was wrong in his assessment this time. In 1941 Ward's was three-quarters the size of Sears, Roebuck, its main competitor; in 1954 it was only one-quarter the size. Avery continually fired Ward's top managers: four presidents and forty vice presidents came and went during his leadership. When Louis E. Wolfson, a Florida promoter, campaigned to assume control of the company, Avery defeated him. Ward's stockholders, however, dismayed by Avery's behavior, forced him to resign as chairman in April 1955.

After the death of his wife the following April, Avery resigned as a member of Ward's board. Despite the firm's subsequent efforts to rebound from the consequences of Avery's postwar management, including the recruitment of new management from Sears, it continued to decline as a major retailer. Avery died in Chicago, leaving a personal fortune estimated at more than $100 million.

Avery's reputation rests on a business genius that masterfully dealt with the challenges of consolidation in the early twentieth century and depression in the 1930s and on an individualism that made him a symbol of the entrepreneur resisting government control. He was so long active and successful that ultimately his refusal to accept changes in government-business relations and the post–World War II marketplace caught up with him and Montgomery Ward.

• For general information on Avery's business career, see *Business Week*, *Time*, and *Newsweek*, 1932–1956. Obituaries are in the *New York Times*, 1 Nov. 1960, as well as in *Time* and *Newsweek*, 14 Nov. 1960.

CARL RYANT

AVERY, Tex (26 Feb. 1908–26 Aug. 1980), director of animated films, was born Frederick Bean Avery in Taylor, Texas. Little is known about his family, except that he was a lineal descendant of Judge Roy Bean, from whom his middle name was derived. Interested in art as a youth, Avery took a three-month summer course in art taught by professional newspaper cartoonists at the Chicago Art Institute a year before graduating, in June 1927, from North Dallas High School, where he was a cartoonist for the yearbook and drew a cartoon strip. Two years later, he headed to California seeking a position as a comic strip artist. Finding no opportunities in that field, he took a job in the inking and painting department at the Walter Lantz Studio, which was producing Oswald the Rabbit cartoons. Remaining at the studio from 1930 to 1935, he painted cartoon backgrounds, worked as an in-betweener completing sequences to bridge the key drawings produced by the animators, wrote gags and stories, and directed two cartoons, although without screen credit.

In 1936 Avery left Lantz for a higher-paying position as a director at Warner Bros., where Leon Schlesinger, head of the cartoon division, gave him a chance to prove himself with a staff of talented animators—Chuck Jones, Bob Clampett, and Bob Cannon. Encouraging their creativity, Schlesinger set them up in what was known as "Termite Terrace," a small shack on the Sunset lot away from the day-to-day activities of the studio, where they developed an exaggerated, distinctive style of animation that was wild, brash, and funny rather than cute. Avery's first directorial effort at Warner Bros., *Golddiggers of '49* (1936), showcased a new star, Porky Pig, whose box-office success assured his appearance in subsequent films. In one of them, *Porky's Duck Hunt* (1937), Avery and his crew introduced the frenetic Daffy Duck, who proved to be a perfect foil for Porky. Other characters followed. Avery directed films featuring Egghead, a silly straight man who was eventually transformed into the character of Elmer Fudd. In 1940 Avery directed *A Wild Hare*, teaming Elmer Fudd with another Warner Bros. character, Bugs Bunny. Although Bugs had appeared in two earlier films, his character under Avery's direction softened: Rather than being obnoxious and annoying, Bugs became clever, smart alecky, and casual. Avery also provided Bugs with his trademark phrase—"What's up, Doc?"—a popular greeting from Avery's hometown. According to animator Michael Maltese, Avery "took Bugs Bunny and instilled into him the character that *made* Bugs Bunny." Nevertheless, Avery downplayed characterization, believing that "what you did with a character was even more important than the character itself. Bugs Bunny could have been a bird."

At Warner Bros., what most defined Avery's style of animation was his use of gags. Fascinated by the possibilities of animation, Avery noted, "We used any kind of distortion that couldn't possibly happen." This often included visual puns involving abnormal size or distortion, such as a surprised character's eyes popping out of his head or his jaw falling to the ground. In all cases, the body parts are restored to their natural state, resulting in no real injury. Avery also proved to be a master of the running gag—fast-paced, perfectly timed successive gags, each one funnier and more outrageous than the one before. Another characteristic of Avery's cartoons was his playful treatment of the conventions of the film medium. In *Porky's Preview* (1941), for example, Porky pens his own cartoon in which he is the star; other Avery cartoons showed characters falling off the frame. In one series of Warner Bros. cartoons, Avery poked fun at travelogs and educational films, featuring, for example, a lizard doing a striptease step as she sheds her skin. All in all, Avery's contributions to Warner Bros. animation were considerable. His films exhibited a fast-paced, freewheeling technique that was the antithesis of Disney's, helping to define the Warner Bros. style and prompting Steve Schneider, in his history of Warner Bros. animation, to say, "More than any other person, Tex Avery was the father of Warner Bros. cartoons."

While at Warner Bros., Avery's films were credited to Fred Avery; however, in 1942, after moving to Metro-Goldwyn-Mayer, Avery was billed by his nickname, Tex Avery. In charge of his own cartoon unit at MGM until 1954, Avery, continuing many of the same themes and techniques that had won him success at Warner Bros., developed several new characters, among them Blitz Wolf, Screwball Squirrel, Dan McGoo, and Droopy. Avery's animation during this period was also characterized by adult themes, especially sex, best exemplified by the character of the Wolf, who, in cartoons such as *Red Hot Riding Hood* (1943) and *Wild and Woolfy* (1945), lusts after a voluptuous woman named Red. His eyes pop, his jaw drops, and his tongue rolls until he finally shatters to the ground, a victim of his own sexual desire. From 1954 to 1955 Avery returned to the studio of Walter Lantz, who had given him his start in animation, and directed four cartoons, two featuring Chilly Willy. He then turned his animation efforts to advertising, making commercials for Cascade Productions and creating such memorable characters as the Raid bugs and the Frito Bandito. In 1979 he began work at Hanna-Barbera Cartoons and remained there until his death in Burbank, California.

Avery's private life has remained very private. There are scant references to his being a "family man" and having a daughter, but beyond that no information is available.

Throughout his career, which resulted in his association with various studios and the creation of over 130 cartoons, Avery became a high-profile animator, recognized more for his gags and directorial style than for his drawings. His detractors denounced his cartoons' frenetic pace, irreverence, violence, sexual innuendos, and corny visual humor. Nevertheless, Avery won many awards as well as praise from audiences, critics, and other animators. His films *Detouring America* (1939), *A Wild Hare* (1940), and *The Blitz Wolf* (1942) were nominated for Academy Awards. He won first prize in the Venice Publicity Festival for *Calo-Tiger* in 1958 and was the recipient of the Television Commercials Council Award in 1960 and the Annie Award from the ASIFA (Association Internationale du Film d'Animation) in 1974. Avery's frenzied, surreal, anarchistic cartoons revolutionized animation and influenced a generation of animators. Studio head Walter Lantz said of Avery, "He was just one of the greats of our industry. I can't praise Tex too much." Likewise, animator Chuck Jones, in his autobiography *Chuck Amuck*, wrote of Avery, "I learned from him the most important truth about animation: animation is the art of timing, a truth applicable as well to all comedy. And the most brilliant masters of timing were Keaton, Chaplin, Laurel and Hardy, Langdon—and Fred (Tex Avery)."

• Two book-length studies of Tex Avery exist: Joe Adamson, *Tex Avery: King of Cartoons* (1975), and Patrick Brion, *Tex Avery* (1984), the latter in French. Useful essays on Avery include Jonathan Rosenbaum, "Dream Masters II: Tex Avery," *Film Comment*, Jan.–Feb. 1975, pp. 70–73; Ronnie Scheib, "Tex Arcana: The Cartoons of Tex Avery," in *The American Animated Cartoon*, ed. Danny Peary and Gerald Peary (1980); and Jeff Lenburg, "Tex Avery," in his *The Great Cartoon Directors* (1993). An interview of Tex Avery by Joe Adamson appears in *Take One* (Montreal), Jan./Feb. 1970. An obituary is in the *New York Times*, 28 Aug. 1980.

KATHY MERLOCK JACKSON

AXIS SALLY. *See* Gillars, Mildred Elizabeth.

AXTELL, Samuel Beach (14 Oct. 1819–6 Aug. 1891), politician, lawyer, and jurist, was born near Columbus, Ohio, the son of Samuel Loree Axtell and Nancy Sanders, farmers. Axtell graduated from Western Reserve College in Hudson, Ohio, and, after studying law, was admitted to the bar. He married Adaline S. Williams in 1840, and in 1843 they moved to Mount Clemens, Michigan, where Axtell established a law practice. The couple had at least one child. In 1851 Axtell migrated to California, where he invested in the booming mining industry and practiced law. Politically active as a Democrat, he helped organize Amador County east of Sacramento in 1854 and was elected as the new county's first district attorney, a post to which he was reelected in 1856 and 1858.

In 1860 Axtell relocated to San Francisco, where he practiced law until 1866, when he was elected to Congress from the First Congressional District. Reelected in 1868, Axtell changed his party affiliation to Republican during his second term in Congress, motivated by his support for President Ulysses S. Grant (and Grant's support for the transcontinental railroad so important to Californians). His service in the Fortieth and Forty-first Congresses lasted from 4 March 1867 to 3 March 1871. Although Axtell did not stand for re-election in 1870, he maintained his political contacts after returning to California.

In late 1874 Grant appointed Axtell governor of the territory of Utah to replace Governor George L. Woods, who had been forced to resign after his refusal to certify a Mormon as the elected delegate to Congress had exacerbated the feud between Mormons and non-Mormons in the territorial Republican party. Within days after taking office in Salt Lake City on 2 February 1875, Axtell, presumably acting on Grant's orders, delivered the certificate of election to its rightful holder. But it was beyond the ability of any federal official to heal the animosity between Mormon and non-Mormon forces. Axtell was quickly engulfed by charges that he was subservient to the Mormon wing of the party, and anti-Mormon forces besieged the president with demands for Axtell's removal. By late May 1875 Axtell was in Washington, D.C., attempting to break the stalemate with a personal lobbying effort. But Grant had no wish to alienate himself from either side in the dispute and when Governor Marsh Giddings of New Mexico died unexpectedly on 3 June, Grant made use of the vacancy to resolve his political dilemma, ordering Secretary of the Interior Columbus Delano on 5 June to "offer Axtell Governorship of New Mexico."

Eager to escape from an untenable situation, Axtell resigned as Utah governor on 20 June and traveled to Santa Fe, where he took the oath of office as territorial governor on 30 July 1875. He was hampered from the start by charges of pro-Mormonism, which persisted even after Mormon leader Brigham Young publicly declared false the rumor that Axtell had been baptized a Mormon. Axtell compounded his problems by openly allying himself with members of the notoriously power-hungry "Santa Fe Ring" of politicians, whose manipulations of the law and the economy outraged many New Mexicans. Having compromised his position by jettisoning any claim to nonpartisan fair-mindedness, Axtell proved singularly ineffective in dealing with the twin evils of political factionalism and rampant lawlessness that beset the frontier territory.

In September 1875 northeastern New Mexico's Colfax County exploded into violence with the murder of a Methodist minister who had denounced the ring's corrupt control of the Dutch-owned Maxwell Land Grant and Railroad Company, which was claiming large portions of the public domain. A company lawyer accused of the murder fled to Santa Fe, where ring members persuaded Axtell to sign a bill moving jurisdiction of the case to another county less antagonistic toward the company. Colfax residents, including reform-minded lawyer Frank Springer, were incensed by the governor's action and pleaded with him to investigate their complaints personally. Axtell refused, insisting he saw no reason to believe the ring or the company had anything to do with the minister's death. By 1876 Axtell himself was involved in the affair: an unpublished letter from Axtell to the territorial district attorney seems to indicate that the governor was planning to have Springer murdered.

Axtell's protestations to Interior Secretary Carl Schurz that he desired nothing but "the just enforcement of the laws" might have saved his administration but for a second eruption of politically and economically inspired violence that took place in southeastern New Mexico's Lincoln County during 1877 and 1878. The Lincoln County War was a deadly competition between rival groups of merchants and cattlemen. The faction headed by Lawrence Murphy and James Dolan was guilty of numerous infractions of the law. Their opponents, led by lawyer Alexander McSween and Englishman John Tunstall, had local support but found themselves hard-pressed to survive. Murphy controlled the sheriff's office and also had strong backing from leaders of the Santa Fe Ring such as the powerful Republican Thomas B. Catron.

Axtell's response to the brutal killing of Tunstall by a sheriff's posse was to accept unquestioningly the sheriff's version of events; to obtain President Rutherford B. Hayes's acquiescence to the use of federal troops to aid the sheriff; and to refuse to meet with county residents, who attempted to present evidence that the county's sole law enforcement agency was under the control of Murphy and Dolan. In violation of a territorial law he himself had signed, Axtell revoked the authority of a justice of the peace, whose issuance of warrants for the arrest of Tunstall's killers had angered Dolan forces. When Dolan complained to the governor about a newly named sheriff, Axtell removed the man from office and appointed a sheriff more acceptable to the Murphy-Dolan faction.

In April 1878 the president and Schurz began receiving detailed reports from a British visitor to Lincoln on Axtell's role in the breakdown of law and order. In May the Justice and Interior departments dispatched federal investigator Frank Warner Angel to New Mexico, where he undertook a thorough assessment of the actions of territorial officials. The report he submitted to the president in August 1878 confirmed the allegations made against Axtell. On 1 September the president suspended Axtell from office; Civil War general Lew Wallace succeeded Axtell. Republican leaders in the territory continued to support Axtell, believing he had been treated unfairly.

Republicans in Ohio, where Axtell settled after leaving Santa Fe, proved less accepting. When it became known in 1881 that President James A. Garfield was considering Axtell for a judicial appointment, party leaders in the Akron area wrote the president that "his reputation as a politician in this community is unsavory to the greatest degree." Nevertheless, on 1 August 1882 President Chester A. Arthur, Garfield's successor, appointed Axtell chief justice of the supreme court of New Mexico. Axtell held the position until 11 May 1885, when his resignation was accepted by President Grover Cleveland. Axtell was a credible justice in a territory still dealing with the complex change from a Spanish-Mexican legal system to one rooted in

Anglo-American law, particularly with regard to land and water use.

After retiring from the court, Axtell remained active in party affairs and in 1890 became chairman of the territorial Republican committee. He died while visiting relatives in Morristown, New Jersey.

Axtell's career reflected the social and economic trends that shaped the nation as a whole in the post–Civil War period. From rural, farming, Democratic roots, Axtell was drawn to the law, as a vehicle for advancement, and to the West, where an ethos of profiting from resource exploitation prevailed. He moved into a Republican party that increasingly subordinated rural, agricultural interests to urban, industrial interests. And he notably embodied the Gilded Age linkage of money and politics through the legislative and judicial processes.

Yet the fact that Axtell's career moved in tandem with these developments does not entirely explain his penchant for repeatedly embroiling himself in political controversies in a manner that discredited him as well as his party. He himself remained convinced that in both Utah and New Mexico he was a victim of faction-based enmities that had existed before his arrival on the scene. While not an atypical Gilded Age politician, Axtell more than most exhibited a blind adherence to the notion that an officeholder might justifiably give more weight to the interests of personal political allies than to the welfare of the general public. Although New Mexico admittedly was one of the more difficult territories to govern as a result of its large foreign-born population and lack of infrastructure, historians agree that the territory experienced a heightening of political divisiveness and an increase in civil strife because of Axtell's actions while governor. Axtell's earlier years as a capable congressman and his later years as a knowledgeable justice restore a degree of luster to his historical reputation.

• Documents pertaining to Axtell, including his nominations and appointments to office during the administrations of presidents Grant, Hayes, Garfield, and Arthur may be found in the governors' papers and the miscellaneous territorial papers, State Records Center and Archives, Santa Fe, N. Mex.; and U.S. Department of Interior, Appointments File, 1849–1879, RG 48, and New Mexico Territorial Papers Collection, RG 233, National Archives, Washington, D.C.

A full biography of Axtell remains to be written, and information concerning his formative years is scant. As a result of the controversial nature of his tenures in several appointive positions, Axtell has been the subject of considerable attention in studies of western frontier history. For information about his political relationships and administrative actions, see Hubert H. Bancroft, *History of Utah* (1889); Maurice Garland Fulton, *History of the Lincoln County War* (1968); Calvin Horn, *New Mexico's Troubled Years: The Story of the Early Territorial Governors* (1963); William A. Keleher, *Violence in Lincoln County 1869–1881* (1957); Robert W. Larson, *New Mexico's Quest for Statehood, 1846–1912* (1968); Carole Larson, *Forgotten Frontier: The Story of Southeastern New Mexico* (1993); Jim Berry Pearson, *The Maxwell Land Grant* (1961); Frank D. Reeve, *History of New Mexico*, vol. 2 (1961); Robert M. Utley, *High Noon in Lincoln* (1987); and Victor Westfall, *Thomas Benton Catron and His Era* (1973). A substantive obituary appears in the *Santa Fe New Mexican*, 7 Aug. 1891.

CAROLE B. LARSON

AYCOCK, Charles Brantley (1 Nov. 1859–4 Apr. 1912), lawyer and governor of North Carolina, was born in Wayne County, North Carolina, the son of Benjamin Aycock and Serena Hooks. The youngest of ten children of a prosperous, slaveholding family whose farmlands by 1863 exceeded a thousand acres, Charles Aycock spent his early years in a rural setting. His father, an active member of the Democratic party, served as clerk of court of Wayne County for eight years and as a member of the North Carolina Senate from 1863 to 1866. Serena Aycock managed the family properties in her husband's absence, but she could not read or write, and her lack of an education profoundly influenced young Charles. Although the Civil War imposed hardships on the Aycocks, their holdings expanded during the Reconstruction era. Benjamin Aycock's support of the Confederacy and disdain for Radical Reconstruction and the enfranchisement of freedmen shaped Charles's own politics.

Aycock completed his secondary training at the Kinston Collegiate Institute in 1877. During a break in his college career, he taught school at Fremont in 1875–1876. The next year he enrolled in the University of North Carolina, where he early demonstrated talent as a debater, an orator, and a student leader. During the summers of 1878 and 1879 he studied at the University Normal School, where a bold, experimental program inspired his enthusiasm for universal education. He graduated after three years and, on completion of his legal studies, was licensed to practice law in 1881. During a Chapel Hill revival he joined the Missionary Baptist church.

In 1881 Aycock joined Frank Arthur Daniels as a law partner in Goldsboro. The same year he married Varina Davis Woodard; they had three children. Varina died in 1889, and Aycock married her sister Cora Lily Woodard in 1891. Seven children were born to that union. In the early years of his law practice, Aycock became active in the Democratic party. He cofounded the Goldsboro *Daily Argus*, a pro-Democratic newspaper, in 1885. An intense and emotional orator, he became a fixture at party rallies. Aycock used strident appeals to white supremacy to rally Democrats of the "black" Second Congressional District, whose large African-American population elected Republican congressmen and county officials. He served as an elector for Grover Cleveland in 1888 and in 1890 campaigned for the U.S. House of Representatives but withdrew before the election. The state Democratic convention in 1892 nominated Aycock as presidential elector at large. Because of his work for Cleveland, he received appointment as U.S. district attorney for eastern North Carolina, an office he held from 1893 to 1897.

For two decades Aycock had also served the public schools in Wayne County and the city of Goldsboro, which were in the vanguard of the North Carolina educational revival. An advocate of local taxation to support schools, he became superintendent of public instruction of Wayne County, 1881–1882. Appointed in 1887 to the board of trustees of the Goldsboro graded schools, he worked with an extraordinary number of gifted teachers and administrators: Edward P. Moses, Edwin A. Alderman, Philander P. Claxton, James Y. Joyner, Julius I. Foust, Eugene C. Brooks, Logan D. Howell, and Charles N. Hunter. Aycock helped secure a normal school in Goldsboro for African Americans and served on its board of directors.

The Populist and Republican parties in North Carolina fused in 1894 and 1896 and gained control of the state legislature and the congressional delegation, as well as the offices of governor and council of state. This political coalition outraged the railroad and corporate interests because of its economic policies. In order to regain power, business interests exploited the issue of white supremacy and in 1898 and 1900 resorted to race-baiting tactics. The recurrent campaign slogan that vilified Radical Republicanism and black "misrule," used so effectively by post-Reconstruction Democrats, stirred racial hatreds. Stumping the state in his effort to restore Democrats to power, Aycock denounced black voting, officeholding, crime, and violence before huge audiences bristling with arms. Populists and Republicans pronounced his charges exaggerated, misleading, and false, but the emotionally charged appeal to white supremacy, accompanied by threats, intimidation, and violence against blacks, contributed to Democratic victory in 1898.

Agitation of the race issue unleashed so much hate in 1898 that Aycock became alarmed about its excesses, yet he and his party employed the strategy aggressively in 1900. Aycock's popularity prompted the 1900 Democratic State Convention to unanimously nominate him for governor. To guarantee Democratic supremacy, the legislature had devised a constitutional amendment, modeled after amendments in Louisiana, Mississippi, and South Carolina, which contained a grandfather clause and literacy requirements that disfranchised illiterate blacks while allowing illiterate whites who voted in 1867 (or whose lineal ancestors had voted in 1867) to register and vote until 1908. Republicans charged that illiterate whites, especially in the western counties, would be disfranchised in future elections, but Aycock seized the issue to promote his campaign for universal education for white children. The amendment was approved, and Aycock was elected by the largest majority in North Carolina history to date.

The responsibilities of the governor's office impressed on Aycock the need for more positive state involvement in social and economic matters. To this end he defended significant tax and spending increases and challenged conservative critics who threatened opposition. Aycock's crusade for public schools was bolstered by the support of northern philanthropists, acting through the Southern Education Board, which financed a meeting of forty-three leading North Carolina educators in the governor's office in 1902. This committee issued a declaration against illiteracy, and afterward its members spoke throughout the state at rallies appealing for local tax levies and bond issues for schools. The campaign to support schools yielded impressive results during Aycock's tenure. Between 1900 and 1904 the length of school terms increased 16 percent, average salaries of white teachers 16 percent, school population 4 percent, enrollment 22 percent, average daily attendance 42 percent, value of school property 65 percent, total school funding 100 percent, and total tax districts for school support 663 percent. Under Aycock's leadership 1,015 new schoolhouses were erected and 877 rural school libraries created. He defeated attempts to divide school funds on the basis of taxes paid by whites and blacks, but black schools did not share equally in school facilities and buildings, teacher salaries, term length, or percentage of students enrolled.

Limited by the state constitution to a four-year term, Aycock returned to his legal partnership with Daniels in Goldsboro in 1905. In 1909 he moved to Raleigh and began a lucrative law practice with the distinguished counsel Robert W. Winston. The lackluster record of Governor William Walton Kitchin after 1908 and the apostacy of U.S. senator Furnifold M. Simmons in supporting Republican measures encouraged Aycock to enter the U.S. senatorial race in 1912. He had moderated his conservative views and supported much of the progressive agenda. He favored a preferential senatorial primary, advocated lower tariffs, proposed adoption of a federal income tax and direct election of U.S. senators, and endorsed dissolution of trusts and monopolies, woman suffrage, and child labor legislation. He reiterated his belief in equality of opportunity for all persons, which he maintained could be achieved through education. Opposing Kitchin, Simmons, and Walter Clark (1846–1924), Aycock did not live to complete his campaign. While delivering his famous oration on universal education before a large audience in Birmingham, Alabama, he collapsed and died of a heart attack. Accolades and testimonials following his death shaped the vast body of literature that depicted his life and public service, and his statue was placed in the U.S. Capitol.

Though rising through white supremacy politics, Aycock had been profoundly influenced by capable, reform-minded educators, journalists, jurists, scientists and conservationists of the state Geological and Economic Survey, good roads advocates, and liberals of the Democratic party. Accordingly, his administration was most noted nationally for its accomplishments in the field of public education.

• The Charles B. Aycock Papers, North Carolina Division of Archives and History, Raleigh, is a small collection of the governor's papers. Oliver H. Orr, Jr., *Charles Brantley Aycock* (1961), is a scholarly treatment of Aycock's career and includes interviews with many of his contemporaries. R. D. W. Connor and Clarence Poe, *The Life and Speeches of Charles Brantley Aycock* (1912), published the year of Aycock's death, is largely eulogistic. Helen G. Edmonds, *The*

Negro and Fusion Politics in North Carolina, 1894–1901 (1951), challenges the exaggerated claims of black voting and officeholding abuses. William E. King, "The Era of Progressive Reform in Southern Education: The Growth of Public Schools in North Carolina, 1885–1910" (Ph.D. diss., Duke Univ., 1970), focuses on the documentary materials relating to public education in N.C. Joseph F. Steelman, "The Progressive Era in North Carolina, 1884–1917" (Ph.D. diss., Univ. of North Carolina, Chapel Hill, 1955), discusses the myriad political, social, and economic developments in N.C. during the Progressive Era. Also see J. Morgan Kousser, "Progressivism—for Middle-Class Whites Only: North Carolina Education, 1880–1910," *Journal of Southern History* (May 1980): 169–94. An obituary is in the Raleigh *News and Observer*, 5 Apr. 1912.

JOSEPH F. STEELMAN

AYDELOTTE, Frank (16 Oct. 1880–17 Dec. 1956), college president, was born in Sullivan, Indiana, the son of William Aydelotte and Matilda Brunger. Aydelotte's relatively comfortable childhood afforded him the opportunity for both intellectual and physical pursuits, and he developed a persistence and competitiveness that would remain lifelong characteristics. He attended Indiana University (1896–1900) and graduated with a B.A. in English literature. A good student, he also joined the Sigma Nu fraternity, played football, wrote for the student newspaper and the senior class book, and at least once appeared on stage. Indiana University's new president, Joseph Swain, encouraged Aydelotte's early academic career, especially his candidacy for the Rhodes Scholarship. Swain, who left Indiana for the presidency of Pennsylvania's Swarthmore College, would later invite Aydelotte to succeed him in that position.

Feeling that his true calling was to teach, Aydelotte earned an A.M. in English at Harvard in 1903, then took a post that combined teaching English and coaching football at Louisville (Ky.) Male High School. The announcement of the Rhodes Scholarships at Oxford University as established in the will of Cecil Rhodes, who died in 1902, fired Aydelotte's imagination. After intensive preparation in Latin and Greek for Oxford's entrance examinations, during which he began a long relationship with Abraham Flexner (who later became known as an educational reformer), the state of Indiana nominated him for the Rhodes Scholarship to attend Brasenose College (1905) in England. While crossing the Atlantic, he met his future wife, Marie Osgood. The time at Oxford was the formative period of his life, but he nevertheless left after two years to marry and to begin his professional career as an associate professor of English at Indiana University (1908–1915). The Aydelottes had one child.

Aydelotte later returned to Oxford for one year to prepare his thesis, *Elizabethan Rogues and Vagabonds* (1913), for publication. His calling, however, was to be an educator rather than a scholar. At Indiana he sought to transform the English composition course into an intellectually formative reading of modern authors. He published an influential text to support the organization of a course combining literature and composition—*College English* (1913). His efforts were snubbed by his Indiana colleagues, but they earned him a professorship at Massachusetts Institute of Technology (1915–1921). Critical of the narrow focus of "engineering English," he developed an English program at MIT designed to broaden the minds of prospective engineers. He edited a book of readings, *English and Engineering* (1917), that gained worldwide acclaim as a text and remained in print for some twenty-two years.

While at MIT Aydelotte gained national recognition. Already founding editor of the *American Oxonian*, an alumni magazine also intended to publicize the Rhodes Scholarships, he became American secretary to the Rhodes Trustees in 1918 and served until 1953. Further national exposure resulted from being named director of the "War Issues" course for the Students' Army Training Corps. After the war, he was sought for several college presidencies but found the situation at Swarthmore especially attractive; he was appointed president of the college in 1921.

The original appeal of the Swarthmore presidency was the opportunity to develop the honors program, thus bringing the Oxford model of a more intellectually challenging degree course to an American institution of higher education. Swarthmore's honors course was somewhat less specialized than the Oxford template and based on small seminars for juniors and seniors rather than tutorials.

The honors program distinguished Swarthmore among American colleges for its devotion to serious undergraduate study. National scholarships attracted a surplus of applications from earnest students and made Swarthmore one of the most selective colleges in the country. Although always a proponent of extracurricular activities and participatory sports, Aydelotte deemphasized the influence of Greek organizations and football. Assistance in meeting the high costs of the honors program was provided by the foundation called the General Education Board, where Abraham Flexner favored Aydelotte's goals.

Aydelotte himself was active in philanthropic circles, not only through the Rhodes Trust but as a director of the Guggenheim Memorial Foundation and as trustee of the Institute for Advanced Studies in Princeton, New Jersey. In 1939 he was asked to replace founding director Flexner as head of the institute. In that capacity he mollified the discontent of Flexner's last years and stabilized operations. His tenure laid the basis for the subsequent achievements of the institute. Aydelotte once reflected that "everything I did before 1920 was preparation for the administration of Swarthmore and that everything I have done since 1940 has been the application of the lessons I learned at Swarthmore to all sorts and kinds of educational situations" (Blanshard, p. 150). After his retirement from full-time responsibilities in 1953, Aydelotte maintained his philanthropic ties, but declining health forced him to reduce his typically energetic pace. He died in Princeton.

Aydelotte made the greatest contributions to the movement in American higher education that sought to elevate the level of undergraduate education. Proponents of liberal education often criticized "Germanic" research or "mass" higher education but rarely offered specific alternatives to the prevailing models. Aydelotte made solid contributions to the development of freshman English, to popularizing Oxonian educational ideals, and to the creation of the first honors program and to the subsequent distinction of Swarthmore College.

• The Aydelotte papers are located in the Swarthmore College Special Collections. Aydelotte first presented his guiding ideas in *The Oxford Stamp and Other Essays: Articles from the Educational Creed of an American Oxonian* (1917). His more retrospective views are presented in *The American Rhodes Scholarships: A Review of the First Forty Years* (1946) and *Breaking the Academic Lockstep: The Development of Honors Work in American Colleges and Universities* (1944). Frances Blanshard has written a full biography, *Frank Aydelotte of Swarthmore* (1970). Aydelotte's contribution to Swarthmore is put into perspective in Burton R. Clark, *The Distinctive College: Antioch, Reed, and Swarthmore* (1970; repr. 1992), and in more personal terms by the Swarthmore College faculty in *An Adventure in Education: Swarthmore College under Frank Aydelotte* (1941).

ROGER L. GEIGER
PATRICIA L. GREGG

AYER, Francis Wayland (4 Feb. 1848–5 Mar. 1923), advertising agent, was born in Lee, Massachusetts, the son of Nathan Wheeler Ayer, a teacher, and Joanna B. Wheeler. Ayer was educated by his father; he began his career at the age of fourteen in a school near Dundee, Yates County, New York, where he was a teacher for five years. Between 1868 and 1869 Ayer attended the University of Rochester in New York but was unable to complete his studies because of a lack of funds.

In 1868 he moved to Philadelphia and became an advertising agent and managed to save $250 from his work for the *National Baptist*. The following year, Ayer—with his father as a silent partner—founded the advertising agency of N. W. Ayer & Son in Philadelphia. The agency began with the business of eleven religious weeklies. Ayer expanded the agency by taking on the representation of additional newspapers, and in 1870 Ayer moved his business to larger premises and hired his first employee, George O. Wallace. By the end of 1871 Ayer was agent for 324 publications. In 1873 Ayer's father died and Wallace became partner in his place, and, henceforth, all partners had to be active in the business.

In 1875 Ayer established his own printing department as part of a policy of vertical integration. He also developed a subsidiary and highly profitable business in printers' supplies. In 1880 a separate merchandise department was established at the agency to handle this business, and Ayer established his own Keystone Type Foundry in 1888. These businesses were sold in 1917. In 1877 Ayer also expanded his business horizontally by taking over the oldest advertising agency in the United States, Coe, Wetherill & Co. of Philadelphia. Ayer had married Rhandena Gilman in 1875; they had two daughters.

Ayer also diversified into publishing and in 1874 founded an annual publication, *Ayer & Son's Manual for Advertisers*, that provided lists of newspapers for which the agency sought business, together with information about rates and circulation. In 1876 a similar publication was founded, the *Advertiser's Guide*. It was followed by the creation of the *American Newspaper Annual* in 1880; this became a standard reference book among newspaper proprietors and advertisers. In 1909 Ayer purchased the name and goodwill of *Rowell's Directory* and combined it with the *Annual* to form the *American Newspaper Annual and Directory*. These publications derived most of their revenue from advertising.

In 1875 Ayer abandoned the existing agency tradition and practice with the introduction of the open contract. Ayer decided that the advertiser and agent would be bound by a contract allowing for a commission sufficient to cover the agent's expenses and a reasonable profit. However, the final version of the open contract and its success was also the result of the contribution to the business made by Henry Nelson McKinney, who became a partner in the agency on 1 January 1878.

Late in 1879 Ayer's agency began to develop new services for its advertisers that were not directly linked with newspaper space-buying, but that were critical to the success of an advertising campaign. He began with market research. Between 1880 and 1895 Ayer developed a second new service, the preparation of copy for its clients. Once again his agency was an industry pioneer. During the period in which Ayer was expanding his agency's services he also adopted new advertising media. His agency had specialized in newspaper advertising. However, in 1896 he began handling magazine advertising and in 1898, outdoor advertising.

Between 1903 and 1911 the Ayer agency opened branch offices in New York, Boston, Chicago, and Cleveland. In 1912 Ayer carried out a final reorganization of the agency during his lifetime to attain further specialization and coordination and also to ensure the survival of the agency after his death.

In addition to the advertising industry, Ayer was involved in other businesses. He became a director of the Merchants' National Bank of Philadelphia in 1888 and later served as its president from 1895 to 1910 when it merged with the First National Bank of Philadelphia. Ayer also became involved in farming after he purchased a farm in Meredith, New York, in 1888. He and McKinney subsequently developed a profitable cattle-breeding and dairy business there. Ayer had also separated the religious-paper advertising business from his main agency in 1882 with the establishment of a separate corporation, the Religious Press Association. In the 1890s he also helped successfully reconstruct two clients in financial difficulty, the Brown

Chemical Company and the Saratoga Spring Water Company.

Ayer joined the North Baptist Church when he moved to Camden in 1869 and, soon after, became Sunday school superintendent, a position he held to the end of his life. For twenty-five years he served as president of the North Baptist State Convention of New Jersey. Ayer was an active member of the Northern Baptist Convention until his death and served one term as president.

During the last part of his life, Ayer was an active philanthropist. He made many substantial donations to favored causes, including the North Baptist Church. Ayer also was involved in the Young Men's Christian Association (YMCA). He was president of the Camden YMCA from 1899 until his death and oversaw the raising of money for the Camden YMCA building. He also served for many years as a member of the Boy's Work Committee of the YMCA's International Committee and as chairman of its State Committee of New Jersey. Ayer also donated money to educational institutions and served as the trustee of the Peddie Institute and Colgate University. His first wife had died in 1914, and in 1919 he married Martha K. Lawson. He died at Meridale Farms, Meredith, New York.

Ayer was one of the pioneers in American advertising. He sought to promote professional standards that were underpinned by his strong commitment to the work of his church. He also supported the temperance movement, and from the 1890s, at considerable personal sacrifice, he eschewed the advertising of alcohol.

• An essay by Ayer, "Advertising in America," can be found in *1795–1895: One Hundred Years of American Commerce*, ed. Chauncey M. Depew (1895). A letter to the editor from Ayer can be found in *Editor & Publisher*, 26 Mar. 1921. *F. Wayland Ayer: Founder* (1923) is a company biography of Ayer. Detail information about Ayer's business career can be found in Ralph Merle Hower, *The History of an Advertising Agency: N. W. Ayer & Son at Work, 1869–1949*, rev. ed. (1949). A biography of Ayer can be found in Edd Applegate, ed., *The Ad Men and Women: A Biographical Dictionary of Advertising* (1994). Obituaries are in the *New York Times*, 6 Mar. 1923; the *Watchman Examiner*, 22 Mar. 1923; and *Forbes*, 21 July 1923.

RICHARD A. HAWKINS

AYER, Harriet Hubbard (27 June 1849–23 Nov. 1903), businesswoman and journalist, was born in Chicago, Illinois, the daughter of Henry George Hubbard, a real estate dealer, and Juliet Elvira Smith. Her father died when Harriet was three years old, but his legacy of valuable land purchases enabled the family to live comfortably. Poor health limited Harriet's early education to private tutors. Although Episcopalian, she entered the Catholic Convent of the Sacred Heart at the age of twelve, graduating three years later.

Harriet, a shy young woman whose facial features paled against those of her attractive mother and sisters, often felt left out of a family whose lives centered on physical beauty. Although Harriet later emerged as a beauty, at the age of fifteen her supposed deficits marked her as an unlikely candidate for suitors. When Herbert Copeland Ayer, son of a prominent iron manufacturer, asked for Harriet's hand, her mother consented. The pair married in 1865 and had three children. An infant died of smoke inhalation in the Chicago Fire of 1871, a disaster that also destroyed their home.

During construction of a new house Harriet Ayer traveled to Paris, where she took French lessons, read extensively, dressed in designer fashions, and acquired a taste for the finest of society's offerings, which included attending the opera and fashionable dinner parties. When she returned to Chicago she retained a taste for the cultured life and entertained lavishly.

Ayer and her husband drifted apart. They separated in 1882, and she moved to New York with her two children. Shortly after she left, her husband lost his business and his fortune on account of unwise speculations. Financially strapped, she obtained employment as a sales clerk with Sypher & Company, an antique and furniture establishment, the owners of which saw the downtrodden socialite as a means to attract clientele. Ayer proved to be an excellent saleswoman, and the company allowed her to work out of her home. Personalizing service for the very rich, she traveled to Europe in search of unusual decorative pieces. In Paris she allegedly visited a chemist, buying from him the formula for a miracle skin cream once used by Madame Récamier, a beauty of Napoleon's era who was said to have retained youthful skin for forty years.

In 1886 Ayer returned to New York City. In that same year, she and her husband divorced. She received financial backing from multimillionaire Jim Seymour to start Récamier Manufacturing Company to produce the skin cream. After experimenting with the formula in her kitchen and finding an attractive jar for packaging, she then rented a factory to start production. She labeled the cream with Récamier's name, her own name, and the Hubbard coat of arms, a combination that went against societal conventions. Claiming that the cream removed facial spots and wrinkles, Ayer employed actresses and famous personalities to endorse her products, including stage star Lily Langtry. She used the endorsements in newspaper advertisements. Emphasizing the cream's healing qualities, she reminded her readers that the cream had kept Récamier's skin flawless for years. Her talent for writing and her tremendous promotional abilities created novel methods for merchandising, and her business quickly became a success.

Tensions began building between Ayer and Seymour, which escalated with her daughter's engagement to his son. Sensing impending trouble, Ayer worked hard and paid off her debt, but complications occurred when a dispute of unknown circumstances erupted with Seymour. He filed a lawsuit charging her with mismanaging business finances. She countersued, claiming her debt to him was paid but that he had not returned the stock certificates, and accused him of trying to poison her. Although she won the suit, Seymour convinced his new daughter-in-law and Ayer's exhusband that Ayer's mental condition was unstable and that she was an alcoholic. Rumors that she took morphine for insomnia added to the scandal. The family committed her to an institution in 1893. Both daughters severed ties with their mother, and Ayer's former husband won custody of their minor daughter.

Lawyers obtained Ayer's release after she had spent fourteen months in the asylum. Her once-thriving business had foundered in her absence, and she had little hope of reviving it. The former beauty, who had advocated the healthiness of being plump, had lost forty pounds. Lackluster skin and gray and brittle hair were hardly advertisements for beauty product sales.

After months of recuperation a rejuvenated Ayer began a successful lecture tour called "Fourteen Months in a Madhouse." She told her audiences of her unwilling incarceration in an airless and padded room, where she was force-fed and made to wear ragged clothes. She wrote an exposé on the horror of asylums, which was handed out at her lectures and later reprinted in newspapers. Her lectures and writings drew attention to the horrible conditions of asylums and the danger of doctors and relatives committing mentally stable people. Sometimes she charged an admission fee, the proceeds of which were used to help other victims.

When Ayer saw an advertisement for the newly created women's page of the *New York World*, she quickly responded and immediately composed a sample health and beauty column. Hired as the beauty advice columnist, she received nearly 20,000 letters a year. She targeted her mass-circulated columns toward the working woman; to identify with her audience, she donned the new working woman's clothes, which included a jacket, shirtwaist, and skirt, with a hem that rose four inches above the floor. She joined the Rainy Daisy moderate-dress reform group and was critical of tightly laced garments. She always advised women to "use common sense" and "never overdo a good thing."

Within a short time Ayer doubled as a reporter and feature story writer. She gathered her articles and advice, publishing them in *Harriet Hubbard Ayer's Book: A Complete and Authentic Treatise on the Laws of Health and Beauty* (1899). In 1902 she traveled to England to write a "Harriet Hubbard Ayer Abroad" series for the paper. She also wrote a pamphlet for the Pond's Extract Company, titled *Beauty, A Woman's Birthright: How Every Woman May Look Her Best* (1904). Eventually she reconciled with her daughters. She died of pneumonia in New York City at the age of fifty-four.

A forerunner of the promotional strategies that would characterize the booming cosmetics industry of the twentieth century, Harriet Hubbard Ayer's innovative advertising techniques set the pace for modern merchandising. Ayer helped change women's thinking regarding healthy eating, proper exercise, and dress reform, while advocating a freer lifestyle. During her final years her contact with women from different socioeconomic levels increased her interest in feminism. But her attitude that wives needed beauty to keep husbands and that working women needed physical appeal to move ahead in the workplace kept her within traditional attitudes of her time.

• Ayer left no papers. A memoir written by Henry E. Hamilton is in the library of the Chicago Historical Society. The best source on Ayer is her biography by her daughter Margaret Hubbard Ayer, with Isabella Taves, *The Three Lives of Harriet Hubbard Ayer* (1957). Other details of her life and career are in Caroline Kirkland, *Chicago Yesterdays* (1919), Albert Payson Terhune, *To the Best of My Memory* (1930), Maggie Angeloglou, *A History of Make-up* (1970), Caroline Bird, *Enterprising Women* (1976), Lois W. Banner, *American Beauty* (1983), Ethlie Ann Vare and Greg Ptacek, *Mothers of Invention* (1987), and Autumn Stephens, *Wild Women* (1992). Obituaries are in the *New York Times* and *Chicago Tribune*, 26 Nov. 1903.

MARILYN ELIZABETH PERRY

AYER, James Cook (5 May 1818–3 July 1878), proprietary medicine manufacturer and entrepreneur, was born in Ledyard, Connecticut, the son of Frederick Ayer, a mill operator, and Persis Cook. His father, who ran water-driven sawmills, gristmills, and woolen mills as well as a blacksmith and wheelwright's shop, died when Ayer was seven. His mother and the children lived for two years with her father in Preston, Connecticut. Ayer spent a winter with his nearby paternal grandfather while attending school; he then returned to Preston and stayed for three years, working long hours at various tasks in a carding mill—eventually under a four-cents-an-hour contract. He insisted on further education and at age twelve was sent to a school in Norwich for six months, after which he clerked for a year for a country merchant.

In 1836 Ayer went to live with an uncle in Lowell, Massachusetts, who sent him for another year of schooling at the nearby Westford Academy. Ayer then continued in grammar school and high school in Lowell, excelling in Latin and the natural sciences. He desired greatly to attend college but could not secure financing. In 1838 he took a job in the Lowell apothecary shop of Jacob Robbins, in four years mastering the apothecary's skills and becoming an expert practical and analytical chemist. Simultaneously he studied medicine with two successive physicians, in time receiving an M.D. from the University of Pennsylvania.

Ayer never practiced medicine but instead turned his knowledge toward devising proprietary formulas. In 1841 he bought the Robbins apothecary shop, and that year he made his first product, Ayer's Cherry Pectoral, promoted to cure pulmonary ailments. Ayer brought his brother Frederick into partnership, moved into a large building in Lowell, and steadily expanded his line of wares to include Ayer's Sarsaparilla (1848), Ayer's Cathartic Pills (1854), Ayer's Ague Cure (1857), and Ayer's Hair Vigor (1858). In 1850 he married Josephine Mellen Southwick; they had three children.

In 1871 Ayer attributed his success to the nation's vast geographic extent and a paucity of physicians: Hence has arisen . . . a necessity for remedies ready at hand with directions for their use—a present recourse for relief in the exigencies of sickness, when no other is near (Cowley, p. 116). Ayer distributed his medicines in the West by horse-drawn wagons. At this time his factory was making 630,000 individual doses a day.

Ayer alerted America and nations around the globe to his medicines by massive and ingenious advertising. In 1871 he placed advertisements in 1,900 newspapers and issued 12 million circulars and 7 million pamphlets. In 1853 Ayer began to issue free almanacs, soon numbering 5 million a year in twenty-one languages. Ayer's slogan boasted that his almanac was "second only to the Bible in circulation." Ayer also conceived and carried out news-making stunts. He sent ornate boxes of his medicines to the czar of Russia, the emperors of China and Japan, the presidents of Mexico and Peru, the king of Siam, the queen of Spain, and other rulers. He bestowed similar gifts on American notables, including William B. Astor, Henry Ward Beecher, Henry Clay, Daniel Webster, and Presidents Franklin Pierce and Millard Fillmore; he then brandished their replies like testimonials in his almanacs. Ayer was credited with being the most lavish patent medicine advertiser of his era and the wealthiest proprietor, with a fortune of some $20 million. He and his family lived in the remodeled historic Stone Tavern on the bank of the Merrimack River near Pawtucket Falls.

Ayer was a driven man, engaging in many endeavors besides pill promotion. He invented several machines, a drug mixer and a drug digester among them, to speed production of his proprietaries, and a paper-folding machine to expedite assembly of his pamphlets. He invested in other industries in his vicinity and publicly charged some corporate officials with malfeasance. Ayer's pamphlet, *Some of the Usages and Abuses in the Management of Our Manufacturing Corporations* (1863), was credited with securing enactment of corporate control statutes by the Massachusetts legislature. Ayer was involved in building the Lowell and Andover Railroad and in a company designed to supply water to Rochester, New York. He owned large timber and milling interests in Florida, and he was involved in a plan to build a canal to link the Atlantic and Pacific oceans by one of eight possible routes near Colombia. He owned a block of stock in the *New York Tribune*. Ayer also secured patents for a means of extracting precious metals from pulverized ores.

In 1874 the Republican state convention nominated him to run for the Seventh Massachusetts District seat in the House of Representatives, but he lost the election. His defeat was blamed on the Republican party's being out of favor and on some local resentment because of Ayer's cold manner. In Ayer, a town named for him, the medicine proprietor was hung in effigy. Worn out from a lifetime of overwork and perhaps brooding over his failed political hopes, Ayer experienced a physical and mental collapse. He spent portions of the two years before his death in Winchendon, Massachusetts, in private asylums. The manufacture of Ayer's proprietary medicines continued under the direction of his brother Frederick.

• Collections of Ayer's almanacs are in the New York Public Library and the Peabody Institute Library in Baltimore. Charles Cowley, *Reminiscences of James C. Ayer and the Town of Ayer* (1879), covers much of Ayer's life. For his activities as a proprietary manufacturer see Henry W. Holcombe, *Patent Medicine Tax Stamps: A History of the Firms Using United States Private Die Proprietary Medicine Tax Stamps* (1979). Brief accounts of Ayer's patent medicine activities appear in *Frank Leslie's Illustrated Newspaper* 5, 15 Mar. 1858; George Presbury Rowell, *Forty Years an Advertising Agent* (1926); and James Harvey Young, *The Toadstool Millionaires* (1961). An obituary is in the *New York Times*, 5 July 1878.

JAMES HARVEY YOUNG

AYER, William Ward (7 Nov. 1892–18 Nov. 1985), Baptist pastor and religious broadcaster, was born in Shediac, New Brunswick, Canada, the son of George Walter Ayer, an employee of a marine construction business, and his cousin Sarah Jane Ayer. The youngest of the Ayers' ten children, William suffered the loss of his mother at age five. After enduring seven years of his father's mistreatment and neglect, he was taken to live in Brooklyn, New York, with one of his older brothers. After about a year there, in 1906 he went to the Boston area to live with other siblings. Ayer quit school in the ninth grade and began to learn the printing trade, leading the life of a roustabout printer's devil for some ten years. In 1916, after attending Billy Sunday's evangelistic meetings in Boston, Ayer experienced a religious conversion.

Feeling called to the ministry, Ayer moved to Chicago and entered the Moody Bible Institute in 1917. By the time he graduated in August 1919, Ayer was already the pastor of a Baptist church 175 miles downstate, in Mason City, Illinois. There he met and married Lucile Woodward in 1919. Ayer's next two pastorates were at Baptist churches in Atlanta, Illinois (1920–1922), and Valparaiso, Indiana (1922–1927). Because of his success as an evangelist, each congregation grew considerably. Nevertheless, Ayer found time to further his education by taking some courses at Lincoln College in Lincoln, Illinois, and the Northern Baptist Theological Seminary in Chicago. In 1927 Ayer entered his first urban pastorate, at Central Baptist Church in Gary, Indiana. There he established an extension program for the Moody Bible Institute and began a weekly radio broadcast.

Ayer's next pastorate took him back to Canada in 1932 to the Philpott Tabernacle, an independent fundamentalist church in Hamilton, Ontario. There he polished his broadcasting skills and hosted many eminent fundamentalist preachers, including Will H. Houghton, who was then pastor of the Calvary Baptist Church in New York City. Houghton left Calvary Baptist in 1934 to become president of the Moody Bible Institute, and Ayer replaced him at Calvary in 1936.

By the time Ayer arrived in New York, radio evangelism had become an integral part of his ministry. Soon he was preaching over New York stations WHN and WMGM and publishing a monthly magazine, the *Calvary Pulpit*, for his listening audience. His preaching was pungent and often laced with controversial opinions on matters religious, social, and political. Ayer claimed, for example, that the station manager of WHN had been pressured by high government officials to silence Ayer's denunciations of the Soviet Union. That incident, plus a campaign led by the National Association of Broadcasters to ban independent religious programs that paid for broadcast time slots and to offer free air time as a public service only to representative religious bodies, such as the Federal Council of Churches, convinced Ayer that conservative Protestants needed a collective voice in public affairs to protect their interests. Ayer became one of the principal organizers of the National Association of Evangelicals, which was constituted in 1943. The following year he became the founding president of the National Religious Broadcasters, which represented the interests of dozens of independent evangelical radio programs. Since local radio stations and the newly formed American Broadcasting Company continued to accept paid religious broadcasting, these independent programs flourished.

Ayer's own radio work brought him great notoriety in the New York metropolitan area. When radio station WOR conducted a listeners' poll in 1947 to name the city's "first citizen," Ayer placed a surprising third behind Francis Cardinal Spellman and Eleanor Roosevelt. Thousands of letters from listeners poured into Calvary Baptist Church every month and so did a growing number of invitations to hold evangelistic campaigns in other cities. In order to focus more intently on his broadcasting and evangelism, Ayer retired from his pastorate in 1949. He then founded a radio program, "Marching Truth," which was broadcast over the ABC network.

These were days of heightened religious interest, when Billy Graham was becoming nationally famous as a citywide evangelistic campaigner, and Ayer aspired to a ministry of comparable scope. His hopes never fully materialized. Graham was at the vanguard of an expansive "new evangelical" movement that was softening some of the hard edges of fundamentalism, and Ayer did not fit in well with this new mood. A controversialist, he felt more at home among militant fundamentalists, such as the leaders of Bob Jones University in Greenville, South Carolina, where he had become a trustee in 1941.

Ayer moved his ministry in 1959 from New York to St. Petersburg, Florida, where he continued to produce "Marching Truth" as a weekly half-hour program until 1968. In that year Ayer's wife died of cancer, and he married his secretary, Barbara Scofield, who had worked for him since 1953; neither of his marriages produced children. Ayer continued to publish his ministry's newsletter, *Marching Truth*, but he gradually decreased the number of speaking engagements on his schedule. He died at his home in St. Petersburg.

Although Ayer never earned a high school diploma or a college degree, he was a prolific writer who published nine books and scores of booklets and religious magazine articles. His most notable books are *Seven Saved Sinners* (1937) and *Christ's Parables for Today* (1949). He traveled widely during his active years as an evangelist and Bible conference speaker, across North America as well as on two international evangelistic tours, to Latin America in 1946 and to Great Britain in 1948. Ayer received two honorary doctorates, and in 1978 he was inducted into the Hall of Fame of the National Religious Broadcasters. Best known for his ministry at Calvary Baptist Church in New York City, Ayer continued to be an important spokesman for the fundamentalist movement until his death. The most significant and lasting of his endeavors, however, were the pioneering evangelical agencies he helped to found in the 1940s, the National Association of Evangelicals and the National Religious Broadcasters.

• Few of the records of Ayer's ministry have survived. Scattered issues of the *Calvary Pulpit* during its first decade are in the files of the Calvary Baptist Church in New York City. Incomplete sets also exist for 1945, 1946, and 1947 at the Northern Baptist Theological Seminary in Oak Brook, Ill., and at the Southwestern Baptist Theological Seminary in Fort Worth, Tex. Bob Jones University in Greenville, South Carolina, holds an incomplete file of *Marching Truth*, but this collection includes most of the issues for the years 1968–1985. The University of Kansas in Lawrence also holds files of *Marching Truth* from 1974 to 1985. Family members possess several scrapbooks of newspaper clippings on Ayer's ministry, a number of audio tapes of his broadcasts, and many sermon manuscripts. The most important published biographical source is Melvin Larson, *God's Man in Manhattan: A Biography of Dr. William Ward Ayer* (1950). Also informative is the chapter on Ayer's pastorate in New York in William R. DePlata, *Tell It from Calvary* (1972). Ayer tells his own story in *Six Decades of Gospel Preaching, 1918–1978* (1978) and *My Thanksgiving for Forty Years of Ministry, 1918–1958* (1958); these two pamphlets are to be found in a clipping file on Ayer in the Fundamentalism Collection, Mack Library, Bob Jones University. An obituary is in *Religious Broadcasting* 18 (Jan. 1986): 14, 46.

JOEL A. CARPENTER

AYERS, Lemuel Delos (22 Jan. 1915–14 Aug. 1955), theatrical designer and producer, was born in New York City, the son of Lemuel Delos Ayers, a physician, and Hazel Carleton Bisland. As a student at Princeton University, he was a member of the Theatre Intime and gained early recognition for his productions of *Peer Gynt* and *The Tempest*. After graduating in 1936, he was awarded a Rockefeller fellowship to attend the University of Iowa, where he received his master's degree in theater in 1938. He then went on to design at summer theaters in Michigan and Massachusetts. In 1939 Ayers married Shirley Osborn, a former actress and costume designer, with whom he had two children.

In 1939 Ayers made his Broadway debut with a revival of *Journey's End*, and within the next two years he designed star vehicles and Shakespearean revivals. Critics were split over his stylized scenery for *As You Like It* (1941), which featured a low mound surrounded by a few trees; some found the show's simplicity attractive, but others were irritated by its sparseness. The same year, however, Ayers received almost universal praise for his setting in *Angel Street*. To simulate the glow of gas lamps in the Victorian parlor and to heighten the sinister mood of the melodrama, the production was dimly lit and shadows on the walls were exaggerated. The patterns on the walls were painted on velour, a technique just beginning to be used at the time, and Ayers was so exacting about the effect that he was granted special permission by the scenic artists' union to work on the scenery himself.

By age twenty-seven Ayers was established as a Broadway designer. During 1942 he had five productions on the Great White Way: *Plan M*, *Autumn Hill*, *The Pirate*, *Lifeline*, and *The Willow and I*. His settings often were described as colorful, attractive, and, occasionally, "the one redeeming thing about the evening." Ayers developed a strong reputation as a scene designer for musicals after supplying the scenery for the Theatre Guild's ground-breaking *Oklahoma!* (1943). Among the shows for which he later designed the settings (and occasionally the costumes) were *Song of Norway* (1944), *St. Louis Woman* (1946), *Inside USA* (1948), *Music in the Air* (1951), *Kismet* (1953), and *The Pajama Game* (1954). In his work outside the theater, Ayers served as art director for the MGM musicals *Meet Me in St. Louis* (1944), *Ziegfeld Follies* (1945), and *A Star Is Born* (1953). He also provided the sets and costumes for Agnes De Mille's ballet *The Harvest According* (1952).

Ayers often employed a painterly approach to scenery, with settings depicted in a stylized realism. For *Oklahoma!* he provided backgrounds of rolling cornfields with running fences and vast skies, in a simplified manner that brought comparisons to painters of American rural life such as Grant Wood and Thomas Hart Benton. His exteriors for *Bloomer Girl* (1944) featured clouds painted with obvious brush strokes and a tree ever bending in the wind and rain of a storm. The backdrop of a town square for the same show resembled a nineteenth-century lithograph with its heavy contours and strong shadows. By using techniques that emphasized the two-dimensionality of the scenery, Ayers gave his settings a graphic quality that acknowledged the artificiality of the stage but at the same time obeyed its realistic conventions.

In 1948 Ayers embarked on his first venture as a producer with Cole Porter's *Kiss Me Kate*. Ayers shared the producing responsibilities with Saint Subber, who had conceived of the modern musical adaptation of *Taming of the Shrew*. The show was an instant hit; it ran for 1,077 performances and earned its producers the Tony award for best musical. Ayers also won awards for both his scene and his costume designs, which fused styles of different periods. The costumes, which won the Tony and Donaldson awards, incorporated both modern and Renaissance silhouettes, substituting the usual Shakespearean ruffles and brocade for bright, contrasting colors, accented with playful stripes and large patterns. The scenery, also given a Donaldson award, was geometric and in linear perspective but had little ornamentation and severe shadows.

Two years later Ayers and Subber produced another Cole Porter musical, *Out of This World*, a modern retelling of the Amphytrion legend. The storyline disappointed reviewers, but Ayers's designs were well received. After he ended his business partnership with Subber, Ayers continued his projects alone, making him, at age thirty-six, one of the youngest independent producers of the era. Ayers attempted to produce adaptations of fictional works, but his plans for dramatizations of William Faulkner's *Requiem for a Nun*, F. Scott Fitzgerald's *A Diamond as Big as the Ritz*, and Rumer Godden's *A Breath of Air* never materialized. In 1952 he succeeded in bringing N. Richard Nash's *See the Jaguar*, for which he provided the costume and scene designs, to Broadway.

Ayers's accomplishments as a producer did not diminish his reputation as a designer. During the 1952–1953 season he received Donaldson awards for both his settings and his costumes for *Camino Real*. Tennessee Williams's surrealistic play presented an unusual collection of characters drawn from history and literature, on a setting with a street and a patio, all surrounded by evocative elements like a fountain, phrenology charts, window dummies, illuminated pawn shop signs, and a staircase "leading nowhere." That same season Ayers garnered a second Donaldson costume award for his brilliant, satiny designs in the musical *My Darlin' Aida*. Ayers earned his sixth Donaldson the following year for his exotic, colorful, and revealing costumes in *Kismet*. During this period he worked on national tours and foreign productions of some of his Broadway successes and served as production supervisor at the New York City Center of Music and Drama.

Ayers was described as urbane and articulate and was a member of the United Scenic Artists and the League of New York Theatres. When he died of cancer in New York City, he was planning to produce the musical *Saturday Night*.

• A clipping file is available at the Billy Rose Collection of the New York Public Library for the Performing Arts at Lincoln Center. See also Orville Larson, *Scene Design in the American Theatre from 1915 to 1960* (1989); Forrest A. Newlin, "The New York Stage Designs of Lemuel Ayers" (Ph.D. diss., Univ. of Nebraska, Lincoln, 1978); Gordon Allison, "Play Producer Lemuel Ayers," *Theatre Arts* (Sept. 1951): 48–49, 96; and *New York World-Telegram and Sun*, 1 Sept. 1951. Ayers's obituary is in the *New York Times*, 15 Aug. 1955.

PHILIP A. ALEXANDER

AYLER, Albert (12 July 1936–c. 5 Nov. 1970), composer and musician, was born in Cleveland, Ohio, the son of Edward Ayler, a semiprofessional violinist and tenor saxophonist, and Myrtle Hunter. Albert and his brother Donald, who later became a professional jazz trumpet player, received musical training early in life from their father. In second grade Albert performed alto saxophone recitals in school. He performed duets with his father (who also played alto saxophone) in church. Together they listened to a great deal of swing and bebop music, both on recordings and at jazz concerts.

From age ten to age eighteen Ayler attended Cleveland's Academy of Music, taking jazz lessons from Benny Miller. Throughout his mid-teenage years Ayler performed in young jazz and rhythm and blues bands. He was a captain of his high school golf team; at the time, Cleveland's courses were largely segregated. Albert also spent two summers while in high school on the blues circuit, performing with Little Walter. According to John Litweiler, the noted avant-garde jazz historian and critic, Ayler's knowledge of jazz standards and his mastery of bebop style gained him the nickname of "Little Bird" after the great Charlie Parker.

Ayler entered the army in 1958, where he switched to tenor saxophone and traveled throughout Europe with a Special Services band based in France. Among the musicians with whom Ayler came into contact during this period were bebop tenor saxophonists Carlos "Don" Byas and Dexter Gordon, as well as King Oliver reedman Albert Nicholas. Europe in the late 1950s and early 1960s was a hotbed of activity in the fledgling free-jazz movement. Innovations such as abandoning chord changes, exploring sound for its own sake, and collective improvising—all recalling music's true roots—were ways of approaching free jazz's goal of "spiritual transcendence." Ayler's proximity to jazz clubs in Copenhagen and Paris allowed him to listen to and practice this emerging style when off duty.

Ayler remained in Europe immediately following his discharge in 1961, performing throughout Sweden with a bebop trio that was recorded live in 1962. That year he returned to Copenhagen, where he experienced his first studio recording date; the recordings that resulted from this session were released as *The First Recordings*, or *Something Different*, on Bird Notes. From that point on Ayler performed only his own music. He sat in with avant-garde pianist Cecil Taylor's group at the Club Montmartre in the winter of 1962–1963. Ayler soon felt constrained by what he termed the "simplicity" of bebop and gravitated toward more free performance. Ayler moved to New York in 1964, where he occasionally performed with Taylor and recorded an album in the winter of 1963–1964. He formed a quartet in New York in the summer of 1964 with bassist Gary Peacock and drummer Sunny Murray, picking up trumpeter Don Cherry in Europe. The quartet toured Sweden and Holland. Ayler married Arlene Benton in 1964; they had one daughter.

Ayler possessed a big, soulful sound very much in the style of rhythm and blues music. Wailing, braying, growling, buzzing—these are just a few terms that have been used to describe his playing. A thorough master of his instrument, Ayler was noted for bringing out multiple overtones in his sound through overblowing and manipulation. Characteristic of his playing were split tones, loud honks in the lower register, shrieks in the upper register, wide harsh vibrato, and extreme interval leaps.

Ayler utilized modes and scales as well as sound for its own sake in his emotional improvisation, which often featured simple motivic repetition based upon initially-stated thematic material that would suddenly deviate from the established harmonic changes to collective improvisation. He played anything that came to his mind that possessed a connection with the material, developing relationships within a free context that were somewhat analogous to free association in psychology and stream-of-consciousness writing in literature. The social and philosophical aspects of his music assumed greater importance for Ayler than strict musical interpretation. He once stated that his goal was to provide an atmosphere of spiritual transcendence for the audience (and for his fellow musicians) that would combine the collective cohesiveness of a New Orleans jazz band with a formal freedom arrived at individually.

Although Ayler received acclaim from critics he was unable to gain a steady audience for his music, resulting in a meager personal income. He performed and toured sporadically with his group throughout the 1960s, both in Europe and the United States. Ayler played in studios and clubs in New York from 1965 to 1968. A member of the short-lived Jazz Composers Guild, Ayler performed his first major United States concert at New York's Town Hall in 1965 with his brother Donald. An appearance at the 1966 Newport Jazz Festival and a European Tour in November of that year highlighted the group's accomplishments.

A 1967 European tour included Ayler and his brother Donald, violinist Michel Sampson, bassist Bill Folwell, and drummer Beaver Harris. Ayler performed college concerts with such musicians as Gary Peacock or Henry Grimes on bass, Beaver Harris, Sonny Murray, or Milford Graves on drums, and Cal Cobbs on piano or harpsichord. Ayler also occasionally performed on instruments such as alto and soprano saxophone, and even the bagpipes.

After returning from a European tour with his quintet in 1970, Ayler was reported missing in New York City. According to his companion at the end of his life, Ayler, in despair over family strife involving his brother Donald, had boarded the ferry to the Statue of Liberty and jumped off before the ferry reached Liberty Island. His body was found on 25 November in the East River near the Congress Street Pier in Brooklyn. The exact cause of death was unconfirmed.

Ayler, together with John Coltrane, Archie Shepp, and Pharoah Sanders, expanded the definition of jazz that was initiated by Ornette Coleman in the late 1950s, creating for future jazz musicians and audiences a much broader concept of improvised music.

• There are significant biographical sketches of Ayler in Len Lyons and Don Perlo, *Jazz Portraits: The Lives and Music of the Jazz Masters* (1989), and Valerie Wilmer, *As Serious as Your Life: The Story of the New Jazz* (1980). Ayler's historical and social context is depicted in John Litweiler, *The Freedom Principle: Jazz after 1950* (1984). Valuable insight regarding Ayler's playing and philosophical views, as well as a select discography, is in Litweiler, "The Legacy of Albert Ayler," *Down Beat* 38, no. 7 (1971): 14–15, 29. An informative interview with Ayler and his brother Donald is Nat Hentoff, "The Truth Is Marching In," *Down Beat* 33, no. 23 (1966): 16–18, 40. See also Frank Kofsky, *Black Nationalism and the Revolution in Music* (1970) and Ralph J. Gleason, *Celebrating the Duke* (1975) for discussions of Ayler's philosophical approach to music. An obituary is in the *New York Times*, 4 Dec. 1970.

DAVID E. SPIES

AYLLÓN, Lucas Vázquez de (1480?–18 Oct. 1526), Spanish judge and founder of the first Spanish colony in North America, was born at Toledo, Spain, the son of Juan Vázquez de Ayllón, a member of a distinguished Mozarabic family, and Inés de Villalobos. Lucas was educated in the law, earning the *bachillero* degree.

In 1504 Ayllón was appointed a district judge (*alcalde mayor*) for the mining district of north central Hispaniola, a position he held until 1509. Returning to Spain to defend his conduct in office, which he apparently did with success thanks to political connections, he seems to have obtained the *licenciado* degree, probably from the University of Salamanca. During this period, Diego Colón, Christopher Columbus's legitimate son and heir, won his lawsuit with the Crown over his father's privileges as viceroy and governor of the lands Columbus had discovered. However, the Crown retained the right to create an appeals court (*audiencia*) to oversee the administration of justice by Colón's judicial appointees. Ayllón was selected as one of the three judges.

Ayllón returned to Santo Domingo in 1512. He rapidly rose to become one of the three most important political figures on the island. By a second marriage, to Ana de Bezerra, daughter of a wealthy miner and landowner from the northern district, and by his own financial dealings, Ayllón grew wealthy. The couple had four children. Among his enterprises was the trade in Indian slaves; according to testimony given in 1517, Ayllón was notorious for not providing adequate provisions for the captives, who often died in large numbers before reaching Hispaniola. He also was active in obtaining slaves from the Bahama Islands, where such trade had been illegal since about 1510. Uninhibited by this prohibition, in the summer of 1521 Ayllón sent Francisco de Gordillo to the Bahamas with orders that if he did not find slaves there he was to sail northwest to a coast where Captain Pedro de Salazar, another of Ayllón's slave raiders, had obtained Indians some years earlier. In company with Pedro de Quejo, who was employed by Juan Ortiz de Matienzo, another of the *audiencia*'s judges, Gordillo made that voyage. Their landfall was on the coast of North America just north of the entrance to Winyah Bay, South Carolina (23 June 1521). Sailing south, they initially anchored in the South Santee River but soon moved the ships to Winyah Bay, where each captain took possession of the new land in the name of his employer. When they departed for Santo Domingo on 15 July, the Spaniards seized sixty Native Americans.

Sent to Spain on official business in late 1521, Ayllón returned to Hispaniola in 1523 with a contract to explore and then settle the new discovery on the mainland. He sent Quejo to the North American coast in 1525 on a voyage that reached from St. Simon's Island, Georgia, on the south, to about Cape Henlopen, Delaware, on the north, and included a return to the Santee–Winyah Bay area. Meanwhile, Ayllón gathered supplies from his estates and through his commercial connections; to pay, he mortgaged his properties. Adventurers gathered in response to the news of the fitting of the expedition.

Ayllón and some 600 persons, including a few women and African slaves, departed Puerto Plata, Hispaniola, in six ships in mid-July 1526. They landed in the Santee–Winyah Bay area early in August, although the flagship and its cargo were lost on a shoal. Francisco, "El Chicorano," a native of the area captured in 1521 and now Ayllón's chief informant and interpreter, quickly deserted, leaving Ayllón without a guide to the rich interior kingdom of "Du-a-e," a land said to contain tame herds of deer and gems. A quick survey of the area revealed little in the way of food resources and no Indians, both essential for the colony Ayllón planned to found. Ayllón and his captains seem to have judged that they could not remain there. Accordingly, exploring parties were sent south by sea and into the interior. Men were set to work building a ship to replace the lost flagship. The results of these activities allowed Ayllón to move his colony to the south, probably in the early days of September.

The site to which Ayllón moved has been disputed, but the best evidence suggests that it was in the area of Sapelo Sound, Georgia. There on 29 September, the festival of the archangel Saint Michael, the town of San Miguel de Gualdape was formally established. The Guale Indians were its neighbors. Although the area provided some land suitable for agriculture, the late summer arrival of the Spaniards meant that they could not plant any crops. Short on supplies of maize and other carbohydrates and unable to obtain large amounts of them from the Guale, although fish and game were abundant, the Spaniards began to sicken and die. Among those buried was Ayllón. San Miguel de Gualdape survived Ayllón's death by only a few weeks. Perhaps only 150 of the 600 persons who had set out from Puerto Plata lived to return to the Antilles.

Contemporary accounts indicate that Ayllón was a talented jurist and politician but inclined to abuse his position and power for personal gain. The chronicler Gonzalo Fernández de Oviedo disparaged Ayllón's effort at leading a colonizing venture by suggesting that such things should be left to soldiers, not lawyers. However, that view ignores the fact that in 1523 Bartolomé de Las Casas and other advocates of Native American rights had persuaded Charles V to insist on peaceful, not violent, contact between Spaniards and Native Americans. A jurist may have seemed the perfect person to lead such an attempt.

• The best account of Ayllón's life and colonial venture is in Paul E. Hoffman, *A New Andalucia and a Way to the Orient: The American Southeast during the Sixteenth Century* (1990). Besides archival materials, it is based on Pietro Martiere d'Anghiera, *Decadas del Nuevo Mundo*, vol. 2 (1965), pp. 594–98, and Gonzalo Fernández de Oviedo, *Historia General y Natural de las Indias*, vol. 3 (1851), pp. 628–30. Earlier and less accurate versions of the story are in Paul Quattlebaum, *The Land Called Chicora: The Carolinas under Spanish Rule with French Intrusions, 1520–1670* (1956); John R. Swanton, *Early History of the Creek Indians and Their Neighbors* (1922); Woodbury Lowery, *Spanish Settlements within the Present Limits of the United States*, vol. 1 (1901); and John G. Shea, "Ancient Florida," in *Narrative and Critical History of the United States*, ed. Justin Winsor, vol. 2 (1886).

PAUL E. HOFFMAN

AYRES, Anne (3 Jan. 1816–9 Feb. 1896), founder of the first Episcopal women's religious order, was born in London, England, the daughter of Robert Ayres and Anne (maiden name unknown). She emigrated in 1836 with her mother to the United States and settled in New York City on the lower west side of Manhattan.

On the strength of letters of introduction to New York merchants, Ayres was able to open a subscription school for the children of wealthy New York families. These connections brought her into contact with William Augustus Muhlenberg, a Philadelphia-born Episcopal priest who was then the head of the short-lived St. Paul's College on Long Island. Muhlenberg was a prominent and innovative dabbler in educational and ecclesiastical projects, and Ayres soon became his devoted admirer. In the summer of 1845, she was deeply moved by hearing Muhlenberg preach on "Jephtha's Vow" and became convinced of "the blessedness of giving one's self undivided to God's service." In the 1840s, however, the Episcopal church offered women none of the formal opportunities for performing the "giving" that Ayres craved; the ordained priesthood remained reserved for males, and only the Roman Catholic church possessed religious orders and houses for women. Nevertheless, Muhlenberg, who had taken note of efforts in Germany in the 1830s to revive orders of female deaconesses for the state Lutheran churches, was persuaded to "consecrate" Ayres for church work on the evening of All Saints Day 1845. The "simple" service involved only Muhlenberg "in his surplice within the chancel" of the chapel at St. Paul's College and Ayres "in her accustomed dress kneeling at the rail."

The immediate object of Ayres's "consecration" was Muhlenberg's new parish, the Church of the Holy Communion, which he opened in New York City in 1846. While Muhlenberg served as rector and made Holy Communion into an ongoing laboratory for liturgical novelties and a rent-free pew system, Ayres became his full-time parish worker. Doing "true Sisters' work in the parish," she directed the Sunday school, an "Employment Society," and a church infirmary and dispensary. In October 1846 Muhlenberg announced his intention to organize a church hospital, which was incorporated in 1850. Building began in 1854, and when St. Luke's Hospital finally opened its doors in 1858, Muhlenberg delegated its administrative oversight to Ayres as "House-Mother." Ayres had become "the church-daughter" to Muhlenberg as well as the "church-sister" of Holy Communion, and the "constant companion of his labors throughout the rest of his consecrated life."

The steady expansion of Muhlenberg's philanthropic projects put greater demands on Ayres's time and labor. Ayres had already begun to assemble a team of female workers at Holy Communion, and in 1852 she formally organized them into the Sisterhood of the Holy Communion, with herself as the "First Sister." Between 1853 and 1857, three other women took full-time vows of service and joined Ayres to live together in the parish house behind the Church of the Holy Communion. In 1858 the Sisters assumed charge of St. Luke's Hospital and took up residence there with Muhlenberg, who resigned as rector of Holy Communion to preside over the hospital.

The organization of the sisterhood did not pass without criticism. Detractors of Muhlenberg's liturgical innovations at Holy Communion accused him of showing sympathy for Tractarianism, or "Puseyism," the Catholic revival movement in the Church of England, which was attracting both support and violent opposition in the Episcopal church. Similar suspicion fell on Ayres's sisterhood, leading to "apprehension of a secret nunnery" at Holy Communion and the hospital. In defense of the sisterhood, Ayres and Muhlenberg collaborated in publishing *Practical Thoughts on Sisterhoods* (1864) and *Evangelical Sisterhoods* (1867), in which Ayres was at pains to distance her sisters from Roman Catholic orders. "A sisterhood . . . is a very simple thing," Ayres contended, "it is a community of Christian women, devoted to works of charity, as the service of their lives, or of a certain portion of them." Unlike Roman Catholic nuns, Ayres's sisters took no lifetime vows (only three-year terms of service), wore no religious habit, and provided the costs of their own support. "Nothing then, is to be feared from a truly Evangelical Sisterhood." Ayres also sought to allay fears that her sisterhood represented an attempt by women to secure power for themselves in church life, and she assured doubters that "any fears or jealousies of a woman-power in the church, which, in fact, would be a priestly power, will have no place."

At the same time, however, Ayres was forced to deal with dissension within her sisterhood precisely because it was not moving in these directions. In 1862 Ayres's third recruit, Harriet Starr Cannon, pressed to have the sisterhood reorganized along just the Roman Catholic lines that Ayres and Muhlenberg deplored, and when Ayres discovered that Cannon had turned the majority of the sisters against her, Ayres resigned as First Sister. Muhlenberg at once intervened and dissolved the sisterhood. Cannon, who had also accused Ayres of "erratic and autocratic" direction of the sisterhood, left St. Luke's Hospital in April 1863, along with three other sisters, to organize the Sisterhood of St. Mary under the pro-Tractarian bishop of New York, Horatio Potter. Ayres, meanwhile, was reinstated at St. Luke's as matron in charge of the hospital, and the remaining sisters were reorganized simply as a "Company of Christian Ladies" under Ayres's direction.

In the mid-1860s Muhlenberg turned his mind to a new project, a "Church Village" on Long Island to be called St. Johnland, which would become an industrial and agricultural settlement for New York City's poor. St. Johnland was incorporated in 1870, and the village church, the Church of the Testimony, was dedicated on 8 October 1870. As with his earlier projects, Muhlenberg turned to Ayres as his manager and administrator, and a new sisterhood—the Sisterhood of St. Luke and St. John—was organized to encompass work at both the hospital and St. Johnland. In 1876 Ayres was named "Sister Supervisor" of St. Johnland, and the aging Muhlenberg came to lean increasingly on "his Sister friend" for "constant attendance and companionship." When Muhlenberg died on 8 April 1877, Ayres resigned all her responsibilities, and, devoting herself to preserving and promoting Muhlenberg's memory, she edited two volumes of his *Evangelical and Catholic Papers* (vol. 1, 1875; vol. 2, 1877) and produced a full-length biography of him in 1880. She remained a "guest" of St. Luke's Hospital until her death. At her request, she was buried beside Muhlenberg at St. Johnland.

• Ayres burned all of the papers of William Augustus Muhlenberg that she held at his death, and did likewise with her own papers before she died. In so doing, she deliberately chose to make Muhlenberg and her loyalty to him the central plot of her life and made herself accessible to historians and biographers only through her connections with Muhlenberg. It is not clear whether she was motivated by personal devotion to Muhlenberg, or whether, as a woman iconoclast in Episcopal religious life, she sought through her association with Muhlenberg protection from criticism. The best sources on Ayres's life, which are mostly devoted to Muhlenberg, include her biography, *The Life and Work of William Augustus Muhlenberg* (1880), and Alvin W. Skardon, *Church Leader in the Cities: William Augustus Muhlenberg* (1971). On the Sisterhood of the Holy Communion, an early and illuminating source is Henry Codman Potter, *Sisterhoods and Deaconesses at Home and Abroad* (1873).

ALLEN C. GUELZO

AYRES, Clarence Edwin (6 May 1891–24 July 1972), economics professor, was born in Lowell, Massachusetts, the son of William S. Ayres, a minister, and Emma Young. He entered Brown University in 1908, obtaining a B.A. in 1912. He was at Harvard in 1913 and then returned to Brown, where he obtained an M.A. in 1914. Ayres married Anna Bryant in 1915; they had three children and were divorced in 1925. He attended the University of Chicago, from which he received a Ph.D. in 1917. His major field of study was philosophy. After graduating he served as an instructor in the Department of Philosophy at Chicago until 1920.

That year Ayres moved to Amherst as an associate professor of philosophy. At that time Alexander Meikeljohn, who had been Ayres's influential teacher at Brown, was the president of Amherst. In 1923, following the firing of Meikeljohn by the Amherst Board of Trustees, Ayres resigned in protest of that action. He then moved to Reed College in Portland, Oregon, as a professor. But in 1924 he returned to the East to become an associate editor of the *New Republic*. During the years from 1924 until 1930 he divided his time among the *New Republic*, ranching in New Mexico, and teaching at the University of Wisconsin. He married Gwendolen Jane in 1926; they had no children. In 1930 he went to the University of Texas as a professor of economics, where he taught until 1968, having been on modified service since his formal retirement in 1961.

The Department of Economics at Texas from the 1920s until the 1960s was a major center in the development of the unorthodox economics called institutionalism, an approach to economics that enjoyed considerable influence in the New Deal era in Washington, D.C., during the 1930s. Ayres was the major factor in this development at Texas. His scholarly work drew on both Thorstein Veblen's institutionalism and John Dewey's instrumentalism. He was a personal friend of both of these men. Another friend, Frank Knight, was also a major economist with a philosophical grounding; he did not, however, stray from mainstream economics to the extent that Ayres did.

Ayres's major work, *The Theory of Economic Progress*, was published in 1944. In the Veblen institutional tradition, Ayres emphasized a pattern of interaction between evolving technological knowledge and static institutions. The distinction might be restated as one between productive industrial and sterile pecuniary types of employment, with the crux of the matter being the nature of the interaction between the two facets and not the mere fact that the distinction exists. As Ayres wrote in a helpful synthesis of his work, *The Industrial Economy* (1952), "Technological and institutional values are never finally (or wholly) opposed. They are not, and cannot be, because institutional values always derive their ultimate sanction from the actual technological experience of the community" (p. 312).

Ayres's technological system of values, on the other hand, owes much to the influence of Dewey. The heart of this system is the concept of the continuum of means and ends. In *The Industrial Economy* he wrote, "Every tool activity is related to every other tool activity in terms of antecedent and consequent. . . . In this continuum there is no qualitative difference between means and ends" (pp. 306–7). In this setting, understanding ongoing process (a process, not a tendency to any identifiable equilibrium) becomes the essence of economics: "The general welfare is not a condition; it is a process" (p. 315).

Ayres is also beholden to Dewey for his conception of the theory of valuation (a more appropriate term than value theory). In this approach it is the nature of the valuation process that is involved, not the identification of value in any quantifiable sense. Here the identification of a welfare maximum is not a meaningful concept. Such an approach leads to a generalization about the meaning of truth. Thus Ayres wrote in *The Industrial Economy*, "As we now realize, knowledge does not consist of a summation of fixed and unchanging truths. There are no fixed, unchanging truths" (p. 315). Nevertheless, Ayres was not a complete cultural relativist: "Moreover, whereas the irrational values are culture-limited, the instrumental (or technological) values are the same for all cultures" (*The Industrial Economy*, p. 26).

The significance of ongoing process is in essence ongoing technological change, which, to be assimilated by the economy, may well require change in the prevailing institutionalized attitudes. Yet an institution is a social pattern that contributes to such resistance. As Ayres recognized, required institutional change is what Veblen called the cultural incidence of the machine process. While technology is dynamic, institutions are static. Ayres, however, points out in *The Industrial Economy* that "there is nothing teleological about the dynamic character of technology. That is, technology is not fated to prevail" (p. 59). And there certainly is no particular conceivable pattern to which society is irresistibly evolving.

In light of Ayres's last major book, *Toward a Reasonable Society: The Values of Industrial Civilization* (1961), the dictum "there are no fixed, unchanging truths" has to be qualified. Ayres deeply believed that something called "progress" is a meaningful and desirable phenomenon and that progress is ongoing. He also was a man of strong moral convictions: "It is generally recognized that certain values have been idealized by all the 'great' religions of history. Those values are universally recognized as the highest of which mankind is capable. . . . That the values of industrial society are real is attested by the eagerness of other peoples to share them, and also by our own common determination . . . to press on to their fuller attainment" (*Toward a Reasonable Society*, p. 168).

These "public" values, as Ayres calls them, are freedom, equality, security, abundance, and excellence. There exist also "the 'private' values of 'personal' morality," including veracity, sobriety, honesty, and decency. A generous, flexible man, Ayres struggled until the end of his life to understand the nature of human existence. He was not dogmatic in espousing his views or in examining those of anyone else, yet he was active and combative in defending the values that were real to him. He died in Alamogordo, New Mexico.

• Ayres wrote innumerable short articles for the *New Republic*, especially during the 1920s, and the book *The Divine Right of Capital* (1946). William Breit and William Patton Culbertson, Jr., eds., *Science and Ceremony: The Institutional Economics of C. E. Ayres* (1976), is a collection of his papers that contains a substantial bibliography and a biographical statement. "In Memoriam: Clarence Edwin Ayres" was published in University of Texas, *Documents and Minutes of the General Faculty*, 17 Sept. 1976, pp. 12150–56.

WENDELL C. GORDON

AYRES, Jacob (c. 1760–c. 1836), Catawba chief, was born in South Carolina into a prominent Catawba kin group. One relative, Hixayoura, was an interpreter and warrior; another was chief in 1763–1764. During the American Revolution, Jacob Ayres (variously spelled Ears or Ayers) served with patriot forces including other Catawbas under General Thomas Sumter. After 1800 Ayres's kin ties to earlier leaders and his credentials as a warrior—both prerequisites for leadership of the Catawbas—brought him to prominence. He came to be called "Colonel," a title that, after the American Revolution, was used to denote the second most powerful person in the Catawba Nation. Confirming this new status, Ayres's mark on official documents rose to second place under that of the Catawba chief, Jacob Scott. Later, after Scott died in 1821, Ayres became chief, or "General," of the Catawbas.

What little can be recovered of Ayres's career points to a firm devotion to the difficult task of defending the Catawbas' independence, lands, and traditional ways. Numbering perhaps 300 people, the tribe was a tiny island in a sea of white settlers and their African-American slaves. Farmers ignored the boundary lines of the 144,000-acre reservation, South Carolina officials whittled away at the Indians' political rights, and federal authorities ignored the tribe altogether. In an effort to prepare the Catawbas to deal with the whites more effectively, Ayres—who, like most Catawbas of the time, was illiterate—joined Scott and other leaders in 1801 to petition the state for funds to educate a few Catawba youths. Although the appeal failed, Ayres and his fellow leaders continued to petition state and sometimes federal officials to keep out trespassers, reinstate the Indians' right to appoint their own agents, and reform the system of leasing land to whites that Catawbas had devised in an effort to make a living while controlling settlement of their lands. "[T]he Wrongs and defrauds that has been Commited upon us by Sharp witted and designing Christians has been many," began one 1805 petition to President Thomas Jefferson. "[I]f we Spoke of the way that they were useing us," Ayres and the other Catawba petitioners charged, "the[y] often Raise Quarrells with our people and commits little Slye Crimes."

Ayres's support of schooling for a handful of Catawba youths and of the leasing of Catawba lands reflected his conservative beliefs that a few literate Catawbas could protect the rest from white schemes and that leasing land kept ultimate control in Catawba hands while mollifying whites eager for land. The best evidence of Ayres's traditionalist stance was his firm resistance to growing pressure from whites and from some Catawbas to sell the entire reservation. He reinforced his opposition by living, with his younger brother John, in King's Bottoms along the Catawba River, traditionally the burial ground of chiefs and the sacred heart of the Catawba Nation. After Ayres died, on 9 November 1838, the Catawbas sold King's Bottoms, and on 13 March 1840 they signed the Treaty of Nation Ford with South Carolina, surrendering the entire reservation.

• Materials on Catawba dealings with the state of South Carolina can be found in the South Carolina Department of Archives and History in Columbia and the York County Public Library in Rock Hill, S.C. Although there are no biographies of Ayres, he is treated briefly in Douglas Summers Brown, *The Catawba Indians: The People of the River* (1966), and James H. Merrell, *The Indians' New World: Catawbas and Their Neighbors from European Contact through the Era of Removal* (1989).

JAMES H. MERRELL

AYRES, Leonard Porter (15 Sept. 1879–29 Oct. 1946), educator, statistician, and economist, was born in Niantic, Connecticut, the son of Milan Church Ayres and Georgiana Gall. His father, a clergyman, author, and journalist, was editor of the *Boston Daily Advertiser*. The family moved to Newton Highlands, Massachusetts, where Leonard received his early education in public schools. An avid bicycle racer, he participated in national matches as a young man. After receiving his Ph.B. degree from Boston University in 1902, he taught school in Puerto Rico, rising rapidly to become general superintendent of the island's schools and chief of the Education Department's Statistics Division in 1906. Returning to the states, he moved to New York City and joined the Russell Sage Foundation in 1908 to conduct investigations of the health and education of schoolchildren under the direction of Luther Halsey Gulick. The results of Ayres's study were incorporated in a book, *Laggards in Our Schools*, which concluded that a child's age at entering school and regular attendance appeared to be the leading factors in satisfactory progress. While doing this work, Ayres also earned M.A. (1909) and Ph.D. (1910) degrees from Boston University.

Ayres was appointed the foundation's first director of statistics (1911) and its first director of education (1912). In his dual capacity he supervised a number of school survey projects; the most extensive was the Cleveland Education Survey, undertaken in 1915 for the Cleveland Foundation. Under Ayres's direction, a comprehensive two-year survey of the city's public school system was made which led to improved methods for testing children's ability in spelling, arithmetic, and reading. Ayres was pleased by nationwide interest in the survey's practical applications.

When the United States entered World War I in 1917, Ayres took a leave from the Russell Sage Foundation to work for the government, organizing a Division of Statistics to chart the growth of the national economy for the Council of National Defense, the War Industries Board, and other agencies. The importance of his work was recognized by the army early in 1918, and he was transferred to the War Department, where a statistical branch of the General Staff was created. Ayres, commissioned a lieutenant colonel, refined the analytical techniques he had developed at the foundation and presented accurate reports on wartime preparation to ranking military officers. He also served as chief statistical officer for the American Commission Negotiating Peace, and received the Distinguished Service Medal in 1919 for his wartime work. Later, in 1924, he was an economic adviser to the Dawes Plan Commission, which reduced the reparations Germany owed to the Allies, extended the repayment period, and provided loans to stabilize that nation's unsound currency.

Ayres returned to the foundation in 1919, but he left the following year to become vice president in charge of statistics at the Cleveland Trust Company and editor of its monthly *Business Bulletin*. Ayres evaluated the business research performed under his direction and converted the results into recommendations for the bank's management. There were few influential business statisticians at that time, and through his widely read *Bulletin*, Ayres gained a nationwide audience for his year-end business reviews and reliable economic forecasts, which appeared in newspapers as well as national periodicals such as *Banker's Magazine* and *World's Work*.

In the December 1927 *Bulletin* Ayres perceptively observed, "It appears likely that we are now in the closing phases of the business cycle that began in the summer of 1924." Like others, however, he was unable to forecast the cycle's catastrophic end in 1929. After the economic downturn and the stock market crash, Ayres predicted in early 1930 that "the bottom of the business slump appears to have been reached"—an assessment publicized throughout a nation anxious for the return of prosperity. At the same time, his lack of confidence in recovery in the durable goods industries largely escaped public notice. Subsequently Ayres recognized the "exceptional character" of the deepening depression, but he criticized Roosevelt's New Deal, particularly the NRA's wage and price policies. He was convinced that the expansion of private long-term financing and increased production of durable goods were the key factors in restoring a sound economy. Ayres's reputation for accurate forecasting remained intact as he charted the uncertain path of recovery, reluctantly accepting the federal government's role in deciding the economic future of the nation. In 1939 the self-supporting economy Ayres sought began to return, as the durable goods industries increased capital spending and output in response to the threat of war in Europe.

Ayres, who had maintained his commission in the army reserve, was recalled to active duty at the rank of colonel in October 1940 and served for two years in the statistics branch of the War Department. Promoted to brigadier general in 1941, he retired a year later, returning to the Cleveland Trust Company.

Calm, logical, and level-headed, Ayres was a confidant of the railroad magnates Orris P. and Mantis J. Van Swearingen, an economic adviser to the president of the Chesapeake and Ohio Railroad and a member of its finance committee, and a vice president and director of the Allegheny Corporation. He never married. He died of a heart attack in Cleveland.

Ayres improved the methods of conducting statistical research and analysis and created the administrative organizations necessary to provide data of practical value to a wide variety of disciplines. Regardless of the milieu he was addressing, his evaluations were delivered clearly, succinctly, and convincingly. His pioneering work in quantitative analysis helped create a foundation for the postwar explosion of statistical measurement and the rapid expansion of his profession.

• Papers from Ayres's career at the Cleveland Trust Company and his *Business Bulletin* are held at the Western Reserve Historical Society, Cleveland, Ohio. For his early work see John M. Glenn et al., *Russell Sage Foundation, 1907–1946* (2 vols., 1947). His monthly business forecasts appeared in the *Cleveland Plain Dealer* (1928–1946) and intermittently in the *New York Times*. An obituary is in the *New York Times*, 30 Oct. 1946.

Ayres's writings on childhood education and the U.S. economy include: *Medical Inspection of Schools*, with Luther Halsey Gulick (1908); *Open Air Schools* (1910); *The Economics of Recovery* (1933); and *Turning Points in Business Cycles* (1939). As a result of his statistical work with the General Staff during World War I, Ayres prepared *War with Germany: A Statistical Summary* (1919).

His numerous monographs and reports on education include: *What American Cities Are Doing for the Health of School Children* (1911); *A Comparative Study of Public School Systems in the Forty-Eight States* (1912); *Scale for Measuring the Quality of Handwriting of School Children* (1912); *Spelling Vocabularies of Personal and Business Letters* (1913); *Fire Protection in Public Schools* (1913); and *An Index Number for State School Systems* (1920). Ayres also wrote eight monographs for the 26-volume study of the Cleveland public schools published by the Survey Committee of the Cleveland Foundation.

MARY B. STAVISH

AYRES, Romeyn Beck (20 Dec. 1825–4 Dec. 1888), soldier, was born at the crossroads of East Creek in Montgomery County, New York. His father was a small-town physician who was dedicated to raising his sons for professional life. He trained Romeyn rigorously in Latin until he was fluent in the language. At age seventeen Ayres received an appointment to the U.S. Military Academy at West Point and graduated twenty-second in the class of 1847. He was subsequently commissioned a brevet second lieutenant in the Fourth U.S. Artillery and was sent to Mexico, where he performed garrison duty at Puebla and Mexico City. Following his return from Mexico, Ayres's service consisted of routine garrison duty at various army posts in Maine, Rhode Island, Texas, New York, California, Minnesota, Kansas, and Virginia.

When the Civil War began Ayres was practicing at the artillery school at Fortress Monroe, Virginia. On 14 May 1861 he was promoted to captain in the Fifth U.S. Artillery. At First Manassas on 21 July 1861 he commanded E Battery, Third U.S. Artillery, and acquitted himself well. On 1 October 1861 he was named chief of artillery of Brigadier General William F. Smith's division, which subsequently became part of the Sixth Army Corps. Ayres served through the Peninsula and Maryland campaigns. General Smith reported that at Antietam, "the artillery, under Captain Ayres's judicious management, assisted very materially in silencing the fire of the enemy." Ayres's cool judgment and competent handling of his artillery command won the notice of his superiors, and on 29 November 1862 he was promoted to brigadier general of volunteers. He served as chief of artillery for the Sixth Corps at the battle of Fredricksburg. Ayres's health was apparently poor; during this period he was absent on sick leave from October to December 1862 and from late January to April 1863. When he returned in April he was assigned to command a brigade of U.S. Regular Army Infantry in the Fifth Corps. He led his command in the battle of Chancellorsville, where it was only lightly engaged. Three days before the battle of Gettysburg, Ayres was promoted to command of the U.S. Regulars division. On 2 July Ayres led his command into action in the "wheatfield" at Gettysburg. Circumstances beyond his control caused his command to be outflanked and driven from the field with a loss of nearly one-third. Following the Gettysburg campaign Ayres accompanied the two regular brigades of his division to New York City to assist in quelling the draft riots. He and his command returned to the army in September and participated in the Rapidan and Mine Run operations.

In the spring of 1864, during the reorganization of the Army of the Potomac, Ayres returned to brigade command, consisting of the regulars reinforced by several Pennsylvania and New York regiments. In the battle of the Wilderness, Ayres's brigade was heavily engaged and suffered severe losses. It was again in the thickest of the fighting at the battles of Spotsylvania Court House and Cold Harbor. In one month of battles the brigade's losses numbered more than 2,000. Ayres's ability in this bloody month earned the notice of Ulysses S. Grant, who wrote that Ayres was "a capital commander . . . one of our best officers." On 6 June 1864 Ayres was selected to command the Fifth Corps division of General John Robinson, who had been wounded at Spotsylvania. Ayres led his new command with quiet efficiency in the operations around Richmond and Petersburg in late 1864 and early 1865. His division helped defeat Confederate forces at Five Forks on 1 April 1865, which precipitated Robert E. Lee's evacuation of the Richmond and Petersburg lines and led to his surrender at Appomattox eight days later.

Following the war Ayres reverted to his prewar regular rank of captain. But on 28 June 1866 he was promoted to lieutenant colonel of the Twenty-eighth U.S. Infantry. He subsequently transferred to the Nineteenth U.S. Infantry in 1869 and on 15 December

1870 to the Third U.S. Artillery. He saw routine garrison and occupation duty in Arkansas, Louisiana, and Florida until November 1872, when he was assigned to Madison Barracks in New York. While at the barracks post he also assisted in suppressing railroad disturbances in Mauch Chunk, Pennsylvania. In 1879 he was promoted to colonel of the Second U.S. Artillery. While on duty at St. Francis Barracks at St. Augustine, Florida, in 1885 his health began to fail, and he took sick leave to Governor's Island, New York. He moved in 1888 to Fort Hamilton, New York, where his second wife's family had a home. Ayres suffered from diabetes and other afflictions. The memory of the war also haunted him. He wrote to a friend about his beloved division of regulars: "Looking back at my command through those years, what an array of splendid fellows—now, alas! no more—rise up before my mind! How they went forth to the harvest of death, as gaily as to a ball!" He succumbed to apoplexy while at Fort Hamilton.

Ayres married twice. He and his first wife had "several children," one of whom was Charles Ayres, a lieutenant in the army at the time of his father's death. He had two daughters with his second wife, all of whom survived him.

Ayres was a large, rough-hewn man, who stood six feet tall by age seventeen. He was strict and tough as a soldier but enjoyed a wonderfully dry sense of humor and a generous dose of common sense. He was meticulous about his personal habits and his dress.

• For Ayres's official reports and correspondence during the Civil War, see *The War of the Rebellion: A Compilation of the Official Records of the Union and Confederate Armies* (128 vols., 1880–1901). His military record is in G. W. Cullum, *Biographical Register of the Officers and Graduates of the United States Military Academy*, vol. 2, 3d ed. (1891). An excellent source on Ayres's service with the U.S. Regulars during the war is Timothy Reese, *The U.S. Regulars in the Army of the Potomac* . . . For his experience at Gettysburg, see Harry Pfanz, *Gettysburg: The Second Day* (1987). Some biographical information is in *Dedication of the New York State Auxiliary State Monument on the Battlefield of Gettysburg* (1926). An obituary is in the *New York Times*, 5 Dec. 1888.

D. SCOTT HARTWIG

B

BAADE, Walter (24 Mar. 1893–25 June 1960), observational astronomer, was born in Schröttinghausen, Westphalia, Germany, the son of Konrad Baade, a schoolteacher, and Charlotte Wulfhorst. Although he was christened Wilhelm Heinrich Walter, he never used his first two names. He was educated at the classical Gymnasium in Herford, where his family moved in 1903, and then at the University of Münster for one year. In 1913 he entered the University of Göttingen, where he studied astronomy.

Baade had a congenital hip defect, which made walking painful and awkward and climbing or running impossible. This excused him from service in the German army in World War I. Baade was a good student, and in 1915 he became a research assistant to the great German mathematician Felix Klein. In 1917 Baade was called up in the auxiliary service and assigned to the army's experimental aerodynamics center at Göttingen. He worked there full time until the end of the war but was allowed to continue his studies. Among his professors, in addition to Klein, were the mathematician David Hilbert, astronomers Johannes Hartmann and Leopold Ambronn, the geophysicist Erwin Wiechert, and the applied mathematician Ludwig Prandtl. Baade completed his doctoral degree in 1919.

An unusually experienced young astronomer, Baade had developed a strong interest in astrophysics and wanted to visit Mount Wilson Observatory near Pasadena, California, with its new 100-inch reflector, and some of the other large American observatories. That was impossible, however, for a German national immediately after World War I. Instead he got a position as assistant at the Hamburg-Bergedorf Observatory, where Richard Schorn was director. He learned to photograph asteroids and comets and soon went on to observational studies of globular clusters, cepheid variables, and the Milky Way. In 1926 he became the first German scientist to receive a Rockefeller Fellowship. With it he worked at the Harvard College, Yerkes, Lick, Mount Wilson, and Dominion Astrophysical observatories. At each he learned more about observational work and forged many links with American astronomers. Baade had a friendly, outgoing, persuasive personality. He quickly learned to speak English fluently and made friends everywhere he worked. On his return to Hamburg in 1927 he was promoted to Observator, traditionally the post for the heir apparent to the director. Baade became an expert in variable-star research—the key to the distances to the globular clusters and star clouds of the Milky Way. In 1928 he was offered a professorship at Jena but declined it because of the better observational research opportunities at Hamburg. For his inaugural lecture as a docent at Hamburg he chose the title "Extragalactic Nebulae as Stellar Systems," the theme of his scientific career.

At Hamburg Baade came to know Bernhard Schmidt, a morose, one-armed Estonian optician who was an expert maker of mirrors for astronomical reflecting telescopes. In 1929 the two were sent to the Philippines to observe a solar eclipse. Although they were "clouded out," they used the long sea voyage to discuss the need for a fast, wide-field reflector, which Schmidt filled with his invention of the revolutionary coma-free system that bears his name. Also in 1929 Baade married Johanna ("Muschi") Bohlmann. They had no children.

In 1931 Baade was offered a permanent research position at Mount Wilson Observatory. He seized it and began his long series of observational programs with the big telescopes in California on variable stars, globular clusters, nebulae, galaxies, and clusters of galaxies. With Fritz Zwicky, a Caltech faculty member, Baade identified supernovae as a distinct class of objects, much more luminous than ordinary novae, and studied their physical properties. Baade had brought news of the new Schmidt reflector with him from Hamburg, and the Pasadena astronomers were quickly persuaded of its potential. Within a few years a new 18-inch Schmidt was in place on Palomar Mountain near San Diego and was used by Zwicky for a supernova search. Baade helped bring Rudolph Minkowski, driven out of Germany by Hitler, to the Mount Wilson staff. They had collaborated in nebular research in Germany and eventually worked together in the United States on comets, nebulae, supernovae, and radio galaxies.

In 1937, when Schorr retired, the Hamburg authorities tried to persuade Baade to return as director of the Bergedorf Observatory. They offered to build a 32-inch Schmidt telescope, but he preferred to stay in California, where excellent telescopes were paired with a fine observing climate.

At Mount Wilson Edwin Powell Hubble was working with Milton Humason on the redshifts of galaxies and the expansion of the universe. Baade worked on accurate measurements of the distances to the nearer galaxies and, hence, values of their absolute magnitudes. During World War II, still a German national, he was officially an enemy alien in the United States and was not permitted to travel; nor could he join the other Mount Wilson astronomers in their wartime weapons development work. The brownout in Los Angeles darkened the skies, and Baade, one of the few left to observe with the 100-inch telescope, used his superb skills to take long exposures, which for the first time resolved M 31, the Andromeda galaxy, and its two smaller companion galaxies, showing the individual red stars in them. This was Baade's great discovery, for which his whole life had prepared him: the recognition of what he called the two stellar populations, young stars and old, characterized by their most luminous stars, blue and red respectively. Word of his observational breakthrough spread through the astronomical community and made him famous. He also obtained excellent direct images of nova and supernova remnants—tiny expanding shells around exploding stars.

Soon after World War II, the new 200-inch Hale reflector and a 48-inch Schmidt, the successor to the 18-inch, went into operation on Palomar Mountain. Baade used them to study the galaxies in detail, carefully measuring the properties of their variable stars, nebulae, and novae. He found that the distance scale then in use was wrong and that, in fact, the galaxies were more distant, and the universe older, than Hubble and Humason had realized. Baade observed the region around the center of our galaxy as well as he could through the thick layers of interstellar dust and compared it with the center of the Andromeda galaxy. He emphasized the importance of the study of color-magnitude diagrams of globular clusters, which his young colleagues Allan Sandage and William A. Baum, and student, Halton C. Arp, carried out. All of Baade's research was based on his thorough knowledge of the observational properties of stars and star systems and well thought out ideas for programs to get at their physical nature and evolution. He inspired such theorists as George Gamow, Martin Schwarzschild, Lyman Spitzer, Fred Hoyle, William A. Fowler, and Geoffrey Burbidge to dig into these subjects.

After World War II, Baade and Minkowski worked closely with the early radio astronomers in identifying the new radio sources with supernova remnants and "peculiar" (active) galaxies. He did not write many papers; he was far more interested in doing the research, understanding the results, and discussing them excitedly with colleagues and students than in writing them up for publication. But he gave numerous talks and lectures at scientific meetings, as well as research courses at the University of Michigan, Caltech, and Harvard. These inspired a generation of graduate students and young research workers. Baade, in his 1953 correspondence with Jan Oort, a Dutch astronomer and theorist, initiated the plan for a cooperative European southern-hemisphere observatory and pushed it with great energy. It came into being after his death as the European Southern Observatory at La Silla, Chile.

Although Baade's research was almost entirely devoted to distant nebulae and galaxies, his direct exposures with large telescopes recorded the images of many faint asteroids in our solar system. Most he merely noted, but among the unusual ones he discovered (at Hamburg) what was for many years the most distant known asteroid, Hidalgo, and (at Palomar) what was then the closest known to the sun, Icarus.

When Baade retired in 1958, he had to give up observing with the big telescopes. He went to Australia as a visiting professor, invited by the radio astronomers, and then returned to Germany. There Baade was appointed the Gauss professor at Göttingen. He planned to publish all the detailed results of his observational programs. But his hip problem had become much worse. It forced him to undergo an operation, and his recovery was very slow. His doctors confined him to bed for a recuperation that stretched out to six months. After that he was allowed up only for brief moments, but within a few days he collapsed suddenly and died. He was one of the most productive observational astronomers of the twentieth century.

• Many of Baade's scientific working papers, drafts, data, charts, etc., are preserved in the Huntington Library, San Marino, Calif., but little of his correspondence has survived. His most important scientific papers were published in the *Astrophysical Journal*. His book, *Evolution of Stars and Galaxies* (1963), edited by Cecilia Payne-Gaposchkin, was prepared by her from tape recordings and notes of the series of lectures he gave at Harvard University. An obituary article by Otto Heckmann in *Mitteilungen der Astronomischen Gesellschaft* 114 (1961): 5–11 contains a complete bibliography of his publications, except for joint papers with Halton C. Arp and with Henrietta H. Swope, his longtime assistant at Mount Wilson, who published them a few years after his death. This obituary, without the bibliography, is reprinted in Otto Heckmann, *Sterne, Kosmos, Weltmodelle* (1976), which is dedicated to Baade and contains many items of information about his life and scientific career. Obituaries that describe other facets of his personality, life, and work are Halton C. Arp, *Journal of the Royal Astronomical Society of Canada* 55 (1961): 113–16; Allan Sandage, *American Philosophical Society Yearbook 1960* (1961): 108–13; Erich Schoenberg, *Bayerische Akademie der Wissenschaften Jahrbuch* (1960): 177–81; and A. A. Wachmann, *Die Sterne* 36 (1960): 204–7. Adriaan Blaauw, *ESO's Early History: The European Southern Observatory from Concept to Reality* (1991) tells of Baade's role in getting this international observatory started.

DONALD E. OSTERBROCK

BABBITT, Irving (2 Aug. 1865–15 July 1933), literary and social critic, was born in Dayton, Ohio, the son of Edwin Dwight Babbitt, a physician and writer, and Augusta Darling. He attended Harvard College from 1885 to 1889 and took a major in classical literature. He returned to Harvard in 1892 and earned a master's degree the next year in the same field, with an additional concentration in ancient Eastern languages. In 1894 he taught in the classics department at Harvard but later joined the Department of Romance Languages, in which he taught French literature. In 1900 Babbitt married Dora May Drew. They had two children and lived in Cambridge, Massachusetts, until Babbitt's death.

While in graduate school Babbitt befriended Paul Elmer More, and the two became leaders of an intellectual movement known as the New Humanism. Stuart Sherman and Norman Foerster, both students of Babbitt, considerably reinforced the movement. More always acknowledged Babbitt's influence on him. "He turned the whole current of my life," he wrote, "saving me from something akin to emotional and intellectual suicide." Babbitt and More displayed contrasting personalities, as reflected in a reference to Babbitt as the

"Warring Buddha of Harvard" and another to More as the "Hermit of Princeton." Babbitt never hesitated to champion his ideas, especially in the classroom, where he became a legendary and controversial figure at Harvard. According to Sherman, "he deluged you with the wisdom of the world; his thoughts were unpacked and poured out so fast you couldn't keep up with them." Babbitt's students at Harvard also included T. S. Eliot, Walter Lippmann, and Van Wyck Brooks.

Babbitt's first book, *Literature and the American College* (1908), brought together a number of essays in which Babbitt had begun to define the New Humanism. *The New Laokoön* followed in 1910 and the *Masters of Modern French Criticism* in 1912. Thereafter came Babbitt's two most important and influential books: *Rousseau and Romanticism* (1919) and *Democracy and Leadership* (1924). Babbitt's humanism centered on a few basic points that he reinforced with greater learning and sophistication in his later writings, but a remarkable continuity of thought nonetheless prevails throughout. As More wrote of Babbitt, he "seems to have sprung up, like Minerva, fully grown and fully armed. . . . There is something almost inhuman in the immobility of his central ideas."

Babbitt's humanism outlined a dualistic view of human nature. He located in each human personality two countervailing instincts. One worked in the direction of liberation from all constraints, an expansionist impulse that sought an indefinite freedom of will and imagination. He associated that norm with the Romantic movement in Western culture and decried the dangerous incidence of Romanticism, personified most particularly by Jean-Jacques Rousseau, in modern life. But Babbitt also posited a principle of control, a force of discipline, restraint, and moderation. This element, he believed, had received its best articulation in classical literature and in later thinkers, such as Samuel Johnson and Joseph Joubert. The value of the great classics of Western writing, Babbitt believed, lay in their ability to assist their readers to glimpse by imaginative insight a high ideal of human nature. Babbitt lamented what he perceived to be the triumph of Romantic notions of individuality and a cult of idiosyncracy over the universal sense of a common humanity. The result was a modern culture lacking in wholeness, tradition, and continuity.

Babbitt also criticized the more recent influence of naturalism, which he believed depicted human beings as the reflex agent of natural forces. Naturalism dissolved the principle of control and explained human behavior by reference to the dominant influence of race and environment. For Babbitt, Romanticism and naturalism reinforced one another, depriving human experience of any center or authority. In the United States he found these tendencies particularly acute. America, he said, had produced a culture that was both mechanistic, worshipping power and force in all aspects of society, and at the same time sentimentalist and emotionally indulgent, as witnessed by the popularity of Hollywood movies and pulp fiction. Not one to mince words, Babbitt warned that America was in danger of producing "one of the most trifling brands of the human species the world has yet seen."

Babbitt's writings applied his standards to a number of categories of American life and letters. On the subject of literary criticism, he led the New Humanists in opposing impressionist criticism, which they associated with Romanticism, and historical criticism, which they related to naturalism. Although Babbitt had a profound distaste for contemporary literature and seldom discussed it, his critical standards led such disciples as Stuart Sherman to attack the literary naturalism best represented by Theodore Dreiser and to engage in polemic such defenders of the new literature as H. L. Mencken.

On the subject of education, Babbitt became an outspoken conservative critic of the elective system, instituted at Harvard by Charles William Eliot after 1869. He believed the elective system to be another concession to individual idiosyncracy and a betrayal of higher education's charge to pass on a cumulative cultural tradition. Under the prevailing liberal curricular practices, Babbitt complained, "the wisdom of the ages is to be naught as compared with the inclination of a sophomore."

In his political views, Babbitt stood self-consciously in the tradition of Edmund Burke. He believed that modern politics had become essentially a contest between the "idyllic imagination" of Rousseau, fostering utopian and egalitarian schemes of social salvation, and the "moral imagination" of Burke. Each society, Babbitt said, must evoke through imagination and symbol a tradition and history that joins past to present. Democracy reduced people to their lowest common selves, Babbitt believed, and only by appealing to an aristocratic element could society be redeemed. But he believed that little help in that effort could come from America's economic plutocracy, and he remained pessimistic about democratic America's ability to generate a true leadership class fitting his aristocratic standards.

Babbitt and the New Humanism attracted many followers but did not gain an ascendant influence in American intellectual life. Nonetheless, Babbitt became one of America's most influential conservative intellectuals. He has been an important influence on such conservative writers as Peter Viereck, Russell Kirk, and George Will. The journal *Modern Age*, founded in 1957, has built on Babbitt's humanist standards.

• Some of Babbitt's papers, including his important correspondence with Paul Elmer More, are privately held by Babbitt's daughter, Mrs. Esther Babbitt Howe, in Washington, D.C. Other letters, as well as lecture and reading notes, may be found in the Harvard University archives. In addition to works cited above, see Babbitt's *On Being Creative and Other Essays* (1932) and his translation, *The Dhammapada* (1936), which contains his important essay, "Buddha and the Occident." An excellent source for Babbitt's character and personality is Frederick Manchester and Odell Shepard, eds., *Irving Babbitt: Man and Teacher* (1941; repr. 1969), with contributions from thirty-nine students and acquaintances. For a useful collection of Babbitt's writings see George A. Panichas, ed., *Irving Babbitt: Representative Writings* (1981).

Thomas R. Nevin, *Irving Babbitt: An Intellectual Study* (1984), is the most complete portrait of Babbitt in the full range of his thought; it contains a useful bibliographical essay. See also Stephan Brennan and Stephen R. Yarbrough, *Irving Babbitt* (1987). Claes G. Ryn, *Will, Imagination and Reason: Irving Babbitt and the Problem of Reality* (1986), examines Babbitt more narrowly. J. David Hoeveler, Jr., treats Babbitt within the context of the New Humanist movement in *The New Humanism: A Critique of Modern America, 1900–1940* (1976). George A. Panichas and Claes G. Ryn, eds., *Irving Babbitt in Our Time* (1986) contains essays about Babbitt and a helpful chronology of Babbitt's life and works by Mary E. Slayton.

J. DAVID HOEVELER, JR.

BABCOCK, Alpheus (11 Sept. 1785–3 Apr. 1842), piano maker, was born in Dorchester, Massachusetts, the son of Lemuel Babcock, a music teacher, singer, and composer, and Sarah Savil. During his youth the family moved to Milton, Massachusetts, where he attended the village school. Babcock learned to make pianos while serving an apprenticeship in Milton with noted musical instrument maker Benjamin Crehore. Crehore's important "Boston School" of pianoforte makers, established around 1792, included Babcock, his brother Lewis Babcock, and John Osborne, teacher of Jonas Chickering.

Babcock is first listed as a pianoforte maker around 1810 when he began his career with his brother Lewis in a small workshop in Boston at 49½ Newbury Street. The Babcock pianofortes were modeled after the imported English squares of this period. The "square" piano of the early nineteenth century was rectangular in shape, with a case made entirely of wood, veneered in mahogany and other fine woods, and had a range of five and one half to six octaves. In 1812 Babcock and Lewis entered into partnership with organ maker Thomas Appleton at 18 Winter Street, making "elegant and excellent toned pianos" that were warranted for ten years. After Lewis Babcock's death in 1814, Alpheus Babcock was joined in business by the merchants Charles and Elna Hayt. The new firm, Hayts, Babcock and Appleton, located at 6 Milk Street, sold "a good assortment of musical instruments and instruction" as well as dry goods, umbrellas, lumber, and fishing poles. After the firm dissolved in 1815, Babcock was self-employed until 1821. During this time he also worked for J. A. Dickson at 34 Market Street in Boston. In 1822 Babcock married Margaret Perkins in Boston; the couple had one son. From 1822 to 1829 Babcock was foreman of the piano company owned by John Mackay, a wealthy sea captain, and his brother George D. Mackay at 7 Parkman's Market on Cambridge Street. On 17 December 1825 Babcock took out a patent for his most important invention, a one-piece cast-iron frame with hitch-pin plate in one casting for a square piano, which was to revolutionize the way pianos would be made. In 1830 Babcock worked in Philadelphia for J. G. Klemm, who had been the agent for his pianos in that city. From 1832 to 1837 he was employed in Philadelphia by William Swift as the superintendent of his piano manufactory. In 1830 Babcock took out a patent for cross-stringing pianofortes, and in 1833 he acquired patents to improve the hammers of the piano and the piano action. In 1837 Babcock returned to Boston, where for the remaining five years of his life he worked for Jonas Chickering & Co.

Babcock's pianos were highly praised by his contemporaries. In 1824 his piano won first prize at the Franklin Institute Exhibition in Philadelphia. The judges noted that "every part of its interior mechanism had the highest finish and its tone and touch are excellent." In 1825 his piano won a silver medal at the second annual Franklin Institute Exhibition. In an account of the institute's fourth annual exhibition in 1827, the judges wrote that "especial mention is made of a horizontal piano made by A. Babcock of Boston of an improved construction, the frame which supports the strings being of solid cast-iron and strong enough to resist their enormous tension."

The significance of Babcock's improved construction was far-reaching. As music in concert halls grew in popularity in the nineteenth century, it became necessary for piano makers to build a stronger piano, an instrument that would not only be capable of a greater volume of sound by supporting greater string tension but would also stay in tune. The problem of how to keep a piano in tune was especially challenging to American makers due to the extreme temperature changes in the New World. In the first decades of the nineteenth century piano makers on both sides of the Atlantic were seeking a solution to this problem. Attempts were made to strengthen the frame with metal plates and bars although metal was traditionally frowned upon as being detrimental to the tone quality. Babcock, however, in a bold move in 1825, patented a one-piece iron-frame with hitch-pin plate in one casting for a square piano. The solid iron frame, "strong enough to resist the enormous tension of the strings," proved to be the solution to strengthening the piano and was a milestone in the development of the piano.

Babcock's invention was not adopted immediately by all piano makers. Many thought the iron frame gave a metallic sound to the tones of the piano, and Thomas Loud, a respected piano maker in Philadelphia, called the invention "worthless." But in Boston Chickering, for whom Babcock was then working, realized the importance of Babcock's invention, and after improving on the design, he patented a one-piece iron frame for a square piano in 1840 and for a grand piano in 1843. In 1852 Chickering's iron-framed pianos won highest honors at the London Crystal Palace Exposition and "proved a veritable sensation." In 1867 both Chickering and Steinway won gold medals for their iron-framed grands, a triumph for the "American system," as it was called, which European makers subsequently adopted.

Babcock was held in high esteem as a master builder. His pianos were praised for their "excellent tone and touch" by those in the trade and for their "beautiful design and workmanship" by Arnold Dolmetch, a noted early instrument authority. Babcock was remembered by local historian Albert Kendall Teele as a craftsman who was constantly working to improve all parts of the piano. "For many years before his death he had a private room to which no one was admitted where he conducted his experiments. His patient study and mechanical ingenuity and skill did much to establish the reputation which Chickering's pianos have long sustained" (Teele, pp. 379–80). Owners of Babcock pianos included John Quincy Adams and Lowell Mason. Although Babcock received little financial remuneration or acclaim during his lifetime for his epoch-making cast-iron frame, the basic principles of his invention helped lay the groundwork for the international triumphs of American piano makers in the second half of the nineteenth century.

• Important documents relating to Babcock are located at the Milton Historical Society, Milton, Mass. The most complete account of Babcock's life is found in Keith Grafing, "Alpheus Babcock: American Pianoforte Maker (1785–1842): His Life, Instruments, and Patents" (Ph.D. diss., Univ. of Missouri, 1972). See Daniel Spillane, *History of the American Pianoforte* (1890; repr., 1969), and Albert Kendall Teele, *A History of Milton, Mass., 1640–1887* (1887), for biographies of the Boston School of pianoforte makers. H. Earle Johnson, *Musical Interludes in Boston 1795–1830* (1942), provides a detailed description of music life in Boston when Babcock started his career. For information on the technical development of the piano in Europe and the United States, see Rosamond Harding, *The Piano: Its History Traced to the Great Exhibition of 1851* (1973), and Arthur Loesser, *Men, Women and Pianos* (1954), for a brilliant social history of the piano and its place in society. For an obituary see the *Boston Evening Gazette*, 9 Apr. 1842.

MARGARET MORELAND STATHOS

BABCOCK, Ernest Brown (10 July 1877–8 Dec. 1954), geneticist, was born in Edgerton, Wisconsin, the son of Emilius Welcome Babcock and Mary Eliza Brown. He developed an early interest in botany by working in his mother's conservatory and his own flower garden. He attended Lawrence College in Appleton, Wisconsin, for one year (1895) and while there became intrigued by the wild plants that flourished along the banks of the Fox River. When his parents moved to California after his freshman year, he accompanied them and attended the state normal school in Los Angeles for two years. In 1898 he took a teaching position in a grammar school in order to earn enough money to complete his education and in 1901 matriculated at the University of California's College of Agriculture with the intention of becoming a plant breeder. Unfortunately, the school offered no such course of study, and so he supplemented the standard agriculture curriculum with as many botany courses as he could take. A series of lectures presented by the visiting Hugo De Vries, the principal promoter of Gregor Mendel's work with plant heredity, piqued his interest in the evolution of plants. He received a B.S. in 1906.

After graduation, Babcock returned to the normal school as its first instructor in agricultural nature study, enrolled for graduate work at the University of California at Berkeley, and began breeding peaches at the Citrus Experiment Station in Riverside. By crossing a little-known Chinese variety with the more common Elberta, he set in motion the development of a peach that produced good fruit in the peculiar conditions of southern California's climate, which his successors named the Babcock peach in his honor. In 1908 he married Georgia Bowen; they had no children. That same year he left the station and the normal school to join the faculty at California's Berkeley campus as assistant professor of plant pathology. In 1910 he became the school's first professor of agricultural education and in 1913, after earning his M.S. in 1911, its first professor and division head of genetics, a position he held until his retirement in 1947.

Babcock's first challenge as division head was to teach his students the implications of what Thomas Hunt Morgan, a future Nobel Prize winner in physiology or medicine, was discovering about chromosomes and heredity in fruit flies. To this end, he and Roy E. Clausen published *Genetics in Relation to Agriculture* (1918) as "an adequate presentation in a single text of the facts and principles of genetics and their practical applications." The book, fully committed to the chromosome theory of heredity and its usefulness in plant and animal breeding, was so widely adopted as a textbook for teaching genetics that Babcock and Clausen put out a second, greatly expanded edition in 1927.

Babcock next set out to probe the universality of Morgan's findings by conducting genetic research similar to his but with plants instead of flies. In 1918 he began to experiment with *Crepis*, a genus of almost 200 species found mainly in north temperate Eurasian settings and known in the United States as hawkweed or hawk's beard. Like Morgan's flies, its species have low chromosome numbers; in addition, they are easy to crossbreed and grow well in a greenhouse. Although he realized by 1925 that the two sets of experiments would not dovetail quite as well as he had hoped, Babcock continued to work with *Crepis* because his experiments were yielding valuable results for studying relationships between species in terms of cellular functions, or cytology, as well as genetics. Most importantly, Babcock showed that new species evolved via gene mutations, structural changes in the chromosomes, and, on occasion, the acquisition of one or more additional sets of chromosomes. In the early 1930s Babcock became convinced that the evolution of *Crepis* could best be understood by studying the cytology of related genera. His efforts in this area resulted in a comprehensive definition of *Crepis*'s standing in both the tribe *Cichorieae* or *Lactuceae*, which includes such plants as lettuce and endive, and the family *Compositae*, which includes asters and daisies.

Babcock's greatest contribution to the field of genetics was the publication of *The Genus Crepis* (1947). This work, the culmination of almost thirty years of research, is the most complete monograph on a genus of flowering plant written to date and "a fascinating classic that no student of taxonomy should fail to read" (Davis and Heywood, p. 67). After throwing out the imposters and including several neglected variations, he ended up with 196 species for which he compiled data on chromosome number, morphology, crossability, and geographic distribution, then traced the evolution and migration of *Crepis* from its origins in Central Asia. His opus was immediately recognized as a milestone in the understanding of plant evolution and inspired similar, though smaller, studies.

After retiring, Babcock helped to form in 1950 the Forest Genetics Research Foundation for purposes of applying genetic research to the breeding of trees. "Future Forests and Heredity" (*American Forests* [Nov. 1953]), his last publication, helped to secure one of the foundation's goals, a congressional appropriation for the Institute of Forest Genetics.

Babcock received a number of awards and honors. He became a research associate of the Carnegie Institution in Washington, D.C., in 1925 and a member of the American Association for the Advancement of Science. He served as president of four professional societies: the Western Society of Naturalists (1929), the California Botanical Society (1940), the Society for the Study of Evolution (1952), and the California Academy of Sciences (1954). He received the University of California's Faculty Research Lectureship in 1944 and was elected to the National Academy of Science in 1946. He died in Berkeley, California.

Babcock made significant contributions to the development of genetics as both a teacher and researcher. His textbook provided the earliest training that many eminent geneticists and plant breeders received. His more than 100 scholarly publications explaining plant evolution primarily in terms of genetics mark him as a pioneer in the application of genetics research.

• Except for a few personal letters located in the Harvey Monroe Hall Papers in Cal-Berkeley's Bancroft Library, Babcock's papers did not survive. George Ledyard Stebbins, "Ernest Brown Babcock," National Academy of Sciences, *Biographical Memoirs* 32 (1958): 50–66, provides a good biography of Babcock as well as a complete bibliography of his publications. P. H. Davis and V. H. Heywood, *Principles of Angiosperm Taxonomy* (1963), discusses the importance of Babcock's work with *Crepis*. An obituary is in the *New York Times*, 9 Dec. 1954.

CHARLES W. CAREY, JR.

BABCOCK, Harold Delos (24 Jan. 1882–8 Apr. 1968), physicist and astrophysicist, was born in Edgerton, Wisconsin, the son of Emilus Welcome Babcock, a general store owner and farmer, and Mary Eliza Brown. Babcock's rural isolation and his frail health (exacerbated by an early attack of rheumatic fever) may have impelled his pursuit of intellectual activities. As a youth, he became interested in science and engineering, and particularly in electricity and photography. In 1896 his family moved to Los Angeles, California, and in 1901 he matriculated at the University of California, Berkeley, in the College of Electrical Engineering. While at Berkeley, Babcock specialized in laboratory physics and concentrated on electricity and spectroscopy (the production and investigation of the spectra of luminous bodies). He completed his studies in 1906 and received a B.S. in absentia the following year. In 1907 Babcock married Mary G. Henderson; they had one son, Horace Welcome, who later became an astronomer and director of the Mount Wilson and Palomar Observatories.

In 1906 Babcock obtained a position as laboratory assistant at the National Bureau of Standards. There he and Edward Bennett Rosa, a bureau physicist, found that small changes in atmospheric humidity were responsible for the variations of the laboratory standards of electrical resistance. Babcock left the bureau in 1908 and returned to the University of California as an instructor in the physics department.

Shortly after his return to Berkeley, Babcock was offered a position at the Mount Wilson Observatory and began work there in February 1909. The staff of the Mount Wilson Observatory, in the southern California mountains near Pasadena, had strong ties with their colleagues at Berkeley's Lick Observatory and were able to hear about someone of Babcock's abilities in a short time. Although his initial research at the observatory was as an assistant in stellar spectroscopy and in Jacobus C. Kapteyn's project of Selected Areas of Stars (wherein the stars in selected samples of the sky were studied in great detail for purposes of learning more about the entire sky from a statistical point of view), Babcock soon concentrated on solar and laboratory spectroscopy. The research that occupied most of his first two decades at Mount Wilson was the determination of accurate wavelengths of the absorption lines in the solar spectrum, using the iron arc spectrum (produced when iron is made luminous in an electric arc) as a standard. Babcock and his colleague at Mount Wilson, Charles E. St. John, realized that the standard reference on solar spectrum wavelengths, Henry A. Rowland's *Preliminary Table of Solar Spectrum Wavelengths* (1895–1897), contained values for the line wavelengths that were too large by .0036 percent, along with erratic fluctuations. With their laboratory experience and the excellent facilities at the observatory's Pasadena Physical Laboratory, Babcock and St. John took into account all of the environmental and instrumental conditions that could affect the spectral line positions and obtained highly accurate and reproducible wavelengths. This work culminated in the publication with St. John, Charlotte E. Moore, Louise M. Ware, and Edmund F. Adams of *A Revision of Rowland's Preliminary Table of Solar Spectrum Wavelengths* (1928), which immediately became the standard reference for wavelengths in studies in astrophysics and proved to be an invaluable tool for astronomers everywhere.

Babcock's study of the solar spectrum led him to investigate the dark bands in the solar spectrum caused by absorption of certain wavelengths of light by oxygen molecules (composed of two atoms of oxygen) in the Earth's atmosphere. Beginning in 1927 Babcock and Gerhard H. Dieke, a research fellow at the California Institute of Technology, examined the structure of the atmospheric molecular oxygen bands. They noted that the main bands were accompanied by faint companion bands. When William F. Giauque and Herrick L. Johnston, chemists at the University of California, suggested that some of the faint bands could be the result of a molecule consisting of one atom of oxygen with the standard atomic weight of sixteen and a hitherto unknown isotope of oxygen with an atomic weight of eighteen, Babcock made a detailed listing of previously unclassified lines and bands. His precise measurements of these unclassified bands led to the discovery that oxygen had isotopes with atomic weights of seventeen and eighteen. This work resulted in the revision of all atomic weights and led other investigators to look for companion bands of additional elements.

In addition to carrying out his regular work, in 1929 Babcock was placed in charge of the observatory's diffraction-grating laboratory after the previous head of the laboratory, John A. Anderson, had transferred to the 200-inch telescope project. By the beginning of the twentieth century, many astronomers had begun to recognize the potential superiority of gratings over prisms for producing the spectra of bright stars and laboratory sources that they used in their research. The advantages of gratings are their ability to disperse a given spectrum to a wider degree than a single prism, their ability to produce a normal spectrum where wavelengths are evenly distributed over the entire spectrum, and their resolving power, which can only be matched by expensive, optically perfect prisms. The observatory's laboratory was established in 1912 to produce diffraction gratings of the highest quality for the researchers at Mount Wilson as there was no place existing that could provide suitable gratings. In 1929 it became apparent that the observatory's grating ruling engine (the "A" engine) was not up to the task of producing the quality of gratings required by astronomers that would be using the 200-inch telescope. For the next five years, Babcock and the observatory's instrument makers built a new ruling engine ("B") which would be capable of making gratings of the desired quality. By the time of Babcock's retirement in 1948, the B machine had just become capable of producing superior gratings for the 200-inch telescope.

Babcock officially retired from the observatory in February 1948 but continued to work there on various postretirement activities. In 1951 he began research on detecting the general magnetic field of the Sun at the observatory's Hale Solar Laboratory in Pasadena. Babcock performed this research with the assistance of his son, Horace, whose expertise in electronics and stellar magnetic fields was indispensable. Horace developed a solar magnetograph that was capable of detecting the low-intensity solar magnetic field. After a few years of mapping the Sun's magnetic field, the Babcocks were able in 1955 to announce that the field was dipolar, with its poles near the Sun's poles of rotation, and that its mean intensity at the poles was one gauss (much less than the fifty-gauss value claimed to have been detected by George Ellery Hale earlier in the century). The Babcocks' work provided the first reliable measurements of the Sun's magnetic field.

Babcock was a member of the National Academy of Sciences and an associate member of the Royal Astronomical Society. In 1953 he received the Bruce Medal of the Astronomical Society of the Pacific. He died in Pasadena, California.

Babcock's demand for precise research resulted in the revision of Rowland's wavelengths and the discovery of the oxygen isotopes, both significant scientific achievements. In addition, his work with his son on the solar magnetic field was a major contribution to solar physics.

• There is no collection of Babcock's personal papers. The best overall assessment of his life is Ira S. Bowen, "Harold Delos Babcock," National Academy of Sciences, *Biographical Memoirs* 45 (1974): 1–19, which also contains a complete bibliography of Babcock's writings. His work on diffraction gratings is discussed in Horace W. Babcock, "Diffraction Gratings at the Mount Wilson Observatory," *Physics Today* (July 1986): 34–42. The Babcocks' significance to solar physics is discussed in Karl Hufbauer, *Exploring the Sun: Solar Science since Galileo* (1991).

RONALD S. BRASHEAR

BABCOCK, James Francis (23 Feb. 1844–19 July 1897), chemist, was born in Boston, Massachusetts, the son of Archibald D. Babcock and Fannie F. Richards. James Francis attended the English High School and then the Lawrence Scientific School of Harvard University from 1860 to 1862 but did not graduate. He established an office and chemical laboratory in Boston, holding sessions for the Massachusetts College of Pharmacy in rooms connected with his laboratory.

Elected to the chair of medical chemistry of the college in 1867, Babcock shortly thereafter became professor. He married Mary P. Crosby in March 1869; they had five children. He resigned his position in 1874 and moved to a similar position at Boston University from 1874 to 1880. According to the memorial notice posted by the college in the *American Druggist and Pharmaceutical Record*, the professor was "kind and sympathetic," had a "sparkling wit," and was loved and respected by his students.

Babcock was a chemist in the Boston Department of Milk Inspection from 1879 to 1884 and inspector of milk and vinegar from 1885 to 1888, during what was an auspicious time for an inventive, articulate chemist specializing in food purity to gain prominence. Two generations of controversy over milk quality climaxed in the 1880s in a series of important laws defining adulteration and governing the manufacture and sale of products related to the dairy industry. The legislation marked a critical turning point in the relationship between government, manufacturers, and consumers and paved the way for the landmark Food and Drug Act of 1906.

The long-widespread practice of watering down milk and subsequently coloring it with chalk, magnesia, or plaster of Paris to make it appear rich and pure posed grave dangers to public health. While an 1868 act had made it unlawful to add foreign substances to milk, and the Federal Food and Health Act of 1882 specifically included deceptive coloring in the list of adulterants, Babcock noted in his Annual Report of 1887 that neither had been enforced because of the lack of analytical methods of detection.

In the dramatic opening remarks of his 1887 report, Babcock illustrated the severity of the problem by citing two cases involving poor children, the group most severely impacted by milk adulteration. A six-month-old baby and a number of children in a day nursery who were given only "heavily watered, skimmed and colored milk" were found to be malnourished and even mortally ill. Expressing his opinion on the adulterator, the impassioned chemist wrote, "Can there be any crime more detestable than the mercenary villainy which would rob the sick and feeble of the indispensable elements of life? . . . And here is a man, if he may be called such, who is willing to steal the food from their lips, and all for a few cents of extra profit. Language fails to properly characterize, and laws are inadequate to properly punish such a villain."

Persuaded "that if the coloring of milk could be prevented, it could but have a marked effect in reducing the quantity of watered and skimmed (sold as whole milk)," Babcock devised two new methods of detecting burnt sugar or caramel and annotto, a yellow coloring agent also used in butter to make it appear of a higher quality and so deceive consumers.

From 1885 to 1888 the percentage of adulterated milk samples tested by the department decreased from 30.64 to 8.49 percent, an improvement Babcock credited to his new analytical methods: "Colored milk and milk impaired by so-called 'preservatives,' as boracic and salicylic acids, has been almost wholly suppressed,—a result due in great measure to improvements in detecting these substances."

Although fraudulent practices were common in the dairy industry, butter speculators, dealers, and dairy farmers raised a great outcry against margarine, introduced in the 1870s, when it was found that the cheaper lard-based product was being deceptively sold as butter or used to adulterate it. In the hopes of stamping out the competitor altogether, the dairy interests claimed that "imitation butter" was full of noxious impurities that endangered public health. In many states, their powerful lobby obtained stringent labeling and licensing laws for margarine, and in 1886 the federal government passed a comprehensive Oleomargarine Act to regulate the manufacture and sale of the product. Many states also passed anticolor laws prohibiting the use of artificial yellow color in margarine.

In 1890 the Federal Committee on Agriculture considered a petition for the further regulation of oleomargarine and called Babcock to testify as an expert witness. Since the agricultural interests could not obtain prohibition, they campaigned for the requirement that the oleomargarine industry manufacture their product with the distinguishing and unappetizing feature of red or black coloring. Thanks to Babcock and other margarine supporters, their petition was rejected. Babcock's dedication to unadulterated food was evident in his paper "Blood Stains" and in his brochure *Laboratory Talks on Infant Foods* (1896). This interest led him to his later presidency of the Druggist Association of Boston in 1894.

In addition to maintaining an overwhelming interest in milk, Babcock was also responsible for the "3 percent limit," defining an intoxicating liquor. He was the state assayer of liquor for Massachusetts from 1875 to 1885 and was responsible for introducing the limit into the Massachusetts statutes. Babcock was also well known for his gift for chemical analysis, and his investigative talents were often called on in criminal cases, food investigations, and patent suits. After his wife's death in 1890, he married in 1892 Marion B. Alden; they had no children. He died of heart disease in Dorchester, Massachusetts.

Babcock, a gifted chemist and inventor, was a well-known lecturer, researcher, and analyst. He gained public recognition while inspector of milk and vinegar for the city of Boston for his success in combating adulteration. As state assayer of liquors, he introduced the 3 percent limit. His patents include a process for clarifying and bleaching fats and fatty oils and the "Babcock fire extinguisher" (patented 4 Aug. 1868), a portable apparatus that required pumping to create pressure. Also considered an expert in many court cases on food adulteration, Babcock used his lifelong obsession with medicine and drugs to his own and society's advantage.

• Some information on Babcock is available in *Historical Registry of Boston University* (1891), p. 25. Obituaries are in the *American Druggist and Pharmaceutical Record* (10 Aug. 1897), and in the *Boston Morning Journal*, 21 July 1897.

CELIA BERGOFFEN
MICHELLE E. OSBORN

BABCOCK, James Woods (11 Aug. 1856–3 Mar. 1922), psychiatrist, was born in Chester, South Carolina, the son of Sidney E. Babcock, a physician, and Margaret Woods. He graduated from Harvard College in 1882 and received an M.D. from Harvard Medical School in 1886. He served as assistant physician at McLean Hospital for the Insane in Somerville, Massachusetts, from 1887 until 1891, when he was appointed superintendent of the South Carolina State Lunatic Asylum in Columbia.

Babcock arrived in South Carolina eager to modernize and improve the asylum. Its physical plant had deteriorated since the Civil War, and its function had become largely custodial. One of his aims was to remodel the institution in ways that would emphasize its role as a hospital. For example, he worked to change its name to South Carolina State Hospital, a goal he achieved in 1895. He also established a training school for nurses with the help of Katherine Guion, a nurse from Lincolnton, North Carolina, whom he had met while at McLean. Guion was a graduate of the Massachusetts General Hospital Training School for Nurses. They married in 1892 and had three children.

Babcock's efforts to improve conditions at the hospital were inhibited by a chronically depressed state economy. The legislature failed to increase the hospital's appropriations in proportion to its rapid growth, and it became badly overcrowded and understaffed. During his years as superintendent (1891–1914), the South Carolina State Hospital spent less per patient than most other American state hospitals, and its mortality rates were well above the average for similar institutions. Black patients, who had first entered the hospital in large numbers after the Civil War, suffered the most from the substandard conditions. Babcock frequently complained about the hospital's deficiencies, including its facilities for black patients, but with little result.

Babcock's personality may have hindered his attempts to improve conditions at his hospital. Several contemporaries referred to him as a shy, gentle man who was reluctant to fight the legislature for appropriations and unable to gain effective control over some of his staff. He stopped having staff meetings and gradually lost touch with life on the wards. He published several articles on medical subjects, but none of them proved of much benefit to the hospital's patients. For example, in an article he published in the *American Journal of Insanity* in 1894, on the prevention of tuberculosis in asylums, he insisted on the need to isolate TB patients; yet he was unable to implement isolation at his own hospital. In 1909 the legislature appointed a committee to investigate the hospital, but the members could not agree as to the extent of Babcock's responsibility for its substandard conditions. After an acrimonious debate in the legislature in 1910, he was retained as superintendent and appointed to chair a new State Hospital Commission charged with purchasing and developing lands for a second state hospital at State Park. In 1913 he clashed with Governor Coleman L. Blease over the governor's attempt to force him to dismiss one of his assistant physicians, Dr. Eleanora B. Saunders. Babcock protested vigorously and successfully demanded a legislative investigation, which met early in 1914. The report of the investigating committee vindicated Babcock, but he resigned a month later and opened Waverley Sanitarium, a private mental institution near Columbia, which he operated until his death.

Babcock's most significant medical contributions were on pellagra. He diagnosed several cases of the niacin-deficiency disease at the state hospital in 1907 and became one of the first physicians to recognize and publicize its existence in the United States. In 1908 he studied pellagra in Italian hospitals and came away convinced that it was the same disease he had seen at his own hospital. Between 1908 and 1912 he published several articles on the nature, prevalence, and history of pellagra. In 1910, along with Dr. C. H. Lavinder of the U.S. Public Health Service, he translated Dr. Armand Marie's *La Pellagre*. He helped to found the National Association for the Study of Pellagra and served as its first president from 1910 to 1912. In 1909 and 1912 he organized national conferences on pellagra, which met at his state hospital. Babcock's writings and organizational efforts regarding pellagra were responsible for attracting national attention and stimulating research that led to Dr. Joseph Goldberger's discovery that the disease was the result of niacin deficiency.

From 1915 to 1922, he also lectured on psychiatry at the Medical College of South Carolina in Charleston. He died in Columbia, South Carolina.

• The Babcock papers at the South Caroliniana Library at the University of South Carolina, Columbia, contain correspondence and other items relating to Babcock's career. Letters to, from, and about Babcock are in the papers of Governors Benjamin R. Tillman, Martin F. Ansel, and Coleman L. Blease at the South Carolina Department of Archives and History, the Benjamin R. Tillman Papers in Clemson University's Special Collections, Robert Muldrow Cooper Library, and the Joseph Goldberger and Patrick L. Murphy Papers in the Southern Historical Collection, University of North Carolina at Chapel Hill. The published annual reports of the South Carolina State Hospital are essential sources on Babcock's career, as are the hospital's records. The latter are in the South Carolina Department of Archives and History. The reports and testimony of the legislative investigations of the South Carolina State Hospital in 1909 and 1914 provide much valuable information about Babcock. They were published under the following titles: *Testimony Taken before the Legislative Committee to Investigate the State Hospital for the Insane at Columbia* (1910); *Report of the Legislative Committee to Investigate the State Hospital for the Insane* (1910); and *Report and Proceedings of the Special Legislative Committee to Investigate the State Hospital for the Insane and State Park* (1914). Many of Babcock's publications, along with the *Transactions of the National Association for the Study of Pellagra* (1909, 1912), are in the Babcock collection at the Medical University of South Carolina, Charleston. Obituary notices are in the *American Journal of Psychiatry* 1 (1921–1922): 709–11, and *Journal of the South Carolina Medical Association* 18 (1922): 338.

PETER MCCANDLESS

BABCOCK, Joseph Weeks (6 Mar. 1850–27 Apr. 1909), U.S. congressman, was born in Swanton, Vermont, the son of Ebenezer Wright Babcock and Mahala Weeks; he was the grandson of Congressman Joseph Weeks of Vermont. When he was five years old Babcock's family moved to Iowa, where his father managed a lumber business in Cedar Falls. After sporadic education in local schools, Babcock attended Mount Vernon College (dates unknown). He entered the lumber trade in 1872, and during the mid-1880s he purchased an interest in what had been his father's company. With extensive holdings of lumber in Iowa and Wisconsin, the firm of Burch and Babcock prospered. In 1867 Babcock married Mary A. Finch, who died in 1899. The couple had one son and an adopted daughter. He later married Katie King.

Babcock moved to Necedah, Wisconsin, in 1881, and he made a successful race for the Wisconsin assembly in 1888. After two terms he ran for Congress as a Republican and won the seat from the Third District in 1892. Because of national GOP losses in 1890 and 1892, Babcock was able to make a name for himself quickly within the shrunken Republican bloc in the House. He helped to organize the Republican Congressional Campaign Committee in 1893 and was named acting chairman during the 1894 election when the sitting chairman resigned suddenly. Babcock supervised the campaign that capitalized on voter discontent after the panic of 1893 to produce record Republican gains in the House. As a result, he held the post of chairman of the congressional committee for the next decade.

In Wisconsin Babcock identified with the conservative wing of the party that opposed the reformist gubernatorial candidacy of Robert M. La Follette during the 1890s. So assiduous did he become in working against La Follette that he placed his own reelection in jeopardy in 1898. Babcock was a candidate for the U.S. Senate in 1899 but lost out to fellow Republican Joseph V. Quarles. Angered at what he deemed a betrayal by party leaders, including Senator John C. Spooner, Babcock made a public peace with the La Follette faction that lasted for several years.

When La Follette ran again for governor in 1900, Babcock arranged for conservatives not to oppose the reformist's candidacy. Newspapers wrote of a "Bob-Bab" alliance. The congressman hoped that La Follette would support his Senate candidacy in 1903 against Spooner. During this brief reform phase of his own career, Babcock sponsored legislation in 1901 that would have lowered tariff duties on the foreign products that competed with those made by large firms such as United States Steel. While emphasizing his overall commitment to the protective tariff, Babcock maintained that trusts should not be allowed to charge higher prices to American consumers. His goal, he said, was to protect labor from foreign competition "but not to a point that would create a monopoly of trade and raise prices to consumers" (*Chicago Tribune*, 15 Nov. 1901). The bill died in Congress, where Republican advocates of high tariffs controlled the agenda. Babcock's initiative did little to help him with the forces of reform, either in Wisconsin or within the emerging progressive coalition in Washington; at the same time it aroused suspicions of his political reliability among his protectionist colleagues within the GOP.

When Speaker of the House David B. Henderson retired in 1902, Babcock was one of the candidates vying to succeed him. He had some support from advocates of tariff reduction within the party, but he had to deny that his election would mean immediate tariff revision. In the end, Babcock's candidacy proved no match for the superior political skills of the winner, Joseph G. Cannon of Illinois.

By 1902 Babcock had ended his flirtation with La Follette and reform. He led the forces opposing the governor's program during the legislative session of 1903. In 1904 Babcock again was in the forefront of those trying to deny La Follette a third term in the statehouse. The intraparty battle raged throughout the entire year, with Babcock active in opposing the seating of a La Follette delegation to the Republican National Convention. Despite support from the Theodore Roosevelt administration, the anti–La Follette forces eventually suffered a series of defeats that left their leadership discredited and the governor in a position of political dominance. La Follette was especially angry at Babcock, and he made a particular point of trying to defeat the congressman for reelection. Babcock survived the challenge in 1904 by fewer than four hundred votes in his normally Republican district. Two years later Babcock again secured the Republican nomination but was unable to withstand the opposition to his reelection of the La Follette wing of the party. His Democratic opponent unseated him.

A stocky man with a full beard, Babcock lived in retirement in Washington, D.C., and Wisconsin until his death in Washington. His career in Congress and in Wisconsin illustrates the conflicting pressures within the Republican party during the transition from the older style politics of the late nineteenth century to the newer emphasis on reform of the Progressive era. Babcock was not able to make the shift successfully, and he became one of the more prominent political casualties of the rise of reform leaders such as La Follette.

• Babcock's papers are located at the State Historical Society of Wisconsin; they reveal more about his family than his public career. The Robert M. La Follette Papers at Wisconsin and at the Manuscript Division, Library of Congress, have information about Babcock. Other Babcock-related items are in the William H. Moody, Theodore Roosevelt, and John C. Spooner Papers at the Library of Congress and in the George D. Perkins Papers at the Iowa State Department of History and Archives, Des Moines. No full-length biography has been published. Among Babcock's published writings are "Lessons of the Recent Elections," *Forum* 26 (Dec. 1898): 403–5; "The Issues of the Campaign," *Independent*, 4 Oct. 1900, pp. 2387–90; and "Statehood Rights of Arizona and New Mexico," *Independent*, 1 Mar. 1906, pp. 505–8. Republican Congressional Campaign Committee, *Republican Text Book for the Campaign of 1902* (1902), is an example of Babcock's political work. Information on Babcock's political career in Wisconsin is in Albert O. Barton, *La Follette's Winning of Wisconsin* (1922); Dorothy Ganfield Fowler, *John Coit Spooner: Defender of Presidents* (1961); and Herbert F. Margulies, *The Decline of the Progressive Movement in Wisconsin, 1890–1920* (1968). An obituary is in the *Washington Post*, 28 Apr. 1909.

LEWIS L. GOULD

BABCOCK, Orville Elias (25 Dec. 1835–2 June 1884), soldier, engineer, and presidential secretary, was born in Franklin, Vermont, the son of Elias Babcock, Jr., and Clara Olmstead. Graduating third in his class from the U.S. Military Academy at West Point in 1861, he was commissioned a second lieutenant of engineers. During the first year of the Civil War he gained promotion to first lieutenant, serving successively in the Department of Pennsylvania and the Department of the Shenandoah. He was then transferred to the Army of the Potomac, where he served on the staff of William B. Franklin during the latter's tenure in charge of the Left Grand Division. Promoted to captain (regular army) and lieutenant colonel (volunteers) in 1863, Babcock joined the staff of the Department of the Ohio, accompanied the Ninth Corps when it reinforced the Union siege of Vicksburg, and later participated in the Knoxville campaign (Oct.–Dec. 1863).

Prominent Union generals, including George McClellan, spoke highly of Babcock's ability, and in 1864 General-in-Chief Ulysses S. Grant added him to his staff. In the year-long campaign that followed, Babcock proved to be a trustworthy aide; he was wounded on 9 August 1864 by an explosion at Grant's headquarters at City Point, Virginia. It fell to Babcock on 9 April 1865 to help select Wilmer McLean's residence as the site of Lee's surrender to Grant at Appomattox Court House.

Babcock remained on Grant's staff after the war, gaining a brevet promotion to brigadier general of regulars for his war service and permanent promotion to major. On 8 November 1866, he married Annie Eliza Campbell in Galena, Illinois; the couple had four sons. He stayed aloof from the debate among Grant's staff officers over Reconstruction and the advisability of a Grant run for the presidency. Nevertheless, when Grant became president in 1869, Babcock was assigned to serve as his assistant private secretary. Charming and personable, he was to be involved in several questionable transactions.

In 1869 Grant sent Babcock to the Dominican Republic on a tour of inspection after lobbyists representing the Dominican government had broached the idea of annexation. Babcock exceeded his instructions and returned with a treaty of annexation for the entire republic, initiating a controversy that was to have a major impact on the Grant administration, as the president pursued first annexation and then vindication. Passionate critics of annexation suggested that Dominican negotiators had promised Babcock rewards for his action, and his behavior became a focal point for the treaty's opponents, led by Charles Sumner.

Appointed superintendent of public buildings and grounds for the District of Columbia in 1871, Babcock oversaw significant construction, including the Chain Bridge and the east wing of the executive offices, as well as important street improvements. However, his association with Alexander R. Shepherd, governor of the district, raised eyebrows when a congressional investigation revealed various fiscal irregularities. In 1876 he was accused of conspiring to set up one of Shepherd's critics by planting on him documents stolen from a safe, but he was acquitted.

Most serious, however, were allegations in 1875 that Babcock was associated with the so-called Whiskey Ring, a conspiracy to defraud the government of revenue from taxes on distilled whiskey. Babcock had befriended John McDonald, supervisor of internal revenue at St. Louis; in turn McDonald, a Grant appointee, had diverted some of the proceeds from his operation to the Republican party at the state and national levels. Telegrams from Babcock to McDonald, many signed "Sylph," a cryptic reference to a certain St. Louis woman, appeared to keep McDonald informed of efforts to investigate the ring. Grant had warmly supported Secretary of the Treasury Benjamin H. Bristow's prosecution of the ring, declaring, "Let no guilty man escape"; thus the president was first shocked, then angered, as Babcock and others tried to convince him that Bristow was seeking to use the case to advance to the White House by assailing the administration. On 9 December 1875, a St. Louis grand jury indicted Babcock for conspiring to defraud the government; his efforts to have a military trial failed. He was acquitted in February 1876, owing in part to Grant's supportive testimony. Aware that Babcock's continued presence in the White House would be counterproductive, Grant named his son, Ulysses Grant, Jr., to replace Babcock as private secretary.

Most historians have judged Babcock guilty of complicity in the Whiskey Ring; however, several people, notably William T. Sherman, joined Grant in believing him innocent. A close examination of Babcock's papers suggests that the president's secretary may have been attempting to conceal some unsavory private matter from public scrutiny, and that he feared members of the ring would tell all if he did not shield them. He proved unsuccessful in preventing Bristow from investigating the fraud or in securing Grant's intervention to halt Bristow. Claims that Grant knowingly protected a guilty man collapsed in light of Grant's subsequent private comments about Babcock, although both Grant and his wife were dissatisfied with his conduct. As the president remarked, "If Babcock is guilty there is no man who wants him so much proven guilty as I do, for it is the greatest piece of traitorism to me that a man could possibly practice" (Brown, p. 90). Nevertheless, as Grant biographer William B. Hesseltine pointed out, "Babcock seems to have had intimate contacts with most of the corrupt men of a corrupt decade. He fished for gold in every stinking cesspool, and served more than any other man to blacken the record of Grant's Administrations" (pp. 380–81). Grant's loyalty blinded him to Babcock's behavior; it proved poor judgment to retain Babcock in office as long as Grant did.

Babcock retained his position as inspector of lighthouses under Grant's successors. He remained in touch with the Grant family and his former White House associates, although he complained bitterly that Grant had not treated him well and that Mrs. Grant kept her distance. Never again was he part of the Grant inner circle. Along with Levi Luckey, another of Grant's White House private secretaries, he drowned at Mosquito Inlet, Florida.

• Babcock's papers are at the Newberry Library, Chicago. Although no biography exists, one can discover much about his controversial career in William B. Hesseltine, *Ulysses S. Grant, Politician* (1935); Allan Nevins, *Hamilton Fish: The Inner History of the Grant Administration* (1936); Dee Brown, *The Year of the Century: 1876* (1966); and C. Vann Woodward, ed., *Responses of the Presidents to Charges of Misconduct* (1974). Obituaries are in the *New York Times* and the Jacksonville, Fla., *Times-Union*, both 4 June 1884.

BROOKS D. SIMPSON

BABCOCK, Stephen Moulton (22 Oct. 1843–1 July 1931), agricultural chemist, was born near Bridgewater, New York, the son of Pelig Brown Babcock and Cornelia Scott, farmers. Babcock worked from childhood on the family farm. His inquisitive mind attracted him to science, and he enrolled in Tufts College, obtaining a bachelor's degree in 1866. He began engineering studies at Renssalaer Polytechnic Institute but returned to the farm after the death of his father. In 1872 he was a student of chemistry at Cornell University and in 1875 an instructor of chemistry. In 1877 he began graduate studies at the University of Göttingen. After receiving a Ph.D. in chemistry in 1879, he resumed his Cornell instructorship. In 1882 he became chief chemist at the newly founded New York Agricultural Experiment Station in Geneva, New York. During his six years there he devised several methods of analysis for food materials.

In 1888 Babcock became professor of agricultural chemistry at the University of Wisconsin and chief chemist at the Wisconsin Agricultural Experiment Station in Madison. From 1901 to 1913 he was the assistant director of the station. Within two years of his arrival he was famous throughout the dairy industry. A major part of the Wisconsin economy, the dairy industry was undergoing a transition from farm to factory production of dairy products. Farmers now sold their milk as a cash crop. Because milk was sold by the pound, many farmers—to increase their income—skimmed off the cream and sold a watered-down product. The determination of the fat content of milk required a trained chemist and special procedures of extraction from milk samples that were slow and tedious. Agricultural scientists responded to the growth of the dairy industry by seeking a simple and rapid method. Babcock was assigned this problem by his dean at Wisconsin. By 1890 he developed a test that used sulfuric acid to release the fat from its suspension in milk followed by centrifugation and collection of the fat in the neck of a calibrated bottle. The milkfat content was read directly as a percentage from the height of the column. This simple method quickly became standard all over the United States, Canada, Europe, Australia, and New Zealand. Babcock never applied for a patent, releasing the test for free use. Several consequences ensued. Because farmers were now paid for milk quality, it was no longer profitable to skim and water milk. The test also enabled cattle testing associations to easily determine the fat production of cows and breed for quality milk production. In addition to herd improvement, the test promoted the campaign waged by the Department of Agriculture for pure foods and drugs, because the test provided a means of analysis and purity control. The test required a centrifuge, pipettes, and graduated test bottles and cylinders. The first laboratory-ware catalog in the United States appeared in 1892. Issued by the Kimble Glass Company, it provided manufactured apparatus affordable to dairymen and was the first example of quantity production of chemical apparatus in the United States. Because Babcock did not patent his invention, unscrupulous manufacturers produced defective models and almost discredited the test.

Babcock made additional contributions to the dairy industry by improving in 1897 the pasteurization process for milk and by inventing in 1902 with Harry Russell the cold curing of cheese, which resulted in a greatly improved quality of cheddar. His final investigation was an important contribution to the physiology of metabolism, a 1906 to 1912 study of how insects living on dry matter produce the moisture necessary to their functioning by their own metabolic processes.

Babcock was most profoundly influential in the field of nutrition. The prevailing ideas on nutrition in 1900 were those of German chemists who claimed that all foods were nothing but protein, fat, and carbohydrate. The protein served to rebuild tissue and the fat and carbohydrate were energy sources. A chemical analysis of food for these components was sufficient to derive the proper protein and caloric balances in the diet. Babcock began feeding experiments along these lines at the New York Agricultural Experiment Station, but he became skeptical when his experiments with cows seemed to reveal nothing of value. In 1901 he began to experiment with single-grain diets using two cows from the Wisconsin herd, feeding one a balanced ration derived from oats and the other from corn. Both cows deteriorated, and when one of them died three months into the experiment, the animal husbandry professor terminated the investigation.

Another opportunity to explore the biological importance of food source arose in 1907 with the hiring of four young scientists: Edwin Hart, George Humphry, Elmer McCollum, and Harry Steenbock. The single-grain experiment resumed with sixteen cows fed over a four-year period, although Babcock did not take part other than providing guidance, advice, and encouragement. The cows, divided into four groups, each got an equivalent food balance from either corn, wheat, oats, or a mixture of the three grains. The corn-fed cows did the best, remaining vigorous and giving birth to healthy calves. The wheat-fed group did poorly and produced premature, sickly calves. The oat-fed and mixed-grain groups were intermediate in health. The four scientists published their report in 1911, concluding that they had demonstrated the lack of biological equivalence in feeds that were chemically equivalent in protein, fat, and carbohydrate. Babcock interpreted the experiment as indicating that there was something in the corn missing from or in insufficient quantity in the other grains that enabled the cows to become sexually mature and bear healthy offspring. Important discoveries followed quickly as McCollum, a close friend of Babcock who was greatly influenced by him, sought a more suitable animal for dietary experiments and developed a white rat colony for this purpose. In 1914 he discovered "fat-soluble A," the first of a complex of substances later dubbed "vitamins." In 1915 he found "water-soluble B," the first of the B-complex vitamins. Babcock's skepticism and feeding experiments had led to the recognition that foods contained not only protein, fat, and carbohydrate, but also many essential trace nutrients.

Babcock married May Crandall in 1896; they had no children. He retired in 1913 and lived in his Madison home until his death. His main characteristics were a lack of seriousness and an earthiness that manifested itself in his love of storytelling, hearty laughter, and merry appearance. Babcock enjoyed life and cared little for gaining credit for his ideas. He loved sports, especially baseball, following the professional teams closely. At seventy-eight he learned to drive a car and indulged himself in long trips through rural Wisconsin.

Babcock, although best known for his work relevant to the dairy industry, made his most profound impact by guiding and inspiring those who took a new approach to nutrition studies at Wisconsin, placing the university at the forefront of the new era of vitamin and mineral research.

• Babcock's personal papers are in the State Historical Society of Wisconsin. There is also a small collection in the Cornell University Archives. Babcock published little; his articles are mostly in the bulletins and reports of the New York and Wisconsin Agricultural Experiment Stations. For accounts of his life by his colleagues, see Harry L. Russell, *Stephen Moulton Babcock* (1943), and with the same title Edwin B. Hart, *Journal of Nutrition* 37 (1949): 3–7. Two fine studies of his scientific accomplishments are by Aaron J. Ihde, "Stephen Moulton Babcock—Benevolent Skeptic," in *Perspectives in the History of Science and Technology*, ed. Duane Roller (1971), pp. 271–82, and Paul de Kruif, *Hunger Fighters* (1926). Edward J. Dies, *Titans of the Soil* (1949), presents a study of agricultural scientists with a chapter on Babcock. For the Babcock milkfat test and the development of chemical apparatus, see F. Kneissl, "A History of the Chemical Apparatus Industry," *Journal of Chemical Education* 10 (1933): 519–23. Obituaries are in the *New York Times*, 3 July 1931, and *Science*, 24 July 1931.

ALBERT B. COSTA

BABSON, Roger Ward (6 July 1875–5 Mar. 1967), businessman, author, and philanthropist, was born in Gloucester, Massachusetts, the son of Nathaniel Babson, a dry-goods merchant and wholesaler, and Ellen Stearns. As a child, Babson spent his summers in Gloucester on his paternal grandfather's farm, an experience that later prompted him to write that he "owed more to that farm than any educational institution." Off the farm, the young Babson, who was a rowdy albeit "nervous" boy, worried his mother by associating not with other middle-class Yankee children but with the "Gould Courters," an Irish street gang.

Babson's days as a gang member ended in 1890 when he entered Gloucester High School and had a religious conversion experience, "the greatest event of my life." After his conversion, Babson became very active in Gloucester's Trinity Congregational Church, where he taught Sunday school. During the week, he was forced by his father, a stern, practical man, to study bookkeeping in school at the expense of required courses, a move that nearly prevented his graduation.

After convincing the Gloucester School Committee to give him a "special" high school diploma in 1894, Babson entertained thoughts of moving west. His father, however, insisted that he attend the Massachusetts Institute of Technology. While enrolled at MIT, Babson studied civil engineering and spent his summers working on road construction projects. But when he graduated from MIT with a B.S. in 1898, his father urged him to take up a trade like banking that involved more "repeat business" than construction.

Heeding his father's advice, Babson got a job in a Boston investment house, from which he was quickly fired because of his independent work style. Afterward he established a bond-selling business in New York City, though he was soon back in Boston, working for a bond firm that specialized in utilities. His income secure, Babson in 1900 married Grace Margaret Knight, a clergyman's daughter whom he had known since childhood. The Babsons had one child.

Babson's career suffered a temporary setback in 1901 when he came down with tuberculosis. Unable to work in Boston, he contemplated ways he could make money from his suburban Wellesley Hills home. From his bond-selling experience, Babson knew that investors would benefit by knowing more about the institutions that issued stocks and bonds. So in 1904 he and his wife set up the Business Statistical Organization, Inc. (BSO; later the Babson Statistical Organization, Inc.), with capital of $1,200. They then proceeded to collect, analyze, and index business information at their home and to disseminate their information among BSO subscribers by means of a publication titled the *Composite Circular*.

After the financial panic of 1907, Babson felt called not only to publish business statistics but also to counsel people on how to invest wisely in stocks, bonds, and commodities. Toward this end, he formulated his "area theory" of the business cycle. Based on Newton's law of action and reaction, Babson's area theory was the inspiration for his *Babsonchart*, which highlighted periods of economic prosperity and depression. Since Babson believed that every period of business prosperity would be followed by an equal and opposite period of depression, he counseled investors to sell in good times and to buy in bad ones, advice that kept many of his clients from going bankrupt in the stock market crash of 1929.

Babson's business services, together with his judicious personal investments in stocks, bonds, and Florida real estate, earned him millions of dollars. But it was not enough for Babson simply to earn money; he also wanted to make the world a better place. To do this he entered politics, serving as assistant secretary of labor in the Woodrow Wilson administration, fighting for U.S. entry into the League of Nations, and running for the presidency of the United States on the National Prohibition party ticket in 1940. He also served a stormy two years (1936–1938) as moderator of the Congregational Christian churches, many of whose members apparently did not appreciate Babson's decidedly old-fashioned views on subjects such as drinking and dancing.

Despite his busy schedule, Babson managed to produce a formidable literary corpus that included more than fifty books on subjects such as religion, business, and labor-management relations. He also founded a number of business schools. The first and largest of these was the Babson Institute (now Babson College). Opened in 1919, this Wellesley, Massachusetts, institution, one of the first privately endowed schools of business administration in the United States, eventually became the repository for the Babson's extensive collection of Newtonian memorabilia.

Eight years after founding the Babson Institute, Babson financed the opening of Webber College for women in Babson Park, Florida. The college was in large part the brainchild of Babson's wife, who wanted to enable women to "assume financial responsibilities." After many years of overseeing the work at Webber College, Grace Babson died in 1956. One year later Babson married Nona Margaret Dougherty, his former nurse.

Toward the end of his life, Babson worked hard to ensure that Protestant values and Yankee ingenuity would emerge intact from a nuclear war. Viewing Eureka, Kansas, as a wholesome site and an unlikely casualty of World War III, he established Utopia College there in 1946. Several years later he chose the comparably safe town of New Boston, New Hampshire, as the site of his Gravity Research Foundation (GRF). Dedicated to harnessing the power of gravity, the GRF was one of Babson's more unconventional projects. Another was his carving of messages into Gloucester's Dogtown Rocks, one of which bears his guiding principle: "Keep out of debt."

Babson knew that his actions struck some as eccentric, but he claimed not to care. Fond of the motto "never try, never win," he viewed his wealth and accomplishments as proof of the value of rugged individualism. Had Babson not been a rugged individualist he might never have realized what was arguably his greatest achievement: success as a pioneer in the field of business statistics. But Babson, who died in Lake Wales, Florida, was not only a pioneer statistician; he was also a shrewd judge of mass psychology, which he viewed as the key to understanding changes in market behavior.

• Babson's papers are in the Horn Library, Babson College, Wellesley, Mass. His autobiography is *Actions and Reactions* (1935). Other notable books by Babson include *Religion and Business* (1920), *Investment Fundamentals* (1930), *Fighting Business Depressions* (1932), *Business Barometers and Investment* (1940), and *Jesus as a Scientist* (1957). For commentary on Babson's life and ideas, see Horace Givens, "Roger W. Babson and His Major Contemporaries" (Ph.D. diss., New York Univ., 1975), and Earl Smith, *Yankee Genius* (1954). An obituary is in the *New York Times*, 6 Mar. 1967.

CLIFFORD PUTNEY

BABY LAURENCE (24 Feb. 1921–2 Apr. 1974), African-American jazz tap dancer, was born Laurence Donald Jackson in Baltimore, Maryland. His parents' names and occupations are unknown. He was a boy soprano at age twelve, singing with McKinney's Cotton Pickers. When the bandleader Don Redman came to town, he heard Jackson and asked his mother if he could take the boy on the road. She agreed, provided that her son was supplied with a tutor. Touring on the Loew's circuit, Jackson's first time in New York was marked by a visit to the Hoofers Club in Harlem, where he saw the tap dancing of Honi Coles, Raymond Winfield, Roland Holder, and Harold Mablin. Jackson returned home sometime later to a sudden tragedy: both his parents had died in a fire. "I don't think I ever got used to the idea," he told Marshall Stearns in *Jazz Dance* (1968). "They always took such good care of me."

Laurence and a brother formed a vocal group called The Four Buds and tried to establish themselves in New York. He worked in the Harlem nightclub owned by Dickie Wells—the retired dancer from the group of Wells, Mordecai, and Taylor—who nicknamed him "Baby" and encouraged his dancing. He frequented the Hoofers Club, absorbing ideas and picking up steps from Eddie Rector, Pete Nugent, Toots Davis, Jack Wiggins, and Teddy Hale, who became his chief dancing rival. "I saw a fellow dance and his feet never touched the floor," the tap dancer Bunny Briggs said, recalling when he first saw Laurence dance in the thirties. Baby worked after-hour sessions, gigged around Harlem, Washington, and Cincinnati and began playing theaters such as Harlem's Apollo in the late thirties. He performed with a group called The Six Merry Scotchmen (in some billings, the Harlem Highlanders), who dressed in kilts, danced, and sang Jimmie Lunceford arrangements in five-part harmony.

Around 1940 Jackson focused on tap dancing and became a soloist. Through the forties, he danced with the big bands of Duke Ellington, Count Basie, and Woody Herman, and in the fifties danced in small Harlem jazz clubs. Under the influence of jazz saxophonist Charlie "Bird" Parker and other bebop musicians, Laurence expanded tap technique into jazz dancing. He performed with jazz pianist Art Tatum, duplicating in his feet what Tatum played with his fingers. Through listening hard to Parker, Dizzy Gillespie, and Bud Powell as well as jazz drummers such as Max Roach, Laurence developed a way of improvising solo lines and variations as much like a hornman as a percussionist. "He was more a drummer than a dancer," Whitney Balliett wrote in *New York Notes* (1976). "He did little with the top half of his torso. But his legs and feet were speed and thunder and surprise . . . a succession of explosions, machine-gun rattles and jarring thumps." Like musicians in a jazz combo, Laurence was also a fluent improviser who took solos, traded breaks, and built on motifs that were suggested by previous hornmen. He was a master of dynamics who would start a thirty-two-bar chorus with light heel-and-toe figures, then drop in heavy off-beat accents and sprays of rapid toe beats that gave way to double-time bursts of rhythm.

Beset by drugs, alcohol, and financial troubles, Laurence stopped performing in the late fifties. After a long illness he returned to Harlem in the early sixties to work again in small jazz clubs. In 1960 he began a long-time engagement with Charlie Mingus at the Showplace and that summer danced with Max Roach and Charlie Mingus in Newport, Rhode Island. He was a sensation at the Newport Jazz Festival in 1962 in a legendary concert that included Nugent, Honi Coles, and Bunny Briggs and marked the revival of tap dancing.

Laurence drifted into near-oblivion in the late sixties, dancing weekends in a restaurant in Gaithersburg, Maryland, with an excellent trio headed by drummer Eddie Phyfe. By 1973 he reappeared in New York City, heading up the successful Sunday afternoon tap dancing sessions at the Jazz Museum. During this time, he took in students, danced at the Palace with Josephine Baker, did some television, and gave one of his last triumphant performances at the Newport–New York Jazz Festival.

Laurence is regarded as an authentic jazz dancer who further developed the art of tap dancing by treating the body as a percussive instrument. "In the consistency and fluidity of his beat, the bending melodic lines of his phrasing, and his overall instrumentalized conception, Baby is a jazz musician," Nat Hentoff wrote in the album notes for *Baby Laurence—Dance Master*, a 1959 recording of Laurence's rhythmic virtuosity that demonstrates the inextricable tie between jazz tap dancing and jazz music.

• Baby Laurence Jackson's tap dancing can be heard on *Baby Laurence—Dance Master* (Classic Jazz CJ30, recorded 1959, released 1977) with liner notes by Nat Hentoff. See also Whitney Balliett, *New York Notes: A Journal of Jazz 1972–1975* (1976), for a vivid recapturing of Laurence's tap dancing style, and Marshall and Jean Stearns, *Jazz Dance: The Story of American Vernacular Dance* (1968), which includes interviews with Laurence from 1960 to 1964.

CONSTANCE VALIS HILL

BACCALONI, Salvatore (14 Apr. 1900–31 Dec. 1969), opera singer, was born in Rome, Italy, the son of Joaquin Baccaloni, a building contractor, and Ferminia Desideri. Young Salvatore attended Rome's San Salvatore in Lauro School, where he received vocal instruction, eventually obtaining a soprano post in 1906 with St. Peter's Sistine Chapel Choir. As a child Baccaloni earned a wage equivalent to that of a government clerk, singing mass litanies and Gregorian chants three times a week. When his voice broke at age twelve, however, he was forced to briefly abandon his singing career until he made the usual transition to bass.

Taking his father's advice, Baccaloni entered the Academy of Fine Arts in Rome in 1915 to study architecture, remaining there until the Italian army drafted him to serve in its signal corps division for one year. When he returned to school in April 1919, Baccaloni finished his degree but soon left architecture for a full-time singing career. Thereafter, he sought every opportunity, both public and private, to practice his singing. In 1921 the operatic baritone Giuseppe Kaschman took him as pupil for two years. With Kaschman's help, Baccaloni made the transition from popular to professional bass singer, debuting in Rome's Teatro Adriano as Bartolo in *The Barber of Seville* in 1922. Unfortunately, during the four years he sang in Italy's small opera houses, he was paid so little that, at one point, he shared a room with eight other aspiring singers.

In 1926 Arturo Toscanini, the conductor of Milan's La Scala Opera, heard Baccaloni sing and encouraged La Scala's director to engage him. Baccaloni joined La Scala and after three years began specializing in the minor but crucial operatic role of *basso buffo*, or comic bass. By virtue of his acting talent, his comedic nature, and his rich bass voice, Baccaloni quickly became a star. He sang regularly at La Scala until 1940, and during that time he debuted in England and the United States. He appeared in Covent Garden from 1928 to 1929 with Timur in *Turandot*. Baccaloni then performed at Glyndebourne from 1936 to 1939 where he was praised as Bartolo in *The Marriage of Figaro* and as Osmin in *The Abduction from the Seraglio*. Baccaloni also occasionally appeared at the Teatro Colón in Buenos Aires from 1931 to 1941, and then again in 1947.

Baccaloni made a brief American debut in 1930 at the Chicago Civic Opera House as Fra Melitone in *La Forza del Destino*. In December 1940 he officially began a twenty-two-year career with the Metropolitan Opera House, settling in New York with his Bulgarian wife, Elena Svilarova, whom he married in 1928. They had no children. Two weeks after debuting as Bartolo in *The Marriage of Figaro*, he performed the title role in an opera restored in his honor, Donizetti's *Don Pasquale*. Maurice Zolotow, writing for the *Saturday Evening Post* in 1947, commented that "within a few weeks he became one of the biggest box-office draws the Metropolitan boasted," winning "audiences by the adroitness of his performance and by his grotesque humor." In fact Baccaloni's repeated performance of Bartolo in *The Barber of Seville* was so superb that it prompted the Metropolitan Opera to reinsert an aria, "A un Dottore," which had been removed years before because of its difficulty.

While at the Met, Baccaloni performed in a number of benefits, and, weighing over three hundred pounds with only a 5′7″ frame, he delighted children by performing comic roles in matinees. Once, following his doctor's orders, Baccaloni reduced his weight to 250 pounds. However, the corresponding drop in his spirit and the quality of his voice convinced him to resume his daily eating schedule of four banquet meals and six snacks, with each snack amounting to an average person's dinner. Though "mountainous," Baccaloni was incredibly "agile," prompting Zolotow to write, "He rolls his eyes, he wiggles his pudgy fingers, he shakes his corpulent body, he waggles his jowls, he stamps all over the stage. He is the funniest thing in opera." Baccaloni felt most honored when one child said he was "funnier than Mickey Mouse." Though some adult critics found his antics heavy-handed, reducing opera to stock comedy, others were impressed by his ability to create comedic effect with the smallest of gestures.

Baccaloni performed 297 times in New York City and gave 146 performances at other opera houses in both America and Europe, making regular appearances at the San Francisco Opera House. By the end of his career, he had taken 170 roles, and despite the fact that most of these parts were minor, Baccaloni often stole the show. He appeared two or three times a week at the Met for a flat rate of $500, making him at that time one of the highest paid singers in opera. He also gave special performances for $2,500. Although Baccaloni sang in five languages and resided in America, because Italian was spoken by performers backstage at the Met, regardless of nationality, he still required the help of phonetic translations to sing arias in English. According to Baccaloni, even when he made an effort to speak English, Americans wanted to practice their Italian with him. Thus he appreciated a 1950 role in the light San Francisco opera *The Chocolate Soldier*, which allowed him to study English and "get paid for it."

With his international comedic fame and enough English under his belt, Baccaloni was offered a number of nonsinging roles in movies. He first appeared as the bossy Italian immigrant father-in-law in the 1957 family comedy, *Full of Life*. A number of movies followed, including *Merry Andrew* (1958), *Rock-a-Bye Baby* (1958), *Fanny* (1961), and *The Pigeon That Took Rome* (1962). Baccaloni retired from the Met in 1962 after performing as Dr. Dulcamara in *L'Elisir d'Amore* and as Fra Melitone in *La Forza del Destino*. Besides singing, Baccaloni painted, read the work of philosophers such as Spinoza, walked his large French poodle, played gin rummy and poker, and attended Catholic mass. Upon his death in New York City's St. Clare's Hospital, he left unfinished an ongoing project to "combine his knowledge of theater, opera and architecture in a new method of stage designing."

• For detailed biographical information about Baccaloni see Maurice Zolotow, "Opera's Funny Man," *Saturday Evening Post*, 29 Nov. 1947, pp. 30–31, 118, 120, 122; and David Ewen, *Musicians Since 1900* (1978). Although written in Italian, R. Celletti, "Baccaloni, Salvatore," in *Le grandi voci* (1964), p. 33, with discography by R. Vegeto, is also a valuable source. See also Ross Parmenter, "Portrait of a Basso," *New York Times*, 24 Nov. 1940; *Opera News*, 2 Dec. 1940, and "Basso Buffo," *Time*, 6 Jan. 1941, p. 34. An obituary is in the *New York Times*, 1 Jan. 1970.

BARBARA L. CICCARELLI

BACHAUER, Gina (21 May 1913–22 Aug. 1976), pianist, was born in Athens, Greece, the daughter of Jean Bachauer, a foreign-car dealer of Austrian descent, and Ersilia Marostica, of Italian descent. Bachauer's father's business was profitable, and she enjoyed a comfortable childhood. Her career may have been determined as early as Christmas of 1917, when she received a toy piano as a present. Young Gina impressed family and friends with her ability to play the tiny instrument; consequently, her mother enrolled her at the Athens Royal Conservatory.

In later life Bachauer recalled that she was not an especially precocious pupil at the conservatory. While studying music there part time, she also attended public school in Athens. At the age of ten she was accepted as a pupil by the virtuoso German pianist Waldemar Freeman, then the preeminent musician on the conservatory faculty; it soon became clear that Bachauer would pursue a musical career. She studied with Freeman for the next six years while completing her secondary education, and in 1929 she graduated with honors from the conservatory.

Soon afterward Bachauer moved to Paris, where she studied for two and one-half years under eminent French pianist Alfred Cortot, the director of the École Normale de Musique. Toward the end of her sojourn in Paris, and on the recommendation of Freeman, she traveled to London in 1932 to play for the Russian composer and pianist Sergei Rachmaninoff, a close friend and associate of Freeman. Encouraged by Rachmaninoff's praise, Bachauer returned to Athens to prepare herself for a state-sponsored musical competition in Vienna. She won first prize and then returned to her studies in Paris. There, in 1933, Bachauer gave her first public recital at the Salle Pleyel to critical acclaim.

Bachauer then stood on the threshold of a major performing career, but her plans changed dramatically within weeks of her first public success: her father's auto dealership collapsed, and the family was rendered virtually penniless. Bachauer returned to Athens to help support her family, in particular her two younger brothers. To help pay for their education she joined the faculty of the Athens Conservatory, where for the next four years she taught elementary piano. Bachauer was able to maintain her performing skills through appearances as a soloist with the conservatory orchestra, which later became the National Orchestra of Greece. She performed with the orchestra under several leading conductors, including Felix Weingartner and Camille Saint-Saëns, and the young conductor Dimitri Mitropoulos. Throughout this period Bachauer received encouragement from Rachmaninoff, and when her schedule and financial situation permitted she traveled to various locations in Europe to receive lessons from him.

In 1937 Bachauer married John Christodoulo. (The couple subsequently divorced; they had no children.) That same year, about the time that her father's business was beginning to prosper again, Bachauer was invited to give several concerts in Egypt. Her successes in Alexandria and Cairo led to a series of orchestral bookings throughout the Middle East during the next two years, as well as recital appearances in Paris and Milan.

Bachauer's rejuvenated career was again interrupted in 1939, when German aggression prevented her from touring in Europe. Because Greece was also threatened, she decided to leave her homeland and settle in Alexandria. During World War II Bachauer gave more than six hundred free recitals for Allied soldiers in the Middle East. She played from a repertory of more than one thousand pieces that included everything from Beethoven to boogie-woogie, and often under circumstances that were far from ideal. On one occasion she arrived at a British military hospital near Tobruk, Libya, to give a concert and discovered that most of the ivory keys had fallen off the only available piano. The resourceful Bachauer used several packs of chewing gum to reattach them, and they remained in place until her last number, the Chopin A-flat Polonaise. As she began to play the opening chords ivories went flying all over the hospital ward, but Bachauer gamely continued to the end.

When the war ended in Europe in May 1945 Bachauer settled in England, hoping to revive her career. After some months she was able to persuade the New London Orchestra, under the direction of Alec Sherman, to engage her for a single performance. The "persuasion" must have been entirely through the language of music: at that time Bachauer spoke no English, and communication at rehearsals occurred through a combination of gestures and Italian musical terminology. Bachauer's first performance with the orchestra, on 21 January 1946 at the Royal Albert Hall, was a success. Sherman rehired her for subsequent appearances, and over the next four years she played with orchestras throughout the British Isles. She also gave several recitals in major European cities.

Bachauer's American recital debut occurred at Town Hall in New York City on 15 October 1950. Although the audience was small—only thirty-five people attended—her performance was a critical success and her career blossomed. During the following season she appeared more than fifty times on the American concert stage and fulfilled dozens of engagements throughout Europe. This active schedule continued unabated for nearly three decades, during which time Bachauer devoted half of each year to coast-to-coast tours of the United States. In 1951 she and Alec Sherman were married. They made their home in London, where Sherman became conductor of the London Symphony Orchestra in the early 1950s. They had no children.

Bachauer specialized in performances of works by Domenico Scarlatti, Mozart, Chopin, and Liszt, as well as concert transcriptions of the organ works of Johann Sebastian Bach. She played with power, volume, and formidable technique and was highly regarded by leading critics in the United States and abroad. At the time of her death longtime *New York Times* music critic Harold Schonberg wrote that from the time of her Town Hall debut in 1950 she was considered part of "the front rank of virtuoso pianists." European critics often compared Bachauer to the great nineteenth-century Spanish pianist Teresa Carreño, who was nicknamed "the Valkyrie of the Pianoforte." Like all great artists Bachauer had some detractors, a small but vocal minority who found fault with her vigorous tempos and disliked her interpretations of works by Brahms and Beethoven, which she played only rarely.

Despite her full schedule, which included five or six hours of practice daily, Bachauer found time to pursue avocational interests in cooking, swimming, reading, and floral decoration; for relaxation she played Bach. Her stamina was the envy of contemporary musicians, many of whom—conductor Mitropoulos and pianists Alicia de Larrocha and Garrick Olson among them—were friends as well as professional colleagues.

Bachauer's honors included membership in both the Order of the Golden Phoenix (1949) and the Order of St. Michael (1950), both conferred upon her by King Paul of Greece, one of her pupils. She died in Athens.

• Accounts of her life and career can be found in "A Pianist with Power," *New York Times*, 30 Oct. 1950; James Lyms, "Perseverance Pays," *Musical America*, 1 Feb. 1954, pp. 8–9; and the entry on Bachauer in *Current Biography 1954*, pp. 53–55. An interview with Bachauer is included in Adele Marcus, *Great Pianists Speak with Adele Marcus* (1979). An obituary, together with an appreciative essay by Harold Schonberg, is in the *New York Times*, 23 Aug. 1976.

ANN T. KEENE

BACHE, Alexander Dallas (19 July 1806–17 Feb. 1867), scientist and educator, was born in Philadelphia, Pennsylvania, the son of Richard Bache, a postmaster, and Sophia Dallas. An elite family history supported Bache's upbringing. He was the great-grandson of Benjamin Franklin and was related to a number of influential men, including his uncle George Dallas, who served as vice president in James K. Polk's administration, and his grandfather Alexander James Dallas, who was appointed secretary of the treasury by President James Madison. Bache entered the U.S. Military Academy at West Point in 1821 at the age of fifteen; four years later he graduated first in his class. He spent one more year at the academy teaching mathematics and natural philosophy before serving for two years as a lieutenant with the Army Corps of Engineers. While working on the construction of Fort Adams in Newport, Rhode Island, Bache met and later, in 1828, married Nancy Clarke Fowler; they adopted one child.

In 1828 Bache made an important decision to accept an appointment as professor of natural philosophy and chemistry at the University of Pennsylvania. Although Bache had broad scientific interests, he was especially interested in geophysical research. In Philadelphia, he built a magnetic observatory and made extensive studies of terrestrial magnetism. During the 1830s Bache became a leader of the scientific community in Philadelphia and played a leading role in administering the American Philosophical Society and the Franklin Institute, seeking to professionalize both institutions by raising the standards of membership and emphasizing original scientific research. At the Franklin Institute, from 1830 to 1835, Bache led the federally funded effort to determine the causes of steam-boiler explosions. This was one of the first uses of technical experts by the federal government to help solve problems involving public policy.

During the 1830s Bache also actively supported educational reform. In 1836 he was asked to help organize the curriculum at Girard College in Philadelphia. He was elected president and spent two years in Europe investigating more than 250 educational institutions. His research resulted in the publication of a 600-page study titled *Report on Education in Europe, to the Trustees of the Girard College for Orphans* (1839). Because of a delay in the opening of Girard College, Bache never had a chance to apply his observations to the organization of the school; instead, he used his *Report* to help organize the curriculum at Philadelphia's Central High School, which he superintended from 1839 to 1842. Bache's *Report* was read by such educational reformers as Henry Barnard and Horace Mann and helped publicize the Prussian educational model in the United States.

During his European tour Bache also met with some of Europe's notable savants, including Alexander von Humboldt, François Arago, and Karl Friedrich Gauss, and he visited key scientific institutions. The trip intensified a commitment to raising the status of science in the United States. Soon after Bache's return, his colleague and friend Joseph Henry, who had accompanied Bache during part of the European trip, wrote Bache that "I am now more than ever of your opinion that the real working men in the way of science in this country should make common cause and endeavour by every proper means to make science more respected at home, to increase the facilities of scientific investigators and the inducements to scientific labours."

Bache saw an opportunity to realize these goals with the sudden death, in 1843, of Ferdinand Hassler, a Swiss émigré who had become superintendent of the U.S. Coast Survey after its establishment in 1807. Bache and his colleagues believed that the coast survey could be used to gain support for American science, especially to obtain federal patronage. After a successful campaign waged by his friends and colleagues, Bache became superintendent in December 1843. He was later appointed a member of the Lighthouse Board (c. 1844–1845) and superintendent of the Office of Weights and Measures (1844). During the two decades after gaining control of the coast survey, Bache transformed it into the most powerful scientific institution in the United States. By the late 1850s Congress annually appropriated approximately $500,000 for the survey, and it supported more scientists than any other institution in antebellum America; Bache thus became the most important patron in this period. His work, which sought to emulate European practices, was praised by European savants. In addition to hiring scientifically trained personnel, Bache employed scientists from outside the survey as consultants. By patronizing such scientific fields as hydrography, geodesy, astronomy, terrestrial magnetism, tidology (the study of the tides), meteorology, and natural history, Bache helped shape a geographical style for antebellum American science.

Bache used his position on the coast survey to become the central leader of the scientific community in the United States. Specifically, he became the "chief" of an elite group known as the "Lazzaroni" or "scientific beggars"; other notable members of this group included Benjamin Peirce, Louis Agassiz, and Joseph Henry. Bache and the Lazzaroni sought to professionalize American science by, among other actions, ensuring that first-class research scientists maintained control of national scientific institutions. Bache and the Lazzaroni attempted to institutionalize these professional ideals by reforming the American Association for the Advancement of Science. Bache served as president in 1850. Bache was also one of the most influential regents of the Smithsonian Institution from its opening in 1846; he stressed that it should be organized to support the advancement rather than merely the diffusion of knowledge. He also helped convince Joseph Henry to become the Smithsonian's first secretary. In 1863 Bache played a leading role in organizing the National Academy of Sciences and served as its first president. During the Civil War Bache used the coast survey to support the war effort, and he became vice president of the Sanitary Commission, a member of the Permanent Commission of the navy in charge of evaluating new weapons, a consultant to the army and the navy advising on battle plans, and a superintendent of the defense preparations for Philadelphia. Bache died in Newport, Rhode Island.

Bache played a central role in establishing professional standards and patterns of patronage for the American scientific community, and his administrative work set an important precedent for government involvement in scientific practice. Bache was a public scientist with social and cultural commitments that motivated a wide range of institution-building activities.

• Bache's private papers are in the Smithsonian Archives, the Library of Congress, and the Rhees Collection of the Huntington Library (San Marino, Calif.). The Records of the U.S. Coast and Geodetic Survey at the National Archives also contain extensive private correspondence. Other sources for Bache letters include the American Philosophical Society and the Franklin Institute in Philadelphia and the Benjamin Peirce Papers at Harvard University. A microfilm collection of some of Bache's letters can be found in the Reingold papers at the Smithsonian Archives. Some of his most important correspondence was republished in Nathan Reingold, *Science in Nineteenth-Century America: A Documentary History* (1964), and in *The Papers of Joseph Henry* (6 vols., 1972–). For a bibliography of Bache's writings, see Joseph Henry, "Memoir of Alexander Dallas Bache," National Academy of Sciences, *Biographical Memoirs* 1 (1877): 205–12. Also see the *Annual Reports of the U.S. Coast Survey* (1844–1866). The only biography of Bache is less than satisfactory: Merle M. Odgers, *Alexander Dallas Bache, Scientist and Educator, 1806–1867* (1947). For a critical study of Bache that focuses on his involvement with the coast survey, see Hugh Richard Slotten, *Patronage, Practice, and the Culture of American Science: Alexander Dallas Bache and the U.S. Coast Survey*

(1994). For a discussion of Bache's activities at the Franklin Institute, see Bruce Sinclair, *Philadelphia's Philosopher Mechanics: A History of the Franklin Institute, 1824–1865* (1974). On Bache's educational activities, see Slotten, "Science, Education, and Antebellum Reform: The Case of Alexander Dallas Bache," *History of Education Quarterly* 31 (Fall 1991): 323–42. On Bache's involvement with the antebellum scientific community, also see Robert V. Bruce, *The Launching of Modern American Science, 1846–1876* (1987). For Bache's views about science and technology, see Reingold, "Alexander Dallas Bache: Science and Technology in the American Idiom," *Technology and Culture* 11 (Apr. 1970): 163–77.

HUGH RICHARD SLOTTEN

BACHE, Benjamin Franklin (12 Aug. 1769–10 Sept. 1798), newspaper editor and publisher, was born in Philadelphia, Pennsylvania, the son of Richard Bache, a merchant, and Sarah Franklin, the daughter of Benjamin Franklin. Richard Bache, who had been trained in a countinghouse in his native Settle in Yorkshire, England, had limited success in business and figured less importantly in his son's life than did his famous grandfather. When Benjamin Franklin left Philadelphia for Paris in October 1776 to serve as one of the new American commissioners to France, his namesake grandson went with him for what became a nine-year stay in Europe. Why Richard and Sarah Bache allowed their seven-year-old son to go has been cause for conjecture: reasons range from the chance to ensure a good education for him away from the uncertainties of Philadelphia during the American Revolution to the desire to please the elderly Franklin, who was fond of the boy and through this arrangement could maintain his customary family dominance.

For three years young Bache attended a school in Passy, the Paris suburb where Franklin lived, and then was sent to an academy in Geneva, Switzerland, because, as Franklin wrote eleven-year-old John Quincy Adams, "as he [Bache] is to live in a Protestant country and a republic, I thought it best to finish his education where the proper principles prevail." When Bache returned to Passy in 1783, his education continued through private tutors and, in a momentous next step, at the hands of the master printer at Franklin's private press. It was Franklin's hope that his grandson might find his path to independence as a printer and publisher. An apt and industrious student, Bache went on to an apprenticeship in typefounding, which was cut short in 1785 when he returned with Franklin to Philadelphia. With European schooling and a cultural experience that included meeting many notable figures in his grandfather's home, Bache completed his formal education at the University of Pennsylvania, from which he received his bachelor's degree in 1787. In that year Franklin gave Bache his start in printing by setting up a business in which the two were nominal partners. Their efforts to furnish type fonts for other printers failed, as did Bache's venture in publishing Greek and Latin texts and Bible stories for use in schools. After Franklin's death in 1790 Bache turned to journalism, using part of his inheritance to establish a newspaper that was to absorb his energies completely.

Bache named his newspaper the *General Advertiser, and Political, Commercial, Agricultural, and Literary Journal*, a title shortened in 1791 to the *General Advertiser*. From the beginning, he made clear his commitment to freedom of the press. In November 1791, when the paper had appeared for a little more than a year, Bache married Margaret Hartman Markoe, who shared his democratic convictions. She had arrived in Philadelphia some years before with her mother, the widow of a sugar planter on the Danish island of St. Croix. Margaret's stepfather was Adam Kuhn, a prominent Philadelphia physician. What had begun as a newspaper of general information quickly became one that focused on important matters at home and abroad, taking full advantage of the fact that as the national capital Philadelphia was a center for incoming news and a source of news in the making. Bache's facility in French served him well in translating foreign documents and dispatches and in learning of the concerns of the large foreign-born population of Philadelphia, many of whom found Bache readily accessible in his newspaper office.

Bache's accounts of all actions of the Congress and his coverage of debates in the House of Representatives (the Senate was as yet closed to reporters), were respected by all factions for their accuracy and were widely reprinted. Thomas Jefferson provided him with copies of the *Leiden Gazette* for reliable news of European developments and, interested in helping Bache as an editor of firm republican principles, wrote him in April 1791 that he wished to see "a purely republican vehicle of news established between the seat of government and all its parts." Jefferson even suggested a makeup that would allow the paper, minus sheets of local advertising, to be mailed economically to distant locations. This plan, Jefferson told George Washington in a letter the following year, was tried but failed for reasons not specified. In the meantime, Jefferson, as secretary of state, had offered Philip M. Freneau "the Clerkship of Foreign Languages." Freneau moved from New York to Philadelphia to establish the *National Gazette*, a partisan republican paper he edited from October 1791 until Jefferson resigned in 1793.

The demise of the *National Gazette* left the *General Advertiser* the dominant republican newspaper, with Bache growing ever more radical in outlook and intemperate in attack. To him the French Revolution was a step taken in pursuit of the rights proclaimed as self-evident in the American Declaration of Independence, and obligations to the French were to be honored according to the terms of the Treaty of Alliance of 1778 despite the change in regime. In this conviction he defended Edmond Charles Genêt (or "Citizen Genêt"), the new French minister to the United States appointed in 1793. Genêt's indiscretions, such as commissioning privateers to operate out of American ports and attempting to launch American-manned military operations against British- and Spanish-held territories in North America, led Washington to demand his recall.

In 1794 Bache renamed his paper the *Aurora and General Advertiser*, announcing that the *Aurora* (as the paper came to be generally known) would "diffuse light, dispel the shades of ignorance, and strengthen the fair fabric of freedom on its surest foundation, publicity and information." Much of the publicity and information in the *Aurora* included unfavorable news about Federalists in general and about George Washington in particular. Enjoying respect bordering on veneration, the president, in Bache's view, provided a convenient shield for Federalists whose interests lay primarily in improving commercial relations with Great Britain rather than in strengthening American sovereignty. Sent by Washington in 1794 to negotiate a final settlement of difficulties arising out of violations of the Treaty of Paris of 1783 and to regulate commerce and navigation, John Jay returned in 1795 with an agreement that yielded so much to Great Britain that Washington was reluctant to send it to the Senate. He finally did so after several weeks but with the demand of a pledge of secrecy from the senators, who ratified the treaty on 24 June 1795.

The Jay Treaty (which Bache always called "the British Treaty") alarmed the supporters of France, who feared a possible military alliance between Great Britain and the United States. On 29 June extracts from the treaty appeared in the *Aurora*, and by 2 July Bache had printed hundreds of pamphlets containing the entire text of the treaty, apparently leaked to him by Senator Stevens Thompson Mason of Virginia. Taking fast stagecoaches, Bache sold these pamphlets at stops between Philadelphia and Boston, where there were public meetings denouncing the treaty. Aggravated by the terms of the treaty, the French refused to receive Charles Coatesworth Pinckney, appointed by Washington as minister to France. Shortly afterward, President John Adams sent John Marshall and Elbridge Gerry to join Pinckney on a peace mission, but Charles Maurice de Talleyrand, the French foreign minister, refused to meet the three-man commission officially. When it became known that Talleyrand suggested that a payment of $250,000 would pave the way for a meeting, with the financial details to be handled by two Swiss citizens and an American banker in Hamburg (designated as X, Y, and Z in commission dispatches), apologists for France were in a difficult position. This was especially true for Bache, who published in the *Aurora* a long letter in which Talleyrand tried to explain the French position. Since the letter appeared in the paper even before the president had received it from the secretary of state, Bache was suspected of being a French agent and was charged with treason. The charge was dropped when he was able to prove that he had received the letter from a resident of Philadelphia; however, remarks made in his defense were used in charging him with seditious libel of the president and the executive branch of the government.

Brought into a federal district court on 29 June 1798, Bache was released on a $4,000 bond, to be tried in October. Recognizing his arrest as an attempt to shut down the *Aurora*, he continued to instruct the public on the importance of a free press. He argued that only state courts could treat cases of libel and predicted that he would be cleared in a federal court on constitutional grounds. The case never came to trial for Bache died in the worst yellow fever epidemic to hit Philadelphia in years. Suspended for a few weeks, the *Aurora* reappeared in November, with Bache's widow as publisher and his able assistant William Duane as editor. In an epitaph, Margaret Bache spoke of her late husband as "a man inflexible in virtue, unappalled by power or persecution, and, who, in dying knew no anxieties but what were excited by his apprehensions for his country—and for his young family." The young family included four children. Margaret Bache and William Duane married in 1800 and carried on with the *Aurora*.

Bache's concern for his country was not overstated in the epitaph. It was this concern that kept Bache at the task of publishing his newspaper six days a week without interruption, building its circulation from 400 paid subscribers in 1790 to 1,700 in 1798. The *Aurora* doubtless reached many more readers than the paid subscribers through copies in public rooms and by being passed from hand to hand. Although he often employed the overheated rhetoric common in the rancorous partisan journalism of the time, he always had political rather than personal ends in view. His persistence in calling for a more open government and greater freedom of the press was important to the existence and endurance of an effective opposition press, of which the *Aurora* was the chief exemplar.

• Books by Bache include *A Specimen of Printing Types Belonging to Benjamin Franklin Bache's Printing Office, Philadelphia* (1790?), *Remarks Occasioned by the Late Conduct of Mr. Washington, as President of the United States* (1797), and *Truth Will Out!: The Foul Charges of the Tories against the Editor of the Aurora Repelled by Positive Proof and Plain Truth, and His Base Calumniators Put to Shame . . .* (1798). Bernard Faÿ, *Bernard Faÿ's the Two Franklins: Fathers of American Democracy* (1933), is a profoundly admiring work. It has been superseded by Jeffery Alan Smith, *Franklin and Bache: Envisioning the Enlightened Republic* (1990), and especially by James D. Tagg, *Benjamin Franklin Bache and the Philadelphia Aurora* (1991). For the larger context of Bache's journalism see Donald H. Stewart, *The Opposition Press of the Federalist Period* (1969), and Smith, *Printers and Press Freedom: The Ideology of Early American Journalism* (1988).

VINCENT FREIMARCK

BACHE, Franklin (25 Oct. 1792–19 Mar. 1864), physician, chemist, and author, was born in Philadelphia, Pennsylvania, the son of Benjamin Franklin Bache, a noted anti-Federalist journalist, and Margaret Markoe. Franklin Bache's grandmother, Sarah, was Benjamin Franklin's daughter. He received a classical education in the academy of the Reverend Samuel D. Wylie and was awarded both his A.B. in 1810 and his M.D. in 1814 by the University of Pennsylvania. He studied medicine privately with Benjamin Rush and James Rush. He joined the Thirty-second Regiment of

Infantry as a surgeon's mate in 1813, was permitted to complete his medical education, and served thereafter on what was then called the frontier until the end of the War of 1812. He remained in military service, as surgeon, until 1816, when he tendered his resignation. He entered medical practice in Philadelphia but never established a prominent or lucrative practice. In 1818 he was appointed "Citizen Surgeon" by the War Department to examine and advise medical recruits. That same year he married Aglae Dabadie, with whom he would have six children before her death in 1835. He was appointed physician to the Walnut Street Prison in 1824 and to the Eastern Penitentiary at Cherry Hill in 1829 and held both posts until 1836, an experience that evoked an interest in penology and led him to advocate "separate confinement" in preference to "gregarious confinement" and to oppose flogging.

He had early shown an interest in chemistry—a newspaper piece on muriatic acid appeared in 1811—and turned his attention in that direction, a move that was accompanied by a decline in his medical practice. In 1819 he published *A System of Chemistry for the Use of Students of Medicine*, a not particularly distinguished work, and later began to lecture on the subject. In 1821 he lectured to the private medical pupils of Thomas T. Hewson and in 1826, in general chemistry as professor of chemistry at the Franklin Institute. In 1831, when George B. Wood, who was to be Bache's lifelong colleague and collaborator, vacated the professorship of chemistry in favor of the professorship of materia medica at the Philadelphia College of Pharmacy, Bache accepted the post of professor of chemistry at the same college. In 1841 he was appointed professor of chemistry in the Jefferson Medical College in Philadelphia and remained in that post until his death.

Bache's work in chemistry was not driven toward the discovery of new truths in science; rather, he criticized, organized, and clarified the work of others. Thus the American edition of Andrew Ure's *Dictionary of Chemistry* (1821) was edited by Robert Hare, "assisted by Franklin Bache." In 1823 Bache wrote a supplement to William Henry's *Elements of Experimental Chemistry*; in 1825, after James Cutbush's death, he edited anonymously and prepared for publication Cutbush's *System of Pyrotechny*; between 1830 and 1840 he edited four (the third through the sixth) American editions of Edward Turner's *Elements of Chemistry* (and contended that his editing and annotations made the U.S. editions "much more correct than the London work"); and in 1836 he edited the third edition of Hare's *A Compendium of the Course of Chemical Instruction in the Medical Department of the University of Pennsylvania*. In 1834 he wrote fifteen articles, all on chemicals, with the exception of one on acupuncture, for the first two, and only, volumes of Isaac Hays's *American Cyclopedia of Practical Medicine and Surgery*. Bache was the most active of Philadelphia physicians experimenting with acupuncture. His translation of J. Morand's *Memoir sur l'Acupuncture* was published in Philadelphia as *Memoir on Acupuncturation* in 1825. He extolled the practice in "Cases Illustrative of the Remedial Effects of Acupuncturation" (*North American Medical and Surgical Journal* 1 [1826]: 211–21). Indicative of Bache's approach and his personal and editorial proclivities was his response to Robley Dunglison's request in 1846 to review the latter's *New Remedies* in preparation for a fourth edition. Bache meticulously listed 159 errors (fourteen others "too trifling") and made five suggestions (mainly to recommend up-to-date terminology of the *London Pharmacopoeia*). In the same vein, Bache compiled and called to the attention of the publisher, on his own initiative, a detailed list of 267 errors he found in the U.S. edition of George Fownes's *Elementary Chemistry* in 1859. From 1826 to 1831 Bache was an editor of and contributor to the *North American Medical and Surgical Journal*. His *Introductory Lecture* to his chemistry classes at Jefferson was published at least six times between 1841 and 1852.

Bache's national recognition derived also, if not mainly, from his work with the *Pharmacopoeia of the United States of America* and the *Dispensatory of the United States of America*. His work with the *Pharmacopoeia* began in 1829 when he was appointed (with George B. Wood) to the committee of the College of Physicians of Philadelphia charged with the revision of the *Pharmacopoeia*. He and Wood became the key figures in carrying out the revisions of the *Pharmacopoeia*. A large portion of Bache's time, a great deal of drudgery, and meticulous attention to detail and to the comments of a good number of prominent collaborators and critics went into some thirty-five years of his work with the *Pharmacopoeia*, all without recompense.

The *United States Dispensatory*, which provided details and commentary that the *Pharmacopoeia* studiously avoided—some so as to provide a market for the *Dispensatory*—did prove profitable. With Wood in the role of chief author, the *Dispensatory* went through eleven editions in Bache's lifetime and proved an indispensable handbook to physicians and pharmacists. Indeed, Bache's income from the work and the proceeds of his appointment at Jefferson placed him in "a position of comparative affluence." Altogether, Bache received proceeds from the sale of 79,000 copies of the book.

Bache was elected a member of the American Philosophical Society in 1820 and was an active and most conscientious member. He chaired various committees, was one of the society's secretaries for eighteen years and its president from 1852 to 1855. He became a Fellow of the College of Physicians of Philadelphia in 1829, was elected vice president in 1855 (a post he held until his death), and presided over the college from 1860 to 1862. He was made a member of the Academy of Natural Sciences of Philadelphia, a corresponding member of the National Institute for the Promotion of Science of Washington in 1840, and an honorary member of the Imperial Academy of Naturalists of Moscow in 1854. He was one of the managers of the Institution for the Deaf and Dumb of Philadelphia and served for a time as president of its board. He was also active in local professional and social groups, the Wistar Club, the Kappa Lambda Society, and the Medical Club. He was an ardent participant in the temperance movement and devoted considerable effort to the Temperance Society. He was a master mason in the Franklin Lodge No. 134. Bache died in Philadelphia.

George Wood, the dominant and more dynamic colleague, described Bache as a man who was slow in reasoning but whose reason and judgment were intellectually superior. Bache possessed very little imagination, although he did have a sense of humor. He was placid in temperament and could not "be said to have been ambitious." He was slow and deliberate in walking and talking. His lectures, like his writing, displayed his sense of orderliness; they were "clear, concise, correct, simple, methodical [and] calculated."

Although he was not a researcher, analyst, or inventor, Bache made a place for himself as one of the most widely known teachers in the field of his time. Benjamin Silliman and Robley Dunglison both asked for his help and advice; Robert Hare and Edward Turner were among his professional correspondents. His very arduous work on the *Pharmacopoeia* and *Dispensatory* earned him the gratitude and respect of U.S. pharmacy and an honorary membership in the American Pharmaceutical Association.

• Bache's papers are distributed among Philadelphia libraries. The Bache papers in the Library of the College of Physicians include his correspondence (mainly professional), holograph lectures, notices of his publications, commentaries on works in chemistry, and the like. Also at the college library are papers pertaining to the *United States Pharmacopoeia* that largely reflect Bache's work, especially for the years 1858–1864. At the Library of the American Philosophical Society, the Bache Papers–Castle Collection contain, among the papers of the Bache family, correspondence with the various institutions with which he was affiliated, a diary he kept for seven months in 1853, and various memorabilia. The Historical Society of Pennsylvania has a letterbook and correspondence of Bache, especially with his brother-in-law and his son on economic and political as well as family matters. There are student notes of Bache's lectures at the Philadelphia College of Physicians Library and at the National Library of Medicine.

George Bacon Wood presented two memoirs of Bache. The first, to the College of Physicians, was published as the *Biographical Memoir of Franklin Bache, M.D.* (1865). The second, to the American Philosophical Society, was published as a lengthy "Obituary Notice" in the *Proceedings of the American Philosophical Society* 10 (1865–1868): 121–36. Bache's chemical contributions are highlighted in Edgar F. Smith's privately published *Franklin Bache, Chemist* (1922). Bache's activity with regard to the *Pharmacopoeia* and *Dispensatory* is described in G. Sonnedecker, *Kremers and Urdang's History of Pharmacy*, 4th ed. (1976), pp. 264–265, 279. His interest in acupuncture is described in J. H. Cassedy, "Early Uses of Acupuncture in the United States," *Bulletin of the New York Academy of Medicine* 50 (1974): 879–906. Bache's interest in penology produced two letters by him in *Hazard's Register of Pennsylvania*, 28 Mar. 1829, pp. 197–99, and 30 Oct. 1830, pp. 282–83.

DAVID L. COWEN

BACHE, Jules Semon (9 Nov. 1861–24 Mar. 1944), financier and art collector, was born in New York City, the son of Semon Bache, a merchant of glass and mirrors, and Elizabeth van Praag. Bache attended the Charlier Institute in New York City and supplemented his studies in Frankfurt, Germany. He worked for a few years in his father's firm before beginning a financial career in the employ of his uncle Leopold Cahn. At the brokerage of Leopold Cahn & Company, Bache worked his way from cashier (1880) to treasurer (1881) to partner (1886). In 1892 he took over the firm, renaming it J. S. Bache & Company. Also in 1892 Bache married Florence Rosalee Scheftel, the daughter of a well-known New York City merchant; they had two children. Bache and his wife were divorced in Paris in 1925.

Under Bache's leadership J. S. Bache & Company prospered, having at the time of his death thirty-seven branches in various cities, all connected by an elaborate wire service. Bache was the first broker to use such a wire service, an innovation soon copied by others. His company held memberships on most stock and commodity exchanges in the United States and had representatives in London, Mexico City, and several Canadian cities.

J. S. Bache & Company accepted deposits, lent money, ran a stock brokerage, and participated in underwriting stocks and bonds. As a result of these activities, Bache became the director of several firms, including American Spirits Manufacturing Company, Empire Trust Company, Cosmopolitan Fire Insurance Company, Ann Arbor Railroad Company, Tennessee Copper Company, and Kelvinator Corporation. He also served as vice president of Chrysler Corporation from 1929 to 1943 and as president of Dome Mines, Ltd., from 1918 to 1943. When the Glass-Steagall Act of 1933 forced a separation of commercial and investment banking, Bache chose to maintain his investment banking and brokerage business, which had generated his greatest profits, giving up the business of making loans and taking deposits.

In most ways Bache was typical of New York financiers of his time. His underwriting activities did not involve uncommon risk, and his impact outside the brokerage business seems to have been minimal. The fortune he made (about $3.5 million in addition to his art collection) was not unusual for bankers at the time. Also like many others, Bache was a philanthropist, founding an orphanage in Paris, France, and supporting medical and scientific research. He donated money to the American Museum of Natural History, the New York Zoological Society, and the Metropolitan Museum of Art. He contributed to the Republican party, serving as a delegate to its national convention in 1920.

Bache occasionally wrote short articles about financial issues, which were published in popular magazines. His writings discussed taxation, railroad reorganization, and Wall Street operations. He wrote in simple but entertaining terms to explain complex ideas to an audience that understood little about finances.

Neither Bache's business career nor his literary efforts proved significant enough to secure lasting fame. However, his activities as an art collector made an enormously important contribution to American culture. Bache, initially influenced by the Lowengard family of Paris, began collecting decorative arts after World War I. He acquired Louis XVI furniture, medieval enamels, French porcelains, English silver, and diverse sculptures in marble, bronze, and terra-cotta. These items were sold when Bache died, with the proceeds going to his granddaughters.

In 1924 Bache began collecting paintings, having become a client of Sir Joseph Duveen. Duveen was an unscrupulous art dealer, more concerned with his commissions than with the quality of the art he sold. Nonetheless, he extended many courtesies to good customers like Bache. Bache's first purchases were from the Flemish and German schools. Duveen subsequently helped Bache and his daughter Kitty furnish and decorate a house in Palm Beach, Florida, including some paintings from the Spanish school. In 1927 Duveen persuaded Bache to begin collecting Italian paintings by arranging a European tour for Bache and Kitty.

By the time the stock market crashed in 1929, Bache had begun to realize that Duveen did not always accurately represent the pictures he sold. Bache then owed Duveen about $4 million, and he arranged a long period of credit. Not until 1937 did Bache completely settle his debt with Duveen, and he made few subsequent purchases.

In 1937 Bache made plans to show his collection publicly in his home at 814 Fifth Avenue. He opened a museum at that location and arranged for the art to be seen by appointment from 1937 to 1942. He continued his corporate work, continued his philanthropy, and traveled. He died in in Palm Beach. Bache bequeathed sixty-three paintings plus other works of art to the Metropolitan Museum of Art. The collection was valued at $12 million in 1944; its worth has increased with time.

Possibly the most important painting Bache donated to the Metropolitan, and certainly the most popular, is Francisco Goya's portrait *Don Manuel Osorio Manrique de Zuñiga* (1788). The work depicts a four-year-old Spanish aristocrat holding a magpie on a string, while three cats in the background stare malevolently at the bird. Bache donated two outstanding religious works to the museum. The first, *Portrait of a Carthusian* (1446), by Flemish painter Petrus Christus, is the earliest-known portrait of a monk. The second is Carlo Crivelli's *Madonna and Child*. Apparently painted in the 1480s, the masterpiece is 15″ ×10″, delicately and precisely executed.

Other significant paintings bequeathed to the Met by Bache include Fra Filippo Lippi's *Madonna and Child Enthroned, with Two Angels* (c. 1437–1444), Luca Signorelli's *Madonna and Child* (c. 1505), Titian's *Venus and Adonis* (c. 1560s), Rembrandt's *The Standard Bearer* (1654), Gerard ter Borch's *Curiosity* (c. 1660), and Jean Honoré Fragonard's *Le Billet Doux* (c. 1769–1773).

Bache's middle-class background instilled in him a respect for financial success and charitable donations. His intelligence and training enabled him to cultivate these values, becoming a well-known millionaire, philanthropist, and art collector.

• There is no publicly accessible collection of Bache papers. Articles that Bache wrote for publication include: "A Fair Deal for the Railroads," *Forum*, Feb. 1924, pp. 198–200; "A Lively Plea for the Sales Tax," *Weekly Review*, 11 June 1921, pp. 554–56; "Profit, Mainspring of Progress," *Forum*, Sept. 1925, pp. 339–45; "The Wall Street of Today," *Moody's Magazine*, Jan. 1911, pp. 8–10; and "Why Not a Sales Tax?" *Review of Reviews*, Jan. 1921, pp. 57–60. Bache also published *A Catalogue of Paintings in the Bache Collection* (1944). The best source of information about his business career is the *New York Times*, which also contains information about his private life and reports on Bache's public speeches in the 1920s and 1930s. "A Typical New York Banking Firm," *Bankers' Magazine*, Aug. 1905, pp. 278–80, provides a description of the offices of J. S. Bache & Company and makes mention of the firm's business matters. "Wall Street Walkout," *Newsweek*, 12 Oct. 1942, pp. 64–66, describes labor union problems at the Bache offices in New York. "Jules S. Bache Dies, Prominent Financier," *Commercial and Financial Chronicle*, 30 Mar. 1944, p. 1325, includes a small amount of information on Bache. There is a considerable amount of information available on the Bache art collection. See Harry B. Wehle, "The Bache Collection on Loan," *Metropolitan Museum of Art Bulletin* 1 (June 1943): 285–90; Mary Fanton Roberts, "The Bache Collection—A Great Gift to New York City," *Arts and Decoration* 48 (May 1938): 13–17, 30; Kathleen Howard, ed., *The Metropolitan Museum of Art Guide* (1984, rev. 1987); Howard Hibbard, *The Metropolitan Museum of Art* (1980); and Colin Simpson, *Artful Partners: Bernard Berenson and Joseph Duveen* (1986). An obituary is in the *New York Times*, 25 Mar. 1944, and a discussion of his will is in the *New York Times*, 30 Mar. 1944.

SUE C. PATRICK

BACHE, Richard (?1737–29 July 1811), merchant and revolutionary leader, was born in Settle in the West Riding of Yorkshire, England, the son of William Bache, a tax collector in Settle, and Mary Blyckenden. With encouragement from his father, Richard, at a young age, pursued a career in business and evidently worked in several British counting houses.

In 1760 Bache went to New York City and became a partner in the business of his older brother, Theophylact Bache. The Bache brothers' firm sold dry goods in New York and engaged in trade with agents in Newfoundland and in the West Indies. Cooperative and easygoing, Richard worked well with his brother and also sold for their firm real estate and marine insurance policies.

In 1762 Richard moved to Philadelphia (but maintained the partnership with his brother), entered the most prominent business and social circles in the city, and became involved with Joseph and William Shippen and Charles and Thomas Willing in the Mount Regale Fishing Company. He did fairly well in 1762 and 1763 with this company, and in 1766 he opened on Chestnut Street a dry-goods store, which sold a "neat assortment of European and East-India goods." In 1766 Bache experienced a business misfortune. With Edward Green he purchased a ship, the *Charleston*, loaded it with merchandise to be sold in Jamaica and in England, but found that his London partner refused to pay his share. The unfortunate Bache was forced to pay the expenses of over £3,600 in the next five years.

In 1767 Bache married Sally Franklin, the only daughter of Benjamin Franklin (1706–1790), despite her father's warning that Bache could not "maintain her properly." They had seven children. Benjamin Franklin Bache, their oldest child, became a prominent journalist. According to Franklin, Bache proved to be "a good Husband" and son-in-law, living in Franklin's home and caring for the affairs of his mother-in-law, Deborah.

Bache in 1769 served as a member of the Committee on Non-Importation Agreements, in 1773 opened a small wine and grocery business, and by 1775 was a member of the Committee of Correspondence. In 1775 the Second Continental Congress appointed Franklin to direct a committee for the creation of a post office, and that year Bache was selected as controller of the new postal system. Between 1776 and 1782 he served as postmaster general. Though his brother was a Loyalist, Bache actively participated in the American Revolution. He was named in April 1777 to the Pennsylvania Board of War and performed routine quarter-mastering activities. Bache also emerged as one of the leaders of the conservative revolutionary movement in Pennsylvania. Between 1776 and 1779 he served as chairman of the Republican Society, calling for the creation of a bicameral state legislature and for efficiency in government (he attributed inefficiency to radicals in the unicameral state legislature) and in the conduct of the war.

Between 1784 and 1792 Bache served as a director of Robert Morris's Bank of North America. He was involved in 1787 in Franklin's Society for Political Inquiries and the next year participated in a parade in Philadelphia to pay tribute to the adoption of the federal Constitution by ten states. With the death of Franklin in 1790, Bache helped to manage family affairs; among other things, Sally and he were left Franklin Court, Franklin's other Philadelphia real estate, and his lands in Ohio. The last years of Bache's life were spent with Sally on their Delaware farm, which was called "Settle" in honor of his English birthplace. He died at the farm. He was a cautious and conservative revolutionary and a merchant who met with limited success. He proved to be a capable and dependable manager and, in the contemporary world, would be perceived as a fairly effective organization man. However, the achievements of his father-in-law and those of his eldest son have done much to eclipse Bache's reputation.

• Several Philadelphia libraries contain primary sources about Bache. The Benjamin Franklin Papers, the Bache Family Papers, and the Benjamin Franklin Bache Papers are housed in the American Philosophical Society. Some of Bache's letters are also in the Historical Society of Pennsylvania. The best accounts of his career appear in James Tagg, *Benjamin Franklin Bache and the Philadelphia "Aurora"* (1991); and Claude-Anne Lopez and Eugenia Herbert, *The Private Franklin: The Man and His Family* (1975). Bache's merchant activities in colonial Philadelphia are mentioned in "The Mount Regale Fishing Company of Philadelphia," *Pennsylvania Magazine of History and Biography* 27 (1903): 88–90. For his role in the Republican Society, consult Richard L. Brunhouse, *The Counter-Revolution in Pennsylvania, 1776–1790* (1971). Bache's connections to Franklin are discussed in Carl Van Doren, *Benjamin Franklin* (1938); and Esmond Wright, *Franklin of Philadelphia* (1986). Bache's ties to his oldest son are examined in Jeffrey A. Smith, *Franklin and Bache: Envisioning the Enlightened Republic* (1990). Comments about Bache appear in J. T. Scharf and T. Westcott, *History of Philadelphia* (1884). Bache's obituary is in the *New York Columbian*, 2 Aug. 1811.

WILLIAM WEISBERGER

BACHE, Sarah Franklin (11 Sept. 1743–5 Oct. 1808), revolutionary war Patriot, was born in Philadelphia, Pennsylvania, the daughter of Benjamin Franklin (1706–1790) and Deborah Read. During her childhood, Sarah, known as Sally throughout her life, resided with her parents and half brother, William, Benjamin's illegitimate son. Deborah directed Sally's upbringing and education, though her father, who was often away from home, wrote a continuous stream of letters containing advice and instruction. Despite Benjamin's earlier written statements supporting Daniel Defoe's desire to develop the intellect of women, Sally's education was typical for a girl of her status in eighteenth-century Philadelphia. She was educated to be "an ingenious sensible notable and worthy woman," and a capable housewife with enough business training to be useful to her future husband. To this end she was taught reading, writing, spelling, arithmetic, and simple bookkeeping. She loved to read, and her many books included Sir Richard Steele's *A Ladies' Library* and Samuel Richardson's novel *Pamela*. She learned the domestic arts of spinning, knitting, and weaving, and her father had a tailor show her how to make buttonholes. She also studied subjects that would help her in social relationships, including French and dancing. Her greatest love was music, and she was known throughout her life as a skilled harpsichordist. Her education also included travels throughout the northern colonies. When she reached young adulthood, she was reported to be sweet tempered, talkative, and well liked. Sally's relationship with her father was affectionate but complex. Though he frequently praised her and sent her presents, he was more likely to lecture her on proper behavior and criticize what he saw as her tendency toward luxury and frivolity. He advised her to be circumspect in her behavior, fearing that his enemies would pounce upon her least indiscretion. Even when she was in her forties his criticism hurt her, though she defended herself and tried to conform to the advice he gave.

When she reached her mid-twenties, Sally fell in love with Richard Bache, a recent immigrant from England who had debts of £3,620, the result of financial setbacks. Sally wished to marry Bache (pronounced "Beech"), but her family had misgivings. Benjamin was in London at the time and at first left the matter in Deborah's hands, but Sally's brother soon wrote that Bache was a fortune hunter, and Benjamin advised Bache that he should not consider marrying Sally until his financial prospects improved. Benjamin then wrote to Deborah suggesting that Sally visit him in London in order to overcome any disappointment. But Sally was devastated. Though a dutiful daughter, she was adamant in her desire to marry Bache, and Deborah allowed the wedding to take place on 29 October 1767. Sally wrote loving, placating letters to her father, but it was eight months before Benjamin acknowledged the marriage. He was not completely reconciled until after the birth of Benjamin Franklin Bache in 1769 and his meeting with Richard Bache in London in 1771. He aided the couple with gifts and loans and helped them set up several stores in Philadelphia. Though Bache's fortunes recovered somewhat, he was never a success in business. Benjamin had to help support Sally and her family for the rest of his life.

Sally and Richard Bache had eight children, whom she raised with the help of a nurse. She cared for her mother and provided hospitality for her father's relatives, friends, and admirers. She worked very hard and never complained about the demands placed upon her. Relatives like her aunt Jane Mecom and visitors like the marquis de Chastellux were uniformly impressed with her kindness and good nature.

Throughout her life Bache was interested in political matters. She supported her father's party in Pennsylvania politics and celebrated its victories. She called herself a committed Whig and closely followed events leading to the Revolution, joining in the revelry over repeal of the Stamp Act even though her father's role in that affair at first had put the family in danger. She supported the war through relief work and applauded the actions of the Constitutional Convention. She is best known for her involvement with the Ladies Association of Philadelphia. In 1780 she was one of the first to heed the association leader Esther Reed's challenge to American women to raise money for the Continental army. Sally was in charge of collections between Chestnut and Market streets. She herself contributed $400 to the cause. When Reed died in September 1780, Sally took over leadership of the association and supervised the sewing of 2,200 shirts for American soldiers. Her father was so proud of her activities that he had an account of the association published in France. On the other hand, her father was deeply angry at her brother William who declared his loyalty to the Crown. Despite her patriotism Sarah remained close to her Loyalist brother and tried unsuccessfully to heal the breach between father and son.

In 1785 her father returned to Philadelphia to live with Sally's family. His last years were loving and companionable. Sally cared for him, entertained his guests, and helped him in some of his activities, such as experimenting with soap manufacture. In her later years she was especially close to her oldest son Benjamin and advised him on his developing political career. She was deeply saddened at his death from yellow fever in 1798. When Benjamin Franklin died, he left most of his estate to Sally and Richard Bache. Richard received land and property, Sally money and stock for her personal use. Among her father's bequests was a portrait of Louis XVI that was surrounded by diamonds. Sally sold the diamonds and used the money for a trip to Europe. She thoroughly enjoyed herself in London but could not visit France because of the political disruption of the French Revolution. In 1794 Richard purchased a farm, named "Settle" after the town of his birth, outside of Philadelphia on the Delaware River. Benjamin's legacy allowed the family to live a comfortable life, but Sally missed the gaiety of Philadelphia. She tried to join the local Quaker community, attending Quaker meetings even though she was an Episcopalian. She could not, however, understand their condemnation of music, which had given her so much pleasure throughout her life. She returned to Philadelphia in 1807 for medical treatment and died there the following year.

Sarah Franklin Bache enjoyed a full and honored life according to the standards of womanhood in late eighteenth-century America. Her primary responsibilities were caring for her family and home, and as Benjamin Franklin's daughter she also had access to the political life of revolutionary Philadelphia. Her patriotism led her to take an active part in colonial resistance to British policy, to aid in the war effort, and to serve as a political hostess for her father.

• Bache's correspondence and other manuscript materials are found in various collections of the papers of Benjamin Franklin, notably that of the library of the American Philosophical Society in Philadelphia. Many are published in Leonard W. Labaree, ed., *Papers of Benjamin Franklin* (1959–). Her grandson wrote a sketch of her life in Elizabeth F. Ellet, *Women of the American Revolution* (1848), and her granddaughter recorded family reminiscences in Elizabeth Duane Gillespie, *A Book of Remembrance* (1901). No modern biography has been written, but many biographies of her father contain accounts of her life; see, for example, Claude-Anne Lopez and Eugenia W. Herbert, *The Private Franklin: The Man and His Family* (1975). An account of the activities of the Ladies Association of Philadelphia is found in Mary Beth Norton, *Liberty's Daughters: The Revolutionary Experience of American Women, 1750–1800* (1980).

ALLIDA SHUMAN MCKINLEY

BACHE, Theophylact (17 Jan. 1735–30 Oct. 1807), merchant, was born in Settle, Yorkshire, England, the son of William Bache, a tax collector, and Mary Blyckenden. In 1751 he arrived in New York City, where he was taken under the wing of Paul Richard, a successful merchant and former mayor, whose wife was a Bache relative. Upon Richard's death five years later, Bache inherited £300, became executor of the estate, and continued the business. His younger brother Richard

Bache arrived in America before 1760 and joined him in business. That relationship continued after Richard moved to Philadelphia in 1765 but ended when the two took different sides during the American Revolution. In 1767 Richard Bache married Sarah Franklin, daughter of Benjamin Franklin, and he later became a prominent Pennsylvania Whig.

As a merchant Theophylact Bache traded with Newfoundland, the West Indies (not all of this apparently legal), and England. In the 1750s he advertised in the New York newspapers an assortment of goods for sale at his store, including cloth, "a great variety of Velvets, Thicksets, Fustians, Jeans, Pillows, and printed Cottons," and "Choice Madeira Wine, Flour, Salt, and Cordage." He was later listed as an owner of the ship *Grace*, participated in the packet trade, and with his brother sold marine insurance.

In 1760 Bache married Ann Dorothy Barclay, the daughter of a wealthy merchant formerly of the West Indies, whose sisters' marriages brought connections to the Van Cortlandts, Jays, Lispenards, and other prominent New Yorkers. The couple had fifteen children, eight of whom survived to adulthood.

By the late 1760s Bache's family ties and business successes made him a member of the colonial establishment, and he began to participate in civic affairs. One of the original twenty-four organizers of the New York Chamber of Commerce in 1768, he was elected treasurer of the organization in 1770, a vice president in 1771 and 1772, and president in 1773. He was also a petitioner for the Marine Society charter in 1770, a governor of the New York Hospital in 1771, and frequently a vestryman of Trinity Church after 1760. Although Bache never sought political office, he was among the merchants caught up in the disagreements with England after the Stamp Act. He served as a member of the committee to enforce the Nonimportation Agreement in 1769 and the Committee of Fifty-one organized in 1774 as part of the response to the Intolerable Acts. After 1775 Bache, along with a substantial number of other New York merchants, was seen as a committed Loyalist, and he has been considered one by historians. One estimate is that, of the 104 members of the Chamber of Commerce in 1775, fifty-seven sided with the king, and twenty-one were neutral.

This simple classification as a Loyalist overlooks Bache's complicated and conflicting ties. Bache initially denied patriot charges of disloyalty but then fled behind British lines, where he remained until the war ended. He avoided an active Loyalist role, managed to keep most of his property at the end of the war, remained in New York, and continued his business activities. Bache had strong ties with family on both sides of the conflict, openly wished for reconciliation, and when war came probably preferred to remain neutral.

However, in many places, particularly the New York City region, neutrality was not an option. His choice of sides was precipitated by the interception of a letter in September 1775 that, although unsigned, indicated Bache as its author. The letter warned his brother-in-law, British major Thomas Moncrieff, in Boston not to return to New York and promised to take care of his wife, Bache's sister-in-law. Alerted, Bache departed town before the Committee of Safety's summons demanding an explanation reached him. The following year, in response to a second demand to appear, Bache wrote a letter in which he refused, denied the accusations, and expressed hope for "reconciliation" and "peace." He justified his absence by the need to care for his wife and large family. In the 1770s he still had at the least a mother and sisters in England, additional ties to that country. On the other hand, his brother Richard and a number of his wife's relations supported independence.

Despite Bache's denials, the patriots regarded him as an important Loyalist. In June 1778, as the object of a raid on the town of Flatbush, he and Major Moncrieff were carried off to Morristown, New Jersey, along with an American prisoner of war, Captain Alexander Graydon. According to accounts, Bache was seized in the middle of the night and removed "without time being given him to put on his clothes," his wife was injured in the fracas, and some of his "plate" was taken. But within a short time Bache and Moncrieff were exchanged for American prisoners, not an uncommon practice at that point in the war.

With the exception of this brief capture, during most of the period from 1776 to 1783, when the British controlled New York City and surrounding areas, Bache stayed in Flatbush and New York City. He was appointed to the city vestry, a civilian group given responsibility for providing city services, including assistance to the poor, street cleaning, and lighting. Although he had been active in the prewar chamber of commerce, between 1779 and 1783 he did not attend a single meeting of this group, which actively assisted the British in obtaining supplies and in police matters. His apparent concern with helping people rather than the war effort is also shown in the report of Captain Graydon. When freed from his captivity in Flatbush, where Bache was seized, Graydon stated that Bache, although "an Englishman and determined royalist," went out of his way to be hospitable and kind to the rebel prisoners. None of Bache's actions indicated bitter hostility to the patriot cause. In 1784, at the first meeting of the chamber of commerce that he attended after the British had withdrawn, he proposed that those who had resigned at the beginning of the war be reinstated.

With the war over, Bache remained in New York City and resumed his business. He reportedly lost £488 in property, only a small part of his holdings, because of the war. His moderate losses, as compared with other Loyalists, are usually explained as a result of the intercession of his patriot relatives but also may have been a recognition of his moderate actions. Along with other Loyalists, he was readmitted to the chamber of commerce in 1787 and the next year was elected to the first of four terms as a vice president. Later he expanded property he owned in the city, building houses and warehouses, and he took his son Andrew Bache into business with him in 1803. The firm traded with England and acted as agents for a London fire insurance company. Bache is listed as one of the original shareholders of the Bank of New York in 1785, although his name is not on the charter of incorporation of 1791. While he supposedly suffered with others from the fluctuations in trade in the 1790s, he continued in business, showing an interest in new enterprises, such as banking, that started after the Revolution.

Bache died in New York City. As a conservative merchant he had helped initiate several of the major commercial institutions in that city. A Loyalist, he remained in New York and participated in the development of the new nation.

• The most complete biographical information on Bache is provided by John Austin Stevens, Jr., *Colonial New York: Sketches Biographical and Historical 1768–1784* (1867). See also Lorenzo Sabine, *Biographical Sketches of Loyalists of the American Revolution*, vol. 1 (1864), and *The Papers of Benjamin Franklin*, ed. Leonard W. Larrabee (1959–). References to Bache and general information on merchants is in Virginia Harrington, *The New York Merchant on the Eve of Revolution* (1935), and Oscar Theodore Barck, Jr., *New York City during the War for Independence* (1931). On the role of the N.Y. Loyalists see Alexander C. Flick, *Loyalism in New York during the American Revolution* (1901), and Oscar Zeichner, "The Loyalist Problem in New York after the Revolution," *New York History* 21 (1940): 284–302. For a more sympathetic view see Robert A. East and Jacob Judd, eds., *The Loyalist Americans: A Focus on Greater New York* (1975), and Philip Ranlet, *The New York Loyalists* (1986). For Bache's business interests in the period see Stevens, *Colonial New York*, and Stevens, *Colonial Records of the New York Chamber of Commerce 1768–1784* (1867); East, *Business Enterprise in the American Revolutionary Era* (1938); and Edward Countryman, "The Uses of Capital in Revolutionary America: The Case of the New York Loyalist Merchants," *William and Mary Quarterly* 49 (Jan. 1992): 3–28.

MAXINE N. LURIE

BACHELDER, John (7 Mar. 1817–1 July 1906), manufacturer and inventor, was born in Weare, New Hampshire, the son of William Bachelder, a lumberman and blacksmith, and Mary Bailey. Bachelder went to public school and to college for training as a teacher. After teaching school for three years, Bachelder left New Hampshire for Boston. There he found employment as an accountant for a Middlesex Canal transportation firm. Soon he formed a partnership that competed with his former employers. The business closed upon the completion of the Manchester railroad, which eliminated the demand for shipping on the Middlesex Canal. In 1843 Bachelder married Adaline Wason; they had three children. With the demise of his transportation enterprise, he worked in Boston's dry-goods business until 1846. During the winter of 1846, he traveled to England in an effort to establish himself as an importer. By 1847 he had established his own firm once again in a partnership called Bachelder, Burr and Company.

Upon returning to Boston, Bachelder encountered his life's major turning point. Elias Howe had developed a sewing machine between 1844 and 1845. Howe displayed the new invention at the Quincy Hall Clothing Manufacturer's building in Boston on Milk Street, which happened to be along Bachelder's customary walk to work. Howe's demonstration of the sewing machine showed Bachelder the possibilities of the mechanism, but he also saw that Howe's sewing machine was not commercially attractive. First, it sewed only straight seams. Tailors who might otherwise use the machine were uninterested because of its limited utility and great expense. In addition, the machine sewed by moving along a baster plate. When the machine came to the end of the baster plate, the plate had to be removed and returned to the beginning of the track and the cloth also needed to be reset. This restricted the length of the seam sewn continuously and therefore the strength of the resulting work. Bachelder recognized that the machine could become a valuable laborsaving device with improvements to the baster plate and in the machine's versatility. Bachelder decided that he could develop a better mechanism and set himself to designing the necessary enhancements.

A short time later Bachelder determined that he should focus his attentions entirely on the sewing machine improvements. He abandoned his importing business, rented a shop, and hired about a dozen employees. He expended his savings and profits from the import business, amounting to about $12,000, entirely on this one project. Ultimately the task necessitated the borrowing of about $4,000. Two years later, Bachelder applied for and received a patent. The patent (No. 6,439), issued on 8 May 1849, represented a major contribution to mechanized sewing and included three significant improvements: the continuous feed, the vertical needle, and the horizontal table. Although Bachelder achieved his goal of improving on Howe's invention, he was not able to use his patent to gain financial success. He did not have control of the additional patents necessary to fabricate a sewing machine on his own or the financial resources to manufacture one. Rather, debts forced him to sell the patent to one of his competitors, inventor Isaac M. Singer, by the mid-1850s.

The importance of Bachelder's work is manifest by the inclusion of his patent in the Sewing Machine Combination, a trust organized by three sewing machine manufacturers to pool the rights to the numerous patents needed to manufacture a single marketable sewing machine. When the combination was formed, no single manufacturer or individual had control over or rights to enough patents to manufacture sewing machines without risking litigation for patent infringement. The industry was crippled by the numerous suits aimed at manufacturers. The combination enabled companies to buy rights to produce sewing machines using the patents included in the combination for a licensing fee of $15. Each of the patent holders received a percentage of the fee and the combination retained fees to cover legal costs. The three Bachelder sewing machine improvements were part of the combination's patent holdings, including the needle moving vertically above a horizontal work plate, a continuous feeding device by belt or wheel, and a yielding presser resting on the cloth. The combination contributed greatly to the popularity of the sewing machine. In 1853 two of the major manufacturers of machines, Singer and Wheeler and Wilson, produced only 1,609 machines, but by 1860 together their production had increased to 33,102. As a result of the combination, Bachelder received royalties for his work until the patent expired on 8 May 1877 after being renewed twice. According to one historian, the patent was worth more than $100 million. The *New York Mail* printed the following on 8 May 1877: "The expiration of the last patent which has linked together the sewing machine companies in a powerful combination is likely to prove a great boon to the public." The *New York Mail* was correct, as, when the patent expired and the combination came to an end, sewing machine prices plummeted by 50 percent. The great reduction in sewing machine prices at the end of the combination enabled the machine to enter into homes and to change garment production forever.

Having failed as a sewing machine manufacturer, Bachelder turned his attentions to cotton manufacturing by purchasing a firm in Lisbon, Connecticut, in 1852. Although his profits from the sewing machine patent proved sufficient to alleviate the debts incurred while developing the invention, they were not enough to buy the mill. Friends stepped in and assisted with the investment. Ultimately, however, Bachelder gained full control of the mill. A fire destroyed the building and, while he was able to rebuild and invest in other textile enterprises, a depression after the Civil War led textile business to fail. Next, Bachelder became a director of the First National Bank of Norwich and a trustee of the Chelsea Savings Bank. In 1875 he left Connecticut for Napa, California, and established another manufacturing enterprise. This was not successful; he had to sell the business in 1880 and he decided to retire.

In retirement Bachelder served as trustee and president of the local library board. He also wrote a book published in 1890, *A.D. 2050: Electrical Advancements at Atlantis by a Former Resident of the Hub*, which portrayed life in a future time through the eyes of the past. He spent his final years in Michigan, where he died. While Bachelder lived an active and vital life to the end, his greatest contributions were to mechanized sewing. His single patent introduced three significant and valuable improvements to a machine called the "Queen of Inventions." The long-term value of the patent is manifest by the use of similar devices in modern sewing machines, which continue to have vertical needles, a yielding presser resting on the cloth, and a continuous feed mechanism.

• Bachelder's life receives treatment in Frederick Clifton Pierce, *Batchelder, Batcheler, Bachelder Genealogy* (1898). His patent and its significance to the development of the sewing machine are detailed in Edward W. Byrn, *The Progress of Invention in the Nineteenth Century* (1900); Grace Rogers Cooper, *The Sewing Machine: Its Invention and Development* (1985); and David Hounshell, *From American System to Mass Production 1800–1932* (1984).

GAIL FOWLER MOHANTY

BACHELLER, Irving (26 Sept. 1859–24 Feb. 1950), novelist and publishing executive, was born Addison Irving Bacheller in Pierrepont, St. Lawrence County, New York, the son of Sanford Paul Bacheller and Achsah Ann Buckland, farmers. Irving attended local schools in Pierrepont, then switched to an academy in Canton, New York, after his family moved there. His secondary education at Clinton Academy was sporadic, however, as he spent long periods during his teenage years working at various jobs—telegraph operator, laborer, post office clerk, bookkeeper, salesman, teacher—to help support the family.

Despite his lack of a high school diploma, Bacheller was admitted to St. Lawrence University, in Canton, as a special student in 1878 and received a bachelor of science degree four years later. Although he majored in the natural sciences, Bacheller served as president of the St. Lawrence literary society and was also an active debater. He began writing verses and short stories for his own amusement, but at this time he did not intend to pursue a literary career.

After college Bacheller moved to New York City, where he worked for several months on the staff of a hotel trade journal. He then joined the *Brooklyn Daily Times*, first as military editor and then as drama editor. Years later he told an interviewer that the *Times* had hired him on the strength of a piece of light verse he had submitted, a poem about an all-too-common tragedy occurring in New York City in the nineteenth century: country visitors had blown out the gaslights in their hotel room, thinking they were candles, and were killed in their sleep by the fumes.

In 1884 Bacheller arranged for the publication in the *Times* of a series of interviews of prominent literary figures by British popular novelist Joseph Hatton. He also arranged for the series to appear in several other big-city newspapers, paving the way for the formation later that year of the New York Press Syndicate, the first major metropolitan press syndicate in the world. Under the management of Bacheller and his partner, James W. Johnson, the syndicate grew rapidly; by the early 1890s it was sending fiction and feature stories to leading newspapers throughout the United States. Bacheller's organization introduced many leading British writers to American readers, serializing works by Arthur Conan Doyle, Rudyard Kipling, and Joseph Conrad, among others. He also published emerging American writers, including Hamlin Garland and Stephen Crane; in 1893 Crane's novel *The Red Badge of Courage* appeared for the first time in print as a serial distributed by Bacheller's syndicate.

Bacheller's financial success enabled him to return to St. Lawrence for part-time graduate study in the sciences; he received a master of science degree in 1892.

Increased self-confidence also led him to launch his own literary career in the early 1890s when he began publishing his verses and short stories in national magazines, including *The Independent* and *Cosmopolitan.* His first two novels, *The Master of Silence*, published in the United States in 1892, and *The Still House of O'Darrow*, which appeared in England two years later, were met with lukewarm response by both critics and the reading public. In 1896 Bacheller sold his syndicate in order to work full time on a third novel but returned to newspaper journalism two years later as Sunday editor of the *New York World.*

Bacheller's third novel, *Eben Holden* (1900), was an immediate bestseller; it eventually sold more than a million copies. A romanticized account of rural life in the St. Lawrence valley, the novel was based largely on Bacheller's childhood memories and offered readers a story that its author characterized as "clean" and "uplifting." Praised by many mainstream American literary figures, including William Dean Howells, *Eben Holden* paved the way for Bacheller's successful career as a popular novelist.

During the next four decades Bacheller wrote more than thirty novels, many of them bestsellers, as well as short stories, essays, and poems; he also published three volumes of personal reflections and memoirs. The subjects and settings of Bacheller's fiction were varied, ranging from a historical romance set in ancient Rome (*Vergilius*, 1904) to a saga of George Washington and the American Revolution (*The Master of Chaos*, 1932). War was a frequent theme in his work; he experienced it firsthand in the late summer and early fall of 1917, when he traveled to France as a guest of the British government to gather material on the world war for a series of magazine articles and was injured by a shell fragment.

The popularity of Bacheller's fiction made him virtually a household name in the first half of the twentieth century. In an interview in the *New York Times* in December 1941, the year Bacheller published his last novel, *Winds of God*, critic Robert van Gelder characterized him as "just about the dean of producing American novelists." Many Americans were introduced to his fiction as teenagers: *A Man for the Ages* (1919), the first in a three-volume series of historical fiction about Abraham Lincoln, was the best known of several Bacheller works required or recommended in U.S. high school English classes from the 1920s through the 1950s. Bacheller's many awards and honors included membership in the National Institute of Arts and Letters.

Bacheller married Anna Detmar Schultz in 1883, and they adopted a son. Bacheller and his family moved to Riverside, Connecticut, from New York City in 1905 and lived there for twelve years. In 1917 they moved to Winter Park, Florida, but returned to Riverside each summer. Bacheller's wife died in 1924, and the following year he married a widow, Mary Elizabeth Leonard Sollace, of Flushing, New York; they had no children. Bacheller died in White Plains, New York.

• Accounts of Bacheller's life, work, and philosophy are in his three volumes of reminiscences: *Opinions of a Cheerful Yankee* (1926), *Coming Up the Road* (1928), and *From Stores of Memory* (1938). Additional biographical information is in Robert van Gelder, "An Interview with Irving Bacheller," *New York Times Book Review*, 21 Dec. 1941. A. J. Hanna, *A Bibliography of the Writings of Irving Bacheller* (1939) includes a list of all of Bacheller's publications up to that date. An obituary is in the *New York Times*, 25 Feb. 1950.

ANN T. KEENE

BACHMAN, John (4 Feb. 1790–24 Feb. 1874), clergyman and naturalist, was born in Rhinebeck, New York, the son of Jacob Bachman, a farmer, and Eva (surname unknown but probably Shop). During his boyhood on a farm in Rensselaer County, New York, Bachman developed a keen interest in natural history and read many books on the subject. Around 1803, after tutoring by the local Lutheran minister, Anton T. Braun, Bachman entered college, evidently somewhere in Philadelphia, but a severe attack of tuberculosis compelled him to leave before he earned a degree. While recuperating, Bachman decided to enter the Lutheran ministry, and by 1810, after briefly studying theology with Braun and then with another minister in the local area, he had returned to Philadelphia for advanced training. During that time he also taught school. Upon the death of Braun in 1813, Bachman assumed his former mentor's pastorate. Soon troubled again by tuberculosis, he decided to move to a warmer climate and accepted a call from St. John's Lutheran Church, in Charleston, South Carolina, where he assumed his duties early in 1815.

In 1816 Bachman married Harriet Martin, a member of his congregation. Of their fourteen children, five died in infancy or early childhood. Although his pastoral duties were demanding, Bachman diligently pursued his interests in natural history. In addition to building a large collection of floral and faunal specimens, he kept and observed many feral and domesticated animals. During a visit to Charleston in 1831, John James Audubon met Bachman, and thus began a friendship and collaboration that lasted until Audubon's death in 1851. Recognizing that Bachman possessed extraordinary knowledge of birds, Audubon relied heavily on him to gather specimens and to describe the character and habits of southern avifauna. Audubon also received considerable assistance from Bachman's sister-in-law Maria Martin, a talented artist who painted background scenery for several of his paintings. The ties of friendship were further strengthened by the marriage of a Bachman daughter to Audubon's younger son in 1837 and again by the marriage of another daughter to Audubon's older son in 1839.

During the 1830s Bachman published a number of original scientific articles dealing with changes of color in birds and mammals, how vultures locate food, the taxonomy of numerous mammals (especially moles, rabbits, and squirrels), regional plants, and the need for applying scientific methods to agriculture. Later in that decade he, Audubon, and Audubon's sons began a work on the mammals of North America, to which

Bachman contributed thirty-one descriptions of previously undescribed mammals, eleven of them in collaboration with Audubon. Audubon and his son John Woodhouse did the paintings and collected most of the specimens outside the South, while Bachman collected regional specimens and furnished nearly all of the text. Thirty parts of five plates each were bound in three volumes (1845–1853) as *The Viviparous Quadrupeds of North America*, and three volumes of text appeared in 1849, 1851, and 1854. The title was changed to *The Quadrupeds of North America* in the later volumes. An edition containing both text and 155 plates was published in 1854. *The Quadrupeds of North America* was the most comprehensive work of its kind for many years. In a lengthy commentary in the December 1846 issue of *American Review*, a well-informed critic noted the excellence of the illustrations and descriptions and placed the work "at the head of Illustrative Mammalogy in the world."

Meanwhile, the burdens of pastoring a large church, collecting specimens, and writing articles had caused Bachman's health to suffer, and in 1838 he traveled to Europe for recuperation. There he found himself highly honored as a naturalist. The trustees of the College of Charleston appointed Bachman professor of natural history in 1848, but he held that position for only five years because of other duties. Bachman had long been active in Charleston's Literary and Philosophical Society, which served as the main organization for the promotion of science in the city. The society was replaced in 1853 by the Elliott Society of Natural History, which Bachman served as its first president.

From 1848 to 1855, Bachman was engaged in a vigorous controversy that pitted him against his fellow scientists in Charleston, the famous naturalist Louis Agassiz, the noted Philadelphia craniologist Samuel George Morton, and the well-known southern physician and racist Josiah Nott over the question of the origins of the black race. Morton contended that blacks represented a separate and inferior creation by God, and Agassiz, who was immensely popular in the South, eventually adopted a similar view. Southern naturalists generally agreed with Morton and Agassiz, but Bachman, although the son of a slaveholder, a slave-owner himself, and a strong supporter of the institution of slavery, argued that the views of Morton and Agassiz were unscientific. In a series of articles and in a book titled *The Doctrine of the Unity of the Human Race, Examined on the Principles of Science*, published in 1850, Bachman demonstrated a superb understanding of the nature of scientific inquiry.

By 1847 Bachman had lost three more of his children (including both daughters who were married to Audubon's sons) and his wife to death, but his religious faith never wavered. In 1848 Bachman married Maria Martin, who had lived with his family for many years. In 1853 he published *A Defense of Luther and the Reformation* . . . , a response to the denunciation of Luther by several Roman Catholics in Charleston. An ardent supporter of his denomination, he was instrumental in organizing the South Carolina Synod of Lutheran Churches and in establishing both a Lutheran seminary and a Lutheran college in South Carolina, and from 1860 to 1862 he served as a coeditor of the *Southern Lutheran*. Bachman was likewise a stout defender of the South, and, as the clamor for secession increased during the late 1850s, he roundly condemned the abolitionists: "my religion bids me forgive, [but] God help me I would rather have them hanged first and forgive them afterwards, . . . [for they would] rob and plunder and bully us in the Union until they had their feet on our necks and their daggers in our throats."

During the Civil War, Bachman devoted considerable time and energy to ministering to wounded soldiers. His second wife died in 1863. On 13 February 1865, shortly before Federal troops occupied Charleston, Bachman fled the city for safety near the town of Cheraw, South Carolina. Confronted by a unit of pillaging Union troops, the old clergyman was severely beaten and suffered permanent injury to his left arm. Bachman preached his last sermon in January 1870 but continued to visit his parishioners for many months thereafter, even after the two strokes he suffered in 1871. Upon his death in Charleston, he was interred in a crypt in the church he had pastored for more than half a century. Eulogists justly acknowledged his exceptional success in promoting Lutheranism in the South and in advancing the study of mammals in the United States.

• The bulk of Bachman's papers are in the library of the Charleston Museum; the Beinecke Rare Book and Manuscript Library, Yale University; the Houghton Library, Harvard University; the Smithsonian Institution Archives; and the Samuel G. Morton Papers, Historical Society of Pennsylvania. William Stanton, *The Leopard's Spots: Scientific Attitudes toward Race in America, 1815–59* (1960), assesses Bachman's views on race (pp. 100–36), but a fuller understanding can be gained by reading the articles by Bachman and Morton published in the *Charleston Medical Journal and Review* in 1850 and 1851 and by Bachman between 1854 and 1856. Most of Bachman's original descriptions of several new species of hares, squirrels, and shrews are in the *Magazine of Natural History* 3 (1839): 113–23, 154–62, 220–27, 378–90; the *Journal of the Academy of Natural Sciences of Philadelphia* 7 (1837): 194–99, 282–403; 8 (1839–1842): 57–105, 280–323; and the *Boston Journal of Natural History* 4 (1842): 26–35. His article "Observations on the Changes of Colour in Birds and Quadrupeds" is in the *Transactions of the American Philosophical Society*, n.s. 6 (1839): 197–239. *John Bachman, D.D., LL.D. Ph.D.: The Pastor of St. John's Lutheran Church, Charleston* (1888), by Bachman's daughter Catherine (based on materials collected and arranged by Bachman's grandson John Bachman Haskell), contains useful but sometimes unreliable information. It also includes many of Bachman's letters, but they are selective. A more objective account of Bachman's life, by Claude Henry Neuffer, is in the *Christopher Happoldt Journal* (1960), pp. 29–118, but it relies heavily on the previously mentioned work and is not comprehensive. Raymond Bost, "The Reverend John Bachman and the Development of Southern Lutheranism" (Ph.D. diss., Yale Univ., 1973), is a substantive treatment of the work of Bachman in behalf of his denomination. Although the biographies of Audubon, of necessity, deal with Bachman, they offer an incomplete picture of the work of Bachman and his relationship to the great artist.

LESTER D. STEPHENS

BACHMANN, Werner Emmanuel (13 Nov. 1901–22 Mar. 1951), organic chemist, was born in Detroit, Michigan, the son of Arnold William Bachmann, a Swiss-born minister, and Bertha Wurster. He developed an early interest in chemistry, and his knowledge was such that his Detroit high school released him from classes for one year during World War I in order to formulate alloy mixtures at a local foundry. From 1919 to 1921 he attended Detroit Junior College. He then enrolled in the University of Michigan, receiving bachelor's, master's, and doctorate degrees in 1923, 1924, and 1926, respectively. In 1927 he married Marie Knaphurst, a childhood friend; they had two children. A 1927 Rockefeller Foundation fellowship enabled him to study in Zurich, Switzerland, with the Nobel prizewinner Paul Karrer, with whom he determined the structure of lycopene, the red coloring matter of tomatoes. From 1929 to 1951 Bachmann was a chemistry faculty member at the University of Michigan, becoming full professor in 1939 and the Moses Gomberg University Professor in 1947. An outstanding teacher, he received in 1933 the Henry Russell Award, the university's highest honor. He divided a 1935 Guggenheim Foundation fellowship between the Royal Cancer Hospital in London, England, and research with Heinrich Wieland in Munich, Germany.

Bachmann's research career began under the director of his doctoral studies, Moses Gomberg, who was famous for his 1900 discovery of free radicals. They collaborated on Bachmann's first publication in 1924, disclosing the discovery of a new reaction, the coupling of two benzene rings to form a biphenyl compound (the Gomberg-Bachmann reaction). Together they published many papers on the chemistry of free radicals and molecular rearrangements. Bachmann was best known for his achievements in organic synthesis, especially of carcinogens and of steroid sex hormones. In the 1920s British scientists showed that the hydrocarbon distillate of coal tar contained cancer-producing substances. Investigating these polycyclic hydrocarbons during his 1927 stay in London and through the 1930s at Michigan, Bachmann found more potent and faster acting carcinogens than hitherto known, synthesized these, and made them available for medical study.

Bachmann's syntheses of natural products employed the traditional approach of deriving the structure of a substance by decomposition reactions, developing a laboratory synthesis, and showing that the synthetic substance was identical to the isolated and purified natural product. His steroid sex hormone syntheses had these features. In the 1920s the steroids were recognized as important physiologically active substances. Bachmann focused on the isolation, characterization, and synthesis of one class of steroids, the estrogens—female sex hormones that had important uses in therapy. But their short supply from natural sources limited their clinical use and made their synthesis imperative. In 1939, with his students Wayne Cole and Alfred Wilds, Bachmann synthesized equilenin, the first total synthesis of an estrogenic hormone. The hormone had two asymmetric carbon atoms and existed in four stereoisomeric forms. He synthesized all four isomers, with every step of the process designed to give high yields. Bachmann's method was immediately widely adopted. His equilenin synthesis marked a milestone in organic synthesis because it represented a synthesis of great complexity and opened the era of total syntheses of complex natural products. For his achievements he was elected to the National Academy of Sciences in 1940.

During World War II Bachmann was under government contract to prepare RDX (cyclonite), the most powerful of nonatomic high explosives. Though known and processed since 1899, RDX had always been too costly to manufacture on a large scale and too sensitive to survive rough handling. In 1940 there were British and Canadian processes but both were inefficient and expensive. Early in 1941 Bachmann conceived a processing method that reduced costs through the production of higher yields of RDX. The consequence was the construction in 1941 of the world's largest munitions plant in Tennessee and the production of RDX in large amounts (peak production was 340 tons per day in 1943). The explosive proved devastatingly effective in torpedoes, bombs, mines, and depth charges. Bachmann received two patents for the RDX process and several high honors, including the Naval Ordnance Award (1946), the Presidential Certificate of Merit (1948), and the King's Medal of Great Britain (1948).

Bachmann also tried to synthesize penicillin during the war. With the discovery in 1940–1941 of penicillin's effectiveness as a therapeutic agent, chemists sought ways to produce the antibiotic. By 1945 Bachmann, along with his student John Sheehan, had synthesized penicillin, but the yield was too low to compete with the fermentation process that pharmaceutical companies had developed, which made penicillin available by 1944. His research was not wasted, however: it contributed considerably to knowledge of the chemistry of penicillin, helping to explicate a natural product of a new type with novel structural features and reactions.

After the war Bachmann was unable to bring his usual vigor and enthusiasm to research. The strenuous exertion of war research had undermined his health and contributed to his death in Ann Arbor of heart failure. Bachmann devoted his leisure time to music and growing orchids, roses, and irises. He so loved music that he seldom missed a musical event at the university. Naturally shy, he was a person of extremely quiet manner and gentleness. To those who were not his friends and associates, he seemed reserved and aloof, characteristics that enabled him to carry out his laboratory research as free as possible from interruption. To those who knew him, however, he was not only an inspiring teacher and creative scientist but a person of charm and wit.

Bachmann was one of the most gifted synthetic chemists of his time. He left a legacy of important syntheses of polycyclic substances and steroid hormones. Developments in physical organic chemistry and instrumentation made organic synthesis far more powerful after 1940. He achieved his syntheses when chemists were unable to control the stereochemistry of reactions for lack of knowledge of reaction mechanisms, and yields were usually low. Although Bachmann did not participate in the postwar advances in synthesis, he passed on to successors an emphasis on understanding and controlling each step in organic synthesis, including a critical attitude toward the experimental procedures and reaction conditions necessary to attain the highest possible yields.

• Bachmann's papers, consisting of correspondence, research notes, and teaching materials, are in the University of Michigan Archives. The only biography other than brief factual accounts is by Robert C. Elderfield in National Academy of Sciences, *Biographical Memoirs* 34 (1960): 1–30, which includes a bibliography of his publications. A considerate and perceptive essay is Alfred L. Wilds, "Werner E. Bachmann (Nov. 13, 1901–Mar. 22, 1951)," *Journal of Organic Chemistry* 19 (1954): 128–30. See James P. Baxter, *Scientists against Time* (1946), for Bachmann's wartime work on RDX and penicillin. See D. Stanley Tarbell and Ann T. Tarbell, *Essays on the History of Organic Chemistry in the United States* (1986), for his carcinogen and steroid hormone research. An obituary is in the *New York Times*, 23 Mar. 1951.

ALBERT B. COSTA

BACHRACH, Louis Fabian (16 July 1881–24 July 1963), portrait photographer and businessman, was born in Baltimore, Maryland, the son of David Bachrach, Jr., a photographer, and Frances Keyser. Bachrach attended public schools and graduated from the Baltimore Polytechnic Institute in 1897. He also took classes at the Maryland Institute of Art and Design and the New York Art Students League; these classes gave him the "sense of line and knowledge of the anatomy of the human figure" that proved invaluable to him as a photographer.

Bachrach's father was not sure there was much of a future in the portrait photography business and encouraged his son to take a job with a maker of fine tools. Bachrach admitted that as a machinist he was not much of a success, and after trying some other types of work he decided to go into the business of portrait photography with his father. Unlike his father, who has been described as dreamy and absent-minded, Bachrach was more like his mother, practical and forward-looking. He realized a method was needed to keep track of day-to-day matters and became interested in the new discipline of business. Intrigued by ideas on salesmanship and efficient business management that were developing at the time, Bachrach involved himself in the new methodology.

From his father Bachrach learned basic photographic principles such as the use of lighting and the positioning of equipment in relation to the subject. Although he thought some of these ideas were old-fashioned, some he continued to use throughout his career. For example, the camera Bachrach and his sons after him used was, except for the lenses, essentially the same camera used by his father. After three years of apprenticeship, making $4 a week and doing everything from dark-room work to printing and finally actually photographing subjects, Bachrach took charge of the family's Washington, D.C., studio for two years. But in 1904 it was time for him to start out on his own. Bachrach purchased, with the help of his father and a number of loans, a small photography studio from William H. Fitton, in Worcester, Massachusetts.

The first years were difficult since there were a number of excellent, established photographers in the city, but Bachrach stated that "competition was a good thing for [him]" and attributed his future success in business to his "training at the hands of the good tough people of Worcester" (quoted in Elie). He also realized that applying some of the principles he had learned about business would give him a "distinct advantage." One of his innovations began with the advent of the automobile, when he started to offer in-home sittings at no additional cost. This brilliant sales tactic immediately set him apart from his competitors. Bachrach traveled to homes throughout Massachusetts, Vermont, and Rhode Island to serve his growing customer base. In 1911 he opened a Boston studio on Boylston Street; in 1916 he and his younger brother Walter opened a studio in New York City. Walter, also a photographer, had expanded a southern chain of Bachrach studios, and in 1925 Bachrach combined all the studios and took over the management. By 1929 he had forty-eight studios in twelve states, extending from Portand, Maine, to Indianapolis, Indiana.

During the depression annual sales fell from $1 million to $400,000. Spread out too far, both geographically and financially, and paying high rents, Bachrach was forced to begin closing studios. By 1935 only eight studios remained. Bachrach remarked that he "would never want to go through such an experience again." He attributed part of the problem to building his business too fast. By 1944, fueled by quality work and imagination, his business had prospered once again, and he opened a ninth studio in Chicago.

Part of Bachrach's success was based on his rules of photography, which would be carried on by his successors. The rules, determined by the gender and age of the subjects, were set down in Bachrach's third article for the *Christian Science Monitor*:

> The pretty woman should be made to look interesting and intelligent. The plain woman should be given an air of beauty and glamour. The older woman needs distinction and an air of experience. The shallow woman should have an air of mystery. The young man should be made to look more grown up. The short man needs dignity and a greater height. The rough-looking man needs an air of breeding. The "pretty" man needs a

look of rugged masculinity. Every man must be graceful, strong and virile. Every woman must be charming, graceful, having distinction and aristocratic bearing.

What Bachrach would do was create portraits of people, making them appear the way they would like to be seen: heightening their good features and lessening the less than advantageous. A method Bachrach perfected to this end was the use of light. In an article he wrote for *American Photography* (July 1942), Bachrach noted that with the proper use of light "a face may be modified greatly, and by intelligent handling, irregular, unattractive features can be modified or even eliminated by light alone." His success in "camouflaging" unattractive features and his growing reputation for distinctive portraits brought him subjects from brides to business leaders to presidents. When discussing photographing presidents, which the family had been doing since the days of Bachrach's father, Bachrach considered Hoover and Kennedy "the least approachable Presidents. Truman and F.D.R. were the most co-operative" (quoted in Hill, p. 81). When he photographed President William Howard Taft at the White House, Bachrach was interrupted while Taft carried on a heated argument by telephone with his predecessor Theodore Roosevelt. Bachrach's sitting with President Calvin Coolidge was characterized by its silence. After thirty minutes, Coolidge was the first to speak, asking, "How's business?" The equally reticent Bachrach replied, "Fine."

In 1909 Bachrach had married Dorothy Deland Keyes. They had three children. The two sons, Bradford Keyser and Louis Fabian, Jr., would also become photographers and join the family business. In 1955 Bachrach became chairman of the board, and Bradford assumed the presidency. While serving as chairman of the board, Bachrach continue to photograph subjects and assumed the difficult task of handling the "adjustment department," a euphemism for complaint. Complaints were few owing to Bachrach's continued insistence on high standards and customer service. His oft-spoken phrase "We can do better than this" became a company motto. The $1.5 million sales for 1963 attest to the success of Bachrach's efforts.

In addition to photography, Bachrach wrote many articles for professional magazines and was an amateur horticulturist. He delighted in growing plants and trees in his yard in West Newton that never, according to the experts, should have survived in the "inhospitable" New England soil. After the death of his first wife in 1956, Bachrach married Marjorie Whitney Callard in 1957. He died in Boston.

Bachrach applied sound business methods to develop a company that continued to prosper under his sons. In addition, he was an employer who inspired loyalty in his employees, many of whom he had trained himself and had been with him for a number of years. But most of all, Bachrach was not simply a photographer of the rich and famous, he was an artist who could capture the essence of his subjects in his portraits.

• Manuscripts of Bachrach's articles, speeches, and interviews, as well as some letters, are at the George Arents Library, Syracuse University. The collection also includes 200 photographs by the Bachrach family. See also the clippings file at the Boston University School of Communication. Bachrach's set of four articles for the *Christian Science Monitor*, 16–19 Jan. 1957, provide biographical information as well as his philosophy on portrait photography. See his three-part interview with Rudolph Elie, "The Roving Eye," *Boston Herald*, 10–12 Aug. 1949. Biographical information as well as information on his business is in Evan Hill, "The Flattering Camera," *Saturday Evening Post*, 19 Aug. 1961, and "Every President since Lincoln Sat for the Bachrachs," *Life*, 8 Aug. 1963. For information on the Bachrach business under his management, see "Capturing the Executive Look," *Business Week*, 18 Jan. 1964. Obituaries are in the *Boston Globe*, 25 July 1963; the *New York Times*, 26 July 1963; and *Popular Photography*, Nov. 1963.

MARCIA B. DINNEEN

BACKUS, Charles (20 Oct. 1831–21 June 1883), actor and minstrel troupe founder, was born in Rochester, New York, the son of a prominent physician. His parents' names are unknown. Backus's grandfather Azel Backus was the first president of Hamilton College and a deeply religious man. Despite the Backus family plans of a literary or professional career for Charley, the young boy's affinity for comedic imitation was apparent from his earliest school days. After completing his public school education, Backus made his acting debut in 1851 in the role of Jerry Clip in *The Widow's Victim* at the Centre Street Theatre in Cleveland, Ohio. Determined to be an entertainer, Backus moved to the rapidly growing theater town of San Francisco, where he joined Donnelly's Minstrels and made his first Gold Coast appearance on 21 September 1853 at the Adelphi Theatre.

By September 1854 leading theater impresario Thomas Maguire had convinced Backus to form his own troupe and to appear at San Francisco Hall. Later that year Christy's Minstrels arrived from New York, and by 23 January 1854 the two troupes had amalgamated to become the Christy Backus Minstrels. It was the first minstrel troupe to include a woman performer, Julia Collins, though this was not the only novelty introduced by the troupe. While other minstrel troupes began their show with "plantation Negroes," attired in colorful rags and mismatched clothing, the Christy Backus Minstrels featured northern, or "dandy," Negroes in the first part of its entertainment, dressed in frilled white shirts, diamond studs, and gold watch chains. Though retaining the traditional burnt-cork makeup and dialectical speech, the Christy Backus Minstrels often included in their act 3 parody a burlesque rendition of a famous play, such as *A Midsummer Night's Dream*, or an opera, like *Fra Diavolo*, assuming audience familiarity with the object of satire. Other minstrel troupes slowly followed suit, shifting the emphasis of the minstrel shows from "Ethiopian delineation" to a format that used broadly based ideas, rather than ethnicity, as the primary source of their humor.

Throughout his career Backus and his various troupes were known for the raucous comedy and rapid-fire ad-libbing that they could create on almost any topic. From the British Blondes to politics, no subject nor any literary masterpiece was safe from the burlesquing of Backus and Company. Backus's imitations of famous personalities were described by the *Golden Era* (1854) as being "as wonderful as they are amusing." One anecdote published in several newspapers, including the *Argonaut* (7 July 1885), recalls the actor Charles Kean, upon seeing Backus perform his imitation of Kean as Hamlet, taking the minstrel aside for private coaching.

In late 1855 Backus broke from the San Francisco troupe and took his own company on the first of many tours. Although he returned to San Francisco periodically, joining various troupes for short periods of time, Backus spent much of 1855–1861 touring to almost every part of the world: Australia, India, Egypt, Gibraltar, Malta, China, England, and the major theatrical centers of the United States. From 1862 to 1864 he played primarily in New York, returning finally to San Francisco, where he joined Billy Birch, W. H. Bernard, and Dave Wambold in a collaboration that became know as the San Francisco Minstrels. With Backus and Birch as the end men, Bernard as the interlocutor, and Wambold as the balladeer, the San Francisco Minstrels dominated the theatrical world of the Gold Coast until 1865, when they permanently moved to New York City. Backus married Leo Hudson, an actress, sometime during the mid-1860s, and they separated shortly thereafter. They did not have children. He married Kate Newton, also a popular actress, in 1868; they also did not have children, and she died in 1873.

On 8 May 1865 the San Francisco Minstrels opened at 585 Broadway and soon became fixtures in the New York world of minstrelsy. Backus and Birch (who would remain his partner until Backus's death), the two end men, closed almost every show, playing off of each other's freewheeling ad-libs. Backus was known as a genial man who could always find the humor in any situation, and the *New York Times* (1883) described him as a performer "who could create a laugh simply by opening his capacious mouth." Backus and Birch, who was quieter and physically smaller than his partner, created skits that held New York audiences captive for the next nineteen years. Some of their more famous sketches include: "Pleasant Companions," "The Phour Candidates," "Les Brigands," "Whar You Gwine," "Laughing Gas," "Big Bananas," "Clothilde; or, The Bruised Heart," as well as parodies of Salvini's *Othello* and Ristori's *Medea*. In 1874 the troupe moved into their newly completed San Francisco Minstrel Hall, where they remained as the sole possessors of New York minstrelsy until the company was sold following Backus's death from Bright's disease in Somans, Connecticut. At the time of his death Backus was married to Elizabeth "Tizzie" Mason of Niagara Falls, whom he had wed in October 1876. They had one daughter.

Backus and his talented partners were considered by many to be the finest minstrel company in the world. Though the comedy was sometimes criticized as "too raucous," the San Francisco Minstrels held the stage when most other minstrel companies had long since failed to captivate. Backus's impersonations, according to the *New York World*, were "wide departures from negro delineations and depended for their effectiveness entirely on the extravagance of the moment" (22 June 1883). A "well known character" in New York with many friends and admirers, Backus helped move minstrelsy from crude ethnic stereotypes to an entertainment of a higher order.

• Playbills and programs can be found in the Harvard Theatre Collection and the Billy Rose Theatre Collection at the New York Public Library for the Performing Arts, Lincoln Center (which also includes a clippings file). The Works Progress Administration Project on *San Francisco Theatre Research*, vol. 13, monograph 25, ed. Lawrence Estaban (1939), is a good resource for Backus's earlier years, as are Edmond Gagey, *The San Francisco Stage* (1950), and the San Francisco editions of *Golden Era*, the *Argonaut*, *McCabe's Journal*, and the *Daily Dramatic Chronicle*. The history of the San Francisco Minstrels in New York can be traced through George C. D. Odell, *Annals of the New York Stage*, vols. 8–11 (1927–1949), and T. Allston Brown, *History of the New York Stage* (1903). Reviews can be found in the *Golden Era* (1854–1860), *New York Tribune* (1882–1883), *New York Clipper* (1871–1883), and the *Spirit of the Times* (1880–1883).

SUSAN F. CLARK

BACKUS, Isaac (9 Jan. 1724–20 Nov. 1806), Baptist clergyman, was born in Norwich, Connecticut, the son of Samuel Backus and Elizabeth Tracy, prosperous farmers. Unlike some members of his extended family, he never attended college and received only seven years of elementary instruction. His father died of measles when Isaac was sixteen years old, leaving a talented youth to begin life as a yeoman farmer. Raised in a household with ten siblings, Backus credited his mother with providing a strong religious influence. He also inherited a tradition of religious dissent from his grandfather Joseph Backus, who was expelled from the Connecticut legislature for opposing the Saybrook Platform, which reorganized Connecticut's churches along Presbyterian lines, and from his mother, who separated from the Backus's home congregation over the same issue. During the Great Awakening, Backus followed his mother's lead, experienced a conversion in 1741, and became a church member the following year. Though he did not hear evangelist George Whitefield preach until after his conversion, Backus heard the fiery James Davenport and other itinerants, who had a great influence on him.

In January 1745 Backus and his mother joined the organizers of a Separatist meeting in Norwich, and soon he felt called to preach. After serving as an itinerant preacher for two years, Backus settled in Titicut parish (a division of the towns of Middleborough and Bridgewater), Massachusetts, where a new Separatist congregation ordained him in April 1748. He immediately challenged Massachusetts laws supporting established churches, and local authorities briefly detained him for refusal to pay parish taxes. Married in 1749 to Susanna Mason of Rehoboth, with whom he eventually had nine children, Backus was perhaps influenced by his new wife's endorsement of Baptist principles. After two years of struggling with the issue of infant versus adult baptism, Backus decided in favor of antipedobaptist beliefs. For the next few years he operated his church under a rule of "open communion" for both Baptists and Separatists but in 1756 brought his flock squarely into the Baptist fold and reconstituted his church as the First Baptist Church of Middleborough.

For the rest of his life Backus organized, itinerated, and wrote pamphlets, newspaper articles, and letters furthering the Baptist cause. He helped mediate conflicts among Baptist congregations and promoted cooperation by convincing individual churches to join the Warren Baptist Association, a key institution founded in 1767 that aided Baptist churches in their battles with the New England establishment and spread Baptist beliefs and organization to Separatist churches throughout the area. He served as a counterweight to more extremist and divisive elements within the faith. If the Baptist movement were to survive in New England, Backus knew, it needed freedom from the taxes that were required to support the established church. From this pragmatic realization, he reasoned his way to the principles of liberty of conscience and separation of church and state. Although influenced by John Locke, Backus's stand for these ideals bore only slight resemblance to the principled and legalistic thinking of Thomas Jefferson and Roger Williams. He showed little sympathy for the plight of other dissenters, and though he came to believe that government should have no influence on church affairs, he never endorsed the reverse proposition, arguing that Massachusetts and later the United States should indeed be Christian entities.

Backus's pamphlet in defense of civil disobedience, *An Appeal to the Public for Religious Liberty* (1773), outlines his philosophy on the separation of church and state, which was based on a pietistic approach, but he also participated in broader public debates. A supporter of the American Revolution, Backus joined together the issues of political and religious liberty, giving Baptists incentive to back the patriot cause. Despite a vigorous public campaign, however, he failed to convince the writers of Massachusetts's new state constitution (1780) to exclude church taxes from their plan. During the argument over the U.S. Constitution, Backus modified his anti-Federalist views and, at the Massachusetts ratifying convention, lent his qualified support to the proposed government, despite united opposition among most other Baptist delegates. He especially praised the bans on religious tests and a hereditary nobility. Backus supported Thomas Jefferson during the 1790s and was happy to see his old adversary, John Adams, who during the Revolution had supported the religious establishment of Massachusetts, voted out of office.

Able to support himself on income supplemented by inherited land in Norwich, the family iron works, and book selling, Backus never suffered the financial hardships often associated with Baptist clerical life. He itinerated extensively, in addition to maintaining his church in Middleborough, traveling at least a thousand miles annually for forty years. A log book of his journeys designates each destination, the dates of departure and return, and the miles covered. The Warren Association sent him to preach throughout Virginia and North Carolina in 1788–1789, giving Backus an important role in sparking the Second Great Awakening in the South. In 1799 he retired as a trustee of the College of Rhode Island (later Brown University), a post he had held since 1765. Despite his own lack of formal schooling, Backus consistently endorsed the principle of a learned ministry. After the death of his wife in 1800, Backus continued as a full-time pastor and remained the leading published author among New England Baptists. Often remembered for his three-volume work, *A History of New England with Particular Reference to the Denomination of Christians Called Baptists* (1777–1796), Backus authored numerous tracts promoting freedom of conscience, justifying the five cardinal points of Freewill Baptists, and discussing other theological and ecclesiastical issues. Having enjoyed a long and influential ministry, Backus died at home in Middleborough.

Backus's career and writings place him among the preeminent religious figures of the eighteenth century, and he stands out as the most important Baptist of his time. Not a rigorous or original thinker, his ideas nevertheless represent the popular understanding of principles that emerged from colonial culture and informed the political rhetoric of the Revolution. Backus's history of New England continues to win praise from modern historians for its thorough research, despite its decidedly sectarian point of view. In the judgment of his friend Dr. Thomas Baldwin, "Few men have more uniformly lived and acted up to their profession" than Isaac Backus, "a burning and shining light" (Backus, "Memoir of the Author," *Church History*, p. 16).

• Backus's papers are scattered in several locations, but the bulk, including his diaries, may be found at Andover Newton Theological School in Newton Centre, Mass., and Brown University. Some manuscripts have been microfilmed and are available at the American Antiquarian Society and at Baylor University. His pamphlets are reproduced in the Early American Imprint Series, and twelve of the most important ones have been edited by William G. McLoughlin and published with a useful introduction as *Isaac Backus on Church, State, and Calvinism: Pamphlets, 1754–1789* (1968). Backus's *A History of New England with Particular Reference to the Denomination of Christians Called Baptists* was republished (based on the second edition) in 1969 as one volume, and his *Church History of New England from 1620 to 1804* (1844) offers a more concise view of the same subject. Alvah Hovey, *A Memoir of the Life and Times of the Rev. Isaac Backus* (1859), remains the starting point for investigating Backus, but the best modern biography is McLoughlin, *Isaac Backus and the American Pietistic Tradition* (1967). McLoughlin updated his view of Backus's importance to church history in *Soul Liberty: The Baptists' Struggle in New England, 1630–1833* (1991). Also useful are T. B. Maston, *Isaac Backus: Pioneer of Religious Liberty* (1962), and Milton V. Backman, "Isaac Backus: A Pioneer Champion of Religious Liberty" (Ph.D. diss., Univ. of Pennsylvania, 1959), which includes a geneaological table on the Backus family. Stanley Grenz, *Isaac Backus: Puritan and Baptist* (1983), places Backus in the broader context of the Puritan and Baptist movements, as well as analyzing his theological and historical works.

ELIZABETH E. DUNN

BACKUS, Jim (25 Feb. 1913–3 July 1989), actor, comedian, and author, was born James Gilmore Backus in Cleveland, Ohio, the son of Russell Gould Backus, a mechanical engineer and president of a local heavy-machinery company, and Daisy Gilmore-Taylor. They lived in Bratenahl, an upper-class borough of Cleveland. Jim attended the Bratenahl School, then as a teenager went to Kentucky Military Institute, but when he tried to enlist, the army rejected him, telling him that he had a vertical stomach and would have to eat six times a day to stay nourished. However, at school he began a lifelong friendship with fellow cadet and future movie actor Victor Mature, who, like Backus, was always getting into trouble. He next enrolled in the preparatory University School back in Ohio and, according to his last autobiography, was expelled for biting his wrestling coach in the groin to free his head from a scissors hold.

Backus recalled in his memoirs that his yen for acting dated back to age nine, when he "directed" *Cinderella* and *The Sleeping Beauty* at the Bratenahl School and "coached" the two leading ladies in his tree house. His father brushed aside talk of a serious acting career, figuring his son would go to college, join the family business, and act to his heart's content in the shows of the local social club. However, even in the throes of the Great Depression, Backus persuaded his parents to give their blessing to his theatrical ambitions. In 1932 he moved to New York City and enrolled in the famed American Academy of Dramatic Arts, from which he graduated in 1933.

With the nation and the theater world enmeshed in the depression, the twenty-year-old Backus was unable to secure a job or an agent. He presently despaired and returned to Cleveland. There he worked briefly with a summer theater until his appendix ruptured. After recovering, he obtained a job, with the help of a distant family connection, as a radio announcer.

In 1938, having lost his radio job, Backus decided to try again for an acting career on Broadway. This time a successful audition earned him a small part in the play *Hitch Your Wagon*, where he shared a dressing room with Keenan Wynn, who became a close friend. In 1941, still poor and struggling, he met actress-model Henrietta Kaye, nicknamed "Henny," who was in better circumstances and happy to come to his aid. They lived together for two years before getting married, and their marriage lasted the rest of his life.

Backus was able to support himself in New York City through radio. ("I like to eat regularly" was how he described the choice to pursue the airwaves even though the live stage was his medium of preference.) A series of successful auditions got him into the ranks of about fifty New York actors who found full employment on radio soap operas, variety hours, and commercials. In the course of this new stage of his working life, he started experimenting with a particular voice characterization that he had been perfecting at parties, described by his wife as the Harvard man who "sounded like he was born with a silver spoon in his mouth and they forgot to take it out." In 1944 that persona became Hubert Updyke III, the delightfully snobbish millionaire on "The Alan Young Show." ("Careful, or I'll have your mouth washed out with domestic champagne" was one classic line.) When Young moved to Hollywood at the beginning of 1946, the show and the Backuses moved with him. Presently, Backus had a radio show of his own in 1947–1948. "The Jim Backus Show," a weekly half-hour of comedy-variety, included his Hubert Updyke characterization. His wife Henny Backus was with him on the writing team.

Having moved to Hollywood, Backus was able to do just what an actor would hope to do there: appear prominently in numerous movies. He played the affluent but ineffectual father of James Dean's character in *Rebel without a Cause* in 1955. Another noted role was that of the glib press agent and friend of silent film star Lon Chaney (portrayed by James Cagney) in *Man of a Thousand Faces* (1957). Backus lamented in a few interviews that he seemed perpetually to be getting cast as somebody's friend. "I can't really blame Hollywood producers. . . . To them, I must look like a St. Bernard. They've done everything but put a keg of brandy around my neck" (United Press story, 13 May 1953). In the late 1940s and throughout the 1950s he provided the voice for the animated cartoon character Mr. Magoo, a myopic, provincial curmudgeon. Backus patterned his characterization affectionately after his father. During this time he also won a brief bout with alcoholism.

On television, Backus distinguished himself with three different roles, all on series that had an afterlife in reruns long after their original inceptions had come and gone. He was the buffoonish Judge Bradley J. Stevens on "I Married Joan" from 1952 to 1954, costarring with Joan Davis. Through the 1960s and even into the 1970s Mr. Magoo came to television in more than one series, always with Backus's voice. And, for three seasons in the mid-1960s, he recycled the voice of Hubert Updyke III into Thurston Howell III, the feisty millionaire marooned on "Gilligan's Island."

The Backuses were popular in the Hollywood social set, and numerous celebrities made their New Year's Eve party an annual appointment. In the last decade of his life Backus wrestled with the degenerative affliction known as Parkinson's disease. This did not stop him from acting, writing, or hosting parties. In the 1984 volume *Backus Strikes Back*, he and his regular coauthor Henny wrote of his travails with a blend of poignancy and their customary risqué humor (as in narrating the time when his legs buckled in the bathtub and he had to be hoisted up nude by a fully outfitted fireman). He was membership chairman of the National Parkinson's Foundation and proved a very successful fundraiser. He died in Santa Monica, California.

• There is a clipping file on Backus in the Billy Rose Theatre Collection at the New York Public Library for the Performing Arts, Lincoln Center. Backus was a prolific writer of autobiographies in addition to his other achievements. His works, mostly co-written with his wife Henny, include *Rocks on the Roof* (1958), *What Are You Doing after the Orgy?* (1962), and *Forgive Us Our Digressions* (1988). Countless articles have appeared about him throughout his career, such as those in the *New York Times*, 17 Nov. 1957 and 30 Mar. 1958.

BEN ALEXANDER

BACKUS, Truman Jay (11 Feb. 1842–25 Mar. 1908), pioneer in female education, was born in Locke, Cayuga County, New York, the son of Jay Spicer Backus, a minister, and Mercy Williams. Backus's early childhood was spent in Groton, Tompkins County, New York, while his father supplied the pulpits of Baptist churches in Auburn and Syracuse, New York. His father eventually became secretary of the Baptist Home Mission Society and moved the family to New York City. After receiving his early education in the public schools of New York, Backus entered the University of Rochester, a Baptist institution, with the intent of following his father into the ministry. After receiving an A.B. with honors (and making Phi Beta Kappa) in 1864, Backus remained in Rochester for a year to pursue postgraduate study. He then relocated to Richmond, Virginia, where, with the city still under martial law following the close of the Civil War, he organized the first school for newly freed slaves. Despite his education and his family's abolitionist background, the school evidently folded shortly after its founding, for Backus returned north and married Sarah C. Glass of Syracuse, New York, in 1866.

Following his return from Richmond, Backus spent some time assisting his father in his work with the Baptist Home Mission in New York. In 1867 he received his A.M. from Rochester and on 7 June of that year accepted an invitation to join the faculty of the recently opened Vassar College in Poughkeepsie, New York. Serving as professor of rhetoric and English language and literature, Backus initially had to overcome resentment from some of the older students, who considered him "unprofessorial" on account of his relative youth and inexperience. He soon won the trust of both faculty and students, however, and proved himself a most effective instructor. Particularly fond of Chaucer, Backus gave outside readings at the Literary Society of Poughkeepsie in addition to his teaching duties. Deeply interested in current affairs (a subject not then generally addressed in college curriculums), Backus began a lecture series for junior and senior students at Vassar in 1872 on the topic and also encouraged his students to read daily newspapers.

College president John Howard Raymond came to rely heavily on Backus, who was serving as department head as well as instructor, for assistance in charting the course of instruction at the pioneering institution. Outside recognition of Backus's efforts came in the form of job offers—a professorship of English at Harvard University and the presidency of Vanderbilt University—that Backus declined. In addition to teaching and outside lecturing, Backus also engaged in much-needed fundraising for the college in 1875. His greatest contribution in the area of administration was his proposal at a special faculty meeting in January 1883 to abolish the college's preparatory department. Founded at the same time as the college, the department had provided badly needed supplementary instruction to the uneven educational background of Vassar's first students but had since become a source of contention. Many claimed that it drained resources needed elsewhere and also hurt the college's reputation. With the abolishment of the preparatory department, Vassar was able to focus all its energies on the education of its undergraduates.

Backus received another benefit from his term at Vassar: following the death of his first wife in 1882, he married Helen Hiscock, a former Vassar student (and later faculty member) in 1883 (between his two marriages Backus had four children). In the latter year Backus left Vassar to assume the presidency of the Packer Collegiate Institute in Brooklyn, New York. The institute, a school for women that (ironically, in view of Backus's efforts at Vassar) provided preparatory and collegiate education, benefited from Backus's effective leadership until his death. Backus also found time to pursue scholarship in his chosen field; he produced a revision of Thomas B. Shaw's *New History of English Literature* (1884) and also authored *The Great English Writers from Chaucer to George Eliot* (1889) and *Outlines of Literature, English and American* (1897).

While in Brooklyn, Backus continued his interest in civic affairs and served his adopted city in numerous capacities. Beginning in 1894 he was a civil service commissioner under Mayors Charles Adolph Schieren and Frederick W. Wurster and from 1896 until 1906 served as a member of the board of managers of the Long Island State Hospital (later becoming president of the board). He also was a trustee of the Brooklyn Public Library and of the Randall's Island House of Refuge. As part of his efforts on behalf of education, Backus served a term as president of the Head Masters' Association of New York City and in 1905 was president of the Association of Colleges and Preparatory Schools of the Middle States and Maryland. He died at his home in Brooklyn.

Although largely forgotten today, Backus deserves to be remembered as one of the early pioneers in women's higher education. Unfettered by tradition at newly founded Vassar, Backus pushed his students to become not only better scholars but better citizens as well.

• The Vassar College archives in Poughkeepsie, N.Y., holds a small biographical file on Backus; his papers do not appear to have survived. Although he receives brief mention in James Monroe Taylor and Elizabeth Hazelton Haight, *Vassar* (1915), the best source of information on his career is Frances A. Wood, *Earliest Years at Vassar: Personal Recollections* (1909). Obituaries are in the *New York Tribune* and the *Brooklyn Daily Eagle*, both 25 Mar. 1908.

EDWARD L. LACH, JR.

BACON, Alice Mabel (6 Feb. 1858–1 May 1918), writer, educator, and lecturer, was born in New Haven, Connecticut, the daughter of Leonard Bacon, a minister, and Catherine Terry. Her father served as the pastor of the Center Church in New Haven for nearly sixty years; he was also a teacher at Yale University and a local civic leader. Bacon was educated at private schools in New Haven and later took the Harvard "examinations for women" in 1880 and 1881.

As a child Bacon spent some time teaching freedmen to read at Hampton Institute in Hampton, Virginia, under the guidance of a General Armstrong. She continued her work at the institute as an adult from 1883 to 1888 and from 1890 to 1899. In 1890 she founded the Dixie Colored Training School for Nurses in Hampton. She also published a survey and assessment of the development of the African-American race in 1896 in association with the Atlanta Exposition.

At the Hampton Institute, Bacon made several Japanese friends, including Princess Oyama, a teacher of English at the conservative and xenophobic Peeress's School in Tokyo, where noble Japanese girls were sent to be educated. Through the princess, Bacon received an invitation to teach for a year at the school, which she did in 1888–1889. During her time in Japan she visited many of the traditional tourist attractions, but she also lived in a house that she described as "half Japanese and half foreign" with three Japanese teachers at the school and a number of Japanese girls. This, together with her teaching, gave her a unique insight into the daily lives of Japanese women, which was augmented by being a guest in other homes.

On her return to the United States, Bacon edited the letters that she had sent from Japan to her brothers and sisters, subsequently publishing them as *Japanese Girls and Women* (1891) and *A Japanese Interior* (1893). In these letters, she described daily life in Japan and the customs, beliefs, and superstitions of the upper classes with whom she associated. As she said of her work, "Whatever views they may give of Japanese life were obtained from the Japanese side, and from the side of the Japanese woman. . . . The letters do not lay claim to deep research or wide knowledge of all subjects touched upon by them. They are simply a daily chronicle of events, sights, and impressions" (preface to *A Japanese Interior*). The books include descriptions of daily life, housekeeping, cooking, education, weddings, funerals, and the social life of the elite. Her writings had immense appeal for the increasingly literate body of white, middle-class American women.

In 1899 Bacon returned to Japan to teach for two years at the Higher Normal School in Tokyo. After returning to the United States, Bacon was in much demand as a lecturer on Japan and Japanese history. She wrote a book of short stories about Japan, *In the Land of the Gods* (1905), and she edited *Human Bullets: A Soldier's Story of Port Arthur* (1907), the autobiography of Tadayoski Sakurai, a participant in the Russo-Japanese War. She ended her teaching career by working from 1908 at Miss Capen's School in Northampton, Massachusetts.

After retiring in 1910 to New Haven, Bacon, who never married, purchased land on Lake Asquam in Holderness, New Hampshire. She developed the property into Deep Haven Camp, were the elite from Boston, New York, and elsewhere could spend their summers as "paying guests" rather than boarders.

Like her father, Bacon was active in the Center Church of New Haven. When she died at her home in New Haven she was the president of the Foreign Missionary Society, a fundraising organization. She had also served as the founder and president of the Center Church Foundation (which subsequently developed into the Women's Church Union) and as the first president of the Women's Civic Club, which later merged with the Civic Federation.

• Information about Bacon's life can be found in Thomas Baldwin, *Michael Bacon of Dedham, 1640, and His Descendants* (1915). A number of reviews of her books are in the *New York Times*; see, for example, 16 Oct. 1891, 17 Aug. 1891, 5 Nov. 1893, and 7 Apr. 1895. An obituary is in the *New Haven Journal-Courier*, 3 May 1918.

CLAIRE STROM

BACON, Benjamin Wisner (15 Jan. 1860–1 Feb. 1932), clergyman and theological professor, was born in Litchfield, Connecticut, the son of Susan (née Bacon) and Leonard Woolsey Bacon, a clergyman. Bacon grew up surrounded by the traditions, habits and the learning of a family of distinguished New England clerics. His paternal grandfather, Leonard Bacon, pastor of First Church in New Haven, Connecticut, for forty-one years before becoming a leader on the faculty of Yale Divinity School, was a particularly strong influence. Young Benjamin studied in private schools in New Haven before a period of travel with his parents. He studied in Europe for two years (1872–1874) at Coburg Gymnasium in Germany and three years (1874–1877) at the Collège de Genève, Switzerland. He entered Yale University in September 1877 and was graduated with the B.A. degree in 1881. Earlier he had considered a career in medicine, but his successes in classical literature and rhetoric, as well as the encouragement of his fiancée, Eliza Buckingham Aiken, in the summer following his graduation, led him to enter Yale Divinity School to prepare for the ministry.

When he completed divinity school in 1884, he married Aiken, with whom he would have two children, and accepted a call to become pastor of First Church, Lyme, Connecticut. While there he began what he would see as his life's work, the introduction of "higher criticism" to the study of the Bible in the United States. In the last decades of the nineteenth century, biblical higher criticism referred to the application of rational and historical questions to the study of the Bible. Bacon thought of his teachers at Yale Divinity School as fearful defenders of tradition against the new historical critical developments taking place in Europe. When the biblical scholar W. Robertson Smith was removed from his position at Aberdeen because his critical interpretation of the Old Testament was judged to be heretical, Bacon's grandfather Leonard Bacon proposed that he be invited to Yale, but opposition from the biblical faculty defeated the proposal. During his tenure at Lyme, Benjamin Bacon studied Smith's *The Old Testament and the Jewish Church*, given to him by his father, as well as the works of Julius Wellhausen, Otto Pfleiderer, and other higher critics. He learned Dutch in order to read the works of Abraham Kuenen, with whom he began a lively correspondence. Most important for his development was the arrival at Yale of William Rainey Harper, the dean of American Old Testament scholars, who would become the first president of the University of Chicago in 1892. Harper invited the young pastor to participate in his seminars and encouraged him to work on the documentary hypothesis of the Pentateuch, the view being widely debated in Europe that the first five books of the Bible had been compiled from several earlier sources, or documents. Bacon's first publications were on that topic, initially articles in Harper's journal *Hebraica* and then *The Genesis of Genesis* (1892) and *The Triple Tradition of the Exodus* (1894). Bacon continued his work in biblical higher criticism in his second pastoral appointment at Oswego, New York (1889–1896), yet he never pursued a doctorate.

When the New Testament chair at Yale became vacant in 1896, Bacon applied for it, but some of the senior faculty were apprehensive about his radical views. He agreed to serve on a trial basis for a year, and after that time he was awarded the chair (1897), which he held until his retirement in 1928. He died less than four years later, in New Haven.

When he joined the Yale faculty, Bacon turned his attention from the Old Testament to the New, but with the same commitment to advance the higher critical interpretation of the Bible. From his student days until the end of his career he battled against fundamentalism and a "scribalism" that relied on church tradition to resolve questions about the origin and meaning of the biblical books. For him, higher criticism was a rigorous historical inquiry into the background of the books themselves that enabled the writers "to speak their own message in their own way, as living men of their own times, not as staged characters sounding their prepared lines through the mask of later convention" ("Enter the Higher Criticism," p. 2). Just as the issue in Old Testament scholarship had focused on the traditional Mosaic authorship of the Pentateuch, the question in his time regarding the New Testament concerned the authorship of the Gospel of John. Bacon was one of the early advocates of the view, later to be taken for granted in biblical studies, that the fourth gospel was not written by John the disciple of Jesus, but by a later figure.

Bacon's contributions to the critical study of the Bible were monumental, both in number and significance. Roy Harrisville, his biographer, counted more than 260 articles, monographs, essays, and books. He was instrumental in developing and securing on the American scene the methods of historical-critical inquiry that went beyond questions of the date and authorship of the biblical books. His "aetiological criticism" paralleled the form critical work of Martin Dibelius and Rudolf Bultmann in locating particular gospel traditions in the situations of the early church. Bacon concluded that many of the traditions in the gospels concerning Jesus developed not out of historical recollections about Jesus, but around the early church practices of baptism and the Lord's Supper. He thought that historical investigation of the life and teaching of Jesus was necessary in order to understand his God-consciousness, that is, his deep awareness of, and his moral identity with, God the Father. His last major work was *Jesus the Son of God* (1930), originally presented as the Shaffer Lectures at Yale the year following his retirement.

Bacon had a taste for controversy and could heap scorn upon those who resisted free inquiry into the origin and meaning of the biblical documents. He confessed that as a teacher he was considered "the worst possible" ("Enter the Higher Criticism," p. 40), but his students described him as gentle and gracious. "Students who were bewildered by his erudition and disturbed by his conclusions were reassured by his prayers" (Bainton, p. 218). He had a sense of humor that enabled him to appreciate a mock trial for heresy conducted by students. For all his accomplishments, at the end of his life he could write, in all humility, that even then he could not pass a Yale Ph.D. examination ("Enter the Higher Criticism," p. 34).

• A complete bibliography of Bacon's publications up to the middle of 1927 is available in the collection of essays honoring him and his close friend and colleague Frank Chamberlin Porter, *Studies in Early Christianity*, ed. Shirley Jackson Case (1928), pp. 443–57. His autobiographical essay, "Enter the Higher Criticism," in *Contemporary American Theology*, vol. 1, ed. Virgilius Ferm (1932), pp. 1–50, lists works published between July 1927 and 1931. A biography by Roy A. Harrisville, *Benjamin Wisner Bacon: Pioneer in American Biblical Criticism* (1976), includes an analysis and evaluation of his contributions to biblical scholarship. Student recollections were published in the *Yale Divinity News* (Mar. and Nov. 1932). See also Roland H. Bainton, *Yale and the Ministry: A History of Education for the Christian Ministry at Yale from the Founding in 1701* (1957), and Ernst W. Saunders, *Searching the Scriptures: A History of the Society of Biblical Literature, 1880–1980* (1982).

GENE M. TUCKER

BACON, Edward Payson (16 May 1834–25 Feb. 1916), grain dealer, was born in Reading Township, near Watkins Glen, New York, the son of Joseph F. Bacon, a tailor, and Matilda Cowles. Edward Bacon was educated at public schools in the vicinity of Geneva, New

York, where his father went to farm in 1838. At fifteen he entered the Brockport Collegiate Institute to prepare for the ministry, but his father's financial reverses caused him to leave after a year. Bacon became a clerk with the newly completed New York & Erie Railroad at Hornellsville, New York, in 1851. After rising to chief clerk of its freight department in New York, he left in 1855 when offered a position in Chicago as head of the freight department of the Michigan Southern & Northern Indiana Railroad, a predecessor of the Lake Shore & Michigan Southern and a major component of the New York Central System's main line.

Feeling strongly that the opportunities for economic advancement were most favorable in what was then considered the Northwest, Bacon joined the Milwaukee & Mississippi Railroad in July 1856 as its chief freight agent in Milwaukee. He became the railroad's general freight agent in March 1857. With this company and its successor, the Chicago, Milwaukee & St. Paul Railway, he worked for nine years, advancing in rank and expanding his authority into passenger traffic and accounting. He made various innovations in administration and accounting, including design of a wooden rack for interline coupon tickets that became widely used on North American railroads. Bacon patented the device in 1863.

Although Bacon seemed assured of a successful career in railroading, he left the industry in 1865 to become a grain merchant in Milwaukee in partnership with Lyman Everingham. He dissolved the partnership in 1874 because of ill health and after a year of recuperation spent two years as a wholesale grocer. In 1877 he reentered the grain trade in partnership with O. E. Britt and M. P. Aitken under the name of E. P. Bacon & Co. The enterprise flourished, expanded its operations from Milwaukee to Chicago and Minneapolis, and was incorporated in 1908. Bacon built the firm into one of the major American grain dealers and remained active in it until his death. He was a member of the Milwaukee Chamber of Commerce from 1865 and served as its president from 1891 to 1893.

Partly because of his business success, but also because of his early familiarity with the institutions of railroading, Bacon was well suited to be a spokesman for the grain trade on transportation issues. Locally, he worked to gain Milwaukee parity in grain rates with Chicago and other rival centers. Nationally, he particularly identified himself with the effort to vest the Interstate Commerce Commission with powers of maximum rate regulation. A Supreme Court decision of 1897 ruled that in the Act to Regulate Interstate Commerce, Congress in 1887 had given the commission only the right to declare an existing rate unlawful, not authority to set a rate for the future. Bacon organized his effort as the Interstate Commerce Law Convention, which first met at St. Louis in October 1900. The convention met again at St. Louis in October 1904 and at Chicago in October 1905. Bacon served as chairman of the convention's executive committee and represented it as a lobbyist in Washington, D.C., while the measure it sought was in Congress. Maximum rate regulation for the future was enacted in the form of the Hepburn Act in June 1906. (President Theodore Roosevelt reportedly offered Bacon membership on the Interstate Commerce Commission while the bill was under consideration, but Bacon declined.) Bacon frequently represented grain dealers in testimony before the commission, however.

Throughout his career Bacon was prominent in Milwaukee local affairs. He was active in the Milwaukee Young Men's Christian Association, of which he served as president from 1889 to 1891. Although not an alumnus, he particularly identified himself with Beloit College, where he served as a trustee from 1892 to his death. He established there a series of scholarships known as the Bacon Fellowships.

Bacon was twice married, first in 1858 to Emma Hobbs of Paterson, New Jersey, who died in 1892; they had four children. In 1895 Bacon married Ella Dey Baird of Pelham Manor, New York, who survived him. He died in Daytona, Florida, where he had gone for the winter to recuperate from an unspecified illness.

• For additional information see Frank A. Taylor, "Edward Payson Bacon," *Dictionary of American Biography*, vol. 1 (1927), p. 476; and *Who's Who in America*, vol. 5 (1908–1909), p. 67. Obituaries are in the *Grain Dealers Journal* 36 (10 Mar. 1916): 385; the *Milwaukee Journal*, the *Milwaukee Sentinel*, and the *Beloit Daily News*, all 26 Feb. 1916; *Beloit Alumnus* 7 (Apr. 1916): 6–7; and *Round Table* (Beloit College) 62 (1 Mar. 1916): 202.

GEORGE W. HILTON

BACON, Ernst (26 May 1898–16 Mar. 1990), composer and pianist, was born in Chicago, Illinois, the son of Charles S. Bacon, a physician, and Maria von Rosthorn. He was also active as a conductor, teacher, and writer. His music education included the study of music theory with P. C. Lutkin at Northwestern University (1915–1918) and with the composers Arne Oldberg and T. Otterstroem at the University of Chicago (1919–1920). While a student at Northwestern and the University of Chicago, he studied piano privately with Alexander Raab (1916–1921). In 1924 Bacon traveled to Vienna, where he studied piano with Malwine Bree and Franz Schmidt and theory and composition with Karl Weigl.

In 1926, after his return to the United States, he taught piano at the Eastman School of Music in Rochester, New York; studied conducting with Eugene Goosens; and was assistant conductor of the Rochester Opera Company. He also studied theory and composition with Ernest Bloch in San Francisco. He completed his formal education at the University of California, Berkeley, where he earned his M.A. in 1935.

Bacon's work as a composer was recognized in 1932, when he was awarded the Pulitzer Prize for his Symphony no. 1 in D Minor. During the 1930s, Bacon's career demonstrated the wide-ranging interests and abilities that were to be his trademark. Not only was he active as a composer, but from 1934 to 1937 he was the supervisor of the Works Progress Administration's Federal Music Project in San Francisco and conductor of its orchestra. In 1935 he founded and directed the Carmel Bach Festival. Simultaneously, he pursued his literary interests by writing music criticism for the *Argonaut*, a weekly newspaper published in San Francisco. His first written work on music, "Our Musical Idiom," was a lengthy article published when he was nineteen years old. It was an early and important investigation of tonality and atonality. Bacon also performed in Europe and the United States as a pianist.

Bacon was professor of piano and dean of the School of Music at Converse College in Spartanburg, South Carolina, from 1938 to 1945 and director of the New Spartanburg Festival. While at Converse, he received two Guggenheim Fellowships (in 1939 and 1942). He was director of the School of Music of Syracuse University from 1945 to 1947 and remained at the university as composer-in-residence until 1963. His two major works on music, *Words on Music* (1960) and *Notes on the Piano* (1963), were published by Syracuse University Press. In his writings, he mostly expressed himself in aphorisms. When he was angry, he was capable of being "fiercely eloquent." These works remain in print after more than thirty years, evidence of their timelessness.

In 1963 Bacon moved to Orinda, California, near San Francisco, where he made his home for the rest of his life. He was married in 1927 to Mary Prentice Lillie, with whom he had two children; in 1937 to Analee Camp, with whom he had two children; in 1952 to Moselle Camp, with whom he had one child, and in 1972 to Ellen Wendt, with whom he also had one child.

Bacon received many commissions, prizes, and awards including the National Institute of Arts and Letters Award, a Louisville Orchestra commission, and a third Guggenheim Fellowship. Many of his compositions were published by major firms, including Schirmer, Fischer, Galaxy, and Peer, and more than twenty-five commercial recordings of his songs and works for orchestra, piano, organ, and other instruments were issued during his lifetime. In 1973 Bacon compiled a list of his existing works that was published with a short introduction by Paul Horgan.

Bacon was a prolific composer who created music throughout his long life. His works include four symphonies, chamber music, cantatas, a folk opera, choral music, band music, ballets, and other instrumental music. However, he is primarily known as a composer of lyric songs that include more than seventy settings of Emily Dickinson's poetry. He also set other poets, including Walt Whitman and A. E. Housman. His vocal pieces possess a gentle, human touch and an awareness of speech rhythms and inflections. His works for the stage demonstrate his ability to catch the natural accent of American speech. He wrote, "I belong to no school or group. My studies in native folk music have played their . . . part in my melody, rhythm, and harmony." He acknowledged that he was considered "eclectic" but proclaimed that he simply honored his musical ancestry. Bacon composed a sonata for viola and piano at the age of eighty-eight when he was nearly blind. He is reported to have been composing, revising earlier compositions, or writing until shortly before he died at his home in Orinda, California.

• Major archival collections relating to Bacon are at the Library of Congress and Syracuse University Library. Additional archival materials are at the New York Public Library, Boston University, the University of California at Berkeley, Stanford University, and the University of Nebraska. For further information, see J. St. Edmunds, "The Songs of Ernst Bacon," *Sewanee Review* 49 (1941); W. Fleming, "Ernst Bacon," *Musical America* 69, no. 8 (1949); and Severine Neff, "An American Precursor of Non-tonal Theory: Ernst Bacon (1898–1990)," *Current Musicology* 48 (1991). An obituary is in the *New York Times*, 17 Mar. 1990.

MARIE J. KROEGER

BACON, Frank (16 Jan. 1864–19 Nov. 1922), actor and author, was born in Marysville, California, the son of Lyddell Bacon, a rancher, and Lehella Jane McGrew. A few years after Frank's birth, the family moved to San Jose, California. Bacon received little formal education and by the age of fourteen had left school to work in a photography studio. Until his early twenties, Bacon was intermittently employed as a photographer, a newspaper advertising solicitor, and a journalist. He started newspapers in Mountain View and Mayfield, California, and was for a time co-owner of the Napa *Reporter*. His various newspaper and photography efforts were never very successful, however, partially because his true interest lay in the theater.

In his autobiography, *Barnstorming* (1987), Bacon traces his passion for the theater to when, at age twelve, he saw a circus show in Bakersfield, California. His curiosity grew into a preoccupation that resulted in his first stage appearance at age fourteen as a "super" (supernumerary) in a San Jose production. Over the next several years Bacon initiated a variety of amateur performances in and around San Jose, many of which included the participation of a leading local elocution student, Jennie Weidman, whom he married in 1885 in San Jose. They had three children, two of whom lived to adulthood.

In 1889 Bacon and his wife accepted positions in a stock company. They continued acting in traveling companies in various western states for several years, performing hundreds of roles, mostly in small towns, to little acclaim and even less money. Bacon and his wife were severely criticized by family members for their extensive traveling, particularly since their children were often left with relatives for months at a time. Eventually, in 1900, Bacon traded the adventure of the road for greater stability by accepting a position with the Alcazar Theater Company in San Francisco, remaining there until 1903; over the years he was cast in increasingly larger roles. The resulting security allowed the Bacons to purchase a small fruit farm near Mountain View, California, in 1904; Bacon lived on the farm, dubbed "Baconia," for the remainder of his life.

The 1906 earthquake and a 1907 railway employees strike in San Francisco made theater employment unpredictable for a time. Consequently, the Bacons decided to look East for positions. Bacon had received his first critical acclaim in San Francisco for his portrayals of old-men comic roles in such plays as *Liberty Hall* and *Tennessee's Partner*. He began honing these characterizations, and with the part of Daddy Graham in a Chicago performance of *The Fortune Hunter*, Bacon established himself in 1910 as an actor to reckon with in the eastern United States.

As early as 1892 Bacon had written a play centered on an elderly Civil War veteran given to drink and exaggeration, with little ambition but enormous charm. During his successful run in *The Fortune Hunter* in Chicago, Bacon began rewriting his play, now called *The House Divided*. Lacking confidence in the play as written, he shared the work with James Montgomery, a highly successful actor and writer who had once boarded with the Bacons in San Francisco. Montgomery, who liked the plot and characters, rewrote the play and renamed it *Me and Grant*. A performance of the Montgomery version in Newark, New Jersey, proved largely unsuccessful, but Bacon persisted, giving the work to writer and producer Winchell Smith. Smith accepted the play, doctored it, and named it *Lightnin'*. Bacon appeared in the first performance of this revised version in Washington, D.C., on 25 January 1918; he played the title role of Lightnin' Bill Jones, the name ironically highlighting the slow and lazy manner of the character. The play opened on Broadway on 26 August and was relatively well received. Bacon went on to play the role in a record run that lasted three years and a day, a total of 1,291 performances. He took the play to Chicago, where he played the title role until a week before his death there from a heart attack.

Bacon's triumph in *Lightnin'* resulted primarily from his acting style. In a speech to the American Academy of Dramatic Art in 1921, Bacon noted, "If you were to ask me what I know about acting, I would say I don't know anything. My advice to young actors would be to learn all about acting and then forget it. I believe absolutely in naturalness—believing in yourself" (printed in the *New York Times*, 20 Nov. 1922). In the *New York Times* review of *Lightnin'* (27 Aug. 1918), Bacon is praised for his underplaying: "Not even the fact that practically all of the humorous lines were his could spoil his performance, for there was never a moment when he appeared conscious of his characterization or tried to hammer a point home."

Well liked by both fellow actors and the public, Bacon secured immediate fame and substantial fortune as a result of *Lightnin'*. His contemporary popularity is underscored by the fact that Presidents Wilson, Taft, and Harding all saw him in the play, and that the largest parade crowd ever assembled in the history of New York City up to that time, over 100,000 people, saw Bacon off as he left for Chicago when the play closed in New York in 1921. Had he lived longer, it is possible that Bacon might have continued to stage the play successfully for many years. His immense popularity was based on a single work that, although played by others after his death, could not command lasting artistic acclaim without its creator. A successful movie version of *Lightnin'*, starring Will Rogers, appeared in 1930. For the most part, however, Bacon has become a forgotten celebrity, as little known today as the play he coauthored.

• The manuscript of Bacon's autobiography, by far the most extensive source available on Bacon, and some other theatrical memorabilia are housed at the San Jose Historical Museum. Besides its value as a source on Bacon, *Barnstorming* provides lively and entertaining insight into theater life on the road in the western United States around the turn of the century. The version of *Lightnin'* coauthored with Winchell Smith was first published by S. French in 1918. It also appears in Bennett Cerf, *S. R. O.: The Most Successful Plays of the American Stage* (1944; 1946). Richard Theodore Glyer, "An Outline of the Life and Work of Frank Bacon" (M.A. thesis, Stanford Univ., 1941), synthesizes useful book, newspaper, and magazine accounts of Bacon's career. Also useful is an interview by Ada Patterson, "A New Rip for the Old," *Theater Magazine*, Nov. 1918, pp. 290–92. One of the finest accounts of Bacon's character and his reaction to his success is Florence Foster, "Frank Bacon as Seen by His Secretary," *Scribner's Magazine*, Mar. 1924, pp. 285–96. Along with the one mentioned in the text, an illuminating review of *Lightnin'* is in the *New York Times*, 8 Sept. 1918. Extensive obituaries are in the *New York Times*, 20 Nov. 1922 (actually a front-page story), and in *Variety*, 24 Nov. 1922.

DELMER DAVIS

BACON, Georgeanna Muirson Woolsey (5 Nov. 1833–27 Jan. 1906), Civil War nurse and philanthropist, was born in Brooklyn, New York, the daughter of Charles William Woolsey, a merchant, and Jane Eliza Newton. Raised on fashionable Sheafe Street in Boston, "Georgy" attended Misses Murdock's School. After her father's death on a river steamer, the *Lexington*, on 13 January 1940, her mother moved the family to 17 Rutgers Place in New York City, where Bacon attended Rutgers Female Institute. In 1850 she began finishing school at Misses Anable's Young Ladies Seminary in Philadelphia, then traveled through Europe. She and her sisters were faithful Presbyterians, readers of Horace Greeley's *New York Tribune*, and staunch abolitionists. They attended lectures on the abolition of slavery by George B. Cheever, Wendell Phillips, and Henry Ward Beecher. After the Civil War commenced, the Woolsey women answered President Abraham Lincoln's call for volunteers. On 26 April 1861 they joined Henry Bellows, pastor of the first Unitarian Church; Elisha Harris, an eminent physician; and other prominent New York women to found the Women's Central Association of Relief for the purpose of providing the army with a consistent flow of supplies and trained nurses. President Lincoln sanctioned the U.S. Sanitary Commission on 9 June 1861.

While her mother and sister Abby transformed their New York home into a center for organizing supplies and sewing bandages, Georgeanna applied for training as a war nurse. She fulfilled the qualifications for health, character, and industriousness outlined by Dr. Elizabeth Blackwell, the first woman in the United States to earn a degree in medicine, and was assigned to attend lectures and observe procedures at the New York Hospital. Georgeanna learned several different ways to wrap a bandage and to cope with minor emergencies on her own. Though she, like the other nurses, "attained a high degree of practical skill" (Nutting, p. 363), the doctors did not want to work alongside women and were "determined to make [their] lives so unbearable that they should be forced in self-defense to leave" (*Letters*, vol. 1, p. 142). According to Georgeanna, "These annoyances could not have been endured by the nurses but for the knowledge that they were pioneers, who were, if possible, to gain standing ground for others" (*Letters*, vol. 1, p. 143).

On 2 July 1861 Georgeanna and her sister Eliza went to serve as nurses in Washington, D.C., where Eliza's husband, Joseph Howland, was stationed at an army camp. After they were introduced to President Lincoln at the White House by their uncle Edward Woolsey, the women were briefed by Dorothea Dix, superintendent of women nurses of the army, on the condition of the hospitals and work of volunteer nurses. Georgeanna inspected the management of the hospitals, helped place trained nurses in hospitals where they were needed, then reported to Dr. Blackwell on their progress. She made use of her vantage point to inform her sister Abby of the specific type and quantity of supplies needed, including bandages, clothing, and food. When Georgeanna reported to Abby that army hospitals were without chaplains, together they petitioned President Lincoln to approve the appointments.

In April 1862 Georgy worked with Frederick Law Olmsted, secretary of the Sanitary Commission, to create a hospital transport system to move wounded soldiers on the Potomac and James rivers to hospitals or their homes. Georgy, Eliza, Katharine Wormeley, and Christine Griffin were permanent staff on several of the steamers, caring for the wounded. Georgy was known for "her constant cheerfulness, her ready wit, her never failing resources of contrivance and management in any emergency" (Brockett, p. 327). In September 1862 Georgy, her sister Jane, and their cousin Sarah Woolsey accepted the request of Katharine Wormeley to be assistant superintendents of nurses at the Portsmouth Grove General Hospital, Portsmouth Grove, Rhode Island, through the spring of 1863.

Thinking her brother was wounded at the Battle of Gettysburg, on 4 July 1863 Georgy joined her mother on behalf of the Sanitary Commission to organize feeding and sheltering for the wounded while they waited for trains to Baltimore and Harrisburg. She wrote about her experience in *Three Weeks at Gettysburg*. Ten thousand copies were distributed to Soldier's Aid Societies and the Sanitary Commission to encourage continued supply of donations.

In August 1863 Georgy and her sister Jane supervised nursing at Hammond General Hospital at Point Lookout, Maryland, and stayed until it became a camp for Confederate prisoners. In November 1863 they moved to Fairfax Theological Seminary Hospital near Alexandria, where as assistant superintendents they oversaw the nursing and allocation of special diets.

On 12 May 1864 Georgy received a furlough from the Fairfax Seminary to go to Fredericksburg for the Sanitary Commission to set up relief stations for soldiers wounded in the battle of Spotsylvania Court House. In a letter to Jane, she reported that the casualties were much worse than she had yet seen and stated that she "would rather a thousand times have a friend killed on the field than suffer in this way" (Jane Woolsey, p. 151). She finished her Civil War work in August 1864 at Beverly, New Jersey, where she helped organize an army hospital with her sister Caroline and Abby Hopper Gibbons, the Quaker abolitionist.

On 7 June 1866 Georgeanna married Francis Bacon, professor of surgery at Yale Medical School and son of the famous antislavery preacher, Leonard Bacon. When the New Haven Hospital was in need of trained nurses, Georgeanna took part with her husband in establishing the Connecticut Training School for Nurses according to Florence Nightingale's principles. Georgeanna Bacon supervised daily operations of the hospital as a member of the school's executive committee and served as secretary of the board of administration and as chair of the Committee on Instruction when the group formed in 1876. Her *Hand Book of Nursing for Family and General Use* (1879) was circulated among hospitals, nursing schools, and the public. In 1905 it was revised and reprinted by demand. She traveled in New Haven and New London counties as a member of the Connecticut State Board of Charities from 1883 to 1893, inspecting state prisons, reform schools, insane asylums, almshouses, and children's homes. Having no children of her own, in June 1901 she donated to the Connecticut's Children's Aid Society her large country cottage, Playridge, at Woodmont, Connecticut, which was safe for use by crippled children from Newington Hospital. Bacon died of heart problems in her New Haven home.

Before the Civil War, doctors took complete responsibility for a patient's medical care. With the enormous number of casualties during the war, however, a need arose for nurses to assist surgeons. As one of the first nurses chosen to be trained for army service, Bacon was a pioneer in the field of nursing by helping to curtail criticisms and gain acceptance for women providing medical care. After the war, she played an important role in the founding of a modern school for the training of nurses.

• Bacon's manuscript "History of the Woolsey Family" and two-volume wartime journal, dating from 25 September 1861 to 14 July 1862, remain in family possession. For Bacon's Civil War nursing experiences, see her *Three Weeks at Gettysburg* (1863) on microfilm in the History of Women Collection at the Schlesinger Library, Radcliffe; her *Letters of a Family during the War for the Union, 1861–1865* (1899), edited with Eliza Woolsey Howland; Jane Woolsey, *Hospital Days* (1968); M. Adelaide Nutting and Lavinia L. Dock, "A Trio of Training Schools," in *A History of Nursing*, vol. 2 (1907); Katharine Prescott Wormeley, *The Other Side of War* (1889); Frederick Law Olmsted, *Hospital Transports* (1863); and L. P. Brockett and Mary C. Vaughan, *Woman's Work in the Civil War* (1867). For Bacon's involvement in philanthropy and professional nursing after the war, see her "Connecticut Training School," *Trained Nurse and Hospital Review* 15 (Oct. 1895); and the *Annual Reports* of the Connecticut State Board of Charities 1884–1890 and the Connecticut Training School for Nurses 1875–1907. Anne L. Austin, *The Woolsey Sisters of New York, 1860–1900* (1971), is a book-length biography of Georgy and her sisters Abby, Jane, and Eliza. A sketch of the sisters, "The Misses Woolsey," appears in L. P. Brockett, *Famous Women of the War: A Record of Heroism, Patriotism, and Patience* (1894). For genealogical history, see John Ross Delafield, "Woolsey Family of Great Yarmouth and N.Y.," in *Delafield: The Family History*, vol. 2 (1945), and Eliza Woolsey Howland, *Family Records* (1900). An obituary is in the *New Haven Morning Journal*, 29 Jan. 1906.

BARBARA L. CICCARELLI

BACON, Henry, Jr. (28 Nov. 1866–16 Feb. 1924), architect, was born in Watseka, Illinois, the son of Henry Bacon, a civil engineer, and Elizabeth Kelton. After repeated moves, in 1876 the family settled in southeastern North Carolina, where Bacon's father had charge of port and channel improvements on the Cape Fear River. They lived at Smithville (now Southport) and later Wilmington, where Bacon attended school.

In 1884 Bacon entered the architecture program at the University of Illinois but left it in 1885 to go to Boston to qualify as a competitor for the Rotch Travelling Scholarship of the Boston Society of Architects. Working as a draftsman first for Chamberlin & Whidden and then McKim, Mead & White, he became involved in the colonial revival and had many perspective drawings of buildings old and new published in architectural journals. In 1889 he won the Rotch scholarship, allowing him to make a two-year study tour of Europe. His itinerary included visits to Rome, Pompeii, Greece, and coastal Asia Minor, where he began to acquire the detailed knowledge of classical, especially Greek, design that became a hallmark of his later work. In this he was influenced by the example of his older brother, Francis Henry Bacon, an architect, furniture designer, and classical archaeologist. In 1893 he married Laura Calvert; they did not have children.

From 1891 to 1897 Bacon worked as a designer for McKim, Mead & White in New York, contributing to such projects as the Rhode Island State House and the Brooklyn Museum and helping turn the firm's work toward its trademark white classicism by applying his extensive, detailed knowledge of Greek precedents to several of the firm's designs of the 1890s. His contribution to some of its designs for monuments and memorials—the field in which the new style is most apparent—is known to have been especially formative. On the strength of noteworthy but unexecuted entries in competitions to design the Philadelphia Art Museum and New York Public Library, Bacon and a friend, James Brite, started a practice of their own in 1897. Brite & Bacon had success in designing city and country residences and public libraries in Madison, Connecticut, and Jersey City and Paterson, New Jersey, but the partnership ended in 1903.

Thereafter Bacon practiced on his own, with a small staff, undertaking a limited number of commissions for small or middle-sized buildings, the design and construction of which he supervised closely. He designed several savings banks and financial houses, including the Union Square Savings Bank, New York City (1905–1907), and served as campus architect for Wesleyan University. For that institution he created a master plan in 1912–1913 and designed two houses for student societies, a dormitory, a swimming pool, an observatory, and a library built to revised designs after his death.

Bacon's specialty, however, was the design of monuments and memorials, usually (but not always) conceived in collaboration with sculptors. On his own he designed many grave markers and mausolea patterned on classical Greek models, such as the marble mausoleum for Mark Hanna in Lake View Cemetery, Cleveland (1904–1906), which has the form of a miniature Doric temple or treasury. He participated in several of Augustus Saint-Gaudens's late projects, including an obelisk in O'Connell Street, Dublin, honoring Charles Stewart Parnell (1900–1911), and collaborated with Karl Bitter several times. Their best-known joint work is a memorial to the German-American leader Carl Schurz in Morningside Park, New York (1909–1913), a platform with an exedra containing a bench, relief panels, and a dignified statue of Schurz.

Bacon's most productive collaboration was with the sculptor Daniel Chester French, whose summer home and studio, "Chesterwood," in Glendale, Massachusetts, Bacon had designed (1897–1901). Together French and Bacon undertook more than fifty monumental projects, including memorials to Francis Parkman in Jamaica Plain, Massachusetts (1902–1907), and to Asa, John, and Samuel Melvin, three brothers who were killed in the Civil War, in Concord, Massachusetts (1897–1908). Both of these were austere exedral monuments with stone benches and figures modeled in "negative" relief emerging from upright slabs. Bacon and French's memorial to Spencer Trask in Saratoga, New York (1913–1915), was a landscape composition with a fountain, pool, and restful walks, whereas the monument to Admiral Samuel Francis du Pont in Washington, D.C. (1917–1921), takes the form of a fountain with allegorical figures in the recesses of its base. In 1921–1924 they planned a large memorial at Saint-Mihiel, France, to those from Massachusetts who had died in World War I, but it was not executed because a federal commission assumed responsibility for building all American battle monuments in Europe.

Thanks to his success with such "ideal" programs, Bacon received the prestigious commission to design one of three open-air courts at the Panama-Pacific Exposition in San Francisco (1915). Consisting of a colonnaded approach and a square containing plantings and a mirror-pool, his *Court of the Four Seasons* was acclaimed by architects and the public as the most reflective and contemplative feature of the fair.

Bacon's career reached its peak when he was invited in 1911 to design the nation's memorial to Abraham Lincoln in Potomac Park, Washington. The memorial, first proposed in the McMillan Plan of 1901–1902, was to terminate the ceremonial axis of the Mall and be a pivot for a new memorial bridge to Arlington. Drawing his inspiration from classical Greek temples, Bacon designed a memorial hall surrounded by Doric columns, raised on a high, stepped podium at the end of a long reflecting basin. His design was selected above others (some for different sites) submitted by architect John Russell Pope and was approved by Congress in 1913. Again, French had a hand in the project, modeling the colossal seated figure of Lincoln within. Dedicated in May 1922, the memorial was a huge public success and has remained one of America's most moving patriotic shrines. For its design Bacon was awarded the gold medal of the American Institute of Architects in 1923, a year before he died in New York City.

Bacon's work, climaxing in the Lincoln Memorial, epitomizes the sophisticated classicism dominant in American civic, national, and commercial design of the early twentieth century.

• Bacon's professional papers, including many drawings and the scrapbooks of his European tour, are in the Olin Memorial Library, Wesleyan University. A reminiscence of him by William Partridge is found in the William R. Ware Collection, Avery Architectural Library, Columbia University. There are large, important collections on the construction of the Lincoln Memorial in the National Archives. For an appreciative early account, see Francis S. Swales, "Henry Bacon as a Draftsman," *Pencil Points* 5 (May 1924): 42–62. On the *Court of the Four Seasons* see *The Architecture and Landscape Gardening of the Exposition* (1915), pp. 124–37. The most comprehensive account of the building of the Lincoln Memorial is Edward Concklin, comp., *The Lincoln Memorial, Washington* (1927). Of modern sources on Bacon, the most complete is Christopher A. Thomas, "The Lincoln Memorial and Its Architect, Henry Bacon (1866–1924)" (Ph.D. diss., Yale Univ., 1990).

CHRISTOPHER A. THOMAS

BACON, John (9 Apr. 1738–25 Oct. 1820), Presbyterian clergyman and public official, was born in Canterbury, Connecticut, the son of John Bacon and Ruth Spaulding. He graduated from the College of New Jersey (later Princeton University) in 1765 in preparation for the ministry. During his stay at the college, Princeton had become noteworthy for the curriculum innovations of its president, John Witherspoon, and the fervor of its student debates over colonial rights. Bacon continued his theological studies after graduation, and on 30 July 1767 he was licensed as a minister by the presbytery of Lewes, Delaware. In 1768 he was ordained as an itinerant Presbyterian preacher and served two separate congregations along the Eastern Shore region of Maryland and Delaware until 1771.

In August 1771 Bacon was released from his duties, allowing him to serve an appointment as co-pastor of the Congregational Old South Meetinghouse in Boston. He was installed as a co-pastor along with the Reverend John Hunt on 25 September 1771, as a measure by the Old South to establish a Boston-based conservative locus of religious views and to counter the liberal Congregational beliefs espoused at Harvard College. Bacon accepted the post only after he made the congregation aware both of his strict adherence to Samuel Hopkins's position on baptism and church membership and of his disapproval of the Old South's acceptance of the Half-Way Covenant. In November 1772 Bacon married Elizabeth Goldthwait Cumming, the widow of former Old South pastor Reverend Alexander Cumming and the daughter of suspected Boston Tory Ezekial Goldthwait. They had one daughter and one son; their son Ezekial would become a prominent lawyer and politician in his own right.

As pastor of the Old South, Bacon was awarded an honorary A.M. in theology from Harvard and named an overseer of the college. Yet his ministerial career began to suffer a series of lethal blows in the 1770s. Boston radicals identified him with the Loyalist cause when in 1771 he read from the pulpit Governor Thomas Hutchinson's Thanksgiving Proclamation, which had been denounced by Samuel Adams. Bacon's political views were furthermore suspected by the radicals owing to his father-in-law's close relations with Governor Hutchinson. Bacon earned the ire of his congregation for theological reasons when he continued to promote strict Hopkinsian beliefs and engaged parishioners in heated debate on theology along the new liberal "New Light" style of preaching made popular by Jonathan Edwards. On 8 February 1775 Bacon was dismissed from his pastorate for doctrinal differences with his parishioners. Unable to procure another pastorate, he moved to Stockbridge, Massachusetts, and became a farmer.

Although he engaged in some sporadic itinerant preaching in Connecticut and some minor church controversies in Stockbridge, Bacon never revived his ministry. With the outbreak of the American Revolution, however, he embarked on a new career as a politician and jurist. In 1777 Bacon was elected to Stockbridge's town Committee of Safety and as a delegate to the Massachusetts House of Representatives. He gained recognition across the state when he fought vehemently in the state constitutional convention of 1778–1779 against a proposed clause in the state constitution that would have denied the vote to "Negroes, Indians, and Mulattoes." Bacon successfully had the racist clause removed from the constitution, which in 1780 was ratified by the electorate.

Throughout the 1780s and 1790s Bacon was among the most prominent political figures in Massachusetts. Beginning in 1779 and ending in 1817, he served twelve separate terms in the state house of representatives. Coincident with this service were his ten terms in the Massachusetts Senate from 1782 to 1807; he was selected the senate's president in 1807. A late student of the law, Bacon also embarked on a judicial career in 1783 with his selection as a justice of the peace in Berkshire County. From 1779 to 1807 he was justice of the Court of Common Pleas in Berkshire County and served as the court's chief justice from 1807 to 1811. In 1780 Bacon was an original incorporator of the American Academy of Arts and Sciences.

Bacon expressed a deep faith in popular democracy that frequently placed him in political skirmishes with more conservative foes. In 1787 he joined the ranks of Massachusetts Antifederalists against the ratification of the U.S. Constitution. Bacon campaigned fervently in the ratification struggle against Federalist Theodore Sedgwick, and he denounced the proposed form of government as one that would favor a wealthy elite at the expense of the agrarian majority and that would establish a repressive standing army. He continued his opposition to the Constitution and the Federalist party throughout the 1790s. He proved an outspoken critic of the Alien and Sedition Acts during the presidency of John Adams, the nationalistic fiscal policies of Treasury secretary Alexander Hamilton, and the federal circuit courts as agents of a blatantly political brand of justice. This staunch opposition to the Federalists led Bacon into the ranks of the Democratic-Republican party of James Madison and Thomas Jefferson.

In 1800 Bacon was defeated in his bid for lieutenant governor of Massachusetts, but in 1801 he gained election to the U.S. House of Representatives. In 1804 he was appointed a presidential elector in Massachusetts and voted for Jefferson's reelection. He died in Stockbridge.

• Primary materials on Bacon are at the Massachusetts State Archives and the Massachusetts Historical Society. Several of Bacon's sermons as pastor of the Old South were published and are available through the Early American Imprints Series. The most complete biographical profiles are in James McLachlan, "John Bacon," in his *Princetonians, 1748–1768* (1976), pp. 479–82; U.S. Government Printing Office, *Biographical Directory of the American Congress, 1774–1971* (1971), p. 537; Franklin Dexter, *Yale Biographies*, vol. 5 (1885–1912), pp. 99–103; and John Sibley, *Harvard Graduates*, vol. 16 (1873–1968), pp. 120–25. For Bacon's later political career see especially R. J. Taylor, *Western Massachusetts in the Revolution* (1954), and Jackson T. Main, *The Antifederalists* (1961).

RONALD LETTIERI

BACON, Leonard (26 May 1887–1 Jan. 1954), poet, literary critic, and teacher, was born in Solvay, New York, the son of Nathaniel Terry Bacon, a chemical engineer, and Helen Hazard. Bacon led a sheltered life at his mother's familial estate in Peace Dale, Rhode Island. His parents enrolled him in 1898 in St. George's at Newport, where he spent seven years preparing to matriculate at Yale, following in the footsteps not only of his father but of some twenty other relatives. Bacon gives candid insight into his college years, remembering colleagues and professors in an amiable light though remarking that "with the exception of English and German, I think we were not particularly well taught, or rather that the conception of teaching was poor" (*Semi-Centennial*, p. 29). This view of institutional education probably arose in Bacon because of his father's eclectic and wide-ranging intellectual pursuits.

In 1906 Bacon's studies were temporarily interrupted by the discovery of a tubercular lesion in his left lung, forcing him to retire to an asylum near Montreux, Switzerland, for six months during his sophomore year. Bacon admitted he never quite accepted the diagnosis (*Semi-Centennial*, p. 51), though he offered no evidence for this belief. Whatever the cause, this enforced isolation allowed Bacon the time and solitude to pursue his own literary interests, reading voraciously among the classics, including Racine, Corneille, and Yeats, and exploring his own poetic abilities. After a brief tour through Italy, he returned to Yale, where he served as one of the editors of the Yale literary magazine, which published several of his earliest poems.

After graduating with a B.A. in 1909, Bacon entered his self-proclaimed "year of wonders," during which he worked briefly under his father's direction on a rubber plantation in Nicaragua, before returning aimlessly to Yale graduate school, where he lasted little more than a semester, "put[ting] on a first-rate imitation of a nervous breakdown" (*Semi-Centennial*, p. 85). During this brief graduate sojourn, however, Bacon was able to publish his first volume of poetry, *The Scrannel Pipe* (1909), at his own expense, reinforcing his belief that above all else he desired to write poetry. He spent the first three months of the following year on a Montana ranch before joining his father on a cotton plantation near Burnsville, Alabama, where he labored as assistant to the manager and foreman to hoe-gangs.

That fall Bacon, largely on the merits of his poetry, received an instructorship at the University of California at Berkeley, where he would remain, except for brief sabbaticals, until his resignation in 1923. Once he overcame his initial awe of lecturing and his mild distaste for the task, he was able to juggle the various demands of reading, research, lectures, and his own poetry writing. In these efforts he had the support of his department chair, Charles Mills Gayley, who had initially rejected Bacon's application for an instructorship before reversing his decision after reading *The Scrannel Pipe*. These busy prewar years at Berkeley affected both Bacon's public and private life. While he gained a larger readership publishing poetry in widely read magazines like *Harper's Weekly*, he also resurrected his interest in languages, translating *Heroic Ballads of Servia* (1913) with his colleague and friend George R. Noyes before completing his own translation of *The Song of Roland* (1914). Despite the fervor with which he threw himself into his profession, he nonetheless found time to woo the daughter of a Berkeley mathematics professor, Martha Sherman Stringham, whom he married in 1912.

Bacon enlisted in the Royal Flying Corps in late 1917 and went through the training camp in Toronto, Canada, where he became convinced of his own military "incompetence and inadequacy" (*Semi-Centennial*, p. 139). He was commissioned a second lieutenant in the Signal Reserve Corps and stationed in Washington, D.C., before being transferred to San Diego, California, and eventually to Columbia University in New York City, to attend radio school. There, "two years at an electrical engineering school were crowded into two months on Morningside Heights" (*Semi-Centennial*, p. 152). Bacon never saw active military duty. In 1919 he returned to Berkeley but was dissatisfied with teaching.

Although he completed the translation of *The Lay of the Cid* with R. Selden Rose that year, his efforts turned more and more toward his own poetry. His satiric "Banquet of the Poets" (1920) "had the superlative luck to win the favor of its principal victim, Miss Amy Lowell" (*Semi-Centennial*, p. 161). This overwhelmingly positive response convinced Bacon to request a sabbatical during the 1921–1922 school year and return to his boyhood home in Peace Dale to concentrate solely on his poetry. By March 1922 *Uleg Beg* was completed. Its popular reception by critics following its publication in 1923 convinced Bacon to retire from teaching permanently.

He moved with his wife and three daughters to Carmel, California, where he eagerly anticipated writing a second book of poetry. Instead, following the publication of his second book of verse, *Ph.D.s* (1925), he was overcome by depression that was severe enough to prompt him to travel to Europe to consult Carl Jung. The Bacon family returned to Peace Dale in 1926 before embarking on a four-year sojourn in Florence, Italy, where Bacon researched and wrote. Following the Italian hiatus, Bacon remained at Peace Dale for eight years prior to returning to the West Coast in 1940, this time to Santa Barbara, California, where he remained until 1952. Bacon finally returned to his ancestral estate in Peace Dale, Rhode Island, where he died.

Despite his prolific corpus of texts of poetry and translations and his frequently published poems in the *Saturday Review of Literature*, *Atlantic*, and the *New Yorker*, Bacon never received overwhelming critical acclaim. Although his *Sunderland Capture and Other Poems* (1940) won the Pulitzer Prize for poetry in 1941, critics generally considered his poems too steeped in academia. He was, however, elected to membership in various prestigious societies, most notably the American Society of Arts and Letters. He delivered an address in 1951 at the 250th anniversary of the founding of Yale University.

• Bacon produced a number of books of poetry and translation not mentioned above, including *Animula Vagula* (1926), *Guinea-Fowl and Other Poetry* (1927), *The Legend of Quincibald* (1928), *Lost Buffalo and Other Poems* (1930), *The Furioso* (1932), *Dream and Action* (1934), *The Voyage of Autoleon* (1935), *The Goose on the Capitol* (1936), *Rhyme and Punishment* (1936), *Bellinger Bound and Other Poems* (1938), *Day of Fire* (1943), and the translation *The Lusiads of Luiz de Camoes* (1950). His autobiography, *Semi-Centennial* (1939), chronicles the first fifty years of his life. His close association with the *Saturday Review of Literature* fostered a number of reviews in that journal, including John P. Marquand, "Life and Opinions," a review of *Semi-Centennial*, 25 Mar. 1939, p. 7; Raymond Holden, "Pulitzer Prize Poems," a review of *Sunderland Capture and Other Poems*, 28 June 1941, p. 11; and a brief statement of appreciation, H. S. Canby, "Leonard Bacon," 16 Jan. 1954, p. 10. His *The Furioso* was reviewed in *Poetry* by Harriet Monroe in "D'Annunzio Complete," Feb. 1933, pp. 275–79, and his *Dream and Action* by R. P. Blackmur in "An Active Poem," *Poetry*, Jan. 1935, pp. 223–26. An obituary is in the *New York Times*, 2 Jan. 1954.

CHRISTOPHER J. NEUMANN

BACON, Leonard, Sr. (19 Feb. 1802–24 Dec. 1881), Congregational minister and reformer, was born in Detroit, Michigan, the son of David Bacon and Alice Parks, missionaries. At the time of his birth Leonard Bacon's parents were Congregational missionaries to Native Americans under the auspices of the Connecticut Missionary Society. After a brief mission in Mackinac that resulted in financial misunderstanding and embarrassment, David Bacon undertook the founding of the town of Tallmadge in New Connecticut in 1807. However, by 1812, plagued again by financial problems, the Bacons were forced to retire to Hartford, Connecticut, where they enjoyed the hospitality of David's brother, a physician for whom his son was named, Leonard Bacon. Despite continuing financial hardships and associated translocations, young Leonard was able to stay with his uncle from the summer of 1812 until the fall of 1817, during which time he attended the Hartford Grammar School. In the fall of 1817, two months after the death of his father, Leonard Bacon entered Yale College.

Although he did not distinguish himself as a student, Bacon showed an early interest in poetry and literature. As graduation approached he entertained the notion of becoming a foreign missionary but was persuaded by his mother (who was living in East Bloomfield, N.Y.) not to go overseas. In the fall of 1820, having graduated from Yale, he entered Andover Seminary. Andover's modified Calvinism suited Bacon, and he flourished, impressed particularly by Moses Stuart, professor of biblical literature. Bacon earned a B.D. in 1823 and continued for another year of postgraduate study, intending to become a missionary to the western frontier. Instead, in 1824 he was called to replace the distinguished Nathaniel W. Taylor at New Haven's First Congregational Church. Taylor had vacated the pulpit at First Church in 1822 in order to teach theology at the newly formed Yale Divinity School.

Formally installed in March 1825, Bacon held the pulpit at First Church for the rest of his career. In addition to his ministerial duties, he was active in a variety of Congregational ministries, such as the Connecticut Missionary Society (later the American Home Missionary Society), the American Board of Commissioners of Foreign Missions, the American Bible Society, the American Tract Society, and the American

Congregational Union; he was also a member of the Yale Corporation. After retiring from First Church in 1866 (remaining as minister emeritus until 1881), he devoted a large part of his energy to Yale Divinity School. Assisting during a troubled and unstable period in the life of the school, he was acting professor of revealed theology from 1866 to 1871 and from then until 1881 was a lecturer in church polity and American church history. In 1870 the Harvard Divinity School conferred on him the degree of LL.D.

Bacon married Lucy Johnson in 1825; eight children were born to them before Lucy, who had suffered many years from poor health, finally died in 1844. In 1847 Bacon married Catherine E. Terry, with whom he had six children. Bacon's son from his first marriage and namesake, Leonard Woolsey Bacon, became an esteemed Congregational clergyman and church historian.

Throughout his career Leonard Bacon, Sr., was a prolific writer. He was a frequent contributor to the *New Englander* (later the *New Englander and Yale Review*) from its inception in 1843 until his death, and he served as editor of the *Christian Spectator* (1826–1838) and as senior editor of the important weekly newspaper of Congregational perspective and social opinion the *Independent* (1848–1861). Bacon's own writings include the *Select Works of Richard Baxter* (1831), *Manual for Young Church Members* (1833), *Thirteen Historical Discourses on the Completion of Two Hundred Years from the Beginning of the First Church in New Haven* (1839), and numerous articles for the *Religious Intelligencer* as well as the publications in which he had an editorial hand. In 1874 he published his most important historical work, *The Genesis of the New England Churches*, an account of New England Congregationalism up to its establishment at Plymouth Colony and Salem.

In his day Bacon had a reputation for being a tough but fair-minded polemicist (known by some as "the fighting parson"). In the social sphere, he was active on behalf of various reform issues, from temperance to slavery. Most of his efforts were directed against slavery. Of his various writings on the subject, *Slavery Discussed in Occasional Essays* (1846) reportedly influenced soon-to-be congressman Abraham Lincoln's thinking on the issue. However, although Bacon vehemently opposed the institution of slavery, he was not an abolitionist. Rather he argued on behalf of a gradual emancipation and for the resettlement of freed slaves in Liberia. Thus he and many like-minded clergymen supported the goals of the American Colonization Society.

Although Bacon favored cooperation among churches, he was a vigilant churchman in his concern for and protection of Congregational autonomy. It is not surprising, therefore, that he came to see the Plan of Union of 1801, a joint Congregational-Presbyterian missionary venture to the Old Northwest, as a threat to Congregationalism in the West and applauded the vote taken in 1852 by a national convention of Congregational churches to remove themselves from the agreement.

Theologically Bacon was a moderate proponent of the New Haven Theology, or Taylorism, a modified Calvinism associated with his predecessor Nathaniel Taylor and the Yale Divinity School. In the Congregational controversy that ensued over this theology, Bacon was influential in stilling the criticisms of conservative Calvinist opponents and in asserting the place of Taylorism in the revered Puritan tradition. Yet in the theological arena he was not so much a creative thinker as an ecclesiastical politician. He died at New Haven.

• For additional information see Theodore D. Bacon, *Leonard Bacon: A Statesman in the Church* (1931); Williston Walker, *Ten New England Leaders* (1901); and the *Congregational Year-book* (1882), pp. 18–21.

DANIEL G. REID

BACON, Leonard Woolsey (1 Jan. 1830–12 May 1907), minister and author, was born in New Haven, Connecticut, the son of Leonard Bacon, a minister, and Lucy Johnson. Bacon graduated from Yale College in 1850. Beginning in September of that year he accompanied his father on a year-long tour of Europe and the East. When he returned to the United States, Bacon spent two years at Andover Theological Seminary and one year at Yale Divinity School, graduating from the latter in 1854. He turned next to medical study and received a degree from Yale Medical School in 1856.

Bacon returned to clerical pursuits and was ordained at the Congregational church in Litchfield, Connecticut, on 16 October 1856. In 1857 he married Susan Bacon. They had ten children before she died in 1887. He served the Litchfield church until June 1860, when he became the state missionary of the Connecticut General Association (Congregational). In the next ten years, he pastored three churches: the First Congregational Church of Stamford, Connecticut (1862–1865), the New England Congregational Church of Brooklyn, New York (1865–1870), and the First Congregational Church in Baltimore, Maryland (1870–1872). Bacon spent the next five years abroad, during which time he pastored the American Church in Geneva, Switzerland (1874–1877). Returning to the United States, from 1878 to 1892 he served four churches: the Park Church in Norwich, Connecticut (1878–1882), the Woodland Presbyterian Church in Philadelphia (1883–1886), the Ancient Independent Presbyterian Church in Savannah, Georgia (1887), and the Second Congregational Church in Norwich, Connecticut. In 1890 he married Letitia Wilson Jordan. They had three children, only one of whom survived to adulthood. From 1892 to 1902 he devoted himself to study and writing and then resumed pastoral work from 1902 to 1906 in Assonet, Massachusetts.

A prolific writer, Bacon published essays on a variety of controversial issues, including temperance, Sabbath observance, and the theater. His books reflect his lifelong association with the Congregational church and his importance to the life of that church. He is especially remembered for his hymnals, *The Church Book: Hymns and Tunes* (1883), *The Congregational Hymn and Tune Book* (1858), and *The Hymns of Martin Luther* (1883), and a 1904 history of the denomination, *The Congregationalists*. He published works on notable Catholics and on Catholicism, including an 1878 essay in *Macmillan's* magazine on St. Francis de Sales. He also translated works from French and German for publication in English and contributed to the *New Englander*, the *Congregational Quarterly*, *Putnam's Monthly*, and other periodicals. Additional noteworthy publications include *Anti-Slavery before Garrison* (1903), *Bearing the Sword as God's Minister* (1887), *Church Papers: Sundry Essays on Subjects Relating to the Church and Christian Society* (1877), *Considerations in Favor of License Laws for Restraining the Liquor Traffic* (1881), *God's Wonderful Work in France* (187?), *The History of American Christianity* (1897), *The Humanity of Christ* (185?), *An Inside View of the Vatican Council* (1872), *Irenics and Polemics* (1895), and *The Simplicity That Is in Christ* (1886). He died at his home in Assonet.

• Several family genealogies are at the Sterling Library at Yale University. See Thomas Williams Baldwin, *Bacon Genealogy* (1915). The *Yale University Obituary Record, 1900–1910* includes an extensive entry on Bacon.

LAURA L. MITCHELL-LORETAN

BACON, Nathaniel (c. 1647–26 Oct. 1676), leader of colonial rebellion, was born in Suffolk County, England, the son of Thomas Bacon, a landed proprietor, and Elizabeth Brooke. His tutor, John Ray, with whom he shared a European grand tour, described him as a young gentleman of "very good parts, and a quick wit," but "impatient of labour, and indeed his temper will not admit long study." A dark side was always present in Bacon's background, as is clear from the fact that when he married Elizabeth Duke, daughter of Sir Edward Duke of Benhall, that gentleman was so angered that he disinherited his daughter and never spoke to her again. Bacon and his wife would have one child. After Bacon became involved in a scheme to defraud a neighboring youth, his father packed him off on a tobacco ship to Virginia where his cousin, Nathaniel Bacon, Sr., served as one of the king's councilors of state.

Not long after his arrival in Virginia in the summer of 1674, Bacon was accorded, on 3 March 1675, the extraordinary honor of being placed on the governor's council, the upper house of the Virginia General Assembly, which consisted of the royal governor, the Council, and the House of Burgesses. The governor, Sir William Berkeley, also was Bacon's cousin, by marriage, through Frances Culpeper, the governor's wife. Virginia in the seventeenth century was a raw, distant, troubled place little resembling the stable eighteenth-century plantation society familiar to most Americans. After having survived two massive Indian uprisings (in 1622 and 1644) that had decimated their numbers, and after surviving diseases that killed many during the "seasoning" process immediately after arrival, the remaining English colonists coexisted in an uneasy peace with Virginia's Indian tribes, some friendly and subordinate, others hostile and independent, who lived in proximity to the scattered colonial habitations.

When Indian troubles again erupted in 1675, Bacon, who had acquired a plantation on the "Curles" of the James River, found himself the favorite of those who wished to take precipitous action against what they perceived to be "the Indian enemy," lumping all Indians in a hostility that existed only in their imagination. They accused Governor Berkeley of coddling and favoring the Indians as well as profiting from the Indian trade, all because he had the job of licensing Indian traders (among them Bacon), a function that his critics easily elevated to the wild charge that he was selling out the colony for the sake of filthy lucre. Both Governor Berkeley and young Bacon had attended the English Inns of Court, where lawyers were trained, but they had diametrically opposed points of view on the rights of the Indians who lived in association with, or on the periphery of, the colony. For Bacon, no Indian had any rights that an Englishman need respect; indeed, one of his articles of indictment against Berkeley was that he sought to protect his "darling" Indians against the wrath of the colonists. Berkeley, for his part, sought to emphasize the distinction between the friendly Indians who lived under English control, and were allies or subjects of the English, and the "foreign" or enemy Indians, sometimes from as far away as Iroquoia, who occasionally committed depredations on English outsettlements in the course of their raids on other Indian tribes.

The resulting conflict, known as Bacon's Rebellion, became a see-saw battle between the governor and the rebel in which first one side and then the other achieved the upper hand. Following a disastrous assault by Maryland and northern Virginia militia against a body of peaceful Susquehannocks (mistakenly thought to be guilty of depredations upon an English plantation), the enraged Susquehannocks attacked a number of outlying plantations, killing, among others, one of Bacon's employees. Bacon and his followers marched to the territory of the Occaneechi in southwestern Virginia, ostensibly to search for the Susequehannocks. The friendly Occaneechi welcomed him and promised to attack the Susquehannocks themselves, which in fact they did with great success, whereupon they were treacherously set upon by Bacon's men in an attempt to seize the booty the Occaneechi had taken from the Susquehannocks. Even though Bacon had killed only friendly Indians on this expedition (and, indeed, throughout the entire rebellion), he was received as a hero on his return. Bacon demanded a commission to go out against "the Indians." Berkeley refused. Bacon and his armed followers surrounded the legislators gathered in the June 1676 assembly and extorted, by threats to kill them all, such a commission. With the commission in hand he and his followers proceeded to march out against other friendly Indians, such as "the good Queen of Pamunkey," as the commissioners, sent by King Charles to investigate the rebellion, called her after the war, attesting to her loyalty.

On 30 July 1676, at a conference at Middle Plantation (now Williamsburg), Bacon issued his bombastic "Declaration of the People," in which he claimed to be acting in behalf of the king against the failure of Berkeley to defend the colony from the Indian threat. Because Bacon was also ransacking the estates of men loyal to the governor, he was able to recruit servants and even slaves who sought to profit from the turmoil. Berkeley was able to retake the capital, Jamestown, on 7 September, but Bacon subsequently laid seige to it and drove Berkeley's forces out; on 19 September he ordered the town to be put to the torch, an act of vandalism that even some of his supporters deplored.

While engaged in his martial activities, Bacon contracted a disease that seems to have been dysentery but which was described at the time as "the bloody flux"; as a contemporary account of the rebellion put it, the disease caused an "honest minister" to write poetically that "Bacon is dead, and I am sorry at my hart, that lice and flux should do the hangman's part." Following Bacon's death at Gloucester County, the rebellion fell apart and Berkeley regained control. Concomitantly, a thousand troops arrived from England, having been sent to put down the rebellion, thus creating additional problems for the governor, who had to find ways to house and feed the troops.

One of the most controversial figures in American colonial history, Bacon has been seen by some historians as a hero who anticipated American independence and by others as a rabble-rousing, Indian-hating frontiersman unconcerned about democracy or independence. Despite the failed and fraudulent character of his rebellion, Bacon was gradually taken up into the pantheon of revolutionary fathers, culminating in the twentieth century in the work of Thomas Jefferson Wertenbaker, whose *Torchbearer of the Revolution* (1940) asserts this theme. Although not all historians have accepted Wilcomb E. Washburn's interpretation in *The Governor and the Rebel* (1957), his view that Bacon did not express the revolutionary impulse of the eighteenth century has generally been accepted in textbooks.

• The papers relating to Nathaniel Bacon and his rebellion are being edited for the Virginia Historical Society. The most important body of such materials is from the papers of Henry Coventry, principal secretary of state for the Southern Colonies, located at Longleat, the estate of the Marquis of Bath in Bath, England. Microfilm copies of this material are in the Library of Congress. Genealogical information on the complicated Bacon family relationships is laid out in Charles Hervey Townshend, "The Bacons of Virginia and Their English Ancestry," *New England Historical and Genealogical Register* 37 (1883): 189–91; of the eight Nathaniels that Townshend discusses, six were members of Gray's Inn. The historical interpretation of Bacon's Rebellion as a forerunner of the American Revolution was the work of Thomas Jefferson Wertenbaker in his *Torchbearer of the Revolution: The Story of Bacon's Rebellion and Its Leader* (1940). Wilcomb E. Washburn, *The Governor and the Rebel: A History of Bacon's Rebellion in Virginia* (1957), categorically rejected Wertenbaker's interpretation of Bacon as a political revolutionary and Governor Sir William Berkeley as an oppressive ruler. Washburn's book includes an introductory chapter on the changing historical interpretations of the rebellion. In a separate publication Washburn considered "The Effect of Bacon's Rebellion on Government in England and Virginia," *Contributions from the Museum of History and Technology*, U.S. National Museum, Smithsonian Institution, Washington, D.C. (1962), bulletin 225, paper 17, pp. 135–52. Stephen Saunders Webb, *1676: The End of American Independence* (1984), attempted to resurrect the Wertenbaker thesis, unsuccessfully in the opinion of Washburn, as noted in his article "Stephen Saunders Webb's Interpretation of Bacon's Rebellion," *Virginia Magazine of History and Biography* 95 (1987): 339–52.

WILCOMB E. WASHBURN

BACON, Robert (5 July 1860–29 May 1919), banker, diplomat, and soldier, was born in Jamaica Plain near Boston, Massachusetts, the son of William Benjamin Bacon and Emily Crosby Low. Raised in an old Massachusetts family long prominent in business, he was educated at Hopkinson's School and at Harvard, graduating in 1880. Although his intellectual abilities were considerable, he won attention for his athletic ability, personality, and good looks, as he would throughout life. After graduation he traveled around the world, then joined the banking firm of Lee, Higginson, and Company. In 1883 he became a member of E. Rollins Morse and Brother. That year he married Martha Waldron Cowdin; they were the parents of three sons and a daughter.

Bacon became a junior partner of J. P. Morgan and Company in New York in 1894. He was J. P. Morgan's trusted assistant in a number of large financial undertakings, among them the loan of millions of dollars in gold to the federal government during the panic of 1895 and the organization of the United States Steel Corporation and the Northern Securities Corporation in 1901. He often represented Morgan in negotiations with his Harvard classmate and friend, President Theodore Roosevelt. Regard for their friendship notwithstanding, the president in 1902 initiated an action that caused Bacon much anxiety. Roosevelt ordered a suit under the Sherman Antitrust Act to dissolve Northern Securities. Bacon found himself in an extremely difficult situation. His health failed, and he resigned from the firm in 1903.

When Secretary of State John Hay died in 1905, Roosevelt appointed Elihu Root as Hay's successor and, upon Root's recommendation, appointed Bacon as assistant secretary of state. During Root's absence on his famous goodwill trip through South America in 1906, Bacon was acting secretary. A crisis developed in Cuba, threatening a government breakdown there, and Roosevelt ordered intervention under the Platt amendment. Bacon personally disapproved of the intervention but carried out the president's orders, going to Havana with Secretary of War William Howard Taft to establish a provisional government.

Early in 1909, when Root resigned as secretary to accept election as senator from New York, Roosevelt appointed Bacon as Root's successor. Bacon was secretary of state from 27 January to 5 March 1909. During this period he persuaded the Senate to approve treaties with Panama and Colombia to resolve the dispute with Colombia that had arisen as a result of the American-backed Panama revolution of 1903, an endeavor that went awry when the Colombian senate refused to ratify.

President William Howard Taft appointed Bacon ambassador to France in December 1909. In Paris Bacon demonstrated skill in social and official matters. When the Seine flooded large areas of Paris, he took an active role in American relief efforts, winning the gratitude of Frenchmen. He resigned in January 1912 to serve as a fellow of Harvard University, explaining that he had received his "field marshal's baton."

When World War I broke out, Bacon's interests again centered on Europe. He went to France in August 1914 to help organize the American Ambulance Hospital and he himself drove an ambulance near the front. Bacon returned to the United States in late 1915 to take part in the preparedness movement. Although fifty-five years old, he trained as a private at the Plattsburg (now Plattsburgh), New York, camp founded by General Leonard Wood. He became president of an important preparedness group, the National Security League, and worked closely with another, the Universal Training League.

Throughout his career Bacon had usually been an assistant to men who possessed more authority than he; rarely had he had opportunities to demonstrate that he possessed leadership abilities. In 1915 and 1916 he found such an opportunity, making speeches warning that the war in Europe was America's struggle and criticizing President Woodrow Wilson for failure to prepare for it and for weakness in response to threats from Mexico. In 1916 Bacon campaigned for the New York Republican senatorial nomination, but he entered the campaign late and was unsuccessful. Winning had not been Bacon's principal objective, however. He used the campaign to urge support for the Allies and a vigorous preparedness program.

When the United States entered the war, Bacon received a commission as a major. He accompanied General John J. Pershing to France, where he was for a time commandant of the general's headquarters at Chaumont. His most important military service was as chief of the American mission at the headquarters of the British commander, General Sir Douglas Haig. According to another liaison officer, Lloyd C. Griscom, Bacon was remarkably effective, winning British agreement with most American policies. While at British headquarters, Bacon was a colonel, but he returned to the rank of major when Pershing assigned him to other duties. He was promoted to lieutenant colonel in the Quartermaster Corps in September 1918, and on 14 November 1918 he was commissioned lieutenant colonel of infantry. He was demobilized on 5 April 1919, less than two months before his death of mastoiditis in a New York hospital.

• The papers of Theodore Roosevelt and Elihu Root in the Library of Congress and James Scott Brown in the Georgetown University Library contain considerable material about Bacon. State Department files in the National Archives contain Bacon's diplomatic correspondence for the period 1906–1912, part of which is printed in the volumes for those years in *Papers Relating to the Foreign Relations of the United States*. A few of Roosevelt's letters to Bacon are in Elting E. Morison, ed., *The Letters of Theodore Roosevelt* (8 vols., 1951–1954). A full-scale biography is James Brown Scott, *Robert Bacon: His Life and Letters* (1923). Scott, Bacon's close associate in the State Department, also wrote "Robert Bacon: Secretary of State, January 27, 1909, to March 5, 1909," in *The American Secretaries of State and Their Diplomacy*, vol. 9, ed. Samuel Flagg Bemis et al. (1928). Ron Chernow, *The House of Morgan: An American Banking Dynasty and the Rise of Modern Finance* (1990), comments on Bacon's role as a Morgan partner. Philip C. Jessup, *Elihu Root* (2 vols., 1938), is invaluable for Bacon's service in the State Department and his leadership during the preparedness movement. John Garry Clifford, *The Citizen Soldiers: The Plattsburg Training Camp Movement, 1913–1920* (1972) is another source for Bacon's involvement with preparedness. Bacon's obituary in the *New York Times*, 30 May 1919, is an excellent commentary on his career.

CALVIN D. DAVIS

BACON, Thomas (1700?–26 May 1768), clergyman and musician, is traditionally said to have been born on the Isle of Man, but his earliest records come from Whitehaven, Cumberland County, England. His parents are unknown. His brother Anthony Bacon, M.P., may have been the same Anthony Bacon who graduated from Trinity College in 1739. Thomas Bacon was in charge of a coal depot in Dublin early in the 1730s. Since his son John Bacon was a lieutenant in the Independent Maryland Foot Company in 1754, he must have been at least eighteen then. Therefore, Thomas Bacon was probably married by 1735. Nothing is known of his wife except a statement by Rev. Jonathan Boucher that while Bacon managed the depot he met "a smart widow, who kept a coffee-house, whom he married." Bacon's *A Compleat System of the Revenue of Ireland* (1737) reveals that he was then "of the Custom-House, Dublin." He decided in 1741 to establish himself as a printer, journeyed to London to arrange for an exchange of newspapers and correspondence, and met Samuel Richardson, who granted him permission to reprint *Pamela*. However, George Faulkner, a rival Irish printer, pirated the book before Bacon could print it. Richardson, in resentment, sent Bacon 250 copies of the genuine edition to sell. Bacon published the *Dublin Mercury* from January to September 1742 and the official Irish newspaper, the *Dublin Gazette,* from September 1742 to July 1743.

Bacon abandoned printing to become a minister. Thomas Wilson, bishop of Sodor and Man, ordained him a deacon on 23 September 1744 and a priest on 10 March 1745. With his wife and son, Bacon arrived in Maryland in the early fall of 1745. He immediately won a reputation as an effective preacher, a praiseworthy clergyman, and a top musician, playing the violin and violoncello better than any of the local performers. He was appointed curate of St. Peter's Church, Talbot County, and was made rector on 31 March 1746. By September he had settled in Oxford, Talbot County, where he, Henry Callister, and Robert Morris often met to play music together. Callister praised Bacon's compositions, especially his "excellent" minuets.

Bacon especially attempted to minister to the poor and to slaves. In 1749 he published *Two Sermons, Preached to a Congregation of Black Slaves*; in 1750, *Four Sermons, upon the Great and Indispensable Duty of All Christian Masters and Mistresses to Bring up Their Negro Slaves in the Knowledge and Fear of God*; in 1751, *Six Sermons on the Several Duties of Masters, Mistresses, Slaves, Etc.* The Society for the Propagation of the Gospel in Foreign Parts paid for the publication in London. They were repeatedly reprinted, appearing as late as 1843. Bacon also undertook to raise money for a charity working school for orphans and poor children in Talbot County. He visited Williamsburg in the summer of 1751 to solicit donations for the school and also staged several benefit concerts in Virginia and Maryland. His sermon at the school's opening on 23 August 1752 was published in London. The dedication to Frederick Calvert, sixth Lord Baltimore, with the support of Bishop Thomas Wilson, was repaid by a gift of 100 guineas from the proprietor.

Elected an honorary member of the Annapolis Tuesday Club on 26 November 1745, Bacon thereafter frequently visited, making special efforts to attend the anniversaries of the elite gentleman's club. Though numerous references in the Callister papers refer to Bacon's own compositions, all his surviving music, except one song, was written for the club and transcribed by Dr. Alexander Hamilton (1712–1756). Hamilton dubbed him "Signior Lardini" in the Tuesday Club history, referring to Bacon's Italianate compositions and last name. Bacon composed six pieces for the Tuesday Club, including several minuets in honor of club members. His major extant composition is music for the club's sixth anniversary, 14 May 1751. It consists of an overture, aria, recitativo, aria con spirto, song, chorus, recitativo, aria dolciment, and aria. It concludes with three pieces that the club later played separately: the "Club March" against Sir Hugh Maccarty, the "Grand Chorus," and the "Grand Club Minuet."

In addition to the works Hamilton transcribed, Bacon's music appears in two other sources. A manuscript music book compiled by John Ormsby in Annapolis in 1758 contains "A Minuet by the Rev. Mr. Bacon," a version of an earlier composition for the Tuesday Club. A catch entitled "See, See My Boys" is preserved in *The Gentleman's Catch Book,* published in Dublin in 1786. Since the songbook was dedicated to the Hibernian Catch Club, Bacon probably belonged to the club when he lived in Dublin, and fifty years later the club still prized one of his songs. John Barry Talley concluded that Bacon "must be regarded as a skilled, if not masterful, composer" (p. 111).

Bacon composed a few poems, one of which is extant in the Callister papers, and he is probably the author of the "Address of the Eastren [*sic*] Shore Triumvirate" to Charles Cole, presented to the Tuesday Club on 16 May 1751. He may be the author of two poems in the *Pennsylvania Gazette* of 1752.

Politically, Bacon was allied with Maryland's proprietary party, and at two ecclesiastical conventions in August and October 1753 he argued for continued proprietary oversight of the clergy. A faction led by Rev. Thomas Chase and Thomas Cradock called for an ecclesiastical jurisdiction over the clergy and wanted the assembly to investigate how the Maryland clergy were supervised. Bacon argued that since the proprietor appointed the clergy, any complaints or questions of ecclesiastical jurisdiction should go to the proprietor or to his representative, the governor. With one more vote than Chase and Cradock could muster, Bacon and the proprietary group prevailed.

The mid-1750s brought Bacon two tragedies. In May 1755 his wife died, and eleven months later his promising young son, John, was killed and scalped near Cumberland, Maryland. In the summer of 1756 Bacon married Elizabeth Bozman Belchier.

In the early 1750s Bacon began compiling the laws of Maryland. In 1758 he petitioned the legislature for encouragement, but since a rival compilation was in progress and because Bacon was identified with the proprietary party, the assembly did nothing. Finally, in July 1762, he produced six folio manuscript volumes of laws from 1637 to 1762, ready for the press. It took four years for Jonas Green to print the tome, the largest and probably most beautiful imprint to come from Green's Maryland press.

At the end of 1758 the proprietor rewarded Bacon, appointing him to All Saints, Frederick, the province's most lucrative parish. In 1760, as Bacon neared the completion of his monumental legal task, Frederick Calvert asked Governor Horatio Sharpe if Bacon could write a history of Maryland defending the proprietary party. Horrified at the idea, Sharpe pointed out that Bacon would have to leave Frederick to do research in Annapolis, that his parishioners would raise an outcry, and that the resulting publicity would embarrass Bacon and the proprietary party. But in 1764, when Stephen Bordley attacked the proprietary party with *Remarks upon a Message, Sent by the Upper to the Lower House of Assembly,* Bacon replied with *An Answer to the Queries on the Proprietary Party.* By the mid-1760s Bacon was in failing health. He died in Frederick, Maryland, survived by his second wife and three daughters.

• Most of Bacon's extant manuscripts are held by the Maryland Historical Society. His correspondence with Henry Callister is in the Callister papers, Maryland Diocesan Society Library, on deposit at the Maryland Historical Society. A few letters are in Lambeth Palace; see William Wilson Manross, *The Fulham Papers in the Lambeth Palace Library* (1965).

Rev. Jonathan Boucher contributed a biographical note on Bacon to William Hutchinson, *History of the County of Cumberland,* vol. 2 (1794). A biographical sketch, together with a primary and secondary bibliography, appears in J. A. Leo Lemay, *Men of Letters in Colonial Maryland* (1972). John Barry Talley edited Bacon's Tuesday Club music: *Secular Music in Colonial Annapolis: The Tuesday Club* (1988). Accounts of Bacon's visits to the club and facsimiles of his music appear in Dr. Alexander Hamilton, *The History of the Tuesday Club,* ed. Robert Micklus (3 vols., 1990). J. A. Leo Lemay recorded his newspaper poetry in *A Calendar of American Poetry in the Colonial Newspapers and Magazines* (1972). See also William E. Deibert, "Thomas Bacon, Colonial Clergyman," *Maryland Historical Magazine* 73 (1978): 79–86. His obituary appeared in the *Maryland Gazette,* 9 June 1768, the *Pennsylvania Chronicle,* 13 June 1768, and Rind's *Virginia Gazette,* 23 June 1768.

J. A. LEO LEMAY

BADEAU, Adam (29 Dec. 1831–19 Mar. 1895), soldier and author, was born in New York City, the son of Nicholas Badeau. He attended a boarding school in Tarrytown, New York, then he worked at an assortment of jobs, including a position with New York City's street department. In 1859 he published a short book, *The Vagabond,* a collection of previously published essays concerning various literary figures and his work as a drama critic. During the Civil War he served in the U.S. Army on the staffs of Quincy A. Gillmore and Thomas W. Sherman. In May 1863, upon the recommendation of James H. Wilson, Ulysses S. Grant, commander of the Army of the Tennessee, added Badeau to his staff. However, Badeau was wounded at Port Hudson, Louisiana, on 27 May, so he did not report for duty until February 1864. When Grant became general in chief the following month, he appointed Badeau as his military secretary with the rank of lieutenant colonel. Badeau remained in that post until the end of the war, and he was present when Robert E. Lee surrendered to Grant. For his war service he was brevetted a brigadier general in both the volunteers and the regular army.

Between 1865 and 1869 Badeau continued on Grant's staff and accompanied the general on his travels through the North and the South Atlantic states. Originally sympathetic to Andrew Johnson's Reconstruction policy, he eventually came to support congressional Reconstruction and the movement to make Grant president. Grant left him in Washington to handle political mail during his election campaign. With Grant's inauguration as president in 1869, Badeau resigned his army commission to accept appointment as secretary of the legation in London.

Badeau spent part of Grant's first year in office in Washington, where he befriended Henry Adams, and he also delivered diplomatic documents to Spain. In 1870 Grant named him consul general to London, which post he held until 1881. Badeau accompanied Grant during the general's travels through Europe in 1877–1879. James A. Garfield attempted to shift Badeau to chargé d'affaires in Copenhagen as part of a complex shuffling of offices, but he declined. He returned home and in 1882 became consul general in Havana, Cuba. He turned down an appointment as minister to Brussels. In 1884 he resigned his position in Havana because the Chester A. Arthur administration refused to investigate frauds he had brought to light.

Badeau spent much of the fifteen years after the Civil War preparing a history of Grant's military career, *The Military History of Ulysses S. Grant.* The work assumed the status of an authorized study. Grant reviewed chapters, and both he and other officers granted Badeau access to materials and documents. The first volume, which appeared in 1868, traced Grant's career through 1863, prior to Badeau's arrival on his staff. Two more volumes, published in 1881, covered Grant as general in chief. While it contains much valuable information, the history is marked by a tendency to eulogize its subject and to assail others. Moreover, Grant's own editorial pen struck out some remarks that might have engendered controversy among soldiers who became politicians.

Thus with some anxiety Badeau heard in 1884 of Grant's plans to write his own memoirs. Although the general had shared his recollections of the war with several writers, he had so far declined to set them down on paper. Badeau agreed to assist Grant in compiling material for the memoirs in return for $10,000, compensation Badeau felt he was owed in part because he believed Grant's book would damage sales of the *Military History.* In this he was correct, as people turned to Grant's own writings to learn his views. Although Badeau also read and slightly revised the general's prose, in point of fact he was a research assistant, not a collaborator or ghostwriter. In April 1885 the partnership abruptly terminated in the wake of the general's near death. Grant, angered by newspaper accounts that Badeau was composing the manuscript, publicly denied it. Badeau, aware that Grant's books would net far more than the originally anticipated sum of $30,000, proposed to complete the volume for $1,000 a month plus 10 percent of the profits. Rejecting this offer, Grant severed their professional association. After the general's death in 1885, Badeau sued the Grant family for the remainder of the $10,000 owed to him. At first the Grants, angered by Badeau's insinuations about the authorship of the *Memoirs,* refused to pay. Eventually, in March 1888, they agreed to pay the original amount plus interest, totaling $11,253.

Soon after Grant's departure from the presidency Badeau drew up plans to compose a history of his administration, and he adhered to these plans despite his falling-out with the general and his family. *Grant in Peace, from Appomattox to Mount McGregor* (1887) covers the last twenty years of Grant's life but concentrates on Grant's relationships with leading politicians and international figures. In the book Badeau reprinted a good number of Grant's letters to him in an effort to prove that at one time the two men had been friends. His other writings, including *Conspiracy: A Cuban Romance* (1885) and *Aristocracy in England*

(1886), reside in oblivion. He died in Ridgewood, New Jersey.

• Badeau's correspondence is at the Library of Congress and in Firestone Library, Princeton University. The latter collection sheds light on his relationship with James H. Wilson. William S. McFeely, *Grant: A Biography* (1981), speculates that Badeau was homosexual.

BROOKS D. SIMPSON

BADGER, George Edmund (17 Apr. 1795–11 May 1866), U.S. senator and secretary of the navy, was born in New Bern, North Carolina, the son of Thomas Badger, a prominent attorney, and Lydia Cogdell. His father died when George was four, and he was raised by his mother. He attended Yale College for two years but left without graduating after a relative withdrew his financial support. He studied law under his maternal cousin, John Stanly, and received his license in 1814. Soon afterward he was appointed solicitor for the New Bern District. He represented the borough of New Bern in the general assembly of 1816.

At the end of the session Badger moved to Hillsborough to take over the law practice of Thomas Ruffin, who had recently been elected to the state superior court. In 1820 Badger himself was elected by the legislature to the state superior court. There he gained a reputation for his "ability, candor, and impartiality as a magistrate" and for the "firm and impartial hand with which he dealt out justice" (*Graham Papers*, vol. 7, p. 165). He resigned in 1825 and moved to Raleigh to engage in the more lucrative practice of law. Appearing frequently before the state supreme court and the U.S. circuit court, he gained wealth and distinction through his power as a speaker, his clear and forceful arguments, and his deep understanding of the law. Badger's great intellect, jocular nature, and fondness for repartee won him numerous friends and admirers. At the same time, a quick temper and a penchant for satire and ridicule brought him his share of enemies.

Like many North Carolina Federalists, Badger was attracted to Andrew Jackson because of his nonpartisan reputation and his tolerant attitude toward members of their party. In 1828 he served as a member of the state Central Jackson Committee, which was chaired by his father-in-law William Polk (1758–1834), and he wrote two important campaign pamphlets. After the election, he was recommended by the Jackson party of North Carolina for the office of U.S. attorney general, a position that Jackson ultimately gave to John Macpherson Berrien of Georgia. In 1834 he broke with the president over the bank issue and became a founder of the North Carolina Whig party. His brilliant organizational efforts and scathing attacks on the financial policies of the Jackson and Martin Van Buren administrations contributed to the landslide Whig victory in North Carolina in 1840.

In 1841 Badger was appointed secretary of the navy in the cabinet of William Henry Harrison. He recommended the establishment of a Home Squadron to patrol the Atlantic coastline—a measure that was enacted into law in July 1841—and encouraged the development of new technology for war vessels. He resigned in September 1841 following the break between the Whigs and President John Tyler (1790–1862).

After his return to North Carolina, Badger remained active in the affairs of the Whig party, delivering the keynote address at the state convention of 1842 and serving as a member of the Whig Central Committee. In March 1844 he was nominated by Whig governor John M. Morehead (1796–1866) to a vacancy on the state supreme court. However, the Council of State, elected by the Democratic general assembly and constitutionally empowered to pass on gubernatorial appointments, rejected the nomination. In 1846 the Whig-dominated legislature chose Badger to serve the remaining two years in the term of Democratic senator William H. Haywood, Jr. A staunch opponent of the Mexican War, Badger denounced the Polk administration on the floor of the Senate, accusing it of prosecuting the war "for the purpose of conquest, and conquest alone." On 8 March 1848 he offered an amendment to the proposed peace treaty of Guadalupe Hidalgo that would have foresworn any territorial acquisitions. He was one of fourteen senators who voted against the ratification of the treaty.

Badger's opposition to the acquisition of territory from Mexico resulted from his reluctance to introduce the issue of slavery expansion into the political arena. Unlike most southern Democrats and many southern Whigs, he believed that Congress had exclusive jurisdiction over the territories and that slavery could not exist there in the absence of positive legislation. That belief led him to conclude that the Wilmot Proviso, which would have excluded slavery from the Mexican cession, was constitutional, although impolitic and unfair to the South.

Badger's controversial position on the territorial issue almost derailed his prospects for a second term in the Senate. Some Whigs refused to support his candidacy, while a majority of Democratic legislators rallied behind Thomas L. Clingman, a Whig congressman who openly solicited Democratic support on the basis of his opposition to the proviso. Badger won election on the fifth ballot by a one-vote majority. After the election Clingman publicly attacked Badger and the other Whig "central managers" at Raleigh for monopolizing the public offices and ignoring the claims of aspirants from remote parts of the state. The bitter contest for the senatorship left scars on the Whig party that were never completely healed.

Badger remained in the Senate until his term expired in March 1855. He voted for most of the provisions of the Compromise of 1850, although he abstained on the California statehood bill and voted against abolition of the slave trade in the District of Columbia. In 1854 he threw his support behind the Kansas-Nebraska Act, a vote that he subsequently characterized as the greatest mistake of his political career. In January 1853 he was nominated as an associate justice of the U.S. Supreme Court, but the Democratic Senate declined to confirm him.

After the demise of the Whig party, Badger reluctantly supported the American party as the "least evil of the alternatives left us." In 1860 he played an active role in reorganizing the state Whig party and served as an elector on the Constitutional Union ticket. He was elected in February 1861 as a Unionist to the state convention, which did not meet because the call was defeated. Later elected to the convention that passed the ordinance of secession in May 1861, he ultimately signed the ordinance but only after the defeat of his own resolution that justified North Carolina's withdrawal from the Union on the basis of the right of revolution rather than the doctrine of secession. Despite his Unionist antecedents, Badger supported the Confederate war effort, declaring in a public letter written in June 1862 that North Carolina would never voluntarily return to the Union. In January 1863 he suffered a paralytic stroke, from which he never fully recovered. He died in Raleigh. Badger was married three times. In 1818 he married Rebecca Turner, who died in 1824. They had no children. In 1826 he married Mary Polk, who died in 1834. They had two children. In 1836 he married Delia Haywood Williams; they had seven children.

Badger's significance lies in his role as a leader of the North Carolina Whig party. His talents as an organizer and strategist helped make the Whigs the majority party in that state during the 1830s and 1840s. Ironically, his image as the embodiment of an arrogant and self-centered "Raleigh clique," together with his allegedly unsound views on the slavery issue, weakened the party during the 1850s and contributed to its loss of power.

• The George Edmund Badger Papers in the Southern Historical Collection, University of North Carolina at Chapel Hill, contain a few items concerning his legal cases as well as microfilm copies of his correspondence while secretary of the navy. Other small collections of his papers are in the North Carolina Division of Archives and History and in the Duke University Library. In addition, numerous items by Badger as well as many references to him can be found among the published letters of Whig leaders Willie P. Mangum and William A. Graham. See Henry T. Shanks, ed., *The Papers of Willie Person Mangum* (5 vols., 1950–1956); and J. G. de Roulhac Hamilton and Max R. Williams, eds., *The Papers of William Alexander Graham* (8 vols., 1957–1992). A detailed discussion of his legal and political career can be found in William A. Graham, "Discourse in Memory of the Life and Character of the Hon. Geo. E. Badger," in *Graham Papers*, vol. 7 (1866). Badger's career in the U.S. Senate is examined in three articles by Lawrence F. London: "George Edmund Badger, in the U.S. Senate, 1846–1849," *North Carolina Historical Review* 15 (1938): 1–22; "George Edmund Badger and the Compromise of 1850," *North Carolina Historical Review* 15 (1938): 99–118; and "George Edmund Badger, Last Years in the United States Senate, 1851–1855," *North Carolina Historical Review* 15 (1938): 231–50. For his tenure as secretary of the navy see London, "George Edmund Badger, Member of the Harrison-Tyler Cabinet, 1841," *South Atlantic Quarterly* 37 (1938): 307–27.

THOMAS E. JEFFREY

BADGER, Joseph (14 Mar. 1708–11 May 1765), portrait painter, was born in Charlestown, Massachusetts, the son of Stephen Badger, a tailor, and Mercy Kettell. He was baptized at the First Church in Charlestown, where he was admitted as a communicant in 1728. In 1731, in Cambridge, he married Katharine Smith Felch, widow of Samuel Felch. They moved to Boston by 1734. They had at least seven children, in addition to Katharine's five children from her first marriage.

Badger earned his living as a painter of houses, signs, and heraldic devices; a glazier; and a portrait painter. He is first recorded as a craftsman in court documents that discuss payment for painting window frames on a house in Dedham in 1737. His earliest portraits date from the 1740s, among them two of James Bowdoin that were later owned by his daughter Elizabeth Bowdoin Pitts and his son James Bowdoin II. His training was probably by observation of the work of other painters. Some of his compositions imitate the portraits of the leading Boston portrait painter John Smibert. Another possible influence was Thomas Johnston, a decorative painter and engraver who, like Badger, was a member of the Brattle Square Church. Badger also imitated poses or background details found in British portrait engravings, as did other American colonial portrait painters.

Around 150 portraits are attributed to Badger, who never signed his work. The few examples documented by inscriptions or sitters' records, including those of wealthy Salem merchant Timothy Orne, his wife Rebecca, and their four children, painted in 1756–1757, provide a firm basis for defining his style. They show that Badger used a subdued technique characterized by thin paint layers applied with little visible brushwork. The figures are usually posed without dramatic modeling and highlighting. Sometimes he used bright colors, especially for backgrounds, and at other times the tones are more somber. His adults have sedate, graceful poses. Children are often shown with playful animals. His canvases often were traditional sizes, suggesting his knowledge of academic practices. Badger's paintings are memorable for a delicate treatment of detail and a quiet charm.

Badger was particularly successful in the late 1740s and early 1750s, after Smibert's retirement. He probably obtained commissions by word of mouth. He apparently never advertised in newspapers. Among his patrons were sea captains, merchants, ministers, and craftsmen from Boston and nearby Massachusetts towns. Often his sitters were closely related; in 1755 he painted five members of the Isaac Foster family. His portraits were not expensive; Orne, for example, paid £6 for his portrait, £6 for his wife's, and a total of £5 5s. for the children's portraits. For Orne, who had lent the artist a sum of money, Badger also executed "a Painted Highlander" and "a Painted Laughing Boy," subject pieces that were probably based on mezzotints. Some sitters paid in goods rather than in cash. For Daniel Rea, who was William Johnston's partner, Badger in 1752 painted fire buckets in addition to his portrait and was paid with "a Hatt and sundrys."

In the mid-1750s Badger's conservative style was eclipsed by the work of younger artists Joseph Blackburn and John Singleton Copley. The lack of dates for Badger's portraits has made a detailed study of his relationship to these artists difficult. It appears that his later work was influenced by theirs. He continued to receive important commissions to at least 1760, when his work included his only life-size full-length portrait, of Captain John Larrabee, commanding officer at Castle William (c. 1760). Among the most charming later portraits are those of Benjamin Badger, probably his son, with a squirrel perched on his arm (c. 1758–1760) and his grandson James Badger (1760). William Scott, a shoemaker, brought fame to Badger in 1764 when he published a poem in the *New-Hampshire Gazette, and Historical Chronicle* (3 Feb. 1764). Accompanying the verses he wrote, "Mr. Scott has his Picture drawn by Mr. Badger, under which is the following Lines, composed by himself." (The portrait has not survived.) No portraits of Badger himself are known to exist.

In 1763 Badger purchased a three-room house and lot on Temple Street in Boston. He died two years later in Boston of "an apoplectic fit" (*Boston Gazette*, 13 May 1765). The probate record that named Badger's widow as the administrator of his estate called him a glazier, whereas his inventory listed him as a painter (rather than a limner or portrait painter). His small estate was valued at £140 10s., of which the house and land were appraised at £120. After selling the property in 1768 his widow may have moved to Charleston, South Carolina, where their sons Joseph and William had opened a painting and glazing business in 1766. Badger's brother Daniel had settled in Charleston in 1735, advertising a similar business of "all sorts of House and Ship paintings very reasonable, and after the best manner." Badger's grandson James settled in Charleston in 1777 and continued the family trade of painting and glazing.

Badger's significance lies with his subtle, charming portraits, which continued the English portrait tradition imported to Boston by Smibert. His decision to take up portrait painting makes him the exception in a family whose other members worked in the craft of decorative painting. Only his nephew Thomas Badger (1792–1868) became a portrait painter, also in the Boston area.

• No letters or papers of Badger's are known to survive. The earliest study of his work is Lawrence Park, *Joseph Badger (1708–1765), and a Descriptive List of Some of His Works* (1918). Another monograph is Richard C. Nylander, "Joseph Badger, American Portrait Painter" (master's thesis, State Univ. of New York, 1972). Studies of aspects of his work include Louisa Dresser, "The Orne Portraits by Joseph Badger," *Worcester Art Museum Bulletin*, n.s., 1, no. 2 (Feb. 1972): 1–16; Phelps Warren, "Badger Family Portraits," *Antiques* 118 (Nov. 1980): 1043–47; and an entry in Richard B. Saunders and Ellen G. Miles, *American Colonial Portraits, 1700–1776*, exhibition catalog of the National Portrait Gallery (1987): 190–91. Jessie Poesch discusses William Scott's poem in "'In Just Lines to Trace'—The Colonial Artist, 1700–1776," in *The Portrait in Eighteenth-century America*, ed. Miles (1993), p. 73.

ELLEN G. MILES

BADGER, Richard McLean (4 May 1896–26 Nov. 1974), physical chemist and molecular spectroscopist, was born in Elgin, Illinois, the son of Joseph Stillman Badger, a manager for General Electric, and Carrie Mabel Hewitt. When Richard was six months old, General Electric assigned his father to supervise the construction of an electric street railway in Brisbane, Australia, so Richard's first six years were spent in Australia with his family; he was then sent back to the United States to attend school. After four years in an Elgin grammar school he went back to Australia, where he completed elementary school and began secondary school. When he was about sixteen, he returned with his family to Elgin and finished high school there; he then attended the junior college of Elgin Academy. In 1916 he enrolled at Northwestern University, but his academic career was interrupted by World War I. From 1917 to 1919 he served in France as a member of the U.S. Army's 311th Field Signal Battalion.

In 1919, after his demobilization, Badger returned to Northwestern, but he decided to transfer to a college in California, where his father intended to retire. He chose the Throop Institute of Technology, even though he knew little about it. This decision began a lifelong association with the school, which in 1920 was renamed the California Institute of Technology (Caltech).

During his junior and senior years at the institute Badger settled on a career in physical chemistry. From his teachers he absorbed an interest in the structures of molecules and how they could be determined. Caltech scientists were using radiations of different frequencies to shed light on these hidden structures, and Badger's undergraduate thesis was an analysis of how X rays could be manipulated to gather information about the surface conditions of crystals. After receiving his bachelor of science degree in 1921, he remained at Caltech to pursue his interest in physical chemistry. His principal mentors were Richard C. Tolman, Roscoe G. Dickinson, Paul S. Epstein, and Arthur A. Noyes. From Tolman he learned the great power of theoretical ideas, particularly when combined with data from high-precision instruments; in 1923 he published a paper with Tolman in which they accurately predicted from spectroscopic data the values of thermodynamic quantities such as the heat capacity of certain gases. From Dickinson, a methodical and meticulous X-ray crystallographer, Badger learned the necessity of being precise and accurate. Epstein, a mathematical physicist, inspired him to choose chemical spectroscopy as his principal field of research, even though Noyes, his thesis supervisor, had him do his doctoral work in the field of thermodynamics. In this ingenious investigation of a high-temperature equilibrium reaction involving ammonia, charcoal, hydrogen cyanide, and hydrogen, Badger used a flow method to determine some important thermodynamic properties of hydrogen cyanide.

After receiving his Ph.D. in 1924, Badger became a research fellow in physical chemistry at Caltech, a position he held for four years. During this time he continued to collaborate with Tolman. In one of their investigations they used experimental data from spectroscopy to verify the predictions of Niels Bohr's correspondence principle. Experimental data on the absolute intensities of spectral lines were at the time very limited, but Badger, a skilled scientific craftsman and instrument maker, devised techniques that permitted him to make spectrometric measurements in regions of low frequencies. This work also strengthened his interest in spectroscopy as a way of determining properties of molecules such as internuclear distances and moments of inertia.

Although Tolman and Badger achieved modest success in their spectroscopic studies, their results also illustrated the unsatisfactory state of physical theory in the period just before the discovery of quantum mechanics. The revolutionary developments of quantum theory attracted several Caltech students and faculty members to Europe. Badger went in 1928–1929 as an International research fellow at the Universities of Göttingen and Bonn, Germany. At James Franck's institute in Göttingen he studied fluorescence in flames. Franck was interested in energy transmissions in atomic systems that fluoresced, and he suspected that fluorescence might be quenched owing to deactivation by high-energy collisions in the flame, but Badger showed that deactivation by collisions was offset by heightened pressure.

Badger spent the second part of his year abroad at Reinhard Mecke's institute in Bonn. There he returned to his interest in the spectra of polyatomic molecules. By utilizing new, highly sensitive photographic plates and improved diffraction gratings, he was able to resolve and analyze the rotation-vibration bands of ammonia, confirming this molecule's symmetrical pyramidal structure.

On his return to Pasadena in 1929 Badger became an assistant professor. Building on his work with Mecke, he established a program for the study of the rotation-vibration spectra of simple polyatomic molecules. In the 1930s he and his coworkers investigated molecules such as iodine, ozone, acetylene, ethylene, and hydrogen cyanide. These researches, done at Caltech and, in 1931, as a visiting lecturer at the University of California in Berkeley, gave Badger and other scientists a detailed understanding of the structures of many important molecules. Now securely ensconced in Pasadena, Badger married Virginia Alice Sherman in 1933; they had two children.

As his understanding of specific polyatomic structures deepened, Badger recognized the importance of certain general regularities in the chemical bonds holding these structures together. In 1934 he published an important paper in the *Journal of Chemical Physics* that explained a relation he had formulated connecting internuclear distances and bond force constants (these constants measured the restoring force when the distance of the two atoms linked by this bond is changed). This relationship, now known as "Badger's rule," resulted from his extensive survey of the force constants and internuclear distances in a large number of diatomic molecules. Despite the empirical nature of his mathematical expression, it proved to be applicable not only to diatomic molecules but also, though less accurately, to polyatomic molecules; it could also be applied to molecules in both normal and excited states. With Badger's rule scientists could calculate approximate values of interatomic distances within molecules from spectroscopic data alone. This was especially valuable in cases where interatomic distances could not be determined from X-ray or electron-diffraction techniques.

In the late 1930s Badger became interested in a special type of chemical bond, the hydrogen bond. Utilizing his excellent spectroscopic facilities, he and a number of graduate and postdoctoral students investigated the spectra of compounds such as alcohols, acetic acid, and urea in which this linkage occurred both within molecules (intramolecular hydrogen bonds) and between molecules (intermolecular hydrogen bonds).

During World War II Badger's research shifted to various war-related projects. He was involved in solving some basic physical problems for the Manhattan Project, the program that built the atomic bomb. He also participated in projects for the Office of Scientific Research and Development and for the Army Air Corps. After his association with the Manhattan Project ended, he worked with Linus Pauling for the Navy Bureau of Ordnance on a study of the properties of smokeless powder. Toward the war's end Badger developed an interest in proteins, substances that had also fascinated Pauling since his work on hemoglobin in the 1930s. Badger used spectroscopic methods in his studies, whereas Pauling used a model-building approach.

Following the war Badger shifted his interest from small molecules to large molecules such as nitrocellulose and proteins. Although his spectroscopic methods were insufficient for discovering structural details of these large molecules, he did find spectral data helpful in eliminating otherwise plausible configurations. Badger, an excellent craftsman in wood and metals, developed mechanical models to aid him in the study of these complex organic molecules. Unlike Pauling's models, which correctly accounted for bond lengths and angles, Badger's models used springs between the atoms, which provided a way to model the force constants for the stretching and bending of particular chemical bonds.

Different approaches to molecular models were not the only difference between Badger and Pauling. During the 1950s and 1960s Pauling's campaign against the testing of nuclear weapons in the atmosphere caused deep divisions among Caltech faculty members. Although Badger was sympathetic to Pauling's overall goals, he did not always approve of the means

Pauling used to accomplish them; for example, Badger believed that Pauling's political activities against nuclear tests were often based on emotion rather than on sound scientific reasons.

After Badger became emeritus professor at Caltech in 1966, he continued to work with graduate and undergraduate students; his final publication was based on his supervision of the research of two undergraduates. He died at his home in Altadena, California.

Badger became a physical chemist whom his teachers Noyes and Dickinson would have admired. Like them he was a painstaking researcher, a dedicated teacher, and a valuable colleague. Whenever new apparatus needed to be built, Badger often helped do it. This manual skill and creativity was also evident in his watercolor paintings of desert scenes and in the jewelry he crafted. In molecular spectroscopy, his studies of polyatomic molecules provided Pauling and other scientists with data for their theoretical studies of the nature of the chemical bond and the structures of important chemical and biological substances. His name will also live on in Badger's rule, a staple of scientific dictionaries.

Badger's work was honored in his lifetime. He was a National Research fellow (1928–1929). He was elected a member of the National Academy of Sciences in 1952 and a fellow of the American Academy of Arts and Sciences in 1961. He was a John Simon Guggenheim Memorial fellow (1960–1961). His dedication to teaching undergraduates was rewarded in 1961, when he received the Manufacturing Chemists' Association Award for Excellence in College Teaching in Chemistry. This pleased him immensely, because it was given to teachers who were "personally responsible over a period of years for awakening in students a genuine interest in chemistry, for inspiring them to serious intellectual effort . . . and for developing that interest into a continuing dedication" (*Engineering and Science* 38: 24).

• Collections of Badger's papers are in the archives of the California Institute of Technology and in the Ava Helen and Linus Pauling Papers at Oregon State University, Corvallis. Many of Badger's scientific publications are listed in Johann Christian Poggendorff, *Biographisch-literisches Handwörterbuch zur Geschichte der exacten Wissenschaften*, vol. 7b (1980), pp. 182–83, and at the end of Oliver R. Wulf's extensive biography of Badger in National Academy of Sciences, *Biographical Memoirs* 56 (1987): 15–20. Shorter biographies include "Richard McLean Badger," in *McGraw-Hill Modern Scientists and Engineers*, vol. 1 (1980), p. 40; and "Richard M. Badger, 1896–1974," *Engineering and Science* 38 (Dec. 1974–Jan. 1975): 24. Badger's work is discussed in many articles and books; representative examples are Gerhard Herzberg, *Molecular Spectra and Molecular Structures*, vol. 2, *Infrared and Raman Spectra of Polyatomic Molecules* (1945); Linus Pauling, *The Nature of the Chemical Bond and the Structure of Molecules and Crystals: An Introduction to Modern Structural Chemistry*, 3d ed. (1960); and George C. Pimentel and Aubrey L. McClellan, *The Hydrogen Bond* (1960).

ROBERT J. PARADOWSKI

BADIN, Stephen Theodore (17 July 1768–19 Apr. 1853), Roman Catholic missionary, was born in Orléans, France, the son of Étienne Badin and Monique Hoüy, a prosperous middle-class couple. Educated at the Collège Montaigu in Paris, Badin entered the Sulpician seminary in Orléans to prepare for ordination to the priesthood in 1789, the year the French Revolution began. When his bishop took the constitutional oath of obedience to the French government rather than to the pope, Badin left the seminary and emigrated to America in 1792 in company with the Sulpician priests Benedict Flaget and John B. David, with whom he would later be associated in Kentucky. After finishing his studies at St. Mary's Seminary in Baltimore, Badin became, at the hands of Bishop John Carroll on 25 May 1793, the first Catholic priest ordained in the United States.

Assigned to serve the Maryland Catholics who had moved to the Kentucky frontier after 1785, Badin and another priest, Michael Barriere, left Baltimore in September 1793, walked to Pittsburgh, and from there traveled by flatboat down the Ohio River to Maysville, Kentucky. They then walked from Maysville to Lexington where Badin celebrated mass for the first time in Kentucky on 30 November 1793.

While Badin settled at White Sulphur in Scott County, north of Lexington, Barriere went farther west to Bardstown. Barriere left for Louisiana in May 1794, leaving Badin as the only priest in Kentucky for the next eleven years, save for the eccentric William de Rohan, who was suspended from the ministry for failing to live up to his ministerial responsibilities. Badin served his flock by riding a circuit among the Catholic families scattered through several central Kentucky counties.

Another priest, Charles Nerinckx, a Belgian, joined Badin on the Kentucky mission in 1805. Later that same year, Dom Urbain Guillet founded a Trappist monastery in Kentucky, but it closed in 1809 because of sickness and death among the monks. In 1806 four Dominican priests made the first American foundation of their order at Springfield, Kentucky. In 1809 a new diocese was formed that included Kentucky, Tennessee, Ohio, and the Northwest Territory with Bardstown, Kentucky, as the seat of the bishop. Badin's contentious personality, his impulsiveness, and his rigorism as a pastor contributed to his being passed over when it came to choosing a bishop for the new diocese. Benedict Flaget was named to the see as its first bishop in 1810. A dispute between Badin and Flaget over who should hold title to church property finally induced Badin to return to France in 1819.

As a parish priest in the diocese of Orléans, France, Badin secured funds and church furnishings for the Kentucky missions and advertised their needs with the publication in Paris in 1822 of a report on "The State of the Missions in Kentucky." Badin grew restless in France and returned to the United States in 1828, intending to join his brother Vincent, also a priest, in Detroit. Badin pastored the Catholics around Monroe, Michigan, for some months, visited Kentucky in

1829, and then went north again in 1830 to establish a mission among the Potawatomi Indians in southwestern Michigan and northern Indiana. Before leaving this mission in 1836, Badin secured title for the bishop of Vincennes, Indiana, to the site whereon the University of Notre Dame would be established in 1842. Badin visited Notre Dame in 1845 and made some donations to the school, but he ended up quarreling over money with Rev. Edward Sorin, the president.

In his later years, Badin was peripatetic, moving at will between Kentucky, Louisiana, and Illinois and being well received by Catholics as the first priest ordained in the United States. In 1850 he settled in Cincinnati, Ohio, where he resided in the house of Archbishop John Baptist Purcell until his death there.

• The Archives of the Archdiocese of Baltimore contain a number of letters from Badin to Carroll describing conditions in Kentucky. Otherwise, Badin manuscripts are scattered in other repositories, a good list of which is to be found in J. Herman Schauinger, *Stephen T. Badin: Priest in the Wilderness* (1956). Badin is known to have published two Latin poems, "Carmen Sacrum" (1811) and "Epicedium" (1843); "Letters to an Episcopalian Friend" (1836), a series of three articles published in the *Cincinnati Catholic Telegraph*, a Catholic newspaper; and the prayer "Sanctissimae Trinitatis, Laudes et Invocatio" (1844). In addition to Schauinger's biography, see Martin J. Spalding, *Sketches of the Early Catholic Missions of Kentucky* (1844), and Benjamin J. Webb, *The Centenary of Catholicity in Kentucky* (1884). Badin's relationship with the University of Notre Dame is described in Edward Sorin, *The Chronicles of Notre Dame du Lac*, trans. by John Toohey, ed. and annotated by James T. Connelly (1992).

JAMES T. CONNELLY

BAEKELAND, Leo Hendrik (14 Nov. 1863–23 Feb. 1944), chemist and inventor, was born in St. Martens-Latem, near Ghent, Belgium, the son of Karel Baekeland, a cobbler, and Rosalia Merchie, a housemaid. A government scholarship enabled Baekeland to enter the University of Ghent, where he studied chemistry in the School of Exact Sciences. He received a B.S. in 1882 and a D.Sc. in organic chemistry in 1884, passing the examination with highest honors. The following year he became an assistant to Theodore Swarts, a professor of chemistry at Ghent. In 1887 Baekeland won a traveling scholarship in an academic competition sponsored by the Universities of Ghent, Liege, Brussels, and Louvain. He postponed travel and instead continued as an assistant professor and then as associate professor from 1888 to 1889 at Ghent and at the nearby Higher Normal School at Bruges from 1885 to 1887. In 1889 he married Swarts's daughter, Céline, an artist; they had two children. The couple used Baekeland's scholarship for travel to France, Britain, and the United States that year.

Inspired by his readings of Benjamin Franklin's autobiography, Baekeland became captivated by the idea of becoming a successful inventor and of traveling to the United States, which, he believed, offered unlimited opportunities for someone with his scientific background. He also found inspiration in the research tradition at Ghent, which chemists August Kekulé and Adolph Baeyer had started and which Swarts continued. Kekulé spent nine years (1858–1867) in Ghent teaching, researching, attracting a first-rate faculty, and refocusing the chemistry curriculum on laboratory work. His famous "dancing snakes" dream that elucidated benzene's ring structure (1865) and his papers on the structure of phenol (1867), a compound obtained from carbonizing coal or partially oxidizing benzene, belong to this period. Baeyer, who came to Ghent with Kekulé but left for Berlin in 1860, was an authority on the chemistry of coal tar compounds, such as benzene and phenol, the study of these compounds at that time dominating much of the chemical research in European universities. He had obtained plastic-like resins from phenol and aldehydes as early as 1871.

Baekeland's 1889 trip abroad complemented his longtime research interest in photographic development, which in its early years required a competency in chemistry. By the 1880s Ghent had become the manufacturing center for the recently introduced dry plate, and encouraged by chemist and dry plate manufacturer Désiré Van Monkhaven, Baekeland experimented with photographic emulsions. He hoped to discover the best silver chloride complex to use in a photographic emulsion and thereby invent a photographic printing paper that, unlike the albumen paper currently available, would not require sunlight for its development. Baekeland also had established close contacts within the photographic industry, and while attending a meeting of the Camera Club in New York City in the fall of 1889, he met Richard Anthony of E. & H. T. Anthony and Company, later Agfa Ansco Company. Recognizing the importance of chemical research to the photographic industry, Anthony and Company had retained Charles F. Chandler, a professor of chemistry at Columbia University, as a consultant to the company. Baekeland favorably impressed Chandler, and when Chandler urged Baekeland to remain in the United States and apply his considerable knowledge to the problems of the chemical industry, Baekeland took Chandler's advice. He resigned from the University of Ghent and in late 1889 accepted a position with Anthony and Company, where he remained for two years before leaving to become an industrial consultant.

The next few years were the most difficult in Baekeland's life. He had neither clients nor money, and he overextended himself mentally to the point of exhaustion. During a rather long recuperation he decided to concentrate exclusively on his earlier idea of inventing a high quality, light-sensitive printing paper. After months of experimenting with several hundred silver chloride emulsions, he achieved success and in 1893 was ready to manufacture Velox, a new emulsified printing paper with increased sensitivity, which permitted its exposure in artificial light.

Velox developed a large commercial following, including George Eastman of Eastman Kodak Company in Rochester, New York, who in 1899 paid Baekeland

and his partner Leonard Jacobi $750,000 for the rights to Velox. Relieved of financial concerns and guided by whim, Baekeland concentrated on small-scale research in his home laboratory in Yonkers, New York, and formulated his lifelong belief that you "commit your blunders on a small scale and make your profits on a large scale."

Throughout his consulting years, Baekeland never lost his interest in the resins that chemists had synthesized by reacting aldehydes with phenol and its derivatives. Formaldehyde's synthesis by the Russian chemist Aleksandr Butlerov in 1859, followed by Kekulé's and Baeyer's researches on phenol in the 1860s and 1870s, had encouraged resin production, but none had held much commercial promise. The best resins were either a gelled mass and a poor substitute for shellac or a hard unstable mass caused by bubble formation during the curing process.

Beginning in 1902 Baekeland tried to produce a shellac by reacting phenol and its derivatives with formaldehyde. Because chemists at the time had no well-developed theories of reaction rates and molecular structure, his research was mainly empirical. Only in 1907 did Baekeland understand how acids and alkalis and the aldehyde-phenol ratio determined the type of resin product thereby enabling him to synthesize Bakelite, the first true plastic. The key reactions he established were that (1) an acid-catalyzed system resulting from an excess of formaldehyde with phenol gave a polymer resin (Novolak) that softened each time on heating and could be molded; (2) an alkali catalyst gave a polymer resin (Bakelite) that softened when first heated but not on subsequent heatings; and (3) the phenol-aldehyde reaction was a condensation process that gave water as a by-product.

Baekeland also developed two techniques that made the molding of Bakelite practical. First, he found that heating it for several hours at 300°F and 50–100 pounds per square inch (psi) prevented bubbles from forming and gave a hard, strong, insoluble, lightweight resin with a tensile strength of 7,000 psi. The application of high pressures to chemical reactions was a new practice that the Russian chemist Vladimir Ipatiev had introduced in 1903. Second, the addition of fillers such as asbestos or wood flour improved Bakelite's resistance to cracking or splitting with age. The final product was a poor electrical conductor that did not melt or burn easily (it charred at around 570°F), and it reproduced the contours of any mold, which made it especially important for industrial purposes.

Baekeland received two patents on 7 December 1909. By that time he already had announced his invention in a paper presented at the February 1909 meeting of the American Chemical Society's New York section. Published later that year, his paper was the first to make a distinction between the older and fairly common word plastic to indicate those compounds upon which you could impress a shape or mold and Bakelite, his phenol-formaldehyde polymer resin.

Remaining cautious as a result of his Velox venture, Baekeland intended to solve any production problems on a small scale. In 1910 he constructed a one-ton capacity plant near his home, from which he determined to manufacture and market Bakelite and convince the skeptics. Previously produced plastics (celluloid), and many natural materials, had limited usefulness because of their tendency to soften when heated, to harden and become brittle when cooled, and to react readily with other chemicals. Bakelite did not have these limitations, and in 1910, with the establishment of the General Bakelite Corporation in Perth Amboy, New Jersey, the age of modern plastics began. Bakelite quickly replaced celluloid as a manufacturing material, particularly for billiard balls. It also became a substitute for hard rubber and amber in switchboards, tabletops, counters, gear wheels, washing machine agitators, and pump housings. The electrical and the new plastics industries were experiencing parallel growth at this time, and Bakelite found extensive use in electrical appliances and insulation. To accommodate Bakelite's different applications Baekeland successfully marketed it as either a powder or a liquid that required little work to give a finished product.

In the early years of its existence, General Bakelite was involved in several patent lawsuits and mergers. One of the disputes was with Thomas Edison, who had begun to experiment with phenolic-aldehyde resins around 1900 in the hope of finding a substitute for the fifty million pounds of shellac used to manufacture phonograph records. Edison collaborated with Jonas W. Aylsworth, whose 1910 patent described a process that converted Novolak-type resins into Bakelite-like resins suitable for phonograph records. The Condensite Company that they established in Glen Ridge, New Jersey, in 1910 put them in legal conflict, and for a time in bitter patent litigation, with Baekeland, ending only in 1922 when Condensite became part of the Bakelite Corporation.

A second dispute, also in 1910, was with University of Kansas chemists Lawrence V. Redman, A. S. Weith, and F. P. Broek, who synthesized the phenolic resin Redmanol by substituting formin (hexamethylenetetramine) for formaldehyde. Redmanol Chemical Products Company, established in 1914, battled with Baekeland over manufacturing rights before accepting a takeover in 1922. Other lawsuits and mergers enabled Baekeland to gain entrance to European markets. Hans Lebach, a chemist with Knoll & Company in Ludwigshafen am Rhein, had obtained European patents for a Bakelite-like thermosetting plastic shortly after Baekeland. Upon coming to the United States in 1912 he established a friendly business arrangement with Baekeland and then returned to Germany to organize the German Bakelite Corporation. Shortly after World War I, Lebach expanded the corporation to Britain, absorbing the Damard Lacquer Company.

The new plastics industry, especially its two largest producers, Bakelite and Condensite, required considerable amounts of phenol and aldehydes. With the outbreak of World War I in 1914, phenol, which European chemical companies such as Badische Anilin- und Soda-Fabrik had supplied for nearly fifty years, was suddenly in short supply. Although phenol was a critical war material used to manufacture picric acid explosives, no commercial production of it existed in the United States. With his supplies of phenol cut, Edison began its manufacture. Other companies soon followed, including Barrett (later Allied Chemical) in 1915 and Dow Chemical in 1917, and by the end of the war the United States had an established phenol industry. Formaldehyde, the other half of the plastics industry, had few practical uses before 1900. Borrowing heavily from German science, Heyden Chemical Works (later acquired by Tenneco) began its production in 1901. The Roessler & Hasslacher Chemical Company in Perth Amboy was Baekeland's supplier. Formaldehyde's importance in making plastics and varnishes led to its increased production after 1910 and established it as a major industrial chemical.

For twenty years after Baekeland's invention, knowledge of polymer phenolic resins was mainly empirical. Chemists frequently confused polymers with colloids and polymerization with molecular association. They knew little about polymer structures until 1929, when Hermann Staudinger of Freiburg, Germany, classified plastics as either thermoplastic or thermosetting and unraveled Bakelite's structure. According to Staudinger, thermoplastics soften on heating (which permits their molding), harden on cooling, and can repeat the heating and cooling sequence many times. This occurs whenever the intermediate compound that first forms provides only two active hydrogen atoms for polymerization, as in an acid-catalyzed system, and consists of linear or partially crossed-linked molecules like Novolak. Thermosetting plastics also soften on heating to allow molding but then set to form a solid cross-linked, three-dimensional polymer that does not soften on further heating. They result when more than two hydrogen atoms are available and an alkali catalyst added. Staudinger showed that in Bakelite's powder form, the methylene groups from formaldehyde linked the phenol molecules into long chains, followed by cross linking of the chains into three-dimensional networks to give a thermosetting plastic. Staudinger received the 1953 Nobel Prize in chemistry for his pioneering work on polymer structures.

Commercial manufacture of Bakelite began in 1911 with a modest output of 2,800 pounds, rising to 700,000 pounds in 1913, 8.8 million pounds in 1922, and 51.5 million pounds in 1939. Price varied with the economy and from 1913 to 1939 increased steadily from $0.35 to $0.65 per pound. Baekeland and his corporation filed over 400 patents from 1911 to 1939, one of which, on the use of Bakelite in General Motors' Delco ignition and starting systems, contributed significantly to the design of the modern automobile.

A successful businessman, Baekeland sold his corporation in 1939, when it numbered 1,350 employees internationally, to Union Carbide and Carbon Corporation for 187,500 shares of Carbide's common stock, which was valued at about $16.5 million. Two factors dictated the sale: Baekeland's son, George, a geologist with the corporation since 1923, did not wish to lead the business; and at age seventy-five Baekeland had lost the interest and energy needed to sustain the corporation through the start of a new era in the plastics industry. The future lay with large, vertically integrated companies with extensive research and technical facilities that converted raw materials into finished products and developed new and diversified markets. The Bakelite Corporation manufactured a comparatively narrow line of products and depended on outside suppliers for many of its raw materials. Consequently, other companies, such as American Cyanamid, Union Carbide, DuPont, Dow, and Monsanto, had moved into the market and waited for Bakelite's key patents to expire. By 1939 the corporation's market share, although considerable, was dwindling, profits were falling, and a massive capital investment or a merger was necessary to sustain the corporation. Baekeland saw the handwriting on the wall, negotiated the sale to Union Carbide, and retired.

Baekeland received many honors for his contributions to chemistry, including the presidency of the Chemists' Club in New York City (1904), the American Electrochemical Society (1909), the American Institute of Chemical Engineers (1912), and the American Chemical Society (1924) and membership in the National Academy of Sciences (1936) and the American Philosophical Society (1936). Among his other awards were the Nichols Medal, New York Section ACS (1909), and Willard Gibbs Medal, Chicago Section ACS (1913); John Scott Medal (1910) and Franklin Medal (1940), Franklin Institute; Chandler Medal, Columbia University (1914); Perkin Medal (1916) and Messel Medal (1938), Society of Chemical Industry.

An active member of his corporation, Baekeland also spent a considerable amount of time lecturing and writing. Publishing fifty-two papers from 1903 to 1940, he focused particularly on the interaction and influence of research and technology on society. He became a crusader for science and education, and his ideas showed the strong influence of Kekulé's theory-guided approach to curriculum design and development. Baekeland championed the patent system, another favorite topic, as the protection of intellectual property and an indispensable stimulus to invention and industrial development. The system also had its drawbacks: "Of all the irritating, time robbing experiences in my life," he once said, "I consider patent suits as some of the worst." But, as many of his competitors discovered, he was an authority on the subject and a master at writing patent specifications.

Baekeland was a man of uneven generosity and curious biases. He provided financially for his parents and once backed a friend in a Bakelite-related moonlighting business. Yet he refused to contribute to a performing arts company when asked by May Sarton, the daughter of Harvard historian of science George Sarton, one of the few people Baekeland revered. He offered a position to an unknown graduate student he met at a dinner party, yet he often rejected his friends' sons when they came to him seeking employment.

In the last years of his life Baekeland increasingly became a loner. His wife, children, and grandchildren spent summers in the Adirondacks, but Baekeland rarely visited them and never stayed long. He spent considerable time at his Coconut Grove, Florida, estate, motoring or sailing along the many waterways of the Florida coast and keys. He led an uncomplicated life, living in spartan rooms and eating from cans. He dressed in white, à la Mark Twain, and often dipped into swimming pools, clothes and all, in search of relief from the Florida sun. He continued to correspond with his many colleagues and to write on topics as diverse as the development of primitive countries, the causes of war, wine making, and solar heating. He made annual pilgrimages to Columbia University, where he was the students' favorite guest lecturer, and while in New York spent much time with friends at the Chemists Club. In Baekeland's final years his mind failed, and he was institutionalized at the time of his death in Beacon, New York.

• A collection of Baekeland's papers is in the Archives Center, National Museum of American History, Smithsonian Institution, Washington, D.C.; other papers are accessible through Union Carbide's Archival Services in Danbury, Conn. A selection of Baekeland's correspondence and documents is in Jan Gillis, *Leo Hendrik Baekeland* (1965); other correspondence is in Letteren en Schone Kunsten van Belgie, Klasse der Wetenschappen, *Verhandelingen van de Koninklijke Vlaamse Academie voor Wetenschappen*, Jaargang 27, Nr. 81, n1. The most complete English-language study is Carl Kaufman, "Grand Duke, Wizard, and Bohemian: A Biographical Profile of Leo Hendrik Baekeland" (master's thesis, Univ. of Delaware, 1968). Published accounts of Baekeland's life include Charles Kettering, "Leo Hendrik Baekeland," *National Academy of Sciences, Biographical Memoir* 24 (1947): 281–302, which contains a complete bibliography of Baekeland's publications and patents; and H. V. Potter, "Leo Hendrik Baekeland," *Chemistry and Industry*, no. 31 (1945): 242–46 and no. 32 (1945): 251–53. A discussion of his work on Velox is in Helmut Gernsheim and Alison Gernsheim, *The History of Photography from the Earliest Use of the Camera Obscura in the Eleventh Century up to 1914* (1955); see also Reese Jenkins, *Images and Enterprise: Technology and the American Photographic Industry 1839–1925* (1975). On Bakelite see Baekeland, "Some Aspects of Industrial Chemistry," *Science* 40 (1914): 179–98; Maurice Holland, *Industrial Explorers* (1928); Williams Haynes, *American Chemical Industry* (1954); G. Dring, "A Plastics Jubilee: 1907–1957," *Chemistry and Industry*, no. 28 (1958): 870–78; Morris Kaufmann, *The First Century of Plastics* (1963); Robert Friedel, *Pioneer Plastic: The Making and Selling of Celluloid* (1983); and Peter Spitz, *Petrochemicals: The Rise of an Industry* (1988). Obituaries are in the *New York Times*, 24 Feb. 1944; *Nature*, 25 Mar. 1944, pp. 369–70; and *Chemistry and Industry*, no. 14 (1944): 134–35.

ANTHONY N. STRANGES
RICHARD C. JONES

BAER, Clara Gregory (27 Aug. 1863–19 Jan. 1938), physical educator, was born in Algiers, Louisiana, the daughter of Hamilton John Baer, a broker/flour merchant, and Ellen Douglas Riley. Algiers, located across the Mississippi River from New Orleans, was undergoing a prolonged Union siege at the time of Clara's birth. She was quickly given "Dixie" as a nickname, perhaps in defiance of the North's aggression. Following her mother's death in 1868, she and her siblings were cared for by their maternal grandmother. Baer was one of a small number of children who attended the few schools in Louisiana during the Reconstruction period. As there were no public Louisiana secondary schools before 1880, she was sent to Louisville, Kentucky, for high school. Following high school she studied first in the late 1880s under S. S. Curry at the Boston School of Expression, then at the Emerson School of Oratory in Boston, and in 1890 at the Posse Normal School of Physical Education in Boston.

Baron Nils Posse, the Swedish-born founder of Posse Normal School of Physical Education, taught his twenty-five select students Swedish gymnastics and other gymnastics popular at the time. Baer was an apt student and, like the other students, also learned anatomy, physiology, hygiene, kinesiology, and physics as these applied to gymnastics along with educational corrective and medical gymnastics, practical exercises, and games. During the 1890–1891 school year she was employed as director of girls' gymnastics at the Episcopal church in Waltham, Massachusetts, and following her graduation in 1891 she returned to New Orleans to create a department of physical culture at Sophie Newcomb Memorial College, an affiliate of Tulane University and the country's first degree-granting coordinate college.

Baer's entire career was spent at Sophie Newcomb College. As director of physical education there she initiated the first certification programs for women in the South in 1893–1894 and instituted the first four-year degree program in physical education in 1907. Her efforts extended beyond Sophie Newcomb, however. From 1891 until 1929 she crusaded for expanded opportunities for children and young women in physical education, was active in professional physical education organizations, and was responsible for the introduction and later modification of basketball rules for women.

During a time, the 1890s, and in a place, New Orleans, where many young women balked at physical activity, Baer championed sports, particularly basketball. She was instrumental in the passage of compulsory physical education in Louisiana in 1894, making her state the third behind California and Ohio to have such a statute. Her efforts to persuade the citizenry of Louisiana to pass this law took various avenues: conducting summer schools in educational institutions in small towns, teaching gymnastics to elite New Orleans socialites one evening a week and two other evenings to working-class women and giving lectures at state professional meetings.

Baer was a pioneer in her state, active in professional organization committees, serving as officer several times, and was a force in shaping physical education not only in Louisiana but also nationally. She lectured frequently on the value of physical education. Her speeches and her published works in professional journals were persuasive and instructional regarding the value of physical education.

The scientific background Baer gained at Posse Normal School prompted her to be the first southern physical educator to apply the science of anthropometry to physical education. In 1899 she also pioneered in the South the teaching of adapted or remedial exercises. In 1896 she authored a physical education text, *Progressive Lessons in Physical Education*, which was widely used by teachers. Baer was an eloquent proponent of exercise. She articulated, both to her students and to the attendees at her lectures, the role of exercise in the achievement of total well-being. She focused on the hygienic objectives of exercise and its connection to mental, spiritual, and emotional aspects in addition to the physical benefits. Like many other early physical educators, Baer did not earn a degree but continued to study under renowned professionals at Columbia College and the University of Wisconsin.

Baer promulgated her philosophy and program as she taught every summer in seven-week-long courses at various educational sessions in small towns, directed the Monteagle Summer School for Higher Physical Culture in the Cumberland Mountains of Tennessee from 1898 to 1910, and taught during the summer of 1892 at the Summer School of Methods in Waynesville, North Carolina, and for the next six summers at the Louisiana Chataqua. She was an energetic and indefatigable spokesperson as she traveled and taught during the years when journeys were arduous and comforts were limited. In recognition of her excellent teaching and all-around educational leadership, she was made a full professor, the first physical educator, male or female, in the South to achieve this rank.

To convince females to exercise and enjoy it was a daunting task at the turn of the century. Physical education was controversial, considered by many middle- and upper-class Louisianians not altogether ladylike. Her students, coming to class sheathed in corsets covered by floor-sweeping dresses that featured elegant bustles, were shielded from the sun by their hats and gloves. Baer's students did their gymnastic drills and exercises and played games in this regalia. Eventually Baer introduced the bloomer outfit. At first the girls, and surely their parents, considered it immodest. By the turn of the century, however, Sophie Newcomb students were doing their gymnastic drills and playing games in bloomer suits. The corsets had been "sweated off," and the students were more comfortable in the below-the-knee voluminous black bloomers and the loosely fitted, long-sleeved middy top. Once they were garbed more appropriately, they enjoyed the activities.

Baer considered enjoyment an important element of exercise. She devised activities that would be more than monotonous, regimented drills. The game that eventually proved to be most popular was basketball. Baer taught it to her students in 1893, less than two years after James Naismith developed it for his class of rowdy male students at Springfield College in December 1891 and a little more than a year after female students first played it at Smith College.

After introducing the game, Baer quickly realized, as did Senda Berenson at Smith, that it was too demanding for her students, most of whom found most exercise too strenuous. Parents and physicians also raised a furor, saying basketball was too rough and physically demanding. Baer did not discard the activity but modified it in January 1894. She overcame the objections by substantially changing the game.

Baer eliminated features that caused overexertion. Berenson also adapted the game, dividing the court into three equal parts. Baer restricted play by greatly reducing the amount of running by sectioning off the court, requiring that a player stay in her own square, which, depending on the number of girls playing, varied from $8' \times 12'$ to $23' \times 25'$. The players were allowed to move only when the ball was in the air. Passing was more important than continual running. The other major change that served to reduce roughness was the elimination of dribbling, all guarding, and interfering with an opponent's attempt to shoot or pass. Even falling down became a foul. Because no more than two players could occupy an area, collisions decreased.

Continuing to modify the game to conform to the Victorian concepts revered by southerners, Baer instituted rules that called for the goal to be changed after every score so players reversed offensive and defensive duties, which countered the possibility of one player being a star. She permitted only one-handed shooting and passing. She did not allow players to shout, yell, or even talk during a game. Although by today's standards Baer's rules and play sound unbelievably limiting, her modified game fit the culture and the era. Her students played the game and enjoyed it immensely. It was essentially played in the same unique manner with the seven-division court until 1914, when the rules were modified. In 1922 Newcomb College began playing the standard Spalding, three-court-division rules used by females across the nation.

Baer also devised the game of Newcomb, a lead-up or practice game for basketball that developed throwing and catching skills. The ball was thrown over a rope, and points were scored by throwing the ball where it could not be caught by an opponent. This simple recreational game similar to volleyball became a popular school and playground game. In some Louisiana public schools and colleges it was a varsity sport for females and males. By 1910 it had spread to all parts of the country. In 1895 Baer patented and published both Newcomb and women's basketball rules, which are still frequently included in modern physical education text and game books.

Clara Gregory Baer is credited with initiating and popularizing basketball and Newcomb along with other physical education activities with her Sophie Newcomb College students and in summer schools for Louisiana and Tennessee teachers. Her basketball rules were published four years before any other rules for women's basketball. She was a prime mover in the sport's early growth as well as in the acceptance of physical education in the total educational program.

At Baer's retirement from Tulane University in 1929 she was conferred the title of professor emeritus in recognition of her remarkable leadership in developing physical training for young women throughout the South.

Baer died in New Orleans. Never having married, her legacy was passed on to the thousands of young women under her tutelage.

• Tulane University holds the records of Baer's employment, publications, and professional services. Baer's published contributions to basketball for women include the first rules on women's basketball, *Basquette* (1895; rev. eds. 1908, 1911, and 1914), *Newcomb-ball: A Game for the Gymnasium and Playground* (1895), *Newcomb College Basketball Guide for Women* (1908, 1911, 1914), and *Progressive Lessons in Physical Education* (1896). Other writings in the field of physical education can be found in *National Education Review*, the *American Physical Education Review*, the *Louisiana School Review*, and the *Advocate*, the official journal of the state of Louisiana. Joan Paul has done extensive research on Baer. Her published works include "Clara Gregory Baer: Harbinger of Southern Physical Education," in the centennial issue of the *Research Quarterly for Exercise and Sport* (Apr. 1985): 46–55, and "Clara Gregory Baer: Catalyst for Women's Basketball," in *A Century of Women's Basketball: From Frailty to Final Four* (1991), pp. 37–52.

JANICE A. BERAN

BAER, George Frederick (26 Sept. 1842–26 Apr. 1914), lawyer and railroad president, was born in Somerset County, Pennsylvania, the son of Major Solomon Baer and Anna Baker, farmers. George spent his early years on the family farm until the Baers moved to the village of Somerset in 1848. Family resources enabled him to acquire his early education at the Somerset Institute. At age thirteen he served as an apprentice at the *Somerset Democrat*, a local newspaper. Over the next few years, Baer attended the Somerset Academy, served as clerk and head bookkeeper for the Ashtola Mills in nearby Johnstown, and spent a year at Franklin and Marshall College.

These experiences proved useful in 1861 when Baer and his brother Henry bought the *Somerset Democrat*, a voice for the county Democratic party. As editor, George Baer acquired the political visibility attached to those who ran local partisan papers but in this case, much to his misfortune. The prosouthern attitude featured in the Baer paper sparked a riot by local readers loyal to the Union, then in the midst of the secession crisis created by the election of Abraham Lincoln in 1860. Baer survived this controversy and in August 1862 gave up his position as editor to raise a local militia. His election as captain by members of the unit demonstrated that he had recovered from the earlier political turmoil and earned respect sufficient to lead the local volunteers. He returned to civilian life in May 1863 and began a legal apprenticeship in the law offices of his brothers William and Herman Baer. George Baer was admitted to the county bar in 1864. Two years later he married Emily Kimmel, the daughter of a prominent Somerset attorney. The couple had five children.

In 1868 Baer moved to Reading, Pennsylvania, in Berks County, which served as a hub for the Philadelphia and Reading Railroad Company (PRR), one of the major anthracite carriers in the country. Baer's legal talents emerged in several cases he successfully prosecuted against the powerful PRR. Impressed by Baer's skills, PRR president Franklin B. Gowen appointed Baer company counsel in 1870. With a firm base in Reading's most powerful company, Baer expanded his community influence as president of the Reading Iron Company and the Reading Paper Mill. His civic activities included terms as president of the board of park commissioners (1887) and organizer of the Reading Hospital (1884) and the Reading Library (1898). Baer's membership in the elite Wyomissing and Berkshire clubs confirmed his position in Reading's upper social strata.

As legal counsel for PRR, Baer participated in the industrywide consolidation movement among the major railroads. In 1891 he worked closely with New York investment banker J. P. Morgan, who was charged with restructuring the bankrupt PRR. Baer's legal and financial skills quickly made him a confidant of Morgan. The former Somerset attorney became president of the Morgan-controlled Reading system, which included the Philadelphia and Reading Coal & Iron Company (PRC&I). These companies also made Baer a dominant force in anthracite mining. At Baer's recommendation, Morgan purchased control of a major competing anthracite carrier, the Central Railroad of New Jersey, in 1901 and made Baer its president. This decision gave Baer's Reading system more direct access to the New York market and ownership of a substantial share of the hard coal industry.

By common agreement of the anthracite company owners, Baer represented the Anthracite Operators Association in the famous 1902 confrontation with the United Mine Workers (UMW), which originated in the attempts of the UMW to organize the anthracite miners. Led by John Mitchell, the UMW had carefully assembled local leaders to hold together, for the first time, ethnically diverse coal miners in their struggles against the coal company and anthracite railroad owners.

In Baer, the UMW confronted an inflexible spokesperson for the companies. He rejected demands for worker participation in wage determination, union recognition, and an eight-hour day as infringements on the owners' absolute right to control what occurred on their property, the anthracite mines. Baer's refusal to negotiate prolonged the strike into the late summer of 1902, which severely tested the capacity of the miners to remain off the job.

At this point, Baer committed an egregious blunder. His 17 July correspondence with a clergyman sympathetic to the miners revealed Baer's true feelings. He declared in the letter that "the rights and the interests of the laboring man will be protected and cared for—not by labor agitators, but by Christian men of property to whom God has given control of the property rights of the country." Released to the public, Baer's letter aroused a storm of criticism against the coal company owners. It also caught the ear of President Theodore Roosevelt, who had carefully monitored the progress of the strike. Pressure from within the Republican party, fears of the growing strength of radicals among the striking miners, and upcoming congressional elections moved Roosevelt to intervene in the labor dispute.

The president convened a White House meeting of Mitchell and the company owners in early October. Infuriated by the arrogance of the owners, and, in particular, Baer, Roosevelt called for an arbitration commission to settle the strike. The March 1903 settlement fell far short of recognition of the UMW by the coal companies. Still, it created an anthracite conciliation board that was designed to settle labor disputes and that included representatives from the miners' organization. The agreement marked a new relationship between the miners and the coal companies, one in sharp contrast to the divine-right management notions of Baer.

Despite his tarnished public image, Baer continued as head of the vast Reading system until his death. Just short of age seventy-two at his passing in Philadelphia, Baer had served beyond the retirement limit for his corporation and was one of the oldest chief railroad executives in the country. Almost until the end, Baer made the daily train ride to his Philadelphia offices, from where he directed the affairs of the Reading company. A veteran public speaker, Baer also maintained his long-standing practice of delivering lectures and addresses and continued to act as president of the Board of Trustees of Franklin and Marshall College (1894–1914).

Baer played a key role in the merger movement that swept through the American economy during the late 1890s. Ironically, the consolidation movement that produced corporate giants such as the Reading system also provoked Roosevelt and Congress to expand federal regulation of large-scale enterprise, a trend bitterly opposed by Baer and others in the corporate world. Firmly committed to a laissez-faire philosophy, Baer assumed that the federal government should protect the corporations as private property and not interfere with their operation. One of the many architects of the new national economy in the early 1900s, Baer still clung to late nineteenth-century notions of the self-made man, believing that the most able succeeded in business throughout life.

• The Baer papers, from the private collection of Walter B. Johnson, are located in the archives of the Reading (Pa.) Public Library. Baer's personal reflections are in William Appel, ed., *Addresses and Writings of George Baer* (1916); Appel was his son-in-law. Baer's daughters gathered newspaper articles on their father's life; the clippings are located in the Historical Society of Berks County in Reading under the title *In Memoriam, George F. Baer*, on microfilm roll 358. For additional biographical information on Baer, see Anna Dora Skirk, "The Rhetoric of George Baer during the Anthracite Coal Strike of 1902" (Ph.D. diss., Temple Univ., 1977). Obituaries are in the *New York Times*, *Philadelphia Inquirer*, and *Reading Eagle*, all 27 Apr. 1914.

EDWARD J. DAVIES II

BAERMANN, Carl (9 July 1839–17 Jan. 1913), pianist and composer, was born in Munich, Germany, the son of Karl Bärmann (1811–1885), a noted clarinetist. His mother's name is unknown. His grandfather, Heinrich Joseph Bärmann, also was a celebrated clarinetist, whose masterly playing inspired both Mendelssohn and Weber to compose works for him; his granduncle Karl Bärmann (1782–1842) was a famous bassoonist. Carl Baermann studied in Munich with Franz Lachner and Peter Cornelius, made his professional debut at age fifteen, playing Mendelssohn's Piano Concerto in G Minor, op. 25, and later studied with Liszt, with whom he formed a lasting friendship. Baermann and Beatrice von Dessauer, from an elite Bavarian family, married in Munich in 1865.

While still a young man, Baermann established a reputation as a rare concert pianist, recognized as one of the most admired performers at the well-known Academy Concerts. He was elected to the faculty of the King's Music School, founded in Munich in 1867 with Hans von Bülow and Karl von Perfall as directors, and in 1876 he received the high rank of king's professor from King Ludwig of Bavaria. Granted leave from his teaching duties, Baermann visited the United States in 1881 and made an enormously successful debut with the Boston Symphony Orchestra on 22 December 1881, playing Beethoven's Piano Concerto no. 4 in G Major, op. 58. The *Musical Record and Review* (1 Feb. 1902) reported that after only a few measures the Boston audience became aware that they were listening to a great interpretation, that Baermann was "too true a musician to show any trace of elocution or mannerism. . . . His technic served him—not for display; it was solely for interpretation." Shortly after his Boston debut, Baermann played Beethoven's Piano Concerto no. 5 in E-flat Major, op. 7 (*Emperor*) and Josef Rheinberger's Piano Concerto in A-flat Major, op. 94, the latter dedicated to Baermann by the composer. The enthusiastic response that Baermann consistently received from both audiences and critics encouraged him to relinquish his Munich position and remain in Boston.

Living in the United States for the rest of his life, Baermann maintained his fame as a pianist and established a reputation as one of the finest teachers of his time. He often performed in Boston, appearing with the Boston Symphony Orchestra more than any other pianist of his day, and also played with orchestras in New York, Washington, D.C., Philadelphia, and Brooklyn. A classicist by training, he was catholic in his musical taste and played a diverse repertoire encompassing works by Bach, Brahms, Beethoven, Chopin, Handel, Johann Hummel, Liszt, Mozart, Anton Rubinstein, and Schumann. Baermann enjoyed performing chamber music and made many appearances with violinists and chamber ensembles. He was noted for his superb readings of Beethoven's Piano Trio in B-flat Major, op. 97, Mozart's Quintet for Piano and Winds, K. 452, and Mozart's Piano Quartet in G Minor, K. 478. The *New England Conservatory Review* (May 1912) describes Baermann as a pianist

> noted, among other things, for his conscientiousness. . . . There is no ostentation or frivolity in his playing, and he is completely satisfied with himself only when he has merged his individuality in that of the composer whose works he is interpreting. . . . In the matter of technique he has no superior, but to him technique is the means and not the end. He is the intelligent, widely experienced artist as well as a pianist, and his fingers are but the means through which his brain and his heart are revealed. . . . It is piano playing at the very best—large, solid, well-considered and noble work.

A teacher highly esteemed by pupils throughout the United States, Baermann taught at his private studio in the Steinert Building, Boston, and from 1897 at the New England Conservatory of Music. He was especially influential in refining the musical taste of the American public; he accomplished this not only through his concert programs, but also through his many students, especially Mrs. H. H. A. Beach (Amy Beach), Frederick S. Converse, and Charles H. Morse, who in turn imbued their pupils with Baermann's high standards of musicianship and pianism. Baermann occasionally returned to Europe to give concerts and once to attend a Munich performance of *Festival March*, an orchestral work he had composed. He wrote mostly for the piano; among his few published works are the magnificent *Etuden*, op. 4 (1877) and the stylish *Polonaise pathétique* (1914). Baermann died in Newton, Massachusetts. The Baermann Society (1908–1913), formed by a group of prominent Bostonians to honor him for his contribution to American music and to foster his high ideals, is witness to the fine reputation Carl Baermann enjoyed during his lifetime.

• The Gunther Schuller Collection at the New England Conservatory of Music includes nineteen documents and letters concerning Carl Baermann and the Baermann Society. Sample programs of his piano and chamber recitals are in George Kehler, *The Piano in Concert* (1982). Jean Parkman Brown, "Carl Baermann," *Musical Record and Review*, 1 Feb. 1902, pp. 40–43, provides an extensive treatment; and an anonymous article, "Carl Baermann," *New England Conservatory Review*, May 1912, pp. 1–2, offers a brief résumé of his life and contributions. Obituaries are in the *Boston Transcript*, 18 Jan. 1913, and the *Boston Sunday Post*, 19 Jan. 1913.

JOHN GILLESPIE

BAGBY, George William (13 Aug. 1828–29 Nov. 1883), journalist and humorist, was born in Buckingham County, Virginia, the son of George Bagby, a merchant, and Virginia Young Evans. A frail constitution forced Virginia Bagby to move to the mountain town of Covington, where she died when George was eight years old. Bagby's father, who owned a general merchandise store in Lynchburg, sent him and his younger sister to live on the Cumberland County plantation of their aunt, Elisabeth Hobson. In 1843, at the age of fifteen, Bagby entered Delaware College. He then studied medicine at the University of Pennsylvania, from which he graduated in 1849.

Though he was now a doctor, Bagby made little or no attempt to establish a practice in Lynchburg, to which he repaired after his graduation. By 1853 he had joined a close friend, George Woodville Latham, in the publication of the *Lynchburg Express*. For the rest of his life he devoted himself exclusively to journalism and to the writing of essays. Even after the failure of the *Express* in 1856, he continued to write for a number of local and national publications, including *Harper's* and the *Atlantic Monthly* magazines.

From 1857 to 1859 Bagby resided in Washington, where he served as correspondent for a number of southern newspapers. During this period, in 1858, he sent the first of eight "Mozis Addums" letters to the *Southern Literary Messenger* in Richmond. The letters are modeled on the speech of backwoods characters Bagby had known as a youth in southside Virginia and are influenced by the well-established tradition of southwest dialect humor. The letters, addressed to a friend named "Billy Ivvins" in "Curdsville, Va.," recounted the rustic and innocent narrator's many burlesque adventures in Washington, D.C., including a trip to see the president that ends up in the disreputable establishment of a faro dealer. They were an immediate success and were no doubt partly responsible for Bagby's being named editor of the *Southern Literary Messenger* in 1860.

Bagby gratefully received the call to Richmond, for he had come to feel increasingly alienated by the antislavery fervor of many of Washington's politicians. The secession that Bagby fervently supported in *Messenger* editorials soon came, but the ensuing war had a disastrous effect on his magazine. After struggling for more than three years to keep the publication alive in the face of dwindling paper and ink supplies and gradually shrinking subscriptions, Bagby resigned his position as editor in January 1864, five months before the *Messenger* ceased publication.

Bagby's fortunes were so closely tied to the Confederacy that he fled Richmond with Jefferson Davis's entourage one day before the city fell to Union troops. He left behind a wife and an infant daughter, having married Lucy Parke Chamberlayne of Richmond in 1863. Within a month, however, he returned to the ruined capital. Faced with the expenses of supporting a growing family, Bagby turned in desperation to lecturing and to reading from his "Mozis Addums" letters and from popular essays such as "Bacon and Greens." Nevertheless, he remained substantially in debt.

From 1867 until 1870 Bagby struggled unsuccessfully in war-impoverished Virginia, first in Orange and later in Gordonsville, to establish a newspaper named the *Native Virginian*. In 1870 he gratefully accepted an appointment as assistant secretary of the commonwealth, acting as custodian of the state library. This position afforded him eight years of relative financial stability, though he was bothered by poor eyesight and chronic dyspepsia. If the years following the Civil War were difficult for Bagby, they were also the years during which many of his most famous essays were written. Of these essays, without doubt the most popular was "The Old Virginia Gentleman." Written for the lecture circuit in 1877, this work has served as the title for the three twentieth-century collections of his essays (1910, 1938, 1943).

The plantation described in "The Old Virginia Gentleman" is much like that of Bagby's earlier and more realistic description, "My Uncle Flatback's Plantation" (1863). In describing the drive that leads to the big house through miles of slash pine and scrub oak, Bagby's meticulous narrative eye does not fail to note the numerous potholes "that make every vehicle, but chiefly the bugback carriage, lurch and careen worse than a ship in a heavy sea." Threading through such realistic descriptions, however, is a strongly elegiac note for a vanished way of life. In the last analysis it is this mourning for such a lost time—for "a beauty, a simplicity, a purity, an uprightness, a cordial and lavish hospitality, a warmth and grace which shine in the lens of memory"—that turns "The Old Virginia Gentleman" into an unabashed celebration of the perfection of antebellum Virginia (Thomas Nelson Page, ed., *The Old Virginia Gentleman* [1910], pp. 4, 44).

Six years after writing "The Old Virginia Gentleman," George William Bagby died at his home in Richmond, leaving a widow and eight children. Though *Richmond Vital Statistics* lists "ulcer of tongue" as the cause of death, contemporary obituaries in the Richmond *State* and *Daily Dispatch* newspapers cited chronic dyspepsia as the cause.

In letters to the Richmond *State* written during the final years of his life, Bagby continued to reveal the abiding tension in his writing between the impulse to see Virginia precisely and accurately and the impulse to sentimentalize and mythologize it. At his best Bagby's observations of plantation life were shaped by an admirable blending of accuracy and objectivity with genuine affection for his subject. "My Uncle Flatback's Plantation," "Fishing in the Appomattox," and "Cornfield Peas" illustrate the skillful combination of nostalgia and humor that made George William Bagby the most popular Virginia humorist of the nineteenth century.

• The Virginia Historical Society has the Bagby family papers (over 53,000 items) and the George William Bagby papers (over 1,600 items, including correspondence and diaries). Both collections are thoroughly catalogued and provide extensive lists of correspondents. Joseph Leonard King, *Dr. George William Bagby: A Study of Virginia Literature, 1850–1880* (1927), remains the only complete biography. Biographical-critical treatments include Ritchie Devon Watson, Jr., *The Cavalier in Virginia Fiction* (1985) and "George William Bagby," in the *Encyclopedia of American Humorists* (1988); and Robert Bain and Joseph Flora, eds., *Fifty Southern Writers before 1900: A Bio-bibliographical Sourcebook* (1987).

RITCHIE DEVON WATSON, JR.

BAGLEY, Sarah George (29 Apr. 1806–?), millworker, reformer, and physician, was born in Candia, New Hampshire, the daughter of Nathan Bagley and Rhoda Witham, farmers.

Bagley grew up in a family whose economic situation became increasingly precarious during the course of the nineteenth century. Nathan Bagley originally farmed land in Candia, which he had inherited from his father, but he later moved on to farming land in Gilford, New Hampshire. After losing litigation in 1822, he sold his land in Gilford and eventually moved to Meredith Bridge, New Hampshire (now Laconia), where he became an incorporator of the Strafford Cotton Mill Company in 1833. However, Nathan Bagley did not own a home after 1824; it was Sarah Bagley who made the down payment on a house for her family in Meredith Bridge in the 1840s. She probably used money she had saved during her stints as a factory worker in Lowell, Massachusetts.

Bagley began work in Lowell in 1837 as a weaver for the Hamilton Company. She moved to the dressing room in 1840 and worked there until 1842, but then returned to weaving, this time for the Middlesex Company. In between stints as a factory operative in the 1840s, Sarah also worked at dressmaking in 1845 and as superintendent of the Lowell telegraph office in 1846.

Her life as a wage earner in Lowell allowed her not only to contribute to the economic well-being of her family but also to participate in a wide variety of reform activities in Lowell and in New England. Bagley was most famous for her leading role in the movement to establish a ten-hour workday in Massachusetts, which she argued would provide working people with the leisure time necessary for moral improvement and thus more sweeping reforms.

Bagley championed the ten-hour cause as president of the Lowell Female Labor Reform Association (LFLRA) from its founding in December 1844 until January 1847. During this time, the organization grew from fifteen members to several hundred. The organization became the voice of many more in its petitioning campaigns to the Massachusetts legislature that garnered thousands of signatures demanding a ten-hour workday at a time when factories commonly ran for thirteen or fourteen hours per day. Under Bagley's leadership, the LFLRA also purchased the *Voice of Industry*, which had been created by the New England Workingmen's Association to press for a shorter workday and to improve the lives of working people. Bagley sat on the editorial board of the *Voice* and briefly served as editor. She was also one of the movement's most important speakers and organizers. At a time when few women spoke publicly, Bagley testified before the Massachusetts legislature on the need for a ten-hour workday. She was also the first woman to publicly address the New England Workingmen's Association, at their meeting in June 1845. When operatives in Manchester, New Hampshire, met to form an association in December 1845, Bagley was there to assist.

As Bagley pushed for a shorter workday, she added an important voice to the labor movement, a voice that blended the concerns of a single wage earner with those of a woman. In critiquing the ten-hour system from a female point of view, Bagley astutely manipulated the language of female benevolence and motherhood. She pointed out that women were supposed to cultivate a virtuous character for their future roles as mothers and yet were denied this opportunity when locked in a factory all day long. She noted that Lowell factory women were supposed to appear well groomed in public, particularly in church, and yet they had no time to clean and repair their clothes. Their physical well-being was also undermined by a lack of time to eat and bathe.

Bagley made her criticisms within a growing tradition of "practical Christianity." She drew on a broad Christian tradition, rather than the specific theology of any particular denomination, and stressed the importance of fundamental Christian values such as brotherly love. This orientation was in line with the anti-institutionalism of radical reformers in other movements such as antislavery and temperance who criticized fellow Christians, particularly clergymen, for their failure to support widespread social reform. Her commitment was summed up in her defense of free expression when speaking in May 1846 to the Circle for Mutual Improvement in Lowell: "We are in no danger of infidelity or fanaticism, by free discussion; and he who would shut up a free soul, within the narrow limits of a creed, in these days of Progress and Reform, has yet to learn, that the mind of man is greater than all parchment, and will not be driven into dark caverns by any theology save that written by the Great Architect, on the blue arch of heaven."

Bagley displayed a broad-based interest in social reform. On a trip to New Hampshire in 1846, she visited a model prison, reporting that it had better hours than a factory. On the same trip she visited an insane asylum, which she praised for its orderliness. She also drew on phrenology to describe some of the inmates. When women from Lowell submitted a petition to the U.S. Congress in 1846 for the creation of an international tribunal to adjudicate disputes and end the need for wars, Bagley's name was at the top. Her commitment to widespread social reorganization was also clear in her Fourierist leanings: she was vice president of the Lowell Union of Associationists and had petitioned the Northampton Association for admission in 1844 (she was turned down).

Bagley's role as a public reformer came to a halt at the end of 1846, precipitated in part by a falling out with the editor of the *Voice of Industry*. She took a job at a telegraph office for a year. Bagley explained the dramatic changes in her life in a letter to Fourierist Marietta Martin. She claimed the editor of the *Voice* had criticized her writing as too radical and the "Female Department" (a weekly column in the newspaper) as undignified. She faced further discrimination at the telegraph office, where she was paid significantly less money than the man who had previously done the same job; she felt this economic bind even more deeply as she tried to support her aging parents.

Commenting that her life in service of the public good was nearly concluded, Bagley added bitterly, "I am sick at heart when I look into the social world and see woman so *willingly* made a dupe to the beastly selfishness of man. . . . I most fervently thank Heaven that I have never introduced into existence a being to suffer the privations that I have endured." Sarah returned to Lowell in 1848 for a final stint as a factory operative. By 1850 she was living in Philadelphia.

Sometime between 1850 and 1851 she married physician James Durno and moved to Albany, New York, where she resided for the next decade. Durno operated a business in Albany selling "Durno's Family Medicines." By the mid-1850s he was primarily engaged in running the business, while Bagley had become the practioner. She advertised her services in the city directory as a rheumatic physician who was willing to travel throughout the countryside and who specialized in the diseases of women and children. Her frustrations with collective struggle for social reform and her growing concerns about the inequitable treatment of women found their expression during the 1850s in her medical practice.

In 1861 Bagley and her husband disappeared from Albany, leaving the circumstances of her death a mystery. Her public life was short but important. She was an innovative reformer who integrated different strands of criticism to forge a wide-ranging critique of inequality and to propose solutions to these problems. Her significance continues to be clear in the analyses of her activities by historians of women and the labor movement.

• Letters by Sarah Bagley are in the Lilly Martin Spencer Papers, 1825–1971, Archives of American Art, Smithsonian Institution, and in the Thomas Dorr Papers of the John Hay Library, Brown University. Most of Sarah Bagley's published work appears in the *Voice of Industry*, 1844–1847. The best biography of her is Helena Wright, "Sarah Bagley: A Biographical Note," *Labor History* 20 (1979): 398–413. The importance of Bagley's thought and activities are also clear in Thomas Dublin, *Women at Work: The Transformation of Work and Community in Lowell, Massachusetts, 1826–1860* (1979); Frances H. Early, "A Reappraisal of the New England Labour-Reform Movement of the 1840s: The Lowell Female Labor Reform Association and the New England Workingmen's Association," *Histoire Sociale* 13 (1980): 33–54; Jama Lazerow, "Religion and the New England Mill Girl: A New Perspective on an Old Theme," *New England Quarterly* 60 (1987): 429–53; David A. Zonderman, *Aspirations and Anxieties: New England Workers and the Mechanized Factory System, 1815–1850* (1992); and Teresa Anne Murphy, *Ten Hours' Labor: Religion, Reform, and Gender in Early New England* (1992).

TERESA ANNE MURPHY

BAGLEY, William Chandler (15 Mar. 1874–1 July 1946), educator and author, was born in Detroit, Michigan, the son of William Chase Bagley, the superintendent of Harper Hospital in Detroit, and Ruth Walker. He enrolled in Michigan Agricultural College (later Michigan State College) in 1891 and received his baccalaureate degree in 1895. Unable to find a suitable position in agriculture during the depression of the 1890s, he took a job in a one-teacher school in Garth, in the Upper Peninsula of Michigan. Bagley began graduate study in the summer of 1896 at the University of Chicago, where he became interested in the scientific study of education. He then returned to teaching but again enrolled in graduate school, this time at the University of Wisconsin, where he received a master's degree in 1898 after studying psychology with Joseph Jastrow and education with Michael Vincent O'Shea. Later, Bagley continued his studies in psychology at Cornell University under E. B. Titchener, earning a Ph.D. in 1900. He was appointed principal at Meramec Elementary School in St. Louis, Missouri, in 1901. That same year he married Florence MacLean Winger of Lincoln, Nebraska, who had been a fellow student at Cornell; they had four children.

Bagley left St. Louis for State Normal College in Dillon, Montana, where he served as director of the training school and professor of psychology. With his first book, *The Educative Process* (1905), Bagley identified himself with social efficiency, a doctrine then just emerging in education. Social efficiency emphasized the importance of teaching useful subjects and advocated a structure of schooling designed to serve the national interest rather than individual purposes. From 1903 to 1906 Bagley served as superintendent of the Dillon public schools. He resigned in 1906 to become superintendent of the training school and instructor in educational theory at the State Normal School in Oswego, New York. After the publication of his popular second book, *Classroom Management* (1907), Bagley was offered three university professorships. In 1908 he accepted an appointment as professor of education at the University of Illinois, where he remained for nine years.

Although Bagley continued to be a proponent of social efficiency as the defining doctrine for American education over the course of his career, his commitment to democratic values kept him from adopting some of the theory's most controversial precepts. In a debate with David Snedden in 1914, for example, he opposed the early division of students according to probable destination and the establishment of separate vocational high schools. Such premature differentiation, he argued, was antithetical to equal educational opportunity.

In 1917 Bagley accepted a professorship at Teachers College, Columbia University, in the areas of teacher training, curriculum development, and school organization and management. His position on certain issues, such as his opposition to the junior high school, earned him a reputation as a conservative in educational matters. Much of his thinking throughout his career was permeated by a desire for greater continuity from one school to the next across the elementary school curriculum, and he saw the junior high school as a threat to the integrity of the eight-year elementary school curriculum.

Bagley was one of a few professional educators of his time who perceived a danger to democratic ideals in some of the tenets of the mental measurement movement. In a farsighted critique set forth in his *Determinism in Education* (1925), Bagley argued that "fatalisic conclusions," such as setting sharp limits on children's educability, were being drawn by proponents of intelligence testing.

During his tenure at Teachers College, Bagley earned a national reputation as an opponent of child-centered education. His identification as a conservative was reinforced when he assumed leadership of the "Essentialist movement" in the 1930s. Essentialists were critical of what they regarded as the soft pedagogy that had been inflicted on American schools by Progressive educators. In 1938 Bagley issued his "An Essentialist's Platform for the Advancement of American Education," a pronouncement designed to herald organized opposition to Progressivism (*Educational Administration and Supervision* 24 [Apr. 1938]: 241–56). Objecting to the lack of rigor and coherence in American education, Bagley argued that an effective democracy required exacting study and mastery of basic subjects. Essentialism, however, attracted few adherents in the educational world of the time and was virtually disbanded by 1942. Bagley died in New York City.

Bagley's opposition to Progressive education in general and his leadership of the Essentialists in particular have served to cast him as an educational conservative who sought to restrict educational reform in the twentieth century. Sometimes forgotten in that characterization is his courage and integrity in espousing unpopular causes, such as opposing the excesses of the mental measurement movement at the height of its public acceptance. As early as 1924, for example, he detected elements of what he called "pro-Nordic propaganda" in some of the implications that were being drawn by some psychologists from the results of intelligence testing. Whatever may have been his stand on particular issues, Bagley never wavered from a genuine commitment to democratic values.

• Bagley's major works not mentioned in the text include *Craftmanship in Teaching* (1911); *Educational Values* (1911); *Human Behavior: A First Book in Psychology for Teachers* (1913), with Stephen S. Colvin; *School Discipline* (1914; repr. 1915); *The History of the American People* (1918), with Charles A. Beard; *The Nation and the Schools* (1920), with John A. H. Keith; *The Professional Education of Teachers for American Public Schools* (1920), with William S. Learned; *The Mastery Speller* (1928), with James H. Smith; *Education, Crime and Social Progress* (1931); *Education and the Emergent Man* (1934); *A Century of the Universal School* (1937); and *America Yesterday and Today* (1938), with Roy F. Nichols and Charles A. Beard. For biographical details, consult I. L. Kandel, *William Chandler Bagley: Stalwart Educator* (1961). A brief assessment of his educational ideas is contained in Morman

Woelfel, *Molders of the American Mind* (1933); his work is discussed passim in Edward Krug, *The Shaping of the American High School* (1964), and in Herbert Kliebard, *The Struggle for the American Curriculum, 1893–1958* (1986).

HERBERT M. KLIEBARD

BAILAR, John Christian, Jr. (27 May 1904–17 Oct. 1991), chemist and educator, was born in Golden, Colorado, the son of John Christian Bailar, an instructor in chemistry at the Colorado School of Mines at Golden, and Rachel Ella Work. His parents were the first married couple to enroll at and graduate from the University of Colorado. His father was a great raconteur, a trait that the son would share. Bailar often accompanied his father to his office-laboratory, where he acquired much chemical knowledge by performing simple laboratory operations, such as folding filter paper and pouring solutions through funnels.

At age thirteen Bailar obtained his first job—constructing shipping crates at the Coors Porcelain Company in Golden, where he later worked on a construction gang and was employed as a chemist analyzing clay. During summers in his high school and college years, he worked at the Coors "bottle house," where near beer (a malt beverage with an alcohol content of less than .5 percent) was bottled and packed (Prohibition was in effect). He attended his parents' alma mater, the University of Colorado at Boulder, from which he graduated in 1924 with a B.A. magna cum laude. During the summer of 1924 he registered as a graduate physics major at the University of Michigan, taking courses in electromagnetism, atomic structure, and X-ray diffraction.

With the aid of a fellowship, Bailar spent a year at the University of Colorado, where he received his M.A. in inorganic chemistry in 1925 with a thesis on nitrogen tetrasulfide and nitrogen selenide. He received a fellowship at the University of Michigan, where he earned his Ph.D. in organic chemistry (1928) with a dissertation on halogen substituted pinacols. His research was supervised by organic chemist Moses Gomberg, famed for his work on free radicals. Later Bailar deliberately eschewed the example of Gomberg, who supervised his students closely. Instead, he gave his research students much freedom and the opportunity to plan and perform their own experiments.

In 1928 Bailar became instructor in organic chemistry at the University of Illinois, Urbana, where he remained for sixty-three years, almost half the time of the school's existence. He became associate in 1930, assistant professor in 1935, associate professor in 1939, professor in 1943, and professor emeritus in 1972. In 1931 he married Florence Leota Catherwood, his former graduate teaching assistant. They had two sons, both of whom would occupy prominent academic positions; the younger one, Benjamin Franklin Bailar, also served as U.S. postmaster general (1975–1978). Bailer's wife died in 1975 and the following year he married Katharine Reade Ross, who had been his babysitter when he was a child.

Although Bailar had been interested in organic isomerism as a graduate student, it was only while teaching a general chemistry course at Urbana that he realized that isomerism, the occurrence of different compounds with the same chemical composition, is a general phenomenon that can also exist among inorganic compounds. In his literature search for examples of inorganic isomers, he encountered coordination chemistry, a field that, like inorganic chemistry itself, had been neglected in the United States. He trained several generations of coordination chemists (ninety doctorates, thirty-eight postdoctoral fellows, and numerous bachelor's and master's degree candidates), making the University of Illinois, already a leading center of organic chemistry in the United States, equally renowned for inorganic chemistry. He soon became universally acknowledged as the "father of American coordination chemistry."

When Bailar began his career at Illinois, inorganic chemistry was languishing in the United States, where, of the small number of inorganic chemists, most, like him, were overburdened with teaching duties in general chemistry. Few inorganic courses existed, little inorganic research was being carried out, and there were few avenues for publication. At the fall 1933 meeting of the American Chemical Society (ACS), five prominent inorganic chemists decided that there was a need for a series of volumes giving detailed, independently tested methods for the synthesis of inorganic compounds in the manner of *Organic Syntheses*, a series founded by Roger Adams, Bailar's Illinois colleague. Bailar joined the editorial board of the new journal *Inorganic Syntheses*, the first volume of which appeared in 1939. He was an active participant and motivating force in its affairs, contributing sixteen syntheses and checking five others and serving as editor in chief of volume four (1953). Similarly, he helped establish the ACS Division of Inorganic Chemistry in 1957 and became its first chairman. In 1962 *Inorganic Chemistry*, the first such journal in the English language, began publication, largely through his efforts.

Bailar considered his most significant achievement to be his first work on coordination chemistry (carried out in 1934 with senior undergraduate student Robert W. Auten), which established the inorganic counterpart of the well-known organic Walden inversion reaction. This work resulted in a 37-part series, "The Stereochemistry of Complex Compounds," issued until 1985. Although stereochemistry (the study of the spatial arrangement of atoms in molecules and its chemical and physical consequences) was his primary interest, he also studied electrochemistry, electrodeposition, electroplating, polarography, homogeneous and heterogeneous catalysis, kinetics, stabilization of unusual oxidation states, dyes, and spectra. In 1959, with later (1990) Nobel laureate Elias J. Corey, he published a classic article on octahedral complexes that led to applications of conformational analysis to coordination compounds. Although an accomplished chemist and administrator, his first love was teaching, and he received the ACS Award in Chemical Education in 1961.

Long active in the ACS, Bailar served as chairman of several of its divisions (Chemical Education, 1947; Physical and Inorganic Chemistry, 1950; Inorganic Chemistry, 1957) and as national president (1959). A member of the editorial or publication boards of twelve journals, he received numerous honors and awards, including the Priestley Medal (the ACS's highest award, 1964) and the only Werner Gold Medal (1966) ever awarded by the Swiss Chemical Society. He was also the first recipient of the University of Illinois's John C. Bailar, Jr., Medal, named in his honor. After retiring in 1972, he continued to spend seven, rather than his previous twelve, hours in his office. He died of a sudden heart attack in Urbana, Illinois. A Bailar Fellowship for chemistry graduate students was established at the university in his honor.

The resurgence of inorganic chemistry after World War II, known as "the renaissance of inorganic chemistry," owed much to the pioneering efforts of Bailar, who also, more than any other person, was responsible for the advancement of coordination chemistry in the United States.

• Bailar's personal papers are in the Archive Library of the University of Illinois, Urbana. In addition to his 338 publications, which include two patents and fifty-eight reviews, Bailar wrote, co-wrote, or edited nine monographs, texts, or laboratory manuals. *The Chemistry of the Coordination Compounds* (1956), written with twenty-four of his former students, summarized almost every aspect of the field. In "The Paradox of Alpha Chi Sigma," *Hexagon of Alpha Chi Sigma* 54 (1963): 3, 4, 11, he discusses his early life and career. An interview with A. B. P. Lever is "A Celebration of Inorganic Lives: Interview of John Bailar," *Coordination Chemistry Reviews* 106 (1990): 1–23. Biographical articles include George B. Kauffman, "Éloge: John C. Bailar, Jr.," *Journal of Coordination Chemistry* 28 (1993): 183–89; Kauffman et al., "John C. Bailar, Jr. (1904–1991): Father of Coordination Chemistry in the United States," *Coordination Chemistry Reviews* 128 (1993): 1–48, which provides six portraits, a complete bibliography, and lists of Ph.D. and postdoctoral students); and Kauffman et al., "John C. Bailar, Jr. (1904–1991): Father of U.S. Coordination Chemistry," in *Coordination Chemistry: A Century of Progress*, ed. Kauffman (1994), pp. 74–80. Obituaries are in *Chemical and Engineering News* 69, no. 43 (28 Oct. 1991): 46–47; and *University of Illinois School of Chemical Sciences Alumni Newsletter* (Fall 1991), insert; and by Stanley Kirschner, "John C. Bailar, Jr.: A Fond Remembrance of the Impact of Personality on Chemical Research and Education," *American Chemical Society Division of Chemical Education Newsletter* (Fall 1992), p. 16.

GEORGE B. KAUFFMAN

BAILEY, Alice Anne La Trobe-Bateman (16 June 1880–15 Dec. 1949), founder of a spiritual movement growing out of the Theosophical tradition, was born in Manchester, England, the daughter of Frederic Foster La Trobe-Bateman, a prosperous engineer and member of a socially prominent family, and Alice Hollinshead. She spent major parts of her early life in Canada and Switzerland because of her father's work. Her mother died when she was six; her father, when she was nine; thereafter she lived on the estate of her grandfather John Frederic La Trobe-Bateman, a wealthy and very well known engineer. She was unhappy as a child, despite mystical tendencies. Her religious upbringing was in the conservative evangelical wing of the Church of England. After finishing school at eighteen, she worked from 1899 to 1907 for the Young Women's Christian Association in a ministry to British troops, which included delivering highly evangelical sermons, first in Ireland and then in India. She met her future husband, Walter Evans, then a soldier, in India. They were married in 1907 in Britain. She then went with him to the United States, where he studied for the Episcopal priesthood in Cincinnati. After his ordination in 1910, they moved to Reedley, California, where he was given a church. They had three daughters. The marriage was not a success, however, and in 1915 they separated, divorcing in 1919. Alice retained custody of the children.

For a time after the separation Alice Evans worked long hours in a fish cannery in Pacific Grove, California. While there she attended a Theosophical lecture. Despite an initial negative reaction, she studied Theosophy and found certain of its ideas appealing: a divine plan for the world, the hierarchy of Masters, karma, and reincarnation. One factor of personal importance was recognizing in a Theosophical portrait a bearded figure, identified as one of the Theosophical Masters, whom she had seen in a vision as a child and had thought was Christ. She joined the Theosophical Society and, in 1917, moved to Hollywood, California, where she worked in the vegetarian cafeteria at Krotona, a Theosophical study center. In 1919 she met Foster Bailey, the national secretary of the Theosophical Society, whom she would marry in 1921.

Alice Evans's relation with Theosophy was soon under strain, however, as a result of her claims to having had a new revelation in the Theosophical tradition. In November 1919, as she was walking in the Hollywood Hills near Krotona, she believed she was contacted by a Master, Djwhal Khul, known popularly as "The Tibetan," who wanted her to serve as his amanuensis. He began dictating to her via telepathy. The first book produced in this way, *Initiation: Human and Solar*, was begun in 1920 and appeared in 1922; it was followed by nineteen others over the next thirty years. Uniformly bound in blue, they comprise the basic texts of the Alice Bailey work.

Resentment of her claims by some Theosophists, and disgruntlement on her part at being denied membership in the Esoteric Section, an elite inner circle of Theosophists, led Alice Evans and Foster Bailey to leave Krotona and Theosophy in 1920. They went to New York, where they established the Lucis Trust to publish her books in 1922. In 1923 they founded the Arcane School, a training organization for students of her teaching. The remainder of her life was spent in writing on behalf of The Tibetan and in running the school. In 1937 she published the prayer called "The Great Invocation," which came to be widely used in occult and "New Age" circles. After Alice Bailey's death in New York, Foster Bailey continued to head the Arcane School and the Lucis Trust until his death in 1977.

In addition to standard Theosophical teaching, Bailey's work advanced two distinctive points. It developed an eschatological emphasis, pointing toward, in the title of one of the books, *The Reappearance of the Christ* (1948). She believed that the exigencies of the twentieth century raised the spiritual yearning and need of humankind to such a pitch that the Christ principle, Christ as a spiritual force, is being brought closer. Its manifestation, however, requires the assistance of group meditation, the second distinctive feature of Bailey's teaching. Adherents form meditation groups that customarily meet at the full moon to focus energies preparing for the return of the Christ.

Bailey's work has taken root throughout the English-speaking world and elsewhere. Although it probably peaked in size and influence in the two or three decades after the Second World War, it remained a potent force in the occult world. Never highly centralized, it has enjoyed the sponsorship of several organizations: the Arcane School, the School of Esoteric Studies in New York, Meditation Groups for the New Age in Ojai, California, and others. Bailey's "Tibetan" books are recognized as occult classics, and directly or indirectly have affected millions of twentieth-century lives.

• Basic sources are Alice A. Bailey, *The Unfinished Autobiography* (1951), and—though an apologia—Sir John R. Sinclair, *The Alice Bailey Inheritance* (1984). Shorter treatments may be found in J. Stillson Judah, *The History and Philosophy of the Metaphysical Movements in America* (1967), and J. Gordon Melton, *Biographical Dictionary of American Cult and Sect Leaders* (1986).

ROBERT S. ELLWOOD

BAILEY, Ann Hennis Trotter (1742–22 Nov. 1825), revolutionary war scout, was born in Liverpool, England. Little is known about her parents, although it is believed that her father had been a soldier under the duke of Marlborough's command. As Bailey was literate, she received an education in Liverpool, although details of it are not recorded. Orphaned as a young adult, she immigrated to America in the wake of relatives named Bell. She arrived in Staunton, Virginia, at the Bells' home, in 1761. In 1765 she married Richard Trotter, a frontiersman and Indian fighter, and they had a son in 1767. Lord Dunmore, the royal governor of Virginia, recruited men in 1774 to fight the marauding Indians who were disrupting the settlers on or near the Scioto River. Richard Trotter volunteered and followed Colonel Charles Lewis to the point where the Kanawha and Ohio rivers meet, known as Point Pleasant. He was killed in the battle there on 10 October 1774.

In order to "avenge" her husband's death, Bailey began her career as a frontier scout, "clad in buckskin pants, with petticoat, heavy brogan shoes, a man's coat and hat" armed with knife and tomahawk and a "long rifle on her shoulder" (Ellet, pp. 249, 251). Nineteenth-century interpretation of Bailey's choice of career is critical of her step beyond the traditional female role. She is described as "short and stout, and of coarse and masculine appearance" while "among her masculine habits" she drank hard liquor and would exercise "her skill in boxing." She scouted for and relayed messages to the existing forts in order to protect the pioneer families in the Shenandoah Valley from hostile Indians. During the Revolution Bailey served as a spy, keenly aware that many of the indigenous population were allied with the British. As she traversed the Shenandoah Valley from one frontier outpost to another, Bailey actively recruited patriots to join the militia.

On 3 November 1785 she married John Bailey, a member of a frontier group called the "Rangers." He spent much of his time "hunting and fighting hostile Indians," and when he was assigned to the garrison at Fort Lee (also known as "Clendenin's Settlement"; now Charleston, W.Va.), they moved there. As they had no children, marriage did not detract from her own duties, and she continued riding horseback between outposts and living a rugged outdoor life.

Bailey's most famous exploit occurred in 1791. The area around Fort Lee had been the site of frequent Indian attacks on families. One particular night, when the outpost was surrounded by Indians and gunpowder supplies were crucially low, Bailey volunteered to ride to Fort Savannah (also called Fort Union) near present-day Lewisberg, West Virginia, to get the needed supplies. Passing stealthily through the Indians surrounding the fort, without harm, she journied a hundred miles through a "track-less forest" and reached Fort Savannah safely. The commandant of the fort gave her two fresh horses, one to ride and the other to carry the gunpowder. Completing her mission within a period of three days, she singlehandedly saved Fort Lee from certain destruction.

Much of the Indian hostility ended in the Kanawha Valley area after the Indian chief Little Turtle signed the Treaty of Greenville with General Anthony Wayne in 1795. The treaty followed Wayne's victory over the Indians at the Battle of Fallen Timbers (in the Ohio Country) in 1794, which firmly established the power of the U.S. government. Bailey continued her frontier life, however. She became well known to the people of West Virginia, who always greeted her warmly as she rode about on her horse "Liverpool." The Shawnee Indians of the area called her "The White Squaw of the Kanawha" and thought the "Great Spirit" protected her. The settlers called her "Mad Ann Bailey" because she knew no fear.

Her son, William Trotter, and his wife settled on the Kanawha River in 1814, and Bailey lived with them for three years. When William sold his property in 1817, Bailey moved with the family to a former French settlement, Gallipolis, Ohio, where she died. Bailey became a legend in Gallia County, Ohio. As the person solely responsible for saving Fort Lee by her famous ride to Lewisberg, she gained prominence as the "Heroine of the Great Kanawha Valley." In 1861 a

U.S. Cavalry man, Charles Robb, wrote a poem entitled "Ann Bailey" to commemorate her famous ride.

• No collection of Bailey papers exists, and little information is available about Bailey's life. A monologue by Frank Hill, "The True Life of Anne [*sic*] Bailey," was donated to the Gallia County Historical Society in 1979. Other works to consult are Elizabeth Ellet, *The Pioneer Women of the West* (1852; repr. 1973); William Oliver Stevens, *Famous Women of America* (1956); and Arnold Dolin, *Great American Heroines* (1960). In addition, Livia Nye Simpson-Poffenbarger edited and published a monograph entitled *Ann Bailey: Thrilling Adventures of the Heroine of the Kanawha Valley, Truth Stranger Than Fiction as Related by Writers Who Knew the Story* (1907). General histories of the battle of Point Pleasant include Lisa Wilson, *Life after Death: Widows in Pennsylvania, 1750–1850* (1992); Simpson-Poffenbarger, *The Battle of Point Pleasant: A Battle of the Revolution* (1909); and Reuben Gold Thwaites and Louise Phelps Kellogg, eds., *Documentary History of Dunsmore's War, 1774* (1989).

HEDDA LAUTENSCHLAGER

BAILEY, Buster (19 July 1902–12 Apr. 1967), jazz clarinetist and saxophonist, was born William C. Bailey in Memphis, Tennessee. Nothing is known of his parents. He attended the Clay Street School in Memphis, where he began studying clarinet at age thirteen. In 1917 he turned professional after joining the touring band of famed blues composer W. C. Handy, and it was during a trip to New Orleans with Handy that he first heard authentic jazz. In early 1919 he left Handy to move to Chicago, where he studied with Franz Schoepp, first clarinetist with the Chicago Symphony, and worked in Erskine Tate's Vendome Theatre Orchestra and doubled in Freddie Keppard's small jazz band at the Lorraine Gardens. In late 1923 or early 1924 Bailey replaced Johnny Dodds in King Oliver's Creole Jazz Band for an extensive tour that concluded with its return to the Lincoln Gardens in June 1924. In August 1922, while working with Carroll Dickerson at the Sunset Cafe, Bailey first met Louis Armstrong, who had just come up from New Orleans to join the Oliver band. Following Armstrong by one week, on 6 October 1924 Bailey left Oliver and joined Armstrong in the Fletcher Henderson Orchestra at New York's prestigious Roseland Ballroom. Bailey and Armstrong both made their first records with Henderson the next day and on or about 16 October backed up blues singer Ma Rainey with a small contingent of Henderson men.

Bailey also recorded as a freelancer from the mid-1920s on; his most enduring association was with Clarence Williams's studio groups sporadically from 1925 to 1937. One of the most active jazz clarinetists of his time, Bailey appeared on hundreds of records throughout the prewar years as accompanist to blues and vaudeville singers such as Bessie Smith, Sippie Wallace, Maggie Jones, Trixie Smith, Alberta Hunter, Eva Taylor, and Coot Grant as well as jazz singers, including Billie Holiday, Mildred Bailey, Maxine Sullivan, Una Mae Carlisle, Jerry Kruger, Midge Williams, and Teddy Grace.

Although working with Henderson enabled Bailey to play with the best jazzmen of the day, including trumpeters Joe Smith and Tommy Ladnier, trombonists Charlie Green and Jimmy Harrison, and tenor saxophonist Coleman Hawkins, he increasingly took time off for engagements with other bands. In April 1929 he left Henderson and in early May embarked on a European tour with singer and band leader Noble Sissle. After Bailey returned to the United States in late 1929, he worked in the bands of Edgar Hayes and Dave Nelson, rejoined Sissle for two years starting in 1931, and then returned to the Henderson fold in January 1934, leaving once more in November to join the Mills Blue Rhythm Band. He stayed with that organization from December 1934 to October 1935, at which time he went back to Henderson and remained until February 1937, when he left permanently to begin a long and fruitful association with former Henderson bassist John Kirby in the latter's newly formed swing sextet.

Unquestionably the result of his formal training, Bailey had developed a fluent clarinet technique early in his career. Indeed, had it not been for the racial temperament of the times, he may very well have gone on to perform in symphony orchestras. As he said many years later in an interview reprinted in *Hear Me Talkin' to Ya*: "One thing I'm happy to see is the integration that's been happening among musicians. . . . Years ago, if it had been like this when I came up I would be able to play with some symphony orchestra. I would have had more of an incentive to study because there would have been more of a prospect of my making a living the way I wanted to. Sure, we played concerts and overtures and numbers like that in the theatres, but when I started you couldn't even think, if you were a Negro, of making symphony orchestras."

On the evidence of his first jazz recordings, Bailey displayed a commendable technical assurance, but he lacked the passion and improvisatory skills of the foremost New Orleans clarinetists—Sidney Bechet, Johnny Dodds, and Jimmie Noone. He progressed rapidly, however, and his best performances of the early period are on the Henderson records of the late 1920s and mid-1930s. He also appeared on scores of records with other bands, most notably the Red Onion Jazz Babies, Erskine Tate, and Dave Nelson, and with a number of small groups in sessions organized by the prolific Clarence Williams. As busy as he was in the 1930s, Bailey always found time to participate in the small-band swing sessions that were common in that period. Thus, much of his characteristic work in those years can be found on the records of Henry "Red" Allen, Lil Armstrong, Leon "Chu" Berry, Roy Eldridge, Lionel Hampton, Wingy Manone, Red Norvo, Stuff Smith, Willie "The Lion" Smith, and a host of others, including those under his own leadership.

It was with the John Kirby small band, though, that Bailey finally found his most symbiotic musical setting. Perhaps no other jazz clarinetist but Bailey, except for Benny Goodman, could have executed the technically demanding parts written by Kirby and his trumpeter Charlie Shavers. The style of this group was as unique as it was well suited for Bailey's particular skills as a reader, a technician, and the possessor of a legitimately trained tone. Alternating swing versions of operatic arias and familiar classical themes with exotic original compositions and jazz standards, the Kirby sextet enjoyed successful engagements at many venues in New York, Chicago, and Los Angeles as well as recording extensively for both commercial labels and the Lang-Worth Radio Transcription Service. For the first time in his long career, the peripatetic, bustling nature of his earlier years with the big bands was now a thing of the past. Bailey remained a regular member of the Kirby band from 1937 through 1944 and occasionally appeared with the group for brief engagements in 1945 and 1946.

Buster Bailey spent most of his later years playing in and around New York. He worked with Wilbur De Paris from September 1947 to April 1949, and after a brief try at leading his own quartet went with trumpeter Red Allen in 1950 and trombonist "Big Chief" Russell Moore in 1952. A rare opportunity to perform theater music again presented itself in late 1953, when he joined the pit orchestra of *Porgy and Bess*. In 1954 he rejoined Allen for a job at the Metropole, but during this period he also started receiving calls for symphony rehearsals and concerts. Jazz festivals were becoming frequent venues in the late fifties and sixties, and Bailey performed at several of them, often in the company of Allen. In 1961 he participated in the film *Splendor in the Grass* and began working with Wild Bill Davison (1961–1963) and then with Red Richards's Saints and Sinners (1963–1964). He joined Louis Armstrong's All Stars in July 1965 and was still with them at the time of his death in Brooklyn, New York.

From the 1940s on, Bailey's most representative recordings were made with Red Allen, Armstrong, the Capitol Jazzmen, Buck Clayton, Wild Bill Davison, Bobby Donaldson, Pee Wee Erwin, Leonard Gaskin, Coleman Hawkins, Claude Hopkins, Jonah Jones, Billy Kyle, Red Richards, Rex Stewart, Joe Thomas, and Trummy Young. Also significant is the one album he made under his own name, *All About Memphis* (1958).

• What is known of Bailey's career must be gleaned from the many references to him in general jazz history books, of which the best accounts of his activities from the 1920s through the 1940s are provided in Gunther Schuller, *Early Jazz* (1968) and *The Swing Era* (1989); Stanley Dance, *The World of Swing* (1974); James Lincoln Collier, *The Making of Jazz: A Comprehensive History* (1978); Nat Shapiro and Nat Hentoff, eds., *Hear Me Talkin' to Ya: The Story of Jazz by the Men Who Made It* (1955); and Samuel B. Charters and Leonard Kunstadt, *Jazz: A History of the New York Scene* (1962). Biographies of major jazz figures who played important roles in Bailey's career are also helpful in determining his importance during these crucial years. These include Max Jones and John Chilton, *Louis: The Louis Armstrong Story* (1971); Collier, *Louis Armstrong: An American Genius* (1983); and Chilton, *Sidney Bechet: The Wizard of Jazz* (1987) and *The Song of the Hawk: The Life and Recordings of Coleman Hawkins* (1990). See also the posthumously published autobiography by Rex Stewart, *Boy Meets Horn* (1991).

Major sources of discographical information are Laurie Wright, *King Oliver* (1987); Tom Lord, *Clarence Williams* (1976); Walter C. Allen, *Hendersonia: The Music of Fletcher Henderson and His Musicians* (1973); Hans Westerberg, *Boy from New Orleans: Louis "Satchmo" Armstrong* (1981); Brian Rust, *Jazz Records, 1897–1942* (1982); and Walter Bruyninckx, *Traditional Jazz Discography, 1897–1988* (6 vols., 1985–1989) and *Swing Discography, 1920–1988* (12 vols., 1985–1989). Abbreviated career notations are found in Chilton, *Who's Who of Jazz* (1972), and Roger D. Kinkle, *The Complete Encyclopedia of Popular Music and Jazz*, vol. 2, *Biographies, A–K* (1974).

JACK SOHMER

BAILEY, DeFord (14 Dec. 1899–2 July 1982), musician, was born in Bellwood, Smith County, Tennessee, the son of John Henry Bailey and Mary Reedy, farmers. Bailey grew up in the rolling hills east of Nashville and as a child listened to what he later called "black hillbilly music" played by his family. His grandfather Lewis Bailey was a skilled fiddler who won numerous local championships, and a family string band often appeared at local fairs and dances. DeFord Bailey's own fascination with the harmonica, an instrument that was especially popular in Middle Tennessee, resulted from a childhood illness. When he was three he was stricken with polio and was bedfast for several years; to amuse himself he practiced the harmonica. Lying in bed and listening to the distant sound of trains, hunting dogs, and barnyard animals, he became adept at working imitations of these into his playing, creating unorthodox "bent" notes and mouthing patterns that would later make his musical style unique. Bailey survived the disease, but it left him stunted and frail.

By 1918 Bailey had moved to Nashville, where he worked at a variety of jobs for wealthy white families. In his spare time he went to local theaters, where he heard his first professional entertainers, including blues singers Bessie Smith and Ma Rainey. He soon adapted their songs to his harmonica and in 1925 entered a harmonica contest broadcast over local radio station WDAD. He won first place, embarrassing the management and forcing them to award two prizes, one for "each race." A short time later he met Humphrey Bate, a fellow harmonica player who was leading a string band that played for a large new Nashville radio station, WSM. Impressed with Bailey's playing, Bate recommended him to the station manager, George D. Hay, who invited him to appear on the new Saturday night "Barn Dance" (later called the Grand Ole Opry). In June 1926 Bailey made his first documented appearance on the show.

Bailey, playing his solo, non-chromatic harmonica, quickly became one of the most popular stars on the show. Radio fans, many of whom were unaware that Bailey was black, wrote hundreds of letters requesting his specialties, such as "The Fox Chase" and "Pan American Blues," in which he imitated a train. Hay made big plans for Bailey and told him that he was "nothing but a gold mine walking around on earth." Hay set up dates with several record companies, and

Bailey did sides for Columbia (1927), Brunswick (1927), and Victor (1928). Surprisingly, the records did not sell well, and some were never even released to the public. The surviving eleven sides preserve the only documentation of Bailey playing in his prime.

Bailey became a familiar figure around Nashville, riding a custom-designed bicycle back and forth to work. In 1929 he married Ida Lee Jones; they had three children.

Also in 1932 the Grand Ole Opry started an Artists Service Bureau to help its radio entertainers set up tours and personal appearances. Bailey overcame his nervousness about traveling and went on tours with other Opry stars like the Delmore Brothers, the Fruit Jar Drinkers, Uncle Dave Macon, Robert Lunn, and later Bill Monroe and Roy Acuff. Though he continued to be a favorite on live shows—he had to play his harmonica through a big megaphone to be heard over primitive public address systems—Bailey often had trouble finding lodging in the segregated South. Hotels that welcomed the other Opry musicians often refused Bailey a room, forcing him to seek accommodations in private homes of local black residents.

At about the time the Opry started winning a national audience on network radio, Bailey left the show. In 1941 he was fired; the official reason was that he refused to learn any new tunes. In truth it was a complex dispute involving a struggle between two song publishing organizations, ASCAP and BMI. In the 1920s Bailey had allowed his producer to publish and copyright his songs with ASCAP, and in 1941 ASCAP songs were banned from the airwaves as a result of a licensing dispute between ASCAP and the major radio networks. Bailey was being told he could not play his old favorites such as "John Henry" and "Fox Chase," songs with which he had made his reputation. Confused, bitter, and angered by the new styles of music he heard on the show, Bailey did not fight the firing, and he totally dropped out of music. During this time, he operated a shoe shine parlor in downtown Nashville, occasionally playing for friends but refusing to talk to journalists or historians about his early days.

By the late 1960s a new generation of fans began to see Bailey as a folk music hero. One of them, Vanderbilt student Dick Hulan, coaxed him into playing at local coffeehouses and festivals. He refused offers to record again, however, and turned down chances to go to the the Newport Folk Festival and to appear in films like Burt Reynolds's *W. W. and the Dixie Dancekings* (1975). In 1974 another young friend, David Morton, who worked with the Nashville Housing Authority, talked Bailey into returning to the Opry stage for an "Old Timers' Reunion." He returned to the Opry several other times before his death in Nashville.

Fans of country and folk music still speak of Bailey as the genre's finest harmonica virtuoso. His songs are still part of the standard repertoire, serving as an important link between rural nineteenth-century folk music and the more commercial music of the twentieth century. His struggle as the first black star in the nearly all-white world of country music has won the respect of generations.

• Bailey's own account of his life and times, dictated through a series of interviews, can be found in David Morton and Charles Wolfe, *DeFord Bailey: A Black Star in Early Country Music* (1991). Some of Bailey's 1920s recordings can be found on compact disc. An account of the early Grand Ole Opry show and Bailey's place in it is in Charles Wolfe, *Grand Ole Opry: The Early Years* (1975; repr. 1996).

CHARLES K. WOLFE

BAILEY, Ebenezer (25 June 1795–5 Aug. 1839), educator, was born in West Newbury, Massachusetts, the son of Paul Bailey and Emma Carr, farmers. Like so many sons of New England yeomanry, he grew up on a small but well-cultivated farm. He was the youngest of four children and the only one sent to college. In 1813, at the age of eighteen, Bailey entered Yale College and graduated with honors in 1817. After graduation he received a gift of $300 from his father, some of which he used to pay his college debts. With $70 remaining, Bailey planned to travel to the American South, but his plans changed as he attempted to help a needy friend who borrowed $50 and did not return it in the agreed time.

His original plans thwarted, Bailey purchased a private school for boys in New Haven. Its poor condition and unpromising prospects for improvement required an extraordinary effort on Bailey's part to improve the school's reputation and attract students. At the same time Bailey began to study law with the intention of making the practice of law his primary profession. The weight of these dual burdensome activities, attempted in less than a year after his graduation, overwhelmed Bailey, and his health began to deteriorate. As a result he sold the school and abandoned the study of law.

Bailey returned to his original plan of traveling to the South and went to Richmond, Virginia, to become a private tutor in 1818 for the aristocratic family of Colonel Carter. While in the colonel's employ Bailey recognized the need to provide a formal education for young women. In the journal that he kept for a few years he noted that "her mind is capable of higher and nobler attainments than to adjust a ribbon or display a gewgaw to the best advantage!" The education of young women became one of Bailey's lifetime goals. He remained in Virginia for little more than a year and returned to Massachusetts in 1819. That year he established a private school for young women in Newburyport.

Bailey was introduced to Allen Dodge, a Newburyport merchant, whose daughters attended Bailey's school. In 1825 he married Adeline Dodge, one of the merchant's daughters. They had five children. In 1823 he left the school for women to become headmaster of the Franklin Grammar School for Boys in Boston.

In February 1826 the first High School for Girls of Boston opened with 130 pupils drawn from an applicant pool of 286 candidates and with Bailey as its principal. The school was the first public high school for girls in the commonwealth and one of the first in the

United States. Previously young women received their education in private academies or seminaries. In many respects the high school was an experiment established by the Boston School Committee "for the instruction of girls in higher departments of science and literature." In the May 1825 report of the committee to consider the establishment of the school, the Reverend John Pierpont had revealed the committee's intent in creating the school: "As to the general expediency . . . of giving women such an education as shall make them fit wives for well educated men, and enable them to exert a salutary influence upon the rising generation . . . your committee . . . will confine themselves to the particular expediency of provision for a higher education of our daughters, at the public expense."

Ironically the school's success as reflected in its rapidly accelerating enrollment statistics led to its demise. The school committee had appropriated $2,000 for annual operating expenses. As enrollment increased, parents placed pressure on the committee to increase expenditures for additional facilities and faculty. In response the committee and Mayor John Quincy, Sr., proposed abolishing the newly founded high school by moving the course of instruction in advanced literature and science to the grammar schools and extending the school-leaving age for young women from fourteen to sixteen. Quincy and others objected to the expense of the school and argued that it was unwarranted when employment opportunities for women were so limited. Within two years after its creation the decision to terminate the girls' high school was made by the mayor with the advice and consent of the school committee.

The school committee and the mayor reasoned that it was better to abolish the High School for Girls because in their judgment an alternative existed in the grammar schools. In addition, they opposed on democratic grounds the recommendation from the school's supporters that admission standards be raised thereby restricting the number of admitted students. They opposed a school supported with public funds for the privileged despite the existence of boys' Latin and English high schools in Boston. On this score they rationalized that the expanding higher educational and professional opportunities for educated Boston boys warranted such expenditures while the opportunities for women were thwarted by tradition.

Bailey's response to the mayor's decision was swift. In 1828 he published a "Review of the Mayor's Report on the Subject of the Schools." In it he stated that though "the High School for Girls was but an 'experiment' it will not be denied that it was a very important one. It was the first institution of the kind. . . . " Yet his most telling criticism was directed at Quincy, whose decision Bailey believed was motivated by the mayor's efforts to placate the powerful grammar school masters who saw the High School for Girls as an institution that might weaken their grammar schools. Apparently the masters were in the process of introducing into their schools the less expensive monitorial system of education, which allowed students in a higher grade to supervise those in a lower grade, and thus wanted to retain the best female students as monitors for the larger student body. So, in addition to opposing the high school based on finances, the clashing interests of the two constituencies and their innovations doomed the high school experiment. A permanent high school for girls was not created until 1872.

Bailey was one of the pioneers in giving women an opportunity for higher education. In December 1827, after leaving the High School for Girls because of a dispute with the mayor, he opened his own Young Ladies High School in Boston. He admitted, without regard for financial means, the most deserving and talented students, expending much of his own money for desks, reference works, literature, and teaching aides imported from Europe that were new features in schoolrooms of the day.

As in many good academies of that era, Bailey's school curriculum included both ancient and modern languages and the sciences. An excellent body of teachers was employed to teach the students. Bailey regarded "the discipline of the mind and the acquisition of knowledge as the two ends of education." In a testament to the school's strength, the young women educated there were frequently sought after for teaching positions in private academies.

When the national financial crisis of 1837 struck, the school collapsed. Families of students hardest hit by the economic panic were unable to meet their tuition payments. As a result, Bailey could not pay salaries or other fixed costs. He sold the school, its furnishings, and books to another educator who died before paying Bailey for the school. The turn of events left Bailey without another buyer and nearly ruined him financially. Undeterred he took the small returns from his book royalties and began anew, opening a school for boys in Roxbury, Massachusetts, in 1838. But this time he limited the school to twenty pupils. In the spring of 1838 he moved it to Lynn but in July of that year he met misfortune once again. Bailey contracted lockjaw after stepping on a large nail. He died shortly thereafter at home in Lynn, ten days after the accident.

Bailey's friends were deeply stirred by his death and the many obituaries written about him speak of his high character as both a man and a teacher. One friend wrote, "I never knew a man . . . so kind and attentive to the feelings and happiness of others. Full of knowledge . . . wit and vivacity, he at once charmed and instructed."

Bailey achieved other noteworthy accomplishments. In 1830 he became one of the founders of the American Institute of Instruction, a nineteenth-century educational clearinghouse that presented programs and lectures on promising pedagogical practices and published proceedings, a journal, and volumes on education for practitioners. He was a frequent contributor of articles to the *Boston Courier*, and his poems often appeared in contemporary journals. In 1825 he was a competitor for the Prize Ode to be delivered at the Boston Theater on the anniversary of George Washington's birthday. He was several times appointed poet for the anniversaries of the Phi Beta Kappa of his alma mater, Yale College. He was a member of the City Council of Boston, director of the Home of Reform, president of the Boston Lyceum, and director of the Boston Mechanics Institute.

Bailey's textbooks include *The Young Ladies' Class Book* (1831), a selection of lessons for reading in prose and verse, and notes and questions for review in Frederick Collier Bakewell's *Philosophical Conversations* (1833), a treatise on English philosophy that was revised and adapted for use in American schools. His best-known work is the very popular *First Lessons in Algebra* (1833), which was designed for use by academies and common schools.

• Bailey's textbooks, including *Key to First Lessons in Algebra* (1844), are available in the Harvard University Gutman Library archives. This archival collection also contains a copy of Frederick Collier Bakewell's *Philosophical Conversations*. Henry Barnard, ed., *American Journal of Education* (1863), also known as *Barnard's Journal of Education*, vols. 12–13, located in the Boston Public Library, is an important source of information on Bailey; vol. 12, pp. 429–52, contains a short biography, and vol. 13 has a commentary on girls in the public schools of Boston and Bailey's response to the mayor's criticism. See also *American Biography*, vol. 9, a Boston Public Library Social Science Reference work.

ANTHONY PENNA

BAILEY, Florence Augusta Merriam (8 Aug. 1863–22 Sept. 1948), ornithologist, was born in Locust Grove, New York, the daughter of Clinton Levi Merriam, a banker, and Caroline Hart. She grew up on the family's country estate, Homewood, in the rural Adirondack foothills. Bailey's father encouraged his children's curiosity about nature and wildlife, camping and exploring with them in the countryside. He had met and corresponded with the naturalist John Muir. Bailey's mother had graduated from Rutgers Female Institute in New York City and taught her children astronomy. Her father's sister, Helen Bagg, promoted Bailey's interest in botany. Bailey often accompanied her older brother, Clinton Hart Merriam, when he collected specimens. She had access to professional opportunities and contacts because her father was elected to Congress in 1871, and her brother later became the first chief of the U.S. Biological Survey.

Bailey attended Mrs. Pratt's Seminary, a private school in Utica, New York, and was also tutored at home. In 1882 she enrolled at Smith College as a special student in a nondegree program because she lacked a formal education. The Smith curriculum emphasized literature and languages with few science courses. Bailey focused on English classwork, which aided her maturation as a gifted communicator.

While at Smith, Bailey read about the killing of birds to secure feathers for hats. Outraged, she organized the college's first Audubon Society to teach young women about birds. Bailey believed that if women were educated about birds they would quit demanding feathers for fashion. She also asked naturalist John Burroughs to lead nature walks for students on campus to expand their awareness of conservation. In 1885 she was invited to be the first "lady associate" member of the all-male American Ornithologists' Union.

Convinced that her purpose was "to leave the world better for my having lived," Bailey considered her talent for writing as the means to achieve her goal of promoting public awareness of nature. She wrote popular articles about birds and wildlife for *Audubon Magazine* while at Smith. Many of the articles, primarily observations of local wildlife in New York, were later collected in her first book, *Birds through an Opera Glass* (1889).

Bailey completed her classes at Smith in 1886 and, like many upper class, educated women of her era, she pursued social work. She focused on such issues as European immigrants living in urban slums and suffering from disease, poverty, and crime. She traveled one summer to Chicago to assist in a school for working girls located near Hull House. Then she helped in a similar women's club in New York City. During this time, she became infected with tuberculosis.

Bailey's physician ordered her to recuperate in a milder climate with fresh air, which was the standard tuberculosis cure because doctors were unaware of the bacterium that caused the disease and therapeutic antibiotics had not yet been discovered. Bailey initially sought tuberculosis treatment in Utah and Arizona. She wrote *My Summer in a Mormon Village* (1894), in which she focused on descriptions of nature she observed and people she met and commented about her travel experiences. Then she traveled to California; she attended classes at the Leland Stanford Junior University in 1893 and stayed at her uncle's ranch in San Diego County, California, through the next year.

Every morning Bailey rode around the ranch, observing migrating birds and noting their nesting patterns. She discovered western varieties, ecstatic over "a new bird world." She collected information about western bird populations, comparing the data with her studies of eastern birds. She wrote two books, *A-Birding on a Bronco* (1896) and *Birds of Village and Field* (1898), chronicling her observations. The latter was a popular guide.

Cured in 1896, Bailey moved to Washington, D.C., where her brother, at the time director of the U.S. Biological Survey, introduced her to area naturalists. Bailey, unlike many women scientists at that time, was not isolated from professional colleagues and facilities. She renewed her friendship with Vernon Bailey, a childhood acquaintance who was a naturalist for the Biological Survey, specializing in mammals, especially mice and moles. They married in 1899, and she accompanied him on government field trips to document southwestern and Plains mammals, reptiles, and plants. Through Arizona, New Mexico, Texas, and the Dakotas, the Baileys traveled by pack train on rutted wagon trails, hiked over mountains, and rode horses across the plains, camping in primitive, isolated and hazardous conditions. During these expeditions, Bailey observed and described indigenous birds, taking elaborate notes about ranges, diets, nests, eggs, and habits, which she transformed into articles, books, and documents at home in the winter.

In Washington, D.C., Bailey was a founding member of the local Audubon Society and taught classes in basic ornithology for area schoolteachers. She especially sought to encourage both professional and amateur birdwatchers and stressed the protection of natural resources in her lectures. The Baileys hosted major naturalists in their home, and she belonged to the Cooper Ornithological Club, the Wilson Ornithological Club, the Biological Society of Washington, and the National Audubon Society. Bailey also was active in the District of Columbia's Women's National Science Club, attempting to start branches elsewhere. Holding firmly to her humanitarian ideals, she also promoted literacy and child welfare.

In about 1900 Bailey began writing scientific books and articles instead of the popular nature pieces she had previously written. She differed from contemporary ornithologists in that she did not use dead specimens for identification and description. She insisted that ornithologists needed only "a scrupulous conscience, unlimited patience, a notebook, and an opera glass" and not a rifle. Bailey worried about birds' loss of habitat and how hunting threatened species. She wrote and lectured on conservation, mostly to Washington-area children. Bailey's affiliation with the U.S. Biological Survey provided her with crucial professional support, including office access and related resources.

Bailey's books were her major achievement. Critics called her a literary ornithologist and lauded her scholarship; hobbyists praised the usefulness of her books. Reviewers said that she was a keen, precise observer, stating that her words were "as sprightly and graceful as the birds themselves." During this time the number of amateur birdwatchers increased. Her guidebook, a *Handbook of Birds of the Western United States* printed in 1902, complemented Frank M. Chapman's *Handbook of Birds of Eastern North America*. Bailey's book was considered a standard reference, and it was reissued in several editions. She also contributed information about birds to her husband's books, *Wild Animals of Glacier National Park* in 1918 and *Cave Life of Kentucky* in 1933. Bailey's articles appeared in *Auk*, *Bird-Lore*, and the *Condor*.

Bailey's *Birds of New Mexico*, published in 1928, secured professional acclaim and acceptance for her. The American Ornithologists' Union had often treated Bailey as a subordinate, angering women ornithologists who disliked less qualified men receiving professional laurels they believed Bailey deserved. Bailey, however, lacked a college degree, specifically a doctorate (Smith awarded her a bachelor's diploma in 1921), or professional position similar to the credentials of most other members.

By 1901 Bailey was elected a full regular member of the American Ornithologists' Union on the basis of her publications. She was nominated for the rank of fellow in 1912 but was not elected until 1929. Two years later, she was the first woman honored with the Brewster Medal, the American Ornithologists' Union's highest award, for her book *Birds of New Mexico* (1928). Bailey's last major work was *Among the Birds in the Grand Canyon National Park* (1939).

Bailey's husband died in 1942. She continued their naturalist work until her death in Washington, D.C. Paul H. Oehser eulogized that Bailey had combined "an intense love of birds and remarkable powers of observation with a fine talent for writing and a high reverence for science." In 1908 Joseph Grinnell had named a variety of California mountain chickadee, *Parus gambeli baileyae*, in her honor, and both during her lifetime and after her death, Bailey inspired and influenced women ornithologists and scientists to pursue research careers.

• The Florence Merriam Bailey Papers are in the Bancroft Library at the University of California, Berkeley; they consist of letters to her brother C. Hart Merriam, field notes, journal notes, correspondence, and autobiographical writings. The Bancroft Library also holds the Harvey Monroe Hall Papers, which contain correspondence between Bailey and botanists Harvey Monroe Hall and his wife Carlotta Case Hall, and the C. Hart Merriam Papers. Smith College holds letters written by Bailey. The Fish and Wildlife Service Collection in the Smithsonian Institution Archives contains Bailey's field notes and reports. The Vernon Bailey Papers at the National Anthropological Archives of the Smithsonian Institution consist of photographs he took during his career that were donated by his wife. Bailey's life is reviewed in detail in Harriet Kofalk, *No Woman Tenderfoot: Florence Merriam Bailey, Pioneer Naturalist* (1989). Several works place Bailey within the context of her profession: Marcia Myers Bonta, *Women in the Field: America's Pioneering Women Naturalists* (1991); Frank M. Chapman and Theodore S. Palmer, eds., *Fifty Years' Progress of American Ornithology, 1883–1933* (1993); and Deborah Strom, ed., *Birdwatching with American Women: A Selection of Nature Writings* (1986). Paul H. Oehser wrote a memorial of Bailey in *Auk* 69 (1952): 19–26.

ELIZABETH D. SCHAFER

BAILEY, Francis (c. 1735–1815), printer and journalist, was born in Lancaster County, Pennsylvania, the son of Robert Bailey and Margaret McDill Barley, farmers. Bailey was apprenticed to Peter Miller, printer at Ephrata, at an early age, and by the time he began publishing the *Lancaster Almanac* in 1771, he had been making and setting type for more than twenty years. He published the almanac, with some assistance in the early years, until 1796. Bailey stayed in Lancaster until late 1778. His most notable achievements there consisted of printing the unremarkable *Das Pennsylvanische Zeitungs-Blat* (4 Feb.–24 June 1778) and his services as coroner for Lancaster County in 1777 and as a brigade-major of Pennsylvania troops at Valley Forge in 1778.

After being persuaded to go to Philadelphia by author Hugh Henry Brackenridge in late 1778, Bailey started the *United States Magazine* there with Brackenridge in January 1779. This publication, which Bailey produced until December 1779, was characterized by a strong affinity for political, economic, and religious themes displayed without stridency or passion. An unabashed supporter of the Pennsylvania Constitution of 1776, Bailey believed in expanding the suffrage, in a legislatively oriented government, in a strong self-sufficient state government, and in an economy in which entrepreneurial activity was open to all citizens. Supported by his political friends, in 1781 he became the official printer of both the Continental Congress and the state of Pennsylvania.

With the announcement that his pages were "open to all parties, but influenced by none," on 25 April 1781 Bailey began to print the *Freeman's Journal or the North American Intelligencer*. He operated the journal until 9 May 1792, all the while maintaining it as a newspaper whose columns were indeed open to all comers. Although he was a moderate Anti-Federalist, during the ratification struggle he nonetheless printed several important pieces authored by James Wilson, a vehement proponent of the popular election of both houses of Congress and the president, and during the newspaper battles of the early 1790s he stayed in the background, disappointing James Madison.

While building a reputation for openness in operating the *Freeman's Journal* during a period of strict partisanship on the part of newspaper editors, Bailey continued to function as official printer of the Continental Congress until its demise and for the state until his death. He also kept up his Lancaster printing business until 1805, doing state business there when that city served as the state capital. After 1797 Bailey ran printing establishments in Sadsbury (on the estate deeded to him by his parents), in Philadelphia, in Lancaster (until 1805), and in Octoraro (fourteen miles east of Philadelphia), employing ten to fifteen printing presses. He thus constitutes a prime example of the few early American printers who became publishing entrepreneurs and managed several establishments sustained by significant capital investment. After 1805 he gradually retired so that by his death he had stopped printing. Bailey had at least one son, Robert, who took over his printing endeavors after his retirement, but the identity of his wife is not known.

Bailey kept his life, like his politics, in perspective and was never a vindictive partisan. Unlike many of his journalistic competitors, who adopted a vociferously narrow editorial style, Bailey pursued his objectives of a gentle egalitarian society without stridency and by exhibiting a generous tolerance. As such he is distinguished as a printer who showed that civility, kindness, and moderation could produce success even in the highly argumentative atmosphere of the early national period.

• The best source for Bailey is his publications, which fortunately exist in large numbers in major repositories throughout the United States, especially at the Philadelphia Library Company and at the Historical Society of Pennsylvania. His life can be traced in part in Isaiah Thomas, *History of the Art of Printing in America* (1816), with William McCulloch's additions in *American Antiquarian Society Proceedings* (1921); E. P. Oberholtzer, *Literary History of Philadelphia* (1906); J. T. Scharf and T. Westcott, *History of Philadelphia* (1884); and Alexander Harris, *A Biographical History of Lancaster County* (1872). His public career can be followed in part in the *Journals of the Continental Congress* (34 vols., 1904–1937), and in the *Pennsylvania Archives and Colonial Records* and the *Pennsylvania Archives and State Records*.

WILLIAM F. STEIRER, JR.

BAILEY, Gamaliel (3 Dec. 1807–5 June 1859), antislavery journalist and political organizer, was born in Mount Holly, New Jersey, the son of Gamaliel Bailey, Sr., a silversmith and Methodist minister, and Sarah Page. As the son of a minister, Bailey enjoyed educational advantages and an early association with evangelical Christianity. Following the relocation of his family to Philadelphia in 1816, Bailey joined with several other adolescents in forming a literary debating society, which stimulated his lifelong interest in literature. He graduated from Jefferson Medical College in 1828, but medicine was never his main interest, and he ceased to practice it by the early 1840s.

Physically frail, Bailey shipped aboard a China trader in 1829 to improve his health. When he returned to the United States in 1830, the nation was entering an era of political upheaval, social reform, and sectional conflict over slavery. Bailey responded by becoming deeply involved in social and political issues. Unlike other northerners who became prominent reformers, however, Bailey worked in the border region between the North and the South. In slaveholding Baltimore, where in 1831 he edited the monthly *Methodist Protestant*, Bailey learned his journalistic craft and expressed mild opposition to slavery.

Bailey left Baltimore in 1832 and settled in Cincinnati, where in 1833 he married Margaret Lucy Shands. They had twelve children, six of whom survived infancy. While lecturing on physiology at Lane Theological Seminary in 1834, Bailey was drawn into immediate abolitionism by the famous student slavery debates. In 1836 he became the assistant editor of James G. Birney's *Philanthropist* and stood with Birney during riots against the newspaper. When Birney left Cincinnati in early 1837, Bailey became editor of the *Philanthropist* and emerged as the dominant figure in western abolitionism. In the late 1830s Bailey guided western abolitionists toward a type of antislavery politics that had broad appeal to northerners who were not themselves abolitionists. As the founder of the Ohio Liberty party in 1840, he pioneered the argument that antislavery political action must be restricted to abolishing slavery within the exclusive jurisdiction of Congress, while relying on moral suasion to encourage indigenous abolitionist movements in the slave states. It was on this platform that Bailey and his associate Salmon P. Chase led the majority of Liberty party voters into the Free-Soil coalition in 1848.

By the mid-1840s Bailey was the major Liberty party journalist and the choice of leading abolitionists to edit a new national antislavery newspaper in Washington, D.C. As editor of the prestigious *National Era* from 1847 until his death, Bailey had continuing influence on national politics. Combining antislavery articles with popular literature, he made the *Era* one of the most important weeklies in the country. He especially encouraged women authors, which led to the original publication of Harriet Beecher Stowe's *Uncle Tom's Cabin* in the *Era* in 1851–1852.

A person of intellect, humor, sophistication, and courage (he weathered a second riot in Cincinnati in 1841 and another in Washington in 1848), Bailey became an influential antislavery lobbyist in Congress and made his home the center of antislavery social life in the capital. His greatest achievement as a lobbyist came in 1854, when, during the struggle over the Kansas-Nebraska bill, he convinced anti-Nebraska Whigs and Democrats to meet in common caucus, which contributed to the founding of the Republican party.

Bailey had been among the first to call for a new major party committed to excluding slavery from the territories. For the rest of his life he struggled to keep the Republican party centered on the slavery issue. Despite failing health, he led campaigns against including antiforeign and anti-Catholic principles in its platform and against downplaying sectional issues in favor of Whig economic policies. At the urging of his doctors, who believed an ocean voyage might be therapeutic, Bailey set out by steamer for Europe in June 1859 only to die at sea. His career exemplifies the continuing impact of abolitionism on the Republican party throughout the 1850s.

• Collections containing the largest numbers of Bailey's letters are the Salmon P. Chase Papers in the Historical Society of Pennsylvania and the Library of Congress, the Joshua R. Giddings Papers in the Ohio Historical Society, the Gerrit Smith Papers in the Syracuse University Library, the Charles Francis Adams Papers in the Massachusetts Historical Society, the James S. Pike Papers in the Calais Free Library, and the Charles Sumner Papers and Palfrey Family Papers in the Houghton Library of Harvard University. Letters from Bailey to James Birney are published in Dwight L. Dumond, ed., *The Letters of James G. Birney, 1831–1857* (1938), and there are numerous letters to Bailey in the Lewis Tappan Papers in the Library of Congress. The only published biography of Bailey is Stanley Harrold, *Gamaliel Bailey and Antislavery Union* (1986).

STANLEY HARROLD

BAILEY, Hannah Clark Johnston (5 July 1839–23 Oct. 1923), philanthropist, reformer, and peace advocate, was born in Cornwall-on-the-Hudson, New York, the daughter of David Johnston, a tanner, and Letitia Clark. In 1853 her father moved the family to Plattekill, New York, where he became a farmer and minister of the Society of Friends (Quakers). She attended public school and a Friends' boarding school and taught in rural New York from 1858 to 1867. Accompanying a female Quaker preacher on a mission to New England churches, almshouses, and prisons, Bailey met her future husband, Moses Bailey, a fellow Society member and prosperous manufacturer of oil cloth. They were married in 1868 and settled at his Winthrop, Maine, home. They had one child.

Bailey and her husband traveled to Quaker churches in other cities. On an 1877 journey to North Carolina they founded a mission to organize schools for the indigent. Bailey believed that "ignorant people are prone to think that 'the way their fathers trod' is good enough for them, hence they do not care to improve. But who can estimate the value of even one advance step?" (Bailey, *Reminiscences*, p. 277). After a number of bouts of pneumonia and hemorrhaging in the lungs, Bailey's husband died in 1882. His example as a Christian inspired her to write his biography, *Reminiscences of a Christian Life* (1884), which she printed and distributed at her own cost.

Although devastated by the loss of her husband, Bailey went forth with conviction, taking over the management of his oil cloth business and retail carpet store in Portland, Maine. In 1889 she sold the manufacturing establishment, and in 1891 her son, Moses, took charge of the Portland business. For ten years she served as treasurer of the Woman's Foreign Missionary Society of the New England Yearly Meeting of Friends. In 1883 she joined the Woman's Christian Temperance Union (WCTU) headed by Frances Willard.

In 1887 Willard gave the support of the WCTU to the Universal Peace Union and appointed the "energetic" Bailey as superintendent of the Department of Peace and International Arbitration. Bailey organized peace bands among children, invited clergymen to preach for peace, and asked teachers to encourage "international goodwill." Her department circulated petitions, Bible readings, leaflets on peace topics for adults and children, and illustrated calendars. It also published two papers devoted to the discussion of peace, the *Pacific Banner* for adults and *Acorn* for children, and two books, *Voices of Peace* and *Gleanings on the Subject of Peace and Arbitration*. As a result of Bailey's leadership, a WCTU Department of Peace and International Arbitration was established in twenty-six states and fourteen countries. In 1888 Willard established the World's Woman's Christian Temperance Union, "the largest international organization of women in the world during the century" (Earhart, p. 270), and in 1891 appointed Bailey the world superintendent of peace. As a representative of the WCTU, Bailey urged President Harrison to opt for arbitration instead of war in his heated negotiations with Chile in 1892.

Bailey lectured extensively in Europe, Asia, and Africa and established her presence in the political milieu of the United States, promoting peace and arbitration. She also continued her struggle for woman suffrage. As long as women were denied the right to vote, Bailey wrote on her check in payment for taxes, "This is taxation without representation" (Stackpole, p. 111). She was president of the Maine Woman Suffrage Association from 1891 to 1897. In her 1896 annual address she stated, "The uplifting of the race is the divine problem for whose solution Christ gave the Golden Rule. Any restriction upon the development of women breaks that rule, and hinders the progress of the race. . . . Whether suffrage be a right or a privilege, if it is of value to one-half of mankind it is of value to all." She closed her address with the statement, "May the time come apace when woman shall be no more weak politically, but when she will be elevated to the highest sphere of her own possibilities."

In 1893 a board of lady managers appointed Bailey one of the judges in the department of liberal arts at the Chicago World's Columbian Exposition. From 1895 to 1899 Bailey was treasurer of the National Council of Women, an organization founded by Willard in support of "international co-operation and work." She was appointed twice to represent Maine on the National Board of Charities and Correction and tried for several years to obtain a reformatory for women in Maine. Throughout her life, Bailey encouraged young men and women to devote themselves to social reform by offering her counsel and financial support toward their college education. Bailey retired as superintendent of the WCTU peace department in 1916; not long after, the organization abandoned its anti-war pledge and supported the United States' entry into World War I. Bailey died in Portland, Maine.

• Bailey's papers are housed in the Swarthmore College Peace Collection. The *History of Women* microfilm collection at Schlesinger Library, Radcliffe College, includes Bailey's *Annual Address of the President of the Maine Woman's Suffrage Association* (1896). Edward Schriver focuses on Bailey's contributions to the suffrage movement in "Hannah Bailey Fought for Women," *Maine Life* (July 1980): 54–55. Bailey's biography of her husband, *Reminiscences of a Christian Life*, includes details on her marriage and religious convictions. For details on her peace work see the *Minutes* (1888–1916) for the National Woman's Christian Temperance Union and chapter sixteen of Mary Earhart's *Frances Willard: From Prayers to Politics* (1944). Merle Curti, *Peace or War: The American Struggle, 1636–1936* (1936), contextualizes Bailey's peace work in light of the larger peace movement in the country. For information on Bailey's place of residence and the oil cloth business of her husband, see Everett S. Stackpole, *History of Winthrop, Maine, with Genealogical Notes* (1925).

BARBARA L. CICCARELLI

BAILEY, Irving Widmer (15 Aug. 1884–16 May 1967), plant anatomist, was born in Tilton, New Hampshire, the son of Solon Irving Bailey, an assistant professor of astronomy at Harvard, and Ruth Elaine Poulter. When he was five years old, his father was sent to Peru to select a site for a high-altitude observatory, which he founded on El Misti at 19,000 feet elevation. Bailey was educated by his parents there, with no playmates of his own age. He wrote of this time:

> I was forced to rely on my own resources for interests and activities. Much of my time was spent in hunting, in exploring the Andes at high elevations, in learning at first hand the traditions and beliefs of Peruvian Indians, and in observing the spectacular activities of Catholic Spanish in peace and in revolution. I developed at an unusually early age, in association with my father and other astronomers, a keenly analytical interest in natural phenomena and in the activities and foibles of the human race under differing hereditary and environmental influences. (*Fiftieth Anniversary Report of the Harvard Class of 1907* [1907], pp. 40–41.)

Together father and son acquired artifacts that were much later presented to Harvard's Peabody Museum.

Bailey entered Harvard College in 1903, graduating in 1907. He sampled history, chemistry, geology, and meteorology, but in his senior year, speeches by pioneering conservationist Gifford Pinchot and President Charles William Eliot inspired him to undertake a career in forestry. Bailey entered the graduate school at Harvard in 1907 as a student of Edward Charles Jeffrey. He received a master of forestry degree in 1909 and, almost simultaneously, an appointment as instructor of forestry in the Graduate School of Applied Science. In 1911 he married Helen Diman Harwood; they had two children. In 1912 the short-lived School of Forestry was formed, with Bailey as an assistant professor. A fellow instructor was Edmund Ware Sinnot, with whom Bailey was to publish several papers. In 1914 the School of Forestry was combined with the now defunct Bussey Institution.

Bailey's study of lumbering and wood-using industries impressed him with the lack of accurate and reliable information regarding the anatomical structure, physical properties, and chemical composition of wood and the processes by which it is formed. During World War I he served as a wood technologist at Wright Field (later Wright-Patterson Air Force Base) in Dayton, Ohio, with the title of chief, Wood Section, of the Materials Engineering Department of the Bureau of Aircraft Production. The methods of cutting, curing, milling, and splicing wood for wing and frame construction of army aircraft were Bailey's responsibilities. When the supply of spruce wood was threatened by insect attacks, Bailey took part in classical studies on the spruce budworm. He resigned in December 1918 and returned to the Bussey Institution, where he was promoted to associate professor in 1920 and to professor of plant anatomy in 1927.

In 1917 Jeffrey published *The Anatomy of Woody Plants*, which contained many ideas and descriptions with which Bailey did not agree, and a conflict in print developed between them on the origin and significance of the "aggregate ray." The rift never healed, but the pattern of much of Bailey's subsequent research was set. He wrote ten significant papers on the cambium and its derivative tissues. An early series, beginning in 1914, was titled "Investigations on the Phylogeny of the Angiosperms," mostly with Sinnot as coauthor; this led to a paper asking the question, "Are *Tetracentron*, *Trochodendron* and *Drimys* Specialized or Primitive Types?" Many papers on the "woody Ranales" and the vesselless dicotyledons followed. These were enhanced by the discovery of a new family of dicotyledons in the Fiji Islands with a previously undescribed type of pistil. Bailey formulated the idea of a conduplicate carpel. He spent several years researching the nature of the primitive leaf and the node, culminating in his final studies, "Comparative Anatomy of the Leaf-bearing Cactaceae."

William Wheeler, a specialist on ants, was the director of the Bussey Institution during Bailey's early years there. He encouraged Bailey to look into the structure of myrmecophytes, plants housing ants. A trip to British Guiana to collect material resulted in the description of several new species of ant plants and a clarification of the pollination mechanism of the genus *Marcgravia*.

When the excavation for the Prudential Insurance building in Boston revealed old fish weirs, Bailey was asked to help identify the woods. The result was studies of cell-wall structure as revealed in deterioration by fungal action.

At the end of World War II, Bailey, as senior staff member in the biology department at Harvard, was asked to review plans for the integration of several botanical institutes, with their budgets, libraries, collections, endowments, and staffs. His report to the dean divided the institutions and their supporters and led to two decades of litigation before concessions were made by all sides. Finally, a ruling of the Massachusetts Supreme Court rendered further discussion moot.

Bailey taught few classes, gave few public lectures, had few graduate students, did not attend international congresses, and published no books beyond a compendium of some of his papers, *Contributions to Plant Anatomy* (1954). His failure to write a book, he once explained, was due to his willingness to let others summarize; he preferred to contribute his original ideas and investigations. His association during many summers with the Desert Laboratory of the Carnegie Institution of Washington gave him productive time to organize papers and outline further research.

Bailey belonged to many professional societies and received several honors, including the Mary Soper Pope Award from Cranbrook Institute of Science (1954), and the Award of Merit from the Botanical Society of America (1956). Bailey retired in 1933 and died in Cambridge, Massachusetts.

• A collection of Bailey's papers is at the Harvard University Archives. Biographical notices after his death include Richard A. Howard et al., "Irving Widmer Bailey," *Harvard University Gazette* 63 (1968): 196; and Howard, "Irving Widmer Bailey, 1884–1967," *Journal of the Arnold Arboretum* 49 (1968): 1–13.

RICHARD A. HOWARD

BAILEY, Jacob (1731–26 July 1808), Anglican missionary and Loyalist, was born in Rowley, Massachusetts, the son of David Bailey and Mary Hodgkins, farmers. The details of Bailey's early education are unknown, but by the age of ten he was able to read and write. Frustrated by the ignorance of the townspeople and a lack of books, he began to devote his leisure time to "scribbling" essays on various topics. One inadvertently came to the attention of the Reverend Jedediah Jewett, pastor of the First Congregational Society, who then offered to tutor Jacob gratis. Bailey matriculated at Harvard in 1751. He depended primarily upon charity for his fees and expenses but successfully graduated in 1755. Bailey then undertook a series of positions as a schoolmaster while preparing for the A.M. degree, which he received in 1758. In June of that year he was approved as a Congregational preacher. He failed to find a permanent parish and continued his precarious career as itinerant teacher and preacher until the end of 1759.

Meanwhile, in August 1758, he had heard from a Mr. Brackett of a vacancy at the mission of the Society for the Propagation of the Gospel in Foreign Parts (SPG) in Portsmouth, New Hampshire. Brackett's proposal that Bailey qualify for this position "wonderfully pleased" him. Bailey's motivation for entering the priesthood of a church regarded as "dissenting" by Massachusetts law is unclear—he probably needed a reliable income—as is his preparation for ordination. He borrowed books, made acquaintances with other Anglican priests, and acquired the patronage of Silvester Gardiner, a prominent member of the Kennebec Proprietors.

Arrangements were made for passage on the British warship the *Hine*. A miserable 28-day journey brought him to Portsmouth on 16 February 1760. Losing no time, Bailey presented his testimonials to Philip Bearcroft, secretary of the SPG, and also presented letters to the bishop of London's assistant on the twenty-seventh. The following day he called upon Thomas Secker, archbishop of Canterbury and president of the SPG, who recommended his ordination. Bailey passed the examinations on the twenty-ninth and was ordained a deacon on Sunday, 2 March, by Zachery Pearce, bishop of Rochester. Two weeks later he was ordained a priest by Richard Terrick, bishop of Peterborough, at St. James' Church, London. Thomas Sherlock, who as bishop of London had oversight of the colonial Anglican church, licensed Bailey on 17 March. The SPG appointed him "Itinerant Missionary on the Eastern Frontier of Massachusetts Bay" on the nineteenth, with a salary of £50 annually, and generously extended its starting date back to Christmas 1759. His congregation was to provide a glebe, a parsonage, and a £20 salary. On the same day he received the royal bounty.

Bailey arrived in Boston on 4 June 1760. Clearly Bailey's friends had arranged to expedite the process, yet despite his youthful dreams of traveling, his sojourn in England was extremely brief compared to that of his fellow American ordinands. His limited personal resources and continued dependence on charity, problems that were to plague him throughout his ministry, are the most plausible explanations.

Concerned about Jesuit missionaries, the people of the Kennebec had petitioned the SPG for a minister in 1754. From 1756 to 1758 they were poorly served by William McClenachan. Bailey took up residence at Pownalborough on 1 July 1760. The following spring he moved across the river to Richmond, where he was granted the right to use land near the fort. In August he married Sally Weeks; they had six children. Bailey held services in the courthouse in Pownalborough from 1761 until St. John's Church was opened on 4 November 1770. A parsonage was erected the following year, and the Massachusetts General Court incorporated the church in 1773. Although finally associated with a legally recognized parish, Bailey continued, as he had done since the beginning of his ministry, to visit the scattered settlements along the frontier. He noted that his auditors came from a variety of ethnic and religious backgrounds, yet the Church of England grew rapidly and, by the time of the Revolution, had three resident ministers in Maine.

Bailey's political problems began in 1774, when he preached about loyalty to the king. He refused to omit prayers for the monarch following the Declaration of Independence and, despite threats and intimidation, continued to perform his religious duties. By July 1778, however, the pressures had become too intense, and Bailey petitioned the General Court to allow his family to move to Nova Scotia. Believing that a plea of conscience would be unsuccessful, he based his appeal on poverty. Permission was granted in November, but the Baileys did not depart Pownalborough until June 1779.

Bailey began to conduct services at Cornwallis, Nova Scotia, in October and resumed teaching to supplement his £70 salary. The SPG appointed him to Annapolis Royal, Nova Scotia, in 1782 and continued his £50 stipend, with another £70 to be paid by the government. The society also hoped that Bailey would be appointed chaplain to the garrison, and he attained that post in 1794. Conditions in Annapolis were primitive. An unfinished church, St. Luke's Church, was opened on Easter 1784 but was not completed until 1789.

Bailey had been a partisan of his friend Samuel Peters, formerly of Connecticut, in the competition to be appointed the first colonial bishop. Charles Inglis won the appointment, and Bailey refused to attend Inglis's 1788 visitation at Halifax, using a pending lawsuit regarding his glebe as a pretext. However, once they met later that year during the bishop's tour of the diocese, they developed cordial relations. Inglis recognized Bailey as one of four hard-working and diligent ministers out of the eleven subject to his authority. He was impressed that Bailey remained strictly orthodox, resisting first Methodism and then New Light enthusiasts, especially the Baptists. The strenuous life of an itinerant missionary took its toll. Inglis noted during his 1803 visitation to Annapolis that Bailey could walk only with the aid of crutches and needed an assistant. Bailey died in Annapolis Royal, Nova Scotia. His widow survived until 22 March 1818.

• The largest collections of Bailey's writings are in the Public Archives of Nova Scotia, Halifax, and at Rhodes House, Oxford, where the letterbooks and journals of the Society for the Propagation of the Gospel in Foreign Parts are deposited. Smaller collections of his writings are in the Fulham Papers at Lambeth Palace Library, London; the Library of Congress, Washington, D.C.; the Archives of the Episcopal Church, Austin, Tex.; the Archives of the Diocese of Connecticut, Hartford; and the Diocesan Library and Archives of Massachusetts, Boston. A full-length biography is William S. Bartlet, *The Frontier Missionary: A Memoir of the Life of the Rev. Jacob Bailey, A.M. Missionary at Pownalborough, Maine, Cornwallis and Annapolis, N.S.; with Illustrations, Notes, and an Appendix* (1853), which is vol. 2 of *Collections of the Protestant Episcopal Historical Society*. Useful contextual material is in Brian Cuthburtson, *The First Bishop: A Biography of Charles Inglis* (1987), and James S. Leamon, *Revolution Downeast: The War for American Independence in Maine* (1993).

SALLY SCHWARTZ

BAILEY, Jacob Whitman (29 Apr. 1811–27 Feb. 1857), naturalist and educator, was born in Ward (now Auburn), Massachusetts, the son of Rev. Isaac Bailey and Jane Whitman. From an early age Bailey was an avid collector and classifier of natural history specimens. Because his family was of modest means, Bailey's formal schooling ended at age twelve, but employment with a bookseller and circulating library in Providence, Rhode Island, permitted him to continue studies on his own. His scholarly habits earned him the patronage of John Kingsbury, secretary of Brown University, with whom he studied Latin. By 1828 he was able to enter West Point, graduating fifth in his class in 1832 and receiving a commission as second lieutenant of artillery in 1833.

The following year Bailey was appointed assistant professor of chemistry at West Point, and by 1838 he had risen to a new chair of chemistry, mineralogy, and geology. He occupied this position until his death. In 1835 he married Maria Slaughter of West View, Virginia. A son, William Whitman Bailey, became a botanist; their only daughter perished along with Mrs. Bailey in the tragic fire aboard the steamer *Henry Clay* near Yonkers in 1852.

Although Bailey was responsible for teaching the chemical and earth sciences at West Point, his principal interests were botany and microscopy, and it was in the latter field that his research was especially concentrated. In his time he was probably America's leading microscopist. His scientific publications, principally in Benjamin Silliman's *American Journal of Science and Arts* and *Smithsonian Contributions to Knowledge*, numbered at least forty. He corresponded with most of the leading scientists in America and many in Europe, including the eminent microbiologist Christian Gottfried Ehrenberg. He was president of the American Association for the Advancement of Science at the time of his death. Augustus A. Gould, eminent physician and scientist, referred to him as the "Ehrenberg of America."

Bailey's brief career spanned two important developments in nineteenth-century science, and his prominence was in part the result of their convergence. In the 1830s, just as Bailey was beginning to establish his reputation, substantial improvements in microscope construction suddenly made this instrument far more useful to science. And in the 1850s surveys for the earliest transoceanic cables yielded the first tangible samples of sediments from the deep-sea bottom. By 1853 sediment samples from a depth of more than two miles were being obtained by the new Brooke Patent Sounding Lead. (Invented by Passed Midshipman John Mercer Brooke, the device consisted of a sampling tube carried down by a cannonball-like weight that detached upon penetration of the bottom, allowing the sample-filled tube to be raised easily.) These and earlier samples were sent to Bailey for microscopical analysis, first by Charles Wilkes of the U.S. Exploring Expedition, and subsequently from the U.S. Navy via Matthew F. Maury and from the U.S. Coast Survey through Alexander D. Bache. Among his last publications were reports of samples from the Sea of Kamchatka (now Sea of Okhotsk). These analyses by Bailey and others led to a lively debate about the origins and significance of the organic constituents of deep-sea sediments. Bailey, supported by Maury, took the now-accepted view that the microscopic protozoans (Foraminifera) whose skeletal remains are common in bottom sediments had lived near the surface and fell to the bottom after death; Ehrenberg, supported by Thomas Henry Huxley, argued that they lived on the bottom.

Bailey was the logical person to carry out these exciting analyses for at least two reasons. He had already devoted the first decade of his career to the microscopic examination of diatoms and other "infusoria" (as microscopic life forms were then called) and to the study of algae. Furthermore, his background in chemistry and mineralogy had prepared him to interpret the inorganic constituents of the samples as well. This combination of botanical and geological expertise may also have made possible one of Bailey's earliest discoveries: the first fossil diatoms to be found in America (1839). Inspired by European samples sent by Ehrenberg, Bailey discovered a substantial layer of fossil infusoria beneath the surface of a peat bog near West Point. More than a quarter of his subsequent publications concerned paleontology.

Bailey was reserved and unpretentious in character, commanding the highest respect from his scientific contemporaries for his quiet industry and breadth of knowledge. His published writings were characterized by brevity and carefulness. He was a skillful scientific artist as well.

Bailey died in West Point, New York.

• The Boston Museum of Science Library holds approximately one and a half linear feet of Bailey manuscripts (formerly held by the Boston Society of Natural History), including one bound volume of indexed notes and drawings and substantial correspondence with Thomas Cole, J. D. Dana, Asa Gray, W. H. Harvey, Joseph Henry, M. F. Maury, E. J. Quekett, Benjamin Silliman, John Torrey, Charles Wilkes, and others. The fullest listing of his publications will be found in the Royal Society's *Catalogue of Scientific Papers*, vol. 1 (1867). The most thorough biographical sketches are by Stanley Coulter in the *Botanical Gazette* 13 (1888): 118–24, and Augustus A. Gould in the *Proceedings of the American Association for the Advancement of Science*, 1857–1858: 1–8. Microscopical and algological collections bequeathed to the Boston Society of Natural History are enumerated by A. A. Gould in the *Proceedings of the Boston Society of Natural History* 6 (1857): 194–200. The scientific context of his deep-sea sediment analyses is best described in Eric L. Mills, "The Problems of Deep Sea Biology: An Historical Perspective," in *The Sea*, vol. 8 of *Deep-Sea Biology*, ed. Gilbert T. Rowe (1983). Useful information also appears in Susan Schlee, *The Edge of an Unfamiliar World: A History of Oceanography* (1973); Margaret Deacon, *Scientists and the Sea 1650–1900: A Study of Marine Science* (1971); Frances Leigh Williams, *Matthew Fontaine Maury: Scientist of the Sea* (1963); and George H. Daniels, *American Science in the Age of Jackson* (1968).

PHILIP F. REHBOCK

BAILEY, James Anthony (4 July 1847–11 Apr. 1906), circus owner, was born in Detroit, Michigan. His surname was McGinness or McGinnis. Details about his parents are unknown. He was orphaned by the age of eight. At eleven or twelve he ran away from his sister's home and began living on his own in Pontiac, Michigan. He began his circus career in 1860, doing odd jobs for Frederick H. Bailey, the advance man of the Robinson and Lake Circus; Bailey took such a liking to the young lad that he not only asked him to become his protégé on the road but had him adopt his name as well.

The facts of James Bailey's early years are vague because the showman, thereafter and for the rest of his life, took great pains to keep his personal history a secret. The antithesis of his last and most flamboyant partner, P. T. Barnum, Bailey shunned personal publicity, even going so far as to have his associates inform any reporters or visiting nabobs who happened to appear on the circus lot that he was not with the show at the time. He would then hide in his private tent until such time as he could move about with complete anonymity. To protect his privacy, he was known to have discharged an employee who claimed to be acquainted with his real family. He married Ruth Louisa McCaddon in 1868 under his assumed name. They produced no children who might have recorded or preserved family history.

Although Barnum always gave Bailey credit for the success of the Barnum and Bailey partnership, Bailey's aversion to personal promotion may explain why his name is so less well known and will forever be in second place.

Bailey's phenomenal rise to the heights of the circus world is, however, well documented. Within weeks of going off with the elder Bailey, and while only thirteen years of age, he found himself in the position of having to make all the necessary arrangements for the arrival of the circus he represented without the help of his mentor. So successful was he at this that he won the respect and admiration of seasoned circus veterans and was given ever more trust and responsibility.

In the winter of 1863 he was working as an usher in a Nashville, Tennessee, theater. One evening when the theater was filled to capacity, a man by the name of Green, a sutler with the Fourteenth Army Corps, tried to bribe Bailey into giving him a seat. Bailey refused to take the money and sent the man back to the box office, mightily impressing the merchant. A week later he offered Bailey a job as his clerk, and the young man spent the rest of the Civil War with Green following Sherman's army.

After the war Bailey reentered show business and at the age of twenty-one became the youngest general agent (purchasing agent) in this field of endeavor. At the close of the 1873 season he took his savings and invested them in a quarter interest in the Hemmings, Cooper, and Whitby Circus. Within two years, at the age of twenty-eight, he had acquired the interests of both Hemmings and Whitby and the show was renamed Cooper and Bailey.

It was Bailey's daring decision to tour that circus through Australia, New Zealand, Java, and South America. The later part of the tour proved to be financially unsuccessful, due to the enormous expenses incurred, but Bailey's logistical and managerial acumen came to the fore. He returned home to buy the Seth B. Howes London Show and thereby became a serious competitor to P. T. Barnum.

During the winter of 1880 one of his circus elephants gave birth to the first such animal known to be born in captivity. The resultant publicity moved Barnum to wire an offer of $100,000 for both mother and offspring. Bailey not only turned down the bid, he publicized the offer in his advertising. The elder showman was so impressed by this masterful stroke of promotion that he decided to join forces with Cooper, Bailey, and their third partner, James L. Hutchinson. Within half a dozen years it was simply Barnum and Bailey.

While Barnum collected all the notoriety, Bailey assumed sole responsibility for the formation and composition of each season's show, its routing, and all the practical details of the day to day management. It was in this capacity that Bailey became responsible for many circus innovations: the introduction of electricity, the purchase of Jumbo, the multiplication of rings, the introduction of theatrical spectacle, and the innovation of transportation and feeding techniques that eventually were copied by the German kaiser for use by his army. Bailey, in fact, was a far better businessman than his partner, and it was that ability, as much as Barnum's gift for publicity, that made their circus truly worthy of being called the Greatest Show on Earth.

A thin man who wore a full beard, Bailey was a collection of nervous habits that included spitting rubber bands and spinning coins. He preferred doing business by telegraph and delegated unpleasant chores, such as the firing of personnel, to his assistants. Although he had no intimate companions or confidants, he visited with all who worked for him with ease and made many of his veteran employees stockholders. He was never known to raise his voice or behave as anything less than a gentleman. Because of the difference in their temperaments, Bailey found working with Barnum difficult, and he went into temporary retirement in 1888. Two years later Barnum persuaded him to return, and he took the mammoth circus to London. After Barnum's death in 1891, Bailey was the sole proprietor of not only the Greatest Show on Earth but also the Forepaugh and Sells Bros. Circus and the Buffalo Bill Wild West Show.

Six years after Barnum's death Bailey took the show back to Europe for a five-year stay. He returned to find a new rival circus owned by the five Ringling Brothers. Always the astute businessman, Bailey worked out a touring compromise with the Ringlings rather than risk a costly face to face competition.

In 1906, while supervising the preparation of the Greatest Show on Earth for its annual spring opening at New York City's Madison Square Garden, Bailey became ill and retired to his home, "The Knolls," in Mount Vernon, New York, where he died of a disease diagnosed as erysipelas.

Although Bailey's reticence has tended to obscure his accomplishments, from 1888 to 1904 he was unquestionably the dominating force during the larger "golden age" of the American circus, and his name will be an enduring part of circus history.

• Bailey's obsession with privacy has resulted in a dearth of biographical studies. During his lifetime he discouraged all such efforts. What remains instead are tangential references to Bailey in the numerous autobiographical and biographical works of and about P. T. Barnum, sources that tend to minimize Bailey's contributions to the partnership. The most reliable and balanced of these is A. H. Saxon, *P. T. Barnum: The Legend and the Man* (1989). Bailey's brother-in-law Joseph T. McCaddon undertook the responsibility of producing what was to be an authoritative biographical work, but it was never published and is now held by the Bridgeport, Conn., Public Library. Clipping files containing some significant contemporaneous pieces can be found in the research library of the Circus World Museum in Baraboo, Wisc., and in the Billy Rose Theatre Collection at the New York Public Library for the Performing Arts, Lincoln Center. Fred Bradna, who was equestrian director of the Greatest Show on Earth while Bailey was still alive, offers a firsthand personal impression of the man on pages 31–34 of his autobiography, *The Big Top* (1952). Earl May Chapin, *The Circus from Rome to Ringling* (1932), charts the subject's circus career in some detail.

ERNEST ALBRECHT

BAILEY, Joseph (6 May 1825–26 Mar. 1867), military engineer, was born probably in Pennsville, Ohio, and moved to Illinois as a child. His parents' names and occupations are unknown. He studied civil engineering and in 1846 married Mary Spaulding. They had one daughter. In 1847 he relocated to Kilbourn City, Wisconsin, where he became a successful lumberman and engineer.

At the advent of the Civil War, Bailey responded to the president's call for volunteers to serve for three years. He raised a company and on 2 July 1861 was mustered in at Racine as captain of Company D, Fourth Wisconsin Infantry Regiment. In mid-July the regiment was sent to Baltimore, where it guarded railroads until February 1862.

In March of that year the regiment was moved to Ship Island, Mississippi, on the Gulf of Mexico. During the next five months, Bailey saw action as a company commander with the Union amphibious force that ascended the Mississippi River, captured New Orleans and Baton Rouge, and threatened Vicksburg. His regiment was then involved in the late July recoil from

Vicksburg and the battle of Baton Rouge, followed by the Confederate occupation and fortification of Port Hudson.

Because of his engineering skills, from mid-December 1862 to January 1864 Bailey was on detached duty to the headquarters of the Department of the Gulf. He performed valuable services in combat at Port Hudson as the Fourteenth Corps's engineer officer, and he oversaw construction projects as chief engineer for the New Orleans defenses. As a result, Bailey steadily moved up through the ranks. He was promoted to major of his unit on 30 May 1863 and to lieutenant colonel on 15 July 1863. On 22 August 1863 his unit was reorganized and designated the Fourth Wisconsin Cavalry. Bailey was made a full colonel in the cavalry on 3 May 1864.

In the spring of 1864 Bailey provided his greatest service to the Union cause during Major General Nathaniel P. Banks's Red River campaign. Success of this joint army-navy undertaking depended on high water on the Red River to facilitate naval operations. Following the battles of Mansfield on 8 April and Pleasant Hill on 9 April, Banks lost his nerve, and the army retreated to Alexandria. In the face of the army's withdrawal and a rapidly falling river, Rear Admiral David D. Porter's fleet retreated downstream. At Alexandria on 26 April the flow of the river over the rapids was too low to permit the passage of the fleet. Colonel Bailey persuaded General Banks that he could extricate the fleet if given the resources. Banks provided 1,000-man fatigue parties, including several hundred lumberjacks from the Twenty-ninth Maine. Bailey oversaw construction of two wing dams from opposite sides of the Red River. The dams constricted the water flow and raised the river enough to allow the fleet to navigate the rapids. On 12 May Porter's thirty-three vessels passed through the spillway. For his ingenuity, Bailey was brevetted a brigadier general. On 11 June Congress, by joint resolution, tendered him the nation's thanks, and he received a handsome presentation sword from Admiral Porter.

In August 1864 Bailey reported to Major General Gordon Granger, commander of the troops attacking the forts that guarded the entrance to Mobile Bay. First Bailey led Union cavalry operating against Fort Gaines and then those operating against Fort Morgan. Following the success of this operation, in November he was made commander of the District of West Florida, with headquarters at Barrancas, in November. This assignment included promotion to brigadier general of volunteers. He led a cavalry division on the Davidson raid from Baton Rouge to West Pascagoula, Mississippi, from 27 November to 13 December. After ten weeks duty at Baton Rouge, he joined the army that Major General E. R. S. Canby had organized to capture Mobile. Bailey built wharves and bridges, opened roads, and kept the fighting men supplied during the ensuing campaign, work that earned him the rank of major general.

After Appomattox, Bailey resigned from the army and settled in Vernon County, Missouri, in an area where violence had been a way of life since the "Border Wars" of the mid- and late 1850s. He was elected sheriff in the autumn of 1866. The following spring Bailey was fatally shot by two bushwhackers whom he had arrested near Nevada, Missouri.

• Information on Bailey is in the Compiled Service Records of Union Soldiers, National Archives, and in Department of War, *The War of the Rebellion: A Compilation of the Official Records of the Union and Confederate Armies* (1880–1901). Also see F. B. Heitman, *Historical Register* . . . (1903); Ludwell H. Johnson, *Red River Campaign: Politics and Cotton in the Civil War* (1958); and James E. Jones, ed., *History of Columbia County, Wisconsin* (1914).

EDWIN C. BEARSS

BAILEY, Joseph Weldon (6 Oct. 1863–13 Apr. 1929), U.S. congressman and senator, was born Joseph Edgar Bailey in Crystal Springs, Mississippi, the son of Joseph B. Bailey, a merchant, and Harriet Dees. As a young adult, he changed his middle name to Weldon. His earliest education came from a local tutor. At age sixteen he studied for one year at the Clinton Academy before matriculating at the University of Mississippi, where he honed his oratorical skills with the Phi Sigma Society. During his study at Oxford, Mississippi, Bailey's political views emerged, and the young man advocated a return to national prominence for southern Democrats. At this time Bailey adopted a style of dress, which later became his trademark, more commonly associated with the antebellum southern planter class. In 1881 Bailey transferred to Vanderbilt University. Unsatisfied, he transferred again to the University of Virginia in October 1881 and studied law. Bailey's mercurial temper hastened his departure the following spring, when the faculty prevented his debating society from considering the topic of its choice. Bailey then enrolled in the law school of Cumberland University at Lebanon, Tennessee. By the summer of 1883 Bailey had secured enough credits that he was able to get his law license. He moved to Hazelhurst, Mississippi, and began a practice. He entered local politics but fell into a controversy that resulted in the Copiah County election riot over whether Democrats or Republicans would control local politics. Bailey marched with other armed Democrats in an attempt to intimidate GOP voters. A leading Republican was shot and killed, and a riot ensued. This episode prompted Bailey's departure for Texas. In 1885 he settled in Gainesville, located near the Red River, and the following year he married Ellen Murray, a woman he had met at the University of Mississippi. The couple had two children.

In his campaign for Congress in 1890 Bailey, a Democrat from the fifth district, lobbied for the free coinage of silver, against the tariff, and for the creation of a state railroad commission and won his race. He was named to the Public Lands Committee. Bailey's fashion habits attracted attention, but his maiden speech demonstrated substance behind his artfully constructed facade. The outgoing Republican Speaker, Thomas B. Reed, had controlled the House with an iron fist, and Bailey, who prided himself on knowledge of parliamentary procedure, interjected constitutional principles in House affairs. His words drew compliments from both sides of the aisle, but as the session progressed his use of the rules of order to kill private bills angered Republicans and Democrats alike.

Bailey broke with Grover Cleveland over the issue of federal patronage when the White House blocked the appointment of a friend of the congressman as customs collector in El Paso. The president's opposition to free silver further shaded the dispute. Bailey declared, "If in pursuing what I believe to be for the best interests of Texas and the entire country I incur the hostility of Mr. Cleveland, I shall regret it, but I shall not alter my course and I do not shrink from its consequences." Bailey's colleagues looked to him for leadership within the Democratic party as they revolted against the administration. In 1894 he fought Cleveland's tariff proposals, urging an income tax instead.

In 1896 Bailey's popularity reached beyond his own congressional district, and he led the anti–William Jennings Bryan forces in the Texas delegation to the Democratic National Convention that year. Upset by Bryan's nomination and possible election, Bailey announced his resignation from Congress but reconsidered when his constituents protested.

With the election of President William McKinley, the Republicans swept control of Congress. Bailey was elected minority leader. He fought the enactment of the protectionist Dingley Tariff. Urging Congress to recognize Cuban belligerency against Spain, his constant pressure helped push McKinley and the Republicans toward war with Spain. In April 1898 he told his colleagues: "If the President wants one day . . . to prepare a message that will be approved by the American people, we will be silent until he sends it here. But if the President of the United States wants two days . . . to continue negotiations with the butchers of Spain, we are not ready to give him one moment longer for that purpose." Constitutional principles dictated his opposition to the annexation of the new territory.

In 1900 Bailey ran for Horace Chilton's seat in the U.S. Senate. He attacked Chilton's support for Cleveland's tariff policy, but the race turned not so much on issues as on questions of character. A U.S. Supreme Court ruling that upheld the ouster of the Waters Pierce Oil Company from Texas because of antitrust violations became the main issue in the contest. Bailey had accepted what he described as a loan from officials with the company, whom he had known for some time. However, his detractors charged the money was in reality payment of legal fees for his representation of Waters Pierce in Austin when that company gained a new operating license. Bailey insisted that in giving advice that helped Waters Pierce return to Texas he had only acted as a friend of the court. These accusations colored Texas politics for many years to come. Bailey, though, overcame the allegations in 1901 and was elected to the Senate by the state legislature.

In the midst of the 1904 elections Bailey endorsed federal regulation of railroad rates. When Theodore Roosevelt advocated similar reforms, Bailey questioned his commitment while vowing Democratic support for a bill in the Senate. He relied on arguments grounded in the Constitution to make his case for the bill, and in 1906 he helped secure the enactment of the Hepburn Rate Bill, which created the Interstate Commerce Commission, a body charged with regulation of railroad rates.

Bailey's race for reelection in 1906 was again fraught with charges of impropriety stemming from the Waters Pierce controversy. The events of 1901 were rehashed after Texas had again sued for the removal of the Waters Pierce Oil Company from the state. Bailey acknowledged the loan but argued that the payments were not a bribe because he had never held public office in the state and thus had not been in a position to decide the company's fate. Nevertheless, in January 1907 the state legislature investigated the matter, and after a month-long inquiry, Bailey was cleared of wrongdoing by a substantial vote. Then the legislature reelected him to the Senate, but the controversy was not abated. Only a statewide poll of the electorate would satisfy the warring factions. Bailey ran for a delegate-at-large slot to the Democratic National Convention in 1908 and promised he would resign from the Senate if defeated. He prevailed in what he termed "the crisis of my life."

After the election of Republican William Howard Taft as president in 1908, Bailey developed a cordial relationship with the new chief executive, despite their difference in party affiliation. Taft even offered Bailey an appointment to the Supreme Court in 1909, but the Texan declined. In April 1909, during debate on the Payne-Aldrich Tariff, Bailey offered an amendment providing for an income tax. A compromise provided for a corporate income tax and submission of a constitutional amendment for a graduated income tax.

Despite this victory Bailey found his party moving in a direction different from his own choosing. When Congress debated the admission of New Mexico and Arizona, the latter with a state constitutional provision for recall of elected officials, Bailey, on 4 March 1911, announced his resignation from the Senate in protest to what he defined as an intolerable encroachment upon the sanctity of the federal Constitution. After hearing the protests of his supporters in Congress and in Texas, Bailey withdrew his resignation, but later that year he declared he would not seek reelection in 1912.

Bailey stayed in Washington and opened a private law practice. The former senator, however, could not remain quiet about his differences with the new president over the specifics of the Federal Reserve Act, which provided banks, not the government, with the authority over currency expansion. His greatest criticisms, though, were reserved for Wilson's foreign policy with Mexico, the war in Europe, woman suffrage, and national Prohibition. Bailey had not given up all hope for the Democratic party, and in early 1920 he announced his candidacy for governor of Texas. Though he lost the race, Bailey returned to Texas, opened a law practice in Dallas, and remained close to the day-to-day affairs of Texas politics. In 1924 he worked for the defeat of the Ku Klux Klan in Texas politics. Ellen Murray Bailey passed away in 1926, and one year later Bailey married Prudence Rosengren, the widow of one of his oldest friends. Bailey died while giving an argument in a Sherman, Texas, courtroom.

• Bailey's papers are available at the Dallas Historical Society in Dallas, Tex., and at the Texas State Library, Archives Division, in Austin, Tex. Information about Bailey can also be found in the Walter Dickson Adams Papers, the Richard Fenner Burges Papers, the Oscar B. Colquitt Papers, and the Martin McNulty Crane Papers, all in the Center for American History at the University of Texas at Austin. The center also has a useful biographical file on Bailey. Further archival materials about Bailey's career can be found in the John Henry Kirby Papers at the University of Houston Library. Bailey wrote a short piece on the Waters Pierce controversy; see E. G. Senter, comp., *The Bailey Case Boiled Down: A Synopsis of the Material Evidence* (c. 1908). For a biographical study see Sam Hanna Acheson, *Joe Bailey: The Last Democrat* (1932). For information on the implications of the Bailey controversy in Tex. politics see Lewis L. Gould, *Progressives and Prohibitionists: Texas Democrats in the Wilson Era* (1973); William L. Crawford, *Crawford on Baileyism: The Greatest Éxpose of Political Degeneracy since the Crédit Mobilier Scandal* (1907); William Alexander Cocke, *The Bailey Controversy in Texas, with Lessons from the Political Life-Story of a Fallen Idol* (1908); and M. L. Johnson, *The Bailey Investigation: Disgrace to Democracy* (1907). See also Bob Charles Holcomb, "Senator Joe Bailey: Two Decades of Controversy" (Ph.D. diss., Texas Tech Univ., 1968); Ruth Emmeline Parks, "Joseph W. Bailey as Defender of State Rights" (M.A. thesis, Univ. of Texas at Austin, 1940); and Jesse Guy Smith, "The Bailey Controversy in Texas Politics" (M.A. thesis, Univ. of Chicago, 1924). For writings about Bailey see Samuel G. Blythe, "The Great Bailey Myth," *Saturday Evening Post* 183 (27 May 1911): 3–4, 34–36; and Victor E. Martin, "The Fight against Baileyism in Texas," *Arena* 40 (July 1908): 51–56. Obituaries are in the *New York Times*, 14,15 Apr. 1929; and the *Dallas Morning News*, 14, 15, 16 Apr. 1929.

NANCY BECK YOUNG

BAILEY, Josiah William (14 Sept. 1873–15 Dec. 1946), U.S. senator, was born in Warrenton, North Carolina, the son of Christopher Thomas Bailey, a Baptist minister, and Annie Sarah Bailey. Bailey spent his youth in Raleigh, North Carolina, where his father edited the *Biblical Recorder*, a weekly Baptist newspaper. He was educated at Wake Forest College (1889–1893), graduating with an A.B. In 1893 his father had a stroke, so Bailey assisted with editing the *Recorder*. When his father died in 1895, Bailey assumed the position of editor. As editor of the state's second largest periodical, he encouraged progressive measures for North Carolina, especially in public education. He advocated financing education through state appropriations, while the state's better known educational reform leaders, Charles D. McIver and Edwin A. Alderman, supported local taxes to finance the state's educational improvements. In 1895 the Republican-Populist governor David L. Russell appointed Bailey, a Democrat, to the state Board of Agriculture, where he served for three years. In 1898 Bailey joined Furnifold M. Simmons, the state Democratic chairman, and Charles B. Aycock, the leading Democratic candidate for governor, in the "white supremacy" campaign, which ended the fusion rule of populists, blacks, and Republicans in North Carolina. To reward Bailey for his part in the campaign, the state legislature wrote his educational proposals into law, and thus the state government, rather than local governments, became responsible for public education funding.

On the issue of alcohol, Bailey took a different stance. As chairman of the state's Anti-Saloon League from 1903 to 1907, he favored the control of alcohol through local options. When the league supported state prohibition and appeared to favor national prohibition, Bailey resigned, believing these approaches unworkable. By 1905 he had become so dissatisfied as editor of the *Recorder* that he began the study of law, seeing that profession as a potentially more gratifying career. He resigned his editorship in 1907 and was admitted to the bar in 1908. His law practice facilitated the rapid expansion of his political activities. From 1909 to 1911 he served on the Wake County Board of Education, and from 1911 to 1913 he chaired the state's Child Labor Committee. Although Bailey was a loyal member of the Simmons machine, he was a progressive. He supported the initiative and referendum, election reform, the commission form of government for Raleigh, and strict child labor laws. In 1913, to reward him for his support in the presidential campaign of 1912, President Woodrow Wilson appointed Bailey collector of internal revenue for eastern North Carolina.

In 1913 Governor Locke Craig selected Bailey to serve on a constitutional commission that recommended reforms in taxes, revenue, and education. With Clarence Poe, editor of the *Progressive Farmer*, Bailey led an unsuccessful effort to persuade the state's 1914 Democratic convention to adopt a progressive platform. In 1916 Bailey married Edith Walker Pou, thus allying himself with one of North Carolina's most distinguished families. They had five children. Although Bailey was a loyal Simmons and party man, he realized that he could further his political ambitions only by running for public office. In 1922–1923 he split with the Simmons machine and, building on his 1914 progressive platform, ran for the Democratic gubernatorial nomination. He lost the nomination fight but in the process built a core of loyal supporters in the Democratic party who saw Bailey as a social and political reformer. The presidential campaign of 1928 was the death knell of the Simmons machine. Senator Simmons deserted the Democratic party and its candidate Alfred E. Smith to support Herbert Hoover. Bailey loyally supported Smith's candidacy, speaking throughout the state on party loyalty and religious toleration. Two years later, in the Democratic senatorial primary of 1930, Bailey defeated Senator Simmons for the party's nomination. In the general election Bailey easily defeated his Republican opponent for the Senate seat, winning election at age fifty-seven.

Bailey's service in the Seventy-second Congress, which began on 7 December 1931, was fairly typical of a freshman senator of the era. He and many others thought the election of Franklin D. Roosevelt in 1932 and the inauguration of the New Deal were necessary to address the nation's economic crisis. However, Bailey, who was philosophically a fiscal conservative and states' rights constitutionalist, rejected many of the liberal economic and nationalist legislative initiatives of the New Deal. He became increasingly suspicious of what he perceived as the New Deal's propensity for centralization of governmental decision making. By the summer of 1934 Bailey stated that he hoped for a "return to reliance upon private enterprise and individual initiatives" as a method of addressing America's economic and business concerns. Nevertheless, Bailey was a political realist who supported President Roosevelt in the 1936 election and in the process won a second senatorial term. Once he was reelected, Bailey's differences with the administration reemerged. In the spring and summer of 1937 he was instrumental in the Senate's defeat of Roosevelt's plan to "pack" the Supreme Court with additional pro–New Deal justices. The coalition of conservative Republican and Democratic senators that fought Roosevelt's court plan evolved into a coalition opposed to what they identified as the "collectivism" of the New Deal. In December 1937, with the country still in recession and amid growing concerns about the government's anticipated intervention in the economy, Bailey and Senator Arthur H. Vandenberg (R.-Mich.) drafted a "conservative manifesto" entitled "An Address to the People of the United States." They outlined a framework for conservatives to employ to counter New Deal initiatives for ending the recession and stimulating economic recovery. Their proposals included a balanced budget, free enterprise, reduced taxes, states' rights, and local unemployment relief.

From 1938 until his death Bailey served as chairman of the Senate Commerce Committee. As one would expect given his political philosophy, Bailey initially tried to curtail New Deal expenditures. However, faced with the European war, he deserted his traditional isolationist posture to support U.S. aid to England and France. Likewise he supported preparedness on the home front by working for increased defense expenditures and for repeal of the arms embargo provisions of the Neutrality Act of 1939.

In early 1941 Bailey supported the "lend-lease" program, which provided vital materials and equipment to Great Britain for the war effort and through which Great Britain granted the United States the use of some of its bases, even though he knew this policy might lead the United States into war. With U.S. entry in the war, Bailey, always an opponent of organized labor, proposed a "work or fight" policy to place men not subject to the draft at work in essential industries. Throughout the war he supported antistrike legislation. Repeatedly he used his chairmanship of the Commerce Committee to work with President Roosevelt and Admiral Emory S. Land of the Maritime Commission and War Shipping Administration to buy and lease merchant ships needed for the war effort. Bailey supported taxes to finance the war effort, but generally he opposed other types of federal economic control.

Bailey, an avid student of political history, saw World War II as the result of the failed peace process after the First World War. In November 1943 he voted for the Connally Resolution, which advocated the creation of a general international organization, and by February 1944 his support of the concept of the United Nations (UN) was clear. He voted for funding of the UN Relief and Rehabilitation Administration. During the last year and a half of his tenure, Bailey was often absent from Senate business because of his declining health. He died in Raleigh, North Carolina.

• Bailey's papers are in the Manuscript Department of Duke University Library, Durham, N.C. John Robert Moore, *Senator Josiah William Bailey of North Carolina* (1968), is a biography of Bailey. See also Robert E. Marcello, "Senator Josiah Bailey, Harry Hopkins, and the WPA: Prelude to the Conservative Coalition," *Southern Studies* 22 (1983): 321–39; James T. Patterson, *Congressional Conservatism and the New Deal* (1967); Elmer L. Puryear, *Democratic Party Dissension in North Carolina, 1928–1936* (1962); Joseph F. Steelman, "The Progressive Democratic Convention of 1914 in North Carolina," *North Carolina Historical Review* 46 (1969): 83–104; and Richard L. Watson, Jr., "A Southern Democratic Primary," *North Carolina Historical Review* 42 (1965): 21–46. An obituary is in the (Raleigh, N.C.) *News and Observer*, 16 Dec. 1946.

W. LEE JOHNSTON

BAILEY, Liberty Hyde (15 Mar. 1858–25 Dec. 1954), horticulturist and botanist, was born near South Haven, in Van Buren County, Michigan, the son of Liberty Hyde Bailey, Sr., a farmer and fruit grower, and Sarah Harrison. From childhood he was interested in nature, observing and making collections of plants and animals in the fields near his home. During his school days he came upon copies of Charles Darwin's *Origin of Species* and *Field, Forest, and Garden Botany* by the renowned American botanist Asa Gray and, profoundly influenced by them, enrolled at Michigan Agricultural College (now Michigan State University) in East Lansing to study botany; he received his B.S. in 1882.

For some months after graduation Bailey, who had been editor of his college paper, the *College Speculum*, worked as a reporter on the *Springfield (Ill.) Morning Monitor*, but an offer from Gray to become his assistant at Harvard University determined his career. By February 1883 he was arranging specimens in the university herbaria and classifying plants in the Harvard gardens. The following year he married a former college classmate, Annette Smith; they had two children. On the expiration of his two-year contract Bailey was offered a professorship of horticulture and landscape gardening at Michigan Agricultural College, the first such chair in the United States.

In those days horticulture and botany were regarded as separate fields; indeed, most horticulturists had little or no botanical training. Countering Gray's fears, for example, that his new post would mean giving up science for mere agricultural business, Bailey defended his vision of a "new horticulture," an applied science in its own right that would base its practical concerns on a knowledge of botany. This view shaped his teaching, which stressed the combination of theory and practice: fieldwork was supplemented by classroom lectures on plant growth, classification, and nomenclature. In 1886 he was awarded a master of science degree by the college. While there he established one of the first laboratories in the United States for the classification of and experimentation on cultivated plants. At the same time, concerned with the improvement of farm life as a whole, the young professor, accompanied by his students, often participated in local National Grange meetings. Significantly, his first published book was an introductory botanical guide designed for farmers, amateur botanists, and young people, *Talks Afield: About Plants and the Science of Plants* (1885). In 1895 he was commissioned to do the revised edition of Gray's *Botany*. Two years later he received the Veitch Memorial Silver Medal of the Royal Horticultural Society, London, "in recognition of his efforts to promote horticulture and to place the cultivation of plants on a scientific basis." In 1927 he received its gold medal. Active in botanical as well as horticultural circles all his life, Bailey was one of the founders of the Botanical Society of America (1892) and was its president in 1926; in 1903 he cofounded the American Society for Horticultural Science and served as its president until 1907.

In 1888 Bailey was invited to Cornell University to take its new chair of horticulture. Before settling in Ithaca, New York, however, he was sent to Europe, where he investigated new methods of agriculture; pursued his study of the genus *Carex* (sedges), on which he became a world authority; and photographed famous gardens and indigenous flora. Bailey was, among other things, a pioneer in the use of photography for botanical illustration. He now began his active writing career: a lifetime total of some sixty-five books and 700 scientific papers. Colorful and crisp in style, the books he wrote and edited remained standard texts for many years. Particularly noteworthy are the four-volume *Cyclopedia of American Horticulture* (1900–1902), revised as *The Standard Cyclopedia of Horticulture* (6 vols., 1914–1917); *The Cyclopedia of American Agriculture* (4 vols., 1907–1909); and the *Manual of Cultivated Plants: A Flora for the Identification of [North American] Species* . . . (1924). In addition, Bailey wrote poetry (a collection titled *Wind and Weather* was issued in 1916) and several volumes on his philosophy of nature. *The Holy Earth* (1915) expresses his conviction that "the earth is good" and that human life should be lived in harmony with the natural environment.

Bailey was appointed dean of the New York State College of Agriculture at Cornell in 1903 and began to lobby actively for state funds for needed additional facilities. In 1904, as a result of his efforts, the state took over maintenance of the school (it was still administered by the university), and it was renamed the New York State College of Agriculture with Bailey as director of the college and its experiment station and as dean of the faculty. Over the next decade his efforts were concentrated on developing the curriculum and designing rural extension courses and a statewide nature-study program for children. By the end of his tenure a small regional college had grown into an institution with a worldwide reputation. One of Bailey's greatest public honors came in 1908 when President Theodore Roosevelt appointed him chair of a commission to make recommendations for the improvement of country life. The commission report, largely written by Bailey himself, was published in 1911. Efforts to persuade him to run for Congress in 1910 or for New York state governor in 1918 were fruitless, however; as he contended, "I will never violate my trust with the farmers by dragging their issues to the political arena" (Rodgers, p. 385).

In 1913 Bailey resigned his posts at Cornell to devote the rest of his life to botanizing and traveling—and continued to write prolifically. In 1917 he went to China to collect plants and study agricultural methods (which he thought to be at the root of China's social and political problems). In later years, becoming particularly interested in New World palms as a primary source of food and fiber, he made numerous collecting trips to the Caribbean and along the Amazon River. His personal collection of 125,000 herbarium specimens of cultivated and wild plants, together with his library of older agricultural books and his botanical photographs—his "hortorium" as he called it—was donated to Cornell University in 1935. Now housed in the agricultural school's Mann Library, the Liberty Hyde Bailey Hortorium continues to acquire specimens and maintains an active publishing program; it ranks as one of the nation's largest herbaria. With his daughter Ethel Zoe, first curator of the hortorium, Bailey compiled his great *Hortus*, a concise dictionary of gardening, general horticulture, and cultivated plants in North America. The first edition, published in 1930, was succeeded by *Hortus Second* in 1941.

With characteristic vigor and enthusiasm, Bailey made his last field trip, to the Caribbean, in 1949. He died in Ithaca. In 1990 Bailey and Gregor Mendel became the first scientists inducted into the new Hall of Fame of the American Society for Horticultural Science. Much honored in his lifetime, he received several doctorates, was a corresponding member of horticultural and botanical societies around the world, and served as president of the American Association for the Advancement of Science in 1926.

• Bailey's correspondence and papers are housed in the Division of Rare and Manuscript Collections, Cornell University Library, Ithaca, N.Y. He is the subject of two full-scale biographies: Andrew Denny Rodgers III, *Liberty Hyde Bailey: A Story of American Plant Sciences* (1950), a detailed account of his life and career in the context of the development of horticultural and agricultural study in the United States; and *Liberty Hyde Bailey: An Informal Biography*, written by an Ithacan and Cornell University alumnus, Philip Dorf. Published two years after Bailey's death, the latter is a lively portrait of a scientist and educator with a great zest for living, and it is valuable for its chronological listing of Bailey's professional honors as well as for its selective bibliography of works by and about him, published and in manuscript. Concise accounts of Bailey's life and career are George H. M. Lawrence, "Liberty Hyde Bailey 1858–1954: An Appreciation," *Baileya* (a publication of the Bailey Hortorium) 3 (Mar. 1955): 26–40; and Harlan P. Banks, "Liberty Hyde Bailey, March 15, 1858–December 25, 1954," National Academy of Sciences, *Biographical Memoirs* 64 (1994): 3–32. Partial listings of Bailey's books, journal articles, and works he edited, as well as others of which he was a joint author, appear in the articles by Lawrence and Banks. Gould P. Colman, *Education and Agriculture: A History of the New York State College of Agriculture at Cornell University* (1963), provides information on Bailey's work as professor and dean. An obituary is in the *New York Times*, 27 Dec. 1954.

ELEANOR F. WEDGE

BAILEY, Lydia R. (1 Feb. 1779–21 Feb. 1869), printer, was born in Lancaster, Pennsylvania, the daughter of Captain William Steele and Elizabeth Bailey. The Steele family was landed gentry, and William Steele, his father, and his brothers served with distinction in the American Revolution. The brothers Steele established a paper mill in Lancaster County after the war, and William also was a prothonotary and a shopkeeper. Elizabeth Bailey was a sister of the printers Francis and Jacob Bailey and assisted them in their work before her marriage. No information is available on Lydia's early life and education.

In the spring of 1797 Lydia Steele married her cousin, Robert Bailey, who was managing his father Francis's Philadelphia printing office at the time; they had four children. She worked alongside her husband in his struggling efforts to run a successful printing enterprise until his death in 1808. Contemporary newspapers reported that Bailey was left impoverished with her family to support, but she began her career resourcefully by immediately paying off her husband's debts. Utilizing the connections already established by her husband and his extended family, she transformed her husband's floundering business into one of the busiest printing establishments in Philadelphia. Although previous generations of printers' widows had continued their husbands' careers, they had done so only long enough to remarry, have a mature son take over, or fold the business; Lydia Bailey made the business a success and never relinquished control of it. She industriously pursued an independent career that brought her continued prosperity and a highly respected social status.

Initially, she turned for help and business to associates such as her uncles Francis Bailey and John Steele (who, as the collector of the Port of Philadelphia and a member of the city's common council, was a man of great influence) and to the publisher Mathew Carey. Philip Freneau, the poet of the Revolution, learned of the young widow's plight and agreed in 1809 to have her publish a third collected edition of his poems, which proved highly successful for both. Favored by the Whig administration, which Steele and Carey in particular supported, she succeeded in getting contracts with a number of government agencies early in her career. In 1813 Bailey obtained the contract to become Philadelphia's official city printer—a post she mostly held until the mid-1850s—further increasing her income and visibility as a printer. Subsequently she acquired steady contracts for job printing with the University of Pennsylvania and various banks and canal companies.

Many of the jobs Bailey obtained were tied to her personal relations and social status in the Philadelphia community. She was a staunch Presbyterian and a member of the Third Presbyterian Church, which she endowed heavily; she printed much material for the church and religious-based charitable organizations such as the Female Tract Society, the Orphan Society, the Indigent Widows' and Single Women's Society, and the Ladies' Liberia School Association. Her father-in-law, Francis Bailey, had helped establish the Swedenborgian church in the United States, and Lydia Bailey for years printed for that church as well.

Although Bailey occasionally published books and pamphlets on her own during the early years, she chose to concentrate her shop's energies on book and job printing for others as she matured. The blank forms, almanacs, annual reports, booksellers' catalogs, broadsides, and chapbooks that she printed constituted a modest body of work but steady, plentiful business. While this focus reflected her practical nature and capabilities, it also demonstrated mid-century developments in the printing trade, as larger and more specialized firms replaced the small family-run general printing shops of the earlier period.

Bailey was the master printer of a shop that at its peak was one of the largest in the city, employing more than forty workers. She organized her staff efficiently on an up-to-date factory basis, though she retained the old hand-press technology long after other printers had modernized. In keeping with her religious nature, she is reported to have run a tight operation, and in her workbooks she repeatedly admonished her employees to attend church regularly and to behave with propriety both inside and outside the shop. Many of her employees went on to respectable careers as bookmen in their own right, among them Alexander Baird, Robert P. King, and John Fagan. Her only son, William Robert, entered the shop around the time of his father's death and eventually became a foreman. Bailey depended on him increasingly over the years, and when he died in 1861, she retired, at the age of eighty-two. By 1861 printing plants of steam-powered presses were churning out more business at lower costs than even the most established, productive hand-press shops; one obituary romantically reported that "steam presses were fatal to her courage and she surrendered to an instrumentality she could neither comprehend nor compete with." For whatever reasons, Lydia Bailey never embraced the new technology and simply closed her business on her retirement. She died in Philadelphia soon after her ninetieth birthday.

The contemporary printing historian William McCulloch reported that Bailey "carried on the printing business with success and reputation." Multiple obituaries noted the respect she had achieved in the printing world and spoke highly of her local reputation. Lydia Bailey was one of nineteenth-century America's few women printers; even by masculine standards, the length, financial success, and abundant output of her 53-year career were noteworthy.

• The only known extant Bailey manuscripts, including business accounts kept with her mother and various ledgers, are at the Historical Society of Pennsylvania, Philadelphia. Additional manuscript information can be found in other printers' and publishers' account books, particularly Mathew Carey's at the Historical Society of Pennsylvania and at the American Antiquarian Society, Worcester, Mass. For contemporary accounts of her printing see the *Printers' Circular*, Aug. 1868, p. 165; Mathew Carey, *Autobiographical Sketches* (1829); and William McCulloch, "Additions to Thomas's History of Printing," *Proceedings of the American Antiquarian Society*, n.s., 31, pt. 1 (1921). William Peden, "Jefferson, Freneau, and the *Poems* of 1809," *New Colophon* 1 (Oct. 1948): 394–400, and Lewis Leary, *That Rascal Freneau* (1941), detail her relationship with Philip Freneau and the printing of his poems. The most comprehensive secondary source is Leona Hudak, *Early American Women Printers and Publishers* (1978), which includes a biography, citations, and a partial bibliography. Obituaries appear in the *Typographic Advertiser*, Apr. 1869; the *North American*, 24 Feb. 1869; the *Philadelphia Daily Evening Bulletin*, 24 Feb. 1869; the *Sunday Dispatch*, 28 Feb. 1869; and the *Philadelphia Inquirer*, 25 Feb. 1869.

KAREN NIPPS

BAILEY, Mildred (27 Feb. 1907–12 Dec. 1951), jazz singer, was born Eleanor Mildred Rinker in Tekoa, Washington, the daughter of Charles Rinker, a farmer of Irish descent, and Josephine (maiden name unknown), who was one-eighth Native American. She attended local schools in Spokane. The Rinkers were a musical family—Mildred's mother, father, and a brother played piano, her father also sang, and another brother played the saxophone. When Mildred was in her teens, her mother died of tuberculosis; She subsequently moved to Seattle to live with an aunt. In Seattle she met and married Ed Bailey; they had no children. Around that time Mildred obtained her first singing job, plugging hit tunes in the back of a Seattle music store. She later divorced her husband and in 1925 moved to Los Angeles, where she found work playing piano and singing in a Hollywood speakeasy. The same year she married Benny Stafford, but the childless marriage did not last.

Mildred Bailey's brother Al often brought the Rhythm Boys—a trio he had formed with Bing Crosby and Harry Barris—to her home in Los Angeles for dinner and conversation. Crosby would later credit Bailey with helping the Rhythm Boys obtain their professional start by introducing the vocal group to a successful theatrical producer (he also cited Bailey's singing as an influence on his own vocal style). The trio eventually took a job with the Paul Whiteman orchestra.

In 1929 Bailey herself was signed to sing with the Whiteman orchestra after the bandleader heard her perform in a San Francisco restaurant. According to some accounts, her brother introduced her to Whiteman; others suggest she sent an audition record to him. In any case, Bailey was the first woman vocalist to appear with Whiteman and the Casa Loma Orchestra, and she toured with the band through 1933. She appeared on nationally broadcast radio programs and recorded independently with musicians such as the Dorsey Brothers, Benny Goodman, Bunny Berigan, and Johnny Hodges. Her songs from this period include "Junk Man," "Ol' Pappy," "Georgia on My Mind," and "Harlem Lullaby."

Bailey fell in love with the Whiteman orchestra's xylophonist, Red Norvo, and in 1934 the pair left the band and married. Initially Bailey tried staying home as a housewife (they had no children), while Norvo performed with various groups. But by 1936 Norvo and Bailey had founded a band and were touring and appearing on radio programs. They became known as "Mr. and Mrs. Swing." The tasteful virtuosity of Norvo and the other instrumentalists showcased Bailey's distinctive vocal style. Influenced by black singers like Bessie Smith, Ethel Waters, and Billie Holiday, Bailey developed a "laid-back" type of phrasing, controlling her vibrato until the end of each phrase, and emulated the black blues singers' vocal inflections and pronunciation. She sang ballads with sincere emotion, and her intonation and natural ear were excellent. Bailey used her voice as an instrument, and, as a more mature singer, her phrasing seemed to emulate a jazz horn player.

During her years with Norvo, Bailey recorded songs such as "Downhearted Blues," "A Porter's Love Song to a Chambermaid," "Smoke Dreams," and "Thanks for the Memory." She was dubbed the "Rocking Chair Lady" after her 1937 recording of Hoagy Carmichael's "Rocking Chair" became popular.

Throughout her career, Bailey was plagued by ill health. In 1939 recurrent sickness caused her temporarily to retire. Consistently overweight, she had a reputation among musicians and friends for overindulgence. Even when ordered by doctors to control her weight, Bailey continued to eat too much. At the same time she blamed obesity for limiting her public appeal. Although seemingly cheerful, she was subject to bad temper. One famous fight with Norvo escalated to the point where both husband and wife were throwing clothing into a fireplace. The fire department had to be called.

In the 1940s Bailey returned to the stage and radio, appearing solo and with Norvo. Even after their divorce in 1945, Bailey and Norvo occasionally teamed up. In later years Bailey lived alone in a New York City apartment with her beloved dachshunds, appearing sporadically in nightclubs. She developed diabetes and eventually retired to a farm she purchased in Stormville, New York. Through this period Bailey became increasingly frustrated with the obscurity into which she had fallen. In 1951, after a nightclub engagement in Detroit, she collapsed. She was taken to Poughkeepsie, New York, where she died, her death attributed to hardening of the arteries, liver malfunction, and a weak heart.

In many ways Mildred Bailey was ahead of her time, bringing elements of classic blues and popular song together in a vocal style that was distinctive in its day. Her sweet, light soprano voice and hornlike phrasing was not what the public expected of early white jazz singers. As talented as she was, though, Bailey did not gain the recognition that other singers with less vocal ability and musicality received.

• A discussion of Bailey can be found in Bruce Crowther and M. Pinfold, *The Jazz Singers* (1986). Other sources include Gunther Schuller, *The Swing Era: The Development of Jazz, 1930–1945* (1989); John Chilton, *Who's Who of Jazz: Storyville to Swing Street* (1978); Henry Pleasants, *The Great American Popular Singers* (1974); Linda Dahl, *Stormy Weather: The Music and Lives of a Century of Jazz Women* (1984); and Leslie Gourse, *Louis' Children: American Jazz Singers* (1984). Also useful are the liner notes by John Hammond, Bing Crosby, Irving Townsend, and Bucklin Moon for *Mildred Bailey: Her Greatest Performances, 1929–1946*, Columbia JC3L22. A sketchy obituary is in the *New York Times*, 13 Dec. 1951; see also M. Jones, "Mildred Bailey, an Appreciation," *Melody Maker*, 22 Dec. 1951, p. 2.

JAN SHAPIRO

BAILEY, Pearce (22 July 1902–23 June 1976), neurologist and federal health science administrator, was born in New York City, the son of Pearce Bailey, a prominent neurologist, and Edith L. Black. Bailey's choice of a career was doubtless influenced by the fact that his physician father was president of the American Neurological Association in 1913 and was a cofounder of the Neurological Institute at Columbia University in New York City. After graduation from Princeton University with an A.B. in 1924, Bailey pursued postgraduate studies at Columbia University, from which he received an M.A. in psychology in 1931. He then studied at the Université de Paris, where he earned a Ph.D. in psychology in 1933; took an honors course in chemistry at the University of London in 1934; and earned an M.D. at the Medical College of South Carolina at Charleston in 1941.

While in Paris in the 1930s, Bailey met and studied with psychiatrists Sigmund Freud, Alfred Adler, Carl Gustav Jung, and Otto Rank. Bailey was cofounder, with Rank, of Le Centre de Psychologie de Paris and served as its associate director from 1933 to 1936. In 1936 he married Georgette Dora Soudry, the Princess Mestchersky, in France; they had no children.

After medical school, Bailey served a rotating internship at Roper Hospital in Charleston, South Carolina, in 1941–1942 and then as chief resident in neurology at Bellevue Hospital in New York City for two years. In 1944 he was commissioned as commander in the Medical Corps of the U.S. Naval Reserve and served as chief of the Neurology Service at Philadelphia Naval Hospital until 1946. Concurrently he was visiting neuropsychiatrist to Bellevue Hospital in New York City.

At the end of World War II, Bailey organized, and became chief of, the Neurology Section of the Veterans Administration Central Office in Washington, D.C. (1946–1948). In 1947 he was certified in neurology by the American Board of Neurology and Psychiatry. From 1948 to 1951 he held the posts of assistant chief of the Psychiatry and Neurology Division and chief of the Neurology Section of the VA Central Office. Over the next three years this became the largest neurological service in the world. Bailey was instrumental in initiating the resurgence of American neurology from its prewar nadir and in establishing neurology as a distinct discipline independent of psychiatry (thus ending the artificial amalgam of neuropsychiatry that had originated in World War I).

In 1950 the Eighty-first U.S. Congress passed Public Law 692, creating the National Institute of Neurological Diseases and Blindness (NINDB) as one of the National Institutes of Health (NIH) headquartered in Bethesda, Maryland. The following year Bailey was appointed the first director of the NINDB (now the National Institute of Neurological Disorders and Stroke), a post he held for the next eight years. In this capacity Bailey was responsible for the further postwar "resurrection" of the field of clinical neurology and for the development throughout the country of highly successful research programs dealing with chronic and disabling disorders of the nervous system—developments that spurred the emergence of the field of neurosciences, a major force in current biomedical research.

In 1959 Bailey became director of the International Neurological Research Programs of the NINDB, in conjunction with the World Federation of Neurology (WFN), which he had cofounded with the Belgian neuroscientist Ludo Van Bogaert in 1957 in Antwerp. From 1957 to 1965 Bailey served as the first secretary-treasurer general of the WFN. His last posts before retirement in 1971 were as special assistant to the director of the NINDB and as chief of Inter-American Activities of the NINDB, with his headquarters in San Juan, Puerto Rico. These latter activities exemplify his many contributions to the development of neurology internationally.

During his career, Bailey held a number of faculty appointments at medical schools and hospitals in the Washington, D.C., area and was a regular or an honorary member of more than twenty-five domestic and foreign professional societies as well as president of the American Academy of Neurology from 1951 to 1953 and of the National Epilepsy Society in 1952–1953. Among his many honors were the bestowals of "Officier de la Santé Publique" of France in 1949; Comendador of "El Sol del Perú" in 1963; and the first Medal and Honorarium from the Epilepsy Foundation of America in 1976 "for exceptional dedicated service in the field of epilepsy." He published some forty-seven papers, chapters, and reviews between 1933 and 1975. His interest in neurological history led him to produce biographical sketches on neurologists Moses Allen Starr (in *The Founders of Neurology*, ed. Webb Haymaker, 1st ed. [1953], pp. 392–95) and Joseph Babinski (in *World Neurology* 2 [1961]: 134–40), and a 1959 translation from the French monograph on neurologist Jean Martin Charcot by Georges Guillain (*J. M. Charcot, 1825–1893. His Life—His Work*). He died in Washington, D.C.

A major force in rescuing neurology from oblivion before World War II, Bailey successfully launched the NINDB at the NIH, producing lasting impacts on clinical neurology and the basic neurosciences. His fund of knowledge was remarkable and his skill as a health science administrator and politician was legendary.

• A curriculum vitae compiled by Bailey in June 1970 is in the NINDS–NIH Archives, Bethesda, Md. Bailey's works include "National Institute of Neurological Diseases and Blindness. Origins, Founding and Early Years (1950 to 1959)," in *The Nervous System*, vol. 1: *The Basic Neurosciences*, ed. Roscoe O. Brady and Donald B. Tower (1975). Obituaries are in the *Washington Post* and the *New York Times*, 28 June 1976; *Surgical Neurology* 6, no. 2 (Aug. 1976): 81; *American Journal of Ophthalmology* 82, no. 3 (Sept. 1976): 510–11; and *Journal of the Neurological Sciences* 30, nos. 2 and 3 (Dec. 1976): 421–22, in French.

DONALD B. TOWER

BAILEY, Pearl (29 Mar. 1918–17 Aug. 1990), actress, singer, and entertainer, was born Pearl Mae Bailey in Newport News, Virginia, the daughter of the Reverend Joseph James Bailey and Ella Mae (maiden name unknown). Her brother Bill Bailey was at one time a well-known tap dancer.

While still in high school, Bailey launched her show business career in Philadelphia, where her mother had relocated the family after separating from Rev. Bailey. In 1933, at age fifteen, she won the first of three amateur talent contests, with a song-and-dance routine at the Pearl Theatre in Philadelphia, which awarded her a $5 prize. In a second contest at the Jungle Inn in Washington, D.C., she received a $12 prize for a buck-and-wing dancing act. After winning a third contest at the famed Apollo Theatre in Harlem, she began performing professionally—first as a specialty dancer or chorus girl with several small bands, including Noble Sissle's band, on the vaudeville circuits in Pennsylvania, Maryland, and Washington during the 1930s; then as a vocalist with Cootie Williams and Count Basie at such smart New York clubs as La Vie en Rose and the Blue Angel, and on the World War II USO circuit, during the 1940s.

Bailey made her Broadway debut as a saloon barmaid named Butterfly in the black-authored musical *St. Louis Woman*, which opened at the Martin Beck Theatre, 30 March 1946, and ran for 113 performances. Although the show was only modestly successful, she was praised for her singing of two hit numbers, "Legalize My Name" and "(It's) A Woman's Prerogative (to Change Her Mind)." For her performance, she won a Donaldson Award as the best Broadway newcomer. After several failed marriages, one to comedian Slappy White, Bailey married the legendary white jazz drummer Louis Bellson, Jr., in 1952; they adopted two children. Their marriage was reportedly a happy one. In later years, she frequently sang with her husband's band, and at one time toured with Cab Calloway and his band.

After appearing in supporting roles in two predominantly white shows, 1950–1951, Bailey's first Broadway starring vehicle was *House of Flowers* (1954), a Caribbean-inspired musical. Bailey played the part of Mme. Fleur, a resourceful bordello madam, whose house of prostitution in the French West Indies is facing hard times, forcing her to resort to desperate measures to save it. The show opened at the Alvin Theatre, 30 December 1954, and had a run of 165 performances. Despite what the *New York Times* (30 Dec. 1954) called "feeble material," she was credited with "an amusing style" and the ability to "[throw] away songs with smart hauteur."

Bailey's most important Broadway role was as the irrepressible Dolly Levi (a marriage broker who arranges a lucrative marriage for herself) in the all-black version of *Hello, Dolly!*, which opened at the St. James Theatre in November 1967 for a long run, sharing the stage with the original 1964 Carol Channing version. The black version provided tangible evidence that roles originally created by white actors could be redefined and given new vitality from the perspective of the African-American experience. Lyndon Johnson, who had used the show's title song as his campaign theme song in 1964, changing the words to "Hello, Lyndon!," saw the show when it came to Washington and was invited, along with his wife Lady Bird, to join Bailey onstage for a rousing finale. For her performance, Bailey won a special Tony Award in 1968.

Bailey's most important film roles included *Carmen Jones* (1954), as one of Carmen's friends; *St. Louis Blues* (1958), as composer W. C. Handy's Aunt Hagar; *Porgy and Bess* (1959), as Maria, the cookshop woman; *All the Fine Young Cannibals* (1960), as a boozing, over-the-hill blues singer; and *Norman . . . Is That You?* (1976), opposite comedian Redd Foxx, as estranged parents of a gay son. Her voice was also used for Big Mama, the owl, in the Disney animated film *The Fox and the Hound* (1981).

A frequent performer and guest on television talk shows beginning in the 1950s, Bailey also hosted her own variety series on ABC, "The Pearl Bailey Show" (Jan.–May 1971), for which her husband directed the orchestra while she entertained an assortment of celebrity guests. She also appeared on television in "An Evening with Pearl" (1975) and in a remake of *The Member of the Wedding* (1982), in the role of Berenice. Bailey released numerous albums and was also the author of several books, including two autobiographies, *The Raw Pearl* (1968) and *Talking to Myself* (1971), and *Pearl's Kitchen* (1973), a cookbook.

In 1975 Bailey was appointed as a U.S. delegate to the United Nations. Other honors and awards included a citation from New York City mayor John V. Lindsay; *Cue* magazine entertainer of the year (1969); the First Order in Arts and Sciences from Egyptian president Anwar Sadat; the Screen Actors Guild Award for outstanding achievement in fostering the finest ideals of the acting profession; and an honorary Doctor of Humane Letters from Georgetown University (1977). She later earned a degree in theology from Georgetown.

During the later years of her life, Bailey was hospitalized several times for a heart ailment. She also suffered from an arthritic knee, which was replaced with an artificial one just prior to her death. She collapsed, apparently from a heart attack, at the Philadelphia hotel where she was staying (her home was in Havasu, Ariz.); she died soon after at Thomas Jefferson University Hospital in Philadelphia.

Bailey was best-known for her lazy, comical, half-singing, half-chatting style, expressive hands, tired feet, and folksy, congenial philosophy of life, which endeared her to audiences both black and white. The *New York Times* obituary (18 Aug. 1990) called her "a trouper in the old theatrical sense," who had "enraptured theater and nightclub audiences for a quarter-century by the languorous sexuality of her throaty voice as well as by the directness of her personality." At her funeral, Cab Calloway, who had starred with her in *Hello, Dolly!*, said that "Pearl was love, pure and simple love"; and her husband called her "a person of love," who believed that "show business" meant to "show love."

• Bailey provided details of her own career up to the 1970s in her two autobiographical writings, *The Raw Pearl* (1968) and *Talking to Myself* (1971). Her life and film career are extensively treated by Donald Bogle in his *Brown Sugar: Eighty Years of America's Black Female Superstars* (1980) and his *Blacks in American Films and Television: An Illustrated Encyclopedia* (1988). Her musicals are described by Bernard L. Peterson, Jr., in *A Century of Musicals in Black and White: An Encyclopedia of Musical Stage Works by, about, or Involving African Americans* (1993). Edward Mapp's *Directory of Blacks in the Performing Arts* (1978) provides a list of her musical compositions and television shows; and Walter Rigdon's *The Biographical Encyclopedia & Who's Who of the American Theatre* (1966) lists her theatrical and nightclub appearances. *Ebony* magazine recorded her career in numerous feature articles, including those in the May 1953, Apr. 1955, Jan. 1957, Apr. 1959, May 1960, and Jan. 1968 issues. Obituaries are in the *New York Times*, 18, 24, and 25 Aug. 1990.

BERNARD L. PETERSON

BAILEY, Solon Irving (29 Dec. 1854–5 June 1931), astronomer, was born in Lisbon, New Hampshire, the son of Israel Carlton Bailey and Jane Sutherland, farmers. Raised in Concord, New Hampshire, he attended the Tilton Academy in Tilton, New Hampshire, and then Boston University, from which he obtained an A.B. in 1881 and an A.M. three years later. In 1883 Bailey married Ruth E. Poulter, who assisted him voluntarily in much of his astronomical work; the couple had two children, one of whom died in infancy.

Upon completing his A.M., Bailey returned to the Tilton Academy as headmaster. Having been intrigued as a boy by the spectacle of the great meteor shower of 1866, he taught introductory astronomy at Tilton and wanted to study the subject in more detail. He wrote to Edward C. Pickering of the Harvard College Observatory but was told that Harvard had no formal graduate program in astronomy. Undeterred, he moved to Cambridge in 1887 to serve as a voluntary assistant at the Harvard Observatory. Pickering was so impressed by Bailey's work that he recommended him for an M.A. in astronomy, which Bailey obtained the following year.

Pickering then hired Bailey to go to South America to investigate possible sites for a southern observing station. For this purpose, Bailey established a string of meteorological stations in Peru. He also made nearly 100,000 observations of the magnitudes of over 7,000 southern stars, extending to the Southern Hemisphere a program Pickering had begun in Cambridge. Examining the evidence Bailey had accumulated, Pickering decided to place Harvard's Boyden station in Arequipa, Peru. When Bailey returned to Cambridge in 1891, he was made an assistant at the observatory and two years later received the rank of assistant professor.

The first director of the Boyden Station was Pickering's brother William. William H. Pickering had expensive tastes and showed little interest in the photographic observations that Edward wished to have made. In 1893 Bailey replaced William Pickering as the director at Boyden. He soon had the instruments in good repair and, from 1896, also observed with a new 24-inch telescope provided by Catherine Bruce, a wealthy New Yorker. Bailey's first term as director ended in January 1898. He would return for a second five-year term in 1899 and more briefly in the 1920s.

In Arequipa, Bailey initially carried out a program of observations that had been laid out in Cambridge. E. C. Pickering soon consulted him, however, about the best use of the telescopes. The photographic plates Bailey sent north, combined with those taken in Cambridge, were measured by a large staff of women there and used for fundamental work in photometry, spectral classification, and the study of variable stars. Bailey himself was particularly interested in galactic clusters. He and his wife counted over 6,000 stars in the cluster Omega Centauri, where only seven had been enumerated previously. He observed the cluster repeatedly and, by 1895, had discovered in it five stars that varied in brightness. By extending these observations over time and to other clusters, he discovered a total of 509 cluster variables, which equaled the total number of previously known variables. Cluster variables were mostly Cepheids, a class of variables whose periods were later shown to be correlated with their magnitudes and indicative of their distance. Bailey thereby provided part of the evidence that a later director of the Harvard College Observatory, Harlow

Shapley, would use in his estimates of galactic dimensions.

In Peru, Bailey also made numerous observations of asteroids and established the period of variation of the light of Eros, observed near the opposition of 1903. He and his associates continued to accumulate meteorological records and even established an observing station atop El Misti, the nearly extinct, 19,200-foot volcano that towers over Arequipa. He published meteorological data for the period 1888 to 1925 in six long articles in the *Annals* of the Harvard College Observatory. Meteorological conditions in Peru, specifically the clouds that made it impossible to see the stars for up to four months of the year, caused Pickering to rethink the location for the Boyden Station. In 1908–1909 he sent Bailey to South Africa to examine possible sites there. Bailey recommended the skies near Bloemfontein in the Orange Free State. A sudden restriction in the observatory's funds delayed the Boyden Station's move to this location until the late 1920s.

Bailey had been named an associate professor in 1898 and was promoted to the rank of Phillips Professor in 1912. From about 1910, he served unofficially as assistant director of the Harvard College Observatory, handling numerous administrative details. When Pickering died in early 1919, Bailey took over as acting director until 1921. The following year, he and his wife made a final trip to oversee affairs at the Boyden Station. While he was there, the University of San Agustin in Arequipa awarded him an honorary Sc.D. degree. When Bailey returned to Cambridge, he resumed his work on cluster variables and began a monograph on the history of the Harvard Observatory. He continued his historical work after his retirement in 1925, and it appeared as *History and Work of the Harvard Observatory 1839–1927* in 1931, the year of his death in Norwell, Massachusetts. Bailey was a fellow of the American Academy of Arts and Sciences and a member of the National Academy of Sciences.

• During his years as director of the Boyden Station, Bailey exchanged numbered letters with Pickering and then Shapley. These letters, as well as other correspondence relating to aspects of Bailey's career, are in the Papers of the Harvard College Observatory in the Harvard University Archives. For accounts of Bailey's work see Annie Jump Cannon, "Biographical Memoir of Solon Irving Bailey 1854–1931," National Academy of Sciences, *Biographical Memoirs* 15 (1932): 193–203; Bessie Zaban Jones and Lyle Gifford Boyd, *The Harvard College Observatory: The First Four Directorships, 1839–1919* (1971); and Howard Plotkin, "Harvard College Observatory's Boyden Station in Peru: Origin and Formative Years, 1879–1898," in *Mundialización de la ciencia y cultura nacional*, ed. A. Lafuente et al. (1993), pp. 689–705.

PEGGY ALDRICH KIDWELL

BAILEY, Temple (1880?–6 July 1953), novelist and short story writer, was born Irene Temple Bailey in Petersburg, Virginia, the daughter of Milo Varnum Bailey and Emma Sprague. Her birth date is uncertain, but when she died she was thought to be in her seventies. The Baileys lived for a time in Richmond, Virginia, before moving to Washington, D.C., when Temple was five. She returned briefly to Richmond, where she attended a girls' school housed in what had been General Robert E. Lee's mansion and which later became the Virginia Historical Association headquarters. When she was frequently unable to attend school because of poor health, she was tutored by her father who paid special attention to her written English. Her only other formal education included some special college courses.

Although Bailey realized as an adult that she had become a careful, competent writer, she had no burning desire to write or to have a career. It was only when, as she said, "a season of stress and sorrow drove me to self-expression" that she began to "scribble" stories. In 1904 she won a prize for a love story that was published in the *Ladies' Home Journal.* Next she wrote children's stories and a children's novel. Soon her stories were being published in many women's magazines, and she began writing serials that later were published as novels. In 1924 *Peacock Feathers* was serialized in *Good Housekeeping* from February to August, followed by *The Blue Window*, which ran from September 1925 to March 1926, with each work published in book form in the year of its conclusion. Sometimes the letters she received during the course of writing a serial helped determine the development of the story. During the writing of *Enchanted Ground*, she was planning to have Peter, one of the two men in love with the heroine, die. But in response to her readers who wrote to her, she changed the plot so it was Boone who died.

Settings were particularly important to Bailey. She said, "I set my characters against a background of Virginia hills, of Boston streets and the blue seas and skies of Old Nantucket." Her love of travel and her belief that people everywhere are basically alike led to settings as widely divergent as Boston, Wyoming, Florida, and the Pacific Coast. Bailey spoke of her love for cities, "the romance of them, the picturesqueness, the charm." Her great admiration for Charles Dickens grew from the way that "he made London a place of dear delights, finding in crowded squares and quiet streets the human stories." Many of her novels were set in Washington, D.C., the place she knew best.

After Bailey had written seven novels and many short stories and had achieved financial success, she tried to explain why she kept writing: "What has kept me at it? That's the question I ask myself. Why do I, in these days when I might be free as air, still stay at my desk, and put black marks on paper. Well, I think that, boiled down to the last analysis, it is because I like to travel. And what I enjoy is not the end of the journey, but the things that happen by the way."

Bailey preferred to write short stories and thought that her stories were her most artistic work, although she found them harder to write than novels. Her stories were published in *Cosmopolitan*, *Harper's*, *Scribner's*, *Outlook*, *Colliers*, *Woman's Home Companion*, and other women's magazines. "White Birches," published first in the *Saturday Evening Post*, was included in *Short Stories for Class Reading* (1925). Some stories were collected in *The Radiant Tree and Other Stories* (1934; repr. 1970). Her Christmas stories appeared each December in *Good Housekeeping* for several years; some were collected in *The Holly Hedge and Other Christmas Stories* (1925) and in *So This Is Christmas and Other Stories* (1931).

Bailey never married, and she lived very privately, spending the last years of her life at the Wardman Park Hotel in Washington, D.C. This hotel was the scene of *Fair as the Moon* (1935), considered one of her better novels. Still, she thought herself "an intensely social person" and was a member of the Authors League in New York, the Authors Club in Boston, and the Chevy Chase Club and the Arts Club in Washington, D.C.

In *Women's Gothic and Romantic Fiction* (1981), Kay Mussell calls Temple Bailey a "fairly obscure but interesting writer." She was far from obscure during her lifetime. Called "innocuous, virginal novels" by the *New York Times* and "escapist fiction for girls and women [that] . . . feature virginal heroines, young love, conventional morality and happy endings" (*The Feminist Companion to Literature in English* [1990]), Bailey's writings were immensely popular. From *Judy* (1907) to *Red Fruit* (1945), she wrote more than thirty novels; each was eagerly awaited and sold through large chain stores such as John Wanamaker's. Her books sold in the millions, almost half of them to libraries. Three of her novels, *Contrary Mary* (1914), *Glory of Youth* (1913), and *The Tin Soldier* (1918), were reprinted in 1975.

Bailey filled the magazines with stories of idealism. In her work, goodness, virtue, and true love triumph over wealth, greed, and selfishness. She wrote for her time, through two world wars and the Great Depression between them, and she seemed to fill her readers' needs to believe in fantasy, in romance, in the possibility of a better life and a happier world. She died in Washington, D.C.

• *Temple Bailey, an Autobiography* (1923?) includes, besides a very brief autobiographical sketch, two short articles, "How I Should Sell My Book If I Were a Bookseller" and "Authorship as a Profession." Excerpts from this work were used in the back or on the book jackets of several of her novels. She was also the subject of one of Grant Overton's columns, "The Women Who Make Our Novels," later published as a book under the same title in 1928. See also a brief sketch in the *Saturday Evening Post*, 5 Nov. 1919, and "Best-Paid Author in the World," *Publishers Weekly*, 24 June 1933, p. 2016. Obituaries are in the *New York Times*, 8 July 1953, and the *Wilson Library Bulletin* 28 (Sept. 1953): 28.

BLANCHE COX CLEGG

BAILEY, Theodorus (12 Apr. 1805–10 Feb. 1877), U.S. Navy rear admiral, was born at Chateaugay near Plattsburg, New York, the son of William Bailey, a judge, and Phoebe Platt. He was the nephew and namesake of Theodorus Bailey (1758–1828), who was a congressman, U.S. senator, and postmaster of New York City. Raised in New York State on the western shore of Lake Champlain, the scion of a prominent family, Bailey attended Plattsburg Academy and joined the U.S. Navy only four years after Commodore Thomas McDonough was victorious over the British in the waters off Plattsburg during the War of 1812.

Bailey was appointed a midshipman in the navy on 1 January 1818, first serving at sea in the frigate *Cyane* on the coast of West Africa and in the West Indies from 1819 until December 1820 engaged in suppressing piracy and the slave trade. In May 1821 he reported on board the ship-of-the-line *Franklin*, the flagship of Commodore Charles Stewart, commanding the tiny U.S. Pacific Squadron operating off the west coast of South America. Returning from the Pacific with *Franklin* in August 1824, he took leave of absence from September 1824 until May 1825, when he returned to active service at the New York Navy Yard. In July 1825 he reported on board the schooner *Shark*, cruising in the West Indies and the Gulf of Mexico. After the schooner's return to New York he again took a leave of absence from September to November 1826, after which he was promoted to lieutenant and served in the receiving ship *Fulton* at New York City until 1829, returning again to leave status. In 1830 he married his cousin Sarah Ann Platt.

Bailey remained awaiting orders until January 1831, when he reported to the sloop of war *Natchez*, serving in the West Indies and along the Atlantic Coast. Only nine months later the navy decommissioned the ship and placed it in ordinary. Awaiting orders until April 1833 he reported to the sloop of war *Vincennes*, then refitting after overhaul at Portsmouth, New Hampshire. On board *Vincennes* he rounded Cape Horn and visited Fiji, the Palau Islands, and Sumatra in search of shipwrecked and stranded American seamen. He was serving on *Vincennes* when it made the first visit of an American warship to Guam, and aboard this vessel circumnavigated the globe, calling en route at Cape Town and St. Helena. After he returned to Hampton Roads, Virginia, he was assigned to special recruiting duty for the U.S. Exploring Expedition, then preparing to sail in 1838 on a scientific expedition to the Pacific under the command of Lieutenant Charles Wilkes.

Detached from recruiting duty in June 1837, Bailey served temporarily on board the receiving ship *Ohio* at New York and then served at the New York Navy Yard until April 1840. After several months' leave he reported to the frigate *Constellation*, the flagship of the East Indies Squadron. After a period of leave awaiting orders, and then at the Naval Rendezvous, New York, Bailey took command of the store ship *Lexington* from May 1846 until October 1848. And after the outbreak of the war with Mexico in the spring of 1846 he transported troops around Cape Horn to California, including such young officers as William Tecumseh Sherman, Henry W. Halleck, and Edward Ord. On the California coast Bailey assisted in blockade duty as well as the capture of La Paz and San Blas.

Bailey returned home in October 1848, at the end of the war. While on leave and awaiting orders, he received a promotion to commander in March 1849. In September 1853 he returned to duty to command the sloop of war *St. Mary's*, then undergoing repair at the Philadelphia Navy Yard. In 1854 Bailey returned to the Pacific Squadron and cruised in the eastern and southern Pacific over the next two years. In 1856 he returned home on leave of absence until May 1861, when he took command of the steam screw frigate *Colorado*. Sailing from Boston in June 1861, Bailey joined the West Gulf Blockading Squadron (WGBS). He cooperated with General Harvey Brown in operations off Pensacola and personally planned and joined several boat expeditions, including the capture of the Confederate privateer *Judah*. On 23 January 1862 the *Colorado* captured the steamer *Calhoun* off South West Pass at the mouth of the Mississippi and a week later engaged four Confederate steamers. In April 1862 Flag Officer David G. Farragut, commanding the WGBS, appointed Bailey his second in command of the attacking force against Fort Jackson, New Orleans, as part of the plan to join the Union forces in the Gulf with those of General Hallack and Flag Officer Foote invading the South down the Mississippi.

Although in poor health and unable to get the *Colorado* over the bar at the mouth of the river, Bailey embarked in the gunboat *Cayuga* and took command of the first division of gunboats. On 24 April Bailey led the attack and took the first division through the chain barrier on the river, past the fire of the forts and flotilla of eighteen gunboats. Above the forts the division attacked the Chalmette batteries and captured the Chalmette Regiment. Anchoring in front of the city of New Orleans in the early morning of 25 April, Farragut ordered Bailey ashore to demand the city's surrender. Accompanied by Lieutenant George Perkins, Bailey landed on the levee in a dramatic scene sketched by William Waud for *Frank Leslie's Illustrated Newspaper* (31 May 1862) and passed through jeering, hostile crowds to place Farragut's demand before Confederate authorities at City Hall.

In early May 1862 Farragut gave Bailey the honor of carrying the official reports on the battle directly to Secretary of the Navy Gideon Welles. Because Bailey was in poor health, this gave him the opportunity to recuperate. He returned to New York, where Welles placed him in command of the Sackets Harbor Naval Station on Lake Ontario. By November he had recovered and with the rank of acting rear admiral took command of the Eastern Gulf Blockading Squadron in the *Cayuga*. In the eighteen-month period of his command, Bailey's squadron captured 150 Confederate blockade runners off the Florida coast. In September 1864 he took command of the navy yard at Portsmouth, New Hampshire, where he remained until he retired from active service in October 1866.

Settling in Washington, D.C., after retirement, Bailey served as a member of the lighthouse board and several other naval boards between March 1869 and April 1873. He died at his home in Washington. Many in his day considered him one of the ablest naval commanders during the Civil War. The U.S. Navy honored him in 1885 by awarding a medal in his memory to an outstanding naval apprentice. The navy also named three successive ships after him: USS *Bailey* (Torpedo boat 21), which served from 1899 to 1918; the Clemson class destroyer USS *Bailey* (DD-269), which served from 1919 to 1940 and was then transferred to Britain as part of the destroyers-for-bases agreement, and the Benson class destroyer USS *Bailey* (DD-492), which served from 1942 until 1946.

• One volume of Bailey's personal letters for the period 1846–1848 is in the Bancroft Library, University of California, Berkeley, and 220 items relating to him covering the period 1828–1885 are in the George Arents Research Library, Syracuse, N.Y. *The Memoirs of General W. T. Sherman*, chap. 2, describes the USS *Lexington* under Bailey's command in 1846. Bailey's official correspondence at sea during the Civil War is published in *The Official Records of the Union and Confederate Navies in the War of the Rebellion* (1894–1927), series 1, vols. 1–3, 9, 12–13, 16–21, 27, and a few letters are also in George E. Belknap, *The Letters of Captain Geo. Hamilton Perkins* (1901). Bailey himself provided information for and approved the sketch in J. T. Headley, *Farragut and Our Naval Commanders* (1867), pp. 224–51. An obituary is in the *New York Times*, 11 Feb. 1877.

JOHN B. HATTENDORF

BAILEY, Thomas Andrew (14 Dec. 1902–26 July 1983), historian, was born in San Jose, California, the son of James A. Bailey, a fruit farmer, and Annie Mary Nelson, a grade-school teacher. Bailey entered Stanford University in 1920, where he was elected to Phi Beta Kappa and received the B.A. (1924), M.A. (1925), and Ph.D. (1927) degrees. In August 1928, while teaching at the University of Hawaii, he married Sylvia Dean, the daughter of the university's former president; they had one child.

When Ephraim D. Adams, Stanford's historian of American foreign relations, died in 1930, Bailey took over his courses. As an undergraduate Bailey had majored in the Greek language and as a graduate student his training had been in American political history, but from this point onward he made foreign relations his own field, speaking of himself at times as an "evangelist of American diplomatic history" or as one who preached the subject. Although shy and introverted, he resembled an evangelical preacher when he delivered his flamboyant lectures, which he had carefully rehearsed and timed. Until the late sixties they were immensely popular.

In his graduate teaching Bailey urged his students to "write, write, write," and his career exemplified that advice. Beginning with articles in 1924 and the publication of his first monograph, *Theodore Roosevelt and the Japanese-American Crises* (1934), his scholarly publications earned him an international reputation along with numerous invitations to teach and lecture. He served as visiting professor at the University of Washington, George Washington University, Harvard University, the Institute for Advanced Study at Princeton, and the National War College, and he delivered the Albert Shaw lectures at Johns Hopkins and the Messenger Lectures at Cornell. He was elected president of the Pacific Coast Branch of the American Historical Association, 1959–1960, the Organization of Historians, 1967–1968, and the Society for Historians of American Foreign Relations, 1967–1968.

Bailey regarded his *Diplomatic History of the American People* (1940), a textbook, which in more than ten editions dominated the field for decades, as his most significant contribution to historiography. His *Woodrow Wilson and the Lost Peace* (1944) and *Woodrow Wilson and the Great Betrayal* (1945) brought him further distinction. But he considered his *Man in the Street* (1948), which examined public opinion as a major force in the shaping of American foreign policy, his pathbreaking work. In it he deplored the record of "appalling ignorance of foreign affairs" in American public opinion but concluded optimistically that in "the last quarter of a century" the public had developed "much greater maturity." His undergraduate survey, *The American Pageant* (1956), went through six editions before he took on a collaborator, David M. Kennedy, and was used by more than two million students in his lifetime. He crafted his writings with care, even those he consciously sprinkled with puns and clichés, a practice he defended as appropriate for attracting nonacademic readers.

Noted for their vivid epigrammatic style, his books and essays on diplomacy dealt mainly with the domestic influences on policymaking rather than on international pressures. His other works focused mostly on politics, or on what he called meat-and-potatoes history, rather than on social or intellectual issues. Although a conservative who rarely attacked the status quo, he regarded himself as a revisionist, maintaining "that all historians worthy of their name are revisionists at heart." His conception of revisionism meant the destroying of historical myths and the correcting of data rather than the challenging of theory or conventional wisdom. He could not, for instance, shake off the attitudes of his white, Protestant, Anglo-American upbringing, which may have contributed to his difficulty in dealing appreciatively with minority groups, or with women in the profession. He believed, as he explained in his memoirs, that history was "essentially a man's subject" that properly dealt with the "movers and shakers—the makers of wars and nations." In his lectures, and some writings also, he lashed out at non-Anglo minorities, reproaching Jewish Americans and Irish Americans, for instance, for allegedly having dual loyalties. Yet when such charges brought protests, he denied having biases. Usually, though, he was tolerant of others who differed from his kind of Americanism.

A love of history and a compulsion to write dominated much of Bailey's life. Even after his retirement in 1968, which he spent in his home and his office on the Stanford campus, he continued to publish approximately a volume each year until ill health kept him from further writing. His best work reveals skillful analysis and a pervasive sense of humor. He was regarded as a great popularizer because of his talent for entertaining thousands while instructing them, either in the classroom or through his books. In the years immediately preceding his retirement, when student activists protested the Vietnam War and questioned authority, his patriotic teaching style lost its popularity. He blamed his disfavor on the widening generation gap between himself and the students and their demand for "relevance." Regardless, he was one of the founding fathers of American diplomatic history as a distinct field of study and a teacher-scholar with a dedication to history matched by few of his contemporaries. He died in a convalescent home in Menlo Park, near Stanford, where he had lived most of his years.

• Bailey's papers are in the Stanford University Archives as is the transcript of an oral history interview of him conducted by Frederic O. Glover, 8 July 1978. Taped "Notes of an Interview with Bailey," 24 Aug. 1977, are in the possession of Allen Wachhold, Santa Barbara, Calif. The best source for Bailey's life and outlook is his autobiography, *The American Pageant Revisited: Recollections of a Stanford Historian* (1982). See also his "Confessions of a Diplomatic Historian," Society for Historians of American Foreign Relations (SHAFR) *Newsletter* 6 (June 1975): 2–11; Alexander DeConde, "Thomas A. Bailey: Teacher, Scholar, Popularizer," *Pacific Historical Review* 56 (May 1987): 161–93; Raymond G. O'Connor, "Thomas A. Bailey—His Impact," *Diplomatic History* 9 (Fall 1985): 303–9; DeConde, "Thomas A. Bailey Remembered," SHAFR *Newsletter* 14 (Dec. 1983): 33–38; and the biographical introduction in *Essays Diplomatic and Undiplomatic of Thomas A. Bailey*, ed. DeConde and Armin Rappaport (1969), pp. vii–xiii. Among his major works not mentioned in the text, particularly noteworthy are *The Policy of the United States toward the Neutrals, 1917–1918* (1942); *America Faces Russia: Russian-American Relations from Early Times to Our Day* (1950); and, with Paul B. Ryan, *The Lusitania Disaster: An Episode in Modern War and Diplomacy* (1975). An obituary is in the *Los Angeles Times*, 5 Aug. 1983.

ALEXANDER DECONDE

BAILLY, Joseph Alexis (21 Jan. 1825–15 June 1883), sculptor, was born in Paris, France, the son of Joseph Philidor Bailly, a maker of cabinet furniture. His mother's name is unknown. As a young man, Bailly studied under Baron Bozio at the French Institute, then worked for his father and in various woodworking shops turning and carving ornamental furniture. Early in his career he carved gargoyles in the castle of the marquis de Lussac in Tourraine. During the 1848 French revolution he was conscripted into the army, but his sympathies lay with the revolutionaries, and after he shot at his own regiment's captain he was forced to flee for his life. In England he studied briefly with Edward Hodges Baily, a member of the Royal Academy. Following sojourns in New Orleans, New York, and Philadelphia, he married Louisa David of Brie, France, in 1850 and settled in Philadelphia. Shortly thereafter he and his wife spent a year in Buenos Aires.

In Philadelphia Bailly quickly gained a reputation for his portraits and decorative sculptures, including wood carvings, cameos, and waxworks. He won prizes for his wood and wax carvings at the Franklin Institute annual exhibitions of 1851 and 1852. During the early 1850s he worked for Gottlieb Vollmer, a German-born cabinetmaker, and he may also have been associated for a time with the large marble yard of Struthers and Son. He briefly had a studio at Earles Gallery but was displaced by fire. In 1854 he opened a sculpture studio with his partner, Charles Bushor (or Buschor). From 1855 to 1857 Bailly and Bushor were primarily occupied with two major commissions. For the Grand Lodge of the Free and Accepted Masons in Philadelphia they carved furniture and eight large wooden female statues that personify the Masonic virtues. They are preserved at the Grand Lodge of Pennsylvania, Masonic Temple, Philadelphia. The second large project to occupy them during this period was the carving of decorative ornamentation for the new Academy of Music on South Broad Street. Bailly and Bushor's studio was in an elaborately festooned building replete with numerous facade statues, at 47 South Eighth Street. A contemporary advertisement touts an attached drawing school.

Bailly was closely associated with the Pennsylvania Academy of the Fine Arts and studied in the rather informal school that existed there during the early 1850s. Between 1851 and 1878 he showed numerous sculptures in wood, wax, plaster, marble, and bronze in the academy's annual exhibitions. He was elected an associate of the Pennsylvania Academy in 1859 and was made an academician in 1860. In the early 1860s he began to teach on a voluntary basis at the academy school and was engaged by the institution as a paid instructor of modeling from 1876 to 1878.

By the late 1860s Bailly was probably Philadelphia's best-known sculptor. Not only was he skilled in many media but his range of subject matter was equally eclectic, running the gamut from flower bouquets and animal sculpture to ideal allegorical figures. A pair of almost life-size marble figurative groups titled *Paradise Lost* (often called *The Expulsion*) and *First Prayer*, which were completed in 1868, are in the collection of the Pennsylvania Academy. *Paradise Lost*, which borrows its title from Milton's epic poem, represents the dejected Adam and Eve after their banishment from the Garden of Eden, and *First Prayer* represents Eve with her children Cain and Abel. The highly polished marble and intricate surface textures of the sculptures are typical of mid-nineteenth-century marbles. Bailly's handling of the themes appears overly sentimentalized to the modern viewer, but their obvious religious and moral narratives were precisely what appealed to his Victorian American audience.

During the 1860s and 1870s Bailly produced several memorials to notable Philadelphians, including a stone figure of Grief for the tomb of General Francis E. Patterson (c. 1868) and bronze effigies of the painter William Emlen Cresson (1869) and of William F. Hughes (1870)—all three in Laurel Hill Cemetery—as well as a statue of John Witherspoon (1876) for Philadelphia's Fairmount Park. Another of his major works, a statue of General John A. Rawlins, was erected in Washington, D.C., in 1874.

At the 1876 Centennial Exposition in Philadelphia, the sculptor's equestrian statue of Venezuelan president Antonio Guzman Blanco stood in the rotunda of Memorial Hall. It was a commission from the Venezuelan government for placement in Caracas. Bailly also exhibited an ideal piece titled *Aurora* (whereabouts unknown) at the Centennial that was highly praised by the art critic Edward Strahan, who called it "a piece of magic . . . a powerful stimulant of our wonder." In his review of the exposition, Strahan noted that if one stood at the corner of Sixth and Chestnut streets in Philadelphia it was possible to see three of Bailly's works: the statue of Benjamin Franklin on the Public Ledger Building, the horses supporting the escutcheon on that same building, and the marble statue of George Washington located in front of Independence Hall. The statue of Washington was later moved inside Philadelphia's city hall and replaced with a bronze copy at its original site.

Bailly seems to have been a shrewd businessman and did a considerable business in more commercial sculpture. He produced several small cabinet busts of American historical figures, including Abraham Lincoln, General Ulysses S. Grant, and General George Meade, which he cast in editions. Bailly died of heart disease in Philadelphia and was buried in Philadelphia's Mount Peace Cemetery.

• Abigail Schade, "Joseph A. Bailly (1825–1883)," in *Philadelphia: Three Centuries of American Art* (1976), pp. 383–84, is a brief, fact-filled biographical account. Other noteworthy sources are William J. Clark, Jr., *Great American Sculptures*, (1878), pp. 105–6; Edward Strahan, *The Art Gallery of the Exhibition: A Selection from the Paintings and Sculpture* (1877), pp. 53–59; and "Joseph Alexis Bailly," in *Biographical Encyclopedia of Pennsylvania of the Nineteenth Century* (1874). A biography of Bailly and information about his partnership with Charles Bushor appears in Henry Houston Hawley, "Charles Buschor: Designer and Manufacturer of Furniture and Interior Decorations" (masters thesis, Univ. of Delaware, 1960). A brief obituary is in the *Philadelphia Public Ledger*, 19 June 1883.

MARY MULLEN CUNNINGHAM

BAINBRIDGE, William (7 May 1774–27 June 1833), naval officer, was born in Princeton, New Jersey, the son of Absalom Bainbridge, a physician, and Mary Taylor. His parents and grandparents sided with the king's forces in the revolutionary war, and Dr. Bainbridge served as surgeon to a Loyalist regiment. This resulted in the confiscation of the family property and probably affected William Bainbridge's view of himself: he was both conservative in politics and touchy—suspicious that, in the eyes of others, his family background cast a shadow on his own loyalty.

In 1789 Bainbridge entered the merchant service; four years later he was captain of the ship *Hope*, a command he retained for five years—not an atypical early career for a young seafarer of good family. During a West Indies voyage in the 1790s he met and married

Susan Heyliger, granddaughter of the former governor general of St. Eustatius; the couple had five children. Unlike many other American merchants, Bainbridge suffered no losses to the French; nevertheless, in 1798 he gladly accepted a lieutenant's commission in the new United States Navy, a choice that implies a preference for prestige over possible fortune. He received one of the rare lieutenant's commands, the schooner *Retaliation*. Within three months he rashly approached two French frigates, and *Retaliation* became the first American warship captured in the Quasi-War.

It seemed an inauspicious beginning for a naval career. Nevertheless, when Bainbridge returned to the United States he was promoted to master commandant and given another command, and in May 1800 he became a captain, a piece of good fortune since the rank of master commandant was temporarily eliminated in 1801. He took the ship *George Washington* with tribute to Algiers, but having somewhat rashly placed his ship under the guns of the city's forts, he found himself forced to sail under the Algerian flag to carry presents and an embassy from Algiers to Constantinople, a humiliation for himself and his country. Still in the Mediterranean, he commanded the frigate *Essex* and then the new *Philadelphia*. Here again bad fortune or bad judgment caught up with him; having sent his consort away, he had no one to assist him when *Philadelphia* grounded on a rock off Tripoli. He surrendered the ship and crew without resistance, and all were imprisoned in Tripoli from 31 October 1803 until the Tripolitan War ended in June 1805. Although no official censure was applied to his conduct, he was always sensitive about the loss of *Philadelphia* and hostile to Stephen Decatur, who gained so much glory by destroying the captured ship in Tripoli harbor.

Bainbridge recouped his finances by making merchant voyages in 1806–1807 and 1810–1812; in the intervening years he participated, as did other naval officers, in the building of gunboats and supervision of naval stations on the eastern seaboard. Returning to the United States in 1812 just before the outbreak of war, he helped persuade the government to fit out the seagoing ships but had to wait for one of his own. He took command of *Constitution* in September 1812, after the ship's successful first war cruise and capture of the British frigate *Guerrière* under Isaac Hull. On 29 December 1812, off Brazil, the *Constitution* under Bainbridge took and sank the frigate *Java*. Twice wounded in this engagement, Bainbridge returned to Boston and the navy yard there, where he superintended the building of the ship-of-the-line *Independence*.

Before *Independence* or any of the new ships of that class could be completed, the war ended. Meanwhile, a resurgence of trouble in the Mediterranean led the U.S. government, as soon as the war ended, to send a squadron to deal with Algiers. Bainbridge made strenuous efforts to obtain the command until he learned that Decatur would take a first squadron and he would follow with a second. After that he was less eager to go; however, when the qualities of *Independence* were questioned, and it was even proposed to cut the ship down to a frigate, Bainbridge hastily sailed for the Mediterranean, only to find that Decatur had already forced peace on Algiers and quieted Tunis and Tripoli as well. Bainbridge not only found himself with nothing to do, but he suffered an attack of measles at Gibraltar, which was followed, on his return to the United States, by influenza.

Bainbridge convinced himself that he had been unwillingly removed from command of the navy yard at Boston and that he was entitled to resume the command. He was furious to find that in his absence Hull had been appointed to Boston and intended to stay there. Unfortunately, the Navy Department permitted Bainbridge to remain as commander afloat at Boston, while Hull commanded the navy yard. There is good reason to suspect that many of the troubles with subordinates that dogged Hull at Boston were fomented by Bainbridge.

In 1819 Bainbridge left Boston to fit out the new ship *Columbus*, and during that winter he was involved in arranging the fatal duel between Decatur and James Barron. Immediately after the duel he sailed for the Mediterranean, returning in July 1821 and again demanding the command in Boston, which he finally achieved in August 1823. From 1825 to 1828 he chaired the Board of Navy Commissioners, then commanded the navy yard at Philadelphia. In 1830 he quarreled with Amos Kendall, the fourth auditor of the Treasury; it was a clash rooted in personalities though expressed in matters financial. The conflict led to Bainbridge's removal from his command. In this difficult period his only son, William Bainbridge, Jr., died.

Reappointed to the Boston yard in January 1832, Bainbridge resigned the command a year later and died in Philadelphia. His last illness seems to have been rooted in earlier diseases and wounds that had undermined his health and complicated by addiction to drugs prescribed by his doctors. Although a loving and beloved family man, he apparently had few close friends. His naval colleagues knew him as moody, humorless, and morbidly sensitive where his own rights were concerned. He called himself "the child of adversity," which suggests that he was too willing to blame unhappy events on luck, or other people, but never on himself. These qualities made him a difficult superior and an impossible subordinate, or as John Rodgers wrote in a famous letter: "if there is any objection to him [for a seat on the Board of Navy Commissioners] it is because he feels the importance of his own abilities [the word "consequence" had been written and lightly crossed out] too sensibly to qualify him as well as he otherwise would be for a subordinate situation." He had a reputation as a draconian commander with whom no seaman would willingly serve. He loved his country and the naval service; within that service he himself was respected, feared, but not beloved.

• Destruction of Bainbridge's papers by his daughter Susan after his death makes primary research a problem; apart from the letterbooks in the U.S. Navy collection at the New-York Historical Society and the official materials in the National Archives (especially RG 45), most remaining Bainbridge correspondence will be found in collections relating to recipients, for example, State Historical Society of Wisconsin, Charles Wilkes Papers and William Compton Bolton Papers; Historical Society of Pennsylvania, James Gibson Papers; Maryland Historical Society, David Geisinger Papers; and Library of Congress, John Shaw Papers. Thomas Harris, *The Life and Services of Commodore William Bainbridge, United States Navy* (1837), and H. A. S. Dearborn, *The Life of William Bainbridge, Esq. of the United States Navy* (1931), a late publication of a work by a friend and contemporary of Bainbridge, have been supplanted by David F. Long, *Ready to Hazard: A Biography of Commodore William Bainbridge, 1774–1833* (1981); see also Long's article "William Bainbridge and the Barron-Decatur Duel: Mere Participant or Active Plotter?" *Pennsylvania Magazine of History and Biography* 103 (Jan. 1979): 34–52. For an unfavorable contemporary view "from the main deck," see John Rea, *A Letter to William Bainbridge, Esqr., Formerly Commander of the United States Ship George Washington* . . . (1802).

LINDA M. MALONEY

BAINTER, Fay (7 Dec. 1893–16 Apr. 1968), actress, was born in Los Angeles, the daughter of Charles Bainter, an inventor, and Mary Okell. Making her stage debut at the age of five in the Burbank Stock Company's production of *The Jewess*, Bainter managed to squeeze in an education between rehearsals and performances of children's roles in stock companies such as the Burbank, the Belasco, and the Grand Theater. She graduated from the Girls Collegiate School in Los Angeles.

Although her fame rests on her screen roles, Bainter had an illustrious stage career for over thirty years. After touring in Missouri, Kansas, and Portland, playing minor roles, she began to receive offers to play the role of ingenue. She made her Broadway debut as Celine in *The Rose of Panama* (1912) and later appeared as Alice in *The Bridal Path* (1913). These plays were not successful, however, and she toured again through Ohio, New York State, and Iowa before she returned to New York City to assume the leading role in *Lady Cristilinda* (1922). During this time she married a naval officer, Reginald S. H. Venable (1921); they had one child.

After a series of roles in minor vehicles in New York City, Bainter starred as Galatea in *Pygmalion* (1927), Kate Hardcastle in *She Stoops to Conquer* (1928), Mrs. Sullen in *The Beaux' Stratagem* (1928), in *Lysistrata* (1930), Lady Mary Lasenby in *The Admirable Crichton* (1931), Mrs. Millamant in *The Way of the World* (1931), Topsy in *Uncle Tom's Cabin* (1933), and Fran Dodsworth in an adaptation of Sinclair Lewis's *Dodsworth* (1934), a difficult portrayal of a shallow woman that earned praise from critics. She appeared in stock companies and touring productions and on Broadway periodically through 1958, crowning her stage career in the national touring company of Eugene O'Neill's *Long Day's Journey into Night* as an especially appealing Mary Cavan Tyrone. She played Eliza Gant in *Look Homeward, Angel* (on tour in 1959) and made her final appearance onstage in *The Girls in 509* (1962) in Miami.

Bainter was over forty years old when she acted in her first film, *This Side of Heaven* (1934), delivering what reviewer Mordaunt Hall described as a "sterling portrait of an affectionate and thoroughly sensible wife and mother." Her mature years and warm personality helped to typecast her in maternal roles, which she patiently accepted while she ruefully acknowledged the difficulty of playing the mother of a young child actor. She remarked, "Kids expect you to be just like their own mothers, which, of course, you aren't, so it takes them awhile to make up their minds about you. I try to treat them sympathetically yet as grown-up people and that wins them over." She was "wholesome and splendid" as Mother Carey in *Mother Carey's Chickens* (1938), played Mickey Rooney's mother in *Young Tom Edison* (1940), and was "quietly effective" as Mrs. Gibbs in *Our Town* (1940). In 1938 she was nominated for an Academy Award both as best actress for her performance in *White Banners* and as best supporting actress for her role as Aunt Belle in *Jezebel.* She won the award for best supporting actress, but Bette Davis won the Oscar for best actress for her role in the same film.

Bainter played supporting roles in *Journey for Margaret* (1942), *Woman of the Year* (1942) with Spencer Tracy and Katharine Hepburn, *Cry Havoc* (1943), *The Human Comedy* (1943), *Presenting Lily Mars* (1943) with Judy Garland, *State Fair* (1945), *The Virginian* (1946), *The Secret Life of Walter Mitty* (1947) with Danny Kaye, *June Bride* (1948), *Give My Regards to Broadway* (1948), and *The President's Lady* (1953). Her performance as Amelia Tilford, an uncompromising woman destroyed by her own manipulations, in *The Children's Hour* (1962) won her another Academy Award nomination as best supporting actress.

Her television credits include *Night Must Fall* (1948), *A Child Is Born* (1952), *All Things Glad and Beautiful* (1953), *They Shall Not Perish* (1954), *The Story of Ruth* (1954), *Belle Fleace Gives a Party* (1955), *Hallelujah* (1955), *Prisoner in Paradise* (1960), *Girl with a Secret* (1960), *The Baby Buggy* (1962), and "Dr. Kildare" (1963).

Bainter's private life was as quiet and dignified as her professional career. Shunning the Hollywood social scene, she lived comfortably with her husband and son in Los Angeles and Palm Springs and described her chief hobby as cooking. Bainter was as modest and candid about her acting roles: "There aren't enough parts to justify stardom for a woman of my type." She was content to excel in supporting roles, always thoroughly professional, patiently enduring rehearsals and retakes, quietly lending her talent and long years of experience to each portrayal. Her dignity and reliability endeared her to her colleagues; her warmth and acting skills made her an ideal "mother." She died in Hollywood.

• Further information on Bainter can be found in the clippings file and the Robinson Locke Scrapbooks in the New York Public Library Theater Collection, Lincoln Center; Walter Rigdon, ed., *Biographical Encyclopedia and Who's Who of the American Theater* (1966); James Vinson, ed., *International Dictionary of Film and Filmmakers*, vol. 3: *Actors and Actresses* (1986); and Anthony Slide, ed., *Selected Theater Criticism*, vol. 1 (1985). An obituary is in the *New York Times*, 18 Apr. 1968.

ELIZABETH R. NELSON

BAINTON, Roland Herbert (30 Mar. 1894–13 Feb. 1984), historian of the Protestant Reformation, was born in Ilkeston, Derbyshire, England, the only son of James Herbert Bainton, a Congregational pastor, and Charlotte Eliza Blackham. Bainton's family moved to Vancouver, British Columbia (1898), and then to Colfax, Washington (1902). He received the traditional British-inspired education in the classics, beginning the study of Latin at twelve and adding German at thirteen. The elder Bainton encouraged his reading and inquiry, and their discussions continued by mail after Bainton entered college. Bainton graduated from Whitman College (B.A. in classics, 1910–1914), Yale Divinity School (B.D., 1914–1917), and Yale University (Ph.D. in Semitics and Hellenistic Greek, 1917–1921).

In 1920 he began a distinguished teaching career at Yale Divinity School, including academic appointments as instructor in church history and New Testament, assistant professor (1923), associate professor (1932), and Titus Street Professor of Ecclesiastical History (1936). While playing a key role in the development of the church history department at Yale, he also delivered German, French, Italian, and Spanish lectures in Europe and South America. After his retirement in 1962 he continued to lecture in the United States and abroad.

Despite his strong training in ancient languages and the New Testament, Bainton became a leading authority on the Protestant Reformation, especially often-neglected heretical personalities and movements. Emphasizing the issues of civil and religious liberty, his research included a study of four heretics who fled Catholic persecution only to fall afoul of the Calvinist regime: Michael Servetus, Spanish physician and anti-Trinitarian; Bernardino Ochino, an Italian theologian and reformer; David Joris, a Dutch Anabaptist leader; and Sebastian Castellio, French theologian, humanist, and translator of the Bible into French. Other scholarly interests in the field included the issues of war, sex, religious liberty, and church unity. Bainton published thirty-two books and more than fifty articles. Outside the academic community he is perhaps best known for *The Church of Our Fathers* (1941) and *Here I Stand: A Life of Martin Luther* (1950). The latter was written, in part, because after the war the publisher wanted to present a great German to the American public. The book, which was translated into many languages and sold more than one million copies, brought Bainton international recognition.

Bainton's professional activities included serving as president of the American Society of Church History (1940) and sitting on the editorial boards of *Archiv für Reformationsgeschichte* (1951–1969) and *Church History* (1955–1963). Numerous honors included a Guggenheim Fellowship (1926, for his research in Europe on the four heretics), British Academy membership (1973), and the Abingdon-Cokesbury Boss Prize for *Here I Stand.* In 1927 he was ordained a minister in the Congregational church (now the United Church of Christ).

Like his father, Bainton exhibited a lifelong commitment to peace and pacifism. He declared himself a conscientious objector in World War I and, taking the ministerial draft deferral, served in a unit of the American Friends Service Committee, a Quaker organization, under the American Red Cross in France from October 1918 to June 1919, helping to relocate refugees and care for wounded soldiers. During World War II he headed a Quaker effort to relocate scholars, finding homes in the United States for German and Italian refugees. In 1948 he and his wife traveled in Germany as religious visitors representing the American Friends Service Committee. His peace activism also led him to close ties with the Society of Friends, Mennonites, Brethren, Hutterites, and the Society of Brothers. In the 1950s, because of his peace efforts, he was the target of investigations by the FBI and the House Committee on Un-American Activities; some citizen efforts were unsuccessfully directed at Yale Divinity School to have him dismissed. He served stints as president of Promoting Enduring Peace and on the council of the Fellowship of Reconciliation. He was an independent voter.

Sketch pad ever in hand, he was famous for his caricatures, and because of his love of bicycle riding, he became known around the Yale campus as a "legend on a bike." He married Ruth Mae Woodruff, a teacher, in 1921. They had two sons and three daughters. She died in 1966. He died in New Haven, Connecticut.

While Bainton wrote and lectured on a wide variety of topics in church history, he is best known as one of the twentieth century's leading scholars of the Protestant Reformation.

• Bainton's books, most of them aimed at scholarly audiences, include *The Travail of Religious Liberty: Nine Biographical Studies* (1951); *The Reformation of the Sixteenth Century* (1952); *The Age of the Reformation* (1956); *What Christianity Says about Sex, Love and Marriage* (1957); *Yale and the Ministry: A History of Education for the Christian Ministry at Yale from the Founding in 1701* (1957, illustrated with line drawings by the author); *Christian Attitudes toward War and Peace: An Historical Survey and Critical Re-evaluation* (1960); *Christendom: A Short History of Christianity and Its Impact on Western Civilization* (1964, vol. 1: *From the Birth of Christ to the Reformation*; vol. 2: *From the Reformation to the Present*); *Erasmus of Christendom* (1969); *Women of the Reformation* (vol. 1: *Germany and Italy*, 1971; vol. 2: *France and England*, 1973; vol. 3: *Spain to Scandinavia*, (1977); *Behold the Christ* (*Christ in Art*) (1974); and *Yesterday, Today and*

What Next? Reflections on History and Hope (1978). Collections of his papers are found in *Collected Papers in Church History*, the three volumes of which are entitled *Early and Medieval Christianity* (1962), *Studies on the Reformation* (1963), and *Christian Unity and Religion in New England* (1964). The last contains a fairly complete bibliography to 1964. A festschrift is entitled *Reformation Studies: Essays in Honor of Roland H. Bainton* (1962). Bainton's affectionate biography of his father is *Pilgrim Parson: The Life of James Herbert Bainton (1867–1942)* (1958). His memoirs, started by him and completed after his death, along with seventy-five of his caricatures, are contained in *Roly: Chronicle of a Stubborn Non-Conformist* (1988). A large collection of his personal papers is in the Yale Divinity School Library.

CALVIN MERCER

BAIRD, Absalom (20 Aug. 1824–14 June 1905), soldier, was born in Washington, Pennsylvania, the son of William Baird, an attorney and local politician, and Nancy Mitchell. His father died when Baird was ten years old, and he served as assistant teacher to his widowed mother, who opened a school in the family home. In 1841 he graduated from the preparatory department of Washington College. He then studied law for three years in the office of one of the city's leading attorneys.

Because war with Mexico seemed inevitable, Baird sought an appointment to the U.S. Military Academy at West Point, arriving in June 1845. He graduated as a second lieutenant four years later, ninth out of a class of forty-three, and was assigned to the Second Artillery Regiment stationed at Fort Monroe, Virginia. Within a few months he was transferred to the First Artillery at Fort Columbus, New York, a post he held until October 1850. That same month he married Cornelia Wyntje Smith; they had one child.

Soon after the wedding, the young couple traveled to Fort Carey, Florida, accompanied by a servant woman who was to remain with the family until her death in 1887. Living conditions were terrible, so Baird sent his pregnant wife and the servant back to Philadelphia in 1851. Baird soon caught a fever that aggravated his chronic liver problems, and he was forced to take sick leave in Philadelphia for six months himself. In March 1852 Commanding General Winfield Scott ordered him to travel to Europe for his health. He remained overseas for more than two months and toured six countries. With his health restored, Baird received orders to become an instructor in the Department of Mathematics at West Point, serving from 1852 to 1859. He enjoyed his duties and the relationships he and his wife developed with the cadets. The artist James McNeill Whistler was a particular favorite, though despite Baird's help, he failed out of the academy because of deficiencies in mathematics.

In August 1859 Baird joined an infantry regiment in Texas to take part in the Indian wars there. After eight months of routine service, he was transferred to Fort Monroe in Virginia. On the eve of the Civil War in April 1861, he was called to Washington to help with the defense of the capital, but in early May he was transferred to the Adjutant General's Office with the rank of brevet captain. On 2 July 1861 he became assistant adjutant general in Daniel Tyler's division. He participated in the battle of Bull Run (Manassas), but after several more transfers, in November he was assigned to the Inspector General's Office as a major.

Because of Baird's growing reputation for efficiency based on his service in the Inspector General's Office, Brigadier General Erasmus D. Keyes, commander of the IV Corps, made him his chief of staff. Baird did so well in the early days of George B. McClellan's (1826–1885) unsuccessful Peninsular campaign that he was named brevet brigadier general on 28 April 1862. In early May he became commanding officer of the Twenty-seventh Brigade of George W. Morgan's Seventh Division of Don Carlos Buell's Army of the Ohio, participating in the successful June 1862 capture of the Cumberland Gap, the important passage through the rugged Appalachian Mountains.

In October 1862 Baird moved to Gordon Granger's Army of Kentucky to form a new division. After several months of uneventful duty in central Kentucky, the division was transferred to William S. Rosecrans's Army of the Cumberland as part of a newly established reserve corps. George H. Thomas, commander of the XIV Corps, asked for his services, and Baird became commander of the First Division in Thomas's corps in late August 1863.

Baird's unit was instrumental in keeping the enemy from breaking through at Chickamauga, helping Thomas gain his nickname, "the Rock of Chickamauga." Despite his heroic activity, Baird found himself relieved from duty so that Major General Lovell Rousseau could regain the command he had earlier given up for a special assignment. This error of judgment was quickly rectified, and Baird returned to his unit. When Thomas replaced Rosecrans as commander of the Army of the Cumberland on 20 October 1863, Baird became commander of the Third Division of the XIV Corps under Major General John McAuley Palmer. He was to retain this post until the end of the war.

At the battle of Chattanooga, Baird's men were among those in Thomas's army who made the legendary charge up Missionary Ridge and broke the Confederate siege of the Tennessee city. Soon after, Baird received two citations and two battlefield promotions for his bravery, becoming a regular army lieutenant colonel.

Baird was part of William T. Sherman's massive force that battled Confederate general Joseph E. Johnston in the Atlanta campaign. It was at Jonesboro, on 1 September 1864, that Baird personally led the charge of Colonel George P. Este's brigade against well-entrenched Confederates. In spite of having two horses shot out from under him and losing 450 of his 1,100 men, Baird routed the Confederate defenders and ensured Union victory. For his valor Baird was awarded the Medal of Honor in 1896. Baird also took part in Sherman's March to the Sea and through the Carolinas, gaining brevet promotion to major general in the spring of 1865.

After the war Baird served as commander of the Department of Louisiana. Because he insisted that the army should stay out of politics, he responded weakly to the infamous antiblack New Orleans riot of 1866 and suffered severe northern criticism as a result. He reverted to his permanent rank of lieutenant colonel and became an assistant inspector general. In following years he served in St. Paul, Louisville, and Chicago. In 1881 he gained the rank of colonel and assignment as assistant inspector general of the entire U.S. Army. In 1885 he became the inspector general, gaining the permanent rank of brigadier general. In 1887 the French invited the United States to send two army officers to view military maneuvers, and President Grover Cleveland sent Baird. There, to his surprise, he received the Legion of Honor.

Retiring to Washington, D.C., in 1888, Baird spent the last sixteen years of his life tracing his ancestry and participating in veterans' activities. A career soldier, he rose through the officer ranks to become head of one of the army's staff bureaus and, in his retirement years, received the Medal of Honor for his leadership of a brigade charge at Jonesboro in 1864. He died near Relay, Maryland.

• Baird's correspondence, orders, and reports are in *The War of the Rebellion: A Compilation of the Official Records of the Union and Confederate Armies* (128 vols., 1880–1901). Material on his stint as inspector general is located in published reports and in manuscript records found in the National Archives and Records Service. The fullest account of Baird's life was written by a relative based on family papers, John A. Baird, *Profile of a Hero: The Story of Absalom Baird, His Family, and the American Military Tradition* (1977). An extended excerpt from the book is Baird, "For Gallant and Meritorious Service: Major General Absalom Baird," *Civil War Times Illustrated* 15 (June 1976): 4–9, 45–48. A brief obituary is in the *New York Times*, 15 June 1905.

JOHN F. MARSZALEK

BAIRD, Charles Washington (28 Aug. 1828–10 Feb. 1887), Presbyterian minister and author, was born in Princeton, New Jersey, the son of Robert Baird, Jr., a Presbyterian minister and author, and Fermine Ophelia Amaryllis du Buisson. Baird's childhood was divided between the United States and Western Europe. His earliest years were spent in Princeton and Philadelphia, but when he was small the family moved to Europe. Robert Baird worked for various evangelical associations to promote religious renewal in Europe; between 1835 and 1843 the Baird family made its home in Paris, France, or Geneva, Switzerland. This wide-ranging experience, very unusual for an American child in the early nineteenth century, combined with the family's evangelical fervor, shaped Charles Baird in ways that would be critical for his most important contributions to American life.

Although considerably impeded by his poor health, Baird's education continued after his return to the United States. Entering New York University in 1846, Baird received his B.A. in 1848; from 1849 to 1852 he studied at Union Theological Seminary in New York City, graduating with a certificate of completion in 1852. In 1860 Baird was awarded an M.A. from New York University. On 14 June 1886 Baird returned to the university to give the Phi Beta Kappa Oration, "The Scholar's Duty and Opportunity," which was published later that year.

Charles Baird's primary life work was that of a Presbyterian minister, both briefly in Europe and then for the rest of his life in the United States. Baird was ordained on 4 October 1853 by the Presbytery of New Brunswick; at the time he was chaplain to the American embassy in Rome, Italy (1852–1854), under the auspices of the American and Foreign Christian Union, for which he continued to work in New York City (1854–1855). Following several years of renewed ill health, Baird was able to return to the pastorate, serving the Reformed Dutch church of Bergen Hill, South Brooklyn, New York (1859–1861), and the Presbyterian church of Rye, New York (1861–1887). In 1861 Baird married Margaret Eliza Strang, with whom he would have two children; they lived in Rye until Baird's death there of a cerebral hemorrhage.

For the majority of Baird's contemporaries, his most attractive writings were historical studies. The most impressive is a two-volume *History of the Huguenot Emigration to America* (1885), for which Baird drew on archives in Europe as well as North America. Several New York local histories, including one about the town of Rye, also were well received. Since his death, however, Baird has become best known for his work in helping American Presbyterians rediscover their historic Reformed (Calvinistic) heritage of worship. His study of early Reformed liturgies, *Eutaxia, or the Presbyterian Liturgies: Historical Sketches*, was first published in New York in 1855 and later, with some additions, in London as *A Chapter on Liturgies* (1856). As a practical complement to the historical work, and drawn primarily from its sources, Baird produced *A Book of Public Prayer* (1856) to provide liturgical resources for pastors.

To understand the motivation for and importance of Baird's liturgical studies, it is necessary to sketch their historical context. When American Presbyterians (re)organized as a national church just after the American Revolution, they adopted, with only a few minor changes, the old Westminster Directory for Worship. This directory was very loosely interpreted, and for practical purposes the ordering of public worship developed without any denominational control. Influenced by the puritan tradition and eighteenth- and nineteenth-century revivals, actual weekly services were centered on the sermon, and there was very strong resistance to "set forms" that might constrict the spontaneity of the Spirit. The result was worship that was dependent almost entirely on the personal resources of the minister, often without a thoughtfully considered plan. By the mid-nineteenth century, this situation was becoming intolerable to some Presbyterians, and a few—Baird among them—unofficially began to address the problem.

Having grown up among the Reformed churches of Western Europe, Baird had become acquainted with their worship patterns, which both emphasized for him the inadequacies of much American Protestant worship and suggested historical models for something different. *Eutaxia* and *A Book of Public Prayer* constituted Baird's plea to American Presbyterians to reconsider the ordering of their worship. Baird invented the title *Eutaxia* ("Good Order") to denote that what he advocated was simply a fulfillment of the biblical precept so popular with Presbyterians (1 Cor. 14:40): that everything should be done "decently and in order [*taxin*]" (p. 1). To counter the view that any set form of liturgy was totally wrong and un-Reformed, Baird aimed "to demonstrate, first, That the principles of Presbyterianism in nowise conflict with the discretionary use of written forms; and secondly, That the practice of Presbyterian churches abundantly warrants the adoption and the use of such forms" (p. 5).

To show that historic Reformed churches had, from the beginning, used written forms to guide worship, Baird conceived *Eutaxia* as a source book of Reformed liturgies from the sixteenth century to the late eighteenth. Included are major figures such as Calvin, Knox, and Baxter as well as significant national liturgies, among them Genevan, French, Dutch, and German Reformed, Scottish Presbyterian, and "Calvinistic forms" in the (English) Book of Common Prayer; it concludes with the (rejected) proposals for American revision of the Westminster Directory in 1787. From the perspective of the late twentieth century, Baird's text is historically inaccurate in several ways, both in sources and method. In its own day, however, *Eutaxia* represented a considerable contribution to liturgical and historical scholarship in North America.

Baird's liturgical writings were welcomed by a few Americans, for example, theologian Charles Hodge of Princeton Seminary, but most Presbyterians regarded these works as too liturgical and too historically oriented. In the century following its publication, however, *Eutaxia* encouraged the exploration of historical worship traditions, and it influenced the move toward officially sanctioned liturgical guides, which American Presbyterians began to use in 1906, with increasing momentum as the century progressed. In the light of modern ecumenical and liturgical renewal movements, Baird's writings on historic Reformed liturgies appear as important pioneering efforts to broaden and deepen American Protestant knowledge and practice of public worship.

• As a young man, Baird translated several works by European Reformed theologians, among them, *Romanism*, by César Malan (1844), and *Discourses and Essays*, by J. H. Merle D'Aubigné (1846). Baird's other historical works include *The Chronicle of a Border Town: History of Rye, N.Y., 1660–1870* (1871), *Civil Status of the Presbyterians in the Province of New York* (1879), and *History of Bedford Church* (1882). Both of Baird's liturgical works were first published anonymously. *Eutaxia, or the Presbyterian Liturgies: Historical Sketches*, "By a Minister of the Presbyterian Church" (1855), then as Charles W. Baird, *A Chapter on Liturgies: Historical Sketches*, with an introductory preface, and an appendix by Thomas Binney (1856); and *A Book of Public Prayer, Compiled from the Authorized Formularies of Worship of the Presbyterian Church, as Prepared by the Reformers Calvin, Knox, Bucer, and Others. With Supplement Forms* (1856, repr. 1857). *Eutaxia* was republished in 1957 by Wm. B. Eerdmans Publishing Co. under the title *The Presbyterian Liturgies*.

A contemporary volume, *Memorials of the Rev. Charles W. Baird* (1888), includes a biographical sketch (pp. 1–12). See also Alfred Nevin et al., eds., *Encyclopedia of the Presbyterian Church in the United States of America* (1884), p. 49. For a modern discussion of Baird's liturgical work and its context in religious history, see chapter 4 of Julius Melton, *Presbyterian Worship in America: Changing Patterns Since 1787* (1967). Obituaries are in the *New York Evangelist*, 17 Feb. 1887, and the *New York Tribune* and *New York Herald*, both 11 Feb. 1887.

ELSIE ANNE MCKEE

BAIRD, Henry Carey (10 Sept. 1825–30 Dec. 1912), publisher and economic pamphleteer, was born at the United States Arsenal, Bridesburg, Pennsylvania, the son of Captain Thomas J. Baird, U.S. Army, and Eliza Carey. Educated in private schools until he was sixteen years of age, he then joined the Philadelphia publishing firm founded by his grandfather, Mathew Carey, which was then operated by his uncles. With the dissolution of the family enterprise (1842), he formed his own business—Henry Carey Baird and Company—which pioneered in publishing technical works on industrial and mechanical topics. He also used his publishing house as a vehicle for disseminating his own writings on economic subjects, many of which he distributed without charge.

Baird is noteworthy for his tireless efforts to recruit converts to the doctrines espoused by his uncle Henry C. Carey, the foremost champion of an American "national" system of economics. Carey's thinking was organized as an attack on the "dismal science" as formulated in Britain under the influence of Malthusian and Ricardian teaching. He rejected totally the orthodox propositions of the classical economists on the gains allegedly generated through specialization under a regime of free trade. Carey substituted a "principle of association," which held that clustering of manufacturing and agricultural activities would generate mutually reinforcing economic growth with benefits to all. In his view, standard British doctrine was misguided as well in its emphasis on conflict between the economic interests of various classes. Instead, he maintained that a "harmony of interests" should prevail—but this happy outcome could be achieved only when home producers were sheltered from foreign competitors. Systematic protection was thus essential to promote harmonious and simultaneous expansion of industry and agriculture.

Baird echoed these themes in his own writings. In 1860, for example, he sought to persuade American farmers to join ranks in support of protective tariffs for manufacturers. Prosperity in agriculture, he insisted, depended on the enlargement of the home market for farm products that would follow from growth in the manufacturing sector. When farmers lacked a "near market" for their output, their real incomes were reduced by the "tax of transportation," which they were obliged to absorb on both what they sold and what they bought. Baird was convinced that farmers, "once . . . their eyes [were] opened to the fact of the entire harmony of all the real interests of the country," would "disregard the specious but false cry of 'free trade'" (*Protection of Home Labor and Home Productions Necessary to the Prosperity of the American Farmer* [1860], p. 16).

In his defense of his uncle's position, Baird aimed at a wide variety of polemical targets. In the 1870s, for example, he chided Yale University for its "folly and inconsistency" in spending large sums to support a "Scientific School," while at the same time teaching free trade in its classrooms. As Baird saw the matter, it was pointless to educate Americans for practical and scientific pursuits if they could not be assured the protection of tariffs (*The Rights of American Producers and the Wrongs of British-Free-Trade Revenue-Reform* [1872]). Baird also did battle against the international establishment in academic economics. When Britain's Alfred Marshall and Austria's Eugen von Böhm-Bawerk attacked Carey's theories, he indicted them as "incompetents" who lacked a "knowledge of even the elementary principles of economic truth" (*Proceedings of the American Philosophical Society* 29 [1891]: 166–73).

In the 1870s Baird was one of the organizers of the Greenback party, which called for an expanded issue of U.S. notes and opposed the resumption of specie payments (which had been suspended during the Civil War). His stance on these matters flowed easily from his intellectual commitment to Carey's style of thinking. The money supply—through the issue of paper greenbacks—should be adjusted to the demands of commerce, thus enhancing "the power of man to associate and combine his efforts" and eliminating the wastage associated with labor and machinery idled for lack of a market. From this point of view, an arbitrary linkage between the nation's circulating medium and its gold stock clearly was wrong (*Atlantic Monthly* 37 [1876]: 345–59). Baird pressed these arguments in testimony to congressional committees in 1876 and 1878. Appearing before the U.S. Monetary Commission in 1876, he endorsed remonetization of silver.

Baird's contributions to economic debate were clearly derivative, but they were marked by a dogged consistency. Even though he had little original to offer, his tracts of advocacy helped to keep Carey's protectionist perspective alive in public discourse.

Baird married Elizabeth Davis Penington in 1850. He died in Wayne, Pennsylvania.

• Baird has been virtually ignored in late twentieth-century commentary. His principal monuments are his own writings, published—with a few exceptions—by his own firm. Among the exceptions are essays appearing in the *American Cyclopedia* (1883), notably those on "Political Economy" and "Money." Even though his doctrinal preferences came through in these works, their contents still indicate that he had a thorough familiarity with the pertinent economic literature of his day.

William J. Barber

BAIRD, Robert (6 Oct. 1798–15 Mar. 1863), Presbyterian missionary and author, was born near Pittsburgh, Pennsylvania, the son of Robert Baird, and Elizabeth Reeves, farmers. After studying at Washington and Jefferson Colleges in his home state, Baird trained for a ministerial career at Princeton Theological Seminary. Graduating from that institution in 1822, he founded a grammar school nearby and served as its principal for five years. In 1824 he married Fermine A. DuBuisson; they had eight children. In 1828 he was ordained by the local presbytery, and for a year he was an agent of the New Jersey Missionary Society. In that capacity Baird traversed the state, distributing Bibles to all who would receive one. During those efforts to place a Bible in every household, he also observed the uneven quality of education among the citizenry. By publishing his observations in major newspapers in Trenton, Morristown, Burlington, and Newark and by lobbying with legislators, he helped lay the foundation for a state-supported system of public schools.

After gathering firsthand information about American religious conditions at the local level, in 1829 Baird enhanced his vantage point by becoming a general agent for the American Sunday School Union. During the next five years he traveled through most of the settled areas of the nation. He reported on moral conditions and religious facilities in every section, establishing Sunday schools wherever he could and informing the general public of needs for providing adequate spiritual guidance throughout the Republic. By 1834 he accepted a new post—he agreed to live in Paris as an agent of the French Association, an association dedicated to advancing the cause of Protestantism in France. His work led to a thorough awareness of Protestant activities in the Catholic countries of Europe, and Baird disseminated these findings.

The European segment of Baird's career spanned almost three decades. The association he served changed its title several times, but it is usually known as the American and Foreign Christian Union. Under its aegis he promoted universal elementary education and Sunday schools, which were merely an extension of his ideal for more specifically doctrinal purposes. Bible distribution reached out to adults as well, simultaneously underscoring the basic Protestant emphasis on Scripture as the source of authority in religion. Baird also became in 1836 an advocate of temperance, probably the only truly American contribution to the many reform programs sponsored by evangelical Protestantism. His efforts to mitigate the use of alcoholic beverages led to three tours of Europe (1836, 1837, 1840) in which he traveled thousands of miles from Rome to Stockholm to Moscow. He lectured, published, preached, and secured interviews with crowned heads, all to persuade his contemporaries that quelling liquor would facilitate physical health and economic prosperity while producing social harmony and spiritual improvement.

In ecclesiastical affiliation Baird was content to remain Presbyterian, but his eclectic interests led him to adopt a more interdenominational viewpoint. In his nineteenth-century version of ecumenism, he considered most Protestant groups to be legitimate branches of Christianity because they shared the same scriptural ideals and moral standards. Thus he became an early advocate of the Evangelical Alliance, frequently attending and addressing that European organization, which sought to nurture cooperation among non-Catholic churches. Besides widespread travels on land, he crossed the Atlantic eighteen times to further the causes of religious tolerance, sobriety, and Protestant evangelicalism. His broad acquaintance with conditions on two continents gave Baird a perspective that could synthesize religious ideals with actual conditions, one that interpreted the past, assessed the present, and spoke knowledgeably about future prospects.

As early as 1840 European colleagues asked Baird to answer questions about religious activities in his native land. His first notable response came the following year with a comprehensive series of lectures delivered in Stockholm. In 1842 while at Geneva he put into book-length form his interpretation of what was new in American religious expressions and what maintained continuity with earlier forms of Christianity. The volume, with the short title of *Religion in America*, was first published in Scotland (1843), then in the United States (1844), and afterward was often reprinted, revised, and expanded (especially 1856). Subsequently it was translated into French, German, Dutch, and Swedish. This work, originally offered as an interpretation of American religion to Europeans, functioned equally well in explaining Americans to themselves. It established a new perspective in American religious studies—that American religious experience, especially with regard to revivals, was respectable—and quickly became a classic among that type of scholarship.

Baird's writing affords some of the best history of major Protestant denominations in the United States of his day. It contains judicious assessments and sound evaluations of their potential for continued growth. Beyond those undoubtedly valuable features, Baird's writing also offers readers a window through which they can learn about the most significant aspects of American culture when it was dominated by Protestant influences. He captured the elemental qualities of pre–Civil War life and displayed their dynamic interaction. His lucid analysis and shrewd judgment has affected studies of American religious phenomena since that time.

In evaluating the religion of his day together with its historical development, Baird harbored negative attitudes as well as positive ones. Among the things he disapproved of were racial tensions stemming from immigration and slavery, dissenting political minorities, and nonevangelicals such as Roman Catholics and Mormons. In these areas he drew from a common store of American notions and articulated many widespread prejudices in force at midcentury. On the positive side Baird singled out the separation of church and state as a hallmark of American achievement. Alongside religious freedom he placed revivalism as another characteristic that made church life distinctive in this country. He spoke at length about permeating all of society with evangelical influences, equating democracy, capitalism, and Protestantism in an amalgam that pointed to ultimate perfection. Of course, the very things that Baird disliked—war over slavery, proliferating dissent, and more immigrants—kept his dream from realization. When he died in Yonkers, New York, the world seemed to be drifting away from his ideals. His life and work epitomized nineteenth-century hopes for a uniform culture in which Protestants controlled both church and state.

• In addition to the classic volume mentioned in the text, Baird's other writings include *A View of the Mississippi Valley* (1832), *Histoire des Societés de Tempérance des États-Unis d'Amerique* (1836), *L'Union de l'Église et de l'État dans la Nouvelle Angleterre* (1837), *Sketches of Protestantism in Italy* (1845), and *The Progress and Prospects of Christianity in the United States* (1851). Biographical information derives primarily from Henry M. Baird, *The Life of the Rev. Robert Baird, D.D.* (1866). An obituary is in the *New York Times*, 17 Mar. 1863.

HENRY WARNER BOWDEN

BAIRD, Spencer Fullerton (3 Feb. 1823–19 Aug. 1887), zoologist and scientific administrator, was born in Reading, Pennsylvania, the son of Samuel Baird, a lawyer, and Lydia McFunn Biddle. He initially attended Reading Grammar School, but after his father died, when Baird was ten years old, his family moved to Carlisle, Pennsylvania. He attended a Quaker boarding school near Port Deposit, Maryland, for six months, then attended the Carlisle grammar school. In 1836 he entered Dickinson College, from which he graduated with an A.B. in 1840. By then, both Spencer and his eldest brother Will had become avid collectors of birds and other natural history specimens. They jointly published their first scientific paper (*Proceedings of the Academy of Natural Sciences* 1 [1843]: 283–85), describing two new species of flycatchers. Correspondence regarding the flycatchers between Spencer and naturalist John James Audubon led to their longtime association. Baird studied medicine in New York for less than a year in 1841–1842 but took advantage of his time there to meet and take drawing lessons from Audubon. Audubon invited Baird to accompany him on his expedition to the Yellowstone River and wrote him a letter of recommendation for a position as curator at the National Institute in Washington. Baird turned down the offer to go west with Audubon and failed to get the position at the National Institute. His brother Will, frustrated with, but understanding of his brother's refusal of his offer to support further medical training told him in essence that he should not do something he did not want to do, but it was time to settle on a career, and "no means of livelihood . . . is to be obtained in America from ornithology." Spencer Baird proved his brother wrong.

In 1843 Baird was awarded a master of arts degree from Dickinson College, and in 1845 he was appointed honorary (unpaid) professor of natural science and curator of the Natural History Cabinet there. In July 1846 he was appointed full professor of natural history at Dickinson at a salary of $400 per year, and the attainment of a paying position enabled him to marry Mary Helen Churchill a month later; they had one child.

During his years at Dickinson, Baird built up large natural history collections through extensive local field work and active exchanges with others. He interacted extensively with scientists at the Academy of Natural Sciences in Philadelphia and elsewhere, building both a reputation as an untiring and thorough systematic zoologist and a cadre of influential friends supportive of his efforts. In 1848 he received a grant to explore the bone caves and natural history of southeastern Pennsylvania, the first grant for scientific exploration given by the new Smithsonian Institution.

In 1850 Baird moved from Pennsylvania to Washington, D.C., when he was appointed assistant secretary and curator at the Smithsonian. Most of his collections went with him, joining other collections in Washington to become the foundation of the U.S. National Museum collections. From his early days at Dickinson, Baird had recognized the need to be familiar with current domestic and foreign scientific literature and had studied major languages to facilitate his efforts. His first major publication was the *Iconographic Encyclopedia of Science, Literature, and Art* (1851), an English translation and expanded version of F. A. Brockhaus's *Bilder Atlas zum Conversations Lexicon*. At the Smithsonian, Baird was in charge of the Department of Explorations, and his reports to the secretary provide particularly systematic accounts of numerous government expeditions of the mid-1800s. In this capacity Baird sought and trained collectors and was able to influence their assignments to get them in favorable localities to provide natural history specimens for the Smithsonian.

Baird came to know the Swiss naturalist Louis Agassiz, whom he met in August 1847, and, following his advice, began arranging exchanges of specimens with major museums around the world. These exchanges rapidly built the young Smithsonian into a major world repository and brought Baird further recognition in the international scientific arena.

Baird's greatest contributions, other than guiding the formative years of the Smithsonian Institution and especially the building of the collections of the U.S. National Museum, were in the fields of ichthyology and systematic ornithology. Fish and birds were major interests from his years at Dickinson and remained dominant interests throughout his life. Recognizing the declining commercial fishery resources of North America, Baird began studying the negative impacts of intensive use of various fish capture methods, unlimited harvest, and restrictions to fish movements, following his studies up with development of techniques for transporting live fishes, hatching fish eggs, and rearing fish in ponds and recommendations for legal restrictions to maintain sustainable fisheries resources. In 1863 Baird first visited the Atlantic coast near Woods Hole, Massachusetts, and recognized it as a site free from pollutants and perfect for studying ocean fisheries. In 1871 he expressed his concerns for American fisheries to the Congressional Appropriations Committee, and in 1871, at Baird's urging and design, Congress authorized the appointment of a commissioner of fish and fisheries to evaluate the status of and protect the economic fisheries of the United States. Baird was appointed to the position, continuing to serve simultaneously as assistant secretary of the Smithsonian. In 1878, following the death of Secretary Joseph Henry, Baird was unanimously elected as the second secretary of the Smithsonian. In 1885, under Baird's direction, the Fish Commission established a laboratory at Woods Hole, where in 1888 it was joined by the university-sponsored Marine Biological Laboratory and in 1930 by the Woods Hole Oceanographic Institution.

Baird's personal research and field work were hampered and essentially ended as a result of his increasing administrative duties, but through his administration and the ability to attract and train young scientists, Baird became the great facilitator that took the Smithsonian, the U.S. National Museum, and American science in general great leaps forward. Even under Joseph Henry, the first secretary of the Smithsonian, Baird was the individual most in touch with and in support of museum collections, constantly seeking to enlarge the collections through purchase or exchange, with specific goals of clarifying species distribution patterns. He was also a great communicator, able to interpret science to the public. He wrote regularly for popular magazines and in 1871 became science editor for *Harper's Weekly*, a post he held for eight years.

Baird knew how to work with people, was an excellent judge of abilities, and had the gifts of knowing when and how to compromise and the perseverance to make bureaucracy work for science. His administrative accomplishments went well beyond science into international relations. For example, Baird assisted with negotiations for the purchase of Alaska, complex negotiations with England and Canada over fishing rights, and with preparations for the Centennial Exposition of 1876, in Philadelphia, commemorating the founding of the nation. The latter efforts, through shrewd planning and hard work, resulted in the Smithsonian's acquisition of many items from foreign exhibits and congressional recognition and funding for the construction of a U.S. National Museum building.

In systematic ornithology, Baird bridged the gap between the Audubon era and modern scientific ornithology, providing a firm systematic foundation that has had a lasting influence. This foundation first appeared as volume nine (1858) of the *Report of Explora-*

tions and Surveys, to Ascertain the Most Practicable and Economical Route for a Railroad from the Mississippi River to the Pacific Ocean. This 1,005-page work, republished in 1860 by Baird, "with cooperation" of J. Cassin and G. N. Lawrence, is best known by the title then given: *The Birds of North America*. In avian biogeography he was able to use the collections of government expeditions to identify broad faunal zones meeting in the vicinity of the 100th meridian. Among his significant publications are *North American Reptiles*, with C. Girard (1853); *Catalogue of North American Mammals* (1857); and *A History of North American Birds*, with T. M. Brewer and R. Ridgway (1874).

In addition to receiving several honorary degrees, Baird was a member or honorary member of leading scientific societies around the world. International recognition included decoration as "Knight of the Royal Norwegian Order of St. Olaf" (1875) and receipt of the silver medal of the Acclimatization Society of Melbourne, Australia (1878), the gold medal of the Société d'Acclimation of France (1879), and the Erster Ehrenpreiz of the Internationale Fischerei Ausstellung, Berlin (1880). He served as permanent secretary of the American Association for the Advancement of Science in 1850–1851, as a trustee of Columbia University, and as an early member of the National Academy of Sciences. He was also prominent among the founders of the American Ornithologists' Union (1883).

Baird's name has been memorialized in the names of numerous vertebrate and invertebrate species, ranging from starfish, mollusks, and butterflies to extant and fossil fishes, reptiles, birds, and mammals. "Baird's sparrow" (*Ammodramus bairdii*), the last bird described, named, and painted by Audubon, was the first species to be named after Baird. Other taxonomic uses of Baird's name include the scientific names of the fish genus *Bairdiella* (some bottom-dwelling croakers) and the Cuban Ivory-billed Woodpecker (*Campephilus principalis bairdi*), as well as the common names of animals such as the Baird's rat snake (*Elaphe obsoleta bairdi*), Baird's sandpiper (*Calidris bairdii*), and the Baird beaked whale (*Berardius bairdi*). To be sure, Baird's influence on systematic zoology was broad and lasting. Lucy's warbler (*Vermivora luciae*) was named after Baird's daughter when she was only thirteen, a "gift" from her father's friend, James G. Cooper. Other unusual tributes to him include a U.S. post office in Shasta County, California, named "Baird" in 1877 by the postmaster-general, and the Baird Ornithological Society (Chevy Chase, Md).

In failing health, Baird stepped down from the Smithsonian Institution in 1887 and retired to the Biological Laboratory at Wood's Hole, Massachusetts, where he died after a lengthy illness. In 1902 the American Fisheries Society attached a bronze tablet in his memory to a granite boulder at Woods Hole.

• The major collection of Baird's papers is at the Smithsonian Institution Archives; depositories of other papers are listed in Dean C. Allard, *Spencer Fullerton Baird and the U.S. Fish Commission. A Study in the History of American Science* (1967). Other biographies include George B. Goode, "The Published Writings of Spencer Fullerton Baird, 1843–1882," *U.S. National Museum Bulletin* 20 (1883): i–xvi, 1–377, which includes a detailed bibliography; John Shaw Billings, "Memoir of Spencer Fullerton Baird, 1823–1887," National Academy of Sciences, *Biographical Memoirs* 7 (1889): 141–60; W. H. Dall, *Spencer Fullerton Baird: A Biography* (1915); E. F. Rivinus and E. M. Youssef, *Spencer Baird of the Smithsonian* (1992); and Barbara and Richard Mearns, *Audubon to Xantus: The Lives of Those Commemorated in North American Bird Names* (1992). Obituaries are by T. S. Palmer in *Auk* 4 (1887): 358–59 (plus frontispiece facing p. 273), and Robert Ridgway, "Spencer Fullerton Baird," *Auk* 5 (1888): 1–14.

JEROME A. JACKSON